HANDBOOK OF PERSONALITY THEORY AND RESEARCH

EDITORS

Edgar F. Borgatta and
William W. Lambert

CONTRIBUTORS

Daniel E. Berlyne, *University of Toronto* · Robert C. Birney, *Amherst College* · John C. Burnham, *The Ohio State University* · Irvin L. Child, *Yale University* · Richard Christie, *Columbia University* · Raymond J. Corsini, *Alcoholism Clinic, Honolulu* · Glen H. Elder, Jr., *Univerversity of North Carolina* · Charles W. Eriksen, *University of Illinois* · Barbara Fleischmann, *Cornell University* · Florence Geis, *University of Delaware* · David C. Glass, *Russell Sage Foundation* · E. P. Hollander, *State University of New York* · Irving Janis, *Yale University* · James W. Julian, *State University of New York* · William Kessen, *Yale University* · Harry Levin, *Cornell University* · Maurice Lorr, *The Catholic University of America* · David T. Lykken, *University of Minnesota* · William McGuire, *University of California, La Jolla* · Roland Radloff, *Naval Medical Research Institute* · William A. Scott, *University of Colorado* · Lee Sechrest, *Northwestern University* · Morris I. Stein, *New York University* · Edwin J. Thomas, *University of Michigan* · W. R. Thompson, *Queens University, Ontario* · Ruth C. Wylie, *Goucher College*

HANDBOOK OF PERSONALITY THEORY AND RESEARCH

Edited by EDGAR F. BORGATTA and
WILLIAM W. LAMBERT

RAND McNALLY & COMPANY
Chicago

Printed in U.S.A. by Rand McNally & Company

Library of Congress Catalogue Card Number 67-14685

Introduction

The social and psychological sciences have had a tremendous growth and proliferation in recent decades, and this development has been neither even nor revealing of a clear and simple basic structure to these sciences. The study of personality, which involves several disciplines, has much of this character of sprawl, of pockets of development, of overlapping and yet uncoordinated concerns, and of the types of challenge that keep research interest vigorous. In such a circumstance, there is great need for a Handbook that can take as its purpose presenting some overview and critical appraisal of the field, albeit necessarily a selected and incomplete one, to help prepare for a hoped-for revolution in the hands of the next generation.

The revolutionary possibilities arise from two resources which have arisen in the past twenty years. The first is that we now have available for the task plenteous human imagination and energy. The second, very new, resource is the availability of increasingly useful computers, which permit quick analysis and data reduction. The next generation, our guess is, will be caught up in an accelerated pace of an Hegelian drama of thesis, antithesis, and synthesis. So we predict revolution, but we don't predict its outcome. The study of personality could end up merely with more incisive and informed "Essays on Man," and deeper literary criticism.

Let us now say something about this Handbook, about the categories into which the proliferation of knowledge in the field of personality study is here placed, about the imagination and effort which this volume represents, and something about the data, the methods and techniques which are involved.

First, a statement about the intentions of the editors and most of the contributors to this Handbook: The goal has been to capture that most exciting and lively of targets, a *research conception* of the topic at hand. Those, therefore, who come to this Handbook for a final compilation of finished and neatly packaged problems may be surprised. That is neither the state of the art, the spirit of the times, nor the sought end. What the reader will find more often is, to paraphrase one of the contributors, writing which is focused upon how to move from some present uncertainties to other future uncertainties, leaving occasional clear areas as by-products, so to speak. Many of the chapters contain, or are actually organized around, diagrams of conceptual schemes which are presented as aids in capturing those ideas, facts, or even speculative hunches that the writer hopes may yield pay dirt when the next "good" study is completed.

The research conceptions of the problems of personality study are the honest reflection of the present wry but hopeful mood in the field, but, more importantly, these research conceptions *should* represent the field. Respect for the bright and increasingly informed undergraduates and graduate students who might turn to a Handbook dealing with personality theory and research requires that they be placed at the frontier of what we *know* as quickly and directly as possible. Experts in personality study who might turn here to read up on another man's area would not be experts in the first place if they expected otherwise than to read a critical account of past research along with adumbrations of future research. And the lack of cumulative, effective development of the area in the past *demands* a research emphasis.

Given, then, the aim for a research conception of personality, the problem of proliferation still deserves a word. Personality is, in its various meanings, a common research heritage of all the behavioral sciences, including biology, and new conceptions and facts about the many topics are used by many attentive and interested people in most fields of knowledge and in most walks of life. But there was a time, not too long ago, when personality research did not gain the attention of the more tough-minded among the biologists, psychologists, sociologists, and anthropologists. The important, basic problems of these disciplines resided elsewhere, and the problems of human psychodynamics and of consistent individual differences were best left to those who had to deal with them face-to-face in the clinic, the school, in industry, or in the mental hospital.

But all this is certainly no longer true, and it is necessary that this Handbook reflect some of the new, tough-minded interest that has helped recently to multiply the proliferation. Behavioral biology has been seen to have more relevance recently, along with behavior genetics—and the physical substrate of bodies must be better understood if we are to obtain improved measures of physiological and biochemical processes because of their possible relationship to cultural, social, and individual dynamics and to consistent differences among individuals. Some of the most technical portions of this Handbook deal with these matters.

This tough-minded dimension of proliferation does not end here. The factor analytic tradition has matured and really come into its own in the age of computers, as has computer simulation as a new and challenging art. And mathematical models have begun to appear, and the old and more limited meanings of the term "experimental psychology" are being moved aside by the rush of laboratory experimental work which focuses upon the study of personality, and by the growth of scientific journals to hold the products.

There is no doubt that the cross-cultural challenge has also arrived to stay, and in every behavioral science. Nothing proliferates like comparative study, and the possibilities for the comparative study of animals will be as nothing compared to multiplicative possibilities in the comparative study of groups, societies, and cultures, with inhabitants of other planets possibly just around the next research corner. We have lived with the comparative study of animals (including man) long enough to know something about where to go in the animal kingdom to study particular problems. We have not yet lived long enough with cross-cultural and cross-societal study of personality, however, to understand many rationally or experientially based limits.

But the study of personality has not merely become tougher-minded and broader-minded. All the problems of self and ego and individuality and creativity and normality and conscience and fear and anxiety are with us still, but in multiplied research forms, and the old philosophical and ethical quandaries still enter into most acts of one person toward another. The old problems are not lost, but are multiplied by the perspectives which have been brought to bear upon them. New data and ideas on how to behave toward clinical patients, how to assess people, and how to change them are always with us. The clinical procedures and the assessment attempts did not stop with Jung and Freud, and both have become self-conscious topics for public and even national debate.

So there has been much done for a Handbook to contain: with what categories have we tried to contain it?

But, here we need another statement regarding intention. Handbooks should have some of the virtues of a liberal education. They should place facts and theories within broad contexts or categories in order that overlooked relationships among those facts and theories may come to light a bit sooner. Not that the generic course titles used in a liberal education, or the broad juxtapositions achieved in a good Handbook, are sufficient. The contents must rest upon basic research papers and upon many summaries of limited problems. Indeed, the student of personality needs contact with all three of these forms of literature for a good education. We now have available in personality study a number of good selections of basic readings and we even have a series of books devoted to research summaries in the kinds of specialized categories which come most naturally to active researchers. What we have needed is a Handbook with some recurrent, generic categories within whose broader confines the partially informed, or the expert, can find suggestions of undiscovered relationships either spelled out or implicit.

Section I of this Handbook is devoted to a discussion of two general bases of personality study, recognizing that personality study has a long history of theories of human nature in its background in Western Culture. These very theories and their modern counterparts are open to the broadening and challenging that comes from cross-cultural test and from consideration of the theories of many *other* traditions and ways of life. Let us acknowledge known *lacunae* in this Section. We had hoped here to directly confront ourselves with the fact that the study of language is *also* one of the general bases for the study of personality. Further we had hoped to have attention to personality study as it dovetails with the great tradition of the basic study of intelligence and the several cognitive abilities. It has been necessary to permit these issues to be treated in a less focused manner in other portions of the Handbook. Possibly the topics are not yet ready to be treated in the way we had hoped—we were not able to find authors prepared to meet the challenge for this Handbook.

Section II is a large category centering on the very important area of personality development. Here it is necessary to bring the very fast-changing literature on genetics, physiology, and comparative behavior study to bear on early (and later) development processes, and to view the emergence of personality from several perspectives. Not all perspectives here are in complete agreement, and the styles of approach, of inference, and of self-conscious criticism differ greatly. The reader should be forewarned, however, that the developmental category is one which cannot be kept down: facets and facts which deal with it abound in all sections of the Handbook.

Section III shifts the focus to the immense but still diffuse data banks that exist on adult personality processes, dispositions, and nature as studied by eye-balling, through inventories and questionnaires, and (with amazing proliferation) with the use of physiological and psychophysical techniques. The very growth of work in this last area demands professional, critical, and technical treatment. What, query these chapters, do we honestly and empirically know about human traits, and how can we assess these and other facets of adult personality?

Section IV would be called by some the "theoretical" section, but despite the fact that it does include some important conceptual schemes of several disciplines of behavioral science, we prefer to call it a section on *Special Emphases.* The treatments here are not intended to be so much more theoretical or research-oriented than many other chapters. They are here to highlight the fact that, as relatively broad areas of interest in research, behavior theory, role theory, self-theory, and balance theories are, and have been, very exciting to many researchers of personality. But, some readers may query: "There's no chapter on Freud!" There are many answers to this, and we will give a few. First, the practical fact must be reported that we did look far and wide, and asked possibly fifteen scholars to undertake the chapter. This all takes time, and the task is not a trivial one that could be undertaken lightly as time became shorter and less available to the author. Another answer may be that in recent years there have been many considerations of the research status of Freudian theory, and certainly there has been no shortage of expressions in print as to why Freud continues to interest personality researchers. In a general way, Freud's influence is present in many chapters of the Handbook. Perhaps we are now emerging into a post-Freud era, where Freud is better treated as part of the heritage, but as a person who served as a provocative stimulus to personality study. New questions and reinterpretations commonly bear little direct relation to his original observations and questions, and in fact often relate more directly to work of others who did not evoke the charismatic image.

Section V provides categories that attempt to capture the tumbling growth of personality study, but with a different cross-cutting. Here the categories are intended to be somewhat restricted. How is it now, and how will it probably be (after the next good study is completed) with "creativity," with "need achievement," "neuroticism," "anxiety"? Of course, as reading this section makes clear, starting with a more restricted category or concept does not mean that it will remain restricted. When "need achievement" or "Machiavellianism" (to pick out one of the exciting newer "variables of personality") are followed in their own right, then the search may end in data from classical Greece, inventory items borrowed from Renaissance politics, or in attempts to predict economic growth functions.

This Section contains something of rather unique value to students and beginners in the area of personality study. When a writer starts at the small end of the funnel, and with a delimited area or variable, it is occasionally possible to make out the sequence of the thinking and action which led an original conception to be shaped into a researchable and researched problem or area. It is difficult to find literature that clearly recounts the natural history of a research problem, since space limits and the formal fashions in presenting evidence work against its appearance. But we should also recall that the natural history of a particular research problem does not necessarily, or even probably, *generalize* to the next new research problem. What *does* generalize is the knowledge that is gained regarding the present canons of proof and the forms of personal and public criticism which documentation and proof of propositions about personality demand.

It is unquestionable that the histories of research on variables and mechanisms of personality vary greatly. Many start in the hurly-burly of everyday life, as when a work supervisor finds himself dividing workers into lazy ones and active ones, or when teachers start discussing how they decide that one child is brighter than another. Many go no farther as research problems, perhaps because they are clear, ubiquitous, and obviously useful for decision making or for communicating about other people. Some concepts have not been researched upon merely because no one has yet decided to try to take out the ambiguity or the confusion residing in the concepts by recourse to rules of evidence. Many research problems on personality have arisen in the psychiatric or psychological clinic. Some are merely age-old and haphazardly analyzed notions, like "creative," "authoritarian," or "of strong conscience." A few concepts, like "culture shock" or "time gestalt" grow out of the experience of meeting different ways of life. A few have come from the experimental laboratories of psychology or of biology, and a few have even come from ethology or from social and psychological ecology. A Handbook should, by exposure to the various standards being used, help us to see more clearly where work needs doing or where work is being repeated over and over, and permit us to induce the function of the measurement and evidence standards which we discover are in general or specific use.

Are all the notions and data regarding personality variables, polar types and personality mechanisms that are being researched captured in Section V? Certainly not! Even in our modest plans we had proposed such additional concepts as "dominance and submission" and "empathy." The intention here is to represent a few important and different *examples* of these things, permitting a different way of cross-cutting the field of personality theory and research. Space simply does not permit exhaustiveness. We hope that some of what is left out in Section V will be found within the larger or more traditional network of chapters and have worked to this end.

Section VI recognizes that the clinic is not the only place where people become changed. Since changing, developing, structuring, forming, or just permitting people to "grow" is so much a part of all other sections of the Handbook, we have singled out for cross-cutting reference only two categories. How do psychotherapists and counselors set about changing people who want and need it? How is change in people achieved through use of the various methods of influence and conformity pressures, as this has been freshly turned over and studied by modern social psychology?

So, then, this is the Handbook. We are grateful to our authors, and we recognize the task of writing Handbook chapters is rarely properly rewarded. If wishing and cajoling would make fact, we would have had a few more chapters, possibly more continuity at points, and possibly it would have appeared earlier. And, if wishing really made it so, probably this Handbook would be too big to be useful, for as we have read and reread chapters we have found that the sprawl of the area still leaves many untouched places, open challenges, in a sense, to go along with that potential for a revolution in knowledge in the area.

It is not possible to close an introduction to a volume on personality study without emphasizing that our experiences in research seem to cumulate so much faster than our knowledge. Problems occur, are bypassed or apparently answered, and then recur again. Laboratory experimentation becomes a central interest inspiring many students, and apparent progress and cumulation is seen as new experiments in an area further the last, but as time passes the magnitude of progress pales with the test of generalization and replication. Particular concepts serve as nuclei of research interest, and a rush of experiments and field research develops a literature, but some years later it fades into the history of single-concept explanations. Quasi-experimental and systematic field studies appear promising, but then prove resistant to improvement, with fallible measures not only in the predictors but also in the criteria. No single approach is satisfactory at this time, and the study of personality must necessarily have its sprawl before the revolution can occur that brings system to the field.

The fact is that the study of personality is vital to all the social sciences, and by implication to *all* the sciences. But, to emphasize the point, in recent sociological writings there is a recurrence of the question of the source of explanation for social phenomena, and the constant recourse to the level of personality for explanation is disconcerting to those who would prefer to keep their analyses at the level of group structures. But, no alternative seems to take such reference to the level of personality out of style. Self-conscious acknowledgment of these limitations in the sciences will aid their advancement. The centrality of the study of personality warrants our constant attention.

EDGAR F. BORGATTA
WILLIAM W. LAMBERT

Contents

PART I General Bases of Personality Study

CHAPTER 1 Historical Background for the Study of Personality[1]

JOHN CHYNOWETH BURNHAM
The Ohio State University

PART I. ANALYTICAL INTRODUCTION

1. Overview

Personality is subject to ambiguous conceptualization. On the one hand, personality connotes the human qualities of a human being, his motivations, why he behaves as he does. On the other hand, personality implies that which is unique about an individual, the thoughts and behavior that differentiate him from his fellow humans and even members of the same social and biological groups within the species. This essay concerns representative writers up to the early twentieth century who contributed to either systematic or scientific thinking about the general nature of human nature or about individual differences. The two facets of the ambiguity are treated together because they cannot be separated. Concepts of human nature have provided basic assumptions and points of departure for the students of individual differences. Reciprocally, inquiries into the origins of individual idiosyncrasies have led to new views of what makes man act the way he does.

From the ancient Greeks to the eighteenth century, the narrative of the rise of systematic thinking about human nature and personality is also the narrative of the rise of naturalism. The Greeks in raising basic questions of the relation of mind and body started a line of thinking that resulted in the first—and most lasting—typology of personality, the doctrine of the temperaments. In attempting to account for the social evil in man, the ancients also gave rise to the theory of human passions. This doctrine, a major formulation of the nature-nurture controversy, fascinated the churchmen who in medieval times succeeded the thinkers of Greece and Rome. The clerics saw in the passions evidence of inherited original sin. Renaissance and Enlightenment examinations of the nature of man represent largely the way in which questions of the nature of man moved from the area of the-

[1] The author would like to express his deep appreciation to colleagues who, in addition to the editors, generously suggested improvements in this history: J. A. Cardno, of the University of Tasmania; Hamilton Cravens, of The Ohio State University; Norman Dain, of Rutgers University; Max M. Levin, of Stanford University; David W. Levy, of The Ohio State University; and James G. Martin, of The Ohio State University.

ology to that of science. The very fact that environmentalism flourished is a token of the extent to which the nature-nurture and, as it turned out, the mind-body problems had outgrown their theological contexts.

During the Renaissance, interest in the individual, his existence and aspirations, led to inquiry as to his nature. Later, political preoccupations, the question of a man's relation to society, gave rise to conceptions of passions and motives on both the individual and social levels of functioning. By the eighteenth century even the passions had taken on social connotations.

While romantic speculation was taking the strictly philosophical writers out of the mainstream of the history of the investigation of personality, science, particularly physiology, was laying the foundation for a materialistic view of man. The ideologues and the phrenologists nourished one line of such thinking; and neurophysiologists and, eventually, association psychologists gave rise to another type of materialism. The former produced the character analysis of Gall and his successors; the latter eventually analyzed all individual differences and even emotional life into reflexes and accidental associations.

The Victorian generations had a penchant to explain both human nature and human individual differences by referring to either a man's heredity or the social group to which he belonged (or, in the concept of race, both). Since heredity was understood both to be Lamarckian in nature and to embrace in practice the "mind" as well as the body, heredity was a fluid concept indeed.

The immediate roots of modern personality theory lie in the post-Victorian period when instinct theories developed as if in reaction to the intellectualism of late nineteenth century psychology. At the same time, partly because Weismann made Lamarckian ideas of heredity untenable, a new environmentalism flourished that embodied a reaction against pessimism both in psychiatry and in social thought in general. Life history replaced racial history as a determining factor. By utilizing both instinct and environment but focusing upon the individual, dynamic psychiatrists, psychoanalysts, psychologists, and social thinkers in effect bypassed the classic nature-nurture formulations. Concurrently, by using the idea of function and adaptation, they circumvented traditional psychological concepts and conceptions and dealt directly with individual differences, particularly in their genetic aspects.

As the theorists broke with established conceptualization, the research workers now had new ways of viewing old problems. There were also increasingly sophisticated physiological data available. After the work of Cannon and others on the physiology of emotion, investigation moved more and more from physiology into the area of social behavior, making use particularly of the culture concept. Researchers were able to devise innumerable ingenious experiments suggestive of patterns of human behavior. Similarly, suggestive clinical testing of the new conceptualizations went on apace. In an area of study in which conceptualization and theory came to play a major role, it was inevitable that philosophical writers should come once again to exert a major influence. While the older formulations of the mind-body and nature-nurture problems seldom had direct applications any more, still personality theory and research more than ever were unable to escape the past.

In spite of the importance of the subject, however, few writers of any epoch have focused on it. As late as 1961 Arthur O. Lovejoy (pp. 12–14) could observe that no one had written a history of man's ideas about his own nature. "We have many works, under various titles," said Lovejoy, "on the history of the idea of God, but none that I can recall on the history of the idea of man." With a few partial exceptions (such as Bain, 1861, ch. 1, and Jastrow, 1915), Lovejoy's observation is still valid and will probably remain so for some time to come. This hiatus in historical and philosophical scholarship reflects the difficulty of synthesizing the implicit opinions of men about their own nature. The difficulty also appears in the concepts and terms that have been used from time to time.

2. Personality

The word "personality" comes from the Latin *persona*. Originally it referred to the masks worn in the theatre; later the term came to include the wearers of the masks. The audience could expect from the wearer of a given mask a more or less consistent pattern of behavior and attitudes, and it is still common to speak of the socially defined role or roles that a person plays in life. Beginning in Roman times the word has taken on many meanings, both denotative and connotative (see Trendelenburg, 1910, and Carus, 1910, for a sample of the literature on this subject).[2]

In 1937 Allport (pp. 26–50) found fifty different definitions connected with the word *persona. The Oxford English Dictionary* lists for the more restricted word, "personality," six main meanings:

1. "The quality, character, or fact of being a person as distinct from a thing."
2. "That quality or assemblage of qualities which makes a person what he is, as distinct from others persons...."
3. "A personal being, a person."
4. "Bodily parts collectively; body, person." [rare]
5. "The fact of relating to an individual, or to particular persons ...," e.g., to resort to personalities in an argument.
6. A rare legal use, derived from the common juristic use of the term "person."

Meanings 1 and 3 have connotations relevant to self psychology. The primary scientific definition of "personality," however, is meaning 2, which emphasizes the distinctive or idiosyncratic quality that distinguishes one human from another.

Allport (1937, pp. 24–50) calls attention to the sociological, biosocial, and psychological meanings that have in recent times accrued to the term "personality." The sociologists, he observes, deny to personality "the attribute of self-sufficiency. In one way or another personality is always considered a reflection of, or dependent upon, the social group." Thus the person is "the ultimate granule of the human group" (Eubank) or "the subjective side of culture" (Faris). Allport also quotes as an example of more synthetic sociological definition Burgess's: "Personality is the integration of all traits which determine the role and status of the person in society.... [i.e.,] social effectiveness."

Biosocial definitions of personality Allport classes as those concerned with external appearance. They are close to the original mask connotation of *persona* and can be summed up in May's view of personality as a man's "social-stimulus value." (This is close to the popular use of "personality" as behavior patterns used to elicit favorable reactions from other people.) As Allport points out, advocates of the biosocial viewpoint implicitly deny that a person's individuality can exist independently of society and can have biological as well as sociological roots and meanings.

Allport distinguishes five types of psychological definitions. The first is the omnibus definition, involving a phrase such as "sum-total," "composite," or "aggregate": "the sum total of all the biological innate dispositions, impulses, tendencies, appetites, and instincts of the individual, and the acquired dispositions and tendencies—acquired by experience" (Prince). Such definitions Allport finds inadequate because their authors omit what he considers to be the vital attribute of mental life: "the presence of *orderly arrangement*."

The second class of psychological definitions, then, is that in which the idea of "organization of personal attributes" pre-

[2] This discussion does not include personality as a philosophical problem, particularly as related to the self. For a discussion of this type of problem, particularly in its metaphysical aspects in post-Kantian philosophy, see Richter (1907).

dominates. MacCurdy, for instance, speaks of "an integration of patterns (interests) which gives a peculiar individual trend to the behavior of the organism." Closely related is a third view of personality, the hierarchical view, of which William James gives a good example in his conception of the four levels of the Self: material, social, spiritual, and Pure Ego (the knower).

Allport's fourth variety of psychological definition of personality is definition in terms of adjustment. This fourth group of definers is concerned with the organism as a whole in action. Allport for instance summarizes Kempf's definition as "the integration of those systems of habits that represent an individual's characteristic adjustments to his environment."

Finally, Allport poses the problem of personality as distinctiveness—the acting, feeling, and thinking that differentiates the individual from the mass. Woodworth provides an example in his conception of the adverbial—rather than substantial—nature of personality. It is not any particular kind of activity but the way in which a person functions, how he talks, remembers, thinks, loves, etc.—his style of life.[3]

There are other emphases that might appear in a discussion of the definitions of personality written since Allport's essay. For example, some writers, perhaps, say, Erik Erikson, might wish to emphasize developmental or epigenetic factors. For historical purposes, however, the best approach to the idea of personality is examining concepts closely related to it. Of particular importance are two terms that not only are close to personality but were for a very long time used functionally as substitutes or partial substitutes, namely, character and temperament (see especially Roback, 1927a).

3. Character

Character is derived etymologically from a Greek word for an instrument used to make a mark or stamp distinctive in nature. The concept of a man's distinctive character was well known in classical times. Character is distinguished from personality because of an element of will that is involved in character but not necessarily in personality. Aristotle [384 B.C.–322 B.C.] (*Nichomachean Ethics* 3.5 1114a7) made the volitional element explicit: "A person's character depends upon the way in which he exercises his powers." Personality, by contrast, is descriptive without the connotation that a man is what he wills to be—and is, therefore, responsibile for the result.

In common usage from Greek times to the present, character has usually been defined in terms of character types—the good man and the bad, the brave and the cowardly. While one can find important examples of characterization in Homer and Greek drama and in other ancient documents such as the Bible, literary characterization as such began with the *Characters* of Theophrastus [372 B.C.–287 B.C.] (ca. 319 B.C.; the edition cited here is 1902). The point of the work is well made in the dedication (which is now believed to be spurious): "Many a time ere now I have stopped to think and wonder ... why it is that we Greeks are not all one in character, for we have the same climate throughout the country and our people enjoy the same education." Yet Theophrastus could see the dissembler, the flatterer, the tactless man, the mean man, the late learner, the avaricious man, the braggart, and so on.

There is another aspect to Theophrastus's *Characters* that distinguishes the work: all of the characters that he described are by and large undesirable. This is, then, truly a work about character, not personality. The tone of his description is satirical: "Garrulity is incessant heedless talk. Your garrulous man is one, for instance, who sits down

[3] This summary is not intended to serve as a substitute for Allport's (1937, pp. 24–50) original essay with its schematic representations of the various meanings and uses of "person" and "personality" and their relationships to each other. Allport's own definition (1937, p. 48) is eclectic, an attempt to utilize all of the meanings, especially the psychological. See below.

beside a stranger, and after recounting the virtues of his wife tells the dream he had last night, and everything he ate for supper. Then, if his efforts seem to meet with favor, he goes on to declare that the present age is sadly degenerate, says wheat is selling very low, that hosts of strangers are in town, and that since the Dionysia the weather is good again for shipping; and that, if Zeus would only send more rain, the crops would be much heavier, and that he's proposing to have a farm himself next year; and that life's a constant struggle, and that at the Mysteries Damippus set up an enormous torch; and tells how many columns the Odeon has, and 'Yesterday,' says he, 'I had an awful turn with my stomach,' and 'What day's to-day?' and 'In Boëdromion come the Mysteries, and in Pyanopsion the Apaturia, and in Poseideon the country Dionysia,' and so on; for, unless you refuse to listen, he never stops."

Character writing, in its proper sense, is analytic, a general description of types. It is thus distinguished from literary portraits (or characterization) of real or fictitious individual (as opposed to typical) persons. The writing of characters had few practitioners after Theophrastus until the seventeenth century, when the art was widely practiced, especially in England. These typologies were known by all literate men and were inevitably incorporated in the descriptive work of the phrenologists and others who later classified personality types (see in general Roback, 1927b, ch. 2, and Aldington, 1924, pp. 1–26; see also below).

4. Temperament

Temperament derives primarily from the medical writings of the ancients. The term came to signify the balance in an individual between the various humors. In the Hippocratic corpus, the earliest systematization of medicine, diseases were ascribed to an imbalance in the body of four humors: blood, phlegm, black bile, and yellow bile. These humors were connected at times with the four basic elements, air, water, earth, and fire, and with attributes of wet, dry, hot, and cold, which were used to describe physical conditions caused by humoral imbalance. Patients of Hippocrates apparently ran in types; according to which humor predominated in a man, he was predisposed to certain diseases. Since to the father of medicine mental diseases also represented the predominance of one humor or another, there was already in Hippocrates the germ of the idea of the influences of the humors on personality.

By the time of the pseudo-Aristotelian *Problems* (perhaps written by Theophrastus), the connection between the humors and personality traits was explicit. The naturally cold black bile if in excess leads to melancholia and even suicide; if overheated, black bile produces in varying degrees cheerfulness, frenzy, or madness (Esper, 1964, pp. 121–123).

The doctrine of temperaments was given its final form by Galen [131–201] in the second century A.D. Within the context of a larger theory of disease causation, Galen described nine types of temperaments, representing the various combinations of predominance and balance among the four humors (along with wet, dry, warm, and cold). Galen's description of each temperamental type included both physical constitution and something of personality: "Cold and dry,—hard—slender—white firm muscles—small joints—little hair—cold to the touch—desponding" (Smith, 1930, pp. 105–110). Galen spoke explicitly about the influence of the humors on individual personality differences: "Those who do not consider that the mind is helped or harmed by the bodily crases can tell us nothing about the differences in children, nor can they explain the help we derive from diet; nor again why there are so many differences in character, some individuals appearing spirited, others spiritless, some intelligent and others not so."

During the Renaissance, physicians, especially, tended to reintroduce Galen's system, usually in the simplified form of only four temperaments: choleric, sanguine, phlegmatic, and melancholic (ignoring Galen's mixtures). The doctrine of humors—as causes of health and ill health as well as of personality traits—persisted in medicine virtually into the nineteenth century (Smith, 1930, pp. 110–124). Renaissance literary men also adopted the idea of temperaments caused by the humors. The notion grew up, for example, that the genius was a man who was melancholy "by nature." Robert Burton's [1577–1640] work is the best known example of this cult of melancholia (Esper, 1964, p. 123; Roback, 1927a, pp. 43–46).

The theory of temperament underwent many changes, not least of which was development independent of specific humors. It shows up in literary character types, in phrenology, and elsewhere in various guises. Allport's (1937, p. 54) definition of temperament, for example, emphasizes the involuntary and persisting elements in temperament that have rendered the concept so useful; the definition also shows the incompleteness of the concept relative to that of personality: "Temperament refers to the characteristic phenomena of an individual's emotional nature, including his susceptibility to emotional stimulation, his customary strength and speed of response, the quality of his prevailing mood, and all peculiarities of fluctuation and intensity in mood; these phenomena being regarded as dependent upon constitutional make-up, and therefore largely hereditary in origin."

5. Disposition

Closely related to temperament is disposition. Sometimes the implication of permanence in temperament is absent in disposition, and any given disposition can be transitory in nature. One interesting theory of the origin of the word is that it refers to the disposition of the stars in the heavens, suggesting, of course, the powerful astrological influences on a man's life. The fault of one's disposition, then, like other faults, to turn Shakespeare around, would lie not in ourselves but in our stars.

More likely disposition is connected to the idea that a person is disposed, or predisposed, to act in a certain way (Dubray, 1905). The relation of disposition to temperament is here apparent in the way in which an individual person—perhaps because of humors—is predisposed to certain diseases. Originally the word indicated order, classification, and arrangement; it came to have the meaning of the end product of regularized procedure, a tendency in the organism to act to the end of producing or reproducing a definite condition. Where a disposition is acquired or learned, it is very close to being a habit (Dubray, 1905, especially pp. 47 ff.).

6. Habit

There still remains to be taken up, then, the concept of habit. The concept of habit was well established in ancient times. Galen (quoted in Brock, 1929, pp. 182–183), for example, quoted Hippocrates and Erasistratus on habits of living. Aristotle (*Categories* 8. 9a 10) contrasted the transitory nature of dispositions (as the word is now confusingly translated) with the permanency of habits, which are otherwise understood to be not only customary actions but also modes of action. "Habits," he (*Eudemian Ethics* 2.2. 1220b 18–20) said, "are such things as are the causes of these things being inherent in us rationally, or irrationally, such for instance as fortitude, timidity, and intemperance."

It is obvious that the synthesis of a man's habits is close to being his personality, if habit be defined relatively broadly, including even, for example, habits of thought. Perhaps the one vital element missing from the idea of habits is their individual uniqueness. Habits can be socially or culturally shared, in which case they also come under the rubric of custom, as is recognized in the German term, *Gewohnheit* (see especially Funke's [1958] exploration of all of the meanings of the German word).

Habits can be understood generally in two senses: passively acquired habits, that is, habits acquired through the operation of innate instincts (the habits of animals) and actively acquired habits (see Hutchins, 1952, II, p. 665). By the late nineteenth century the distinction was usually made between instincts (innate) and habits (acquired). As a matter of fact, most writers have spoken of habits as learned, and the ability to acquire habits is generally referred to as very close to memory (Dubray, 1905, pp. 6–9). Hume (1896, pp. 178–179) believed that the ability of organisms to form habits is "but one of the principles of nature, ... [deriving] all its force from that origin."

The subject of habit brings up directly the subject of human nature as such, for traditionally "Habit is a second nature."[4] Aquinas, for example, defined *habitus* as an influence upon the will to some end, and he observed that a man is the kind of man he is because of his habitual inclination or "second nature" (R. R. Baker, 1941, pp. 132–134; Dubray, 1905, pp. 31–32). The great influence on a man of this "second nature" has also long been recognized. Aristotle (quoted in Hutchins, 1952, II, p. 665) quoted an ancient poet who said that "Habit is but long practice, and this becomes men's nature in the end." Lord Monboddo [1714–1799] (quoted in Greene, 1961, p. 203) raised in clear terms the question of whether, in practice, the original nature of man is of great importance, since the "second nature" of habit incorporates and alters it: "And if we rightly consider the matter, we shall find that our nature is chiefly constituted of acquired habits, and that we are much more creatures of custom and art than of nature. It is a common saying that habit (meaning custom) is a second nature. I add, that it is more powerful than the first, and in a great measure destroys and absorbs the original nature: For it is the capital and distinguishing characteristic of our species, that we can make ourselves, as it were, over again, so that the original nature in us can hardly be seen; and it is with the greatest difficulty that we can distinguish it from the acquired."[5]

PART II. LEGACY OF THE ANCIENTS

1. The Pre-socratics

Systematic conceptions of the nature of man and his individuality, in the form of personality, character, humor, disposition, or habit, have in general come from two sources: philosophy and science (including the antecedents of science). The existence of these two sources of man's notions about himself was clear even in the writings of the pre-Socratic Greeks. On the one hand the early Ionian philosophers believed that there is order in the universe, that it is governed by regularities or laws. These philosophers believed that all phenomena are functions of natural principles—air, fire, water, and earth—and of matter, without any supernatural interference. The Ionians believed that man, like the animals, belongs to the world. This was the naturalistic viewpoint. Contemporaneously, on the other hand, the Pythagoreans introduced a philosophical version of the soul: it is part of a spiritual world. Knowledge of the soul and its spir-

[4] This concept or a variety of it has been much quoted; this particular version is from Bartlett's *Familiar Quotations,* quoting Montaigne; see also Funke (1958). See also below.

[5] Shakespeare (*Hamlet,* Act III, Scene 4) had put the same idea forward in a different age:

Assume a virtue, if you have it not.
That monster, custom, who all sense doth eat
Of habit's devil, is angel yet in this;
That to the use of actions fair and good
He likewise gives a frock, or livery,
That aptly is put on: Refrain to-night;
And that shall lend a kind of easiness
To the next abstinence; the next more easy:
For use can almost change the stamp of nature,
And master even the devil, or throw him out
With wondrous potency.

(Carlson and Simpson, 1965, suggested this quotation.)

itual world is not based upon sensory impressions, nor are its operations subject to the laws regulating the material universe. In opposition to the materialism of the Ionians, the Pythagoreans emphasized abstract form and relationships. Their work gave rise to the idealistic viewpoint (H. C. Baker, 1947, ch. 1).

2. Plato

Plato [428/427 B.C.–348/347 B.C.], partly in reaction against the relativism of this-worldly Sophists, rejected sensation and opinion as bases for truth. Instead, he turned to generalized philosophical (and non-naturalistic) concepts that would transcend the errors inherent in the specific and changeable. The soul, by means of reason, according to Plato, can have knowledge of the ideal world. Plato believed that the individual's soul includes three elements: reason, or the tendency toward the ideal; desire; and spirit, which is a distinct entity but still the agent used by reason to overcome and harness and use the passions; the passions can, however, initiate motion on their own. Men in whom rational powers have not been cultivated will be ruled by their appetites (hence the need for the notorious controlling state of *The Republic*).

Plato located each element in a different part of the body—the lower part of the irrational soul, for example, below the diaphragm, the better part above, in the heart—establishing a tradition of anatomical localization of mental faculties that was to reach full flower in phrenology. The relation between the mind-soul and the body was not clear: how, for example, the desires that represent organic needs find representation in the soul. (See Wilm, 1925, pp. 18–19; Peters, 1953, pp. 68–69; in these psychological expositions Plato's emphasis was upon harmonizing the body and soul rather than denying the body, however inconsistent such an emphasis is with the rest of his writings; see H. C. Baker, 1947, ch. 3.)

3. Aristotle

In contrast to Plato's contempt for the material, Aristotle conceived all of the universe, including man, to be both matter and form. Possessing a soul he believed to be an attribute of life, i.e., the soul gives life to matter or is the life form of matter. Aristotle (not entirely unlike Plato) described a hierarchy of souls suitable for different types of life. Plants possess a nutritive soul and animals possess in addition a sensitive soul, he said; he considered sensation to be the basis of knowledge. Man's soul, Aristotle said, is not only nutritive and sensitive but rational, and the attribute of reason therefore distinguishes humans from the animals. The rational soul as conceived by Aristotle is characterized by various faculties: common sense (the ability to classify sense data), imagination, memory, and reason. Reason, Aristotle believed, derives ultimately from sensations, but when actively used it partakes of the universal and, unlike the faculties, cannot perish with the body (H. C. Baker, 1947, ch. 3).

Aristotle assumed that all actions are basically hedonistic: a man avoids pain and seeks pleasure. Their capacity to reason permits human beings to postpone their gratifications, to suit their actions to expectations of gaining pleasure or avoiding pain in the future. Thus, prudent moderation in life, said Aristotle, leads to the maximum amount of happiness (Dickinson, 1922, pp. 27–31).

Much of the more specific part of Aristotle's conception of human nature is vague, inconsistent, or lost in the ambiguities of language. The faculties are both higher and lower, and a man feels pleasure in the proper exercise of any of his faculties. Even in the case of the lowest faculties, there seems to be in Aristotle no sense of mechanical, automatic behavior in man. All conduct would appear to be, at least theoretically, under control, although the means of control is not always clear. Most significantly, however, Aristotle recognized the existence of character, the habitual level at which an individual has regulated the function of his faculties and specifically the extent to which he controls his passions. (See Gardiner, Metcalf, and Beebe-Center, 1937, ch. 2; Wilm, 1925, pp. 21–27, and section above on habit.)

Aristotle did not show clearly what he meant by the passions, although they are obviously related to the physical correlations of feelings and emotions. The affections—a term often synonymous with passions, or nearly so—he once listed in pairs: anger and mildness, friendship and enmity or hatred, fear and boldness, shame and shamelessness, favor or gratitude and ingratitude, pity and indignation, emulation and envy. Even this list, however, constitutes only an incomplete sample of Aristotle's views of motivation, for it leaves out, for example, pecuniary motivations of which we know he was vividly aware (Dickinson, 1922, pp. 32–33).

4. The Greek Ideal and Education

The ancient Greeks not only formulated the classic mind-body problem but also formulated and explored the nature-nurture problem. Their interest grew out of the conflict between their increasingly naturalistic view of man, on the one hand, and, on the other hand, the idealism inherent in their political philosophy. Even some of the ancient post-Homeric poets were attempting to suggest, for example, that the natural tendency to save one's own life is more commendable than an artificial and dogmatic sacrifice to the aristocratic social ideal of honor (Jaeger, 1939–1944, I, pp. 116–117, 131–132).

At the height of Athenian civilization the intellectual and social conflict between the natural and the ideal continued, and thinkers attempted to synthesize the two viewpoints. The goal of the Athenians was the harmonious functioning of society. In Plato's writings the social ideal reached the point where the idea of the perfect state defined the idea of the perfect man both in society and in nature. Evil in a man, according to Plato, is unnatural and unhealthy as well as anti-social.

The most striking synthesis of the time is that formulated by a group of educators, the Sophists. They viewed the human as a natural being, but they did not accept him as complete in his natural state. They saw in man potential for acquiring character. By practice and learning a man could develop a second nature (see above). The Athenians, therefore, cultivated a sense of correctness, particularly in the form of urbane modes of behavior. As Jaeger puts it, through child rearing and other social institutions, "men were, for the first time, engaged in deliberately forming human character in accordance with a cultural ideal." This character formation was essentially political in its nature. Emphasizing ideal behavior was aristocratic. The idea that citizens could be shaped and formed was democratic. Thinkers who synthesized the two represent the best of Hellenic culture (based generally on Jaeger, 1939–1944, especially I, pp. 272–273, 302–303; II, pp. 54, 320–322).

While Athenian society was politically oriented, nevertheless, as the great philosophers show, even in this cultural bent naturalism played an important role. Aristotle, for instance, is easy to classify in the naturalistic tradition because he accepted fully the material world. Even Plato made use of the ancient physicians' ideas when, for example, he equated evil with unnatural. But it was more directly from those ancient physicians that later naturalistic and scientific views of man were derived.

5. The Physicians

Despite their preoccupation with teaching and character building, the philosophers were interested primarily in metaphysics and ethics, not in the internal life of man as such (see Gardiner, Metcalf, and Beebe-

Center, 1937, pp. 1–2, 26). The physicians approached the problem from the point of view of the influence of bodily conditions upon behavior. Two concepts are of primary importance: the humors and the pneuma (vital spirits), both of which have historical roots back as far as ancient Egypt (Keele, 1957, p. 4).

The humoral theory that gave rise to the concept of temperament was for either Hippocrates [460 B.C.–377 B.C.] or Galen—or their successors for a millennium and more—only a part of a medical theory of life. These excellent physicians posited the pneuma (related to the basic element or principle, air, and to life itself) to explain many physiological processes, including mental activity. In some writers' views, the humors exert their influence through the mediation of the pneuma. (See in general Allbutt, 1921, pp. 224–264, 296–297.)

In one of the Hippocratic treatises the pneuma or vital spirit is supposed to circulate through the blood vessels and carry sensation itself. Later, Aristotle, for example, spoke of the vital spirit that brings life to all parts of the body, and, indeed, he did not distinguish clearly between pneuma, soul, energy, and vital heat (Allbutt, 1921, p. 240; Keele, 1957, pp. 29, 32–34). Like the humoral theory, the doctrine of pneuma or vital spirits or animal spirits found its classical expression in Galen's works.

Galen distinguished between the vital spirits, located in the blood vessels and primarily nutritive in function, and the psychic or animal spirits, upon which nervous functioning (sensation and movement) depends. This distinction was still alive many centuries later, and Galen's ideas are of importance primarily in foreshadowing the later model of the nervous system. Galen supposed the nerves to be hollow and the psychic spirits to pass through them. Building upon the work of Alexandrian dissectors, Galen localized the mind in the brain and distinguished the efferent and afferent nerves (Keele, 1957, pp. 46–53). But it was more than a thousand years before there was any improvement on Galen's model, and meantime it was much corrupted. (See Allbutt, 1921, pp. 260–264.)

6. End of the Ancient World

In reading the ancients the hazard of reading back is always present. How, exactly, did the humors and animal spirits affect a man's behavior, for example? Are these concrete descriptions of real or imagined substances to be taken literally or more or less figuratively? And if figuratively, on the level of the shadows of Plato's cave or, say, on the level of analogy, as the action of the humors is compared to the action of intoxicating beverages upon thought, feeling, and behavior (Esper, 1964, p. 122)? In general, since these ideas were used empirically, they must often have been taken literally. Those who came after the ancients, however, even those in the naturalistic tradition, often used classical concepts in a very different context. It was a long time before a recognizable sequence of successors could be picked up.

In medieval times the naturalistic view of man was in fact lost; those who recorded their opinions were churchmen who gloried in mysticism. Where the Greeks had valued reason most in the nature of man, medieval writers followed Augustine, the Bishop of Hippo [354–430], in emphasizing the will. According to Augustine man in a primeval state (i.e., Adam) had willed to disobey God. As a result, all men, i.e., the wills of all men, are evil and corrupt by nature. Men can be saved not by their own intelligence or actions but only by the will of God, who may infuse certain individual members of the corrupt race with the knowledge and goodness that mean salvation in heaven. The evil nature of man—understood in terms of slavery to bodily pleasures, especially sex—makes necessary coercive social institutions such as the church and state. In this Augustinian synthesis, the passive nature of a man, as opposed to his use of intelligence, is notable.

Likewise the extreme to which the classical distinction between the mind-soul and matter (the body) was taken is remarkable.

PART III. AQUINAS AND THE RENAISSANCE

1. Aquinas

In the thirteenth century Thomas Aquinas [1225–1274] undertook to reconcile faith and reason, resuscitating the active intellect of Aristotle by which men could know God. Aquinas also reestablished the Aristotelian notion that the body and soul are merely different aspects of the same thing—the soul the form of the material body. He asserted the necessity and good of all that which is—spiritual, social, and material. The spiritual soul needs the material body to operate, he pointed out, for example.

Man, according to Aquinas, is endowed with appetites, which have their ultimate source in the inclination of all things, both animate and inanimate, to act in accordance with their natures, to realize themselves. In man, Aquinas saw operative the Aristotelian scheme of proper motivations (i.e., will) and reason working together in a complementary way toward the perfection of each person. A man's faculties so engaged (and here Aquinas still followed Aristotle) produce pleasure. Since it is natural to do good, when a man fails to follow his reason, that is an unnatural act (and a sin, incidentally). It upsets the natural order that God has instituted.

The natural order of Thomistic theology has relevance in several ways. Aquinas visualized the individual as incomplete without participating in mutual relationships with society and God, relationships analogous to the mutual obligations undertaken by lord and vassal. Original sin, according to Aquinas, disrupted this natural order and weakened all of the faculties—especially the will—involved in inclining a man to do good. A man is thus at the mercy of his lowest appetites. Moreover, according to Aquinas, giving way to sin against right reason further disrupts nature, primarily by giving precedence to the individual at the expense of God, society, and nature. This continued disruption of nature further weakens the tendency of the individual to do what is right. Whatever the tendency, Aquinas believed that habits and modes of behavior can be learned. (See in general Snell, 1942, pp. 3–74; R. R. Baker, 1941; and H. C. Baker, 1947, pp. 194–199.)

2. The Rise of Naturalism

Aquinas's synthesis lasted almost untouched until the sixteenth century. Then came questioning and revision and finally the full-fledged flowering of the Enlightenment in the seventeenth and eighteenth centuries; these later events constitute "the rise of naturalism," which turned out to be more than just a renaissance of the naturalism of the ancients. The most important aspect of the rise of naturalism was the fact that the basis of man's study of man changed. In medieval times, and even largely in ancient times, the approach to studying man had been external. One started with the universe, or with society, or with God, and then approached man. In the Enlightenment there were the first beginnings of approaching the world through man—the depths of the individual mundane human—and working outward. (See Lovejoy, 1955.)

3. The Elizabethan Prelude

In a classic study, Theodore Spencer (1949) describes how, in the time of Shakespeare, three and a half centuries after Aquinas, a stable, hierarchical, and mostly Thomistic view of man and the universe continued to prevail in Western Europe. Spencer then goes on to show how in those years "the Renaissance conflict" developed that destroyed the Thomistic synthesis and ultimately led to the Enlightenment.

The revival of classical learning brought with it a great deal of attention to the physical influences of the stars, the humors, and the vital spirits (see Robin, 1911) on an individual's conduct as well as his uncontrollable fate (like the astrological incompatibility of Romeo and Juliet or the humoral determinants of Burton's melancholy). Beyond that, the European's view of man and the universe tended to be optimistic in that all phenomena were seen to be orderly. God had created man in order that human beings would know and love Him. Knowledge of God was available from the Bible and from nature. Nature was understood to be the book, as Montaigne [1533–1592] (quoted in Spencer, 1949, p. 2) put it, "of the universal order of things." These sixteenth century thinkers saw order in the three types of law they discovered in the universe: the laws of nature, natural law applicable to all men, and civil law as found in each country. This faith in the naturalistic order of the world —an ancient idea—turned out in the sixteenth century and after to be one of the bases for the development of naturalism.

The Elizabethans saw man in terms of three largely traditional hierarchies, each one parallel to the others. Leaving out the social hierarchy, the hierarchies of nature and man were (Spencer, 1949, p. 12n):

God—pure actuality
angels—pure intellect
man—reason
animals—sense
plants—growth
stones—being.

Here was man in the critical position, neither material nor heavenly but partaking of both. "Man is made of two natures," said Gelli [1498–1563], an Italian humanist (quoted in Spencer, 1949, pp. 11–12), "one corporeal and terrestrial, the other divine and celestial; in the one he resembles beasts, in the other those immaterial substances which turn the heavens." Man, from another viewpoint of the time, is but the microcosm reflecting the order of the macrocosm of the universe in general.

4. Pessimism and Doubt

The Renaissance conflict that Spencer (1949) describes grew out of two currents, both of which contradicted the prevailing optimistic assessment of man's situation. The first was based on a belief that there was then so much sin that the hierarchies were all out of order; that, as a result, increasing conflict was developing and that Judgment Day was close at hand. Godfrey Goodman [1583–1656] (quoted in Spencer, 1949, pp. 26–27) mourned in 1616, "When I consider the diseases of these times, together with all the signs, tokens and symptoms: alas, alas, I fear a relapse, I fear a relapse." He believed that the elements were engaged in civil war, the faculties of man "in an uproar." John Calvin [1509–1564] (quoted in Torrance, 1957, pp. 108, 111), for example, who was not untypical of contemporary thinking, viewed the individual human as "misframed by nature.... Perverse passions rule within which lead us to rebellion ... and our will is carried away by a sort of insane impulse to resist God."

The second source of conflict was doubt, doubt about the entire scheme whereby, in spite of original sin, God's grace might move men into the realm of the angels. The doubts were of two varieties. One type reflected the impact of the growth of both intellectual and geographical discovery to the detriment of traditional views—the first uneasy glimmerings of Copernican ideas, on one level, and, on another level, excitement following in the wake of Henry the Navigator and Christopher Columbus. In the seventeenth century men used science to build upon these doubts a series of new beliefs.

Doubt of another but similar kind grew out of skepticism about the traditional hierarchies and especially man's place in them. Thomas More [1478–1535], the English humanist, in his *Utopia* manifested one type of questioning of the hierarchies. Instead of upholding the social order, he used the words meaning noble and gentle in an ironic, even pejorative way. He saw the stable social order as "a kind of conspiracy of the rich aiming at their own interests under the name of commonwealth" (Hexter, 1964, pp. 961–964). The prince of the underminers of the Thomistic scheme, however, was Montaigne. He attacked almost all of the conventional beliefs of his day with avowed skepticism: "Before the principles which Aristotle introduced were in repute, other principles satisfied human reason, as his satisfy us at the moment. What letters-patent, what special privilege have these, that the course of our discoveries should stop at them, and that they should for all time to come possess our belief? They are no more exempt from being thrust out of doors than their predecessors" (Montaigne, 1927, II, p. 15). Montaigne emphasized the evil in human nature, and he made a devastating comparison between beasts and human beings to the disadvantage of the latter. The great essayist (Montaigne, 1927, I, p. 441) pictured man as proud and at the same time slave to his most ignoble passions. "Is it possible to imagine anything more ridiculous than that this miserable and puny creature, who is not . . . master of himself, exposed to shocks on all sides, should call himself Master and Emperor of the universe, of which it is not in his power to know the smallest part, much less to command it?" (See Spencer, 1949, pp. 32–40.)

Montaigne was not just repeating the usual indictment of man's evil nature and unworthiness; he was suggesting that man as he is has little celestial about him. Another influential thinker who saw man without reference to traditional hierarchies and notably, in this case, outside any moral order, was Machiavelli [1469–1527]. A worthy precursor of Hobbes, as Hexter (1964) has shown, Machiavelli turned right and wrong, virtue, the commonwealth, all into terms subordinate to a prince's getting what he wants (rather than what he should according to traditional standards). Social activity, according to Machiavelli (quoted in Becker and Barnes, 1961, I, p. 303), is motivated by the insatiability of human desires: ". . . as human desires are insatiable (because their nature is to have and to do everything whilst fortune limits their possessions and capacity of enjoyment), this gives rise to a constant discontent in the human mind and a weariness of the things they possess; and it is this which makes them decry the present, praise the past, and desire the future." In practice, Machiavelli's conception of the will was not unlike that of Augustinian theologians: it is ruled by evil and animal impulses rather than, as most men of the time optimistically supposed, acting as the instrument of reason and virtue (H. C. Baker, 1947, p. 290). Machiavelli accepted without elaboration this conception of man; the theologians, of course, implicitly could not.

5. The Individualizing of Self

By the end of the sixteenth century, many educated people were beginning to assert openly that man is willful, even rebellious against God's order. The idea of man's willfulness developed in two directions. First, the will was considered to be evil and to reflect man's basically corrupt nature, which he should not pretend is angelic. (This general view of human nature was reflected in the satirical literature of the period making fun of men's weaknesses.)[6] The second aspect of willfulness was an increasing recognition that was being given to the interest—if not the worth and virtue—inhering in the individual human who willed. (Such

[6] John Marston [1575–1634] (1856), in his "Scourge of Villanie," gives a good example:

> Seest thou yon gallant in the sumptuous clothes,
> How brisk, how spruce, how gorgeously he shows?
> Note his French herring-bones: but no more,
> Unless thou spy his faire appendant whore. . . .
> Is this a man? Nay, an incarnate devill,
> That struts in vice and glorieth in evill.

an attitude, as Iago shows, had not long before been considered sinful [Spencer, 1949, p. 135].) In the sixteenth century the characters in drama tended to get away from the types of the morality plays, such as Gluttony; instead, writers created complex, emphatically individual characters such as Hamlet (Spencer, 1949, p. 69). On a philosophical level, a cult of neo-Stoicism flourished, emphasizing self-realization (H. C. Baker, 1947, p. 301). In Machiavelli's *Prince* self-realization was carried to the extreme of self-aggrandizement. Evidence of the growing importance of the individual appeared even in the language itself; in English the very words that begin with "self" and a hyphen began to come into use: "self-conceit, self-liking, self-love" (Barfield, 1954, p. 165). The stage was set for a study of the individual that began not with the universe or God or society but with the individual man. The agent of this *Zeitgeist* was the great thinker, René Descartes [1596–1650], who began his philosophy with the thinking of one single person, namely, himself.

6. Descartes

The epistemology and much else in the philosophy of Descartes are not directly relevant to his views of human nature. Philosophy changed profoundly after Descartes, who tried to dispense with all authority except his own thought processes. But his psychological ideas contained very little that could be characterized as radical.

Descartes believed in innate ideas, that is, that in the mind there are certain ideas, such as pure perfection, that do not depend upon sensation and that cannot be learned. Experience calls up these ideas, but no image derived from the senses can be the same as the corresponding idea as it preexists in the mind (Peters, 1953, pp. 355–357). Descartes, in other words, advocated a thoroughgoing mind-body dualism that was widely adopted and copied as a consequence of his work.

The most startling aspect of Descartes' dualism was his contention that the body is a mere machine. He wrote after Harvey had demonstrated the mechanics of the circulation of the blood, and Descartes had seen the mechanical statues that were built for amusement at the time (Peters, 1953, p. 349; his idea was of course not without precedent; see Rosenfield, 1941, ch. 1). While the world overlooked the erroneous specific details of his description of the machinery of the body, it remembered his general idea. Mind Descartes limited to thought (intellect) and will, which are independent of the brain. Other mental processes, including sensation and motor impulses, he described in terms of the movement of the animal spirits. The human body is, he said, as much subject to the mechanistic laws regulating the universe as is an animal or a material substance. Although remembered for his dualism, Descartes was also an interactionist. He believed that the soul-mind, lacking the quality of extension, is located in a single point, the pineal gland. There the animal spirits affect the soul-mind and in turn are affected by it. The will Descartes believed to be absolutely free, and the object of life, therefore, is not unlike that suggested by Aristotle: to free the will from the obfuscating influence of the animal spirits and to bring the passions, feelings, and emotions under the influence of reason.

Descartes' descriptions of the mechanics of emotion and feelings are very complicated and not entirely consistent. Of central interest is the place he made for the development of patterns of reactions. Early in life, he contended, certain characteristic motions become associated with certain feelings and emotions by means of repetition; once the animal spirits move a given way, repetition of the movement is facilitated. Thus, there is a material basis for individual temperaments ("natural inclinations, various temperaments and characters, desires, habits, and inborn dispositions"), which can be formed without the intellect or will (Gardiner, Metcalf, and Beebe-Center, 1937, p. 157). Included in individual temperament also, however, is the characteristic reaction of the free will—but again operating through the animal spirits.

Descartes, then, in spite of his disdain of empiricism represents an attempt to describe and account for personality in terms that, insofar as they were mechanistic, were also therefore essentially scientific. (See in general Wilm, 1925, ch. 7; Gardiner, Metcalf, and Beebe-Center, 1937, ch. 6; and Peters, 1953, pp. 355–360.) In spite of his making a place for a mind-soul, Descartes was contributing substantially to the naturalistic view of man.

PART IV. THE ENLIGHTENMENT

1. The Rise of Neurophysiology

In the Enlightenment period both science and philosophy contributed to establishing a naturalistic view of man's nature. Unlike other areas of science, medicine and especially physiology can be differentiated from philosophy early in the period, and this physiological medicine provided one set of explanations for men's feelings and actions. Beginning with Thomas Willis [1621–1675] there has been an unbroken line of attempts to relate physiological mechanisms and events to behavior and personality. Although at first influenced by the thought of Descartes and others, by the nineteenth century physiological explanations tended to ignore all major contemporary philosophy and to evolve within a relatively isolated scientific milieu.

Willis (1684), one of the founders of the Royal Society, was a physician who, like Descartes, envisaged a fully mechanical explanation for thinking and feeling in terms of mechanical action of the animal spirits in the nervous system. Although Willis still included the humors, which he said affect and are affected by the action of the animal spirits, he spoke, like the ancients, of passions and instincts that have their origin in the praecordia and viscera. The purpose of the instincts, Willis explained, is to indicate what would serve for self-preservation. Like others at the time, Willis located reason in the brain. A man's reason, he said, can control his corporeal (brute) soul only part of the time, and the two are often in conflict. Willis's attention to motivation and feeling is of great interest in itself, but he was most remarkable because of the consistently physiological basis of his mechanism. He refused to discuss the spiritual soul and argued, for example, against Descartes' idea of the pineal gland as the body-soul connection, because both animals and men have such glands. (Willis's ideas are significant insofar as they show the extent to which naturalistic thinking could go in his time. His originality was largely lost on his contemporaries because he failed to make corresponding innovations in therapy; see Veith, 1965, p. 135.)

2. The End of the Idea of Animal Spirits

Throughout the seventeenth and eighteenth centuries the nature of the animal spirits became more and more vague in physiological thinking (Keele, 1957, p. 87). Finally the English medical authority, Robert Whytt [1714–1766] (1763, pp. iv–viii, 1–11), declined to discuss how the subtle fluid that he imagined pervades the nervous system might work unless, he hypothesized, it perhaps acts merely to convey what we would now call a nervous impulse. Whytt also contributed two other elements to the development of modern neurophysiology: the idea that each nerve is separate from all other nerves, from its origin to its terminus, and a rudimentary conception of the sympathetic nervous system (Keele, 1957, pp. 94–95). The significance of these contributions for views of human nature was not appreciated at the time, however.

Contemporaneous with Whytt was Albrecht von Haller [1708–1777], who by means of animal experiments showed that only nerves manifest the quality of sensitivity and that only muscle tissue shows irritability (or contractility) (Temkin, 1936; see also below). But it was only after the Enlightenment that the discovery of the difference between sensory and motor nerves permitted the postulation of a purely mechanistic nervous system. The philosophers of the Enlightenment had no need of such reductionism to develop naturalistic views of human nature.

3. The End of the Humoral Doctrine

Having brought the animal spirits under the purview of science, it only remained for Enlightenment writers to investigate the humors and put them into scientific terms. After Willis's bypassing of the humoral doctrine and the resulting temperaments—which is what he essentially did—a number of writers explored modifications of the traditional humoral explanation of temperaments and even modifications of the traditional scheme of the temperaments. This activity lasted well into the nineteenth century but was essentially Enlightenment in spirit and conception.

Von Haller used the traditional four temperaments but related them to general bodily conditions of irritability and contractility. François Joseph Victor Broussais [1772–1838], a French physician working upon contemporaneous physiological ideas, devised six temperaments, primarily upon the basis of which physiological system predominated in a man. The temperaments that he suggested were the gastric, bilious, sanguineous, lymphatico-sanguineous, anemic, and nervous.

Cabanis, followed by Richerand (on Cabanis and Richerand see below), attempted to combine three principal systems of temperament that had developed by their time: that based on humors, that based on a mechanical physiology such as von Haller's, and that based upon physiological function. Cabanis ended up with six types of temperament, four of them the usual sanguine, melancholic, choleric, and phlegmatic, each one caused by a different set of physiological influences: "the tone of the solids ... the quantity and quality of the several healthy fluids ... [and] their relative proportion ... the size and power of the lungs, heart, liver, &c.; and ... the sympathetic communication subsisting between all these parts. His fifth and sixth temperaments are the muscular and the nervous, which he said result from the reciprocal predominancy of these two systems, the one above the other" (Blatchford, 1848, pp. 55–56).

These attempts of physiological writers to maintain humoral dispositions were almost entirely speculative, or at best only crudely empirical. The nervous temperament had a long life in literature and psychiatry (see below), but humoral dispositions were superseded and overshadowed by an enormously popular and influential movement in the nineteenth century, phrenology, and, except for a physiological vogue in literature (see below), served for the most part only as ghostly precursors of the glandular determinants of personality discovered in the twentieth century. The lively interest of Enlightenment thinkers in conceptions of human nature grew out of considerations far removed from physiology.

4. Interest in Human Nature

During the seventeenth century the quantity and intensity of interest in the nature of man grew, reaching a sustained high level in the eighteenth century. In Elizabethan times the question, while interesting, was more or less tangential, but beginning with Hobbes, who was contemporary with Descartes, the question of human nature became explicitly a central issue in Western thought. In England, at least, this interest grew out of a shift of social power and the manner of exercising it which, along with economic, religious, and scientific changes, demanded new formulations of old problems. In contrast to the ancient Greek view that the conception of an ideal society should give rise to a national character, in England questions of both public and private virtue were seen to hinge upon conceptions of human nature. Attention to them, therefore, grew with the diffusion of social responsibility and changing intellectual climate. (See Rich, 1935, pp. 5–8.)

In England in the seventeenth century in literature Theophrastian character writing gave way to a remarkable flowering of the art of characterization. Most memorable were the changes in historical writing, often on the model of Plutarch and Tacitus, that gave an occasion to Edward Hyde, Earl of Clarendon [1609–1674], and others to emphasize the individuality of men, as opposed to Theophrastian general types. On the continent, where politics was not as influential as the new science in stimulating interest in characterization, the French took the lead in character depiction in the memoir. The memoir was designed to present not the true and objective world but events and persons as they were seen through the eyes of the writer, that is, subjectively. All over Europe writers produced a huge volume of memoirs before they were superseded by the biography and novel in the eighteenth century (Smith, 1920, pp. ix–xxx). The latter two implicitly involve the development of character, an idea that Rousseau, for example, was to take up later. The earlier characterizations had simply called attention to the particular qualities that distinguish an individual.

As Enlightenment thinking developed, along with improved physiological work came a freedom from physiology. Writers showed a remarkable boldness in treating psychology by itself in a system of cause and effect that gradually became more and more irrelevant to the particles, spirits, and humors that had spawned it. (See Foucault, 1965, pp. 119 ff., 129–130.)

5. Hobbes

Thomas Hobbes [1588–1679] was the first major thinker about human nature to employ the notion that became widespread in the seventeenth century, that all phenomena are subject to scientific laws (in a more modern sense than the Greeks' similar idea). He accounted for all of man's thought, action, and, incidentally, society in terms of mechanistic materialism. Unlike Descartes, Hobbes described all mental powers in terms of physical motion. Sensations, he said, cause mental images just as a blow on the head might make one "see stars." Mental processes, specifically passions and the will, that have their origins inside the body grow out of the motions of the vital spirits. Man, in Hobbes's eyes, therefore, is a helpless animal responding automatically to internal and external stimuli.

Two details of Hobbes's scheme are of special interest. The first is why the will chooses one course of action over another. Hobbes described the human animal as hedonistic—seeking pleasure (i.e., motivated by appetites) and avoiding pain (motivated by aversions). In any given situation the particular combination of appetites and aversions called up by that situation determines absolutely how the will will act. Up to this point Hobbes sounds not unlike Aristotle.

The nature of pleasure and pain, Hobbes continued, is determined by what is beneficial to the organism. Good and evil, he said, are words used to describe individual aspirations; what is good for one man may be evil (i.e., undesirable) for the next. In general, life is a war, man against man, or a race in which the object is to get ahead and stay ahead of one's fellow man. Men fear and avoid punishment, said Hobbes, but otherwise they get as much power as possible for purposes of hedonistic gratification. In addition to "nutritive, generative, and motive" gratifications, Hobbes (1839–1845, IV, pp. 37–38) mentioned intellectual pleasures. Beyond those, he continued, a man's power consists of such things as "riches, place of authority, friendship or favour, and good fortune." All of this power is to the end of self-aggrandizement at the expense of others (those preoccupied with sensual pleasures would of course be exceptions here). Hobbes's (1839–1845, III, pp. 153–154) whole scheme was aimed at justifying the necessity of a strong state to control with terror "our natural passions, that carry us to partiality, pride, revenge, and the like." Indeed, according to Hobbes, without the state men would naturally rob each other and gain thereby not only spoils but honor. (See in general Hobbes, 1839–1845, especially IV, pp. 1–76; III, pp. 38–70, 110–116; Wilm, 1925, pp. 87–88; Gardiner, Metcalf, and Beebe-Center, 1937, pp. 183–192.)

A second point of interest in Hobbes is his attention to individual differences. He noted the subjective nature not only of good and bad but necessarily therefore of the appetites and aversions. Men differ, said Hobbes (1839–1845, IV, pp. 54–55), in two ways. First of all, their physical constitutions—the vital spirits—that are inherited differ. Some men, consequently, have more wit than others; similarly, some are dull and sensual, others vainglorious and imaginative (all of this physically determined). The second way that men differ is in experience. After all, said Hobbes (1839–1845, III, p. 40), what men desire and avoid must be known to them, and specific appetites and aversions must therefore reflect the experiences of the individual (except for the desire to try a new experience).

Hobbes presents a key to Enlightenment views of human nature. From him run two lines of development in thinking about the causes of human action: sensationalism and environmentalism, on the one hand, and, on the other hand, notions of the subtle self-serving tendencies of men that were basic in the thinking of the late seventeenth and eighteenth centuries.

6. Sensationalism

One of Hobbes's ideas was that repetition of specific movements of the vital spirits tends to imprint such patterns of movements, either individually or in groups. On a psychological level this line of thinking led to John Locke's [1632–1704] emphasis on the association of ideas, later developed by Hartley and Mill. Locke (see 1961 edition) wrote explicitly to combat the notion that there are pre-existing in the mind innate ideas, or, more accurately, innate principles. He pictured the mind as endowed with the ability to think (reflect) and to will, but all specific knowledge and ideas, both simple and complex, he argued, derive ultimately from sense impressions. What impels the will to choose one alternative or another, Locke said, is a hedonism very similar to that described by Hobbes (see Hudson, 1911, pp. 24–25). Unlike Descartes and Hobbes, Locke kept his description on the psychological level, saying that he did not know how the mind and body were related. (See in general Hudson, 1911, ch. 2 and especially pp. 18–19.)

Locke's work was carried one step further by Étienne Bonnot de Condillac [1714–1780], who showed that a thoroughgoing sensationalist did not need to assume even the faculty of reflection as long as he assumed that each sensation was accompanied by a feeling tone of pleasure or displeasure. Even instincts Condillac (1930, pp. 233–235) believed to be merely habits built up by repetition: ". . . *natural impulses, mechanical actions, instincts,* . . . we falsely suppose to have been born in us. We shall avoid this error, if we judge these habits by others which have arisen naturally and the acquisition of which we very distinctly remember" (see Schaupp, 1926, pp. 34, 41, 91–92, 99). This developmental approach to personality led Condillac to assert that one's entire temperament is acquired. Bizarre aspects of an individual's character Condillac referred in part to very early life when a person's first associations are formed (Schaupp, 1926, p. 42). Condillac believed, however, that man is not entirely a helpless creature at the mercy of the emotions and impulses that grow out of the fundamental moving power of pain and pleasure. On the contrary, he held that because of his intelligence (physical endowment), a person can learn through experience "to control his desires, direct his movements, hold the balance. . . ." Such autonomy animals, for example, cannot possess (Condillac, 1930, p. 250; Schaupp, 1926, pp. 91, 98–99).

In this line of development that began with Descartes, the final step, represented most notoriously by the French physician, Julien Offray de LaMettrie [1709–1751], was asserting, without any of Hobbes's reservations about a soul, that man is indeed entirely material and his actions purely mechanical (Rosenfield, 1941). LaMettrie's work is particularly important because so many naturalistic trends converged in it (although he was, for instance, unaware of Hobbes's work). In addition to Cartesian mechanism, freethought of the time and the doctrines of the iatrophysical school of medicine clearly contributed to LaMettrie's thinking. Building upon the doctrine of irritability, LaMettrie asserted that there is in the body a natural force sufficient to account for all life phenomena, including thinking. He viewed the body as a self-contained, self-regulating unit. A sophisticated precursor of twentieth century behaviorism, LaMettrie was father to the ideologues (see below) and a whole school of deterministic physiologists (based on Vartanian, 1960).

Such materialistic philosophers as LaMettrie simply eliminated the soul, leaving only a psychological or physiological mind that operates entirely according to natural law. They were trying to carry Newton's description of the natural laws of the physical universe over to man, but it was another century before physiology developed sufficiently to permit a relatively undoctrinaire, physicalistic conception of mental functioning.

7. The Direction of Enlightenment Thinking About Human Nature

The increasing acceptance of sensationalism during the late seventeenth and eighteenth centuries was evidence of another facet of the development of naturalism. That is, men came more and more to trust and accept their senses and, therefore, the importance of the world around them. They not only accepted nature but took great interest in it. Enlightenment thinkers therefore tended more than their predecessors to look to man's natural environment for the forces shaping his personality. Not only did the *philosophes* frequently follow Locke and Condillac in emphasizing man's potential to change, presumably, of course, for the good, but they often found in man's environment the forces making for his transformation. There was, in short, a strong stream of environmentalism in Enlightenment thought. In the hands of late Enlightenment psychiatrists, for example, this environmentalism represented a version of von Haller's physiological doctrine of irritability: defective social institutions (such as crowded cities) lead to an excess of irritation, which in turn produces strong psychological effects, including mental illness (Foucault, 1965, pp. 157–158). In the hands of Jean Jacques Rousseau [1712–1778] the capacity for perfectibility in eighteenth century environmentalism represented an aspect of early romanticism.

It is commonplace to observe that the Enlightenment was a time of contrasts, an observation particularly true of the *philosophes'* opinions of man. They took keen interest in the individual person and his inner workings, as indicated in literary character writing and the modern novel with its individualized heros and heroines.[7] Further changes in language show the thinking that was going on. The internal feelings of people became especially subject to discussion, with the introduction of more "self" words (self-confidence, self-knowledge, self-pity) and the shift in meanings of a number of words that had been objective and were now transferred to the realm of inner feelings: agitation, disappointment, excite-

[7] Insofar as interest in the individual coexisted with environmentalism, Enlightenment thinking presented a marked contrast to the environmentalism of later behaviorism in which there was little room for a self concept.

ment. At the time when many men were toying with environmentalism, the English language added a large number of a class of words that describe things not in terms of themselves but in terms of the effects that they produce upon people: affecting, amusing, boring, charming, diverting, entrancing, fascinating, interesting, pathetic (Barfield, 1954, pp. 165, 169–170).

8. The Potential of Reason

The main contrast arising from this new interest in the individual man or woman lay in the fundamental question of whether a man is basically good or evil. One current of opinion is described by Becker (1932, especially pp. 63–65) in his classic essay on *The Heavenly City of the Eighteenth-Century Philosophers*. Becker starts with the idea that the belief in the universal application of natural law that became widespread after Newton's work led to an attempt to integrate human behavior into a naturalistic world view. Locke had repudiated not only innate ideas but in effect the earlier ideas of man's depravity, and the task of man became therefore to get himself into harmony with the world order of natural law: "This was Locke's great title to glory, that he made it possible for the eighteenth century to believe with a clear conscience what it wanted to believe, namely, that since man and the mind of man were shaped by that nature which God had created, it was possible for men, 'barely by the use of their natural faculties,' to bring their ideas and their conduct, and hence the institutions by which they lived, into harmony with the universal natural order. With what simple faith the age of enlightenment welcomed this doctrine! With what sublime courage it embraced the offered opportunity to refashion the outward world of human institutions according to the laws of nature and of nature's God!" If the mind is indeed free of built-in contents, it is also free of built-in limitations, and that age had hopes of man's not only bringing himself into harmony with nature but in effect reaching some sort of heaven on earth.

The disconcerting problem here was that of determining what is natural, for anything natural must be good. Somehow evil in the world—and specifically in man—had to be accounted for. By inspection of society and its history the *philosophes* found that certain human institutions and customs go contrary to natural law (such as those violating "natural rights"); under such circumstances undesirable human actions are inevitable. Man, then, is only potentially good or perhaps, in the eyes of these thinkers, he is the neutral *tabula rasa* of sensationalism. The most important belief of such writers was that man's reason is a powerful and effective instrument for changing both the individual and the world. Such a view is not incompatible with the idea that there is much room for improvement.

9. The Efficacy of Evil Passions

Contemporaneous with this essentially sensationalistic optimism was, as Lovejoy (1961) has shown, another current of opinion, to the effect that man is governed not by his reason but by his passions. Like Hobbes, Enlightenment men typically saw man as evil and self-serving, not as the master of himself and the world through the use of reason. Reason is the chart by which we sail the ocean of life, wrote Alexander Pope [1688–1744] (1913, II, line 108), "but Passion is the gale. . . ." One of the themes of literature of the day was the degraded nature of man. Robert Gould (1708, quoted in Lovejoy, 1961, p. 17) wrote bitterly:

> What beast beside can we so slavish call
> As *Man?* Who yet pretends he's lord of all.
> Whoever saw (and all their classes cull)
> A dog so snarlish, or a swine so full,
> A wolf so rav'nous, or an ass so dull?
> Slave to his passions, ev'ry several lust
> Whisks him about, as whirlwinds do the dust;
> And dust he is, indeed, a senseless clod

That swells, and yet would be believ'd
a God.

Many men of that time believed that reason is but the tool of the passions, serving to deceive man into thinking that his motives are rational. (As Lovejoy, 1961, p. 25, points out, it was Enlightenment writers, not the Freudians, who discovered "hidden motives.")

One of the distinguishing features of literature in the late seventeenth and early eighteenth century was the fact that satire flourished. There had been some notable satire in the sixteenth century, but one needs only mention Molière [1622–1673] and the Restoration in the seventeenth century and Swift [1667–1745] and Voltaire [1694–1778] in the eighteenth century to suggest the quality and quantity of the wit of this later period devoted to exposing the foibles and weaknesses of mankind. Blackening the character of man and then ridiculing it enjoyed a popularity that testifies to the power of the belief of the age that man is indeed ruled primarily by evil passions (Lovejoy, 1961, pp. 18–21).

10. Revulsion from Pessimism

By the mid-eighteenth century, satire was no longer so much in vogue. Boileau [1636–1711], Grimm noted in 1755, was because of this change little read (C. L. Becker, 1932, p. 84). The main difficulty with stressing the weaknesses of humanity, Vauvenargues [1715–1747] (quoted in Lovejoy, 1961, pp. 20–21) pointed out at the time, is that it "does not tend to improve human nature but to deprave it." Even the *philosophes* most convinced of the weaknesses of mankind were devoted to trying to counteract them. It was a time of projects to improve the world, practical schemes to establish an earthly paradise, and, as Addison [1672–1719] (quoted in Lovejoy, 1961, p. 19) observed, while satire might have some moral value, such devastating satires as he was seeing "are of no use to the world. . . ." In the place of satire came sentiment. Pity for the evil in man and determination to do away with his corruption replaced irritation and scorn (C. L. Becker, 1932, pp. 39–43).

Questions not only of nature and Newtonianism underlay the Enlightenment views of man: political questions, as earlier, were omnipresent. Hobbes, for example, wrote in part under the inspiration of the English Civil War. In contrast to ancient Athens, eighteenth century political man was almost by definition evil in nature, and it was political man whom the writers of the Enlightenment centuries found especially susceptible to satire. Voltaire was no doubt thinking of politics when he described the history of great events as scarcely more than the history of crimes. Yet the men of the age, we have noted, were determined to improve society, including politics. As Lovejoy (1961) has shown, their solution was not only to admit the frailties of man but to use them to the advantage of society.

11. Turning Evil into Good

Hobbes provides the clearest example of the Enlightenment solution. He believed that in a model society a system of countervailing forces could be set up so that each man for his own selfish reasons would contribute to social stability and the commonweal. Over a century later Adam Smith [1723–1790] suggested that natural law in the field of economics was so ingeniously contrived by the Author of the Universe that each man's acting in his own interest in the end benefits society as a whole. One of the most famous tracts of the times was Bernard Mandeville's [1670–1733] *The Fable of the Bees,* written in 1714, in which he (Mandeville, 1924, I, p. 369) believed that he had "demonstrated that, neither the Friendly Qualities and kind Affections that are natural to Man, nor the real Virtues he is capable of acquiring by Reason and Self-Denial, are the Foundation of Society; but that what we call Evil in the World, Moral as well as Natural, is the grand Principle that makes us sociable Creatures, the solid Basis, the Life and Support of all Trades and Employments without Exception: That there we must look for the true Origin of all Arts and Sciences, and that the Moment Evil ceases, the Society must be spoiled, if not totally dissolved."

Not the least eminent of the *philosophes* who suggested that by skillful mixing and counterbalancing of men's separate impulses a social system could be devised that "counter-works each folly and caprice," as Pope (1913, II, line 239) put it, were the authors of the American system of checks and balances (Lovejoy, 1961, ch. 2). The *Federalist Papers* are expositions of Pope's (1913, II, lines 247–248) belief that it is proper to

> . . . build on wants, and on defects of mind,
> The joy, the peace, the glory of mankind.

Men of an earlier era had seen in human failures tokens of eternal damnation and the end of the world; the Enlightenment saw in man's evil proclivities a key to blissful existence on earth.

12. Emphasis Upon the Spiritual Passions

Enlightenment thinkers saw the passions of mankind as of two varieties: the passions of the flesh, long traditional, and the passions of the spirit. What is distinctive about this period is the stress that its thinkers put upon the spiritual passions. The discussions centered around a passion peculiar to man, namely, pride (Lovejoy, 1961, especially ch. 4). "It came to be a widely accepted premise that all men are incapable of being actuated by any other motive in their social conduct, that the craving for admiration or applause is not only universal in the human species but also that it was ingeniously implanted in man by his Creator as a substitute for the Reason and Virtue which he does not possess, and is the sole subjective prompting of good conduct, and the motive of virtually all the modes of behavior necessary for the good order of society and the progress of mankind" (Lovejoy, 1961, p. 157).

In an earlier day man's distinctive pride was understood to be his rebelliousness against God. Enlightenment men, however, meant, by pride, desire for esteem, love of fame, the "passion of glory." Closely related and usually included were the desire for self-esteem and for a feeling of superior social rank, or distinction of some kind. (See Lovejoy, 1961, ch. 4.)[8] What made the greatest contrast between the seventeenth and eighteenth century view of pride and that of earlier centuries was the Enlightenment belief that love of reputation has—or can have—desirable social consequences. Christian Wolff [1679–1754] (quoted in Lovejoy, 1961, p. 167), the German philosopher, asserted that "Nothing pre-eminently great has ever been done in the world which did not flow from glory as its source. . . ." As Adam Smith (quoted in Lovejoy, 1961, p. 191) drew the lesson, "The great secret of education is to direct vanity to proper objects."

13. Hume

David Hume [1711–1776] provides a sophisticated version of this complex of Enlightenment beliefs and assumptions. He is of particular interest not because he differed from Mandeville or Smith or the founding fathers who believed that men's evil and selfish passions should be used to effect social virtue but because he worked the idea

---

[8] There was divided opinion as to whether men are conscious or unconscious of these motives. Edward Young [1683–1765] (*Love of Fame the Universal Passion,* 1726–1728, quoted in Lovejoy, 1961, pp. 138–139) spoke of

> The *Love of Praise,* howe'er conceal'd by art,
> Reigns, more or less, and glows in ev'ry heart. . . .

Malebranche [1638–1715] (1674, quoted in Lovejoy, 1961, p. 133) recognized that "vanity . . . is so natural to man that he is not sensible of it; and though it is this that gives . . . life and movement to most of his thoughts and designs, it often does so in a manner which to him is imperceptible."

out both in its social versions and in a detailed individual psychology.

In the tradition of naturalism, Hume attempted to establish morals on an empirical basis so that they could not be overturned by a sudden shift in *a priori* philosophical fashions. Explicitly following Newton, Hume attempted to gather evidence—for conclusions that were always tentative, pending the accumulation of more facts—about the nature of human nature (see Ross, 1942, and Hume, 1896). He argued that custom—at least on a statistical basis—provides substantial evidence of what is "natural," even though very complex social behavior might be involved. "Nature," Hume (1896, I, p. 179) said, "may certainly produce whatever can arise from habit;" as noted above he believed that habit has both a natural basis and natural force. The conclusion followed, therefore, that customary morals are "natural."

Hume's individual psychology is quite similar to Hobbes's except that Hume, save for passing references (e.g., Hume, 1896, II, p. 424) to the animal spirits and the common assumption that passions have a somatic basis, maintained as Locke did a psychological level of description without Hobbes's materialistic explanations. Men are motivated, according to Hume (1896, II, pp. 438–439), by their passions, which is merely a specific way of saying that they seek pleasure and avoid pain. He denied the traditional view that reason opposes passion: "Reason is, and ought only to be the slave of the passions" (Hume, 1896, II, p. 415). All actions, he asserted, are motivated by passions, and when two or more passions are influential, the stronger will prevail and, indeed, absorb and transform the weaker.[9]

It is in the working out of how passions can result in civilized behavior that Hume was so typical of his age. In the process of socialization, Hume contended, the human being develops learned secondary instincts, often formed by transformation of the weaker passions. These socially conditioned passions are precisely the pride and associated aspects of self-esteem with which we are familiar. Hume also believed that man has "a fellow-feeling" for other humans that aids his establishing social institutions through which men cooperate with each other (Ross, 1942, p. 32; Bryson, 1945, pp. 156–159; Adam Smith worked out a more famous version of these feelings of sympathy for other humans). In such a context Hume, like others of his age, found in individual selfish motives the origins of all social virtues. Self-love, for example, gives rise to justice, and greed to honesty, because men judge that in the long run practicing such virtues will bring them more gratification than a more direct expression of their passions. Human nature is neither good nor bad, men are merely either wise or foolish, said Hume (1896, III, pp. 487–492): "For whether the passion of self-interest be esteemed vicious or virtuous, 'tis all a case; since itself alone restrains it: So that if it be virtuous, men become social by their virtue; if vicious, their vice has the same effect."

14. Primitivism

Still one final current in the development of naturalism has to be taken up, namely, the primitivism that had its origins in the Enlightenment and its full development in the romantic movement. The origin of this current of primitivism lay in the desire of many thinkers to discover a true picture of nature not only in the world around them but in the human being himself. Hume represented one facet of this desire in his study of humans and their institutions as he could observe them. Primitivism, how-

[9] Hume assigned to reason the role of judging what actions are appropriate to maximize the amount of gratification. This hedonistic calculation can of course make mediating judgments very important in determining a man's actions, even though the reasoning is in the service of a passion. Habitual character and momentary disposition both affect the struggle for dominance among the passions and the role reason plays in their expression. (See especially Kydd, 1946, chs. 3–5.)

ever, developed out of a belief that the civilized, adult man represents much that is artificial, that is, unnatural, and therefore bad, and but little that is natural, and therefore good. The major problem of these thinkers was to find people in a natural state so that a human being could be observed whose true nature had not been distorted by acquired habits, secondary social instincts, and other marks of civilization.

One possibility was to find a human being who had grown up without any human environment, and indeed the eighteenth century took particular notice of "feral children" who were supposed to have been reared in a naive and wild state. Buffon [1707–1788] (quoted in Greene, 1961, p. 204), the great naturalist, speculated in 1749: "An absolute savage, such as the boy educated among the bears, as mentioned by Conor, the young man in the forests of Hanover, or the little girl in the woods of France, would be a spectacle full of curiosity to a philosopher: in observing this savage he might be able precisely to ascertain the force of the appetites of nature; he might see the soul undisguised, and distinguish all its natural movements. And who knows whether he might not discover in it more mildness, more serenity and peace than in his own; whether he might not perceive, that virtue belongs more to the savage than to the civilized man, and that vice owes its birth to society."

Since most feral children turned out to be frauds, a more promising approach was to look for men who lived in "a state of nature," that is, uncorrupted by traditional social institutions. From ancient times existed the tradition of a Golden Age of man, sometime in the distant past, from which man's condition had degenerated. In Christian times the Golden Age was identified with the Garden of Eden, and the fall of man was believed to correspond to a primitive social condition in which human society was very much like that of beasts of the field; the violence of it supposedly served as punishment for Adam's descendents. Writers of the social contract school of the Enlightenment continued these views, utilizing a hypothetical or imagined actual state of human society prior to the development of civilization to explain the existence of political institutions. In general such writers showed man to be naturally evil—and thus in need of government as a matter of self-defense—or naturally social and thus able to establish government as a natural fulfillment of human nature. Hobbes is the best known exponent of the first view. Locke represents a variety of the second. Because of their political preoccupations social contract writers did very little to furnish any specific information about man's original nature by means of his condition in an historical "state of nature." (See Barnes, 1923, pp. 33–73.)

15. Empirical Natural Man

With the Age of Exploration and the opening up of the "uncivilized" areas of America, Africa, and the South Pacific, philosophers found men who were actually, if not in a state of nature, at least in another state of civilization. At first the natives of these distant parts of the globe were considered to be crude, cruel savages. Occasionally they appeared in satires to contrast the virtues of the cannibals with the evils of European society, much as Montaigne used beasts and Tacitus used the barbarians (Fairchild, 1928, ch. 1). But man as the explorers saw him in a savage state generally confirmed the assumptions of the observers that man's nature is bestial. The "horrid salvages" surprised no one who knew Hobbes and other writers.

With the approach of romanticism and the glorification of nature, the late Enlightenment and early romantic period writers developed a new concept, the Noble Savage. Compounded from (1) the ancient literary device of showing that the simple, naive, unpretentious peasant or other humble person is morally superior to his social betters; (2) the idea of the aboriginal sage; and (3) the idea of unspoiled natural man, the Noble Savage concept enjoyed considerable vogue. In 1784 Helen Maria Williams [1762–1827] (quoted in Fairchild, 1928, p. 76) in *Peru* pictured the Indian:

> In Ataliba's pure, unsullied mind
> Each mental Grace, each lib'ral Virtue shin'd,
> And all unfultur'd by toils of Art,
> Bloomed the dear genuine offspring of the heart. . . .

As Fairchild (1928) has shown, there was considerable confusion between the natural savage and the wise wilderness sage. Yet all of the exponents of the Noble Savage concept shared a significant common tendency: they related the idea to exactly those social vices that Lovejoy describes as the special objects of Enlightenment writers' attention. Primitive characters in literature gained their admirability and happiness from their freedom from pride, greed, and the associated civilized vices.

16. The Child

There is still one more phenomenon in which human nature might appear in its pure form: childhood. Rousseau (1892) in his *Emile* wrote several striking passages about how civilization changes the growing child from a natural person into a social person. "Compelled to oppose nature or our social institutions," declared Rousseau (1892, p. 5), "we must choose between making a man and a citizen, for we can not make both at once."[10]

Aries (1962) has shown how the idea of childhood changed between medieval and Enlightenment times. In the middle ages the child either simply was not admitted to exist or was seen as an adult; painters, indeed, depicted children merely as adult figures drawn on a small scale. The idea of childhood was largely absent. By the seventeenth century the child had become, "on account of his sweetness, simplicity, and drollery," an appropriate object to be cuddled and to be indulged—the child, in other words, was innocent (Aries, 1962, p. 129). This natural innocence of the child was of much the same order as the natural innocence of the Noble Savage.[11] By the eighteenth century the child had ceased to be an object of amusement and indulgence for adults and was recognized as a person, to be taken seriously. Children were seen to be fragile, needing "to be both safeguarded and reformed." Not only did the child's health become of concern but also the course of his general development and especially the development of his reason. (See Aries, 1962, especially p. 133.)

In Rousseau's work it is possible to explore the Enlightenment view of childhood as it was turning into romanticism. At times Rousseau spoke in terms of radical environmentalism, describing how the child's personality is the product of his environment. At other times he (Rousseau, 1892, e.g., pp. 14–15, 28, 193) formulated a genetic view of childhood: a child evolves naturally from stage to stage, and rather than trying "to control Nature and reform the work of God," the child's natural inclinations should be used to good purpose. Rousseau, in other words, accepted the passions and frailties of human nature as givens, but he believed that man could, by ingenious use of these natural givens in any stage, move toward perfection.

17. The Perfectibility of Man

This idea of the perfectibility of human beings was the hallmark of the late Enlightenment (when reason was often invoked as an effective force to that end) and of the early romantic period. The idea that man is

[10] Rousseau has often been interpreted as exalting the child and the natural man at the expense of the civilized; see on this subject Lovejoy, 1955, ch. 2.

[11] Aries (1962) notes the parallel between the development of what came to be the romanticization of the simple lower classes and the child and how each at the same time gained increasing recognition from society.

malleable did not express naive environmentalism, although there was an irreducible minimum of optimism present compatible with the idea of progress (see Greene, 1961, ch. 7). Jefferson (quoted in Curti, 1953, p. 360), for example, observed, "The brier and bramble can never become the vine and the olive; but their asperities may be softened by culture, and their properties improved to usefulness in the order and economy of the world." Children—and men—even with much evil in their natures, might use the evil to gain perfection. By the late romantic period the optimism and reformism had died out, replaced by a repressive conservatism that still recognized the evil nature of man but despaired of doing more than holding it back from working further evil in society.

PART V. THE EARLY NINETEENTH CENTURY

1. Romanticism

With the growth of romanticism and the partial eclipse of the Enlightenment, naturalism had largely run its course, and the search for the antecedents of a scientific approach to human nature and personality must turn away, for the most part, from the mainstream of philosophical thought. Moral philosophy still remains to be taken up, but it was a side eddy; increasingly during the nineteenth century the nature of science and the growth of specialization in science precluded the unity of philosophy and science and even the relevance of the one to the other (e.g., see Dillenberger, 1960, p. 185).

In the romantics subjectivism, which in the Renaissance had raised naturalistic queries about man's nature, now removed these romantic thinkers from the lineage of scientific investigations of personality. The essence of science is gaining knowledge in order to predict; and it was exactly the unpredictability of man in which romantic writers gloried. To them the Newtonian mechanism of the Enlightenment provided an arid and inadequate basis for the description of man. But in their attempt to be realistic, the romantics in their treatment of man discarded the naturalistic level of explanation. Even madness took on a specially individual character. Indeed, many romantics explicitly denounced attempts to apply science to the analysis of the human being (although, of course, not necessarily to nature). (See Barzun, 1943, especially pp. 77–78, 277; Foucault, 1965, p. 234; Dillenberger, 1960, especially p. 207.) It was a century before the individualism implicit in romanticism bore fruit in the field of personality, and meantime two schools of philosophers associated with the romantic movement, the ideologues and the moral philosophers, powerfully affected Western conceptions of human nature.

2. Ideology[12]

Ideology, the doctrine of the ideologues, was one important romantic philosophy that for a time maintained a connection between philosophy and science. The ideologues followed Condillac in a radical sensationalism and insisted on analyzing all ideas into sensations and habits (which latter are in turn reducible to sensation). Where analysis of empirically observed facts leaves gaps, the ideologues—unlike many of their predecessors—were perfectly content to profess their ignorance in an agnostic way. The chief exponents of the school were Antoine Louis Claude Destutt de Tracy [1754–1836] and the eminent physician, Pierre Jean George Cabanis [1757–1808]. The ideologues flourished in the 1790's and after, until suppressed by Napoleon, but their direct influence was very great well into the nineteenth century. (See especially Boas, 1925, chs. 1 and 2.)

Like LaMettrie, the ideologues were ma-

[12] This term refers to a school of thought, not to the technical meaning given it by Mannheim.

terialists except that they believed that life cannot be reduced to physical and chemical processes but includes a life force; they were, as Temkin (1946b) shows, vitalistic materialists. Unlike Descartes, they tended to reject the idea of a soul as unnecessary; biological principles, they said, can explain thought, instincts, and emotions. The ideologues held the mind to be a function of the body. Destutt de Tracy (quoted in Temkin, 1946a, p. 13) summarized their attitude: "One has but an incomplete knowledge of an animal if one does not know its intellectual faculties. Ideology is a part of zoology, and it is particularly in man that this part is important and deserves to be examined thoroughly." Cabanis (quoted in Temkin, 1946a, p. 14) was responsible for a famous passage in which he suggested that the brain produces thought just as the glands secrete vital juices.

Cabanis represents a departure in psychology from Condillac in that, although otherwise a follower, he attempted to avoid the subjectivism implicit in the sensationalism of Condillac. Cabanis viewed the will as predetermined, that is, perfectly passive, but nevertheless capable both of ascertaining what material actuality is and of generating an ego (surely a symptom of romantic modifications of an Enlightenment idea). When the will is resisted, said Cabanis, as when one's extended hand meets a wall, the mind gains not only the impression of material actuality but a sense of ego, differentiation of the self from external reality. In the hands of Laromiguière [1756–1837] and Maine de Biran [1766–1824] the will became a more and more active entity in this process (and these writers eventually contributed greatly to Schopenhauer's idea of the will; see Boas, 1925, especially pp. 35–44; and Temkin, 1946a, p. 21). In its later philosophical stages ideology represents the separation and specialization of science and philosophy and becomes irrelevant to our subject.

All of the earlier ideologues gave prominent attention to the influence of the body on the mind and especially the importance of temperament and disposition. (Rosen, 1946, p. 334, for example, compares Cabanis's ideas with modern psychosomatic medicine.) Since a number of the physicians most important in the development of French medicine and physiology were ideologues, their influence was profound. The temperaments of Cabanis (see section on temperament above), for example, were utilized consistently by the novelist, Henri Beyle [1783–1842], who also tried to suggest—by ideological analysis—the critical sensation connected with an important dramatic action. Destutt de Tracy's theory of the will likewise appeared in Beyle's works (Boas, 1925, pp. 65–68).

Anthelme Balthasar Richerand [1779–1840], a physician and close follower of Cabanis, gives in his classic book on physiology a good example of how the ideologues believed that physiological influences affect psychology and personality. Although Richerand (1821, p. 21) distinguished between contractility and sensibility, neither he nor his successors for some time had any idea of the difference between motor and sensory nerves or any exact sense of the functioning of the nervous system as it was adduced later. Gall's phrenology Richerand (1821, p. 357) thought based on insufficient observation. He (Richerand, 1821, p. 278) viewed the functioning of the nervous system in large part in terms of adaptation, tending "to the preservation of the Individual, by establishing his relations with the beings that surround him." While giving a large place to internal sensations that cause instinctive behavior, Richerand (1821, pp. 359–360, 528) believed that external sensations, except in savage men, get more attention than the instincts. In addition, "... age, sex, temperament, health, disease, climate, and habit, which modify our physical organization ... [help account for] the diversity of humours, of opinions, of characters, and of genius." Even inherited physical dispositions, Richerand made clear, can be modified or changed altogether by "... education, manner of life, climate, acquired habits."

Temperaments, as visualized by Richerand, are as firmly rooted in the body as those pictured by Galen and are typical of ideology. "We give the name of temperaments," wrote Richerand (1821, p. 518), "to certain physical and moral differences in men, which depend on the various proportions and relations among the parts that make up their organization, as well as upon different degrees in the relative energy of certain organs. There is, besides, in each individual, a mode of existence which distinguishes his temperament from that of any other, to whom, however, he may bear great resemblance. We express by the term *idiosyncrasy,* these individual temperaments, the knowledge of which is of no small importance in the practice of medicine. The predominance of any particular system of organs, modifies the whole economy, impresses striking differences on the results of the organization, and has no less influence on the moral and intellectual, than on the physical faculties." (For Richerand's classification of the temperaments, see above.)

The influence of ideological medicine such as that of Cabanis and Richerand was very great, especially in France. Among the most interesting purveyors of ideology were a number of major French literary figures like Beyle who drew on medical sources for characterization. The problem of literary characterization in France, however, needs separate treatment after a consideration of two other early nineteenth century movements, moral philosophy and phrenology, that, like ideology, have been connected with romanticism and yet had other, independent determinants.

3. Moral Philosophy

One variant of what may be considered partly romantic philosophy was the Scottish common sense philosophy or moral philosophy, which was extremely important, especially in the United States in the first half of the nineteenth century. Unlike the mainstream philosophers, the Scottish school is particularly relevant to the study of personality because of the effort that all members of the school devoted to determining what human nature is. Moreover, the formulations of the Scottish philosophers influenced the way that phrenology and other scientific ideas were subsequently developed and understood.

The Scottish school flourished in the eighteenth century and can be considered to include Hume and Adam Smith as well as Ferguson, Reid, Stewart, and later American followers such as Noah Porter. The Scottish philosophers attempted to refute the mechanism and rationalism of Descartes and Hobbes and to base their opinions upon empirical observation (see the section on Hume, above). Although they were thus in the naturalistic tradition, they emphasized that which is common to mankind and so were marked as part of the Enlightenment. That is, the human nature that they described is the ideal toward which all men tend, in contrast to the way at least some romantics stressed individual variation. This issue of the tendency of variation became important again in the idea of degeneracy (see below).

The emphasis of the Scottish school upon feelings and instincts, however, reveals a close kinship to romanticism, or at least early romanticism. In general the moral philosophers, like Enlightenment figures, saw in the passions and emotions the basis for good; unlike Mandeville and others, however, and more like romantic writers, moral philosophers found in man impulses toward the good and so did not need to envisage a system in which countervailing evil forces balanced each other to produce good. The Scots saw in man impulses of both the selfish and the unselfish variety; their philosophy embodied the assumption that the latter could be effective in determining behavior. (See Bryson, 1945, especially p. 27.)

The two preoccupations of the Scottish school were ethics—the goal of these philosophers—and human nature—the starting point of their systems. In searching in experience for the motives that make men what they are, the Scottish philosophers each recorded a list of inborn propensities observable in human kind, and the propensities included "intuitive, irresistible ... self-evident truths of knowledge and morals.... implanted in our constitution by God" (Olin McKendree Jones, quoted in Bryson, 1945, p. 134). This emphasis upon the moral sense of man, observable for example in the form of conscience, gave the school its name, moral philosophy.[13]

With this common base, still the different moral philosophers each emphasized distinctive elements. Nor did these writers appear original in any way except in their emphases, only some of which they held in common. The faculties and other concepts they employed were taken from others. Adam Ferguson [1723–1816] (1792), for example, used Aristotle's classification of the faculties. Like previous, mostly ancient, thinkers Ferguson believed that man shares basic needs and instincts with the animals but can act on the basis of future expectations and is in general "let loose from the trammels of instinct." Beyond that, Ferguson suggested that man's inclinations are based on self-preservation and social instincts. With Hobbes and Condillac, Ferguson shared the belief that the formation of habits is central in establishing a man's patterns of behavior.

Ferguson (1792, I, pp. 232–233) was distinctive in emphasizing the malleability of the human, as shown in his ability to acquire and lose habits. And Ferguson consequently de-emphasized inborn propensities. True to the Scottish school, he still invoked the special sense that enables all men to distinguish between right and wrong. Ferguson's belief in man's ability to change was not environmentalism as, say, in the case of Condillac, but an explicitly optimistic belief that man, by his willing to exercise his virtues, could develop not only desirable faculties but desirable habits. Man responds not only to his instincts and environment, said Ferguson, but to his inborn moral propensities.

The fact that moral conduct was the conscious goal of the Scottish philosophers meant that their orientation was, in addition to being empirical, at least on one level scientific: they wanted to be able to predict behavior in order to control it (Bryson, 1945, ch. 1, especially pp. 16–17; Wilson Smith, 1956, ch. 2). Needless to say, contemporaries for whom scientific predictability was important could find in an organically based analysis of human nature a more reassuringly "scientific" characterology. Such was precisely the role played by phrenology, which not only included many of the standard human propensities suggested by the moral philosophers but used them so as to emphasize the individuality of each person in a way that harmonized with a similar emphasis of the romantic movement.[14]

4. Physiognomy

The romantic source of phrenology lay in the science of physiognomy. Physiognomy was originated by Johann Kaspar Lavater [1741–1801], a Swiss clergyman and litterateur associated with the romanticists. Lavater (1789, III, pp. 62–74) avowed his independence of the technical medical works on temperament, although he had read enough of such literature to understand parts of it. He explicitly rejected the physiological theories of personality, including those based on the humors and on irritability.

Lavater instead chose to emphasize sense

[13] The alternative description of the moral philosophers as the common sense philosophers derives from an ambiguous reference to their appeal to common sense for vindication of their opinions (for example, that man is a social animal) and their idea that the senses, and especially the moral sense, are common to all men.

[14] Much of the similarity of the propensities adduced by the moral philosophers and the phrenologists at first derived from the use of a common intellectual heritage; later on the influence of moral philosophy on some of Gall's followers was direct.

perception and to declare that "There is no object in nature the properties and powers of which can be manifest to us in any other manner than by such external appearances as affect the senses" (Lavater, 1789, I, pp. 11–12). Lavater concluded, therefore, that the superfices of the human being would reveal the invisibles that lie inside a man: his animal, moral, and intellectual natures. Although superficially empirical, his argument is basically an appeal to analogy—we read the physiognomy, so to speak, of grain to see if it is growing blighted or not—and to common sense and experience: "... evil eyes ... honesty in his looks ... unhealthy countenance ... insidious smile...." (Lavater, 1789, I, p. 27). Lavater's argument is, therefore, essentially literary. The only points at which it becomes at all like science are, first, where he invoked sense perception and, second, where he (Lavater, 1789, I, p. 23) suggested that actions can cause looks: "Anger renders the muscles protuberant; and shall not therefore an angry mind and protuberant muscles be considered as cause and effect?"

Lavater wrote in the belief that men are uniquely individual. No person, he held, will have either the character or countenance of another. This represents a substantial departure from the limited number of temperamental types (although one writer cited by Lavater [1789, III, pp. 69–70] had gotten the number of temperaments up to eight). The door was now open for the use in scientific physiognomy of all of the words possible for characterization: the satiric types of the books of characters and also the more praiseworthy qualities known to exist in the human race; and the terms of description of the memoirs, histories, and novels.

5. Phrenology

It was at this point that Franz Joseph Gall [1758–1828] came along and turned Lavater's work upside down—or right side up. Where Lavater had seen the physical countenance as an expression of character, Gall viewed character as an expression of cerebral physiology (Temkin, 1947, pp. 276–278). Gall's phrenology, therefore, represents the confluence of (1) the growing idea that neurophysiology could explain human actions with (2) romantic concepts of personality.

Gall was a well-known Austrian physician who resided during most of his adult life in Paris. He himself made some lasting contributions to the anatomy of the brain, and his method of anatomical demonstration of the brain was widely adopted.

As much as Lavater, Gall was self-consciously original. He rejected earlier attempts at personality analysis and classification. Reviewing both traditional and contemporary systematizations of the temperaments and faculties, he denied that they provided useful terms of description. The temperaments, he said, are of bodily origin, but he was convinced that the brain was the source of all behavior. Moreover, said Gall (1835, II, p. 104), the temperamental descriptions of individual people are after-the-fact rationalizations and do not stand up empirically. The influence of temperament ought to be consistent, yet "... there is scarcely anyone, who is not passionately fond of some things, and wholly indifferent in regard to others.... How does it happen, that a person has astonishing power in one department, and extreme weakness in another, which he has cultivated even with greater assiduity?"

Likewise, the senses and faculties, Gall (1835, VI, pp. 245–255) said, are not useful categories but are common to all general tendencies to behavior. In the attribute of bravery, for example, perception, recollection, memory, judgment, imagination, and attention all play their parts, or, more accurately, are all attributes, in one sense, of bravery. These traditional faculties had been abstracted by the philosophers, said Gall, and were just that, abstractions. Gall, like Lavater, was interested in individual differences that depend upon a set of fundamental powers or propensities that he defined as elemental. Gall (1835, I, p. 60) said that early in his life he had noticed that even members of his own family and schoolmates, all reared in the same environment, manifested personalities of vastly different types. The behavior that expresses a man's personality, said Gall, is not determined by any one single influence but by the whole pattern of predominances of the fundamental powers and propensities.

6. The Fundamental Powers

Gall's list of fundamental powers was empirical. His first method of discovering the different behavior tendencies of man was to observe animals. It seemed obvious to Gall (1835, IV, p. 226) that a pigeon circling a cote is doing so "for the purpose of ascertaining whether there is any thing to fear from birds of prey or martins, as well as to give the signal of return to other pigeons, which might have been forgotten in the fields." This to Gall was clear evidence of circumspection or foresightedness. Several of the fundamental attributes, however, he found exclusively in the behavior of the human animal.

The second empirical basis of Gall's system was his correlation of observed behavior tendencies with specific brain configurations. He (Gall, 1835, IV, p. 156) for example tells how he discovered the cerebral organ of the attribute of pride when he examined the head of an enormously proud beggar and found "on the upper and back part of the middle line, a prominence extending from above downwards, which could arise only from the development of the brain beneath." Although an experienced brain anatomist, Gall usually used cranial inspections to infer the configuration of the brain underneath.

Gall's approach involved two basic naturalistic assumptions: that the fundamental attributes are innate in man as much as in animals, and that each attribute is represented by an organ of the brain. Although most of Gall's localizations of brain function proved to be baseless, such attempts at specification continued with increasing sophistication in neurophysiology throughout the nineteenth century. Unlike many of his successors, Gall was not at all a materialist and considered the cerebral organs "but the instruments through which the basic qualities manifested themselves" (Temkin, 1947, p. 283).

The exact nature of Gall's conceptualization of personality traits he never made clear except that they are behavioral. He referred to them variously and collectively as moral qualities and intellectual faculties; propensities and faculties; instinctive forces, moral and intellectual; instincts, propensities, aptitudes, talents, and faculties. At times Gall (e.g., 1835, I, p. 160) noted that internal impulses act to excite the fundamental qualities, and the distinction between a propensity and an instinct is not clear. It would be easy to maintain that the fundamental qualities that Gall elucidated are, like those of Lavater, merely a list of more or less literary terms of characterization. At the same time, Gall's attempt to systematize human personality is impressive. He listed twenty-seven basic traits or propensities for which he found "organs."

1. Instinct of generation, of reproduction; instinct of propagation
2. Love of offspring
3. Attachment. Friendship
4. Instinct of self-defence, disposition to quarrel, courage
5. Carnivorous instinct; disposition to murder
6. Cunning, trick, tact
7. Sense of property, instinct of providing, covetousness, propensity to steal
8. Pride, hauteur, loftiness, love of authority, elevation
9. Vanity, ambition, love of glory
10. Cautiousness, circumspection, foresight
11. Memory of things, memory of facts, sense of things, educability, perfectibility
12. Sense of locality, sense of the relations of space
13. The faculty of distinguishing and recollecting persons
14. Faculty of attending to and distinguishing words; recollection of words, or verbal memory

15. Faculty of spoken language; talent of philology, &c.
16. Faculty of distinguishing the relation of colors; talent for painting
17. Faculty of perceiving the relation of tones, talent for music
18. Faculty of the relations of numbers
19. Faculty of constructiveness
20. Comparative sagacity, aptitude for drawing comparisons
21. Metaphysical depth of thought; aptitude for drawing conclusions
22. Wit
23. Talent for poetry
24. Goodness, benevolence, gentleness, compassion, sensibility, moral sense, conscience
25. Faculty of imitation, mimicry
26. God and religion, the religious sentiment
27. Firmness, constancy, perseverance, obstinacy

(Compiled and quoted from Gall, 1835, III, IV, V, *passim*.)

7. The Impact of Phrenology

Gall spoke widely in behalf of phrenology, and his doctrines were popularized all over Europe and America by him and by his followers, the best known of whom were Johann Gasper Spurzheim [1776–1832] and George Combe [1788–1858], a Scotsman. In spite of considerable opposition, the science of phrenology was widely studied and used in the first half of the nineteenth century, and very much less so in the second half. Temkin (1947, pp. 275–276) notes that among those whom phrenology influenced significantly were, for example, Broussais, Herbert Spencer, Balzac, Baudelaire, Poe, Horace Mann, and Cobden.

To a large part of the educated classes in the Western world—even those who disapproved of materialistic phrenology—the human personality could be described in terms of the thirty-seven or so basic qualities and tendencies that Gall and his successors (who added ten or so more to the list) used (see Ackerknecht and Vallois, 1956, pp. 82–86).[15] The later phrenologists, moreover, came to believe that the faculties or propensities could be cultivated, much as the moral philosophers had suggested. This conception of self-improvement underlay much of the thinking of the nineteenth century. Social reformers, especially, hoped to improve the world by inducing people to exercise desirable propensities.

The "scientific" basis of phrenology in later years, therefore, became an aid to reformist propaganda, but phrenologists in all periods in their public expositions were careful to cover themselves with the mantle of science. In the beginning Spurzheim, Combe, and others achieved this effect, like Gall, by beginning their lectures with a public dissection of a brain. Although in later years phrenology became popularized and debased—the reading of bumps on the head—the faculties and propensities persisted independently in European languages. (See especially Davies, 1955.)

Those who attacked Gall's beliefs were not usually concerned directly with his classification of characteristics. Some critics, it is true, did object because he ignored and denied the traditional psychological categories. But the bulk of his adversaries took issue with his materialism, or at least the materialistic implications of his work. Appropriately, then, the most important thinker whom Gall influenced deeply, Auguste Comte [1798–1857], advocated Gall's views precisely because of their materialism and the dynamic (as opposed to traditional) nature of his psychology. Throughout the nineteenth century, phrenology received important advocacy in Comtean positivism.

8. Comte

Comte, a social philosopher, reformer, and founder of positivism, understood that

[15] The later phrenologists assumed that human beings came in general humoral dispositional types; rather than four types, however, the number was reduced to three: the mental, the motive, and the vital types. These types formed the basis for Sheldon's later typology (see Davies, 1955, 4n).

Gall's attempted cerebral localizations were premature, but Gall's conception meant to Comte that there is a discoverable material basis for the elements of human nature. Moreover, by adopting Gall's original corollary idea that the traits of human nature are not only biological but specifically innate, Comte (Martineau, 1858, pp. 387–388) established a stable, "scientific" foundation for his derivative social analysis.

Comte followed Gall in making antimentalistic statements that sound like behaviorism of about a century later.[16] Although accepting irritability and sensibility as attributes of animal life, Comte (Martineau, 1858, p. 370) emphasized the organization of behavior and denied the relevance of the inquiry into the mechanisms of the basic phenomena of irritability and sensibility. As Martineau (1858, p. 383) renders one passage, "No function can be studied but with relation to the organ that fulfils it, or to the phenomena of its fulfilment...." Comte, like Gall, used empirical observation of behavior to learn the nature of human nature and interdicted as epistemologically unacceptable the philosophers' study of intellect, which he characterized as mind observing itself. Lévy-Bruhl (1903, p. 193) quotes Comte: "Against all evidence man has been represented as essentially reasoning, as being continually performing unaware a multitude of imperceptible calculations with scarcely any spontaneity, even from tenderest childhood." Comte (Martineau, 1858, pp. 376, 397) went further than Gall in positing the necessary internal nervous system and proprioceptions that could explain how the force of internal drives works. The traditional psychologies, according to Comte (Martineau, 1858, p. 384), emphasized the importance of the intellect; he wanted to show that "the affections [i.e., affects], the propensities, the passions are the great springs of human life."[17]

Gall and Spurzheim showed Comte that determinism in the realm of human actions is extremely complex. Even in animals instincts need not be limited to operating in simple, stereotyped behavior but can result in varied and complicated activities (see Martineau, 1858, pp. 386–387). Because of the complexity of the combination and interaction of the moral faculties and propensities, it would be "a great mistake to accuse cerebral physiology of disowning the influence of education or legislation...." (Martineau, 1858, pp. 390–391). Comte understood the requirements of the character analysis that phrenology made possible; namely, the development of more minute systems of categories. Instead of talking about mathematical genius as such, he (see Martineau, 1858, pp. 393–394) said, it is possible to explore the "compass and variety of faculties ... required to constitute mathematical genius, and how various are the forms in which that genius manifests itself. One great geometer has shone by the sagacity of his inventions; another by the strength and extent of his combinations; a third by the happy choice of his notations, and the perfection of his algebraic style, etc."

9. Social Instincts

Comte's major modification of phrenology was introducing the social instincts, as opposed to the selfish. His concept of altruism is the lasting legacy of this innovation.[18] One of Comte's chief concerns was to show that human society had its origins in the social instincts rather than in a social compact. He held that the lower, more organic,

[16] The resemblance has been noted also by Boas (1925, p. 284) and Cardno (1958, p. 427).

[17] Later Comte incorporated more of the traditional psychologies; see Cardno, 1958; Lévy-Bruhl, 1903, pp. 203 ff. From the beginning Comte divided all thought processes into intermittencies or habits—which could be innate—and associations as such; see Martineau, 1858, pp. 377 ff., 395–396.

[18] Social instincts were of course not new; they were important in moral philosophy, and both the moral philosophers and Comte were anticipated, for example, by Grotius (see Dickinson, 1922, pp. 34–35). On the other hand, Comte's emphasis upon social sympathy, as opposed to the gratification that one gets from social functioning, was essentially an innovation.

primitive, and selfish instincts determine the aim and direction of a person's social actions, in a way very reminiscent of the socially beneficent balance of evil impulses envisioned by Enlightenment thinkers. But Comte went on to assert that selfish propensities are balanced not only by each other but by the demands of social impulses and natural benevolence. (See Martineau, 1858, pp. 498–502.)

The combination of social instincts with the social environment is the secret, according to Comte (1953, pp. 24–25), of the strength of the unselfish propensities. "The social instincts would never gain the mastery [over self-love] were they not sustained and called into constant exercise by the economy of the external world, an influence which at the same time checks the power of the selfish instincts." Man alone would be a selfish animal; in society his unselfish and social tendencies are necessarily called into play. Comte's conception of the interaction of instinct and social environment was, accordingly, relatively sophisticated.

10. Social Versus Individual Levels of Discussion

Comte is best known for his sociology as such; relatively little attention has been devoted to his underlying concept of human nature. The reason probably is that he very seldom connected either his theory of personality or his concept of human nature to his grand generalizations about society (and, indeed, in a way denigrated the connection; see Martineau, 1858, pp. 486–488). In only one place did the two meet explicitly, namely, where Comte discussed the dynamics of the family. The family he saw as the basic institution of society in general, on the one hand, and, on the other hand, the mechanism the operation of which socializes each person. It is based upon primitive sexual instinct and yet is overwhelmingly social (Martineau, 1858, pp. 502–508).

With all of this effort to relate social theory to personality, still Comte asserted the adequacy of a sociological plane of discussion without reference to other levels of discussion. He represents an attempt to combine an interest in individual psychology with a preoccupation with a more or less organic view of society. His work on personality (including his later "Cerebral Table"), however, is in fact largely unconnected with his more famous ideas (see Lévy-Bruhl, 1903, pp. 201 ff.). In his writings the social preoccupation overwhelms the individual (Karpf, 1932, pp. 20–21). Gunn (1922, p. 35) maintains that Comte "even goes to the extent of regarding the individual man as an abstraction; for him the real being is the social being, Humanity." It was empirically evident to Comte (quoted in Boas, 1925, p. 291) that society is not reducible to individual human atoms. "The scientific spirit," he said, "does not permit us to look upon society as being really composed of individuals."

In some ways, then, Comte belongs in another section, with thinkers who emphasized personality as an expression of collective rather than individual traits. Actually Comte is best classified as one of the French writers who during the nineteenth century took a lively interest in individual personality and the classification of character traits. The most notable of such writers, aside from post-ideological physicians, were literary men who, like Comte, tended to see a physiological basis for personality traits. One who was not literary as such and yet who serves as a good example of this French propensity is Charles Fourier [1772–1837], the eccentric communitarian reformer. He is particularly interesting because he was so much more successful than Comte, his contemporary, in combining the social and individual levels of character functioning.

11. Fourier

Fourier's concept of social "associationism" gained much attention throughout the world in the early nineteenth century and inspired a number of utopian communitarian experiments. He believed that the human race should organize itself into self-governing communities of workers (phalansteries) so planned that each community contained precisely the number of persons necessary to carry out all of the functions of the community. One of the major aspects of Fourier's plan was his belief that there are exactly 810 types of human temperament. Since each type is suitable for one function in the community, the ideal community consists of 1620 persons whose various complementary temperaments will establish absolute social equilibrium.

Fourier's (1851, II, pp. 292–293) doctrine of temperaments, he made it quite clear, is not based on a pseudo-science like Gall's but is purely phenomenological, that is, described entirely in terms of behavior. The general system itself is radically unempirical. He derived it largely from his own version of numerology and made it analogous to music, as if men could, like musical notes, be brought into harmony by bringing them together in the right combinations. He (Fourier, 1851, I, ch. 1) asserted that all schemes of enumerating the passions that motivate men are defective because they are simple and mutually exclusive. Fourier incorporated all such enumerations by asserting that previous writers had merely written on different levels; avarice and ostentation, for example, are simply variants on a more detailed level of the general passion of ambition.

According to Fourier (1851), most men have one dominant passion; he called them monogynes. A few men, the polygynes, have two or more dominant passions. He (Fourier, 1851, II, pp. 298–299) figured the proportions to be: one dominant, 288; two, 48; three, 12; four, 4; five, 1. His characterization (Fourier, 1851, II, p. 337) of the concrete population distribution of the various passions among the monogynes gives an excellent picture of his conception of the passions:

Monogynes with sensual dominants		
Of smell	24	
Of hearing	36	
Of sight	48	240
Of touch	60	
Of taste	72	
Monogynes with affectuous dominants		
Of friendship	40	
Of ambition	56	
Of parentism	32	192
Of love	64	
Monogynes with distributive dominants		
Of composite	32	
Of papillon	48	144
Of cabalist[19]	64	
		576

Even this summary does not suggest the varieties of groupings, subdivisions, and complementary classifications into which Fourier worked the basic passions.

The passions of Fourier's system are in content and action entirely commonsense and obvious. Any complication arises only in further analysis; for example, is friendship manifested in its individual or group variety? That the passions act as they do is given, implicitly on the basis that the working of the passions in human life was well known at the time.

12. Fulfillment of Individual Character

Where Fourier is most interesting is in his belief that civilization does not permit the full expression of a person's special temperament. Especially when a person is dominated by two or more passions, society enables such a polygyne to express and utilize only one. According to Fourier (1851, II, p. 357), "Every civilizee polygyne is compelled from infancy to undergo spiritual mutila-

[19] Composites are unrealistic optimists; papillons, while not basically attractive, tend to be the life of every party and group; cabalists are given to intrigue.

tion, to reduce his soul from the composite to the simple, at least in appearance. He is compelled to regard one of the two gamuts which he possesses as vicious; to throw himself headlong into the other, and carry it to excess, in order to smother and forget the inward promptings of that which has been silenced. . . ." The result of such suppression, in addition to unhappiness, is a tendency of the suppressed passion to erupt violently. Most social evil in civilization Fourier (1851, II, pp. 395–396) traced to this suppression or perversion of natural temperament. His utopia was based on the idea that men should be assigned social functions that harmonize with their passions and permit them to "develop their characters" fully, which in turn, according to Fourier, results in virtuous behavior. This idea showed up again later in Marxian thinking.

The main line of development from Fourier leads into Marxism. Nevertheless he does reflect, on another plane, the major French lines of interest in personality, which were literary and medical. In the way in which physiology, in addition to classification, came to dominate both the literary and medical lines, the two lines became essentially identical.

13. Physiology and Character in Literature

As the novel and short story developed, questions of characterization and motivation became more and more important. In the wake of the ideologues' influence on literature—exemplified by Beyle—came a whole literature of "physiologies." The term was used loosely but it did indicate the influence of physical, bodily factors upon motivation and behavior. The instincts and appetites, especially sexual desire, were the object of several writers such as Beyle and Sénancourt. The first explicitly named was Jean Anthelme Brillat-Savarin's [1755–1826] *Physiologie de Goût* [1825] (1949), which was based—insofar as it contained any physiology—on Richerand. The most famous example of these literary physiologies was Balzac's satirical *Physiologie du Mariage,* in which the chief *motif* is how to evade the marriage bond and at the same time prevent one's spouse from doing the same. Balzac in his writings also gave a great deal of attention to the role of food in thought and behavior, suggesting (apparently out of Brillat-Savarin), for example, that "A nation's fate depends on the food it consumes." Still another aspect of the close connection between body and mind that the writers of the physiologies tended to explore was physiognomy or even phrenology. Balzac, for example, made extensive use of physiognomy and employed phrenology to characterize *Père Goriot.* (See Fess, 1924, especially pp. 10–12 and ch. 2; King, 1929, p. 113.) Describing physiognomical or phrenological expressions of character was both an economical and convincing way of characterizing and a use of commonly accepted belief to communicate ideas.

Beginning with the physiologies, literary characterization tended in two directions, each one representing a major current in the thought of the late nineteenth century, as will be seen below. Both of them involved a strong tendency to determinism—again a characteristic of late nineteenth century literature. The first was the use of physiology in a very literal way, especially those aspects of it that involve morbid developments in character. Physiological literature, as it evolved, came to represent in literature and in thought in general a diverting of interest from accidental and environmental factors and to the crediting—or, more likely, blaming—of heredity for an individual's temperament and behavior.

The other type of determinism that showed up as an important tendency both in general intellectual trends and in literature was economic determinism. The later physiologies themselves tended to emphasize economic motives. A random example is Louis Huart's (1841) *Physiologie du Tail-*

leur, in which no action of the tailor is to be understood except as in some way connected with his desire for monetary gain.[20] There was good reason for the acquisitive instinct to appeal to writers of fiction. The novel and short story in the nineteenth century were no longer directed toward an upper class (or those who aspired to identify with the upper class). Fiction's clientele became the growing numbers of middle class people and reflected their preoccupations. It was no wonder that "Courtship would give place to marriage, exploits to possessions, and happy endings would combine the two" (Levin, 1963, p. 33). As fiction matured, characterization improved. As characterization improved, it complemented the growing individualism of bourgeois society. So, correspondingly, economic motives harmonized with it. Economic man eventually contributed one stream to realism and naturalism, the emphasis on material environment (Levin, 1963, pp. 34–35 ff.). In France the work of Zola and others included much economic determinism (see below); in England it tended to be social-climbing economic man who was characterized. These most conspicuous of the currents that converged in the Victorian-Bismarckian-Republican *fin de siècle* contributed each in its way to the neglect of the study of human nature, at least in its individual manifestations.

PART VI. THE LOW POINT OF INTEREST IN PERSONALITY

1. The Late Nineteenth Century

The late nineteenth century was a period in which Darwinism presented a general intellectual diathesis. In part, at least, the dominance of the model of organic evolution reflected the general nineteenth century interest in development and historical thinking, but Darwin's work went beyond development. On the one hand, the pattern of evolutionary process dominated thinking; on the other hand, man was more freely and systematically treated as an animal than previously. Specifically biological laws (and imagined laws) were applied to human behavior.

Within this general evolutionary context, however, the study of human nature in general and personality in particular can be traced along several leitmotivs that were often relatively independent of the Darwinian revolution. These currents of thinking were often also independent and even contradictory of each other. As economic and social individualism flourished, so also did types of collectivistic thinking. Both sides of the nature-nurture controversy had their days, and just when intellectualistic psychology held the field, instincts made a comeback. In the period when the individual seemed to be lost, the psychology of individual differences was in utero. The complexity of the pattern woven by these intellectual threads at any one time in the Western world defies analysis. They must, therefore, be lifted out, each in turn, to be examined independently, showing but few traces of the larger fabric of history from which they are drawn.

Having noted the diversity of these strands of thought, it is possible now to go on and point out that around the middle and later part of the century the spirit of the times was in general not congenial to a study of individual personality. An English philosopher and writer, W. L. Courtney, as late as 1890 concluded that a real "science of character"—given the science, psychology, and social thought that he knew—is impossible. He reflected the fact that interest in the elemental human nature to be found in any single person had

[20] In this book the artisan is still an object of comic derision, and such comedy was the chief source of fictional characterization. Later this type of characterization was applied to non-comic figures in literature (Levin, 1963, pp. 36–37).

reached a nadir not attained since medieval times and not duplicated afterwards. This lack of interest was reflected particularly in three currents: intellectualistic association psychology, from which the instincts were pretty well eliminated; a remarkably thoroughgoing belief in the heredity of personality traits, which led to impersonal, purely theoretical classification; and occasional devotion to group interpretations of character, which social, geographic, racial, and national categories were believed to determine.

2. Marxism

Marxism, i.e., the doctrines of Karl Marx [1818–1883] and Friedrich Engels [1820–1895], provides not only an outstanding but the most influential example of a viewpoint in which, like Comte's, the social level of analysis predominates over the individual. "The human essence...," said Marx (quoted in Venable, 1945, p. 20), "is no abstraction inherent in each separate individual. In its reality it is the *ensemble* of the social relations."

The Marxist conception of human nature is distinctive in two ways. First, Marx and Engels visualized man without any enduring, unchanging nature. Man, they held, is the product of his history, his institutions, the way in which he interacts with nature (Venable, 1945, pp. 4–5, 202 ff.). If men have instincts, the instincts are conscious, for, unlike animals, humans' activities on even the most primitive level are marked by the presence of some plan or goal. Essentially, "Consciousness takes the place of instinct or ... [a human] instinct is a conscious one" (quoted in Venable, 1945, p. 67). True, Marx and Engels recognized the existence of human needs but not their importance as such in the final determination of human behavior. Needs are strictly biological and have no place in Marxist social science; moreover, the material production that satisfies such needs in and of itself generates new needs that are not part of the biological givens. Discussion of needs is therefore quite futile (Venable, 1945, pp. 82–85).

In the Marxist scheme, the way men labor and the institutions within which they produce determine their actions (Fromm, 1961, p. 12). This belief contains within it an assumption that, given certain factors, human behavior is on the whole predictable —not in each individual instance, but on the whole (Venable, 1945, pp. 202 ff.). Marx and Engels supposed that at one time each man had labored only for himself, for his own needs. As soon as production became social, men became divided into two groups, the exploiters and the exploited. The basis of production then changed from the needs of the individual to the needs of the ruling class. The actions and the goals of an individual became determined, therefore, by his actual work, on the one hand, and by his function as a member of a class, on the other hand. This combination of forces determines not only a man's life but the course of human history. (See Venable, 1945, especially pp. 52–54.)

The process of division of labor, therefore, is of crucial importance in Marxism. In the shop a man is restricted to one monotonous routine and is brutalized in the process. "How much human feeling, what abilities can a man retain in his thirtieth year," asked Engels (quoted in Venable, 1945, p. 127), "who has made needle points or filed toothed wheels twelve hours every day from his early childhood, living all the while under the conditions forced upon the English proletarian?" The worker, in short, is turned into a machine, or, more accurately, a part or almost literally a cog in a machine, for, according to Marx and Engels, it is not the worker but the shop, in an organic sense, that is the producer. The individual in bourgeois society, even a member of the ruling class, is completely conditioned. His actions are blind and unthinking; and his conscious motives are but reflections, direct or indirect, of his class and place in the institutions of production. (See Venable, 1945, especially pp. 54, 76–78, 116–117, 132–139.)

3. Needs and Their Expression

The criticism that Marx and Engels made of bourgeois society and the aim of their utopia point up their conception of human nature. Both primary needs (biological) and secondary needs (resulting from the process of production) of men are denied satisfaction by bourgeois institutions. The system that reduces a worker to a mere cog in the machine makes of the worker, said Marx (quoted in Venable, 1945, p. 133), "a cripple, a monster, by forcing him to develop some highly specialized dexterity at the cost of a world of productive impulses and faculties. . . . Not merely are the various partial operations allotted to different individuals; but the individual himself is split up, is transformed into the automatic motor of some partial operation." (Fromm, 1961, pp. 38 ff., emphasizes the alienation of man from his self, using Marxism as an expression of modern concepts of self-alienation.)

The promise of Marxism is a system in which, according to Marx (quoted in Venable, 1945, p. 190), man "initiates, regulates and controls the material reactions between himself and nature. . . . By thus acting on the external world and changing it, he at the same time changes his own nature. He develops the potentialities that slumber within him, and subjects them to his own control." Starting out, like Fourier, with a belief that society forces men to suppress their own real natures, Marx and Engels used a sophisticated analysis of the interactions between humans, their material environment, and their history as a basis for supposing that recognizing the determining power of social forces, as opposed to the individual, could lead to a society in which the individual can be true to his nature—not a fixed nature but a set of potentialities. Fromm (1961, p. 38) asserts explicitly that Marx's aim was "the development of the individual personality" in a social utopia.

4. Social Collectivism in General

Marxism was deeply influenced by Hegelian thinking, and insofar as Hegel caused and/or represented the idea of a social entity with its own reality—or soul—nineteenth century philosophy had some connection with theories of personality. Hegelianism particularly complemented the growth of nationalism by suggesting that in history nations rather than individuals are the meaningful units; individual interests are, therefore, secondary and tributary to those of the spiritual, if not actual, nation. This viewpoint ties in not only with Marxism (in which class substitutes for nation) but with cultural nationalism. Late in the century, the statistical study of human behavior, traditionally connected with the name of Adolphe Quetelet [1796–1874], added a new dimension to the study of humankind in the mass. Statistical units of humanity, however, fit better into Comtean rather than Hegelian ideas of man in the aggregate.

Comte's work represents a second major type of collectivism, namely, the belief that society as such is the proper focus of an analysis to discover the best way for men to live. Hegel and Marx especially emphasized that reality lies in process and history; yet collectivist thinkers tended, like Comte and even Marx, to neglect the specific and actual connection of the individual and his personality with the superorganic social unit.

5. Spencer

Another major intellectual figure and force in the late nineteenth century West was Herbert Spencer [1820–1903], the English writer and evolutionist. Like Marx, he emphasized process and development. And like both Comte and Marx he failed to explore thoroughly the connection between the individual personality and the social entity. Spencer's failure is particularly remarkable because he advocated in detail an individualistic economic philosophy and associationist psychology (not to be confused with Fourier's social "associationism"; see below).

Spencer conceived society to be organic in nature, and he concentrated on the evolution of societies and the factors involved in that evolution. The deaths of individual members of the group he compared to the replacement of cells in the organism. "Integrity of the whole as of each large division is perennially maintained, notwithstanding the deaths of component citizens," he (Spencer, 1900, I, pp. 456–457) wrote. "The fabric of living persons which, in a manufacturing town, produces some commodity for national use, remains after a century as large a fabric, though all the masters and workers who a century ago composed it have long since disappeared. . . .. Hence arises in the social organism, as in the individual organism, a life of the whole quite unlike the lives of the units; though it is a life produced by them."[21]

At one point Spencer (1899, pp. 228–229) talked about "social forces," parallel to physical forces and vital forces. Both vital and social forces, he said, are derived, by reduction, from physical forces (that is, energy in the universe): "Not only is the force expended by the horse harnessed to the plough, and by the labourer guiding it, derived from the same reservoir as is the force of the falling cataract and the roaring hurricane; but to this same reservoir are eventually traceable those subtler and more complex manifestations of force which humanity, as socially embodied, evolves." Obviously the energy of life is the element from which social activity is made; in Spencer, however, the conception of social forces remained relatively undefined. Nevertheless, he devoted considerable space (Spencer, 1900, I) to climate and geographical factors that embody natural forces operating directly upon social institutions.

The individual units in society—people—form into an aggregate, Spencer (1900, I, pp. 459–460) said, because they are interdependent and can communicate. Unlike the biological organism, the social organism does not have its consciousness concentrated in one organ, or institution (as Marx might have held), but consciousness "is diffused throughout the aggregate." The social organism, therefore, exists teleologically for the good of the units, and individual units are not to be sacrificed "for the benefit of society" (Spencer, 1900, I, pp. 461–462).

The individual person in society Spencer took surprisingly for granted. Those social units, he (Spencer, 1900, I, p. 461) admitted, are not insensible; occasionally they show traces of differentiation: "Human beings are unlike in the amounts of sensation and emotion producible in them by like causes: here callousness, here susceptibility, is a characteristic. The mechanically-working and hard-living units are less sensitive than the mentally-working and more protected units." Units differ also, Spencer (1900, I, p. 9) noted, in strength, energy, and intelligence. But just as a biological organism has regulative processes, so society has control factors built into it, namely, the social environment of the person. "The control exercised by the aggregate over its units," Spencer (1900, I, pp. 11–12) pointed out, "tends ever to mould their activities and sentiments and ideas into congruity with social requirements; and these activities, sentiments, and ideas, in so far as they are changed by changing circumstances, tend to re-mould the society into congruity with themselves." Spencer (1900, I, pp. 571–574) noted only one major determinant of the characterization of the social unit that seriously differentiates the pattern of evolution of one society from another: the factor of race. And

[21] Essentially both Spencer's psychology and his sociology were descriptive and taxomonic rather than explanatory, and it is difficult to find his theory in the midst of his often over-detailed classification of human institutions and psychological relations. The problem is that Spencer's inquiries usually were aimed at ascertaining the direction of social evolution, not the dynamics of individual behavior.

the contemporaneous conception of the temperaments of various races, another type of collectivistic thinking, requires separate treatment (see below).

6. Ward

Lester Frank Ward [1841–1913], an American social philosopher whose thinking was largely derivative, serves as an excellent example to indicate how social collectivist thought was tending as the nineteenth century progressed. His work might be viewed as an attempt at a higher synthesis of Comte and Spencer. But where Comte and especially Spencer (e.g., 1899, pp. 248–249) had neglected the interrelationships between individual dynamic psychology and social processes, Ward's most interesting work was in just this area.

Each person, said Ward (1893, especially p. 54), has desires—detectable through manifestations of the emotions. Like other writers, Ward believed that men avoid pain and seek pleasure. "All animated nature is burning and seething with intensified desires," he (Ward, 1893, p. 53) said, and all human activity is aimed at fulfilling these desires. Moreover, he (Ward, 1893, pp. 22–23) continued, these desires have an organic basis in the nervous system, especially the sympathetic nervous system. Desire is, therefore, a true natural force. "Human phenomena, or, as they are popularly called, social phenomena, differ . . . from geological and other phenomena only in the nature of the forces which produce them. In these it is the psychic forces . . . [i.e., desires]. Man is the instrument through which these forces operate and the immediate cause of the phenomena is human action" (Ward, 1893, p. 97). Man has been almost entirely social, and his activities have been social, or cooperative, too. Therefore, Ward concluded, the desires are the social forces that Spencer first described. They operate like other forces and can be opposed to each other (as in competition) or can reinforce each other, as, for example, in two people sexually attracted to each other. (See in general Ward, 1893, ch. 15.)

Ward introduced conventional modifications of this idea, such as secondary desires derived in the course of social evolution and the idea that intelligence could be used to direct the social forces as they determine the course of social action. But he stood true to his contention that society does not literally have "wants and passions" but is directed by the aggregate of the directions of the desires of the individual members.

With Ward, then, what started out as the organic view of social units was analyzed reductively back into the nature of the individual. (Ward's scheme of individual motivation was very simple and resolved essentially into self-preservation and race preservation.) Social analysis, therefore, put Ward into another stream of thought, and one that will be taken up in its place, namely, the resurgence of the instinct concept in late nineteenth century thinking. First, other types of group character determinants must be taken up.

7. Climatic and Geographical Determinism

Almost all of the social collectivists recognized the influence of climatic and geographical factors on the social units they posited; Marx and Spencer, with their materialistic biases, especially mentioned such determinants. For some thinkers, however, these physical influences were not just contributory, but central. Yet they, too, represent a type of collectivistic thinking: all of the people subject to a given climate and geography tend to have the same personality characteristics. As Friedrich Ratzel [1844–1904] (quoted in Thomas, 1925, pp. 138–139), the leading advocate of geography in the late nineteenth century, put it: "Lands, no matter how distant from one another they may be, whenever their climates are similar, are destined to be scenes of analogous historical developments. . . . Man, in spite of all racial and national differences, is fundamentally quite as much of a unity as the soil upon which he dwells."

8. Antecedents

The idea that climate and geography are important determinants of character is an ancient one. Hippocrates (1849, I, pp. 205–222), in his famous *Airs, Waters, and Places,* made the classic statement of the influence of climate and geography on temperament as well as physical appearance. Those who live in rugged, infertile country in which changes of season are violent are likely "to be naturally of an enterprising and warlike nature." Those from the warm lowlands are not given naturally to "courage and laborious enterprise," but their institutions may engender those traits. Poor country and extremes of climate also cause "haughty and opiniative . . . morals and passions" in the inhabitants. Hippocrates apparently believed that the climate acts on the semen at the time of conception as well as continuously on a man's humors in a direct way, both types of influence affecting temperament. In addition, he believed that physical environment occasions generally corresponding activity, as stimulation and excitement of the mind result from a harsh climate in which survival demands more activity than in a milder climate.

One writer, in particular, represents an extreme in ascribing the character of groups of people to the climate in which they dwell. This was Jean-Baptiste Du Bos [1670–1742], the Abbé Du Bos, secretary of the French Academy. Du Bos assumed that the quality of the air was a major physical influence on the body, not only on the humors but on the spirit and, from childhood on, the actual conformation of the organs. Du Bos recognized that changes in climate brought about changes in mood or disposition, and he mentioned, for example, how warm weather is known to increase crimes of violence. But his main concern was with the permanent and palpable, but still unmeasurable, differences in the air between one area or country and another. "All nations," he (quoted in Koller, 1937, p. 79) said, "differ more in inclinations and mind than in make and color of body." Du Bos believed that the differences in modes of thinking between a Chinese and a European are infinitely greater than their physical differences. Perhaps his most interesting observation was that regardless of demographic or racial changes, the people of a particular geographic area tend to have the same traits as their ancient predecessors who were not necessarily their ancestors. (See in general Koller, 1937, especially pp. 64–93.)

One of the classic statements of the influence of geography upon group character is that of the Baron de Montesquieu [1689–1755]. He drew upon the work of a Scottish physician, John Arbuthnot [1667–1735], who believed that climate, especially temperature, affects the tensions of the body fibers and so affects the physiology, which in turn affects temperament (Thomas, 1925, pp. 59–63, 67–69). Montesquieu's primary interest was in political institutions. If climate has produced obstinate and willful citizens, their political organization tends toward tyranny, and likewise the opposite with mild and gentle peoples. As Thomas (1925, pp. 64–65) summarizes Montesquieu's beliefs, "The inhabitants of cold countries tend to be brave, vigorous, insensible to pain, devoid of sex passion and possessed of relatively strong physical frames and phlegmatic temperaments. The people of warm climates are weak, timid, apathetic toward physical exertion, vivacious, sensitive to pleasure or pain, inordinate in their sexual indulgences, and utterly lacking in mental ambition."

The significance of Montesquieu lies in his acceptance of the determining power of environment. Like subsequent environmentalists, in spite of his physiological theories he found geography to be mostly an indirect rather than a direct determinant of social institutions. "Fertile countries," for example, "are usually flat without any natural protective barriers, which makes them an easy prey to foreign powers, for a fertile country invites invasion and is conducive to ease and effeminacy. Barrenness, on the other hand, stimulates industry" (Thomas, 1925, p. 125).

9. Climatology and Geography in the Late Nineteenth Century

Beliefs about the influence of geography and climate upon character continued into the twentieth century and were, of course, well known and influential in the late nineteenth century, on both the folk and scientific levels. An excellent example of extreme nineteenth century belief in physical environmental influences is John W. Draper [1811–1882] of Cornell. He asserted (Draper, 1867, I, p. 110) that "for every climate, and, indeed, for every geographical locality, there is an answering type of humanity." Draper traced as the basic factor in the coming of the Civil War the character differences between the North and the South that grew out of geographical and climatic factors, such as dispersion of population in the South and its concentration in the North. He suggested that the alternation of seasons in the North makes for periods of intense work, followed by enforced leisure when reflection on one's actions takes place. In the South, one can procrastinate, because the seasons are all mild; at the same time, weather permits activity all of the time, which leads to impulsiveness because there is no time for reflection. (See Draper, 1867, pp. 100–101.)

One of the most frequently quoted statements of the efficacy of geographical factors is that of the English writer, Henry Thomas Buckle [1821–1862]. In an introductory chapter to his *History of Civilization in England* Buckle (1863, ch. 2) explored the effects of "climate, food, soil, and the general aspect of nature" on civilization in general. He (Buckle, 1863, pp. 29–30) discounted race as an "altogether hypothetical" factor in the differences between peoples. Climate, food, and soil, he maintained, have powerful influences on the accumulation of material wealth and its distribution. Very hot climate, for example, is not conducive to labor, and long cold seasons with enforced idleness of the working class prevent their forming good working habits (Buckle, 1863, p. 32). Likewise the type of food consumed in some climates is more costly than in others, thus inhibiting the accumulation of wealth, which is, of course, a requisite of any considerable degree of civilization. Mostly Buckle, like Draper, concentrated on the indirect effects of climate and geography, many of which he held do affect character tendencies of peoples. The general aspects of nature, however, according to Buckle (1863, pp. 85 ff.), affect the mind directly; specifically they conduce to the power of either the understanding or the imagination. Thus in Europe, where nature is relatively kind and unspectacular, reason has been able to flourish. In non-European areas, where nature induces terror in the inhabitants, the imagination is stimulated. Earthquakes, for example, tend to cause superstition and bigotry in the population.

By the mid-nineteenth century, nationalism had grown so virulently that most nonindividual character tended to be described in terms of nationality. The nation, of course, tended to have some geographical and climatic unity. Since there was almost universal belief in the inheritance of acquired characteristics, it was easy for people of the time to see how a constant environmental factor like geography and climate would over several generations develop common behavior tendencies in the inhabitants of a given area. These people might even be sufficiently differentiated to be designated a race, thus permitting the identifying of nation with race.

10. Race

Race is presumably inherited; if race involves personality traits, they are, consequently, inherited. Such was the earliest scientific conception of the nature of racial character.[22] Linnaeus [Carl von Linné, 1707–1778] provides an excellent example of the way in which early raciologists conceived of racial characteristics. He described four varieties of man: American, European, Asian, and African. The American is not only "reddish, choleric, erect" and has black hair, wide nostrils, and no beard, but is "persevering, content, free.... Governed by customs." The European is "White, sanguine, muscular," with blue eyes and yellow hair and is "Easy-going, keen, ingenious.... Governed by law." The Asiatic is "yellow, melancholic, inflexible. Black hair. Dark eyes. Severe, haughty, miserly.... Governed by opinion." The African is "black, phlegmatic, indulgent," with black, kinky hair, smooth skin, flat nose, and protuberant lips. Linnaeus characterized him as "Crafty, lazy, negligent.... Governed by whim." (Scheidt, 1950, pp. 355–358; von Linné, 1758, pp. 20–21.)

Buffon, too, employed psychical traits as a basis for distinguishing one human race from another, and the idea crops up occasionally in other writings of the eighteenth and early nineteenth centuries. In general, however, after Linnaeus the scientific students of race used strictly anatomical criteria for differentiating the races. (See Scheidt, 1950, p. 357; Count, 1946, pp. 150–151.) As head measurement became increasingly the criterion for distinguishing races, phrenology provided an opportunity to suggest that racial character, as well as cranial conformation, could be measured (Barzun, 1937, pp. 53–63). This was only a side eddy, however.

11. Gobineau

In 1853 Arthur de Gobineau [1816–1882] (1915), a French aristocrat, introduced again in an important way the idea of character traits as a concomitant of race. Although he spoke largely outside of the scientific community, he represented many important intellectual currents of the time that persisted both in and out of science.

Unlike earlier writers on race, the approach of this child of the nineteenth century was fundamentally historical and developmental. The problem that he set out to solve was why in the course of time a civilization would degenerate. His answer was: the race whose superior qualities established the civilization intermarried with inferior races—many of which are incapable of being really civilized—and lost its superiority. Six years before Darwin suggested evolution by the process of survival of the fittest, Gobineau envisaged one race overcoming another—which was to Gobineau clear proof of its superiority—but, of course, in contrast to the model of progressive evolution, scheduled for inevitable intermarriage and decline. One of the great contributions of the romantic period, philology, Gobineau used as other writers on race had, arguing that language provided a very close—if not exact—indication of race.

Gobineau explicitly denied that the influence of climate and soil, institutions, or even religion could change the hereditary character of a race. But, like others who talked in terms of humanity in the aggregate, Gobineau neglected, even explicitly ignored (e.g., Gobineau, 1915, p. 180), the connection between the individual's personality and the group's character. Indeed, his final chapter, in which he (Gobineau, 1915, pp. 205–207), for example, characterized the negroid variety of human as of "animal character ... [with] powerful energy ... inordinate desires ... mental faculties are dull or even nonexistent" and

[22] In the early treatises it is not clear to what extent racial characteristics are really inherited; this is the more doubtful not only because of Lamarckian beliefs but because of the tendency to give the races geographical, i.e., environmental names. (See Scheidt, 1950, pp. 358–363.)

the whites as having "energetic intelligence ... love of liberty," and so on, is not implicitly connected to the rest of his essay and represents no essential progress from Linnaeus. What had been added in Gobineau is the element of nationalism. He (Gobineau, 1915, pp. 152–153), for instance, spoke of the nationalities of Europe, "different groups within the white race," virtually as races themselves. Gobineau shows as well as any writer that a consideration of racial thinking in the nineteenth century belongs with a discussion of cultural nationalism.

12. Persistence of Racial Thinking

Nevertheless, the idea of racial characteristics persisted on its own in the late nineteenth century. It had been common, as Barzun (1937, especially p. 118) has shown vividly, that when a man's race did not reveal his temperament, his temperament had been used to infer his "race." ("Napoleon felt on one occasion that all great men of letters were French.") For a long time the idea of aristocracy had racial connotations, explicit in the Abbé Sieyès, obvious in Gobineau (Barzun, 1937, p. 30). The lingering effect of the ideologues and the physiological school of character reinforced the conception that character was hereditary (see below), and who could doubt that traits such as skin color or head shape signaled an inheritance that included temperament?

It was usual for late nineteenth century thinkers to use the idea of race. Spencer (1900, I, pp. 294–295, 571 ff.) casually referred to "the inferior races" and their opposites, the Aryans and Semites, and noted that each different race evolves different institutions suitable for itself and not other races. Likewise the pioneer social psychologist and advocate of the collective mind concept, Gustave Le Bon [1841–1931] (1898), in writing about *The Psychology of Peoples* assumed that each people has a soul, built up by inherited acquired characteristics, although by the time he wrote, he said, the European races had such a heavy stock of inherited characteristics and mixed so little that few further changes in them were likely.

"The moral and intellectual characteristics, whose association forms the soul of a people," said Le Bon (1898, pp. 6–7), "represent the synthesis of its entire past, the inheritance of all its ancestors, the motives of its conduct. They appear to be very variable in individuals of the same race, but observation proves that the majority of the individuals of a given race always possess a certain number of common psychological characteristics, which are as stable as the anatomical characteristics that allow of the classification of species, while, like these latter characteristics, the psychological characteristics are regularly and constantly reproduced by heredity. This aggregate of psychological elements observable in all the individuals of a race constitutes what may rightly be called the national character."

13. National Character

While both racial and geographic thinking contributed to the idea of national character, that concept has its own history and, indeed, for the most part in the nineteenth century it biased and absorbed the racial and physical environmental streams of thought, as Le Bon suggests. The idea of national character as it developed in the nineteenth century had two sources: the romantic idea of a folk soul and virulent patriotism.

14. Herder

While the concept of national character was far from new—Herodotus had spoken of the customs and manners of the Egyptians, and Tacitus had generalized similarly about the distinctive behavior of the German tribes—the earliest major writer to articulate folk psychology in a more or less modern form was Johann Gottfried von Herder [1744–1803], a German clergyman and writer. Herder's basic approach was historical and developmental. Further, he believed that man's behavior is a natural phenomenon and is therefore subject to investigation that will yield generalizations or scientific laws. With some reservations Herder believed that psychology has a physiological basis and that humans have instincts like the animals. In this historical and naturalistic context, Herder was able to take into account fully the influence on various peoples of climate, geography, and physical environment in general, as well as social environment. That is, by assuming that both culture and hereditary traits are developed over a period of time, Herder was able to explain both diversity and change. The Kalmucks and Mongolians, for example, have ears that stick out—like animals listening for distant sounds—and projecting incisors for gnawing bones because they listened and gnawed for so many generations that the relevant features became inherited. Racial or national character is, therefore, according to Herder, physiologically based psychology, at least indirectly caused by environment but for practical purposes largely invariable. (See in general Wells, 1959, especially p. 14, ch. 2.)

The critical concept in Herder's writings is that of the *Volk*. The *Volk* represents a group distinctive because of its collective personality. It is essentially national in character because the basic defining character is language. Although there are variations from the *Volk* character, individuals in the group tend to approach the *Volk* ideal rather than vary away from it. On at least some levels, and perhaps all, the *Volk* is a real, functional entity.

The *Volk* also carries connotations of primitivistic purity. It does not include the ruling classes, nor the rabble, both of which have been corrupted by civilization. The *Volk* is the largest and best part of the people, largely untutored, with untainted moral and intellectual traits. At times Herder compared the *Volk* to children, formed directly by nature. These are the blessed people, the ones for whom Luther wrote. Like Tacitus, Herder glorified the primitives and tried to define their character and virtue with folk songs, folk sayings, and the like. The attractiveness of the *Volk* derives from its connotations of the good "common people," generous, virtuous, humble, brave. (See Simpson, 1921, *passim.*)

Although a patriot who occasionally spoke in terms of German nationalism, Herder (who was typical of early romanticism), was not nationalistic as such. He was ready to praise any *Volk* that could maintain its integrity, not just the Germans. To him the French Revolution symbolized the pitting of class against class. For such a dangerous situation he believed the antidote to be cultural nationalism. The national character of any people, i.e., *Volk,* was therefore good in Herder's eyes. In contrast to others, Herder did not glorify the state, for the rulers are, of course, apart from the *Volk*. (See Simpson, 1921, pp. 54–57; Wells, 1959, pp. 153–154, 189–190, 197.)

15. Virulent Nationalism and National Character

With the coming of the French Revolution, modern patriotic nationalism was born. This emphasized the involvement of the individual in the fate of the nation, his duty to it and fulfillment in it. Beginning with the French, intellectuals in Europe advocated nationalism of this variety until nationalism as a phenomenon became a major, if not the major, force in world history. It found cultural expression in Hegel and in the national historians who turned to political affairs as the truest expression of the important and real in historical development. Likewise, advocates of Burkean conservatism emphasized institutions, i.e., national institutions, which had existence and validity because they were the historical creations of a people and could not be created at a given moment in time. (See in general Kohn, 1955, chs. 2–4.)

Patriotic nationalists of the nineteenth

century sought, therefore, to find in the past the true essence of national character and to exclude foreign elements. Fichte, for example, suggested closing off foreign trade and other contaminating contacts in order to strengthen national character (Wells, 1959, p. 197). National character, moreover, took on a metaphysical aspect and was believed, in and of itself, to be a determining force in history. This type of belief usually resulted, in the end, in glorification of the state. In the works of such thinkers the individual's relation to the nation became as tenuous as in other collectivists. During the later years of the century, Wilhelm Dilthey, Eduard Meyer, and Wilhelm Wundt spoke out strongly against a mystical "national soul," and until later, in the twentieth century, the idea tended to die out. (See Wells, 1959, pp. 195–205.)

The persistence of the idea of national or national racial traits in general thinking in the Victorian period is remarkable. A writer (quoted in Barzun, 1937, p. 152) in the 1860's, for example, declared that during the prolonged Irish crisis "five out of six English writers and political speakers were discoursing gravely on the incurable idleness and lawlessness of the Celtic race and the Irish peasant." It was an unusual writer who, during the nineteenth century, did not at one time or another invoke the idea of national character—even in one's self, where, of course, national traits, like any other virtues, are easily seen. It was a long time before sociocultural views of personality overcame the imprecisions of late nineteenth century ideas of national character.

16. Association Psychology

At the other extreme from collectivist thinking lay individualistic association psychology; yet associationism and its derivatives in the late nineteenth century were as effective as collectivist thinking in distracting attention away from what later became the study of personality.

Aristotle was the first to systematize the idea of learning by association of ideas; by the time of Locke, Hume, and Hartley, the conception was both familiar and traditional, and John Stuart Mill [1806–1873], for example, could do little more than make new variations on old themes when he formulated another version of the laws of association. What was new about the associationists was the way in which they used associationist ideas to make a total explanation of man's behavior.

The associationists shared with the moral philosophers a preoccupation with ethical and political questions; hence the origins of nineteenth century associationism lay very close to the moral philosophers (see Davidson, 1916). One of the underlying assumptions of the associationists goes back directly to Jeremy Bentham [1748–1832], a wealthy English moral philosopher who contributed much to the social thinking especially of James Mill [1773–1836] and John Stuart Mill. Bentham (1843) drew up a "Table of Springs of Human Action," and the assumption that there were such springs of human action is evident in the works of James Mill (1878, II, p. 185) and his successors. Bentham (1843) found that the springs of human action fall into fourteen general categories:

1. Hunger etc.
2. Sexual Desire etc.
3. Physical want, need ....
4. Desire, want, need, hope .... of [means]
5. Ambition
6. Curiosity
7. Opinion .... aid from certain others
8. Opinion & services of public at large
9. Sense of Religious Duty
10. Sympathy
11. Antipathy
12. Love of ease, aversion to labor
13. Self Preservation
14. Personal interest

These motives, Bentham noted, either can give rise to action or can act to restrict action. That he was closely allied to traditional thinking can be seen in his designation of sympathy as interest of the heart and antipathy as interest of the gall bladder. All except (10) and (11) were, he noted, as one might expect of an Enlightenment man, related to the pleasure of self-regard.

Bentham spelled out clearly the pleasures and pains associated with each of the springs of action. Hunger, for example, is associated with pleasures of the palate, ambition with the pleasure of power, love of ease with the pain of toil and fatigue. The later associationists distinguished themselves by their reduction of explanations of human conduct to the level of pains and pleasures, each of which can, by practice, be associated with an idea and thus lead to action because of anticipation of consequences of the action, namely, either obtaining pleasure or avoiding pain (or both).

17. Mill

The standard work of the associationist school is the annotated edition of James Mill's (1878) *Analysis of the Phenomena of the Human Mind*.[23] In addition to Bentham's list of hedonic tendencies, which Mill assumed, Mill (1878, II, ch. 21) classified sources of pleasure and pain as either sensual or else: wealth, power, and dignity; social and familial relationships; and appreciation of beauty. According to Mill (1878, II, pp. 258–259), when the idea of future pleasure or pain is associated with the idea of a man's action (or specific inaction), he has a *motive*. In order for a motive to be translated into action, however, the man must have a specific *disposition* to obey that motive. A man, for example, with the motive of eating will have a disposition of either temperance or intemperance which will in turn decide whether his motive to eat results in nourishment or is carried to the point of gluttony (Mill, 1878, II, pp. 260–262; Cardno, 1955).[24]

Mill suggested that the will can be analyzed into associations (see Warren, 1921, pp. 93–94). Involuntary actions he believed to be easily understood as reactions built upon association (yawning after someone else does); but voluntary actions, he continued, always have connected to them a desire either to avoid pain or to obtain pleasure (Mill, 1878, II, pp. 350–351). The ability of an idea to excite muscular contraction the associationists explained by the fact that at first a sensation by itself will somehow automatically call forth muscular movement, but that, with practice, the idea of the sensation can set off the movement. The process is analogous to developing the ability to play a musical instrument, in which intermediate associations, once conscious, become so rapid as to appear automatic (Mill, 1878, II, pp. 354–356n). All voluntary action, then, can be explained in terms of a man's figuring ways to maximize pleasure and minimize pain; he acts always in the light of self-interest, hopefully enlightened self-interest. The concept of enlightened self-interest, of course, received much attention in nineteenth century economic theory (see below).

The associationists conceived of personality as the sum total of congeries of habitual patterns built up by association. Specific reactions to specific stimuli, built up by association, are clearly part of personality (e.g., Mill, 1878, II, p. 347). Since dispositions, likewise, have their origin in habitual attempts to maximize pleasure, change, according to the associationists, is best effected by changing one's intellectual conceptions of what actions will lead to the most pleasure and least pain.

Associationist hedonism gave rise not only to the idea of economic man but to a psychology that permitted a very different analysis of human motivation than had theretofore been common. First of all, by reducing all motives to feelings of pain and pleasure, the associationists, unlike Hobbes and even Aristotle, avoided the traditional concepts of emotion and instinct. The traditional affec-

[23] The text was the same as that published in 1829; the annotations were first published in 1869.

[24] Disposition in this sense is of course present in earlier works, notably Bentham's.

tive element in thought was simply analyzed—by association—into pain and pleasure, and all action into hedonism (see especially Warren, 1921, p. 94). (The instinct psychologies of the early twentieth century [see below] in general represented a reaction to this over-intellectual view of human nature.) Where the associationists started out with pain-pleasure hedonism as the mechanism of achieving satisfaction of basic motivations, they ended up with a psychology in which pain-pleasure hedonism is in itself the goal of human behavior. Unlike a simple hedonism, in which men do what is pleasurable and pleasurable actions are circularly defined as what men do, the associationists moved the level at which the pleasure or pain is effective to the psychological level rather than the behavioral level. (See Dickinson, 1922, pp. 98–99.)

The second departure of the associationists lay in their analysis of the will, reducing it to merely a special case of association. The analysis in this case involves an assumption that there were at first, in the individual, automatic reactions to sensations that later, because of associations learned over a period of time, were modified by the interposition of ideas of various types between the sensation and the reaction in the association process. Associationism, in other words, was mechanistic in tendency and overtly mechanistic in the work of James Mill (see Warren, 1921, pp. 87–88).

18. The Neurophysiological Model

Such a reductionistic, mechanistic psychology was entirely suitable to be adapted to the model of the nervous system that the physiologists had evolved in the nineteenth century. Clinical neurologists contributed the knowledge not only that organic brain diseases produce profound alterations of personality but that certain types of localized diseases of the nervous system and brain produce, precisely because of their localization, certain characteristic symptoms. Experimental physiologists, for their part, took up the question of exactly how the nervous system functions. They quickly ran head-on into the phenomenon of reflex action, which also parallels in a striking way association psychology.

The first man systematically to introduce into a psychological discussion a physiological base taken from the new neurophysiologists was Bain, in 1855 (Hearnshaw, 1964, pp. 11–12). (Most of Bain's psychology is associationist, except for his introduction into association psychology of Kant's threefold division of mind—knowing, feeling, willing —but Bain's importance to personality theory lies in another direction, and so he must be discussed later.) By the late nineteenth century the materialists, especially, utilized an association psychology as the psychological counterpart of the new neurophysiology. Spencer (1903, I, p. 432), for example, dealt with the concept of instinct by asserting that "Instinct may be described as—compound reflex action."

In the second and third decades of the nineteenth century Sir Charles Bell [1774–1842] and François Magendie [1783–1855] distinguished afferent and efferent nerves and established the schema of a nervous system with sensations traveling to the brain, followed by appropriate motor impulses returning from the brain and activating the muscles. The distance of this conception of the nervous machinery from that of Gall is illustrated by Bell's (quoted in Fearing, 1930, p. 117) early criticism of phrenology: "It is sufficient to say, that without comprehending the grand divisions of the nervous system, without a notion of the distinct properties of the individual nerves, or having made any distinction of the columns of the spinal marrow, without even having ascertained the difference of cerebrum and cerebellum, Gall proceeded to describe the brain as composed of many particular and independent organs, and to assign to each the residence of some special faculty." Probably more than most early neurophysiologists, Bell recognized the potential of the new schema for an automatism that was infinitely more closely based on scientific fact than the implicit determinism of Gall (Fearing, 1930, pp. 119–120).

Interestingly enough, Magendie, like Bell, departed from his teachers, in this case French ideologues, in the direction of reductionism. Where they were thoroughgoing vitalists, Magendie devoted himself to experiment and visualized, far more than they, the analysis of life processes into physical and chemical events. While he died a vitalist, Magendie, both by his discoveries in neurophysiology and by his attitudes, had contributed to the monistic deterministic materialism of the late nineteenth century, in which the new neurophysiological model played an important role. (See Temkin, 1946.)

19. Refinements of Neurophysiology

Before the neurophysiological model could be perfected, several questions had to be settled. First, the nature of the nerve cell and the courses along which nervous impulses traveled had to be clarified. With major improvements in the microscope and in staining techniques, by late in the century investigators adopted the neurone theory of the structure of the cells. With the development of the synapse theory in the early 1890's, the connections—or the relationships—between individual nerve cells became understood. The nature of the nervous impulse—descendant of the animal spirits—took less time to settle. The long-standing prejudice that nervous impulses are electrical discharges was never seriously challenged, although many details were left to be filled in. When, in 1850, Helmholtz measured the velocity of the nervous impulse, the slow speed that he found showed that the nerves were not just simple wires transmitting electricity. But the mechanical model of nervous system functioning still held good. (See in general Liddell, 1960, chs. 1–3.)

If the reflex arc was the microcosmic model for all thinking processes, the different views of what constitutes a reflex contributed greatly to the total pictures that various scientists held of the mechanisms that cause behavior. For a long time the issue was confused by the idea that any action must involve consciousness and/or the soul. In discussions of what happened in the spinal cord to cause a reflex action, the question invariably came up of how far, if at all, the soul extended down into the spine. Or the problem could be put the other way around: how much of thinking and behavior is the result of pure reflex action—before the will intervenes? (See Liddell, 1960, *passim;* Fearing, 1930, chs. 9–12.)

From the eighteenth century, the phenomenon of habit had been referred at times to reflex action, depending upon how one defines reflexes. By the late nineteenth century materialistically minded neurologists and physiologists were entirely prepared for the idea of the learned or transferred response, formulated in its classical version by Pavlov and constituting essentially a physiological association psychology. Likewise the work of Sherrington and others who emphasized the ability of the nervous system to carry out on a reflex level extremely complicated activity that involves not only integration but, as it was termed later, feedback, was presaged by a number of sophisticated workers. (See in general Liddell, 1960, especially ch. 4; Fearing, 1930, especially ch. 16.) One of the least anticipated heirs of the neurophysiological reflex schema was Sigmund Freud, who based his psychological theory upon a simple afferent-efferent circuit model, with, of course, some complex layering of the circuitry in the brain, but still basically an association psychology. (See Freud, 1955, ch. 7; Amacher, 1965.)

20. Wundt and Physiological Psychology

To a great extent, association psychology survived relatively intact. But insofar as it did not, its chief heir in the late nineteenth century was the new experimental psychology, whose most orthodox advocate was Wilhelm Wundt [1832–1920]. Wundt, who also wrote in the field of philosophy, attempted to apply logic in the most rigorous way in order to separate different aspects of psychology. He therefore advocated essentially a psychophysical parallelism, on the one hand, carefully adhering to the psychological level of description; on the other hand, Wundt explicitly utilized the neurophysiological model, "the organic interconnection of nerve-fibres and nerve-cells," to explain the association of "mental elements." (See, e.g., Wundt, 1894, p. 384; 1902, p. 8.) So thoroughgoing was Wundt's associationism, including the association of reflexes, that although eschewing materialism, he was close to at least psychological mechanism (e.g., Wundt, 1894, pp. 120–123, where he used clockwork as analogous to the operation of psychological processes).

Wundt in his psychology concentrated on what could be known by experiment. Only processes, he said, and in this case, psychological processes, can be investigated by the experimental method.[25] And of the processes, only those into which a controllable external factor can enter are suitable for precise research. He limited himself, therefore, to investigating the psychological processes affected directly by sensory perception. (See Wundt, 1894, pp. 12–13; 1902, pp. 24–25.) Since the degree of sensitivity of each individual to sensory stimuli differs, by utilizing a standard stimulus, any individual differences could be compensated for and therefore eliminated. Wundt (1894, p. 21) and his followers, in other words, were interested in general psychological principles and were not interested, as such, in individual differences.[26]

Yet as the years went on, Wundt modified his original rigorous associationism that tended to derive all mental elements from sensory perceptions. Like Bain, he utilized Kant's three categories: ideas, feelings, and volition. Ideas and feelings he employed in a pain-pleasure scheme similar to Mill's. Wundt's emphasis on affect and instinct, however, reflected a changing intellectual temper as the twentieth century approached. He connected volition explicitly with emotions and assumed that a system of instincts, therefore, underlay non-reflex action. An affect, he asserted, is always followed by bodily action of some kind. But Wundt's analysis of conflicting emotions and intellectual inhibition and control of them represented little advance over the ideas of the seventeenth century. (See, e.g., Wundt, 1894, pp. 13, 383; 1902, p. 209.)

21. Economic Man

Just as Wundt started out with an intellectualistic pain-pleasure psychology and was moving toward a psychology of motivations, so the economic theory that dominated nineteenth century thinking ended up moving in a dynamic direction that its advocates did not anticipate. The founder of classical economics was Adam Smith [1723–1790], who as a moral philosopher held a systematic view of man's motivations but as an economist held a not necessarily consistent view of the economic man whose actions are governed essentially by economic hedonism. From Smith came two lines of economic thought: one represented by economists such as Malthus or Ricardo, on the

[25] Wundt also devoted time to the study of mental products, as opposed to processes: language, myth, and custom. His more or less Lamarckian folk psychology belongs with that of Herder and his successors, but it is worth noting that behavior in general could well be considered a mental product in Wundt's system. Mental products, however, Wundt said, such as animal behavior, are not susceptible to experiment but only to observation as in other non-experimental natural history observation. (See Wundt, 1902, pp. 26–27.)

[26] Wundt (e.g., 1902, p. 30) recognized like Mill that the psychological processes over time developed associations and formed together into a personality; likewise he saw that personalities became associated together into groups. He himself had little interest in genetic or child psychology, but he did have a great deal to say about social psychology, as has been alluded to.

one hand, and, on the other hand, that represented by the utilitarian philosophers emphasizing associationist psychology. Both lines found expression in the work of John Stuart Mill and were carried further by Spencer.

Smith's economic psychology, like association psychology and Wundtian psychology, tended to emphasize the uniformity of human nature, not its variety and particularity. Smith based his ideas heavily upon the concept of human wants and the methods of satisfying them. The wants Smith considered essentially nutritive in character and therefore similar in all men. The methods of satisfying them, Smith said, were labor and exchange—again more or less, on a general or abstract level, the same for all men. Men labor and trade for as great a share of the "necessaries and conveniences of life" as possible. Each man, Smith supposed, by pursuing a natural interest fulfills God's plan that production and distribution be maximized. (See Veblen, 1948, pp. 252–258.)

With the utilitarians, Bentham and his successors, came a shift in emphasis. Gone was the teleology of God's plan, visualized by Smith; Bentham, as we have seen, went a long way toward reducing the springs of human action to an automatic hedonism. A man was supposed to exercise a "felicific calculus" to determine which course of action would maximize his pleasure (and, incidentally, material gain) and minimize his pain. By the time of James Mill, the calculating was thought to be often unconscious, but the effect of the psychology was the same, with the mechanistic tendency noted already in Mill. (See Veblen, 1948, pp. 257–259; Dickinson, 1922, pp. 76–77.) Economic man, like association psychology man, operated, whether consciously or unconsciously, automatically or volitionally, according to enlightened self-interest.[27]

22. Social Darwinism

The utilitarian economists, having shifted away from the nutritive emphasis of Smith, found themselves stressing the exchange of goods rather than their production. Their hedonism could be read largely in terms of seeking pecuniary gain. (See Veblen, 1948, pp. 262–265.) With the advent of large-scale capitalism, the accumulation of wealth tended to become an end in itself, both in economic life and in economic theory (the bourgeois novel has been noted above). At the same time, the overwhelming influence of evolutionary thinking led a number of intellectuals and businessmen to conceptualize traditional capitalistic economic theory in terms of Darwinism. The particular concept of Darwin's that these writers appropriated was "survival of the fittest." This commandeering was particularly seemly because Darwin had borrowed the idea from Malthus.

The social Darwinists, chief of whom was Spencer, were primarily concerned with the idea of competition, how competition contributes to social efficiency by weeding out the "unfit" and elevating the able. "The price which society pays for the law of competition," wrote Andrew Carnegie [1835–1919] (1962, p. 16), who rose from poor immigrant boy to industrial millionaire, "... is great; but the advantages of this law are also greater still than its cost—for it is to this law that we owe our wonderful material development, which brings improved conditions in its train.... It is best for the race, because it insures the survival of the fittest in every department." Of course the measure of fitness became vulgarized into the amount of wealth a man could accumulate, and when great corporate enterprises, involving economic cooperation, came to dominate capitalism, the conception of individual economic man, fighting for survival in the economic jungle, came into serious question. Nevertheless, it was through the efforts of Spencer's successors that social psychology developed (Karpf,

[27] John Stuart Mill finally suggested that a science of characterology—or as he called it, ethology, in which ethics was involved—was needed to supplement association psychology; but he never developed it.

1932, pp. 147–151).[28] And through helping to bring about the realization that Darwinism is biological, not economic, the social Darwinists unwittingly contributed, like other descendants of association psychology, to the rise of the new instinct psychologies of the turn of the century.

23. The Vogue of Heredity

The belief in heredity as the most important determinant of man's thought and action was connected with three diffuse currents of nineteenth century thought. One was the growing knowledge of how physiological processes operate, particularly in their pathological form, to bring about changes in both physique and behavior. A second current was the interest, stirred up by Darwin, in heredity and variation from type. Finally, there was a long-standing conviction that heredity gives a better explanation of behavioral phenomena in both humans and animals than any other explanation that had, until then, been offered.

24. Heredity as a Dictum: Lucas

The critical document in understanding the overwhelming belief in heredity is Prosper Lucas's [1808–1885] *Traité philosophique et physiologique de l'hérédité naturelle* (1847). Lucas was a French physician of considerable eminence in the field of mental illness. Although—or because—his book only summarized and synthesized common opinions about heredity, it remained the standard work on the subject for many decades. Lucas made a distinction between the passive mechanism of the body and its dynamism, or the quantity and direction of its actions. In its formulation this distinction is similar to that of Aristotle. Lucas contended that both the mechanism and the dynamism ("the moral form of our existence") of the individual are inherited. The precise physiological means of inheritance he never dealt with clearly, but they are the same for both form and function. (See Lucas, 1847, I, *passim* and pp. 7, 43.)

The moral nature that Lucas pictured as innate consists of an unremarkable group of attributes, not necessarily mutually exclusive: touch, taste, sight, hearing; motor faculties, vocal faculties; vital force; conscience, impulses, disposition; inclinations, qualities, defects; propensity to criminality (two varieties: against property and against persons); intelligence (in a broad sense). These attributes are of course, loosely speaking, also the units of inheritance in Lucas's scheme. He devoted half of his treatise to exploring the quantitative influences of mother, father, and other blood relations in the inheritance of various combinations of traits.

The most extraordinary aspect of Lucas's work is the evidence that he offered to prove his statements. It is of two kinds: proofs by authority and proofs by experience. Both amount to the same thing: casual observations of instances of resemblance assumed to be caused by heredity. Lucas used examples of heredity in animals—known especially from the well-established practices of breeding—as valid demonstrations of human inheritance.

The legacy of Lucas was threefold. First, he provided a relatively dogmatic statement that not only mind and body but character and disposition are inherited and innate. Second, he provided authority for such a position. That such authority was accepted until almost 1900 is a comment on the desire of nineteenth century thinkers to believe in innate character traits. Third, the Aristotelian distinction between the mechanism and the dynamism of the human being was compatible with the prevailing psycho-physical parallelism of the day and

[28] Another version of social Darwinism was the competition of one social group with another. The chief heir of collective social Darwinism was virulent militaristic nationalism, often in the form of racism—the superior Europeans dominated the world because they were superior (as their military strength proved) to "lesser breeds without the law."

resulted in a most extraordinary assumption: that "mind" as well as body can be inherited. In spite of the progress of neurophysiology, for decades the inheritance of character, even of criminality and insanity, was accepted without serious thought about how it was all possible in a material, physiological way—by men whose orientation, often, was materialistic. (See, for example, Ribot, 1875; Gold, 1957, pp. 20–21.)

25. Morel and Degeneration

Added to Lucas's authority for a general belief in the efficacy of heredity as a factor in human affairs was another widespread idea: degeneration. Degeneration was introduced by a Paris physician (born in Vienna) Bénédict Auguste Morel [1809–1873], in 1857. Morel traced abnormal characteristics, both physical and psychic, to a hereditary factor of degeneration. As a pre-Darwinian, he (Morel, quoted in Gold, 1957, p. 9) defined degeneracy in an individual as "the morbid deviation from a primitive type." That is, the tendency of variation is toward a savage or backward type of human, often marked by arrested development, and away from the ideal. After Darwin wrote, degeneration was understood to be atavism, a "throwback" or reversion to one's primitive or animal ancestry. Such an idea was not uncommon in post-Victorian writings, such as Jack London's *Before Adam* and Jung's expositions of the concept of a "racial unconscious."

In practice, degeneration was understood to be a process progressive through generations: "*First Generation:* Nervous temperament; moral depravity; excesses. *Second Generation:* Tendency to apoplexy and severe neuroses; alcoholism. *Third Generation:* Mental derangements; suicide; intellectual incapacity. *Fourth Generation:* Hereditary imbecility; deformities; arrested development. With this last generation the race comes to an end by sterility" (Hirsch, 1896, pp. 118–119). In degeneration what start out as personality traits end up as serious mental illnesses and physical changes.

Degeneration is not, according to Morel, hereditary in the conventional sense. Inferior hygiene and even diet, he believed, can cause the biological deviation that constitutes degeneration. Moreover, in Morel's thinking this deviation is a corporeal expression of original sin—deviation from the perfect—and at the same time a biological or at least medical version of the Enlightenment belief that social corruption (environmental influence) is the cause of evil in the individual. Where degeneration is most like original sin is in the fact that, even though possibly acquired, it is transmissible from generation to generation. (See Genil-Perrin, 1913, pp. 49–54.) This hereditary aspect of degeneracy became the most conspicuous in late nineteenth century thinking.

Like the phrenologists, the Morelians believed that degenerate mental changes are accompanied by significant modifications of the body, the so-called stigmata of degeneracy such as anomalies of the ear lobe. The most famous writer to utilize these ideas was Cesare Lombroso [1836–1909], an Italian physician who ascribed a large fraction of criminal behavior to the presence of atavistic personality—along with physical stigmata—in the population. According to Lombroso (1918, pp. 365–366), atavistic persons are marked by sexual precocity, laziness, "a passion for gambling and alcoholic drinks," excitability, etc.

26. Psychiatry

Morel's most important influence was in the field of psychiatry. There degeneration came to be confused with the inheritance of insanity. That is, the idea of degeneration had the effect of making mental illness appear less a disease than a biological fact. (See Genil-Perrin, 1913, pp. 69, 79–80.) Within psychiatry were two streams of physiological thinking, and the idea of a degenerate personality affected both of them deeply.

Writers in the French ideologue tradition in physiology had absorbed Lucas's work and fearlessly connected not only personality characteristics but mental diseases with bodily processes or just with inheritance in general. That is, the form, i.e., the body, possibly with physical stigmata, the physiological processes, and the spirit, or the mind, connected with physiology by material connection or Aristotelian assumption, all were fundamentally interdependent and in general inherited. The precise mechanisms of interconnection were, of course, almost never made clear.

Writers in the German tradition in physiology (materialistic mechanism) emphasized the new neurophysiology. Mental diseases, they asserted dogmatically, are brain diseases.[29] The neurophysiological determinism characteristic of the psychiatric profession in that period led to physical explanations of the behavior that grew out of nervous system activity; suggested treatments, likewise, were often organic: the best way to treat a sick organ is to attain general bodily health and so minimize the malfunctioning. The weakness of the organ, in this case the nervous system, clearly results from a flaw in one's heredity, just like a defective heart, for example.

The common term of the late nineteenth century to describe hereditary degeneracy affecting the nervous system was "the neuropathic constitution." Any finding of unusual or vicious behavior in a relative was used as evidence of the presence in a patient of a hereditary weakness of the nervous system (sometimes understood as degeneracy, sometimes not). Charcot, who opened up the field of hysteria to modern investigation, believed strongly that both hysteria and the ability to be hypnotized were clear behavioral stigmata of hereditary neuropathic degeneration which, because of its organic and constitutional basis, can only be relieved, not cured.

27. Krafft-Ebing

Probably the best example of a psychiatrist who embodied these trends was Richard von Krafft-Ebing [1840–1902], who introduced Morel's ideas of degeneration into psychiatry.[30] Like others of his day, Krafft-Ebing (1904, p. 22), professor of psychiatry at Vienna, believed that mental disease is a diffuse brain disease and that it is largely hereditary: "the laws of origin of mental diseases are essentially the same as those of other diseases of the brain and nerves, where the biologic law of heredity, which can be conceived only as resting on an organic basis, is of the greatest importance."

Krafft-Ebing (1904, pp. 280–281) divided mental illnesses into two kinds: cases in which the disease is more or less accidental and acute, and cases in which there has been evidence of a predisposition to mental illness. These latter he called degenerate, the outgrowth of an inherited neuropathic or "neuropsychopathic" constitution. Although the signs of neuropathic constitution vary widely with individuals, he (Krafft-Ebing, 1904, p. 359) said, in general "in such abnormally organized persons the central nervous system shows small resistive power, abnormal impressionability, and is prone to exhaustion, and . . . the cerebral functions, including those of mind, manifest themselves partly with abnormal force, partly in a distorted or perverse manner."

Actually Krafft-Ebing (1904, pp. 360–364) described a series of personality and behavior traits that could usefully be employed to describe persons predisposed to mental illnesses: developmental irregularities; exaggerated nervous symptoms in disease; unusual sensitivity and reactivity to sensory stimuli; abnormal tendencies to blush, faint, etc., and to react abnormally to physiological stimuli such as alcohol; motor defects such as strabismus and stuttering; either very

---

[29] A good example of the place of this idea in medicine of the day is provided by Wilhelm Griesinger (1867) who made such an assertion in the theoretical part of his influential book and then with utter abandon contradicted it implicitly in his section on treatment.

[30] Krafft-Ebing is useful for examination because he was so typical. Virtually all of the same general ideas, for example, are found in briefer form in the widely used work of the English psychiatrist, Henry Maudsley (1896).

weak or very strong sexual propensities; and a general tendency to emotionality and impulsiveness. All of these traits Krafft-Ebing tied to the functioning of an abnormal nervous system, although he admitted that the pathologic anatomy of degeneracy had not been established. He (Krafft-Ebing, 1904, p. 23) had no hesitation in asserting that degeneracy or any "diffuse disease of the cerebral cortex must necessarily induce a change of consciousness and of the psychic personality. Hence the psychosis appears not simply as a disease of the brain, but also as an abnormal alteration of the personality."

If character traits are biologically determined, the most confusing aspect of the conception of heredity and degeneracy held by Krafft-Ebing and others is their belief in the inheritance of acquired characteristics. Any behavior produced by the environment might well show up in the next generation as an inherited personality trait. The distinction between heredity and environment is therefore almost impossible to make, and Lamarckians in psychiatry—or in other fields of endeavor—can stand on both sides—or above—the classical nature-nurture controversy.[31] In practice advocates of such views simply traced inherited traits—or degenerative processes—back to either one's animal heritage or the influence of the environment of his more immediate ancestors. That thinkers of the Victorian era, however, tended to emphasize the aspect of heredity is significant of the trends of the times.

28. Literary Realism and Inherited Personality Traits

The French realists provide in their fiction an indication of the impact of hereditary and physiological thinking in general on late nineteenth century civilization. Although there was already a history of the influence of physiology on French fiction (see above), in the middle of the century a writer's use of physiology was one of the stigmata of the school of realists (King, 1929, p. 126). From contemporaneous hereditarian physiology the realists could draw both the documentary case histories that they needed to portray things as they actually are and the element of determinism that marked the school.

The Goncourt brothers, Edmond [1822–1896] and Jules [1830–1870], leaders of mature (or, as some believe, decadent) realism, were well acquainted with a number of eminent French physicians, including Claude Bernard, founder of experimental medicine and frequenter of literary salons (Jarman, 1939, p. 9; King, 1929, pp. 244–245). Other eminent medical figures, such as Pasteur and Charcot, often talked to literary men and presumably exerted a direct influence on their works. Where a writer such as Flaubert included medical detail in his novels for the sake of the flavor of authenticity, later authors such as the Goncourts included the medical history in order to explain the characters and actions of the principals of their novels.

The Goncourts claimed to base their novels upon nervous disorder in modern society.[32] They therefore studied the abnormal rather than the normal in their search for material for their novels. (See Jarman, 1939, p. 5.) In actual practice Charles Demailly, for example, the main character of the Goncourts' novel by that name, was taken from a case described by the famous alienist, Esquirol (King, 1929, pp. 253–254; Jarman, 1939, p. 35).

What the Goncourts were interested in primarily was the mental effects of disease processes. In *Madame Gervaisais,* for example, the characterization depends upon the psychological effects of tuberculosis, as suggested to the Goncourts by their friend, Dr.

[31] Such views no doubt expressed the practical judgment of the experienced clinician that a theoretical distinction between nature and nurture has not been justified by scientific investigation.

[32] There was widespread belief at the time that civilization itself was a cause of certain diseases, notably neurasthenia; see below.

Charles R. Robin (Jarman, 1939, p. 11). An abnormal childbirth disturbs the humors—and therefore personality—of the main character of *Germinie Lacerteux,* who already had a neuropathic constitution (King, 1929, p. 260). This interest in the effect of disease upon character resulted in a morbid irony as Edmond recorded the phenomena of Jules de Goncourt's terminal illness, which had spectacular effects on his personality and psychological state (King, 1929, pp. 247–248).[33]

29. Zola

Émile Zola [1840–1902], who now appears as a dominant figure in *fin de siècle* French literature, in his first novels used physiological, if somewhat unscientific, ideas for both plot and characterization. The plot of the earliest book revolves around the belief that the man who first impregnates a woman has (in a sense) power always to attract her, and she does not understand this physiological force that drives her. Zola's second novel, *Thérèse Raquin,* explores the fact that when two people of dissimilar physiological temperaments live together, the dissimilarity can in a purely materialistic way transform, even destroy, either partner. "These modifications," said Zola, "which have their origins in the flesh, are speedily communicated to the brain and affect the entire individual." In these early novels the supposed laws of physiology serve as fate, analogous to the supernatural forces and ghosts in the earlier—and similar—gothic novel. (See Hemmings, 1953, pp. 27–33.)

As Zola prepared to write the multivolume *Rougon-Macquart* epic of a French family, he came across Lucas's work and adopted "the laws of heredity" as the deterministic force in his novels (possibly through the influence of the great critic, Hippolyte Taine [1828–1893]). From Lucas, Zola took the idea of certain types for his characters, just as the Goncourts searched for suggestive medical cases to use as raw material. Zola also used Lucas's laws of heredity to suggest what proportion of any given trait he should assign to different blood relatives. (See Hemmings, 1953, pp. 39–43.)

At the same time, Zola did not forget the force of environment; he had one of his characters say, "She was unmistakably of the blood of the Rougons. He recognized the greed for gain, the love of intrigue that characterized the family; only, in her case, thanks to the environment in which she had grown old, . . . the common temperament had been warped to produce this strange hermaphroditism of the unsexed woman, at one and the same time business man and procuress." Here is a determinism of both heredity and the force of civilization upon the personality (quoted in Hemmings, 1953, p. 43; see also p. 34).

In large part the emphasis on social environment in Zola reflects his heritage, which was also the heritage of realism, namely, social criticism (an ironic outcome of the bourgeois, economic-motive-oriented novel) (see Hemmings, 1953, pp. 180–181; Levin, 1963, pp. 70–73). Such an attitude involves emphasizing the cumulative effect of the determinism of heredity and of historical and social circumstance. As Zola (quoted in Hemmings, 1953, p. 46) said of his cycle, "My study is the ambitions and appetites of a family rushing headlong through the modern world, making superhuman efforts, failing through its own nature and the influences that act on it. . . ." Determinism in literature to Zola was the counterpart of determinism in science. He recognized that the predictability of man was anathema to the romantics, and he opposed the romantics. His attempt to portray human nature, as well as circumstance, was therefore consciously scientific. He (Zola, 1927, p. 12) compared his work in exposing the passional and intellectual life

[33] He died of progressive general paralysis, which causes major personality disturbances and increasing mental disability; it was later found to be a true organic disease of the brain, of syphilitic origin.

of man with that of Bernard in physiology.[34]

30. Kraepelinian Psychiatry and Psychology

Such determinism also infected psychiatric thinking. The German psychiatrists, of whom Emil Kraepelin [1856–1926] of Munich was the most famous, tended to combine the pessimistic idea of organic inheritance of insanity with a basically physiological (and anti-individualistic) association psychology. Kraepelin was the psychiatrist who finally worked out a clinically practical nosology of mental illnesses, based mostly on clinical prognosis. His work (often parodied unintentionally by his followers) reinforced the view that heredity was the chief cause of mental illness. Who could have foreseen then the ways in which Kraepelin was to be, in effect, father of several aspects of modern personality study?

In addition to his medical training, Kraepelin was a student of Wundt's and in the 1890's started a series of studies on thinking processes. Since he was interested in differential diagnosis, he and his co-workers took up association processes in both normal and abnormal subjects. There is, in fact, a direct line of intellectual descent from the experiments of Kraepelin and Aschaffenburg (who differentiated, for example, between internal and external—Klang—associations) to Jung and the association test to modern diagnostic psychological testing (see Menninger, Rapaport, and Schafer, 1947). Wundt (1902, p. vii) recognized correctly that Kraepelin had taken upon himself to develop a psychologically orthodox study of "individual characterology." (Kraepelin's efforts, interestingly enough, for the most part contributed little to the mainstream of the development of psychology.)

Again, Kraepelinian psychiatry was relatively free of theory. While emphasizing proper diagnosis and prognosis, it was utterly devoid of any active therapy (except, perhaps, eugenics). This terribly pessimistic psychiatry became intolerable, and a number of conscientious and optimistic physicians began advocating psychotherapy on purely empirical grounds (see below). They were revolting, essentially, against the aridity of a belief in the inheritance of mental illnesses. Their reaction was not unlike that of Zola—toward a sophisticated environmentalism.

31. Neurasthenia

In a striking parallel to Zola's invoking modern society as a determining cause of character and behavior was the late nineteenth century medical vogue of the diagnosis of neurasthenia in psychiatry/neurology. The disease was first described definitively by an American physician, George M. Beard [1839–1883]. It is literally the result of the exhaustion of the nervous system in fast-moving modern civilization. Beard (1880, p. 189) ascribed the disease essentially to the "nervous diathesis," apparently acquired at least in part by the effects that modern living can have on the nervous system: "The prime cause of nervous disease is, without any doubt, nervous development and activity; which activity in our higher forms of civilization, especially in modern times, is carried to a degree from which nervous diseases must be the inevitable results." Beard's (1880, p. 3) dictum that the neurasthenias "are all diseases of civilization, and of modern civilization, and mainly of the nineteenth century, and of the United States," was widely quoted. (See in general Rosenberg, 1962.)

In discussions of neurasthenia, as in Morel, Zola, and Kraepelin, the idea of heredity became indistinguishable from environment. The organic viewpoint which neurasthenia in large part embodied was

[34] Heredity and environment are complicated in Zola as they are in physiological psychiatry by the presence of Lamarckian ideas (as in the apparently acquired and now inherited love of the French peasants for their land: "They love their plots of land so much they would fornicate with them" [quoted in Hemmings, 1953, p. 206]).

bankrupted by Weismannism, except for the implicit and empirical environmental manipulation that was occasionally used to supplement drug and hydrotherapy (see, for example, Mitchell, 1884).

32. Darwinism and Weismannism

As the idea of evolution received more and more attention in the decades after Darwin's *Origin of the Species,* many emphases and scientific conceptions within the general idea changed. Undoubtedly the greatest change was Weismann's introduction of the idea of inviolate germ plasm and the end of the idea of the inheritance of acquired characteristics.

Through most of the nineteenth century man was viewed both individually and as a race in terms of an organism adapting to its environment. The emphasis on heredity in the period grew in part out of an indifference to the environment as such because, as noted above, in the Lamarckian view when the environment affects the organism significantly, the effects are essentially incorporated and passed on by heredity.

After Weismann, the historical and accidental factors that affect man as an individual and as a member of a society took on a new meaning. Social institutions, especially, had to be studied on a cultural rather than a biological level, and the importance of environmental factors in explaining social processes became very great. (See Thomas, 1925, pp. 5–6.)

The Lamarckian beliefs of Darwin and his followers permitted the development of the idea that society and especially civilization had developed because moral and civilized behavior had been inherited (just as the moral philosophers believed moral propensities to be innate) because it was practiced for so long. Thus Lombroso, for example, believed that the specimens of human atavism that he found represented a reversion not to the original man but to the partly socialized savage who, having never practiced civilization, was inherently inclined to what civilized persons would consider criminal behavior. (See deQuirós, 1911, pp. 12–15.) In general the inheritance of moral characteristics guaranteed that civilization would progress and, at the same time, gave good reason for society to demand moral behavior: it is self-perpetuating and cumulative.

When, around the turn of the century, the work of Weismann, deVries, and others on the actual mechanisms of inheritance gained recognition, certain basic changes occurred in Western thinking. First, and most important, it became clear that there is an enduring, basic, inherited human nature. It does not shift and change as various groups undergo and assimilate different experiences. Second, the question of inheritable traits came up. For a long time there had been no basic improvement over the commonsense view or that of Lucas as to precisely what personality elements could be transmitted from parent to child. The gene and chromosome theory demanded much greater precision of thinking. Finally, the new views of inheritance tended to emphasize both the primitive, animal nature of the unimproved organism that comes from the womb, on the one hand, and the importance of stimuli in its environment, on the other hand. Environment was no longer seen as the cause of variation as much as it was the focal factor in adaptation. (See Thomas, 1925, p. 27.) In the emphases on well articulated ideas of both instinct and environment lay the origins of modern thinking about human nature and personality.

PART VII. THE SEED BED OF MODERN PERSONALITY THEORY AND RESEARCH

1. Instinct Theories

The foregoing narrative has suggested how the intellectual streams that underlay the neglect of the study of the individual personality developed in directions that contributed to an exactly opposite current of thought. The most striking example is the way in which both social collectivists and adherents of heredity were led to an embryonic dynamic psychology in the form of a belief in instincts.

Renewed interest in instincts grew naturally out of the Darwinian and biological climate of late nineteenth century thinking. Spencer, in attempting to show how mind had evolved, asserted that reflex actions develop into instincts, from which the higher mental functions evolve (by means of Lamarckian cumulation). (See Boring, 1950, p. 242.) Likewise the idea that man is an animal led to a great increase in attention to animal psychology, including, inevitably, both the instincts and "higher processes" of animals (see Boring, 1956).

2. Bain

One of the major roots of human instinct psychology, however, lay in the work of a Scottish philosophical psychologist, Alexander Bain [1818–1903], who began writing before Darwin published (see Cardno, 1958). Bain was a direct follower and exponent of classical association psychology, but he was troubled by its mechanistic deterministic tendency (Boring, 1950, p. 239). Since he started his psychology with an account of neurophysiology, he (Bain, 1868, p. 64) was able to go on and point out that the nervous system contains energy that leads to "movements and actions, anterior to, and independent of, the sensations of the senses." Thus muscle tonicity, random movements of the infant, and perhaps involuntary physiological activities show that central innervation is important in and of itself and that sensory stimuli are not, as suggested by the pure associationists, the only source of stimulation. "The nervous system," he (quoted in Hearnshaw, 1964, p. 12) said, "may be compared to an organ with bellows constantly charged, and ready to be let off in any direction, according to the particular keys that are touched. The stimulus of our sensations and feelings, instead of supplying the inward power, merely determines the manner and place of the discharge." This primordial nervous energy Bain (1868, p. 296) of course saw as an important element in volition. The rest of his discussion of will and motive follows Mill's closely.

Bain distinguished between the appetites and the instincts (see Cardno, 1956). The appetites, he (Bain, 1868, p. 240) said, are sensations or feelings. They appear as "the cravings produced by the recurring wants and necessities of our bodily, or organic life." Essentially, the appetites are a special class of sensation. Instinct, or "untaught ability to perform actions," by contrast, said Bain (1868, pp. 246–247), involves action and is, therefore, connected with the spontaneous innervation of the nervous system. The details of his exposition emphasize movement and expression, especially reflex actions, both simple and complex. Bain represents an interesting and influential attempt to introduce dynamics. It was just unfortunate that he was still transitional, and his plan suffered badly from competition with his lingering loyalty to intellectualistic pain-pleasure hedonism.

Bain is also notable because in 1861 he published a book *On the Study of Character*. This was the only major work on personality for many decades. How much of a pioneer Bain was is shown by his recognition that the last serious students of character before him were the phrenologists. Although Bain (1861) made excellent criticisms of the classifications of characteristics put forward by the phrenologists, he himself was unable to effect the escape—which Gall had—from thinking in terms of conventional faculties. Bain's own classification of behavior tendencies, therefore, represents no substantial improvement, but it was a long time before he had any major successors in this line of development. Even the many contemporary and later French classifications of character (such as Paulhan, 1922) did not make any serious progress, either.

3. Darwin

Another pioneer of the renewed interest in instincts was Darwin himself. His work is the best example of how evolutionary thinking led to the study of animal psychology in order to learn more about the psychological aspects of man's biological givens. In writing on *The Descent of Man,* Darwin (1896a, pp. 66, 71) included a chapter "to show that there is no fundamental difference between man and the higher mammals in their mental faculties. . . . Most of the more complex emotions are common to the higher animals and ourselves." Darwin (1896a, pp. 98 ff.) found even the social instincts to exist in animals. While Darwin's object was to prove the biological continuity between man and his non-human relatives by anthropomorphically endowing them with human characteristics, obviously it was easy enough—as his critics remarked—to turn the argument around and suggest that mere animal instincts operate in mankind.

Unlike other good Victorians, who appealed to the inheritance of acquired moral character, Darwin hedged on this issue. He did believe in the inheritance of social habits after some generations; yet at the same time he held that most fundamental instincts are not acquired but strictly part of one's native inheritance (Wilm, 1925, pp. 170–171). In general, Darwin emphasized how difficult it is to distinguish between habits built up by association in the individual and inherited habits (that is, automatic complex patterns of behavior differing but little from reflex actions). (See Darwin, 1896b, ch. 1.) In either case, however, the habits, innate or learned, Darwin (1896b) argued, are adaptive in function, that is, contribute (or at one time contributed) to the survival of the animal.

4. James

By the end of the nineteenth century a number of writers were suggesting the importance of instincts in human behavior. Probably the early systematist most widely cited was the American psychologist, William James [1842–1910]. James's (1890) theory has much to recommend it. He recognized that "cerebro-mentally" determined body movements can be set off by volition, by emotion, and by instinct or impulse. "All instinctive performances and manifestations of emotion," he (James, 1890, II, pp. 381, 384) asserted, although organized patterns of behavior, "are reflex acts." But every instinct has some purpose, he added, and human beings, unlike animals, have some idea of the end they seek in their instinctive behavior.

Our instincts can be controlled, said James (1890, II, pp. 392–394), by developing habits (that is, limiting the objects that will excite an instinctual impulse) and by the natural developmental process by which an instinct, having served its function of engendering a certain habit, will fade away. For every instinct, moreover, James asserted, somewhat like traditional thinkers, there is an exactly contrary instinct, and experience and reason decide which one, in any given case, will win out. Because a man has so many more instincts than an animal, he has more choices and his life therefore has more possibilities. (See James, 1890, II, especially p. 393.)

James, like Bain, was a seminal thinker and was, in addition, not at all consistent. While adhering to traditional ideas, he stands as a precursor of such modern concepts as imprinting. The place where his inadequacies show up at their worst is in his list of specific instincts and the casual, anecdotal evidence that he cited for their existence. He seems never to have conceived of the idea that a universally observed phenomenon might be culturally rather than biologically determined. His list runs to forty-four or forty-nine, depending on how one counts, and includes such diverse instincts as biting, pointing at desired objects, play, curiosity, hunting, grinding the teeth, imitation, and an anti-sexual instinct (Bernard, 1924, p. 144).

5. McDougall

The most influential list maker, whose work represents a high point in the revival of instinct, was the English psychologist, William McDougall [1871–1938]. His *Social Psychology* was first published in 1908 and then repeatedly reprinted and widely studied for many years thereafter. McDougall's (1916, pp. 8 ff.) aim was avowedly to refute the mechanistic pain-pleasure hedonism of association psychology and its cognate versions that suggest that reason and/or will direct the instincts. McDougall's method of refutation was to trace to their instinctual roots human behavior and institutions. His scheme is as mechanistic as the Mills' except for the elements of cognition and purposiveness that are involved in the operation of an instinct. (An instinctive action is not just a reflex action, declared McDougall, because the stimulus that activates it must have meaning, in terms of purpose, to the animal.) (See McDougall, 1916, pp. 27–29, 44.)

In harmony with post-Weismann thought, McDougall (1916, pp. 19–20) believed that social science is impossible unless one assumes as a basis for it a stable human nature which, except for racial and circumstantial variation, "has everywhere and at all times . . . [a] common native foundation . . ." of a set of instincts. Habits, McDougall (1916, pp. 43–44) said, grow out of instincts, and so all human behavior is at base instinctual. The habits do not appear in infancy; rather, various stages of maturity activate them. The higher animals modify instincts in various ways—blending, organizing, modifying and complicating reactions to them, substituting the idea of an exciting object for the actual object—but empirically one can still usually recognize the instinctual roots of actions by the types of emotions that accompany them. (See McDougall, 1916, pp. 31–32, 41, 49.)

McDougall's treatment of instincts was a great improvement over most previous expositions, even though his list contains mostly the same impulses that are based on circular logic: man has an "instinct of pugnacity" that shows up in his pugnaciousness, which is caused by the instinct of pugnacity. The place where McDougall's scheme breaks down is in his vagueness as to the mechanism by which instincts operate (he having concentrated on their phenomena and taxonomy) and, closely related, accounting for individual differences in temperament. These difficulties are pinpointed where he (McDougall, 1916, ch. 5) introduced "general or non-specific innate tendencies" such as habit forming, imitation, and even temperament (!). Not only are there no clear emotional signs of these "tendencies" (relating emotions and instincts is one of the strengths of his conception of instinct) but McDougall violated his previous careful adherence to a psychological and phenomenal level of description and invoked the nervous system, general health, and even glands.

6. Early Freud

A far more successful instinct theorist was Sigmund Freud [1856–1939], the Viennese neurologist who founded psychoanalysis. Freud's success grew out of his ability to maintain an organic and hereditary basis for instincts but escape the idea of the inheritance of either mind or complicated specific patterns of behavior. Freud in the 1890's found it necessary to account for some apparently unlearned wishes and desires in his patients and for psychological tendencies that he unearthed in dream content. He therefore posited a complex psychical apparatus in which organically derived tendencies and needs find expression in the form of instinctual drives. Freud, unlike many others, provided conceptually for both an object and for the results of the satisfaction of the drive. Eventually he worked out a method of at least partial empirical validation of his system, a considerable improvement over the circular definitions that had largely been used theretofore.

Although Freud's instinctual theory was not fully understood and appreciated for many years, he gained recognition very early for showing how instinctual drives could be understood to motivate action. Primarily he suggested the "vicissitudes" to which a drive is subject—deviation to another object and indirect methods of satisfaction, on the one hand, and, on the other hand, repression and blocking (in contrast to thinkers who believed that instincts could only be guided, not controlled). Secondarily, Freud sketched the specific mechanisms by which drive expressions are possible—symbolization, reaction formations, etc. He was understood in the early twentieth century as a major thinker who believed that there is a basic human nature.[35]

7. The Vogue of Instincts and Its Demise

At the turn of the century, advocates of various instinct psychologies flourished. One very important type, for example, appeared in those writers who found in imitation the explanation of much or all of human activity. Imitation is an exclusively social influence that derives from an apparently overwhelming innate tendency. The outstanding proponent of imitation was the French jurist and criminologist, Gabriel Tarde [1843–1904]. In addition to a basic biological inheritance built up by Lamarckian means, Tarde used the human tendency to imitate in order to explain all social phenomena. He based his individual psychology of imitation on the contemporaneous psychopathological idea of suggestion and suggestibility (see below). Many thinkers used Tarde's seminal ideas, and systematic instinctivists almost always included imitation as an instinct. (See in general Karpf, 1932, pp. 93–107.)

The era of instincts ended pretty effectively in the early 1920's with the work of L. L. Bernard [1881–1951], an American sociologist. Bernard (1924, pp. 8 ff.) traced to the influence of biology many of the shifts in attitudes toward instinct theory. The dominance of a biological approach led to the use of a biological model for the study of human behavior and institutions, he said. Then Weismann and his successors destroyed the undergirding of the instinctivists' ideas of inherited acquired characteristics which had, as noted above, included, indirectly, environmental factors. Instead of readjusting their theories, the biologists doggedly avoided environmental factors, and because of the continuing prestige of biology, many psychological and sociological writers followed their lead. So strong was this bias that for years, for example, there was no serious criticism of McDougall. (See Bernard, 1924, pp. 8–9, 12–13, 15–16, 19.)

Bernard represented and advocated a pragmatic and logical use of environmentalism and operationally viable concepts such as habit (reminiscent of Condillac) in order to study and explain character formation and social phenomena. His strongest argument was his devastating dissection of current and recent instinct theories. He found the term instinct misused and loosely used. He drew up hilariously funny lists of the various instincts that serious writers had described in man. He made basic distinctions, as between instinct as fundamental psychic energy and instinct as an inherited pattern. He questioned instincts with objects and instincts without them. He explored the almost impossible distinctions between instinct and, on the one hand, emotion, and, on the other hand, reflex action and learned habit. All of these problems appeared in damning abundance in writers, good and bad, who wrote about instincts around the turn of the century.

---

[35] Apparently Freud always believed that most of his patients had inherited neuropathic constitutions. He was misunderstood often to believe in environmentalism because he advocated psychotherapy (see below).

The impact of Bernard's work was to reinforce attitudes like that of Knight Dunlap (quoted in Bernard, 1924, p. 4), whom Bernard himself believed went too far: "Practically, we use the term instinctive reaction to designate any reaction whose antecedents we do not care, at the time, to inquire into; by *acquired reaction* on the other hand, we mean those reactions for whose antecedents we intend to give some account." The net effect of the anti-instinctivists was more destructive than Bernard, at least, desired (see below). Yet they did cut away a great deal of intellectual underbrush. The fact that heredity rather than imprecise thinking was the victim of their attacks simply reflected a predilection of the day—to emphasize environmentalism.

8. Environmentalism

When Weismannism became fully comprehended, the search for the explanations of complicated human behavior turned from past moral and social development to events in the lifetime of the individual. Freud's emphasis on the importance of the early life of the child was eagerly seized upon and had, indeed, been anticipated to some extent, for example, by genetic psychology (related to educational reform) as it developed in the 1890's.[36] The cult of the child grew in part out of the belief that he would not inherit moral instincts but would have to be taught them. Indeed, since the field in which environmental factors could operate was very much wider than had theretofore been realized, many intellectuals saw a tremendous potential to effect social change through manipulation of the environment.

There was in the twentieth century a resurgence of the Enlightenment belief that the individual human is to a significant, perhaps great, extent malleable. On the popular level this environmentalism expressed itself in reform movements in which education on all levels was to be the chief means of solving the problems of the world. On the technical level, two significant developments embodied this faith in the power of nurture: in psychology, behaviorism; in medicine, the psychotherapy movement. (See in general Burnham, 1960.)

9. The Psychotherapy Movement

Late in the nineteenth century the leading physicians dealing with nervous and mental diseases avowed a dogmatic adherence to the belief that all such illnesses are physical, usually understood as strictly organic brain diseases (see above). Even neurasthenia, caused by civilization, was understood to be a physical disease. At this very time, however, various currents in medicine were combining to change the physical bias of the treatment, if not the theory, of such diseases.

First were the empirical observations that faith cures often worked, occasionally in a striking manner. Thus grew the belief that mind—often the "power of the imagination"—could produce strong effects on even the body (e.g., see Tuke, 1873). At about the same time, hypnotism came under scientific scrutiny and was found to produce more spectacular effects that could be understood as the effect of the mind on the body. In addition, in hypnotism the influence of the hypnotist in effecting powerful changes in both mind and body was evident. Many physicians treated psychoneurotic diseases—even when, like Charcot, they believed the illnesses to be physical in nature—by hypnotic suggestion. (See Bromberg, 1954, pp. 177–195; Veith, 1965, ch. 10.)

Traditionally, and empirically, every physician knew the importance of what was referred to as "the influence of the physician." In mental illnesses systematic attempts to communicate with the patient

[36] Genetic psychology is best followed in the works of G. Stanley Hall and the publications he edited.

or in some way to change his mental attitude by environmental manipulation were known as moral treatment. Moral treatment had a long and honorable history but had fallen out of favor theoretically (see especially Dain, 1964, *passim*), although in practice all good psychiatrists and neurologists still supplemented any therapy with some "moral means." Organically oriented neurology first showed its inadequacies in the treatment of the psychoneuroses. Its practitioners tended to do little but dispense gloomy prognoses, because the diseases were, after all, supposed to be the result of a hereditary neuropathic constitution. Worst of all, physicians were losing patients to the faith healers, who were in fact relieving the agonizing symptoms from which neurotic patients suffer. The time had come, it was clear, to throw theory to the winds and establish some sort of mental treatment, or at least revive and systematize moral treatment. The result was the psychotherapy movement.

The basic assumption that was necessary to launch the psychotherapy movement was the belief that real illnesses sometimes grow out of mental processes. By the 1890's hypnotism, faith healing, and the study of hysteria had effected sufficient change—or at least open-mindedness—in the medical profession to permit the large-scale introduction of one kind of psychotherapy or another.

10. Hypnotism and Suggestion

At first hypnotism was widely used, and the term psychotherapy was understood to be a synonym or euphemism for hypnotism. The transitory nature of its effects, however, led many of its practitioners to modify their techniques and to develop a whole theory, that of the psychology of suggestion. The psychology of suggestion was extremely influential in both medicine and thought in general around the turn of the century, and it constituted in itself the chief environmental theory of personality.

Suggestion was usually a version of association psychology. Where suggestion psychology represented an innovation was in the emphasis its advocates put on suggestibility. They recognized that many associative connections are not conscious and that patterns of association (one version of which Jung popularized as the "complex") can affect behavior deeply. Suggestibility is the ability of a person to absorb into his systems of associations suggestions made, usually, by the social environment. Treatment by suggestion was aimed at changing patterns of association by replacing noxious ideas and unhealthy associations with healthy ideas and associations. (Virtually all precision in suggestion psychology was derived directly from association psychology; mostly the ideas of the advocates were at best not systematic.)

The discovery of the subconscious by many of the suggestion psychologists gave a great deal of flexibility to their school: one can accept any psychology he wishes and still account for a wide range of phenomena by invoking the power of the subconscious. A person contains, according to this theory, two selves, the conscious self with personality formed conventionally by, usually, association, and the subconscious self. Most suggestion psychologists believed that the subconscious self is that aspect of a person that can and will respond to suggestion. (The extent to which a person's subconscious can affect his life depends upon individual differences between people —some are more suggestible than others— and the particular theorist speaking.) The subconscious self was understood by most of these writers to be purely reflex in nature (e.g., Bernheim, quoted in Sidis, 1898, pp. 20–21). As the American psychopathologist, Boris Sidis (1898, pp. 245–246, italics removed), put it, the "subwaking self lacks personality"; its chief characteristic is its "extraordinary plasticity." Here was environmentalism in an extreme form, subject only to the at least partial control of the conscious self.[37]

On an empirical rather than a theoretical level, the effectiveness of suggestion in changing one's well-established personality patterns was ascribed to both authority and the basic law of association, namely, repetition of presentation. Vulnerability to repetition of the same stimuli implies that a person is relatively passive in nature, as suggested by one popularizer (Münsterberg, 1909, p. 87): "Every advertisement in the newspaper, every display in the shop-window, every warm intonation in the voice of our neighbor has its suggestive power, that is, it brings its content in such a way to our minds that the desire to do the opposite is weakened. We do buy the object that we do not need, and we do follow the advice which we ought to have reconsidered."

One of the most obscure parts of suggestion theory is why some people have the power to influence others, i.e., convey suggestions in such a way as to modify existing associations. The authority of the physician, seen at its extreme in deep hypnosis, was one of the most important assumptions of the physicians who used suggestive treatment. On the popular level it helped account for "psychic contagion"—at least where there was a charismatic suggester.

11. Re-Education and Persuasion

Obviously, educational theory of various kinds, in which one person attempts to influence another in order to change his thinking and behavior, was very close to theories of psychotherapy. One version of psychotherapy was actually called re-education. It developed out of the idea of retraining to remedy physical disabilities (relatively well established, for example, in cases of paralysis). In an early stage of knowledge hysterics with muscular disabilities received training to regain the use of their muscles by turning their attention fully to moving the arm or leg, say, affected. Habit modification very quickly came to include not only physical habits but mental habits. (See Janet, 1925, II, ch. 12.) The emphasis in re-education is upon what the patient can do to develop objective skills and use his own mental apparatus to confront the illness; the influence of the personal authority of the physician or teacher is played down.

Another major version of psychotherapy was persuasion, whose most influential advocate was an eclectic Swiss physician, Paul Dubois [1848–1914] (1909). Persuasion sometimes degenerated into mere exhortation of the patient to change his ways and get well. In the best hands, however, it is a long, tedious series of talks with the patient to bring every influence possible to bear to effect a change in the patient's thinking. Dubois (1909, p. ix) differentiated persuasion from suggestion by saying that in suggestion the suggestions are external and foreign to the patient, whereas in a successful treatment by persuasion the patient incorporates fully and permanently as his own the curative changes of mental attitude. The patient in suggestion is passive; in persuasion he has to take an active part.

Although widely used, re-education and persuasion were basically empirical medical treatments and did not involve explicit and well worked out psychological theories or ideas of personality; that field was left to suggestion psychology on one level and psychoanalysis on another. All of the psychotherapies, however, were significant—indeed, under the circumstances, dramatic—manifestations of a belief in the potential of the environment to effect changes in people. The physicians were not slow to see some of the social implications of their

[37] One source of both evil and psychopathological symptoms was held to be autosuggestion, the willful repetition by the individual of poisonous thoughts. Obviously the opposite idea, of repeatedly thinking salutary thoughts, developed into a version of mental healing, the most famous advocate of which was Emile Coué.

work. If by environmental therapy they could cure extremely difficult mental diseases, why could not the same environmental manipulation on a social scale effect changes in the masses of men, in all society? (See Burnham, 1960.)

12. Behaviorism

During the great instinct controversy, the chief anti-instinctivists were associated with the behaviorist school. Their work of destruction was not merely negative but involved the substitution for an instinct psychology of a psychology that, like psychotherapy, tended to a radical environmentalism. As one of them (Lashley, 1938, p. 130) later pointed out, the behaviorists' criticism of instinct was aimed primarily at thinkers who postulated imaginary forces to explain behavior. The anti-instinct movement missed its mark, however, and discredited and maligned the idea of the inheritance of behavior patterns or tendencies, thus for a generation discouraging psychological theorists from investigating genetic transmission of the various drives and other instinct substitutions that rushed in to fill an intellectual vacuum.

Behaviorism represented on its positive side more than just an attempt to eliminate subjectivism from scientific psychology. The behaviorists were attempting to make psychology practical, to discover ways of controlling behavior. Their hope was to discover which patterns of stimulation of the organism would produce certain behavioral reactions. If successful, behaviorism would permit the institution of complete social control through the manipulation of environmental stimuli. John B. Watson [1878–1958] (1919, p. 2, italics removed), the founder and high priest of behaviorism, explicitly anticipated that out of scientific prediction of behavior would grow the "formulation of laws and principles whereby man's actions can be controlled by organized society. Psychology endeavors to guide society as to the ways in which the environment may be modified to suit the group or individual's way of acting; or when the environment cannot be modified, to show how the individual may be moulded (forced to put on new habits) to fit the environment."

In its details behaviorism is essentially adaptive in viewpoint. The emphasis of study was upon the process of the organism's adapting to its environment. Eventually Watson employed primarily the model of conditioned reactions that Bechterev had adapted from Pavlov. Watson went further than this reduction of all behavioral reactions to reflex action, however. He suggested a complicated model composed of a few basic instinctive/emotional responses, methods of verbalization, and the layering that develops from the interplay of complex interrelationships built up from such relatively simple elements (see, e.g., Goss, 1961). Popularly, however, Watson, at least, was better known for his polemical claim (almost always cited out of context) that if he could specify the environment in which a child grew up, he could make the child into any sort of person he pleased.

13. The Rise of the Psychology of Individual Differences

Although Darwinists had been giving increasing attention to adaptation to environment, with the impact of Weismannism came, for the first time, the idea that the modes of individual adaptation might be of central importance in human and animal behavior. Alfred Russel Wallace (1875, pp. 311 ff.) as early as the 1860's had pointed out that the appearance of the human brain had changed the application of the process of natural selection to man, and the idea grew that man, unlike animals, had means other than physical endurance to win the battle of survival. Here, then, was a new test of fitness—how well the individual adapts by manipulating his environment. In contrast to the scheme of the social Darwinists, the fit were now those most intelligent, not rich; in contrast to the hereditarians, traits appeared to be randomly distributed in the population, not limited to an aristocracy. Boring (1956, pp. 274–275) has suggested the compatibility of this new view with an egalitarian society.

14. Mental Testing

The interest in individual differences was most effectively embodied in two movements: mental testing and dynamic psychiatry. Mental tests originated long before Weismann's work. At first they were usually designed to test the elements of consciousness of conventional psychology. They were, therefore, of two basic kinds: those testing the sensory and motor functions of an individual and those testing the higher mental functions. James McKeen Cattell [1860–1944], a student of Wundt's whom the master considered *ganz Amerikanisch* because he wanted to work on the problem of individual differences, in 1890 proposed ten such tests dealing with (1) strength of grip, (2) quickness of hand movement, (3) perception of the distance between two stimuli on the skin, (4) pressure-pain threshold, (5) discrimination of weights, (6) speed of reaction to sound, (7) speed of naming a number of colors in miscellaneous order, (8) accuracy of halving a fifty centimeter line, (9) determination of a ten-second interval, (10) memory of a series of consonants.

Cattell and his students undertook to test such mental and physical traits. By 1899 it was becoming clear that individual variations in quickness of reaction, muscular strength, and other attributes of sensory and motor ability do not have any meaningful relationship to scores in tests of such higher mental functions as memory and imagination. This was extremely valuable work in a negative way: it showed the necessity of a new approach to mental testing, and interest in mental tests dropped off for some years. (See in general Freeman, 1926, ch. 2; Boring, 1950, especially pp. 532–540.)

The mental test was brought back to life by Alfred Binet [1857–1911]. Many investigators had attempted to measure—in some sense—the higher mental functions. Herman Ebbinghaus (1884), for example, by the ingenious use of nonsense syllables had discovered the learning curve, but the factor of individual differences was first put into a scale by Binet in 1906–1908. He showed that one can measure the performance of an individual in a battery of tests of progressive difficulty against an ideal standard. This widely adopted, expanded, perfected, copied, and applied intelligence test measured one area of individual differences and inspired a great deal of interest in the concept of intelligence. One of the reasons that it was so exciting was that in scaling children Stern, Terman, and others found that a performance rating relative to age changed very little in an individual over the years. The idea grew that these tests must be measuring something very close to one aspect of the native human nature that Weismannism suggested must exist. (See Murphy, 1949, chs. 12 and 24; Boring, 1961, p. 249.) Indeed, for some time intelligence was believed to have a real connection with character because it was discovered that so many juvenile delinquents were mental defectives.

The development of statistics in the nineteenth century gave the measurement of individual differences its initial—and most important—impetus. Quetelet had formulated the normal law of error (the bell-shaped curve of normal distribution) and validated it with measurements of the chests and heights of soldiers. Sir Francis Galton [1822–1911], a cousin of Darwin, took over the idea and applied it crudely to the incidence of genius. The problem here was the Darwinian problem of variation. Cattell, for example, used Galton's ideas of the incidence of measurable traits (Boring, 1961, pp. 239, 251–253).

The idea that sensation, memory, and learning could be measured and scaled to show how an individual stood in a normal human population had obvious potential for the measurement of character and personality. Galton (1883, pp. 56–61) spoke—but did little—about the possibility of measuring character, but most such experimental work was stymied because of adherence to traditional psychological faculties. Attempts (such as that of Downey, 1923) to measure the will, for example, were not very promising because it was not clear exactly what was being measured. When the Würzburg school discovered the "intervening variable" in supposedly purely intellectual processes, a new field of measurement was opened up. Another early approach to the personality test was the questionnaire and inventory, used especially by G. Stanley Hall and his students, mostly on children, to find out what normal behavior really is—for example: do boys really naturally collect things? Other early workers attempted, without much success, to devise commonsense tests of traditional categories of characterization, such as "honesty." Personality testing made considerable progress only when new categories and ways of looking at human behavior that could be used to devise meaningful tests were suggested by psychiatrists and original minds in psychology and sociology (see the systematic history of objective personality testing by R. I. Watson, 1959).

15. Dynamic Psychiatry

One of the most profitable applications of biological viewpoints to the study of human nature was that of dynamic psychiatry, associated with the name of Adolf Meyer [1866–1950]. Meyer was a Swiss physician who came to the United States in the 1890's and by the 1900's represented a new and extremely profitable approach to psychiatry (see Lief, 1948, especially pp. 121–123). Like most psychiatries, dynamic psychiatry had implications far beyond the clinic in its application to questions of human nature.

A pioneer in recognizing the contributions of Kraepelin in classifying mental patients, Meyer was also one of the leaders in denouncing sterile classification of patients. Reacting against a tendency merely to pin labels on patients, Meyer insisted on starting the study of mental illness—and man—with the individual life history.

Meyer viewed each human being as a biological organism, with certain internal givens, including instincts, attempting to adapt to the environment in which he finds himself. Both the constitution and the environment, however, are uniquely individual. The pattern of inherited givens—physique, drives, defects, metabolism—is unique in every person. Likewise his circumstances are unique. To these already complex unique external givens, Meyer added a most important dimension: life history.

It was precisely in the most individual aspect of a person's existence that Meyer found a meaningful way of generalizing about human kind, and he found it by his insistence on focusing on the person as an adaptive animal. Given his nature and nurture, said Meyer, what are the animal's patterns of adaptation—using the language of psychology of the day, how effective are his reactions and habits in meeting the challenges of life? Meyer was famous for his early observation that a slowly cumulative history of habit deterioration in the patient was ascertainable in cases of schizophrenia.

By studying patterns of adaptation, Meyer and his school avoided many of the traditional views of man. Nature-nurture was no longer a meaningful or profitable distinction in reconstructing the reaction patterns of the whole man. "The best medical standard is that of adequate or efficient function...," he (Meyer, in Lief, 1948, p. 105) said as early as 1903. "In the process of emancipation from traditional and untenable views of man, an iconoclastic attitude toward all attempts at practical characterology and theories of constitution ... [is] probably the only safe procedure." Lists of instincts, classifications of faculties had little place in the Meyerian view of man except as they could be used to describe process and mode in an individual. Meyer tried to indicate the focus of his work by calling it psychobiology.

Psychobiology was long in developing, and the dynamic psychiatrists had to learn from Freud, for example, the importance of early childhood experiences and psychosexual patterns. But unlike others, they could easily absorb and use such new viewpoints as Freud's and even such disturbing innovations as the work on glandular and other physiological determinants of temperament that grew out of the increasing sophistication of experimental physiology.

16. The New Physiology of Personality

In the early twentieth century, the organic biological basis of human personality gained new students. Two discoveries, especially, were believed at the time to carry in them much potential for the future: the influence of glands on personality and Cannon's work on the physiological concomitants of emotion. As the popularizer of the former (Berman, 1921, p. 21) exclaimed, "The future belongs to the physiologist."

The internal secretions of various glands became relatively well known in the nineteenth century. The behavioral effects of excision of gonads in domestic fowl and exotic eunuchs was well known, and the medical effects of glandular dysfunction, as in Addison's disease and acromegaly, aroused great interest. The potentials of the glands for rejuvenation were publicized by the aged Brown-Séquard late in the century. (See in general Garrison, 1922.) By the 1920's the possibilities of gland regulation were arousing great popular interest. One extremist (Rubin, 1925, pp. 54–56) asserted flatly that "not only individuals, but families, nations, and races exhibit definite traits referable to the character of their internal secretions, which distinctly classify these individuals, families, or races with this quality of difference. In fact, the index of the internal secretion of any given individual may, at some not distant time, constitute the means of measurement, which will fit him into a distinct niche of our social, ethnological, and physical system.... We are rapidly coming to the conclusion that the mystery of human personality ... is, in large measure, due to the differences that exist in the character and quality of ... [individuals'] secretions." The ideologues and their physiological successors seemed to be reincarnated.

The other physiological effort to throw light on the organic bases of personality was the famous work of W. B. Cannon [1871–1945] (1915), who showed in experimental animals that there are surprisingly undifferentiated physiological effects accompanying strong emotions. Variations in various physiological processes in connection with affect had been known for some time. Galton (1884, pp. 183–184), for instance, had suggested the use of a pneumocardiograph to study character differentiation. Cannon's work, however, like Meyer's, suggested new categories of classification and proved very fruitful for his successors. (Kempf, 1918, for example, a student of Meyer's, made an ingenious combination of the work of Cannon, Sherrington, and Freud.)

PART VIII. SUMMARY AND POSTSCRIPT

By the early twentieth century, students of human behavior, with the help of increasingly sophisticated work in science, medicine, and psychology, had reached either approaches to or resolutions of the classical problems of human nature, mind-body and nature-nurture, that permitted the development of modern personality theory and research. In addition, new interest in individual differences—in terms of either modes of adaptation or measurable abilities —demanded useful and sophisticated conceptualization of both the uniqueness of the individual and his interrelationships with his society.

The study of personality as such was not formalized until the mid-1930's (see Murphy, 1949, p. 420). It is instructive to contrast the work of Gardner Murphy and Friedrich Jensen, *Approaches to Personality,* published in 1932, with the works of Gordon Allport [1897-] (1937), Henry A. Murray [1893-] (1938), and others later in the decade. Murphy and Jensen covered primarily the well-established schools of psychology and psychiatry: Gestalt; mental elements and dissociation; behaviorism; Freud; Jung; Adler; plus the genetic and child guidance approaches. Allport and Murray used approaches and materials from all of the psychological and psychiatric schools. In addition, they both knew sociological approaches to personality, such as that represented by W. I. Thomas [1863–1947]. But Allport and Murray also synthesized, Allport in terms of self, Murray in terms of type. Out of their labors and other contemporaneous work developed the present field of study.

In spite of the synthesis and creative conceptualization of the late 1930's and since, much of the innovation of the first decades of the twentieth century is still contemporary. No student of psychoanalysis dares ignore as purely historical Freud's papers of the 1890's. Expositors of field theory still carry one back, if not to the Würzburg School, at least to the 1920's. Cultural approaches to personality still have to take account of the early formulations of Franz Boas's students. George Herbert Mead [1863–1931] and even Charles Horton Cooley [1864–1929] are still commonly read for current relevancies. Those advocating the study of correlations between somatic and personality types still have to be familiar with work done in this field decades ago. All of these writings that are both historical and yet contemporary our immediate forebears produced in the first two or three decades of this century.

While this narrative must stop before it becomes contemporary, still it is appropriate to inquire as to what it was that occurred in the years between *fin de siècle* and the Great Depression that brought the study of personality to fruition. The answer, briefly put, is that investigators were able to utilize new approaches to the problem and introduce new classifications.

Psychoanalysis provides the best and most important example of the breakthrough that fathered the present subdisciplines dealing with personality. Freud's contribution, in addition to overcoming limitations in the traditional formulation of the mind-body problem (noted above), consisted of suggesting new ways of viewing motivation and new categories for typing people.

Psychoanalytic theories of motivation caught hold because they were demonstrably useful in explaining human behavior, both in general through instinctual drive concepts (sketched above) and in a specific way through the psychological mechanisms by means of which identifiable motives are expressed. By the 1930's the instinctual drive concept, derived essentially from psychoanalysis, had proved its fitness by surviving the assaults of Bernard and other anti-instinct writers and coming to dominate motivology.[38]

Psychoanalytic typology had its origin in Freud's description of the anal erotic character structure in 1908. By adding to well-established psychiatric clinical syndromes (such as schizophrenia) that can be utilized as paradigms for personality types, the psychoanalysts opened the field for the articulation of new modes of behavior that, like the oral-passive, for example, could be general in genetic development and at the same time individual in the incidence of the pattern at any stage of life. However used, such typologies broke conventional limita-

[38] Where so much contemporary literature is involved, no detailed documentation will be offered.

tions and permitted now the systematic description of "styles of life," the verisimilitude of which had theretofore been the property of literary rather than scientific writers. It was not until the time of Freud and his colleagues, such as, for example, Hermann Rorschach [1884–1922], that Gall's aspiration to overcome the traditional psychological categories and characterizations was actually fulfilled.

The contribution of Freud and other psychopathologists, as Foucault (1965, p. 198) points out, is that they re-established communication with the thinking of the mentally ill and in so doing discovered important human truths. One of the remarkable achievements of the nineteenth century pioneers of modern psychiatry had been to render thinking of the mentally ill irrelevant to their society. By making "insanity" *merely* a disease, the early modern psychiatrists had stripped mental maladies of any significance. The later psychopathologists not only established a "dialogue with madness" but saw its relevance to the interior workings of humanity in general. As Pierre Janet (quoted in Veith, 1965, p. 249) noted, "We find it neither useless nor wearisome to write down the wandering speeches of a lunatic."

One approach of psychopathologists (exemplified best by Janet and the American, Morton Prince [1854–1929]) was that of suggestion (or dissociation) psychology (see above). These men saw within a person's association systems areas of functioning that could be detached, most spectacularly in the form of autonomous multiple personalities existing in the same person. (Insofar as these areas of functioning were conceived to be layered, they resembled in part the dynamic unconscious of the Freudians.) This idea represents an extreme form of the classical association psychologists' analysis of the category of will into meaninglessness. The new unit was a given, more or less accidental personality. Because it was incomplete or influenced by accidental associations, one could hardly expect such a personality to be either rational or predictable. But one could take it seriously.

When Freud, too, began listening to his patients and even his dreams and discovered that they all made sense, he was able to go far beyond conventional categories also, no matter how much he depended upon classical association processes in his conceptualization. Freud's psychological theories and even psychoanalytic typologies worked well enough in individual cases; but when Freud and others went on to apply psychoanalytic ideas to social processes (as in *Totem and Taboo*), they ran headlong into other contemporary ideas. Reconciling these various approaches has been one of the major tasks of modern personality theory.

The task has been easier because the anthropologists followed the lead of the psychopathologists as well as the internal logic of the discipline. Anthropological writers, too, turned from formal, conventional, and drily historical patterns of classification, such as kinship patterns, to search for the consistent style of human behavior within a culture. Emphases tended to shift to the processes and away from the structures of society. The anthropologists in their new interests succeeded in raising questions about the determinism of culturally distinctive behavior that have focused attention on two areas: the interrelationship of the individual and his culture and the same question in its genetic form: child rearing.

Franz Boas [1858–1942] and his students gave the greatest impetus to this movement (see White, 1965, especially pp. 24–27). As he (quoted in White, 1965, p. 26) asserted as late as 1930, "Problems of the relation of the individual to his culture . . . have received too little attention. The standardized anthropological data that inform us of customary behavior, give no clue to reaction to his culture, nor to an understanding of his influence upon it. Still, here lie the sources of a true interpretation of human behavior. It seems a vain effort to search for sociological laws disregarding what should be called social psychology, namely, the reaction of the individual to culture. They can be no more than empty formulas that can be imbued with life only by taking account of individual behavior in cultural settings." Such investigators as Boas did not escape—nor usually tried to—from the traditional line of thinking that embodies the use of group characteristics, especially as in national character. The devotion of anthropologists and the social psychologists closely allied with them to the idea of group character seemed now to be viable, however, because of conceptions of personality and personality formation current in that sophisticated discipline.

Many other intellectual streams have contributed to the breaking of old patterns of thinking and characterization. One need mention only such terms as myth and ideology (in its modern sense) to suggest how important even writers in a speculative tradition are in recent conceptualization. (See Hughes, 1958.)

It is ironic but instructive that this essay should have to terminate with a recognition that modern personality theory and even research have been deeply influenced by philosophy. The history of the field of personality before the twentieth century is clearly the story of how questions about both individual behavior patterns and general human nature came more and more under systematic study either by scientists or by men, like Comte, influenced by the standards of science. With the rise of evolutionary thinking, at one extreme of generality, and, at the other extreme of specific practicality, the immediate need of medical clinicians to treat mental illnesses, science in one form or another led to inquiries that set up the intellectual and scientific environment in which modern personality theory could flourish. The re-entry of philosophy into the field surely appears paradoxical.

The philosophy relevant to personality is, however, of a special variety. It is mostly social philosophy—and not surprisingly, since research into personality has often had the same political urgency as in the times of the Greeks or the moral philosophers and utilitarians. The particular social philosophies most important in personality theory have been those of the pragmatists, and their ideas, it must be pointed out, have been derived essentially from science. On the one hand, they are adaptive and functional (and thus anti-traditional) in the general evolutionary diathesis of the period. On the other hand, pragmatism is supposed to be either a way of doing without philosophy or, more relevantly, a philosophical version of the scientific method. In either case, the use of the work of Dewey, Mead, and others in the scientific investigation of personality can hardly be considered to be on the same level with the dominance that formal philosophy held over the consideration of human nature and personality for so many centuries.

The modern use of philosophy is, nevertheless, vital, particularly in the conceptualization of investigators concerned with the precision of their work. The present essay suggests some of the pitfalls in the area of precision and conceptualization that surround all workers in the field of personality. More than most scientific endeavors, therefore, the study of personality can profit from the experiences of its antecedents. It behooves the behaviorist to know Condillac and LaMettrie; the field theorist, Marx; the culturalist, Du Bos; the constitutionalist, the ideologues; the Freudians, Hobbes, Mandeville, and the founding fathers; and every student of personality, Hippocrates, Lucas, and McDougall. And every investigator in the personality field should have a lively awareness of how often, in all ages, conceptions of man have appeared to both scientists and philosophers to be in harmony with the particular biases of Western culture dominant at any particular time, from Hellenic ideal man to the impersonal, mechanical man of late nineteenth century industrialism and literary realism. In the 1920's the public was learning how to use a man's motives to manipulate his behavior. "Personality" became acting in such a way as to influence the behavior of others. (See Burnham, 1968.) It is encouraging that the present study of personality had its origins at a time when, in the face of the rapid expansion of totalitarianism, intellectuals were reasserting the worth and dignity of the individual person.

REFERENCES

Ackerknecht, E. H., & Vallois, H. V. *Franz Joseph Gall, Inventor of phrenology and his collection*. Madison: Dept. of Hist. of Med., Univer. of Wisconsin Medical School, 1956. Tr. Claire St. Léon.

Aldington, R. *A book of 'characters.'* London: George Routledge, 1924.

Allbutt, T. C. *Greek medicine in Rome*. London: Macmillan, 1921.

Allport, G. W. *Personality; A psychological interpretation*. New York: Holt, 1937.

Amacher, M. P. *Freud's neurological education and its influence on psychoanalytic theory*. New York: International Universities Press, 1965.

Aries, P. *Centuries of childhood; A social history of family life*. New York: Knopf, 1962. Tr. Robert Baldick.

Bain, A. *On the study of character, Including an estimate of phrenology*. London: Parker, Son and Bourn, 1861.

Bain, A. *The senses and the intellect*. London: Longmans, Green, 1868.

Baker, H. C. *The dignity of man, Studies in the persistence of an idea*. Cambridge, Mass.: Harvard Univer. Press, 1947.

Baker, R. R. *The Thomistic theory of the passions and their influence upon the will*. Notre Dame, Ind., 1941.

Barfield, O. *History in English words*. (2nd ed.) London: Faber and Faber, 1954.

Barnes, H. E. The natural state of man. *Monist,* 1923, 33, 33–80.

Barzun, J. *Race, A study in modern superstition*. New York: Harcourt, Brace, 1937.

Barzun, J. *Romanticism and the modern ego*. Boston: Little, Brown, 1943.

Beard, G. M. *A practical treatise on nervous exhaustion (neurasthenia), Its symptoms, nature, sequences, treatment*. New York: William Wood, 1880.

Becker, C. L. *The heavenly city of the eighteenth-century philosophers*. New Haven: Yale Univer. Press, 1932.

Becker, H., & Barnes, H. E. *Social thought from lore to science*. New York: Dover, 1961. 3 vols.

Bentham, J. Table of the springs of action. In J. Bentham, *Benthamiana*. London: Semphin, Marshall, 1843. Vol. 1, pp. 195–219.

Berman, Louis. *The glands regulating personality; A study of the glands of internal secretion in relation to the types of human nature*. New York: Macmillan, 1921.

Bernard, L. L. *Instinct, A study in social psychology*. New York: Holt, 1924.

Blatchford, T. W. History of the temperaments. *Trans. Med. Soc. N. Y.,* 1848, 7, 39–59.

Boas, G. *French philosophies of the romantic period*. Baltimore: Johns Hopkins Press, 1925.

Boring, E. G. *A history of experimental psychology*. (2nd ed.) New York: Appleton-Century-Crofts, 1950.

Boring, E. G. The influence of evolutionary theory upon American psychological thought. In S. Persons (Ed.), *Evolutionary thought in America*. New York: Braziller, 1956. Pp. 268–298.

Boring, E. G. The beginning and growth of measurement in psychology. *Isis,* 1961, 52, 238–257.

Brillat-Savarin, J. *The physiology of taste, or, Meditations on transcendental gastronomy*. New York: Limited Editions, 1949. Tr. M. Fisher.

Brock, A. J. *Greek medicine, Being extracts illustrative of medical writers from Hippocrates to Galen*. London: J. M. Dent & Sons, 1929.

Bromberg, W. *Man above humanity, A history of psychotherapy*. Philadelphia: Lippincott, 1954.

Bryson, Gladys. *Man and society, The Scottish inquiry of the eighteenth century*. Princeton: Princeton Univer. Press, 1945.

Buckle, H. T. *History of civilization in England*. (2nd ed.) New York: D. Appleton, 1863.

Burnham, J. C. Psychiatry, psychology and the Progressive movement. *Amer. Quart.,* 1960, 12, 457–465.

Burnham, J. C. The new psychology: From narcissism to social control. In J. Braeman,

R. H. Bremner, & D. Brody (Eds.), *Modern America: The twenties*. Columbus: The Ohio State Univer. Press, in press, 1968.

Cannon, W. B. *Bodily changes in pain, hunger, fear and rage; An account of recent researches into the function of emotional excitement*. New York: D. Appleton, 1915.

Cardno, J. A. The notion of 'attitude': An historical note. *Psych. Rep.*, 1955, 1, 345–352.

Cardno, J. A. Bain, Lewes, and hunger. *Psych. Rep.*, 1956, 2, 267–278.

Cardno, J. A. Auguste Comte's psychology. *Psych. Rep.*, 1958, 4, 423–430. (a)

Cardno, J. A. Instinct: Some pre-experimental landmarks. *Aust. J. Psychol.*, 1958, 10, 329–340. (b)

Carlson, E. T., & Simpson, Meribeth M. Benjamin Rush's medical use of the moral faculty. *Bull. Hist. Med.*, 1965, 39, 22–33.

Carnegie, A. *The gospel of wealth*. Cambridge, Mass.: Belknap, 1962.

Carus, P. Person and personality. *Monist*, 1910, 20, 364–401.

Comte, A. *A general view of positivism*. Stanford, Calif.: Academic Reprints, 1953. Tr. J. H. Bridges.

Condillac, E. B. de. *Condillac's treatise on the sensations*. Los Angeles: Univer. of Southern California, School of Philosophy, 1930. Tr. Geraldine Carr.

Count, E. W. The evolution of the race idea in modern Western culture during the period of the pre-Darwinian nineteenth century. *N. Y. Acad. Sci. Trans.*, 1946, 8, 139–165.

Courtney, W. L. Can there be a science of character? *National Rev.*, 1890, 15, 29–38.

Curti, M. Human nature in American thought, The age of reason and morality, 1750–1860. *Polit. Sci. Quart.*, 1953, 68, 354–375.

Dain, N. *Concepts of insanity in the United States, 1789–1865*. New Brunswick: Rutgers Univer. Press, 1964.

Darwin, C. *The descent of man and selection in relation to sex*. New York: D. Appleton, 1896. (a)

Darwin, C. *Expression of the emotions in man and animals*. New York: D. Appleton, 1896. (b)

Davidson, W. L. *Political thought in England*. New York: Holt, 1916.

Davies, J. D. *Phrenology: Fad and science, A nineteenth century crusade*. New Haven: Yale Univer. Press, 1955.

Dickinson, Z. C. *Economic motives, A study in the psychological foundations of economic theory, With some reference to other social sciences*. Cambridge, Mass.: Harvard Univer. Press, 1922.

Dillenberger, J. *Protestant thought and natural science*. Garden City: Doubleday, 1960.

Downey, June E. *The will-temperament and its testing*. Yonkers-on-Hudson, N. Y.: World Book, 1923.

Draper, J. W. *History of the American Civil War*. New York: Harper, 1867–1870. 3 vols.

Dubois, P. *The psychic treatment of nervous disorders*. New York: Funk & Wagnalls, 1909. Tr. S. E. Jelliffe & W. A. White.

Dubray, C. A. The theory of psychical dispositions. *Psychol. Rev. Monog. Suppl.*, 1905, 7, No. 2.

Ebbinghaus, H. *Memory; A contribution to experimental psychology*. New York: Teachers College, 1913. Tr. H. A. Ruger & Clara E. Bussenius.

Esper, E. A. *A history of psychology*. Philadelphia: Saunders, 1964.

Fairchild, H. N. *The noble savage, A study in romantic naturalism*. New York: Columbia Univer. Press, 1928.

Fearing, F. *Reflex action: A study in the history of physiological psychology*. Baltimore: Williams & Wilkins, 1930.

Ferguson, A. *Principles of moral and political science, Being chiefly a retrospect of lectures delivered in the College of Edinburgh*. Edinburgh: A. Strahan & T. Cadell, London, and W. Creech, 1792. 2 vols.

Fess, G. M. *The correspondence of physical and material factors with character in Balzac*. Philadelphia: Univer. of Pennsylvania, 1924.

Foucault, M. *Madness and civilization, A history of insanity in the age of reason*. New York: Pantheon, 1965. Tr. R. Howard.

Fourier, C. *The passions of the human soul, And their influence on society and civilization*. London: Hippolyte Baillierre, 1851. Tr. H. Doherty. 2 vols.

Freeman, F. N. *Mental tests, Their history, principles and applications*. Boston: Houghton Mifflin, 1926.

Freud, S. *The interpretation of dreams*. New York: Basic Books, 1955. Tr. J. Strachey.

Freud, S. Character and anal erotism. In J. Strachey (Ed. & Tr.), *The standard edition of the complete psychological works of Sigmund Freud*. London: Hogarth, 1959. Vol. 9, 167–175.

Fromm, E. *Marx's concept of man*. New York: Frederick Ungar, 1961.

Funke, G. Gewohnheit. *Arch. Begriffsgeschichte*, 1958, 3.

Gall, F. J. *Origin of the moral qualities and intellectual faculties of man, and the conditions of their manifestation*. Boston: Marsh, Capen and Lyon, 1835. Tr. W. Lewis, Jr.

Galton, F. *Inquiries into human faculty and its development*. London: Macmillan, 1883.

Galton, F. The measurement of character. *Fortnightly Rev.*, 1884, 36, 179–185.

Gardiner, H. M., Metcalf, Ruth C., & Beebe-Center, J. G. *Feeling and emotion, A history of theories*. New York: American Book Company, 1937.

Garrison, F. H. History of endocrine doctrine. In L. F. Barker (Ed.), *Endocrinology and metabolism, Presented in their scientific and practical clinical aspects*. New York: D. Appleton, 1922.

Genil-Perrin, G. *Histoire des origines et de l'évolution de l'idée de dégénérescence en médecine mentale*. Paris: Alfred Leclerc, 1913.

Gobineau, A. de. *The inequality of human races*. London: William Heineman, 1915. Tr. A. Collins.

Gold, M. Nordau on *Degeneration*: A study of the book and its cultural significance. Unpublished doctoral dissertation, Columbia Univer., 1957.

Goss, A. E. Early behaviorism and verbal mediating responses. *Amer. Psychologist*, 1961, 16, 285–298.

Greene, J. C. *The death of Adam, Evolution and its impact on Western thought*. New York: New American Library, 1961.

Griesinger, W. *Mental pathology and therapeutics*. London: New Sydenham Society, 1867. Tr. C. L. Robertson and J. Rutherford.

Gunn, J. A. *Modern French philosophy: A study of the development since Comte*. London: T. Fisher Unwin, 1922.

Hearnshaw, L. S. *A short history of British psychology, 1840–1940*. New York: Barnes & Noble, 1964.

Hemmings, F. W. J. *Émile Zola*. Oxford: Clarendon Press, 1953.

Hexter, J. H. The loom of language and the fabric of imperatives: The case of *Il Principe* and *Utopia*. *Amer. Hist. Rev.*, 1964, 69, 945–968.

Hippocrates. *The genuine works of Hippocrates*. Vol. 1. London: The Sydenham Society, 1849. Tr. F. Adams.

Hirsch, W. *Genius and degeneration, A psychological study*. New York: D. Appleton, 1896. Tr. anon.

Hobbes, T. *The English works*. London: John Bohn, 1839–1845. 11 vols. Ed. W. Molesworth.

Huart, L. *Physiologie du tailleur*. Paris: Aubert et cie., Lavigne, 1841.

Hudson, J. W. *The treatment of personality by Locke, Berkeley and Hume; A study, in the interests of ethical theory, of an aspect of the dialectic of English empiricism*. Columbia: Univer. of Missouri, 1911.

Hughes, H. S. *Consciousness and society, The reorientation of European social thought, 1890–1930*. New York: Knopf, 1958.

Hume, D. *A treatise of human nature*. Oxford: Clarendon Press, 1896. Ed. L. A. Selby-Bigge.

Hutchins, R. M. (Ed.) *Great books of the Western world*. Vol. 2. New York: W. Benton, 1952.

Jaeger, W. *Paideia: The ideals of Greek culture*. New York: Oxford Univer. Press, 1939–1944. 3 vols. Tr. G. Highet.

James, W. *The principles of psychology*. New York: Henry Holt, 1890. 2 vols.

Janet, P. *Psychological healing, A historical and clinical study*. New York: Macmillan, 1925. 2 vols. Tr. E. and C. Paul.

Jarman, Laura M. The Goncourt brothers: Modernists in abnormal psychology. *Univer. New Mexico Bull., Language Ser.*, 1939, 6, No. 3.

Jastrow, J. Antecedents of the study of character and temperament. *Pop. Sci. Mo.*, 1915, 86, 590–613.

Karpf, Fay B. *American social psychology; Its origins, development, and European background*. New York: McGraw-Hill, 1932.

Keele, K. D. *Anatomies of pain*. Springfield, Ill.: Charles C Thomas, 1957.

Kempf, E. J. *The autonomic functions and the personality*. New York: Nervous and Mental Disease Publishing Company, 1918.

King, D. L. *L'influence des sciences physiologiques sur la litterature française de 1670 à 1870*. Paris: Société d'édition:—Les Belles Lettres, 1929.

Kohn, H. *Nationalism: Its meaning and history*. Princeton: D. Van Nostrand, 1955.

Koller, A. H. *The Abbé Du Bos—His advocacy of the theory of climate*. Champaign, Ill.: Ganard Press, 1937.

Krafft-Ebing, R. von. *Text-book of insanity based on clinical observations, For practitioners and students of medicine*. Philadelphia: F. A. Davis, 1904. Tr. C. G. Chaddock.

Kydd, Rachael. *Reason and conduct in Hume's treatise*. Oxford: Oxford Univer. Press, 1946.

Lashley, K. S. Experimental analysis of instinctive behavior. *Psychol. Rev.*, 1938, 45, 445–471.

Lavater, J. C. *Essays on physiognomy; For the promotion of the knowledge and the love of mankind*. London: G. G. J. and J. Robinson, 1789. 3 vols. Tr. T. Holcroft.

Le Bon, G. *The psychology of peoples*. New York: Macmillan, 1898. Tr. anon.

Levin, H. *The gates of horn*. New York: Oxford Univer. Press, 1963. Tr. R. Fitzgerald.

Lévy-Bruhl, L. *The philosophy of Auguste Comte*. London: 1903. Tr. F. Harrison.

Liddell, E. G. T. *The discovery of reflexes*. Oxford: Clarendon Press, 1960.

Lief, A. (Ed.) *The commonsense psychiatry of Dr. Adolf Meyer. Fifty-two selected papers*. New York: McGraw-Hill, 1948.

von Linné, Carl. *Systema naturae. Regnum animale. Editio Decima, 1758*. Lipsiae: Sumptibus Guilielmi Engelmann, 1894.

Locke, J. *An essay concerning human understanding*. London: J. M. Dent & Sons, 1961. 2 vols. Ed. J. W. Yolton.

Lombroso, C. *Crime, Its causes and remedies*. Boston: Little, Brown, 1918. Tr. H. P. Horton.

Lovejoy, A. O. *Essays in the history of ideas*. New York: George Braziller, 1955.

Lovejoy, A. O. *Reflections on human nature*. Baltimore: Johns Hopkins Press, 1961.

Lucas, P. *Traité philosophique et physiologique de l'hérédité naturelle dans les états de santé et de maladie du système nerveux avec l'application méthodique des lois de la procreation au traitment général des affections dont elle est le principe*. Paris: J. B. Baillièr, 1847–1850. 2 vols.

McDougall, W. *An introduction to social psychology*. Boston: John W. Luce, 1916.

Mandeville, B. *The fable of the bees, or, Private vices, publick benefits*. Oxford: Clarendon Press, 1924. 2 vols. Ed. F. B. Kaye.

Marston, J. *The works of John Marston*. Vol. 3. London: John Russell Smith, 1856.

Martineau, Harriet. (Ed. and Tr.) *The positive philosophy of Auguste Comte*. New York: Calvin Blanchard, 1858.

Maudsley, H. *Responsibility in mental disease*. New York: D. Appleton, 1896.

Menninger, K., Rapaport, D., & Schafer, R. The new role of psychological testing in psychiatry. *Am. Jour. Psychiat.*, 1947, 103, 473–476.

Mill, J. *Analysis of the phenomena of the human mind*. (2nd ed.) London: Longmans, Green, Reader, and Dyer, 1878. 2 vols. Ed. J. S. Mill.

Mitchell, S. W. *Fat and blood: An essay on the treatment of certain forms of neurasthenia and hysteria*. (3rd ed.) Philadelphia: Lippincott, 1884.

Montaigne, M. *The essays of Montaigne*. New York: Oxford Univer. Press, 1927. 2 vols. Tr. E. J. Trechmann.

Münsterberg, H. *Psychotherapy*. New York: Moffat, Yard, 1909.

Murray, H. A., *et al. Explorations in personality, A clinical and experimental study of fifty men of college age*. New York: Oxford Univer. Press, 1938.

Murphy, G. *Historical introduction to modern psychology*. (2nd ed.) New York: Harcourt, Brace, 1949.

Murphy, G., & Jensen, F. *Approaches to personality, Some contemporary conceptions used in psychology and psychiatry*. New York: Coward-McCann, 1932.

Paulhan, F. *Les caractères*. (5th ed.) Paris: Librairie Félix Alcan, 1922.

Peters, R. S. (Ed.) *Brett's history of psychology*. London: George Allen & Unwin, 1953.

Pope, A. *Essay on man*. Cambridge: Cambridge Univer. Press, 1913. Ed. H. Thompson.

DeQuirós, C. B. *Modern theories of criminality*. Boston: Little, Brown, 1911. Tr. A. de Salvio.

Ribot, T. *Heredity: A psychological study of its phenomena, laws, causes, and con-*

sequences. London: Henry S. King, 1875. Tr. anon.

Rich, Gertrude V. B. *Interpretations of human nature, A study of certain late seventeenth and early eighteenth century British attitudes toward man's nature and capacities.* New York: Columbia Univer., 1935.

Richerand, A. *Elements of physiology.* Philadelphia: Jesper Harding, 1821. Tr. G. J. M. De Lys.

Richter, A. *Geschichtsphilosophische Untersuchungen über den Begriff der Persönlichkeit (Zweiter Teil einer Schrift über "Die Persönlichkeit als noëtisches Lebensideal").* Langensalza: Hermann Beyer & Söhne (Beyer & Mann), 1907.

Roback, A. A. *Bibliography of character and personality.* Cambridge, Mass.: Sci-Art, 1927. (a)

Roback, A. A. *The psychology of character, With a survey of temperament.* New York: Harcourt, Brace, 1927. (b)

Robin, P. A. *The old physiology in English literature.* London: Dent, 1911.

Rosen, G. The philosophy of ideology and the emergence of modern medicine in France. *Bull. Hist. Med.,* 1946, 20, 328–339.

Rosenberg, C. E. The place of George M. Beard in nineteenth-century psychiatry. *Bull. Hist. Med.,* 1962, 36, 245–259.

Rosenfield, Leonora C. *From beast-machine to man-machine, Animal soul in French letters from Descartes to LaMettrie.* New York: Oxford Univer. Press, 1941.

Ross, W. G. *Human nature and utility in Hume's social philosophy.* Berea College [Berea, Ky.: the author], 1942.

Rousseau, J. J. *Emile, or Treatise on education.* New York: D. Appleton, 1892. Tr. and ed. W. H. Payne.

Rubin, H. H. *The mysterious glands; How your glands control your mental and physical development and moral welfare.* Philadelphia: Milo, 1925.

Schaupp, Zora. *The naturalism of Condillac.* Lincoln: Univer. of Nebraska, 1926.

Scheidt, W. The concept of race in anthropology and the divisions into human races from Linneus to Deniker. In E. W. Count (Ed.), *This is race, An anthology selected from the international literature on the races of man.* New York: Henry Schuman, 1950.

Sidis, B. *The psychology of suggestion, A research into the subconscious nature of man and society.* New York: D. Appleton, 1898.

Simpson, Georgiana R. *Herder's conception of "Das Volk."* Chicago: Univer. of Chicago Libraries, 1921.

Smith, D. N. *Characters from the histories & memoirs of the seventeenth century, With an essay on the character and historical notes.* Oxford: Clarendon Press, 1920.

Smith, May. The nervous temperament. *Brit. J. Med. Psychol.,* 1930, 10, 99–174.

Smith, W. *Professors and public ethics, Studies of Northern moral philosophers before the Civil War.* Ithaca: Cornell Univer. Press, 1956.

Snell, Roberta. *The nature of man in St. Thomas Aquinas compared with the nature of man in American sociology.* Washington: Catholic Univer. Press, 1942.

Spencer, H. *First principles.* New York: D. Appleton, [1899]. 2 vols.

Spencer, H. *The principles of sociology.* New York: D. Appleton, [1900]. 2 vols.

Spencer, H. *The principles of psychology.* Vol. 1. New York: D. Appleton, [1903].

Spencer, T. *Shakespeare and the nature of man.* (2nd ed.) New York: Macmillan, 1949.

Temkin, O. (Ed.) Albrecht von Haller. A dissertation on the sensible and irritable parts of animals. *Bull. Inst. Hist. Med.,* 1936, 4, 651–699.

Temkin, O. Materialism in French and German physiology of the early nineteenth century. *Bull. Hist. Med.,* 1946, 20, 322–327. (a)

Temkin, O. The philosophical background of Magendie's physiology. *Bull. Hist. Med.,* 1946, 20, 10–35. (b)

Temkin, O. Gall and the phrenological movement. *Bull. Hist. Med.,* 1947, 21, 275–283.

[Theophrastus]. *The characters of Theophrastus.* New York: Longmans, Green, 1902. Tr. C. E. Bennett & W. A. Hammond.

Thomas, F. *The environmental basis of society: A study in the history of sociological theory.* New York: Century, 1925.

Torrance, T. F. *Calvin's doctrine of man.* Grand Rapids, Mich.: Wm. B. Eerdmans, 1957.

Trendelenburg, A. A contribution to the history of the word "person." *Monist,* 1910, 20, 336–363.

Tuke, D. H. *Illustrations of the influence of the mind upon health and disease, Designed to elucidate the action of the imagination.* Philadelphia: Henry C. Lea, 1873.

Vartanian, A. *La Mettrie's* L'Homme machine, *A study in the origins of an idea.* Princeton: Princeton Univer. Press, 1960.

Veblen, T. The preconceptions of the classical economists. In M. Lerner (Ed.), *The portable Veblen.* New York: Viking, 1948. Pp. 241–274.

Veith, Ilza. *Hysteria, The history of a disease.* Chicago: Univer. of Chicago Press, 1965.

Venable, V. *Human nature: The Marxian view.* New York: Knopf, 1945.

Wallace, A. R. *Contributions to the theory of natural selection, A series of essays.* London: Macmillan, 1875.

Ward, L. F. *The psychic factors of civilization.* Boston: Ginn, 1893.

Warren, H. C. *A history of the association psychology.* New York: Scribner's, 1921.

Watson, J. B. *Psychology from the standpoint of a behaviorist.* Philadelphia: Lippincott, 1919.

Watson, R. I. Historical review of objective personality testing: The search for objectivity. In B. M. Bass and I. A. Berg (Eds.), *Objective approaches to personality assessment.* Princeton: D. Van Nostrand, 1959. Pp. 1–23.

Wells, G. A. *Herder and after: A study in the development of sociology.* Gravenhage: Mouton & Co., 1959.

White, L. A. Individuality and individualism, A culturological interpretation. In G. Mills (Ed.), *Innocence and power, Individualism in twentieth-century America.* Austin: Univer. of Texas Press, 1965. Pp. 3–35.

Whytt, R. *An essay on the vital and other involuntary motions of animals.* (2nd ed.) Edinburgh: Hamilton, Balfour, & Neill, 1763.

Willis, T. *An essay of the pathology of the brain and nervous stock: In which convulsive diseases are treated of.* London: S. Roycroft, 1684.

Wilm, E. C. *The theories of instinct, A study in the history of psychology.* New Haven: Yale Univer. Press, 1925.

Wundt, W. *Lectures on human and animal psychology.* London: Swan Sonnenschein, 1894. Tr. J.E. Creighton and E. B. Titchener.

Wundt, W. *Outlines of psychology.* Leipzig: Wilhelm Engelmann, 1902. Tr. C. H. Judd.

Zola, E. *Le roman experimental.* Paris: François Bernouard, 1927.

CHAPTER 2 Personality in Culture

IRVIN L. CHILD
Yale University

The terms "culture" and "personality" have been linked primarily in anthropology, to designate a special field of interest within that discipline. Writings by anthropologists on culture and personality turn out, naturally enough, to be of great interest to psychologists. Even without this powerful stimulus, however, the work of psychologists would lead, if not so directly and pressingly as the work of anthropologists, to considering the relation between these two concepts. While I will draw on anthropological work, I will make no attempt to review it thoroughly; that is accomplished in several recent books and articles (Honigmann, 1959; Wallace & Fogelson, 1961; Kaplan, 1961; Hsu, 1961; LeVine, 1963). My orientation here will be toward the interests of psychology, as the title "Personality in culture" indicates. How is our knowledge of personality modified, supplemented, clarified by awareness of the concept and phenomena of culture?

Each of these two terms may, of course, be used in various ways. For personality, two common meanings will be adopted here: one provides the framework for the first and smaller part of the paper; the other, for the larger second part. In the first meaning, personality refers to the complex psychological processes occurring in a human being as he functions in his daily life, motivated and directed by a host of internal and external forces. A distinction is implied between the complexity of these processes as they normally occur and the simplicity of the processes which are attended to in studying the same human being as a laboratory subject. The experimental subject is cut off from the outside world by closed doors, soundproof walls, and the attention-getting novelty of the apparatus he confronts, and has agreed to hold his various personal motives temporarily in abeyance in order that the experimenter may observe the influence on him, in these constrained conditions, of variations deliberately introduced. Among experimental findings, some offer special promise of being directly applicable to the complexly determined behavior of everyday life, or result from experiments especially planned to have this value; in referring to them the term "personality" is likely to be used. But the student of personality is not generally content with what can be learned by experiment, and seeks his data also in ordinary life and its echo in the therapeutic chamber. *Personality* in this sense is simply human psychodynamics.

The other and narrower meaning of personality refers to a more restricted subject matter within this wider range—to the internally determined consistencies underlying a person's behavior, to the enduring differences among people insofar as they are attributable to stable internal characteristics rather than to differences in their life situation. Where personality has been given a narrower meaning by psychologists, it has generally been in just this way; see for example Allport (1937) or Child (1963). Personality, in this sense, consists of all those more or less stable internal factors that make one person's behavior consistent from one time to another, and different from the behavior other people would manifest in comparable situations.

And what of culture? Where Allport filled a chapter (1937, pp. 24–54) with diverse meanings of *personality,* Kroeber and Kluckhohn's corresponding efforts for *culture* occupied a whole monograph (1952). Here, too, is a variation in meaning that we need to consider, but it is more a variation in emphasis than a real distinction in subject matter.

The culture of a group consists of the modes of acting, knowing, and feeling customary in the group. A culture may be thought of as a descriptive statement of uniformities found in the observation of many particular incidents, as abstractions formulated either by a participant in the culture or by an observer from outside. Alternatively, a culture may be thought of as a set of norms or ideals which in some way regulate or determine what occurs in particular incidents. This difference in conception of culture, fundamental though it may be to some issues, does not seem important for present purposes. The variation in emphasis that does seem important here is that *culture* is sometimes viewed as stressing uniformity and sometimes as stressing difference. Wallace (1961a, pp. 26–41) puts it very clearly, though creating in my opinion too sharp a dichotomy: The culture concept, he says, sometimes stresses replication of uniformity, and sometimes organization of diversity. That is, culture involves consistency in the action of a number of people; for example, a man who is getting married must perform certain rituals in a specified way. But culture also involves differing consistencies for differing sets of people, and the organization of these diversities into a social system is, in part, what culture is about. The man who is getting married cannot perform his expected role unless his bride and representatives of the families and of the community are all present and performing their very different but complementary roles. The distinction is especially important here because much writing on culture and personality emphasizes too strongly replication of uniformities and gives too little recognition to organization of diversity. A functioning culture necessarily involves both features; neglect of either in talking about culture may well lead to error.

PERSONALITY AS HUMAN PSYCHODYNAMICS

When personality is taken to mean the general psychodynamics of human behavior, to ask what bearing considerations of culture have upon personality leads directly to fundamental questions of human behavioral science, such as "What is universally true of human nature?" or "How much of our general psychology is valid for our culture only?" To scan an introductory textbook in psychology is to see how slow is progress toward reaching satisfactory answers to these questions. I shall attempt here little more than to try to show that such questions are indeed sensible ones to ask in a scientific context, that they deal with problems to which the methods of psychology and anthropology are applicable, and that information bearing on their answers has actually been obtained by these methods.

First, though, I will illustrate the positive contribution that awareness of culture can make to understanding specific instances of human action. Then I will turn to the question of what is universally true of human nature.

Culture and the Meaning of an Act

Psychologists often use for an act the paradigm S→O→R; the stimulus impinges on the organism and the organism responds. In the laboratory the stimulus may be as simple and isolable as a buzzer in a quiet room; the response, an eye blink or knee jerk. Within the context of the experiment these may be defined physically as vibrations of certain intensity or contractions of certain muscles. Gestalt psychology has taught the artificiality of such a definition of an act's elements. What functions as a stimulus is likely to be characterized by spatio-temporal structuring: not just the buzzer, but its sudden appearance where all was quiet; not just a circle of light, but its relation to a black field surrounding it. And on the response side, what functions as a response is for most purposes appropriately defined not physically but with reference to its significance for interaction with the physical and social environment. The words, "I love you," and appropriate movements of the face may be equivalent responses in leading up to a tender kiss, though having nothing in common physically. The words, "I love Sue," constitute quite a different response even though physically very similar to "I love you."

Patterns that function as effective stimuli and responses arise in part by cultural definition, and knowledge of the culture may be necessary or at least helpful in understanding what these patterns are and thus in knowing what a person is doing and why. The psychologist is less likely than the anthropologist to appreciate this, because he is ordinarily working entirely within his own culture. Should a psychologist be suddenly transported to a South Seas island where, peeking through the jungle underbrush into a clearing, he sees a group of natives busy at a community task with one person on a raised platform chanting, it would take him some time to decide—and then perhaps quite uncertainly—whether the chanter is directing, timing the work, invoking supernatural blessings upon it, singing to make a tedious job more bearable, or any of several other possibilities or combinations of them. Only because he knows his own culture well is he not puzzled when he looks into a factory and hears a song coming over a loudspeaker while people work.

So long as the psychologist works entirely within the culture he knows well, his understanding will perhaps not come to serious error through unawareness of the cultural sources of the meaning of stimuli and responses. He may automatically, as a member of the culture himself, draw fully upon his cultural knowledge and give to the people he sees behaving the same meaning for their surroundings and responses that he would imagine for himself in the same setting. Error may come only at a higher level of abstraction when he asks himself why the person's world is seen as it is and why the response potentialities are gathered together into acts in the way they are. Then the culturally naive psychologist may answer with an oversimplified nativism rather than an appropriately complicated cultural relativism.

At the other extreme of knowledge, the psychologist may be in little danger of error when he is completely alien to the culture. Economics and politics aside, a clinical psychologist in the United States would hardly think he could move to Tanzania and immediately practice psychotherapy with normal efficacy. He would realize that a lengthy period of learning about the alien culture is required. The real danger of concrete error through lack of cultural awareness comes, of course, at some intermediate point where one is dealing with people whose cultural background is different in subtle ways from one's own, so that one does not realize the difference or its importance. Here the American psychologist is at a great disadvantage in comparison with his imaginary colleague in a small society;

living in a very large and complex society in which people over a wide area have an astonishing similarity of appearance and manners, the American is ever in danger of overgeneralizing from his own experience.

The Psychic Unity of Mankind

Anthropologists generally assume some kind of "psychic unity of mankind" (*cf.* Wallace, 1961c, pp. 144–147). That is, they assume that certain basic psychological processes are the same in man everywhere regardless of his cultural milieu. To many a reader of anthropology in the days of the "white man's burden," this must have seemed a bold and dubious assertion. How could the dispassionate decisions of a colonial agent representing the rational power of a benevolent worldwide empire, and the crazy mumblings of a sorcerer's victim approaching his last frightened breath, possibly grow out of the same basic processes? But to the psychologist, the assumption of the psychic unity of mankind seems very modest indeed. He is well accustomed to the fact that many of his fellow psychologists, if not he himself, make the much bolder assumption of the psychic unity of the animal world including man, and regard it as not at all dubious. (Psychologists would, of course, not generally phrase the assumption that way; since there is no means of being sure that an earthworm or even a rat or a pigeon has any functions that deserve to be called psychic, they would rather forget that man may, and prefer to regard the name of their discipline as merely an unfortunate historical accident.)

But if psychologists naturally take for granted the psychic unity of mankind, it by no means follows that their methods are adequate for arriving at an apt characterization of that unity—for arriving, that is, at a satisfactory picture of what is universal in human nature. The orientation of psychology toward comparison with other animal species can help. Basic processes that experimental subjects in our society genuinely share with the rat and pigeon may be safely assumed to be shared with men of all times and places. To be sure, there is still room for self-deception about their importance. If we seek in the rat and pigeon only those processes that Western culture finds it congenial to emphasize in its view of man, our view of rats and pigeons may, for all its objectivity of detail, have a curiously Western bias.

The outcome of the comparative quest, devastating though its implications are for man's old tendency to regard himself as quite outside the animal world, still has not been altogether compatible with the psychologists' once-bland assumption of a psychic unity of the animal or even the mammalian world as a whole. The processes shared throughout must, however basic, be very limited. Evolutionary development of the nervous system brings important new potentialities even if they are a continuous growth out of those present earlier. Ethology finds important differences in the innate psychological makeup of even closely related species. We have today as much reason as ever—indeed, better reason—to believe that a proper characterization of the psychic unity of mankind will be in part distinctively human and will therefore require for its formulation and testing an adequate comparison of widely differing human groups, as well as a comparison between man and other species.

In this quest, a careful survey of the respects in which cultural rules differ from one society to another, and the respects in which they are the same, is of some help. A casual reading of some anthropological writing may give the outsider the impression that human societies are infinitely variable in the rules they have arrived at to govern social life. An account of the remarkable number of universalities in human culture, such as Murdock's (1945), is a useful corrective. But knowing about a universality of culture does not necessarily tell us what kind of process lies behind it, nor does recognition of a particular variation in culture necessarily pinpoint the exact nature of the corresponding variation in basic psychological process. Facts about how cultures are alike and different help shape our thought about the psychic unity of mankind, help us pose fruitful questions about human nature, but do not themselves tell us all we want to know about it.

To know about basic psychological processes we must get closer to them. One promising way is through field work directed at asking about uniformities or differences in psychological process. Margaret Mead (1946, p. 671) appeals to evidence of this sort in field work of her own when criticizing the generalization that frustration leads to either substitute behavior or aggressive behavior. Dollard, Doob, Miller, Mowrer, Sears, *et al.* (1939) put forth this hypothesis as applicable to all mankind. No doubt it comes from clinical and other observations in Western society, though Dollard *et al.* cite anthropological observations from other societies to argue for its probable universal validity. Mead argues that her observations on the Balinese are not compatible with this view. The underlying notion that behavior is oriented toward goals, with a temporal sequence of action normally terminating in the satisfaction of goal attainment, she claims is not valid for the Balinese, who "see their own behavior either as an infinite continuum leading nowhere, or else as separate atomic pieces." A more appropriate view of the general behavioral process, Mead suggests, would use some such term as "time gestalt" for various patterned sequences of acts; orientation toward a goal is the time gestalt characteristic of our society but may be rare or absent in some others. For the notion that frustration leads to either substitution or aggression, Mead substitutes a more general statement which might be valid for all mankind:

> . . . it is now possible to look at the goal-seeking and at the aggressive behavior in terms of this new abstraction and to see that both are alike in their punctuation, in that both end in climax. (Mead, 1946, p. 671)

This leads Mead to a broadened version of the original generalization by Dollard *et al.*:

> If an individual has been conditioned to a certain time gestalt, and if a sequence of his acts is interrupted, he will turn toward some other sequence in which a similar gestalt is implicit. (Mead, 1946, p. 671)

I, for one, am not convinced that the difference in basic process between Balinese and Americans is anything like as great as Mead would have us believe. But sitting in an office at an American university is not a very good way of finding out. Psychologists frequently rely on anthropologists who have made field trips to alien cultures to answer this sort of question. The quotations from Mead illustrate a claim sometimes made by anthropologists that the psychologists' picture of human nature grossly exaggerates the degree to which processes we think of as basic are indeed basic and universal.

On some issues of this sort, psychologists and anthropologists tend to differ from each other in quite the opposite direction. Many psychologists seem to believe that objective rational judgment about abstract questions is a special attainment of civilized man, impossible except in a person who has developed to maturity in a complex society where rational inquiry, because it is a positive value in the society, is trained into him. An alternative view is that such rational judgment can be readily developed out of universal human potentialities, so that it will sometimes be found in people who lack the upbringing of civilized men. This seems to be Pospisil's opinion (1963), supported with evidence he obtained while studying a primitive stone-age people within a few years of their first contact with the civilized world. His study of the world view of the Kapauku Papuans leads him to the conclusion that

> .... in his religious philosophizing, a Kapauku is basically logical; he refuses to accept dogmas that either oppose clear empirical

evidence or that contradict his common sense and logic. On this subject an incident in the year 1955 was illuminating to me. A very old man from the Mapia region, supported by his two sons, managed to come to see me in the Kamu Valley. As he explained to me, his main purpose in coming was a problem he wanted to have clarified before he died. The problem concerned the white man. He could not understand how it was possible that the white man could be so clever and ingenious in designing such amazing contrivances as aeroplanes (which the old man could see flying over his valley), guns, medicines, clothes, and steel tools, and at the same time could be so primitive and illogical in his religion. "How can you think," he argued, "that a man can sin and can have a free will, and at the same time believe that your God is omnipotent, and that he created the world and determined all the happenings? If he determined all that happens, and (therefore) also the bad deeds, how can a man be held responsible? Why, if he is omnipotent, did the creator have to change himself into a man and allow himself to be killed (crucified) when it would have been enough for him just to order men to behave?" (Pospisil, 1963, p. 85)

Psychologists, if they are willing to venture away from their usual haunts, can also contribute to this mapping of the psychic unity of mankind. An example is provided by Kilby's recent article (1964). Kilby's concern was with what he calls self-processes, i.e., emotional reactions connected with a person's conception of himself—reactions such as feeling embarrassed, proud, guilty, insulted, or hurt. Westerners are accustomed to thinking of such reactions as a universal part of human nature; but if an anthropologist were to tell us that in a society he had studied, such reactions were not to be found, we would probably be easily persuaded (at least more easily than in the case of goal orientation) that what we had believed to be universal was in fact not. Kilby determined to make what relevant observations he could during a stay in India. Using a variety of techniques, he ended up convinced (as his reader is likely to be) that self-processes essentially the same as ours are equally a part of human nature in India. To be sure, this is just one other society, and probably not one in which we could easily be persuaded that self-processes ought to be absent. But the inquiry needed to be started, and is usefully started here.

Both Mead's negative conclusion and Kilby's positive one suffer somewhat from being based solely on observation summarized in words, either by the local informant or by the visitor from outside. Dependence on how a member of the group verbalizes his experience, or on how the outsider verbalizes what he observes, is likely to offer more difficulty in interpreting negative findings than positive. Why should a group consistently speak of feelings having to do with evaluation of the self unless they indeed experience such feelings? It is easy, on the other hand, to imagine many reasons why feelings or a type of orientation might not be mentioned even though very much present and perhaps even accessible to awareness. Maybe the Balinese really do, as much as Westerners and the animals in Western laboratories, engage in sequences of acts oriented toward goals, despite the fact that their ways and Mead's ways of talking about their actions are discrepant with that assumption. How to resolve the question?

The answer is the same for trans-cultural investigations as for the usual psychological investigations within our own society. Try to formulate the issues and to devise methods so that the scientific meaning of terms is embodied in statements which predict observations and which are therefore vulnerable to disproof. To be short in words and long in suggestions: develop psychology through coordinated research in highly diverse cultural settings, so that its terms and statements as they develop will be known to be trans-culturally valid. Every bit of psychological knowledge, however, hardly needs to be tested in every cultural setting. Here, as elsewhere in science, the investigator's judgment must be relied on to choose what lines of research are most likely to be especially useful in confirming or upsetting doubtful generalizations, and in opening the way to better understandings.

Systematic research which tests psychological generalizations in different cultural groups is now well under way. On the cognitive side of human nature, a good example is the anthropologists' inquiry into how other peoples classify colors. Studies by Ray (1952, 1953) and by Conklin (1955) show that our own folk traditions about the major grouping and labeling of colors are not inevitable consequences of human nature, and Ray argues that trans-cultural variation here constitutes important evidence bearing on the validity of theories of color vision. Whatever the eventual conclusion, one thing that surely emerges is an effective critique of the implicit generalization by layman and psychologist alike, that our traditional classification of color is the natural one.

In imagery, careful methods of inquiry have been applied by Doob (1964, 1965) to test whether eidetic imagery is as rare among adults in two African societies—the Ibo and the Kamba—as it is among European groups. He finds a very much higher frequency of eidetic imagery in the African societies. The basis is puzzling. Doob's evidence suggests that this and related forms of imagery are a less efficient alternative to verbal methods of storing information, and that European societies somehow favor the development of the verbal alternatives. It is likely, then, that culture influences modes of storing information to an extent quite unsuspected from research limited to a European setting. A similar conclusion is reached by Gladwin (1964) in comparing Trukese and European modes of thinking. His account of Trukese navigation calls attention to the astonishing level of intellectual performance which may be found in cultures where the logical thinking we take for granted appears to be relatively weak, and where cognitive strategies of a quite different sort predominate.

Perceptual illusions were long treated in psychology as uniformities of human nature. Awareness of variation has in this instance come more or less simultaneously for comparison of individuals and comparison of cultures. Person-to-person variation in illusion plays a major part in the investigation of cognitive aspects of personality by Gardner, Holzman, Klein, Linton, and Spence (1959). Cultural variation in visual illusion was demonstrated by Allport and Pettigrew (1957) and has been investigated in a number of African societies by Segall, Campbell, and Herskovits (1966). These studies too suggest that cognition varies with culture to a degree far exceeding what the laboratory psychologist is likely to dream of, yet underneath this diversity cognition everywhere shows a basic constancy of process.

Valuable studies of uniformity and variation in the patterning of connotative meaning have been initiated by Osgood (1962) and various colleagues. His early summary of these studies suggests a very important degree of constancy in patterning from one cultural setting to another, yet probably some variation that calls for explanation. Triandis (1964, pp. 39–40) has described a Japanese study of connotative meaning by Sagara, Yamamoto, Nishimura, and Akuto (1961) which illustrates the possibility of arriving at a useful explanation of the discrepancies. Along with what may be modifications of the evaluation, potency, and activity factors repeatedly encountered in many of the studies, Sagara *et al.* report the presence of a sensory pleasure factor and point out a possible linkage with the presence of many sensory words in Japanese.

These are but samples in a rapidly expanding field of inquiry. Two recent reviews, by French (1963) and by Triandis (1964), are extremely valuable. The former draws rather more upon the work of anthropologists, and the latter, upon that of psychologists; but both are concerned with the interaction of contributions from the two sources. Both reviews seem to agree on some general implications. The details of knowledge here are just beginning to be filled in. It seems safe to predict this much about the general outcome. On the one hand, the easy assumption of universal validity of whatever is learned about cognitive processes from studying laboratory subjects in the United States or Europe is grossly in error. On the other hand, what is learned in this way is going to be universally valid in many more ways than the extremest statements of cultural relativism would have led us to believe. Some of what we readily take as "human nature" is just that and some is not, and we will know the difference only by investigation and study, not by mere reflection.

There are no comparable summaries of recent research on motivation and action directed at problems of universality and cultural variation. Of course no sharp distinction exists here, and some of the work on cognition could be classified under motivation as well. But systematic replication of psychological research in diverse cultural settings does seem to be further advanced on more strictly cognitive issues. An example on the motivation and action side is Milgram's comparative study (1961) of conformity in several Western nations. There is an urgent need for carefully selected psychological research to be replicated in highly varied settings while great cultural diversity still exists. If we wait too long, some of the psychic unity we find may be suspected of being an importation as recent as Coca-Cola.

PERSONALITY AS CONSISTENT DIFFERENCE AMONG INDIVIDUALS

The first definition of personality is concerned with generalities of human behavior —with how the typical human being acts and feels. The second definition shifts attention to differences among individuals. It is not concerned with all variations, but only with stable ones, and only with those which somehow characterize the person himself rather than the situation he is in.

Given this meaning of personality, the first great and most obvious question about its relation to culture is whether, and in what ways, personality differences among people result from differences between the cultures in which they participate. Presumably no one would ever take the extreme position of arguing that all differences among individuals are a product of culture. Against this extreme a sufficient argument is sometimes sought in the obvious fact that there are vast differences in personality among the people living within a single culture; this argument is based, however, on too narrow a concept of culture, emphasizing exclusively its significance for uniformity within a society. A more valid argument can be made by pointing out that psychological theory and research give us ample reason to believe that personality is greatly influenced by such non-cultural factors as heredity, disease and physical accident, order of birth, etc. (While these factors may themselves be an outcome of cultural regulation, they need not be.) An argument based upon understanding of culture itself is that a viable society requires the performance of various functions likely to be most congenial to people of differing personalities, and that the culture of a society, through its definition of a variety of interacting roles, can be counted on to produce diversity among its members as well as uniformity.

We may also confidently reject the other extreme view that culture's influence on personality is of slight importance. Here the most compelling argument at present is based on general psychological and anthropological knowledge. The flexibility of human personality, the amount of potential variation still left open by a person's genetic make-up, seems clearly to be great enough so that many of the distinctive cultural characteristics of each separate society are bound to have considerable influence on the developing personalities of its members. But direct evidence, the fact that individuals can be seen to behave differently, is less compelling here than it is in establishing the fact of personality differences within a society. That one person lives in a certain cultural milieu and another in a different one makes it very difficult to be confident in ascribing differences between them to personality rather than to other factors. The methodological difficulty is so great that this section will begin with attention to it.

Difficulties in Getting Evidence

Research on how personality varies with culture obviously involves some comparison between personalities in one culture and personalities in another. These comparisons must be based on some kind of observation. Initially they may be based upon a traveler's or ethnographer's general impressions of persons in the society he is visiting. Such impressions, organized into generalizations about the modal personality of a people, play a very important role in research; but they do not escape the uncertainties which characterize even more objective and precise methods, and they introduce risks of their own. At times, to be sure, the more objective and precise methods involve special risks not found in the impressionistic observational method, such as the risk of irrelevancy to the phenomena chosen for study.

By whatever method, formal or informal, comparable information needs to be gathered about personality in the various societies to be compared. And whatever the method chosen, there are very basic difficulties not easily resolved that limit the confidence to be placed in conclusions drawn. If each study to be mentioned here were carefully evaluated with respect to all these difficulties, the lengthy discussion required for each would distract from the points the studies are intended to illustrate. Instead, attention will be called at the beginning to the difficulties; and the reader is urged to apply them critically to the studies he is especially interested in, both to the facts given here and to the fuller accounts to be found elsewhere. The researcher planning to gather cross-cultural data will find particularly helpful a similar discussion by Hudson, Barakat, and LaForge (1959), for it is built around the problems encountered in a single cooperative enterprise of collecting comparable data in several societies.

Linguistic Translation

First of all there is the problem of linguistic translation. This may be essential to evaluation of responses when the method is one in which people make statements that must subsequently be judged in relation to a dimension of personality. The problem may be sufficiently illustrated with the simple case of translating questionnaire items to which the subject responds by checking one of several standard alternatives. Though the individual subject's responses do not in this case need translation, the problem of translation remains a serious one in the preparation of items. There is generally no one most obviously appropriate translation, but a number of possibilities—in sufficiently complicated cases, almost an infinity. The psychologist knows well from the experience of personality-test construction and public-opinion polling that slightly different versions of what may seem essentially the same idea can yield very different distributions of response. How then to choose among the possible translations the one which would come closest to evoking in each person the same response he would make to the original version if it were intelligible to him? A moment's consideration of the diversity of meaning from one person to another within the same culture would immediately yield the answer that there can in general be no such unique translation, for the most appropriate translation would vary from one person to another. Moreover, even in the case where the statement to be translated is so simple that there is indeed one best translation, we have no guarantee that this one most appropriate translation will be identical in meaning throughout a society, and indeed there is every reason to suppose that it can not be.

The careful researcher can reduce the difficulties connected with translation. He can check on the degree of ambiguity in translation from Language A to Language B by having another person independently translate the version of Language B back into Language A. In response to the results of this back-translation, he may then be able to achieve a more appropriate version in Language B. Especially large discrepancies in the meaning of the original and the translated versions, if they escape such preliminary cautions, may come to light in the interpretation of results. A good example is provided by Morris's detection (1956, p. 36) of inadequate translation of one part of the material he used in the study of variations in values from one society to another. And occasionally, of course, cultural comparisons are made within the body of users of a single language. English is the most conspicuous case in the literature of culture and personality thus far; personality tests have been applied in order to compare Britain and the United States and to compare sub-cultural groups within each of these countries. Here we need only be concerned with whether the statements in a single language will be understood in the same way by members of diverse societies or groups who all share the language. Greater difficulties may occur where some of the people with whom the instrument is used have only a partial or marginal use of the language—as for example when American questionnaires are given to students from abroad who are only in process of learning English, or are used in a country where English is a language of scholarship and business but is not the vernacular.

In developing new instruments especially for comparison of societies, awareness of the translation problem may help lead the investigator to useful invention. A good example is Dennis's development (1957b, 1960a) of a "uses" questionnaire for cross-cultural comparison of values, orientations, and modes of thought. The questions are extremely simple: "What is so-and-so for?" or "Why does a person do so-and-so?", asked about things and acts common everywhere. The reduction of stimuli to such bareness would hardly have been thought of in working within a single culture—though to be sure even such simple questions do not entirely avoid the difficulties of translation. Yet stimuli of such simplicity can if well chosen—as Dennis shows—be astonishingly productive of significant material.

Cultural Translation

A second difficulty has to do with what may be called cultural translation. In some instances the stimulus material used in a personality test consists partly of nonlinguistic elements; Rorschach ink blots and Thematic Apperception Test pictures are the most familiar examples. Ink blots might seem ideal for escaping this difficulty since, after all, the particular forms of the ink blots chosen by Rorschach for his test material are not culturally distinctive. Yet it must be recognized that in some societies, such as our own before the invention of ball-point pens, almost everybody had had the experience of making ink blots and seeing them, while in other societies not only ink blots but ink itself may be quite unfamiliar. Conceivably this differential in what the stimulus material is and how it was derived might have an important influence on response to it. More obvious is the problem of cultural translation of stimulus material in the case of TAT pictures. To Americans, the people on the original cards are more or less their own kind of people. If their skin or eyes do not match those of some Americans, at least their clothing and the background indicate that they share the same general culture. We could certainly not use these same TAT cards in a society with different geographical setting, clothing, and physique and reasonably expect that the meaning of all these elements would be equivalent. For this reason, researchers using the TAT in very different cultural settings have prepared a special version of the pictures aimed at having something like the same fit to the life of the people studied that the original TAT cards have for us. But just as for linguistic translation, there can be no one-to-one correspondence here. The extent to which, and precise ways in which, responses of differing peoples to differing stimulus materials can be compared remains a question to be considered separately for each case.

Varying Reactions to Being Observed or Tested

A third difficulty is that variations in the meaning to a person of the situation in which he is being interviewed, observed, or tested may be so great as to invalidate the usual use of the observations in judging general personality. Even within our own society, in which testing is common in school and knowledge of testing for other purposes is widespread, variations in the meaning of the test situation for the subject, either created by him or produced by variations in the way the examiner presents the task, are known to have a very appreciable influence on performance (Sarason, 1954). In experimental and social psychology the importance of comparable elements has recently been demonstrated by Rosenthal (1964).

In obtaining personality information from members of other societies, the field worker often labors under great difficulty and has little control over the situation in which he observes, interviews, or tests. It is likely to vary more from one subject to another than if the researcher were collecting similar data within his own society. And even if the researcher is able to control the situation, how can he make it truly comparable with that available in the other societies with which he is making a comparison? Can one meaningfully compare results of a personality test given in a society where tests have never been heard of, with results of a test given in a society where personality tests are commonly believed to reveal whether a person is insane?

Other Unintended Influences on Performance

A fourth difficulty is that even if the instructions and accompanying stimuli have been appropriately translated and the meaning of the test situation rendered fairly comparable, responses which in our society might be sufficiently determined by personality characteristics to serve as a useful index of personality may in another society instead be dominated by some causal factor irrelevant to personality. A striking example of this is provided by the work of Dennis (1960b) on drawings of the human figure by Bedouin Arabs. Dennis finds that drawings made by his Bedouin subjects are uniformly small. Principles used in interpreting figure drawings as personality expression within our society, if extended to the Bedouin drawings, might lead us to see their small size as indicating social constraint or personal constriction. Dennis reports the general reputation of Bedouins to be rather the contrary of this. The small size of their drawings, however, as well as a number of other stylistic features, are in complete harmony with the very limited visual art made and widely used by Bedouins—non-representational decorations which tend to be "low in detail, geometric in form, simple and small." The drawing experience of Dennis's subjects had probably been extremely slight, perhaps in some instances completely absent. Faced with a novel task, the Bedouin may have been strongly influenced toward a uniform sort of product by the rather limited and repetitious artistic experience he had had. The American subject, with a diversity of visual experience in art and some drawing experience, at least in school, would be more susceptible to influence by his own internal characteristics.

This interpretation by Dennis of his findings is inevitably subject to the same kinds of uncertainties being reviewed here, but it seems very likely to be correct.

Validity Specific to the Culture

Another possible difficulty is that the responses the psychologist is looking at are indeed related to personality variables and may usefully serve as an index of them, but the relationship is distinctive to the particular culture. That is, a single response variable may be significant for personality in two compared cultures, but what it signifies may be quite different in the two. A hypothetical example will have to be provided here. Let us suppose that among American subjects, the size of a human-figure drawing is a direct index of social outgoingness. If the Bedouins Dennis studied uniformly made small drawings because their experience with visual art was principally of small isolated decorations, then variation in size among the Bedouins might be indicative of degree of freedom from constraint by experience. Thus size of human-figure drawing among the Bedouins might indicate originality or spontaneity, a variable there seems no reason to consider relevant to size of drawing among Americans. Some of the substantive research to be treated later, dealing with variation among cultures in pattern of inter-variable relationships, will illustrate at a more complex level the very real existence of difficulties such as this one.

Sampling of a Society

A difficulty of quite another kind pertains to the sampling of people within each of the societies to be compared. The comparison is often thought of as relevant to the modal personality of the entire society. But getting a representative sample of a large and diverse population is a very difficult undertaking, often prohibitive in cost even for the researcher's own society. Obtaining a representative sample during a brief visit as an alien compounds the difficulties. While the problem may be somewhat reduced in studying small and less differentiated societies, it remains serious. We know that position on personality variables may vary systematically with social position within our own society, and indeed may itself be an influence on how likely it is that a person may volunteer to be a subject in a psychological study. The same factors may be operating, though perhaps in quite different ways, in another society with which a comparison is being made. If a significant difference is found on a personality variable between, let us say, Americans and Algerians, are we safe in viewing the difference as indicative of a general difference between the modal personality of members of these two societies? Or should we suspect that it is more likely related to the social status, the educational level, and the motives appealed to in obtaining subjects in the two countries? The alert investigator can reduce the probability that his findings are due to such factors irrelevant to his main purposes, but clearly the possibility can never be completely eliminated.

Difficulties in obtaining samples truly representative of a society, and in inferring that characteristics of samples obtained are attributable to the national culture, are well indicated in a careful piece of research by Butcher, Ainsworth, and Nesbitt (1963). In certain ways their study offers the minimum of difficulties. They were able to compare two countries which speak the same language—the United Kingdom and the United States—with a test especially prepared for both countries, that avoided items distinctively relevant to one national culture and not the other. They used school samples, which can more readily be made representative of some large segment of the population than any easily obtained adult samples. They found some highly significant differences between the scores of two American school samples—an urban and a rural group from the same state—and apparently also between two British samples, one from an academically selected secondary school and the other from the residual student population found in "secondary modern" schools. A comparison of the total American sample with either of the two British samples would lead to some significant findings which would be missing if the other sample instead had been used. The same is probably true, though not reported, for separate comparisons of two American samples with either of the British samples or the total British sample. Despite such difficulties, however, when the several samples from each society are put together so that real cultural consistencies may appear, some consistent differences between the two societies seem to emerge. What stands out especially is that British children manifest a higher average on assertion and American children, on conscientiousness.

Difficulties of generalizing from even large samples to the society as a whole also appear when this study is viewed against one by Cattell and Warburton (1961) that compares adults in the above two countries by means of a basically similar personality questionnaire. Here an American university sample is compared with a British university sample and with a British technical-college sample. On a number of variables the American sample is distinguished in the same direction from both the British samples, often significantly so. But on two variables the American sample lies between the two British samples, showing a highly significant difference from each of the latter. Distressingly, one of these variables, called dominance or assertion, is one of the two on which the secondary-school study had apparently shown evidence of a consistent difference between American and British samples. The only clear uniformity in the results of the two studies is that on conscientiousness or superego the American sample is significantly higher than both British samples at both educational levels. Of course, differences in comparative personality characteristics at various age levels may be a very real phenomenon. Until it is made theoretically meaningful, however, a more reasonable inference seems to be that differences between variously selected groups within any complex society are likely to far outweigh the average or over-all difference between the societies in determining scores on a personality variable. The wisdom of Butcher, Ainsworth, and Nesbitt in choosing to study children, since children can more readily be sampled in a way representative of the entire society, is thus confirmed.

Group Character Constructed from Cultural Data

Some topics I want to take up require that an important distinction be held clearly in mind. The terms I will use for making the distinction—*group character* vs. *modal personality*—are almost identical with those used by Wallace (1961a, p. 21) in a very stimulating discussion which should help bring order where usage has been confused. Both terms, as I will use them, refer to personal characteristics of individuals typical of a cultural group. We might reasonably expect, then, that when a single group is involved, the group character and modal personality should be much the same. But in fact that is a matter to be determined by observation; the two concepts are arrived at by different routes, often from quite separate observations, and might not agree well or at all.

What is the distinction, then? Group character is a concept derived by complex inference from a description of a culture; modal personality is a concept derived by generalizing from descriptions of individual personalities. This can be most clearly elucidated by sticking for the moment to data gathered by methods most typical of anthropology and of psychology, respectively. (When other sources of data are considered, the distinction is still important but is not always so clear-cut.)

An anthropologist typically inquires into

the culture of a people by asking an informant what is customarily done. Many of the cultural rules that the anthropologist learns about may seem to have no relation to one another, or a relation only of common historical origin, or a relation only of fitting together in a social system (making the performance of one role, for example, complementary to the performance of another interlocking role). But some of the cultural rules may seem to go together psychologically, in the sense that a person who follows certain of them would be imagined to like following—or to feel constrained to follow—certain others. Where this is true, the picture anthropology draws of the culture suggests a picture of the typical kind of person who would fit into that culture, would find it congenial, and would perhaps have come to be what he is as a way of adjusting to the pressures exerted by that culture. Now this is a purely hypothetical person, and it is useful to have a distinct term for his hypothetical characteristics to constantly remind us that we are not talking about the personality of an actual individual. For this usage the term *character* is adopted. Where used thus, the term has most often been incorporated (as it is by Wallace) into the phrase, *national character;* I prefer the more general phrase, *group character,* recognizing that the group involved is not necessarily a nation or even a close approximation of one.

An inference from culture to characteristics of the typical participant is most likely to be made—and to be made with most confidence—where a number of cultural features appear to have a psychological coherence of the sort I have described. But inferences of the same kind are sometimes made from separate cultural features, and the term *group character* still seems appropriate. Many features of culture do not ordinarily tempt us to make inferences of this kind. If we do speculatively find a significance for personality in customary rules of etiquette or tool-making, or in speaking a language with or without clicks among its phonemes, we are going to be very uncertain about the validity of our inferences. But in some we may feel more confidence. Suppose we read that a particular society has a very stable economy, with ample food for a long period always on hand, and efficient and equitable techniques of distributing it. We are strongly tempted to believe that the typical member of that society has little if any anxiety about getting enough to eat. If we read that young children in another society see little of adult men, we will easily believe that some aura of early-instilled femininity will cling to the typical male child there as he grows up. In these instances the cultural feature is seen as producing certain characteristics in the person influenced by it. The reverse sequence of thought may also be persuasive. Reading about the system of competitive examinations in scholarly subjects which was at the heart of the imperial Chinese civil service, we can easily imagine that for such a system to have worked successfully, strong achievement needs must have been present in many youths to have motivated their arduous study.

Such isolated inferences are very risky, and must often be quite mistaken. Probably no one would want to defend them as providing, without further test, any sound knowledge. But they can be valuable as sources of hypotheses, and it is useful to recognize them as involving the same kind of inference—from culture to personality of the typical participant—as the more complex inferences based on coherence of many features of a culture. So here too the term *group character* is appropriate to designate what is inferred about the typical person from some characteristic of the culture.

The concept to be distinguished from group character, modal personality, is a much simpler construct, growing directly out of the ordinary meaning of personality. Psychologists concerned with personality are most likely to gather data by tests designed to measure the motives, values, cognitive styles, etc., of specific individuals.

If a set of measurements have been made on individuals representative of some cultural group, then it is possible to generalize about the personality traits characteristic of the group. For such a generalization the term *modal personality* seems appropriate. It should not be taken literally in its statistical sense as the mode rather than the mean or median of a set of measurements. All that is intended by the term is that some personality variable or set of variables has been assessed, and the central tendency or value typical of the group is referred to. I will return later to this concept of modal personality, and for the present just consider group character.

What I am calling group character has ordinarily, as I have indicated, been called national character. As this term suggests, it has often been applied to inferences about the typical member of a large and complex society, a modern nation. Such inferences have one serious flaw or limitation so fundamental that, though already implied, it needs reiteration and expansion; this difficulty, moreover, is also a potential danger even in more modest inferences to group character. All actions of one person result from processes occurring in a single nervous system. While it is an empirical question how much consistency there is among his actions, whatever consistency there is has potentially a psychological or physiological source. Consistencies found in a culture do not have any such simple basis. All elements of a culture are not shared by any one person; a culture involves regularities in the behavior expected in a variety of roles, some complementary to each other in a specific situation and others performed in very different situations out of context with each other. No one person even knows about all the culture. Thus the idea of a "typical person" is a fiction whose usefulness may vary radically from one instance to another. Societies doubtless vary in the extent to which their culture approaches the never-realized extreme of being shared in its entirety by all members; complete sharing can never be expected, since sex and age must supply a quite irreducible minimum of differentiation. But in even the most highly differentiated society, some aspects of culture might conceivably be shared so widely that the notion of a typical person with corresponding personality characteristics would be very useful; it would be important, however, to recognize that the group character portrayed on this basis emerged from consideration not of the entire culture but of only a few especially widespread elements. In a highly differentiated society, a group-character construct probably would more often be useful for a restricted group within the society.

The resulting limitation is not so severe as might appear at first glance, for the analogy to individual personality is not necessarily pursued in detail. In the case of the individual, *personality* is thought of as the internal consistencies responsible for the behavior observed. In the case of the typical member of a group, *group character* may be thought of in the same way, but it may also be considered the consequences of a person's behaving over and over again in the way the culture requires. The basis for the consistencies, that is, may lie in the functioning of the society, and consistencies in the individual may only be the result of his behaving in the way required by his society. Or—in a more complicated sequence to be considered in the next section of the chapter—some aspects of the culture might shape the typical person into a certain form, and then some other features of the culture might be thought of as being selected because of their psychological compatibility with that form. The looseness of the analogy leads some anthropologists to abandon it altogether, and to substitute for *group character* some such concept as *ethos,* which is completely at the group level and makes no analogy between group and individual. Into this anthropological controversy I will not enter. For psychology the concept of group character is of special interest because it does have implications for individual personality, implications whose validity needs to be tested; and hence it, rather than ethos, is the concept considered here. The same anthropological writings could, in some instances, be considered in the one light or the other, and it is not always clear whether their authors intended to suggest direct implications for individual personality.

Probably the most widely known instance of group-character construction is Ruth Benedict's book *Patterns of Culture* (1934). Though also concerned with other aims, she constructs, for each of the three cultures examined, a picture of the most general and abstract tendencies lying behind it. These tendencies are represented as unifying principles which integrate the diverse elements of the culture (Benedict suggests that the cultures studied are probably high in degree of integration). They are also portrayed as characteristics of the typical person in the society. The personality variable to which Benedict gives special attention—Nietzsche's distinction of Apollonian *vs.* Dionysian—is thought of as partly determined by heredity or accident; but, as Benedict says, "Most people are shaped to the form of their culture because of the enormous malleability of their original endowment" (p. 254).

A group-character study based entirely on data at a societal level—in contrast to Benedict's use of individual as well as cultural data—is by McGranahan and Wayne (1948). They compare in two countries—Germany and the United States—themes, characters, and outcomes of the 45 most popular plays presented in 1927. The plays were, of course, written by a few highly specialized individuals; it is choice by the public that makes them possibly representative of group character. Viewing the plays as expressing the values of the playgoing public, McGranahan and Wayne infer a number of very marked differences between the two countries, such as, "the American orientation is essentially moralistic, the German orientation idealistic." That the findings pertained to stable group character rather than passing fad could be confirmed in some instances by referring to plays of other periods, by comparing relative success in Germany and the United States of a few plays produced in both, and by noting consistency with recurrent opinions of various observers about other aspects of the two countries' cultures.

Several studies of group character appear in a volume edited by Mead and Métraux (1953). They were begun because of possible practical value in wartime; war heightens awareness that government policy toward other nations might usefully be guided in part by information about general personality tendencies in their members, yet makes inaccessible for study most members of enemy nations. At least a few individuals, however, are likely to be available. Some of the reports in the Mead and Métraux volume synthesize social data obtained from newspapers, films, etc., with data from selected individuals regarded both as psychological subjects and as anthropological informants. Some are examples of what can be done with a single one of these approaches. The studies serve as examples of method and theory presented by writers who took a leading role in developing the group-character approach.

In individual psychology we may look for especially interesting case studies from clinicians whose practice is greatly varied. In the study of group character as well, unusually broad experience may make comparisons sounder and new insights more likely; and skillful writing may give the outsider some fruitful access to both. Two examples are conspicuous. Margaret Mead has had something of a group-character approach from her earliest days of field work and has used her highly varied experience with great ingenuity in writing numerous books and articles designed to give the intelligent layman as much of her trans-cultural understanding of personality as can be conveyed in this way. In *Male and Female* (1949) this approach is dominant. The author draws on her own field experience in several societies for suggestions about how biology and the social order interact to produce psychological differences between the sexes. A number of Mead's papers, several of which are included in her recent paperback (1964), are concerned with possible implications for personality in our society of comparisons with personality development in other societies. Where Margaret Mead draws especially on field experience in societies less complex than ours, Francis L. K. Hsu (1963) has made comparisons between our society and two others of at least equal complexity, India and China. Applying the group-character approach to social units so large that it might have been feared to be entirely fruitless, Hsu shows at the very least that a person may be led by such a route to new and convincing insights about personality problems within his own society.

The concept of group character, when based entirely on data at a social level and left with no further test of its value, is of very questionable status. Perhaps the various elements of a culture do not create or express personality characteristics. Psychological hypotheses appealed to in group-character analyses suggest that they should. These hypotheses, however—even the ones of whose validity we can be most confident in the realm of individual behavior—may lead us astray if extended in an analogical manner to the "individual" imagined as "typical" of a society. The only way to find out is by directly testing this application of such hypotheses.

To the extent that a study of group character is based on data about individuals as well as data on a group level, there is a built-in empirical test. Bateson and Mead in their study of Balinese character (1942) offer interpretations about what typical character tendencies could explain major features of Balinese culture. But they are in effect saying that these interpretations partly grew out of and partly are confirmed by observation of consistencies in the behavior of particular individuals and in the socialization experiences undergone by particular individuals. Gorer, presenting a picture of American group character (1948), interprets mass phenomena with greater confidence since his acquaintance with individual Americans confirms the appropriateness of his interpretations for at least some of them. Appeal to the observation of individuals is at least implicit in all studies based directly on field work and in some studies based principally on documents. Careful, systematic evaluation of such observation, however, requires methods quite different from the interpretative skill of the group-character approach itself. Attention will be turned to it in a later section of this paper.

Testing Hypotheses about Personality Integration of Culture

Constructing a picture of group character is sometimes based on the assumption that much of the culture of a group is integrated through personality processes. Asking why the typical member of the group behaves in the various ways indicated by an account of the culture, the answer offered by this approach is that he must have a pattern of personality tendencies which reconciles and makes consistent the variety of actions. Construction of such a picture of group character has a certain similarity to the construction by the clinician, in seeking to understand a patient as fully as possible, of a picture of that patient's individual personality. But this "idiographic" approach of the clinician, directed at understanding a specific individual, is complemented by the "nomothetic" approach aimed at abstract knowledge about personality in general. In the nomothetic approach attention may, for example, be directed at some particular dimension of variation among individuals and at testing hypotheses about the sources of this variation. The nomothetic approach, too, has its parallel at the cultural level.

Some of the group-character studies have themselves been nomothetic in emphasis even though idiographic in method. The clearest case is in the two volumes written by Kardiner and several collaborators (1939, 1945). For five different cultures—Marquesan, Tanala, Comanche, Alorese, and an American town—group-character pictures are presented. A consistent theoretical approach underlies each one, and as a result they can be readily compared. Aspects of culture given major attention are divided into two categories. *Primary institutions* are the basic aspects centering around the established social organization and means of subsistence but including the child-training practices. *Secondary institutions* are the aspects of culture probably most susceptible to influence by personality characteristics that most people in the society share—for example, artistic and other recreational customs, and certain aspects of religion and magic. These are the aspects of culture which "must satisfy the needs and tensions created by the primary or fixed ones" (Kardiner, 1939, p. 476). The link between primary and secondary institutions is provided by a theory that explains how needs and tensions are generated or modified by interaction with family and community, and how they may be expressed projectively. The theory used in the Kardiner books is psychoanalysis.

Psychoanalysis was at the time the most obviously useful theory for this purpose because it was quite explicitly concerned with the effect of childhood experience on personality and with the projective expression in adult life of the personality so formed. Behavioristic theory, however, lends itself to the effort to recast psychoanalytic hypotheses into conceptually sharper and hence more readily testable form. A combination of psychoanalytic and behavioristic influence thus guided the first attempts at adequate testing of nomothetic principles through application of nomothetic methods. The methods applicable here are those of cross-cultural correlation, first applied to personality phenomena by Horton (1943) in a study of the motivational significance of use of alcoholic beverages, and by Whiting and Child (1953) in a test of the influence of child-training practices on adult reactions to fear of illness and death.

The theoretical side of such studies has followed essentially the same reasoning as that of Kardiner, though without adopting his terminology. Certain aspects of culture are selected as more basic or primary, as the "givens" for the particular study. Often these are aspects which would be generally agreed to have a socially basic quality either in their immediate impact on survival (as in the case of economy) or in their probable stability and pervasiveness (as in the case of social structure). Most often stressed are child-training practices, considered basic because of the early and hence pervasive and persistent formative influence which psychological theories ascribe to them in the development of individual personality. Aspects of culture selected for attention as basic are then hypothesized—generally by derivation from psychoanalytic or behavioristic theory or both—to have some effect on the personality of the typical individual subjected to their influence. The resulting personality characteristic is then considered to modify or influence some less basic aspect of culture, which can be thought to have its maintenance appreciably affected because it satisfies needs characteristic of people in the society.

This reasoning has been most commonly applied to the consequences of socialization practices. For example, sudden and punitive techniques of weaning are hypothesized—because of theories of personality development arising out of clinical observations in our society—to give rise to high anxiety about oral matters. If the typical individual in a society has high anxiety about oral matters, then when confronted with the vague anxieties produced by illness and the threat of death, he may be considered likely to project his concern with orality onto these dangers over which he has little realistic control. Thus he will tend selectively to adopt or maintain theories of illness and death which attribute them to oral origins.

Here the approach differs from the group-character approach of Kardiner in what is done with this theoretical reasoning. Kardiner's approach is directed at understanding a particular culture, bringing together whatever assemblage of theory and data will best contribute to constructing a coherent and plausible picture of the implications of the culture for the personality of the typical individual participating in it. The cross-cultural approach focuses instead on a particular hypothesis. It deals with a number of cultures, hopefully a sample which can be taken as representing some larger population of cultures. In each of these, aspects are selected for analysis which the hypothesis leads us to expect to be correlated. A test is then made of whether they are in fact correlated. To continue the example cited in the previous paragraph: A hypothesis presented there predicts a positive correlation between the degree to which a society's weaning practices are traumatic and the extent to which its explanations of illness and death refer to oral activities. This is one of the hypotheses actually tested by Whiting and Child (1953). They obtained ratings for a number of societies of the severity of weaning and of the orality of explanations of illness. The two sets of ratings are found to have a very significant positive correlation.

Most studies of culture integration concerned with personality effects of child-training practices, except those published very recently, have been summarized and reviewed by Whiting (1961). They provide impressive evidence (which has continued to accumulate since) for the view that personality processes in the typical individual in a group provide one important linkage between fundamental cultural variables of economy and social structure and those aspects of culture most capable of being influenced by the typical personality characteristics resulting from the basic culture pattern. This research has been principally directed at two general problems which stand rather apart from the concern of the present paper. One has to do with theory of culture, where the question arises: What kinds of bonds are there between various elements of a culture? The answer given by these studies is that personality processes in the typical individual seem to constitute one kind of bond, one of appreciable importance. The other problem develops from psychological rather than cultural theory. It is disturbing that psychological theory has in general been verified only by studies within our society. Use of a psychological hypothesis to predict correlations over the whole range of known societies permits a universal test of its validity. Such a test is subject to all the limitations of correlational studies, but has the great advantage of not being culture-bound. It provides a way of searching for what is universally true of human nature as against what is true only within our own society or others like it. The second problem is, therefore, relevant to the first section of the present paper.

In this section, however, we are concerned with the role of culture in determining the personality characteristics of individuals. From this point of view, cross-cultural hypothesis-testing research has another interest. Predictions from psychological theory to cultural correlations are made on the assumption that basic aspects of culture produce certain personality characteristics in typical members of the society. To the extent that the predictions are confirmed, the research may be taken as indicating that the personality of typical members is indeed probably shaped in the way that these hypotheses specify. In short, these studies dealing entirely with evidence at a cultural level may be thought to provide indirect evidence about phenomena at the level of individual personality—evidence for believing that personality characteristics of individuals are to an appreciable extent shaped by pressures inherent in their society's customary ways of rearing children and of providing gratifications and frustrations at later periods of life. With respect to this conclusion of special interest here, however, the evidence of this sort of study is clearly very indirect. Nor in such research, as in group-character writings, does the typical approach involve any informal use of evidence from observation of individuals. Even more pressingly than the group-character writings, therefore, the cross-cultural studies make us wish for systematic work directed specifically at assessing how individual personality varies as a function of culture. Cross-cultural studies of the sort considered here, in short, imply important modal-personality tendencies but in themselves provide only very indirect evidence for or against them.

When viewed in this light, cross-cultural studies of personality integration of culture may greatly invigorate attempts to develop transculturally valid measures of individual personality through offering tantalizing suggestions of important potential discoveries about modal personality. An example is Allen's application (1962) to cultures of the concept of ego strength. He analyzes the concept as it has been used by various writers on mental health within Western culture, and especially as it has been applied in efforts at measurement. He then shows that the various features of individual behavior united by this concept may be paralleled by features of culture. In a subsequent paper (Allen, 1967), the same author also reports that such features of culture, complex though some of them are, can be rated with a usable degree of inter-judge agreement and thus provide a group-character measure akin to ego-strength. Most important, he finds evidence that this measure is correlated with child-training practices in ways suggested by clinically derived theories of ego strength. Here is a challenge, then, for students of culture and mental health. Their attention has been principally directed at trying to get comparable information about mental *disease* in various cultural settings. Allen's research offers promise that a positive measure of degree of mental *health* of the individual, valid transculturally, would also—if it can be developed—be of great value.

Testing the Relation between Group Character and Modal Personality

If a picture of the group character of some cultural group is constructed on the basis of inferences from cultural data, and then the personalities of a representative sample of members of that group are actually assessed, the modal-personality tendency found may or may not agree with the picture of group character. If there is agreement, this finding confirms the validity of the picture of the group character and of the procedures by which that picture was drawn, and also tends to confirm the validity, for use within this group, of the methods used in assessing individual personality. If, on the other hand, there is no fit, then the particular picture of group character is questioned; or the procedures involved in constructing group character, or in assessing individual personality, or both, become doubtful.

The same variety of outcomes is possible with respect to the inferred position of members of a group on some personality dimension used as a linkage between two aspects of culture in the manner considered in the previous section. Suppose a test designed to measure oral anxiety were applied to members of the societies used in obtaining the cross-cultural correlation between weaning trauma and oral explanations of illness. Members of societies with traumatic weaning and oral explanations of illness should tend to get high scores on this test. Members of societies with mild weaning and without oral explanations of illness should tend to get low scores. If this is not the outcome, the discrepancy is a serious challenge to the claim that personality processes are involved in culture integration.

Interest in measuring personality in various cultural groups and determining whether there is variation from one group to another does not, however, depend solely on its bearing on the validity of the two procedures we have thus far considered. It is also the direct and only appropriate way for answering the empirical question of whether, and in what ways, personality does in fact differ from one cultural group to another. In this perspective, confirmation or lack of confirmation of those expectations arising from the culturally based inferences we have reviewed is of interest primarily because it provides information about whether the personality-measuring procedures are valid when employed in this new way in a culture different from the one in which they were first applied. It is mainly because of this quite independent origin of interest in the question that most studies have been done which provide any evidence. The portrayal of group character and the personality measurements of individuals have usually been undertaken independently of each other, by different people. Thus the data available do not provide as adequate a test of the validity of procedures as if they had been collected primarily with that purpose in mind.

The challenge here comes from discrepancies, so that discrepancies are a good place to begin. One emerged from Dennis's observations of children from a pueblo society, the Hopi, of the American Southwest (1955; data gathered in 1941). In pueblo societies, including the Hopi, ethnographic studies have repeatedly reported, as Dennis says, "a minimum of overt displays of rivalry and a comparative lack of aggressiveness and of competition for prestige." This might well lead to a group-character picture which would portray the Hopi as low in motivation for competitive achievement. Generalizing to individual personality, then, if Hopi children were tested for competitive motivation, they should have a low distribution of scores. Dennis used two measures. One was cheating to get a better test score; here the Hopi children averaged lower (less cheating) than American norms. The other measure consisted of expressing interest in a competitive response (e.g., saying one would rather run a race for a prize than just for fun). On this measure the Hopi children were significantly more competitive than the American children with whom they could be compared. Why the discrepancy? We don't know. But, as Dennis puts it,

> The findings illustrate the hazard involved in assuming that traditional patterns of behavior provide a simple clue to the motivation of persons who display these patterns. (Dennis, 1955, p. 100)

An article by Turner (1960) provides another clear instance of contradiction between group character and modal personality. Turner begins by citing anthropological and semi-anthropological writings on the English and American national characters. The writers cited seem to agree that American culture is more preoccupied with competition and striving for social acceptance than English culture, which may even suppress these tendencies. He concludes that "there seems relatively little basis for doubting the general observation that American culture affords more overt approval to competitive and popularity orientation than does the English culture." He then reports scales for measuring preoccupation with competition and with social acceptance. A person's level of preoccupation is measured by his endorsement of statements ranging from a small degree of preoccupation, which almost anyone would admit, all the way to a degree of preoccupation admitted by only a small proportion. These scales were administered to several different groups of college students of both sexes in the United States and in the United Kingdom. On the scale of preoccupation with competition there is a large sex difference, and on both scales there are differences, probably genuine and meaningful, from one college population to another. Both these kinds of differences appear in each country. There is practically no suggestion, though, of any over-all difference between the two countries. Turner concludes:

Within the limitations of the method used, the results one-sidedly favor the view that surface cultural differences in competitive attitude and in striving to be liked by everyone do not fundamentally alter the private preoccupation with these matters induced by a similar social and economic structure. (Turner, 1960, p. 322)

Another instance of disagreement between individual and group generalizations is of special interest because at both levels careful quantitative analysis was used. McClelland (1961, pp. 76–79) reports for seven countries measures of concern with achievement derived separately from group and individual sources. The group source consisted of stories in children's readers used as school textbooks; the individual source, of TAT stories told by samples of college or high-school students. The two kinds of material were analyzed by the same scoring procedure. Each measure showed considerable differentiation among the countries sampled. But there was no sign of any relation between the two measures. There is no way at present of deciding among the various reasons for this discrepancy, but it stands as a useful reminder that a single measure of a variable of either group character or modal personality may not adequately predict the other kind of measure and indeed—as McClelland points out—may not be adequately representative of the culture or society even for its own kind of measure.

Such instances of discrepancy between group character and modal personality may, of course, be balanced—and, perhaps, in broad outcome though not for particular cases may be outweighed—by instances of agreement. Agreement can occur in almost direct parallel with disagreement. I began an account of the latter with Dennis's finding of a remarkable amount of achievement orientation in children reared in a culture presumably lacking such an orientation. Murphey and Nolan (1963), on the other hand, make a similar comparison with a very different outcome. They argue that children of an Indian pueblo (Jemez) should, on the basis of group-character interpretations, show less tendency than Mexican-American or Anglo-American children to choose the more-difficult-to-get of two rewards. The choice was tested for in a small sample in each of the three groups and, as predicted, it occurred least often among the pueblo Indian children.

A particular personality variable for which several studies have reported agreement of modal personality with group character is authoritarianism. Some societies appear to be more authoritarian than others in political structure, intrafamily relationships, patterns of informal social influence on the job and in recreational life, etc. Such differences in culture, when consistent, may lead to different pictures of group character. Distributions of scores on a measure of authoritarianism as a personality characteristic were first obtained in the United States, where the F-scale for measuring this variable was developed by Adorno, Frenkel-Brunswik, Levinson, and Sanford (1950). Comparison has been made with distributions of scores on the F-scale (or translations of it) in several societies which appear to be more authoritarian culturally than the United States. One is Germany, where Cohn and Carsch (1954) report a higher distribution of scores than for comparable American samples. Another is Arab society of the Middle East, where Prothro and Melikian (1953) and Melikian (1956, 1959) have applied the F-scale. The mean scores of various groups of Middle Eastern college students, they find, exceed comparable means for United States groups by amounts varying from about one standard deviation up to as much as two full standard deviations—a group difference of extraordinary magnitude.

In his cross-national study of values, Morris (1956) uses data at the personality level to make generalizations which he then, in some instances, compares with statements at a cultural level. The data consisted of ratings, by several hundred students in each of several nations, of personal preference for thirteen different ways of life described in detail. The mean rating given to each of the ways is compared for various national groups, and this comparison—together with other information emerging from the study —is used as a basis for characterizing the values of the students sampled in each nation. A comparison (not entirely confirmatory in outcome) with cultural generalizations previously made is suggested by the statement (p. 50) about the American sample that "The situation as revealed in the analysis as a whole is complex, and none of the common generalizations concerning American youth does it full justice." Taking the results from the personality data as partly confirming generalizations derived from cultural data is more clearly implied by the following statement (p. 60) about the Chinese sample: "While there is hardly a trace of a demanding possessive self, there is some evidence that the ancient Chinese stress on the cultivation of the self was still a living force." Prothro (1958) has applied Morris's "ways of life" questionnaire to Arab university students, and he too interprets some of the personality findings as consistent with group-character conceptions. Prothro's subjects averaged higher than any of Morris's groups except the Chinese in their willingness "to be used by cosmic forces," and he points out (1958, p. 6) that this is consistent with "the classical interpretation of 'Islam' as meaning submission to fate."

Sometimes the group-character concept with which personality measurements may be compared is rather hazy in origin—the sort of concept often referred to as a stereotype. The stereotype of a group character may be partly derived from knowledge about its culture and hence correspond closely to the meaning I give to the technical concept *group character*. But the stereotype may be also derived in part from experience of individuals in the group. Some studies already mentioned draw on popular stereotypes as well as on more technically derived pictures of group character. A study where the group-concepts are presented as stereotypes is that by Fenz and Arkoff (1962), who applied the Edwards Personal Preference Schedule in a Hawaiian high school to boys and girls of five different racial origins. The motivational profile of each racial group is considered in relation to the local stereotype of its group character. Correspondence is on the whole good, but it ranges from excellent agreement for Caucasians to disagreement for Filipinos. In an earlier study with the same questionnaire, also done in Hawaii, Arkoff (1959) compared second- and third-generation Japanese-Americans with the American test norms. Both generations deviate from the test norms in ways Arkoff considers consistent with the general stereotype of the Japanese. The third generation deviate from the norms less than do the second, as should be expected if a steady process of acculturation is influencing the personality variables measured by this questionnaire.

Another example of agreement between personality measurement and stereotype is provided by Cattell and Warburton (1961). They find that American undergraduates, compared with British university students, are on the average about half a standard deviation higher on anxiety and on extroversion, and they regard this as confirmation of their own experience and that of other observers. Yet even here caution is appropriate in examining how close the fit really is: Students of industrial administration in a British technical college were found in this same study to be significantly less anxious than their university compatriots, and just as extroverted as the American subjects. This evidence of major variation within a society from one student group to another is disconcerting in view of the fact that the university samples for the two countries do not seem at all likely to be comparable; the Americans were undergraduates, presumably assorted, while the Britishers were all graduate students in education. Greater similarity of sample seems to characterize Tsujioka and Cattell's comparison (1965a, 1965b) of Japanese and American students. Differences they find in modal personality are regarded by them as generally consonant with group-character formulations. For example:

> The higher score of the Americans on Cortertia (activation level) and of the Japanese on Pathemia (feeling, emotional sensitivity) is . . . . highly significant on both forms . . . . This difference is in accord with the greater emphasis on passive artistic appreciation in the everyday life values of the Japanese and on the unusually high-stimulation level (activation, excitation) in American culture. (Tsujioka & Cattell, 1965a, p. 217)

Some investigations into personality traits of members of a cultural group produce no clear confirmation or disconfirmation of expectations based on group-character notions. They may, instead, simply add their own substantial findings to the accumulating knowledge about the particular group, eventually permitting integrated interpretation of findings on individual and on group levels. Such claims can be made principally for studies done with special methodological care, so that exactly what is learned is readily seen and recorded for the future. A good example is Rainwater's analysis (1960) of themes in the personalities of German men. The data derive from market-research interviews, with the sample carefully defined and much more nearly representative of the entire population than can be true of research on college students. The data are stories told in response to three pictures. The stories were analyzed to arrive at a portrayal of main themes. Rainwater offers some comparison of these with cultural observations, but for the most part the findings are simply recorded and summarized. They obviously provide an important resource for later and fuller comparison with other relevant information about either German personalities or German culture.

Certain kinds of research on personality in relation to culture have a special interest for their bearing on recent trends in personality research within our society. A prime development in American personality research in recent years has been its extension, much more successfully than before, into cognitive aspects of individual differences, and this is beginning to be paralleled in studies of group differences. For example, Mercado, Diaz, and Gardner (1963) have reported a first attempt to compare Mexican and American children on variables in the concept formations evoked by an object-sorting test. Interesting differences were found on such variables as preferred level of abstraction. The authors are wisely reluctant to generalize from a first study on groups uncertainly representative of the societies from which they were drawn, using a single method whose findings are—as the authors take care to point out—subject to alternative explanations so long as they stand alone. But their findings suggest that variables of cognitive style may show important differences of distribution in various cultural groups. Though Mercado, Diaz, and Gardner do not discuss the relation of their tentative conclusions to group-character observations, it seems clear that the problem arises for cognitive as for motivational aspects of personality. Popular conceptions of group-character obviously include both. If technical accounts of group character have tended to stress motivational aspects, that may be only because of the neglect of cognitive aspects by the individual psychologies which provided the theoretical background of those accounts.

A relation between individual cognitive-style measures and generalizations about group character is made explicit by Goodman (1962), who compared American and

Japanese children on conceptualizing habits revealed in a story-recall procedure. Goodman believes her findings justify the conclusion that the Americans are somewhat more "systematizing" than the Japanese. For example, they are more prone to recall elements in the story especially crucial to its logical development, and to modify items in the direction of making the logic of the story explicit. This finding, she says,

> . . . is in accord with what was anticipated in view of the nature of the two cultures, e.g., the systematizing influence stemming from American cultural emphasis on ideologies both religious and scientific—emphases not paralleled in Japan. (Goodman, 1962, p. 383)

Exactly the same comparison, Goodman points out, consistent at individual and group level, had emerged from Nadel's earlier application (1937) of the same story-recall procedure in two African societies, the Yoruba and Nupe. Of these two, the Yoruba subjects brought more systematic meaning into their story recall, by a very wide margin; they showed a corresponding difference from Nupe subjects in their description and later recall of what they saw in photographs. This variation in modal personality is portrayed by Nadel as consistent with group-character inferences from culture. The Yoruba have highly developed visual art and drama, and a complex, rationalized religious system; the Nupe have little art, and their religion centers on vague magical principles. Goodman notes that the Yoruba show even more systematizing than the American subjects, although the cultural or group-character difference is presumably in the reverse direction. Quite probably, as she points out, this surprising finding is merely a consequence of uncontrolled differences in age; Goodman's subjects were 11 to 12 years old, while Nadel's varied from 12 to 18. In some other detailed findings, Goodman shows more definite lack of obvious fit between group-character and modal-personality observations, though on the whole the agreement is close.

Of very general interest in personality study is the question of what effects a child's experiences have on his lasting personality characteristics. One way to investigate this involves a special kind of comparison between group-character and modal-personality concepts. A cultural group treats its children in a particular way. Some hypothesis about personality development predicts that a certain trait will therefore be part of the group character. Personality observations may then be made on members of the group to check whether they will tend to agree with this picture of the group character. Such research could, of course, play an important role in relation to theories of personality integration of culture, as a partial verification of those theories. But studies of modal personality in groups varying in child-training practices need not be planned with that particular end in view; they are valuable in other ways even if personality integration of culture should turn out to be of no importance.

One instance is Grinder and McMichael's comparison (1963) of Samoan and American children. American culture has been asserted to socialize children in ways calculated to develop guilt and guilt-anticipation as internalized mechanisms of social control; Samoan culture has been said to socialize children in ways depending primarily upon external sanctions and not leading to the development of guilt. Grinder and McMichael compared children of Samoan and mainland-United States origin living in the same Hawaiian community to see whether measures of individual guilt-tendency would distinguish the two groups. Two kinds of measures were used: mention of guilt in stories told by the children, and refusal to cheat in situations tempting them to cheat. On each measure there is a large and statistically significant difference in the expected direction.

Research following this pattern is especially interesting, I have already pointed out, as a source of evidence on the relation between the way children are reared and the personalities they develop. But many uncertainties affecting the interpretation of the findings are likely to arise—for instance, were the particular persons studied actually reared in accordance with the cultural norm supposedly characterizing their group? This uncertainty would be eliminated if good information could be obtained about the rearing of each person under study. Formidable difficulties stand in the way of this, as those studying personality development in our society well know. The uncertainty can at least be reduced by checking the culture-norms or even deriving them from information supplied by the group of persons whose individual characteristics are being assessed.

Exactly this procedure is followed by Scofield and Sun (1960) in a study of 40 Chinese students at Oklahoma State University. All had been reared in a Chinese cultural setting, and almost all had arrived in the United States not more than two years before the data were collected. All knew English well enough to permit use of an American personality questionnaire, Cattell's test for 16 personality factors. In addition to taking this test, the subjects were asked to write about "their knowledge of child-training practices among their own Chinese families." Information supplied was read by three graduate students in psychology to judge whether training in each of several areas was more or less severe than the training of American middle-class children. Scofield and Sun report that the agreement among the 40 subjects in their description of Chinese practices was very high. The inter-cultural comparison of socialization which emerged was used as a basis for predicting how the Chinese subjects' personality characteristics should differ from those of an American university group. Child-training practices were judged to be more severe than American ones in moral, sexual, and aggression training, and in dependence training in the sense that very strong pressures for dependence were reported both in infancy and in childhood. No difference appeared in toilet training, except that it was reported to begin at a somewhat later age in Chinese culture. From these differences in child-training practices, through hypotheses which are not made explicit about their effects on personality, Scofield and Sun say they would predict that the Chinese would be, in comparison with American students, "more withdrawn, more shy, more emotionally insecure, more introverted, more sensitive, more suspicious, more cold and aloof," and that a difference between the two groups would not be expected "in compulsivity, curiosity, sociability, or laxity." The pattern of similarities and differences obtained on the 16 PF test follows these predictions very closely. Despite the various uncertainties that remain—connected with the choice of sample, implicitness of hypotheses, etc.—this appears to be an impressive instance of confirmation by personality-test procedures of differences in modal personality such as would be predicted from differences in child-training practices.

Differentiation Within a Society

So far we have considered group character or modal personality with respect to differences between one society and another, contrasting either two entire societies or corresponding segments of them. But parallel phenomena and problems are relevant to group differences within a single society. This has already been implied when pointing out that the concept of group character might need to be restricted to some segment of a society rather than to the society as a whole; the concept of modal personality likewise seems to be the more certainly useful the more homogeneous the group.

Any society, even the simplest, consists of segments which may be markedly different.

The segments may be of several sorts. Every society must have groups whose members interact with one another with especially high frequency or in distinctive ways; the household is such a grouping, and usually neighborhood and community are. A society may also include segments whose membership has distinctive internal interaction but yet is distinguished primarily by characteristic kinds of interaction with non-members (many occupational groups, for example). But every society also includes segments whose membership is defined exclusively by characteristic interaction with non-members, with little or no tendency toward special interaction within the segment; a clear example is provided by fathers in our society. Any segment of society, whether or not it is an interactional grouping, may conceivably have special implications for the personality of its members.

In discussions of this question, Linton's (1936) terminology of status and role have long been helpful. Goodenough (1965) has recently made a new analysis of culturally patterned interaction which is a valuable clarification, and I shall begin by summarizing the most relevant parts of his analysis. To act at one moment as a member of any segment of a society is, in Goodenough's terms, to select an *identity* (e.g., father, student, lawyer). *Select* is used here in a technical sense not implying conscious choice; to select an identity is to have it activated, to have it operative. To avoid confusion, I shall sometimes use these alternate terms. Behavior at a moment is not culturally regulated just by an identity—this is one major point of Goodenough's analysis—but by an *identity-relationship*. Thus the rights and duties of a policeman in relation to an ordinary citizen differ from those he has in relation to a fleeing criminal, and both differ from those he has in relation to the lieutenant of his division. For each identity a person must or may select, then, there are a number of possible identity-relationships with other people—generally only one in relation to each possible person or group. In interacting with another person, however, cultural regulation of behavior does not come only from a single identity-relationship. This is the second major point of Goodenough's analysis. Of necessity, each person in an interaction normally has several identities operative at once; the policeman may be white, male, middle-aged, with an Irish accent, and in responding to the inquiries of a passing citizen who is an elderly woman with an obvious Irish brogue he may well be influenced by several identity-relationships implicit here. The composite of the identities selected by one person in a given interaction is referred to by Goodenough as his *social persona* in that interaction.

Goodenough's concern is with understanding culture. If we turn, with his analysis in mind, to understanding individual behavior, how should we relate *identity, identity-relationship,* and *social persona* to concepts ordinarily used in psychology? They are odd concepts for psychology, perhaps, at least for a psychology whose conventional units are stimulus and response. Goodenough's concepts do not refer to the external situation. Nor do they refer to what the person brings to the situation as a residue of previous experience. They refer to something that is already an emergent from the interaction of an individual with what is at the moment outside him. Predicting what will emerge—what identity-relationships will arise when two people meet in certain circumstances—is, then, one problem for the psychologist as it is for the anthropologist. But the appeal to such concepts also implies a belief that knowledge about the identities, etc.—either by prediction or by observation of what emerges—can play an important part in predicting the further course of the interaction. The concepts are not, then, so unusual for psychology as they may first appear. They are the same in general nature as the concept of role, and are a clarification of it.

Goodenough proceeds to show how such concepts may be efficiently and fruitfully applied to the analysis of culturally patterned social interactions. My purpose here is to present these concepts as the background for consideration of how a person's belonging to various differentiated segments of a society is likely to influence his personality. If a person has so many potential identities, each varying in its behavioral demands according to the reciprocal identity selected by another person, and if he can readily slip in and out of them, how can they be of any importance for the fairly durable characteristics we call personality? For personality study, certainly, attention will be on the potential identities a person can select from, rather than on those he does select at a particular moment. What are the effects on personality of the fact that a person has the biological, psychological, or social characteristics that qualify him (or, perhaps, require him) to act at times in a particular identity? To the extent that such effects are inferred from the cultural rules, the concept of group character is applicable (though the term *group* may be an unfortunate one except where those sharing the identity do also form an interacting segment of the society). To the extent that such effects are known to be present through personality measurement of individuals, the concept of modal personality is applicable.

We need first to recognize that many of the identities a person can and does select are not important as influences on his personality, not least because of the diversity of the many identities available and the transient qualities of some. But certain identities are likely to be important for personality.

1. Some of a person's identities are inevitably operative in a large proportion of his interactions with others. A sufficient example here is sex. It is hard to imagine social situations in which a person's sex has absolutely no relevance to cultural regulation of his interactions with others. For identities such as sex, this high frequency of activation in a great variety of situations sets the stage for marked influence on personality if additional conditions are met.

2. Some of a person's identities, even if their activation is less frequent, involve interactions which by cultural regulation can be counted on to be at times especially gratifying or especially frustrating and stressful. Psychological theory leads us to expect that such relationships will be particularly influential in personality formation, and such concepts as identity are useful in recognizing the culturally predictable elements in these relationships. The identity of husband, for example, though operative less frequently than some others and in only a single identity-relationship, may well have general significance for personality because of the high degree of motivation and satisfaction or frustration. The identity of accused murderer might be expected to have a decided effect on an individual's personality though only once and quite involuntarily activated.

3. Some identities are associated with conditions of a non-cultural nature which may also influence personality. This may make it difficult to trace accurately the multiple lines of causation, but may increase the importance of those identities as indices or clues. Again, a sufficient example is sex, where the identity is accompanied by the even more stable and continuous fact of distinctive anatomy and physiology. The multiplicity of routes of influence is indicated in the rare cases where a person is reared as a member of one sex while having wholly or partly the biological features of the other. Miles (1942) studied such a case, a pseudohermaphrodite who was found at the age of 20 to be a male but had been reared as a girl. Though limited knowledge of the case does not permit certainty, it appears probable that a variety of masculine tendencies deriving from glandular function were effective even while the child's social identity was feminine.

4. Where an identity seems to be important for lasting, inner characteristics of personality, the lasting quality may be due to the stability of cultural regulation of social interactions quite as much as to stability of

internal response-tendencies. We do not ordinarily have a good basis for relative evaluation of these two sources of stability because a person's life-situation cannot be freely altered. When a radical change is made in an identity normally stable, personality sometimes appears surprisingly flexible. The same study by Miles (1942) is again pertinent here; shortly after abandoning feminine identity at the age of 20, the patient was able to be masculine in personality to a greater extent than might have been guessed. There is, however, little information about effects on general personality of changes in major identities. The relative extent to which the effects of a major identity become imbedded in a stable personality structure and influence behavior at times when that identity is not selected; the extent to which such internalized effects are resistant to change; or the extent, on the other hand, to which an identity influences behavior only at the times when that identity is selected in interaction with others—these are questions of theoretical interest which must be settled empirically, and probably have no one general answer. For many practical purposes, however, they are not important questions since many of the major identities are not normally subject to abrupt change.

5. That a person repeatedly acts in a particular identity in ways important for him may have diverse and possibly unique effects on his personality. In individual case study, whether by clinician or biographer, we expect to encounter distinctive consequences of a person's sex, age, occupation, religion, etc. Generalizations can also be sought about personality effects of individual variation in an identity-relationship—amount of conflict between father and son, for example—and in a later section I will consider these. My discussion here, however, will be focused on the uniformities among people who in a given society share an identity, and on how they differ from compatriots who do not share that identity. This emphasis parallels that of earlier sections. Though recognizing that the general culture of a society has differing effects on various individuals, I dealt mainly with the central tendency of those effects, represented in the concept of modal personality (or group character) of a society. Here I will be concerned with the modal personality (or group character) of a segment of a society.

6. Some of a person's identities are, both in themselves and in relation to the particular ways he acts during their activation, crucial to his general self-esteem. At this point the concept of social identity becomes relevant to the concept of personal identity stressed in recent years by Erikson (1963) among others. Here is still another route, then, by which a person's social identities have a critical influence on personality. Goodenough (1963, pp. 176–251) has made an excellent analysis of this implication of social identity, in the context of considering why deliberate efforts to produce social change vary greatly in outcome.

An excellent illustration of personality in relation to social differentiation is Dollard's application (1937) of the psychodynamic ideas of psychoanalysis to the problem of race relations in a southern town in the 1930's. Dollard studied the town in much the way that an anthropologist might study a primitive community. In doing so, however, he made a special effort to understand the psychodynamic meaning of the individual's position within the society and placed great emphasis on those interviewing methods most promising for this purpose. His principal attention is given to the implications for personality of membership in the white or the Negro caste, and he summarizes his main conclusions about this in the following passage:

> The white caste have the satisfactions that go with mastery, superiority, control, maturity, and duty well-fulfilled. They have the pleasure also of despising the Negroes who are inferior in self-renunciation and self-esteem. The Negroes, on the other hand, get much more and much freer direct impulse satisfaction. The

internal checks on gratification are less, and the social organization among lower-class Negroes does not put a great strain on its members. For example, the sexuality of white men is superior since they have access to two classes of women, but it is internally checked by prohibitions set up in developing this personality for the masterful role. The Negro man, as we have seen, is limited to sexual choices within his own caste, but there they may be more numerous and less burdened with inner or outer restraints. Whites must organize action with respect to remote goals; Negroes may live from day to day and make the most of passing opportunities for gratification. (Dollard, 1937, pp. 431–432)

Identity as Negro or white, this passage implies, is very pervasive in that it is—in the community and time referred to—inevitably selected as a part of a person's *social persona* on practically every occasion of interaction. It is, moreover, a powerful influence on personality, because major frustrations and rewards result from social interactions in ways predictable from this aspect of the identity-relationship. Within each of the two caste groups, Dollard also gives some attention to the implications of membership in middle class vs. lower class. Interaction between caste and class is also recognized in the observation that one implication of membership in the Negro caste is greatly increased probability of being, within one's caste, in the lower rather than in the middle class.

The relation to culture of behavioral tendencies such as outlined by Dollard for specific caste and class groups may be regarded in two ways. On the one hand, the culture of the entire community or entire society may be seen as regulating the identity-relationship of Negro and white. For example, the general culture of the community defines the Negro-white relationship in such a way that a white can always act toward a Negro in a manner that confirms and reasserts his own superiority, while a Negro must inhibit any outward show of the hostility which this behavior on the part of whites must arouse in him. Some of the implications of identity, on the other hand, may be seen as a more immediate consequence of the distinctive sub-culture of one of the groups. Consider the Negroes, since we more readily think of the general culture as being defined by the sub-culture of the dominant group. Lower-class Negroes seem relatively free in the expression of both sexual and aggressive impulses within their own group. This may be viewed as part of the distinctive sub-culture of this one segment of the society. It is a part, indeed, that other segments—say middle-class whites—may not very clearly understand; aware of this side of Negro behavior, they may well see it as an inevitable racial tendency rather than as a culturally regulated characteristic of only one segment of the Negroes. Negro sub-cultures within an American community are in considerable part an adjustment to the position of Negroes in American society now and in the past. There are other sub-cultural groups within the United States, such as a recently arrived immigrant group, whose distinctive culture may come largely from perpetuation of cultural characteristics they possessed before they came.

Two kinds of differentiation with implications for personality, every society must have: differentiation by age and by sex. Though a person's age identity at any part of his life span is only temporary, its effects may be quite stable enough to warrant using the term *personality*. That the behavior of children looms large in modern accounts of national character and modal personality is not ascribable entirely to Freudian bias. Sarnoff, Lighthall, Waite, Davidson, and Sarason (1958), for example, compared British and American children on general anxiety and on anxiety about tests, predicting that the latter would be markedly higher in British children because they know that test performance at the age of 11 will determine their whole life-course. Just this difference was found. Earlier travelers between the United States and Britain seem also to have been impressed with differences in modal personality between children of the two societies, differences somewhat specific to childhood and not just a foreshadowing of adult personality. Much of the inter-cultural variation in child personality may, of course, be just such a foreshadowing. An instance is reported by Lambert and Klineberg (1963) on a specific aspect of personality, the extent to which a boy's occupational aspirations reach above his father's status. This "filial-aspiration index" was available on a sample of boys at three ages (6, 10, and 14) in 11 nations. For nine of the nations, a group-character measure of achievement motivation was available in McClelland's analysis (1961) of stories in children's textbooks. The correlation between these two measures was +.87. Yet even here, evidence appeared of variation among the societies in the degree or way in which the foreshadowing of adult character occurred at different age levels. French boys, generally low in the filial-aspiration index, were lower at 14 than at 10. For Japanese and German boys, also generally low, the change from 10 to 14 was instead upward. Among nations high on the index, Israel alone showed a reliable change with age, an increase. Lambert and Klineberg suggest that

> . . . transmitters of the French culture curtail any inappropriate aspirational ventures by the time a boy reaches his teens whereas Japanese and German socializers may lose some type of control over their children's aspirations after the early years. . . . In Israel, there apparently is social support for high filial-aspirations which gets progressively stronger at each age level. (Lambert & Klineberg, 1963, p. 64)

Further on in the life cycle, too, age may have varying implications for personality; the modal personality of the aged in a society where age carries high prestige may be expected to be very different from that in a society where old people are looked on as unfortunates. Though all societies must deal with such basic uniformities as the maximum physical vigor of the young adult and the sterility of children and older women, the personality implications of membership in an age group may clearly vary a great deal from one society to another. In fairly extreme contrast with our society, for example, are those peasant groups where full adulthood, marked by marriage and succession to independent economic status, comes very late. An ethnographic analysis of two such instances, in Ireland and Norway, has been made by Park (1962). The analysis is also of interest in raising the question of how the great shift of behavior involved in an abrupt change at a mature age from "boy" to "man" is related to the stable quality we suppose (perhaps erroneously) any mature personality to have. Extension of knowledge beyond our culture will be invaluable at just this point if the outcome is to show that stability of adult personality is much more a product of stability of identity-relationships than psychologists have generally supposed. Our impressions that adult personality is an internal structure very difficult to change may be too greatly influenced by evidence from a special and unrepresentative situation, that of psychotherapy.

Implications for personality of being male or female likewise vary widely, yet everywhere they must constitute a major influence. Margaret Mead (1949) stresses both these points in reviewing the significance of sex in the several societies with which she has direct acquaintance. Her book is an invaluable document for getting a feel of the range of possible variation, even though her methods involve no adequate guarantee against exaggeration. Attempt at unbiased assessment of ethnographic evidence from a variety of field workers in a general sample of human societies (Barry, Bacon, & Child, 1957) indicates that variation from one society to another in the implications of sex, though certainly real and important, is perhaps not so great as Mead seems to suggest. Evidence of surprisingly consistent sex-differences appears also in a personality study (Gough, 1966) using the femininity scale of the California Psychological Inventory in six nations which vary considerably in general culture and sex-role differentiation (France, Italy, Norway, Turkey, United States, and Venezuela).

On such evidence, and according to circumstances, we must decide whether to emphasize cultural constancy or diversity in differentiation of personality by sex. If there is some constancy, diversity too is surely present. An example emerging in quantitative psychological research is found in Lindgren and Lindgren (1965). They had previously studied in U.S. college students the relation between two kinds of personality measures: (1) creativity and number of responses in a task of composing captions for cartoons; (2) tendency to ascribe to oneself the adjectives which Barron (1952) found to characterize the self-descriptions of subjects scoring high on the Barron-Welsh Art Scale. (The Art Scale measures preference for designs liked by artists over those liked by non-artists; people scoring high on it tend to ascribe to themselves many traits not conventionally desirable.) In their United States study, Lindgren and Lindgren had found their two kinds of measures to be positively correlated in each sex. This seems very reasonable, since both measures look as though they might sample some part of a general creativity domain. But when the study was repeated with university students in the Middle East, a sex difference appeared. The same correlations found in the United States appeared in women, two out of four large enough to be statistically significant despite the small number of women. Correlations in men, however, were so small as to lack significance despite there being almost three times as many men. Lindgren and Lindgren view this discrepancy of outcome as reasonable in view of a cultural variation in sex differentiation. They report a tendency for men in Middle Eastern societies "to inhibit the expression of any self-derogatory attitudes" such as those involved in scoring high on their adjective measure. In the United States, they imply, there is greater frankness of this sort in both sexes, and such frankness is found also in Middle Eastern women. Self-descriptions have different significance in atmospheres of frankness or restraint, and hence the sex difference in correlation in one culture and not in the other.

Societies may vary in amount of differentiation by sex. Two studies of children, using quite different techniques, provide evidence for lesser sex differentiation in children in the United States than in a comparison country. Rabin and Limuaco (1959) show that Filipino children drawing human figures distinguish between the sexes more than do American children. Mercado, Diaz, and Gardner (1963) report, using a measure of preferred level of abstraction, a difference between the sexes in mean score in Mexico but not in the United States. In both studies, the modal personality findings, of greater sex differentiation in another country than in the United States, are presumably compatible with group-character inferences from cultural observations.

A hierarchy of prestige and of access to resources is perhaps as ubiquitous as age and sex as a basis of differentiation with implications for personality. In our society, certainly, speculations are frequent about group-character of social-class segments; such speculations, moreover, are often asserted with great confidence. When standard personality tests of clinical origin have been applied to people differing in social class, as Auld (1952) shows in a review of such studies in the United States, differences in modal personality are often found, though they are not so large or consistent as might have been expected. But the tests were not developed primarily to check on beliefs about the group character of social classes, and they may not be measuring the most pertinent variables. The evidence is persuasive, though not completely definitive, that class identity greatly influences kind of mental illness; see, for example, Hollingshead and Redlich (1958). If valid, this indicates an important effect of class identity on at least one highly general personality characteristic.

Another characteristic of a fairly pervasive nature which seems to be regularly associated with socio-economic position is authoritarianism, as measured by the *F*-scale. The original study by Adorno, Frenkel-Brunswik, Levinson, and Sanford (1950, pp. 265–269) found that the groups averaging highest were of largely working-class origin, though there was otherwise no obvious regular relation between average class identity and average F-score of the other groups they tested. Later studies which treat class more systematically have confirmed this direction of relation. MacKinnon and Centers (1956) sampled the adult population of Los Angeles County with a brief *F*-scale, and used three separate indices of class position: education, occupation, and self-ascribed class. For each index they find a regular negative relation between authoritarianism and class position, except that the last two indices show a slight upturn of authoritarianism at the highest class level. Similarly Rhodes (1960, p. 102), in a study of Tennessee high-school seniors, presents data which indicate a very consistent tendency for children of "blue-collar" workers to score higher (more authoritarian) on the *F*-scale than children of "white-collar" workers. Could such findings be artifacts of the particular scale, or be a purely local phenomenon? Lipset (1959) presents evidence that they agree with more fragmentary social-survey data from other countries and also with a variety of reasonable group-character inferences. He argues that the rearing of children varies by class in a way that should theoretically produce authoritarian group-character in lower-class groups, and that many facts about the adult culture of various classes confirms this expectation.

Analysis of the class system is a special interest of sociology, and we may look to that discipline for comparative studies on implications for personality in different societies. Systematic comparative work of this sort seems to be fairly new, and direct measures of individual personality have not yet been widely used. An instance is, however, Rosen's comparative study (1962) in Brazil and the United States, of boys' achievement motivation (as measured by the TAT) in relation to social class. In each country there was a fairly regular positive relation except for a possible dip at the top level.

Sociologists also use indices based on facts about individual behavior which have significance for personality. Inkeles (1960) shows that such indices used in comparative studies of social hierarchy may yield results of great psychological interest. He brings together material derived from social surveys in several modern industrial nations, including nations so diverse in some ways as the United States, the USSR, Japan, and Italy. Inkeles shows that the social forces created by industrial society, despite the cultural diversity of these nations, tend to produce some decided uniformities in how attitudes and values vary with social position. The qualities considered most important about a job, for example, vary in the same way in the United States and the Soviet Union: the higher a person is in the hierarchy, the less important are pay and security and the more important is the interest of the work. Higher levels in the hierarchy are associated with greater job satisfaction and with a higher standing on general indices of happiness (how recently one has laughed, how long it has been since one cried, a judgment about the balance of pain and joy in one's life). Some child-training values vary systematically with social standing; emphasis on obedience is less at higher levels. Inkeles views several of these findings as indicating a mastery-optimism complex in those of relatively high position in industrial societies.

Assessment of personality may ultimately be incorporated in multi-national studies of social structure, and thus give us a good basis for generalizing about variables in addition to those reflected in the survey data

Inkeles used. An example of this possibility is Storm's use of personality tests in studying differentiation between the dominant group in a society and marginal ethnic groups not fully integrated and having a relatively low position. With various associates, he has made somewhat comparable studies of children's personality in two nations, including in each instance a marginal group—the Maori of New Zealand and Indians in Canada. Each marginal group was compared with middle-class and lower-class children of the dominant group. In New Zealand, Storm, Anthony, and Porsolt (1965) tested for motivational value of material and non-material rewards. In children aged 5 or 6, they found higher performance with the non-material reward among the dominant group, with the superiority greater in the middle class than in the lower class, and higher performance with material reward in the Maori children. Among 10- and 11-year-olds, there were no significant differences between groups. In Canada (British Columbia), Cameron and Storm (1965) used other measures of the child's motivation to work for a non-material reward, or to tolerate delay of reward, and a TAT measure of achievement motivation. In an elementary school, results were similar to those for the young children in New Zealand, except that the lower class of the dominant group resembled the marginal group rather than the middle class. Storm and Cameron describe briefly other related studies which, put together, suggest—more adequately than a single study could—the beginnings of a theory about the general implications of membership in a marginal group low in the social hierarchy.

Sometimes a differentiated segment of a society may be especially interesting to students of personality because of conditions which distinguish it from the rest of mankind generally, rather than just from the rest of its society. This is true of some of the Israeli kibbutzim, cooperative communities of several hundred people where many usual functions of the family are assumed by the community and its specialists. Among these functions are the major burden of child rearing. In a kibbutz of this type, a child is taken soon after birth to a nursery to be reared with other children by specialists in child care. After weaning, a child spends only about two hours a day with its parents, and this time is primarily for relaxation and social enjoyment. Some people in other societies might think such child rearing would lead to a high frequency of maladjustment. A survey of childhood behavior problems by Kaffman (1961) indicates clearly that this is not the case.

A more reasonable hypothesis is that children reared by the community method of these kibbutzim might develop distinct modal personality tendencies. Spiro (1958) combined ethnographic and psychological techniques in studying one kibbutz intensively to test this hypothesis. He presents a picture of personality tendencies in the children of the kibbutz at all ages—including the first of its children, who were in their twenties at the time of the study. His analysis is cautious and rich in detail, and does not lend itself to brief summary. On many variables the children of the kibbutz differ in central tendency from United States children, but on few if any of them is the difference easily ascribable to the single influence of lessened parental share in child rearing. A number of variables in their environment, rather, are shown as contributing to their modal personality. Closest, perhaps, to a direct consequence of group rearing by professionals rather than parents is the tendency for the internalized superego to be relatively mild and centered on anticipation of external punishment rather than internal—on anticipation of shame rather than of guilt.

The fact that kibbutz rearing does not lead to personalities outside the range of those found elsewhere calls attention to the desirability of sharpening the comparison by finding a control group which shares some features of kibbutz life but does not share those especially interesting as possible influences on personality. Rabin (1965) has sought to do just this. He uses a variety of personality tests in comparing children and young adults from kibbutzim with age-mates who share general Israeli culture and an agricultural economy but not the community life and special child-rearing customs of the kibbutzim. Despite this sharpening of the comparison, Rabin points out that a number of possibly influential variables distinguish the background of his two groups. His findings and interpretation agree substantially with Spiro's on the mildness of conscience (neither reports any inadequacy of conscience). He reports evidence of some initial intellectual retardation in kibbutz children, later completely wiped out, and says that homosexuality appears to be completely absent. Both are plausibly explained, but not confidently predictable, from general principles.

Like the tracing of a very unusual case history, these studies convince us that environmental forces are powerful shapers of personality, but normally operate in such complex combinations that the single case defies confident interpretation. If other societies too develop differentiated communities resembling the kibbutzim in one or another way, perhaps the effects on personality of different variables involved may eventually be disentangled. The existence of the kibbutzim and their willingness to be studied offer the promise of radical gain in man's effort to rear children so as to achieve rational aims.

Group Character and Historical Change

If the internal differentiation of a society means variation in group character among its component parts, just so the variation of a society through time may mean alteration of group character—both of the society as a whole and of its components. Picturing the group character of a nation and its changes through history has been a part of the traditional task assumed by historians. This task has in recent decades been avoided, one historian indicates (Potter, 1954), because of the excesses and errors associated with the earlier attribution of group character to racial inheritance. But it constitutes an important part of historical work, a part to which the psychologist and the social scientist may make some contribution.

In the recent literature of social science, the most widely known effort to relate group character to historical change is that of Riesman in *The Lonely Crowd* (1950). Riesman argues that over the last century Americans have tended to become less inner-directed and more other-directed, that this change has economic origins in the shift from predominantly individual enterprise to predominantly bureaucratic organization, and that the pressures toward other-directedness rather than inner-directedness are felt at various stages of the individual's life—from infantile training through formal education, occupational activity, and constant adult exposure to mass-communication media. Riesman's stress on the dimension of inner-directed vs. other-directed is one instance of a general recent concern with psychological mechanisms of social control. His application of this concern to a thesis about social change has been extensively debated. Many objections raised by the sociologist Lipset (1961) illustrate the difficulties in making confident inferences about shifts in group character on the basis of the limited sort of information at a social level ordinarily available in historical documents. Even within these limitations, however, the concept may be essential to developing an adequate history of a nation, as Potter (1954) seems to feel in his attempt to integrate social-science contributions such as Riesman's with the writings of historians.

Psychologists are perhaps less likely to engage in this kind of research than in the other kinds we have been considering. Since past times are under scrutiny, people are not present to be assessed as individuals, and the group-character approach must dominate, rather than the modal-personality approach. When psychologists do decide to enter this field, they are more likely than sociologists and anthropologists to attempt quantification. A very stimulating example of the consequences is McClelland's endeavor (1961) to trace the interrelation of economic growth and changes in group character. On both sides of this interaction he relies on objective quantitative indices. For economic growth he uses whatever most suitable measure of energy or volume of trade is available for a particular society through the appropriate period. For the aspect of group character with which he is concerned—strength of motive for achievement—he uses scoring methods derived from study of individual differences in our society, applying them to samples of the literary or artistic products of the societies in question. For comparable periods of economic growth, peak, and decline in several societies, he finds some remarkable uniformities. In general, motive for achievement seems to be the first index to rise, followed with a lag of at least a couple of generations by the economic index; decline seems to show the same time-relationship. From such evidence he argues that the roots of economic change lie partly within the group character, rejecting the view that group character arises only from economic conditions. Position on this question has obviously important practical implications for efforts to influence economic growth. McClelland's attempts (1965) to develop techniques for strengthening an individual's achievement motive, and to apply them in economically underdeveloped countries, illustrate the practical value that knowledge of group character may have.

Application of the group-character approach to studies of change in the past highlights the need to determine the validity of the methods of inference used in moving between concepts at individual and group levels. When a contemporary society is studied, the validity of personality inferences derived from information at the societal level may be checked against information about individuals. But such a procedure is inapplicable to historical research. Even where we have some limited data about individuals in the past, we have little opportunity to compare this sample of their behavior with other samples. Thus we can be confident in inferring group character through analyzing historical documents only to the extent that the application of comparable procedures within groups available for study has been verified by parallel study of other indices of individual personality. Venturesome research into urgent social problems should not, however, be delayed for years to await perfect validation and refinement of method.

There are advantages in studying social change as it occurs, avoiding some of the methodological limitations of historical research. An interest in general processes of social change may thus lead to studying a contemporary society, viewing present behavior as a cross-section of historical processes in action. To the extent that understanding social change is specific rather than general, there is also a practical advantage in examining changes in progress. These are the changes whose course we may hope to alter, to help shape the world in which we and our descendants hope to live.

All these reasons seem to underlie the current great interest in the world-wide acculturation or inter-culturation now proceeding so rapidly. Theory of personality will probably play an increasing role in efforts to utilize intellectual resources to deal with the ongoing transformation of the world. An outstanding example of this attempt at synthesis is Hagen's book, *On the Theory of Social Change* (1962). It is so broad in its coverage that only a part of the data pertains to contemporary change, but the problem is one of special urgency today. Hagen, who is an economist, draws upon a wealth of ideas from psychology, anthropology, and sociology in attempting to account for the transition, at different times in different places, from traditional society to society undergoing rapid economic growth. He believes the social changes involved in economic growth to be appreciably dependent upon the innovative activities of individuals who have the "innovational personality," which he contrasts with the "authoritarian personality" predominant in traditional society. The characteristics of innovational personality have much in common with those of the creative personality as pictured in recent psychological research (cf. Barron, 1965), and are regarded by Hagen as typically occurring in groups whose position in the social hierarchy has declined. The personality of members of a society, then, is directed by earlier social events into motivating technological innovations and thus into radically altering the later history of the entire society.

Somewhat less general in intent and more closely linked to empirical research on individual behavior is Doob's *Becoming More Civilized* (1960). Doob uses his own research and that of others on several acculturating groups to seek the psychological correlates of degree of acculturation. Some psychological accompaniments of high acculturation may most plausibly be considered as consequences, others as antecedents of the acculturation. But generally the most probable view is what Doob calls a *spiraled explanation*. The most independent members of a community, for example, may be the most likely to venture beyond the traditional and gain knowledge of the new and alien culture. The power they gain through this knowledge, if the new culture is technologically advanced, makes possible more effective independence, which in turn permits them to become more acculturated. If satisfied with the life to which their independent tendencies have led, they may rear their children to value independence even more strongly, and the circle may start in the new generation at a higher level.

Psychologists are most numerous in the United States, and the acculturating persons most immediately available for study here are foreign students. It is not surprising, then, that these rather highly selected subjects have provided some of the very interesting evidence about personality and social change. An instance is a study of students from India, done by Zajonc and Wahi (1961). The focus was on differential conformity to features of American culture, according to whether the particular feature was shared by Indian culture. On features where the two cultures differed, pressure on students to express acceptance of American culture came not only from their being in the United States, but also from their being deliberately exposed in the experiment to apparent endorsement of some features of American culture by fellow Indians. The personality measure studied in relation to conformity was motive for achievement, as determined by a Thematic Apperception Test. Students high on motive for achievement showed more conformity to American culture on those items where American culture differs from Indian than on those where the two cultures agree. For the students low in motive for achievement the reverse was true; i.e., they were more acceptant of American culture where it agrees with Indian culture than where the two differ. If the finding may be generalized and extended to persons living within their own society, it suggests the following: People high in motive for achievement, and exposed to situations in which there is some pressure toward cultural change consistent with personal advancement, will tend to accept or promote the change, whereas people low in motive for achievement will tend to react to the pressures for change by an ever-firmer attachment to those elements in their traditional culture which are also acceptable in the new situation but which do not in themselves signify change.

For Each Cultural Group, A Distinct Personality Type?

It is useful to think about differences among cultural groups in the modal personality of their members. How can one best conceptualize the modal personality of a group and the ways in which it differs from that of other groups?

A seemingly simple answer is provided by folk terminology, which gives to the typical personality of any group an appropriate label, thereafter employed as though it greatly facilitated understanding. Latin temperament, Anglo-Saxon character, Oriental inscrutability, today's teenager—such stereotyped terms have wide currency but are often scorned by the scholar. One reason for the scorn is that they have often been used—"Aryan" is a good example—as a pseudo-intellectual façade for a structure quivering with malice. Another reason is that such terms are empty labels (a fact that facilitates their use for evil ends), yet often give a false impression of conveying important knowledge.

The emptiness, in themselves, of such personality-type labels may be seen by considering their parallel at the individual level. What is conveyed by saying that there are as many personalities in a city as there are entries in the city directory, bearing names all the way from Abby Aachen to Zechariah Zucker? The concept of an Abby-Aachen personality is empty unless we know Abby; and if we have met her only once, the concept may mislead us into overgeneralizing our first impressions. The concept of a typical Swedish personality is empty unless we know some Swedes; and it carries with it the danger that we may too readily conclude that the few we know are typical.

Easy misuse of such concepts must not lead us to disregard them, for we might then lose sight of an important objective. To understand a unique person as adequately as possible is sometimes the goal of a psychologist, and to leave the person without a label—his own name or a pseudonym, according to the situation—would be obvious foolishness. Sometimes the goal is to understand as adequately as possible the shared or typical personality tendencies of members of a cultural group; and an appropriate name is equally handy here as a label for what one is seeking to understand. But the label may in this case turn out to correspond to very little in reality. If we take any two individuals and compare them, we may be sure of finding interesting differences. If we take two cultural groups, we cannot be so sure of finding interesting differences between their modal personalities. And, just as in the case of individuals, the name does not give us the right personality picture; that can come only from study of the person or the people, or from communication of systematic knowledge based on such study.

In the quest for this systematic knowledge, other terms will be more crucial than the label of the group to be studied. They are the constructs used in measuring, describing, and interpreting personality tendencies. Such constructs generally refer to dimensions of variation. If the ultimate objective is to understand fully one particular group—to deal with the social parallel of what Allport (1937) calls the individual trait—a comparison of this group with other groups on various dimensions may be only an analytic preliminary to the final synthesis. Indeed, there may be only an implicit appeal to the idea of dimensions of variation. If the objective is to formulate or verify generalizations about why group differences have arisen, then attention to dimensions of variation will probably be primary and continuous. But how should the dimensional concepts be chosen and used? That is the next question.

Dimensions of Personality: The Same or Different?

Many a measure of personality is based on a number of items which each contribute to a single measurement. Thus M, on the Rorschach test, is a count gotten by scoring 1 for each response classified as human movement and 0 for each response not so scored. Anxiety, on the Manifest Anxiety Scale, is a count obtained in the same way from a set of questionnaire responses, scoring 1 for each response considered to be indicative of anxiety. For most purposes some consistency is desirable among the items so pooled, and the degree of consistency is usually measured by some kind of reliability coefficient. The relation between one variable so measured and other variables measured by other sets of items is often, in its turn, subject to inquiry. If several variables tend to be consistent with one another, they may be taken to define a general dimension of variation; if a variable stands alone, not related to others, it may be taken to define by itself a dimension of variation. Statistical techniques of correlation and factor analysis are commonly used to assess the degree and patterning of the consistencies found.

Should we consider the same dimensions to be ideally applicable to persons in all cultures, and should we select dimensions so as to increase the probability that they will in practice be universally applicable? Or should dimensions of personality variation be considered specific to a particular culture? Holding always to the first extreme would risk neglect of variables highly important at one time and place because there were no corresponding consistencies at other times and places. An example may well be degree of alienation—a variable important in distinguishing among individuals in a complex society undergoing rapid change, and yet perhaps irrelevant to individual differences within a simple traditional society. But to hold to the other extreme and define each personality variable in a way likely to restrict its usefulness to a single time and place would greatly hinder the advance of comparative knowledge. The desirable position is likely to shift according to the purposes of the research.

The first step in inquiry here is to determine whether inter-item consistency is reasonably constant from one cultural setting to another. Do questionnaire items that form a cluster in American college students also do so when the questionnaire is translated into Hindi and administered to college students in India? If the Rorschach test is given to Eskimo and Australian aborigines, will a factor analysis of the scores lead in each case to factors similar to those which emerge from studies of European and American samples? Uniform meaning of tests across cultures is too often taken for granted, and such questions fail to be asked. But sometimes they have been.

By some the questions are raised in general theoretical discussions. The sociologist Turner (1961) has presented a very stimulating argument for expecting that the important dimensions of personality would vary from one culture to another. Among a number of interesting suggestions he makes are the following: (1) Major personality differences are likely to develop in connection with areas of free choice for individuals in a society, and since cultures differ in what they leave open to individual choice, the resulting dimensions of variation should differ. (2) Consistency in behavior means predictability; since predictability has practical value in social interaction, we might expect interaction in a given society to create pressures shaping consistencies in ways especially relevant to the specific values and hence practical interests predominant in that society. (3) Occupation is likely to have a pervasive influence on personality, and dominant occupations are likely to "establish a fundamental set of dimensions which serve as a reference in the organization of personality" (p. 60). Such reasoning, however, as Turner clearly realizes, does not establish whether in fact the important dimensions of personality are different in various cultural settings. It merely suggests possibilities to watch for.

By others the same questions have been raised in a more empirical context, that of developing personality tests usable in diverse cultural settings. An excellent example is the research done by Comrey, Meschieri, Misiti, and Nencini (1965) with an Italian version of a personality test previously used by Comrey with United States subjects. An attempt was made to measure with multiple-choice questionnaire items 28 variables measured in Comrey's American questionnaire. For each of these variables, six items were prepared in Italian, and responses were obtained from about 500 Italian subjects. The variables were then grouped (12 or fewer variables in a set) for calculating correlations among all items in the group and then factor-analyzing this matrix. The outcome is a remarkable confirmation of the original variables; every one is to some extent sustained, though usually not with all of its original six items. The authors do not attempt any detailed comparison with the American results, though such a comparison might provide very interesting material for assessing the impact of each culture on personality. They are more concerned with a higher level of abstraction—with the factors that would emerge from relations between variables—to which I shall turn in a moment.

Cattell, Pichot, and Rennes (1961) have reported a similar outcome for a French translation of Cattell's 16 PF questionnaire. They consider the intercorrelations of 44 items, four chosen to represent each of 11 factors in the American version, and conclude that essentially the same 11 factors appear in factor analyses of two separate French studies. Unlike the authors previously cited, Cattell, Pichot, and Rennes then proceed to consider specific items whose relation to the factors differs between the two countries, and to relate these discrepancies to cultural impressions. Of special interest is the similarity of these discrepancies, as pointed out by Cattell, Pichot, and Rennes, to those found in an unpublished comparison of American and Italian responses to this same questionnaire. Where French and Italian results differ in the same way from the American, explanation seems likely to be found in common characteristics of the two Latin cultures.

Concern with whether items fall into the expected pattern of relationship is always appropriate if the intent is to measure a variable with a number of items which ought to be intercorrelated. The items comprising a variable need not be correlated at all; that depends upon the logic and purpose of measuring the variable (see Child, 1963, pp. 613–614). But if correlated items are wanted, the fact that they are correlated in one setting does not guarantee that they will be in another.

Sometimes, of course, each single item is in itself a meaningful variable, not intended in advance to be pooled with a set of other items. Yet the quest for broader variables may lead to looking for consistencies among the items, and of interest is the variation from one cultural setting to another. This is true, for example, of Morris's questionnaire on ways of life (1956), where each item is a fairly lengthy description of a philosophy of life, and the subject is asked to rate its personal appeal to him. Morris studied the inter-item consistency of ratings by students in the United States, India, and China. Three factor analyses (two of which are reported in greater detail by Morris and Jones, 1955) showed a very good agreement among national groups in the patterns that emerged. The agreement was close enough, Morris felt, to justify his using five factors as variables on which to compare the values of students in these three countries and in additional countries where he later collected data. Indication that agreement will not always be equally good comes from Prothro's (1958) application of factor analysis to data he collected from Arab students with Morris's questionnaire. He obtained three factors which clearly corresponded to three of Morris's, but two additional factors seemed entirely different from the other two obtained by Morris.

Usually, psychologists pool several items to measure a variable and then ask about its relation to comparably derived measures of other variables. If the same measures are obtained in diverse cultural settings, will the relation among them vary, or will it remain constant? This question is raised by Comrey, Meschieri, Misiti, and Nencini (1965). Having established that they could measure in their Italian subjects 28 variables corresponding to those previously measured in an American sample, they then did a factor analysis on the matrix of correlations among these (and some additional) variables. Comparing it with the factor analysis on the U.S. data, they conclude:

> Hostility, Compulsion, Neuroticism, Dependence, and Social Desirability were the most prominent factors in the study with American subjects. They were also the most prominent factors in the present analysis based upon Italian subjects. Although the correspondence between these factors is by no means perfect, the similarity of factor structure in the two investigations is unmistakable. (Comrey, Meschieri, Misiti, & Nencini, 1965, p. 261)

The authors are able to cite other comparisons between Italian and American subjects, using different items, that also indicate similarity of factor structure, and are encouraged to believe more generally

> ... that if a well-substantiated factor structure of personality can be worked out for American subjects, it probably will apply reasonably well to Italians and perhaps other western Europeans. (Comrey, Meschieri, Misiti, & Nencini, 1965, p. 261)

To the extent that this prediction is fulfilled, certain kinds of research on personality will be greatly facilitated. On the other hand, instances where the prediction is not fulfilled, where difference in culture is associated with difference in factor pattern, may turn out to be equally or even more interesting. Such instances will be cited in the next section of this chapter.

Inquiry into similarity of factor structure found in personality measurements in different cultural settings has been recently pursued on a large scale by Cattell and collaborators in several countries. I have already cited the French study by Cattell, Pichot, and Rennes (1961), which concentrates on the structure of inter-item correlations. Other articles in this series proceed to higher levels of abstraction from item response. In the following section I will use the Cattell and Warburton article (1961) to illustrate the interest of finding differences as well as similarities between nations. Here is a very substantial foundation for comparative knowledge about personality dimensions in different cultures. Perhaps the most comprehensive summary so far is that given by Tsujioka and Cattell (1965a) while discussing Japanese and American findings with Cattell's 16 PF questionnaire. Some of the modal-personality differences emerging from that study have been mentioned much earlier in this chapter. They are offered by Tsujioka and Cattell (1965a, 1965b) only with the justification that close similarity of factor structure warrants a comparison of means between national samples. Comparable similarity is also asserted for other studies not yet published, and is regarded as clearly sufficient to justify intercultural comparison of modal personality through the various versions of the 16 PF questionnaire.

Peterson (1965) has raised the question of whether at the highest level of abstraction, when factors are themselves analyzed to yield second-order factors such as Cattell's extroversion and anxiety, the structure is any longer specific to personality. Perhaps factors of such broad generality may be best identified with the very general dimensions of connotative meaning which Osgood (1962) finds to have considerable stability from culture to culture. Whatever the outcome of this very stimulating criticism of second-order factors of personality, it should not distract attention from the cross-national findings of great interest at a level of abstraction closer to the data.

That certain items, or sets of items, are similarly correlated in different cultural settings does not conclusively prove that the variable they measure is the same. Where possible, we would like to know next how this variable is related, in each culture, to some external criterion of validity. If the variable is found to have very similar relationships to relevant criteria in different cultural settings, then we can be confident about the consistent meaning of what it measures. If the relation of a single measure to an appropriate criterion is radically different from one cultural setting to another, the implication is not so clear. Perhaps the measure simply does not get at the same variable in the several cultural settings, or indeed the variable may not even be relevant in all. Perhaps a single variable is in fact being measured, but its relation to potential criteria genuinely differs from one setting to another. Further methods would have to be found, perhaps with great difficulty, to determine which interpretation was more nearly correct.

The best work of this sort so far, admirably displaying the general pattern such work must follow to be most useful, has been done by Gough and various associates. The basic instrument is the California Psychological Inventory (CPI), one especially created to be applicable in various cultural settings. It is a questionnaire designed to measure variables derived from folk concepts and presumed to be universally important. A subject responds to each statement by checking whether it does or does not describe himself. The test was first developed and applied in the United States; several translated versions have now been used in other countries. Studies thus far available relating its variables to external criteria are centered on predicting two criteria: high-school performance and degree of delinquency.

The cross-cultural study of the relation of variables on the CPI to high-school performance (Gough, 1964) compares students in the United States and Italy. For a large sample of over 1,300 students in American high schools, a regression equation was constructed for predicting grade-point average from the best combination of six variables out of the 18 measured by the CPI. The predictions made by the equation are, in a cross-validation sample of similar size, correlated .56 with actual grade-point average. Precisely the same regression equation was then applied to a sample of 341 Italian students who had taken the CPI in an Italian version, and the predicted grade averages were correlated .39 with the actual grade averages. This highly significant value is well below the accuracy of prediction obtained in the United States, but high enough to confirm to a remarkable extent the relative constancy, with conditions differing very substantially, of the variables' meaning and of their bearing on high-school performance. So far as we share the general bias of recent times toward expecting great cultural variation, we are likely to be surprised by finding this much constancy, and to suppose that the decline of predictive accuracy from one national sample to the other is of course to be attributed to a cultural difference in which of the personality variables are relevant to academic performance. Another analysis of some of the same data (Gough, 1965b) gives us a very different view. Here Gough calculates the best equation for the Italian data alone, based on the total sample of 341. The correlation between actual grades and grades predicted from the personality variables is .47 for boys and .43 for girls. The Italian-derived equation is then applied to the American cross-validation sample. Instead of falling, the correlation actually rises a bit, to .48! The pattern of relationship between personality measurements and school grades, then, is much more similar for the two countries than appears from the first stage of the study considered alone.

A comparable finding of constancy in different cultural settings has been obtained with a particular scale within the CPI, the socialization scale. This scale is intended to measure position along a continuum "from behaviors of greater waywardness and recalcitrance at one end, through an intermediate zone of partial balance and adaptation, to an extreme of archetypal virtue and probity." An appropriate criterion for such a variable would seem to be delinquency vs. non-delinquency, or degree of delinquency. For various kinds of samples in the United

States, correlations with such a criterion range from .73 to .83. Gough and Sandhu (1964) report for samples of subjects in India correlations of .70 and .73. Comparison of exact values seems likely to be less appropriate here than for high-school performance since it is likely that various samples differ considerably in the range of delinquency covered. But it is impressive again that the values attained are close to those in the original culture, despite the fact that—in addition to great change in general culture—the items had to be translated into two languages (Hindi and Punjabi), 10 per cent of the items had to be dropped as untranslatable, and about half the Indian subjects required oral presentation because of illiteracy. While Gough and Sandhu's findings pertain directly only to one measuring instrument developed with special care for cross-national use, there is already evidence for believing the outcome will be far from unique. Shirasa and Azuma (1961) have applied to Japanese subjects a translation of a brief questionnaire developed by Quay and Peterson (1958) to differentiate delinquents and non-delinquents in the United States and reported by its authors to have a correlation of about .70 with Gough's socialization scale (from which it was, in part, derived). The power of the scale to discriminate between delinquents and non-delinquents was as high in Japan as it had been in the United States.

More recently Gough (1965a) has extended to a total of ten countries, with subjects tested in eight different languages, the finding that CPI socialization score is highly related to delinquency vs. non-delinquency. Despite the obvious presence of several of the difficulties I reviewed earlier—especially linguistic and cultural translation of items, and questionable comparability of samples—not one of the delinquent groups has a mean socialization score as high as that of any of the non-delinquent groups. These findings, moreover, apply to female groups as well as male, except that in this case data are available from only six countries instead of ten. For females, indeed, it looks as though the socialization scale developed in the United States may in several other countries distinguish more sharply between delinquents and non-delinquents than it does in the United States.

Wherever we have such impressive evidence of a constancy of meaning for a measured variable in different cultural settings, the measurement can then be used as a basis for substantive investigation of the relation between this variable and others with greater confidence than would have been proper without this evidence of validity. Gough's comparative findings on predictors of high-school performance in Italy and the United States, for example, permit some tentative inferences about differences in personality determiners of high-school grades in the two countries. One conspicuous difference is that the variable of intellectual efficiency is more closely related to grades in the American sample than in the Italian. The socialization scales for which such striking evidence of validity has been obtained in several countries seem not yet to have been used in published research on the antecedents of degree of general socialization in different cultural settings. But an invaluable tool is obviously now at hand for use in such research.

I have thus far discussed the problem of personality consistency with reference to psychological measurement, where it most often arises. An ingenious anthropologist (Valentine, 1963) has shown that one can also deal with this problem through field work on ethnopsychology, and make a unique contribution in doing so. *Ethnopsychology* refers to the conceptions of behavior and experience indigenous to a particular culture. Valentine has studied these conceptions among the Lakalai of New Britain (a Melanesian people), and has presented a detailed analysis of their understanding of individual differences in personality, which he then compares with the personality-type concepts of Western psychology.

The Lakalai are attentive to individual

differences in personality and speak about them a great deal. Valentine reports that some of the terms used fall into two sets. The terms within a single set are often applied to the same person. Terms from the two sets rarely are applied to the same person, and when they are, an inconsistency is usually recognized. Thus Valentine's observations on Lakalai ethnopsychology establish that their folk traditions embody, and imply a belief in the existence of, a typology or bi-polar dimension.

What is this dimension or typology? In one set of terms appear—in the Melanesian pidgin current in the group along with their own Lakalai language—*man bilong shem* (man of shame), *man bilong save* (man of knowledge), and terms translatable as man of silence, of art, and of good conduct. The contrasting set includes *man bilong kros* (man of anger), *man bilong ple* (man of play), *man bilong pushpush oltaim* (man of sexuality), as well as man of movement and man of diffuse attention. Valentine makes a persuasive case, on the basis of very careful analysis of these concepts and their use, for identifying this contrast with the introversion-extroversion distinction in our psychological tradition. This conclusion is extremely provocative in a variety of ways for the planning of future work on personality and culture, as Valentine shows in discussing its implications at some length. The special point I would make here is that in starting with the conceptions indigenous in a society, and their spontaneous application to people in ordinary conversation, Valentine has been able to show a relevance of the dimension of introversion-extroversion which could not have been shown through psychological tests. He demonstrates not only that the dimension can be abstracted from the patterning of individual differences among Lakalai persons, but that the dimension has in fact already been abstracted by the Lakalai and their ancestors in their own development of ways of talking about those individual differences. If this finding is paralleled in other ethnopsychologies yet to be studied, it would appear that the concept introversion-extroversion is more nearly demanded or required for comprehending a much greater variety of everyday behavior than most psychologists realize.

All the approaches we have considered so far in this section involve separate analysis of observations in each cultural setting. Where the observations are numerous enough in each cultural setting to permit adequate assessment of their interrelations, this certainly seems the approach to choose, at least for determining whether the interrelations vary from one setting to another or remain the same. If the observations from each cultural setting are too few to permit this, ordinarily nothing very satisfactory can be done. But in the special case where the observations from various cultural settings are highly comparable and their interrelations have a good chance of remaining constant, there is another approach to studying those interrelations. This is the technique of pan-cultural factor analysis used by Minturn, Lambert, *et al.* (1964). They were dealing with interviews obtained from a small number of mothers (about 20) in each of six societies. The interviews were closely comparable in the six societies because the field workers deliberately took care to obtain uniformity. The ratings of all the interviews were also comparable, having been done simultaneously without separation of the societies. In this special case, it was feasible to put together the six small sets of data, treat them as one larger set, and apply factor analysis to identify the major strands of consistency underlying the numerous variables rated. Here the test of whether the interrelations were sufficiently uniform from one culture to another consists only of observing whether the approach yields generally sensible results. There was enough uniformity from culture to culture so that reasonable factors emerge and factor scores based on them, when used to compare individuals and societies, yield results that seem to fit the impressions of the field workers and analysts. Perhaps such an approach will also be useful in other special cases.

Differing Relations among Personality Variables in Different Cultures

Where the relations among variables differ from one culture to another, the meaning of the relation within any given culture is likely to be seen differently from the way it would be if only the facts about it alone were known. Development within a single culture of knowledge about a set of variables may be followed by an appeal to knowledge from another culture as a basis for altering the initial understanding. Research on authoritarianism provides an example.

Authoritarianism was first studied in relation to other personality variables by Adorno, Frenkel-Brunswik, Levinson, and Sanford (1950) in the United States. Melikian (1956) subsequently made a comparative study of correlates of authoritarianism in American college men and in Middle Eastern college men studying in Lebanon. Authoritarianism as measured by the *F*-scale is an internally consistent measure of a personality dimension in both cultural settings. In the Middle Eastern sample, authoritarianism had little or no relation to measurements of the extent to which a person considers his parents or ideal parents as acceptant or rejecting. Higher and more consistent relationships with such variables were found for the American sample, where authoritarianism is associated with a view of parents as rejecting. A questionnaire measure of the subject's general hostility showed the same pattern of relationships. The relation between hostility and conception of parents, moreover, was linked in the American sample to the relation of each with authoritarianism; there, partialing out the relation to authoritarianism appreciably reduces the correlation between hostility and conception of parents, as is not true for the Middle Eastern sample. Melikian suggests the following interpretation:

> Where authoritarianism is a commonly accepted character ideal which stresses conformity, it does not apparently contribute to relationships that have a significant psychological function. Hence even though authoritarianism as a personality dimension is established for different cultural conditions, generalizations as to its psychological correlates as well as to its effect on relationships between other psychological variables, are valid only when made within a specific cultural context. (Melikian, 1956, p. 245)

In a later study conducted in Egypt, Melikian (1959) found that deviations from other United States findings on correlates of authoritarianism were not large but tended to be in a consistent direction. The tendency was for authoritarianism to show a slight positive relation to indices of good adjustment in the more authoritarian cultural setting of Egypt, and to show a slight negative relation or none at all in the more liberal setting of the United States. Such findings direct our attention to the local cultural meaning of a behavior tendency as an element that needs to be considered in evaluating its significance for personality.

Sometimes a number of variables may be measured in individuals in order that their interrelations may contribute to constructing a picture of modal personality or group character. An example is a comparison of German and American boys between 16 and 19, of the educational elite—that is, boys preparing to go on to college—by McClelland, Sturr, Knapp, and Wendt (1958). Here the difference in factorial pattern obtained in two cultural settings plays a crucial role in working from individual personality data toward a single coherent picture of modal personality and group character. A parallel questionnaire, devised in English and translated into German, was given to an appropriate sample in each of the two countries. The matrix of correlations among items was obtained for each country, and separate factor analyses were performed. Two main factors emerged which were in part loaded on the same items in both countries. Factor A could be labeled, on the basis of the items heavily loaded on it in both countries, as rational striving. Factor B could, on the same grounds, be labeled as resignation and cynicism. A third set of items had loadings on Factor A in Germany, but on Factor B in the United States. These items all have to do with concern for propriety or for the welfare of others. From these factors the authors formulate the statement that rational striving in Germany

. . . is definitely sociocentric: conscientious striving is included in a network of idealistic sentiments relating to decent social behavior. In the United States, rational striving is part of no such framework. (McClelland, Sturr, Knapp, & Wendt, 1958, p. 249)

In the United States, indeed, concern for decent social behavior appears to be related to resignation and cynicism.

An attempt is then made by these authors to interpret various other findings on the TAT and questionnaire responses of the same subjects in relation to this basic finding of differing factorial pattern. In doing so, the authors relate their findings to statements on a cultural level, particularly to the analysis by McGranahan and Wayne (1948) of themes of successful drama in Germany and the United States as a basis for inferences about group character, and to the common attribution of authoritarian elements to German culture. The major interpretation is that

. . . in the United States obligation to self appears as a strong unconscious need for Achievement, and obligation to society as participation in many group activities, and that in Germany obligation to the self appears as a stress on the ego as a separate, unique, willing entity and obligation to society as a moral imperative to place obligation to the "impersonal other" as an abstract code above particularistic, "selfish" considerations. (McClelland, Sturr, Knapp, & Wendt, 1958, p. 255)

This conclusion about difference in national character has thus developed from an insight apparently originally suggested by the varying factorial pattern of relationships among items and then verified, extended, and modified by comparison with other personality and cultural data.

In several studies of the correlates of introversion-extroversion, Siegman (1963) neatly demonstrates cultural variation in pattern of correlation among personality variables. One study deals with two subcultural groups, Protestants and Jews of comparable socio-economic background (medical students). Extroversion was measured by a single questionnaire, Eysenck's Maudsley Personality Inventory; religiosity was measured by several different scales. Each of the religiosity scales is positively correlated with extroversion in the Protestant students, and negatively correlated in the Jews. The author interprets this to mean that religiosity differs in personality meaning within the two subcultural settings, sociability and social conformity tending to motivate it among Protestants, and introversion tending to motivate it among Jews. The interpretation could be stated another way: religiosity, while superficially the same in the two cultural settings, actually is a different variable psychologically. Defining variables objectively, however, we see clearly that the pattern of relationship among them differs for the subcultural groups.

A second and similar observation in Siegman's study involves variation with sex within a single cultural group. Here we are concerned with cultural definition of complementary roles, rather than a multiplicity of cultural groups within a single society. The major variable related in this instance to extroversion is anti-social behavior, as measured by a questionnaire devised by Nye and Short (1957). In a group of male students there is a significant positive correlation between extroversion and anti-social behavior, whereas in a female group there is a tendency toward a negative correlation. Siegman interprets this difference on the assumption that extroversion is probably an index of general sociability or social conformity. Since anti-social behavior is to some extent a part of the masculine role, it might be expected in men to be correlated positively with extroversion; conformity to the female role, on the other hand, might be expected to lead to lack of anti-social behavior. This interpretation is strengthened also by a parallel finding that the sexes differ in how religiosity (of Protestants) is related to extroversion. In men, religiosity is positively correlated with extroversion; in women, the correlation is close to zero. Introverted, reflective motivations for religious participation, which might interfere with the extroversion-religiosity correlation, are presumably freer to operate in women, since they are more compatible with the stereotyped female Protestant role. This interpretation makes the finding similar in significance to that on anti-social behavior.

One especially important study of cultural variation among personality variables involves fairly similar cultures—those of the United States and the United Kingdom. Cattell and Warburton (1961) applied Cattell's 16 PF questionnaire to about 600 American college students and to 200 British students, the latter almost evenly divided between students of industrial administration and graduate students of education. The questionnaire was scored for the 16 personality variables it is intended to measure, and Cattell and Warburton make no report about relative item consistency in the two cultural settings. Their report is concerned instead with consistency and difference at a higher level, the interrelations among the 16 variables. Separately for each national sample, the 16 variables were intercorrelated and factor analysis was applied to the resulting matrix. The question then is: Are the factors identical or different in the two countries? The discussion centers mainly on two factors in each analysis, labeled by the authors as anxiety and extroversion. Basically these two factors are clearly the same in the two countries; the correlation of United States and United Kingdom factor-loadings is +.88 for anxiety and +.61 for extroversion. But for each factor, certain variables are definite exceptions to the general positive relation, and to these Cattell and Warburton give special attention.

Loadings on the anxiety factor are substantial and very similar in the United States and United Kingdom for variables labeled paranoid tendency, guilt proneness, id pressure, low ego strength, and low self-sentiment. (I have modified the labels where necessary so that the loadings will all be positive.) These facts, together with the nature of the variables with low loadings, seem to make the label *anxiety* very appropriate. Now what are the variables which yield inconsistent results for the United States and the United Kingdom? One, which Cattell calls Autia or Bohemianism, is viewed as measuring tendency "to think autistically and to have an inner productivity and tenacity of phantasy that has little relation to external realities" (Cattell & Warburton, 1961, p. 9). Its loading on the anxiety factor is +.40 for the United Kingdom sample and almost zero for the United States. In considering why this tendency forms a part of the anxiety pattern in one national sample and not in the other, Cattell and Warburton suggest as the best hypothesis that phantasy is a more likely channel for expression of anxiety in British culture than in American because the culture imposes greater inhibition and provides less opportunity for "acting out." Another variable shows an opposite pattern of inconsistency, in that it is related to anxiety much more strongly for the American sample than for the British (loadings of .66 vs. .18). This is timidity, or lack of adventurousness (Parmia). The authors conjecture that

> . . . the British culture is more inhibited and introvert, so that anxieties arise more from conflicts in the complex mazes of the culture, and less from realistic threats of the environment. It seems reasonable to suppose that dispositional timidity would play a greater role in magnifying anxieties in an extravert culture. (Cattell & Warburton, 1961, p. 9)

Thus these two differences in factor pattern are both tentatively explained by reference to a single hypothesized difference in group character having to do with inhibition or introversion, a difference evidently regarded as confirmed by cultural observation and confirmed also by the fact (mentioned already in an earlier reference to this study) that these British students average decidedly more introverted than do these Americans.

For the extroversion factor there are more variables on which the loadings are appreciably different for the two countries. Two of the differences are tentatively explained by appeal to the same hypothesis used in explaining the difference in anxiety loadings; for the others, separate tentative explanations are offered. The rather simpler case of the anxiety factor is sufficient illustration for our purpose here. It is clear that inquiry into similarities and differences between cultural groups in the interrelation of personality variables has led Cattell and Warburton to plausible interpretations, based on integration of their findings with concepts at a cultural level, and susceptible of eventual test because richly suggestive of diverse implications. Greater attention to selecting groups of subjects truly representative of each society compared, or closely corresponding segments, and systematic inquiry into facts about the cultures, are features that might be borrowed from the method of sociologists and anthropologists to make this type of psychological research even more valuable.

Antecedents of Personality Variables in Different Cultures

Where differences are found among cultural settings in the relationships between personality variables, explanation is usually sought in hypotheses about variation among settings in the causal factors affecting the several variables. In the previous section we have reviewed several such explanations. Where the relationships among variables are the same in different cultural settings, on the other hand, the influences on them are generally assumed to be more or less constant. Of this reasoning too we have seen examples, in the section before last. In both instances, reference to antecedents of the personality variables remained hypothetical. The evidence obtained in such research concerns the relation among current personality variables, not the relation of these variables to possible causal factors which operated at an earlier time. But similar theoretical reasoning may of course lead to direct empirical test of the relation personality variables have to antecedent variables upon which their development may have depended. Such research is a common part of inquiry into personality variation within our own society; extension to comparative inquiry is now beginning.

At the outset we should note that some comparative research of this sort has already been considered: among important antecedents of personality is membership in some differentiated segment of a society—possession of one rather than another identity. In the present section I will turn to antecedents which consist of variations in an identity-relationship or which are defined independently of identities or identity-relationships.

It happens that several variations in the father-son relationship are among the first antecedents of personality to undergo comparative study. Mussen, Young, Gaddini, and Morante (1963) have reported on one such variation, amount of affection expressed by father toward son. They studied adolescent boys of Italian descent in a United States city and in three Italian cities. An interview with each boy's mother provided evidence for sorting the boys into those receiving "sufficient" or "insufficient" paternal affection. This was the antecedent variable, and a number of variables deriving from interview and story-productions of the boys were related to it. Results were similar in the several cities sampled; the authors review pertinent previous research and conclude

> . . . that the present data generally confirm the findings of other studies, based exclusively on American subjects, that show that affectional parent-child relationships are important antecedent conditions of strong identification, and that such identification makes for greater degrees of sex-typing, conscience-development and good social adjustment. The present findings suggest that the antecedents and consequents of the identification process are very much alike in other cultures, such as the Italian, where the family structure is more authoritarian and paternalistic. (Mussen, Young, Gaddini, & Morante, 1963, pp. 14–15)

Another variable in the father-son relationship is presence of the father and opportunity for interaction. Bradburn (1963) included this variable in a study of achievement motivation, as measured by the TAT, in three groups of Turkish men. Specifically, the variable was age at which the son had first lived apart from his parents or had lost his father. Achievement motivation was correlated with this variable; sons separated from their fathers relatively early (the dividing line used was 18 years in two groups, 14 in the other) averaged higher in achievement motivation. Turkish culture calls for vigorous domination of son by father. Bradburn therefore views this outcome as consistent with Rosen and D'Andrade's finding (1959) for United States boys that achievement motivation tends to be higher in boys whose fathers are relatively non-dominant and non-authoritarian in observed interaction with them. In this interpretation, interaction with a father who dominates relatively little is held, very plausibly, to be similar in some way to non-interaction with a very dominant father. The confirmation by Bradburn of United States findings is, however, only at a theoretical level. If his results are instead compared with United States results on an empirical variable more nearly like his, the comparison leads to an apparent contradiction. As Bradburn points out, Veroff, Atkinson, Feld, and Gurin (1960) related achievement motivation in American men to whether absence of one or both parents (because of divorce, separation, or death) occurred before they were 16. The correlation obtained is the reverse of the one Bradburn found in Turkey. Such a discrepancy is even more interesting than simple confirmation, for it leads us (if we think useful the hypothesis of a psychic unity of mankind) to search for the causal processes peculiar to each cultural setting. We are thus prevented from easy acceptance of a possibly superficial conclusion based on the external facts observable in a single culture. Bradburn offers a plausible interpretation:

> In the United States, where the father may play a more encouraging role, setting high standards for the boy in encouraging him to achieve, loss of the father means the removal of a positive masculine model for achievement. In Turkey, on the other hand, where the father is a much more dominating figure, loss of the father represents an escape from restraining influences which are associated with low n Ach [need for achievement], and leaves the boy free to respond to any positive forces which may reward him for achievement-related behavior. Thus the same set of objective circumstances may lead to different results depending on the cultural context. (Bradburn, 1963, p. 468)

However plausible, such a *post hoc* interpretation must remain very uncertain until its further implications are tested. Without the cross-cultural research out of which it grows, however, a much longer time would be required to arrive at an understanding of personality processes in any one cultural setting sufficiently basic to be generalizable to other cultural settings. Failures of replication in different settings provide impetus for improving understanding of what goes on within a single culture.

Father-absence has been studied for possible influences on personality during childhood by Lynn and Sawrey (1959) in Norway, and by Mischel (1961) in several Caribbean groups. Somewhat comparable results are available from earlier studies on individual differences within the United States.

Lynn and Sawrey (1959) investigated Norwegian boys and girls, aged 8 to 9½, whose father's occupation as sailor or whaler kept him away for at least nine months per year, and compared them with other children carefully matched on a number of background characteristics. Personality variables were assessed through interview of the mother and play-interview with the child. General confirmation is obtained for the hypotheses that father-absence in boys makes for immaturity, strong strivings toward father-identification, compensatory masculinity, and poor peer adjustment, and that in girls father-absence makes for dependence on the mother.

Mischel (1961) concentrates on a single psychological variable, but pools several items to measure it. The variable may be called tolerance for delay of gratification. It is measured by two questionnaire items and the child's actual choice between a small gift immediately available and a larger one promised for a week later. Father-absence was measured by answer to the single question, "Does your father live at home with you?" In Negro children 8 and 9 years old in Trinidad and in Grenada, father-presence is positively correlated with tolerance for delay of gratification, as it had been in some earlier research by Mischel. While he cites no data on precisely the same relationship from cultures other than the Caribbean, he points out the consistency of his findings with the general conclusion from American and Norwegian studies, that maturity of personality is favored by presence of father. To this extent, then, an objectively defined variable is found to have a similar effect in diverse cultural settings even though circumstances giving rise to it differ radically. (The United States data pertain to father-absence for wartime military service; the Norwegian, absence of sailor-fathers on long voyages; the Caribbean, father-absence as part of a general cultural pattern of informal and unstable marriage.) This uniformity of finding, however, is not complete. Mischel notes that Lynn and Sawrey establish different effects in each sex, while Mischel's studies find an effect common to both sexes. Furthermore, Mischel also studied a group of older children (age 11 to 14) and in them found no relation between father-presence and tolerance of delay—an age effect not predicted by hypotheses developed from United States experience. This presumed difference from the United States, Mischel suggests, may result from other cultural differences such as earlier attainment of independence and exposure to stronger formative influences outside the family in the Caribbean cultures. Again, then, both agreements and disagreements between findings in different cultural settings may serve to clarify how personality develops in each one.

An instance of parallel personality study in different cultures, on an antecedent not defined in relation to a specific identity-interaction, is provided by birth-order—specifically, a contrast between first-born and later-born children. In some societies—Japan, for example—"eldest son" is a clearly separated identity. In the United States it is not, and it probably is not in Uruguay, the other country compared below. Capra and Dittes (1962) had reported from research on college men in the United States that first-born sons are more likely to volunteer to take part in psychological experiments on group interaction. Varela (1964) obtained the same finding in a study of high-school boys and girls in Uruguay. Neither finding by itself, nor the two together, can identify very definitely the personality variable reflected in the volunteering and the processes linking it with birth-order. As both authors indicate, however, a possible explanation lies in hypotheses developed by Schachter (1959) in research among United States students on birth-order in relation to affiliative response to anxiety. Deciding what to make of the transcultural confirmation of Capra and Dittes's findings is complicated by the fact that similar studies on United States students, published about the same time as Varela's Uruguayan research, find no consistent relation between birth-order and volunteering (Ward, 1964; Brock & Becker, 1965). For anyone who is inclined to regard cultural differences as always of overwhelming magnitude, it is instructive to see here that seemingly minor differences of procedure affect results more than does a major cultural difference.

Testing a Basic Hypothesis in Different Ways

Studying personality in relation to culture has a special value to anyone interested in understanding personality origins. Our most direct knowledge of these origins must be derived from correlational studies. (Experimental work can of course contribute valuable evidence about basic principles. But when extrapolated to understanding personality origins in the ordinary life-situation, this evidence acquires its own uncertainties.) We observe that individuals who have been exposed to a particular set of influences tend to have a certain personality trait, and that those who have not had this exposure tend to lack the trait. We infer that exposure to these influences is the antecedent or cause of the trait. This reasoning is obviously risky; perhaps the trait existed earlier and was responsible for the exposure, or perhaps both are separate consequences of some common cause. Suppose, for example, that aggression toward peers is found in boys to be positively correlated with the severity with which their aggression toward their parents gets punished. We are likely to infer that boys who are prevented by punishment from expressing the hostility they feel toward their parents are thereby led to express it toward their peers instead. But perhaps these boys are hyper-aggressive to start with; the observer sees this characteristic directly in peer interaction, but in interaction between boy and parents all that is visible is the punitiveness the parents, in their position of greater power, have developed to squelch the boy's aggression toward them. Or perhaps the high aggression common to boy and parents is an outgrowth of selective mating and shared genes. For another example of radically different explanations for correlational findings in this field, see the discussions by Young (1962) and Whiting (1962) on how to interpret cross-cultural studies of initiation ceremonies.

One hope for disentangling these assorted threads of possible causation is to test the same hypothesis in very different situations. Theoretical interest is likely to direct special attention to the hypothesis embodying one particular causal sequence. But an alternative explanation highly likely in one situation may be less likely in another. The more varied the tests leading to confirmation of a single hypothesis, the greater is the confidence that can be placed in its general validity. If it is confirmed in some situations and not in others, this may lead to its rejection, to a decision that it is valid in a limited sphere, or to its replacement by some more general hypothesis that can account for both its successes and its failures. Such a process is involved, of course, in simply replicating a correlational study with subjects drawn from a slightly different population, or with slightly different measures or procedures. But special value inheres in testing implications a single hypothesis can yield for predictions of great diversity, such as: correlations between antecedents and consequences in individuals within a single group (or, separately, within several groups); co-variation of antecedents and consequents for the modal personality of differentiated groups within a society (or, within several separate societies); co-variation of antecedents and consequents in the course of historical change in a society (or, in parallel changes in several societies); correlation of antecedents and consequents in the group character or modal personality of discrete societies. I have already presented examples of some replication within one of these kinds—testing whether class position has similar effects on personality in different societies, for instance, or whether father-absence does. Here I would like to consider the question of submitting the same hypothesis to two or more different *kinds* of test.

The earliest cross-cultural hypothesis-testing research involved such a broadening of test conditions, though this may not be immediately apparent because the initial test had for the most part not been systematic. When Horton (1943), by group-character application of cultural data, investigated whether use of alcohol is motivated by anxiety, he was testing a hypothesis already confirmed in our society by unsystematized clinical observation. Whiting and Child (1953), in predicting cross-cultural correlations from hypotheses of negative and positive fixation, were attempting to extend the application of hypotheses which many psychoanalysts already regarded as well confirmed by clinical observation. In their chapter on the origins of guilt (1953, ch. 11), moreover, they were able to cite correlational studies of individual differences confirming two of the hypotheses for which the cross-cultural study provided some evidence.

Since that time, personality research has advanced on all fronts, and there is now hope of finding for many hypotheses considerable evidence already on record. Thus when Bacon, Child, and Barry (1963) explored cross-culturally the correlates of frequency of crime, they were able to compare several of their results with the outcome of previous intra-societal research on individual and group differences. They find crime to be more frequent in those primitive societies where the young child's opportunity for intimate contact with his father is limited; this is paralleled by sociological findings that a disproportionate number of United States delinquents are from broken or fatherless homes. This similarity of finding for individual differences in the United States, where intact nuclear family is the rule, and for cross-cultural comparisons of varying rules, strengthens the likelihood that each result is properly explained by a hypothesis dealing with what is common to the crime-producing circumstances identified in the two studies, i.e., absence of, or reduced contact between, child and father.

Comparisons with other sources of evidence are likewise possible for a more recent cross-cultural study of alcohol use, by Bacon, Barry, and Child (1965). They report a number of correlations confirming the hypothesis "that high levels of use of alcohol are in part motivated by a need to relieve frustrated or conflicted dependency needs" (p. 46). High frequency of drunkenness tends to characterize societies that place strong pressures on their children toward achievement and assertion, and that offer adults relatively little satisfaction for dependency needs. Now, as these authors point out, essentially the same hypothesis is used by McCord and McCord (1960) to explain why some individuals in our society become alcoholics and others do not. If we attribute the relative absence of immoderate drinking among Jews to the relative lack of dependency conflict in Jewish family life, this interpretation is a special instance of the same hypothesis. The identical hypothesis would lead, moreover, to the expectation that immoderate drinking would very generally be found in men more than in women, since conditions creating conflict about dependence are likely to be almost universally stronger in men. This expectation that sex identity would tend to have elsewhere the same significance for drinking that it has in our society is amply confirmed by Child, Barry, and Bacon (1965) in a cross-cultural survey of sex differences in drinking. Thus the mutual fit of these various types of finding and of the theoretical interpretation which has grown out of some and led to others gives added plausibility to each. Obviously, however, such added plausibility is not an acceptable long-run substitute for more thorough critical investigation of each type of correlation.

Sometimes, of course, an important relation among different studies may not be noted at the time by any of the researchers, but may appear to the interested reader. Here is an instance that occurred to me while preparing this chapter. In a cross-cultural study, Whiting and Child (1953) used explanations of illness as possible indices of personal conflicts and found strong evidence that attribution of illness to possession by a spirit is typically an outcome of conflict about dependency. However impressive the evidence, though, a single finding of this sort must remain subject to considerable doubt. Recently Freed and Freed (1964), reporting a study of individual cases of spirit possession in a village in India—without, so far as their paper indicates, any knowledge of these cross-cultural findings—conclude that the conditions which in that village tend to precipitate illness by spirit-possession

> . . . have two general characteristics: (1) the victim of spirit possession is involved in difficulties with relatives of the nuclear or joint family, and (2) he is often in a situation where his expectations of mutual aid and support are low. (Freed & Freed, 1964, p. 170)

The clear focusing here on problems of dependence, and the cross-cultural finding, serve to strengthen each other as reason for believing that spirit-possession probably has a special relation to dependence.

As the value of testing the same basic hypothesis in several ways becomes better appreciated, research may be deliberately planned to gain this advantage, as may be seen from some of the research on father-child relationship partially presented in the preceding section. I have already reported there that Mischel (1961) finds father-presence to be correlated with tolerance for delay of gratification among young children in several Caribbean groups where father-absence is common. In the same research, he finds that Negroes of Grenada are more tolerant of delay than are Negroes of Trinidad, but that fathers are not appreciably more often present in one group than in the other. Difference between these societies in tolerance of delay, then, cannot be attributed to the variable identified as influential on individual differences within each of them. Mischel seeks an explanation in other aspects of the culture, especially in Grenadians' placing a higher value on personal autonomy. He observes, too, that the difference in tolerance between Trinidadians and Grenadians is accounted for entirely by the children with fathers; a comparison of those without fathers in the two groups shows no difference in tolerance of delay. He suggests the possibility that transmittal of such a cultural value as autonomy, in cultures possessing it, is dependent upon the father's presence. Thus the very processes by which tolerance of delay is brought about within a society may eventually be more fully understood because a single set of processes failed to account for both intra-cultural and inter-cultural findings.

Bradburn's exploration (1963) of the father-son relation also involved comparison between societies as well as among individuals within Turkish society. Turkish fathers customarily dominate their sons more than American fathers; Bradburn carefully verified this proposition by interviewing his subjects. Turks should then average lower in achievement motivation than comparable Americans, if societal differences here are predictable from the antecedent variable Bradburn had identified as important for intra-societal variation. He compared TAT achievement scores of junior executives in the two countries, and found the predicted difference. Here then we gain some increased confidence in the general validity of the proposition that domination of son by father makes for low achievement motivation. Research of other kinds, or in other cultural settings, may establish limits to its validity and carry us on to a still fuller analysis of how father-son interaction influences achievement motivation.

Related in theory and technique to Bradburn's work is that by Rosen (1962), also mentioned earlier. He, too, tested a single hypothesis two ways. Rosen compared social classes within and between two countries, Brazil and the United States. Samples from each show, as I have reported earlier, a similar tendency for achievement motivation to vary positively with class position; achievement motivation is also higher in the United States sample than in the Brazilian. Rosen studied, as a probable antecedent of achievement motivation, earliness of child-training emphases on independence and achievement. The presumed connection is strengthened by the fact that this measure varies in much the same way as the achievement measure, both between societies and among classes.

A final example comes from recent research on the psychological significance of games. In an initial cross-cultural study, Roberts, Arth, and Bush (1959) considered three categories of games—strategy, physical skill, and chance. Exploring the correlations of each game type with other features of culture, they find some reason to infer that all might function as exercises in mastery, with special concern about mastering the social system (strategy), the physical environment (physical skill), or the supernatural (chance). In a subsequent cross-cultural study (Roberts & Sutton-Smith, 1962) relating these game categories to socialization practices, evidence is found which in part confirms the initial proposals and in part supplements or replaces them with evidence of additional motivational themes. The cross-cultural findings were then used to predict differences between groups in our society. Where groups could be held to differ on the dimensions found significant cross-culturally for game preference, they were predicted to show the corresponding difference in game preference. Predictions were made in this way for boys vs. girls (Roberts & Sutton-Smith, 1962, pp. 176–178) and, among adults, for differentiation by sex, education, and occupation (Sutton-Smith, Roberts, & Kozelka, 1963). In general, the predictions are confirmed. For example, games of strategy are associated cross-culturally with "severe primary socialization, psychological discipline, high obedience training, and complex culture" (Sutton-Smith, Roberts, & Kozelka, 1963, p. 29). Because these characteristics tend to be found more in the background of girls, women, and high-status groups, the authors believe, they predict that preference for games of strategy will average higher there than in the contrasting groups. All these predictions are confirmed.

Several of the studies or arguments I have cited deal with a comparison between two instances—Brazil vs. the United States, Trinidad vs. Grenada, Jews vs. non-Jews, males vs. females in one society. In an excellent discussion of the methodological relevance of anthropology and psychology to each other, Campbell (1961, pp. 344–345) points out very forcefully that a single comparison between two things cannot be interpreted confidently because alternative explanations cannot be ruled out. We need this reminder in the present context. When, as in some of this research, a single comparison of two groups is linked with a more adequate test of the same hypothesis applied to individual differences, it is easy to forget how indecisive the comparison of two instances is. There is still greater value in combining, when possible, several kinds of test which are each separately capable of yielding a reliable conclusion.

On the other hand, the agreement of several predictions about contrasting pairs, based on a single theory, as in the research on games, greatly increases confidence in the theory. Rosenblatt (1962) derived from the initial cross-cultural research on games some predictions about inter-individual relationships, between frequency of participation in games of strategy and chance and several personality characteristics apparently relevant to the theory that games are exercises in mastery. Obtaining data from college students, he finds no consistent relationships. Combined with only the initial cross-cultural study, this negative evidence might make me doubt the whole theory. With the addition of the later cross-cultural study and confirmation of several two-group predictions, I am more inclined to think that perhaps this first inter-individual test may turn out to be unrepresentative. But we will not know until the enquiry is further ahead. Such uncertainties really characterize, to greater or lesser degree, all the topics I have reviewed here. All invite the further study that alone will permit us to clarify them and, through the knowledge thus gained, move on to new uncertainties.

Interaction between Biological and Cultural Variables

In an earlier day, when the importance of learning and the role that cultural background plays in determining what is learned were not well understood, differences between cultural groups were often one-sidedly attributed to heredity. Clear demonstration in recent times of the importance of culture on the social level and of learning on the individual level, together with the coupling of hereditarian doctrine with social mischief as in Germany and the American South, has led to a one-sided neglect of possible biological factors determining differences among cultural groups. The redress of this balance has begun, and we may hope it will lead to a valid synthesis somewhere between two equally false extremes.

Reappearance of biological elements in the interpretation of cultural phenomena may be seen in a recent paper by Lynn and Gordon (1962) comparing England and the United States with respect to differences between middle and lower class on certain variables. The ones measured in the study have to do with maternal attitudes toward child socialization, attitudes presumably correlated with maternal behavior toward children. Scales prepared by Sears, Maccoby, and Levin (1957) were used. The mother interviewed was presented with items describing, in the actual words of another mother, a child's behavior and maternal reaction to it; the interviewee rated on a scale her agreement or disagreement with the reaction. Items were designed to measure, among other variables, permissiveness of aggression and punishment of aggression. Significantly greater permissiveness toward aggression was found in the American mothers, and punitiveness in the British mothers.

These results are not very substantial and serve only to raise questions. But the authors' interpretation is of interest for the novelty of their speculating as freely about biological as about social influences. Lynn and Gordon argue that current notions about experiential influences on aggression would require that with this background of childhood experience English adults should be more aggressive than Americans. Common experience points to an opposite difference. The authors regard their study, therefore, as "something of a challenge to the theory linking maternal punitiveness to the aggression of the child," and they suggest that consideration of hereditary factors may resolve the difficulty. They assert that aggression is positively-correlated with extroversion, and then cite some evidence that extroversion is considerably influenced by heredity.

> The fact that Americans are more extraverted than the English may therefore be due to the fact that they are genetically a more extraverted strain. When it is considered that Americans are descended from ancestors who have emigrated it seems not improbable that they are selected for some personality factor; and in view of the findings that people with extraverted characteristics are intolerant of monotonous stimuli (Petrie, Collins, & Solomon, 1960) it seems not implausible that extraversion might be a factor in emigration. Such a hypothesis could, of course, be easily checked. Now it has been shown that extraverted mothers are less punitive towards their children than introverted mothers (Lynn, 1961) and this finding is consistent with the finding that American mothers are less punitive than English mothers. It is, therefore, suggested that the hereditary factor of extraversion accounts for both the non-punitiveness of American mothers and the aggressiveness of their children, and that the hereditary factor is a more important determinant of aggression than the mother's punitiveness. (Lynn & Gordon, 1962, pp. 54–55)

This interpretation involves several untested or inadequately tested assumptions. Perhaps it is a defect of hereditarian hypotheses that at the present stage of our ignorance about behavioral genetics they may encourage proliferation of sheer speculation. But when tested, the assumptions may turn out to have some validity and importance. It is encouraging, therefore, to see the prospect of advances in this field. Naturally enough, advances are most likely for psychological characteristics whose genetic basis is partially identified and reasonably simple.

An example is deficiency of color vision. Here is a psychological characteristic which must be supposed to have an influence on personality, though an influence never investigated. There seems no reason to expect a general personality syndrome growing out of color defect, but individuals with defective color vision are likely to develop characteristics determined in part by their sensory deficiency. The reasons which lead us to this expectation lie especially in the fact that color deficiency hampers a person in some practical endeavors such as hunting and the recognition of certain signals, and alters the kinds of stimulus diversity which can have esthetic meaning for him. Red-green color blindness is the particular defect for which, because of its greater frequency, the best comparative information is available. Recent work, reviewed by Post (1962a) and Pickford (1963), indicates strongly that this defect varies in incidence in different populations as a result of their ancestors' culture. Here is the theoretical reasoning. When a society is dependent for survival upon hunting and gathering, there is a steady process of selection against color defects. A person with color deficiency is less often successful in these activities; therefore, the probability of his having children and bringing them to adulthood is appreciably decreased. When agriculture, herding, and other more settled forms of economy are adopted, the probability that defective color vision will affect a person's having and rearing children is lessened. An assumption of a steady rate of mutations producing the gene for color defect, combined with this increased possibility of reproduction, predicts a gradual increase in the proportion of the population defective in color vision. The observed distribution of population differences, both Post and Pickford conclude, agrees well with expectation based on this prediction. Other recent research pointing in the same direction is that of Best (1963) and Dronamraju and Meera Khan (1963). In a variety of such comparisons from various parts of the world, a substantial relation is claimed between the probable period since a population abandoned a hunting and gathering economy and its present incidence of red-green color defect.

With considerably less confidence, a parallel interpretation has been offered for population differences in visual acuity (Post, 1962b). Comparable observations on different populations are harder to obtain for acuity than for color deficiency; the genetic mechanisms are more complicated than for red-green color deficiency, and experiential influences are likely to be greater.

Such difficulties are multiplied many times over when speculation is shifted to other possible ways in which personality might be influenced by genetic differences among groups. The examples of color blindness and perhaps acuity are especially interesting because they demonstrate an effect of culture on personality mediated by genetics. The culture influencing the characteristics of the gene pool is the culture of a person's ancestors. The culture determining the impact of the genetically determined characteristic on personality is of course the current or recent culture in which a person has lived.

Culture may also influence personality by way of biological mediating processes other than genetic. Some of these may be yet unknown; a surprising one has apparently been discovered recently by Landauer and Whiting (1964). They find that members of societies which customarily subject their infants to some stressful procedure (e.g., piercing the skin or shaping the head) tend to be taller in adulthood than members of societies which do not stress their infants. The average difference is over two inches; Landauer and Whiting suggest that an influence of stress on growth is the most likely causal process involved. The uncertainty about this finding is only that which attaches to any relatively isolated correlational result (though parallels in animal experimentation offer support). There is further uncertainty, though, in my connecting the finding speculatively with personality. Obviously, height differences of this magnitude within a society can have significant effects on personality; for everyone in a society to be taller or shorter may well be of no importance for personality.

A connection with personality may be more confidently claimed, though other doubts may still remain, in the case of two recent suggestions that basic economy has an influence on personality by way of physiological effects of the diet it provides. Wallace (1961b) presents a reasoned argument that calcium deficiency may be a major factor in the specialized mental illness (pibloktoq) of Thule Eskimo, and follows this by a more speculative extension of the same interpretation to the hysteria common in an earlier generation in Europe. Wallace takes off from the specific hypothesis of calcium deficiency to argue more generally the need for truly integrated consideration of biological and cultural factors as interacting in the etiology of mental illness.

A second suggestion, made by Whiting (1964), is concerned with protein deficiency. The long taboo of some cultures on sexual relations between husband and wife after the birth of a child is the central point. This taboo has the effect of permitting the child to be breast-fed for a long time. The taboo might be viewed as an adjustment to an economy which otherwise provides a diet unsafe for a young child. Whiting finds that long post-partum sex taboo is indeed associated with economies providing a low-protein diet, source of the often-fatal childhood disease kwashiorkor. Previous research had already shown an association between long post-partum sex taboo and a variety of customs which could be seen as products of sexual anxiety, latent conflict about sex identity, or other residues of a close relation of infant with mother resulting from her sexual deprivation (Whiting, Kluckhohn, & Anthony, 1958; Burton & Whiting, 1961; Stephens, 1962). The uncertainty inherent in all correlational research is multiplied when so many steps are involved, but the interpretation Whiting offers traces a connection between economy and personality by way of diet, biological effects of diet, and cultural adjustments to these.

Even where biological differences between peoples are not present, the biological uniformities need to be considered in relation to culture. This point is well illustrated by variations among groups in developmental sequences where a biological difference is unlikely to be the major source of variation. Development of behavior through childhood is sometimes thought of as determined simply and directly by biological growth processes. Such a view is oversimplified, and plausible only so long as environmental events are not unusual enough to produce marked deviation from the standard sequence. (Just as the opposite oversimplification of viewing a developmental sequence as 100 per cent environmentally determined remains plausible only so long as the environmental pressures occur in a manner well adapted to growth processes.)

A probable case of differences in development related to differing cultural pressures is presented by Torrance (1962). He gave a group of non-verbal tests of originality to approximately 1,000 pupils in grades 1 through 6 in each of six cultural settings: general United States public schools, segregated Negro schools in Georgia, schools in Australia, Western Samoa, Germany, and India. In these tests the child is encouraged to give original responses, and his responses are scored for their unusualness in the particular cultural setting. The average score differs among the various cultural groups at first-grade and at sixth-grade level, and in all instances the sixth-grade level is higher than the first. But the year-by-year course of development differs. At one extreme, in Western Samoa, there is a steady but slow and almost rectilinear increase. At the other extreme, in the general United States sample, there is a marked decline from third to fourth and fifth grades, reaching almost down to the level of first-grade performance, before an abrupt rise at the sixth-grade level. The difference between these two extreme cases Torrance plausibly relates to differences in general culture and in the particular culture of the schools. In Western Samoa there is relatively continuous socialization with general pressure against creativity and independence at all times—pressure not sufficient to counter-balance completely the maturational or other environmental influences making for increased creativity, and continuous enough to produce no abrupt changes. In the United States originality is consciously encouraged, but pressures for conformity disrupt and abate the development of originality during certain periods of progress through school. One of these is at the time of moving from third to fourth grade. Retrospective accounts by gifted sixth-graders indicate many factors "which they feel coerced them to become less imaginative, curious, and original in their thinking at about this time" (Torrance, 1962, p. 6).

Another instance of cultural influence on rate of development is in Dennis's comparison (1957a) of maturity of human-figure drawing in several Near Eastern groups and an American standardization group. At age 5, the various Near Eastern groups are at approximately the same maturity level as the American group. At age 10, most of the Near Eastern groups are well below the maturity of the American group. The one Near Eastern group which is an exception consists of children from upper-middle-class homes in Beirut, pupils in a school whose curriculum and methods resemble those of the United States more than do the schools attended by any of the other groups. The families of these children probably resemble Americans and Europeans culturally more than do the others'. Dennis's interpretation of the difference is that the other Near Eastern groups to some extent share the influence of the former Moslem taboo on representational art, so that the children lack the wealth of experience with visual representation which is evidently a necessary condition for what we think of as the normal developmental sequence of drawing behavior. On the other hand, those portions of the development occurring before the age of 5 may require no more than a minimum of instigation from the presence of pictures in the environment, or may even require no such environmental influence at all.

REFERENCES

Adorno, T. W., Frenkel-Brunswik, Else, Levinson, D. J., & Sanford, R. N. *The authoritarian personality*. New York: Harper, 1950.

Allen, M. G. The development of universal criteria for the measurement of the health of a society, *J. soc. Psychol.,* 1962, 57, 363–382.

Allen, M. G. Childhood experience and adult personality: A cross-cultural study using the concept of ego strength. *J. soc. Psychol.,* 1967, 71, 53–68.

Allport, G. W. *Personality*. New York: Holt, 1937.

Allport, G. W., & Pettigrew, T. F. Cultural influence on the perception of movement: The trapezoidal illusion among Zulus. *J. abnorm. soc. Psychol.,* 1957, 55, 104–113.

Arkoff, A. Need patterns in two generations of Japanese Americans in Hawaii. *J. soc. Psychol.,* 1959, 50, 75–79.

Auld, F., Jr. Influence of social class on personality test responses. *Psychol. Bull.,* 1952, 49, 318–332.

Bacon, Margaret K., Barry, H., III, & Child, I. L. A cross-cultural study of drinking: II. Relations to other features of culture. *Quart. J. Stud. Alcohol,* 1965, Suppl. No. 3, 29–48.

Bacon, Margaret K., Child, I. L., & Barry, H., III. A cross-cultural study of correlates of crime. *J. abnorm. soc. Psychol.,* 1963, 66, 291–300.

Barron, F. Personality style and perceptual choice. *J. Pers.,* 1952, 20, 385–401.

Barron, F. The psychology of creativity. In F. Barron, W. C. Dement, W. Edwards, H. Lindman, L. D. Phillips, J. Olds, & Marianne Olds, *New Directions in Psychology II*. New York: Holt, Rinehart & Winston, 1965.

Barry, H., Bacon, Margaret K., & Child, I. L. A cross-cultural survey of some sex differences in socialization. *J. abnorm. soc. Psychol.,* 1957, 55, 327–332.

Bateson, G., & Mead, Margaret. *Balinese character*. New York: New York Academy of Sciences, 1942.

Benedict, Ruth. *Patterns of culture*. Boston: Houghton Mifflin, 1934.

Best, R. H. "Colorblindness" distribution in Britain, France, and Japan: A review, with notes on selection relaxation. *Eugenics Quart.,* 1963, 10, 110–118.

Bradburn, N. M. N Achievement and father dominance in Turkey. *J. abnorm. soc. Psychol.,* 1963, 67, 464–468.

Brock, T. C., & Becker, G. Birth order and subject recruitment. *J. soc. Psychol.,* 1965, 65, 63–66.

Burton, R. V., & Whiting, J. W. M. The absent father and cross-sex identity. *Merrill-Palmer Quart.,* 1961, 7, 85–95.

Butcher, H. J., Ainsworth, M., & Nesbitt, J. E. Personality factors and school achievement: A comparison of British and American children. *Brit. J. educ. Psychol.,* 1963, 33, 276–285.

Cameron, Ann, & Storm, T. Achievement motivation in Canadian Indian, middle- and working-class children. *Psychol. Rep.,* 1965, 16, 459–463.

Campbell, D. T. The mutual methodological relevance of anthropology and psychology. In F. L. K. Hsu (Ed.), *Psychological anthropology: approaches to culture and personality*. Homewood, Ill.: Dorsey, 1961. Pp. 333–352.

Capra, P. C., & Dittes, J. E. Birth order as a selective factor among volunteer subjects. *J. abnorm. soc. Psychol.,* 1962, 64, 302.

Cattell, R. B., Pichot, P., & Rennes, P. Constance interculturelle des facteurs de personnalité mesurés par le test 16 P.F.: II. Comparaison franco-américaine. *Revue Psychol. appliquée,* 1961, 11, 165–196.

Cattell, R. B., & Warburton, F. W. A cross-cultural comparison of patterns of extraversion and anxiety. *Brit. J. Psychol.,* 1961, 52, 3–15.

Child, I. L. Problems of personality and some relations to anthropology and sociology. In S. Koch (Ed.), *Psychology: A study of a science*. New York: McGraw-Hill, 1963. Vol. 5, pp. 593–638.

Child, I. L., Barry, H., III, & Bacon, Margaret K. A cross-cultural study of drinking: III. Sex differences. *Quart. J. Stud. Alcohol,* 1965, Suppl. No. 3, 49–61.

Cohn, T. S., & Carsch, H. Administration of the F scale to a sample of Germans. *J. abnorm. soc. Psychol.,* 1954, 49, 471.

Comrey, A. L., Meschieri, L., Misiti, R., & Nencini, R. A comparison of personality factor structure in American and Italian subjects. *J. Pers. soc. Psychol.,* 1965, 1, 257–261.

Conklin, H. C. Hanunoo color categories. *Sthwest. J. Anthrop.*, 1955, 11, 339–344.

Dennis, W. Are Hopi children noncompetitive? *J. abnorm. soc. Psychol.*, 1955, 50, 99–100.

Dennis, W. Performances of Near Eastern children on the Draw-a-Man Test. *Child Develpm.*, 1957, 28, 427–430. (a)

Dennis, W. Uses of common objects as indicators of cultural orientations. *J. abnorm. soc. Psychol.*, 1957, 55, 21–28. (b)

Dennis, W. Arab and United States children: some psychological comparisons. *Trans. N. Y. Acad. Sci.*, 1960, ser. II, 22, 589–605. (a)

Dennis, W. The human figure drawings of Bedouins. *J. soc. Psychol.*, 1960, 52, 209–219. (b)

Dollard, J. *Caste and class in a southern town.* New Haven: Yale Univer. Press, 1937.

Dollard, J., Doob, L. W., Miller, N. E., Mowrer, O. H., Sears, R. R. *et al. Frustration and aggression.* New Haven: Yale Univer. Press, 1939.

Doob, L. W. *Becoming more civilized: A psychological exploration.* New Haven: Yale Univer. Press, 1960.

Doob, L. W. Eidetic images among the Ibo. *Ethnology,* 1964, 3, 357–363.

Doob, L. W. Exploring eidetic imagery among the Kamba of central Kenya. *J. soc. Psychol.*, 1965, 67, 3–22.

Dronamraju, K. R., & Meera Khan, P. Frequency of colour blindness among the tribal and nontribal peoples of Andhra Pradesh. *Ann. hum. Genet.*, 1963, 27, 17–21.

Erikson, E. H. *Childhood and society* (2nd ed.). New York: Norton, 1963.

Fenz, W. D., & Arkoff, A. Comparative need patterns of five ancestry groups in Hawaii. *J. soc. Psychol.,* 1962, 58, 67–89.

Freed, S. A., & Freed, Ruth S. Spirit possession as illness in a North Indian villiage. *Ethnology,* 1964, 3, 152–171.

French, D. The relationship of anthropology to studies in perception and cognition. In S. Koch (Ed.), *Psychology: A study of a science.* New York: McGraw-Hill, 1963. Vol. 6, pp. 388–428.

Gardner, R., Holzman, P. S., Klein, G. S., Linton, Harriet, & Spence, D. P. Cognitive control: A study of individual consistencies in cognitive behavior. *Psychol. Issues,* 1959, 1, No. 4.

Gladwin, T. Culture and logical process. In W. H. Goodenough (Ed.), *Explorations in cultural anthropology.* New York: McGraw-Hill, 1964. Pp. 167–177.

Goodenough, W. H. *Cooperation in change.* New York: Russell Sage Foundation, 1963.

Goodenough, W. H. Rethinking 'status' and 'role': Toward a general model of the cultural organization of social relationships. In *The relevance of models for social anthropology,* A. S. A. Monographs 1. London: Tavistock, 1965. Pp. 1–24.

Goodman, Mary Ellen. Culture and conceptualization: a study of Japanese and American children. *Ethnology,* 1962, 1, 374–386.

Gorer, G. *The American people.* New York: Norton, 1948.

Gough, H. G. A cross-cultural study of achievement motivation. *J. appl. Psychol.,* 1964, 48, 191–196.

Gough, H. G. Cross-cultural validation of a measure of asocial behavior. *Psychol. Rep.*, 1965, 17, 379–387. (a)

Gough, H. G. La predizione del successo scolastico attraverso il California Psychological Inventory. *Bolettino di Psicologia applicata,* 1965, No. 67–68, 29–38. (b)

Gough, H. G. A cross-cultural analysis of the CPI Femininity Scale. *J. consult. Psychol.*, 1966, 30, 136–141.

Gough, H. G., & Sandhu, H. S. Validation of the CPI socialization scale in India. *J. abnorm. soc. Psychol.*, 1964, 68, 544–547.

Grinder, R. E., & McMichael, R. E. Cultural influence on conscience development: resistance to temptation and guilt among Samoans and American Caucasians. *J. abnorm. soc. Psychol.*, 1963, 66, 503–507.

Hagen, E. E. *On the theory of social change: How economic growth begins.* Homewood, Ill.: Dorsey, 1962.

Hollingshead, A., & Redlich, F. C. *Social class and mental disease.* New York: Wiley, 1958.

Honigmann, J. J. Psychocultural studies. *Biennial Rev. Anthrop.*, 1959, 67–106.

Horton, D. The functions of alcohol in primitive societies: A cross-cultural study. *Quart. J. Stud. Alcohol,* 1943, 4, 199–320.

Hsu, F. L. K. (Ed.) *Psychological anthropology: approaches to culture and personality.* Homewood, Ill.: Dorsey, 1961.

Hsu, F. L. K. *Clan, caste, and club.* Princeton: Van Nostrand, 1963.

Hudson, B. B., Barakat, M. K., & LaForge, R. Problems and methods of cross-cultural research. *J. soc. Issues,* 1959, 15, No. 3, 5–19.

Inkeles, A. Industrial man: The relation of status to experience, perception, and value. *Amer. J. Sociol.,* 1960, 66, 1–31.

Kaffman, M. Evaluation of emotional disturbance in 403 Israeli kibbutz children. *Amer. J. Psychiat.,* 1961, 117, 732–738.

Kaplan, B. (Ed.) *Studying personality cross-culturally.* Evanston: Row, Peterson, 1961.

Kardiner, A. *The individual and his society.* New York: Columbia Univer. Press, 1939.

Kardiner, A. *The psychological frontiers of society.* New York: Columbia Univer. Press, 1945.

Kilby, R. W. Universals in the self-processes. *J. soc. Psychol.,* 1964, 62, 253–272.

Kroeber, A. L., & Kluckhohn, C. Culture: A critical review of concepts and definitions. *Pap. Peabody Mus.,* 1952, 47, No. 1.

Lambert, W. E., & Klineberg, O. Cultural comparisons of boys' occupational aspirations. *Brit. J. soc. clin. Psychol.,* 1963, 2, 56–65.

Landauer, T. K., & Whiting, J. W. M. Infantile stimulation and adult stature of human males. *Amer. Anthrop.,* 1964, 66, 1007–1028.

LeVine, R. A. Culture and personality. *Biennial Rev. Anthrop.,* 1963, 107–145.

Lindgren, H. C., & Lindgren, Fredrica. Creativity, brainstorming, and orneriness: A cross-cultural study. *J. soc. Psychol.,* 1965, 67, 23–30.

Linton, R. *The study of man.* New York: Appleton-Century, 1936.

Lipset, S. M. Democracy and working-class authoritarianism. *Amer. sociol. Rev.,* 1959, 24, 482–501.

Lipset, S. M. A changing American character? In S. M. Lipset & L. Lowenthal, *Culture and social character: The work of David Riesman reviewed.* New York: Free Press of Glencoe, 1961. Pp. 136–171.

Lynn, R. Personality characteristics of the mothers of aggressive and unaggressive children. *J. genet. Psychol.,* 1961, 99, 159–164.

Lynn, R., & Gordon, I. E. Maternal attitudes to child socialization: Some social and national differences. *Brit. J. soc. clin. Psychol.,* 1962, 1, 52–55.

Lynn, D. B., & Sawrey, W. L. The effects of father-absence on Norwegian boys and girls. *J. abnorm. soc. Psychol.,* 1959, 59, 258–262.

McClelland, D. C. *The achieving society.* Princeton: Van Nostrand, 1961.

McClelland, D. C. Toward a theory of motive acquisition. *Amer. Psychologist,* 1965, 20, 321–333.

McClelland, D. C., Sturr, J. F., Knapp, R. H., & Wendt, H. W. Obligations to self and society in the United States and Germany. *J. abnorm. soc. Psychol.,* 1958, 56, 245–255.

McCord, W., & McCord, J. *Origins of alcoholism.* Stanford: Stanford Univer. Press, 1960.

McGranahan, D. V., & Wayne, I. German and American traits reflected in popular drama. *Hum. Relat.,* 1948, 1, 429–455.

MacKinnon, W. J., & Centers, R. Authoritarianism and urban stratification. *Amer. sociol. Rev.,* 1956, 61, 610–620.

Mead, Margaret. Research on primitive children. In L. Carmichael (Ed.), *Manual of child psychology.* New York: Wiley, 1946. Pp. 667–706.

Mead, Margaret. *Male and female.* New York: Morrow, 1949.

Mead, Margaret. *Anthropology, a human science: Selected papers, 1939–1960.* Princeton: Van Nostrand, 1964.

Mead, Margaret, & Metraux, Rhoda (Eds.), *The study of culture at a distance.* Chicago: Univer. of Chicago Press, 1953.

Melikian, L. H. Some correlates of authoritarianism in two cultural groups. *J. Psychol.,* 1956, 42, 237–248.

Melikian, L. H. Authoritarianism and its correlates in the Egyptian culture and in the United States. *J. soc. Issues,* 1959, 15, No. 3, 58–68.

Mercado, S. J., Diaz, G. R., & Gardner, R. W. Cognitive control in children of Mexico and the United States. *J. soc. Psychol.,* 1963, 59, 199–208.

Miles, Catharine C. Psychological study of a young adult male pseudohermaphrodite reared as a female. In *Studies in personality contributed in honor of Lewis M. Terman.* New York: McGraw-Hill, 1942. Pp. 209–227.

Milgram, S. Nationality and conformity. *Sci. Amer.,* 1961, 205, No. 6, 45–52.

Minturn, Leigh, Lambert, W. W., *et al. Mothers of six cultures: Antecedents of child rearing.* New York: Wiley, 1964.

Mischel, W. Father-absence and delay of gratification: cross-cultural comparisons. *J. abnorm. soc. Psychol.,* 1961, 63, 116–124.

Morris, C. *Varieties of human value.* Chicago: Univer. of Chicago Press, 1956.
Morris, C., & Jones, L. V. Value scales and dimensions. *J. abnorm. soc. Psychol.,* 1955, 51, 523–535.
Murdock, G. P. The common denominator of cultures. In R. Linton (Ed.), *The science of man in the world crisis.* New York: Columbia Univer. Press, 1945. Pp. 123–142.
Murphey, R. M., & Nolan, E. G. Irrelevant goal-seeking behavior as a function of culture. *Psychol. Rep.,* 1963, 13, 449–450.
Mussen, P. H., Young, H. B., Gaddini, R., & Morante, L. The influence of father-son relationships on adolescent personality and attitudes. *J. child Psychol. Psychiat.,* 1963, 4, 3–16.
Nadel, S. F. A field experiment in racial psychology. *Brit. J. Psychol.,* 1937, 28, 195–211.
Nye, F. I., & Short, J. F. Scaling delinquent behavior. *Amer. sociol. Rev.,* 1957, 22, 326–331.
Osgood, C. E. Studies on the generality of affective meaning systems. *Amer. Psychologist,* 1962, 17, 10–28.
Park, G. K. Sons and lovers: Characterological requisites of the roles in a peasant society. *Ethnology,* 1962, 1, 412–424.
Peterson, D. R. Scope and generality of verbally defined personality factors. *Psychol. Rev.,* 1965, 72, 48–59.
Petrie, A., Collins, W., & Solomon, P. The tolerance for pain and sensory deprivation. *Amer. J. Psychol.,* 1960, 73, 80–90.
Pickford, R. W. Natural selection and colour blindness. *Eugen. Rev.,* 1963, 55, 97–101.
Pospisil, L. *The Kapauku Papuans of West New Guinea.* New York: Holt, Rinehart, & Winston, 1963.
Post, R. H. Population differences in red and green color vision deficiency: A review, and a query on selection relaxation. *Eugen. Quart.,* 1962, 9, 131–146. (a)
Post, R. H. Population differences in vision acuity: A review, with speculative notes on selection relaxation. *Eugen. Quart.,* 1962, 9, 189–212. (b)
Potter, D. M. *People of plenty: economic abundance and the American character.* Chicago: Univer. of Chicago Press, 1954.
Prothro, E. T. Arab students' choices of ways to live. *J. soc. Psychol.,* 1958, 47, 3–7.
Prothro, E. T., & Melikian, L. The California Public Opinion Scale in an authoritarian culture. *Publ. Opin. Quart.,* 1953, 17, 353–362.
Quay, H., & Peterson, D. R. A brief scale for juvenile delinquency. *J. clin. Psychol.,* 1958, 14, 139–142.
Rabin, A. I. *Growing up in the kibbutz.* New York: Springer, 1965.
Rabin, A. I., & Limuaco, Josefina A. Sexual differentiation of American and Filipino children as reflected in the Draw-a-Person Test. *J. soc. Psychol.,* 1959, 50, 207–211.
Rainwater, L. Some themes in the personalities of German men. *Genet. Psychol. Monogr.,* 1960, 61, 167–195.
Ray, V. F. Techniques and problems in the study of human color perception. *Sthwest. J. Anthrop.,* 1952, 8, 251–259.
Ray, V. F. Human color perception and behavioral response. *Trans. N. Y. Acad. Sci.,* 1953, ser. II, 16, 98–104.
Rhodes, A. L. Authoritarianism and fundamentalism of rural and urban high school students. *J. educ. Sociol.,* 1960, 34, 97–105.
Riesman, D. *The lonely crowd.* New Haven: Yale Univer. Press, 1950.
Roberts, J. M., Arth, M. J., & Bush, R. R. Games in culture. *Amer. Anthrop.,* 1959, 61, 597–605.
Roberts, J. M., & Sutton-Smith, B. Child training and game involvement. *Ethnology,* 1962, 1, 166–185.
Rosen, B. C. Socialization and achievement motivation in Brazil. *Amer. sociol. Rev.,* 1962, 27, 612–624.
Rosen, B. C., & D'Andrade, R. The psychosocial origins of achievement motivation. *Sociometry,* 1959, 22, 185–218.
Rosenblatt, P. C. Functions of games: An examination of individual difference hypotheses derived from a cross-cultural study. *J. soc. Psychol.,* 1962, 58, 17–22.
Rosenthal, R. Experimenter outcome-orientation and the results of the psychological experiment. *Psychol. Bull.,* 1964, 61, 405–412.
Sagara, M., Yamamoto, K., Nishimura, H., & Akuto, H. A study on the semantic structure of Japanese language by the semantic differential method. *Japan. Psychol. Res.,* 1961, 3, 146–156.
Sarason, S. B. *The clinical interaction, with special reference to the Rorschach.* New York: Harper, 1954.
Sarnoff, I., Lighthall, F., Waite, R., Davidson, K., & Sarason, S. A cross-cultural study of

anxiety among American and English school children. *J. educ. Psychol.*, 1958, 49, 129–136.

Schachter, S. *The psychology of affiliation.* Stanford: Stanford Univer. Press, 1959.

Scofield, R. W., & Sun, Chin-Wan. A comparative study of the differential effect upon personality of Chinese and American child training practices. *J. soc. Psychol.*, 1960, 52, 221–224.

Sears, R. R., Maccoby, Eleanor E., & Levin, H. *Patterns of child rearing.* Evanston: Row, Peterson, 1957.

Segall, M. H., Campbell, D. T., & Herskovits, M. J. *The influence of culture on visual perception.* Indianapolis: Bobbs-Merrill, 1966.

Shirasa, T., & Azuma, T. The applicability of an American delinquency scale to Japanese subjects. *J. clin. Psychol.*, 1961, 17, 291–292.

Siegman, A. W. A cross-cultural investigation of the relationship between introversion-extraversion, social attitudes and anti-social behavior. *Brit. J. soc. clin. Psychol.*, 1963, 2, 196–208.

Spiro, M. E. *Children of the kibbutz.* Cambridge: Harvard Univer. Press, 1958.

Stephens, W. N. *The Oedipus complex: Cross-cultural evidence.* New York: Free Press of Glencoe, 1962.

Storm, T., Anthony, W. S., & Porsolt, R. D. Ethnic and social class differences in performance for material and nonmaterial rewards: New Zealand children. *J. Pers. soc. Psychol.*, 1965, 2, 759–762.

Sutton-Smith, B., Roberts, J. M., & Kozelka, R. M. Game involvement in adults. *J. soc. Psychol.*, 1963, 60, 15–30.

Torrance, E. P. Cultural discontinuities and the development of originality of thinking. *Except. Child.*, 1962, 29, 2–13.

Triandis, H. C. Cultural influences upon cognitive processes. *Adv. exper. soc. Psychol.*, 1964, 1, 1–48.

Tsujioka, B., & Cattell, R. B. A cross-cultural comparison of second-stratum questionnaire personality factor structures—anxiety and extraversion—in America and Japan. *J. soc. Psychol.*, 1965, 65, 205–219. (a)

Tsujioka, B., & Cattell, R. B. Constancy and difference in personality structure and mean profile, in the questionnaire medium, from applying the 16 P.F. Test in America and Japan. *Brit. J. soc. clin. Psychol.*, 1965, 4, 287–297. (b)

Turner, R. H. Preoccupation with competitiveness and social acceptance among American and English students. *Sociometry*, 1960, 23, 307–325.

Turner, R. H. The problems of social dimensions in personality. *Pacific sociol. Rev.*, 1961, 4, 57–62.

Valentine, C. A. Men of anger and men of shame: Lakalai ethnopsychology and its implications for sociopsychological theory. *Ethnology*, 1963, 2, 441–477.

Varela, J. A. A cross-cultural replication of an experiment involving birth order. *J. abnorm. soc. Psychol.*, 1964, 69, 456–457.

Veroff, J., Atkinson, J. W., Feld, S. C., & Gurin, G. The use of thematic apperception to assess motivation in a nationwide interview study. *Psychol. Monogr.*, 1960, 74, No. 12.

Wallace, A. F. C. *Culture and personality.* New York: Random House, 1961. (a)

Wallace, A. F. C. Mental illness, biology, and culture. In F. L. K. Hsu (Ed.), *Psychological anthropology: approaches to culture and personality.* Homewood, Ill.: Dorsey, 1961. Pp. 255–295. (b)

Wallace, A. F. C. The psychic unity of human groups. In B. Kaplan (Ed.), *Studying personality cross-culturally.* Evanston: Row, Peterson, 1961. Pp. 129–163. (c)

Wallace, A. F. C., & Fogelson, R. D. Culture and personality. *Biennial Rev. Anthrop.*, 1961, 42–78.

Ward, C. D. A further examination of birth order as a selective factor among volunteer subjects. *J. abnorm. soc. Psychol.*, 1964, 69, 311–313.

Whiting, J. W. M. Socialization process and personality. In F. L. K. Hsu (Ed.), *Psychological anthropology: approaches to culture and personality.* Homewood, Ill.: Dorsey, 1961. Pp. 355–380.

Whiting, J. W. M. Comment [on Young, 1962]. *Amer. J. Sociol.*, 1962, 67, 391–394.

Whiting, J. W. M. Effects of climate on certain cultural practices. In W. H. Goodenough (Ed.), *Explorations in cultural anthropology.* New York: McGraw-Hill, 1964. Pp. 511–544.

Whiting, J. W. M., & Child, I. L. *Child training and personality: a cross-cultural study.* New Haven: Yale Univer. Press, 1953.

Whiting, J. W. M., Kluckhohn, R., & Anthony,

A. S. The function of male initiation ceremonies at puberty. In Eleanor E. Maccoby, T. Newcomb, & E. Hartley (Eds.), *Readings in social psychology*. New York: Holt, 1958. Pp. 359–396.

Young, F. W. The function of male initiation ceremonies: A cross-cultural test of an alternative hypothesis. *Amer. J. Sociol.,* 1962, 67, 379–391.

Zajonc, R. B., & Wahi, N. K. Conformity and need-achievement under cross-cultural norm conflict. *Hum. Relat.,* 1961, 14, 241–250.

PART II Personality Development

CHAPTER 3 Development and the Biophysical Bases of Personality

WILLIAM R. THOMPSON
Queens University, Ontario

Personality has been defined in very many ways. Since these will be more fully covered elsewhere in this handbook, only a brief overview will be given here. During the 1930's, many attempts were made to articulate comprehensive theories that were epic in scope and intended by their authors to supply unique and final answers to the set of phenomena with which they dealt. Like most monolithic enterprises, such theories attracted their dedicated disciples, whose lively, if sometimes futile, debates gave strong impetus to the growth of personality study. Today, most psychologists are more eclectic (Koch, 1959). They feel no necessity of opting for a trait theory as opposed to a psychoanalytic position; for a need theory as opposed to a factor theory; for a typology as opposed to a behavioristic point of view. They appear to be content, instead, to study carefully limited segments of behavior and personality and to construct modest theoretical schemas that deal particularly with these (cf. Jenness, 1962). It must be pointed out, of course, that such work would not be now going on were it not for the comprehensive theory-builders of the past, such as Freud, Jung, Allport, Murray and others. Current studies on such mechanisms as identification, on such needs as *n* Achievement, *n* Aggression, and *n* Affiliation, or on such traits as introversion have strong roots in the writings of these and other similar figures.

The empirical orientation of present research on personality, precisely because of its lack of commitment to any general theoretical scheme, might be expected to yield a more permissive attitude to data and concepts that stem from other disciplines in psychology, in particular the comparative, physiological, and developmental areas. But such does not appear to be the case. Although the relevance of these fields to personality theory is continually being pointed up by various workers (for example, the contributors to Eysenck's *Handbook of Abnormal Psychology;* Eysenck, 1961), this does not seem to have produced any marked change in the theorizing or experimentation of those identified with personality study. Presumably this is due to the rootedness in past conceptualizations to which we have already referred. Certainly, it does seem unreasonable that we should try to study, let us say, need achievement in rats, or even in monkeys. The degree of abstraction necessary to do this would strip this segment of behavior of its most interesting, unique, and vital qualities. And the great

Preparation of this manuscript was assisted by grants from the National Research Council of Canada and the Queen's Arts Research Committee.

appeal of psychoanalytic constructions from which most theories of personality derive lies in their rich, almost literary style—a style seemingly necessary to capture the individual person. While this may have merit, particularly in face-to-face dealings between the therapist and his patient, it is not an approach that encourages much consideration of some of the more rigorous and more biologically oriented points of view in psychology.

To examine the biophysical bases of personality, it will be necessary to consider closely relevant work in other areas, in particular, those disciplines mentioned above, namely, behavior genetics and comparative, physiological, and developmental psychology. Of those, the last will be used as the thread by which we can relate all of them to personality theory.

Thus, it is the basic notion of this chapter that whatever general or particular theoretical schemata we may wish to use to treat of personality, these must be incomplete *unless they take development as a dimension of primary concern.* Werner (1957) has understated the case in pointing out:

> Another developmental aspect of individuality that is in need of experimental and clinical study concerns what one might call the genetic stratification or the developmental heterogeneity of a person. Developmental stratification means that a person is structured into spheres of operations which differ in regard to developmental level (Werner, 1957, p. 145).

We regard these not merely as developmental aspects of individuality which may be chosen for study or not, but rather as fundamental properties of all personality variables. Any trait or character possesses, to modify slightly Werner's terminology, *developmental stratification,* and can only be properly understood in these terms. This viewpoint is shared, of course, by many other psychologists, particularly those of a psychoanalytic persuasion. Thus Schachtel says of Freud:

> Freud's emphasis on the ontogenetic past was so strong that he tended to see in man nothing but the power of his past over his present life and that he often failed to see in the past the seeds and portents of the future (Schachtel, 1959, p. 8).

We are not committed here to such an extreme position. Organisms live in time and interact with an environment all through their lives from conception to death. Thus it cannot be correct to assert that the individual is totally a prisoner of his past history. The past can be undone and the present can have an influence. The basic question concerns the relative influence of each in setting the qualitative and quantitative characteristics of behavior. For example, we can ask, will some harsh parental treatment have the same kind and intensity of effect on the 8-year-old child as it does on the 1-year-old infant? What will be the modifications of adult personality produced by each? Such problems are crucial ones. For all living organisms, despite their immense diversity in form and function, grow up, grow older, and in some sense die. Whatever their genotype, whether they are unicellular or multicellular, whether they have a simple or a complex nervous system or none at all, all of them show development. And development refers to more than merely increments in age; rather it refers, as we will show, to certain crucial processes that accompany aging. It is with these processes that we shall mainly deal.

The mere fact of being alive and possessing a genotype, then, produces development. But the particular manner in which it proceeds in a given individual of a certain species is determined by particular genes and by particular environments, and by the interaction of these two sets of factors. Both of them operate ultimately on behavior through complex biochemical and physiological pathways. The situation is depicted graphically in Figure 1. This indicates, first of all, that the horizontal slice we take of the individual and call adult personality has a stratification that relates to different stages of development; secondly, that the occurrence of such stages and the process of development itself are dependent on having a genotype; and thirdly, that what happens during any one of these stages is determined by (a) what has happened during some previous stage, (b) particular genes having an action that is timed to this particular developmental stage, and (c) the environment occupied by the organism during this stage. At this point of the discussion, the use of three stages is quite arbitrary, though, in point of fact, we will later make use of three for reasons that will be explicitly stated.

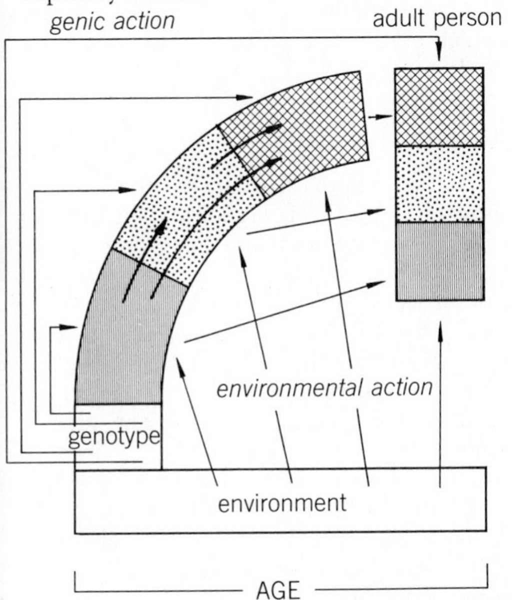

Figure 1. The divisions in the figure refer to hypothetical stages in development and to corresponding developmental strata in the adult personality.

The graph above essentially summarizes the plan of this chapter. It will attempt to deal with adult personality in terms of a stratification derived from a close consideration of development, and then to account for variations in personality structure between different individuals by reference to the effects of environmental and genic agents acting on these strata. We might remark in parenthesis at this point that although the framework we are using is somewhat idiosyncratic, it is broad enough to permit a compilation and review of data from a wide variety of sources, employing both human and animal subjects, and of a behavioral and physiological character.

THE DEVELOPMENTAL STRATIFICATION OF PERSONALITY

The proposition to be considered here is that any segment of personality, such as a trait or a need, is stratified into components, each of which has its origin in a particular stage or period of development. If this is so, we may expect to find that a gross phenotypic score on some personality measure, such as a projective test of achievement or some other need, can be generated in a variety of different ways according to the relative contribution made by each of the component parts of which it is comprised. It is obvious that a knowledge about such qualitative differences should allow predictions of a far higher order of precision than those that are possible from the use of a single over-all measure. Thus our task is an important one. The first step in its execution is, of course, the delineation of developmental stages according to some rational criteria, and to carry this out, we will first have to consider in some detail the nature of development.

THE NATURE OF DEVELOPMENT

As indicated already, the most primitive feature that characterizes the progression from youth to maturity is an increment in age. Older things have lived longer than younger things. By itself, however, aging means very little. It is the various processes that accompany it that must interest us. What are these? Many different ones have been defined by different writers. Thus

Piaget has made use of such concepts as assimilation, accommodation, and equilibration (cf. Flavell, 1963). Werner (1948) has dealt with development chiefly in terms of differentiation and hierarchization, and Gesell (1946) has referred to reciprocal interweaving, developmental direction, and functional asymmetry. We will make use here of only three principles. These are: differentiation, growth, and organization. We will now attempt to show how an analysis of these can allow us to make some interesting statements about the stratification of adult personality.

Differentiation

This describes the fact that, as it gets older, the living system progresses from something that is unitary, in the sense of its having relatively few distinct parts, to one that is made up of many parts. It refers at the physiological and morphological level to such processes as regionalization, histogenesis, and morphogenesis whereby qualitative differences in form and structure appear in a system. Thus the zygote becomes a multicellular organism, with groups of cells having different appearance and staining properties and being dedicated to different functions, such as body support, movement, sensory reception, neural conduction, and circulation. At the behavioral level, the situation is similar. Motor behavior, for example, becomes less global and diffuse and more articulated and individuated. Limbs become capable of independent movement and respond to stimuli as separate units. On the input side, the organism becomes capable of making discriminations it could not make previously, and more centrally, particular abilities and cognitive functions may differentiate out from each other. Bridges' classical treatment of emotional development (Bridges, 1932) is based on the notion that the highly specialized emotions, such as delight, jealousy, and disgust, gradually differentiate out from an initial diffuse excitement. It must be remarked that although her schema has some intuitive appeal and may, in fact, be true, it is based on data that are far from being precise. However, this need not disturb us unduly for the moment.

More formally, the increment in differentiation that occurs with development may be defined as an *increment in discontinuity* (Waddington, 1957). There is perhaps no greater advantage to be gained from using such a phrase. But it does suggest a more abstract mode of conceptualization that may be of some value to us.

The mechanism by which differentiation occurs is obscure. However, at the behavioral level, at least, it must involve some kind of inhibiting process or processes which give greater selectivity to both input and output.[1]

Growth

As they approach maturity, most organisms and parts of organisms increase in size. For many animals, this process ceases at maturity; for others, such as fish, and for many plant forms, such as sequoias, it goes on until death. This is fairly obvious for gross physical size, but it also is true for different subsystems. Figure 2 shows two examples of central nervous system growth and decline, one on the number of fibers in the spinal root in humans (Zubek & Solberg, 1954), the other on total brain weight (Himwich, 1962). It is clear that a sharp increment occurs first, followed by a gradual decline in quantity. The same applies to density of neural and glial cells elsewhere in the central system, and also to cell mitochondria. The quantity of chemical compounds per unit mass of tissue also shows increases with age. This applies probably to all such substances, for example, glutamic acid, cholinesterase, acetylcholine, gamma-aminobutryic acid, to name a few. Claude Villee (1962) has suggested that the age of a tissue be partly defined in this way:

[1] For an excellent review and analysis of the concept of inhibition, cf. Diamond, Balvin & Diamond (1963).

A tissue might be regarded as immature if it does not have an adequate number of enzyme molecules to carry on its metabolic processes efficiently. (Villee, 1962, p. 266)

An example of biochemical growth is shown in Figure 3, taken from Roberts (1960). He and Himwich (1962) have speculated that, during the rapid initial spurts shown by these substances, the organism may be peculiarly susceptible to environmental pressures of various kinds. Such a speculation—and it is one often made about immature organisms—is generally based on the notion that "plasticity" is a basic property of young systems, though the reason for this being the case is seldom made clear. However, a more formal definition of growth, analogous to the one given to differentiation, may be suggestive. Growth is essentially an *increment in redundancy of a system*. By reason of growth, more mature systems or subsystems have more redundancy than less mature systems or subsystems. That is to say, they contain a larger number of replicated parts subserving the same function. As Kascer has pointed out (cf. Waddington, 1957) in an interesting explication of this problem, this should give to them greater, or at least different, buffering properties. Any system that has more redundancy in it can withstand stress or "noise" more successfully. Language systems exemplify this principle. The probability of a message being communicated is known to be greater if it contains some redundancy than if it contains none. The same is true for different physical (e.g., mechanical and electrical) systems. The actual evidence on this point in respect to living organisms is both scanty and complex. We will present some of it later in the chapter.

Organization

Mature systems may be said to be more organized than young systems in the sense that, independently of degree of differentiation of parts, or number of parts, they show a *greater degree of reliable relatedness between parts or subsystems*. The definition given suggests that the term has some similarity of meaning to Werner's hierarchization (Werner, 1957) and to Lewin's "organization" (Lewin, 1951), though it does not contain within it the dimension of relative importance, or degree of subordination, that is an integral part of these other concepts. The kinds of empirical data which may be subsumed under the category of organization are not so easily specified. Broadly, however, they are of this sort: the transition from diffuse, uncoordinated action; the acquisition of learning sets, or of what Piaget has called "intellectual structures," or "schemas"; the formation of aptitudes and abilities; and the development of master traits of personality. Changes in degrees of organization might thus be inferred from shifts, during development, in the factorial structure of a correlation matrix, or from transfer data taken at different ages. At a physiological level, certain genetically controlled organizations build up simply with the passage of time. Thus as Sperry has shown (1959) in various species, different fibers inevitably migrate during growth, according to some principle of chemical affinity, to specified loci. This occurs despite drastic surgical interventions. Likewise, if Hebb's formulations (Hebb, 1949) are correct, organized arrangements of neural cells—cell assemblies—are gradually built up over time as the maturing organism interacts with its environment. At the level of behavior—particularly that type of behavior that we would associate with personality—documentation is meager. Such data as are available we will consider later on.

The three dimensions discussed above, differentiation, growth, and organization, represent the basic parameters of an approach to development. Explication of them will permit us to deal directly with the central problem of the developmental stratification of personality. Since we will employ some degree of formalization in presenting

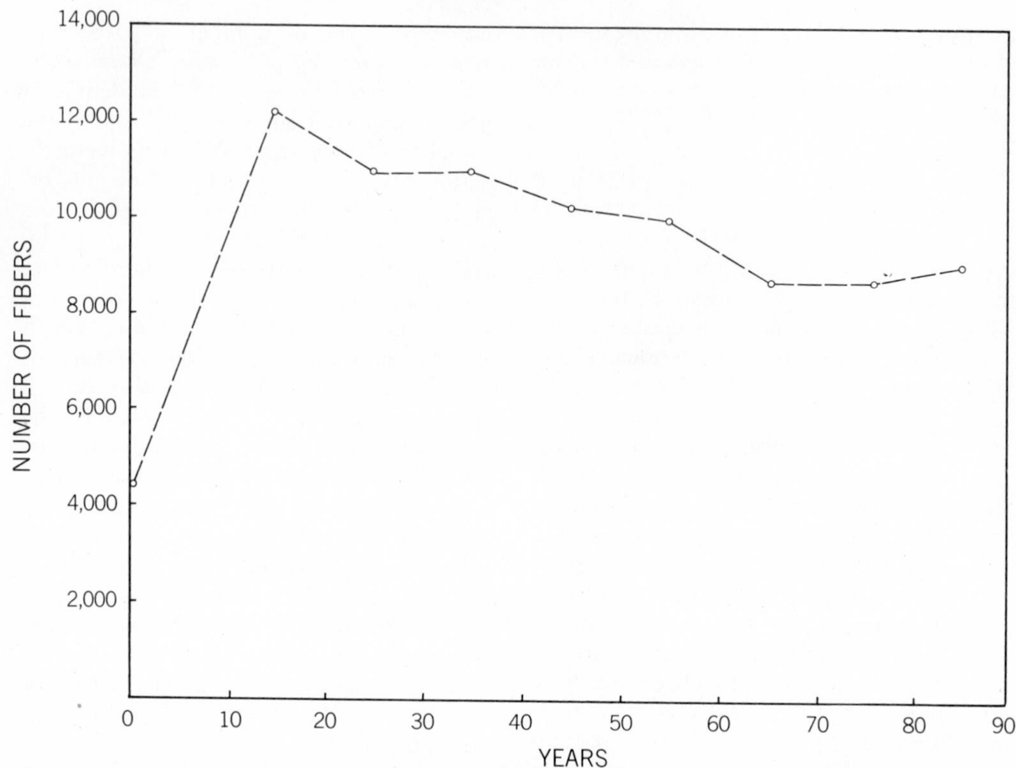

Figure 2a. Age changes in number of fibers in human spinal nerve (Zubek & Solberg, 1954, p. 67, and Gardner, 1940).

this approach, we will refer to it as a "model," though it is clear that it only lays the groundwork for a model, as the latter is usually conceived.

We will now deal with the implications of the three developmental dimensions, taking each one separately.

A Model of Behavioral Development

Outcomes of Changes in Differentiation

In our treatment of differentiation, we made an implicit distinction between the response and perceptual side. We will now attempt to make this explicit, since the major aspects of the model rest on it. Every animal has both input and output systems, and, with development, differentiation occurs in respect to both of these. We can state this broadly in terms of the increasing ability of the organism to discriminate the parts of its environment, and to respond to these discriminanda (more precisely, discriminata) in a coordinated and well-articulated manner. The paradigmatic test of differentiation on the input side involves experimental variation of stimuli and the holding of response constant. Its occurrence is then indicated by alterations in the intensity characteristics of the response produced by alterations in the stimulus. Two experiments can serve as examples. The first of these was done by Thompson and Solomon (1954) using rats. Subjects were permitted to explore either black and white striations or a triangle for ten minutes. Fol-

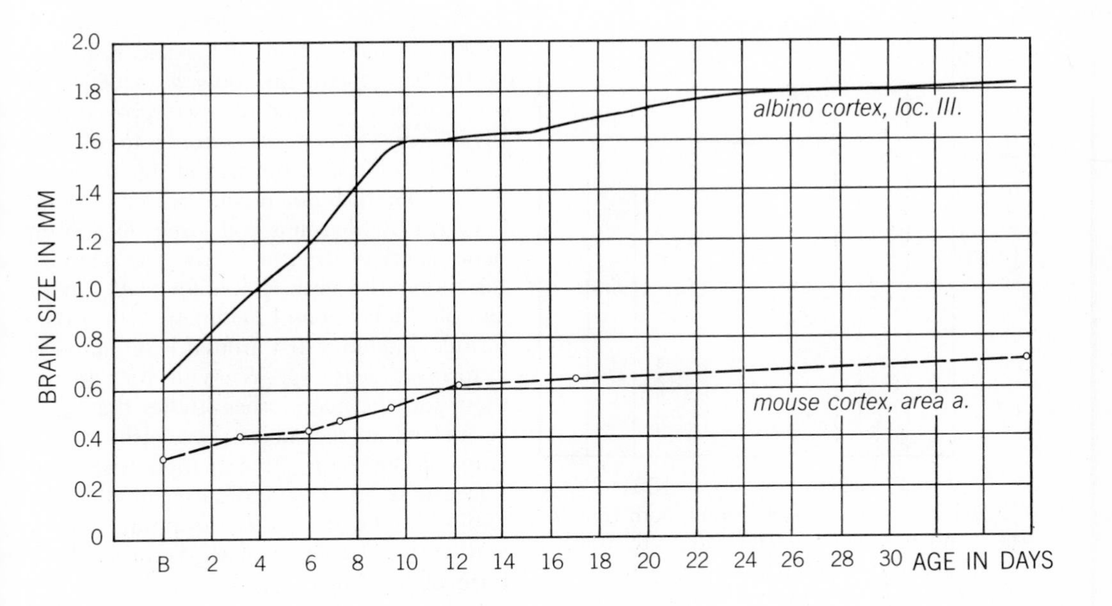

Figure 2b. Age changes in brain size in rat and mouse (Himwich, 1962).

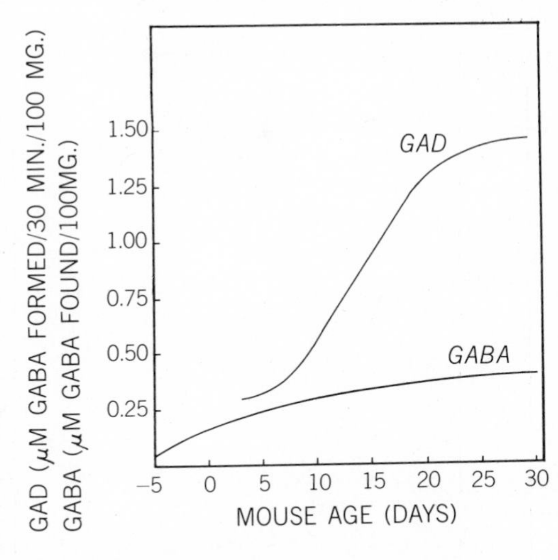

Figure 3. Age changes in glutamic decarboxylase activity (GAD) and gamma-aminobutyric acid (GABA) levels of whole mouse brain (Roberts, 1960, and Roberts, Harman, & Frankel, 1951).

lowing a short rest period, these groups were each split in half. Experimental groups then were exposed to a different figure, control groups to the same figure again. Comparisons were made between controls and experimentals in respect to amount of exploratory activity. Results are shown in Figure 4. It is clear that animals presented with new figures showed more exploration than animals exposed to the same figure a second time. In other words, the exploratory response which had habituated to one stimulus with time, now showed dehabituation when the stimulus was altered. This dehabituation provided a fairly clear indication of discrimination or perceptual or input differentiation.

The second example is a study by Bartoshuk (1962). This investigator used 60 full-term human neonates, tested between 48 and 96 hours after birth. These were presented with 80 decibel tones of one-second

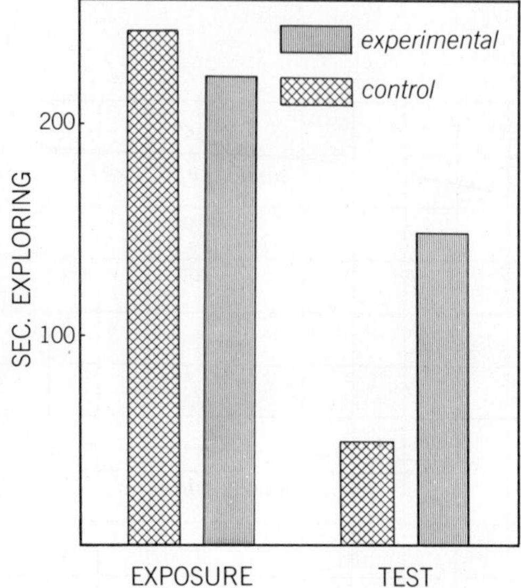

Figure 4. In the exposure session both controls (C) and experimental (E) rats were exposed to an identical pattern. In the test session, C's are exposed again to the same pattern, E's to a new one. E's now explore significantly more than C's (Thompson & Solomon, 1954).

duration given at one-minute or six-second intervals for a certain number of trials, following which a tone of 91 decibels was presented. Major results are shown in Figure 5. Presentation of the new tone produced prompt dehabituation of cardiac response. A further experiment using a sequence of tones, which was then reversed, proved that the effect was not due simply to the increased loudness of the second signal. From a discussion of his own data, as well as those obtained by Sharpless and Jasper (1956) on habituation of arousal in the cat reticular formation, the work of Sokolov *et al.* (1961) and of Glickman and Feldman (1961), Bartoshuk concludes that arousal habituation is a form of learning. We will not discuss these and the many other studies that have been done on the subject; we wish only to point up the fact that habituation-dehabituation can serve as an indication of differentiation in the perceptual or input system, and that habituation itself is probably a form of learning.

It must be pointed out here that our use of differentiation applied to perceptual development is the same as that of Gibson and Gibson (1955); that is, it refers to the progressive increase in correspondence between

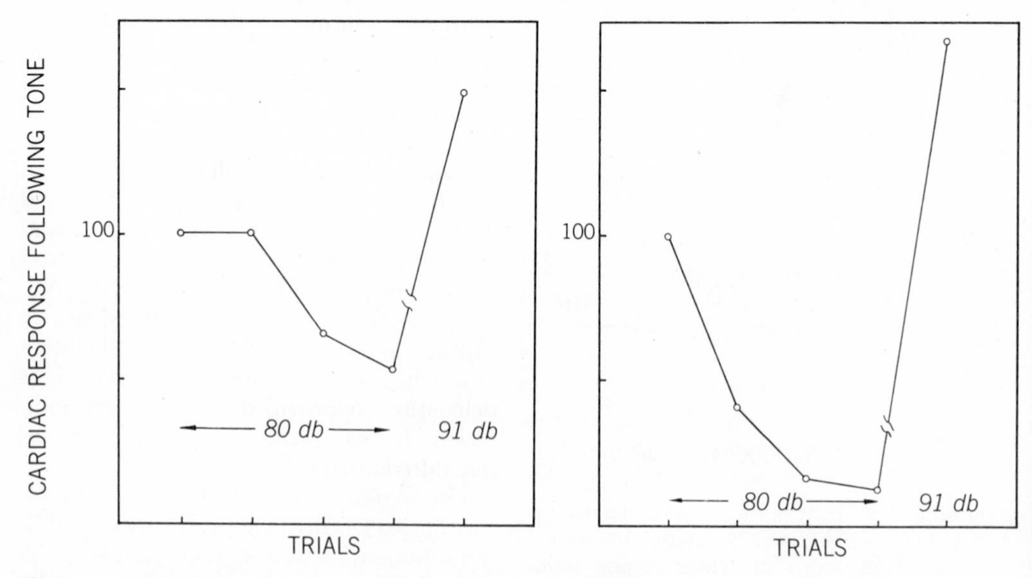

Figure 5. Habituation occurs in neonates on repeated presentation of a tone. When the tone is then changed, dehabituation takes place as indicated by the jump in cardiac response. This indicates a discrimination of tonal intensity has occurred.

environmental stimulation and an organism's perception of it that occurs with aging until maturity. The Gibsons have contrasted this view with another set of theories which they term "enrichment" theories. These latter account for perceptual development in terms of additions made to an initially meager and fragmentary sensory input. Stimuli become distinct by acquiring associations with other stimuli or with responses —they are, in other words, enriched. The evidence on either side is not definitive, but, logically, it is difficult to envisage the possibility of part of the environment becoming more distinct by virtue of association enrichment unless it is already differentiated in the first place. Probably both occur, though it seems likely that differentiation must take place first. We will return to this point later on.

That discrimination of the world does improve with age, whatever the reason for it, is fairly obvious. Documentation has been provided by Gibson (1964), Piaget & Inhelder (1956), Piaget (1961), Bevan (1961), Francès (1962), Wohlwill (1960), and many others. It is also likely that, in most species, it develops at a very fast rate, at least in relation to most of the ordinary dimensions of the world with which that species has to deal, for example, parents, predators, and foodstuffs. It also may continue developing during the whole lifetime of an organism. The complexity of the world many animals occupy, especially man, may demand finer and finer degrees of perceptual differentiation. Thus it is of little importance for most human beings to be able to distinguish minute differences in hue. But it may be of great importance to an artist working with paints or to a geneticist working with *Drosophila* eye-colors. Connoisseurship, as Gibson has pointed out (1964), involves a high degree of perceptual differentiation in respect to some sensory dimensions. The wine-taster, by virtue of long practice, is able to distinguish subtle variations in bouquet, taste, body, and color that are lost on the novice. The yields in enjoyment are, of course, great.

Hebb (1949), on the basis of work by Riesen (1947), Van Senden (1932), Mishkin and Forgays (1952), and others, has argued that the infant's perception of the world is not immediate as some psychologists previously supposed, but is built up gradually. Only unities, but not identities, are initially seen. Haynes, White, and Held (1965) have added notably to our information on the subject. Using a technique known as dynamic retinoscopy, they have shown that the human infant can focus on objects only at a particular distance (median 19 centimeters). Apparently objects closer or further away will appear blurred. Good, flexible accommodation does not appear until around the fourth month—a time not long before infants commence to discriminate familiar from unfamiliar faces.

Let us now look at the response or output side. The situation here is not so clear. As we have already stated above, response differentiation refers, in broad terms, to the increasing independence of responses or response systems. It is obvious enough that, initially, an infant can respond to stimulation only in a very diffuse, global manner. With increasing age, output becomes progressively refined, proceeding in cephalocaudal and proximodistal directions. Thus more mature systems can do more than less mature systems. Documentation of such increments in response repertory is truly extensive. But it is not so obvious how this can be demonstrated clearly at an experimental level. On the perceptual side, it is easy enough to hold response constant and to vary stimuli, as was discussed above; but on the output side, the converse is not so easily accomplished, that is to say, the holding of stimulus constant, and the experimental variation of responses. Something like it is seen in the typical avoidance-conditioning experiment, in which a rat gradually learns to avoid shock by progressing from a gross level of responding to a very economical level involving a minimum of surplus action. In such a situation, we might say that there has occurred a reduction of noise on the output side. In human beings, we can point to similar examples. Professional ballerinas, athletes, and many others with such vocations or avocations are all concerned with control of movements and responses. They are quite analogous to the wine-taster already mentioned. While the second has achieved a high degree of differentiation in respect to input from the external world, the former have achieved a high level in respect to output and can respond quickly and efficiently in a beautifully articulated manner.

Now we would assume that perceptual differentiation precedes in time and partly produces response differentiation. Organisms are so constructed that input must come before output, and they start gaining information about the world before they can do very much with this information. Furthermore, there appears to be, in most animals, a longer lag-phase in the rate of differentiation of output or response. That is to say, *differentiation is slower on the output than on the input side*. When we say "slower," we refer to the speed with which some hypothetical capacity or physiological limit is approached in each case. Direct evidence for this assertion is, of course, difficult to obtain, since we cannot really know what the physiological limits of input and output are. We must consequently be content to take it as a hypothesis based only on rather loose and indirect data. These latter relate mainly to developmental norms of the kind supplied painstakingly for human infants by Gesell, and summarized for lower animals by Cruikshank (1954). Thus it is well established that the human infant can make a variety of fairly fine sensory discriminations at and even before birth, but it cannot crawl until about 34 weeks, creep until about 35 weeks, and walk until around 12 months. Likewise, the rat, soon after birth, shows differential responses to sound in a classical conditioning situation (Caldwell & Werboff, 1962), but it is not able to stand, walk, sit, or climb until around 12–14 days. It will be obvious that the lag in response differentiation is characteristic mainly of the voluntary motor system, that is, the skeletal musculature. If the animal is to survive at all, most of the efferent components of the autonomic system must be functioning early; the same applies to many basic reflexes, such as sucking, grasping, righting, and others. In fact, infants may not be very different from adults in respect to most measures of autonomic function. But in some species, at least, maternal care compensates for the immaturity of somatic development. The infant rat, mouse, or chimp does not need to be able to do much for itself, since the mother takes care of all its basic needs. However, this is not true in other animals, such as gallinaceous birds, or some grazing species, for example, horses, sheep, or cattle, all of which are born in rather open, exposed situations that place a premium on immediate independence. Thus we find marked variation attributable to genotype in degree of lag between input and output differentiation.

We suggested above that differentiation on the response side may be partly dependent on perceptual differentiation. More complex inputs usually demand more complex outputs. However, it must also be true that the sensory feedback from the motor systems acts to refine and articulate perception. Hebb (1949) has implied this in his concept of phase-sequence, as has also Drever (1961) and Piaget (cf. Flavell, 1963), in his discussions of the modifications of schemata produced by active movements. On the experimental side, Held and his associates (Held & Schlank, 1959; Held & Bonsom, 1961; Held & Heim, 1963) have shown the importance of reafferent stimulation from self-produced or active movement for spatial discrimination in kittens. When movements are passive, or "experimenter-produced," perceptual ability suffers. Undoubtedly, both input and output systems reinforce each other. After all, both involve perceptual components, and though they develop independently to some extent, we should expect to find, on the response side, some analogue to what has been called perceptual learning. Equally, each must aid in the further differentiation of the other.

The above discussion of differentiation has emphasized essentially three points. We will now state these in the form of axioms.

1. Differentiation increases in organisms as they increase in age up to maturity. Such increments are partly dependent on maturation and partly on learning.
2. The curve representing this increment in differentiation is probably sigmoid, having the usual three component phases—the lag, the logarithmic, and the stabilization phases.
3. Differentiation occurs both on the input or perceptual side and on the output or response side. Each has a facilitatory effect on the development of the other.
4. Input differentiation increases at a faster rate than output differentiation.

As we have already indicated, the evidence for affirming these propositions is not precise but of a rather general nature. It is for this reason that we refer to them as axioms rather than as empirical statements. Nonetheless, they can readily be explicated into testable hypotheses, many of which, as we shall show below, have empirical support in extant data. Let us now examine the immediate consequences of the statements above.

Figure 6 shows a graphical plot of input and output differentiation against age according to the four propositions. It will immediately be obvious that we may divide development into three distinct age zones, according to their input-output characteristics. These are as follows:

a. Undifferentiated input—undifferentiated ouput;
b. Relatively differentiated input—undifferentiated output;
c. Differentiated input—differentiated output.

Since the zones are defined in terms of quantitative parameters, they cannot be taken as being completely discrete or discontinuous with each other. As we hope to show, each represents a kind of critical

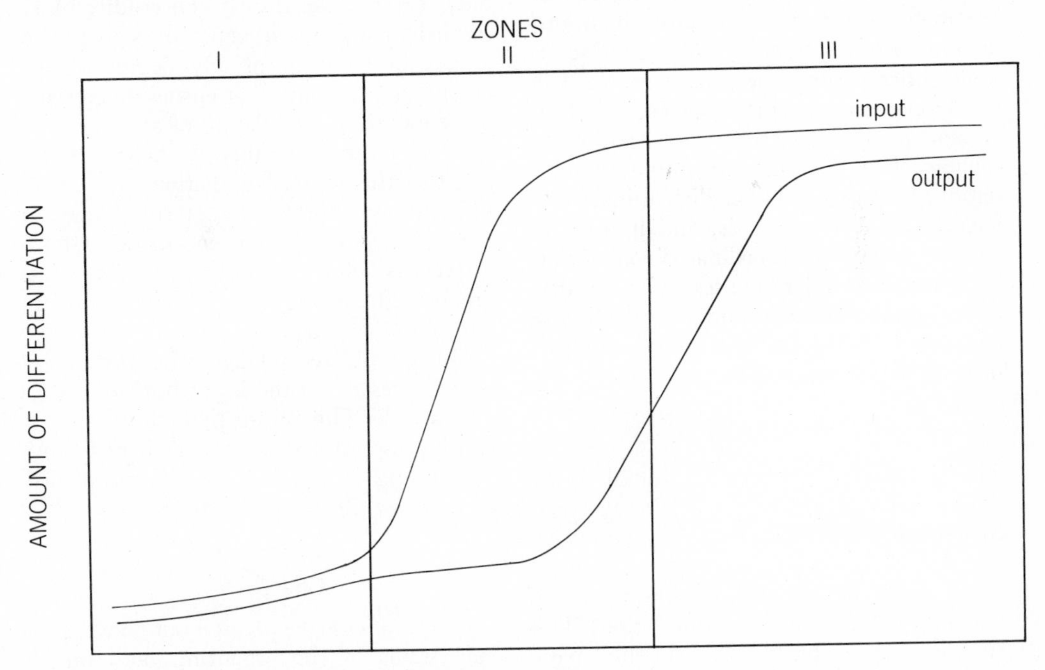

Figure 6. Hypothetical rate of input and output differentiation as a function of age.

period during which a certain type of behavior has a maximal chance of being set.

Now our major concern here is with the manner in which events occurring at any particular age can affect adult personality—that is, with what can be taken in by the developing organism and stored or remembered. In short, we are directing our attention to the *residua of early learning*. For the most part, learning situations can be conceptualized in terms of S-R relationships, or, in our terms, input-output relationships. Consequently, the three zones of development we have demarcated above also define three types of storage or learning mechanisms. Let us now attempt to identify these. A usual paradigm for many complex types of learning, for example, instrumental conditioning, is as follows:

US——UR

CS——CR

Thus, lack of food produces hunger and general arousal responses from which differentiated particular reinforcement-producing behaviors occur in response to some differentiated cue. Whatever may be the special mechanisms involved, this kind of storage demands that the organism be capable of both input and output differentiation. It must be able to discriminate relevant from irrelevant cues, and it must be able to make well-coordinated and articulated instrumental responses. Now by definition, these have a minimal probability of occurrence during the first age zone. Therefore, all that remains is the relationship:

US——UR

That is to say, the general arousal or reflexive behavior elicited, in the first instance, by general conditions of stimulation. What learning occurs must then refer to changes in strength of general responsiveness to general, undifferentiated stimulation. This simple situation fits the experimental paradigm commonly used to study habituation learning (cf. Harris, 1943). Some stimulus that reliably elicits some response is repeatedly presented and observations are made of the waning or waxing of response strength. An example is afforded by the experiments of Hinde (1954). This investigator studied changes in the strength of mobbing responses of finches made to an owl surrogate continuously exposed to them for various periods of time. Typically, there occurred gradual diminution in the number of to-and-fro flights per unit of time; removal of the surrogate led to a partial recovery in response-strength on its replacement in the enclosure. Amount of recovery became less with repetition of the removal-replacement procedure, suggesting both long- and short-term habituation effects. Now although studies of habituation like this one have generally dealt with the changes in strength of rather specific instinctive responses to rather specific releasing stimuli, there is no reason why the term habituation itself should be taken to refer only to cases like this. It can readily be regarded as descriptive of changes in the intensity of behavior of any degree of specificity or generality that ensues on repeated presentation of stimulation of any degree of specificity or generality (Thorpe, 1959). Used in this sense, habituation may be applied to any short- or long-term changes in neural, biochemical, or endocrine systems, as well as behavioral systems provided they are brought about by some environmental stimulus.

During the second age-zone, differentiation is present on the input but not on the output side. This means that stimuli or cues can be discriminated, but that instrumental responding is still minimal. Consequently, in respect to learning, we have:

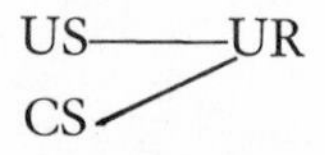

Since, as we have pointed out above, some subsystems of the organism, both on the input and on the output side, differentiate faster than others, we may expect to find some overlap between the three types of learning at any age level. During any age-zone, each will have a certain degree of *dominance,* or *probability of occurrence,* ranging from very high to very low. The value at any age level will represent a kind of average, for the total organism, of sub-system probabilities. Figure 7 graphically illustrates the point being made. It indicates that during the first age-zone most of the changes that can be brought about in the young animal will be referrable to habituation. A limited number of changes will be possible via classical conditioning through the use of special procedures, but probably almost no instrumental learning will be possible, though, of course, this can never be proved categorically. Similar statements can be made in respect to the two other age zones. As indicated also in the figure, we have labeled the three age-zones, respectively, *temperament-adaptation zone, affective-meaning zone,* and *instrumental-meaning zone.* The use of the term "meaning" in the last two represents a bow but not a commitment to cognitive theory. Thus although our development of the model has so far been made in terms drawn from behaviorism, we do not wish to enforce too strict restrictions on its explication. Table 1 offers a summary of what we have discussed up to this point.

Several features of the figure should be emphasized. First of all, the age-zones are defined in terms of degree of differentiation that has occurred in the organism, not in terms of chronological age itself. Thus, if we take birth as a reference point, we will find that its exact designation on the abscissa in Figure 7 will vary considerably

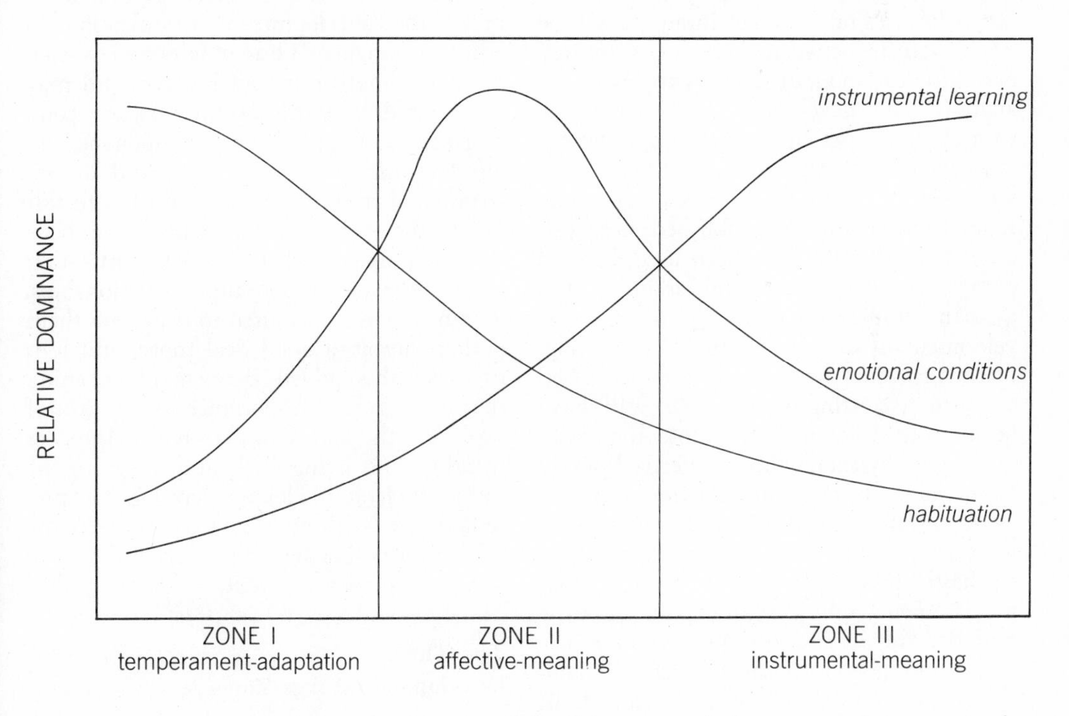

Figure 7. Critical zones during development defined in terms of three types of storage mechanisms.

TABLE 1

SUMMARY OF THE MODEL

Zone	Differentiation Input	Differentiation Output	Dominant Type of Learning	Behavior Mainly Changed
Temperament-adaptation	Low or absent	Low or absent	Habituation	Temperament
Affective-meaning	High	Low or absent	Classical or emotional conditioning	Affective relations with specific cues
Instrumental-meaning	High	High	Instrumental conditioning	Instrumental responses to cues

with the species under consideration. For precocial species, like the guinea-pig, the chick, and the monkey, it should probably be placed around the intersection point of the habituation and emotional conditioning curves. For a rat or a mouse or a marsupial, however, it will be placed much closer to the ordinate. For a human infant, it will be somewhere in between these two extremes. Secondly, the model is based entirely on an analysis of development. Conveniently enough, the types of input-output relationships we have postulated happen to coincide with already established types of learning. Had they not so been established, however, other names might have been used, but the picture would not be any different. This is a further indication of the primacy of development in understanding behavior. The directions taken by learning theories based on such a starting-point might well have been quite different from those that have been taken by extant theories derived purely from the study of adult behavior. But it is quite certain that they would be equally interesting. Thirdly, development is a stochastic process, in the broad sense that its parameter values at any point in time will depend on previous values. Thus the shape and height of the classical or emotional conditioning curve will depend, in any particular case, on what has happened during the first age zone. Likewise, instrumental learning will depend on experience during the two age-zones preceding it. A very emotional or temperamental animal will learn differently from a very stable one. This point was, of course, emphasized a long time ago by Pavlov (1960).

Fourthly, and most importantly, it is the residua of these three age-zones that comprises the developmental stratification of adult personality. Thus it is our view that any need, motive or trait involves and may be assessed in terms of three major components—a temperament component, an affective meaning component, and an instrumental meaning component. Up to this point, these three components have been defined only in rather abstract terms—that is, in terms of input-output relationships. The names we have used to designate them perhaps imply a good deal more, and it is precisely this added richness of meaning that is of greatest importance to our task of exploring the nature of personality. In order to add some living flesh and blood to the rather skeletal model we have so far presented, we will now survey some of the evidence that is relevant to each of the three age-zones of development.

The Three Developmental Age-Zones

The temperament-adaptation zone—As it has been defined above, the character of organism-environment interactions during this age-zone and the residua resulting from these interactions are a consequence of lack of differentiation on the input and on the output side. The very young animal cannot make very clear discriminations between the objects in his world, and he cannot emit well-coordinated or articulated responses. We have therefore suggested that any storage or learning that occurs must relate to level of general reactivity to the world in general, that is, to temperament. Such learning may be designated as habituation, negative or positive, or habituation-sensitization. The environmental conditions that are necessary to produce these kinds of changes are very simple: they merely involve the repeated presentation of some form of stimulation, of an intensity sufficient to elicit some general arousal or reflexive response. For example, we expose the young animal to an intense sound over repeated trials and it reacts with some general arousal responses. As a result of this procedure, we may later find that the subject's general responsiveness to any alteration in stimulus conditions is different from what it would have been had there been no exposure to early stimulation. Such terms as nervous, stable, phlegmatic, docile, jumpy, overreactive, excitable, and emotional are commonly used to describe the kinds of behavioral changes that eventuate from such procedures. Let us now consider some relevant experimental data. As a matter of convenience only, we will divide our discussion into a section concerned with prenatal treatments and one concerned with postnatal treatments.

The effects of prenatal stimulation—It has been a traditional folk-belief that the qualitative experience of a mother during pregnancy could have striking effects on her unborn child. For example, it was considered quite plausible that the spilling of a glass of wine on the mother during her pregnancy could produce in her child a wine-colored blemish, or that a bad experience with a dog could produce an offspring constitutionally disposed to fear dogs. Such anecdotal material is of sociological interest but has no scientific validity. Embryology has conclusively established that there are no neural connections between mother and fetus. Thus the transfer of qualitative experience between the two is not possible. There are, however, intimate humoral bonds via the placenta. By diffusion or by active transport, or both, a great variety of different substances can pass from the maternal to the fetal circulation, as well as in the other direction. The number and nature of the agents that can so cross are not fully established as yet. Many factors affect placental permeability, such as the quantity and molecular characteristics of the agent involved, the stage of gestation, and the genotype or genotype make-up of the animal (Flexner & Gellhorn, 1942; Hooker, 1952; Nalbandov, 1958; Page, 1957; Montagu, 1963). There is no doubt, however, that the number of chemical compounds that can cross is very large (Page, 1957). Under normal conditions, placental transfer simply serves the basic fetal functions of nutrition and excretion. Often, however, it permits the passage to the fetus of undesirable effects produced in the mother by abnormal agents or stresses. Around this fact has grown up the science of teratology—that is, the study of monsters. The classic case is that of the rubella virus, or German measles, which, when contracted by the mother early in pregnancy, produces among other things congenital blindness in the infant (Gregg, 1941). It is now known that the range of agents that can produce malformations, and the range of these malformations themselves, is very large. Atmospheric changes producing hypoxia or anoxia, poisons of various kinds, ionizing radiations, various hormones and chemical compounds, antibiotics, nutritional deficiencies or imbalances, infections, and many other such agents can produce in young animals such abnormalities as cleft palate, spina bifida, hernia, absence of limbs or eyes, cranial malformations, and similar defects (Fraser, 1958; Fraser, Fainstat, &

Kalter, 1953; Kalter & Warkany, 1959; Montagu, 1962). It is therefore obvious that the fetus is very far from being insulated from the effects of maternal stress. This being so, it is not unreasonable to suppose that slighter or less drastic alterations of the physiology of the mother might well be reflected in changes in offspring behavior. Such indeed seems to be the case. In a number of different species, changes in the maze-learning ability, motivation, emotionality, and activity have been found to result from a variety of maternal treatments administered during pregnancy, for example, drugs, alcohol, x-irradiation, audiogenic seizures, adrenalin injection, and conditioned anxiety (cf. Thompson, Watson, and Charlesworth, 1962; Montagu, 1962; Werboff, 1963; Werboff & Gottleib, 1963). The exact nature of the effects, and their size, duration, and direction, appear to depend on type of agent, size of dosage, or amount of stress, trimester of administration, and conditions of testing (Thompson *et al.,* 1962). Since all of these factors interact in a complex manner, it is difficult to draw firm generalizations about their separate contribution. Data obtained with human beings are less precise. They have usually involved the comparison of pregnancy records of mothers of children having some kind of abnormality with those of mothers of normal children. In a large number of publications, Pasamanick, Lilienfeld and their colleagues (Pasamanick & Knobloch, 1961; Lilienfeld *et al.,* 1955) were able to establish a relationship between incidence of complications during the mothers' pregnancy or parturition and various behavioral and physical defects in the offspring. These disorders included mental deficiency, cerebral palsy, epilepsy, tics, speech defects, and various behavior abnormalities. Sontag (1941) claimed to have found a relation between severe anxiety suffered by mothers during pregnancy and "neuroticism" (excessive crying, vomiting, etc.) in the infants, but his evidence is meager. Stott (1958, 1959) on the basis of data obtained mostly from retarded or mongoloid children, attempted to establish a causal relation between pregnancy stress, early illness, malformation, and "unforthcomingness," the last being a syndrome measured by the Bristol Social Adjustment Guides and defined as "absence of that natural assertiveness and will to effectiveness which induces temperamentally normal children to seek new experience and to overcome reasonable difficulties. . . ." Since his control of other variables was loose and his sample very atypical, we must view his positive conclusions with skepticism, the more especially since it has been shown that mongolism or Down's syndrome is due to a chromosomal anomaly (cf. Fuller & Thompson, 1960). In short, the work with human subjects on the effects of pregnancy-stress is suggestive but not entirely convincing. It is plausible mainly because its conclusions make physiological sense and because they are strongly supported by the animal studies referred to above.

The effects of postnatal stimulation—During the early part of their postnatal life, the young animals of many species more closely resemble the fetus than they do the adult animal. Because of the relative lack of differentiation on both the input and output side, most of the residua of experience are therefore still carried by habituation learning. Repeated stimulation, depending on its intensity characteristics, produces in the animal an increasing tendency to be less easily aroused by stimulus change, or more easily aroused by it. During the last ten years, a massive amount of evidence has accumulated showing this in a number of different species, particularly the rat and the mouse. Some of the first observations were made by Bernstein (1952) who speculated that the improvement in maze-learning ability found in rats that had been home-reared as pets, as reported by Hebb (1949), might be due not so much to a richer perceptual experience but to the larger amount of "gentling" they had received. He investigated this point by giving to his experimental animals special handling for 10 days starting at 50 days of age, or for about 40 days starting at 21 days. Both groups, but particularly the earlier-handled, were later found to be superior to controls in maze-learning ability, and also more exploratory. Much subsequent work has essentially verified these results and extended them in many directions. It has also been shown that the term descriptive of the procedure—"gentling"—is a misnomer. It is not necessary to be "nice" to the animal or "gentle" with it. Any form of massive stimulation, electrical, mechanical, thermal or auditory, can produce effects. Thus placing a young rat on ice, or giving it a series of fairly strong shocks can result in behavior changes of the same kind as those resulting from petting or simply holding the animal for a minute or two.

With human infants, the evidence is again less incisive than that obtained with lower animals. However, the studies of Ribble (1944), Spitz (1945), Fischer (1953), Provence and Lipton (1962) and others are suggestive and do show agreement with the animal work. All of them have made the point that sensory stimulation in the form of "mothering" is very important for the welfare of the infant. Thus Ribble (1944) speaks of the "stimulus feeding" which the mother supplies the neonate by talking to it, stroking and holding it, rocking it, and moving in front of it. She has claimed that the lack of such stimulation often produces eventually a kind of "wasting away" syndrome which she has called "marasmus."

Full summaries of all the work in this area, both with human infants and with animal subjects, have been made by Thompson and Schaefer (1961), Denenberg (1962), Bovard (1958), Levine (1962), and others. We will now attempt simply to present a number of salient points that arise out of all the work on early stimulation and that seem of major importance to the model being explicated.

Major points arising out of work on effects of early stimulation—It seems clearly established that stresses of various kinds imposed on animal mothers during pregnancy can alter offspring behavior but that there does not seem to be any close relationship between the kinds of effects produced and the specific characteristics of the stress used. Such agents as anoxia, radiation, tranquilizing drugs, intense sound, and conditioned anxiety all have effects on similar kinds of behavioral measures. Some typical results obtained by the writer (Thompson, 1957) and by Ader and Belfer (1962) on the effects of pregnancy anxiety on open-field behavior of rat offspring are shown in Figures 8 and 9. Low activity-level is generally taken to indicate high emotionality, since it is assumed that fear of the new and strange situation inhibits activity. In human beings, Stott (1957) has claimed a relationship between incidence of pregnancy stress and/or early illness and later mental retardation. The fact that incidence in sibs of the retardates is about the same as that in an unrelated group suggests that genetic factors are not involved here at least.

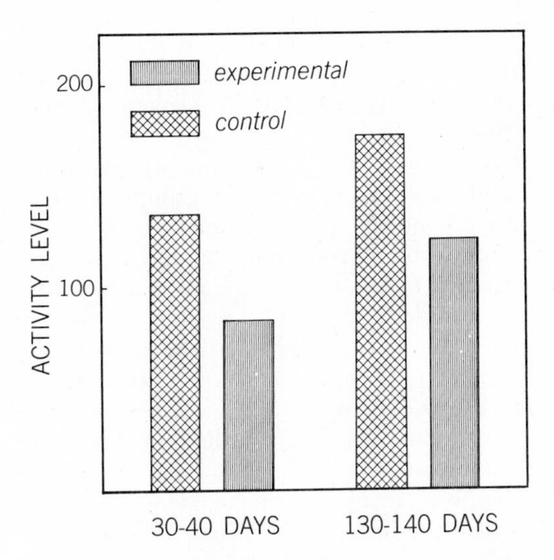

Figure 8. Open-field activity levels in rat offspring from mothers made anxious during pregnancy (E's) and normal mothers (C's). Low activity is taken to mean high emotionality (Thompson, 1957).

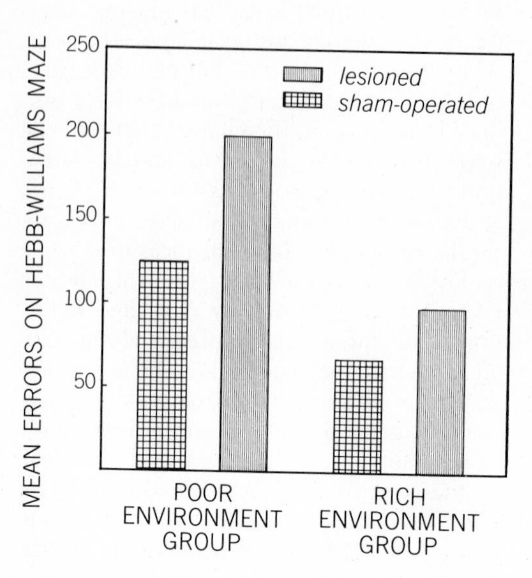

Figure 9. Results of Ader and Belfer (1962) replicating those of Thompson shown in Figure 8, percentage of animals venturing into the center of the open field in the two test trials.

Results of work done on early postnatal stimulation may be exemplified by studies by Levine (1956), and by Denenberg and Morton (1962a; 1962b). Levine compared on several tests of emotionality given at adulthood (71 days) three groups of rats: early handled (EH), commencing the day after birth and continuing until day 21; late handled (LH), handling from day 50 to 71; nonhandled group. His results are shown in Table 2. It is clear that the early treatment group is the least emotional on all measures. The nonhandled is the most emotional, and the late handled in between. Levine suggested that handling is equivalent to a "fear-producing noxious stimulus" which produces in the young animal some form of adaptation to later stress. That these kinds of changes are fairly long-lasting is shown by the work of Denenberg and Morton (1962a). They found that young rats handled for the first 24 days of life were

TABLE 2

RELATION BETWEEN EARLY AND LATE HANDLING AND SUBSEQUENT BEHAVIOR (LEVINE, 1956)

	Early Handled	Late Handled	Control
Hurdle crossing	7.25	6.92	4.95
Defecation (%)	0	38	58
Freezing (%)	18	93	65
No. trials freezing	.44	1.69	2.37

significantly more active and defecated less in an open-field, i.e., were less emotional than nonhandled controls, both at 76 and 180 days of age.

In human neonates, the effects of early stimulation, or lack of it, are less well documented, as we have already pointed out. Thus the observations of Ribble and Spitz, for example, are open to criticism (cf. Pinneau, 1950, 1955). A most useful survey of all the material on the effects of maternal deprivation has recently been made by Casler (1961). He points out that almost all of the studies in this area have confounded two kinds of causal factors, first, perceptual or sensory deprivation, and secondly, maternal deprivation. He says:

Although the roles of maternal deprivation and of perceptual deprivation are not always easy to separate, they *are* separable. If it is true that ill effects encountered when the maternal separation occurs during the first six months of life are attributable to perceptual deprivation, while ill effects found in cases where the separation occurs later on are the result of perceptual deprivation plus certain affective components of maternal deprivation accompanying the breaking of an established reciprocal bond, we would expect there to be a difference between the two reactions. (Casler, 1961, p. 18)

This distinction was made explicitly by the writer in several publications (Thompson, 1958, 1960; Thompson & Schaefer, 1961) (as noted by Casler), and is, of course, crucial to the model being developed here. Schaffer (1958) has suggested that perceptual deprivation may have its effects up to about the age of 7 months in the human infant, whereas maternal deprivation will become the important agent thereafter. He attributes this, in anticipation of the thesis of this paper, to increasing perceptual differentiation. From data he gathered on 76 infants, hospitalized for various reasons at ages from 3 to 51 weeks, he and Callender (1959) were able to distinguish two syndromes. These were: (a) "Global," characterized mainly by "unfocussing inspection of his surroundings"; (b) "overdependent," characterized by "an overly strong tendency to demand maternal attention." The first of these tended to be associated with hospitalization during the first half year, the second with hospitalization after this time. Such results as these, together with those of other studies summarized by Casler, are perhaps not as incisive and clear-cut as they might be. Nonetheless, they do fit well with the animal data, and are, in themselves, very suggestive.

There has been somewhat less attention paid to the effects of unusually large amounts of stimulation. We may cite three studies in this connection. Hopper and Pinneau (1957), using a genuine experimental approach—rather unusual in the area of child development—instructed one group of mothers to give to their babies ten minutes of extra handling or cuddling prior to regular feeding periods. The control mothers gave only a "regular" amount. At the end of a five-week period, the babies in the two groups were compared in respect to frequency of regurgitation. It was found that both had declined, but the experimentals more than the controls. The difference was not at a level of statistical significance, but did approach it. Replication of this study would be of great value. An entirely different approach was taken by Geber & Dean in a series of papers on children in Uganda (Geber, 1958a, 1958b; Geber & Dean, 1957a, 1957b). These focus on the fact that the average Uganda baby is, by Western standards, extraordinarily advanced in developmental rate. He can sit without support by seven weeks, walk to a Gesell box and look inside by seven months, and so on. Geber has attributed this precocity to the fact that the mother and baby are in almost continual contact until weaning, so that it receives continual stimulation in unusual amounts. After weaning, this is sharply reduced, whereupon developmental progress slows down.

The third study, by Landauer and Whiting (1963), has also made use of anthropological material. Having noted the results of animal experiments on the physical effects of early stress, these investigators located, in the Human Relations Area Files, societies in which various stressful procedures were or were not involved in the customary infant-rearing practices. The particular procedures were as follows: (1) piercing; (2) molding, usually for cosmetic reasons; (3) extreme heat; (4) extreme cold; (5) internal stressors, e.g., emetics, enemas, etc.; (6) abrasions, e.g., rubbing with sand, scraping with shell, etc.; (7) unusually intense general stimulation, e.g., massaging, painting, exposure to loud noises; (8) binding, e.g., swaddling, etc. Their next step was to obtain average stature measurements on these societies. As shown in Table 3, in which are presented data for 36 societies, the presence of piercing or molding is associated with greater stature —on the average, almost two inches. The difference is statistically significant. Of further interest is an age effect. Part *b* of Table 3 shows data based on 63 societies. These indicate that the effects on adult stature are produced maximally during the first two years of life. Stress between 6 to 15 years appears to decrease growth. Genetic, climatic, and nutritional variables were at least partly controlled in this study. However, the actual numbers of individual height measurements in any given society on which the final averages were based appear to be very small (the authors state

TABLE 3 (a)

EFFECTS OF STRESSFUL INFANT-REARING PRACTICES ON ADULT STATURE (INCHES) (LANDAUER & WHITING, 1963)

Nonstressful (N = 30)	Stressful (N = 7)
63.1	65.0

TABLE 3 (b)

STATURE AS RELATED TO AGE AT FIRST STRESS

	Under 2 wk.	2 wk.–2 yr.	2–6 yr.	6–15 yr.	After 15 yr.
No. of societies	19	16	11	6	11
Mean stature (in.)	65.4	65.9	63.6	61.7	63.0

"at least 25"). Furthermore, although the authors discount this, it seems very possible that stressful infant-rearing customs, while probably not themselves often responsible for increasing the mortality rate, might nonetheless tend to occur in and be symptomatic of societies in which hardship and stress are generally common enough to result in a strong selection against small size and physical weakness. In view of such difficulties, we must treat the results of Landauer and Whiting with some caution.

We may thus conclude from the above survey that, in lower animals and in human infants, the amount of massive stimulation imposed is an important variable affecting physical and psychological development.

The second major point relates to the behavioral and physiological functions primarily affected by early stimulation. There seems little question but that at least some components of intelligence as well as temperament and emotionality can be affected by early stimulation. This has been demonstrated for the prenatal period in cats and rats by such workers as Meier *et al.* (1960), Werboff *et al.* (Werboff, Broeder, Havlena, & Sikov, 1961; Werboff, Gottlieb, Dembicki, & Havlena, 1961; Werboff, Gottlieb, Havlena, & Word, 1961; Werboff, Havlena, & Sikov, 1962, 1963), and Thompson *et al.* (Thompson, Watson, & Charlesworth, 1962; Thompson, Goldenberg, Watson, & Watson, 1963) using a variety of different types of mazes and puzzleboxes. The work of Pasamanick and his associates and of Stott referred to above indicates that this is also true for human beings. Consequently, our use of the term temperament in the label we have given to this age-zone must be qualified somewhat. It must take in some aspect of intelligence, perhaps its chemical or physiological basis, or what Hebb (1949) described as Intelligence A. This may be different from, or more limited than, what is generally meant by intelligence and may be measured in varying degree by different tests. There is also, however, evidence that suggests intelligence is not usually affected by treatments very early in life. Thompson and Kano (1965) found that large amounts of phenylananine administered to female rats during pregnancy produced clear changes in offspring emotionality, but had no effect on performance in the Hebb-Williams maze, once emotional differences had been minimized by the training procedure. It is a matter of speculation whether the Hebb-Williams maze actually measures something different from what is measured by other standard mazes. However, it does have special features, these being, first, a rather long pretest training period, and secondly, the use of a number (twelve) of different problems. It would be of great interest to know whether, because of these characteristics, performance on it is relatively immune to the effects of very early environmental stimulation, though still susceptible to alteration by treatments at a later age.

Treatments administered to rats and mice in early postnatal life clearly affect all those forms of behavior that can be defined as pertaining to temperament, for example, activity-level, defecation frequency, latency to enter a strange place (e.g., open alley-way), conditioned avoidance behavior, resistance to stress and others (cf. summaries cited above). At the physiological level, these must relate to the pituitary-adrenal axis. Some evidence for this notion has been presented by Levine, Alpert, and Lewis (1957, 1958). They found that rats manipulated in infancy showed significantly earlier and greater adrenal ascorbic acid depletion in response to severe cold stress than nonmanipulated controls. A summary of these results is shown in Figure 10. Likewise, Levine, Cohen, and Anderson (cf. Levine, 1962) demonstrated that rats stimulated in early life as against controls characteristically react more sharply to distinctly noxious situations, but much less to mild stresses. Data bearing on this point are shown in Figure 11. In the graph, low values for leukocyte (white blood cell) count mean more reaction to stress. Levine suggests that nonstimulated animals not only are hyperreactors but are also much less able to withstand extreme situations than animals stimulated in infancy.

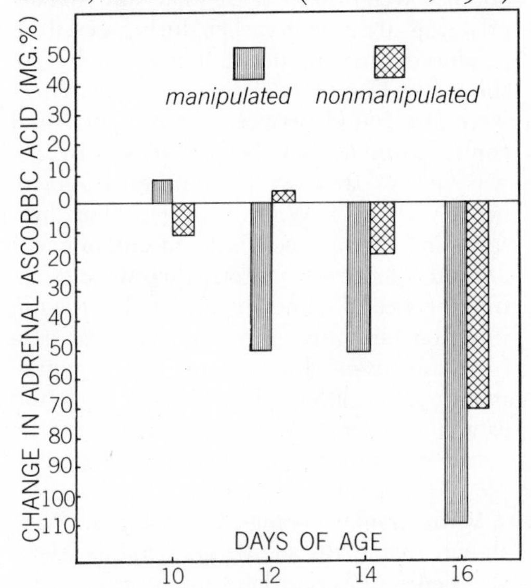

Figure 10. Adrenal abscorbic-acid depletion in manipulated and nonmanipulated infant rats, manipulation carried out up to day prior to test day (Levine, *et al.*, 1958).

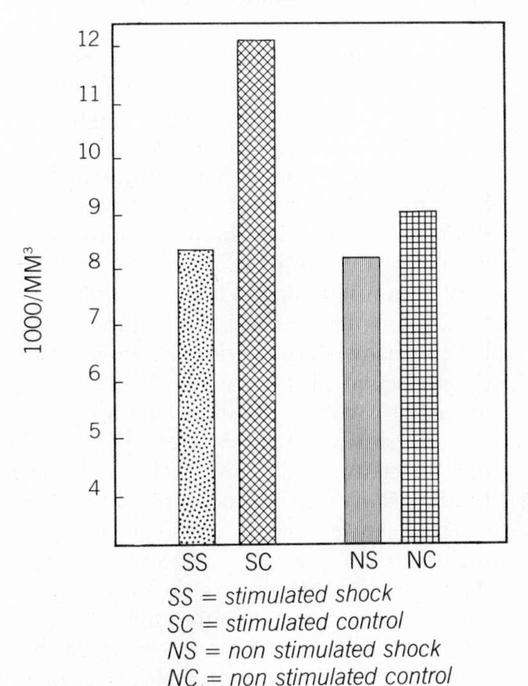

Figure 11. Leukocyte counts in various groups of stimulated and nonstimulated rats. Nonstimulated animals react as much to the nonshock or neutral condition as they do to shock (Levine, 1962).

While there is no doubt that early postnatal stimulation affects temperamental characters and their physiological bases, there is some doubt about its relationship to intellectual behavior. Denenberg and Morton (1962b) and Schaefer (1957) have found that performance on the Hebb-Williams maze is not altered by early handling. Other results obtained by Winston (1963) have supported this conclusion. Likewise, Perez (personal communication) failed to find any intellectual deficits (Lashley III maze) in rats which had been given intraperitoneal injections of phenylalanine during early infancy, although it is well known that animals given such treatment later in life do characteristically show losses on various maze and discrimination problems (cf., e.g., Louttit, 1962; Perez, 1963).

In human beings, the evidence on primary target systems of early stimulation is hard to evaluate. Most investigators have dealt only with the short-term effects of mothering or lack of it, and many of these may wane with age. Those attempting to look at long-term effects, on the other hand, have usually started with grown-up children, assessed in some way, and have then looked at the available information relating to early rearing of these cases. Apart from the difficulty of drawing tight inferences by the use of such a procedure, interest has oriented more towards personality abnormalities than towards intellectual deficits. Nonetheless, some reports do indicate that performance in the cognitive sphere can be altered. Goldfarb (1955), for example, has noted, besides some peculiarities of personality that appear in orphanage-reared children, failures in problem-solving and ability to abstract. If such effects do occur, however, it is by no means certain that they can be referred to events in the first age-zone. It is therefore fair to say that the human data are ambiguous (cf. Casler, 1961; Yarrow, 1964; Caldwell, 1964).

Perhaps the safest conclusion we can reach regarding the kinds of residua left by experiences during this early developmental stage is as follows: the primary target will be whatever system underlies general and reflexive responsiveness to general stimulation, together with its central components. Physiologically, this will probably relate to: (a) general input to the brain-stem reticular formation; (b) the reticular formation itself and the limbic system with which it connects; (c) the adrenal-pituitary axis and the autonomic system. Psychologically, this must relate directly to those types of behavior that may be classified under the nomenclature of temperament, and only indirectly to those behaviors defined as intellectual.

The third point is as follows: We have asserted that the nature of effects produced appears to be independent of the type of stimulation imposed on the young system. What do appear to be crucial, however, are the intensity characteristics of the stress, the age at which it is administered, and the genotype of the animal. Thus Werboff, Havlena, and Sikov (1962, 1963) found that prenatal X-irradiation with dosages of 25, 50, or 100 r had profound effects on emotional behavior and maze performance in rats. Dosages of 5, 10, 15, and 20 r, however, produced no changes. An age effect is illustrated by data of Thompson and Goldenberg (1962) on the influence of prenatal maternal adrenalin injection on offspring adrenal weights. In both male and female offspring, treatment earlier during gestation produced greater effects. These results are shown in Figure 12. Behavioral differences were also found between experimental and control animals, but the part played by age was not so striking (Thompson, Goldenberg, Watson, & Watson, 1963). There was some indication that effects on emotionality and on intellectual performance were maximal for second trimester maternal adrenalin injection, but this cannot be regarded as a firm conclusion. In the same set of experiments, some differential effects were found as a function of the intensity characteristics of the stress, but again these were too complex to be easily interpreted.

With human beings, teratologists have shown that many of the congenital defects are dependent on the time during pregnancy at which the stress occurs, the rubella virus and thalidomide being good examples. Less is known regarding intensity effects, though undoubtedly these are im-

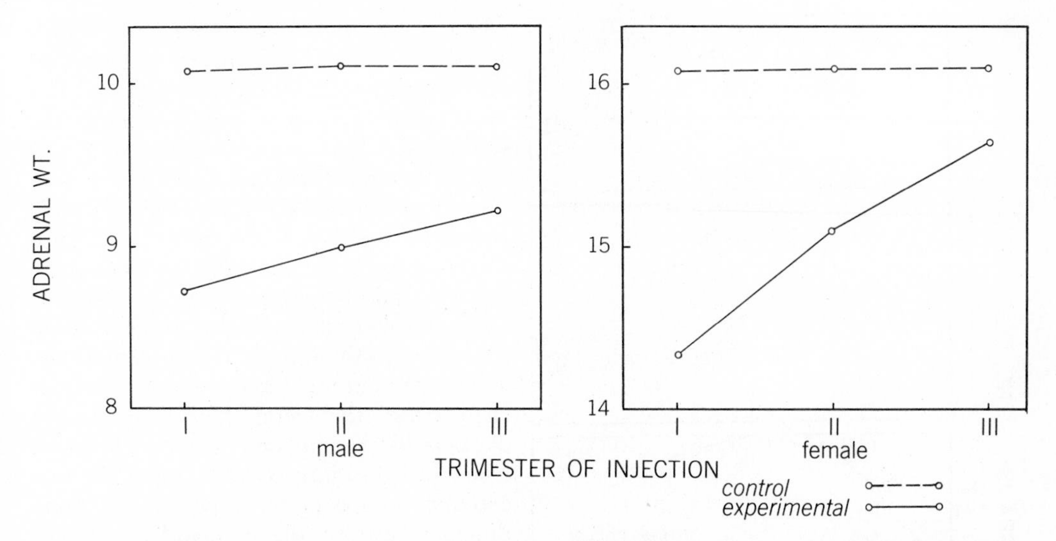

Figure 12. Adrenal weights of male and female rat offspring from mothers injected with adrenalin at one of the three trimesters of pregnancy (Thompson & Goldenberg, 1962).

portant. Almost no evidence exists about the relevance of these parameters to behavioral characteristics.

Age of the organism and intensity of stress also govern the effects of early postnatal stimulation. However, the relationships are far from simple. Under some circumstances, it appears that the earlier the stress is applied, the greater are the effects. Thus Seitz (1959), working with kittens, has shown that deprivation of handling brought about by maternal separation produces more drastic changes the earlier it is imposed. Kittens deprived at 2 weeks of age showed the most ill effects, but there was not much difference between those deprived at 6 weeks and those deprived at 12 weeks. A great deal of work in this regard has been done by Denenberg and his associates using rats and mice. It is clear enough from their experiments that age and intensity are crucial factors, but the complex manner in which they interact makes formulation of any simple generalizations rather difficult. Some typical results obtained by Denenberg (1962) are shown in Figure 13.

A number of experiments have now shown that genotype is also important in determining the direction and size of effects resulting from early experience. Lindzey, Lykken, and Winston (1962) have demonstrated this with several strains of mice, as have also Levine and Wetzel (1963) with three rat strains. The writer and Olian (Thompson & Olian, 1961) have shown that activity-level in mice altered in a manner that is dependent on genotype. As shown in Figure 14, offspring of mice from the genetically high-active strains show decreased activity-level as a result of prenatal treatment; those from genetically low-active mothers show increased activity; and finally, those of medium-active genotypes show little change in either direction. We will come back to a fuller discussion of genetic influences later on. The last experiment mentioned above suggests another important point relating to the effects of very early stimulation. We will turn to this now.

Our fourth point is that it is quite common in experimentation in this area to find bidirectional changes. Again, these are usually a function of age, intensity of stimulation, or testing conditions. Thus the writer has found that offspring emotionality may

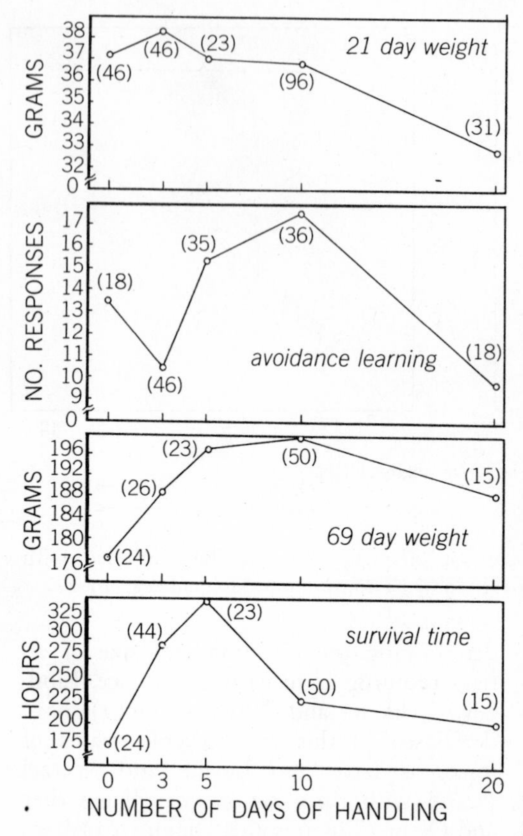

Figure 13. The effects on rats of varying amounts of early handling. Four measures are shown (Denenberg, 1962).

be raised or lowered as a result of conditioned anxiety undergone by the mother during pregnancy (Thompson, Watson, & Charlesworth, 1962).

Similarly, two independent investigations, by Meier *et al.,* (1960) and by Werboff, Havlena, and Sikov (1962), using anoxia and X-irradiation respectively, have shown that treatment early during gestation has a facilitating effect on maze-learning of offspring, whereas treatment during the last part of gestation has deleterious consequences for this behavior. The relevant data are summarized in Figure 15. It is clear by now that these bidirectional effects are not spurious. They have also been found by Thompson and Goldenberg (1962) and Thompson and Olian (1961), Furchtgott, Echols, and Openshaw (1958), and by Vincent (1958), to mention a few. They also occur with early postnatal stimulation as well.

Two examples of bidirectional effects produced as a function of intensity of early postnatal stimulation are shown in Figure 16. These are based on studies by Denenberg (1959) and by Denenberg and Karas (1960). Taken at face value at least, these data seem to show that no stimulation or a great deal of stimulation produce an equivalent effect, this being high emotionality of a mildly stimulated group. However, Denenberg has insisted (1964) that the two extreme groups perform poorly for quite different reasons—the nonhandled animals because they are indeed very emotional, but the high-stimulation subjects because they are very unemotional and docile. This interpretation follows from the rather radical assumption made by Denenberg that later emotionality is reduced as a monotonic function of intensity of early stimulation. It would be inappropriate in such a paper as this to enter into a critique of this hypothesis and the evidence upon which it is based. This will be done elsewhere. All that needs to be said here is that a different position is held by the writer—namely, that the relation between emotionality and stimulation intensity is a U-shaped rather than a monotonic function, and that data of the kind shown in Figure 16 directly reflect this.

This position states essentially that understimulation and overstimulation have equivalent effects in the sense that both treatments produce highly emotional animals. Whether the "emotionality" of each is the same, however, is questionable. To take a simple example, it may well be that low activity-level shown by a nonhandled rat is produced by different mechanisms than those which are responsible for the equally low activity-level of our overstimulated animal. Insofar as Denenberg's hypothesis is aimed at elucidating this difference, it has distinct merit. It is only his designation of

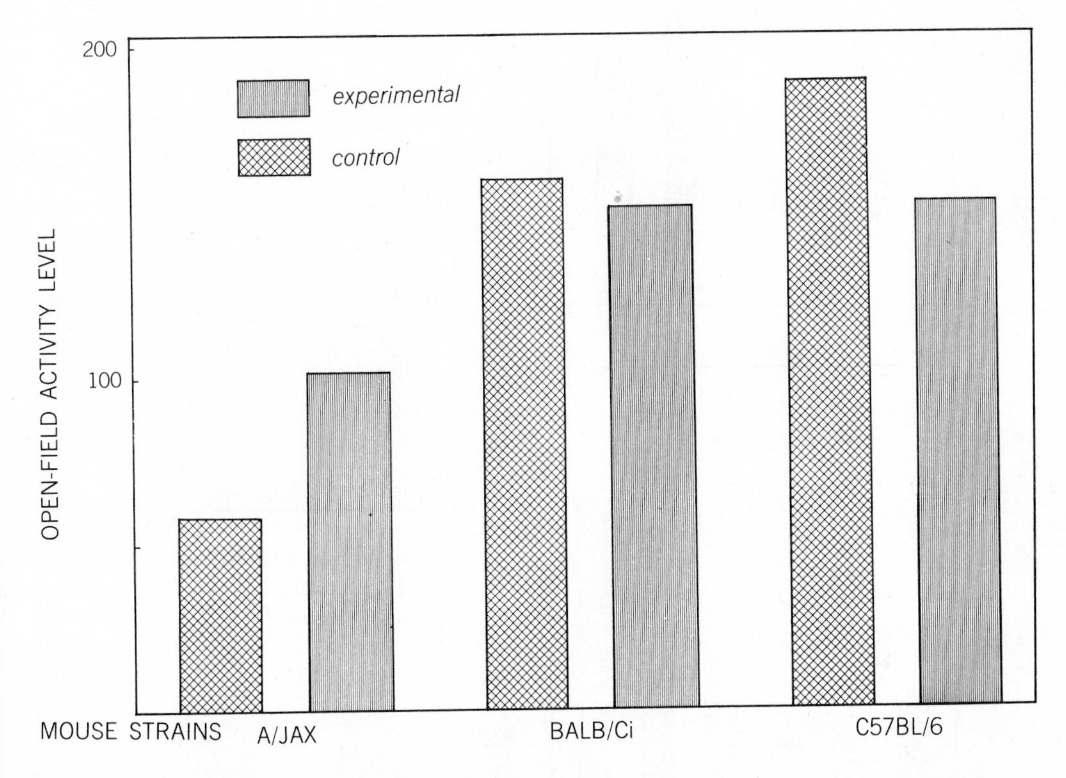

Figure 14. Activity levels in offspring mice from mothers treated with adrenalin during pregnancy. Under normal conditions, A/Jax are genetically low-active, BALB/Ci's are medium-active, and C57BL/B's are high-active (Thompson & Olian, 1961).

what the difference consists in that may be mistaken.

The affective-meaning zone—At a certain age, by hypothesis, input starts to differentiate at a rapid rate—that is, it enters the log-phase of its development, while the output curve is still in its lag-phase. This combination allows a type of storage which we have associated with classical or emotional conditioning. In the paradigm case, a neutral stimulus can come to evoke some relatively massive response that was formerly elicited by another stimulus—the unconditioned stimulus. What is therefore learned at this stage is the affective meaning of the world. At first, these may be very broad categories, for example, for children, female adults, male adults, or peers. An affective relation set up to one of them, for example, the mother, may then generalize readily to all females. It is obvious that it must be during this age-zone that the Oedipus complex occurs. It is probably true, as Melanie Klein and her followers (cf. Klein, 1950) have put forward, that its origins are a good deal earlier—perhaps in the first year of life. But further differentiation must take place before a child can perceive parental figures as unique entities distinct from everything else. Consequently, there is no real contradiction between the Kleinian and the classical Freudian position. Klein appears to be dealing with emotional responsiveness conditioned to very broad stimulus categories. The terms "depressive position," "manic position," and "paranoid position" are so global as to be close to what we have defined as temperament. However,

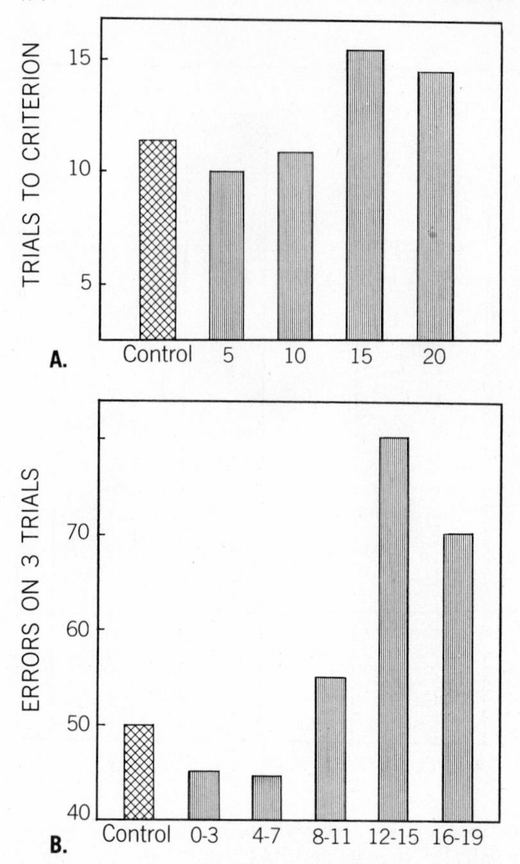

Figure 15. (A) Maze-learning ability of offspring rats from mothers treated with X-irradiation on different gestation days (Werboff *et al.*, 1962); (B) Maze-learning of offspring from mother rats made anoxic at varying gestation days (Meier *et al.*, 1960).

as the behavioral resultants of experience involving specific cues—e.g., the mother's breast—they must be set by classical conditioning albeit during the first age-zone. Let us now look at some of the data that have a bearing on what can happen during the affective-meaning zone.

One of the most striking sets of data relating age to ease of classical conditioning is that obtained in several studies on mice by Denenberg (1958, 1960). Using a buzzer plus shock as the conditioned stimulus (CS) and unconditioned stimulus (US), respectively, he recorded conditioned responses (CR's) ("any gross movement") following

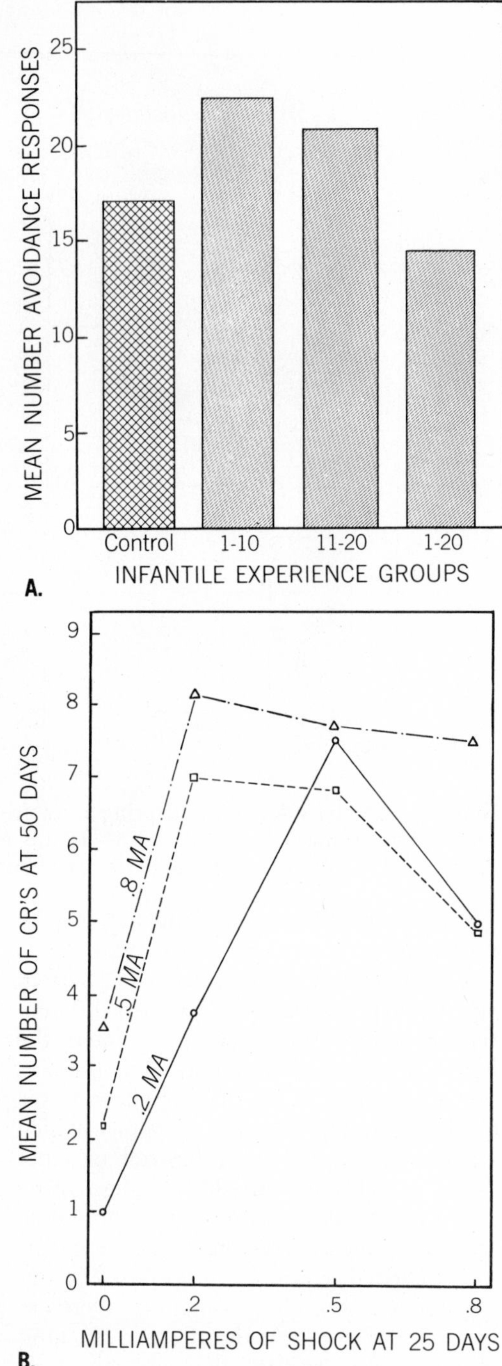

Figure 16. Bidirectional effects of early manipulation of rats. (A) Number of days of handling (Denenberg & Karas, 1960); (B) Intensity of early shock (Denenberg, 1959).

the onset of the buzzer but preceding shock. The relation between age and number of conditioned responses is shown in Figure 17.

The peaking that occurs between 20 and 25 days is striking. It would be interesting to know, however, why performance is lower in younger and older mice. The reasons must be different in the two cases and should, if our hypothesis is correct, have much to do with differences in degree of differentiation. Denenberg's findings have been supported by a study of Lindholm (1962). Lindholm showed that emotional response of rats to a bell and buzzer combination at 49 days was greatest in animals which had previously been exposed to it together with shock at 21–30 days of age. Subjects treated earlier showed a smaller response. Since no rats older than 30 days were used in the experiment, the data do not permit the conclusion that the 21–30 day period is critical in the sense that Denenberg found it to be. Furthermore, recency effects were not controlled. The time interval between initial experience and test was greater for animals manipulated younger. Consequently the study should be repeated. One finding of particular interest was that the 21–30 day group, though showing the most emotional response to the cues in whose presence they had been shocked, were very unemotional in a general situation. Thus it appears to be possible, at a particular age, to produce by a single treatment an organism that is unemotional in general but highly emotional in particular. The age at which this happens must be at the intersection of the habituation and classical conditioning curves of Figure 7.

It should be mentioned parenthetically at this point that the age-function for classical conditioning appears to differ sharply from that of avoidance learning. As measured by a savings method, a simple conditioned avoidance response (CAR) appeared to be directly related to age (Campbell & Campbell, 1962)—that is, older animals retained the response more readily than younger subjects, contrary to what might be expected. The same seems to be true for acquisition of the conditioned avoidance response according to work on monkeys by Green (cited by Campbell & Campbell, 1962). On the other hand, Henderson (1964) has shown that in mice, early experience (shock and handling) has maximal effects on improving avoidance conditioning when im-

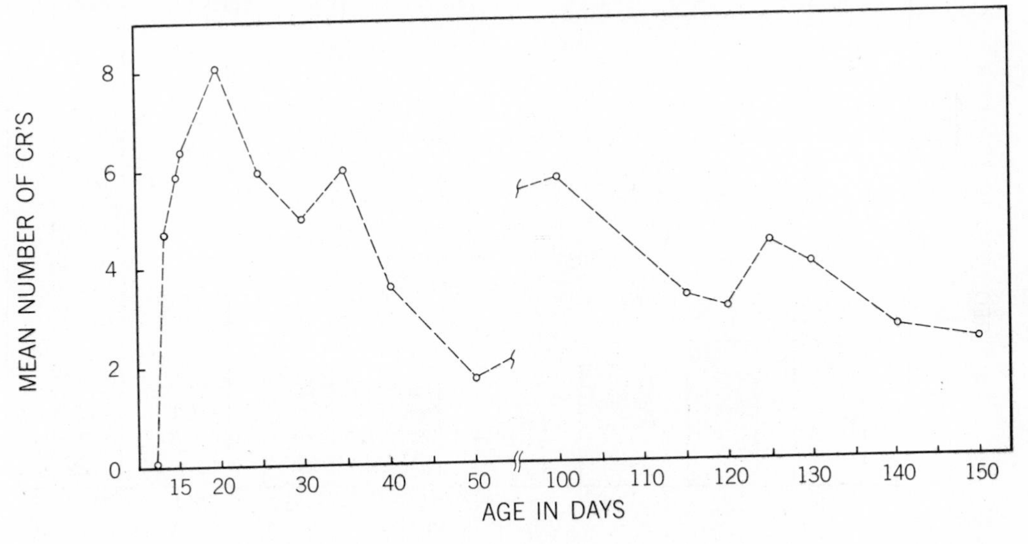

Figure 17. Relationship between age and ease of conditioning a startle response (classical conditioning) (Denenberg, 1960).

posed at 30 days of age rather than earlier or later. His data are shown in Figure 18. If we assume with Mowrer (1960) and others a dual factor theory of learning, it would be interesting to see whether this improvement was due to an alteration of the stimulus (classical) rather than the response (or instrumental) component of the avoidance training. The former would be implicated by our model and also by Denenberg's findings cited above. We should emphasize in passing that some classical conditioning is certainly possible very early. This has been demonstrated for rats by Caldwell and Werboff (1962) and for dogs by Stanley *et al.* (1963). However, it is probably a good deal less stable at this age than later on.

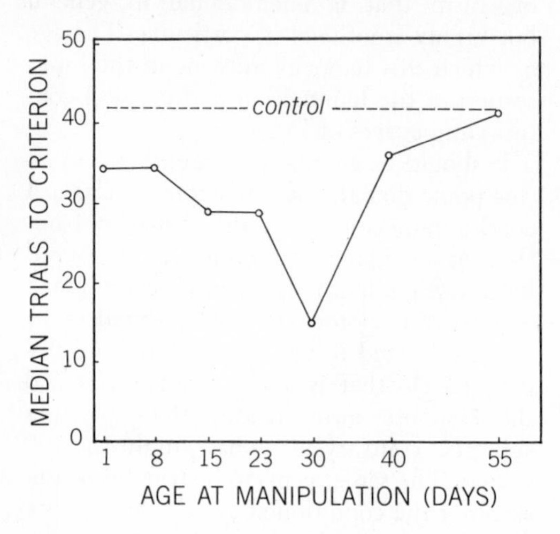

Figure 18. Mean trials to criterion of avoidance conditioning as a function of age at manipulation (shock or handling) in mice (Henderson, 1964).

In human beings, conditioning ability (of the classical type) appears to be fragile and uncertain during the first part of life, then gradually increases. There may be a peak somewhere between 5 and 8 years of age before a subsequent decline occurs, according to Razran's summary of some Russian studies (Razran, 1935). The data are shown in Figure 19. Razran suggests that the inflection after the 4–5 year old level is due to the increasing ascendancy of symbolic ability and voluntary control. In any case, the developmental curve is remarkably similar to that obtained by Denenberg (1960) for mice (as Denenberg himself pointed out), though we cannot say for sure that the 4 or

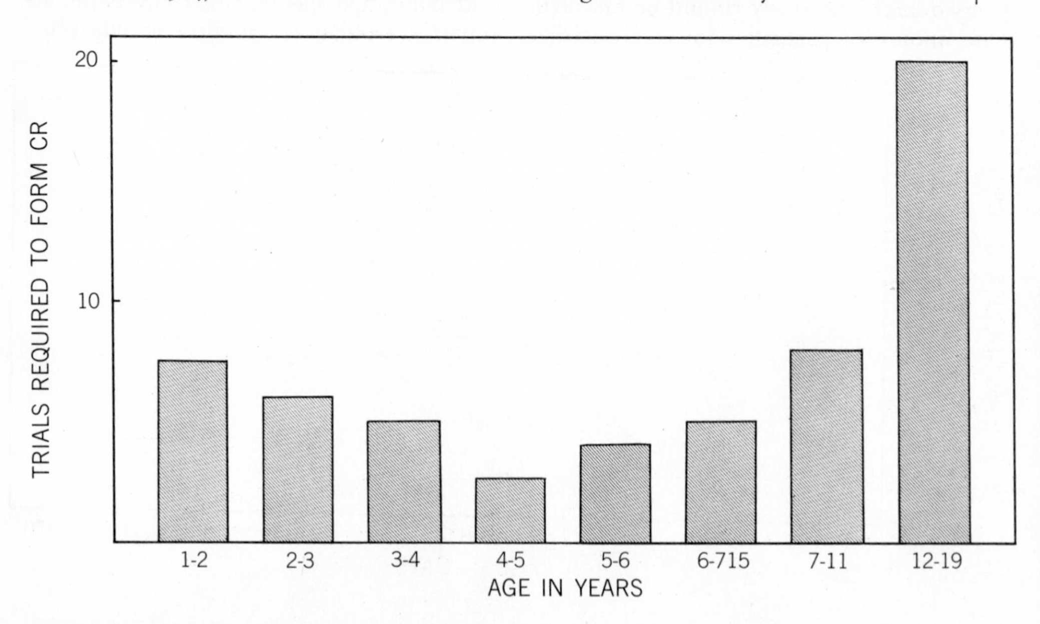

Figure 19. Ability to be classically conditioned as a function of age in children (Razran, 1935).

5 year old child is quite comparable in developmental age and maturity to the 20–30 day mouse.

It should be noted, of course, that the course of operant behavior is probably quite different and follows a normal growth curve of the kind depicted for instrumental learning in the graphical summary of the model (cf. Figure 7). However, until around 6–7 years behavior is postulated as being dominated by a more primitive type of learning or cognitive structure, of which classical conditioning is at least prototypic. Many child psychologists have noted the occurrence of a "shift" between ages 5 and 7, notably Sheldon White (1965) who has attributed its occurrence to an increment in some inhibitory processes that permit a delaying of responding and also reduce tendencies to over-rapid generalization. Similarly, the view of various Russian workers (e.g., Luria, 1960) has been that the second signal system—that is, language, as opposed to classical conditioning—starts to emerge. This and several other points of view have been summarized by White (1965) in a paper to which we will return shortly. All of them seem to be in agreement on the empirical facts though they describe them by somewhat different nomenclatures. But none of them offers any *developmental* explanations as to why the shift should occur. The model put forward in this paper, however, attempts to do this quite directly.

The material summarized above provides some direct evidence bearing on the storage mechanism that operates maximally during the second age-zone. In addition, there are a great many studies, using both human beings and animals, that provide further elucidation of its main characteristics. These deal with it not directly but rather inferentially inasmuch as they arrive at a delineation of its properties by a consideration of later outcomes of certain treatments imposed at this age-level. These treatments have to do mostly with the addition or removal of physical or social components of the environment considered to be important.

With animals, a typical example is afforded by the work of Scott and his colleagues using dogs at Bar Harbor. The age-zone we are considering appears to be identical with that Scott has called "the socialization period." Thus, he has considered it a critical time for formation of all social relationships—though his reasons for doing so are empirical rather than theoretical. The kind of data that indicate this are shown in Figure 20. These show the amount of emo-

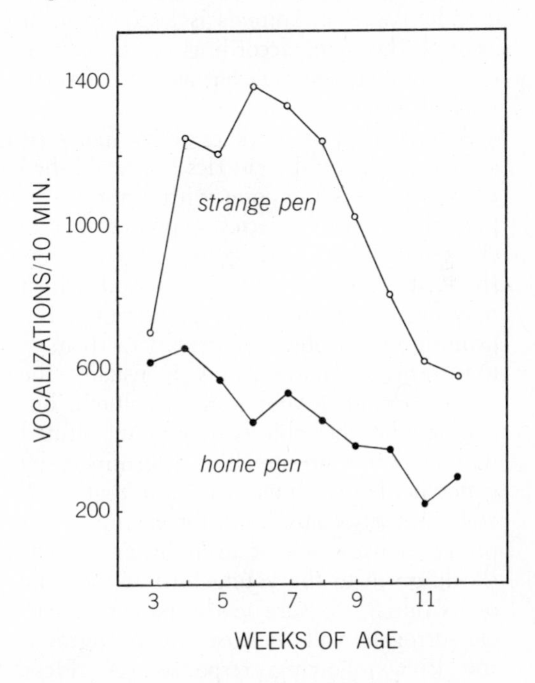

Figure 20. Average number of vocalizations in puppies in their home pen and when placed alone in a strange pen as a function of age (modified from Elliot & Scott, 1960).

tional distress, as measured by vocalization occasioned by placing a puppy in a strange pen away from its mother and siblings. It can be clearly seen that distress is greatest at around 6–7 weeks of age. Note that the curves are not simply a function of their magnitude in a normal situation—that is, in the home pen. The inference, then, is that it is around this time when dogs (and other animals) are maximally prone to forming strong attachments to others of their own or even of different species. Otherwise, separation would not produce such strong emotional arousal. More direct evidence on this point has been provided by Freedman, King, and Elliot (1961). They found that the extent to which a dog would socialize with other dogs or with human beings was diminished in direct proportion to the amount of contact it was permitted with them between about 4 and 14 weeks. Animals isolated up to or beyond this age, according to Freedman *et al.* (1961), were never able to develop normal social relationships.

A great deal of work done by many researchers in several countries has established essentially the same point with a number of precocial bird species, predominantly chickens, ducks, and geese. All of these show, at a certain critical age period, which may be only a few hours in duration, imprinting on an object presented to them at that time. In nature, this is usually the mother or other young in the clutch, but a variety of other objects may be substituted within limits presumably determined by genotype. It is of interest to note that moderate arousal of any kind, for example, that produced by a bell or even by an electric shock, given to the young bird at the time of its initial exposure to the parent or parent-surrogate will increase the strength of the later following response (cf. Hess, 1962). Complementing these data are those of C. W. Tolman (1963) showing that the age function of arousal in chicks, as measured by "wakefulness," peaks sharply at 12 hours. Since a small number of animals was involved, the observations could be repeated with profit.

Hess has developed a model, not unlike the one presented here, which predicts that the critical period occurs as a result of the intersect of the developmental curves, one for locomotor ability (increasing), the other for tameness (decreasing). It is graphically depicted in Figure 21.

The model explicitly makes locomotion important for imprinting and, in line with this notion, Hess (cf. Hess, 1962) has postulated a "law of effort" whereby the vigor of the following by the young chick of the surrogate is directly correlated with effectiveness of imprinting. Some workers, however, for example Klopfer and Hailman (1964), have disagreed with this and have suggested instead that imprinting is largely a matter of perception or of "conspicuousness" of the surrogate (Bateson, 1964). In our own model, the characteristics of input and output during the affective-meaning zone are such as to suggest that instrumental activity is not a critical feature and that only the establishment of a relation between a discriminated cue and general arousal is really important. However, the matter is still open to further experimental test.

A final study of relevance done by Thompson and O'Kieffe (1962) showed that chicks which had been imprinted showed less emotional response to a stress (auditory signal) than did chicks that had not been imprinted. It did not appear to make much difference whether the surrogate was present at the time or not. The study indicates fairly clearly that an already formed emotional attachment may yield distinct advantages in respect to the handling of stress.

The studies in imprinting in birds suggests strongly that a critical period occurs some time after birth during which social attachments can readily be formed. This conclusion is further borne out by work on monkeys done mainly in the Wisconsin Primate Laboratory under the direction of Harlow. He and his colleagues have shown very clearly that young rhesus monkeys reared away from their real mothers will develop strong affection for surrogate mothers made of terry-cloth or even of wire —though less so for the latter. When grown

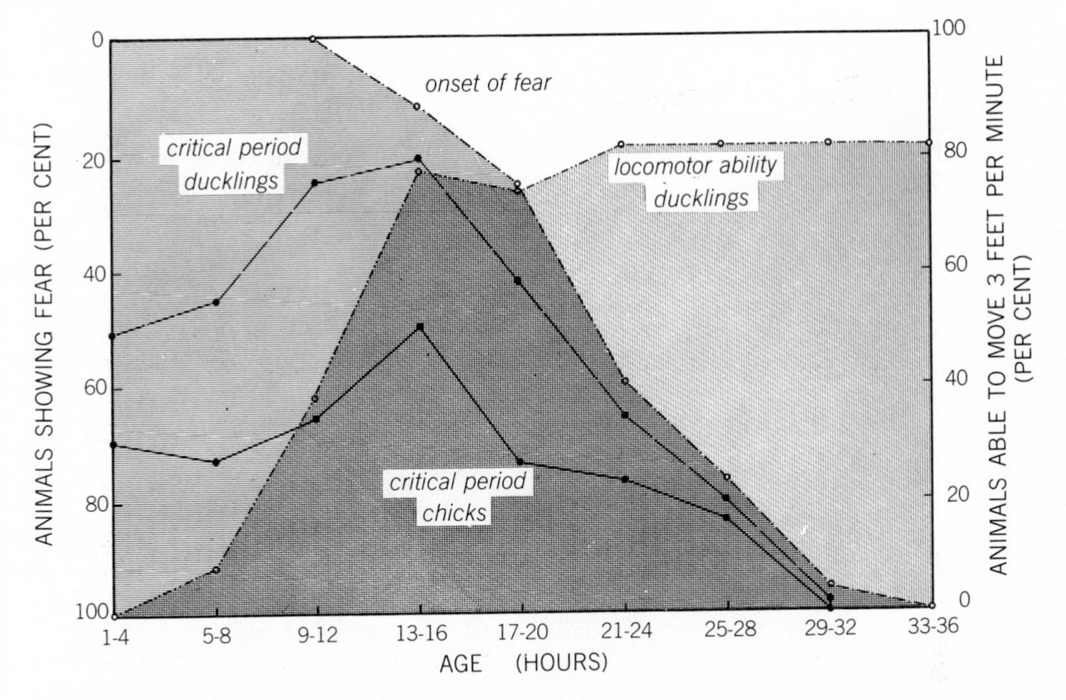

Figure 21. The hypothetical period of imprinting sensitiveness as determined by the superposition of the fear and locomotion curves, together with actual curves of imprintability in chicks and mallard ducklings as a function of age, as shown by mean test scores (Hess, 1959).

up, monkeys reared in this manner show lack of interest in other monkeys and mate only with a great amount of encouragement. Those that do mate and have young turn out to be extremely poor and even hostile mothers (Harlow, 1963). However, in spite of continued and savage rebuffs, the young show a pathetic devotion to these poor mothers, thus demonstrating again, in a converse way, the importance of this early socialization period. (For evidence contrary to Harlow's, see Meier, 1965).

Finally, there is supportive evidence at the human level. In the last ten to twenty years, much has been made of the so-called separation-experience. Bowlby (1951), one of the first to emphasize its importance, noted peculiar symptomatology developing in children who were separated from their parents—usually because of hospitalization —during the 2–4 year old period. Much of this and subsequent work has been reviewed by Casler (1961) and Gewirtz (1961). In general, it is in fairly good agreement with the animal studies that we have discussed above. There seems little doubt that children go through a socialization period and that this coincides in time with what has been designated, in rather broader terms, as the affective-meaning zone.

While it is true that few would dispute the facts that the severity of the effects of maternal deprivation must imply that a strong and important affective bond is set up between mother and child, it is also true that there is disagreement as to how this bond is set up. Thus Bowlby (1957, 1958) has emphasized possible genetic or instinctive components. In his 1958 paper he reviews several theories of the "nature of the child's tie to his mother," and offers a combination of two of them which he labels "the theory of component instinctual responses." This involves the supposition that the attachment of the child to the mother emerges from a number of unlearned behavior patterns—specifically, *sucking, clinging,* and *following,* which mature at different times during the first year of life and develop at different times. Crying and smiling on the baby's part seem to activate or "release" maternal behavior. This point of view has the advantage of explicitly relating affective behavior in human children to that demonstrated in young monkeys and young birds in those studies of the kind discussed above. To offer such a biological basis for mother-child relations and relate it successfully to psychoanalytic theory is quite a *tour de force*. The writer, being himself genetically oriented, is quite prepared to believe that certain components of infant appetitive behavior are under strong genetic control. Nonetheless, it still appears to be true, as Gewirtz points out (1961), that although broad directions may be so set, the specific attachments that occur may also involve some learning components. This is the case with chicks, ducks, and monkeys; it is in all probability even more true of human infants. It should be noted that although the model presented here has suggested classical conditioning as the general mechanism whereby particular stimuli acquire emotional significance, it does not in its nature preclude the possibility that certain parts of the environment—at a time when the animal is capable of differentiating them—can elicit innate emotional responses. Indeed, this point is made quite explicitly in Figure 1. There is no doubt that chicks and other gallinaceous birds respond positively to and imprint on only certain kinds of surrogates; likewise, that the preference of a young rhesus monkey for a furry or cloth mother is innately determined rather than learned. Many other examples could be given. However, since genotypic influences in development will be discussed more fully later on, they will not be considered further at this point. Let us sum up the major points that have been made in regard to the affective-meaning zone.

The model predicts that at a certain age level the situation in regard to differentiation in input and output will be such as to allow the formation of classical conditioning—that is, the formation of bonds between specific cues and massive arousal. Thus pleasant feelings will come to be generated by some parts of the world, unpleasant feelings by others, simple excitation by still others. Some objects may elicit different feelings under different circumstances. Thus a mother smiling may evoke only mild arousal whereas a frowning mother may produce fear. This ambivalent character of important figures in the social environment of a child is, of course, very well documented in the clinical literature.

A brief survey of studies on various developmental processes in animals and human beings suggests that the prediction made by the model is accurate. There does appear to be a period during which the world—now coming to be perceptually well articulated—is given affective coloring. To call this age-zone a "socialization period" as Scott has done (cf., e.g., 1962) is certainly correct, but such a designation is not inclusive enough. Approach and avoidance predispositions will be learned not only in respect to other living organisms of the same or of different species, but also in respect to inanimate objects. Indeed, it should be emphasized that many of the phobias and philias that are part of the psychoanalytic framework deal with objects or places or even acts, for example, agoraphobia, scoptophilia, and the many phobic responses to specific objects. It is significant that these are usually discussed (cf., for example, Fenichel, 1945) in precisely the terms we have used, namely the affective reactions elicited by specific stimuli. Little attention is given by analysts to the many ways in which persons attempt to cope with these associations. Skinnerian therapy and the conditioned-reflex theory of Wolpe and others (Wolpe, Salter, & Reyna, 1964), on the other hand, deal mainly with such coping responses. For this reason, they do not find it necessary, as do orthodox psychoanalysts, to attempt to produce in the patient a psychic regression to the Oedipal age and earlier so that personality can be rebuilt. They are dealing with a different age-zone, that is, in our schema, the third rather than the second. Which is of more importance in therapy is a moot point and will depend not only on the contingencies of the individual case but also on a postulate relating age to the enduringness of events that are stored independent of the nature of the storage. This postulate relates to the developmental parameter of growth, and we will discuss it later. Let us turn now to the third age-zone.

The instrumental-meaning zone—During this age-zone, due to the gain in output or response differentiation, complex learning gains ascendancy. Affective cues can now come to elicit coping or instrumental responses. Thus a phobia or a fixation, before simply a fact about the affective relation of the organism to some part of the world, will now start to involve a component of behavior aimed at reducing the unpleasantness or promoting the pleasantness that the relation may involve. A person suffering acutely from his stage-fright, for example, may, in his avoidance of contact with things theatrical, show great skill and rationality. He may cleverly circumvent all occasions for public speaking, or avoid all larger groups in which he might possibly be forced into a solo performance. He may associate with friends, male or female, who will act as substitutes for him in such circumstances and seek a vocation in which he is able to remain well hidden. Similarly, a rat in an instrumental avoidance situation, in the absence of obvious escape routes, may show a remarkable degree of ingenuity in discovering ways of avoiding or reducing shock. We will now consider some of the data bearing directly on the transition from the second to the third age-zone.

It is worth noting that although some behaviors remain relatively constant in structure or topography with aging, they may shift from being reflexive to being instrumental. A good example is the smiling response in infants which is first elicitable by various stimulus configurations (Ambrose, 1961) but later comes to have the properties of an instrumental activity in the sense that it is used by the child to produce or elicit rewards (Brackbill, 1958). The same is probably true of exploratory behavior which at first may oppositely be designated as an *orienting reflex* (as Russian psychologists have called it) but at a later time becomes deliberate and spontaneous. The transition from involuntary to voluntary behavior is well known, having been emphasized some time ago by McGraw (1943) in her studies of the development of behavior in human infants. She designated, for such behaviors as swimming movements, three phases: (a) reflexive; (b) disorganized; (c) voluntary, attributing the shift from one phase to another to a progressive increase of "cortical inhibitory control." The curve representing the manner in which development proceeds for another behavior—the suspension-grasp—is shown in Figure 22. It shows that the ability of an infant to suspend its own weight from a bar does not develop at all in a linear fashion. After reaching a high point during the initial phase of development, it declines during the next two phases. After the transition phase, between 100 and 400–600 days, voluntary behavior commences to lock in and the ability improves sharply.

Some important work done by Margaret Vince (1959, 1960) on birds seems to relate rather closely to the above. In studying the learning behavior of juveniles and adults of several species, Vince found evidence to suggest that although the younger birds are more highly motivated, in the sense that they will respond more vigorously than older subjects to an unfamiliar or slightly unfamiliar object, they are less able to in-

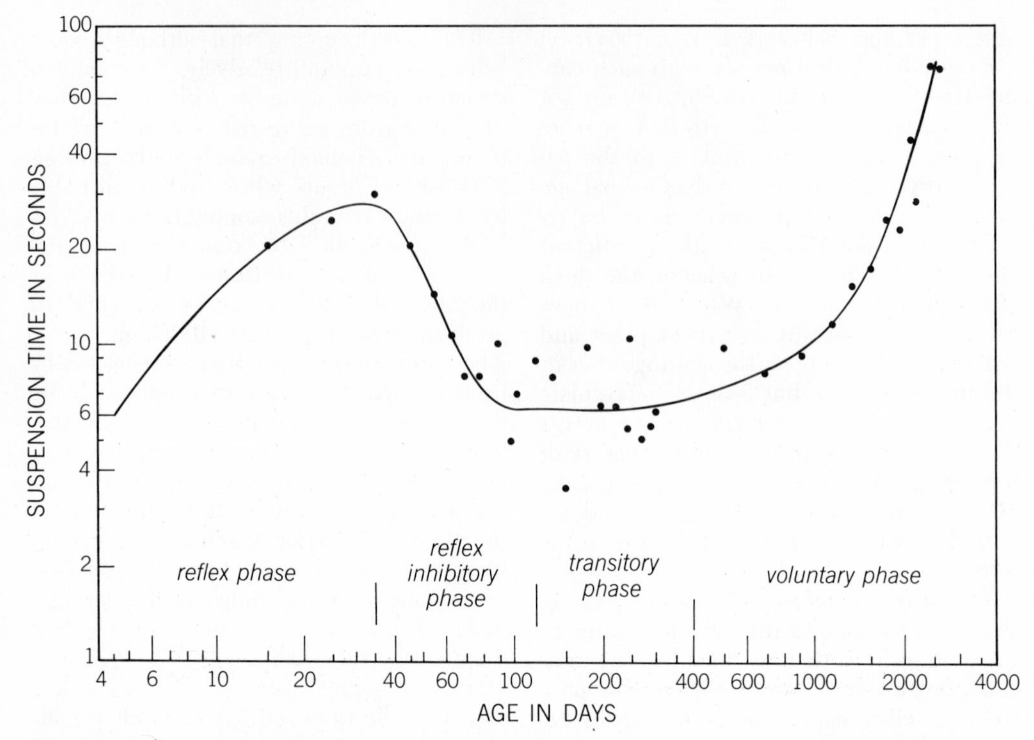

Figure 22. Suspension time for children plotted on a log scale against age. Note transition phases (McGraw, 1943, and Dennis, 1951).

hibit responses that are not rewarded. This indicates that internal inhibition becomes more "stable" with age, at least up to a point, beyond which it appears to decline again. Interpretation of these data is difficult, since other factors such as fear inevitably affect responsiveness. Vince fully discusses this and several other possibilities (Vince, 1960, 1961). As such, however, her studies do show some agreement with the notion suggested above that development of inhibition contributes a great deal to the development of adequate voluntary instrumental activity.

Also relevant are observations of affectional responses in young rhesus monkeys made by Mowbray and Cadell (1962). These investigators showed a gradual acquisition of voluntary control over movements involved in affectional behavior. For example, "clasping" remained reflexive or involuntary until about 10 days of age, was partially voluntary for two days, and became fully voluntary at about 19 days of age. Their results are very similar to those of McGraw discussed above.

The evidence suggests, then, that increasing differentiation may be accompanied by an increment in inhibition. Another study bearing on this point is one carried out by Richard F. Thompson (1962). This investigator found that bilateral destruction of auditory cortex in adult cats resulted in complete generalization to a range of tones other than that used in training. Normals, by comparison, showed sharp fall-off from the training tone. Thompson concluded with the suggestion that "removal of auditory cortex prevents the characteristic development of response inhibition, seen in the normal animal, to stimuli other than the training tone" (1962, p. 286).

A final experiment of relevance is that of Tempone (1965). This investigator showed with 8 year old children that generalization is inversely related to mental age. There appear to have been certain ambiguities in regard to the instructions given to the subjects prior to the task which make it difficult to know exactly what the results mean. However, taken at their face value, they nicely complement those of Thompson.

The studies briefly discussed above indicate that there occurs, during development, a transition from so-called involuntary to voluntary activity. Another way of putting this may be to say that there is an increase in "central autonomous processes" (Hebb, 1949). They suggest, in addition, that this transition may have something to do with cortical development and the inhibitory influence this exerts. This will result in sharp changes not only in intelligence and coping behavior, but also in personality. The organism will become less impulsive, less sweeping in its likes, dislikes, and general attitudes, more ready to accept delayed rewards, and so forth. Mischel (1958, 1961) has shown that the lack of capacity to prefer larger later rewards rather than smaller immediate ones is correlated with delinquency and immaturity. It is characteristic of the psychopath or the young child (before the "shift") that he is unable to delay gratification and acts on impulse.

This and many other features that distinguish what the writer has designated as the instrumental-meaning zone have been recently summarized for humans in a most useful manner by White (1965). He lists five categories of shifts:

a. *Changes in learning,* including a shift from narrow to broad transposition, easier reversal shifts, growing resistance to classical conditioning, growth of interference, and several others.
b. *Perceptual changes,* including shift from tactual to visual exploration, and from color to form dominance.
c. *Transition in orientation and localization,* including the development of a personal left-right, decreases in form, word, and letter reversals, increased ability to hold spatial information through disorientation, and increased tactual ability.
d. *Change in general intellectual measures,* including an IQ score that better predicts later performance and the emergence of more "abstract" behavior.
e. *Miscellaneous other transitions,* including internalization of speech, shift from syntagmatic to paradigmatic associations, increased influence of delayed auditory feedback, or shift toward planning, a better appreciation of maxima and minima, and a transition from a concern with social to more abstract forms of reward.

For a detailed exposition of the above points, the interested reader should consult White directly. One more point worth noting here is that the shift may involve, at least initially, some losses in performance. The older child, because of his increased awareness, may be more liable to the interfering effects of irrelevant components of a task. This will be, of course, prefatory to substantial gains later on.

It is obvious that the changes that occur give the appearance of a qualitative shift and make very difficult the interpretation of developmental data based on a consideration of such simple measures as error time or latency scores. Vince (1961) in her review of studies on learning as a function of age has already pointed this out. Thus, results such as those obtained by Ball and Warren (1960), in which maze-learning in chicks was found to be a direct monotonic factor of age, are probably the exception rather than the rule. However, it is possible that the variation of the Hebb-Williams maze procedure used by these investigators may have successfully dampened out all but the component of instrumental learning.

Likewise, the studies of Campbell and his associates at Princeton (Campbell & Campbell, 1962; Kirby, 1963) on the development of learned fears showed that retention of responses reflecting these was again a direct function of age. However, they found no differences between age groups in rate of acquisition. It seems likely, however, that had more complex, or more simple, responses been examined than those studied by these investigators, age changes might have emerged.

In general, the direct data we have available suggest that personality during the third age-zone has shifted considerably in emphasis. Whereas before there was a dominance of the affective, the thematic, the intuitive, and the involuntary, now there is a dominance of the instrumental, the logical, the abstract, and the voluntary in the organisms' approach to the world. Such a change, though appearing qualitative in character, must simply be the resultant of the alteration in relative importance of a set of continuous developmental curves (cf. Figure 1). Let us now consider more indirect data bearing on the third age-zone.

These deal with the effects that can be obtained by environmental manipulation of organisms during the third age-zone. Unfortunately, there are no data that give us information as specific as we might wish. Most so-called "enrichment" or "restriction" experiments have dealt with large blocks of early development more or less indiscriminately, though usually they have commenced after the earliest age-zone, for example, in animals, the post-weanling period. However, it is also true that these experiments have not deliberately involved attempts to manipulate arousal or emotionality; rather they have attempted to provide the animal with increased or decreased amounts of exposure to "rich" sensory environments and practice in behaving in such environments.

One of the first experiments done specifically on the topic was by Hebb (1949), reported by him in his book, *The Organization of Behavior*. The purpose was essentially to test Hebb's postulates that early manipulation of experience or brain have larger effects than similar manipulations later in life. A group of rats blinded at birth were compared to a group blinded at 3 months of age, two months after the latter group were blinded. The early-blinded group turned out to be much worse on Hebb-Williams maze performance than the late-blinded group. However, it is uncertain whether such an effect was due to the greater age of the late-blinded group or the fact that they had had more experience, or both factors in interaction. Furthermore, the absence of a nonblinded control group prohibited the possibility of knowing how much the late-blinded animals had been affected.

In spite of these difficulties, the study did show that some treatment could affect intellectual capacity more readily if it was administered some time in early life and, for this reason, was of importance. It led, in fact, to a large number of studies concerned with the effects of enriched or restricted early environment on later behavior. J. McV. Hunt (1961) has made an excellent critical summary of many of these. By and large, they agree with Hebb's findings. They have also added a good deal of more specific information that is relevant to our discussion here.

In the first place, it seems to be true that, whatever effects having to do with complex intellectual activity ensue on some treatment (e.g., enrichment of environment), these cannot be obtained before a certain period. Thus Denenberg and Morton (1962) have shown that intelligence is most readily altered in rats by a post-weanling treatment. Before that period, some experimental treatment affected mostly temperamental or motivational characteristics. Winston (1963) using mice obtained data agreeing with this conclusion as did also Thompson and Kano (1965). Likewise, Woods (1959) has shown that treatments applied *after* a certain period appear to have a smaller effect, in terms of their reversibility. Thus we seem again to have a critical period during which residua relating to instrumental learning may optimally be set in the organism. Note, however, that the reason for the post-critical-period decline may be more complicated than that for the earlier periods. Previously, this lay in the fact that differentiation proceeded to the point where global stimulation and global responding were less dominant in the organisms' behavior. During the instrumental-meaning zone, however, further maturation brings only increasing dominance of the characteristics that define the zone. Thus it cannot be the "availability" of the input-output relation that declines. Rather, the increasing difficulty of producing changes in instrumental behavior with increasing age must be mainly due to a diminishing plasticity. This factor we have not considered in any detail, so far, since we have defined it more as a property of the dimension of growth rather than of the dimension of differentiation. We will return to it later.

A second point of information obtained by the studies on enriched and restricted early experience relates to the kinds of dimensions that may be involved in the treatment effects. Evidently, both perceptual and motor components are important. Though Hymovitch (1952) originally argued that perceptual experience alone was crucial, both Forgays and Forgays (1952) and Forgus (1955a, 1955b) have shown that particularly in a test in which visual cues are reduced to a minimum, animals reared with plenty of opportunity for actual motor exploration of objects are superior to those reared with enriched visual experience alone. Some of Forgus' data (1955a) are summarized in Table 4.

TABLE 4

PERFORMANCE ERRORS ON LATER MAZE-TESTS OF RATS GIVEN VISUAL OR VISUAL-MOTOR EXPERIENCE IN EARLY LIFE (FORGUS, 1955a)

	Visual	Visual-Motor
With visual cues	33.36	27.79
Visual cues reduced	83.14	60.50

It is clear that perceptual experience alone is apparently inferior to perceptual and motor exploration together. Just what part the exploration plays is uncertain. The opportunity to explore directly the enriched environment might simply promote better perceptual learning; that is, the purely motor component could be irrelevant. Held's studies (Held & Bonsom, 1961; Held & Heim, 1963) on reafferent feedback, however, suggest that the afferent aspects are important. There is a need for more work that satisfactorily separates the various dimensions of enriched or restricted early experience so as to specify the contribution that each makes to later behavior.

Observations on human beings are even more uncertain. Since no experimental manipulation of the environments of young children is ethically feasible, it is difficult to sort out causes of the often dramatic effects produced by such treatments as orphanage rearing, or the extreme confinement occasionally imposed in aberrant families. There seems little doubt that intellectual ability as well as sociability and temperament may suffer, as Goldfarb (1955) has pointed out. Deficits are commonly found in abstract reasoning, playfulness, capacity to delay or inhibit responses, and ability to concentrate. What aspects of the restriction are responsible, however, is not really known, since not only the initial experience but also the later assessment of it are both highly complex. Some of the relevant literature has been summarized by Bowlby (1951), Casler (1961), and Gewirtz (1961), as well as by writers of a number of chapters in Solnit and Provence (1963) and in Hoffman and Hoffman (1964).

Before leaving the topic of differentiation, one final aspect of it must be discussed. Almost all we have said so far has related to the *nature of early experience*—that is, to the kinds of things that are most likely to happen to an organism, given a certain state of differentiation. The other aspect of this dimension concerns the *importance* of a given experience. The term "importance" is taken to refer to the *size, duration, generality,* and *reversibility* of the residua of the experience. Now one reason why some event impinging on the organism when it is young has a greater effect than when the organism is old must be because it is less differentiated. At an early age, the categories of experience and action are few in number. An influence exerted on one of these categories so as to change it in a certain direction may then affect all subcategories that later differentiate out from the original one. Thus development has, like evolution, a branching character whereby the earlier categories have a higher or broader taxonomic rank and the more recent categories have a lower taxonomic rank. This is to say that a decision taken earlier has many more outcomes than a decision taken later, other things being equal. To give a concrete example, we may consider a boy of 4 who is treated cruelly by a father as compared to a boy of 16 similarly treated. In the former case, it is likely that the outcome of such treatment may result in an adult who dislikes or is afraid of all men or even all people; in the latter case, however, it is probable that only that particular father will be disliked and then perhaps only in specific situations. Thus an early fear-provoking situation tends to result in generalized fear later on. Development is a complex stochastic process. Few alternatives are open to an organism when it is young and a choice among them must influence all subsequent choices. This is not to say that reversals cannot occur. For example, a young person may decide, at an early age, to be a physician, and this decision may affect many aspects of his life. But he may still change his mind later on and become an artist instead, though this may now be much more difficult to do.

We will now leave the dimension of differentiation and turn to the factors of "growth" and "organization." Much less is known about these. All we will be able to do is to suggest certain kinds of research strategies that may usefully contribute to a better understanding of the biophysical basis of personality.

Outcomes of Changes in Growth

Growth has been defined as an increment in the amount of a system. Increases occur in the number of parts and in the size or mass of parts. We have suggested that this may result in greater redundancy and that for this reason the adult may have better buffering and greater efficiency than the young system. It should be emphasized that the relationship between growth and buffering characteristics is hypothetical. It is obviously true, however, that in purely physical terms the inertia of a large mass is greater than that of a small mass. In other words, it takes more energy to effect changes in the former than in the latter. Living systems are homeostatic, or self-correcting. We might thus deduce that young organisms can be readily influenced but can also readjust rather quickly by homeostasis, provided the stress is not too great; whereas, older systems should be less readily influenced but, once they are, be less able to realize a normal state again.

These notions appear to square with common observation. Young children catch diseases or break bones more easily than adults. However, at least up to a point, their bodies quickly repair themselves. Adults, on the other hand, are much more resistant to disease or bodily damage, but once they contract something, take longer to recuperate. Some of the reasons for these differences, of course, relate to experience rather than mainly to the intrinsic properties of young versus adult systems. For example, adults, by exposure to disease or by inoculation, may *acquire* active immunity of resistance to many diseases. But it is also likely that the expression of *natural* immunity is different in the two cases for the reasons we have discussed.

Other evidence indicates some degree of instability in young animals compared with adults. Temperature control, for example, is notoriously poor in infant rats. When the mother leaves her young, the ambient temperature falls and body temperature decreases. Oxygen consumption first rises and then falls (Hahn *et al.,* 1961). The data are summarized in Figure 23. It is for this rea-

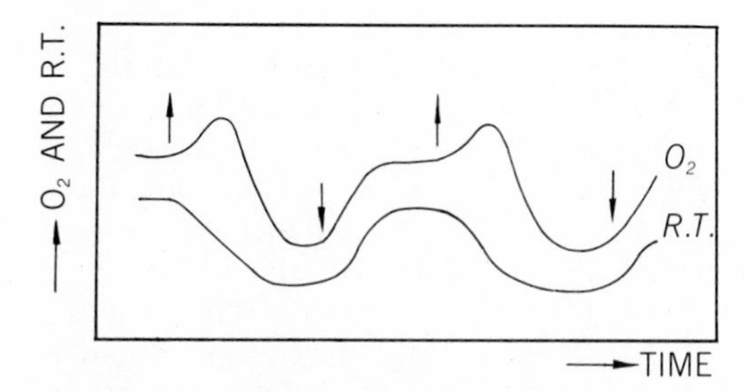

Figure 23. Diagrammatic representation of changes in body temperature (R.T.) and oxygen consumption (O_2) in infant rats which are dependent on the presence and absence of the mother animal. Upward arrows indicate that mother is leaving nest (Hahn *et al.,* 1961).

son that Schaefer (1963) has suggested that the effects of handling or stimulation in neonatal rats may be due partly or entirely to the temperature changes ensuing on the treatment.

Many other similar deficiencies of homeostasis in the newborn have been noted. An excellent discussion of them can be found in the volume edited by Wolstenholme and O'Connor (1961). R. A. McCance, in the first chapter in the book, states the general problem succinctly:

Experience has taught us that in surroundings which would not upset an adult, the body temperature and chemical composition of the newly born often exhibit wide deviations from the conventional steady states of infancy or later life. It is often said in consequence that the newly born animal is "unstable." The causes of these departures from the normal are many and various, but there would appear to be a general principle underlying them all.

Any biological stimulus which provokes a departure from the conventional "normal" initiates responses, which are designed to restore the original steady state. The responses tend to be much weaker in the newly born than they are in adults, though, as in the adult, they may become stronger as the departure from the "normal" increases. If this is so, and if the stimulus persists, a new steady state may be established when the response has become sufficiently effective to prevent further departure from the conventional normal, although not adequate to correct the abnormality (1961, p. 1).

The situation is undoubtedly very much more complex than we have depicted it. At present, however, in terms of research strategies, it would probably not be profitable to attempt any closer articulation of the problem than that already presented. Investigation simply of the mechanism of adaptation in young as compared to adult systems should yield interesting and useful data.

Apart from the changes that some environmental event may produce immediately in a young animal, we must also be concerned with long-term residual effects. Thus we must ask, for a given type of situation, whether its importance, as the term has been defined, varies inversely with age. In more specific terms, does the replication of neuronal and glial cells, their greater mass, and the larger amounts of inhibitory and excitatory chemical substances that ensue from growth, also mean a change in the degree to which some experience may be retained? The notion that sheer brain size is important in this respect has been put forward forcefully by Rensch (1957). He has attempted to document this point in a series of experiments comparing learning and retention in an assortment of animal species varying in body and brain size, for example, mice, dogs, horses, and elephants. His data appear to indicate that the larger species are superior, though admittedly there are great difficulties in this kind of comparison. He attributes this to the greater size and density of neurons in the larger brains and the greater richness of interconnections. If Rensch's conclusion is correct, we might expect to find that older systems, with their larger brains, are superior to younger in respect to learning and memory. The data of Campbell and his associates, cited above, are in agreement with this idea, at least for the fairly complex kind of situation that these workers examined. Though it is a very commonly held view that many kinds of learning and retention are superior in the young, language being perhaps the prime example, the evidence for this is anecdotal and ambiguous. Indeed, it is just as likely that, given the total and intensive level of exposure which the child gets to language and other forms of learning, the adult would show faster acquisition and better retention. The writer's own experience accords with this view. He was exposed only to French for the first four and a half years of his life and having moved then to England, forgot this language and spent the next fourteen years relearning it. McClelland (1965) has taken somewhat the same position, asserting that many important segments of human personality, for example the achievement need, can be altered as easily in adulthood as in childhood. Citing other workers of this persuasion, he says: "They retain a simple faith in the infinite plasticity of human behavior in which one response is just like any other and any one can be 'shaped up' (strengthened by reward)—presumably even an 'achievement' response as produced by a subject in a test" (1965, p. 322). In support of this view, he has presented the results of a practical experiment in which he was able to produce, by means of a relatively short-term program, radical changes in the need structure of members of a different culture. Whether these alterations were permanent, however, remains to be seen. It is the writer's feeling that the kinds of long-lasting changes allegedly produced by missionaries are probably via mission schools and manipulation of the young of that culture rather than by manipulation of the adults. We have offered above some theoretical reasons for this hypothesis, these having to do with the lack of differentiation and relatively poor buffering or instability in young systems. Both of these properties imply that events occurring earlier in life should have a more long-lasting influence than those occurring later. Actual data bearing on this problem are slim and, in addition, it has been conceptualized at a level that is rather broad. Let us look at a few examples.

Many studies have been done on the effects of early stimulation. But, it is unfortunate that very few of them have employed adult control groups. They do not, therefore, really allow any statement to be made about *early* experience, though most of them infer that it is essentially with this that they are dealing. Several exceptions to this are the studies of Dolittle and Meade (1957), Brookshire, Littman, and Stewart (1961), and Ader (1959). The results of these have been negative. That is to say, they demonstrated that a variety of experiences given prior to testing could indeed alter performance, but that this effect was independent of age. Some of Ader's results are summarized in Table 5. It is clear from

TABLE 5

Effects of Manipulation Early as Against Late in Life on Emotionality (Open-Field Activity) in Rats (Modified from Ader, 1959)

	Handled	Nonhandled
Early	34.60	26.67
Late	20.08	16.64

these that the earliness at which an experience is imposed has little effect.

On the other hand, several experimenters have obtained positive results. Among these are Hunt (1941), Wolf (1943), Hebb (1947), Hymovitch (1952), and Woods (1959). Consequently, the whole matter must be regarded as still being in some doubt. It is highly likely that there are genotypic components operating in respect to young-adult differences in responsiveness to stimulation and that variation in respect to these may be responsible for some of the differences between studies. Indeed, there is great variation in the rates of normal development of physiological function in different species (cf. Himwich, 1962). This fact alone would suggest that the same treatment applied to such different genotypes as represented by the guinea-pig and the rabbit at the same age after birth may have quite different effects, since the target systems in each case will have quite different levels of stability. Within one species such as the rat, the variation is likely to be less but may still be considerable enough to contribute significant variance to any results obtained. Furthermore, within one single individual separate parts develop at different rates. Again, this makes any general statement about the whole organism rather suspect.

A good example of the difficulties involved is afforded by the work on the effects of early brain injury. This is a complex field, since apart from anything else, the problems of control over lesion size are great. We will now discuss briefly the few studies done on this subject.

Hebb, reviewing some of the work on brain injury a number of years ago (1942), noted that in the adult human clean surgical removal of brain outside the speech area appeared to have little effect on psychometric IQ. This led him to formulate the hypothesis that:

In any test performance, there are two factors involved, the relative importance of which varies with the test: one factor being present intellectual power, of the kind essential to normal development; the other being the lasting changes of perceptual organization and behavior induced by the first factor during the period of development.

Hebb finds that early brain injury, however, has rather larger and unselective effects on measured intelligence, notably vocabulary scores. Thus, the first factor—which corresponds to a capacity to develop new patterns of response—is more readily alterable by injury in young than in mature humans, this probably being because development of this kind of ability requires more cerebral efficiency than does its functioning at a later level. In our terms, the infant brain is much less well buffered than the adult brain. There is less of it, and the amounts of critical chemical substances per unit mass of tissue are smaller. Work done on animals, on the other hand, for example, that of Kennard (1936) and of Tsang (1937) appears to show a lack of agreement with Hebb's findings. These studies show that infant animals have a much greater resistance to brain damage. Thus Kennard's infant monkeys with injury to cortical areas 4 and 6 showed better recovery of motor function than adults. Likewise, Tsang's study showed that striate area ablations had less effect on the problem-solving ability of rats if imposed early in life.

Thus the evidence appears to be contradictory. It is possible that the difference lies in the fact that most laboratory animals, unlike human beings, are reared in semi-restricted conditions. Were they to be raised in enriched environments, it is possible that greater protection against the effects of brain injury might be afforded the adult. Indeed, this notion is suggested by work of Schwartz (1964) who found that early brain lesions in rats produced significant effects only if coupled with restricted environmental rearing. His results are shown in Figure 24. There is clearly a rich area for investigation here. More work is needed particularly on the effects of brain stem and limbic area lesions in neonatal animals as compared with the already well-known residua in adults.

Little else can be added to this section beyond one cautionary note. The kind of work described above only partially gets at the differences due to growth, since young animals are different from adults not only in respect to their mass but also in respect to their degree of differentiation. To unconfound these two variables may be difficult or impossible. Perhaps the only way may be by comparisons of young-adult differences in several species which show variation in respect to developmental characteristics. For example, a neonatal rat is

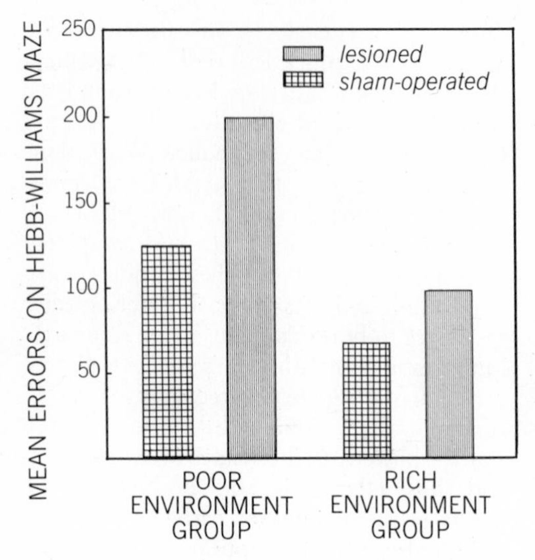

Figure 24. Learning deficits in rats as a result of neonatal cortical lesions (posterior surface). The effect varies as a function of environmental rearing conditions (Schwartz, 1964).

relatively poorly differentiated and also small as compared to its adult counterpart; whereas a newborn guinea-pig or a newly-hatched chick is rather well differentiated but much smaller than the mature animals of the species. It may be for this reason that chicks, at a relatively young age, are quite capable of most of the repertory of responses of the adult, for example, crowing, male copulatory behavior, special courtship patterns and fighting, and will show these if injected with suitable dosages of androgens (Hamilton, 1938; Andrew, 1963). Thus the difference between young and adult in this case is apparently due less to the absence of differentiation in the young, but rather to the lack of sufficient quantities of a specific chemical compound—in this case, the male sex hormone. It is very doubtful whether similar treatment would produce such precocial behavior in the young rat of comparable age, though, to the knowledge of the writer, such a comparison has not been made. The problems facing the investigator in this area are certainly formidable but any answers obtained will represent a basic contribution to our understanding of the origins of personality and intelligence.

Outcomes of Changes in Organization

Given that aging involves increments in growth and differentiation, it is hypothesized that there also occurs an increasing relatedness between parts of the developing system. Both Lewin (1951) and Werner (1960) have suggested concepts that designate essentially such a process. Thus Lewin states (1951, p. 100) in rather an elaborate discussion:

> If development in behavior led merely to an increased variety of behavior, one might expect the conduct of an individual to become more and more chaotic or at least more and more unconnected. This is obviously not the case. Parallel to the increasing differentiation goes a development according to which an increasingly greater variety of parts is included in *one* unit of action.

He goes on to distinguish three aspects of the organizational process as follows:

a. *Complexity of units*—This is similar to what has been defined here under the rubric of growth—that is, an increase in the number of subparts contained in one unit of action. Thus perceptually and motorically, for example, the child, as he gets older, comes to be able to handle more blocks at one time for playing, and also becomes able to play or work for longer durations of time.

b. *Hierarchical organization*—The way in which subunits are united becomes hierarchical, in the sense that units connected by one principle or goal may be under the indirect control of a higher principle or goal. Thus the subgoals of moving the legs in unison and moving the arms a certain way may both be governed by the general goal of swimming.

c. *Complicated organization*—By this concept, Lewin means the increasing ability of the developing child to stop and later resume some unit of activity and also to intermingle and still keep separate two consequences. For example, a book may be read for a while, then put aside to be taken up again later. Likewise, a child may be able to hum a tune while playing with blocks.

This brief resume hardly does justice to Lewin's long and subtle analysis of development. However, the level of abstraction at which he writes is rather remote (as many psychologists have found) from the possibility of empirical test. The simple definition given here of organization as relatedness of differentiated subunits is perhaps sufficient as a starting point.

It is true that relatedness is, on the other hand, a concept so broad as to require at least some further specification, particularly at the empirical level. Two approaches that may have the possibility of opening up research seem worth comment.

The first is that of neuropsychology. Hebb (1949) in his book, *The Organization of Behavior,* had as his major concern the problem of precisely how stable organizations are built up in the brain. His solution to it represented a kind of compromise between the field theorists such as Lashley and Kohler who were nicely able to explain perceptual generalization but had trouble with memory, and the S-R theorists, such as Hull, who could explain memory but had difficulty with generalization. Both of these problems are very basic ones and deal with the degree of predictability in a living system, memory being predictable over time with situation constant and generalization being predictable across stimulus situations with time constant. They both therefore involve organized behavior. Note, however, that a distinction must be drawn between predictability that arises simply from a failure to differentiate stimuli and one that involves a perceived equivalence at a higher level of previously differentiated stimuli. An infant is highly organized in the sense that many aspects of the world will evoke the same response. But, as we have already suggested, such simple generalization occurs less readily with increasing cortical development. Thus, in a sense, differentiation works against organization. As fast as one level of stability is reached, it is liable to be broken up again by the other factor. The work of McGraw cited above shows this quite clearly in respect to motor organizations in young children. It is also clearly implied by Gesell's principle of self-regulatory fluctuation. He says:

> The organism at times seems to retreat from a locus of maturity which it has already attained. Temporarily, such a retreat may look like an abandonment. It would be an abandonment if it continued on one tangent. The course of development, however, being spiral, turns back toward the point of departure; and it does not return precisely to this point. It returns to the same region but at a higher level. (Gesell, 1946, p. 317)

In attempting to deal with the growing organization of brain cells during development, Hebb formulated the concept of "cell assembly"—the spatial arrangements of neural elements, and the "phase sequence"—that is, the temporal characteristics of the cell assemblies as they fire off over time. These are interesting notions and may square well with reality. Furthermore, the two-phase process by which in Hebb's theory such organizations are laid down suggests a gradual transition from less to more organized behavior. The check on overorganization, whereby, if the process continued, everything in the brain would become linked to everything else, is given by the concept of inhibiting cells. Not much was known about these when Hebb wrote, so that it was left to Milner (1957) to see their usefulness in formulating a more realistic concept of the fluctuating manner in which organization proceeds.

The second possible approach to understanding the concept of organization is that of psychometrics. It arises from the fact that organization implies covariation or correlation. Empirically, this means examining the manner in which the elements in a correlation matrix change with age. An example of such a study is afforded by Balinsky (1941). He administered the ten different subtests of the Wechsler-Bellevue intelligence scale to age groups of 9, 12, 15, 25–29, 35–44, and 50–59. For each age level, he computed intercorrelations between subtests. As shown in Figure 25, the results indicate that the average intercorrelation declines from 9 to 25–29 years and then

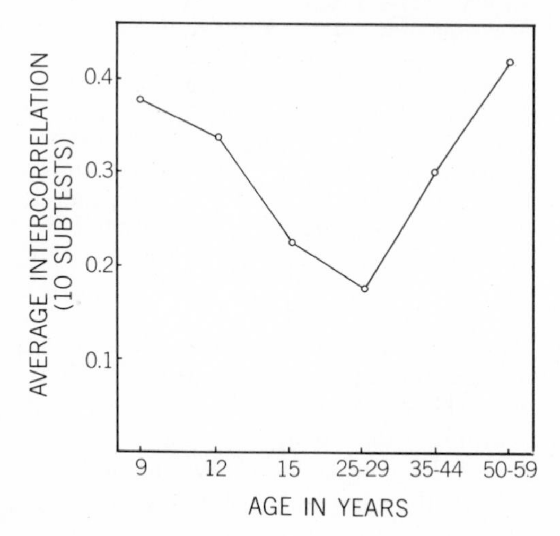

Figure 25. Change in the average size of intercorrelations between Wechsler-Bellevue subtests as a function of chronological age (Balinsky, 1941).

rises again to beyond its initial level. Likewise, the proportion of total variance accounted for by the first factor extracted followed the same relationship with age. This suggests that between 9 and 27 there is increasing specialization of ability and after this there occurs a reorganization to a new kind of general ability which permits the more flexible utilization of various abilities for different tasks. General ability at an early age represents the fact that the individual makes use of several abilities in order to solve a particular problem because, as yet, he has no specialized method for attacking it; but general ability in the adult represents a more integrated organization. This is an appealing formulation and fits well with the ideas of McGraw and Gesell.

In addition, Balinsky showed that the factorial composition of the correlation matrices was also qualitatively different at each age-level. This is summarized in Table 6. It is clear that a Wechsler-Bellevue score

TABLE 6

Factor Structure of Wechsler-Bellevue at Different Ages

Age	Factor Structure
9	G, Verbal
12	Verbal, Performance, Social Perception
15	Verbal, Performance (another not interpretable)
25–29	Verbal, Performance, Memory (Restriction in solution)[a]
35–44	Verbal, Performance, Memory
50–59	G, Performance, Reasoning

[a]This factor has high loadings for Information, Object Assembly, and Block design. The interpretation is uncertain.

is going to mean qualitatively different underlying structures at different ages. Further evidence on this point at the preschool level has recently been summarized by Meyers and Dingman (1960). It is very clear from their survey of a large number of studies that personality and ability are organized quite differently at different age-levels. What seems to be lacking, however, is any demonstration that two or more performance or ability variables, measurable in an equivalent fashion at different age-levels, show a systematic change in their covariation from the very young organism to the adult. Balinsky's data do provide such information, but unfortunately do not deal with age-levels below 9 years. Inspection of his correlational tables for the range he covers, however, show no simple increments with age in the degree of relationship between any small groups of specific variables.

The above discussion of the organization

parameter and work relating to it clearly does not take us very far. It is intended merely to pinpoint some modes of attacking the problem of development at a more specific level than that which characterizes most work in the field. Current work of the Piaget-Bruner variety on cognitive structure in children and language acquisition is interesting and original. But it does not appear to be predicated on models that involve basic developmental variables, that are capable of empirical explication, and that at the same time are abstract enough to allow a contrast to be made between youth and maturity across a broad range of species. The concepts of organization, plus differentiation and growth, as they have here been defined, may well represent suitable building-blocks for such models. For one thing, they are genuinely developmental parameters and are common to both psychological and biological development (cf., e.g., Weisz, 1959), and for another, they are relevant to the development of any phenotypic character in almost any species. Furthermore, they do appear to be as empirically tractable in psychology as they have proved to be in embryology.

Let us now attempt to summarize the major points that have emerged from our discussion of differentiation, growth, and organization, and explore the manner in which they may complement each other.

Summary of the Model

The problem which we initially considered was the determination of personality and ability structure by events occurring during the biophysical development of the organism. We suggested that development may involve stages or zones during which certain kinds of functions are maximally dominant and hence most available to environmental influences. The dimension used to define these age-zones was *differentiation*. By separating input as against output differentiation it was possible to demarcate three age-zones, each characterized by a certain kind of input-output relation and storage mechanism. These were: the temperament-adaptation zone, involving mainly habituation learning; the affective-meaning zone, involving mainly classical conditioning; and the instrumental-meaning zone, involving mainly instrumental or complex learning. Increments in differentiation—and hence the transition from one zone to the next—were postulated to arise from an increase in some inhibitory process.

Such a schema appears to fit a good deal of diverse data on both lower animals and human beings. Furthermore, not only does it predict what an organism should be like at a given age, but, in addition, it predicts the kinds of alterations that should ensue from some environmental contingency impinging on the organism at a particular age-level.

It must be emphasized again that the differentiation concept tells us mainly about the broad modes in which the young organism can perceive the world, respond to it, and store such information. It says only a little, however, about relative degree of plasticity as a function of age-level—a problem made quite explicit in the common phrase—"the *importance* of early experience." The parameter relating to this we have postulated to be mainly *growth,* this being defined in terms of size, mass, or redundancy. According to this definition, growth must have something to do with buffering, or plasticity. From this arises the general postulate that younger organisms, at least beyond a certain threshold, are more readily influenced than mature organisms. Not all have supported this idea, however, commonsensical as it may seem. In addition, the empirical evidence available is by no means conclusive. Whatever the case, the concept of growth relates to the manner in which size, duration, and reversibility of some effect resulting from experience relate to the physical age of the organism.

The final dimension of *organization* was defined in terms of relatedness of subparts of the living system. We suggested that, in general, this increases with age, though any simple incremental change must be constantly being disturbed by parallel alterations in degree of differentiation. The continued dialectic between the two during development must thus produce the spiralling kind of fluctuation that Gesell noted (Gesell, 1946). Taken by itself, at a fairly simple level, however, organization must relate to the particular content that is stored by an organism at a certain age, given the mental equipment characteristic of this age. For example, two components of experience may be strongly associated. An environmental experience that affects one of them may then come to affect the other also. One might be a father who is cruel to his child. The strong fear that comes to be generated by him through classical conditioning may then generalize to something associated with him, for example, a pipe, his slippers, his dog, and so on. If the experience is sufficiently intense, it may leave relatively permanent effects on the child, generalizing to other components of experience that come to be added to the initial organization, as he gets older. It must be noted, of course, that many organizations—particularly those of an intellectual variety ("cold cognitions") are undoubtedly dependent on both learning and maturation. This seems to be the view of Piaget and many others who follow an epigenetic approach to the problem of development.

The analysis we have made, then, attempts to specify in terms of three dimensions what an organism should be like at certain ages and the residua that should result from environmental impingements at such ages. It must be strongly emphasized that, although the specifications and predictions made fit well with both human and subhuman developmental data, they are not based directly on the latter but rather on an explication of the three basic characteristics of development. These deal with the broad categories of input-output relationships, the stability and plasticity of the organism, and the structure or content of the organism's experience. Our treatment of them is perhaps of a rather crude and preliminary character. Nevertheless, it does contain in it certain directives for future research and theorizing that may turn out to be profitable. One indication of this is that it does bear a close similarity to at least three other schemas that have been derived by other investigators from quite different starting points. Let us now look at these briefly.

The first has been put forward by Scott (1962). Although he bases it mostly on empirical observations of puppy behavior, he has suggested its general applicability to a wide variety of living forms. Table 7 summarizes his schema for the dog and compares it with that of Nice (1943) for the song sparrow.

It is clear that there is a fairly close correspondence between these empirically established stages and the theoretically defined age-zones suggested here. Scott cites a large number of studies on many species to support his notions and hence this particular article (Scott, 1962) is worth a careful reading.

A second schema is that of Brookshire, Littman, and Stewart (1961). On the basis of an interesting study of the residua of early trauma in rats, to which we have already referred, they have offered a "three-factor thesis." The three factors are "pure shock effect," "acquired fear," and "instrumental-habit." These obviously represent special cases of the broader categories of input-output relations that we have postulated as having a certain degree of dominance at each of the three age-zones. Again, Brookshire *et al.*'s three factors are empirically derived, and, in fact, suggested rather than demonstrated by their data. Nor were they able to relate them separately to particular age-levels. However, their set of six experiments represents a most interesting line of work certainly deserving to be followed up.

The final analogue to the model presented here is that of Gray Walter (1956). By gathering EEG records on several hun-

TABLE 7

PERIODS OF DEVELOPMENT FOR THE DOG AND THE SONG SPARROW
DATA ARE BASED ON STUDIES OF SCOTT (1962) AND NICE (1943)

PUPPY Name of Period	Period Length (Weeks)	Initial Event	SONG SPARROW Name of Period	Period Length (Days)	Initial Event
I Neonatal	0–2	Birth, nursing	Stage 1 (nestling)	0–4	Hatching, gaping
II Transition	2–3	Eyes open	Stage 2	5–6	Eyes open
III Socialization	3–10	Startle to sound	Stage 3	7–9	Cowering—first fear reactions
			Stage 4 (fledgling)	10–16	Leaving nest—first flight
			Stage 5	17–28	Full flight
IV Juvenile	10–	Final weaning	Stage 6 (juvenile)	29–	Independent feeding

dred children, he has plotted the relative prominence at different age-levels of delta, theta, and alpha rhythms. "Prominence" is defined in terms of both "amplitude and abundance of activity together as a product" (1956, p. 134). His results are shown in Figure 26. The resemblance these graphs have to our own (cf. Fig. 7) will be obvious. Walter next attempts to educe properties of personality at each age level, given the psychological correlates of the different wave forms. He delineates three age-periods. The first of these, involving a predominance of delta waves, he characterizes as being governed by a "search for peace" or "equilibration." During the second period, with its prominence of theta rhythms, he suggests the personality is concerned pri-

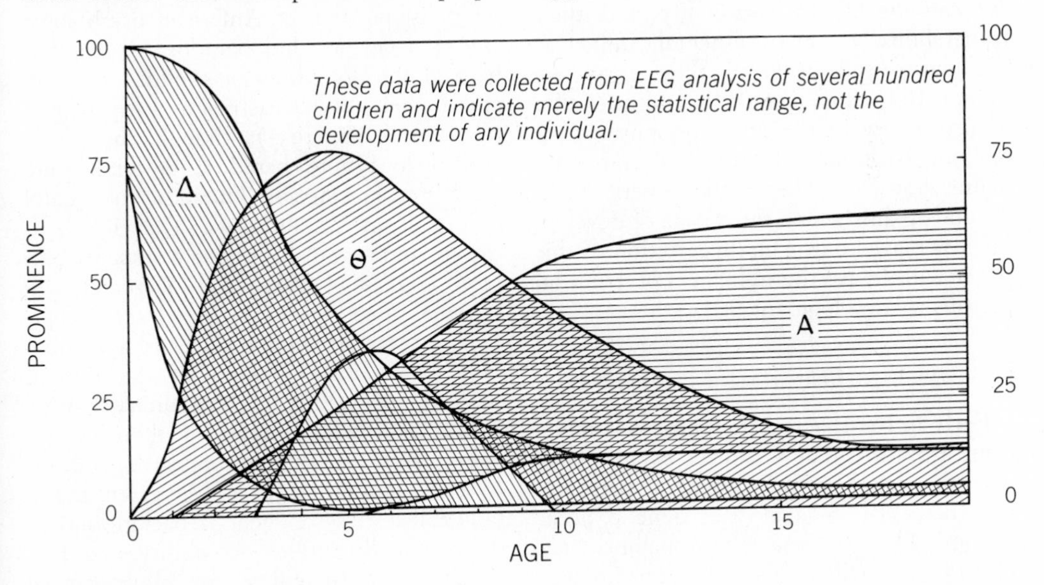

Figure 26. "Prominence" of EEG wave forms as a function of age (Walter, 1956).

marily with pleasure as a specific entity. In the normal adult, according to Walter, theta waves can be obtained by the withdrawal of some pleasing stimulus. Thus the dimension of major relevance involves equilibration or arousal-level in respect to particular stimuli. Finally, the dominance of the alpha rhythm during the third period indicates, according to Walter, a primary concern with pattern—or, in our terms, with instrumental activity independent of emotional involvement. It must be said that Gray Walter's schema goes a good way beyond the actual data he has collected. The amount of interpretation is high. There are serious difficulties involved in measuring relative dominance of types of EEG wave as well as in assessing the supposed personality correlates of these, to say nothing of putting the two together. In spite of such ambiguities, however, the general ideas are interesting ones and suggest potentially productive areas of research.

These three schemata taken together agree with our own notion that there may be fundamental age-zones occurring during development, and that transition from one to the other produces a rearrangement of the components of personality and their vulnerability to environmental influence. Without consideration of these facts, we cannot fully understand the organization of personality in the adult organism. One additional category of great importance remains, however. This is the genetic background against which the drama of development is played out. The final section of this paper will discuss the influences of genes on personality development.

Genotype and Personality Development

Early in the chapter, the point was made quite explicitly that whatever events influence the structure and content of personality, these operate against a genetic background. Heredity sets the probability that an organism will respond in a certain way not only across a wide range of environments, but also in particular environments. Behavior is a phenotype and like any other organismic character can be related *in at least some of its aspects* to genotype. The fact that a person speaks German may be quite independent of heredity; but the fact that he was able to learn it quickly, the fact that he can pronounce it aptly, and the fact that he uses it with literary skill call in part for a genetic explanation.

Such a point of view has been, up till recently, rather inimical to American psychology. Less than two decades ago, in fact, Pastore (1949) argued that a positive attitude toward hereditary influences was correlated with authoritarian attitudes. This rather extreme suggestion was perhaps understandable at the time it was made, following the extravagances of the Nazi position on race. There is little else to commend it, however. We must assume, if we are to operate as scientists, that although biases may exist in respect to the work we do, they are less crude than those on which Pastore has written, and emerge slowly from a subtle unfolding of historical and sociological influences. To look at the other side of the coin, it may be profitable at this point to trace the origins of the environmentalist position of American psychology.

It is a curious and paradoxical fact that both of the disciplines of scientific psychology, namely, psychometrics and experimental (Cronbach, 1957), though they have tended to ignore heredity, descend quite directly from Darwin. The father of mental testing, Francis Galton, was Darwin's half-cousin, and two of his major works, *Hereditary Genius* (1869) and *Inquiry into Human Faculty and Its Development* (1883), were attempts to describe systematically behavioral variation of the human species and specify its hereditary causes. Those men who followed Galton in England, such as Pearson, Spearman, Burt, Eysenck, and others, to a large extent maintained his stress on genetic background as the major determiner of ability and personality. The mental testing movement in America, however, abandoned this tradition, opting instead for a position that was at least implicitly environmentalist. This is not to say that there has been going on within the testing movement no work concerned with hereditary influences on abilities and aptitudes. On the contrary, there has been a great deal. But it has been scattered in character and has not been part of the mainstream of theoretical and empirical activity.

Experimental psychology, likewise, has antecedents in Darwinian thinking. In particular, the evolutionary associationism of Herbert Spencer was an important forerunner of early American functionalism and its later offshoots. Associationism, prior to Spencer, had contented itself simply with describing the rules by which simple elements of the mind became compounded into complex ideas. Spencer added a utility principle by suggesting that those associations which were useful to survival and progress were more likely to be formed and, in fact, would be passed on, in Lamarckian fashion, to succeeding generations. It is obvious that some of the currents of modern behaviorism have employed the same notion, notably Hullian theory which postulated in its initial form that those S-R units are selected that contribute to the survival of the organism by reducing its basic needs (Hull, 1943). In spite of having an ancestry so grounded in biology and heredity, experimental psychology, as Hirsch (1962) has forcefully pointed out, has leaned strongly to an environmentalist position. It was perhaps John Watson, preeminently, who set the climate for this with his emphasis on the almost limitless shapability of behavior.

Psychoanalytic psychology and its many descendants have also tended to disclaim hereditary influences in favor of early experience. Freud obviously did not deny hereditary influences, but his general orientation was in a different direction. Most of modern personality theory, with the possible exception of the constitutional psychologies of Kretschmer and Sheldon, has followed and reinforced this viewpoint.

There are signs today of a resurgence of interest in genetic influences on behavior. Many active programs have been initiated at such centers as those at Berkeley, Colorado, Alberta, Minnesota, Cleveland, Illinois, and Bar Harbor in North America, Birmingham, Cambridge, and London in the United Kingdom, and Stockholm, Oslo, and Munich in Europe, to mention a few. A good deal of active collaboration between geneticists and psychologists is taking place with the result that each is achieving a degree of sophistication in both fields well beyond that attained by most earlier workers. It is still true that much of the data collection is of an exploratory kind. But in the opinion of the writer, we may look forward to the establishment in the not-too-distant future of some theoretical foci on which will concentrate research of a kind that relates directly to basic problems in psychology (cf. Thompson, 1965).

We will now discuss briefly the concept of trait heritability and then summarize some of the empirical data dealing with the relation between genotype and personality.

The Meaning of Heritability

This concept refers essentially to the relative influence of heredity and environment in determining the trait variance in a given population. It is thus not a property of a character in abstract, but of the character as it occurs in a given set of individuals living under certain conditions. It should not surprise us then to find that heritability estimates obtained by different investigators on the same trait may vary widely. This fact is expressed in the components of variation equation:

$$V_P = V_G + V_E + V_G V_E$$

where V_P = phenotypic variance of the trait.

V_G = variance of trait due to genetic causes.

V_E = variance of the trait due to environmental causes.

$V_G V_E$ = genotype-environment interaction effects.

Heritability is broadly defined as follows:

$$h^2 = V_{G(A)} / V_P$$

where h^2 = heritability.
$V_{G(A)}$ = additive portion of genotypic variance.
V_P = phenotypic variance.

In natural populations, due to correlations between genotypic and environmental factors, the variance model is difficult to apply. For example, it may be that in human societies, on the average, brighter children more frequently grow up in a rich environment, duller children more frequently in a poorer environment. In animal populations, however, this can be controlled by randomly assigning different genotypes to particular environments and then applying variance analysis. Under such conditions, if all individual animals representing a genotype are in fact genetically identical as is the case with inbred strains, it is theoretically possible for all of the variation to be due to genes and none to environment. In practice, this is unusual, especially with behavior traits. Since we cannot control environment perfectly, fairly large nongenetic within-strain variation tends to appear, this being treated as error. On the other hand, genotype may not contribute significantly to the variation at all if the environments are very disparate and rather heterogeneous within themselves. Finally, we may find that some genotypes react sharply to change in environment while others show no change in behavior. In other words, some are better "buffered" than others. Such an effect, if present, will show itself in the interaction variance. A good example, taken from a review article by Gottesman, is shown in Table 8, based on the data of Cooper and Zubek (1958). This shows the maze-learning of two strains of rats bred originally by the writer (Thompson, 1954) in a cage environment for maze-brightness and maze-dullness. If the strains are reared either in enriched or in restricted conditions, the large difference that appears as a result of the selection under the "natural" rearing condition almost vanishes.

TABLE 8

Maze-Learning (Errors in Hebb-Williams) as a Function of Genotype and Early Experience (Cooper & Zubek, 1958)

Experience	Strain: Bright	Dull
Enriched	111.2	119.7
Restricted	169.7	169.5
Normal	117.0	164.0

Such data illustrate one of the more interesting and crucial problems in behavior genetics. They also document rather aptly the point made above that there is little absolute about heritability estimates. These approach absoluteness only when measures of the trait are taken on a representative sample of all of the organisms under study in a sample of all possible environments. Let us now turn to empirical data dealing with the relation of genetic factors and personality.

Empirical Data

Studies on the inheritance of personality and temperament up to around 1960 have been summarized by Fuller and Thompson (1960). With a few important exceptions, not a great deal has been done since this review. It is fair to say that much of the work done has not controlled adequately for environmental influences and hence has not yielded firm conclusions. Consequently, only a few researches will be discussed here.

One early study in the field was done by Carter (1935) using the Bernreuter Personality Inventory on 133 pairs of twins made up of 55 monozygotic and 78 dizygotic pairs. His results are summarized in Table 9. It is clear from these data that, assuming equal amount and direction of environmental influence between pairs, all of the scales measured show a dependence on genotype. Heritability estimates, though not calculated, would undoubtedly be high—for some of the scales on the order of 60–80 per cent. The scale showing the lowest heritabil-

TABLE 9

TWIN SIMILARITIES IN PERSONALITY AS MEASURED BY THE BERNREUTER SCALE (CARTER, 1935)

	No.	Bernreuter Scale					
		Neuroticism	Self-sufficiency	Introversion	Dominance	Self-confidence	Sociability
MZ	55	.63	.44	.50	.71	.58	.57
DZ							
Like-sex	44	.32	−.14	.40	.34	.20	.41
Unlike-sex	34	.18	.12	.18	.18	.07	.39

ity (ratio of *MZ* to like-sex *DZ* correlations) is introversion, a finding in disagreement with some later work to be discussed shortly. We should note in passing that heritability estimates based on one-egg versus two-egg twins deal with the influence of genotype as against environment within families only. Consequently, since dizygotic twins already have an average genetic correlation of 0.5, such values underestimate hereditary effects in the general population by approximately a factor of 2.

A more recent series of studies done by Cattell and his associates examined hereditary and environmental effects on traits defined by means of factorial methods. It has been Cattell's view that psychological factors should have heritabilities larger or smaller than that of composite tests (Cattell, 1960). Although this position is not demonstrated by his own data, the latter are interesting in themselves. The first of the two studies by Cattell, Blewett, and Beloff (1955) used 12 personality factors derived from "life record" behavior (L factors) and "questionnaire" data (Q factors). In the second study by Cattell, Stice, and Kristy (1957) 11 factors from objective tests (T factors) were examined. In both cases, the multiple abstract variance analysis method of Cattell (1960) was used to obtain nature-nurture ratios. Results from the two studies are shown in Table 10. Out of all 23 factors, only five showed a predominance of hereditary determination, and 11 a predominance of environmental determination. The variance of those remaining was determined by both about equally. Heredity-environment correlations were also calculated, these being mostly negative and somewhat larger between families than within families. Cattell *et al.* interpreted this to mean that both society and the family tend to constrain hereditary differences inward to a "biosocial norm," though the family is more permissive in this respect. This is an interesting notion and deserves further exploration.

A final study on the heritability of human personality that should be mentioned is by Gottesman (1963). This investigator examined the similarity of 34 identical and 34 fraternal twin pairs of the Minnesota Multiphasic Inventory (MMPI) and on Cattell's High School Personality Quiz (HSPQ). His zygosity determination was done carefully and involved a number of different measures including blood types, fingerprint ridge counts, and photographs. Significant heritability estimates were found on four of the MMPI scales and on three of the HSPQ factors. These are shown in Table 11. It is of some interest that factors F and Q_2 together provide a measure of intraversion-extroversion as a large second-order factor. The fact that these both showed considerable heritability agrees nicely with an earlier conclusion of Eysenck (1956) that this dimension represents a basic component of personality heavily influenced by genotype. It disagrees, however, with Carter's findings (1935). In addition, the high H value found for the "schizophrenia" scale is in line with

TABLE 10

Hereditary versus Environmental Determinations of L, Q, and T Personality Factors (Cattell et al., 1955, 1957)

L & Q factors	H predominantly	E predominantly	H & E equal
1. Tender-mindedness vs. tough-mindedness		+	
2. Nervous tension vs. autonomic relaxation		+	
3. General neuroticism vs. ego strength		+	
4. Will control		+	
5. Impatient dominance, immaturity vs. sthenic emotionality			+
6. Cyclothymia vs. schizothymia	+		
7. Adventurous cyclothymia vs. withdrawn schizothymia	+		
8. Socialized mode vs. boorishness			+
9. Dominance independence vs. submissiveness			+
10. Energetic conformity vs. quick eccentricity			+
11. Surgency (i.e., cheerful optimism) vs. desurgency		+	
12. General intelligence	+		
T data			
1. General intelligence	+		
2. Assertiveness		+	
3. Inhibition			+
4. Critical practicality			+
5. Convention (gregariousness)	+		
6. Exuberance			+
7. Corticalertia (speed of response)		+	
8. Neural rescue vs. neuroticism		+	
9. Self-sentiment control		+	
10. Asthenia		+	
11. Immediate over-responsiveness		+	

an extensive amount of work done already on individuals showing this disease and its incidence in their relatives (cf. Fuller & Thompson, 1960).

These three studies must be taken as representative of work in this difficult field. It is not possible to draw any general conclusions from them at present. Some unex-

TABLE 11

STATISTICALLY SIGNIFICANT HERITABILITY ESTIMATES ON MMPI SCALES AND HSPQ FACTORS (GOTTESMAN, 1963)

MMPI		HSPQ	
Scale	H[a]	Factor	H[a]
1. Depression	.45	F. Serious vs. enthusiastic	.56
4. Psychopathic deviate	.50	O. Confidence vs. guilt-proneness	.46
8. Schizophrenia	.42	Q_2. Group dependency vs. self-sufficiency	.56
0. Social intraversion	.71		

[a] All H values statistically significant ($p < .05$).

pected traits show high heritability, for example, sociability or gregariousness. On the other hand, the bipolar factor of Cattell, phlegmatic vs. excitable temperament, which might be naively supposed to be rather close to genotype, has an H value of zero. It should be mentioned, finally, that some wide differences were found by Gottesman between male and female H values. For example, Factor E of the HSPQ—submissiveness vs. dominance—showed zero heritability in females, but yielded a value of .74 in males. Such a result is undoubtedly due to a cultural suppression of the trait in girls but the provision, for boys, of environments allowing maximal expression of genetic differences.

The human data are fairly well backed up by a number of animal studies using the methods of selection and strain differences. Hall (1938) was able to select for emotionality in rats, as were also Broadhurst (1962) and Bignami (1964). These studies indicate clearly that rat temperament, to the extent that the phenotypic response reflects it, is highly responsive to selection and hence under close genetic control. Similarly, numerous studies on different dog breeds, and rat and mouse strains, have yielded the same conclusions (cf. Fuller & Thompson, 1960; Broadhurst, 1960; McClearn, 1962; Lagerspetz, 1964). Again, it must be emphasized that such genotypic differences may often be suppressed by one mode of rearing, expressed under another, and they may be maximal at one age and minimal at another. These two problems—the gene-environment relationship and the gene-development relationship—are worth exploring a little further. Let us consider the first of them.

Gene-Environment Relationship

We suggested above that different genotypes may respond differently to the same environment. Thus the data in Table 8 showed that dull rats become much brighter when reared in a rich environment, whereas bright rats remain about the same. Conversely, a restricted environment pulls the brights down but does not alter the performance of the dulls. This seems certainly reasonable and points to the conclusion that in the two strains some physiological limits of high and low intelligence have been reached by selection so that environment can only exert effects in one direction. Although this is not emphasized by Cooper and Zubek (1958), it is clear that with each strain there is *variation* with respect to the impact of a new environment. In other words, even in rather homozygous lines, there occurs a differential sensitivity to environmental change. We spoke of this before as "buffering" which may be defined as the general capacity to resist environmental influence.

An experiment of considerable interest in this connection is that of Waddington (1952, 1953) on so-called genetic assimilation. He subjected a base-population of *Drosophila* pupae to a heat-shock. About 30 per cent of the individuals responded with an absence of cross-veins in the wings. This abnormality did not occur without the heat-shock. Waddington then selected in both directions for 14 generations. The incidence of the character in the responding group accordingly rose to 80 per cent, and in the originally nonresponding group it was only 8 per cent. By generation 16, the cross-veinless character began to appear spontaneously in about 1–2 per cent of the responding line. Further selection resulted finally in the appearance of the character without treatment in about 95 per cent of the individuals of one subline. Lerner (1954, p. 70), in discussing this experiment, suggests that what may have been involved was selection for strong or weak buffering. Obviously, some animals in the base population were capable of responding in the manner described given a special kind of environmental treatment. Selection apparently lowered the threshold of expression of the genes involved in one line while raising it in the other, that is, produced weak and strong buffering, respectively.

An analogue to these data in psychology is the differential responsiveness of different animals or genetic strains to early manipulation. A number of experiments have shown this, for example, those of King and Eleftheriou (1959), Levine and Wetzel (1963), and of Lindzey, Lykken, and Winston (1960). Evidence with human beings appears to be lacking at present. It has been suggested by Kallman (1953) that schizophrenia—a disease considered by him to be determined by a single recessive gene—may be expressed or not, depending on a nonspecific constitutional defense mechanism carried by a polygenic system. Thus a heterozygote with a low defense might break down under a severe stress more readily than a homozygote with a strong defense system. This is an interesting idea and well worth following up. Bentley Glass (1954) has discussed the same notion under the rubric of "adaptability," this being defined as the general process by which living organisms make or undergo appropriate adjustments to changing conditions. In the same paper, Glass presented some preliminary though exciting data on the similarity between members of an identical twin pair in adaptability to simple stresses. The task consisted of a visual-motor precision test—hitting a small target with a needle—and the environmental stress consisted of drinking five cups of hot or cold coffee. In Figure 27 are shown performance of the twins under normal and control conditions (hot or cold water) and following caffein intake. The similarity of the two subjects under all conditions is striking and suggests that both the quantity and quality of the adapting response have a genetic basis, though, as Glass points out, more data will be needed before an environmental etiology can be ruled out.

If buffering or adaptability is indeed genetic, its exact basis is still something of a puzzle. As Lerner (1954) has suggested, there appear to be two main possibilities: one, that it is a property of degree of homozygosity either in general or at specific loci, the other that it is a character dependent on specific genes. At present, we do not have sufficient data on behavioral characters to decide between these alternatives. Data gathered by Winston (1964) comparing the amount of early trauma-induced behavioral changes in inbred mouse strains and their hybrids indicated that the latter were more resistant. This result would indicate that buffering is a heterotic effect accruing to more heterozygotic genotypes. On the other hand, as we have already indicated, inbred strains that are considered to be about equally homozygous still differ among

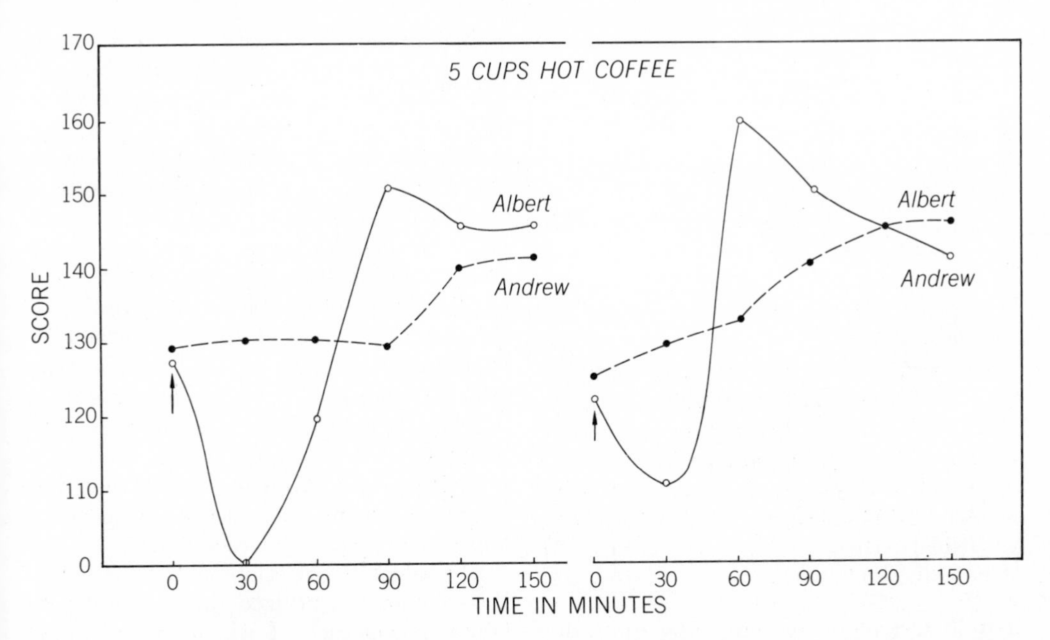

Figure 27. The similarity of effects of a mild stress on visual-motor performance in a pair of identical twins. In the left graph, Albert drank the coffee, on the right Andrew drank it (Glass, 1954).

themselves in respect to their sensitivity to environmental treatment. Consequently, the matter is an open question and well deserving of concentrated research effort.

The Gene-Development Relationship

The second problem area to which we will now turn concerns the relationship between genetic expression and development. The original classical Mendelian models were based on relatively fixed phenotypic characters assessed independently of the age of the plant or organism in which they occurred. Many traits, however, and particularly behavioral ones, vary a great deal with development and, in fact, show different degrees of heritability when measured at different stages. A character as apparently straightforward as human weight has a heritability of about 50 per cent or more at maturity, but only about 18 per cent at birth (Falconer, 1960). Likewise, human intelligence, if we are to trust its measurement early in life, shows low correlation at this time with that of parents, but a good deal more later on. An example in animals is afforded by the work of Scott on the development of barking in five dog breeds (Scott, 1964). Percentage of animals of each breed showing barking as a function of age is shown in Figure 28. It is likely, judging from the graphs, that genetic analysis would yield quite different results if done at different ages. Scott chose the age of maximal differences (11 weeks) as optimal for further work. At this time, the two breeds, cocker and basenji, differ by a factor of somewhat greater than 3. F1 and F2 and backcross hybrids showed thresholds of barking that gave a good fit to a one-factor dominance model. This is suggested by the fact that hybrid means approximate the mean of the parents with a low threshold for barking—that is, the cocker breed. It is uncertain, however, whether this would also fit the barking phenotype taken at other ages. What looks like the same character

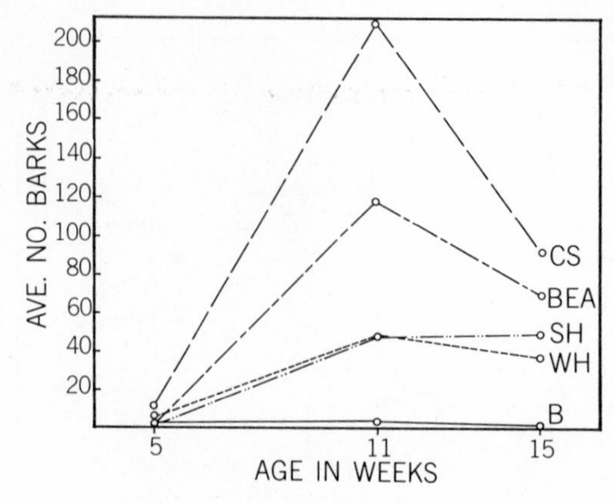

Figure 28. Average number of barks in five dog breeds as a function of age. Cockers (CS), beagles (BEA), Shetland sheep dogs (SH), wirehaired terriers (WH), and basenjis (B) were used (Scott, 1964).

may in fact represent something quite different at different times. For example, it is conceivable that barking at a young age reflects general arousal, but at a later age means specific aggressiveness or fear. The same may well be true of human personality and intelligence.

These possibilities imply that selection can act on characters at specific developmental stages, and this implies, in turn, that genes act sequentially in time, some determining events early in the life of an organism, other different ones determining later events. Such a point of view, espoused by most modern geneticists (cf., e.g., Waddington, 1962), is backed up by the data of Mechelke (1961) showing that different gene loci on a chromosome manifest activity in the form of "puffing" at different developmental ages. This puffing presumably has to do with the initiation of some specific protein-synthesizing function which can then keep going independently via instructions transmitted to the cytoplasm (Waddington, 1962, p. 56). We should therefore be prepared to find, as suggested above, that similar phenotypes at two ages do not depend on the same genes and may therefore have quite different functions. Thus personality, in lower animals or human beings, may be somewhat discontinuous throughout development, some dimensions of it showing high heritability at one time and low heritability at another. This is not so unreasonable if we consider that organisms must adapt to different problems at different stages during development, and must have evolved on this basis.

The above sketch hardly does justice to the empirical work and evolving theoretical conceptualizations in the study of genotype and personality. It is hoped, however, that it will give something of the flavor of ongoing work and suggest to the reader the interesting and intimate connections that exist between the study of behavior genetics and that of behavior development.

The schema of development suggested in this chapter has utilized three critical age-zones during each of which the organism has a character such as to allow certain kinds of residua to eventuate from environmental contacts. The basic parameters which were used to define the whole development of the organism, including these age-zones, were differentiation, growth, and organization. These must certainly be dependent on genetic influences which then control, though less directly, the progressive changes in psychological make-up of the developing individual. A good example is given by the work of John A. King (1958) on the behavioral development of two subspecies of deermouse, *Peromyscus maniculatus bairdii* and *Peromyscus maniculatus gracilis*. These do not interbreed in nature and occupy rather different environments. P.m. gracilis are arboreal and rarely leave a woodland habitat, whereas P.m. bairdii are ground-dwelling. King's studies have shown that bairdii develop more rapidly than gracilis on both the sensory and motor side. Their eyes open sooner and they can fight and climb efficiently at an earlier age. Presumably, this difference in developmental rate (differentiation) is due to the increased pressure for survival that the more exposed habitat of bairdii places on them. Much the same contrast can be found in many other species, for example, chickens and ducks as against robins, thrushes, and other nidifugous species, or such plains-dwelling mammals as deer and antelope compared with carnivores like lions and leopards. Nature affords a wide spectrum of differences in genetically controlled developmental sequences. These variations should be of prime interest to the comparative psychologists. Adult organisms of different species show astonishing diversity of form and function. But this diversity is achieved gradually. Infant animals are much more alike and only through maturation ultimately manifest their latent differences. The study of development thus represents a crucial wedge into the understanding of species differences and, for that matter, individual differences within one species.

SUMMARIZING STATEMENT

The basic notion that has been explicated is that one important way of understanding personality is by examining its developmental stratification. Any measure of it, whether this be in terms of a purely clinical and intuitive assessment made by a counselor or an analyst or in terms of a formal psychometric device, must generate scores which confound different developmental components. Consider the personality trait, achievement need. It is our view that any measure of this must involve separable aspects—specifically, the basic temperament of the subject and how he reacts to any general stress such as that occasioned by competitive situations, secondly, the affect, positive or negative, that is aroused in him by the specific complex of cues that surround competition and achievement, and thirdly, the instrumental capabilities of the person when placed in a situation where achieving behavior is called for. Clearly, as we pointed out in the first part of the chapter, a certain score on some test designated to measure need achievement could be generated by a large number of permutations and combinations of these three factors weighted differentially. The same must be true of any aspect of behavior we wish to consider. If a sports instructor wishes to teach a child tennis, for example, it is clear that he will have to deal, in one way or another, with the fact that his pupil may be lethargic, with the fact that he may be generally suspicious of adults, and with the fact that he may have poor sensorimotor coordination. The business of radically altering behavior through therapy can also be viewed in this way, and the arguments between the psychoanalytic, the conditioning, and the chemical or surgical approaches may be at least partly resolvable by reference to the developmental-components model of personality espoused here.

It must be recognized, of course, that other theories of personality have offered similar constructions, notably Freudian psychoanalysis. In the latter, the structured division of the personality is ontogenetically defined, ego and super-ego being regarded as differentiating out of id. But such a definition is largely an empirical one made without real reference to any of the basic characteristics of development. Our own model, on the other hand, explicitly starts with development as one of the fundamental properties of all living systems. This allows it to encompass a broad range of data dealing with the biophysical and biosocial basis of personality, and we have, in fact, made use of the model as a way of summarizing such data. It is true that such a breadth of approach may be dangerous, since any theoretical construction that explains everything is often empty of predictive power. It does seem to the writer, however, that the present model does make at least certain broad directives for research; and, in addition, it has some features that are capable of precise experimental study at the human or at the animal level. The postulate concerning rate of differentiation on the input versus the output side is certainly amenable to such analytic treatment, and the writer now has in progress a series of experiments relevant to this problem, using mainly young chicks and rats. These promise to yield some fruitful empirical data. Likewise, at the human level, the recent work by Bloom (1964) and by Witkin *et al.* (1962) on stability, consistency, and differentiation in personality seems to represent a general research direction quite consonant with that suggested by the conceptualizations of this chapter.

Underlying all changes occurring during development is genotype. For any trait of personality or intelligence, we may derive an estimate of heritability by partitioning the observed variance into genetic, environmental, and interactional components. The values of these terms are not absolute but vary with the population studied and the environment which the subjects occupy. A large number of empirical studies have been done to demonstrate genetic factors in human personality, notably those of Carter, Cattell, and Gottesman. Likewise, experiments on animals have shown that such traits as emotionality and general reactivity vary between inbred strains and in heterogenous genetic populations will respond readily to artificial selection.

Perhaps the most interesting problems, however, are posed by the gene-environment and the gene-development relationships. There is some evidence to suggest that the responsiveness of a given genotype to the impact of an environment is itself genetically controlled either as a heterotic effect or as a property of specific genes or gene-combinations. Similarly, genetic factors control the major parameters of development and hence the susceptibility of an organism to certain kinds of early experience and the types of residua that may ensue from these. If there is such differential sensitivity of genotype at different developmental periods, it is then logical that heritability estimates of a trait will also vary considerably from one age to another in the same individual. It may well be that at a period during which the genetic code underlying the disposition of a character is being transmitted to cytoplasmic control, this trait has a maximal environmental-sensitivity, but that before or after such a period, it is relatively well buffered. This whole notion of plasticity of a genotype to environmental influence at different stages of development is of great interest and well worth some intense research effort.

Little more remains to be said. The chapter has been something of a protest against the prototypic gene-less, age-less organism that has dominated so much of behavior theory for so many years. It is hoped that the emphasis given here to these basic dimensions of development and genotype will stimulate a fresh and more integrated approach to the understanding of personality in lower animals and man.

REFERENCES

Ader, R. The effects of early experience on subsequent emotionality and resistance to stress. *Psychol. Monogr.*, 1959 (73, Whole No. 472).

Ader, R., & Belfer, M. L. Prenatal maternal anxiety and offspring emotionality in the rat. *Psychol. Rep.*, 1962, 10, 711–718.

Ambrose, J. A. The development of the smiling response. In B. M. Foss (Ed.), *Determinants of infant behavior.* New York: Wiley, 1961.

Andrew, R. J. Effect of testosterone on the behavior of the domestic chick. *J. comp. physiol. Psychol.*, 1963, 56, 933–940.

Balinsky, B. An analysis of the mental factors of various ape groups from nine to sixty. *Genet. Psychol. Monogr.*, 1941, 23, 191–234.

Ball, G. G., & Warren, J. M. Maturation of umweg learning in white Leghorn chicks. *J. comp. physiol. Psychol.*, 1960, 53, 273–275.

Bartoshuk, A. K. Human neonatal cardiac acceleration to sound: habituation and dishabituation. *Percept. Mot. Skills,* 1962, 15, 15–27.

Bateson, P. P. G. Relation between conspicuousness of stimuli to their effectiveness in the imprinting situation. *J. comp. physiol. Psychol.*, 1964, 58, 407–411.

Bernstein, L. A note on Christie's "Experimental naivete and experiential naivete," *Psychol. Bull.*, 1952, 49, 38–40.

Bevan, W. Perceptual learning: an overview. *J. gen. Psychol.,* 1961, 64, 69–99.

Bignami, G. Selection for fast and slow avoidance conditioning in the rat. *Bull. Brit. psychol. Soc.,* 1964, 17, 5A (abstract).

Bloom, S. Stability and change in human characteristics. New York: Wiley, 1964.

Bovard, E. W. The effects of early handling on viability of the albino rat. *Psychol. Rev.,* 1958, 65, 257–271.

Bowlby, J. *Maternal care and mental health.* Monogr. Series, No. 2, Geneva: World Health Organization, 1951.

Bowlby, J. An ethological approach to research in child development. *Brit. J. med. Psychol.,* 1957, 30, 230–240.

Bowlby, J. The nature of the child's tie to his mother. *Int. J. Psychoanal.,* 1958, 39, 350–373.

Brackbill, Y. Extinction of the smiling responses in infants as a function of reinforcement schedule. *Child Develpm.,* 1958, 29, 115–124.

Bridges, K. M. B. Emotional development in early infancy. *Child Develpm.,* 1932, 3, 324–334.

Broadhurst, P. L. Experiments in psychogenetics. In H. J. Eysenck (Ed.), *Experiments in personality.* London: Routledge & Kegan Paul, 1960.

Broadhurst, P. L. A note on further progress in a psychogenetic selection experiment. *Psychol. Rep.,* 1962, 12, 65–66.

Brookshire, K. H., Littman, R. A., & Stewart, C. N. Residue of shock-trauma in the white rat: a three-factor thesis. *Psychol. Monogr.,* 1961, 75 (10, Whole No. 514).

Caldwell, B. M. The effects of infant care. In M. L. Hoffman & L. W. Hoffman (Eds.), *Review of child development research.* New York: Russell Sage Foundation, 1964.

Caldwell, D. F., & Werboff, J. Classical conditioning in newborn rats. *Science,* 1962, 136, 1118–1119.

Campbell, B. A., & Campbell, E. H. Retention and extinction of learned fear in infant and adult rats. *J. comp. physiol. Psychol.,* 1962, 55, 1–8.

Carter, H. D. Twin similarities in emotional traits. *Charact. & Pers.,* 1935, 4, 61–78.

Casler, L. Maternal deprivation: a critical review of the literature. *Monogr. Soc. Res. Child Develpm.,* 1961, 26, No. 2.

Cattell, R. B. The multiple abstract variance analysis equations and solutions: For nature-nurture research on continuous variables. *Psychol. Rev.,* 1960, 67, 353–372.

Cattell, R. B., Blewett, D. B., & Beloff, J. R. The inheritance of personality: a multiple variance analysis determination of approximate nature-nurture ratios for primary personality factors in Q-data. *Amer. J. hum. Genet.,* 1955, 7, 122–146.

Cattell, R. B., Stice, G. F., & Kristy, N. F. A first approximation to nature-nurture ratios for eleven primary personality factors in objective tests. *J. abnorm. soc. Psychol.,* 1957, 54, 143–159.

Cooper, R. M., & Zubek, J. P. Effects of enriched and restricted early environment on the learning ability of bright and dull rats. *Canad. J. Psychol.,* 1958, 12, 159–164.

Cronbach, L. J. The two disciples of scientific psychology. *Amer. Psychologist,* 1957, 12, 671–684.

Cruikshank, Ruth M. Animal infancy. In L. Carmichael (Ed.), *Manual of child psychology.* New York: Wiley, 1954.

Denenberg, V. H. Effects of age and early experience upon conditioning in the C57BL/B mouse. *J. Psychol.,* 1958, 46, 211–226.

Denenberg, V. H. Interactive effects of infantile and adult shock levels upon learning. *Psychol. Rep.,* 1959, 5, 357–364.

Denenberg, V. H. A test of the critical period hypothesis and a further study of the relationship between age and conditioning in the C57BL/10 mouse. *J. genet. Psychol.,* 1960, 97, 379–384.

Denenberg, V. H. The effects of early experience. In E. S. E. Hafez (Ed.), *The behavior of domestic animals.* Baltimore: Williams & Wilkins Co., 1962.

Denenberg, V. H. An attempt to isolate critical periods of development in the rat. *J. comp. physiol. Psychol.,* 1962, 55, 813–815.

Denenberg, V. H. Critical periods, stimulus input, and emotional reactivity: a theory of infantile stimulation. *Psychol. Rev.,* 1964, 71, 335–351.

Denenberg, V. H., & Karas, G. G. Interactive effects of age to duration of infantile experience on adult learning. *Psychol. Rep.,* 1960, 7, 313–322.

Denenberg, V. H., & Morton, J. R. C. Effects of environmental complexity and social grouping upon modification of emotional behavior. *J. comp. physiol. Psychol.,* 1962, 55, 242–246. (a)

Denenberg, V. H., & Morton, J. R. C. Effects of preweaning and postweaning manipulations upon problem-solving behavior. *J. comp. physiol. Psychol.,* 1962, 55, 1096–1098. (b)

Dennis, W. *Readings in child psychology.* New York: Prentice-Hall, 1951.

Diamond, S., Balvin, R. S., & Diamond, F. R. *Inhibition and choice.* Harper & Row, New York, 1963.

Dolittle, R. F., & Meade, R. The effect of gambling on some psychological and physiological phenomena. Paper read at the meetings of the Eastern Psychol. Assn., New York, April, 1957.

Drever, J. D. Perception and action. *Bull. Brit. psychol. Soc.,* 1961, 45, 1–9.

Elliot, O., & Scott, J. P. The development of emotional distress reactions to separation in puppies. *J. genet. Psychol.,* 1961, 99, 3–22.

Eysenck, H. J. The inheritance of extraversion-introversion. *Acta Psychologica,* 1956, 12, 429–432.

Eysenck, H. J. *Handbook of abnormal psychology.* Basic Books, Inc., New York, 1961.

Falconer, D. S. *Introduction to quantitative genetics.* New York: Ronald, 1960.

Fenichel, O. *The psychoanalytic theory of neurosis.* New York: Norton, 1945.

Fischer, L. K. Hospitalism in six-month old infants. *Amer. J. Orthopsychiat.,* 1953, 23, 803–814.

Flavell, J. *The developmental psychology of Jean Piaget.* Princeton, Van Nostrand & Co., 1963.

Flexner, L. B., & Gellhorn, A. The comparative anatomy of placental transfer. *Amer. J. Obstet. Gynecol.,* 1942, 43, 985.

Forgays, D. G., & Forgays, Janet W. The nature of the effect of free environmental experience in the rat. *J. comp. physiol. Psychol.,* 1952, 45, 322–328.

Forgus, R. H. Influence of early experience on maze-learning with and without visual clues. *Canad. J. Psychol.,* 1955, 9, 207–214. (a)

Forgus, R. H. Early visual and motor experience as determiners of complex maze-learning ability under rich and reduced stimulation. *J. comp. physiol. Psychol.,* 1955, 48, 215–220. (b)

Francès, R. *Le Developpement Perceptif.* Presses Universitaires de France; Paris, France: 1962.

Fraser, F. C. Recent advances in genetics in relation to pediatrics. *J. Pediat.,* 1958, 52, 734–757.

Fraser, F. C., Fainstat, T. A., & Kalter, H. The experimental production of congenital defects with special reference to cleft palate. *Neonatal Stud.,* 1953, 2, 43–57.

Freedman, D. G., King, J. A., & Elliot, O. Critical period in the social development of dogs. *Science,* 1961, 133, 1016.

Fuller, J. L., & Thompson, W. R. *Behavior genetics.* New York: Wiley, 1960.

Furchtgott, E., Echols, M., & Openshaw, J. W. Maze learning in pre- and neonatally X-irradiated rats. *J. comp. physiol. Psychol.,* 1958, 51, 178–180.

Galton, F. *Hereditary genius.* London: Macmillan, 1869.

Galton, F. *Inquiry into human faculty and its development.* London: Macmillan, 1883.

Gardner, E. D. Decrease in human neurons with age. *Anat. Rec.,* 1940, 77, 533.

Geber, M. The psychomotor development of African children in the first year, and the influence of maternal behavior. *J. soc. Psychol.,* 1958, 47, 185–195. (a)

Geber, M. Tests de Gesell et de Terman-Merrill appliqués en Uganda. *Enfance,* 1958, 11, 63–67. (b)

Geber, M., & Dean, R. F. A. The state of development of newborn African children. *Lancet,* 1957, 272, 1216–1219. (a)

Geber, M., & Dean, R. F. A. Gesell tests on African children. *Pediatrics,* 1957, 20, 1055–1065. (b)

Gesell, A. The ontogenesis of infant behavior. In L. Carmichael (Ed.), *Manual of child psychology.* New York: John Wiley & Sons, 1946. Ch. 6.

Gewirtz, J. L. A learning analysis of the effects of normal stimulation, privation and deprivation on the acquisition of social motivation and attachment. In B. M. Foss (Ed.), *Determinants of infant behaviour.* New York: Wiley, 1961.

Gibson, E. J. Unpublished manuscript. Center for Advanced Studies in Behavioral Sciences, May, 1964.

Gibson, J. J., & Gibson, E. J. Perceptual learning: differentiation or enrichment. *Psychol. Rev.,* 1955, 62, 32–41.

Glass, H. B. The genetic aspects of adaptability. *Proc. Ass. Res. nerv. ment. Dis.,* 1954, 23, 367–377.

Glickman, S. E., & Feldman, S. M. Habituation of the arousal response to direct stimulation of the brainstem. *EEG Clin. Neurophysiol.*, 1961, 13, 703–709.

Goldfarb, W. Emotional and intellectual consequences of psychological deprivation in infancy: a revaluation. In P. H. Hoch & J. Zubin (Eds.), *Psychopathology of childhood.* New York: Grune & Stratton, 1955.

Gottesman, I. I. Genetic aspects of intelligent behavior. In Ellis, N. R. (Ed.), *Handbook of mental deficiency.* New York: McGraw-Hill, 1963.

Gottesman, I. I. Heritability of personality: a demonstration. *Psychol. Monogr.*, 1963, 77, Whole No. 572.

Gregg, N. McA. Congenital cataracts following German measles in the mother. *Trans. opth. Soc. Aust.*, 1941, 3, 35–46.

Hahn, P., Koldovsky, O., Krecek, J., Martinek, J., & Vacek, Z. Endocrine and metabolic aspects of the development of homeothermy in the rat. In G. E. W. Wolstenholme & Maeve O'Connor (Eds.), *Somatic stability in the newborn.* Ciba Foundation Symposium. Boston: Little, Brown & Co., 1961.

Hall, C. S. The inheritance of emotionality. *Sigma Xi Quart.*, 1938, 26, 17–27.

Hamilton, J. B. Precocious masculine behavior following administration of synthetic male hormone substance. *Endocrinology*, 1938, 23, 53–57.

Harlow, H. F. The maternal affectional system of rhesus monkeys. In H. Rheingold (Ed.), *Maternal behavior in mammals.* New York: John Wiley, 1963.

Harris, J. D. Habituatory response decrement in the intact organism. *Psychol. Bull.*, 1943, 40, 385–422.

Haynes, H., White, B. L., & Held, R. Visual accommodation in human infants. *Science*, 1965, 148, 528–530.

Hebb, D. O. The effect of early and late brain injury upon test scores, and the nature of normal adult intelligence. *Proc. Amer. Phil. Soc.*, 1942, 85, 275–292.

Hebb, D. O. The effects of early experience on problem-solving at maturity. *Amer. Psychologist*, 1947, 2, 306–307.

Hebb, D. O. *Organization of behavior.* New York: Wiley, 1949.

Held, R., & Bonsom, J. Neonatal deprivation and adult rearrangement: complementary techniques for analyzing plastic sensory-motor coordinations. *J. comp. physiol. Psychol.*, 1961, 54, 33–37.

Held, R., & Heim, A. Movement-produced stimulation in the development of visually guided behavior. *J. comp. physiol. Psychol.*, 1963, 56, 872–876.

Held, R., & Schlank, M. Adaptation to disarranged eye-hand coordination in the distance-dimension. *Amer. J. Psychol.*, 1959, 72, 603–605.

Henderson, N. D. Behavioral effects of manipulation during different stages in the development of mice. *J. comp. physiol. Psychol.*, 1964, 57, 284–289.

Hess, E. H. Two conditions limiting critical age for imprinting. *J. comp. physiol. Psychol.*, 1959a, 52, 515–518.

Hess, E. H. Imprinting. *Science*, 1959b, 130, 133–141.

Hess, E. H. Ethology: an approach to the complete analysis of behavior. In *New directions in psychology.* New York: Holt, 1962.

Himwich, Williamina A. Biochemical and neurophysiological development of the brain in the neonatal period. In C. C. Pfeiffer & J. R. Smythies (Eds.), *Int. Rev. Neurobiol.*, 1962, 4, 117–159.

Hinde, R. A. Factors governing the strength of a partially inborn response, as shown by the mobbing behavior of the Chaffinch (*Fringella coelebs*). I & II. *Proc. Roy. Soc. B*, 1954, 142, 306–31, 33–58.

Hirsch, J. Individual differences in behavior and their genetic basis. In Bliss, E. L. (Ed.), *Roots of behavior.* New York: Harper, 1962.

Hoffman, M. L., & Hoffman, L. W. (Eds.) Review of child development research. New York: Russell Sage Foundation, 1964.

Hooker, D. *The prenatal origins of behavior.* Lawrence: Univer. of Kansas Press, 1952.

Hopper, H. E., & Pinneau, S. R. Frequency of regurgitation in infancy as related to the amount of stimulation received from the mother. *Child Develpm.*, 1957, 28, 229–235.

Hull, C. L. *Principles of behavior.* New York: Appleton-Century, 1943.

Hunt, J. McV. The effects of infant feeding frustration upon adult hoarding in the albino rat. *J. abnorm. soc. Psychol.*, 1941, 36, 338–360.

Hunt, J. McV. *Intelligence and experience.* New York: Ronald Press Co., 1961.

Hymovitch, B. The effects of experimental variations in early experience on problem-solving in the rat. *J. comp. physiol. Psychol.*, 1952, 45, 313–321.

Jenness, A. Personality dynamics. *Ann. Rev. Psychol.*, 1962, 13, 479–514.

Kallman, F. J. *Heredity in health and mental disorder*. New York: Norton, 1953.

Kalter, H., & Warkany, J. Experimental production of congenital malformations in mammals by metabolic procedure. *Physiol. Rev.*, 1959, 39, 69–115.

Kennard, M. A. Age and other factors in motor recovery from precentral lesions in monkeys. *Amer. J. Physiol.*, 1936, 115, 138–146.

King, J. A., & Eleftheriou, B. E. Effects of early handling upon adult behavior in two subspecies of deermice, *Peromyscus maniculatus. J. comp. physiol. Psychol.*, 1959, 52, 82–88.

King, J. A. Maternal behavior and behavioral development in two subspecies of *Peromyscus maniculatus. J. Mammal.*, 1958, 39, 177–190.

Kirby, R. H. Acquisition, extinction and retention of an avoidance response in rats as a function of age. *J. comp. physiol. Psychol.*, 1963, 56, 158–162.

Klein, Melanie. *Contributing to psycho-analysis*. London: Hogarth Press, 1950.

Klopfer, P. H., & Hailman, J. P. Perceptual preference and imprinting in chicks. *Science*, 1964, 145, 1333–1334.

Koch, S. (Ed.) *Psychology: a study of a science*. Epilogue, Vol. 3. New York: McGraw-Hill, 1959.

Lagerspetz, Kirsti. Studies on the aggressive behaviour of mice. *Suomalaisen Tiedeakatemian Toimituksia Annales Academiae Scientiarum Fennicae*, 1964, B, 131.

Landauer, T. K., & Whiting, J. M. Infantile stimulation and adult stature of human males. *Amer. Anthropologist*, 1964, 66, 1007–1028.

Lerner, I. M. *Genetic homeostasis*. New York: Wiley, 1954.

Levine, S. A further study of infantile handling and adult avoidance learning. *J. Pers.*, 1956, 25, 70–80.

Levine, S. Psychophysiological effects of early stimulation. In E. L. Bliss (Ed.), *Roots of behavior*. New York: Hueber, 1961.

Levine, S. Psychophysiological effects of infantile stimulation. In E. L. Bliss (Ed.), *Roots of behavior*. New York: Harper & Bros., 1962.

Levine, S., Alpert, M., & Lewis, G. W. Infantile experience and the maturation of the pituitary adrenal axis. *Science*, 1957, 126, 1347.

Levine, S., Alpert, M., & Lewis, G. W. Differential maturation of an adrenal response to cold stress in rats manipulated in infancy. *J. comp. physiol. Psychol.*, 1958, 51, 774–777.

Levine, S., & Wetzel, A. Infantile experience, strain differences, and avoidance learning. *J. comp. physiol. Psychol.*, 1963, 56, 879–881.

Lewin, K. *Field theory in social science*. (Ed. by D. Cartwright.) New York: Harper & Bros., 1951.

Lilienfeld, A. M., Pasamanick, B., & Rogers, M. E. The relationship between pregnancy experience and the development of certain neuropsychiatric disorders in childhood. *Amer. J. Publ. Health*, 1955, 45, 637.

Lindholm, B. W. Critical periods and the effects of early shock on later emotional behavior in the white rat. *J. comp. physiol. Psychol.*, 1962, 55, 597–599.

Lindzey, G., Lykken, D. T., & Winston, H. D. Infantile nature, genetic factors, and adult temperament. *J. abnorm. soc. Psychol.*, 1960, 61, 7–14.

Lindzey, G., Lykken, D. T., & Winston, H. D. Maze learning and the effects of pretraining in inbred strains of mice. *J. comp. physiol. Psychol.*, 1962, 55, 748–752.

Louttit, R. T. Effect of phenylalanine and isocarboxazid feeding on brain serotonin and learning behavior in the rat. *J. comp. physiol. Psychol.*, 1962, 55, 425–428.

Luria, A. R. Verbal regulation of behavior. In M. A. B. Brazier (Ed.), *The central nervous system and behavior*. 3rd Macy Conference; Madison, N. J.: Macy Foundation, 1960.

McCance, R. A. Characteristics of the newly born. In G. E. W. Wolstenholme & Maeve O'Connor (Eds.), *Somatic stability in the newborn*. Boston: Little, Brown & Co., 1961.

McClearn, G. E. The inheritance of behavior. In L. Postman (Ed.), *Psychology in the making*. New York: Knopf, 1962.

McClelland, D. C. Toward a theory of motive acquisition. *Amer. Psychologist*, 1965, 20, 321–333.

McGraw, M. *The neuromuscular maturation of the human infant*. New York: Columbia Univer. Press, 1943.

Mechelke, F. Das Wandern des Aktivitätsmaximums im BR_4-Locus von *Acricotopus lucidus* als Modell für die Wirkungsweise eines komplexen Locus. *Naturwissenschaft,* 1961, 48, 29.

Meier, G. W. Other data on the effects of social isolation during rearing upon adult reproductive behavior in the Rhesus monkey (*Macaca-mulatta*). *Animal Behavior,* 1965, 13, 228–231.

Meier, G. W., Bunch, M. E., Nolan, C. T., & Scheidler, C. H. Anoxia, behavioral development and learning ability: a comparative-experimental approach. *Psychol. Monogr.,* 1960, 74, No. 1 (Whole No. 488).

Meyers, C. E., & Dingman, H. F. The structure of abilities at the preschool ages: hypothesized domains. *Psychol. Bull.,* 1960, 57, 514–532.

Milner, P. M. The cell assembly: Mark II. *Psychol. Rev.,* 1957, 64, 242–252.

Mischel, W. Preference for delayed reinforcement: an experimental study of cultural observations. *J. abnorm. soc. Psychol.,* 1958, 56, 57–61.

Mischel, W. Preference for delayed reinforcement and social responsibility. *J. abnorm. soc. Psychol.,* 1961, 62, 1–7.

Mishkin, M., & Forgays, D. G. Word recognition as a function of retinal locus. *J. exp. Psychol.,* 1952, 43, 43–48.

Montagu, M. F. A. *Prenatal influences.* Urbana: University of Illinois, 1962.

Mowbray, J. B., & Cadell, T. E. Early behavior patterns in rhesus monkeys. *J. comp. physiol. Psychol.,* 1962, 55, 350–357.

Mowrer, O. H. *Learning theory and the symbolic process.* New York: Wiley, 1960.

Nalbandov, A. V. *Reproductive physiology.* San Francisco: Freeman, 1958.

Nice, M. M. Studies in the life history of the song sparrow. II. The behavior of the song sparrow and other passerines. *Trans. Linnaen Soc. N. Y.,* 1943, 6, 1–329.

Page, E. W. Transfer of materials across the human placenta. *Amer. J. Obstet. Gynecol.,* 1957, 74, 705–718.

Pasamanick, B., & Knobloch, H. Epidemiologic studies on the complications of pregnancy and the birth process. In G. Caplan (Ed.), *Prevention of mental disorders in children.* New York: Basic Books, Inc., 1961.

Pastore, N. The genetics of schizophrenia. *Psychol. Bull.,* 1949, 46, 285–302.

Pavlov, I. P. *Conditioned reflexes.* Translated by G. V. Anrep. New York: Dover Publications, 1960.

Piaget, J. *Les Mecanismes Perceptifs.* Paris: Presse Universitaires de France, 1961.

Piaget, J., & Inhelder, Barbel. *The child's conception of space.* Trans. by F. J. Langden & J. L. Lunzer. London: Routledge & Kegan Paul, 1956.

Pinneau, S. A critique on the articles by Margaret Ribble. *Child Develpm.,* 1950, 21, 203–228.

Pinneau, S. The infantile disorders of hospitalism and analclitic depression. *Psychol. Bull.,* 1955, 52, 429–452.

Perez, V. J. Experimental phenylketonuria: effects of excessive amounts of L-phenylalanine upon maze learning ability of the albino rat. *Amer. Psychologist,* 1963, 18, 430 (abstract).

Provence, S., & Lipton, R. C. *Infants in institutions.* New York: International Universities Press, Inc., 1962.

Razran, G. H. S. Conditioned responses: an experimental study and a theoretical analysis. *Arch. Psychol.,* 1935, No. 191, V. 28.

Rensch, B. The intelligence of elephants. *Sci. Amer.,* 1957, 196, 44.

Ribble, Margaret A. Infantile experience in relation to personality development. In J. McV. Hunt (Ed.), *Personality and the behavior disorders.* New York: Ronald Press, 1944. Ch. 20.

Riesen, A. H. The development of visual perception in man and chimpanzee. *Science,* 1947, 106, 107–108.

Roberts, E. Biochemical maturation of the central nervous system. In M. Brazier (Ed.), *The central nervous system and behavior.* Macy Foundation Symposium, 1960.

Roberts, E., Harman, P. J., & Frankel, S. Gamma-amino-butyric acid content and glutamic decarboxylase activity in developing mouse brain. *Proc. Soc. Exper. Biol. & Med.,* 1951, 78, 799–803.

Schachtel, E. G. *Metamorphosis: on the development of affect, perception, attention, and memory.* New York: Basic Books, 1959.

Schaefer, T. The effects of early experience: Infant handling and later behavior in the white rat. Unpublished doctoral dissertation, Univer. of Chicago, 1957.

Schaefer, T. Early "experience" and its effects on later behavioral processes in rats: II. A critical factor in the early handiing phenomenon. *Trans. New York Acad. Sci., Ser. II,* 1963, 25, 871–889.

Schaffer, H. R. Objective observations of personality development. *Brit. med. Psychol.,* 1958, 31, 174–184.

Schaffer, H. R., & Callender, W. M. Psychologic effects of hospitalization in infancy. *Pediatrics,* 1959, 24, 528–539.

Schwartz, S. Effect of neonatal cortical lesions and early environmental factors on adult rat behavior. *J. comp. physiol. Psychol.,* 1964, 57, 72–77.

Scott, J. P. Critical periods in behavioral development. *Science,* 1962, 138, 949–958.

Scott, J. P. Genetics and the development of social behavior in dogs. *Amer. Zoologist,* 1964, 4, 161–168.

Seitz, P. F. D. Infantile experience and adult behavior in animals. *Psychosomat. Med.,* 1959, 21, 353–378.

Sharpless, S., & Jasper, H. Habituation of the arousal reaction. *Brain,* 1956, 79, 655–680.

Sokolov, E. N., Paramonova, N. P., & Lomonosov, M. V. Extinction of the orienting reaction. *Pavlov J. higher nerv. Activity,* 1961, 11, 1–8.

Solnit, A. J., & Provence, S. A. (Eds.) *Modern perspectives in child development.* New York: International Universities Press, Inc., 1963.

Sontag, L. W. The significance of fetal environmental differences. *Amer. J. Obstet. Gynecol.,* 1941, 42, 996–1003.

Sperry, R. W. The growth of nerve circuits. *Sci. Amer.,* 1959, 201, 68.

Spitz, R. A. Hospitalism: an inquiry into the genesis of psychiatric conditions in early childhood. *Psychoanal. Stud. Child,* 1945, 1, 53–74.

Stanley, W. C., Cornwell, Anne, Poggiani, Constance, & Trattner, Alice. Conditioning in the neonatal puppy. *J. comp. physiol. Psychol.,* 1963, 56, 211–214.

Stott, D. H. Physical and mental handicaps following a disturbed pregnancy. *Lancet,* 1957, 1006–1012.

Stott, D. H. Some psychosomatic aspects of casualty in reproduction. *J. psychosomat. Res.,* 1958, 3, 42–55.

Stott, D. H. Evidence for prenatal impairment of temperament in mentally retarded children. *Vita Humana,* 1959, 2, 125–148.

Tempone, V. J. Stimulus generalization as a function of mental age. *Child Develpm.,* 1965, 36, 229–236.

Thompson, R. F. Role of the cerebral cortex in stimulus generalization. *J. comp. physiol. Psychol.,* 1962, 55, 279–287.

Thompson, W. R. The inheritance and development of intelligence. *Proc. Res. Ass. nerv. ment. Dis.,* 1954, 33, 209–231.

Thompson, W. R. Influence of prenatal maternal anxiety on emotionality in young rats. *Science,* 1957, 125, 698–699.

Thompson, W. R. Motivational factors in development. *Austral. J. Psychol.,* 1958, 10, 127–143.

Thompson, W. R. Early environmental influences on behavioral development. *Amer. J. Orthopsychiat.,* 1960, 30, 306–314.

Thompson, W. R., & Goldenberg, L. Some physiological effects of maternal adrenalin injections during pregnancy on rat offspring. *Psychol. Rep.,* 1962, 10, 759–774.

Thompson, W. R., Goldenberg, L., Watson, J., & Watson, M. Behavioral effects of maternal adrenalin injection during pregnancy in rat offspring. *Psychol. Rep.,* 1963, 12, 279–284.

Thompson, W. R., & Kano, C. Effects on rat offspring of maternal phenylalanine injection during pregnancy. *J. Psychiat. Res.,* 1965, 3, 91–98.

Thompson, W. R., & O'Kieffe, M. Imprinting: its effect on the response to stress in chicks. *Science,* 1962, 135, 918–919.

Thompson, W. R., & Olian, S. Some effects on offspring behavior of maternal adrenalin injection during pregnancy in three inbred mouse strains. *Psychol. Rep.,* 1961, 8, 87–90.

Thompson, W. R., & Quinby, S. Prenatal maternal anxiety and offspring behavior: parental activity and level of anxiety. *J. Genet. Psychol.,* 1964, 106, 359–371.

Thompson, W. R., & Schaefer, T. Early environmental stimulation. In D. W. Fiske & S. R. Maddi (Eds.), *Functions of varied experience.* Homewood, Ill.: Dorsey Press, 1961.

Thompson, W. R., & Solomon, L. M. Spontaneous pattern discrimination in the rat. *J. comp. physiol. Psychol.,* 1954, 47, 104–107.

Thompson, W. R., Watson, J., & Charlesworth, W. R. The effects of prenatal maternal stress on offspring behavior in rats. *Psychol. Monogr.,* 1962, 76, Whole No. 557.

Thorpe, W. H. Learning. *Ibis,* 1959, 101, 337–353.

Tolman, C. W. A possible relationship between the imprinting critical period and arousal. *Psychol. Rev.,* 1963, 13, 181–185.

Tsang, Y. C. Visual sensitivity of rats deprived of visual cortex in infancy. *J. comp. Psychol.,* 1937, 24, 255–262.

Van Senden, M. *Raum und Gestultaufassung bei operiernten Blindgeborenen vor und nach der Operation.* Leipzig: Barth, 1932.

Ville, C. A. Enzymes in the development of homeostatic mechanisms. In G. E. W. Wolstenholme & Maeve O'Connor (Eds.), *Somatic stability in the newborn.* Ciba Foundation Symposium. Boston: Little, Brown & Co., 1961.

Vince, Margaret A. Effects of age and experience on the establishment of internal inhibition in finches. *Brit. J. Psychol.,* 1959, 50, 136–144.

Vince, Margaret A. Developmental changes in responsiveness in the great tit (*Parus major*). *Behaviour,* 1960, 15, 219–243.

Vince, Margaret A. Developmental changes in learning capacity. In W. H. Thorpe & O. L. Zanewill (Eds.), *Current problems in animal behaviour.* Cambridge: Cambridge Univer. Press, 1961.

Vincent, N. M. The effects of prenatal alcoholism upon motivation, emotionality and learning in the rat. *Amer. Psychologist,* 1958, 13, 401 (abstract).

Waddington, C. H. Selection of the genetic basis for an acquired character. *Nature* (London), 1952, 169, 278.

Waddington, C. H. Genetic assimilation of an acquired character. *Evolution,* 1953, 7, 118–126.

Waddington, C. H. *The strategy of the genes.* London: Allen & Unwin, 1957.

Waddington, C. H. *New patterns in genetics and development.* New York: Columbia Univer. Press, 1962.

Walter, G. Electroencephalographic development of children. In J. M. Tanner and Barbel Inhelder (Eds.), *Discussions on child development.* Vol. I. Proc. 1st meeting W. H. O. study group on the psychological development of the child, Geneva, 1953. London: Tausboek Publications, 1956.

Weisz, P. B. *The science of biology.* New York: McGraw-Hill, 1959.

Werboff, J. Prenatal factors determining later behavior. *Bull. Merrill-Palmer Inst.,* 1962, 98–105.

Werboff, J., Broeder, J. D., Havlena, J., & Sikov, M. R. Effects of prenatal X-ray irradiation on audiogenic seizures in the rat. *Exp. Neurol.,* 1961, 4, 189–196.

Werboff, J., & Gottleib, J. S. Drugs in pregnancy: behavioral teratology. *Obstet. Gynecol. Survey,* 1963, 18, 420–423.

Werboff, J., Gottlieb, J. S., Dembicki, E. L., & Havlena, J. Postnatal effects of antidepressant drugs administered during gestation. *Exp. Neurol.,* 1961, 3, 542–555.

Werboff, J., Gottlieb, J. S., Havlena, J., & Word, T. J. Behavioral effects of prenatal drug administration in the white rat. *Pediatrics,* 1961, 27, 318–323.

Werboff, J., Havlena, J., & Sikov, M. R. Effects of prenatal x-irradiation on activity, emotionality and maze-learning ability in the rat. *Rad. Res.,* 1962, 16, 441–452.

Werboff, J., Havlena, J., & Sikov, M. R. Behavioral effects of small doses of acute x-irradiation administered prenatally. *Atompraxis,* 1963, 9, 103–105.

Werner, H. *Comparative psychology of mental development.* New York: International Universities Press, 1948.

Werner, H. The concept of development from a comparative and organismic point of view. In D. Harris (Ed.), *The concept of development.* Minneapolis: University of Minnesota Press, 1957.

White, S. H. Evidence for a hierarchical arrangement of learning processes. In L. Lipsett & C. C. Spiker (Eds.), *Advances in child development and behavior.* Vol. II. New York: Academic Press, 1965.

Witkin, H. A., Dyk, R. B., Paterson, H. F., Goodenough, D. R., & Karp, S. A. *Psychological differentiation.* New York: John Wiley, 1962.

Winston, H. D. Influence of genotype and infantile trauma on adult learning in the mouse. *J. comp. physiol. Psychol.,* 1963, 56, 630–635.

Winston, H. D. Heterosis and learning in the mouse. *J. comp. physiol. Psychol.,* 1964, 57, 279–283.

Wohlwill, J. F. Developmental studies of perception. *Psychol. Bull.,* 1960, 57, 249–288.

Wolf, A. The dynamics of the selective inhibition of specific functions in neurosis: a preliminary report. *Psychosom. Med.,* 1943, 5, 27–38.

Wolpe, J., Salter, A., & Reyna, L. J. *The conditioning therapies.* New York: Holt, Rinehart & Winston, 1964.

Wolstenholme, G. E. W., & O'Connor, Maeve (Eds.) *Somatic stability in the newborn.* Ciba Foundation Symposium. Boston: Little, Brown & Co., 1961.

Woods, P. J. The effects of free and restricted environmental experience on problem-solving behavior in the rat. *J. comp. physiol. Psychol.,* 1959, 52, 399, 402.

Yarrow, L. J. Separation from parents during early childhood. In M. L. Hoffman & L. W. Hoffman (Eds.), *Review of child development research.* Vol. I. New York: Russell Sage Foundation, 1964.

Zubek, J. P., & Solberg, P. A. *Human development.* New York: McGraw-Hill, 1954.

CHAPTER 4 Childhood Socialization

HARRY LEVIN AND BARBARA FLEISCHMANN[1]
Cornell University

Typically, personality development during childhood is discussed in terms of the socialization of certain drives or behavior systems. The antecedent or independent variables are parental child-rearing practices or demographic variables such as sex of the child, ordinal position, or social class; the consequent, dependent variables are drive systems—aggression, dependency, affiliation, achievement—and the ubiquitous complex of behaviors which, for the moment, we may call identification. Not to break with tradition, and because it is difficult to find another organizational scheme for the masses of data which have been organized in this traditional fashion, this chapter will treat the "drives" named above. First, we will discuss those benchmarks of personality theory, sex-role typing and moral development, and then take up dependency and aggression.

Our appraisal of the state of the field was inevitably influenced by our conception of personality. In other parts of this handbook the nature of personality theories is the focus of concern, and indeed there may be as many points of view as there are chapters. We believe, first, that personality variables should be residual variables. Insofar as behavior can be explained by situational variables, personality theory is superfluous. Suppose someone shouts "fire!" and everyone in earshot makes for the exit. One can, we suppose, talk about the arousal of fear as a motivating state, but this does not really help to explain the invariant behavior that the warning has created. Now, imagine that the same warning is shouted and the behaviors vary. Some people run pellmell to the exit, elbowing their friends at the door; others jump out of a window; still others walk naturally to the door; and a final small knot of people remain in their seats continuing their conversation. We are tempted now to introduce personality-like concepts. Some people panicked, others were calm; some were ruthless, more were altruistic; and so on. The point is that it is inter-individual variation to a common stimulus which forces us into personality theory.

The usual personality concept has been a trait concept, and indeed this approach to explaining behavior has more or less dominated the research in developmental psychology. Let us go back to the trivial fire example. One young man ran toward the door until he saw his girl friend walking calmly and watching him. He turned back,

[1] The preparation of this chapter was supported in part by Grant MH-07226-03 from the National Institutes of Health.

joined her, waited for the crowd to squeeze through the door, and then walked to safety. We would argue that he was faced with two situations, which elicited different behaviors. To say that he was a panicky type does not make sense in terms of his later behavior. Trait theory makes the explanation difficult. We would suggest, therefore, that personality theory must make statements about the interaction between a disposition or potential for behavior and the instigation of that potential. Trait theory is justified when a range of instigating conditions all lead to the same behaviors. The disposition is so strong that almost any stimulus leads to the behavior, although even here we could think of conditions which would be out of the scope of the particular disposition. It is as though the person had a chip on his shoulder so that, regardless of what happened to him—mild stimulus or strong, relevant or irrelevant—we predict aggressive behavior.

These notions lead to examination of the antecedents of three classes of events in personality theory. The first are the conditions which determine the strength of the behavioral disposition. Another is the relevance of specific situations to this disposition, and the third is the interaction between the disposition and the correlated instigators. For example, the investigation of dependent behavior should, ideally, concern the strength of disposition toward dependency and the conditions which elicit such behavior. More often, the assumption has been that if the potential for the behavior is strong, specification of the instigators is not important. Dependent behavior will out if the child is given the opportunity, and hence the indexing of the behavior in doll play or in the classroom without attention to the nature of the setting.

The senior author was involved with a series of studies which made use of the above paradigm to study shame in children (Baldwin & Levin, 1958; Levin & Baldwin, 1958, 1959; Levin, Baldwin, Gallwey, & Paivio, 1960). Shame was treated as a hypothetical construct—an emotional state aroused by the public disclosure of failure. Various studies were designed to test the interactions between the disposition or potential for the arousal of shame and the conditions which trigger the disposition. The strength of the disposition was indexed by a variable we called "self consciousness," measured by a brief pencil and paper inventory. Variations of the situation included performance alone or to audiences of various kinds, and success or failure in a variety of tasks. The behavior most responsive to these variations was hesitations in children's speech. In one study, hesitations were differently predicted by the disposition than by the situational conditions (Levin *et al.,* 1960). Speech hesitations, characteristic of stress, responded to the situational variation of public or private performance and those indicating care in the task were related to self consciousness (Levin & Silverman, 1965). A further study in this program appraised the child-rearing antecedents of self consciousness (Paivio & Lambert, 1959).

This program of research illustrates a strategy whose main characteristic is the study of behavior across a number of situations. The disposition was independently indexed and the focus of concern was the interaction of this characteristic with the nature of the task and the social setting in which the task was performed. No claims were made for the predictive value of the disposition alone, but for the consequences of the "arousal" of the personal characteristic by external conditions.

A flow diagram indicating the categories of variables which might be treated in research on socialization is presented below. This scheme is intended as a guide to the classes of variables which might profitably be treated by research on socialization. Some of these classes, e.g., relationships between parents' and child's behaviors, have been studied frequently. We call attention particularly to the child's behavior as an antecedent to the parents' child-rearing practices. A theory which includes such interaction would be truly dyadic, a type of theory which, even after Sears's (1951) admonition about its necessity, has not often been achieved in the study of socialization. The use of theory in the research on socialization has been largely opportunistic. Psychoanalytic and behavior theories have been the major conceptual frameworks for research. Cognitive and interaction theories have had little influence, and, in fact, a serious lack is research on the socialization of cognitive and interpersonal behaviors.

In this chapter we have chosen to concern ourselves with moral development, sex typing, aggression, and dependency. For each of these topics we have selected research that seems to us to be representative or to present issues of consistent findings or of interpretation. In some cases, particularly in respect to dependency, we have emphasized recent work on the behavior itself which may point to new directions in the study of child-rearing antecedents. There is no dearth of excellent extensive reviews of the literature. We particularly call attention to the following: moral development, Kohlberg (1963b, 1964); sex role typing, Kagan (1964); dependency, Hartup (1963); aggression, Berkowitz (1962).

The usual research strategies in studying socialization are to relate child-rearing practices to child or to adult behavior. The assumption is often implicit that childhood characteristics are in some fashion related to what the person will be like as an adult.

Is the child the father to the man? Will the tallest child be the tallest adult, the most intelligent child the most intelligent adult, or the most aggressive child the most aggressive adult? Most psychologists believe, implicitly or explicitly, that childhood characteristics and experiences do predict adult behavior.

So far as physical characteristics are concerned, the question of consistency is reasonably easy to answer. By taking standard measurements of a group of individuals at

TABLE

PARENTAL AND CHILD BEHAVIOR ANALYSIS

Remote Antecedents to Parental Behavior	Intermediate Antecedents to Parental Behavior	Parental Behaviors	Situational Variables	Child's Characteristics	Child's Disposition	Child's Behavior
Grandparents' child-rearing practices Nature of parents' family origin	Behavior of child Personality characteristics of parents Parental attitudes Size family Social class Ecological characteristics of home Parental relationships	Rewards Punishments Modeling	Instigation Real Fantasy Home School	Social class Ordinal position Sex	Anxiety Aggression potential Threshold	Dependency Aggression

different ages, we can determine accurately the consistency of physical traits. Assessing the development and consistency of mental abilities, however, is more difficult. It is necessary to use different tests, and therefore different definitions, of mental ability at different ages. Bayley (1933, 1949) has done the most careful and comprehensive research on the consistency and variability of mental development. In infancy she used tests of sensorimotor ability on the assumption that rapid maturation in these areas would be predictive of later, more complex, development. Such tests when given to adults, however, have low correlations with intelligence, making the assumption tenuous.

Bayley did, in fact, find that the scores on intelligence tests administered before 2 years of age did not correlate with mature (18 or 20 years) intelligence test scores. Intelligence tests given beyond 2 years of age correlate significantly with mature intelligence and with each other. That is, any intelligence score beyond 2 years of age is predictive of adult intelligence, and intellectual functioning shows high consistency from one year to the next, after infancy. It must be noted, however, that although the correlations are significant, they do not preclude a good deal of change over time.

An interesting finding to come out of the work on intelligence is the observation that the size of the standard deviation changes over time. Variability in scores decreases until age 2 years, increases steadily until ages 9, 10, 11 when it is maximum, and then decreases until maturity (18 years). Although much of the variability may be due to the test used, there are indications that more is involved. Bayley concludes, after surveying the available data, that:

> The test scores are reflecting actual changes in variability which are inherent in the processes of development of any given function (Bayley, 1949, p. 179).

This implies that, as a function or structure develops, there are periods of high variability due both to differences in ability and to differences in rate or direction of growth. As individuals become more stable, the effects of different rates of change on the standard deviation become less. That is, during the period of rapid growth for a particular function, there will tend to be a larger range of scores.

This sort of finding is one indication that the concept of "critical periods" (to be discussed below with respect to dependency) may be applicable to human development. While a function is in a period of rapid growth, it is easily influenced by the environment. The ways in which the environment interacts with the organism during this period will have a greater influence than will later interactions. (For a detailed discussion of this notion, see Bloom, 1964.)

When attempting to demonstrate similar consistencies in personality development, the problem of definition becomes crucial. It is necessary to assume that we are looking for genotypic similarities throughout life, but that these genotypic similarities will be manifested in phenotypically different behaviors at different times. This sort of assumption may result in postdictive explanations, for almost any later behavior can then be said to derive from the same genotypic drive or habit as an earlier behavior. In some cases, where significant relationships are found between childhood and adulthood, the question arises as to whether this is an indication of consistency or of prediction. Although either relationship would be useful, "consistency" implies more understanding than we may actually have. In addition to the problem of defining the "same" behavior over time, there is also the problem of measuring this behavior when it has been defined. There are few well-accepted personality tests, and the problems inherent in observation and interview methods are manifold.

The ambitious work which has been done on personality development over time is valuable, not so much because of specific, conclusive findings, but because of the consistent, but often not individually significant, positive relationships which have been found. Although we cannot say that any one personality trait is significantly stable, the high percentage of positive correlations is suggestive that there is some behavioral consistency over time.

Tuddenham (1959), using a wide range of personality variables, in spite of the fact he did not demonstrate many significant correlations, found that the number of positive correlations obtained (92 per cent) differed significantly from the expected number (50 per cent).

Kagan and Moss (1962) also found moderate stability in dependency, aggression, and achievement. Achievement behavior showed adequate consistency for both sexes. In dependency, however, only for girls was childhood dependency highly stable and predictive of adult dependency. An opposite relationship held for aggression—boys showing greater consistency during childhood and more predictability to adulthood than girls. It would seem that sex-role training reduces unacceptable adult dependency in males and unacceptable adult aggression in females. Although there are childhood differences with respect to aggression and dependency in both sexes, the differences in aggression are decreased in girls and the differences in dependency are decreased in boys. It is interesting that for girls the range in dependency remains and that boys retain their differences in aggression. Sex-role training then does not seem to encourage the unaggressive boy to be more aggressive, nor does it encourage the independent girl to be more dependent.

In a follow-up study of the children studied by Sears, Maccoby, and Levin (1957), Sears (1961) also found low consistency of aggressive behavior from 5 to 12 years of age. He explains the finding by noting the changing role of punishment from facilitating to inhibiting. Sears points out, however, that those high in antisocial aggression at 5 but not at 12 were significantly higher in prosocial aggression at 12 than those high in antisocial aggression on both occasions, giving some indirect evidence for general behavioral consistency.

There seems to be some underlying consistency in personality behaviors between childhood and adulthood, although the evidence is difficult to obtain and is meager. For personality characteristics, the experiences intervening between the two age levels are important and are essential to understanding the ways in which behavior remains stable or changes. In discussing consistencies from childhood to adulthood it is, therefore, necessary to determine the consistency of parental treatment. The data available relate to maternal behavior, and even here there is little material on maternal behavior toward the same child over time.

Kagan and Moss (1962) suggest that a mother's behavior toward the infant will be qualitatively different from her later behavior toward the same child. It is their belief that early in the child's life the mother "acts upon" him, and later she "interacts with" him. Although they offer no direct evidence for this, they do present data suggesting some general stability of maternal behavior.

Bayley and Schaefer (1960) attempted to find the relationships of social class to maternal behavior, and in doing so took measures of maternal behavior when the child was 0 to 3 years and again when the child was 9 to 14. They found that socio-economic status had a significant effect and, more relevant, that there was consistency over time with respect to the dimensions of their study, autonomy versus control and love versus hostility.

Kagan and Moss (1962) studied maternal consistency with respect to protection, restriction, acceleration, and hostility. Protection showed moderate stability for males, none for females; acceleration, slight consistency for males, none for females; restriction, high stability for females, little for males; and hostility, moderate stability for females, none for males. Once more, sex differences seem to have a great effect on the stability of the variables studied. Maternal variables were also found to be more closely related to childhood behavior than to adult behavior. The child's own behavior during childhood was a better predictor of his adult behavior than were maternal practices.

This finding suggests that ratings of maternal behavior may not be optimal predictors of the child's behavior. Studies by Radke-Yarrow (1963) and Wenar and Coutler (1962) have found that mothers' reports of their child-rearing practices during a certain period do not show stability over time. The seeming lack of predictive validity may then be in part due to the mother's unwillingness or inability to report her behavior correctly, since data on maternal behavior are conventionally obtained by interviews.

Robbins (1963) interviewed the same group of mothers twice, separated by three years, and found that discrepancies in recall of a past period tended to move toward agreement with the opinions of experts. The trends often noted in child-rearing practices can be thought of as an interaction between actual practices and expert opinion. The evolution of child-rearing practices, then, is probably slower than it appears, for people report certain practices after the experts advise them, but before they are in use.

Several psychologists (Bronfenbrenner, 1958; Escalona, 1949; Wolfenstein, 1951, 1953; Miller & Swanson, 1958) have described and attempted to explain the trends over time in child-rearing practices. Bronfenbrenner (1958), integrating studies done at different times, which dealt with social class differences in child-rearing practices, noted that there has been a tendency in this country toward permissiveness in child training, especially in the middle class. The middle classes are more exposed and more receptive to the advice of the experts, and are probably the first to adopt the practices advocated.

Wolfenstein (1951, 1953) suggests that the increased permissiveness and indulgence, once thought harmful and now viewed as innocuous, is a result of the development of a "fun morality." The goodness morality, in which anything which was fun was necessarily immoral, has been replaced by a fun morality in which everything must be fun. Escalona (1949), on the other hand, claims that, having lost our naive faith in technology, we have all become guilt-ridden about the state of the world and try to make it up to the children by "letting" them have fun while we punish ourselves. Both Wolfenstein's driven fun and Escalona's masochistic insistence that only children should have fun seem unnecessarily pessimistic, but, in this realm of discourse, speculation has no limits.

SEX TYPING

The consequences of identification, according to psychoanalytic theory, are self-control and mature behavior. Of the latter, we shall discuss the child's acquiring behavior appropriate for his sex. Bronfenbrenner (1960) describes the two Freudian theories of identification: aggressive and anaclitic identification. The first results from the threat of the Oedipal situation; the second is based on the love or dependency relationship between the child and adult. It is doubtful that they are different processes basically. Anaclitic identification occurs when the love object is not available, which can be thought of as a situation of threat to the child. In fact, the conditions of anaclitic identification are similar to the conditions forerunning dependency, as we discuss below.

Another theory of identification has been advanced by Whiting and his students (1960). According to this status-envy theory of identification, a child will identify with the person who successfully controls or consumes a desired resource. This theory subsumes the Oedipal theory in that the child will identify with the same-sexed parent who is receiving the love of his spouse desired by the child. The status-envy theory makes certain assumptions about the child's perception of the subtleties of resource control within the family and the maintenance of behavior by vicarious satisfaction.

By far the simplest explanation of how a child learns to behave like members of his own sex is offered by Kagan (1964b). From a child's birth, adults are obviously aware of his sex and thus respond to him in certain ways. They treat girls like girls and boys like boys. Girls may like dolls better than guns simply because they receive dolls and are encouraged to play with them. The boy, likewise, is encouraged to be masculine.

The large initial range in both aggression and dependency, found by Kagan and Moss (1962), which decreased greatly with time, is an indication that the child learns to behave in ways which society believes are appropriate for his sex. The Sears, Maccoby, and Levin (1957) study on child-rearing practices does, in fact, indicate that parents allow more aggression in boys and more dependency in girls.

The desire not to be socially rejected seems, as Kagan points out, sufficient reason for sex-appropriate behavior. It is, then, not a desire to win the love of a parent which "drives" a child to identify, but instead, the desire to be accepted.

There are indications that children are able to discriminate masculinity and femininity very early in life. An experiment by Kagan, Hosken, and Watson (1961) showed that by at least 6 years of age, children of both sexes are able to make the conventional delineation of the sexes.

With some understanding of the sex role he would like to assume and having a model of that role in his home, it is reasonable that the child would choose to model himself after, or identify with, the same-sexed parent. The child will have learned, also, that inappropriate behaviors will produce negative responses in others. Having been called a "sissy" a few times, a boy will want to be more masculine and will learn how by watching his father and practicing similar behaviors. The development of identification with one's own sex is also dependent on the parents' encouraging the child to behave in sex-appropriate ways and upon their rewards or punishments for his attempts.

Several other possibilities about sex-role typing have been suggested by Lynn (1959). The early dependency on the mother and her more constant presence make it easier for the girl to identify with the same-sexed parent. Boys, on the other hand, have to rely upon the mother's training and the societal stereotype, more than upon the father as a model. Boys, however, should have the advantage of being more secure in sex-role preference, for, in our society, more status and opportunities are available to males. It may be for this reason that Lynn also suggests that there is less pressure placed upon girls than on boys to acquire sex-appropriate behaviors. Boys are quickly punished for being feminine, but a "tom-boy" is accepted.

From the very dramatic tenets of Freudian theory, then, we have moved to the common-sense notions that a child behaves in sex-appropriate ways because he is encouraged to do so by his parents and peers and wants to so that he will be accepted.

MORAL DEVELOPMENT

It is vital to society that the young child learn the rules of behavior for his society, understand these rules so that he can extend them to novel situations, and behave in accordance with these rules.

Freud first suggested that the human conscience is a learned and not an innate phenomenon, dependent primarily upon the teachings and behavior of the parents. Although his original description of the dynamics of moral development is rarely used without modification, his thinking has influenced the research and theory in this field to a greater extent than any other theorist's. Freud's concern and hence a great deal of subsequent research was with the development of moral feelings and moral behavior.

The one aspect of morality which Freud did not discuss is moral knowledge or judgment. Piaget (1932) and his followers have done the primary research in this area. Using clinical interviews and observation of children's games, Piaget observed that the moral judgments of children progress from the absolute to the relative. At first the child sees rules as absolute and authoritative—they have existed for years and are inviolate. The wrongness of a deviation is measured by the amount of harm done. From this absolute position, the child then moves to a more relative or cooperative one, in which the child realizes that rules are for the service of the participants and can be changed by mutual consent. The intentions of the wrong-doer are considered in any judgment of deviation and the punishment becomes relative to the crime. According to Piaget, by 8 or 9 years of age, all children have attained this second, cooperative stage.

Piaget's findings concerning attention to motivation or intention have been well replicated in this country (Boehm, 1962a, 1962b; Boehm & Nass, 1962; Durkin, 1959a, 1959b, 1959c, 1961). Consistently, children of 9 or older respond with "equity." Durkin (1959a, 1959c, 1961) found, however, that strict reciprocity increased and then decreased, contrary to Piaget's notion of consistent increase. She does suggest, however, the possibility that "a definition of reciprocity as being a return of identical behavior is too narrow in that it fails to include the more subtle forms of reciprocity" (Durkin, 161, pp. 12–13).

The findings with respect to social class are more definite. Boehm (Boehm, 1962a, Boehm & Nass, 1962) finds consistently that the higher the social class, the more quickly the child will adopt a morality based on equity. This difference in moral judgment related to social class is believed to be mediated by both differences in the value of material goods and differences in child-rearing practices. The fact that the lower-class family cannot replace damaged items as easily may make absolute judgments by the parents more common, and the practice of using reasoning, found in the upper classes, is thought to facilitate the change from absolute to relative judgment by the child.

The findings on the relationships between intelligence and moral judgment are contradictory. Boehm (1962a, 1962b) consistently found that, although intelligence is not so important as social class, within any social class, the more intelligent child will acquire the concept of equity before those of lower intelligence. Durkin (1959b), however, concluded from her data that "although not always statistically significant, there is a trend toward no relationship between a child's particular concept of what is just and his level of intelligence" (Durkin, 1959b, p. 256).

Although all of Piaget's observations have not been completely replicated, the change from absolute to relative moral judgment seems to be valid. Kohlberg (1963a) has developed additional stories containing intriguing moral dilemmas and has extended the development of moral judgment to six stages, adding four more complex stages to Piaget's original two.

The ability to judge situations, weigh alternatives, and make moral decisions, while not sufficient to insure moral behavior, will facilitate the production of moral conduct. The development of moral judgment proceeds as the child gains more experience and develops his language and cognitive abilities. The other two aspects of morality—behavior and feeling—although facilitated by understanding, can to an extent be learned without understanding.

When a child transgresses and is punished, the concomitant anxiety becomes associated with the transgression. Subsequently, the anxiety will follow the response prior to punishment, even when there is no objective reason to fear punishment. This anxiety-like feeling following wrongdoing is known as "guilt," and since its strength has, in much research, been considered to vary with the strength of conscience, it has been used as an index of conscience. "Guilt" can be measured in various ways: physiological measures, self-report, or observers' judgments.

Guilt following transgression would not be adaptive unless the behavior could be controlled before the actual transgression. We may assume, from the usual findings on avoidance learning, that the feelings of guilt will move forward in the behavior sequence to become associated with the instigation to transgression. This anxiety may then be reduced by "resistance to temptation." In fact, both measures, guilt following wrongdoing and resistance to temptation, have been studied as indicators of conscience development. The assumption, however, that they are, in fact, measures of the same process is not tenable.

An early experiment by MacKinnon (1947) put college students in a position in which they could cheat or not on a group of problems. He found that 50 resisted temptation and that 43 cheated. In a later interview, 22 of those who had cheated were given a chance to confess; only six of them did confess. Confessed deviators were asked whether they had felt any guilt; all others were asked whether they thought they would have felt guilty if they had cheated. A quarter of those who had cheated reported that they had (or would have) felt guilt; 84% of those who resisted reported that they would have felt guilt. This postdictive reporting would probably have been influenced by what they had actually done, but it is some indication that guilt and resistance to temptation are, in fact, associated. MacKinnon also asked his subjects what form of punishment they remembered receiving as a child. A higher proportion of cheaters recalled physical punishment, and those who resisted were more likely to recall psychological punishment.

Sears, Maccoby and Levin (1957), relying on mother interviews for information about both child-rearing practices and "evidence of conscience" found that maternal warmth and acceptance were related positively to the development of conscience. The use of withdrawal of love as a means of punishment was also associated with conscience development, but only when the mother was warm. Although these investigators cited the various responses of the child which may be considered "evidence of conscience," their rating of conscience was a global one, based, as mentioned previously, on the mother interview and concerned mostly with evidence of guilt after transgression.

Burton, Maccoby, and Allinsmith (1961) correlated 15 parental variables, rated from mothers' interviews, with children's resistance to temptation in a game situation. The resistance to temptation was an all-or-none measure; either the child did or did not conform to the rules when the experimenter was not present. No measure was taken of possible guilt feelings after cheating.

The behavioral phenomenon which they measured—a child's resistance to temptation when there seems to be no danger of being caught—is potentially quite different from the behavior measured by Sears, Maccoby, and Levin. Sears, Maccoby, and Levin asked the mothers about the child's response after transgression; Burton, Maccoby, and Allinsmith determined whether or not the child would transgress. Burton, Maccoby, and Allinsmith did find that the child-rearing practices related to their measure of conscience were different from those which had been found by Sears, Maccoby, and Levin, an indication that "guilt" and "resistance to temptation" are not as closely associated as had been assumed. They found that, for boys, early severity was related to high resistance to temptation. Punishment timing and technique were also related to resistance. Scolding and physical punishment were positively related to resistance; reasoning and deprivation of privileges, negatively related. These results indicate that the antecedents of resistance to temptation are not the same as those which MacKinnon and Sears, Maccoby, and Levin found for guilt.

Grinder (1964), using a similar game situation, and children from the Sears, Maccoby, and Levin sample, found that for girls, resistance to temptation at 12 years was significantly related both to telling about deviation and to "evidence of conscience" at the age of 5; for boys, resistance to temptation at 12 was significantly related to admission of deviation when asked at 5.

It appears that by middle childhood, experiences of guilt feelings after transgression and resistance to temptations of wrongdoing are related. In early childhood, the two behaviors are independent. Why should this be so? After the fact, the child's deviation may be either ignored or punished; it is unlikely that the parent will reward the child. The cues are reasonably clear for guilt in that he has the memory of his behaviors plus occasional physical evidences of his behavior, such as a broken dish or a bawling playmate. The acquisition conditions for resistance to temptation are more amorphous. The parent may reward or ignore him for something he has not done. The parents, however, may have guessed wrong. Even though the temptation may exist in their eyes, the move to transgression may never have entered the child's mind. They, in effect, are guessing at his intentions.

At the age of 5 it is possible that some children who have "learned" to be guilty after transgression have not yet learned that resistance to temptation is a means to avoid this guilt. Conversely, it is possible that a child may perform resistance to transgression behaviors at 5, but may not have yet acquired the understanding or been given the opportunity for experience which would enable him to understand this resistance as an avoidance of guilt.

Once the child has learned to experience guilt after transgression, we can assume that he will probably learn to avoid this guilt by resisting deviation. However, it is possible that the child may learn to resist temptation without associating this resistance with avoidance of guilt. Since the learning conditions for the two behaviors are so diverse, we may expect them to be separate behaviors to the child. When he grows older they may share a common domain, probably through the mediation of language. The concept "transgression" encompasses a single semantic category for the two behaviors so that they are responded to similarly.

As indicated by the Grinder study (1964) reported earlier, the pattern of moral development is different for girls and boys. Because of the important role that verbal mediation plays in the association of guilt and resistance to temptation, it could be hypothesized that girls, whose verbal behavior develops earlier than that of boys, would be able to make this association sooner. A look at the research findings may determine whether or not such a hypothesis is plausible.

Burton, Maccoby, and Allinsmith (1961) found that resistance to temptation in boys was related to: high activity level, severity of weaning, early sex education, high anxiety level, the use of withdrawal of love, and warmth of the mother and father. For girls, however, none of the above relationships was found, and there was a tendency for girls whose mothers thought that their daughters understood about honesty to cheat. Mothers who reported that they frequently played with their daughter also tended to have daughters who cheated.

The sex differences found in this study have been somewhat cleared up by a later study by the same researchers (in press). In this later study, again with 4-year-olds in a game situation, the sex of the experimenter and the amount of attention given to the subject before the game were varied. Subjects who were tested by an adult of the opposite sex showed less deviation. The amount of prior attention had no effect on the girls' behavior, but interrupted rather than continuous attention produced more deviation among the boys.

As the authors point out, all studies on moral development assume that if the child wishes to please the experimenter, who is never present during the game, he will conform to the rules. It is also possible that the child will want to achieve a high score in order to please the adult. Boys, then, because of past training, might feel that females would reward honesty and males, achievement. The opposite would be true for girls. There is, in fact, evidence which supports the notion that parents expect and encourage more achievement in their children of the same sex (Baldwin, Kalhorn, & Breese, 1945).

On the basis of these few studies, no conclusions about the process in which resistance to temptation and guilt are associated can be made. The process is much more complex than it first appeared. Further research in this area could contribute much to our understanding of moral development, concept formation, and child rearing variables.

In summary, then, all three components of morality—knowledge, conduct, and feeling—are necessary for the development of "moral character." The association of affect with different responses facilitates moral behavior, and an understanding of common features prevents moral behavior from being only a series of isolated responses.

DEPENDENCY

The performance of appropriate responses to organisms of the same species is necessary for species survival. The infant must be able to recognize his own species, to recognize rival species, and to develop the appropriate patterns for food getting, mating, shelter building, and protection. Heinroth (cited in Brown, 1965) observed that geese, raised without contact with members of their own species, would, while young, follow their human caretakers and, as adults, make their sexual responses to humans. This phenomenon, called "imprinting" by Lorenz, suggests that much of what was once thought to be instinctive includes a large component of learned behavior. Fortunately, the contact with another which directs this essential learning is usually with the infant's own species because of his early dependency on the mother.

Hess (1958, 1962), working with infant mallard ducks and using decoy ducks as the objects of imprinting, found that the strength of the imprinting response can be changed by varying several conditions. In ducks, imprinting is strongest when it occurs between 13 and 16 hours after birth. This indicates that there is, in some sense, a critical period for dependency. Before or after this critical period, it is more difficult to establish similar responses. The strength of imprinting was also found to be affected by the amount of effort which the infant ducklings exerted—the more effort necessary, the stronger the imprinting—but not by the duration of the imprinting period.

The phenomenon, then, occurs during a specific, critical period in the infant's life and requires only short exposure to be effective. Imprinting is a unique type of learning because of its rapid acquisition and resistance to forgetting. Imprinting experiments with other species indicate that the critical period is a common feature of animal life—a useful mechanism for species survival. It has been observed that the beginning of the critical period for imprinting is usually marked by the beginning of locomotion. The time at which the organism begins to fear strangers usually marks the end of the period during which imprinting is possible.

Since, in humans as in animals, there is a specific time when the fear response is observable (5½ to 6 months), it is possible that there is also in humans a critical period for the development of the psychological attachment necessary for the acquisition of adaptive social responses. Since human infants cannot be reared under conditions of isolation, it is necessary to get information about possible critical periods, and more generally about the nature of dependency on others, indirectly. One method of obtaining such related evidence is to work with nonhuman primates.

Harlow's program of research (Harlow, 1959; Harlow & Zimmermann, 1959) determined the nature of affectional responses in rhesus monkeys. It had long been assumed that the attachment between mother and infant developed out of the mother's properties as a secondary reinforcer—after the infant had learned to associate the mother with reduction of biological drives, her presence itself would be reinforcing. To challenge this belief, Harlow placed newborn monkeys with surrogate mothers, either a cone covered with terry cloth or one made of wire. Both "mothers," or one or the other in some experiments, were equipped to provide milk. He found that the monkeys consistently showed a strong preference for the terry cloth mother, even when it did not provide milk. Although it is possible that a wire mother is, not neutral, but actually pain-producing, Harlow's work does indicate that the theory that attachment is based on secondary reinforcement acquired during nursing is inadequate. Harlow suggests that it is the contact comfort, usually present during nursing, which promotes the development of a psychological bond. Monkeys reared solely with wire mothers did not use the surrogate to reduce their anxiety in novel field tests, whereas monkeys reared with the terry cloth mother found it to be a source of security and anxiety reduction.

It might be expected that something similar would be true of institutionalized human babies, and these data are the second source of information about the development of affectional relationships in the human. Institutionalized babies are generally given less, and more impersonal, attention than children reared by their mothers. Unfortunately, institutionalization is often associated with deprivations other than maternal deprivation and is often preceded by the destruction of close ties under traumatic circumstances. For these reasons, and because these children may be institutionalized because of congenital deficiencies, much of the data relating to "hospitalism" in children must be considered tentative.

There are, however, indications that children raised in institutions are intellectually and socially subnormal (Rheingold, 1956; Yarrow, 1961; Zigler & Williams, 1963). The fact that institutionalized children who had experienced a close relationship with another, although they later lost it, are more capable of later forming affectional ties than are children institutionalized from birth suggests that there may be a critical period for the formation of those ties which enable the individual to respond socially and to become socialized (Yarrow, 1961).

A third source of information about dependency comes from studies of the temporary isolation of normal subjects. It has been suggested that social isolation is anxiety-producing, and also that many individuals respond to anxiety from various sources by affiliating with others. This second proposition has been tested by Schachter (1959). Schachter used female college students and manipulated their anxiety by the instructions given. One group was told, in part:

> I am Dr. Gregor Zilstein of the medical school's Department of Neurology and Psychiatry . . . We would like to give each of you a series of electric shocks. Now, I feel I must be completely honest with you and tell you exactly what you are in for. These shocks will hurt, they will be painful . . . It is necessary that our shocks be intense . . . They will do no permanent damage. (Schachter, 1959, p. 13).

These instructions were designed to create high anxiety. The low anxiety group were given instructions designed to put them at ease.

After hearing either the neutral or the threatening instructions, the subjects were told that there would be a delay before the start of the experiment and were asked whether they would prefer to wait alone or with others. Most of those who had been given the low anxiety instructions did not care; those who had been given the high anxiety instructions, however, more often chose to wait with others.

Schachter then went on to show that this affiliative response was a highly specific one. Girls under the high anxiety conditions preferred to wait with others, but only with others who were also taking part in the experiment. He also found indications that forbidding verbal communication among subjects did not decrease the number choosing to wait with others.

Anxiety does seem to produce a desire for social contact, but does social isolation produce anxiety? The effectiveness of social isolation in producing anxiety is usually measured by determining the effectiveness of social reinforcement after periods of isolation. Since it has been shown that affiliation is a response to anxiety, the assumption is that subjects who had been isolated would be more responsive to affiliation.

The studies of Gewirtz and Baer (Gewirtz & Baer, 1958a, 1958b; Gewirtz, Baer, and Roth, 1958), done with young school children, indicated that isolation periods of 15 to 20 minutes do, in fact, increase responsiveness to social reinforcement, especially when the reinforcer is of the opposite sex. The work of Stevenson and Odom (1962) tentatively confirms the notion that it is social deprivation and not the more general stimulus deprivation which facilitates affiliation. This was established by the use of three conditions—one group with no isolation, one with isolation, and one provided with toys and games but socially isolated. The toy group was consistently, but not significantly, more responsive to social reinforcement than those in the control condition, but also less responsive than the isolation group. In all of the social isolation experiments, the responsiveness of the children was measured by improvement in the performance of a simple task under social reinforcement. Gewirtz and Baer (1958a) have also found that after conditions of social satiation—approval and attention for 20 minutes—children are less responsive to social reinforcement.

The effectiveness of either the technique of isolation in developing anxiety or the alleviation of possible anxiety by social reinforcement is consistently contingent upon the age and sex of the subject and the sex of the experimenter. Lewis, Wall, and Aronfreed (1963) have found that the older the subject, the less effective are social reinforcements generally, and this is presumably also true after isolation. Stevenson (1961) has found that, even without conditions of isolation, an adult of the opposite sex is a more effective reinforcing agent. The amount of anxiety aroused is probably also dependent upon the age and sex variables, although there is no direct evidence to support this.

Schachter has uncovered one other variable which mediated differences in anxiety aroused and the response to this anxiety. First born and only children, although not usually more sociable, choose to be with others significantly more than later born children when anxious. First born and only children are also significantly more anxious after the threatening instruction than are later borns.

These studies tell us something about the nature of the affiliative response, but little about its origin. As far as child-rearing practices are concerned, there is no consensus about which practices relate to later dependency. There is some indication (Sears, Maccoby & Levin, 1957; Sears, Whiting, Nowlis & Sears, 1953) that maternal warmth and acceptance of the dependency overtures of the child are related to a "healthy" amount of dependency. Failure to help or nurture the child and failure to let the child do things for himself both produce a lack of dependency. Other than these general statements, little can be said about the origins of dependency.

Since the manipulation of love and praise is a frequent and effective means of child training, however, the reactions of others do have reinforcement value for the human.

The seeking of praise, attention, support, or nurturance are all manifestations of "dependency." How do others acquire this reinforcement value for the individual? Is dependency an innate drive, is it an acquired drive derived from the biological needs whose satisfaction is mediated by others early in life, or is dependency a learned response to others' drives—notably anxiety?

Walters and Ray (1960) compared the effectiveness of social reinforcement in four groups—one isolated and made anxious, one isolated and not made anxious, one not isolated and made anxious, and one neither isolated nor made anxious. They found that anxiety, and not isolation, was the more important variable. That is, regardless of whether there was isolation, if the subject was anxious he would respond to social reinforcement; if not anxious, he would not. Social isolation, then, according to Walters and Ray, does not arouse a drive to affiliate, but may often be accompanied by anxiety, a learned response to which is affiliation.

In contrast to this experiment, Byrne (1961) divided his subjects into those with high and low need for affiliation as measured by the TAT. He then put them into a condition in which they knew that their affiliative behaviors were being rated. Those with high need affiliation were significantly more anxious than those with low need affiliation. This indicates, according to Byrne, that affiliation is indeed a drive, which will be aroused by appropriate stimulation. Neither of these experiments offers unequivocal support for dependency as a habit or as an acquired drive, although the work of Walters and Ray seems to us more convincing.

The findings on the nature of dependency behavior permit us, we believe, to make sense of some child-rearing antecedents of dependency. One point of view has been that the "dependency drive" grows out of nurturance and positive reinforcement of the child by his parents. However, if we agree with Harlow that the affectionate bond between mother and child has its antecedents in contact comfort it is reasonable to suppose that the original sources of comfort and others via stimulus generalization take on secondary reinforcing properties for the child. Hence, under stress, as in Schachter's or Walters and Ray's experiments, the person exhibits dependent behavior. In turn, if the dependent behavior, as a system of responses, is reinforced, the person should continue such behaviors. In other words, it makes sense to us to think of dependency as a set of responses having their origins in the instinctual relationships between mother and child. Later these behaviors are learned as escape responses from anxiety and so are instigated by anxiety. Finally, they may be autonomously reinforced when adults accept or encourage them.

The results reported by Sears, Maccoby, and Levin (1957) are in line with this view of the development of dependency. Both withdrawal of love and the mother's acceptance of dependent actions were related to the amount of dependent behavior which the child exhibited.

Our analysis of aggression will also follow the rationale that such behaviors are better understood as habits rather than drives.

AGGRESSION

Next to identification, aggression is probably the most frequently researched topic in socialization. Aggression is behavior whose goal response is evidence of pain or injury to a person or object. To separate this behavior from accidental injury, intention is sometimes added to the definition of aggression, although intent is difficult to infer (Levin & Wardwell, 1962). Interesting basic and applied questions have been asked about aggression. Is violence in the mass media encouraging or teaching children to be more aggressive? Will punishment for aggression only make a child more angry and thus more aggressive? Is aggression a hydraulic system—given some level of pressure will aggression out regardless of the circumstances? The questions are endless; the answers, scarce, and when present often unconvincing.

Freud's postulation of the innate nature of aggression was based on his belief that the goal of organisms is to achieve reduction of stimulation. Subsequent research has failed to substantiate this position and has shown, in fact, that organisms frequently behave in ways which serve to increase stimulation (Berlyne, 1960). Although there are theorists who still contend that aggression is innate, few believe that it is based on a drive toward self destruction. Most of those who feel that aggression is an innate tendency also believe that the form it takes will be determined by learning experiences (Berkowitz, 1962). Implicit also in an instinctual theory is the notion that aggression must be expressed if the organism is to remain sound. The impulses to aggression, if not expressed, become so strong that they will produce aggressive behavior even without appropriate external stimulation. This latter proposition has been somewhat discredited by the animal studies which have consistently shown that animals must be trained to behave aggressively. There is no natural selection of opponents nor is there any aggressive behavior without some form of learning (as discussed in Berkowitz, 1962). As we will discuss below, we believe that there is an unlearned basis for aggression, as there is for dependency, but that its form is quite different from the conventional view of instinctive behavior.

The most influential publication on aggression is still the monograph, *Frustration and Aggression* (Dollard, Doob, Miller, Mowrer, & Sears, 1939). It was the contention of the Yale group that aggression was a consequence of frustration, and that all frustrations led to aggression. Frustration was defined as those circumstances which interfere with goal-directed behavior. Both postulates have been faulted for being too broad. When frustration does not lead to aggression the inhibition against aggressive behavior may be strong. Then again, frustration often will produce constructive behavioral change, regression in goal choice, regression in behavior, or stereotyped behavior. If frustration does not necessarily produce aggression, can we say that all aggression is the result of frustration? This question is difficult to answer, for any time an aggressive act is observed, it is possible to find antecedents which might be considered frustrating. The definition of frustration then becomes: any behavior preceding aggression, including pain and threats to an individual's self-esteem. Such a circular definition has no predictive value, and we are left with the uninformative statement that frustration may produce aggression and aggression may be anteceded by frustration.

The original work of Dollard *et al.* has also been criticized for its failure to consider the affective state of the organism. It has been suggested by several psychologists, including Berkowitz (1962), that frustration gives rise to an emotional state—anger—which may be responded to by behaving aggressively. This formulation is similar to that used in this paper for dependency; that is, frustration, like social isolation, produces physiological arousal. The response to this arousal is in large part a function of past learning.

Aggression, defined as behavior whose goal is to do intentional harm, is a general term, covering behaviors which could be instigated in many ways. Further, aggression may be divided into two categories: instrumental aggression and goal aggression. Instrumental aggression is concerned with those aggressive acts whose purpose is to achieve some goal. One may be aggressive to obtain possession of a certain object, to win a football game, to win a war, or to achieve power and control. The aggressive behaviors in these cases are performed with intention to harm, not for the sake of harm, but because it is the most efficient way of obtaining the desired goal. If there were some other way to obtain the same ends which was also effective, the individual might be expected to choose this other method. In other words, aggressive acts have been effective in reaching various goals and so are continued.

Goal aggression, on the other hand, has as its purpose injury to another, and it is for such behavior that researchers have postulated an aggressive drive. The distinction is muddy, and we question the usefulness of the drive concept applied to aggression. Following Berkowitz (1962), it makes sense to us to think of emotional arousal as an unlearned response to frustration, in much the same way that pain and fear are connected. Aggressive acts which are instigated by frustration are reinforced if they reduce the aroused state. Such responses, may, of course, be attacks on the frustrators, and these are the behaviors which have often been called "goal aggression." Or, the person may adaptively respond to the frustration, thus serving two purposes: the reduction of emotion and the attainment of some goal. These are the acts which are labeled instrumental aggression. In other words, we see no need for the concept, aggressive drive, as earlier we were prepared to do away with the dependency drive. Aggressive behaviors are used either as habitual means of goal attainment or as learned responses to the arousal associated with frustration.

During socialization, aggressive acts may be punished, and the inhibition may extend to the feelings themselves. The extent and the intensity of overt aggression, then, are a function of both the strength of instigation and that of inhibition.

Before reviewing the research on aggression, it is useful to inspect the typical methods of measuring aggression. When observation is used, there are several cautions which must be noted. To score a behavior as aggressive, the observer must distinguish the behavior from accidental injury. It is also necessary to take the setting and the instigating conditions into account. Fantasy measures of aggression have been used frequently under the assumption that inhibitions to aggression will be minimized.

When studying aggression in young children, the conventional measure has been fantasy aggression in doll play (Levin & Wardwell, 1962). It has been found that, by not punishing the child for aggressive actions during doll play, he will show more aggression across sessions. Decreased inhibition has been used to explain this phenomenon. A study by Siegel and Kohn (1959), however, indicated that the presence of a permissive adult experimenter may be more encouraging than neutral. Siegel and Kohn measured the aggressive behavior of two groups, one with an adult present and one with none present, for two sessions. The adult present group increased in aggressiveness from the first to the second session; the adult absent group showed decreasing amounts of aggression. A similar study by Levin and Turgeon (1957) was designed to investigate further the amount of inhibition or facilitation in the doll-play situation and to test Miller's displacement model. Miller (1948) contends that aggression will be displaced onto noninstigating objects to the extent that they are similar to the original instigators. It had been assumed that doll play was similar enough to the home to instigate aggression, but different enough to decrease inhibition. Levin and Turgeon, however, found that a child was more aggressive in the second doll-play session when his mother was present than when a stranger was present. That is, the expected increase in inhibition did not occur. This finding along with that of Siegel and Kohn suggest that the freedom of the doll-play setting does not simply reduce inhibition, but may instigate aggressive acts as well.

The Thematic Apperception Test (TAT) is commonly used as a measure of fantasy aggression for older children and adults. The use of fantasy measures of aggression raises the issue of the relationship of such behavior to overt aggression. Some support for the notion that the TAT measures the individual's wished-for but inhibited aggressive behavior is found in the work of Lesser (1957). By dividing his subjects into those whose mothers were permissive of aggression and those whose mothers punished aggression, Lesser found that for the children whose mothers allowed aggression, the fantasy aggression scores were positively related to the amount of overt aggression. If the mother discouraged aggression, the fantasy aggression score was negatively correlated with overt behavior. Mussen and Naylor (1954) have also found that by considering a subject's TAT aggression score in relation to his expectancy for punishment, as also measured by the TAT, the prediction to overt behavior is increased.

On the other hand, a study by Kagan (1956) has shown that the more realistic and appropriate the TAT card, the better it is able to predict overt behavior. This can be explained if we consider that the individual may be responding in terms of his past learning experiences and not necessarily reflecting his wished-for, but prohibited aggression. Doll play also appears to tap replication of real experiences rather than being a measure of wish-fulfillment. Kagan's study points out clearly the value of varying the instigation conditions for understanding aggression. Attempts to quantify aggression in terms of the number of overt or fantasy aggressive acts in a standard situation are inadequate. It is unrealistic in many cases to say that one person is more aggressive than another, for while in one situation he may be, he might be less aggressive in a different situation. As mentioned earlier, it is necessary to study both the situation and the individual. If we could determine the amount of aggression generally produced by different situations and also look at individual differences in responding to a set of situations, we would be much closer to understanding and predicting the behavior in question.

A fairly recent concern in the study of aggression has been the effects on the observer of seeing aggressive behavior, especially in the mass media. Bandura, Ross, and Ross (1961) conducted an experiment in which 3- to 5-year-old children were exposed to models who behaved either aggressively or nonaggressively. They found that the subject exposed to the aggressive models imitated many of their actions, but it is unclear whether there were changes in the amount of total aggression. A subsequent study by the same authors (Bandura, Ross, & Ross, 1963b) made use of aggressive models of three types—real-life human models, human models on film, and a cartoon film. Here they found that all three experimental groups showed significantly more total aggression than did a control group. There were, however, no significant differences in total aggression among the experimental groups. Also, the real-life model was more effective in producing imitative aggression than the other two presentations, although the difference was significant only from the cartoon condition. This experimental work indicates that the observation of aggression may, in fact, increase its incidence.

A study by Walters, Llewellyn, and Acker (1962), using adults and employing a procedure in which the person was asked to shock another (who was actually unharmed), found an increasing willingness to hurt the other after viewing an aggressive film. This study, using victims capable of experiencing pain, seems to be a strong indictment against aggressive movies and suggests that the observation of aggression is indeed inducing to aggressive behavior.

There is, however, an alternative theory regarding the effects of observing aggression. Basing their opinions on either Freud's catharsis hypothesis or Miller's displacement model, many theorists believe that fantasy aggression will serve as an outlet and will decrease the probability of future overt aggression. There has been some evidence against this theory obtained by Mussen and Rutherford (1961) who exposed their subjects to aggressive and nonaggressive films after frustration or without frustration. They found that frustration had no effect on the amount of aggression shown in doll play. The type of film viewed, however, did affect the resulting aggression.

Feshbach (1955) has obtained results with college students which are seemingly opposite to those of Mussen and Rutherford. After insulting his subjects, he either allowed them to express their aggression in fantasy or prevented them from doing so. Afterwards, a measure of aggression toward the experimenter was obtained. The group who had expressed their aggression showed significantly less aggression toward the investigator than did the other group.

Feshbach explains these divergent results by suggesting that the expression of aggression allowed to one group may increase their guilt or anxiety and not lower their aggression. Since his subjects were involved in active fantasy production—writing answers to TAT cards—and Mussen and Rutherford's subjects merely viewed a film, this seems a plausible explanation. Watching an aggressive film, then, would tend to increase the individual's aggression whether or not he had been frustrated, but performing aggression, even in fantasy, might increase guilt and therefore decrease future aggressive behavior. A further source of the differences between the two studies is that in the Mussen and Rutherford study, the post-fantasy measure of aggression was doll play—which is itself a fantasy measure. They have, then, actually shown that passive fantasy aggression will increase the amount of active fantasy, whereas Feshbach's work indicates that active (and in a later study, passive) fantasy will decrease overt aggression. Experiments in this problem must, it seems, take into account the active or passive nature of the expression of aggression as well as the final appraisal of aggression by overt and fantasy indices.

These studies, in addition to telling us something about the effects of violence in the mass media, also provide useful information concerning the nature of aggression. If, as the Bandura (Bandura, Ross, & Ross, 1961, 1963b) studies indicate, aggression is often imitated, it is probable that children with aggressive parents will be aggressive. The research of Sears, Maccoby, and Levin (1957) has, in fact, shown that children who have parents high on both permissiveness and punishment of aggression will themselves be aggressive. A punishing parent becomes a model for the child and his punishing behavior then defeats its own purpose when the child emulates his actions (Levin & Sears, 1956).

The association between aggressive behaviors and imitation is strengthened by the additional finding that physical punishment for aggression will produce more aggression (Sears, Maccoby, & Levin, 1957).

The original Sears, Maccoby, and Levin data were collected when the children were 5 years old. Later information obtained by Sears (1961) on some of the children who had been in the original sample indicates that, at age 13, the effects of high punishment have reversed somewhat. This change in the effect of punishment may be related to the child's changing ability to understand and learn and to his changing perception of the parents.

Aggressive behaviors are learned responses to arousal induced by frustration or are instrumental acts in the service of various goals. Aggressive behaviors are easily imitated, so that the conditions for imitation are important determiners of the circumstances under which aggressive behaviors are learned.

As we reviewed the various topics in this chapter, we formed the following impressions:

1. Research on socialization is dominated by a trait approach to personality so that variations in behavior across situations receive relatively little attention. Following the trait assumptions, the behaviors are appraised by projective devices such as the TAT or doll play. At the same time, experimental research on the behaviors indicates their variation as a function of various manipulated conditions. We suggest that uniting the experimental and child-rearing-antecedent approaches would be fruitful. There are nascent indica-

tions of this combination when, for example, the sex of the experimenter is varied or when the eliciting qualities of various TAT cards are taken into consideration.

2. The research on socialization, despite its volume, does not seem to be cumulative. We tried to order studies by common problems or by common measures and were unsuccessful. Aggression, to take one example, has numerous definitions and, in turn, is measured in still more ways. There is somewhat more consensus on child-rearing variables. Until there is more agreement on variables and measures, socialization will be a field of many interesting studies which cannot be summed to a significant body of science.

These pessimistic impressions led us to speculate about the conditions of research on personality which might achieve cumulative results. The procedures by which the physical sciences achieve consensus on definitions are informative, although we do not wish to imply that the behavioral sciences need unequivocally model themselves on the more precise disciplines. The measurement of the velocity of light provides a good example. When various measurements do not agree, the interim accepted value is some combination of the measures. There is a general skepticism about any published value so that an accepted part of the scientific endeavor is to check the previously announced findings. Occasionally, a method is so obviously clear and striking (as the measurement by radar in this case) that the new findings are generally, yet provisionally, accepted. Sometimes, an elder scientific statesman appoints himself the "keeper of the constants" and his judgment is accepted by the scientific community. Finally, international congresses are convened to decide on the appropriate measures.

Obviously, this analogy is only grossly applicable to the behavioral sciences. Yet, we have had instances where a generally agreed upon measure (e.g., the measurement of need achievement by the TAT) has forced cumulative and comparable results. We see another, albeit indirect, implication. If for any domain of variables—aggression, dependency, achievement, etc.—the psychological community decided on a basic indexing measure—a bench mark—all other measures could be calibrated against it. In a sense, the Stanford-Binet serves this function for the study of intelligence. At any rate, we see a substantial problem and suggest these several approaches toward its solution.

SUMMARY

In this chapter we have discussed the selected topics of sex-role typing, moral development, dependency, and aggression.

1. Sex-Typing

The child learns to behave in ways appropriate to his sex because he is encouraged to do so. Parents have different expectancies for boys and girls—they treat them differently and expect different behaviors from them. The child's successful identification with his own sex is dependent mainly upon the adequacy of the models presented to him and the amount of encouragement he receives from parents and peers.

Following Kagan (1964b), we believe that the primary reason for identifying with one's own sex is the desire to be accepted. Attributing complex motivation to the child's sex-appropriate behaviors, as most theories of identification tend to do, has not been fruitful.

2. Moral Development

The development of "moral character" can be thought of as the development of three overlapping components—moral judgment, moral feeling, and moral behavior. Moral judgment is a cognitive process that undergoes change with age. The individual matures in his moral judgments as he develops the abilities to generalize from his own experience and knowledge, to consider the intentions and wishes of others, and to perceive the implications of his own actions. If the individual is capable of mature moral judgment, we expect that he will be capable of moral conduct. The production of consistent moral behavior without the ability to generalize and to anticipate the future is difficult to imagine. It makes sense, therefore, to say that the ability to form moral judgments in novel situations is a necessary but not a sufficient condition for the development of moral character.

Moral feeling, too, is necessary if moral behavior is to be consistent. The association of guilt, or anxiety, with transgression enables the individual to later learn to resist temptation so as to avoid this anxiety. Although certain acts of resistance to temptation could be performed, not to avoid anxiety, but to be rewarded, these behaviors would not form a "moral category." The resistance to temptation behaviors and the guilt associated with transgression must eventually be understood by the child as occupying a common domain.

3. Dependency and Aggression

Aggression and dependency can be discussed together, because the mechanisms we have chosen to explain them are similar. The basis of both of these types of behavior is emotional arousal. Dependency behaviors have their origin in the intricately instinctual mother-child relationship. From these early experiences the child comes to associate mother, and later others, with security and comfort. He will then perform dependency behaviors when anxious. Aggression, also, can be seen as a response to arousal. In this case, there is an innate association between frustration and arousal. From the cues offered by other people or by the situation in which frustration has occurred the organism learns to respond aggressively. The aggressive acts serve as instrumental to reduction of arousal and/or to goal attainment.

In reviewing the literature on these two topics, it was difficult to reach firm conclusions on the child-rearing antecedents or situational determinants of the behaviors. In these areas, problems of definition and measurement seem especially acute.

REFERENCES

Aronfreed, J. The effect of experimental socialization paradigms upon two moral responses to transgression. *J. abnorm. soc. Psychol.*, 1963, 66, 437–448.

Aronfreed, J. The origin of self-criticism. *Psychol. Rev.*, 1964, 71, 193–218.

Aronfreed, J. The nature, variety, and social patterning of moral responses to transgression. *J. abnorm. soc. Psychol.*, 1961, 63, 223–240.

Baldwin, A. L., Kalhorn, Joan, & Breese, Fay H. Patterns of parent behavior. *Psychol. Monogr.*, 1945, 58, Whole No. 268.

Baldwin, A. L., & Levin, H. Effects of public and private success or failure on children's repetitive motor behavior. *Child Develpm.*, 1958, 29, 363–372.

Bandura, A. Social learning through imitation. In M. R. Jones (Ed.), *Nebraska Symposium on Motivation.* Lincoln, Neb.: Univer. of Nebraska Press, 1962. Pp. 211–274.

Bandura, A., & Huston, Aletha. Identification as a process of incidental learning. *J. abnorm. soc. Psychol.*, 1961, 63, 311–319.

Bandura, A., & McDonald, F. J. The influence of social reinforcement and the behavior of models in shaping children's moral judgments. *J. abnorm. soc. Psychol.*, 1963, 67, 274–282.

Bandura, A., Ross, Dorothea, & Ross, Sheila A. Transmission of aggression through imitation of aggressive models. *J. abnorm. soc. Psychol.*, 1961, 63, 575–582.

Bandura, A., Ross, Dorothea, & Ross, Sheila A. A comparative test of the status envy, social power, and secondary reinforcement theories of identificatory learning. *J. abnorm. soc. Psychol.*, 1963, 67, 527–534. (a)

Bandura, A., Ross, Dorothea, & Ross, Sheila A. Imitation of film-mediated aggressive models. *J. abnorm. soc. Psychol.*, 1963, 66, 3–11. (b)

Bandura, A., & Walters, R. H. Aggression. In H. W. Stevenson (Ed.), *Child psychology.* Chicago: National Society for the Study of Education, 1963. Pp. 364–415.

Bayley, Nancy. Mental growth during the first three years. *Genet. Psychol. Monogr.,* 1933, 14, 1–92.

Bayley, Nancy. Consistency and variability in the growth of intelligence from birth to eighteen years. *J. genet. Psychol.,* 1949, 75, 165–196.

Bayley, Nancy. Some increasing parent-child similarities during the growth of children. *J. educ. Psychol.,* 1954, 45, 1–21.

Bayley, Nancy, & Schaefer, E. Relationships between socioeconomic variables and the behavior of mothers toward young children. *J. genet. Psychol.,* 1960, 96, 61–77.

Berkowitz, L. *Aggression.* New York: McGraw-Hill, 1962.

Berlyne, D. E. *Conflict, arousal, and curiosity.* New York: McGraw-Hill, 1960.

Bloom, B. S. *Stability and change in human characteristics.* New York: Wiley, 1964.

Boehm, Leonore. The development of conscience: a comparison of American children of different mental and socioeconomic levels. *Child Develpm.,* 1962, 33, 575–590. (a)

Boehm, Leonore. The development of conscience: a comparison of students in Catholic parochial schools and in public schools. *Child Develpm.,* 1962, 33, 591–602. (b)

Boehm, Leonore, & Jones, H. Environmental correlates of mental and motor development. *Child Develpm.,* 1937, 8, 329–341.

Boehm, Leonore, & Nass, M. L. Social class differences in conscience development. *Child Develpm.,* 1962, 33, 565–574.

Brim, O. Family structure and sex role learning in children. *Sociometry,* 1958, 21, 1–16.

Bronfenbrenner, U. Socialization and social class through time and space. In Eleanor E. Maccoby, T. M. Newcomb, & E. L. Hartley (Eds.), *Readings in social psychology.* New York: Holt, Rinehart, and Winston, 1958. Pp. 400–425.

Bronfenbrenner, U. The changing American child. Paper read at the White House conference on children and youth, 1960. (a)

Bronfenbrenner, U. Freudian theories of identification and their derivatives. *Child Develpm.,* 1960, 31, 15–40. (b)

Bronfenbrenner, U. Developmental theory in transition. In H. W. Stevenson (Ed.), *Child psychology.* Chicago: National Society for the Study of Education, 1963. Pp. 517–542.

Bronson, Wanda C., Katten, Edith S., & Livson, N. Patterns of authority and affection in two generations. *J. abnorm. soc. Psychol.,* 1959, 58, 143–152.

Brown, J. S. Problems presented by the concept of acquired drives. In M. R. Jones (Ed.), *Current theory and research in motivation.* Lincoln, Neb.: Univer. of Nebraska Press, 1953. Pp. 1–23.

Brown, R. *Social psychology.* New York: The Free Press, 1965.

Burton, R. V., Maccoby, Eleanor E., & Allinsmith, W. Antecedents of resistance to temptation in four-year-old children. *Child Develpm.,* 1961, 32, 689–710.

Burton, R. V., Maccoby, Eleanor E. & Allinsmith, W. Resistance to temptation in relation to sex of child, sex of *E,* and withdrawal of attention. *J. pers. soc. Psychol.,* in press.

Byrne, D. Anxiety and experimental arousal of affiliation. *J. abnorm. soc. Psychol.,* 1961, 63, 660–662.

Caldwell, Bettye. The usefulness of the critical period hypothesis in the study of filiative behavior. *Merrill-Palmer Quart.,* 1962, 8, 229–242.

Dollard, J., Doob, L., Miller, N., Mowrer, O., & Sears, R. *Frustration and aggression.* New Haven: Yale Univer. Press, 1939.

Durkin, Dolores. Children's concepts of justice: a comparison with the Piaget data. *Child Develpm.,* 1959, 30, 59–67. (a)

Durkin, Dolores. Children's concepts of justice: a further comparison with Piaget data. *J. educ. Res.,* 1959, 30, 252–257. (b)

Durkin, Dolores. Children's acceptance of reciprocity as a justice principle. *Child Develpm.,* 1959, 30, 289–296. (c)

Durkin, Dolores. The specificity of children's moral judgments. *J. genet. Psychol.,* 1961, 98, 3–13.

Escalona, Sibylle. A commentary upon some recent changes in child rearing practices. *Child Develpm.,* 1949, 20, 157–162.

Feshbach, S. The drive-reducing function of fantasy behavior. *J. abnorm. soc. Psychol.,* 1955, 50, 3–11.

Feshbach, S. The catharsis hypothesis and some consequences of interaction with aggressive and neutral play objects. *J. Pers.,* 1956, 24, 449–462.

Feshbach, S. The stimulating versus cathartic effects of a vicarious aggressive activity. *J. abnorm. soc. Psychol.,* 1961, 63, 381–385.

Gewirtz, J. L., & Baer, D. M. Deprivation and satiation of social reinforcers as drive conditions. *J. abnorm. soc. Psychol.,* 1958, 57, 165–172. (a)

Gewirtz, J. L., & Baer, D. M. The effect of brief social deprivation on behaviors for a social reinforcer. *J. abnorm. soc. Psychol.,* 1958, 56, 49–56. (b)

Gewirtz, J. L., Baer, D. M., & Roth, Chaya H. A note on the similar effects of low social availability of an adult and brief social deprivation on young children's behavior. *Child Develpm.,* 1958, 29, 149–152.

Gilmore, J. B., & Zigler, E. Birth order and social reinforcer effectiveness. *Child Develpm.,* 1964, 35, 193–200.

Grinder, R. Parental child rearing practices, conscience, and resistance to temptation in sixth grade children. *Child Develpm.,* 1962, 33, 803–820.

Grinder, R. Relations between behavioral and cognitive dimensions of conscience in middle childhood. *Child Develpm.,* 1964, 35, 881–891.

Harlow, H. F. Love in infant monkeys. *Sci. Amer.,* 1959, 200, 68–74.

Harlow, H. F., & Zimmermann, R. R. Affiliative responses in the infant monkey. *Science,* 1959, 130, 421–432.

Hartup, W. W. Nurturance and nurturance-withdrawal in relation to the dependency behavior of preschool children. *Child Develpm.,* 1958, 29, 191–201.

Hartup, W. W. Dependence and independence. In H. W. Stevenson (Ed.), *Child psychology.* Chicago: National Society for the Study of Education, 1963. Pp. 333–363.

Hartup, W. W. Patterns of imitative behavior in young children. *Child Develpm.,* 1964, 35, 183–191.

Hess, E. Ethology. In R. Brown, E. Galanter, E. Hess, & G. Mandler (Eds.), *New directions in psychology.* New York: Holt, Rinehart, & Winston, 1962. Pp. 157–256.

Hess, E. Imprinting in animals. *Sci. Amer.,* 1958, 198, 81–90.

Jensen, A. R. Aggression in fantasy and overt behavior. *Psychol. Monogr.,* 1957, 71, Whole No. 445.

Jones, H., & Bayley, Nancy. The Berkeley growth study. *Child Develpm.,* 1941, 12, 167–173.

Kagan, J. The measurement of overt aggression from fantasy. *J. abnorm. soc. Psychol.,* 1956, 52, 390–393.

Kagan, J. The concept of identification. *Psychol. Rev.,* 1958, 65, 296–305.

Kagan, J. American longitudinal research on psychological development. *Child Develpm.,* 1964, 35, 1–32. (a)

Kagan, J. Acquisition and significance of sex typing and sex role identity. In M. L. Hoffman and L. W. Hoffman (Eds.), *Review of child development research.* New York: Russell Sage Foundation, 1964. Pp. 137–167. (b)

Kagan, J., Hosken, Barbara, & Watson, Sara. Child's symbolic conceptualization of parents. *Child Develpm.,* 1961, 32, 625–636.

Kagan, J., & Moss, H. *Birth to maturity.* New York: Wiley, 1962.

Kagan, J., & Moss, H. The stability of passive and dependent behavior from childhood through adulthood. *Child Develpm.,* 1960, 31, 577–591.

Kagan, J., & Moss, H. Stability and validity of achievement fantasy. *J. abnorm. soc. Psychol.,* 1959, 58, 357–364.

Kagan, J., Sontag, L. W., Baker, C. T., & Nelson, Virginia L. Personality and I.Q. change. *J. abnorm. soc. Psychol.,* 1958, 56, 261–266.

Kohlberg, L. The development of children's orientations toward a moral order. *Vita hum.,* 1963, 6, 11–33. (a)

Kohlberg, L. Moral development and identification. In H. W. Stevenson (Ed.), *Child psychology.* Chicago: National Society for the Study of Education, 1963. Pp. 277–332. (b)

Kohlberg, L. Development of moral character and moral ideology. In M. L. Hoffman & L. W. Hoffman (Eds.), *Review of child development research.* New York: Russell Sage Foundation, 1964. Pp. 383–431.

Lesser, G. S. The relationship between overt and fantasy aggression as a function of maternal response to aggression. *J. abnorm. soc. Psychol.,* 1957, 55, 218–221.

Levin, H., & Baldwin, A. L. The choice to exhibit. *Child Develpm.,* 1958, 29, 373–380.

Levin, H., & Baldwin, A. L. Pride and shame in children. In M. R. Jones (Ed.), *Nebraska Symposium on Motivation.* Lincoln, Neb.: Univer. of Nebraska Press, 1959. Pp. 138–173.

Levin, H., Baldwin, A. L., Gallwey, Mary, & Paivio, A. Audience stress, personality, and speech. *J. abnorm. soc. Psychol.,* 1960, 61, 469–473.

Levin, H., & Sears, R. R. Identification with parents as a determinant of doll-play aggression. *Child Develpm.,* 1956, 27, 135–153.

Levin, H., & Silverman, Irene. Hesitation phenomena in children's speech. *Lang. Speech,* 1965, 8, 67–85.

Levin, H., & Turgeon, Valerie F. The influence of the mother's presence on children's doll-play aggression. *J. abnorm. soc. Psychol.,* 1957, 55, 304–308.

Levin, H., & Wardwell, Elinor. The research uses of doll play. *Psychol. Bull.,* 1962, 59, 27–56.

Lewis, M., Wall, K. M., & Aronfreed, J. Developmental change in the relative values of social and nonsocial reinforcement. *J. exp. Psychol.,* 1963, 66, 133–137.

Lovaas, O. I. Effect of exposure to symbolic aggression on aggressive behavior. *Child Develpm.,* 1961, 32, 37–44.

Lynn, D. A note on sex differences in the development of masculine and feminine identification. *Psychol. Rev.,* 1959, 66, 126–135.

Maccoby, Eleanor E. Role-taking in childhood and its consequences for social learning. *Child Develpm.,* 1959, 30, 239–252.

Maccoby, Eleanor E. The taking of adult roles in middle childhood. *J. abnorm. soc. Psychol.,* 1961, 63, 493–504.

MacKinnon, D. Personality differences between violators and nonviolators of prohibition. In H. A. Murray (Ed.), *Explorations in personality.* New York: Oxford Univer. Press, 1947. Pp. 491–501.

MacRae, D. A test of Piaget's theories of moral development. *J. abnorm. soc. Psychol.,* 1954, 49, 14–18.

Miller, D. R., & Swanson, G. E. *The changing American parent.* New York: Wiley, 1958.

Miller, N. E. Theory and experiment relating psychoanalytic displacement to S-R generalization. *J. abnorm. soc. Psychol.,* 1948, 43, 155–178.

Mussen, P. H., & Naylor, H. K. The relationships between overt and fantasy aggression. *J. abnorm. soc. Psychol.,* 1954, 49, 235–240.

Mussen, P. H., & Rutherford, E. Effects of aggressive cartoons on children's aggressive play. *J. abnorm. soc. Psychol.,* 1961, 62, 461–465.

Mussen, P. H., & Rutherford, E. Parent-child relations and parental personality in relation to young children's sex role preferences. *Child Develpm.,* 1963, 34, 586–606.

Paivio, A., & Lambert, W. E. Measures and correlates of audience anxiety ("stage fright"). *J. Pers.,* 1959, 27, 1–17.

Piaget, J. *The moral judgment of the child.* New York: Free Press, 1932.

Radke-Yarrow, Marian. The elusive evidence. Presidential address to the Division on Developmental Psychology, Amer. Psychol. Assoc., 1963.

Rheingold, Harriet L. The modification of social responsiveness in institutional babies. *Monogr. Soc. Res. Child Develpm.,* 1956, 21, No. 2.

Robbins, Lillian C. The accuracy of parental recall of aspects of child development and child rearing practices. *J. abnorm. soc. Psychol.,* 1963, 66, 261–278.

Schachter, S. *The psychology of affiliation.* Stanford: Stanford Univer. Press, 1959.

Sears, Pauline S. Doll-play aggression in normal young children: influence of sex, age, sibling status, father's absence. *Psychol. Monogr.,* 1951, 65, Whole No. 323.

Sears, R. R. Relation of fantasy aggression to interpersonal aggression. *Child Develpm.,* 1950, 21, 5–6.

Sears, R. R. A theoretical framework for personality and social behavior. *Amer. Psychologist,* 1951, 6, 476–483.

Sears, R. R. Relation of early socialization experiences to aggression in middle childhood. *J. abnorm. soc. Psychol.,* 1961, 63, 466–492.

Sears, R. R. Dependency motivation. In M. R. Jones (Ed.), *Nebraska Symposium on Motivation.* Lincoln, Neb.: Univer. of Nebraska Press, 1963. Pp. 25–65.

Sears, R. R., Maccoby, Eleanor E., & Levin, H. *Patterns of child rearing.* Evanston, Ill.: Row, Peterson, & Co., 1957.

Sears, R. R., Whiting, J. W. M., Nowlis, V., & Sears, Pauline S. Some child-rearing antecedents of aggression and dependency in young children. *Genet. Psychol. Monogr.,* 1953, 47, 135–234.

Siegel, Alberta E. Film-mediated fantasy aggression and strength of aggressive drive. *Child Develpm.,* 1956, 27, 365–378.

Siegel, Alberta E., & Kohn, Lynette G. Permissiveness, permission, and aggression: The effect of adult presence or absence on aggression in children's play. *Child Develpm.*, 1959, 30, 131–141.

Stevenson, H. W. Social reinforcement with children as a function of chronological age, sex of *E*, and sex of *S*. *J. abnorm. soc. Psychol.*, 1961, 63, 147–154.

Stevenson, H. W., Keen, Rachel, & Knight, R. M. Parents and strangers as reinforcing agents for children's performance. *J. abnorm. soc. Psychol.*, 1962, 65, 429–430.

Stevenson, H. W., & Odom, R. D. The effectiveness of social reinforcement following two conditions of deprivation. *J. abnorm. soc. Psychol.*, 1962, 65, 429–430.

Stone, A. A., & Onque, Gloria C. *Longitudinal studies of child personality.* Cambridge: Harvard Univer. Press, 1959.

Tuddenham, R. D. The constancy of personality ratings over two decades. *Genet. Psychol. Monogr.*, 1959, 60, 3–29.

Walters, R. H., & Karal, Pearl. Social deprivation and verbal behavior. *J. Pers.*, 1960, 28, 89–107.

Walters, R. H., Llewellyn, T. E., & Acker, C. W. Enhancement of punitive behavior by audio-visual displays. *Science*, 1962, 136, 872–873.

Walters, R. H., & Parke, R. D. Dependency and susceptibility to social influence. In L. Berkowitz (Ed.), *Advances in experimental social psychology.* New York: Academic Press, 1964. Pp. 231–276.

Walters, R. H., & Ray, E. Anxiety, social isolation, and reinforcer effectiveness. *J. Pers.*, 1960, 28, 358–367.

Wenar, C., & Coutler, Jane B. A reliability study of developmental histories. *Child Develpm.*, 1962, 33, 453–462.

Whiting, J. W. M. Resource mediation and learning by identification. In I. Iscoe and H. W. Stevenson (Eds.), *Personality development in children.* Austin: Univer. of Texas Press, 1960. Pp. 112–126.

Wolfenstein, Martha. The emergence of the fun morality. *J. Soc. Issues*, 1951, 7, 15–25.

Wolfenstein, Martha. The emergence of the *Amer. J. Orthopsychiat.*, 1953, 23, 120–130.

Yarrow, L. Maternal deprivation: toward an empirical and conceptual reevaluation. *Psychol. Bull.*, 1961, 58, 459–490.

Zigler, E., & Williams, Joanne. Institutionalization and the effectiveness of social reinforcement. *J. abnorm. soc. Psychol.*, 1963, 66, 197–205.

CHAPTER 5 Adolescent Socialization and Development

GLEN H. ELDER, JR.
University of North Carolina, Chaple Hill

This chapter uses a developmental perspective to examine processes of socialization and personality between childhood and the adult years. Throughout these years, the course of development is formed by transactions among past, present, and anticipated properties of the individual and his social setting. Within the limits of available data, the antecedents of socialization and personality in adolescence are traced to factors in the childhood years. The scope of the review is extended to adulthood in order to identify conditions predictive of continuity and discontinuity in adolescent behavior.

Through socialization, the adolescent learns his position in the social matrix and the ways of the larger community in which he will eventually assume adult roles. These ways include required skills, codes of behavior, and social privileges. Through interaction with others, the adolescent learns to know and accept himself in sex role, physique, and talents; develops interpersonal skills and meaningful friendships with agemates of the same and opposite sex; acquires confidence, judgment, inner controls, and personal values which enable mature independence; and becomes oriented toward occupational roles.

Children actively shape the form of their socialization; this is particularly true of the adolescent who brings to encounters physical, cognitive, and social capacities which approach those possessed by an adult. The adolescent's cognitive abilities enable self-evaluations and decisions to be made within the context of the anticipated future. The growth of abstract reasoning during adolescence enables more thorough understanding of principles conveyed through experiences and training. Participation in activities and relationships is particularly instrumental in the preparation of youth for contemporary and future roles.

Socialization includes intended as well as naturally occurring processes. The home and school provide formal training, but they also expose youth to experiences that may weaken the impact of this instruction. Both of these aspects of socialization are revealed in the everyday behavior of adults as models and participants in the family, school, and community. A parent with a grade-school education who encourages academic achievement in his son may not be able to minimize

I am indebted to John Clausen, M. Brewster Smith, and Norma Haan for reading sections of the manuscript at various stages of completion, and to the Institute of Human Development for providing clerical and typing assistance.

the contrary message conveyed by his level of educational attainment. The daily behavior of parents—their conversations, disagreements, priorities, and language—are a large element of adolescent socialization. The greater freedom from family and the physical mobility of youth, compared to children, increase their exposure to experiences that may conflict with the goals and intentions of parents and other authority figures. The growth of activities and involvement with age-mates during early adolescence is a prominent feature of these experiences. Early and contemporary family and school relations are generally manifested in the kinds of social interactions and options adolescents select. Electronic media are another source of information and influence which may compete with the training and example provided by parents, teachers, and religious authorities.

In this chapter, we shall use the concept of development to refer to changes that normally occur in an adolescent's behavior over time periods which are generally defined by age. Viewed from a developmental perspective, the content and form of socialization usually vary in relation to the age of the child and are altered by changes in family status. The history of a family's social class and residential mobility describes the degree of homogeneity or diversity encountered by a child in cultural patterns and in social relationships. Frequently, role transitions are coordinated with the adolescent's age and achievements to produce appropriate change in socialization.

Individuals, groups, and the larger society have timetables for growth and status passage which structure, through their interaction, the pace and pattern of personality development from childhood to the adult years. The child's developmental timetable, initially structured by genetic factors, is subject to varying degrees of modification, depending on the particular characteristic and environmental influences. Variations in physical maturation—observable in early childhood and most clearly manifested during the adolescent growth spurt—result in significant individual variations among youth of the same age during early adolescence in readiness for social experiences common to the age group. Rate of cognitive maturation—influenced by genetic factors, environment, and rate of physical maturation—determines the adolescent's readiness for particular types of role and task learning. Cognitive maturation, according to data presented in this chapter, is intimately related to identity formation, growth of moral judgment, performance in school, and to conceptions of self in an occupational role within the context of future possibilities and self characteristics.

The social timetable, defining rate of passage for children from one status or role to another, is structured largely by norms that specify behavior or performances appropriate to age, sex, and achieved status. Relatively standardized schedules for status passage are indicated by societal and institutional timetables. Of all institutions in the United States, schools have been most instrumental in establishing a standardized schedule for the passage of children from early childhood to adulthood and in defining paths and points of role transition. Minimum performance standards for promotion from one grade to another vary across schools and by the criteria emphasized. Movement from home to grade school, from the sixth to the seventh grade, and from high school to either college or occupational roles represent potentially critical points in the life course for growth or regression. The psychological continuity or discontinuity across these transitions depends on the nature of the change in environment and on the characteristics of the adolescent, both social and psychological. In this chapter, we shall examine how variations in degree of coordination between individual and social timetables affect growth and development during adolescence.

A developmental perspective of socialization and personality development between the childhood and the adult years is largely dependent on data obtained from the same sample of persons at two or more points in time. Studies of this type have generally obtained repeated measurements during the preadult years, followed by one or more data collection periods in adulthood. Longitudinal research spanning the years between childhood and maturity has many disadvantages as well as strengths: it is time-consuming and slow in the determination of outcomes, costly to administer, and is subject to numerous methodological flaws.[1] Only in the last decade have findings from longitudinal studies been sufficient to permit explorations of socialization and personality processes. However, most of the emphasis has been on age-related characteristics of the individual, rather than on socialization. Other research designs that enable assessments of individuals at two points in time include follow-up studies in which data were collected in adulthood from subjects originally included in a cross-sectional survey or in the records of social agencies and institutions. Though we shall rely heavily upon longitudinal and follow-up studies in this chapter, limitations in the availability of such data require the inclusion of cross-sectional studies as well. Research trends indicate a growing awareness of socialization and personality development as lifelong processes subject to considerable differentiation and modification in relation to the individual's position and movement within the social structure.

We shall begin the chapter with a brief survey of historical change in status passage to adulthood and of the effects of environmental change during adolescence on socialization. The association between change in environment and in personality is a basic hypothesis in role theory. In the next chapter section, data are examined that bear upon this hypothesis as it applies to the years between childhood and adulthood and the kinds of personality consequences which result from different combinations of personal and environmental properties.

As an introduction to personality and cognitive processes in adolescence, we shall describe the currently influential theories of development authored by Harry Stack Sullivan, Erik H. Erikson, and Jean Piaget. Each of these theories provides a stage-analytic formulation of development—Sullivan in interpersonal relations, Erikson in ego strength, and Piaget in cognitive structures—and at least implies social influences that promote or thwart movement from one stage to another.

General psychological themes such as competence and self-esteem are reflected in transactions between personality and environment in adolescence. These themes find expression in aspects of adolescent development, such as behavior associated with physical maturation, cognitive development, autonomy, moral development, achievement, and vocational behavior. Recent research and theory are reviewed in sections devoted to each of these. Although some cross-national studies and research are included in the chapter, our primary focus is on longitudinal and cross-sectional studies of American youth. The extensive literature on heterosexual relationships—dating, courtship, sexual behavior, and marriage—is not surveyed in this chapter, since competent reviews are provided by Burchinal (1964) and Ehrmann (1964).

SOCIALIZATION IN THE PASSAGE TO ADULTHOOD

Concepts of the pre-adult and forms of social institutions have been influential

[1] Some of the methodological limitations in long-term longitudinal studies are inherent in this type of research design, while others reflect the state of research techniques and economic resources available at the time they were launched. The former are illustrated by changes in project staff, sample attrition, and the effects of frequent measurement and study participation on test responses; the selection of small, atypical samples and dependence on measurement devices which are improved in subsequent years are examples of the latter type of limitation (see Kessen, 1960, and Schaie, 1965, for critical evaluations of longitudinal studies).

throughout history in defining age-groups and social timetables for status passage. Some evidence suggests that from medieval society in Europe to the present, passage from child to adult status has moved from an early, rapid transition soon after birth to an ambiguously defined point of transition after puberty. Though historical analyses of age distinctions and child rearing are very limited, studies by Ariès in France (1965) and Musgrove in England (1965) indicate that evolution of a prolonged pre-adult stage was a consequence of the following conditions: concepts of the distinctive nature of the child that called for special treatment such as protection, discipline, and education; the concept of modern schooling, establishment of educational institutions, and social legislation which were associated with the above concept of the child; and societal needs, both economic and military.

From documents and iconography in France, Ariès (1965) found a concept of childhood to be nonexistent in medieval society: the child belonged to the adult community as soon as he could live without the constant nurturance of his mother, nanny, or "cradle-rocker." In the sixteenth and seventeenth centuries, the child was viewed as a charming toy for the amusement of adults on account of his simplicity and sweetness. A second concept of childhood emerged in the seventeenth and eighteenth centuries among a small number of religious leaders, lawyers, and moralists who defined the child as a delicate creature needing protection and reformation. Belief in a long childhood—beyond the first six or seven years—appeared with a modern concept of schooling among moralists and pedagogues in the seventeenth century. In the ancien régime, adolescence was not clearly defined but did appear with military conscription for boys in the late eighteenth century, while schooling and conscription were outside the lives of most girls who continued to enter the adult world as soon as they could talk and walk.

In England, Musgrove found that the educator, social reformer, tailor, and publisher "... began in the late eighteenth and early nineteenth centuries to cater for a specific age-group of 'young persons,' neither children nor adults" (1965, p. 33). Youth began to wear clothes that distinguished them from adults; penal and labor legislation called for differential treatment of young persons; some areas and activities were defined as inappropriate for young persons, and redefinition of the public school in the nineteenth century segregated adolescents from children and adults.

The setting in which status passage is socially prescribed varies according to whether youth are socialized for life outside or within the wider kinship group. Yehudi Cohen finds that societies in which children are brought up for social interdependence within the wider kin group tend to mark points of transition by rites of passage in the first stage of puberty—late childhood—and in the second stage several years later (1964). Boys are commonly extruded from the household and brother-sister avoidance rules are imposed during the first stage, while initiation ceremonies are used to symbolize a more permanent disruption of child-family ties in the second stage. Each of these transitions involves a significant disruption of relationships and hence, marks a change in identity. By contrast, modern industrial societies establish a series of transition points outside the nuclear family in which status passage is governed by nonfamilial authorities, i.e., schools and the labor market.

Currently, the average age of entry into secondary school in the United States appears to mark the lower social boundary of adolescence, while the upper boundary, less uniform and clearly marked, is generally symbolized by departure from home, economic independence, and especially marriage. Youth from the middle classes generally leave school and assume occupational and marital roles at a later age than do children from the lower classes. The transition between elementary and secondary school seems to represent a turning point at which youth move increasingly toward dependence on age-mates for companions in activities, affective security and support, and aid in problem solving (cf. Bowerman and Kinch, 1959). One consequence of delayed status-passage is seen in the influence of spontaneous youth groups. In a cross-national survey of age groups, the youth groups' influence in socialization was found to be positively correlated with formalization of the educational system, extension of the preparatory period for youth, and the number of years between leaving parents and assuming full status in a family of procreation (Eisenstadt, 1956, p. 177).

Within the school environment, student stratification by ability and other criteria (gradepoint averages, test scores, and conduct evaluations) differentiates a variety of career patterns that vary in culture, socialization, and future opportunities. Student stratification identifies both positive and negative reference groups, and youth placed in low-ability groups frequently learn to define themselves as their evaluators have. Among students similar in ability, the likelihood of entrance into college is associated with enrollment in a college preparatory curriculum (Nam & Cowhig, 1962).

Status transitions, regardless of their degree of institutionalization, vary in the extent to which they facilitate successful passage and psychological continuity in skills and expectations. The transition from single status to marriage is an experience common to most Americans, yet upon entering marriage many youth find that the skills, expectancies, and attitudes acquired in prior socialization sharply conflict with the demands of their new role. Though much socialization in the pre-adult years is oriented toward the future roles of youth, often inappropriate timing, insensitivity to the perspectives of youth, lack of specificity in coverage, and the low credibility of socializing agents reduces its value. The relevance of career similarity in the pre-adult years between an adult and adolescent for the effectiveness of the former's instruction is sometimes seen in the credence which delinquents ascribe to the "coaching" (on the coaching function in status passages see Strauss, 1959, pp. 109–118) offered by a young adult who has been through comparable encounters with legal authorities and "made good" in job, income, and family.

Between childhood and the adult years, changes in a child's environment are frequently associated with change in the techniques and content of socialization. Some of these changes occur as a result of family mobility through the class structure, changes in residence, and the adolescent's progress within the educational system. Movement into the middle class by a working-class family might increase the attractiveness of parents as behavior models, alter the pattern of family friendships, and increase emphasis on middle-class standards of behavior. Contrary modifications in the adolescent's environment are a probable consequence of downward mobility, resulting from paternal unemployment, alcoholism, or physical illness. At different points in the life histories of youth, parents may be viewed as positive and negative behavior models.

The residential history of a youth's family may include a series of discontinuities in culture and socialization. The developmental significance of such disjunctures would depend partly on the frequency and the timing of such moves in relation to the child's chronological age and abilities. For instance, a residential change that results in an improved educational environment is likely to have a more beneficial effect on the intellectual development of six-year-olds than of adolescents (see Bloom, 1964a, pp. 74–75). On the other hand, frequent residential changes that introduce discontinuities in the experiences of a child may create feelings of insecurity, social isolation, and identity confusion.

During childhood and adolescence,

changes in social environment differentiate a variety of paths to adult roles, each of which is characterized by a particular history of socialization and cultural patterns, experiences with adults and peers, public and personal definitions of self and others, and of decisions made in varying degree by the adolescent, his family, and social institutions. In the approach to adulthood, learning becomes more specific and organized around anticipated roles and situations. It increasingly involves the integration of learned responses as well as new learning, and becomes more reality-oriented. At each choice-point, the breadth and variety of alternatives narrow; of all their initial options, adolescents must eventually settle on only a few by choice or circumstance.

ROLE TRANSITIONS AND PERSONALITY CHANGE

At least two-thirds of a person's life is characterized by role engagement in an ever-widening world, the building of a role repertoire and a pronounced orientation toward the environment; the remainder of life is focused relatively more toward self and involves the shedding of peripheral roles and commitments. As a period of emerging identity, the years between childhood and adulthood are characterized by a marked increase in the complexity of role relationships, growth of independence from authority figures, often coupled with intense involvement with peers, by unusual sensitivity to the evaluations of others, and by role transitions varying in degree of social and cultural discontinuity. Inner change and uncertainty is likely to increase dependence on others and a need for consensual validation. A pronounced change in environment is experienced by youth at the time they leave their home to establish economic independence, marry, or enter college. A new matrix of relationships brings new expectations, socialization, and opportunities which may require a substantial reassessment of self, a change in identity, and modifications in object attachments.

That pronounced role transitions result in personal change, of either a positive or regressive nature, is a central hypothesis of self or role theory and has been expressed in the writings of numerous other theorists as well (cf. Sarbin, 1964). One of the clearest statements is provided by Clara Thompson in her sympathetic appraisal and interpretation of Sullivan's theory of the self: "Alteration of the self ... occurs when the significant people in our lives change and, in adapting to the new situation, certain characteristics may be pushed aside and others allowed to emerge. ... This change can be either in a constructive or destructive direction" (see Green, 1964, p. 40). J. P. Scott has proposed a similar hypothesis: "the time at which any new social relationship is normally formed tends to be a critical period for the socialization of the individual" (1958, p. 184). Mannheim suggests that the lack of vested interests of youth in the social and economic order, in contrast to the commitments and obligations of adults, accounts for the "'peculiar' fact that persons in adolescence and prolonged adolescence ... are ardent revolutionaries or reformers, whereas very often the very same people, as soon as they accept a settled job and found a family, are on the defensive and plead for the *status quo*" (1943, p. 36). Likewise, Piaget has explained the decline in egocentric idealism in terms of the transition from adolescence to adult roles and responsibilities (Inhelder & Piaget, 1958). Since large numbers of juvenile lawbreakers without serious psychiatric disorders become respectable, law-abiding citizens when they take on adult roles, an examination of this transition might increase our understanding of adolescent deviance.

Among the potentially important social continuities from childhood to the adult years are norms defining modes of sex-appropriate behavior, except sexual behavior (Benedict, 1938). It is apparent from longitudinal studies at the Institute of Human

Development and from the Fels study[2] that aggression and dependence-independence vary in stability between the sexes (Honzik, 1965). Aggression appears to be more stable among males than among females, while the reverse is true for dependence-independence. As a *post hoc* interpretation of these sex differences in the Fels study, Kagan and Moss emphasized sex-appropriateness as a factor in behavioral stability: "The individual's desire to mold his overt behavior in accordance with the culture's definition of sex-appropriate response is a major determinant of the patterns of continuity and discontinuity in his development" (1962, p. 269). In a perceptive criticism of this interpretation, Honzik shows that it does not adequately account for the high degree of stability in nonpassive behavior among females in the study; a correlation of .48 was obtained between a seven-point rating of passivity during the grade-school years and withdrawal behavior in adulthood. Since the low end of these ratings indicates nonpassive behavior, this behavior was also relatively stable between childhood and early adulthood. It is not possible to determine whether the females who were nonpassive in grade school moved toward more passive response tendencies during adolescence and young adulthood since Kagan and Moss reported correlation coefficients and not means or variances for the ratings. Among the possible explanations for sex differences in the stability of aggression and dependency, Honzik suggests the strong influence of constitutional or genetic factors, the continuous but differential support provided by the environment, and the powerful impact of early experiences in establishing the response patterns of males and females.

The impact of environmental changes in personality would depend on interaction between two sets of characteristics: the degree of discontinuity in the transition, and the skills, values, and ego strength of the adolescent. While some incongruence between environmental and personal properties is necessary for personal change to occur, a pronounced discrepancy is apt to result in failure, and attempts to leave the field. The most detailed empirical analyses of psychological consequences resulting from the fit between personal and environmental properties have been conducted on college students and the college environment (Sanford, 1962a). Role transitions may be one or a combination of several types which indicate variations in the relevance of past learning, experiences, and acquired skills for effective performance and fulfillment in the new situation (cf. Biddle & Thomas, 1966). Thirty years ago, Benedict (1938) identified three cultural discontinuities that American youth encounter as they enter adult roles: from a nonresponsible to a responsible role, from submission to dominance, and from inhibited sexual behavior to sexual activity in family roles. In each of these transitions, youth are required to unlearn much of what they learned during childhood and adolescence. The following general description of role transitions by the author focuses on continuity and discontinuity in role demands:

I. *Intra-role change*—In this change, new role demands are acquired. As the child attains higher levels of biosocial maturation, behavior

[2] Perhaps the most serious methodological limitation of the Kagan-Moss study (1962) is that 19 families contributed two or more children to the sample of 89 subjects. As Honzik (1965) notes, this defect in sample composition could significantly inflate correlation coefficients if siblings are more alike in behavior than randomly selected children. Longitudinal data between birth and the middle years of adolescence were obtained from observations of the subjects in the home, nursery school, public school, and in summer camps. Moss rated 29 dimensions of behavior in four age periods: birth to 3 years, 3 to 6, 6 to 10, and 10 to 14 years. Seventy-one of the 89 subjects were interviewed by Kagan between the ages of 19 and 29 years. The wide variation in age at follow-up and the relatively short time-period between preadult and the young adult ratings (based on the interviews) are two other important limitations to the study. Although the subjects varied substantially in marital and educational experiences, these differences were not included as variables in the analysis.

expectations are generally increased. Parents generally expect more in autonomy and responsibility from a 14-year-old son than from a younger son. A teacher during a school year is likely to increase her expectations regarding the role performance of her students. In any developmental or socialization setting, institutionalized sequences of intra-role change are integral signposts of progress. Change of this kind *maximizes continuity of experience and socialization*. Since each new demand assumes acceptable mastery of preceding demands, status passage is regulated according to evidence of mastery of age-appropriate requirements.

II. *Acquisition of a new role*—This change is more abrupt than the former since the child assumes a new role and enters a new set of relationships. The first day of school, changes in school due to promotion or geographic mobility, and a youth's first full-time job are a few examples. Acquisition of a new role and role set is frequently coupled with gradual changes of an intra-role nature. The relevance of experience and learning in other situations, both antecedent and contemporary, for learning and performance in the new situation differentiates conditions of high and low role discontinuity within this general pattern of environmental change. The greater the relevance of past learning and acquired skills for the new role, the lower the degree of discontinuity.

Role discontinuity is consequently least probable in sequential patterns of intra-role change, is somewhat more likely in transitions which involve the acquisition of a new role in which skills and past experiences are relevant, and is greatest in the assumption of a new role which has little, if any, relevance to past learning and skills. These gradients could also be applied more broadly to degrees of environmental change. As the degree of role discontinuity for an adolescent increases, successful adaptation to the new set of role relationships becomes more problematic.

From analyses of longitudinal data, Bloom found that personal change was most pronounced when individuals entered a new environment that differed sharply from their prior environment. Most of the change occurred soon after entrance into the new environment (1964b, p. 128). Entry into college is one such change, and a recent longitudinal study of college freshmen found that attitudinal change was so rapid and pervasive during the first few weeks of college experience that a single measurement was unlikely to be representative of the first-year students (Wallace, 1964).

At times a desired role transition may be blocked entirely by commitments to others which cannot be broken by unilateral action (cf. H. S. Becker, 1963). A street gang's power over a boy may commit him to group loyalty and participation, despite his desire to leave. The binding power of commitments to the gang would be influenced by his degree of estrangement from social institutions and the group's perceived utility in providing means to achieve status needs and goals (Sherif & Sherif, 1964, p. 248). The greater the youth's dependency on the group, personally and/or situationally induced, the higher his stakes in meeting group obligations. Under these circumstances, the reduction or termination of group involvement and commitments might be facilitated by appeals to a higher priority, and by role changes which appear to be caused by external forces. Higher priorities are encountered in full-time employment and especially in marriage. The latter role often has a stabilizing effect on youth, and legitimates as well as forces the surrender or weakening of earlier ties. The pressure of responsibilities associated with marriage is illustrated in the observation of a dance band musician on his transition from single status to marriage. "You know, when you're married, it's a little different. Before it was different. I worked, I didn't work, all the same thing. If I needed money, I'd borrow five from my mother. Now those bills just won't wait. When you're married you got to keep working or else you just can't make it" (H. S. Becker, 1963, p. 118). Role changes which are externally caused, such as induction into the Armed Services and residential change, facilitate the breaking of undesired commitments by attributing responsibility to forces beyond the adolescent's control. Some youth may escape a commitment to undesired relationships with minimal psychological and social costs by changing schools and communities.

Environmental change may produce immobilizing anxiety, psychological disorders, and regression as well as growth and development. Studies have found mental disorders and behavioral problems to be unusually common at points of sharp role or environmental discontinuity. For instance, results from the Midtown Manhattan study indicate that the rate of incidence of mental disorders was particularly high at points of role transitions and loss, such as the change from a maternal to a post-maternal role (Srole, Langner, Michael, Opler, & Rennie, 1962). Data on social mobility suggest that role changes which involve a decline in status or role loss markedly lower self-esteem and may lead to suicide (Breed, 1963). The emergence of behavior problems in children at points of role change is suggested by a longitudinal sample of subjects in the Guidance Study at the Institute of Human Development (Macfarlane, Allen, & Honzik, 1954). The disruption of behavior patterns occurred around points which seemed to the authors "to coincide with the ages at which children are called upon to make major adjustments in their school life, the year of kindergarten entrance, the last year of elementary school, and the year of entrance to junior high school" (1954, p. 174).

A successful status passage and mastery of new requirements are probably a complex function of the interacting effects of the transition—the degree of role and cultural discontinuity and the availability of supportive individuals—and the adolescent's personality. The same change viewed with anxiety by an insecure, depressed youth may be seen as a challenge by an active, self-confident adolescent. A recent study of the interacting effects of instructional methods in the classroom and student characteristics found that children who are highly anxious are more likely to achieve in a structured than in an unstructured setting (Grimes & Allinsmith, 1961, p. 269). Sullivan notes that except under conditions of extreme pressure, defensive and insecure youth are unlikely to feel "the necessity for change." These youth "expect to go on indefinitely as they are" (1953, p. 301).

Mastery of a new situation is partly contingent on the appropriate meshing of organismic and social timetables. A dilemma is posed by the necessity for relatively standardized schedules in the socialization of youth and significant individual differences. Unevenness in development presents unusually difficult problems in the school setting. When an adolescent is moved ahead of his age group because of unusual intellectual talents, he enters a system of social demands that are likely to exceed his social skills and maturity. Social consequences from this experience could undermine the benefits that might otherwise accrue from more advanced academic instruction. There are also problems associated with the practice of linking chronological age of the child with class placement; these include the early maturing youth's advantage over the late maturer in passing age-bound examinations and in social maturity (Tanner, 1961, p. 121).

Since role discontinuity may bring to the surface latent pathology as well as strengths previously unrecognized by the individual, points of frequent and pronounced role transitions, such as during late adolescence and early adulthood, may have diagnostic and predictive value for disclosing the course of subsequent development. Conclusions drawn from two studies differing in research design are suggestive on this point. In the Guidance Study, a correlational analysis of behavior clusters in the pre-adult years with adult psychological health (Livson & Peskin, 1967) found characteristics in the junior-high period to be more predictive than similar variables in childhood and in the midadolescent period (ages 14, 15, and 16). Livson and Peksin interpret these findings as possibly indicating "that the manner in which the child responds to [the transition between grade school and junior high]—actively inviting or withdrawing from the new experience—tells us something about how healthy an adult he will turn out to be. It may be heuristic, then, to look upon these years as a microcosm of adult life, anticipating its requirements for active and effective adaptation" (forthcoming, p. 517). In *Mental Health in the Metropolis,* Srole suggests that the profound impact of role discontinuity on vulnerable personalities, which he inferred from age-trend data in the study and observed in the lives of psychiatric patients, may be considered partly due to "cultural failure to provide a bridge of training for the individual, preparatory to assuming, changing, or departing an important social role" (1962, p. 361). Since indications of potential mental illness may emerge at points of role discontinuity, he suggests that parents and adults in youth-serving positions should be encouraged to be especially sensitive to youth having difficulties in these situations and that educational agencies could be designed to provide anticipatory training for the requirements of the new role in the form of group discussion and psychological counseling. While services of this kind are available on a limited scale, they are frequently not available or are not used by adolescents who most need such help on a voluntary basis.

Longitudinal studies indicate that predictions of adult competence and conformity from similar variables in childhood or adolescence appear to be more accurate than predictions of adult pathology and deviance from pre-adult data on delinquency, antisocial behavior, and psychiatric disorders. Generally, capable, healthy children turn out to be capable, healthy adults, but a significant number of children with psychiatric problems, school difficulties, and antisocial behavior confound predictions by turning out as effective, well-adjusted adults (see Robins, 1966, p. 70). In reference to these results, Lee Robins concludes, "Perhaps social scientists have concentrated on the difficulties of predicting deviant behavior to the exclusion of recognizing how well they can predict conforming behavior" (1966, p. 70). It is conceivable that there is much greater variation among deviant youth in personal resources and in vulnerability to role discontinuity than among competent, conforming adolescents. Some variation is likely also in the degree of social support and access to resources during periods of role transition. The following two studies illustrate the wide variability and often successful adult outcomes achieved by youth who gave every indication in adolescence of poor adjustment and performance in adulthood.

In a large longitudinal study of children between the ages of 9 and 17 who were followed up five to seven years later, Anderson found the prediction of later adjustment to be least accurate for children who were poorly adjusted at an early age (1960). Youth showing incompetence in their adolescent roles often improved markedly after they stepped into a new harness of responsibilities and challenges. An interpretive summary of these results is suggestive concerning the role change hypothesis:

> As the person grows, he changes and the demands made upon him change. As he moves into new zones of experience, some of his earlier difficulties seem to get straightened out. For example, a fair number of adolescents were having difficulties in their homes and difficulties in school when they were first examined. But six years later, when they were accepting the responsibility of their own homes and their vocations and were really out on their own in the community, they seemed to be doing quite well in meeting their obligations and responsibilities. Putting them on their own brought out qualities which had not appeared to the same degree in their earlier school and home experience (Anderson, 1960, p. 68).

Striking improvement in psychological health and competence was also observed by Jean Macfarlane in the adult follow-up of

166 persons in the Guidance Study at the Institute of Human Development (1964). Many individuals in the study were able in time to bypass early barriers and difficulties, secured compensatory satisfactions, or experienced changed situations which enabled them to resume or change the direction of their growth.

> In fact, many of the most outstandingly mature adults in our entire group, many who are well integrated, highly competent, and/or creative, who are clear about their values, who are understanding and accepting of self and others, are recruited from those who were confronted with very difficult situations and whose characteristic responses during childhood and adolescence seemed to us to compound their problems (Macfarlane, 1964, p. 121).

THEORIES OF DEVELOPMENT IN ADOLESCENCE

Three theories provide differing, though complementary, analyses of development during adolescence: Harry Stack Sullivan's interpersonal theory of personality development (1953), Erik H. Erikson's psychosocial theory of ego development (1963), and Jean Piaget's stage-analytic theory of cognitive development (Inhelder & Piaget, 1958; Flavell, 1963). We have selected these theories for special emphasis, from among others, because they have made highly significant contributions to the conceptualization of developmental processes during adolescence and are a rich source of hypotheses. Piaget's theory, a product of over four decades of experimental research with children and adolescents, is currently an unrivaled influence in the field of cognitive development. Erikson's and Sullivan's theories are widely admired as two of the first truly developmental formulations of personality structure and processes. The contemporary psychosocial problems of selfhood, mastery, and fidelity among youth in complex, rapidly changing societies are assessed in Erikson's analysis of the identity crisis at the point where life history and social history intersect.

Sullivan's essays and lectures describe developmental epochs defined by particular interpersonal tasks and explore the effects of sequential social experiences on the development of the self and feelings of personal worth. His rich clinical insights have particular relevance to our subsequent consideration of the effects of physical maturation and social experiences on the adolescent self-image. Erikson's psychosocial theory of ego development covers the entire life span, although identity formation and role confusion in late adolescence have been most fully elaborated.

Piaget's theory describes the growth of formal thinking in adolescence and explores the implications of cognitive maturation for aspects of personality development. As a determinant of the capacity to envision and act upon future possibilities, the maturation of formal thinking strongly influences the process of identity formation, growth in autonomy and moral judgment, achievement, and vocational development. Although we shall not review Havighurst's theory of adolescent development (1953), his concept of developmental tasks has become part of the vocabulary of a number of developmental theories, such as Donald Super's self-concept theory of vocational development. A brief review of other theories of adolescent development is provided by Muus (1962).

Piaget's descriptive-developmental theory presents the ontogenetic development of "thought and perception of a relatively passionless, non-need oriented variety. ... Excluded are the realms of feeling and affect, of affectively toned, 'warm-blooded' cognitions, of social interpersonal interactions, and the like" (Flavell, 1963, pp. 419–420). These aspects of personality and interpersonal relationships are stressed by Sullivan and Erikson; though both were trained in psychoanalysis, they have moved far from Freud's biological bias. Sullivan's intellectual development includes the influence of Freud, Adolf Meyer, and William A. White in psychiatry; George Herbert Mead, Charles H. Cooley, and W. I.

Thomas in sociology; and Edward Sapir and Ruth Benedict in anthropology. Sullivan became increasingly more oriented toward sociological social psychology, as reflected in the essays of G. H. Mead, during his professional life, in contrast to the consistent ego-psychological perspective in Erikson's writings. Piaget, unlike Sullivan and Erikson, does not emphasize the interplay between environmental variations and developmental processes. "Piaget's theory, as it now stands, appears to be geared exclusively to the normative, 'in-general' aspects of cognitive ontogenesis" (Flavell, 1963, p. 440). Despite this emphasis, Piaget does describe how the child's encounter with new role sets and experiences results in more differentiated, higher-order cognitive structures. Also in moral development, the increase in complexity and demands in childhood are considered significant factors in bringing about the transition from egocentrism to moral realism (see Kohlberg, 1966a). Genetic potential and maturation of the nervous system are viewed as specifying the total range of potentials. A facilitative environment is essential for their development: "... their realization can be accelerated or retarded as a function of cultural and educational conditions. This is why the growth of formal thinking as well as the age at which adolescence itself occurs ... remain dependent on social as much as and more than on neurological factors" (Inhelder & Piaget, 1958, p. 337).

The stage concept of development theoretically implies the following set of assumptions: development within each stage is fundamentally different from development in other stages; each stage of development assumes a relatively invariant order in the course of development such that stage A appears in a child before stage B, and B before C; development follows the same sequence, though varying in level by age of child, across different environments; and structures specifying earlier stages are integrated with and reworked into succeeding stages. Success and failure in resolving developmental problems and requirements thus influence the path of subsequent developments. Criticisms of the stage hypothesis of human development and its underlying assumptions are examined in the subsequent section on intellectual development. When inappropriately defined by age groups, developmental stages are vulnerable to the criticism that they ignore sociocultural variations in development. However, Sullivan and Erikson have consistently warned readers not to affix ages to the boundaries of each stage. The age at which children pass through each stage varies markedly by social and cultural environments (see Kohlberg, 1966a). For instance, in Sullivan's theory, the boundaries of a number of the developmental epochs are defined by institutionalized role transitions and consequently vary across societies.

Sullivan's eras of development include infancy, childhood, the juvenile era, preadolescence, early adolescence, late adolescence, and adulthood or maturity (1953). Each stage is identified by distinctive biological and social pressures. Successful accomplishments in each era, as manifested in the individual's developmental history, are not likely if earlier crises are not successfully resolved. The further one moves from infancy, the less fixed is each era by biological factors and the greater the influence of environment—such as transitions in school—in defining the boundaries. The self, in Sullivan's theory, develops primarily in response to the approval and disapproval of significant others. Anxiety avoidance or the pursuit of security is the central motivational force. That part of the self which is largely protective and defensive in function is described as the self-system. While the self changes in relation to significant change in the social environment, the self-system is viewed as rigid and relatively resistant to change. The human organism encounters the world and internally elaborates it in three types of experiences, from the prototaxic (uncommunicable state characteristic of infants) to the parataxic mode or partially communicable state, to the syntaxic mode representing wholly communicable experience which appears with the acquisition of language. The seven stages are defined as follows:

> *Infancy* extends from a few minutes after birth to the appearance of articulate speech, however uncommunicative or meaningless. *Childhood* extends from the appearance of the ability to utter articulate sounds of or pertaining to speech, to the appearance of the need for playmates—that is, companions, cooperative beings of approximately one's own status in all sorts of respects. This ushers in the *juvenile era,* which extends through most of the grammar-school years to the eruption, due to maturation, of a need for an intimate relation with another person of comparable status. This, in turn, ushers in the era that we call *preadolescence,* an exceedingly important but chronologically rather brief period that ordinarily ends with the eruption of genital sexuality and puberty but psychologically or psychiatrically ends with the movement of strong interest from a person of one's own sex to a person of the other sex. These phenomena mark the beginning of *adolescence,* which in this culture (it varies, however, from culture to culture) continues until one has patterned some type of performance which satisfies one's lust, one's genital drives. Such patterning ushers in *late adolescence,* which in turn continues as an era of personality until any partially developed aspects of personality fall into their proper relationship to their time partition; and one is able, at *adulthood,* to establish relationships of love for some other person, in which relationship the other person is as significant, or nearly as significant, as one's self. This really highly developed intimacy with another is not the principal business of life, but is, perhaps, the principal source of satisfactions in life; and one goes on developing in depth of interest or in scope of interest, or in both depth and scope from that time until unhappy retrogressive changes in the organism lead to old age (Sullivan, 1953, pp. 33–34).

Personality growth at each stage of development is indicated by the achievement of *integrated* relationships in which needs for security and intimacy are satisfied. Achievement of a oneness with others and belongingness are viewed as essential elements of this process in Sullivan's clinical analyses of development in preadolescence and early adolescence. The problem of achieving positive relations with others, particularly with youth of the same sex, is indicated as the major developmental task of preadolescence. Interpersonal intimacy in this kind of relation provides the opportunity for validation of personal worth. In this context, Sullivan describes at length loneliness, isolation, and the fear of social ostracism experienced by youth during the junior-high-school years. Interpersonal competence in adulthood is largely contingent on interpersonal developments in this stage. The onset of puberty adds sexual desires to the need to achieve interpersonal intimacy and creates difficulties for achieving relationships with persons of the opposite sex in which both needs are met.

In *Childhood and Society* (1963), Erikson outlined a sequence of eight psychosocial stages of ego development. Each stage represents a critical period of conflict and possible crisis for the development of an ego quality such as trust, initiative, and so on. Erikson postulates that ego development unfolds according to a "ground plan" (epigenesis) and is contingent on the interplay between accrued ego strength at each stage and role demands. Ego qualities that emerge at a particular stage or step of development have their origins in the earliest periods of life, and seem to reach a critical stage in development according to generally compatible personal and social timetables. Ego strength in each is achieved by integrating "the timetable of the organism with the structure of social institutions" (1963, p. 246). The probability of successful ego integrations at each of the stages is dependent on the person's history of ego achievements and failures. The eight basic ego conflicts are: trust vs. mistrust, autonomy vs. shame and doubt, initiative vs. guilt, industry vs.

inferiority, identity vs. role confusion, intimacy vs. isolation, generativity vs. self-absorption, and integrity vs. disgust and despair. The first three ego conflicts are experienced by the preschool child, while conflict between industry vs. inferiority is pronounced during latency. Demands imposed on the school-age child stress achievement and skills of all kinds. The challenges of these years, as set forth by Erikson, closely resemble basic features of the juvenile era in Sullivan's formulation. Both stress the importance of the period for developing self-esteem and appraise the psychological effects of social discrimination and segregation for achieving this quality.

With the advent of puberty, and particularly late adolescence, emerges the ego problem of articulating values, fantasies, and identifications with plans, ideals, and expectations in the process of identity formation. The individuation of self in the midst of new freedoms and the anticipated future is frequently accompanied by serious examination of self, parents, and society which seeks to distinguish their contrasts and similarities, worthy qualities from those not deserving of acceptance and commitment. Self-examination and self-definition in the historical context raise questions that are likely to have profound emotional significance. Some adolescents may avoid the risks of this experience by refusing to probe, preferring instead to define themselves on society's terms. In contrast, those who raise questions are likely to become preoccupied with the issue of "fidelity," with a determination of the things, persons, and institutions to which they can be loyal (Erikson, 1962). A mature sense of fidelity constitutes "the strength of disciplined devotion" and is achieved by youth when they involve themselves in experiences that represent the "essence of the era they are to join —as the beneficiaries of its traditions, as the practitioners and innovators of its technology, as renewers of its ethical strength, as rebels bent on the destruction of the outlived, and as deviants with deviant commitments" (Erikson, 1962, p. 23).

Conflict between intimacy and isolation centering around heterosexual relations occurs in the late adolescent and young adult years. The remaining two ego conflicts emerge during middle and late adulthood. While the various conflicts theoretically appear in developmental sequence, this does not imply that earlier achievements and retardations are permanent developments. Ego qualities achieved on each stage are not "impervious to new inner conflicts and to changing conditions" (Erikson, 1964, p. 274).

Erikson's theory emphasizes individual uniqueness in the process of identity formation: "... the development of a healthy personality depends on a certain degree of *choice,* a certain hope for our own individual *chance,* and a *conviction* in freedom of self-determination" (1959, p. 93). Sense of ego identity is the acquired confidence that inner continuity developed in the past is similar to the continuity of the individual's meaning for others; these components of ego identity are similar to personal and public definitions of a career. Some degree of correspondence between the inner and outer world is thus essential for a sense of identity. The term is freighted with multiple meanings on the conscious and unconscious levels of personality, and by implication includes the self as object and as subject, as observed and as observer. Helen Lynd provides a brief critical analysis and elaboration of the ego identity concept in *On Shame and the Search for Identity* (1961). While social demands and role changes in late adolescence tend to force an identity crisis, identity formation in Erikson's theory is a lifelong process from infancy to death. Failure to achieve a sense of identity may result in role confusion and personal disorganization. The flavor of individualism and the process of individuation in Erikson's theory strongly reflect ideals embedded in Western culture.

One of Erikson's major interests is the interrelation between life history and social history. His justly famous work in this area is *Young Man Luther* (1958), and he is presently engaged in research on the life of Mahatma Gandhi. Erikson's influence in this type of analysis is seen in the research and writing of Robert Lifton, whose essay in "Youth and History: Individual Change in Postwar Japan" (1962) examines the psychological consequences in contemporary Japanese youth of the absence of nourishing ties to their heritage as manifested in conflict between group affiliation needs and the ideal of individualism reflected in the dual aspects of *shutaisei,* selfhood and social commitment. More recently Erikson has developed ideas that have considerable relevance to analyses of the socialization, development, and outlook of individuals in different age groups or generations (cf. Ryder, 1965). He describes the "historical logic" common to lives lived interdependently in a particular historical period (1964, p. 207), in an analysis similar to Mannheim's formulation of a "political generation" (1952, p. 286). Much of this shared orientation, he suggests, is a consequence of the imagery of reciprocal identifications between men, their institutions, and their leaders. All of the historical events and forces of immediate relevance to the identity formation of the individual constitutes his "psycho-historical actuality." This psychologically relevant experience "contributes to the prevalent sense of space-time in a given population. And what becomes most relevant to individuals as they live their individual life-histories will also determine their influence on future history" (1964, p. 207).

A comparison of Sullivan's and Erikson's formulations of personality development during adolescence indicates differences as well as significant points of complementarity. Erikson's conception of personality more closely approximates a *developmental model* in which personality resides "within the skin" and attains greater order, complexity, and differentiation of parts over time (Allport, 1964, pp. 39–54). In Sullivan's writings, personality is virtually equated with a person's recurring interpersonal relationships. In the essay "Illusion of Personal Individuality" (1950), Sullivan dealt directly with the question of whether a "unique individual self" exists. He excluded as relevant data the private mode of personal existence, one that cannot be observed or is not expressed in social relationships.

The interpersonal or role theory of personality assumes substantial variability of behavior across roles and situations. In an essay on role learning in personality development, Brim writes that "the learned repertoire of roles is the personality. There is nothing else. There is no 'core' personality underneath the behavior and feelings; there is no 'central' monolithic self which lies beneath its various external manifestations" (1960, p. 141). In the essay, Brim compared the assumptions of this theory with those of traditional trait theory. Traits are high-level abstractions from repeated occurrences of behavior, and thus the stability of personality characteristics across situations and roles is assumed to be large. In presenting the case for personal continuity across situations, Gordon Allport has urged that the personality theorist not ignore the fact that there is a subjective and internal patterning of acts in particular situations and roles. "A traveler who moves from culture to culture, from situation to situation, is none the less a single person; and within him one will find the nexus, the patterning, of the diverse experiences and memberships that constitute his personality" (1964, p. 48). The issues posed by role-theoretical and general trait theories are especially controversial in the area of moral behavior and development. The Hartshorne and May studies have been interpreted as support for the position that a large share of moral conduct is situation specific (see Kohlberg, 1966). Kohlberg's research on moral development shows a high degree of continuity in moral judgment across verbal moral situations within particular stages, although the general pattern of correlations indicates considerable variability by situation as well. Consistent with the role-theory position, Donald Fiske suggests that "the persistence of a major theme is a matter of degree: a person who is characterized as assertive is assertive only a small part of the time, namely, in interpersonal situations. Even there, he is typically assertive only towards some kinds of people, and only some of the time" (1961, p. 350). However, he also notes that the characterization of a person as having a strong tendency or showing a particular theme *may* appropriately describe him in relation to other people, even though a detailed analysis would indicate that the tendency, as recurring behavior, was highly variable.

The most complete summary and evaluation of the research and theory which Jean Piaget and his Genevan colleagues have produced during the last thirty or so years are provided in Jean Flavell's *The Developmental Psychology of Jean Piaget* (1963). Piaget's primary theoretical and empirical interests are in the "qualitative development of intellectual structures" (Flavell, 1963, p. 15). The content or raw material of intelligence changes drastically with age, while the general dimensions of cognitive activity —assimilation of the new and accommodation of the old to the new—are similar for all ages. Cognitive structures develop through encounters with new experiences and requirements. The stages are assumed to form an invariant sequence; structures defining earlier stages are integrated into the cognitive organization of successive stages. The stage model of intellectual development covers three main periods of development between infancy and adolescence: Sensory-Motor Intelligence (0–2 years), Concrete Operations (2–11 years), and Formal Operations (11–15 years).

The most significant property of formal-operational thought is the emphasis on the *possible* rather than on the *real,* the world of "as if," expressed in abstract, propositional statements. The adolescent is continually engaged in hypothesis formulation, testing, and elimination. Formal thought is basically hypothetico-deductive and is propositional in the sense that propositions are manipulated, rather than raw data. Formal operations represent propositions-about-propositions.

Formal operations enable the adolescent to think beyond the present, to consider things hypothetical and distant, to commit himself to possibilities that may subsequently lead to commitments. The adolescent's theories represent the "cognitive and evaluative bases" for entering the adult matrix of roles and responsibilities. His view of the future includes a life schedule and expectancies as well as plans for changing the society he perceives. Ideals tend to become autonomous in adolescence. Though the child rarely has feelings about ideals, the adolescent's emotional life is profoundly influenced by the ideals of humanity, equality, and social justice. Reformist tendencies noted at this stage of development are a manifestation of adolescent egocentrism, a phase in which the adolescent "attributes an unlimited power to his own thoughts so that the dream of a glorious future or of transforming the world through Ideas ... seems to be not only fantasy but also an effective action which in itself modifies the empirical world" (Inhelder & Piaget, 1958, pp. 345–346). The transition from this idealistic crisis to greater realism is described as a process of "decentering." Initial tendencies in this direction may result from interaction with peers which provides a social medium in which hypotheses are promoted, tested, refuted, and modified. Entrance into the occupational world constitutes the focal point of decentering. "It is then that he is transformed from an idealistic reformer into an achiever" (Inhelder & Piaget, 1958, p. 346).

From a developmental standpoint, formal operations may be a precondition for the acquisition of highly cognitive ego mechanisms such as discrimination and detachment (see Haan, 1963). Formal operations also enable youth to acquire orientations toward future roles and to reconstitute content and structures acquired earlier in life in the light of new perspectives, role demands, and opportunities. Cognitive development associated with passage through increasingly more demanding self-other systems may thus be seen as having consequences for the process of identity formation. Contemplation of the future provides an opportunity for reworking past learning and identifications.

Together these theories provide a complex, multi-faceted view of development during adolescence which results from continual interaction between properties of the individual and his environment. In Erikson's terminology, "ego strength develops from an interplay of personal and social structure" (Erikson, 1964, p. 175). However, successful mastery may not occur if these requirements greatly exceed personal capacities or if new encounters are not sufficiently challenging. For example, the youth who is slow in maturing is likely to experience serious difficulties in managing relationships with youth who are more mature, socially and physically. On this latter point, Sullivan observes that "If the (peer) group includes some members whose development is delayed, the social pressure in the group, in the gang, is extremely hard on their self-esteem and may lead to very serious difficulties of personality ..." (1953, p. 265).

From Piaget, we acquire an understanding of the transition from concrete to formal thinking and of the implications of formal thought processes for other domains of development. The stage assumptions in Piaget's theories of cognitive and moral development, a source of much controversy at present, are discussed in subsequent chapter sections. Erikson's theory of psychosocial development in adolescence describes the growth of ego identity, the identity crisis, and the intersection between life history and social history in late adolescence. One of the few longitudinal analyses designed to test hypotheses on ego development in adolescence derived from Erikson's theory is currently in progress on subjects from the Oakland Growth and Guidance studies at the Institute of Human Development.

The quality of interpersonal relationships from childhood to the adult years is a central aspect of personality development in Sullivan's theory. Preadolescence, in particular, is viewed as a crucial period for establishing relationships with peers of the same and opposite sex. He suggests that failure to develop close ties with an age-mate increases the likelihood of subsequent isolation and interpersonal handicaps in adulthood. Longitudinal studies have found a moderate degree of continuity between social isolation, turbulent interpersonal relations, antisocial behavior in adolescence or earlier, and interpersonal difficulties in adulthood (see Roff, 1961, and Robins, 1966). However, since there is also substantial discontinuity, research is needed which identifies personal and social conditions associated with levels of stability and the direction of change in these behavior patterns. Relevant to Sullivan's theory are Lowrie's writings (1948) which define dating as a vital experience in personality development. Though some of the socially incompetent youth in high school may be among the nondaters, as Burchinal suggests (1964, p. 632), this may be even more true of youth who date frequently as compensation for failures and difficulties in school and family (see Stinchcombe, 1964, and Morris, 1964). A well-designed longitudinal study on the qualitative and quantitative dimensions of heterosexual relations during adolescence is needed to determine the developmental significance of heterosexual experiences for subsequent courtship and marriage.

PSYCHOLOGICAL THEMES IN ADOLESCENCE

One of the most visible features of adolescence experience is its changeful character, both within the organism in physical and psychological growth and in social relationships with authority figures and age-mates. Another feature is its anticipatory quality, especially in the later years. As Inhelder and Piaget (1958) have noted, youth are equipped to think about the future and to commit themselves to possibilities; their view of the future influences activities in the present (Douvan & Adelson, 1966). The changeful and anticipatory quality of adolescence experience centers the attention of youth on concerns that seem to reflect psychological themes. The pace of physical development and intense social pressures make more problematic the ability to show competence and be accepted by significant others. Uncertainty and low personal worth are associated with vulnerability to the judgments of others (Rosenberg, 1965). Related to competence and self-esteem are orientations toward the future and the general process of identity formation, both of which have special relevance to vocational development.

Technical and Interpersonal Competence

Competence may be defined as the demonstration of effectiveness on tasks such as class assignments or gainful employment (technical), or in relations with age-mates and adults (interpersonal). In a series of important essays on competence motivation, Robert White has emphasized the developmental and motivational significance of the child's successful manipulation of his environment. "When action is focalized, intended, and effortful, and when it produces effects on the bit of environment toward which it is aimed, the consequent experience includes a feeling of efficacy, a feeling of power to be an effective agent" (1965, p. 206). He suggests that this emotion is one of our most important human affects, the force that "lies behind our unceasing attempts to enlarge the sphere of our competence" (1965, p. 206). Potential variations in competent behavior include differences between interpersonal and task performance. A bright, self-motivated student may have little skill in relating to others; in some cases exemplar technical performances could serve as compensation for interpersonal failures and difficulties. Inability to show competence in one role is likely to have consequences for behavior in other relationships.

The likelihood of competent performances is influenced by interaction between personal resources and the environment. The array of personal characteristics that enable rewarding exploration and mastery of the environment would include specific talents, intelligence, curiosity, resourcefulness, self-confidence, and the desire to excel. Opportunity to show competence, the nature of the task and relationship, and the response of others appear in research studies as important determinants of conditions favorable to the production of desirable outcomes and a feeling of efficacy. For instance, an experimental study found that moral learning was greatest among sixth-graders presented with hypothetical conflict situations one level above their moral development, in comparison to children presented with situations one level below or two levels above their own level (cited in Kohlberg, 1966a, p. 24). Torrance's studies of creative thinking show teacher respect for the products of the students to be one of the most facilitative conditions (1965). If it is assumed that effort to maximize a feeling of efficacy is a general motivational tendency, the behavior of some dropouts and delinquents would be appropriately interpreted in this context. Youth with accumulated frustrations and failures in the school setting are inclined to leave the field for alternatives such as employment which appear to offer improved possibilities for mastery. Those who do not leave may escape through the vicarious enjoyment of mastery in fantasy. Likewise, juvenile deviance committed 'for kicks' may be viewed as an expression of mastery rather than as hedonism.

The extent to which competent role performance is a function of transactions between personal resources and environment is shown in the behavior of a small group of Peace Corpsmen who served as teachers in Ghana (M. B. Smith, 1966). The 44 Peace Corpsmen were rated on a variety of predictive variables by psychiatrists on the basis of two 50-minute appraisal interviews before leaving the States. Smith found that the psychiatrists' mental health ratings (i.e., "predicted psychological effectiveness") to be uncorrelated with measures of competent performance in the field. "Within the admittedly restricted range of volunteers actually sent overseas, the degree to which a person's adjustment as appraised by the psychiatrists approximated the 'optimal' pattern simply had nothing to do with the adequacy with which he performed in the Peace Corps role" (1966, p. 563). However, this relationship varied strikingly in three groups of volunteers classified by their teaching setting in Ghana. In comparison to an overall correlation of —.02 between psychiatric ratings and the second-year administrative evaluations, Smith obtained correlations of .54 for the city teachers, —.02 for volunteers in intermediate settings, and —.36 for those located in the "bush." These results suggest that the ratings of psychological competence were situationally specific, restricted principally to the functioning of teachers in an urban setting. Urban assignments also departed sharply from the expectations of the volunteers, creating morale problems for the city group.

Situational influences on role performance shown in the Peace Corps study suggest that a general competence factor with predictive efficiency across situations, roles, and sociocultural groups is most unlikely. This point is further illustrated by the experience of a research psychiatrist in the Civil Rights Movement. Concerning young student workers in the South, Coles observes that he has seen "quiet, even timid young men become vigorous teachers, shrewd organizers, and adaptive fighters in what has often been, in many senses, a real war—between sheriffs and the police on the one hand and students on the other, between angry white mobs and determined Negro and white demonstrators" (1966, p. 27). He expressed doubt as to whether he would ever have been able to predict the stamina, courage, and ability shown by these youth under fire.

A variable that seems to represent a central component of competence behavior is internal vs. external (I-E) control of reinforcement, a concept based on Julian Rotter's social learning theory (Rotter, 1966). Belief in internal control is manifested when an individual perceives reinforcement following from his action to be due to his behavior or ability, and not to other forces. When reinforcement is not seen as contingent on the individual's action but on the action of others, the outcome is likely to be interpreted as due to chance or luck. Conditions favorable to a belief in internal control would also tend to elicit a sense of efficacy if the requirements of the situation are challenging and necessitate considerable, genuine effort. The literature on alienation and powerlessness in mass society and complex organizations is especially relevant to this concept and to the sense of powerlessness experienced by delinquents, school failures, and both Negro and white youth from the lower classes; Seeman's essays and field studies have linked the I-E variable with the concept of powerlessness in research on alienation (1959; 1966).

A central hypothesis in the research of Rotter, Seeman, and others is that learning is greater under skill than under chance conditions. Experimental and field research has generally supported this hypothesis; the results have far-ranging significance for the socialization and learning experiences of youth. In summarizing the results of experimental studies, Rotter concludes that a subject in a chance condition tends to be less attentive to environmental cues, places less reliance on past experience, learns less and may in fact learn the "wrong things," and is apt to develop a pattern of superstitious behavior (1966, p. 8). An external orientation is also associated with a tendency to blame others rather than self (Clark, 1963). From four field studies including a comparative study of work alienation in Sweden, France, and the United States, Seeman found that an individual's sense of mastery over his destiny was related to membership in an organization, such as a union, which had some control over his occupational future, that members of such organizations were more likely to be internal in orientation if they were active participants, and that the tendency to learn and retain knowledge relevant to the individual's future was directly influenced by membership in a "relevant" organization and by his sense of mastery (1966).

This relation of membership and active involvement in organizations to a sense of competence corresponds to results in a study of the effects of large and small schools on the behavior of high school students (Barker & Gump, 1964). Students in the small schools, in comparison to those in a large school, performed in 2.5 times as many responsible and important positions, assumed crucial positions such as chairmen of meetings six times as often, and were more likely to fill important positions in school activities. Furthermore, students who did not possess abilities and backgrounds that enable school success were four times as likely to be encouraged to participate than were marginal students in the large school. These membership and participation differences largely account for differences in the satisfactions reported by students in the two types of schools. Youth in the small schools expressed more satisfactions related to being challenged, to the development of interpersonal competence, to being valued, to participation in important activities and group involvement, and to the acquisition of cultural and moral values. Students in the large school may have had some advantages in experiences that develop academic or technical competence (this was not investigated), but the small schools offered more participation opportunities and experiences relevant to the development of interpersonal competence. In this context we should note that one of the most consistent characteristics of students who leave school early is their lack of membership and involvement in group activities (see S. M. Miller, Saleem, & Bryce, 1964, for annotated bibliography of research on dropouts). This is possibly a reflection of the interdependence between academic and interpersonal competence.

Self-esteem

Feelings of personal worth are influenced by performances, abilities, appearance, and the judgments of significant others. Self-perceptions not infrequently differ from the evaluations and attitudes of others as illustrated in the person who regards himself more highly than do others. Commonly used techniques for measuring self-esteem include self-report indexes and the discrepancy between actual and preferred self qualities, as measured by the *Q*-sort technique (Wylie, 1961). Another useful methodological approach employed by Stanley Coopersmith is the assessment of self-esteem feelings and behavior (1959). Coopersmith's research is especially noteworthy in the imaginative use of different sources of data on self-esteem.

The dependency of self-estimates on the judgments of others is subject to the requirements of inner needs and external conditions. During adolescence, the instability and uncertainty generated by both rapid internal and external change increase the likelihood of dependence on the evaluations of others as a response to feelings of insecurity and anxiety. The conformity of youth to peer group norms on appearance seems to reflect this intensification of social dependence (see Tryon, 1944, p. 223). In a large sample of high-school seniors, Ralph Turner found that the conformity of youth to the norms and values of youth culture generally represented "ritualistic" compliance which served to protect insecure youth from one another, rather than personal commitment and opposition to the world of adults (1964a, pp. 168–169).

If social dependence is intensified, at least temporarily, in adolescence, we might expect to find marked variations in self-esteem and mood across situations and time. No study to my knowledge has charted the level and variability of self-esteem in adolescents across different life circumstances and relationships, or over time by a series of daily measurements. A clinical study of mood and variability in a small sample of male college students during a six-week period is suggestive of the potential value of this type of research design (Wessman & Ricks, 1966). Comparisons made between only two points in adolescence indicate that self-esteem is relatively stable (see Carlson, 1965), yet research of this type has not adequately measured variations in self-esteem over time nor variations across situations and roles. Assessment of self-esteem in a specific role is illustrated by research on the self-concept of ability (Brookover, Thomas, & Paterson, 1964).

Feelings of personal worth and competent role performance are interrelated and tend to be mutually reinforcing. The Peace Corps volunteers with a high sense of personal worth in Smith's research were likely to perform competently in the teaching role, and the results of these successful efforts presumably reinforced their self-confidence and sense of agency (1966). On the other hand, youth with low self-esteem expect to fail in their efforts and tend to avoid situations that are demanding and involve competitive or power relations (Rosenberg, 1965). Such expectancies are likely to have a self-fulfilling effect by resulting in behavior that confirms negative feelings about self. Research findings are consistent with clinical observations in showing low self-esteem, feelings of depression, and anxiety to be highly intercorrelated, and a decrease in self-esteem to be associated with change toward a more negative image of self with no modification in the ideal concept of self. In a clinical study of 18 Harvard students over a six-week period, Wessman and Ricks correlated a large number of personality measurements with variations in mood, as indicated by an Elation-Depression factor (1966). Self concepts varied considerably across the two emotional states, elation and depression, while personal ideals remained relatively constant. In depression, self concepts tended to become more derogatory, indicating social isolation and self-preoccupation. The self failed to meet ideals primarily on progress toward important life goals and intellectual ability; these deficiencies were more acutely experienced in periods of depression. Elation was generally accompanied by a substantial increase in self-esteem, while the reverse trend was observed in relation to depression.

A recent cross-sectional study of dimensions of the adolescent self-image obtained results that are generally consistent with those obtained by Wessman and Ricks (Rosenberg, 1965). The sample included approximately 5,000 eleventh- and twelfth-grade students in 10 randomly selected schools in the state of New York. Self-esteem was measured by a ten-item self-report scale. Low self-esteem was correlated with depressed feelings, anxiety, and a low grade average. Low and high self-esteem adolescents were similar in desiring occupational success, but the former were more likely to feel that they would never attain such success, to prefer an occupation which they believed they would never enter, and to feel that they did not have the assets essential for success in their chosen fields. The high self-esteem adolescents were significantly more likely than those low in personal worth to consider the following qualities as personal assets: ability for self-expression; self-confidence; hard work and effort; leadership potential; talent, intelligence, or skill; ability to make a good impression; feeling at ease with different people; practical knowledge; and being sure of oneself.

Low self-esteem adolescents in Rosenberg's study were characterized by a sense of incompetence in social relationships (1965). These adolescents frequently put on "false fronts," were socially isolated and preoccupied with self, and felt that other people neither really understood nor respected them and were not to be trusted. Their reactions to classmates were likely to elicit responses that confirmed their apprehensions and feelings of rejection. Relevant to this circular, reinforcing process is Sullivan's observation that "one can find in others only that which is in the self" (1947, p. 22). Thus a youth with low self-esteem tends to reject offers of friendliness, continues to be hostile and distrustful, and resists change. The happy and unhappy men in the Wessman and Ricks study closely resemble the high and low self-esteem adolescents in Rosenberg's sample.

The changing form of the body during early adolescence enhances its salience as an object of self-feelings and as a source of variation in self-esteem. The effect of physique on self-esteem is apt to be most pronounced among girls since they tend to express greater concern than boys over their appearance when it departs markedly from preferred ideals (see Douvan & Adelson, 1966, p. 372). Ideals of the female and male figure in American culture are transmitted to youth in parental judgments, in the evaluations of peers, and in the mass media. Through this process they acquire emotional significance and influence body- and self-image when used as standards for the evaluation of physical characteristics. The greater the deviation of physical characteristics from preferred dimensions or aspects of the body, the greater the likelihood of negative feelings toward these body-parts and the self (see Gunderson, 1965). The relation between body-image and self-feelings has been noted by Freud, Adler, and other personality theorists (see Fisher & Cleveland for a review of this literature, 1958). Paul Schilder's original work in this area, published in 1935, is especially noteworthy as a source of hypotheses. Despite Cooley's (1902) seminal observations on the relation between self-feelings and appearance, sociologists in the area of socialization have been inclined to ignore the human body and its stimulus properties (see, for instance, Benne's critique of an essay by John Seeley, 1965). This neglect is illustrated by two large-scale investigations of the adolescent self-image (Rosenberg, 1965; Kemper, Brim, & Cottrell, 1962), neither of which collected data on physical characteristics and their social stimulus value, on real-ideal images of the body, or on feelings about the body. Substantial additions to knowledge in this area would have been likely if these studies had employed or improved upon the techniques used by Secord and Jourard to measure body-cathexis and real and preferred dimensions of body-parts (1953).

In a sample of college students, Secord and Jourard found satisfaction with body-parts to be strongly correlated with positive attitudes toward the self and low body-cathexis to be associated with anxiety and insecurity (1953). The satisfaction of males with body-parts such as height, chest, and muscular strength varied by extent or size, in accord with the value of these characteristics in the ideal image of masculinity in our culture (Jourard & Secord, 1954). These findings are supported by results obtained in a study of body-size and self-image in a sample of young Navy men (Gunderson, 1965). Deviation from preferred height and weight was directly correlated with dissatisfaction with these body-parts. Height in particular had a pervasive effect on general self-evaluations, with short-underweight and short-overweight men having the most negative self-images. Similar psychological correlates of deviations from preferred size of body-parts were obtained by Jourard and Secord in a sample of college women (1955). Deviations from estimated and measured size of hips, height, weight, and waist were highly correlated with satisfaction with these body-parts. Average self-ratings of preferred size for these physical attributes were significantly smaller than their mean actual size, while their preferred size of bust was larger than their self-reported size. None of the women had physical dimensions that equalled measurements they considered desirable. The data suggest that women share an image of the ideal female figure and that deviations from this ideal may be a source of low self-esteem and insecurity. Whether physical deviations lead to emotional distress and a low sense of personal worth depend partly on the responses and attitudes of parents. If the adolescent is confronted by unfavorable comparisons with the ideal physique in his family and is ridiculed or teased about physical deficiencies, the likelihood of extreme self-consciousness, insecurity, and low self-esteem is markedly increased (MacGregor, Abel, Bryt, Laner, & Weissman provide a comprehensive review of the literature on the relation between family patterns and body-image, 1953).

Although the self-esteem of an adolescent who has been accepted unconditionally by his parents would vary less by the presence or lack of accomplishments than the self-feelings of other youth (see Rosenberg, 1965, pp. 119–121), experiences that facilitate the child's successful transactions with his environment are undoubtedly a major factor in the growth of a positive self-image. Parental respect and interest were related to a positive sense of worth in Rosenberg's study. Wessman and Ricks conclude that the happy men in their study "were able to make positive identifications with respected and approachable role models, which favored the establishment and development of a worthwhile sense of self. Begun in the family, this continuing process was furthered as they moved into the world" (1966, p. 248).

Orientation Toward the Future

The adolescent's conception of his future life is influenced by current and anticipated transactions between personal resources and the attractions, opportunities, and requirements characteristic of his environment. Studies examined in the preceding sections indicate that planful, goal-directed behavior and an optimistic exploration of future possibilities are highly related to a sense of competence and personal worth. The developing vision of the future includes formation of a tentative life plan, which establishes goals and means priorities within a time sequence and may be characterized by the degree to which it shows complex differentiation, is demanding, and describes the individual as a primary cause of the evolving pattern (cf. M. B. Smith, 1966; Inhelder & Piaget, 1958, p. 350). In a study of the biographies of 300 persons during the thirties, Bühler noted the directive quality of the life plan and described the process whereby provisional formulations in adolescence become more focused during the twenties (1933). A life plan seems to include what Everett Hughes has called a subjective career, "the moving perspective in which the person sees his life as a whole and interprets the meaning of his various attributes, actions, and the things which happen to him" (1958, p. 63). Throughout life, the content of this orientation is influenced by the position of the individual's age cohort in the historical process and is subject to modification as he moves from one position to another in the social structure.

To the extent that the life plan represents an anticipated series of definable and related activities through which a group of individuals move in a particular sequence toward a goal, it is likely to result in the formulation of timetables that vary in length of time covered and in specificity (cf. Roth, 1963). These timetables are structured by age norms, personal desires, and rules governing status passage in complex organizations. The general life plan and associated timetables are likely to be correlated with activity priorities for the allocation of time and energy. A life plan may also encompass *a unifying philosophy of life* which may or may not be articulate in words. Any mature person, suggests Allport, "participates and reflects, lives and laughs, according to some embracing philosophy of life developed to his own satisfaction and representing to himself his place in the scheme of things" (1937, p. 214).

In Smith's study of Peace Corps volunteers, the content of the varimax factor,

Intellectualizing Future-Orientation, seems to describe young persons with a well-formulated life-plan (1966). This factor was the second one extracted in a factor analysis of personality *Q*-items. The volunteer with a high score was likely to have "a highly articulate intellectual formulation of his situation and problems," long-term goals and a complex, well-differentiated picture of a challenging personal future, thought well of himself and believed that what he did with his life mattered, and was actively searching for a "clearer, more complex, or mature sense of identity."

Identity Formation

The role transitions and commitment pressures youth experience in middle and late adolescence generate the developmental task of achieving a sense of unity, independence, purpose in life, and an acceptable identity in the social matrix. The process of identity formation involves decisions and commitments regarding future alternatives and their assimilation and integration with selves in contemporary and past relationships. The eventual identities of youth are products of transactions between their active search for selfhood and acceptable roles, on the one hand, and the directive pressures applied by institutions and socializing agents toward approved identities in the social matrix, on the other. Yehudi Cohen observes that an intricate balance between these forces is essential to the developing individual. "Unless the society's institutional organization can work with the child's needs to mature, it cannot make its indelible impressions on the growing person. Similarly, the child's need to find a personal identity or sense of self would be aimless without the orienting targets of social goals, without the reality of a sense of social belonging, and without the meaningfulness of a particular life with other people" (1964, p. 60). The adolescent's feeling of efficacy and personal worth affect his willingness to encounter the future, to select goals, make decisions and commitments, and enter new relationships, while the orienting effect of social goals are evident in his life plan. The assimilation and integration of the youth's selves and commitments depend in large measure on the integration of his social environment; the unity of the self reflects, according to Mead, the "unity and structure of the social process as a whole" (see Strauss, 1956, p. 219). Instead of unity in the social process, the late adolescent is likely to experience social discontinuities, status inconsistency, and cross-pressures which complicate the formation of an integrated sense of identity.

One of the difficult phases of growing up occurs when youth become aware of the subterranean side of life, at a time when, as idealists, they desire models of honesty and justice and a society which lives its democratic values. Helen Lynd observes that conflict between self and society tends to increase self-consciousness and poses questions of personal significance. This confrontation

> . . . sharpens awareness that it is one's society, as well as oneself, that stands uncovered. Values, ways of life that one has accepted without question may appear in this new light to be cruel, hypocritical, destructive of the individual freedoms and possibilities they proclaim. . . . Just as shame for one's parents and shame for others may be an even more searing experience than shame for oneself, so the questioning of certain dominant values presented by society can for some people be more disquieting than the questioning of one's own adequacy in living up to these values (Lynd, 1961, p. 215).

The adolescent's public identities, his recognized status in various relationships, are formed through contact and involvement with peers in social groups and by the perceived and actual evaluations of the adult community. Since the activities and settings in which youth interact with peers and adults differ, as does the frequency of interaction, the public identities of adolescents formed by these age groups are likely to differ substantially. The contrasting social positions, investments in the social order, and cumulative experience of the two age groups would also increase the likelihood of discrepancies between their respective definitions of the same individual.

The desire of youth to be known and recognized in the adolescent community reflects their interest in achieving a clearcut identity. Unusual performances in visible activities, whether legitimate or illegal, tend to result in recognition, a reputation, and an identity. The status rank of activities among youth determines whether the resulting reputation and identity are favorable or negative. Leadership in conventional activities which earn recognition and an identity generally includes social and athletic events. A youth who commits a highly visible deviant act may be admired for his courage by the conventional crowd in school but be labeled as a delinquent. Public identities of youth acquired through unusual performances in conventional and deviant activities are also influenced by their friends and companions in the form of guilt or fame through association. Requirements in the peer group for loyalty and membership character may influence a member's image and reputation by further crystallizing his identity in the minds of youth outside the group. The realness of involvement in peer activities constitutes a prime target for testing; this is particularly true of cohesive youth groups. Sounding is one technique employed for this purpose in delinquent gangs. "Sounding," according to Matza, "is a probing of one's depth, taking the form of insult. One's depth is never definitely certified. It is sounded almost daily. ... Most sounding is a probing of one's manliness and one's membership. Are you really a man, or just a kid? Are you really one of us, or just faking it?" (1964, p. 53). This control technique in conventional and delinquent groups stirs basic anxieties that strengthen tendencies toward conformity in dress, action, and overt thinking. The influence of public identities in establishing approach and avoidance patterns in the peer system contributes to the formation of groups of youth with similar identities and shared problems.

In the act of recognizing and labeling youth, adult society potentially influences the content of their developing identity. Teachers and particularly guidance counselors are in a particularly strategic position for influencing the life course and identity of their students by classifying them within the classroom and assigning them to different ability groups. Law enforcement agencies are in a similar position to influence a boy's identity by the differing treatments accorded juveniles who commit a misdemeanor or felony. Conviction for these acts is a form of status degradation which may have a continuing influence on youth throughout life (cf. Garfinkel, 1956). Adult suspicion, distrust, and the expectation of trouble may encourage a young person to become "exactly what the careless and fearful community expects him to be and make a total job of it" (Erikson, 1959, p. 164). Adolescents in Great Britain (Musgrove, 1965, Ch. 5) and in the United States generally perceive adults as hostile, lacking understanding, and as having little respect for them as persons (Hess & Goldblatt, 1957). These perceptions may be partly a consequence of age segregation in the community that minimizes interaction between old and young.

The average adolescent appears to be a different person to youth and adults. In three upper-middle to lower-middle class school districts in a large midwestern city, Goldman investigated the images high-school students, noneducators, and high-school teachers had of the typical high-school graduate (1962). A set of ten descriptions of the ideal and actual high-school graduate were ranked by 153 high-school teachers, 224 noneducators drawn from various civic and school related clubs, and by 956 high-school students. The statements represented a set of orientations: religious, economic, political, aesthetic, altruistic, social, hedonistic, physical, ethical, and theoretical. The correlation between characterizations of the real and ideal image was —.53 for educators, .15 for noneducators, and .46 for students. The three groups showed little agreement on the image of the actual high-school graduate but relatively high agreement on the ideal image. The first three qualities chosen by the educators describe the graduate as one who "feels that the prime goal in life is to make as much money as possible" (economic), who is "able to make friends easily" (social), and whose "prime goal in life is to have as much fun as possible" (hedonistic). Noneducators, who were primarily parents, did not rank "hedonistic" as high and substituted in place of it the theoretical orientation, "has some knowledge of many things and a desire to learn more." According to students, the foremost orientations of the contemporary high-school graduate were theoretical, social, and ethical; they described him as interested in learning, capable of making friends, and as both honest and trustworthy. All three groups saw the high-school graduate as not likely to know the "political issues of the day, to be willing to be involved in political activity," and to be "willing to sacrifice personal comfort for the comfort of others." This "privatistic" image probably reflects the concerns of youth in the 1950s more accurately than the attitudes of urban youth in the late 1960s.

For the ideal graduate, adults assigned greater importance to religious and ethical orientations than to theoretic interests, whereas students reversed the order. Physical, hedonistic, and economic orientations were the lowest ranked qualities in each group. Parents and teachers saw the typical graduate as materialistic, personable, and a pursuer of pleasure but would prefer him to have moral character and religious interests. Students, on the other hand, differed very little in their real and ideal images of the graduate.

Role confusion, selection of a negative identity (Erikson, 1959), and alienation from self are potential alternatives in the process of forming one's identity. Role confusion, experienced as lack of direction, unity, and identity, is commonly experienced in late adolescence, a time when self-definitions in relation to a vocational future, marriage, and intimate social ties are changing and uncertain. The feeling that things are all mixed up becomes most acute, Erikson suggests, when the adolescent is exposed to a "combination of experiences which demand his simultaneous commitment to *physical intimacy* (not by any means overtly sexual), to decisive *occupational choice,* to energetic *competition,* and to *psychosocial self-definition*" (1959, p. 123). Commitment of an adolescent to a life that is counter to that pressed upon him might be termed choice of a negative identity. Erikson has brilliantly analyzed the psychodynamic and social forces associated with the formation of a negative identity (1959). For example, an upper-middle class boy, in bitterness toward his parents' world and their unwillingness to let him decide what he wants to be and do, may become a beatnik. Alienation from self refers to the state associated with self-contempt in which an adolescent has rejected ties and identifying symbols which relate him to his family and ancestry. This option, likely among youth with low self-esteem, is most evident in the reactions of Negro youth to the stigmatizing effect of black skin in a predominantly white society. Attempts to alter their hair and skin color to become more like white youth reflect a rejection of racial features and heritage. Kardiner writes that "low self-esteem leads to self-contempt and idealization of whites, which, in turn, nourishes the future wish to become white by magical means. Since magic is unattainable, the result is hatred of the whites, as well as self-hatred" (1959, p. 417).

DIMENSIONS OF DEVELOPMENT: AGE-RELATED CHANGES AND ENVIRONMENTAL INFLUENCES FROM CHILDHOOD TO ADULTHOOD

The four psychological themes are expressed in a wide array of developmental processes and behavior patterns during adolescence, including physical and intellectual development, autonomy, moral judgment, achievement, and vocational behavior. The stimulus value of the body, as indicated on the preceding pages, has a potentially significant effect on self-esteem. Size and strength determine a youth's ability to perform competently in athletics. Self-esteem and a sense of competence result from and facilitate future-oriented vocational behavior, a high level of school performance, and satisfying interpersonal relations. Formation of a life plan and a sense of identity are processes inherent in the developing vocational orientations of youth.

Although each of the above six dimensions will be examined one at a time, we should note the degree to which they are interrelated and form a configuration of processes within the developing person. Measured intelligence, for instance, is correlated with level of moral judgment (Kohlberg, 1966a), with vocational maturity (Super & Overstreet, 1960), achievement, and even with height (Tanner, 1962). One study found a correlation of .15 between test scores and height among youth in the same sex, age, stage of sexual development, social class, and family size category (Douglas, Ross, & Simpson, 1965). The relation between physique and temperament, a source of interest for many centuries, has been explored in considerable detail in the United States by William Sheldon in *The Varieties of Temperament* (1942). Sheldon's three somatotype ratings —endomorphy, mesomorphy, and ectomorphy—were correlated with ratings of temperament on 200 young men. The endomorphs were characterized by a set of traits (labeled viserotonia) such as relaxation, love of comfort, pleasure in digestion, and greed for affection; mesomorphy was correlated with somatotonic traits such as assertive posture, high energy, and love of risk and chance; and ectomorphy was highly associated with cerebretonic variables such as love of privacy, introverted tendencies, mental oversensitivity, and need of solitude when troubled. The correlations between the types of morphology and temperament were exceedingly high, averaging close to .80. Sheldon has interpreted this close association as mainly a consequence of the same genetic factors, although other explanations, such as the stimulus value of different body-types, are equally plausible, as critics have pointed out. The credibility of Sheldon's research has been seriously jeopardized by numerous methodological weaknesses such as the subjectivity involved in somatotyping individuals from photographs and the lack of independence between ratings of morphology and temperament. However, more recent studies on the relation between somatotypes and temperament among adolescent boys have obtained results that generally confirm Sheldon's findings; the degree of association is much lower, however. In a study of this relationship among boys in the Oakland Growth Study, all of whom were somatotyped by Sheldon from photographs at physical maturity, Hanley found peer ratings of bossy, daring, and active-in-games to be significantly correlated with mesomorphy, and unhappy related to ectomorphy (1951). In a comparison of matched groups of delinquent and nondelinquent boys, the Gluecks' found mesomorphy to be twice as common among the former; also their data on the relation between physique and temperament tend to correspond with Sheldon's initial findings (1956). Since these results are a likely product of the interplay among genetic factors, environment, and the stimulus value of physical variations, this research area would benefit from a carefully designed cross-cultural study employing objective techniques of somatotyping (see Parnell, 1958).

Physique, temperament, and intelligence —characteristics Allport has termed the three principal raw materials of personality —develop early in the human organism and are relatively stable, compared to other characteristics, throughout the life span (1937, p. 78). Boys, on the average, attain 54 per cent of their mature height by age 3 and 86 per cent by age 11; height at age 7 correlates .81 with height at age 16 (Bloom, 1964a, pp. 23–26). Measured intelligence develops at a somewhat slower rate; Bloom estimates that approximately half of a child's intelligence measured at age 17 is developed by the age of 4, with intelligence measured at age 5 and age 17 correlated .80 (1964a, pp. 61–68). Temperament qualities such as activity level show a high degree of stability from early childhood to adolescence (Yarrow, 1964). A recent study at the Institute of Human Development found that the most stable cluster of personal characteristics between childhood and midadolescence (ages 5–7 and 14–16) included traits such as reserved-expressive, reactive-phlegmatic, and explosive-calm (Bronson, 1966).

I. Physical Growth and Maturation

Over the past 35 years, three growth studies at the Institute of Human Development (Berkeley) have been a major source of carefully executed studies on physical growth and maturation in the United States. The Berkeley Growth Study, begun with children at birth in 1928–29, has focused on motor, physical, and mental development from infancy to the present date, and is directed by Nancy Bayley. The Guidance Study under the direction of Jean Macfarlane began in the same year and was designed to assess parent-child relationships and their effects on personality development from 21 months to maturity. The Oakland Growth Study, directed by Harold E. Jones until his death in 1960, began with a sample of approximately 212 children from the fifth grade in Oakland, California. All three studies are currently engaged in an analysis of adult follow-up data; an overall description of these studies along with selected papers are included in the *Course of Human Development* edited by Jones, Bayley, Macfarlane, and Honzik (forthcoming). An outstanding, critical summary of the Institute's studies of physical growth and maturation as well as research throughout the world is provided by James Tanner, a well-known British biologist, in *Growth at Adolescence* (1962).

The Oakland Growth Study, in particular, has produced a series of significant investigations on the process of physical development during adolescence. The subjects in this study were born in 1921–22, are white, and most came from Protestant, middle-class families; approximately 40 per cent of the families were working class. Annual seriatum measurements were obtained during junior and senior high on physical development, personality, and social behavior. As a developmental psychologist, H. E. Jones considered adolescence to be basically "a biological phenomenon." In a 1939 essay, he posed a general research hypothesis that indicates (as well as any single statement could) a guiding principle of the longitudinal study. As paraphrased, it states that physiological and anthropometric development in adolescence influences an individual's behavior through modifications or alterations in physiological equilibria, drives, growth and pattern of abilities, and in social status among peers (1939, p. 157). Over the past thirty years studies in this research program have examined age-related patterns of physical development, interrelations among indicators of physiological and physical growth, the relation between skeletal maturation and the development of physical characteristics, and the effects of early and late maturation on social development, personality, and achievement from early adolescence to middle-age. The following review relies heavily on these studies and on James Tanner's work.

The Adolescent Growth Spurt and Behavior Patterns

One of the most striking aspects of human development during adolescence is the sharp saccadic pattern of physical growth (Tanner, 1962; Bloom, 1964a). In general, the velocity of growth decreases from birth on through the lifespan, though it tends to be checked during the latency years (6 to 8 years) and reversed from 13 to 15. The adolescent spurt in growth occurs in most children, although there are variations in intensity and duration between the sexes and among children of the same sex. In boys it generally takes place between the ages of 12.5 and 15 with the peak velocity of growth usually around the age of 14. The spurt for girls tends to come approximately 2 years earlier and is less pronounced with respect to gains in height.

> Every muscular and skeletal dimension of the body seems to take part in the adolescent spurt. Even the head diameters, practically dormant since a few years after birth, accelerate somewhat in most individuals. The cartilages of the wrist grow and ossify more rapidly (Shuttleworth, 1938). The heart grows faster; so also do the abdominal viscera. The reproductive organs in particular enlarge, strength increases, and the face noticeably changes. Only the brain seems probably unaffected by this activity, and that only in size; structural changes may well be accelerated in it. Lymphatic tissue decreases, however, and in boys the subcutaneous fat on the limbs decreases, at least for the duration of the spurt (Tanner, 1962, p. 10).

Growth in stature and development of reproductive organs are highly correlated in both boys and girls (Nicolson & Hanley, 1953). The appearance of pubic hair and other secondary sex characteristics are less strongly interrelated with these two growth rates. Nevertheless, physical growth occurs in a relatively uniform pattern; an early maturing boy, for instance, shows an early growth spurt in all of these areas (Tanner, 1962). Sex differences in physical growth result in greater height and wider shoulders for boys and, for girls, larger hips. At age 13, sex differences in static dynamometric strength are relatively small; however at this age boys have achieved less than half of their mature strength. By age 16, distributions in strength among boys and girls show very little overlap; virtually no girls attain the average performance level of boys (H. E. Jones, 1949). A pronounced fat increase is experienced by some boys early in the pubertal growth period. These boys in the Oakland Growth Study tended to have a more feminine build when physically mature than boys with a slight fat increase (Stolz & Stolz, 1951, Ch. 3). Although the growth spurt results in dramatic physical changes, it only adds, in Tanner's words, "the finishing touches to a physique which is recognizable years before" (1962, p. 104).

In the most rapid phase of physical growth, spanning 1.5 to 3 years, staff members in the Oakland Growth Study observed pronounced changes in the social behavior and self-attitudes of boys and girls. Caroline Tryon has described this period as the "excited phase" of social development, the "age of conformity to peer group standards" (1944, p. 223). "The apparent egocentric interest in their own persons ... indicates that they are working on one of the most important developmental tasks, that of accepting the reality of their own appearance; in this process they are trying to make that reality as attractive as possible" (1944, p. 223). In attempting to meet these standards and their personal ideal of an attractive, feminine appearance, girls devoted hours daily in manicuring themselves, in experimenting with hair arrangements, clothing styles, and cosmetics. Boys likewise became preoccupied with their appearance and disapproved of the "unkempt" qualities that were accepted as part of the male appearance several years before. They began to carry combs, kept their clothes neater and their shoes more polished, and were frequently observed smoothing their hair. Tryon suggests that "probably at no time during the lifespan for most individuals is there such great striving for conformity to the group pattern as there is in this middle phase of adolescence" (1944, p. 223). This social dependence and conformity seems to represent an adaptation to inner feelings of uncertainty and insecurity emanating from rapid change in physique within the context of sex-role and heterosexual pressures.

In the community of age-mates, being "different" in physique from most classmates is a potentially significant barrier to social acceptance when it represents a deficiency in sex-appropriate physical characteristics that elicit social rewards. The greater this perceived deficiency, the greater the likelihood that the body will assume negative stimulus value to the self and to others. On the other hand, deviations in the opposite direction, which accentuate valued characteristics, may enhance positive feelings toward the body. Studies by Secord and Jourard, reviewed in the preceding section of this chapter, suggest that actual and perceived deficiencies in physical characteristics would tend to elicit negative feelings to the extent the adolescent feels that they deviate from his own preferred image of his body. These body-images are influenced by cultural uniformities on ideal male and female body-types but may vary from these cultural ideals as a result of family influence and attitudes. In the case of physical deformities, results from one study indicate that a child's liking and acceptance of a girl or boy tends to increase as a function of the distance of the disability from the face (Richardson, Goodman, Hastorf, & Dornbusch, 1961).

For an adolescent boy, a physique that enables success in athletic ability, is attractive to girls, and lacks feminine features is particularly status-conferring. Data from the Oakland Growth Study suggest that this appearance and physique include a tall, angular, muscular build coupled with a handsome face unblemished by acne (Stolz & Stolz, 1944). In a study of boys above and below average in muscular strength, Harold Jones found that the former scored significantly higher in athletic tests, were rated higher by staff members in social prestige, popularity, emotional buoyancy, appearance, masculine behavior, and in masculine physique (1949). The strong boys were less likely to report feelings of inferiority, anxiety, social difficulties, and physical symptoms. Some boys who achieved popularity were not equipped with desired physical attributes, but these were generally youth who relied upon other talents and were resourceful and aggressive. It is assumed that training programs in endurance and skills develop physical abilities, although very little competent research with controls for age-related processes of physical development as well as other influences extraneous to the training program has been conducted. A well-designed longitudinal study is much needed on this research problem (see Cureton, 1964).

In the Oakland Growth Study, physical examination records for 93 boys during junior and senior high school indicated that 29 were definitely disturbed by aspects of their physique at one time or another (Stolz & Stolz, 1944, p. 86). Twenty-two expressed concern over lack of size and muscular strength, fatness, or a poor physique. Although many of these disturbances reflected actual deficiencies in relation to statistical norms in the sample, there were exceptions. Some short boys were less concerned about their height than classmates who were appreciably taller.

Physical ideals and attitudes toward the body acquired in the family may have accounted in part for these differences in sensitivity. At present we know relatively little about the degree to which parental socialization policy and practices are influenced by the developing physiques of their sons and daughters (some data on this problem are reported in Glueck & Glueck, 1956).

While the stimulus value of the body among boys stemmed from associated physical skills as well as its appearance to others, the perceived appearance of the face and figure were of primary concern to girls in the Oakland Growth Study. Forty-one per cent of the 83 girls with physical examination records gave evidence of being disturbed at some point with one or more physical characteristics. Twenty-one of the girls expressed concern about being too tall or too heavy, and 16 were disturbed about their facial appearance. Peer ratings of girls in the study during high school indicate the liability associated with these characteristics. One of the most status-conferring constellations of qualities described a girl who was attractive in face and figure, well-groomed, and sophisticated (Tryon, 1944, p. 229). Studies by Coleman (1961) and Gordon (1957) of status systems and values among high-school students indicate the extent to which personal attractiveness, along with the social skills and self-confidence it facilitates, influences the status of girls.

Variations in Physical Maturation: Social and Psychological Effects

Physical characteristics such as height, weight, strength, and body conformation during adolescence are related to marked variations in physical maturation, especially in the pubescent growth cycle. Physical maturation rate has been defined by the relation of developmental age to chronological age. The former index has most frequently been measured by skeletal age, indicated by X-ray examination of bone development and also by secondary sex character age. Using skeletal age as a measure of developmental age on adolescents in the Oakland Growth Study, Bayley obtained a range of about four years in the age at which the boys attained skeletal maturation, and an estimated range of approximately 3.5 years among girls (1943). She assigned the boys and girls to three maturation groups, early, average, and late; the early and later maturers differed from the average group by approximately one year in physical maturation. Thirty-five per cent of the girls were classified as early maturers, 38 per cent as average, and 27 per cent as late in maturation. Twenty-seven per cent of the boys were assigned to each of the deviant maturation groups.

A series of studies at the Institute of Human Development indicate that physical characteristics which closely approximate sex-appropriate ideals for body-types are most common among early maturing boys and late maturing girls (see Eichorn's review, 1963). These studies have generally compared boys and girls who were consistently accelerated and retarded in skeletal maturation on staff-, peer-, and self-ratings. The primary research question has concerned the extent to which behavior patterns and personality characteristics are associated with different rates of maturation. Unfortunately data were not obtained on the adolescent's perception of his rate of physical and social maturation relative to the average rate among his classmates. Whether objectively measured differences in rate of maturation are defined as both real and important differences would depend on family experience, cultural patterns, and peer pressures.

The first analysis of the social and psychological correlates of rate of maturation was conducted by Jones and Bayley (1950). From boys in the Oakland Growth Study they selected 16 who were most consistently accelerated in physical maturation, and an equal number who were most consistently retarded during adolescence; neither group represented pathological extremes in skeletal maturation. The two groups differed in skeletal maturation by two years, but did not differ significantly in SES and IQ. The late maturers were relatively small, slender, and long-legged in body-build; were weak in strength tests during their growth lag; and were below average in tests of athletic ability. The early maturing, on the other hand, were generally large, broad-built, strong, and demonstrated above average skills in athletics. Differences in strength and physical skills were greatest between ages 13 and 15. Data assembled by Tanner show the early maturing boy to be higher in degree of masculinity in body form (1962, p. 102). Adult follow-up data on the physical characteristics of males in these two extreme groups are incomplete at this point. However, a comparison of 11 early maturers with 9 late maturers produced no significant differences in height, weight, and body-build (Eichorn, 1963, p. 42).

Ratings by adult staff members and by peers of behavior were made between the sixth and twelfth grades. The staff ratings were made independently by at least three observers on the behavior of the adolescents in small, same-sex groups in the waiting room at the Institute and on the playground when they came for their physical examinations; the average rater-reliability for these "free-play" ratings was .87. Behavior ratings made by classmates once or twice a year on a "guess who" instrument provided data on the reputations of the adolescents among their peers. The early maturing boys differed most strikingly from the late maturers in attractiveness of physique, as rated by staff observers. The late maturers were rated as more expressive and active than the early maturers, a finding which Jones and Bayley (1950) interpret as a continuation of "little boy" behavior and perhaps a compensatory striving for attention and acceptance. The attention-seeking behavior of the late maturers was also evident to their classmates; peers rated them as more bossy, attention-getting, and restless. Since the early maturers were more athletic and masculine in build than the late maturing, it is especially surprising that this difference was not registered in higher social prestige. No significant differences between these groups were obtained on adult ratings of popularity, leadership, prestige, poise, assurance, cheerfulness, and social effect on group. Similar peer ratings also did not differentiate the two groups. At the end of senior high, earlier differences between the extreme groups on the adult ratings were appreciably smaller. In high school the early maturers were more likely to have achieved recognition through athletics and social leadership. Mary Jones found a significant correlation between the rank order of boys on number of mentions in the school newspaper and skeletal maturation (1958). Kinsey's retrospective data on males shows a relationship between rate of physical maturation and sexual activity (Kinsey, Pomeroy, & Martin, 1948, Ch. 9).

The late maturing boys tended to have a more negative self-image and were more likely to report strained relations with parents than were the early maturers (Mussen & Jones, 1957). TAT protocols were used to measure self-image and relations with parents. The stories of the late maturers disclosed more feelings of inadequacy, a negative self-image, and feelings of rejection; they described their parents as forcing them to do things they did not want to do, and expressed rebellious attitudes toward parents. On inferred ratings of motivational tendencies, the late maturers tended to have stronger needs for social acceptance and aggression (Mussen & Jones, 1958). Though seeming to be opposite in character, these drives frequently stem from feelings of insecurity. The data on relations with parents suggest that some parents may have forced their late maturing sons to keep pace with the interests and abilities of boys more advanced in maturation and may have teased or ridiculed them about their physical deficiencies. The ratings and self-report data show a discrepancy between the observed and subjective status of the late maturers; their perceptions and feelings regarding self show greater concern with acceptability and status among peers than seem warranted by adult and peer ratings of their social prestige. Perhaps as a response to their body-image, these boys seem to have achieved status through intensely active, recognition-seeking behavior or by entering activities that were compatible with their physical abilities; status was earned more easily by the early maturers, as suggested by their relaxed, contented, calm manner, and they more readily achieved prominence in highly visible activities during high school.

In adulthood, personality differences between men who developed early and late resemble group differences obtained in adolescence (Mary C. Jones, 1965). Twelve early and 15 late maturing men were compared on scales from the California Personality Inventory, on measures from interviews when the subjects were in their mid-thirties, and on items from an adult *Q*-sort. The early maturers were characterized by the CPI scales as more conventional, controlled in impulse expression, concerned with making a good impression, responsible, and inclined toward achievement through conformity. The late maturers were significantly higher in flexibility and were more oriented toward inner feelings and achievement through independence. The *Q*-item characterizations of the two groups generally correspond to those shown by the CPI. Men who developed early perceived themselves as practical, objective, and conventional, while the late maturers were described as having a sense of humor. In personality, the early and late maturing men tend to resemble rather closely the college men with stable and variable moods in Wessman and Ricks' study (1966, pp. 249–250). They describe these two types as persons of "solid character" and of "lively passions." Like the early maturing subjects, the stable men were characterized as objective, cautious, rational, and controlled, not given to imaginative thinking, and oriented toward occupational achievement by conformity to external standards. The variable men resembled the late maturers in their impulsiveness, flexibility, activism, intense inner life, emphasis on originality, and inclination toward occupational achievement via independence and inventiveness. The stability of the mood and personality characteristics of men who developed early and late between adolescence and adulthood points to relatively potent genetic influences. At present there is no conclusive evidence on differences in adult attainments between the two groups of men (Mary C. Jones, 1957), although research on this problem is currently in progress at the Institute of Human Development.

Among girls, the physical and behavioral correlates of maturation rate are similar in many respects to those obtained for boys. However, for girls, the slender, feminine body-build of the late maturing is a feature of the ideal physique. Similar to the analysis of boys, an equal number of the most consistently accelerated and retarded girls (16) were selected from the Oakland Growth sample (Everett, cited in Eichorn, 1963, pp. 45–46). The two groups did not differ in chronological age, IQ, or in SES. Compared to the total sample of girls, the early maturers were taller up to age 13.5, while the late maturers were shorter until they reached the age of 15. The early maturers tended to carry more weight for their height throughout adolescence than the average and late maturing girls. In the middle period of adolescence, the large size of girls accelerated in maturation placed them at a distinct social disadvantage. Mary Jones observes that "they are conspicuously large in relation to other girls in their classroom and decidedly so in relation to boys of their own age. Boys, on the other hand, find that early maturity puts them on a par with the majority of the girls in their peer group in size and in the accompanying changes of interests" (1958, p. 93). The heightened self-consciousness resulting from accelerated proportions in height, weight, and bust may encourage a tendency to slouch and avoid situations which increase visibility.

Late maturing girls were rated by adult observers as more active and expressive, more sociable and prominent among their peers, and as higher on attention-seeking (Eichorn, 1963, pp. 45-46). By the high-school years the early maturers appeared to be just as buoyant and sociable as the late maturers, and were even rated somewhat more popular and good-natured. Girls in the two extreme groups did not differ significantly in attractiveness of physique, unlike the sizable difference obtained between comparable groups of boys. Peer ratings on popularity did not vary significantly between the accelerated and retarded groups, although the late maturing girls were more likely to have achieved social prominence in the high school, as indicated by number of mentions in the school newspaper (Mary C. Jones, 1958). The self-image of girls in the two extreme maturation groups did not vary markedly. The early maturing girls tended to give more TAT responses indicating negative characteristics and a need for recognition than the late maturers (Jones & Mussen, as cited in Eichorn, 1963, p. 46). However, these results are challenged by data from other samples summarized by Eichorn which show more positive social experiences and self-feelings among early than among late maturers (1963). In general, the social and psychological effects and correlates of maturation rate appear more pronounced among boys than among girls. At present there is little evidence of significant differences in adulthood between the maturation groups of females in the Oakland Growth Study, although this analysis is still in progress at the Institute.

There are a number of unexplored questions concerning the social and psychological effects and correlates of physical maturation. Rate of maturation refers to a loose complex of developing characteristics, and yet we have little information on their relative contributions to the overall effect of early or late maturation. Though height and body-build among boys are related to skeletal maturation, comparison of subgroups defined by these two measurements before the early maturers start their growth spurt might produce sharper variations in self-image and behavior patterns than a comparison of extreme maturation groups. Further exploration of environmental variations in the behavior correlates of skeletal maturation would be desirable in cultural contexts outside of the United States, since these correlates probably vary markedly by the stimulus value attached to differing physiques. Another problem worthy of attention is the known fact that extreme maturation groups in adolescence show many of the same physical differences in childhood, especially in height, that are evident during early adolescence. Is the early maturing boy's self-confidence, acceptance of body, and prestige among peers well established in middle childhood, and thus only reinforced by experiences during the growth spurt? No study has used both objective and subjective measures of physical maturation. Discrepancies between objective and subjective measures, as well as indications of the meaning to adolescents of deviations above and below preferred group standards, might provide valuable insight regarding the sources of different reactions to the same type of physique. One study has found a curvilinear relationship between the reactions of young men to physical deviations above and below preferred ideals (see Gunderson, 1965).

The Secular Trend in Growth and Maturation

Since at least the 1850's, a pronounced upward trend in the height and weight of adolescents and in the growth rate, as indicated by age at menarche, has been noted by scientists. This secular trend, according to James Tanner, "is one of the most considerable phenomena of human biology at present and has, into the bargain, a host of medical, educational and sociological consequences" (1961, p. 119). From a review of studies showing secular trends in physical growth, Tanner found the average gain in height and weight between 1880 and 1950 (North American, British, Swedish, Polish, and German data show very similar trends) to be approximately 2½ centimeters and 2 kilograms per decade during adolescence (1962, p. 145). Maximal height some 50 years ago was not attained until about the age of 26 in comparison to the current ages of 18–19 and 16–17 for boys and girls in the United States (Tanner, 1962, p. 149). Children today are generally taller and heavier than children of the 1930's at the same age, and the increase has been equivalent to four months per decade; thus, children of age 11 in 1930 would be similar in size to children of age 10 today. Although youth from upper- and middle-class families are taller and heavier than those from the lower classes, the secular trend in size is pronounced on all class levels. A number of explanations for this trend have been proposed; these include an improvement in nutrition and in environmental conditions, and a decrease in the tendency for individuals to marry within the same village. There is considerable support for the former theory. For example, Tanner reports a study by Ito in 1942 which found that Japanese who migrated to the improved environment of California as children became larger and more linear than those who remained at home (1962, p. 141). For a critical evaluation of evidence relevant to these theories, the reader should refer to Tanner (1962, Ch. 5).

The secular trend in age at menarche, as an indication of growth acceleration, is similarly pronounced. As with height and weight, we find age at menarche has decreased by about four months per decade over the last 100 years (Tanner, 1962, p. 152). Trends in Western Europe and in the United States are relatively similar. Using British data, Tanner shows this decrease in a striking comparison: a sample of middle-class women in Manchester, England, in 1820 averaged 15.7 as of age at menarche, whereas 12.9 is the average figure for a comparable group of women at present (1962, p. 152). There is no conclusive evidence of a similar trend among males. Recent data on American girls (between 1940 and 1955) show the average age at menarche to be between 12.5 and 13 years, depending on class and regional variations (Tanner, 1962, p. 159). Tanner finds no evidence that the upward trend in earlier age at menarche and in maturation in height and weight is leveling out, although reason would suggest an end in the near future.

II. Intellectual Development

The ascendance of conceptual over perceptual processes is generally considered the central feature of development toward mature intellectual functioning. The pace and form of this development is in large measure a consequence of the child's experiences, the richness and variety of stimuli presented by his environment. As noted earlier, a child's encounter with a new environment and set of role expectations is considered by Piaget as a significant determinant of the acquisition of new logical structures. In reference to Inhelder and Piaget's research on the growth of logical thinking, Jerome Bruner observes that "logical structures develop to support the new forms of commerce with the world. . . . So the concretely operational child need not manipulate the world of potentiality (save on the fantasy level) until pressure is placed upon him, at which point propositionalism begins to mark his thinking" (1959, p. 369). Similarly, Hunt observes that "change in circumstances is required to force the accommodative modifications of schemata that constitute development" (1961, p. 258). Experience and its requirements thus induce differentiation of cognitive structures, and variations in environment under favorable circumstances generally foster the desire for new experiences. The development of logical structures in adolescence enables youth to order objects in their world in an abstract, relativistic, and less stereotyped fashion; to think in terms of multiple alternatives rather than in terms of dichotomous categories; to transcend information; and to develop abstract relations from objects encountered and to order them in terms of their relations. The differentiated conceptual matrix provides a means for locating oneself in social time and space and enables the articulation of an identity.

> Concepts, in their matrix of interrelatedness, serve the critical cognitive function of providing a system of ordering by means of which the environment is broken down and organized, is differentiated and integrated, into its many psychologically relevant facets. In this capacity, they provide the medium through which the individual establishes and maintains ties with the surrounding world. It is on the basis of the web of these conceptual ties that one is able to place oneself stably and meaningfully in relation to time, space, and other objects and dimensions of his psychological universe. It is on this basis, hence, that one's self-identity and existence are articulated and maintained (Harvey, Hunt, & Schroder, 1961, p. 11).

Three testable assumptions are implied by the stage-analytic concept in Piaget's theory of cognitive development: the acquisition of cognitive structures or levels of moral judgment follows an invariant series of steps—A must be mastered before B, and B before C; the stage sequence is similar across sociocultural environments, while the relation between developmental and chronological age is subject to environmental variations; and level of cognitive development is consistent across situations and roles. Joachim Wohlwill notes that there is a surprising lack of sound evidence on the first principle and that a convincing test of the invariant stage concept necessitates a longitudinal study (1963). Lawrence Kohlberg's studies of the development of moral judgment among preadolescent boys and adolescent boys in the United States and in other cultures generally support the first two hypotheses, although they are not based on a longitudinal design (1966a). On the intertask consistency hypothesis, Wohlwill's review of studies indicates considerable variability in the responses of children to tasks supposedly requiring the same level of cognitive development, and thus suggests a need for refinements of theory and method. Although Kohlberg's studies—reviewed in the subsequent section on moral development—indicate a relatively high degree of consistency in level of moral judgment between verbal moral situations, they also show substantial variability. On available evidence, the consistency hypothesis is less firmly supported than the first two principles.

The sequence of developmental stages in cognitive functioning from late childhood to adolescence is suggested by a recent series of cross-sectional studies on concept attainment and role-taking ability. Elkind tested 469 junior and senior high-school students for their conceptions of mass, weight, and volume (1961). The proportion of students with abstract conceptions of volume increased significantly between age 12 and 18; the percentage of boys with an abstract conception generally exceeded the percentage of girls. Yudin and Kates examined the process of concept attainment across three age groups of 40 boys each: 12-year-olds, 14-year-olds, and 16-year-olds (1963). Three aspects of maturity of cognitive functioning were examined: *perceptual error,* an inability to handle data presented directly and perceptually; *consistent strategy,* skill in dealing with data by modifying or maintaining guesses without a systematic integration of previous information; and *ideal strategy,* consistent strategy coupled with an ability to integrate previous data systematically. All subjects were presented with two practical problems and six experimental problems on slides. The problem was considered solved when the correct answer was offered twice in succession without subsequent wrong responses. The 12-year-old boys differed from the 14- and 16-year-old boys by making more perceptual errors and showing fewer consistent and ideal strategies. No difference was observed between the two older age groups.

In a series of experiments on the ability of children to assume different social perspectives regarding the same event, Feffer found role-taking skill (tested by projective role-taking tasks) to be correlated with age and intelligence in a sample of children ranging from age 6 to age 13 (Feffer, 1959; Feffer & Gourevitch, 1960). In a related study, Wolfe selected 136 boys from 910 sixth- through twelfth-grade students who represented extremes in conceptual level, from abstract to concrete, measured by a self-report instrument (1963). Cognitive performance on role-taking (measured by Feffer's projective tasks) and impression formation tasks were directly related to conceptual level, age, and intelligence. Level of conceptual abstractness was similarly related to age.

A number of studies have shown that boys tend to out-perform girls on mathematics tests and that girls generally perform better on verbal than on mathematics tests (see Carlsmith, 1964). On the basis of these findings, Carlsmith suggests that boys tend to employ an "analytic" conceptual style characterized by "clear discrimination between stimuli, a direct pursuit of solutions, and a disregard for extraneous material"; girls, on the other hand, seem to employ a "global approach" characterized by "less discrimination of stimuli and a greater influence from extraneous material" (1964, p. 17).

In samples of high-school students and Harvard freshmen, Carlsmith found verbal ability to be correlated with father-absence. Among males, early separation from father was significantly correlated with higher performance on verbal than on mathematics tests. In the high-school sample, results for girls corresponded to those obtained among boys. These findings could be interpreted as indicating that father-absence and a correlated strengthening of emotional ties between mother and child fosters the development of verbal skills. The presence of father, on the other hand, would tend to weaken these ties, perhaps enabling the acquisition of analytic and number skills that require concentration and autonomy. From an experimental study of the familial correlates of verbal, numerical, and spatial ability in fifth-grade children, Elizabeth Bing concluded that

> The essential condition for the development of verbality is probably the close relationship with an adult, and verbal ability is fostered by a high degree of interaction between mother and child. In contrast, the development of number ability requires, above all, concentration and ability to carry through a task by oneself. Similarly, spatial ability is probably developed through interaction with the physical rather than the interpersonal environment. A marked pattern of help-seeking and help-giving interferes with the development of an independent and self-reliant attitude, which may be the intervening con-

dition for a high degree of development of spatial and numerical ability (Bing, 1963, pp. 646–647).

From Thurstone's research, we find considerable variation in the development of these cognitive abilities from childhood to adolescence (cited in Bloom, 1964a, p. 58). Absolute scales of different abilities were constructed from sets of cross-sectional data on Primary Abilities tests obtained from samples of children in the age span of 5 to 19. Using 80 per cent of adult performance as an index with which to compare development, he found that the Perceptual Speed factor reached this level at age 12, and Space and Reasoning factors by age 14, Number and Memory factors by age 16, Verbal Comprehension by age 18, and Verbal Fluency after age 20.

Age-Related Change in IQ Test Performance: The Effects of Heredity and Personality

Longitudinal studies indicate that the percentage of measured intelligence at age 17 developed by age one is approximately 20 per cent; by age 4, 50 per cent; by age 8, 80 per cent; and by age 13, 92 per cent. Thus from birth to 4 years, children develop about half of their mature intelligence, another 30 per cent is added between ages 4 and 8, and the remaining 20 per cent is gained between 8 and 17 years (Bloom, 1964a, p. 58).

In the Fels longitudinal study, stability of intellectual performance among 36 males and 35 females was examined across five periods from birth to adulthood: I, birth to 3 years; II, 3 to 6 years; III, 6 to 10 years; IV, 10 to 14 years; and V, early adulthood (Kagan & Moss, 1962). The subjects in the adult period ranged in age from approximately 19 to 29. Intellectual achievement represented the child's skill in mastering language and numbers, his desire to perform well in school situations, his interest in the acquisition of knowledge, and his interest in reading and in scientific projects. From Period I to the adolescent period, the average correlation of intellectual achievement among boys and girls was only .19. Correlations were much stronger between Periods II and IV, .54, and between Periods III and IV, .78. Intellectual performance in adolescence and early adulthood was highly related, .66. Thus, intellectual mastery in adolescence, actually early adolescence in the Fels study, was a relatively accurate predictor of adult orientation toward educational matters, cultural sophistication, and curiosity. On most measures of adult functioning, the gifted child in Terman's longitudinal study became a competent adult (Terman & Oden, 1959).

A large proportion of the variance in intellectual development from childhood to adulthood is accounted for by hereditary and personality factors. Since genotype and environment interact in the developmental process, "a question that inquires as to the proportional contribution of genetic and environmental sources of variance can receive only a relative answer. Estimates of heritability refer to a specifically defined trait in a particular population at a certain time and under certain environmental conditions" (McClearn, 1964, p. 463). Thus it is not surprising that estimates of the proportion of intelligence attributable to heredity have ranged as much as 28 per cent, from 60 to 88 per cent (cited in Bloom, 1964a, p. 71). Studies show an increasing resemblance in intelligence between children and their biological parents from infancy to adolescence, regardless of whether the child is reared by his real parents or by adoptive parents (Honzik, 1963). Bloom's analysis of data on separated identical twins shows that variations in family environment strongly influence the degree of twin resemblance in IQ. The more similar the two environments, the closer the resemblance (Bloom, 1964a, p. 70).

Several studies indicate that IQ acceleration is associated with a competitive, coping personality. Increases in IQ between age 6 and 10 in the Fels sample were more common among children who were overtly competitive and independent with peers as well as with adults (Sontag, Baker, & Nelson, 1958). In the Oakland Growth Study, Haan assessed the relation of coping and defense mechanisms to IQ change between adolescence and the mid-thirties among 49 men and 50 women (1963). A coping orientation was significantly correlated with IQ acceleration, and defense with IQ deceleration. An insecure, defensive student is likely to feel threatened by a school environment that encourages open questioning of teachers and freedom for exploration of unstructured problems. One consequence of this type of incongruence between personality and environment is shown in a study of a small sample of undergraduate students enrolled at the University of Chicago. The authoritarian student was similar to other students at the university in level of intelligence, although he felt particularly threatened by the relatively high degree of freedom and lack of structure in academic life at the university. Stern describes his academic approach as

> ... somewhat obsessive-compulsive, stressing detailed organization and structure. A distinct minority group at Chicago, the authoritarians contributed most heavily to the withdrawal rate, complaining of the lack of professional courses and the looseness of a pedagogical approach that tolerated smoking in the classrooms, did not require attendance, and expected students to answer their own questions (1962, p. 694).

The association of aggressive, competitive attributes with the utilization of mental ability in adulthood has been well documented by data from Lewis Terman's sample of "gifted children" (Terman & Oden, 1947). This sample includes approximately 1500 subjects who, in 1921, were in the top one per cent of the population in IQ. In the early 1940's a detailed comparison was made of biographical data on the 150 most successful men and on a similar number of the least successful men. These groups were selected according to criteria such as eminence, reputation in the community, and professional status. The highly successful men differed most significantly from the least successful men on four traits: persistence in the accomplishment of ends, freedom from inferiority feelings, self-confidence, and integration toward goals. "In the total picture the greatest contrast between the two groups was in all-round emotional and social adjustment, and in drive to achieve" (Terman & Oden, 1959, p. 149).

Environmental Influences

Environments may be classified by the degree to which they facilitate or retard intellectual development. Numerous studies have shown that families, neighborhoods, and schools tend to vary in educative influence according to their social-class status and composition (see, for instance, Douglas, 1964). The higher the social-class status of these environments, the more likely they are to facilitate the intellectual development of children. A conservative estimate of the effect of an extremely deprived environment on intelligence is considered by Bloom to be about 20 IQ points. "This could mean the difference between a life in an institution for the feeble-minded or a productive life in society. It could mean the difference between a professional career and an occupation which is at the semiskilled or unskilled level" (1964, p. 89; see also Skeels, 1966). And since the largest increments in IQ gain are achieved before children enter school, deprived home environments constitute a major factor in retarding the development of verbal, reasoning, and numerical abilities. A study described by Bloom found family environment to have the least effect on skills taught principally in school and the greatest influence on language development (1964, p. 124). Frequency of parent-child interaction, verbal training, reading instruction, and the educative influence of parental skills and interest in learning are known to facilitate the development of linguistic skills. In Douglas's longitudinal study of children in Great Britain, education of parents, parental interest in the child's intellectual progress, and the provision of reading lessons before the child entered primary school were highly intercorrelated (1964, Ch. 7). These facilitative conditions are least likely to be found in lower-class families with a large number of children and crowded living conditions. The full effect of these negative conditions on mental ability in Douglas's study was manifested among children in the sample by the age of 8. Just as children with aggressive, competitive personalities are most likely to develop their intellectual potential, the Fels study found that high performing boys and girls were likely to have competitive, aggressive mothers (Kagan & Moss, 1962, pp. 221–222).

The deprived learning environment represented by some schools in the slum areas of our large cities is characterized by relatively poor facilities, a lack of qualified and motivated teachers, and by low faculty expectations concerning the ability of their students to learn (Sexton, 1961). The effect of this climate on the student's concept of his ability to learn is suggested by a study in the Harlem schools which found a decline in test performance among children from grade school to junior high school (*Youth in the Ghetto,* 1964). In Douglas's study (1964), gains in test scores among children between the age of 8 and 11 were highly correlated with the quality of the educational environment provided by their primary schools; this relationship was found when school size, the quality of the building and educational equipment, student social background, and the school's past accomplishments in getting students into grammar schools were used as indexes.

Within schools varying in quality, the practice of stratifying students according to ability or other criteria tends to create both facilitative and deprived environments. The resulting student strata are commonly associated in the minds of teachers and students with different meanings. The bright or clever students have elite status, while the slow or poorly performing students become a negative reference group. Eventually, students in these various strata tend to see themselves as they are publicly defined. In doing so, even misplaced children are likely to confirm the classifiers' judgment by meeting expectations experienced in the school environment. Teachers may encourage such congruence by structuring anticipatory socialization in ways relevant to "manual-minded" and "college-ability" students. In the low-ability groups the absence of intellectual models may result in a climate of dullness, boredom, and alienation from school. In an experimental project with slow learners in junior high-school, Bowman and Liddle found that both students and teachers outside the program negatively defined the slow learners and their teachers. It was the "dumb bunny" class to some students. Some teachers believed that the teacher of slow children was not as bright as the teacher of gifted children (Bowman & Liddle, 1959). Studies of ability grouping in Sweden (Johannesson, 1962) and Great Britain (Jackson, 1964) generally find this practice to have a negative effect on youth in the low-ability groups, while not appreciably benefiting the brighter students. The effects of tracking in American schools on measures of ability and achievement are less clear. By reducing student heterogeneity in ability, ability-grouping may provide relatively greater benefits for teachers than for students (Goldberg & Passow, 1962). In her study of a large urban school system Patricia Sexton[3] offered the following observation concerning the effect of student stratification:

> The teacher learns that he has a low I.Q. rating and puts him into a slow-moving group where he is not expected to do much or given much attention. He is bright enough however to catch on very quickly to the fact that he is not considered very bright. He comes to accept this very unflattering appraisal because, after all, the school should know. Now he is in his pigeonhole. He can't get out and, what is more, he doesn't try; he accepts his fate. His parents also accept it, since, after all, the school should know. Intellectually he is lost. He has accepted this low appraisal of himself, and both he and society must suffer the consequences (1961, p. 52).

In Great Britain, stratified secondary education shows on a broader scale the effects of grouping students by ability. Selection for qualitatively different levels of secondary education in Great Britain illustrates the institutionalization of facilitative and deprived school environments. Since the Education Act of 1944, different types of secondary education have been provided British youth according to test performance, interviews, and personal evaluations upon completion of primary schooling. Generally, the top quintile of students are selected for grammar school, while most of the remainder are enrolled in the more vocational modern school. Grammar school is more highly esteemed since it is linked to the universities, the professions, and white-collar work, while placement in a modern school is typically equivalent to selection for manual work. The impact of failure in the 11-plus examination and the lower set of expectations experienced by the student entering a modern school appear to encourage a lowering of self-estimates of ability, academic motivation, and of test performance from the first to the last year of modern school (Elder, 1965b). Grammar-school students, on the other hand, tend to increase in performance.

When deprived school and family environments are improved, this change is frequently registered in subsequent improvements in the intellectual performance of youth. Improvement in the educative environment of the family is one possible consequence of adult programs in developing basic literacy skills. A mother who learns to read and write becomes able for the first time to answer communications from her children's school, to understand messages written by her children, and to at least appreciate, if not understand, their learning problems. One likely consequence of entering her children's world of the written word is greater respect toward herself and from her children. The educational model presented by this mother may initiate a series of changes in the family which increase the academic motivation and aspirations of her children. A study in progress at the Institute of Human Development is exploring the effects of adult education on family relations and socialization among adults, mostly women, in a day school. Three-fourths of the adults over 25 years of age who had children at home indicated that their return to school had a positive effect on their children. They noted that they could now help their children in their schoolwork and that their visible sacrifices in getting an education encouraged their children to put forth greater effort. Often mother and child did their homework together. An increased sense of competence and respect was the primary personal change mentioned. The comings and goings of the adults during the school day as well as their homework at night also presented educational examples to other adults in their generally deprived neighborhoods; 40 per cent of the

[3] From *Education and Income* by Patricia C. Sexton.

adults felt that their return to school had an uplift effect on the educational interest of people in their neighborhoods. The preliminary findings from this study indicate a need for research on the implications of adult education for changing family environments.

The gain in test scores experienced by Negro children who migrated from the South to northern school systems is one well-known example of the relation between environmental and test score improvements. Young children have the greatest potential for intellectual growth, and this research shows the size of test score gains to be inversely correlated with the age of the migrant child (Bloom, 1964a, pp. 74–75). The impact of increased parental and faculty interest in the academic progress of students on intellectual achievement is demonstrated in the Banneker Project under the direction of Samuel Shephard, a Negro educator in the St. Louis public school system (see Pettigrew, 1964, p. 124). The Banneker section of the city includes 23 elementary schools and over 16,000 slum and low-income housing project children, 95 per cent of whom are Negro. Operating under the principle that ghetto children can learn and can overcome economic disadvantage, Shephard forcefully challenges teachers, parents, and students to achieve high standards of excellence:

> ... he appeals to race pride and resorts to continuous exhortations, rallies, contests, posters, and meetings with teachers and parents. Students who make good grades are asked to stand in assemblies for the applause of their classmates. Teachers are asked to visit the homes of their charges. And parents are asked to provide their offspring with encouragement, study space, a library card, a dictionary, and other books as gifts (Pettigrew, 1964, p. 126).

The results of this stimulating environment are seen in the tripling of percentages of Banneker graduates who were accepted for high-ability programs in St. Louis high schools (Pettigrew, 1964, pp. 126–127). The median IQ of students increased from the mid-80's to the 90's during the first four years of the program.

III. Autonomy

In adolescence, growth of independence from family may occur on at least four dimensions: achievement of freedom of movement and participation in making personal decisions; shedding of binding, infantile attachments to parents; development of internal controls; and determination of acceptable personal values (Douvan & Adelson, 1966). In late adolescence and early adulthood, autonomy in relation to family also includes the issue of economic independence. In developmental sequence, behavioral independence is presumably achieved in some measure before emotional, moral, and value autonomy, since it provides opportunity for testing, evaluating, and differentiating self from parents. The transition from home to a college environment provides an experience conducive to growth in all aspects of autonomy by weakening affective ties to family in a new context of different values, people, and situations.

Conflict resulting from differential growth in the various autonomies is frequently manifested between behavioral independence and a lingering need to be dependent on parents. Such conflict is apt to be particularly intense and produce emotional ambivalence among family dependent boys reared in cultures that emphasize toughness and courage in males. As a protective device, social camouflage of inner dependencies may take the form of aggression and bravado. In his study of lower-class boys, many of whom were reared in female-based families, Walter Miller observed that "the pose of tough rebellious independence often assumed by the lower-class person frequently conceals powerful dependency cravings" (1958, p. 13). Some youth may transfer their dependence from parents to peers, especially those with a strong need for social acceptance.

In the following pages, we shall examine patterns of change and stability in behavioral and emotional autonomy during adolescence, the socialization of these types of autonomy in the family, and behavioral expressions of adolescent rebellion. The development of internal controls and moral judgment is the subject of the following chapter section.

Stability of Behavioral and Emotional Autonomy

Patterns of change and stability in behavioral and emotional dependence between childhood and early adolescence are shown by four ratings from the Fels longitudinal study (Kagan & Moss, 1962, pp. 52–54). Affectional dependence included evidence of the child seeking emotional reassurance, acceptance, and affection from mother. Instrumental dependence indicated requests for assistance in difficult or stressful situations. Independence behavior represented the frequency of autonomous behavior in situations requiring problem solving. The fourth rating, passivity, was based primarily on incidence of withdrawal to frustration.

The overall pattern of correlations between these ratings in Periods I and II, ages birth–3 and 3–6, and the same ratings in early adolescence, ages 10–14, showed much greater instability among boys than girls in passive behavior, in dependence on emotional support from mother, and in reliance on others for help in difficult situations. Between the grade-school period (ages 6–10) and early adolescence, measures of both types of autonomy were relatively stable for both boys and girls in the sample. Those who tended to withdraw to frustration or acted autonomously in problem-solving situations during the grade-school period showed similar behavioral tendencies in early adolescence. However, sex differences in the stability of dependence-independence again appeared in correlations between ratings in each of the four pre-adult periods and ratings of analogous behavior in adulthood. Correlation coefficients were strongest from the grade-school and early adolescent periods to early adulthood. For instance, withdrawal to frustration as indicated by the passivity rating in the grade-school period was correlated .27 and .48 for males and females with an adult rating on withdrawal from stress. Between early adolescence and adulthood, correlation coefficients on this relationship were .36 for males and .67 for females.

As noted earlier in the chapter, Kagan and Moss hypothesized that this sex difference was a consequence of the "differential cultural expectations" regarding independence and dependence for males and females in American culture. Passive or dependent behavior is rewarded and independence permissively accepted in the behavior of girls; boys, on the other hand, are pressed toward independence in sex-role socialization and are often subject to social punishment for showing dependence. This interpretation would be convincing if Kagan and Moss had shown that dependent males in childhood achieved higher scores in adolescence and adulthood on ratings of independence and if males who were high in autonomy in childhood remained relatively stable in this behavior pattern. Since a correlational analysis does not show kinds of behavior change, the hypothesis on differential sex-role expectations remains only one of several hypotheses which might explain the results they obtained.

Socialization and the Development of Autonomy

The following conditions have proven to be especially instrumental in the development of behavioral and emotional autonomy: models of competent autonomy in mother and father, guided opportunities and training for self-reliance, and emotional support. The interaction between these conditions and personality is a central feature of this developmental process. Independence opportunities may be viewed as threatening to some youth and lead to flight from one dependency relation to another. In late adolescence, the expression of independence or dependence may be influenced by interaction and conflict between the youth's childhood experiences and the larger society. It is at this point, according to Erikson (1962), that fidelity of self, parents, and society is seriously questioned by some youth in an attempt to identify objects worthy of personal commitment. For youth brought up in a sheltered environment, awareness of reality in the latter part of adolescence may result in feelings of apprehension and distrust toward the parental generation and social institutions.

1. *Warmth and respect in the modeling process.* One of the important areas in which parents may demonstrate competent autonomy is in their occupational roles. The desire for youth to model their parents depends partly on the emotional quality of the parent-adolescent relationship and on reciprocal feelings of respect. The influence of warm parent-son relations on the modeling process is illustrated by a comparison of two groups of boys (Oakland Growth Study subjects) defined by extreme Masculine-Feminine scores on the Strong Vocational Interest inventory (Mussen, 1961). In response to the TAT, boys with strong, appropriate sex-typed interests tended to describe relations with their fathers as more rewarding and favorable than the low-masculine group and were less likely to tell stories in which father acted in punitive or controlling ways. The highly masculine group exceeded the other group in overall adjustment as well; they were rated by observers as more carefree, contented, exuberant, and smoother in social relations. In a related study of adolescents, desire to model parents was found to be most common among youth with opportunities to interact in decision making with parents who explained rules not understood (Elder, 1963).

The perceived competence of father in the home and on the job as a determinant of role model attractiveness is illustrated by findings from a study of 184 adolescent boys in Flint, Michigan, and their families (Gold, 1963). The sample was composed of 92 delinquents and 92 controls. Over one fourth of the boys mentioned high occupational status as a factor that would make a man an attractive adult. In questioning mother, father, and son, Gold found the influence of father directly related to the prestige rank of his occupation. The desire of boys in both samples to be like their fathers when they grow up was directly related to the amount of influence which father was perceived as exercising in the family.

Fathers may demonstrate competent independence to their sons and daughters by a willingness to assume responsibilities and risks on their own. The occupational activities of fathers who run their own business represents a particularly visible example of independence. The industry and drive shown by upwardly mobile fathers are another example of behavior patterns that may be emulated by sons. A longitudinal analysis of father's work-life mobility in relation to the independence and mastery behavior of sons illustrates this source of paternal influence. Smelser related the work-life patterns of 93 fathers with boys in the Guidance Study between 1928 and 1946 to the personality development of their sons who were born in 1928 (1963). The boys were placed in five social status and mobility groups on the basis of father's occupational status during son's childhood and adolescence: high status–upwardly mobile, low status–upwardly mobile, high status–stationary, low status–stationary, and downwardly mobile. The groups were compared on intellectual development, adult perception of self and parents, and other personality variables. An emphasis on competence, autonomy, and power was most common among sons in the following groups ranked from high to low: high status–upwardly mobile, high status–stationary, low status–

upwardly mobile. Boys in these groups tended to perceive their fathers as strong, competent persons. In intellectual ability, the sons from downwardly mobile families ranked highest in mean IQ score at age 6 and last in ability at age 18. They saw themselves as relatively weak, stressed affection more than power in perception of father, and were more likely, on the average, to see mother as stronger than father.

Mother's occupational behavior is likely to foster self-reliance in girls when it demonstrates competent autonomy. Data showing these results were obtained from a large national sample of adolescent girls who ranged in age from 11 through 18 (Douvan, 1963). Family interaction and training in middle-class families in which mother worked either full- or part-time appeared to foster self-reliance in girls. These adolescents admired their mothers more than girls with unemployed mothers, were relatively independent in judgment and free of external authority, and were active in organized and informal leisure activities. Working-class girls, particularly those with mothers working full-time, were found to differ in several respects from their middle-class counterparts. They carried heavy household responsibilities, were expected to fend for themselves in the family, and were emotionally dependent on their mothers. These class differences may be explained by two conditions. Middle-class mothers, compared to those in the working class, are likely to have jobs that require high-level skills, and to have a choice in whether to work or not. The employment of the working-class mother, on the other hand, may reflect a family condition rather than personal competence and independence.

2. *Opportunities and training for self-direction*. Experience and skills acquired through participation in decision making are instrumental in the growth of self-confidence and autonomy. Using retrospective data from samples of adults in five nations —Mexico, Italy, Great Britain, the United States, and Germany—Almond and Verba found participation in decision making and the chance to voice criticisms in the home and school during adolescence to be related in each nation to degree of social involvement and to competence in political affairs (1963). The index of civic competence included items indicating the adults' perceived ability to do something about an unjust regulation, the likelihood that they would do something to correct it, and the extent to which they had ever acted to change or influence a local regulation. Adults with high scores participated in more voluntary associations, were more willing to cooperate with others in a common venture, were more trustful of others, and were higher in education in each nation. With level of education controlled, participation in family decision making and the opportunity to complain about unjust treatment in family and school were correlated with civic competence primarily among adults with a primary education or less.

Independence opportunities are also influenced by task experiences. In current research on the effects of economic deprivation in the Great Depression, the author found that boys in the Oakland Growth Study were most likely to have behavioral autonomy, as reported by themselves and by their mothers, if they were gainfully employed, did not have chores to do in the home, and were brought up in a home in which mother made the important decisions. Boys who were working at the end of junior high were likely to gain more in autonomy between junior and senior high than unemployed youth. Though boys encountered lower parental strictness in families that were dominated by mother rather than by father, a reverse tendency was indicated in the socialization of girls. Maternal dominance and heavy household chores were most frequently experienced by girls in economically deprived families, and they were significantly more dependent on their family than other girls.

Independence training, which includes the provision of opportunities as well as autonomy demands, has been viewed primarily within the context of family socialization, although it may also apply to relations with peers and other authority figures. In social and delinquent gangs, the accomplishment of group objectives may require independence opportunities for members coupled with the expectation and demand that they successfully perform the assigned task. These two aspects of independence training may not always be present to the same degree. Some adolescents may have abundant opportunities to gain experience in self-reliance and yet not experience parental expectations and demands that they engage in certain activities and perform tasks on their own. On the other hand, strong independence demands may be imposed without adequate opportunities to fulfill them. Marian Winterbottom's frequently used index of independence training measures autonomy demands and assumes that adequate autonomy opportunities are provided (1958). In this technique, mothers are provided with a list of activities and are asked to indicate the age at which they expect their child to do them. These activities include making "friends among children of his own age" and "decisions like choosing his own clothes or deciding to spend money by himself." Using an adaptation of Winterbottom's index, Bernard Rosen obtained a significant inverse relationship between mean age at independence training, as reported by mothers of preadolescent boys, and social class (1962). The mean age reported by Class I mothers, indicated by the Hollingshead index, was 6.4 in comparison to an average age of 8.2 for mothers in the lower working class (Class V). In a cross-national analysis, Rosen found that American mothers tended to train their sons for independence at an earlier age than Brazilian mothers on all but one of the five class levels (1962).

3. *Variations in parental control and warmth.* Studies on the development of autonomy during adolescence have examined the independent and interacting effects of varying levels of parental control and warmth. This research has generally found the effects of level of parental control to vary by level of parental warmth, and that similar patterns of control and warmth have different consequences in the behavior and attitudes of boys and girls.

The influence of parental domination in a context of warmth on adolescent behavior and feelings of political trust are shown in a cross-national study of high-school and university students in Belgium and Holland (Pinner, 1965). Data were obtained from questionnaires. Pinner observed from largely impressionistic evidence that Belgian parents prize "restrained behavior" in their children, whereas the Dutch encourage children to explore their social world, to assume independence, and develop friendships with different youth. He noted that Dutch youth are more "independence-minded" than Belgian adolescents; they travel more on their own and are more likely to prefer to live away from their families when attending the university even though it may be in their home town. Belgian students prefer to live at home even if it means commuting long distances to the university. On the basis of these data and impressions, Pinner hypothesized that parental overprotection would be more common among Belgian than Dutch students and that overprotected youth would tend to be apprehensive and distrustful of politicians and politics.

From a factor analysis of similar items on family relations in the Belgian and Dutch samples, Pinner constructed a scale indicating high parental warmth and control (Social Confinement) and a measure of sponsored social independence (Guidance). A high score on Social Confinement describes a youth who felt that his family was too affectionate, was prevented from doing things on his own, was not often allowed to go out at night, and who submitted to parental decisions on most of the important issues pertaining to his future. A high score on the Guidance scale describes an adolescent who felt he has always gotten along well with his parents, is allowed some independence but relies primarily on parental advice, and is permitted to have friends with different social backgrounds. Comparison of the Belgian and Dutch students on individual items and on the scales indicated that Belgian parents were significantly higher in control and protectiveness, while Dutch parents were more likely to sponsor social independence and involvement. Strong emotional dependence on family and a feeling of excessive parental control were significantly more characteristic of Belgian than Dutch students. This difference in dependency was indicated also in the way Belgian and Dutch students with separate income handled their money. Belgian students were more than three times as likely as their Dutch counterparts to turn over all of their scholarship stipends or earnings to their parents and to receive from them an allowance. Despite these cross-national variations, the social confinement scale was significantly correlated with measures of political distrust and disaffection in both samples.

Pinner's study primarily shows the behavioral effects of high levels of both parental control and warmth. An indication of behavior associated with other patterns is provided by a recent summary of research on parental discipline (W. C. Becker, 1964). Becker organized the behavioral outcomes obtained in studies of child rearing which employed measures of both control and warmth in a four-fold table defined by restrictiveness-permissiveness and warmth-hostility (p. 198). Similar to Pinner's results, the warm-restrictive pattern was associated with compliant, dependent, submissive, and low-aggression behavior. A warm-permissive condition was related to active, outgoing, low self-blame, friendly, and independent behavior. Children who experienced parental hostility and restrictiveness were characterized by the various studies as shy, inhibited, anxious, and high on self-aggression, while delinquency, noncompliance, and high aggression were correlated with hostility and permissiveness. It should be noted that restrictiveness in the above typology refers primarily to disciplinary practices and not to limit setting or to the regulation of independence opportunities. High parental control over a child's behavior does not necessarily imply the use of punitive or restrictive discipline. An adolescent's parents could strictly limit independence opportunities without using punitive discipline.

In addition to the importance of considering the emotional context of parental control, it has also been recognized that finer distinctions than high or low should be made on the continua of control and warmth. During adolescence, the development of self-confidence in self-direction seems to be associated with moderate rather than either high or low control by mother and father. In the case of parent-youth decision making, a study of adolescents found both high and low parental control to be correlated with feelings of rejection; youth who felt most accepted by parents were those who experienced moderate control and guidance in self-direction (Elder, 1961). In a subsequent analysis of these data, three levels of parental control were defined (1963): autocratic control in which parents were described as generally telling the adolescent what to do; democratic control in which the adolescent participated in decision making but did not have the final word; and permissive control in which the youth reported that he could make up his own mind, although his parents wanted him to consider their advice. These levels of control were then correlated with items indicating confidence in ability to make wise decisions and the tendency to make decisions with or without prior consideration of advice and ideas from others. Among boys and girls, level of reported parental control was directly related to a tendency to let others make decisions; a feeling of confidence in self-direction was most prevalent among youth with democratic parents and least common among those who had no voice in making their own decisions. Upon further analysis, the effects of parental control were found to vary by the frequency with which parents explained rules or decisions that were not understood. This latter variable was related to perceptions of parental warmth and appeared to increase the perceived legitimacy of parental restraints. Dependence on others in decision making situations and low self-confidence were directly related to level of parental control only among adolescents who received frequent explanations. Frequent explanations and autocratic control thus resemble the high warmth-control pattern in fostering dependent, submissive behavior. Both permissiveness and democratic relations were associated with self-confident independence when explanations were frequently offered by parents. These and other data reported in the study indicate that adolescents who received explanations from parents and were provided with experience in decision making under parental supervision were most likely to be confident and independent, to want to be like their parents, and to associate with parent-approved peers. By maximizing parent-adolescent interaction, increasing trust and the legitimacy of rules, and providing experience in self-reliance, this type of relationship provides a facilitative environment for acquiring autonomy and learning adult standards of behavior.

In a provocative analysis of the familial correlates of adolescent responsibility and leadership, Bronfenbrenner found that parental control and warmth had different consequences in the behavior of boys and girls (1961). Data on parental practices were obtained from a questionnaire administered to 192 tenth-grade boys and girls; ratings on responsibility and leadership were made by teachers. Among boys, high ratings of leadership and responsibility were prevalent among those who experienced warm relations with parents, especially with mother, and moderately strong discipline from father. Extremes in paternal discipline, either too little or too much discipline, were correlated with low ratings on both types of behavior. Lack of discipline, associated with both neglect and rejection, was most strongly correlated with irresponsibility and lack of leadership ability in boys. However, among girls the general pattern of outcomes differed strikingly by level of control and warmth. The highest ratings of responsibility were found among girls who experienced warm relations with parents, but a low-moderate level of paternal discipline, in contrast to the high-moderate pattern among boys. The effects of lack of discipline on girls were generally similar to those observed in boys. On the basis of these results, Bronfenbrenner suggests that there are different *optimal* levels of affection and control for the two sexes.

> While an affectional context is important for the socialization of boys, it must evidently be accompanied by and be compatible with a strong component of parental discipline. Otherwise, the boys find themselves in the same situation as the girl who, having received greater affection, is more sensitive to its withdrawal, with the result that a little discipline goes a long way and a strong authority is constricting rather than constructive (1961, p. 260).

4. *Maternal restrictiveness and protectiveness in developmental periods.* The Fels study offers a suggestive picture of change in the effects of maternal restrictiveness and protectiveness in the socialization of boys and girls from the first few years of life to late childhood and identifies potentially critical periods for the development of behavioral and emotional autonomy (Kagan & Moss, 1962, Ch. 7). In the Fels program of research, observations in home visits and interviews with the mothers were obtained during the first twelve years of their child's life. From these materials four types of maternal behavior were rated on a seven-point scale: maternal protection, restrictiveness, hostility and criti-

cism, and acceleration. These ratings were averaged for three developmental periods: birth–3 years, 3–6 years, and 6–10 years.

Maternal protection indicated the extent to which the mother rewarded and encouraged dependence and limited independence opportunities. The restrictiveness scale is poorly named since it measures the use of external enforcement techniques, such as physical punishment and threats, rather than control in limit setting. Hostility measured the mother's dissatisfaction with her child: her tendency to criticize the child's skills and performance and to show favoritism toward a sibling. Acceleration described the mother's tendency to impose high-achievement and independence demands on her child, to express concern over the age at which the child was able to demonstrate skills.

Since maternal protectiveness and restrictiveness showed only a slight positive correlation for boys and girls in each of the three periods, the mothers could have been classified according to whether they were above or below average on the two scales. This procedure might have provided a valuable test of the interacting effects of these socialization practices on the development of autonomy between early childhood and adolescence. Some evidence of these potential effects is suggested by intercorrelations among the four maternal practices in each developmental period. From the early to late childhood period, restrictive mothers of boys were increasingly more likely to be rated hostile and critical of their sons and generally did not attempt to accelerate their development in cognitive and motor skills. In the socialization of girls, restrictiveness became increasingly more associated with maternal hostility and criticism as they approached adolescence. These restrictive mothers, in contrast to those with sons, were more likely to be accelerators in each of the developmental periods, and this relationship was most pronounced after their daughters entered school. Maternal protectiveness and hostility were negatively correlated among boys and girls, especially in the school-age period.

These maternal practices were correlated with ratings of emotional and behavioral independence or dependence in four periods: 3–6, 6–10, 10–14, and in adulthood. The adult data, obtained from interviews, included ratings of dependence on love objects, parents, and others. The data on boys are presented first. If mothers were highly protective during the first three years, their sons were generally dependent, emotionally and behaviorally, highly conforming, achievement-oriented in adolescence and adulthood, and not inclined to criticize father in adulthood. In adolescence they tended to be fearful and expected rejection from others, a result that corresponds with Pinner's data on the correlates of parental overprotection among Dutch and Belgian students. Nonmasculine sex-role interests were particularly common among those boys in childhood and adolescence. Despite these childhood correlates of maternal overprotection, this rating was not significantly associated with measures of dependency in adulthood. The effects of leaving home and other role changes were probably important in this behavioral change. In later years, rewards for dependency and discouragement of independence had a less inhibiting effect on independence behavior in adolescence.

Early restrictiveness was less strongly correlated with dependent behavior in childhood and adolescence than maternal protectiveness and in fact was more predictive of independence in adulthood than any other maternal behavior. During the 3–6 year period and especially the grade-school years, on the other hand, maternal restrictiveness was associated with dependence. In adolescence, boys whose mothers were highly restrictive during the grade-school period were likely to be dominant though not independent, to express aggression toward mother and peers, and to be high on retaliation and anger arousal in adulthood. Maternal acceleration during the 3–6 year period most strongly facilitated a conforming, low aggression-type of independence.

From these findings we arrive at a general picture of the sequence of socialization patterns resulting in responsible independence and rebelliousness in adolescence and adulthood. The former outcome appears most likely when mother is moderately restrictive but not overprotective during the first three years, encourages achievement and independence behavior during the years just prior to entrance into school, and rewards independence behavior during the remainder of childhood on into adolescence. While early protectiveness is most predictive of subsequent emotional and behavioral dependence, as well as achievement, the data suggest that both achievement and independence result from moderate levels of warmth and nurturance. A high level of rejecting, punitive restraint after the age of 5 is most predictive of rebelliousness and hostility in adolescence and adulthood (cf. Schaefer & Bayley, 1963).

The developmental pattern for girls in the Fels study differed from that of boys primarily in relation to maternal restrictiveness. In the first three years, maternal protectiveness and restrictiveness were significantly correlated with emotional and behavioral dependence in adolescence and adulthood. For boys and girls, a high level of maternal protective and nurturance during this initial developmental period was associated with feminine sex-role interests and dependency in adolescence. However, boys from this type of family environment were more achievement-oriented than girls in subsequent periods. Girls observed in early adolescence as relatively independent were most likely to have had critical and demanding mothers in Period I. In the remaining years of childhood, independence in adolescence was less influenced by each type of maternal behavior. Girls with strict, punitive mothers after the age of 3 were *less* likely than boys to be emotionally and behaviorally independent, aggressive toward mother and peers, dominant, and nonconforming in adolescence and adulthood. These data suggest that boys were more inclined than girls to resist the controls imposed on them. Standards of sex-appropriate behavior among peers in grade and junior high-school may partially explain this sex difference as well as discontinuities in autonomy between adolescence and adulthood; boys in the study appear to have been drawn toward independence and girls toward emotional dependence regardless of the degree of autonomy achieved in early adolescence.

5. *Social class and historical variations.* Class differences in the socialization of adolescents indicate variations in the timing and patterning of independence from family. The Fels study and a number of cross-sectional surveys show that parental restrictiveness is inversely related to parental education and social class (Kagan & Moss, 1962, p. 210; Psathas, 1957; Elder, 1961; Rosen, 1962). In the Fels study, maternal education in Period I was significantly correlated with hostility and acceleration in the socialization of boys in Period II, and with low restrictiveness in rearing girls during the grade-school period. These patterns suggest that middle-class mothers become less controlling and coercive at an earlier age in rearing boys and girls than mothers from the working class. Such changes in the middle-class family may be supplanted by a form of sponsored independence and continued awareness of children's activities (Psathas, 1957). In the rearing of adolescent boys, working-class parents appear more restrictive toward independence in the family and less outside the home, than middle-class parents (Psathas, 1957; Gans, 1962).

From a historical perspective, a number of studies have reported a significant decline in authoritarian ideology and restrictive child-rearing practices among American parents, a trend evident in modernizing and industrial countries as well (Elder, 1965a). In a survey of family patterns throughout the world, William Goode observes that "the modern doctrine that members of the nuclear family should love one another, that permissive love is 'psychologically healthful' for the child, has given ideological support to the normal pressures of children toward greater choice in all matters and to the greater opportunity to be free economically at an early age" (1963, p. 77). Bronfenbrenner's review of American research on child rearing since the Great Depression shows the trend toward greater permissiveness to be most pronounced among middle-class parents (1958). Social conditions that may account for this secular trend include increasing urbanization, industrialization, educational attainment, and affluence; a decline in institutional and cultural support for authoritarian ideology; and the exposure of parents to democratizing child-rearing literature (Elder, 1965a, p. 176).

Expressions of Independence and Rebellion

The assertion of independence by testing and evaluating authority in adolescence is a common feature of increasing autonomy. This strain toward independence may be coupled with rebellious attitudes when it is frustrated by rigid constraints or uncovers falseness and deception in parents and society. This resentment or disillusionment may be expressed by adopting a "negative identity" (Erikson, 1959), by engaging in behavior proscribed by parents and other authority. For example, in an early study of parental control of adolescent courtship behavior, all of the secret marriages came from highly autocratic families in which parents severely regulated and restricted heterosexual relationships (Bates, 1942). Of the numerous ways in which youth may express their rejection of parental authority and societal norms, we shall briefly review research on two: the adoption of adult consumption privileges such as drinking, and deviation from parental political views.

The expression of rebellion against parental and other authority may take the form of early claims on adult consumption rights, such as approval of early marriage, smoking, drinking, and car ownership. In a high-school sample, Stinchcombe (1964, p. 112) found rebellion against school authority most common among unsuccessful students. These students generally considered a car to be necessary to have fun, did not reject the idea that smoking is the personal business of the student, and believed a girl to be ready for marriage before the age of 18. Students with high scores on these three indicators of an adult-orientation were more apt than other youth to report low grades, placement in a noncollege preparatory track, stronger allegiance to peers than to parents, and heavy dating. An ongoing analysis on cigarette smoking from adolescence to the midforties in the Oakland Growth Study by John Clausen shows compliant dependence on parents who did not smoke to be one of the most powerful predictors of nonsmoking in adulthood among men and especially women.

Youth who accept parental abstinence policy on drinking and smoking should be less subject to contrary peer pressures than rebellious or alienated youth. Relevant to this hypothesis is Campbell's analysis of the internationalization of an abstinence norm in a large sample of adolescent boys (1964). Internalizers (defined by responses to story completion items) were more likely to come from families in which the parents did not drink and were religious. These youth more frequently remained abstainers during the transition from home to college than other adolescents. Moreover, differences between internalizers and noninternalizers were most pronounced in situations that provided opportunities to drink, such as in fraternities on the college campus and in "wet" home communities. A more direct test of peer group support for drinking was made by Alexander on the same sample of adolescents. The 5,200 senior boys in this analysis were selected from schools in an area of North Carolina in which social and religious norms strongly prohibit alcoholic consumption of any kind (1964). About half of the students reported that they believed that God would punish them for using alcohol, and a majority of those who drank indicated that their parents would never permit them to use alcohol. Thirty-seven cliques were identified in a sociometric analysis of friendship choices. Each clique included four or more members, and the relation between any two members was defined by at least two connecting paths that did not include the same reciprocal choices. All members in seven of the cliques drank, all members of 15 groups were abstainers, and the remaining groups included abstainers and drinkers. Nine groups included one youth who deviated from the group pattern in drinking or abstaining; in eight of these groups the deviant received fewer choices than the average member, thus suggesting a tendency for cliques to reject youth who do not go along with group norms and behavior. Among youth whose parents did not permit the use of alcohol, those in drinking groups were more likely to legitimate drinking than were members of groups composed of abstainers and drinkers. Unfortunately, data on relations with parents were not included in the study. Since this study is not longitudinal, there are two possible interpretations of trends toward group uniformity; the cliques were formed by adolescents with similar drinking habits, or clique uniformity in drinking resulted from group pressures. Both of these social processes appear to be reflected in the data. Although Alexander's analysis did not include information on the internalization of an abstinence norm, Campbell's data indicate that internalizers were less likely than other youth to enter groups or situations that encouraged drinking and were also more resistant than noninternalizers to group influences in drinking situations.

Adolescent rebellion from parents has been explored over the years by numerous researchers as one of many potential sources of generational change in political views (Hyman, 1959). Political ideology and expression in late adolescence are influenced by evaluations of society and parents and by patterns of behavior acquired through family socialization. Thus, deviation from parental views may be accompanied by a generally rejecting or accepting attitude toward societal values and norms. Likewise, a student who has generally maintained the liberal or conservative position of parents may be oriented in either direction toward social institutions and values. This crude fourfold typology is not sensitive to the complexity of adolescent orientations but does identify variations in family upbringing associated with different types of adolescent rebellion and student political behavior.

Several studies suggest that rebellion from parents and parental overprotection are prominent experiences among students who deviate from parental political views and reject political institutions. Keniston selected 12 Harvard undergraduates who gave extreme "alienation" responses in a battery of psychological tests, and studied them over a three-year period (1965). All of these students were from upper middle-class homes. Although the students were sufficiently committed to traditional academic pursuits to remain in good standing at Harvard over the three-year period, they were bitter toward the "dehumanizing" influence of technological society, rejected adult roles and associated responsibilities, and strongly opposed pursuits valued in the Protestant Ethic. Keniston suggests that the rebellion of these youth was directed at society rather than at parents; nevertheless the typical mother was generally domineering and protective, and the students expressed strong resentment of this control even though they desired an intimate, dependent relationship with her. The fathers were recalled as cold, rigid, and withdrawn men who were oriented toward traditional success values.

A similar but less extreme pattern of estrangement from parents and society, coupled with emotional dependence on family, is described by Pinner's study of Belgian and Dutch students (1965). He developed two scales indicating ideological conflict and distance between the parental and student generations: (a) Ideological Detachment—students with high scores felt that their opinions on social and political issues differed widely from their parent's views and believed that age and social distance between the generations made mutual understanding unlikely; and (b) Ideological Opposition, indicating social estrangement from parents. Dutch and Belgian students who experienced high control and warmth in their families (Social Confinement scale) were likely to have high scores on both of these scales. In contrast, sponsored social involvement and parental guidance (Guidance scale) were negatively correlated with ideological detachment and opposition in both samples. Pinner's data further suggests that the effects of parental overprotection on attitudes toward parents and political institutions are not dependent on a climate of political distrust and conflict. This climate is more characteristic of Belgian than Dutch politics, yet the Social Confinement scale was highly correlated with measures of political distrust and disaffection, ideological opposition and detachment in the Dutch sample. These findings, and the significant correlation between fears in adolescence and early maternal protectiveness in the Fels sample, suggest that a sheltered upbringing fosters emotional dependency which, in the context of greater social freedoms and increasing awareness of "reality" in adolescence, may result in distrust toward self, parents, and society.

Family socialization that fosters emotional independence and rebellion against parental authority would tend to increase the political influence of experiences and individuals outside the family, especially among youth who enter college. These conditions might result in deviation from parental views and a general acceptance of social and political institutions. There is little substantial evidence relevant to this hypothesis which includes student orientations toward both society and parents, although a recent study by Middleton and Putney is suggestive (1963). In a large sample of American college students, they found emotional estrangement from father to be correlated with extremes in paternal discipline, either very strict or lax, and with deviation from father's political views only when he was interested in politics. Similar, but less significant, findings were obtained on the effects of mother-student relations.

In societies undergoing rapid social and economic change, youth who rebel against the authority and "old" ways of their parents become a significant "revitalizing agent" in society when they are encouraged in their dissent by political leaders (Mannheim, 1943, p. 34). Morroe Berger[4] observes that

> the victorious revolts in Egypt, Syria, and Iraq were led by young men and have found their most enthusiastic supporters among the youth. Indeed, recent political and social conflict have taken on the aspect of a struggle between generations rather than between social classes. The new regimes have given younger men greater opportunities to serve their countries and to advance themselves at the same time. The rhetoric of revolution and the ideologies of governments that come to power through it are studded with tributes to youth and criticism of both 'old politicians' and the "old ways" (1962, p. 312; see also Lipset, 1966, for cross-national surveys of student political protest).

Despite striking differences between Depression-reared parents and their college offspring in social and economic experiences, political continuity is more the rule than discontinuity. Studies by Katz and Sanford suggest that the majority of contemporary college students in the United States accept society as well as their parents' political orientations (cited in Block *et al.,* forthcom-

[4] From *The Arab World Today* by Morroe Berger. Copyright © 1962 by Morroe Berger. Reprinted by permission of Doubleday & Company, Inc.

ing). They are preoccupied with career, marriage, and success concerns rather than political and social processes. Student activists represent the other extreme on involvement and in attitudes toward society. These youth have selectively rejected major values and goals in American society but, contrary to popular belief, seem to have maintained in an intensified fashion a large share of the political beliefs and ideals of their parents (Block, Haan, & Smith, forthcoming). Various studies summarized by Block and her colleagues show consistent differences in the family experiences of students engaged in social protest and of the politically apathetic. The parents of student activists are higher in educational attainment and are more permissive in child rearing. The activists have strong intellectual interests and, at least on the Berkeley campus, have academic records superior to those of the average student.

A recent comparison of a random sample of students at the University of California with a sample of students in the Free Speech Movement who were arrested at the Sproul Hall sit-in shows in more detail the above differences in family background between Activists and generally inactive students (Block, Haan, & Smith, forthcoming). All students selected for the study were enrolled during the fall term of 1964 and were sophomores or upperclassmen. The samples were compared on biographical information and on Q-sort descriptions of self, ideal self, and parents. The Activists were more likely than students in the random sample (hereafter described as Cal students) to have been reared outside of any religious tradition, and their parents were appreciably more liberal in political views, although not significantly more active in politics. Humanities majors, choice of a creative profession, and an interest in the Peace Corps or similar types of programs were more prevalent among the Activists than other Cal students. On all measures of political and social involvement—precinct work, soliciting funds, peace marches, tutoring and so on—the FSM students exceeded the "Cal" students.

Parents and close friends were considered important in forming the political and social orientations of most students in each of the samples; but the Activists appeared somewhat more liberated from direct parental influence and were more influenced by friends than Cal students. Significant sample differences were not found in political orientations between the student and parental generations. On the contrary, FSM students appear to have identified with many of the beliefs and ideals of their liberal parents.

The differing outlook and socialization of these two groups of university students are strikingly portrayed in self and family characterizations. The FSM men were significantly more likely than men in the random sample to describe themselves as critical, curious, rebellious, idealistic, restless, and impulsive; the latter group pictured themselves as responsible, conventional, practical, ambitious, and considerate of others. Comparison of women in the two groups indicated many of the same differences. Parents of the male Activists were described as permissive, encouraging independence, praising more than punishing, showing affection, and encouraging exploration and wonder about the world. In all of these respects the FSM sample differed significantly from the random sample. The mothers of these men were pictured as loving but at times angry. The costs of the permissiveness and individuation afforded by family life were manifested in reports of conflict with both parents. Men in the random sample tended to experience a more structured and protected environment in their socialization. Their parents were more apt to be seen as encouraging achievement, as relying more on physical punishment and strict limits than love-oriented control, and as sheltering them from "different values." These youth were more likely than the Activists to claim that they knew what was expected of them and where they stood at all times. The upbringing experienced by women in the two groups resembled differences obtained among the men.

IV. Moral Development

Increasing moral maturity is an integral dimension of growth toward mature independence. Autonomy of moral judgment is expressed when a position on "right or wrong behavior" is maintained in the face of strong counter-influences. In his Piaget-type research on moral development, Kohlberg has defined moral judgment as evaluative decisions about the good and correctness of behavior; according to philosophers these judgments are generally "universal, inclusive, consistent," and based on "objective, impersonal or ideal grounds" (1964, p. 405). Level of moral judgment—conceptualized as the individual's ability to make judgments in relation to an internalized humanistic standard and to justify adherence to the standard to himself and to others—is moderately related to moral autonomy; both measures are correlated with age and appear in moral thinking during early adolescence (1964, p. 409).

In sociological and psychological theories, moral development is viewed generally as a process of decreasing reliance on external constraints manifested by evidence of internalized standards. But there is a significant difference between Kohlberg's developmental theory and sociological theories on the specific content of these standards. Kohlberg emphasizes the universal nature of humanistic standards and shows that moral development follows a comparable stage-sequence in a variety of cultures. Sociologists, on the other hand, have stressed the cultural content of internalized standards; this includes norms and values specific to a particular society or subgroup as well as standards common to all subgroups in society or to a large number of cultures.

In a thorough review of research on the development of moral behavior, Kohlberg distinguished three indicators of internalization (1964): judgmental evidence in moral thinking; emotional response to the violation of norms which indicate recognition of the "wrongness" of the act, such as remorse and self-blame; and conformity to norms which is intrinsically motivated. Researches on moral judgment in children and adolescents have as their primary source Jean Piaget's stage-analytic model of moral development (see especially *The Moral Judgment of the Child,* 1948). Lawrence Kohlberg's studies are noteworthy examples of research based on this conception of moral development (1964). George H. Mead's stage-theory of moral learning through role taking is particularly compatible with Piaget's theory (see Strauss, 1956).

In Piaget's stage-theory, the child acquires an "autonomous" regard for rules as products of group agreement in place of a concept of adult rules as sacred and unchangeable as he leaves childhood and enters adolescence. Other evidence of moral realism, such as duty defined as obedience to authority, absolutism, and moral wrongness defined by sanctions, are replaced by internally-patterned moral judgments that are relatively independent of sanctions. Sense of duty becomes internally rather than externally determined. Concepts of a sense of justice change in a similar direction. This pattern of moral development is associated with cognitive development in the child's perceptions and conceptual understanding of his world. Social participation in the peer group and moral role-taking are viewed as the primary means by which the child learns to make sense of his world and acquires internal moral principles. The stage-sequence is considered invariant across cultures, although developmental variations occur in relation to differences in social and family experiences. Lack of social experience, it is assumed, retards role-taking experience and moral learning. In an evaluation of research tests of Piaget's theory, Kohlberg concludes that it is "validated only in its description of the young child's morality as oriented to obedience and to punishment and as ignoring subjective ends and values, and in its assumption that these features of child morality decline with age and development in various cultural settings" (1963b, p. 320).

In a series of well-designed studies in the United States and in other cultures, Kohlberg has found that moral judgment is sequentially patterned from childhood to adolescence and follows the same sequence in various cultures; that moral decision making within a particular level generally shows consistency across verbal moral situations; and that moral conduct is significantly related to level of moral judgment (1966). His initial study included 72 boys, ages 10, 13, and 16 (1963a; 1966a). Half of the boys in each age group were upper middle-class, and all groups were similar in IQ. Data were collected in lengthy two-hour tape-recorded interviews centered on ten hypothetical moral dilemmas. In each situation, acts of disobedience to legal-social rules or to the commands of authority conflicted with the human needs or welfare of other individuals. Each child was asked to select one of two acts as the most desired solution and was then questioned about the reasons for the particular choice. These reasons were used to construct stages of moral thinking. From an intensive analysis of individual cases, three moral levels were delineated, and two ideal types of moral orientation were distinguished within each level: I. Premoral level, (1) punishment and obedience orientation, and (2) naive instrumental hedonism; II. Morality of conventional role-conformity, (3) good-boy morality of maintaining good relations, approval of others, and (4) authority maintaining morality; and III. Morality of self-accepted moral principles, (5) morality of contract and of democratically accepted law, and (6) morality of individual principles of conscience. Each type of moral orientation was defined according to its position on 32 aspects of morality, such as Concepts of Rights and Basis of Respect for Social Authority. Premoral thinking sharply declined from the younger to the older age groups, the next two types increased until age 13 and then stabilized, and the remaining types increased from ages 10 to 16.

The data generally support the stage-theory assumption that each level of moral judgment is a prerequisite for the attainment of the next level. Attainment of a high level of moral judgment appeared to involve the reworking of earlier thought patterns rather than simply an additive process of development. Lastly, moral development seemed to follow an invariant sequence among children in various sociocultural groups; "in middle- and working-class children, in Protestants and Catholics, in popular and socially isolated children, in boys and girls, and in Formosan, Chinese, and American children" (Kohlberg, 1964, p. 406). Developmental variations were obtained by social class and antisocial behavior. Middle-class and nondelinquent youth were generally more mature in judgment than working-class and delinquent children. Also teachers' ratings of "conscience" and of "fairness with peers" were significantly correlated with level of moral judgment (Kohlberg, 1964). Kohlberg explains these developmental differences in terms of variations in role-taking experience, social participation, and social responsibilities. The working-class adolescent and the delinquent have less of these kinds of experiences than conforming, middle-class youth.

Moral emotion, as a measure of internal control, is indicated by research that has inferred moral characteristics of youth from their responses to transgression stories. Bandura and Walters used this approach in their analysis of the relation between family socialization and strength of conscience in highly aggressive and normal boys (1959). Desire to be like parents and strength of conscience were significantly associated with consistent discipline and the use of reasoning (see also Miller & Swanson, 1960). Recently there has been increasing emphasis on defensive and adaptive ego-functions in moral development. This view is expressed in Douvan and Adelson's interpretation of moral development during adolescence (1966). They hypothesized that the more intact adaptive functions remain, "the more effective will control be; conversely, loss or failure of these functions will in most cases interfere with control. The loss of the reality-testing capacity ordinarily makes good control impossible to achieve ..." (1966, p. 92). The intensification of drives in adolescence may lead to failures in ego control, they suggest, by "activating superego forces." "The ego then defends itself not against the id but against the superego, using impulse-expression in a flight from guilt" (Douvan & Adelson, 1966, p. 99). A similar orientation toward moral development was emphasized by Peck and Havighurst in their longitudinal study of 35 adolescent boys in a small midwestern community (1960). A general rating of ego strength was highly correlated with indices of moral character, such as responsibility and honesty.

Moral judgment theory, as developed by Kohlberg, places much greater emphasis on peer than family experiences as stimuli of development. One consequence of this orientation is a tendency to ignore the interdependence and continuity of family and peer experiences. Ego theory, as developed by Nevitt Sanford (1962b), attributes somewhat greater primacy to family relations, but within the context of social experiences outside the family. Both theories define the years between childhood and adolescence as a significant period in moral development. This perspective differs from research on the development of "conscience" which has generally defined early family experiences as critical. Nevertheless, even research findings in this tradition suggest that the more mature emotional reactions to transgression, such as self-blame, are not common in the responses of children until the ages of 12 or 13 (see Kohlberg, 1964, p. 411). From an ego-theory perspective, Nevitt Sanford observes that "for values to be internalized they must be reflected on, and made the object of the individual's best efforts at judgment and decision making; they must find their way into the personality structure through the activity of the conscious and developed ego rather than through automatic conditioning or unconscious mechanisms" (1962b, p. 263). A developmental view of impulse control is suggested by a theoretical curve which Sanford inferred largely from the writings of Anna Freud (Sanford, 1962b, p. 259). According to estimated values applied to the curve by Bloom, the average 15-year-old has reached about 70 per cent of mature development in impulse control; by the age of 19 the value is approximately 95 per cent (1964a, p. 135). A number of studies have found development during the college years to be characterized by a gradual achievement of flexible controls; college seniors tend to be more flexible and tolerant than they were as freshmen (see Sanford, 1962, p. 261b). Thus, the general process of moral development during adolescence outlined by ego and moral judgment theories involves increasing maturity of moral thinking and decision-making abilities.

Mastery and Moral Learning

Belief in personal mastery is likely to facilitate moral learning, understanding, and self-control. The results of experimental and field studies, briefly discussed in the chapter section on competence, indicate that effective learning is most likely to result when the individual feels that he has control over the outcomes of his behavior, when he is in a situation that requires skills rather than acquiescence to "chance" circumstances. Experimental studies have found that individuals in "chance" conditions pay less attention to environmental cues, are unlikely to rely on past experience, accomplish less as well as poorer learning, and tend to develop superstitious behavior (Rotter, 1966). Consequently, one would expect a child's continued exposure to "chance conditions," to result in qualitatively poor moral learning. Presumably behavior in this situation would be governed largely by fear and anxiety concerning punishments and rewards and thus would be highly responsive to situational pressures and variations. An adolescent who has grown up in a "chance" environment is likely to be insensitive to moral cues provided by individuals in family and school settings, to "go along" with standards he encounters rather than try to "make sense" of them, and to have little ability in role taking. An environment not understood would appear mysterious, threatening, and punitive. Since a feeling of mastery is a potential cause and consequence of social participation, this factor may be an intervening condition in the relationship Kohlberg obtained between social involvement and the development of moral judgment (1964). In Kohlberg's studies, the relation between moral judgment and a sense of mastery is clearly indicated in the moral thinking of youth in the highest level (1966a). If confronted by a rule which they did not believe in, they would be inclined to try to get it changed rather than to violate it.

Socialization and family relations which resemble "chance" more than "skill" conditions for learning appear to be relatively prevalent among families in the lower class (Bowerman & Elder, 1962); these practices include erratic discipline and inconsistent rules, greater reliance on physical than on verbal methods, and infrequent attempts by parents to explain rules and discipline to their adolescent sons and daughters. Greater reliance on external than on internal control techniques might result from the pressures associated with a large family in crowded living conditions, inadequate verbal and reading skills on the part of parents, and conditions in life situations which engender a belief in obedience as a highly desirable quality in children.

A lack of precise meaning in parental communications, and its adverse consequence for the development of cognitive control among children from the lower classes is suggested by the work of Basil Bernstein at the University of London (1964). Language, according to Bernstein, patterns what and how the child learns, and establishes limits within which future learning may occur. He identified two communication codes; restricted and elaborated. The restricted code is a language of implied meaning in which the speaker's mode of discourse is highly restricted in individual selection and permutation and is dependent on tacit understandings, inflection, gestures, and facial expressions. In the elaborated code, there is much greater individual variation in mode of expression enabled by complex, differentiated possibilities in syntax and sentence organization. Qualification and meaning are transmitted through relationships and structure within and between sentences. This language provides the speaker with greater flexibility, precision, and subtlety in communication. Though middle-class parents can use both forms of language, lower-class parents are more or less limited to public language. A phrase such as "you know what I mean" in response to a child's question—an expression common in lower-class speech—inhibits conceptual development. Obedience thus becomes a means of avoiding punishment, rather than a response motivated by understanding.

Working-class parents tend to prefer "obedience" over "independent self-control" as a desired quality in their children, while the order of these values is generally reversed among parents of middle-class status. This finding has been obtained in samples of fifth-grade children in the United States and in Turin, Italy (Pearlin & Kohn, 1966). In order to explain this class difference, Pearlin and Kohn (1966) examined the effects of three aspects of the Italian father's occupational life which seemed likely to emphasize either obedience or self-direction: closeness of supervision, degree of autonomy in the work setting, and the nature of the work—whether it involved primarily working with ideas, people, or things. Close supervision, low autonomy, and work involving things were found to be correlated with belief in the value of obedience to rules rather than of self-direction, and these features of occupational life were most prevalent among Italian fathers in the working class.

The implications of these class-linked family circumstances, language patterns, training and values for moral learning are suggested by data which show significant relationships between social class and both moral judgment (Kohlberg, 1966) and "internality" (Battle & Rotter, 1963) in samples of adolescents. In a sample of sixth-grade children, Aronfreed found that middle-class children showed more independence of external events in responding to transgression, while working-class youth were more external in orientation (1961). Fatalism, distrust, and apathy appear to be particularly common in the lower classes. Also, limited social experiences of the lower-class youth outside his family and neighborhood, and negative encounters with a middle-class school would further reinforce an external orientation.

Moral Learning and the Internal Control of Behavior: Effects of Family Socialization

Role and cultural transmission theories suggest three general aspects of socialization in the context of parent-child relations as significant determinants of moral learning: the intensity and frequency of interaction; rules of conduct—the quality of presentation and enforcement practices; and the availability of independence opportunities in which the adolescent can both test and evaluate moral principles. In Sutherland's theory of differential association, which outlines conditions that facilitate both moral and criminal learning, the impact of a relationship is said to vary according to its priority, duration, intensity, and frequency (see Sutherland & Cressey, 1966; for a stimulating restatement of propositions in differential association theory in terms of operant conditioning see Burgess & Akers, 1966). A powerful relationship for socialization would be one that is initiated early in a child's life, is long in duration, is characterized by emotional involvement, and consumes most of the child's time.

The last two aspects—intensity and frequency—have particular relevance to parent-youth relations and to the likelihood and kind of learning that occurs in the family. The intensity of a parent-youth relationship may be defined as a product of reciprocal patterns of affection and respect. Parental warmth develops dependency needs that constitute a critical lever for parental influence and a primary condition for the modeling of parents and moral socialization (Mussen & Distler, 1959). In adolescence, respect for parents becomes a particularly important basis of attraction and mutual involvement. In a warm emotional context, respected parents are likely to be admired and modeled by youth (Bowerman & Elder, 1962). Perceived expertise, power in the family, and status in the community are among the most important factors that have been found to influence the respect and admiration adolescents have for their parents (Gold, 1963). In the presentation and enforcement of behavior standards, a favorable learning situation is provided by parents who make rules clear and meaningful, are moderately strict in setting behavior limits, are consistent in presenting and enforcing rules, and rely upon corrective rather than controlling techniques of enforcement (Elder, 1961). Frequent interaction between parents and adolescent offers opportunities for the communication of values and norms that are seen as meaningful and legitimate by the adolescent, but the quality of this exchange depends partly on the type of involvement. A one-sided form of interaction, such as an autocratic or an extremely permissive pattern, is associated with poor communication between parent and adolescent.

1. *Independence opportunities.* Opportunities to acquire experience in self-reliance, to associate with peers from different backgrounds, and to participate in school activities allow youth to test and evaluate behavior standards obtained from parents in a variety of social relationships. Kohlberg, in particular, has emphasized the importance of diverse social experiences among peers as a facilitative condition for moral learning and development (1966a). Douvan and Adelson, in their study of moral development during adolescence, make a similar point (1966). They found the development of inner controls and moral autonomy to be markedly slower among girls than among boys and interpreted this result in terms of the stronger autonomy and identity pressures experienced by boys. They showed more concern than girls about developing independent controls and expressed less unquestioned identification and acceptance of parental restraint. Dependence on family controls was correlated with indications of social incompetence and deficient ego functioning among boys, but not among girls. The highly internalized boys exhibited strong achievement tendencies, autonomous judgment, and self-confidence coupled with realistic self-criticism. A relationship between sex differences in independence training and moral development was also found by Kohlberg. Adolescent boys were significantly more mature in moral judgment than girls (1964, p. 406). This finding, he suggests, is "consistent with the notion that roles entailing more participation and responsibility should stimulate greater maturity" (1964, p. 406).

The effects of overstrict control depend partly on the emotional quality and consistency of family life, as indicated in the section on autonomy. In adolescence, overstrictness, as well as indifference, has been found to be associated with low parental warmth (Elder, 1961). In Bronfenbrenner's analysis of family socialization, adolescent boys who were exposed to excessively strict discipline were likely to be rated low on responsibility by teachers (1961). In the Gluecks' well-known comparative analysis of 500 delinquent and 500 nondelinquent boys, maternal overstrictness was significantly more prevalent in the former group and was correlated with ratings on hostility, feelings of isolation, and feelings of resentment (1962). Paternal overstrictness, in contrast to Bronfenbrenner's findings, was not correlated with indicators of irresponsibility and lack of conscientiousness. The amount of cruelty associated with paternal domination may be a crucial determinant of behavioral outcomes (Robins, 1966, p. 161).

2. *Explanations and cognitive control.* The effect of parental explanations on moral learning and the internalization of standards was analyzed in an Ohio and North Carolina study of adolescents (Bowerman & Elder, 1962). Parents reported as usually explaining rules and decisions that were not understood were more likely than other parents to be perceived as consistent in their rules, as willing to discuss and possibly change rules that seemed to be unreasonable or inappropriate, as allowing youth to participate in making decisions, and as expecting standards to be obeyed. During interviews with approximately 60 adolescent boys and girls, youth who recalled that they had always received explanations from parents and were reasoned with in disciplinary situations frequently could not recall specific rules which their parents wanted them to obey, but they were more likely than other adolescents to report that they followed very general behavior principles which they had learned over the years. These findings were obtained among girls and boys in the middle and lower classes. Middle-class parents were, however, more likely to offer explanations than parents in the lower classes. That frequency of parental explanations en-

hanced the quality of moral learning is suggested by its behavioral correlates. Adolescents who usually received explanations were more likely than other youth to state that they knew what their parents expected of them, usually obeyed rules of conduct, respected their parents, valued parental advice, and wanted to be like their parents in many respects.

The stage at which explanations were offered by parents seemed to make a significant difference in the response of adolescents to rules of conduct. Those who received explanations primarily in disciplinary situations, instead of in the transmission process, were less likely to know what their parents expected of them, to feel that parental policy was reasonable, and to obey rules of conduct than youth who received explanations in the transmission stage. Interview data indicated that some youth in the former situation felt that they were disciplined at times for violating a rule they never thoroughly understood. Additional evidence on the significance of parental explanations in moral learning was obtained by Miller and Swanson in their study of adolescent boys. Those with parents who explained their rules were more likely to "write stories in which heroes resist temptation" (1960, pp. 171–172).

The explanation of rules assumes of course that there are limits and standards. Lax or minimal standards and enforcement have been found in numerous studies to be associated with delinquency (see, for instance, Glueck & Glueck, 1950, and McCord & McCord, 1959). In a large probability sample of British adolescents, level of sexual experience among boys and girls was significantly correlated with an absence of parental regulations on time to be home on weekends and with parental indifference concerning their activities (Schofield, 1965, pp. 139–150). Likewise the moral significance of behavior standards, as well as their effective enforcement, depends on parental awareness of adolescent behavior. Delinquency studies have consistently found low parental awareness and supervision of adolescent behavior to be correlated with delinquency and noncompliance in general (Glueck & Glueck, 1950; Dinitz, Scarpitti, & Reckless, 1962). The effects of these family patterns on moral learning would presumably be most acute during childhood for all children and during adolescence for youth dependent on external constraints.

3. *Inconsistency and cognitive control.* Parental inconsistency in rules and in discipline defines, perhaps as well as any parental behavior, a "chance" environment for learning, one which appears erratic, arbitrary, and leads to fear and superstitious learning. From the adolescent's perspective, at least, a generally inconsistent parent is one who does not make rules of conduct clear and meaningful (Elder, 1961). Although a parent may vary in consistency on rules and discipline, youth tend to see this characteristic as a relatively general feature of parental behavior. Moreover, the probable consequences of one highly inconsistent parent are differences *between* parents in administering discipline, making decisions, and setting behavior limits. In general, the various types of inconsistency in the home and their behavioral consequences have not been thoroughly examined in socialization research. In a family in which one parent is consistent and the other highly erratic in both rules and discipline, do the effects vary according to the sex of the child and the power of the parent? Also, are there significant differences in the behavioral consequences of erratic rule transmission and limit setting, on the one hand, and inconsistent enforcement, on the other? Effective moral learning would be most unlikely in the former situation but might occur if parents are inconsistent only in enforcing behavior standards.

A number of studies have found intra- and interparent inconsistency associated with delinquency and behavior disorders (Bandura & Walters, 1959; Peck & Havighurst, 1960; Glueck & Glueck, 1950, 1952;

McCord & McCord, 1959; Nye, 1958; Rosenthal, Finkelstein, Ni, & Robertson, 1959; Rosenthal, Ni, Finkelstein, & Berkwits, 1962). Bandura and Walters compared 26 adolescent boys with a history of antisocial behavior, and an equal number of controls matched on age and occupation of father, on family socialization (1959). Inconsistency between parents in setting behavior standards was significantly more common among parents of the aggressive boys. Some of the most rebellious youth came from homes in which father was generally restrictive and severe and mother was protective and lenient. Rosenthal and his colleagues compared the father- and mother-child relations of 450 children who were brought to a clinic at the Institute of Juvenile Research at Chicago (Rosenthal *et al.,* 1959, 1962). The behavior problems of the children (most of whom were in grade school through senior high-school) were disobedience, hostility, temper outbursts, restlessness, excitability, bullying, aggressiveness, and domineering behavior. Conflict between parents in child rearing, which is likely to result in child-rearing differences between parents, was found to be associated with a similar set of behavior problems. The permanence of behavioral disorders associated with this parent syndrome seemed to be corrected in large measure after the parent's behavior was changed in therapeutic sessions.

Consistency in setting standards and administering discipline, in contrast, has been found to be correlated with ratings of maturity of moral character and may counteract the effects of low parental affection in the development of internal controls. In a longitudinal study of the character development of 35 children in the Prairie City study, consistency in family life was significantly related to maturity of character (Peck & Havighurst, 1960). Lack of consistency was most common in the families of "amoral" children (one of five character types delineated in the study). These youth seldom experienced "consistency in moral standards, were unlikely to be rewarded for adopting moral values, and were not consistently punished for not obeying" (p. 110). In addition, their parents were extremely distrustful and disapproving toward them. In a follow-up study of boys from the Cambridge-Somerville Youth Study, erratic discipline was highly related to criminality under certain conditions (McCord & McCord, 1959). Erratic discipline was less likely to produce antisocial behavior if the home was cohesive and parents were nondeviant and affectionate. In families in which parents were low on affection, consistent discipline seemed to be an adequate substitute for eliciting conformity. The McCords suggest that

> affection establishes the base; the parents' model furnishes the content of conscience; and consistency insures the internalization of this content. If affection is missing, the child lacks the rewards for conformity; if the parental model is antisocial, the child becomes confused with respect to values; if values are inconsistently enforced, he becomes uncertain as to their worth (p. 200).

4. *Discipline and moral learning*. The value of discipline for moral learning appears to vary according to the technique of enforcement used, the level of affection between parent and adolescent (see W. C. Becker, 1964), and the quality of communication between parent and adolescent prior to and associated with the disciplinary episode (Bowerman & Elder, 1962). The Fels research (Kagan & Moss, 1962) and other studies indicate that physical punishment in adolescence tends to elicit disobedience and aggressive behavior among boys (see Bandura & Walters, 1959), especially in a context of low parental warmth (W. C. Becker, 1964). In childhood and in adolescence boys are more likely to be disciplined physically than are girls (W. C. Becker, 1964). During adolescence, physical discipline seems to reflect an external-control orientation in parental behavior. In the Ohio and North Carolina study, the use

of physical discipline on boys and girls from the seventh to the twelfth grade was associated with autocratic control, infrequent explanations, and erratic rules and discipline (Bowerman & Elder, 1962). Parental regulation of the behavior of children is more difficult in large families, and a study of seventh-grade boys and girls found physical discipline and negative verbal techniques such as scolding and nagging, autocratic control, and infrequent explanations to be more common in large than in small families (Elder & Bowerman, 1963). Although these external control techniques were also correlated with low socioeconomic status, variations by family size were stronger.

A situation in which reasoning or praise is used to correct or reinforce behavior tends to enhance learning. In the North Carolina and Ohio study, parents reported as using these techniques frequently were also likely to explain and be consistent in their rules and discipline; youth from these homes were more apt to feel that they knew what their parents expected of them, to consider parental policy reasonable, and to comply in most situations with behavior standards (Bowerman & Elder, 1962). In the Bandura and Walters' study (1959), reasoning was more frequently experienced by the control boys than by their aggressive counterparts and was more strongly correlated than any other parental practice with guilt responses to transgression stories (1959). Delinquency studies have generally found that delinquent boys receive more physical discipline, especially from father, and less reasoning than nondelinquents in samples matched on background factors (Gold, 1963; Glueck & Glueck, 1950).

Parental training practices that facilitate moral learning and an internal patterning of behavior could transmit deviant as well as culturally-approved values. The approval or disapproval that parents attach to behavior may be communicated verbally, by facial expressions, and by the behavior models presented by parents in the family as well as in other roles. Two longitudinal studies of boys have found criminal or antisocial behavior on the part of fathers to be a significant antecedent of deviant behavior in adulthood (Robins, 1966; McCord & McCord, 1959). In a thirty-year follow-up of children—mostly from lower-class homes—who were referred to a clinic for antisocial and other reasons in the 1920's, Robins found antisocial behavior of father to be significantly correlated with deviance in adolescence and in adulthood (1966). Furthermore, it was the most significant childhood predictor of high stability in antisocial behavior between adolescence and the mid-40's. Faulty socialization indicated by erratic, punitive, and lax child-rearing practices as well as emotional conflict were generally associated with the presence of an antisocial father. As in the McCord study, consistently firm discipline and supervision markedly weakened the effects of deviant behavior on the part of father. Though Robins found that early separation from an antisocial father did not reduce the effects of this family condition, the greatest impact of this type of family situation probably occurs very early in a child's life. Thus, with an aggressive pattern initially established, departure of the antisocial father from the home would leave control problems which the mother might not be able to handle.

Socialization practices by which the parents, whether antisocial or not, foster aggressive tendencies in boys, have been explored intensively by Bandura and Walters (1959; 1963). In the study of aggressive and control boys, parents of the former, particularly father, were more likely to use physical techniques of discipline and to reward or condone aggression toward peers (1959). In a more recent analysis of socialization experienced by preadolescent aggressive and inhibited boys, Bandura found that parents of the latter were more firm and had a nonpunitive attitude toward aggression (cited in Bandura & Walters, 1963, p. 119). Parents of aggressive boys, especially mother, tended to reward aggression toward siblings and other children but were punitive and non-permissive concerning aggression directed toward themselves. "The aggressive boys expressed considerably more physical and verbal aggression toward their peers, more oppositional behavior toward their teachers, and less inhibition of aggression than inhibited boys" (cited in Bandura & Walters, 1963, p. 122). Consistent with this parental training, the aggressive boys showed no more aggression toward parents than their inhibited counterparts. The expression of severe, aggressive control and discipline by father toward his son may represent a displacement of hostility generated by close supervision in the work-setting (McKinley, 1964).

Family socialization is undoubtedly conditioned by the personality characteristics of children as well as by social conditions and values, yet few studies have assessed the effects of parental training techniques on children differing in personality. In a complex and frequently ambiguous analysis, the Gluecks (1962) obtained interrelationships among three sets of factors in their matched samples of delinquent and nondelinquent boys: somatotype ratings; personality traits; and indicators of family structure and socialization. The analysis is severely limited by its cross-sectional design, and readers should quarrel with many of the authors' interpretations of causal sequence. However, the results are suggestive regarding the complexities involved in analyzing the interacting effects of personal and environmental properties. Consider, for instance, characteristics associated with maternal supervision. Mesomorphs—a majority in the delinquent sample—were more likely than boys with other body-types to be closely supervised and firmly disciplined by mother. They conclude that "evidently youngsters of this body build (characterized as they are by greater energy, more extraversiveness, and less conventionality) invite attention from their parents ..." (1962, p. 60). A boy's vitality, they suggest, is not a consequence of parental socialization or family conditions, but rather it "conditions in some measure the behavior of parents toward him" (Glueck & Glueck, 1962, p. 60). However, high energy might also frustrate the efforts of mother to provide supervision. In fact, without having seen the data, one might expect, especially in the working class, that mothers with high energy, muscular sons would be more inadequate in supervision than mothers of endomorphs or ectomorphs. Low maternal supervision was most likely to enhance the delinquency potential of boys who felt able to be independent and were not characterized by masochistic tendencies. It is apparent that a well-designed longitudinal study is essential for clear-cut interpretations of results from this type of analysis.

Deviance and Conformity: The Effects of Personal and Environmental Factors

Moral development theories assume that properties of the individual are more important in determining the likelihood of deviance or conformity than characteristics of the larger social context or specific situation. They also assume that the influence of situational conditions in patterning behavior is greater among children on a relatively low level of moral development. In Kohlberg's theory, the adolescent who has achieved mature moral judgment and autonomy is by definition less subject to variations in external constraints and pressures than a youth markedly lower on the scale of moral development. Adolescents with mature moral judgment are apt to be resistant to norm violation, regardless of the particular situation, whereas, behavioral predictions for youth in the premoral stage are likely to be highly inaccurate unless made within the context of specific relationships and situations. The Hartshorne and May study of moral character in children and Kohlberg's evaluation of it in a developmental context generally support this expectation (see Kohlberg, 1966a).

A number of studies have achieved much less success in predicting deviance than in predicting conformity from data on the adolescent and family socialization (Hathaway & Monachesi, 1963; Robins, 1966, p. 70; Dinitz, Scarpitti, & Reckless, 1962; Toby & Toby, 1962). In a sample of children referred by teachers for antisocial behavior, Tait and Hodges used the Glueck delinquency prediction tables (which include indicators of positive family relations and socialization) to make predictions of delinquent and nondelinquent status (cited in Robins, 1966, p. 70). Prediction of delinquency was accurate in only a third of the cases in comparison to a success rate of 95 per cent in predicting no delinquency. The effect of a positive self-image and effective moral socialization on resistance to deviance pressures is illustrated by results from a longitudinal study of white boys in high delinquency areas of Columbus, Ohio (Dinitz, Scarpitti, & Reckless, 1962). All sixth-grade teachers in the highest delinquency areas of Columbus, Ohio, were asked to nominate boys they thought were headed for "trouble with the law" and those most likely to stay out of trouble. Seventy of the 101 vulnerable boys were contacted at age 16; 103 out of the 125 boys considered insulated from delinquency were also contacted at this time. The "insulated" boys were much more likely than their "vulnerable" counterparts to report that they enjoyed school, thought well of themselves, got along with teachers and other adults, felt accepted by parents and expressed acceptance of them, and felt able to stay out of trouble and avoid delinquent peers. Parental interest, affection, and effective supervision were significantly more prevalent among parents of "insulated" than of "vulnerable" boys. At age 16, four of the "good" boys had encounters with legal authorities (a warning was sufficient for three of them, while the other persisted in delinquency); in contrast, slightly less than 40 per cent of the vulnerable boys from the same slum areas of the city averaged more than three contacts with the court.

Environmental conditions that increase the likelihood of deviation from norms in the community have been specified by sociological anomie, cultural transmission, and group process theories. Excellent critical reviews of both psychological and sociological theories of deviance have been provided by Martin and Fitzpatrick (1965) and by Albert Cohen (1966). The sociological concept of anomie, as originally formulated by Durkheim, refers to a state of normlessness in society. Robert Merton has defined an anomic environmental condition as "a breakdown in the cultural structure, occurring particularly when there is an acute disjunction between the cultural norms and goals and the socially structured capacities of members of the group to act in accord with them" (Merton, 1957, p. 162). Extreme anomie creates a "chance" environment that is likely to foster poor learning, superstition, deviant norms, and deviant behavior. The psychological counterpart to social anomie includes, among other aspects, a sense of powerlessness, a belief in external control (see Seeman, 1966; Rotter, 1966). Psychological strain and tendencies toward deviance are assumed to be greatest among youth who have internalized, or at least value, widely extolled success-goals but do not have the opportunity to achieve them, i.e., the ambitious, lower-class boy. Merton's well-known types of individual adaptations to a pronounced disjuncture between culture and social structure—such as conformity, innovation, and rebellion—have inspired subsequent formulations such as Albert Cohen's delinquent subculture theory (1955) and Cloward and Ohlin's opportunity theory (1960), both of which attempt to explain the emergence of delinquent subcultures.

1. *Delinquent subcultures: etiology and themes.* Cohen suggests that a collective solution to a shared condition of status deprivation among working-class boys is achieved by substituting an alternative status system for the middle-class system through a process of reaction formation; the resulting delinquent subculture is characterized by hedonism and negativism. Cohen writes that "the hallmark of the delinquent subculture

is the explicit and wholesale repudiation of middle-class standards and the adoption of their very antithesis" (1955, p. 129). Data from recent studies of lower-class male gangs indicate a need for some modification of this hypothesis (Short & Strodtbeck, 1965; Sherif & Sherif, 1964). In their Chicago study of gang, lower-class, and middle-class adolescent boys, Short and Strodtbeck (1965) found that middle-class prescriptive norms were equally likely to be endorsed "in principle" by youth in each of the samples. However, gang boys differed most from their middle-class counterparts in their greater tolerance of behavior proscribed by the middle-class.

Although very little research has focused on middle-class delinquency, severe psychological effects of academic failure and the need for face-saving devices would seem greatest among youth who have internalized achievement standards and are committed to high goals by parents. Middle-class boys who fail in school are confronted by few status-maintaining alternatives to college. The ambitious working-class boy, on the other hand, is less apt to be committed to mobility goals by the expectations of parents, peers, and teachers. In a provocative analysis of adolescent rebellion in a high school, Stinchcombe (1964) found rebellion such as truancy and especially "expressive" alienation—hedonistic and negativistic attitudes—most common among lower- middle-class boys who were academic failures. Compared to working-class youth, upper- and lower- middle-class boys were more likely to maintain college aspirations despite below-average school achievement and were also more committed to a college preparatory curriculum and to college plans by parents. The apparently less severe effects of academic failure among upper middle-class boys may have been due to the ability of their families, through economic resources and social influence, to make aspirations seem feasible regardless of school achievement.

In cultural transmission theories, exemplified by Sutherland's theory of differential association (see Sutherland & Cressey, 1966), the deviant differs from other youth only in his special knowledge, skills, and values; he does not differ from conforming youth in basic personality structure. A number of studies have found that boys who associate with greatest frequency, duration, and intensity with delinquent peers are more likely than other youth to report delinquent behavior (see, for instance, Glaser, 1962). A high rate of delinquency in a neighborhood provides numerous opportunities for youth to learn deviant skills and values and offers support for deviant activities (Reiss & Rhodes, 1961). High delinquency areas may also be characterized by a high level of police surveillance which increases the likelihood of being arrested for suspicion or actual participation in deviant activities. Treatment of the offender by law enforcement officials varies according to his demeanor and the quality of his home life; as a consequence, the lower-class offender is more likely than his middle-class counterpart to be processed through the courts and to be sentenced to correctional institutions (see Robins, 1966, p. 205; H. S. Becker, 1963).

Cloward and Ohlin have drawn upon anomie and cultural transmission theories in their analysis of the ways in which available illegitimate opportunities determine the content of delinquent subcultures among lower-class boys who have identified with middle-class success-goals, do not have the means to achieve them, and are indifferent to membership in the middle class (1960). This theory and Cohen's formulation are focused on the emergence of delinquent subcultures rather than on the actual distribution of deviant acts. Ohlin points out that the factors which explain the etiology of delinquent subcultures and activities are "likely to be quite different." "The distribution of clearly defined subcultures in our society probably does not correspond with the distribution of delinquent acts, yet the explanation of the former is often criticized because it does not explain the latter" (see Spergel, 1964, p. viii).

In Cloward and Ohlin's theory (1960), the lower-class youth's response to limited opportunities for achieving "entitled" economic rewards depends on the availability of illegitimate means. Such opportunities—not equally available to all deprived youth—vary according to the degree of integration among carriers of criminal and conventional values. A high degree of integration facilitates criminal learning from adult models and provides opportunity for advancement toward economic goals within the criminal subculture. When legitimate and illegitimate opportunities are not available to youth in unintegrated urban areas, a conflict subculture characterized by expressive behavior and violence as a mode of gaining status is likely to emerge. The third mode of adaptation described is the retreatist, drug-oriented culture which is considered most likely among lower-class youth who are unable to succeed in either legitimate or illegitimate avenues. Some research on delinquent and drug-using gangs (Chein, Gerard, Lee, & Rosenfeld, 1963) shows considerable change in gang-orientations of this type by community reactions and control.

An attempt to find male, lower-class gangs characterized by these orientations was made by Short and Strodtbeck in their Chicago project (1965). Conflict gangs were easily located; more than one year was required to locate a drug-oriented gang, and no success was achieved in finding a gang specializing in criminal activities. Sixteen lower-class Negro and white gangs were selected for intensive study. Measures of gang activities were obtained from ratings of 69 types of behavior made by detached workers after they had had at least six months contact with the respective gang. Most boys were rated by only one worker. These ratings were combined into 39 items, then intercorrelated and the matrix was factor analyzed. Five Varimax patterns were obtained: (I) *conflict,* such as individual fighting, group fighting, and assault; (II) *stable-corner pattern,* such as individual and team sports and social activities; (III) *stable-sex maturity pattern,* which included sexual intercourse, petting, and work experience; (IV) *retreatist,* defined by narcotics, pot, homosexuality, common-law marriage, and attempted suicide; and (V) *authority protest,* indicated by driving without a license, auto theft, and running away from home. The items which loaded similarly on more than one factor were typically low on delinquency content, i.e., baby sitting, running errands, joy riding, hanging out on the corner, and truancy. Short and Strodtbeck suggest that these items describe a "parent delinquent subculture" characterized by the problems common to adolescence—interpersonal difficulties and needs for status—and imply "recognition of the moral validity and legitimacy of adult and middle-class prescriptive norms" (1965, p. 93). Although a "criminal" behavior factor was not extracted from the correlation matrix, robbery, theft, and forgery tended to load most heavily on Factor V, Authority Protest, next on the Conflict Factor, and least on Factors III and IV. Since lower-class Negro boys generally have less access to legitimate and illegitimate economic opportunities than white youth, Short and Strodtbeck predicted that Negro gangs would have higher scores on the Conflict Factor than white gangs. This expectation was strongly supported by the data: all of the gangs above average in conflict-orientation were Negro. White gangs clearly ranked higher than Negro gangs only on Authority Protest. Although none of the gangs was characterized by a criminal orientation, this emphasis was found among some cliques within conflict gangs.

2. *Group and situational influences.* The emergence and type of delinquent subcultural orientation may be predicted from knowledge of anomie and the pattern of legitimate and illegitimate opportunities, but these conditions are of little assistance in predicting how a particular youth will

act in the social context. On the other hand, psychological theories—what Albert Cohen has termed "kinds of people" theories (1966)—indicate personal characteristics that make the adolescent susceptible to deviant pressures and opportunities but are severely limited in predicting the likelihood of a particular deviant act, which is always subject to situational influences. These situational or group influences have been most fully explored by field research on adolescent gangs or groups which has examined conditions related to group formation, structure and functioning, as well as the consequences of interaction between group and individual properties for group and member behavior. One of the most significant developments in research on delinquency and adolescent behavior has been the increase in theoretically-grounded field studies of adolescent groups and gangs. In addition to the Chicago study, these include the Sherifs' imaginative field investigations of naturally formed adolescent groups—high, moderate, and low in SES—in several Southwestern cities (1964); Chein and associates' studies of delinquent and drug-use gangs in the New York area (1963); and Walter Miller's research on lower-class gangs in Boston (1962). In the Chicago project, group process variables such as status maintenance were found to be the most important determinant of "what happens in the gang, of who becomes involved and in what type of behavior, and with whom. This *level* of explanation 'washes out' variations in perception of opportunities related to social structure as a determinant of individuals' behavior in the gang context" (Short *et al.*, 1965, p. 67). Both the Sherif and Chicago study have obtained many similar findings on group influences which have wide significance for small group and role theory.

The Sherifs' research, initiated in 1958, included 12 groups of adolescent boys—6 to 15 in each—in several Southwestern cities. The groups were selected from three status areas of the cities—high, middle, and low—and were intensively observed by young staff members recruited from each area and trained by the Sherifs in the skills of participant observation. With the exception of low-status Mexican-American youth, the groups were composed of white boys. In contrast, most of the lower-class groups in the Chicago study were Negro. In the Sherif study, hypotheses were drawn from the literature on reference group theory and from the authors' prior research on intergroup conflict and norms. From a methodological standpoint, the study is noteworthy on at least two points: in the utilization of a wide variety of measurement techniques to measure the same variable and in the policy of adapting research technology whenever possible to the flow of behavior, rather than modify behavior by extraneous measurement procedures. The analysis is focused primarily on how conditions in the group and in the larger setting influence adolescent conformity to group norms and to social norms in the community. The one major difference between low SES boys in the Sherif and Chicago studies is in interpersonal competence. Even in low SES groups in the Sherif study, members appear to have been more competent and self-assured than the lower-class boys in the Chicago study. In part, this difference may be due to greater economic and social deprivation experienced by youth in the Chicago study. Though gratification of dependency and status needs was a significant motivational force in the formation of low-status groups in both studies, member satisfactions and group solidarity appear to have been much greater in the Sherifs' low-status groups.

In the Sherifs' study, boys who contributed most to "delinquent" or "nondelinquent" activities were more highly endowed with talents valued by the group and tended to have higher status than other members. Attributes and performances indicating sex-role competence—virile manliness—appeared to be the most important requisite for high status and leadership.

Sexual prowess and bragging about sexual activities were viewed a "proof" of manliness in all of the groups; and in a large number of the gangs, the leader was highly successful with girls. Short and Strodtbeck obtained similar findings on the characteristics of leaders (1965). Among boys from the lower class, compulsive striving to demonstrate manliness may reflect a sex-identity conflict resulting from socialization in a female home environment in a culture that emphasizes toughness as a masculine trait. Among Negro males drawn from *The Children of Bondage* study, Rohrer and Edmonson found a pervasive rejection of femininity: the gang member sees it "in women and in effeminate men, in laws and morals and religion, in schools and occupational striving" (1960, p. 163; see also W. Miller, 1958).

Violation of community codes of behavior was strongly supported by group norms among low-status boys in both the Sherif and Chicago study when it served the welfare of members and the group as a whole. This was particularly evident in attitudes toward theft. Boys in several low-status gangs in the Sherif study frequently stole things when they were broke, "usually selling articles other than clothing, and often using the money for group entertainment and treats" (Sherif & Sherif, 1964, p. 174). Though only two or three members stole together, the whole group was generally informed of the act, and when successfully accomplished, it elicited praise and admiration. Several conflict-oriented gangs in the Chicago study charged small amounts of money from small boys for "protection," stole purses, shoplifted, and committed burglaries; group norms defined these activities "as acceptable ways of acquiring a little 'bread' to buy a bottle of wine, a bite to eat, one's share of the cost of a game of pool, and the like" (Short & Strodtbeck, 1965, p. 97). In the Sherif study, the latitude of permissible behavior was inversely related to the importance of the activity in all groups. Conformity to norms in matters involving the security and survival of the group was most rigorously enforced, such as contact with police and situations of intergroup conflict. Youth suspected of betrayal, of squealing to the police, were rejected by their fellow members. One leader offered the following rule on the expected behavior of members when flight from another gang was necessary: "'If you have to run, run like mad, but if one of your boys is caught by the opposition, then you have to stop and help him. If you don't, you're a punk'" (Sherif & Sherif, 1964, p. 178). Since greater wisdom and performance was expected from the group leader, he was generally allowed less leeway in relation to important norms than other members. In activities relatively unimportant to group maintenance, the range of allowable behavior was broad for all group members, and was even greater for the leader. Relevant to these differential expectations for leader and member behavior is a finding from the Chicago study on the status implications of "joining the action." "For any given incident a good proportion of the boys do stay aloof, but those who are leaders, or are within striking distance of leadership roles, are particularly responsive to the immediacy and implications of the group response for their status" (Short & Strodtbeck, 1965, p. 264).

The Chicago and Sherif studies obtained relatively consistent results on interrelations among, and factors related to, four conditions: group solidarity; sense of belonging to group; relative investment in group, conventional groups, and institutions; and participation in deviant as well as conflict activities. In both studies, group solidarity was intimately related to the sense of belonging of group members. In the Sherif study, sense of belonging was inferred from the variety, regularity, and duration of activities in which the member participated, and by the length of time members had been together. Degree of group solidarity was indicated by the extent members maintained consistent patterns of behavior with and without the presence of the leader, by group exclusiveness regarding the involvement of nonmembers, by the effectiveness of group functioning in situations of moderate stress such as provided by intergroup competition, and by degree of group secrecy indicated in reactions to outsiders. Consistent with the Sherifs' previous work and the observations of Thrasher, intergroup competition in athletics and fights tended to increase group solidarity. Data obtained in the Chicago study suggest that participation of gangs in delinquent and nondelinquent activity was motivated by an attempt to increase group solidarity and a sense of belonging on the part of members. From observations of the activity of a white gang, a detached youth worker found that group activities of all kinds and deviant acts committed by members occurred most often in periods following low points on a group solidarity index. An increase in group solidarity was noted following these activities (Short & Strodtbeck, 1965, p. 245). The most active participants in these activities were probably the boys who felt most threatened by the decline in group solidarity, i.e., the high-status members.

In the Sherif study, the commitment of a member to his group was found to be contingent on the importance of the gang relative to other groups such as family, school, church, and formal clubs. The group's importance sharply increased from high- to low-SES boys, and this trend was paralleled by increasing group solidarity. Boys from high-status areas felt closer to family, were more positive toward school, got along better with adults, and participated more frequently in programmed activities than boys from low-status neighborhoods; their groups tended to mean less to them and were more loosely knit than the groups to which low-status youth belonged. However, economic success-goals were shared by youth in all class levels, and the low-status boys were at least as ambitious, from a relative standpoint, in their aspirations as high-status youth. Findings from the Chicago studies also suggest that a youth's personal commitment to a relationship reflects the proportion of basic satisfactions derived from it. The estrangement of lower-class gang boys from family, school, law enforcement agencies, and adults in general was correlated with their dependency on the gang for interpersonal satisfactions and status. Thus peer-group influence, whether deviant or conventional in design, is likely to be greatest relative to adult agents of socialization and control among youth who are most dependent on external constraints in patterning their behavior. These youth are also likely to experience stronger feelings of shame and guilt from violating group than societal norms.

Deviant Youth in Adulthood

The implications of deviance in adolescence for adult careers, achievement, and role performance vary significantly between psychological and sociological theories. A high degree of continuity in antisocial behavior between adolescence and adulthood would be expected if it is assumed that recurring deviance in adolescence is a reflection of retarded moral judgment and erratic impulse control. A similar prediction of stability would be made for youth who participated in criminal gangs according to Cloward and Ohlin's opportunity theory (1960). However, in this case, continuity is attributed to criminal learning and opportunity rather than to defective personality development. For youth in criminal gangs, illegitimate career opportunities are provided through the integration of carriers of conventional and criminal values involving patterns of cooperation among police, businessmen, residents, and others. Criminal learning is facilitated by integration among offenders in different age-grades. "Each age-level is connected to a higher level so that young offenders are, through intervening age-grades, ultimately linked to the adult criminal system. Knowledge, values, skills, and attitudes are transmitted through this age hierarchy. For those who excel in learning, upward passage is assured, and a position in a stable adult criminal enterprise may be the eventual reward" (Cloward, 1963, p. 81). Cloward suggests that socialization for adult criminal careers is most likely in close-knit, lower-class communities.

Outside of the environment described by Cloward, role theory would lead to predictions of considerable discontinuity in deviant behavior between adolescence and adulthood; however, these predictions would be specific to particular person-environment patterns. In adolescence, the stigma acquired through recognized deviance, a court record, and strong commitments to the gang generally limit opportunities to obtain an education and a good job. However, the adult prognosis for a boy with these experiences would depend on his success in leaving the system of expectations represented by his gang and in acquiring commitments to meaningful adult roles through employment and marriage. The effect of the role transition on prior behavior patterns would depend partly on characteristics of the new environment. For a highly aggressive boy, an environment likely to elicit commitments to conventional roles might include a wife and employer who are able to tolerate occasional hostility and erratic behavior. The role viewpoint on the patterning of conforming and deviant behavior through the life span is cogently stated by Albert Cohen in what he terms an interaction process perspective:

> The deviant act develops over time through a series of stages. Some individual, in the pursuit of some interest or goal, and taking account of the situation, makes a move, possibly in a deviant direction, possibly with no thought of deviance in mind. However, his next move—the continuation of his course of action—is not fully determined by the state of affairs at the beginning. He may, at this juncture, choose among two or more possible directions. Which it will be will depend on the state of the actor and situation at this point in time, and either or both, may in the meantime have undergone change (Cohen, 1966, p. 44; see also H. S. Becker, 1963).

Data that bear upon these hypotheses were obtained in a recently completed follow-up of three samples of subjects who were adolescents during the 1920's; children who were referred to a clinic for antisocial and other reasons and a matched sample of normal children (Robins, 1966). This study, spanning the years between early adolescence and the mid-40's, collected data on a broad range of life areas from an intensive adult interview and records and obtained assessments of the subjects' psychiatric status in adulthood. The primary objective of the study was to examine the natural history of the sociopathic personality, defined by *gross,* recurring nonconformity to norms in various areas of life. From the records of a defunct psychiatric clinic in St. Louis, Robins selected 524 individuals who entered the clinic for behavior problems between 1924 and 1929 and who met the following qualifications: white, under 18, and an IQ of 80 or above. The average age of referral for the sample was 13. Three-fourths of the cases were referred for antisocial reasons such as theft, incorrigibility, and aggression; the remainder for psychological problems such as learning difficulties and temper tantrums. Boys outnumbered girls three to one in the total sample, but there were no significant sex differences between the antisocial and "other" sample. Forty-four per cent of the subjects came from families with an occupational status of semiskilled or lower, and only a third were living with both parents at the time of referral. The average IQ of the subjects was 97, half were retarded at least one year in school at the time of referral, and a similar proportion did not even complete grade school. One hundred control subjects—selected from the records of elementary schools in the city—were matched, as a group, with the patient sample on race, age, sex, IQ, and socioeconomic status. This sample excluded children who had repeated a grade or more in elementary school, who had records of suspension from school, or who transferred to a correctional institution. Since high-school data were not used, a small proportion (two per cent) were later found to have appeared in juvenile court during adolescence.

The adult follow-up involved the difficult task of locating and interviewing all of the subjects in the control and patient samples. For subjects who had died after the age of 24, Robins tried to obtain an interview with a close relative. The success which Robins and her interviewers achieved is remarkable considering the characteristics of her subjects; adult records were obtained for 93 per cent of the cases, and interviews were obtained on 82 per cent. A comparison of data obtained in the interview with record data indicated that between 14 and 18 per cent were dishonest in a large portion of the interview. From life history, psychiatric, and record data, the health of the subjects was assessed by two psychiatrists; they were not given information on the years prior to age 19. In 71 per cent of the cases, the psychiatrists were able to place the subject in a diagnostic category such as alcoholism, sociopathic personality, and anxiety neurosis. The criteria for sociopathic classification was failure to conform to societal norms in at least five life areas; 80 men and 14 women were so classified. Only a fifth of the patient sample was diagnosed as free of disease in comparison to slightly more than half of the controls.

On measures of conformity to societal norms, competence and attainments in adult roles, and health, the control sample ranked first, the sample of subjects referred for reasons other than antisocial behavior was a close second, and the antisocial subjects a distant third. Almost all of the adults diagnosed as sociopathic were in the antisocial sample during adolescence. Non-traffic arrests and incarceration were primarily concentrated in the antisocial group, especially among men. Half of these male subjects had been arrested three or more times and 43 per cent had been imprisoned, in comparison to percentages of 4 and zero for male controls. These sample differences were also reflected in the behavior of the subjects' children: a significantly larger proportion of children of antisocial subjects had court or police records. Failure to maintain stable relationships in marriage and in the occupational system was strikingly more common among antisocial subjects than in the other samples; the former were less likely to be living with a spouse at the time of interview and were more likely to have obtained at least one divorce (request generally coming from the spouse). Childlessness was significantly more common among women antisocial subjects who ever married than among women in the other samples. Unemployment, frequent job changes, low-status jobs, financial dependency, and social isolation were significantly more prevalent among men referred for antisocial reasons than among men in the other samples. An antisocial father was the most significant correlate of antisocial behavior in adolescence and in adulthood among subjects from the middle and lower class. Though only one of the adult men had connections with organized crime, Robins's data do not support the assumption in cultural transmission theory that the primary difference between deviant and nondeviant individuals is in values and learned criminal skills rather than in personality disorders; 60 per cent of the robbers, burglars, and thieves, as well as two-thirds of the white-collar criminals—forgers and embezzlers—were diagnosed as sociopaths.

At first glance these adult outcomes seem to describe a high degree of continuity in antisocial behavior patterns from adolescence to the mid-40's. However, Robins points out that the prevalence of adult effectiveness and competence in the control sample is even more striking than the degree of continuity in nonconformity among subjects referred to the clinic in adolescence for antisocial reasons. Continuity in antisocial behavior was somewhat higher between adolescence and the 20's than between adolescence and the mid-40's; this was especially evident among the most seriously disturbed adolescents later diagnosed as sociopaths. Twelve per cent of the sociopaths were found to have given up their antisocial behavior at the time of the adult interview and another 27 per cent had improved substantially; most of these subjects improved between ages 30 and 40 after many role failures. Not having an antisocial father was the only childhood correlate of improvement. Two conditions in particular seemed to support improvement by pressing toward stable role commitments and acceptable behavior: fear of more severe punishment from legal authorities which in a number of cases resulted from brief sentences, and rewarding marital, work, and community relationships. The social integration of improved subjects could be attributed to prior change in personality, although this outcome was probably a consequence of concurrent improvements in behavior patterns and social environment. A number of findings were suggestive of ways in which the environment could be structured to enhance the development of stable role commitments and improved behavior in adulthood among individuals diagnosed as sociopathic in adolescence. For instance, among male sociopaths success in holding a job was related to low supervision in the work setting.

Achievement

There are at least two general forms in which achievement behavior may be expressed in adolescence: the quality of task performance and status-goals. In the school setting, a high quality performance in relation to standards of excellence is shown in the academic role by outstanding grades and membership in an Honor Society, in social activities through the demonstration of leadership ability in student organizations and committees, and in athletics through record performances in track and field events. In later years, marital and occupational roles are other potential areas for high quality performances. The desired levels of educational, occupational, and economic achievement in adulthood are prominent status-goals. Since promotions based on merit depend on the quality of task performance, the latter constitutes a potential means for advancement. However, the two types of achievement behavior need not be highly related. For instance, girls tend to achieve higher grades than boys in high school, but are less likely than boys to have college plans. In a sample of adolescents, Turner (1964a, p. 173) distinguished modes of ambition similar to these forms of achievement behavior. Two craftsmen, he noted, may be equally ambitious but have substantially different objectives. One strives to employ his skills in an effort to advance into a supervisory position within the firm, while the other takes pride in his skills as a craftsman and strives to achieve excellence in his work.

The usual indicators of adolescent educational and occupational goals in sociological research involve measurement of the desired *level* of achievement. The psychological significance of the chosen level would depend in large measure on the intensity and relative priority of a youth's orientation toward the goal. Intensity is indicated by the strength of personal commitment, and goal priority by the profile of a youth's commitments to all relatively salient goals. Thus the goal of attending college could be accompanied by personal commitments ranging from strong to weak and represent only one of several equally attractive objectives. Personal commitment to a goal should be distinguished from being committed by the expectations of significant others; a youth may or may not strongly desire to achieve goals to which he is committed by parents and friends. A discrepancy between personal and public commitment to an educational goal is likely between a low-ability boy and his ambitious middle-class parents.

In Turner's study (1964a), several types of ambition were measured, in addition to the distinction between quality of performance and status goals. For boys, these included level of occupational and educational goals, preference for working alone or under supervision in adulthood (ownership), desired possessions in adulthood expressed in terms of car and home ownership (material), and desire to become outstanding in an occupation (eminence). In addition to educational and material goals, girls were also asked to indicate the level of education and minimum occupation they would like their prospective husbands to have. The single-item index of eminence ambition was relatively uncorrelated with other forms of ambition among girls and boys in the sample. In this study at least, a boy's mobility goals did not indicate the reputation he expected to achieve in his occupation. Occupational, educational, and material goals were highly interrelated among boys and girls and were combined in a general measure of ambition.

A number of experimental studies have found achievement motivation, measured by fantasy elicited to stories on the TAT, to be related to quality task performance and to realistic goals (Klinger, 1966). However, there is no substantial evidence from longitudinal research that high *n* (need) Achievement in adolescence significantly predicts intergenerational upward mobility among males (see Skolnick, 1966). In this context, we should note that the psychological relationship between the content of TAT imagery and corresponding action—whether direct or substitutive—is subject to measurement, personality, and situational variations (see Birney "Research on the Achievement Motive" in Chapter 14 of this volume). In *The Achieving Society* (1961), McClelland took the position that achievement fantasy was an indication of *n* Achievement and that *n* Achievement under favorable conditions would be expressed in achievement behavior. More recently, however, he has revised this view in a commentary on Skolnick's analysis by stating the more defensible position that fantasy elicited by the TAT is a "sample" of thought (1966).

Performance evaluations, standards of excellence, and achievement goals are initially presented and reinforced by parents through rewards and punishments in the socialization process. Under favorable conditions, these judgments and standards are eventually internalized and elaborated. Depending on the setting, internalized standards and goals may be congruent or at variance with group norms and values. To the extent that achievement behavior of both types is internally patterned, it should be fairly resistant to external influences and stable across situations in which required skills are functionally related. Some evidence on this hypothesis was obtained by Coleman and his colleagues in a large nationwide study of educational achievement and opportunity (1966, pp. 304–325).[5] In grades 6, 9, and 12, the school achievement of children from educationally disadvantaged homes—who were more likely to feel in-

[5] This study is one of the largest ever to be completed on education in the United States. Initiated by the U.S. Office of Education, the main survey included over 600,000 students enrolled in grades 3, 6, 9, and 12 of approximately 4,000 schools, along with first graders in 2,000 schools. Schools enrolling minority children were purposively overrepresented, although they were generally representative of all public schools in the United States. The students were tested on achievement and on verbal and nonverbal ability inventories and completed a questionnaire which included self-image, attitude, future plans, and family items. Questionnaires were also filled out by teachers, principals, and superintendents, and teachers were asked to complete a short verbal-ability test. There are numerous flaws as well as strengths in the technical aspects of the survey. For example, approximately 30 per cent of the schools selected for the study were unwilling to participate. It should be noted, however, that estimates of measurement and sampling reliability were more than satisfactory. The prevalence of missing data also posed a serious problem; these blanks were filled in by average scores.

competent and fatalistic than other youth—was more strongly influenced by characteristics of fellow students and teachers than the achievement of children oriented toward internal control and reared in educative families. Other relevant data are examined subsequently in the context of school effects on student achievement.

Given internally patterned standards and goals, stability in achievement behavior across situations and time would be contingent on the degree of continuity in required skills, opportunities and role priorities. In some respects the transition between student roles in high school and college is relatively continuous, since skills, priorities, and obligations are functionally related. Thus, it is not surprising that grade achievement in high school is the most effective predictor of academic performance in college (Lavin, 1965, p. 57). Achievement behavior in areas other than the academic role in high school, such as social prominence, appears to be unrelated to similar types of behavior in adulthood. In an eight-year follow-up of high-school students, Hess (1963a) found very little relationship between social prominence in high school and either occupational status or social participation and prominence in adulthood. A comparison of the 20 most popular and socially prominent members of the senior class with a matched group of students indicated that they did not maintain their relative position in social achievement. "Some of the high school wallflowers are now leading very active social lives, and some of the sociometric queens of the prom now have little social interaction outside of their family" (Hess, 1963, p. 411). Change in role priorities and situations associated with the demands of marriage and an occupation is presumably a major factor in this discontinuity. Social activities are a major preoccupation of girls in high school, but are pushed far down the priority list in young adulthood by marriage and family responsibilities. Social experiences and achievements may have an enduring effect through acquired skills, but the role settings of adulthood determine opportunities to express these abilities and interests. Status factors in adulthood in Hess's study were significantly correlated with involvement in formal associations and with the acquisition of role commitments.

Sex Differences in Achievement Behavior

The contrasting occupational perspectives of males and females are reflected in the achievement concerns of youth. In the academic role, boys encounter strong achievement imperatives, while girls have other options and, in contrast to boys, invest more of their self-esteem in social relationships than in academic success (Douvan & Adelson, 1966; Stinchcombe, 1964). For the majority of girls primarily oriented toward marriage rather than a career, the kinds of boys they date and their progress in courtship have greater importance for their adult status and style of life than how well they do in course work during high school. In Turner's study of high school seniors (1964b), ambitious girls who planned to be only a homemaker expressed life goals in terms of their prospective husbands' achievements and emphasized material ambition over their own educational goals; career girls, on the other hand, stressed their own educational goals over material expectations.

Sources of achievement worries and satisfactions among boys and girls vary in relation to sex-appropriate paths to anticipated adult roles. In their nation-wide survey of adolescents, Douvan and Adelson (1966) found very little overlap in the worries of boys and girls; boys were primarily concerned about school achievement and vocational problems, while girls were equally worried about achieving acceptance by friends, boys, parents, and others. Assets for achieving popularity and social acceptance, such as appearance and personality inadequacies, were mentioned three times as often by girls as by boys. Corresponding sex differences on achievement and interpersonal concerns were obtained in a nation-wide survey of adults (Gurin, Veroff, & Feld, 1960, pp. 52–83).

As requisites for social mobility, attractiveness and charm are likely to be as important to the mobility chances of girls as grades are to the mobility prospects of boys. Only a few studies have explored the relation between the attractiveness of girls and subsequent mobility through marriage. In the New Haven study of family patterns and mental illness, Myers and Roberts (1959) found that female patients in the lower middle-class frequently used their physical assets to get ahead. Compared to male patients, they were "more active in extracurricular activities for meeting high status persons, particularly boys. Whenever possible, they utilized their physical assets in their mobility strivings. They flattered and charmed male teachers in high school and college. Later on, they used the same technique with the men they met in business" (Myers & Roberts, 1959, p. 156).

Parents in the middle and working class appear to be at least equally interested in the academic progress of daughters and sons, but they are less likely to insist that their daughters obtain a college education (Elder, 1962). These differences in socialization and expectations are reflected in the academic performance and the college attendance rates of girls and boys. Girls surpass boys in grades earned in high school (Coleman, 1961) but are much less likely to enter college (Sewell & Shah, 1967). Low parental educational expectations, relatively greater dependence on family, and marital interests may largely account for this lower rate of college attendance. At least one longitudinal study has found that family social class has a stronger effect than ability on the educational level achieved by girls, whereas the reverse pattern was obtained for boys (Sewell & Shah, 1967). In a randomly selected cohort of high school seniors followed from 1957 to 1964, Sewell and Shah obtained these sex differences on college plans, entrance into college, and on graduation from college.

Sources and Correlates of Variations in Achievement Behavior

Variations in task or role performance, goals, and goal-attainment can be traced in large measure to two general sources: genetic and environmental. A third source, the developed characteristics of the child, is an outcome of transactions between genetic and environmental factors; in time sequence, environmental and personality influences are antecedent and consequent to achievement behavior in the developmental process. Although the relative genetic influence in achievement behavior is a controversial issue, the hereditary component in measured intelligence is presumably larger than in any other characteristic related to or indicating achievement behavior and status-goals. One indication of this is shown in a comparison of developmental rate and stability from birth to adulthood: measured intelligence develops earlier and is more stable over time than general achievement behavior (Bloom, 1964a). In a review of the research literature on academic performance, Lavin (1965, p. 56) reports an average correlation of .60 between intelligence tests in high school and grades. This relationship is generally stronger than correlations between IQ and measures of achievement motivation; in Turner's study, a correlation of .46 was obtained between a general index of ambition and IQ among boys (1964a, p. 184). Of the major environmental influences—family, peers, teachers, and school facilities—family status, structure, and socialization explained by far the largest proportion of variance in the academic achievement of children in grades 1, 3, 6, 9, and 12 in Coleman and associates' survey of American schools and students (1966, p. 325).

Personal characteristics and resources that facilitate or result from high academic performance include, in addition to achievement motivation and goals, measures of social maturity in the student role such as responsibility and compliance (Lavin, 1965, p. 107; Stinchcombe, 1964); sense of personal worth, low anxiety, and high morale (Rosenberg, 1965); cognitive skills and style manifested in curiosity, originality, and flexibility (Lavin, 1965, p. 107); and general beliefs, especially belief in internal rather than in external control of one's environment (Rosen, 1956; Coleman *et al.,* 1966, p. 325). Both self-esteem and belief in internal control are indicators of a sense of competence and thus have particular relevance for academic performance and mobility goals. The variable time order of these characteristics in relation to academic achievement is illustrated by Stinchcombe's analysis of behavioral rebellion in the high school (1964). Low IQ boys were more likely to be rebellious—truant and being sent out of the classroom—than high-ability boys, and the relatively low achievement of the former group was probably due in part to their noncompliant behavior. On the other hand, school failure undoubtedly reinforced their rebelliousness. "Failure, then, tends to be a self-confirming process among boys: failure leads to rebelliousness which leads to more dramatic and irrevocable failure" (Stinchcombe, 1964, p. 158). A similar self-confirming process has been observed in the relation of self-concept of ability to academic performance (Brookover *et al.,* 1964).

The relation of anxiety to achievement behavior has received considerable attention since Allison Davis's initial essay (1944) on the development and implications of social anxiety for effective learning and mobility strivings. According to Davis, "the behavioral manifestations which teachers and psychologists would regard as 'anxious' are associated with striving behavior. Anxiety leads to striving because only thus can anxiety be reduced to a tolerable level. Thus, it may be said that, in our kind of society, if a child wishes to be rewarded, he must learn to mobilize and bear that degree of anxiety which will serve to make him strive most effectively for the goals of his group" (1944, pp. 208–209). Davis does not clearly specify the level of socialized anxiety which motivates achievement striving nor the form of the relationship between anxiety and achievement. Nevertheless, a number of studies using a variety of general and specific measures of anxiety consistently show anxiety level to be negatively correlated with school performance and test scores (Hill & Sarason, 1966; Kagan & Moss, 1962; Rosenberg, 1965). High anxiety is also associated with low self-esteem, unhappiness, dependence on adults, and social withdrawal (Rosenberg, 1965; Hill & Sarason, 1966, p. 17) and with low achievement motivation (Kagan & Moss, 1962). In Sarason's provocative work on test anxiety, the highly anxious child has been found to experience the "greatest difficulty in evaluative situations in which he is required to function independently" (Hill & Sarason, 1966, p. 61). For instance, in a sample of grade-school children, Hill and Sarason found the negative effect of high test-anxiety to be less on mathematical than on reading tasks, which are less structured and require greater independence.

A five-year longitudinal study conducted by Hill and Sarason (1966) clearly shows the educational consequences of test anxiety. Approximately 1,100 children were selected from the first and second grades of elementary schools during 1958–59 in a middle-class suburb. The students were administered Test Anxiety, Defensiveness, and Lie Scales in the first, third, and fifth years; intelligence tests were given every year and a standard achievement test was administered in the second, fourth, and fifth years. Teachers' ratings of school performance and average grades were obtained at the end of the fifth year. Scores on the Test Anxiety Scale were highly unstable between the first and fifth year of the study for boys and girls (r's $=$ .15 and .20 on subjects initially selected from the first grade). Most of the instability occurred during the first three grades, since correlations of .58 and .49 were obtained between the fourth and sixth grades on boys and girls respectively. Due perhaps to fluctuations during the first several years of grade school, cross-sectional negative correlations between anxiety and test performance were found to increase in strength over the five-year period. The negative effects of high anxiety on test performance were similar on all ability levels. From the first to the fifth years, change in test anxiety was correlated meaningfully with change patterns in test performance and in defensiveness; children, especially boys, who increased in test anxiety gained less in test performance and expressed greater defensiveness than students who decreased in anxiety.

Hill and Sarason (1966) did not empirically examine factors that might explain anxiety and test-performance patterns as well as the changing relationship between these two variables during the grade-school period. However, they discussed at length the potential significance of situational factors in the school environment, such as the degree of discontinuity experienced by children as they move from one grade to another. At each point, they encounter an array of new, demanding, and "varied tasks of a cognitive and interpersonal nature" (1966, p. 70). Paralleling the change in teachers are transitions and discontinuities in learning tasks varying in content and level of difficulty both within and between particular grades. "There are probably wide variations in the degree of abruptness of these transitions, and informal observations have suggested that many such changes or transitions might more accurately be termed discontinuities, for example, the way in which the 'new math' has at times been introduced" (1966, p. 70). The effects of these transitions or discontinuities on school performance are likely to vary in relation to the student's test anxiety, sense of mastery, ability, and family environment. Hill and Sarason's study shows that successful negotiation of transitions between social and academic tasks among highly anxious children was more common among high- than low-ability students; similar variations are probable in relation to the student's belief in his ability to control his environment. Change in grades and in reading or math groups, as well as the often abrupt change between the sixth and seventh grade, are transitions of potential significance, as they interact with the personal characteristics of the student. To assess the effects of the elementary or any other school environment on anxiety level and school performance, it is necessary, as Hill and Sarason point out, to identify points at which discontinuities appear, "to what extent they involve social-personality and academic-learning adaptations, the manner in which children are prepared for them, the rationale for the timing of their introduction [and] the variations that exist among teachers and schools" (1966, p. 72).

Research and theory on values and beliefs indicating an orientation toward achievement have identified a number of dimensions in addition to a belief in mastery (Rosen, 1956; Strodtbeck, 1958; Kahl, 1965). They include trust in others, degree of independence from family, and the relative primacy of occupational commitments. These studies are indebted to Florence Kluckhohn's well-known formulation of dominant and variant value-orientations (Kluckhohn & Strodtbeck, 1961). She identified five problems common to all human societies which require solution. The alternative solutions are not random or infinite but are considered variable within a range of possibilities. The five proposed problems and the range of variation in each respective orientation are: (a) the character of human nature—the Human Nature orientation includes the categories of Evil, Neutral Mixture of Good-and-Evil, and Good; (b) the relation of man to nature and supernature—the Man-Nature Orientation includes the relations of Subjugation, Harmony, and Mastery; (c) the temporal forces of Life-Time Orientation includes Past, Present, and Future perspectives; (d) the modality of human activity—the Activity Orientation includes Being, Being-in-Becoming and Doing; and (e) the modality of man's relationship to other men—the Relational Orientation includes Lineality, Collaterality, and Individualism. From a factor analysis of value statements obtained from samples of Mexican and Brazilian men and a review of other research, Kahl (1965) suggests that an achievement orientation includes at least four dimensions, three of which closely parallel dimensions in Kluckhohn's theory: Activism or Mastery indicating belief in a controllable future; Trust in People; Independence of Family expressed in rejection of statements such as "Nothing in life is worth the sacrifice of moving away from your parents"; and Occupational Primacy in which occupational demands have priority over other considerations. Only the first three dimensions were found to be positively correlated with each other and with high social status.

Research on the relation of achievement values to the academic performance and goals among youth has used indices constructed from items loading on one or more of the dimensions in Kahl's analysis. In a study of the determinants of academic performance and mobility aspirations among high-school boys, Rosen (1956) constructed an index of achievement values which included items on mastery, deferred gratification, and independence from family. This index was moderately related to college aspirations. Strodtbeck (1958) constructed an eight-item value scale in a study of family patterns associated with the achievement behavior of high-school boys in New Haven. The *V*-scale measures primarily two achievement dimensions: planning for the future and belief in a controllable environment; and independence from family as expressed in greater loyalty to self and occupational career than to family (Kahl, 1965). All items in the *V*-scale predicted achievement behavior. Low achievers were more likely than other boys to believe in external control and to feel more strongly committed to family than to occupational striving. Similar results on the achievement correlates of mastery values were obtained in a nationwide study of children in grades 6, 9, and 12 (Coleman *et al.,* 1966). An index of external control was constructed from three items: "good luck is more important than hard work for success"; "every time I try to get ahead, something or someone stops me"; and "people like me don't have much of a chance to be successful in life" (1966, p. 320). Fatalistic responses to the three items were significantly more common among Negro than among white students. In each grade and across white and minority groups, correlations between this index and a test of verbal skills ranged from .40 to .50. The relationship was strongest among Negro students and weakest among whites, whereas a measure of student self-image was more strongly correlated with verbal skills among whites than among Negroes. These differences held up even with background factors statistically controlled. Color barriers to achievement encountered by Negro youth undoubtedly contribute to their perception of the environment as problematic and unresponsive to their efforts. The environment experienced by white youth, on the other hand, is more conducive to developing an internal patterning of achievement behavior; as a result, their concepts of self more directly reflect and facilitate their academic performance than is the case among Negro youth. Coleman and his colleagues tentatively suggest that "children from advantaged groups assume that the environment will respond if they are able to affect it; children from disadvantaged groups do not make this assumption, but in many cases assume that nothing they will do can affect the environment—it will give benefits or withhold them, but not as a consequence of their own action" (Coleman *et al.,* 1966, p. 321).

In research on environmental determinants of academic achievement and goals, considerable attention has centered on the anti-intellectual values of youth culture evident in large coeducational high schools and on the influence of family and school on school performance and goals. The character of youth culture is generally assumed to be similar in all social strata. The remainder of this chapter section is devoted to a review of theory and recent research on these two topics.

Coeducation, Youth Culture, and Academic Performance

There are divergent views regarding the influence of youth culture on the academic performance and goals of youth in American high schools. Turner (1964a) found little evidence of an "effective youth conspiracy against academic excellence" in his sample of high-school seniors. Contrary findings have been reported by James Coleman in his ten-school study (1961). In Talcott Parsons's (1953) original description of youth culture, two features stand out: its oppositional stance in relation to the adult world and the influence of sex-role standards in defining status-conferring activities and characteristics. Athletic skills, attractiveness to the opposite sex, and a well-rounded "personality" are status-conferring assets for boys; together, these aspects define manliness and appropriate avenues for demonstrating masculinity in youth culture. The "glamour girl" pattern of sexual attractiveness and popularity represent a status-conferring means for girls to affirm their femininity. In Parsons's brief description of youth culture, academic excellence has little relevance for status achievement and appears to be valued or tolerated only if it is accompanied with specifically sex-appropriate assets. Academic excellence might not be a detriment to status achievement if the boy is an athlete and not effeminate or overly studious. Other observers have suggested that "mediocrity" and the gentleman's C are rewarded patterns in youth culture (cited in Turner, 1964a, p. 139).

The results of Coleman's study consistently document these features of youth culture (1961). Each adolescent in ten high schools was asked how he would like to be remembered in high school: boys favored athletic star and most popular over being remembered as a brilliant student, while girls preferred the social leader and popular student image over the brilliant student. In schools where scholarship was of little value for getting into the leading crowd, high academic achievers were less likely to be those with the highest ability. The negative effects of an antischolarship climate were most evident among girls. High-ability girls in schools with a negative scholarship climate were less likely than boys of similar ability to be high achievers. One of the most extreme illustrations of sex-role influences on the values of girls is shown in the image preferences of 49 girls in a leading crowd; not one wanted to be remembered as a brilliant student. That scholarship among boys is not a detrimental quality when shown by well-rounded youth who possess valued sex-role skills is indicated by the sociometric status of athlete-scholars in Coleman's study (1961); of the elite boys in the sample, the athlete-scholars received a disproportionate number of peer choices.

The dominant sex-role and heterosexual features of youth culture in the United States are undoubtedly a major consequence of coeducational junior and senior high-schools, and this structural condition may be the primary difference between youth cultures in the United States and in European countries which have largely sex-segregated secondary schools. Coeducation is spreading in both Great Britain and France and is currently a highly controversial issue from both educational and moral perspectives. In the United States, opposition to the coeducation concept by the Catholic church is based on the "moral dangers" of sex-integrated schools and not on the academic consequences. In this respect, it is noteworthy that a large survey of British adolescents found no difference in sexual experience between youth from coeducational and same-sex schools (Schofield, 1965).

The extent to which scholarship is viewed by adolescents within the context of manly or womanly characteristics is also shown by an experimental study of adolescent attitudes toward brilliance in a sample of eleventh-grade students in New York City (Tannenbaum, 1962). Brilliance was most negatively evaluated as a male characteristic when it was combined with "bookish," effeminate characteristics. A set of eight stimulus characters were created from three dichotomous attributes (academic ability, effort in school work, and sportsmindedness), and the adolescents were asked to indicate which desirable and undesirable traits in a list (e.g., serious, dresses well, etc.) were most typical of each stimulus character. Rated most favorably by boys was the brilliant-nonstudious athlete; this type was closely followed by three athlete combinations: average-nonstudious-athlete, average-studious-athlete, and brilliant-studious-athlete. Girls tended to rate any stimulus character with the attribute of brilliance lower than the rating given by boys. The brilliant-studious-nonathlete was rated well below all other stimulus characters by boys and girls. The potent characteristic was clearly athletic-mindedness, the extent to which the imaginary character was described as a participator in athletic events. Tannenbaum notes that "it doesn't matter whether the student is brilliant or average so long as he is also athletic-minded" (1962, pp. 39–40). When adolescents were asked to indicate the sex of each of the stimulus characters, both boys and girls were more apt to designate the athlete combinations as "boys." Males more often saw the brilliant-studious-nonathlete as a girl than any other type.

On the college level, Riesman has noted the inhibiting effects of sex-role norms and pressures on girls in coeducational colleges (1956). In visits to a large number of campuses, he found students in women's colleges were less self-conscious in their sex-role and showed greater individuality in talents and appearance. The greater conformity among coeds, he suggests,

> is understandable, because the girls in the classroom worry not only about what the boys would say about what they said, but also about what the other girls would think about what the boys would think—a feedback to daunt all but the most courageous and insensitive. While from the perspective of Smith and Vassar, the coed schools cultivate easy-going camaraderie with boys as against the artificiality of week-end visits and proms, what the camaraderie seems to me often to accomplish is to anticipate by four years the girl's marriage to a boy whom she will assist in his career by sacrificing hers (1956, p. 154).

A somewhat different view of youth culture and its effects on scholarship is presented by Turner on the basis of his study of seniors in ten high schools in the Los Angeles area (1964a). He found widespread antischolarship values among students in all schools, but this public climate had little effect on their friendship choices. In a sociometric analysis of friendship choices, students nominated as "brains" were more likely than other students to be chosen as "friends" and as "wheels." In noting the high status of male and female academic achievers, Turner tentatively concluded that "the antischolastic values in youth subculture are of ritual character and are at variance with private preference and the determinants of peer-group social prominence" (1964a, p. 155). Although the causal direction is ambiguous, other data suggest that the antischolarship content of youth culture was most frequently endorsed by youth low on ambition. For example, three-fourths or more of the adolescents endorsed the item "talks about popular music and sports vs. talks about foreign policy and politics," and this item was significantly related in a negative direction to a general index of ambition. Other values of a similar nature, such as performing no better than friends, were related in a similar fashion to ambition. The most negative influence of youth culture on ambition and academic values appeared in middle-status schools. It is possible that stronger evidence on the negative effects of antischolarship values would have resulted if Turner had examined the influence of academic climate on the relation between the ability and grades of "brains" and "wheels." Some of the most significant results in Coleman's study (1961) were obtained from this kind of analysis. Since both studies found that college-oriented youth were accorded high status by peers, it is apparent that the style used to achieve good grades and the sex-role character of the achiever are primary targets of youth culture.

Social Class Variations in Academic Achievement and Goals

Research studies in the United States and in other countries have consistently reported sizable and statistically significant differences in grades, achievement motivation, IQ, test scores, and mobility goals by the social-class origins of children and adolescents (Floud, 1961; Douglas, 1964; Lavin, 1965). Youth from the lower and working classes are less likely to complete high school, receive scholarships, enter college, and complete their college education (Lavin, 1965; National Merit Scholarship Corporation, 1961; Sewell & Shah, 1967). Characteristics associated with achievement behavior, such as belief in internal control, language skills, and a sense of personal worth, as well as conditions in the home and school which develop achievement motivation and abilities, are also less common in the personalities and social worlds of children from the lower classes (Lavin, 1965). Even within the lower-lower class, children with unemployed fathers do more poorly on achievement tests than the children of unskilled fathers (Douglas, 1964, p. 41). In Douglas's longitudinal study of British children (1964), the difference in school performance between children from the middle and lower classes increased from the age of 8 to 11 years. Socioeconomic variations across regions in the United States are reflected mainly in the significantly lower test performance of children living in the South. Coleman and associates (1966) found educationally deprived children to be primarily those living in the South and in nonmetropolitan areas of the North. Regional variations were particularly large among Negro youth, with those in the rural South lowest and in the metropolitan North highest in mean test scores. Large regional variations in educational quality and achievement have also been reported in England (Floud, 1961), France, and Italy; the contrast between educational opportunities in northern and southern Italy is particularly striking.

These class variations are also reflected in the school achievement of children from minority groups predominantly low in socioeconomic status. On a variety of mean test scores, Coleman and associates (1966) obtained the following rank order from high to low achievement: Whites, Oriental Americans, American Indians, Mexican Americans, Puerto Ricans, and Negroes. Approximately 85 per cent of the Negro scores were below the average score for white students (1966, p. 219). At least in the South and Southwest, the gap between white and Negro children tended to increase by grade-level.

Class differences in college aspirations do not appear to have changed appreciably since 1939. A survey of high-school students at the end of the Depression decade found that 62 per cent from professional and managerial families "planned on going to college" in comparison to only a third of the students from manual families (Jaffe & Adams, 1964). By 1959, these percentages had increased about five per cent. Both social class and ability determine who will enter college, but ability has a relatively stronger effect on the likelihood of graduating from college than socioeconomic status (Sewell & Shah, 1967). The kind and quality of post high-school institution entered also varies by the class background of students, as well as by ability. Elite private schools in the East recruit most of their students from the upper middle-class, while junior and state colleges draw a large proportion of their students from the working and lower classes.

Despite the strong relationship between family social class and adolescent achievement, there is considerable intraclass variation due to variations in the educative environment of family, neighborhood, peer relations, and school. In a large random sample of high-school seniors in Wisconsin, Sewell and Shah (1967) found that only 7.5 per cent of the boys from low SES families graduated from college; however, completion of college was many times more likely among high than low ability boys with this kind of family background (0.3 vs. 20.1 per cent). On the following pages, our focus is on selected aspects of family, peer, and school environments which are instrumental in developing academic achievement and motivation. Though similar environmental conditions and contexts generally have comparable effects on achievement on all class levels, there are also markedly different sources of achievement and educational goals in the middle and lower classes. For instance, a deprived family environment may be partially counteracted in its effects by the positive influence of ambitious relatives and a high quality school environment. The contextual influence of the school environment has received considerable attention from sociologists during the last ten years (Sewell & Armer, 1966a).

1. Family Status, Structure, and Socialization

Three general dimensions of the family status and environment have been explored as explanations of class variations in school achievement and status-goals: economic factors, the cultural climate of the home, and specific training practices. Low income, by imposing limitations on potential residential areas, generally determines the quality of housing, neighborhood, and schools. There is a tendency for residential areas in large and small communities to be occupied by families similar in social, economic, and ethnic characteristics. Low-income families are less likely to have access to adequate medical care; their homes tend to be crowded and noisy, provide little privacy for reading or studying, are deficient in educational materials such as books, encyclopedias, and quality magazines, and frequently lack adequate sanitary facilities (Fraser, 1959; Douglas, 1964). In addition to learning and language disabilities produced by this type of environment, economic need may require youth to leave school early to help support the family. For adolescents who manage to do well in school, limited family resources usually lessen their opportunities to go on to college, even though scholarships and loans have enabled large numbers of low SES youth to attend college. Even among middle-class families, level of family income is a significant factor in determining chances for education beyond high school. In a large, national sample of high-school seniors, Nam and Cowhig (1962) found that approximately three-fifths of the adolescents from white-collar homes with family incomes of $6,000 and over actually enrolled in college, compared to only 45 per cent of the white-collar students from families reporting less income.

Of the many aspects of cultural climate and socialization related to achievement behavior, our review includes four that have received considerable attention in research: achievement and independence training, parental goals and parental models.

1. Achievement and independence training. Research by Winterbottom (1958), Rosen (1959), and others on family patterns that transmit standards of excellence and develop achievement motivation has identified three important socialization practices: warmth, achievement training, and independence training. In achievement training, parents establish high goals for the child, emphasize competence in performing well on tasks and in roles, and impose standards of excellence even where such standards are not explicit (Rosen, 1959). In Rosen's research (1959) based on Winterbottom's earlier study of middle-class mothers and sons, achievement training has been measured by asking mothers the age at which they expect their son to do particular activities well. These include school performance, leadership in activities with other children, and achievement in competitive games and sports. The index does not include items on what the mother does to encourage her son to perform tasks well. Independence training includes the communication of expectations that the child perform autonomously when competing with a standard of excellence and the provision of independence in task and decision-making situations which forces the child to assume responsibility for his actions. The index that Rosen has used to measure independence training primarily measures parental expectations concerning self-reliance; the provision of independence is implied, but no items on actual training in self-reliance are included. Mothers are asked to indicate the age at which their son should do such things as entertain himself, make his own decisions, and work on hard things without assistance.

Separate indexes on actual training procedures that parents use to implement their achievement and independence expectations would be a useful addition to the measures Rosen has employed in his research. Though demands and training are undoubtedly related, the kind of training is apt to differ markedly between middle- and working-class parents, with the latter relying more on external regulation and control. On the basis of Rosen's findings in a large sample of mother-son pairs, McClelland suggests that lower-class mothers tend to emphasize reduction of parental care in getting their son to take care of himself, while middle-class parents place relatively greater emphasis on genuine training in independence and mastery (1961, p. 345). Lower-class mothers in Rosen's study (1959), particularly Negro mothers, expected earlier independence than mastery, while the reverse pattern was more common in the training practices of middle-class mothers. In two samples of American preadolescents and their mothers, Rosen (1962) found the mean age of achievement and independence training to be significantly higher in the working class than in the middle class. Less pronounced differences in the same direction were obtained in a Brazilian sample of preadolescent boys and their mothers (1962). In both countries, achievement motivation was higher among middle- than among working-class boys.

In a large sample of adolescents from Ohio and North Carolina (Elder, 1962), a five-item index was constructed which indicates both the provision of independence and training for self-reliance. Parents high on the index were moderate in control, had decreased control as the child became older, frequently explained rules of conduct and discipline which were not understood, and used reasoning as the primary technique of discipline. These practices structure an environment that can be understood and mastered through the use of skills. In the section on moral development, it was noted that these socialization practices were associated with knowledge of parental expectations, the belief that parents meant what they said, a feeling that demands and restrictions were reasonable, and a tendency to comply with parental requests. Though lower-class adolescents (defined by manual occupational status) less often placed parents high on the index, youth in the middle and lower classes with parents high on the index were more likely than other adolescents to have achieved a grade average of "B" or higher, to be highly motivated to excel in school work, and to have high educational goals. Adolescents who reported strong parental pressure to do well in school were generally low in scholastic achievement, and this technique was positively associated with academic motivation only among low achievers. Although training in meeting standards of excellence was not specifically included in the index of independence training, learning facilitated by this form of socialization appears likely to result in the internalization of achievement standards.

In an experimental study, Rosen and D'Andrade (1959) found training in mastery and warmth by both parents to be instrumental in developing achievement motivation in boys, and encouragement of independence by father to be more critical than independence training by mother. This study was designed to compare what parents report on training practices with what they actually do. Rosen and D'Andrade observed parent-child interaction in 20 families with a son in the highest quartile of *n* Achievement scores and an equal number of families with a son in the lowest quartile. The boys were matched on social class, race, and intelligence, and were between the ages of 9 and 11. Each boy was assigned several experimental tasks—such as block stacking in which he was blindfolded and could use only one hand—and both parents and the boy were told the performance norm for a "typical boy." Parents were instructed to talk if they wanted to, but that they could not physically assist their son on the task. The observers obtained measures of parental level of aspiration in relation to the task norm, of parental warmth expressed through happiness, laughter, and other positive evaluative responses, and of parental authoritarianism manifested in rejecting behavior, specific directions, pressures, and dominance in decision making. Preadolescent boys with a strong desire to achieve were more likely than other boys to be encouraged by their fathers to demonstrate self-reliance in a series of tasks and were trained in achievement by both parents. Mothers of highly motivated boys placed greater emphasis on achievement than independence training; they also applied stronger pressures on their sons than mothers of boys with low motivation. This pressure, however, was accompanied by high standards of excellence, and observers noted that these mothers appeared to be competent, aggressive persons who demanded similar characteristics in their sons. Longitudinal data from the Fels study generally correspond with Rosen and D'Andrade's findings on maternal socialization of sons (Kagan & Moss, 1962). Boys who were high on various ratings of intellectual achievement from grade school to young adulthood were closely protected by mother during the first three years of life but thereafter were subjected to strong achievement demands and training. Maternal acceleration in the grade-school period was highly correlated with the achievement behavior of sons.

Neither too early nor too late independence and achievement training appears to be effective in generating high *n* Achievement. "What is desirable," concludes McClelland, "is a stress on meeting certain achievement standards somewhere between the ages of six and eight (at least according to the mothers' reports), neither too early for the boy's abilities nor too late for him to internalize those standards as his own" (1961, p. 345). In samples of mother-son pairs in Brazil, Japan, and Germany, McClelland found early and late achievement training to be related to low *n* Achievement in sons (1961, p. 347). Data obtained from Japanese and German mothers on their level of *n* Achievement suggest that mothers with little desire to excel do not set high achievement standards, while those very high in *n* Achievement stress mastery at too early an age.

Socialization practices most unfavorable for developing mastery and self-reliant behavior in sons were found by Rosen in a large number of Brazilian families (1962).

Rather than encouraging autonomy, the authoritarian father severely thwarted "his son's efforts to be self-reliant and autonomous. The child learns that toward a severely authoritarian father only revolt or submission is possible" (Rosen, 1962, p. 623). Neither did this type of father stress mastery for his son, since this represented a potential threat to his power in the family. The Brazilian mother tended to be highly authoritarian but also excessively indulgent and overprotective. The effect of this type of family socialization, as well as cultural pattern, was strikingly indicated in *n* Achievement scores; on each class level, Brazilian boys were markedly lower in achievement motivation than their American counterparts (1962). Similar family patterns are described by Madsen (1964) in an ethnographic study of Mexican-Americans in Texas. An 11-year-old boy observed that "I learned that my mother can feel sympathy, but my father only demands and demands and demands" (Madsen, 1964, p. 52).

The relation between parents and youth is presumably more relevant to the provision of autonomy than the conjugal relationship, although these two relationships have not been clearly distinguished in research on achievement motivation and performance. For instance, in Rosen's study of Brazilian family patterns references are made to paternal power in the conjugal and father-son relationship. The implicit assumption seems to be that a father who is dominant in family matters is also likely to dominate his son. Although power structures in the two types of relationships, as perceived by youth, are moderately related, there is considerable variation (Elder, 1961). The boy who perceives his father as dominant in the family may also report that his father gives him considerable freedom to make decisions. It is also conceivable that a father in a wife-dominated family may try to convince his son that he is boss, through coercive domination. A number of studies have found achievement among American boys highest in the equalitarian home and lowest in the wife-dominant household (Elder, 1962), although contradictory findings have been reported by Devereux (1962). These findings are also complicated by the usually strong association between marital conflict and wife dominance. Since marital conflict has not been controlled in research on the effect of conjugal power relations, we cannot be certain whether variations in achievement by husband-wife power are a consequence of marital conflict or wife-dominance. Harmonious family relations are instrumental in developing achievement motivation (Rosen & D'Andrade, 1959; Elder, 1962). In a study of the family relations of highly intelligent boys who were either high or low in academic achievement, Morrow and Wilson (1961) matched 49 boys in each group for grade in high school, socioeconomic status, and intelligence. The high achievers more often described their parents as approving, trusting, affectionate, encouraging, but not pressuring with regard to achievement, and as relatively nonrestrictive. Parents of low-achieving boys, on the other hand, tended to disagree more frequently on standards of behavior, and the level of tension was generally higher (cf. Douvan & Adelson, 1966, Ch. 3).

In one study of adolescents, the effects of parental power in the child-rearing relationship accounted for a significantly larger portion of the variance in academic motivation (a self-report scale) than differences in conjugal power, a result which corresponds with the theoretical significance of independence training (Elder, 1962). Academic motivation was generally lowest among boys in husband-dominant families in which father was highly dominant in the father-son relationship, a pattern resembling the Brazilian father's influence in the family. Boys who were highest in academic motivation perceived their fathers as dominant in the family but reported that they had considerable freedom in decision making. In this type of family, father is likely to be seen by his son as an attractive role model by virtue of his demonstrated influence on important family matters (cf. Gold, 1963). It is significant, therefore, that adolescent boys from the working and lower classes are more likely than their middle-class counterparts to report both wife-dominance in conjugal relations and authoritarian control by father in child rearing (Elder, 1961).

2. *Goals, training, and ability*. The influence of parental goals on achievement motivation and performance depends on the personal and social context. Instead of generating achievement motivation and a sense of competence, high parental aspirations may produce rebellion or withdrawal through fantasy when not accompanied by training in mastery and self-reliance, when the goals far exceed the adolescent's ability or when opportunities are not available. High goals for a low-ability youth accompanied by training in standards of excellence—a combination most likely in the homes of proud, successful middle-class parents—would presumably intensify the psychological consequences of failure as expressed in an excessive fear of failure, low self-esteem, and withdrawal through fantasy. High aspirations without achievement training seem most probable among parents who, because of family and personal circumstances, are unable, unwilling, or do not know how to implement their goals effectively.

In a comparison of achievement and independence training experienced by American and Brazilian preadolescents, Rosen (1962) found that Brazilian parents in the middle and working class expected their sons to do things well and to be independent at a significantly later age than American parents; however, the Brazilian boys were more likely to report high parental aspirations concerning their accomplishments. For instance, over half of the Brazilian boys agreed that "My mother thinks I'm going to be an important person someday" compared to only one-fifth of the American boys. The Brazilian boys were also more likely to report that their parents considered them "somebody special." High goals were accompanied with maternal indulgence, emotional responses to failure, and a general tendency to praise performances regardless of quality. These conditions were characteristic of only a portion of the Brazilian families, but they were significantly more common in this sample than in the sample of American parents. Rosen suggests that the combined effect of deficient achievement and independence training and high aspirations foster inflated self-images of ability and future accomplishments which magnify the likelihood of frustration, failure, and a tendency to fantasize about success, when confronted with the "realities" of competitive achievement situations. On all class levels, the Brazilian boys were significantly lower in achievement motivation than their American counterparts.

Variations in achievement values between the two samples of mothers may partially account for differences in mastery training; belief in a controllable future, less common in Brazilian culture, is conducive for the establishment of high standards of excellence and independence demands. In German and Japanese samples, McClelland found that mothers who were optimistic and believed in a controllable future were more likely to stress early responsibility training manifested in expectations that their son do chores in the home and dress himself; they tended "to bring up sons who are conscientious, hard-working, and optimistic, if somewhat restricted or 'unspontaneous' in their expressive behavior" (McClelland, 1961, p. 348). The same mastery index on boys was not positively correlated with *n* Achievement on Japanese, Brazilian, German, and Indian samples, although the two achievement indicators appear to be related in the United States, according to Rosen's findings from samples of preadolescent boys (1959).

The Brazilian family pattern has some

relevance to the socialization of Negro youth. A number of studies have found Negro boys to have unrealistically high aspirations, higher than white youth on the same class level (Sexton, 1963), and a similar racial difference has been found in parental aspirations for the child's success in education (Coleman *et al.,* 1966). In a sample of boys ranging in age from 8 to 14 and their mothers, Rosen found that 83 per cent of the Negro mothers expected their sons to go to college (1959). Jewish and Protestant mothers were more likely to have college aspirations for their sons, but they were also more apt to train their sons in standards of excellence and self-reliance. In Coleman and associates' study, Negro youth in grades 6, 9, and 12 tended to report greater parental interest in academic progress and higher educational aspirations than white youth similar in family background (1966, p. 302). However, parental interest accounted for a much larger portion of the variance in school achievement among whites than among Negroes. In a large-scale study of adolescents in the South (Cramer, Bowerman, & Campbell, 1966), parental practices and goals relevant to achievement training were much less related to the educational goals of Negro than of white youth. Assuming that these reports of parental behavior are valid, the data suggest that Negro parents are less effective than white parents in translating their interests and goals into training practices that foster achievement motivation and academic achievement. This ineffectiveness is probably most common among Negro parents who lack a sense of competence and mastery over the environment (see Coleman *et al.,* 1961, p. 321). Rosen's earlier study of Negro parents and their sons (1959), as well as studies listed above, indicate that ineffective achievement training coupled with high aspirations may account for the sizable discrepancy between the inflated goals and low academic performance of Negro adolescents.

Even if parents train their offspring in standards of excellence and in self-reliance, goals excessively high in relation to developed ability and skills would tend to generate unrealistic ambition and increase the psychological impact of academic failure. In Stinchcombe's study of adolescent rebellion (1964), these conditions were most prevalent among low-ability boys from lower-middle class families. A large proportion of their parents expected them to take college preparatory courses and to enter college. Many of these boys had internalized the high academic standards and aspirations of their parents and continued to believe that they could attend college despite poor performance and flunk notices in their academic courses. Possibly as a defensive reaction to their failures and status deprivation, these youth were more likely than any other subgroup of boys to violate school rules—were truant or sent out of class—and to downgrade the significance of school achievement. In similar circumstances, other youth might respond by dropping out of school or by leaving the field through fantasy. These alternatives appear most likely among youth who have either not internalized high achievement standards and goals or were able to lower their goals. In a survey of factors associated with media use among tenth-grade students, heavy viewing of television was most prevalent among adolescents who perceived parental aspirations for themselves to be much higher than their own aspirations (Schramm, Lyle, & Parker, 1961, p. 125). Moderate or high conflict was most frequently reported by low-ability youth and by boys. The greater the discrepancy, the more the adolescent watched television, listened to the radio, attended movies, and the fewer books and magazines he read. Excessively high goals appear to have encouraged low-ability boys, in particular, to change the world of reality for the world of fantasy in which family tensions and pressures could be temporarily forgotten.

3. Parents as achievement and educative models. What parents say and do in training their children are frequently not compatible with what they represent in family and occupational roles. Though working-class parents may be keenly interested in developing achievement skills in their children, they cannot readily alter their educational deficiencies and low occupational status. A father with an unskilled job cannot easily change or disguise the fact that he failed to complete the ninth grade and does not have the skills for a better job. Also parents who have little more than basic literacy skills can encourage their children to read but are limited in showing good reading habits and interest. This discrepancy between what parents say and what they do could undermine their achievement demands. It is perhaps in behavior models that lower- and working-class parents are most handicapped in developing a desire to excel and school achievement in their children.

The achievement model is most clearly illustrated in the ambition and occupational success of a father who has been able to improve the lot of his family by obtaining increasingly better jobs. In particular, one would expect the strivings and success of upwardly-mobile parents to elicit future-oriented achievement behavior in their children. Two longitudinal studies have analyzed data relevant to this research problem. In a sample of 93 fathers and their sons who were born in 1928 (Guidance Study subjects), Smelser (1963) assessed the relation of paternal work-life between 1928 and 1946 to the personality development of sons. Using the Warner occupational index for these two years, Smelser defined five mobility groups: high-status upwardly mobile; low-status upwardly mobile; high-status stationary; low-status stationary; and downwardly mobile. It is unfortunate that data on the entire work-life were not included in defining these patterns, since the time period includes both the Great Depression and World War II, years of widespread unemployment and economic affluence. Even so, Smelser found that sons from the first three groups chose higher status occupations at age 15½ and were more inclined to perceive themselves as strong, powerful, autonomous, and distant from others. In Douglas's nation-wide sample of British children born in 1946, 43 per cent of the families moved out of their occupational group over an 11-year period; however, only 5 per cent of the families moved across the manual-nonmanual line, while 3 per cent moved down from the middle to the working class (1964, p. 40). The attributes and characteristics of upwardly-mobile families were found to resemble more those of families in the stratum of destination than of origin. The achievement orientation of mobile parents was also reflected in the academic performance of their children between the ages of 8 and 11; these children improved in test scores during the three-year period, whereas the performance of children in downwardly-mobile families declined.

There are a number of questions left unanswered by these two studies. Douglas's large sample of children offers an unusual opportunity to examine socialization and personality correlates of different types of work-life patterns, yet his monograph barely touches this problem. Does mobility within the middle or working classes have an effect on the achievement of children similar to that of mobility across the manual-nonmanual line? Although relatively few working-class families moved into the middle class during the 11-year period, this transition would seem to have the greatest impact on family life and socialization. If all data in the work-life histories had been used to identify orderly and disorderly movements both up and down in the occupational structure, it is probable that Douglas would have found much greater movement between the middle and working class. The direction, degree, and orderliness of work and intergenerational mobility warrant investigation in relation to achievement training and parental goals, and Douglas's longitudinal study has the potential for this kind of analysis.

A study of this type might resolve an apparent contradiction between the achievement outcomes related to downward mobility in Smelser's and Douglas's studies and other research findings that show that working-class parents brought up in middle-class families have middle-class aspirations for their children. Wilensky and Edwards found that men with this mobility pattern identified with the middle class and held middle-class aspirations for themselves as well as for their children (cited in Krauss, 1964, p. 871). Relatively similar findings are suggested by results from two other studies (E. Cohen, 1958; Krauss, 1964).

Despite high aspirations for children, a downwardly mobile or low-status father would be unable to demonstrate achievement and success for his son's emulation. He may, in fact, be seen as a negative example of occupational life. Several studies suggest that lower-class boys with college ambitions tend to reject their father's occupational role and are encouraged to take this attitude by parents (Kahl, 1953; Beilin, 1956; E. Cohen, 1958). In addition to the motivational implications of father's job as a negative reference object, studies indicate that at least two other factors in the lower and working classes are instrumental for developing achievement motivation and high educational and occupational goals: the competence and ambitions of mother and support from individuals outside the family (Warner & Abegglen, 1955; Krauss, 1964; Ellis & Lane, 1963). If father has less than a high-school education and an unskilled job, educational achievement and ambition are most likely among youth when mother has more education than father, is interested in education, and aggressively encourages achievement; when relatives have some college education or are in the middle class; and when the school attended is of high quality, and teachers offer support, encouragement, and direction with respect to preparation for college. All of these individuals and experiences provide socialization according to mobility goals rather than by social origins.

In a sample of working-class adolescents, Krauss (1964) found the most significant determinants of college aspirations to be mother's educational and occupational experience, the education of siblings, and influences outside the family, when father had neither a skilled job nor a high-school diploma. College aspirations among youth from these families were most likely to be correlated with one or more of the following conditions: maternal employment in a nonmanual job, mother's education higher than father's education, at least one middle-class grandparent, at least one brother or sister who had gone to college, and some friends of the family who had a college education. These youth were also more likely than other students to have college-oriented friends and to participate in extracurricular activities.

Additional data on the significance of mother as a primary motivational influence on lower- and working-class youth are shown in a longitudinal study of 194 Stanford students (Ellis & Lane, 1963). Only 31 per cent of the lower-class students reported that father was the most important parental influence on college plans, compared with two-thirds of the students in the random sample. Three-fourths of the lower-class students cited mother as the dominant parental influence, in contrast to half of the regular students. The influence of mother on the educational plans of the lower-class student was associated with her educational status relative to that of father; mothers with more education were likely to be more influential than their husbands. The significance of outside influences was also greatest among the lower-class students. Support and encouragement by teachers were particularly noteworthy and were probably a reflection of the students' outstanding ability. A third of these students considered teachers to be the most important influence on their college plans, compared to only four per cent of the regular students. Other adults were also more instrumental in supporting the educational ambitions of lower-class students. Similar to Krauss's finding (1964), the lower-class students developed close peer-group affiliations with middle-class youth through course work and extracurricular activities in high school.

The major social class difference in these studies is the behavior model and educative influence of father. Due to low occupational status, educational deficiencies, and other class-linked factors, fathers in the lower classes, especially those who are unskilled, are much less likely to represent a significant source of achievement motivation and high aspirations than middle-class fathers. For the capable adolescent from a low-status environment, the void due to paternal default is filled, if at all, by the initiative of mother, successful siblings, teachers, and other adults outside the immediate family. Feedback from competence in school work, teacher appraisals, and the positive image of the college preparatory program tends to increase his motivation to enter college and his interest in extracurricular activities. Through these experiences, the working-class student develops friendships with middle-class students which reinforce his goals. The tendency for ambitious working-class youth to have high-status friends with similar goals is a potential result of many factors (Turner, 1964a; Simpson, 1962), including school policy on student stratification and the desire of youth to have friends with similar interests and goals. Using data obtained from 600 students in their freshmen and senior years, McDill and Coleman (1965) found that membership in a high-status group was more strongly predictive of college plans among senior boys and girls than the educational status of their mothers and fathers. Status in school during the senior year was only slightly less related to college plans than parental educational goals when the students were freshmen. The effects of social status were strongest in schools where college-going was highly valued.

At first glance, these results seem to conflict with findings on father's influence in Kahl's well-known exploratory study of 24 working-class boys and their parents (1953). All of the high-school boys were drawn from the Harvard Mobility sample of 3,971 boys and were similar in background and ability. Only half of the boys planned on college, even though all were capable of doing college work. Through intensive interviews, Kahl found that paternal behavior differed most strikingly between the two groups. By and large, the father of noncollege boys displayed a just "getting by" philosophy and were oriented toward the present; they were interested in a stable, secure, congenial work-setting for their sons. Fathers of college-oriented sons, on the other hand, were ambitious for themselves and their sons; they valued education, realized its importance for acquiring the good things of life, and encouraged their sons to take school seriously. The contrast between these findings on the important role of father and studies showing the working- and lower-class mother to be the dominant influence may be due partly to variations in family socioeconomic status. Although different indices of social class make comparisons uncertain, Kahl's sample of families (1953) appears to be generally higher in SES than lower-class families in the Ellis and Lane sample (1963) and similar to the social status of skilled-manual families in Krauss's sample (1964). These variations are important, since the father who values education, encourages quality performance, and has high aspirations is a positive influence on the academic performance of sons on all class levels (Douglas, 1964), but decreases markedly in prevalence from the middle to the lower class. In Douglas's study of British children, middle-class parents were much more likely to show interest in their children's academic progress and to visit their school and teacher, but this class difference was most striking among fathers. Both measures of parental interest were positively correlated with the test scores of middle- and working-class children at ages 8 and 11 (1964, pp. 52–53).

4. Father absence. A problematical issue relevant to the role of father in achievement training concerns the effect of broken families. The theoretical and empirically demonstrated effects of the fatherless home are markedly clearer on sex-role than achievement socialization. A number of studies have reported that boys reared in fatherless homes, particularly during the preschool years, show more infantile characteristics, greater dependency, and conflict over sex-identity expressed in overly aggressive behavior than boys from intact families (Whiting & Burton, 1961). The markedly greater prevalence of fatherless homes among lower-class Negro than white children has drawn attention to the possibility that these variations in household structure contribute to the substantial racial difference in academic achievement and to the fact that Negro girls are more likely to enter college than Negro boys. The presumed effect of father-absence on boys has been hypothesized as occurring through two conditions: the lack of a male model and maternal socialization. In noting the prevalence of broken homes among lower-class, urban Negro families, Deutsch has suggested that the boy from this type of family environment "often has no experience with a 'successful' male model or thereby with a psychological framework in which effort can result in at least the possibility of achievement" (1963, p. 167). But is a lower-class Negro child from an intact family more likely than his fatherless counterpart to be exposed to a "successful" male model? An unskilled father with less than a high-school education represents a most unlikely source of educational stimulation and achievement training for white and Negro boys. Indeed, father-absence might even improve the developmental potential of the family environment if father had been authoritarian, punitive, and erratic in relation to the child, or was a source of quarrels and violence in the family; these characteristics are especially prevalent among lower-class fathers. Another adverse effect of father-absence in the family on socialization is thought to occur through maternal indulgence and failure to set standards of excellence (see McClelland, 1961, p. 375).

Two types of data have been related to household structure: measures of achievement motivation and indices of academic performance or ability. In several studies reviewed by McClelland, *n* Achievement is shown to be significantly lower among American boys and men from broken than from intact families (1961, p. 374). McClelland suggests that this is due to overindulgence among mothers in broken families, although no study to my knowledge has directly examined the relation between father-absence and achievement training. Failure to set standards of excellence may also result from feelings of apathy and fatalism among mothers who are without husbands in the home. Dependence on public welfare is likely to reinforce such feelings through the external and often capricious requirements imposed by this condition. In Coleman's study, students from fatherless homes were more likely to report a low sense of mastery than students from intact families, with economic status and other aspects of the family environment controlled (1966, p. 324).

One problem of research in this area is that the effects of father-absence are frequently confounded with economic and cultural factors. In the lower class, a very large percentage of Negro families headed by women are on welfare and thus may be significantly lower on both economic and cultural status than intact families within the same general stratum. The importance of adequate controls is illustrated by one of the few studies that has found a difference in test scores between children from father-absent and intact families (Deutsch & Brown, 1964). The sample included 543 urban Negro and white children in the first and fifth grades on three general class levels. Appropriate levels of the Lorge-Thorndike Primary Battery were administered to children in each grade. The only statistically significant effect of household structure was obtained when SES was not controlled; in a four-way analysis of variance design with sex, grade, race, and father in home as independent variables, children from father-absent families were significantly lower in mean test score than children with fathers living at home. Due to relatively few lower-class, fatherless families in the white sample, Deutsch and Brown were able to assess the effects of household structure independent of social class only among Negro children. Mean test scores were slightly lower among children from father-absent homes, but the difference was not statistically significant. Even this variation may be due primarily to the general SES categories used in the analysis.

When socioeconomic variations are satisfactorily controlled, available data indicate that household structure has little, if any, effect on the academic performance and test scores of children and adolescents. In a sample of approximately 4,000 adolescents, Wilson (1967) found that household structure had no significant effect on grade average and achievement test scores when the following variables were statistically controlled in a multivariate analysis: supervision by mother, number of objects in the home, reading materials, and parental educational interest and goals were statistically controlled. A similar result was obtained in Coleman and associates' sample of school children (1966, p. 302). Urbanism and education of parents, family size, number of objects in the home, reading materials and parental educational interest and goals were statistically controlled. The only relationship of any size between father-absence and relatively low scores on verbal ability tests occurred among minority group children other than Negro and Oriental Americans. In order to resolve conflicting assertions and data concerning the effects of father-absence on achievement, the following procedures within a longitudinal design seem necessary: adequate control of confounding variables such as socioeconomic status, specification of the time-span and developmental period in which father was absent from the home, and thorough exploration of the intervening variables between household structure and performance outcomes.

2. Class Variations in the Effects of Family Size and Birth Order

A large number of studies have found academic performance, achievement motivation, aspirations, and educational achievement to be inversely correlated with the number of children in the family (Nam & Cowhig, 1962; Clausen, 1966; Schachter, 1963). In the middle and working classes, these variations by family size can be partially explained by related socialization and environmental factors. James Bossard's work (Bossard & Boll, 1956) represents the most fully developed formulation of variations in socialization and relationships by family size. As the number of children increase, Bossard noted the tendency toward a more centralized form of leadership structure expressed in parental dominance, less contact of parents with each child, more directive, one-sided communication from parent to child, and the increasing role of older children in rearing their younger siblings. Simmel's theory of group-size effects on intragroup relations is another provocative source of relevant hypotheses (see Elder & Bowerman, 1963). Family limitation may also reflect higher mobility aspirations among parents for themselves and for their children. Only recently have studies attempted to test these hypotheses on family-size effects. In one study of this kind based on a large sample of adolescents, family size in the middle and working class was found to be related to authoritarian behavior control, frequent use of physical discipline, infrequent explanations of rules and discipline, and low parental aspirations for children (Bowerman & Elder, 1962; Elder, 1962; Elder & Bowerman, 1963). In Douglas's study of British children (1964), mothers in the middle and working classes were more likely to provide inadequate care for their children during infancy and early childhood and to show little interest in the school work of their children (rated by teachers) as the number of children in the family increased. Large families in the working class frequently lived in shabby, crowded, and generally undesirable homes. With poor housing, lack of parental interest in academic progress, and quality of elementary school controlled, the negative effects of a large family on school achievement were reduced but still remained sizable (Douglas, 1964, p. 98). Perhaps the greatest impact of family size occurs during the formative years of cognitive and language development; it is at this point that burdens posed by a large number of children severely limit the mother's contact with the child and verbal training, factors instrumental in developing linguistic skills. Early maternal socialization in a large family is apt to be more devoted to behavior control than to instruction and training.

Family size is more strongly correlated with low school-achievement among children from the working than middle classes. Upper-middle-class children in Douglas's study (1964) decreased noticeably in test scores at the ages of 8 and 11 in families of four or more children, but the decline was pronounced only in the six-child family. A decline in test scores occurred progressively with each additional child in the working class. This differential effect may be partially explained by the correlates of a large family. Douglas found that low parental interest in education, poor housing, and deficient care-taking were more associated with family size in the working than middle class.

Both resulting limitations on economic resources and the early effect of family size on academic performance presumably contribute to the negative effect of a large family on the working-class adolescent's chances for going to college (Elder, 1962). But even in a subgroup of capable high-school students—those reporting at least a "B" average—college plans were negatively related to family size; family-size effects were particularly strong in the working and lower classes.

The meaning of variations in family size for socialization may also vary significantly by parental age at first marriage, the time-span between marriage and birth of the first child, spacing between births, and parental age at completion of family. These factors have not been adequately explored. Two completed families with a similar number of children may differ strikingly in socialization as a result of variations in the above factors. For instance, parents in one family might have married in their late teens, borne their first child within a year after marriage, and had their fourth and last child in the seventh year of their marriage. This contrasts to parents who married in their early 20's, gave birth to their first child five years after marriage, and completed their family of four children twenty years after marriage.

Within families varying in number of children, order of birth and the sex ratio of siblings structures each child's experiences. Freud and Adler, in particular, have argued from clinical data that social experiences associated with birth order have significant personality consequences. Adler (Ansbacher & Ansbacher, 1956) described the pathological effects of status loss which the first-born experiences at the birth of the second child, as expressed in an intensified quest for power and prestige. Partly in response to the long-noted disproportionate number of first-borns among men of eminence, a number of studies during the past ten years have examined the effects of birth order on educational achievement. (For a useful bibliography and selected abstracts of these studies, see SSRC Work Group, 1965.) Although the results of this research are not entirely consistent, it generally shows that the first-born boy and girl achieve higher grades and test scores in school than later-born children, with family size and social class controlled. With controls on family size and demographic variations in births by ordinal position, Schachter (1963) found a disproportionate number of first-borns and only children in samples of undergraduate and graduate students. Explanations offered for the achievement-orientation of the first-born include their exclusive socialization by adults before the birth of siblings, status displacement, sibling rivalry, and higher parental standards for the behavior of the first-born (see Clausen, 1966, and Sampson, 1965). The former condition is likely to foster acute sensitivity to adult cues and an adult orientation toward achievement goals.

Methodological limitations of birth-order studies on achievement include inconsistent measurement of ordinal position and inadequate statistical controls.

There are significant differences between the social environments experienced by only, first-born, middle-, and last-born children, yet some studies have grouped only with first-born children and compared them with all later-born children. Koch's research (1956) shows pronounced effects of spacing and sex composition as well as birth order on the behavior patterns of 5- and 6-year-old children in two-child families, yet few if any studies of birth-order variations in achievement have examined the independent effects of these factors within families varying in size and social class. The family experiences of the youngest child depend partly on the sex of his siblings; the only boy in a family of girls who is also the youngest child is likely to be the object of parental indulgence and favoritism (see Rosenberg, 1965, pp. 107–127). Although some parental and family characteristics may change between the birth of the first and last child, this change is seldom explored as an explanation of differences between these children in personality and performance. For instance, the last-born has older parents at birth than the first-born and family status may have changed over this time span.

Perhaps the most serious deficiency of birth-order research is the lack of studies that attempt to explain the relationship between ordinal position and educational achievement by socialization variables. At present, not a single study has used socialization variables as test factors in explanatory analyses of this type. Thus, despite the methodological weaknesses of available studies on this topic, we know much more about the effects of birth order on educational achievement than about factors which explain them. This deficit is most apparent in studies that have obtained contrasting birth-order effects in different cultural contexts. For instance, the younger child in the working class was higher in *n* Achievement than the eldest child in Rosen's sample of preadolescent boys (1961), while the reverse pattern was found among middle-class boys. In Douglas's sample of British children, the youngest child averaged higher test scores at ages 8 and 11 than the first-born only in three-child, lower-working-class families (1964, p. 167). In a sample of high-school students in the Los Angeles areas, Turner (1964a) found ethnic differences in the prevalence of first-born children. A strikingly disproportionate number of first-born adolescents were found only among Anglo students in the sample, and this difference was most pronounced for boys. As an explanation, he suggests that Negro and Mexican-American families—largely concentrated in the lower class—tend to withdraw their eldest sons from school in order to have them help support the family. Boys from these families are also more likely than other youth to fail in school, but there is little evidence which indicates this to be more probable among first-born males. In any case, such ad hoc explanations are largely based on educated speculation rather than adequate data.

Available studies of birth order variations in socialization are primarily based on middle-class families. These include longitudinal studies by Lasko (1954) and Douglas (1964); Douglas's study includes middle- and working-class families, but findings on birth-order variations in socialization are reported mainly for middle-class parents. Sibling influences are another dimension of socialization which has relevance to birth-order variations, and Koch's series of studies are a valuable source of such information, although her findings are limited to two-child families (Koch, 1956; SSRC Work Group, 1965). In their initial experience as parents, middle-class parents tend to be anxious, uncertain, cautious, and concerned with the performance of their first child, more so than with subsequent children. Changing patterns of birth-order variations in maternal socialization were reported by Lasko (1954) in a longitudinal sample of 46 pairs of first- and second-born children drawn from the Fels sample. The children ranged in age from 15 months to over ten years. Maternal behavior was measured by twenty-one home ratings. From a cross-sectional analysis, Lasko found that mothers were significantly more critical and demanding of the first-born, talked more, and more actively stimulated his verbal development. Mothers were rated higher on protectiveness and "babying" in relation to the second-born. On age trends, she found that the eldest child experienced a pronounced decrease in maternal warmth and "child-centeredness" during the late preschool years. The second-born received less warmth initially than the first-born, but maintained his position from the preschool to the grade-school period. Thus the second-born tended to receive more maternal warmth, "babying," and protectiveness than the first-born in the late preschool period, a time at which the average first-born was encouraged to meet standards of excellence and to do things by himself. However, all birth-order differences evident in the preschool period decreased to insignificance in the grade-school period. This trend suggests that a longitudinal study would be required in order to correlate parental training linked to birth-order with indicators of achievement behavior in grade and secondary school. Nevertheless, Douglas (1964) found pronounced differences during grade school in maternal behavior by birth order; in the middle class, mothers were more likely to visit their eldest child's school, to show interest in his academic progress (as rated by teachers), and to be anxious that he obtain a place in grammar school and remain there beyond the age of sixteen (1964, p. 89).

The relatively stronger orientation toward adults than toward peers which studies have reported for first-borns (McArthur, 1956) may be associated with unusual sensitivity to adult cues and dependence on rewards offered by teachers, which in turn enhances their performance in school. Koch suggests that this responsiveness is a reflection of status-sensitivity resulting from displacement in the family (1956). In a sample of five- and six-year-old children in two-child families, she found that first-borns were higher in curiosity and were more inclined than younger siblings to associate with adults who encouraged their questions and stimulated their interests. As a result, one might expect first-borns to be more appreciated by teachers than children in other ordinal positions. The greater prevalence of interpersonal difficulties in relations with peers among first- than later-born children reported by two studies (Schachter, 1963; Douglas, 1964) could be both a consequence and a reflection of their predominant orientation toward adults and achievement.

Although sibling competition and influence have not been directly related to educational achievement, Koch (1956) suggests that the status-sensitivity of the first-born is reinforced by sex rivalry; first-borns in mixed-sex pairs had a greater number of interests and showed greater enthusiasm than those in same-sex pairs. In his sample of British children, Douglas (1964) offers sibling competition as a possible explanation for the relatively higher academic achievement of first-borns than of only children. First-borns did better on secondary school examinations and on placement in grammar school than would be expected according to their measured ability, whereas no discrepancy of this kind was obtained among only children. Measures of sibling competition and sex composition were not included in the analysis.

3. Socioeconomic Contexts.

Outside the family, socioeconomic properties of the adolescent's neighborhood, school, and peers define accessible and approved behavior models, interpersonal networks, normative climates varying in standards of excellence and expectations, and both cultural and economic resources. In numerous studies (see Sewell & Armer, 1966a), aspects of the nonfamilial environment, though related to family status, appear to have a significant independent effect on student achievement and goals. Two assumptions in particular are indicated in this research; the effects of neighborhood, school, and peers are *similar, or vary* across subgroups of adolescents differing in personal and family characteristics. Studies based at least implicitly on the first perspective—especially common in psychological research—assume that the main effect of independent variables is generally similar in different subgroups and that statistical interaction between two or more variables is minimal. For example, it might be assumed that the school environment has the same influence on the performance of boys and girls, Negro and white youth, and that the relative effects of family background and IQ on college attendance are comparable among students from upper-, middle-, and working-class schools. If these conditions do not apply—that is, if there is considerable variation in factor effects and interaction across subgroups—a multiple regression analysis may result in highly misleading findings. In this case, specification of the effect in the various subgroups would be required to adequately represent the data. Lavin concludes that the disappointing results on personality factors as predictors of academic performance are due to the tendency for most studies to conceive of the student as if "he were operating in a social vacuum. It might be, however, that personality characteristics are useful in predicting academic performance only when the social setting in which that performance takes place is conceptualized and used as a significant variable" (Lavin, 1965, p. 111).

1. *The school environment.* A controversial study by Sewell and Armer (1966a) illustrates how failure to assess fully the effects of independent variables in specific subgroups when data show the need for such analysis results in misleading conclusions. This study examined the influence of sex, ability, family social-class, and the socioeconomic status of neighborhoods on the college aspirations of seniors in 20 high schools located in Milwaukee County. The neighborhoods were classified according to socioeconomic status by the proportion of white-collar workers residing in the school district. As a major hypothesis, Sewell and Armer proposed that "the socioeconomic status of the high-school district—since it presumably reflects the shared norms and aspirations of its members—would have an important effect on the educational aspirations of its youth over and above that of family socioeconomic status" (1966a, p. 708). Controlling for the effects of IQ, sex, and family SES in a multiple regression analysis, neighborhood status was found to account for less than 2 per cent of the variance in college aspirations. The effects of ability and family status were most significant, but all factors explained only 25 per cent of the variance in college aspirations. Some critics have

questioned the use of IQ as a control rather than an outcome factor (Sewell & Armer, 1966b), but a more serious weakness of this type of analysis is that it obscures the substantial interaction variations across subgroups. These variations are clearly shown in cross-tabular analyses and are briefly described by the authors. For instance, school and family background effects were appreciably stronger on the college aspirations of girls than of boys and were particularly significant among students who are normally borderline prospects for college—the bright student from an upper-working class family and the low-ability youth from a wealthy family. This study, as well as others, clearly indicates the need for analyses sensitive to potential subgroup variations in the effects of school environments and individual properties on student achievement.

One of the weaknesses of most studies on the contextual effects of school environment is that they have relied upon very limited information concerning the educational setting and family environment. As a measure of educational climate or environment, most have used simply the proportion of middle- or working-class students in the school. With the exception of Coleman's study (1966) and Project Talent, none has used school facilities, curriculum, and teacher characteristics to construct a typology of the educational quality of the school. There is a strong relationship between the socioeconomic characteristics of the student body and both the quality of teachers and facilities (see Sexton, 1961), but there is value in obtaining separate measures of each dimension. Schools can improve the quality of their teachers but have little control over the initial quality of their students. The value of more detailed information on the composition and structure of school environments is shown in Coleman's assessment of the relative effects of school facilities and curriculum, teacher characteristics, and student-body characteristics (1966). School facilities and curriculum included such items as volumes per student in the library, science laboratory facilities, and the presence of an accelerated curriculum; teacher characteristics included the average educational attainment of teachers' families, average years of teaching experience, average score on a self-administered vocabulary test, and preference for teaching middle-class students; and indicators of student-body quality included the proportion of families owning encyclopedias, attendance, proportion of students planning to attend college, and teacher perception of student-body quality. With background factors controlled in a multiple regression analysis, quality of the student body accounted for the greatest proportion of the variance in verbal ability scores of ninth- and twelfth-grade students, and the effects of teacher quality were substantially greater than the influence of school facilities and curriculum. The overall effect of differences between schools on student achievement was much less than the influence of variations within the student body of each school. More than 70 per cent of the variation in student achievement was due to within school conditions.

Despite countless studies on schools, little attention has been given to the process by which new students are socialized into the system by teachers and peers, on how they learn the student role, official and unofficial standards, and strategies for coping with particular teachers. How do orientations toward adults—teachers and parents—and peers change as students move from the first to the last years of junior or senior high school? Although Coleman did not thoroughly analyze grade variations in student values and commitments in his study of schools in the Chicago area, some data presented in his monograph suggest that the influence of students' value climates is greatest in the middle years of high school (1961). From an observational learning and reference-group perspective, one might expect new students to be primarily oriented toward parental models, with a change in orientation toward student exemplars and emersion in youth culture most evident in the middle years, followed by a gradual upswing in the salience of adult models, especially parents and teachers, as students enter the last grade of high school and anticipate the realities of future lines of action. Uncertainties in the transition from high school to future roles would tend to increase the value of guidance from adults who have passed through the same status sequence which youth expect to follow.

Another deficiency of research on school effects is failure to statistically control variations in the inital quality of students. Such information would necessitate measurement of ability on a cohort of children before or soon after they enter grade, junior, and senior high-school in a longitudinal study. There is only one study of this type, and we shall describe it shortly (Wilson, 1967). The value of studies which have analyzed the effects of the high-school environment in samples of seniors (Turner, 1964a; Sewell & Armer, 1966a) is significantly reduced by the fact that an important aspect of the effect—in the form of dropouts—was excluded from the analysis.

Reliance on socioeconomic status as the sole index of family environment in research on school effects has several important implications. These studies have found that working- and middle-class youth are more likely to have college aspirations if they attend a middle- rather than a working-class school (Wilson, 1959; Sewell & Armer, 1966a). But one does not know how much of this effect is due to school environment and how much to the characteristics of families differing from neighborhood families in social class. From family data on residential and occupational histories, mobility aspirations, and socialization practices, one could determine whether working-class parents who send their adolescents to middle-class schools are upwardly mobile in status and aspirations or whether middle-class parents with children in working-class schools are downwardly mobile through loss of job or income. Since a middle-class father with a daughter or son in high school should be nearing his peak earning capacity, there is reason to suspect that middle-class parents with adolescents in a working-class school are atypical in important respects.

2. *Student vulnerability to the school environment.* Earlier we noted that social influences on achievement behavior would depend on the degree to which such behavior is externally, rather than internally, patterned. An external orientation is indicated by agreement with the statement that "good luck is more important than hard work for success." In the chapter section on moral development, erratic and unresponsive environments, particularly common in lower- and working-class families, were considered as possible explanations for the greater prevalence of external orientations among youth from these social classes than from the middle class. These conditions and racial discrimination also produce "chance" environments for many Negro youth. In their nation-wide study, Coleman and associates found that Negro youth were much less likely to feel that they could control their environment than white adolescents (1966, p. 321). In a small sample of sixth- and eighth-grade students, Negro children were significantly more "external" on a projective measure of the internal-external variable than white children with social class and IQ controlled (Battle & Rotter, 1963). Within race and IQ subgroups, middle-class children were higher than working-class students on "internality." Although no study has directly assessed school influence on students who vary on the internal-external dimension, several studies have compared the effects of school environment on subgroups of students defined by social class and race.

Hilde Himmelweit (1966) followed up approximately 600 boys at ages 23–24 who were originally selected for a cross-sectional study from the third forms of five grammar and four secondary modern schools in London. The academic progress and educational attainment of boys from the working-class, in comparison to their middle-class counterparts, were more strongly influenced by aspects of the school environment. Working-class boys tended to stay in school if they experienced significant academic success and felt accepted; the simple lack of failure was of little consequence in their decision to stay in or leave school. By contrast, the middle-class boy was likely to remain in school regardless of the degree of academic success experienced and left only when difficulties and failure in school, intensified by problems at home, were extreme and overwhelming. Both placement in a stream (similar to a track in American schools) and academic evaluations by teachers tended to have a stronger effect on the decision to leave school among working- than middle-class boys. Himmelweit provides several striking illustrations of this result. In an A stream of one school, working-class boys not evaluated by teachers as highly industrious left school at a significantly earlier age than middle-class boys comparable in evaluative status. Over 90 per cent of the students in this stream who remained in school were either "industrious" working-class boys or middle-class boys. On the other hand, 93 per cent of the working-class boys who were placed in the C stream left early, and teacher evaluations had little, if any, effect on their decision. Similar class differences are reported by Douvan in an experimental study (1956). She found *n* Achievement scores to be significantly higher among middle- than working-class students after they were made to fail in an achievement situation when no material reward was provided for the best performance. When a ten-dollar reward was promised, students from both social classes were just as high in *n* Achievement after failure.

Teacher characteristics and student body quality in Coleman's study accounted for a significantly larger portion of the variance in verbal achievement among Negro than among white adolescents with family background statistically controlled (1966, pp. 304–305). School influence was particularly striking among Negro youth in the South, a region where disadvantaged family environments are especially prevalent. Another test of the differential effects of school environment on the academic achievement of Negro and white students is provided in a noteworthy longitudinal analysis by Alan Wilson of both neighborhood and school influences (Wilson, 1967). The secondary school population in an urban county was stratified by race, sex, school, and grade level, and random samples were drawn from each stratum. The approximately 4,000 students in the total sample completed a detailed questionnaire. Through an exhaustive search of school records, Wilson was able to obtain an average measure of the racial and class composition of neighborhood and school in four periods: Primary Grades, 1–3; Intermediate Grades, 4–6; Junior High, 7–9; and Senior High, 10–12. In all twelve grades, the residence of each student was located in enumeration districts. The percentage of families which were Negro and lower-class in occupational status were aggregated across each three-year period for students living in the enumeration district or in contiguous districts not separated by major highways or other physical barriers. Classification of the school environment according to racial and class composition followed a similar procedure on data aggregation for percentage Negro and lower class in each of the four periods. Though many students changed residence and schools within each of the three-year periods, the aggregate measures provided an average index of their school and neighborhood environment defined by racial and class composition. The racial and class compositions of elementary schools were found to be highly related ($r = .77$).

The longitudinal design enabled Wilson to specify the time-order of variables in a causal model: family socialization and genetic factors as antecedent to measured ability in the Primary Grades, and this factor as antecedent to school achievement in the higher grades. Neighborhood was viewed as influencing both Primary Grade ability and subsequent school achievement. In order to assess the effects of neighborhood and school environments independent of variations in student ability upon entrance into school, Primary Grade ability measured by the California Mental Aptitude test was statistically controlled throughout the analysis. Supervision by mother, number of objects in the home, family size, and social class were employed as indicators of the family environment.

Neighborhood composition did not have a significant independent influence on achievement in the four time periods with the social-class composition of the school, family environment, and mental ability controlled. The primary independent effect of the school environment stemmed from its social-class rather than racial composition. Although the two factors were highly related, neither neighborhood environment nor the racial composition of the school made any significant difference in the achievement of students who attended schools similar in socioeconomic status. Coleman and associates obtained a similar finding (1966, p. 307); the achievement of minority group students was highly correlated with the proportion of white students in their schools, but this relationship was due largely, if not entirely, to the educational goals and background of the student body.

In Wilson's study, school status in the Intermediate Grades most strongly influenced student achievement, particularly on verbal reasoning scores in the eighth grade. With family environment and mental ability in the Primary Grades controlled, status of the Intermediate School had twice the effect of school status in the Primary and Junior High periods. As in Coleman's study, Wilson found the performance of Negro students to be more strongly affected by school environment than the achievement of white students. Allowing for the influence of family background and mental ability in the primary grades, the social-class composition of the intermediate school environment had a significantly stronger effect on the eighth-grade verbal reasoning scores of Negro than of white students. Even in a subgroup of junior high students who came from a predominantly lower-class intermediate school, the adverse consequences of this background were substantially greater on the test performance of Negro than of white students, with family background and mental ability controlled.

These data suggest that discontinuities in social and academic demands between the neighborhood elementary school and junior high school are greater than in any other educational transition between the first and twelfth grades (in a 6-3-3 system). Furthermore, due to residential segregation by race and socioeconomic status, the discontinuity between a low quality elementary school and the higher educational requirements of junior high school is experienced most frequently by children who are least equipped to survive the more stringent demands—those from lower-class Negro families. For the average Negro child in Wilson's study (1967), the percentage of Negro and lower-status classmates declined appreciably as he moved from grade school to senior high. For the average white child who started school in a higher quality school, each successive level of education increased the proportion of Negro and lower-status classmates. As a result, the Negro child began his education in a school environment which failed to prepare him for the more rigorous demands of junior high, while the reverse condition was generally experienced by white students.

VI. Vocational Development

It is appropriate to conclude our coverage of adolescent socialization and development with vocational behavior, since the work-role represents a primary source of identity in adult society. Despite an imposing number of studies on factors associated with the occupational choice of adolescents, there is currently a surprising dearth of information on the process whereby children and adolescents become oriented toward particular prestige levels and occupations. In addition, there is little consensus on the kinds of behavior which should be included within the vocational domain.

Variations in definition and measurement range from specific elements of occupational choice to comprehensive formulations of vocational development which include all behavior relevant to work (see Borow, 1966). Sociologists have tended to focus upon occupational choice among adolescents, including preferences for occupations and qualities of work, commitment to occupational goals, and expected achievements. A developmental analysis might include the following types of behavior: concepts of tasks, occupations, and self; vocational knowledge and values; performance on tasks; judgment and decision-making skills; and occupational choice, including the prestige level of the choice, specific characteristics of the preferred occupation, and goal-orientation. Although a primary focus on occupational choice excludes much that is relevant to vocational development and has been criticized in this respect, there is also a danger of diffuseness in a formulation that encompasses a broad spectrum of behavior.

In this chapter section, a general developmental perspective is employed, with particular emphasis on the acquisition and modification of occupational concepts, values and goals as influenced by cognitive abilities, personality, and environmental factors. Since the development of status-goals was included within the context of achievement, this subject receives little attention in this section.

Vocational behavior viewed as a consequence of person-environment interactions related to work is evident in the writings of at least two psychologists in the vocational field (Super, 1963a; Holland, 1966) and is a relatively common theme in the research of sociologists (Lazarsfeld, 1931; Sewell & Orenstein, 1965). However, psychologists generally have emphasized personality as a determinant of vocational choice, while sociologists have stressed the effects of environmental factors. For example, vocational choice is viewed as an "expression of personality" by Holland (1966) and as an act of implementing the self-concept by Super (Super & Overstreet, 1960). On the other hand, Paul Lazarsfeld proposed on the basis of the vocational behavior of pre-Hitler Austrian and German youth that "the nature of occupational choice is not determined primarily as an individual decision, but rather is a result of external influences. For the occupational impressions offered by daily life are proportional to the actual occupational distribution" (cited in Lipset & Bendix, 1959, p. 221). Research on the occupational choice of youth supports each of these interpretations under certain conditions. Occupational choice as primarily an expression of personality and decision making implies freedom to choose and the availability of occupational alternatives. For many lower-class and Negro boys these alternatives do not exist or are severely restricted, and the same is generally true for youth in totalitarian and traditional societies. On the other hand, unfavorable environmental influences would be least among capable, upper-middle-class youth in the United States who have a variety of attractive occupational options and must choose among them. A large share of the research on vocational choice conducted by psychologists in the United States has focused on white, middle- and upper-middle-class boys. Up to the mid-50's, much of this research was devoid of theory and isolated from the mainstream of developments in personality and developmental psychology. Although atheoretical studies are still a prominent feature of this research literature, approximations of a developmental theory have been formulated by Ginzberg, Super, and Tiedeman (Holland, 1964).

The interaction of personal and environmental properties in patterning vocational behavior is a central theme in Holland's theory of vocational choice (1966). From a background of experience as a vocational counselor, a review of the research literature in vocational psychology, and an analysis of occupational titles, Holland constructed a theory of vocational choice which includes six types of personality—Realistic, Intellectual, Social, Conventional, Enterprising, and Artistic—and a similar typology of environments defined by characteristics that parallel the six personality types. In research on samples of National Merit Scholars, Holland has used a variety of techniques to measure the personality types, including his Vocational Preference Inventory which contains sets of occupational titles, and scales from the Strong Vocational Interest inventory. The Environmental Assessment Technique was constructed to assess the "psychologically important features of the environment" by measuring the vocational characteristics of its population, i.e., preferences and field of training. This device has been used primarily to measure college environments. The individual's "pattern of personal orientations" is defined by his scores on the six personality types, and a similar type of profile analysis has been used to characterize the dominant feature of environments.

Holland hypothesized that persons attempt to select environments which are consonant with their modal orientation; a number of studies have found that college students are more apt to remain in a field of study when personal and environmental characteristics are similar (Holland, 1966, p. 74). Holland also proposed the hypothesis that stability of vocational behavior would be correlated with the degree of integration (consistency) represented by the individual's pattern of orientations. Internal conflict and uncertainty associated with personal inconsistency are likely to result in vulnerability to external influences. For example, the Realistic-Social orientation includes a wide range of opposing tendencies such as "an orientation toward things versus an orientation toward people, masculinity versus femininity, poor interpersonal skills versus verbal skills" (Holland, 1966, p. 44). In a sample of college students, personal consistency was found to be related to persistence in a major field over a four-year period (1966, p. 75). Holland has proposed a number of other hypotheses on the effects of person-environment interactions in patterning vocational behavior and personality which are suggestive for future research.

Age-Related Patterns of Vocational Behavior

During the preadult years, the acquisition of three concepts progressively narrows vocational alternatives and orientations: a sex-role concept influenced by cognitive maturation and socialization in early childhood; the child's concept of self as a person with particular values, abilities, reference-group ties, and goals; and the adolescent's concept of future possibilities in the context of family status and perceived self-characteristics. Borow (1966) has reviewed a number of studies on children and adolescents which suggest that this narrowing process occurs through aversive learning in which undesirable activities and occupations are rejected. The evolving self-concept, perceived opportunities, ability, and cognitive maturation appear to structure the pace and form of occupational foreclosure. In a sample of approximately 600 elementary- and secondary-school students, Nelson found acceptance of all 16 occupations presented in a list most common among children who were young, low in ability, and low in socioeconomic status (cited in Borow, 1966, p. 414).

During the grade-school years, sex-role concepts and preferences presumably structure and reflect conceptions of unattractive and appealing vocational activities, although little substantial research has examined the relation between sex-role and vocational development during these years. Tests used to measure masculinity and femininity in children are based on activity and interest preferences that are relevant to subsequent vocational roles and tasks. In a theory of the development of sex-role concepts and attitudes, Kohlberg has proposed that "cognitive learning of sex-role concepts leads to the development of new values and attitudes ..." (1966b, p. 111). The content learned is assumed to be consistent with the child's image of his sex-identity: objects unlike self are rejected and those like self accepted. Boys become oriented toward sex-appropriate images that have vocational significance such as power, competition, and strength, while girls select the feminine qualities of attractiveness, interpersonal skills, goodness, and social approval. Attachment to like-sex parents reinforces sex-appropriate learning and structures attitudes toward tasks in the home and community. The vocational thinking of the grade-school child is restricted by the limitations of concrete operations; vocational preferences are not related to personal resources or to future opportunities (E. Ginzberg, S. Ginzberg, Axelrod, & Herma, 1951). In these years, selection of an occupation is assumed to be sufficient for entering that position.

Data from a longitudinal study by Tyler (1964) suggest that crystallization of vocational preferences in adolescence develops out of sex-role concepts and interests acquired in early childhood. Data were collected on the abilities, interests, and personal-social attributes of 145 children in four grades: 1, 4, 8, and 12. The subjects were in the first grade in 1946. From profile patterns on the Strong Vocational Interest Inventory obtained during the twelfth grade, she selected for comparison purposes two groups of boys, defined by Scientist and Nonscientist profiles, and two groups of girls with clearly differentiated Career and Noncareer interests. The groups did not differ on father's occupational status. The Scientist boys and Career girls achieved slightly higher scores than their comparison groups on ability tests in secondary school but the difference was not statistically significant. In grades 1 and 4, Scientist boys made more masculine choices on interest tests, but did not differ in vocational interests from the Nonscientist group. These differences were reversed in adolescence; in the eighth and twelfth grades, boys with Scientist interests differed significantly from the Nonscientists in vocational profile but did not differ on Masculine-Feminine measures. Similarly the earliest difference between the two groups of girls occurred on sex-typed interests; in grade 1 the Career girls made more masculine choices than Noncareer girls, but did not differ in vocational interests. In adolescence, pronounced differences between the groups occurred only on vocational interests. Distinct vocational patterns in boys and girls appeared for the first time in the eighth grade, a time when youth become increasingly aware of future requirements and opportunities, and begin to appraise themselves within this context. Growth in formal thinking during these years is probably a major determinant of future-oriented vocational behavior. In addition, an attractive future is likely to encourage vocational planning and motivate behavior that has relevance for subsequent goal-attainment; a pessimistic view, on the other hand, may lead to escapist, aggressive, or apathetic behavior.

Two theories have been instrumental in stimulating research on age-related aspects of vocational behavior during adolescence; Ginzberg's formulation of age-related changes in conceptions of self within the context of vocational decisions and goals (E. Ginzberg, S. Ginzberg, Axelrod, & Herma, 1951); and Super's self-concept theory (1963a). These formulations are only approximations to a theory of vocational development and have been developed as well as tested primarily on samples of males limited in both size and representativeness. Super's research and the Harvard Studies in Career Development (Tiedeman, O'Hara, & Baruch, 1963) represent the most intensive programs of research on vocational development during adolescence. A review of major programs of psychological research on vocational behavior is provided by Holland (1964).

Currently the most detailed psychological formulation of vocational development from childhood into the adult years is provided by Donald Super's self-concept theory. Super's stage-analytic, developmental perspective can be traced to Charlotte Bühler's original work on the course and life periods of human development (1933) and to Harold Carter's research on the vocational interests of boys in the Oakland Growth Study at the Institute of Human Development (1944). Vocational behavior, defined as "any interaction between the individual and his environment which is related to work" (Super & Overstreet, 1960), is conceptualized as becoming increasingly more complex, differentiated, and reality-oriented during adolescence through successive transactions between personal attributes of vocational relevance, particularly aspects of the self-concept, and environmental conditions. Exploration and establishment are the major stages of vocational development in adolescence and early adulthood. The exploratory stage includes three phases of vocational development in adolescence: the tentative phase in which vocational decision-making and interests are highly diffuse and unrealistic, the transition phase, and the trial phase characterized by minimal commitment. The establishment stage, generally spanning late adolescence and early adulthood, includes two phases: trial with commitment and stable advancement. Individuals in each stage are confronted by a sequence of developmental tasks. In the exploratory stage, the adolescent is involved in crystallizing, specifying, and implementing a vocational preference; in the establishment stage, during the 20's and early 30's, tasks include stabilization of self in a vocation, consolidation of status, and occupational advancement.

Vocational development represents growth, differentiation, and integration of vocationally relevant self-concepts, and thus measurement involves describing and defining the vocational self-concept on a variety of dimensions such as self-esteem, clarity, abstraction, refinement, certainty, stability, and realism (Super, 1963a). Factors relevant to vocational development include the internal differentiation and consistency of the self-concept, the variety, complexity, and number of self-characteristics, openness to new information and to subsequent modification of the self-image, and the relative prepotency of the self-concepts.

Factors associated with vocational maturity have been explored by Super and Overstreet in a small sample of ninth-grade boys (1960).[6] Vocational maturity in these boys was indicated by how they were thinking about goals and what they were doing about them; it did not include "having consistent or realistic vocational preferences, having clear-cut interests or work values, or having had independent work experience. It is not, at this stage, characterized by preferences which are consistent with each other or with the realities of the self or of the occupational world, by any initial achievement of a place for oneself in the working world" (1960, p. 63). Even by these criteria of vocational maturity, Super and Overstreet found many of the ninth-grade boys in their study to be immature. These boys, many of whom were relatively low in intelligence, SES, and achievement, tended to know very little about the choices they would be called upon to make, were not aware of the implications of these

[6] Reprinted with permission of the publisher from Donald E. Super and Phoebe L. Overstreet, *The Vocational Maturity of Ninth-Grade Boys* (New York: Teachers College Press, 1960). © 1960 Teachers College, Columbia University.

choices for later educational and occupational choices, and did not recognize factors and conditions that should be considered in decision making.

A follow-up of Project Talent youth one year after high school supports Super's findings on the vocational development of ninth-grade boys; only 17 and 26 per cent of boys and girls in the ninth grade in 1960 held the same occupational plan one year after high-school graduation (Project Talent, 1966). Instability varied substantially across occupational categories; the most stable choices were occupations in the professions, journalism, and art, and in fields that require college and postgraduate study. The implications of vocational instability would depend, however, on the proportion of changes within the same general occupational field or between neighboring fields. The personal consequences of these variations would be less than the effects of movement between fields completely dissimilar in required academic records and skills. No data were presented on types of change. An ability profile based on a series of aptitude tests in high school proved to be a more accurate predictor of adolescent occupational plans after graduation than either earlier plans or measures of vocational interests. It is probable that aptitude profiles are more stable in adolescence than interests or plans, while the latter are more indicative of developmental level in vocational behavior.

Two extreme types of vocational patterns have substantially different psychological and vocational implications: *premature vocational choice* and a *lack of vocational commitment.* Vocational choice and commitment might be premature if they are made without self-appraisals, experience, and learning gained from exploration and trial. In some cases, early formation of a vocational identity may precede the crystallization of other identities and thus require considerable adjustment in subsequent years. Since the relation between self-estimated and tested aptitudes tends to increase markedly over the high-school years, vocational choice early in high school is likely to be uninformed by accurate self-appraisals (O'Hara & Tiedeman, 1959). The necessity of coming to terms with an occupational choice incompatible with developing interests and abilities is an experience relatively common to college freshmen.

The other extreme in vocational development is manifested by persons who are young adults by legal criteria but are confused, dilatory, and indecisive in their vocational behavior. Indecision and lack of direction in vocational behavior among college and university students are a potential source of personal instability and scholastic failure. Beardslee and O'Dowd observe that students who feel uncertain and confused about their vocational future "frequently defend themselves against a sense of self-diffusion by devices that are of little value to the institution or to the preparation of the students for future activities. One common contemporary solution is the development of a 'beatnik' pattern; another consists of shifting from one career goal to another in search of some sense of security. The students often envied by those who are unable to settle on an identity are the premedical students. These men have a goal reached by a series of graded steps that are visible to all from the very beginning of college" (1962, p. 603). The professional student role is another alternative to vocational choice and commitment for students with independent wealth or adequate financial support from other sources. For students who have made a choice regarding graduate education, a latent function of abundant fellowships and other types of support has been to encourage graduate students to prolong their predoctoral education in lieu of assuming the responsibilities of the professional role. Vocational uncertainty and undue prolongation of status as a student may be viewed as evidence of inadequate vocational progress.

Occupational Goals and Values: The Effects of Social Structure and Socialization

The socialization of occupational goals and work-values has received little attention from sociologists and psychologists in comparison to the amount of research on personality and social structure effects. There is a large and growing sociological literature on variations in occupational goals and ambition by social class, race, residence, and religion (see Sewell & Orenstein, 1965). By contrast, little is known about the process of occupational socialization in the family and school. Relatively unexplored problems include the source and transmission of work values and habits, the vocational significance of task experiences in the home, school, and community, and the process by which parental and other work models acquire negative and positive valence to children. In what follows, three types of influences on the formation of occupational choice are examined: community structure, family social class, and work values transmitted within the family. Other environmental influences of relevance to the process of occupational socialization were discussed in previous chapter sections; these include the educative influence of the home and school, achievement training, and the behavior models as well as achievement orientations presented by parents, teachers, and peers.

1. *Social class and occupational choice.* In an analysis of the occupational choices of Austrian and German adolescents, Paul Lazarsfeld found that "local variations in occupational choice tended to correspond with variations in the economic structure" (cited in Lipset & Bendix, 1959, p. 221). The larger the proportion of persons employed in a particular kind of job in a city, the larger the proportion of 14-year-old youth who desired to go into that occupation. Lipset and Bendix have suggested that variations in the occupational structure and the resulting impressions of job opportunities most strongly influence the occupational goals of working-class youth (1959, p. 222). They point out that middle-class parents, even in a context of highly restricted job opportunities, would be more able than the working-class family to develop broad vocational interests, an awareness of opportunities beyond the local community, and high aspirations in sons through their greater cultural and economic resources. On this point, Lazarsfeld observes that "the socially disadvantaged adolescent has seen less, read less, heard about less, and has experienced less variety in his environment in general, and is simply aware of fewer opportunities than the socially privileged young person" (cited in Lipset & Bendix, 1959, p. 199). As a result of their limited environment and outlook, low SES boys are inclined to take "'the only job they know about' at the time they enter the labor market" (Lipset & Bendix, 1960, p. 198). The interplay of these class-linked factors is evident among college students as well. A study of occupational values and choice among Cornell undergraduates found that the sons of high-income fathers had an accumulation of advantages: "they receive the best early training, go to the outstanding colleges, and go on for professional training (if necessary); when they go to work, they can either enter flourishing businesses owned by their fathers, or they can enter large organizations in which their fathers are on the managerial level, or their families have contacts which make coveted jobs available to them, or they have family capital or credit to engage in their own ventures" (Rosenberg, 1957, p. 57).

Several studies have used data on community size to infer variations in occupational structure and assessed the effects of the former variable on occupational aspirations (see Sewell & Orenstein, 1965). These studies do not offer a precise test of the "class-effect" hypothesis, since they have not obtained data on the actual and perceived distribution of specific occupations and job opportunities.

In a sample of senior boys drawn from public as well as private schools in Wisconsin during 1957, Sewell and Orenstein analyzed the influence of community size, IQ, and socioeconomic status on occupational aspirations (1965, data on girls were also included but are not reported here). Boys planning to farm were deleted from the analysis. Residence included five categories: farm, village, small city, medium city, and large city. High aspirations (professional or managerial) were significantly related to community size with social class and IQ statistically controlled. However, results on social class variations did not support the Lipset-Bendix hypothesis. Social class and IQ were strongly related to high aspirations, with the greatest variation by community size found among low IQ and high SES boys. The data suggest that strong parental and school support for high aspirations is more strongly associated with ability level in small than in large communities characterized by a complex division of labor. In farming areas or small villages, low-ability boys on all class levels resembled each other in having relatively low occupational aspirations (between 10 and 21 per cent planned on professional or managerial jobs). On the other hand, family social class in large communities made a sizable difference in the occupational goals of low-ability boys; in this group, 19 per cent from low-status homes reported high occupational aspirations compared to 53 per cent of the boys high in SES. In the limited environment of a small rural community, bright boys were more likely than boys with low ability to have high aspirations in low, middle, and high SES groups, and the discrepancy increased by class level. These findings suggest that level of general ability significantly determines how strongly a boy will be influenced by the attractions and limitations of his environment. The reading experiences, interests, and broad horizons of a bright boy, coupled with an ability and desire to assert personal interests, even in the face of parental opposition, may partially account for this result. In addition, ability grouping in secondary school and the attention of guidance counselors as well as teachers would tend to channel this type of boy toward occupations appropriate to his talents whether available in the community or not. The vulnerability of low-ability and -status boys to the limitations of their immediate environment is illustrated by a report on Negro and white dropouts in Syracuse, New York (Miller & Harrison, 1964). One Negro boy who was asked for his idea of a good job answered, "wash dishin' machine" (dishwasher). When asked why, he replied, "because it's what I figure I could get" (pp. 476–477).

2. *Family patterns and work values.* Cultural patterns, parental personalities, family relationships and socialization, the kinship system, and the work-setting of father are potential sources of the work values transmitted to children within the family. A recent cross-national study of the relation between the characteristics of father's work and parental values among American and Italian parents of fifth-grade children is suggestive of the kind of research needed in the area of vocational socialization (Pearlin & Kohn, 1966). Three prominent features of father's occupational experience were measured: closeness of supervision, autonomy on the job, and the kind of work, indicated by whether the job involved working primarily with people, things, or ideas. As noted earlier in the chapter, these variables were significantly related to parental preference for qualities desired in children.

Kinnane and Pable (1962) found the work-value orientations of 121 high-school boys to be strongly related to the social and cultural environment of their home. Family background was measured by five relatively independent scales drawn from a Biographical Inventory: cultural stimulation, family cohesiveness, social mobility, adolescent independence, and materialistic emphasis.

These scales were correlated with six work-value scales: security-economic-material, social-artistic, work conditions and associates, heuristic-creative, achievement-prestige, and independence. Cultural stimulation—highly correlated with social class—was most strongly related to social-artistic and heuristic-creative work values. Boys frequently exposed to cultural and scientific experiences at home tended to prefer work that offered opportunities to develop their own scientific and creative ideas. In contrast, a materialistic emphasis in the home was most strongly associated with preferences for security, economic, and material aspects of the job. Other intercorrelations were relatively low.

Anne Roe's theory of the development of vocational orientations emphasizes the quality of the parent-child relationship as a potential source of occupational values or interests (Roe & Siegelman, 1964). A primary thesis is that "one of the earliest and greatest differentiations in interest develops from the degree to which attention is focused on persons and that this difference in focus of attention develops very early in life and primarily as a result of early experiences" (Roe & Siegelman, 1964, p. 4). Since vocational development is considered a lifelong process, such interests are viewed as undergoing further differentiation throughout the life cycle. The person-oriented individual may be submissive, or power-oriented, succorant or nurturant. "The non-person-oriented individual may be oriented toward living things other than persons, toward ideas" (Roe & Siegelman, 1964, p. 4). Persons with loving, demanding, and protecting parents were hypothesized as likely to acquire a person-orientation, and persons with rejecting, casual, and neglecting parents, non-person-orientations of various sorts. Studies in which these aspects of parental behavior have been correlated with classifications of interests or occupations according to the person and nonperson dimensions have generally not supported these hypotheses. The six category model of parental behavior appears to be inadequate to account for the complexity of parent-child interaction, and the same conclusion applies to the dichotomy between orientations toward and away from persons. Reliance on retrospective reports of parental attitudes and family experiences is also a serious weakness in much of this research.

The complexity of family influence is suggested by the fact that men from stressful families may prefer occupations which offer interpersonal satisfactions they were deprived of in childhood and adolescence (Roe & Siegelman, 1964). Roe and Siegelman offer the suggestive hypothesis, partially supported by their data, that the farther an occupational choice is from sex-appropriate patterns, the greater the likelihood that there have been specific pressures in childhood and adolescence, especially in the family of origin, which have influenced the choice. This seems to apply to male social workers and female engineers in their samples. For these individuals, deficient family relations resulted in a drive to secure experiences missing in their lives, "in the case of the men social workers, love and understanding; in the case of the women engineers, a lost father" (Roe & Siegelman, 1964, p. 67).

Education of Women, Heterosexual Experiences, and Marriage

The vocational socialization and development of most American girls are in some respects more complex and less programmatic than among boys, in that their adult status and life style is generally determined by whom they marry rather than by their own personal achievements. Although most girls who intend to marry will work at some point in their adult lives, such employment is usually more an optional choice than a necessity. In a sample of high-school senior girls, Turner found that only four per cent planned on a life-time career, 48 per cent intended to become a homemaker, and a similar proportion wanted to combine both homemaking and a career (1964b). The career-oriented girls tended to stress their own educational goals more than material ambition, while the reverse set of preferences was found among girls with primary interests in homemaking. Thus, differentiation between heterosexual and occupational experiences in adolescence is probably greatest among girls who intend to go to college and have career interests, and least in the lives of noncollege girls oriented toward marriage.

The educational status and orientation of girls are highly correlated with the character of their dating, courtship, and marriage patterns. Age at termination of formal schooling is closely associated with age at first marriage. In the fall of 1962, a U.S. Census survey found that two-fifths of the girls 18 and 19 years old who were not in school were married and living with spouse compared to less than two per cent of the girls enrolled full-time in college. Girls who perform poorly in their classwork and are dissatisfied with school are more likely than other girls to date frequently and to be adult-oriented (Stinchcombe, 1964). Unsatisfactory experiences in school could reinforce involvement in heterosexual relations and represent a consequence of such involvement. On the college level, girls who marry are likely to sacrifice their education in order to support their husband and manage the home. For instance, a fourth of the senior class of 1964 was married, but four-fifths of these students were male. Married coeds were primarily enrolled on a part-time basis (Pop. Ref. Bur., 1964).

In three American studies (Burchinal, 1964, p. 630), and in a recent survey of British youth (Schofield, 1965), two sets of conditions appear most strongly associated with accelerated heterosexual development: alienation from school, poor academic progress, and low educational goals (see Stinchcombe, 1964); and an unhappy, conflicted home which may be associated with inadequate parental supervision and control. Schofield's (1965) sample of adolescent girls and boys in London, England, is one of the very few studies of adolescent sexual behavior based on a probability cross-section of youth; approximately 1,900 adolescents, 15 to 19 years of age, were interviewed in the field. The sample was equally divided between boys and girls, older (17–19) and younger adolescents. From interview data, three levels of sexual experience were identified among older adolescent girls: *Experienced*—those who had sexual intercourse with at least one partner; *Inceptives*—those who reported the experience of breast stimulation under clothes, genital opposition and/or genital stimulation; and the *Non-experienced*—the remaining subjects. The three groups of girls did not differ significantly on socioeconomic variables. The Experienced girls were less likely to get along with and to receive sex information from parents; their homes were also more likely to be unhappy than the homes of the Inexperienced girls. Sexual experience was correlated with lax parental supervision, lack of behavior limits such as what time to be in at night, and with opportunities to entertain friends at home in the absence of parents. Not surprisingly, the Experienced girls spent less time with parents and reported much greater freedom to be alone with their boy friends; they were also higher on reported misconduct, were more often drunk, and smoked more than the other girls. The Experienced girls were also less likely to do well in their studies, to appreciate school, and tended to leave school at an earlier age than the Inexperienced girls. Although Schofield did not analyze marital plans in relation to the sexual experience groups, nearly all sexual partners of the Experienced girls were steady boy friends, thus suggesting that premarital pregnancies and early marriage would be most likely among these girls. A well-designed longitudinal study is needed to test the relationship between heterosexual experiences in adolescence and marriage patterns (see Burchinal, 1964, p. 632). The high risk of failure in teenage marriages may be partially a consequence of the conflict, unhappiness, and poor parent-youth communication common in the family backgrounds of girls accelerated in heterosexual development.

Sex-Roles, Values, and Vocational Orientations During the College Years

From early childhood socialization, most girls acquire a predominant orientation toward persons rather than things, while the reverse pattern is more characteristic of boys. These orientations are further reinforced by peer pressures, and are manifested in qualities desired in a job. This pattern of socialization and resulting vocational orientation differs among the small minority of women students oriented toward a full-time career; they tend to resemble career-oriented men in some of the qualities desired in a job. These sex differences in occupational values and their relation to career intentions are shown in a study of students enrolled at Cornell University (Goldsen, Rosenberg, Williams, & Suchman, 1960).

Women were more likely than men to rate self-expression and relations with people as highly important aspects of a job, while men tended to emphasize monetary rewards more than did women. Coeds more often than men considered opportunity to use their special talents, to be "creative and original," to work with people rather than with things, and to "be helpful to others" highly important in a job or career (an average difference of approximately 11 per cent). College men in the study were decidedly more interested in the extrinsic reward features of the job, such as whether it provided a "stable, secure future" and a "chance to earn a good deal of money."

Virtually all of the women planned to marry and relatively few expressed strong interest in a career. However, few of the coeds agreed with the traditional view that "a woman's only career should be her family." Most expected to marry between the ages of 20 and 25; slightly more than half did not expect to work ten years after graduation. The general plan was to prepare for an occupational career, to follow it before marriage and up to the birth of the first child, to give up the job while the children were young, and possibly to resume the job after the children were older. Coeds who indicated that a career would give them the greatest satisfaction in life were more likely to value the opportunity for self-expression in a job and tended to rank "people" values lower than noncareer coeds. This finding corresponds with the results of Turner's analysis (1964b) of types of ambition and values which distinguished career-oriented high-school girls from noncareer girls: the former were higher on educational ambition and placed greater emphasis on self-expression and esthetic values. In the Cornell study, only self-expression values were associated with career-orientation among the men. Of the three sets of occupational values—self-expression, people-centered, and reward—the former was more strongly correlated with career-orientation, while the latter two were more highly associated with sex-role patterns. Similar sex differences in occupational values were obtained by James Davis in the NORC sample of more than 30,000 college seniors in the spring class of 1961 (1963).

These sex differences are reflected in the sex composition of occupational fields: people-oriented fields such as Education and Social Work tend to attract more women than men, while Engineering, Medicine, Law, Business, and Physical Science are largely male in student composition. In the NORC study the greatest sex contrast was found in Engineering, 99 per cent male, and in Education, 70 per cent female (1963). Davis found that initially masculine fields, such as the Physical Sciences and Engineering, had a masculine trend in recruitment and retention, while a feminine trend characterized initially feminine fields such as Education and the Humanities

(1963, p. 147). Since the study is not longitudinal, these trends are indicated by retrospective data. Over four years of college, approximately half of the students changed their career choice. Most of these changes seemed to reflect an attempt to make occupational choice consonant with occupational values. Students with people-oriented values tended to enter fields which satisfied this preference (Social work, Nursing, and Education), and the same was true for self-expression values (Humanities) and reward values (Business and Law). The hypothesis that a student's persistence in a field of study in college is associated with the degree of congruence between his personality—self-concept, abilities, and values—and environment has been documented by a large number of studies (see Holland, 1966, p. 74).

The combined influence of work values and sex role on occupational choice is clearly shown by comparing senior women with service interests in the NORC study with senior men oriented toward money (Davis, 1963). Seventy per cent of the former were headed for public school teaching compared to only 5 per cent of the men. In contrast, approximately one-third of the men with service interests and of women with monetary interests intended to teach. Sex role and a service orientation were by all standards the most significant predictors of student choice of Education as a career.

It is apparent from studies of predominantly female professions—social work, nursing, and teaching—that few women in these fields are primarily motivated by career interests. A study of nursing students found that professional education had little effect in producing change toward career commitment and professional values (Davis & Oleson, 1965). The class of 1963 expressed a highly orthodox stance on issues pertaining to the status of American women at entry and showed no appreciable change over the three-year period to graduation. An example of an orthodox statement in the ten-item index is "There is something unnatural and unattractive about women who seem to be more preoccupied with their work and careers than they are with their families." On the relative value the students attached to different aspects of the feminine role, over 87 per cent at both time periods ranked "home and family" over three other thematic components. Even more surprising was the finding that the proportion ranking "work and career" second actually decreased from time of entry to graduation. Over the three-year period vocational concerns—for instance, the desire for good pay and regular hours—increased at the expense of professional perspectives toward nursing. These changes occurred despite vigorous efforts by the institution to develop "strong professional commitments in its students" (1965, p. 340). Davis and Oleson found no evidence that the desire to seek graduate education in nursing increased from entry to graduation.

OTHER DIMENSIONS OF ADOLESCENT SOCIALIZATION

The process by which youth form attachments to and comprehend political and religious figures and systems has lately received increasing attention. Some noteworthy studies in this area and a brief review of research on the relative achievement of Protestant and Catholic youth are presented below.

A comprehensive review of research on political socialization up to the mid-fifties has been provided by Herbert Hyman (1959). Recent studies of political socialization and development during childhood and adolescence include Almond and Verba's five-nation survey (1963); among other aspects of the study, retrospective reports from adults in each sample on participation in decision making in family and school during adolescence were analyzed in relation to measures of political competence and involvement. Variation among children in learning political concepts and orientations has been assessed by age, sex, and family variables by Greenstein (1965) and by Hess and Torney (1967). Hess found that political learning begins early in the preschool years and that the basic acquisition of political concepts and preferences is largely accomplished by the age of 13. Research in progress includes a large-scale, nation-wide study of civil education at the University of Michigan. On this subject, Lawrence Kohlberg's application of research and theory on the development of moral judgment to civic education in the classroom (1966) is suggestive of the ways in which such instruction could be made more effective. Recent student activism in the United States and in other countries has brought forth a large number of research publications on this topic. Surveys of this research are provided by Block and her colleagues (1967), and by Lipset (1966). At present no longitudinal study has related the political socialization and development of individuals during childhood and adolescence to their adult political behavior. This research design would be necessary to accomplish what Pinner has termed the "long-term objective of any student of political socialization," that of indicating "how experiences account for personality orientations, and in what way the latter explain specifically political dispositions and actions. We are still a long way from this goal" (1965, p. 59).

Important sociological studies of religious socialization include Rosen's analysis of peer and family influences on the religious beliefs and practices of Jewish youth (1965), and Lenski's comparative analysis of the socialization practices of Protestant and Catholic parents (1961). One of the significant aspects of these studies is that they operationalize a multi-dimensional conception of religiosity. Charles Glock has identified five dimensions of religiosity which are suggestive for future research on religious socialization (Glock & Stark, 1965): experiential (religious feeling), ritualistic (church attendance and other forms of religious behavior), ideological (beliefs), intellectual (knowledge), and consequential (the effects of the other four dimensions manifested in secular domains). Glock and Stark's research is based on samples of adults and does not deal directly with religious socialization in the preadult years; however, their findings are a source of provocative hypotheses. A comprehensive review of psychological research on religious development is provided by David Elkind (1966).

Research on the educational and occupational achievements of Protestants and Catholics in relation to family socialization has as its main source of inspiration Max Weber's hypothesized association between the Protestant Ethic and the rise of capitalism (1958). In *The Protestant Ethic and the Spirit of Capitalism,* Weber characterized the Protestant personality type as individualistic, ascetic in the use of time and money, inclined to assume responsibility for personal deeds, and committed to productive work as the highest calling in life. According to McClelland, the Protestant Reformation could have produced family patterns conducive to the development of achievement motivation, since "it stressed perfection (high standards of excellence) in every detail of performing one's duty in the world, tending to be anti-authoritarian in its initial impulse" (McClelland, 1961, p. 357).

Recent comparisons of Protestant and Catholic youth and adults in the United States have disclosed no significant differences in educational and occupational achievement and values, with ethnicity and social class controlled (Greeley, 1963). On the other hand, several studies of Protestant and Catholic youth in the middle and working classes in Germany generally show educational achievement to be higher among the former (McClelland, 1961, Ch. 8). Differences in the sociocultural context and tradition of Protestant and Catholic religious groups in these two countries may be important factors in these contrasting results. In the United States, one of the major weaknesses of comparative studies of Protestant and Catholic families has been the failure to distinguish between the effects of religious affiliation, ethnicity, and social class (see Greeley's review, 1963). The relatively low educational and occupational achievement of Catholics during the first half of the twentieth century may have been due in large measure to ethnic and socioeconomic factors rather than to religious beliefs and practices. Another potential explanation for these cross-national differences is the greater denominational homogeneity of German than American Protestants. In the United States, wide variations in religious practices and beliefs among Protestants similar in socioeconomic and ethnic status indicate a need for typologies of parents defined by measured beliefs, knowledge, practices, and experiences. At present, we do not have a well-designed comparative study of socialization in Protestant, Catholic, and Jewish families which takes into account intragroup variations in religious beliefs and practices and employs adequate controls. A wealth of information on the effects of education in Catholic secondary schools in the United States is provided by the Notre Dame Survey of Catholic education (Neuwein, 1966) and by a more analytic survey by Greeley and Rossi (1966).

SOME METHODOLOGICAL ISSUES AND PROBLEMS

Most research on socialization has employed either interviews or questionnaires in the collection of data. Excessive reliance on verbal responses is particularly common in studies of youth and adults. In a survey of approximately 430 studies of youth between 1890 and 1958, Wright found only three in which adolescents were observed in their natural settings (cited in Barker, 1963, p. 7). Of the studies reviewed in this chapter, only a few are even partly based on observations in the family and school. More than one source of perceptions regarding the same variable and observational records would facilitate measurement of the important distinction between what parents and teachers do and what they say they do, between, for example, verbalized values and practices. The implications of total reliance on self-report data from one source is clearly shown in the research literature; different methods used to measure the same variable do not correlate highly, and available evidence on the reliability and validity of single measurements leaves much to be desired. Donald Fiske's observation on the current status of personality measurement is appropriate to the field of socialization research: "... no one test can be accepted as a really adequate measure of the variable at which it is aimed. The reverse of that conclusion is even more important: no major variable in current personality theory is adequately measured today, and certainly not by any one test" (1966, p. 74).

Two outstanding examples of the potential value of a multi-method approach are Short and Strodtbeck's research on lower-class male gangs in Chicago (1965), and the Sherifs' research on adolescent groups (1964). These studies employed different devices to obtain information from youth on relevant variables, and also compared measurements of the same variable based on data obtained from different individuals —participant observers, youth, adults, and the respondents themselves. The richness of these data enable a portrayal of youth and their social environment which contrasts markedly with the results of analyses limited to questionnaire or interview data. The cost and sheer complexity of using a variety of methods and social sources are limiting factors, but it would seem strategic at this point to allocate a greater share of project resources to these problems.

For the most part, research on socialization has centered on the context and techniques of training and has paid relatively little attention to the messages or content transmitted in this process. The familial context of socialization is defined by structural features and the emotional tone of the family. Techniques of training include supervision, frequency of explanations, response to disobedience, and methods of enforcement such as physical discipline. Exclusive emphasis on techniques of training ignores the possibility that they could be used to transmit deviant as well as conventional messages and skills. During the past ten years, an increasing number of studies have examined both family values and training techniques in the socialization process. Kohn's studies of fifth-grade children and their parents (cf. 1959) are a noteworthy example of this kind of research.

CONCLUDING OBSERVATIONS

In this chapter, two general sources of behavior patterns were examined from childhood to the adult years: change in environments and socialization. Role transitions may be very gradual as in the addition of role requirements for children with each passing year, or they may represent graded but moderately discontinuous transitions in which past learning and experiences have some relevance for the new role, or they may be markedly discontinuous, in which past learning has little relevance to the new situation. In the United States, the timing of these transitions for an age cohort of children is largely structured by norms concerning behavior appropriate to age and achieved status. Universal education has defined three transitions which are encountered by a majority of American youth: home to entrance into school, elementary to secondary school, and secondary school to college, marriage, or job.

Whether environmental change fosters growth or regression is contingent on the degree of discontinuity and on the specific combination of environmental and personal attributes. Encounters with increased requirements represent a potentially important stimulus of growth, but extreme discontinuity or role demands which greatly exceed personal resources substantially increase the possibility of failure, loss of personal worth, and regression. The psychological significance of the same type of environmental change to adolescents similar in age depends in large measure on their personal resources. For instance, studies in the school setting have found that highly anxious children perform better on academic tasks in structured rather than in unstructured environments, and are more adversely affected than other children by transitions between tasks and social environments. Low ability and a belief in external control are other personal characteristics which increase both dependence on the environment and vulnerability to transitions between roles and tasks. In one study, the negative academic consequences of a deprived grade-school were most evident when the student changed environments by entering junior high-school; this was especially true for Negro students. Within the course of human development, transitions of a discontinuous nature elicit responses which appear to disclose the organism's potential for health and illness and thus have predictive value for subsequent personality development.

Successful passage through transition points is made problematic for some youth by a lack of coordination between individual and social timetables. Standardized schedules for status passage generally ignore substantial variations in rate of physical and intellectual maturation. The problem of coordination is further complicated by intra-person variations in the development of particular characteristics. Students who are advanced intellectually may be slow in physical maturation and consequently not prepared for the social demands in an older age group.

The transition from adolescent to adult roles and the specific character of the adult environment appear to be important and largely unexplored determinants of the adult consequences of socialization and personality in the preadult years. Longitudinal studies indicate that competent, healthy adolescents generally show similar characteristics in adulthood; on the other hand, antisocial patterns in adolescence frequently do not persist as youth enter adult roles. It is plausible that the former group is less vulnerable to role discontinuities and problems in adult, family, and occupational roles. These youth may also have greater access to external resources. Robins's longitudinal study (1966) suggests that environmental conditions are a particularly crucial determinant of adult effectiveness and adjustment among persons who were seriously antisocial during adolescence. For instance, a tolerant wife and a job allowing considerable freedom from supervision could make the difference between a stable or erratic home and work life for an individual with a preadult history of interpersonal conflicts and aggression.

Socialization entails the transmission of cultural traditions, new knowledge and values, the development of skills, and the utilization of training techniques to ensure appropriate learning. These techniques include training procedures such as the enforcement of standards and the establishment of task experiences. Learning resulting from interpersonal and task experiences is both conscious and unconscious. In socialization from childhood to the adult years, learning generally becomes more specific and focused around roles, tasks, and situations. Some change in the form and content of socialization is associated with passage from one environment to another, and with family mobility. Though few studies have examined the relation between father's work-life and socialization, available evidence suggests that the personal strivings of parents in motive and accomplishment are transmitted to their children. The effectiveness and implications of preadult socialization are most fruitfully assessed within the context of adult personality and careers. Longitudinal studies have made important contributions to our understanding of change and stability in the human organism, but have added very little to knowledge on the relation between socialization and personality development. The long-term study of socialization is a promising, unexplored field of inquiry for sociologists. Due to the inherent limitations of cross-sectional and age-specific analyses for studying lives in process, it is hoped that more research in the future will be addressed to questions concerning the complex interplay between socialization and personality processes between childhood and the adult years.

REFERENCES

Alexander, C. N., Jr. Concensus and mutual attraction in natural cliques: A study of adolescent drinkers. *Amer. J. Sociol.,* 1964, 69, 395–403.

Allport, G. *Personality: a psychological interpretation.* New York: Holt, 1937.

Allport, G. *Personality and social encounter.* Boston: Beacon Press, 1964.

Almond, G., & Verba, S. *The civic culture.* Princeton, N.J.: Princeton Univer. Press, 1963.

Anderson, J. E. The prediction of adjustment over time. In I. Iscoe & H. W. Stevenson (Eds.), *Personality development in children.* Austin, Tex.: Univer. of Texas Press, 1960. Pp. 28–72.

Ansbacher, H., & Ansbacher, Rowena. *The individual psychology of Alfred Adler.* New York: Basic Books, 1956.

Ariés, P. *Centuries of childhood.* Robert Baldick (Transl.). New York: Vintage Edition, 1965.

Aronfreed, J. The nature, variety, and social patterning of moral responses to transgression. *J. abnorm. soc. Psychol.,* 1961, 63, 223–240.

Bandura, A., & Walters, R. H. *Adolescent aggression: A study of the influences of child-training practices and family interrelations.* New York: Ronald Press, 1959.

Bandura, A., & Walters, R. H. *Social learning and personality development.* New York: Holt, Rinehart & Winston, 1963.

Barker, R. G. (Ed.) *The stream of behavior.* New York: Appleton-Century-Crofts, 1963.

Barker, R. G., & Gump, P. V. *Big school,*

small school. Stanford, Calif.: Stanford Univer. Press, 1964.

Bates, A. Parental roles in courtship. *Soc. Forces,* 1942, 20, 483–486.

Battle, Esther S., & Rotter, J. B. Children's feelings of personal control as related to social class and ethnic group. *J. Pers.,* 1963, 31, 482–490.

Bayley, Nancy. Skeletal maturing in adolescence as a basis for determining percentage of completed growth. *Child Develpm.,* 1943, 14, 1–46.

Beardslee, D. C., & O'Dowd, D. D. Students and the occupational world. In N. Sanford (Ed.), *The American college.* New York: Wiley, 1962. Pp. 597–626.

Becker, H. S. *Outsiders.* New York: Free Press, 1963.

Becker, W. C. Consequences of different kinds of parental discipline. In M. L. Hoffman & Lois W. Hoffman (Eds.), *Review of child development research.* New York: Russell Sage Found., 1964. Pp. 169–208.

Beilin, H. The pattern of postponability and its relation to social class mobility. *J. soc. Psychol.,* 1956, 44, 33–48.

Benedict, Ruth. Continuities and discontinuities in cultural conditioning. *Psychiatry,* 1938, 1, 161–167.

Benne, K. D. Something there is that doesn't love a wall. *J. appl. behav. Sci.,* 1965, 1, 327–335.

Berger, M. *The Arab world today.* London: Weidenfeld & Nicolson, 1962.

Bernstein, B. Elaborated and restricted codes: their social origins and some consequences. *Amer. J. Anthro.,* 1964, 66 (1), 55–69.

Biddle, B. J., & Thomas, E. J. (Eds.) *Role theory: concepts and research.* New York: Wiley, 1966.

Bing, Elizabeth. Effect of child rearing practices on development of differential cognitive abilities. *Child Develpm.,* 1963, 34, 631–648. Copyright © The Society for Research in Child Development, Inc.

Block, Jeanne H., Haan, Norma, & Smith, M. B. Activism and apathy in contemporary adolescents. In J. F. Adams (Ed.), *Contributions to the understanding of adolescence.* New York: Allyn & Bacon, forthcoming.

Bloom, B. S. *Stability and change in human characteristics.* New York: Wiley, 1964. (a)

Bloom, B. S. Stability and change in human characteristics. In J. E. Birren (Ed.), *Relations of development and aging.* Springfield, Ill.: Charles C Thomas, 1964. Pp. 121–147. (b)

Borow, Henry. Development of occupational motives and roles. In Lois W. Hoffman & M. L. Hoffman (Eds.), *Review of child development research.* Vol. 2. New York: Russell Sage Found., 1966. Pp. 373–422.

Bossard, J. H. S., & Boll, Eleanor. *The large family system.* Philadelphia: Univer. of Pennsylvania Press, 1956.

Bowerman, C. E., & Elder, G. H., Jr. The adolescent and his family. Unpublished manuscript, 1962.

Bowerman, C. E., & Kinch, J. W. Changes in family and peer orientation of children between the fourth and tenth grades. *Soc. Forces,* 1959, 37, 206–211.

Bowman, P. H., & Liddle, G. P. *Effect on slow learners of special school classes.* National Institutes of Health, Res. Grant No. M-1319. Bethesda, Md.: Authors, May 1, 1959.

Breed, W. Occupational mobility and suicide among white males. *Amer. sociol. Rev.,* 1963, 28, 179–188.

Brim, O. G., Jr. Personality development as role-learning. In I. Iscoe & H. W. Stevenson (Eds.), *Personality development in children.* Austin: Univer. of Texas Press, 1960. Pp. 127–159.

Bronfenbrenner, U. Socialization and social class through time and space. In Eleanor E. Maccoby, T. M. Newcomb, & E. L. Hartley (Eds.), *Readings in social psychology.* New York: Henry Holt, 1958. Pp. 400–424.

Bronfenbrenner, U. Some familial antecedents of responsibility and leadership in adolescents. In L. Petrullo & B. Bass (Eds.), *Leadership and interpersonal behavior.* New York: Holt, Rinehart, & Winston, 1961. Pp. 239–271.

Bronson, Wanda C. Central orientations: a study of behavior organization from childhood to adolescence. *Child Develpm.,* 1966, 37, 125–155.

Brookover, W. B., Thomas, S., & Paterson, Ann. Self-concept of ability and school achievement. *Sociol. Educ.,* 1964, 37, 271–278.

Bruner, J. S. A psychologist's viewpoint. Review of B. Inhelder & J. Piaget's *The growth of logical thinking. Brit. J. Psychol.,* 1959, 50, 363–370.

Bruner, J. S. *The process of education*. Cambridge, Mass.: Harvard Univer. Press, 1961.

Bühler, Charlotte. *Der Menschliche Lebenslauf als Psychologishes Problem*. Leipzig: Hirzel, 1933.

Burchinal, L. G. The premarital dyad and love involvement. In H. T. Christenson (Ed.), *Handbook of marriage and the family*. Chicago: Rand McNally, 1964. Pp. 623–674.

Burgess, R. L., & Akers, R. L. A differential association-reinforcement theory of criminal behavior. *Soc. Problms.*, 1966, 14, 128–147.

Campbell, E. Q. The internalization of moral norms. *Sociometry*, 1964, 27, 391–412.

Carlsmith, Lyn. Effect of early father absence on scholastic aptitudes. *Harvard educ. Rev.*, 1964, 34, 3–21.

Carlson, Rae. Stability and change in the adolescent's self-image. *Child Develpm.*, 1965, 35, 659–666.

Carter, H. D. The development of interest in vocations. In N. B. Henry (Ed.), Adolescence, *Yearb. nat. Soc. Stud. Educ.*, 1944, 43, Part I. Pp. 255–276.

Chein, I., Gerard, D. L., Lee, R. S., & Rosenfeld, Eva. *The road to H*. New York: Basic Books, 1963.

Clark, J. P. Acceptance of blame and alienation among prisoners. *Amer. J. Orthopsychiat.*, 1963, 33, 557–561.

Clausen, J. Family structure, socialization, and personality. In Lois W. Hoffman & M. L. Hoffman (Eds.), *Review of child development research*. Vol. 2. New York: Russell Sage Found., 1966. Pp. 1–53.

Cloward, R. A. The prevention of delinquent subcultures: Issues and problems. In W. R. Carriker (Ed.), Role of the school in prevention of juvenile delinquency. *Coop. Res. Monogr.*, No. 10, Washington, D.C., 1963.

Cloward, R. A., & Ohlin, L. E. *Delinquency and opportunity*. Glencoe, Ill.: Free Press, 1960.

Cohen, A. K. *Delinquent boys: the culture of the gang*. Glencoe, Ill.: Free Press, 1955.

Cohen, A. K. *Deviance and control*. Englewood Cliffs, N.J.: Prentice-Hall, 1966.

Cohen, Elizabeth. Parental factors in educational mobility. Unpublished doctoral dissertation, Radcliffe College, 1958.

Cohen, Y. A. *The transition from childhood to adolescence*. Chicago: Aldine, 1964.

Coleman, J. S. *The adolescent society*. New York: Free Press of Glencoe, 1961.

Coleman, J. S., Campbell, E. Q., Hobson, Carol J., McPartland, J., Mood, A. M., Weinfeld, F. D., & York, R. L. *Equality of educational opportunity*. Washington, D.C.: U.S. Government Printing Office, 1966.

Coles, R. A psychiatrist joins the movement. *Trans-action*, 1966, 3, 21–27.

Cooley, C. H. *Human nature and the social order*. New York: Scribners, 1902.

Coopersmith, S. A method for determining types of self-esteem. *J. abnorm. soc. Psychol.*, 1959, 59, 87–94.

Cramer, M. R., Bowerman, C. E., & Campbell, E. Q. *Social factors in educational achievement and aspirations among Negro adolescents*. Chapel Hill, N.C.: Inst. for Res. in Soc. Sci., mimeo, 1966.

Cureton, T. K. Improving the physical fitness of youth. *Monogr. Soc. Res. child Develpm.*, 1964, 29 (4), Serial No. 95.

Davis, Allison. Socialization and adolescent personality. In N. B. Henry (Ed.), Adolescence, *Yearb. nat. Soc. Stud. Educ.*, 1944, 43, Part I, Pp. 189–216.

Davis, F., & Oleson, Virginia L. The career outlook of professionally educated women. *Psychiatry*, 1965, 28, 334–345.

Davis, J. H. *Great aspirations*. Vol. 1. Chicago: Nat. Opinion Res. Center, 1963.

Davis, K. The sociology of parent-youth conflict. *Amer. sociol. Rev.*, 1940, 5, 523–535.

Deutsch, M. P. The disadvantaged child and the learning process. In A. H. Passow (Ed.), *Education in depressed areas*. New York: Bureau of Publications, Columbia Univer. Teachers Coll., 1963. Pp. 163–179.

Deutsch, M. P., & Brown, B. Social influences in Negro-white intelligence differences. *J. soc. Issues*, 1964, 20, 24–35.

Devereux, E. C., Jr. Children of democracy: on the consequences for children of varying patterns of family authority in the United States and Germany. Summary of research report read at the 7th International Seminar on Family Research, Washington, D.C., September, 1962.

Dinitz, S., Scarpitti, F. R., & Reckless, W. C. Delinquency vulnerability: a cross group and longitudinal analysis. *Amer. sociol. Rev.*, 1962, 27, 517–522.

Douglas, J. W. B. *The home and the school*. London: MacGibbon & Kee, 1964.

Douglas, J. W. B., Ross, J. M., & Simpson, H. R. The relation between height and measured education ability in school children of the same social class, family size, and stage of sexual development. *Human Biol.,* 1965, 37, 178–186.

Douvan, Elizabeth. Social status and success strivings. *J. abnorm. soc. Psychol.,* 1956, 52, 219–223.

Douvan, Elizabeth. Employment and the adolescent. In F. I. Nye & Lois W. Hoffman (Eds.), *The employed mother in America.* Chicago: Rand McNally, 1963. Pp. 142–164.

Douvan, Elizabeth, & Adelson, J. *The adolescent experience.* New York: Wiley, 1966.

Ehrmann, W. W. Marital and nonmarital sexual behavior. In H. T. Christenson (Ed.), *Handbook of marriage and the family.* Chicago: Rand McNally, 1964. Pp. 585–622.

Eichorn, Dorothy H. Biological correlates of behavior. Child Psychology, *Yearb. nat. Soc. Stud. Educ.,* 1963, Part 1, 4–61.

Eisenstadt, S. N. *From generation to generation: Age groups and the social structure.* New York: Free Press of Glencoe, 1956.

Elder, G. H., Jr. Family structure and the transmission of values and norms in the process of child rearing. Unpublished doctoral dissertation, Univer. of North Carolina, 1961.

Elder, G. H., Jr. *Adolescent achievement and mobility aspirations.* Chapel Hill: Institute for Res. in Soc. Sci., mimeo, 1962.

Elder, G. H., Jr. Structural variations in the child rearing relationship. *Sociometry,* 1962, 25, 241–262. (b)

Elder, G. H., Jr. Parental power legitimation and its effect on the adolescent. *Sociometry,* 1963, 26, 50–65.

Elder, G. H., Jr. Role relations, sociocultural environments, and autocratic family ideology. *Sociometry,* 1965, 28, 173–196. (a)

Elder, G. H., Jr. Life opportunity and personality: some consequences of stratified secondary education in Great Britain. *Sociol. Educ.,* 1965, 38, 173–202. (b)

Elder, G. H., Jr. Children of the Great Depression. Unpublished manuscript, 1967.

Elder, G. H., Jr., & Bowerman, C. E. Family structure and child-rearing patterns: The effect of family size and sex composition. *Amer. sociol. Rev.,* 1963, 28, 891–905.

Elkind, D. Quantity conceptions in junior and senior high school students. *Child Develpm.,* 1961, 32, 551–560.

Elkind, D. The developmental psychology of religion. In Olive H. Kidd & Jeanne L. Rivoire (Eds.), *Perceptual development in children.* New York: International Universities Press, 1966. Pp. 193–225.

Ellis, R. H., & Lane, W. C. Structural supports for upward mobility. *Amer. sociol. Rev.,* 1963, 28, 743–756.

Erikson, E. H. *Young man Luther.* New York: Norton, 1958.

Erikson, E. H. Identity and the life cycle. *Psychol. Issues,* 1959 (Whole No. 1).

Erikson, E. H. Youth: fidelity and diversity. *Daedalus,* 1962, 91, 5–27.

Erikson, E. H. *Childhood and society.* (Rev. ed.) New York: Norton, 1963.

Erikson, E. H. *Insight and responsibility.* New York: Norton, 1964.

Feffer, M. H. The cognitive implications of role-taking behavior. *J. Pers.,* 1959, 27, 152–168.

Feffer, M. H., & Gourevitch, Vivian. Cognitive aspects of role taking in children. *J. Pers.,* 1960, 28, 383–396.

Fisher, S., & Cleveland, S. E. *Body image and personality.* New York: Van Nostrand, 1958.

Fiske, D. W. The inherent variability of behavior. In D. W. Fiske and S. R. Maddi (Eds.), *Functions of varied experience.* Homewood, Ill.: Dorsey Press, 1961. Pp. 326–354.

Fiske, D. W. On the coordination of personality concepts and their measurement. *Human Develpm.,* 1966, 9, 74–83.

Flavell, J. H. *The developmental psychology of Jean Piaget.* New York: Van Nostrand, 1963.

Floud, Jean. Social class factors in educational achievement. In A. H. Halsey (Ed.), *Ability and educational opportunity.* New York: Organization for Economic Cooperation and Development, 1961. Pp. 91–109.

Fraser, E. *Home environment and the school.* London: Univer. of London Press, 1959.

Friedenberg, E. Z. *The vanishing adolescent.* Boston: Beacon, 1959.

Gans, H. J. *The urban villagers.* New York: Free Press of Glencoe, 1962.

Garfinkel, H. Conditions of successful degradation ceremonies. *Amer. J. Sociol.,* 1956, 61, 420–424.

Ginzberg, E., Ginzberg, S. W., Axelrod, S., & Herma, J. L. *Occupational choice.* New York: Columbia Univer. Press, 1951.

Glaser, D. The differential-association theory of crime. In A. M. Rose (Ed.), *Human behavior and social processes.* Boston: Houghton Mifflin, 1962. Pp. 425–442.

Glock, C. Y., & Stark, R. *Religion and society in tension.* Chicago: Rand McNally, 1965.

Glueck, S., & Glueck, Eleanor. *Unraveling juvenile delinquency.* New York: Commonwealth Fund, 1950.

Glueck, S., & Glueck, Eleanor. *Delinquents in the making: paths of prevention.* New York: Harper, 1952.

Glueck, S., & Glueck, Eleanor. *Physique and delinquency.* New York: Harper, 1956.

Glueck, S., & Glueck, Eleanor. *Family environment and delinquency.* Boston: Houghton Mifflin, 1962.

Gold, M. *Status forces in delinquent boys.* Ann Arbor, Mich.: Inst. for Soc. Res., Univer. of Michigan, 1963.

Goldberg, Miriam L., & Passow, A. H. The effects of ability grouping. *Education,* 1962, 82, 482–487.

Goldman, S. Profiles of an adolescent. *J. Psychol.,* 1962, 54, 229–240.

Goldsen, Rose K., Rosenberg, M., Williams, R., Jr., & Suchman, E. A. *What college students think.* Princeton, N.J.: Van Nostrand, 1960.

Goode, W. J. *World revolution and family patterns.* New York: Free Press of Glencoe, 1963.

Gordon, W. C. *The social system of the high school: a study in the sociology of adolescence.* Glencoe, Ill.: Free Press, 1957.

Greeley, A. M. *Religion and career.* New York: Sheed and Ward, 1963.

Greeley, A. M., & Rossi, P. H. *The education of Catholic Americans.* Chicago: Aldine, 1966.

Green, M. R. (Ed.) *Interpersonal psychoanalysis: The selected papers of Clara M. Thompson.* New York: Basic Books, 1964.

Greenstein, F. I. *Children and politics.* New Haven, Conn.: Yale Univer. Press, 1965.

Grimes, J. W., & Allinsmith, W. Compulsivity, anxiety, and school achievement. *Merrill-Palmer Quart.,* 1961, 7, 247–271.

Gunderson, E. K. E. Body size, self-evaluation, and military effectiveness. *J. Pers. soc. Psychol.,* 1965, 2, 902–906.

Gurin, G., Veroff, J., & Feld, Sheila. *Americans view their mental health.* New York: Basic Books, 1960.

Haan, Norma. A proposed model of ego functioning: coping and defense mechanisms in relationship to IQ change. *Psychol. Monogr.,* 1963, 77 (Whole No. 571).

Handlin, O. *The uprooted.* New York: Grosset & Dunlap, 1951.

Hanley, C. Physique and reputation of junior high school boys. *Child Develpm.,* 1951, 22, 247–260.

Harvey, O. J., Hunt, D. E., & Schroder, H. M. *Conceptual systems and personality organization.* New York: Wiley, 1961.

Hathaway, S. R., & Monachesi, E. D. *Adolescent personality and behavior—MMPI patterns of normal, delinquent, dropout, and other outcomes.* Minneapolis: Univer. of Minnesota Press, 1963.

Havighurst, R. J. *Human development and education.* New York: Longmans Green, 1953.

Hess, R. D. High school antecedents of young adult achievement. In R. E. Grinder (Ed.), *Studies in adolescence.* New York: Macmillan, 1963. Pp. 401–414.

Hess, R. D., & Goldblatt, I. The status of adolescents in American society: A problem in social identity. *Child Develpm.,* 1957, 28, 459–468.

Hess, R. D., & Torney, Judith V. *The development of political attitudes in children.* Chicago, Ill.: Aldine, 1967.

Hill, K. T. & Sarason, S. B. The relation of test anxiety and defensiveness to test and school performance over the elementary-school years: a further longitudinal study. *Monogr. Soc. Res. child Develpm.,* 1966, 31(2), Serial No. 104.

Himmelweit, Hilde T. Social background, intelligence, and school structure: Interaction analysis. *Eugenics society symposia,* 1966, 2, 24–42.

Holland, J. L. Major programs of research on vocational behavior. In Henry Borow (Ed.), *Man in a world of work.* Boston: Houghton Mifflin, 1964. Pp. 259–284.

Holland, J. L. *The psychology of vocational choice.* Waltham, Mass.: Blaisdell Publications, 1966.

Honzik, Marjorie P. A sex difference in the age of onset of the parent-child resemblance in intelligence. *J. educ. Psychol.,* 1963, 54, 231–237.

Honzik, Marjorie P. Prediction of behavior from birth to maturity, a book review of

Birth to maturity: a study in psychological development, by Jerome Kagan and Howard Moss (New York: Wiley, 1962). *Merrill-Palmer Quart.,* 1965, 11, 77–88.

Hughes, E. C. *Men and their work.* New York: Free Press of Glencoe, 1958.

Hunt, J. McV. *Intelligence and experience.* New York: Ronald Press, 1961.

Hyman, H. H. *Political socialization.* Glencoe, Ill.: Free Press, 1959.

Inhelder, Barbel, & Piaget, J. *The growth of logical thinking.* New York: Basic Books, 1958.

Jackson, B. *Streaming: An education system in miniature.* London: Routledge & Kegan Paul, 1964.

Jaffe, A. J., & Adams, W. College education for U.S. youth: The attitudes of parents and children. *Amer. J. Econ. & Sociol.,* 1964, 3, 269–284.

Johannesson, I. School differentiation and the social adjustment of the pupils. *Educ. Res.,* 1962, 4, 133–139.

Jones, H. E. Principles and methods of the adolescent growth study. *J. consult. Psychol.,* 1939, 3, 157–159.

Jones, H. E. *Motor performance and growth.* Berkeley: Univer. of California Press, 1949.

Jones, Mary C. The later careers of boys who were early- or late-maturing. *Child Develpm.,* 1957, 28, 113–128.

Jones, Mary C. A study of socialization patterns at the high school level. *J. gen. Psychol.,* 1958, 93, 87–111.

Jones, Mary C. Psychological correlates of somatic development. *Child Develpm.,* 1965, 36, 899–911.

Jones, Mary C., & Bayley, Nancy. Physical maturing among boys as related to behavior. *J. educ. Psychol.,* 1950, 41, 129–148.

Jones, Mary C., Bayley, Nancy, Macfarlane, Jean W., & Honzik, Marjorie H. *The course of human development: Selected papers from the Berkeley longitudinal studies.* Forthcoming.

Jourard, S. M., & Secord, P. F. Body-cathexis body-cathexis. *J. consult. Psychol.,* 1954, 18, 184.

Jourard, S. M., & Secord, P. F. Body-cathexis and the ideal female figure. *J. abnorm. soc. Psychol.,* 1955, 50, 243–246.

Kagan, J., & Moss, H. A. *Birth to maturity.* New York: Wiley, 1962.

Kahl, J. A. Educational and occupational aspirations of "common man" boys. *Harvard educ. Rev.,* 1953, 23, 186–203.

Kahl, J. A. Some measurements of achievement orientation. *Amer. J. Sociol.,* 1965, 170, 669–681.

Kardiner, A. Explorations in Negro personality. In M. K. Opler (Ed.), *Culture and mental health.* New York: Macmillan, 1959.

Kemper, T. D., Brim, O. G., & Cottrell, L. S., Jr. Beyond self-esteem: The social structure of the adolescent self-image. Paper read at American Sociological Association, Washington, D.C., August, 1962.

Keniston, K. *The uncommitted.* New York: Basic Books, 1965.

Kessen, W. Research design in the study of developmental problems. In P. H. Mussen (Ed.), *Handbook of research methods in child development.* New York: Wiley, 1960. Pp. 36–70.

Kinnane, J. F., & Pable, M. W. Family background and work value orientation. *J. counsel. Psychol.,* 1962, 9, 320–325.

Kinsey, A. C., Pomeroy, W. B., & Martin, C. E. *Sexual behavior in the human male.* Philadelphia: Saunders, 1948.

Klinger, E. Fantasy need achievement as a motivational construct. *Psychol. Bull.,* 1966, 66, 291–308.

Kluckhohn, Florence R., & Strodtbeck, F. L. *Variations in value orientations.* New York: Row, Peterson, 1961.

Koch, H. L. Children's work attitudes and sibling characteristics. *Child Develpm.,* 1956, 27, 289–310.

Kohlberg, L. The development of children's orientations toward a moral order: I. Sequence in the development of moral thought. *Vita Humana,* 1963, 6, 11–33. (a)

Kohlberg, L. Moral development and identification. Child Psychology, *Yearb. nat. Soc. Stud. Educ.,* 1963, Part 1. Pp. 277–332. (b)

Kohlberg, L. Development of moral character and moral ideology. In M. L. Hoffman and Lois W. Hoffman (Eds.), *Review of child development research.* New York: Russell Sage Found., 1964. Pp. 383–431.

Kohlberg, L. Moral education in the schools. A developmental view. *Sch. Rev.,* 1966, 74, 1–30. (a)

Kohlberg, L. A cognitive-developmental analysis of children's sex-role concepts and attitudes. In Eleanor E. Maccoby (Ed.), *The development of sex differences.* Stanford, Calif.: Stanford Univer. Press, 1966. Pp. 82–173. (b)

Kohn, M. L. Social class and parental values. *Amer. J. Sociol.,* 1959, 64, 337–351.

Krauss, I. Sources of educational aspirations among working-class youth. *Amer. sociol. Rev.,* 1964, 29, 867–879.

Lasko, J. K. Parent behavior toward first and second children. *Genet. Psychol. Monogr.,* 1954, 49, 96–137.

Lavin, D. E. *The prediction of academic performance.* New York: Russell Sage Found., 1965.

Lazarsfeld, P. F. *Jugend und beruf.* Jena: C. Fischer, 1931.

Lenski, G. E. *The religious factor.* Garden City, N.Y.: Doubleday, 1961.

Lifton, R. J. Youth and history: Individual change in postwar Japan. *Daedalus,* 1962, 91, 172–197.

Lipset, S. M. (Ed.) Student politics. A special issue of *Comp. Educ. Rev.,* 1966, 10 (Whole No. 2).

Lipset, S. M., & Bendix, R. *Social mobility in industrial society.* Berkeley: Univer. of California Press, 1959.

Livson, N., & Peskin, H. The prediction of adult psychological health in a longitudinal study. *J. abnorm. Psychol.,* 1967, 72, 509–518.

Lowrie, S. H. Dating, a neglected field of study. *Marrg. fam. Liv.,* 1948, 10, 90–91, 95.

Lynd, Helen M. *On shame and the search for identity.* New York: Science Editions, 1961.

Macfarlane, Jean W. Perspectives on personality consistency and change from the guidance study. *Vita Humana,* 1964, 7, 115–126.

Macfarlane, Jean W., Allen, Lucille, & Honzik, Marjorie. *A developmental study of the behavior problems of normal children between 21 months and 14 years.* Berkeley: Univer. of California Press, 1954.

MacGregor, F. C., Abel, T. M., Bryt, G., Laner, E., & Weissman, S. *Facial deformities and plastic surgery.* Springfield, Ill.: Charles C Thomas, 1953.

MacKinnon, D. W. The nature and nurture of creative talent. *Amer. Psychologist,* 1962, 17, 484–495.

Madsen, W. *Mexican-Americans of South Texas.* New York: Holt, Rinehart & Winston, 1964.

Mannheim, K. *Diagnosis of our time.* London: Routledge and Kegan Paul, 1943.

Mannheim, K. The problem of the generations. In P. Kecskemeti (Ed.), *Essays on the sociology of knowledge.* New York: Oxford Univer. Press, 1952.

Martin, J. M., & Fitzpatrick, J. P. *Delinquent behavior.* New York: Random House, 1965.

Matza, D. *Delinquency and drift.* New York: Wiley, 1964.

McArthur, C. Personalities of first and second children. *Psychiatry,* 1956, 19, 47–54.

McClearn, G. E. Genetics and behavior development. In M. L. Hoffman & Lois W. Hoffman (Eds.), *Review of child development research.* Vol. 1. New York: Russell Sage Found., 1964. Pp. 433–480.

McClelland, D. C. *The achieving society.* Princeton, N.J.: Van Nostrand, 1961.

McClelland, D. C. Longitudinal trends in the relation of thought to action. *J. consult. Psychol.,* 1966, 30, 479–483.

McCord, W., McCord, Joan, with Zola, I. *Origins of crime: A new evaluation of the Cambridge-Somerville youth study.* New York: Columbia Univer. Press, 1959.

McDill, E. L., & Coleman, J. Family and peer influence in college plans of high school students. *Sociol. Educ.,* 1965, 38, 112–126.

McKinley, D. G. *Social class and family life.* New York: Free Press of Glencoe, 1964.

Merton, R. K. *Social theory and social structure.* Glencoe, Ill.: Free Press, 1957.

Middleton, R., & Putney, S. Political expression of adolescent rebellion. *Amer. J. Sociol.,* 1963, 68, 527–535.

Miller, D. R., & Swanson, G. *Inner conflict and defense.* New York: Holt, 1960.

Miller, S. M., & Harrison, I. E. Types of dropouts: The unemployables. In A. B. Shostak & W. Gomberg (Eds.), *Blue-collar world: Studies of the American worker.* Englewood Cliffs, N.J.: Prentice-Hall, 1964. Pp. 469–484.

Miller, S. M., Saleem, Betty L., & Bryce, H. *School dropouts: A commentary and annotated bibliography.* Syracuse, N.Y.: Syracuse Univer., 1964.

Miller, W. B. Lower class culture as a generating milieu of gang delinquency. *J. soc. Issues,* 1958, 14, 5–19.

Miller, W. B. The impact of a "total-community" delinquency control project. *Soc. Problms.,* 1962, 10, 168–191.

Morris, Ruth R. Female delinquency and relational problems. *Soc. Forces,* 1964, 43, 82–89.

Morrow, W. R., & Wilson, R. C. Family relations of bright high-achieving and under-achieving high school boys. *Child Develpm.,* 1961, 32, 501–510.

Musgrove, F. *Youth and the social order.* Bloomington, Ind.: Indiana Univer. Press, 1965.

Mussen, P. H. Some antecedents and consequents of masculine sex-typing in adolescent boys. *Psychol. Monogr.,* 1961, 75, No. 2 (Whole No. 506).

Mussen, P. H., & Distler, L. Masculinity, identification, and father-son relationships. *J. abnorm. soc. Psychol.,* 1959, 59, 350–356.

Mussen, P. H., & Jones, Mary C. Self-conceptions, motivations, and interpersonal attitudes of late- and early-maturing boys. *Child Develpm.,* 1957, 28, 243–256.

Mussen, P. H., & Jones, Mary C. The behavior-inferred motivations of late- and early-maturing boys. *Child Develpm.,* 1958, 29, 61–67.

Muus, R. E. *Theories of adolescence.* New York: Random House, 1962.

Myers, J. K., & Roberts, B. H. *Family and class dynamics in mental illness.* New York: Wiley, 1959.

Nam, C. B., & Cowhig, J. D. *Factors related to college attendance of farm and nonfarm high school graduates: 1960.* Washington, D.C.: U.S. Government Printing Office, Bureau of the Census, Farm Population Series, P-27, No. 32, 1962.

National Merit Scholarship Corporation. *A pledge to the future.* 1960 Annual Report. Evanston, Ill.: Author, 1961.

Neuwien, R. G. (Ed.) *Catholic schools in action.* Notre Dame, Ind.: Univer. Notre Dame Press, 1966.

Nicolson, A. B., & Hanley, C. Indices of physiological maturity: Deviation and interrelationships. *Child Develpm.,* 1953, 24, 3–38.

Nye, F. I. *Family relationships and delinquent behavior.* New York: Wiley, 1958.

O'Hara, R. P., & Tiedeman, D. V. The vocational self-concept in adolescence. *J. counsel. Psychol.,* 1959, 6, 292–301.

Parnell, R. W. *Behavior and physique.* London: Edward Arnold, 1958.

Parsons, T. Age and sex in the social structure of the United States. In C. Kluckhohn, & H. A. Murray with the collaboration of D. M. Schneider (Eds.), *Personality in nature, society, and culture.* (2nd Ed. Rev.) New York: Knopf, 1953. Pp. 269–281.

Pearlin, L. I., & Kohn, M. L. Social class, occupation, and parental values: A cross-national study. *Amer. sociol. Rev.,* 1966, 31, 466–479.

Peck, R. F., & Havighurst, R. J., with Cooper, Ruth, Lilienthal, J., & More, D. *The psychology of character development.* New York: Wiley, 1960.

Pettigrew, T. F. *A profile of the Negro American.* New York: Van Nostrand, 1964.

Piaget, J. *The moral judgment of the child.* Glencoe, Ill.: Free Press, 1948.

Pinner, F. G. Parental overprotection and political distrust. *Ann. Amer. Acad. polit. soc. Sci.,* 1965, 361, 58–70.

Population Reference Bureau. Marriage and the coed. Washington, D.C., June 1, 1964.

Project Talent. One year follow-up studies. Bulletin No. 5, July, 1966.

Project Talent News. Univer. of Pittsburgh, 1964, 3 (No. 1).

Psathas, G. Ethnicity, social class, and adolescent independence. *Amer. sociol. Rev.,* 1957, 22, 415–423.

Reiss, A. J., Jr., & Rhodes, A. L. The distribution of juvenile delinquency in the social class structure. *Amer. sociol. Rev.,* 1961, 26, 720–732.

Richardson, S. A., Goodman, N., Hastorf, A. H., & Dornbusch, S. M. Cultural uniformity in reaction to physical disabilities. *Amer. sociol. Rev.,* 1961, 26, 241–247.

Riesman, D. *Constraint and variety in American education.* Lincoln, Neb.: Univer. of Nebraska Press, 1956.

Robins, L. N. *Deviant children grown up.* Baltimore: Williams & Wilkins, 1966.

Roe, Anne, & Siegelman, M. *The origin of interests.* Washington, D.C.: American Personnel and Guidance Assoc., 1964.

Roff, M. Childhood social interactions and young adult bad conduct. *J. abnorm. soc. Psychol.,* 1961, 34, 333–337.

Rohrer, J. H., & Edmonson, N. S. *The eighth generation grows up: Cultures and personalities of New Orleans Negroes.* New York: Harper, 1960.

Rosen, B. C. The achievement syndrome: a psycho-cultural dimension of social stratification. *Amer. sociol. Rev.,* 1956, 21, 203–211.

Rosen, B. C. Race, ethnicity and the achievement syndrome. *Amer. sociol. Rev.,* 1959, 24, 47–60.

Rosen, B. C. Family structure and achievement motivation. *Amer. sociol. Rev.,* 1961, 26, 574–585.

Rosen, B. C. Socialization and achievement motivation in Brazil. *Amer. sociol. Rev.,* 1962, 27, 612–624.

Rosen, B. C. *Adolescence and religion.* Cambridge, Mass.: Schenkman, 1965.

Rosen, B. C., & D'Andrade, R. The psychosocial origins of achievement motivation. *Sociometry,* 1959, 22, 185–218.

Rosenberg, M. *Occupations and values.* Glencoe, Ill.: Free Press, 1957.

Rosenberg, M. *Society and the adolescent self-image.* Princeton, N.J.: Princeton Univer. Press, 1965.

Rosenthal, M. J., Finkelstein, M., Ni, E., & Robertson, R. E. A study of mother-child relationships in the emotional disorders of children. *Genet. Psychol. Monogr.,* 1959, 60, 65–116.

Rosenthal, M. J., Ni, E., Finkelstein, M., & Berkwits, G. K. Father-child relationships and children's problems. *Amer. Arch. gen. Psychiat.,* 1962, 7, 360–373.

Roth, J. A. *Timetables.* Indianapolis, Ind.: Bobbs-Merrill, 1963.

Rotter, J. B. Generalized expectancies for internal versus external control of reinforcement. *Psychol. Monogr.,* 1966, 80 (Whole No. 1).

Ryder, N. B. The cohort as a concept in the study of social change. *Amer. sociol. Rev.,* 1965, 30, 843–861.

Sampson, E. E. The study of ordinal position: Antecedents and outcomes. In B. Maher (Ed.), *Progress in experimental personality research.* Vol. 2. New York: Academic Press, 1965. Pp. 175–228.

Sanford, N. (Ed.) *The American college.* New York: Wiley, 1962. (a)

Sanford, N. Developmental status of the entering freshman. In *The American college.* New York: Wiley, 1962. Pp. 253–282. (b)

Sarbin, T. R. Role theoretical interpretation of psychological change. In P. Worchel and D. Byrne (Eds.), *Personality change.* New York: Wiley, 1964. Pp. 176–219.

Schachter, S. Birth order, eminence and higher education. *Amer. sociol. Rev.,* 1963, 28, 757–768.

Schaefer, E. S., & Bayley, Nancy. Maternal behavior, child behavior, and their intercorrelation from infancy through adolescence. *Monogr. Soc. Res. child Develpm.,* 1963, 28(3), Serial No. 87.

Schaie, C. W. A general model for the study of developmental problems. *Psychol. Bull.,* 1965, 64, 92–107.

Schilder, P. *The image and appearance of the human body.* London: Kegan Paul, Trench, Trubner, 1935.

Schofield, M. *The sexual behavior of young people.* Boston: Little, Brown, 1965.

Schramm, W., Lyle, J., & Parker, E. B. *Television in the lives of our children.* Stanford, Calif.: Stanford Univer. Press, 1961.

Scott, J. P. *Animal behavior.* Chicago: Univer. Chicago Press, 1958.

Secord, P. F., & Jourard, S. M. The appraisal of body-cathexis: Body-cathexis and the self. *J. consult. Psychol.,* 1953, 17, 343–347.

Seeman, M. On the meaning of alienation. *Amer. sociol. Rev.,* 1959, 24, 783–791.

Seeman, M. Antidote to alienation—learning to belong. *Trans-action,* 1966, 3, 35–39.

Sewell, W. H., & Armer, J. M. Neighborhood context and college plans. *Amer. sociol. Rev.,* 1966, 31, 159–168. (a)

Sewell, W. H., & Armer, J. M. Reply to Turner, Michael, and Boyle. *Amer. sociol. Rev.,* 1966, 31, 707–712. (b)

Sewell, W. H., & Orenstein, A. M. Community of residence and occupational choice. *Amer. J. Sociol.,* 1965, 70, 551–563.

Sewell, W. H., & Shah, V. P. Socioeconomic status, intelligence, and the attainment of higher education. *Sociol. Educ.,* 1967, 40, 1–23.

Sexton, Patricia C. *Education and income.* New York: Viking Press, 1961.

Sexton, Patricia C. Negro career expectations. *Merrill-Palmer Quarterly*, 1963, 9, 303–316.

Sheldon, W. H. *The varieties of temperament.* New York: Harper, 1942.

Sherif, M., & Sherif, Carolyn. *Reference groups: exploration into conformity and deviation of adolescents.* New York: Harper & Row, 1964.

Short, J. F., Jr., Rivera, R., & Tennyson, R. A. Perceived opportunities, gang membership, and delinquency. *Amer. sociol. Rev.,* 1965, 30, 56–67.

Short, J. F., Jr., & Strodtbeck, F. L. *Group process and gang delinquency*. Chicago: Univer. of Chicago Press, 1965.

Shuttleworth, F. K. Sexual maturation and the physical growth of girls age six to nineteen. *Monogr. Soc. Res. child Developm.*, 1938, (5), Serial No. 18.

Simpson, R. L. Parental influence, anticipatory socialization and social mobility. *Amer. sociol. Rev.*, 1962, 27, 517–522.

Skeels, H. M. Adult status of children with contrasting early life experiences: A follow-up study. *Monogr. Soc. Res. child Develpm.*, 1966, 31, (3), Serial No. 105.

Skolnick, Arlene. Motivational imagery and behavior over twenty years. *J. consult. Psychol.*, 1966, 30, 463–478.

Smelser, W. T. Adolescent and adult occupational choice as a function of family socioeconomic history. *Sociometry*, 1963, 26, 393–409.

Smith, M. B. Explorations in competence: A study of Peace Corps teachers in Ghana. *Amer. Psychologist*, 1966, 21, 555–566.

Social Science Research Council Work Group on Family Size and Birth Order. Family size and birth order as influences upon socialization and personality: Bibliography and abstracts. Prepared by J. A. Clausen, July, 1965.

Sontag, L. W., Baker, C. T., & Nelson, V. L. Mental growth and personality development: A longitudinal study. *Monogr. Soc. Res. child Develpm.*, 1958, 23 (2), Serial No. 68.

Spergel, I. *Racketville, Slumtown, and Haulberg*. Chicago: Univer. of Chicago Press, 1964.

Srole, L., Langner, T. S., Michael, S. T., Opler, M. K., & Rennie, T. A. C. *Mental health in the metropolis: The Midtown Manhattan study*. Vol. 1. New York: McGraw-Hill, 1962.

Stern, G. G. Environment for learning. In N. Sanford (Ed.), *The American college*. New York: Wiley, 1962. Pp. 690–730.

Stinchcombe, A. L. *Rebellion in a high school*. Chicago: Quadrangle Books, 1964.

Stolz, H. R., & Stolz, Lois M. Adolescent problems related to somatic variations. In N. B. Henry (Ed.), Adolescence, *Yearb. nat. Soc. Stud. Educ.*, 1944, 43, Part 1. Pp. 80–99.

Stolz, H. R., & Stolz, Lois M. *Somatic development of adolescent boys*. New York: Macmillan, 1951.

Strauss, A. (Ed.) *The social psychology of George Herbert Mead*. Chicago: Univer. of Chicago Press, 1956.

Strauss, A. L. *Mirrors and masks: the search for identity*. Glencoe, Ill.: Free Press of Glencoe, 1959.

Strodtbeck, F. L. Family interaction, values and achievement. In D. C. McClelland (Ed.), *Talent and society*. Princeton, N.J.: Van Nostrand, 1958. Pp. 135–194.

Sullivan, H. S. *Conceptions of modern psychiatry*. New York: Norton, 1947.

Sullivan, H. S. Illusion of personal individuality. *Psychiatry*, 1950, 13, 317–332.

Sullivan, H. S. *The interpersonal theory of psychiatry*. H. S. Perry & Mary L. Gawel (Eds.). New York: Norton, 1953.

Super, D. E. Toward making the self-concept theory operational. In D. E. Super, R. Starishevsky, N. Matlin, & J. P. Jordaan (Eds.), *Career development: Self-concept theory*. Princeton, N.J.: College Entrance Exam. Board, 1963. Pp. 17–32. (a)

Super, D. E. Vocational development in adolescence and early adulthood: Tasks and behaviors. In D. E. Super, R. Starishevsky, N. Matlin, & J. P. Jordaan (Eds.), *Career development: Self-concept theory*. Princeton, N.J.: College Entrance Exam. Board, 1963. Pp. 79–95. (b)

Super, D. E., & Overstreet, Phoebe L. *The vocational maturity of ninth grade boys*. New York: Columbia Univer. Teachers Coll., Bur. of Publications, 1960.

Sutherland, E. H., & Cressey, D. R. *Principles of criminology*. (7th Ed.) New York: Lippincott, 1966.

Tannenbaum, A. J. *Adolescent attitudes toward academic brilliance*. New York: Columbia Univer. Teachers College, Bur. of Publications, 1962.

Tanner, J. M. *Education and physical growth*. London: Univer. of London Press, 1961.

Tanner, J. M. *Growth at adolescence*. (2nd Ed.) Springfield, Ill.: Charles C Thomas, 1962.

Terman, L. M., & Oden, Melita H. Genetic studies of genius. *The gifted child grows up*. Stanford, Calif.: Stanford Univer. Press, 1947.

Terman, L. M., & Oden, Melita H. *The gifted group at mid-life*. Stanford, Calif.: Stanford Univer. Press, 1959.

Tiedeman, D. V., O'Hara, R. P., & Baruch, R. W. *Career development: Choice and adjustment.* Princeton, N.J.: College Entrance Exam. Board, 1963.

Toby, J., & Toby, Marcia L. *Low status as a predisposing factor in subcultural delinquency.* New Brunswick, N.J.: Rutgers State Univer., Coop. Res. Monogr. with United States Office of Education, 1962.

Torrance, E. P. *Rewarding creative behavior.* Englewood Cliffs, N.J.: Prentice-Hall, 1965.

Tryon, Caroline M. The adolescent peer culture. In N. B. Henry (Ed.), Adolescence, *Yearb. nat. Soc. Stud. Educ.,* 1944, 43, Part 1. Pp. 217–238.

Tyler, Leona E. The antecedents of two varieties of vocational interests. *Genet. psychol. Monogr.,* 1964, 70, 177–227.

Turner, R. H. *The social context of ambition.* San Francisco: Chandler Publishing, 1964. (a)

Turner, R. H. Some aspects of women's ambition. *Amer. J. Sociol.,* 1964, 70, 271–285. (b)

Wallace, W. L. Institutional and life-cycle socialization of college freshmen. *Amer. J. Sociol.,* 1964, 70, 303–318.

Warner, W. L., & Abegglen, J. C. *Big business leaders in America.* New York: Harper, 1955.

Weber, M. *The Protestant ethic and the spirit of capitalism.* Transl. by T. Parsons. New York: Charles Scribner's Sons, 1958.

Webster, H., Freedman, M., & Heist, P. Personality changes in college students. In N. Sanford (Ed.), *The American college.* New York: Wiley, 1962. Pp. 811–846.

Wessman, A. E., & Ricks, D. F. *Mood and personality.* New York: Holt, Rinehart & Winston, 1966.

White, R. W. The experience of efficacy in schizophrenia. *Psychiatry,* 1965, 28, 199–211.

Whiting, J. W. M., & Burton, R. The absent father and cross-sex identity. *Merrill-Palmer Quart.,* 1961, 7, 85–95.

Wilson, A. B. Residential segregation of social classes and aspirations of high school boys. *Amer. sociol. Rev.,* 1959, 24, 836–845.

Wilson, A. B. The educational consequences of segregation in a California community. In U.S. Commission on Civil Rights, *Racial isolation in the public schools.* Vol. 2. Washington, D.C.: U.S. Government Printing Office, 1967 Appendix C3, pp. 165–206.

Winterbottom, Marian. The relation of need for achievement to learning experiences in independence and mastery. In J. W. Atkinson (Ed.), *Motives in fantasy, action and society.* Princeton, N.J.: Van Nostrand, 1958. Pp. 445–479.

Wohlwill, J. F. Piaget's system as a source of empirical research. *Merrill-Palmer Quart.,* 1963, 9, 253–262.

Wolfe, R. The role of conceptual systems in cognitive functioning at varying levels of age and intelligence. *J. Pers.,* 1963, 31, 108–123.

Wylie, Ruth. *The self-concept.* Lincoln, Neb.: Univer. of Nebraska Press, 1961.

Yarrow, L. J. (Ed.) Symposium on personality consistency and change: perspectives from longitudinal research. *Vita Humana,* 1964, 7 (Whole No. 2).

Youth in the ghetto. New York: Harlem Youth Opportunities Unlimited, Inc., 1964.

Yudin, L., & Kates, S. L. Concept attainment and adolescent development. *J. educ. Psychol.,* 1963, 54, 177–182.

General References

Brim, O. G., Jr., & Wheeler, S. (Eds.) *Socialization after childhood.* New York: Wiley, 1966.

Child, I. L. Socialization. In G. Lindzey (Ed.), *Handbook of social psychology.* Vol. 2. Reading, Mass.: Addison-Wesley, 1954. Pp. 655–692.

Christenson, H. T. (Ed.) *Handbook of marriage and the family.* Chicago: Rand McNally, 1964.

Clausen, J. A. (Ed.) *Socialization and society.* Boston: Little, Brown, 1968.

Hoffman, Lois W., & Hoffman, M. L. *Review of child development research.* New York: Russell Sage Found., Vol. 1—1964, Vol. 2—1966.

Mussen, P. H. (Ed.) *Handbook of research methods in child development.* New York: Wiley, 1960.

Worchel, P., & Byrne, D. (Eds.) *Personality change.* New York: Wiley, 1964. Pp. 489–523.

CHAPTER 6 Comparative Personality Development

WILLIAM KESSEN
Yale University

The common metaphors through which we often indicate variation in human personality testify to man's preoccupation with the relation between the animal and the human being. We are sly as foxes, wise as owls, busy as bees, playful as monkeys, dirty as pigs, and silly as geese. But metaphors will not provide a theory of personality—we are also bright as buttons and sharp as tacks. Over a period of two thousand years, men have sought to build a systematic and relevant account of the behavioral links between animal and man. A necessary assumption in the construction of comparative psychology, whether of learning or of development or of personality, is that man and animal are in some sense of one substance. Aristotle had no doubt about the fundamental similarity nor about its complex character and in *Historia Animalium* he also stated the relation between animal and child that has been a continuing concern of psychologists through the years.

> In the great majority of animals there are traces of psychical qualities or attitudes, which qualities are more markedly differentiated than the case of human beings. For just as we pointed out resemblances in the physical organs, so in a number of animals we observe gentleness or fierceness, mildness or cross temper, courage or timidity, fear or confidence, high spirit or low cunning, and, with regard to intelligence, something equivalent to sagacity. Some of these qualities in man, as compared with the corresponding qualities in animals, differ only quantitatively . . .; other qualities in man are represented by analogous and not identical qualities. . . (Aristotle, 1910, 588a).

These words set out the central question that must be addressed to any treatment of comparative personality development: in comparing the behavior of animal and man, and particularly in comparing the behavior of animal and child, how can we go beyond analogy, beyond the metaphorical ascription of human characteristics to animals and, characteristic of more recent times, the metaphorical ascription of animal characteristics to man? Certainly Aristotle's remarkable recognition of phylogenetic continuity and his observations on animal nature did not produce a comparative psychology. Animals were studied because of their importance to human economy and human entertainment but the examination of behavioral similarities between animals and men degenerated into inventive moralizing. Not only were

The author wishes to express his gratitude to Robert T. Brown and Marshall M. Haith for reading this manuscript well and critically.

remarkable characteristics assigned to animals, but, when the need was great enough, animals were invented to contain the required characteristics. White has translated a twelfth-century bestiary which represents relatively well the status of comparative personality psychology in the years between Pliny and Darwin.

> They are called MONKEYS (Simia) in the latin language because people notice a great *similitude* to human reason in them. Wise in the lore of the elements, these creatures grow merry at the time of the new moon. At half and full moon they are depressed. Such is the nature of a monkey that, when she is giving birth to twins, she esteems one of them highly but scorns the other. . . .
>
> Admitting that the whole of a monkey is disgraceful, yet their bottoms really are excessively disgraceful and horrible. In the same way, the Devil had a sound *foundation* when he was among the angels of heaven, but he was hypocritical and cunning inside himself, and so he lost his cauda-caudex [tail-scripture] as a sign that he would perish in the end (White, 1954, pp. 34f).

The modern age of comparative psychology began in 1871 with the publication of Darwin's *The Descent of Man*. In addition to his speculations on sexual selection, Darwin's book presented an extended statement on the common psychology of animals and man. As he wrote in his chapter on the mental powers of animals, "My object . . . is to shew that there is no fundamental difference between man and the higher mammals in their mental faculties" (Darwin, 1897, p. 66). Darwin fully recognized the enormous distance that separated the "most highly organized ape" and the "lowest savages" but with anecdotes from field, zoo, and home, he insisted on the continuity of mentality and morality as well as on the continuity of structure from species to species. "The fact that the lower animals are excited by the same emotions as ourselves is so well established, that it will not be necessary to weary the reader by many details" (Darwin, 1897, p. 69). Darwin wrote of the common emotions of terror, suspicion, courage, and fear; he also told stories of animal wonder, curiosity, imitation, attention, imagination, reason, progressive improvement (that would today be called learning), the use of tools, language, and the sense of beauty in animals. There can be no doubt that for Darwin the direction of comparative study was to see man in animals. "It is a significant fact, that the more the habits of any particular animal are studied by a naturalist, the more he attributes to reason and the less to unlearnt instincts" (Darwin, 1897, p. 75). The sentence anticipates Jennings' enthusiastic remarks on the variability of amoeba.

> The writer is thoroughly convinced, after long study of the behavior of this organism, that if Amoeba were a large animal, so as to come within the everyday experience of human beings, its behavior would at once call forth the attribution to it of states of pleasure and pain, of hunger, desire, and the like, on precisely the same basis as we attribute these things to the dog (Jennings, 1906, p. 336).

For Darwin, animals were tied to man not only by the bonds of common emotion and cognition but also by the common bonds of social responsibility. He forecasts our contemporary interest in relations between parent and offspring and on social organization when he writes " . . . any animals whatever, endowed with well marked social instincts, the parental and filial affections being here included, would inevitably acquire a moral sense or conscience, as soon as its intellectual powers had become as well, or nearly as well developed, as in man" (Darwin, 1897, p. 98). The reservation is crucial; even at his most enthusiastic, Darwin never lost sight of the profound difference between animal and man in the possibility of abstract thought expressed in flexible language. He has "anthropomorphous" apes, in hypothetical introspection, "admit, that though they could make other apes understand by cries some of their perceptions and simpler wants, the notion of expressing definite ideas by definite sounds had never crossed their minds" (Darwin, 1897, pp. 125f.). It is important to note that Darwin's interest in animal behavior derived from a theoretical attitude; the naturalist was in search of signs of evolution in behavior just as he was in search of signs of evolution in anatomy and physiology. Concern with the evolution of behavior has been a leading theme in the work of one group of Darwin's heirs—the ethologists. As Lorenz put it "psychologically as well as organically, all living creatures are historical entities and it is impossible to understand all their traits without a historical perspective" (Lorenz, 1939, in Schiller, 1957, p. 239).

Darwin saw variation among different animals as only one of the sources of information about the way man came to what Aristotle had called his "most rounded-off and complete" nature. Another source was in the study of children. Here too one could see the change from primitive to polished, from instinctive to intellectual, and from cared for to caring for. The "analogies of development" or "genetic analogies," as James Mark Baldwin (1895, 1902) called them, provoked the parallel development of animal psychology and child psychology in the years following the publication of *The Descent of Man*. Boring (1950) has written of the impact of evolutionary theory on American psychology and he demonstrates the parenthood of Darwin in our study of animals and in our study of children. G. Stanley Hall was the evangelist of evolution—". . . I must have been almost hypnotized by the word 'evolution,' which was music to my ear and seemed to fit my mouth better than any other." (Hall, 1923, p. 357)—and Baldwin was its theorist, attempting to go beyond the metaphor to provide a general structure for the analogies of development. Baldwin saw four epochs in animals and children:

> First, the epoch of rudimentary sense processes, the pleasure and pain process, and simple motor adaptation, called for convenience the 'affective epoch': second, the epoch of presentation, memory, imitation, defensive action, instinct, which passes by gradations into, third, the epoch of complex presentation, complex motor co-ordination, of conquest, of offensive action, and rudimentary volition. These, the second and third together, I should characterize, on the side of consciousness, as the 'epoch of objective reference': and, finally, the epoch of thought, reflection, self-assertion, social organization, union of forces, co-operation; the 'epoch of subjective reference,' which, in human history, merges into the 'social and ethical epoch' (Baldwin, 1895, p. 16).

The study of animals and the study of children by American psychologists continued apace but the ties to evolutionary theory fell away. Animals—rather, rats and monkeys (Beach, 1950; Bitterman, 1960)—were seen by psychologists as conveniently reduced forms for the study of learning and motivation. Child psychology came increasingly to depend on psychoanalysis and on animal learning to provide its conceptual footings. To be sure, some psychologists (notably Katz, 1937, and Werner, 1948) continued to exploit the analogies of development but, between the two world wars, the study of animals and the study of children in the United States developed procedures and attitudes independent of their origins in evolutionary theory. The notion of instinct, so critical for a psychology of phylogeny, fell into disrepute and attempts to understand variation and change in behavior were based almost exclusively on models for conditioning and the learning of skills.

About 1950, European work on comparative psychology—the investigations of ethology—found a wider audience with the publication of a symposium on physiological mechanisms in animal behavior by the Society for Experimental Biology and with the appearance of Tinbergen's *The Study of Instinct* (1951). The aim of the ethologists was not the aim sometimes attributed to psychologists—"to work with animals rather than with men largely on account of their lesser complexity and greater tolerance of the indignities of experiment!" (Thorpe &

Zangwill, 1961, p. x)—but, rather, the ethologists aimed to investigate the phylogeny of behavior, to return to the Darwinian comparisons of evolutionary variation in behavior. During the last decade or so, psychologists have learned a new language (or a dialect of an old language) about fixed action patterns, critical periods, sign stimuli, imprinting, overflow activity, releasers, and so on. Of course, as ethological observations have been assimilated into animal psychology, there has been a tendency for psychologists to subject the observations of the new naturalists to experimental analysis and the theoretical language of ethology to sceptical scrutiny. Running parallel with a revived interest in the comparative study of animal behavior has been a striking increase of interest among psychologists in child development. It is a conjunction that would have delighted Darwin. The parallel development of research and speculation in animal psychology and child psychology has produced an area of common interest and theory. Students of children and of animals alike speak of imprinting and the critical period, of the effects of early stress, of the results of being raised in an enriched or deprived environment, and, in the clearest case of circling back to the problems of 90 years ago, of the development of social attachments between parent and offspring and among members of the social group. The present chapter will present a selection from the vast literature of animal studies directed to issues of early experience and attachment. First however some consideration should be given to the fundamental issue of the relevance of animal study to the understanding of human personality.

THE RELEVANCE OF ANIMAL WORK TO THE STUDY OF HUMAN PERSONALITY

All serious students of animals agree with Bowlby that "direct extrapolation of findings from one species to another is not permissible" (Barnett, 1962, p. 49) and it is common for students of comparative psychology to write justifications for the systematic investigation of animal behavior. Two important reasons for studying animals are by and large irrelevant to the problem of generalization to man. Animals have a central place in human economy and, at least since the first hominid crushed the skull of a baboon, men have had an acute interest in the habits of animals that provide them with food, clothing, and transportation. Easily as obvious a reason for studying animal behavior derives from scientific curiosity. Quite regardless of the implication of animal behavior for human behavior, the systematic study of animals holds an ancient and respected place in biological science. The flight of bees, the attack patterns of squids, the language of dolphins, the arboreal movement of monkeys—there is an integrity and beauty in constructing a science of animal behavior that needs justification by its direct relevance to human beings as little as does systematic study of dwarf stars and the compounds of noble gases. The problem of justification—or, better, the problem of theoretical rationale—becomes acute when we consider how we are to link what we see in animals and what we see in men. Difficult as this question is when we consider comparative studies of drive or comparative studies of simple learning, the problem of indicating the relevance of animal to man in the study of personality development is depressingly short of solution. Surely it is not enough to note with Thorpe (1963, p. 469) ". . . the extraordinary superficial similarity between much animal and much human behaviour." And, although one may be in sympathy with Carpenter's (1964, p. 358) assumption that " the kinship of non-human primates to man makes it reasonable to assume that the study of these types may yield data which can be readily employed in understanding basic kinds of human motivation," *reasonableness* has had little status as a justification for scientific conclusions for many centuries. Moreover, what Ratner and Denny (1964) call "capricious comparisons" lure and can entrap the student of animal behavior. There is so much variety in the behavior of man and in the behavior of animals that a keen analogist could write a rather convincing twentieth-century bestiary from the last fifty years of comparative psychology. Serious treatments of the relation between animal behavior and human behavior fall into one or another of three categories—*the study of the phylogeny of behavior, the observation of parallels (the animal as model),* and *the animal as inspiration.*

The Phylogeny of Behavior

Perhaps the most ambitious view of the relation between animal behavior and human is Darwin's own—that a science of the evolution of behavior could be built comparable to the science of the evolution of structure. One of his most provocative works, *The Expression of the Emotions in Man and Animals* (1872) was addressed to this school and a central thesis of the recent ethological movement has been "a phyletic comparison of different species" (Lorenz, 1939, in Schiller, 1957, p. 240). The study of the phylogeny of behavior does not tend toward mere taxonomic listing of variation among animals although a behavioral taxonomy is the starting point of phyletic study; a true evolutionary theory of animal behavior requires attention to the mechanisms of selection. Consider Lorenz's discussion of "symbolic fights."

> A remarkable group of ritualized motor patterns are the so-called "symbolic fights," which are quite frequent among bony fish (teleosts), reptiles, birds and mammals. These innate reactions originally served to harm rivals of the same species. They have developed along one of two lines of differentiation. Some have turned into perfectly harmless, rigid "ceremonies" (sham fighting among mandarin ducks and game cocks), which serve to allure the female rather than to drive off a rival. Others are so changed that, although the rival is exhausted and finally "gives up," he is not annihilated. Lines of differentiation as well as ontogenetic development leave no doubt that symbolic fighting has evolved by ritualization from primary destructive fighting. Its survival value is evident: it must be of advantage to the species if the strongest animals are selected for reproduction without involving an unnecessary sacrifice of individuals (Lorenz, 1952, in Schiller, 1957, pp. 304f.).

Recently, Lorenz has presented a full-dress survey of the phyletic natural history of aggression from Blue Angelfish to Man, in part "to explain the causes of many of the ways in which aggression in man goes wrong" (Lorenz, 1966, p. xiii).

A similar commitment underlies Carpenter's statement that "the study of the phylogenesis of behavior and social relations on the nonhuman primate level will facilitate the understanding and control of human activities. This approach is likely to reveal archaic behavior mechanisms which are organically functional on the human level" (Carpenter, 1964, p. 358). The program of a phylogeny of behavior, however, suffers from several disabilities, some particular to it and some more generally applicable to the problem of comparison. In the first place, there have been until recently relatively few data collected in a comparable fashion for comparable processes across a wide range of species variation. There are quite a few data on interspecies variation in sex behavior, the older literature on maternal behavior is being steadily added to, we know a great deal about learning in rodents, there is a growing literature on social attachment in precocial birds and social organization in primates, but comparative psychology is still a long way from the array of data on interspecies variation that will be necessary to establish even a primitive taxonomy. Another difficulty in the program of a phylogeny of behavior derives from man's peculiar position as a creature of evolution. Man has existed as a separate species for half a million years and apparently no significant change in structure has taken place during that period. The remarkable adaptations that have taken us from Olduvai to Manhattan have been adaptations based on mechanisms other than classical selection. Finally, although it is not a fatal flaw, the study of the phylogeny of behavior can rarely be subjected to experimental tests, at least among mammals.

The older hopes for an evolutionary theory of development that was contained in the slogan "ontogeny recapitulates phylogeny" can no longer be maintained and a true phylogeny of personality development, comparable in scope and depth to the study of comparative anatomy, has not been presented even in outline.

The Observation of Parallels (The Animal as Model)

The arguments most frequently advanced to underwrite the relevance of animal studies to human behavior center on the animal as a model for man, the animal as an opportunity to study in finer detail or in simpler form processes which are relevant to the study of man. This rationale typically has two components—the animal as presenting simpler process or function and the animal as permitting more precise (specifically, experimental) analysis. The argument of simplification of method, on the face of it, is unassailable. We can far more easily control the experience of rats and cats and macaques than we can control the experience of human infants; we can subject the behavior of nonhuman animals to more precise analysis, varying their environment in a systematic way and measuring their behavior with some precision, while the possibility of doing comparable investigations with human beings is forever barred. But the argument of the simplification of method rests altogether on the prior argument of the simplification of function. To put it bluntly, the most elegant method for the study of animal behavior is of little interest to the psychologist of man if the relevance of the *theoretical relation* of animal behavior to human cannot be well defended. Unfortunately for our confidence in extrapolations from animal to man the gravest deficiency of comparative psychology, particularly as it relates to personality development, is the infrequency of formal statements relating assumed common process, species-specific adaptation, and the relevant parameters of the environment under study. All animals feed and fight and mate and adapt to changing circumstances; the fact that men learn and rats learn scarcely justifies the generalization of findings on rat learning to learning in man. The most sensitive of modern students of comparative psychology, T. C. Schneirla, has indicated some of the complexities of the problem of interspecies study in a discussion of the appearance in development of apparently instinctive behavior.

> Our premise consequently is that the hypothetical genic effects are mediated at each ontogenetic stage by systems of intervening variables characteristic of that stage in that species under prevalent developmental conditions, and that from initial stages these variables include both factors indirectly dependent on the genotype and others primarily dependent on the situation and environs of development (Schneirla, 1960, pp. 307f.).

By his emphasis on the fact that, at each point in development, the organism's adaptation depends on prior adaptation, maturation, and an environmental demand for change, Schneirla indicates the basic problems for a psychology of comparative personality development. There are two dimensions along which comparative research varies, each of which contains a paradox and both of which are important to an understanding of the research to be reported later in this chapter. Ethologists and psychologists influenced by the ethological movement have emphasized the importance of species-specific behavior and a central theme of comparative psychology continues to be the variation in solution of "problems" presented to different species. Yet, to the degree that a solution is species-specific, to that degree it becomes difficult to specify the characteristics of a common process underlying the variation from animal group to animal group. A parallel difficulty, also reflected in the differing traditions of ethology and classical comparative psychology, appears in the distinction between study in a natural environment and experimental study with "artificial manipulation of stimuli." Natural observation typically results in a more highly organized description of the animal's relation to its environment but it also leads to an exaggeration of the efficiency of the animal's adaptation. The animal in its normal environment selects that environment for that set of environmental conditions for which it has a readily available and adaptive response. The laboratory experimental investigation of animal behavior permits a better estimate of the animal's ability to adapt to unusual—truly unnatural—circumstances but the laboratory may remove the animal so far from his expectable environment as to distort the efficiency, even the forms, of his adaptation. Animals raised in laboratories and in zoos apparently vary a great deal from the behavior of their species mates in the wild. The fact that scores of generations of laboratory rats have been raised without access to the earth which is the normal habitat of this animal group illustrates well the special circumstances of laboratory studies of comparative psychology. Neither the conflicting demands of species-specific analysis and the analysis of underlying process nor the conflicting demands of natural and experimental study are fixed obstacles in the development of a comparative psychology of personality. However, these problems are indicative of the difficulties that lie in the way of setting up rule-functions relating the behavior of animals to the behavior of other animals and to the behavior of man. Only as such rule-functions or theories are elaborated with consideration of common processes and specialized differences will animal psychology become truly comparative.

The task of the comparative psychologist of personality is not made easier by the diversity of current personality theory. It is not as though we had a well-formed psychology of human personality from which animal psychologists could draw their questions and toward which they could address their answers. The variety and diversity of animal behavior which have been mentioned already and which support capricious comparison are matched by the variety and diversity of human views of human behavior.

The Animal as Inspiration

The least pretentious and currently most valuable use of the animal in the understanding of human behavior is as a source of ideas to thoughtful students of man. Neither as a way station on the evolution of man nor as a form of man writ small, the variety of animal behavior provokes the psychologist to consider anew some of his old problems. The dance of the bees, the family structure of baboons, the mothering activities of cats, the fighting behavior of some small fish, the behavior of rats in conflict—by their apparent relevance to human behavior and by their desensitizing distance from it—can start the personality psychologist toward a new principle or toward the design of a new study in the only setting which can properly test the relevance of animal behavior to man—observations on man himself. It is a truism worth repeating that, however suggestive observations on animals may be, it is only by testing their application to men that their relevance to human psychology may be completed. The animal as inspiration can be the first step in the process that leads to the elaboration and test of useful principles about human personality. It is a modest role for comparative study but, in our present ignorance of the dimensions of animal and of human personality, research on animals which in a sense serves to declare "behold the phenomenon!" the most restrained and perhaps the most scientific use of animals in the study of human personality.

THE RANGE OF ANIMAL STUDY

From anecdote to monograph, in field study and in experiment, almost any observation of animal behavior can be brought to bear on a discussion of personality. After a look at two general problems in the study of development—the issue of universality and the embryological analogy—the present chapter will draw from the sea of recent animal research a group of studies relevant to the basic theme of *early experience in animals.* Under discussion will be the *following response in precocial birds,* the *song of chaffinches and sparrows,* the *socialization of dogs and monkeys, early enrichment, early restriction,* and the *effects of early handling and early trauma.*

TWO SCHOOLS, TWO PROCEDURES

The student of early development faces a curious choice when he examines human behavior in the first years of life. On one hand he can see early development as *universal in the species.* There is remarkable regularity in the timing and form of infantile smiles, in the timing and succession of responses that lead to walking, in the timing and apparently in the structural sequence of language acquisition, to name just a few of the characteristics that identify human development. Consideration of infancy as universal (Bijou & Baer, 1965) has been a central theme in the study of the child; the regularity of developmental patterns across history and across cultures and the obvious vast differences between human development and the development of any other animal have produced theories of psychological growth which emphasize the species-specific and universal character of early development. In the theories of Freud (1905, 1940) and Piaget (1936, 1946), and unambiguously in the theories of Gesell (Gesell & Amatruda, 1947; Gesell, 1952), inevitable sequences of behavior or of underlying process are specified for man. Although regularities of development have been postulated for adolescents and even for later parts of the lifespan, the implication of relative emphasis has been that the regularities—the universals—of development are greater the younger the child. No one has done a systematic study of variants in timing of critical life events but it seems an unstated assumption of developmental theory that the variation from child to child in age of first smile is less than the variation in age of first heterosexual encounter, that the variation from child to child in locomotor patterns preceding walking is less than the variation in skill at driving an automobile, that the variation in the structure of language in the 2-year-old is less than the variation in the communicative use of language among adults, and so on. Put briefly, variability among persons increases with increasing age. The assumed inevitability of early development has made the first years of life a period of central theoretical interest for the developmental psychologist and substantial research effort has been devoted to the description of the early course of motor, linguistic, social, and cognitive development. As a result, the *normal* development of the human being is undoubtedly more fully documented than the normal development of any other animal species.

But the student of development may come to his data not with an eye for the regularities that separate man from the other animal groups but with an eye for the variation that lies behind statements of typical age or of typical behavior forms. From this point of view—the within-species view, if you like—*early development is often seen as critical for variation* among persons. The early years are not of great empirical and theoretical interest as much for their regularity and stability as they are for the implications of their variation for later growth and personality. Commitment to the proposition that early childhood is a period of particular importance for the development of personality is as least as old as Solomon but more recent theorists have been led to an interest in early development for more than traditional reasons. In the first place, the major theories influencing child psychology in this century—psychoanalysis, learning theory, and Piaget's postulates about cognitive development—all contain, though for different reasons and with different emphasis, propositions about the special importance of early years. Perhaps as important as theory to students of personality development in the first decades of this century was their being caught between an inability to understand human variation in adult environment and an unwillingness to accept the notion of genetic variation in personality. As a consequence, the roots of adult variability were sought in earlier and earlier stages of childhood. Finally, some empirical observations began to suggest a factual base for the special relevance of early experience. A number of investigations have shown that there is a tendency for individual characteristics to stabilize over time. Although it is by no means a universal proposition, it seems to be the case that for some important characteristics of human beings, the older the child is the more like his adult self he will be. Bloom (1964) has summarized these findings and his survey confirms the proposition that—in contrast to the case of comparisons *among* people—there is less variability within the same person as he grows older. Such individual stabilization suggests the relatively greater importance of early experience. In addition to the data on stabilization, there have been a number of observations over the last several decades on the distortions of development that follow on the child's confinement to certain types of institutions. These data have come under some critical examination but they serve to revive interest in the dimensions of early experience relevant to the development of personality.

These two points of view about human development—that early development is stable and regular and that the early years are critical for human variation—are clearly neither exclusive nor incompatible; the regularities of man's development when taken as species-characteristic are truly awesome but no less so is the variability one confronts in examining the behavior of a group of human beings. Unfortunately, the two points of view toward developmental data have sometimes hardened into psychological dogma and become protected by particular social groupings of investigators. The enthusiasts of regularity have dealt with individual variation as reflecting variation in the maturation of important processes and the enthusiasts of variability have seen the regularities of development either as uninteresting or as the consequences of regularities in the environment. With the attitude toward data and the attitude toward theory went a characteristic attitude toward method, with the regularists emphasizing a descriptive-normative procedure and with the idiosyncrasists much more strongly bent toward manipulative experiment. The last decade has seen the steady dissolution of the barrier between these two attitudes toward development. Nonetheless, research on development continues to be marked by the heritage of the dichotomy and, of some consequence to the comparative study of personality, the disjoint traditions of the naturalist-descriptive nativist and the laboratory-experimental environmentalist persist in recent animal work on early development. There are signs of a healthy reconciliation (Schneirla, 1960; Moltz, 1963, 1965) and in the last section of this chapter some recent speculations born of compromise will be presented.

THE EMBRYOLOGICAL ANALOGY

Embryology has long served as a source of analogy for the developmental psychologist. Gesell (e.g., 1952) had a particular interest in the behavior of fetal and premature children and often drew on the ideas of a developmental morphology for his discussion of changes in behavior during the child's development. Although Gesell recognized, as has every serious student of development, the interactive effects of what the child is given and what the child encounters, he returned often to the images of embryology—"the genes initiate the process of development and determine its sphere and limits; but the process continuously creates its own inner control" (Gesell, 1928, p. 358). More recently Lorenz has made explicit his recognition of "a striking analogy between the origin of the system of instinctive behavior patterns and processes familiar from developmental morphology" (Lorenz, 1935, in Schiller, 1957, p. 105).

The analogy with embryology, in the ways it reflects the study of behavior and in the ways it does not, warrants closer attention. The concepts of embryological study which have been brought to bear on the study of development of behavior are chiefly *determination, competence,* and *induction*. The notion of determination is drawn from the observation of the decreasing plasticity of the embryo.

> At an early stage during the development of any given region of the egg, its future fate becomes more or less fixed, so that it can only be altered within a narrow range by any known experimental means; thereafter, that region will always develop into one fairly definite end-product, provided of course that the conditions are such that it can develop at all (Waddington, 1956, p. 13).

Waddington makes a distinction between determination and differentiation. "During determination something occurs which decides which, out of a number of possible types of development, will actually be realised; during the later phases of differentiation, this realisation comes to pass" (Waddington, 1956, p. 13). It is a truism of both popular and academic psychology that a corresponding process occurs in the development of behavior with determination of important psychological processes relatively early in the lifespan. The embryologist, like the psychologist, is concerned with the further analysis of differentiation; he seeks to learn the circumstances under which determination and differentiation take place. For a long time confined to such empty notions as "developmental potency," embryological analysis took a great step forward several decades ago in a series of studies of the determinants of embryological change. Reported in detail by Spemann (1938), these studies indicated that some parts of the developing embryo were more consequential to its further differentiation than others. Working with species of the newt, Spemann and his colleagues found that the blastopore region of the early gastrula was essential for the continued growth of the embryonic newt and he went on to suggest that all growth was organized around such critical parts—the *organizers* of the embryo. In a crucial study, Spemann and Mangold (1924) grafted blastopore regions of gastrulae of one species of newt into gastrulae of another. Not only did the transplanted sections of tissue develop according to their "presumptive fate" but they also differentially determined the development of close-by tissue. This process of developmental control was called *induction* and the search for inducers of embryonic development was on. The search was productive; one of the most interesting findings was that of Waddington and his colleagues who showed that "artificial" inducers such as methylene blue were effective in embryonic differentiation. The parallel with developmental psychology is clear; in order to understand the regularities of human development, one must find those events, in nature or in the laboratory, which induce a change in behavior or in underlying process. But, of course, even the embryological case was not a simple one. Inducers did not operate on undifferentiated inert tissue. Again, from

Waddington, in describing another series of experiments, "This region of the gastrula must not . . . be considered as completely neutral and characterless. It has one most important property; namely the readiness to react to the organiser stimulus. This property shows no sign of being in existence before the onset of gastrulation, and is certainly no longer present by the end of it; organiser grafts into old gastrulae . . . no longer produce inductions. During the stage when the gastrula ectoderm can react, it is said to be *competent* . . . and the period when the reaction is possible is the period of competence. . . . Competence can be thought of as a state of unstable equilibrium; the tissue is poised between two or more alternative paths of development, and may follow one or the other according to the organiser stimuli acting on it" (Waddington, 1956, pp. 178f.). The notion of competence remains of interest to embryologists even after the biochemical discoveries of the last decade that have so changed the study of genetics and organic development.

These then are the embryological notions that have influenced so strongly the thinking of developmental psychologists about maturation and early experience. Of increasing interest over recent years has been the notion of competence or, as it has typically been expressed in writings of students of behavior, the *critical period,* the *sensitive period,* or the *susceptible period* of development. Just as is the case for embryological investigation, it has been proposed that there are periods in the life of the developing organism during which, and only during which, certain determining events can have their influence. We shall see that the notion of competence has been drastically transformed in its translation to the study of behavior, but one characteristic of the embryological model that is not yet relevant to its psychological application can be mentioned here. The embryologist generally knows toward what goal the growth of his material is directed; the structure of the completed newt or pig or human being is quite well known. Slight aberrations in that development, so important for experimental study, can be detected readily and often understood in terms used to describe normal development. No such precise formulation can be given to the terminal state of human personality, of course, and, as noted earlier, one of the difficulties of understanding personality development is the absence of a coherent and fully worked through description of adult personality.

In spite of the fact that embryologists have used the notions of determination, induction, and competence to suggest valuable research about embryonic development, many of the problems posed by the notions will sound familiar indeed to the developmental psychologist who attempts to understand the development of behavior in terms of the analogous notions of maturation, structure, and critical period. Waddington asks his fellow embryologists a series of questions which are directly relevant to current psychological concern with early experience. ". . . [H]ow far does the arising of a later competence, for example, to develop into lens or cornea, depend on the previous performance of an earlier step, such as, beginning to develop in the direction of epidermis rather than mesoderm? If an inducer for a late-appearing tissue is allowed to act at an early stage and then removed, can it perform its induction, or must it operate during the phase of competence? If it can induce, what is happening in the cells in the period between the inducer's action and the manifest response of the cells?" (Waddington, 1962, p. 82). The lament that we know "disappointingly little" about competence will be loudly echoed in a review of studies of critical periods in the development of behavior.

The psychologist concerned with the comparative development of behavior has addressed three kinds of questions that mirror the embryological enquiry. How is behavior regularly related to age? Are there periods in development when the organism is particularly sensitive? How does early experience affect later behavior? The latter two questions have received great attention in recent years with research inquiry and speculation directed to the issues of *critical periods* and the effects of *early experience* in animals and in men. The first more classical question about the regularities of behavioral development remains important and a number of natural historical studies of animals, particularly primates in the wild, have carried our knowledge in giant steps beyond the beginnings made by Yerkes (R. M. Yerkes, 1929; R. M. Yerkes & A. W. Yerkes, 1943) and Carpenter (e.g., 1934).[1] But, in attempting to draw on research with animals to assist our understanding of human development, it will be found that more is known of the relation between behavior and age in man than in any other species. Developmental tests, whatever their deficiencies in thoughtfulness and relevance to later behavior, have provided a reliable inventory of the human march toward maturity. The comparative psychology of development, in the traditions of testing, will not be discussed in this chapter. Necessary as it is to establish baseline values, the description of development as it normally occurs in a species is a poor guide to the conditions and their variations that influence development. And not only because the emphasis of the maturationalists has been normative. As Schneirla points out, not only is the behavior of animals adaptive; each species also occupies an adaptively established environment and the regularities of development may be ascribable as much to the regularities of the species-selected environment as to its "natural unfolding of behavior." For this reason, among others, the interest of clinical psychologists and comparative psychologists alike have turned to enthusiastic consideration of what may be called, most generally, early experience. A key to the puzzle of personality variation is being sought simultaneously in the distortion of the institution and the manipulation of the laboratory.

THE EARLY EXPERIENCE OF ANIMALS

The literature on early experience in animals was first brought together in an excellent review by Beach and Jaynes in 1954; since that time a number of attempts have been made to bring the vast array of new studies into coherent theoretical or summary-descriptive form. The papers by King (1958), Denenberg (1962), Fuller and Waller (1962), and Thompson and Schaefer (1961) are of particular interest. No attempt will be made in the present chapter to duplicate their work of review. Rather, the effects of early experience will be examined by treating a few representative animal studies in some detail.

It must be noted at the outset that the term "early experience" hides great variation in species studied, methods, stimulus variation, and response measures. Rats, cats, dogs, mice, guinea pigs, and monkeys have been isolated, deprived, shocked, enriched, and weaned while psychologists studied their perception, learning, emotionality, exploration, and their social and sexual behavior. It is little wonder that Beach and Jaynes were constrained to write, after asserting their conviction of the importance of studies of early experience, ". . . an equally strong impression is that much if not most of the presently available evidence

[1] The variety of "natural" studies of animal development is awesome. Laymen have written unsystematically about "Toto and I" (Hoyt, 1941) and about "My friend the chimpanzee" (Oberjohann, 1957); zoologists have attempted to describe whole groups of animals (e.g., Bourlière's [1964] beautiful book on mammals) and to draw together all available information on a single species (e.g., Barnett's [1963] study of the rat); Riesen and Kinder (1952) have put together a Gesell-based test for chimpanzees; and these citations can only suggest the range of studies of animal development. Recently, observations of primates in the wild (e.g., Jay, 1962; Schaller, 1963; Devore, 1963) and in the laboratory (e.g., Harlow, 1961; Mowbray & Cadell, 1962; Mason, 1963) give promise of a coherent comparative study of development in anthropoids.

bearing upon this problem is equivocal and of undetermined reliability" (Beach and Jaynes, 1954, pp. 256f.). King found so much variation in experimental procedure in some two dozen studies of early experience in rodents that he was able "to accept only the general hypothesis that some early experiences affect later behavior" (King, 1958, p. 56). It is revealing of this variation to compare Fuller and Waller's (1962, p. 236) ideal design for studies of early experience shown in Figure 1 with King's summary of the available data from rat studies up to 1958, shown in Figure 2. With the addition that these studies represent some eleven different kinds of manipulation of early experience and at least four different classes of test task, the problem of drawing firm conclusions even for the rat are clearly seen. In examining studies of early experience, it is well to bear in mind two distinctions among the several hypothesized relations between age and effect of treatment. Thompson and Schaefer have presented three curved forms to represent the possible relations between age and effect. These curves are shown in Figure 3. The first curve in Figure 3, which assigns a greater effect to treatments at early ages, in fact represents two possible relations. As Ader (1959) has pointed out, it is

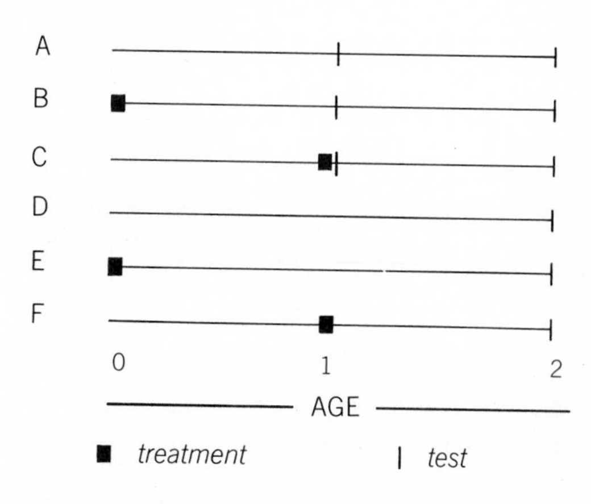

Figure 1. A six-group design for analyzing the effects of treatment at two stages (from Fuller and Waller, 1962). The scheme is designed to assess the effects of treatment age, test age, and treatment-test interval.

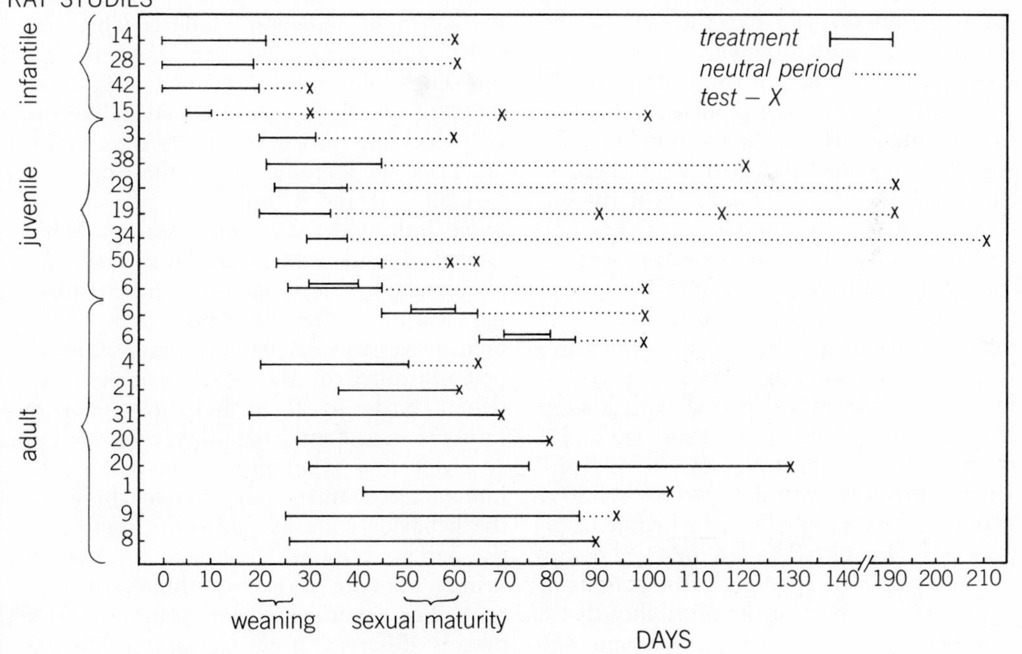

Figure 2. Selected empirical studies of early experience in rats. From King, 1958.

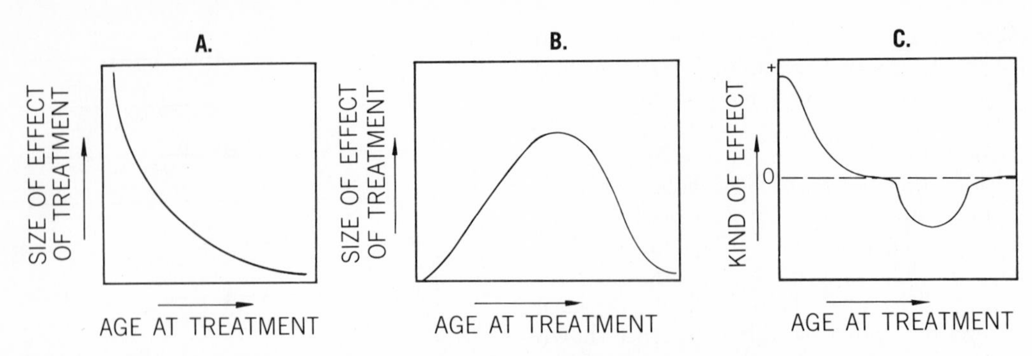

Figure 3. Possible relations between age at treatment and size or kind of effect produced, either immediately or later in life. From Thompson and Schaefer, 1961.

essential to distinguish between *early* experience and *merely prior* experience, between the importance of an event occurring early in development as against the importance of an event occurring first. Thus, if the abscissa in Thompson's first figure is fixed at particular age values then it represents truly the effects of early experience. If the abscissa represents a floating variable with a value at the left being only *prior* to a value at the right then the function represents the greater effect of prior experience. The distinction is an important one; there is great theoretical and practical implication in the difference between saying, for example, that human infants are attached to human adults because they encounter them first or because they encounter them at a particularly susceptible time of the infants' lives. The second curve in Figure 3 represents an expression of the critical period hypothesis—that a certain treatment will have its effect only during a bounded period of the organism's life. This curve too can be seen as representing an absolute critical period with a steep rise from zero effect at an early age and a steep fall to zero effect at a later or as representing a relative critical period or "sensitive period" (Thorpe, 1963) or a "schedule of experience" (Fuller & Waller, 1962). Thompson and Schaefer, apparently for reasons of symmetry, also present the possibility that a treatment may have one effect at one age and an inverse effect at another but hardly any data exist to support the postulation of such a relation. Finally, of course, the possibility of a null relation between age and effect of experience must be admitted.

The Following Response in Precocial Birds

Some thirty years ago, Lorenz reviewed the observations of earlier workers and added some of his own to illustrate a remarkable phenomenon in birds which he called *imprinting*. No one doubted that ducklings followed ducks and that goslings followed geese—fictional anomalies like the ugly duckling only emphasize the regularity of conspecific identification in these developmentally advanced birds who are able to move independently after hatching. What Lorenz found remarkable was that the phenomenon was apparently neither innate nor learned. That identification of one's own species was not innately organized was best illustrated by the attachment of hand-reared birds to their human caretakers rather than to members of their own species. ". . . if a greylag gosling is taken into human care immediately after hatching, all the behavior patterns which are slanted to the parents respond at once to the human being" (Lorenz, 1935, in Schiller, 1957, p. 103). The argument that imprinting was a process different from learning contained two components. First, imprinting can only take place within a brief critical period in the life of an individual and, second, the effects of imprinting during this critical period early in life are irreversible—adult forms of social and sexual behavior are directed toward members of the species on whom the animal is imprinted, whether these are conspecifics or not. A paper on imprinting by Ramsey and Hess (1954) and a series of papers by Jaynes (1956, 1957, 1958a, 1958b) opened the way to a flood of American studies on patterns of following in precocial birds. Hess and his colleagues have published papers reporting studies on thousands of animals and a variety of species have been examined although most studies have been on domesticated mallards (Peking ducks) and on domestic chicks. The phenomenon of imprinting as reported by Lorenz has great apparent relevance to the wider study of relations between parent and offspring and to the identification of one's own kind in species very different from nidifugous birds and, as we shall see, the notion has been used in attempts to understand early human behavior. The appeal of imprinting as an explanatory notion rests in part on its neat compromise of the issue of innateness and learning and in part on the suggestive implication of the notions of critical period and irreversibility. Data collected by Goldfarb (1945, 1955), by Spitz (1945), by Spitz and Wolf (1946), and by Provence and Lipton (1962), among others, on the debilitating effects of early institutionalization could facilely be cast into the language of critical periods and irreversible effects. Voices of caution have been heard—Hinde (Thorpe and Zangwill, 1961, p. 190) reminds us that the ancestors of men and the ancestors of mallards parted evolutionary company sometime during the Permian—and many psychologists have rejected the notion that imprinting represents a process fundamentally different from conditioning and instrumental learning. A consideration of the relevance of the notion of imprinting to human behavior can be postponed; in the next paragraphs, a group of studies will be reported in illustration of the complexities of the imprinting phenomenon even among its favorite practitioners, the fowls.

In the typical procedure for the laboratory study of imprinting, animals are isolated shortly after hatching and housed alone until their imprinting trials. The young animal is then introduced into a runway which contains a moving model. The tendency of the young animal to follow the object (e.g., to stay within one foot of it) is measured and, oftentimes, later tests are run to determine the preference of the young animal for the model on which it was imprinted. Within this general definition of procedure there has been wide variation in detail. Birds are sometimes held on a light-dark cycle before imprinting tests, they are sometimes housed with another bird, the model is sometimes a decoy of the species and sometimes a colored cube or triangle or ball, the model may be silent or talking (e.g., "gock, gock, gock" or "come, chick, chick, chick" or the recorded natural call of the birds' species), and both timing and measure of strength of imprinting have varied from study to study. Available evidence indicates that none of these variations is inconsequential for an understanding of imprinting and some of them may be critical for arguments about reversibility and innateness.

The critical period

Jaynes (1957) exposed New Hampshire Red chicks for 30 minutes to a green cardboard cube that moved and paused in a journey up and down a ten-foot-long alley. An animal was considered to be imprinted if he stayed within one foot of the cube for 60 seconds or more during the last 5 minutes of the session. The intensity of imprinting was measured by the length of time the animal stayed within one foot of the object. Jaynes' findings during the imprinting sessions themselves are shown in Figure 4. He also observed the behavior of the animals when placed in the alley with the model ten days after the initial imprinting session. The results of this observation are shown in Figure 5. The reduced tendency

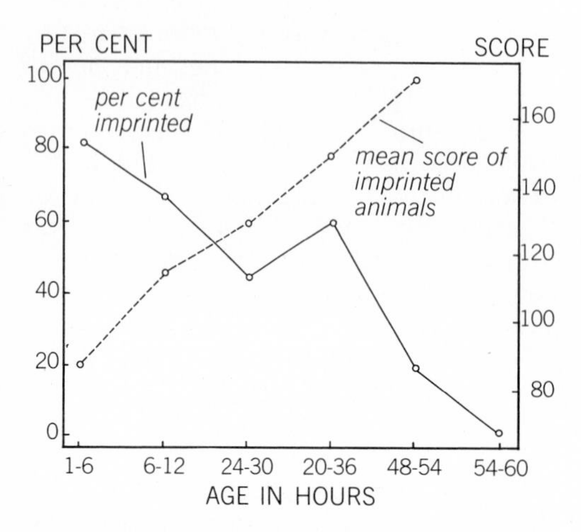

Figure 4. The "critical period for imprinting" in young New Hampshire Red chicks. From Jaynes, 1957.

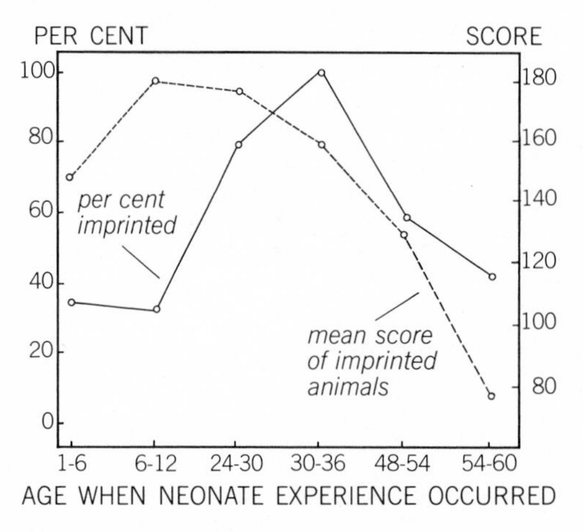

Figure 5. Following of model 10 days after exposure in New Hampshire Red chicks. From Jaynes, 1957.

to follow in young animals Jaynes called "forgetting" and the increased tendency of animals imprinted between 6 hours and 54 hours to follow he called "latent imprinting." Jaynes also pointed out the tendency of the chicks to flee from the model when they were first exposed to it after 30 hours of age. In an often-quoted study of critical period in mallards, Hess (1959) isolated the ducklings shortly after hatching and maintained them in the dark until imprinting trials. At ages of from 1 hour to 32 hours the ducklings were placed in a circular runway with the model of an adult male mallard who called "gock" and they followed the model for approximately 150 to 200 feet around the runway during a 10-minute period. Sometime after the imprinting experience, the ducklings were given four preference tests with two duck decoys. The decoy which they had followed, silent, was pitted against a female decoy, silent; one minute later, the male model began "gocking" and the female gave the natural call of mallards; in the third test only the female called; in the fourth test the male was stationary and silent and the female moved and called. A positive score was a move toward the male decoy; a perfect score was to remain with the male decoy through all four tests. Figures 6 and 7 present the results of this study. Subsequent studies by Hess and his colleagues (e.g., 1964) as well as observations in other laboratories have in general confirmed the finding of a period of time early in the lives of chicks and ducklings when they are most likely to follow an object presented and to prefer the presented object during a later test. There has been less consensus on the interpretation of the phenomenon and recent research on imprinting in precocial birds has turned on attempts to understand the dimensions of the critical period and the persistence of initial attachment.

The boundaries of the critical period

Hess has proposed that the strength of imprinting varies with the effort expended by the bird and that the slowly developing ability of animals to move and to follow an object vigorously accounts for the ascending limb of the function relating strength of imprinting to age. As the bird is able to follow more vigorously, his greater expendi-

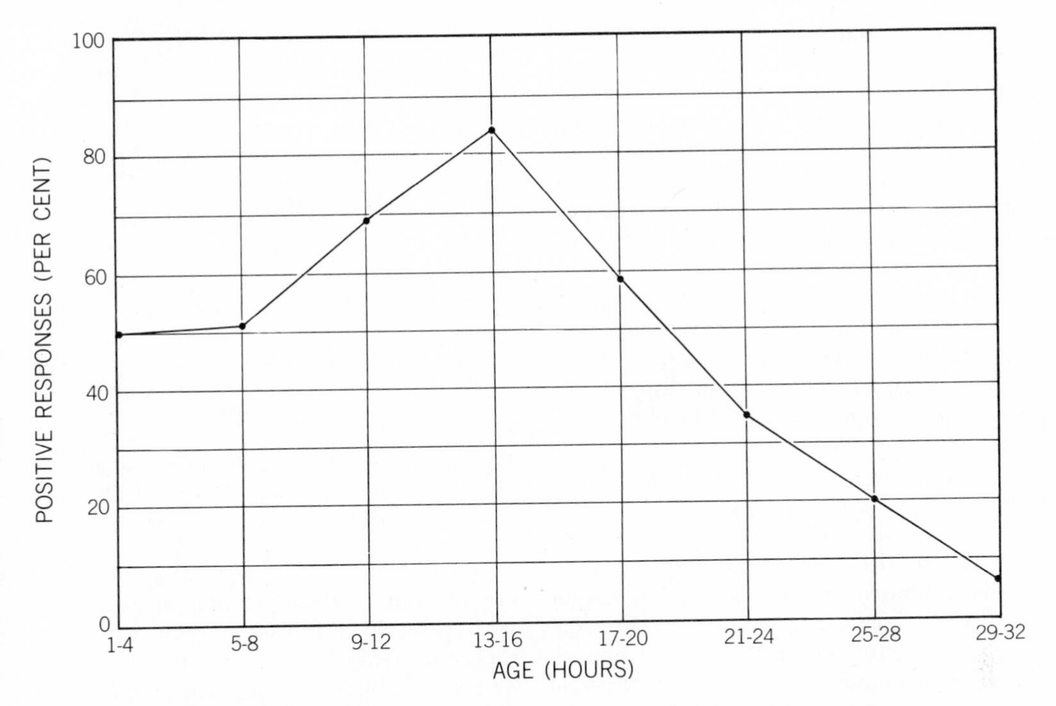

Figure 6. Preference scores of ducklings during tests of imprinting. From Hess, 1959.

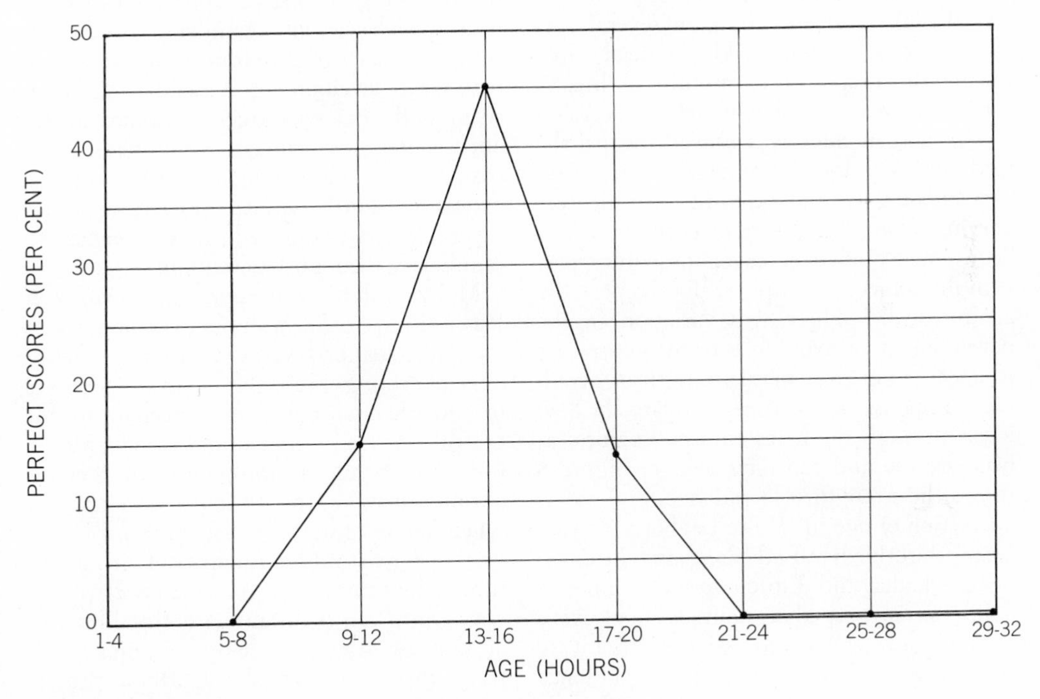

Figure 7. Percentage of perfect preference scores of ducklings during tests of imprinting. From Hess, 1959.

ture of effort results in stronger imprinting. Far more research has been carried out on the descending limb of the imprinting-age function. Why does imprinting apparently become more difficult with increasing age past a certain point and, a closely related question, how can susceptibility be extended past its usual time of appearance? Jaynes' observations on flight responses in his chicks suggested that, after 30 hours of age, animals would begin to flee rather than to approach the presented object. Hess and Schaefer (1959) observed the distress calls and flight of White Rock chicks of different ages and found evidence of fear that ran from very low levels at ages under 12 hours to very high levels at ages above 32 hours. Hess concluded from this pair of studies that the critical period for imprinting in birds is limited on one side by locomotor ability and on the other by the development of fearful responses to novel objects. The development of avoidance in precocial birds has recently been studied in some detail by Schaller and Emlen (1962) who observed flight and crouching in several species of domestic and wild precocial birds during the first 5 to 12 months of life. A cardboard rectangle that varied on occasion in size and in color was moved toward the birds and withdrawn several times; intensity of avoidance was measured in seven degrees varying from "no avoidance response" to "runs wildly all over cage, sometimes past stimulus objects; jumps or flies repeatedly against wall." There was variation in the development of avoidance from one species to another but in general strength of avoidance response rose from a relatively low level through high asymptotic values at between 100 and 140 days of age. Figure 8 shows the strength of avoidance response as a function of age in White Leghorn X New Hampshire birds raised alone and in darkness. Schaller and Emlen found some evidence to suggest that animals who were isolated but who could see the laboratory showed somewhat lower levels of avoidance after 100 hours. And, on the basis of their

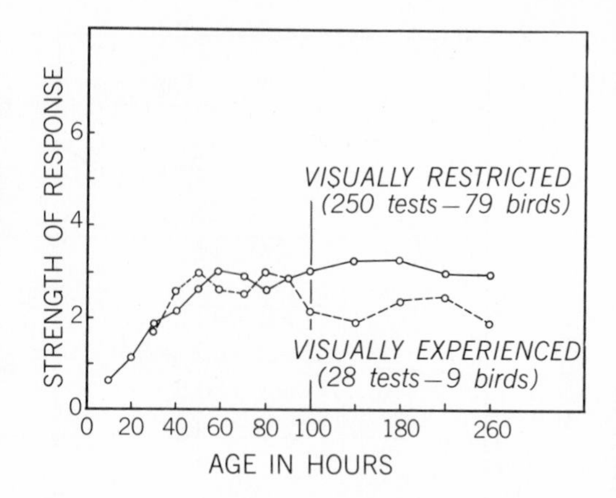

Figure 8. Strength of avoidance response in chicks raised in isolation. From Schaller and Emlen, 1962.

observations of the reduction in avoidance with repeated stimulation, these investigators concluded that "the property of strangeness in an object is thought to be the essential factor which elicited avoidance behavior in our young chicks. It is proposed that objects which become familiar to a chick through repeated or continuing exposure before the development of avoidance responsiveness do not subsequently induce avoidance; objects which are encountered after that stage of development tend to induce avoidance until repeated exposure under favorable conditions reduces strangeness to familiarity through habituation."

Moltz and his colleagues (e.g., Moltz & Rosenblum, 1958; Moltz & Stettner, 1961) have also studied variation in the fearfulness of young precocial birds in attempts to provide an explanatory mechanism for critical periods in imprinting. Briefly, Moltz, following Schneirla, proposes that there is a time early in the animal's development when he is almost exclusively sensitive to variation in stimulus intensity. During this time, when imprinting is most effective, the young bird can maintain an optimal level of arousal by staying a short distance away from the presented object. By a process much like contiguity conditioning, aspects of the object become cued to the state of optimal arousal. Later on, when the animal's developing perceptual abilities make it more responsive to the detail of its environment and thereby more fearful of novel stimulation, its fear is reduced by approach to the model and the model's cues of fear reduction and an optimal state of arousal. Several studies have lent support to this position. In one of these Moltz and Stettner (1961) studied Peking ducklings whose visual experience was limited by the use of latex hoods until their first exposure to a model (in this case a green cardboard object), a procedure which was meant to postpone the time at which the animal would be sensitive to and thereby fearful of environmental novelty. To be sure, although there was little difference in the following of the model between the visually deprived and visually experienced animals at 12 hours, the visually deprived animals followed the object more than the normal controls at both 24 hours and 48 hours of age. In a test of the notion that imprinted birds would follow more the more fearful they were, Moltz and Rosenblum (1958) exposed a group of animals to the imprinting alley *without* the model for one hour each day between Days 4 and 10 of the animals' lives. In confirmation of expectation, these habituated animals followed the model significantly less than did controls who were not given the habituation experience. Recent studies on the effects of rearing in the presence of another chick prior to imprinting (Hess, 1964), on the effects of handling (Thompson & Dubanoski, 1964), and on the effects of shock (Kovach & Hess, 1963) all testify to the importance of considering the level of fearfulness or arousal in studies of imprinting. Consider one of the studies of Kovach and Hess. Vantress broiler chicks were placed in a circular runway at 14 hours, 18 hours, and 32 hours of age. For 25 minutes, they followed a blue sphere which said "Come, chick, chick, chick." A control group was run in the conventional fashion; three experimental groups were given either 27 light shocks (approximately one milliampere for one-half second delivered to electrodes on the chicks' wings), 11 heavy shocks (approximately 3 milliamperes for one-half second), and 27 heavy shocks, all during the imprinting period. Figure 9 shows the dis-

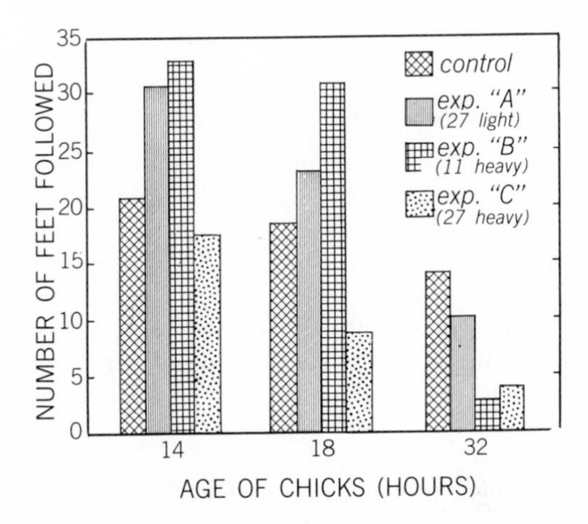

Figure 9. Following of model by Vantress broilers after shocks of different value during imprinting. From Kovach and Hess, 1963.

tance in feet the sphere was followed by each group of animals. For the two younger groups of chicks, light shock and infrequent heavy shock facilitated the following while frequent heavy shock depressed it; for the older group all levels of shock had a depressing effect on following. The conclusion of the authors approaches that of Moltz and Schaller and Emlen in spirit if not in detail: ". . . while the critical age for acquisition of the following response corresponds to the maturational state at which the particular excitability implicated in following behavior is at its optimum, the actual following performance is the combined result of excitability and the intensity of external stimulation" (Kovach & Hess, 1963, p. 464).

Studies of the critical period in precocial birds, varying as they do in procedure, species, and response measure, tend to support the conclusions that the upper age of susceptibility to following and attachment is not fixed but varies with perceptual experience of a quite general kind (e.g., reduction to patterned light alone as against full visual experience) and according to level of arousal both during imprinting and during test, both by raising the level of arousal through shock or by lowering it through habituation to the environment.

The stability of imprinting

As noted earlier, one of the most striking characteristics assigned by Lorenz and by Hess to true imprinting is its remarkable stability. Exposure to a model in early life predisposes the animal's later social and sexual identifications. By and large support for this position has been drawn from informal accounts; the hard data available were from animals tested in a limited range of circumstances, and not long after the initial imprinting session. Klopfer and Hailman (1964) and Klopfer (1965) cast doubt even on the short-term stability of attachment in both ducklings and chicks. Animals were trained during the peak of the normal critical period to follow one of two lifesize mallard decoys both of whom said "Kom, kom, kom, kom." The plain decoy was flat white in color; what Klopfer and Hailman call the "striking" model was yellow with patches and stripes of red, green, blue, and brown. When chicks were trained to moving models and tested with stationary models 24 hours later, the expected clear preference for the training model was found. When chicks were trained to stationary models and tested with stationary models, much less following was shown in both training and test and the preference of the birds for the training model was reduced and statistically unstable. Their truly surprising finding, however, was that when birds were trained to moving models and tested with moving models 24 hours later, the striking model was clearly preferred by both groups. Thus, birds who followed a plain model during the imprinting session chose the striking model when given a preference test on the next day. This finding raises a question about the simplicity of the imprinting phenomenon and suggests, among other possibilities, that the initial imprinting session may serve to get the animal following and that other circumstances (for example, the perceptual characteristics of the presented objects) may determine what specific object is followed later on. Results in support of this suggestion were obtained by Waller and Waller (1963). Using somewhat smaller groups than are typical for imprinting studies, they performed three experiments on the general question of the object specificity of imprinting. In the second and perhaps most revealing of these, Peking ducks were exposed for an hour each day to a green cardboard cube or to a sibling duckling. In Group C-D the animals were exposed for the first five days after hatching to the cube and for Days 6 through 10 to their sibling; Group D-C was exposed to a sibling on Days 1 through 5 and to the cube on Days 6 through 10; Group O-C had no exposure during the first five days of life but was exposed to the moving cube during Days 6 through 10. On Day 11 all animals were presented with a preference test pitting the cube against a live duckling of the subject's age. Figure 10 shows the results of the preference test; although both Group D-C and Group C-D spent more time with the stimulus duckling than did Group O-C, they did not differ significantly from one another and it is interesting that both of them spent more time with the duckling than with the cube even though Group C-D did not see a duckling until well into the period which normally produces avoidance to normal stimulation. Although the Waller and Waller experiments give support to the operation of imprinting they also demonstrate the importance of varying potency of objects and suggest, like the Klopfer studies, that "imprinting" sessions may serve to make later following more likely regardless of the object followed.

Systematic studies of the persistence into

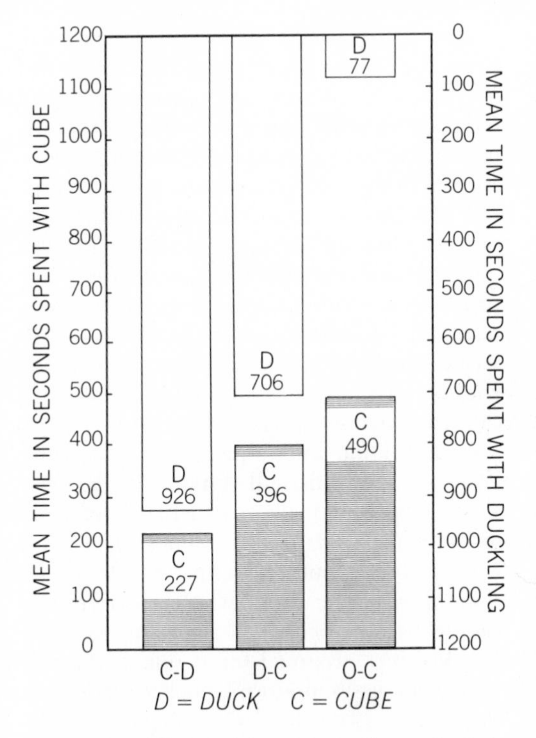

Figure 10. The preference for cube or duck in tests of animals imprinted under three conditions. From Waller and Waller, 1963.

adult life of the effects of early imprinting experience hardly exist and a study by Guiton (1961) of the aggressive and sexual sequelae of imprinting in the Leghorn is valuable in spite of the small number of birds observed. Brown Leghorn males spent one hour a day on the second, third, fourth, and fifth days after hatching with either a triangular box or a rectangular box, both of which played a recording of broody-hen clucking. In addition to 17 birds trained individually on these models, some nine birds were trained to follow the models in groups of four or five. Imprinting was weak in these communally trained birds and they will not be discussed further here. Two small control groups were habituated in the test situation during their six-week period. Following, aggressive behavior, and sexual displays were observed. The individually imprinted birds continued to follow the correct model through the first 8 weeks of life; when tested at 8 weeks 12 of the 17 birds responded correctly whereas none of the habituated birds did although the duration of following at 8 weeks was much less in the imprinted birds than it had been at 7 days. Observations of aggressive behavior at 8 weeks found the rectangle-trained birds responding more frequently to the rectangle model than to the triangle model and the triangle-trained birds preferring the triangle model for their aggression. No significant effects of imprinting on sexual display or "tidbitting" or "waltzing" was found at 8 weeks or at 24 weeks although two birds clearly waltzed to the appropriate training model. Only six birds were kept for further study after sexual maturity at 24 weeks and these included the two consistent waltzers. Only in these two birds did signs of discriminating response to the appropriate model persist and for both of them there was differential responding at 14 months of age. However, when presented with a stuffed cockerel or hen as well as with their models even these two persistently imprinted birds made more vigorous responses toward the stuffed animals. The effect of imprinting on the following response in the first 8 weeks is clearly demonstrated by Guiton's observations but, as he concludes, ". . . though the Brown Leghorn cockerel's behaviour is influenced by early experience [it is probable that] neonatal experience during the first 5 days of life . . . is yet not in itself sufficient to have effect[s] as irreversible and drastic on subsequent adult behaviour as those reported to occur in some other species" (Guiton, 1961, p. 175). For contrasting positive evidence of persistent effects Guiton, like everyone else, calls on Lorenz's informal and unsystematic observations.

There have been hints in the data on imprinting that some stimuli are more potent to the animal than others and that the precocial bird may not be willing to accept as species member any stimulation presented to him during the typical critical period for imprinting. These hints have been confirmed with the force of data in a group of excellent studies by Gottlieb (1965) on the response of naive birds to the parental calls of their own species. The first two experiments in Gottlieb's series will serve to illustrate his procedure and his findings. In the first experiment 224 Peking ducks of known developmental age[2] were exposed to a moving model of an adult Peking duck for a 20-minute period. Each of three groups heard a different message from the model; for the fourth group the model was silent. One group heard the exodus call (i.e., the call that the mother bird makes in nature as she leads her young from the nest) of the mallard, Peking duck's wild conspecific; the second group heard the exodus call of the wood duck hen; the third experimental group heard the exodus call of the domestic chicken. In a second experiment domestic chicks of the White Rock breed were divided into four groups parallel to those of Experiment 1. Table 1 shows the incidence, latency, and duration of following of the ducklings in Experiment 1 and the chicks in Experiment 2. It is clear from these data that, quite without prior experience of parental call, ducklings and chicks responded more vigorously and more often to the parental calls of their own species than to the calls of other species. Gottlieb properly points out that such findings require mechanisms other than imprinting or learning. He also showed in an analysis of the relation between age and incidence of following that "critical period" for this relation depends in part on species and in part on presented stimulation. Later studies in this series (Gottlieb, 1965) showed that the tendency of ducklings to follow the parental call of their own species is strongly resistant to modification by "imprinting" experience although the birds will respond in the classically expected way to experience of calls other than one natural to their species.

It is ironic, but altogether in the tradition of scientific analysis, that imprinting should partake neither of the regularity and stability first proposed for it nor of the full independence of preformism that made it so

[2] Gottlieb (1963) has presented evidence that a cold shock procedure permits accurate identification of incubation age in birds and that this true "developmental age" is a more stable indication of maturation than post hatch age.

TABLE 1

INCIDENCE, LATENCY, AND DURATION OF FOLLOWING RESPONSE OF NAIVE BIRDS EXPOSED TO A MODEL EMITTING THE PARENTAL CALL OF THEIR OWN AND OTHER SPECIES (FROM GOTTLIEB, 1965)

Experimental Condition	*N*	Percentage Following	Latency (in sec.)		Duration (in sec.)	
			M	*SD*	*M*	*SD*
Ducklings from Experiment 1						
Mallard	60	85	290.9	253.1	589.6	370.5
Wood duck	59	63	421.7	250.5	468.6	322.9
Chicken	57	40	468.2	307.7	367.9	336.7
Silence	48	4	607.0	151.3	300.5	181.7
Chicks from Experiment 2						
Chicken	79	72	297.4	204.6	371.0	293.8
Mallard	71	37	401.6	220.9	238.6	215.4
Wood duck	75	26	517.7	267.0	117.3	160.1
Silence	63	25	595.9	272.5	89.4	163.2

appealing as a model of human behavior. Nonetheless, there can be little doubt that precocial birds are particularly sensitive during a relatively short period of their early lives to stimulation which produces following and, further, that the object followed during this sensitive period remains consequential for the animal for some time. Perhaps it is appropriate to speak of the analogy between imprinting and its critical period on one hand and the phenomena of developmental morphology on the other—to see the process underlying attachment as *competence* during a bounded period of time and to see stimulation provided during that time as an *organizer* of further development. But we are hardly beyond the analogy; we have only glimmerings of indexes of competence independent of age, and the nature of the hypothesized organizer becomes, if anything, less certain with the accumulation of systematic data.

Our knowledge of imprinting is based almost altogether on observations of precocial birds (see Sluckin, 1965, for a recent review) although a few studies suggest the relevance of the notion to the developmentally precocious guinea pig (Shipley, 1963) and to maternal behavior in sheep and goats (Hersher, Richmond, & Moore, 1963). Social and sexual behavior in altricial birds—those who cannot leave the nest shortly after hatching—has recently been put under systematic observation by Klinghammer (Klinghammer & Hess, 1964; Klinghammer, in press). One group of ring doves was removed from the nest on Days 4 through 14, reared by hand until weaning, and then isolated. A second group was removed from the nest, hand-reared until weaning, and then returned to a cage with other ring doves. A third group was isolated only after they had been raised and weaned by their parents. A fourth group was raised by their parents and kept in a cage with other doves until tested. When presented after sexual maturity (that is, when the birds were at least 8 months old) with a choice between a human being and a conspecific, birds in the four groups behaved quite differently. Hand-reared isolated birds removed from the nest before 10 days of age tended to select the human being, birds raised to weaning by their parents and then isolated behaved in a highly inconsistent fashion, and both groups which spent all of their post-weaning lives with other doves invariably chose a dove instead of a human being. Evidence from the hand-reared isolated animals suggests that a sensitive period for imprinting may exist between Days 7 and 9 (a period near the onset of fear in this bird), but the results from birds returned after isolation to the community of their own specifics indicates quite clearly that whatever imprinting takes place on human beings during hand-rearing is reversible later in life. This preliminary finding with one species of altricial birds emphasizes again how highly specialized the imprinting phenomenon in precocial birds may be.

The Song of Chaffinches and Sparrows

The complexities of what is given and what is got in animal development are neatly demonstrated in research on acquisition of species-specific song by altricial birds. Thorpe (1958a, 1958b) demonstrated three characteristics of song learning in the chaffinch (*Fringilla coelebs*): (1) birds raised without an opportunity to hear the characteristic song of their species developed a reduced and irregular form of the characteristic song; (2) birds who hear the characteristic song of their species, even though they do not produce it themselves in their first few weeks of life, are able to produce the song in the next singing season even though isolated; (3) further changes take place in the details of the chaffinch's song during the first singing season, apparently as a consequence of hearing the song of his neighbors. Clearly, the fully formed song of the adult chaffinch in nature is determined by the interlocking of some preformed "program" of appropriate duration and number of notes, juvenile experience that sets the common outline of the species-song, and early adult experience that adds somewhat more individualized components.

The findings of the English group on song learning in birds have been extended by Marler and Tamura (1964) and their colleagues. They have made use of the fact that the white-crowned sparrow (*Zonotrithia leucothyrs*) not only shows a species-specific song but, in addition, shows variation in song "dialect" from one geographical center to another. Like other song birds, the white-crown hears the singing of adults from about his twentieth day of life to his hundredth; he sings himself normally only after the molting layoff of summer and fall. Marler and Tamura have examined a number of white-crown sparrows raised under different circumstances and, in a preliminary report, demonstrate how inappropriate is any dichotomous treatment (learned versus unlearned, for example) of song acquisition. Like Thorpe's chaffinches, young white-crown sparrows captured after having heard the song of their fathers and other adults developed the dialect of their home area in the following spring. Males taken in the first two weeks of life and isolated developed a peculiar song pattern that is only barely recognizable as the white-crown song. Marler and Tamura have found further that exposure of isolated birds to recorded bird song of an alien dialect had little influence prior to the second week after hatching and after about 100 days of age. As one would guess from the condition in nature, male white-crowns are sensitive to the learning of dialects between the tenth and hundredth day of life. Experimental birds exposed to a recorded song of the species, whether of their own geographical dialect or another, during this period produced a good though not perfect copy of the training song during their first singing season. But the effects of exposure to dialectical variation seemed to be constrained in the following interesting fashion. White-crown males exposed to the song of their own species and alternately to the song of a different sparrow sing the song appropriate to their own species. Moreover, isolated birds who are exposed only to the song of another species are unaffected by the exposure and sing the peculiar reduced song of naive isolated birds. Thus, bird song for chaffinches and sparrows is a multiply determined phenomenon with at least four components. The listing of them will illustrate the complication of apparently simple cases of animal behavior and will further illustrate how seductive is the analogy between bird song and aspects of human development (for example, the acquisition of language or of sex-role).

1. Even without specific exposure the birds will develop a primitive song recognizably of the shape of the species.
2. Experience appears to be more effective at certain times than at others although there is evidence of further change past the "sensitive period."
3. There is a species-specific *sensitivity* to experience; that is, only experience of the dialects of conspecifics has an effect on developing bird song.
4. Within the domain of species-specific dialectical variation, it appears that the bird will learn whatever song he hears during the "sensitive period" and will refine this song in response to his experience as a young adult.

The Socialization of Dogs and Monkeys

The attachment of dogs to human beings has been studied in detail in a series of studies at the Jackson Laboratory in Bar Harbor, Maine. Much of this work, together with observations of genetic variation among different breeds of dogs, has been summarized recently by Scott and Fuller (1965). The investigators at Bar Harbor are convinced that there is a critical period for the socialization of dogs (Scott, 1962, 1963). They maintain that, near the end of the third week of life, marked by a startle response to sound and the first eruption of teeth as well as systematic decrease in heart rate, the dog is peculiarly sensitive to the social partner. Freedman, King, and Elliot (1961) carried out what has been called a "wild dog" experiment in which animals were kept in large fields with no exposure to human beings except during an experimental period of one week. The exposure to human beings was carried out for different animals at different ages—at 2, 3, 5, 7, and 9 weeks, with some puppies (the so-called control animals) isolated from human contact until 14 weeks of age. The dogs were given a series of standard tests in the fourth month of life. Animals who encountered human beings at 5, 7, and 9 weeks responded best to leash control and responded more positively to a human handler. Table 2 summarizes the data on six behavioral measures taken from the dogs. Figure 11 (as reported in Scott and Fuller, 1965) presents data on two measures—attraction of the dog to an active handler and fear of an inactive handler—which are strongly reminiscent of Hess's two-factor system for understanding imprinting in chicks. Scott and Fuller conclude from a review of the investigations of dogs and of studies of other animals that ". . . a young animal automatically becomes attached to individuals and objects with which it comes into contact during the critical period. The capacity to do this need not be lost at later stages, but the process can be slowed down or prevented by the development of interfering behavior, particularly fear responses" (Scott & Fuller, 1965, p. 147).

Since 1958, Harlow and his associates at Wisconsin have reported a number of provocative observations on the development of what they call the "affectional systems" (Harlow, 1963) of macaques. Early observations of infant monkeys raised with dummies ("mother surrogates") provided evidence in support of the proposition that nursing was not the critical encounter between infant and mother and, further, that contact with the body of the dummy was essential to the establishment of an attachment by the infant (Harlow, 1958; Harlow & Zimmermann, 1959). For example, infant monkeys raised with a dummy made largely of wire mesh were compared with infants raised with a similar dummy covered with terrycloth. To heighten the contrast between the mother surrogates, Harlow installed a feeding bottle only in the wire-mesh dummy. Over the course of the first months of life, monkeys showed several different patterns of response to the different dum-

TABLE 2

RANK ORDER OF DOGS ON TESTS GIVEN AFTER 14 WEEKS OF AGE
(FROM SCOTT & FULLER, 1965)
(AFTER FREEDMAN, KING, & ELLIOT, 1961)

Test	Age Socialized, Weeks					
	2–3	3–4	5–6	7–8	9–10	Controls
Handling:						
Initial attraction to handler	5	4[a]	3[a]	2[a]	1[a]	6
Leash-control:						
Eating in strange situation	4	3	1.5[a]	1.5[a]	5	6
Fewer balks	4	5	3[a]	1[a]	2[a]	6
Reactivity test:						
Total activity	2	4	3	1	6	5
Heart rate	6	3	4	1	2	5
Vocalization, panting, and tail wagging	2	3	4	1	5	6

[a]Distinctly superior ranks.

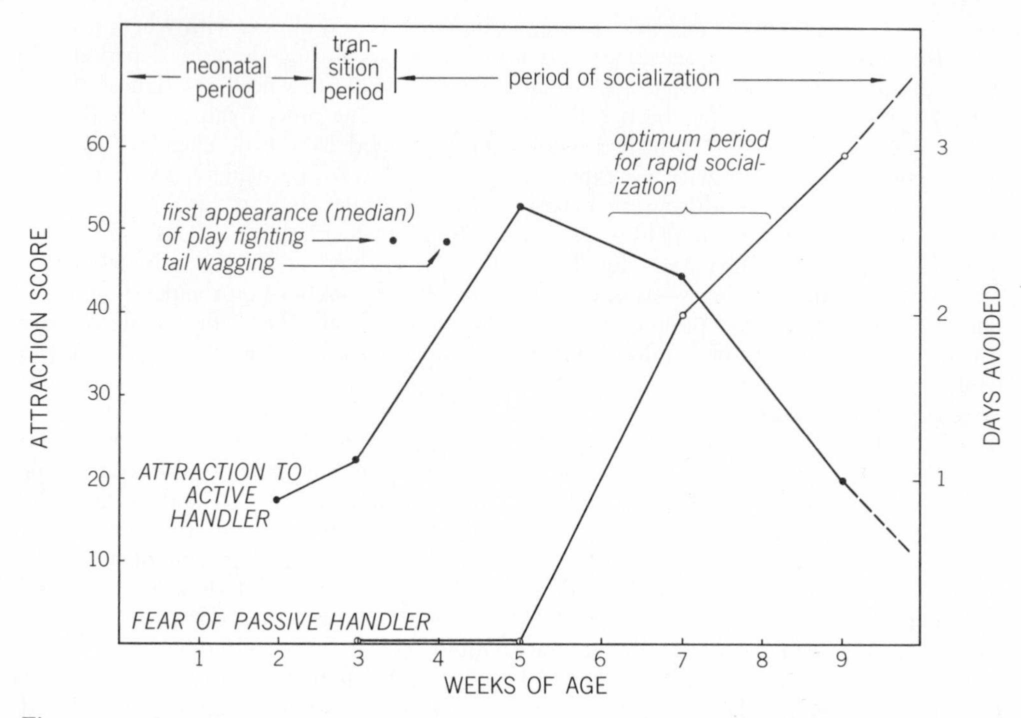

Figure 11. Attraction to active handler and fear of passive handler in dogs as related to age. From Scott and Fuller, 1965.

mies. The results shown in Figure 12 are representative. After rearing with the surrogates, animals were given an opportunity to press a lever that opened a window in their cage and permitted a glance at the dummy on which they had been raised. Clearly, the cloth-mother-raised animals worked harder to see their "mother" than did the wire-mother-raised animals. The cloth-raised infants also spent more time on their dummies, showed relatively less fear to a disturbing stimulus, and more frequently approached their dummy in a fearful open field. These data led Harlow to the conclusion that "contact comfort" was of great importance in the establishment of infant-mother attachments and he was moved to speculate about human beings that ". . . in the foreseeable future neonatal nursing will [come to be regarded] as a luxury . . . a form of conspicuous consumption" (Harlow, 1958, p. 685).

More recent observations by Harlow (1961, 1963) have complicated the first simplicities. As his surrogate-reared animals have grown, it has become evident that they are not the same sort of monkeys as those raised by natural mothers. Their sexual behavior is badly organized; no surrogate-raised male has been reported to breed and the few pregnancies induced in surrogate-reared females have been ascribed to "simply incredible feats of motor skill on the part of the [normally reared and sexually experienced] male" (Harlow, 1963, p. 28). Of even greater interest to the student of developmental analogies are Harlow's observations on the *maternal* behavior of four macaques who were raised with surrogates. These "unmothered mothers" were "either completely indifferent or violently abusive" toward their infants and, in a passage that tells a great deal about the role of the active infant in the establishment of infant-mother

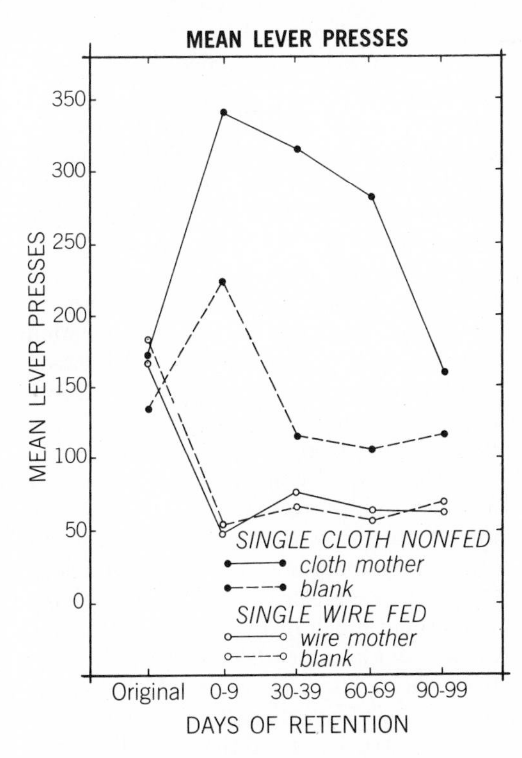

Figure 12. Lever-presses to obtain a glimpse of surrogate or empty chamber in monkeys raised with cloth dummies and wire dummies. From Harlow and Zimmermann, 1959.

attachment, Harlow describes the approach of infant monkeys to their unmothered (and obviously unmothering) mothers.

> [The mother] would beat them and knock them down; they would come back and make contact; the mothers would rub their face into the floor; they would wriggle free and again attempt contact. The power, insistence, and demandingness of the infant to make contact and the punishment the infant would accept . . . [made] . . . strong men . . . [hardly able to] . . . observe this unmaternal behavior (Harlow, 1963, p. 25).

There can be no doubt that, in the macaque at any rate, the relation between mother and child is more than an elaboration of contact comfort; some of Harlow's observations on the exchange between natural mother and infant are revealing of the intricacy of the responses and of the timing of responses that link mother and infant. For example, Harlow has shown that the mother macaque retrieves and clasps the newborn in the first days of its life but that such positive caretaking begins to drop off after the second month. Moreover, the mother begins at about the same time to make negative responses toward the infant —almost literally pushing him away from her. Figures 13 and 14 summarize the Wisconsin observations on the responses of macaque mothers to their infants during the first seven months of life.

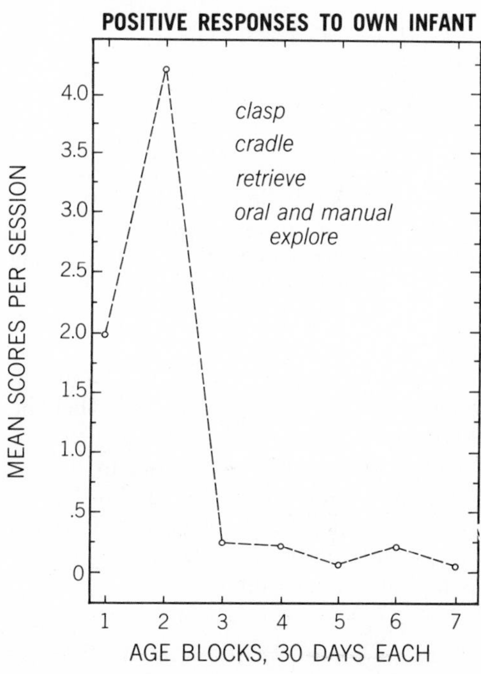

Figure 13. Summary of positive responses of macaque mothers toward their infants during the first seven months of life. From Harlow, 1963.

Harlow's data on the relation between the behavior of the infant and the behavior of the mother have received elegant confirmation and extension by Rosenblatt (1965) in studies of the rat. He has shown the inti-

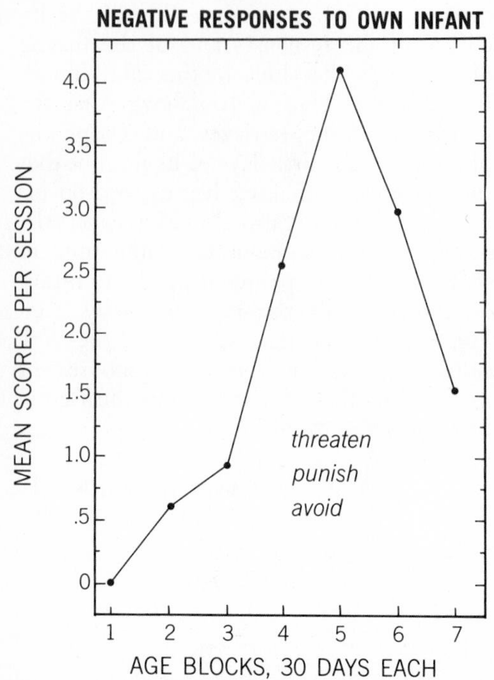

Figure 14. Summary of negative responses of macaque mothers toward their infants during the first seven months of life. From Harlow, 1963.

mate and interactive relation that binds together what the mother does and what the infant does. Figure 15 shows a synchrony of maternal and infantile responses in the rat that warrants the use of "system" or "structure" to describe the development of attachment and separation between animal mother and animal infant.

The Consequences of Early Enrichment in Rats

At least since the time of Comenius (1633) it has been a Western truism that the early years of human life are of particular consequence for proper development. Freud wrenched conventional attitudes about early experience from their educational context and, as three decades of research on early human development testify, he transformed our view of the child. The interest of animal psychologists in early experience, however, was not so obviously awakened by Freud's speculation. The intellectual origin of most research on early experience in animals, published in mounting quantities over the last decade and a half, was the publication of Hebb's *The Organization of Behavior* (1949). Hebb maintained that changes that took place in the early life of the animal—changes in perceptual structure, in the interpretation of drive states, and in strategies of learning—constrained all later development. Development was, for Hebb, rather like an endlessly branching tree; the earlier an experience forced a "decision" for one branch or another, the greater the effect on the animal's fully grown condition. Hebb reported some preliminary observations of the effects of early experience on problem-solving (1947) and much of the consequent experimental work on early experience derived from these observations and Hebb's reading of their theoretical consequence. Two studies carried out in the McGill laboratories and published in 1952 (Hymovitch, 1952; Forgays & Forgays, 1952) set the pattern of much subsequent research on the relation between early enrichment and the behavior of animals. A description in some detail of the procedure and results of the study by Hymovitch will illustrate the key characteristics of research on early enrichment.

In one of Hymovitch's studies (1952), hooded rats lived from their twenty-seventh day of life until their seventy-ninth in one of four different environments. The "free-environment box" was 24 square feet in area and contained "a number of blind alleys, inclined runways, small enclosed areas, apertures, et cetera." This enriched environment was expected to provide optimal conditions for later problem-solving. Other animals were confined to small mesh cages but the cages were moved through the apparatus and about the experimental room to vary the animals' visual experience. A third group of animals was confined to

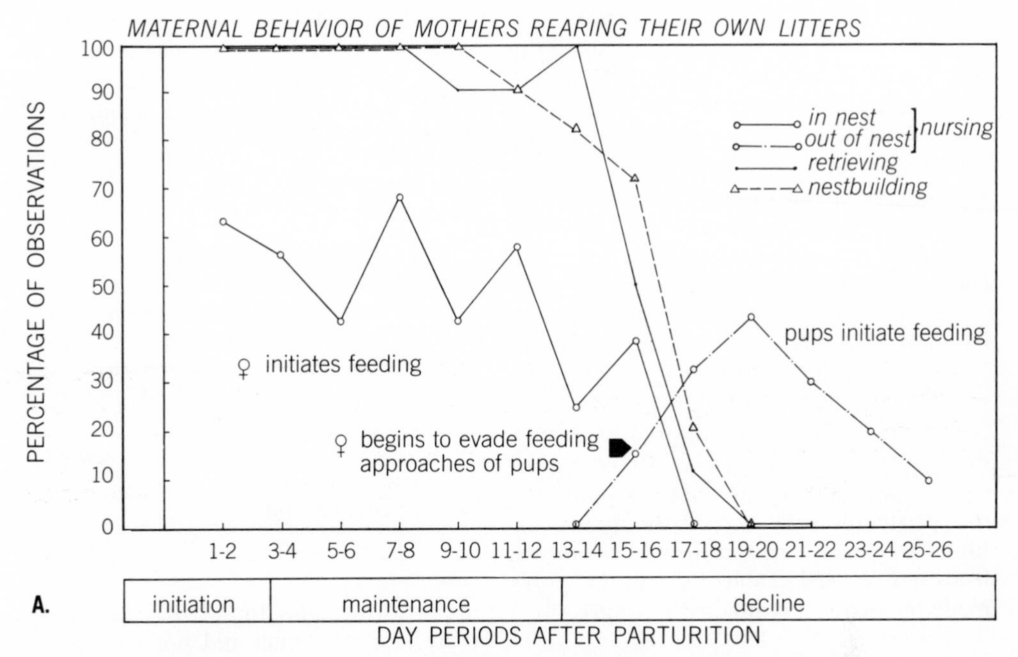

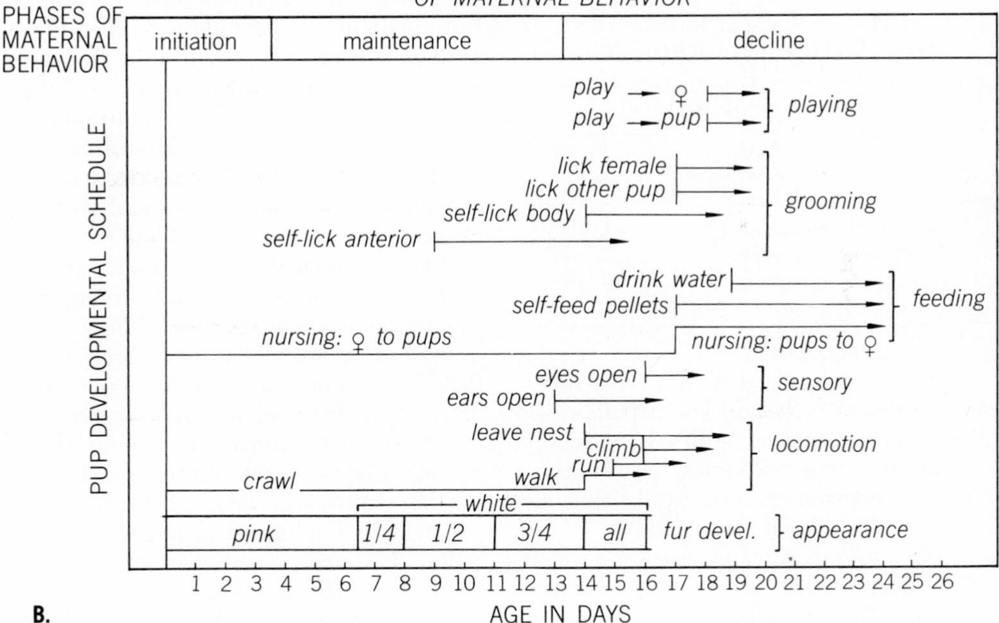

Figure 15. The relation between behavior of mother rats and the behavior of their infants during early life. From Rosenblatt, 1965.

"stovepipe cages" that permitted little visual exposure, and a fourth group was reared in fully enclosed activity wheels. The testing device used by Hymovitch to assess problem-solving ability in the rat also set a style for studies of early enrichment. In the Hebb-Williams closed-field test (Hebb & Williams, 1946; Rabinovitch & Rosvold, 1951), the rat must find his way from one corner of a square field to the corner diagonally opposite (where he finds food). After an animal masters a series of training problems in which he finds his way past barriers placed through the field, he is given a number of test problems. In the test problems, the animal is scored for his effectiveness in getting past barriers in different positions; the specific measure taken is the number of times he enters "error zones" as he moves from start to goal. Table 3 shows the scores made by each of Hymovitch's groups.

TABLE 3

ERRORS MADE BY RATS IN HEBB-WILLIAMS CLOSED-FIELD TEST AFTER DIFFERING EARLY EXPERIENCE (FROM HYMOVITCH, 1952)

	Number of Subjects	Mean Error Scores
Free environment	20	137.3
Mesh cages	8	140.1
Stovepipe cages	6	233.1
Activity wheels	4	235.0

Hymovitch also tried to assess the differential effect of early and late experience in the free-environment. Animals were exposed to the free-environment box on many occasions between 30 and 75 days of age while another group was confined to the stovepipe cages. After a brief return to normal cage rearing, these two groups were reversed, the free-environment animals going into stovepipes and the stovepipe animals going into free environments. These animals were then tested in the Hebb-Williams closed-field as were comparison animals raised throughout the rearing period in free environment and a group that spent their early life in normal laboratory cages. Table 4 presents the outcome of this study.

TABLE 4

ERRORS MADE BY RATS IN HEBB-WILLIAMS CLOSED-FIELD TEST AFTER DIFFERING EARLY EXPERIENCE (FROM HYMOVITCH, 1952)

	Number of Subjects	Mean Error Scores
Early free environment	6	161.3
Late free environment	5	248.8
All free environment	3	152.6
Normal cages	4	221.5

Hymovitch also found that his differentially reared animals did not vary in their performance on a t-maze and that the animals raised in free-environments were more disturbed by a rotation of the Hebb-Williams closed-field than were restricted animals. He concluded from the several results that the difference in problem-solving ability in free-environment animals and restricted animals should be ascribed to "the differential opportunity presented the various groups for perceptual learning . . ." and he suggested that the effects might be "relatively permanent and possibly irreversible."

The Hymovitch study is representative of a large number of studies of enrichment that have appeared since its publication. There have been variation in character of the rearing environment, variation in breed of rat, variation in the timing and duration of the experience, and, not surprisingly, variation in results and in interpretation of results. No review of this literature will be attempted here; in general, rats who spend part of their early lives in a large and complicated environment perform better in such tests of "problem-solving" as the Hebb-Williams closed-field (e.g., Woods, 1959; Woods, Ruckelhaus, & Dowling, 1960;

Brown, 1966). Of greater interest for the study of comparative personality development are questions about (a) the existence of sensitive periods for the effect of early enrichment and (b) the generality of the effects of enrichment, even for the rat. Forgays and Read (1962) exposed five groups of animals to an enriched environment with "playthings" for three weeks of their lives and tested them all for general activity and performance in the Hebb-Williams closed-field when the animals were approximately 4 months old. Table 5

TABLE 5

ACTIVITY SCORES AND HEBB-WILLIAMS ERROR SCORES FOR ANIMALS EXPOSED TO ENRICHED ENVIRONMENTS AT DIFFERENT AGES (FROM FORGAYS & READ, 1962)

Time of Enriched Experience (Days of Age)	*N*	Mean Entries of Y-Maze	Mean Error Score on Hebb-Williams
0–21	8	74.88	174.25
22–43	17	73.59	153.29
44–65	9	67.67	160.33
66–87	9	63.67	160.56
88–109	9	61.00	176.67
No enriched experience	8	69.52	195.75

shows the time in the rats' lives when they were placed in the complex environment and it shows, as well, their activity scores (entries into sections of an elevated y-maze) and mean error scores on the Hebb-Williams. None of the differences in activity scores was statistically stable; the group given enriched experience in the second three weeks of life, however, made significantly fewer errors on the Hebb-Williams test than either the early-exposed group (0–21 days) or the late-exposed group (88–109 days), as well as being strikingly different from the control group. These results replicate in part the findings of other investigators and support the postulation of a sensitive period for the effects of early experience.

In order to assess the basis of the effects of early enrichment, a number of studies have been carried out to determine the generality and the correlates of the apparent superiority of enriched-environment animals. For example, Bell and Felbinger (1962) found that rats raised in a complex environment for the first 42 days of life showed more sexual curiosity and activity than did animals raised in a restricted environment. Animals who were shifted from an enriched to a restricted environment or from a restricted to an enriched environment at 21 days of age showed intermediate values of sexual activity, with some suggestion that the variation in environment had a greater effect when it occurred prior to weaning. A number of investigators (Forgus, 1958; Gibson, Walk, Pick, & Tighe, 1958; Gibson, Walk, & Tighe, 1959; Baird & Becknell, 1962; among others) have studied, with somewhat ambiguous results, the effects of experience with particular visual forms—metal cutouts of circles and triangles, two-dimensional forms, and parts of plane figures. Research on the effect of particular perceptual experience is important in analyzing the larger issue of enrichment; one of the most productive general proposals made to explain the effects of early experience rests on the premise that differential early experience critically affects the animal's perceptual competence or his ability to process information (Bruner, 1961; Melzack & Burns, 1963). Hymovitch (1952) presented evidence that enriched-environment animals were learning something more about distant visual cues than their restricted-environment counterparts; enriched-environment animals were more disturbed by rotation of the Hebb-Williams closed-field after training than were the restricted-environment animals. Brown (1966) has shown that the superiority of free-environment animals over restricted-environment animals can be demonstrated only when the Hebb-Williams closed-field is maintained in the stationary position during problem-solving tests. Yet another attempt to comprehend the effects of early enrichment has been based on variation in exploratory tendencies by animals with very early experience. Zimbardo and Montgomery (1957) showed that animals raised in a restricted environment showed more exploration than free-environment animals; Woods, Ruckelhaus, and Dowling (1960) have confirmed this finding and demonstrated a negative correlation between Hebb-Williams closed-field performance and amount of exploration. Although the results of the many studies of early enrichment in rats are by no means congruent, it is plausible to believe that animals raised in complex environments develop perceptual skills or strategies for processing information or (and the alternatives are not mutually exclusive) animals raised in restricted environments are unable to handle the discrepancy between the limited range of their early experience and the typical variety and complexity of test environments such as elevated y-mazes and the Hebb-Williams closed-field. Put in exaggerated brevity, enriched-environment animals solve the presented problems in much the same way that they explore their early complex surroundings while the restricted-experience animals, in the midst of new confusions, engage in somewhat agitated exploration and consequent inferior problem-solving.

The investigation of the effects of early enrichment has recently been broadened to include consideration of the physiological and anatomical correlates of early experience. Bennett, Diamond, Krech, and Rosenzweig (1964) raised animals under (a) environmental complexity (Group ETC)—the animals were in social groups with access to "toys" and they were exposed to varying closed-fields—and under (b) isolated conditions (Group IC)—the animals were housed alone and in a dimly lit and quiet room. Animals were exposed to these contrasting environments from about the twenty-fifth day of their lives until about the one-hundred-and-fifth day. The experimenters then made systematic determinations of brain weight and of acetylcholinesterase activity of brain for the two groups. Table 6 summarizes their results.

All of the indicated differences, including the greater weight of noncortical brain in the IC group, reach conventional levels of statistical significance. Bennett *et al.* recognize that ". . . finding these changes in the brain consequent upon experience does not prove that they have anything to do with storage of memory. The demonstration of such changes merely helps to establish the fact that the brain is responsive to environmental pressure . . ." (Bennett *et al.*, 1964, p. 618). A neat demonstration of the interaction of anatomical change with environmental variation has been presented by

TABLE 6

BRAIN WEIGHT AND ACETYLCHOLINESTERASE ACTIVITY IN RATS RAISED UNDER ENVIRONMENTAL COMPLEXITY (ETC) AND IN ISOLATION (IC) (FROM BENNETT ET AL., 1964)

	Brain Weight (Mg.)			Acetylcholinesterase Activity (10^{-8} Mole/Min.)		
	Cortex	Rest of Brain	Total Brain	Cortex	Rest of Brain	Total Brain
Mean ETC	700	939	1639	631	1825	2455
Mean IC	669	951	1620	614	1787	2401
ETC/IC	62/77	33/77	51/77	53/74	50/76	52/73

ETC/IC: number of littermate pairs in which the ETC value exceeded the IC value.

Schwartz (1964). He made posterior cortical oblations in newborn rats and introduced them, together with their sham-operated controls, either into a restricted environment or into an enriched environment—one that added three ping pong balls to the usual array of rat toys and games. At the end of about three months of life, the animals were tested in the Hebb-Williams closed-field. Figure 16 shows Schwartz's

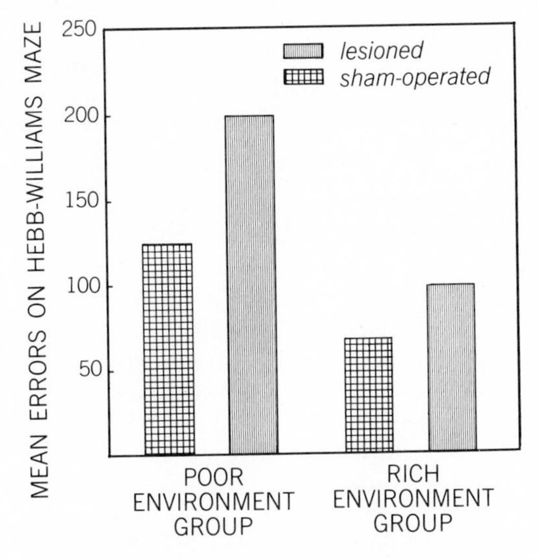

Figure 16. Errors on Hebb-Williams closed field by rats lesioned or sham-operated as newborns. From Schwartz, 1964.

results. Clearly, the newborn lesion had a consequential effect on behavior in the Hebb-Williams apparatus but so did environmental enrichment. In fact, the lesioned animals raised in an enriched environment made fewer errors (though apparently not significantly fewer) than did the sham-operated animals raised in a poor environment.

The Effects of Early Restriction

Yet another empirical technique for the study of early experience derives from the attempt to reduce the animal's "normal laboratory experience" by drastic restriction of his environment. The range of environmental variation from restriction to enrichment may, of course, represent a continuum; however, so few values along this hypothetical continuum are examined in the typical study that no single set of functions can be drawn on the present data.

Studies of early visual restriction (e.g., Lashley & Russell [1934] on rats; Riesen & Aarons [1959] on cats; Lindsley, Wendt, Lindsley, Fox, Howell, & Adey [1964] on monkeys; Solomon *et al.* [1961] for a general review) have examined the anatomical, physiological, and discriminatory consequences of restrictions in light and patterning of stimulation. Perhaps more interesting for the student of human development are the small group of studies that have examined "temperamental" variation, changes in social response, and changes in response to pain as consequences of early deprivation in animals.

Again, the first studies on the noncognitive effects of early deprivation came from the McGill Laboratories. A preliminary report by Clarke, Heron, Fetherstonhaugh, Forgays, and Hebb (1951) described the striking differences between a group of three dogs raised as home pets and three dogs raised together in a small cage which prevented their seeing outside and from which they were not removed until they were over 7 months old. The cage-reared dogs were more submissive than home-reared dogs, they were less responsive to unfamiliar animals, they responded to stress by decrease in activity or by freezing, and they showed, in exposure repeatedly to the same situation, less tendency to become satiated. As the investigators put it, the dogs showed "differences in capacity for 'boredom'" (Clarke *et al.,* 1951, p. 154). A number of more systematically designed studies on the early restriction of dogs followed on these initial provocative observations (e.g., Thompson & Heron [1954] on levels of exploration after restriction; Melzack & Thompson [1956] on variation in social behavior); among these studies, the findings of Melzack and Scott (1957) on the response of restricted dogs to painful stimulation stand out as among the most impressive evidence available on the effects of early restriction. Ten dogs raised in complete isolation from weaning until 8 months of age were compared in a number of tests with twelve dogs raised as pets. The restricted dogs required longer to learn to avoid a pursuing toy car that gave them a shock; the restricted animals took longer to learn to avoid shock in a shuttlebox (some of them apparently learned nothing at all); the restricted dogs did not tend to avoid an experimenter who pricked them with a pin; most dramatically, the restricted animals did not avoid an experimenter who burned their noses with a lighted match. In this last case, the home-reared dogs spent about 45 per cent of their time near the experimenter before he tried to burn them and about 33 per cent after presentation of the match; the restricted animals, on the other hand, increased the percentage of time they spent near the experimenter from 28 per cent before to 51 per cent after being burned. Even so, the numbers do not adequately testify to the peculiarity of the restricted animals. Melzack and Scott's description of the behavior of the dogs when the experimenter tried to burn them warrants quotation in detail.

> To the astonishment of the observers, seven of the ten restricted dogs made no attempt to get away from *E during* stimulation, and it was not even necessary to hold them. . . . They moved their noses into the flame as soon as it was presented, after which the head or whole body jerked away, as though reflexly; but then they came right back to their original position and hovered excitedly near the flame. Three of them repeatedly poked their noses into the flame and sniffed at it as long as it was present . . . Only three of the initial dogs squealed on making contact with the flame and tried subsequently to avoid it by moving their heads . . . In contrast, the normal dogs moved their heads so rapidly that it was often impossible to hit their noses with the flame. (Melzack & Scott, 1957, p. 158)

These remarkable observations appear to justify the conclusion that "perceiving and responding to pain . . . requires a background of early, prolonged, perceptual experience" (Melzack & Scott, 1957, p. 160). To be sure, we remain in ignorance of the precise timing and character of the experience necessary to develop normal pain sensitivity in these strange animals.

Mason has reported a number of comparisons between a group of six rhesus monkeys raised alone for the first two years of their lives (but with visual and auditory access to other animals) and a group of six feral animals (Mason, 1960, 1961a, 1961b; Mason & Green, 1962; summarized in Mason, 1963). In almost every measure taken—free social behavior, systematic tests of gregariousness, sexual behavior, dominance—striking differences were found between the two groups of animals. The restricted animals were sexually ineffective, rarely chosen as social partner either by other restricted animals or by members of the feral group, and unusually aggressive in dominance tests. Mason's conclusions about his observations illuminate somewhat the nature of the effect of restriction. He points out that the restricted male monkeys showed almost all of the components of appropriate sex behavior but were not able to tie them together in an effective and integrated pattern. Similarly, although the restricted animals in Mason's study showed most of the postures, gestures, and vocalizations that make up rhesus communication, they were unable to coordinate these communicative acts in a way that permitted smooth sexual and social functioning. Even though the "units" of a complicated response may be present in the animals, temporal integration of the units and, particularly, their organization into a chain of communication with another animal appear to require specific (though as yet unknown) experience.

Mason and Sponholz (1963) have reported preliminary observations on animals raised in complete social isolation; the two animals described neither saw nor heard any other being until testing began at about 15 months of age. Mason and Sponholz describe the behavior of the isolated monkeys "as a form of traumatic withdrawal." The isolates showed no behavioral constriction when they were observed in their original isolation cages but, throughout a thousand hours of exposure to various tests, their primary response was to crouch in a corner and "the most common reactions to social contact were submission or flight" (Mason & Sponholz, 1963, p. 305).

There can be little doubt, in the range of conditions that run from enrichment to restriction and across a wide variety of animal species, that the effects of general early experience can be detected in later life. It is frustrating, in the face of so clear a generalization, that so little can be said about the particular dimensions—situational, social, or temporal—that are relevant to the effects of early experience.

The Effects of Gentling, Handling, and Stress

How does handling or "gentling" of the infant rat affect his later behavior and development? A number of studies have shown that the handled animal grows fatter and withstands deprivation of food and water better than his ignored brothers (Weininger, 1954, 1956; Levine & Otis, 1958; Denenberg & Karas, 1959). Many of these studies have been summarized by Bovard (1958) who has presented a hypothesis about physiological functioning to account for the empirical findings. Recent research has concentrated on two closely related questions. How do early handling and shock affect later emotionality and physiological response of the animal? How do early handling and shock affect later avoidance learning in animals? Again, a few studies will be drawn from the proliferating literature on these questions in order to illustrate typical procedures and the overall shape of obtained results.

Levine, Alpert, and Lewis (1958) showed that handling infant rats (a procedure which involved removing the rat pup from its nest and mother for three minutes each day) produced significant effects in the animal's adrenal response to cold stress. Handled animals showed an earlier and greater physiological response to stress—the measure Levine and his associates employed was adrenal ascorbic acid depletion—than animals who were not handled. Later studies in a long series by Levine and his associates (summarized by Levine, 1962) suggest that handled animals develop faster, are less reactive to stress in adulthood, are less likely to show seizure under electro-convulsive shock, and are far less emotional after septal lesions. Somewhat surprisingly, handled animals were somewhat more susceptible to a pathogenic agent that produces leukemia.[3] For the person who thinks of animal analogs to human experience, the Levine findings on physiological response to early handling are ambiguous. Is the animal who is handled in infancy "over-anxious" or better prepared for the stresses of adult life? Studies by Levine and other investigators on the later response of rodents to early handling and shock have led to the somewhat remarkable conclusion that animals who are given hard times in early infancy are better able to handle the stresses of adult life than are "ignored" animals.

Studies of the behavioral effects of early experience of handling and shock show the now-expected variation in age and technique of inducing early experience, age and procedures of later testing, and measures of emotionality and learning. It is difficult,

[3] Evidence is beginning to accumulate that the operative variable in studies involving the separation of the infant rat from its nest, whether it is handled or not, is a relatively sudden change in temperature (Fairfield, 1948; Schaefer, 1963; Hutchings, 1965).

therefore, to cite representative studies. The studies that follow are, rather, a sample from diversity. Denenberg and Morton (1962) compared rats that were not handled for the first 24 days of life with animals who were removed from their cage and placed apart for three minutes each day. In addition, as a "therapeutic" maneuver, Denenberg and Morton placed half of each early-experience group in a large free environment for 25 days; the rest of the animals were kept in ordinary laboratory cages. All groups were tested at 180 days of age. It was found that handled animals were significantly more active than nonhandled animals in a large empty box; handled animals also defecated much less than did the nonhandled animals. Assuming low activity and high defecation to be measures of emotionality, Denenberg and Morton conclude that subjects "handled in infancy were . . . significantly less emotional . . ." (Denenberg & Morton, 1962, p. 244). Some evidence for the effectiveness of post-weaning "therapy" appeared in the finding that animals in the free environment for 25 days after weaning defecated less than animals raised in cages. Denenberg and Morton also assessed the effect of mixing handled and nonhandled animals during open-field testing. The results were striking and the investigators' description of the behavior of the rats is reminiscent of descriptions we have already heard of different species after early isolation.

> When first placed in the box, the non-stimulated . . . subjects immediately huddled together in one or two corners of the box. When they moved, it was usually along the walls. The handled subjects, on the other hand, moved about freely and explored the complete box. They also engaged in much play behavior, including wrestling and nipping each other (Denenberg & Morton, 1962, p. 245).

So far, so good. If we see the nonhandled animals as similar to isolated monkeys and dogs, then we may see the early experience of handling as a beneficent sort of supermothering. However, there is noteworthy evidence that the more intense the early experience, the less emotional the animals will be in adulthood. Consider the large-scale study by Denenberg and Smith (1963) which, among other independent variables and other measures, assessed the effects of early handling and early shock on behavior in an open-field and avoidance learning in adult animals. In addition to the usual handled group and a nonhandled control, Denenberg and Smith subjected one group of animals to daily shocks. From the eleventh through the twentieth day of life, each animal in the shock group spent three minutes on a scrambling grid that delivered .25 milliamperes of shock, an early experience that would be difficult to justify as maternal! Both experimental groups, whether handled or shocked, were more active in the open-field and showed less defecation. Table 7 presents the results on defecation; nonhandled control subjects are significantly more emotional by this index than either of the experimental groups and the difference between merely being handled and being shocked approaches conventional levels of statistical significance. Results on activity in the open-field were not quite so clear-cut

TABLE 7

PERCENTAGE OF RATS IN THREE CONDITIONS OF EARLY EXPERIENCE WHO DEFECATED DURING OPEN-FIELD TESTING (FROM DENENBERG & SMITH, 1963)

Group	*N*	Preavoidance	Postavoidance
Control	52	61.5	57.7
Handle	53	30.2	24.5
Shock	49	24.5	8.2

but, after 15 days of avoidance training, nonhandled animals were significantly less active than either handled or shock animals and the latter two groups were not different. Measures of avoidance learning seemed to vary most with age of testing but Denenberg and Smith found a marginally significant tendency for the shocked animals to show longer response time in the avoidance situation. Denenberg (1964) has attempted to bring the results of these studies and many others on early handling and shock under a single set of explanatory principles. He maintains that, contrary to the expectation of a critical period hypothesis, emotional reactivity in adults will be a simple inverse function of stimulus input in infancy. However, Denenberg recognizes that the results of a number of studies on adult behavior cannot be reconciled to this position without an intervening assumption. He maintains, therefore, that quality of adult performance will vary, not only as a function of emotional reactivity, but also as a function of difficulty of task. This statement of the relations between performance and reactivity or arousal is a familiar one (e.g., Hebb, 1955) and it permits Denenberg to predict several different relations between early experience and adult performance. Figure 17 presents Denenberg's position in schematic form.

Denenberg's two-premise theory permits him to account for many of the diverse findings on the effects of early handling and shock in rats and mice but it is appropriate to emphasize that diversity without prejudice to Denenberg's ability to account for it. Levine and Broadhurst (1963) and Levine and Wetzel (1963) have shown that the adult response to early handling clearly varies from one breed of rat to another. Baron, Brookshire, and Littman (1957) found that animals subjected to high levels of unavoidable shock (1.25 milliamperes for three continuous minutes on two successive days!) were more effective learners in escape and avoidance training as adults but their weak age-of-experience effects led them to the conclusion that their results did ". . . not strongly [substantiate] the hypothesis that traumatization at an early age has broader consequences than traumatization at maturity" (Baron, Brookshire, & Littman, 1957, p. 534). Ader (1959) found that few of his dozen or so indexes of emotionality differentiated groups varying in early experience (Ader threw his animals in the air, rolled them across the floor in a container, exposed them to electric shock, among other indignities) although most of the measures showed the same pattern of differentiation of groups. Handled animals and animals subjected to distributed emotion-provoking stimulation either just after weaning or as adults showed less adult emotionality than did nonhandled animals. For some reason, animals given massed emotion-provoking stimulation were more emotional than the other experimental groups. Spence and Maher (1962a, 1962b) and Brookshire, Littman, and Stewart (1961) have shown rather striking differences between stimulation prior to weaning and stimulation after weaning. Two studies by Henderson (1964, 1965) on mice have shown a *higher* level of defecation and a *lower* level of activity in animals given half-second one-milliampere shock eight times on each of two days; he confirmed earlier findings, however, that handled or shocked animals were superior in a later avoidance-learning task. Hender-

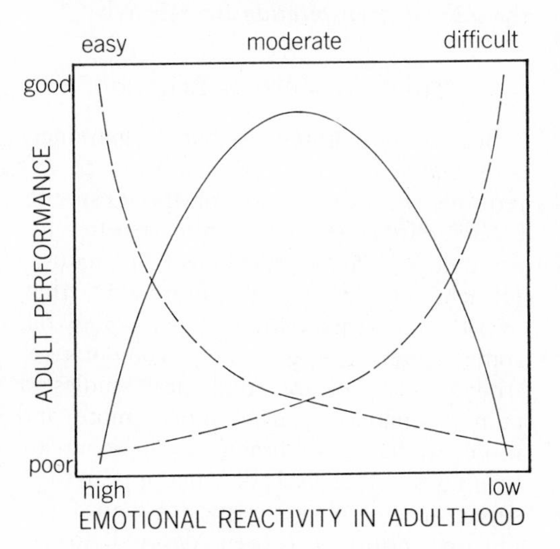

Figure 17. Denenberg's proposal linking emotional reactivity in adults (based on varying infantile stimulation) to performance on tasks of varying difficulty. From Denenberg, 1964.

son (1965) also presents evidence to suggest that the age differences in avoidance learning which he had found earlier and which suggested the existence of some sort of critical period could not be ascribed to variation in the ability of animals to learn but must rather be a function of differential arousal.

Denenberg's search for a simple theoretical account to encompass the diversity of empirical outcomes in studies of early handling and shock is ambitious and, for seekers of analogy between the behavior of animals and the behavior of children, provocative. His primary postulation (shared with Levine, 1956) that adult emotionality *decreases* with increasing stimulus input in infancy "may not appear reasonable at first glance because of our knowledge of conditioned fears, traumatic experiences in childhood, etc." (Denenberg, 1964, p. 347). Denenberg is careful to point out the limitation of most experimental data to rodents but his theoretical notions have the power of predicting variation in adult *behavior* as a function of the match between emotionality induced by infantile experience and the level of emotionality required by any particular task in adult life. The data available on the effects of early experience, even from rodents alone, require at least this degree of predictive flexibility.

FROM ANIMALS TO CHILDREN

We may still be sly as foxes and wise as owls but the careful research on early experience in animals which is represented in the foregoing pages has, in a sense, cast doubt on the slyness of foxes and the wisdom of owls. The neat and persuasive simplicities—the analogies of development that would permit us to talk of duck, monkey, and human infant in a single simple conceptual language—have not appeared. The following response in precocial birds, surely the most popular genetic analogy of our time, is seen to be a complicated and fascinating function of breed, intensity and relevance of the stimulus provoking early following, age, and conditions of test, to name only a few of the considerations relevant to our understanding of following in chickens, ducks, and geese. Studies of early enrichment, restriction, and stress in animals, while they have begun to accumulate in depth and sophistication adequate to permit meaningful comparison one with another, have not led to patterns of explanation which will encompass the diversity of findings on rats and mice, to say nothing of the implications for enrichment, restriction, and stress in human infants. The work of the Wisconsin group has taught us that we have not yet extracted the essence of rhesus maternality and affection. What are the implications of comparative study for human personality, even for the limited domain of early experience? Clearly, the variety of animal behavior makes a serious answer to the question impossible in our time. Rather, the present condition of the genetic analogies can be best assessed by a brief second look at the categories of relevance of animal study for human development—the *phylogeny of behavior,* the *animal as model* of man, and the *animal as inspiration* for research.

The Phylogeny of Behavior

Beach has maintained that "a genuinely comparative science" (Beach, 1960, p. 17) requires the examination of species-specific behavior in hopes of "reaching a better understanding of [man's] place in nature" (Beach, 1960, p. 17). There are signs that, over the last years, American psychology has come closer to "genuinely comparative" study. Not only are ethological studies of animals increasing in number; more and more, students of human development are turning to an analysis of what appear to be species-specific characteristics of man. Great research effort has been devoted to the human smile (Ambrose, 1961; Gewirtz, 1965; Laroche & Tcheng, 1963, among others). Language, perhaps man's most differentiating characteristic, has begun to receive close study (e.g., Bellugi & Brown, 1964). The study of species-specific behavior, of course, encloses a paradox; to the degree that some pattern of behavior is peculiar to a particular species, to that degree will systematic comparison among different species be difficult. Nonetheless, students of animal and human development are confronting one another with the results of their investigations in search of common ground. *Determinants of infant behavior* (Foss, 1961, 1963, 1965) have illustrated many of the difficulties of comparative analysis and some of its intellectual values. Although there are few works, in the tradition of Darwin's *Expression of emotion in animals and men,* that range in description and speculation widely across different animal groups, studies aiming for comparison have appeared on sexual behavior (Ford & Beach, 1951), on maternal behavior (Rheingold, 1963), on learning (Hess, Rheingold, & Stevenson, in press), and, most ambitiously and in greatest comparative detail, on aggression (Lorenz, 1966). The prospect of a comparative analysis of personality development, however, is dimmed by a restatement of Beach's requirements for comparative study. The pattern of each animal's behavior, studied in its own right and understood in its natural setting, forms the *basic data* from which a comparative description or, ultimately, a comparative theory can be constructed. We are at some distance from a description of the development of human personality that would take its place in a possible comparative analysis.

The Animal as Model of Man

The use of animal behavior as a model of human behavior is easier and more risky than the pursuit of comparative analysis. If the analogy turns out to hold when tests are made of its application to the human case, a clear gain in knowledge is made. If the analogy does not hold, *or if its application to human beings cannot be assessed,* there is a danger that further analysis will be postponed by the illusion of explanation. Spitz' (1965) use of the embryological notion of "organizer" in his discussion of infant development, Gray's (1958) assertion that human socialization is a form of imprinting, Scott's (1963) theory of critical periods in human socialization, Bowlby's (1958) elaborate treatment of attachment to the mother as a result of "instinctual response systems," Freedman's (1961) conclusion that human fear of strangers is homologous with animal flight—such proposals, however provocative and plausible, must meet two groups of criterial questions before they can be accepted as more than provocative and plausible. First, the human behavior to be explained must be related in some detail to its animal model. It is not enough, in the face of the diversity of animal behavior, to say that human socialization is like imprinting or fear of strangers like animal flight. Imprinting under what circumstances? Animal flight under what conditions? If the human smile is like the clinging of anthropoids, what is the nature of the similarity? To what aspects of the monkey mother-infant exchange should we compare aspects of the human mother-infant exchange? Second, the implications of the asserted analogy for the study of human behavior should be stated. Again, it is hardly sufficient to rewrite a human phenomenon poorly understood (e.g., early smiling, the response to separation) in the language of animal behavior. The critical questions for the usefulness of the animal as model are: What predictions are possible that are not possible without the analogy, and What observations would lead to the abandonment of the analogy? The animal model must, like all others in psychology, reveal its power and its limitations. Although many students of human development who are fond of animal analogies are also sensitive to the traps such models pose, the criteria of usefulness are not always respected. Perhaps the most suitable corrective to a search for animal simplicity to explain human complexity is the recognition of animal complexity.

THE ANIMAL AS INSPIRATION FOR RESEARCH

The interest in species-specific behavior, the revival of concern with the role of unlearned responses, the new emphasis on observations in a natural setting—characteristics of the recent comparative study of animals—have had obvious effects on the course of research in human development. Speculations about the nature of the child's tie to his mother have been productive of Ainsworth's (1963) observational studies of children in Uganda, of Robertson and Bowlby's (1952) work on separation, and of Schaffer and Emerson's (1964) longitudinal study of attachment to the mother. The study of the effects of institutionalization, which grows from humane concern and from the implications of separation for the formation of ties to the mother, has produced several new analyses of the relevant data (Yarrow, 1961, 1964; Clarke & Clarke, 1960). A number of studies of human development are focusing on the naturally occurring exchange between parent and child (e.g., Wolff, 1963). Discussions of critical periods in animals have led to a reexamination of the timing of human development (Caldwell, 1962). Whatever reservations must be entered about the overenthusiastic application of the animal as model of man, there can be no doubt that *research* on the early months of human life has been broadened in method and in relevance to comparative analysis by the inspiration of studies of animal development.

REFERENCES

Ader, R. The effects of early experience on subsequent emotionality and resistance to stress. *Psychol. Monogr.,* 1959, 73, Whole No. 472.

Ainsworth, M. D. The development of infant-mother interaction among the Ganda. In B. M. Foss (Ed.), *Determinants of infant behavior.* II. New York: Wiley, 1963.

Ambrose, J. A. The development of the smiling response in early infancy. In B. M. Foss (Ed.), *Determinants of infant behavior.* I. New York: Wiley, 1961.

Aristotle. *Historia Animalium.* Trans. D'A. W. Thompson. Oxford: Oxford Univer. Press, 1910.

Baird, J. C., & Becknell, J. C., Jr. Discrimination learning as a function of early form exposure. *Psychol. Rec.,* 1962, 12, 309–313.

Baldwin, J. M. *Mental development in the child and the race.* New York: Macmillan, 1895.

Baldwin, J. M. *Development and evolution.* New York: Macmillan, 1902.

Barnett, S. A. (Ed.) *Lessons from animal behaviour for the clinician.* London: Nat. Spastics Soc., 1962.

Barnett, S. A. *A study in behaviour.* London: Methuen, 1963.

Baron, A., Brookshire, K. H., & Littman, R. A. Effects of infantile and adult shock-trauma upon learning in the adult white rat. *J. comp. physiol. Psychol.,* 1957, 50, 530–534.

Beach, F. A. The shark was a boojum. *Amer. Psychologist,* 1950, 5, 115–124.

Beach, F. A. Experimental investigations of species-specific behavior. *Amer. Psychologist,* 1960, 15, 1–18.

Beach, F. A., & Jaynes, J. Effects of early experience upon the behavior of animals. *Psychol. Bull.,* 1954, 51, 239–263.

Bell, W., & Felbinger, R. J. Effects of free and restricted environmental experience on the development of socio-sexual behavior in the rat. *Psychol. Rep.,* 1962, 10, 351–356.

Bellugi, U., & Brown, R. The acquisition of language. *Monogr. Soc. Res. Child Develpm.,* 1964, 29, Whole No. 92.

Bennett, E. L., Diamond, M. C., Krech, D., & Rosenzweig, M. R. Chemical and anatomical plasticity of brain. *Science,* 1964, 146, 610–619.

Bijou, S. W., & Baer, D. M. *Child development.* II. New York: Appleton-Century-Crofts, 1965.

Bitterman, M. E. Toward a comparative psychology of learning. *Amer. Psychologist,* 1960, 15, 704–712.

Bloom, B. *Stability and change in human characteristics.* New York: Wiley, 1964.

Boring, E. G. The influence of evolutionary theory upon American psychological thought. In S. Persons (Ed.), *Evolutionary thought in America.* New Haven: Yale Univer. Press, 1950, pp. 267–298.

Bourlière, F. *The natural history of mammals.* (3rd ed.) New York: Knopf, 1964.

Bovard, E. W. The effects of early handling on viability of the albino rat. *Psychol. Rev.,* 1958, 65, 257–271.

Bowlby, J. The nature of the child's tie to his mother. *Internat. J. Psychoanal.,* 1958, 39, 1–23.

Brookshire, K. H., Littman, R. A., & Stewart, C. N. Residue of shock-trauma in the white rat: A three-factor theory. *Psychol. Monogr.,* 1961, 75, Whole No. 514.

Brown, R. T. Early experience and problem-solving ability. Unpublished doctoral dissertation, Yale Univer., 1966.

Bruner, J. S. The cognitive consequences of early sensory deprivation. In P. Solomon, P. E. Kubzansky, P. H. Leiderman, J. H. Mendelson, R. Trumbull, & D. Wexler (Eds.), *Sensory deprivation.* Cambridge: Harvard Univer. Press, 1961.

Caldwell, B. M. The usefulness of the critical period hypothesis in the study of filiative behavior. *Merrill-Palmer Quart. Behavior Develpm.,* 1962, 8, 229–242.

Carpenter, C. R. A field study of the behavior and social relations of howling monkeys (*Alouatta palliata*). *Comp. Psychol. Monogr.,* 1934, 10, No. 2.

Carpenter, C. R. *Naturalistic behavior of nonhuman primates.* University Park, Pa.: Pennsylvania State Univer. Press, 1964.

Clarke, A. D. B., & Clarke, A. M. Some recent advances in the study of early deprivation. *J. Child Psychol. Psychiat.,* 1960, 1, 26–36.

Clarke, R. S., Heron, W., Fetherstonhaugh, M. L., Forgays, D. G., & Hebb, D. O. Individual differences in dogs: Preliminary reports on the effects of early experience. *Canad. J. Psychol.,* 1951, 5, 150–156.

Comenius, J. A. *The school of infancy.* 1633. Chapel Hill: Univer. of North Carolina Press, 1956.

Darwin, C. *The descent of man and selection in relation to sex.* (First published in 1871.) New York: D. Appleton, 1897.

Darwin, C. *The expression of the emotions in man and animals.* London: J. Murray, 1872.

Denenberg, V. H. The effect of early experience. In E. S. E. Hafez (Ed.), *The behaviour of domestic animals.* London: Balliere, Tindall, & Cox, 1962.

Denenberg, V. H. Critical periods, stimulus input, and emotional reactivity: A theory of infantile stimulation. *Psychol. Rev.,* 1964, 71, 335–351.

Denenberg, V. H., & Karas, G. G. Effects of differential infantile handling upon weight gain and mortality in the rat and mouse. *Science,* 1959, 130, 629–630.

Denenberg, V. H., & Morton, J. R. C. Effects of environmental complexity and social groupings upon modification of emotional behavior. *J. comp. physiol. Psychol.,* 1962, 55, 242–246.

Denenberg, V. H., & Smith, S. A. Effects of infantile stimulation and age upon behavior. *J. comp. physiol. Psychol.,* 1963, 56, 307–312.

Devore, I. Mother-infant relations in free-ranging baboons. In H. L. Rheingold (Ed.), *Maternal behavior in mammals.* New York: Wiley, 1963.

Fairfield, J. Effects of cold on infant rats: Body temperatures, oxygen consumption, electrocardiograms. *Amer. J. Physiol.,* 1948, 155, 355–365.

Ford, C. S., & Beach, F. A. *Patterns of sexual behavior.* New York: Harper & Bros., 1951.

Foss, B. M. (Ed.) *Determinants of infant behavior.* New York: Wiley, 1961, 1963, 1965.

Forgays, D. G., & Forgays, J. W. The nature of the effect of free-environmental experience in the rat. *J. comp. physiol. Psychol.,* 1952, 45, 322–328.

Forgays, D. G., & Read, J. M. Crucial periods for free-environmental experience in the rat. *J. comp. physiol. Psychol.,* 1962, 55, 816–818.

Forgus, R. H. The effect of different kinds of form pre-exposure on form discrimination learning. *J. comp. physiol. Psychol.,* 1958, 51, 75–78.

Freedman, D. G. The infant's fear of strangers and the flight response. *J. Child Psychol. Psychiat.,* 1961, 2, 242–248.

Freedman, D. G., King, J. A., & Elliot, O. Critical period in the social development of dogs. *Science,* 1961, 133, 1016–1017.

Freud, S. *Three essays on the theory of sexuality.* 1905. In J. Strachey (Ed.), *Standard Edition of Sigmund Freud.* VII. London: Hogarth Press, 1953.

Freud, S. *An outline of psychoanalysis.* 1940. New York: Norton, 1949.

Fuller, J. L., & Waller, M. B. Is early experience different? In E. L. Bliss (Ed.), *Roots of behavior.* New York: Hoeber, 1962.

Gesell, A. *Infancy and human growth.* New York: Macmillan, 1928.

Gesell, A. L. *Infant development: The embryology of early human behavior.* New York: Harper, 1952.

Gesell, A. L., & Amatruda, C. S. *Developmental diagnosis.* (2nd ed.) New York: Hoeber, 1947.

Gewirtz, J. L. The course of smiling by groups of Israeli infants in the first eighteen months of life. *Scripta Hierosolymitana,* 1965, 14, 9–58.

Gibson, E. J., Walk, R. D., Pick, H. L., Jr., & Tighe, T. J. The effect of prolonged exposure to visual patterns on learning to discriminate similar and different patterns. *J. comp. physiol. Psychol.,* 1958, 51, 584–587.

Gibson, E. J., Walk, R. D., & Tighe, T. J. Enhancement and deprivation of visual stimulation during rearing as factors in visual discrimination learning. *J. comp. physiol. Psychol.,* 1959, 52, 74–81.

Goldfarb, W. Effects of psychological deprivation in infancy and subsequent stimulation. *Amer. J. Psychiat.,* 1945, 102, 18–33.

Goldfarb, W. Emotional and intellectual consequences of psychologic deprivation in infancy: A re-evaluation. In P. H. Hoch and J. Zubin (Eds.), *Psychopathology of childhood.* New York: Grune & Stratton, 1955.

Gottlieb, G. Refrigerating eggs prior to incubation as a way of reducing error in calculating developmental age in imprinting experiments. *Animal Behavior,* 1963, 11, 290–292.

Gottlieb, G. Imprinting in relation to parental and species identification by avian neonates. *J. comp. physiol. Psychol.,* 1965, 59, 345–356.

Gray, P. H. Theory and evidence of imprinting in human infants. *J. Psychol.,* 1958, 46, 155–166.

Guiton, P. The influence of imprinting on the agonistic and courtship responses of the Brown Leghorn cock. *Animal Behavior,* 1961, 9, 167–177.

Hall, G. S. *Life and confessions of a psychologist.* New York: D. Appleton, 1923.

Harlow, H. F. The nature of love. *Amer. Psychologist,* 1958, 13, 673–685.

Harlow, H. F. The development of affectional patterns in infant monkeys. In B. M. Foss (Ed.), *Determinants of infant behavior.* I. New York: Wiley, 1961.

Harlow, H. F. The maternal affectional system. In B. M. Foss (Ed.), *Determinants of infant behavior.* II. New York: Wiley, 1963.

Harlow, H. F., & Zimmermann, R. R. Affectional responses in the infant monkey. *Science,* 1959, 130, 421–432.

Hebb, D. O. The effects of early experience on problem-solving at maturity. *Amer. Psychologist,* 1947, 2, 306–307.

Hebb, D. O. *The organization of behavior.* New York: Wiley, 1949.

Hebb, D. O. Drives and the C.N.S. (conceptual nervous system). *Psychol. Rev.,* 1955, 62, 243–254.

Hebb, D. O., & Williams, K. A method of rating animal intelligence. *J. gen. Psychol.,* 1946, 34, 59–65.

Henderson, N. D. Behavioral effects of manipulation during different stages in the development of mice. *J. comp. physiol. Psychol.,* 1964, 57, 284–289.

Henderson, N. D. Acquisition and retention of conditioned fear during different stages in the development of mice. *J. comp. physiol. Psychol.,* 1965, 59, 439–442.

Hersher, L., Richmond, J. B., & Moore, A. U. Modifiability of the critical period for the development of maternal behavior in sheep and goats. *Behavior,* 1963, 20, 311–320.

Hess, E. H. Imprinting. *Science,* 1959, 130, 133–141.

Hess, E. H. Imprinting in birds. *Science,* 1964, 146, 1128–1139.

Hess, E. H., Rheingold, H. L., & Stevenson, H. W. (Eds.) *Learned and unlearned behavior in immature organisms.* New York: Wiley, in press.

Hess, E. H., & Schaefer, H. H. Innate behavior patterns as indicators of the "critical period." *Z. Tierpsychol.,* 1959, 16, 155–160.

Hoyt, A. M. *Toto and I: A gorilla in the family.* Philadelphia: Lippincott, 1941.

Hutchings, D. E. Early handling in rats: The effects of body-temperature reduction and stimulation on adult emotionality. *Proc. 73rd Annual Convention Amer. Psychol. Assn.,* 1965, 183–184.

Hymovitch, B. The effects of experimental variations on problem solving in the rat. *J. comp. physiol. Psychol.,* 1952, 45, 313–321.

Jay, P. Aspects of maternal behavior in langurs. *Proc. N. Y. Acad. Sci.,* 1962, 102, 468–476.

Jaynes, J. Imprinting: The interaction of learned and innate behavior. I. Development and generalization. *J. comp. physiol. Psychol.,* 1956, 49, 201–206.

Jaynes, J. Imprinting: The interaction of learned and innate behavior. II. The critical period. *J. comp. physiol. Psychol.,* 1957, 50, 6–10.

Jaynes, J. Imprinting: The interaction of learned and innate behavior. III. Practice effects on performance, retention and fear. *J. comp. physiol. Psychol.,* 1958, 51, 234–237. (a)

Jaynes, J. Imprinting: The interaction of learned and innate behavior. IV. Generalization and emergent discrimination. *J. comp. physiol. Psychol.,* 1958, 51, 238–242. (b)

Jennings, H. S. *Behavior of the lower organisms.* New York: Columbia Univer. Press, 1906 (Reprinted 1915).

Katz, D. *Animals and men: Studies in comparative psychology.* New York: Longmans Green, 1937.

King, J. A. Parameters relevant to determining the effect of early experience upon the adult behavior of animals. *Psychol. Bull.,* 1958, 55, 46–58.

Klinghammer, E., & Hess, E. H. Imprinting in an altricial bird: The blond ring dove (*Streptopelia risoria*). *Science,* 1964, 146, 265–266.

Klinghammer, E. Sexual imprinting in altricial birds. In H. Rheingold, E. H. Hess, & H. W. Stevenson (Eds.), *Learned and unlearned behavior.* New York: Wiley, in press.

Klopfer, P. H. Imprinting: A reassessment. *Science,* 1965, 147, 302–303.

Klopfer, P. H., and Hailman, J. P. Perceptual preferences and imprinting in chicks. *Science,* 1964, 145, 1333–1334.

Kovach, J. K., & Hess, E. H. Imprinting: Effects of painful stimulation upon the following response. *J. comp. physiol. Psychol.,* 1963, 56, 461–464.

Laroche, J. L., & Tcheng, F. *Le sourire du nourrisson.* Louvain: Publications Universitaires, 1963.

Lashley, K. S., & Russell, J. T. The mechanism of vision. XI. A preliminary test of innate organization. *J. genet. Psychol.,* 1934, 45, 136–144.

Levine, S. A further study of infantile handling and adult avoidance learning. *J. Pers.,* 1956, 25, 70–80.

Levine, S. Psychophysiological effects of infantile stimulation. In E. L. Bliss (Ed.), *Roots of behavior: Genetics, instinct, and socialization in animal behavior.* New York: Hoeber, 1962, pp. 246–253.

Levine, S., Alpert, M., & Lewis, G. W. Differential maturation of an adrenal response to cold stress in rats manipulated in infancy. *J. comp. physiol. Psychol.,* 1958, 51, 774–777.

Levine, S., & Broadhurst, P. L. Genetic and ontogenetic determinants of adult behavior in the rat. *J. comp. physiol. Psychol.,* 1963, 56, 423–428.

Levine, S., & Otis, L. S. The effects of handling before and after weaning on the resistance of albino rats to later deprivation. *Canad. J. Psychol.,* 1958, 12, 103–108.

Levine, S., & Wetzel, A. Infantile experiences, strain differences, and avoidance learning. *J. comp. physiol. Psychol.,* 1963, 56, 879–881.

Lindsley, D. B., Wendt, R. H., Lindsley, D. F., Fox, S. S., Howell, J., & Adey, W. R. Diurnal activity, behavior and EEG responses in visually deprived monkeys. *Ann. N. Y. Acad. Sci.,* 1964, 117, 564–587.

Lorenz, K. Companionship in bird life. 1935. In C. H. Schiller (Ed.), *Instinctive behavior.* New York: Internat. Univer. Press, 1957.

Lorenz, K. Comparative study of behavior. Report given in Rostock, 1939. In C. H. Schiller (Ed.), *Instinctive behavior.* New York: Int. Univer. Press, 1957.

Lorenz, K. The past twelve years in the comparative study of behavior. Report given in Freiburg, 1952. In C. H. Schiller (Ed.), *Instinctive behavior.* New York: Int. Univer. Press, 1957.

Lorenz, K. *On aggression.* Trans. M. K. Wilson. New York: Harcourt, Brace, & World, 1966.

Marler, P., & Tamura, M. Culturally transmitted patterns of vocal behavior in sparrows. *Science,* 1964, 146, 1483–1486.

Mason, W. A. The effects of social restriction on the behavior of rhesus monkeys: I. Free social behavior. *J. comp. physiol. Psychol.,* 1960, 53, 582–589.

Mason, W. A. The effects of social restriction on the behavior of rhesus monkeys: II. Tests of gregariousness. *J. comp. physiol. Psychol.,* 1961, 54, 287–290. (a)

Mason, W. A. The effects of social restriction on the behavior of rhesus monkeys: III. Dominance tests. *J. comp. physiol. Psychol.,* 1961, 54, 694–699. (b)

Mason, W. A. The effects of environmental restriction on the social development of rhesus monkeys. In C. H. Southwick (Ed.), *Primate social behavior.* New York: Van Nostrand, 1963.

Mason, W. A., & Green, P. C. The effects of social restriction on the behavior of rhesus monkeys: IV. Responses to a novel environment and to an alien species. *J. comp. physiol. Psychol.,* 1962, 55, 363–368.

Mason, W. A., & Sponholz, R. R. Behavior of rhesus monkeys raised in isolation. *J. Psychiat. Res.,* 1963, 1, 299–306.

Melzack, R., & Burns, S. K. Neuropsychological effects of early sensory restriction. *Boletín del instituto de estudios médicos y biológicos,* 1963, 21, 407–425.

Melzack, R., & Scott, T. H. The effects of early experience on the response to pain. *J. comp. physiol. Psychol.,* 1957, 50, 155–161.

Melzack, R. A., & Thompson, W. R. Effects of early experience on social behavior. *Canad. J. Psychol.,* 1956, 10, 82–90.

Moltz, H. Imprinting: An epigenetic approach. *Psychol. Rev.,* 1963, 70, 123–138.

Moltz, H. Contemporary instinct theory and the fixed action pattern. *Psychol. Rev.,* 1965, 72, 27–47.

Moltz, H., & Rosenblum, L. A. The relation between habituation and the stability of the following response. *J. comp. physiol. Psychol.,* 1958, 51, 658–661.

Moltz, H., & Stettner, L. J. The influence of patterned-light deprivation on the critical period for imprinting. *J. comp. physiol. Psychol.,* 1961, 54, 279–283.

Mowbray, J. B., & Cadell, T. E. Early behavior patterns in rhesus monkeys. *J. comp. physiol. Psychol.,* 1962, 55, 350–357.

Oberjohann, H. *My friend the chimpanzee.* London: Hale, 1957.

Piaget, J. *The origin of intelligence in the child.* 1936. New York: Int. Univer. Press, 1952.

Piaget, J. *The psychology of intelligence.* 1946. London: Routledge & Kegan Paul, 1950.

Provence, S., & Lipton, R. C. *Infants in institutions.* New York: Int. Univer. Press, 1962.

Rabinovitch, M. S., & Rosvold, H. E. A closed-field intelligence test for rats. *Canad. J. Psychol.,* 1951, 5, 122–128.

Ramsey, A. O., & Hess, E. H. A laboratory approach to the study of imprinting. *Wilson Bull.,* 1954, 66, 196–206. Cited in Hess, 1959.

Ratner, S. C., & Denny, M. R. *Comparative psychology.* Homewood, Ill.: Dorsey, 1964.

Rheingold, H. L. (Ed.) *Maternal behavior in mammals.* New York: Wiley, 1963.

Riesen, A. H., & Aarons, L. Visual movement and intensity discrimination in cats after early deprivation of pattern vision. *J. comp. physiol. Psychol.,* 1959, 52, 142–149.

Riesen, A. H., & Kinder, E. F. *Postural development of infant chimpanzees.* New Haven: Yale Univer. Press, 1952.

Robertson, J., & Bowlby, J. Responses of young children to separation from their mothers. *Courrier Centre International de l'Enfance,* 1952, 2, 131–142.

Rosenblatt, J. S. The basis of synchrony in the behavioral interaction between the mother and her offspring in the laboratory rat. In B. M. Foss (Ed.), *Determinants of infant behavior.* III. New York: Wiley, 1965.

Schaefer, T., Jr. Early "experience" and its effects on later behavioral processes in rats: II. A critical factor in the early handling phenomenon. *Trans. N. Y. Acad. Sci.,* 1963, 25, 871–889.

Schaffer, H. R., & Emerson, P. E. The development of social attachments in infancy. *Monogr. Soc. Res. Child Develpm.,* 1964, 29, Whole No. 94.

Schaller, G. *The mountain gorilla: Ecology and behavior.* Chicago: Univer. of Chicago Press, 1963.

Schaller, G. B., & Emlen, J. T. The ontogeny of avoidance behaviour in some precocial birds. *Animal Behavior,* 1962, 10, 370–381.

Schneirla, T. C. Instinctive behavior, maturation-experience and development. In B. Kaplan & S. Wapner (Eds.), *Perspectives in psychological theory: Essays in honor of Heinz Werner.* New York: Int. Univer. Press, 1960, pp. 303–334.

Schwartz, S. Effect of neonatal cortical lesions and early environmental factors on adult rat behavior. *J. comp. physiol. Psychol.,* 1964, 57, 72–77.

Scott, J. P. Critical periods in behavioral development. *Science,* 1962, 138, 949–958.

Scott, J. P. The process of primary socialization in canine and human infants. *Monogr. Soc. Res. Child Develpm.,* 1963, 28, Whole No. 85.

Scott, J. P., & Fuller, J. P. *Genetics and the social behavior of the dog.* Chicago: Univer. of Chicago Press, 1965.

Shipley, W. U. The demonstration in the domestic guinea pig of a process resembling classical imprinting. *Animal Behavior,* 1963, 11, 470–474.

Sluckin, W. *Imprinting and early learning.* Chicago: Aldine, 1965.

Solomon, P., Kubzansky, P. E., Leiderman, P. H., Mendelson, J. H., Trumbull, R., & Wexler, D. (Eds.) *Sensory deprivation.* Cambridge: Harvard Univer. Press, 1961.

Spemann, H. *Embryonic development and induction.* New Haven: Yale Univer. Press, 1938.

Spemann, H., & Mangold, H. Über Induktion von Embryonalanlagen durch Implantation artfremder Organisatoren. *Arch. mikr. Anat. Entw. Mech.,* 1924, 100, 599–638. Cited in Spemann (1938).

Spence, J. T., & Maher, B. A. Handling and noxious stimulation of the albino rat: I. Effects on subsequent emotionality. *J. comp. physiol. Psychol.,* 1962, 55, 247–251. (a)

Spence, J. T., & Maher, B. A. Handling and noxious stimulation of the albino rat: II. Effects on subsequent performance in a learning situation. *J. comp. physiol. Psychol.,* 1962, 55, 252–255. (b)

Spitz, R. A. Hospitalism: An inquiry into the genesis of psychiatric conditions in early childhood. *Psychoanal. Study Child,* 1945, 1, 53–74.

Spitz, R. A. *The first year of life.* New York: Int. Univer. Press, 1965.

Spitz, R. A., & Wolf, K. M. Anaclitic depression: An inquiry into the genesis of psychiatric conditions in early childhood. *Psychoanal. Study Child,* 1946, 2, 313–342.

Thompson, W. R., & Dubanoski, R. A. Early arousal and imprinting in chicks. *Science,* 1964, 143, 1187–1188.

Thompson, W. R., & Heron, W. The effects of early restriction on activity in dogs. *J. comp. physiol. Psychol.,* 1954, 47, 77–82.

Thompson, W. R., & Schaefer, J. T. Early environmental stimulation. In D. W. Fiske & S. R. Maddi (Eds.), *Functions of varied experience.* Homewood, Ill.: Dorsey, 1961.

Thorpe, W. H. The learning of song patterns by birds, with especial reference to the song of the Chaffinch (*Fringilla coelebs*). *Ibis,* 1958, 101, 535–570. Cited in Thorpe and Zangwill, 1961. (a)

Thorpe, W. H. Further studies on the process of song learning in the Chaffinch (*Fringilla coelebs gengleri*). *Nature* (London), 1958, 182-1, 554–557. (b)

Thorpe, W. H. *Learning and instinct in animals.* (new ed.) Cambridge: Harvard Univer. Press, 1963.

Thorpe, W. H., & Zangwill, O. L. *Current problems in animal behavior.* Cambridge: Cambridge Univer. Press, 1961.

Tinbergen, N. *The study of instinct.* Oxford: Oxford Univer. Press, 1951.

Waddington, C. H. *Principles of embryology.* London: Allen & Unwin, 1956.

Waddington, C. H. *New patterns in genetics and development.* New York: Columbia Univer. Press, 1962.

Waller, P. F., & Waller, M. B. Some relationships between early experience and later social behavior in ducklings. *Behavior,* 1963, 20, 343–363.

Weininger, O. Physiological damage under emotional stress as a function of early experience. *Science,* 1954, 119, 285–286.

Weininger, O. The effects of early experience on behavior and growth characteristics. *J. comp. physiol. Psychol.,* 1956, 49, 1–9.

Werner, H. *Comparative psychology of mental development.* Chicago: Follett Pub. Co., 1948.

White, T. H. *The book of beasts: Being a translation from a Latin bestiary of the twelfth century.* London: Jonathan Cape, 1954.

Wolff, P. H. The natural history of a family. In B. M. Foss (Ed.), *Determinants of infant behavior.* II. New York: Wiley, 1963.

Woods, P. J. The effects of free and restricted environmental experience on problem-solving behavior in the rat. *J. comp. physiol. Psychol.,* 1959, 52, 399–402.

Woods, P. J., Ruckelhaus, S. J., & Dowling, D. M. Some effects of "free" and "restricted" environmental rearing conditions upon adult behavior in the rat. *Psychol. Rep.,* 1960, 6, 191–200.

Yarrow, L. J. Maternal deprivation: Toward an empirical and conceptual reevaluation. *Psychol. Bull.,* 1961, 58, 459–490.

Yarrow, L. J. Separation from parents during early childhood. In M. L. Hoffman & Lois W. Hoffman (Eds.), *Review of child development research.* I. New York: Russell Sage Foundation, 1964.

Yerkes, R. M. *Chimpanzees: A laboratory colony.* New Haven: Yale Univer. Press, 1943.

Yerkes, R. M., & Yerkes, A. W. *The great apes: A study of anthropoid life.* New Haven: Yale Univer. Press, 1929.

Zimbardo, P. G., & Montgomery, K. C. Effects of "free-environment" rearing upon exploratory behavior. *Psychol. Rep.,* 1957, 3, 589–594.

PART III Adult Behavior and Personality

CHAPTER 7 Neuropsychology and Psychophysiology in Personality Research

DAVID T. LYKKEN
University of Minnesota

Not many years ago it was still possible for theoretical psychologists to defend an ignorance of neurophysiology on the grounds that this molecular discipline had as yet failed to develop many facts, concepts, and principles which could be usefully translated into the language of psychology. Most psychologists assumed, then as now, that it is the nervous system that mediates the relationship between stimulus and response, between input and output, and therefore that any adequate theory that claims to account for these relationships must, in some ultimate sense, be a theory about the nervous system. Although the language of such a theory might be exclusively psychological, making no direct reference to neurons, synapses, or nuclei, any adequate theory of, say, the emotions must be structurally homeomorphic with the description that an omniscient neurophysiologist would give of the aspect of the nervous system which in fact mediates emotional phenomena, i.e., the psychological theory must in principle be reduceable to the corresponding physiological account (although such a reduction may be difficult and inexpedient). But the concepts of psychology were so molar, and the building-blocks of physiology so molecular, that there seemed to be little common ground on which a mutually rewarding interchange might be established.

However, developments within and communication between these two disciplines have accelerated greatly in the past ten or twenty years. It is permissible to infer that the basic unit of current statistical learning theories or of the structural theories proposed by Blum (1961), Deutsch (1960), or Hebb (1949) may be identified with the single neuron or synapse. Physiologists, in their turn, are identifying complex systems that clearly seem to constitute the substrate for such psychological states or processes as sleep, dreaming, arousal, pleasure, reward, pain, fear, rage, memory, and the like. The present extensive use of physiological techniques on the part of psychologists and the equal popularity of psychological or behavioral techniques among many physiological researchers (including pharmacologists) is probably both symptomatic of and facilitating to this greatly increased interchange at the level of theory.

The study of sensation and perception provides just one of many possible examples

Original manuscript of this chapter was completed in 1965.

of this kind of development. Psychologists of the "softer" variety have known since before the time of Freud that what a man perceives and even senses can be considerably influenced by the nature of his attitudes, expectations, and beliefs ("Such tricks hath strong imagination that, if it would but apprehend some joy, it comprehends some bringer of the joy; or in the night, imagining some fear, how easy is a bush suppos'd a bear!"—*Midsummer Night's Dream*). Psychologists of the "harder" type have understood much the same thing at least since the work of Bruner and Goodman (1947). It is possible that these admittedly imprecise notions of the psychologists helped to motivate or guide the physiological research of Golambos, Hernández-Peón, and many others on the centrifugal control of afferent processes (*vide infra*), research which has written a new and exciting chapter of molar neurophysiology in just the past ten or fifteen years. These developments, in turn, should be of heuristic value to psychologists working with such phenomena as perceptual defense and the like and should give impetus as well as guidance to attempts to elaborate a psychological theory of perception.

But the relevance of modern physiology to psychology in general, and to personality research in particular, is technological as well as theoretical. An increasing proportion of studies in the personality field make use of experimental techniques—independent or dependent variables—derived from the physiological laboratory. Some examples: In the study of temperament, autonomic responses such as heart rate changes or the galvanic skin response (GSR) are used as indicants of the intensity of emotional responses shown by different types of individuals or in reaction to different types of stimulus conditions. So-called psychotropic drugs, like adrenalin, amphetamine, or the various tranquilizers, may be used to manipulate states of arousal or emotional reactivity as an aid in the study of the defense mechanisms or other affective-cognitive or affective-sensory interactions. There are areas of personality research which already demand some familiarity with these technological developments, and it is difficult to imagine an area in which some such competence would not prove to be an asset to the investigator.

A convention has recently been proposed (Stern, 1964) aimed at clarifying and stabilizing a distinction already implicit in our use of the designations *physiological psychology* and *psychophysiology*. It is suggested that we characterize as "physiological psychology" research in which the independent variables are physiological manipulations—surgical procedures, brain stimulation, drugs—while the dependent variables are psychological—test performance, Skinner box behavior, subjective report, behavioral observations or ratings, and so on. Obversely, "psychophysiological research" will imply the use of psychological manipulations and the measurement of physiological effects, e.g., a study of fear conditioning using the GSR as an indicant, research on stage fright as monitored by heart rate changes, the use of pupillary dilation to measure the interest value of stimuli. By this definition, a few personality researches qualify as "physiological psychology," studies using drugs, principally, like Schachter and Singer's (1962) experiment (a mixed case, really, since psychological manipulations were also used) in which *S*s pretreated with adrenalin became angry in the presence of an angry-acting stooge or, with equal readiness, gay and light-hearted in the presence of a frivolous stooge. But personality researchers seldom employ surgery or stimulate the brain (no pun intended), so that the relevance here of physiological psychology is mainly theoretical or heuristic, whereas, as suggested above, the use of physiological dependent variables is already widespread in the personality area. The present chapter is organized in accord with this distinction, the first part being devoted to a discussion of some recent research in physiology and physiological psychology which would seem to be of interest to the personality theorist, while the second part is primarily technological, concerned with problems of measuring and interpreting certain psychophysiological dependent variables which have been and will continue to be profitably employed in personality research.

PART 1. PHYSIOLOGICAL PSYCHOLOGY AND PERSONALITY THEORY

Rather than attempt a comprehensive survey, which would be both superficial and incompetent, I shall give only passing mention to several important areas which the interested reader can follow up elsewhere on his own, and then essay a more detailed examination of recent work on the reticular activating system and the physiological psychology of arousal, perception, and attention.

Biochemical Individuality

A collection of stomachs or livers or hearts, obtained from a random sample of normal, healthy human beings, may appear so extraordinarily diverse in size, shape, and internal structure as to lead the uninitiated to conclude that they must have been obtained from several different species of animals. Some normal hearts can pump 11 liters of blood per minute and others only 3; the size, capacity, and branching pattern of the blood vessels to the brain show a similar variability. In a summary of the 19 enzymes for which data are available, the "normal" range of interindividual variation in enzyme efficiency was found to be never less than twofold, typically three- or fourfold and, in some instances, differences of 1,000 to 5,000 per cent were recorded. Healthy human thyroids range in weight from about 8 to 50 gm., and stable measures of thyroid activity vary between individuals over at least a fivefold range. Normal variation in pituitary weight is from about 350 to 1,100 mg., while individual levels of secretion of the eight or more hormone products of this gland appear to be at least equally variable.

In a fascinating monograph, Roger Williams (1963) has assembled a multitude of such illustrations of anatomical and biochemical variability, mostly constitutional and some actually genetic in origin. That these are all "normal" subjects, each coping reasonably successfully with rather similar environmental demands, emphasizes the extraordinary capacity of the organism to compensate for idiosyncratic patterns of biological endowment by suitable adjustments in its pattern of activity and of nutrition. Williams's thesis, in part, is that individual differences in neurophysiological—microstructural, biochemical—endowment, while less well documented thus far, may be expected to be of similar magnitude, that no single pattern of *nutrition*—defined broadly enough to include vitamins and drugs at one extreme and special patterns of training and experience at the other—can be expected to produce optimum development and function in all cases, and that special patterns of nutrition, rationally derived from an improved understanding of neurophysiological individuality, may enable different individuals to approach the same goals in different ways or, at least, different goals of equal value.

In spite of its polemical overtones, Williams's book is the best compensation I can think of for those psychologists not fortunate enough to have been able to hear the late D. G. Paterson discourse on the nature, extent, and importance of individual differences. All students of personality would benefit from reading it. Psychologists who tend to assume that if a characteristic does not clearly run in families, it must be learned; clinicians who refuse to consider possible constitutional etiology of a condition on the grounds that this implies "therapeutic nihilism"—in the face of the manifest difficulties of modifying a lifetime of mislearning and the many successes of organic medicine in compensating for constitutional defects by surgical, pharmaceutical, or nutritional means—should take Williams's data and his message under serious advisement.

Motivation and Reward

Just over ten years ago, W. R. Hess (1954) reported the elicitation of voracious eating behavior in cats by electrical stimulation in the hypothalamus, and in the same year, Olds and Milner (1954) showed that brain shocks in similar locations also had the properties of behavioral reward, that rats would learn new responses and work almost untiringly at old ones if such stimulation was provided as a reinforcer. In that same productive year, Delgado, Roberts, and Miller (1954) found that stimulation of certain regions in the thalamus and hippocampus could produce the behavioral effects of normal pain or fear, viz., punishment, emotional arousal, and the learning of escape and avoidance behavior. These exciting discoveries have precipitated a flood of research, much of which can be found ably summarized by Olds (1962).

It is now clear that stimulation in many brain regions will produce the reinforcing effect in varying degrees. In some areas the effect is subject to satiation, but it appears that rats, cats, and monkeys will work for stimulation in the lateral hypothalamus without any sign of satiation until exhaustion supervenes. At least some of these areas seem to be related to specific primary drives, e.g., shocks in some regions are rewarding when the animal is hungry but less so or not at all when he is satiated for food. There is considerable overlap between the motivating and reinforcing effects; in many areas where the animal will work for stimulation, that same stimulation will also lead him to consume food if it is available or to emit previously acquired food-finding responses. In at least some loci, rewarding brain stimulation also provides its own motivation. Animals will not begin again to self-stimulate if interrupted for a brief interval but must be "primed" by one or more brain-shocks which seem to reinstitute the "drive" for additional stimulation (Deutsch, 1963). In addition to other brain regions where stimulation is unequivocally nociceptive, producing emotional and escape or avoidance behavior, there are loci at which both the onset and the offset of stimulation have been shown to be reinforcing, i.e., the animal will learn one response to turn the brain-shock *on* and a different response with which he then promptly turns it *off*. There is also evidence for reciprocal inhibition between these "plus" and "minus" centers with some dispiriting indications that the latter tend to dominate the former (although cf. Brady & Conrad, 1960).

Emotion

The pioneering work of Hess (W. R. Hess, 1954) on the technique of electrical stimulation in the depths of the brain substance led also to an acceleration of research on the related problems of the neurophysiology of emotional behavior. The anatomical substrate of emotion appears to reside in a kind of shell of tissue which surrounds much of the innermost core of the hemispheres, made up of such structures as the hippocampus, the amygdala, the cingulate gyrus, the hypothalamus, fornix, mammillary bodies, and anterior thalamus, and which has come to be known as the *limbic system* or "visceral brain" (MacLean, 1955). The intimate relation between the emotions and the systems of drive and reward is illustrated anatomically by the fact that the medial forebrain bundle, the region in which stimulation seems to produce the most potent reinforcing effects, is also the major line of communication between the limbic lobe on the one hand and the hypothalamus, midbrain, and other brain stem structures on the other.

The lesion studies of Klüver and Bucy in the late 1930's demonstrated that bilateral ablation of the amygdala converted wild monkeys into tame and docile, unemotional creatures, showing compulsive orality and a bizarre hypersexuality—the "Klüver-Bucy syndrome." MacLean (1963) has emphasized the anatomical proximity in the amygdala of centers concerned with oral or eating behavior—salivation, chewing movements—and those concerned with sexual responses, including penile erection. Noting that stimulation in the nearby region of the anterior commissure may produce angry or fearful vocalization and the showing of fangs, MacLean suggests that these anatomical linkages may help explain the behavioral interrelation of sexuality, orality, fear, and aggression.

Rage-like or aggressive behavior can be elicited by stimulation in several brain areas. Roberts and Kiess (1964) showed that stimulation in the anterior hypothalamus not only produces in cats hissing and other affective displays but also leads the animal to attack a rat that it had hitherto ignored, even turning away from the food dish to do so, and most importantly, under the influence of such stimulation these animals would learn to run a Y-maze to obtain a rat that they could attack; without stimulation, performance deteriorated and there were no attacks. "It was concluded that the performance of the attack was rewarding, and the central readiness for attack elicited by the stimulation possessed motivational and cue properties salient in the evocation of the learned responses leading to prey." (Roberts & Kiess, 1964, p. 187).

Stimulation of the Human Brain

The sparse literature so far available on the effects of stimulation of these regions in unanesthetized human subjects (e.g., Delgado & Hamline, 1960; Heath & Mickle, 1960; Sem-Jacobsen & Torkildsen, 1960; King, 1961) indicates that electrical excitation of roughly the same areas that are concerned with positive reinforcement in animals produces in humans feelings of well-being, euphoria, and sometimes even a kind of erotic ecstacy; the temptation to refer to the Olds "plus" centers as "pleasure" or "joy" regions thus finds some additional justification. In contrast, Penfield (1958) was able to elicit feelings of fear, sorrow, loneliness, or disgust by stimulating the anterior and inferior temporal cortex. Penfield and Roberts's (1959) reports of the hallucinatory effect of temporal lobe stimulation are particularly arresting. As described by the patients afterwards, these experiences are vivid evocations apparently of the veridical past which begin and end with the switching of the current and can sometimes be rerun or restarted where they ended by stimulating again in the same area. This truly seems to be the "stuff that dreams are made of" and, taken together with a considerable quantity of less dramatic but equally essential work on the role of the hippocampus in learning and recall, focuses attention on the hippocampal zone as the probable storage site for long-term memory, either "the actual repository of ganglionic patterns or the mechanism of reactivation of the record (of the stream of consciousness)" (Roberts, 1961).

One way of dramatizing the significance of these developments is to contemplate this fact: It is now quite within the purview of established technology to implant a small cluster of electrodes deep within a human brain, attached to a small power cell and radio receiver screwed to the skull—small enough to hide under one's hat—and then by telemetry to produce in that subject an intense, protopathic feeling of terror, or an equally intense experience of euphoria, ecstacy, or exhaltation, or (probably although localization here may be less certain) a feeling of implacable hatred or a frenzy of rage—at the whim of the experimenter and the press of a button. It is a sobering thought.

Schachter's Contributions

I shall devote this section to a review of some recent work by a *social* psychologist using *physiological* techniques (among others) to produce findings which are of great interest to the personality theorist and to the student of emotion in particular. It is well known that the peripheral sympathetic arousal produced by the injection of adrenalin most commonly yields a state of "as if" emotion—"I feel as if I ought to be scared, but I'm not"—although a real emotional reaction (fear) sometimes does "break through" (Marañon, 1924; Hawkins, Monroe, Sandifer, & Vernon, 1960). This ability to experience the usual visceral accompaniments of fear without subjective fear was a principal basis for Cannon's (1927; 1929) refutation of the James-Lange theory of emotion. However, a recent study of human paraplegics, deprived by high spinal lesions of most peripheral sympathetic activity, suggests that the subjective emotional experience of these individuals is also distorted—weaker, more superficial, rather passionless; "It's a mental kind of anger; I say I am afraid ... but I don't really feel afraid" (Hohmann, quoted in Schachter, 1964).

Schachter (1964) sees these two sets of introspections as "... opposite sides of the same coin. Marañon's subjects report the visceral correlates of emotion but in the absence of veridical cognitions do not describe themselves as feeling emotion. Hohmann's subjects describe the appropriate reaction to an emotion-inducing situation but in the absence of visceral arousal do not seem to describe themselves as emotional. It is as if they were labeling a situation, not describing a feeling." Schachter and Singer (1962) found that they could produce apparently genuine subjective emotions (euphoria, anger) in normal subjects after epinephrine injection, providing (1) the subjects were misled as to the effects to be expected from the drug and thus not allowed to attribute their visceral sensations to the injection and (2) an identifiable emotional context was provided by having the subject, after the injection, sequestered with another "subject" (a stooge) who behaved either in a gay or in an angry fashion. Schachter (1964) concludes, "given a state of physiological arousal for which an individual has no immediate explanation, he will 'label' this state and describe his feelings in terms of the cognitions available to him. To the extent that cognitive factors are potent determiners of emotional states, it could be anticipated that precisely the same state of physiological arousal could be labeled 'joy' or any of a great diversity of emotional labels depending on the cognitive aspects of the situation. Given the same cognitive circumstances, the individual will react emotionally or describe his feelings as emotions only to the extent he experiences a state of physiological arousal."

These experiments provide the most striking empirical support yet available for Lindsley's (1951) *activation theory* of emotion—the notion that there is a single dimension of activation or arousal common to all at least of the 'excited' emotions—although Schachter emphasizes rather more than Lindsley does the role of the visceral as well as the central components of arousal. Arousal, however, is a necessary but not sufficient condition for emotional behavior or experience. The "other side of the coin" is the cognitive activity of the subject who will feel emotion only if he labels his aroused condition as emotional. The quality of the emotion he then feels depends also on the particular emotional label he chooses. But, surely, neither cognitive activity nor labeling is a *sine qua non* for emotional experience. One supposes that the presence of a particular emotion implies the activity of some particular center or assembly in the diencephalon which is reciprocally interconnected with the "higher" centers subserving perception, symbolic activities, and the like; thus do we know how we feel and thus feel what we know. The activation theory implies further (or so it would seem to me) that each such *primary emotion* center is also reciprocally connected with the brain stem activating system; nonspecific arousal however induced, whether naturalistically or by epinephrine injection, would seem to lower the thresholds of the primary excited emotions, such as joy, fear, and rage. (Is *grief* a primary emotion, and does it share the activation component? *Depression,* at least, seems to involve reduced central nervous system [CNS] arousal.) Thresholds lowered, the primary centers wait upon centrifugal activation from above. Clinical evidence strongly suggests that there must be some sort of mutually inhibitory process interlinking the primary centers or at least a positive feedback mechanism so that, e.g., fearful cognitive content activates the (potentiated) fear center which in turn provides stimulus support for continued fearful mentation, and so on; once fear holds sway, it is surely difficult to elicit euphoria or rage. By the same token, anger is an inhibitor of fear, and one suspects that self-induced rage is one of the more popular tranquilizers.

If fear is a chief inhibitor of antisocial or psychopathic behavior, and if undifferentiated arousal is a *sine qua non* for fear, then normal subjects in the presence of ethical conflict should be more inclined to yield to temptation if their autonomic arousal is somehow artificially damped. Schachter and Latené (1964) found that some 20 per cent of a control group of college girls cheated while correcting their own answer sheets in a psychology course quiz, but that nearly 40 per cent of another group cheated in the same situation after premedication with the tranquilizer chlorpromazine. The present writer had found some years ago that the true primary psychopath of the Cleckley type shows low clinical anxiety, deficient anxiety conditioning, and negligible *avoidance learning* in a task motivated in normal subjects by fear of a painful shock (Lykken, 1957). After replicating the latter finding on two sets of prison inmates selected to meet criteria of "primary psychopathy," Schachter and Latené then found that the psychopaths showed a sharp increase in avoidance learning after premedication with epinephrine. The implication here, of course, is that the poor avoidance learning of the psychopath, manifested both in the laboratory and in the antisocial activities leading to his incarceration, is the consequence of a relative lack of fear resulting from a relative deficiency in nonspecific arousal; artificially augmenting arousal by means of epinephrine injection produces an evanescent display of normal avoidant behavior.

Schachter and Latené, however, noted that their psychopathic subjects had actually higher heart rates than did their nonpsychopathic prisoners at the start of the experiment and also a greater elevation in heart rate during the avoidance task under the epinephrine condition. Similarly, in their college girl sample referred to above, subjects scoring below the median on the Lykken (1957) scale of anxiety reactivity showed significantly *higher* heart rates after taking the examination than did those whose anxiety scores were above the median. Finally, Valins (1963), also using college students, found that subjects with low Lykken anxiety scores gave a significantly greater increase in heart rate in response to a stress situation than did high-anxious subjects as defined by the same test. These findings led Schachter and Latené to speculate along the following lines. Perhaps some psychopaths tend to be hyperreactive to virtually any titillating event, to be autonomically aroused by circumstances which would be frightening to others and also by events which most people would consider harmless. "Such generalized, relatively indiscriminant reactivity is, we would suggest, almost the equivalent of no reactivity at all. If almost every event provokes strong autonomic discharge, then, in terms of internal autonomic cues, the subject feels no differently during times of anger than during relatively tranquil times. Bodily conditions which for others are associated with emotionality are, for the sociopath, his 'normal' state. It would appear from the data on the effects of adrenaline on avoidance learning that only intense states of autonomic reaction, presumably stronger than and differentiable from his normal reactions, acquire emotional attributes for the sociopathic subject." Schachter and Latené do not reject the notion that some psychopaths are relatively hyporeactive but argue rather that a similar behavioral phenotype may result, under certain circumstances of, e.g., childhood experience, from the obverse condition of autonomic hyperreactivity and, indeed, were able to report that their psychopathic prisoners gave a cleanly bimodal distribution of heart rates, one mode well above and the other symmetrically below the single mode of the heart rate distribution given by the nonpsychopathic prisoners.

This idea that there may be important individual differences in the ability to discriminate different emotional or other subjective states is provocative and has implications for other phenomena beyond psychopathy. Thus, Schachter is currently following up the suggestion of the psychoanalyst Hilde Bruch (1961) that the root problem in chronic obesity is a failure to discriminate between the feeling of hunger and the feelings of anxiety or emotional stress, a confusion due perhaps to a parental habit of feeding the infant in response to every indication of distress whether hunger-related or not. Alternatively, however, Schachter's finding that the psychopathic subject displays accelerated heart rate in stress situations may possibly be related to the interesting report of Lacey *et al.* (Lacey, Kagan, Lacey, & Moss, 1963) —treated more fully later in this chapter— that nociceptive stimulation tends generally to accelerate the heart. This, Lacey believes, decreases cortical arousal and attenuates exteroceptive input via an inhibitory feedback circuit from the carotid sinus. Perhaps Schachter's "hyperreactive" psychopaths were really individuals in whom this cardioacceleratory-CNS-inhibitory mechanism is unusually well developed, allowing them to damp stressful input or the distress response which it produces in them. In any event, it seems clear now that heart rate does not vary monotonically with arousal or emotional excitement and heart rate alone cannot be safely used as an indicant of emotional reactivity. Similarly, Schachter's analysis of the interrelation of anxiety and oral stimulation in obesity should be contrasted with the compelling proposal of Kessen and Mandler (1961) that oral stimulation is an innate inhibitor of undifferentiated distress; it seems very possible that the obese individual eats not because he misinterprets anxiety for hunger but because eating actually quells his emotional discomfort, at least temporarily.

The Executive Functions of the Brain Stem Reticular Formation

One of the most active and exciting areas of neuropsychological research during recent years has been the study of the reticular activating system (RAS) in the brain stem, which, together with related higher structures, appears to govern such basic functions as sleep, wakefulness, and cortical arousal, the modulation or filtering of sensory input, and the orientation of awareness or attention. As early as 1937, Bremer had shown that cutting the brain stem just above the level of the pons (this is the *cerveau isolé* preparation) produced, in the cat, a state of coma together with a pattern of EEG activity characteristic of normal sleep. The real surge of research into these matters, however, waited upon the demonstration by Moruzzi and Magoun in 1949 that direct electrical stimulation of the midbrain reticular formation in the sleeping animal produces immediate behavioral awakening together with the EEG arousal reaction that would normally accompany arousing the animal by means of sensory stimulation. There followed a crescendo of research which still continues in laboratories all over the world. Discussion and resumés of subsequent developments which are of particular interest to psychologists may be found in the excellent review by Samuels (1959), in Lindsley's authoritative chapter in the *Handbook of Physiology* (1960), in Magoun's elegant little book, *The Waking*

Brain (1963), and in a wide-ranging and important monograph by Berlyne (1960).

Anatomical Relationships

The reticular formation is a strip of nervous tissue, including nerve cells of many types and sizes with diffusely branching or *reticulated* nerve fibers, which extends upward through the central core of both sides of the brain stem from the level of the medulla to the thalami (see Figure 1). All sensory pathways which run from the peripheral receptor organs or from the interoceptors via the thalamus to the primary projection areas in the cortex give off in addition collateral fibers into this reticular substance. Significantly, in view of the role played by the reticular mechanism in arousing the cortex, tracts subserving pain sensation are especially widely interconnected in these regions; indeed, about two-thirds of the fibers in the classical lateral "spinothalamic" tract appear to terminate within the upper brain stem (Magoun, 1963). Higher brain centers, including many regions of the cortex, the cerebellum, and the structures of the limbic system thought to be concerned with emotional experience, send fibers into the reticular substance through which they can influence its activity. The most important sources of cortico-reticular influence appear to be regions of the frontal poles, the sensorimotor cortex and the cingulate gyrus. Thus, the reticular formation (RF) is equipped to monitor the entire flux of sensory input, to

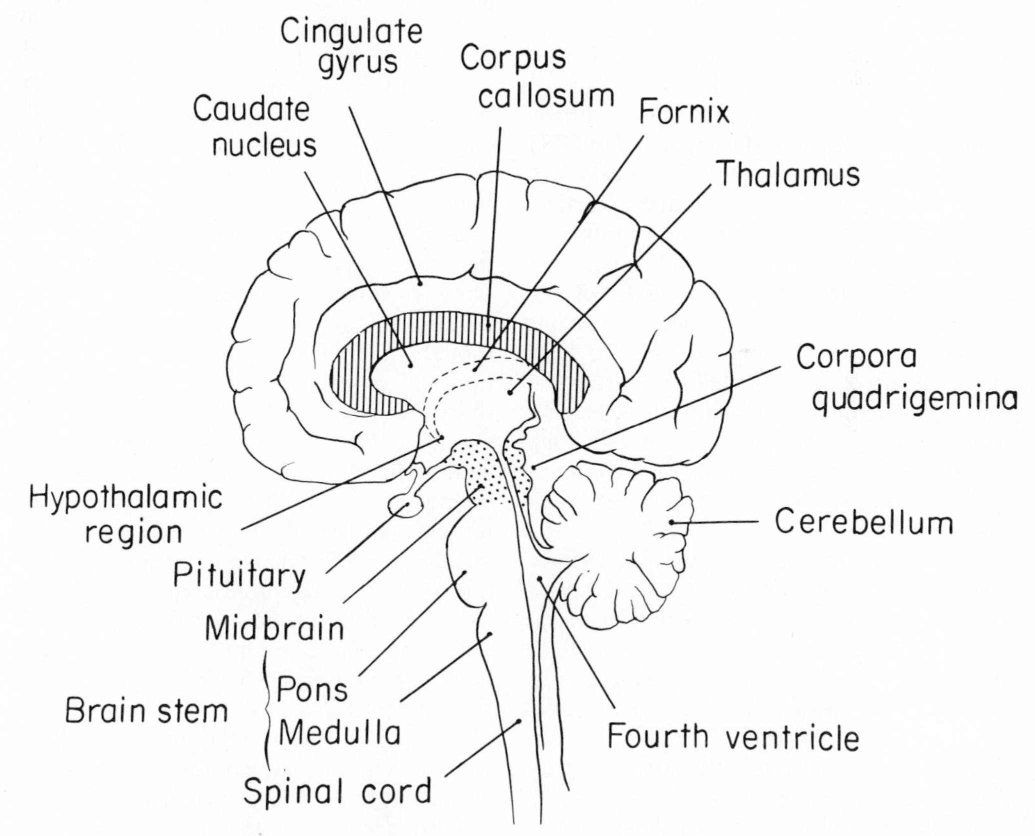

Figure 1. Median view of right cerebral hemisphere.

receive excitation, information, or commands from other regions, and, presumably, to subject this incoming information to some degree of analysis and integration, as indicated by the rich interconnections of the myriad reticular neurons and the fact that single units have been shown to be responsive to stimulation from different parts of the body and even through different modalities.

The outgoing or efferent connections of the RF are equally complex and ubiquitous. In the upward direction, there is an extensive reticulo-cortical pathway involving fibers which radiate diffusely to nearly all areas of the cerebral cortex from origins in the midbrain reticular substance; this is the ascending reticular activating system (ARAS) of Moruzzi and Magoun. Another and relatively independent system appears to originate somewhat higher in the intralaminar nuclei of the thalamus, considered to be the rostral extremity of the reticular formation. This is the diffuse thalamo-cortical projection system (DTPS) which is now known to be anatomically distinct from the specific thalamo-cortical system (STPS) over which sensory information is transmitted in a specific, point-to-point fashion from the relay nuclei of the thalamus to the sensory projection regions of the cortex. There appears to be at least one synaptic relay in the DTPS, since cortical destruction does not lead to degeneration within the intralaminar nuclei, but the site of this relay and origin of the final common path of the DTPS has not yet been definitely located.

Stimulation of the midbrain ARAS produces a long-lasting and very general *activation* of the cortex coupled with behavioral arousal—waking of the sleeping animal or an increase in alertness or excitement in a subject already awake. High-frequency electrical stimulation of the DTPS can produce similar results, although the activating effects of this system appear to be more phasic and delicate in character, with shorter latencies and briefer duration, and, unlike the ARAS, the DTPS appears capable of activating localized regions of the cortex with some selectivity. The DTPS is known to be capable also of an opposite, inhibitory influence on the cortex. Low-frequency stimulation of the nonspecific thalamic nuclei can produce synchronization rather than activation of cortical areas which, if sufficiently widespread, may be accompanied by behavioral relaxation, lassitude, or sleep. Centers capable of driving this inhibitory mechanism of the DTPS have been localized in limbic system structures and in the hypothalamus (Magoun, 1963). The initial and lighter stages of sleep may result from influences arising in an inhibitory center in the lower, bulbar portion of the RF which tends to deactivate the ARAS. Still another inhibitory center, situated in the tegmental region of the pons, has recently been shown to be responsible for the deepest level of normal sleep in which midbrain and diencephalic structures are inhibited and the cortex, while cut off from the ARAS excitation, is also freed from the inhibitory influences of the DTPS.

In the downstream direction, there are first the classical reticulo-spinal efferent fibers capable of both facilitating and inhibiting spinal motoneurons and which are thought to be concerned with the integration and coordination of striped-muscle activity. Secondly, there is the complex gamma-efferent system of fine, myelinated gamma fibers which lead off to the receptor organs of the proprioceptive system, the muscle spindles. By means of this mechanism, the RF is capable of either augmenting or attenuating proprioceptive feedback, thus providing an additional and versatile means of controlling motor activity. Even more generally, it has now been established that the reticular formation sends efferent fibers outward to the relay nuclei of all incoming sensory pathways as well as to the peripheral receptor organs themselves.

Thus, deep within the very stem and core of the brain, we find a kind of inner brain or communications center which is equipped to monitor all incoming sensory information and to deliver some sort of commands to the peripheral pathways carrying that information and which is richly interconnected with the higher brain structures and with the cortex itself. Included here are systems for controlling sleep and wakefulness and the level of tonic activation of the cortex generally as well as the phasic fluctuations of excitability of more localized cortical areas. The mechanism of attention appears to reside here as well as an apparatus for screening sensory input which, as we shall see, seems to be capable of crude perceptual analysis in its own right. In collaboration with the (not necessarily activated) cortex, this mechanism may be capable of complex pattern recognition as well and may primarily determine which information is to be passed on to the higher executive system.

Cortical Activation and Behavioral Arousal

The EEG and the arousal continuum—Much of our understanding of the reticular system depends heavily upon the use of the EEG as an indicant of the level of cortical arousal. Table 1 (modified from Lindsley, 1960) summarizes some of the principal relationships. EEG tracings recorded from the occipital and parietal areas of an awake but relaxed subject tend to be dominated by the *alpha* rhythm which consists of waves with a frequency in the range from 8 to 13 per second and an amplitude of some 20 to 50 microvolts. When the subject is aroused, as by emotional stimulation or by some task demanding concentration, these alpha rhythms give way to a pattern of low-voltage fast activity (often called *beta* waves) which represents the *activated* or *desynchronized* EEG. Unexpected or novel stimuli, presented to a relaxed waking subject, produce a transitory interval of fast activity sometimes called *alpha blockade*. Conversely, as the subject drifts off into sleep, the alpha fades out and is replaced by irregular 14-per-second bursts known as *sleep spindles,* often punctuated by large, slow oscillations called *K-complexes*. Deeper sleep is signalled by an increasing proportion of slow, large waves, called *theta* waves in the range from 4 to 7 per second or *delta* waves when slower than 4 per second. Finally, in deep sleep, the record is dominated almost entirely by still larger, slower delta activity. Several methods of classifying the EEG stages of sleep have been proposed, the most commonly used being a letter system (Loomis, Harvey, & Hobart, 1937) and the number system more recently employed by Dement and Kleitman (1957). The two schemes can be roughly equated as indicated in Table 1.

As arousal increases above the level of drowsiness, marked by the low-voltage irregular activity of Stage 1, there is both an increase in the amount of alpha present in the record ("percent-time alpha") and also an increase in the amplitude of the alpha waves. Further increase in arousal decreases alpha once again as the record approaches the completely "desynchronized" pattern characteristic of excitement. This inverted U-shaped relationship of alpha amplitude to arousal has been specifically supported by Stennett (1957) using palmar conductance as an indicant of arousal.

One can see here a rough trend for the brain waves to decrease in voltage but increase in frequency as the subject moves from deep to light sleep to relaxed wakefulness and finally to more alert activity. This picture has been complicated, however, by recent evidence that normal sleep is punctuated by intervals in which the EEG reverts to the low-voltage irregular activity characteristic of activation but during which the subject is substantially more difficult to awaken than even in the high-voltage slow-wave sleep of Stage 4 (Jouvet, 1961; H. L. Williams, Hammack, Daly, Dement, & Lubin, 1964). During these intervals of "paradoxical sleep," rapid eye movements (REM) can be detected and

TABLE 1

THE AROUSAL CONTINUUM: EEG AND BEHAVIORAL CORRELATES (MODIFIED FROM LINDSLEY, 1960)

Arousal Continuum	EEG	State of Awareness	Electrocortical Response	Behavioral Characteristics
Strong, Excited Emotion; Fear, Rage, Anxiety	Desynchronized: low to moderate amplitude; fast mixed frequencies	Restricted awareness, narrowed attention span, confusion, strong sensory suppression	Probably widespread inhibition of evoked potentials	Disorganized, poor discrimination and coordination, may be increased strength and endurance for primitive "flight-fright" functions
Alert Attentiveness	Partially synchronized (periods of alpha activity): mainly low-voltage, fast activity (beta waves)	Selective attention, concentration, anticipation	Selective inhibition and facilitation of evoked potentials	Efficient, fast reaction time, optimum discrimination and coordination. May be too well focused for optimum creativity
Relaxed Wakefulness	Synchronized: mainly alpha rhythm at moderate voltage (8–12/sec, 30 microvolts)	Attention wanders, not forced, favors free association	Either alpha blockage or evoked potentials in alpha background	Broadened attention span, quickly activated, capable of routine activities, perhaps optimal for reflection and creative thought
Drowsiness	Stage 1 (D & K), Stages A and B (Loomis). Alpha fades out; low-voltage, irregular fast frequency. Transition phase only	"Dreamy," hypnogogic state, partial awareness, imagery and reverie		Reduced awareness, slower to arouse, poor sensorimotor function. GSR suppression
Light Sleep	Stage 2 (D & K), Stage C (Loomis). Low-voltage background with 14/sec sleep spindles and K-complexes	Loss of consciousness but rather easily awakened	Evoked potentials changed from waking wave shape	Capable of simple conditioned motor responses, Sidman-avoidance. Responds selectively to own name. Graded EEG and vascular response to graded intensity of auditory stimuli. GSR reappears

Arousal Continuum	EEG	State of Awareness	Electrocortical Response	Behavioral Characteristics
Moderate Sleep	Stage 3 (D & K), Stage D (Loomis). Intrusion of random high-voltage, slow waves (1–4/sec, 50–100 mV), some spindling	Sound sleep	Evoked potentials further modified in wave shape, especially K-complexes	
Deep Sleep	Stage 4 (D & K), Stage E (Loomis). Mainly large, random slower delta waves (1–2/sec, 50–150 mV). No K-complexes	Deep sleep, high arousal thresholds	Evoked potentials similar to Stage 3	Intermittent simple motor response to stronger stimuli, Sidman avoidance, reduced EEG responsiveness but vascular response to noise stimulus unaffected
	Stage 1_{REM} (H. L. Williams *et al.*, 1962). Identical appearance to Stage 1 (desynchronized, low voltage) but accompanied by rapid eye movements (REM), occasional jerky movements, reduced muscle tone. (Jouvet's "rhombencephalic sleep")	Highest arousal thresholds, frequently or always accompanied by dreaming	Evoked potentials markedly attenuated, considerable cortical activity	Motor and vascular responsivity as in Stage 4, heart rate slows and blood pressure drops, reduced EMG activity, penile erection, possibly random variation of palmar conductance, increased general metabolism
Barbiturate Narcosis, Coma	Large, slow waves (delta) with periods of no activity in deeper stages	Complete loss of consciousness, little or no response to stimulation, amnesia	Evoked potentials present and strong	As in deep sleep?

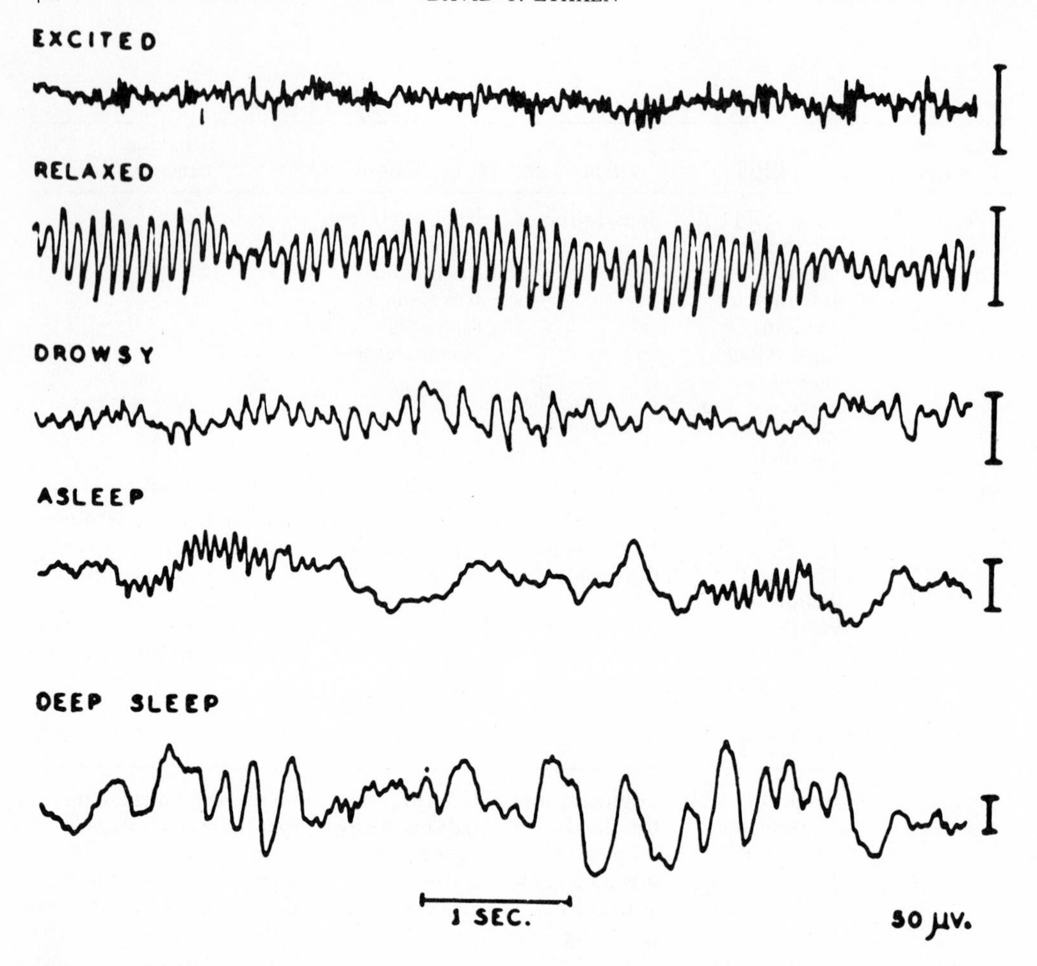

Figure 2. Characteristic EEG tracings from a normal human subject during various excitatory states from sleep to wakefulness (Jasper, 1941).

there is a general lowering of muscle tone and electromyographic (EMG) activity, although occasional jerky limb movements may be seen. Systolic and diastolic blood pressure is sharply reduced during these periods (Guazzi & Zanchetti, 1965). The work of Kleitman and his students (e.g., Kleitman, 1961) indicates that it is during these intervals when most or all of normal dreaming occurs. This deepest sleep level has been referred to as Stage 1REM (Williams *et al.,* 1964) because its EEG pattern seems to be identical to the low-voltage, irregular activity of the transitional Stage 1 which follows the disappearance of alpha in drowsiness and precedes the onset of sleep spindling and delta activity. Although "deeper" even than Stage 4, in the sense of higher thresholds of arousal, Stage 1REM is associated with higher metabolic rates (oxygen consumption) than even Stage 2 (Brebbia & Altshuler, 1965), and it is likely that Stage 1REM is less restful or restorative than Stage 4 and is thus, in that different sense, a "lighter" sleep.

Jouvet (1961) has shown in the cat that Stage 1REM which occurs only after periods of lighter sleep (often Stage 2), is controlled by a center in the pontile tegmentum which appears to exert inhibitory control over the nonspecific systems of both the thalamus and midbrain. Pontile inhibition of the synchronizing mechanisms of the DTPS releases the cortex into desynchrony (it may be this effect which allows the presumably cortical activity of dreaming during Stage 1REM, as Magoun [1963] suggests), and pontile inhibition of the ARAS increases by several times the intensity of sensory stimulation required to arouse the sleeper. Cortical evoked potentials produced by sensory stimuli, which are modified as to shape in the deeper stages of synchronized sleep but not reduced in amplitude, are very much smaller during Stage 1REM (H. L. Williams, Tepas, & Morlock, 1962) which may reflect the absence of the normal supplementary feedback from the now inhibited reticular mechanisms. Huttenlocker (1960) reports that evoked potentials recorded from the midbrain RF and elicited by auditory click stimuli are large and undiminished even after 1,000 repetitions in the waking animal but rapidly diminish to about half-amplitude during slow-wave sleep. During Stage 1REM sleep there is almost complete suppression of midbrain response to these repeated clicks.

An important investigation by H. L. Williams, Hammack, Daly, Dement, and Lubin (1964) provides additional evidence that cortical and behavioral arousal can vary to some extent independently of the state or stage of the EEG. Subjects were stimulated by repeated acoustical noise bursts of varying intensities during all EEG sleep stages both before and after 64 hours of sleep deprivation. Three types of response to these sounds were recorded: EEG changes, including K-complexes and alterations in frequency, finger vasoconstriction, and an operant response (pressing a microswitch) which the subject, while in the waking state, has been instructed to emit after each sound. It was found that the amplitude or frequency of response increased systematically with increasing

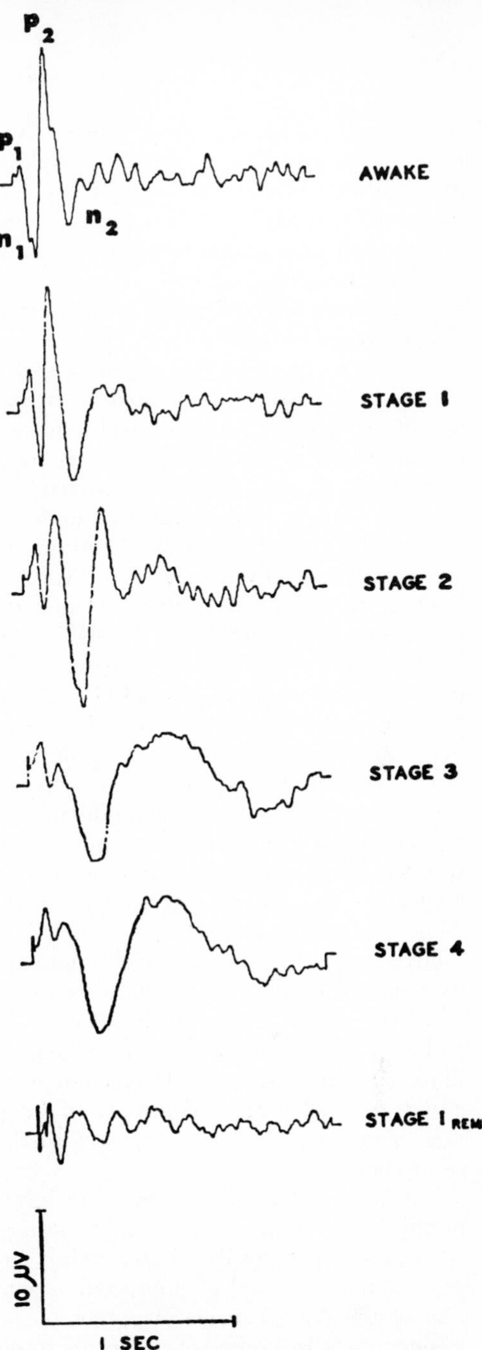

Figure 3. Averaged evoked cortical responses to auditory clicks as a function of the stage of sleep. EEG recorded between an electrode on the vertex and another in the left occipital region. Each response represents an average of 100 EEG segments, each 1,536 mSec long following the presentation of the click stimulus (H. L. Williams, Tepas, & Morlock, 1962).

sound intensity at all sleep stages. Even noise levels near the subjects' waking threshold of audibility produced fairly consistent EEG and vasoconstrictor responses during both light and deep sleep. Response amplitudes were considerably diminished at all sleep levels after extended sleep deprivation, however, indicating that depth of sleep as defined in terms of the *reactivity* of the brain is not perfectly correlated with electrocortical activity. As additional evidence, responsiveness to stimulation during moderate Stage 2 sleep (which occurred frequently enough throughout the night to allow such tabulation) was found to decrease systematically as the night wore on in the case of both the behavioral and the vascular responses, although the EEG reactivity did not systematically change. While these subjects showed less EEG and behavioral reactivity to the stimuli during Stage 4 and Stage IREM, consonant with other evidence that these stages represent deeper sleep levels, there was no differential responsiveness in vasoconstriction. One wonders whether this latter finding may be related to the activated condition of the diencephalon during Stage IREM sleep (Jouvet, 1961) and to the labile emotionality which is thought to be characteristic of dreaming. The recent demonstration by Fisher, Gross, and Zuch (1965) that in human male subjects penile erection is an almost invariable accompaniment of Stage IREM sleep intervals seems relevant in this connection.

Finally, some indication must be given of the limits of this concept of an arousal *continuum*. It is possible, but certainly not proven, that the level of nonspecific excitation of the ARAS increases monotonically as one moves from the bottom to the top of Table 1, but clearly "behavioral efficiency" does not do so, falling off at the high end, nor does "cortical activation" which is apparently higher in Stage IREM than in presumably lighter stages of sleep. Moreover, the inflection in psychological functioning at the junction of sleep and waking is so abrupt that this schema is potentially misleading. Indeed, the existence of so many interrelated excitatory and inhibitory mechanisms, both neural and hormonal, counterpoised in a still poorly understood manner, makes the notion of an unidimensional arousal continuum seem somewhat precarious, except perhaps as a temporary working hypothesis subject to prompt reformulation as the steady flow of new evidence may require.

Sleep[1]—Although some of the most basic questions still remain unanswered, many facts about the properties and mechanisms of sleep have been uncovered in the course of the last two decades. First of all, it seems fairly well established that sleep is the stage which supervenes when the cortex is deprived of the energizing influence of the ARAS. There is a reciprocity in the connections between cortex and midbrain so that the cortex can control its own activation to a certain extent by corticifugal excitation or inhibition of the ARAS. The onset and lighter stages of sleep begin with a synchronization of the cortex via the inhibitory mechanism of the DTPS followed by a cortically induced inhibition of the ARAS. The synchronized cortex apparently drives the ARAS into parallel slow-wave activity, thereby lowering its reactivity (Jouvet, 1961). Perhaps equally important, the inhibited cortex transmits less tonic excitation over the cortico-reticular circuits. An inhibitory center in the bulbar RF appears also to inhibit the ARAS during sleep either directly (Moruzzi, 1964) or indirectly by driving the DTPS as Magoun (1963) suggests. Once sleep has been attained, the inhibitory center in the pons is somehow triggered into action periodically (perhaps at about 90-minute intervals in man) during which time the ARAS is directly and powerfully

[1] An excellent and detailed survey of the recent work in this area may be found in U.S. Public Health Service Publication #1389, "Current Research on Sleep and Dreams," available from the Superintendent of Documents, U.S. Government Printing Office, Washington, D.C., 20402, for $.65.

inhibited together with the thalamic mechanisms (Jouvet, 1961).

A segment of the midbrain tegmentum is known to be strongly responsive to adrenalin (Rothballer, 1956) so that built-up epinephrine concentrations resulting from excitement and high arousal tend to retard the deactivation and inhibition of the ARAS. It has long been supposed that there must be a symmetrical hormonal mechanism having an inhibitory effect which, once in action, would act to damp the more labile neural mechanisms and help maintain uninterrupted sleep. A recent article (Monnier & Hosli, 1964) reports the discovery of such a substance, although its chemistry and site of action are not yet known, which when concentrated from the blood of a sleeping animal can be injected into the bloodstream of a waking animal thereby causing it to fall asleep.

Magoun (1963) tends to regard the cortical inhibitory mechanism of the DTPS as the agent involved in those phenomena which Pavlov grouped under the heading of *internal inhibition:* Any stimulus associated with the withholding of reinforcement may come to produce spindle bursting and synchronization in cortical regions—a conditioning stimulus (CS) during extinction trials; a discrimination stimulus which is never reinforced; a conditioned inhibitory stimulus whose presentation together with the CS means that reinforcement will be withheld on the trial; or the early portions of a protracted CS-US interval in the "inhibition of delay" experiment. Similar effects have been observed on the EEG of experimental animals for intervals following copulation or feeding, and it seems probable that stimuli associated with satiety and with sleep or relaxation can become able through conditioning to produce similar inhibitory responses of the DTPS. Bonvallet, Dell, and Hiebel (1954) demonstrated that distention of the carotid sinus, as might result from an increase in blood pressure, acts through the bulbar inhibitory center to drive the DTPS mechanism, producing cortical deactivation and slow waves. This finding is the basis of Lacey's conjecture, discussed further in a later section, that blood pressure increase following noxious stimulation may serve to attenuate sensory input, while blood pressure decrease in situations requiring attention to the environment may have the opposite effect.

These phasic and relatively localized inhibitory effects upon the cortex by the DTPS must serve specialized adjustive functions during the waking state, but whenever they are unusually strong or occur against a background of reduced ARAS excitation, their influence can spread. Heads nod during the Sunday sermon not because of the excesses of the night before (at least, not in every case) but because sensory input is minimized and proprioceptive feedback as well, while inhibitory activity is maximized; *stop* coughing, *quit* squirming, *don't* look around. Add to this, postprandial inhibition following a large breakfast, a regular, hypnotic rhythm in the speaker's voice, insufficient content in the sermon to support cortical activity, and spreading inhibition of the cortex must result. Trying *not* to go to sleep under these conditions is notoriously ineffectual, possibly because *trying not* to do anything involves inhibitory processes. A better solution, although not without risk, is to yield to drowsiness in the hope that one will catch one's self just as the head falls limply forward; the orienting reflex and adrenalin secretion which this narrow escape produces can be counted upon to counteract somnolence for as long as half an hour.

The loss of adaptive function during sleep is probably relatively much greater for man than for other animals because the capabilities most affected are precisely those which are distinguishingly humanoid. The sleeper cannot perform any sort of logical analysis of a complex stimulus nor enrich his interpretation by means of recollections or association of ideas. Much of our waking commerce with the environment involves a continual process of learning—one learns something about the identity of the speaker and interprets what he says accordingly; one notes and remembers that no one else is in the room so that what is said must be addressed to one's self, etc.—and it appears that at least this kind of learning ceases during sleep (Lindsley, 1960).

However, the contrast between sleep and coma is considerable also. First, of course, the sleeper can awaken reasonably quickly in reaction to almost any strong stimulus, the exceptions being those recurrent disturbances to which the subject has become habituated after long experience: the traffic noises, the passing train, the moderate and chronic pains. The sleeper can still make use of his biological clock to awaken at the accustomed time just before his alarm goes off or to be disturbed in his sleep if the Midnight Limited *fails* to rumble past on schedule. After some practice while awake, he can continue to perform on a Sidman-avoidance schedule even during deep sleep, regularly pressing a key which delays an electric shock another three seconds (Granda & Hammack, 1961). The same subjects also pressed a second key with their other hand, being rewarded after a fixed number of responses by a five- to eight-minute "time-out" period, during which shock was stopped so they could sleep undisturbed, and this behavior showed much the same regularity found with waking subjects. A conditioned stimulus previously associated with electric shock can produce partial or complete arousal (Rowland, quoted in Magoun, 1963), although that same tone at that same loudness would not affect a naive animal. The human sleeper can be selectively aroused by stimuli having special significance for him. Oswald, Taylor, and Treisman (1961) instructed subjects to press a key during sleep in response to hearing their own names. When a long list of spoken names was played over and over during the night, most subjects showed selective partial arousal to their own names and did press the key appropriately on a high proportion of trials. Considerable research will be required before the true limits of behavior under sleep can be established, and one cannot help but think that such information must make an important contribution to our understanding of the waking organism also.

Dreaming—The work of Kleitman and his students (reviewed in Kleitman, 1961) inaugurated a new era in the scientific study of dreaming. At intervals of about 70 to 90 minutes during the night, a normal subject displays a minutes-long period of desynchronized EEG activity coupled with frequent rapid eye movements (REM). Wakened during such periods, most subjects report that they were dreaming, whereas dreaming is seldom reported when the sleeper is awakened during other EEG stages (Dement & Kleitman, 1957a, 1957b). It appears that some 20 per cent of one's sleeping hours are occupied with dream activity, and this value holds with surprisingly little variation across individuals. When subjects were deprived of the opportunity to dream by awakening them within a minute or two after the start of each REM period, they showed a striking increase in the number of such dream periods initiated and a considerable increase in "dream time" measured during undisturbed nights following the four- to seven-night deprivation interval (Dement, 1960). However, both Berger and Oswald (1962) and H. L. Williams *et al.* (1964) find that when subjects are deprived of *all* sleep for a lengthy period (e.g., 64 hours), the first recovery night shows a sharp increase in time devoted to Stage 4 sleep with perhaps even a small decrease in time devoted to (Stage I REM) dreaming. Stage 4 time is reduced by the second recovery night while Stage I REM time increases, leading H. L. Williams *et al.* to infer that, with total sleep deprivation, the need for Stage 4 sleep is dominant and must be partly compensated before the lesser need for dreaming can assert itself.

Getting coincident results with several methods of recording, Fisher, Gross, and

Zuch (1965) have recently shown that nearly all Stage IREM periods are accompanied by partial or complete penile erection in the human male. Combined with other reports of decreased heart rate and blood pressure with labile "spontaneous" GSR activity, this suggests that dreaming may be commonly accompanied by a condition of generalized parasympathetic activation, probably related to the disinhibition of limbic system mechanisms during "rhombencephalic" sleep (Jouvet, 1961). Fisher *et al.* speculate that the need for these Stage IREM intervals and the distress and irritability shown by Dement's subjects after deprivation may be related to some sort of emotional tension discharge which normally occurs at these times.

Before leaving the topic of sleep, one must ask why it is that we must spend a third of our lives in this curious condition? Muscle fatigue can be relieved by rest without sleep. The brain itself *may* be less active and therefore "resting" during sleep, but it is strange that its metabolism does not, in that case, seem to slow; Kety (1961) reports that cerebral blood flow and oxygen consumption are not reduced during sleep, indicating that the brain continues to consume its customary 20 watts of energy. Other contributors to the same symposium provide electrographic evidence that during sleep the activity of cerebral neurons changes in pattern but does not diminish in total amount. On the other hand, the majority of cortical neurons are too small to be studied individually by present microelectrode techniques, and it is possible that these smaller units do, for some reason, "rest" during sleep.

Not only is it uncertain as to *why* we sleep but also the mechanism that initiates normal sleeping is still largely a mystery. In a recent authoritative review, Moruzzi (1964) points out that there must be some process which, during the waking hours, gradually increases the need for and the probability of sleep, but this process has not yet been identified. One would think that electronarcosis, the induction of sleep by application of mild, rhythmic electrical stimulation of the brain, would be a valuable experimental technique in this connection, e.g., the amount or duration of electronarcotic stimulation necessary to produce sleep might serve as a dependent variable in the study of factors thought to be related to sleep susceptibility. Although much used in the USSR in sleep therapy with psychiatric patients (Obrosow, 1959), the electrosleep method seems to have not yet found its way into Western research laboratories (although see Forster, Post, & Benton, 1963).

Cortical excitability cycles—The low-voltage high-frequency EEG characteristic of the alert, waking subject is referred to as "desynchronized" because of the belief, for which there is some support from microelectrode studies, that the excitability of individual cortical cells fluctuates at a fairly constant frequency and that the activity of these individual units is brought into phase or synchronized through the influence of the DTPS to yield the regular and relatively large ten-per-second voltage waves of the alpha rhythm. ARAS stimulation disrupts this synchrony so that local regions cycle independently of their neighbors. Figure 4 (from Lindsley, 1961) illustrates how a number of such cortical regions operating out of phase but at similar frequencies would produce an EEG picture of low-voltage, irregular activity with the usual sort of bipolar scalp recording. Lansing, Schwartz, and Lindsley (1959) have shown that warning signals shorten reaction times when they occur early enough to produce desynchronization of the EEG before the advent of the critical stimulus. EEG activation typically requires about 250 mSec, and warning intervals shorter than this seem to have little or no facilitating effect. Lansing (1957) demonstrated that visual signals which reach the occipital cortex during a critical portion of the alpha cycle (the interval when the wave changes from positive to negative) produce shortened reaction

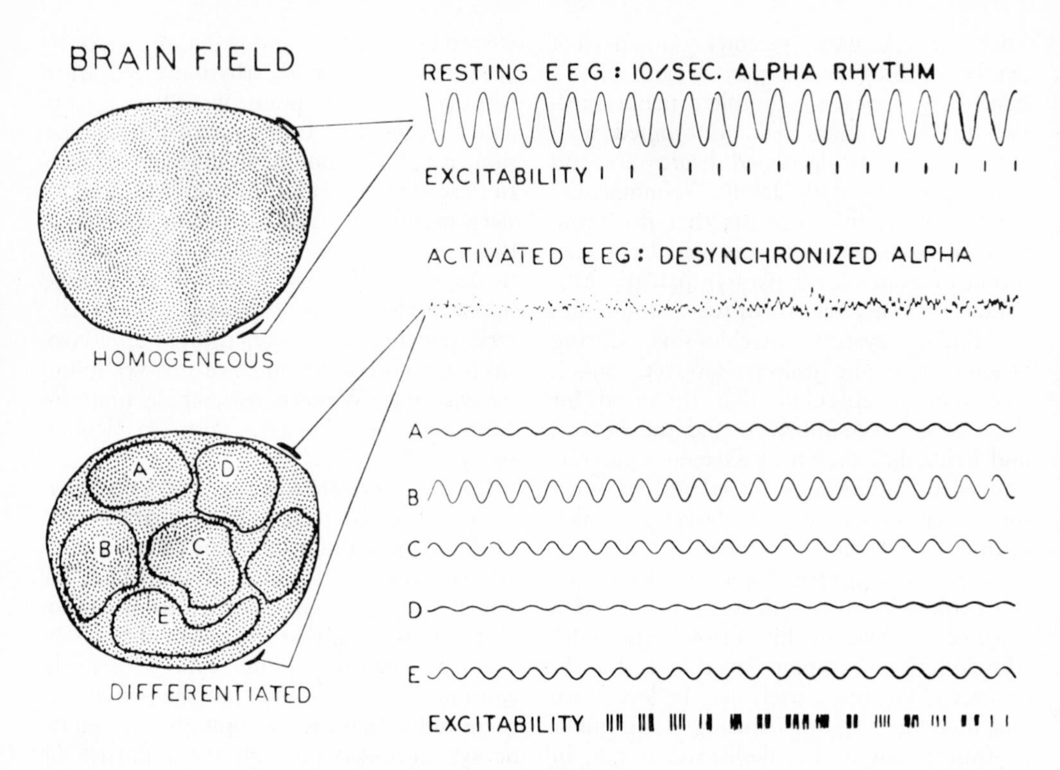

Figure 4. Hypothetical brain fields, illustrating Lindsley's theory of EEG desynchronization. Resting alpha at 10/sec characterizes the "homogeneous," or relaxed, condition. A desynchronized, activated EEG is associated with a "differentiated" state of brain function. According to the concept that an excitability cycle is associated with the waxing and waning phases of the waves, it is evident that alternating periods of excitability and inexcitability could occur only ten times per second in the case of the resting EEG, whereas almost continuous excitability is represented in the case of the desynchronized EEG resulting from a differentiated brain field (Lindsley, 1961).

times, and similarly it appears that response commands are reacted to more quickly when they reach the motor cortex at the corresponding point in its "alpha excitability cycle." Lindsley (1961) argues that these hypothetical excitability cycles in cortical units or in synchronized aggregates of units provide a kind of scanning or gating mechanism for sensory input and that desynchronization of a receiving area increases the probability that a given signal will find some unit(s) in a state of maximum receptivity at the moment of its arrival. (Perhaps the very slow delta waves of deep synchronized sleep work in the opposite direction, reducing sensory excitability. It would be interesting to compare arousal thresholds to brief sounds or shocks presented at different points in the delta wave cycle during Stage 4 sleep.)

Quite recently, Surwillo (1963; 1964) has reported some striking relationships between brain-wave frequency and reaction time in human subjects. Using careful measurements of the number of brain-wave cycles intervening between the stimulus (a tone) and the motor response (a switch closure), he divided this number into the S-R time interval, getting average brain-wave *period*—the reciprocal of frequency.

This concurrent EEG period was found to correlate +.72 with simple reaction time across a sample of 100 normal males ranging in age from 29 to 99 years. Partialing out the correlation between reaction time and age raised this value to +.76. Moreover, *P*-type or within-subject correlations between average EEG period and reaction time were almost all positive and averaged +.30. In a second study (Surwillo, 1964) involving 54 normal males, EEG period correlated +.76 with simple reaction time and also +.76 with "disjunctive" or choice reaction time. In both studies, EEG frequency was found to decrease with age.

Surwillo proposes "that the EEG cycle is the basic unit of time in terms of which events are programmed by the central nervous system, [which] means simply that *time* in this domain is reckoned by the brain-wave cycle. Hence, the speed with which a response may be elicited will be determined by the number of cycles required for organizing the particular events leading to the response" (Surwillo, 1963, p. 105). One possible difficulty in these experiments lies in the fact that EEG period is computed from a ratio in which reaction time figures as the numerator; the EEG is sampled for a shorter interval when reaction times are shorter, a procedure which conceivably might lead to a spurious correlation. These data have such important implications that one would like to see them confirmed, possibly by measuring EEG frequency during a *constant* time interval just preceding the stimulus.

Cortical activation and speed of perception—Lindsley (1958; 1961) reports that pairs of brief light flashes produce discrete evoked responses in the visual cortex of the cat or monkey when the flashes are separated by 100 mSec, but only a single evoked response when the separation is shortened to 50 mSec; with similar light intensities, human observers can perceive both flashes at the 100 mSec interval but only one at the 50 mSec interval. During about 10 seconds following electrical stimulation of the animal's midbrain reticular system, the 50 mSec flash pair evoked two distinct responses in the visual projection area, suggesting that reticular activation had increased the temporal resolving power of the cortex and, presumably, that a similar effect in a human subject might allow him to perceive the 50 mSec pair as a double flash.

At least two investigators have since employed the *two-flash threshold* (TFT) as an indicant of individual differences in cortical activation in experiments with human subjects. Venables (1963a) studied the relationship between TFT and performance on a card-sorting task with a sample of schizophrenics. Although there was no correlation with amount of learning during the first four trials (and, apparently, no relationship with average performance, although the report is unclear), the disruption in performance caused by changing the basis for scoring on the fifth trial correlated about +.60 with the TFT, which the author regards as evidence that selectivity of attention—freedom from distraction by the now irrelevant sort criteria—increases with greater cortical arousal. Rose (1964) found correlations between two-flash thresholds and a measure of palmar skin conductance of −.53, −.70, −.72, and −.76 in four different samples and a correlation of −.47 in a single patient tested on 16 occasions over a period of three months. When 38 normal subjects were retested after several days, but at the same time of day, the test-retest correlation for the TFT was +.81, indicating favorable psychometric properties for this variable. Rose found that the TFT was significantly higher in a sample of psychiatric patients receiving some form of tranquilizer than in samples of normals or drug-free patients. Interestingly, the correlation between the TFT and palmar conductance for the tranquilized patient group was only −.26 (not significant). Finally, in a sample of drug-free psychiatric patients, the TFT was found to correlate −.63 with the scale of anxiety proneness described by Lykken (1957). Clinicians judged the MMPIs of patients showing low thresholds to indicate high anxiety, agitation, or depression, while patients with high thresholds were judged to be less anxious, more impulsive, more hysteroid or psychopathic.

It may be noted in passing that this finding of lower two-flash thresholds in drug-free (than in tranquilized patients) and in anxious patients, while consistent with the idea that lower thresholds result from increased reticulo-cortical activation, appears to conflict with earlier reports that critical flicker fusion frequencies (CFF) are *lower* in anxious subjects (Krugman, 1947; Goldstone, 1955). As Lindsley (1961) has pointed out, visual flicker provides in its rhythmic character a kind of information to the brain not available from a single pair of flashes, which may be responsible for the fact that continuous trains of flashes can be perceived as flicker at inter-flash intervals far below those necessary for the resolution of a single pair. The matter is still unclear, but there does appear to be sufficient basis for assuming that the CFF implicates perceptual mechanisms not involved in the TFT. King's (1962) finding of zero-order correlations between TFT and CFF measured in samples of normal and schizophrenic subjects further indicates that these two variables should properly be treated as reflecting different, though related, parameters of brain function. (One would like to think that measuring CFF with *irregular* inter-flash intervals, by eliminating rhythmic information, would lower fusion frequency to a value nearer that found with two flashes. Lindsley (1961) found that, e.g., alternating 35 mSec and 65 mSec intervals gives flicker at light intensities for which a steady 50 mSec interval is seen as fused, i.e., the more complex pattern raises rather than lowers CFF. However, the 35–65 alteration does still constitute a pattern and the prediction that *random* inter-flash intervals—varying, say, from 35 to 65 mSec—should lower the CFF remains to be tested.)

The oft quoted experiment by Fuster (1958), more recently extended by Fuster and Uyeda (1962), was concerned with the effect of electrically stimulating the midbrain reticular formation on performance in a previously learned tachistoscopic discrimination problem. Monkeys were trained to find food in a compartment under one of two stimulus figures. Then a series of trials were run in which the stimuli were flashed for durations of from 10 mSec, where performance fell to chance levels, up to 40 mSec, where performance averaged about 85 per cent correct. On half of these trials, mild reticular stimulation was given, beginning two seconds before the flash and continuing until the animal had made its choice. Both numbers of errors and mean reaction time were reduced under reticular stimulation at all exposure times. Stimulation higher in the reticular system, in the midline nuclei of the thalamus, may also facilitate learning of a similar two-choice problem. Mahut (1964) found such facilitation when her monkeys were stimulated while looking at the test stimuli. Stimulation just before presentation of the stimuli had no effect while stimulation during the ten seconds right after a response disrupted learning.

Activation and sedation tolerance—It is well established that the reticular system is particularly sensitive to barbiturate anesthesia (French, Verzeano, & Magoun, 1953; Gellhorn, 1953; Killam & Killam, 1957). Therefore, the amount of barbiturate, per unit of body weight, necessary to produce sedation should provide an index of the level of pre-existing reticular activation. In an extensive series of investigations (summarized in Shagass, 1962), Shagass and his co-workers have developed a measure of sedative susceptibility using paced, cumulative intravenous doses of barbiturate and a rather complex EEG criterion of the point at which "sedation" has occurred. Using this measure, Shagass has reported remarkable discriminations between various clinical groups; thus, patients with neurotic depression have much higher sedation tolerance than patients with psychotic depression (Shagass, Naiman, & Mihalik, 1956), and sedation tolerance is strongly associated with degree of manifest anxiety (Shagass & Naiman, 1956). Other investigators have reported considerable difficulty in using Shagass's EEG criterion for sedation, however, and the procedure developed by Rose (1964) is both simpler to use and more reliable.

In Rose's method, a brief electric shock is presented every 30 seconds concurrently with the administration of 1 cc of thiopental, diluted to 0.25 mg/kg body weight and injected via an indwelling intravenous apparatus without disturbance to the subject. The sedation criterion is based on the decreasing amplitude of the palmar GSR elicited by the shock; viz., sedation tolerance is defined as the amount of thiopental required to reduce the shock-GSR to 10 per cent of its average value during the three shocks given before starting the drug. Using this method, Rose tested a small group of ten male interns on two occasions, finding a retest rank correlation of +.96. Since the sedation tolerance test presumably measures the increment in arousal produced by the subject's reaction to the test conditions *added to* the basal level characteristic of him, i.e., both *state* and *trait* in Cattell and Scheier's (1961) sense, such remarkably high stability suggests that these interns adapted more readily to the injection situation than would be expected of most subjects. In another study, using the less reliable "sleep threshold" criterion, Rose tested 10 male chronic schizophrenics on three occasions, finding a retest stability of +.57 for tests I vs. II and +.86 for tests II vs. III; corresponding stability coefficients for palmar conductance measured before each test were +.38 and +.83. If we can assume from the stability found between test II and test III that these patients had adapted to the circumstances of the testing situation by the end of the first session, so that tests II and III represent real trait values which are therefore more stable, then it appears that there was considerable variability in their reaction to the unfamiliar and somewhat threatening circumstances of the first testing which was *not* correlated with their basal or trait values, e.g., some normally low-activation subjects showed high *state* arousal on the first test, while other high-activation patients reacted relatively less. This finding, although it clearly should be extended under other conditions, suggests an important methodological caution. Wherever possible, when one is interested in assessing some *trait* which one expects to be reasonably stable over time, one should carefully consider the possibility that the testing procedure itself may induce considerable change in the variable being used to estimate that trait. When, as in this instance, it appears reasonable to expect that even subjects all having the same trait value might produce considerable score variability due to variations in their reaction to the unfamiliar test conditions, then one should attempt to repeat the testing on at least a second occasion, regarding the first testing merely as an adaptation trial.

The arousal reaction and the orienting reflex—In their now classical paper, Sharpless and Jasper (1956) demonstrated that "repetition of a specific tone, which initially produces long-lasting arousal of a sleeping cat, fails to do so after 20 or 30 trials." This habituation of the arousal reaction was found to be specific to the quality, modality, or pattern of the stimulus used. Thus, after habituation to a 500-cycle tone, a tone of 100 cycles still produced EEG activation and behavioral arousal. Arousal caused by a particular sequence or pattern of tones could be selectively habituated in some animals, but this was no longer possible after destruction of the auditory cortex; cortical damage did not, however, affect the efficiency or specificity of habituation to a particular tonal pitch. Specific evoked potentials recorded from the intact cortex were, if anything, larger after habituation of the arousal reaction, indicating that the effect cannot involve interference in the specific afferent pathways.

It was possible by means of surgical procedures to show that the arousal reaction consists of two components. One, mediated by the nonspecific nuclei of the thalamus and the DTPS, responds rapidly to relatively weak stimulation and is exceedingly resistant to habituation, recovering quickly with rest. The other, mediated by the ARAS, responds relatively slowly, requires stronger or repeated stimulation, and habituates quite rapidly. DTPS activation can be described as phasic, producing an EEG desynchronization which begins rapidly but does not outlast the eliciting stimulus for more than a few seconds. ARAS activation, more sluggish, endures longer so that the animal may remain aroused for many minutes after the stimulus has been removed. In the intact animal, EEG activation is observed nearly simultaneously in the cortex, thalamus, and midbrain and is initiated by signals transmitted directly to the RF over the collateral afferents without the participation of the specific sensory systems.

This *arousal* of Sharpless and Jasper seems to parallel in many respects the *orienting reflex* (OR) described by Pavlov and elaborated in the work of the contemporary Russian neuropsychologist, E. N. Sokolov (1960; 1963). The OR is thought of as a central-nervous-system event, signaled by such observable phenomena as behavioral arrest, "propriomuscular" changes (Berlyne, 1960, p. 84) producing orientation and increased sensitivity of the receptors, increased muscle tonus, EEG activation, and by a characteristic pattern of autonomic changes which includes the GSR and a combination of vasoconstriction in the fingers with vasodilation in the blood vessels of the head. The OR may be initiated by an increase, decrease, or qualitative change in a stimulus and is subject to habituation on repeated presentation of the stimulus. The functional significance of the OR is thought to be that it produces an increase in the "discriminatory power of the analyzers," lowering sensory thresholds, increasing resolving power, and the like.

Just as Sharpless and Jasper found with sleeping cats, Sokolov finds in his work with waking human subjects that the habituation of the OR to a particular tone is frequency specific (see Figure 5). Should a stimulus occur at regular intervals until the OR habituates, then the withholding of that stimulus will elicit an OR. (This recalls the story of the man, living near the railroad tracks, who had so adapted to the roar of the Midnight Express, that, on a night when the train was unaccountably late, he awoke with a start in the midnight stillness and asked, "What was that?") Such findings lead Sokolov to conclude that repeated

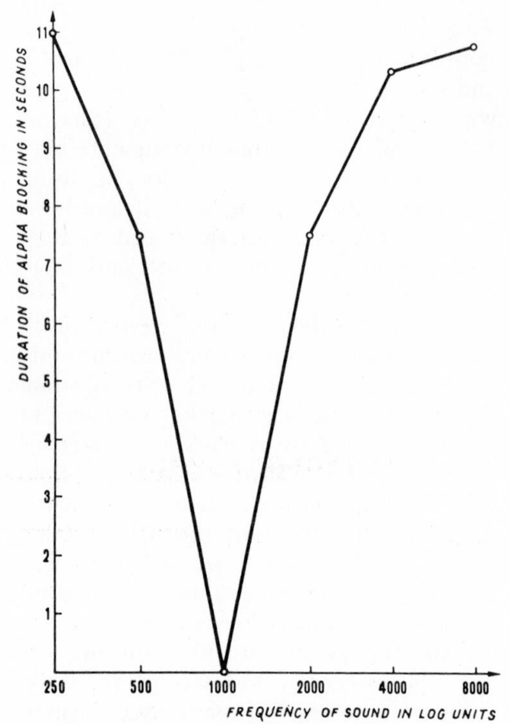

Figure 5. Amplitude of orienting reflex (duration of alpha blocking) following presentation of tone stimuli at various pitches above and below the pitch (1,000 cps) to which the subject had become accustomed. The OR seems to vary as a function of the degree of mismatch between the characteristics of the stimulus and the characteristics of the neuronal model (i.e., "expectation"?) built up in the subject by prior habituation to a particular stimulus (Sokolov, 1960).

experience with a stimulus leads to the formation within the nervous system of a *neuronal model,* embodying the salient features of that stimulus, against which the signal resulting from each new stimulation is compared. The orienting reflex then is a function of the discrepancy obtaining between the current signal and this model (see Figure 6). Making use of the fact that neural transmission is faster in the specific afferent pathways to the cortex than it is in the nonspecific reticular afferent system, Sokolov proposes that signals found to be concordant with the neuronal model in the cortex initiate inhibitory cortico-reticular impulses which tend to block transmission of that signal through the collateral fibers to the RF.

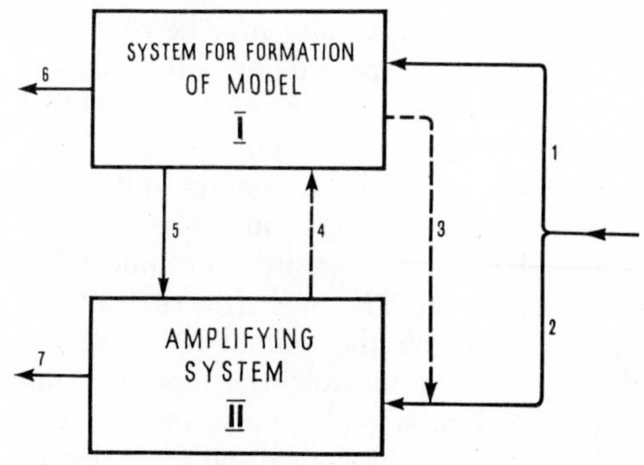

Figure 6. Sokolov's "neuronal model" for the orienting reflex. I. Modeling system. II. Amplifying system. 1 indicates specific pathway from sense organs to cortical level of modeling system; 2, collateral to reticular formation (represented here as an amplifying device); 3, negative feedback from modeling system to synaptic connection between collaterals from specific pathway and reticular formation; 4, ascending activating influences from the amplifier (reticular formation) upon modeling system (cortex); 5, pathway from modeling system to amplifying system (this is the pathway through which the impulses signifying concordance are transmitted from the modeling system to the amplifying system); 6, to the specific responses caused by coincidence between the external stimulation and the neuronal model elaborated in the cortex; and 7, to the vegetative and somatic components arising from the stimulation of the amplifying system (reticular formation) (Sokolov, 1960).

That the cortex is capable of powerful and selective inhibition of RF activities has been shown by the work of Hugelin and Bonvallet (quoted in Berlyne, 1960). In the decorticate animal, RF stimulation tonically facilitates spinal motor reflex activity; with the cortex intact, this initial increase in reflex strength dissipates within a few seconds, even though the RF is continuously stimulated. This indicates that, at least in its motor function, the RF receives selective inhibitory regulation—negative feedback—from the cortex. Significantly, Hugelin and Bonvallet found no reflex facilitation at all when the stimulation to the RF was increased gradually from zero, which seems to show that cortical inhibition can keep pace with slow changes in RF activation, neutralizing them before they can have any effect. More speculatively, Sokolov assumes that *any* RF activation, such as might be initiated by a novel stimulus as part of an OR, immediately elicits inhibitory feedback from the waking cortex so that the recovery phase of an OR is not merely the result of the withdrawal of excitation but an active corticifugal inhibitory process. Moreover, he assumes that this inhibitory response can be conditioned, so that, e.g., it begins earlier with each repetition of the stimulus.

As evidence that habituation of the OR is a cortical process, that the "neuronal model" resides in the cortex, Sokolov describes two experiments in which an OR was readily habituated in a waking subject only to return as the subject became drowsy; moreover, it was found to be impossible to rehabituate the OR while in this drowsy state, because, Sokolov argues, cortical function is lost in this state and with it the specific cortical inhibition upon which OR habituation depends.

But this finding is paradoxical in the light of the Sharpless and Jasper results which clearly show that arousal—reticular activation—produced by a particular stimulus *can* be selectively habituated during actual sleep.

The key to this difficulty may be contained in the results reported by Huttenlocker (1960) concerning specific evoked responses recorded from the midbrain RF during repeated auditory click stimulation in both the waking and sleeping conditions. It was found that these responses continue undiminished in the RF long after the OR has habituated when the animal is awake but that they are rather quickly suppressed during sleep. This would seem to indicate that OR habituation does not result from disruption of transmission through the afferent collaterals, as Sokolov has supposed, but rather from a change in the responsiveness of the RF to the signal. Huttenlocker's data suggest that habituation of the arousal reaction during sleep involves an entirely different mechanism than does habituation of the waking OR. With specific cortico-reticular inhibition lost, the sleeping animal apparently resorts to filtering or blocking afferent input to the RF, probably in the afferent collaterals rather than more peripherally, since the cortical evoked potentials are undiminished. During drowsiness, as the subject fluctuates between sleep and waking, perhaps neither mechanism can establish full control so that habituation is difficult in this transition phase. Dumont and Dell (1960) provide further evidence that this phase is "special," showing that the effect of reticular stimulation upon cortical evoked potentials is very markedly enhanced during the crossing-over from sleep into wakefulness.

It is possible that OR habituation will reflect itself also in habituation of the arousal reflex provided that sufficient presentations of the stimulus are experienced while the subject is awake. There seems to be reason for supposing that considerable *overlearning* is required for selective performance during sleep. We may distinguish between stimuli that can be responded to automatically while awake and those that require that one focus one's attention upon them; practice continued long after we first "learn" to identify a new stimulus pattern or to organize some new response can often render these reactions automatic and capable of being run off without conscious awareness. Perhaps it is at this point that a function becomes capable of operating under sleep conditions. Could subjects who responded to their own names during sleep (in the study by Oswald *et al.*, 1960, cited above) have performed as well had their instructions been to react only to "dit-dit-dah," from a list of letters sounded in Morse Code? One suspects not and yet it is likely that experienced telegraphers *could* do so.

Functions of the orienting reflex—The orienting reflex, as instanced by finger vasoconstriction coupled with vasodilation in the head, is to be distinguished from a specific *adaptive reflex,* exemplified by a vasodilation in both loci upon presentation of a warm stimulus, and also from a *defensive reflex,* which might be a vasoconstriction in both loci in response to an electric shock. Typically, a new stimulus first elicits the OR. Thus, before starting a tone-shock conditioning series, the CS and US were first presented singly until the OR to the tone habituated (after 17 presentations) and the OR to the shock gave way to a defensive reflex (after 47 presentations). When now the CS and US were combined, the first effect was a return of the OR, and it required 35 CS-US pairings before a conditional defensive reflex was elaborated, as indicated by vasoconstriction in both head and hand to the presentation of the CS alone. Thus, "stabilization of a conditional reflex is connected with the habituation of the orienting reflex and all *changes* in the conditional reflex are connected with an increase in activation of the orienting reflex" (Sokolov, 1960, p. 223).

In another experiment, the CS was a 500-cycle tone, and the vasomotor reactions to other tone frequencies were sampled after increasing numbers of reinforcements with shock. During the earlier stages, frequencies from 300 to 900 cycles all evoked the defensive reflex (vasoconstriction, both hand and head) while frequencies outside this range produced ORs (dilation in the head). After many more reinforcements, the defensive reflex was obtained only in the range from 490 to 510 cycles and the OR from about 450 to 490 cycles and from about 510 to 550 cycles with negligible response of any kind outside these limits. Thus, as discrimination improves, the OR serves to demarcate the zones of stimulus uncertainty, a result which, incidentally, Sokolov's neuronal model theory seems unable to encompass.

However mediated, the OR seems to correspond in amplitude to some joint function of the intensity and the predictability of the eliciting stimulus. This is very nicely illustrated in an experiment by Kimmel (1960) in which five groups of subjects were exposed to 20 presentations of a 1,000-cycle tone at a constant intensity of 35, 55, 75, 95, or 115 db. (Twenty shocks were also given, either paired or unpaired with the tones, for reasons unrelated to the present point.) Following these 20 experiences of the tone at some given intensity, each subject then received a single test trial in which the tone was sounded at either the same or a different intensity and his GSR to that test tone was measured. The results were analyzed in terms of the disparity between the loudness of the test tone and the loudness to which that subject had been exposed on the previous trials and presumably had come to expect. The findings are illustrated in Figure 7. The GSR, which we can interpret as an

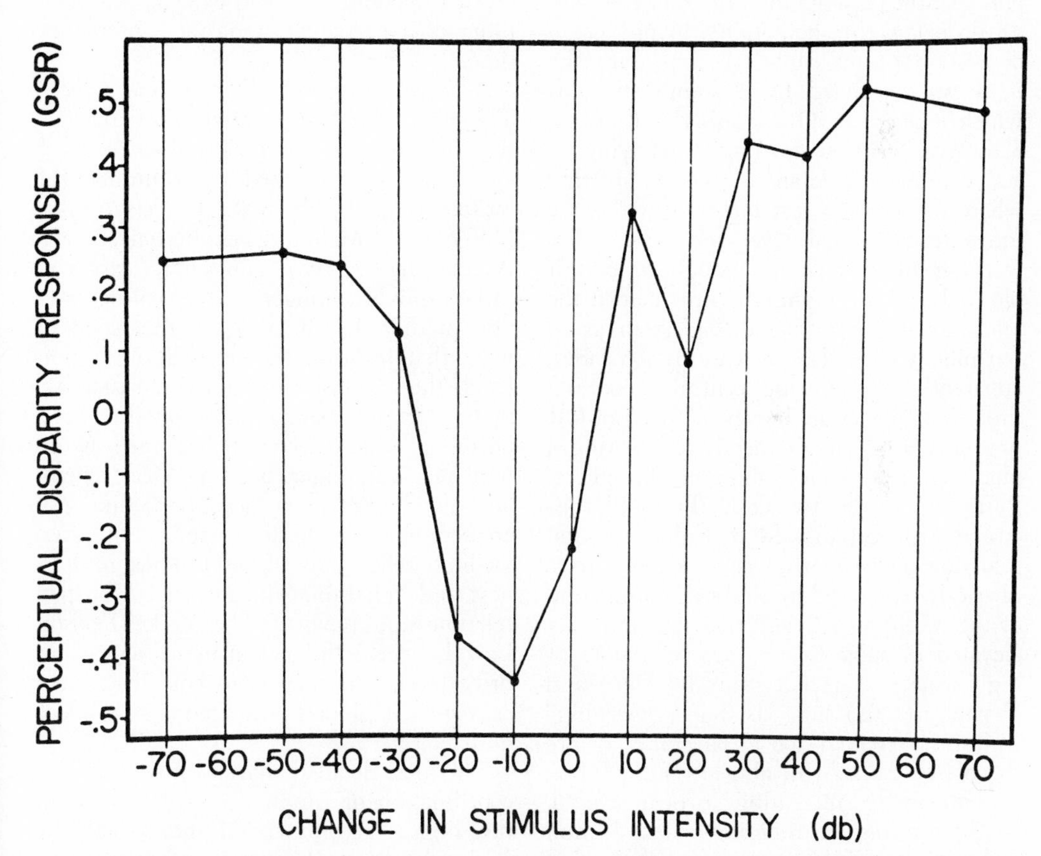

Figure 7. Amount of "perceptual disparity response" (GSR) as a function of the amount of change in the intensity (loudness) of the stimulus from the value to which the subject had become accustomed (Kimmel, 1960).

indicant of the orienting reflex, was minimum for small changes in the stimulus and larger when the test tone was either louder *or* softer than expected; however, a given increase in loudness produced a greater GSR increment than a decrease of the same size. Discussing this together with other similar studies from his laboratory, Grings (1960) shows that the size of such "perceptual disparity responses" increases with the number of prior exposures to the standard stimulus (e.g., with the strength and specificity of the subject's expectation concerning the nature of the stimulus on the test trial).

The ability of the orienting reflex to "increase the discriminatory power of the analyzers" is illustrated by Sokolov's (1960) report that the presentation of a light intensity 0.8 db below threshold failed to produce a depression of the alpha rhythm until the light was preceded by a sound stimulus which evoked an OR. Similarly, Lansing, Schwartz, and Lindsley (1959), studying reaction times in human subjects, found that where the average reaction time without a forewarning signal averaged 280 mSec, warning intervals long enough to permit blockade of the alpha rhythms before the reaction stimulus occurred (e.g., from 300 to 100 mSec) yielded a decrease to 206 mSec, apparently by reducing central processing time. It is not clear, however, that the OR produces these effects merely by eliciting a phasic, transitory activation of the cortex. Research on the two-flash threshold, discussed earlier, indicated that the temporal resolving power of the visual cortex can be phasically enhanced by electrical stimulation of the midbrain RF and that it is tonically elevated in subjects who are in a state of high arousal. A recent study by Horn and Venables (1964) suggests that a "warning" stimulus presented 300 to 600 mSec before the paired flashes will also lower the TFT, presumably by increasing cortical arousal, i.e., by evoking an orienting reflex. Stimuli occurring less than 200 mSec before the first of the paired flashes markedly elevate the TFT; the interval here is too short for activation to develop. The fact that such short intervals raise the TFT rather than simply not affecting it may have to do with the distraction of attention (see the discussion of the single-channel theory of attention below).

If the effect of the OR upon perception were due *only* to its nonspecific activating of the cortex, then a subject with moderate arousal should perform as well without warning signals as a low-arousal subject does with them and the performance of a subject already aroused should actually be better when no warnings are provided. As its name implies, the orienting reflex undoubtedly provides something more than nonspecific arousal, information which allows the organism to orient or tune its perceptual apparatus so as to expedite the handling of a particular signal at a particular time.

Arousal, energy mobilization, and drive—The close relationship between reticular activation and the psychological concept of *drive* has been marked by a number of writers (e.g., Hebb, 1955; Lindsley, 1957; Duffy, 1957; Malmo, 1962; Berlyne, 1960). As Berlyne (p. 166) points out, "excess of carbon dioxide, hunger, and sexual deprivation modify the chemistry of the blood in ways that sensitize the reticular formation [and] the responsiveness of the reticular formation to adrenaline and nonadrenaline, hormones whose secretion has much to do with fear and anger, has been clearly demonstrated." Reticular activation, like increased drive, may reduce response latencies, facilitate reflex activity, and produce restlessness and agitation. The inverted *U*-shaped relationship known as the Yerkes-Dodson Law, between efficiency of performance and drive level, also appears to hold true when *activation* is plotted on the abscissa in place of *drive*.

The most detailed analysis thus far of this coordination of concepts is to be found in the highly recommended monograph by Berlyne (1960). Berlyne first analyzes the drive notion into three components: $drive_1$, representing the energizing aspect as in Hull's *D; $drive_2$*, representing the directional or cue aspect as in Hull's *SD;* and *drive*$_3$, representing the "condition whose termination or alleviation is rewarding." He then defines *arousal tonus* as the minimum level of RF activation of which the individual is capable at a particular time. "The location of the tonus level will depend on the pattern of cortico-reticular interaction, with, no doubt, other subcortical structures playing their part also. This interaction will, in its turn, depend on internal factors, such as how often the environment has been issuing calls for urgent action" (p. 193). Having identified drive$_1$ with arousal level, drive$_3$ is related to any increase in arousal above the prevailing level of arousal tonus; in these circumstances, a decrease in arousal back toward the tonus level is assumed to be rewarding.

We know that most of the classical methods for increasing drive also increase reticular activity (at least under certain conditions of measurement; see below), and we have seen that satiation of such needs as hunger and sex is followed by a decrease in cortical and RF arousal. The problem which Berlyne's or any drive-reduction theory of reinforcement has to face is that of dealing with behavior that appears to arise out of a state of low arousal, and behavior which is learned and maintained even though it seems to result in an actual increase in drive or arousal. In the case of boredom, the consequence of minimal or unvarying stimulation which ought to lead to decreased arousal and even sleep, Berlyne suggests that monotonous stimulation disorganizes the cortex, thus presumably disrupting both its excitatory and its inhibitory cortico-reticular influences. The initial result in a fatigued individual may indeed be sleep, but this must eventually be followed by awakening and increasing restlessness and agitation. Deprived of its usual cortical restraints, the RF becomes more and more aroused, stimulus-seeking behavior is initiated, and the attainment of novel or excitatory stimulation is experienced as rewarding because, by activating the cortex and re-establishing cortico-reticular inhibitory control, such stimulation results in an actual decrease in arousal. Outside the context of monotony and boredom, the "aperitif phenomenon," the seeking out of stimuli whose immediate effect is an undeniable increase in drive or arousal—eating salted nuts, precoital sex play, riding the roller-coaster, i.e., what Hebb (1955) refers to as "the positive attraction of risk-taking and of problem solving"—is handled by assuming that the eventual result of such behavior is an even larger decrease in arousal.

Laying out so starkly the bare bones of Berlyne's position does a serious injustice to the ingenuity of his argument and the wealth of evidence which he has brought together in provocative array. Still, this oversimplification does highlight certain genuine difficulties. For example, one suspects that Berlyne sought out a secluded (i.e., unstimulating, monotonous) environment in which to do his writing but was not *bored* therein (nor did he, obviously, go to sleep). The extent to which the cortex can maintain its functional integrity independent of exteroceptive stimulation varies widely from person to person and from time to time, and one would like to know why. Berlyne's hypothesis, that boredom is a state of agitation resulting from a failure of cortical control, is plausible and suggestive but needs further elaboration. More seriously, the maneuver of assuming that drive *increase* is not punishing, although drive *decrease* is always rewarding, which Berlyne employs in the attempt to save the drive reduction theory from drowning in the flood of his own collection of evidence, seems like supererogation. Hebb's (1955) notion that some intermediate level of arousal is hedonically optimum and that increases below that level are rewarded and those above that level punishing appears to be both simpler and more reasonable on current evidence. Indeed, retaining the identification of activation with drive$_1$ or *D,* it really seems most probable that reinforcement is only contingently and incidentally related to drive reduction. The reinforcement associated with the presentation of an appropriate stimulus seems to increase monotonically with the level of arousal. With aversive drives, such as pain or fear, the "appropriate" stimulus will probably produce a decrease in arousal, but this clearly need not follow when the arousal has a nonaversive basis. In the case of sexual excitement, although objective measurements seem to be lacking, appropriate stimuli *do* appear to be more rewarding as arousal increases and levels of activation *can* be attained which seem as high or higher than those involved in common aversive experiences.

Berlyne and others have pointed out that autonomic and EEG indicators of arousal tend to increase during sleep deprivation (e.g., Malmo & Surwillo, 1960) and have found in this support for the identification of arousal and drive$_1$ or D. Although the *need* to sleep can be real enough, one might feel uncomfortable about thinking of the *sleep drive* in the same conceptual category as, say, the hunger or the sex drive. More importantly, these findings of increased activation during sleep deprivation are typically obtained only when the subject is tested during the periodic performance of some task. Since many aspects of task performance do not deteriorate even with fairly extended deprivation (e.g., Williams, Lubin, & Goodnow, 1959; Wilkinson, 1961), it is possible that the subject expends more energy, producing higher concurrent levels of arousal, in order to maintain his performance as the vigil progresses and that continuous monitoring would show that his intercurrent levels of arousal actually do *decrease* with deprivation. Alternatively, Berlyne might expect that arousal would consistently increase, due to decreased cortical inhibition, given only sufficiently strong and varied stimulation to keep the subject awake but without requiring any organized response from him. The research necessary to resolve this question does not appear to have been done.

The only other direct test of the arousal-drive$_1$ linkage which seems to be available is the study by Belanger and Feldman (1962) in which it was found that heart rate in the rat increases monotonically with from 24 to 72 hours of water deprivation. Again, however, the relationship held true only for heart rate measured during the time when the animals were actually working for and receiving water reinforcement. The more thirsty animals did not show elevated heart rates while resting in their cages nor even when placed in sight of the lever and water magazine but separated from it by a transparent screen. Granted that heart rate is one of the more dubious indicants of activation, it seems unreasonable to argue from these results that arousal is identifiable with drive level which *is* normally expected to increase monotonically with deprivation.

Lykken and Meisch (1965) found that when brief electric shocks are presented at random intervals to rats busy pressing a lever for food reinforcement, the rate of pressing increases for some 30 to 60 seconds following each shock. Both pre- and post-shock rates decreased as the shocks were made stronger until pressing ceased entirely and the behavior was no longer under appetitive control. These results could mean that the shock produced a transitory increase in nonspecific activation which, acting like D in Hull's formula for reaction potential, augmented whatever behavior was then dominant, e.g., lever pressing. But why does the overall rate decrease as the random shocks get stronger? A conventional explanation would be that the shocks produce a state having drive$_2$ or cue properties different from those of the hunger state which tend to channel the combined drive$_1$ components into different activities which are incompatible with lever pressing.

Central Modulation of Afferent Input: Perception and Attention

The major sense organs, the specialized receptors of the skin, the interoceptors and proprioceptors, combine to inundate the central nervous system with a never-ending

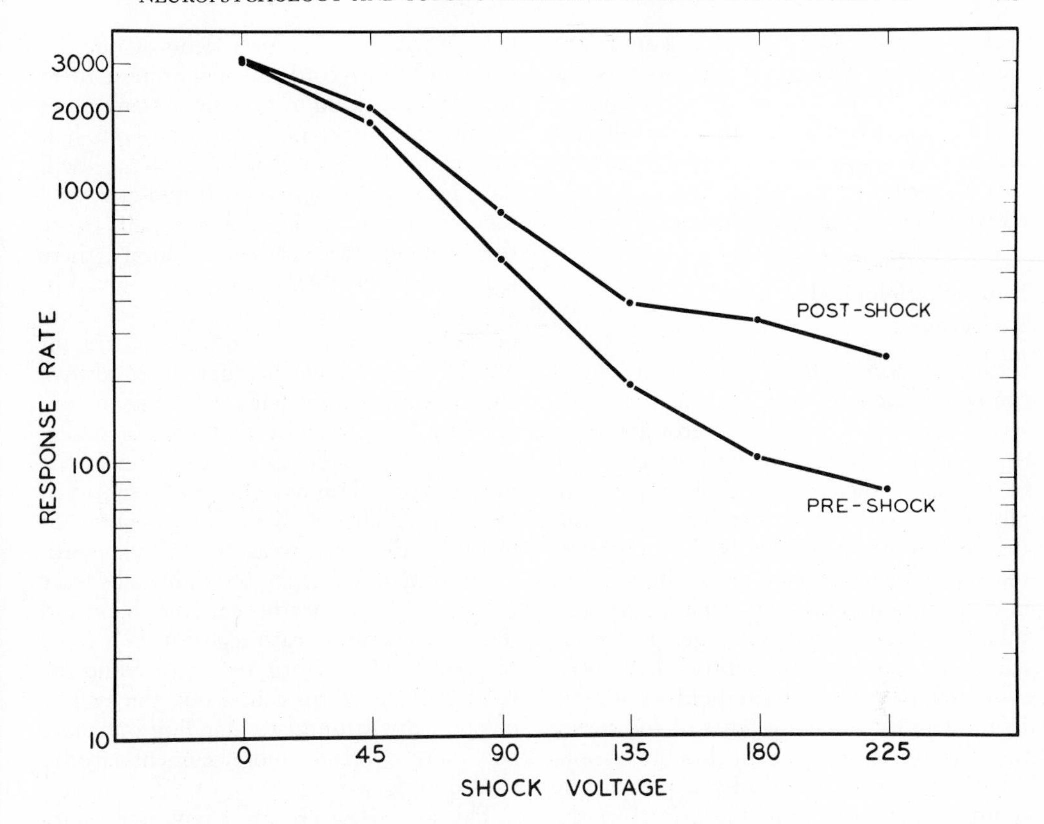

Figure 8. Logarithm of response rate (lever pressing) as a function of the intensity of aperiodic, noncontingent shocks. Each point is the mean of three one-hour sessions for four rats. Lower curve represents rate during the 30 second periods *preceding* shocks. Upper curve represents rate during 30 seconds *following* shocks and illustrates apparent activation of response rate produced by the presentation of the shock (Lykken & Meisch, 1965).

flood of raw sense data. How the brain can cope with this embarrassment of riches, selecting what it needs and ignoring what it doesn't, has been a perennial problem for students of perception. The discovery that the reticular system sends efferent fibers to all peripheral afferent relay stations as well as to the receptors themselves suggested that part of the answer might lie in a system of afferent filtering under central control. One example has already been described; the sleeping subject apparently can selectively inhibit transmission of specific sensory impulses across the collaterals linking the reticular formation to the afferent pathways, thus preventing arousal. The perceptual analysis required for this is accomplished subcortically, perhaps in the RF itself, in the case of simple stimuli; habituation to more complex stimuli requires some participation of the (sleeping) cortex, although it may be that complex patterns can also be handled by lower structures when these patterns have been sufficiently overlearned.

When the subject is awake, afferent modulation might serve to (a) help determine which signals are admitted to or retained in the focus of attention and (b) modify the affective quale of the signal by, e.g., attenuating noxious sensations or amplifying pleasurable ones. It appears that such "perceptual tuning" may be either *anticipatory,* evoked by some sort of warning signal, or *reactive,* being elicited by the onset of the stimulus itself. As to specificity, evidence of varying quality suggests that the afferent system can selectively amplify (or attenuate) a specific signal, all signals in a given modality, or the entire flux of sensory input.

Neurophysiological Background

Evoked potentials—The afferent signal can be followed on its way to the brain as a series of evoked potentials recorded from electrodes placed near the nerve tract or one of its relay nuclei. The evoked potential represents a composite of the many individual neuron action potentials. At each relay, the postsynaptic potential may be smaller, if transmission across the synapse has been inhibited in some way, or larger, if, for example, the postsynaptic neurons have been subjected to prior subthreshold excitation. In the sensory receiving areas of the cortex the evoked potential is a much more complicated waveform; it includes a presynaptic component, representing the arrival of the impulse through the ascending axons; a postsynaptic component, representing the reaction of the intracortical neurons to this impulse; and normally, an after-discharge, which consists of a complex and variable series of waves related to persisting local activities and to reverberating impulses traveling back and forth between the cortex and distant structures, particularly in the thalamus.

Intracranial recording is not always feasible with human subjects (!) so it is fortunate that the cortical evoked potential is also present in the EEG activity recorded from properly positioned electrodes on the scalp. In the raw EEG recording, these evoked potentials are typically hidden amidst the fluctuations of the spontaneous brain rhythms; during recent years, however, techniques have been developed for eliminating this background "noise" by an averaging process. To illustrate the method, suppose one were to take 100 one-second segments at random from an EEG record and superimpose them so as to get a kind of average. At any point within this one-second interval, about half the segments making up the average will have been in the positive half of a cycle and the remainder in the negative half (since the segments were chosen randomly, there is no reason for them to be synchronized in any way). Therefore, the average or composite record will tend toward a straight line of zero voltage because these positive and negative components will tend to cancel out. Now suppose that these 100 segments had all been chosen to begin at the instant that a flash of light was presented to the subject. Then each EEG segment would include within it a weak trace of the cortical potential evoked by the light; this trace would have very nearly the same shape and the same latency in each segment. When the 100 segments now are averaged, while the noisy EEG rhythms cancel out, the evoked potentials will summate, standing out more and more clearly as more segments are included in the average.

This averaging process is now done automatically by means of a specialized computer; the EEG is recorded on magnetic tape which is later played back into the computer which in turn draws out the averaged wave on an X-Y recorder. Averaged cortical evoked responses have been shown to correspond quite well with what would have been obtained recording directly from the cortex (Domino, Matsuoka, Waltz, & Cooper, 1964). Examples of evoked responses to auditory click stimuli in a waking subject and at various levels of sleep are illustrated in Figure 3.

Significance of the cortical evoked response—Geisler, Frishkopf, and Rosenblith (1958) reported that averaged cortical responses to auditory clicks first appear as the stimulus rises above the auditory threshold. Shagass and Schwartz (1961) obtained similar results with somatic and visual stimuli. A careful parametric study by Wicke, Donchin, and Lindsley (1964) shows that it is the first of the two diphasic waveforms in the visual evoked response which decreases with decreasing luminance and disappears at or near the threshold. Moreover, these authors find that this component varies with the perceived brightness of the stimulus rather than with its physical intensity (luminance). Haider, Spong, and Lindsley (1964), studying averaged cortical responses to dim signal light flashes in a protracted vigilance experiment, found that the average response to signals detected by their subjects was substantially larger than that evoked by undetected signals. However, it is well known that the cortical response is actually enhanced during sleep and under anesthesia; hence, the presence of the response cannot guarantee that the subject will be aware of the stimulus or have it influence his behavior. Davis (H. Davis, 1964) reports that when a subject is required to make a difficult discrimination in, say, pitch between the second and third of a sequence of four tone bursts presented to him, the cortical response evoked by the *third* tone is sharply augmented, although that tone neither is nor does it sound any louder to the subject; hence, perceived intensity does not always vary with the amplitude of the cortical evoked response. Similarly, Chapman and Bragdon (1964) found that a *meaningful* stimulus evokes a larger response than does an interpolated stimulus that is not relevant to the task set for the subject. Electroretinographic responses (ERGs) produced by the two stimuli did not differ. Most recently, Spong, Haider, and Lindsley (1965) report consistent changes in the relative amplitude of evoked responses from temporal and occipital areas, produced by alternating clicks and flashes, as the subjects were required to attend to the clicks while ignoring the flashes, and vice versa.

These findings are the first gleanings of a rich harvest of research in which traditional psychophysical measurement is being supplemented by electrocortical recording. Much remains to be learned about the significance of the several components of the complex cortical response; it is already plain, for example, that to speak of the "amplitude of the response" is an oversimplification, since its components can vary in size independently of one another. It would appear that the initial diphasic wave does vary with perceived intensity of the stimulus in a situation where the subject is attending about equally to all stimuli in the series. Since giving special attention to a stimulus amplifies its cortical evoked response without increasing its perceived intensity, it would appear that the intensity property may be separately decoded, perhaps subcortically. Another reasonable speculation is that the amplitude of an evoked response, figured in relation to the activity evoked by concurrent competing stimuli, determines the probability that the evoking stimulus will be attended to at all.

Evoked potentials in the midbrain reticular formation can only be recorded from implanted electrodes and are correspondingly more difficult to study. We know that these responses are reduced or absent during pontile sleep and also when the waking subject's attention is distracted (e.g., Winters, 1964). Jouvet, Benoît, and Courjon (1956) have found cortical regions at which stimulation inhibits evoked potentials in the ARAS without affecting activity in the specific sensory system. We have already seen that evoked responses in the ARAS diminish rapidly with repeated stimulation during sleep but not when the animal is awake (Huttenlocker, 1960) and therefore attributed habituation of the orienting reflex to a corticifugal mechanism which inhibits reticular reactivity without blocking sensory transmission to the RF (Dell, Bonvallet, & Hugelin, 1961).

It is tempting to suppose that one of these inhibitory mechanisms, that which reduces reticular reactivity to stimulation or that which attenuates sensory impulses transmitted to the RF, is employed by the cortex under special circumstances to deprive stimuli of the disturbing or excitatory effects they might normally have upon the ARAS. It is quite clear that the intensity of a stimulus and its arousing or excitatory quality, while normally correlated, are not the same thing and can sometimes vary independently. Even in the case of pain, for example, we know that individuals under hypnotic suggestion, morphine analgesia, or after frontal lobotomy often show intact capacities for discriminating pain intensities and unaltered pain thresholds while at the same time experiencing little of what Kessen and Mandler (1961) have called the "distress" component of the usual pain response. This distress reaction includes reticular activation which, in the absence of cortical influence, is probably proportional to the strength of the signal transmitted to the RF over the collateral afferents.

Tonic reticular afferent inhibition—It is now generally established that cortical potentials evoked by natural receptor stimulation tend to increase in amplitude as the gross activity of the midbrain and pontile RF *decreases*. Thus, cortical potentials are larger in deep than in light anesthesia (Derbyshire, Rempel, Forbes, & Lambert, 1936), larger in sleep than during waking (e.g., H. L. Williams, Tepas, & Morlock, 1962), and diminished in the waking animal by electrical stimulation of the RF or by exciting the animal by naturalistic methods (e.g., Bremer, 1961).

Normally, reticular activation also depresses evoked potentials recorded earlier in the afferent pathway, and it was at first believed that reticulofugal inhibition of the afferent relays as early as the first sensory synapse was responsible for these effects and, through them, for the depression of the cortical responses (e.g., Hernández-Peón, 1961; 1964). Later it was found that cutting the tympanic muscles of the middle ear or paralyzing them with curare prevented RF stimulation from reducing auditory evoked potentials in the dorsal cochlear nucleus, although the diminution of the cortical response persisted (Hugelin, Dumont, & Paillas, 1960). In the visual system, RF stimulation actually increases peripheral evoked responses, although at the same time decreasing the cortical response; the peripheral effect was shown to be due to the pupillary dilation which regularly accompanied cortical activation (Naquet, Regis, Fischer-Williams, & Fernandez-Guardiola, 1960). Thus, it appears that the peripheral effects of nonspecific arousal may be limited to essentially mechanical changes in the receptor and that these effects vary with modality and cannot be responsible for the consistent diminution observed in the cortical evoked response. The latter effect, however, seems enough to justify the claim (Hernández-Peón, 1961) that the RF tonically inhibits sensory transmission—or at least the registration of sensory input at the cortex—and that this generalized inhibition is roughly proportional to the level of arousal.

Attention and distraction—In a series of studies summarized in Hernández-Peón (1964), using freely moving cats with electrodes implanted in various afferent pathways, it was observed that evoked potentials elicited by stimuli in one modality are immediately reduced or blocked when the animal's attention is distracted by a stimulus presented to some other sense modality. Thus, cochlear potentials evoked by auditory clicks disappear when a container of mice is placed before the animal or when a delightfully fishy odor is wafted into his cage. The same sort of inhibition produced by the presentation of a "more significant" stimulus in some other modality has been demonstrated in the optic tract and for tactile and pain stimuli. Conversely, associating the click or flash with a "significant" stimulus like food or pain yields an enhancement of the respective evoked potentials. In human subjects, stimulated by flashes of light, evoked potentials coursing up the optic radiations toward the visual cortex were reduced or abolished when the subject's attention was diverted by, e.g., pricking him with a pin, and intensified when he was asked to count the flashes (Hernández-Peón & Donoso, 1959; Jouvet, 1957). Jouvet and Lapras (1959) reported that potentials evoked in the thalamus by tactile stimulation of the face were diminished by distraction of attention.

Using scalp recording and averaging techniques, Garcia-Austt, Bogacz, and Vanzulli (1964), as well as Spong, Haider, and Lindsley (1965), confirm that the amplitude of the cortical evoked response varies with the extent to which the subject's attention is focused upon the stimulus. The studies by H. Davis (1964) and by Chapman and Bragdon (1964), mentioned earlier, show that more meaningful or task-relevant stimuli, both auditory and visual, produce stronger cortical responses than do less meaningful stimuli of the same intensity. Using microelectrodes to record the activity of individual cells in the auditory cortex of unrestrained cats, Hubel, Henson, Rupert, and Golambos (1959) reported finding some units which responded to sounds only when the animal appeared to be paying particular attention to the stimuli. Some of these "attention" units responded only during the first few presentations of a stimulus, although other more typical auditory units responded faithfully to each sound even during sleep. One "attention" unit responded to the noise of paper rustled in the experimenter's hand if—but only if—the cat also turned its head to look toward the source of the sound. As any cat-lover knows, the ears of these creatures—the external meatus —have an extraordinary capacity to orient, independently of one another, toward novel noises to the side or the rear. This easily monitored "orienting reflex" should be a delicate indicant of the momentary fluctuations of the animal's attention and an interesting correlate of electrocortical events.

Habituation of evoked responses—We have already seen that habituation of the arousal reaction and the orienting reflex can be accomplished after some 20 to 40 repetitions of the stimulus and that such habituation is not accompanied by any significant reduction in the amplitude of evoked potentials recorded from the specific afferent system. However, a series of studies by Hernández-Peón and others (reviewed in Hernández-Peón, 1964) seemed to indicate that these evoked potentials also can be habituated by continuing to present the stimulus repeatedly for perhaps hundreds of trials. This phenomenon, which has been called *afferent neuronal inhibition* (Hernández-Peón, 1961), was thought to depend upon the development of stimulus-specific negative feedback in the reticulofugal circuits to the sensory relays of the afferent pathway concerned. However, in a recent and careful attempt to replicate some of these observations, Worden and Marsh (1963) presented click stimuli (1/sec or 10/sec) continuously for six hours to cats both waking and asleep without finding any consistent changes in the responses recorded at the dorsal cochlear nucleus. Fernandez-Guardiola, Roldán, Fanjul, and Castels (1961) did obtain consistent habituation of visual evoked responses; after about two hours of flash stimulation all of their cats showed a diminution of evoked responses in the optic chiasm, the lateral geniculate body, and in the visual cortex. However, cortical habituation *preceded* changes in the periphery, and their animals also displayed progressive relaxation, sleepiness, and general deactivation accompanied by increasing constriction of the pupils; when the pupils were dilated and fixed by topical application of atropine, habituation was no longer observed in the peripheral pathway (although the cortical responses did still habituate to some extent). These authors believe that the rhythmic flashes have a kind of hypnotic effect, reducing reticular activation accompanied by pupillary constriction; this in turn diminishes the peripheral afferent signal.

Thus, habituation of peripheral evoked responses is secondary to more central changes in the visual system and may not occur in the auditory system at all. Habituation of cortical evoked responses, however, seems to be a reliable finding (Bogacz *et al.*, 1962; Garcia-Austt *et al.*, 1964).

Conclusions—There is a tonic attenuation of afferent input, effected somewhere above the first sensory relay, which is greater during reticular arousal and less when RF activation is decreased during relaxation, sleep, or anesthesia. Both cortical and peripheral evoked responses are at once reduced or disappear when attention is diverted; at least the cortical component is phasically augmented when the evoking stimulus is at the focus of attention. Although these effects of attention and distraction may involve phasic changes in peripheral afferent transmission, it is clear that the role of peripheral modulation has been exaggerated. The alternative picture which seems to be emerging is that much of the "peripheral" afferent modulation may be accomplished in the cortex itself by the interplay of specialized units influenced from below by the structures of the nonspecific sensory system.

Related Psychological Research

Arousal, fatigue, and tonic afferent inhibition—That the reticular system maintains a tonic inhibition of afferent input implies that sensory thresholds as ordinarily measured should be, paradoxically, *lower* in a relaxed or even drowsy subject than in one who is more aroused. This surprising result has in fact been obtained in pilot work by Rosenblith (quoted by Bremer, 1961, p. 46). In a series of studies reported nearly forty years ago, Spencer and Cohen (1928a, 1928b; Spencer, 1928) found very high correlations (.8 to .9 and higher) between the simple sensory threshold and the *increase* in that threshold measured in the presence of an additional, "inhibitory" stimulus. These findings, obtained both across a sample of 50 subjects (R-correlation) and also across 50 daily measurements on the same subject (P-correlation), were interpreted to support the theory advanced earlier by Heymans (1899) that the sensory threshold is normally greatly elevated above its physiological minimum by an active process of inhibition and that the inhibition is a function of the aggregate intensity of all ambient stimulation. The higher a subject's simple threshold, the higher his immediate capacity for inhibition and therefore the more will his threshold be further elevated by increasing ambient stimulus levels. In their study of the single subject over 50 days, Spencer and Cohen also correlated his simple (brightness) threshold against the amount of sleep the subject had on the preceding night (all measurements were made first thing in the morning). This correlation was about +.60 over all 50 days and about +.80 over just the final 25 days when the threshold data were presumably most reliable. Correlations between thresholds and the subject's self-ratings of "freshness" were of about the same magnitude.

These findings are impressive and deserve to be extended. It is at first surprising that fatigue lowers sensory thresholds rather than raising them; on the other hand, most people would agree that they are more irritable, more distractable, more sensitive to pain and the like at the end of a tiring day than when they are well rested. Assuming that one's normal protection from the continuing noise, discomfort, and distraction in the environment is provided by an active inhibitory process which necessarily would be effortful and energy consuming, it is reasonable that this protection should be diminished by fatigue. Although arousal probably tends to decline with fatigue, sleep deprivation research has shown that arousal can be at least phasically elevated to meet the demands of some task even under conditions of extreme fatigue. It may be that Spencer and Cohen's subject showed lower thresholds when more fatigued because he was also then less aroused, or it may be rather that thresholds vary with fatigue independently of arousal.

Another related phenomenon is that of *audio analgesia* in which high levels of auditory noise stimulation have been found capable of inhibiting the pain of dentistry and other surgical procedures. The relevant data, as reviewed by Licklider (1959), are quite interesting. Among other things, it appears that pain suppression is most effective if the noise is turned up before the pain begins, which may be related to another observation, that the method generally works less well with patients who are already tense or anxious. Some patients report that they do feel pain but that "it doesn't hurt," suggesting that the noise has suppressed the secondary elaboration or distress component of the primary pain. The extreme individual differences in response to this procedure are of special interest; one feels that there must be important temperamental differences between persons who experience full analgesia with only moderate noise levels and those who feel pain even with intense noise, or between those for whom white noise is most effective and others who respond better to music. Reasoning from the Spencer and Cohen findings, one would expect that the effectiveness of audio analgesia should vary directly with the simple sensory threshold and inversely with fatigue.

A different but related phenomenon was observed in the course of a study of individual differences in fear conditioning in neurotic and "primary" psychopaths (Lykken, 1957). A number of subjects failed to show any appreciable conditioned GSR to a buzzer CS in spite of repeated pairings with a painful electric shock; most of these were "primary" psychopaths who showed abnormally little anxiety reactivity either clinically, in their prison and earlier records, or in other psychometric findings. Four subjects with low conditioning scores, however, were clearly anxious individuals, with neurotic-looking histories and test scores, who seemed genuinely frightened of the shock and responded strongly to it but not to the associated CS. Absolute or tonic palmar skin resistance had been recorded at intervals during the 40-minute session, and these data, reflecting changes in general level of arousal before, during, and after the conditioning trials, proved to differentiate these four anxious, but strangely unreactive, subjects from all the other individuals tested. As shown in Figure 9, the four "primary" psychopaths with the lowest conditioning scores showed a gradually decreasing palmar resistance during the session; this was typical also of most of the other subjects tested. Three of the four anxious but unreactive "neurotic" psychopaths showed very elevated resistances with a unique tendency for the resistance to increase still further during part of the session. The fourth subject's resistance was not high overall, but he was the only subject tested whose resistance increased sharply after he experienced the first shock (given alone prior to the conditioning trials) and then remained higher throughout the stressful conditioning series. Apparently, then, these four individuals reacted to the stress of the conditioning trials with *decreasing* arousal and under these conditions, although they showed about normal GSRs to the shock, they gave remarkably little GSR to the CS which warned that the shock was to follow.

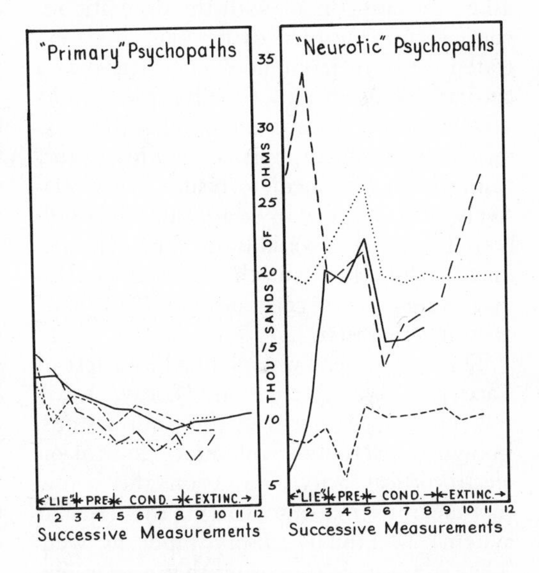

Figure 9. Individual curves of tonic skin resistance (SR) before and during conditioning trials involving painful electric shock. Subjects on the left are "primary" psychopaths showing very poor GSR conditioning and little clinical anxiety. Subjects on the right also showed reduced conditioned GSR, anticipating shock, but were clinically anxious or neurotic. These subjects, alone of those tested, showed anomalous tendency for tonic SR to *increase* (in the direction of decreased alertness or sleep).

Selective afferent inhibition—Lacey, Kagan, Lacey, and Moss (1963) have reported that stimulus conditions which encourage or require the subject to attend to or "take in" the external environment will tend to elicit *cardiac deceleration,* while noxious stimuli, or tasks which are facilitated by a focusing of attention inward, "shutting out" the environment, elicit cardiac *accelerations*. Thus, a mental arithmetic task, a reverse spelling task, and another involving sentence production were expected to be intratensive stimuli for which a lowered reactivity of the sensorium would be adaptive; as predicted, all three tasks produced cardiac *acceleration* as did a painful cold pressor stimulus. Conversely, a task requiring detection of colors and patterns in visual flashes and another in which the subject was asked to "empathize" with the dramatic recorded soliloquy of a dying man, both extratensive in their intended effect, produced cardiac *deceleration*. Finally, two tasks which required careful attention both to external input and to internal cognitive processing gave intermediate results with relatively little change in heart rate, although both produced elevations in skin conductance, as did all tasks in the series, thus demonstrating their generally excitatory or arousing character.

This experiment was planned as a test of Lacey's earlier speculation (Lacey, 1959) that pressure receptors in the carotid sinus, known to exert tonic inhibitory control on electrocortical activity and on the spinal motoneurons, may also act (via the reticular system) to inhibit sensory input as well. That is, Lacey is supposing that a set to exclude external input may, by some unspecified mechanism, generate excitation of the cardiovascular system, increasing heart rate and blood pressure which, in turn, will cause the baroreceptors of the carotid sinus to feed back impulses which result in inhibition of afferent transmission. In a recent replication, Obrist (1963) reports that each of his three extratensive tasks (e.g., a hidden pictures test) produced cardiac deceleration in all 28 of his subjects. However, blood pressure did not change significantly, suggesting that baroreceptor reflex inhibition was not operative. Conversely, the intratensive cold pressor and mental arithmetic situations elevated both HR and systolic BP.

The inductive leap to this neurophysiological hypothesis, from the observation that the two classes of stimuli produce opposite heart-rate reactions, is a long one, as Lacey would no doubt be the first to admit. But it has the compensating virtue of directly suggesting a whole series of related and potentially important studies. At the physiological level, one might investigate whether afferent evoked potentials wax and wane with experimental variations in baroreceptor activity. Do sensory thresholds increase with increasing heart rate? Is the subjective intensity of a noxious stimulus, as assessed by magnitude estimation or by GSR, decreased when heart rate and blood pressure rise? Do persons scoring toward the hysteroid end of the hysteria-psychasthenia continuum and who show repressive behavior in the perceptual defense situation show higher heart rates and blood pressures in that situation than their opposite numbers, the "sensitizers"? This research of the Lacey group offers a good example of a way in which the methods, problems, and concepts of personality research, experimental psychology, and physiology can be commingled with mutual facilitation.

The provocative finding reported by Hess and Polt (1960), that pupil size varies with the interest value of visual stimuli, would seem to provide another instance of selective modulation of afferent input, in this case by means of a change in receptor sensitivity. A later study, however, rather complicates the picture (Hess & Polt, 1964; Hess, 1965). Here it was found that the pupils dilate while the subject is solving a mental arithmetic problem, with more difficult problems producing greater dilation. Since it would seem more adaptive to attenuate sensory input while solving problems in one's head, one might have expected pupillary constriction in this case. As Naquet *et al.* (1960) showed in the cat, pupil size varies directly with cortical activation; one suspects that Hess and Polt's findings are not teleologically concerned with afferent modulation at all. "'What big eyes you have, Grandmother!' said Red Riding Hood. 'A mere epiphenomenon of my general state of arousal,' replied the Wolf." In any case, these experiments do underscore the significance of pupil size as a dependent variable of interest to the personality researcher.

Preception—When a noxious stimulus, such as a brief electric shock, is made predictable in time by the use of a warning signal, the GSR elicited by that stimulus is reduced in amplitude, suggesting that there has been a reduction in the subjective intensity of the sensation. Similarly, if several shocking electrodes are attached to different parts of the body, it will be found that shocks always presented through the same electrode will yield smaller GSRs than when the site of the shock is unpredictably varied from trial to trial. I have suggested (Lykken, 1959a; 1962) that such findings illustrate a kind of anticipatory afferent tuning or *preception* which, in the case of a noxious or interfering stimulus, attenuates the afferent signal in proportion to the subject's ability to predict the source, quality, and time of occurrence of that stimulus. It is assumed that such tuning is effortful and cannot be maintained at peak efficiency for more than a brief time. Thus, vigilance, which exemplifies "positive preception," is more efficient over brief intervals and fatiguing if continued too long. Negative preception, as indicated by decreased shock-GSR amplitudes, was greater in human subjects for 5-second than for 30-second warning intervals (Lykken, 1959a) and in the rat showed a sharp optimum with constant warning intervals of one second (Lykken, 1962).

One must also assume that the direction of the effect—whether the afferent system is tuned to amplify or to attenuate the expected stimulus—must depend on the subject's expectations as to whether the stimulus will be stronger or weaker than he wishes it to be. If one is sipping a fine wine, one's gustatory system should show positive preception; while taking a dose of castor oil, negative preception is indicated. When sampling your first fried grasshopper, a little afferent attenuation will protect you while still permitting you to discover that, well salted, grasshoppers can be tasty. Positive preception would be expected in a subject whose auditory threshold is being determined, but one would expect negative preception to supervene, and the threshold to rise, if one began giving a 100 db tone on a few of the trials at the moment when the subject was expecting a tone at near-threshold intensity.

An interesting aspect of this research has to do with the remarkable range of individual differences in "preception ability" which are observed in even the relatively homogeneous population of male college students. Some subjects cease responding altogether to the predictable shocks (those preceded by the warning tone) within 10 to 15 trials, although continuing to respond consistently to the interpolated shocks given without warning. Other subjects, although their average GSRs to the predictable shocks may be smaller than those produced on the shock-alone trials, still continue to emit sizeable GSRs under both conditions even after 100 or more repetitions of the stimulus. This ability to ignore or attenuate unavoidable noxious stimuli has such adaptive significance that it seems important to inquire into the possible causes of such marked individual variability, both situational (e.g., fatigue) and also constitutional. One is led to wonder what effect extreme over- or underendowment in "preception ability" might have upon the course of personality development.

The mechanism of attention—Any harried housewife will tell you that she "can't do two things at once!" She can, of course; she can tell Johnny to tie his shoes while at the same time hurrying across the kitchen to the stove, without neglecting to breathe, blink her eyes, or dodge the cat. What she can't do, it appears, is to perform two functions absolutely simultaneously, both of which require her conscious attention. That highest level of cerebral processing, wherein seems to reside the seat of awareness, is apparently a single-channel mechanism which can admit, process, and respond to only one input, one "chunk" of information, at a time. Experimental evidence for this is illustrated by the work of R. Davis (1956; 1957; 1959). The general paradigm is to provide a subject with two response keys with instructions to press one key with the left hand upon seeing the first signal, S_1, and the other key with the right hand upon seeing S_2. When the time interval between S_1 and S_2 is more than 250 mSec, the reaction time is about the same to both signals (e.g., 150 mSec for visual signals). As the interval between S_1 and S_2 is shortened below 250 mSec, the reaction time to S_2 starts to lengthen; for intervals of less than 150 mSec, shortening the interval by 50 mSec lengthens the reaction time to S_2 by about 50 mSec. Even if the subject is not required to respond to S_1 at all, the effect is very nearly as great; most of the delay arises "as a result of paying attention to the first signal, rather than the performance of any overt response to it" (R. Davis, 1959, p. 220).

Many details remain to be filled in. This "psychological refractory period" (Welford, 1952) seems to be longer than the estimated time required for central processing of a single reaction. In one of R. Davis's experiments (1957), the single central channel appeared to be blocked, unable to begin processing S_2, for some 180 mSec after the signal of S_1 reached the cortex, even though the motor impulse for R_1 was initiated within about 100 mSec and the response actually completed 50 mSec later. It is known that S_1 and S_2 may be in different modalities without changing the effect, i.e., a subject cannot begin processing a visual signal *or* an auditory signal until the end of a refractory period of, say, 180 mSec after a preceding visual signal first captures his attention (R. Davis, 1959). Although individual differences appear not to have been studied systematically as yet, subjects do seem to differ in the length of their refractory periods, and one suspects that this parameter should vary inversely with arousal. It is natural to think of some sort of scanning operation here; the attention channel may open briefly at regular intervals so that S_1 must wait until the next "opening" and S_2 must wait in its turn until the first "opening" after S_1 has been processed and the attention channel is released to accept a new input. Is the cortical alpha rhythm related to this scanning process? At an alpha frequency of 10 per second, S_1 would have to wait 50 mSec on the average to capture the attention channel (assuming one "opening" per cycle, perhaps during the downward crossing of the equipotential axis as implied by Lansing's study [1957], mentioned earlier); allowing then one full cycle for processing, this would yield a "psychological refractory period" of about 150 mSec, which is perhaps close enough to the values estimated in Davis's experiments to be worth investigating.

Of special interest is the question of whether even greatly overlearned automatized reactions to moderately strong signals would also display this refractory period effect. Perhaps any signal, no matter how mundane, familiar, and highly practiced, will capture the attention of a quiescent subject who has nothing better to do; such a signal figuring as S_1 in the paradigm might be followed by the usual refractory interval. But used as S_2, a signal for an automatized reaction *might* not show a lengthened latency even when closely following S_1, indicating that $S_2 \rightarrow R_2$ was being processed at a lower level.

What constitutes a single signal for this mechanism? How much perceptual information can be admitted to the single attention channel at one time? Undoubtedly, as Miller (1956) has suggested, the information-handling limitations of the channel can only be defined in relation to the past learning of the individual. Thus, one can identify a familiar printed word at tachistoscopic presentation speeds too fast to allow one to spell out all the letters of a nonsense word of equal length. Just a little information about a familiar gestalt or "chunk" is adequate to trigger the appropriate schemata already present in one's mind. The activated schemata add information to that provided by the senses in the same manner that a scientific hypothesis adds to the information contained in the experimental facts which suggested it; in either case, of course, one may be wrong.

As the Deutschs (1963) have argued, it appears to be the case that a great deal of complex perceptual processing takes place outside of awareness, before the perceptual signal even becomes a candidate for admission to the attention channel. We have seen that one can respond selectively to one's own spoken name during sleep (Oswald, Taylor, & Treisman, 1961). Moray (1959) found that when a subject is fed different messages to the two ears simultaneously (this is called "dichotic" listening) and has "tuned out" on one channel in favor of the other, speaking his name on the rejected channel may cause him to switch his attention back to this channel. Thus, the complex pattern analysis required to identify one's name can clearly be accomplished outside of attention. Other data on dichotic listening, summarized by Deutsch and Deutsch (1963), support the belief that what might be called the "preconscious analyzers" (corresponding to Broadbent's [1957] "filter"), must be capable of very high-level analysis (discrimination, identification) indeed. Thus, we may reasonably suppose that the raw flux of sensory input is analyzed preconsciously, not just for such primitive attributes as intensity, figure-ground properties, and the like but also into patterns and, to a certain extent, for "meaning." Patterns are identified as familiar or not, as salient or not, and we may assume that patterns having some immediate emotional significance can initiate the appropriate emotional reaction or at least that such patterns receive a special increment in their attention-getting power.

At each interval at which the attention channel opens, we can thus imagine an array of partially predigested signals, all competing for admission. It seems reasonable to assume that the signal gaining admission will be the one which is at that moment in some sense the strongest; but, as a result of the preconscious analysis, the "strength" of a signal at this level will depend less on the intensity of the original physical stimulus involved and more on the modulation resulting from the "significance" which has already been attributed to that signal by the analyzers. As in the theory suggested by Blum (1961), we might also expect to find that a continuing signal which has already achieved admission to the attention channel will be given an advantage in this competition at each successive "opening," by means of some kind of positive feedback or "reverberation" as Blum calls it, in order to maintain a better continuity of action of this highest level analyzer.

Since we are assuming a very large number of competing inputs, the problem arises of how the attention mechanism can determine the "strongest" without running through an impossibly large number of paired comparisons. The Deutschs (1963) suggest that some intensity mechanism, perhaps in the reticular activation system, may have its level determined, preconsciously, by the "strength" of the strongest competing input; the attention channel is then able to ignore all inputs whose "strengths" are less than this level. This device, however, seems merely to push the problem back one step; how then does the *intensity mechanism* determine which input is "strongest"? Perhaps one should not be too quick to reject the paired-comparison idea (brains and computers make such comparisons easily; it is selecting one from many *directly* that is difficult to engineer); with its notoriously large number of interconnected units, the brain may do just that, perhaps in some hierarchical sequence in which all "winners" advance to the next higher level. Although the present writer is most sympathetic to Deutsch's (1960) structural approach to theory building—"how might I build a machine which would behave this way?"—it is perhaps pushing the limits of respectable speculation too far to carry this problem any further at the moment.

PART II. PSYCHOPHYSIOLOGICAL TECHNIQUES AND PERSONALITY RESEARCH

More and more research in the personality field qualifies as "psychophysiological" by Stern's (1964) definition, in that physiological measures are employed as dependent variables. The remainder of this chapter is devoted to a discussion of some of the more important of these experimental tools and to associated problems of methodology and interpretation.*

Biochemical Indicators

Emotional arousal is accompanied by hormonal changes which, especially if the arousal is intense or prolonged, may be detected through biochemical analysis of body fluids. Adrenal secretion is particularly important in the emergency emotions of fear and rage, and methods are now available for measuring the products (or their metabolic end-products) of adrenal cortex and adrenal medulla in the blood plasma or in the urine.

Hormones of the Adrenal Cortex

The pituitary hormone ACTH or corticotropin stimulates the adrenal cortex to secrete *hydrocortisone* which circulates in the blood plasma and metabolizes to produce at least 11 different steroids (Persky, 1962). Several of these metabolic products are referred to collectively as the *hydroxycorticoids,* and another group constitutes the 17-*ketosteroids*. Elevated levels of hydrocortisone are found in the blood plasma of acutely disturbed or anxious patients, and the levels can also be reliably increased by the stress of a disturbing interview or the like. Hypnotic induction of anxiety in normal subjects can also produce a marked elevation in plasma hydrocortisone (Persky, Grosz, Norton, & McMurtry, 1959). Stress associated with the conditioned emotional response (CER) and the Sidman avoidance procedures produce marked elevations of plasma 17-hydroxycorticoid levels in experimental monkeys (Brady, 1964). Handlon (1962) was able to produce a significant *decrease* in plasma 17-hydroxycorticosteroid levels in normal subjects through relaxing hypnotic suggestion or by having his subjects watch a "bland" motion picture or engage in an absorbing but nonstressful perceptual discrimination task. Urinary excretion of hydroxycorticoids was markedly elevated in anxious psychiatric patients (Persky, 1962) and also in medical students just after taking an important final examination (Schwartz & Shields, 1956).

Fox *et al.* (Fox, Murawski, Bartholomay, & Gifford, 1961) attempted a longitudinal study of healthy college students combining interviews and Rorschach testing with daily measurements of urinary hydroxycorticoid and 17-ketosteroid excretion. These authors were not able to relate the manifest anxiety levels of their subjects to the biochemical indices but do report that the highest hydroxycorticoid excretors showed relatively poor control of their feelings and impulses, while the lowest hydroxycorticoid excretors were characterized by emotional overcon-

* After this chapter had gone to press an excellent compendium of psychophysiological principles and methods was published; for a more detailed treatment of some of the topics in Part II the interested reader should consult P. H. Venables and Irene Martin (Eds.), *Manual of psycho-physiological methods*. New York: John Wiley, 1967.

trol. In a cross-sectional study with normals, Fiorica and Muehl (1962) found a correlation between score on Taylor's Manifest Anxiety Scale and the level of free 17-hydroxycorticosterone (17-OH-CS) in the venous blood. Long-term longitudinal studies of individuals in psychotherapy have produced conflicting results; Schwartz and Shields's (1965) patient showed *lower* steroid excretion during periods of high tension, whereas the psychoanalytic patient studied over a three-year period by Fox *et al.* (Fox, Murawski, Thome, & Gray, 1958) showed an elevation of urinary hydroxycorticoid excretion during the first year or two of treatment followed by a decrease both in mean level and in variability during the final year as the treatment was brought to a successful conclusion. Like 17-hydroxycorticoid excretion, the level of 17-ketosteroids in the urine increases with stress or anxiety level and, in normal subjects, seems to be a predictor of anxiety proneness. Persky (1962) has demonstrated that the adrenal cortex of the anxious patient is unusually responsive to ACTH, and he found elevated levels of this pituitary hormone in the plasma of these patients as well. He suggests that patients, or normals under extreme stress, may show a change in their pattern of metabolizing hydrocortisone, from a primary output of hydroxycorticoids to a relative increase in the production of 17-ketosteroids.

Detailed biochemical methods for determining the levels of these substances in plasma or in urine may be found in McCarthy, Brodsky, Mitchell, and Herrscher (1964); Peterson (1963); Quesenberry and Ungar (1964); Silver (1963); and Vanden Heuvel, Creech, and Horning (1962).

Secretions of the Adrenal Medulla

The chemical mediator released by sympathetic nerve-endings is the catecholamine *norepinephrine* (NE) which is closely related to the great emergency hormone *epinephrine* (E), or *adrenalin,* which stimulates metabolism and promotes blood flow to the skeletal muscles, preparing the organism for "fight or flight." Epinephrine is secreted into the bloodstream by the adrenal medulla. It has been estimated that as much as 20 per cent of the total catecholamine content of adrenomedullar product consists of norepinephrine, and it is said that stimulation of different hypothalamic areas varies the proportions of NE and E released (Goth, 1964). Although chemically very similar, the two differ greatly in many of their effects; e.g., in physiological quantities, both increase systolic blood pressure while diastolic pressure is raised by NE (which increases peripheral vascular resistance) but lowered by E; E sharply increases heart rate while NE produces a reflex slowing of the heart secondary to vasoconstriction and increased blood pressure. Although the catecholamines are believed to be largely blocked by the blood-brain barrier, it is known that a region of the upper midbrain reticular formation is sensitive to E and may mediate the cortical arousal effects of that hormone (Jasper, 1958a), and it appears that NE may play a role in hypothalamic activity (Vogt, 1954).

Funkenstein and his co-workers (Funkenstein, Greenblatt, & Solomon, 1952; Funkenstein, King, & Drolette, 1957) showed that there are wide individual differences in the pattern of blood-pressure response following the injection of mecholyl. Pre-injection of NE in normals yields a marked hypertensive reaction (brief decrease and then pronounced, overshooting elevation of blood pressure) while pre-injection of E produces an exaggerated hypotensive reaction (persisting fall in blood pressure lasting many minutes). The NE-like mecholyl response in psychiatric patients was characterized by aggressiveness and outward expression of anger, while the E-like response was associated with inward-directed anger or anxiety and fearfulness. Silverman and

Cohen (1960) obtained similar findings from a more homogeneous group of seven military aviators and were also able to show that the ratio of NE to E excreted in the urine of their subjects tended to accord with expectations; i.e., the three men rated as anxious but not angry had low NE/E ratios and gave hypotensive mecholyl reactions, while the three men rated to be most aggressive and least anxious gave high urinary NE/E ratios and hypertensive mecholyl reactions. In another experiment, these same authors attempted to make their aviator subjects angry during a centrifugation test for g-tolerance; the subjects who seemed to be frightened by this stress were found to have the least tolerance for rotational acceleration and showed the highest levels of excreted E and the lowest levels of NE. Conversely, the men who reacted to the stress with overt anger and aggression had the highest g-tolerance, the lowest stress levels of E, and the highest stress levels of NE.

Elmadjian, Hope, and Lamson (1957) measured the urinary E and NE levels of a group of professional hockey players, before and after a typically extrapunitive display of their art, finding an average five-fold increase in NE and a two- to threefold increase in E after the game. The goalie, whose duties limit his aggressive opportunities, and two injured players who watched from the sidelines showed only slight NE increments but a considerable rise in E excretion. A group of amateur boxers were found to have very high NE levels both before and after their encounters in the ring. In a preliminary report of findings from a study of a group of Formosan children, Wolf and Lambert (personal communication) indicate a similar tendency for high incidence of interpersonal aggressiveness to be associated with high ratios of NE to E as excreted in the urine.

Although the mechanisms involved are not well understood, it thus seems clear that either the absolute or the relative levels, or both, of secretion or excretion of these two catecholamines must bear a close and important relationship to emotional arousal and to temperamental differences in fear or anger readiness. Although various biochemical techniques are available for assessing E and NE levels in plasma and in urine (e.g., Anton & Sayre, 1962; Crout, 1961; Fales & Pisano, 1962; Vendsalu, 1960; Euler & Lishajko, 1961), normative data are not yet available which would allow one to compare the quantitative findings of different investigators. One eagerly awaits the technological improvements which may make these promising dependent variables available to the personality researcher and the psychiatric clinician.

The Electroencephalogram (EEG)

The electroencephalogram is a graph against time of rhythmic variations in the minute electrical potentials recorded between two electrodes on the scalp (bipolar recording) or between a single scalp electrode and an "indifferent" or reference electrode attached to the ear lobe or to the back of the neck (monopolar recording). These voltage waves vary in amplitude from a few microvolts (near the residual noise level of most recording systems) up to as high as 200 microvolts, and in frequency from near-DC to 50 cps or more. Experience has made it possible to divide the EEG spectrum into bands of frequencies having special significance. In his original paper in 1929, Berger described the *alpha* waves, which include frequencies in the range from 8 to 13 cps, and *beta* waves, in the range from 18 to 30 cps. Alpha waves tend to dominate EEG tracings recorded from occipital, parietal, and temporal locations on the resting subject, especially when the eyes are closed. Electrodes placed over the frontal regions commonly show more low-voltage, fast activity in the beta range. Slow waves having a frequency of 3.5 cps or below and generally of large amplitude, characteristic of sleep, are known as the delta rhythm. The intermediate frequencies from 4 to 7 cps, known as *theta* waves, are common in the EEG of the young child. Other EEG correlates and their relation to the arousal continuum are discussed elsewhere in this chapter.

The origin of these "brain waves" is still not definitely established. The earlier view was that these rhythms were produced by spreading waves of firing of cortical neurons, i.e., that the slow EEG wave is a kind of average envelope of many brief axon spikes. It is now much more widely believed, however, that the slower, graded activity of the apical dendrites of the pyramidal cells of the cortex may be the primary source; i.e., that the rhythmic activity of many of these units, waxing and waning in synchrony, may produce the waves that are recorded on the scalp. Actual cell firing also contributes to the recorded electrical activity as in the case of the cortical evoked potentials. Epilepsy, focal and diffuse brain damage, anesthetic agents, and other pathological conditions may produce bizarre or characteristic electro-cortical activity, and therefore the EEG is an important clinical tool for use in diagnosis, localizing irritative cerebral lesions, monitoring anesthesia, and the like.

Techniques of Recording

EEG electrodes are most commonly small silver disks, sometimes chlorided electrolytically before use, which are either attached to the scalp by a special cap or harness or else individually cemented in place. Subcutaneous needle electrodes are also frequently used but may not be worth the discomfort which they cause to the subject. The electrode site should be lightly abraded and rubbed well with electrode paste to insure minimum electrode resistance. For clinical purposes and to insure a comprehensive coverage of all cortical areas, as many as 20 individual electrodes may be used at a time, placed over the head in a more or less standard arrangement suggested by Jasper (1958b).

The standard electroencephalograph allows for the recording of as many as eight or more channels simultaneously, each channel representing the signal developed between one scalp electrode and the reference, in the case of monopolar recording. Bipolar recording, between two scalp electrodes, is more difficult to interpret since the result is an algebraic difference between the activities of the two sites. However, bipolar recording is especially useful in localizing tumors or lesions. Because EEG potentials are so small, EEG amplifiers must be very sensitive, and this in turn presents a considerable problem of interference from electrical noise. Amplifiers must have a high capacity for rejecting in-phase signals appearing at both electrodes, and the subject must be well grounded. In electrically noisy environments, a shielded room may be required.

For psychophysiological research purposes, fewer channels or even a single channel may be used. A common practice now is to record the EEG on magnetic tape, using an oscilloscope or a standard ink-writer for on-line monitoring. Once stored on tape, the record can be later reviewed by playing back to an oscilloscope; important segments can be saved by playing back to an ink-writer without the need for writing out yards of unessential record, and the tape-recorded data can also be easily subjected to various types of automatic analysis. For example, the tape can be played back repeatedly into an electronic frequency analyzer or a bandpass filter in order to determine the amplitude of various frequency components in each channel, or other specialized electronic analyzers may be used to compare phase relationships between channels, compute autocorrelations, and the like. Cortical evoked potentials may now be obtained from EEG recordings by computer averaging techniques, providing that the eliciting stimulus can be repeated at least 50 to 100 times; this method is explained more fully elsewhere in this chapter.

Of the many useful references available on EEG method and theory, attention may be directed to the symposia edited by Hill and Parr (1963) and by Glaser (1963).

The Electrocardiogram

The electrocardiogram (EKG or ECG) is a graph against time of the electrical activity of the heart as it is picked up between two electrodes on the surface of the body. Like all muscle fibers, those of the heart muscle are electrically polarized in the normal state; that is, the surface of each muscle fiber is some 50 millivolts positive with respect to the interior of that fiber. When stimulated into contraction, the muscle fiber *depolarizes* and the surface loses its positive potential and even becomes momentarily negative with respect to the interior of the muscle cell. Immediately thereafter, the cell begins to repolarize back to its normal resting condition. When a large number of such fibers contract nearly simultaneously as they do in the mass of the heart muscle, their changing surface potentials may summate in the form of a rather considerable wave of voltage.

Within the heart muscle, contraction spreads in a regular wave of excitation originating in the auricles and spreading into the more massive ventricles. These waves of excitation are initiated by a cardiac pacemaker mechanism which is situated in the sino-auricular node in the right atrium. Excitation spreads through both auricles until it reaches the bundle of His near the upper margin of the ventricular mass. The bundle of His is a two-branched system of specialized conductive tissue whose branches course downward and laterally to the walls of the right and left ventricles and guide the spreading wave of excitation smoothly through these regions. Because the ventricles comprise most of the mass of the heart, ventricular contraction generates the larger waves of electrical activity recorded in the EKG.

An electrode placed on or near the heart itself will record maximum electrical activity at the moment that the wave of excitation passes directly under the electrode site. This relatively short, large amplitude deflection will normally be followed by a second wave of smaller amplitude but longer duration representing the spread of repolarization of the muscle tissue. Repolarization will ordinarily spread in the same direction as the original depolarization and should then produce a wave of opposite polarity. The shape of the wave produced by depolarization will depend upon the placement of the electrode relative to the course of the excitatory process. In *bipolar* recording, where the second or reference electrode is placed upstream from the first (with respect to the wave of contraction), the first or recording electrode will appear to go positive as the wave of depolarization passes under the reference electrode and then negative again as its own region depolarizes, returning both electrodes to the same potential. Should the reference electrode be situated downstream from the recording electrode, this same spread of excitation will be recorded as a negative voltage wave rather than as a positive wave.

In electrocardiography, the recording electrodes are placed at some distance from the contracting muscle mass and separated from it by the fairly complex conducting pathway represented by the intervening tissue. Potentials at the heart surface radiate and interact so that a small electrode on the surface of the body will tend to behave rather like a much larger electrode in direct contact with the heart.

Electrode Placement

Clinical electrocardiography normally employs three fixed electrodes situated on both arms and the left leg together with one or more exploratory electrodes located in anatomically standardized positions on the chest. In the early days of electrocardiography, recording was entirely bipolar between various possible pairs of these standard electrode positions. Unipolar recording, developed during the 1940's, is a technique in which each standard electrode site is compared against a reference point obtained by tying the remaining standard electrodes together through 5,000 ohm series resistors (all standard electrodes may also be tied together in this way to form the common reference, including the lead from which one is recording). Since all electrodes or leads are thus compared against a standard and less changeable reference point, unipolar recording provides relatively simpler results in which the recorded electrical phenomena are easier to rationalize with respect to the underlying physiological events.

A standard nomenclature has evolved for describing these various electrode arrangements. In the case of bipolar recording, the comparison of the right arm electrode against the left arm electrode is known as Lead I, the right arm against the left leg as Lead II, the left arm against the left leg as Lead III, and an exploring electrode on the chest wall compared to an indifferent electrode on the left leg is known as Lead CF_4. In the case of unipolar recording, where the three standard electrodes are tied together through resistors to a common reference terminal, the comparison against this common terminal of the right arm electrode is known as Lead VR, use of the left arm electrode gives Lead VL, and use of the left leg electrode gives Lead VF. A list of standard locations for unipolar chest electrodes has also been agreed upon. Finally, there are the so-called augmented standard unipolar leads, designated aVR, aVL, and aVF, respectively, in which the electrode from which one is actively recording is disconnected from the common reference terminal. This system increases the amplitude of the recorded deflections (hence the designation "augmented"), but since the reference terminal is to some extent electrically different for each lead, this method may also lead to certain distortions of the resulting EKG.

EKG Waveform

One cycle of the typical EKG as might be recorded by bipolar Lead II is represented in Figure 10. There are a total of five waves in the cycle, designated by the letters P, Q, R, S, and T, respectively. The initial low-amplitude *P-wave* represents the contraction of the auricles. Following the *P-wave* is the *QRS complex* which is the largest deflection in the EKG and represents depolarization and contraction of the ventricles. The final component in the record is the relatively small *T-wave* which is associated with the process of repolarization of the heart muscle.

The actual wave shapes of the normal EKG may vary greatly from this standard pattern depending upon the leads employed and also upon the anatomical position of the heart relative to the rest of the body, which may vary considerably even among healthy subjects and thus cause variation in the pattern of electrical activity picked up at the standard lead positions. The usual clinical EKG will include recordings from the extremities, usually bipolar leads I, II, and III and the augmented unipolar leads aVR, aVL, and aVF together with a set of unipolar precordial (chest) leads V_1 through V_6. Most abnormalities of heart function produce more or less characteristic changes in the patterns recorded from these standard leads, changes in the amplitude, shape, duration, or polarity of one or more of the five waves or changes in the timing of the intervals between waves. At the present time, electrocardiography is a semitheoretical discipline in the sense that certain inferences about heart position, structure, or function can be made from the EKG by deduction from a theoretical understanding of the anatomical, physiological, and electrical principles involved. However, most clinical diagnostic usage is still largely empirical; previous clinical or laboratory investigations have shown that certain physiological ab-

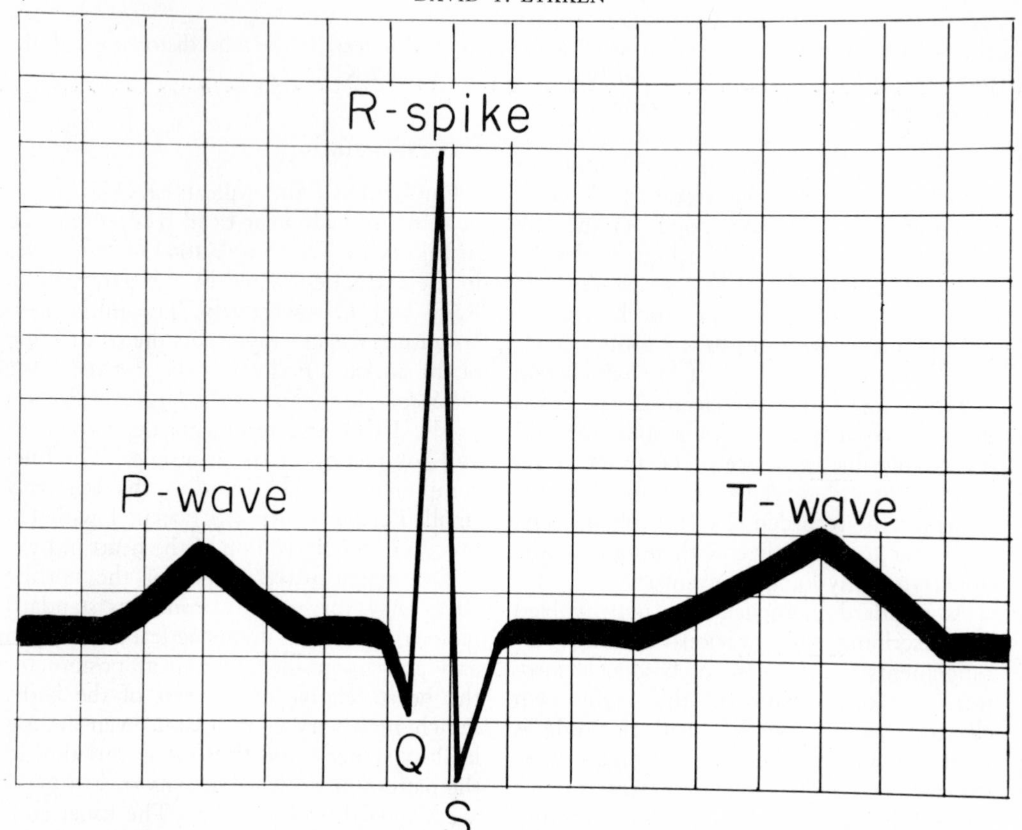

Figure 10. Typical electrocardiographic (EKG) cycle. P-wave represents contraction of auricles, QRS complex results from ventricular contraction, and T-wave represents repolarization of heart muscle. Shape and relative size of EKG components may vary greatly from lead to lead or from subject to subject. Each vertical division represents 0.5 mV while each horizontal division represents 100 mSec.

normalities yield characteristic changes in the electrical record, although the details of the mechanism involved may be somewhat obscure.

There are many competent texts on clinical electrocardiography. Two good examples are Bernreiter (1963) and Burch and Winsor (1960).

The various waves that are the phenomena of interest in the EKG may range in amplitude from a few hundredths of a millivolt to a few millivolts as measured from the skin surface. The duration of the QRS complex is characteristically less than 100 milliseconds, although the slower *P* and *T-waves* may last as long as 200 milliseconds. Since the steady-state potential difference between the recording electrodes has no significance relative to the heart, EKG recording is normally done by means of an AC recording system having good low-frequency response. Because of AC recording, electrode polarization is not a serious problem, and large German silver electrodes are commonly used together with a convenient, nondrying saline jelly to insure a good contact with the skin surface. Large or variable skin resistances under the several electrodes may be a problem, however, and a common practice is to include fine pumice granules in the electrode paste and to rub this paste thoroughly into the skin before applying the electrode. Alternatively, the electrode site can be lightly abraded with fine sandpaper. Standard EKG recording is on a strip chart from 4 to 5 centimeters wide, moving at a speed of 5 centimeters per second and with the amplifier calibrated to yield a deflection of one centimeter per millivolt.

Measurement of Heart Rate (HR)

Heart rate can be obtained from the EKG record by measuring the average time between corresponding waves in successive heart cycles (the average interbeat interval) in seconds and dividing this value into 60 to get heart rate in beats per minute. Because it is normally the largest and most sharply peaked of the five waves, the R-wave of the QRS complex is the usual reference point for this measurement. Measurement of heart rate is done automatically by an instrument called the *cardiotachometer* in which the amplified EKG signal is filtered in such a way as to produce a single pulse corresponding to each successive R-wave. These pulses are then electrically molded into a standard shape and amplitude and fed into an integrating circuit whose output is a voltage inversely proportional to the last one or several interbeat intervals, i.e., directly proportional to the momentary rate. Less expensive instruments for clinical use integrate over a number of successive beats and display the average heart rate either on a meter or on a moving chart recorder. More sensitive (and expensive) instruments may integrate over only one cycle at a time, reporting out each successive interbeat interval to a strip chart recorder or to a high-speed digital printer. Since all cardiotachometers identify each heart cycle by the relatively large spike of the R-wave, it is essential that the other waves in the EKG signal shall be sufficiently small relative to the R-wave so that the filtering circuits in the cardiotachometer can differentiate between them. This implies that, although only one pair of bipolar leads are required for heart rate measurement, these leads should be so located as to produce a relatively large R-spike. A chest-to-leg connection normally will be the best in this respect followed by the right arm-left leg (Lead II) and the right arm-left arm (Lead I) connections, in that order. Failure to provide an adequate R-spike or the presence of spiky electrical noise in the record may cause the cardiotachometer to miss beats or to count each beat more than once, producing over- or underestimation of the true heart rate.

Blood Pressure

Arterial blood pressure (BP) is a complex function of heart rate, the volume of blood pumped at each stroke, the force of the stroke, and the resistance of the circulatory system. Arterial pressure is maximum during the *systole* or contraction of the heart muscle and minimum during the *diastole,* the period in which the heart relaxes and refills with blood. Accurate continuous measures of arterial BP are obtained in animal research by cutting a vessel and inserting a strain gauge pressure transducer. With humans, periodic measurements of BP are made by wrapping a pneumatic pressure cuff (a *sphygmomanometer*) about the upper arm while monitoring flow sounds in the brachial artery just below the cuff with a stethoscope. The cuff is inflated to a pressure which occludes flow, and then the pressure is slowly bled off until the sharp pulse of the systole is first heard; the pressure reading of the sphygmomanometer at this point is the *systolic blood pressure*. As more pressure is released, a point is reached at which the characteristic sound of the diastole is heard; this is the *diastolic blood pressure*.

No wholly satisfactory method of obtaining accurate continuous measures of systolic (or diastolic) pressure without cannulation have been developed. Conventional "lie detectors" measure a somewhat ambiguous quantity known as "relative BP" by applying a cuff pressure midway between systolic and diastolic and then recording changes in cuff pressure (the pen is commonly driven by direct pneumatic connection with the cuff). Rather elaborate systems have been described (Darrow, 1937; R. C. Davis, Seldon, & Stout, 1954) which automatically inflate and deflate the cuff at intervals, using the appearance and disappearance of the peripheral pulse to identify the systolic level. At least one such sytem is available commercially. R. C. Davis (1957) describes another method of applying a strain-sensitive transducer above the radial artery in such a manner as to record pressure variations without occlusion of the vessel at any time.

Blood Volume

The *plethysmograph* is a device for measuring changes in the volume of a part of the body (e.g., a finger) as an index of the volume of blood in the peripheral small vessels. Mechanical plethysmographs contain the member in a volume of air or water while changes in the size of the member are measured as changes in the volume of air or water displaced under constant pressure. The *impedance plethysmograph* measures variations in the impedance of a portion of the body to moderately-high-frequency alternating current; under proper conditions, impedance variations will reflect variations in local blood volume. A typical impedance plethysmograph is described by Sheer and Kroeger (1961). Brown, Giddon, and Dean (1965) provide a comprehensive discussion of plethysmographic techniques, including the promising new method of *optical* plethysmography.

Electromyography

Electromyography is concerned with the recording and interpretation of the electrical activity involved in the contraction of muscle fibers. Each motor unit, consisting of a single motor neuron and all the individual muscle fibers innervated by that neuron, generates a *motor unit potential* immediately before fiber contraction, which typically consists of a two- or three-phase voltage wave several hundred microvolts in amplitude and lasting some few milliseconds. In clinical electromyography, the behavior of individual motor units is studied, by means of needle electrodes inserted into the muscle, as an aid in the diagnosis and treatment of neurogenic and myogenic disease. The amplitude and wave form of the single motor unit response changes in characteristic ways in various nervous and muscular disorders, and clinical electromyography can also be used to measure changes in motor nerve conduction velocity, to specify accurately the effects of motor nerve lesions, and the like.

The psychophysiologist will employ electromyography as a means for measuring tonic muscle tension and sometimes also to detect incipient or inhibited motor movements. For these purposes, surface electrodes similar to those used in EEG recording are usually employed, localized on the skin over the "belly" of some large muscle mass. Surface electrodes pick up simultaneously from large numbers of individual motor units and typically produce a complex, "spiky" record in which the chief interest is its average amplitude, indicating the tonic level of tension in that muscle and any marked changes in amplitude which may indicate phasic muscle activity.

EMG recording commonly employs standard EEG equipment, since the sensitivity and frequency characteristics required are very similar in the two cases. For psychophysiological purposes, an electronic integrating system is often used, the output of which provides a continuous, smoothed average of EMG amplitude. As is true in EEG work also, the electromyographer must frequently cope with serious problems of electrical noise, consisting mainly of 60-cycle AC interference in his records. By avoiding the proximity of fluorescent lights, electrical motors, diathermy machines, and the like, and by using modern differential-input amplifiers with an active and a reference electrode plus a separate ground electrode on the patient, these noise problems can usually be overcome. In some environments, a special shielded room may be required for EEG and EMG recordings.

A good discussion of clinical applications of electromyography may be found in the handbook by Pearson (1961), while a standard reference for psychophysiological work is the manual by J. F. Davis (1959).

Eye Movements and Pupil Size

A number of methods have been described for measuring movements and position of the eye. One approach involves mounting a tiny mirror on a contact lens and projecting a light beam onto the mirror from a stationary source while recording the position or movements of the reflected beam on a target (Ditchburn, Fender, & Mayne, 1959). A similar technique employs a tiny light source on the contact lens (Byford, 1960). A commercial system is available which uses goggles on which an infrared light source and a photo-cell are mounted. Due to the lower reflectance of the pupil, the amount of red light reflected to the photo-cell varies with the position of the eye, generating a relatively large electrical signal unencumbered by most of the usual artifacts. Another method employs corneal reflection without goggles and can be used to track the area of the stimulus target being viewed by the subject (Mackworth & Mackworth, 1958). One of the simplest methods, although prey to various artifacts and problems, is *electro-oculography.* Each eyeball functions as a small battery, maintaining a constant potential of many millivolts from front to back, the pupil being positive. If electrodes are attached to the skin above and below the eye or, to record lateral movements, one on either side of the eyes, any deviation of the eyeball from the position of direct forward gaze will produce a voltage difference between the electrodes, the one toward which the pupil turns going positive. A system of two pairs of electrodes, one in vertical and the other in horizontal alignment, will make it possible to determine eye position with considerable exactitude. The signals produced are in the range of from 10 to 40 microvolts per degree of eye movement. The technique of electro-oculography is described in admirable detail by Shackel (1961).

Pupil size is most commonly measured semicontinuously by photographic methods (Hess & Polt, 1960; Hess, 1965). An automatic camera operating at about two frames per second gives adequate temporal resolution for most purposes, and the system can be arranged so as not to interfere with the subject's vision of stimulus material, using mirrors and infrared illumination of the eye. A highly sophisticated (and expensive) instrument is available commercially which provides accurate and continuous measures of pupil size by means of an infrared scanning system.

Electrodermal Phenomena

The skin of the palms and soles (i.e., the *volar* regions) has the curious property of altering its electrical characteristics in concert with changes in the psychological status of the subject. Other skin regions, especially the backs of the hands and areas about the face and chest, may also participate in these psychological reactions, particularly if the subject is highly aroused or if the ambient temperature is elevated. The palmar and plantar regions, however, seem to be consistently reactive across subjects and conditions. Since, as we shall see, the sweat glands appear to be a principal effector organ for these electrodermal phenomena, it is significant that the volar sweat glands are unique in that they do not participate in thermoregulation (except at high temperatures), but respond to *psychological* excitation, while glands in nonvolar areas participate in such "emotional" sweating only under conditions of high temperature or high arousal. Darrow (1936) suggested that volar sweating serves the function of preparing the organism for action, moistening the relatively thick epithelium of the palms and soles and thereby increasing the adhesiveness and the tactual sensitivity of these manipulative surfaces. Although there is an increase in touch sensitivity during palmar sweating, Edelberg (1961) found that this change occurred both when the skin is dry and when it is immersed in water and inferred that some mechanism other than the sweating itself must be responsible for these effects. Wilcott (1966a) confirmed an observation by Edelberg and Wright (1962) that, during sweating, palmar skin is toughened and becomes unusually resistant to cutting or abrasion. Thus, emotional sweating anywhere on the body seems to have the adaptive value of protecting the skin against mechanical injury while volar sweating, except in excessive quantities, also helps prepare for action by increasing the pliability and adhesive qualities of these skin areas.

Skin Conductance Phenomena

If two suitable electrodes are affixed to the skin surface and a battery is used to drive a weak "exogenous" electric current between them, then one can calculate the apparent electrical resistance of the tissue from the ratio of the applied voltage to the current passed; i.e., by Ohm's law, $R = E/I$. If the current (I) is held constant, then the voltage (E), measured between the two electrodes, will vary linearly with the apparent resistance of the tissue through which the current flows. Most of this resistance is contained within the two transverse sections of epidermis which are in contact with the two electrodes; piercing the skin under one electrode so as to make direct electrical contact with the moist and highly conductive subdermal tissue reduces the apparent resistance nearly in half, whether the electrodes are located on opposite hands or on the same hand. If, instead, the voltage applied across the electrodes is held constant, then the current flowing in the circuit will vary linearly with the reciprocal of the apparent skin resistance, the skin *conductance* (SC). The unit of electrical conductance is the *mho;* a skin resistance (SR) of 100,000 ohms is equivalent to a skin conductance (SC) of 10 micromhos.

The tonic SC of the volar regions displays marked diurnal variations. It is lowest during sleep and rises sharply when the subject is awakened. Tonic SC tends to increase gradually during the morning hours and to decrease again toward evening, falling somewhat faster as the subject goes to sleep again. In the waking subject, SC will be lowest during quiet relaxation, higher during attentive listening or active work, and higher yet during excitement. Thus, there is considerable support for the view that tonic SC varies with some dimension of psychological arousal (Darrow, 1936; Freeman & Giffin, 1939; Malmo, 1958; Richter, 1926; Rose, 1964; Woodworth & Schlosberg, 1961).

Superimposed upon these relatively slow, tide-like changes of the tonic SC may be seen the wave-like or phasic changes known as the galvanic skin reflex or GSR. If a subject is stimulated by a brief shock, a sudden noise or signal, or by an internal stimulus such as a cough or an itch or an idea, then following a latency of about two seconds from the onset of the stimulus will be seen a sharp increase in conductance which reaches a peak in from two to five seconds and falls off again, roughly exponentially, toward the original SC value during the ensuing five to ten seconds. If a series of stimuli of different subjective intensities are administered, the amplitude of the GSRs produced will tend to vary in proportion to these intensities (e.g., Hoveland & Riesen, 1940; Kimmel, 1964; McCurdy, 1950; Plutchik, 1963). However, since the subjective intensity of a stimulus appears to depend in part on the subject's expectations (Lykken, 1959a), a novel or unexpected stimulus will commonly produce an unusually large GSR or "orienting reflex"

(Sokolov, 1960). Many subjects under conditions of excitement will show a fairly high frequency of *nonspecific* GSRs presumably elicited by internal stimuli. There is some evidence (Burch & Greiner, 1960; Cohen, Silverman, & Burch, 1956) that the rate of such spontaneous responding, like tonic SC level, varies with psychological arousal.

Skin Potential Phenomena

If an electrode on the palm and a reference electrode on an inactive region are connected to a sensitive high-impedance voltmeter, one will normally observe an endogenous potential difference with the palm being from about 5 to 60 millivolts (mV) negative with respect to the reference. In man, this palm-negative tonic skin potential (SP) appears to vary also, like SC, with some dimension of arousal. Treating the skin with atropine, which inhibits sweat gland activity, decreases both SC and SP (note: in my usage, "decreasing SP" means to render the palm less negative), as shown by Wilcott (1964). [In the cat, curiously, pad potentials seem to vary inversely with the level of sudomotor stimulation. Lloyd (1961) reports that the resting and also the denervated foot pad show a low SC and high SP; sudomotor stimulation produces pad sweating together with an increase in SC, while the SP goes less negative.] Venables and Sayer (1963) report moderate R-type correlations (i.e., across subjects) (+.68 and +.51 for two samples of schizophrenics) between SP and SC. In my own laboratory, we have observed SP and SC varying closely together within individual subjects over time, yielding high *P*-type correlations. In some subjects, however, certain experimental treatments appear to have a much stronger effect upon SP than SC, while other treatments affect SC more strongly. While we cannot yet specify which treatment will have what effect nor be sure how general this differentiation is, it is worth suggesting here that SP and SC may be related to two different aspects of arousal which are themselves correlated but can be "pulled apart" by appropriate experimental manipulations.

Like tonic SC, the tonic level of skin potential (SP) also shows wave-like, phasic changes which resemble and are related to the more familiar conductance GSR. These phasic changes in SP are often designated by one of the various labels applied to phasic SC changes—GSR; "psychogalvanic response" or pgr; "electrodermal response" or EDR, etc.—but the two phenomena are not identical and this practice is to be discouraged. Alternative locutions such as "skin potential GSR" or "endogenous GSR" seem awkward. In spite of a reluctance to add a further neologism to an already overburdened glossary, we shall employ the expression "skin potential reflex" or SPR in the following discussion.

The SPR is frequently a biphasic response consisting of an initial *alpha wave* of increased negativity at the active site, followed by a *beta wave* during which the potential swings in the positive (i.e., less negative) direction (Forbes, 1936; Forbes & Bolles, 1936). A more relaxed subject or one who has become better adapted to the stimulus or the experimental setting may show only the negative-going alpha wave, while a highly aroused subject may produce uniphasic positive or beta-wave SPRs (Wilcott, 1958a). Thus, the presence of the beta component, other things equal, will normally suggest either a more excited subject or a stronger eliciting stimulus. However, the exact significance of these variations in the wave-form of the SPR, although much debated, is still something of a mystery.

The Biophysics of Electrodermal Phenomena

The electrical activity of skin seems to be concentrated in (a) the sweat glands and (b) the cutaneous "barrier membrane." As shown schematically, in Figure 11, the epidermis consists of an outer "horny" layer, a dry porous cornified epithelium which is relatively thick (0.5 to 1.5 mm in volar skin) and an inner mucus layer which is moist and electrically conductive, the two being separated by one or two thin layers of densely packed cells, the granular layer and at least in volar skin the *stratum lucidum,* only a few microns thick. Somewhere at the base of the horny layer, probably coextensive with the stratum lucidum, is a membrane (consisting perhaps of the semicontinuous membranes of the cells of this layer) which has primary responsibility for limiting the transfer of water and other matter through the skin and for resisting the invasion of the body by harmful chemicals, bacteria, ultraviolet radiation, and the like (Griesemer, 1959; Rothman & Lorenze, 1963).

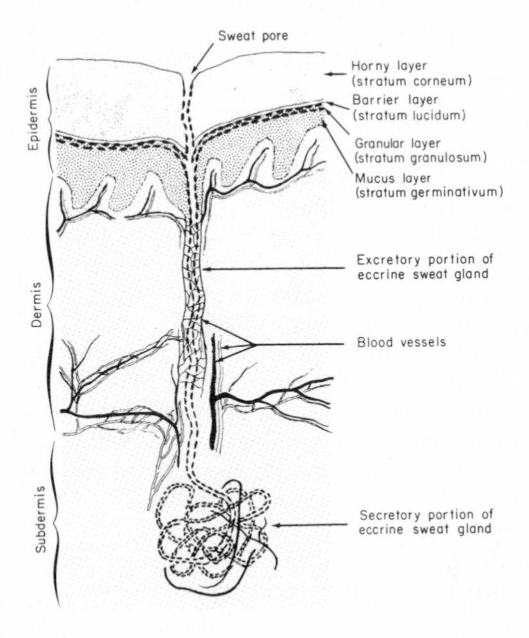

Figure 11. Semi-schematic representation of section of palmar epidermis showing eccrine sweat gland.

In human skin, this barrier membrane is penetrated at intervals by the excretory ducts of the eccrine sweat glands which spiral downward some 3 mm or more to the coiled, secretory portion of the gland, located in the moist regions of the dermal-subdermal boundary. A cross-section of the upper or excretory portion of the tubule shows a lumen of some 15 microns diameter with a two-layer cell wall surrounded by a "basement" or limiting membrane. The secretory portion has a somewhat larger lumen, a single layer of secretory cells, and, between this and the basement membrane, a single layer of muscle cells, disposed longitudinally and called the *myoepithelium* (Weiner & Hellmann, 1960). The myoepithelial lining is rhythmically activated, by some as yet unknown mechanism, in a manner which narrows the lumen of the lower portion so that the level of sweat in the tubule periodically rises and falls (e.g., Kuno, 1956). The density of eccrine sweat gland distribution in man varies from about 100/sq cm on the skin of the trunk to as high as 2,000/sq cm on the palms and soles (Weiner & Hellmann, 1960). On the palm, the density of active glands is greater on the protuberant grasping surfaces, especially the volar surfaces of the distal phalanges (Kuno, 1956) where the glands are distributed along the dermatoglyphic ridges. If the average diameter of the sweat duct is about 15 microns in the epidermis (Kuno, 1956), then these openings through the barrier membrane constitute as much as 1 per cent of its area on portions of the palms and fingertips.

Under normal conditions, there is a slight but continuous loss of water outward through the cutaneous membrane ("insensible perspiration"), amounting to perhaps 0.5 kg or more per day (Kuno, 1956). Active sweating, in contrast, releases some 3 kg per day (up to as high as 15 kg per day in extreme conditions), part of which may first diffuse from the sweat pores into the dry surface epithelium, thus providing a larger area for evaporation. Sweat contains a variety of salts and organic compounds in small or trace amounts, but its principal constituents include chloride, sodium and potassium ions, urea, and lactic acid. The concentrations of chloride and sodium are lower than in plasma, while potassium and urea are somewhat more concentrated in sweat than in blood (Kuno, 1956). Sweat also contains an enzyme which, upon exposure to protein materials in skin tissue, synthesizes the active polypeptide bradykinin, which apparently is responsible for active dilatation of cutaneous blood vessels (Fox & Hilton, 1958) and which, since it is a potent smooth muscle stimulant, may also be implicated in sweat gland myoepithelial activity.

The cutaneous barrier membrane is negatively charged (Rothman, 1954); amphoteric proteins in the membrane adsorb a layer of negative ions and thereafter repel other anions, so that the skin tends to be selectively permeable to cations. This property is maintained only at normal pH; acidifying the skin will discharge the membrane or even reverse its charge. The permeability of skin has not been well studied, and it is quite possible that, as is true for other biological membranes, skin permeability to particular ionic species may be independently variable, e.g., that certain chemical or hormonal influences may alter permeability to Na^+ without affecting permeability to Cl^- or K^+. Larger ions generally are blocked by the membrane so that SO_4^{--} and large organic ions are unable to pass the barrier in appreciable quantities.

An interesting possibility is that, like cell membranes, the cutaneous barrier or the sweat glands themselves possess a "sodium pump"—a metabolically energized mechanism which actively transports sodium ions inward against the existing concentration gradient. Such a mechanism is well known in frog skin (e.g., Whitfield, 1964) where it is required to prevent the loss of vital sodium by outward diffusion into the fresh water in which this amphibian normally lives. Since man is capable of a considerable sodium loss through his 1 to 4 million sweat glands (Weiner & Hellmann, 1960), active inward sodium "pumping" would seem to be adaptively appropriate, and such a mechanism might well explain the fact that the skin surface is normally some tens of millivolts negative with respect to the interior. Brusilow and Gordes (1964) report that human sweat obtained directly from the secretory portion of the sweat gland is hypertonic, indicating that sodium and chloride are in fact reabsorbed after secretion, possibly by active pumping. Since surface sweat from the cat foot pad is hypertonic and the cat's sweat gland has a shorter, simpler excretory duct, these authors suppose that in man the duct may be the principal site for reabsorption of these salts.

Biophysics of Skin Potential

Palmar SP is properly measured between an active electrode on some palmar surface and a reference electrode on an inactive, nonvolar area such as the forearm. The skin at the reference site is first treated so as to rupture the cutaneous membrane, by drilling (Shackel, 1959), sanding, or repeated stripping with Scotch tape, or so as to greatly increase the membrane's permeability, as by soaking with a strong solution of salt or detergent. Under these conditions, the potential observed between the two electrodes can be regarded as an estimate of the potential that exists across the intact membrane under the active electrode. As explained in the later section on electrode properties, however, differences between the salt concentration in the electrode fluid on the outside of the membrane and in the body fluids on the inside can generate sizable membrane potentials which may seriously confound these estimates of the endogenous skin potentials. Much of the published research on SP is difficult to interpret because of a failure to use isotonic electrolyte or else to specify clearly what was used.

In man, as we have seen, volar SP increases with increasing sweat gland activity (the outside surface becoming more negative with respect to the inside or to the reference site), whereas the reverse holds true for the pad SP in the cat (Lloyd, 1961).

These species differences are possibly related to the fact that pad sweat in the cat is slightly hypertonic with respect to plasma, while sweat at the skin surface in the human contains a much lower concentration of Na^+ and Cl^- ions than does human blood. According to the data of Brusilow and Gordes (1964), about 25 per cent more Na^+ than Cl^- ions are apparently reabsorbed from human sweat after secretion, which might account for the surface-negative potential of the skin and for the increase in SP with increased sweating. The relevant data are so scanty, however, that the true source of these negative SPs and of their tonic variations cannot be identified at present for either species.

Takagi and Nakayama (1959) inserted a microelectrode into the lumen of individual human sweat glands, finding that only the negative component or alpha wave of the SPR could be recorded from within the gland even while the subject was concurrently showing typical biphasic SPRs at the site of a conventional macroelectrode on the other hand. Similar findings in the cat have been reported by Shaver, Brusilow, and Cooke (1962; 1965) who were able to localize the source of this alpha response in the outer or epidermal portion of the sweat duct. The response decreased and vanished as the electrode was lowered into the dermal duct or when the epidermis was dissected away, even though the secretory portion of the gland continued to pour forth sweat in response to stimulation.

Similarly, a positive-going SPR may be observed if one removes the horny layer of cornified cells and touches a microelectrode to the exposed epithelium at some distance from any sweat duct. In the cat, this is a slow, weak positive deflection with a latency of several seconds following continuous stimulation of the sudomotor nerve (Shaver *et al.,* 1962; Wilcott, 1964) while in man it is a more rapid response, more like the beta component of the normal human SPR but apparently still weaker in amplitude than one might expect of the beta wave (Takagi & Nakayama, 1959; Wilcott, 1964).

Thus, one might conclude that the alpha wave is a response of the sweat glands, albeit of the excretory duct rather than of the secretory portion of the gland, and that the beta wave is a response of the epithelial cells, unrelated to sweating. These conclusions, however, may be premature. Shaver *et al.*'s localization of the alpha wave to the distal portion of the duct, for example, might be explained by the rising of fluid in the duct to the level of the electrode. It is likely that cat sweat as secreted is negatively charged with respect to plasma, and it is known that sudomotor stimulation causes contraction of the smooth muscle lining the secretory portion of the duct, narrowing the lumen and causing the fluid contents to rise and then fall again if stimulation is insufficient to produce secretion of additional fluid. Also, the positive deflections recorded from human epithelium seem too small to be confidently identified with the human beta wave. There is clearly a very slow positive response which results from strong stimulation in the cat and possibly in man but this is not the usual beta response. Wang (1957) denies the existence of the beta wave in the cat, and Lloyd's (1961) data show only the sluggish positive deflection. Takagi and Nakayama (1959) observed only uniphasic-negative SPRs in a monkey under conditions where one would expect a diphasic response from a human subject. However, Wilcott has published what appears to be a typical diphasic SPR from a cat (1964, p. 64, Fig. 1: C1), and I have observed the same on rare occasion in some unpublished work.

In any case, even if the beta wave is shown certainly to be a response of epithelial tissue, this would not prove that it is independent of the primary activity of the sweat glands. A factor which has been overlooked by most students of this problem is the presence in at least human sweat of a bradykinin-forming enzyme which has been found both in the subcutaneous space around the stimulated gland as well as in sweat collected from the skin surface (Fox & Hilton, 1958). Bradykinin is a potent smooth-muscle stimulant which appears to be responsible for the vasodilation of the cutaneous blood vessels which accompanies local sweating. Fox and Hilton show that this peptide can be produced from the gland prior to visible sweating when the stimulus is weak, or even after the sweat response has been abolished by atropinization. With strong stimulation, the appearance of visible sweat may coincide with vasodilation. Although study of the possible electrical effects of bradykinin has not yet been reported, it would be surprising if this highly active substance does not have such effects, e.g., activating the myoepithelium of the gland, increasing the permeability of the duct wall, and, where sweating is sufficient to perfuse the outer, cornified layer, perhaps affecting the interductal epithelium as well.

It has been suggested that the phasic beta-wave of the SPR may be secondary to increased surface negativity of the skin, e.g., the result of a partial rupture of a membrane overstressed by too strong a surface-negative potential (Trehub, Tucker, & Cazavelan, 1962). Wilcott's (1964) ability to produce apparent beta-waves by driving the skin surface negative with an exogenous current source seems to lead toward a similar conclusion. However, Wilcott's findings may have been an artifact of the effect of phasic changes in skin conductance (GSRs) concurrent with the SPRs he was recording. With a constant-current circuit such as he used, a phasic increase in apparent skin conductance will appear as a decrease in the voltage across the skin under the active electrode. Where the active electrode is given positive polarity, this will look like an alpha wave or negative SPR while under the negative electrode this effect may be confused with the positive-going beta wave. Surwillo (1965) has made the same point to which Wilcott (1966b) replied that, with modest elevations of SP by an external current, one can observe "beta" responses with the characteristic latency, longer than that of the alpha response recorded simultaneously from a control site. However, the only example Wilcott has published (Wilcott, 1964, p. 62, Fig. 3C) appears to have the short latency of the response at the control site. In any case, if the leading edges of the concurrent alpha and GSR waves have appropriate slope and amplitude characteristics, their superimposition in the situation Wilcott employed could easily result in a mutual cancellation of apparent voltage change for the first second or so of the response, thus giving the appearance of a beta wave with a delayed latency. Wilcott's claim that the waveform of the SPR depends directly upon the existing SP level—that the latter directly determines the former in some causal sense—remains to be proven. (There is no dispute about the association of SPR waveform with SP level, uniphasic alpha waves being most common with low negative SPs and biphasic or uniphasic-beta wave occurring more frequently with high negative SPs; what is at issue is the question of the explanation of this relationship.) Moreover, the beta response disappears with, e.g., exsanguination (Wilcott, 1958b) which does not systematically decrease negative SP nor eliminate the negative-going alpha wave.

Biophysics of Skin Conductance

Since the flow of electric current through tissue is almost entirely by means of ionic movement, the apparent electrical resistance of tissue is determined mainly by (a) the availability of charge carriers (ions), (b) frictional or inertial factors (e.g., large ions move more slowly, semiporous membranes may prevent large ions from passing at all and impede a proportion of the smaller ones as well), and (c) electrostatic forces (e.g., a negatively charged membrane repels anions and hence limits current flow to cationic charge carriers). Apparent resistance is very low for moist tissue, body fluids, and the column of sweat in the duct of a sweat gland. The external, cornified epithelium is porous but is permeated by a lipid film (Griesemer, 1959) and may have a fairly high apparent resistance, especially when dry. The chief barriers to the flow of unidirectional or low-frequency alternating current through the skin are the cutaneous barrier membrane and the cell layers or membranes that line the sweat gland tubules. The principal current pathways in skin are diagrammed in Figure 12.

If a brief (say, 10 mSec) square wave of constant voltage (say, 0.5 volt) is applied across the skin while the current flow is observed on an oscilloscope, the current will be found to decrease roughly exponentially during the first 0.2 mSec or so to a fraction of its instantaneous initial value, e.g., from 50 microamps/sq cm to about 10 microamps/sq cm. At the end of the applied voltage pulse, one can observe briefly a voltage

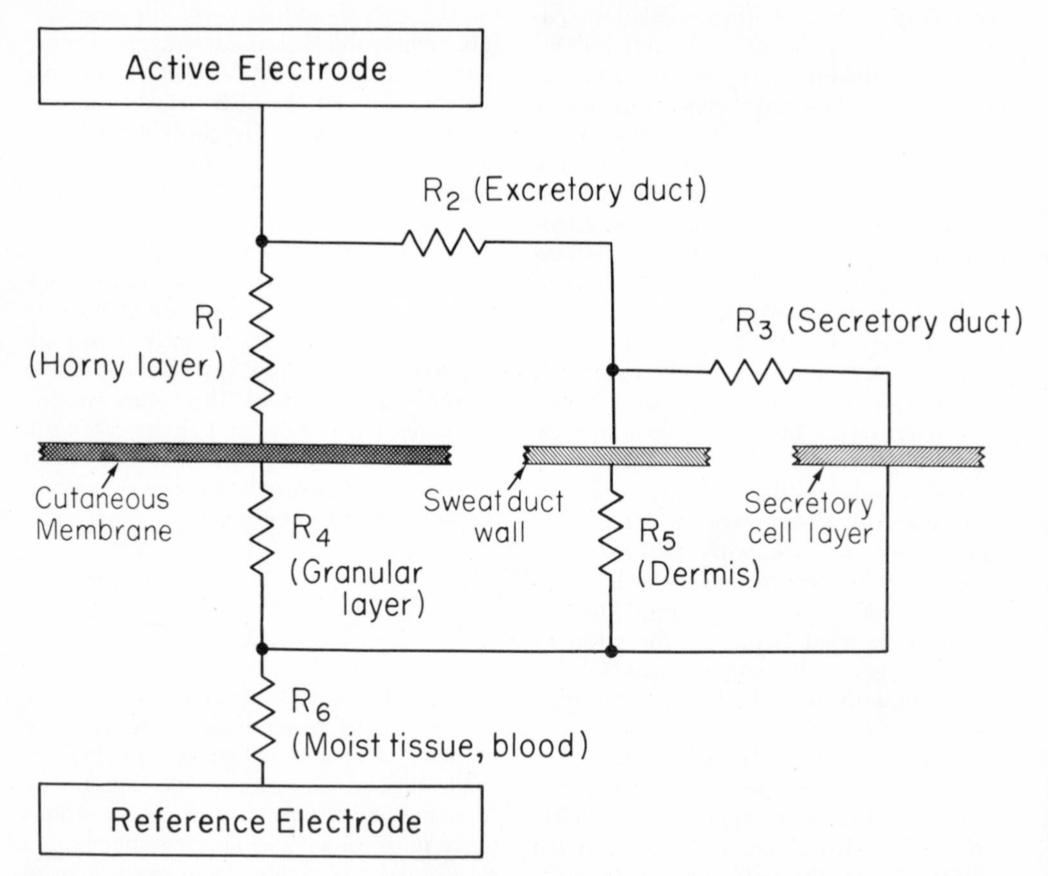

Figure 12. Schematic diagram of principal current pathways through the skin. It is assumed that the reference electrode is in direct electrical contact with subdermal tissues. R_1, the resistance of the dry horny layer, will normally be very high, while the resistance of the lower, more moist layers will be lower (R_4, R_5, and especially R_6). The resistance of the current path down the excretory duct of an eccrine sweat gland (R_2 and R_3) will be very low when the duct is filled with saline sweat but may be high when the duct is empty. All tissue layers, but especially the compact cutaneous membrane and the walls of the sweat gland, may generate potentials in opposition to the flow of current.

of opposite polarity across the skin, nearly as large as the original pulse, which decays exponentially to zero within 0.1 mSec or so. These observations indicate a *polarization* phenomenon, a rapid build-up of a voltage or "counter emf" across the membrane which acts in opposition to the applied voltage in such a way as to reduce the flow of current.

Rein's experiments (quoted in Rothman, 1954) showed that skin membranes (either the cutaneous barrier membrane or those lining the sweat glands or both) are negatively charged; this is interpreted to mean that the membrane adsorbs a number of anions which become fixed negative charges in or near the pores of the membrane (Sollner, 1955). The "counter ions" of these fixed wall charges, small cations held in proximity to the fixed anions by electrostatic attraction, have some freedom of movement through the pores of the membrane in either direction. A possible explanation of the membrane polarization phenomenon is that the application of an external voltage across the membrane causes these counter ions to move through the pores in the direction of the negative pole until the backward attraction of the fixed wall charges prevents further movement. This results in the formation of an ionic double-layer with the fixed anions on the side toward the positive pole of the applied voltage gradient and the counter-cations forming a layer facing the negative pole of the applied gradient. Such a double-layer would act as a battery in series-opposition to the applied voltage. The initial surge of current would then represent the conductivity of the membrane as limited only by the size of its pores, its resistance to anionic flow, and the like. The 200 microseconds or so required for this initial surge to fall nearly to its steady state value would be interpreted as the time required for the counter-cations to move into the orientation of the double-layer.

This polarization hypothesis (which, in one form or another, goes back to Gildemeister [cf. Forbes & Landis, 1935]) helps to account for the failure of skin resistance to obey Ohm's law at higher current densities. At low current levels, the counter emf of polarization might be expected to increase as a constant fraction of the applied voltage, yielding a correspondingly linear increase in current. But the polarization capacity of any membrane is limited; when all available counter-cations are optimally arrayed in the ionic double-layer, the counter emf can increase no further so that an additional increase in applied voltage must be accompanied by a sharp increment in current flow. Moreover, it is likely that high external voltages would actually discharge the membrane, stripping away the adsorbed anions and thus reducing its polarization capacity until normal metabolic processes are able to restore the initial conditions. It is for this reason, perhaps, that apparent skin resistance decreases with increasing current density above a level of about 10 microamperes/sq cm (Edelberg, Greiner, & Burch, 1960).

If, while observing current flow through palmar skin using the experimental arrangements described above, one then stimulates the subject so as to produce a GSR, it will be found that this phasic increase in apparent conductance is observed only as a transitory increase in the asymptotic level to which current falls after polarization; the GSR affects neither the maximum amplitude of the initial current pulse nor the rate at which the current falls during the ensuing 200 microseconds or so. This would seem to indicate that the local effect of GSR activity is one of momentarily decreasing the polarization capacity of the skin membrane. A similar conclusion was drawn by McClendon and Hemingway in 1930 and again by Forbes and Landis in 1935 as a result of observing that the GSR, in the form of a decrease in apparent impedance to a sinusoidal applied voltage, seemed to disappear when the frequency of the applied waveform was increased beyond about

10,000 cps. Their observations, however, might be accounted for merely in terms of capacitative shunting. The thin, relatively nonconductive membrane is thought to function as a capacitor to alternating current, shunting an increasing proportion of the applied current as frequency increases. Even if the GSR were some sort of decrease in the ohmic component of apparent impedance (e.g., an increase in the level of sweat in the ducts or an increased permeability of the membrane), this increase in parallel conductance would be of less and less importance—i.e., less observable—at high frequencies due to the great decrease in capacitative reactance of the membrane. The square wave analysis described above indicates, however, that there is no decrease in parallel impedance during the GSR but rather only a decrease in apparent polarization capacity.

One locus of this variable polarization capacity in skin is probably in the membranes of the sweat gland secretory cells. However, at higher rates of sweating, GSR activity (i.e., a phasic increase in sudomotor innervation) may quickly increase sweat concentration in the horny layer, which may in turn affect the polarization capacity of the cutaneous membrane perhaps via bradykinin activity. Thus, the conductance GSR accompanying a typical biphasic SPR may consist, first, of a depolarization of secretory cells, providing additional high-conductance pathways for current flow through the skin, followed by a partial depolarization of the cutaneous barrier, which would increase the conductivity of the direct pathway. After exsanguination of the limb, sudomotor innervation may continue to produce secretory cell depolarization accompanied by the alpha wave; however, the lack of sweat would prevent any effect upon the cutaneous membrane and hence would abolish the beta wave and greatly reduce conductance change. When the residual sweat in the ducts has all been reabsorbed, depolarization at the base of the sweat gland would no longer provide a low resistance shunt through the skin, and the conductance GSR may be then entirely eliminated.

Conclusions

This relatively brief review of the voluminous and controversial literature concerned with electrodermal phenomena will have illustrated at least that this technology has not yet stabilized; nearly every investigator uses some unique combination of electrodes, electrode placement, signal conditioner and recording method, current level, electrolyte constituents and concentration, and so on—and we have seen that each such variation can influence, sometimes drastically, the measurements obtained. In spite of these complexities, and although many investigators have employed such poor techniques as to render their findings difficult to interpret, electrodermal phenomena continue to be widely used by psychologists in psychophysiological researches, in studies of classical conditioning, in studies of emotional reactivity, arousal, reactivity to pain, habituation, in the study of perceptual defense, and in a host of practical applications. The fact that this dependent variable has provided so many provocative results in such a diversity of applications, in spite of the lack of a standard technology and in the face of so many examples of clearly inadequate technique, implies that these phenomena must be unusually rich in psychological significance to have survived so much careless handling so well. The mass of findings available supports quite firmly the general conclusion that skin conductance (and presumably also skin admittance, negative palmar potentials, and frequency of nonspecific GSRs) varies monotonically with some basic dimension of psychological activation or arousal. Similarly, it seems clear that the phasic conductance change or GSR (and presumably the negative-going skin potential change or SPR) varies in amplitude directly with what can best be called the *subjective intensity* of the eliciting stimulus or, alternatively, the *attention-value* of that stimulus.

The problems of electrodermal methodology have been gone into here in some detail (although a really adequate discussion of this extensive literature would have required a volume to itself) for two reasons. First, these phenomena appear to comprise the most important psychophysiological variables currently available for use in general psychological research (the electrical activity of the brain—the EEG, evoked potentials, and the like—are no doubt the *most* important in an absolute sense but not as they are currently accessible to and interpretable by the average psychologist). Secondly, it seems necessary to remind some psychologists, who find themselves in increasing numbers turning away from paper-and-pencil techniques to the more promising tools of the experimental laboratory, that these procedures are complex and cannot be correctly used merely by following cookbook formulas. The psychological investigator, as his colleagues in the other experimental sciences have long since done before him, must adapt himself to the need for mastering an increasingly elaborate research technology. At the other end of the continuum of scientific evolution, nuclear physics has produced a division of labor between the experimenter on the one hand and, on the other, the theoretician, whose laboratory is his blackboard; one wonders whether present-day psychology can afford that luxury.

A Method for Direct Measurement of Apparent Skin Conductance

Although the partial account of the biophysics of skin conductance phenomena given above seems plausible on the existing evidence, it should be re-emphasized that it is largely speculative and that most of these issues are still quite unsettled. (Wilcott [1967], for example, provides a closely reasoned analysis leading to rather different conclusions.) Considerable additional research will be required to determine which, if any, of these speculations may be true and to answer the remaining questions before one can expect workers in this field to settle upon a standardized technology. Meanwhile, the nonspecialist might be wise to avoid the major mysteries of the skin potential methods. Alternatively, the direct measurement of apparent skin conductance recommends itself as relatively easy to instrument, quite simple to use, and reasonably immune to major artifacts.

The usual practice of measuring apparent skin resistance and then converting the resistance values into units of conductance is both onerous and subject to considerable error under certain conditions (Lykken and Roth, 1961). A better approach is to measure SC directly by applying a small constant voltage to the skin and measuring variations in current. Since this tissue obeys Ohm's law to a reasonable approximation, as long as current densities are maintained below about 10 microamps/sq cm, current in this range will vary linearly with conductance in such a constant-voltage circuit. A suitable signal conditioner for this purpose is diagrammed in Figure 13. This circuit is designed for use with a single active finger electrode and a typical high-gain DC pre-amplifier of the chopper-stabilized type (*vide infra*). The amplifier should be equipped with a zero-suppression control (with which one can subtract a calibrated amount from the input voltage) and the usual step-type input attenuator switch (which adjusts the amplification of the net input signal to various calibrated fractions of the maximum gain of the amplifier). The voltage across the subject is set by adjusting P_1 to a value which will insure that the current density will never exceed the limit of 10 microamps/sq cm for the particular electrodes used. With a single 1 sq cm finger electrode and the skin punctured at the reference site, minimum skin resist-

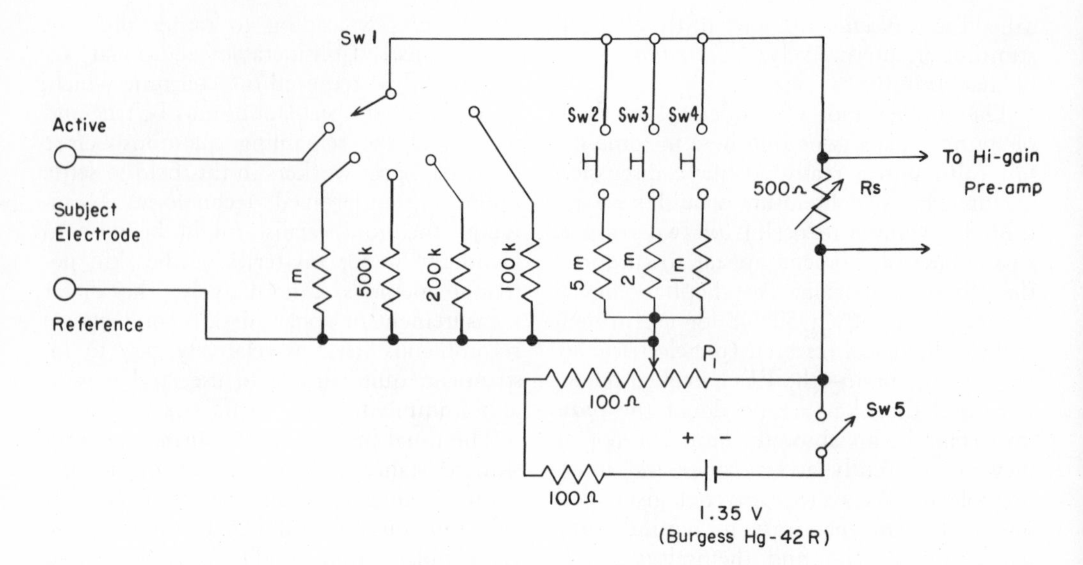

Figure 13. Sensor or signal conditioner for use in the direct measurement of skin conductance (SC). Voltage across subject, determined by setting of P_1, remains essentially constant so that current through subject, producing output voltage across R_s, will vary linearly with subject's apparent conductance. Details of operation are given in text.

ance to be expected is about 50 K-ohms; hence, a proper subject voltage would be about

$$E_s = (50 \times 10^3) \text{ ohms} \times (10 \times 10^{-6} \text{ amperes} = 0.5 \text{ volt.}$$

If skin drilling is not feasible for some reason, the reference may be replaced by a second active finger electrode. This will reduce both the tonic SC level and the GSR amplitude by about half.

Because the output signal is the voltage dropped across the small series resistance, R_s, rather than across the subject, the preamplifier is not required to have a high input impedance.

Calibration of the system is accomplished in two steps. First, a known conductance is substituted for the subject by appropriate setting of Sw1 and then the size of the output signal, determined by the setting of R_s, is adjusted so that the zero-suppression control on the pre-amplifier (usually a 10-turn potentiometer calibrated to read from 0.00 to 10.00) can be read directly in micromhos or in even multiples thereof. For example, with $E_s = 0.5$ V and Sw1 set at 200 K-ohms (5 micromhos), current flowing through R_s will equal 2.5 microamps; thus, the voltage across R_s can be varied from zero to $(500)(2.5 \times 10^{-6}) = 1.25$ mV. If the zero-suppression on the pre-amplifier can be set to suppress 1 mV at the maximum setting of 100.00, then—to make this control read directly in micromhos—R_s should be adjusted downward to give an output of 0.5 mV for this 5 micromhos conductance (which will then be just cancelled by a zero-suppression setting of 05.00).

Secondly, the gain of the pre-amplifier must be adjusted so that a given change in conductance will produce a known deflection of the recording pen. Amplifier input-attenuator switches are typically calibrated "X1, X2, X5, X10, . . . , X1000"; set at X1, the gain is maximum, while set at X10, the gain is one-tenth maximum, and so on. Therefore, it is convenient to adjust the gain control of the pre-amplifier so that a conductance change (e.g., a GSR) of 1 micromho produces full-scale pen deflection at X1, half-scale at X2, and so on. This may be done using the push-button switches Sw2, Sw3, and Sw4 on the signal conditioner. Thus, with the amplifier attenuator at X1, pressing Sw3 adds a conductance of 0.5 micromhos to that already in the circuit and should produce half-scale deflection of the recorder once the amplifier gain control has been properly adjusted.

In use, the subject is inserted in the circuit by means of Sw1, and the zero-suppression control is adjusted so as to bring the recorder pen to some convenient position on the chart. One then writes down the setting of this control (e.g., "03.64 micromhos") together with the setting of the attenuator (e.g., "X2") directly on the chart paper. From this information, one can determine with precision the subject's exact momentary SC value for any position of the pen on the chart. Another important advantage of recording SC directly is that the variations in the subject's tonic conductance during the experimental session tend to be much smaller than his corresponding variations in tonic resistance, relative to the amplifier sensitivity required for measuring phasic changes. This means that the pen is not continually drifting off the chart, requiring range-changing or manual resetting of the zero-suppression.

Electrodes for Bio-Electric Measurement

Measurement of most bio-electric phenomena requires that a connection be made between the measurement apparatus and the tissue at two or more junctions which are known as *electrodes*. At the electrode, the manner in which current is transported changes from electronic in the wires to principally ionic conduction in the tissue. This transition necessarily implies that chemical processes occur at both electrodes, resulting in the production of electrode potentials or resistances which may seriously distort the measurements one is attempting to make. From the standpoint of the psychophysiologist, such problems are of greatest importance in relation to electrodermal measurement, although poor electrode technique can also create difficulties in EEG and EMG recording as well as in the administration of electrical stimulation or shock.

Electrode Potentials

When any metal is immersed in an electrolyte, the metal tends to discharge cations into the solution, this tendency being stronger for the more active metals. At the same time, metal cations in the solution tend to transmit their positive charge to the metal electrode in proportion to their concentration. If the "dissolving pressure" of the metal is greater than the osmotic pressure of the cations in solution, the metal shows a net loss of positive charges to the solution and thus becomes relatively negative; if the osmotic pressure predominates, the electrode potential will be positive. Although it is not possible to eliminate such electrode potentials entirely, two identical metals immersed in identical electrolytes will show no voltage difference with respect to one another. However, any difference in concentration of the ions in solution at the two electrodes will produce a net "concentration potential" between them which can be calculated from the equation

$$E_c = \frac{RT}{nF}\left[\log_e \frac{c_1}{c_2}\right] \qquad (1)$$

where R is the gas constant, T the absolute temperature, n the ionic valency, F is the faraday, and c_1 and c_2 are the respective concentrations of the relevant ion in the two solutions. Converting to Briggsian logarithms and simplifying:

$$E_c = 60.6 \text{ mV } (\log \frac{c_1}{c_2}) \text{ at } 30^\circ \text{ C.} \qquad (2)$$

Thus, for example, if the electrode paste used at the active electrode on the skin contains 0.1 N NaCl while the electrolyte at the reference electrode contains 0.01 N NaCl, then the active electrode (having the more concentrated solution) will prove to be some 60 mV positive with respect to the reference due to concentration potential alone, even if the tissue is electrically inert.

Liquid-Junction Potentials

At the junction between any two liquids containing salts in different concentrations, ions will tend to diffuse in the direction of lower concentration, the more mobile ions diffusing more rapidly. As a rule, the diffusion of either positive or negative ions will be faster, resulting in an imbalance of electric charge across the liquid-junction. If a solution of 0.1 N NaCl is connected to a solution of .01 N NaCl by a "salt-bridge" made of cotton wick soaked in the latter solution, there will be a voltage between the two solutions which can be computed from the formula:

$$E_d = \frac{u-v}{u+v} E_c = \frac{u-v}{u+v}$$

$$(60.6 \text{ mV}) \log \frac{c_1}{c_2} \text{ at } 30° \text{ C} \qquad (3)$$

where v and u are the mobilities of the negative and positive ions respectively. The mobility of Na^+ (u) is about 4.5 while the mobility of Cl^- (v) is 6.8; therefore,

$$E_d = \frac{-2.3}{11.3} [60.6 \log \frac{0.1}{0.01}] = -12.4 \text{ mV}$$

(i.e., the more dilute solution negative).

Since the mobilities of the potassium and chloride ions are so nearly equal, salt-bridges saturated with a solution of KCl are commonly used as a means of avoiding liquid-junction potentials. If these same NaCl solutions had been connected by a saturated KCl bridge, the diffusion of K^+ and Cl^- into solution at both ends of the bridge would have occurred at about the same rate leading to a negligible net junction potential on the order of 1 mV.

Membrane Potentials

When two solutions are separated by a semipermeable membrane, differences in ionic concentration will produce a "diffusion" potential across the membrane as at any liquid junction. However, the membrane may greatly alter the effective mobilities of the various ionic species involved. Thus, a membrane with small pores may be far less permeable to the Na^+ ion, which is hydrated and large, than to the K^+ or Cl^- ions, so that different dilutions of NaCl will yield a much higher potential across such a membrane than the same dilutions of KCl. A negatively charged membrane such as skin is relatively impermeable to anions regardless of their size. Therefore, only cations will diffuse across the membrane, and the potential will depend only on cationic concentrations; since, in equation (3), $v = 0$, we get:

$$E_m = \frac{u}{u} [60.6 \log \frac{c_1}{c_2}] \text{ mV}$$

$$= 60.6 [\log \frac{c_1}{c_2}] \text{ mV at } 30° \text{ C.} \qquad (4)$$

If the membrane separates salts having different cations, the membrane potential can be calculated from the somewhat more general formula:

$$E_m = 60.6 [\log \frac{u_1 c_1}{u_2 c_2}] \text{ mV at } 30° \text{ C,} \qquad (5)$$

where u_1 and u_2 are the mobilities in the membrane of the two cations and c_1 and c_2 are their respective concentrations. In the negatively-charged collodion membrane, the mobility of K^+ is some 7.5 times the mobility of Na (Bures *et al.,* 1960), so that such a membrane separating solutions of NaCl and KCl in equal concentrations will produce a membrane potential of about 60.6 [log 7.5] mV = 53 mV at 30° C. The relative mobilities of various cations in skin have not been determined; the possibility of active sodium pumping suggests that these mobilities may not be the same in both directions, and it must also be expected that the mobility of (i.e., permeability for) different cations in skin may vary considerably with local conditions. The basic point to remember is that any difference in ionic (especially *cationic*) concentration between the local body fluids inside the skin and the electrode fluid used on the skin surface will in general produce a membrane potential which may be on the order of tens of millivolts.

Types of Electrodes

Even with the same metals and identical electrolyte concentrations, it proves to be quite difficult in practice to produce pairs of electrodes whose potential difference remains low (e.g., less than a few millivolts) and stable over time. Minute impurities in the metal or in the electrolyte, producing complex and cumulative chemical reactions, are probably responsible for these problems. When current is passed between any electrode pair, as it must be even in the measurement of potentials, the difficulties are compounded. The flow of current sets up diffusion potentials within the electrolyte, due to local variations in ionic concentration. Most important, chemical reactions occur at both metal-electrolyte junctions which may bring about marked and cumulative changes in the apparent resistance of the electrodes due, e.g., to progressive changes in electrolyte composition or the deposition (plating) of insoluble metallic salts upon the surface of the electrode metal. So-called nonpolarizing electrodes have the property that such reactions are completely reversible when the direction of current flow is reversed; i.e., no reaction products are lost through precipitation or the evasion of gas. Most nonpolarizing electrodes consist of two types: (a) a metal plate separated from the tissue by a solution containing a salt of that metal (e.g., a zinc plate used with a zinc-sulfate electrolyte) or (b) a metal plate coated with an insoluble salt of that metal and separated from the tissue by a solution containing the same anion (e.g., a silver electrode coated with silver chloride and used with a KCl or NaCl electrolyte.

However, not all metal-salt combinations yield suitable electrodes; the processes involved are surprisingly complex in detail so that electrode design is based to a considerable extent upon trial and error. Measuring electrodermal potentials probably presents the most difficult problem, requiring electrodes having stable bias potentials of about a millivolt or less. EEG, EKG, and EMG potentials are essentially AC phenomena so that fairly large electrode potentials can be tolerated; the main desiderata here are convenience, secure contact with the tissue to prevent movement artifacts, and low electrode resistance. The latter is accomplished by breaking or discharging the cutaneous membrane; i.e., by puncturing the skin or by rubbing in a strongly hypertonic electrode paste (one commercial EKG paste contains pumice grit which seems to facilitate this process). Skin conductance measurement requires stable electrodes with relatively low bias potentials and the ability to pass a small unidirectional current without excessive build-up of apparent electrode resistance. The use of the so-called dry electrode, in which the electrode metal is placed directly against the skin, depends upon the tissue fluids to supply the necessary electrolyte, with its composition, concentration, and amount being outside the control of the experimenter. This practice is naïve and to be avoided in any kind of careful work. Most of the electrode systems which have proven useful in psychophysiological applications are described briefly below.

The calomel electrode—This is a high quality nonpolarizing electrode widely used by neurophysiologists for recording nerve action-potentials and the like. Distilled mercury is covered by a layer of calomel (Hg_2Cl_2) which is covered in turn by a solution of KCl. Contact with the tissue is commonly made by means of a wick soaked in an isotonic NaCl solution. Detailed instructions for constructing calomel electrodes may be found in Bures *et al.* (1960) or in Whitfield (1964), and they are also available commercially.

The silver-silver chloride electrode—Perhaps the best quality electrode suitable for direct attachment to the skin, the Ag-AgCl electrode is made by electrolytically depositing a layer of silver chloride on a pure silver base and is employed with an isotonic (or slightly hypotonic) NaCl electrolyte. In one version, a helix of platinum wire is coated with silver oxide which is then reduced by baking, leaving a porous "sponge" of silver having a very large surface area. After plating with silver chloride, such electrodes may show extremely low bias potentials and excellent stability. Detailed instructions can be found in Feder (1963) and in O'Connell and Tursky (1960), and commercial versions are also available (e.g., from Beckman or Lexington Instruments).

A disadvantage of the silver-sponge type electrode is that it is somewhat fragile and difficult to clean and re-chloride in the event of drying or contamination. Although their bias potentials may be on the average somewhat higher, chlorided silver discs have the advantage of being easier to make in the first place and easier to repair when damaged. Venables and Sayer (1963) describe a technique in which a pure silver disc, set in a rubber grommet, is chlorided by being made the anode in an electrolytic bath of 0.5 per cent KCl through which a current of 0.5 milliamps is passed for one hour. These electrodes commonly show a bias potential of less than 0.1 mV, but the chloride coat is rather fragile and must be protected from injury or drying. A more durable version, developed by Ralph Miller, may be made by mounting the silver disc permanently in a plastic housing prior to plating. The finished electrode is then inserted into a collar of soft plastic tubing which projects slightly beyond the chloride surface, thus affording some protection to it. This assembly, having an outside diameter of 3/8 inch, is then filled with electrode paste and inserted into the opening of a felt corn pad mounted on the skin. The whole assembly can then be secured with surgical tape. If damaged, the electrode is easily disassembled, sanded clean, and re-plated. These electrodes should be stored in small groups, short-circuited in .07 N NaCl. Before using, it is best to check the bias potentials of various pairs, selecting that pair showing the lowest potential difference. Still another disc-type Ag-AgCl electrode, used in the NASA *Mercury* program for EKG recording, is described in detail by Day and Lippitt (1964).

The zinc-zinc sulfate electrode—This electrode is most commonly made in the form of a pure zinc disc sealed in plastic, sanded bright and clean before each use, and coated with a paste containing zinc sulfate. For electrodermal recording, the zinc sulfate electrolyte has the disadvantage that the zinc cation tends to depolarize the tissue, decreasing apparent skin resistance and affecting skin potential as well. One way to minimize this difficulty is to separate the zinc sulfate from the skin by a layer of KCl or NaCl paste or by a sponge soaked in a dilute solution of one of these chlorides. Another method is to use only one active electrode which is connected to the negative pole of the external current source; the skin being highly impermeable to the sulphate anion, the only ionic movement at the active site will be migration of cations outward from the body fluids, while depolarization at the reference site can be accomplished at the outset by puncturing the skin. In the case of skin potential recording, the active or palmar site is normally negative, attracting cations, so the zinc sulfate electrode is less satisfactory. This type of electrode typically has a somewhat higher electrode potential and electrode resistance than the best examples of the silver chloride electrode, but is considerably easier to make and to use. As a general practice one should have a number of pairs of such electrodes available and use a pair having a minimum electrode potential when immersed in physiological saline.

The lead electrode—A very simple electrode for electrodermal recording and one which is also useful for EKG and EMG work can be made from a disc of high purity lead. As with the other disc electrodes mentioned above, the metal disc with the lead wire soldered to its back side should be cemented tightly into some type of plastic housing so that only the single metal surface is exposed, surrounded by a collar of plastic. The exposed lead surface should be sanded bright before each use and may contact the skin surface through a standard KCl or NaCl electrode paste. One can usually find pairs of such simple electrodes which will maintain bias potentials of less than three millivolts in saline over a period of several hours. In electrodermal work, the single element lead electrode should be considered only for potential recordings, where the flow of current is negligible; even a few microamperes of current will soon build up a substantial amount of polarization on these electrodes, giving high electrode resistances and potentials. Whitfield (1964) describes a nonpolarizing lead-lead chloride electrode which may also have applications in electrodermal measurement.

The two-element electrode—Another type of electrode has been described (Lykken, 1959b) for use in measuring skin resistance, consisting of a small metal disc surrounded by, but electrically isolated from, an annular ring element made from the same metal. After separate lead wires have been attached, the disc and ring elements are cemented flush into a plastic housing, the face of which exposes the central metal disc, a ring of plastic, the metal ring element, and then a final outer ring of plastic. As used for skin resistance measurements, the ring elements of a pair of these electrodes are connected to the external source of current; the center disc elements are connected to a separate, high impedance voltage measuring instrument (e.g., a DC amplifier and associated strip-chart recorder). Since all the significant current flow in this arrangement is between the ring elements, electrode polarization effects are largely limited to the surfaces of these rings and to the immediately adjacent portion of the electrode paste. The potential registered between the relatively uncontaminated central discs is therefore a very accurate representation of the voltage (IR) drop through the skin. With such electrodes made of high-purity lead, and used with an ordinary saline electrolyte, one can measure skin resistance accurately but at the expense of providing an electrically isolated constant-current supply.

Other electrode considerations—Since contact with the skin is made through the electrolyte rather than by the electrode metal proper, the effective area of an electrode is determined not by the size of the metal disc but by the area of skin surface wet with electrolyte. Since apparent electrical conductance of the skin varies directly with effective area, this parameter must be held constant in SC measurement. Some electrodes are enclosed in a cup-like plastic housing, the lips of which press against the skin to contain the spread of the electrolyte. This arrangement is subject to artifacts from movement and pressure variation, however; a better method is to demarcate the effective skin area with a piece of wide surgical adhesive tape having a hole punched in its center. Then an ordinary corn pad is used between the skin and the electrode proper as described by Lykken (1959b). (I have found that the adhesive supplied on one side of the corn pads is not really sticky enough to assure a good seal to the skin and so have resorted to using the surgical tape in addition.) It would be a help if investigators would follow the practice of reporting the exact location of their active electrodes in SC measurement and specifying the apparent skin conductance *per square centimeter* of effective skin area. In measuring skin potentials, as well as in

EKG work and the like, controlling electrode area is of much less importance, except where the skin surface might become saturated with saline sweat and thus be "short circuited" over a broad expanse.

The best electrolyte for most electrodermal work will be a chemically inert, nondrying paste or cream, somewhat thinner in consistency than ordinary cold cream, and containing a 0.07 molar solution of NaCl, which will be approximately isotonic with the principal ionic constituents of surface sweat. Such a paste can be made by boiling the salt solution with a small quantity of agar (about 4 per cent), stirring the mix as it cools. A still easier method is to add sufficient water and salt to a neutral ointment base (e.g., Parke-Davis's "Unibase") to produce a mixture of suitable consistency and salt concentration. For use with zinc electrodes, zinc sulfate may be substituted for the NaCl or, better, the electrode metal can be coated with a stronger $ZnSO_4$ paste (say, 0.5 N) while the skin is coated with the usual isotonic NaCl paste. For EEG, EKG, and EMG work, minimum skin resistance is desirable so that a strong, depolarizing electrolyte is appropriate. An agar or Unibase paste containing a 3.0 N KCl solution should be a good choice (see also Day & Lippitt, 1964).

Reference electrodes should always be located in electrically inactive regions and should show minimum apparent resistance. For electrodermal recording, both inactivity and low resistance can be insured by puncturing the skin under the reference electrode using the skin-drilling technique described by Shackel (1959). If the barrier region cannot be broken by puncturing or sanding, its apparent resistance can be reduced by soaking in saturated KCl or a weak acid (e.g., vinegar) and using a large effective electrode area. Generally the best location for the active electrode in electrodermal work is on the palmar surface of the distal phalanx of the fingers, where sweat gland distribution is most dense and GSR activity is maximal. (The second phalanx, a site recommended by Edelberg & Burch (1962), has the advantage that this skin is less likely to show cuts or other damage but it also contains many fewer sweat glands.) Alternatively, the palms, the soles, or even the forehead or chest might be employed, but since individual differences in sweat gland distribution and GSR activity are so great, the finger location recommends itself wherever possible.

The proposed site should be examined, preferably under low-power magnification, for tiny cuts or abrasions which might provide a short-circuit pathway for current through the epidermis. The skin may be rubbed lightly with alcohol or ether to remove surface oils before application of the electrodes (recent soaking in strong detergents may sharply alter SC and GSR findings). One difficulty with the finger location is the necessary restriction imposed upon electrode area. Other things being equal, a larger electrode area will contact a larger and more stable population of sweat glands, minimize errors resulting from small variations in area, and also allow for a reduction in average current density when measuring SC directly (see above). One way to obtain larger areas with finger electrodes is to use separate electrodes on two or more fingers. Each finger can be tested separately against the reference as a check on possible artifacts (each active electrode should show about the same apparent SC); all of them can be tied together electrically to serve jointly as the active electrode.

Electrode technique is particularly critical in skin potential measurement. The electrodes themselves must of course have negligible (and stable) bias potentials. Moreover, as implied by the foregoing discussion of concentration and membrane potentials, the potential actually measured may be strongly affected by the salt used in the electrolyte, its concentration, and the relative permeability of the skin at the active and reference sites.

Electrodes for Shock Stimulation

The administration of electric shock stimulation through skin electrodes has been greatly illuminated by the recent work of Tursky and Watson (1964). These authors have shown that variations in apparent skin resistance, including those produced by the passage of the shock current itself, produce changes in the subjective intensity of the stimulus no matter what sort of control is applied to the physical stimulus (e.g., maintaining the shock current or voltage constant). Their solution is to employ a concentric disc electrode applied to a skin area previously treated by rubbing with a depolarizing electrode paste, which reduces skin resistance to a low and stable level. Thereafter, either constant-voltage or constant-current stimulation will produce stable subjective stimulus intensities. The Tursky and Watson method can be recommended as a standard procedure and the above reference should be consulted for details.

Instrumentation for Psychophysiological Research

Sensors or Transducers

The kymograph, with its smoked drum and its styli driven by mechanical or pneumatic linkages to the preparation, has gone to an honorable retirement along with the string galvanometer and those many giants of physiological research who somehow managed to discover so much with such primitive tools. Modern electronics has made it possible to amplify, record, and analyze electrical signals with extraordinary ease and fidelity. The first step (and frequently the weak link) in almost all current physiological measurement is to convert or *transduce* the phenomenon of interest into an electrical signal having corresponding amplitude or temporal characteristics. A *thermister* can be used as a temperature transducer because its electrical resistance varies with temperature over a wide range. A *strain gauge* is a carbon or semiconductor element whose resistance changes as a function of mechanical strain and, suitably mounted, can be used to convert pressures, positions, and movements into electrical signals. A *pH meter* uses a conductivity cell to transduce the acidity (hydrogen ion concentration) of a test solution into an electrical potential. (Technically, recorders of all kinds are transducers also, converting the amplified electrical signal back into readable or storable form, but convention reserves the term for transducers whose output is electrical.) The term *sensor* includes transducers and applies also to the measurement of phenomena which are intrinsically electrical in nature, including the electrodes and *signal conditioners* which may intervene between the preparation and the amplifier-recorder.

Amplifiers

The *power amplifier* is designed to drive whatever recording equipment is to be used —oscilloscope, tape recorder head, recording galvanometer—and normally has a high-impedance input of some 1 to 10 volts sensitivity. The *pre-amplifier* drives the power amplifier and is designed with input and amplification characteristics to match appropriate transducers. *AC-coupled pre-amplifiers* are relatively inexpensive and can combine high sensitivity with good stability but cannot handle DC levels or very low frequency signals. Until recently, stable DC pre-amplifiers of high (e.g., 1 mV) sensitivity were difficult to obtain. A common solution to the problem of designing stable DC amplifiers is to use a "chopper" input circuit; the DC signal is "chopped" by an electrical or mechanical switch and the resulting "AC" signal is fed to the primary of an input transformer from whence it passes to a conventional AC-coupled amplifier. The amplified signal is then converted back again to DC at the output. Chopper-type amplifiers have the limitation that their input impedance is normally too low for some applications (e.g., from about 5 K-ohms). Unless the input impedance of the amplifier is high relative to the impedance of the signal source, an appreciable fraction of the signal voltage will be dropped across the source impedance and, hence, not recorded. Where the signal source consists of a pair of skin electrodes (as in SR or SP recording), the pre-amp input impedance must be at least one megohm to prevent degradation of the signal.

Electrometer amplifiers are especially designed to have the very high input impedance (10^9 ohms and above) required for use with high-impedance micro-electrodes.

An important property of physiological amplifiers is the ability to reject in-phase signals or noise. Electrostatic fields in the surround commonly induce AC voltages at the electrodes or in the connecting cables, voltages which may be large in relation to the small signals one wishes to record. An analogous problem arises in attempting bioelectric recording from a subject who is also being electrically stimulated or shocked. Frequently these "noise" potentials, although large with respect to ground, may be instantaneously identical or nearly so at the active and the reference electrodes, provided neither is grounded. If neither amplifier input is grounded (i.e., "floating" inputs) or if the amplifier is of the differential or "push-pull" input type, such in-phase noise can be rejected although many times greater in amplitude than the desired signal. Useful discussions of methods of eliminating stimulus artifact and noise may be found in Becker, Peacock, Heath, and Mickle (1961) and in Guld (1960).

Recorders

Because it paints its picture with an almost inertia-less electron beam, the *oscilloscope* provides the most accurate representation of high-frequency electrical activity. Long persistence cathode-ray tubes can be used to retain the image for several seconds or the image can be photographed for permanent storage. Recording galvanometers using light-sensitive paper and mirror galvanometers that reflect an intense light beam upon the moving paper can accurately record signals up to 10,000 cps. Many channels of information can be recorded simultaneously on a single 10-inch chart, and a useful characteristic of the light-beam recorders is that one or more channels can be interlaced—i.e., one or more of the galvanometers can be allowed to write over the full chart width rather than remaining in their respective narrow tracks. Most *oscillographs* or "direct writers" draw their graphs of voltage against time by means of galvanometer-driven pens or heated styli writing on conventional or heat-sensitive paper that is driven at a constant speed beneath them. Typical oscillographs of the type used for EEG, EKG, and GSR recording may be obtained with from 1 to 12 pens, a frequency range of from DC to about 100 cps, and a suitable range of chart speeds. Older oscillographs have the disadvantage that the written wave-form is distorted as a result of the pen's being mounted on a stationary pivot and moving in an arc. Rectilinear coordinates are provided by systems using a heated stylus that wipes the paper as it is pulled over a straight-edge and also by modern pen-writers employing special linkages between the pens and the pen-motors. The simplest oscillographs are *recording milliammeters* in which the pen-motor is simply a robust one-milliampere meter movement; these instruments commonly have a fairly wide chart and a low frequency capability but are quite adequate for, say, GSR recording.

The *potentiometric recorder* employs a servomechanism which automatically adjusts an internal potential to match the applied signal until zero input current flows. A pen is simultaneously driven across the recording paper to a position corresponding to the setting of this internal voltage. Like the recording milliammeter, the potentiometric recorder is a relatively low-speed device, requiring from about 0.1 to as much as 2 seconds for full-scale excursion of the pen. However, the potentiometric recorder has very high input impedance (nearly infinite at balance), compared to about 1,000 ohms for the recording milli-ammeter, and a high enough sensitivity (often as high as 1 mV full-scale) to be used without additional amplification. The *X-Y recorder* uses a single rectangle of stationary chart paper over which the pen is moved both vertically and horizontally by two independent servo-systems. This instrument is frequently used as a computer-output device.

An important recent improvement in psychophysiological instrumentation is the use of magnetic-tape data recording. Most commonly, the input signal—which may vary in frequency from DC to several thousand cps—is amplified and then used to frequency-modulate a carrier signal that is recorded on the tape. During playback, this FM signal is de-modulated to reproduce the original input exactly. As many as seven or more separate channels may be recorded on a single tape, usually with an audio channel also provided, at a recorder cost of about $1,000 per channel complete with input and output electronics. Thus equipped to store and reproduce the "raw data" in its original form, the experimenter is able after the experiment to review the data at his leisure, using, e.g., an oscilloscope; to make written records of only those aspects which prove to be of interest by feeding the tape output to an oscillograph; to make convenient use of electronic methods of data analysis; and to recapture aspects of the data which might have been lost with more limited methods of on-line recording. When the recorder is equipped with both low and high tape speeds, high-frequency signals can be slowed down for oscillograph recording—by recording at high speed and played back at low speed—or, conversely, slow or intermittent phenomena can be speeded up.

A resumé of the more important transducer and amplifier requirements for some common psychophysiological dependent variables is provided in Table 2.

More detailed treatment of psychophysiological instrumentation can be found in Brown and Saucer (1958), Bures *et al.* (1960), and Donaldson (1958). An excellent primer of basic electrical theory and circuits is Cornsweet (1963). More advanced general texts include Malmstadt and Enke (1962) and Prensky (1963).

Interpreting Psychophysiological Response Data

The Problem

The most common—although not the best—method for monitoring GSR activity is to make continuous recordings of skin resistance (SR). Wave-like decreases in the SR curve are the skin-resistance GSRs. But we could also choose to measure skin conductance (SC) instead, either directly or by taking the reciprocals of SR measurements, and we could express the GSR in units of *conductance change*. Since this transformation is nonlinear, one choice of unit may give us different results than another. Suppose, for example, that a drug supposed to produce increased arousal yields tonic SC values of 1, 1, 10, and 10 micromhos in four experimental subjects, while a placebo yields SC values of 5, 5, 5, and 5 micromhos in four control subjects. The mean SC for the drug group (5.5 micromhos) is higher than for the controls, suggesting that the drug has indeed produced a stimulating effect. But expressed in SR units, these results are reversed; the experimental group shows SRs of 10^6, 10^6, 10^5, and 10^5 ohms, i.e., a mean of 550,000 ohms, while the control group has a mean SR of 200,000 ohms. Although conductance and resistance are reciprocals of one another, the experimental group has both a higher mean SR *and* a higher mean SC!

TABLE 2

INSTRUMENTATION REQUIREMENTS FOR RECORDING VARIOUS AUTONOMIC PHENOMENA

		Amplifier Requirements		
Phenomenon	Transducer or Signal Conditioner	Frequency Range	Input Impedance	Full-Scale Sensitivity
EEG	Electrodes on scalp	DC to 250 cps	100 K or higher	10–100 microvolts
EMG	Electrodes on or inserted into skin	10 cps to 5 K cps	1 Megohm or higher	5–100 microvolts
Averaged Evoked Potentials	As for EEG	As for EEG		
EKG	Electrodes on arms, leg, and chest	.05–100 cps	1 Megohm or higher	10 microvolts to 10 mV
Heart Rate (HR)	As for EKG	Special: a cardiotachometer		
GSR, Skin Resistance (SR)	Palmar electrodes with external constant-*current* source. Calibrated zero suppression	DC to 100 cps although DC to 10 cps adequate for most purposes	1 Megohm or higher	50 mV to 10 V
GSR, Skin Conductance (SC)	Palmar electrodes with external constant-*voltage* source. Calibrated zero suppression		5 K-ohms	250 microvolts to 5 mV
SPR, Skin Potential (SP)	Palmar electrode with reference on arm. Electrode temperature compensation. Calibrated zero suppression		1 Megohm or higher	1–100 mV
Blood Pressure (BP): Continuous absolute BP	Pressure transducer with: —vein cannula;	DC to 100 cps	Carrier-type pre-amplifier for pressure gauge	
Intermittent absolute BP	—automatically inflating arm cuff;			
Continuous relative BP	—arm cuff at below systolic pressure.			
Skin or Core Temp.	Thermister probe with associated bridge circuitry	Amplifier generally not required		
Eye Movements: Electro-Oculography	EEG electrodes either side of orbit	As for EEG		
Infrared Photocell	Commercial goggles with light source and pre-amplifier	As for EKG		
Pupil Size	Cinematography	None		
	Infrared reflection	Commercial instrument (expensive)		

This particular problem will arise only if the groups differ for some reason in their variances, but it is clear that nonlinear transformations of scale can play havoc with group comparisons and summary statistics of many kinds; the product-moment correlation, for example, may be considerably changed if one variable is transformed to its reciprocal. Note, too, that reciprocal units are naturally available for other response systems as well; one can express the rhythm of the heart in terms of beats-per-minute or, equally logically, in terms of the period or average inter-beat interval.

A different kind of problem has to do with the relationship of the poststimulus change in some response measure to the tonic or prestimulus value. For example, Smith and Jones show resistance GSRs of 10 K-ohms and 1 K-ohm, respectively, to the same shock stimulus; which subject has been more disturbed by the shock, which has shown the larger *psychological* reaction? With no other evidence available, we should have to say "Smith," but suppose that his prestimulus SR was 1,000 K-ohms, while Jones's was only 100 K-ohms, and suppose also that we know from other evidence that resistance GSRs have a high positive correlation with prestimulus SRs (as they almost always do). Then, clearly, we must assume that Smith's response would have been smaller had the stimulus been administered when his SR was as low as Jones's. One obvious solution might be to use the known regression of GSR on SR to *correct* Smith's GSR value; that is, we could partial-out the effect of SR so that the resulting transformed GSRs could be compared in the same way that we could compare the raw scores if all subjects happened to show that same SR at the moment of stimulation. This, in fact, is the principle of Lacey's *autonomic lability score* (Lacey, 1956) which will be discussed below.

Note, however, that it is not at all clear that one should always *want* to remove all correlation between prestimulus values and change or response scores. It may be, for example, that Smith, with his high SR, was relaxed and rather sleepy when the shock was administered, while Jones was alert and "ready for it"; it seems likely that in this case Smith might really have been more disturbed by the sudden shock, that it actually felt stronger to him than it did to Jones, and that Smith's GSR was therefore validly larger than Jones's. If the prestimulus value has some meaning concerning the physiological and psychological state of the subject at that moment (and we do usually interpret it so), then some *valid* relationship between this value and the subsequent response is to be expected; this is after all just another way of stating the usual formula that behavior is some joint function of the stimulus *and* the state of the organism at that time. If one rushes to transform away *all* correlation between prestimulus and change scores, assuming it to be some sort of statistical artifact, one may distort the proper psychological interpretation of one's data.

Some Relevant Considerations

One can distinguish some four stages in the causal sequence underlying an observed psychophysiological response: (A) An initial central event or psychological process (e.g., the perception and analysis of the stimulus, identifying it as intense or threatening or painful), followed by (B) the central initiation of a response to the stimulus (subsequent to the perceptual process itself, e.g., reticular arousal, central sympathetic discharge, initiation of activity in the sudomotor pathways to the palms); this central physiological reaction leads to (C) a peripheral physiological change at the site of our electrodes or other transducer (e.g., increased heart rate, desynchronization of cortical dendritic potentials, increased palmar sweating), some aspect of which produces (D) the observed change in the physical variable which we are actually recording (changing electrical potentials between arm and arm or between two points on the scalp, a change in current flowing through the palmar skin). As we shall see, there are times when one might wish to talk about either *A* or *B* or *C*—e.g., about how strong the subject perceived the stimulus to be, about how disturbed or aroused he was by it, or about how much faster it caused his heart to beat—but in any case one has only the observed value, *D,* upon which to base one's inference about *A, B,* and *C.*

Now the relationship between *D,* the observed datum, and *C,* the local physiological change, in this example will depend on the characteristics of the transducer and recording system used. Thus, if *C* is "a 10 per cent increase in the number of active sweat glands per unit area of palmar skin," then *D* might be a change in conductance of from 1.0 to 1.1 or 0.1 micromhos. But if our measuring circuit gives us readings of resistance instead, then *D* would in this case be a resistance change of from 1,000 to 909 or 91 K-ohms. Now there is fairly good reason to think that the main effect of sudomotor innervation really is to increase the density of active sweat glands which would amount to adding more conduction paths in parallel to those already present. In this event, conductance would be the logical unit to employ since it would be linearly related to the density of active glands. Moreover, if this model of the peripheral process, *C,* is approximately correct, increments in SC (the conductance GSR) would not in general be correlated with prestimulus values (since adding more conductors in parallel produces the same increase in conductance no matter how many are already present), whereas in this same situation resistance GSRs would be strongly correlated with the prestimulus SR! (For example, the same 0.1 micromho conductance GSR would give resistance GSRs of 91, 24, 4, and 1 K-ohms, respectively, as the prestimulus SR varies from 1,000 to 500 to 200 to 100 K-ohms.) Here would be an example of a correlation between prestimulus and change scores which *is* entirely an artifact of the choice of unit; given resistance units, the relation of transducer to peripheral physiology forces such a correlation quite apart from any valid relation there may be between the state of the subject and the way in which he responds to stimulation. This kind of correlation is entirely spurious for the psychologist's (or physiologist's) purposes and should (and can) be eliminated by, in this case, using the proper units in the first place.

The relationship between *C,* the local change, and *B,* the central physiological response, in this example will depend upon the current state of the local effector "organ" or mechanism and, hence, upon its recent history or prestimulus activity. Floor or ceiling effects may enter in here; e.g., if most of the sweat glands are already active, a given sudomotor impulse will not yield as great a change in *C* (or in *D*) as it otherwise would. Homeostatic or negative feedback influences may also complicate the picture. The electrodermal mechanism seems to be unique in its lack of any apparent peripheral homeostatic control; there seems to be no mechanism to monitor the rate of palmar sweating and adjust sudomotor outflow so as to maintain some stable intermediate rate. But the heart is of course under strong homeostatic restraint so that, as Lacey (1956) has argued, the same cardio-accelerating stimulation will be opposed by greater vagal inhibition when heart rate and blood pressure are already high and so will yield a smaller acceleration than it would had the previous heart rate been slower.

The local response, *C,* may also vary with respect to its source of excitation, *B,* due to fatigue of the effector mechanism or changes in its reactivity related to nutritional factors and the like. In the case of the EEG, a given increment in reticular arousal, *B,* might produce an increase in alpha amplitude, *C,* if the subject is drowsy, or a decrease in alpha amplitude if the subject is already wide awake. Thus, even if our observed variable, *D,* is a faithful, linear measure of the local process, *C,* we cannot be guaranteed that *D* will measure *B* with equal fidelity. Sometimes our interest is in *C* specifically; we want to know the heart rate, the amount of palmar sweating, the alpha amplitude. But in other cases we are concerned with *B* instead, and we require that our observations tell us something about the "degree of sympathetic arousal" or the "amount of reticular activation"; if this is the kind of question one chooses to ask, then one must be concerned not only about the relation of *D* to *C* but also about the relation of *C* to *B*. That is, the farther back in the causal sequence is the variable we wish to assess, then the more nuisance factors there may be to complicate and distort the relationship between that variable and the end effect which we can actually observe.

Finally, the relation between the perceptual process, *A*, and the central response, *B*, which it initiates must be considered. For present purposes, I have included under *A* the entire process of evaluation of the stimulus situation; after *A* has been completed, the subject has assigned whatever meaning he can to the stimulus and commands have been initiated for appropriate changes in arousal, emotional reactions, and the like. But again we know that there can be both inter-subjective and intra-subjective variability in the response to such "commands." An exhausted subject may identify a new stimulus as "an emergency," calling for increased activation—just as he would at any other time—and yet be unable to muster the degree of central arousal that he normally would show. We know that stimuli can be identified as "painful" and even ordered for degree of painfulness by subjects, who, for some reason, are not experiencing the usual "distress" concomitant of pain; in such cases one would speak of a disruption of the expected relation of *B* to *A*. In an experiment concerned with GSR conditioning in the psychopathic personality (Lykken, 1957), a few psychopaths who seemed to have pathologically little susceptibility to normal anxiety gave negligible GSRs to signals which had been repeatedly paired with a painful electric shock. It was assumed that these subjects were perfectly aware of the CS-shock contingency but that they "didn't much care"; perceiving the CS and realizing that it meant shock was to follow [A], failed in these individuals to initiate the expected central and peripheral pattern of emotional arousal [B]. A few other, apparently neurotic, subjects gave almost as little GSR to the CS, and other evidence was found which gave some support for the hypothesis that these individuals might actually not have been fully "aware" of the CS-shock contingency. Their tonic conductance levels were uniquely depressed, suggesting that they might have reacted to the general stress of the situation by a kind of defensive "turning out the lights" so that the rather similar response observation, *D*, was in their case tentatively attributed to a peculiarity at the level of perception, state *A*, rather than to an abnormality in the relation of *B* to *A*.

The psychologist will be interested in events at level *A*, of course, frequently in events at level *B*, and much less frequently in events at level *C* (he may have an intrinsic interest in the rate of heartbeat, for example, because the proprioceptive feedback from a pounding heart may have important psychological stimulus effects, but *qua* psychologist his usual concern is with the central events for which he is using heart rate as an indicant). There is interest for the physiologist in events at levels *B* and *C* and perhaps to some extent at level *A* as well. The relation of *D* to *C* represents mainly a measurement problem, of little general scientific interest but having great methodological significance. These problems are sometimes negligible as in the case of heart rate again where the "local" effector mechanism is clearly specifiable and where modern techniques permit us to be confident that, e.g., Smith's and Jones's hearts are in fact both beating at 70 per minute if the cardiotachometer reads "70" in both instances. At the other extreme, the local mechanism for electrodermal phenomena is still not well understood, and it is certain that a variety of extraneous factors can exert considerable effect upon our observations [*D*]. Thus, the observed value of SC is affected by the chemistry and concentration of the electrolyte, the current density, the location of the electrode, the thickness and hydration of the skin, racial differences in skin characteristics, hormonal effects relating to the menstrual cycle, and so on, and all such factors would normally be regarded as "noise" in one's measurements.

Evaluating Measures of Tonic Level

Most of the response systems presently under consideration are alike in that one can distinguish a *tonic* level of activity, determined by the subject's general physiological status, his current level of arousal, the average excitatory value of the environmental situation, and the like, on which may be superimposed *phasic* fluctuations elicited by specific stimuli. Both kinds of measures involve special problems of interpretation. In considering these problems in their turn, we shall use skin conductance—the tonic SC level and the phasic GSR—as a fairly typical response system for purposes of illustration.

The Choice of the Best Physical Unit of Measurement

The first step is to choose among alternative physical units in which to express the observations to be made. There is adequate evidence that skin conductance increases with increasing sudomotor activity over at least most of the range. Although we do not yet know the form of this increasing monotonic function, we can at least be confident that it will be somewhat simpler than that obtained by expressing our measurements in resistance units. For similar reasons we would choose heart *rate* in preference to heart *period* on the grounds that the former will be more simply related to cardioaccelerator excitation.

Correction for Individual Differences in Range

We cannot expect the effector organ to exhibit the same absolute level of activity in all individuals for the same level of central activity. In their study of cardiac activity in infants, Bridger and Reiser (1959) observed "that babies in the same activity state—from profound sleep to violent crying—may have different heart rate levels, and that babies with the same heart rate levels may be in different states of excitability" (p. 274). Individual differences in the range of SC values are probably still greater. Where one subject's SC ranges from 1 micromho during sleep to 5 micromhos in high excitement, we may find another subject showing SC values of 5 and 20 micromhos under the same conditions of measurement.

Even with no sudomotor innervation, the skin displays a certain minimum conductance, $SC_{i(min)}$, which will vary among individuals in relation to local anatomical and physiological peculiarities. Similarly, the maximum conductance $SC_{i(max)}$, produced under the condition of maximal central activation, will vary from person to person due to characteristics of local effector reactivity. More generally, it seems reasonable to say that neither the minimum nor the maximum absolute level of an autonomic response system (measured under conditions of zero or maximum activation, respectively, of the central process which controls this system) will normally be correlated with the properties of this central process nor with any other variable of direct psychological interest.

Therefore, we can say that the tonic level, T_{ij}, observed in individual i under stimulus condition j, is the sum of that individual's minimum tonic level, $T_{i(min)}$, plus a component of increased activity, $\hat{T}_{ij}$, due to his reaction to the stimulus situation:

$$T_{ij} = \hat{T}_{ij} + T_{i(min)} \quad (1)$$

Now this increase in tonic level above the physiological minimum results from the reaction of the local effector to some central process, ψ; e.g., ψ might be a measure of central arousal. If we let ρ_i represent the "activity potential" of the local effector for individual *i*, then we could say that the measured increase in tonic level above the physiological minimum equals the product of ρ_i, the reactivity of the local effector, times some function of the relevant central state of individual *i* in situation *j*:

$$\hat{T}_{ij} = \rho_i f(\psi_{ij}) \quad (2)$$

What we are working toward is a means of estimating $\phi_{ij} = f(\psi_{ij})$ from the measurements which can actually be observed. We shall arbitrarily assume that $f(\psi_{ij})$ varies from zero to 1.00 as ψ_{ij} varies from minimum to maximum. Then, for example,

$$T_{i(max)} = \rho_i f(\psi_{i(max)}) + T_{i(min)} \quad (3)$$

and, therefore,

$$\rho_i = T_{i(max)} - T_{i(min)}. \quad (4)$$

If $\phi_{ij} = f(\psi_{ij})$, then $\hat{T}_{ij} = \rho_i \phi_{ij}$ and $T_{ij} = \rho_i \phi_{ij} + T_{i(min)}$. Solving this last expression for ϕ_{ij} and substituting for ρ_i its equivalent from Equation 4, we get, finally:

$$\phi_{ij} = \frac{T_{ij} - T_{i(min)}}{T_{i(max)} - T_{i(min)}}. \quad (5)$$

This suggests that, after choosing what seems to be the most rational physical unit in which to express the tonic level of a response system, the next step should be to convert one's absolute measurement, T_{ij}, into the corrected index, ϕ_{ij}, from which the influence of individual minima and maxima has been removed, i.e., into a unit representing one's best available estimate of $f(\psi_{ij})$. This index, ϕ_{ij}, which varies between 0 and +1.00, expresses the tonic level produced in person *i* by stimulus situation *j* as a proportion of the maximum increment over *his* minimum tonic level of which *this* individual is capable.

To illustrate, suppose that Jones and Smith show tonic SC values of 10 and 7 micromhos, respectively, in an experimental situation, X, and assume that we know Jones's minimum and maximum SCs to be 5 and 20 micromhos compared to 1 and 10 micromhos for Smith. We compute corrected indices according to the formula

$$\phi_{ix} = \frac{SC_{ix} - SC_{i(min)}}{SC_{i(max)} - SC_{i(min)}}. \quad (6)$$

For Smith,

$$\phi_{sx} = (7 - 1) / (10 - 1) = 0.67.$$

For Jones,

$$\phi_{jx} = (10 - 5) / (20 - 5) = 0.33.$$

Thus, although Jones's absolute conductance level was higher than Smith's, we must conclude that in fact our stimulus condition produced a relatively larger tonic level in Smith. Knowing that the central process, ψ, which controls intra-individual variation in SC is some component of psychological *arousal* or of CNS *activation*, we can further conclude that Smith's arousal or activation in our situation X was greater than Jones's.

It should be possible to devise relatively simple and feasible means for estimating the limits of the tonic range. One or two inhalations of CO_2 may elevate heart rate to a near approximation of the individual's normal upper limit; a brief standardized exercise might do the same for blood pressure. In the case of skin conductance, local sweat gland activity can be eliminated by iontophoretic application of atropine and maximized by application of pilocarpine. It is possible, but requires experimental proof, that the low and high SC values thus produced might be fair estimates of the individual's normal range of variation.

Even much cruder estimates can be an improvement over the use of uncorrected absolute values. Rose (1964) correlated the two-flash threshold, which varies inversely with arousal, with tonic SC in four separate samples. He also "corrected" his SC values by the method described above using as his estimate of minimum SC simply the lowest SC value shown by the subject in the session, while to estimate maximum SC he used the highest value reached while the subject was blowing up a balloon to bursting. As shown in Table 3, these "corrected" SC values correlated more highly with the two-flash threshold than did the raw SC scores in all four samples. If the two variables are indeed both measures of arousal, then their unshared variance must be largely due to their combined errors of measurement; correcting the SC scores even by means of such crude estimates of the individual SC ranges decreased the total unshared or "error" variance by some 26 per cent on the average (and increased their common variance by an average of 76 per cent).

Determining the Relationship Between the Corrected Index of Tonic Level, ϕ, and the Underlying Variable of Interest, ψ

The above procedure for deriving the corrected index, ϕ, from the raw measurements of tonic level is designed to eliminate the effects of individual differences in peripheral effector characteristics (which are usually irrelevant) and thus to eliminate what may be a sizable component of error-of-measurement in the estimation of the underlying variable of interest, ψ. Uncertainty will still remain, however, as to the exact form of the relationship between this derived index and the underlying variable; i.e., the form of the function $\phi = f(\psi)$ remains unknown. In the case of skin conductance, a considerable accumulation of imperfect (and imperfectly analyzed!) data provides reasonable empirical support for the conclusion that the function $\phi_{sc} = f(\psi)$, where ψ represents some aspect of arousal or CNS activation, is at least monotonic-increasing and probably negatively accelerated. The curve in Figure 14, based upon the hypothetical data of Table 4, illustrates a possible finding—that ϕ_{sc} is a growth function of ψ, viz., $\phi_{sc} = 1 - e^{-3\psi}$.

One possible method of determining the relationship of ϕ to ψ, which could be used when one has measures of two (or more) variables both of which are believed to be related to the same underlying variable, is illustrated below. Suppose that ϕ_{sc} is some function of activation, $\phi_{sc} = f(\psi)$, and that the two-flash threshold is some other func-

TABLE 3

Improvement Obtained in the Correlation Between Two Putative Measures of Arousal, Tonic Skin Conductance (SC) and the Two-Flash Threshold (TFT), When One Variable (SC) is Corrected for Individual Differences in Range (Yielding the Index ϕ_{SC}) by the Method Described in the Text (Data from Rose, 1964)

Sample	*N*	Correlation between TFT and: SC	ϕ_{sc}	Reduction in "Error" Variance
1. Normal males	22	−.54	−.76	.29 (41%)
2. Normals, both sexes	36	−.41	−.53	.11 (13%)
3. Psychiatric patients, males	20	−.61	−.70	.12 (19%)
4. Psychiatric patients, females	20	−.50	−.72	.27 (36%)

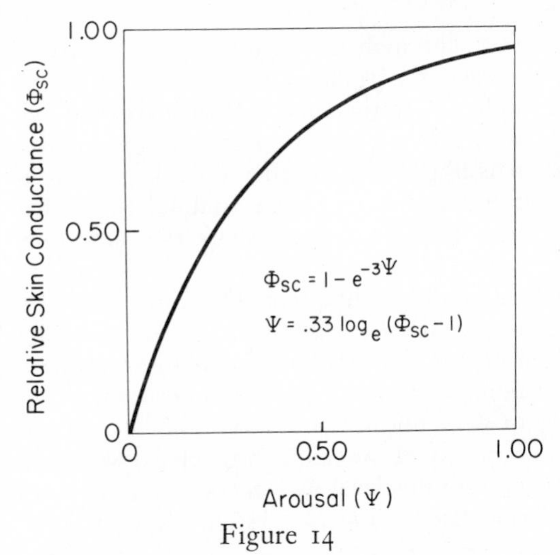

Figure 14

Figure 14. Growth function relating ϕ_{SC} to ψ, based on hypothetical data in Table 4 (see text).

TABLE 4

HYPOTHETICAL VALUES OF ACTIVATION (ψ) CORRESPONDING TO VARIOUS CORRECTED SC LEVELS (ϕ_{SC}), ON THE ASSUMPTION THAT THE CURVE-FITTING PROCEDURE DESCRIBED IN THE TEXT MIGHT SHOW THAT ϕ_{SC} IS A GROWTH FUNCTION OF ψ, $\phi_{SC} = 1 - e^{-\alpha\psi}$, WITH $\alpha = 3$.

$\phi_{SC} = 1 - e^{-3\psi}$	ψ (Arousal)
0	0
0.1	0.035
0.2	0.078
0.3	0.119
0.4	0.170
0.5	0.231
0.6	0.305
0.7	0.401
0.8	0.536
0.9	0.768
0.95	0.999
1.00	

tion of activation, $\phi_{tft} = g(\psi)$. (Note: the TFT is first corrected for range differences as are the raw SC scores.) Then the linear correlation between the two *inverse functions*, $f^{-1}(\psi)$ and $g^{-1}(\psi)$, will approach unity, limited only by errors of measurement of the two variables. Although both functions (with their inverses) are unknown, one could specify a small number of families of functions which would be likely to include both $f(\psi)$ and $g(\psi)$ to a reasonable approximation: e.g., $\alpha\psi$, $\log \alpha\psi$, etc. Assume that we stipulate six such functions for trial. We then obtain a representative sample of, say, 1,000 people who can be assumed to show a reasonable range of arousal at the time of measurement and obtain from them measures of ϕ_{sc} and ϕ_{tft} (by using corrected values of both variables we are then entitled to study their relationship across individuals in a R-type rather than a P-type design). We now require our computer to obtain the inverse of each of the six functions of both variables and to compute all 36 correlations. For example, the inverse of $\phi_{sc} = 1 - e^{-\alpha\psi}$ is

$$\psi_{sc} = \frac{1}{\alpha} \log_e(\phi_{sc} - 1);$$

the inverse of $\phi_{tft} = \beta/\psi$ is $\psi_{tft} = \beta/\phi_{tft}$. If these two functions, respectively, provide a good approximation of the true relationship between ϕ_{sc} and ψ and between ϕ_{tft} and ψ, then the correlation between $[\frac{1}{\alpha} \log_e (\phi_{sc} - 1)]$ and $[\beta/\phi_{tft}]$ should be larger than that between the inverses of any other pair of functions that we test.

Until some such method of analysis is actually applied to real data, we shall have no adequate empirical grounds for specifying the function relating the corrected measures of tonic level to the underlying variable of interest. However, the simple step of correcting the raw measures for individual differences in range will generally provide a large improvement in the accuracy and utility of measures of tonic level (and, one might add, this step alone is a considerable improvement over most current practice). Moreover, there *is* some evidence and considerable rational justification for assuming that the function relating tonic level to central state must be at least negatively accelerated and therefore likely to be better approximated by a logarithmic or a growth function than by a linear one. Indeed, although the data of Table 4 are wholly hypothetical, it would be surprising if they do not give a better approximation to the real state of affairs than the linear function implicity assumed when one uses ϕ alone. In analyzing an experiment in which tonic SC level figures as a dependent variable, I should be inclined to use ϕ_{sc} first and then to repeat the analysis using estimates of ψ from Table 4 $[\psi = .33 \log_e(\phi - 1)]$ to see whether this transformation did not help to clarify my findings.

Evaluating Measures of Phasic Change

One must first of all be careful to distinguish phasic changes, those wave-like fluctuations in the output of a response system which are generally elicited by specific stimuli, from more lasting changes in tonic level, such as may occur when the overall stimulus situation changes. Thus, the start of an experimental task may elicit a GSR or phasic increase in SC that returns within seconds to a relatively stable level which itself may be higher than the previous or resting level, reflecting the higher level of arousal necessitated by the demands of the task. Similarly, the termination of that task period might elicit another GSR, again a phasic increase in SC which, however, returns this time to a level lower than before; i.e., here the phasic *increase* is accompanied or followed by a *decrease* in the tonic level. Increments in tonic SC have a relatively long latency, persist far longer, and seem to represent a generalized response of the organism to the total situation, while the GSR has a shorter latency, a much faster rate of recovery, and is typically identifiable as a differentiated response to a specific stimulus. These contrasts are reminiscent of the differences Sharpless and Jasper (1956) observed between cortical arousal effects of midbrain reticular stimulation and the more phasic and specific effects of stimulation of the rostral thalamic reticular regions. However, although the significance of these two kinds of peripheral changes seems to be different, in the sense that they appear to be related to somewhat different central events, it is likely that the efferent linkage and effector mechanism is the same for both—that both response systems share the same final common path.

On this assumption, the GSR is an increase in ϕ_{sc}, $\Delta\phi_{sc} = \phi_1 - \phi_0$, resulting from an increment in sudomotor innervation, $\Delta\psi = \psi_1 - \psi_0$. If the relation of ϕ_{sc} to ψ is linear, then $\Delta\phi_{sc}$ will be a linear function of $\Delta\psi$ and uncorrelated with the prestimulus level ϕ_0 (except insofar as $\Delta\psi$ is correlated with ψ). But, if $\phi_{sc} = f(\psi) = 1 - e^{-\alpha\psi}$, then:

$$\Delta\phi = (1 - e^{-\alpha\psi_1}) - (1 - e^{-\alpha\psi_0}) = e^{-\alpha\psi_0} - e^{-\alpha\psi_1}. \tag{7}$$

Therefore,

$$\Delta\phi = e^{-\alpha\psi_0}(1 - e^{-\alpha(\Delta\psi)}) \tag{8}$$

or

$$\Delta\phi = (1 - \phi_0)(1 - e^{-\alpha(\Delta\psi)}). \tag{9}$$

Thus, if ϕ is a growth function of ψ, then $\Delta\phi$ will be a growth function of $\Delta\psi$ (with ψ_0 or ϕ_0 held constant) and an inverse linear function of ϕ_0 (with the increment, $\Delta\psi$, held constant). In this event, one's best estimate of underlying change, $\Delta\psi$, would be the index (obtained by solving equation 9 for $\Delta\psi$),

$$\hat{\Delta}\psi = \frac{1}{\alpha}[\log_e(1-\phi_0) - \log_e(1 - \phi_0 - \Delta\phi>], \tag{10}$$

which would be uncorrelated with prestimulus level, ϕ_0. This index could be computed more easily directly from raw conductance measurements thus:

$$\hat{\Delta}\psi = \frac{1}{\alpha}[\log_e(SC_{mx} - SC_0) - \log_e(SC_{mx} - SC_1)], \tag{11}$$

where SC_{mx} is the upper limit of that individual's conductance range, SC_0 is the prestimulus tonic level, SC_1 is the peak poststimulus conductance ($SC_1 = SC_0 + \Delta SC$), and α is the parameter of the function $\phi_{sc} = 1 - e^{-\alpha\psi}$. That is to say that, *if* the relationship of the corrected tonic level, ϕ, to the underlying process, ψ, is nonlinear (e.g., a growth function), then the change in the tonic level brought about by a given change in the underlying process will necessarily be dependent upon the level preceding the change. A given increment, $\Delta\phi$, from a high prestimulus level will not indicate the same change in the underlying process that is indicated by that same increment from a low prestimulus level. If one knows the function $\phi = f(\psi)$, then one can compute from $\Delta\phi$ an index which will provide an estimate of the underlying process change, $\Delta\psi$, which *is* independent of prestimulus level (e.g., by using Equation 11 in the case of a growth function, provided one has not only a measure of the increment, $\Delta\phi$, but also a measure of the prestimulus value, ϕ_0).

However, since the relation of ϕ to ψ has yet to be determined empirically, it would be academic to develop such possible correction methods any further here. Although there are many published studies reporting correlations between, e.g., GSRs and prestimulus levels, it should be noted that such findings do not provide the data we require. The correlation across subjects between raw measures of tonic level and GSR (or change in tonic level), uncorrected for individual differences in range, is so contaminated by various extraneous influences as to be largely meaningless as a basis for inferring $\Delta\phi = f(\phi_0)$. Indeed, the reported values vary greatly from one experimental situation to another, as the present analysis would lead one to expect. Even if the range correction is employed, the observed relationship between $\Delta\phi$ and ϕ_0 will be ambiguous, since it will confound the effects of a nonlinear relation of ϕ to ψ (which effects one will want to remove) with the effects of any possible relation of $\Delta\psi$ to ψ_0 (which *are* psychologically relevant and the elimination of which would not ordinarily be desirable). That is, the same stimulus may be perceived differently or produce a different central reaction at a low level of prestimulus arousal, ψ_0, than at a high level, and one would normally want one's peripheral change measure, $\Delta\phi$, to reflect that real and psychologically meaningful difference.

For immediate practical purposes, the present analysis indicates that raw conductance GSRs should be expressed as changes in the individual's corrected index of tonic SC level, which can be done by means of the formula

$$\Delta\phi_{ij} = \frac{\Delta SC_{ij}}{SC_{i(max)} - SC_{i(min)}}. \quad (12)$$

Since it is free of the "noisy" influence of individual differences in range of SC, this index must provide a more accurate estimate of $\Delta\psi$ than any algebraic function of ΔSC_{ij} alone. Pending determination of the true relation of ϕ to ψ, one must keep in mind that an unknown portion of any observed correlation between $\Delta\phi$ and ϕ may be due to nonlinearity in that relationship and hence artifactual. If one is willing to gamble that $\phi = 1 - e^{-3\psi}$ is not far from correct, then the index given in Equation 11 may be used.

The Interpretation of Changes in Tonic Level

Consider the following experimental problem which is typical of many possible applications of psychophysiological techniques in the broad domain of personality research. There is some evidence that children with specific reading problems perform less well than do normal children in discriminating letter-like forms. Some authorities will infer from this that the reading disability is a consequence of a primary defect in perception—that these children actually see the figures differently or fail to perceive those attributes which are essential for discriminating similar forms from one another. An alternative view is that the reading disability is secondary to a conditioned anxiety reaction which has been developed in the child by unfortunate or inept handling and which manifests itself in all reading and test-like situations. This anxiety interferes with both learning and performance in school and, by easy generalization, to the school-like circumstances of the laboratory. The latter hypothesis suggests that children with reading problems should be more anxious—and hence more aroused or excited—in the laboratory than control children, matched for age, sex, IQ, and the like, both in a task involving discrimination of letter-like forms and *a fortiori* in a task involving discrimination of actual letters. The perceptual-defect hypothesis, on the other hand, suggests that, while the problem-readers may indeed show higher autonomic arousal while working with letters (by this time many of them *will* have become emotional about letters, whatever the etiology of their problem), any increase in arousal, due to generalization, when they are working with the novel letter-like forms will not be great enough to explain their discrimination defect. (This is not a very good experiment since the most probable outcome, slightly greater arousal in the problem-reader group, will not permit a clear conclusion. It is not, however, in this respect atypical of contemporary psychological research!)

Suppose, then, that the average reading-disabled child and his normal control mate displayed corrected tonic SC levels as shown in Table 5. As the anxiety-psychogenesis hypothesis predicted, the problem readers show substantially higher arousal than the normals during the letter-discrimination task and somewhat higher arousal during the task-involving forms. However, we note that they were also much more aroused during the "rest" or prestress period at the start of the experiment. "Therefore," argues the exponent of the perceptual-defect view, "one surely cannot attribute all of the arousal shown by these children during the letter task to the effects of that task; the increment in arousal due to the letter task itself, estimated by the difference between the prestress level and the level during the task, is actually the same for both groups. Therefore, one must conclude that problem-readers are no more frightened by letter tasks than normal readers."

"The fact remains," rejoins the defender of the anxiety hypothesis, "that the problem-readers were much more aroused—and the circumstances here permit us to attribute this arousal to anxiety—than were the normals. The prestress differences indicate either that they are generally more anxiety reactive than normals or else that the labo-

TABLE 5

RESULTS OF HYPOTHETICAL EXPERIMENT DESCRIBED IN TEXT. READING-DISABLED CHILDREN SHOW MUCH HIGHER TONIC SC LEVELS THAN NORMALS IN DISCRIMINATION TASK WITH LETTERS, SOMEWHAT HIGHER IN TASK INVOLVING LETTER-LIKE FORMS. BUT IN TERMS OF THE INCREMENT IN TONIC LEVEL OVER PRESTRESS LEVELS, THE TWO GROUPS WERE IDENTICAL ON THE LETTER TASK AND THE PROBLEM READERS ACTUALLY SHOWED LESS RELATIVE AROUSAL THAN THE NORMALS ON THE FORMS TASK. (THE VALUES IN PARENTHESES ARE ESTIMATES OF AROUSAL LEVEL, ψ, BASED ON THE ASSUMPTION THAT $\phi = 1 - e^{-3\psi}$.)

	Corrected Tonic Levels, ϕ			Change in Tonic Level, $\Delta\phi$		
	Prestress ϕ_0	Letters ϕ_1	Forms ϕ_2	Letters $\phi_1 - \phi_0$	Forms $\phi_2 - \phi_0$	Forms $\phi_2 - \phi_1$
Reading-disabled	.70(.40)	.80(.54)	.60(.31)	.10(.14)	−.10(−.09)	−.20(−.23)
Normals	.40(.17)	.50(.23)	.50(.23)	.10(.06)	.10(.06)	.00
Differences	.30(.23)	.30(.21)	.10(.08)	0(.08)	−.20(−.15)	−.20(−.23)

ratory situation was 'school-like' enough to trigger their specific phobias by generalization."

We shall have to concur with this latter interpretation and endorse the use of tonic levels rather than increments in tonic level in this case. Obviously the fact that the problem-readers had higher tonic levels in all three experimental conditions does not prove that their reading problem is psychogenic or anxiety based—as we acknowledged at the onset, the design of this experiment is inadequate, albeit not unrepresentative. But we can at least deny with some confidence the claim that these results *disprove* the anxiety hypothesis on the grounds that the specific letter task does not show a larger *increment* in arousal in the problem-readers.

Autonomic level scores are very commonly analyzed in this way using as the dependent variable the difference between poststress and prestress values; i.e., changes in tonic level are treated like phasic changes elicited by fleeting stimuli. But by definition a change in tonic level is a relatively enduring change brought about by a persisting alternation in the stimulus situation. The subject has time to take stock of the new situation, and there is opportunity for his psychophysiological mechanisms to adjust themselves accordingly. Whereas phasic reactions to novel stimuli are usually transient *increases* in activity, changes in tonic level may be either positive or negative. Thus, an apprehensive subject may discover, after the start of the experimental task, that its demands are not as great as he had expected so that the poststress level may actually be lower than the prestress level for him. The problem readers in our hypothetical experiment had a tonic level of .70 at the start of the experiment, which decreased to .60 during the task of discriminating letter-like forms; under the same conditions, the control children showed an increase from .40 to .50. Clearly one must conclude that this task was more stressful for the problem readers even though it produced a decrease in their tonic level, indicating, perhaps, that it was not as stressful as they had anticipated.

The argument in favor of using increments in tonic level, rather than the actual "poststress" levels themselves, is based on the notion that part of the arousal during the stress situation must be attributable to factors other than the stimuli being manipulated in the experiment; the subject with a high prestress level is already aroused for extraneous reasons, hence it is only the *increment* to the poststress level that can rightfully be attributed to the effects of the stress. But surely this conception is too great an oversimplification. The introduction of the task or stressor does not merely *add* a stimulus to the stimuli already present; rather it *changes* the total situation. Normally, the prestress or resting situation is relatively unstructured. The subject has little to occupy him and is free to worry apprehensively or to think pleasant thoughts, as his fancy and his temperament may predispose him. The experimental task or stressor, in contrast, is typically engrossing, so that the subject's average tonic level during the experimental manipulation can usually be taken as a fair index of *his* reaction to *that* controlled, external situation.

Some illustrative examples—The reader will already have become convinced that interpreting physiological response data can sometimes be a rather tricky business. One must first acquire an adequate grasp of the specific technological problems involved in measuring the response systems one wishes to employ as dependent variables. The next step is to formulate very carefully the questions one wishes to answer. Some of the more common types of experimental questions are illustrated in the following examples.

1. *Individual Differences in Autonomic Reactivity*—Example: Jones shows a more elevated heart rate than does Smith while giving a speech before a class. We know that Jones is more susceptible to "stage fright" than is Smith, and we hypothesize

that this may be partially explained by the fact that Jones has the more labile autonomic nervous system; his stronger responses to the "same" stress produce more insistent proprioceptive feedback which disrupts his concentration on what he is trying to say. Our experimental question is therefore a physiological one. To prove that Jones's heart rate is more labile requires us to show that his tonic heart rate is higher under a wide variety of stressors (allowing for the possibility that Smith's heart rate may be higher in certain situations which, for some reason, have special significance for him). The appropriate unit of measurement is the raw physical unit *rate,* since our question is concerned with the absolute activity of the effector organ—which will determine the level of visceral afferent feedback—rather than with the psychological state which that level implies for the particular individual. The same demonstration for a number of autonomic response systems would allow us to speak of individual differences in general autonomic reactivity.

As a rule, we may expect to find that Jones is more labile in some autonomic response systems, while Smith is more labile in others. This generalization is what Lacey (Lacey, Bateman, & Van Lehn, 1953) has called "the principle of autonomic response specificity." We might still ask whether Jones does not show greater lability at least in those systems which most easily disrupt performance in the public speaking situation: e.g., hyper- or hyposecretion of the salivary glands, greater hand tremor, and the like. Note that if one is asking a psychological question—e.g., which subject is more aroused in this situation?—autonomic response specificity need not pose a problem of interpretation *provided one employs the unit of measurement corrected for individual differences in range* as has been discussed above.

2. *Individual Differences in the Character of the Psychological Response*—Example: Remaining in the stage fright context, it has been argued that serious stage fright may result when an individual is for some reason angry at his audience; such anger is said to lead by the mechanism of projection to the conviction that the audience is angry with him, which in turn makes him afraid. To test this *psychological* hypothesis, we might employ autonomic measurement to determine whether Jones but not Smith betrays the peripheral accompaniments of anger at the start of his performance. Thus, we might expect to find in Jones's record evidence of the autonomic pattern which Ax (1953) has shown to be characteristic of anger. A difficulty here is that Ax's results were given in terms of absolute physical units; e.g., his subjects averaged more spontaneous GSRs, higher diastolic blood pressure, and a smaller increase in respiration rate during anger than during fear. Now suppose that Jones shows 12 GSRs per unit time, a diastolic blood pressure increase of 18 millimeters of mercury, and a respiration rate increase of less than two per minute—these values are about equal to the means of Ax's subjects under the anger condition. Can we therefore conclude that Jones is in fact angry?

One suspects that Ax himself would be uneasy about such an application of his findings. Suppose, for example, that Jones tends to be unusually labile with respect to both number of spontaneous GSRs and diastolic blood pressure and unusually stabile with respect to respiration rate; the "principle of autonomic response specificity" tells us that such might well be the case. Jones might then tend to show an "anger-like" pattern in response to nearly any stimulus and, in our particular experiment, to show an anger pattern when he is in fact afraid.

Clearly, this problem devolves from a lack of intra-subjective standardization of units. Suppose Ax had expressed each individual's levels in both emotional conditions in relation to the maximum and minimum levels of which that individual was capable in each autonomic response system

—i.e., in terms of the range-corrected units advocated herein. Then his results might have read something like this: "average diastolic blood pressure was .50 under anger and .30 under fear, the relative index of spontaneous GSRs was .60 under anger and .30 under fear, and relative respiration .10 under anger and .40 under fear." Now suppose that Jones's relativized scores on these three variables are .60, .65, and .20, respectively. Noticing first of all that these scores are somewhat higher than the means for Ax's *anger* group, can we attribute this difference merely to the possibility that Jones has a generally higher autonomic reactivity? Probably not, since these are relativized scores from which differences in physiological reactivity have been already partialed out. We *can* conclude that Jones reacted *psychologically* more intensely to the situation we are using than did Ax's average subject to his anger stimulus, either because our situation was effectively stronger or because Jones is *psychologically* more reactive than the average person. Secondly, we note that the pattern of Jones's response is similar to the pattern of the mean anger response of Ax's subjects. Can this be again an artifact resulting from Jones's being hyperreactive in the first two channels and hyporeactive in the third? Probably not, again because these *relativized* scores are independent of mean reactivity differences, channel by channel.

Suppose that we had expressed Jones's responses as standard scores relative to the *inter*-subjective norms provided by the (absolute) responses of Ax's subjects, giving him scores of, say, +2.0, +1.5, and −1.5, respectively. This would give us somewhat more precise information as to how Jones's levels compared with those of Ax's subjects; for example, we might now be able to say that Jones's diastolic blood pressure was 0.5 sigma greater than the mean of Ax's subjects under the anger condition and 2.5 sigma greater than their mean under the fear condition. However, the advantages of this intersubjective relativization are more apparent than real; upon reflection, one can see that these data will still be very nearly as ambiguous with respect to our hypothesis as they were in their original raw score form. The question we are asking is a psychological one—having to do with the character or quality of the subject's *psychological* response to the situation—and for this we require that our data be expressed in units relativized with respect to *intra*-subjective variability.

3. *Individual Differences in Tonic Psychophysiological Level*—Example: Judging from the autonomic response record, was the stage fright situation more psychologically disturbing for Jones than for Smith? This typical problem calls for the use of range-corrected units of tonic level. We are not concerned with whose skin conductance or heart rate is higher in absolute terms, but rather we wish to evaluate the relative intensities of the underlying psychophysiological states. Nor do we measure the *increment* in corrected tonic level when the subject walks to the front of the room to give his speech, because our interest is in his degree of arousal while speaking. We realize that his arousal level just before he is called on to perform may depend upon a variety of uncontrolled factors—whether he was expecting to be called on just then, how effective his psychological defense mechanisms may be, and the like—so that including even a range-corrected measure of "prestress" level in the process of computing increments will probably add only error to our assessment.

In some response systems which are under strong homeostatic control, the function relating tonic level to the underlying variable of interest may actually be nonmonotonic so that increases in the latter above some critical value, ψ_p, may actually produce a *decrease* in the former, ϕ [Wilder's (1962) "paradoxical response"]. This phenomenon was apparently regularly observed in Bridger and Reiser's (1959) study of heart rate in neonates (although one would like to have seen independent evidence that the infants showing heart rate decrease *were* actually more aroused after stimulation than before). However, it is much less commonly seen in work with older subjects when one is careful to identify those cases where the subject was for some reason actually more aroused under the "prestress" condition so that his negative "pre-post" stress increment is actually a proper indication of his change in state rather than a "paradoxical" response. When $\phi = f(\psi)$ is actually nonmonotonic—i.e., not single-valued—no simple range-correction or other transformation can solve the problem and one's only recourse is the plotting of individual regressions of $\Delta\phi$ on ϕ_0 as recommended by Bridger and Reiser (1959).

Suppose we find that Jones's tonic SC was higher than Smith's but his tonic blood pressure was lower, even when both are expressed in range-corrected units? If we were using absolute physical units, such a result might be attributed to "autonomic response specificity." A common practice in such cases is to convert both scores into *inter*-subjective standard scores. Thus, relative to measures obtained for the total sample, Jones's SC level might be +2.0 sigma and his BP level +1.0 sigma, while corresponding scores for Smith might be −1.0 and +1.5. Then such scores are averaged—Jones's mean being +1.5 and Smith's being +0.25—leading to the conclusion here that Jones was more disturbed by the situation than was Smith. However, finding such differences among autonomic response channels *when levels are expressed in individual range-corrected units* implies simply (and reasonably) that these two dependent variables are not measuring the same thing—that the psychophysiological process underlying variation in (corrected) skin conductance is not identical to the process governing variations in (corrected) measures of blood pressure. Extrapolating from the interesting findings of Lacey *et al.* (Lacey, Kagan, Lacey, & Moss, 1963), we might speculate that, while Jones's higher SC indicates that he experienced greater general CNS arousal, Smith's higher BP shows that he was more actively inhibiting exteroceptive input so as to better concentrate on his speech.

4. *Individual Differences in Phasic Response to Specific Stimuli*—Finally, let us suppose that we have arranged for a series of disturbances to occur at intervals while each subject is delivering his speech; e.g., after three minutes, a voice from the back calls, "Speak louder," after five minutes a bell rings; two minutes later, a member of the audience gets up and leaves; etc. We measure the phasic autonomic response—e.g., the GSR—to each of these "standard" disturbing stimuli. We wish to know which subject is more distracted by such stimuli on the average as indicated by a greater phasic response. We assume that a subject may react differently to, e.g., a bell, while giving a speech than he might under other circumstances, and therefore we must expect some sort of relationship between his phasic response to the bell and his tonic level under the stage fright condition. We wish and expect this relationship to display itself in the final results of the experiment, from which we intend to draw our inferences about the psychological processes which were at work. But we realize that these phasic and tonic output variables may also be related in some manner for other, extraneous reasons—such as homeostatic restraint or the biophysical peculiarities of the peripheral effector organ—and we do not wish to retain the influence of *this* sort of relationship in the data as finally analyzed. In particular, if the function relating the measure of tonic level to the underlying variable of interest is nonlinear, then we know that measures of phasic response will necessarily display a spurious relationship to prestimulus level. If this function, $\phi = f(\psi)$, is known, then one can compute from $\Delta\phi$ an index which estimates $\Delta\psi$ independently of any spurious correlation with initial level, ϕ_0, as illustrated for the case of the GSR above in equations 11 and 12.

Other Approaches

Normalizing Transformations

An approach to the problem of finding the "correct unit" in which to express psychophysiological data which was popular some years ago involved trying various algebraic transformations on the raw measures, searching for one which would yield a normal distribution of the sample values. For example, since GSR distributions are often positively skewed, logarithmic or square-root transformations were frequently applied. Such scalar changes may be useful if one plans to employ statistical methods which involve distributional assumptions, but it is clear that the data should *not* be transformed for this purpose unless and until it has first been adjusted to provide the best possible index of the underlying variable of interest, along the lines suggested above. GSR data, for example, should first be expressed in units of conductance-change, ΔSC, then adjusted for individual differences in SC range [by applying the formula $\Delta\phi = \Delta SC/(SC_{mx} - SC_{mn})$], and then finally adjusted for nonlinearity in the relation of ϕ to ψ so as to provide a linear estimate of $\Delta\psi$ [e.g., by application of equation 11 or 12, if $\phi = f(\psi)$ is a growth function]. If *now* the sample distribution of $\hat{\Delta}\psi$ is skewed and one wishes to employ ANOVA or some other normality-assuming procedure, an appropriate transformation or scale may be applied to the $\hat{\Delta}\psi$ values.

In some of the earlier literature it is implied that if the transformation $Y = g(X)$ normalizes the sample distribution of the raw autonomic measures, X, then the transformed variable, Y, must be a better estimate of the true underlying variable, ψ. This particular *non sequitur* has tended to infect psychometric thinking since the days of Quetelet and is to be sedulously avoided. The so-called Normal Law of Variation which Quetelet introduced was never ratified by the Almighty, and one has no *a priori* assurance whatever that the population distribution of *any* individual difference variable has any particular form. Similarly, the notion that a transformation of some measure of autonomic change, which eliminates any correlation between the adjusted change score and the initial tonic level, must therefore be a better measure of the true change in the underlying variable of interest is also specious though seductive. We shall repeat one last time that, if the initial tonic level has some significance concerning the state of the organism at the time of stimulation, then clearly it is usually to be expected that a measure of the organism's response to stimulation at that time will be in some way related to the tonic level; a "blind" algebraic procedure which is designed specifically to eliminate any vestige of correlation between change and initial level must in general serve to distort the data and to increase the error variance.

Lacey's Autonomic Lability Score

In a thoughtful and widely quoted analysis of the problems of autonomic measurement, Lacey (1956) proposed what was intended to be a general method of evaluating measures of autonomic change, both phasic changes and changes in tonic level. Lacey is specifically concerned with the difficulties imposed by the action of the so-called Law of Initial Values (Wilder, 1962), which asserts that an excitatory stimulus evokes smaller increments when prestimulus activity already is high while an inhibitory stimulus produces greater decrements from elevated tonic levels than when prestimulus activity is already low. In the terms of the present analysis, at least the first part of this alleged "Law" is contained in the proposition that the function $\phi = f(\psi)$ is nonlinear. For example, if $\phi = f(\psi)$ is a growth function, then the LIV will hold as stated; a given increment in ψ will yield a smaller increment in ϕ as the initial tonic level, ϕ_0, increases. That is, the increment, $\Delta\phi$, produced by a given change in the underlying process, $\Delta\psi$, will be a function of the prestimulus level, ϕ_0, viz., $\Delta\phi = (1-\phi_0)g(\Delta\psi)$, and the correlation between $\Delta\phi$ and ϕ_0 thus produced will be spurious in the sense that it will detract from the accuracy of $\Delta\phi$ as an index of $\Delta\psi$ when initial level, ϕ_0, is allowed to vary.

Now the actual relation of ϕ to ψ has yet to be determined for any psychophysiological response system. There are adequate grounds for confidence that the nature of this function will vary from one system to another. We have suggested above methods by which the form of this relationship might be determined empirically from appropriate measures of activity in a given system. Lacey's Autonomic Lability Score (ALS) was designed to deal with this problem in a very general way by means of regression analysis. Specifically, the ALS is the difference between the observed poststimulus level, TL_1, and the value predicted from the prestimulus level, TL_0, on the basis of the observed regression of TL_1 on TL_0, this difference being expressed in T-score units (with mean = 50 and SD = 10).

To illustrate this method, we shall return to the earlier example of assessing individual differences in stage fright from measures of SC obtained while the subject is giving a speech. To compute the ALS, one would measure each subject's SC_0 before he gets up to perform and his SC_1 while performing and correlate these two values across the sample. One would then compute the usual linear regression equation for estimating SC_1 from SC_0, i.e.,

$$\widehat{SC}_{1(i)} = (\overline{SC}_1 - r_{01}\frac{s_1}{s_0}\overline{SC}_0) + (r_{01}\frac{s_1}{s_2})\ SC_{0(i)}.$$

From this, one computes the ALS,

$$ALS_{(i)} = 10\,\frac{SC_{1(i)} - \widehat{SC}_{1(i)}}{s_1\sqrt{1 - r^2_{01}}} + 50.$$

Thus, by converting the "poststress" SC_1 values to Autonomic Lability Scores, we can be assured that these scores will be uncorrelated (across subjects, R-type correlation) with their SC_0s obtained prior to performing. But one can argue that the arousal (or anxiety) shown by a subject while performing *should* be correlated with his level of arousal while waiting to perform; we have repeatedly inveighed against "blind" statistical procedures designed to eliminate such correlations from the data. In fact, the ALS procedure eliminates any R-type correlation between SC_0 and SC_1 but does not eliminate the correlation between the better measures of pre- and post-stress level, ϕ_0 and ϕ_1; the ALS assumes that the regression *across subjects* of SC_1 and SC_0 is a close estimate of the regression of poststress on prestress conductance which one would observe in repeated measures of the same subject, and this assumption does not generally hold due to individual variation in the range parameters. Without attempting a detailed critique here, these considerations alone may be sufficient to suggest that the ALS has outlived its usefulness.

REFERENCES

Anton, A. H., & Sayre, D. F. A study of the factors affecting the aluminum oxide—trihydroxyindole procedure for the analysis of catechol amines. *J. Pharmacol. exp. Ther.*, 1962, 138, 360–375.

Ax, A. F. The physiological differentiation between fear and anger in humans. *Psychosom. Med.*, 1953, 15, 433–442.

Becker, H. C., Peacock, S. M., Jr., Heath, R. G., & Mickle, W. A. Methods of stimulation control and concurrent electrographic recording. In D. E. Sheer (Ed.), *Electrical stimulation of the brain*. Austin: Univer. of Texas Press, 1961.

Belanger, D., & Feldman, S. Effects of water deprivation upon heart rate and instrumental activity in the rat. *J. comp. physiol. Psychol.*, 1962, 55, 220–225.

Berger, H. Über das Elektrenkephalogramm des Menchen. *Archiv für Psychiatrie und Nervenkrankheiten*, 1929, 87, 527–570.

Berger, R. J., & Oswald, I. Effects of sleep deprivation on behavior and subsequent sleep and dreaming. *EEG clin. Neurophysiol.*, 1962, 14, 297.

Berlyne, D. E. *Conflict, arousal and curiosity.* New York: McGraw-Hill, 1960.

Bernreiter, M. *Electrocardiography.* (2nd ed.) Philadelphia: Lippincott, 1963.

Blum, G. S. *A model of the mind.* New York: Wiley, 1961.

Bogacz, J., Vanzulli, A., & García-Austt, E. Evoked responses in man. IV. Effects of habituation, distraction and conditioning upon auditory evoked responses. *Acta neurol. Latinoamer.,* 1962, 8, 244–252.

Bonvallet, M., Dell, P., & Hiebel, G. Tonus sympathetique et activité electrocortical, *EEG clin. Neurophysiol.,* 1954, 6, 119–144.

Brady, J. V. Behavioral stress and physiological change: a comparative approach to the experimental analysis of some psychosomatic problems. *Trans. N.Y. Acad. Sci.,* 1964, 26, 483–496.

Brady, J. V., & Conrad, D. G. Some effects of limbic systems self-stimulation upon conditioned emotional behavior. *J. comp. physiol. Psychol.,* 1960, 53, 128–137.

Brebbia, D. R., & Altshuler, K. Z. Oxygen consumption rate and electroencephalographic stage of sleep. *Science,* 1965, 150, 1621–1623.

Bremer, F. L'activité cérébrale et la problème physiologique du sommeil. *Boll. Soc. It. Biol. Sp.,* 1938, 13, 271–290.

Bremer, F. Neurophysiological mechanisms in cerebral arousal. In G. E. W. Wolstenholme and Maeve O'Connor (Eds.), *The nature of sleep.* London: Churchill, 1961.

Bridger, W. H., & Reiser, M. O. Psychophysiologic studies of the neonate: an approach toward the methodological and theoretical problems involved. *Psychosom. Med.,* 1959, 21, 265–276.

Broadbent, D. E. A mechanical model for human attention and immediate memory. *Psychol. Rev.,* 1957, 64, 205–215.

Brown, C. C., Giddon, D. B., & Dean, E. D. Techniques of plethysmography. *Psychophysiology,* 1965, 1, 253–266.

Brown, C. C., & Saucer, R. T. *Electronic instrumentations for the behavioral sciences.* Springfield, Ill.: Charles C Thomas, 1958.

Bruch, Hilde. Transformation of oral impulses in eating disorders: a conceptual approach. *Psychiat. Quart.,* 1961, 35, 458–481.

Bruner, J. S., & Goodman, C. C. Value and need as organizing factors in perception. *J. abnorm. soc. Psychol.,* 1947, 42, 33–44.

Brusilow, S. W., & Gordes, E. H. Solute and water secretion in sweat. *J. clin. Invest.,* 1964, 43, 477–484.

Burch, G. E., & Winsor, T. *A primer of electrocardiography.* (4th ed.) Philadelphia: Lea and Febiger, 1960.

Burch, N. R., & Greiner, T. H. A bioelectric scale of human alertness: concurrent recordings of the EEG and the GSR. In L. J. West and M. Greenblatt (Eds.), *Explorations in the physiology of emotions.* Washington, D.C.: Amer. Psychol. Assoc., 1960.

Bureš, J., Petráň, M., & Zachar, J. *Electrophysiological methods in biological research.* Prague: Czech. Acad. Sci., 1960.

Byford, G. H. Eye movement recording. In the "Proceedings of the Second International Conference on Medical Electronics," Paris, 1959. In C. N. Smyth (Ed.), *Medical electronics.* London: Elliffe & Sons, Ltd., 1960.

Cannon, W. B. The James-Lange theory of emotions: a critical examination and an alternative theory. *Amer. J. Psychol.,* 1927, 39, 106–124.

Cannon, W. B. *Bodily changes in pain, hunger, fear and rage.* (2nd ed.) New York: D. Appleton, 1929.

Cattell, R. B., & Scheier, I. H. *The meaning and measurement of neuroticism and anxiety.* New York: Ronald, 1961.

Chapman, R. M., & Bragdon, H. R. Evoked responses to numerical and non-numerical visual stimuli while problem solving. *Nature,* 1964, 203, 1155–1157.

Cohen, S. I., Silverman, A. J., & Burch, N. R. A technique for the assessment of affect change. *J. nerv. ment. Dis.,* 1956, 124, 352–360.

Cornsweet, T. N. *Design of electric circuits in the behavioral sciences.* New York: John Wiley & Sons, 1963.

Crout, J. R. Catechol amines in urine. In D. Seligson (Ed.), *Standard methods of clinical chemistry,* Vol. 3. New York: Academic Press, 1961.

Darrow, C. W. The GSR (sweating) and blood pressure as preparatory and facilitatory functions. *Psychol. Bull.,* 1936, 33, 73–94.

Darrow, C. W. Continuous records of systolic and diastolic blood pressure. *Arch. Neurol. Psychiat.,* 1937, 38, 365–370.

Darrow, C. W., Wilcott, R. C., Siegal, A., Wilson, J., Watanabe, K., & Vieth, R. The mechanism of the diphasic skin potential response. *EEG clin. Neurophysiol.*, 1957, 9, 169–173.

Davis, H. Enhancement of evoked cortical potentials in humans related to a task requiring a decision. *Science*, 1964, 145, 182–183.

Davis, J. F. *Manual of surface electromyography*. WADC Technical Report 59–184, 1959.

Davis, R. The limit of the "psychological refractory period." *Quart. J. exp. Psychol.*, 1956, 8, 24–38.

Davis, R. The human operator as a single channel in the information system. *Quart. J. exp. Psychol.*, 1957, 9, 119–129.

Davis, R. The role of "attention" in the psychological refractory period. *Quart. J. exp. Psychol.*, 1959, 11, 211–220.

Davis, R. C. Continuous recording of arterial pressure: an analysis of the problem. *J. comp. physiol. Psychol.*, 1957, 50, 524–530.

Davis, R. C., Seldon, G. F., & Stout, F. G. Apparatus for recording autonomic states and changes. *American J. Psychol.*, 1954, 67, 343–356.

Day, J. L., & Lippitt, M. W., Jr. A long-term electrode system for electrocardiography and impedance pneumography. *Psychophysiology*, 1964, 1, 117–182.

Delgado, J. M. R., & Hamline, H. Spontaneous and evoked seizures in animals and humans. In E. R. Ramey and D. S. O'Doherty (Eds.), *Electrical studies on the unanesthetized brain*. New York: Paul B. Hoeber, Inc., 1960.

Delgado, J. M. R., Roberts, W. W., & Miller, N. E. Learning motivated by electrical stimulation of the brain. *Amer. J. Physiol.*, 1954, 179, 587–593.

Dell, P., Bonvallet, M., & Hugelin, A. Mechanisms of reticular deactivation. In G. E. W. Wolstenholme and Maeve O'Connor (Eds.), *The nature of sleep*. London: Churchill, 1961.

Dement, W. The effect of dream deprivation. *Science*, 1960, 131, 1705–1707.

Dement, W., & Kleitman, N. Cyclic variations in EEG during sleep and their relation to eye movements, body motility, and dreaming. *EEG clin. Neurophysiol.*, 1957, 9, 673–690. (a)

Dement, W., & Kleitman, N. The relation of eye movements during sleep to dream activity; and objective method for the study of dreaming. *J. exp. Psychol.*, 1957, 53, 339–346. (b)

Derbyshire, A. J., Rempel, B., Forbes, T., & Lambert, E. F. Effects of anesthetics on action potentials in the cerebral cortex of the cat. *Amer. J. Physiol.*, 1936, 116, 557–596.

Deutsch, J. A. *The structural basis of behavior*. Chicago: Univer. of Chicago Press, 1960.

Deutsch, J. A. Learning and electrical self-stimulation of the brain. *Theoret. Biol.*, 1963, 4, 193–214.

Deutsch, J. A., & Deutsch, D. Attention: some theoretical considerations. *Psychol. Rev.*, 1963, 70, 80–90.

Ditchburn, R. W., Fender, D. H., & Mayne, S. Movements of retinal image. *J. Physiol.*, 1959, 145, 98–107.

Domino, E. F., Matsuoka, S., Waltz, J., & Cooper, I. Simultaneous recordings of scalp and epidural somatosensory-evoked responses in man. *Science*, 1964, 145, 1199–1200.

Donaldson, P. E. K. (Ed.) *Electronic apparatus for biological research*. London: Butterworth Scientific Publications, 1958.

Duffy, Elizabeth. Psychological significance of the concept of "Arousal" or "Activation." *Psychol. Rev.*, 1957, 64, 265–275.

Dumont, S., & Dell, P. Facilitatión reticularie des mecanismes visuels corticalux. *EEG clin. Neurophysiol.*, 1960, 12, 769–796.

Ebbecke, V. Pflügers Arch., 1951, 253, 333–350.

Edelberg, R. The relation between the galvanic skin response, vasoconstriction and tactile sensitivity. *J. exp. Psychol.*, 1961, 62, 187–195.

Edelberg, R., & Burch, N. R. Skin resistance and galvanic skin response: influence of surface variables and methodological implications. *Arch. gen. Psychiat.*, 1962, 7, 163–169.

Edelberg, R., Greiner, T., & Burch, N. R. Some membrane properties of the effector in the galvanic skin response. *J. appl. Physiol.*, 1960, 15, 691–696.

Edelberg, R., & Wright, D. J. Two GSR effector organs and their stimulus specificity. Paper read at the Society for Psychophysiological Research, Denver, October, 1962.

Elmadjian, F., Hope, J. M., & Lamson, E. T. Excretion of epinephrin and norepinephrin in various emotional states. *J. clin. Endocrinol.*, 1957, 17, 608–620.

Euler, U. S. v., & Lishajko, F. Improved technique for the fluorimetric estimation of catechol amines. *Acta Physiol. Scand.,* 1961, 51, 348–356.

Fales, H. M., & Pisano, J. J. Gas chromatography of biologically important amines. *Analyt. Biochem.,* 1962, 3, 337–342.

Feder, W. Silver-silver chloride electrode as a nonpolarizable bioelectrode. *J. appl. Physiol.,* 1963, 18, 397–401.

Fernandez-Guardiola, A., Roldán, E., Fanjul, L., & Castels, C. Role of the pupillary mechanism in the process of habituation of the visual pathways. *EEG clin. Neurophysiol.,* 1961, 13, 564–576.

Fiorica, V., & Muehl, S. Relationship between plasma levels of 17-hydroxycorticosteroid (17-OH-CS) and a psychological measure of manifest anxiety. *Psychosom. Med.,* 1962, 24, 596–599.

Fisher, C., Gross, J., & Zuch, J. Cycle of penile erection synchronous with dreaming (REM) sleep. *Arch. gen. Psychiat.,* 1965, 12, 29–45.

Forbes, T. W. Skin potential and impedance responses with recurring shock stimulation. *Amer. J. Physiol.,* 1936, 117, 189–199.

Forbes, T. W., & Bolles, M. M. Correlation of the response potentials of the skin with "exciting" and non-"exciting" stimuli. *J. Psychol.,* 1936, 2, 273–285.

Forbes, T. W., & Landis, C. The limiting A.C. frequency for the exhibition of the galvanic skin ("psychogalvanic") response. *J. gen. Psychol.,* 1935, 13, 188–193.

Forster, S., Post, B. S., & Benton, J. G. Preliminary observations on electrosleep. *Arch. phys. med. Rehab.,* 1963, 44, 481–489.

Fox, H. M., Murawski, B. J., Bartholomay, A. F., & Gifford, S. Adrenal steroid excretion patterns in eighteen healthy subjects: tentative correlations with personality structure. *Psychosom. Med.,* 1961, 23, 33.

Fox, H. M., Murawski, B. J., Thome, G. W., & Gray, S. J. Urinary 17-hydroxicorticoid and uropepsin levels with psychological data. *AMA Arch. intern. Med.,* 1958, 101, 859.

Fox, R. H., Goldsmith, R., & Kidd, D. J. Cutaneous vasomotor control in the human head, neck and upper chest. *J. Physiol.,* 1962, 161, 298–312.

Fox, R. H., & Hilton, S. M. Bradykinin formation in human skin as a factor in heat vasodilation. *J. Physiol.,* 1958, 142, 219–232.

Freeman, G. L., & Giffin, L. L. The measurement of general reactivity under basal conditions. *J. gen. Psychol.,* 1939, 21, 63–72.

French, J. D., Verzeano, M., & Magoun, H. W. An extralemniscal sensory system in the brain. *Arch. Neurol. Psychiat.,* 1953, 69, 505–518.

Funkenstein, D., Greenblatt, M., & Solomon, H. C. Norepinephrine-like and epinephrine-like substances in psychotic and psychoneurotic patients. *Amer. J. Psychiat.,* 1952, 108, 652.

Funkenstein, D. H., King, S. H., & Drolette, M. E. *Mastery of stress.* Cambridge: Harvard Univer. Press, 1957.

Fuster, J. M. Effects of stimulation of brain stem on tachistoscopic perception. *Science,* 1958, 127, 150.

Fuster, J. M., & Uyeda, A. Facilitation of tachistoscopic performance by stimulation of midbrain tegmental points in the monkey. *Exp. Neurol.,* 1962, 6, 384–406.

García-Austt, E., Bogacz, J., & Vanzulli, A. Effects of attention and inattention upon visual evoked responses. *EEG clin. Neurophysiol.,* 1964, 17, 136–143.

Geisler, G. D., Frishkopf, L. S., & Rosenblith, W. A. Extracranial responses to acoustic clicks in man. *Science,* 1958, 128, 1210–1211.

Gellhorn, E. The hypothalamic-cortico system in barbiturate anesthesia. *Arch. int. Pharmacodyn.,* 1953, 93, 424–432.

Glaser, G. H. (Ed.) *EEG and behavior.* New York: Basic Books, 1963.

Goldstone, S. Flicker fusion measurements and anxiety level. *J. exp. Psychol.,* 1955, 49, 200–202.

Goth, A. *Medical pharmacology.* (2nd ed.) St. Louis: Mosby, 1964.

Granda, A. M., & Hammack, J. T. Operant behavior during sleep. *Science,* 1961, 133, 1485–1486.

Griesemer, R. D. Protection against the transfer of matter through the skin. In S. Rothman (Ed.), *The human integument.* American Association for the Advancement of Science, 1959.

Grings, W. W. Preparatory set variables related to classical conditioning of autonomic responses. *Psychol. Rev.,* 1960, 67, 243-252.

Guazzi, M., & Zanchetti, A. Carotid sinus and aortic reflexes in the regulation of circulation during sleep. *Science,* 1965, 148, 397–399.

Guld, C. The reduction of stimulus interference in electrophysiology. *Proc. int. Conf. med. Electronics,* 1960, 3, 103–105.

Haider, M., Spong, P., & Lindsley, D. B. Attention, vigilance, and cortical evoked potentials in humans. *Science,* 1964, 145, 180–182.

Handlon, J. H. Hormonal activity and individual responses to stresses and easements in everyday living. In R. Roessler and N. S. Greenfield (Eds.), *Physiological correlates of psychological disorder.* Madison: Univer. of Wisconsin Press, 1962.

Hawkins, D. R., Monroe, J. T., Sandifer, M. G., & Vernon, C. R. Psychological and physiological responses to continuous epinephrine infusion—an approach to the study of the affect, anxiety. In L. J. West and M. Greenblatt (Eds.), *Explorations in the physiology of emotion.* Washington, D.C.: American Psychiatric Association, 1960.

Heath, R. G., & Mickle, W. A. Evaluation of seven years experience with depth electrode studies in human patients. In E. R. Ramey and D. S. O'Doherty (Eds.), *Electrical studies on the unanesthetized brain.* New York: Paul B. Hoeber, Inc., 1960.

Hebb, D. O. *The organization of behavior.* New York: Wiley, 1949.

Hebb, D. O. Drives and the conceptual nervous system. *Psychol. Rev.,* 1955, 62, 243–253.

Hernández-Peón, R. Reticular mechanisms of sensory control. In W. A. Rosenblith (Ed.), *Sensory communication.* Boston: The M.I.T. Press, 1961. Ch. 26.

Hernández-Peón, R. Attention, sleep, motivation and behavior. In R. G. Heath (Ed.), *The role of pleasure in behavior.* New York: Harper and Row, 1964.

Hernández-Peón, R., & Donoso, M. Activités sous-corticaux du cervu humain en état de veille evoquée par stimulation photique. In *First Internatl. Congress of Neurological Sciences: Brussels, 1957, III.* Pp. 385–396. London: Pergamon, 1959.

Hess, E. H. Attitude and pupil size. *Sci. Amer.,* 1965, 212, 46–54.

Hess, E. H., & Polt, J. M. Pupil size as related to interest value of visual stimuli. *Science,* 1960, 132, 349–350.

Hess, E. H., & Polt, J. M. Pupil size in relation to mental activity during simple problem solving. *Science,* 1964, 143, 1190–1192.

Hess, W. R. *Diencephalon: autonomic and extra-pyramidal functions.* New York: Grune, 1954.

Heymans, G. *Z. Psycol. Physiol. Sinnesorg.,* 1899, 21, 357 f.

Hill, J. D. N., & Parr, G. (Eds.) *Electroencephalography.* (2nd ed.) London: McDonald Co. Ltd., 1963.

Horn, G., & Venables, P. H. The effect of somaesthetic and acoustic stimuli on the threshold of fusion of paired light flashes in human subjects. *Quart. J. exp. Psychol.,* 1964, 16, 289–296.

Hoveland, C. I., & Riesen, A. H. Magnitude of galvanic and vasomotor response as a function of stimulus intensity. *J. gen. Psychol.,* 1940, 23, 103–121.

Hubel, D. H., Henson, C. O., Rupert, A., & Galambos, R. "Attention" units in the auditory cortex. *Science,* 1959, 129, 1279–1280.

Hugelin, A., Dumont, S., & Paillas, N. Tympanic muscles and control of auditory input during arousal. *Science,* 1960, 131, 1371–1372.

Huttenlocker, P. R. Effects of state of arousal on click responses in the mesencephalic reticular formation. *EEG clin. Neurophysiol.,* 1960, 12, 819–827.

Jasper, H. H. Electroencephalography. In W. Penfield and T. C. Erickson (Eds.), *Epilepsy and cerebral localization.* Springfield, Ill.: C. C. Thomas, 1941. Ch. 14.

Jasper, H. H. Reticular-cortical systems and theories of the integrated action of the brain. In H. F. Harlow and C. N. Woolsey (Eds.), *Biological and biochemical bases of behavior.* Madison: Univer. of Wisconsin Press, 1958. (a)

Jasper, H. H. The ten twenty electrode system of the International Federation. *EEG clin. Neurophysiol.,* 1958, 10, 371. (b)

Jouvet, M. Etude neurophysiologique chez l'homme de quelques mécanismes sous-corticaux de l'attention. *Psychol. Francois,* 1957, 2, 254–260.

Jouvet, M. Telencephalic and rhombencephalic sleep in the cat. In G. E. W. Wolstenholme and Maeve O'Connor (Eds.), *The nature of sleep.* London: Churchill, 1961.

Jouvet, M., Benoît, O., & Courjon, J. Action de l'êpilepsie experimental par stimulation cortical sur le résponse de formation specifique et non specifique des signaux acoustiques. *Rev. Neurol.,* 1956, 94, 871.

Jouvet, M., & Lapras, C. Somesthésiques au niveau du thalamus chez l'homme au cours de l'attention. *C. R. Soc. Biol.,* 1959, 153, 98–101.

Kessen, W., & Mandler, G. Anxiety, pain and the inhibition of distress. *Psychol. Rev.,* 1961, 68, 396–404.

Kety, S. S. Sleep and the energy metabolism of the brain. In G. E. W. Wolstenholme and Maeve O'Connor (Eds.), *The nature of sleep.* London: Churchill, 1961.

Killam, E. K., & Killam, K. F. The influence of drugs on central afferent pathways. In W. S. Fields (Ed.), *Brain mechanisms and drug action.* Springfield, Ill.: Charles C Thomas, 1957.

Kimmel, H. D. Amount of conditioning and intensity of conditioned stimulus. *J. exp. Psychol.,* 1959, 58, 283–288.

Kimmel, H. D. The relationship between direction and amount of stimulus change and amount of perceptual disparity response. *J. exp. Psychol.,* 1960, 59, 68–72.

Kimmel, H. D. Adaptation of the GSR under repeated applications of a visual stimulus. *J. exp. Psychol.,* 1964, 68, 421–422.

King, H. E. Psychological effects and excitation in the limbic system. In D. E. Sheer (Ed.), *Electrical stimulation of the brain.* Austin: Univer. of Texas Press, 1961.

King, H. E. Two-flash and flicker fusion thresholds for normal and schizophrenic subjects. *Percept. motor Skills,* 1962, 14, 517–518.

Kleitman, N. The nature of dreaming. In G. E. W. Wolstenholme and Maeve O'Connor (Eds.), *The nature of sleep.* London: Churchill, 1961.

Krugman, M. Flicker fusion frequency as a function of anxiety reaction: an exploratory study. *Psychosomat. Med.,* 1947, 9, 269–272.

Kuno, Y. *Human perspiration.* Springfield, Ill.: Charles C Thomas, 1956.

Lacey, J. I. The evaluation of autonomic responses: toward a general solution. *Ann. N.Y. Acad. Sci.,* 1956, 67, 123–164.

Lacey, J. I. Psychophysiological approaches to the evaluation of psychotherapeutic process and outcome. In E. A. Rubenstein and N. B. Parloff (Eds.), *Research in psychotherapy.* Washington, D.C.: Amer. Psychol. Assoc., 1959.

Lacey, J. I., Bateman, D. E., & Van Lehn, R. Autonomic responses specificity. *Psychosomat. Med.,* 1953, 15, 8–21.

Lacey, J. I., Kagan, J., Lacey, B. C., & Moss, H. A. The visceral level: situational determinants and behavioral correlates of autonomic response patterns. In P. H. Knapp (Ed.), *Expressions in the emotions in man.* New York: International Universities Press, 1963.

Lansing, R. W. Relation of brain and tremor rhythms to visual reaction time. *EEG clin. Neurophysiol.,* 1957, 9, 497–504.

Lansing, R. W., Schwartz, E., & Lindsley, D. B. Reaction and EEG activation under alerted and non-alerted conditions. *J. exp. Psychol.,* 1959, 58, 1–7.

Licklider, J. C. R. On psychophysiological models. In W. A. Rosenblith (Ed.), *Sensory communication.* Cambridge, Mass.: M.I.T. Press, 1959. Ch. 3.

Lindsley, D. B. Emotion. In S. S. Stevens (Ed.), *Handbook of experimental psychology.* New York: Wiley, 1951.

Lindsley, D. B. Psychophysiology and motivation. In M. R. Jones (Ed.), *Nebraska symposium on motivation.* Lincoln: Univer. of Nebraska Press, 1957.

Lindsley, D. B. The reticular system in perceptual discriminations. In H. H. Jasper *et al.* (Eds.), *Reticular formation of the brain.* Boston: Little, Brown, 1958. Ch. 25.

Lindsley, D. B. Attention, consciousness, sleep and wakefulness. In *The handbook of physiology,* Sect. I. Neurophysiology, III, 1960. Ch. 64.

Lindsley, D. B. The reticular activating system in perceptual integration. In *Electrical stimulation of the brain.* Austin: Univer. of Texas Press, 1961. Ch. 23.

Lloyd, D. P. C. Action potential and secretory potential of sweat glands. *Proc. nat. acad. of sci.,* 1961, 47, 351–358.

Loomis, H. L., Harvey, E. N., & Hobart, G. A. III. Cerebral states during sleep, as studied by human brain potentials. *J. exp. Psychol.,* 1937, 21, 127–144.

Lykken, D. T. A study of anxiety in the sociopathic personality. *J. Abnorm. Soc. Psychol.,* 1957, 55, 6–10.

Lykken, D. T. Preliminary observations concerning the 'preception' phenomenon. *Psycholphysiol. meas. Nwsltr.,* 1959, 5, 2–7. (a)

Lykken, D. T. Properties of electrodes used in electrodermal measurement. *J. comp. physiol. Psychol.,* 1959, 52, 629–634. (b)

Lykken, D. T. Preception in the rat: autonomic response to shock as a function of the length of warning interval. *Science,* 1962, 137, 665–666.

Lykken, D. T., & Meisch, R. Postshock "activation" of operant behavior. *Psychiat. Res. Rep.* No. PR-65-1. Minneapolis: Univer. of Minnesota, 1965.

Lykken, D. T., & Roth, N. Continuous direct measurement of apparent skin conductance. *Amer. J. Psychol.,* 1961, 74, 293–297.

MacLean, P. D. The limbic system ("visceral brain") and emotional behavior. *AMA Arch. Neurol. Psychiat.,* 1955, 73, 130–134.

MacLean, P. D. "Phylogenesis." In P. H. Knapp (Ed.), *Expressions in the emotions in man.* New York: International Universities Press, 1963. Ch. 20.

Mackworth, G. J., & Mackworth, M. H. Eye fixations recorded on changing visual scenes by the television eye marker. *J. Optical Soc. Amer.,* 1958, 48, 429–435.

Magoun, H. W. *The waking brain.* (2nd ed.) Springfield, Ill.: Charles C Thomas, 1963.

Mahut, Helen. The effects of subcortical electrical stimulation on discrimination learning in cats. *J. comp. physiol. Psychol.,* 1964, 58, 390–395.

Malmo, R. B. Measurement of drive: an unsolved problem in psychology. In M. R. Jones (Ed.), *Nebraska symposium on motivation.* Lincoln: Univer. of Nebraska Press, 1958.

Malmo, R. B. Activation. In A. J. Bachrach (Ed.), *Experimental foundations of clinical psychology.* New York: Basic Books, 1962. Ch. 11.

Malmo, R. B., & Surwillo, W. W. Sleep deprivation: changes in performance and physiological indicants of activation. *Psychol. Monogr.,* 1960, 74, 15. (Whole No. 502.)

Malmstadt, H. V., & Enke, C. G. *Electronics for scientists.* New York: W. A. Benjamin, 1962.

Marañon, G. Contribution a l'étude de l'action émotive de l'adrénaline. *Rev. franc. Endocrinol.,* 1924, 2, 301–325.

McCarthy, J. L., Brodsky, A. L., Mitchell, J. A., & Herrscher, R. F. Thin-layer chromatography of adrenal corticoids: observations on change in mobilities. *Analyt. Biochem.,* 1964, 8, 164–170.

McClendon, J. F., & Hemingway, A. The psychogalvanic reflex as related to the polarization-capacity of the skin. *Amer. J. Physiol.,* 1930, 94, 77–83.

McCurdy, H. G. Consciousness and the galvanometer. *Psychol. Rev.,* 1950, 57, 322–327.

Miller, G. A. The magical number seven, plus or minus two: some limits on our capacity for processing information. *Psychol. Rev.,* 1956, 63, 81–97.

Monnier, M., & Hosli, L. Dialysis of sleep and waking factors in blood of the rabbit. *Science,* 1964, 146, 796–798.

Montagu, J. D. The psychogalvanic reflex: a comparison of A.C. skin resistance and skin potential changes. *J. Neurol. Neurosurg. Psychiat.,* 1958, 21, 119–128.

Moray, N. Attention in dichotic listening: affective cues and the influence of instructions. *Quar. J. exp. Psychol.,* 1959, 11, 56–60.

Moruzzi, G. Reticular influences on the EEG. *EEG clin. Neurophysiol.,* 1964, 16, 2–17.

Moruzzi, G. & Magoun, H. W. Brainstem reticular formation and activation of the EEG. *EEG clin. Neurophysiol.,* 1949, 1, 455–473.

Naquet, R., Regis, H., Fischer-Williams, M., & Fernandez-Guardiola, A. Variations in the responses evoked by light along the specific pathways. *Brain,* 1960, 83, 52–56.

Obrist, P. A. Cardiovascular differentiation of sensory stimuli. *Psychosom. Med.,* 1963, 25, 450–458.

Obrosow, A. N. Electrosleep therapy. In S. Licht (Ed.), *Physical Medicine Library: Vol. 4. Therapeutic electricity and ultraviolet radiation.* New Haven, Conn.: Eliz. Licht, 1959.

O'Connell, D. N., & Tursky, B. Silver-silver chloride sponge electrodes for skin potential recording. *Amer. J. Psychol.,* 1960, 73, 302–304.

Olds, J. Hypothalamic substrates of reward. *Physiol. Rev.,* 1962, 42, 554–604.

Olds, J., & Milner, P. M. Positive reinforcement produced by electrical stimulation of septal area and other regions of rat brain. *J. comp. physiol. Psychol.,* 1954, 47, 419–427.

Oswald, I., Taylor, Anne M., & Treisman, M. Cortical function during human sleep. In G. E. W. Wolstenholme and M. O'Connor

(Eds.), *The nature of sleep*. Boston: The Ciba Foundation, Little, Brown, 1961.

Pearson, R. B. *Handbook on clinical electromyography*. El Monte, Calif.: Meditron, 1961.

Penfield, W. Functional localization in temporal and deep sylvian areas. *Res. Publ. Assoc. nerv. ment. Dis.*, 1958, 36, 210–226.

Penfield, W., & Roberts, L. *Speech and brain-mechanisms*. Princeton, N.J.: Princeton Univer. Press, 1959.

Persky, H. Adreno cortical function during anxiety. In R. Roessler and N. A. Greenfield (Eds.), *Physiological correlates of psychological disorder*. Madison: Univer. of Wisconsin Press, 1962. Ch. 9.

Persky, H., Grosz, H. J., Norton, J. A., & McMurtry, M. Effect of hypnotically induced anxiety on the plasma hydrocortisone level of normal subjects. *J. clin. Endocrinol. Metab.*, 1959, 19, 700.

Peterson, R. E. Determination of urinary neutral 17-ketosteroids. In D. Seligson (Ed.), *Standard methods of clinical chemistry*. New York: Academic Press, 1963. Ch. 4.

Plutchik, R. Physiological responses to high intensity intermittent sound. *Psychol. Record*, 1963, 13, 141–148.

Prensky, S. D. *Electronic instrumentation*. Englewood Cliffs, N.J.: Prentice-Hall, 1963.

Quesenberry, R. O., & Ungar, F. Thin-layer chromatographic systems for adrenal corticosteroids. *Analyt. Biochem.*, 1964, 8, 192–200.

Richter, C. P. Significant changes in the electrical resistance of the body during sleep. *Proc. Nat. Acad. Sci.*, 1926, 12, 214–222.

Roberts, L. Activation and interference of cortical functions. In D. E. Sheer (Ed.), *Electrical stimulation of the brain*. Austin: Univer. of Texas Press, 1961.

Roberts, W. W., & Kiess, H. O. Motivational properties of hypothalamic aggression in cats. *J. comp. physiol. Psychol.*, 1964, 58, 187–193.

Rose, R. J. Preliminary study of three indicants of arousal: measurement, interrelationships, and clinical correlates. Unpublished doctoral dissertation, Univer. of Minnesota, 1964.

Rothballer, A. B. Studies of the adrenaline sensitive component of the reticular activating system. *EEG clin. Neurophysiol.*, 1956, 8, 603–622.

Rothman, S. *Physiology and biochemistry of the skin*. Chicago: Univer. of Chicago Press, 1954.

Rothman, S., & Lorenze, A. L. Defense mechanisms of the skin. *Annu. Rev. Med.*, 1963, 14, 215–242.

Samuels, Ina. Reticular mechanisms and behavior. *Psychol. Bull.*, 1959, 56, 1–25.

Schachter, S. The interaction of cognitive and physiological determinants of emotional state. In L. Berkowitz (Ed.), *Advances in experimental social psychology*, Vol. 1. New York: Academic Press, 1964.

Schachter, S., & Latené, B. Crime, cognition, and the autonomic nervous system. In *Nebraska symposium on motivation*, Vol. 12. Lincoln: Univer. of Nebraska Press, 1964.

Schachter, S., & Singer, J. E. Cognitive, social, and physiological determinants of emotional state. *Psychol. Rev.*, 1962, 69, 379–399.

Schwartz, T. B., & Shields, D. R. Urinary excretion of formaldehydrogenic steroids and creatinine. *Psychosom. Med.*, 1956, 18, 158.

Sem-Jacobsen, C. W., & Torkildson, A. Depth recording and electrical stimulation in the human brain. In E. R. Ramey and D. S. O'Doherty (Eds.), *Electrical studies on the unanesthetized brain*. New York: Paul Hoeber, Inc. 1960.

Shackel, B. Skin-drilling: a method of diminishing galvanic skin potentials. *Amer. J. Psychol.*, 1959, 72, 114–121.

Shackel, B. Electro-oculography; the electrical recording of eye position. In *Proc. 3rd Int. Conf. Med. Electronics*. Springfield, Ill.: Charles C Thomas, 1962.

Shagass, C. Explorations in the psychophysiology of affect. In J. Sher (Ed.), *Theories of the mind*. New York: Free Press, 1962.

Shagass, C., & Naiman, J. The sedation threshold as an objective index of manifest anxiety in psychoneurosis. *J. psychosom. Res.*, 1956, 1, 49–57.

Shagass, C., Naiman, J., & Mihalik, J. An objective test which differentiates between neurotic and psychotic depression. *AMA Arch. Neurol. Psychiat.*, 1956, 75, 461–471.

Shagass, C., & Schwartz, M. Evoked cortical potentials and sensation in man. *J. Neuropsychiat.*, 1961, 2, 262–270.

Sharpless, S., & Jasper, H. H. Habituation of the arousal reaction. *Brain*, 1956, 79, 655–680.

Shaver, B. A., Brusilow, S. W., & Cooke, R. E. Origin of the galvanic skin response. *Pro. Soc. exp. Biol. Med.*, 1962, 110, 559–564.
Shaver, B. A., Brusilow, S. W., & Cooke, R. E. Electrophysiology of the sweat gland: intraductal potential changes during secretion. *Bull. Johns Hopkins Hosp.*, 1965, 116, 100–109.
Sheer, D. E., & Kroeger, D. C. Recording autonomic responses as an index of stimulation effects. In D. E. Sheer (Ed.), *Electrical stimulation of the brain*. Austin, Tex.: Hogg Foundation, 1961.
Silver, H. Free and conjugated 17-hydroxycorticosteroids in urine. In D. Seligson (Ed.), *Standard methods of clinical chemistry*. Vol. 4. New York: Academic Press, 1963.
Silverman, A. J., & Cohen, S. I. Affect and vascular correlates to catechol amines. In L. J. West and M. Greenblatt (Eds.), *Explorations in the physiology of emotions.* Washington, D.C.: Amer. Psychiatric Assoc., 1960.
Sokolov, E. N. Neuronal models and the orienting reflex. In M. A. B. Brazier (Ed.), *CNS and behavior III*. New York: Josiah Macy, Jr. Foundation, 1960.
Sokolov, E. N. *Perception and the conditioned reflex*. New York: Macmillan, 1963.
Sollner, K. The electrochemistry of porous membranes. In T. Shedlovsky (Ed.), *Electrochemistry in biology and medicine*. New York: Wiley, 1955.
Spencer, L. T. The concept of the threshold and Heymans' law of inhibition. *J. exp. Psychol.*, 1928, 11, 88–97.
Spencer, L., & Cohen, L. H. Correlation of the visual threshold and Heymans' coefficient of inhibition in a single individual, with uniocular vision. *J. exp. Psychol.*, 1928, 11, 194–201. (a)
Spencer, L., & Cohen, L. H. The relation of the threshold to estimates of daily variation in freshness. *J. exp. Psychol.*, 1928, 11, 281–292. (b)
Spong, P., Haider, M., & Lindsley, D. B. Selective attentiveness and cortical evoked responses to visual and auditory stimuli. *Science*, 1965, 148, 395–397.
Stennett, R. G. The relationship of alpha amplitude to the level of palmar conductance. *EEG clin. Neurophysiol.*, 1957, 9, 131–138.
Stern, J. A. Toward a definition of psychophysiology. *Psychophysiology*, 1964, 1, 90–91.
Surwillo, W. W. The relation of simple response time to brain-wave frequency and the effects of age. *EEG clin. Neurophysiol.*, 1963, 15, 105–114.
Surwillo, W. W. The relation of decision time to brain wave frequency and to age. *EEG clin. Neurophysiol.*, 1964, 16, 510–514.
Surwillo, W. W. On the effects of artificial variation of the basal level of skin potential. *Psychophysiology*, 1965, 2, 83–85.
Takagi, K., & Nakayama, T. Peripheral effector mechanisms of G.S.R. *Jap. J. Physiol.*, 1959, 9, 1–7.
Trehub, A., Tucker, I., & Cazavelan, Jane. Epidermal b-waves and changes in basal potentials of the skin. *Amer. J. Psychol.*, 1962, 75, 140–143.
Tursky, B., & Watson, P. D. Controlled physical and subjective intensities of electric shock. *Psychophysiology*, 1964, 1, 151–162.
Valins, S. Psychopathy and physiological reactivity under stress. Unpublished master's thesis, Columbia Univer., 1963.
Vanden Heuvel, W. J. A., Creech, B. G., & Horning, E. C. Separation and estimation of the principal human urinary 17-ketosteroids as trimethylsilyl ethers. *Analyt. Biochem.*, 1962, 4, 191–197.
Vendsalu, A. Studies on adrenaline and nonadrenaline in human plasma. *Acta Physiol. Scand.*, 1960, 49, Suppl. 173.
Venables, P. H. Selectivity of attention, withdrawal, and cortical activation. *Arch. gen. Psychiat.*, 1963, 9, 92–96. (a)
Venables, P. H. The relationship between level of skin potential and fusion of paired light flashes in schizophrenic and nomal subjects. *J. psychiat. Res.*, 1963, 1, 279–287. (b)
Venables, P. H., & Sayer, E. On the measurement of the level of skin potential. *Brit. J. Psychol.*, 1963, 54, 251–260.
Vogt, M. The concentration of sympathin in different parts of the central nervous system under normal conditions and after the administration of drugs. *J. Physiol.*, 1954, 123, 451–481.
Wang, G. H. The galvanic skin reflex. A review of old and recent works from a physiologic point of view. Part I. *Amer. J. phys. Med.*, 1957, 36, 295–320.

Weiner, J. S., & Hellmann, K. The sweat glands. *Biol. Rev.,* 1960, 35, 141–186.

Welford, A. T. The "Psychological Refractory Period" and the timing of high speed performance as a review and a theory. *Brit. J. Psychol.,* 1952, 43, 2–19.

Whitfield, I. C. *Manual of experimental electrophysiology.* Oxford, N.Y.: Pergamon Press, 1964.

Wicke, J. D., Donchin, E., & Lindsley, D. B. Visual evoked potentials as a function of flash luminance and duration. *Science,* 1964, 146, 83–85.

Wilcott, R. C. Correlation of skin resistance and potential. *J. comp. physiol. Psychol.,* 1958, 51, 691–696. (a)

Wilcott, R. C. Effects of local blood removal of the skin resistance and potential. *J. comp. physiol. Psychol.,* 1958, 51, 295–300. (b)

Wilcott, R. C. The partial independence of skin potential and skin resistance from sweating. *Psychophysiology,* 1964, 1, 55–66.

Wilcott, R. C. Adaptive value of arousal sweating and the epidermal mechanism related to skin potential and skin resistance. *Psychophysiology,* 1966, 2, 249–262. (a)

Wilcott, R. C. A reply to Surwillo on artificial skin potential basal level variation and skin potential response wave form. *Psychophysiology,* 1966, 2, 377–378. (b)

Wilder, J. Basimetric approach (law of initial value) to biological rhythms. *Ann. N.Y. Acad. Sci.,* 1962, 98, 1211–1228.

Wilkinson, R. T. Effects of sleep-deprivation on performance and muscle tension. In G. E. W. Wolstenholme and Maeve O'Connor (Eds.), *The nature of sleep.* Boston: The Ciba Foundation, Little, Brown, 1961.

Williams, H. L., Lubin, A., & Goodnow, J. Impaired performance with acute sleep loss. *Psychol. Monogr.,* 1959, 73, No. 14 (Whole No. 484).

Williams, H. L., Hammack, J. T., Daly, R. L., Dement, W. C., & Lubin, A. Responses to auditory stimulation, sleep loss and the EEG stages of sleep. *EEG clin. Neurophysiol.,* 1964, 16, 269–279.

Williams, H. L., Tepas, D. I., & Morlock, H. C., Jr. Evoked responses to clicks and electroencephalographic stages of sleep in man. *Science,* 1962, 138, 685–686.

Williams, R. J. *Biochemical individuality.* New York: Wiley, 1963.

Winters, W. D. Comparison of the average cortical and subcortical evoked responses to clicks during various stages of wakefulness, slow wave sleep and rhombencephalic sleep. *EEG clin. Neurophysiol.,* 1964, 17, 234–245.

Woodworth, R. S., & Schlosberg, H. *Experimental psychology.* (Rev. ed.) New York: Holt, 1954.

Worden, F. G., & Marsh, J. T. Amplitude changes of auditory potentials evoked at cochlear nucleus during acoustic habituation. *EEG clin. Neurophysiol.,* 1963, 15, 866–881.

Yokota, T., Tarahashi, T., Kondo, M., & Fujimori, B. Studies on the diphasic form of the GSR. *EEG clin. Neurophysiol.,* 1959, 11, 687–696.

CHAPTER 8 Traits and Persons

EDGAR F. BORGATTA
The University of Wisconsin

Probably the most common tendency in speaking of personality is to make reference to particular personality traits of an individual. The trait approach is ubiquitous and finds its way even into the most complicated of theories. When one looks at definitions of personality traits, the reasons for this become relatively obvious. How else can a person be described except in terms of certain of his characteristic behaviors?

This chapter will be relatively limited in its approach to the description of personality, and while it is labeled generally as concerned with "traits," the approaches to be considered are primarily those that may be described as *direct* and systematic. The attempt here will be to cover certain approaches and point to a few particular emphases. No attempt will be made to be exhaustive, for the literature in this area amounts to thousands of items.

What is to be included in a definition of "traits" is not self-evident. For example, if the common definition is used of a characteristic tendency to behave in a given way, this could include all classes of behavior. Thus, a trait like aggressiveness could be appropriate. The next question is, would a trait like "latent aggressiveness" be equally appropriate in our consideration? And, with some degree of facetiousness one may go further and ask, should repressed latent aggressiveness also be considered as a trait under this definition? Further, are things that are called values appropriately considered under this heading? And, if values are appropriate, are attitudes, as more specific responses, to be included?

Obviously, these are just a few questions that may be raised, and the answers are not, to repeat, self-evident. Different researchers and theoreticians involve different kinds of content in what they would consider to be appropriate for a personality inventory. There has been, however, some tendency to distinguish among personality tests which in theory are oriented toward categories that may be labeled personality traits. The differentiation has occurred in a number of different ways. For example, there is a distinction between a personality inventory and studies of values, mood check lists, aptitude tests, achievement and intelligence tests, and other special tests. There is little or no distinction made, however, between what are called personality tests and some other kinds of tests, such as social adjustment tests and personal preference schedules. This is not, therefore, an area in which language for designating the subject matter is clear.

FACTOR ANALYSIS OF PERSONALITY INVENTORIES

In the development of techniques for describing personality traits, the inventory of items and its component scores have had an important place. The notion that there are many personality traits appears general today, but of course occurs implicitly in languages through the many different adjectives for the description of persons and peoples. Classifications of such traits have been common, but some have had more visible places in the recent history of social psychology than others. Whether these were described as "instincts" or as "tendencies to behave in a given way," the fact is that notions of traits have been important, if not unavoidable. For example, in describing the age of onset of emotions, lists of differentiable emotions had to be described.

There is no question, however, that the description of personality through traits can be moved in two directions. On the one hand, description can be concerned with characteristics that are relatively rare and therefore tend to identify relatively unique characteristics. Sometimes such an approach is associated with the description of pathological conditions. On the other hand, emphasis may be placed on selecting characteristics on which the entire population distributes well, that is, with a substantial degree of variation and possibly even with the convenient characteristics of a normal curve. These two emphases may also be viewed in terms of objectives associated with building a theory of personality. The approach that emphasizes relatively idiosyncratic characteristics may be directed towards elaboration of a taxonomic approach. The approach associated with more general characteristics may be directed towards the building of a theory emphasizing the regularities in the population.

It is not the purpose of this presentation to dwell on different approaches to personality theory, but since these appear to be implicit in the method of test construction, some attention must occur incidentally. The differences in approaches may be characterized in part by reflecting on the issue of "clinical vs. statistical" prediction. It may be acknowledged that in the absence of good tests, a clinician may be more efficient than tests that are not good. However, if good clinicians assist in building good tests, then the tests should contain variables appropriate to assess all the regularities associated with the criterion. Assuming that this is done, then the test should be at least as good as the clinician, but various factors should actually militate for the test to become better than the clinician. This should occur because (a) once the test is established, statistical procedures may be utilized to purify it and establish the sources of predictive variance. This permits the elimination of irrelevant variance in the test but also makes possible the addition of more information gathering which would improve the reliability of the test. (b) Then, an improved test would be competing not only with good clinicians but also with less good ones, and on this basis the statistical procedures would have an edge over the clinical procedures. Now, it must be noted that, in argument against such an analysis, emphasis is often placed on the unique characteristics of individuals which are not encompassed by the tests. This, however, is not an allowable argument, since it suggests that unique characteristics may be used in differentiating individuals. Actually only *regularities* have use in a predictive system. If anything, paying attention to idiosyncratic materials should make a clinician less efficient.

The development of tests may proceed from two directions related to the above distinctions. On the one hand, tests may be devised to correspond to criterion groups. For example, a diagnostic category may be designated as important, and a considerable amount of agreement may exist among clinicians. Thus, a criterion group may be established, and the next question that is raised is: What are the characteristics which distinguish this group from the rest of the population? Such an approach has many inherent problems. Groups that are selected as extreme may be extreme in very many ways. Are persons who are described as having the characteristics invariably placed within the group? This latter question is an extremely important one in the definition of criterion groups, as persons who come to the attention of clinicians may do so by peculiar social routes. Persons come to the attention of clinicians, generally speaking, not because they have certain characteristics but because their characteristics have become objectionable to some section of society, whether this be the spouse, the parent, children, the neighborhood, or others. People arrive for treatment either because they have come to the attention of authorities through any of myriad routes or because they have volunteered themselves as requiring attention. Thus, persons who may be classified by clinicians into a particular category may represent a small proportion of persons having such characteristics, and presumably the rest of the persons having such characteristics are operating in an acceptable way for society. The problem of diagnostic categories is admittedly a difficult one, and procedures for test development according to these categories may be relatively resistant to development.

By contrast, on the other hand, should the alternative approach that emphasizes differentiation of characteristics of persons within the total population be of little relevance to clinicians? Certainly this issue is not decided, but there is some appropriateness in raising the question of whether or not the hesitancy of clinicians to use these tests is such an indictment. Clinicians may indicate, for example, that the verbal basis of these tests, and the fact that they are written and long, makes them inapplicable for many of their cases. In fact, there is the perennial anecdote of the use of the MMPI in order to test "readiness for discharge" among mental patients. When a mental patient can complete the test, he has demonstrated sufficient virtues to be discharged, independently of what the test scores are. Aside from this, there is also the question of whether the content of any test built on the general population will involve sufficient attention to the types of behaviors that may indeed be associated with diagnostic categories.

Attempts at developing systematic and inclusive personality inventories from factor analytic procedures were summarized over a decade ago by French (1953). Generally speaking, the factor analytic approaches concern themselves with allocating to a parsimonious set of variables the content involved in the larger inclusive set of items within a test. Thus, the approach generally is to find a number of scores within a large set of items which will summarize most of the information that is included through all the items. In brief, French found about 70 factor analytic studies, including clinical observation, interest inventories, attitude scales, personality questionnaires, behavioral ratings, and objective test scores. These generated some 450 factors that were loosely classified in about 50 categories. The exercise was most impressive, but certainly not definitive. The question of how many factors indeed were located in these many analyses was left to speculation, as a reasonable set of additional questions could be phrased. For example, if a sufficient number of items could be placed into a single test and a subsequent factor analysis, would there be roughly 50 factors that would come out and would they have the characteristics in the classification in French's work? How many of the factors could be attributable to what may be called method bias, or differences in methods of getting data? How many of the factors are differences in rotation locations on two factor planes? And so forth.

The issue of whether subtests and personality inventories should coincide or align, whether they are based on factor scores or on more intuitive procedures, is an important one conceptually. On the other hand, there is some notion that, if there is order to the phenomena studied, there should be convergence also in the tests that describe the phenomena. On the other hand, more subtle and general theories imply that ordering of characteristics through one medium, say self-report personality inventories, should parallel the structures found through another medium, say peer ratings. This latter issue will be discussed briefly later, but it is noted at this point because an emphasis on convergence of measures at the level of personality inventories relates to the more general problem. Examination of the concepts associated with some of the more generally used personality inventories leads to little confidence about the current generality of structures. For example, in an exercise designed to examine directly the coincidence of subtests, the findings left much to be desired (Borgatta, 1962). The importance of this issue is crucial if one is concerned with generality of findings. In using a personality test, a researcher must raise the issue of whether he would get the same findings if he used another personality test. And, what may happen is that the tests do not involve similar content even though they may have similar names for subtests. Additionally, some tests may omit some aspects of content entirely.

In the exercise comparing the Guilford-Zimmerman Temperament Survey, the Thurstone Temperament Schedule, the Cattell 16 Personality Factor Questionnaire, and the Edwards Personal Preference Schedule, the summary of conclusions was as follows: two main clusters were found and several minor ones for the subscores. One of the main clusters that appeared was concerned with the content generally associated with a concept of extroversion, and a simplex type arrangement of the scores seemed to range from a notion of activity at one pole to dominance at the other. The second main cluster involved content of emotional stability, with a simplex type arrangement possible locating measures of affiliation at one pole and measures of conventional behavior or controlled behavior at the other. Gross differences between the personality inventories become visible in such exercises. For example, the Edwards Personal Preference Schedule appeared not to include any of the major content of emotional stability. On the other hand, the other tests did not appear to involve the content of affiliation and nurturance as much.

The reasons for the apparent lack of coincidence in tests are multiple. For example, there has been some tendency to move away from the old social adjustment inventories that had only two or three scores, emphasizing the many ways in which individuals may differ from each other. The development of tests adding more subscores may not correspond to the empirical experience of sampling of items but may indicate pursuit of particular avenues of cluster construction. Indeed, the concept of "semantic clusters" often arises, indicating the notion that correlated items may be found corresponding to language clusters. The question the test designer always faces is whether these semantic clusters correspond to important aspects of personality or whether they are relatively unimportant. Answering such questions, of course, raises issues that must be embedded in more general personality theories.

Other factors that militate for the construction of subtests may involve tendencies contrary to those of being parsimonious. For example, it may be that in a sample of items the content associated with two general factors may be spread in terms of joint loadings on the two factors. Thus, there is a possibility for construction of scores associated not only with pure factors but also with locations between these pure factors, or joint loadings. Additionally, it may occur that important concepts such as leadership, initiative, hostility, and others may be associated with these joint loadings, and thus there is a reinforcing tendency to build additional scores. Generally speaking, personality inventories have been constructed not on the basis of factor analyses so much as they have been based on experience drawn from factor analyses. This would be demonstrably true if the statement were based merely on the fact that most of the popular personality inventories have 10 or more factors and 200 or more items, more than could be handled by the sophisticated factor analytic procedures available at the time that the tests were constructed.

The above comments are not meant to be critical of existing tests, as the existing personality inventories reflect a tremendous amount of investment of effort. On the other hand, it would be a great error to suggest that personality inventories currently available represent the best that can be developed.

One of the disconcerting aspects of more general examination of the personality inventories is the fact that out of "second order" factor analyses or analyses of scores (rather than items), major concepts arising tend to have much the flavor of the older and simpler tests that emphasize such concepts as extroversion-introversion, ascendence-submission, emotional stability, and social and emotional adjustment. With the current development of computers we may expect new and more systematic investments in the development of personality inventories. When these are executed, we may also expect that considerable attention will be given to some of the theoretical problems that have been raised about such inventories in past years. However, some problems may be viewed as more relevant than others. For example, concern with notions of social desirability, acquiescence, response style, and other such concepts may actually have less importance for future developments than concerns with such notions as convergent and discriminant validation (Campbell & Fiske, 1959).

It is appropriate to give some attention to concepts like social desirability, acquiescence, response style, and the like. It is difficult to trace how interests in particular variables develop in the area of personality, but obviously the popularization of a particular concept may not have an appropriate reflection of the problems out of which it arose. Thus, it may well be that the popularization of concepts like social desirability arise because of a milieu of dissatisfaction with personality inventories rather than because of particular virtues in the concepts themselves. And, historically, a considerable amount of dissatisfaction may be found with personality inventories. They tend to predict very little. Generally, because they predict very little, people usually raise the question of what is the matter with the personality inventory rather than examining whether or not they have established an appropriate prediction task. The factor of social desirability has been particularly emphasized by Edwards (1957), and the Edwards Personal Preference Schedule is indeed designed to take into account this concern with social desirability. A major presumption has been that social desirability accounts for a considerable amount of the variance in personality inventories and thus must be taken into account. In the construction of the Edwards Personal Preference Schedule, items are balanced with regard to social desirability and then presented in balanced pairs, presumably permitting the individual respondent to choose between the equally socially desirable contents (paired comparisons would be made for the 15 scores). From the point of view of test construction, this creates two kinds of problems. First, if items are really balanced and paired comparisons are carried out systematically, then, in theory, persons who are high on everything would get the same scores as persons who are low on everything. Or phrased differently, a person cannot be high on everything or low on everything. Second, obviously, items are used in the creation of more than a single score. The latter difficulty, of course, may be most important in analyses involving the scores when correlated to external variables. Additionally, some justification for such a test appears to be that it may discourage "faking," but the test intrinsically is no less liable to this abuse than other personality inventories.

If one begins with the factor analytic model of analysis, then a notion like social desirability is untenable. In particular, if social desirability is an overriding factor, then it should be present in the factor analysis of a set of items as a general or dominant factor. If, on the other hand, from a factor analysis a set of scores is derived which tend to be relatively well defined with regard to orthogonal axes, the possibility of there being a social desirability factor is immediately and conclusively excluded. Generally speaking, the objectives of test construction along factor analytic lines thus bypass the problem of social desirability completely. There continues to be some possible relevance, but only in a very peculiar sense. That is, scores constructed from factor analytic procedures ordinarily are not pure factor scores but scores corresponding to items maximally loaded in the factors. The problem of using items in more than one score is usually a sufficient deterrent in test construction, so that scores ordinarily are not built with "suppressors." Thus, it is quite possible that if a substantial number of scores are developed, there will be a real possibility that "second-order" factors may be derived from the matrix of scores, or, if other procedures are used, from a matrix of angular measurements of oblique factors. As noted, common experience is that when such factors arise, they are likely to be in either of two areas, either involving a general concept of extroversion-introversion or one of social-emotional adjustment. Indeed, these two "super factors" are not generally orthogonal either, so a concept suggesting a possible alignment of *all common variance* is possible, and such a score would be highly correlated to what Edwards has called social desirability. *It is a peculiar notion theoretically, however, to begin with a concept of such a score as a form of "bias" that needs to be taken into account.*

A quite striking attack on the question of "social desirability" is found in a research by Norman (in press). Of particular interest is his analysis of data using 24 short content scales (3-10), which when factor analyzed yielded 5 factors. A desirability scale composed of 50 items drawn from the same pool of items was then developed. Each of the 24 component measures was correlated with the desirability scale, and then the desirability was partialled out. The residual relationships among the 24 measures were then factor analyzed in parallel to the original analysis. The results indicated that "a comparison of the sum of the communalities for the original analysis with that based on the desirability-regressed residual measures indicates a drop of less than 15% (11.05/12.89 = .857) in the total common variance for these scales when desirability is partialled out. What is perhaps more striking is the fact that the factor structures are extremely similar for the two analyses and could hardly be accounted for in either case by the operation of any single general response tendency." Among other conclusions, the author indicates that individual differences in social desirability responses "may well be a far less salient source of variance in questionnaire measures of personality than has been widely assumed in recent years." Another rather general consideration of the problem is to be found in the paper by Rorer (1965).

Problems of such concepts as response style, acquiescence, extreme response set, and so forth are conceptually related to those of social desirability. If the construction of test scores has proceeded from factor analytic study and if researchers have been concerned with even a reasonable amount of caution with regard to item analysis, such factors may be expected to be minimal. For example, if items within an inventory have high variance and if items within the scores of the inventory are all aligned in their response categories, then persons who are high on all scores or low on all scores both come out with the highest scores on extreme response set, by definition. If the items within scores are balanced so that half are positively stated and half are negatively stated, again persons who are high on all scores or low on all scores would have the high scores on extreme response set. However, in this circumstance one could distinguish between those who are inclined to be agreeing from those who are inclined to be disagreeing. That is, in order to emphasize a tendency to agree, individuals would have to be inconsistent within the scores. Examination of the possibilities of meaning associated with such derivative scores as extreme response set, acquiescence, and the like is likely to lead the investigator to conclude that, theoretically, such tendencies may not be particularly important traits. From the point of view of test construction, certainly, such concepts raise caution in test development rather than lead test developers to introduce ways of getting at these concepts in their tests.

SELF-REPORT AND EXTERNAL OBSERVATION

Personality inventories generally get at self-reports and expressions of preference. These may range from direct self-evaluation on traits to responses of orientation toward highly specific situations or, by contrast, to highly abstract principles. The responses of any individual on a personality inventory may involve various types of inaccuracies. For example, subjects may be deluded about their characteristics or may misperceive their own preferences, and may unintentionally err in other ways. Additionally, test conditions may vary in ways that systematically affect the responses of the subject. Further, and this becomes an issue with regard to some applications, subjects may "fake" their responses in order to create particular impressions. In the use of personality inventories, there is some hesitancy to take scores at face value, particularly when a motive for attempting to misrepresent one's characteristics may exist. There are myriad demonstrations that, under instruction, subjects can "fake" their responses in the directions instructed. On the other hand, there is no systematic evidence that indicates that subjects indeed do "fake" their responses when given the ordinary instructions for completing the personality inventories. However, the known potential for "faking" when coupled to the low level predictive value of most personality inventories appears to have served to keep general applications of the inventories to a minimum, and the inventories remain suspect. Under these circumstances, emphasis on systematic validation becomes focal.

The question of "to what" should personality inventories be validated is not easily answered. In general, the answer is to more "objective" measures. The notion of what is a more objective measure in some cases is difficult to describe. For example, who but the person is the best judge of what feelings he is undergoing? So, at the level of indicators of mood or feeling states, external observers are inferring while the respondent may answer directly. While there may be physiological concomitants to certain feeling states, the physiological concomitants that may be measured objectively are not the feeling states themselves. Of course, we now raise the definitional question of whether such feeling states are personality characteristics. The answer must be that if individuals tend to hold such feeling states characteristically, and if they vary among individuals, they would certainly fit the inclusive definition of personality traits. However, in general, traits of individuals which are described in the discussion of personality tend to be interpersonal rather than intrapersonal.

Persons trained in the tradition of the "symbolic interactionists" and familiar with the work of such persons as James, Baldwin, Cooley, Dewey, and Mead have little difficulty in moving to the arena of interpersonal relations to locate criteria of validation for personality inventories. Indeed, from such a tradition one may draw such principles as the individual's concept of himself is derived from responses of others; and, the characteristics of an individual are those aspects of behavior to which others respond. In such a view, direct observation becomes the "objective" way of gathering information. However, even here there is some question about what kind constitutes objectivity. We may postulate a situation of a subject, others who are his co-participants, and observers who are excluded from participating in the interaction. The subject acts and perceives the impact of his actions. The others respond to him. The observer observes the interaction. The question is, how did the subject behave? Obviously, the subject may have had particular intentions in his action, and these may color his perception of the effect on others. Other factors may enter into the situation to distort the accuracy of his perception. The others respond to the subject, and they in this sense determine what the action of the subject was, not its intention. The observer, not being a part of the interaction, infers what the action has been and what the response has been. The observer who can be objective may also be in the position where he can misperceive both the action and the response to it. In one sense, the observer is inferring the most! So, it may be that peer ratings of an individual on a characteristic may be more valid than those of an "objective" observer.

The use of ratings, defined loosely, is as ancient as attempts of one individual to describe the characteristics of others. At the same time, there always has been a sense of concern about such descriptions. Raters may have systematic biases, tending to view all people in a given way. They may respond to particular individuals in a holistic manner, displaying the "halo" effect. They may respond excessively to particular stimuli or idiosyncratic characteristics. And other biases, of course, may enter into ratings. At the same time, in the light of the question of criteria, ratings are hard to disregard, notwithstanding the inaccuracies of supervisers, teachers, and others.

The limitations of ratings and rankings are well known, and various techniques have been developed in order to improve the gathering of information under given circumstances. Still there are intrinsic problems that will remain, and these will not be discussed here. Rather, we will move to examination of at least one point of convergence with the use of ratings.

Convergence of findings is sufficiently infrequent to make the publication of an article emphasizing replicated factor structure in peer nominations notable (Norman, 1963). While this paper did not cover the full literature in the area, it did emphasize that in the area of peer assessments, a factor structure tended to recur in the work of independent researchers. Relating his own work to that of Cattell and subsequent workers, Norman identifies the five factors as:

I. *Extroversion*
II. *Agreeableness*
III. *Conscientiousness*
IV. *Emotional Stability*
V. *Culture*

He concludes that a relatively orthogonal and highly stable structure of personal characteristics has been identified and that reasonably good measures of these characteristics are available in situations where the peer nomination method of data collection can be reasonably employed. The current author in a series of researches drawn from a quite different tradition, but cognizant of the Cattell tradition, arrived at a similar set of categories. Here, rather than beginning with a broad variety of trait names as was the case originally in the work of Cattell, the progression was from interest in the distinction between the criteria of socio-group and psyche-group in the Moreno (1934) and Jennings (1943; 1947) tradition, through the accumulated studies summarized by Carter (1954). Carter concluded that three factors appear sufficient to account for most of the variance of individual assessments. Beginning with the research reported by Borgatta *et al.* (1958), evidence became available in this series of studies that more than three factors were required, factors being erroneously aligned in Carter's summary in the absence of overlap studies or marker variables.

From the point of view of lag in social-psychological science, it should be noted that more restricted views of factorial structure with regard to ratings persists. For example, Foa (1961) presents a two-factor system in context of a theoretical formulation, and more recently Longabaugh (1966) relates his work to that of Carter (1954) and Leary (1957) without apparent influence from the several sources noted above.

The design reported in the final study of the series (Borgatta, 1964) followed the design of the multitrait-multimethod approach elaborated by Campbell and Fiske (1959) and replicated the prior systematic studies in the series having such a design. In the final study five factors were utilized, named as follows:

I. *Assertiveness*
II. *Likeability* (or Sociability)
III. *Emotionality*
IV. *Intelligence*
V. *Task Interests* (or Responsibility)

It should be noted incidentally that the tendency to use a continuum of hostility-sociability appears to require active resistance on the part of researchers in this area. If *Assertiveness* is one reference vector, at 90 degrees from that vector the concept that will be located is *Likeability*. Sociability and even Friendliness involve some content of *Assertiveness*. Similarly, at the opposite pole of *Likeability,* one does not find Hostility but concepts like Sour or Surly and other notions associated with being unlikeable in the relative absence of *Assertiveness*. Hostility tends to be in the negative quadrant of *Likeability,* but the major loading is likely to be on *Assertiveness*. The incidental comment on structure is noted immediately above to emphasize that in order to carry out research on parallelism through methods, the structure of the traits must be well defined and stable and *cannot come from* ad hoc *speculation or theory*.

The design in the final study of the series utilized five methods (of data collection). Self-ratings were the basis for one method, and self-rankings and peer-rankings, gathered under two criterion specifications, were the basis for the four additional methods. Sample sizes were large, and the study was designed to have an internal replication by separate analysis of female and male subjects. The conclusions of the study were, simply stated, that peer-rankings predict other peer-rankings; self-rankings predict self-rankings; self-ratings predict self-rankings; and self-rankings and self-ratings predict peer-rankings. The findings were well ordered, and two points may be emphasized. The first is the correspondence to the convergent findings on the five-factor structure of ratings reported by Norman (1963). The second and possibly the more important point, however, is the fact that the different methods utilized in data collection establish the connection between paper-and-pencil tests, such as inventories represent, and peer assessment procedures. Cattell (1946; 1957) has long emphasized the theoretical importance of aligning tests corresponding to different methods of data gathering. While his assertions about success in this regard have been challenged, there has been no quarrel with his emphasis on the theoretical importance he ascribes to the problem. In fact, Becker (1960) concludes: "It is suggested that *behavior ratings factors* (as orthogonal as possible) be used as the criteria in developing questionnaire measures of personality." In the context of the research reviewed immediately above, self-ratings may be viewed as a form of direct self-assessments in questionnaires, which is the actual form in which these data were gathered. Other questions commonly asked in personality interviews which relate to preferences thus may be placed in a different context from that in which they are ordinarily found. They may, indeed, be defined as indirect ways of assessing one's own behavior. When this is done, some explanation is provided for the low predictive validity that is ordinarily associated with paper-and-pencil personality inventories. Also, some question is raised about how concepts should be developed in constructing paper-and-pencil tests, and some guidelines for further development of the inventories may therein be provided.

The emphasis thus far has been on ratings, and implicitly the reference point has been with adults or persons who have reached a stage of development in which concepts involved in peer assessments are viable. It should be noted that special and different problems are associated with the description of characteristics of children, and especially of infants. For example, descriptions of infants almost necessarily are observer ratings, as infants cannot report their feelings or preferences, and similarly, peer reactions are nonsensical theoretically. As the social person develops, of course, self-report and peer reactions become more intelligible and interpretable. Concern with observation of infants and children also is productive in the sense that it points to other types of limitations in the study of personality characteristics. For example, characteristics associated with the early ages tend to be general in nature and *not* involved with deviant or pathological conditions, or diagnostic categories. It is only when notions of appropriate behavior become relevant that such categories may be used. Thus, studies of the socialization process may be intimately connected with the more static descriptive problems with regard to traits at later periods.

SYSTEMATIC OBSERVATION SYSTEMS

Since a general presentation on systematic observation systems, particularly related to social interaction, has recently been published (Borgatta & Crowther, 1965), comments on the use of external observer systems will be restricted here.

As we have noted above, external observers are usually identified as the most "objective." What is observed, however, may range from categories that are highly interpretative to relatively specific behaviors that may require little or no interpretation. Chapple's (1940) scoring system, for example, required relatively little inference on the part of observers and thus could be viewed as highly objective. The question that one is left with, however, is whether or not the highly objective scoring procedures lead to summary information on traits that are important in the description of persons. At one level, the answer has to be positive. In particular, the amount of interaction an individual displays, which can be scored relatively objectively, appears to be a most important characteristic in terms of correlates. However, other objectively scored characteristics do not seem to have, either on theoretical grounds or on subsequent empirical analysis, high relevance with regard to understanding the behavior of persons in terms of correlates with variables external to the observation system.

Alternatives available in the development of systematic observation systems are many, but the fact of the matter is that once they are constructed, the utility of the system must be judged in either of two arenas. Either the system must be useful for the analysis for social process and structure, or the system must provide scores for individuals which involve important traits relative to the interaction of the individual and consequences measured in terms of concepts drawn from outside the observation system. Our concern here is with the latter application, and implicitly a criteria of "socially relevant behavior" becomes emphasized.

In the last two decades possibly the most visible and influential scoring system is the one developed by Bales (1950). This system involves greater interpretation than is the case with Chapple's system, and indeed the structure of categories provides symmetries designed especially for analysis of interaction process. In the use of the system over time, however, the categories have been associated with scores attributable to participants, or derivatively, to "roles." Much productive research has emanated from this type of application, but limitations similarly have become visible. Among these are questions that have to do with the articulation of the scores on the objective observer system and peer- and self-ratings that individuals may make. Questions may be raised as to why, if the observer system is not coordinated to the ratings or rankings, there should be expectations of high predictability from the system variables to the other variables. Similarly, the attempts to predict interaction behavior on the basis of paper-and-pencil personality inventories have had only negligible success. There is a real question that must be asked, thus, of whether any more success than has been found should have been expected.

At this point materials noted as presented elsewhere will not be duplicated. However, emphasis is given to the notion that category systems, to be useful in the construction of systematic theory that ranges from the level of personality theory through the analysis of social structures, must take cognizance of problems of parallel measures. Analysis in the areas of personality and social structure is difficult enough without involving problems of conceptual inconsistency of measures. The specifications of operations used in measurement are not sufficient conditions, but merely minimal conditions involved. Ordinarily, in science, establishment of relevance and appropriateness of measures involves the satisfaction of additional criteria, including the specification of domains in which the measures lie and appropriate differentiation of measures into parsimonious sets. Such a comment leads us transitionally to consideration of an additional problem that is crucial to the analysis of characteristics of persons. Namely, what are the characteristics of persons, and how are they differentiated from the characteristics of the social order in which the persons exist? It is in order to emphasize this question that the next section is presented here. The approach is to examine if emergent group properties may be considered as appropriate or well defined concepts. This consideration leads to an important—but not answered—question. How are individual characteristics to be distinguished from the group properties? Since we constantly tussle with notions of reality of individual characteristics and of group characteristics, what kinds of bases do we have for analyses of personality and social structure? The following section may indicate the rather *ad hoc* assumptive basis for definitions at both the group and individual level.

SYNTALITY VS. PERSONALITY VARIABLES

Another issue that arises in research which is confusing to many is not unrelated to the insight of the early symbolic interactionists who placed stress on the situational determinants of behavior. In essence, the distinction was made that an individual is known only through the reactions of others to him. But, and this is the dilemma placed into our heritage, then how is the individual described separately from his fellows? Actually, a more interesting set of questions raised later by psychologists, and emphasized in the work of Cattell, ask how characteristics of groups are related to the characteristics of individuals. The questions go much beyond the simple notions of "group intelligence" which were in vogue earlier. Here we shall proceed to examine some of the more sophisticated theory, and a critique and an example are provided which seem to point to a psychologistic approach.

In a recent review, Cattell defines three classes of variables representing the exhaustive set applicable to group description as follows:

By population characteristic measures ... we refer to the mean and sigma of the population, measures on attributes of individuals which can be and are normally considered as individual characteristics and are not measures of the total groups as such. ... By group structure characteristics, we refer to the patterns of interactions of individuals, out of which, by analysis, group traditions, roles, association patterns, hierarchies, cliques, status dimensions, etc., are inferred as constructs. ... By group syntality characteristics we refer to the attributes describing the group when it acts as an organic whole (Cattell, 1961, pp. 210–211).

These definitions are similar to earlier ones (Cattell, 1951). Cattell is aware of problems of conceptualization, and some shift of his position is noticeable in his publications. In his more recent work little attention is actually given to the distinction between the panels, but Cattell says:

Before proceeding further, it may be necessary to point out that although the population, structure and syntality panels can be conceptually separated and independently measured, this is not the same thing as stating that they are functionally and statistically independent. On the contrary, it is our assumption ... that any one of these panels should ultimately be inferable ... from the remaining two, when the laws of group dynamics are known. For example, the performance of a group in building a house can be predicted (as yet imperfectly) from the mean intelligence of its members and the form of leadership structure, particularly in relation to intelligence distribution. But causation runs both ways, e.g. the mean population level on an information test may be a function of syntality, e.g. the national decision to require for its children an extra year of schooling (Cattell, 1961, p. 212).

Here we shall focus on the definition of the syntality characteristics following the argument previously outlined (Borgatta *et al.*, 1956). Let us assert that if a group syntality characteristic is an attribute describing the group when it acts as an organic whole, it is not a population variable. Thus, group talking rate (average rate of talking for the group) is a syntality characteristic only if it is not the direct measure of the *characteristic* talking rates of the members, which is a population variable. Then: (a) if group talking rate has no correlation to the average characteristic talking rate of the members, we could suspect and expect that it is a syntality variable; and (b) if group talking rate is perfectly correlated to the average characteristic talking rate of the members, it could be reasonably asserted that it is not a syntality characteristic at all. The more difficult ground arises in the more likely circumstance, namely: (c) if group talking rate is imperfectly correlated to the average characteristic talking rate of members, it *may* be a syntality variable. It becomes necessary to ask further questions. Can the group talking rate be accounted for by additional characteristics of the group members? A conditional restriction appears logically necessary for this question, however. The group talking rate should not be accounted for on the basis of *concomitant* group measures but on measures that can be shown to be predictive. Thus, the group talking rate should be demonstrable as a *product* of some input of group members. (This is true for *a*, also.)

Input may refer to (*1*) characteristic measures on the members or (*2*) measures taken in the early performance of the group. If the measures are of type *1*, they are clearly population measures, and only a few additional questions need to be answered about them. For example, it should be demonstrated that the input measures are not correlated to the average characteristic talking rate of the group members, because if this were the case, then the interpretation of the additional prediction of the group talking rate may well involve two independent predictors of the same characteristic with independent errors of measurement rather than prediction of an emergent quality. If the variables are of type 2, not only must the questions of association with the other population variables be taken into account but also the relationship of the variables to the group talking rate at the time the individual measures were assessed. If it turns out that the relationship of the individual measures to group talking rate is similar at the early point and the subsequent point, then for all practical purposes all that is demonstrated is the stability of the concomitant measures, not the consequent development of emergent properties. In short, what is evident here is that accounting for what is not accounted for by the parallel population measures in the group talking rate *must* involve a demonstration of the prediction *as a consequence of the early measures.* Concomitant measures cannot be used to explain the group (emergent) measures. Similarly, utilization of additional measures that can be interpreted as providing direct measure of parallel population variables with independent errors of measurement cannot be used to demonstrate emergent properties but only to improve the unreliable population measure in the same way that one builds more reliable tests.

It has been noted that population characteristics are not only averages or means but can be other moments of the distribution. Thus, in examining the ability to predict the group talking rate, characteristics of the distribution other than the average may be utilized. These quite obviously include the variance, but there is no reason why the additional common characteristics of the distribution such as flatness or skewness of the distribution should not also be considered directly as population variables. It must be emphasized, however, that these additional moments are not necessarily independent of the average. Thus, a high average characteristic talking rate for a group of small size commonly might have a small variance with a high peak and a large skew. On the other hand, if it should turn out that these additional moments add to the predictability of group talking rate, such facts are not trivial. To the contrary, *they constitute important formal properties for the description of group behavior.*

These considerations place a burden on the profession not to theorize about the relationships among syntality characteristics and population characteristics but to demonstrate the existence and, if possible, to provide a classification of syntality characteristics. *What, in fact, are group products?* It is, of course, appropriate to theorize about the kinds of things that might be group products.

Let us examine first what population variables constitute. It is simple to think of the average IQ of group members and even such things as the average "dominance" personality score of the members as population variables. For a simple aggregate group task such as the provision of recalled nonsense stimuli, is there a direct set of measures that can be taken on the individual members prior to the group participation which would constitute a population measure? It seems relatively obvious that the individual recall ability of the members can be assessed and a population measure described in parallel to the group ability to recall the nonsense syllables. If the population measure would account for the group performance, the group performance could hardly be called a syntality characteristic.

The above statement is inadequate, however, as a specification of how individual recall ability of members should be assessed to be parallel to the group measure. Consider the following ways: First, in accord with common procedures of individual testing the person may be tested "alone" in some laboratory setting. Second, the individual may be tested in groups of "random" composition, and the average contribution of the subject in such groups could be assessed. Third, the individual may be tested in groups of "random" composition, and the average *impact* on the group product could be assessed. Further, the relevance of the testing situation could be considered explicitly. Whatever variables would systematically affect the individual scores would be taken into account. For example, if group size affects the performance of particular members, would not the appropriate measure of individual performance be one in which the quality is assessed in groups of appropriate size? And further, and here the problem gets sticky, if the statement can be made that the participation of the type of members in the group bears a direct relationship to the characteristic performance of the other members, should the performance of the individual be assessed over all possible combinations of other members (or some other notion of sampling), or should it be assessed only in the relevant class of members in which his characteristic performance is to be entered as a component part of a population variable?

The last question can be phrased relative to personality characteristics (and abilities) a little more simply. If we deal with a concept such as assertiveness, and by assertiveness we mean the way an individual behaves towards others which is recognized (or responded to) by others as assertive behavior, and other behaviors are distinguishable (an orthogonal factor can be described), then shall this be the personality variable that is to be utilized in the construction of a general theory of behavior? This question is an appropriate one here because of the additional question that immediately follows: If it can be demonstrated that in different situations persons make predictably different responses (relative to others) in regard to assertive behavior, then are there as many variables that should be called assertiveness as there are different situations? Should we have, for example, assertiveness-Sit_1, assertiveness-Sit_2, . . ., assertiveness-Sit_n? If so, how do we proceed to specify the Sit_i?

Illustration of the Definitional Alternatives

Suppose we have a two-person situation, with subjects S_A and S_B given the task X_1, which can be reliably evaluated by some objective criterion. The score on X_1 is a score given jointly to the two-person unit. The question that we face is to examine the relationship of inputs based on subjects S_A and S_B and the score X_1.

For convenience, let us assume that there is no practice effect in the score X_1. (That is, after the product emerges, improvement in practice does not occur.)

Suppose that S_A and S_B on task X_1 are repeatedly observed. Then, if the same score of X_1 is attributed in each successive observation to S_A and to S_B, the prediction of the performance of S_A and S_B on the next task X_1 will be identical to the prediction that S_A and S_B will continue to perform as they have, and the limitations of the prediction are determined entirely by the reliability of the "test," the measurement of X_1. In other words, since the scores of S_A and S_B are perfectly correlated, any combination of these two scores will add no information to the prediction of the X_1 score.

Let us note that if for each observation the input S_A and S_B are identical, there should be no variation on the score X_1 except that attributed to the limitations of measurement. Obviously, we would not take such a radical position as to assert that S_A and S_B are identical at each observation, nor similarly that the task situation X_1 is identical in each observation. However, we must then distinguish between random factors that might affect the score of X and those that are systematic. Before discussing this, let us note, however, additional extensions on the above tautology.

For S_A it may be possible to substitute other persons who are equivalent, S_{A_i}. When this is done the effect on the prediction of X_1 should be determined entirely upon the effectiveness of the classification of the S_{A_i}. Obviously, if the S_{A_i} are identical to S_A, no effect should occur on the prediction of X_1. Again, such perfect classification is not expected, and again the classification errors can be seen as being either random or systematic relative to the performance of X_1. From the point of view of measurement, the performance of the S_{A_i} must be assessed to determine equivalence relative to S_B in the performance of X_1. The assumption is that each S_{A_i} will fall into this classification, because his performance with S_B would lead to the same characteristic performance as S_A with S_B on task X_1. Similarly, S_{B_i} should be capable of definition, and the extension of this procedure is that in examination of all possible combinations of persons relative to the task X_1, a classificatory system would develop. It is possible to define S_{A_i}, S_{B_i}, and to determine further that $S_{A_i} = S_{B_i}$ or $S_{A_i} \neq S_{B_i}$, and that there is further a classification S_{I_i} into which all others fit.

It should be emphasized that such a classificatory system could be extremely complex. There is no necessary assumption that persons fall into discrete classes, and thus the property relative to the performance of X_1 might involve a continuous rather than a discrete classification. In addition, there is no implication involved that any arrangement is linear, so that a set of persons S_{I_i} might be ordered in one way to another subset S_{J_i} and in quite a different way to a third subset S_{K_i}, and the ordering of S_{J_i} to S_{K_i} might be independent of the two prior orderings. The fact is, however, that if knowledge is available of every S relative to every other S, then the prediction of X_1 is in each case equivalent in form to our example of S_A and S_B.

Note, then, that the question of random variation vs. systematic variation is already implicitly taken into account. If systematic variation is involved in the definition of S_A, he no longer belongs to the class of S_A but belongs to some other class. This leads immediately to the question of what it is about S_A that has changed to move him from one class relative to another. Here care needs to be given to the implications of this statement. The question of what changes have occurred in S_A to change his classification is identical to the question of what changes have occurred in S_A that affect the product X_1.

This, of course, brings us to a point where a serious dilemma in the study of personality arises. We have been dealing with a characteristic of S_A associated with the performance of task X_1. What other characteristics can be measured? The answer, simply stated, is the performance of S_A on all other tasks X_i. We must again remind ourselves that the task X_1 we have been considering is defined in the situation of two persons, and thus the tasks X_i have the characteristic that they are defined by the situations that can elicit a differential response from S_A, and more generally from any S.

Discussion of the Illustration

The procedure described thus is a conceivable method for the accumulation of information about characteristics of individuals relative to their response in highly specific situations. In particular, the situations defined ultimately would be those that accumulate on a notion of just noticeable (measurable) differences. Assumptions of any such approach would be that if there are modular categories, these would dominate the location of the points involved in the just noticeable differences. Obviously, if the variables involved are linear and simple, a method of simplification for classification would arise, but initially no such assumption could be made that there is linearity or that the dimensions involved are simple rather than complex. By complex here is not necessarily meant merely a compounding of additive factors but the possibility that some variables might have the identical positive pole and quite different negative poles, and other such situations that might occur in the definitions.

To reiterate, the method described would be conceivable but not practical. If practicality were to be utilized in conjunction with the method, all sorts of *ad hoc* assumptions would need to be brought to the fore, including assertions about appropriateness of dimensions of observation, existence of modular categories, and so forth. We are in a state of knowledge where, in essence, to ask the kinds of questions suggested by the method we must imply more assumptions that influence the outcome than the method as a pure form allows.

It is important to note, however, what the meaning would be of a classification system that would be devised having the characteristics suggested. First, there would be as many variables as there are ways in which individuals differ. Concomitantly there would also be as many variables as there are situations to which individuals differentially respond. With this kind of knowledge, the prediction of composition of groups with regard to their products would be a direct extension of measurement. Thus, the group product would be merely a function of the individual components *with no implication of emergent quality,* since the emergent quality would already be associated with the characteristic of the individual. The limitations on the prediction of the group product would arise merely from the unreliability of the assessment of individuals or from inappropriate prediction based on an assessment of the situation which does not take into account all relevant factors. In other words, the prediction may be based on incorrect input when the consequences are observed.

Alternatives in the Composition Problem

The discussion of group products emphasizes the nature of measurement that is to be carried out for the individuals involved. We may at this point suggest some of the alternatives that exist in developing a prediction problem in the composition of groups with regard to a group product.

First, a method of composition which is not uncommon is to preselect individuals on ability for the task of the group. Thus, for example, on the basis of evaluation criteria, an aircraft commander might be chosen as high performing or low performing, and expected behavior on a new assignment would be in accord with the choice. If all members of a crew are chosen with high ability, the prediction would be that the crew would be a high performing crew. The assumptions in this type of operation should be clarified. Evaluation has occurred on a highly complex task in which the end result is observed. Factors concerned in the completion of the end result involve many discriminable characteristics of the individual. Most simply, his abilities and social-psychological characteristics and his training are involved. While in the process of training, there may be tests of a general nature which are predictive of efficiency on the ultimate criterion. The prediction of performance is on the basis of a test that attempts as closely as possible to simulate the actual conditions of performance. Thus, prediction is based on some notion of an average situation in which the performer is tested. Prediction under these circumstances is merely the extension of individual performance, although error in prediction would not necessarily be simple. For example, in a group with differentiated tasks (and positions), performance on one task may more directly affect the group product than performance on another task. The function, in other words, might not be a simple additive one. Similarly, performance on the group product may be of such a nature that if performance of particular individuals falls below a given threshold, the completion of the group product is negated. On the other hand, it may be that the nature of the task for the group is of such an order that compensatory mechanisms develop as long as the performance of an individual does not fall below a given point. The consequences in selection on the social-psychological characteristics need to be noted. In the process of training and selection, it may very well be that all of the persons having characteristics at the social-psychological level (personality) which would negatively affect task completion have already been eliminated, or the range of inclusiveness has been narrowed to a point that the relevance of such factors is very small. This does not mean, however, that differences among individuals on such characteristics are not discernible. It may be that one person is more assertive than another, but no person is included whose assertiveness is either so low or so high that it affects the task completion in a noticeable and significant way. Composition on personality characteristics, thus, is relatively unlikely to pay off in improving task performance when participants have already been prescreened to remove negative aspects with regard to the task. On the other hand, there may persist a notion that "ideal" composition should improve performance. Again, if this is the case, it should have already been reflected in the performance characteristics assessed in advance of the composition with regard to task performance.

Comment may also be added on the question of the reported finding that in groups where sociometric choice level is high, task performance is higher. Here there are a number of problems. An immediate one is that the sociometric choice level may be a reflection of success, an indication of morale in success. At a slightly more subtle level it may also be the assessment of favorable performance of other members, and most generally morale as reflected therein.

In short, under these circumstances of composition, prediction of group success becomes a problem for several reasons. The criterion variable is attenuated in the sense that most groups are at the level of success rather than ranging from failure to success in a well-distributed way. Prediction on the basis of the individual components is based on an extension of prior experience and includes in a complex way most of the variables that could be dealt with separately in some notion of improvement of composition.

A second alternative in the composition problem arises in the attempt to separate the assessment of ability with regard to the task from other relevant factors that include the social-psychological. Thus, it might be possible to devise tests of mechanical ability with regard to a task which are relatively devoid of the social-psychological factors, except to the extent that the latter are not overriding factors of the type that would become noticeable even in the independent testing. It is conceivable, for example, that there would be design of a three-location (person) task, each with its control requirements that are dependent upon the abilities of the participants capable of being ordered in a hierarchy or in any combination of dependencies, and also capable of independent assessment of the performer if the positions can be detached physically. It should be possible, subsequently, to place the three positions in proximity or otherwise introduce the social interaction that presumably would elicit individual responses at a social-emotional level that might affect performance. Again, here it would be important to discriminate between types of characteristics that might be implied in the manipulation of the individual. For example, would the concern with regard to characteristics center on such notions as resistance to stress and endurance under task conditions? Or, would they relate to such characteristics as assertiveness, sociability, activity, and so forth, perhaps ordered in some complementary or some antagonistic way to affect the group product?

The experimental manipulation suggested here is one that has a high liability in that the task has the element of realism removed in part. The participants do not, for example, have their lives depend upon the participation, as might be the case when they are crew members. The risks involved would generally be known, and these would constitute important values determining performance.

Experimental manipulation can proceed in the direction of making the task more abstract and less directly related to the life situation of the individual. Thus, for example, mechanical tasks would be devised which involve learning and achievement of a given performance level that could be independently assessed from group participation. Then, in some additive way with the ability of developing methods for increasing dependencies among participants, "group products" could be assessed. If a sufficient control could be developed on the task in order to standardize measurement independently and prior to participation, it would then be possible to measure responses to input personality characteristics that traditionally are of interest but practically have been eliminated from the researchability in the composition problem.

THE GROUP PRODUCT NOTION AND TRAITS

The major question raised relates to the definition of what a group product is. The emphasis that develops may appear to stress the psychologistic interpretation, but this is a consequence, rather than the intent, of the analysis. The existence of group products is not a matter of definition so much as of demonstration. On the other hand, this places equal emphasis on notions of personality traits. What a personality characteristic is can be defined in the operations of measurement, but it also needs to be defined as a part of a systematic science within the context of all measurement for the science.

There is circularity and lack of productivity implicit in any analysis that proceeds on the assumption that personality is something to be "understood" in levels of organization if the analyses do not imply systematic structuring of variables at each level. The *ad hoc* quality of much personality theory, even when it makes "good sense," is no substitute for systematic rigor. When less than systematic empirical approaches are used, the self-deception can be practiced of appearing to understand "in depth" when all that is involved may be a set of poorly defined variables.

It is relatively obvious that definitive studies in the area of group products will not be carried out full-blown in the immediate future. Examination of theoretical questions with regard to notions of group products place emphasis on limitations of knowledge in the area of personality. Here we would conclude that, indeed, many theoretical questions about how measurements of personality should be developed and what the nature of personality theory should be have yet to be faced.

REFERENCES

Bales, R. F. *Interaction process analysis: A method for the study of small groups.* Cambridge, Mass.: Addison-Wesley, 1950.

Becker, W. C. The matching of behavior rating and questionnaire personality factors. *Psychol. Bull.,* 1960, 57, 201–212.

Borgatta, E. F. The coincidence of subtests in four personality inventories. *J. soc. Psychol.,* 1962, 56, 227–244.

Borgatta, E. F. The structure of personality characteristics. *Behav. Sci.,* 1964, 9, 8–17.

Borgatta, E. F., & Crowther, Betty. *Social interaction processes.* Chicago: Rand McNally, 1965.

Borgatta, E. F., *et al.* The spectrum of individual interaction characteristics. *Psychol. Rep.,* Monograph supplement 4, 1958, 4, 279–319.

Borgatta, E. F., *et al.* On the dimensions of group behavior. *Sociometry,* 1956, 19, 223–240.

Campbell, D. T., & Fiske, D. W. Convergent and discriminant validation by the multitrait-multimethod matrix. *Psychol. Bull.,* 1959, 56, 81–105.

Carter, L. F. Recording and evaluating performance of individuals as members of small groups. *Personnel Psychol.,* 1954, 7, 477–484.

Cattell, R. B. *Description and measurement of personality.* New York: World Book, 1946.

Cattell, R. B. New concepts for measuring leadership in terms of group syntality. *Hum. Relat.,* 1951, 4, 161–184.

Cattell, R. B. *Personality and motivation; Structure and measurement.* New York: World Book, 1957.

Cattell, R. B. Group theory, personality and role: A model for experimental researches. In *Defense psychology.* New York: Pergamon Press, 1961.

Cattell, R. B. Theory of situational, instrument, second order, and refraction factors in personality structure research. *Psychol. Bull.,* 1961, 58, 160–174.

Chapple, E. D. Measuring human relations: An introduction to the study of interaction of individuals. *Genet. Psychol. Monogr.,* 1940, 22, 3–147.

Edwards, A. L. *The social desirability variable in personality assessment and research.* New York: Dryden Press, 1957.

Foa, U. G. Convergences in the analysis of the structure of interpersonal behavior. *Psychol. Rev.,* 1961, 68, 341–353.

French, J. W. *The description of personality measurements in terms of rotated factors.* Princeton, N.J.: Educ. Testing Serv., 1953.

Jennings, Helen H. *Leadership and isolation.* New York: Longmans, 1943.

Jennings, Helen H. Sociometric differentiation of the psychegroup and sociogroup. *Sociometry,* 1947, 10, 71–79.

Leary, T. *Interpersonal dimensions of personality.* New York: Ronald Press, 1957.

Longabaugh, R. The structure of interpersonal behavior. *Sociometry,* 1966, 29, 441–460.

Moreno, J. L. *Who shall survive?* New York: Beacon House Press, 1934.

Norman, W. T. Toward an adequate taxonomy of personality attributes: Replicated factor structure in peer nomination personality ratings. *J. abnorm. soc. Psychol.,* 1963, 66, 574–583.

Norman, W. T. Relational questions and unrelated answers: Social desirability and self report. *Psych. Bull.,* in press.

Rorer, L. G. The great response-style myth. *Psychol. Bull.,* 1965, 63, 129–156.

CHAPTER 9 Testing, Measuring, and Assessing People

LEE SECHREST
Northwestern University

Except for occasional instances in which they may be used as "filler" or decoy activities in experiments, tests or quasi-tests are given for the purpose of acquiring information about people, presumably information about their response tendencies. It should be obvious, but is perhaps often forgotten, that the only response tendencies about which direct information can be obtained from tests is response tendencies toward the (total situational) test stimuli themselves. When a person responds "bat" to a reproduction of an inkblot, we can know directly only that the inkblot aroused the verbal response "bat." There is more than ample evidence by now that personality tests may often elicit responses which seem to indicate only how the individual will respond to similar test stimuli. In fact, with one administration of one item, we cannot even be certain that we have information about a response "tendency" if we mean by that term a consistency of responding, for the response obtained may be in some manner fortuitous and not indicative of the individual's response *tendency*.

However, it is scarcely ever the case that we are interested in an individual's test responses as such. They will be of interest only to the extent that they are indicative in some manner of the way in which the individual will respond in an inferential chain which leads in some manner to predictions and decisions that have to be made. There are a number of ways in which the inferential process may proceed. In some instances it may be possible to infer more or less directly from a test response what an individual might do in an extratest situation. For example, if a person responds "True" to the statement "I often read detective stories," it can be assumed that he in fact does so. That is not to say that all persons who respond "True" to that item do often read detective stories, but in general the inference will almost certainly be supportable. Probably more often, however, the inferential process involves the summarizing of a test performance or a part of it by invoking a test construct, i.e., something very like the "intervening variable" (MacCorquodale & Meehl, 1948) in behavioral theory. The test construct may be arrived at in a variety of ways, and its implications for extratest behavior may be quite evident or may involve extra inferential steps. An individual responding to the items of the Manifest Anxiety Scale (MAS) responds either "True" or "False" (or, to be perfectly accurate, the response may consist of marking one or the other of two spaces on an answer sheet), and on the basis of his responses, it is inferred that he is an "anxious" person, and it is predicted that in other situations he will respond as an anxious person would. Note that the test construct "anxious" is an inference from test responses, but it is quite unrelated to the actual character of the responses made. It need not be and is not assumed that the MAS respondent's behavior is anxious while he is taking the test. It will be seen that the inferential step from test construct anxiety to behavioral anxiety is a direct one.

On the other hand, consider the example of the inferential process beginning with a respondent's long reaction-time and poor response to a Rorschach card, and which goes from there to the test construct "color shock," from there to "anxiety," and finally ends in an extratest behavioral prediction. In this instance there is a direct relationship between the individual's test behavior and the test construct. However, note that there is an extra inferential step necessary to get from the circumscribed construct "color shock" to the extratest prediction. Other things being equal we may take it as being almost certain that the more steps there are in an inferential process, the greater the probability of error.

It appears to the writer that there are three types of statements which may ensue from an analysis and interpretation of a personality test or assessment procedure. Ultimately most testing must be pointed toward the assessment and prediction of what Campbell (1963) has termed *behavioral dispositions,* although the behavioral implications may be only implicit in some of the outcomes or decisions stemming from testing. It should be clear that when on the basis of a personality test or any other information an individual is described, for example, as "dependent," it is being implied that he probably will respond in a "dependent" manner in a variety of situations or to an exceptional degree. Even a "diagnostic" statement, which is to say a categorical relegation, such as "schizophrenic," can only mean that the person to whom it is applied can be expected to *behave* more or less like schizophrenics in a variety of situations. Of course, the behavioral prediction may be qualified in any one of a number of ways so that the disposition is described more completely. Forer (Carr, Forer, Henry, Hooker, Hutt, & Piotrowski, 1960) suggests that statements about behavior may be of four kinds: (a) statements about the kind of response which will occur, (b) statements about the intensity of the response, (c) statements about the situations in which the response will occur, and (d) statements about the degree of instigation or environmental pressure necessary to elicit the response. Such specifications would be most valuable any time that they are possible.

It is often argued that personality tests, particularly those of a projective nature, are not directed toward the assessment of overt behaviors or toward behavioral prediction. Rather, they are meant to focus on the structure of the personality, the conflicts and motives which underlie behavior, and the like. Thus, Forer (Carr *et al.,* 1960) makes a distinction between the use of tests for *extrinsic* as opposed to *intrinsic* prediction. By the former he refers to behavioral prediction and by the latter to the more covert, underlying elements of personality. However, it is apparent that at some point the underlying elements, the structure of the personality, the conflicts, must articulate with the ongoing behavior of the individual. Otherwise they lose all meaning. If, for example, we consider a person who smiles a great deal, who describes himself to others as happy and successful, who is regarded by his family as a good husband and father, who is often rewarded by his employer, and who has many friends—all of these being overt, operational traits—the question of his underlying personality, of what he is really like, becomes trivial. If conflicts exist, if there are weaknesses in the personality structure, then they will have to be revealed at some time in behavior that can be observed. This is not to say that statements about what are viewed as dynamics of personality can be validated or invalidated for every individual case. It is perfectly possible that one might develop the hypothesis that a particular individual has a personality weakness that will make him unusually vulnerable if he encounters a special kind of stress, and if the stress is never encountered, the prediction can never be tested. However, such predictions or extrapolations from intrinsic diagnostic statements must be open to validation across a sample of persons about whom they are made.

A second very common but questionable use of personality tests is for the purpose of reconstructing some aspect of an individual's life history, i.e., for post-dictive purposes. For example, on the basis of a TAT a clinician may attempt to state the kind of relationship the subject had with his father. Often what is meant by giving a "dynamic" interpretation of a test is the facile construction of a past history which would account for current behavior. That many such histories may be possible, and that many such histories may even be constructed from the same test protocol, calls into serious question the use of tests for such purposes. In fact, some of the severest critics of personality test interpretations cite as a major criticism the dreary *sameness* of the so-called dynamics which are developed for different cases (Meehl, 1956). In any case, the use of tests to reconstruct the past history of a patient certainly does not involve the assessment or prediction of overt behaviors which could be used in some manner to verify the statements made.

A third and theoretically, if not empirically, more defensible use of tests is in the diagnosis of organic brain injury (or some other neurological or anatomical state). In the case of brain syndromes there is a more or less well-defined neurological structure or anomaly to be identified, and the outcome of the test is a prediction at some (implicit) level of confidence that neurological pathology will or will not be found (or could be found) regardless of the future behavior of the subject. That is, it is not necessary that a patient continue or discontinue acting like an "organic" patient in order for the prediction to be demonstrated as having substance.

If psychopathologists knew of pathological anatomical or physiological changes associated with schizophrenia, then the diagnosis of schizophrenia would consist at least in part of the prediction that such physical pathology would be found. At the present time, though, the diagnosis can refer only to gross behavioral events.

There are two somewhat distinct prediction or assessment problems involved in psychological testing which have been termed *bounded* and *unbounded* prediction by Levy (1963). A bounded prediction problem refers to the familiar use of tests to make some specific, limited prediction about the individual, a prediction which might be limited in time, situationally, or behaviorally. Examples of such predictions would be the prediction of grade point average, of response to psychotherapy, or of the possibility of an individual's becoming psychotic. For bounded prediction problems it is ordinarily a reasonably simple matter to establish the validity or utility of any particular prediction device, whether it be a formal test or an interview. Unbounded assessments are those, so common in clinical practice, in which a test is given with the aim of making a general assessment of a patient which can be used in the future to make predictions which have not been specified at the time the test is given. Thus, for example, a clinical patient may be given a test or battery of tests in order that the clinician may arrive at some general "understanding" of the case, but without the aim of making any particular predictions at that time. Later, however, the clinical examiner may be called upon to make a wide variety of statements about the patient, some of which may be unique to that patient. It is apparent that to the extent that a test is used repeatedly to make the same prediction or statement about patients, e.g., possibility of psychosis, the problem is essentially that of the bounded prediction, and the test may be validated in the usual way. But to the extent that the test is used to make statements about a patient of a kind which the test interpreter may seldom have made before about other patients, e.g., will patient *A* regard his discharge as a rejection, then the problem of establishing the validity, let alone the utility, of a test is difficult. At a later point, the latter problem will be considered.

WAYS OF ASSESSING BEHAVIORAL DISPOSITIONS

There are, of course, many conceivable ways in which one might appraise the behavioral dispositions of any given person, and tests of one sort or another must be judged for their validity and utility along with all other alternatives. Campbell (1963) has suggested seven ways in which information about behavioral dispositions might be acquired, and we will add here possible variants on his seven plus a different one.

1. *Tailing* involves following an individual about for a sufficient period of time to enable us to make an assessment of his predominant modes of response. While tailing is conceivable, it is apparent that it would, under most circumstances, be an expensive method of acquiring information, and it could yield quite misleading information unless care were taken to sample in some adequate manner from the universe of situations in which an individual might be observed. However, it is worth noting that the method is in wide use in situations in which important information must be obtained and in which errors are scarcely tolerable, e.g., marital fidelity, employee honesty, trustworthiness of responsible officials.

2. *Episodic recall* is a method in which an individual is asked to recall portions of his past with emphasis on the ways in which he has behaved. The length of the probe into the past might be anywhere from a few hours or days to years. This often is the method of the anamnestic data gatherer, and it is also infrequently used in personality assessment by way of the technique of the autobiography. In many respects episodic recall may be considered a variant of tailing, but one dependent upon self-report. The anamnesis or other episodic recall procedure is probably not used so often in research as a predictive assessment procedure as it is used as a criterion operation in such studies as that by Little and Shneidman (1959).

3. *Situational sampling.* Rather than following an individual in the persistent but somewhat aimless manner required for tailing, it is probably more efficient and nearly as informative to decide ahead of time the situations in which it would be most fruitful to make observations—presumably those situations exemplifying most clearly the relevant stimuli—and then to sample from those situations by observing only a portion of the total time or sites in which observations could conceivably be made. A military officer who makes surprise inspections of the facilities under his command may be said to be engaging in situational sampling. Gore and Rotter (1963) were interested in whether their subjects believed in their own power to modify their environment so they noted whether Negro subjects volunteered for "sit in" demonstrations. Craddick (1961, 1962) and Sechrest and Wallace (1964) have obtained figure drawings from children before and after such important, naturally occurring events as Halloween and Christmas.

4. *Contrived situations* is a variant of situational sampling and requires the invention of special situations in which responses of interest have a high probability of being elicited. Given a sufficient number of reasonably homogeneous situations to permit the estimate of the interesting S-R possibilities, this should be a relatively powerful diagnostic technique. Certainly it has a rea-

sonableness that is difficult to deny. Probably the most obvious and major use which has been made of contrived situations in personality assessment is the famous O.S.S. assessment efforts during World War II (Murray, MacKinnon, Miller, Fiske, & Hanfmann, 1948), but the technique was also used systematically in the well-known assessment program carried out with Veterans Administration clinical psychology trainees (Kelly & Fiske, 1951). However, a little reflection will suggest that contrived situations are widely used in personality research to assess response dispositions in a rather direct way. Research on conformity, for example, has made extensive use of such contrived situations as the autokinetic phenomenon (Sherif, 1935), judgment of length of lines (Asch, 1955), expression of personal beliefs in the face of contradictory group opinion (Crutchfield, 1955), etc. Other investigators have employed contrived situations to study hostility (Hokanson & Gordon, 1958), anxiety (Feshbach & Feshbach, 1963), frustration (Barker, Dembo, & Lewin, 1941), honesty (Hartshorne & May, 1928), and a wide variety of other traits.

There is a less obvious but even more extensive use made of contrived situational estimates of behavioral dispositions in the common clinical practice of noting not only the specific response of the subject to the test stimulus but of noting his response to the entire testing situation as a contrived interpersonal or stress situation in which characteristics of a presumably general nature may be observed. Thus, for example, an intelligence testing procedure may provide a situation in which a subject's reactions to ego threats may be seen. Handing a subject a Rorschach plate provides an opportunity to see the manner in which he customarily relates to his surroundings. To the extent that the examiner giving a test is interested in the response of his subject to the test situation, and to the extent that he considers the testing materials useful in eliciting interesting responses over and above the responses to the test stimuli per se, the test situation partakes of the character of a contrived situation of the same order as, for example, situations in which anxiety or hostility are to be induced intentionally.

5. *Symbolic stimulus tests* constitute a category into which many psychological tests fall, particularly many of those which utilize an indirect (or projective) approach to the assessment of behavioral dispositions. In symbolic stimulus tests the test stimuli themselves represent at a symbolic level the extratest stimuli to which any person is presumably exposed. Thus, for example, it has been alleged that certain Rorschach cards represent at a symbolic level "Mother" and "Father" stimuli, and therefore that something about an individual's response tendencies toward his own parents may be inferred from his responses to the cards (Allen, 1954; Phillips & Smith, 1953). Similarly, TAT cards may be assumed to symbolize various stimulus situations to which an individual might be exposed, and thus the subject's responses should in some degree be representative of more important and interesting behavior tendencies. Presumably it should be possible to diagnose contingent relationships between stimuli and responses by the employment of symbolic stimulus materials. If a Rorschach inkblot really is a symbolic representation of the subject's world or some part of it, i.e., if that is the way things look to him "out there," then his response to the inkblot should reflect his view, or perception, of that part of the world symbolized by the blot. If, on the other hand, the inkblot symbolizes the self or some part of it, then the subject's response should indicate not his view of the world but his characteristic response to it. These alternatives represent an issue of considerable importance in the theory and practice of projective testing, and they will be considered in more detail in a later section (see "Concepts of Projection and Personality Assessment").

6. *Respondent's report on his own dispo-*

sitions. A much disparaged but hardy method of diagnosing behavioral dispositions is simply to ask a person about them. If one would like to know how an individual acts toward other persons, e.g., whether he frequently is hostile toward them, it is possible to ask the individual directly, perhaps requesting that he rate himself on some number or graphic scale or even in relation to other persons in some reference group.

There are obvious reasons why one might be suspicious about or at least cautious in accepting at face value the responses which subjects make to a direct request for a self-report, but there is no reason to suppose that the method might not be quite useful for some dispositions or with some subjects. As a matter of fact, as will be evidenced later, on the basis of extant research findings, the self-report is probably the method of choice under most circumstances.

The most common type of personality test—that involving a series of statements which the individual is to rate as being applicable or descriptive of himself or inapplicable or undescriptive of himself, i.e., the personality "inventory"—is obviously a self-report, but the question is, a self-report on what? Can an individual who takes the MAS be said to be making a self-report on his disposition to display anxiety? Can an individual who takes the MMPI be said to be making a self-report on his disposition toward hysteria or paranoia? Certainly not in such direct terms. It seems rather improbable that an individual who is otherwise capable of responding to the MAS or MMPI does not have a rather good idea of just what it is he is reporting about himself, at least, for example, that he is revealing some degree of personal disturbance when he makes certain responses. On the other hand, for many of the items an individual is making a self-report, but a considerable degree of inference is necessary in order to get from the particular response to the more general disposition that is presumed to underlie it. Nonetheless, for most persons such tests as the MMPI and MAS are self-report measures, and it is to be expected that they will correlate well with even more direct self-reports, e.g., "Rate yourself on 'anxiety.' "

7. *Respondent's report on his view of the stimulus* is yet another way of arriving at some conclusion about an individual's behavioral dispositions. A report by a respondent about his environment is not taken as a direct report of his behavioral dispositions, but his report is likely to be suggestive of them. If an individual describes another person as hostile, selfish, and domineering, the probable behaviors to be expected in relation to that person are considerably narrowed. Often it is of critical importance to make the distinction between a respondent's report of his own disposition and his view of the stimulus. For example, if an individual responds, "A terrible monster" when shown Card IV of the Rorschach, are we to suppose that he is reporting on his own disposition and that he would tend to be (or think of himself as) threatening, or might we suppose that the individual is reporting on the way the world looks to him, i.e., "filled with frightening things" and that he is, therefore, an anxious person? Schafer (1948, p. 36) suggests that *anxiety* of the hysterical patient is likely to be reflected in such responses as dragons, monsters, spiders, slimy snakes, and the like. Such an interpretation is clearly based on the supposition that the subject's verbal response is descriptive of the stimulus and not of his own disposition. One can invoke here either the principle of *isomorphism of experience and action* or, as Campbell (1963) suggests, the reverse principle as a basis for the interpretation of such responses. Some of the specific considerations involved in the interpretation of projective responses will be discussed in a later section of this paper (see particularly *complementary projection*).

The foregoing set of seven approaches to

diagnosing behavior dispositions exhausts the list suggested by Campbell, but there are two potentially important variants on his list, and there is one additional category of measurement operations which is of considerable importance in personality assessment. First, the two variants:

a. Four of the procedures outlined above utilize a verbal report by the subject (2, 5, 6, and 7), and at least conceivably the other three might be approximated by a verbal report. Thus, one might, instead of *tailing* a subject, ask him to give an exhaustive report on his activities over a period of time. While such a report would come close to being an episodic recall, it might be somewhat more complete. Assuming a cooperative, intelligent subject and a short, recent time period, one might get a report of some value and at much less cost than *tailing*. If the kinds of episodes one were interested in were not especially likely to be forgotten or suppressed, the technique might be useful. Verbal report is a more likely, and actually employed, variant on *situational sampling*. For example, one may by means of some such technique as sentence completion items attempt to sample situations in which an individual might find himself and use his response as an indication of his probable actual response when in such situations (Forer, 1960). Obviously such a procedure is very close to No. 6, *respondent's report on own dispositions*. In fact, one might argue that most such items as are on the MAS or MMPI are "situational samples" and that only direct self-ratings on traits represent a report on own disposition. Finally, one could ask an individual to say how he would respond in some contrived situation(s) in which he might never have found himself. For example, the Rosenzweig *Picture-Frustration Study* (1935) might be so used. The subject may be asked to write a response characteristic of the one he might make *if* he were in such a situation. Presumably one might describe the Asch conformity situation to subjects and ask them to report how they might respond if they were actually exposed to it, although that seems never to have been done.

b. A second and even more important variant on Campbell's procedures is *report by others,* and in theory at least it is relevant to all seven of the basic methods, although its use would be somewhat unusual for some of the seven procedures. As a variant of *tailing* or *episodic recall, report by others* is probably fairly common. For example, nurses and hospital attendants are often relied upon to report on the behavior of a patient during a specified period of time, and depending upon the completeness of the observations and the report, the method may approximate either *tailing* or *episodic recall.* And it is common practice for relatives or friends of a patient to be interviewed on the patient's background or history. Often social workers can contribute greatly by history from an informant which may be unavailable from the patient himself. A similar extension of *report by others* is possible for *situational sampling*. One need only ask "How does he behave when ..." in order to approximate the information obtained from actual observations in the situations in question. It is considerably less credible that *report by others* would be used as a substitute for actual observations in *contrived situations* or *symbolic stimulus tests,* but the possibility exists. Actually a more likely research use of *report by others* for *contrived situations* or *symbolic stimulus tests* is in investigations in which the predictive ability of the informant is at issue. On the other hand, *report by others* may well be used as a substitute for both *respondent's report on own dispositions* and *respondent's view of stimulus*. Such a substitution produces the widely used *peer* or *reputational ratings*. In fact reputational ratings are sufficiently common and have achieved such good standing in personality research that they would seem to merit a separate category as a method of diagnosing behavioral dispositions. It is only to point out the breadth of their applicability, i.e., that the method cuts across all other category lines, that reputational ratings have not been accorded separate status here. An important consideration in determining the status of reputational ratings is whether they simply substitute for self-ratings or other procedures or whether they contribute information not otherwise available. The correlation between self-measure and reputational measures is usually relatively high, but it is far from unity, and there is evidence that reputational measures often get at something quite different from self-reports, e.g., Murstein's (1963, pp. 112–113) finding that subjects who both rate and are rated high on hostility differ from subjects who rate themselves friendly but who are rated as hostile. Certainly it is commonly believed that people can "see through" each other, and when a number of opinions are available, many errors may cancel out and leave a reasonably veridical picture of the individual being rated (see also Wallace & Sechrest, 1963, for additional discussion of these issues).

There is one additional method of diagnosing behavioral dispositions which is of considerable importance in personality assessment.

8. *Behavioral trace*. It is often the case that behavioral dispositions are diagnosed not by observing directly a response being made but by noting some trace, residue, or after-effect which the response has produced or might have produced. Thus, for example, we enter an office, note that the inhabitant's desk is tidy to the point of exaggeration, and from that behavioral trace arrive at the conclusion that the inhabitant of the office is compulsive. It is obvious that there are certain dangers in the process of inferring a behavioral disposition from a behavioral trace rather than from direct behavioral observations. For one thing we must know whose behavior is represented in the trace we note. In our previous example, the tidiness of the desk may reflect the compulsivity of the inhabitant's secretary or it might even reflect an imposed orderliness stemming from a trait of the inhabitant's boss. Second, we must also make the assumption that the behavioral trace could have arisen only in the way we surmise. Very likely there are many traces which could have resulted from any number of rather diverse behavioral dispositions. Again, to take the example of the tidy desk which could have been engendered by a compulsive need for order, such a desk could also have been engendered by a slavish conformity to and imitation of another person, probably a superior.

Personality assessment devices may be regarded as *behavioral trace* devices to the extent that they are based on analyses not of actual behavior but of the impact that some behavior has left on the environment of the individual in whom we are interested. It is patently true that we very often have no more than a behavioral trace. When a subject has finished an MMPI, all we have are the traces of all the responses, covert and overt, which he made during the course of the test. However, because the response options are limited and because of occasional observations of subjects taking the MMPI, we ordinarily treat the marks on the answer sheet as if they represented direct responses rather than their traces. It is true that an individual *might* have responded with the test booklet upside down and with his eyes closed, but it is scarcely likely. But for many other assessment devices when we happen upon the final product of an individual's response(s) without being in a position to know what his responses actually were like, our attempts to reconstruct his responses from their traces may go sadly awry. Take, for example, a Mosaic Test (Lowenfeld, 1954) production of a design which may be presented to a clinician for evaluation. Unless there are specific notations of the test subject's behavior during the construction of the design, the design itself represents only a somewhat ambiguous trace of the actual responses. Even though a particular outcome might strike the clinician as highly original and creative, the possibility remains that the design is the outcome of a careless, idle approach to the task. It would make a good deal of difference in the inference made about behavior to know whether a design was the product of a careful, reasoned, and intent attack or whether it resulted from a casual, thoughtless performance. Indeed, for some purposes it may be far more important to have knowledge of the behaviors than of the trace they leave. (Lest it might be thought that that is always the case, it must be understood that as outcomes, traces may be important in their own right, e.g., in distinguishing the effective creative person from the ineffective.)

From the standpoint of assessing personality, perhaps the most important traces which behaviors leave are those they produce on other persons, e.g., reputation. In a very real sense most of the interpersonal rating procedures which are used in collecting personality data represent a reliance on the impressions left by behaviors. For example, when a fraternity man is asked to rate one of his brothers on the trait "dependency," his rating reflects the trace which the behavior of the person he is rating has left. The rating item might just as well be phrased, "Has he impressed you as being a dependent person?" The distinction between behaviors and their traces is an important one, and it is one whose nature is revealed rather well in a consideration of behaviors, reputations, and peer ratings (see Wallace & Sechrest, 1963).

In order for behavioral traces to be left, (a) the behaviors must be sufficiently flinty to make a trace; (b) the environment must be sufficiently plastic to register the impression; and (c) the environment must be sufficiently solid to retain the impression. Translating these requirements into the area of peer ratings, we can see that an individual's behavior must be salient, remarkable in some degree, and faithful in some manner to the underlying intent in order for enduring and veridical trace to be produced. Thus, for example, if an individual has strong feelings of hostility toward other persons and yet is unable to produce a behavior which would impress others as being hostile, his reputation for hostility may not reflect well that important characteristic. Such a person might very well regard himself as considerably more hostile than he is regarded by his associates. (The preceding is an entirely different issue from that of obscuring or dissimulating about some undesirable trait, in which case reputation might or might not register the trace of the unwanted behavior.) However, even though an individual engages in fairly strong forms of some behaviors, i.e., shows a behavioral disposition to a marked degree, it is quite possible that his environment may itself be flinty and immune to the trait. One might think of associates forming such an environment as being "insensitive." Probably not all traits can be rated equally well by peers because of their differing sensitivity to various behavioral dispositions. It is quite possible to imagine a group of peers who would not recognize the signs of "creativity" or even of "anxiety" sufficiently well to be able to rate the trait reliably. Finally, the environment must in some manner retain the trace left by the behavior, or in this instance, one's associates must have some way of remembering so that a stable reputation is possible. The simplest example of a nonretentive environment might be of a "casual company" in a military organization in which there is a constant and high level of turnover of transient personnel so that even though one man might have the misfortune to remain in such an organization for a considerable period of time, he might never acquire a "reputation." (It might be noted that Jacobs and Campbell [1961] have shown how even a very unstable laboratory culture can transmit its values, and a reputation is something that can be passed on to persons who never have had personal contact with the subject of the reputation.)

With respect to other kinds of personality assessment devices and procedures which depend more upon traces left by behaviors than upon notations of the behaviors themselves, the considerations given above apply equally well. If obsessiveness is to be assessed by the effect which a disposition to obsessiveness has on the environment, then obsessiveness must be manifested in a rather strong and unequivocal way, the environment in which the response occurs must have a good possibility of being affected by obsessiveness, and the record left must be preservable.

We have reviewed here a variety of approaches to the assessment of behavioral dispositions, all of them applicable to the field of personality, but only a few really systematically exploited in research. The field of personality might well profit from a more open and creative look at the possibilities for assessing the constructs with which it deals.

PERSONALITY ASSESSMENT IN RESEARCH

There are three ways in which personality tests and assessment procedures may enter into research. Most obviously the construction and validation of personality measures may be the focus of research. In fact, the bulk of research which is ordinarily thought of as pertinent to personality measurement consists of attempts to develop, improve, or substantiate some procedure by means of which a correct picture of some (set of) personality trait(s) may be obtained. Since it is primarily such research which is the principal topic of this chapter, its further discussion will be deferred to later sections.

Personality measurement very frequently enters into other research when subjects are categorized on the basis of personality trait measurement, e.g., anxious-nonanxious, sensitizer-represser, n achievement-n affiliation. In such research personality variables operate as independent variables in classical experimental work, although they are often called "subject" (Underwood, 1957) or "organismic" (McGuigan, 1960) variables to indicate that they are not, strictly speaking, manipulable variables. (If the personality variable is manipulated in the research, e.g., by inducing anxiety, then it is truly an independent variable, and personality measures may not enter into the research.) A seldom employed variant on the use of personality variables to establish subject differences is their use as "control" variables for purposes of statistical manipulation, e.g., in partial correlation or analysis of co-variance.

It is well beyond the scope of this paper to do a systematic review of the use of personality characteristics as subject variables in research, but some of the problems and issues are worth pointing out, and examples will illustrate the typical uses and results. Quite evidently many of the problems that plague developers of personality measures and their clinical consumers must also be of concern to those who propose to use these measures in order to differentiate among subjects in experimental research. A measure that is lacking in either reliability or validity or both can scarcely enhance any research in which it is used. Moreover, both the convergent and discriminant validity (Campbell & Fiske, 1959) of a measure must be considered before it is used as a basis for categorizing subjects. To categorize subjects on an erroneous basis, e.g., intelligence rather than the intended variable *ego strength,* is perhaps an even more serious error than categorizing subjects randomly as would occur with an unreliable measure.

On the other hand, there are some problems that probably do not pose as serious an issue to the researcher as to the clinician. All good research designs have as their basis the gathering of multiple observations under conditions that permit errors, but random errors that can and should cancel each other out. If the researcher is somewhat in error and misclassifies one subject, any error thereby introduced will probably be compensated for or rendered trivial under the comforting cloak of large numbers of observations. That cloak does not extend to the clinician, however, for he can scarcely take comfort in the fact that an error that has led to the mistreatment of a patient will probably be made up at some future time by an equally fortuitous error resulting in favorable treatment of some other patient. Thus, a validity coefficient of, say, .40 which would be a very infirm ground on which to base decisions about individual patients, e.g., whether or not to send a given patient on home visits, might be satisfactory for a research project requiring only that two groups of subjects with a clear mean difference be identified. The researcher may even have the option of discarding those subjects who fall at or near the midpoint of his scale and thus take even greater advantage of the discriminatory power of the instrument he is using.

Moreover, the researcher who wishes to employ a subject variable design need not concern himself so much with incremental validity (Sechrest, 1963) or utility (Cronbach & Gleser, 1957) considerations, because he is ordinarily employing only one operation in differentiating among his subjects, and the decision process is an extremely simple one.

The principal problem for the researcher with a subject variable design is to employ a measure with at least a modest degree of convergent validity plus a substantial level of discriminant validity. In fact, it is probably the latter problem that constitutes the major source of error in the use of personality measures in experimental research. The demonstration that a group of subjects differed only, or at least primarily, on the trait denoted by the experimenter is a difficult task, but it is one which usually could and should be undertaken. There are, to be sure, an infinite number of variables from which a given one might be differentiable, and it cannot seriously be proposed that a researcher demonstrate that his subject variable measure is absolutely different from all other variables, but he might at least be expected to eliminate the obvious and frequently troublesome ones. The recommendation of Campbell (1960) that measures should be shown to be *more than,* e.g., intelligence or response set measures, is certainly a reasonable one. Of course, when an experimenter is using a thoroughly researched measure that has been shown by others to have discriminant validity, his responsibility is lessened. But when he is using a new measure, perhaps one which has been developed especially for his purposes, he would do well to establish the discriminant, as well as the convergent, validity of his measure. In particular the problem of social desirability (Edwards, 1957) is proving a difficult one, and those measures susceptible to desirability sets, e.g., all self-report measures and many reports made by interested informants, should be shown to be more than social desirability measures.

Fortunately, in many instances the experimenter's own results reflect positively on the personality measure he employed. If the results make good sense in terms of the assumed subject variable and do not make such good sense in terms of the alternative possibilities, the experimenter's procedures are considerably justified. Grimes and Allinsmith (1961), for example, report an investigation into school achievement under two different kinds of teaching regimens as a function of compulsivity (and anxiety). The measure of compulsivity depended upon the report of the child's parent, and considering the types of behaviors subsumed under compulsivity, there was certainly a possibility that the scale might be an equally good measure of some other characteristic, e.g., intelligence or adjustment. However, the compulsivity measure proved not to correlate with an anxiety questionnaire measure also used, and the results of the investigation seem scarcely plausible when viewed solely in terms of intelligence. Thus, considerable credence is lent to the supposition that the compulsivity measure was a valid one. It should be clear that the experimenter runs some risk in depending upon the results of his experiment to bear out his earlier judgment, and it is a risk that is usually avoidable by the wise provision for independent measures of such important subject characteristics as intelligence, social desirability bias, and socio-economic status.

A variant of subject variable research is the design in which personality measures are obtained at some point during the procedure and are used later to elucidate the findings. This category of research actually consists of two somewhat distinct designs, the experimental and the correlational, although viewed strictly from the standpoint of the use of personality measures, there would seem to be little difference. Typical of the experimental type of research is an investigation by Berkowitz and Lundy (1957) in which subjects more susceptible to influence by authority figures differed in personality from those subjects more susceptible to influence by peers. Of a basically correlational and R-R nature is an investigation by Scodel, Ratoosh, and Minas (1959) of the personality correlates of risk-taking preferences. After dividing a group of subjects into those who were inclined to take long-shot bets as opposed to those with a preference for a smaller but surer payoff, the investigators determined the differences between the two groups on a number of personality measures.

Obviously the same considerations of validity and reliability for research involving correlations between personality and other response measures obtained for the subjects. Nothing is to be gained and much will be lost by utilizing faulty personality measures. In fact, one can make a case for using only well-tested, proven personality measures for a design that depends on the elucidation of some new or theoretically important variable. There is a minimum of elucidation provided by the use of personality measures that are themselves poorly understood. There is, however, another important aspect of the personality measures to be taken into account in correlational studies. The response measure to be elucidated and the personality measure to be employed in doing so should be methodologically as distinct as possible. The gain in knowledge from the research is directly and substantially related to the methodological separateness of the response and personality measures employed.

A third main category of research in which personality assessment plays a part is research in which performance on some assessment device is a dependent variable, i.e., in which the interest is in the effect of some experimental manipulation on personality. However, dependent variable research involving personality assessment may be of either the R-R, correlational type, or of the S-R, experimental variety (K. W. Spence, 1944). If there is only one group of subjects who have been exposed to some experimental treatment, and if the experimenter looks for co-variance in degree of response to treatment and in personality test scores expected to reflect effects of treatment, the research is not different from other correlational research. However, if there is an experimental treatment whose effects can be compared with those of a different treatment, the research is of the S-R type. Outcome research in psychotherapy provides the best instances of research in which scores on personality measures are a dependent variable. Research of the correlational type is exemplified in investigations in which all subjects are exposed to psychotherapy, and some judgment about the degree of response to or improvement in therapy is related to scores on some personality measure or, more convincingly, to *changes* in personality scores (Butler & Haigh, 1954; Dymond, 1954).

Experimental research involving effect on personality measures of two or more treatments is not especially frequent in personality and related areas, but there are a number of notable examples. Without becoming embroiled in the controversies over the nature and adequacy of controls for psychotherapy, a number of examples of the effects of psychotherapy can be noted which meet the requirements of an experimental investigation. (An experiment is still an instance of the experimental model whether or not the control groups or measures are adequate.) Rogers and Dymond (1954) in particular have reported a series of investigations in which personality measures, viz., *Q* sorts descriptive of self and ideal self, and TAT measures of adjustment, have been employed as dependent variables. Other investigators have employed similar measures with varying results (e.g., Cartwright & Vogel, 1960; Shlien, Mosak, & Dreikurs, 1962).

However, not all examples of use of personality measures as dependent variables are in the area of psychotherapy. Recently Wallach and his associates (Wallach & Gahm, 1960; Wallach, Green, Lipsitt, & Minehart, 1962) have been using a free drawing (doodling) measure of social expansiveness and constriction, and they have found that enforced social isolation or social participation is reflected in the types of doodles produced (Wallach & Thomas, 1963). A number of investigators have used various Rorschach indices as dependent variables in investigations of the effects of examiner and situational influence on test performance (see Masling's, 1960, review). And Singer and Meltzoff and their associates (Meltzoff, Singer, & Korchin, 1953; Singer, Meltzoff, & Goldman, 1952) have used the Rorschach *M* score in studying the effects of inhibited movement. Finally, Ross *et al.* (Ross, Adsett, Gleser, Joyce, Kaplan, & Tieger, 1963) have tried several projective tests to assess the effects of two active drugs and a placebo. Four of twelve hypothesized effects on the Rorschach were substantiated, but the other measures do not fare as well.

Although it was stated above that various researches have employed personality measures as dependent variables, it is obvious that there will be differences in the degree to which the investigator is interested in the independent manipulations and the dependent measures. For example, most psychotherapy researchers are not very interested in personality test scores per se, but they might be quite interested in length of hospitalization. On the other hand, other investigators may not have any substantial interest in the independent manipulations but may be interested in the capacity of their personality measure to reflect manipulations of various kinds.

THE TEST SITUATION

There are a number of decrepit assumptions about testing people which should long ago have been discarded and which usually are rejected verbally when the issue arises. Nonetheless, some of the assumptions are probably more often honored in practice than not, and it is time that psychologists became generally more sophisticated in their practices with respect to testing.

First, it once seems to have been implicitly assumed that the stimulus for a test response was the test item. However, once psychologists discovered that the "stimulus" was something to be sought in research rather than to be defined (Baughman, 1958a), it became evident that test responses are the net result of a variety of factors operating in the total test situation. In an especially helpful article, Goss and Brownell (1957) examine and elaborate the total stimulus situation which eventuates in a particular "test response." It is now very clear that such factors as the context in which the test is given (E. M. Henry & Rotter, 1956; Rabin, Nelson, & Clark, 1954), the characteristics of the examiner (E. Lord, 1950; Rabin, Nelson, & Clark, 1954; Veroff, 1961), set induced by prior activities of the testee (Crandall, 1951; Hedwig, 1963; Leventhal, 1956), and even immediately preceding test responses (Atkinson, 1958; Murstein, 1963) operate to determine the particular response that is given on a particular occasion. Masling (1960) should especially be consulted for an overview of examiner influences on test performance. It becomes very clear that the task of standardizing conditions of test administration is not to be approached casually. However, the best that one can recommend at this time is that the experimenter be aware of the importance of the conditions of administration and that he take precautions to ensure that there are not factors that will differentially affect the test performance of various experimental groups. For example, suppose it is desired to employ some test as an outcome measure for an experimental treatment, and both an experimental and an untreated control group are to be tested. At the time of the postexperimental measurement will both groups be equally familiar (or unfamiliar) with the person doing the testing, with the laboratory or other situation in which the test is to be administered, with other persons with whom he might find himself during the administration of the test, etc.? It becomes evident that for many types of experiments the notion of an "untreated" control group leads inexorably to inequalities prejudicial to the scientific status of the experiment. If experimental subjects have had several sessions of experimental "handling" (and an analogy to experiments on handling of animals may be appropriate, e.g., see Spence and Maher [1962a, 1962b]), they may be quite different from "unhandled" control subjects, no matter what the nature of the treatment. Moreover, in order to provide for replicability across experiments, it is quite necessary that conditions of test administration be carefully specified. Dimensions of greatest relevance would appear to be: sex and status of examiner, demeanor of examiner (warm, neutral, aloof), activity immediately preceding testing, context of examination (laboratory, classroom, private office, etc.), and emphasis of instructions (casual, matter-of-fact, demanding). Present descriptions, e.g., "Then the subjects were given an individually administered Rorschach," are clearly insufficient.

In view of increasing evidence that projective test responses are susceptible to verbal or even postural reinforcements (Simmons & Christy, 1962; Wickes, 1956), it is necessary to exercise greater control over the conditions of test administration, even to the extent of insisting upon test administrators who are unaware of the hypotheses of the experiment.

It should also be pointed out that an examiner may not only not always be necessary, he may sometimes represent an obstacle to the obtaining of the most meaningful test responses. Bernstein (1956) found it possible to administer both oral and written TATs without the intervention of an examiner by employment of written instructions and a tape recorder. Moreover, he found that stories given with the examiner absent were judged higher in emotional tone (Eron, Terry, & Callahan, 1950) and other seemingly desirable response measures.

However, it is probably also the case that the scoring or categorization of responses after testing needs to be better described. Masling's review and other research (Masling, 1957, 1959) indicates clearly enough that characteristics of the experimenter may bias the scoring of a response or the determination of the category to which it belongs. If there is some interest in absolute levels of responding, then it is not enough to show that two scorers correlate reasonably well in scores they assign. It must also be demonstrated that their means and standard deviations are approximately equal. Such a demonstration is rare in personality research.

STIMULUS FACTORS AS RESPONSE DETERMINANTS

As is demonstrated by Murstein (1963), many investigations point conclusively to the fact that the *strongest* determinant of a test response is the stimulus. By far the greatest proportion of the variance in hostile responses to a set of TAT cards is contributed by the characteristics of the cards themselves rather than by differences among subjects or among conditions of administration of the test. Given a card with the appropriate structure and subject matter, a hostile response has a very high probability of occurrence no matter who the subject. Unquestionably the same is true of the Rorschach inkblots as is evidenced by "popular" responses given by so many subjects. And in a way even the "social desirability" factor in more structured tests is a reflection of the stimulus characteristics of the item. Therefore, we can safely predict that by using appropriate stimuli any group can be made to appear more or less hostile, dependent, sexy, or achievement-oriented than any other group. Thus, unless stimuli are quite well equated for what has been called "stimulus pull" for relevant responses, comparisons between groups or between experiments are meaningless. Murstein (1963) has shown that some troublesome differences in results between separate experiments are almost certainly the result of nonequivalent stimuli.

The question to be answered, then, is what kind of a stimulus is best for eliciting a particular response tendency? One can certainly find somewhat contradictory recommendations. Kagan (1959), for example, believes that reliability of TAT measures is likely to be better when the stimuli are clearly structured for a particular motive—a likely possibility because of the fact that across periods of time the same needs, motives, or other dispositions would be tapped by structured stimuli, whereas less structured cards might be expected to tap different dispositions at different times. Kenny (1954), on the other hand, finds that medium ambiguity cards have the highest transcendence indices. Weisskopf (1950) and Kenny and Bijou (1953) found a similar superiority for medium ambiguity cards for level of "personality revealingness." Presumably degree of projection is related to transcendence, which is the degree to which cards elicit responses going beyond simple description, and therefore, Kenny's findings may be taken as a recommendation of medium-structured cards. Murstein (1958b) has also found that TAT cards at a medium level of ambiguity elicit a wider variety of themes, and he has concluded (Murstein, 1959, 1961a, 1961b) that cards at that level are best. But Epstein and Smith (1956), Fenz and Epstein (1962), Leiman and Epstein (1961), and Murstein (1963, p. 191) have all found some superiority for TAT cards at a rather low level of structure for a particular disposition in that they are superior for revealing that disposition. Certainly the common clinical folklore also favors less structured cards. Comparable research findings are not available for other tests, but it seems likely that whatever considerations apply to TAT stimuli would apply to other instruments also.

Is there any sense to be made out of the contradictions above? First, Murstein (1963) has contributed a valuable distinction between stimulus structure and stimulus ambiguity. By structure he refers to the stimulus properties of the cards, i.e., how much agreement there would be in describing it, while by ambiguity he refers to disagreement or variability in the *meaning* attached to the stimulus. Thus, at the conclusion of his careful review of stimulus properties of TAT cards he concludes that rather highly *structured* cards are desirable, i.e., it should be clear just what the card is a picture of. Next, let us note that the less ambiguous a card is, i.e., the clearer it is just what is supposed to be going on, and why it is going on, and how it will end, the more certain it is that the card is relevant to one rather limited response disposition. If that is the case, then Kagan's (1959) recommendation concerning the reliability of highly structured (i.e., low in ambiguity) cards makes sense. A card that is very high in ambiguity will tap a number of dispositions more or less equally well, and rather minor changes in response strength could be expected to produce major shifts in response. Therefore, if one is interested in the relative strengths among individuals of a particular disposition, it would seem that a moderate to low ambiguous stimulus would be superior. In this regard the research of E. J. Murray (1959) on sleep deprivation may be mentioned, for he found that only cards highly structured for sleep themes showed a difference between sleep-deprived and control subjects, a finding somewhat to be anticipated since sleep themes would undoubtedly have a very low a priori probability of occurrence.

Second, it should be noted that cards differing in pull for different responses represent a considerably different task for the subject, depending upon (a) the strength of his disposition and (b) his willingness for other persons to know about it. Thus, for example, Leiman and Epstein (1961) found that subjects high in self-reported sexual drive produced more sex responses only to pictures low in pull for sex imagery. On the other hand, subjects with a high level of self-reported guilt over sex produced less sex imagery for high sex-pull pictures. Murstein (1963) found similar relationships for hostility. Murstein concludes that low-pull pictures are probably better for assessing the strength of such dispositions as sex and hostility, but that while it has been suggested that high-pull, i.e., unambiguous, pictures are more useful for assessing defensive operations, the evidence there is more equivocal. Clearly, if stimuli are too unambiguous for a given theme, there will be little variability among subjects in frequency of the theme. But for more ambiguous stimuli the strength of the disposition may be greater than unaroused defenses, and the response will occur if its inherent strength is high. It would seem almost certain that stimuli of only a moderate level (whatever level that is) of ambiguity for a particular theme should be best for assessing such factors as guilt, denial, etc., since at a moderate level reality factors would still allow for the play of defensive responses.

Third, there are probably some kinds of response dispositions which are unpleasant and more threatening to the subject himself than to his social image. The best way to deal with such dispositions may often be denial. Such a conclusion is suggested by a rather long history of research on hunger and its effects on thematic responses. Early research suggested a more or less direct relationship between hunger and food and related imagery in response to ambiguous stimuli (Sanford, 1936, 1937), but it soon became evident that the case was more complex than that. McClelland and Atkinson (1948) found that with increasing levels of hunger, food imagery did not increase, but deprivation themes did. Epstein and Smith (1956) found that hungry subjects produce significantly more hunger themes and hunger-related responses to pictures ambiguous for hunger themes, but they produce significantly *fewer* hunger themes when the pull for food responses was high. A remarkably similar finding was obtained by Murray (1959) for sleep deprivation. He found that subjects deprived of three nights of sleep gave fewer sleep themes than control subjects, but it was only on cards with a high pull for sleep themes that the difference was manifested. His conclusion was that the very sleepy subjects who thought it important to stay awake could not indulge themselves in sleep imagery because of the threat it constituted to their continued wakefulness. A similar suggestion has been made with respect to hunger, i.e., that in order to control it as a disposition it must be denied (Murstein, 1963). Rather curiously, it was quite evident, despite their test responses, that subjects in the well-known Minnesota study on long-term semistarvation engaged in elaborate food fantasies (Brozek, Guetzkow, & Baldwin, 1951). However, in that situation there were many external controls that ensured that the men would not suddenly abandon everything they were doing and run to seek food. It might be of interest to study the fantasies and test responses of serious dieters, for whom nearly all controls are internal, to determine whether they are afflicted with many elaborate fantasies of food or whether they tend vigorously to push such thoughts aside. Finally, some of the above speculations and findings are nicely confirmed by the imaginative study by Fenz and Epstein (1962) of sports parachutists. They found that while on the day of a jump the parachutists made significantly more "approach" responses to pictures highly relevant to jumping, the over-all quality of their stories went down and they showed a stronger GSR, thus suggesting the probability that their responses to the high-pull cards represented a "mastery" attempt over their fear of jumping. The above findings all suggest that certain dispositions, probably those which are not in themselves reprehensible but which are unpleasant to experience, may when they reach a given strength be dealt with largely by denial, and the result will be that stimuli highly relevant to the disposition will tend to elicit either irrelevant responses or exaggeratedly positive responses. However, other response indicators less susceptible to deliberate control, such as GSR or formal characteristics, are likely to reveal the nature of the disposition involved. It is most unfortunate that in such studies as Murray's (1959) other response characteristics than themes were not recorded and scored.

Finally, distinctions must be made among the various uses to which a measure may be put. Probably many clinical uses of a test are somewhat akin to a dredging operation in which one is interested in whatever may turn up. In such a case a "broad band" test such as the Rorschach or the TAT may be appropriate, although it should by now be clear that neither of those instruments taps anything like the full scale of dispositions in which one might be interested. However, certainly for research purposes and probably for more pointed clinical inquiries a broad band instrument is a considerable handicap. It can definitely be recommended that for more pointed inquiries a more pointed instrument be used. As others have recommended (Kagan, 1956; Lazarus, 1953; Murstein, 1963), what would seem to offer the best chance of success in assessing a particular disposition would be a set of stimuli representing a considerable range of ambiguity or pull with respect to the disposition. Murstein (1963) in particular offers many valuable suggestions for the development of a good series of stimuli.

DO-IT-YOURSELF TESTS

There are many tests currently available commercially and many others entered into the research literature and probably available on an informal basis, and conglomerately the available stimuli probably tap a rather wide variety of dispositions. However, it is probably also the case that few of the available measures will fit precisely and neatly into very many research plans, and there are many other plans for which no measure is available. Then the researcher must decide whether to use a known and available measure that is perhaps about 20° off course or whether to try to build his own. With the exception of only a very few dispositions, e.g., perhaps hostility (Murstein, 1963), n achievement (McClelland, Atkinson, Clark, & Lowell, 1953), and possibly sex (Auld, Eron, & Laffal, 1955), it can heartily be recommended that the researcher do-it-himself. A study of available research reports will reveal at least as many significant and replicable findings for homemade measures as for the more standard ones, probably for some of the reasons mentioned in the preceding section, i.e., the broad-bandedness of most published materials. Thus, for example, needs for achievement, affiliation, and power (McClelland *et al.,* 1953; Shipley & Veroff, 1952; Veroff, 1957), fear (Fenz & Epstein, 1962; Walker, Atkinson, Veroff, Birney, Dember, & Moulton, 1958), sleepiness (E. J. Murray, 1959), and sex (Leiman & Epstein, 1961) have all been profitably studied with specially developed sets of pictures similar to TAT stimuli. Sentence completion items have also been used successfully in custom-built or modified forms (Burwen, Campbell, &

Kidd, 1956; Efron, 1960; Maher, Watt, & Campbell, 1960). Inkblots are probably more difficult to produce from a technical standpoint, but it has been done, and the results were satisfactory for the purposes of the experimenter (Wickes, 1956). Baughman (1954, 1958a, 1958b) has produced very useful modifications of the Rorschach blots for his research and clinical purposes. In any case there are now available well over 120 commercially prepared inkblots of more or less the same size and quality from which one might select subsets appropriate for particular purposes (Behn-Eschenberg, 1931; Holtzman, 1958a, 1958b; Howard, 1960; Rorschach, 1942).

There is, of course, the objection that homemade tests lack the research foundation that exists for the older, better-known instruments, but that objection is scarcely supportable. There is no special reason to suppose that research on TAT pictures or on Rorschach inkblots would not be generalizable to similar pictures or inkblots except insofar as the research is pointed toward specific characteristics of the stimuli. In fact, we must of necessity suppose that the research is generalizable. Therefore, if an experimenter is reasonably careful in constructing his stimuli, whatever research there is that would support the use of the TAT, Rorschach, or any other instrument would support the use of derivations therefrom. There are no special rules for the personality development do-it-yourselfer, but helpful discussions of the problems involved may be found (Forer, Rabin, Goldstein, & Lesser, 1961; Murstein, 1963; Symonds, 1939).

THE RESPONSE IN PERSONALITY ASSESSMENT

In their S-R analysis of the projective test situation Goss and Brownell (1957) note that the overt verbal response is usually the only one recorded, but they also note that there are other aspects of the total response of the individual which might be of equal or greater importance. Thus, in addition to the words he utters, the subject probably also engages in a good bit of implicit vocalization, he makes various observable motor responses, and he also responds autonomically. Various aspects of the autonomic response may or may not be observable without special instrumentation, e.g., blushing, trembling, perspiring, GSR, peristalsis. Obviously we are limiting ourselves severely by recording only the verbal response, although there are serious obstacles to more complete recording.

There are certainly good grounds for supposing that our understanding of our variables, measures, and subjects would be increased by expanding the scope of our observations. Fenz and Epstein (1962) found that although sports parachutists responded quite positively to pictures suggestive of jumping, they also showed a stronger GSR to the same pictures than did control subjects. The fact that they actually made more fear responses to cards of low jump-relevance suggests rather strongly that the GSR revealed a negative reaction not indicated by the content of the verbal response. GSRs have also proven to be valuable in Rorschach (see Hertz, 1962) and word association research (Jacobs, 1955; Levinger & Clark, 1961). In laboratory investigations when subjects are being subjected to obviously experimental procedures anyway, a GSR recording could be a very worthwhile addition.

Another way in which considerable improvement in research might eventuate would be in a somewhat finer grained analysis of verbal responses obtained. The findings of McClelland and Atkinson (1948; Atkinson & McClelland, 1948) concerning effects of food deprivation are instructive here. It will be remembered that food deprivation did not result in an increase in food themes and food-related themes. However, themes of deprivation did show the influence of deprivation. Examples of similar findings could be cited at length, and they all suggest the necessity for a more careful analysis but probably only an analysis based on good theoretical or other a priori considerations.

Auld (1954) has indicated a number of very definite ways in which behavior theory may be relevant to projective testing, and among these is the analysis of the response component. He suggests that the usual measures of habit strength, viz., frequency of response, vigor of response, and latency of response, are quite applicable to the projective response. Thus, the more frequently a theme occurs, the stronger the underlying disposition is assumed to be, an assumption identical with Lindzey's (1961) and with the recommendation of Piotrowski (1950, p. 116) to "proceed on the assumption that the chances of a TAT thema being manifested in the subject's overt behavior are positively correlated with the frequency of the thema's appearance in the TAT ...." Probably frequency is the most often utilized basis for interpretation of test responses, although much remains to be known about the relationship between test response frequency and extratest behavioral frequency. There have been few experiments, for example, reporting any substantial data at more than two levels of frequency, i.e., high and low. There is a definite possibility that frequency relationships might not always be linear or even monotonic.

Another important aspect of responses which can certainly be scored and which is theoretically sound is intensity (or vigor). As Auld and others have pointed out, it is quite possible that a single, intense response, e.g., a response involving a brutal murder, is of greater significance than almost any number of milder responses. Jackson (1962) found that clinicians are quite sensitive to the intensity dimension in their interpretations, and they tend to place more reliance on extreme responses than upon larger numbers of less extreme responses. But at present there is almost no research on the intensity dimension. Some scoring schemes have incorporated intensity as a basis for assigning weights (Holtzman, Thorpe, Swartz, & Herron, 1961; Stone, 1956) but thus far the intensity dimension of responses to personality measures remains largely unexplored.

There are, of course, some reasons to suppose that frequency of response and intensity of response should be related. As an example, a Guttman scale can be achieved only if individuals endorsing the most extreme (intense) items also endorse the most items, i.e., those at lower degrees of intensity. Various theoretical deductions would lead to the conclusion that frequency and intensity of response should be redundant. Nonetheless, it seems unlikely that such would be the case in personality—the frequency with which meek, mild-mannered persons have committed single brutal crimes, i.e., without committing lesser violent offenses, would argue otherwise. More research is needed.

Latency also may be taken as an attribute of responses in two senses. First, one can measure the elapsed time between onset of stimulus and onset of response, and that is usually done for word associations and Rorschach responses. As indicated earlier there is some evidence for the usefulness of latencies obtained in that way. However, for more complex stimuli and for more complex responses, e.g., hostility as measured by the TAT, it would seem that latencies would have limited usefulness at best. Auld (1954), however, suggests that there is another aspect of latency as elapsed time which may apply to test responses, viz., the total elapsed time from beginning of a test until the response in question appears. Thus, for example, of two individuals exposed to the same sequence of cards, the one emitting a hostile response first would be assumed to have the strongest disposition to hostility. Actually latency could be measured either in terms of time or number of stories told. Such a measure has never been used to the best of the writer's knowledge. Finally, Auld suggests that there is a rather completely different sense in which the idea of latency may be relevant to test responses. One may regard a response from the standpoint of the power or amount of stimulus needed to evoke it. A response that is evoked by a very mild stimulus is assumed to reflect a stronger disposition than one requiring a stronger stimulus. Forer (1960) has suggested a very similar idea. One may view the provocation for a response either in terms of the judged or demonstrated "pull" of a stimulus, or in terms of the total number of stimuli needed. Thus, in a series of TAT cards which are more or less suggestive of hostility, the provocation for a hostile story would seem to get stronger later in the series. Viewing provocation in terms of judged pull or relevance of the stimulus has, of course, been done by numerous researchers as has been noted above, although the concentration has usually been on the pull of the stimulus rather than upon the readiness of the response.

Another way of improving response analysis, and a way that has been too often ignored for thematic tests, sentence completions, and the like, is to pay more attention to the formal aspects of the response. Again, there is a sound research foundation for making such a recommendation (see the summary by Murstein, 1963), but an example provided by Fenz and Epstein (1962) in their study of sports parachutists will suffice. They found that parachute jumpers actually made more "approach" or positive responses to highly relevant pictures on the day of a scheduled jump, and it could be naïvely assumed that their responses disconfirmed the suspicion that they would show fear. However, when the quality or "goodness" of their responses was examined, they showed a decrement in performance as indicated by such features of their responses as: inaccurate perceptions, poor integration, illogical story development, speech faults, etc. Thus, it can firmly be recommended that formal as well as content features of responses be analyzed in research.

One aspect of the total response system which must be considered and which merits considerable additional investigation is what Goss and Brownell (1957) refer to as "response produced cues." That is to say that responses produced sequentially to test stimuli are by no means independent. Thus, for example, Balken and Masserman (1940) note their impression that "good" or "revealing" TAT stories are often followed by defensive ones, and Reitman and Atkinson (1958) have described a "saw-tooth" phenomenon in which stories high and low in achievement imagery alternate. An unpublished analysis of the data of Jackson and Sechrest (1962) shows the same sort of finding for the pleasantness of early memories; relatively pleasant and unpleasant memories tend to alternate. Undoubtedly similar findings would obtain for other tests with multiple responses, e.g., Rorschach, sentence completion.

However, response produced cues seem capable of affecting response output in an even more important way. One ordinarily would assume that longer response sequences would show greater stability and hence greater validity than shorter sequences. But, Atkinson (1958) reports that "Current evidence shows a loss in predictive validity of stories late in a series of eight or more .... This suggests that until more definitive results are available, thematic apperceptive measures of motivation should probably not exceed about six pictures in length" (p. 831). Moreover, Lindzey and Heinemann (1955) found some evidence, for a group administration of the TAT with written responses, that a five-minute response period was preferable to a longer period. Thus, it appears necessary to have more research that will indicate the limits within which the best possible responses will be obtained, and it seems quite possible, if discomfiting, that some of the outcomes are going to point to considerable complexity. At the present time the evidence would suggest that written response periods should be about five minutes and that only a few cards be used to assess a given disposition, at least when the cards are given "massed," as is usual.

A final and very important point about response analysis is that an emitted response probably is the net result of both excitatory and inhibitory processes, and it is often difficult to know of a particular response in what proportions response strength and defensive components are represented (Lazarus, 1953). Thus, a response may be weak because the strength of the underlying disposition is weak or because defensive, inhibitory dispositions are strong. It has been suggested that many failures of projective test validation are accounted for by failure to take avoidance or defensive motives into consideration (Kagan, 1956; Purcell, 1958), and various research has shown that there is improvement in validity of measures when defensive processes are properly accounted for (Clark, 1952; Clark & Sensibar, 1956; Ericksen, 1951; Lesser, 1958, 1959; Nelson & Epstein, 1962; Purcell, 1956; Saltz & Epstein, 1963). Defensive aspects of response dispositions are apparently thought to be implicit in Rorschach scoring and analysis (e.g., Schafer, 1948), but adequate research on the problem seems never to have been done, and at this point one must conclude that the possibility of increasing Rorschach validity by consideration of defensive processes is in need of investigation. Much the same may be said for other measures such as sentence completions and word associations, although for the latter there is some evidence suggesting that a long reaction-time is indicative of a negative affective response and that GSR is not (Jacobs, 1955).

INTELLIGENCE AND VERBAL FLUENCY

Among the largely extraneous variables that can be expected to contribute to variance in responses to tests, even of the projective variety, are intelligence and verbal fluency (Webb & Hilden, 1953). Obviously, while such procedures as figure drawing are not particularly likely to be sensitive to intellectual variables, at least for the middle range of their values, all verbal response measures are potentially vulnerable. Yet, surprisingly little is known about the relationship between intelligence and/or verbal fluency and test performance.

There are several possible ways in which intellectual variables might operate to affect performance on tests, aside from the possibility that some personality dispositions, e.g., cynicism, might be linked to intelligence. For example, intelligence and verbal fluency might be related to an individual's ability to articulate both his stimulus field and his response to it so that he would be able to describe aspects of his experience not available to others. Thus, on the Rorschach, an individual's ability to respond to various aspects of the blots and *to describe* the stimulus might well be related to intellective factors. Lotsoff (1953) found that certain categories of Rorschach scores are influenced by verbal fluency, color and shading being particular instances. And Levy (1955) has presented similar findings for M, indicating that it is to some extent a stylistic variable consisting of a "rhetorical embellishment."

However, intellectual variables, particularly ideational and verbal fluency, may also affect performance on tests by the sheer fact of being related to the amount of material produced. The more responses or the longer the response the more possibilities for entries in any scoring category. Perhaps the effect on gross, global evaluations would be limited if systems of response evaluation were unbiased, for if longer responses give a greater opportunity for undesirable, negative responses, they also give more opportunity for positive interpretations. However, it seems probable that many of our response evaluation systems are unequally sensitive to positive as opposed to pathological personality dispositions, and the net result of longer responses will tend to be more negative conclusions. In any case, in many research problems unipolar scoring is typical, e.g., in scoring n achievement, scores can range only from 0 up. The other pole of the dimension, n failure, would seem to have only very limited usefulness. MacIntosh and Maher (1955) found that the "conflict" score (Rotter & Rafferty, 1950) for Rotter's Incomplete Sentences Blank correlated .79 with a measure of verbal fluency which was largely independent of a measure of verbal reasoning. While their result may seem somewhat paradoxical in view of the fact that the ISB conflict score makes provision for the "positive" scoring of responses, longer responses are more likely to be scored for conflict since they are more likely to express opposing motivations, outlooks, etc. Although there is provision for the modification of a positive response in the direction of a conflict score, e.g., "*Most women* are nice, but some are not" would be scored for conflict, there is no provision for the modification of a negative response in a positive direction, e.g., "*Most women* are bad, but some are good" would be scored about as negatively as if the qualification had not been added. Certainly when one takes into account the apparent bias toward the perception of psychopathology by clinical interpreters (e.g., Cox & Sargent, 1950; Little & Shneidman, 1959) one can scarcely hope that conclusions drawn from test responses will be independent of intelligence and verbal fluency.

On the other hand, it should be recognized that much of the research work that psychologists do is accomplished on rather homogeneous groups of subjects, and intellectual differences may not be of special importance in some situations. For example, Atkinson (1958) concludes that the correlation between number of words per TAT story and motive scores is likely to be negligible in homogeneous college groups when leading questions are employed and only four minutes are allotted for each story. However, when shorter time periods are used or when the population is heterogeneous, some correction for story length must be made (e.g., Veroff, 1961).

Thus far it appears that a rather straightforward correction for length of response is most justifiable for most verbal tests. The typical procedure is to divide each raw score by some measure of total productivity, in this way providing a response index independent of productivity. However, there has been some question about the proper corrections to be made for the Rorschach, since it appears that the relationship between the various raw scores and Total R are different from one score to another, and many are probably not linear (Cronbach, 1949; Fiske & Baughman, 1953). But even an imperfect correction may be preferable to no correction at all, and it seems likely that for values of Total R in the usually encountered ranges an index score with Total R as the denominator is the best alternative. If the Rorschach is to be of future value in scientific psychology, more research is plainly needed on some of these fundamental problems.

CONCEPTS OF PROJECTION AND PERSONALITY ASSESSMENT

The idea of projection is so firmly fixed in the realm of personality and personality assessment that it seems wise to view it at least briefly for what it implies about the field. Projection has what is called a *classical* definition that stems back to Freud and which, put simply, suggests that impulses or ideas which are unconscious but repugnant to the individual may be attributed to other persons, thus relieving the projecting individual of anxiety about the unpleasant material. There have been many attempts to study projection, many of them falling under the general rubric of "trait attribution," and out of these investigations there has come an improved and more sophisticated understanding of projection and, ultimately, the necessity for an expanded list of concepts or types of projection. In the discussion that follows we lean heavily on

Campbell (1959) and Murstein and Pryer (1959).

One of the first departures from the classical conception of projection was a now well-known investigation by H. A. Murray (1933), in which a group of boys around nine years of age were given a party during which they made judgments about some photographs. Later they played a game designed to frighten them, and they judged additional photos. Somewhat surprisingly from a classical point of view, the second set of photos was judged higher in maliciousness but not in anxiety. With Campbell (1959) we prefer the term *similarity projection* to refer to the situation in which an individual attributes to others traits which he, himself, has. Had the boys judged the photographs as more anxious, they would be said to be engaging in similarity projection. However, their judgments were of such a nature as to be consistent with or to justify their outlook at the time of the second judging, and Murray used the very satisfactory term *complementary projection* to refer to the attribution of a trait which complements rather than being identical to one's own. Campbell points out, however, that similarity and complementary projection lead to the same expectation about trait attribution for many traits, and it will often be difficult to disentangle them, e.g., by similarity projection the hostile person will see others as hostile, but hostility in others is also complementary to, i.e., justifies hostility. Complementary projection is related to what is sometimes called "rationalized projection" (Murstein & Pryer, 1959; R. D. Singer, 1963), but the latter seems to be thought of more as similarity projection, but of such a nature as to mitigate one's own trait. Thus, if hostile people think of others as hostile, that tends to excuse their own hostility. Thus, rationalized projection should lead always to similarity, whereas complementary projection may lead to a prediction of a difference.

Similarity projection is far and away the most commonly recommended basis for interpretation of projective responses on any test. Such writers as Schafer (1948) rely quite heavily on the assumption that the responses which appear on a test are those characteristic of the subject himself. Piotrowski (1950) suggests explicitly that interpretations be made on the basis of similarity, and Lindzey (1952, 1961) points out that similarity is an assumption underlying the use of the TAT. Lindner (1950) has discussed the interpretation of the Rorschach and has presented 43 content "signs" whose meaning he believes is more or less well understood. According to the count of the present writer, 31 of 56 recommendations he makes are based on the similarity assumption, and another 13 are ambiguous with respect to the assumption underlying them. Thus, only 12 recommendations involve any other assumption, nearly all of those having to do with complementarity.

In spite of the rather lengthy history of the concept of complementary projection there is relatively little research bearing on the distinction between complementary and similarity projection. Feshbach and Singer (1957; R. Singer & Feshbach, 1962) found evidence for similarity projection of anxiety, i.e., others perceived as anxious, but one study yielded positive evidence for complementary projection, i.e., others perceived as threatening, and one did not. On the other hand, Hornberger (1960) studied projection via photo judgments of both sex and fear arousal and found evidence only for complementary projection of fear. Finally, in one of those all too rare "definitive" experiments, Feshbach and Feshbach (1963) repeated H. A. Murray's (1933) experiment with improved methodology. They reasoned that the characteristics of the photos shown to frightened children in the photo judgment task is of essential importance. They noted that Murray had used pictures of men and suggest that it may not be reasonable to expect children, fear-aroused children, to judge adult male pictures as more anxious. Therefore, the Feshbachs deemed it important to include a variety of photos, viz., photos of men, women, boys, and girls. In their first experiment they more or less replicated Murray's party situation with a group of boys 9–12 years old who were asked to make some photo judgments and then after a "scary" game of "murder" were asked to make them again. In that experiment, fear arousal produced an increase in judgments of the maliciousness of men but no changes for the other photos, i.e., there was complementary but no similarity projection. The Feshbachs had some residual concern about the adequacy of their manipulations, so they did a second experiment in a YMCA with boys 8–12 years old who were exposed to a fear-arousing situation involving a good bit of spooky laboratory equipment including a large hypodermic syringe. In that way they hoped to maximize the arousal of fear and minimize arousal of hostility. The fear arousal again produced an increase in judged maliciousness of photos of men, but there was also an increase in fear attributed to the photos of boys. Thus, it would seem that, at least for anxiety, similarity of the object person or stimulus to the respondent is a critical variable for similarity projection. There was no increase in fear attributed to girls. And probably similarity of the object person or stimulus to an actual or probable threatening person is critical for complementary projection. There was no increase in maliciousness attributed to women. It is probably the case that boys 8–12 years old are far less often seriously threatened by women than by men, and certainly their fantasies, both personal and "borrowed," are more fully occupied by male than female villains. It would be of interest to determine what would happen should a female experimenter do an experiment in which boys were similarly threatened. At any rate, it would seem that there is sufficient evidence for the occurrence of complementary projection to justify additional research on the problem, particularly research directed toward determining just when similarity and complementary interpretations are to be made where they conflict. Although actual similarity between a subject and a stimulus person may eventually prove to be an important factor, the evidence to date shows that similarity is not an especially powerful determinant of overall projection (see, e.g., review by Murstein, 1963).

A third variety of projection described by Campbell is "Panglossian projection" which is the tendency to attribute motives to others which would be gratifying to oneself, i.e., to see things as "rosy," better than they really are. Murstein and Pryer (1959) use the term "autistic projection" to refer to an apparently similar process. There seems to be no research evidence for Panglossian projection, but it is not unknown at a clinical level. Lindner, for example, bases two of his recommended interpretations on what seems to be an understanding of a Panglossian process. However, it does seem likely to be an infrequent phenomenon, and Panglossian projection is not likely to bother society very much. Few persons are so very modest that they object to being thought especially well of.

A fourth process in trait attribution which has been suggested by Campbell and which is certainly of considerable potential importance is *reactivity*. There is probably a rather general inclination to suppose that when a paranoid individual describes other persons as hostile he is simply projecting his own hostility. However, it is rather likely that paranoid people live in somewhat more hostile environments than most other people, i.e., hostility engenders hostility. Therefore, when the paranoid describes others as hostile, there may be considerable truth in his remarks. Probably a similar reactive process operates for a number of traits. It is not unthinkable that meek, fearful people live in a capriciously malicious world, for they invite by their defenselessness the displaced hostile attacks that cannot be made upon stronger persons. Some very careful research in this area is badly needed. It may show that what appear to be aberrant judgments of other persons are more than a little justified.

The processes just discussed above may not always operate in different directions, and when they operate in the same direction they may produce an augmented response. When they do not operate in the same direction, it is important to know which processes are operating and in what strengths. Perhaps the validities of test interpretations would not be so distressingly low if more were known about different types of projection and about reaction-producing dispositions.

THE CONCEPT OF PROJECTION IN PERSONALITY ASSESSMENT

The idea of projection as a basis for test responses has been common for a long time, although L. K. Frank (1939) is usually given credit for what is called the "projective hypothesis," a rather general statement of the assumption that whatever an individual does when exposed to an ambiguous stimulus will reveal important aspects of his personality. Obviously there are problems with such a statement as a hypothesis, for it would be quite difficult to disprove that something important was being revealed. As it is usually accepted and interpreted, the projective hypothesis very nearly rules out of projective testing the notion of error so dear to psychometric theory. However, there is every reason to suppose that responses to projective tests may be interpreted in terms of error theory (Murstein, 1963). If an individual may misunderstand some such command as "Add 6 and 9," and if he may for reasons of distraction or whatever give a wrong response even if he understands the command, so it would seem possible for an individual to tell a story or describe an inkblot in a manner quite inconsistent with his usual performance. In this connection it is worth pointing out that there is apparently no kind of pathological Rorschach response which is not found with notable frequency in normal and even diagnosed healthy populations (Wittenborn & Sarason, 1949). One or two odd responses are probably as poor a basis for assuming something about personality as they are for assuming something about intelligence.

One of the possible sources of confusion in interpretation of projective test responses, a confusion denied by the projective hypothesis, is that a subject may not be creating his own responses but may be "borrowing" them, e.g., from paintings, movies, TV shows, etc. Ardent defenders of projective testing are wont to reply that it will be significant that subjects "remember" certain themes or responses to borrow and report. Coleman (1947) has shown that a movie shown to boys the evening before they were given a TAT does not necessarily affect their performance, but the movie he used was a rather immemorable one in all probability. In the only investigation that seems to have been directed specifically toward the borrowed fantasy notion, Wylie (Wylie, Sisson, & Taulbee, 1963) had subjects read both "dependency" and "aggression" stories as alternative interpretations of TAT pictures. In a carefully counterbalanced design subjects were either asked to give "creative" or "memory" stories to TAT cards. Later correlations were obtained between subjects' scores for dependency and aggression for the creative and memory stories. The correlation reached significance for aggression but not for dependency. Thus, the evidence would indicate that borrowed fantasies may, but then they may not, be generally congruent with an individual's other responses.

If we take "projection" to refer generally to an unwarranted, but not necessarily incorrect, assumption either that others are similar to oneself or that they have traits which justify one's own dispositions, then we may ask what the circumstances are which facilitate or lead to projection. Surprisingly enough, projection has not always been producible when it might have been expected (e.g., Rosenthal, 1959). There are good studies that indicate rather definitely that conflict (Zimmer, 1955) and inhibition of feeling (Feshbach, 1963; Zimbardo, 1964) are important determinants of projection. Thus, there is likely to be more projection for traits about which the individual feels conflicted—incidentally, it seems not to matter whether the traits are positive or negative in value—and there is likely to be more projection when, for some reason, the individual refrains from the expression of his feelings.

A point which is well worth emphasizing is that Freud's assumption that only undesirable traits would be projected seems to be wrong. It now appears to be sufficiently established that positive dispositions may be projected in the same way as negative ones (Feshbach, 1963; Wright, 1942; Zimmer, 1955). Therefore, the analysis of projective test responses should take into account the possibility of projection of positive characteristics. There has long been a problem about the utilization of positive material obtained from projective responses, and a good bit of evidence points to the bias of clinicians toward pathological interpretations (Cox & Sargent, 1950; Little & Shneidman, 1959). Clearly the research that has been done points to the necessity for research on the interpretation of positive traits appearing in projective test responses. A general theoretical analysis of projection has been made from the standpoint of dissonance theory (Bramel, 1962), and it has been suggested that dissonance theory will account for the projection of desirable traits (R. D. Singer, 1963).

A question of truly overriding importance is whether all the effort of projective testing is really worthwhile or even necessary. Do we gain anything by the utilization of such complex and expensive procedures that could not be obtained by more direct means (the problem of incremental validity, Sechrest, 1963)? Straightforward investigations into the validity of personality measures would suggest not (e.g., Barger & Sechrest, 1961; Wallace & Sechrest, 1963). However, it has long been believed that projective measures tap a level of response not amenable to more direct assessment, a belief that may be labeled the "levels hypothesis" (see Murstein, 1963). There have been very few methodologically adequate studies that have really demonstrated that projective measures get at something beyond what is tapped by direct methods (e.g., see Murstein's, 1963, pp. 66–67; criticism of Stone and Dellis, 1960). However, Davids (1955) has shown that in comparison with an anonymously tested control group, an experimental group that believed that they were taking tests in order to qualify for employment showed greater homogeneity on self-report measures of personality. Moreover, Hanfmann and Getzels (1953) obtained results suggesting that third-person stems in a sentence-completion test reflect a somewhat different aspect of personality than do first-person stems. Zimbardo (1964) used a photo judgment projective measure of fear arousal along with a direct measure of fear arousal in an experimental setting in which there were conditions of high and low fear-arousal. Zimbardo had previously classified his subjects as either likely or unlikely to express pain on the basis of their self-reports. The photo judgment and direct measures of fear arousal correlated .75, but those subjects who had reported that they were unlikely to tell others when they were in pain obtained significantly higher scores on the projective measure of fear arousal and significantly lower scores on the direct measure. Thus, there is a modicum of evidence supporting the hypothesis that projective measures may get at something rather different from more direct measures, although there is scarcely any evidence to suggest that the material tapped is at a different level or that it is something of which he is unaware. We would agree with others (e.g., Lindzey, 1961; Murstein, 1963) that the current evidence does not strongly support the conclusion that projective measures get at "unconscious" dispositions.

ASSUMPTIONS UNDERLYING THE USE OF PROJECTIVE TECHNIQUES

Various writers, including Murstein (1963) and Piotrowski (1950), have listed some of the assumptions which underlie projective measures, but Lindzey (1961) has compiled the most complete list. There is not space here to go over all of his points, but the interested researcher will find them a veritable mine of testable hypotheses. It will be noted that similarity projection is dignified by assumption No. 9, and other assumptions relate to the importance of repeated responses, rare or unusual responses, omitted responses, and to such issues as the influence of the examiner and the test situation. The assumptions stated do not appear to be well supported by evidence, but they are certainly common in the projective test movement. It is curious that there is as yet so little research evidence bearing on such issues as failure to give expected responses (omitted responses) or giving responses that are infrequent to the particular stimulus used (rare responses). One rather clever investigation by Ericksen and Lazarus (1952) did suggest that failure to give appropriate Rorschach percepts when subjected to a modification of "testing of limits" might be associated with aggression or succorance, but not homosexuality. And various work cited by Murstein (1963) is relevant to the interpretation of responses emitted to stimuli for which they are infrequent, but the data thus far do not lend themselves to any very straightforward conclusions. What is most evident is the need for a more extensive and systematic testing of assumptions such as are stated by Lindzey.

In order to complete the list we might point out that one reasonable assumption for stimuli such as TAT cards is what has been called the "hero assumption" (e.g., Lindzey & Kalnins, 1958), i.e., the assumption that the central character or hero of a story is particularly likely to represent a projection. The evidence for such an assumption is very limited, but what there is (Lindzey & Kalnins, 1958) is quite supportive of it.

A second, and closely related, assumption is that characters other than the central one may represent the subject's view of the world, i.e., they are to be interpreted in the light of complementary projection. As was suggested earlier, there is a good bit of evidence for the existence of complementary projection and what is needed is research which will result in specifications for its employment in response interpretation.

THE PSYCHOMETRIC PROPERTIES OF PERSONALITY MEASUREMENTS

The Scoring of Responses

In order to reduce to manageable proportions the mass of possible data which might eventuate from a single subject taking a test on a single occasion (e.g., think of the 555 discrete responses which a subject makes in taking a MMPI), and in order to make precise comparisons with other persons who have taken the same test, it is highly desirable to be able to "score" a test. By scoring a test we mean the quantifying of the responses, or more precisely, the assigning of a particular weight to a response according to some set of rules.

There are many ways in which a response can be weighted for the purpose of developing a scoring system for a test. Probably the most common system is to use arbitrary unit weights based on an assumption of a simple monotone relationship between the number of "positive" responses and the characteristic being measured, e.g., as when a "true" response is weighted 1 and a "false" response is weighted 0. A simple scoring system involving unit weights is used for most personality tests and is thought of especially in connection with self-report inventory tests of the true-false type, e.g., MMPI, MAS, CPI. However, most other tests are scored in the same manner. The Rorschach, for example, utilizes a simple scoring system for most variables in which each response is given a unit weight and the total score is equal to the number of responses. One M or D response counts the same as another in determining the total score. Similarly, a TAT scoring system that counts themes is a simple, monotonic, unit-weight system. It is possible to have a scoring system of the same type utilizing integral rather than unit weights so that more values than 0 and 1 are employed. Tests that permit the respondent to choose a degree of intensity of responding ordinarily employ integral weights of a monotonic nature. The California *F* scale, which permits responses ranging across six values from *Strongly Agree* to *Strongly Disagree* weights the response with integers ranging from 1 to 6.

A response may be weighted in a manner proportional to the frequency with which it is given on the assumption that the more unusual a response is, the more significant it is likely to be. Thus, if a response indicative of hostility is given by relatively few persons it might be taken to indicate a more extreme degree of hostility than a response given by many, and it could, therefore, be weighted more heavily. Such a scoring system has been used for weighting items in attitude tests (Green, 1954), but it has not achieved any great popularity in personality measurement in the development of formal scoring systems. However, it should be recognized that underlying much so-called clinical use of tests, for which no standard scoring systems are used, are implicit scoring systems in which responses may certainly be weighted more heavily because of their rarity in the experience of the test user. If a Rorschach interpreter who is interested in estimating a subject's tendency to use the whole blot in his response weights a given response more heavily because it is given to a card for which whole responses are relatively infrequent, he is using an imprecise version of Likert scoring. It is also the case that many scoring systems do, in fact, operate as Likert-type scales even though the rationale is inexplicit or may even be quite different. For example, weighting "color" responses on the Rorschach in such a manner that FC = .5, CF = 1.0, and C = 1.5 (Beck, 1949) almost certainly results in an approximation to a Likert scale inasmuch as weighting is inversely proportional to frequency.

Finally, an item may also be weighted on the basis of its discriminating power, i.e., its validity. It might be thought that the better an item discriminates, the more heavily it should be weighted. If an opportunity is available to do a good validational and cross-validational study on individual test items, the weighting of items in proportion to their validities can be justified. Some tests do use such a weighting system, notably the Bernreuter Personality Inventory (Bernreuter, 1935) and the Strong Vocational Interest Blank (Strong, 1951). But there is a cautionary note to be entered concerning the differential weighting of test items based on their discriminating power. The discriminating power of an item can only be judged against some particular criterion. It is not always desirable, however, to direct a test toward the prediction of some one single criterion, especially if a measure of some trait or disposition is desired, rather than the prediction of some specific behavior. By weighting the items in a trait measure on the basis of their power to discriminate on some criterion, it is quite possible to develop a test that is a better predictor of the criterion behavior and a poorer measure of the trait. For example, nearly everyone would agree that persons scoring high on a measure of need for achievement should make better grades than persons scoring low on the same measure, assuming, that is, equal intelligence. However, it would be unwise to weight the items in a need-for-achievement scale on the basis of their ability to discriminate students with high grades from students with low grades. There are many other variables that contribute to the grade point average than need for achievement and intelligence.

Generally it has been found that the simpler a scoring system is, the more useful it is likely to be in the long run. Complex scoring systems, especially those with nonintegral weights or with an excessive range of values, tend to capitalize on chance in the original construction process, and they often do not hold up so well in subsequent research efforts. Moreover, complex scoring systems introduce expenses and opportunity for error which may outweigh any advantage gained by more precise weighting of responses.

Even after a scoring system for a test or assessment procedure has been developed, there remains the problem of evaluating the scores against some standard. There are two general classes into which test scores may fall. These have been called *normative* and *ipsative*. By far the most common type of measurement operation is to get a score with a normative group, i.e., with the scores of some other persons. If an individual has a larger score than most other persons, then he is thought of as having a relatively great amount of the trait or characteristic in question. A person who has a small score relative to other persons is assumed to have little of the characteristic. Thus, if a student scores higher than 95 per cent of other students on a measure of dependency, it would be expected that he would show many more signs of dependency than other persons.

However, it is also possible to order an individual's responses relative to his own mean and without regard for the performances of other persons. This is referred to as *ipsative* measurement. One example of an ipsative procedure would be to rank an individual's characteristics for their prominence. For example, consider the three characteristics (a) intelligence, (b) cheerfulness, and (c) honesty. We might try for a particular person to decide which of the three traits most characterized him, which second, and which least. If we did so, we would have achieved an ipsative ordering of his traits. The implications of ipsative type measurements for behavioral predictions are not at all clear, particularly if it is desirable for some purposes to make comparisons among samples of persons. If an individual is particularly characterized by cheerfulness in comparison with his other traits, may we expect that he will be generally cheerful or that other persons will regard him as cheerful? Despite the conceptual interest of ipsative scores, it is to be doubted that in practice they can be considered to be different in their implications from normative measures. Block (1957) compared ipsative and normative *ratings* and was led to conclude that there is necessarily a normative basis for ipsative descriptions and that the two types of descriptions are substantially equivalent. The one personality measure that makes a serious gesture toward ipsative measurement is the Edwards Personal Preference Schedule (Edwards, 1954). In responding to the EPPS the subject indicates for each of a pair of need-related statements which best describes him, and by accumulating responses across a series of such items, it is presumably possible to order an individual's needs according to their relative strengths. Theoretically a given person might have achievement as his strongest need without being particularly high in that need in the population from which he was drawn. However, it is to be noted that the EPPS is interpreted in a normative manner with percentile scores indicating the subject's standing on each need measure relative to a general normative sample. At the present time it has not been demonstrated that it is possible to develop a meaningful personality measure that does not take into account the standing of test subjects in some normative group.

Test Norms and Standardization

Once a score on a test has been obtained in some manner, and it does not matter whether the "score" is a precise numerical representation of the performance or whether it is only a quantitative estimate such as "much" or "few," it is ordinarily desirable, even necessary, to have some basis for comparison of the score with other scores so that it may be known whether the score is an unusual one or not. Norms provide a basis for a systematic comparison of test scores with some standard. However, it is necessary to keep in mind that not just any sort of norms will do. Obviously the norms must be relevant to the comparisons which are to be made, but it is seldom the case that any personality test provides sufficient normative data that it is possible to compare an individual with either very precisely defined or meaningful groups. As a result, many tests do not permit more than the grossest distinctions. For example, if the only norms available for a test are for "people in general," all hospitalized psychiatric patients are likely to appear quite deviant, and very few distinctions among them will be possible. It would almost certainly be far more meaningful to have separate norms for hospitalized patients.

Norms, at least formal norms, are most inadequate, if they exist at all, for projective techniques. While there have been some few normative studies for the TAT (Eron, 1950, 1953), the Rorschach (Ames, Learned, Metraux, & Walker, 1952; Ames, Metraux, & Walker, 1959; Carlson, 1952; Hertz, 1951a), and various sentence completion tests (Rohde, 1957; Rotter & Rafferty, 1950), the norms available are typically for rather narrowly defined groups such as college students or "eight-year-old children" and are often untrustworthy by reason of other sampling considerations. It is probably the case that few clinical psychologists really pay much attention to published norms in any case, with the possible exception of norms for scoring popular vs. original Rorschach responses, and most normative comparisons in clinical practice are made on the basis of the individual clinician's own experience. Tutko (1962) found some evidence suggesting that one of the important differences between experienced and inexperienced clinical psychologists in the interpretation of projective tests is the greater normative sophistication of the former. Although the collection of normative data is probably not highly regarded and greatly rewarded in the research hierarchy today, it is no less necessary than ever, and when a really superior effort in that direction comes along, such as the Holtzman Inkblot Test (Holtzman, Thorpe, Swartz, & Herron, 1961), it deserves commendation and emulation.

It certainly should not be—but it probably is—necessary to say that there is no relationship between test norms and test validity. Norms only provide a basis for systematic comparison of an individual's performance with the performance of other persons, but the performance may still be either unreliable or invalid as an indicator of other behavior, or both. It is perfectly possible to have a superb set of norms for a measure whose validity is .00. This point may be seen clearly by regarding height as a possible measure of intelligence. The available norms for height are unquestionably better than the norms for any of our tests, but the validity of height as a measure of intelligence would be very nearly .00 in an adult population. The normative tables for tests, inadequate as they may be, are nearly always far more impressive than the tables presenting evidence for validity. A prospective user of a test should make a clear distinction between the two kinds of test information.

The Validity of Tests

At the present time "validity" seems to be another one of those psychological constructs that has been used in so many ways to mean so many things that its usefulness as a concept is imperiled (see, e.g., Ebel, 1961; Loevinger, 1957; Renner, 1962). Exactly what is meant by validity of a test is often quite uncertain. Strictly speaking, of course, a test is valid as a predictor for anything with which it correlates. Such a conception of validity has been termed *empirical* validity by Anastasi (1954) and viewed in such a way the validity of a measure can be expressed precisely by a correlation coefficient. However, it becomes quite evident that, if validity is approached in a strictly empirical manner, there is no such thing as *the* validity of a test. As Guilford (1946) and Loevinger (1957) have pointed out, a test has as many "validity" coefficients as there are things with which it might be correlated, X situations in which it might be given, and X groups of subjects for whom it might be used. To ask the simple question without further specification, "Is this test valid?" is at best naïve.

In more general terms, the question of the validity of a test is whether the test does, in fact, measure what it purports to measure, but just how it may be established that a test is measuring some trait or characteristic is the crux of the problem. Unquestionably the simplest conception of validity is *face* validity which is the extent to which a test *seems* to measure what it purports to measure. One would suppose that a test such as the Manifest Anxiety Scale (Taylor, 1953) would have a relatively high degree of face validity (strangely enough, no exact operations for determining face validity seem ever to have been specified), for the scale was originally established on the basis of the face validity of the individual items, taking as face validity the extent to which the items seemed to clinical psychologists to measure anxiety. Whether the MAS would have equal face validity for other groups, e.g., lay persons, is an empirical matter. Probably they would. Tests with a high degree of face validity are likely to be rather transparent by definition, but they need not have much of any other sort of validity as has been amply demonstrated by the history of attempts to validate empirically instruments with a great deal of face validity. Perhaps because of repeated disappointments in attempts to validate self-report measures of personality, disappointments stemming in part from the expectation that moderate to high correlations would be the order, face validity has fallen into very nearly complete disrepute in the field of test construction, and certainly face validity is rarely a sufficient justification in itself for the use of a test. Nevertheless, the literature on validation of personality tests justifies the conclusion that face validity is probably a good starting point in test construction, especially if for estimates of face validity the judgments of psychologically sophisticated persons are sought.

Anastasi (1954) lists *content* validity as one of the four basic kinds of validity. It refers to the adequacy with which a test samples the relevant behavioral domain. The examples of content validity are usually chosen from the area of achievement testing where it is obvious that if a test is supposed to be a measure of "arithmetic ability," it should contain problems requiring use of all the basic arithmetic operations. However, the concept is applicable to personality test construction and evaluation. If a test purports to be a measure of "hostility," to take one instance, and all the items refer to responses to frustrations by authority figures in recognition situations, the test would not be regarded as having adequate content validity. Again, however, there are no unusual and explicit specifications for content validity, and its assessment is a matter of judgment and perhaps theory. It should be noted that Loevinger (1957) questions severely the relevance of concept validity to personality measurements.

At present the two most influential conceptions of validity are unquestionably *construct* validity (Cronbach & Meehl, 1955; Loevinger, 1957) and the *convergent-discriminant* validity conceptions of Campbell and Fiske (1959), advanced in their paper on the multitrait-multimethod matrix. Cronbach and Meehl noted that tests are infrequently validated against any criterion in which we are really interested. An excellent example of that point is the persistent practice of establishing that personality measures will distinguish hospitalized psychotics from normals. (It will be noted that if the procedure were to validate tests against the actual *pre*diction of becoming psychotic, the issue would be quite different.) In fact, it is very infrequent that psychologists can ever specify any definite or ultimate criterion of the trait in which they are interested. It has been stated that construct validity is "ordinarily studied when the tester has no definite criterion measure of the quality with which he is concerned and must use indirect measures. Here the trait or quality underlying the test is of central importance, rather than either the test behavior or the scores on the criteria" (Technical Recommendations for Psychological Tests and Diagnostic Techniques, 1954).

Although Cronbach and Meehl discuss construct validity in terms of a "nomothetic net," by which they mean a series of theoretical propositions and experimental operations which would relate a given construct to other constructs and other operations, in actual practice most attempts at construct validation of tests have proceeded pretty much along the lines of what Campbell and Fiske (1959) have referred to as convergent validity. That is, it is shown that the test either does or does not relate to some other variable which one would, on a priori grounds, expect it to relate to. Consequently, as the idea is actually used in test validation research, it does not seem to represent a large departure from higher work in test validation particularly of the trait measure variety. However, some writers, notably Jessor and Hammond (1957), have suggested that construct validity must mean something more than a simple demonstration of empirical relationship between a test and a criterion and have insisted that theoretical considerations must play a part in the construction of a test as well as in the attempts to validate it. Although other writers (e.g., Bechtoldt, 1959) have implied that the notion of construct validity is but another excuse for careless and unthinking experimentation, it would seem that only the stern one-concept, one-operation view of philosophy of science could take issue with the proposals of Cronbach and Meehl.

It should be quite obvious that the construct validity of a test cannot be represented by a coefficient and probably not even by a series of coefficients, for there is no reason to suppose that any given correlation or experimental difference represents the ultimate level of the validity of the instrument. At the very best, we can get only approximations of the level of the validity of a test, perhaps to the point of being able to state roughly the upper and lower bounds of a measure's probable validity.

Campbell and Fiske (1959) have stated a somewhat simpler conceptual and more exact methodological model for establishing test validity. Notable in their suggestion is that it is important not only to establish what it is a test measures, i.e., its convergent validity, but also what a test does *not* measure, i.e., its discriminant validity. They point out that a test can be invalidated by disappointingly high correlations with other variables as well as disappointingly low correlations. In some respects, much of the controversy surrounding the so-called response set variable in the development of self-report measures of personality concerns the very fact that measures may be invalidated not only by showing that they correlate poorly with some criterion but also by showing that they correlate highly with some conceptually simpler variable, such as the tendency to respond true, or in a socially desirable manner, to all items. Campbell (1960) has made a number of suggestions regarding the establishment of discriminant validity for tests which should certainly be considered by anyone proposing a new measure of a trait. For example, Campbell suggests that every new trait measure should be correlated with intelligence, measures of response set, and the like. If it is shown that new trait measures correlate very highly with intelligence or very highly with some response set such as social desirability, then the discriminant validity of the test is impaired and the necessity for new measures is open to question.

Campbell and Fiske point out that in order to establish the trait validity of a measure, a minimum context is a correlation matrix in which two or more traits are measured by two or more methods. If, then, the correlation between methodologically independent measures of the same trait is exceeded by methodologically independent measures of different traits, the convergent validity of the measure is doubtful. Similarly, although it has been shown by Humphreys (1960) not to be an absolute requirement, it is desirable to be able to demonstrate that the correlation between methodologically independent measures of the same trait is higher than the correlation between two traits measured by the same method. If it occurs that two traits measured by the same method correlate more highly than when either of them is measured by two different methods, then we can suspect that the discriminant validity of the traits is open to question, i.e., that methods variance obscures the valid measurement of the trait.

In a related approach to the problem of the validity of measures, Sechrest (1963) has suggested that the incremental validity needs to be considered. This problem arises from the fact that in most situations, particularly clinical situations in which tests are used, it is scarcely ever the case that prediction is really at a chance level without the test. In a typical clinical situation, for example, there is a substantial amount of biographical information, knowledge of the patient's family, his appearance, etc., which can obviously contribute to accurate predictions about him. Even though there may be available a test which has a demonstrated validity in the sense of permitting accurate predictions above chance, it is not necessarily the case that the addition of the test would improve the predictions over what Cronbach and Gleser (1957) have called the *a priori model*. It will not always be easy to demonstrate that a test actually permits an increment in the accuracy of some prediction. As has been found by a number of investigators using clinical instruments or projective tests, the validity of such measures over and above general clinical stereotypes or simpler forms of information is doubtful. For tests which are intended to have some practical value, it ought to be a requirement that their incremental validity over and above simpler, cheaper, quicker methods be established (see also Meehl, 1959).

Sechrest (1962) has also pointed to the need for consideration of the "relative" validity of personality measures. Similar considerations have been outlined by Cronbach and Gleser (1957) under the general rubric of *utility functions* for predictive instruments, while Loevinger (1957) has criticized utility considerations as stemming directly from consideration of the predictive validity of tests rather than their construct validity. Nonetheless, in practical situations, i.e., in situations in which tests are actually used for decision-making purposes, one must consider the actual value of an instrument as related to its cost expressed in some terms. As pointed out by Cronbach and Gleser (1957) and also by others (Rimm, 1963; Sechrest, 1962, 1963), one must take into account the utility of a decision in terms of the savings consequent to being correct and the losses consequent to being wrong and in terms of the cost of the operations involved in the decision-making process. There are a variety of criteria by which one may seek to establish the utility of those measures, one being what Brogden and Taylor (1950) have referred to as the "dollar criterion." Additional important criteria may be the amount of time required by highly trained personnel, the amount of time required of the subjects, the time which may elapse between the decision to resort to psychological testing and the moment at which the results become available.

Of considerable theoretical and research interest is the value of the clinical instrument expressed in terms of some measure or unit of verbal productivity by the subject (Sechrest, 1962). It is obvious and implicit in the attempts which have been made to construct special personality instruments that some stimuli are better for eliciting verbal responses from which predictions may be made than are others. If tests are really only ways of eliciting verbal responses, then one might ignore specific stimulus properties, specific instructions, and conditions of administration. Quite evidently the constructors of various clinical instruments did not mean for such aspects of the test situation to be ignored. Therefore, it should be apparent that some stimuli are supposed to be better than other stimuli. Occasionally one encounters controversies concerning the validities of various clinical instruments, and it may be alleged that one instrument has a greater validity than another instrument. Such a statement has meaning, however, only with respect to some supposed equation of the two tests. Thus, for example, should someone make the statement that a 100-item test has greater validity than a two-item test, we would scarcely experience any surprise. Should we, then, experience surprise or concern were it to be demonstrated that, for example, the TAT which elicits perhaps 1,500 words has a greater validity in the prediction of some criterion than the incomplete sentences blank which elicits perhaps 300 words? In many respects one might be surprised were the TAT not shown to have a higher degree of validity. Certainly for research and theoretical purposes, it would be desirable to have validity expressed in an index as some function of verbal productivity, time required, or expense, etc.

While considering this matter it might be well to point out that we are scarcely yet at any degree of understanding concerning what constitutes clinical information or any other information about personality. It should be clear that not just any increment in knowledge can be considered to be information in the true sense of the term. This stems from the fact that it is quite possible to acquire information that is redundant to some degree with information that has already been attained. For example, should it be known that an individual is 68 inches tall, it scarcely could be considered to be "information," or at least additional information, to discover that he is also 173 centimeters tall. An important research problem, then, is to discover the relationship between "information" that can be obtained from various personality instruments and the decisions that may be made on the basis of such information. It may be argued that if "information" does not facilitate the making of decisions, does not alter them in some respect, then it is not information at all. At what point the information contained in personality tests begins to become relevant is not known at this time. However, there is very strong suggestion in research which has been done that the point of redundancy is reached relatively early (Cohen, 1962; Kostlan, 1954; Meehl, 1960; Sines, 1959). In fact, some of the research suggests very definitely that the relationship between amount of material available and accuracy of predictions is not even monotonic. That is, there is a point beyond which predictions not only cease to become better but they even begin to be worse (e.g., Sines, 1959). In this sense, then, it may be questioned what is actually meant by having "more information" about an individual.

The Reliability of Personality Measures

Generally when speaking of reliability we mean the extent to which a test is likely to yield a consistent score. Essentially we want tests that do not elicit random responses or give us randomly derived information for whatever reason. The problem of reliability of tests boils down to the question of how much faith we can have that the information obtained from a test is true and not erroneous information. It might be noted that this is distinctly different from the question of validity, for we may have absolutely true information about an individual that is absolutely invalid for whatever purpose it was intended. On the other hand, it should be equally as apparent that in order to get valid results, a test must also give consistent, i.e., reliable results. If we have a valid test it is, of necessity, reliable in some degree (Guilford, 1946). Sometimes it may be possible to increase the validity of a test by increasing its reliability. Thus, statistical adjustments in correlations between measures, known technically as corrections for attenuation, are estimates of the degree of correlation between two measures to be expected should one or both of the measures have some specified, ordinarily perfect, reliability. On the other hand, Guilford (1946, 1954) points out that under some, by no means unusual, circumstances it may be possible to increase the reliability of a test and simultaneously to decrease its validity. This rather paradoxical result may be achieved if the criterion to be predicted is of a rather heterogeneous nature and by increasing the reliability we increase its homogeneity. Thus, for example, should we attempt to predict grades in college by means of an intelligence test, we might refine an intelligence test to the point at which it became more and more reliable and yet discover that its correlation with college grades became lower and lower because of the fact that we purified the test and removed variance attributable to such factors as motivation and personality which are, themselves, very likely associated with achievement of high grades in college.

It is evident that the final output of an assessment effort is a deceptively simple index or score which represents the net result of the operations of several complex determinants. It may be nearly impossible to separate the various contributions to error or inconsistency in the final score except at a conceptual level. It is worthwhile, however, to consider the sources of inconsistency in test scores in order that the operations necessary to increase "reliability" become evident.

There are sources of inconsistency or error which reside in the individual responding to the test items and, thus, which are not inherently a fault of the measure. However, it may be possible to obviate some such sources by proper design of the entire test system. First, it is characteristic of human subjects to have competing response dispositions or response dispositions at intermediate levels of strength. Therefore, a certain amount of behavior similar to "oscillatory" behavior can be expected in response to test items, i.e., as the strength of a disposition waxes and wanes in an epicyclic fashion, test items with a threshold value at or near the mean level of the disposition can be expected to elicit inconsistent responses. This will particularly be the case when the items require an "all or none" response, e.g., true-false items, or when they are scored in an all or none manner, e.g., presence or absence of a theme. If many of the test items have thresholds for response at a value close to the mean value of a disposition in a population, the test will appear to be highly unreliable even though it might, from another point of view, be regarded as reflecting a "true" state of affairs. At the present time it would probably be a rather simple matter to write opinion items about the responses that the United States should make to Communist countries which would produce highly unreliable scores for Americans, in part because there is a middle ground of opinion within which both individuals and groups fluctuate from time to time or from one context to another. Only by including fairly extreme items in both directions, i.e., tough and conciliatory, will substantial "consistency" be produced. As has been suggested by Kagan (1959), when a stimulus such as a TAT card taps more than one disposition, a certain amount of inconsistency in responses can be expected because of fluctuations in the relative strengths of the dispositions, inconsistency which is not implicitly attributable to the test. Rotter (1960) has made a related point in indicating that the usual assumption that the strongest response will always occur is possibly wrong; the frequency of occurrence of responses may be in proportion to their relative strengths.

A second source of inconsistency residing in the subject rather than in the test is a tendency toward random responding (Sechrest & Jackson, 1963). No matter how carefully constructed a test may be, it will not yield reliable results if subjects respond randomly to it. Why people should respond randomly is a question worthy of empirical study, but several possibilities occur. First, motivation may be so low that the subject desires only to complete the test performance and escape the situation. Or motivation may not be high enough to support the careful and thoughtful behavior that is necessary for some complex procedures. One point worth noting is that motivation of the subject is not entirely an attribute of the subject divorced from any context. In part, low motivation may be a result of the context in which the test is given or even of the test itself if the test is long, arduous, difficult, etc. Second, it is possible that certain test procedures and stimuli may be anxiety arousing and that anxiety may interfere with performance, e.g., by increasing errors of reading or marking responses. Finally, for a variety of reasons some subjects may be inclined to approximate a random performance by responding humorously, deviantly, or otherwise inconsistently, perhaps for their own amusement. Such subjects will almost certainly lower the reliability of any test or measure.

Some researchers have proposed that improvement in measurement might eventuate from repeated administration of measures. Osterweil and Fiske (1956) found that sentence completion responses changed markedly over different administrations of the test, two to three weeks apart. A very interesting aspect of their findings was that "popular" responses were significantly more likely to be repeated than unique ones and that there was a significant positive correlation between the number of unique responses by a subject and the number of responses changed. Fiske and Van Buskirk (1959) showed that interpretations of sentence completion protocols for the same patient but obtained on different occasions were often strikingly different. They concluded that it might be necessary to obtain more than one protocol from a subject in order to get a stable, consistent picture of his personality. K. I. Howard (1962; Howard & Diesenhaus, 1965) has shown that for self-report measures the first administration is psychometrically inferior (less reliable) than later administrations of the same measures and better differentiation of subjects is achieved on second and third administrations. It should also be noted that Kaplan (1963; Kaplan & Berger, 1956) has amply demonstrated the fact that it is possible to obtain multiple Rorschach protocols from the same subject without damaging the integrity of the test. All of the above lines of evidence converge on the conclusion that repeated administrations of the same stimuli may be desirable or even necessary in order to achieve a stable and useful picture of personality, not necessarily because of limitations of the tests.

There are characteristics of tests which also contribute to inconsistency in responses. There may be perturbations in response dispositions produced by ambiguously worded or difficult items, or the structure of the test may require such care about the nature of the response, e.g., preciseness about where the mark should be placed, that inconsistencies are inevitable. It should be noted that it is random errors across items or occasions that are referred to here. There may also be constant errors produced in much the same way, e.g., by use of ambiguous or difficult words, but while constant errors lower validity, they do not affect reliability of response. It is probably not possible to develop a test format for which errors are impossible, but careful attention to structure of tests can probably eliminate many problems. No matter what care is taken in the construction of a test, it is also possible that it will be administered or otherwise used erroneously and thus that atypical responses will be elicited. Finally, inconsistency of response may result from variations in the situation or conditions of administration of the test. For example, if it is true that such transient states or occurrences as hunger, social isolation, task failure, and the like can affect test responses, then to the extent that conditions of administration are not rigidly standardized, inconsistency of response will be an inevitable consequent.

With respect to changes in response resulting from oscillations in response dispositions and from changes in conditions of administration, test developers are caught in something of a dilemma. Ordinarily we do not want tests to be so sensitive that the results fluctuate quite freely with the changing of the mood of the subject and the situation. Rather more typically in psychology we want tests to tap the more enduring aspects of behavior. On the other hand, we want tests sufficiently sensitive that they will reflect important changes in the status of the subject. Not all inconsistencies in test behavior are likely to be attributable to error. Thus, for example, there is a limit within which we might expect the reliability of good measures to lie. For example, if over a period of five years we found a test-retest correlation for a group of subjects on the order of .90, we might be very suspicious that the test was tapping some spurious response characteristic of the subject in which we were not genuinely interested. For most personality characteristics we would hardly expect a high degree of consistency over a period of five years. On the other hand, if the reliability over that period went to .00, we would conclude that we were not dealing with an aspect of behavior with really enduring implications.

In the same sense in which engineers may speak of a "man-machine system," one may think of the test-user system, and it becomes meaningful to think of the dependability of various aspects of the system rather than of a single part, viz., the test. We discover, then, that undependability may reside in the user of a test rather than in the test itself. It is important for many reasons to distinguish among sources of unreliability. Very often in the case of personality measures considerable attention is paid to what is called scoring "reliability." It should be clear that the agreement between two scorers of a test in no way reflects upon the reliability of an instrument. It reflects only the reliability of the scoring system. One might just as well refer to the reliability of an IBM test scoring machine as to the reliability of two clinicians in scoring a test. In fact, it is questionable whether the term *reliability* should even be used when referring to the agreement with which clinicians can score clinical instruments. Conceptually, scoring a TAT protocol for hostility is in no way different from scoring an achievement test on an IBM machine. The problems are exactly the same, that is, making sure that a particular response is scored the same way on one occasion as on another or from one scoring machine to another. The demonstration of adequate agreement between scorers is in no way a substitute for demonstration of instrument reliability, although some may imply otherwise (e.g., Dana, 1959).

In clinical situations, the importance of a test performance or a score is slight in comparison with the interpretation and use that is made of it by the clinician. For such uses of personality instruments it is appropriate to determine the consistency of interpretation or even of decisions that are made on the basis of the tests rather than scorable properties of the test itself. While the test may give very consistent quantitative scores from time to time, the interpretation or the use made of those scores may vary rather greatly or vice versa. Fiske and Van Buskirk (1959) showed that the consistency of clinical interpretations of sentence completion protocols is not high when separate protocols are obtained on different occasions. On the other hand, various investigators have found moderately good agreement between different clinical interpretations of the same protocol, e.g., for the Rorschach (Krugman, 1942; Palmer, 1951) and the TAT (Horowitz, 1962; Silverman, 1959). It is probably more typically the case in personality research that tests are used because of more or less objective indices or scores which they yield. Thus, the usual practice in using tests as independent variables or separate variables in research is to separate subjects into groups on the basis of scores or indices that are derived rather directly from the test performance. In such a case the clinician who scores the test operates very much as a scoring machine, simply counting up the particular number of responses which occur.

A statistical problem that often arises in attempts to estimate agreement between clinicians scoring or interpreting the same responses stems from the fact that in the personality area, test performances often seem to have more qualitative than quantitative properties. If responses are quantitative and if they have suitable metric characteristics, the agreement clearly is best expressed in terms of correlation. However, under other circumstances there may be an inclination to express agreement in terms of percentage of responses classified in the same manner. As Murstein (1963) demonstrates, there are times when per cent agreement may give a better indication of the actual level of agreement than correlation. One instance in which great caution must be exercised, however, is when marginal frequencies are markedly skewed. If, for example, a particular sign is judged to be absent in 90 per cent of all protocols by both judges, then the *minimum* per cent agreement possible is 80. Such a figure is meaningless for a problem analogous to the base rate problem in prediction (Meehl & Rosen, 1955) obtains. A seemingly satisfactory solution to this problem has been given by Winer (1955) who has developed a technique for representing in correlational terms agreement between categorizations which takes into account only the agreement for the less frequent response. Winer's technique is probably very often applicable in personality assessment research. It was employed with good effect by Jackson and Sechrest (1962). Another way of eliminating the influence of marginal discrepancies is to bias the selection of materials to be scored by presenting equal numbers of previously classified positive and negative instances to a second scorer (e.g., see Wallace & Sechrest, 1963). By such a procedure there can be no spurious agreement introduced by marked judging biases.

APPROACHES TO THE ESTIMATION OF RELIABILITY

If we take the problem of reliability to be centered around the question of consistency of measurement, in assessing the reliability of a measure we want to know whether, or to what degree, the test would give the same results if it were administered again under the same conditions. It is because we can never be certain that conditions are, in fact, the same—in fact, we can usually be certain that they are not the same—that we can at best estimate the reliability of a test.

An obvious approach is, of course, to give the test two or more times which results in the well-known test-retest reliability coefficient. There are, however, serious problems concerning retesting as an approach to reliability. First of all, it is necessary to specify what the time interval between administrations of the test should be. It may obviously vary anywhere from a few seconds, in the case of a simple item or a simple task, on up to as many years as the researcher and his subject are willing to wait. Many factors, such as the fatigue induced by the testing procedures, must be taken into account as determining what the proper interval ought to be. Moreover, if the time interval becomes very extensive at all, it becomes questionable whether one is assessing the reliability of the instrument or the stability of the characteristic being measured. For example, if it is found that the test-retest correlation between measures of anxiety taken over a period of one year is .40, should this be taken as an indication of the characteristic? This question can only be answered by multiple assessment of the test-retest reliability at varying periods of time. If it is found that the reliability is .40, whether the interval of time is one hour or one year, it would seem relatively plausible that it is the instrument that is lacking in reliability. On the other hand, if the correlation between the two measures drops off rather gradually as a function of time, it may very well be that the characteristic being measured is unstable. The interpretation of test-retest reliabilities could be enhanced if reliability indices were available at several points in time. Finally, one must then decide what level of reliability is desirable over a period of time. Although it may seem paradoxical, it is quite clearly the case that reliability can be too high as well as too low, as suggested above.

One can take the position, as some do (Holzberg, 1960; Macfarlane & Tuddenham, 1951), that inconsistencies in a subject's responses to projective stimuli, even over a relatively short period of time, are the result of changes in the subject's personality. Or one can take the position that responses to projective stimuli tap the enduring and deep-lying levels of personality. However, one is on shaky ground in attempting to maintain both positions simultaneously as do the above authors.

A further weakness in the test-retest reliability operation, as with all "other things being equal" procedures, is that it is almost certainly impossible ever to know whether the conditions of two administrations of the test are, in fact, equivalent. There may be practice effects, sensitization effects, fatigue effects, as well as many external environmental changes which would operate to reduce the equivalence of the two administrations.

Retesting is often thought to be meaningless in the case of most, if not all, projective tests. The usual argument is that the situation is so drastically changed by reason of the first administration that the retesting is quite incomparable. Tomkins (1961) has likened a second exposure to projective stimuli to a second hearing of a joke, suggesting that the quality of response is markedly altered. Such contentions depend from the notion that novelty is an important aspect of the stimuli. However, such an argument could as easily be made for other kinds of measures, e.g., the MMPI. It is true that the demonstrably low correlations usually obtained for test-retest projective measurement are interpretable as evidence for the changes in the meaning of the testing situation and of the stimuli, but low correlations are also interpretable as evidence for unreliability. One's choice of interpretations cannot be supported on grounds other than prior conviction.

It has even been questioned whether the

concept of reliability is relevant for projective techniques (Hertz, 1951; Rosenzweig, 1951), but such a view can be dismissed summarily insofar as it is intended that projective stimuli are intended to provide a basis for measurement.

Most of the considerations involved in test-retest reliability apply equally as well to parallel forms measures of test reliability. There still is no way of determining exactly what the time interval between administrations of the two forms of the test should be, nor is there any way of determining the equivalence of the relevant conditions of test administration. Moreover, practice effects, important ones, are not necessarily eliminated by the use of parallel forms of the test. Of even greater importance is the circularity described by Loevinger (1957) which becomes apparent when the correlation between tests is used to establish the reliability of the measurement. A low correlation may be just as well interpreted as a lack of equivalence of the two forms as of the unreliability of the instrument.

One of the most widely used indices of reliability is the correlation between two halves of the same test, known as split-half reliability. The correlation between two halves of the same test obviously may be viewed as a special instance of test-retest reliability. However, in the case of split-half reliability, usually based on the correlation between odd and even items, both "tests" are given simultaneously and thus the problems having to do with the equivalence of conditions and the passage of a time interval are resolved. Actually, of course, no time interval exists, which is advantageous as ordinarily we are not interested in unreliability due to the passage of time alone. A serious problem that does remain for many personality instruments concerns the particular way in which the test is to be split into two halves to be correlated. Ordinarily the splitting of a test into odd and even halves is a satisfactory solution for tests involving a great number of discrete items. However, for tests in which the number of items is small, as for the Rorschach and the TAT, and for which it is exceptionally difficult to make a split of the stimuli into equivalent halves, it is difficult to be confident that any particular split gives a good estimate of the reliability of the instrument. If the number of items is very small, it is not difficult to make a random split of the items for every subject and then to correlate the resultant scores. In the case of the Rorschach, rather than attempting to split the card stimuli into two equivalent halves, it has been suggested that a reasonable alternative may be to deal with halves made up of alternate responses. The Holtzman Inkblot Test (Holtzman, Thorpe, Swartz, & Herron, 1961) has an obvious psychometric advantage in that the larger number of stimuli provides a better possibility of splitting the test into two equivalent halves for purposes of establishing reliability.

Split-half reliability coefficients are, of course, usually corrected by means of the well-known Spearman-Brown prophecy formula to correct the estimate for the length of the test involved (Guilford, 1954). Ordinarily a correction involves estimate for a test twice the length. One methodological caution that should be noted is that when split-half reliabilities are being done on tests of short length and an odd number of items, the two halves into which the test is split will not contain an equal number of items. It is, then, not correct to use the Spearman-Brown prophecy formula to estimate the reliability of a test of doubled length. For example, if a five-item test is split into halves of three and two items and a correlation between the two halves of .40 is obtained, the use of all five items would obviously not result in doubling of the length of the test. Horst (1951) has developed a general solution for estimating total test reliability when for reasons of necessity or convenience the separate parts must be of different length.

Gulliksen (1950) maintains that split-half reliability coefficients are almost certain to result in an overestimate of reliability since variability attributable to normal quotidian variation, minor variations in conditions, etc., is eliminated. And from a practical standpoint, Gulliksen is certainly correct. However, one may wish to know what the purely instrumental reliability is, and split-half correlation probably gives a good estimate of that. Once again, however, such considerations point to the possible value of multiple estimates of consistency.

Another way of estimating the reliability of tests is by use of one of the well-known Kuder-Richardson formulas (Kuder & Richardson, 1937). These formulas estimate the mean reliability for all possible split halves of the items in the test. Thus, many of the problems involving estimation of reliability of the test are solved. For example, the time lapse is zero, the conditions of administration are presumably the same for nearly all of the split halves (the conditions obviously may not be exactly equivalent for the first half of the test as opposed to the last half of the test), and since all the items come from the same test, the form is presumably as equivalent as it can be. However, all of the forms of the Kuder-Richardson formulas which are easily computable involve a number of assumptions which serve to limit the interpretations that may be placed upon them. In particular, Kuder-Richardson formulas 20, 21, and 22 assume that the test is measuring but a single factor: i.e., that all items are measuring the same thing. If they are not, then the Kuder-Richardson formulas 20, 21, and 22 will give a low estimate of the reliability of the instrument. In fact, the Kuder-Richardson reliability estimate has been described as a lower bound estimate of reliability (Guilford, 1954). That is, the reliability of the test is at least as high as obtained and probably somewhat, but indeterminately, higher. There are unquestionably tests of considerable value which could scarcely be described as single factor tests. For these instruments, Kuder-Richardson reliability estimates would be lower than would split-half reliability.

Some test construction theorists have preferred to deal with the concept of "homogeneity" rather than the concept of reliability (Loevinger, 1947). Homogeneity represents the idea that all items in a test should be measuring the same dimension, i.e., they should be positively intercorrelated. Total test scores are frequently used to order people along some presumed underlying dimension, and it is certainly true that the results are ambiguous for nonhomogeneous tests when tests are multidimensional or multifactored. Then two people with the same scores are not necessarily alike in any important respect. This is seen with clarity on intelligence tests in which two persons, each with an IQ score of 110, may be extremely different in the abilities that apparently characterize them. Homogeneity theorists say that to order persons in a meaningful way, the responses on the test must occur in such a way that each subject's total score is the result of a unique configuration of responses. That is, a given total score should be obtainable in only one way. In a perfectly homogeneous test if all the items are arranged in order of increasing difficulty, and then if any given item is known to be passed, the probability is unity that all the previous items will have been passed. Thus, the concept of homogeneity is related very closely to the concept of reproducibility (White & Saltz, 1957). To some extent, measures of homogeneity and reproducibility are measures of redundancy in test items (Cronbach, 1951). For example, given a perfectly homogeneous test with all items at the .50 level of difficulty, then the items are completely redundant. Presumably an individual will either pass all of the items or fail all of the items (the so-called attenuation paradox: Loevinger, 1954; F. M. Lord, 1955).

The requirements for reproducibility and single trial or single item reliability are, in fact, quite stringent, and the proponents of reproducibility in particular have been criticized for their "rigidity" in this respect (White & Saltz, 1957). Perfect reproducibility and perfect single trial reliability will occur only when: (a) factors determining subject's responses to the test do not change during the testing period; (b) the factors determining responses to the test are the same for all subjects; and (c) all the items in the test are identical in the factors determining the responses they elicit.

The homogeneity of test items is a theoretical desideratum, and it may be achieved, at least in part, by psychometric iterative procedures (Wherry & Gaylord, 1943). However, the homogeneity of a set of test items cannot be used to demonstrate the unidimensionality of a trait or construct. Unidimensionality is a property of the measure and not of the trait that underlies it. Typically the constructor of a test or of some trait, say, dominance, assumes that he is getting at a unidimensional characteristic of behavior. Then, he derives a series of measures or items to measure the characteristic. If, upon giving the items, he discovers they are not homogeneous, he throws out the "bad" ones and writes new ones to take their place. He may continue this process of purifying his scale either until he succeeds in developing a unidimensional measure or until he is forced to give up. The fact that it is possible to develop a relatively homogeneous measure is not a sufficient demonstration of the unitary nature of a trait. Nevertheless, there is a great deal to be said for the development of homogeneous tests as long as it is not presumed that they necessarily reflect reality better than other kinds of tests.

Actually, somewhat different interpretations may be made of identical coefficients by reliability and homogeneity theorists. Reliability theorists interpret coefficients in terms of error variance attributable to the unreliability of the item. That is, it is assumed that error tendencies of a random nature affect performance on the items. On the other hand, homogeneity theorists interpret the same coefficients in terms of the homogeneity or lack thereof of the items. There is still another possible way of looking at the same phenomenon which has not yet been extensively applied. We might think of coefficients of homogeneity in terms of homogeneity of subjects rather than homogeneity of items. Perhaps some of the lack of homogeneity is attributable to lack of homogeneity in the response characteristics of the population or sample. That is to say, a measure that proves to be homogeneous in one population will not necessarily prove to be homogeneous in all populations (see White & Saltz, 1957, for further discussion of this point).

A concept fundamental to psychometric theory is "error of measurement," it being assumed that any given score or performance is some combination of true and error variance (Gulliksen, 1950; F. Lord, 1952). It is clear enough how the concept of error of measurement applies to multi-item self-report type measures, e.g., MMPI. A given score may be in error in some degree because the subject misread the item, because he accidentally marks the wrong space, because the scoring machine (or clerk) is fallible, etc. However, there often seems to be a failure of understanding of the applicability of error theory to projective measures. For example, if a child is asked the sum of 8 and 7, and he replies "13," it will be conceded that the erroneous response may not indicate really poor arithmetic ability. It might indicate carelessness, poor hearing, poor motivation, or a desire to fool the examiner. But when a child replies that he sees a "horrible monster" on a projective test, there is not likely to be such caution in interpreting the results. Yet there could certainly be any number of processes in operation to produce a response not really characteristic of the subject. Responses to ambiguous stimuli are interpretable only in terms of the normative expectations for similar subjects, and the establishment of "norms" presupposes a substantial uniformity in conditions of administration, set on the part of the subjects, and the like. Thus, if for some reason a subject has come to understand that he should "make up" the most exciting responses he can, his responses will not be comparable to those of other persons operating under more restricting sets. The responses given under unique sets are equally as much "in error" as responses given in order to play a joke on the examiner. It does not preserve much to argue that the fact that the set is different or that such responses can be made is important unless there is some established basis for comparing the particular subject to some relevant population. Quite clearly, then, responses to projective stimuli, or any other kind of stimuli, are interpretable in terms of test theory.

THE VALIDATION OF PERSONALITY MEASURES

It is only apparently a simple task to validate a personality measure. In fact, the problem is exceedingly complex, and it begins with a decision about the concept of validity to be represented in the research. To be sure, if one chooses to try to predict some distinct criterion, e.g., success in selling insurance, by means of an objectively scored measure, then only the ordinary problems must be solved, i.e., operational definition of the criterion, representativeness of the sample, possible nonlinearity of relationships, and possible interactions with other variables. But when one ventures into the realm of construct validity with any test, but most especially with one requiring a sophisticated and nonobjective scoring, the problems begin to form a thicket that may barely be penetrable.

We need not detail the problems and their solutions, particularly those having to do with construct validity, for they have been dealt with most admirably in other places (see especially Campbell, 1960; Cronbach & Meehl, 1955; Loevinger, 1957). We would suggest that the recommendations of Campbell and Fiske (1959) concerning convergent and discriminant validity will go a long way toward resolving the residual uncertainties in considerations of construct validity.

We would, however, like to point to some other questions fundamental to test validation which are often ignored. First, when validating a test, scores, or conclusions based on inferences rather than direct counting operations, three separate questions must be posed (Meehl, 1959). First, it must be asked whether the information desired is intrinsically contained in the test behavior. Second, it must be asked whether the information can be retrieved by the best interpreters available, and third, whether the information can be retrieved under the circumstances in which the test is likely to be used. The first two issues are not easily disentangled if the initial results of an investigation are discouraging. Thus, if clinical interpretations of the Rorschach do not relate well to seemingly reasonable criteria, is it because the desired information is simply not in the responses or because the information is not properly retrieved by the clinicians using the instrument? And even if it is possible for certain persons, e.g., experts, to retrieve the information, is it likely that other clinicians will be able to do so? It is obvious that efforts to validate complex measures must themselves be complex and that the conditions of validation or invalidation must be carefully specified, e.g., along the lines proposed by Shneidman (1959).

A first recommendation for the route to be followed in validating any personality measure is that first it be shown that the measure can do the easy things. For example, if a personality measure shows no differences between psychotics and normals, is it likely that it will be sensitive to really subtle forces? Holtzman *et al.* (1961) began their program of validating a new inkblot test by initial demonstrations of its capacity to do obvious things. Baughman and Guskin (1958) make the point that a supposedly sensitive personality instrument should reveal such a simple fact as the sex of the respondent, and if the instrument does not do so, it is inadequate in some important respects. That they found no male-female differences in Rorschach responses is suggestive of the results to be expected in other investigations with that instrument.

A second recommendation for the initial stages in test validation is that both positive and zero values of relevant stimuli be investigated. It is not necessarily an achievement to show that "authority figures" in a projective test elicit hostile responses from delinquent youths, unless it is also shown that hostility indices decrease when authority figures are not portrayed. Dana (1954), for example, found that patients who made poor responses to Card IV of the Rorschach also responded poorly in psychotherapy and interpreted his findings in terms of the supposed status of Card IV as a "father" or "authority" card. However, there was no demonstration that the same kinds of poor responses would not have occurred to any other card, father card or not. In one persuasive demonstration of the issue at hand, Sullivan and Adelson (1954) showed that a supposed measure of hostility specifically toward foreigners, ethnocentrism (Adorno, Frenkel-Brunswik, Levinson, & Sanford, 1950), was in fact a measure of misanthropy. A related recommendation that could have spared psychology countless controversies had it been followed is that both positive and zero values of the disposition being measured be represented. Not only must it be shown that certain test responses characterize deviants, for example, but it must be shown that such responses do not characterize normal groups. Thus, the demonstration of various Rorschach responses thought pathogenomic for the diagnosis of schizophrenia is considerably vitiated by the discovery that the same responses occur among normals (Wittenborn & Sarason, 1949). Similarly, any demonstration that an expected response does occur in any particular group is not persuasive unless it is also shown that the response does not occur in groups in which it is not expected.

Both in evaluating test performances and in predicting extratest behaviors, account needs to be taken of the threshold for performance of any given behavior (Campbell, 1963). It is obvious that thresholds for various responses indicative of the same disposition are likely to be widely disparate. Take, for example, the ways in which "hostility" might be indexed: sarcasm, self-admission of hostility, public admission of hostility, public verbal attack, striking with the fist, striking with a club, etc. Thus, one would not expect that all persons scoring high on a privately administered hostility scale would be openly hostile in behavior. Moreover, thresholds for different responses are likely to differ greatly from individual to individual so that what is an easily made response for one person may be made only with difficulty by another. Attempts have been made to take such differences into account on objective tests such as the MMPI via the "correction" scales (Dahlstrom & Welsh, 1960), but little has been done about such response variables as "plus getting tendencies" for most tests. Perhaps the surprising "pathology" in projective test protocols of normal and even superior subjects is attributable to a low threshold for recognition and emission of superficially unacceptable personal responses, especially those of a strictly verbal nature. There must be some way of telling the difference between the responses of a healthy person who is "letting himself go" and those of a tortured soul.

Validation of Unbounded Predictions

We noted earlier that a distinction has been made between "bounded" and "unbounded" use of tests (L. H. Levy, 1963). Validation of tests for a specific purpose or prediction, i.e., bounded use, is straightforward, if not always simple. However, if tests are used in an unbounded way, i.e., to make unique predictions or predictions not anticipated at the time of test administration, it is considerably more difficult to achieve any confidence about validity. There are, it seems to the writer, two approaches which can be taken. First, tests may gain validity credence because they make good sense theoretically. There probably are very few tests that can stand close examination for theoretical soundness, but to the extent that a test articulates well with a good general theory, it does merit some degree of confidence.

A second, necessary, and more convincing approach to validation of tests for unbounded use is the route of inductive proof. The greater the variety of predictions for which a test has proven valid, the greater our justified confidence in additional prediction. It is very difficult to establish validity for every prediction, but we can sample from the universe of predictions to be made and validate a test for that sample of predictions. When a test is validated against *Q* sorts, for example, the *Q*-sort items represent a sample, even if not randomly drawn, of the possible statements that might be made about a person. If the test proves valid for inferring the kinds of things represented in the items, then it gains validity generally, even for untried items. Quite obviously inductive validity is never going to reach 100 per cent, but it can get pretty high. Intelligence measures are probably often used for predictions or in situations for which they have not specifically been validated, and such use stems from confidence engendered by induction from many previous validations.

Criteria for Validation of Personality Measures

There are many criteria that may be useful for establishing validity of personality measures. Essentially, however, we believe that the process must involve the demonstration of convergence among multiple measures of the same disposition (Campbell & Fiske, 1959). Thus, there is no one and final criterion. However, it is desirable that measures used mutually to validate each other be as distinct as possible in terms of the operations employed. Therefore, less confidence ensues when tests are merely shown to correlate with each other than when they are found to correlate with measures of a very different kind. Peer reputation measures afford a particularly convenient, available, and valuable measure for many dispositions, and as argued elsewhere (Wallace & Sechrest, 1963), they may often be quite sensitive. Viewed in terms of convergent and discriminant validation, we would suggest that there is more evidence of both kinds of validity for peer reputations than for any other category of measurement. It is rare (in fact, to this writer unknown) to find a study involving multiple methods in which operationally distinct measures of a trait correlate higher with each other than either does with a reputational measure of the same trait.

Other measures such as "real life" behavior, expert judgment, and objective status, e.g., psychiatric patient vs. nonpatient status, may also be used, and should be used when available. In many ways it is true that there is safety in numbers.

NEED FOR NONREACTIVE MEASURES

It has been noted frequently in the field of measurement that the very operation of measuring a phenomenon may change that phenomenon in fundamental ways (Selltiz, Jahoda, Deutsch, & Cook, 1959). Although it is only rather recently that researchers in personality assessment have become particularly aware of the problem, cautions have been voiced for quite some time about the problems involved in repeated administrations of the same test, especially in the case of projective tests (e.g., L. K. Frank, 1948; Holzberg, 1960). In general terms, the problem may be referred to as the *reactivity* of a test or measurement operation (Campbell, 1957; Campbell & Stanley, 1963). We mean by a reactive measure one which in some way affects subsequent relevant responses of the subject. There seem to be two senses in which measures may be reactive. First, they may alter a person's response(s) to experiences subsequent to the measurement operation. For example, giving a test for "anxiety" prior to an experimental manipulation may affect the subject's response to the experimental treatment. Such an effect has been found for pretesting in experiments on teaching spelling (Solomon, 1949), on education about the United Nations (Campbell, 1957; Star & Hughes, 1949–50), and on persuasion (Hovland, Lumsdaine, & Sheffield, 1949), and has been suggested (Campbell, 1957) as an alternative hypothesis for effects of a movie on prejudice (Rosen, 1948). Second, a measurement operation may change an individual's response to subsequent measuring operations so that scores from later measurements are not comparable to those which were obtained or would have been obtained earlier (see, e.g., Campbell, 1957; Crespi, 1948; Underwood, 1957).

Quite apparently it would be highly desirable to have available a stock of nonreactive measuring techniques for a wide variety of psychological variables. If we wish to do research requiring repeated measurements or repeated experimental manipulations, it is necessary to discover operations that are nonreactive or at least minimally reactive. Thus, for example, it would appear that the Rorschach would be unsuitable for the purpose of plotting progress in psychotherapy because each administration presumably changes subsequent responses in subtle, complex, and seemingly unpredictable ways. In order to achieve nonreactivity of measurement it will probably be necessary to get beyond the standard "test" kind of operation into the observation of behavior *in situ* and by means which conceal not only the nature of the measurement being conducted but the fact that measurement is occurring at all. Webb, Campbell, Schwartz, and Sechrest (1966) have collated successful instances from the literature of behavioral sciences of nonreactive measurements.

Although it is obvious why psychology very early and quickly became addicted to tests, particularly those of a pencil-paper variety, it is not so easy to understand why their use has persisted and even proliferated in the face of uniformly disappointing results ensuing from their application. It is difficult enough to obtain consistently significant validity correlations, let alone correlations consistently higher than .40 or so. Certainly it is doubtful that the pioneers of the testing movement envisioned what appears to be a nearly impassable validity barrier at $r = .50$.

What is remarkable is that the disenchantment with test predictiveness has not led to more attempts to break through the confining boundaries of the artificial, sterile test situation into areas of observation which are at least potentially more fruitful, i.e., what have at least not been *shown* to have limited validity, such as "real life" behaviors represented especially by tailing, situational sampling, and, perhaps, trace measures. Perhaps a part of the reluctance to become involved in observations of extratest behaviors stems from the well-publicized failure of the O.S.S. assessment program which relied so heavily on contrived situations (H. A. Murray, MacKinnon, Miller, Fiske, & Hanfmann, 1948). However, an unquestionably greater obstacle is the conviction that real-life behaviors are complex, difficult to interpret, and even "messy." Moreover, the fairly elaborate procedures that have been used in some investigations (again, notably, the O.S.S. assessment program) have probably contributed to a belief that the collection of data about "real" behavior is a truly formidable task.

A good, nonreactive measure has three important qualities. First, it should bear a fairly evident relation to the disposition that it presumably reflects. Ideally, very few inferential steps should be required to interpret the measure as an index of a disposition. For example, eye blink rate would seem to have a rather direct and theoretically sound relationship to anxiety or tension level. Second, a measure should be observable in a nonlaboratory setting, or at least possibly observable, and without instrumentation which would suggest the fact and nature of the measurement to the subject. And, third, the measurement operations should not affect the disposition being assessed. It should be possible to make a series of observations all interpretable on the same basis.

Admittedly the above criteria are not easily met, but they are not impossible of approximation either, and they are worth striving for. Space here does not suffice for a detailed and thorough presentation of methods that have been used, and the review by Webb *et al.* (1966) makes that unnecessary. Thus, a few examples will serve to illustrate the interesting possibilities that arise when psychologists step outside their laboratories but do not leave behind their imaginations. First, the concept of anxiety or tension has long been considered important in psychology, and numerous attempts have been made to measure it, most of them consisting of either paper-and-pencil self-report devices such as the MAS (Taylor, 1953) or of some special analysis of a projective-type instrument. Such attempts at measurement have never been notably successful, although the MAS has proven rather consistently to have some degree of validity. However, there are approaches to assessment of anxiety which do not possess the disadvantages of tests. Eye blink rate has been found to have considerable promise as a measure of emotionality (Kanfer, 1960). It has the very obvious advantage of providing for a continuous and current assessment of tension, something which a paper-and-pencil test or a projective instrument probably cannot do. Moreover, it requires no elaborate apparatus or special conditions to observe blink rate. It is available as a measure in a very wide variety of situations. Perturbations in normal speech have been found to correlate with GSR responses (Panek & Martin, 1959), thus suggesting the possibility that various flaws in speech might indicate concern or anxiety about a topic of conversation. Again, special apparatus is not necessary, and a wide variety of situations become open to observation. And, as with blink rate, the measurement operations can scarcely be said to affect the disposition or the measure. Finally, a particular nervous mannerism, leg-jiggling, has been shown to have some promise as a measure of tension (Sechrest & Flores, 1965), and many other mannerisms or gestures could equally well be observed.

A second variable which has been studied by way of direct behavioral observation is "social distance." Sommer (1959, 1960, 1962) established the fact of reliability for measures of linear distance between participants in social interactions and presented data suggesting the validity of linear distance as a measure of social distance. Leipold (1963) showed that preference for a particular distance in social interaction was a function of both introversion-extraversion as a personality trait and anticipated stress in the interaction. Both introversion and anticipated stress tended to increase social distance as reflected in linear distance. Sechrest, Flores, and Arellano (1965) have also used such a measure and have found that social distance is greater in unacquainted pairs of persons when they are of opposite sex. Moreover, in a sample of Filipino students an English-speaking female tended to produce especially great social (i.e., spatial) distance.

Many other indices have been used successfully: manner of dress to index response to psychotherapy (Kane, 1958, 1959, 1962); crossing against a traffic light to index willingness to violate prohibitions (Lefkowitz, Blake, & Mouton, 1955); toilet wall "graffiti" to index sex attitudes in two cultures

(Sechrest & Flores, 1965); and mailing of a "lost" envelope apparently containing money to index pecuniary honesty (Merritt & Fowler, 1948) being interesting examples.

SOME CURRENTLY AVAILABLE MEASURES

In spite of our earlier recommendations of homemade test, peer reputation ratings, and nonreactive, cooperation-free measures, there is still a place for the more conventional, established tests. It is beyond the scope of this paper to review in detail the research on even one of the commonly used instruments, and to do so would probably be unnecessary, for there are many sources which the interested reader may consult for good summaries of nearly all the tests to be mentioned. The intent of this section is merely to describe briefly some of the more common tests of a nonobjective, nonself-report kind, and some of the newer and promising tests of the same variety.

Inkblot Tests

After many years of complete pre-eminence of the *Rorschach Inkblot Test* and abortive attempts to establish an alternative inkblot format (Behn-Eschenberg, 1931; Harrower & Steiner, 1945; Howard, 1953, 1960), it now appears that there is another inkblot test to be reckoned with in the *Holtzman Inkblot Test* (Holtzman *et al.,* 1961). It is likely to be many years before the Holtzman test becomes established in the clinical cupboard, but the lag may prove to be more a function of dogmatic conservatism or undogmatic inertia than of the demonstrable superiority of the Rorschach itself. Since at the present time there does not seem to be any basis for distinguishing at a conceptual level between the two tests, it would appear that research findings should be more or less generalizable from one test to another except insofar as they refer to specific features of either test. Obviously most of the research to date has been accomplished with the Rorschach, but many of the findings should be applicable to the Holtzman as well as to other inkblot tests.

In an inkblot test the subject is shown an inkblot and is asked to say, "What it looks like. What it might be." Then, at some later point he is questioned further in order to establish just which aspects of the blot gave rise to his response. In the case of the Rorschach the subject is permitted—and probably implicitly encouraged—to give more than one response per card. There are no constraints placed on him. And that is one of the sources of serious psychometric problems with the Rorschach. Subjects may differ radically in the number of responses they have given, and, therefore, they are almost certain to differ in many other important ways, e.g., in the number of responses determined by "color." Although one might suppose that it would be possible to "correct" for the response total by dividing any measure by the total number of responses, available evidence (Fiske & Baughman, 1953) suggests strongly that such indices are imprecise because the relationships between various response measures and total number of response are not uniform and linear. The Holtzman test obviates such a problem by employing a larger number of stimuli (45 to the Rorschach's 10) and recording only one response per blot. Therefore, subjects should be equal, or nearly so, in their total number of responses.

It will be noted that the response on the Rorschach is limited, often markedly so, in length. Often no more than a few words are elicited for each blot. Therefore, one must suppose that just about each word is fraught with significance if one is to achieve insight into personality, a supposition that apparently is not at all discomfiting to many users of the test. Nonetheless, the greater number of responses elicited by the Holtzman test can be seen to be a probable advantage. A similar contention can be made for the greater number of stimuli in the

Holtzman test. Certainly ten stimuli seem a rather scant collection from which to make inferences about the total personality. We have already noted that inkblot tests can be viewed as symbolic stimulus tests, and as such it would seem that they should constitute a good sample of the stimuli to which one might want to generalize. Otherwise, interpretations may be based on what amounts to one-item tests. It is asking rather too much of any technique to expect it to be so powerful that a few words given in response to one item can lay bare the personality or any important aspects of it.

By and large the basis for interpretation of inkblots is similarity projection, i.e., it is assumed that the characteristics indicated in the response are those that characterize the subject himself, but probably complementary projection plays a considerably more important role than in any other test. For example, when the subject gives "sex" responses, it is likely to be assumed that he is the one who is "sexy." That is similarity projection interpretation. On the other hand, if the subject sees "threatening monsters," many clinicians are likely to infer that the subject is himself afraid rather than threatening. Or if he often sees human figures as "statues," clinicians may be inclined to suppose that that is his view of other people rather than his view of himself, i.e., that he feels rejected in an aloof and impersonal world rather than that he, himself, is cold and aloof. However, there are certainly many, many instances in which similarity and complementarity stand in opposition and in which there is no a priori way of deciding which is the correct interpretation, e.g., is "blood" to be interpreted as a hostile or an anxious response? Many of the percepts often scored as hostile (DeVos, 1952; Elizur, 1949) could just as sensibly be scored for anxiety. The writer's own count of 56 suggestions for content interpretation made by Lindner (1950) indicated that 31 were based on similarity and 10 on complementary projection. For the remainder, two seemed to involve "autistic" interpretation and 13 were ambiguous as to basis.

In addition to the usual Rorschach scoring that is intended primarily for clinical use, a number of special scales or scoring systems have been developed for individual dispositions. Notable among the special scales is the Elizur (1949) scale for hostile content, a scale which has been used in original or modified form in a sizable number of studies with fair results (Finney, 1955; Goodstein, 1954; Murstein, 1956, 1958a; J. R. Smith & Coleman, 1956; Towbin, 1959; Wolf, 1957). At least one other similar content scale has been developed for dependency (Levitt, Lubin, & Zuckerman, 1962), but it should be noted that the Holtzman scales include anxiety and hostility scales closely resembling the Elizur method. Of course, in many instances the Rorschach is "scored" simply by reliance on the global judgment of clinical raters, e.g., global ratings of "adjustment" (Grant, Ives, & Ranzoni, 1952).

Surprisingly little research has been done on the properties of Rorschach scores, but there are disturbing suggestions of their inadequacy, at least when not used with great caution. Wittenborn (1949, 1950) was able to show that internal consistency justified the quantification of M and the combining of color responses into a total score interpreted differently from M. However, he found no basis for the common practice of ascribing personality differences on the basis of small differences in C, M, W, and D. Ledwith (1959) found marked skewness for most measures in a large sample of children, and deviations would have to be quite extreme in most categories to be of any clear importance. Other investigators (Cronbach, 1949; Fiske & Baughman, 1953) have pointed to numerous difficulties inherent in Rorschach scores.

Many of the serious problems with the Rorschach as a psychometric instrument stem directly from the fact that the total number of responses may vary greatly from person to person. In clinical practice there is scarcely any problem because the individual clinician makes his own subjective corrections for total number of responses. However, for research purposes such a state of affairs is grossly unsatisfactory. The Holtzman Inkblot Test seeks a way out of the dilemma by establishing a standard number of responses to be elicited from each person, i.e., one per card. Various other scoring problems are resolved for the user of the Holtzman test. An example of the scoring revisions made by Holtzman is provided by the scoring of "movement." In the usual Rorschach scoring there are three varieties of movement—human, animal, and inanimate—but there are no degrees of movement. Holtzman scores on a single dimension the degree of implied movement in the response. Thus, the highest score is reserved for "violent" movement, and lower scores are given to lesser movement down to the point of no movement implied at all. At least from a psychometric point of view Holtzman's revisions seem eminently sensible. The scoring system does have the advantage of simplicity and an apparently high level of scorer agreement (Holtzman *et al.*, 1961) even for those not trained in the system (Barger & Sechrest, 1961).

At the time of publication of the Holtzman test, explicitly in an experimental form, there were 23 variables of a motley nature, many having been chosen because they seemed promising empirically rather than because they were derivable from any a priori considerations. Some of the variables are familiar from the Rorschach, e.g., "populars," some appear to be Holtzman's own inventions, e.g., "pathogenomic verbalizations," and some were borrowed from other investigators, e.g., Fisher and Cleveland's (1958) barrier and penetration scores.

One of the advantages often attributed to the Rorschach, a capacity exemplified in the likening of the test to a psychological X-ray, is that since the subject is ignorant of the nature and purposes of the test, he cannot censor his responses or defend himself in any way. Moreover, the standardization and objectivity of the Rorschach procedure, perhaps along with the professional standing of the people who use it, were supposed to be quite a sufficient safeguard against any biases of the examiner himself. Unfortunately, but quite predictably, both the above suppositions have proven wrong. Early studies have shown that different examiners produce different Rorschach responses (Baughman, 1951; Gibby, 1952) and the differences appear attributable to differences in examiner personality (Berger, 1954; E. Lord, 1950; Miller, 1953; Sanders & Cleveland, 1953). Rorschach responses have been shown to be influenced by conditioning procedures involving both verbal and motoric response reinforcements (Gross, 1959; Simkins, 1960; Wickes, 1956), and other experiments have shown the Rorschach to be susceptible to response sets to fake either good or bad impressions (Carp & Scharizen, 1950). Different results may be obtained depending on whether the subject believes that the test is a measure of intelligence or "nervousness" or "insanity" (Calden & Cohen, 1953; Henry & Rotter, 1956), and a set may even be produced by having subjects spend a waiting period in a room containing sexually interesting pictures (Rabin, Nelson, & Clark, 1954). Finally, Tutko (1962) found that chronic psychiatric patients selected so as to be high in need for approval (Crowne & Marlowe, 1964) produced records quite different from those low on the same need, the difference lying not so much in ability to obscure the level of pathology as in tendency to give a record unrevealing of personality by the high need-approval subjects. Thus, we must conclude that inkblot tests require a good bit of openness and cooperation on the part of the subject.

Reliability

Satisfactory measures of the reliability of the Rorschach have not proven easy to obtain. Holzberg (1960), in reviewing the problem, specifically disavows the psychometric aspects of the Rorschach, stating that the problem is how to study the personality synthesis that emerges from the test rather than how to study its isolated parts. As stated above, agreement among judges or scorers is not a substitute for reliability, but it is a necessary condition. Some findings showing substantial agreement among judges are difficult to interpret because they were expressed in percentages (Sicha & Sicha, 1936) or contingency coefficients (Ramzy & Pickard, 1949), providing for biases in an unknown degree. Satisfactory agreement has been reported for specific Rorschach content categories such as hostility (DeVos, 1952) and dependency (Levitt, Lubin, & Zuckerman, 1962), but an attempt to obtain global ratings of "adjustment" indicated little agreement among three supposedly expert judges (Grant, Ives, & Ranzoni, 1952). Moreover, the judges were not especially consistent in their own ratings. A rather interesting investigation from the standpoint of agreement between judges was an attempt (Moos, 1962) to increase agreement of student Rorschach and MMPI interpretations with those of experts by a one-semester training course on the two tests. The MMPI training did produce an increase in agreement, but instruction in the Rorschach was to no avail. Whether the Rorschach was taught improperly, the Rorschach cannot be taught anyway, or the experts were wrong is a question for further research. The reader's attention should be given to the ample demonstration of both inter- and intrascorer agreement for the Holtzman Inkblot Test (Holtzman *et al.,* 1961).

In view of the small number of diverse stimuli, estimating the internal consistency of the Rorschach is bound to be difficult. Moreover, ratio scores with small denominators are inherently unreliable (Cronbach, 1949). Nonetheless, reasonably good split-half reliabilities were reported by Hertz (1934), the values ranging from .66 to .97 for specific scores. Although other investigators have not always found such good reliabilities as Hertz (Vernon, 1933), her findings are not unique (Ford, 1946). The multiple-choice form of the Rorschach (Harrower & Steiner, 1945) is somewhat more amenable to internal consistency estimates, and it appears reasonably satisfactory (Lawshe & Forster, 1947; Singer, 1950).

It will certainly occur to many readers that with the plethora of Rorschach scores and indices the task of establishing reliability is a sizable one. Not all the findings are especially generalizable to other indices, e.g., the apparently good reliability of total number of responses (Wirt & McReynolds, 1953) probably has limited significance for the reliability of W or M except insofar as they reflect R. That leads to the point that any split-half or other technique which utilizes scores uncorrected for R may reflect the reliability of R more than of the scores themselves. The larger the number of responses, the larger most raw scores will be from either half of the test or from one test to another. The only recommendation that can be made at this point is that scores should be expressed as percentages rather than as raw scores.

There is no problem involving total R for the Holtzman test, of course, and the greater number of cards make split-half or other internal consistency measures quite appropriate. There is ample evidence for the reliability of all the scores utilized on the Holtzman Inkblot Test, and generally speaking, the reliabilities are satisfactory, although there are occasional differences between samples that are troublesome. Most of the unexpectedly low values appear to be attributable to the marked restriction of range for some of the samples. However, it is important to note that it is often the normal samples for which reliability is lowest, which suggests that great caution should be exercised in ordering persons within a normal sample on the basis of inkblot test scores.

The problem with test-retest reliability, i.e., consistency over time, for the Rorschach is that, according to the usual views of the test, the pressures of the situation and the "surprise" afforded by each of the blots are an important part of the total testing situation. Presumably a good bit is lost when the subject knows what is coming next. Once again the small number of stimuli contribute greatly to the difficulty. Nonetheless, test-retest studies have been done, and the results are reasonably satisfactory. Ford (1946) found reliabilities for determinants between .38 and .86 over a one-month period with small children, and Holzberg and Wexler (1950) report reasonably good reliabilities for schizophrenics. Troup (1938) followed a somewhat different tack and had judges try to match pairs of protocols obtained from the same person on two occasions and found quite good matching. There is a serious problem with such matching studies, however, and that is that the basis for matching is unknown, and there is the possibility that the matching is done on the basis of one or two outstanding features and that the remainder of the protocol might be quite different. Such a problem is the same as exists for matching in validity studies (Cronbach, 1949). Test-retest reliabilities have also been shown to be satisfactory, or mainly so, for the group Rorschach over a three-month interval (Blanton & Landsman, 1952) and for both one-week and ten-month intervals (Rychlak & Guinouard, 1960), the latter period producing estimates ranging from .11 to .75.

A somewhat different and clever approach to obtaining retest data was employed by Kelly, Margulies, and Barrera (1941). Capitalizing on the temporary amnesia produced by electro-convulsive therapy, they administered the Rorschach to patients before and after their treatments and found that the tendency was for the psychograms to be approximately equivalent and for the clinical diagnosis to be the same.

Again the greater number of stimuli on the Holtzman test would tend to decrease the influence of memory as a factor in test-retest studies. However, no studies involving readministration of the same form of the test are reported for the Holtzman, a fact which is accounted for by the fact that there are parallel forms available for test-retest purposes.

We might inquire about the consistency of a Rorschach interpretation over time, i.e., the same protocol interpreted by the same judge on two occasions. However, memory would play a very important role in such an investigation. Perhaps a lucky investigator will on some occasion encounter some Rorschach interpreters who are undergoing shock therapy. Krugman (1942) made a study of the agreement between judges in interpreting the same protocols. She was able to show that interpretations made by different judges can be matched quite accurately and that Rorschach records can be matched with interpretations made of them. However, the same cautions previously voiced about matching studies apply in this instance. The matching occurred, but just what its import is for agreement between judges in Rorschach interpretation is not known. The judges who were attempting to match the interpretations thought that there was "essential agreement" in about 90 per cent of the pairs of interpretations.

There is, finally, reliability as estimated by agreement between different forms of the same test. There is, however, a fundamental dilemma facing the researcher who attempts to estimate reliability from equivalent forms. As Loevinger (1957) notes, it is indeterminate whether a low correlation results from poor reliability or from nonequivalence of forms. A good example of the dilemma occurs in Holzberg's (1960) discussion of the results obtained when correlating the Behn-Rorschach with the Rorschach and in which he attributes poor results to lack of equivalence of tests rather than to poor reliability. Actually, it would appear that while the Behn blots are not exactly equivalent to the Rorschach blots, they produce highly similar results (Buckle & Holt, 1951; Eichler, 1951; Rosenwald, 1947; J. Singer, 1952). A study is needed in which interpretations from the two sets of blots are compared.

The combined test-retest, equivalent forms reliabilities of Holtzman variables are reasonably good even when the time period is as much as one year. Intraclass correlation estimates for elementary students retested after one year range from .28 to .75, the median being about .48, and for college students the range was from .15 to .64 with a median of .43.

Validity

Considering the emphasis which has been placed on the "holistic" nature of the Rorschach (e.g., Holzberg, 1960), a surprising amount of attention has been devoted to the possible validity of specific and isolated Rorschach "signs." It should be a rather simple matter to settle once and for all the validity of any given sign, but the facts have proven otherwise. The problem, it seems, is that the possible number of signs on a complex instrument such as the Rorschach is very large, and one sign is no sooner stamped out than another one or more arise, like the heads of a hydra, to take its place. Unfortunately, the evidence against a sign may be equally as poor as the evidence for it. A good case in point is the study by Fromm and Elonen (1951) of *one* female homosexual on the basis of whose responses they cast doubt on previous signs of homosexuality and propose two new ones!

Another study of "homosexual signs" illustrates several general problems in sign research. Fein (1950) studied 9 homosexual, 10 neurotic, and 24 normal college males. Aside from the small number of cases of questionable representativeness, the study is marred by innocence of statistical tests. Moreover, by the very fact of selecting clear-cut cases of homosexuality, the findings lose considerable force when applied to the usual run of clinical diagnostic problems, e.g., detecting homosexual tendencies in apparently nonhomosexual persons. For example, Fein suggests that content involving feminine apparel is more common among the homosexuals, but would that response occur at all among nonself-confessed homosexuals? Somewhat paradoxically the methodological solution to the problem is to include a research group not clear-cut as to diagnosis, i.e., "suspected" homosexuals or individuals showing other relevant characteristics such as excessive femininity. Then if it were shown that signs occurring in the confessed homosexual group occurred also in the suspected group but not in the normal group, confidence in the diagnostic utility of the signs would be enormously increased. It should be noted that similar considerations suggest the inclusion of ambiguous groups such as suspected organic cases, schizophrenics, and the like in other research. Finally, in empirical research it is important to provide for cross-validation of findings. One can probably find signs which distinguish *any* two groups, no matter how selected, but the apparent validity of the signs may evaporate when exposed to the hot light of subsequent investigation.

Still another example of what can happen when proper elaboration of a research problem occurs is found in investigations of so-called neurotic signs originally suggested by Harrower-Erickson and later refined by Miale and Harrower-Erickson (1940). Harrower-Erickson (1942) reported considerable success in distinguishing neurotics from normals, but Ross (1941) showed that the supposed neurotic signs were characteristic also of persons with low socio-economic status, and he suggested that rather than neuroticism the signs reflect general insecurity. Then Berkowitz and Levine (1953) attempted to use the signs to differentiate 25 neurotics from 25 schizophrenics. Of nine signs only one proved valid, the schizophrenics showing more "shading shock." Other studies of the Rorschach in objective psychiatric diagnosis have been largely negative (Hamlin, Albee, & Leland, 1950; Knopf, 1956a, 1956b; Kobler & Steil, 1953; Rubin & Lonstein, 1953; Wittenborn & Holzberg, 1951), have lacked cross-validation (S. Cox, 1951), or have shown something of doubtful utility. Reiman (1953) culled 86 scores with replicated samples of "neurotic" and "ambulatory" schizophrenics and found six scores significant at the .10 level in both samples. It might also be noted that some findings are too good to be easily accepted, e.g., Hughes (1948) found that a system of differential weights for a sizable number of signs would correctly identify 82 per cent of organic cases without *any* false positives! Cross-validation would take care of the skepticism one has about such excellent results.

Diagnosis of suicidal inclinations is another problem to which sign research has been directed with both positive (Daston & Sakheim, 1960; Hertz, 1948, 1949; White & Schreiber, 1952) and negative (Fisher, 1951) results, but without any attention given to base rates or the utility of the signs. Prognosis in psychotherapy has also been studied with a predominance of negative evidence either for signs (Filmer-Bennett, 1952; Knopf, 1956a; Lessing, 1960; Roberts, 1954; L. S. Rogers & Hammond, 1953) or for global clinical judgment (Lessing, 1960; L. S. Rogers & Hammond, 1953; L. S. Rogers, Knauss, & Hammond, 1951), although there have been some successful efforts, including those of Siegel (1948), unfortunately not cross-validated, and Kirkner (Kirkner, Wisham, & Giedt, 1953). While L. S. Rogers and Hammond (1953) failed to validate previous findings, they were able empirically to derive and cross-validate some new rules. Prediction of continuation in treatment met with early failure (L. S. Rogers, Knauss, & Hammond, 1951), but there have been some subsequent mild successes (Auld & Eron, 1953; Gibby, Stotsky, Miller, & Hiler, 1953; Gibby, Stotsky, Hiler, & Miller, 1954; Kotkov & Meadow, 1953). The Rorschach has also been used to assess the effects of treatment (Carr, 1949; E. Lord, 1950b; Mintz, Schmeidler, & Bristol, 1956; Muench, 1947; Pacella, Piotrowski, & Lewis, 1947; Rioch, 1949), but the significance of the research for Rorschach validity is open to question, especially since negative findings would be totally inconclusive and would undoubtedly be far more likely to remain unpublished.

Undoubtedly more critical from the standpoint of evaluating Rorschach validity in clinical use are studies of the test in the hands of clinicians who ordinarily use it. It is quite difficult to design and carry out an investigation which would satisfy those already committed to a belief in the validity of the Rorschach and only awaiting the inevitable scientific proof (e.g., Hertz, 1959). Certainly it is easy to be critical of some of the early failures of the Rorschach in prediction situations (e.g., Holtzman & Sells, 1954; Jensen & Rotter, 1947) on the grounds of the unfamiliarity of the task, the peculiar nature of the criterion, etc., although it should be noted that Holtzman and Sells (1954) selected a group of flight trainees who failed because of adjustment difficulties. But it should be noted that if the failures are disavowed on such grounds, the successes (e.g., Abt, 1947) are difficult to acknowledge. Advances in methodology have answered many previous objections; recent efforts to demonstrate Rorschach validity demand more careful attention, and they can be rejected only with the greatest caution.

Krugman (1942) merits credit for one of the earliest sophisticated efforts at validating clinical interpretations of the Rorschach, and she obtained some fairly impressive levels of matching between Rorschach-derived personality descriptions and abstracts of clinical charts. However, as noted earlier, there are deficiencies in straightforward matching procedures, and her study was made additionally equivocal by the fact that the matching procedure made possible the solving of some problems by elimination. Nonetheless, her results were impressive and stand, unfortunately, nearly alone. Hunter (1939) found very little correct matching of Rorschach personality sketches with those made by teachers. Palmer (1951) found that therapists could pick the Rorschach interpretation for their own patient from a group of five at a level better than chance, but the fact that very few additional correct choices were made when a second choice was allowed indicates that patients are either transparent on the Rorschach, i.e., reveal themselves pretty clearly, or they are not. How to know whether a patient has revealed himself? Holsopple and Phelan (1954) utilized a complex matching design in which solution by elimination was precluded and found that the highest number of correct matches among TAT's, self-report test batteries, and Rorschachs occurred for the Rorschachs, but still 67 per cent of all judgments were wrong, and only one-half of a group of experienced clinicians were below a chance level.

The two most damaging investigations from the standpoint of the clinical validity and utility of the Rorschach are those of Little and Shneidmen (1959) and Sines (1959). Employing only expert clinicians, a prediction situation much like that involved in normal clinical practice, and a realistic criterion consisting of material carefully culled from case histories, Little and Shneidman found only minimal evidence for validity of the Rorschach. Certainly the level of validity established for Little and Shneidman's expert clinicians would not support the routine use of the Rorschach (or MMPI, TAT, or MAPS) in clinical practice. Sines (1959) employed a criterion consisting of descriptive statements *Q*-sorted by therapists working with patients, and his clinicians were trainees. Not only did the use of the Rorschach not improve upon predictions made with a stereotype key but the addition of the Rorschach to such information as a biographical data sheet and an interview actually resulted in a decrement in validity of predictions. Horowitz (1962) also found a battery of projective tests to yield predictions no better than the base rate, but the design did not provide for separate estimates of the validity of the tests which were the Rorschach, TAT, and a sentence-completion test. Silverman (1959) found better than chance *Q*-sorting of statements against a therapist-sorting criterion, but he did not use a stereotype or base rate predictor, and his design also did not permit assessment of validities of individual tests.

A rather large and diverse group of studies either has dealt with the correlates of specific Rorschach scores or has constituted attempts to find in the Rorschach correlates of other constructs. By far the most thoroughly studied area has been "aggression." Buss (1961) has pointed out that two kinds of scoring, viz., hostile content and formal elements, are used for scoring Rorschach aggression, but unquestionably the former is more common. Much of the work on aggressive tendencies as revealed by the Rorschach seems to have started with the attempt by Elizur (1949) to develop a hostile content scale. In view of the importance attached to the Rorschach as a peep-hole into the unconscious, it is of great interest that Elizur's chosen criteria were a self-report questionnaire, a brief interview, and a self-rating on hostility. The correlations between the Rorschach and the criteria were .74 for the questionnaire, .60 for the interview, and .45 for the self-rating. Hostility on the Rorschach would seem to be related to hostility of which the subject is quite aware. Other investigations do not alter that impression. Counts and Mensh (1950) and Pattie (1954) reported attempts to induce hostility through hypnosis, and while there were some behavioral changes suggestive of hostility, there were no differences in any of the Rorschach scoring categories. Murstein (1956) used a modification of the Elizur scale and found that Rorschach hostile content was significantly higher for fraternity men labeled as hostile-insightful on the basis of agreement in peer and self-ratings of hostility. A number of other investigators have had some success in finding relationships between Rorschach hostility and overt hostile aggressions such as physical aggression, verbal aggression, and quarrelsomeness (J. R. Smith & Coleman, 1956), assaultiveness (Finney, 1955; Storment & Finney, 1953; Towbin, 1959; Wolf, 1957). Hafner and Kaplan (1960) found that Rorschach and TAT hostility did not correlate at all, and Barger and Sechrest (1961) and Wallace and Sechrest (1963) got negative results for validity of inkblot hostility measures.

Obviously many other variables have been studied in relation to the Rorschach. The investigations have been at varying levels of methodological sophistication although the over-all level is not impressive. Both positive and negative studies are easy to criticize, although it is not easy to remain consistent in doing so. For example, Holtzman (1950a, 1950b) failed completely to substantiate hypotheses concerning certain Rorschach scores and their relation to impulsivity and the dimension of shyness-gregariousness, the criterion in each instance being peer ratings. It is perfectly true that peer ratings are imperfect as criteria, but if they are poor for impulsivity and shyness, in the absence of a prior rationale, we must conclude that they are poor for other traits as well, and such positive results as those obtained by Elizur are meaningless. On the other hand, there are innumerable "positive" studies that could be criticized on the grounds of a small and unrepresentative sample, but one must note that some "negative" results (e.g., Counts & Mensh, 1950) are equally or more at fault.

We come, at last, to what to the writer is by far the most interesting and promising set of investigations. These are studies or experiments which seem to fall most readily under the rubric of construct validity. They are not directed toward any special predictions of validation; rather they are attempts to achieve understanding of basic processes underlying the Rorschach response, if there are any such processes. Most are limited in their immediate applicability, but they are more promising than other investigations from a longer view.

The techniques for accomplishing construct validity research are diverse and difficult to prescribe. Much depends upon the imagination of the experimenter in devising the research procedures. One general way in which such research is occasionally attempted in the field of personality assessment validations is by the artificial or temporary induction of response tendencies highly similar (hopefully) to those that are at issue. We have already mentioned attempts to induce "hostility" by means of posthypnotic suggestion (Counts & Mensh, 1950; Pattie, 1954) which produced partially conflicting results. Hypnosis is certainly an important research procedure under many circumstances, but its psychological status is still sufficiently uncertain (Orne, 1962) to make any findings open to serious question. Other investigators have attempted to induce desired states by special manipulations prior to or during the testing period. One of the first to do so was Williams (1947) who used rather elaborate apparatus and instructions to lead his subjects to believe that they would receive strong electric shocks. He then examined their Rorschachs for indices of anxiety. While his results were predominantly positive, they have not proven especially replicable (Carlson & Lazarus, 1953; Ericksen, Lazarus, & Strange, 1952). Eichler (1951b), however, also reported some positive findings from a shock-induced anxiety experiment. Of 15 putative anxiety indicators, 4 were found to provide significant differentiation of a control and the experimental group. Four of 15 is not at all a bad score, but 11 of 15 clinical signs left unvalidated cannot be cause for contentment. It is important to note that research on anxiety indicators (and other multiple signs or indices) validates only those that prove significant. It does not validate the others. On the whole, however, the procedure of inducing a state which one wishes to study is worth serious consideration in many areas, a judgment which is well supported by the successful use of the technique in TAT research (Atkinson, 1958).

Of course it is not always possible to know just what specific state is being induced by any particular experimental manipulation. A good case in point is the pair of experiments devised by Meltzoff, Singer, and Korchin (1953) and Singer, Meltzoff, and Goldman (1952) in which they persuaded subjects to inhibit bodily movement either by standing as still as possible for five minutes or by writing a phrase as slowly as possible. The subsequent increase in Rorschach M responses probably would make good sense to most Rorschach theorists and probably to many other theorists as well. But could it honestly be said that either no increase in M or a decrease in M would not have made sense? The complexities of both the research and the theoretical situation are strongly emphasized by the finding of Goldman and Herman (1961) that strapping subjects in a chair so that they were immobilized for 15 minutes did *not* produce an increase in M or M responses. And to demonstrate that, apparently, dispositions of either a congruent or a compensatory nature (as well as no disposition at all) may be produced by a particular manipulation, we may refer to the ingenious experiment by Leventhal (1956). He administered either a figure-closure test or an embedded figures test to subjects prior to giving them the Rorschach. The first test presumably requires the subject to make an integrative response, while the second requires an analytic response. Leventhal found that subjects given the two different tasks differed markedly in the number of W responses given on the Rorschach. Thus, the state induced was one resulting in a response disposition congruent with the manipulation. Just why a fairly demanding task requiring close attention to detail should result in a disposition to continue in the same manner rather than in a compensatory relaxation analogous to relief from inhibited movement is not clear. Nonetheless, the experiments as they stand do at least provide a beginning basis for understanding of the processes underlying Rorschach responses. It will be noted that the Rorschach is not at all impervious to rather mild, transitory environmental effects, and most directly the experiments just described lend weight to the assumption that Rorschach responses are determined by momentary dispositional states rather than by longer, more enduring dispositions.

A very different approach to the Rorschach has been taken by Baughman in a series of carefully devised and executed investigations. Starting from the observation that there is a large hiatus between psychoperceptual theory and Rorschach theory and noting that the stimulus properties of the Rorschach cards have been little investigated (Baughman, 1958a), Baughman has developed variations in the Rorschach and procedure for using it which cast a good bit of light in a previously murky domain. He has been able to show that most Rorschach responses are in fact form determined (Baughman, 1959a). There are relatively few color or shading responses. Therefore, systems that place a predominant emphasis on color and shading are doomed to suffer from inherent unreliability. It can be noted here that the Holtzman Inkblot Test is likely to prove quite different from the Rorschach, inasmuch as it was devised specifically in order to increase the number of color and shading responses. Baughman (1959b) has developed a paired-comparison technique for eliciting color and shading responses, and he has found that his procedure produces more shading responses but no more color responses than the usual procedure. Such findings suggest the great importance of the stimulus in producing Rorschach responses and are cause for some reflection about the assumption that the responses are determined by some deep-lying inner state.

Finally, a series of fine experiments by

Kagan (1961) remains to be reported. Kagan began with the basic hypothesis that the human movement response "reflects a pre-potent tendency to interpret the environment in terms of human motives" (p. 201). Therefore, it was predicted that ascription of activity to inkblots would be related to tendencies to attribute affect states to social stimuli and to the sorting of human figures on the basis of affect. Moreover, it was expected that all measures would be related to interview ratings of introspectiveness. The subjects were 64 adults, both male and female. Kagan's predictions were well substantiated by his findings. A very important aspect of his findings from the standpoint of Rorschach theory is the fact that the predictions held only for human movement responses. The correlations with animal movement responses were negligible. From the standpoint of the discriminative validity of the test it is also important that Kagan found that his results were not attributable to intelligence to any marked degree. In a second study the long-term stability of his measures was investigated, and he found that over a period of eight years (!) human movement responses were predictive of an introspective attitude as rated from an interview. Moreover, human movement responses were related to a subject's ability to talk about motives, conflicts, and sources of anxiety over a 12 (!) year period. In the third study the number of human movement responses was correlated with ability to attain concepts based on sex and anger relevant responses, but they were not related to ability to attain number, texture, and "happy" concepts. Clearly Kagan's investigations contribute to an understanding of the Rorschach, and they lend some support to those who might wish to use the instrument in their clinical practice.

It seems a pity that after so many years of its existence one cannot say something more favorable about the Rorschach than that now and then the research findings are in the right direction. To be sure, there are spectacular successes, but they are balanced by the failures or marginal successes. One can only express astonishment at what is undoubtedly even now the pre-eminent clinical position of the Rorschach (Sundberg, 1961) when one reviews the research history of the instrument and the research itself. In 1948, Rotter (1948) and Thurstone (1948) were warning that the Rorschach had distinct limitations and were pleading for Rorschachers to bring their practice and beliefs within the realm of scientific psychology. Yet in 1956 Cronbach (1956) was led to conclude that "there is nothing in the literature to encourage reliance on Rorschach interpretations" (p. 184), and in 1958, A. R. Jensen (1958) produced a severe indictment of the Rorschach, even as a research instrument. Alas, the writer cannot find much to suggest grounds for more than the most modest of hopes for the theoretical validity of the Rorschach, and evidence for its actual utility in clinical situations is completely lacking. Whether the Holtzman Inkblot Test will prove better remains to be seen. Psychometrically it is almost certainly incomparably superior to the Rorschach. Whether it will prove clinically useful remains to be seen. One can concur heartily, most heartily, with Hertz's (1959) statement that "Therefore a fair statement of the status of the scientific worth of the Rorschach today would be, not that it is an invalid method, but that developments with the method and validating studies to date have not demonstrated its validity" (pp. 34-35). One would only wish to add that after 40 years or so, it's about time someone made an honest producer out of this perennially *enceinte* test.

Storytelling Methods

Fortunately there are several excellent surveys of both substantive issues and research. The reader should find Murstein's (1963) book very helpful, and books edited by both Atkinson (1958) and Kagan and

Lesser (1961) contain excellent treatments of important questions concerning storytelling test theory and methodology.

There is a sizable group of tests and techniques that have as a common element the fact that the response made by the subject is constituted by a story which he either completes or tells in entirety in response to some stimulus. The best known of these techniques is, of course, the Thematic Apperception Test, which has precedence, at least in terms of date of publication. It was introduced to psychology in 1935 (Morgan & Murray, 1935) and was published in its present form in 1943 (H. A. Murray, 1943). Since the publication of the TAT there have been numerous announcements of other storytelling tests, many of them obviously derivatives of the TAT. The best known variants are the Symonds Picture Story Test (Symonds, 1948), Make-A-Picture Story Test (MAPS) (Shneidman, 1949), Children's Apperception Test (Bellak & Bellak, 1949), Michigan Picture Test (Hartwell, Walton, Andrew, & Hutt, 1955), and the Thompson TAT (Thompson, 1949). However, lesser known variants such as the Adult-Child Interaction Test (Alexander, 1955) and the Vocational Apperception Test (Ammons, Butler, & Herzig, 1949) would extend the list of TAT derivatives considerably.

Four other tests merit some mention in this section, since, in one way or another, they involve a storytelling response. However, only one of the four is clearly derivative from the TAT. Sargent (1953) described the development of a story completion test which required the subject to finish a story briefly set by what were called "armatures." Although the Insight Test of Sargent has not been the subject of much research, it would seem to be similar to other storytelling tests, and Sargent's armatures are probably not so very different from the brief verbal descriptions of TAT cards which have been used successfully by Lebo (Lebo & Harrigan, 1957; Lebo & Sherry, 1959). Moreover, French (1955, 1958) has found the form of the Insight Test quite useful in assessing n achievement. The Four Picture Test seemingly was devised some years ago by Lennep, but it was actually published only in 1948. The Four Picture Test (Lennep, 1948) consists of four water-color drawings which may be arranged by the subject to suit himself and about which he is then asked to tell a story. While it is possible to note the ordering of the pictures as a response, principal emphasis is placed on the story. The Tomkins-Horn Picture Arrangement Test (Tomkins & Miner, 1957) is clearly not a derivative of the TAT, and it is a storytelling test only insofar as the subject is asked to arrange the pictures in order to make a story, and for clinical use of the test the respondent may be asked to relate the story. There has been relatively little research on the PAT, but early findings suggested that it could successfully discriminate among psychiatric groups. Finally, the Blacky Test (Blum, 1950) while perhaps partially derived from the thinking that had gone into the TAT, is in considerable proportions a hybrid, consisting as it does of both structured and unstructured phases. In fact, it is difficult to classify the Blacky Test, and it is included in this section partly for convenience.

As a response to be analyzed and from which to predict, the telling of stories would seem to offer many advantages. From a response standpoint, storytelling would easily meet all the criteria suggested by Lindzey (1961) for projective tests. That is not to say that stories when told *will* reflect unconscious or latent aspects of personality or that they *will* be rich in material for analysis, but certainly in comparison to many other types of responses, the limitations inherent in stories would seem to be few. The problems with stories all center around the question of what to do with the stories once one has them. They are not directly countable; they cannot be measured against any scale (save, perhaps, for such formal characteristics as length and verb-adjective ratio). But in the opinions of many clinical psychologists and researchers the clear advantages of storytelling responses have definitely outweighed their disadvantages.

In the original proposal for the TAT and for most similar techniques, oral responses clearly were anticipated, and in clinical use of the tests it is quite rare to encounter any other practice than to have an individual examiner administer the test to one subject, laboriously recording his spoken responses, verbatim if possible. Probably the initial fears were that written responses would lack spontaneity and that they would be unusually guarded and defensive. However, neither assumption is especially justified. Eron and Ritter (1951) and Lindzey and Heinemann (1955) found some differences between protocols obtained under group-written and individual-oral administrations, but there was no basis for concluding that one method or the other gave superior results. In fact, in the latter investigation the reliabilities for all scores were so low that it is correct to say that both methods were equally unsatisfactory. Weisskopf-Joelson and Wich (1961) found that simple instructions to "tell a story" and a verbal description of TAT cards both elicited longer responses than the usual visual TAT, and Bernstein (1956) found that results were apparently better without an examiner actually present, whether the responses were oral or written. Additional results of Lindzey and Heineman (1955) suggest that a writing period of five minutes per card is about right and that projecting the pictures on a screen is satisfactory. Whether the pictures are exposed to the subjects for 20 or 5 minutes makes no difference (Lindzey & Silverman, 1959). Such results are heartening for the efficiency-minded researcher.

A question of considerable theoretical importance for projective tests is the source of the responses actually emitted, it being equally naïve to suppose that they have no antecedents in the experience of the subject or that they are generated randomly. Coleman's (1947) results suggested that the TAT may be relatively impervious to recent experience of a movie, but it should be noted that a similar investigation has never been done with adults as subjects and Coleman's movie was a rather innocuous one. There is the argument that all responses are determined by personality dispositions and that all stories are revealing of personality. Even when fantasies are borrowed, those themes will be remembered and used which are meaningful and important to the person (Morgan & Murray, 1935). However, a recent experiment by Wylie, Sisson, and Taulbee (1963) is at best equivocal for the "significant memory" hypothesis. In their experiment subjects working under varying conditions were asked both to write "creative" stories to TAT cards and to write stories either from free memory or from memory of stories to which they had previously been exposed in the experiment. All stories were scored for the two themes of aggression and dependency. The correlations between the creative set condition (corresponding to the usual TAT instructions) and either of the two memory conditions were approximately zero for dependency. In other words, when asked to draw stories from memory, the subjects did not give stories consistent with those they created. For aggression the correlations were low, but they did reach significance and thus suggested that memories which subjects had for aggressive themes were somewhat selective. Another possibility is that rather than being fantasy responses TAT stories are actually autobiographical, a possibility strongly supported by the work of Combs (1946). Autobiographical stories may be "significant" in the same sense as memory stories, and the technique of assessing personality by means of earliest memories involves the interpretation of autobiographical material (Mosak, 1958).

Storytelling techniques partake of the characteristics of *symbolic stimulus* tests, but with some subjects they may also be pretty straightforward self-reports either of his own dispositions or of his view of the stimulus. However, a more usual view of storytelling stimuli is that they stand for a class of stimulus conditions in an individual's life. Thus, for example, TAT Card 1 is an "achievement" stimulus; Card 6BM is a "Mother-son" card, etc. Ability to interpret stories depends in part on the adequacy of understanding of the symbolic quality of the stimulus. However, some investigators have chosen to concentrate on the response, sometimes nearly to the exclusion of consideration of the stimulus. Balken and Masserman (1940), for example, in concentrating on the purely formal aspects of language ignore the stimulus. By their very nature formal analyses tend to be independent of the stimulus, and the testing situation is viewed more or less as a contrived situation in which certain systematic observations of behavior might be made. But in the usual approach to TAT interpretation little attention is paid to the subject's actual responses, e.g., it is not supposed that an individual is actually angry when he gives a "hostile" response; rather the response is considered at an abstract level. It is worth noting that first order, actual behaviors may be most significant from the standpoint of predicting how the respondent is going to behave in some other situation. Thus, Jensen (1957) found that overt hostility and other violations of social proprieties during testing were more predictive of antisocial aggression than the content of any of the stories told.

Murstein (1963) has been especially concerned with the role of the stimulus in TAT responses, and he has been able to show that the stimulus is, in fact, a powerful determinant of the responses obtained. There is far more variance attributable to differences among stimuli than to differences among persons. Clearly, then, the user of projective tests must be careful that his choice of stimuli does not bias his findings in such a way as to make them uninterpretable. There is a definite danger of bias leading to the selection of stimuli that are likely to substantiate whatever hypothesis the experimenter (or clinician) has in mind. Ullmann (1957) and Gurel and Ullman (1958) note that clinicians tend to use TAT cards with the greatest pull for emotional words and with the highest transcendence indices, and Simmons and Christy (1962) make the point that it is a mistake for the examiner who has a hypothesis about a subject to select TAT cards with a high pull for the expected characteristics. Similarly, if a researcher has a hypothesis about some group, e.g., only children, convicts, or Japanese, he should ensure that his selections of stimuli do not bias the results they will obtain. The obvious solutions are either to select a range of stimuli or to test other groups for control purposes.

An early expectation was that projection would be enhanced if stimuli were more similar to the subject, although the dimensions of similarity which would maximize projection have never been specified. In the original development of the TAT, dual forms for males and females were provided, but evidence has shown that females respond just as well to the male as to the female series and probably the opposite is true (Weisskopf, 1950). Other evidence on projection supports such a position (McIntyre, 1954; Lubetsky, 1960). After a review of considerable research Murstein (1963) concludes that modification of stimuli to produce greater similarity to the subject is not only not effective but possibly detrimental.

For research purposes it is desirable, even necessary, to derive a score from the storytelling response so that data can be subjected to statistical analysis. The major exception is when global matching techniques are used, i.e., in which a judge matches a response or set of responses to some criterion material. There are numerous ways in which stories may be scored, the various procedures probably being suitable for different kinds of research questions.

One way of dealing with stories is to have them judged on a global basis by some (usually) expert or trained person. For example, either individual stories or an entire protocol might be judged for "level of adjustment" reflected in it. The distinguishing feature of this approach is that the judge is not required to restrict himself to some objective feature of the response itself. He is free to make whatever inferences at whatever level he can. Typical examples of the global judgment procedure are investigations by B. Cox and Sargent (1950) and Magnusson (1959). In the former investigation, protocols were given to clinician judges who were simply asked to state whether the protocol had been given by a well-adjusted or a poorly adjusted child. The "scoring" then consisted of a binary scale of adjustment. On the other hand, Magnusson asked his judges to rate each subject from his TAT protocol on 16 traits, such as "dominant," "scrupulous," and "warm-hearted." In neither study were judges urged to pay attention to any particular aspects of the response. The adequacy of such a scoring system depends completely upon the adequacy of the judges to make the correct inferences. Unfortunately it would appear that considerable caution must be exercised in relying on judgments even of experts. Often research findings show that judges do not agree particularly well in the ratings they make (Hartman, 1949; Little & Shneidman, 1959; Magnusson, 1959), or, when they do agree, they do so merely by shared error tendencies (B. Cox & Sargent, 1950; Magnusson, 1959). However, there have been some successful efforts to use global judgments (Lindzey, Tejessy, & Zamansky, 1958; Silverman, 1959), and for some kinds of variables requiring an inference the method is indispensable.

A second scoring procedure for stories concentrates on a characteristic of the response itself rather than upon some disposition inherent in the respondent, although rather typically it is assumed that the response characteristic is in fact characteristic of the subject. For example, themes of any kind may be looked for in stories as reasonably objective aspects of responses. Achievement imagery, as a notable instance, has been defined in response terms, and a manual for its scoring has been developed (Atkinson, 1958). Other themes of a wide variety have been successfully scored: food imagery (Atkinson & McClelland, 1948; McClelland & Atkinson, 1948), fear imagery (Walker, Atkinson, Veroff, Birney, Dember, & Moulton, 1958), aggression (Kagan, 1956; Stone, 1956), affiliation (Shipley & Veroff, 1952), and power (Veroff, 1957), to name but a few. To reiterate, in scoring themes the emphasis is on the response. Whether the response can be related to some underlying disposition is an empirical matter.

At a still simpler level than counting themes, it is possible to count words falling into a particular category, words related to the disposition in which the investigator is interested. One can easily count "aggressive" or "achievement" related words once one has decided what words fall into each category. Wallace and Sechrest (1963) used such a scoring procedure and obtained very high agreement between scorers, as might be expected, and word counting has also been used by Bellak (1944), MacBrayer (1959), and Matarazzo (1954).

A more recent proposal for objective scoring of the TAT has been advanced by Dana (1955, 1959). In its most recent form Dana's system (1959) has been reduced to three variables, two of which are clearly formal. *Perceptual organization* refers to the ability to follow the standard directions to "tell a story," and *perceptual personalization* refers to deviations from a coherent, organized TAT story, e.g., out-of-place words and phrases. The third variable, *perceptual range,* is less clearly formal, since it is indexed by adherence to normal content in stories, but it should be noted that the nature of deviations from normally expected content is ignored and *perceptual range* partakes of the nature of a formal variable. Dana's system seems to be sufficiently objective to produce very satisfactory agreement between independent scorers, and none of the variables seems to be related either to verbal productivity or to intelligence taken across normal, neurotic, and psychotic groups.

Except for scoring based on global clinical impressions, most of the approaches to scoring seem to be based at least implicitly on the frequency hypothesis, i.e., the hypothesis that the more frequently a particular response occurs, the stronger the underlying response disposition. Thus, for example, three achievement themes indicate a stronger disposition than two such themes; six anxiety "signs" indicate higher anxiety than five similar signs. To state a point made before, the frequency hypothesis is appealing in its rationale and simplicity, but it remains to be investigated in several of its ramifications.

There are other possible hypotheses concerning the scoring of responses which could provide a partial basis for quantitative analysis of stories and which should receive further investigation. Two of special interest would be the intensity and rare response hypotheses. Would superior scoring be achieved if themes were scored for intensity as well as for frequency? And would superior scoring be achieved if responses were differentially weighted according to the rarity of their occurrence in a normative population? These are provocative questions. There are other hypotheses which should be investigated, e.g., the omitted response hypothesis, the bizarre response hypothesis, for their import for the understanding of both response processes and scoring, but they have, as yet, limited applicability to the analysis of research data.

A fourth way of scoring stories, and again one that is directed toward a more or less objective analysis of the response, is to examine stories for the occurrence of "signs" that are of either theoretical or empirical importance. This has been a commonly employed technique in storytelling research with both theoretical and purely empirical approaches being employed. For example, the misinterpretation of the sex of a TAT figure would seem to have a theoretical justification as a sign of "problems in sex identification." On the other hand, such a specific sign as "hypnotism" on TAT 12BM as a sign of homosexuality is of a more empirical nature. (Why specifically hypnotism of all the themes involving subordination?) For the most part the sign approach is likely to minimize problems of agreement among scorers, since the rationale of the signs is in part that they are objectively determinable. The list of TAT investigations into signs of some disposition or another would be quite long, but good examples are provided for clinical deviations by Ritter and Eron (1952); for anxiety by Mandler, Lindzey, and Crouch (1957) and Lindzey and Newburg (1954); and for homosexuality by Davids, Joelson, and McArthur (1956) and Lindzey, Tejessy, and Zamansky (1958).

A final approach to the scoring of storytelling responses has been termed "formal," by which is meant that rather than concentrating on the content of the stories, what corresponds to the grammar and syntax of the stories becomes the focus of attention. It has been suggested that formal aspects of TAT responses are deserving of more attention (Holt, 1958), and that may indeed be true. Certainly scoring of formal characteristics just about eliminates the problems of achieving scoring agreement. Some of the formal characteristics of responses which have been studied are grammatical structure and parts of speech (Balken & Masserman, 1940; Mandler, Lindzey, & Crouch, 1957), story length (Balken & Masserman, 1940; B. Cox & Sargent, 1950; Mandler, Lindzey, & Crouch, 1957), and vagueness and hesitation in speech (Lindzey & Newburg, 1954).

Validity of Storytelling Measures

The TAT was first and is still primarily a clinical instrument, and it seems reasonable to begin with a consideration of its validity in the hands of clinical users. One of the earliest and, upon casual examination, most promising clinical validation studies is one that illustrates both an early methodological sophistication and an early and basic deficiency of design of which current experimenters are still too often guilty. Harrison (1940) made rather free interpretations of TAT protocols of 40 patients, and another psychologist checked his predictions against clinical case materials. Although by far the majority of the statements made by Harrison could not be checked in any way, those that could proved to be correct with remarkable frequency (82.5 per cent), even when the interpretations were made blindly (74.6 per cent). However, Harrison and Rotter, his coworker (Rotter, 1940), saw an important issue in the study of prediction, for they realized that Harrison's predictions might have been correct simply because they were true of most patients rather than because of any differential accuracy. What resulted is almost certainly the first experiment on clinical prediction with any control for accuracy of stereotype statements. By randomly matching Harrison's interpretations for 15 cases with 15 case histories, and by matching a "guessed" (stereotype) write-up with 10 actual case histories, it was possible to show that Harrison's predictions were considerably higher than would be expected on a "chance" basis. Despite the generally positive results of Harrison's experiment, it has the critical defect, as we can see now, of failing to sample from the population of clinical psychologists to whom generalizations might be made. Since Harrison was the only clinician studied, we are left with the rather likely possibility that he was an especially astute clinician, which was, perhaps, why his study was done in the first place. Perhaps his investigation could be added to that of Little and Shneidman (1955) who found considerable accuracy across clinicians but only for one case!

Other early studies by Henry (1947), Hartman (1949), and B. Cox and Sargent (1950) were methodologically flawed, and at best the outcomes were only mildly encouraging. The latter study in particular, however, pointed to a serious bias in the direction of overestimating degree of pathology, a bias which has consistently proven a problem (Little & Shneidman, 1959). More (1957) found some slight evidence for validity of TAT interpretations in the sense that they agreed with those from an interview and a biographical summary, but Winch and More (1956) found that while the TAT may have some validity in the sense that predictions from it were "better than chance," it did not add anything to the accuracy of predictions that could be made from a brief interview. In general the interview had higher validity than the TAT, and the multiple correlation with the criterion decreased as often as it increased with the addition of the TAT.

A spate of clinical validity studies appeared during 1959, and only one was grounds for any special optimisim at all. In what is by now surely the currently most cited work in clinical test validation, Little and Shneidman (1959) elicited the cooperation of an outstanding group of clinical psychologists, gave them a clinically realistic task, and had a well-conceived and carefully verified criterion consisting of data from case histories, and were forced to a very pessimistic conclusion about the validity of the TAT. Judgments from the TAT scarcely exceeded chance validity, and the TAT generally came off the worst of the tests studied. The experiment of Little and Shneidman is difficult to rationalize away. Silverman (1959) utilized a criterion consisting of *Q*-sorts in six areas which had been made by therapists of patients being studied. Unfortunately Silverman's clinicians were given access to a whole battery of tests, including the TAT, so it is difficult to assess the import of his findings specifically for the TAT. The average correlations with the criterion Q-sorts ranged from .14 to .41, and five of the six correlations were better than a stereotype prediction. Such correlations are mildly encouraging, but they do not establish TAT validity.

Magnusson (1959) published a study indicating clearly that the woes of the TAT devotee are not to be resolved by running off to Sweden. Working with Swedish high school students, he obtained peer ratings for 16 traits. In general the reliabilities for the traits were high. All 63 of the students had been given an individual TAT, and the protocols were interpreted by four experienced clinicians who rated each subject on each trait. There was *no* trait for which all four of the judges achieved significant validity, in spite of the fact that the validity coefficients were corrected for attentuation in the criterion variable. Only for two traits, "sensitive" and "warmhearted," were the mean validity coefficients even significant, and they were only .28 and .26 respectively. Magnusson's work bears a strong resemblance to the pioneering work of Sanford *et al.* (Sanford, Adkins, Miller, & Cobb, 1943), who scored TAT protocols of children for a number of Murray's needs. The scorers did not agree especially well, split-half reliabilities were disappointingly low, and the average validity coefficient against ratings of overt behavior was only .11.

It is possible to close this discussion of 1959 clinical interpretation of the TAT on a mildly positive note. W. E. Henry and Farley (1959) developed a research method to meet the suggestions of Cronbach (1948) for validational studies. A set of 27 criterion statements was developed, and these statements covered most of the critical areas of clinical description. The applicability of each statement to each target object was determined separately for overt, subjective, and projective levels of description. The target objects were 36 adolescents. The task of the judge was to match TAT summaries (not, it will be noted, the protocols themselves) with the criterion statements. The matching was done in triads of cases. Henry and Farley analyzed the data separately for two kinds of errors: (a) errors consisting in failure to make proper discriminations among subjects, and (b) errors consisting in failure to identify or recognize a trait where it occurs.

From their results Henry and Farley conclude that the TAT was valid as a predictor, although, as in so many studies, it is impossible to determine just what the degree of accuracy was in a way that would be very meaningful for the utilization of the test in decision-making situations. Nonetheless, their results are to be considered evidence that the TAT can, under some circumstances, produce judgments at an accuracy level better than chance. On the other hand, the individual judges did not agree particularly well, for they tended to have "specialties" in which they excelled. While the experimenters concluded that the TAT reflects consistent aspects of personality, they also concluded that it is better for some aspects than for others, viz., peer group and emotional adjustment vs. family relations and mental functioning. Their general conclusion was that the TAT tends more to reflect current conscious and unconscious concerns than the unconscious and deeply repressed sources of these concerns. Apparently the X-ray does not penetrate to the skeleton of the personality.

Validity of the TAT for assessing a variety of personality traits has been studied. Normals and various clinical groups do show some differences on the TAT, although not as striking as might be supposed (B. Cox & Sargent, 1950; Dana, 1955, 1959; Friedman, 1957; Ritter & Eron, 1952; Rosenzweig & Fleming, 1949). Still, such findings represent a legitimate first step. Homosexuals have also been studied and their responses compared with those of normal males. Davids, Joelson, and McArthur (1956) included a group of presumably heterosexual but neurotic males as a control sample and found that homosexuals did produce a larger mean number of homosexual signs on the TAT, but the most distinguishing feature of their performance was the larger number of frankly sexual responses. Lindzey, Tejessy, and Zamansky (1958) did a similar study with less encouraging findings, especially in studying cases of supposed latent homosexuality.

Taking somewhat more ordinary instances of traits on which TAT research has been done, anxiety has been studied in the form of "test anxiety" with largely negative results (Mandler, Lindzey, & Crouch, 1957) and as clinically rated anxiety, again with mostly negative findings (Lindzey & Newburg, 1954). In both studies the only significant indicators were formal rather than content in nature. Kagan and Mussen (1956; Mussen & Kagan, 1958) have related group conformity to both dependency and parental attitudes as measured by the TAT, but Fitzgerald (1958) found no evidence for the validity of a TAT dependency measure in a study employing both interview and peer rating techniques, which did correlate with each other ($r = .59$). Wallace and Sechrest (1963) found only minimal evidence of TAT validity for four traits, but Davids and Rosenblatt (1958) concluded that the TAT would be of some value in assessing the "alienation syndrome."

The one trait for which the TAT has been most extensively studied is hostile aggression, and that body of research is of interest because of what it suggests about the need for and the possibility of assessing defensive or inhibitory processes. A number of investigations showed that the TAT is sensitive to feelings or motives which *might* provide a basis for hostile action (Bellak, 1944; Ericksen, 1951; Feshbach, 1955). However, Mussen and Naylor (1954) noted the probable complexity of the problem of relating TAT responses to overt aggression and found a predicted positive relationship for lower-class boys where aggression is presumably relatively more permissible. Where there is concern for punishment, the relationship is lower. Lesser (1957) actually found a positive correlation of .43 and a negative correlation of −.41 between TAT and overt hostility, depending upon whether the mothers of his young male subjects were relatively tolerant or intolerant of their son's aggressions. Other investigators have found positive relationships (Kagan, 1956; Purcell, 1956) when the subjects fairly uninhibited for overt aggression are studied, but with most subjects some measure of anxiety about expression of aggression would probably improve the findings (Lesser, 1958), and where no such measure has been used they often prove negative (Gluck, 1955; Lindzey & Tejessy, 1956).

One conceptual advance would seem to be Jensen's (1957) idea of dividing the aggressive group into those who express aggression in socially unacceptable ways and those who manage to express their aggressions in ways that do not transcend the bounds of acceptability, both groups being contrasted to a passive group. A methodological development that could help considerably is Stone's TAT Aggressive Content Scale (Stone, 1956) which presents an objective scoring system for different types of aggressive and nonaggressive responses. His scale differentiated successfully between groups of assaultive and nonassaultive Army prisoners. It is worthwhile to review the conclusions of Buss (1961) after his extensive consideration of the TAT as a measure of tendencies toward aggression. He concludes that (a) the TAT is a relatively good measure of antisocial aggression (assaultiveness) but not of milder forms; (b) the population to be studied is an important variable; (c) the relationship between TAT and behavioral aggression is direct; (d) the nature of the scoring system is important, and the addition of an anxiety measure helps; and, (e) the more ambiguous the picture, the less the tendency to emit aggression. Unambiguous pictures are best for yielding indications of behavioral aggression.

The TAT in Motivational Studies

One way of studying the validity of an assessment technique is to manipulate in some way the variables that one is interested in measuring and then to look for changes in the manifestation of the variable on the assessment procedure. This is a potentially powerful and convincing operation, involving as it does the direct manipulation of one variable (hopefully) while holding all others constant (hopefully). In the best of all possible worlds it would be possible to be quite confident of the precision of one's manipulations and of the constancy of the unwanted or irrelevant variables. Moreover, it would also be possible to show that the manipulation had a direct effect on the variable being measured, and the effect would be a dependable function (not necessarily linear) of the degree of manipulation. Perhaps it is part of the human tragedy that the world of experimenters is, alas, imperfect.

In two of the earliest investigations into the effect of strength of motive on "imaginal processes," Sanford (1936, 1937) showed that hungry subjects are biased in their responses in the direction of producing more "food relevant" responses. While subsequent investigations (e.g., Atkinson & McClelland, 1948; McClelland & Atkinson, 1948; Postman & Crutchfield, 1952) have shown that the effect is rather a complicated one, nonetheless, biases in responses are seemingly producible by manipulation of level of hunger. However, to keep the record straight, it is not quite true that hunger was actually manipulated in all instances in which it has been studied. A typical procedure, for example, is to test subjects at varying lengths of time since their last meal, but that also results in a difference in other cues than hunger associated with eating, e.g., time of day. A more clear-cut manipulation is exemplified in an experiment by Klein, Salomon, and Smith (1959) who manipulated level of thirst by feeding subjects very salty food. They subsequently obtained size estimates for thirst-related objects and found results related to the thirst manipulation only when a general perceptual style was taken into account.

Although hunger as a motive is of only incidental interest to the study of personality and personality assessment, it has been studied rather extensively in its effects on various judgmental and imaginative tasks, probably because of the fairly clear-cut manipulations that can be expected to produce hunger and because of the ease of defining appropriate response outcomes. This is not the place to survey all the research on the effects of hunger on various responses, and the interested reader can find excellent summaries elsewhere (e.g., Sherif & Sherif, 1956). Briefly, the findings seem to show that there is an initial increase in food-relevant responses with increasing food deprivation. However, at some point, perhaps when hunger becomes acute, there seems to be a decrease in food-relevant responses. McClelland and Atkinson (1948) found that only deprivation responses showed the expected increase. Food imagery did not. Moreover, the results may be quite different depending upon whether one is studying temporary induced hunger or prolonged deprivation. In the study of volunteers undergoing prolonged semi-starvation (Keys, Brozek, Henschel, Mickelson, & Taylor, 1945), it was found that preoccupation with food became so complete that it pervaded nearly all activities of the subjects. Their fantasies about food were intense and vivid, and they remained high in frequency of occurrence. On the other hand, in spite of the subjects' constant preoccupation with food, there was no evidence of increased hunger associations when they were formally tested (Brozek, Guetzkow, & Baldwin, 1951). The argument advanced by Lazarus (1961) that the men may have found such release in all their talking about food that fantasy gratifications were unnecessary is not particularly persuasive in view of the reports by the subjects themselves of continuing fantasies about food and food-related activities. That different motives may require very different control processes and may result in different manifestations on projective tests is indicated by a study by E. J. Murray (1959) of subjects who had undergone 86 hours of sleep deprivation. When tested with the TAT for sleep themes, the sleep-deprived subjects gave *fewer* sleep themes than a control group, and they produced no greater number of fatigue or hostility themes. The results are interpreted in terms of avoidance by the very sleepy subjects of thoughts or verbal responses that might arouse overpowering sleepiness. Presumably the subjects were highly motivated to stay awake, and to abandon themselves to their fantasies could produce an irreversible lapse from the behavior expected of them. However, for hungry subjects to engage in food fantasies does not represent a threat to their experimental role. It would be of interest to test very hungry subjects undergoing voluntary abstinence from food in the presence of a plentiful supply. And it would be interesting to test a group of sleep-deprived subjects like Murray's at the very end of the experiment after they were prepared for falling asleep.

Even though the hunger motive did not prove to be related in a simple manner to food fantasies and other food responses, the early work on the hunger motive did provide the impetus for subsequent investigations into other motives that seemed to be amenable to experimental manipulation. The first and most intensively explored variable has been motivation for achievement, or need achievement as it is customarily called. McClelland and his associates have investigated the measurement of n achievement and many of its ramifications in personality development and personality theory (Atkinson, 1958; McClelland, Atkinson, Clark, & Lowell, 1953). However, important beginnings have been made in the development and exploration of measures of other seemingly important motives such as affiliation (Shipley & Veroff, 1952), power (Veroff, 1957), and fear (Walker, Atkinson, Veroff, Birney, Dember, & Moulton, 1958). A distinguishing feature of the work done by McClelland and his associates and students has been the experimental arousal of a motive together with the appropriate operations (TAT-type cards) for assessing the strength of the motive.

In the development of a measure of n achievement pains were taken to specify the manifestations of the motive which could be expected in storytelling responses, and the score for a given subject was then obtained simply by counting the number of themes falling into various achievement-related categories (McClelland, Clark, & Roby, 1949). Although the scheme that has been developed can be and has been criticized on both procedural and empirical grounds (McArthur, 1953), n achievement research has exposed a fruitful vein for both motivation researchers and personality assessers. A study of the investigations included by Atkinson (1958) in his collection of readings on motivation research will be rewarding to those persons who are looking for positive results in psychology. Moreover, there are numerous other investigations in the psychological journals which are supportive of the claims for validity of the n achievement measure (e.g., Atkinson, 1953; Marlowe, 1959). On the other hand, the evidence has not been uniformly positive, and there are some investigations that have been interpreted somewhat negatively for the validity of n achievement measurement (Bendig, 1957; Broverman, Jordan, & Phillips, 1960; Murstein & Collier, 1962). An interesting development in n achievement technology has been the French Test of Insight (French, 1955, 1958), a paper-and-pencil test presenting brief descriptions of behavior which the subject is to explain. The test is patterned after the Sargent Test of Insight (1953). Evidence now available would suggest that the French TI is probably about as valid as the storytelling measure based on the TAT, and it has the advantage of being considerably less cumbersome (Atkinson & Litwin, 1960; French & Thomas, 1958).

Although a fair appraisal at the present time must lead to the conclusion that the experiments relating manipulations in motive strength to storytelling responses have been successful and valuable, it is not by any means true that they lead inevitably to the conclusion that the TAT is valid for any purpose for which one might wish to use it. In fact, the experiments referred to above point to some very serious problems that remain to be solved. One that has already been mentioned is that to the extent that storytelling responses prove to be susceptible to the fairly casual and transient kinds of manipulations used in some studies, doubt is cast on their validity for inferring more enduring states. However, various lines of evidence do converge to suggest that at least in the case of n achievement the TAT taps a rather stable disposition. When it is shown that the initial manipulation produces differences in scores and then that the scores differentiate groups of subjects who will perform differently in a variety of situations, the case for the measure becomes considerably strengthened.

There have been ample demonstrations of both scorer agreement and reliability (Atkinson, 1958; McClelland *et al.,* 1953) for n achievement and the other variables for which similar scoring systems have been developed. In fact, the objectivity of scoring is a major attraction of the systems developed by McClelland and his associates. It is noteworthy that both scorer agreement and reliability appear to exceed the values obtained by Sanford *et al.* (Sanford, Adkins, Miller, & Cobb, 1943) in their early attempt to develop and apply a "need" scoring system for the TAT. A desideratum if not a necessity for the n achievement and other measures would be to determine the function relating test scores and the manipulations used to arouse the need in experimental groups. For example, does a stronger arousal situation produce higher need scores? Or does the arousal situation operate in an "all or none" fashion so that a stronger arousal increases the number of subjects showing an effect without increasing the mean score of those who are susceptible at all? And it may well prove to be the case that the function is not linear, i.e., that at some point in the dimension of arousal an increase in scores is no longer produced or even that a reversal occurs.

At present most of the investigations that have been accomplished have utilized college students as subjects. Unfortunately it is quite unsafe to generalize to the findings that can be expected with other populations. Hence, the implications of the research for the over-all validity of the TAT, e.g., in clinical use, are quite limited. There is already serious question about the use of n achievement scoring with female subjects (Atkinson, 1958, p. 831), and nearly all the investigations of other needs have been done with male subjects. Whether the difficulties arise because of the differential validity of the TAT with male and female subjects or because of the different strengths and manifestations of the needs being studied is not known, and both problems may, in fact, occur. But if differences exist between college males and females, then they may certainly exist between college males and other groups with whom one might want to use the TAT.

The Arnold Approach to the TAT

Finally, an approach to the TAT described by Arnold (1962) and supported by several studies reported by her must be considered separately because of the startlingly favorable results of the method in validity studies. Arnold suggests that instead of regarding each story as simply an aggregation of themes, a story is a creative reorganization of past sense impressions and a new product of human imagination.

She insists that it is necessary to take into account not only the story action and the outcome but the relationship between the action and the outcome. Arnold's scoring scheme does not depend on the picture on which the story is based. She states that the stimulus value of the picture is irrelevant. It is the story "import" that is scored and not story elements. Scoring story imports instead of story themes equalizes story length, since only one import is scored for each story. "Whether long or short, every story is reduced to an import which is usually contained in one sentence. Imports make it possible to score and to evaluate meager as well as rich records which is a decided advantage when testing children, low status adults, or mental patients" (p. 15).

By an import Arnold seems to refer to the meaning or significance of a story rather than to its specific content. "The story import will usually show how the story teller thinks people usually act and how he feels they should act; what opinions he thinks right and which wrong; what will lead to success in his opinion and what to failure; what can be done when danger threatens and what are the things to strive for" (p. 51). It seems to the writer that the diagnosing of an import in a story requires a good deal of plain, old-fashioned intuition on the part of the clinician and that it might be exceptionally difficult to achieve any degree of agreement in scoring. However, Arnold suggests that the imports may be placed into one of four categories, depending upon the problems with which they are concerned. The four categories are (a) achievement, success, happiness, active effort; (b) right and wrong; (c) human relationships; and (d) reaction to adversity. After that categorization the imports are scored on a five-point scale ranging from "strongly positive" to "strongly negative." Arnold ultimately arrives at a "motivational index" which is simply the algebraic sum of the scores of all the imports. Thus, the seemingly complex scoring system eventuates in a single dimension that probably relates to such characteristics of the story as optimism, reasonableness, and adequacy of responses to the central character. She reports interscorer agreements of 97 per cent and 94 per cent between herself and two other scorers for 1,200 stories. And she reports reliabilities in the neighborhood of .80 for the motivational index.

Arnold reports several investigations relevant to the validity of her motivational index. In one study teachers were rated by their pupils for seven questions relating to their adequacy as teachers. For 50 elementary and 50 secondary teachers Arnold reports phi coefficients ranging from .96 down to .37 for the 14 computed relationships. (Why phi rather than some more satisfactory correlation coefficient was used is not clear.) The correlations she obtained are so high, so deviant from those usually found in such research, as to defy belief. However, just to show that her findings are no fluke, it may be noted that Arnold reports additional studies. Twenty-nine naval disciplinary offenders were paired with nonoffenders, and 27 of the 29 offenders obtained scores more negative than those of their matched nonoffenders. Arnold reports correlations between the motivational index and grade point averages of .75 for seventh graders, .83 for college women, and .85 for college men. And finally she reports a study of seminarians for whom correlations of .59 and .61 were obtained for the variable "promise in the order" as rated by peers and superiors respectively.

All these investigations add up to the most favorable picture ever obtained for the validity of any method of scoring the TAT. Even though it is a bit difficult to comprehend Arnold's system, e.g., why the imports are categorized into four categories prior to being scored on the motivational index, it is difficult to quarrel with success. Her system is simple. It is based almost exclusively upon similarity projection ("Both the type of problem a man sets himself and the kind of outcome he prefers are characteristic for him" [p. 13]) and the cumulation of scores across a series of items. Up to this point the writer does not know of investigations with Arnold's system done in laboratories other than her own, but such investigations are not only merited, they are imperative.

Research on TAT Variants

The research on variants of the TAT has not been extensive, and as indicated earlier, since the variants involve the same procedures and the same assumptions as the TAT, they probably stand or fall on the basis of TAT research. In fact, it is difficult to see what the advantages of the variants are. The MAPS Test (Shneidman, 1949) permits a bit more participation by subject, perhaps, but an analysis of what the subjects actually do during the test might suggest that the number of options actually used by them is rather limited. That schizophrenics use more deviant test figures (Goldenberg, 1951; Shneidman, 1948) is to be expected since they are deviant in so many respects. Moreover, such responses as placing the figures in midair, on the margins, etc., are as easily explained by the motivational impairment hypothesis (Cofer & Hunt, 1944) as by any reference to the "dynamics" of such behavior. General descriptions of the MAPS responses of clinical groups without specification of control groups, significance levels, etc., such as have been given by Shneidman (1948) and Goldenberg (1951), cannot be considered evidence for the validity of the test. At present it would seem incumbent upon exponents of the MAPS Test to demonstrate something about its reliability and validity in a methodologically acceptable manner.

The Thompson TAT for Negroes (Thompson, 1949) might have seemed a good idea, but probably it is a bit too obvious to be used in a society with heightened sensitivity to racial differences. At least the study of Riess, Schwartz, and Cottingham (1950) provides no basis for using the Thompson TAT with Negroes, and with Northern Negroes the Murray cards seem preferable. On the other hand, it is quite likely that special sets of cards might be better in other countries where Caucasian features stimulate curiosity or negativism. There is a Japanese version of the TAT (Hisama, personal communication), and a special set of cards is being constructed for use in the Philippines (Lagmay, 1964).

Still another variant on the TAT is a special version for use with children entitled the Children's Apperception Test (Bellak & Bellak, 1949). Its distinguishing feature is the substitution of animal figures for humans on the ground that children will identify more readily with animals. However, as in so many ways children prove recalcitrant to adult notions about their behavior, and the evidence suggests the inferiority for most children of the animal pictures (Budoff, 1960; Light, 1954).

The Sargent Insight Test (Sargent, 1953) is not clearly a TAT derivative, but it is related in the kind of response it requires. The writer knows of no bona fide empirical research on the test, but it should work if other techniques do. A mark in favor of Sargent's test is the fact that French's Insight Test (French, 1958) seems to be working rather well for the measurement of achievement motivation (Atkinson & Litwin, 1960; French, 1955).

The Blacky Test

Blum (1950) attempted to develop a test specifically out of psychoanalytic theory, and although there has been some telling criticism of the logic and methods involved in its development (Seward, 1950), the Blacky Test remains as the best example of a test stemming directly from a comprehensive theory of personality. The test is designed to produce scores for 13 psychoanalytic constructs from four sources of information: stories about the cards, answers to multiple choice questions, spontaneous comments, and supplementary questions.

Ideally the reliability of each of the 13 variables measured in four ways should be determined, but the usual reliance on generalizations from a limited number of tested relationships has to be permitted.

Although most of the Blacky variables probably have reliabilities greater than zero, they are probably not high enough to inspire much confidence (Charen, 1956a) in spite of Blum's (1956) denial of the relevance of test-retest reliability for the Blacky Test. The findings of Berger and Everstine (1962) are more positive, if irrelevant, but their conclusion that "These results are indicative of reasonably good test-retest reliability ..." (p. 226) is not as prudent as the somewhat contradictory statement on the same page that "the test-retest reliability measures of this instrument, although favorably comparable with other instruments, are not very high."

An early review of studies on validity of the Blacky Test (Blum & Hunt, 1952) was undoubtedly overoptimistic, and some methodological problems were ignored. For example, paranoids were shown to be higher on certain dimensions presumably consistent with psychoanalytic theory (Aronson, cited by Blum & Hunt, 1952), but they were not shown to be lower on other dimensions thus admitting the possibility that they might have been higher on many of the variables. Similarly, the study by Lindner cited by Blum and Hunt which showed that sex offenders were higher on 9 of 13 variables is hardly persuasive for the differential validity of the test.

Charen (1956a, 1956b) found that changes in Blacky Test responses of tuberculosis patients studied over a period of physical recovery indicated that they were regressing in personality. Since the Rorschach and 15 other paper-and-pencil tests gave no evidence of change, Blum's (1956) criticism of Charen for assuming the correctness of the Rorschach is not especially convincing.

The clinical validity of the Blacky Test was studied by Ellis (1953) in an investigation marred only by the fact that there was only one patient being rated by 22 different clinicians. The patient was in psychoanalysis and had had about 200 hours of treatment. The dual criterion consisted of a description of the female patient on a standard scale by both her analyst and herself, agreement between the two being quite high. The clinicians agreed rather well among themselves in the predictions they made, and they agreed well with Blum, who was serving as guest expert clinician in the study. However, agreement with the criterion was not impressive in spite of the fact that the clinicians knew that the patient was a female analytic patient and several of the statements were rather obvious. Moreover, the diagnoses made by the clinicians were pretty far off.

Finally, Blum (1954, 1955) succeeded in two studies in producing evidence for "perceptual defense" by showing that subjects made biased guesses about the presence or absence of tachistoscopically presented Blacky Pictures representing areas in which they had repressed conflicts or to which they were sensitized. However, the failure of Smock (1956) to replicate Blum's findings and his pointing to the similarity in the operations used to demonstrate both repression and perceptual defense, i.e., in both cases the tendency of the subject to "undercall" a given card was noted, largely vitiates the importance of Blum's investigations.

At present the verdict on the Blacky Test is about the same as for other tests; its validity has not been demonstrated. However, the absolute quantity of data is not yet large, and optimism is likely to persist.

Sentence Completion Method

A technique in which a respondent is encouraged to respond to a brief stimulus consisting of the initial words of a sentence (stem) in such a manner as to complete the sentence, usually to express his own feelings, defines a sentence-completion test.

There are several varieties available including the Rotter Incomplete Sentences Blank (Rotter & Rafferty, 1950), the Make a Sentence Test (Borgatta, 1961), the Michigan Sentence Completion Test (Kelly & Fiske, 1951), Rohde's Sentence Completion Method (Rohde, 1957), the Forer (Forer, 1950), and the Stein (1949) Sentence Completion Tests. The different forms are of different lengths and differ in the particular stems used, but there is no empirical basis for supposing that any one form is better than another. Many investigators have created their own set of stems in order to meet some specific research need. The technique is well adapted to the do-it-yourself researcher.

Stems may obviously differ along a dimension of directness or specificity. Again, there is no evidence to suggest which form is superior. Some researchers and test developers (e.g., Stein, 1947) have used both first and third person stems in the belief that third person stems might tap dispositions at a lower level of awareness, and Hanfmann and Getzels (1953) did find some aspects of their data that supported that contention. However, Sacks (1949) in a direct comparison found that six of seven clinical interpreters thought the first person form to be preferable, and predictions from the test to ratings were better for the first person form. The research justification for distinctions often made between first and third person stems (e.g., Forer, 1960) is lacking.

As with nearly all other personality measures, for sentence completions one must opt to achieve either "bandwidth" or "fidelity" (Cronbach, 1954). The published forms of sentence-completion tests, being intended for general clinical use, obviously go in the direction of bandwidth, since they must, of necessity, be able to afford information about a wide variety of personality characteristics. The Rotter ISB, for example, seems to have been constructed to provide an opportunity for the subject to reveal anything that might be bothering him. The scoring of the Rotter ISB (Rotter & Rafferty, 1950) produces a single score for "conflict." Even such a general purpose instrument as Rotter's can be used for fairly specific research purposes by scoring it for particular kinds of completions. For example, Sechrest and Hemphill (1954) scored Rotter ISB protocols for Air Force personnel for a number of different content categories such as somatic complaints and satisfactions with the Air Force; Fitzgerald (1958) scored it for dependency; and Renner, Maher, and Campbell (1962) scored for anxiety, dependency, and hostility. Still, for accuracy of assessment, it would seem that materials had better be constructed specifically for the dispositions to be measured. Moreover, the construction of more focused instruments usually allows for more stimuli for a particular disposition and hence, greater reliability of measurement. The Make a Sentence Test (MAST) devised by Borgatta (1961) is something of a compromise in that a 54-item test is scored for 11 discrete variables, and the 54 items were selected empirically in order to provide for good coverage of the variables.

There are many ways of scoring sentence completions, probably about as many as for other kinds of responses, but in practice global clinical judgment and content frequency are most common. In the clinical use of sentence completion it is almost certainly true that clinical judgment is the usual way of dealing with the protocols, whether the instrument is used for clinical "dragnet" operations or for the assessment of specific dispositions. However, for research purposes responses are more likely to be categorized and counted (frequency scoring). Some judgment is usually required to score individual completions, but a high degree of agreement can be achieved (Borgatta, 1961; Renner, Maher, & Campbell, 1962). An important feature of the scoring system employed by Rotter and Rafferty is that intensity is also taken into account, a seven-point scale ranging from high conflict to positive adjustment being utilized. A high degree of agreement between scorers is possible (Churchill & Crandall, 1955).

Whether global clinical judgment and more meticulous item-by-item scoring are different is an empirical question, and Jackson (1962) made up special brief sentence completion protocols, using Rotter and Rafferty scoring as a guide. She was able to show that clinicians are affected in their over-all judgments of the protocols by the number of conflict completions and by their intensity. They differed from more objective scoring in weighting "positive" completions less heavily, in weighting extreme conflict responses relatively more heavily, and in showing a "primacy" bias, i.e., they were biased by conflict responses that occurred in the first part of the protocol.

Sentence-completion methods have been shown to permit reasonable internal consistency ($r_{tt} = .69$) for attitudes toward authority (Burwen, Campbell, & Kidd, 1956), and for anxiety, dependency, and hostility (Renner, Maher, & Campbell, 1962). Churchill and Crandall (1955) obtained test-retest reliabilities for the Rotter ISB of from .38 to .54, the higher figure obtaining for adult females (as opposed to college students), but Burwen, Campbell, and Kidd (1956) found a retest reliability of only .12 over a period of one year. Borgatta and Meyer (1962) studied retest reliability of MAST scales over a period of eight months for a group of tenth-grade girls in a vocational high school and found median correlations in two groups of only .35 and .33. However, the long time period and the nature of the population, presumably one changing rapidly in many characteristics, should be taken into account. In addition Borgatta and Meyer point out that their scales are not highly correlated with each other, only a very few of the between-scale correlations being as high as corresponding reliabilities. Stephens (1960) reanalyzed the data of Churchill and Crandall in order to study reliability of individual stems of the Rotter ISB, and in spite of considerable variation in reliabilities, many of which were quite good, there was no obvious pattern that would indicate rules for creating good sentence stems. In a review of sentence-completion techniques, Benton, Windle, and Erdice (1957) find a number of studies showing that the reliability of the method is probably as great as or greater than the reliability of any other unstructured test.

Another approach taken to reliability of sentence completions is to determine the consistency of the content of individual responses over a period of time. Osterweil and Fiske (1956) found that over a period of two to three weeks the great majority of responses given by subjects changed in some degree, but individual differences in number of responses changed were reliable. In other words, some subjects consistently changed more responses than did others. That finding is of interest in the light of our earlier assertion that variance in reliability may be contributed by persons as well as by items or tests. There was also a reliable difference between stems in the tendency to produce changed responses, a finding consistent with Stephens' discovery of great variation in reliabilities of individual stems. Fiske and Van Buskirk (1959) also studied the agreement in interpretations of the same person's sentence-completion protocols obtained on different occasions. Their results showed that there are distinct difficulties in distinguishing between persons and occasions, i.e., protocols obtained on different occasions may be mistaken for protocols obtained from different persons. The conclusion of Fiske and Van Buskirk that it may be necessary to obtain more than one protocol from a subject in order to get a stable, consistent personality picture would seem to be justified.

The validity of sentence-completion method has not been as extensively studied as it should be. Benton *et al.* (1957) survey a number of validity studies and show that there are wide discrepancies in values obtained, but many of the studies are of questionable relevance for validity, particularly since many present *post hoc* findings never cross-validated. However, over-all level of personality disturbance, or, conversely, adjustment seems to be assessed with about as much validity as can be obtained from any other measures, and in view of the economy of the method, it would seem difficult to justify more complex expensive procedures. Hiler (1959) developed and cross-validated a scoring system to predict continuation in psychotherapy which worked rather well and which equaled the validity for global clinical judgment. Efron (1960) was not successful in obtaining correct clinical predictions of suicidal attempts from a special sentence-completion test constructed so as to elicit depressive themes.

Nearly all investigations of personality measures involve normative scoring or judging of protocols, but K. I. Howard (1962) asked clinical judges to rank order the strengths of 10 needs for each of 10 patients after studying their test protocols. The average agreement between different raters rating the same test for the same patient was only .30, and the validities, as represented by correlations for the same patient rated from different tests by different raters, were not significantly different from chance. Even the same raters did not differentiate patients across tests.

Various investigators have reported significant validity figures for sentence-completion measures of specific traits and behaviors. Sechrest and Hemphill (1954) found it useful for measuring social responsibility, satisfaction with the Air Force, and somatic complaints in an Air Force population. Campbell and his associates have reported a series of studies in which attitudes toward authority (Burwen, Campbell, & Kidd, 1956), attitudes toward home and parents and law and justice (Maher, Watt, & Campbell, 1960), and anxiety, dependency, and hostility were successfully measured in various populations. Fitzgerald (1958) also developed a sentence-completion dependency scale which correlated significantly with interview and peer reputational measures of the same trait. And Wallace and Sechrest (1963) found some evidence for validity of hostility, somatic concern, achievement orientation, and religiosity, the latter scale correlating .43 with peer reputation for religious interest.

The MAST devised by Borgatta yields scores on 11 scales such as (a) paranoid, suspicious, (b) hostile, (c) assertive, (d) avoidance, and (e) anxiety. Thus, it is necessary to validate the scales separately. The initial validational efforts consisted of correlations with self-report measures of comparable traits along with direct self-ratings, peer-ratings, and behavior or in small discussion groups. In general the scales yielded correlations with the self-report measures, the Guilford-Zimmerman Temperament Survey, the Thurstone Temperament Schedule, the Edwards Personal Preference Schedule, and the Cattell 16 PF, which were consistent with the traits presumed to be measured by the various scales. Most of the correlations were of modest size, but correlations of .40 and even .50 occurred with some frequency. Several of the scales also correlated well with direct self-ratings. However, significant correlations with either peer ratings or the measures from discussion groups were infrequent. Borgatta's results support the contention that sentence completions are best viewed as self-report measures, but that they are probably as good as or better than most other such measures.

Quite apparently the validity of sentence completions cannot be considered impressive in absolute terms; indeed, there is ground for discouragement. Yet, so much of what one must face is relative, and the validity of sentence completions must be regarded in the rather dismal context of demonstrated validity of other similar measures such as the Rorschach and the TAT. Coupled with the recognition of the temporal and monetary economy of the sentence-completion method, the relative validity of the method becomes more impressive.

Certainly a dispassionate appraisal of empirical findings plus considerations of utility would lead to the conclusion that the sentence-completion method is preferable to many others if for no other reason than that it is desirable to err as cheaply as possible.

Rosenzweig Picture-Frustration Study

A test with a considerably narrower focus than most other unstructured personality tests is the Picture-Frustration Study (Rosenzweig, 1944) which has a special form for children (Rosenzweig, Fleming, & Rosenzweig, 1948). The test was developed in order to assess responses to frustration. It consists of 24 line drawings, cartoon-like pictures in which something presumably frustrating is happening to one of the persons portrayed, and the task of the subject is to write in the response which the frustrated person makes, the emphasis being placed on writing down the first response thought of. Obviously the expectation is that the response is representative at some level of the response that would be made by the subject, although it has been suggested that the subject might identify with the frustrating rather than the frustrated figure (Winfield & Sparer, 1953). The test is scored for the direction of aggression: extrapunitive, intropunitive, and impunitive; and it is scored for type of response: need persistent, ego defensive, and object dominant, the latter referring to a concern with the fact of frustration rather than with a means of meeting it.

Norms are available (Rosenzweig, 1950; Rosenzweig *et al.,* 1948), even for different racial and cultural groups (McCary, 1956). However, other research has been sparse in spite of the fact that the test is simple, economical, relatively objective, and pointed in content. The successes of the test have not been many, but there are some suggestions that it has some slight degree of validity at least (e.g., Kaswan, Wasman, & Freedman, 1960; Lindzey, 1950). A number of other studies, although interesting, are equivocal with respect to validity (Brown & Lacey, 1954; Winfield & Sparer, 1953). It is of interest that very few modifications in the test or procedure have ever been tried although Moore and Schwartz (1963) have shown that alterations in sex of the frustrated figure makes no difference.

Drawing Techniques

The inclination of this writer is to give pretty short shrift to drawing techniques as measures of personality, since there is little persuasive evidence of their validity. In spite of numerous speculative articles (Montague, 1951; Napoli, 1951; Wolff, 1942; Wolff & Precker, 1951), almost nothing is known about the relationship between free drawings and personality. Aronson (1958) obtained evidence that certain variables in "doodle" drawings might be related to need achievement, and his results received presumptive support from further data given by McClelland (1958). However, the most convincing studies in the whole drawing area relate to the expansion-constriction dimension as it cuts across both drawings and social situations. Berger (1954) examined doodles in lecture notebooks of college students and obtained some support for the notion that graphic constriction might be related to personality constriction. More recently Wallach and his associates (Wallach & Gahm, 1960; Wallach, Green, Lipsitt, & Minehart, 1962; Wallach & Thomas, 1963) have produced good evidence to show that graphic expansiveness-constriction in a free-drawing task is related to social interaction among both children and college students. General defensiveness was found to interact with the drawing measure to determine whether the expansiveness-constriction scores would be positively or negatively correlated, and enforced social isolation and interaction were also found to affect the drawing measure. Wallach's results are impressive and deserving of intensive additional study.

Aside from findings cited above, it is difficult to find a series of investigations producing consistent positive results, and even isolated positive findings are difficult to come by. Swenson (1957) reviewed evidence on the Draw-a-Person Test (Machover, 1951) several years ago and uncovered very little positive evidence, especially if one excludes the expected and obvious findings that grossly abnormal clinical cases differ from normals. The Bender-Gestalt (Bender, 1938) lacks evidence for validity, and one of the more positive findings, it seems to the writer, only shows that an expert with long experience and training may use it to make some fairly low-level distinctions, i.e., between clear-cut cases of organic brain damage and normals (Goldberg, 1959).

Attempts to demonstrate the validity of the DAPT have been numerous and varied. Quite a number of studies have centered on such obvious characteristics as sex of the first-drawn figure and size of figure. However, Brown and Tolor (1957) reviewed the evidence relating sexual identification and figure drawings and concluded that the meaning of the drawing of an initial figure of the opposite sex is unknown. Most persons draw a figure of their own sex first (Armstrong & Hauck, 1961; Bieliauskas, 1960; G. Frank, 1955; Mainord, 1953; Weider & Noller, 1950), even when they are psychiatric patients (Fisher, 1961; Smith, 1953; Wisotsky, 1959). Starr and Marcuse (1959) found that the sex of the first drawn figure was not a reliable occurrence for females. Size of drawing has not been established as a predictor either (Bennett, 1964; Goldstein & Rawn, 1957; Silverstein & Robinson, 1961). Other investigations have represented attempts to verify various "signs" taken from the many hypotheses suggested by Machover (1948, 1951). Those investigations have also been predominantly negative, e.g., for homosexuality (Barker, Mathis, & Powers, 1953; Grams & Rinder, 1958); anxiety (Hoyt & Baron, 1959); paranoid tendencies (Fisher & Fisher, 1950; Reznikoff & Nicholas, 1958; Ribler, 1957). In one departure Goldstein and Rawn (1957) found some support for hostile indicators in an experimental setting inducing hostility in normal subjects.

Global clinical judgments from drawings also give no great cause for enthusiasm about the method. Investigations showing some positive evidence (Royal, 1949; Schmidt & McGowan, 1959; Tolor, 1955) are easily offset by negative results (Blum, 1954; Fisher & Fisher, 1950; Silverstein & Robinson, 1956; Stolz & Coltharp, 1961). Probably the most hopeful note is provided by D. C. Murray and Deabler (1958) who demonstrated that improvement in accuracy of sorting drawings into five diagnostic categories followed systematic feedback about accuracy of initial predictions. No very high level of accuracy was achieved, but the experiment points to direction that subsequent efforts might take.

There are probably several reasons for the inaccuracy that results from interpretation of figure drawings, but Strumpfer and Nichols (1962) present a sizable amount of data casting doubt on the communicability and reliability of a number of figure drawing indices. Fisher and Fisher (1950) even found that raters could not agree on such simple matters as describing the stance and facial expression of the drawings. However, an even more important source of error lies unquestionably in the fact that a major part of the variance in figure drawings is contributed by drawing ability (Nichols & Strumpfer, 1962), and clinician judges are too much biased by artistic quality (Feldman & Hunt, 1958; Levy, Lomax, & Minsky, 1963; Sherman, 1958; Whitmyre, 1953). Whether that bias could be corrected, and whether anything would be left if it were, is open to demonstration.

Many other drawing tasks and variations on the above exist. Little sound research exists for any of them. However, if the reader has a persistent interest in the possibility of extracting something from drawings, the work of Buck (1948) on the House-Tree-Person Test; Caligor (1952,

1957) who has a clever method of obtaining repeated drawings of human figures; Harrower (1950) who suggests that subjects be asked to draw something quite unpleasant; and of Franck and Rosen (1949) and Pikunas and Carberry (1961) on tasks involving completion of a drawing, might prove the most stimulating.

Word Association

Word association as a technique in personality assessment has never justified the initial enthusiasm displayed for it by Jung (1910) who made it the topic of one of his invited lectures at Clark University. However, word association has continued to be used throughout the years for one purpose or another in personality research. It is used infrequently in clinical situations (Sundberg, 1961), and it is obviously not likely to prove of any great value as a broad-band assessment device. Nonetheless, it has persisted in the literature because there is some reason to believe that variability in associations might be related to some personality dimensions or to areas of conflict. Davids (1956), for example, found that two groups of subjects previously identified as "high alienation" and "low alienation" individuals differed in word associations in that they produced words falling into different personality dispositional categories.

Most commonly, long latency of response and inability to repeat associations have been taken as indices of conflict. Jacobs (A. Jacobs, 1955) was able to show that long latencies are indicative of emotional reaction, whereas a GSR was not, and Levinger and Clark (1961) obtained evidence for the emotional arousing nature of words whose associations are later forgotten, although the longest interval, four months, was somewhat longer than is likely to be used in most investigations. Siipola, Walker, and Kolb (1955) concluded that speed of association is related to adjustment, but that the relationship takes the form of poorly adjusted subjects responding at the same speed whether they are under instructions to respond rapidly or not, while better adjusted subjects adjust their speed of association according to instructional sets.

In research, word association is likely to have its greatest value when the investigator can use it more with the finesse of the rapier than with the power of the broadsword. When he wishes to identify emotional or conflict-laden stimuli for other use, or when he wishes to determine whether or not conflict exists for a subject in a particular area that is predetermined, word association may be useful.

The Hand Test

A recent addition to the stock of projective tests is the Hand Test (Bricklin, Piotrowski, & Wagner, 1962; Wagner, 1962), consisting of a set of ten line-drawings of hands in various positions, to each of which the subject is supposed to respond with a guess as to what the hand might be doing. Very apparently the Hand Test resembles the Rorschach in numerous ways. The evidence on the test is limited to date, but the principal research efforts thus far have been directed toward the prediction of antisocial or aggressive behavior, and the findings are mildly encouraging (Bricklin, Piotrowski, & Wagner, 1962; Wagner & Medvedeff, 1963). Sexual maladjustment (Wagner, 1963), schizophrenia (Wagner, 1961), and satisfactory employment in Goodwill shops (Wagner & Copper, 1963) have also been studied with encouraging results. By this time there would seem to be no reason to expect miracles, but the Hand Test could prove to be better than many others for some types of assessments.

The IES Test

Another test based in large part on psychoanalytic theory is the IES Test by Dombrose and Slobin (1958), IES standing for "impulse," "ego," and "superego." The test consists of four subtests, each of which yields a score for I, E, and S components of personality. The tests are varied in nature, but all are relatively brief and seemingly scorable in a manner that permits good agreement between scorers. Only one of the subtests is not completely objective. The materials include a Picture Title test that requires the subject to make up a title for each of a set of pictures which portray scenes of such complexity that the title presumably might reflect any of the three personality components; a Picture Story Completion test somewhat like the Picture Arrangement Test from the Wechsler intelligence tests (Wechsler, 1944) but which requires the subject to pick one of three pictures to complete a cartoon story; a Photo Analysis Test in which the subject chooses a phrase that he thinks best describes a man portrayed in a photo; and an Arrow-Dot test in which the subject is asked to draw lines from an arrow to a dot but in such a way as to avoid breaking certain rules but also so as to avoid unnecessary prohibitions. There is, as yet, only a limited amount of evidence for validity and reliability of the IES, but some of the early results are promising. Findings reported in their monograph by Dombrose and Slobin (1958) indicate that the test probably has moderately good test-retest and internal consistency reliabilities. Evidence for validity reported by them consisted mostly of demonstrations of differences among preselected groups, but the results were mostly quite consistent with expectations. Additional investigations by Bortner (1963, 1964), Herron (1962), and Rankin and Wikoff (1964) are also mostly encouraging for the validity of the IES. Very apparently this test merits additional and intensive study.

IN CONCLUSION

It is the contention of the writer that what is needed in the field of personality assessment is more imagination and inventiveness, which is not a way of saying that what is needed is more of the same thing we already have. As an example of the kind of thinking which should be encouraged, the writer would offer the work by Zamansky on the assessment of homosexuality by indirect means. In his initial study Zamansky (1956) reasoned that homosexual inclinations should produce a greater interest in pictures of persons of the same sex than in pictures of persons of opposite sex or in pictures of a neutral character. The problem was, however, that if subjects knew that their interest was being measured, results would be affected. Therefore, Zamansky developed a device involving one-way glass by means of which he could observe the time that subjects spent looking at each member of a pair of stimuli without the subject being aware that his eye movements could be seen. Then by presenting appropriate pairs of pictures in the guise of a judgment task, Zamansky was able to obtain "time spent looking" measures that confirmed the prediction that male homosexuals would be attracted to male pictures and would avoid female pictures. Using the same device, he was able to study homosexual interests of paranoid patients and show that they differed from homosexuals in having weaker avoidance reactions to females (Zamansky, 1958). A similar "time spent looking" measure was used by Martin (1964) in an intriguing study of sex arousal under permissive and inhibiting conditions.

There are, in contrast, many other available measures that represent only changes on the themes provided by other tests: a three-dimensional projective test (Twitchell-Allen, 1948); a nonverbal design-building test (Schaie, 1963); a TAT-like set of pictures (Phillipson, 1955); and a photo-judgment task (Meer & Amon, 1963). While some such measures may be mildly interesting, it seems unlikely that any will provide a badly needed breakthrough in personality assessment methodology. In the estimation of the writer, the individual with an assessment problem will do well to think about it from many different angles before he adopts one of the currently available, standard measures. A fair appraisal of the research literature would justify the conclusion that any reasonably well thought out new method would not be likely to be measurably worse. It would not have to be remarkable to be better.

REFERENCES

Abt, L. E. The efficiency of the group Rorschach in the psychiatric screening of Marine Corps recruits. *J. Psychol.,* 1947, 23, 205–217.

Adorno, T. W., Frenkel-Brunswik, Else, Levinson, D. J., & Sanford, R. N. *The authoritarian personality.* New York: Harper, 1950.

Alexander, T. The adult-child interaction test. *Monogr. soc. Res. Child Develpm.,* 1955, 17, 2.

Allen, R. M. *Elements of Rorschach interpretation.* New York: International Universities Press, 1954.

Ames, L. B., Learned, J., Metraux, R. W., & Walker, R. N. *Child Rorschach responses: Developmental trends from two to ten years.* New York: Hoeber, 1952.

Ames, L. B., Metraux, R. W., & Walker, R. N. *Adolescent Rorschach responses.* New York: Hoeber, 1959.

Ammons, R. B., Butler, Margaret N., & Herzig, S. A. *The Vocational Apperception Test: Plates and manual.* New Orleans: R. B. Ammons, 1949.

Anastasi, Anne. *Psychological testing.* New York: Macmillan, 1954.

Armstrong, R. G., & Hauck, P. A. Sexual identification and the first figure drawn. *J. consult. Psychol.,* 1961, 25, 51–54.

Arnold, Magda B. *Story sequence analysis.* New York: Columbia Univer. Press, 1962.

Aronson, E. The need for achievement as measured by graphic expression. In J. W. Atkinson (Ed.), *Motives in fantasy, action, and society.* Princeton, N.J.: Van Nostrand, 1958. Pp. 249–265.

Asch, S. E. Opinions and social pressure. *Sci. Amer.,* 1955, 193 (5), 31–35.

Atkinson, J. W. The achievement motive and recall of interrupted and completed tasks. *J. exp. Psychol.,* 1953, 46, 381–390.

Atkinson, J. W. (Ed.) *Motives in fantasy, action, and society.* Princeton, N.J.: Van Nostrand, 1958.

Atkinson, J. W., & Litwin, G. H. Achievement motives and test anxiety conceived as motive to approach success and motive to avoid failure. *J. abnorm. soc. Psychol.,* 1960, 60, 52–63.

Atkinson, J. W., & McClelland, D. C. The projective expression of needs. II. The effect of different intensities of the hunger drive on thematic apperception. *J. exp. Psychol.,* 1948, 38, 643–658.

Auld, F., Jr. Contributions of behavior theory to projective testing. *J. projective Tech.,* 1954, 18, 421–426.

Auld, F., Jr., & Eron, L. D. The use of Rorschach scores to predict whether patients will continue psychotherapy. *J. consult. Psychol.,* 1953, 17, 104–107.

Auld, F., Jr., Eron, L. D., and Laffal, J. Application of Guttman's scaling method to the TAT. *Educ. psychol. Measmt,* 1955, 15, 422–435.

Balken, Eva R., & Masserman, J. H. The language of phantasy. III. The language of the phantasies of patients with conversion hysteria, anxiety state, and obsessive-compulsive neuroses. *J. Psychol.,* 1940, 10, 75–86.

Barger, Patricia M., & Sechrest, L. Convergent and discriminant validity of four Holtzman Inkblot Test variables. *J. psychol. Stud.,* 1961, 12, 227–236.

Barker, A. J., Mathis, J. K., & Powers, C. A. Drawings characteristic of male homosexuals. *J. clin. Psychol.,* 1953, 9, 185–188.

Barker, R. G., Dembo, T., & Lewin, K. Frustration and regression: an experiment with young children. *Univer. of Iowa Stud. Child Welfare,* 1941, 18, No. 1.

Baughman, E. E. Rorschach scores as a function of examiner difference. *J. projective Tech.,* 1951, 15, 243–249.

Baughman, E. A comparative analysis of Rorschach forms with altered stimulus characteristics. *J. projective Tech.,* 1954, 18, 151–164.

Baughman, E. The role of the stimulus in Rorschach responses. *Psychol. Bull.,* 1958, 55, 121–147. (a)

Baughman, E. A new method of Rorschach inquiry. *J. projective Tech.,* 1958, 22, 381–389. (b)

Baughman, E. An experimental analysis of the relationship between stimulus structure and behavior on the Rorschach. *J. projective Tech.*, 1959, 23, 134–183. (a)

Baughman, E. The effect of inquiry method on Rorschach color and shading scores. *J. projective Tech.*, 1959, 23, 3–7. (b)

Baughman, E., and Guskin, S. Sex differences on the Rorschach. *J. consult. Psychol.*, 1958, 22, 400–401.

Bechtoldt, H. P. Construct validity: A critique. *Amer. Psychologist*, 1959, 14, 619–629.

Beck, S. J. *Rorschach's test. II. A variety of personality pictures.* New York: Grune and Stratton, 1949.

Behn-Eschenburg, H. *Behn-Rorschach Tafeln.* Bern: Hans Huber, 1931.

Bellak, L. The concept of projection, an experimental investigation and study of the concept. *Psychiatry*, 1944, 7, 353–370.

Bellak, L., & Bellak, S. S. *Children's Apperception Test and manual.* New York: C.P.S. Co., 1949.

Bender, L. A visual motor Gestalt test and its clinical use. New York: American Orthopsychiatric Association, 1938, Research Monograph No. 3.

Bendig, A. W. Manifest anxiety and projective and objective measures of need achievement. *J. consult. Psychol.*, 1957, 21, 354.

Bennett, Virginia D. C. Does size of drawing reflect self-concept? *J. consult. Psychol.*, 1964, 28, 285–286.

Benton, A. L., Windle, C. D., & Erdice, E. *A review of sentence completion techniques.* Iowa City: State Univer. of Iowa, 1957.

Berger, C. S. An experimental study of doodles. *Psychol. Newsltr*, 1954, 138–141.

Berger, D. Examiner influence on the Rorschach. *J. clin. Psychol.*, 1954, 10, 245–248.

Berger, L., & Everstine, L. Test-retest reliability of Blacky Pictures Test. *J. projective Tech.*, 1962, 26, 225–226.

Berkowitz, L., & Lundy, R. M. Personality characteristics related to susceptibility to influence by peers or authority figures. *J. Pers.*, 1957, 25, 306–316.

Berkowitz, M., & Levine, J. Rorschach scoring categories as diagnostic "signs." *J. consult. Psychol.*, 1953, 17, 110–112.

Bernreuter, R. G. *The personality inventory: manual.* Stanford, Calif.: Stanford Univer. Press, 1935.

Bernstein, L. The examiner as an inhibiting factor in clinical testing. *J. consult. Psychol.*, 1956, 20, 287–290.

Bieliauskas, V. J. Sexual identification in children's drawings of the human figure. *J. clin. Psychol.*, 1960, 14, 42–44.

Blanton, R., & Landsman, T. The retest reliability of the group Rorschach and some relationships to the MMPI. *J. consult. Psychol.*, 1952, 16, 265–267.

Block, J. A comparison between ipsative and normative ratings of personality. *J. abnorm. soc. Psychol.*, 1957, 54, 50–54.

Blum, G. S. *The Blacky pictures and manual.* New York: The Psychological Corp., 1950.

Blum, G. S. An experimental reunion of psychoanalytic theory with perceptual vigilance and defense. *J. abnorm. soc. Psychol.*, 1954, 49, 94–98.

Blum, G. S. Perceptual defense revisited. *J. abnorm. soc. Psychol.*, 1955, 51, 24–29.

Blum, G. S. Reliability of the Blacky Test: A reply to Charen. *J. consult. Psychol.*, 1956, 20, 406.

Blum, G. S., & Hunt, H. F. The validity of the Blacky Pictures. *Psychol. Bull.*, 1952, 49, 238–250.

Blum, R. H. The validity of the Machover DAP technique. *J. clin. Psychol.*, 1954, 10, 120–125.

Borgatta, E. F. Make a Sentence Test: an approach to objective scoring of sentence completions. *Genetic Psychology Monographs*, 1961, 63, 3–65.

Bortner, R. W. Research cooperation in older institutionalized males. *Percept. motor Skills*, 1963, 16, 611–612.

Bortner, R. W. Personality preferences for skill- or chance-determined outcomes. *Percept. motor Skills*, 1964, 18, 765–772.

Bramel, D. A dissonance theory approach to defensive projection. *J. abnorm. soc. Psychol.*, 1962, 64, 121–129.

Bricklin, B., Piotrowski, Z., & Wagner, E. E. *The Hand test.* Springfield, Ill.: Charles C Thomas, 1962.

Brogden, H. E., & Taylor, E. K. The dollar criterion—applying the cost-accounting concept to criterion construction. *Personnel Psychol.*, 1950, 3, 133–154.

Broverman, D. M., Jordan, E. J., & Phillips, L. Achievement motivation in fantasy and behavior. *J. abnorm. soc. Psychol.*, 1960, 60, 374–378.

Brown, D. G., & Tolar, A. Human figure drawings as indicators of sexual identification and inversion. *Percept. motor Skills,* 1957, 7, 199–211.

Brown, R. L., & Lacey, O. L. The diagnostic value of the Rosenzweig P-F Study. *J. clin. Psychol.,* 1954, 10, 72–75.

Brozek, J., Guetzkow, H., & Baldwin, Marcella V. A quantitative study of perception and association in experimental semistarvation. *J. Pers.,* 1951, 19, 245–264.

Buck, J. N. The H-T-P technique: A qualitative and quantitative scoring manual. *J. clin. Psychol., Monogr. Suppl. No. 5,* 1948.

Buckle, D. F., & Holt, N. F. Comparison of Rorschach and Behn inkblots. *J. projective Tech.,* 1951, 15, 486–493.

Budoff, M. The relative utility of animal and human figures in a picture-story test for young children. *J. projective Tech.,* 1960, 24, 347–352.

Burwen, L. S., Campbell, D. T., & Kidd, J. The use of a sentence completion test in measuring attitudes toward superiors and subordinates. *J. appl. Psychol.,* 1956, 40, 248–250.

Buss, A. H. *The psychology of aggression.* New York: Wiley, 1961.

Butler, J. M., & Haigh, G. V. Changes in the relation between self-concept and ideal concepts consequent upon client-centered counseling. In C. R. Rogers & Rosalind F. Dymond (Eds.), *Personality changes and psychotherapy.* Chicago: Univer. of Chicago Press, 1954. Pp. 55–75.

Calden, G., and Cohen, L. B. The relationship between ego involvement and test definition to Rorschach test performance. *J. projective Tech.,* 1953, 17, 300–311.

Caligor, L. The detection of paranoid trends by the Eight Card Redrawing Test (8CRT). *J. clin. Psychol.,* 1952, 8, 397–401.

Caligor, L. *A new approach to figure drawing: based upon an interrelated series of drawings.* Springfield, Ill.: Charles C Thomas, 1957.

Campbell, D. T. Factors relevant to the validity of experiments in social settings. *Psychol. Bull.,* 1957, 54, 297–312.

Campbell, D. T. *Five varieties of projection in trait attribution.* Progress Report. NIMH Research Grant M-1544 (C1). January, 1959.

Campbell, D. T. Recommendations for APA test standards regarding construct, trait or discriminant validity. *Amer. Psychologist,* 1960, 15, 546–553.

Campbell, D. T. Social attitudes and other acquired behavioral dispositions. In S. Koch (Ed.), *Psychology: A study of a science.* Vol. 6. New York: McGraw-Hill, 1963. Pp. 94–172.

Campbell, D. T., & Fiske, D. W. Convergent and discriminant validation by the multitrait-multimethod matrix. *Psychol. Bull.,* 1959, 56, 82–105.

Campbell, D. T., & Stanley, J. C. Experimental and quasi-experimental designs for research on teaching. In N. L. Gage (Ed.), *Handbook of research on teaching.* Chicago: Rand McNally, 1963. Pp. 171–246.

Carlson, R. A normative study of Rorschach responses of eight-year-old children. *J. projective Tech.,* 1952, 16, 56–65.

Carlson, V. R., & Lazarus, R. S. A repetition of Meyer Williams study of intellectual control under stress and associated Rorschach factors. *J. consult. Psychol.,* 1953, 17, 247–253.

Carp, A. L., & Scharizen, A. R. The susceptibility to falsification of the Rorschach psychodiagnostic technique. *J. consult. Psychol.,* 1950, 14, 230–233.

Carr, A. C. Evaluation of nine psychotherapy cases by the Rorschach. *J. consult. Psychol.,* 1949, 13, 196–205.

Carr, A. C., Forer, B. R., Henry, W. E., Hooker, Evelyn, Hutt, M. L., & Piotrowski, Z. A. *The prediction of overt behavior through the use of projective techniques.* Springfield, Ill.: Charles C Thomas, 1960.

Cartwright, Rosalind D., & Vogel, J. L. A comparison of changes in psychoneurotic patients during matched periods of therapy and no therapy. *J. consult. Psychol.,* 1960, 24, 121–127.

Charen, S. Reliability of the Blacky Test. *J. consult. Psychol.,* 1956, 20, 16. (a)

Charen, S. A reply to Blum. *J. consult. Psychol.,* 1956, 20, 407. (b)

Churchill, R., & Crandall, V. J. The reliability and validity of the Rotter Incomplete Sentence Test. *J. consult. Psychol.,* 1955, 19, 345–350.

Clark, R. A. The projective measurement of experimentally induced levels of sexual motivation. *J. exp. Psychol.,* 1952, 44, 391–399.

Clark, R. A., & Sensibar, Minda R. The relationships between symbolic and manifest projections of sexuality with some incidental correlates. *J. abnorm. soc. Psychol.,* 1956, 50, 327–334.

Cohen, A. J. Clinical judgment as a function of the complexity of the judge's cognitive system. Unpublished doctoral dissertation, Northwestern Univer., 1962.

Coleman, W. The Thematic Apperception Test: I. Effects of recent experience; II. Some quantitative observations. *J. clin. Psychol.,* 1947, 3, 257–264.

Combs, A. W. The use of personal experience in Thematic Apperception Test story plots. *J. clin. Psychol.,* 1946, 11, 358–363.

Counts, R. M., & Mensh, I. N. Personality characteristics in hypnotically induced hostility. *J. clin. Psychol.,* 1950, 6, 325–330.

Cox, B., & Sargent, H. TAT responses of emotionally disturbed and emotionally stable children. *J. projective Tech.,* 1950, 14, 60–74.

Cox, Shelagh M. A factorial study of the Rorschach responses of normal and maladjusted boys. *J. genet. Psychol.,* 1951, 79, 95–115.

Craddick, R. A. Size of Santa Claus drawings as a function of time before and after Christmas. *J. psychol. Stud.,* 1961, 12, 121–125.

Craddick, R. A. Size of witch drawings as a function of time before, on, and after Halloween. *Amer. Psychologist,* 1962, 17, 307. (Abstract)

Crandall, V. J. Induced frustration and punishment reward expectancy in Thematic Apperception stories. *J. consult. Psychol.,* 1951, 15, 400–404.

Crespi, L. P. The interview effect in polling. *Publ. opin. Quart.,* 1948, 12, 99–111.

Cronbach, L. J. A validation design for qualitative studies of personality. *J. consult. Psychol.,* 1948, 12, 365–374.

Cronbach, L. J. Statistical methods applied to Rorschach scores. *Psychol. Bull.,* 1949, 46, 393–429.

Cronbach, L. J. Coefficient alpha and the internal structure of tests. *Psychometrika,* 1951, 16, 297–334.

Cronbach, L. J. Report on a psychometric mission to clinicia. *Psychometrika,* 1954, 19, 263–270.

Cronbach, L. J. Assessment of individual differences. *Ann. Rev. Psychol.,* 1956, 7, 173–196.

Cronbach, L. J., & Gleser, Goldine C. *Psychological tests and personnel decisions.* Urbana: Univer. of Illinois Press, 1957.

Cronbach, L. J., & Meehl, P. E. Construct validity in psychological tests. *Psychol. Bull.,* 1955, 52, 281–302.

Crowne, D. P., & Marlowe, D. A new scale of social desirability independent of psychopathology. *J. consult. Psychol.,* 1960, 24, 349–354.

Crowne, D. P., & Marlowe, D. *The approval motive.* New York: Wiley, 1964.

Crutchfield, R. S. Conformity and character. *Amer. Psychologist,* 1955, 10, 191–198.

Dahlstrom, W. G., & Welsh, G. S. *MMPI handbook: A guide to use in clinical practice and research.* Minneapolis: Univer. of Minnesota Press, 1960.

Dana, R. H. The effects of attitudes towards authority in psychotherapy. *J. clin. Psychol.,* 1954, 10, 350–353.

Dana, R. H. Clinical diagnosis and objective TAT scoring. *J. abnorm. soc. Psychol.,* 1955, 50, 19–24.

Dana, R. H. Proposal for objective scoring of the TAT. *Percept. motor Skills, Monogr. Suppl. No. 1,* 1959.

Daston, P. G., & Sakheim, G. A. Prediction of successful suicide from the Rorschach Test, using a sign approach. *J. project. Tech.,* 1960, 24, 355–361.

Davids, A. Comparison of three methods of personality assessment: direct, indirect, and projective. *J. Pers.,* 1955, 23, 423–440.

Davids, A. Personality dispositions, word frequency and word association. *J. Pers.,* 1956, 24, 328–338.

Davids, A., Joelson, M., & McArthur, C. Rorschach and TAT indices of homosexuality in overt homosexuals, neurotics and normal males. *J. abnorm. soc. Psychol.,* 1956, 53, 161–172.

Davids, A., & Rosenblatt, D. Use of the TAT in assessment of the personality syndrome of alienation. *J. project. Tech.,* 1958, 22, 145–152.

DeVos, G. A. A quantitative approach to affective symbolism in Rorschach responses. *J. project. Tech.,* 1952, 16, 133–150.

Dombrose, L. A., & Slobin, M. S. The IES Test. *Percept. motor Skills, Monogr. Suppl.,* 1958, 8, 347–389.

Dymond, Rosalind F. Adjustment changes over therapy from Thematic Apperception Test ratings. In C. R. Rogers & Rosalind F. Dymond (Eds.), *Personality changes and psychotherapy.* Chicago: Univer. of Chicago Press, 1954. Pp. 109–120.

Ebel, R. L. Must all tests be valid? *Amer. Psychologist,* 1961, 16, 640–647.

Edwards, A. L. *Edwards Personal Preference Schedule.* New York: Psychological Corp., 1954.

Edwards, A. L. *The social desirability variable in personality assessment and research.* New York: Dryden, 1957.

Efron, H. Y. An attempt to employ a sentence completion test for the detection of psychiatric patients with suicidal ideas. *J. consult. Psychol.,* 1960, 24, 156–160.

Eichler, R. A comparison of the Rorschach and Behn-Rorschach Inkblot Tests. *J. consult. Psychol.,* 1951, 15, 185–189. (a)

Eichler, R. M. Experimental stress and alleged Rorschach indices of anxiety. *J. abnorm. soc. Psychol.,* 1951, 46, 344–355. (b)

Elizur, A. Content analysis of the Rorschach with regard to anxiety and hostility. *J. project. Tech.,* 1949, 13, 247–284.

Ellis, A. The Blacky Test used with a psychoanalytic patient. *J. clin. Psychol.,* 1953, 9, 167–172.

Epstein, S., & Smith, R. Thematic apperception as a measure of the hunger drive. *J. project. Tech.,* 1956, 20, 372–384.

Ericksen, C. W. Some implications for TAT interpretation arising from need and perception experiments. *J. Pers.,* 1951, 19, 282–288.

Ericksen, C. W., & Lazarus, R. S. Perceptual defense and projective tests. *J. abnorm. soc. Psychol.,* 1952, 47, 302–308.

Ericksen, C. W., Lazarus, R. S., & Strange, J. R. Stress and its personality correlates. *J. Pers.,* 1952, 20, 277–286.

Eron, L. D. A normative study of the Thematic Apperception Test. *Psychol. Monogr.,* 1950, 64, No. 9.

Eron, L. D. Responses of women to the Thematic Apperception Test. *J. consult. Psychol.,* 1953, 17, 269–282.

Eron, L. D., & Ritter, Anne M. A comparison of two methods of administration of the Thematic Apperception Test. *J. consult. Psychol.,* 1951, 15, 55–61.

Eron, L. D., Terry, Dorothy, & Callahan, R. The use of rating scales for emotional tone of TAT stories. *J. consult. Psychol.,* 1950, 14, 473–478.

Fein, Leah G. Rorschach signs of homosexuality in male college students. *J. clin. Psychol.,* 1950, 6, 248–253.

Feldman, M. J., & Hunt, R. G. The relation of difficulty in drawing to rating of adjustment based on human figure drawing. *J. consult. Psychol.,* 1958, 22, 217–219.

Fenz, W. D., & Epstein, S. Measurement of approach-avoidance conflict by a stimulus dimension in a test of thematic apperception. *J. Pers.,* 1962, 30, 613–632.

Feshbach, S. The drive-reducing function of fantasy behavior. *J. abnorm. soc. Psychol.,* 1955, 50, 3–11.

Feshbach, S. The effects of emotional restraint upon the projection of positive affect. *J. Pers.,* 1963, 31, 471–481.

Feshbach, S., & Feshbach, Norma. The influence of the stimulus object upon the complementary and supplementary projection of fear. *J. abnorm. soc. Psychol.,* 1963, 66, 498–502.

Feshbach, S., & Singer, R. D. The effects of fear arousal and suppression of fear upon social perception. *J. abnorm. soc. Psychol.,* 1957, 55, 283–288.

Filmer-Bennett, G. Prognostic indices in the Rorschach records of hospitalized patients. *J. abnorm. soc. Psychol.,* 1952, 47, 502–506.

Finney, B. C. Rorschach correlates of assultive behavior. *J. project. Tech.,* 1955, 19, 6–16.

Fisher, F., & Fisher, R. Test of certain assumptions regarding figure drawing analysis. *J. abnorm. soc. Psychol.,* 1950, 45, 727–732.

Fisher, G. M. Nudity in human figure drawings. *J. clin. Psychol.,* 1961, 17, 307–308.

Fisher, S. The value of the Rorschach for detecting suicidal trends. *J. project. Tech.,* 1951, 15, 250–254.

Fisher, S. Body reactivity gradients and figure drawing variables. *J. consult. Psychol.,* 1959, 23, 54–59.

Fisher, S., & Cleveland, S. E. *Body image and personality.* Princeton, N.J.: Van Nostrand, 1958.

Fiske, D. W., & Baughman, E. E. Relationships between Rorschach scoring categories and the total number of responses. *J. abnorm. soc. Psychol.,* 1953, 48, 25–32.

Fiske, D. W., & Van Buskirk, C. The stability of interpretations of sentence completion tests. *J. consult. Psychol.,* 1959, 23, 177–180.

Fitzgerald, B. G. Some relationships among projective test, interview and sociometric measures of dependent behavior. *J. abnorm. soc. Psychol.,* 1958, 56, 199–203.

Ford, M. The application of the Rorschach test to young children. *Univer. of Minnesota*

Institute of Child Welfare Monogr., 1946, No. 23.

Forer, B. R. A structured sentence completion test. *J. project. Tech.*, 1950, 14, 15–30.

Forer, B. R. Sentence completions. In A. C. Carr *et al.* (Eds.), *The prediction of overt behavior through the use of projective techniques*. Springfield, Ill.: Charles C Thomas, 1960. Pp. 6–17.

Forer, B. R., Rabin, A. I., Goldstein, F. J., & Lesser, G. S. Custom-built projective methods: A symposium. *J. project. Tech.*, 1961, 25, 3–31.

Franck, K., & Rosen, E. A projective test of masculinity-femininity. *J. consult. Psychol.*, 1949, 13, 247–256.

Frank, G. A test of the use of a figure drawing test as an indicator of sexual inversion. *Psychol. Rep.*, 1955, 1, 137–138.

Frank, L. K. Projective methods for the study of personality. *J. Psychol.*, 1939, 8, 389–413.

Frank, L. K. *Projective methods*. Springfield, Ill.: Charles C Thomas, 1948.

French, E. G. Some characteristics of achievement motivation. *J. abnorm. soc. Psychol.*, 1955, 50, 232–236.

French, E. G. Development of a measure of complex motivation. In J. W. Atkinson (Ed.), *Motives in fantasy, action, and society*. Princeton, N.J.: Van Nostrand, 1958. Pp. 242–248.

French, E. G., & Thomas, F. H. The relation of achievement motivation to problem-solving effectiveness. *J. abnorm. soc. Psychol.*, 1958, 56, 45–48.

Friedman, I. Characteristics of the Thematic Apperception Test heroes of normal, psychoneurotic, and paranoid schizophrenic subjects. *J. project. Tech.*, 1957, 21, 372–376.

Fromm, Erika, & Elonen, Anna. The use of projective techniques in the study of a case of female homosexuality. *J. project. Tech.*, 1951, 15, 185–230.

Gibby, R. G. Examiner influence on the Rorschach inquiry. *J. consult. Psychol.*, 1952, 16, 449–455.

Gibby, R. G., Stotsky, B. A., Miller, D. R., & Hiler, E. W. Prediction of duration of therapy from the Rorschach test. *J. consult. Psychol.*, 1953, 17, 348–354.

Gibby, R. G., Stotsky, B. A., Hiler, E. W., & Miller, D. R. Validation of Rorschach criteria for predicting duration of therapy. *J. consult. Psychol.*, 1954, 18, 185–191.

Gluck, M. R. Relationship between hostility in the TAT and behavioral hostility. *J. project. Tech.*, 1955, 19, 21–26.

Goldberg, L. R. The effectiveness of clinician's judgments: the diagnosis of organic brain damage from the Bender-Gestalt Test. *J. consult. Psychol.*, 1959, 23, 25–33.

Goldenberg, H. C. A resume of some Make-A-Picture-Story (MAPS) test results. *J. project. Tech.*, 1951, 15, 79–86.

Goldman, A. E., & Herman, J. L. Studies in vicariousness: The effect of immobilization on Rorschach movement responses. *J. project. Tech.*, 1961, 25, 164–165.

Goldstein, A. P., & Rawn, M. L. The validity of interpretive signs of aggression in the drawing of the human figure. *J. clin. Psychol.*, 1957, 13, 169–171.

Goodstein, L. Interrelationships among several measures of anxiety and hostility. *J. consult. Psychol.*, 1954, 18, 35–39.

Gore, Pearl M., & Rotter, J. B. A personality correlate of social action. *J. Pers.*, 1963, 31, 58–64.

Goss, A. E., & Brownell, Marjorie H. Stimulus-response concepts and principles applied to projective test behavior. *J. Pers.*, 1957, 25, 505–523.

Grams, A., & Rinder, L. Signs of homosexuality in human-figure drawings. *J. consult. Psychol.*, 1958, 22, 394.

Grant, Marguerite Q., Ives, Virginia, & Ranzoni, Jane H. Reliability and validity of judge's ratings of adjustment on the Rorschach. *Psychol. Monogr.*, 1952, 66, 1–20.

Green, B. F. Attitude measurement. In G. Lindzey (Ed.), *Handbook of social psychology*. Cambridge, Mass.: Addison-Wesley, 1954. Pp. 335–369.

Grimes, J. W., & Allinsmith, W. Compulsivity, anxiety and school achievement. *Merrill-Palmer Quart.*, 1961, 7, 247–272.

Gross, L. Effects of verbal and nonverbal reinforcement in the Rorschach. *J. consult. Psychol.*, 1959, 23, 66–68.

Guilford, J. P. New standards for test evaluation. *Educ. psychol. Measmt*, 1946, 6, 427–438.

Guilford, J. P. *Psychometric methods*. New York: McGraw-Hill, 1954.

Gulliksen, H. *Theory of mental tests*. New York: Wiley, 1950.

Gurel, L., & Ullmann, L. P. Quantitative differences in response to TAT cards: The relationship between transcendence score and number of emotional words. *J. project. Tech.*, 1958, 22, 432–439.

Hafner, A. J., & Kaplan, A. M. Hostility content analysis of the Rorschach and TAT. *J. project. Tech.*, 1960, 24, 137–143.

Hamlin, R. M., Albee, G. W., & Leland, E. M. Objective Rorschach "signs" for groups of normal, maladjusted and neuropsychiatric subjects. *J. consult. Psychol.*, 1950, 14, 276–282.

Hanfmann, Eugenia, & Getzels, J. W. Studies of the Sentence Completion Test. *J. project. Tech.*, 1953, 17, 280–294.

Harrison, R. Studies in the use and validity of the Thematic Apperception Test with mentally disordered patients. II. A quantitative validity study. III. Validation by the method of "blind analysis." *Charact. Pers.*, 1940, 9, 122–138.

Harrower, Molly R., & Steiner, Matilda E. *Large scale Rorschach techniques: a manual for the group Rorschach and multiple-choice test.* Springfield, Ill.: Charles C Thomas, 1945.

Harrower-Erickson, M. R. The value and limitations of the so-called 'neurotic signs.' *Rorschach Res. Exchange,* 1942, 6, 109–114.

Harrower, Molly R. The Most Unpleasant Concept Test: a graphic projective technique. *J. clin. Psychol.*, 1950, 6, 213–233.

Hartman, A. A. An experimental examination of the Thematic Apperception Technique in clinical diagnosis. *Psychol. Monogr.*, 1949, 63, No. 8.

Hartshorne, H., & May, M. A. *Studies in deceit.* New York: Macmillan, 1928.

Hartwell, S., Walton, R. E., Andrew, G., & Hutt, M. L. *The Michigan Picture Test.* Chicago: Science Research Associates, 1955.

Haskell, R. J., Jr. Relationship between aggressive behavior and psychological tests. *J. project. Tech.*, 1961, 25, 431–440.

Hedwig, Eleanor B. Stability of early recollections and thematic apperception stories. *J. individ. Psychol.*, 1963, 19, 49–54.

Henry, E. M., & Rotter, J. B. Situational influences on Rorschach responses. *J. consult. Psychol.*, 1956, 20, 457–462.

Henry, W. E. The Thematic Apperception Technique in the study of culture-personality relations. *Genet. Psychol. Monogr.*, 1947, 35, 3–135.

Henry, W. E., & Farley, Jane. The validity of the Thematic Apperception Test in the study of adolescent personality. *Psychol. Monogr.*, 1959, 73, No. 17.

Herron, W. G. IES Test patterns of accepted and rejected adolescents. *Percept. motor Skills,* 1962, 15, 435–438.

Hertz, Marguerite R. The reliability of the Rorschach Inkblot Test. *J. appl. Psychol.*, 1934, 18, 461–477.

Hertz, Marguerite R. Suicidal configurations in Rorschach records. *Rorschach Res. Exchange & J. project. Tech.*, 1948, 12, 3–58.

Hertz, Marguerite R. Further study of 'suicidal' configurations in Rorschach records. *Rorschach Res. Exchange,* 1949, 13, 44–73.

Hertz, Marguerite R. *Frequency tables for scoring responses to the Rorschach Inkblot Test.* Cleveland: Western Reserve Univer. Press, 1951. (a)

Hertz, Marguerite R. Current problems in Rorschach theory and technique. *J. project. Tech.*, 1951, 15, 307–338. (b)

Hertz, Marguerite R. The use and misuse of the Rorschach method: I. Variations in Rorschach procedure. *J. project. Tech.*, 1959, 23, 33–48.

Hertz, Marguerite R. Current problems in Rorschach theory and technique. In M. Wirt (Ed.), *Rorschach Science*. Glencoe, Ill.: Free Press, 1962. Pp. 391–430.

Hiler, E. W. The sentence completion test as a predictor of continuation in psychotherapy. *J. consult. Psychol.*, 1959, 23, 544–549.

Hokanson, J. E., & Gordon, J. E. The expression and inhibition of hostility in imaginative and overt behavior. *J. abnorm. soc. Psychol.*, 1958, 57, 327–333.

Holsopple, J. Q., & Phelan, J. G. The skills of clinicians in analysis of projective tests. *J. clin. Psychol.*, 1954, 10, 307–320

Holt, R. R. Formal aspects of the TAT: a neglected resource. *J. project. Tech.*, 1958, 22, 163–172.

Holtzman, W. H. Validation studies of the Rorschach test: Impulsiveness in the normal superior adult. *J. clin. Psychol.*, 1950, 6, 348–351. (a)

Holtzman, W. H. Validation studies of the Rorschach test: shyness and gregariousness in the normal superior adult. *J. clin. Psychol.*, 1950, 6, 343–347. (b)

Holtzman, W. H. *Holtzman Inkblot Tech-*

nique. Form A. New York: Psychological Corp., 1958. (a)

Holtzman, W. H. *Holtzman Inkblot Technique*. Form B. New York: Psychological Corp., 1958. (b)

Holtzman, W. H., & Sells, S. B. Prediction of flying success by clinical analysis of test protocols. *J. abnorm. soc. Psychol.*, 1954, 49, 485–490.

Holtzman, W. H., Thorpe, J. S., Swartz, J. D., & Herron, E. W. *Inkblot perception and personality: Holtzman Inkblot Technique*. Austin: Univer. of Texas Press, 1961.

Holzberg, J. D. Reliability re-examined. In Maria A. Rickers-Ovsiankina (Ed.), *Rorschach psychology*. New York: Wiley, 1960. Pp. 361–379.

Holzberg, J. D., & Wexler, M. The predictability of schizophrenic performance on the Rorschach test. *J. consult. Psychol.*, 1950, 14, 395–399.

Hornberger, R. H. The projective effects of fear and sexual arousal on the rating of pictures. *J. clin. Psychol.*, 1960, 16, 328–331.

Horowitz, Miriam J. A study of clinician's judgments from projective test protocols. *J. consult. Psychol.*, 1962, 26, 251–256.

Horst, P. Estimating total test reliability from parts of unequal length. *Educ. psychol. Measmt*, 1951, 11, 368–371.

Hovland, C. I., Lumsdaine, A. A., & Sheffield, F. D. *Experiments on mass communication*. Princeton: Princeton Univer. Press, 1949.

Howard, J. W. The Howard Ink Blot Test. *J. clin. Psychol.*, 1953, 9, 209-255.

Howard, J. W. *The Howard Ink Blot Test.* Brandon, Vt.: Journal of Clinical Psychology, 1960.

Howard, K. I. The convergent and discriminant validation of ipsative ratings from three projective instruments. *J. clin. Psychol.*, 1962, 18, 183–188.

Howard, K. I. Differentiation of individuals as a function of repeated testing. *Educ. psychol. Measmt*, 1964, 24, 875–894.

Howard, K. I., & Diesenhaus, H. 16PF item response patterns as a function of repeated testing. *Educ. psychol. Measmt*, 1965, in press.

Hoyt, T. E., & Baron, M. R. Anxiety indices in same-sex drawings of psychiatric patients with high and low MAS scores. *J. consult. Psychol.*, 1959, 23, 448–452.

Hughes, R. M. Rorschach signs for the diagnosis of organic pathology. *Rorschach Res. Exchange*, 1948, 12, 165–167.

Humphreys, L. G. Note on the multitrait-multimethod matrix. *Psychol. Bull.*, 1960, 57, 86–88.

Hunt, J. McV., & Cofer, C. N. Psychological deficit in schizophrenia. In J. McV. Hunt (Ed.), *Personality and the behavior disorders*. Vol. 2. New York: Ronald Press, 1944. Pp. 971–1032.

Hunter, M. E. The practical value of the Rorschach test in a psychological clinic. *Amer. J. Orthopsychiat.*, 1939, 9, 287–294.

Jackson, Marilyn. The effects of frequency, extremeness, consistency, and order of the stimulus on clinical judgment. Unpublished doctoral dissertation, Northwestern Univer., 1962.

Jackson, Marilyn, & Sechrest, L. Early recollections in four neurotic diagnostic categories. *J. individ. Psychol.*, 1962, 18, 52–56.

Jacobs, A. Formation of new associations to words selected on the basis of reaction-time-GSR combinations. *J. abnorm. soc. Psychol.*, 1955, 51, 371–378.

Jacobs, R. C., & Campbell, D. T. The perpetuation of an arbitrary tradition through several generations of a laboratory microculture. *J. abnorm. soc. Psychol.*, 1961, 62, 649–658.

Jensen, A. R. Aggression in fantasy and overt behavior. *Psychol. Monogr.*, 1957, 71, 1–13.

Jensen, A. R. Personality. *Annu. Rev. Psychol.*, 1958, 9, 295–322.

Jensen, M. B., & Rotter, J. B. The value of 13 psychological tests in officer candidate screening. *J. appl. Psychol.*, 1947, 31, 312–322.

Jessor, R., & Hammond, K. R. Construct validity and the Taylor Anxiety Scale. *Psychol. Bull.*, 1957, 54, 161–170.

Jung, C. G. The association method. *Amer. J. Psychol.*, 1910, 21, 219–270.

Kagan, J. The measurement of overt aggression from fantasy. *J. abnorm. soc. Psychol.*, 1956, 52, 390–393.

Kagan, J. The stability of TAT fantasy and stimulus ambiguity. *J. consult. Psychol.*, 1959, 23, 266–271.

Kagan, J. Stylistic variables in fantasy behavior: The ascription of affect states to social stimuli. In J. Kagan & G. S. Lesser (Eds.), *Contemporary issues in thematic apperceptive methods*. Springfield, Ill.: Charles C Thomas, 1961. Pp. 196–220.

Kagan, J., & Lesser, G. S. *Contemporary issues in thematic apperceptive methods.* Springfield, Ill.: Charles C Thomas, 1961.

Kagan, J., & Mussen, P. H. Dependency themes on the TAT and group conformity. *J. consult. Psychol.,* 1956, 20, 29–32.

Kane, F. Clothing worn by outpatients to interviews. *Psychiat. Commun.,* 1958, 1, No. 2.

Kane, F. Clothing worn by an outpatient: a case study. *Psychiat. Commun.,* 1959, 2, No. 2.

Kane, F. The meaning of the form of clothing. *Psychiat. Commun.,* 1962, 5, No. 1.

Kanfer, F. H. Verbal rate, eyeblink, and content in structured psychiatric interviews. *J. abnorm. soc. Psychol.,* 1960, 61, 341–347.

Kaplan, B. Projective techniques and the theory of action. *Merrill-Palmer Quart.,* 1963, 9, 3–10.

Kaplan, B., & Berger, S. Increments and consistency of performance in four repeated Rorschach administrations. *J. project. Tech.,* 1956, 3, 304–309.

Kaswan, J., Wasman, M., & Freedman, L. Z. Aggression and the Picture-Frustration Study. *J. consult. Psychol.,* 1960, 24, 446–452.

Kelly, D. M., Margulies, H., & Barrera, S. E. The stability of the Rorschach method as demonstrated in electric convulsive therapy cases. *Rorschach Res. Exchange,* 1941, 5, 35–43.

Kelly, E. L., & Fiske, D. W. *The prediction of performance in clinical psychology.* Ann Arbor: Univer. of Michigan Press, 1951.

Kenny, D. T. Transcendence indices, extent of personality factors in fantasy responses, and the ambiguity of TAT cards. *J. consult. Psychol.,* 1954, 18, 345–348.

Kenny, D. T., & Bijou, S. W. Ambiguity of pictures and extent of personality factors in fantasy responses. *J. consult. Psychol.,* 1953, 17, 283–288.

Keys, A., Brozek, J., Henschel, A., Mickelson, O., & Taylor, H. L. *Experimental starvation in man.* Minneapolis: Laboratory of Physiological Hygiene, Univer. of Minnesota, 1945.

Kirkner, F. J., Wisham, W. W., & Giedt, F. H. A report on the validity of the Rorschach prognostic rating scale. *J. project. Tech.,* 1953, 17, 465–478.

Klein, G. S., Salomon, Ann D., & Smith, J. W. G. Studies in cognitive style and the regulation of need. Unpublished manuscript, 1959. Cited in R. Stagner. *Psychology of personality* (3rd ed.) New York: McGraw-Hill, 1961.

Knopf, I. J. The Rorschach test and psychotherapy. *Amer. J. Orthopsychiat.,* 1956, 26, 801–806. (a)

Knopf, I. J. Rorschach summary scores in differential diagnosis. *J. consult. Psychol.,* 1956, 20, 99–104. (b)

Kobler, F. J., & Steil, Agnes. The use of the Rorschach in involutional melancholia. *J. consult. Psychol.,* 1953, 17, 365–370.

Kostlan, A. A method for the empirical study of psychodiagnosis. *J. consult. Psychol.,* 1954, 18, 83–88.

Kotkov, B., & Meadow, A. Rorschach criteria for predicting continuation in individual psychotherapy. *J. consult. Psychol.,* 1953, 17, 16–20.

Krugman, J. I. A clinical validation of the Rorschach with problem children. *Rorschach Res. Exchange,* 1942, 6, 61–69.

Kuder, G. F., & Richardson, M. W. The theory of the estimation of test reliability. *Psychometrika,* 1937, 2, 151–160.

Lagmay, A. Preliminary report: Development and construction of the Philippine Thematic Apperception Test. Paper delivered at annual convention of The Psychological Association of the Philippines, 1964.

Lawshe, C. H., & Forster, M. H. Studies in projective techniques: I. The reliability of a multiple choice group Rorschach test. *J. appl. Psychol.,* 1947, 31, 199–211.

Lazarus, R. J. Ambiguity and nonambiguity in projective testing. *J. abnorm. soc. Psychol.,* 1953, 48, 443–445.

Lazarus, R. S. A substitutive-defensive conception of apperceptive fantasy. In J. Kagan & G. S. Lesser (Eds.), *Contemporary issues in thematic apperceptive methods.* Springfield, Ill.: Charles C Thomas, 1961. Pp. 51–71.

Lebo, D., & Harrigan, Margaret. Visual and verbal presentation of TAT stimuli. *J. consult. Psychol.,* 1957, 21, 339–342.

Lebo, D., & Sherry, P. J. Visual and verbal presentation of TAT descriptions. *J. project. Tech.,* 1959, 23, 59–63.

Ledwith, Nettie H. *Rorschach responses of elementary school children: a normative study.* Pittsburgh: Univer. of Pittsburgh Press, 1959.

Lefkowitz, M., Blake, R. R., & Mouton, J. S. Status factors in pedestrian violation of traffic signals. *J. abnorm. soc. Psychol.,* 1955, 51, 704–706.

Leiman, A. H., & Epstein, S. Thematic sexual responses as related to sexual drive and guilt. *J. abnorm. soc. Psychol.,* 1961, 63, 169–175.

Leipold, W. D. Psychological distance in a dyadic interview as a function of introversion-extraversion, anxiety, social desirability and stress. Unpublished doctoral dissertation, Univer. of North Dakota, 1963.

Lennep, D. J. *Four-picture test.* The Hague: M. Nijhoff, 1948.

Lesser, G. S. The relationship between overt and fantasy aggression as a function of maternal response to aggression. *J. abnorm. soc. Psychol.,* 1957, 55, 218–221.

Lesser, G. S. Conflict analysis of fantasy aggression. *J. Pers.,* 1958, 26, 29–41.

Lesser, G. S. Population differences in construct validity. *J. consult. Psychol.,* 1959, 23, 60–65.

Lessing, Elise E. Prognostic value of the Rorschach in a child guidance clinic. *J. project. Tech.,* 1960, 24, 310–321.

Leventhal, H. The effects of perceptual training on the Rorschach W and Z scores. *J. consult. Psychol.,* 1956, 20, 93–98.

Levinger, G., & Clark, J. Emotional factors in the forgetting of word associations. *J. abnorm. soc. Psychol.,* 1961, 62, 99–105.

Levitt, E. E., Lubin, B., & Zuckerman, M. A simplified method of scoring Rorschach content for dependency. *J. project. Tech.,* 1962, 26, 234–236.

Levy, B. I., Lomax, J. V., & Minsky, R. An underlying variable in the clinical evaluation of drawings of the human figure. *J. consult. Psychol.,* 1963, 27, 508–512.

Levy, L. H. Movement as a "rhetorical embellishment" of human percepts. *J. consult. Psychol.,* 1955, 19, 469–471.

Levy, L. H. *Psychological interpretation.* New York: Holt, Rinehart and Winston, 1963.

Light, B. H. Comparative study of a series of TAT and CAT cards. *J. clin. Psychol.,* 1954, 10, 179–181.

Lindner, R. M. The content analysis of the Rorschach protocol. In L. E. Abt & L. Bellak (Eds.), *Projective psychology.* New York: Knopf, 1950, 75–90.

Lindzey, G. An experimental test of the validity of the Rosenzweig Picture-Frustration Study. *J. Pers.,* 1950, 18, 315–320.

Lindzey, G. Thematic Apperception Test: Interpretive assumptions and related empirical evidence. *Psychol. Bull.,* 1952, 49, 1–25.

Lindzey, G. *Projective techniques and cross-cultural research.* New York: Appleton-Century-Crofts, 1961.

Lindzey, G., & Heinemann, Shirley H. Thematic Apperception Test: Individual and group administration. *J. Pers.,* 1955, 24, 34–55.

Lindzey, G., & Kalnins, D. Thematic Apperception Test: Some evidence bearing on the "Hero Assumption." *J. abnorm. soc. Psychol.,* 1958, 57, 76–83.

Lindzey, G., & Newburg, A. S. Thematic Apperception Test: A tentative appraisal of some "signs" of anxiety. *J. consult. Psychol.,* 1954, 18, 389–395.

Lindzey, G., & Silverman, M. Thematic Apperception Test: Techniques of group administration, sex differences, and the role of verbal productivity. *J. Pers.,* 1959, 27, 311–323.

Lindzey, G., & Tejessy, C. Thematic Apperception Test: Indices of aggression in relation to measures of overt and covert behavior. *Amer. J. Orthopsychiat.,* 1956, 26, 567–576.

Lindzey, G., Tejessy, C., & Zamansky, H. Thematic Apperception Test: An empirical examination of some indices of homosexuality. *J. abnorm. soc. Psychol.,* 1958, 57, 67–75.

Little, K. B., & Shneidman, E. S. The validity of the thematic projective technique interpretations. *J. Pers.,* 1955, 23, 285–294.
among interpretations of psychological test

Little, K. B., & Shneidman, E. S. Congruencies among interpretations of psychological test and anamnestic data. *Psychol. Monogr.,* 1959, 73, No. 6.

Loevinger, Jane. A systematic approach to the construction and evaluation of tests of ability. *Psychol. Monogr.,* 1947, 61, No. 4.

Loevinger, Jane. The attenuation paradox in test theory. *Psychol. Bull.,* 1954, 51, 493–504.

Loevinger, Jane. Objective tests as instruments of psychological theory. *Psychol. Rep., Monogr. Suppl. No. 9,* 1957, 3, 635–694.

Lord, Edith. Two sets of Rorschach records obtained before and after brief psychotherapy. *J. consult. Psychol.,* 1950, 14, 134–139. (a)

Lord, Edith. Experimentally induced variations in Rorschach performance. *Psychol.*

Monogr., 1950, 64, No. 10. (Whole No. 316 (b).

Lord, F. M. A theory of test scores. *Psychomet. Monogr.*, 1952, No. 7.

Lord, F. M. Some perspectives on "the attenuation paradox in test theory." *Psychol. Bull.*, 1955, 52, 505–510.

Lotsoff, E. J. Intelligence, verbal fluency and the Rorschach test. *J. consult. Psychol.*, 1953, 17, 21–24.

Lowenfeld, Margaret. *The Lowenfeld Mosaic Test.* London: Newman Neame, 1954.

Lubetsky, J. Assimilative projection as measured by trait attribution. Unpublished doctoral dissertation, Northwestern Univer., 1960.

McArthur, C. The effects of need achievement on the content of TAT stories: a re-examination. *J. abnorm. soc. Psychol.*, 1953, 48, 532–536.

MacBrayer, Caroline T. Relationship between story length and situational validity of the TAT. *J. project. Tech.*, 1959, 23, 345–350.

McCary, J. L. Picture-Frustration Study normative data for some cultural and racial groups. *J. clin. Psychol.*, 1956, 12, 194–195.

McClelland, D. C. The use of measures of human motivation in the study of society. In J. W. Atkinson (Ed.), *Motives in fantasy, action, and society.* Princeton, N.J.: Van Nostrand, 1958. Pp. 518–552.

McClelland, D. C., & Atkinson, J. W. The projective expression of needs: I. The effect of different intensities of the hunger drive on perception. *J. Psychol.*, 1948, 25, 205–222.

McClelland, D. C., Atkinson, J. W., Clark, R. A., & Lowell, E. L. *The achievement motive.* New York: Appleton-Century-Crofts, 1953.

McClelland, D. C., Clark, R. A., & Roby, T. B. The effect of the need for achievement on thematic apperception. *J. exp. Psychol.*, 1949, 37, 242–255.

MacCorquodale, K., & Meehl, P. E. On a distinction between hypothetical constructs and intervening variables. *Psychol. Rev.*, 1948, 55, 95–107.

Macfarlane, Jean W., & Tuddenham, R. D. Problems in the validation of projective techniques. In H. H. & Gladys Anderson (Eds.), *An introduction to projective techniques.* Englewood Cliffs, N.J.: Prentice-Hall, 1951.

McGuigan, F. J. *Experimental psychology.* Englewood Cliffs, N.J.: Prentice-Hall, 1960.

Machover, Karen. *Personality projection in the drawing of the human figure.* Springfield, Ill.: Charles C Thomas, 1948.

Machover, Karen. Drawing of the human figure: a method of personality investigation. In H. H. & Gladys Anderson (Eds.), *An introduction to projective techniques.* Englewood Cliffs, N.J.: Prentice-Hall, 1951. Pp. 341–369.

MacIntosh, Shirley P., & Maher, B. A. The relationship of verbal fluency to sentence completion series in anxious and non-anxious subjects. Unpublished manuscript, Northwestern Univer., 1955. (Mimeographed)

McIntyre, C. J. Sex, age and iconicity as factors in projective film tests. *J. consult. Psychol.*, 1954, 18, 475–477.

Magnusson, D. *A study of ratings based on TAT.* Stockholm: Swedish Council for Personnel Administration, 1959.

Maher, B. A., Watt, N., & Campbell, D. T. Comparative validity of two projective and two structured attitude tests in a prison population. *J. appl. Psychol.*, 1960, 44, 284–288.

Mainord, Florence R. A note on the use of figure drawings in the diagnosis of sexual inversion. *J. clin. Psychol.*, 1953, 9, 188–189.

Mandler, G., Lindzey, G., & Crouch, R. G. Thematic apperception test: Indices of anxiety in relation to test anxiety. *Educ. psychol. Measmt,* 1957, 17, 466–474.

Marlowe, D. Relationships among direct and indirect measures of the achievement motive and overt behavior. *J. consult. Psychol.*, 1959, 23, 329–332.

Martin, B. Expression and inhibition of sex motive arousal in college males. *J. abnorm. soc. Psychol.*, 1964, 68, 307–312.

Masling, J. M. The effects of warm and cold interaction on the interpretation of a projective protocol. *J. project. Tech.*, 1957, 21, 377–383.

Masling, J. M. The effects of warm and cold interaction on the administration and scoring of an intelligence test. *J. consult. Psychol.*, 1959, 23, 336–341.

Masling, J. M. The influence of situational and interpersonal variables in projective testing. *Psychol. Bull.*, 1960, 57, 65–85.

Matarazzo, J. D. An experimental study of aggression in the hypertensive patient. *J. Pers.*, 1954, 22, 423–447.

Meehl, P. E. Wanted—A good cookbook. *Amer. Psychol.,* 1956, 11, 263–272.

Meehl, P. E. Structured and projective tests: some common problems in validation. *J. project. Tech.,* 1959, 23, 268–272.

Meehl, P. E. The cognitive activity of the clinician. *Amer. Psychol.,* 1960, 15, 19–27.

Meehl, P. E., & Rosen, A. Antecedent probability and the efficiency of psychometric signs, patterns or cutting scores. *Psychol. Bull.,* 1955, 52, 194–216.

Meer, B., & Amon, A. H. Photos preference test (PPT) as a measure of mental status for hospitalized psychiatric patients. *J. consult. Psychol.,* 1963, 27, 283–293

Meltzoff, J., Singer, J. L., & Korchin, S. J. Motor inhibition and Rorschach movement responses: a test of the sensory-tonic theory. *J. Pers.,* 1953, 21, 400–410.

Merritt, C. B., & Fowler, R. G. The pecuniary honesty of the public at large. *J. abnorm. soc. Psychol.,* 1948, 43, 90–93.

Miale, Florence, & Harrower-Erickson, Molly R. Personality structure in psychoneuroses. *Rorschach Res. Exchange,* 1940, 4, 71–74.

Miller, D. R. Prediction of behavior by means of the Rorschach test. *J. abnorm. soc. Psychol.,* 1953, 48, 367–375.

Mintz, Elizabeth E., Schmeidler, G. R., & Bristol, M. Rorschach changes during psychoanalysis. *J. project. Tech.,* 1956, 20, 414–417.

Montague, J. A. Spontaneous drawings of the human form in childhood schizophrenia. In H. H. and Gladys Anderson (Eds.), *An introduction to projective techniques.* Englewood Cliffs, N.J.: Prentice-Hall, 1951. Pp. 370–385.

Moore, M. E., & Schwartz, M. M. The effect of the sex of the frustrated figure on responses to the Rosenzweig P-F Study. *J. project. Tech. Pers. Assessment,* 1963, 27, 195–199.

Moos, R. H. Effects of training on students' test interpretations. *J. project. Tech.,* 1962, 26, 310–317.

More, D. M. The congruence of projective instruments in personnel assessment. *J. appl. Psychol.,* 1957, 41, 137–140.

Morgan, C. D., & Murray, H. A. A method for investigating fantasies. *Arch. Neurol. Psychiat.,* 1935, 34, 289–306.

Mosak, H. H. Early recollections as a projective technique. *J. project. Tech.,* 1958, 22, 302–311.

Muench, G. A. An evaluation of non-directive psychotherapy by means of the Rorschach and other indices. *Appl. Psychol. Monogr.,* 1947, 13, 163.

Murray, D. C., & Deabler, H. Drawings, diagnoses and the clinician's learning curve. *J. project. Tech.,* 1958, 22, 415–420.

Murray, E. J. Conflict and repression during sleep deprivation. *J. abnorm. soc. Psychol.,* 1959, 59, 95–101.

Murray, H. A. The effect of fear upon estimates of the maliciousness of other personalities. *J. soc. Psychol.,* 1933, 4, 310–339.

Murray, H. A. *Thematic Apperception Test Manual.* Cambridge, Mass.: Harvard Univer. Press, 1943.

Murray, H. A., MacKinnon, D. W., Miller, J. G., Fiske, D. W., & Hanfmann, Eugenia. *Assessment of men.* New York: Rinehart, 1948.

Murstein, B. I. The projection of hostility on the Rorschach and as a result of ego threat. *J. project. Tech.,* 1956, 20, 418–428.

Murstein, B. I. The relationship of stimulus ambiguity on the TAT to the productivity of themes. *J. consult. Psychol.,* 1958, 22, 348. (a)

Murstein, B. I. Some determinants of the perception of hostility. *J. consult. Psychol.,* 1958, 22, 65–69. (b)

Murstein, B. I. A conceptual model of projective techniques applied to stimulus variations with thematic techniques. *J. consult. Psychol.,* 1959, 23, 3–14.

Murstein, B. I. Assumptions, adaptation-level, and projective techniques. *Percept. motor Skills, Monogr. Suppl.,* 1961, 12, 107–125. (a)

Murstein, B. I. The role of the stimulus in the manifestation of fantasy. In J. Kagan & G. S. Lesser (Eds.), *Contemporary issues in thematic apperceptive methods.* Springfield, Ill.: Charles C Thomas, 1961. (b)

Murstein, B. I. *Theory and research in projective techniques.* New York: Wiley, 1963.

Murstein, B. I., & Collier, H. L. The role of the TAT in the measurement of achievement as a function of expectancy. *J. project. Tech.,* 1962, 26, 96–101.

Murstein, B. I., & Pryer, R. S. The concept of projection: a review. *Psychol. Bull.,* 1959, 56, 353–374.

Mussen, P. H., & Kagan, J. Group conformity and perception of parents. *Child Develpm.*, 1958, 20, 57–60.
Mussen, P. H., & Naylor, H. K. The relationships between overt and fantasy aggression. *J. abnorm. soc. Psychol.*, 1954, 49, 235–240.
Napoli, P. J. Finger painting. In H. H. & Gladys Anderson (Eds.), *An introduction to projective techniques*. Englewood Cliffs, N.J.: Prentice-Hall, 1951. Pp. 386–415.
Nelson, J. T., & Epstein, S. Relationships among three measures of conflict over hostility. *J. consult. Psychol.*, 1962, 26, 345–350.
Nichols, R. C., & Strumpfer, D. J. W. A factor analysis of draw-a-person test scores. *J. consult. Psychol.*, 1962, 26, 156–161.
Orne, M. T. On the social psychology of the psychological experiment. *Amer. Psychologist*, 1962, 17, 776–783.
Osterweil, J., & Fiske, D. W. Intra-individual variability in sentence completion responses. *J. abnorm. soc. Psychol.*, 1956, 52, 195–199.
Pacella, B. C., Piotrowski, Z., & Lewis, N. D. C. The effect of electric convulsive therapy on certain personality traits in psychiatric patients. *Amer. J. Psychiat.*, 1947, 104, 83–91.
Palmer, J. O. A dual approach to Rorschach validation: A methodological study. *Psychol. Monogr.*, 1951, 8, 1–27.
Panek, D. M., & Martin, B. The relation between GSR and speech disturbances in psychotherapy. *J. abnorm. soc. Psychol.*, 1959, 58, 402–405.
Pattie, F. A. The effect of hypnotically induced hostility on Rorschach responses. *J. clin. Psychol.*, 1954, 10, 161–164.
Phillips, L., & Smith, J. G. *Rorschach interpretation: advanced technique*. New York: Grune & Stratton, 1953.
Phillipson, H. *The object relations technique*. Glencoe, Ill.: The Free Press, 1955.
Pikunas, J., & Carberry, H. Standardization of the graphoscopic scale: the content of children's drawing. *J. clin. Psychol.*, 1961, 17, 297–301.
Piotrowski, Z. A. A new evaluation of the Thematic Apperception Test. *Psychoanalyt. Rev.*, 1950, 37, 101–127.
Postman, L., & Crutchfield, R. S. The interaction of need, set and stimulus-structure in a cognitive task. *Amer. J. Psychol.*, 1952, 65, 196–217.
Purcell, K. The TAT and antisocial behavior. *J. consult. Psychol.*, 1956, 20, 449–456.
Purcell, K. Some shortcomings in projective test validation. *J. abnorm. soc. Psychol.*, 1958, 57, 115–118.
Rabin, A., Nelson, W., & Clark, Margaret. Rorschach content as a function of perceptual experience and sex of the examiner. *J. clin. Psychol.*, 1954, 10, 188–190.
Ramzy, I., & Pickard, P. M. A study in the reliability of scoring the Rorschach Inkblot Test. *J. genet. Psychol.*, 1949, 40, 3–10.
Rankin, R. J., & Wikoff, R. L. The IES Arrow Dot performance of delinquents and nondelinquents. *Percept. motor Skills*, 1964, 18, 207–210.
Reiman, G. W. The effectiveness of Rorschach elements in the discrimination between neurotic and ambulatory schizophrenics. *J. consult. Psychol.*, 1953, 17, 25–31.
Reitman, W. R., & Atkinson, J. W. Some methodological problems in the use of thematic apperceptive measures of human motives. In J. W. Atkinson (Ed.), *Motives in fantasy, action, and society*. Princeton, N.J.: Van Nostrand, 1958. Pp. 664–683.
Renner, K. E. Must all tests be valid? *Amer. Psychologist*, 1962, 17, 507–508.
Renner, K. E., Maher, B. A., & Campbell, D. T. The validity of a method for scoring sentence-completion responses for anxiety, dependency, and hostility. *J. appl. Psychol.*, 1962, 46, 285–290.
Reznikoff, M., & Nicholas, Alma L. An evaluation of human-figure drawing indicators of paranoid pathology. *J. consult. Psychol.*, 1958, 22, 395–397.
Ribler, R. I. Diagnostic prediction from emphasis on the eye and the ear in human figure drawing. *J. consult. Psychol.*, 1957, 21, 223–225.
Riess, B., Schwartz, E. K., & Cottingham, Alice. An experimental critique of assumptions underlying the Negro version of the TAT. *J. abnorm. soc. Psychol.*, 1950, 45, 700–709.
Rimm, D. Cost efficiency and test prediction. *J. consult. Psychol.*, 1963, 27, 89–91.
Rioch, Margaret J. The use of the Rorschach test in the assessment of change in patients under psychotherapy. *Psychiatry*, 1949, 12, 427–434.
Ritter, Anne M., & Eron, L. D. The use of the Thematic Apperception Test to differen-

tiate normal from abnormal groups. *J. abnorm. soc. Psychol.,* 1952, 47, 147–158.

Roberts, Lynn K. The failure of some Rorschach indices to predict the outcome of psychotherapy. *J. consult. Psychol.,* 1954, 18, 96–98.

Rogers, C. R., & Dymond, Rosalind F. *Personality changes and psychotherapy.* Chicago: Univer. of Chicago Press, 1954.

Rogers, L. S., & Hammond, K. R. Prediction of the results of therapy by means of the Rorschach test. *J. consult. Psychol.,* 1953, 17, 8–15.

Rogers, L. S., Knauss, J., & Hammond, K. R. Predicting continuation in therapy by means of the Rorschach test. *J. consult. Psychol.,* 1951, 15, 368–371.

Rohde, A. R. *The sentence completion method.* New York: Ronald, 1957.

Rorschach, H. *Psychodiagnostics.* Bern: Hans Huber, 1942.

Rosen, I. C. The effect of the motion picture, "Gentleman's Agreement," on attitudes toward Jews. *J. Psychol.,* 1948, 26, 525–537.

Rosenthal, R. The experimental induction of the defense mechanism of projection. *J. project. Tech.,* 1959, 23, 357–364.

Rosenwald, A. K. A comparison of the Rorschach and Behn-Rorschach tests based on a study of chronic alcoholic subjects. *Amer. Psychol.,* 1947, 2, 270. (Abstract)

Rosenzweig, S. A test for types of reaction to frustration. *Amer. J. Orthopsychiat.,* 1935, 5, 395–403.

Rosenzweig, S. *Rosenzweig P-F Study.* St. Louis: the author, 1944.

Rosenzweig, S. Revised norms for the adult form of the Rosenzweig Picture-Frustration Study. *J. Pers.,* 1950, 18, 344–346.

Rosenzweig, S. Idiodynamics in personality theory with special reference to projective methods. *Psychol. Rev.,* 1951, 58, 213–223.

Rosenzweig, S., Fleming, Edith E., & Rosenzweig, L. The children's form of the Rosenzweig Picture-Frustration Study. *J. Psychol.,* 1948, 26, 141–191.

Rosenzweig, S., & Fleming, Edith E. Apperceptive norms for the Thematic Apperception Test: II. An empirical investigation. *J. Pers.,* 1949, 17, 483–503.

Ross, W. D. The contribution of the Rorschach method to clinical diagnosis *J. ment. Sci.,* 1941, 87, 331–348.

Ross, W. D., Adsett, Nancy, Gleser, Goldine, Joyce, C. R. B., Kaplan, S. M., & Tieger, M. E. A trial of psychopharmacologic measurement with projective techniques. *J. project. Tech.,* 1963, 27, 222–225.

Rotter, J. B. Studies in the use and validity of the Thematic Apperception Test with mentally disordered patients: I. Method of analysis and clinical problems. *Charact. Pers.,* 1940, 9, 18–34.

Rotter, J. B. The present status of the Rorschach in clinical and experimental procedures. *J. Pers.,* 1948, 16, 304–311.

Rotter, J. B. Some implications of a social learning theory for the prediction of goal directed behavior from testing procedures. *Psychol. Rev.,* 1960, 67, 301–316.

Rotter, J. B., & Rafferty, J. E. *Manual for the Rotter Incomplete Sentences Blank, College Form.* New York: Psychological Corp., 1950.

Royal, R. E. Drawing characteristics of neurotic patients using a drawing of a man and woman technique. *J. clin. Psychol.,* 1949, 5, 392–395.

Rubin, H., & Lonstein, M. A cross validation of suggested Rorschach patterns associated with schizophrenia. *J. consult. Psychol.,* 1953, 17, 371–372.

Rychlak, J. F., & Guinouard, D. Rorschach content, personality and popularity. *J. project. Tech.,* 1960, 24, 322–332.

Sacks, J. M. Effect upon projective responses of stimuli referring to the subject and to others. *J. consult. Psychol.,* 1949, 13, 12–20.

Saltz, G., & Epstein, S. Thematic hostility and guilt responses as related to self-reported hostility, guilt and conflict. *J. abnorm. soc. Psychol.,* 1963, 67, 469–479.

Sanders, R., & Cleveland, S. E. The relationship between certain examiner personality variables and subjects' Rorschach scores. *J. project. Tech.,* 1953, 17, 34–50.

Sanford, R. N. The effect of abstinence from food upon imaginal processes: A preliminary experiment. *J. Psychol.,* 1936, 2, 129–136.

Sanford, R. N. The effect of abstinence from food upon imaginal processes: A further experiment. *J. Psychol.,* 1937, 3, 145–159.

Sanford, R. N., Adkins, M. M., Miller, R. B., & Cobb, E. A. Physique, personality and scholarship: A cooperative study of school children. *Monogr. soc. Res. Child Develpm.,* 1943, 8, No. 1.

Sargent, H. D. *The insight test.* New York: Grune & Stratton, 1953.

Schafer, R. *The clinical application of psychological tests.* New York: International Universities Press, 1948.

Schaie, K. W. The color pyramid test: A nonverbal technique for personality assessment. *Psychol. Bull.,* 1963, 60, 530–547.

Schmidt, L. D., & McGowan, J. F. The differentiation of human figure drawings. *J. consult. Psychol.,* 1959, 23, 129–133.

Scodel, A., Ratoosh, P., & Minas, J. S. Some personality correlates of decision making under conditions of risk. *Behav. Sci.,* 1959, 4, 19–28.

Sechrest, L. On the relative validity of psychological tests. Northwestern Univer., 1962. (Mimeographed)

Sechrest, L. Incremental validity: a recommendation. *Educ. psychol. Meas.,* 1963, 23, 153–158.

Sechrest, L., & Flores, L. A nervous mannerism in two cultures. Paper read at Convention of Psychological Association of the Philippines, 1965.

Sechrest, L., Flores, L., & Arellano, Lourdes. Language and social interaction in a bilingual culture. Northwestern Univer., 1965. (Mimeographed)

Sechrest, L., & Hemphill, J. K. Motivational variables in the assuming of combat obligation. *J. consult. Psychol.,* 1954, 18, 113–118.

Sechrest, L., & Jackson, D. N. Deviant response tendencies: their measurement and interpretation. *Educ. psychol. Measmt,* 1963, 23, 33–53.

Sechrest, L., & Wallace, J. Figure drawings and naturally occurring events: elimination of the expansive euphoria hypothesis. *J. educ. Psychol.,* 1964, 55, 42–44.

Selltiz, C., Jahoda, Marie, Deutsch, M., & Cook, S. W. *Research methods in social relations.* New York: Holt, Rinehart, and Winston, 1959.

Seward, J. P. Psychoanalysis, deductive method and the Blacky Test. *J. abnorm. soc. Psychol.,* 1950, 45, 529–535.

Sherif, M. A study of some social factors in perception. *Arch. Psychol.,* 1935, 27, No. 187.

Sherif, M., & Sherif, Carolyn W. *An outline of social psychology.* New York: Harper, 1956.

Sherman, L. J. The influence of artistic quality on judgments of patient and non-patient status from human figure drawings. *J. project. Tech.,* 1958, 22, 338–340.

Shipley, T. E., Jr., & Veroff, J. A projective measure of need for affiliation. *J. exp. Psychol.,* 1952, 43, 349–356.

Shlien, J. M., Mosak, H. H., & Dreikurs, R. Effect of time limits: A comparison of two psychotherapies. *J. counsel. Psychol.,* 1962, 9, 31–34.

Shneidman, E. S. Schizophrenia and the MAPS Test: a study of certain form and psychosocial aspects of fantasy production in schizophrenia as revealed by performance on the Make-A-Picture-Story (MAPS) Test. *Genet. Psychol. Monogr.,* 1948, 38, 145–223.

Shneidman, E. S. *The Make-A-Picture-Story Test.* New York: Psychological Corp., 1949.

Shneidman, E. S. Symposium: current aspects of the problem of validity: Suggestions for the delineation of validity studies. *J. project. Tech.,* 1959, 23, 259–261.

Sicha, K., & Sicha, M. A step towards the standardization of the scoring of the Rorschach test. *Rorschach Res. Exchange,* 1936, 1, 95–101.

Siegel, Miriam G. The diagnostic and prognostic validity of the Rorschach test in a child guidance clinic. *Amer. J. Orthopsychiat.,* 1948, 18, 119–133.

Siipola, E., Walker, W. N., & Kolb, D. Task attitudes in word association, projective and nonprojective. *J. Pers.,* 1955, 23, 441–459.

Silverman, L. H. A Q-sort study of the validity of evaluations made from projective techniques. *Psychol. Monogr.,* 1959, 73, No. 7.

Silverstein, A. B., & Robinson, H. A. The representation of orthopedic disability in children's figure drawings. *J. consult. Psychol.,* 1956, 20, 333–341.

Silverstein, A. B., & Robinson, H. A. The representation of physique in children's figure drawings: *J. consult. Psychol.,* 1961, 25, 146–148.

Simkins, L. Examiner reinforcement and situational variables in a projective testing situation. *J. consult. Psychol.,* 1960, 24, 541–547.

Simmons, W. L., & Christy, E. G. Verbal reinforcement of a TAT theme. *J. project. Tech.,* 1962, 26, 337–341.

Sines, L. K. The relative contribution of four kinds of data to accuracy in personality assessment. *J. consult. Psychol.*, 1959, 23, 483–492.

Singer, J. L. The Behn-Rorschach Inkblots: a preliminary comparison with the original Rorshach series. *J. project. Tech.*, 1952, 16, No. 2, 238–245.

Singer, J., Meltzoff, J., & Goldman, C. Rorschach movement responses following motor inhibition and hyperactivity. *J. consult. Psychol.*, 1952, 16, 359–364.

Singer, M. The validity of a multiple-choice projective test in psychopathological screening. *Psychol. Monogr.*, 1950, 64, No. 8.

Singer, R. D. A cognitive view of rationalized projection. *J. project. Tech.*, 1963, 27, 235–243.

Singer, R., & Feshbach, S. Effects of anxiety arousal in psychotics and normals upon the perception of anxiety in others. *J. Pers.*, 1962, 30, 574–587.

Smith, Elgie. A study of sex differentiation in drawings and verbalizations of schizophrenics. *J. clin. Psychol.*, 1953, 9, 83–85.

Smith, J. R., & Coleman, J. C. The relationship between manifestations of hostility in projective tests and overt behavior. *J. project. Tech.*, 1956, 20, 326–334.

Smock, C. D. Replication and comments: an experimental reunion of psychoanalytic theory with perceptual vigilance and defense. *J. abnorm. soc. Psychol.*, 1956, 53, 68–73.

Solomon, R. W. An extension of control group design. *Psychol. Bull.*, 1949, 46, 137–150.

Sommer, R. Studies in personal space. *Sociometry*, 1959, 22, 247–260.

Sommer, R. Personal space. *Canad. Architecture*, 1960, 76–80.

Sommer, R. The distance for comfortable conversation: a further study. *Sociometry*, 1962, 25, 111–116.

Spence, Janet T., & Maher, B. A. Handling and noxious stimulation of the albino rat: I. Effects on subsequent emotionality. *J. comp. physiol. Psychol.*, 1962, 55, 247–251. (a)

Spence, Janet T., & Maher, B. A. Handling and noxious stimulation of the albino rat: II. Effects on subsequent performance in a learning situation. *J. comp. physiol. Psychol.*, 1962, 55, 252–255. (b)

Spence, K. W. The nature of theory construction in contemporary psychology. *Psychol. Rev.*, 1944, 51, 47–68.

Star, S. A., & Hughes, H. M. Report on an educational campaign: the Cincinnati plan for the United Nations. *Amer. J. sociol.*, 1949–50, 55, 389.

Starr, S., & Marcuse, F. L. Reliability in the Draw-A-Person Test. *J. project. Tech.*, 1959, 23, 83–86.

Stein, M. I. The use of a sentence completion test for the diagnosis of personality. *J. clin. Psychol.*, 1947, 3, 47–56.

Stein, M. I. The record and a sentence completion test. *J. consult. Psychol.*, 1949, 13, 448–449.

Stephens, M. W. Item validity and response sets in sentence completion tests. Paper given at MPA meeting, 1960.

Stolz, R. E., & Coltharp, Frances C. Clinical judgments and the Draw-A-Person Test. *J. consult. Psychol.*, 1961, 25, 43–45.

Stone, H. The TAT aggressive content scale. *J. project. Tech.*, 1956, 20, 445–452.

Stone, H. K., & Dellis, N. P. An exploratory investigation into the levels hypothesis. *J. project. Tech.*, 1960, 24, 333–340.

Storment, C. T., & Finney, B. C. Projection and behavior: a Rorschach study of assaultive mental hospital patients. *J. project. Tech.*, 1953, 17, 349–360.

Strong, E. K. *Vocational Interest Blank for Men: Manual.* Stanford, Calif.: Stanford Univer. Press, 1951.

Strumpfer, D. J. W., & Nichols, R. C. A study of some communicable measures for the evaluation of human figure drawings. *J. project. Tech.*, 1962, 26, 342–353.

Sullivan, P. L., & Adelson, J. Ethnocentrism and misanthropy. *J. abnorm. soc. Psychol.*, 1954, 49, 246–250.

Sundberg, N. D. The practice of psychological testing in clinical services in the United States. *Amer. Psychol.*, 1961, 16, 79–83.

Swenson, C. H., Jr. Empirical evaluations of human figure drawings. *Psychol. Bull.*, 1957, 54, 431–466.

Symonds, P. M. Criteria for the selection of pictures for the investigation of adolescent fantasies. *J. abnorm. soc. Psychol.*, 1939, 34, 271–274.

Symonds, P. M. *Symonds picture-story test.* New York: Columbia Univer., Teachers College, Bureau of Publications, 1948.

Taylor, Janet A. A personality scale of manifest anxiety. *J. abnorm. soc. Psychol.*, 1953, 48, 285–290.

Technical recommendations for psychological tests and diagnostic techniques. *Psychol. Bull. Suppl.*, 1954, 51, 2, Part 2, 1–38.

Thompson, C. E. The Thompson modification of the Thematic Apperception Test. *Rorschach Res. Exchange,* 1949, 13, 469–478.

Thurstone, L. L. The Rorschach in psychological science. *J. abnorm. soc. Psychol.*, 1948, 43, 471–475.

Tolor, A. Teachers' judgments of the popularity of children from their human figure drawings. *J. clin. Psychol.*, 1955, 11, 158–162.

Tomkins, S. Discussion of Dr. Murstein's paper. In J. Kagan & G. S. Lesser (Eds.), *Contemporary issues in thematic apperceptive methods.* Springfield, Ill.: Charles C Thomas, 1961. P. 279.

Tomkins, S. S., & Miner, J. B. *The Tomkins-Horn Picture Arrangement Test.* New York: Springer, 1957.

Towbin, A. P. Hostility in Rorschach content and overt aggressive behavior. *J. abnorm. soc. Psychol.*, 1959, 58, 312–316.

Troup, E. A comparative study by means of the Rorschach method of personality development in twenty pairs of identical twins. *Genet. Psychol. Monogr.*, 1938, 20, 461–556.

Tutko, T. A. Need for social approval and its effect on responses to projective tests. Unpublished doctoral dissertation, Northwestern Univer., 1962.

Twitchell-Allen, Doris. *Three-dimensional apperception test.* New York: Psychological Corp., 1948.

Ullmann, L. P. Productivity and the clinical use of TAT cards. *J. project. Tech.*, 1957, 21, 399–403.

Underwood, B. J. *Psychological research.* New York: Appleton-Century-Crofts, 1957.

Vernon, P. E. The Rorschach Inkblot test. II. *Brit. J. med. Psychol.*, 1933, 13, 179–205.

Veroff, J. Development and validation of a projective measure of power motivation. *J. abnorm. soc. Psychol.*, 1957, 54, 1–8.

Veroff, J. Thematic apperception in a nationwide sample survey. In J. Kagan & G. S. Lesser (Eds.), *Contemporary issues in thematic apperceptive methods.* Springfield, Ill.: Charles C Thomas, 1961. Pp. 83–110.

Wagner, E. E. The use of drawings of hands as a projective medium for differentiating normals and schizophrenics. *J. clin. Psychol.*, 1961, 17, 279–280.

Wagner, E. E. *The Hand Test: Manual for administration, scoring and interpretation.* Akron, Ohio: The Mark James Co., 1962.

Wagner, E. E. Hand test content indicators of overt psychosexual maladjustment in neurotic males. *J. project. Tech.*, 1963, 27, 357–358.

Wagner, E. E., & Copper, J. Differentiation of satisfactory and unsatisfactory employees at Goodwill Industries with the Hand Test. *J. project. Tech.*, 1963, 27, 354–356.

Wagner, E. E., & Medvedeff, E. Differentiation of aggressive behavior of institutionalized schizophrenics with the Hand Test. *J. project. Tech.*, 1963, 27, 111–113.

Walker, E. L., Atkinson, J. W., Veroff, J., Birney, R., Dember, W., & Moulton, R. The expression of fear-related motivation in thematic apperception as a function of proximity to an atomic explosion. In J. W. Atkinson (Ed.), *Motives in fantasy, action, and society.* Princeton, N.J.: Van Nostrand, 1958, 143–159.

Wallace, J., Jr., & Sechrest, L. The frequency hypothesis in the analysis of projective tests. *J. consult. Psychol.*, 1963, 27, 387–393.

Wallach, M. A., & Gahm, Ruthellen C. Personality functions of graphic construction and expansiveness. *J. Pers.*, 1960, 28, 73–88.

Wallach, M. A., Green, L. R., Lipsitt, P. D., & Minehart, J. B. Contradiction between overt and projective personality indicators as a function of defensiveness. *Psychol. Monogr.*, 1962, 76, No. 1 (Whole No. 520).

Wallach, M. A., & Thomas, Helen L. Graphic constriction and expansiveness as a function of induced social isolation and social interaction: experimental manipulations and personality effects. *J. Pers.*, 1963, 31, 491–509.

Webb, E. J., Campbell, D. T., Schwartz, R. D., & Sechrest, L. *Unobtrusive measures: Nonreactive research in the social sciences.* Chicago: Rand McNally, 1966.

Webb, W. B., & Hilden, A. H. Verbal and intellectual ability as factors in projective test results. *J. project. Tech.*, 1953, 17, 102–103.

Wechsler, D. *The measurement of adult intelligence.* (3rd ed.) Baltimore: Williams & Wilkins, 1944.

Weider, A., & Noller, P. A. Objective studies of children's drawings of human figures: I. Sex awareness and socio-economic level. *J. clin. Psychol.,* 1950, 6, 319–325.

Weisskopf, Edith A. A transcendence index as a proposed measure in the TAT. *J. Psychol.,* 1950, 29, 379–390.

Weisskopf, Edith A., & Dieppa, J. J. Experimentally induced faking on TAT responses. *J. consult. Psychol.,* 1951, 15, 469–474.

Weisskopf-Joelson, Edith, & Wich, R. An experiment concerning the value of a "pictureless" TAT. *J. project. Tech.,* 1961, 25, 360–362.

Wherry, R. J., & Gaylord, R. H. The concept of test and item reliability in relation to factor pattern. *Psychometrika,* 1943, 8, 247–269.

White, B. W., & Saltz, E. Measurement of reproducibility. *Psychol. Bull.,* 1957, 54, 81–99.

White, Mary Alice, & Schreiber, Hana. Diagnosing "suicidal risks" on the Rorschach. *Psychiat. quart. Suppl.,* 1952, 26, 161–189.

Whitmyre, J. W. The significance of artistic excellence in the judgment of adjustment inferred from human figure drawings. *J. consult. Psychol.,* 1953, 17, 421–424.

Wickes, T. A. Examiner influence in a test situation. *J. consult. Psychol.,* 1956, 20, 23–26.

Williams, M. An experimental study of intellectual control under stress and associated Rorschach factors. *J. consult. Psychol.,* 1947, 11, 21–29.

Winch, R. F., & More, D. M. Does TAT add information to interviews? Statistical analysis of the increment. *J. clin. Psychol.,* 1956, 12, 316–321.

Winer, B. J. A measure of interrelationship for overlapping groups. *Psychometrika,* 1955, 20, 63–68.

Winfield, D. L., & Sparer, P. J. Preliminary report of the Rosenzweig P-F Study in attempted suicide. *J. clin. Psychol.,* 1953, 9, 379–381.

Wirt, R., & McReynolds, P. The reliability of Rorschach number of responses. *J. project. Tech.,* 1953, 17, 493–494.

Wisotsky, M. A note on the order of figure drawing among incarcerated alcoholics. *J. clin. Psychol.,* 1959, 15, 65.

Wittenborn, J. R. Statistical tests of certain Rorschach assumptions. *J. consult. Psychol.,* 1949, 13, 257–267.

Wittenborn, J. R. Statistical tests of certain Rorschach assumptions; the internal consistency of scoring categories. *J. consult. Psychol.,* 1950, 14, 1–19.

Wittenborn, J. R., & Holzberg, Jules D. The Rorschach and descriptive diagnosis. *J. consult. Psychol.,* 1951, 15, 460–463.

Wittenborn, J. R., & Sarason, S. B. Exceptions to certain Rorschach criteria of pathology. *J. consult. Psychol.,* 1949, 13, 21–27.

Wolf, I. Hostile acting out and Rorschach test content. *J. project. Tech.,* 1957, 21, 414–419.

Wolff, W. Projective methods for personality analysis of expressive behavior in pre-school children. *Charact. Pers.,* 1942, 10, 309–330.

Wolff, W. W., & Precker, J. A. Expressive movement and the methods of experimental depth psychology. In H. H. & Gladys Anderson (Eds.), *An introduction to projective techniques.* Englewood Cliffs, N.J.: Prentice-Hall, 1951. Pp. 457–497.

Wright, B. A. Altruism in children and the perceived conduct of others. *J. abnorm. soc. Psychol.,* 1942, 37, 218–233.

Wylie, R. C., Sisson, B. D., & Taulbee, E. Intraindividual consistency in "creative" and "memory" stories written for TAT pictures. *J. consult. Psychol.,* 1963, 27, 145–151.

Zamansky, H. S. A technique for assessing homosexual tendencies. *J. Pers.,* 1956, 24, 436–448.

Zamansky, H. S. An investigation of the psychoanalytic theory of paranoid delusions. *J. Pers.,* 1958, 26, 410–425.

Zimbardo, P. G. Relationship between projective and direct measures of fear arousal. *J. abnorm. soc. Psychol.,* 1964, 68, 196–199.

Zimmer, H. The roles of conflict and internalized demands in projection. *J. abnorm. soc. Psychol.,* 1955, 50, 188–192.

PART IV Special Emphases

CHAPTER 10 Behavior Theory as Personality Theory[1]

D. E. BERLYNE
University of Toronto

CHARACTERIZATION OF BEHAVIOR THEORY

It is extremely difficult to say exactly what "behavior theory" is and to delineate its boundaries. Is it a branch of psychology, a school of psychology, a theoretical position, a methodological approach? It is certainly not quite any of these, and yet it is all of them to some extent. What is the relation of behavior theory to the rest of psychology? In fact, what kinds of psychology, if any, lie outside its boundaries? All sorts of answers to these questions have been put forward at one time or another. There are those who have felt that behavior theory is destined to assimilate more and more of psychology as time goes on, so that everything in psychology will eventually be marked with its stamp, and the sooner the better. Others, of course, have felt that behavior theory is a transitory aberration whose pernicious influence will soon be seen for what it is and annihilated. Some have maintained that all psychologists are behavior theorists, but that some realize it and some do not; the implication is that those who are aware of what they are doing will do it better.

The term "behavior theory" has been used fairly interchangeably with the term "learning theory." "Learning theory" seems to have come into use rather earlier, and some writers, notably Mowrer, have strongly favored it. Hull and Spence have preferred to speak of "behavior theory." There have been some not very happy attempts to distinguish between the theory of learning and "behavior theory" as the theory of performance, but, although, according to most theories, there are differences between the principles that determine the acquisition of habit-strength and those that determine the probability and vigor of responding, it is certainly impracticable to separate the two completely, let alone to assign them to two distinct bodies of theory. The term "behavior theory" is perhaps to be preferred, on the grounds that "learning theory" has come to encompass much more than a statement of the principles that govern learning. It has, for example, coalesced in large part with motivation theory. It has encroached on vast areas of social, abnormal, and developmental psychology. As the work of the ethologists (Tinbergen, 1951; Thorpe, 1956) has

[1] The preparation of this chapter was supported by Research Grant MH-06324 from the National Institute of Mental Health of the U.S. Public Health Service.

abundantly demonstrated, many of the principles governing learned behavior apply equally to unlearned or instinctive behavior. The content of this chapter may help the reader to decide whether or not behavior theory will eventually contain personality theory.

Behavior theory can safely be identified with the behaviorist movement and more particularly with its later or neo-behaviorist phase. So a brief review of the course of development through which this movement has gone seems called for at this point, if the positions of its contemporary exponents are to be understood.

The Early Behaviorism of J. B. Watson

Watson is now often regarded as a figure of fun, as a bogey-man, or as a straw man to use in attacking contemporary psychologists with behaviorist proclivities. Their position is often assumed to resemble his in all important respects. It is true that Watson wrote in a racy style, which was not conducive to meticulous phrasing and precise wording, and that he tended to be carried away by his iconoclastic fervor. He was not highly trained as a philosopher, and, in the 20th century, philosophy has become, if anything, more of a professionalized and esoteric vocation than in previous centuries. It has certainly become much more self-conscious about language, so that an amateur can hardily hope to enter that domain without showing himself for what he is as soon as he opens his mouth. Pulling Watson to pieces—laying bare the inconsistencies and oversights in his pronouncements—was, at one time, a favorite limbering-up exercise of philosophers, and an elementary one at that. Now we can arrive at a sounder evaluation and separate the wheat from the chaff in his contribution better than his contemporaries, and no doubt better than he himself, could have done.

Watson maintained that psychologists should no longer concern themselves with conscious mental events and should no longer rely on introspection as their prime source of data. The psychological Establishment of the time was bound to react to this as astronomers would do if told that, from now on, stars were no longer their business and that they must dispense with the telescope. From our present vantage-point, we can see that to follow Watson's advice means to preserve all the worthwhile problems of his predecessors, while evading much of the haze that sometimes enveloped them. Watson set off his revolution before psychologists became cognizant of the logical-empiricist philosophy-of-science movement, with its attempts at a sophisticated characterization of the aims of science and the kinds of linguistic formulae that it uses. But he saw the essential point that there is a great difference between the study of "public" or "intersubjective" phenomena, which are accessible to everybody's sense-organs so that a consensus about them can rapidly be reached, and the study of private, subjective experiences that everybody can, and no doubt should, pursue for his own benefit but that can hardly become part of a collective enterprise. He made rash and ultimately untenable statements with regard to the philosophical problems of body-mind relations. But he made us see that it is important for a psychologist to decide whether he is pursuing an explanation of behavior or an explanation of conscious experience. Confusion can hardly be avoided if the two are pursued together, and, unless one subscribes to the interactionist view that conscious experiences determine behavior, why should one want to pursue them together?

These lessons have, of course, not by any means permeated the whole of contemporary psychology. It is far from clear whether some current writers are trying to account for conscious experiences or for publicly observable responses. It is, in fact, far from clear that these writers themselves have decided which they would attempt. If it were not for vestiges of interactionism, why should there have been so much stir when stimuli appeared, in certain conditions, to evoke galvanic skin responses but not verbal responses?

Watson did not reject verbal reports once and for all from psychology. Indeed, he put onerous responsibilities on them himself, e.g., in his analysis of perception. Present-day social psychologists and psychophysicists would certainly be hard pressed if they were not allowed to listen to what subjects say. But our whole attitude to the verbal report has changed since Watson. We are now unlikely to hold that the verbal report gives a complete and thoroughly accurate specification of the processes within the subject that underlie his behavior.

We can now afford to smile superciliously at Watson's naïvete in believing that the brain works through structures very much like the spinal reflex arc, that all human behavior can have developed out of an inaugural stock of a few hundred specific innate reflexes and three innate emotional patterns through the operation of classical conditioning, at his truculent refusal to attach much importance to inherited individual differences, and at his insistence on belittling the differences between what human beings and lower animals can do. If, however, we disregard the literal content of much that he said, we can discern with more sympathy what he was really after. He was committing himself, and trying to commit psychology, to a strategy that had paid off in other branches of science, namely that of taking up the study of simple phenomena first and seeking in them clues that will later facilitate the study of more complex phenomena. He believed that the most elaborate and uniquely human activities must have grown, both phylogenetically and ontogenetically, out of the simplest adaptive response mechanisms and that they cannot be understood unless the process of development has been traced. He appreciated that, in any case, a scientific discipline has not completed its task unless it has related the complex to the simple and laid bare the common threads that string them together. He saw that, since most of the behavior of the higher mammals is learned, psychologists should give the highest possible priority to the task of working out the laws that govern learning.

A methodological position that, in its essentials, was the same as Watson's was being simultaneously established in Russia by Pavlov, extending the tradition founded by the 19th-century Russian physiologist, Sechenov. It is true that Pavlov turned to the study of behavior not for its own sake but as an indirect means of ascertaining what goes on in the brain. Nevertheless, he demonstrated the fruitfulness of carefully observing behavior and especially the modifications that combinations of environmental events impose on behavior.

The First Generation of Neo-Behaviorism

By the early 1930's, Watson's behaviorism had died while giving birth to an heir. The heir, while showing unmistakable signs of its parentage, has had enough individuality to deserve a name of its own, and it has accordingly been christened "neo-behaviorism." The event evidently received insufficient publicity, since many psychologists outside the family appear to believe either that behaviorism passed away long ago without issue or that the original bearer of the name is still hale. European psychologists, especially those working in the Soviet Union, are apt to see in Watson's ill-considered assertion that, given the response, it should be possible to predict the stimulus and vice versa the substance of contemporary "S-R behavior theory."

A publication that is often held to mark the changeover is Hull's (1929) article, "A functional interpretation of the conditioned reflex," which, in discussing the biological significance of familiar conditioning phenomena, strikes a new note in its emphases rather than in what it actually says. Tolman's book, *Purposive Behavior in Animals and Men* (1932), was the first large-scale contribution to neo-behaviorism, and he very definitely intended it to mark a break-away. Holt, although a philosopher rather than a psychologist, gave the budding neo-behaviorist movement a substantial fillip with his book *Animal Drive and the Learning Process* (1931), and had, in fact, adumbrated some of the themes that were to characterize neo-behaviorism much earlier in his book *The Freudian Wish and its Place in Ethics* (1915).

The principal differences between early behaviorism and the neo-behaviorism of the 1930's and 1940's can be summed up briefly as follows.

1. The neo-behaviorists were deeply influenced, directly or indirectly, by the logical-empiricist movement in philosophy, with its feeling that the boundaries of scientific activity and the scientific use of language need to be sharply delineated to avoid mutual interference between what lies inside them and what lies outside. Accordingly, the neo-behaviorists kept themselves aloof on the whole from such extra-scientific questions as the nature of conscious experiences, their relation to bodily events, and what it "means" to possess a mental process.

Either a mental event can possess no correlation at all with observable behavior—to outward view (even if aided by special recording equipment), the subject behaves in all respects as he would if the mental event were absent—or there is some degree of correlation or correspondence between mental events and overt behavior. In the former case, science, regarded as a social activity concerned with public phenomena, can have no interest in the mental events and could lose nothing by disregarding them. In the latter case, there must be a *logical equivalence* between statements about the mental events and statements about overt responses. In the new logic whose chief founders were Whitehead and Russell (1910–12), statements p and q are "logically equivalent" when p is true if and only if q is true. It follows that a set of statements about mental events can be replaced by a corresponding set of statements about overt responses without loss as far as the aims of science are concerned, i.e., with respect to antecedent and consequent conditions or, in other words, with respect to what the statements imply and are implied by. Whether statements that are logically equivalent in this way must be identical in "meaning" or "empirical content" is a contentious question that the neo-behaviorist psychologist can safely leave to the analytic philosopher.

In short, therefore, the neo-behaviorists took over the behaviorist methodology from Watson while holding aloof from his provocative stance over the nature of mind. They saw no reason to eschew verbal reports. They regarded verbal responses, including those elicited by questioning, as deserving of study like any others and perhaps especially valuable because of the unique potentialities for information transmission that their variety confers on them. They took care, however, not to regard a verbal report as a peephole affording a grandstand view of the subject's internal workings.

2. The neo-behaviorists were generally more interested than Watson or Watson's predecessors in the construction of systematic and rigorous theories. They were influenced by the lively discussions on the nature and desiderata of scientific theories that the logical-empiricist philosophers of science carried on in the 1920's and 1930's. They were self-conscious about their theorizing. Not only did they learn that they must make clear exactly what their theoretical statements mean in terms of empirical implications. They realized that the onus was on them to demonstrate that they have any meaning at all of the sort in which science is interested.

3. The neo-behaviorists were fully aware that there is no one-to-one correspondence between stimulus conditions and response conditions. They recognized that the overt response depends jointly on the external stimulus situation and on conditions inside

the organism. To take care of this difficulty, their theories tend to be replete with references to intervening variables, mediating processes, and implicit stimulus-producing responses, the function of all these devices being to make manageable the conceptual treatment of intricate input-output relations. Some neo-behaviorists, notably Skinner and his associates, have looked askance at all this talk about unobservable events inside the organism and at the constructs to which it has given rise, but even Skinner has been unable simply to list external stimulus conditions and specify the behavioral consequences of each. His early writings (e.g., 1938) mentioned such intervening variables as "reflex reserve," while his later works, particularly those dealing with human verbal behavior and cognate processes (1953, 1957), contain copious references to such hypothesized entities as "covert speech."

4. Most neo-behaviorists were intensely interested in motivational problems. This is partly because what we call motivational variables are obviously among the most important of the conditions whose variations cause changes in behavior when the external situation is held constant. But it was also part of an eagerness to place the facts about behavior in a biological setting, i.e., to show the relevance to biological adaptation of the characteristics of behavior that are disclosed.

5. This increased emphasis on the biological setting of behavior went together with a sharply reduced interest in its physiological underpinning. One of the few things that Watson took over unchanged from his introspectionist predecessors was the belief that to explain a psychological phenomenon means to relate it to the data of physiology. In the early 1930's, it became apparent that neurophysiology had so far contributed little to the understanding of learning, which was the neo-behaviorists' main preoccupation, so that there was no point in waiting for knowledge about the nervous system to catch up. The current view of science implied, furthermore, that there could be such a thing as an adequate theory of behavior making no reference to events in the nervous system. The psychologist would be carrying out his task quite adequately if he worked out the laws that enable responses to be predicted when pertinent facts about the external environment and the organism's internal condition are known. The internal condition (which, it seemed, need not be described in physiological terms) could be inferred either from previous behavior or from previous external stimulus conditions.

The neo-behaviorists had learned from Pavlov, Watson, and Thorndike to concentrate on the experimental study of learning as the best hope of placing psychology on a firm footing and, above all, of providing a language in which the various fields of psychology, including social psychology, developmental psychology, abnormal psychology, and the study of complex processes, can be discussed and interrelated. There was, however, an important difference in that early behaviorism placed its main hopes in the classical or Pavlovian conditioning paradigm. In contrast, the neo-behaviorists have set greater store by the kind of learning known as "instrumental conditioning" or "operant conditioning" or "selective learning."

Although there have been disputes over the precise relations between classical and instrumental conditioning, the latter appears to differ from the former insofar as it enables a new response pattern to be acquired, while classical conditioning is mainly a matter of associating old responses with new stimulus conditions. This is, however, something of an oversimplification, since the new response patterns must be put together out of components that were already in the organism's behavior repertoire and since the classically conditioned response, as has often been pointed out, is not always identical with what the unconditioned stimulus elicited. A more crucial distinction is perhaps to be found in the forms of reinforcement to which these two kinds of learning are susceptible: in both cases, the presence of a reinforcing agent is necessary to establish learning and ward off extinction, but in classical conditioning it takes the form of the unconditioned stimulus which originally evoked the response, and in instrumental conditioning it is a rewarding condition that closely follows the response.

The earliest experiments on instrumental conditioning may with some justification be held to be the puzzle-box experiments of Thorndike and the earliest experiments on maze learning in the rat, which were roughly contemporaneous with the first studies of classical conditioning in Pavlov's laboratory. Nevertheless, a number of experimenters working in different countries (e.g., Skinner, 1935, in the United States; Grindley, 1932, in England; Ivanov-Smolenski, 1927, in Russia; Miller & Konorski, 1928, in Poland) devised experimental situations that enabled the similarities and dissimilarities between classical and instrumental conditioning to be clearly shown.

The neo-behaviorists have never formed a coherent school, let alone a group subscribing to an explicit set of tenets. Those of the first generation seemed clearly more conscious of their disagreements than of any commonly held position. The points of dispute were, after all, interesting ones and stimulated feverish experimentation. Nevertheless, whereas the spokesmen of the various factions felt themselves to be poles apart, their opponents saw them as purveyors of slightly different brands of the same dubious product. Those who believe in the product's essential soundness can now recognize that, although the behavior theorists of the 1930's spent relatively little time marking out their areas of agreement, these were more extensive than they, in the heat of battle, were inclined to acknowledge.

The most prominent schism within the first echelon of neo-behaviorists was that between the "cognitive theorists" and "S-R theorists." The latter, when they accepted mediating processes (and some like Skinner have been vehemently averse to them), thought of them as implicit or internalized "responses," i.e., as derivatives of overt responses whose acquisition and performance follow essentially the same principles as those of overt responses. The cognitivists were somewhat more eager to find room for mediating processes and to conceive of these (expectations, cognitions, etc.) as subject to essentially different principles from those that apply to overt responses. The cognitivist mediating processes were thus closer in structure and content (to be precise, in "informational correspondence"—see Berlyne, 1965) to perceptual processes, whereas those of the S-R theorists came closer to motor processes.

There were other divisions within the S-R wing, bearing notably on the relations between classical and instrumental conditioning. For some, particularly Hull and his associates, all learning conformed to the instrumental pattern, while for others, particularly Guthrie, all learning was governed by contiguity and consisted essentially of classical conditioning. Some like Skinner and, for one period of his career, Mowrer maintained that classical and instrumental conditioning were two distinct kinds of learning applicable to different responses. In the Soviet Union, classical conditioning has always been taken as a model for learning in general, although it has been viewed rather flexibly. Pavlov had a theory of instrumental conditioning, which is little known in the West but was actually outlined in an article in the *Psychological Review* in 1932. He felt that contiguity learning could account for instrumental conditioning, provided that the formation of two-way connections between sensory and kinesthetic-motor areas of the cortex was accepted. Konorski (e.g., 1948) has, on the other hand, consistently emphasized the gulf between Type I (i.e., classical) and Type II (i.e., instrumental) conditioning.

Although neo-behaviorism has never denied its Watsonian parentage, and it would be disingenuous for it to do so, its origins were far from parthenogenetic. One far from insignificant contributor to it was psychoanalysis. As we shall see later in this chapter, efforts at synthesis between psychoanalysis and behavior theory took up a great deal of energy at one time. Quite apart from this explicit influence, there is no mistaking the similarity between the view of behavior, most clearly expressed in the writings of Hull and his followers, as a collection of devices for getting rid of internal or external disturbances and the motivational theory outlined by Freud at one stage in his career (1915).

McDougall's work also helped to make the neo-behaviorists realize, unlike Watson, that motivational questions must be faced. The neo-behaviorists were eager to crystallize within their theories the fruits of the thought and experimental work on motivation that began during the 1920's. This work and its continuation by the neo-behaviorists were inspired in no small measure by a desire to do what McDougall had shown to be necessary and yet overcome the objectionable features of his instinct theory. Tolman's book *Purposive Behavior in Animals and Men* (1932) was intended to show that behaviorists could accept McDougall's (1923) contention that "purposive" behavior has important characteristics marking it off sharply from reflex behavior and could handle the problems that goal-directedness raises in a manner fully consonant with the principles of behaviorism.

The influence of the American functionalism of the turn of the century (e.g., Dewey, 1896) is evident in the much greater importance that the neo-behaviorists, as compared with Watson, attached to chains of responses organized for the fulfillment of biological purposes.

Biases taken over from Gestalt psychology were most noticeable in the cognitivist wing (cf. Tolman's "sign-gestalt-expectations"), but some of the chief points on which the Gestalt school insisted were taken to heart to some extent by all the neo-behaviorists. Razran (1939) and Hull (1943) found quite congenial to learning theory the view that wholes or combinations have effects other than those of their components. They pointed to the substantial evidence that had been collected in both Russian and American laboratories for what they call "configural conditioning" or "patterning," such that an animal learns to perform a response to a combination of stimuli but to inhibit the response when the elements of the combination appear separately, or vice versa. Hull deliberately introduced his not too successful principle of "afferent neural interaction" to account for the special effects of combinations. The influence of Gestalt psychology was, however, most clearly evident in the wider connotation that neo-behaviorists began to give to the notion of a "stimulus." A "stimulus" came to mean virtually any kind of distinguishable property that can mark off a class of stimulus situations. We find, for example, Miller and Dollard (1941) recognizing that a response can become associated with a particular pitch of sound, with the existence of a difference in pitch between two sounds, with the direction of such a difference, with the extent of such a difference, etc.

The Second Generation of Neo-Behaviorism

Some marked changes in emphasis and atmosphere became apparent in the beginning of the 1950's. The first major publication sounding some of the new notes was Hebb's *The Organization of Behavior* (1949). The year 1949 was actually a remarkable one for psychology in many ways. It saw the appearance of the article by Moruzzi and Magoun (1949) that focused attention on the brain-stem reticular formation. This was the year when Shannon and Weaver's (1949) *The Mathematical Theory of Communication* presented the intellectual revolution of information theory to a potentially wide audience. It was also about then that investigators in the United States, the United Kingdom, and the Soviet Union had begun independently to treat exploratory behavior as a phenomenon worth intensive examination. All of these developments have left their stamp on the second phase of neo-behaviorism.

I was tempted to propose a new term, e.g., "ceno-behaviorism" (Greek *kainos*, recent), to denote the behaviorism of the 1950's and 1960's and to distinguish it from the neo-behaviorism of the 1930's and 1940's, but there have actually not been such violent breaks with the general aims and outlook of the first-generation neo-behaviorists as would justify this neologism. The changes that have occurred are simply of kinds that are to be expected as inquiry progresses, and they are certainly not comparable with those that divided the first neo-behaviorists from Watson. So it would be prudent to keep the term "ceno-behaviorism" for some more sweeping transformation that will undoubtedly come at the beginning of a future odd-numbered decade.

The main thing that marks off the work of contemporary neo-behaviorists from that of their predecessors is the abundant influence of new lines of inquiry that have taken shape outside the neo-behaviorist mainstream.

Among such sources of influence have been:

(1) the cybernetic notion of gravitation towards a goal by negative feedback and correction of deviation,

(2) the concepts and measures introduced by information theory,

(3) the concepts, theoretical models, and research data supplied by computer simulation,

(4) Piaget's findings and theoretical ideas concerning the development of perceptual and intellectual activities in the child,

(5) experimental findings and theoretical ideas originated by Russian investigators of conditioning and of complex intellectual processes, these having been made available by the rapid growth of translation from Russian and of mutual contact between East and West that has occurred since the death of Stalin.

Behavior theories are, needless to say, not the only ones to have felt these influences. Psychologists not identified with the neo-behaviorist movement have, however, either confined their attention to circumscribed areas of interest opened up by these new trends or proposed, more or less, that psychology should be built up anew with one of these new approaches as its main foundation. Behavior theorists have, in contrast, confronted these new lines of investigation with the belief that the psychology of the past, including the behavior theory of the past, had some solid achievements to its credit. The most urgent need, it seems to them, is to establish some synthesis between the new complexities introduced by these recent developments and what was learned in the past with the help of established experimental techniques and theoretical concepts.

The most impressive contrast between present-day neo-behaviorism and the neo-behaviorism that existed before 1950 is in the attitudes of its proponents to neurophysiology. The first neo-behaviorist generation kept aloof—in some cases intransigently aloof—from reference to what might go on in the brain and were wont to use "neurologizing" as a defamatory term. Their recent successors have been faced with a veritable cloudburst of neurophysiological advances that has poured forth since shortly after World War II and shows no sign of abating. These advances were made possible by growing use of the electroencephalograph, supplemented before long by implanted recording and stimulating electrodes, microelectrodes, stereotaxic instruments for aiming these electrodes at specific structures, and a variety of new techniques for recording and processing torrents of data. One of Hebb's avowed aims in his book *The Organization of Behavior* (1949) was to warn psychologists, and behavior theorists in particular, that, since they were last in touch with neurophysiology, that discipline had undergone changes with which they would do well to acquaint themselves. He argued that even those who proclaimed their indifference to brain function were, whether they realized it or not, apt to show the influence of outmoded neurophysiological conceptions. Insofar as his case rested on the accomplishments of neurophysiology before 1949, it may or may not have been found convincing. But within a few years, neurophysiological laboratories began to emit such a spate of significant new findings as must sooner or later break down any open-minded behavior theorist's skepticism regarding their pertinence to his interests. So present-day contributions to behavior theory are commonly formulated in terms that make contact with the latest neurophysiological discoveries. At the time of such head-spinning flux, any hypothesis suggested by the latest neurophysiological picture is apt to require revision within a very short time. But there is no reason why this should matter. The attempt to keep up with the tide is exhilarating, and experimental techniques for testing any neuropsychological speculation either are available already or can confidently be expected before long. The old arguments of the 1930's and 1940's about the dispensability of physiological knowledge for the behavior theorist are as valid as ever. It is certainly possible to study relations between external events and observable behavior without any concern for what occurs in the brain, just as somebody who is unfamiliar with watches could arrive at a notion of what one does, and how its user can control it, by looking at the face and manipulating the crown. If, on the other hand, he professes to be interested in how a watch works but refuses to listen to what a friend who has succeeded in prising off the back has to tell him, he is being pigheaded.

There has been a feeling in some quarters that psychological and neurophysiological subject matters are fundamentally incapable of synthesis, because they represent different "levels of discourse." It has been held that psychology and physiology differ in that the latter breaks things down into smaller units. It would, however, be hard to maintain that, say, a physiological condition of high arousal, with manifestations pervading the whole body, represents a finer scale of analysis than, say, the response of pressing a key with the right index finger, as in a traditional psychological experiment on reaction time. Some have felt that psychology, and especially behavior theory, should rigorously espouse a "black-box" point of view with the single-minded objective of analyzing relations between inputs and outputs. According to this view, reference to happenings in the brain is out of order, because it makes reference to processes that go on within the black box and are thus not embraced by that objective. This is surely a misunderstanding. Devices that provide us with clues to the working of the nervous system are not giving us a view of what is occurring within the black box. By definition, whatever occurs within the box is unobservable. As soon as an event becomes accessible to observation, it no longer belongs to the interior of the black box but to the output. Psychophysiological and neurophysiological recording techniques thus add to the outputs that the behavior theorist must take into account. And this information supplies additional guidance for our theoretical divagations by cutting down the number of alternative formulations that can be entertained, since the more numerous the outputs that must be predicted, the fewer the hypotheses regarding input-output relations that become tenable.

Apart from the reinstatement of brain physiology into a major advisory function, the latest phase of neo-behaviorism continues to show the traditional behaviorist biases with regard to content. Learning still has pride of place, although ethology has cautioned against underestimating the possible significance of unlearned behavior even in the higher mammals. There is still heavy reliance on animal experiments, with deliberate concentration on a few intensively studied species such as the rat and the pigeon, although the informative potentialities of human children and of computers are receiving more and more recognition.

However, despite the behaviorist insistence that it is best to start with the simplest phenomenon, behavior theorists are beginning to muster the confidence to attack the most complex symbolic processes. There is, in fact, an increasing readiness, both in the English-speaking countries and in the Soviet Union, to realize that there are vast differences between the simplest kinds of behavior of which animals and human beings are capable and the activities that we describe as "voluntary," "rational," and "accompanied by awareness." Yet recognition of the gulf between them does not preclude a naturalistic treatment of the differences or a search for principles common to them all. As another earnest of this willingness to face greater intricacies, let us note J. G. Taylor's book (1962), *The Behavioral Basis of Perception,* which, in aspiring to annex the domain of perception to behavior theory, revives some of the delicate problems regarding the function of consciousness that Watson and Lashley (1923) boldly took up, that Tolman (1932) toyed with, but that most neo-behaviorists steadfastly shunned.

Finally, the most recent neo-behaviorists have maintained their predecessors' concern for motivational problems, but several new doors have been opened by their steeply mounting interest in "intrinsic" or "collative" motivation. Earlier neo-behaviorists hoped to trace all behavior back to external annoyances or organic needs affecting tissues other than the sense organs and the nervous system. Now, it has become apparent that activities pursued "for their own sake," without any practical consequences of an obvious and immediate nature, take up a large part of the time and energy of higher animals. These activities appear to be self-motivating and self-reinforcing, which must mean that the motivational factors to which they are subject depend on their structure or, in other words, on the relations, harmonious or discordant, between simultaneous internal psychophysiological processes.

The attention of behavior theorists was first drawn to these matters by experimental work on exploratory behavior and attention. Similar lessons have been hammered home, in different guises, by recent trends in developmental psychology, social psychology, attitude change, the psychology of thinking, the psychology of humor, and aesthetics (Berlyne, 1960, 1963a, 1965).

The discrepant reactions that form the motivational basis for the kinds of behavior in question arise largely from "collative" properties of stimulus patterns, i.e., properties such as novelty, surprisingness, complexity, ambiguity, vagueness, and puzzlingness. The operative element common to all these properties may well be conflict, i.e., initiation of processes that would, if completed without hindrance, lead to incompatible motor responses. Several kinds of evidence point to a close relation between the motivational effects of collative variables and the psychophysiological dimension of "arousal," which evidently depends on the degree of activity of the brain-stem reticular formation and its modes of interaction with other brain structures. As close affinities emerge between the new concept of "arousal" and the older concept of "drive," which has for so many decades dominated the psychology of motivation, new light promises to be shed on the fundamentals of motivation in general.

RELATIVE NEGLECT OF PERSONALITY THEORY BY BEHAVIOR THEORISTS

Reasons for Neglect

It can hardly be overlooked that problems of personality have figured much less prominently in the writings of the behavior theorists than in psychological literature as a whole, although Pavlov and Watson, the joint founders of the behaviorist current, were by no means tight-lipped on the topic.

One difficulty has been finding a conception of "personality" that would cover everything with which psychologists have concerned themselves under the aegis of that word. Most would agree to allot all study of individual differences to personality theory, but some might object to this on the grounds that "personality" implies some coherent pattern of individuality. Some matters that have at times been accepted as part of personality theory have no direct bearing on individual differences at all. They relate rather to general principles governing the nature and interrelations of the complex psychological processes contributing to the "integration" of the "self." Psychology students have not infrequently been encouraged to feel that "personality" is another name for those areas of psychology that are most "interesting," that have the widest immediate appeal. Writers can even be found who appear to be using the word "personality" simply as a pusillanimous substitute for what psychologists used to discuss without qualms as the "mind." For the purposes of this chapter, we had better simply identify "personality theory" as the theory of individual differences, while recognizing that this definition would not win universal assent.

Some of the reasons why behavior theory has neglected personality, in the sense of individual differences, are historical, which means that their validity for the present day would bear some reexamination. The behavior theorist has always committed himself to the goals of basic research and pure science, with all that they entail in the way of patience and relative aloofness from practical social problems. Most work on individual differences has, on the other hand, been actuated by the pressing needs of those engaged in clinical practice, education, or industry, which has all but equated it with applied psychology. There have therefore been the inevitable suspicions and disparagements that the ivory tower and the market place inspire in each other. Applied psychologists have, for example, been obliged to concern themselves with individual differences pertaining to extremely complex processes about which, the pure psychologist feels, little is known. One has only to think of the long-standing lack of contact between the theory of intelligence testing and the experimental psychology of thinking.

Further, behavior theorists have inherited from their empiricist and associationist forebears of previous centuries a bias towards environmentalism. Watson was evidently determined not to be outdone by any 17th-century *tabula rasa* theory, as witness his famous claim (1924) that any normal child can be turned into "any type of specialist I might select—doctor, lawyer, artist, merchant, thief, and yes, even make a man and a thief, regardless of his talents, penchants, tendencies, abilities, vocations and race of his ancestors." No neo-behaviorist has assumed this position, but the fact remains that behavior theorists spend most of their time studying learned behavior and feel that to understand the behavior of the higher mammals means, above all, to understand how learning works. Specialists in individual differences have, however, devoted much effort to considering and investigating how far personality may be predetermined by heredity. In recent years, the ethologists have made apparent the scope of elaborate unlearned behavior patterns in lower animals, and although it can hardly be doubted that such "instinctive" behavior is far less prominent in man than in the birds, fishes, and insects on which the ethologists have concentrated, the possibility that they play more part than we think in human life cannot be dismissed. Specialists in genetics (e.g., Hirsch, 1962; Darlington, 1963) have lately protested that hereditary factors may be responsible for characteristics of behavior that psychologists rarely consider from this angle. Nevertheless, the behavior theorist feels that personality theorists have all too often assumed something to be constitutional that is actually a product of learning and have, in any case, not paid nearly enough attention to the role of learning processes in the creation of individual differences.

Preoccupation with learning may lead

one to disregard innate differences, which must seem the logical starting point to anyone who wishes to throw light on the dissimilarities among human beings. Nevertheless, interest in learning does not preclude interest in individual differences. One might well think that it must sooner or later compel attention to them. First, what is learned varies with the environmental conditions to which an individual is exposed and, since different individuals encounter different combinations of external stimulus conditions, they will inevitably acquire different behavior through learning. It has, in fact, been a commonplace among behavior theorists who have maintained contact with other social scientists that the contrasting child-rearing practices and economic circumstances that characterize different social groups must inevitably produce contrasting forms of learned behavior. Precisely because of the infinite variety that learning can exhibit, it has been difficult to find appropriate classificatory schemes to impose the necessary conceptual order on them, and this has certainly been an obstacle to progress in this direction. Secondly, individuals can differ in how they learn. Such differences might well be hereditary even though they affect behavior in conjunction with learning. Factors of this sort have long been discussed in Russia, but they have received little study, and most of what they have received has been recent, in the West.

This last point is connected with an issue of research strategy on which behavior theory is firmly committed to one side. It is perfectly obvious that human beings are different from one another in some respects but alike in other respects. The question is whether we should first look for statements that apply to all of them or whether we should first try to describe and explain their differences. The behavior theorist feels that research for common principles of human and animal behavior must take precedence. This, he would point out, is how scientific inquiry must proceed, and this is how other branches of science have had the spectacular successes that have so far eluded psychology. The urge to fashion order out of chaos and to catch sight of the homogeneities that underlie diversity has always been one of the mainsprings of the human quest for knowledge and understanding. Until we can see what individuals of a class or species have in common, we cannot hope to understand how their dissimilarities have come about or even to find the most fruitful way to describe and classify these dissimilarities.

The chemical elements, a behavior theorist would recall, are certainly distinct in behavior and in outward appearance, but could their differences have been described unless we were clear about the dimensions —color, density, melting point, etc.—along which any material substance can be located? Unless we had the general concept of a chemical reaction and knew the kinds of outcome that one could have, could we say anything worth saying about chemical behavior? Now physicists and chemists are in a position to relate the findings of chemistry to principles of atomic structure and quantum mechanics that are applicable to all atoms. The properties of the different elements can now be understood in terms of differences in the number of protons and neutrons in the nucleus, differences in the numbers of electrons occupying particular "shells," etc. Likewise embryology has advanced by working out the general scheme of development from zygote to mature adult that is followed by all sexually reproducing metazoa. Yet there are undoubted differences. For example, there are contrasts between the chordates, including vertebrates, and the echinoderms on the one hand and most invertebrates on the other hand. One of them relates to the location from which mesodermal cells begin to proliferate after gastrulation. Could such a difference have conceivably been characterized before the existence and nature of gastrulation, as something found throughout the animal kingdom apart from its very lowest phyla, were known?

It is true that this line of argument has limitations. Before the different properties of chemical elements could be related to universally applicable principles of atomic structure, their manifest differences had to be noted and recorded, which took a number of centuries before the modern study of the atom was begun. So when the behavior theorist feels ready to add personality differences to the phenomena that he aspires to explain and to utilize in predicting behavior, he must acknowledge his debt to those psychologists of other orientations who have done the spade-work of delineating personality differences.

The Place of Personality Traits in Behavior Theory

Hull (1945) felt the need to establish "a genuine junction between pure and applied psychology, which of late seem to be drifting farther and farther apart." He saw that a prerequisite of this aim was to find some way of handling inter-individual and inter-species differences within the bounds of "a strict quantitative natural-science approach to the theory of behavior." He offered the hypothesis that this could be achieved by "assuming that the *forms* of the equations representing the behavioral laws of both individuals and species are identical, and that the differences between individuals and species will be found in the empirical constants which are essential components of such equations."

In 1948, Spence introduced a useful and much discussed distinction between S-R and R-R laws, as they have come to be called. The former type of law takes the form of a statement or equation that identifies a response variable as a function of stimulus-variables. The latter type defines a response variable as a function of other response variables. In other words, the S-R law enables one to predict properties of behavior from a knowledge of stimulus conditions, whereas the R-R law enables one to predict one property of behavior from a knowledge of other properties of behavior or to predict how a subject will behave in one situation from how he has behaved in other situations. Now, it is clear that specialists in personality theory have expended the bulk of their effort on working out R-R laws. In attempting to disclose the fundamental dimensions of personality, they have had to ascertain what forms of behavior tend to be found together and what characteristics can be predicted from one another. They have accordingly made great use of correlational studies and techniques such as factor analysis for analyzing correlations among traits. They have contrived measuring instruments that can be used to diagnose psychological abnormalities or to specify the educational or occupational positions to which individuals are best suited. The use of such instruments depends on R-R laws that enable patterns of behavior in a wide range of everyday situations to be inferred from behavior in the test situation.

This has undoubtedly been a further factor tending to turn behavior theorists away from the study of personality. Experimental psychologists, and behavior theorists no less than others, have always given priority to the formulation of S-R laws. They are dissatisfied with R-R laws for a number of reasons. The R-R law expresses a correlation, and it has long been realized that the existence of a correlation does not identify a causal relation: if x is significantly correlated with y, x may determine y, y may determine x, they may both influence each other, or x and y may be determined by some third factor, z. If we think of the principal aims of science as control (in the sense of making particular events more or less probable than they would otherwise have been), prediction (in the sense of anticipating future events with a greater probability of being correct than if one were to guess at random), and explanation (the aim that is hardest to characterize and the one with regard to whose achievement it is hardest to obtain agreement), we can see that, whereas an S-R law must contribute to all three of these, the R-R law can contribute only to the second. Moreover, R-R laws can be deduced from an adequate set of S-R laws, but the converse is not true.

These arguments in favor of S-R laws are powerful, but some reservations must not be overlooked. As Cattell (1957) among others has pointed out, techniques like factor analysis that have traditionally been used to analyze intercorrelations of test scores and to reveal R-R laws can be used to analyze correlations between properties or events occurring in succession, such as stimulus variables and response variables. They can thus contribute to the formulation of S-R and R-R laws simultaneously. Moreover, an adequate behavior theory must yield R-R laws as well as S-R laws. Hull's theory (1943, 1951, 1952), for example, certainly incorporated both assumptions about S-R relations and assumptions about correlations among different response properties, particularly measures of response strength. During Hull's lifetime and since, a great deal of experimentation has been devoted to the testing of the S-R predictions, and little time has been spent in testing the R-R predictions. Yet the latter stand in need of verification and many of them are, in fact, highly questionable.

In any case, the division of psychological laws into the S-R and R-R categories is an oversimplification. Contemporary psychologists, and especially behavior theorists, make copious use of "intervening variables," as we have noted. These are essentially mathematical devices to make cumbersome relations between inputs (stimulus-variables) and outputs (response-variables) conceptually manageable. There must be some sort of correspondence, but not necessarily a one-to-one correspondence, between values of these variables and conditions within the organism that are not directly observable. Spence recognizes this and mentions two additional types of psychological laws, the one (O-R laws) identifying response variables as functions of "organic variables" (i.e., "measurements of neuroanatomical or neurophysiological properties of the organism") and the other (S-O laws) identifying organic variables as functions of stimulus variables. Most psychological laws must surely be placed in a fifth category, containing what we may call "S,O-R laws," stating how response variables are determined jointly by stimulus and organic (i.e., intervening) variables.

A number of distinctions among the organic or intervening variables are worth drawing. First, we have what we might call *transient intervening variables* (O_T), whose values change within a matter of minutes or hours, e.g., motivational condition, emotional state, mood, degree of fatigue. A second important class is *age* (O_A): developmental psychology has the responsibility of providing laws of the O_A-R and the S, O_A-R types. It tells us, in other words, how the probabilities of certain kinds of behavior over a random sample of stimulus situations will vary from age to age, and it tells us how the probabilities of particular kinds of behavior in specifiable stimulus situations change with age. Thirdly, there are intervening variables whose values may change abruptly or gradually but can remain relatively fixed thereafter for many years (O_L). These represent the results of learning processes. They comprise what we call *habits,* but factors known by many other names, e.g., "attitude," "disposition," or "motive" often qualify for this category. Finally, we have variables that take on different values for different individuals but maintain the same values throughout the lifetime of one individual (O_C). These consist, of course, of *constitutional* or *congenital predispositions* to particular kinds of behavior. The variables of concern to personality theory must clearly include those of the last category. Many individual differences, however, i.e., acquired personality traits, belong to the third category, which is one reason why some behavior theorists have been led to doubt whether personality theory requires separate treatment, feeling it to be inseparable from the study of the formation and nature of learned behavior patterns in general. Be that as it may, we must recognize as the ultimate objective of behavior theory the formulation of laws that will enable the contribution of all of these kinds of variables in the determination of behavior to be taken into account. In other words, the only fully adequate laws of psychology will be of the S, O_T, O_A, O_L, O_C-R variety.

We shall now review the main bodies of work carried out within the behavior-theory movement that are relevant to personality theory. They can be divided from the outset into two groups. First, there are investigations concerned with factors, presumed to be mostly hereditary, that affect how an individual learns. Secondly, there are investigations concerned with differences in the learning experiences to which individuals have been exposed, creating differences in what they have learned.

INDIVIDUAL DIFFERENCES IN LEARNING CAPACITY

Pavlov's Theory of Types of Nervous System

Although the concept of "behavior theory" is not current in the U.S.S.R., we shall begin with Russian work belonging to the Pavlovian tradition, because its general aims and methodology are fully consonant with those of Western behavior theory.

Pavlov's Early Theory

In the two translated books, *Conditioned Reflexes* (1927, Lecture XVII) and *Lectures on Conditioned Reflexes* (1928, Chapter XL), Pavlov put forward a classification of "types of nervous system" that is fairly well known in the West. He describes four types of dogs, corresponding to the four types of human temperament in the Hippocratic scheme, representing different segments of a continuum going from extreme predominance of excitatory processes to extreme predominance of inhibitory processes.

At one pole, there is the highly "excitatory" dog, corresponding to the choleric temperament, which is aggressive and hard to discipline. Such dogs form positive conditioned associations easily but have difficulty in acquiring inhibitory associations. At the opposite pole, there is the "inhibitory" type, corresponding to the melancholic temperament, with a marked preponderance of inhibitory processes, as shown by the difficulty of establishing positive conditioned responses and the ease of training in inhibition. "Everybody who sees such an animal would immediately judge it a great coward." Between these two extreme types, there are the two "central" or "equilibrated" types, in which excitatory and inhibitory processes are less disproportionate in strength, so that such dogs are less prone to neurotic breakdown. Equilibrated dogs can, however, be divided into the "sanguine" type, with a slight preponderance of excitation, and the "phlegmatic" type, with a slight preponderance of inhibition. Sanguine dogs are "extremely vivacious, always sniffing at everything, gazing at everything intently, and reacting quickly to the minutest sounds." They are satisfactory subjects for conditioning experiments as long as they receive a variety of stimuli in close succession. If left unstimulated for long, they are apt to become drowsy and go to sleep. The "phlegmatic" dog is, in contrast, "self contained and quiet—a persistent and steadfast toiler in life."

Pavlov's Later Theory

As time went on, Pavlov became more and more dissatisfied with this one-dimensional classification and, after his thinking on the subject had gone through several vicissitudes, arrived at a scheme (1935a, 1935b) that is not well known in the West but has been the accepted basis for most Soviet work on individual differences ever since. He now recognized three criteria by which nervous systems could be distinguished, namely, *strength, balance,* and *mobility*. Theoretically, a nervous system could be strong or weak; it could possess equilibrium between excitatory and inhibitory processes, disequilibrium with predominance of excitation, or disequilibrium with predominance of inhibition; it could have mobile or inert excitatory processes and mobile or inert inhibitory processes. This means that there could be twenty-four different types, even if simple presence or absence of a particular property were noted. If differences of degree were introduced, the number of possible types would become, of course, much greater.

In spite of the theoretical admissibility of more numerous types, Pavlov continued to insist that most dogs fall clearly into one or other of four types, corresponding to the four temperaments of Hippocrates. His accounts of the differences separating these types had, however, undergone great changes since he formulated his earlier theory. He now identified the "choleric" with a *strong, unbalanced* nervous system, having a preponderance of excitation over inhibition, the "sanguine" type with a *strong, balanced, mobile* nervous system, the "phlegmatic" type with a *strong, balanced, inert* nervous system, and the "melancholic" type with a *weak* nervous system.

The *strength* of the nervous system is manifested by an animal's resistance to "passive" forms of inhibition. Western psychologists are generally familiar with the "active" or "internal" forms of inhibition that were fully described in the most familiar translated writings; this is the kind of inhibition responsible for extinction, differentiation, conditioned inhibition, and inhibition of delay. However, Pavlov also recognized "passive" inhibition, representing not simply temporary weakening of conditioned associations but temporary suppression of them by competing factors. An example of this is "external inhibition," which occurs whenever a novel, extraneous stimulus is presented at a time when an animal would otherwise be performing a conditioned response. In later writings (e.g., 1928), he attributed external inhibition to "negative induction" (i.e., the induction of inhibition in neighboring parts of the cerebral cortex when a strong excitatory process is generated at one locus) due to the powerful "orientation reaction" (i.e., exploratory and attentive activities) evoked by the extraneous stimulus. He also paid increasing attention to "transmarginal" or "supramaximal" inhibition. This is a protective process that intervenes when the nervous system is subjected to excess excitation, e.g., by inordinately intense, novel, or prolonged stimuli. It results in the paradoxical appearance of weaker responses to stronger conditioned stimuli (contravening the usual trend, which was called the "law of strength") or by the absence of any response at all to a stimulus productive of intolerable levels of excitation.

Pavlov (1935b) outlined the following procedures as methods for gauging the strength or weakness of the nervous system:

1. An attempt is made to establish a conditioned salivary response to the extremely loud sound of a rattle as well as to other, more moderate stimuli. Strong dogs will respond to the rattle as intensely, if not more intensely, as to the other stimuli. In weak dogs, the response to the rattle will be weaker or it will be absent altogether, and it may even give rise to a neurotic breakdown.

2. Excitatory processes are strengthened by starving the dog before the conditioning session begins. This will give rise to more pronounced conditioning responses than usual in animals of strong types, but it will diminish conditioned salivation in animals of the weak type.

3. The third technique (which has become the standard test for strength of the nervous system among Pavlov's successors studying animal behavior) depends on administration of caffeine, and this likewise heightens conditioned responses in strong

nervous systems but produces decreased responding, indicative of supramaximal inhibition, in weak nervous systems.

4. The dog is conditioned to a conditioned stimulus which, in early trials, is followed by the presentation of food after a second or two. The delay is then increased to 20–30 seconds. In a strong nervous system, the amount of salivation will increase steadily from the onset of the stimulus to the moment when food is due, but, in weak nervous systems, there will be a steady decline in salivation or else irregular fluctuations.

Although imbalance could in principle take the form of either a deficiency of inhibition or a deficiency of excitation, Pavlov insisted that the latter was rarely if ever encountered; so estimating the degree of balance amounted to measurement of the *strength of inhibitory processes*. Pavlov described a number of ways of doing this:

1. An inhibitory conditioned stimulus is prolonged in order to ascertain the duration of inhibition that the nervous system can stand. If inhibitory processes are strong, unheralded prolongation of the stimulus up to 5–10 minutes will produce little or no disturbance. If inhibitory processes are weak, the continuation of a stimulus that has usually lasted 15 seconds for an additional 15 seconds may be seriously disruptive; a duration of 5 minutes, introduced even once, leads to a "collapse of all conditioned-reflex activity, in the form of a lasting neurosis."

2. According to Pavlov, both excitatory and inhibitory processes, having been set up in one location in the cerebral cortex, will first irradiate over a wide expanse of cortical regions and then concentrate, producing opposite processes ("negative induction" and "positive induction" respectively) in adjacent regions. Animals with strong inhibitory processes will show great capacity for rapid and narrow concentration. So if a positive conditioned stimulus is presented shortly after a negative or inhibitory stimulus, an unbalanced nervous system, weak in inhibition, will show an inhibitory after-effect, whereas strength of inhibition will be manifested through positive induction, i.e., the positive stimulus will evoke a more intense response than usual.

3. A nervous system that is weak in inhibition will form inhibitory associations slowly, and they will always be somewhat unstable.

4. An unbalanced nervous system will be unable to develop inhibitory associations if attempts are made to establish these concurrently with positive conditioned responses.

5. In an animal with an unbalanced nervous system, anything more than a small dose of a bromide will cause conditioned-reflex activity to disappear, whereas animals with stronger inhibitory processes will withstand larger doses.

The *mobility* factor had been little studied when Pavlov wrote the article (1935b) whose content we are reviewing. But he mentions three ways in which degree of mobility might be measured.

1. If the conditioned stimulus is made to act for a long time before the unconditioned stimulus appears, an inert nervous system will have difficulty in forming a delayed conditioned response; the necessity of changing over from inhibition to excitation at the appropriate moment will exceed its capacity.

2. The inert nervous system has difficulty in responding appropriately when a positive conditioned stimulus closely follows a negative conditioned stimulus or vice versa. The process of excitation or inhibition induced by the first stimulus tends to persist during the application of the second. One particularly effective test is to subject the animal to a situation in which the same conditioned stimulus is presented four times consecutively, being reinforced with food after the last of the four presentations. The inert nervous system is unable to refrain from salivation at the first three presentations and then to salivate during the fourth. Animals with low mobility will likewise be disturbed by a "change in stereotype," i.e., a change in the habitual order of presentation of a series of intermingled positive and negative

stimuli. The change may cause all conditioned salivary responses to disappear for days, whereas the dog with high mobility will regularly respond or not respond to a stimuli, as appropriate, despite the order in which they appear.

3. If a positive conditioned stimulus is to be turned into a negative one, by ceasing to pair it with the unconditioned stimulus, or vice versa, the mobile nervous system will acquire the new association quickly and easily whereas the inert nervous system will do so slowly and imperfectly.

More Recent Work With Dogs

During a visit to the Pavlov Institute of Experimental Psychology at Kol'tushi near Leningrad, in 1961, the writer found the study of individual differences in dogs continuing to be assiduously pursued. A conversation with Professor Krasuski disclosed that the caffeine test is now the standard procedure for measuring strength, and attempting to turn positive into negative conditioned stimuli and vice versa is the usual method for measuring mobility. There is no one procedure in use for measuring balance, but, in general, the ease of establishing differential and other inhibitory associations is examined. The bromide test for inhibitory processes and the sudden replacement of a positive by a negative conditioned stimulus or vice versa as a test for mobility have both been given up as insufficiently reliable.

In a recent article, Krasuski (1963) describes 48 types of dogs that his investigations have led him to distinguish. He recognizes four levels of "strength," depending on the dose of caffeine that is necessary to produce supramaximal inhibition, and three levels of "balance," depending on the ratio of the amplitude of response to a differential stimulus and the amplitude of response to a positive conditioned stimulus. "Mobility" has four levels: when a positive conditioned stimulus is turned into a negative one and vice versa, the changeover may be successful or unsuccessful, and the reversal of effect may be equal or unequal for the two stimuli involved. Finer distinctions can be made with regard to the "mobility" dimension by taking into account exactly how effective the changeover is for the two stimuli, how permanent it is, and how many trials are required to establish it. In this way, a tenfold classification can be made along the "mobility" dimension, resulting in 120 types.

One topic of concentration at Kol'tushi is the role of genetic factors in the determination of type of nervous system. It had been found that environment could modify behavior so as to produce behavior characteristic of a particular type. For example, dogs reared in restricted environments behave like animals with weak nervous systems even if born of strong parents. They do not actively investigate novel stimuli but show arrested movement and widespread inhibition (what Pavlovians called the "passive-defensive reflex"). The findings of Melzack (1954) and Melzack and Scott (1957), who likewise studied differences in emotional behavior between normally reared and restricted dogs, may be compared.

Similarly, nutrition makes a difference. If better-than-usual food is fed to the mother during pregnancy and to the offspring for the first year of life, strength will be increased in both constitutionally strong and constitutionally weak individuals. Nevertheless, the next generation will revert to type, showing that these environmentally induced changes have simply masked constitutional characteristics.

Experiments were under way to ascertain whether heredity effects in underlying strength and mobility are dominant or recessive. It was conjectured that they must be recessive, since weak or inert nervous systems are maladaptive.

Then, physiological correlates of the Pavlovian traits were under investigation. It had been found that mobile adults are more generally active, as shown by a stabilimeter test, than inert dogs, and balanced slightly more active than unbalanced, but there was little difference between strong and weak animals. In strong dogs, inflammation of the skin induced by cantharides or by ultraviolet rays occurs more rapidly, the effects of ACTH are more pronounced, and abscesses are produced much more slowly by turpentine. This suggests that, in strong animals, the corrective reactions of the body are prompter and more efficient.

Extension to Human Beings

Among Pavlov's students, the pioneers in applying conditioned-response techniques to human subjects were Krasnogorski and Ivanov-Smolenski. Both specialized in child subjects, but they made use of different experimental techniques. Krasnogorski devised a variant of the original salivary conditioning technique used with dogs. The unconditioned stimulus consisted of an edible substance, usually some sort of cranberry puree, delivered into the child's mouth through a spout. The responses investigated consisted of mechanically recorded masticatory movements and the secretion of saliva, collected through a metal device placed in the child's mouth. Ivanov-Smolenski and his followers originated a "motor-conditioning" procedure. The response consisted of pressing a rubber bulb, connected with a kymograph by means of a rubber tube so that the slightest variations in pressure could be registered, and the unconditioned stimulus consisted of hearing the word "Press!" uttered by the experimenter. Inhibitory associations were set up by having the experimenter say "Don't press!" immediately after the presentation of the stimuli that were to be negative. Various events—visual, auditory, etc.—were used as conditioned stimuli in both laboratories.

Both Krasnogorski (1958) and Ivanov-Smolenski (Briks, 1956) applied their conditioning methods to the investigation of individual differences in children. In Ivanov-Smolenski's laboratory, the method of free association to verbal stimuli was also tried out. Four types of children, corresponding to the four types of nervous system figuring in Pavlov's later classificatory scheme, were found to exist in both laboratories.

The descriptions given by Krasnogorski and by Briks were in agreement with each other and with Pavlov's descriptions of the corresponding types of dogs, except for a few details. For example, Briks writes that children of the weak type are characterized by an absence of generalization whereas Krasnogorski mentions "generalized irradiation" and "reduction in processes of concentration" as typical of them. In general, however, both writers depict the strength of the nervous system as manifested by a resistance to passive forms of inhibition and a capacity for connected speech of high quality. Krasnogorski mentions emotional reactions, signifying relative lack of dominance by the cortex of subcortical centers, as an additional manifestation of weakness, as well as the proneness to neurotic symptoms mentioned by Pavlov. Strength of excitatory and inhibitory processes is revealed through the speed with which positive or negative associations are established, stability of these associations, and response latency. Children of the choleric (strong, unbalanced) type tend to give several words as a response in the free-association test and to engage in motor activity at the same time. Mobility is shown by the capacity to change abruptly from inhibition to excitation, e.g., when a prolonged conditioned stimulus is at last accompanied by the unconditioned stimulus.

Rabinovich (1961) has related Pavlov's concept of mobility to that adopted by the St. Petersburg University school of physiologists led by Vvedenski and Ukhtomski. Vvedenski regarded mobility as a matter of the number of electrical "oscillations" that neural tissue can support within a unit of time. Rabinovich measures mobility with the help of an apparatus that presents a light repeatedly for a brief period. The subject is instructed to turn off the light with a switch before it goes off by itself. By varying the frequency with which the light appears, the rate at which the subject can respond is ascertained.

Rogov *et al.* (1964) have related the Pavlovian typology to vasomotor reactions. Their investigations indicate that strong balanced individuals have plethysmograms with steady base-lines and that both their conditioned and unconditioned vasoconstrictions (cold being the unconditioned stimulus) are high in amplitude and stable. When the nervous system is strong but unbalanced, the base-line is wavy, and conditioned and unconditioned vasomotor reflexes fluctuate in amplitude. Subjects with weak nervous systems have flat base-lines; their unconditioned reflexes are "inert and small," while their conditioned reflexes are slight and unstable.

The most thoroughgoing effort to study human individual differences with the guidance of Pavlov's classificatory concepts was headed by Teplov (1956, 1961) at the Institute of Psychology of the Academy of Pedagogical Sciences in Moscow. An extremely helpful compilation of material in English on the work of this group and on the development of the Pavlovian approach to individual differences has appeared under Gray's (1965) editorship. Teplov deliberately rejected the motor-conditioning method adopted by Ivanov-Smolenski, following Pavlov's criticism that this method must involve the intervention of thought processes, as the child tries to puzzle out what is required of him in this situation, and thus does not represent typical conditioning. There is actually evidence (Paramanova, 1956) that this is true of older children, whereas, at about the age of three, a direct conditioned association between the conditioned stimulus and motor response is set up. There are some interesting and striking differences, e.g., in latency, stability, and speed of forming associations, between the two cases.

At any rate, Teplov argued in favor of involuntary responses as indices of the characteristics in which he was interested. His group relies heavily on the "conditioned proto-chemical reflex" discovered by Dolin. The unconditioned response is the decrease in visual sensitivity brought on by brief exposure to an intense, uniform patch of light. If an auditory stimulus is immediately coupled with exposure to the light, it may come to evoke a conditioned rise in threshold. All the standard conditioning phenomena can, it is claimed, be detected and measured with this method. Other procedures are used to supplement it, and, more recently, conditioned EEG alpha blocking, with a flashbulb light as the unconditioned stimulus and a tone as the conditioned stimulus, has been used.

The assumption that the processes under study can be accounted for in terms of Pavlov's dimensions and the assumption that the various aspects of behavior regarded as indices of a particular dimension are actually intercorrelated seem to call for statistical tests. Recently, members of Teplov's group have begun to make use of the kinds of statistical techniques that Western psychologists would apply in these circumstances. They have examined the hypothesis that " 'strength' of a nervous system is correlated with low reactivity, hence with low sensitivity to peripheral stimulation" (Nebylitsyn, Rozhdestvenskaia, & Teplov, 1960), finding that persons with strong nervous systems (ascertained by measuring supermaximal inhibition, with or without caffeine, in a conditioned-photochemical-response situation) have significantly higher visual and auditory absolute thresholds. Significant positive correlations have been found among certain measures of EEG activity assumed to be indices of balance, e.g., the speed with which alpha waves return after the presentation of a tone alone or of a tone that has been paired with light, the rapidity with which repeated presentation of a tone produces extinction, duration of alpha blocking to the tone before or after conditioning, and the speed with which differentiation between tones of two pitches is set up (Nebylitsyn, 1961). A Thurstone-type factor analysis of intercorrelations among 21 suspected indices of strength of nervous system (Rozhdestvenskaia, Nebylitsyn, Borisova, & Ermolaeva-Tomina, 1960) revealed a factor on which thirteen of the measures have significant loadings. On the other hand, four indices, relating to amplitude and speed of extinction of vasomotor orientation reactions, which have traditionally been regarded by Pavlovians as indices of strength, had small loadings on the first factor but high loadings on the second factor, identified with balance. A more recent factor analysis of 18 EEG variables (Nebylitsyn, 1963) produced four centroid factors. The first three were identified with "balance," "excitatory strength," and "alpha-reactivity" respectively, while the fourth was found difficult to interpret and left unnamed.

Finally, Teplov and his collaborators have attempted to identify the general psychological characteristics that go together with the variables on which the type of nervous system depends, which means extending the Pavlovian theory of individual differences to the elucidation of temperament (Leites, 1956). Strength of excitatory processes is said to go together with a capacity to handle complex materials perceptually and intellectually, as well as with ability to withstand prolonged tension and to recover quickly from fatigue. Persons with strong inhibitory processes tend to concentrate their attention effectively, terminate and restrain their activities where appropriate, write and speak concisely, and generally exercise self-control. Weakness in both excitation and inhibition means inability to concentrate, lack of capacity for intellectual work, lack of initiative and perseverance. The signs of a balanced nervous system include placidity, freedom from impetuosity in thought, speech, and action, and immunity to neurotic disturbance. High mobility implies adaptiveness and flexibility in rapidly changing conditions. Teplov's group recognizes, however, that innate properties of the nervous system interact with learning to produce "character," so that "genotypes" must not be confused with "phenotypes."

Later findings led Teplov (1963) to the conclusion that the strength of excitatory processes and the strength of inhibitory processes should be recognized as separate traits rather than lumped together under the label of "strength of nervous system" in accordance with the traditional practice. Furthermore, factor-analytic data compelled him to distinguish two kinds of lability, one pertaining to the ease with which excitatory stimuli can become inhibitory and vice versa, the other to the speed with which neural processes are set off and arrested.

Nebylitsyn (1966), Teplov's successor, now regards equilibrium as a "secondary property of the nervous system," depending on primary properties (strength, mobility, dynamism) of both excitation and inhibition. Dynamism is now regarded as a separate parameter, distinct from strength. It is reflected in the speed with which conditioned (excitatory or inhibitory) connections are formed and in the magnitude and rate of extinction of EEG desynchronization and of the components of the orientation reaction.

Psychological Abnormalities

One of Pavlov's most celebrated contributions to personality theory is his inauguration of the study of experimental neurosis. In *Conditioned Reflexes* (1927), he tells of a number of ways in which behavior apparently analogous to human neurotic breakdowns can be induced in dogs. They comprise (1) exposure to a stimulus midway between a positive conditioned stimulus (a circle) and a differential inhibitory stimulus (an ellipse), (2) the use of an excessively intense electric shock as a conditioned stimulus reinforced with food, (3) the sudden replacement of a positive conditioned stimulus (24 tactual stimulations per minute) by an inhibitory stimulus (12 tactual stimulations per minute), (4) extreme prolongation of the conditioned stimulus (a buzzer) before delivery of food, (5) training in extremely difficult discriminations, (6) exposure to "powerful and unusual stimuli" due to a flood.

It is evident that individual dogs will vary widely in susceptibility to experimental neurosis and in the kinds of behavior shown when experimental neurosis occurs. In accordance with his first typology, Pavlov began with the view that neurosis is most likely in animals representing extreme proponderance of excitation (the choleric type) or extreme proponderance of inhibition (the melancholic type). In the former, neurosis meant a loss of inhibitory associations and violent motor activity, which he compared with neurasthenia. Dogs at the opposite extreme showed weakening of excitatory associations and abnormal immobility, which he compared with hysteria (Pavlov, 1928, p. 375).

Later, his typology changed, as we have seen, and, in the final years of his life, he became intensely interested in psychological abnormality. He spent a great deal of time observing human patients exhibiting various disorders and attempting to interpret their symptoms with reference to his concepts (Pavlov, 1941; Ivanov-Smolenski, 1954). He still regarded choleric and melancholic nervous systems as those most prone to psychopathological disorders, regarding imbalance and weakness as relatively maladaptive properties. He related these two types, in fact, to Kretschmer's *cyclothymia* and *schizothymia* respectively.

In *schizophrenia,* he noted an intense susceptibility of the cerebral cortex to passive inhibition producing, in extreme cases, symptoms like mutism and catatonia. Through disinhibition and positive induction, older processes which had long been subject to inhibition are restored. Infantile behavior and automatism appear, or unconditioned postural reflexes may be liberated from cortical control to produce catalepsy. Focal disturbances at various points in the cortex create disintegration. *Paranoia* results from pathological inertness of excitation together with a decline in active inhibitory processes, which are responsible for correction of tendencies to delusion in normal persons. As for *manic-depressive psychosis,* there was held to be extreme excitation in the manic phase, with an insufficiency of the "abating and restorative process" that normally comes from supramaximal inhibition.

In interpreting neurotic syndromes, Pavlov refers to an additional dimension of personality that he came to recognize as he turned his attention late in life to human behavior. "Life," he writes, "definitely uses two categories of people—artists and thinkers ... the artists ... comprehend reality as a whole, as a continuity, as a complete living reality, without any divisions, without any separation. The other group, the thinkers, pull it apart, kill it, so to speak, making out of it a temporary skeleton and then only gradually putting it together anew, occasionally ..." (Pavlov, 1941, pp. 113–114). The character of the thinker reveals dominance of the "second signal system" (i.e., verbal behavior and responses to verbal stimuli) over "the first signal system" (i.e., behavior involving nonverbal stimuli and responses), whereas, in the artist, the first signal system is on top.

Pavlov regarded *neurasthenia* as the kind of disturbance to which dogs and human beings with weak or unbalanced nervous systems are liable, but he distinguished a "hypersthenic" form, with a preponderance of excitation, from a "hyposthenic" form, with a preponderance of inhibition, as well as cases in which periods of excitation and activity alternate with periods of "weakness and temporary wear." Then, in addition, there are the two uniquely human conditions of *psychasthenia* and *hysteria,* representing accentuations of the "thinking" and "artistic" types respectively. Psychasthenia may include compulsive actions and obsessive thoughts, showing, in their perseveration, psychological inertness with inadequate inhibition, but there may also be obsessive fears (phobias) and inabilities to act, which means that inhibition has overstepped normal bounds. Hysteria involves inhibition of particular functions or of widespread systems of conditioned associations (e.g., amnesias). Subcortical functions may be manifestly out of control due to weakness of the higher parts of the central nervous system. Hysterics are prone to suggestion and to hypnotism, in which a focus of excitation is allowed free play as potentially interfering processes are disabled through negative induction.

Pavlov, as well as his collaborators and successors, paid some attention to therapeutic measures. He recommended administration of bromide as a means of strengthening inhibitory processes and thus overcoming either pathologically inert excitation or unbalanced conditions in which inhibition is unduly overwhelmed by excitation. Prolonged narcosis and other conditions conducive to rest were widely used for the treatment of cases in which the protective effects of supramaximal inhibition, whose restorative power Pavlov continually stressed, were deficient. In the early years of conditioned-response research, a period of respite from experimentation had been found the best way to deal with dogs suffering from an excess of inhibition (Pavlov, 1927, p. 317).

Eysenck and the Maudsley Group

Taxonomic Studies

Early in his research career, Eysenck (1947, 1952a) was a personality theorist in the tradition of Spearman and Burt, believing that the highest priority should be assigned to taxonomic problems and that factor analysis and related statistical techniques form the most valuable aids to their solution. His first major study (1947) was one in which information about the presence of symptoms and other traits and about previous life-history was collected for 700 neurotic patients in a military hospital and the data were factor-analyzed. The outcome was the identification of two major personality factors labeled *neuroticism* and *introversion-extraversion*. The Maudsley Medical Questionnaire and, later, the Maudsley Personality Inventory (MPI) and Eysenck Personality Inventory (EPI) were subsequently published as means of measuring these factors.

Neuroticism was conceived as a dimension on which neurotics have higher scores than normal persons. It seemed to be close to the "*w*" factor that Webb (1915) had introduced in the early days of factor analysis and described as "prominent on the 'character' side of mental activity," reflecting "persistence of motives," "consistency of action resulting from deliberate volition or will"; low "*w*" corresponds, of course, to high neuroticism. Persons tending towards the two poles of the introversion-extraversion dimension were characterized as follows (Eysenck, 1947): "(a) the introvert has a more subjective, the extravert a more objective outlook; (b) the introvert shows a higher degree of cerebral activity, the extravert a higher degree of behavioral activity; (c) the introvert shows a tendency to self-control (inhibition), the extravert a tendency to lack of self-control." Introverts high in neuroticism tended to develop "dysthymic" disorders, i.e., anxiety state, obsessive-compulsive neurosis, or reactive depression, whereas hysterics and psychopaths appeared to be high in neuroticism and extraversion.

A review of the previous literature on personality classification (Eysenck, 1953) showed that, despite wide differences in the kinds of data collected and in methods of analysis, dimensions close to neuroticism and introversion-extraversion had emerged time after time under different names. Sometimes investigators appeared to have discovered the same factor space with the reference vectors rotated. At other times, typologies had been suggested that could readily be related to Eysenck's two-dimensional scheme. For example, the fourfold Hippocratic classification that so many psychologists of recent times (including Pavlov) have felt unable to reject has been assimilated by Eysenck (1963a) by identifying the melancholic type with unstable (i.e., relatively neurotic) introverts, the choleric type with unstable extraverts, the phlegmatic type with stable introverts, and the sanguine type with stable extraverts.

Studies subjecting normal and psychologically abnormal subjects to a variety of experimental situations have brought to light several significant differences separating neurotics from normal individuals and introverts from extraverts. As this work proceeded, it became apparent that a third dimension, labeled *psychoticism* since it distinguished psychotics from both neurotics and normals, should be added (Eysenck, 1952a; S. B. G. Eysenck, H. J. Eysenck, & Claridge, 1960).

Personality and Conditioning

In the mid-1950's, Eysenck became committed to the enterprise of relating differences in personality to concepts of behavior theory, with the aim of giving personality theory a firm footing in general psychology (1955, 1957). After turning to the works of Pavlov and Hull for guidance he formulated a *Postulate of Individual Differences* stating that:

Human beings differ with respect to the speed at which excitation and inhibition are produced, the strength of excitation and inhibition produced, and the speed at which inhibition is dissipated. These differences are properties of the physical structures involved in making stimulus-connections (Eysenck, 1957).

He added a *Typological Postulate,* according to which

Individuals in whom excitatory potential is generated slowly and in whom excitatory potentials so generated are relatively weak, are thereby predisposed to develop extraverted patterns of behavior and to develop hysterical-psychopathic disorders in cases of neurotic breakdown; individuals in whom excitatory potential is generated quickly and in whom excitatory potentials so generated are strong, are thereby predisposed to develop introverted patterns of behavior and to develop dysthymic disorders in case of neurotic breakdown. Similarly, individuals in whom reactive inhibition is developed quickly, in whom strong reactive inhibitions are generated, and in whom reactive inhibition is dissipated slowly, are thereby predisposed to develop extraverted patterns of behavior and to develop hysterical-psychopathic disorders in case of neurotic breakdown; conversely, individuals in whom reactive inhibition is developed slowly, in whom weak reactive inhibitions are generated, and in whom reactive inhibition is dissipated quickly, are thereby predisposed to develop introverted patterns of behavior and to develop dysthymic disorders in case of neurotic breakdown.

It was deduced from these postulates that introverts will acquire conditioned responses more quickly than extraverts and take longer to show extinction when a conditioned response ceases to be reinforced.

The hypothesis that extraverts have more inhibition than introverts must seem rather paradoxical, since introverts are generally thought of as more "inhibited," i.e., more reserved and restrained, less likely to express themselves easily or to behave impulsively. Eysenck overcomes this difficulty by postulating that the introvert is more "socialized." He has learned more effectively than the extravert to conform to social norms and to avoid behavior that might incur social disapproval. He has a relative preoccupation with "social duties, ethics, guilt, and similar moral notions." In his opinions on moral, social, and political matters, he is apt to be "tender-minded," i.e., to be governed by ethical and religious ideals and to be opposed to overgratification of sexual and aggressive impulses (Eysenck, 1954, 1957). Since moral training and socialization depend largely on the acquisition of instrumental avoidance responses and conditioned fear responses, the presumption is that the introvert's superior aptitude for rapid and effective conditioning will make him acquire these behavior patterns to a fuller degree than the extravert. Thus, "a smaller degree of reactive inhibition" makes for "a greater degree of social inhibition." The proneness of the dysthymic, or introverted neurotic, to anxiety is claimed as corroboration of this hypothesis.

The postulate of individual differences was tested in two experiments performed by Franks. The first of them (1956) showed the frequency of conditioned eyeblink responses during conditioning and subsequent extinction to be significantly higher for dysthymics than for hysterics. GSR was also recorded and yielded the same results. Normal subjects came between the two neurotic groups in eyelid responses but were not significantly different from hysterics. They were quite close to the hysterics in GSR incidence. The second experiment (1957a) used non-neurotic subjects throughout. The number of conditioned eyeblink responses was found to be significantly higher in introverts than in extraverts but not significantly related to neuroticism.

Criticisms and Queries

Eysenck (e.g., 1957) claimed strong support for his Postulate of Individual Differences from Franks's findings, as well as from investigations of other forms of behavior, e.g., kinesthetic figural after-effects and dark adaptation. His position underwent, however, a number of quite vituperative attacks (e.g., Hamilton, 1959; Lykken, 1959; Storms & Sigal, 1958), to which Eysenck retorted no less forthrightly (1959b, 1959c, 1960b).

Some criticisms were aimed at ambiguities in Eysenck's assertions. They brought up such questions as which of several possible parameters descriptive of excitatory and inhibitory processes are to be regarded as crucial, whether more frequent responses during conditioning can be said to indicate a high rate of conditioning, whether dysthymics may have shown more conditioned blinking because they were more reactive from the start. With regard to these points, Eysenck could be defended on the grounds that he was opening up new and long overdue lines of research and that what was needed at that juncture was a set of hypotheses precise enough to indicate empirical relations worthy of investigation but imprecise enough to be progressively filed down as research progressed. That a strategy of gradual zeroing-in may be conducive to the advancement of science can be justified on information-theoretic grounds (Broadbent, 1956; Berlyne, 1964).

More substantive questions were, however, raised as well:

1. Differences in the rate at which inhibition is accumulated should affect the ease of acquiring any kind of learned response. Should it not first have been established that subjects tend to be consistently high or low in conditionability and resistance to extinction over a wide variety of conditioning situations? Campbell (1938) failed to find significant correlations between measures of the strength of conditioned eyeblink and patellar reflexes. Davidson, Payne, and Sloane (1964) examined conditioned finger-withdrawal responses and GSRs to a tone, with electric shock as the unconditioned stimulus, and found a negligible correlation between the strengths of the two kinds of conditioned response. If there is not a general factor of conditionability, might not the differences between introverts and extraverts observed by Franks be restricted to eyelid conditioning? Davidson, Payne, and Sloane obtained no significant correlations between any of their conditioning measures and either neuroticism or extraversion.

On the other hand, significant tendencies for extravert normals and alcoholics to show less GSR conditioning have been found by Vogel (1960, 1961). Franks (1956), it will be remembered, obtained more GSR conditioning from dysthymics than from hysterics, and Halberstam (1961) obtained a comparable difference between subjects scoring high on the Psychasthenia and Hysteria scales, respectively, of the MMPI.

Willett (1960) found a significant negative correlation between extraversion and salivary-conditioning scores in a pilot experiment, but, in a large-scale study conducted subsequently, only a small, insignificant negative correlation was obtained. There was an insignificant negative correlation between extraversion and the rate of progress towards probability matching in a binary guessing situation, while a "spatial-conditioning" procedure, designed to find out how far sound would be wrongly localized in the direction of a simultaneously presented light, yielded a significant negative correlation between extraversion and tendency to perceive the sound displaced towards the light. Willett concludes, however, that these last two tasks did not represent true conditioning. It cannot, however, be denied that they measured either learning in the experimental situation or the effectiveness of previous learning, and the Postulate of Individual Differences should presumably apply to learning in general. Nevertheless, there may well have been all sorts of complicating factors in these less automatic forms of behavior.

2. Do dysthymics and hysterics form suitable criterion groups for introversion and extraversion respectively? Might they not differ in other respects that could account for the differences that distinguish them in eyeblink conditioning? Hysterics have been found to occupy intermediate positions between dysthymics and normals on measures of neuroticism in studies by Claridge and Herrington (1960) and Sigal, Star, and Franks (1958). Might dysthymics and hysterics differ in drive level, which would certainly be expected to affect rate of conditioning? Has the predicted difference between introverts and extraverts been established in normal populations?

Some of the force of these questions was removed by Franks's (1957a) experiment in which introverted normals performed more conditioned eyeblinks than extraverted normals. However, Willett (1960) cites four experiments, including his own, in which correlations between extraversion in normal subjects and eyeblink conditioning were examined. He notes that Franks (1957a) was the only experimenter to find a significant correlation in the predicted direction.

Two more recent experiments (Spence & Spence, 1964; Franks, 1963b) could be added to those that failed to confirm Franks's original finding to a statistically significant extent. Eysenck (1965) has since reviewed studies relating level of conditioning to extraversion. He reports a significant confirmation of his hypothesis in six out of eleven partial-reinforcement eyeblink-conditioning studies, in two out of four continuous-reinforcement eyeblink-conditioning studies, and in five out of nine GSR-conditioning studies. No significant differences or correlations in the opposite direction are reported, and all but one of the nonsignificant correlations specified are negative. He discusses variations in procedure that might account for those results that fail to demonstrate a negative relation between conditioning and extraversion. Franks (1963b), in a recent article summing up the current status of this line of research, reviews several attitudinal and other factors that are known to affect conditioning scores in human subjects and whose independent fluctuations must tend to lessen correlations between conditioning measures and measures of basic personality factors.

3. Willett expresses doubt that the MPI is a satisfactory instrument for measuring extraversion, mentioning that differences between extraverts and introverts in experimental tasks have sometimes turned out to be more clear-cut when subjects are placed in these two categories on the basis of ratings of behavior rather than of MPI scores alone. A study by Franks, Holden, and Phillips (1961) revealed that ratings by external observers and self-ratings in the form of answers to items from the MPI were reliably correlated in normal subjects. In an abnormal population, external ratings, while showing a high inter-judge reliability, tended to be uncorrelated with MPI self-

ratings. Eysenck and Eysenck (1963) have recently acknowledged that the extraversion scale derived from the MPI can be regarded as measuring two oblique factors with a .5 correlation between them and reflecting "impulsiveness" and "sociability" respectively. These are reminiscent of the two forms of extraversion that Guilford and Guilford (1934) differentiated some time ago. So there is clearly room for more progress to be made in analyzing the introversion-extraversion dimension and in devising measures for it.

4. The one distinguishing mark of internal inhibition (Pavlov, 1927) or reactive inhibition (Hull, 1943) is the fact that it dissipates, producing spontaneous recovery, after a rest. Is not therefore reminiscence (the improvement in performance that appears immediately after a rest period) the crucial test of the postulate of individual differences? Should not Franks have brought back his subjects after, say, an interval of 24 hours and measured spontaneous recovery if he wished to demonstrate decisively that differences of inhibitory potential were responsible for his findings? Franks (1963a) has found that subjects performing more conditioned eyeblink responses during training are likely to have higher reminiscence scores. He did not compare introverts and extraverts in this study, but some corroboration is provided for the assumption that differences in performance during conditioning reflect differences in the quantity of inhibition accumulated.

Recent Developments

Since the publications that embroiled him in these controversies, Eysenck and his associates have conducted further studies from which they claim further substantiation of their taxonomic scheme (Eysenck, Eysenck, & Claridge, 1960; Eysenck & Claridge, 1962), making use of the new technique of canonical variate analysis. They have, moreover, come to rely on pursuit-rotor and other skilled manual tasks, rather than on conditioning, in seeking empirical support for their hypotheses. Eysenck (1962) cites twenty investigations using techniques of this kind, some, but not all, of which verify that extraverted normal subjects show greater reminiscence. Claridge (1960) confirmed expectations derived from the hypothesis that hysterics are more susceptible to inhibition than dysthymics, obtaining from them a poorer over-all performance and a steeper decline in a vigilance task, greater reminiscence in a pursuit-rotor task, and shorter-lasting after-effects of fixating a rotating spiral.

Complications have arisen, however, with respect to the role of differences in drive or arousal. Eysenck and his colleagues (Eysenck & Maxwell, 1961) were compelled, as their work with the pursuit-rotor continued, to recognize the validity of a theory originally presented by Kimble (1949), according to which there must be a close relation between drive level and the amount of inhibition that is acquired. According to the theory, amount of inhibition is limited by the fact that subjects give themselves brief rest pauses whenever inhibition reaches a critical level and thus prevent inhibition from going higher. The critical level—the maximum amount of inhibition that will be tolerated—is, in its turn, held to vary directly with the level of drive. In view of evidence for processes of this kind, Eysenck has recently (1962) modified his Postulate of Individual Differences. He now maintains that extraverts generate reactive inhibition more quickly than introverts and dissipate it more slowly but that they do not necessarily accumulate more inhibition.

As Eysenck (1962) concedes, we might expect introverts to have higher prevailing levels of drive, since most motivation in human beings must be secondary or acquired motivation and introverts, being more conditionable, should be more susceptible to the kinds of conditioning that engender secondary drive. Evidence that dysthymics exceed hysterics in their prevailing level of drive or arousal has come from Claridge's (1960) study, already mentioned, from an investigation of sedation threshold (Claridge & Herrington, 1960), and from an investigation of performance on a paced five-choice serial reaction-time task (Claridge, 1961). Claridge suggests that the "excitation-inhibition balance assumed to underlie the dimension of extraversion" may undergo shifts dependent on arousal level. "If this were true," he writes, "then it would mean that, for example, the lower arousal (excitation) level in hysterics would result in a relatively speedier growth of inhibition in these patients than would be predictable from their position on the extraversion-introversion continuum."

Physiological Speculations

Guided by a study of Wenger's (1948), showing that persons diagnosed as neurotics significantly surpass normals on a number of indices of sympathetic-nervous-system activity, Eysenck proposes the identification of his neuroticism factor with "autonomic lability," meaning predominance of sympathetic functions. He concludes from this that neurotics are distinguished from normals by a higher level of drive. This may be a slightly precarious step, since, although there is some evidence (see Berlyne, 1960, 1963a; Malmo, 1959) that indices of sympathetic activity are increased by some recognized drive conditions, it has by no means been established that high sympathetic activity always means a rise in drive with all its connotations. There is some apparent tendency for states of high drive to be experienced and reported as unpleasant. Neurotics are frequently unhappier than normals, but are they always? The "*belle indifférence*" of the hysteric is well-known, and some unpleasant states, e.g., depressions, may well go together with lowered drive. Injections of adrenalin, which produce most of the manifestations of high sympathetic activity, may in some conditions give rise to euphoria (Schachter & Singer, 1962).

As for the introversion-extraversion dimension, Eysenck (1963a, p. 7) asks "Is it possible to locate any structure within the nervous system which may be responsible for individual differences in these mysterious processes of excitation and inhibition? I would suggest that the ascending reticular formation may fit this prescription reasonably well." This speculation is supported by studies suggesting that stimulant drugs shift behavior in an introverted direction, whereas depressive drugs, e.g., amytal, have the opposite effect. For example, d-amphetamine sulfate raises performance during eyeblink conditioning and slows down extinction, while amytal depresses performance and hastens extinction (Franks & Trouton, 1958; Eysenck, 1963b).

This physiological interpretation raises some interesting questions. The two orthogonal dimensions of neuroticism and introversion-extraversion are assumed to depend on sympathetic activity and reticular activity respectively. There is evidence that the sympathetic nervous system and the reticular formation normally act in close concert (Bonvallet, Dell, & Hiebel, 1954; Bloch & Bonvallet, 1960; Harris, 1958). Positive correlations have been found between measures of sympathetic activity and measures of EEG activation (the most direct indices of reticular-system activity available in the intact organism) when subjects are stimulated (Darrow *et al.*, 1942; Sherman & Jost, 1942). On the other hand, these correlations have been reported as negative when subjects are awake but unstimulated (Darrow, Pathman, & Kronenberg, 1946), and a variety of evidence has recently been accumulating to show that the electrocortical manifestations of high arousal, dependent on the reticular formation, and the vegetative manifestations of high sympathetic activation, dependent on the hypothalamus, are separable (Feldman & Waller, 1962; Lacey, 1966).

Eysenck and Pavlov

To relate Eysenck's classificatory scheme to Pavlov's is difficult. As Eysenck has repeatedly pointed out, his view of introversion-extraversion as a dimension characterized by relative predominance of excitation and inhibition fits, and was in fact partly inspired by, Pavlov's early (1927) theory of individual differences. But as we have seen, Pavlov later felt obliged to abandon this linear model and to postulate three factors that can vary independently, viz., the strength of excitatory processes, the strength of inhibitory processes (these two determining "strength" and degree of "balance"), and degree of mobility. He made use of these three criteria, for example, to explain the four Hippocratic types, whereas Eysenck identifies them with the four quadrants marked out by the two axes corresponding to his principal dimensions. Pavlov later believed that individuals with a predominance of inhibition are not common, so that balance became essentially a matter of whether inhibitory processes are commensurate with excitatory processes or not. Finally, we recall that, according to Eysenck, dysthymics and hysterics differ in their locations along the extraversion-introversion dimension, which means, according to his hypotheses, that they differ in susceptibility to inhibition and maybe in arousal also. Pavlov, on the other hand, depended on the thinker-artist dichotomy to account for the contrasts between psychasthenia (which Eysenck would presumably include under dysthymia) and hysteria.

There surely must be some way of integrating what is valid in Pavlov's and Eysenck's contributions, especially since the Pavlovians have recently taken to factor analysis and Eysenck has come to lay more and more stress on learning processes as the best indicators of what lies behind personality differences.

Both introversion (Eysenck, 1963) and weakness of nervous system (Gray, 1965) have been equated with relatively high arousability, which suggests a close affinity between the two. It is noteworthy that, according to Eysenck's statements, introverts are more prone than extraverts to find stimulation excessive and therefore distressing. Similarly, the Pavlovians regard high susceptibility to supramaximal inhibition and to the "passive defensive reflex," both processes affording protection against excessive excitation, as the prime distinguishing marks of the weak type. Introverts, according to Eysenck's account, form conditioned eyeblink and GSR responses rapidly, but there is so far no demonstration that they are particularly quick at acquiring "appetitive" conditioned responses, with pleasant or rewarding forms of reinforcement, such as conditioned salivary responses. The eyeblink is clearly an action that wards off irritating external stimulation, whereas the GSR is a component of the orientation reaction and thus an index of momentarily increased arousal. Eysenck (1967) has, in fact, recently identified his extraversion factor with the Pavlovian strength factor on the basis of evidence that he has collected. He finds, for example, that introverts, like "weak" individuals, have lower absolute sensory thresholds and are more prone to supramaximal inhibition. Rozhdestvenskaia (1966) has found that subjects with stronger nervous systems show more signs of fatigue and inhibition in the course of performing monotonous mental work. This seems at first sight surprising in view of the conception of the strong nervous system as one with a superior "working capacity." But it fits in with Eysenck's evidence that "strong" individuals are more extraverted and that extraverts are particularly susceptible to reactive inhibition and boredom.

On the other hand, there would seem to be some resemblance between the individual with an unbalanced nervous system and an individual with high neuroticism. It was recognized quite early by Pavlov's school (see Ivanov-Smolenski, 1952) that experimental neuroses can be produced most easily in the unbalanced type. Furthermore, we have Nebylitsyn's (1964) review of reasons for believing that, in the unbalanced nervous system, the brain-stem arousal system is subject to comparatively weak restraint by the cerebral cortex, while Eysenck believes that high-neuroticism subjects are characterized by chronically high drive. Nebylitsyn stressed the role of the reticular formation in this regard, but he might well have considered the possible importance of the hypothalamus and the autonomic processes dependent on it, especially in view of the recent contributions cited above.

To sum up, a view that might be worth investigating further is that the stable (high-neuroticism) or unbalanced individual is high in prevailing level of arousal, while the introvert or weak individual is high in arousability, i.e., in the ease with which his arousal can be increased. These two attributes could be more or less independent of each other. However, it is hardly necessary to say that the ultimate truth is unlikely to be so simple.

As for the psychoticism dimension, might this approximate Pavlov's mobility dimension? Eysenck (1952a, p. 217), summing up his findings, states that psychotics are "less fluent, ... perform poorly in mirror drawings, show slower oscillation on the reversal of perspective test, are slow in tracing with a stylus, ..." This sounds as if these traits might well have something to do with low mobility. Mirror drawing, in particular, involves abandoning one set of habits and replacing them with another set, which resembles the process of turning a positive stimulus into a negative stimulus or vice versa that is the main Pavlovian test for mobility. Pavlov mentioned "inertia" as a characteristic of psychotic behavior patterns, and Eysenck (1962) concludes, on the basis of studies of reminiscence in psychotics, that psychotics dissipate inhibition very slowly. He mentions the "*general slowness* of psychotics," i.e., their inability to adjust to environmental conditions gradually, which is likewise similar to the Pavlovian notion of inertia. Payne and Hewlett (1960), in a factor-analytic study of thought-disorder tests, found psychotics to be differentiated significantly from neurotics and normals by a "retardation" factor, manifested by slowness in a variety of intellectual, perceptual, and motor tasks. Rabinovich (1961), using the test of mobility mentioned earlier (pp. 647-48), found the maximum rate of responding to be much lower in schizophrenics than in normal subjects.[1]

Spence and the Iowa Group

Since the beginning of the 1950's, Spence, J. A. Taylor, and their students have been engaged in a series of experiments (summed up by Spence, 1956, and Taylor, 1956), designed to test some of the assumptions about drive embodied in the Hull-Spence theory. Anxiety is the drive on which they have chosen to concentrate, and, instead of the more usual procedure of experimentally manipulating the drive level, they have sought to compare groups of subjects in whom different degrees of anxiety can be presumed to exist naturally. Their instrument for distinguishing high-anxiety from low-anxiety subjects has been the Taylor Manifest Anxiety Scale (MAS) (Taylor, 1953). This consists of items from the Minnesota Multiphasic Personality Inventory (MMPI) judged by clinical practitioners to indicate anxiety. So, although this research is not aimed primarily at the understanding of personality differences but rather at the furtherance of basic behavior theory, it investigates correlates of individual differences, using a personality test and a personality variable, anxiety, that has long been of interest to personality theorists.

The predictions tested have been derived from the postulated multiplicative influence of drive on response strength (reaction potential): an increase in drive (D) is assumed to entail an increase in the strength (E) of all instigated responses by a certain proportion (Spence, 1956, p. 147, adapted from Hull, 1943). It follows that an increase in drive

[1] G. S. Glaridge (*Personality and arousal.* London and New York: Pergamon, 1967) has proposed an alternative interpretation after studying arousal processes in psychiatric disorders. He identifies introversion-extraversion with an "arousal modulation" dimension, to which a "tonic arousal" dimension is orthogonal. Neuroticism (obsessoid-hysteroid) and psychoticism (cycloid-schizoid) dimensions are orthogonal to each other and oblique to the other two.

will raise the difference in strength between any two responses by the same proportion, since $kE_1 - kE_2 = k(E_1 - E_2)$.

The effects of an increase in drive on learning will depend on how complex the situation is, and particularly on how the "correct" response, i.e., the response to be learned, stands in relation to competing responses. If the correct response is instigated virtually alone or at least stands higher than its competitors from the start, the number of reinforced trials necessary for it to reach the criterion of mastery should be less when drive is higher. If, on the other hand, the correct response is initially in competition with erroneous responses of comparable strength or is even overshadowed by them, it will take longer under higher drive to make up the leeway and attain the required degree of predominance.

These predictions have been confirmed with fair consistency in several experimental situations. Blinking is a response with a high rate of spontaneous occurrence, and it has no serious competitors as a reaction to a puff of air. So we should expect high-anxiety subjects to acquire a conditioned eyeblink response more rapidly than low-anxiety subjects, which has been found repeatedly to be the case (e.g., Spence & Taylor, 1951; Taylor, 1951). When, however, some tendency for errors to replace correct responses can be expected, as in stylus-maze learning (Farber & Spence, 1953), verbal-maze learning (Taylor & Spence, 1952) and paired-associate verbal learning (Ramond, 1953), high anxiety has been found, as predicted, to slow down learning. In one informative crucial experiment on serial nonsense-syllable learning by Montague (1953), high-anxiety subjects performed better with lists composed of items with low mutual similarity and high association value and worse with lists whose items had high mutual similarity and low association value.

As Spence and Taylor have acknowledged, there are two possible interpretations of the characteristics underlying difference in MAS scores. High-anxiety subjects may differ from low-anxiety subjects in having a higher prevailing level of anxiety drive most of the time regardless of environmental conditions. On the other hand, high-anxiety subjects may be subjects whose level of anxiety drive receives a larger increment when they are exposed to threat. The latter interpretation is favored by the fact that speed of salivary conditioning apparently bears no relation to anxiety level (Bindra, Patterson, & Strzelecki, 1955) and by the results of experiments (Lucas, 1952; Gordon & Berlyne, 1954) in which the performance of high-anxiety subjects in verbal-learning tasks deteriorated when fear of failure was introduced in them but not otherwise.

The Iowa group has accumulated an impressive measure of corroboration for its hypotheses, but their theoretical analyses have by no means won universal assent. Among the alternatives mooted have been the following:

1. Child (1954) lays stress on interfering responses, evoked by internal anxiety stimuli, which impede performance of their correct response. Mandler and Sarason (1952) obtained some evidence for the existence of such responses in studies comparing test performance of subjects with high and low scores on a measure of test anxiety. It is conceivable that complex tasks, which, unlike eyeblink conditioning, present a threat of failure, may produce such interfering responses in high-anxiety subjects and that these may be responsible for their inferior performance.

2. Several investigators, particularly Bélanger and his students, have provided indications that the strength of a learned response does not increase monotonically with drive level but rather reaches a maximum and then declines as drive rises above an optimum point (e.g., Ducharme & Bélanger, 1961; Bélanger & Feldman, 1962). The hypothesis that the decline is due to the emergence of competing responses has been tested by Dufresne-Tassé (1963), but the findings tend to refute it. It seems quite possible that the optimum level of drive is

lower for more complex tasks, and this may have had something to do with the difficulties that such tasks present for high-anxiety subjects.

3. The most vehement counterblast against the Iowa position has been set off by Eysenck (1957). Having found that MAS score is positively correlated with both neuroticism and introversion, he suggests that the greater susceptibility to eyeblink conditioning of high-anxiety subjects simply reflects the higher conditionability of introverts, attributable to their lower capacity for acquiring reactive inhibition.

In support of his criticism, Eysenck cites Franks's (1956) finding that, whereas dysthymic neurotics acquire conditioned eyeblinks more easily than normal subjects, hysteric neurotics acquire them less readily. Since in his view, neurotics in general have a higher drive level than normals, both neurotic groups should, he maintains, show more conditioning than normals if Spence's hypotheses about the role of drive are valid. Although Eysenck refers to this as a "crucial" experiment (p. 115), the argument depends on Eysenck's assumption that prevailing drive level is the main thing that distinguishes high-neuroticism from low-neuroticism individuals. As we have already noted, this may be called in question. Further, as Eysenck (1962) has conceded, introverts can be expected to have higher levels of at least acquired drives than extraverts because of their superior conditionability. So a difference in drive may well contribute to the differences in the behavior of introverts and extraverts in eyeblink conditioning.

Eysenck even goes so far as to dispute the long-established principle that response strength in the conditioning situation is affected by drive. He cites an experiment by Franks (1957b), in which subjects who had abstained from eating, drinking, and smoking for 18 hours before the experimental session were found not to differ from control subjects in eyeblink conditioning and subsequent extinction. This result is rather surprising, since there is a large body of literature (see Brown, 1961; Kimble, 1961) showing the strength of a variety of learned responses to increase with the level of drive, relevant or irrelevant. Brown gives reasons why Franks's experiment may not have constituted a fair test of the hypothesis.

On the other hand, Eysenck's argument that the MAS test is not a very satisfactory instrument for the purpose to which it was applied, since its score is likely to reflect several different things, is well taken and has been posed by other writers also. Manipulation of anxiety, which is not difficult to contrive, might have yielded less equivocal answers to the questions that actuated the Iowa experiments.

Spence and Spence (1964) have recently retaliated with a study in which the number of conditioned eyeblink responses was positively correlated with MAS scores and with the MPI neuroticism scale but bore no significant relation to either the MPI extraversion scale or the MMPI hysteria scale. They point out that the practice of the Iowa group is to exclude, or study separately, the records of subjects who tend to give responses of a "voluntary form." The failure of Eysenck's group to follow this practice would, they claim, depress the correlation between MAS scores and measures of conditioning.

Reviewing eyelid-conditioning experiments performed in his own laboratory and elsewhere, Spence (1964) has found differences in favor of high-anxiety *S*s appearing in 21 out of 25 independent comparisons, the majority being sufficiently significant. Whether or not a significant difference emerged has depended, he suggests, on the number of *S*s, the presence or absence of "voluntary-form" responders, the degree of experimental naivete of *S*s, and "the extent to which the experimental situation is designed to arouse some degree of apprehensiveness."

DIFFERENCES IN WHAT HAS BEEN LEARNED

In the laboratories directed by Pavlov and Eysenck, interest has focused on characteristics of the nervous system that determine how quickly and in what manner learned responses will be acquired. The differences uncovered by these studies appear to be genetically determined in large part. In Spence's laboratory, it has been shown that anxiety or, at any rate, something reflected in MAS scores affects ease of learning in various situations, but there has been no commitment to a position on whether or not hereditary differences are involved.

The studies that we shall take up now have been directed at differences in behavior resulting from different environmental conditions to which individuals have been exposed in the past and which have caused them to learn different things. It is a familiar truism that one of the ways in which learned behavior contrasts with unlearned behavior, and one source of its advantages over unlearned behavior, is the fact that, when external conditions vary from one member of a species to another, the response patterns adopted to cope with them can vary accordingly. Yet learned responses are of interest to personality theory only when they are relatively broad in scope and are manifest in a wide sample of an individual's behavior. The fact that one animal has learned to go left in a T-maze while another has learned to go right or the fact that one person has mastered a particular skill or learned a certain poem off by heart is not in itself regarded as a feature of personality.

How the theory of learning, and especially the S-R or neo-associationist conception of learning, fits in with the interests of personality theorists can, however, be seen from the hierarchical scheme (Fig. 1) that Eysenck (1947) has presented to reflect the basic notions on which factor analysis depends. The figure shows four levels. As one ascends from the lowest to the highest level, smaller correlations are found but larger samples of behavior are involved. The lowest or *specific-response* level stands for the particular responses that a subject makes in specific stimulus situations. The next or *habitual-response* level represents the close similarities that exist among the ways in which a subject responds when confronted with similar stimulus situations, making it relatively easy to predict how he will behave in that kind of situation in future once one knows how he has behaved in such a situation once. The *trait* level represents the cor-

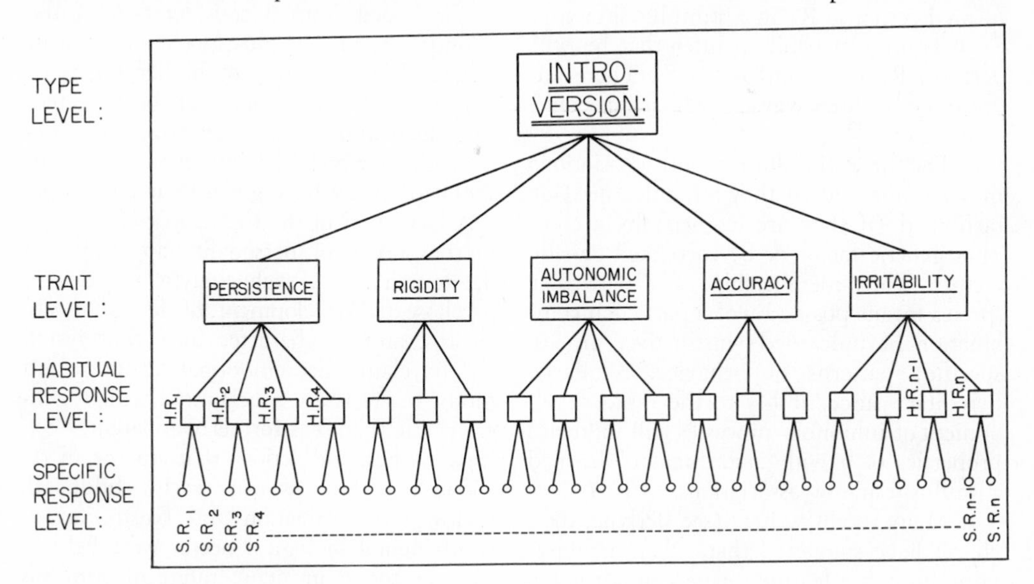

Figure 1. Hierarchical organization of levels of behavior. Reproduced with permission from H. J. Eysenck: *Dimensions of personality*. London: Routledge, 1947.

relations that exist between responses performed in a variety of distinct but related situations, e.g., "persistence" means a relatively high correlation between duration of effort in different tasks even though the stimuli with which the subject is faced in the two tasks and the forms of response required of him may be very dissimilar. Finally, there is the highest or *type* level, representing the correlations that exist among virtually all facets of an individual's behavior in all the situations in which he finds himself, so that, if he behaves, say, in a manner characteristic of introverts in one situation, an observer can infer something about how he is likely to behave in any other situation that could be specified.

The two highest levels are, of course, those that interest personality theorists. There have been bitter controversies over the precise meaning of the factors, corresponding to traits and types, that are revealed by factor analysis, some maintaining that they are merely classificatory devices while others argue that there must be a unitary causal agent underlying each of them. To revert to learned behavior, it is undoubtedly true that, on knowing that a subject has performed response R_A in a stimulus situation, S_1, it is often possible to infer that he will perform R_B in S_2 and R_C in S_3. There are presumably three ways in which this could come about:

1. The three stimulus-response associations may be inherited (if they are unlearned) or facilitated (if they are learned) by a common genetic factor or by correlated genetic factors. Thus membership of a particular species means possession of a particular combination of unlearned (instinctive, species-specific) patterns of behavior. Similarly, hereditary susceptibility to the rapid development of inhibitory processes will influence properties of a wide assortment of learned stimulus-response associations.

2. Many recent writers (see Berlyne, 1965, ch. 7) have suggested that, when a subject goes through a learning experience, it is not acquiring a particular response, to be performed in a particular kind of situation, but something like a "rule" or "principle" that is manifested by the performance of a number of different responses in different situations, all having something structural in common. An alternative, but currently less popular, way of making the same point is to say that there is a tendency to widespread stimulus-response generalization.

3. A number of specific learned responses may have been acquired quite separately and independently of one another, and yet they may tend to occur together not because of the way that the nervous system is constituted but because of the way that the external environment is constituted. If the world is so made that individuals who have one kind of experience are likely also to have another kind of experience, then there will be a correlation between attributes of the behavior, appearing in different stimulus situations, to which these experiences give rise.

4. Some forms of learning may occur with an extraordinarily wide capacity for stimulus generalization.

Of these four cases, the first is evidently the one to which Pavlov and Eysenck have attached importance. Little of concern to personality theory other than vague talk has so far issued from a consideration of the second case, and we must presumably await advances in the study of higher forms of learning before any more can be expected. The third and fourth cases cover the phenomena to which the investigators we are about to review have given their attention.

A large part of the Freudian contribution to the theory of personality appertains to the fourth case. Psychoanalytic theories of psychosexual development, of defense mechanisms, and of character formation rested on the claim that emotional attitudes and motor patterns are much more widely generalizable than was formerly apparent. Feelings, wishes, and actions that emerge in response to the crises of early childhood, relating to satisfaction and frustration of fundamental biological needs, were held to transfer to an immense range of stimulus conditions encountered in later life. These conditions are ones that possess links, sometimes extremely remote, with the original critical situations, through resemblances, through being among their incidental accompaniments, or indirectly through chains of words or thoughts. This psychoanalytic view is thus, in principle, fully in tune with the notions of primary and secondary stimulus generalization, first-order and higher-order conditioning. The only point at issue is whether, in fact, generalization can span such vast distances. Dollard and Miller (1950) argue that generalization may well run riot and follow trivial resemblances and associations within the realm of the "unverbalized," which they identify with a Freudian "unconscious." When intellectual processes are in charge of behavior, a restriction of generalization to "rational" resemblances and associations is, they hold, assured mainly by processes of secondary generalization and discrimination that work through verbal labels.

Motivation Theory

The advent of neo-behaviorism brought with it a keen interest in motivational processes, a predilection for relatively elaborate (and therefore relatively versatile) theoretical structures with copious reference to inferred internal mediating processes, and a feeling of readiness to confront human behavior in its full complexity. Psychologists identifying themselves with this current inevitably found themselves turning to problems that Freud had been the first, or one of the first, to raise and about which psychoanalysts have had much more to say than any other group of psychological thinkers. The Institute of Human Relations at Yale University was expressly set up to foster interaction among diverse lines of inquiry into human behavior, and, in the 1930's, Hull presided over a series of seminars at which the ideas of prominent social theorists were critically examined. The participants included a most impressive sample of those who bore responsibility for the subsequent course of behavior theory. It was only natural that the prospect of establishing a synthesis between the kind of psychology represented by Hull and the kind represented by Freud should be irresistibly alluring. There were such obvious points of contact right from the start, and what union could be more propitious than that between the rich insights of psychoanalysis and the methodological fastidiousness of behavior theory?

It has often been asserted that Freud was primarily interested in understanding behavior, even though he might have thought of himself as a student of mental processes, conscious and unconscious. His pleasure principle had much in common with the law of effect that assumed larger and larger responsibilities as the wide scope of the instrumental-conditioning paradigm came to be appreciated. Both could, after all, be traced back to the hedonism of the 18th and 19th centuries and earlier. The reality principle, according to which the older child and adult tempered the pursuit of pleasure with a sense of expediency, evidently depicted the operation of the laws of effect when a great deal of discrimination learning had taken place.

The view that behavior is motivated by uncomfortable drive states, resulting from conditions of biological need or disturbances of homeostasis, came close to the view that Freud had developed, i.e., in his article on "Instincts and their vicissitudes" (1915). There, he held behavior to be initiated either by *Reize* (stimuli) or by *Triebe* (commonly translated "instincts" but actually etymologically related to the English word "drive"), holding the only differences between these two kinds of disturbance to be that the former are external in origin and intermittent, whereas the latter are internal and recurrent. At this stage, he represented behavior as a collection of devices for keeping stimulation, whether external or internal, to a minimum and thus maintaining or restoring quiescence. Hull's postulate (1943), according to which responses are reinforced when followed by "the diminuation of the receptor discharge characteristic of a need" had much the same implications. The similarity became even closer when Miller and Dollard (1941) replaced need-reduction by drive-reduction, a change in which Hull acquiesced (1951), although many critics of the drive-reduction position have failed to notice the far-reaching differences this made. Miller and Dollard maintained that a drive is nothing but a strong stimulus. In fact, every stimulus was held to have a drive property in proportion to its intensity. So reinforcement became a matter of reducing net stimulation for them, as for Freud in his middle period.

Secondary Motivation

The links between behavior theory and Freudian theory became firmer as the theory of secondary motivation was developed.

Secondary Reinforcement

The principle of *secondary reinforcement* postulated that neutral stimuli accompanying primary rewards (i.e., conditions in which primary drives are reduced) would acquire a conditioned reward-value in their own right. This principle had much in common with Freud's account of how external events or thoughts associated, by contiguity or by similarity, with biological gratifications would become objects of cathexis and sources of symbolic or substitute satisfaction.

Fear

Even more to the point was the concept of "anxiety" or "fear" as a *secondary* (or *acquired*) *drive*. Mowrer (1939) offered a stimulus-response analysis of the biological and psychological role of anxiety, pointing out the convergences between the view that had grown out of the experimental study of learning and the view at which Freud eventually arrived (e.g., 1926). Both Mowrer (1940b) and Miller (1941, 1948) applied the theory of secondary drive to the analysis of avoidance learning in the rat. "Anxiety," as Mowrer called it, or "fear" as Miller called it, was assumed to be evoked as a consequence of conditioning by any stimulus (warning signal) that has habitually preceded or accompanied pain. The avoidant response, which, if performed during the interval between the onset of the warning signal and the delivery of an electric shock, averts the shock, was assumed to be reinforced by reduction of the secondary drive.

It was recognized that relatively little human behavior, at least in civilized societies, is controlled by primary drives and primary rewards alone. Secondary drives and secondary reinforcement will virtually always be playing some part, whether alone or in conjunction with primary drives and rewards. Fear has been by far the most thoroughly investigated of all presumed secondary drives, and this is justified by the pervasive part that learned fear must play in all departments of human behavior. Social motives, such as the desire for acceptance as a member of a group, for prestige and power, for money, must presumably contain at least a large admixture of fear. Fear reduction, it is argued, must be responsible for the reinforcement of learning to inhibit actions that are followed by punishment, for the learning of an action governed by foresight in the sense of anticipation of consequences delayed by more than a few minutes, for learning to adhere to group mores and to ethical principles. In this way, many personality traits, both normal and abnormal, can be interpreted as behavior patterns that have been learned because of their effectiveness in relieving or preventing fear. They may do this by affording access to stimulus conditions indicative of safety and thus conditioned to some kind of relaxation response or by terminating or forestalling the impact of stimuli conditioned to a fear response.

Aggression

The next most important secondary drive, especially in relation to social interaction and personality, is *anger* or *aggressiveness*.

Despite the publicity given to Freud's emphasis on sexual motivation, it has been pointed out (e.g., Mowrer & Kluckhohn, 1944) that Freud saw many neurotic symptoms and other irrational forms of behavior as defences against aggressive impulses and all the adverse consequences that their expression would entail.

A treatise on the principles governing aggressive behavior was published under the title *Frustration and Aggression* in 1939. Its authors—Dollard, Doob, Miller, Mowrer and Sears—were five leading figures among Hull's younger associates and constituted the nucleus of what came to be called the "Yale group." The first half of the book is concerned with laying down some basic postulates about aggressive behavior, all hinging on the basic assumption, as stated on the first page, that "aggression is always a consequence of frustration." The strength of instigation to aggression was held to depend on (1) the strength of instigation to the frustrated response, (2) the degree of interference with the frustrated response, and (3) the number of frustrated response sequences. Direct expression of aggressiveness, being frequently punished, is subject to inhibition. This inhibition leads to indirect expression, with either the object or the form of the aggressive behavior changed. Experiments using a heterogeneous assortment of situations to test predictions from the theory were reported, and a great deal of space was devoted to the relations between aggressive components of personality and the experiences typical of childhood and adolescence in various societies. A few years earlier, Seward (1945a, 1945b, 1945c, 1946) had drawn on conditioning principles to predict how experiences of success and failure in fighting would give rise to dominant and submissive behavior patterns, and he had performed a series of experiments with rats that contributed relevant data.

The determinants of aggressive behavior have received a high degree of attention from experimenters. Berkowitz (1962) and Buss (1961) have written books reviewing the findings that have accrued to date. As was to be expected, the simple formulations that guided early work on this topic have proved inadequate. In particular, many writers have found reason to doubt that frustration always gives rise to aggression or that aggression results only from frustration. There have, in fact, been suggestions from animal experiments that aggressive behavior can be innately evoked by a variety of aversive or punishing stimuli (e.g. Ulrich & Azrin, 1962).

Conflict and Frustration

The two outstanding pioneers in the study of neurotic behavior, Pavlov and Freud, both came, despite their vastly different approaches, to underline the etiological role of conflict. Pavlov regarded "collision" between excitatory and inhibitory processes as the principal cause of neurotic breakdown, whereas Freud's theory went through a number of stages, culminating in his emphasis on conflict between the ego and the id, with the super-ego joining in sometimes on the one side and sometimes on the other (Freud, 1923; Fenichel, 1945).

Lewin (1935) realized that conflicts of a less spectacular nature must be a recurrent feature of normal everyday life and have effects on behavior that are important even though they may not have the duration and gravity of neurosis. He distinguished three special cases of conflict and deduced what kind of behavior would result from each. First, there is the situation in which a subject finds himself between two attractive objects or regions. Conflict of this sort is resolved relatively easily and quickly, since approach toward one attraction is in itself often sufficient to give it predominance. Secondly, the subject may find himself between two repulsive objects or regions, and the consequences are then more serious: he will have a tendency to "go out of the field," i.e., to move away from both of them, or, if this is prevented by a barrier of some nature, he will remain trapped midway between the two. Thirdly, the subject may find himself within sight of a region that has both attractive and repulsive qualities; he is then likely to advance part of the way towards this region and then to remain at this distance, unable to approach nearer or to retreat (Lewin, 1931, 1935). Lewin pointed out, however, that what behavior actually emerges will depend not only on the type of conflict but also on the relative strength of the attractive and repulsive forces in the situation.

N. E. Miller (1944, 1951) built on Lewin's theory of conflict and translated it into the language of behavior theory. Besides the three types of conflict—approach-approach, avoidance-avoidance, and approach-avoidance—described by Lewin, Miller recognized a fourth important type. This was the double approach-avoidance conflict, which occurs when a subject finds himself between two regions, each of them having attractive and repulsive aspects. He laid down four postulates, viz., (1) that the strength of the tendency to approach a positive incentive increases with nearness to it, (2) that the strength of the tendency to avoid a negative incentive increases with nearness to it, (3) that the strength of the avoidance tendency diminishes with increasing distance more steeply than that of the approach tendency, and (4) that the strength of an approach or an avoidance tendency at a given distance from the incentive object varies directly with the strength of the relevant drive. From these postulates, which paralleled assumptions formulated by Lewin in his own peculiar terminology, a number of predictions regarding behavior in conflict situations were deduced. Since Miller's theory was first presented, it has given rise to a large mass of experimental work, which has provided substantial confirmation for both the postulates and some of the predictions derived from them (Miller, 1959).

Since, whenever an organism is in conflict, the two competing response tendencies cannot complete themselves as each of them would if it were acting alone, frustration of at least one may result. Frequently, both response tendencies and their corresponding motives will be frustrated. In addition, it seems likely that conflict itself will be a source of discomfort and drive. This being so, an organism will need to acquire behavior patterns that are capable of averting or resolving conflict, and many personality traits can be explained as behavior patterns that have been learned thanks to the reinforcement value of conflict reduction. In recent years, the concept of conflict has been broadened by recognizing the possibility of incompatibilities among implicit response-tendencies, including those of a perceptual or symbolic nature. The assumption that conflict is in itself an aversive or drive-raising condition has proved especially promising for the study of stimulus-seeking, attentive, and intellectual behavior patterns. For reviews of relevant literature, see Berlyne (1960, 1963a, 1964).

Although conflict must entail frustration, frustration can occur without conflict, if one defines it as a state of affairs in which an instigated response is prevented from completing itself, e.g., because some external condition required for its completion is missing (see Rosenzweig, 1944). Amsel (1958, 1962) has built up a powerful theory, centering round the hypothesis that stimulus conditions associated with frustration (by which he means absence of an expected reward) will produce an increase in drive and emotional disturbance. This theory, which has prompted a great deal of experimental work, explains why lack of reward sometimes leads to the abandonment of an accustomed response but sometimes favors prolonged persistence. It has been applied mainly to animal behavior, but its applicability to behavior patterns that shape human personalities is obvious.

Brown and Farber (1951) proposed a quantitative conceptualization of conflict (although they called it "frustration") as the principal determinant of emotion. They postulated that its degree will be greater

(1) the more nearly equal two competing response stimuli are in strength, and (2) the greater their absolute strength. Berlyne (1954), extending this treatment to cases where three or more response tendencies may be in conflict and to cases where competing response-tendencies may be less than fully incompatible, added (3) a number of competing response-tendencies and (4) degree of compatibility, as determinants of degree of conflict. The list of four determinants thus produced has proved suggestive for the theoretical analysis and experimental investigation of collative motivation in general and, in particular, of the forms of curiosity that underlie exploratory and epistemic behavior (see Berlyne, 1960, 1963a). Further, they make fruitful contact with concepts belonging to information theory (Berlyne, 1957) and with the list of factors on which the degree of "cognitive dissonance" (Festinger, 1957), a concept that has been highly influential in recent social psychology, is held to depend.

Temporal Integration

Mowrer and Ullman (1945) have drawn attention to, and analyzed, the problems that arise from the fact that responses commonly have several consequences, some of which are immediate and some of which occur after a considerable delay. There is reason to believe that the direct reinforcing effect of a reward declines steeply as the time interval between the response and the rewarding event increases, reaching zero if the delay is longer than a few seconds (Spence, 1947). Much the same probably applies to the inhibiting effects of punishment. On the other hand, rewards and punishments can be effective after much longer delays if some intermediary stimulus with secondary reward value or conditioned fear-inducing power, as the case may be, occurs immediately after the response and can thus act as a representative of the impending, but temporally remote consequences. Particularly in human life, a response will often have immediate consequences that are rewarding but long-term consequences that are punishing or vice-versa. The long-term consequences will, more often than not, be more serious than the immediate consequences, and yet the reinforcement-gradient principle (Hull, 1943) will tend to give them much less weight in determining how the organism will behave. In fact, they will have no weight at all unless an intermediary stimulus can bridge the gap. In human beings, such intermediary stimuli will preponderantly be internal and result from implicit symbolic responses. Thoughts about the uninviting prospect of a penurious old age may induce a man to contribute to a pension plan, and, although there will be no monetary return for several decades, immediate reinforcement will be furnished by relief from fear and the secondary reward-value of the knowledge that a retirement income is assured.

Mowrer and Ullman carried out an experiment with rats to illustrate some of the factors that are involved. The limited symbolic capacities of the rat make it necessary to provide an external stimulus representing a delayed consequence, but the authors took care to underline the analogies between the behavior shown by some of the rats in their experiment and human personality disorders. In their experiment, food pellets were delivered into a trough but, if the food was eaten within 3 seconds of its appearance, the rat was condemned to receive an electric shock. For different groups, the shock was administered at the end of the 3-second "taboo period," 3 seconds after its end, and 9 seconds after its end. In all cases, a buzzer sounded from the time the food appeared until the end of the taboo period. After the first day or two, most rats in the first two groups learned to refrain from eating until it was safe to do so. This was designated "normal" behavior. But a minority of animals engaged in "delinquent" behavior, i.e., eating during the taboo period, and suffered the punishment when it became due, or "neurotic" behavior, i.e., not eating at all.

In the third group, the one with the longest delay of punishment, most rats behaved "delinquently."

What Mowrer and Ullman called "integrative learning," i.e., learning that takes short-term and long-term consequences into account in proportion to their intrinsic importance, has obviously much in common with what Freud called the "reality principle," which he held to govern behavior once a child became capable of "reality testing" and "delay of gratification."

Bixenstine (1956) has carried further the work of Mowrer and Ullman. In his experiments, rats in an experimental group had not only a danger signal during the taboo period (a blinking light that appeared whenever they came within 3 inches of the trough) but also, in case they ate during the taboo period, a second stimulus (a steady light) that remained on until 3 seconds before the punishment was due and was then replaced by the blinking light which lasted until the punishment was administered. A control group was deprived of the blinking light immediately before punishment, so that there was no stimulus condition accompanying both the "delinquent" act and the imminence of shock. The experimental group showed appreciably more integrative learning than the control group, even when the taboo period lasted for 40 seconds and the shock was delayed for 110 seconds after the taboo period terminated.

Eysenck (1963b) has compared performance in Mowrer and Ullman's situation of rats belonging to emotional and non-emotional strains, which he likens respectively to human beings high and low in neuroticism. He found non-integrative responses to be more frequent in more emotional rats, "delinquent" reactions (which Eysenck prefers to call "psychopathic reactions") were commoner than "neurotic" reactions (which he prefers to call "dysthymic reactions"). When the shock was made more intense, "integrative" reactions became more frequent in both strains. Eysenck predicts that when ways of placing rats along the introversion-extraversion dimension have been devised, introverted rats will turn out to be more prone to "dysthymic" reactions and extraverted rats more prone to "psychopathic" reactions in these conditions.

Sidman and Boren (1957) have demonstrated how a stimulus that warns of impending punishment can be more intolerable than the punishment itself. When rats are able to choose between terminating a visual stimulus associated with shock, at the expense of suffering a shock, and preventing shock, at the expense of prolonging the stimulus, there is a tendency for them to prefer the former. Kamin (1956) had earlier shown that a running response would be learned by rats whether it led to avoidance of shock without termination of a stimulus associated with shock or to termination of the stimulus without avoidance of the shock.

Defence-Mechanisms and Other Adaptive Behavior Patterns

One of the most celebrated and piquant parts of Freud's contribution was his description of "defence-mechanisms" or devices for staving off anxiety. They served to protect the subject against exposure to situations or thoughts that were productive of anxiety, e.g., by preventing the expression in action or in consciousness of forbidden impulses. They were apt to become so pervasive and distinctive as to constitute major ingredients of personality. Neurotic and psychotic symptoms amounted to exaggerated variants of these defence-mechanisms.

As means of allaying or averting anxiety, defence-mechanisms were easily recognized as complex avoidance responses, and it was impossible to overlook the linkages between Freud's conception of them and the more recently launched theory of fear (anxiety) as a secondary drive supplying the main motivation for avoidance conditioning. So in the 1940's, one major objective of behavior theorists was to show how the occurrence of the kinds of behavior that Freudians attributed to defence-mechanisms could be inferred from principles of learning. Support for these analyses was drawn from animal experiments, either already in the literature or expressly designed for this purpose, in which apparently analogous behavior patterns were observed. The simplicity of the organisms under study and the experimentally controlled conditions could presumably afford a more reliable view of the underlying processes and the determining factors to supplement descriptions and interpretations of everyday human reactions. Books given over in large part to discussions of this kind were written by Dollard and Miller (1950), Masserman (1943), Mowrer (1950), and Sears (1943). Psychotherapy, concerned basically in Freudian terms, was analyzed as a special kind of learning process by these writers and by Shoben (1949). Others who showed interest in reconciling elements of Freudian theory with behavior theory were Guthrie (1938), Skinner (1953), and Tolman (1942), although this was not a primary target of experimental research for them.

Fixation and Regression

Freud (1916–17) indicated a close relation between *fixation* and *regression* with the help of an apt analogy. "If you think of a migrating people who have left large numbers at the stopping-places on their way, you will see that the foremost will naturally fall back upon those positions when they are defeated or when they meet with an enemy too strong for them. And again, the more of their number they leave behind in their progress, the sooner will they be in danger of defeat" (Freud, 1920). This view could easily be translated into the language of behavior theory. When one behavior pattern is given up in favor of another as the result of extinction or counter-conditioning, the earlier pattern will not be obliterated but merely inhibited (Mowrer & Kluckhohn, 1944). The subject will possess a hierarchy of responses, ordered according to their strength, with the most recently acquired response on top if it has received sufficient reinforcement to supplant its predecessors. If this response, in its turn, meets with frustration or inhibition, the consequent reduction in its strength may relegate it to a lower position in the hierarchy, with the result that a previously abandoned response becomes uppermost and reemerges. The more strongly reinforced the earlier responses were, the more serious the competition they will offer, the more precarious the hegemony of the most recently acquired response, and the more easily it can be weakened to the point of being submerged.

Sears (1943) was able to cite a large number of pertinent animal experiments and several factors that, according to established principles of learning, should affect the degree to which instrumental responses can resist inhibition. "Object fixation," as distinct from "instrumental act fixation," could be interpreted in terms of the conditioning processes that produce secondary reward-value.

A number of studies had apparently shown that an animal is particularly apt to become stereotyped in its behavior when it has just been punished. Maier (1949) reported a series of experiments in which rats were subjected to an insoluble discrimination problem in a Lashley jumping-stand and developed an astonishingly consistent habit of jumping in one direction repeatedly, which was extremely difficult to eliminate even if the conditions of the experiment changed. He concluded from the phenomenon of "fixation" that frustration released behavior from the normally operating laws of motivation and reinforcement and transferred it to the control of an altogether different kind of mechanism. A number of writers, notably Mowrer (1950), Wilcoxon (1952), and Eglash (1954), objected to this conclusion. They pointed to the probable role of intermittent reinforcement (which is known to generate extraordinary resistance to extinction) in an insoluble-problem situation and of the reinforcement that the response of jumping in any direction would receive through termination of the electric shock, air blast or prodding with whose help Maier forced his rats to leave the stand.

Experiments by Farber (1948) and Whiteis (1956) verified implications of the hypothesis that removal from cues associated with pain provide reinforcement through fear-reduction and thus account for the peculiar strength that punished locomotor responses often exhibit. More recently, experiments by Amsel and Ward (1965) show how conditioning to internal cues connected with frustrative non-reward can contribute to persistence. Experiments with rats by Mowrer (1940) and Whiting and Mowrer (1943) demonstrated a tendency to regress to an earlier response when the more effective or less strenuous response that has replaced it is weakened by punishment, non-reward or a physical barrier. Child and Waterhouse (1952, 1953) discussed the more complicated kind of regression, sometimes known as "primitivation," that frustration may engender in the child (Barker, Dembo, & Lewin, 1941). They argued that this kind of regression, taking the form of a qualitative decline to a point characteristic of immaturity, is due to interference from responses associated with frustration.

Imitation and Identification

Experiments designed to find out whether animal learning can be speeded up by *imitation* have been performed since the beginning of the 20th century, and although their findings have been open to debate, evidence for imitative learning in primates seems fairly good. For reviews, see Miller and Dollard (1941) and Masserman (1943). A Russian experimenter, Pen (1934), showed that 10-year-old children could acquire a response (pressing a rubber bulb when a bell sounded), and also show conditioned inhibition (withholding the response when a white light accompanied the bell), as a result of imitation. They would respond correctly on seeing another person demonstrate the response, after witnessing the demonstration, and even when the stimuli and manipulanda were changed somewhat. In the West, the behavior-theoretic analysis of imitation was initiated by Miller and Dollard (1941), whose experiments showed that rats and children would learn to perform responses observed in a model, that this imitative behavior conformed to acknowledged principles of learning, and that, once an imitative habit had been acquired, it would be generalized to other situations, other responses, and other models. Differential reinforcement could bring about discrimination, so that certain models were imitated but not others.

Mowrer (1950) discussed the more far-reaching forms of imitation that Freud had in mind when he introduced the concepts of *identification* and *introjection*. The relations between imitation and identification have been vigorously argued over ever since. If a useful distinction is to be made, it would seem that the word "identification" should be used when extensive sectors of behavior, as distinct from isolated response sequences, are taken over from the model and when implicit responses—attitudes, values, etc.—are taken over as well as overt behavior. There will, in such cases, be what Piaget (1945) has called "deferred imitation," i.e., performance of responses characteristic of the model when the model is no longer present. When these conditions are met, we come close to what social psychologists have frequently called "role-playing." It can be expected to occur only when stimuli coming from behavior characteristic of the model have an intrinsic or secondary reward-value in their own right, so that the behavior in question is not reinforced solely by some extrinsic reward whose attainment it facilitates.

Lair (1949) has recommended a distinction between "developmental identification" or identification with liked persons, i.e., persons productive of stimulation with secondary rewarding properties, and "defensive identification" or identification with a person at whose hands punishment or frustration is being suffered, i.e., a person in whose place one would prefer to be (the "identification with the aggressor" of Anna Freud, 1936). The role of identification, especially with one or the other parent, in the formation of personality and the conditions that favor it have received copious discussion (e.g., Sears, 1957; Whiting, 1959, 1960). Bandura, Ross, and Ross (1963) found that children are more likely to imitate adults who control the dispensation of reward rather than those who are recipients, thus corroborating some of the theories of identification that have been propounded (e.g., Whiting, 1960) and rebutting others. The growing mass of experimental work on imitation and identification in animal and human subjects has been reviewed by Mowrer (1960) and by Bandura (1962).

Repression

Shaw (1946) worked out a stimulus-response analysis of repression. Thoughts associated with actions that have incurred social disapproval come to evoke anxiety. Stimuli habitually preceding such thoughts thus come to act as warning signals, and the response of inhibiting, or not entertaining, a frightening thought will be learned as an instrumental avoidance response, reinforced by anxiety-reduction. Essentially the same interpretation was given by Dollard and Miller (1950).

Reaction Formation

In the course of one of his experiments concerned primarily with regression, Mowrer (1940a) observed behavior that he regarded as an instance of reaction formation. Rats that had been accustomed to press a pedal as a means of terminating electric shocks began to receive a shock from the pedal whenever they pressed it. Mowrer reports: "After discovering that the pedal was charged, these animals would frequently *retreat* from the pedal end of the apparatus soon after they began to feel the grill shock, i.e., as soon as they began to have an impulse to press the pedal. In effect, they were thus *running away from the pedal because they wanted to go toward and touch it.*"

Displacement

Miller (1948b) has presented a rather ambitious theory of displacement. A response will, it is predicted, undergo displacement to some target other than its original one, if the original target is absent or if the aiming of the response at the original target is inhibited by fear. In the former case, the displacement target will be whichever object, out of those that are available, most resembles the original target. In the second case, there will be conflict. Miller deduced, with the help of the kind of diagram shown in Figure 2 that the displacement target would bear some intermediate degree of resemblance to the original target. This diagram is reminiscent of those that Miller had used in his analysis of approach-avoidance conflict. There is, however, the difference that the horizontal axis of the diagram illustrating the theory of conflict represents a set of points ordered according to their spatial or temporal distance from the goal-object, while, in the diagram illustrating the theory of displacement, the horizontal axis represents a set of alternative goal-objects ordered according to their degree of resemblance to the original goal-object. In approach-avoidance conflict, it was predicted that the subject would take up a location corresponding to the point at which the gradients crossed, but, when displacement occurred, the object chosen as displacement target would correspond to the point at which the distance of the approach gradient above the avoidance gradient is at a maximum. As with conflict, the changes that would occur if the approach or avoidance gradient were raised or lowered, i.e., if the drive motivating the response (e.g., aggres-

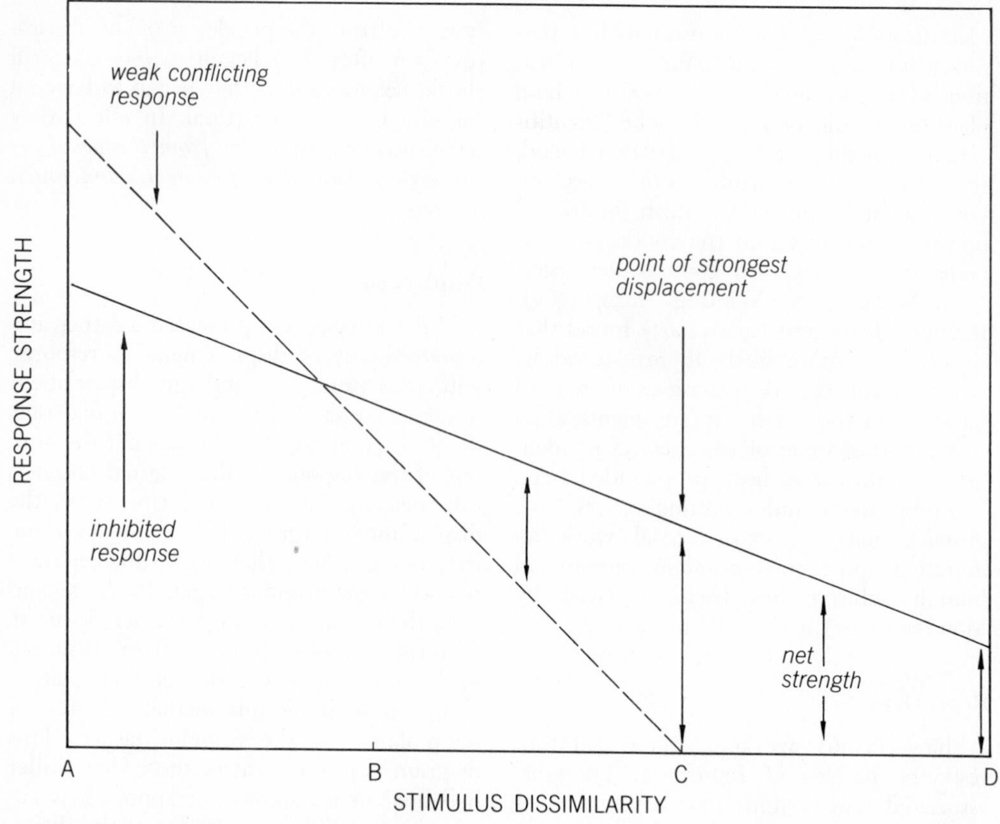

Figure 2. N. E. Miller's Theory of Displacement. Reproduced from N. E. Miller: Theory and experiment relating psychoanalytic displacement to stimulus-response generalization. *J. abnorm. soc. Psychol.*, 1948, 43, 155–178.

siveness) or the fear leading to its inhibition were heightened or moderated, can be deduced from the diagram.

Various implications of the theory have received experimental support (reviewed by Miller, 1959). Brush *et al.* (1952) extended Miller's theory of displacement in a direction of greater mathematical rigor, linking it with the Bush-Mosteller mathematical model for learning (1951). It is interesting that, like several other phenomena characteristic of learned behavior, a tendency to displacement is prominent among the unlearned "instinctive" or "species-specific" behavior patterns studied by the ethologists (Tinbergen, 1951): frustration (absence of the normal goal-object) or conflict causes consummatory responses to be directed towards unusual targets, including, at times, no target at all ("vacuum activity" or "explosion activity") or else to be replaced by responses appropriate to a quite different drive from the one that is aroused.

Child-Rearing Practices

Psychoanalytic theory held that the main lineaments of personality are determined by experiences during the first few years of life and that the most decisive factors are the satisfactions, frustrations, and conflicts that occur in the course of "psychosexual development." These conflicts center in turn on oral functions (with which dependency problems were thought to be connected), anal problems (with which problems relating to aggression were thought to be connected), and genital functions (with which many problems concerning inter-personal relations were thought to be connected). The behavior theorists of the Yale group were eager to build up a theory of child development that could account for the effects of variations in child-rearing practices and childhood experiences on lasting characteristics of behavior.

Freud's depiction of psychosexual development was generally taken as a starting-point, and much energy was spent on efforts to translate psychoanalytic statements into a language from which unequivocal and testable predictions could be derived, as well as to designing experiments and correlational studies to verify them. There was, however, a tendency during the 1940's to assume that the Freudians had gathered at least *prima facie* evidence for their assertions, so that at times the grounds for considering them received meager critical scrutiny.

McClelland (1951) argued that primacy, relative lack of symbolic processes, opportunities for frequent repetition, and absence of conditions that favor forgetting should make the learning that accrues from experience in early childhood particularly enduring. Konorski and Szwejkowska (1952), working with salivary conditioning in the dog, studied the effects of making a stimulus a positive and a negative conditioned stimulus in turn a number of times. They found that it was generally easier to restore the property—excitatory or inhibitory—that a stimulus had first acquired than to give it the opposite property, which led them to lay down a principle of "the primacy of first training." Nevertheless, a behavior theorist is bound to hold that learning can induce profound changes in behavior at any age.

Accounts of the course of child development and of ways in which early experiences can affect the motivational foundations of later personality were offered by Mowrer and Kluckhohn (1944), Dollard and Miller (1950), and McClelland (1951), drawing both on findings from experiments on learning and from Freudian delineation of critical problem areas. Neo-behaviorists of the first generation, especially those belonging to the Yale group, were often in close contact with anthropologists and sociologists, which made them keenly aware of the wide variations that distinguish the child-rearing practices of different societies. They were inevitably interested in studying, with the help of learning principles, the bearing that these have on the relations between culture and personality. Whiting (1941) presented an analysis of one group of which he had made a field study, the Kwoma of New Guinea, from this point of view.

Whiting and Child (1953) applied the cross-cultural method to the verification of some predictions derived from psychoanalytic theory, regarding the effects on personality of the degree of severity applied to various sectors of childhood training. They regarded a "custom" as a "*characteristic habit* of a typical member of a cultural category" and spoke of "custom potential" as a measurable variable analogous to "habit strength." They felt, however, obliged to propose some modifications of psychoanalytic theory. Defining a "system of behavior" as "a set of habits or customs motivated by a common drive and leading to common satisfactions," they recognized five such systems. Dependency and aggression, which they held to be chiefly motivated by secondary or acquired drives, were regarded as distinct from oral, anal, and sexual behavior, which are presumably motivated by their corresponding primary drive. Moreover, they drew a distinction that the Freudians slurred over, in that "positive fixation," i.e., the acquisition of secondary reward-value as a consequence of a high degree of gratification, was discussed separately from "negative fixation," i.e., the acquisition of secondary drive as a consequence of a high degree of frustration. A similar amalgam of themes taken from behavior theory and psychoanalysis informs Whiting's more recent cross-cultural studies (Whiting, Kluckhohn, & Anthony, 1958; Whiting, 1959, 1960) on the connections between childhood experiences and identification.

In a thesis directed by Sears, McKee introduced yet another methodological outgrowth from the Yale group's position. He found that overt aggressiveness bears a concave-downward curvilinear relation, and fantasy aggression, judged by behavior in a doll-play situation, a monotonic inverse relation, to the degree of severity with which aggressive behavior is punished at home. Extreme frustration of aggressiveness evidently inhibits overt aggression but intensifies aggression in fantasy (McKee, 1949; Sears, 1950).

Experimental investigations of learning in infants and children multiplied apace in the late 1950's. Relations between early learning and personality continue to receive intensive discussion (e.g., Bandura & Walters, 1963; Gewirtz, 1961; Lundin, 1961; Staats & Staats, 1963). Some new trends are, however, in evidence. More emphasis is given to imitation and identification than ever before. Under the influence of recent work on exploratory behavior and related topics, as well as of Piaget's work, the power of a great variety of biologically neutral but "interesting" stimulus changes to reinforce responses is recognized and acknowledged to have a profound influence. Following Skinner's (1953) lead the effects of various schedules of intermittent reinforcement receive increasing emphasis. Harlow's (1962) experiments with monkeys yielded findings that made stimulation from bodily contact appear more important than feeding in the establishment of the mother-child bond. These last three developments have led to a relative devaluation of primary organic drives and physiological gratifications in child development, which loosens some of the principal links between behavior theory and psychoanalytic theory. Secondary drives and secondary reinforcers are accorded more prominence. The possibility that uncertainty, surprise, and predictability may play more critical roles in child rearing and therefore in personality development than has generally been appreciated offers itself for consideration (Berlyne, 1963a).

The Behavior-Therapy Movement

Apart from the trends just mentioned, the attraction that psychoanalytic theory had for the behavior theorist interested in motivation and personality suffered some hard blows at the beginning of the 1950's. Among these were Orlansky's (1949) article, in which evidence of hypotheses linking the treatment of infants with later personality was examined and largely negative conclusions were reached. In particular, hypotheses stemming from psychoanalytic theory were found to have little, if any, support. Secondly, there was Eysenck's (1952b) article, in which available statistics on the effectiveness of psychotherapy were scrutinized. Apparently, the proportion of patients recovering spontaneously without treatment, recovering after treatment by general practitioners, and recovering after psychotherapy were about the same, all being in the neighborhood of two-thirds. Psychoanalytic therapy seemed a little, but not markedly, less effective. There was clearly room for a great deal of debate over the adequacy of some of the studies reviewed by Eysenck and over possible differences of criteria of recovery. However, Eysenck's main point that evidence conclusively vindicating the effectiveness of psychoanalysis is insufficient could hardly be disputed. Thirdly, there have been some trenchant scrutinies of the evidence on which some psychoanalytic hypotheses are based (e.g., Wolpe & Rachman, 1960).

The most recent phase of behavior theory is marked by attitudes to psychoanalysis ranging from skepticism to acrimony. This contrasts with the high hopes that were placed in the prospects of integrating behavior theory and psychoanalytic theory during the 1940's.

Much of the hostility is connected with the appearance of new methods of psychotherapy, which are firmly and expressly rooted in the theory of learning and are put forward as superior alternatives to traditional kinds of psychotherapy, derived with greater or lesser orthodoxy from psychoanalysis.

The new kind of therapy, for which Eysenck (1959a, 1960a) has proposed the name "behavior therapy," is not merely different from psychoanalysis but, in some of its features, diametrically opposed to it. The belief, largely due to Freud, that it is useless to attack the symptom directly, on the grounds that a recurrence of the same symptom or the substitution of another symptom will result unless the underlying personality disturbance is remedied, is challenged. Behavior therapists regularly report absence of confirmation for it in follow-up studies, and they claim that the removal of a symptom often has widespread beneficial effects on other aspects of behavior. They feel it to be unnecessary to probe back into early childhood to find events that are responsible for the neurosis; it is enough to uncover the factors that are producing neurotic behavior in the patient at present. Finally, the patient can be taken into the therapist's confidence, and hypotheses about the nature and etiology of the trouble, as well as plans for its treatment, can be discussed fully and frankly with him. The symptom is represented as the product of unfortunate learning processes, which must be undone with the help of future learning processes.

Behavior therapy makes contact with a line of research that was started by Watson but subsequently overlooked or held to be of little value as behavior theory lost confidence in its self-sufficiency. Watson and Rayner (1920) built up a conditioned fear of a rat in an 11-month-old boy by exposing him to a loud noise (listed by Watson as one of the innate determinants of fear) while the rat was in sight. The resulting fear apparently conformed to the Pavlovian principles of conditioning, including stimulus generalization to a wide variety of furry animals and a fur coat. Watson and Rayner suggested that emotional disturbances in adults could be traced back to "conditioned and transferred responses set up in infancy and early youth." They intended to use further conditioning procedures to remove the conditioned phobia, but they lost contact with the subject before they could do so. This missing part of the investigation was, however, realized in experiments by Mary Cover Jones (1924a, 1924b). She discovered a number of children from 3 months to 7 years of age who were already afraid of rabbits and other animals. Various methods of eliminating their fears were tried out, two of which were successful. These were (1) counter-conditioning by presenting the feared animal, in the distance at first and then gradually nearer, while the child was eating and (2) allowing the child to see the feared animal in the company of children who were not afraid of it. Both of these methods evidently worked by forming conditioned responses to the fear-inducing stimulus that were incompatible with fear and eventually became strong enough to inhibit it.

The foremost developer, advocate, and practitioner of the new kind of therapy has been Wolpe (1958). Having originally been interested in psychoanalysis and then become skeptical about it, he conducted some experiments in which neuroses were induced in cats. These resembled some experiments in which Masserman (1943) had made cats neurotic by exposing them to electric shocks or blasts of air just when they were beginning to eat. Wolpe found, however, that the simultaneous application of stimuli evoking conflicting approach and withdrawal responses was not necessary. It was enough to induce strong fear by administering electric shocks while a cat was confined in a cage, so that the fear could become conditioned to the stimuli presented by the interior of the cage. He proceeded to remove the conditioned fear by first placing the cat in a situation in which (1) the conditioned fear was weakened through a generalization decrement (the cat was placed in a room that slightly resembled the room in which shocks had been experienced), and (2) responses incompatible with fear were associated with surrounding stimuli by presenting food. The animals were then fed in rooms bearing closer and closer resemblances to the original room, until finally they would eat with no sign of disturbance in the room where they had been made neurotic.

Wolpe believes human neurotic behavior, like neurotic behavior in animals, to consist of "any persistent habit of unadapted behavior acquired by learning in a physiologically normal organism" (1958, p. 32) and to result invariably from anxiety. He relies principally on "reciprocal inhibition," i.e., on training procedures that inhibit anxiety by associating incompatible responses with anxiety-inducing stimuli. Among the incompatible responses that he uses are assertive and sexual responses, but his main resource is conditioned relaxation. By questioning the patient, he discovers what kinds of stimulus situation produce anxiety and to what degree. He then takes a situation that is mildly frightening and robs it of its power to induce anxiety by having the patient imagine it repeatedly while relaxed. Other situations, associated with greater and greater intensities of anxiety, are handled in the same way, until the patient is able to face the stimuli that he used to find most daunting with calm and assurance. Various subsidiary techniques, such as application and termination of electric shock, hypnotism, and inhalation of a mixture of oxygen and carbon dioxide, have been tried from time to time and found to have utility for certain cases.

Wolpe reports that 90 per cent of the patients that he has treated with these methods were "apparently cured" or "much improved." The median number of interviews was 23, stretching over a mean time span of 10.7 months. After following up some of his patients for periods of up to 12 years, he finds that relapses are extremely rare.

An increasing number of psychologists in various countries are trying out therapeutic procedures based on conditioning. Several of them have made rigorous statistical analyses of results and found grounds for concluding that their treatments were successful. Many of these reports are printed in a book edited by Eysenck (1960a), and they continue to appear in the journal *Behavior Research and Therapy* (founded 1963). Methods of "behavior modification," inspired largely by Skinner's work, are being applied with apparent success to a growing variety of abnormalities (Krasner & Ullman, 1965).

Eysenck (1960a) has suggested that different methods will have to be used with different syndromes characteristic of different personality types. Dysthymic disorders, involving undesirable habits and maladaptive fears depend, he contends, on "surplus conditioned reactions," so that training procedures productive of inhibition are indicated for them. Other patients, such as those suffering from hysteria, psychopathy, and enuresis, seem to have "deficient conditioned reactions," so that positive conditioning procedures may be what they require.

Certainly, although Wolpe and others have offered a theory explaining how neurosis in general comes about, more will be needed in the way of an account of the conditions that engender different symptoms. This will, of course, link up with personality theory and make it possible to prescribe specific treatments in accordance with individual differences.

It is worth noting that the view of neurosis espoused by Watson and the recent behavior therapists is quite different from that put forward by Pavlov. Pavlov believed that neurosis represented a breakdown of normal conditioning processes due to subjection of the nervous system to extraordinary stresses. According to the newer view, neurotic behavior results from the operation of normal conditioning processes, which give rise to abnormal and maladaptive responses, particularly emotional and avoidance responses, because the patient has been exposed to unusual circumstances. The responses in question may have been, or may continue to be, quite effective means to an immediate reduction in fear, which explains why they have been so strongly reinforced and are thus so persistent. They are, however, maladaptive when the feared stimuli are no longer dangerous or have never been dangerous enough to warrant the patient's violent reaction to them and when the responses have long-term undesirable consequences that are serious enough to outweigh the immediate comfort that they yield. In the latter case, there must be some deficiency in the symbolic mechanisms, discussed earlier, through which the selection of behavior is made to take delayed consequences into account (Mowrer & Ullman, 1945).

AROUSAL PROCESSES AND COLLATIVE MOTIVATION

One conspicuous trend in the neo-behaviorism of the 1950's and 1960's has been, as was mentioned earlier, a growing interest in exploratory behavior, "collative" stimulus properties, and psychophysiological arousal processes and in the relations that link these with one another and with a variety of psychological phenomena. There will indubitably be wide inter-individual variations in the ways in which these factors function and in their interconnections. Their ramifications are seen to pervade more and more regions of behavior as research progresses, and so differences in reaction to novel, surprising and complex stimulus patterns, and especially in such reactions as are mediated by the arousal system, must form salient components of personality. Many of the measures that are pertinent in this connection belong to physiological correlates of personality or to other well-established approaches and will therefore be receiving due consideration in other chapters of this Handbook. All we can do here is to touch on some points cursorily, since this is one sector in which behavior theory and other approaches show promise of establishing valuable junctions in coming years.

First, there will presumably be differences in prevailing level of arousal. Since the concept of "arousal" comes close to some connotations of the concept of "drive," this will amount to much the same as prevailing level of drive, whose role the Iowa group has been pursuing with the help of the Manifest Anxiety Scale. We also noted Eysenck's speculations linking extraversion and neuroticism with deactivation of the reticular arousal system and with overall drive level respectively. Since an active reticular formation apparently mobilizes, and renders more excitable, extensive tracts of the cerebral cortex, arousal (see Beritov, 1961; Berlyne, 1960; Ellingson, 1956) seems closely related to the Pavlovian state of "excitation" that could spread over part or all of the cortex and thus with the strength of excitatory processes that is, according to the scheme inherited from Pavlov by contemporary Russian investigators, a prime determinant of temperament.

Lát has devoted a great deal of study to a dimension of "excitability" in the rat (Lát, 1956, 1957, 1960; Lát & Weisz, 1958). Indices of excitability, which are found to be intercorrelated and intraindividually consistent, are speed of acquiring a bar-pressing response rewarded with food, speed of acquiring an instrumental avoidance response, number of spontaneous responses performed while the conditioned stimulus is absent, amount of exploratory behavior, rate of growth, food intake, and relative preference for carbohydrates over proteins and fats. Rats that are intermediate on the scale of excitability have the highest body weights when fully grown and the smallest adrenal glands. Whereas number of spontaneous (inter-signal) responses is a good index of excitability, the time interval between the disappearance of the conditioned stimulus and the first such response was taken to be indicative of differential inhibition, being significantly correlated with performance in a differential-conditioning situation involving a positive and a negative tone of different pitches and intensities. By this criterion, an intermediate degree of excitability makes for best discrimination. This is interesting in view of the numerous studies with human subjects showing performance at intricate tasks, especially tasks that make heavy demands on information-processing capacities, to be an inverted U-shaped function of arousal.

In human verbal-learning experiments, subjects with moderate arousal, as judged by skin conductance, show the best retention 6 minutes after training, but, with a one-week interval between training and test, the retention increases monotonically with skin conductance (Berry, 1962; Kleinsmith, Kaplan, & Tarte, 1963). Findings with other indices of arousal are, however, more complicated. According to data collected by Berry and Davis (1958), both good and poor learners show more intense action potential in forehead (*frontalis*) and jaw (*masseter*) muscles than moderate learners. Good learners show decreases in the activity of these muscles when they see that their anticipations have been correct but little change when they find that they have anticipated wrongly. This difference is reversed in moderate learners. Poor learners show a decrease after confirmation but a sharp increase after finding their anticipations to be incorrect. The authors suggest that the relatively high muscular activity at the two extremes of learning speed may be associated with different kinds of responses, especially since the curvilinearity is particularly evident when subjects find out that they have made errors. In good learners, the activity may reflect pronunciation of the syllable, but, in poor learners, it may represent "tendencies to escape, to combat *E*, to make subvocal ejaculations of surprise or dismay," etc. A later experiment (Berry & Davis, 1960) revealed a monotonic positive relation between *masseter* activity and learning speed, but the procedure was such that extremely slow learners were eliminated from consideration. Moderate learners showed the greatest decreases in electrocardiographic level during the information interval, while the reduction in finger-pulse during the learning session, as compared with the resting level, was directly related to learning proficiency.

Novel, and particularly surprising, stimulation evokes the transient rise in arousal that constitutes a major part of the "orientation reaction" (Sokolov, 1958; Berlyne, 1960). There is great variation among human beings in the magnitude of the orientation reaction to a particular kind of stimulus event, the speed with which arousal returns to the vicinity of its original level after the initial impact of the event, the time taken for the orientation reaction to habituate as the event is repeated, and the indices of arousal that display the greatest changes. There have been suggestions that individuals who take longest to recover from an orientation reaction and who show the greatest resistance to habituation have traits indicative of emotional instability or neuroticism. In them, the degree of restraint exercised by the cerebral cortex over brainstem structures may be relatively limited in its effectiveness. Most of the investigations aimed at sorting out the personality correlates of EEG characteristics have, however, been less than fully convincing and insufficiently precise in their descriptions of behavior (see Ellingson, 1956; Berlyne, 1960). Nebylitsyn's factor-analytic study (1961) showed the duration and resistance to extinction of EEG alpha blocking, another component of the orientation reaction, to have high loadings on a factor identified with Pavlov's balance dimension.

Gray (1965) has suggested an identification of the Pavlovian strength dimension with "arousability." He relates the characteristics of the weak nervous system, as reported by Teplov's group, to what is known about the workings of arousal, the orientation reaction, and the reticular formation. This results in an impressive case for the view that a tendency for a given stimulus to raise arousal more markedly can account for the peculiarities distinguishing the weak individual from the strong individual.

In a complementary vein, Nebylitsyn (1964) has reviewed a considerable body of literature supporting the view that the "dynamism" of excitatory processes depends on the activity of the reticular formation while the "dynamism" of inhibitory processes depends on the moderating influence of the cerebral cortex. The balance factor would therefore depend on how the reticular formation and the cortex interact.

Eysenck's attempts to relate his taxonomy, especially the introversion-extraversion dimension, to the functioning of the reticular formation, have already been mentioned.

It seems that human beings generally strive to keep arousal potential (by which is meant the properties, particularly the informational and collative properties, of the external environment that affect arousal) in the vicinity of an intermediate, optimal level and that they are uncomfortable and distressed whenever arousal potential rises far above, or falls far below, this level (Berlyne, 1960, 1963a; Fiske & Maddi, 1961). The precise influx of arousal potential that is experienced as optimal must show considerable inter-individual fluctuation, but there has been a dearth of work on the conditions that govern it. Several experiments have indicated that human beings and higher mammals will, if given the choice, be less inclined than otherwise to expose themselves to novel, complex or ambiguous stimulation when they are anxious or more generally when their arousal is driven above its normal level by some extraneous agent (Smock, 1955; McReynolds & Bryan, 1956; Brim & Hoff, 1957; Thompson & Higgins, 1958; Haywood, 1962; Berlyne & Lewis, 1963).

When arousal potential is distressingly low, there is no remedy but to seek additional stimulation. Subjects differ enormously in how much they are disturbed by sensory deprivation (see Kubzansky, 1961), but little attention has been paid by experimenters to the determinants and personality correlates of susceptibility to boredom. When, on the other hand, a subject is beset by extremely novel, surprising, complex, or puzzling stimulus patterns, he can relieve the discomfort resulting from innordinately high arousal in either of two ways. He can remove himself from the disturbing stimulation or withdraw attention from its disturbing features. Alternatively, he can seek further and intensified exposure to it (i.e., exploratory behavior) or otherwise seek additional information about it (e.g., by thinking or asking questions) as a means of robbing it of its novelty and relieving the uncertainty and conflict that derived from it. Individuals must differ in their degrees of inclination towards one or the other of these two recourses. Which they resort to may well be a matter of how disturbing they find a given amount of arousal potential. Luborsky, Blinder, and Mackworth (1963), exposing subjects to a succession of interspersed "neutral" and "threatening" pictures, found pictures evoking more intense GSRs to occasion more inspection of "ground" rather than "figure," and to be more likely to be forgotten.

Among personality dimensions that have come into prominence in recent years, those distinguishing persons high and low in intolerance of ambiguity (Frenkel-Brunswik, 1949), persons preferring simple and complex patterns (Barron & Welsh, 1952), and "repressers" and "intellectualizers" (Lazarus, Eriksen, & Fonda, 1951) seem to reflect degrees of preference for withdrawal and inattention on the one hand and for exploration and intellectual analysis on the other. Smock and Holt (1962) found that the extent to which children spent longer looking at more complex or incongruous visual patterns than simple patterns was correlated with their scores on a test of intolerance of ambiguity or rigidity. Luborsky *et al*. report differences in looking behavior between subjects prone to the defence mechanism of isolation (as judged from previous tests) and subjects prone to repression. Films of eye movements show that the former "look around" more when facing pictures of sexual, aggressive, or neutral content. Unlike the repressers, they look at the ground as well as the figure. Their fixations are more scattered and separated by longer leaps. Berlyne and Lewis obtained a significant positive correlation between tendency to prefer complexity, as measured by the Barron-Welsh Art Test, and tendency to choose more complex rather than simpler patterns to look at in a test of exploratory choice. Day (1965) found the Barron-Welsh score (reflecting the degree to which expressed preference tends towards the complexity pole) to possess significant positive correlations with tendency to choose exposure to more complex patterns, with time spent fixating more complex patterns when they are paired with less complex ones, with tendency to rate more complex patterns more pleasing, and with tendency to rate more complex patterns more interesting. The tendency to fixate more complex patterns was positively, but not quite significantly, correlated with the tendency to rate complex patterns more pleasing, while the tendency to choose more complex patterns was significantly correlated with the tendency to rate more complex patterns interesting.

Eysenck (1963c) mentions the inverted-U-shaped function that, in the light of several pieces of evidence, relates hedonic tone to "level of stimulation." He postulates that the peak—the point at which stimulation is most pleasant—will occur at a lower level in introverts than in extraverts, so that the way he envisages the situation is depicted in Figure 3. The variables connoted by "level of stimulation" include intensity, whose effects on judgments of hedonic tone were studied in a number of early experiments. Presumably, they will also include such variables as degree of novelty, surprising-

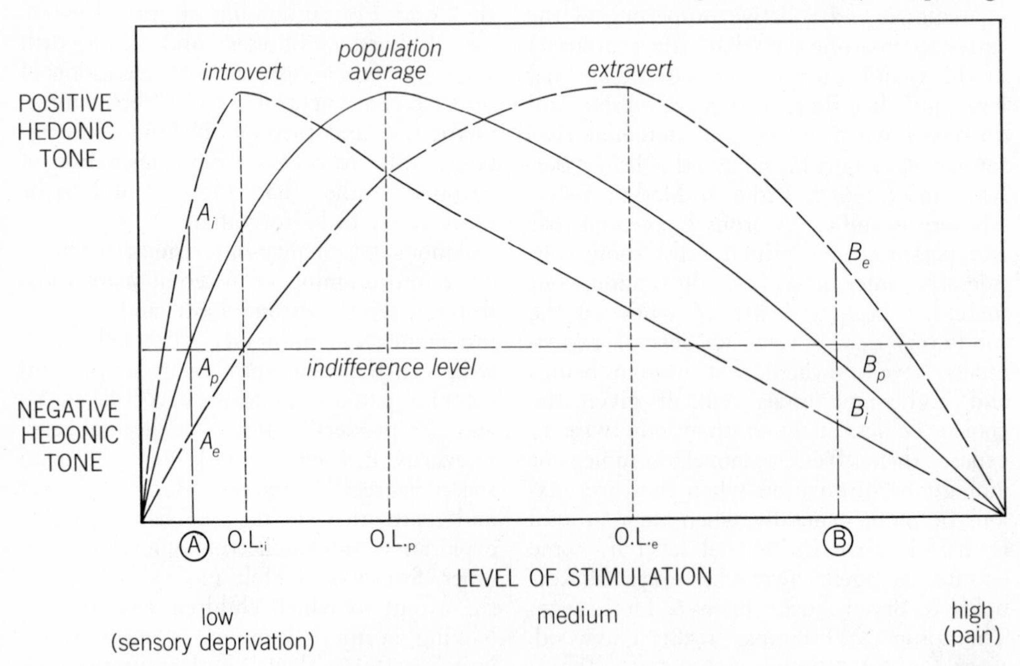

Figure 3. Graph depicting level of stimulation relationships.

ness, and complexity, so that "level of stimulation" means, in fact, arousal potential. If the optimal influx of arousal potential is lower for introverts than for extraverts, this may mean that a given stimulus will induce more arousal in an introvert than in an extravert, perhaps, in line with Eysenck's speculations, because he has a more excitable reticular formation or because the neural mechanisms that restrain and dampen reticular activity are less effective.

From this hypothesized picture, Eysenck deduces several predictions and cites evidence in support of all of them:

1. Extraverts will be more tolerant of pain than introverts.

2. Extraverts will be less tolerant of stimulus deprivation than introverts.

3. Relatively speaking, extraverts will be characterized by stimulus hunger and introverts by stimulus avoidance. "We would predict that extraverts would be likely to smoke more, drink more, and eat more, particularly spicy food; have intercourse more frequently; take more risks ...; and enjoy parties and social intercourse generally because of the considerable stimulation provided" (Eysenck, 1964, p. 99).

In an earlier book (1954), Eysenck had suggested, on the basis of rather indirect evidence, that introverts should tend to prefer more complex stimulus patterns than extraverts. The hypotheses just discussed would surely favor the opposite belief. Day (1964) actually obtained a significant positive correlation between extraversion and degree of preference for complex patterns in the Barron-Welsh test. Eysenck (1963c) now cites unpublished studies indicating that extraverts prefer more highly colored, and introverts less highly colored, pictures.

There are grounds for conjecturing that introverts may be more inclined towards information-gathering and extraverts towards selective attention as ways of coping with environmental novelty, complexity or ambiguity. If so, this may be due to the differential sensitivity or proneness to arousal that we have just been discussing. Extraverts are supposed to be relatively impulsive, whereas introverts possess the self-restraint that is necessary for "looking before leaping." Foulds (1951) found that dysthymics hesitate longer than hysterics before embarking on a pencil maze. Lynn and Butler (1962) report that extraverts express willingness to gamble larger sums of money than introverts. Repression, it has long been believed, is a major element in the makeup of the hysteric, whereas the doubts and brooding of the obsessive seem like morbid travesties of normal exploratory and epistemic activities.

Other facts are, however, not quite so straightforward. According to data collected by Hamilton (1957), both obsessives and conversion hysterics are less willing than normal subjects or persons suffering from anxiety states to accept ambiguity, as shown by use of a "can't decide" category in making psychophysical judgments. One would suspect that individuals of the first two types have different ways of avoiding indefiniteness. Obsessives may well look for trivial cues as pretexts for positive classification, whereas hysterics may arrive at positive judgments by ignoring external stimulus properties. Day found no significant correlations between, on the one hand, the strength of the tendency to fixate complex patterns, to choose exposure to them, or to rate them as pleasing or interesting, and, on the other hand, extraversion as measured by the MPI or intolerance of ambiguity as measured by Budner's (1962) test. So more work is evidently needed before these fragmentary clues can be sorted out.

Students of personality have hitherto concentrated on differences in overt behavior and in the mediating perceptual, affective, and judgmental processes that define a subject's internal condition and determine the form of his response to a particular external stimulus configuration. But a piece of behavior, as behavior theorists have recently come to realize more than previously, usually begins with activities that direct sense organs towards particular features of the external environment. This is often the first point at which a particular human being selects a different alternative from his fellows and begins to impart biases to his behavior that will culminate in a coherent individuality.

It is noteworthy that, in discussing these latest, inchoate developments, we have found it remarkably hard to separate work done under the aegis of behavior theory from other work. This is surely indicative of how things will go henceforth. We can surely expect a progressive coalescence between behavior theory and other psychological currents, including those that make up the main body of personality study. If behavior theory as personality theory belongs largely to the future, the same future may present us with personality theory as behavior theory!

REFERENCES

Amsel, A. The role of frustrative nonreward in noncontinuous reward situations. *Psychol. Bull.,* 1958, 55, 102–119.

Amsel, A. Frustrative nonreward in partial reinforcement and discrimination learning: some recent history and a theoretical extension. *Psychol. Rev.,* 1962, 69, 306–328.

Amsel, A., & Ward, J. S. Frustration and persistence: resistance to discrimination following prior experience with the discriminanda. *Psychol. Monogr.,* 1965, 79, No. 4.

Anokhin, P. K. *Vnutrennee tormozhenie kak problema fiziologii* [*Internal inhibition as a physiological problem*]. Moscow: Medgiz, 1958.

Bandura, A. Social learning through imitation. In M. R. Jones (Ed.), *Nebraska symposium on motivation,* 1962. Lincoln: Univer. of Nebraska Press, 1962. Pp. 211–269. (a)

Bandura, A., Ross, D., & Ross, S. A. A comparative test of the status envy, social power, and secondary reinforcement theories of identificatory learning. *J. abnorm. soc. Psychol.,* 1963, 67, 527–534.

Bandura, A., Walters, R. H. *Social learning and personality development.* New York: Holt, Rinehart, & Winston, Inc., 1963.

Barker, R. G., Dembo, Tamara, & Lewin, K. Frustration and regression: An experiment with young children. *Univer. Ia. Stud. Child Welf.,* 1941, 18 (Whole No. 386).

Barron, F., & Welsh, G. S. Perception as a possible factor in personality style: its measurement by a figure preference test. *J. Psychol.,* 1952, 33, 199–207.

Bélanger, D., & Feldman, S. M. Effects of water deprivation upon heart rate and instrumental activity in the rat. *J. comp. physiol. Psychol.,* 1962, 55, 220–225.

Beritov, I. S. [Morphological and physiological bases of temporary connections in the cerebral cortex.] *Trudy Inst. Fiziol. Beritashvili,* 1956, 10, 3–72.

Beritov, I. S. *Nervnye mekhanizmy povedeniia vysshikh pozvonochnykh zhivotnykh* [*Neural mechanisms of the behavior of higher vertebrates*]. Moscow: Acad. Sci. U.S.S.R., 1961.

Berkowitz, L. *Aggression: a social psychological analysis.* New York: McGraw-Hill, 1962.

Berlyne, D. E. A theory of human curiosity. *Brit. J. Psychol.,* 1954, 45, 180–191.

Berlyne, D. E. Uncertainty and conflict: a point of contact between information-theory and behavior-theory concepts. *Psychol. Rev.,* 1957, 64, 329–339.

Berlyne, D. E. *Conflict, arousal, and curiosity.* New York: McGraw-Hill, 1960.

Berlyne, D. E. Exploratory and epistemic behavior. In S. Koch (Ed.), *Psychology: A study of a science.* Vol. 5. New York: McGraw-Hill, 1963. (a)

Berlyne, D. E. Psychology in the U.S.S.R. *Canad. Psychologist,* 1963, 4, 1–14. (b)

Berlyne, D. E. Emotional aspects of learning. *Annu. Rev. Psychol.,* 1964, 15, 115–142.

Berlyne, D. E. *Structure and direction in thinking.* New York: Wiley, 1965.

Berlyne, D. E., & Lewis, J. L. Effects of heightened arousal on human exploratory behaviour. *Canad. J. Psychol.,* 1963, 17, 398–411.

Berry, R. N. Skin conductance levels and verbal recall. *J. exp. Psychol.,* 1962, 63, 275–277.

Berry, R. N., & Davis, R. C. Muscle responses and their relation to rote learning. *J. exp. Psychol.,* 1958, 55, 188–194.

Berry, R. N., & Davis, R. C. The somatic background of rote learning. *J. exp. Psychol.,* 1960, 59, 27–34.

Bindra, D., Patterson, A. L., & Strzelecki, J. On the relation between anxiety and conditioning. *Canad. J. Psychol.*, 1955, 9, 1–6.

Bixenstine, V. E. Secondary drive as a neutralizer of time in integrative problem solving. *J. comp. physiol. Psychol.*, 1956, 49, 161–166.

Bloch, V., & Bonvallet, M. Le déclenchement des résponses électrodermales à partir du système réticulaire facilitateur. *J. Physiol.*, Paris, 1960, 52, 25–26.

Bonvallet, M., Dell, P., & Hiebel, G. Tonus sympathique et activité électrique corticale. *EEG Clin. Neurophysiol.*, 1954, 6, 119–144.

Briks, Z. N. [Experimental investigations of the typological characteristics of the higher nervous activity in school age children.] *Trudy Inst. Vys. Nerv. Deiat. Pavlova*, 1956, 2, 149–174. English translation in *The central nervous system and behavior*. Bethesda, Md.: U.S. Public Health Service, 1960.

Brim, O. G., & Hoff, D. B. Individual and situational differences in desire for certainty. *J. abnorm. soc. Psychol.*, 1957, 54, 225–229.

Broadbent, D. E. The concept of capacity and the theory of behaviour. In C. Cherry (Ed.), *Information theory*. New York: Acad. Press Inc., 1956.

Brown, J. S. *The motivation of behavior*. New York: McGraw-Hill, 1961.

Brown, J. S., & Farber, I. E. Emotions conceptualized as intervening variables with suggestions toward a theory of frustration. *Psychol. Bull.*, 1951, 38, 465–495.

Brush, F. R., Bush, R. R., Jenkins, W. O., John, W. F., & Whiting, J. W. M. Stimulus generalization after extinction and punishment: an experimental study of displacement. *J. abnorm. soc. Psychol.*, 1952, 47, 633–640.

Budner, S. Intolerance of ambiguity as a personality variable. *J. Pers.*, 1962, 30, 29–50.

Bush, R. R., & Mosteller, F. A mathematical model for simple learning. *Psychol. Rev.*, 1951, 58, 313–323.

Buss, A. H. *The psychology of aggression*. New York: Wiley, 1961.

Campbell, A. A. The interrelations of two measures of conditioning in man. *J. exp. Psychol.*, 1938, 22, 225–243.

Cattell, R. B. *Personality and motivation structure and measurement*. Yonkers, N.Y.: World, 1957.

Child, I. L. Personality. *Annu. Rev. Psychol.*, 1954, 5, 149–170.

Child, I. L., & Waterhouse, I. K. Frustration and the quality of performance: I. A critique of the Barker, Dembo, and Lewin experiment. *Psychol. Rev.*, 1952, 59, 351–362.

Child, I. L., & Waterhouse, I. K. Frustration and the quality of performance: II. A theoretical statement. *Psychol. Rev.*, 1953, 60, 127–139.

Claridge, G. The excitation-inhibition balance in neurotics. In H. J. Eysenck (Ed.), *Experiments in personality*. Vol. 1. *Psychodiagnostics and psychodynamics*. London: Routledge & Kegan Paul, 1960.

Claridge, G. S. Arousal and inhibition as determinants of the performance of neurotics. *Brit. J. Psychol.*, 1961, 52, 53–63.

Claridge, G. S., & Herrington, R. N. Sedation threshold, personality, and the theory of neurosis. *J. ment. Sci.*, 1960, 106, 1568–1583.

Darlington, C. D. Psychology, genetics, and the process of history. *Brit. J. Psychol.*, 1963, 54, 293–298.

Darrow, C. W., Jost, H., Solomon, A. P., & Mergener, J. C. Autonomic indications of excitatory and homeostatic effects in the electroencephalogram. *J. Psychol.*, 1942, 14, 115–130.

Darrow, C. W., Pathman, J., & Kronenberg, G. Level of autonomic activity and electroencephalogram. *J. exp. Psychol.*, 1946, 36, 355–365.

Davidson, P. O., Payne, R. W., & Sloane, R. B. Introversion, neuroticism, and conditioning. *J. abnorm. soc. Psychol.*, 1964, 68, 136–143.

Day, H. Exploratory behavior as a function of individual differences and level of arousal. Unpublished doctoral dissertation, Univer. of Toronto, 1965.

Dewey, J. The reflex arc concept in psychology. *Psychol. Rev.*, 1896, 3, 357–370.

Diamond, S., Balvin, R. S., & Diamond, F. R. *Inhibition and choice*. New York: Harper & Row, 1963.

Dollard, J., Miller, N. E., Doob, L. W., Mowrer, O. H., & Sears, R. R. *Frustration and aggression*. New Haven: Yale Univer. Press, 1939.

Dollard, J., & Miller, N. E. *Personality and psychotherapy*. New York: McGraw-Hill, 1950.

Ducharme, R., & Bélanger, D. Influence d'une stimulation électrique sur le niveau d'activation et la performance. *Canad. J. Psychol.*, 1961, 15, 61–68.

Dufresne-Tassé, C. La compétition des résponses et l'activité instrumentale. Unpublished doctoral dissertation, Univer. of Montreal, 1963.

Eglash, A. Fixation and inhibition. *J. abnorm. soc. Psychol.,* 1954, 49, 241–245.

Ellingson, R. R. Brain waves and problems of psychology. *Psychol. Bull.,* 1956, 53, 1–34.

Eysenck, H. J. *Dimensions of personality.* London: Routledge, 1947.

Eysenck, H. J. *The scientific study of personality.* New York: Macmillan, 1952. (a)

Eysenck, H. J. The effects of psychotherapy: an evaluation. *J. consult. Psychol.,* 1952, 16, 319–324. (b)

Eysenck, H. J. *The structure of human personality.* London: Methuen, 1953.

Eysenck, H. J. *Psychology of politics.* London: Routledge, 1954.

Eysenck, H. J. A dynamic theory of anxiety and hysteria. *J. ment. Sci.,* 1955, 101, 28–51.

Eysenck, H. J. *The dynamics of anxiety and hysteria: an experimental application of modern learning theory to psychiatry.* London: Routledge & Kegan Paul, 1957.

Eysenck, H. J. Learning theory and behavior therapy. *J. ment. Sci.,* 1959, 105, 61–75. (a)

Eysenck, H. J. Anxiety and hysteria: a reply to Vernon Hamilton. *Brit. J. Psychol.,* 1959, 50, 64–69. (b)

Eysenck, H. J. Scientific methodology and the dynamics of anxiety and hysteria. *Brit. J. med. Psychol.,* 1959, 32, 56–63. (c)

Eysenck, H. J. *Behavior therapy and the neuroses.* New York and London: Pergamon Press, 1960. (a)

Eysenck, H. J. Eysenck on Lykken. *Cont emp. Psychol.,* 1960, 5, 106–107. (b)

Eysenck, H. J. Reminiscence, drive and personality—revision and extension of a theory. *Brit. J. soc. clin. Psychol.,* 1962, 1, 127–140.

Eysenck, H. J. Biological basis of personality. *Nature,* 1963, 199, 1031–1034. (a)

Eysenck, H. J. Emotion as a determinant of integrative learning: an experimental study. *Beh. Res. & Therapy,* 1963, 1, 197–211. (b)

Eysenck, H. J. Personality and drug effects. In H. J. Eysenck (Ed.), *Experiments with drugs.* New York: Macmillan, 1963. (c)

Eysenck, H. J. *Crime and personality.* Boston: Houghton Mifflin, 1964.

Eysenck, H. J. Extraversion and the acquisition of eyeblink and GSR conditioned responses. *Psychol. Bull.,* 1965, 63, 258–270.

Eysenck, H. J., & Claridge, G. The position of hysterics and dysthymics in a two-dimensional framework of personality dimension. *J. abnorm. soc. Psychol.,* 1962, 64, 46–55.

Eysenck, H. J. *The biological basis of personality.* New York: Charles C. Thomas, 1967.

Eysenck, H. J., & Maxwell, A. E. Reminiscence as a function of drive. *Brit. J. Psychol.,* 1961, 52, 43–52.

Eysenck, S. B. G., & Eysenck, H. J. The validity of questionnaire and rating assessments of extraversion and neuroticism, and their factorial stability. *Brit. J. Psychol.,* 1963, 54, 51–62.

Eysenck, S. B. G., Eysenck, H. J., & Claridge, G. Dimensions of personality, psychiatric syndromes, and mathematical models. *J. ment. Sci.,* 1960, 106, 581–589.

Farber, I. E. Response fixation under anxiety and non-anxiety conditions. *J. exp. Psychol.,* 1948, 38, 111–131.

Farber, I. E., & Spence, K. W. Complex learning and conditioning as a function of anxiety. *J. exp. Psychol.,* 1953, 45, 120–125.

Feldman, S. M., & Waller, H. J. Dissociation of electrocortical activation and behavioral arousal. *Nature,* 1962, 196, 1320–1322.

Fenichel, O. *The psychoanalytic theory of neurosis.* New York: Norton, 1945.

Festinger, L. *Theory of cognitive dissonance.* Evanston, Ill.: Row, Peterson, 1957.

Fiske, D. W., & Maddi, S. R. *Functions of varied experience.* Homewood, Ill.: Dorsey, 1961.

Foulds, G. A. Temperamental differences in maze performance: I. Characteristic differences among psychoneurotics. *Brit. J. Psychol.,* 1951, 42, 209–217.

Franks, C. M. Conditioning and personality: a study of normal and neurotic subjects. *J. abnorm. soc. Psychol.,* 1956, 52, 143–150.

Franks, C. M. Personality factors and the rate of conditioning. *Brit. J. Psychol.,* 1957, 48, 119–126. (a)

Franks, C. M. Effect of food, drink, and tobacco deprivation on the conditioning of the eyeblink response. *J. exp. Psychol.,* 1957, 53, 117–120. (b)

Franks, C. M. Ease of conditioning and spontaneous recovery from experimental extinction. *Brit. J. Psychol.,* 1963, 54, 351–358. (a)

Franks, C. M. Personality and eyeblink conditioning seven years later. *Acta. Psychol.,* 1963, 21, 295–312. (b)

Franks, C. M., Holden, E. A., & Phillips, M. Eysenck's "stratification" theory and the questionnaire method of measuring personality. *J. clin. Psychol.,* 1961, 17, 248–253.

Franks, C. M., & Trouton, D. Effects of amobarbital sodium and dexamphetamine sulphate on the conditioning of the eyeblink response. *J. comp. physiol. Psychol.,* 1958, 51, 220–222.

Frenkel-Brunswik, Else. Intolerance of ambiguity as an emotional and perceptual personality variable. *J. Pers.,* 1949, 18, 108–143.

Freud, Anna. *Das Ich und die Abwehrmechanismen.* Vienna: Internationaler Psychoanalytischer Verlag, 1936. [*The ego and the mechanisms of defense.* London: Hogarth, 1937.]

Freud, S. Triebe und Triebschicksale. *Inter. Z. f. ärztl. Psycholanal.,* 1915, 3, 84–100. [Instincts and their vicissitudes. In *Collected Papers,* Vol. IV. London: Hogarth, 1925.]

Freud, S. *Vorlesungen zur Einführung in die Psychoanalyse.* Leipzig and Vienna: Heller. 1. Teil, 1916; 2. & 3. Teil, 1917.

Freud, S. *A general introduction to psychoanalysis.* New York: Boni and Liveright, 1920. (Trans. of Freud, 1916–1917.)

Freud, S. *Das Ich und das Es.* Vienna: Internationaler Psychoanalytischer Verlag, 1923. *The ego and the id.* London: Hogarth, 1927.

Freud, S. *Hemmung, Symptom und Angst.* Vienna: Internationaler Psychoanalytischer Verlag, 1926. [*Inhibitions, symptoms and anxiety.* London: Hogarth, 1936.]

Gewirtz, J. L. A learning analysis of the effects of normal stimulation, privation, and deprivation on the acquisition of social motivation and attachments. In B. M. Foss (Ed.), *Determinants of infant behavior.* New York: Wiley, 1961.

Gordon, W. M., & Berlyne, D. E. Drive-level and flexibility in paired-associate nonsense-syllable learning. *Quart. J. exp. Psychol.,* 1954, 6, 181–185.

Gray, J. A. *Pavlov's typology.* New York: Macmillan, 1965.

Grindley, G. C. The formation of a simple habit in guinea-pigs. *Brit. J. Psychol.,* 1932, 23, 127–147.

Guilford, J. P., & Guilford, R. B. An analysis of the factors in a typical test of introversion-extroversion. *J. abnorm. soc. Psychol.,* 1934, 28, 377–399.

Guthrie, E. R. *The psychology of human conflict.* New York: Harper, 1938.

Halberstam, J. L. Some personality correlates of conditioning, generalization, and extinction. *Psychosom. Med.,* 1961, 23, 67–76.

Hamilton, V. Perceptual and personality dynamics in reactions to ambiguity. *Brit. J. Psychol.,* 1957, 48, 200–215.

Hamilton, V. Eysenck's theories of anxiety and hysteria: a methodological critique. *Brit. J. Psychol.,* 1959, 50, 48–63.

Harlow, H. F. The heterosexual affectional system in monkeys. *Amer. Psychol.,* 1962, 17, 1–9.

Harris, G. W. The reticular formation, stress, and endocrine activity. In H. H. Jasper *et al.* (Ed.), *Reticular formation of the brain.* Boston: Little, Brown, 1958.

Haywood, H. C. Novelty-seeking behavior as a function of manifest anxiety and physiological arousal. *J. Pers.,* 1962, 30, 63–74.

Hebb, D. O. *The organization of behavior.* New York: Wiley, 1949.

Hirsch, J. Individual differences in behavior and their genetic basis. In E. L. Bliss (Ed.), *Roots of behavior.* New York: Harper, 1962.

Holt, E. B. *The Freudian wish and its place in ethics.* New York: Holt, 1915.

Holt, E. B. *Animal drive and the learning process.* Vol. I. New York: Holt, 1931.

Hull, C. L. A functional interpretation of the conditioned reflex. *Psychol. Rev.,* 1929, 36, 498–511.

Hull, C. L. *Principles of behavior.* New York: Appleton-Century-Crofts, 1943.

Hull, C. L. The place of innate individual and species differences in a natural-science theory of behavior. *Psychol. Rev.,* 1945, 52, 55–60.

Hull, C. L. *Essentials of behavior.* New Haven: Yale Univer. Press, 1951.

Hull, C. L. *A behavior system.* New Haven: Yale Univer. Press, 1952.

Ivanov-Smolenski, A. G. On the methods of examining the conditioned food reflexes in children and in mental disorders. *Brain,* 1927, 50, 138 (4).

Ivanov-Smolenski, A. G. *Essays on the pathophysiology of the higher nervous activity.* Moscow: Foreign Langs. Publ. House, 1954.

Jones, Mary C. The elimination of children's fears. *J. exp. Psychol.,* 1924, 7, 383–390. (a)

Jones, Mary C. A laboratory study of fear: the case of Peter. *Pedagog. Sem. & J. Genet. Psychol.,* 1924, 31, 308–315. (b)

Kamin, L. J. The effects of termination of the CS and avoidance of the US on avoidance learning. *J. comp. physiol. Psychol.*, 1956, 49, 420–424.

Kimble, G. A. An experimental test of a two-factor theory of inhibition. *J. exp. Psychol.*, 1949, 39, 15–23.

Kimble, G. A. *Hilgard and Marquis' conditioning and learning*. (2nd ed.) New York: Appleton-Century-Crofts, 1961.

Kleinsmith, L. J., Kaplan, S., & Tarte, R. D. The relationship of arousal to short- and long-term verbal recall. *Canad. J. Psychol.*, 1963, 17, 393–397.

Konorski, J. *Conditioned reflexes and neuron organization*. New York: Cambridge Univer. Press, 1948.

Konorski, J., & Szwejkowska, E. Chronic extinction and restoration of conditioned reflexes. IV. The dependence of the course of extinction and restoration of conditioned reflexes on the "history" of the conditioned stimulus. (The principle of the primacy of first training.) *Acta. Biol. Exp.* 1952, 16, 95–113.

Krasner, L., & Ullmann, L. P. *Research in behavior modification*. New York: Holt, Rinehart & Winston, 1965.

Krasnogorski, N. I. *Vysshaia nervnaia deiatel'nost' rebenka* [*The higher nervous activity of the child*]. Leningrad: Medgiz, 1958.

Krasuski, V. J. [Method of estimating properties of nervous processes in dogs, accepted by the Laboratory of Physiology and Genetics of Higher Nervous Activity Types.] *Zh. Vys, Nerv. Deiat.*, 1963, 13, 165–176.

Kubzansky, P. E. The effects of reduced environmental stimulation on human behavior: a review. In A. D. Biderman & H. Zimmer (Eds.), *The manipulation of human behavior*. New York: Wiley, 1961.

Lacey, J. I. Somatic response patterning and stress: Some revisions of activation theory. In M. H. Appley & R. Trumbull (Eds.), *Psychological stress: issues in research*. New York: Appleton-Century-Crofts, 1967.

Lair, W. S. Psychoanalytic theory of identification. Unpublished doctoral dissertation, Harvard Univer., 1949.

Lashley, K. S. The behavioristic interpretation of consciousness. *Psychol. Rev.*, 1923, 30, 237–272; 329–353.

Lát, J. The relationship of the individual differences in the regulation of food intake, growth and excitability of the central nervous system. *Physiol. Bohemoslovenica,* 1956, 5, 38–42.

Lát, J. [The problematics of the study of the higher nervous activity of freely moving animals and research into so-called spontaneous reactions.] *Česk. Psychol.*, 1957, 1, 25–38.

Lát, J. [On the importance of different analyzers for the elaboration of conditioned motor reflexes.] In E. A. Asratian (Ed.), *Tsentral'nye i perifericheskie mekhanizmy dvigatel'noi deiatel'nosti zhivotnykh* [*Central and peripheral mechanisms of motor activity in animals*]. Moscow: Acad. Sci., 1960.

Lát, J., & Weisz, P. [On the relation between individual differences in the excitability of the central nervous system and adrenal activity.] *Česk. Fysiol.*, 1958, 7, 293–294.

Lazarus, R. S., Eriksen, C. W., & Fonda, C. P. Personality dynamics and auditory perceptual recognition. *J. Pers.*, 1951, 19, 471–482.

Leites, N. S. [An attempt at psychological characterization of temperaments.] In B. M. Teplov (Ed.), *Tipologicheskie osobennosti vysshei nervnoi deiatel'nosti cheloveka* [*Typological characteristics of higher nervous activity in man*]. Moscow: Acad. Pedag. Sci., 1956.

Lewin, K. Environmental forces in child behavior and development. In C. Murchison (Ed.), *A handbook of child psychology*. Worcester, Mass.: Clark Univer. Press, 1931.

Lewin, K. *A dynamic theory of personality*. New York: McGraw-Hill, 1935.

Luborsky, L., Blinder, B., & Mackworth, N. Eye fixation and recall of pictures as a function of GSR responsivity. *Percept. mot. Skills,* 1963, 16, 469–483.

Luborsky, L., Blinder, R., & Schimek, J. Looking, recalling and GSR as a function of defense. *J. Abn. Psychol.*, 1965, 70, 270–280.

Lucas, J. D. The interactive effects of anxiety, failure and intra-serial duplication. *Amer. J. Psychol.*, 1952, 65, 59–66.

Lundin, R. W. *Personality: an experimental approach*. New York: Macmillan, 1961.

Lykken, D. T. Turbulent complication. *Cont. emp. Psychol.*, 1959, 4, 377–379.

Lynn, R., & Butler, J. Introversion and the arousal jag. *Brit. J. soc. clin. Psychol.*, 1962, 1, 150–151.

McClelland, D. C. *Personality*. New York: Sloane, 1951.

McDougall, W. *Outline of psychology*. New York: Scribner, 1923.
McKee, J. The relationship between maternal behavior and the aggressive behavior of young children. Unpublished doctoral dissertation, State Univer. of Iowa, 1949.
McReynolds, P., & Bryan, J. Tendency to obtain new percepts as a function of the level of unassimilated percepts. *Percept. mot. Skills,* 1956, 6, 183–186.
Maier, N. R. F. *Frustration, the study of behavior without a goal*. New York: McGraw-Hill, 1949.
Malmo, R. B. Activation: a neurophysiological dimension. *Psychol. Rev.,* 1959, 66, 367–386.
Mandler, G., & Sarason, S. B. A study of anxiety and learning. *J. abnorm. soc. Psychol.,* 1952, 47, 166–173.
Masserman, J. H. *Behavior and neurosis: an experimental psychoanalytic approach to psychobiological principles*. Chicago: Univer. of Chicago Press, 1943.
Melzack, R. The genesis of emotional behavior: an experimental study of the dog. *J. comp. physiol. Psychol.,* 1954, 47, 166–168.
Melzack, R., & Scott, T. H. The effects of early experience on the response to pain. *J. comp. physiol. Psychol.,* 1957, 50, 155–161.
Miller, N. E. An experimental investigation of acquired drives. *Psychol. Bull.,* 1941, 38, 5–34.
Miller, N. E. Experimental studies in conflict. In J. McV. Hunt (Ed.), *Personality and the behavior disorders*. Vol. I. New York: Ronald, 1944.
Miller, N. E. Studies of fear as an acquirable drive: I. Fear as motivation and fear-reduction as reinforcement in the learning of new responses. *J. exp. Psychol.,* 1948, 38, 89–101. (a)
Miller, N. E. Theory and experiment relating psychoanalytic displacement to stimulus-response generalization. *J. abnorm. soc. Psychol.,* 1948, 43, 155–178. (b)
Miller, N. E. Learnable drives and rewards. In S. S. Stevens (Ed.), *Handbook of experimental psychology*. New York: Wiley, 1951.
Miller, N. E. Liberalization of basic S-R concepts: extension to conflict behavior, motivation, and social learning. In S. Koch (Ed.), *Psychology: a study of a science*. Vol. 2. New York: McGraw-Hill, 1959.
Miller, N. E., & Dollard, J. *Social learning and imitation*. New Haven: Yale Univer. Press, 1941.
Miller, S., & Konorski, J. Sur une forme particulière des réflexes conditionnels. *C. R. Soc. biol.,* 1928, 99, 1,155–1,157.
Montague, E. K. The role of anxiety in serial rote learning. *J. exp. Psychol.,* 1953, 45, 91–96.
Moruzzi, G., & Magoun, H. W. Brain stem reticular formation and the activation of the EEG. *EEG Clin. Neurophysiol.,* 1949, 1, 455–473.
Mowrer, O. H. A stimulus-response analysis of anxiety and its role as a reinforcing agent. *Psychol. Rev.,* 1949, 46, 553–565.
Mowrer, O. H. An experimental analogue of "regression," with incidental observations on "reaction formation." *J. abnorm. soc. Psychol.,* 1940, 35, 56–87. (a)
Mowrer, O. H. Anxiety reduction and learning. *J. exp. Psychol.,* 1940, 27, 497–516. (b)
Mowrer, O. H. *Learning theory and personality dynamics*. New York: Ronald Press, 1950.
Mowrer, O. H. *Learning theory and the symbolic processes*. New York: Wiley, 1960.
Mowrer, O. H., & Kluckhohn, C. Dynamic theory of personality. In J. McV. Hunt (Ed.), *Personality and the behavior disorders*. Vol. I. New York: Ronald, 1944.
Mowrer, O. H., & Ullman, A. D. Time as a determinant in integrative learning. *Psychol. Rev.,* 1945, 52, 61–90.
Nebylitsyn, V. D. [Some electroencephalographic indices of the equilibrium of neural processes.] *Doklady Akad. Pedag. Nauk.,* 1961, 2, 115–120.
Nebylitsyn, V. D., Rozhdestvenskaia, V. I., & Teplov, B. M. Concerning the interrelation between absolute sensitivity and strength of the nervous system. *Quart. J. exp. Psychol.,* 1960, 12, 17–25.
Nebylitsyn, V. D. The electroencephalographic study of the characteristics of strength of nervous system and balance of neural processes in man using factor analysis. In B. M. Teplov (Ed.), *Tipologicheskie osobennosti vysshei nervnoi deiatel'nosti cheloveka* [*Typological peculiarities of higher nervous activity in man*]. Vol. III. Moscow: Acad. Pedag. Sci., 1963.
Nebylitsyn, V. D. [Cortico-reticular relations and their role in the structure of properties

of the nervous system.] *Vop. psikhol.* 1964, 1, 1–24.
Nebylitsyn, V. D. Some questions relating to the theory of properties of the nervous system. *Proc. XVIII Int. Cong. Psychol.,* 1966.
Orlansky, H. Infant care and personality. *Psychol. Bull.,* 1949, 46, 1–48.
Paramanova, N. P. [On the formation of the two signal systems in the normal child.] In A. R. Luriia (Ed.), *Problemy vysshei nervnoi deiatel'nosti normal'nogo i anomal'nogo rebenka* [*Problems of the higher nervous activity of the normal and abnormal child*]. Vol. I. Moscow: Acad. Pedag. Sci., 1956.
Pavlov, I. P. *Conditioned reflexes.* Oxford: Oxford Univer. Press, 1927.
Pavlov, I. P. *Lectures on conditioned reflexes.* New York: International, 1928.
Pavlov, I. P. The reply of a physiologist to psychologists. *Psychol. Rev.,* 1932, 39, 91–126.
Pavlov, I. P. The conditioned reflex. In *Conditioned reflexes and psychiatry.* New York: International, 1941. First published 1935. (a)
Pavlov, I. P. General types of higher nervous activity in animals and man. In *Selected works.* Moscow: Foreign Lang. Publ. House, 1955. First published 1935. (b)
Payne, R. W., & Hewlett, J. H. G. A thought disorder in psychotic patients. In H. J. Eysenck (Ed.), *Experiments in personality,* Vol. II, *psychodiagnostics and psychodynamics.* London: Routledge & Kegan Paul, 1960.
Pen, R. M. [The formation of new conditioned connections through imitation.] In A. G. Ivanov-Smolenski (Ed.), *Na puti k izucheniia vysshikh form neirodinamiki rebenka* [*Towards the study of the higher forms of neurodynamics in the child*]. Moscow: Medgiz, 1934.
Piaget, J. *La formation du symbole chez l'enfant,* Neuchâtel & Paris: Delachaux & Niestlé, 1945. [*Play, dreams and imitation in childhood,* New York: Norton, 1951.]
Rabinovich, M. [Electrophysiological analysis of the activities in different layers of the cortex during the formation of a conditioned reflex.] *Zh. Vys. Nerv. Deiat.,* 1961, 11, 463–473.
Ramond, C. K. Anxiety and task as determiners of verbal performance. *J. exp. Psychol.,* 1953, 46, 120–124.
Razran, G. H. S. Studies in configural conditioning: I. Historical and preliminary experimentation. *J. gen. Psychol.,* 1939, 21, 307–330.
Rogov, A. A., Gorlanova, T. T., Kantorovich, M. M., & Kovaleva, N. T. Changes in vascular conditioned reflexes in man as a function of typological features of the nervous system. *Zh. Vys. Nerv. Deiat.,* 1964, 14, No. 4 (Translation in *Sov. Psychol. Psychiat.,* 1965, 3, 25–28.)
Rosenzweig, S. An outline of frustration theory. In J. McV. Hunt (Ed.), *Personality and the behavior disorders,* Vol. I. New York: Ronald, 1944.
Rozhdestvenskaia, V. I., Nebylitsyn, V. D., Borisova, M. N., & Ermolaeva-Tomina, L. B. [A comparative study of different indices of strength of nervous system in man.] *Vop. Psikhol.,* 1960, 6 (5), 41–56.
Rozhdestvenskaia, V. I. A study of mental capacity for work in relation to typological characteristics of the nervous system. *Proc. XVIII Int. Cong. Psychol.,* 1966.
Schachter, S., & Singer, J. E. Cognitive, social and physiological determinants of emotional state. *Psychol. Rev.,* 1962, 69, 379–399.
Sears, R. R. *Survey of objective studies of psychoanalytic concepts.* New York: Social Science Research Council, 1943.
Sears, R. R. Relation of fantasy aggression to interpersonal aggression. *Child Develp.,* 1950, 21, 5–6.
Sears, R. R. Identification as a form of behavioral development. In D. B. Harris (Ed.), *The concept of development.* Minneapolis: Univer. of Minnesota Press, 1957.
Seward, J. P. Aggressive behavior in the rat. I. General characteristics, age and sex differences. *J. comp. Psychol.,* 1945, 38, 175–197. (a)
Seward, J. P. Aggressive behavior in the rat. II. An attempt to establish a dominance hierarchy. *J. comp. Psychol.,* 1945, 38, 213–224. (b)
Seward, J. P. Aggressive behavior in the rat. III. The role of frustration. *J. comp. Psychol.,* 1945, 38, 225–238. (c)
Seward, J. P. Aggressive behavior in the rat. IV. Submission as determined by conditioning, extinction, and disuse. *J. comp. Psychol.,* 1946, 39, 51–76. (d)
Shannon, C. E., & Weaver, W. *The mathemati-*

cal theory of communication. Urbana: Univer. of Illinois Press, 1949.

Shaw, F. A stimulus-response analysis of repression and insight in psychotherapy. *Psychol. Rev.*, 1946, 53, 36–42.

Sherman, M., & Jost, H. Frustration reactions of normal and neurotic persons. *J. Psychol.*, 1942, 13, 3–19.

Shoben, E. J. Psychotherapy as a problem in learning theory. *Psychol. Bull.*, 1949, 46, 366–392.

Sidman, M., & Boren, J. J. The relative aversiveness of warning signal and shock in an avoidance situation. *J. abnorm. soc. Psychol.*, 1957, 55, 339–344.

Sigal, J. J., Star, K. H., & Franks, C. M. Hysterics and dysthymics as criterion groups in the study of introversion-extroversion. *J. abnorm. soc. Psychol.*, 1958, 57, 143–148.

Skinner, B. F. Two types of conditioned reflex and a pseudo-type. *J. gen. Psychol.*, 1935, 12, 66–77.

Skinner, B. F. *The behavior of organisms: an experimental analysis*. New York: Appleton-Century-Crofts, 1938.

Skinner, B. F. *Science and human behavior*. New York: Macmillan, 1953.

Skinner, B. F. *Verbal behavior*. New York: Appleton-Century-Crofts, 1957.

Smock, C. D. The influence of psychological stress on the "intolerance of ambiguity." *J. abnorm. soc. Psychol.*, 1955, 50, 177–182.

Smock, C. D., & Holt, B. G. Children's reactions to novelty: an experimental study of "curiosity motivation." *Child Develpm.*, 1962, 33, 631–642.

Sokolov, E. N. *Vospriiate i uslovny refleks*. Moscow: Univer. of Moscow Press, 1958. [*Perception and the conditioned reflex*, New York & London: Pergamon, 1964.]

Spence, K. W. The role of secondary reinforcement in delayed reward learning. *Psychol. Rev.*, 1947, 54, 1–8.

Spence, K. W. The postulates and methods of "behaviorism." *Psychol. Rev.*, 1948, 55, 67–78.

Spence, K. W. *Behavior theory and conditioning*. New Haven: Yale Univer. Press, 1956.

Spence, K. W. Anxiety (drive) level and performance in eyelid conditioning. *Psychol. Bull.*, 1964, 61, 129–139.

Spence, K. W., & Spence, J. T. Relation of eyelid conditioning to manifest anxiety, extraversion, and rigidity. *J. abnorm. soc. Psychol.*, 1964, 68, 144–149.

Spence, K. W., & Taylor, J. A. Anxiety and strength of the UCS as determiners of the amount of eyelid conditioning. *J. exp. Psychol.*, 1951, 42, 183–188.

Staats, A. W., & Staats, C. K. *Complex human behavior*. New York: Holt, Rinehart & Winston, 1963.

Storms, L. H., & Sigal, J. J. Eysenck's personality theory with special reference to 'The dynamics of anxiety and hysteria.' *Brit. J. med. Psychol.*, 1958, 31, 228–246.

Taylor, J. A. The relationship of anxiety to the conditioned eyelid response. *J. exp. Psychol.*, 1951, 41, 81–92.

Taylor, J. A. A personality scale of manifest anxiety. *J. abnorm. soc. Psychol.*, 1953, 48, 285–290.

Taylor, J. A. Drive theory and manifest anxiety. *Psychol. Bull.*, 1956, 53, 303–320.

Taylor, J. A., & Spence, K. W. The relationship of anxiety level to performance in serial learning. *J. exp. Psychol.*, 1952, 44, 61–64.

Taylor, J. G. *The behavioral basis of perception*. New Haven: Yale Univer. Press, 1962.

Teplov, B. M. (Ed.), *Tipologicheskie osobennosti vysshei nervnoi deiatel'nosti cheloveka* [*Typological characteristics of higher nervous activity in man*]. Moscow: Acad. Pedag. Sci., 1956.

Teplov, B. M. *Problemy individual'nykh razlichii* [*Problems of individual differences*]. Moscow: Acad. Pedag. Sci., 1961.

Teplov, B. M. New data in the study of the characteristics of the nervous system in man. In B. M. Teplov (Ed.), *Tipologicheskie osobennosti vysshei nervnoi deiatel'nosti cheloveka* [*Typological peculiarities of higher nervous activity in man*]. Vol. III. Moscow: Acad. Pedag. Sci., 1963.

Thompson, W. R., & Higgins, W. H. Emotion and organized behavior: experimental data bearing on the Leeper-Young controversy. *Canad. J. Psychol.*, 1958, 12, 61–68.

Thorpe, W. H. *Learning and instinct in animals*. London: Methuen; Cambridge, Mass.: Harvard Univer. Press, 1956.

Tinbergen, N. *The study of instinct*. Oxford: Clarendon Press, 1951.

Tolman, E. C. *Purposive behavior in animals and men*. New York: Appleton-Century, 1932.

Tolman, E. C. *Drives toward war*. New York: Appleton-Century, 1942.
Vogel, M. D. The relation of personality factors to GSR conditioning of alcoholics: an exploratory study. *Canad. J. Psychol.,* 1960, 14, 275–280.
Vogel, M. D. GSR conditioning and personality factors in alcoholics and normals. *J. abnorm. soc. Psychol.,* 1961, 63, (2), 417–421.
Watson, J. B. *Behaviorism*. New York: W. W. Norton & Co., Inc., 1924.
Watson, J. B., & Rayner, R. Conditioned emotional reactions. *J. exp. Psychol.,* 1920, 3, 1–14.
Webb, E. Character and intelligence. *Brit. J. Psychol., Monog. Supp.,* 1915, 1, part 3.
Wenger, M. A. Studies of autonomic balance in army air forces personnel. *Comp. Psychol., Monogr.,* 1948, 19, 1–111.
Whiteis, U. E. Punishment's influence on fear and avoidance. *Harv. Educ. Rev.,* 1956, 26, 360–373.
Whitehead, A. N., & Russell, B. *Principia mathematica*. Cambridge: Cambridge Univer. Press, Vol. I, 1910; Vols. II & III, 1912.
Whiting, J. W. M. *Becoming a Kwoma*. New Haven: Yale Univer. Press, 1941.
Whiting, J. W. M. Sorcery, sin, and the superego. In M. R. Jones (Ed.), *Nebraska symposium on motivation,* 1959. Lincoln: Univer. of Nebraska Press, 1959, 174–195.
Whiting, J. W. M. Resource mediation and learning by identification. In I. Iscoe & H. W. Stevenson (Eds.), *Personality development in children*. Austin: Univer. of Texas Press, 1960, 112–126.
Whiting, J. W. M., & Child, I. L. *Child training and personality*. New Haven: Yale Univer. Press, 1953.
Whiting, J. W., Kluckhohn, R., & Anthony, A. The function of male initiation ceremonies. In E. E. Maccoby, T. M. Newcomb, & E. L. Hartley (Eds.), *Readings in social psychology*. New York: Holt, Rinehart & Winston, 1958.
Whiting, J. W. M., & Mowrer, O. H. Habit progression and regression—a laboratory study of some factors relevant to human socialization. *J. comp. Psychol.,* 1943, 36, 229–253.
Wilcoxon, H. C. "Abnormal fixation" and learning. *J. exp. Psychol.,* 1952, 44, 324–333.
Willett, R. A. Measures of learning and conditioning. In H. J. Eysenck (Ed.), *Experiments in Personality,* Vol. II, *Psychodiagnostics and Psychodynamics*. London: Routledge & Kegan Paul, 1960.
Wolpe, Joseph. *Psychotherapy by reciprocal inhibition*. Stanford: Stanford Univer. Press, 1958.
Wolpe, J., & Rachman, S. Psychoanalytic "evidence": a critique based on Freud's case of little Hans. *J. nerv. ment. Dis.,* 1960, 141, 135–148.

Ulrich, R. E., & Azrin, N. H. Reflexive fighting in response to aversive stimulation. J. exp. anal. Behav., 1962, 5, 511-520.

CHAPTER 11 Role Theory, Personality, and the Individual

EDWIN J. THOMAS
School of Social Work and Department of Psychology
The University of Michigan

INTRODUCTION

Theories of personality and social role are ordinarily addressed to sufficiently different subject matters so that one does not expect the two perspectives to be simultaneously applicable to the same topic. By and large, the fields of personality and role have considerable substantive integrity, with few of the concepts, theories, and research inquiries being claimed by both. There is an important interface between the two fields, however, and here they have equal claims to the topics and similar stakes in the results of further inquiry. Using the familiar expressions of the fields, the overlapping topics concern (a) the effects of personality on role behavior and on role phenomena in general, (b) the effects of role factors on personality and, more generally, on individual behavior, and (c) the joint effects of personality and role factors.

In thinking about these topics of mutual interest it soon became apparent that they implicated more fundamental problems. Thus, to pursue any of the topics, one must face the question of what is "personality" and what is "role." If viable distinctions cannot be made between the phenomena of personality and role, then intelligible commentary is precluded. Because distinctions between the phenomena of personality and role are basically matters of conceptual clarification, this was called *the definitional problem*. The second more fundamental issue relating to these topics is that of locating the source of variance—either in personality or role factors—for behavior displayed by individuals or groups. This was called the *problem of explanation*. The third more basic issue was the *problem of personal change,* so identified because assumptions about the degree of plasticity and fixedness of personal characteristics are typically implicated in discussions of these topics.

These three problems and the topics to which they relate are the concerns of this essay. The literature of personality and role is rich in commentary and assumption about these matters, despite the existence of a growing empirical literature. Actually, only the problem of definition is conceptual and strictly nonempirical; the other two involve matters of fact for which the relevant empirical literature may be informative. The significant empirical literature is scattered over writings in many disciplines, however, and it appears under diverse and sometimes deceiving titles. It is therefore easy to understand why the majority of writers who have touched upon aspects of the empirical problems have drawn little from the empirical reports and—more lamentably—that many of the writers have not conceived of the problems as factual matters at all. Part of the accomplishment of this paper—if achievement it be—was simply to recognize the relevance and nature of these three general problems for the interface of personality and role theory; and the more important part was the marshalling of idea and fact, as pertinent, to various facets of the problems and the formulation of hypotheses from this effort. Because this review is based upon a little known, scattered and largely unreviewed literature, the conclusions presented must necessarily be viewed as more tentative than might otherwise be the case.

THE DEFINITIONAL PROBLEM

All fields of scientific study demark their domains of inquiry by agreed upon definitions of the subject matter. Personality and role theory differ from many of the more mature scientific fields in that the subject matters of both are not as easy to identify concretely and there is considerable disagreement concerning what the subject matters are. The disagreements about what personality or role are would be much less problematic were there objectively compelling guidelines to specify the subject matters. In the absence of such objective specifications, one must resort to the definitions and their referents.

A review of the definitions of personality in that field would probably serve more to highlight the range and degree of disagreement than a modal view. The common features of the definitions, in any event, would probably turn out to be abstract elements of the definitions rather than specific, substantive assertions. Thus Sanford observed the following in connection with his introduction to a survey of the field of personality: "I have assumed—in company, I believe, with most theorists in this field—that personality exists as an organized whole (system), that is constituted of parts or elements (subsystems), and separated somehow from an environment with which it interacts (1963, p. 489)." Sanford went on to observe that the fundamental questions for the theorists and, we might add, the fundamental points of disagreement among them as well, have had to do with the nature of the elements, the principles of organization, the delimitation of the personality from the phenomena of the environment, and the relations between personality and other phenomena.

Reviews of role definitions have revealed a striking diversity of definition (cf. Neiman & Hughes, 1951; Rommetveit, 1954; Gross, Mason, & McEachern, 1958). Indeed, there is probably more disparity in the definitions of role than in those of personality, this being attributable to the fact that the term "role" has had to denote an even more diverse range of phenomena than has the word "personality." If there is a most common definition it is that role is the set of prescriptions defining what the behavior of the position member should be. The definition of Parsons and his associates (1951) is probably among the more exemplary here: "The role is that organized sector of an actor's orientation which constitutes and defines his participation in an interacting process. It involves a set of complementary expectations concerning his own actions and those of others with whom he interacts (p. 23)." These authors go on to assert that roles are institutionalized when they are congruent with existing cultural patterns and when they conform with morally sanctioned patterns of value-orientation shared by members of the social collectivity in which the role functions.

The common denominators in the definitions are also very general. The first such common feature is that the concept pertains to the particular behavior of particular persons. The referents of the role concept are almost always persons *and* behaviors, each partitioned in a specific way. As a consequence, there are numerous, subtle, and complex combinations of partitioned behaviors and persons that may be formed from the entire person-behavior matrix (Thomas & Biddle, 1966). There are many intersections of the whole person-behavior matrix from which particular specifications may be drawn, and most existing definitions of role merely denote one or another given intersection of this large matrix. Thus there are distinctions that pertain mainly to the person segments. Notions of an individual role, such as "subjective role," "personal role," and "total individual role," would be cases in point; and so would conceptions of aggregate role, such as "group role," "cultural role," and "total aggregate role." Similarly, there are conceptions of role that pertain mainly to behavioral segments, these denoting particular partitions of behavior rather than the persons in question. Examples might be an overt role ("public role," "objective role," "role behavior," "role performance"), covert role ("private role," "subjective role," "implicit behavior"), and the prescriptive, descriptive, evaluative, active, and sanctioning role. There are also various complex person-and-behavior distinctions to be found in the literature. (The reader is referred to Thomas and Biddle [1966] for an explication of the person-behavior matrix and of its segments pertaining to persons, behaviors, and persons-and-their-behavior; and to Kemeny, Snell, and Thompson [1956] for details involving sets and partitions.) In a recent analysis of the conceptual structure of role theory it was concluded that the single concept of role was inadequate to capture with any denotative precision the diversity and complexity of the phenomena in question (Thomas & Biddle, 1966).

A second common denominator in conceptions of role is that most writers have defined role in connection with position, following Linton's (1936) influential conceptualization of these ideas. Common to most conceptions of position is the idea that it refers to a collectively recognized *category* of persons. The basis for differentiating the collectively recognized category, however, may be such diverse factors as the individuals' common attributes (e.g., age, sex, or skin color), their common behavior (e.g., teaching, healing), or the common reactions of others toward them (e.g., "victims," "outcasts," "scapegoats") (Thomas & Biddle, 1966). By linking role with position, most writers have endeavored to retain the import of Linton's original distinction. In Linton's view, positions and the attending roles were elements of the structure of social systems; role concepts provided a linkage to individual personality and behavior; and in this way, the concepts of position and role provided analytic means to connect social structural phenomena with individual behavior.

Additional insight into the definitional problem may be gained by considering not only the denotative aspects of the definitions but the connotative aspects as well. When one examines what is intended when the terms "role" and "personality" are used, there appear to be five axes with respect to which intended meanings may be ordered. The differentia below were derived largely from writings in which the authors were addressing particular problems involving the interface between personality and social role. The five differentiating axes follow:

1. Internal *Versus* External Controlling Variables

In Cattell's discussion of personality and role we find role defined "as that which causes a characteristic change in response to a whole complex ... of situations from the values characteristic of the person when he is not in the role ... or of others who are never in the role ..." (1963, p. 3). Cattell indicates also that two conditions are necessary for locating and defining any particular role. The first is that for any wide sample of behavior measures and of people, one must locate the modal behavior pattern itself; and the second is that for the sample of persons thus characterized, the role behaviors are typically significantly shifted, in the case of a role, from what would be expected from the particular personality endowments of this group of individuals. Although the behaviors of a group thus located may well have been learned earlier and "internalized," we may infer that the modal behaviors become identified as indicative of role by virtue of being reliably emitted when the individuals in question display the behaviors in response to role-related cues. It is in this sense, then, that Cattell's conception tends to emphasize external controlling factors.

If Cattell's conception of role is exemplary of an emphasis upon role as involving external controlling variables, then Child's conception of personality is equally exemplary of an emphasis upon personality as involving internal controlling variables. Child said "for the present discussion, personality will be defined as comprising consistencies of individual differences in behavior which are internally determined (1963, p. 593)." Such conceptions make the determination between personality and role an essentially empirical matter, for with proper information at any particular time it is possible, in principle, to decide whether or not external controlling variables are operative. For purposes of explanation, as we shall see, this is a very useful perspective. But many would be dissatisfied with this as the sole distinguishing criterion. One is constrained by this criterion to relegate all acquired behavioral dispositions that function autonomously of external controlling variables to the personality sphere, making that which has been internalized in connection with conforming to role expectations the domain of personality and not of role. Thus, according to this distinction, acquired behavioral dispositions associated with one's sex role must be classified as personality, not as social role.

2. Particularity *Versus* Commonality

Conceptions of personality typically emphasize the particular, if not unique, complex of dispositions and traits of an individual. In contrast, conceptions of social role tend to emphasize the sharedness and commonality of behavior. Thus we find McClelland defining role as follows: "A role is a cluster of traits (or pattern of behavior) which serves as the culturally normal or modal solution to recurrent, usually social problems peculiar to a particular status or position in society (1951, p. 293)." Most writers, again, would reject this criterion as the sole basis for distinguishing between personality and role. One problem is that particular personal dispositions may be shaped largely by external social conditions and, in some cases, entire groups of individuals may share particular dispositions, these being culturally prescribed and formed.

3. Covert Tendencies *Versus* Overt Action

For most writers, personality is not behavior, but rather it is a particular organized disposition to behave conceptualized in terms of such factors as motives, habits, memories, and cognitive-perceptual styles. Such conceptions of personality are prebehavioral. For some writers, personality is a conceptualization of a sum total of the individual's behavior. In this respect, personality is metabehavioral. And for still others, personality is in and of the mind, a particular neural organization. It is thus that personality is postbehavioral. Most conceptions of role, in contrast, are not restricted to covert tendencies and a large portion of the concepts of role deal expressly with overt behavior. For example, the notion of role performance (or "role behavior") is a common term for the overt actions of members of a position.

Although we surmise that fewer personality theorists than role analysts would be offended by this distinguishing criterion, by itself it is misleading and incomplete. In addition to predicting from external role factors to behavior, role analysts are as concerned with relating internalized role phenomena to behavior as are the personality theorists with predicting from personality to behavior.

4. Persistence *Versus* Transitoriness

Appositions and definitions of the personality and role frequently turn, in part, upon the extent to which the personal dispositions are persistent or short-lived. More personality theorists, however, would accept the persistence criterion than role analysts accept the transitoriness standard. Indeed, for most role analysts, the question of the persistence of the role behavior is an independent problem, irrelevant to the conception of role itself. As one individual changes from one position to another, his role and behavior may change rapidly; but in instances where an individual has been a member of a social position all of his life, as in the case of the sex role, selected dispositions and behavior may be remarkably persistent. Similarly, some personality theorists would regard the persistence of a personal characteristic as a variable of personality, not as a defining feature.

5. Person *Versus* Position Centeredness

Personality characterizes a given individual, typically, whereas role generally has reference to the behavior of particular persons who are members of a position. This is perhaps the single most important axis with respect to which writers distinguish between personality and role. For the personality theorist, dispositions and behavior as well are bounded essentially by a given biological individual, whereas the dispositions and behavior associated with role are generally particular to a given position and its prescribed behaviors.

Because the personality theorist is person-centered and the role analyst position-centered, each tends to study different samples of human behavior. The differences in the samples emphasized here do *not* relate necessarily to the depth or superficiality of behavior or to alleged contrasts between the descriptive or dynamic features of behavior. Although there may be such differences in data preferences between some personality theorists and role analysts, there are enough exceptions in the research literature to invalidate this distinction as a differentiating factor. The more telling difference, we believe, is that which attends whether the behavior sample, whatever the "level" or content, is person- or position-centered. The personality theorist tends to draw a sample from the common data pool of human behavior by selecting relatively large groupings of such data for given individuals, often doing so at various points in time. With such data, the researcher might then infer and characterize the relatively enduring behavioral dispositions particular to given individuals. The role analyst, in contrast, is much more likely to sample restricted segments of this behavior pool (such as prescriptions, descriptions, or performances) in given areas of content, drawing these data from many members of a position over either brief or long periods of time. The objective of the role analyst is more to characterize and understand the role associated with a given social position, generally without considering all the other behavior engaged in by the individuals in question.

It is clear, then, that at best there is generally only a limited subset of human behavior implicated in the samples that personality and role analysts draw from the common pool. The entire sample of behavior that is person-centered for the personality theorist is mainly different from the entire sample of behavior that is position-centered for the role analyst. This is to say nothing of the very different inferences drawn from the diverse behavior samples. From his sample, the personality analyst tends to conceptualize relatively enduring behavioral dispositions of individuals, whereas the role analyst generally employs his sample to infer patterned uniformities of behavior associated with particular social positions. Because of these differences in data samples and conceptualizations it may be said that that which *is* the personality is virtually never all that *is* the role; and only in the special instance of drawing a small subset of common behavior as part of different, larger samples may it be said, in this most restricted sense, that that which *is* personality *is* also role.

THE EXPLANATORY PROBLEM

The question of whether behavior is attributable to the personality factors of individuals involved or to their role or social position arises frequently in explanatory accounts. There are essentially three types of information that give rise to such explanatory queries: the existence of commonalities in the behavior of position members, variations in the adequacy with which individuals perform their roles, and differences in the reactions of individuals to problematic social conditions. Explanations generally take two forms. The "personalistic" view accounts for the behavior mainly in terms of developmental factors and personality characteristics of the individuals involved, whereas the "sociologistic" perspective accounts for the behavior in terms of the roles, positions, and social conditions prevailing for these individuals. Explanations that combine the personalistic and the sociologistic are not uncommon, but in most accounts, one may detect a bias toward one sort or the other.

Appraisal of the scattered literature relating to these issues soon reveals that sweeping generalizations in either the personalistic or sociologistic mode are oversimple. The studies pertinent to these issues reveal, on balance, that there is some evidence for both explanatory modes, but that the documentation and corroboration of the operation of either personality factors or role factors virtually never also rule out the operation of the factors not considered. The problem is simply that a study which indicates the operation of personality factors rarely precludes the possibility that role factors may not also be operating, and vice versa. Thus the evidence at hand does not readily allow one to draw firm conclusions concerning the extent to which personality or role factors enter into given behaviors. The literature does indicate, however, that there are complex and subtle means by which personality factors and role factors shape behavior, and it is along these lines that the analysis will proceed.

BEHAVIORAL COMMONALITIES

Commonalities in the dispositions, behavior, and human activities of members of given social categories are one of the nearly ubiquitous and perplexing facts of social life. The large literature indicating relationships between intelligence, childhood experience, personality, and interests, on the one hand, and vocational preference, choice, and membership, on the other hand (cf. Roe, 1956; Holland, 1959; Nachmann, 1960; Segal, 1961; Super, 1957; Bordin, Nachmann, & Segal, 1963), is illustrative of such commonalities in the occupation sphere. More specifically, the literature is abundant with such challenging findings as the following: that there is a positive association between socioeconomic status and intelligence (Haller & Thomas, 1962); that female schizophrenics display more activity and dominance in their interaction profiles than do normal females, and that schizophrenic males produce profiles indicating relative withdrawal, inactivity, and passivity (Cheek, 1964); that persons who eventually enter entrepreneurial occupations provide higher need achievement scores in their college years than their fellows who eventually entered nonentrepreneurial occupations (McClelland, 1965a); that attendants and student nurses have higher scores on custodial mental-illness ideology than their staff colleagues who are trained nurses and physicians (Gilbert & Levinson, 1956).

In addition to such relatively specific behavioral commonalities, writers have documented the association of clusters of dispositions with positional memberships. These patterns of behavior have frequently been called role orientations. Thus Argyris (1954) found that a bank tended to employ workers who were quiet, passive, obedient, and cautious. In order to analyze and classify the role orientations of union intellectuals, Wilensky (1956) examined the motives, values, and sources of satisfaction for these employees. This author then identified the role orientations of "missionary," "professional service worker," "careerist," and "politico," each orientation tending to be associated with a particular functional activity in the union. Thus missionaries were most strongly represented in the internal communications specialty; the professional service orientation was strongly associated with the facts and figures function; the careerist orientation was most strongly represented in the facts and figures function, but also in the contact and internal communications specialties; and the politico role orientation most strongly related to the functional type of contact man.

Presthus (1962) isolated three types of role orientation in formal organizations: the upward-mobile, the indifferents, and the ambivalents. Reismann (1949) classified civil servants as "functional bureaucrats," "specialist bureaucrats," "service bureaucrats," or as "job bureaucrats." Etzioni (1964) identified three types of executive in decision-making positions: the "specialists" (people in charge of one kind of activity), the "segmentalists" (people in charge of a multifunctional subunit), and the "generalists" (people recruited to positions in which decisions about objectives are made, such as top executives, or to positions from which extensive qualities are directly controlled). Etzioni observed further that these three types of positions could be construed as personality types. He said "no assumption is made about a one-to-one relationship between a personality type and a role. We assume only that the people typically found in each type of role differ systematically from those in others ..." (Etzioni, 1964, pp. 212–213).

An even more extreme and general fusion of diverse personality characteristics with membership in a social category would be a society in which all or most members had a basic underlying personality.

Behavioral commonalities of the sort cited here exist despite the fact that there are variations in the extent to which the particular personal characteristics are displayed by all the persons involved and in the degree to which an individual's entire behavioral repertoire and personality are encompassed in the commonality.

These behavioral commonalities may be accounted for in terms of personalistic or sociologistic explanations, but without further specification of the particular means by which such commonalities are achieved, these explanations are too general. In his discussion of organizational recruitment, Etzioni (1964) has emphasized the processes of selection and socialization but, again, the processes are too general. To achieve the proper specificity, one must distinguish between the "mechanisms" by which commonality is accomplished and the "agents" who act by and through a mechanism. There are two mechanisms to be considered, the first being *selection*. It is through selection that persons are either selectively entered (in-selection) or selectively excluded (out-selection) from a social category. The other mechanism is *change,* by which persons are altered or the role factors are modified. The agents which act through a mechanism may be the individual in question, another person, or external process or structure. The former is called the *personal agent,* and the latter the *social agent.* We can readily see that a commonality may be achieved (or not achieved) by six distinct, alternative routes. These "commonality routes" are personal in-selection, personal out-selection, personal change (by the person as the agent), social in-selection, social out-selection, and social change (by the social factors as agents).

The commonality routes serve to explicate, in this context, the personalistic and sociologistic viewpoints. A personalistic explanation typically attributes a commonality of personal characteristics to personal selection into the social category of given individuals who already possess the requisite personal characteristics, to the voluntary withdrawal from the category of those lacking the desired characteristics, or to personal change of the social factors in a direction more compatible with the individual behavioral dispositions. The sociologistic viewpoint, in contrast, typically attributes commonality to social selection into the category of individuals having the personal characteristics in question, to social selection out of the social category of those lacking given personal characteristics, or to social change by which the persons are modified in desired directions. But the six routes may operate singly or in various combinations to achieve a commonality, and they are consequently more articulate analytically than the general explanatory viewpoints. We now turn to a more detailed consideration of the six commonality routes.

Personal In-Selection

Personal in-selection consists of all ways in which the individual himself, as opposed to external social factors, may behave so as to increase the likelihood of entering one social category as opposed to another. The actions in question may range from sheer calculation, in which choice and intent are fully apparent, to the unwitting commitment to social alternatives. Ingratiation to obtain a job or engaging in proper study needed to enter an occupation are general intentional "staging actions." There are also staging actions where choice and intent are more obscure, but the behavior of the individual is nonetheless equally influential in committing a course of action. Consider the findings of a recent study by Hare and Bales (1963). These investigators found that individuals high rather than low in dominance and males as opposed to females tended to select central seats at the beginning of discussion sessions. The central seats, in turn, made it possible for the individuals so located to communicate more directly to others and, thereby, to become "leaders." Similarly it has been found that students with particular occupational interests tend to enter these occupations rather than others (Roe, 1956), and that specific childhood experiences and associated personality tendencies were consistently related to the choice of law, dentistry, or social work as professions (Nachmann, 1960). In general, the unintentional staging of future behavior may be achieved through the formation of motives, interests, and skills that increase the probability of certain future actions and choices over others.

One of the most thoroughgoing personalistic conceptions of occupational choice and commitment is that of Bordin, Nachmann, and Segal (1963). This view illustrates the extent to which commonality of behavior of position members, in this case of members of an occupation, may have its roots in early formative experiences. The assumptions of this approach have been stated well by the authors:

1. A continuity in development which links the earliest work of the organism in food getting and mastery of the body and coping

with the stimulations of the environment to the most highly abstract and complex of intellectual and physical activities.

2. That the complex adult activities retain the same instinctual sources of gratification as the simple infantile ones.

3. That although the relative strengths and configurations of needs are subject to continual modification throughout the life span, their essential pattern is determined in the first six years of life. The seeking out of occupational outlets of increasingly precise appropriateness is the work of the school years, but the needs which will be the driving forces are largely set before that time (p. 110).

The approach of these authors establishes a series of pivotal personal dimensions, forming a matrix into which occupations can be set. They identify the gratifications that diverse work experiences can offer and attribute the gratifications to the physiological functions necessary to their achievement. The physiological factors are discussed in terms of the dimensions of nurturants (feeding and fostering); aggressiveness (cutting, biting, devouring); manipulation (physical, interpersonal); sensual (sight, sound, touch); anal (acquiring, time-ordering, hoarding, smearing); genital (erection, penetration, impregnation, producing); exploratory (sight, touch, sound); and flowing-quenching; exhibiting; and rhythmic movement.

Personal Out-Selection

Quitting school and resigning from a job or an organization are among the common examples of personal out-selection. Personal out-selection is said to occur when the individual behaves so as to decrease the likelihood of retaining membership in a social category, independently of the operation of external social factors. Again, the staging and committing behavior ranges from actions involving obvious choice and intention to less "rational" determining behavior. The more subtle operation of personal out-selection is well illustrated in a study by Ross and Zander (1957). In this study, 169 women who resigned from a large private utility were investigated. These women were compared with a matched group who remained on the job. It was found that those who resigned from the company were much more likely than those who stayed to have received less gratification of needs for recognition, achievement, and for autonomy.

Personal Change

By personal change we mean any alteration by the individual of the role factors so as to produce more congruence with the behavioral dispositions of the individual involved. In the extreme case, the individual creates his role and position in his own image. In various ways such individuals as Schweitzer, Christ, Hitler, and Napoleon created their own roles and positions. Outstanding professors are sometimes hired without teaching, administrative, or research obligations, thus allowing them much freedom to construct their roles. Along more mundane lines, we find the same phenomenon occurring with husbands or wives who because of their needs, create tailored and sometimes unusual marital roles for themselves. The businessman who combines his hobbies with part-time employment might be illustrative as well. In the above, we have examples of how an individual may shape the role that he comes to play. Equally illustrative, however, would be instances in which an individual eliminates a position from the set that he occupies or stops performing various role activities.

The intriguing findings of the early study by Merei (1952) provide relevant insights. In this study, children who were demonstrated leaders in a nursery school situation were placed, as newcomers, into a group of demonstrated followers who had had time to establish a firm group tradition in their own right. One of the ways in which the erstwhile leaders came to assert leadership was through "diplomacy." This was a roundabout course of action by which the newcomer first accepted the group tradition in order then to change it to suit himself. The author documented the steps in this process as follows:

1. He tries to do away with the group traditions and lead it on to new ones.

2. He is rejected.

3. He accepts the traditions and quickly learns them.

4. Within the frame of those traditions he soon assumes leadership, and, though reluctantly, the group follows him because he does a good job.

5. He introduces insignificant variations, loosening the tradition.

6. He then introduces new elements into the ritual already weakened by variations (p. 529).

It is apparent that the "diplomat" operated indirectly, but so did the vast majority of the other leader-newcomers, no matter what particular means they chose to accomplish this end. The direct overthrow of the group's traditions and the creation of a group climate for one's self was not found. Rather, it was the following: "In the overwhelming majority of our cases the leader was forced to accept the group's traditions —that is, he proved weaker than the group but still managed to play the role of leader (Merei, p. 526)."

The other early and intermediate stratagems illustrated in this study were also relatively subtle. In addition to what one might call "playing the game" by going along temporarily with the tradition of the group, as illustrated above, we have what Merei called order giving, all done on behalf of the group's traditions; proprietary acquisition of all valued objects with which the children played, again the newcomer controlling the objects in behalf of serving the established traditions of the group in its customary activities; and ingratiation.

Another indirect means by which an individual may create his own role is through how he casts the role of others with whom he is in a complementary relationship. Weinstein and Deutschberger (1963) have discussed this process as "altercasting," defined "... as projecting an identity, to be assumed by other(s) with whom one is in interaction, which is congruent with one's own goals (p. 454)." The authors identify six a priori dimensions by which such altercasting may be achieved. Thus, in terms of these dimensions, an individual may cast the role of alter as being distant or close in relative authority, in evaluation, or in emotional affinity; and, furthermore, the role of the other may be shaped as supportive or nonsupportive, as interdependent or as autonomous, or as free or restricted.

Still another indirect means for individuals to achieve personal change in their roles is through what Merton has called goal displacement. In his discussion of personality and bureaucracy, Merton (1940) noted that there was often a tendency in bureaucracies for the means intended originally to serve the attainment of the organization's goals to acquire special salience and importance and, ultimately, to displace the original objectives.

In addition to these more elusive and indirect role-shaping behaviors, individuals of course make use of the more obvious and direct influence techniques of coercion, constraint, and reward (including bribes).

Social In-Selection

We speak of social in-selection when the social unit of which the individual may be a part exercises control over the individuals allowed to enter that social unit. Personnel-selection practices are of course a highly developed institutionalized form of social in-selection, but again this process, like the others discussed earlier, may be devoid of apparent rational choice and intent.

We see the operation of both intentional and unintentional factors in Argyris' (1954) report of the process of selecting employees in a bank. One management person put it this way: "I usually like a certain kind of youngster—a quiet youngster, slightly on the nervous side. Oh, I don't mean that he or she should be completely upset, but I think that's the kind of person we are looking for. They should have a certain amount of poise and not do too much talking" (p. 66). Another official noted the way the person talked, how he was dressed, and whether or not his fingernails were clean. The modulation of the voice, the use of grammar, and how the person would appear at the window in meeting the public were also gauged. Argyris concluded that as a consequence of these selection procedures, a "right type" was recruited, this being a person who was quiet, passive, obedient, cautious, and careful. This right type appeared to have strong desires for security, stability, predictability, and autonomy; and a dislike of aggressiveness or hostility in himself or others. The main consequence was that there was a relative homogeneity in the employee group, all persons having personalities compatible with the demands of the organization. Among the effects of keeping a cadre of the right types, the author noted, were that few persons quit, the bank was not unionized, and there were virtually no informal groups.

Although personal and social in-selection are analytically distinct and empirically distinguishable, both appear frequently to occur simultaneously. Whenever there are options for both individuals as well as the social categories, one would generally expect to find an admixture of personal and social in-selection. The two are typically involved, for example, in the sorting of individuals into jobs.

Social Out-Selection

The selecting out of undesirable individuals by various social units in which the selection is controlled by the social unit and not by the individual, is commonly recognized in its terminal and extreme forms. Dismissal from jobs is a case in point. Even more extreme but less common in this country is the execution of undesirables. Other more benign methods include promotion "upstairs," demotion, transfer from one department to another, or "encapsulation," this being the strategic isolation of the individual along with granting him only limited responsibilities and authority (cf. Etzioni, 1964, and Lemert, 1962).

Social Change

Social change involves alteration of the individual through social agents so as to achieve commonality of the personal characteristics in question. A large literature relates to this subject. Indeed, a sizable portion of the literature in the behavioral sciences documents various ways in which individuals are influenced by their social environment. Studies of political and socialization processes, the social psychology of influence, psychotherapy and planned change, of hypnosis, and of behavior under extreme conditions are among the bodies of inquiry pertinent to the problem at hand. If there is an overemphasis upon social change as a route to behavioral commonality and a prevailing viewpoint that Wrong (1961) has characterized as the "oversocialized conception of man," it is probably attributable to the sheer mass of research and theory on this problem. The extensive contributions to this subject cannot possibly be detailed here. Instead, we shall make use of the literature to highlight four important aspects of social change, these being the areas, modes, social loci, and group agents of change.

Areas of socialization—It is not enough to observe that virtually all aspects of human behavior may be subject to social influences. By way of being more specific, Caplow (1964) has identified what socialization does in the context of transforming a new member of an organization into a successful incumbent, and his observations are pertinent to the present question of the effects of role factors upon personal changes. The four areas of socialization are the development of a new self image, engagement in a new network of individuals with whom one interacts, the acquisition of new values, and new accomplishments. Although all of these may be directly instrumental to the accomplishment of the tasks of a given social position, the new accomplishments are most clearly instrumental. In contrast, the development of a new self image, of new involvements and values, while partly instrumental, is also expressive as well. The socialization of both expressive and instrumental behaviors is typically involved in the socialization into new organizations, as Etzioni (1964) has emphasized.

Modes of change—The specific content involved in the socialization process is typically more diverse than the modes by which the content is transmitted. Indeed, Caplow has observed that the modes of socialization appear repeatedly in societies and organizations of diverse types. In this connection, Caplow identifies the following recurring and common modes of socialization: schooling, training, apprenticeship, mortification, trial and error, assimilation, co-option, anticipatory socialization, screening, and nepotism (1964).

Social loci of change—We might add that the social locations of socialization for positional incumbents are likewise few in number. Thus socialization may be accomplished in the peer group, the family, the organization, the occupation and profession, the community, or by society at large. These loci may employ diverse modes and, in turn, the modes of socialization may be directed toward such areas as the acquisition of the new self image, new involvements, new values, and new accomplishments—and all of these, likewise, may encompass different specific content.

Group agents of change—All of this is a prelude to what is perhaps the heart of our subject. We have identified three group agents that operate irrespective of the area, mode, or locus of change. The first of these is the *prescriptive system,* which includes the entire set of statements that define positional behavior as obligatory, forbidden, or permitted. Prescriptions occur in diverse forms —as norms, officially codified rules, group standards, role expectations, and many others. The particular form of the prescription, whether formal or informal, obligating or forbidding, covert or overt, should not obscure the behavior delimiting function shared by all prescriptive phenomena. The prescriptive system defines that which is acceptable and unacceptable through indicating such details as how, when, and in what context given behaviors may be obligatory, forbidden, or permitted.

The second group agent is the *sanctioning system* and this involves the set of reinforcements and punishments that attend and operate in conjunction with the prescriptive system. Sanctions may consist of reinforcements for engaging in the prescribed behavior, of punishments for failure to engage in the desired behavior, and both may vary in magnitude and in probability of application. It is by means of the sanctioning system that the prescriptive system is "policed" and controlled.

The third agent by which social change is achieved is the *performance system,* this being composed of two parts. The first involves the particular behaviors engaged in by the persons themselves, these tending to be delimited, prescribed, and patterned in relationship to the performances of others in the role network. The second aspect of the performance system consists of the behavior of others as they may facilitate or hinder the role performance of the individuals in question. When in interdependence with others, an individual may have his behavior made easier to perform (in which case it is facilitated) or it may be impeded in part or fully blocked (in which case we speak of hindering).

These three systems—the prescriptive, the

sanctioning and the performance—typically operate in concert to achieve social change, although the literature documents also the various ways in which these agents may often work at cross purposes.

In the study by Merei (1952) cited earlier, we find an example of the operation of the prescriptive system. When the leaders joined established groups of followers, it was found that in most cases, the leader had to adopt the norms and standards of the group in order to get along with the other members and, eventually, to achieve leadership status again. The operation of the sanctioning system is illustrated in an experiment by Schachter (1951). Here it was found that members expressing deviant opinions, following the exertion of pressures upon them to change their views, were often rejected from the group. The operation of that aspect of the performance system involving one's own role enactment is seen in the findings of a study by Sarbin and Allen (1964). This experiment, again corroborating the findings of Janis and King (1954), indicated that in role-playing in which one is obligated to espouse an opinion contrary to one's private beliefs, there is more attitude change than that which occurs when not engaging in such role enactment. These attitude changes are mainly dispositional and are but one possible effect of role enactment. In a recent review of the psychological effects of role enactment, Sarbin (1964) has marshalled documentation for additional influences on somatic processes, on the deployment of attention and on performance itself. The reader is referred to Sarbin's review for additional details.

Postscript

The six routes to behavioral commonality outlined above encompass two distinct phases of positional membership. Personal and social in-selection operate mainly in the pre-entry phase, whereas personal and social change and personal and social out-selection occur during the individual's membership in the position. Because each of these six routes may function differently to achieve commonality in the personal characteristics of positional members and because the various types of selection and change occur in one or another of the two phases of positional membership, it is clear that a proper understanding of the relative contribution of the commonality routes necessitates scrutiny of their operation, for any cohort of potential position members, at both the pre-entry and incumbency phases. Only in this way will it be possible to obtain understanding of the relative contributions of all six commonality routes.

There is very little known presently concerning the conditions under which the diverse selection and change processes occur. Future research on these problems, however, will undoubtedly inform us concerning the particular limits constraining their operation. Change is a process that occurs necessarily within given bounds. In principle, there is a limit in the extent to which various personal characteristics are changeable, under given conditions, and, similarly, there are bounds upon the extent to which the role and positional factors in a social situation are subject to alteration. Selection processes, like those of change, are also subject to constraints. In-selection by the individual himself occurs necessarily from among some set of available social positions. In-selection processes controlled by agents external to the individual himself are necessarily restricted to an available pool of persons who might enter the position. Departure from social positions is governed in part by the availability of alternative positions for the individual and, analogously, the exclusion of members from a social position is certain to be affected by the availability of substitutes.

Throughout the above discussion, we have assumed the functional equivalence of selection and change. This general inverse relationship between the two mechanisms should not obscure the fact that they are not necessarily otherwise similar or equivalent. Thus there may be important differences in efficiency and cost among the six commonality routes.

Performance Adequacy

Another aspect of the explanatory problem involves accounting for the adequacy of performance of individuals occupying a social position. By performance we mean the behavior displayed by position members which relates to the role expectations placed upon them. Such behavior is generally goal directed, voluntary as opposed to "reflex," and has been previously acquired. There are various terms found in the literature for such performance, among them being "role enactment," "role behavior," and sometimes "behavior." The "adequacy" of role performance is almost invariably determined by its approximation to qualitative or quantitative standards of excellence. What the particular criterion of excellence is, of course, depends upon the content of performance for the given position. Thus academic achievement may be an indicator of a student's performance adequacy in an educational context, or the amount of a product sold by a salesman may indicate performance adequacy in this occupation.

Role Factors

The studies of the effects of role factors on performance reveal that there are at least three classes of role-related change agents that may be operative. These change agents —mentioned earlier—involve the prescriptive, sanctioning, and performance systems.

The set of prescriptions that constitutes the prescriptive system affects role performance in diverse ways. In the first place, the level of role demands, assuming that the performance standard is within the range of the individual's performance capacities, is itself a basic determinant. In a study of the relationship of role playing specification, personality, and performance, Borgatta (1961) found that role-playing specifications to be assertive or submissive related directly to the total interaction scores. More specifically, it was found that the difference between the total behavioral output between the assertive and the submissive conditions, for those with high prior assertiveness scores, was in the magnitude of two to one, that for those with medium prior assertiveness scores it was over three to one, and for those with low prior assertiveness scores it was over two to one. In a study by Smelser (1961), subjects were assigned roles to be demanding or submissive in the performance of a two-person cooperative task that required the coordinated running of miniature trains. Here it was also found that there was a productivity outcome consistent with whether individuals were assigned to demanding or submissive roles—all in contrast with subjects who had no role assignment at all. These findings from laboratory studies are further corroborated by the results of field inquiries in which the level of posthospital performance of discharged mental patients was found to be positively correlated with the level of the role expectations held for such performance by the patient's family members (Dinitz *et al.,* 1962; Freeman & Simmons, 1963).

Role expectations are generally placed upon position members by more than one "role sender" and these "senders" do not always agree. Disagreement concerning role expectations may be polarized around essentially two distinct and different desired behaviors or, in the nonpolarized case, the aggregate of role expectations may display near maximally diverse disagreement. The former is generally called "role conflict," and the latter, when it is distinguished at all, is generally termed "dissensus." In either case, however, the disagreement makes conformity to all of the role expectations difficult or impossible. In contrast to consensus, where conformity to the single behavioral standard is at least possible, the existence of polarized or nonpolarized disagreement presents the person with multiple standards of desired behavior. And when the adequacy of performance is determined in terms of conformity to such behavioral standards, the existence of multiple standards and the impossibility of performing consistently with all of them at the same time means that the individual's performance is defective by at least some of the competing behavioral standards. It is clear that under these conditions when performance adequacy is related to conformity to role expectations—and it most frequently is—the more disagreement there is in the set of role expectations for an individual, the more likely it is that his performance will be deemed inadequate by some of those placing the conflicting expectations upon him. This adverse effect of role-expectation disagreement is straightforward logically, but we are not familiar with adequate empirical corroboration.

Still another feature of prescriptions is the extent to which they are complete in specifying desired behavior. An incomplete prescription may fail to indicate such matters as the means by which performance is to be engaged in or the conditions of performance (for example, time, place, and condition). The terms "role ambiguity," "expectation ambiguity," or "norm ambiguity" have often been employed when referring to various aspects of an incompletely specified prescription. The effect of incomplete or ambiguous prescriptions is, in general, either to increase the variance of productivity or, in certain instances, to reduce the level of productivity. The latter effect is illustrated in an experiment by Smith (1957) in which it was found that the problem-solving productivity of five-man groups having two silent members with ambiguously specified roles was less than that of similar groups in which silent members had clearly specified roles. Another effect of ambiguity is to reduce the satisfaction of the group members, this finding being supported by the research of Raven and Rietsema (1957) in a study in which the clarity of group paths and goals were varied for individuals. The reduced satisfaction associated with ambiguous role specification should generally reduce the level of member productivity, although the latter was not examined in this experiment.

The reinforcements and punishments that comprise a sanctioning system also affect the adequacy of performance. Reinforcement for performance includes such tangibles as money and material goods and such intangibles as approval and attention. The withdrawal of privileges, criticism, disapproval, incarceration, dismissal and group rejection are various forms that punishment may take. Whatever the form, however, punishment typically involves either the presentation of an aversive stimulus or the withdrawal of a positive reinforcer for failure to perform at a desired level. The potency of such sanctioning measures has been amply demonstrated in various bodies of research. Thus the inquiries into industrial productivity have shown the effectiveness of selected incentive systems, on the one hand, and of informal group sanctions, on the other hand (for example, see Viteles, 1953). A significant portion of the extensive research on operant and aversive conditioning indicates the potency of various reinforcing and punishing conditions in affecting performance.

The performance system involves the role performance engaged in by the person himself as well as the performances of others. The operation of the performance system is perhaps most graphically illustrated by the effects of the hindering and facilitative efforts of others as they affect the performance of individuals. When engaging in interdependent task activities, the individual's performance exercises means control over the performance of others. If in such situations the performance of the individual is impeded by others, we speak of means-controlling hindrance and, analogously, if the performance of others readily makes possible the role performance of the individual, we speak of means-controlling facilitation.

The effect of means-controlling interdependence on the role performance of others is shown in an experiment by Thomas (1957). In its high means interdependence condition, participants constructed portions of a miniature house in a modified assembly line in which each person's constructive effort was dependent upon the prior task accomplishment of others. The productivity of complete houses in this condition greatly exceeded the output of participants in the low means-controlling condition where each member constructed all component parts of the houses himself. A related experiment by Raven and Eachus (1963) indicates the adverse effect on productivity of means-controlling hindrance, as well as the beneficial effect of facilitation. In a clever spirit-leveling task in which the performance of each member was entirely determined by the other two co-workers, facilitation was induced by instructions that members should work as rapidly as possible to level all three carpenter's spirits on the board; and hindrance was induced by instructions to triads to try to level each individual's spirit as rapidly as possible. The cooperating triads leveled the spirits much more rapidly than did the competing groups. Considering the findings of both of these studies it would thus appear that hindrance in means-controlling role relationships not only decreases the adequacy of role performance, but that facilitation in means-controlling relationships increases the adequacy of role performance above that which obtains under conditions of independence of the task activities.

So much for the operation of role factors. It is clear that the systems of prescription, sanction, and performance may operate singly as well as in concert to affect greatly the adequacy of role performance.

Personal Factors

In Sarbin's (1964) recent review of the correlates of effective role enactment, he singled out role-relevant skills and aptitudes among the significant determinants. Turning first to the skills component, it is clear that if one lacks the requisite skills for performing a role, his chances of performing well are obviously small. And it is equally apparent that the possession of the required skills will at least make possible adequate performance, although they will not necessarily guarantee it. Many of the role-relevant skills go beyond the technical and instrumental skills that are patently pertinent. For example, some of the skills relating to leadership are relatively divorced from any particular instrumental area of leadership activity. The fact that there are such general leadership skills has been suggested by many studies, among them being the study of Merei (1952), cited earlier. One recalls that in this inquiry, established leaders in one situation, when placed in a new ongoing group of followers, emerged again as leaders, although they had to accommodate and work through the norms and traditions of the group to accomplish this. In a study bearing upon the "great man" theory of leadership, Borgatta, Couch, and Bales (1954) selected a sample of distinguished individuals from the top tenth of a total sample on the criteria of task ability, individual assertiveness, and social acceptability. Two significant results emerged: individuals designated as great men appeared in subsequent sessions as great men; and the groups in which the great men participated, as compared with those not so characterized, displayed higher product rates of giving suggestion, agreement, of showing solidarity and tension release, and lower rates of showing tension—leading the authors to say that "great men make great groups."

Aptitudes for role performance, like role-relevant skills, undoubtedly involve specific, particular aptitudes related to one type of performance and not others, and, possibly also, more general aptitudes that enter into many varieties of role performance. Research on the aptitudes for role performance, however, does not explicate this speculation. However, if there is a general aptitude entering into many different role performances, an excellent candidate for it is a capacity for role taking. In the early work of George Herbert Mead (1934), the ability of the person to ascribe meaning and to communicate, and thereby take the role of others, was emphasized as one of the central features of human social interaction. More recently, Sarbin (1954, 1964) and others (e.g., Rose, 1962) have emphasized role taking as an aptitude with respect to which individuals may display differences and those possessing this aptitude in high degree are viewed as being able to perform their roles more effectively. Sarbin and his associates (Sarbin, 1954) have conducted various studies which indicate specific relationships between measures of role-taking ability and effective role enactment. In order to demonstrate that role-taking ability is indeed a general aptitude positively related to the adequacy of most all role performance, it will be necessary, however, to study the relationship between measures of role-taking aptitude in many more performance areas than have now been examined.

There are other personality characteristics than role-taking aptitude, however, that have been found to be impressively related to various aspects of group behavior. In a review of the relationships between personality and performance of small groups, Mann (1959) found that the best predictor of an individual's performance in groups was intelligence. In order of the proportion of positive results, it was found in this appraisal that intelligence was positively related to total activity rate, leadership, and popularity. Even the other personality predictors examined in this review, although less powerful predictively, related to various aspects of performance in groups. Thus adjustment was found to be positively related to leadership, popularity, and total activity rates; extraversion was positively related to popularity, total activity rate, and leadership; dominance was directly related to the total number of task contributions initiated and to leadership; masculinity had a low positive relationship to leadership and popularity; and conservatism was negatively related to leadership, but positively associated with popularity.

The number of personality predictors and their diverse correlates, however, should not be construed as indicating that personality factors were powerful predictors. On the contrary, where it was possible in Mann's review to estimate the magnitude of relationships between personality factors and performance, the average correlations between aspects of personality and performance were never higher than .25, and most of the median correlations were in the neighborhood of .15. Furthermore, despite the general tendencies referred to above, there were numerous confirming relationships between personality and indices of performance. The general, low magnitude of the associations may be due simply to the fact that many of the personality measures, being at least one step removed from direct behavioral indicators of the phenomena measured, bear only a remote relationship to some of the more complex group activities examined.

In the discussion above it has been implied that a personality effect, whatever its magnitude, is relatively noncontingent; i.e., the implication was that a personal characteristic would affect behavior of members without qualifying and mediating conditions. Personality effects, however, may be highly contingent upon such additional conditions as the particular persons with whom one interacts or the position of which one is a member. Indeed, there may be no truly noncontingent personality effects, only effects that are contingent in varying degrees.

The relevance of this distinction between the contingent *versus* the noncontingent personality effects is highlighted by a report of Haythorn (1958), in which some of the effects of varying combinations of leaders and followers were examined. In this study, discussion groups were composed of four members; in some the appointed leaders were authoritarian and in others they were equalitarian, with both leader types working with either authoritarian or equalitarian followers. This design made it possible to examine the effects of leader personality and follower personality, independently of the personalities of their followers or leaders, respectively; and to examine the effects of homogeneity of leader and follower personalities. Some of the effects were relatively noncontingent. For example, it was found that authoritarian leaders were more autocratic, efficient, and formal, achieved a lower degree of equal participation of followers, were less highly motivated toward group goals and had fewer differences of opinion—all as compared with groups having equalitarian leaders. Other "noncontingent" effects were found for equalitarian leaders, and for authoritarian and equalitarian followers. It should be noted that although these results were noncontingent with respect to the personalities of followers for leaders or of leaders for followers, they were all contingent upon whether the individuals in question were in the positions of leader or follower. Furthermore, contingent effects of personality were revealed when the data were analyzed in terms of the homogeneity of leader and follower personalities. If the followers and leaders were either authoritarian or equalitarian, it was found that in these homogeneous groups the leaders were less submissive, more aggressive and more autocratic than the leaders of heterogeneous groups. The followers in the homogeneous groups showed more striving for group approval and withdrew more into extraneous activity. But considering all the findings, the author concluded that the differences in personalities between the leaders and followers seemed to have created conflicts in the groups, detracting from the group morale.

It is likely that most personality effects are contingent in one way or another, but it is difficult to draw firm conclusions concerning the particular personality characteristics that display more rather than less noncontingency and to stipulate the conditions upon which the effects are contingent, for there are simply exceedingly few studies in which personality characteristics and the potential contingency conditions are simultaneously varied.

Role Factors and Stress

A third significant set of explanatory problems involves accounting for stress reactions of individuals who face role problems. In this connection, the stress factors may be attributed to role factors, to the particular personality characteristics of the individuals thus exposed, or to various combinations of the role factors and the personality dispositions of members. There have been instances in the common experience of most everyone that illustrate one or another of these explanations. Thus an employed mother is observed to be emotionally upset, apparently as a consequence of the demands of her job, on the one hand, and those placed upon her as a mother and spouse, on the other hand. Or it is observed that a husband who has been physically handicapped makes a remarkable psychological adjustment to his disablement whereas another becomes withdrawn, dependent, and emotionally incapacitated.

The problems of role are not simple and unitary. Analysis of the various role factors that may dispose individuals to stress reveals that there are at least these five distinguishable and different problems: role conflict, role ambiguity, role overload, role discontinuity, and role incongruence. The diverse reactions of individuals in the face of these role problems are taken up below.

Role Conflict

Most conceptions of role conflict pertain to incompatibilities of the prescriptions placed upon a position member. Our conception is consistent with this community of thought. Role conflict is said to exist for an individual when the role expectations placed upon him are incompatible, making it impossible for him to conform to both sets of expectations at the same time. It is important to observe that the incompatible role prescriptions may be externally imposed, may involve some prescriptions external to the person which conflict with other internalized role expectations, or in extreme cases, may involve sets of internalized incompatible expectations in which the external sources of these expectations are either no longer visible or even currently operative.

Role conflict of these various forms is perhaps one of the most common and widespread of all role difficulties. In a national survey of 725 individuals representing a portion of the labor force in the United States employed in 1961, Kahn and his associates (Kahn, Wolfe, Quinn, & Snoek, 1964) found that nearly half of the male wage and salary workers were confronted with role conflict, that 48 per cent reported that at various times they were caught in the middle between two sets of people who wanted different things from them—15 per cent revealing this to be a frequent and serious problem—and that 39 per cent indicated that they were bothered at times by thinking that they were not able to satisfy the conflicting demands of various people over them.

Although there have been many studies of role conflict, relatively few have dealt with the emotional reactions and social costs of such conflicts. Consequently, there is insufficient information upon which to base a comprehensive picture. One of the few studies focused expressly upon role pressures and the emotional tensions of persons exposed to role difficulties is that already mentioned by Kahn and his associates (1964). In this study, an intensive series of case studies of 53 selected individuals in six industrial locations was undertaken. The focal persons completed questionnaires and personality inventories, and were interviewed twice. Information was obtained concerning the focal person's over-all evaluation of his role in terms of conflict, ambiguity, and tension; and the focal person's major role senders were located. In the interviews with the role senders—namely, those persons identified by the focal person as those whose expectations were relevant to their work—information was obtained concerning the magnitude and direction of pressures that each sender was trying to exert upon the focal person.

Measures of role conflict consisted of the following indices: the role sender's desire to have the focal person perform differently, the role sender's desire to have the focal person perform more or less of what he was then engaging in, the role sender's desire for the focal person to be different, and the role sender's ideal for the focal person. Indices for these were normalized and combined into role-conflict scores.

A balanced picture of the numerous effects of role conflict may be garnered from the authors' summary of their findings on this problem:

> Contradictory role expectations ... give rise to opposing role pressures (role conflicts), which generally have the following effects on the emotional experience ... of the focal person: intensified internal conflicts, increased tension associated with various aspects of the job, reduced satisfaction with the job and its various components, and decreased confidence in superiors and in the organization as a whole. ...
>
> The strain experienced by those in conflict situations leads to various coping responses—social and psychological withdrawal (reduction in communication and attributed influence) among them.
>
> Finally, the presence of conflict in one's role tends to undermine his relations with his role senders, to produce weaker bonds of trust, respect, and attraction. ... It is quite clear that role conflicts are costly for the person in emotional and interpersonal terms. They may also be costly to the organization, which depends on effective coordination and collaboration within and among its parts (Kahn *et al.,* 1964, p. 171).

The findings cited above pertain to the effects of role conflict irrespective of the personality characteristics of the focal persons. The authors went ahead in their analysis to examine how individuals with different personality profiles reacted to role conflict. On the basis of a broad battery of objective personality tests, the investigators conducted a factor analysis, rotating by the Varimax criterion, from which six factors were derived, these accounting for 99 per cent of the common factor variance. Factor I was called "neurotic anxiety *versus* emotional stability" and this contained high factor loadings on anxiety, guilt proneness, inner conflict intention, depression, lack of will power, neuroticism, and physiological correlates of anxiety. Although other important factors were isolated and analyzed, the results for the neurotic anxiety factor are perhaps best illustrative of the various ways in which a personality characteristic may combine with role conflict in the determination of effects.

Focal persons who had high and low objective role conflict and for whom the personality tests indicated either high or low neurotic anxiety were analyzed in terms of the various indicators of emotional tension. Because neurotic anxiety implies a heightened sensitivity to environmental pressures and a low degree of stress tolerance, one would anticipate that individuals with high neurotic anxiety would experience more conflict than those with low neurotic anxiety. Although this was borne out in the analysis, the findings turned out to be more complex; namely, that individuals with high role conflict and high anxiety experienced the greatest intensity of conflict, whereas individuals with low conflict, irrespective of their anxiety, experienced considerably less conflict. These findings illustrate the contingent personality effect discussed earlier. But other findings illustrated the noncontingent personality effect. Thus it was found that individuals high in neurotic anxiety compared with those not so characterized displayed higher levels of attention, lower job satisfaction, higher sense of futility, irrespective of whether objective role conflict was high or low.

A still different personality effect is illustrated by the findings of this study for the factor of flexibility-rigidity. The flexibility factor was composed of traits of other-directedness, openmindedness and interpersonal relations emphasizing colleagueship instead of authoritarian relations; whereas, the rigid syndrome involved innerdirectedness, dogmatism, and authoritarian interpersonal relations. It was found that the flexible individuals exposed to high objective role conflict experienced much greater tension than did the inflexible individuals; the rigid individuals, in contrast, experienced only a moderate amount of tension irrespective of whether objective role conflict was high or low. The authors speculated that the other-directedness of the flexible person exposes him to role conflict more than the rigid one, and, because of his reluctance to reject such overtures from diverse role senders, the flexible person commits himself excessively and beyond his capacity to fulfill obligations. Consequently, the flexible person with high role conflict is likely to experience a very high level of anxiety. And by contrast, the rigid person is able to shut off overtures from various role senders who might create conflict. Although these speculations were not sustained by sufficient corroborating evidence, the point here is that personality characteristics such as flexibility-rigidity may themselves function to dispose persons to various role problems which, in turn, may produce difficulties for the individual.

Role Ambiguity

Role ambiguity, like role conflict, is a condition of the prescriptive system that may generate stress for individuals. The incompleteness of prescriptions for behavior defines role ambiguity. This lack of specificity is what is emphasized here, not the personal confusion that is a highly plausible consequence of the role ambiguity. Of the few studies that have examined the emotional effects of role ambiguity, the inquiry by Kahn and associates (1964) is again one of the most informative.

In their measure of role ambiguity, these investigators obtained the focal person's judgment of the clarity of what various role senders expected, their certainty of how they were evaluated, and their subjective appraisal of the clarity of their jobs. Three indices were derived: one for ambiguity, another for role expectations, and a third for evaluations. It was found that all three indices correlated positively with the emotional reactions of tension and futility, and were negatively related to job satisfaction and self-confidence. They found, furthermore, that these ambiguity indices were negatively related to trust in, respect for, and communication frequency with role senders. The effects of role ambiguity were similar to those for role conflict, although it was found that the conditions of ambiguity and conflict occurred independently of one another. It was largely by chance, the authors observed, that a person may find himself in a work environment that is both ambiguous and conflictful. But when this occurs, these researchers found that the degree of tension was highest for those exposed to high ambiguity and role conflict and lowest for those exposed to low role ambiguity and conflict. In general, the mediating effects of personality factors found for role conflict were not found for role ambiguity.

Role Overload

Role overload occurs when the role demands are in excess of the individual's capacity to meet such demands. Although role conflict may create role overload, overload may occur independently of conflict. In Goode's (1960) theory of role strain, he has indicated that excessive demands—indeed, the mere fact that demands for regular performance are made at all—is one of the determinants of role strain. Clinical inquiries abound with illustrations of role overload as a precipitating condition for emotional disturbance and studies of stress under extreme environmental conditions also reveal the adverse effects of role overload. However, we are not familiar with adequate research indicating the effects of role overload proper on the emotional reactions of individuals, nor of the personality factors that may mediate these effects.

Role Discontinuity

Ruth Benedict (1938) introduced the concept of role discontinuity to characterize the lack of order and smooth sequence in the cultural role training of the life cycle. She documented how various primitive cultures provided for more continuity in the training for responsibility, dominance, and sexuality than was characteristic in the United States. The "storm and stress" of adolescence so often attributed only to physiological changes, she concluded, was in fact due to the particular discontinuities resulting from prior role training.

Although Benedict used the term in connection with age-graded transitions universal for all mankind, it is but a simple step to realize that discontinuities may also occur for specific groups and individuals whenever there is a transition from one position to another in which the role behaviors associated with each are different. The transitions associated with movements into positions indexed by such terms as "divorcee," "aged," "patient," "retiree," "disabled," "unemployed," "breadwinner," and even "parent," all may involve discontinuities to varying degrees. Role discontinuity may be said to exist for a transition between any two positions when (a) that which is learned in the first position does not provide an ordered bridge for performance in the second position, or (b) the performances required in the second position necessitate the unlearning of a portion or all of that which was learned in the prior position. Both aspects of discontinuity may vary in degree and pattern.

Davis (1940) has attributed some of the problems of parent-youth conflict to discontinuity; Sayres (1956) has associated certain disoriented states to status changes; Landy (1960) has conceived of halfway houses and similar transitional facilities in terms of the essential desirability of having graded and ordered socialization experiences in moving from one facility to another; Donahue and associates (Donahue, Orbach & Pollack, 1960) have emphasized the importance of preretirement planning and anticipatory socialization to help ease the transitions into retirement; Strauss (1959) has analyzed elements of regularized status passage; and Wilson, Trist, and Curle (1952) reported a pioneering social experiment in which transitional facilities were used to bring prisoners of war back into civilian life. These are among the more prominent discussions of continuity proper. But there are few systematic treatments and, to our knowledge, no reviews of the effects of discontinuity.

In order to learn more about the possible effects of various role discontinuities, writings in the diverse areas have been examined. Among the bodies of literature examined in this connection were inquiries into the emotional correlates of disability, unemployment, retirement, and of family role changes. A mosaic of results emerged, but this search for uniform, common effects was fruitless. In fact, the task of isolating reliable correlates in any one of these particular areas turned out to be most difficult. In the research on the effects of retirement, for instance, investigators have been concerned with the adjustmental correlates of the transition from productive employment to retirement. Although Phillips (1957) found that retirees scored lower on a test of adjustment than did a comparable group of employed persons, examination of the various studies and reviews in this area compels the conclusion that researchers have not established that the simple transition from work to nonwork, leaving aside matters of health, economic deprivation, and willingness to work or retire, is reliably associated with various indices of emotional health and adjustment (for example, see Kutner, Fanshel, Togo, & Langner, 1956; Thompson & Streib, 1958; Donahue, Orbach, & Pollack, 1960). For example, Thompson and Streib, in one of the few more fine-grained examinations of this problem, did not find that a sense of subjective deprivation was associated with whether retirement was voluntary or administratively determined by the employer.

The findings in the area of the psychological correlates of physical disability, when reviewed by Barker in 1948, led that writer to conclude that physically disabled persons more frequently than the physically normal exhibited behavior commonly termed maladjusted (Barker, 1948). It was noted, however, that 35 to 45 per cent of disabled subjects were reported to be as well or better adjusted than the average nondisabled person. In a more recent review of the literature on this and related problems, Wright (1960) concluded her assessment of the field of somatopsychology as follows: "... somatic abnormality as a physical factor is not linked in any direct or simple way to psychological behavior" (p. 373). The scholars who have reviewed the scientifically reputable studies concerning the effects of disability upon adjustment have not found that there is presently any known, general, consistent adverse effect upon adjustment attending disablement (in addition to Wright, 1960, see Barker, Wright, Meyerson, & Gonick, 1953; Meyerson, 1957; Cowen, Underberg, Verrillo, & Benham, 1961).

Unemployment is clearly typically an abrupt status change and there have been various inquiries into the social, psychological, and economic effects attending this change. Among the more revealing of the studies on the psychological effects is the early inquiry of Zawadski and Lazarsfeld (1935). The findings of this study were based upon 57 autobiographies collected from unemployed individuals by the Government of Poland. The authors described four stages that the workers went through. At first, the workers appeared to be unbroken, during which time they were active, enterprising, and still looked for work; a second stage was that of resignation in which their needs seemed to be limited and there was a relative absence of plans and hopes; a third stage was characterized as that of apathy, during which the individuals were relatively idle and indolent; and the final stage was termed distressed, characterized by hopelessness, bitterness, rage, and sometimes by suicidal feelings. Furthermore, feelings of degradation and superfluousness were widespread, as were feelings of hostility and aggression.

Another area of inquiry relating to discontinuity involves the consequences of membership loss in families. Among the most searching of the inquiries in this area is the exhaustive analysis of Hill (1949) in which 139 Iowa families were studied. The focus of this study—an examination of the factors associated with adjustment to separation and to reunion—was restricted to families in which the husband had been inducted into war service. In general, neither the exhaustive statistical analysis nor the more insightful qualitative case analyses revealed any strong influence of role factors. Thus it was found that adjustment to separation was not related to the flexibility in shifting roles nor to the "closing of ranks" and reallocation of roles and duties of the absent one to the remaining members of the family. It was found, however, that previous success in handling crises was highly related to the adjustmental indices, as was the tendency not to be crisis prone.

In all of the above areas of discontinuity —retirement, disability, unemployment, and family member loss—there are many factors associated with the position transitions. Thus, when an employee retires from work, he may be in poor health, he may be relatively incompetent, he may desire to stop working, to name but a few of the plausible correlates. The problem, clearly, is that in any inquiry into the adjustmental effects of such position changes, there may be diverse associated conditions not part of the discontinuity proper that may condition the effects found. There are at least the following six associated conditions: deprivation, as in unemployment; reduced interpersonal contact, this typically being associated with prolonged unemployment, and with retirement and aging in general; loss of power and authority; loss of pride and self-respect; response interference; and strangeness. Role discontinuity will be associated with one or more of these component conditions. Furthermore, there is even some evidence concerning the specific effects of each of these. But the problem is that each of these associated conditions may appear in complex combination with a given role discontinuity and the general effects found are likely to depend upon this particular complex and the extent to which each of the components enters into it.

As further research is conducted to isolate the particular effects of discontinuity proper, attention should be given to dimensions that condition the extent to which the discontinuity produces deleterious effects. We have in mind the abruptness of change, the amount of change, the type of learning and unlearning required, as well as the sanctions and reinforcement associated with the discontinuity; for all of these should determine the extent to which the changes have impact.

Role Incongruence

Virtually everyone has had the experience of being out of fit with his social role. Person-role malfit is particularly common in the early period of membership in social positions and, sometimes, individuals retain membership in malfitting positions for long periods, even lifetimes. The existence of role congruence derives from two facts. The first is that the range and variety of individual differences greatly exceed society's mold of positional alternatives, and the second is that the processes of selection and change do not always operate sufficiently well to achieve a fit between given positions and particular persons.

Although problems of role congruence are often discussed in the abstract, as if role congruence were unitary and unambiguous, there are numerous personal dispositions that may or may not be congruent with one's role. The varieties of person-role incongruence have not been articulated in the literature, to our knowledge, although an appraisal of the writings on this subject suggests examples of generic types. On the basis of this analysis, the following seven distinct types of person-role malfit are offered:

1. *Motive malfit,* defined by the arousal of motives that are irrelevant to, or interfere with, the requisite performance in a position. This type of incongruence is illustrated by inquiries into the types of motives suited to given occupational callings. Thus Atkinson and Hoselitz (1958) have indicated the compatibility of high motivation to achieve and entrepreneurial activity.

2. *Incentive malfit,* defined by a discrepancy between the incentives sought by an individual and those available through performance in a position. For example, in Wilensky's (1956) analysis of the rewards primarily sought by various types of union intellectuals, he distinguished such factors as ideological objectives, community and social prestige, money, professional recognition, power over others, and the intrigue of meeting interpersonal challenges.

3. *Skill malfit,* defined by the individual's lack of skills requisite to perform adequately in a position or the possession of valuable skills not made use of in the position. Almost any armed-service veteran can detail extreme cases of skill malfit alleged to have been visited upon him or his buddies.

4. *Capacity malfit,* defined by either the underuse or overtaxing of the individual's capacity to perform in a position. Argyris (1957), in his analysis of personality and large-scale organizations, concludes that there are basic incongruences between the growth trends of a healthy personality and the requirements of many formal organizations. He argues that if the principles of formal organization are used as traditionally defined, most employees will tend to work in an environment which serves to deny their abilities, their desires to be independent, self-fulfilling, and to anticipate life over the long haul rather than the short term. The basic incongruency will be increased, he further argues, to the extent that employees are mature, the organization is made more formal, as one occupies a lower rather than a higher position in the chain of command, and as the activities become more and more mechanized.

5. *Identify malfit,* defined by the discrepancy between an individual's identity and that provided by membership in a social position. This requires elaboration. Following Miller (1963), identity may be viewed in terms of two connotations: the organization of observable or inferable attributes by which a person becomes identified to himself and others; and his identity as a socially labeled object. One aspect of an individual's public identity is the portrait of the individual associated with the positions he occupies; and associated with these positions, there will be various objective public identities defined by the person's pattern of traits as they appear to members of the various groups. An individual's subjective public identity may not be consonant with the objective public identity of a position he occupies, or the incongruence may attend the individual's self-identity as it relates to either his subjective public identity or the objective public identity. Self-appraisal of these various identities may involve differences between one's actual identity, potential identity, or ideal identity, for all of these may be components of either a public or a subidentity.

6. *Performance malfit,* defined by performance demands of a position that are inconsistent or interfere with the performance

dispositions of an individual. Thus a demonstrably assertive individual may be constrained to meet role demands that he be submissive, or a nonassertive person may be expected to perform in a position requiring much assertive behavior (cf. Borgatta, 1961).

7. *Value malfit,* defined by an inconsistency between the individual's values and the ideological commitments associated with the position he occupies. For instance, the union intellectuals whom Wilensky (1956) identified as missionaries tended to be committed to radical, leftist ideologies. But these intellectuals generally did not fit well into the union's work as the functions of the union changed and the missionaries were later confronted with a union purge of Communists and other leftists.

Because there may be congruence or incongruence for all of the above factors, the concept of "total role congruence" becomes relevant. This refers to the extent to which there is congruence for all these component forms in the position the individual occupies. Clearly, there may be highly diverse profiles considering all the congruence components, and the elements may themselves be more or less important for the individual, some having much more weight than others in affecting behavior.

There are many outcomes of person-role incongruence, perhaps the most common being the achievement of the increased congruence. There are different alternatives here. First, the person himself may change so as better to fit the demands of the position. Thus, if the incentives offered in the position are too low, an individual may lower his aspiration level; if the individual lacks the requisite skills to perform his role well, he may achieve additional training; and performance preferences, identities, values, and even motives may be changed. This latter type of change has been demonstrated by the results of a program to train management executives in motivation to achieve. In McClelland's (1965a) report, he indicated that such training produced about double the spontaneous rate of unusual entrepreneurial activity, the latter being unrelated to training. Second, whether or not the individual himself changes, the role factors may be altered so as better to accommodate the individual. Thus in some occupations, incentives may be adjusted to fit more adequately the individual's desires; the role demands may be altered so as to make use of the particular skills and capacities of the person; and so on. A third alternative consists of vacating the position. For instance, a person may quit, resign, be dismissed, or promoted. Fourth, the individual may sustain the incongruence while remaining in the position. From the perspective of the present discussion, this is the most important alternative.

Argyris (1957) has elaborated various psychological effects of conflict between the person and the role, all of these being pertinent to the effects of continued person-role incongruence. The first of these effects is frustration, which may take the form of regression, aggression, hostility, or attack. Another consequence is the experience of failure and this, in turn, may be associated with loss of interest in work, of self-confidence, lower work standards, fear of new tasks, the anticipation of future failure, or a tendency to blame others. A final correlate is a shortened time perspective associated with which are feelings of uncertainty and insecurity, with attending increases in tension.

These individual effects described by Argyris are illustrative of one of two essential costs that writers have attributed to sustained person-role incongruence. In addition to these individual costs are those that may best be called social. Here individuals are used inefficiently and uneconomically. Margaret Mead (1948), for example, has enumerated the waste of male and female talent in societies having limiting, constraining, and traditional sex roles. The social costs attending person-role incongruence are largely axiomatic and are easily demonstrated as compared with the alleged individual costs. The latter involve hypotheses, like those of Argyris, concerning such effects as frustration, failure experiences, and a reduced time perspective—all empirical matters. We are familiar with only a few studies on these individual costs. The studies are most relevant, however, and they deserve careful review.

In one of the more systematic of the inquiries, Borgatta (1961) varied role-playing specifications and personality characteristics of individuals, creating all combinations of person-role congruence. The personality characteristic in this study was assertiveness, derived from peer rankings following five-man discussion sessions, based upon the extent to which the person was active, took initiative, made many suggestions, and displayed assertiveness. Then, in a subsequent 20-minute role-playing session, individuals were placed into three-person groups, one member being high, the other medium, and the last low on the prior assertiveness scores. Three roles were played in the sessions: an assertive, a submissive, and an emotional role. The role-playing sessions were observed using a revision of Bales' scoring categories called Interaction Process Scores, and then following the sessions, participants rated how well they enjoyed playing the role and how adequately the other persons performed. This study was replicated in such a way that each of the persons in the design classified as high, medium, and low on prior assertiveness played the three different role specifications.

The results revealed the effects of both personality and role specification. Thus the means on the total interaction scores correlated positively with the prior assertiveness scores and the mean level corresponded with the role-playing specifications to be assertive or submissive. It is clear from inspection of the data that the variation in total interaction was more a function of role specification than of personality. Other findings pertained to a so-called facilitation effect for the subjects in the replicated series as opposed to the initial series. Here it was found that the role specifications were followed more clearly in the second as opposed to the first series. A third set of findings related directly to the congruence problem. First, with respect to the criterion of satisfaction—derived from self-ratings—it was found that all subjects, regardless of prior assertiveness scores, enjoyed the assertive more than the submissive role. However, the degree of assertiveness was directly associated with satisfaction in performing the emotional role. Of particular significance was that no congruence effect was found for the criterion of satisfaction.

It was found for the criterion of role-playing ability that the moderates on assertiveness did best in performing the assertive role, and the lows were rated lowest. And on performing the submissive role, it was found that the high assertives were best and the moderates and lows performed less well. In general, the highs played all roles best. These findings suggested that assertiveness may be related to a general role-playing skill, rather than being a particular behavioral propensity only associated with assertive and submissive behaviors. Considering the judgments of the observers, in contrast to the findings for peer ratings mentioned above, there was some minor support for a congruency hypothesis, but in general the highs and the mediums were rated much better than the lows. On balance, considering the criteria of satisfaction and role-playing ability, there was no clear evidence that incongruence produced low satisfaction or poor role playing.

Moos and Speisman (1962) examined the relationship between personality and role compatibility as they relate to productivity in group problem solving. Personality compatibility was said to exist "... when one member of a group expresses behavior that the other member of the group wants, or when one member 'pulls for' behavior which the other habitually expresses" (p. 190). The concept of role compatibility was defined as follows: "When the roles given the individual group members are congruent with their preferred behaviors" (p. 190). The general prediction of the study was that both forms of compatibility would facilitate group problem solving. Personal compatibility, it was said, contributes to the ease of interaction between members, since each participates in a desired or at least habitual way; and role compatibility permits expression of habitual modes of behavior through the function of task assignment. The compatibility of personality was based upon scores for three different personality tests (FIRO-B Scale of Schutz, CPI Dominance Scale of Gough, and the Interpersonal Check List of Leary). Personality compatibility, in general, consisted of pairing persons so that what one member expressed the other one wanted, whereas incompatibility obtained when what one member expressed the other did not want. Role compatibility, in general, consisted of a member rated as displaying more dominant behavior being one whose personality tests were higher than the other on dominance. A total of sixty groups were formed, with ten being high and low on compatibility of personality and role, and half the groups being males and the other half females. These pairings were done separately for each of the personality tests. The tasks involved transferring five rings, differing in size, from one peg to others, under certain restrictions. The dependent variables were the number of moves and the time required to transfer the rings.

There were no strong consistent results, although on four out of the twelve comparisons there were statistically significant results in favor of the general compatibility hypothesis. The qualifications are also important. The first is that for personality compatibility it was found that four out of the six comparisons favored the compatible groups, two of these for the criterion of the number of moves and the other two for the criterion of time. For role compatibility, however, the trends of the results, as we view them, were considerably more favorable; here it was found that six out of the six comparisons favored role compatibility over role incompatibility—two of these being statistically significant. Thus there was a small compatibility effect, this being stronger for role than for personality compatibility—all for the criterion of moves rather than that of time. More gross groupings of the data were also analyzed, none of these revealing any noteworthy compatibility effects. Of some incidental significance is the finding that with respect to the criterion of time, the males performed more rapidly than the females.

In a study of dominance as a factor in achievement in cooperative problem-solving interactions, Smelser (1961) varied the personality characteristics of being demanding and assertive as well as role assignments to be dominant or submissive. Congruent and incongruent combinations of personality and role assignments were made. The task required cooperation in running trains. The results revealed that the dominant subjects, irrespective of role, tended to perform more effectively than did the submissive subjects. In general, however, there was a beneficial effect of role assignment as compared with having no role definition. There were no adverse effects of incongruence on the performance criteria. And, as we interpret the findings, the most impressive result was that in the course of running the trains on six trials, all subjects were performing at about the same high level of efficiency in the final trials as compared with the initial trials, irrespective of personality, role congruence or incongruence. It would appear that repeated performance overcame any temporary dislocations resulting from person-role malfit or lack of role assignment.

An experiment by Trow (1957) provides results concerning satisfaction and motive-role congruence. In this experiment individuals high and low in need for autonomy were placed in three-person communication structures in which prewritten notes were employed to effect the illusion of centrality (or peripherality) and of autonomy (or dependence). The participants performed a simple task requiring the coordination of their activities. Job satisfaction was unrelated to the centrality or peripherality in the communication network, but high autonomy was related to higher job satisfaction than was dependence. Furthermore, a congruence effect was clearly demonstrated in that the job satisfaction of the individuals high in need autonomy was lowest when placed in the dependent position, and was high in the autonomous position; but there were no differences in the job satisfaction scores of individuals who had low need for autonomy, whether in autonomous or dependent experimental treatments. Thus the contingent operation of motive and position is illustrated here in that job satisfaction was directly related to need for autonomy for persons high in this need, but not for those who scored low.

A complex picture emerges when the results of all of these studies are appraised. With respect to the criterion of member satisfaction, there was no evidence for a straightforward incongruence effect in either the Trow or Borgatta inquiry. Rather, a more complex contingent effect was demonstrated in the Trow study, in which satisfaction was related to role demands only for individuals scoring high on the personality characteristic in question. And in the Borgatta study, in contrast to an incongruence effect, the assertive role was enjoyed more than the submissive role, irrespective of the assertiveness scores. Considering the criterion of adequate role performance, again there was found to be little evidence for a straightforward incongruence effect. Only in the study by Moos and Speisman was there suggestive evidence for any adverse effect of incompatibility upon productivity. In both the studies by Borgatta and Smelser, however, there was evidence that independently of compatibility, the personality characteristics and role specifications were directly related to performance. And Moos and Speisman found that one's sex role, occupied independently of the experimental role specification, affected productivity. Furthermore, it is noteworthy that in both the studies by Borgatta and Smelser there was evidence for a practice effect, suggesting that the longer one engages in the activities requisite to a role, the more adequate the performance.

It is clear from these inquiries that, in general, the presumed adverse effects of person-role incongruence on member satisfaction and productivity have not been demonstrated. These experimental inquiries have the distinct advantage over field studies of offering the opportunity to vary personality and role specification systematically and under controlled conditions. They have the noteworthy disadvantage, however, of dealing with individuals in relatively brief encounters that have less personal relevance than many real life activities. And moreover, inquiries into the effects of person-role incongruence almost of necessity require the measurement of personality and it is very possible that the inner states measured on the personality tests do not relate directly enough to behavior manifested by individuals in experimental situations and, consequently, the failure to obtain incongruence effects is inconclusive. An interesting exception is that the effects of personality alone were most clearly revealed in Borgatta's study where personality was measured by peer rankings of prior behavior, not by the typical pencil and paper test to measure inner states.

PERSONAL CHANGEABILITY

Most explanations of problems in the area of role and personality involve implicit or asserted assumptions about personal changeability. Such assumptions generally pertain to the extent of personal changeability for given personal characteristics, at particular times, and under specified conditions. Reliable information on these matters would necessarily have important implications for specific explanatory accounts as well as for general perspectives concerning problems of personality and role. Thus, to take two extremes, if personality is stabilized and fixed in the early years of life, particular personalistic accounts of later behavior would generally be favored over sociologistic views; but if personality is changeable beyond the years of childhood, then sociologistic accounts would be more tenable.

Researches on problems of personal change are beset by uncommonly formidable problems. The limitations of current information cannot be fully appreciated without acknowledging these difficulties at the outset. In the first place, the data required to assess the extent of personal changeability points one primarily toward longitudinal rather than cross-sectional studies, and there have been relatively few longitudinal studies. And furthermore, considering all of the data that one might marshal, there is altogether simply insufficient evidence to arrive at firm, wide-ranging generalizations. In the studies available, moreover, there are at least two biases that tend to color most of the results. The first of these is that investigators have been much more favorably disposed to employ reliable measures in their efforts to chart individual changes through time and, consequently, they may have selected precisely those personal characteristics which are least subject to environmental influence. A second bias is toward a conceptionalization and measurement of inner processes as opposed to overt behavior. To the extent that the presumed inner processes have ambiguous or indeterminate relationships to overt behavior, the relevance of the stability of such processes, in the context of some questions about role behavior, is open to question. But even assuming that personal characteristics can be measured properly, there are additional problems. Many of the changes in personal characteristics are cumulative in the sense that, like intelligence, any change depends mainly upon cumulative accretions up to that time. Thus for certain personality characteristics, the extent and type of change at any given time is largely dependent upon what has occurred at earlier periods.

The environment associated with any personality change is itself virtually never unitary or fixed. Environments are typically diverse and changing such that for no cohort of individuals may one safely assume that any personality changes are independent of at least some environmental influences. Most data on personal change reflect a heavy but largely unknown environmental impact. Furthermore, the socialization demands themselves vary at different points in the life span, with the demands generally decelerating through the life cycle. Although these factors do not preclude informative inquiry into problems of personal change, they caution one sharply against expecting many definite and conclusive generalizations.

In recent reviews that have attempted to come to the grips with the problem of personal consistency, we encounter many pertinent conclusions. Thus in Kuhlen's (1964) review of personality change and aging, one finds for the years of adulthood to old age that there are different levels of motivation, goals, interests, drive levels and degrees of involvement, amounts of happiness, self-confidence, and susceptibility to stress and threat. Most of the studies on which these findings are based, however, are not longitudinal and, consequently, they do not show whether individual changes are responsible for the results or whether different socialization experiences particular to the age cohorts are operative.

In the review of Yarrow and Yarrow (1964) we find an appraisal of many longitudinal studies relating to the problem of personal consistency in childhood and adolescence. The authors sum up as follows:

> Clearly no simple conclusions about personality consistency are possible from the existing research. There is some evidence of continuity in personality characteristics, and there are also data which point to changes over time. On the whole, the research which has dealt with global personality characteristics, personality style, indicates a moderately high degree of consistency over time, whereas the research which has focused on more specific traits

shows little consistency. Although the findings are not precise or clear-cut, the periods of greatest stability appear to be between infancy and the early preschool period and between late adolescence and adulthood; the greatest degree of variability seems to occur between middle childhood and adolescence. The findings on sex differences indicate different degrees of stability over time for boys and girls in different characteristics, e.g., girls show greater consistency in dependent behavior and social prestige, boys in drive aggression. On the whole, there seems to be a greater degree of stability for girls than for boys (p. 500).

These conclusions seem to be consistent with the findings reviewed by the authors, but because base rates—either age cumulative or normative—were not used in appraising the differential magnitudes of change in the various studies, one may not conclude reliably concerning the true extent of consistency. In a recent comprehensive reanalysis of data from longitudinal studies against either normative or age-cumulative base rates, Bloom (1964) provides one of the most comprehensive and valid sets of findings in the literature. These and other findings serve to explicate and qualify the conclusions of Yarrow and Yarrow. The research of Bloom and others suggests the plausibility of selected general statements about personal consistency, these being offered below.

The first such generalization is that for most personal characteristics, changes occur at differential rather than at uniform rates. To elaborate: "for each stable characteristic there is usually a period of relatively rapid growth as well as periods of relatively slow growth. Although it is not invariably true, the period of most rapid growth is likely to be in the early years and this is then followed by periods of less and less rapid growth" (Bloom, 1964, p. 204). Bloom has documented differential rates of growth in terms of the half-development of selected characteristics, taking the ages 18–20 as the criterion of the level of growth. The estimated ages for half-development are 2½ for height, 4 for general intelligence, 3 for aggressiveness in males, 4 for dependence in females, 4 for intellectuality in males and females, and grade 3 for general school achievement. Equally pertinent were results reported for the development of such characteristics as intellectual interest, dependency and aggression. For these it was found that at about the age of 5 as much as one-half of the variance at adolescence is predictable. Although there were limitations of the data here and numerous qualifications were voiced by Bloom, he observed that his findings were in essential agreement with personality theories—such as the psychoanalytic—that emphasize the significance of rapid, formative development in the early years of life. Attempts to measure personality characteristics on the basis of cognitive-perceptual tasks revealed, in contrast, that there was at least as much stability in the period ages 10–21 as would be expected on the basis of an age curve of development. Furthermore, the longitudinal evidence on interests and attitudes revealed that there is change in these throughout life and that this change is very close to estimates based upon an age curve of development. The longitudinal data derived from self-report instruments to measure interests, attitudes, and personality characteristics intended primarily for use with high school juniors, seniors, and college students revealed that, for the most part, there were more changes taking place on these instruments in the first two years of college than in the remaining college years and that more change takes place in these two years than in the next ten to twenty years.

A second generalization is that personal characteristics are themselves differentially changeable. One may imagine a hypothetical continuum ranging from high to low changeability in terms of which all personal characteristics may be ordered. Darley's (1938) conclusions on this topic provide such an ordering. Considering all "attitudes," "adjustments," and "opinions," as to whether they are directed toward the self or toward objects external to the self, Darley proposed a continuum of stability with each of the following being decreasingly subject to change: statements remote from the self; "opinions" based upon misinformation and unfamiliarity with the facts; statements in the form of superstitions; "opinions" related to deep-seated prejudices; ethical, religious, and moral views; and, finally, opinions toward the self as intimate self-evaluations—the latter generally being construed as "adjustment," "personality traits," or "characteristics." In Kelly's (1955) longitudinal study of the consistency of the adult personality, he estimated the long-term consistency of five domains of personality variables. Using the coefficient of determination as the index of consistency, Kelly reported the following indices: 48 per cent for values; 45 per cent for vocational interests; 31 per cent for self-ratings; 30 per cent for such characteristics as self-confidence, sociability (Bernreuter) and Strong's Masculinity-Femininity, Interest Maturity, and Occupational Level; and 8 per cent for attitudes.

A third generalization involves the differential impact of environmental presses. Environments may be characterized as nurturant or deprived, as demanding or permissive, and so on. The diverse effects of such environments upon the development of intelligence have been reported in many inquiries and Bloom has estimated that approximately 20 per cent of measured intelligence may be attributable to such environmental variations. Role demands are an important special case of environmental press. As one moves from infancy to old age, there are correspondingly different role demands. Thus in childhood, there are particular role demands associated with the positions of male-female, child, sibling, and student; in adulthood, marital, family, and occupational roles are singularly influential; and in old age, role obligations associated with familial, occupational, and associational positions generally tend to become less pressing. Despite important differences in role demands and some exceptions, it is probably correct that the general burden of role demands decelerates with age, reaching a general plateau in adulthood.

The constraint of role demands would appear to be particularly acute in the individual's transition from one position to another. Entry into school or college, into marriage, or a new job would be illustrative as would such position departures as those associated with retirement, divorce, or leaving a mental hospital. The effects of position changes on attitudes are clearly shown in Lieberman's (1950) unusual study of workers in a factory. Following the administration of questionnaires to rank and file workers, some workers were promoted to foreman and still others were elected as union stewards. The later administration of a second questionnaire to the entire sample revealed that the foreman changed toward more pro-management attitudes, the stewards became more pro-labor, whereas those who remained as workers either did not change their attitudes or changed very little. The questionnaire was given still another time, this being after some of the foremen had to be demoted to worker status following a recession and after many of the union stewards had not been re-elected again. The demoted foremen were now less pro-management than their counterparts who had not been demoted and the former stewards, as compared with workers who had remained stewards, became less pro-labor following their stewardships. Larger changes were generally found for worker-foreman transitions than for worker-steward shifts, these being attributed to by the author to larger changes necessitated by the foreman's job as compared with the steward's.

Evidence from scattered sources suggests that if there are changes in personal characteristics associated with membership in a position, these changes will occur early rather than later in one's tenure in the position. In a related context, Bloom has observed the following: "the effect of environment on general intelligence is also demonstrated by the significant increases in measured intelligence during the first year of college in contrast with the smaller increments over the next three years of college, suggesting that new and intensive learning experiences have a more powerful effect than the continuation of these same experiences" (Bloom, 1964, p. 90). Findings reported by Bloom on changes in values and attitudes indicate that there is considerable change during the period of late adolescence and early adulthood. This researcher also reported that aggression is established early as a characteristic for males, whereas there is considerably less stability in this area for females; and in contrast, dependence and passivity appear to become stabilized in the very early years for females but not for males. This "early tenure effect" has been shown in an analysis conducted by Brim (1958) in which he examined the extent to which cross-sex siblings had traits of the opposite sex. He found that in contrast to same-sex siblings, younger cross-sex siblings displayed more traits of the opposite sex than did older cross-sex siblings. The effect of early tenure here was probably counteracted by sex-role differentiation as the children grew older.

Also pertinent are findings deriving from Kelly's (1955) exploration of changes in 38 personality variables for 116 spouses to whom the battery of tests had been administered on two occasions, separated by twenty years. Because the paired individuals had presumably been subject to common social forces, Kelly analyzed the data to determine whether there was any inter-spouse effect. Correlations were computed between each set of changed scores and the original scores of the spouse. For both cross-spouse comparisons, the correlations were all relatively low, revealing, at best, a negligible tendency either for the husband to change toward the original score of his wife or the wife to change toward that of her husband. In this context, Kelly said: "In fact, although the magnitude of most of the correlations was not large enough for them to be individually significant, nearly three out of four were negative, indicating a slight trend for changes for both the husband and the wife to be away from the original score of the other" (1955, p. 680). Thus changes in the later tenure of marriage positions, to the extent that they occur, tend to be somewhat toward divergence rather than convergence.

A fourth generalization is suggested by research in personality and social psychology in which personal change has been found to be contingent upon selected variables of personality and role. Many of these variables pertinent here to the impact of positional membership upon personal change have been reviewed elsewhere for other purposes (cf. Blake & Mouton, 1961; Campbell, 1961; Janis *et al.,* 1959). Examples will be sufficient in this context. Self-esteem has been found to be among the more significant personality variables associated with changeability, the relationship being negative (see Janis *et al.,* 1959, for example). Individual dispositions, such as attitudes, habits, knowledge, beliefs, and response tendencies, when these oppose the direction of change demanded in a position, will tend to retard compliance (cf. Campbell, 1961). The more individuals interact with others in a new position, the more likely it is that they will be susceptible to personal changes associated with the position (e.g., see Newcomb, 1943; Wheeler, 1961). When reinforcements and incentives are made conditional upon the achievement of personal change, such change becomes more probable. In general, unambiguous and unified prescriptive systems, combined with strong sanctioning systems and with performance systems that are more facilitative than hindering, will achieve greater personal change than those not so characterized.

SUMMARY AND CONCLUSIONS

Throughout this analysis of problems of mutual interest in personality and role theory, an analytic approach was employed in which definitional problems were separated from empirical questions and the latter issues were subjected to a conceptual analysis and to the test of data and research findings, where such information was available. At present, it would appear that most problems at the interface of the fields of personality and role involve (a) matters of definition, these centering mainly about what personality is and what role factors are; (b) explanatory differences in accounting for the commonality of personal characteristics of position members, the adverse effects of role difficulties, or the adequacy of role performance; and (c) the changeability of personal characteristics.

Definitions of personality and role were analyzed and most conceptions were found to distinguish personality from role in terms of one or more of five differentiating axes. These differentia were internal *vs.* external controlling variables, particularity *vs.* commonality, covert tendencies *vs.* overt action, persistence *vs.* transitoriness, and person *vs.* position centeredness. In general, when the terms personality and role are used, they differ denotatively and connotatively; but important minor exceptions were noted.

Personalistic and sociologistic explanatory modes of accounting for commonalities of the personal characteristics of position members were explicated in terms of six functionally equivalent but different "routes to commonality." Four such commonality routes involved selection, these being personal in-selection and out-selection and social in-selection and out-selection. Personal change and social change were the other two routes. In the analysis of each, their operations were documented with available research findings. Abundant evidence for both personalistic and sociologistic accounts was reviewed, considering each commonality route separately, but the review was limited by lack of information about the combined operation of all six routes. Because all six may contribute differentially and in diverse combinations to achieve behavioral commonality, the six must all be examined as they operate in either the premembership or incumbency phases of positional tenure.

Role and personality influences on the adequacy of role performance were reviewed. The role factors could be divided conveniently into the systems of prescription, sanctions, and performance. If the levels of prescribed performance are low, or if the prescriptions are in conflict or are incomplete, the research indicated that performance adequacy would be adversely affected. Performance adequacy was found to be beneficially affected by suitable sanctions and by facilitative performance conditions.

Among the personal characteristics affecting performance adequacy were the possession of role-relevant skills and role-taking ability. Small but consistent correlations with various indicators of performance were found for such additional characteristics as intelligence, adjustment, extraversion, dominance, masculinity, and conservatism. Some personality variables were found to relate noncontingently to performance, whereas others operated contingently, in conjunction with role and social factors. This and the uncertain relationship between inner personality states and their manifestation in overt behavior contributed to the complexity of the problem, and to an inconclusiveness of the review.

Five problems of role potentially conducive to stress were identified and discussed, these being role conflict, role ambiguity, role overload, role discontinuity, and role incongruence. There was more research on the effects of some of these than of others, although there was generally insufficient information to sustain firm conclusions. Despite these shortcomings, however, where there was pertinent research, a surprising mosaic emerged. Thus no clear adverse effects of role incongruence were found, although there were direct effects of such factors as role specifications, personality, performance experience, and of prior positional membership. Nor were the effects of the very diverse forms of role discontinuity clearly or uniformly adverse. While some adverse effects of unemployment were noted, clear-cut effects were less apparent for disability, retirement, and for family dismemberment. Many of the extraneous factors typically associated with such discontinuities may have obscured any true effects of the discontinuity proper. In contrast, role conflict and, to a smaller extent, role ambiguity were associated with numerous stress and emotional consequences. These effects of conflict and ambiguity were similar except that some personality factors were found to operate independently of, or contingently with, role conflict, while no such results were found for role ambiguity. Additional research may alter this picture substantially.

In connection with an examination of the problems of personal change and consistency, numerous methodological and substantive problems were discussed. These problems and the relative paucity of pertinent research, considering the complexity of the general question, were sufficient to preclude the formulation of definite and conclusive generalizations. There were many informative researches and reviews, however, the findings from which were marshalled in support of four general propositions.

The first pertained to the differential rather than uniform rates of change for personal characteristics, with many characteristics—but significantly not all—displaying much more change in the early childhood years than in later periods. The second involved the differential changeability of personal characteristics, some apparently being much more alterable than others at given time periods. The third pertained to the differential impact of environmental presses, with particular emphasis on role demands. Here the general deceleration of total role demands over the life cycle was noted, along with the heightened role demands attending the individual's transition from one position to another and, especially, the heightened press in the early as contrasted with the later stages of position tenure. The final generalization concerned the contingency of personal change upon selected variables of personality and role. Some salient variables here were identified and discussed.

Throughout this essay the author has been impressed with how the simple and sovereign views on matters of personality and role turned out to be wanting in the face of conceptual analysis and data. The apparently simple problem invariably was disclosed to be subtle and complex. The plausible, if naive, hypothesis, when confronted with pertinent facts, was not often corroborated and, in more than a few instances, was incomplete or not supported. The interface between personality and role is a fertile and challenging area of inquiry in which further research and conceptualization will undoubtedly force revision of many favored but heretofore uncorroborated views in both personality and role theory.

REFERENCES

Argyris, C. Human relations in a bank. *Harvard Business Rev.,* 1954, 32, 63–73.

Argyris, C. *Personality and organization.* New York: Harper, 1957.

Atkinson, J. W., & Hoselitz, B. F. Entrepreneurship and personality. *Explorations in Entrepreneurial Hist.,* 1958, 10, 107–112.

Barker, R. G. The social psychology of physical disability. *J. soc. Issues,* 1948, 4, 28–35.

Barker, R. G., Wright, Beatrice A., Meyerson, L., & Gonick, M. R. *Adjustment to handicap and illness: a survey of the social psychology of physique and handicap.* (2nd ed.) New York: Social Science Research Council, Bulletin 55, Revised, 1953.

Benedict, Ruth. Continuities and discontinuities in cultural conditioning. *Psychiatry,* 1938, 1, 161–167.

Blake, R. R., & Mouton, Jane S. The experimental investigation of interpersonal influence. In A. D. Biderman & H. Zimmer (Eds.), *The manipulation of human behavior.* New York: Wiley, 1961. Pp. 216–277.

Bloom, B. S. *Stability and change in human characteristics*. New York: Wiley, 1964.

Bordin, E. S., Nachmann, Barbara, & Segal, S. J. An articulated framework for vocational development. *J. counsel. Psychol.*, 1963, 10, 107–117.

Borgatta, E. F. Role playing specification, personality, and performance. *Sociometry,* 1961, 24, 218–234.

Borgatta, E. F., Couch, A. S., & Bales, R. F. Some findings relevant to the great man theory of leadership. *Amer. sociol. Rev.*, 1954, 19, 755–759.

Brim, O. G. Family structure and sex role learning by children: a further analysis of Helen Koch's data. *Sociometry,* 1958, 21, 1–17.

Campbell, D. T. Conformity in psychology's theories of acquired behavioral dispositions. In I. A. Berg & B. Bass (Eds.), *Conformity and deviation*. New York: Harper & Bros., 1961. Pp. 101–143.

Caplow, T. *Principles of organization*. New York: Harcourt, Brace and World, 1964.

Cattell, R. B. Personality, role, mood, and situation-perception: a unifying theory of modulators. *Psychol. Rev.*, 1963, 70, 1–18.

Cheek, Frances B. A serendipitous finding: sex roles and schizophrenia. *J. abnorm. soc. Psychol.*, 1964, 69, 392–400.

Child, I. L. Problems of personality and some relations to anthropology and sociology. In S. Koch (Ed.), *Psychology: a study of a science*. Vol. 5. *The process areas, the person, and some applied fields: their place in psychology and in science*. New York: McGraw-Hill Book Co., 1963. Pp. 593–63.

Cowen, E. L., Underberg, R. P., Verillo, R. T., & Benham, F. G. *Adjustment to visual disability in adolescence*. New York: American Foundation for the Blind, 1961.

Darley, J. G. Changes in measured attitudes and adjustment. *J. soc. Psychol.,* 1938, 9, 189–199.

Davis, K. The sociology of parent-youth conflict. *Amer. sociol. Rev.*, 1940, 5, 523–535.

Donahue, Wilma, Orbach, H. L., & Pollack, O. Retirement: the emerging social pattern. In C. Tibbitts (Ed.), *Handbook of social gerontology: societal aspects of aging*. Chicago: Univer. of Chicago Press, 1960. Pp. 298–330.

Etzioni, A. *A comparative analysis of complex organizations: on power and involvement and their correlates*. New York: The Free Press of Glencoe, 1964.

Gilbert, Doris C., & Levinson, D. J. Ideology, personality, and institutional policy in the mental hospital. *J. abnorm. soc. Psychol.,* 1956, 53, 263–271.

Goode, W. J. A theory of role strain. *Amer. sociol. Rev.*, 1960, 25, 483–496.

Gross, N., Mason, W. S., & McEachern, A. W. *Explorations in role analysis: studies of the school superintendency role*. New York: Wiley, 1958.

Haller, A. O., & Thomas, S. Personality correlates of the socio-economic status of males. *Sociometry,* 1962, 25, 398–405.

Hare, A. P., & Bales, R. F. Seating position and small group interaction. *Sociometry,* 1963, 26, 480–487.

Haythorn, W. The effects of varying compositions of authoritarian and equalitarian leaders and followers. In Eleanor Maccoby, T. M. Newcomb, & E. L. Hartley (Eds.), *Readings in social psychology*. (3rd ed.) New York: Holt, 1958. Pp. 511–522.

Hill, R. *Families under stress: adjustment to the crises of war separation and reunion*. New York: Harper, 1949.

Holland, J. L. A theory of vocational choice. *J. counsel. Psychol.*, 1959, 6, 35–44.

Janis, I. L., Hovland, C. I., Field, P. B., Linton, Harriet, Graham, Elaine, Cohen, A. R., Rife, D., Abelson, R. P., Lesser, G. S., & King, B. T. *Personality and persuasibility*. New Haven: Yale Univer. Press, 1959.

Janis, I. L., & King, B. T. The influence of role playing on opinion change. *J. abnorm. soc. Psychol.*, 1954, 49, 211–218.

Kahn, R. L., Wolfe, D. M., Quinn, R. P., & Snoek, D. J. *Organizational stress: studies in role conflict and ambiguity*. New York: Wiley, 1964.

Kelly, E. L. Consistency of the adult personality. *Amer. Psychologist,* 1955, 10, 659–682.

Kemeny, J. G., Snell, J. H., & Thompson, G. L. *Introduction to finite mathematics*. Englewood Cliffs, N.J.: Prentice-Hall. Pp. 54–113.

Kuhlen, R. G. Personality change with age. In P. Worchel & D. Byrne (Eds.), *Personality change*. New York: Wiley, 1964. Pp. 524–557.

Kutner, B., Fanshel, D., Togo, A. M., & Langner, T. S. *Five hundred over sixty*. New York: Russell Sage Foundation, 1956.

Landy, D. Rehabilitation as a sociocultural process. *J. soc. Issues,* 1960, 16, 3–7.

Lemert, E. M. Paranoia and the dynamics of exclusion. *Sociometry,* 1962, 25, 2–21.

Lieberman, S. The effects of changes in roles on the attitudes of role occupants. *Hum. Relat.,* 1950, 9, 385–403.

Linton, R. *The study of man.* New York: Appleton-Century-Crofts, 1936.

McClelland, D. C. *Personality.* New York: Dryden, 1951.

McClelland, D. C. N achievement and entrepreneurship: a longitudinal study. *J. pers. soc. Psychol.,* 1965, 1, 389–392. (a)

McClelland, D. C. Toward a theory of motive acquisition. *Amer. Psychologist,* 1965, 20, 321–334. (b)

Mann, R. D. A review of the relationships between personality and performance in small groups. *Psychol. Bull.,* 1959, 56, 241–271.

Mead, G. H. *Mind, self and society from the standpoint of a social behaviorist.* Chicago: Univer. of Chicago Press, 1934.

Mead, Margaret. *Male and female: a study of the sexes in a changing world.* New York: Wm. Morrow, 1948.

Merei, F. Group leadership and institutionalization. In G. E. Swanson, T. M. Newcomb, & E. L. Hartley (Eds.), *Readings in social psychology.* (2nd ed.) New York: Holt, 1952. Pp. 318–328.

Merton, R. K. Bureaucratic structure and personality. *Soc. Forces,* 1940, 18, 560–568.

Meyerson, L. Special disabilities. In P. R. Farnsworth & Q. McNemar (Eds.), *Annual review of psychology.* Vol. 8. Palo Alto, Calif.: Annual Reviews, 1957. Pp. 437–457.

Miller, D. The study of social relationships: situation, identity, and social interaction. In S. Koch (Ed.), *Psychology: a study of a science.* Vol. 5. *The process areas, the person, and some applied fields: their place in psychology and in science.* New York: McGraw-Hill Book Co., 1963. Pp. 639–738.

Moos, R. H., & Speisman, J. C. Group compatibility and productivity. *J. abnorm. soc. Psychol.,* 1962, 65, 190–196.

Nachmann, Barbara. Childhood experience and vocational choice in law, dentistry, and social work. *J. counsel. Psychol.,* 1960, 7, 243–250.

Neiman, L. J., & Hughes, J. W. The problem of the concept of role—a resurvey of the literature. *Soc. Forces,* 1951, 30, 141–149.

Newcomb, T. M. *Personality and social change.* New York: Dryden Press, 1943.

Parsons, T., Shils, E. A., Allport, G. W., Kluckhohn, C., Murray, H. A., Sears, R. R., Shelden, R. C., Stouffer, S. A., & Tolman, E. C. Some fundamental categories of the theory of action: a general statement. In T. Parsons, & E. A. Shils (Eds.), *Toward a general theory of action.* Cambridge: Harvard Univer. Press, 1951. Pp. 3–30.

Phillips, B. S. A role theory approach to adjustment in old age. *Amer. sociol. Rev.,* 1957, 22, 212–217.

Presthus, R. *The organizational society: an analysis and a theory.* New York: Knopf, 1962.

Raven, B. H., & Rietsema, J. The effects of varied clarity of group goal and group path upon the individual and his relation to his group. *Hum. Relat.,* 1957, 10, 29–44.

Raven, B. H., & Eachus, H. T. Cooperation and competition in means-interdependent triads. *J. abnorm. soc. Psychol.,* 1963, 67 307–317.

Roe, Anne. *The psychology of occupations.* New York: Wiley, 1956.

Rommetveit, R. *Social norms and roles.* Minneapolis: Univer. of Minnesota Press, 1954.

Rose, A. M. A systematic summary of symbolic interaction theory. In A. M. Rose (Ed.), *Human behavior and social processes.* Boston: Houghton Mifflin, 1962. Pp. 3–20.

Ross, I., & Zander, A. Need satisfactions and employee turnover. *Personnel Psychol.,* 1957, 10, 327–339.

Sanford, N. Personality: its place in psychology. In S. Koch (Ed.), *Psychology: a study of a science.* Vol. 5. *The process areas, the person, and some applied fields: their place in psychology and in science.* New York: McGraw-Hill Book Co., 1963. Pp. 488–593.

Sarbin, T. R. Role theory. In G. Lindzey (Ed.), *Handbook of social psychology.* Cambridge, Mass.: Addison-Wesley, 1954. Pp. 223–259.

Sarbin, T. R. Role theoretical interpretation of psychological change. In P. Worchel & D. Byrne (Eds.), *Personality change.* New York: Wiley, 1964. Pp. 176–220.

Sarbin, T. R., & Allen, V. L. Role enactment, audience feedback, and attitude change. *Sociometry,* 1964, 27, 183–194.

Sayres, W. C. Disorientation and status change. *Southwest. J. Anthrop.*, 1956, 12, 79–86.

Schachter, S. Deviation, rejection, and communication. *J. abnorm. soc. Psychol.*, 1951, 46, 190–207.

Segal, S. J. A psychoanalytic analysis of personality factors in vocational choice. *J. counsel. Psychol.*, 1961, 8, 202–210.

Smelser, W. T. Dominance as a factor in achievement and perception in cooperative problem solving interactions. *J. abnorm. soc. Psychol.*, 1961, 62, 535–542.

Smith, E. E. The effects of clear and unclear role expectations of group productivity and defensiveness. *J. abnorm. soc. Psychol.*, 1957, 55, 213–218.

Super, D. E. *The psychology of careers: an introduction to vocational development.* New York: Harper, 1957.

Thomas, E. J. Effects of facilitative role interdependence on group functioning. *Hum. Relat.*, 1957, 10, 347–366.

Thomas, E. J., & Biddle, B. J. Basic concepts for classifying the phenomena of role. In B. J. Biddle & E. J. Thomas (Eds.), *Role theory: concepts and research.* New York: Wiley, 1966.

Thompson, W. E., & Streib, G. F. Situational determinants: health and economic deprivation in retirement. *J. soc. Issues,* 1958, 14, 18–35.

Trow, D. B. Autonomy and job satisfaction in task-oriented groups. *J. abnorm. soc. Psychol.*, 1957, 54, 204–210.

Viteles, J. S. *Motivation and morale in industry.* New York: Norton, 1953.

Weinstein, E. A., & Deutschberger, P. Some dimensions of altercasting. *Sociometry,* 1963, 26, 454–467.

Wheeler, S. Socialization in correctional communities. *Amer. sociol. Rev.*, 1961, 26, 697–712.

Wilensky, H. L. *Intellectuals in labor unions: organizational pressures vs. professional roles.* Glencoe, Ill.: The Free Press, 1956.

Wilson, A. T. M., Trist, E. L., & Curle, A. Transitional communities and social reconnection: a study of the civil resettlement of British prisoners of war. In G. E. Swanson, T. M. Newcomb, & E. L. Hartley (Eds.), *Readings in social psychology.* (2nd ed.) New York: Holt, 1952. Pp. 561–581.

Wright, Beatrice A. *Physical disability—a psychological approach.* New York: Harper, 1960.

Wrong, D. The oversocialization conception of man in modern sociology. *Amer. sociol. Rev.*, 1961, 26, 183–193.

Yarrow, L. J., & Yarrow, Marian R. Personality continuity and change in the family context. In P. Worchel & D. Byrne (Eds.), *Personality change.* New York: Wiley, 1964. Pp. 489–523.

Zawadski, B., & Lazarsfeld, P. Psychological consequences of unemployment. *J. soc. Psychol.*, 1935, 6, 224–250.

CHAPTER 12 The Present Status of Self Theory[1]

RUTH C. WYLIE
Goucher College

I. INTRODUCTION

A. Brief Historical Overview of Interest in Constructs Concerning the Self

Early in the history of American psychology, there was considerable interest in the self. For example, William James (1890) accorded this topic an important place in his psychological thinking, and to a certain extent the study of the self was pursued by introspectionists (Calkins, 1915).

During the second, third, and fourth decades of the twentieth century, constructs concerning self did not receive much attention from the behaviorist and functionalist psychologies which were dominating the American scene. As Hilgard (1949) points out, the introspectionists were unable to handle the self, and of course such a "mentalistic" construct as the self concept was anathema to behaviorists. Meanwhile the psychodynamic postulates which were being developed by Freudians and neo-Freudians necessarily implied a self-referent in order to make them plausible and understandable. For at least two reasons these theories did not immediately bring constructs concerning the self to the forefront of American psychology. First of all, Freud himself, in his early theorizing, strongly emphasized the role of the id. He did not explicitly formalize a self construct nor assign the closely related ego functions much importance, in comparison to the id. Secondly, his theory was being denied or ignored by many American general psychologists who found it lacking in rigor, in susceptibility of empirical test, and in comparability with the theoretical models then in favor.

Recently, however, there has been a marked proliferation of self theories, traceable to a number of influences. In his later writings, Freud himself assigned greater importance to ego development and functioning; and of course the neo-Freudians stressed the importance of the self picture and the ego-ideal. At the same time, American psychologists who were beginning to work in clinical areas found behavioristic models apparently too limited to account for the phenomena they were observing, and they were ready to entertain psycho-

[1] I wish to thank Goucher College for partially defraying the costs of preparing this chapter, and the University of Nebraska Press for allowing me to draw upon my recent book, *The Self Concept,* in preparing certain portions of the chapter. I am also grateful to Dr. Cecille Gold, Dr. Georgiana Wylie, and Miss Patricia Wienert who read the manuscript and made useful suggestions.

analytic ideas, particularly of the revised variety. Since their interests were somewhat different from those of students of the general experimental psychology of cognition and motivation, the clinicians may have felt less need for neat, philosophically sophisticated, operationally circumscribed theorizing. They may have been less distressed to depart from such theorizing in their search for conceptual schema to account for their observations.

Throughout this period the functionalists never gave up introspective methods, and the gestalt psychologists injected their phenomenological methods and theories into the stream of general psychology. Meanwhile, the possibility of an operational behaviorism involving complex cognitive and motivational intervening variables was being explored within the domain of general psychology. All of these facts implied the possibility of fusing general psychological theories of cognition and motivation with the psychoanalytic or psychodynamic theories originating in the clinic. And so we find that all the theories of personality which have been put forth within the last two decades assign importance to self-referent constructs. These theories include the phenomenal and/or nonphenomenal self concepts, with cognitive and motivational attributes.

B. Scope of the Chapter

In the immediately following section (Section II) we attempt to summarize the role in personality theory of constructs referring to "self." Following this, we consider in Sections III and IV problems of measuring the self concept, and problems of research design in studies which attempt to relate the self concept to antecedent or consequent variables. Finally, in Section IV we outline briefly the major classes of published empirical research and examine studies from three of these classes from the viewpoint of methodological problems and substantive conclusions.

II. THE ROLE IN PERSONALITY THEORY OF CONSTRUCTS REFERRING TO "SELF"

A. Meanings of the Term "Self"

The scientific utility of a term such as self is vitiated when various psychologists who employ it do not offer even literary or denotative definitions, let alone operational ones, but instead simply talk about the construct to which they wish to assign the specified label. Any given theorist often seems to include several quite disparate ideas under one "self"-referent label, while using several different labels to indicate what appears to be the same idea. Moreover, there is no consistency in usage among theorists. Consequently, one task in this chapter is to try to discern and delimit the various classes of meanings of "self," distilling what is useful without distorting the authors' intentions.

It is commonly said that usages of the term self may be classified roughly into those which refer to *self as agent* and those which refer to *self as the object of the person's own knowledge and evaluation* (English & English, 1958; Symonds, 1951). Under the agent category, for example, Adler (Ansbacher & Ansbacher, 1956, p. 177) says, "Who moves the mental life . . .? The mover is always the self." Jung applies the term self to that part of the mental life which carries out psychic, mental, or psychological acts (English & English, 1958); and Hilgard (1949) speaks of the "healthy self" achieving integrative organization; while Horney (1942, p. 269) describes the self as dealing with the forces of resistance in therapy, and Rogers (1951, p. 40) indicates that "there are many elements of experience which the self cannot face . . . ."

It is impossible to get a clear meaning from these quotations. Some of them might be clearer if one read "person" for "self." In others, "self" seems to refer to restricted classes of behavior.

Under the second or self-concept category falls Snygg and Combs's (1949, p. 58) *phenomenal self* which "includes all those parts of the phenomenal field which the individual experiences as part or characteristic of himself." Jung's *conscious ideal* of personality (part of the *persona*) (Progoff, 1953, p. 84); and Adler's *self ideal* which becomes available to consciousness after psychotherapy are further instances (Ansbacher & Ansbacher, 1956, p. 233). So are Munroe's *self-image* (1955, p. 609); Rogers's *self concept* (1951, p. 136); and McClelland's *symbolized portion of the self schema* (1951, p. 544).

Following an assumption of unconscious perception and knowledge, some psychologists have posited self pictures or self ideals which are partially or entirely unavailable to awareness. These constructs, which presumably also belong under the second or self-concept heading, are exemplified by Fisher and Cleveland's *body image* (1958, p. x); Horney's *idealized image* (1945, p. 96); and McClelland's *unsymbolized portion of the self schema* (1951, p. 544).

This dichotomy of "self as doer" and "self as known to oneself" proves to be an inadequate basis for classifying the self constructs used by personality theorists. First, as English and English (1958) point out, many authors attribute behavior-influencing characteristics to the self concept or to the ideal-self concept. This moves these constructs back toward the category of "doer," blurring the original distinction. For example, Snygg and Combs's most basic postulate states, "All behavior, without exception, is completely determined by and pertinent to the phenomenal field [including the phenomenal self] of the behaving organism" (Snygg & Combs, 1949, p. 15). Rogers (1951, p. 140) quotes with approval Angyal's (1941) statement that the "conscious self often tends to take over the government of the total personality, a task for which it is not qualified ..." (p. 118).

Second, some authors postulate processes which seem to involve self in both the doer and the conceived sense, but which go beyond both senses and are not clearly related to either. For example, Horney (1950) suggests that growth tendencies of a "real self" are present in everyone; Maslow (1954) postulates an inborn motive to develop one's potentialities (self actualization). (These postulated processes in no sense constitute a unified third category, however.)

A third reason why the dichotomous classification is inadequate is that its categories cannot be meaningfully related to such concepts as motivation, learning, perception, traits, or attitudes which have been found useful in general behavior theory and personality theory. Later in this chapter we try to classify uses of the word self according to some of these more familiar concepts.

B. Range of Theorists Using Self-Referent Constructs

Some theories such as that of Rogers are labeled self theories, while others such as Freud's are not. Following these labels, one might choose to summarize the status of theorizing in the so-called self theories, ignoring the others. However, constructs concerning self play some role in all personality theories. Therefore, it seems more enlightening to consider here the self-referent constructs from any and all theories, and to present them and their theoretical roles in comparative fashion.

C. Reasons for Postulating Self-Referent Constructs

Why have various theorists deemed it necessary or desirable to invent self-relevant constructs? Some of their reasons reflect scientific goals and opinions as to the most appropriate strategies in theory construction. Other reasons seem more closely related to the theorists' personal opinions as to what constitutes a palatable, optimistic, or ethical view of human nature.

From the former, or scientific, standpoint, what sorts of observations appear to some theorists to require self-referent constructs?

First, it seems clear that, in the present state of knowledge about what to observe and how to measure the selected observable dimensions, we cannot predict group or individual behavior accurately from a combination of observable antecedents external to the subject and observable characteristics of the subject. Of course, this generally accepted fact does not of itself necessitate the invention of constructs concerning processes within the organism. Skinner (1950) has made this point eloquently. Nevertheless, many theorists of various persuasions feel that constructs have a useful role to play in enhancing the ultimate predictiveness of psychological laws. Self-referent constructs are included among those which have been invented with the general aim of improving the accuracy of our behavior laws.

As a case in point, motivated or goal-seeking behavior seems to some theorists to require postulation of self-referent constructs. It is obvious that behavior persists after external stimulation stops, that many alternate paths or behavior patterns may be used enroute to a specified goal, that a given objectively defined goal may or may not be approached. These kinds of observations led Tolman (1932) and more recent purposive behaviorists to the formulation of explanatory intervening variables in their learning theories. But their schemes have been rejected by many personality theorists as too rigid or limited to account for the complexity and apparent paradoxes in the purposive behaviors of human beings.

For example, Allport (1943) emphasizes the common sense and clinical observations that success in one area may compensate for failure in another, in that the person appears to have achieved goal satisfaction. McClelland (1951, p. 541) suggests that "there appears to be an over-all sense of self-potency which may be raised or lowered by actions or frustrations in different areas of life." Experimental psychologists have observed that results of an experiment may differ, depending on whether the instructions lead the subject to think that the experimental task tests some valued ability or personal characteristic. Hilgard (1949) declares that defense mechanisms are not understandable except in terms of a unifying self to which feelings of guilt can be attached. He suggests that other overtly dissimilar, apparently paradoxically motivated behaviors may be explained and unified in terms of a similarity in underlying motives, especially motives centering around a self. Allport (1943) calls attention to a particular kind of apparent contradiction among motivated behaviors in which behavior antithetical to "segmental tensions" is seen. That is, drives such as hunger and thirst are sometimes superseded by behaviors which must be interpreted as serving a self or *proprium* according to Allport (1955). In short, the apparent unrelatedness or even the apparent contradictions among goal-directed behaviors may be resolved by postulating unifying self-referent constructs. The predictability of human behavior will thus be enhanced, presumably.

We note parenthetically that self theorists are sometimes hoist on their own petard when offering the above argument. They often scorn the alleged tendencies of other theorists to offer an oversimplified view of man. In their derision, they disregard the justifications for parsimony in theorizing. They criticize learning theorists, for example, for offering "caricatures of human nature," apparently being under the wrong impression that the goal of scientific theorizing is to represent everything about the phenomena under study, to re-create reality, as it were. Yet at the same time that they criticize other psychologists for oversimplifying their analysis of man, the typical alternative offered by the self theorists is a single, overriding motive (e.g., self-actualization, enhancement of the phenomenal self). Such an alternative, if taken literally, provides too few parameters to account for complex behaviors. Some *ad hoc* way must be found to stuff many diverse observations into one or two pigeonholes, yielding serious distortions and omissions of observations of behavior. This issue has been generally discussed by McClelland (1951); and Munroe (1955) has repeatedly leveled the criticism of reductionism at self theorists in particular.

We have spoken of the way in which self-referent constructs are supposed to be useful in presenting a unified account of superficially diverse behaviors. Curiously enough, an apparently opposite justification for self-referent constructs is also frequently offered: It is said that a behaving human organism is so obviously unitary that explanations in terms of "segmental tensions," separate habits, and the like will not account for this obvious unity or patterning. Self theorists criticize Freudians and learning theorists for offering no conceptual tools or rules for interrelating the separate dimensions postulated in their theories. Personal reports of identity and continuity of reported memories are cited as relatively simple examples of obvious behavioral unity requiring explanation (Hilgard, 1949). More complex patternings and consistencies in behavior are also alluded to often, and other psychological theorists are berated for failing to note them and to offer principles to account for them. But unfortunately, no specific criteria are given for identifying the "consistency" and "patterning" which are alleged to be obvious at the behavioral level (Rogers, 1951; Lecky, 1945). A search of self theories and related research does not reveal any adequate conceptual tools or methods for encompassing and representing the alleged patterning or unity.

Self theorists often say that the observed *uniqueness* of each individual person can be explained only in terms of self-referent constructs, not by other scientific theories (see, for example, Allport, 1955). Here we have a case of the general question about which there has been much confused thinking: What is the difference between general behavior theory and personality theory? Klein and Krech (1952) among others, have pointed out that any personality theory must also be a general behavior theory and vice versa. If personality theory extends beyond general behavior theory, it is by way of concern with the problems of explaining the organized whole person, individual differences, and developmental trends in these.

It is true that most psychological theories are avowedly nomothetic, i.e., concerned with general or nomological laws. But there seems to be a serious confusion in the thinking of self theorists between: (1) what *has* been accomplished by general psychological theories and (2) what *could in principle* be accomplished by them. There is no reason in principle why general psychological theories could not introduce specifications for combining predictive variables to make predictions for unique individuals. Hence, the fact that each person is unique does not constitute necessary *a priori* grounds for postulating self-referent constructs, as opposed to other types of constructs. *In principle* we cannot see how one can scientifically discuss organization or unique patterns without some specification as to what dimensionalized attributes are organized and patterned. And individual differences presumably occur along these to-be-specified dimensions, as well as with respect to overall organization or patterning. *In practice,* some general or nomothetic theorists have actually gone farther than have self theorists in attempting to write regression equations to predict behavioral outcomes for individuals. Meanwhile, the self theorists who attempt to represent patterned individuality by means of such devices as *Q*-sort correlations have not as yet achieved an index of personal uniqueness.

While self theorists deplore the alleged limitations of nomothetic laws in accounting for the uniqueness of each person, their own laws and principles are *in practice* quite nomological, in most if not all instances. For example, *all* human beings are striving for superiority, according to Adler (Ansbacher & Ansbacher, 1956), or are striving for self-consistency, according to Lecky (1945); or are enhancing their phenomenal selves, according to Snygg and Combs (1949). No explicit theory is offered as to how such general processes yield uniqueness of individuals.

Self theorists have called attention to the fact that rational problem-solving and conscious choice behaviors have received little attention in current behavior theories, and presently are beyond the scope of the more rigorous theories. It is said that a concept such as the "creative self" of Adler (Ansbacher & Ansbacher, 1956) needs to be introduced to explain these behaviors among others.

Self theorists have generally been aware that self-referent postulates may seem to reintroduce the scientifically untenable and unfruitful idea of the homunculus inside the man. They are careful to point out that they do *not* subscribe to this homunculus viewpoint (see, for example, Allport, 1955). Nevertheless, such concepts as Jung's self, Adler's creative self, Allport's proprium, and Horney's real self still seem to many tough-minded psychologists to retain some of the qualities of the "little man inside the head." These concepts remove the explanatory problems one or more steps from the level of observation without providing means for avoiding reification of the homunculus.

Mention of the creative self brings us to the nonscientific or personal considerations which seem to have influenced self theorists strongly. For example, Adler (Ansbacher & Ansbacher, 1956, p. 179) says, "The child, then, is not a simple, passive creature molded exclusively by external [and hereditary] forces; he is very much a creature in his own right, moving through his own experiences and creating his own world." In the same vein Lecky asserts (1945, p. 75) that "There is a coherence in the behavior of any single organism which argues against explanation in terms of chance combinations of determiners and points to an organized dynamic subsystem which tends toward self-determination. . . ." Murphy (1947, p. 645) declares that "soft determinism," that is, the participation of the person as cause, is one of the most valuable working concepts available; but Hall and Lindzey (1957, p. 125) believe that the creative self is "not unlike the older concept of soul." Thus, although these theorists sometimes laud science and claim that they themselves are working toward scientific theories, their feelings about the scientific method and its implications seem to be markedly ambivalent. Furthermore, their concepts are sometimes inconsistent with scientific assumptions. The assumption of determinism stressed by Freud and modern behaviorists is interpreted by self theorists as robbing man of dignity and creativity, and as inadequate to the task of understanding man. The positivistic approach which modern behavior theorists find congenial is based on the assumption that our knowledge is always a function of our methods, and that therefore we have no way of knowing the "ultimate reality" of any event, including human behaviors and mental processes. Some self theorists are extremely critical of positivism and operationism, claiming that it has moved psychology away from studying the "reality of man," "the nature of man's being." However, no conclusive rational or empirical arguments against positivism and determinism are presented, nor can they be. Of course the fact that we cannot now predict human behavior accurately leaves open the possibility that the assumption of determinism is incorrect. But such a fact cannot definitely disprove the assumption either. It seems that these theorists want to have their cake and eat it too. They want to have the advantages of being scientific. At the same time, they want to reintroduce assumptions which are inappropriate to the scientific method, and to bring into psychology concepts which by definition operate in a nondeterministic way and are indescribable by scientific operations. While their unscientific assumptions and personal intuitions about man may be correct, trying to bring these into science itself only confuses different procedures for trying to understand man, to the detriment of each procedure.

In short, self theorists offer many plausible reasons for postulating self-referent constructs in trying to account for human behavior. These theorists contend that the higher thought processes, the apparent contradictions and unities in motivated behavior, and the uniqueness of each person require self-referent constructs to make them understandable. On the other hand, few if any scientific observations *necessitate* this sort of construct (or necessitate any particular class of theoretical constructs for that matter).

We return later to the important question whether self-referent constructs have led to fruitful research. Meanwhile, let us examine further the variety of self-referent constructs which have been proposed, in an attempt to see whether any "synthetic" ideas and principles can be formulated from the available theoretical writings.

D. A Synthetic Set of Behavior Principles Formulated from Theorists' Statements Concerning Self-Referent Constructs

Personality theorists have written thousands of pages expressing their ideas about the self, and there appears to be considerable overlap among their central points. It also appears that much of what they are saying about the self refers to the already familiar concepts and principles of general psychology concerning motivation, learning, and perception. We think it might be useful to students of psychology to have a brief, "synthetic" statement of the various theorists' major tenets concerning self, together with a "translation" of these tenets into the better known terminology and principles of general psychology. It is the purpose of this section, therefore, to attempt such a synthesis and translation.

Some may doubt that anyone could succeed in such an attempt, or that it would be useful to the field of psychology even if one could succeed. For one thing, the innumerable obscurities and polemics over straw men make the undertaking undesirably dependent on one reader's interpretations. Then, too, some psychologists (e.g., Munroe, 1955) think that what is enlightening about a particular construct of a theorist can be understood only by considering the full discussion of the construct in the unique context of the total theory. However, we have acted on the adage, "Nothing ventured, nothing gained." Only the future applications of such a synthesis in theory and research will indicate whether what follows is merely a futile intellectual game.

Let us begin with the broadest relevant concept, the *person,* by which we mean a single, living human being. *Personality* is harder to define—some would say it is undefinable.

Yet all "definitions" agree that: (a) personality is characteristic of persons, but is not as broad a concept as person; (b) personality is a set of inferences about a person. For example, Lazarus (1961, p. 49) says that "personality is the organization of stable structures within a person that disposes him to act in certain ways. These structures are in reality hypothetical constructs that are inferred from behavior." McClelland (1951, p. 69) defines personality as "the most adequate conceptualization of a person's behavior in all its detail that the scientist can give at a moment in time." For some reason, Allport (1961, p. 27) seems to feel that McClelland's definition is too "positivistic" to do justice to the "real" processes within a person and to their organization. But Allport's definition (1961, p. 28) appears to be formally quite similar to McClelland's and Lazarus's, viz: "Personality is the dynamic organization within the individual of those psychophysical systems that determine his characteristic behavior and thought." For Allport, as for Lazarus, organization which cannot be directly observed is an important inferred characteristic of personality. Allport's "systems" include habits, sentiments, traits, concepts, and styles of behaving, all of which are hypothetical constructs.

Even though there are formal similarities in the definitions, an agreement on the meaning of personality can be reached only if psychologists agree on the most useful conceptual dimensions or constructs to employ. This time is far away. However, we can see now that self constructs may be one class of the conceptualizations defining personality; and we can examine this particular class of constructs for signs of emerging agreement among theorists.

We come now to the word *self*. Its nontechnical uses sometimes make it equivalent to the broader concepts "personality" or "person." Even some of its technical usages are this inclusive. Rank, according to Munroe (1955, p. 578) sometimes seems to equate personality-as-a-whole and self. Jung in his earlier writings used self as equivalent to total personality (Hall & Lindzey, 1957, p. 85); Horney's "actual self" is defined by English and English (1958) as "the total psychophysical being at a given moment"; and Lecky states in one place (1945, p. 188) that self is the same as personality. When Freud speaks of self-preservative drives, he apparently refers to the maintenance of the person's life.

However, most psychological usages of self seem to refer to a certain restricted class of constructs which are only part of the system of constructs defining personality. For instance, Hilgard (1949) indicates that the "inferred self" may be thought of as a pattern of persisting habits and attitudes, while Allport (1961) says that for him personality is a broader concept than self.

How, then, do we find the various more limited meanings of self fitting into the broader system of constructs, personality? And how do the proposed principles concerning the development and functioning of self-referent processes fit into a general set of proposals concerning behavior and personality development?

In attempting to answer these questions, we have chosen two intimately interrelated sets of reference constructs (motivational and cognitive) which came originally from general psychology and general behavior theory. Our justification for this choice stems from the argument we presented earlier that a personality theory must be a general behavior theory and vice versa. Pursuing that argument, we think that the meaningfulness, usefulness, and limitations of self constructs can probably be better evaluated if the thinking concerning such constructs is "translated" into a more familiar set of reference dimensions which are more widely used and empirically explored. However it does not seem necessary or possible at this point to choose any one of the more specialized behavior theories as a source of reference dimensions.

1. Motivational Constructs, with Special Reference to Inborn Needs and Drives

There is wide agreement among psychologists that human beings are born with certain physiological needs for objects and activities necessary to sustain life or to facilitate the organism's characteristic activities. It is also thought that there are inborn "drives." Unfortunately, no agreed-upon theory of motivation exists which adequately classifies and "explains" needs, relates needs to drives, characterizes drives, or accounts for the acquisition of new drives through learning. Nevertheless, it is agreed that observed variations in degree of activity or arousal, and variations in directedness and selectiveness of behavior must someday be accounted for. (The paradox of "compensatory" goal substitutions and the hierarchies of goal-directed behaviors mentioned earlier are special cases of the problem of directedness and selectiveness of behavior.)

There is also some consensus about assigning arousal properties to the construct "drive"; and in postulating that certain events, activities, or objects will lower the arousal state on an unlearned basis. The idea of a general drive state, contributed to by separate drives, has been postulated by some, e.g., Hull (1951).

It is widely assumed that selectivity and directedness can be explained partly on an innate basis, partly as resulting from learning. There is some agreement that secondary drives may be acquired through learning based on primary drive.

It is obviously impossible for us to go into detail here about controversies over theories of motivation. Instead we use the above statements as a set of reference assumptions for analyzing certain self-referent constructs and their assumed characteristics.

In some cases, the term "self" seems to be used to refer to most or all of the energy or force attributed in general behavior theory to drives (both inborn and learned drives). For example, Horney (1942, p. 290) describes the "real self" as "What I really feel ... want ... believe ... decide. It is, or should be, the most alive center of the psychic life." English and English (1958, p. 488) say that Horney's real self comprises "the source of the energy that, in each individual can be mobilized in the direction of constructive, healthy growth." Jung describes the self as a newly created focusing point where libido lost to the unconscious comes to rest in the mature adult (Progoff, 1953, p. 152). This kind of use of the term self seems to be vague and mystical, and does not appear to clarify or extend in a useful way the general notions of "arousal," and "general drive state."

Many theorists have postulated inborn drives or needs of the person to develop his generic and personal potentialities, i.e., to develop his abilities, his motivational characteristics, and the like. For instance, Horney postulates that a person strives toward self-realization "by his very nature and of his own accord" (1950, p. 15). Maslow (1954) posits a self-actualization need, according to which one strives to develop one's capacities, self-understanding, and self-acceptance along the lines dictated by one's "inner nature." Maslow assumes that the person must put first the satisfaction of survival and other more basic needs; and that the trend toward self-actualization may also be "overcome by habit, cultural pressure, and wrong attitudes toward it," but that it nevertheless persists "underground." Goldstein postulates that self-actualization is the person's only motive (Hall & Lindzey, 1957, p. 304); while Rogers (1951, p. 487) says, "The organism has one basic tendency and striving—to actualize, maintain, and enhance the experiencing organism."

Concerning a related kind of allegedly inborn motive, Lecky (1945, p. 137) asserts "all pleasure appears to trace back to the primary motive of unification, instinct theories to the contrary notwithstanding."

Although theorists apparently vary as to the degree to which they believe a person is aware of these inborn self-referent drives, their opinions of this matter are obscure. We return later to the problem of the conscious-unconscious dimension when we consider the partly cognitive constructs such as self concept and self-esteem.

In criticizing the hypothesized drive toward self actualization (or self realization or self unification), we note first that the "definitions" are far from being operational, since no alleged connections with observable antecedents or consequents are specified.

Presumably the idea that such a drive is inborn counteracts the unpalatable Freudian view that man is inherently "evil," or tragically at the mercy of inescapable destructive forces, or is a "neutral machine." However, no evidence or relevant arguments are offered to support the assertion that a drive of the self-actualizing variety is an inborn, biological "given."

Even if there is such a "given," merely to postulate it does not advance the explanation of motivated behavior. For one thing, the possible biological mechanisms or characteristics of such a drive are left entirely obscure.

We noted earlier that postulating a single "master" motive is insufficient theoretically to account for all the complexities of direction and selectivity in behavior which it is supposed to explain. Possibly in recognition of this limitation, the self-actualization drive is assigned the function of integrating "segmental" drives, which are thus reintroduced into the theory, but presumably included within the self-actualization drive itself. However, no explanation is offered as to how the self-actualization drive relates to the supposedly subordinated segmental drives, either with respect to biological origins or mechanisms of operation. And, as Munroe points out (1955, p. 607) "The undeniable fact that the individual perishes when integrative functions fail does *not* imply a positive, organismic or psychological urge toward integration *as such*."

Another point of criticism centers around the apparently teleological qualities assigned to such inborn drives as the need for self-actualization. Munroe (1955, p. 640) states that the increasing evidences of purposiveness and integrativeness as human beings grow into adulthood has been offered by some theorists as support for such telic motivational constructs. She comments, however, that these developmental observations do not "justify a telic version of the 'total personality' any more than a selective observation of progressive advance in flexible mastery of the environment from ameba to man justifies the concept of entelechy, of an intrinsic purposiveness in the evolutionary process."

Since the most prominent motivational theories have concerned themselves with the relationships among drives, consummatory behaviors, pleasure, and tension reduction, it is of interest to examine the supposed relation of self-actualizing and self-unifying drives of these other constructs. To a certain extent, self-actualization needs and their fulfillment seem to involve tension and tension-reduction respectively. Self theorists seem to feel that tensions are probably associated both with the segmental drives subordinately included in the self-actualization drive, and with distance from achieving the over-all goal of self-actualization. On the other hand, these theorists sometimes seem to be denying a tension-reduction theory of drive and reinforcement; that is, persons are said sometimes to seek increased tension and pain. But at still other places in these theorists' writings, it appears that seeking pain and tension is simply an instrumental phase on the way to the goal of self-actualization which itself is associated with tension-reduction and pleasure. For example, Lecky (1945, p. 139) says, "pleasure demands the continuous solution of new problems, rather than a condition of relief and passivity . . . (but) the generalization that pleasure consists in the removal of conflict by some means or other appears to hold true in all cases." Rogers, after apparently subscribing to a tension-reduction theory of anxiety and of drives like hunger and thirst, qualifies this by saying that "there might be some question as to whether absence of psychological discomfort or tension is synonymous with adjustment" (1951, p. 182).

Not only are the antecedents of these inborn drives not specified, as we said above; but also their observable consequents are not stated. No clear specifications are given for defining "goal," or for telling how one can recognize the directionality and selectivity which defines that behavior which is supposedly motivated by self-actualization. Also, no means are given by which one may distinguish the influence of self-actualizing drives on behavior from the influence of other drives, or from the influence of habits, cognitive determinants, or situational determinants.

Other allegedly inborn self-referent motives are subject to the same sorts of critical comments. These motives include Adler's (Ansbacher & Ansbacher, 1956, p. 104) striving for superiority, and Horney's less intrinsically competitive need for self-esteem which is a "given" of human nature (Munroe, 1955, p. 346).

2. Self-Referent Constructs as Related to Perceptual and Learning Processes

What important relationships can be seen between self-referent constructs as discussed by personality theorists and the perceptual and learning processes as discussed in general psychology? As a basis for discussing this question, we review briefly some major points of widespread agreement in general psychology concerning these functions and their manifestations. This broad class of processes includes perceptual discrimination, perceptual-motor learning, memorizing, verbal learning, concept formation, and symbolic problem-solving. Through learning, new drives are acquired, and more or less stable response dispositions such as habits, concepts, skills, attitudes, and traits develop. The perceptual, remembering, and symbolizing processes have objects or events as their referents, e.g., we perceive groups of stimuli, remember words or sentences.

It is also generally agreed that these processes and acquired dispositions have functional significance. That is, they enable a person to deal with internal and external events in such a way as to maintain life, to optimize physiological functioning. Related to this, but not synonymous with it, is the idea that cognitive processes and acquired dispositions are useful to the organism in maximizing positive reinforcement and minimizing negative reinforcement. (We use the term reinforcement here in the empirical, weak, or operational sense for two reasons: [1] it is obviously impossible to resolve theoretical controversies concerning a "strong" or theoretical definition of reinforcement; and [2] the self theorists' statements which imply learning through reinforcement are not classifiable under any one "strong" definition of reinforcement.)

How can self-referent constructs be related to this class of psychological processes and acquired dispositions, and to the alleged functional utility of the cognitive processes? Can some of the statements concerning self-referent constructs be understood in terms of laws of perception or learning?

a. *Freud's Ego*—The first self-referent constructs which obviously are related to this group are the ego functions of Freud. These functions are comprised in a "special organization (which) ... acts as an intermediary between the id and the external world" (1949, p. 15). The ego capacities of perception, cognition, and manipulation are assumed to be inborn; but "the ego" as an organization arises "under the influence of the real external world," i.e., through learning. Freud offers no principles of perception or learning as such, but a tension-reduction, law-of-effect principle is implied. That is, lack of automatic discharge of id tensions, overpowering and painful stimuli from the environment, and anxiety signals which come to be associated with these states force the ego to develop means for appraising "reality" and coping with it. It is clear that Freud had in mind the general notion of cognitive-manipulative processes having adaptive significance.

It is also obvious that Freud's term "the ego" implies more than a modern psychologist's cognitive and manipulative processes and acquired dispositions. "The ego" as Freud uses the term sometimes seems to mean "the person." But Freud himself assigns the name Ego to a postulated "region of our mental life."

He may be criticized first for failing to distinguish clearly between (a) acquired behavioral dispositions and (b) the perception and learning processes by which these dispositions are acquired. Furthermore, he assigns unifying, executive functions to the Ego which go beyond the cognitive processes and acquired dispositions themselves. All this suggests that he has reified a little man within the person. He disclaims such naive intentions, but his actual writings do not clear him of this criticism of naive reification.

The confusions and naivete in the Freudian Ego concept are well indicated by the defense mechanisms. In these, the ego (agent) appraises internal and external events in terms of their threat to the ego (person?); and the ego (agent) learns to avoid this threat by use of intellectual (ego) processes such as rationalizing.

b. *The self concept*—Returning to a general consideration of cognition, we find agreement that among the classes of objects and events known to a person are some of his own physical characteristics, thoughts, feelings, and behaviors. It is these to which many self-referent constructs refer. We cite some representative examples.

At the beginning of modern psychological interest in self, James (1890, p. 371) said "... personality implies the incessant presence of two elements, an objective person, known by a passing subjective Thought and recognized as continuing in time. *Hereafter let us use the words ME and I for the empirical person and the judging Thought.*" (James's famous material, social, and spiritual selves actually referred to characteristics, possessions, and processes of the person, and to reactions the person gets from others, not the person's self concept per se). *Ego* is for Jung (1923, p. 540) the "complex of representations which constitutes the centrum of my field of consciousness and appears to possess a very high degree of continuity and identity." Allport (1961, p. 113) stresses the "*sense of bodily self,*" and asserts its importance in the overall sense of self. The *body image* of Fisher and Cleveland (1958) seems to overlap the self concept or at least the "sense of bodily self." However, it is said to refer roughly to "the body as a psychological experience, and focusses on the individual's feelings and attitudes toward his own body" (p. x). It is also said to be largely unconscious. Allport (1961, p. 114) picks up James's idea of continuing self-identity; and Hilgard (1949, p. 378) refers to the "continuity of memories as binding the self, as maintaining *self-identity.*" The latter is an important aspect of Hilgard's construct "*self awareness,*" the other important aspect being *self-evaluation*. Rogers (1951, p. 136) writes that "The *self-concept* or self-structure may be thought of as an organized configuration of perceptions of the self which are admissible to awareness. It is composed of such elements as the perceptions of one's characteristics and abilities; the percepts and concepts of the self in relation to others and to the environment; the value qualities which are perceived as associated with experiences and objects; and goals and ideals which are perceived as having positive or negative valence." With a slightly more behavioristic flavor, McClelland (1951) speaks of the *self schema* as "a cluster of memories centered around a common element (the person)" (p. 542); "an organized hierarchy of response tendencies of different strengths" (p. 543). Its main dimensions are *self-potency* (a sense of what is included as part of the self), *consistency,* and *evaluation*. Munroe (1955, pp. 273 f.) assigns considerable importance to the *self image,* saying that "people build up a rather clear-cut picture of themselves .... Typically there are important sub-images which may have a high degree of autonomy. Most of us have several pictures of ourselves, not always logically compatible with one another, which serve as a dynamic focus under varying circumstances" (Munroe, 1955, p. 611).

Additional possible examples are Horney's *self image* and *idealized self image* (1945, pp. 96 f.); Snygg and Combs's (1949) *phenomenal self;* and Angyal's (1941) *symbolic self*. Sullivan (1953) speaks of personifications, referring to the images one has of himself or of another. So far as personifications of self are concerned, Sullivan especially stresses the evaluative processes, i.e., he emphasized the *good-me* and *bad-me* divisions of the self concept. (His famous term *self-dynamism* seems sometimes to refer to certain habit systems adopted to avoid the anxiety associated with the disapproval of "significant others," sometimes to one's view of self. Executive functions are also occasionally attributed to the self dynamism, it appears to us.)

What do we find in common among these "definitions" and descriptions? They all refer to complex concepts or systems of concepts within a person, and as such they must be inferred from behavior. In one or more of the statements, these concepts are described by the theorist in the following ways:

1. A person as an entity separated from others is experienced.
2. A sense of being the same person continues over time.
3. Physical characteristics as experienced are included in the concept.
4. One's behaviors as experienced and remembered are included, especially if associated with feelings of intent or being under the control of the experiencing person.
5. A degree of organization or unity among items included in the self concept is experienced. On the other hand, some theorists postulate semi-autonomous subdivisions which can be logically incompatible with one another. There is no statement as to how to reconcile these two views on the internal organization of the self concept.
6. Self percepts and self concepts are not distinguished by the theorists. That is, no particular theoretical attempt is made to conceptualize separately distal stimulating events, proximal stimulating events, central events, and behavioral events. Nor has the desirability of doing so been recognized. (In describing "perceptions" of self and others, there is considerable borrowing from gestalt terminology of visual perception, e.g., Rogers (1951), Snygg & Combs (1949), and Murphy (1947) use the terms gestalt, configuration, figure and ground. But no connection is made between stimulating characteristics and the alleged "perceptual" experiences. In short, the gestalt perceptual terms constitute loose figures of speech rather than expressions of a theory of self-referent perception.)
7. The self concept includes a person's evaluations as well as his cognitions.
8. The self concept is described as involving degrees of consciousness or unconsciousness.

The above listing makes more evident the enormous complexity and inclusiveness of the "definitions." The self concepts as described in the inclusive listing we henceforward call the *generic self concept.*

It seems that the generic self concept might become more theoretically and empirically useful if at least the following possibilities for subclassification and analysis are recognized. It must be understood that there can be considerable overlap in content between the self-concept divisions which we think should be conceptually subdivided by theorist and researcher. The suggested subdivisions are schematized in Figure 1.

(a) The evaluative aspects of the generic self concept rest partly on an assumed division into an ideal-self concept and the actual-self concept. This is true since discrepancies between these two aspects of the generic self concept are supposedly partly at the base of the evaluative aspects. Consequently, we need to examine the person's ideal-self concept as a separate classification, considering separately the ideals the person has for himself and his concepts of others' ideals for him. We return below to a discussion of this analysis.

(b) The person often differentiates between the social effects of his behavior as he sees it (his social-self concept) and his own view of his characteristics (private-self concept).

(c) The social-self concept itself is typically multiple, corresponding, for example, to different social roles, to the different parts of the *persona* of Jung, to James's various *social selves,* or to different reactions one gets from various other individuals and

THEORISTS' ALL-INCLUSIVE DESCRIPTIONS AND "DEFINITIONS" OF SELF CONCEPT:

SUGGESTED CONCEPTUAL SUBDIVISIONS OF THE GENERIC SELF CONCEPT:

FURTHER SUBDIVISIONS, ACCORDING TO SUBJECTIVE CONTENT OR REFERENCE DIMENSIONS:

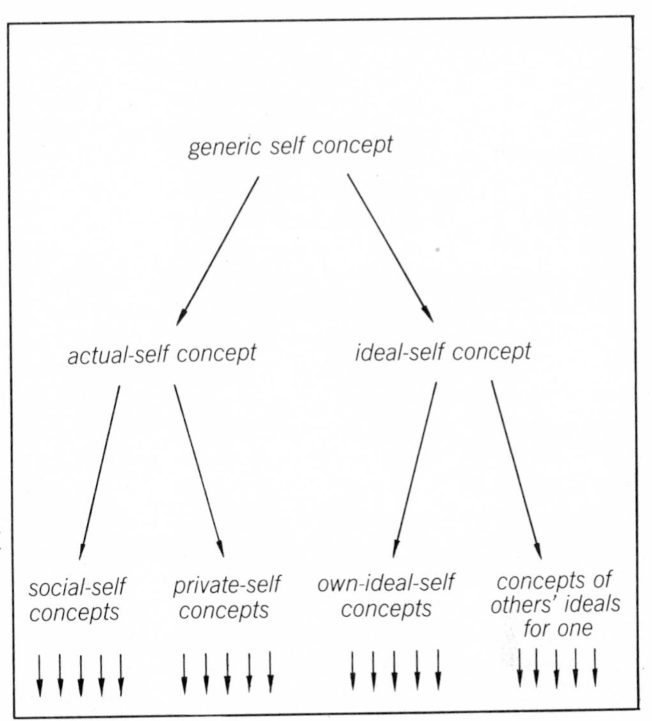

groups. Subcategorization is definitely needed here.

The suggested subdivisions of the generic self concept imply a number of possibilities for conflict within the generic self concept, viz.: among aspects of the actual-self concept, among aspects of the ideal-self concept, or between aspects of the ideal-self concept and aspects of the actual-self concept. However, little theoretical attention has been given to the first two of these kinds of implied conflict.

(d) Some systematic relation of self concept to the unconscious-conscious dimension is needed.

That the person's ideal for himself and his picture of his actual self should be separately conceptualized has been recognized by a number of psychologists. Concerning the ideal for self, Freud discussed the ego ideal, conscience, and superego; but the relationships among these terms are not clear (Healy, Bronner, & Bowers, 1930). McClelland (1951, pp. 572 f.) has suggested that ego-ideal applies to the "conscious (or symbolized) self-potent realistic cluster of values within the self schema," while the term superego labels the "unconscious (unsymbolized) ego alien, irreal, rigid cluster of values within the self schema." For Adler (Ansbacher & Ansbacher, 1956, p. 95) "The self-ideal has been created as a guiding point by the safeguarding tendency and fictionally carries within itself all abilities and gifts of which the so-disposed child considers himself deprived." The self ideal of Adler may in various respects be conscious and unconscious. The persona of Jung is partly the ideals, goals, and social roles the person has taken over from society and made his own (Munroe, 1955, p. 559). (It also seems to include role behaviors, and part of the actual-self concept.) Rogers's idea of the ideal-self concept is implied in the *Q*-sort instructions given to Butler and Haigh's (1954) *Ss*. They were asked to keep in mind "how I would most like within myself to be."

As in the case of the actual-self concept, the ideal-self concept is obviously a complex, widely inclusive construct or group of constructs. Clearer theorizing and research should result if we could set up subconstructs. For example, "how I would most like within myself to be" is not necessarily synonymous with "how I think others wish I were." Depending on my own characteristics such as sex and age, and upon the person or group with which I am interacting, each of the above sets of ideals may differ. This is analogous to the manner in which variations in social-self concept depend on variations in the other group or person with whom I am interacting.

Much of the research and theorizing in this area implies a number of very doubtful assumptions about the ideal-self concept and related evaluation of self, viz.: (1) There is a stereotyped cultural ideal or norm of the ideal person with respect to specified characteristics or behavior. (2) A given person has accepted this cultural norm as his own personal ideal-self concept. (3) Self-esteem (e.g., congruence between actual-self concept and ideal-self concept, self-favorability) is somehow "global." That is, there is a strong general factor in self evaluation, with little or no need to consider degrees of self-regard with respect to conceptually separate dimensions or characteristics. Little or no attention has been given to the fact that discrepancies or conflicts might occur among aspects of the ideal-self concept just as they may among aspects of the actual-self concept. A further examination of some of these problems is found in Wylie (1961). Also, we should not assume that the evaluative aspects of the self concept involve only the degree of congruence between actual-self concept and ideal-self concept, no matter how we subdivide the latter two constructs. This becomes apparent when we examine the meaning of "self acceptance." Although definitions of this term vary widely, some being essentially synonymous with self-esteem or with congruence between actual-self concept and ideal-self concept, a common usage refers to how much one respects one's characteristics, including one's admitted faults.

We suggested that, in addition to needing more analytical subdivisions of the generic self concept, we need a systematic statement of the relationships of various classes of self concept to the dimensions of consciousness-unconsciousness. Theorists have not been systematic in their statements on this matter, but in general many self theorists lay great stress on the role of conscious cognitions concerning self, and the associated motives such as the motive to increase self esteem.

Apparently this trend is partly due to the theorists' personal distaste for the Freudian stress on unconscious factors. It seems that consciousness is more congruent with self theorists' personal belief in the rationality and dignity of man, and his powers of "free choice." As part of his emphasis on man's upward strivings and creative self, Adler's swing toward emphasizing consciousness caused Freud to criticize him erroneously for denying the existence of the unconscious (Thompson, 1950). Rank (1932), in explaining the development of the highest ("creative") stage in the development of individuality, assigns to consciousness a very important role. The person can "develop his standards beyond the identification of the super ego morality to an ideal formation which consciously guides and rules this creative will in terms of personality" (p. 212). Although Rogers (1951) postulates an inherent striving of the organism in the direction of "self-enhancement and growth," he feels that "factors of choice (must) be clearly *perceived* in order for this forward-moving tendency to operate" (p. 491). Moreover, the emphasis on unconscious motivation seemed incongruent with the self theorists' observation that persons could frequently describe their own feelings and emotions in a way which would agree with a clinician's inferences.

The trend toward emphasizing consciousness has been carried so far by some recent theorists (e.g., Snygg & Combs, 1949; Rogers, 1951) that self psychology is sometimes referred to as phenomenological psychology.

In stressing the conscious-unconscious aspect of cognitions and motivations, it may seem that certain philosophical problems are implied. The question arises whether conscious processes (or unconscious processes which supposedly have characteristics analogous to conscious ones) belong to a different realm, a mental one in contrast to the physical realm of behavioral events. Whether stressing the unconscious or conscious pole, personality theorists have not discussed the mind-body problem systematically. However, this need not be a serious difficulty since we can subsume conscious and unconscious mental processes into a "neutral monistic" viewpoint consonant with scientific psychology. That is, self theorists agree that both conscious and unconscious mental processes must be inferred from behavior which is observed by the scientist or other person. (Only certain existentialist psychologists seem to be saying that one can literally enter the phenomenal world of another person—see May [1958]). Accordingly, all the data of psychology are observational, and the inference of conscious or unconscious mental processes need not raise the pseudo-problem of mind and body.

But how are the data from conscious processes to be theoretically articulated with the data from unconscious ones and with other behavioral and environmental data in order to predict behavior? This problem has not been handled as yet by self theorists.

We have said that perception and learning processes have functional significance. What does this mean in the case of the self concept (using that term in its widest sense)?

What principles does self concept *development* allegedly follow? Can these be seen as exemplifying the general principles of adaptive learning? In particular, can the origin of those self-concept characteristics which theorists stress be accounted for in terms of reinforced learning? At any given stage of development, what is the role of the self concept in initiating or guiding further adaptive perception and learning?

c. Learning of the generic self concept. Although some philosophers such as Descartes and Kant assumed that a sense of self is inborn, most modern theorists take for granted that the conscious and unconscious self concepts are learned. However, self theorists' statements implying learning are scattered and incomplete, and are not consistently phrased in terms of any one theory of learning. For instance, Rogers's assertions about learning seem to be a mixture of views characteristic of Tolman, Bruner, Miller and Dollard, and Wertheimer.

Is it possible, on the basis of an overview of self theorists' writings, to make any definite statements about acquisition of the generic self concept, and to "translate" them into some very general and eclectic conceptualizations concerning reinforced or functionally adaptive learning? In the paragraphs which follow we have freely synthesized and adapted ideas on self-concept development, and in the process of attempting such a "translation" have added some ideas beyond those found in self theories as such.

Our main point here is to suggest a rapprochement between self-concept theory and learning theory; and to identify possible sources of reinforcement which may account for learning of various aspects of the self concept. Eventually, if it seems possible to conceive of self-concept development following principles of reinforced learning, attempts to make more detailed statements may be fruitful. For example, paralleling Hill's (1960) suggestions in his proposed application of learning theory to the acquisition of values, detailed hypotheses concerning self-concept learning may usefully involve such variables as number, percentage, magnitude, and delay of reinforcement; distribution of practice; and discriminability of stimuli. To the extent that a translation into more detailed principles is possible, new research is suggested based on the present state of laws of learning. To the extent that translation seems impossible, gaps in both self-concept theory and learning theory would be revealed, to the benefit of each.

But even if more detailed principles may eventually be feasible, it is not our purpose here to try to go that far beyond the formulations of self theorists. And before beginning our general statements, we warn the reader that the fact that a statement below is made as a positive assertion does not mean that it has an empirical referent or can presently be related to research findings.

Our order of presentation follows that of the numbered statements about the generic self concept given earlier.

Sense of being a separate entity—The sense that one is separate from other persons and objects is presumably learned by experienced discontinuities in the perception of other objects and persons, and by failure to be able to manipulate them to obtain reinforcements at all times. Probabilities of attaining many kinds of positive reinforcements and of avoiding many kinds of negative reinforcement are increased when this fundamental discrimination has been learned. For example, biting a teething ring can yield positive reinforcement while biting one's own finger is painful.

But the reinforcement pattern associated with this discrimination may be mixed. For example, certain satisfactions through fantasy are thwarted, and feelings of isolation and helplessness may be increased. Perhaps these negative reinforcements are part of what Rank is referring to when he speaks of the "life fear ... that is the fear of realizing the own ego as an independent individuality" (1945, p. 82). In an apparently similar vein Fromm says "This separation from a world which in comparison with one's own individual existence is overwhelmingly strong and powerful, and often threatening and dangerous, creates a feeling of powerlessness and anxiety" (1941, p. 29). The implications of the mixed reinforcement patterns have not been worked out.

Along with a sense of separateness, one also develops a sense of being an entity, with an accompanying tendency to react to oneself as a unit. Presumably this is learned partly through the continual and intimate interassociation of one's experienced characteristics and behaviors. In addition, other persons foster the development of this sense of being a unit by reacting to one as a whole, and by labeling one with a name which becomes attached to all one's characteristics and behaviors. For example, sometimes rewards and punishments are meted out to "John," or to "a good boy," or "a bad boy." Even when parents try to tell a child that only a certain aspect of his behavior is being evaluated or reacted to, he may be incapable of making a clear discrimination.

Perhaps our culture with its stress on the value and responsibility of the individual and on the need to be continually aware of others' reactions to one's behavior provides especially great opportunities for learning a consciousness of one's self as a unique individual (Murphy, 1947, p. 521; Munroe, 1955, pp. 610 f.).

Self theorists often note not only that one develops a sense of being a separate entity at any one point in time but that a "sense of identity" endures over time, despite changes in the objective person which would make him unrecognizable to others. For example, in referring to the generic self concept, Rogers says, "This configuration, this gestalt, is in its details a fluid and changing thing, but it is decidedly stable in its basic elements ... (1951, p. 191). And Allport (1961) remarks, "even an oldster of eighty is sure that he is the same 'I' as at the age of three, although everything about him—including the cells of his body and his environment—has changed many times over" (p. 114). This is most plausibly explained in terms of continuity and overlap among the accumulating memories, all of which are associated with common and continuing referents such as the person's name, his characteristic bodily sensations, his overall level of self evaluation, his continuing sex role characteristics, and the like. Murphy suggests that a converse process may also occur in such conditions as aging when "changes in organic and kinesthetic sensations may alter the bodily matrix of selfhood so that one does not recognize himself . . ." (1947, p. 519).

Bodily referents of the actual-self concept—Presumably, bodily contents of the actual-self concept are among the first to be learned, as opportunities to observe one's body parts and their functions are always available, and the child can carry out all kinds of explorations continually, whether or not other persons are present. In the Freudian view, libidinal discharge may be gained through exploration and manipulation of one's own body, providing a source of reinforcement. A number of more recent theorists (e.g., Nissen, 1954; White, 1959) stress that exploration of various kinds may occupy so much of the child's time because exploring *per se* is positively reinforcing. Exercise of muscles and use of sense organs and brain are said to be intrinsically positively reinforcing. In any case it is understandable how formation of an accurate concept of one's body would probably maximize the occurrence of positive reinforcements and minimize the occurrence of negative reinforcement. For example, one learns that one's lips are pleasurably stimulable by one's finger, but that one's fingernail can cause pain to one's lip.

Actual-self concept of physical and social competencies—A concept of one's physical and social competencies is also learned, presumably through sensory exploration and manipulation. White (1959) feels that developing a sense of competence is inherently reinforcing, thus accounting for exploration and manipulation through primary reinforcers intrinsic to the activity, in addition to the usual ones of food, water, etc. In a broader sense, it seems likely that developing an accurate knowledge of the kind of reactions one can elicit in the physical environment and in others increases the chances of attaining many kinds of primary and secondary positive reinforcements and avoiding many kinds of primary and secondary negative reinforcements. On the other hand, if one is in fact incompetent in some respect, accurate recognition of this may be negatively reinforcing, because one anticipates failure in the process of trying to manipulate people and things. This anticipation of negative reinforcement supposedly arouses anxiety. Consequently a conflict arises in which the self concept may not include the anxiety-provoking features. But then the person increases the possibility of negative reinforcement in the long run, since he loses some possibility of developing ways of manipulating others to attain his goals. We return to this issue later when discussing inaccuracies in the self concept.

The "extended self concept"—The self concept is said eventually to include more than one's recognition that one is a separate entity with certain bodily characteristics, behaviors, thoughts, and feelings. As James (1890, p. 291) vividly pointed out, the "ME" which is known to the judging "I" is the "*sum total of all that (a person) can call his,* not only his body and his psychic powers, but his clothes and his house, his wife and children, his ancestors and friends, his reputation and works, his lands and horses and yacht and bank-account."

On what grounds can one claim that all these objects and processes may be included in the self concept? James justified his statement by recourse to introspection: "All these things give (a person) the same emotions. If they wax and prosper, he feels triumphant; if they dwindle and die away, he feels cast down—not necessarily in the same degree for each thing, but in much the same way for all" (1890, pp. 291–292). This vague criterion seems still to be tacitly accepted without asking for an empirical translation of it. Persons are also alleged to behave toward other objects and persons as they would behave toward themselves, and this is sometimes offered as a criterion of the degree to which others are included in one's wider self concept. For example, one may apologize or rationalize for the behavior of another. All in all, however, the criteria for telling what is included in the "extended self concept" are vague and scientifically unsatisfactory.

James's description seems to connote what McClelland (1951) called the "areal" characteristic of the self concept. McClelland associates this areal characteristic with what he calls self potency. According to his idea, a person comes to include things in his wider self concept in proportion to the degree to which these things have proven to be under the person's control, or even to be associated with the person's "feelings of intent."

There are also other plausible ways in which reinforcement may be involved in extending the self concept. Early incompleteness in discriminating oneself as a separate entity may be involved at first. Later, through classical conditioning, certain originally neutral sensory cues produced by another who is in pain, for example, may arouse unpleasant reactions in a person, since the person has previously produced and perceived these sensory cues himself when the pain was in his own body. In part, the "extension of the self concept" seems to be essentially similar to one meaning of "identification." It is commonly assumed that one may receive positive reinforcement by considering the other's power, skills, or other desirable attributes to be partly one's own. This attitude may be fostered by parents helping the child to do things beyond his own abilities, then praising the child for "his" accomplishments. And there are other circumstances in which one may be directly rewarded or punished for reacting to another's behaviors as if they were his own. For example, a child might be praised for guiding a little brother's behavior so that the brother was successful or socially approved. The child is rewarded for learning to label his own body and actions as "mine," and at the same time he is instructed to consider that the concept "mine" should include family, community, country, etc. It is made clear that "my" family's and "my" country's welfare are important to one's own more limited goals; and one is positively reinforced for accepting this idea, or threatened with loss of approval if one does not.

Furthermore, if developing a sense of separateness is anxiety-provoking as some theorists maintain, extension of the self concept (or identification with others) may be reinforcing in that it helps a person to avoid or escape anxiety from this source.

Internal organization of the generic self concept—Thus far we have said that the generic self concept allegedly has many aspects, and we have speculated concerning the ways in which some of them are learned. But amidst the ever increasing inclusions within the generic self concept there is supposedly an internal organization, consistency, or coherence which is part of the person's experience of himself. We shall not attempt to account for this consistency here, as we consider its possible origins below when talking about "inaccuracies" in the self concept. On the other hand, the possible origins of the internal contradictions or semi-autonomous subimages are not too difficult to imagine. There is no reason to expect internal logic or consistency within a given person's learning opportunities. For example, it seems obvious that even within the family one is reinforced for reacting differently when with different persons, and that other persons react differently toward one. These possibilities for differing reactions are multiplied when one encounters new persons outside the family. As a group, self theorists stress more than did Freud the continuing possibilities for new learning about one's characteristics. For example, Sullivan (1953), in his outline of stages of development, stresses the influence of the peer group. And in discussing psychotherapy, many self theorists emphasize the possibility of revising parts of the self concept at any age. All things considered, there seem to be plenty of opportunities to learn internally contradictory parts within the generic self concept.

The ideal-self concept—A number of theoretical statements concerning the origins of the ideal-self concept are exceedingly vague and of questionable usefulness to a scientific analysis. They seem to imply the operation of processes which by definition are beyond description by natural law (e.g., Adler's creative self), or to intimate that part of the ideal self-concept may be biologically inherited. Exemplifying the first point, the Ansbachers assert that for Adler the "self creates the personality ideal" (Ansbacher & Ansbacher, 1956, p. 286). And Rank states, "... he evolves his ego ideal from himself, not merely on the ground of given, but also of self-chosen factors which he strives after consciously" (1945, p. 212). As to the second point, Healy, Bronner, and Bowers (1930) say "(The Superego) has a great many points of contact with the phylogenetic endowment of each individual—his archaic inheritance" (p. 44).

Whatever the meaning of these examples, most theorists seem to imply that acquiring an ideal-self concept is mostly or entirely a matter of reinforced *social* learning. Even the physical characteristics and competencies which one idealizes seem to be largely determined by social learning (e.g., to be athletic if a boy, to have a certain kind of figure if a girl).

Theorists vary, however, as to what kind of reinforcement is stressed. Actual or threatened withdrawal of physical satisfactions such as food and water are most probably involved in early life at least. Freud, of course, emphasizes the role of castration threats and positive rewards for modeling after the father as reinforcing factors in the development of the superego, especially the conscience aspects of the superego. Then he speaks of the child's narcissism being disturbed by parental criticisms and admonitions so that the child "seeks to recover the early perfection thus wrested from him in the new form of an Ego-ideal" (quoted in Healy, Bronner, & Bowers, 1930, p. 256). Also, reduction of homosexual libidinal tensions is suggested as a reinforcer involved in formation of the Ego-ideal.

Sullivan feels that the mother's displeasure or pleasure communicates itself to the child by an innate process of empathizing, creating anxiety or euphoria in the child. These states constitute primary negative and positive reinforcers, and the child learns to want to behave in ways which are associated with escaping or avoiding anxiety (or increasing euphoria). All self-evaluations, as well as all self dynamisms are developed with this kind of reinforcement, according to Sullivan (1953).

Giving and withholding of expressions of love are sources of reinforcement in learning the ideal-self concept. This is true not only within the home, but in larger groups as well. To what extent expressions of love originally acquire this reinforcing value by being associated with positive reinforcers such as food, water, or bodily contact between mother and child is not clear. Horney (1950) seems to feel that the child is directly sensitive to expressions of love, and particularly to expressions of hostility which are negative reinforcers. The child is positively reinforced, too, not only for setting up ideals but for controlling himself by them. This positive reinforcement takes the form of direct praise, of being allowed increasing freedom from supervision, and of being given to understand that he is fulfilling expectations for his own development and thus pleasing his parents and others. Adler (Ansbacher & Ansbacher, 1956, p. 144) noted that, in the neurotic personality, one might see in extreme form another kind of reinforcement for establishing an exaggeratedly raised self ideal: "... to shine through modesty, to conquer with humility and submission, to humiliate others with one's own virtue, ... to make oneself small in order to appear big ...." This analysis follows, of course, from Adler's stress on the striving for superiority.

Hill (1960) considers the possible applicability of learning theory to conscience development. The reader may wish to refer to this for more detailed suggestions concerning patterns of reinforcement in acquiring the prohibiting aspects of the ideal-self concept.

We noted earlier the possibility that mutually conflicting ideals could be learned, depending upon contradictions between or within sources from which the ideal-self concept is learned. In his views on the three stages in the development of individuality, Rank (1945) lays major emphasis on the conflict between "willing" what parents and society compel one to want and accepting the ideals created by one's own will. Horney (1945) sees a major conflict in neurosis between self-realization and self-idealization. By this she apparently means a conflict between what the person "really" wants or believes, and what the person thinks he wants or believes because accepting these "external" ideals seems necessary in order to preserve his basic "sense of security." This general notion is found in the writings of many theorists.

In the type of conflict within the ideal-self concept described by Rank and Horney, one gets the idea that reinforcement for adopting external standards involves many positive reinforcements, and, in addition involves escape from anxieties such as the "life fear," or the anxiety created from feeling alone in a hostile world. Just what the reinforcements are for adopting or creating one's own self-ideals is not made clear. It may possibly be related to a biological trend toward individuation, but this idea is too vague to be useful to our present account. Perhaps some positive reinforcement for learning "one's own" ideals may occur when the personal ideals entail relaxing somewhat society's prohibitions toward gratification of primary drives and hostility, or lowering standards for one's personal appearance, or academic achievements. Another possibility for positive reinforcement may occur if one is taught that "thinking for oneself" is valued by one's parents and society. Thus, setting up one's own ideals may imply reinforcement from social and self approval.

Or we may speculate that learning "one's own" ideals might entail resolving contradictions among the earlier acquired social expectations, since parental and societal teachings are internally contradictory, as has often been noted. This reduction of conflict is presumably positively reinforcing. Finally, Rogers (1951) has suggested that behavior stemming from consciously thought-out ideals may lead to a greater sense of being able to predict and control one's own behavior, so that one avoids the anxiety associated with feeling out of control, and with creating unexpected effects in others.

Of course, all of these speculative statements imply that some way is available for identifying empirically which are really the person's "own" ideals and which are only ostensibly his. Whether this distinction can ever be empirically classified remains to be seen.

Inaccuracies in the self concept—An outstanding feature of the self concept is that it does not correspond to objective appraisals of the person. A thorough analysis of this situation would involve the degree of correspondence between the conscious self concept and "reality," *and* between the unconscious self concept and "reality." Theorists have not been thorough and logically consistent in their statements, however. They have mainly stressed the degree of correspondence between conscious self concept and reality, and their partial analysis leads to equivocalities and contradictions which we examine later.

Can we apply learning principles to explain the lack of correspondence between the self concept and objective appraisals of a person?

One hypothesis is related to the fact that acquiring a self concept begins before the child has language. Thus the child may not identify clearly what aspects of himself are arousing displeasure in others, and he may overgeneralize, thinking he is generally a bad boy; or he may try to exclude a behavior from his repertoire and from his conscious self concept when it is in fact irrelevant to the disapproval he received. (See, for example, McClelland [1951], and Sullivan [1953], who stresses the importance of parataxic thinking in the development of the self dynamisms.) Thus his conscious self concept may be a quite vague and inaccurate conceptualization of his characteristics. In order to extinguish the original learning and replace it by more accurate conscious self conceptualizations, the original learning situation should be reinstated. But in the case of pre-verbal learning in infancy, this seems manifestly impossible, so the long-term retention of inaccurate self concepts is partially understandable in these terms.

A second hypothesis as to why the conscious self concept is incongruent with the person's objective characteristics stems from the alleged fact that the conscious self concept tends to be a simplified, "shorthand" or stereotyped conception. In functional or adaptive learning terms, why might this be? We assume that forming of any kind of complex concept is difficult for a learner. Therefore, development of a realistic self concept might be beyond the capacities of some learners. And in any case, if we assume that expenditure of effort beyond a certain point is negatively reinforcing, it seems understandable that persons would learn and retain a self concept which is simpler than reality warrants.

Closely related to the alleged oversimplicity of the conscious self concept is its supposed internal consistency. The "fact" of internal consistency is in turn related to the lack of correspondence between the self concept and objective characteristics, since one's objective characteristics are not necessarily internally consistent.

It is not possible to specify what is meant by internal consistency, unfortunately. Apparently one important kind of internal consistency involves the degree of congruence between the ideal-self concept and the actual-self concept. We return later to a consideration of this kind of evaluative inconsistency. But supposedly there are other "kinds" of consistency. A hypothetical example might be that if a person considered himself to be strongly interested in forestry he would not tend to regard himself simultaneously as a sedentary person. Let us assume that internal consistencies of this kind may be a factor in making the self concept discrepant from the person's objective characteristics. Why should one plausibly be expected to acquire a concept having such internal consistencies?

Although he does not consistently maintain this position, Murphy asserts in one place (1947, p. 532) that "The urge to consistency can indeed be accepted as a primary mechanism ..."; and Lecky (1945) postulates a striving for consistency *per se*. According to this viewpoint, attaining and maintaining consistency yield primary positive reinforcement. No evidence is offered, however, to support the contention that such a drive exists or is innate.

Another line of reasoning supposes that inconsistencies within the conscious self concept lead to conflicting behavior tendencies. This conflict would lessen the possibility of getting the positive reinforcement attainable from carrying out any one tendency. Additionally, some would say that conflicting behavior tendencies are inherently frustrating or anxiety-producing since goal-directed behavior is interfered with. But this argument for the positively reinforcing value of "unrealistic" internal consistency in the *conscious* self concept runs into trouble when one simultaneously examines the theoretical view that behavior is influenced by the unconscious self concept as well as by the conscious one. The inconsistent items relegated to the unconscious self concept may still supposedly influence behavior in conjunction with the influences from the conscious self concept, and conflicting behavior tendencies would still be produced.

Self theorists think that by far the most important influence leading to incongruities between the self concept and the objectively judged characteristics of a person is the need to preserve approval and affection from others and from self. If one's actual characteristics and behaviors lead to loss of approval, anxiety becomes attached to them. To minimize this anxiety, one ignores the characteristics or behaviors, so one acquires a conscious self concept which is incomplete. Then as the ideal-self concept is acquired, the person may see himself as having characteristics inconsistent with the ideal-self concept. To maximize the positive reinforcement of self-approval, and to avoid or escape the anxiety associated with self-disapproval, the person ignores the inconsistent behavior, and again the conscious self concept becomes discrepant from objectively judged behaviors or characteristics.

This sort of reasoning was introduced into psychological theorizing by Freud, in some of his discussions of narcissism, the development of the ego ideal, and the defense mechanisms of the ego. The general principle now seems to have been accepted by all personality theorists as applying to all persons. Exaggerated versions of this process seem to be at the basis of numerous theories of neurosis as well. We find Adler (Ansbacher & Ansbacher, 1956) saying, "In the anxious person we shall meet again the well-known type who feels forced by necessity to think more of himself ..." (p. 277).

Horney gives a central position in her theory of neurosis to the unrealistic idealized self image which originates in a need to escape basic anxiety. This self image coincides with what pride says one should be, and not only increases feelings of superiority, but preserves longed-for unity which is being threatened by contradictory neurotic trends. Horney's discussion is quite confused as to whether the person is unaware of the idealized image itself (in which case her concept would not be an illustration of our general discussion here), or whether he is unaware of how unrealistic his idealized image is (1945, pp. 96–114).

In sum, then, we must say that theorists' descriptions of the self concept and its characteristics are very sketchy, incomplete, and apparently contradictory in places. If we have correctly understood their descriptive and explanatory intentions, however, plausible interpretations can be made in terms of very general ideas concerning reinforced learning. Neither the theoretical writing nor available empirical research is definite enough to justify more refined applications of learning principles at this time.

3. The Effects of Self Concept on Behavior

In discussing how the acquisition of the generic self concept may exemplify adaptive learning, we have inevitably referred several times to the supposed adaptive role of the self concept in influencing further behavior. To the self theorists this role of the self concept is of paramount importance, and we turn now to a more systematic discussion of it.

For all self theorists, the generic self concept is said to be at least *a* determiner of behavior. Snygg and Combs attempt to defend the extreme view that "All behavior, without exception, is completely determined by and pertinent to the phenomenal field [including the self concept] of the organism" (1949, p. 15). Rogers (1951) represents a more common view in that he feels the necessity for two "systems" in determining behavior: (1) the person's perceived world and self, and (2) organismic processes and automatic adjustive behaviors, learned or unlearned. Thus there is general agreement that the determinants of behavior cannot all be classified under self concept, or even under phenomenal field. But how, in building a personality theory, are other classes of behavioral determinants to be systematically articulated with the determining role assigned to the self concept? This awkward question has not even been faced, let alone clearly formulated or answered.

To consider only what is said about the self concept, then, we note that most theoretical statements are extremely general and extravagant in nature. As representative examples of this type of assertion, we cite the following: "Our conscious and unconscious memory and its individual structure function in accordance with the personality ideal and its standards" (Adler, in Ansbacher & Ansbacher, 1956, p. 215). "One's feelings, thoughts, and actions are almost entirely determined by one's idealized self image" (Horney, 1942, p. 291). "[The self concept] is constantly used as a frame of reference when choices are to be made. Thus it serves to regulate behavior and may serve to account for observed uniformities in personality" (Rogers, 1951, p. 191).

Considering the importance assigned to the self concept in accounting for such a wide variety of behavior, it is amazing to be able to find so few statements saying anything definite or potentially operational about the relationship of the self concept to behavior. The major points seem to be these:

1. At any given stage in the development of the self concept, the person tends to perceive or learn more readily things which are consistent with the self concept, while tending to not perceive or learn things which are inconsistent with the self concept.

One class of such inconsistencies involves further learning about one's own personality, as we have discussed earlier. Failing to note or remember items about one's personality occurs when these items are inconsistent with the ideal self; but even when items about the personality are consistent with the ideal-self concept, they may be excluded because they are inconsistent with the actual-self concept. For example, if a person wishes he were bright, but believes he is stupid, he may reject a teacher's favorable opinion of his ability, or believe a high test score is in error. We have already discussed the difficulties in specifying this sort of "consistency" operationally, and considered possible reasons why maintaining self-concept consistency of both types may be reinforcing.

We note here that this general principle of the effects of the self concept on perception and learning supposedly applies not only to further learning about one's own personality, but also to other kinds of learning and perception such as verbal learning, and tachistoscopic word recognition and learning about characteristics of others. We cannot be more specific as to the alleged mechanisms by which this influence operates. There may well be factors of familiarity and positive transfer from past encounters with the stimuli, or with similar stimuli, and the influence of expectancy.

2. As we explained earlier, a person with an inaccurate self concept is said to be vulnerable because he is continually exposed to the possibility of receiving unexpected reactions from others. These reactions may be ones to which he cannot respond in a way leading to positive reinforcement; and furthermore they may force upon him a negatively reinforcing revision of the self concept. Thus anxiety and defensive reactions are supposedly the ultimate outcome of inaccuracies in the self concept. Theorists seem to differ, however, in their description of this chain of events.

In the classical Freudian and neo-Freudian views, complete "lack of insight" is alleged to be accompanied by defensive behaviors. Sometimes phenomenal theorists seem to espouse this view, too. But in other places we find such statements as this: "[Although the individual whose self concept is incongruent with reality may be vulnerable] the extent to which he dimly perceives these incongruences and discrepancies is a measure of his internal tension and determines the amount of defensive behavior" (Rogers, 1951, pp. 191–192).

3. Evaluation of others is a positive function of one's own level of self-evaluation.

Neo-Freudians and self theorists depart from Freud's views on this matter. Consistent with his views concerning a fixed amount of available libido, Freud thought that a person could love others only by withdrawing libido from himself, so that in effect there is an inverse relationship between self love and love for others. But Fromm (1939), for example, argues vigorously that the capacity to love others and the exercise of that capacity depend on the development of positive regard for oneself.

The chain of events in the development of positive regard for others has not been clearly specified, and is doubtless extremely complex. Presumably a person comes to love others partly by generalization from loving his parents, and the latter would be partly a function of how much they manifest love for him. If they manifest love for him, he learns to regard himself highly, this being one aspect of his acquisition of their values. Here may be one source of positive correlation between level of self regard and level of regard for others, a source which does not involve the level of self-regard as an antecedent to the level of regard for others.

Then, if a person perceives himself as loved and lovable, he need not be preoccupied with the possibility of receiving such negative reinforcements as rejection and isolation in a hostile world. Thus he is less apt to behave defensively, and in turn less apt to elicit through his defensive behavior negatively reinforcing behaviors from others, which would lower his regard for them. If others behave toward him in a positively rather than in a negatively reinforcing fashion, his regard for them increases. In this hypothetical sequence of events, level of self regard does play an antecedent role.

We may further postulate that stimulus generalization occurs between learned information and attitudes about oneself and learned information and attitudes about others. As a special case of this, one's level of self regard might generalize to others, and in this hypothesis we again deal with a supposed antecedent influence of level of self regard upon level of regard for others.

III. MEASURING SELF-REFERENT CONSTRUCTS

To do effective research in any area, we must of course use valid and reliable measures and appropriate research designs. In this section we discuss problems of measuring self-referent constructs, and briefly describe and evaluate the kinds of instruments which have been used for this purpose.

A. Classification and Description of Measures

In Table 1 we proposed a possibly useful scheme for subclassifying self-referent constructs, but we have already pointed out that theorizing and measurement have not, in practice, been analytical. For purposes of discussion, the measures actually used may be roughly grouped as follows: (1) measures of conscious self-regard, either over-all self-regard or evaluation along a specified dimension; (2) measures of configurational properties of the self concept; (3) measures of the unconscious self concept, usually some evaluative aspect of it.

1. Evaluative Measures

The most commonly studied class of aspects of the conscious self concept includes such attitudes as self-satisfaction, self-acceptance, self-esteem, self-favorability, congruence between actual-self concept and ideal-self concept, and discrepancies between actual-self concept and ideal-self concept. As we pointed out earlier, all these terms are not synonymous, even in the literary sense. For some authors, self-acceptance means respecting one's self, including one's admitted faults, while self-esteem or congruence between the actual-self concept and the ideal-self concept means being proud of one's self or evaluating one's attributes highly. If the terms had more clearly differentiated literary meanings and correspondingly differentiated operational definitions, it would be desirable to classify our discussion of the instruments according to the construct involved (e.g., self-esteem as contrasted to self-acceptance). However, the terms are so intertwined and overlapping in the literature that the constructs must be considered as a group. For convenience of discussion we use here the word self-regard as a generic term to include self-satisfaction, self-acceptance, self-esteem, self-favorability, congruence between actual-self concept and ideal-self concept.

There seems to be a tacit assumption that an over-all or global level of self-regard characterizes a given person. Only on such an assumption does it make sense that so many investigators, using a wide variety of instruments, have labeled any or all of the obtained scores "self-esteem" or some variation of this term. However, there are as yet no empirical grounds for accepting this assumption of a general factor in self-regard. Its uncritical acceptance is a partial explanation of the fact that research findings frequently cannot be meaningfully compared and psychologically interpreted.

Space precludes our discussing in detail the instruments which have been used purportedly to measure over-all level of self-regard. Instead we briefly describe here the general types, referring the reader to Wylie (1961) for more detailed information.

a. *Q sorts*—One of the most commonly used techniques for assessing phenomenal self-regard is the *Q* sort or slight modifications thereof. In the typical application of this technique a large number of personality-descriptive items are sorted by *S* into nine piles which are arranged on a continuum according to the degree to which they are characteristic of *S*'s actual-self concept. *S* is forced by the instructions to place a specified number of items in each pile so as to yield a quasi-normal distribution of items. *S* then sorts the same items once more into nine piles which are arranged on a continuum according to the degree to which they are characteristic of his ideal for himself. Again, the instructions force him to produce a quasi-normal distribution of the items.

Each item in the self-sort may be assigned a value from one to nine, according to the pile in which *S* has chosen to put it. Correspondingly, each item in the ideal sort may be assigned a value from one to nine, according to the pile in which *S* has chosen to put it. For the individual *S*, a Pearson correlation coefficient may then be computed across items. This so-called self-ideal correlation may be considered to be a score for the *S*, and from the magnitude of that score the degree of that *S*'s self-regard is inferred. In another less frequently used way of obtaining a self-regard score from an individual *S*'s self-descriptive *Q*-sort, one compares the pile number of each statement, as *S* has sorted it, with the independently judged self-favorability value of each item. This type of score introduces a possible theoretical confusion. To be consistently phenomenological, a self-concept theorist must be concerned with the relationship between *S*'s conscious actual-self concept and his conscious ideal-self concept, rather than relating *S*'s conscious self-concept to an objective judgment or cultural stereotype of an ideal person. Of course *S*'s idiosyncratic ideal-self concept may overlap considerably or entirely with the culturally accepted view of an ideal person. Nevertheless, it is not empirically safe to assume that this is the case. And if *S*s do vary from one another with respect to the coincidence between the phenomenal ideal-self concept and the cultural norm, scores based on objectively judged ideals cannot be interpreted in a theoretically consistent way from *S* to *S*.

The set of *Q*-sort items used by Butler and Haigh (1954) has been used most frequently and explored most extensively. The 100 items are an "accidental" sample of statements from "available therapeutic protocols," reworded for clarity (p. 57). This set of items is open to numerous criticisms in the light of specifications for construct validity which we present below.

Many sets of *Q*-sort items have been used only once. For 90 per cent of the 22 sets of *Q*-sort items described in Wylie (1961), no information on construct validity for inferring the conscious self concept is available in published scores. For three-fourths of these item sets, no published reliability information is available. (Of course in those studies in which the author's hypothesis was confirmed, this confirmation offers some very indirect and ambiguous support to the idea that the measure used has some relevant construct validity. We discuss this more fully below.)

b. Rating scales, questionnaires, adjective check lists—The most frequently used types of instruments for inferring over-all self-regard are the questionnaire, rating scale, and adjective check list. In terms of the operations used as a basis for inferring self-regard, several main categories of such instruments may be roughly distinguished: (1) those which purport to tap self-acceptance directly, i.e., by asking *S* how he feels about his standing on the stated characteristics; (2) those which use this direct approach and also derive a discrepancy score between separately obtained actual-self ratings and ideal-self ratings, answers or checks; (3) those which utilize mainly a self-minus-ideal discrepancy score; (4) those which rely on *S*'s reports of actual-self concept only, with the ideal end of the scale being assumed by *E,* or the favorability of the terms being defined in terms of external judges' opinions of desirability.

Bills's Index of Adjustment and Values (Bills, Vance, & McLean, 1951), a well-known example of the second type, has been most frequently used and widely explored. In this instrument, 49 trait names were selected from Allport and Odbert's (1936) list of 17,953 traits as representative, in the opinion of the test's designer, of items which occur frequently in client-centered interviews. For each adjective, *S* rates self, ideal self, and self-acceptance, each on a five-point scale. The instrument is open to numerous criticisms in the light of specifications for construct validity which we present below.

Many of the instruments of this type have been used only once. For two-thirds of some 80 instruments of this variety described by Wylie (1961), *no* published reliability information is available; while for 80 per cent of these instruments, *no* information on construct validity for inferring the conscious self concept is available in published sources (except for confirmation of the author's research hypothesis, which was based on self-concept theory plus the assumption that the self-concept measure has relevant construct validity). Also, no systematic application of scaling techniques has been made in constructing these instruments.

Another possible way to conceptualize and measure conscious or phenomenal self regard is along more limited dimensions. This has been relatively little used in practice, but it seems potentially a more interpretable approach. (A description of some of these instruments is given in Wylie, 1961.)

2. Configurational Properties of Self Concept

We saw above that configurational properties of the self concept have received much theoretical emphasis, and that they have been theoretically differentiated from the level of self regard per se. Nevertheless, little empirical work has been done to define these properties operationally and relate them to theoretically relevant variables. This is probably due in part to the vagueness of the theoretical formulations concerning such constructs as "organization," "configuration," "differentiation," and "consistency."

In an earlier publication (Wylie, 1961) we reviewed five measures each purporting to index a different "configurational" construct, each using different operations. Information on relevant construct validity was not available for any of these measures. In some cases, it seems that constructs other than the gestalt properties of the self concept could parsimoniously account for individual differences in the scores. For example, level of self-regard is sometimes confounded with the "configurational" influences upon the index. We raised the question whether configurational properties can ever be represented by a single score.

3. Measures of the Unconscious Self Concept

Some researchers have attempted to measure such processes as unconscious aspects of the self concept and other nonphenomenal variables which they believe to be pertinent to self theories. Those who do this seem to base their work implicitly and/or explicitly on two lines of reasoning: (1) It is obvious that the phenomenal self, at least as measured by currently used instruments, is far from providing a sufficient basis for accurate predictions of *S*s' behaviors. This lack of predictive power may stem in part from the fact that instruments which purport to measure the phenomenal field will provide an incomplete inventory of relevant variables, no matter how highly perfected they may eventually become for the purpose of measuring the phenomenal field. (2) Because of theoretical reasons one might expect that important characteristics of *S* and his relation with his environment would be unavailable to his phenomenal field. Theorists point out that much important learning occurs pre-verbally, and the need to maintain self-esteem will lead to repression and denial.

With the measurement of such unconscious determinants, we are presented with the question of construct validity. The specifications presented in Section B below for establishing such validity could and should be applied to these instruments. With few exceptions, however, these specifications have been almost entirely ignored by users of indices purporting to measure unconscious determinants and such measures have remained almost entirely unvalidated.

In particular there is a unique and difficult requirement of discriminant validity for this type of measure which has received little or no recognition: If one is to say that a certain projective response or score represents an *un*-conscious attitude toward the self, one must prove not only that *S* holds this attitude, but that he is unaware of it. At the very least one should check to see whether the same attitude might be consciously present, as inferred from a self-report. If the inferences from the self-report and the projective measure differ, one may then have grounds for exploring the more complex assumption that the projective measure is revealing an unconscious self-attitude. Almost universally, however, this measurement problem has been overlooked by workers interested in indexing the so-called unconscious self concept.

The instruments used thus far in an attempt to measure the unconscious self concept are picture judgments, storytelling (including TAT stories), Rorschach records, and some miscellaneous devices. Many of these, together with the studies in which they were used, are described in Wylie (1961). Since theory, measurement, and research design in this area are in a parlous state, no interpretable pattern of results has emerged to date, and we do not consider further in this chapter research on the unconscious self concept.

B. Construct Validity of Measures of the Conscious Self Concept

We have deplored the lack of information on reliability and construct validity of the many measures used to index the conscious self concept. We turn now to a consideration of the problems and specifications which should be considered in this area of measurement. In a recent publication (Wylie, 1961) we discussed in detail the problem of reliability. For brevity, we restrict ourselves here to considering construct validity; and in Section C we consider the intimately related topic of scaling.

1. Specifications for Establishing Construct Validity

Problems of measuring the phenomenal field may be seen as essentially those of establishing "construct validity," in Cronbach and Meehl's (1955) sense of this term. Construct validity is necessary because self-concept theories explicitly require that we measure a stated class of variables, *S*s' conscious processes; and, by definition, *S*s' phenomenal fields are private and beyond direct observation by the experimenter. It is *not* sufficient to demonstrate that one's self-concept measures have "predictive" or "concurrent" validity in the sense that an MMPI scale, for example, may be shown to discriminate nosological categories without an explanation of why the association between MMPI scores and diagnostic labels is obtained.

In order to index constructs involving *S*s' phenomenal fields, *E* must use some form of self-report response made by *S* as a basis for his inferences. In practice this self-report behavior has usually taken the form of a verbal response or some sort of a choice response when *S* is instructed to indicate specified conscious processes. These methods seem to be the only kinds appropriate to this type of construct. That is, if we obtain motor, autonomic, or projective test responses from *S* without telling him of our intent to infer his conscious processes, we have no way of knowing whether such responses reflect conscious or unconscious cognitions and feelings.

We would like to assume that *S*'s self-report responses are determined by his phenomenal field. However, we know that it would be naïve to take this for granted, since it is obvious that such responses may also be influenced by (a) *S*'s intent to select what he wishes to reveal to the *E;* (b) *S*'s intent to say that he has attitudes or perceptions which he does not have; (c) *S*'s response habits, particularly those involving introspection and the use of language; (d) a host of situational and methodological factors which not only may induce variations in (a), (b), and (c) but may exert other more superficial influences on the responses obtained.

We believe that self-concept theorists could profit by examining and applying relevant analyses made by psychologists working in other areas. For example, the difficulties and requirements encountered in measuring the phenomenal field seem to be similar to those already encountered and to some extent analyzed by experimental psychologists working in the field of perception. Garner, Hake, and Eriksen (1956) have noted the fundamental problem of identifying the influence of *perceptual* processes on responses made in perceptual experiments, as opposed to other influences on response availability and production. (For example, in a perception experiment, the question arises whether higher tachistoscopic threshold measurements for taboo words as compared to neutral words are attributable to differential ease of recognition per se, or to differential willingness to guess out loud on the two types of words.) Garner, Hake, and Eriksen say,

> The necessary condition which makes possible the determination of particular characteristics of any concept (including the concept of perception) is the use of what have been called converging operations. Converging operations may be thought of as any set of two or more experimental operations which allow the selection or elimination of alternative hypotheses or concepts which could explain an experimental result. They are called converging operations because they are not perfectly correlated and thus can converge on a single concept" (1956, pp. 150–151).

(Thus, to continue our earlier example, if a series of experiments varies such things as the sex of *E,* or the instructions given to *S,* and differential threshold measurements are still obtained for taboo and neutral words, one increases one's confidence that the difference in measured response may represent different perceptual processes associated with the two classes of words.)

In Cronbach and Meehl (1955) and Campbell and Fiske (1959) we find what amounts to more particularized specifications for appropriate "converging operations" for establishing the construct validity of measuring instruments:

a. We may make observational, including mathematical, analyses of the measuring process to determine what variables other than the construct in question might be influencing our results (Cronbach & Meehl, 1955).

b. We may ascertain that there are intercorrelations among measures presumed to index the same construct (Cronbach & Meehl, 1955). Campbell and Fiske (1959), in their discussion of trait validity, state an additional specification along this line. (In paraphrasing their ideas, we shall use the word "construct" instead of their word "trait.") Using the word "method" to refer to variations in instrument form or procedure for collecting data, they point out that data from a given method can be used to infer different constructs (e.g., the questionnaire form can be used to infer self-esteem or test anxiety). On the other hand, different methods can purport to measure the same construct (e.g., either a questionnaire or an interview might reveal self-esteem). They give the following specifications concerning correlations between scores obtained from differing methods which purport to measure the same construct: (i) Ideally, such correlations should exceed correlations between scores which are obtained by a given method, but which purport to index different constructs. (ii) Such correlations should exceed correlations between scores which are obtained by different methods and which purport to index different constructs. Thus, for example, scores from a rating scale and a True-False questionnaire which both purport to measure over-all self esteem should correlate with each other more highly than do scores from (i) two True-False questionnaires, one purporting to measure self-esteem, the other purporting to measure test anxiety; (ii) a rating scale purporting to measure self-esteem and a questionnaire purporting to measure test anxiety. (Humphreys [1960] has argued that the specification stated under (i) is desirable, but not necessary. He believes that "the degree of importance to be attached to it is simply a function of the number of different methods that can be used to measure the trait" [p. 86].)

c. It is pertinent to make internal item analyses and factor analyses of an instrument to determine how many basic processes must be postulated to account for response variance on the instrument as a whole (Cronbach & Meehl, 1955). We may include here the following, but more limited, statement of Campbell and Fiske (1959). They specify that correlations between scores obtained from a given method which purports to measure the same construct should exceed: (i) correlations between scores which are obtained by a given method but which purport to index different constructs; (ii) correlations between scores which are obtained by different methods and which purport to index different constructs; (iii) correlations between scores which are obtained by different methods but which purport to index the same construct.

For example, the correlation between scores from two True-False questionnaires, both purporting to measure self-esteem, should exceed: (i) the correlation between scores from two True-False questionnaires, purporting to measure self-esteem and test anxiety respectively; (ii) the correlation between scores from a rating scale purporting to measure self-esteem and a True-False questionnaire purporting to measure test anxiety; (iii) the correlation between a rating scale and a True-False questionnaire, both purporting to measure self-esteem.

d. Cronbach and Meehl (1955) have suggested that, in the absence of suitable external validating criteria, we may examine results obtained from studies in which responses on the instrument in question are related to other stimulus and response variables. That is, we may design a study on the basis of certain theoretical premises coupled with an assumption concerning the construct validity of the instrument we are using to measure one of the variables. Positive findings from such a study offer support simultaneously to the construct validity of the instrument and to the theory behind the study. In general, such investigations would involve: (i) successful prediction of group differences, and (ii) studies of predicted changes over occasions (especially after controlled experimental intervention). We must bear in mind, however, that such findings offer ambiguous support at best, since the ratio of unknown to known variables does not preclude alternate interpretations. We are not, therefore, warranted in bypassing validating procedures of the types (a) to (c) above. The appearance of face validity of our instruments coupled with studies of type (d) will never suffice to establish the construct validity of a newly devised instrument.

Thus far, the requirements we have stated are applicable to the study and measurement of any sort of construct, and we have indicated particular similarity to the problems of psychologists studying perceptual processes. However, we face an additional problem not encountered by psychologists studying perception. In the case of a perception experiment, *E* usually is dealing with *S*'s response to a stimulus, the properties of which can be agreed upon by a number of observers. Therefore, insofar as *S*'s reports agreed with *E*'s independent knowledge of stimulus attributes, *E* can establish that *S*'s verbal report is most probably validly indexing his percept. If *S*'s report does *not* reveal that he has seen the stimulus characteristics *E* expects, *E* is faced with an ambiguous situation, thus: (a) *S* may be missing something, or experiencing something different from other observers who have examined the stimulus under comparable conditions, but his report is nevertheless a valid index of what *he* is seeing; *or* (b) *S* may be withholding what he sees, or may not have the necessary verbal skills to report accurately, etc. (i.e., his report is *not* a valid index of his percept). The self-concept researcher, although dealing with phenomenal fields in much the same way as the perception experimenter, has the disadvantage of having no way of independently checking *S*'s reports, since there is no immediate stimulus and hence no way of getting agreement of other observers about what *S* should presumably be experiencing under specified conditions. So the self-concept researcher's method problems are much more complicated than those of the experimental psychologist studying perception.

2. Evaluation of the Construct Validity of Extant Instruments

In an earlier publication (Wylie, 1961) we applied the above specifications to each of the many instruments actually used in research on the conscious self concept, and we present here a brief summary of that discussion.

a. Analysis of irrelevant response determiners—Among the variables other than the phenomenal field which might be influencing the observed response on a self-report instrument are those listed below. With the exception indicated, there is some evidence to suggest at least indirectly that each of these may have a distorting influence, i.e., may diminish construct validity. Social Desirability (in the sense described in Edwards, 1957); the content area of the self concept *E* is trying to index; whether or not *S* is anonymous to *E* (no evidence); lack of rapport between *S* and *E;* the form of the measuring instrument (e.g., rating scale, check list), with associated possibilities for the operation of response sets; degree of restriction of *S*'s response as in forced choice inventories or *Q* sorts; set or expectation induced by instructions or otherwise; past frequency of the response with associated variations in response availability; scoring or statistical procedures which mask complicated and psychologically quite varying responses. The latter source of distortion warrants some elaboration here.

The most serious and frequently recurring difficulties seem to be those associated with two-part indices. We find, for example, that authors often obtain discrepancies between actual-self rating and ideal-self rating on each of several items, and sum these discrepancies to make a single self-regard score. Or, in a *Q* sort, a correlation is obtained between the pile numbers *S* assigns to the items when sorting them to describe his actual-self concept and the pile numbers he assigns to the same items when sorting them to describe his ideal-self concept. So far as check lists and rating scales are concerned, two-part indices have been widely used without sufficient prior exploration of such pertinent questions as the following: (a) How much variance is contributed by each part to variance in scores on the dual index? (b) How much is independently contributed by each part to the correlation between the dual index and theory-relevant behavior? (c) By any standard for relevant construct validity, is the dual index superior to a "simpler" score? For example, would the level of self-regard experienced by the *S* be expressed just as effectively by a direct report of self-acceptance as it is by an experimenter's derived discrepancy score obtained from two of *S*'s reports? Or, alternately, might one infer the level of self-regard from the "actual self" report alone? (d) Is the apparently simpler "actual self" score really less complex than the self-minus-ideal discrepancy, or does it imply that we are obtaining another kind of dual index, one part of which may be nonphenomenal? That is, in assigning a self-regard value to a self-concept score, are we in fact assuming a discrepancy between *S*'s phenomenal self and a cultural norm which *S* may or may not have accepted as his phenomenal ideal for himself? In the case of *Q*-sort correlations, questions (a) and (b) should be examined. And when the actual-self sort is correlated with a self-favorability sort prepared by judges (rather than with *S*'s own ideal-self sort), the question again arises whether we are assuming a discrepancy between *S*'s phenomenal self concept and a cultural norm which *S* may or may not have accepted as his phenomenal ideal for himself.

Insofar as there is any evidence on the above questions, we find considerable stereotypy in ideal-self ratings and ideal-self sorts, implying that the ideal-self responses contribute less than the actual-self responses to variance in two-part scores and to correlations between two-part scores and outside criteria. But the stereotypy is not great enough to warrant unthinking substitution of a cultural norm for the personally stated ideal-self concept.

There are also two other closely related difficulties associated with two-part scores, when self-minus-ideal discrepancies are summed across many items to yield a composite score or a single value of *r*. Summing implies that each item has equal salience for *S*'s self-regard, a most questionable and unsupported assumption. And a single score or *r* of any given value can be made up by innumerable combinations of item discrepancies. In the case of absolute summing across item discrepancies (a common practice), one even loses track of whether *S*s' ideal-self report is "above" or "below" his actual-self report (when "above" refers to the culturally stereotyped "good" end of the scale). In short, use of a global index such as a sum or a Pearson *r* buries individual differences we ought to be identifying for further study. We agree with Cronbach and Gleser's (1953, p. 459) statement that "combining many traits into any sort of composite index, whether it be a *D* measure, a *Q*-correlation or a discriminant function, or any of the other methods presently used, involves assumptions regarding scales of measurement which cannot usually be defended."

In practice, none of the possibly irrelevant response determiners we have listed above has been systematically studied with reference to self-concept measures. Certainly adequate precautions have not been taken to eliminate or control for them. (The reader should also note that the problems in scaling are intimately related to problems of irrelevant response determiners. Scaling problems are considered in Section C, below.)

b. Intercorrelations among measures presumed to measure the same construct—When we survey self-concept measures from the viewpoint of our second criterion, "intercorrelations among measures presumed to measure the same construct," we find that this standard has only rarely been applied, even to a limited degree. Certainly no investigator has satisfied Campbell and Fiske's (1959) minimum requirements for assuring that construct, not method variance, is making the major contribution to variance in the scores.

c. Internal factor analysis—So far as our third criterion is concerned, few persons have internally factor-analyzed their instruments to throw light on the number of basic processes which must be postulated to account for response variance. Of course, even when factors are obtained, this does not reveal whether any of the factors represent subregions of the phenomenal field. However, such a procedure might help us to see that our *a priori* guesses as to the number of variables involved were accurate or erroneous. It might also help to make more obvious the presence of some irrelevant variables.

d. Predictable relation of alleged self-concept measures to other variables—In most investigations of the self concept, the only evidence which might be adduced for the construct validity of the self-concept measures is that implied by Cronbach and Meehl's (1955) fourth criterion—positive findings in studies relating alleged self-concept measures to some other variables in a manner predicted by self theory. Since most investigators have proceeded to use their self-concept instruments for such studies without systematically applying any of the other previously mentioned forms of analysis, the results of their studies can be considered to support, rather than to demonstrate unambiguously, the construct validity of their self-concept measures. At present no general conclusion can be drawn concerning any one instrument or type of instrument, because the array of such studies is too widely scattered across instruments.

C. Scaling in Self-Concept Measurement

Scaling problems are closely related to problems of construct validity. In particular, the precision of inference can be increased when proper scaling techniques are applied, while inappropriate scaling procedures can be among the irrelevant response determiners which eliminate construct validity.

Scaling problems arise in connection with all those instruments on which *S* describes himself by choosing among several degrees of an adjective or descriptive phrase. Examples of such instruments include the semantic differential scales, graphic rating scales, rating scales with descriptive adjectives to demarcate scale ranges, and questionnaires in which *S* says how frequently the item characterizes him.

With reference to a single item in such an instrument, *E*'s problem is to assign numbers to *S*s to reflect magnitudes on a subjective dimension. As a first step *E* defines the dimension verbally for *S*. *E* then, in effect, asks *S* to regard himself as a "stimulus" and to place this "stimulus" on the subjective dimension *E* has described. To follow these directions, *S* has to do two things: (1) develop a conception of what content and situation the item refers to; (2)

develop some psychological metric of the dimension on which he is going to place himself.

In the typical instrument, *S* has to decide for himself to what situations the items refer. For example, is he supposed to rate his degree of self-confidence with reference to dating, participation in sports, or getting along on his job? Is he to take into account both the situations where it would be appropriate and those where it would be inappropriate to feel depressed? Since the instructions typically do not answer these questions for *S,* he supposedly places his self-rating on the item with reference to an unknown combination of situational referents. It remains to be demonstrated that scales with such ambiguities yield meaningful scores or ones which are optimally reliable and/or valid indices of self concept.

Assuming that problems of situational ambiguities were satisfactorily resolved, we would still need to explore further the meaning of successive scale steps. How can *E* interpret *S*'s placement of himself in meaningful numerical terms if he knows nothing of *S*'s psychological metric for the dimension used? How can he interpret the difference between the self placements of two *S*s if he does not know that they were using the same psychological metric? Similarly, how can *E* interpret a difference between *S*'s self placement and his ideal-self placement if he does not know about *S*'s psychological metric? To the extent that we can move from ordinal to ratio scales, we can make our laws involving the scale scores more precise.

Although Guilford (1954), Torgerson (1958), Stevens (1957), and Stevens and Galanter (1957) have discussed how psychophysical methods can be used to derive scales for subjective dimensions, none of the instruments covered in the present review has been refined by the application of such techniques.

Most relevant to the type of scales used by self-concept researchers is work done by Dudek (1959) and by Cliff (1956), who scaled nine common adverbs of degree (e.g., rather, quite, very) in combination with certain evaluative adjectives (e.g., immoral, charming). Dudek used the constant-sum method, while Cliff employed a successive-intervals method. Although each technique was aimed toward achieving a ratio scale, Dudek (1959) reports that the two sets of scale values resulting from the different scaling procedures were not linearly related. Stevens and Galanter (1957) have also noted that for certain kinds of dimensions, "category" scales yield scale values that are curvilinearly related to those derived from methods involving ratio estimations more directly.

The important implications for self-concept measurement seem to be these: (1) It is possible and desirable to refine rating scale instruments and get more precise knowledge about such subjective continua by applying psychophysical methods. There is available in the literature information which would be useful for devising scales with logical rationales and sound empirical bases. (2) Until we determine why different methods lead to somewhat different scales, "a rigorous operational approach in interpreting and using variously derived scales seems indicated" (Dudek, 1959, p. 547).

IV. RESEARCH DESIGN IN SELF-CONCEPT STUDIES

A. Research Designs Appropriate for Tests of Phenomenological Personality Theories

Of course adequate research includes much more than valid measuring instruments. We turn now to some of these broader methodological issues.

Some persons feel that the methodological requirements of phenomenological theory are peculiar to that type of theory. That is, they feel that the scientific methods of the phenomenologist *must* differ from those which can be used and are appropriate to testing other kinds of psychological theory (see Spence, 1944).

In examining this controversy, we assume that theoretical propositions in psychology are always of the *if-then* variety, in which observable behavior is predicted or "explained" as a function of observable variables that are external to the subject and/or characteristic of the subject. The behavior variables are often called the observable consequents, or dependent variables; and the environmental or subject variables of which the behavior is supposedly a function are often called observable antecedents, or independent variables. The word antecedent seems to imply a variable which is temporally prior to the behavior, a variable which in imprecise, ordinary speech might be called a "cause" of the behavior. This implication is correct in some instances, e.g., presenting a light of specified physical characteristics is temporally prior to and is a "cause" of *S*'s response "I see a light." However, in all areas of psychology, variables are sometimes called antecedents when their temporal priority or "causal" status cannot be unequivocally demonstrated. That is, a variable is sometimes called an observable antecedent when its usefulness as a mathematical (rather than a temporal) predictor has been established through correlational techniques.

Preceding the observable consequent behaviors, most psychologists find it necessary or desirable to insert inferred variables or theoretical constructs into the predictive "equation." From the viewpoint of theory building, the theoretical constructs or inferred variables of the phenomenological personality theorist fulfill the same role as any other sort of theoretical construct. That is, these constructs are introduced to help explain behavior variations which occur when observed environmental and objective subject characteristics are constant; and to help explain similarities of behavior which occur when external stimulation and objective characteristics of the subject are varying. And, like the theoretical constructs in any theory, those of the phenomenological personality theorist must be defined in terms of relationships between observables, if they are to be scientifically useful.

On the antecedent side, it is common in psychological theorizing to divide the observables into several classes: (1) observable characteristics of the environment, or stimuli (contemporary and past); (2) observable characteristics of the subject (contemporary and past).

Behaviorists, gestalt psychologists, and phenomenological personality theorists have all assigned importance to contemporary "stimuli." But problems arise in the definition of "stimulus," and to some it has seemed that this is one point at which the appropriate method for phenomenological personality theory becomes unique (e.g., Spence, 1944).

The argument on that point goes as follows: The phenomenological personality theorist has made it clear that he is interested in the "stimulus" from self or from environment *as the subject sees it,* rather than being concerned with the "stimulus" as it is physicalistically defined. This means that the "stimulus" *must* be inferred from *S*'s response. The necessity of defining stimuli by means of response inferences seems to some psychologists to imply that the phenomenologist must employ R-R (response-response) designs instead of the more usual S-R (stimulus-response) designs.

An overview of the studies actually done in the area of self-concept theory quickly reveals that R-R designs are, indeed, the most common. What does this situation imply?

Can one unequivocally infer "cause-effect" relationships from such R-R correlational designs? The answer is clearly negative. If phenomenological personality theorists are limited by the nature of their theory to correlations between two contemporary responses of their subjects, their theory can never lead to "cause-effect" laws.

Does the fact that stimuli must be response-inferred by phenomenological theorists necessarily restrict these theorists to such response-response correlations, so that they will never be able to state "cause-effect" relationships in the same sense as the behaviorist does?

There are two methodological problems here for any theorists, behavioristic or phenomenological. One is whether environment or subject antecedents can be specified in data language. Assuming the first problem is solvable, the second is whether the experimenter can control conditions of observation well enough to establish the temporal priority of the observable antecedents, i.e., whether he can justify the interpretation that the observable antecedent "causes" the observable consequent.

Verplanck (1954) has offered an analysis of the "stimulus" which is helpful in comparing phenomenological theory and general behavior theory with reference to these methodological problems. He has outlined four definitions of stimulus: Stimulus I is a part of the environment or a change in part of the environment. Stimulus II adds to Stimulus I the qualification that the environmental change becomes a stimulus only when a response of some kind is produced. Stimulus III refers to a class of environmental events which cannot be identified independently of the observation of lawful activity of the organism. This is Skinner's "stimulus" term. Stimulus IV adds to Stimulus II hypothetical or inferential stimuli such as the movement-produced stimuli of Guthrie, or of Dollard and Miller. Verplanck remarks (p. 286), "Such inference-backward to quasi-independent variables in behavior seems to be characteristic of the work of many behavior theorists. . . . It is not impertinent to ask whether, since this is so regularly the case, will it ever be possible to develop a science of behavior in which laws relating data-language stimuli to data-language responses can be found. Is it necessarily the case that 'stimuli' become response-inferred concepts, bearing no necessary relationship to what is put in front of the organism?"

Verplanck's (1954) analysis of the stimulus in behavioristic learning theories makes it clear that the phenomenological theorist is not unique in having difficulties in defining his antecedents in terms of data language. Stimuli are, it seems, response-inferred constructs in all sorts of psychological theories. Thus, no fundamentally new methodological problems for phenomenology seem to be implied by our analysis of the antecedent up to this point.

Let us carry the analysis further, however. First let us note, as Jessor (1956) has pointed out, that "stimulus" characteristics can be defined (inferred) from the responses made by two classes of persons. (1) The experimenter defines the stimulus through his own observing responses, and such defining observations can presumably be repeated by other experimenters. In this instance we say that the stimulus antecedent is defined in data language. Let us call this stimulus inferred from the experimenter's response $Stim_E$. (2) The "stimulus" values which variations in $Stim_E$ have for the subject must be inferred from the subject's perceptual responses. Let us call the stimulus as inferred from the subject's response $Stim_S$. One way of looking at classical perception experiments is to say that we relate $Stim_E$ (stimulus as defined by the experimenter's response) to $Stim_S$ (stimulus as inferred from the subject's response). Both psychophysicists and gestalt psychologists have done many experiments of this sort. It is obvious that we usually call them "stimulus-response" experiments. Although the antecedent is response-inferred, it is called "stimulus" because it is inferred from the experimenter's, not the subject's, response. We certainly have here a situation in which both the antecedent ($Stim_E$) and the consequent (subject's response, from which $Stim_S$ is inferred) can be given in data language.

Consider now that the behavioristic psychologist has actually established "stimulus"-

response laws of the sort just described, e.g., he has obtained *S*'s subjective brightness responses to a series of light stimuli of measured energy value. Now he is in a position to go on to use $Stim_E$ in further experiments, involving other predicted behavioral consequents in which he is theoretically interested. For example, he can present *S* with one value of $Stim_E$ and condition him to give a galvanic skin response (GSR) to it. From learning theory he predicts that, if he presents other values of $Stim_E$, the generalization of the galvanic skin response will follow a gradient of similarity along the $Stim_E$ dimension. He feels that it is sensible to make the prediction partly on the basis of the already established function which relates $Stim_E$ to $Stim_S$. If his prediction is confirmed, he feels that he has another "stimulus"-response, "cause-effect" law. Only to the extent that he has carried out such procedures can he correctly speak of "cause-effect" relationships between separately defined stimuli and responses.

How does this apply to the questions in which the phenomenologist is interested? Typically, the gestalt psychologist interested in perception has not carried his procedure beyond the first kind of "stimulus"-response experiments, establishing relationships between $Stim_E$ patterns and $Stim_S$ as inferred from *S*'s verbal response. There is nothing in his theoretical orientation which would prevent him from going on to the second kind of experiment described above, however.

A hypothetical example will illustrate how necessary it can be to establish a $Stim_E$-$Stim_S$ relationship before trying to predict relationships between $Stim_E$ and other behaviors. Suppose the experimenter has established a discriminative GSR to patterns containing curved lines as contrasted to patterns containing only straight lines. To test generalization, he presents two parallel straight lines with radiating additional straight lines. $Stim_E$ is defined in terms of the *E*'s responses in preparing and measuring the stimulus pattern of straight lines. *S* gives a GSR to the straight line pattern. Why? To explain or predict *S*'s behavior in this instance one must utilize $Stim_S$, *not* $Stim_E$, i.e., one needs to know that the *S* would say these parallel lines ($Stim_E$) look curved to him ($Stim_S$). If that had been established prior to the conditioning experiment, one could, as in the case of the brightness conditioning experiment, say that one had demonstrated cause-effect relationships between independently defined stimuli and responses. And in this case it would be particularly pertinent to use $Stim_S$ as the basis of prediction.

But what about the phenomenological personality theorist? Insofar as he is interested in the subject's phenomenal view of the environment, it seems that the logic of the perception experiments would apply to him. The difference lies in the practical difficulties in implementing this logic.

First of all, there are probably greater practical problems in establishing useful $Stim_E$ categories for the sorts of complex environmental patterns in which the phenomenological personality theorist is interested. Secondly, the practical difficulties of making the experimenter's stimulus-defining responses public and repeatable may be greater, due to the complexity of the environmental patterns which seem theoretically relevant (e.g., parental treatments of the subject). And of course the practical difficulties of systematically presenting various values of any $Stim_E$ category would be much greater for the phenomenological personality theorist than for the psychophysicist or for the gestalt psychologist who is interested in visual perception. Nevertheless, such studies should be undertaken. Nothing about the theory necessarily implies that such studies are theoretically irrelevant or impossible in principle.

When we turn to the second kind of experiment in which $Stim_E$ antecedents (and therefore $Stim_S$) are related to theoretically relevant responses of the subject, we find again that the practical difficulties are greater for the phenomenological personality theorist. For one thing, individual differences may be much greater and may occur more commonly in the $Stim_E$-$Stim_S$ relationships of the complex sort which interest the phenomenological personality theorist. Furthermore, it is not clear how one can set up general criteria (comparable to the establishment of *S*s' visual normality prior to the conditioning experiment described above), by which one can know that the $Stim_E$-$Stim_S$ function obtained on one subject will quite probably apply to another subject. It seems, therefore, that the phenomenological theorist must use the same subject in exploring the $Stim_E$-$Stim_S$ relationship that he uses in a further study which tests an hypothesis about the relationship between $Stim_E$ (therefore $Stim_S$) and a theoretically relevant response.

For example, the experimenter might first establish that Stimulus Person 1 ($Stim_{E1}$) and Stimulus Person 2 ($Stim_{E2}$) are regarded by the subject as respectively a friend of his ($Stim_{S1}$) and a mere acquaintance ($Stim_{S2}$). The experimenter could then test the hypothesis that a subject's self-rating behavior on a stated instrument is more affected by evaluations of him which allegedly come from Person 1 (friend) than by evaluations of him which allegedly come from Person 2 (acquaintance). One cannot safely assume that the same actual stimulus persons, $Stim_{E1}$ and $Stim_{E2}$ would be viewed as friend and acquaintance by another *S*. Therefore the $Stim_E$-$Stim_S$ relationship would have to be separately established for a second subject before going on to test the hypothesis with him.

Contemporary Characteristics of the Subjects

The behaviorist, if he wishes to, can enter into his *if-then* statements some observable characteristics of the subject such as age, sex, or IQ. In the learning equations of Hull (1951), for example, individual or species differences are to appear as constants. Such variables would be consistent with an objective, behavioristic approach.

The phenomenologist, on the other hand (if he is consistently phenomenological) must use the *subject's view* of his own characteristics in his lawful *if-then* statements. This point has sometimes been said to differentiate the methodology required by phenomenological theories from the methodology required by behavioristic theories. Does it?

First, we note that in either case an R-R design is implied, i.e., a subject's characteristic or response is correlated with a behavior of that subject. But in the case of the objectively observable subject characteristic used by the behaviorist as an antecedent, it may seem that the experimenter defines it by his own responses; while the subject's view of himself which the phenomenologist uses as antecedent is defined in terms of the subject's responses. This differentiation cannot be defended, however, because the operations used to define subject antecedents are essentially the same for the phenomenologist and the behavior theorist. In both cases the experimenter specifies what observations of the subject he has made and under what conditions. For example, in determining an objective characteristic like IQ, the behaviorist asks specified questions and records and scores the subject's replies. In determining the subject's view of his own ability, the experimenter also asks specific questions and records and scores the subject's replies. If the behaviorist wishes to infer that IQ indexes ability, or if the phenomenologist wishes to infer that the subject's description of himself indexes his self concept of his ability, both are faced with the requirement of establishing the construct validity of their instrument. In any event, neither the R-R design of the behaviorist nor the R-R design of the phenomenologist is sufficiently controlled to permit the conclusion that "cause-effect" relationships have been established. Underwood (1957) has made very clear that the use of subject variables as antecedents necessarily involves ambiguities in interpreting the obtained results.

In addition to the necessary ambiguities associated with R-R designs, there is much danger of artifactual contamination between the two measures being correlated. Probably such contamination has occurred frequently and is more difficult to avoid in the studies of the phenomenological personality theorist than in studies of behavioristic psychologists. This merely implies the need for greater precaution in establishing operationally independent measures for the antecedent responses (from which *S*'s self concept is inferred), and the consequent responses. It does not seem to imply that a fundamental difference must obtain between behavioristic and phenomenological research.

Past Environmental Conditions, Stimuli, or Subject Characteristics

Phenomenological personality theorists have often been labeled "ahistorical" with the implication that studies involving past antecedents for present behavior are inappropriate to these theories. However, it is clear from an examination of these theories that they are by no means ahistorical, so genetic research designs are in order.

The problems of defining past environmental or past subject characteristics in historical studies are in principle the same as those we have already discussed in connection with defining contemporaneous antecedent environmental or subject characteristics.

One fact about the studies which have actually been done to test genetic propositions should be noted. Most researchers who are interested in historical propositions have used R-R research designs in which two *contemporaneous* responses are correlated. For example, the young adult's current view of his parents' opinions of him is correlated with his present report of his self concept. Such a design is an inappropriate expedient for exploring the influence of the parents' earlier opinions upon the child's self concept. The design may yield interesting exploratory information on *S*'s current view of parent and self, but it does not test an historical hypothesis in which the researcher was primarily interested.

All in all, we do not believe that *in principle* the testing of phenomenological theories requires a methodologically distinct approach from that which is appropriate to testing more behavioristic theories. Although R-R correlational designs may be easier, and may even be the only possible kind for a given proposition, controlled antecedent-consequent studies are as necessary and appropriate in testing phenomenological theory as in testing behavioristic theories.

B. Common Faults in Research Designs Used in Self-Concept Studies

Specifications for controlled research design have been discussed in numerous places. Among the most recent and directly applicable to this area of research are Underwood's (1957) and Campbell's (1957) analyses. The former covers a wide range of research designs, and as we said above, it demonstrates effectively the limitations and difficulties encountered when trying to use subject variables as independent variables. Campbell's analytical summary of experimental designs has been developed with special reference to investigations performed in social settings.

There are so many particular ways in which research designs can be inadequately controlled that space does not permit a detailed analysis here. However, one can make the general statement that the designs of the majority of researches in the area of self-concept theory have been uncontrolled in one or more important respects. In addition to unsolved problems of measurement already discussed, we list below the most common classes of methodological difficulties found in studies concerning the self concept.

1. The method used is often so vaguely indicated as to prevent analysis and make replication impossible.

2. In some studies there are not enough different control groups to hold constant or account for all the important irrelevant variables, so one cannot conclude that the dependent variable is a function of the alleged independent variable. Frequently no information is given as to matching or randomizing of groups. Thus in many studies one cannot pinpoint just which factors may afford alternate interpretations of the findings.

3. The use of demographic or sociological independent variables which have unknown relevance to psychological variables precludes clear psychological interpretations of obtained associations.

4. In many studies there is a strong possibility of artifactual contamination between independent and dependent variables, due to overlapping instruments, failure to use blind judgments, effects of common response sets, etc. Artifactual contamination is especially likely to occur when two-part scores are used to measure either or both variables.

5. Various types of overgeneralization occur. In their conclusions and discussions, *E*s sometimes do not respect the limitations imposed by their restricted hypotheses, measuring instruments, groups, and procedures. In some studies it appears that psychological generalizations are based on findings of unclear statistical significance. This is due to *E*'s failure to adhere to commonly accepted statistical conventions.

6. Most studies have been one-shot affairs with no replication or even cross-validation of instruments. It is probable that some of the statistically significant findings are actually due to chance and could not be replicated. Perhaps some of the significant findings may depend on particular idiosyncrasies of procedure and instrument which are theoretically irrelevant. And of course null findings obtained from a single study are uninterpretable.

7. Even though cross-sectional R-R studies cannot support "cause-effect" inferences, they could, if properly controlled and based on enough responses, afford a factor-analytic interpretation. Unfortunately, such an ideal situation rarely occurs among the actual studies.

For a detailed discussion of how these faults manifest themselves in many different studies, the reader should consult Wylie (1961). Unfortunately, in looking over the researches on the self concept which have come out since that book was published, we cannot conclude that a significant improvement in research designs has occurred.

V. RESEARCHES ON THE SELF CONCEPT[1]

A. MAJOR CLASSES OF PUBLISHED STUDIES

We turn now to a consideration of the research bearing on self-concept theories. As we have stressed, the theories are in many ways ambiguous, incomplete, and overlapping. Therefore it is not possible to organize the relevant empirical studies according to an outline of major theoretical principles. Instead, in our earlier review (Wylie, 1961) we found it convenient to group the avail-

[1] This chapter was written in the summer of 1963. The author has examined the published literature up through January, 1965, especially as it pertains to the three empirical topics discussed in detail in this chapter, viz., sex differences and the self concept; effects on the self concept of experimentally induced success or failure; and insightfulness of the self concept and "adjustment." These more recent publications which have come to the author's attention do not materially affect the generalizations and conclusions presented in this section.

able studies of the conscious self concept according to the following outline, which we present here to give the reader an idea of the range of published research.

1. Descriptive studies of the development of the self concept.

2. Studies of the variables which are presumed to influence the development and current characteristics of the self concept (i.e., studies in which the self concept is the inferred consequent).

a. parent-child interaction
b. social interaction (other than parent-child)
   i. sex and role as related to self concept
   ii. peer interaction and the self concept
   iii. self concepts and friendship choice
   iv. self-regard and susceptibility to persuasion
c. body characteristics
d. counseling and psychotherapy
e. lobotomy
f. experimentally induced success and failure
   i. experiments in which *S*'s personality characteristics are devaluated
   ii. experiments in which *S*s are made to fail on experimental tasks
g. learning

3. Studies in which the self concept is related to behavior. This category includes studies of behaviors which are presumed to depend on the self concept (i.e., the self concept is inferred as the intervening variable immediately preceding the behavior), and studies in which the direction of influence between the self concept and other behavior variables is not specified.

a. performance in learning tasks
b. performance under experimentally induced success and failure
c. self-regard and "adjustment," using the following criteria of adjustment:
   i. degrees of diagnosed pathology
   ii. behavior ratings and measurements (by teachers, authorities, peers, etc.)
   iii. projective test scores
   iv. scores on self-report instruments
d. self-acceptance and acceptance of others
e. self-regard and ethnocentrism or authoritarianism
f. self-regard and level-of-aspiration behavior

4. In addition to the studies of the self concept per se, a considerable number of researches on insightfulness of the self concept have appeared. In these studies, "insight" is usually defined as the degree of agreement between some kind of self report by the subject and a report by another observer concerning the same attribute of the subject. Insight has been related to the following major classes of dependent variables. It is apparent that all these dependent variables may plausibly be considered to be varying indices of the degree of *S*'s personal "adjustment."

a. adjustment (or personality variables associated with adjustment) as inferred from:
   i. *S*'s self-reports
   ii. an external observer's diagnosis
   iii. a score based on a combination of *a* and *b*
   iv. *S*'s having undergone psychotherapy
b. defensive behavior, inferred from *S*'s responses on a nonprojective instrument or a projective technique
c. competence as a therapist
d. success in a vocation

B. Consideration of Some Published Studies in Three Areas

Altogether, hundreds of studies have appeared. But substantive findings have been disappointing because serious flaws in measurement and research design render a great many studies inconclusive; and wide variations in instruments and other aspects of procedure make it impossible to compare researches directly and synthesize their results. Since we cannot attempt a comprehensive review and evaluation here, we selected a few of the above categories for discussion, our choice being based on two considerations:

There are enough studies in the area to yield at least preliminary conclusions, *and/or*

Studies in the area illustrate well some methodological difficulties which should be guarded against in future research.

Our discussion is organized around the following categories, and where enlightening we introduce research more recent than that in our earlier review.

1. sex differences in self concept
2. experimentally induced success and failure
3. insightfulness of the self concept and "adjustment"

1. Sex Differences and the Self Concept

The studies of sex differences in the actual self concept and in self-regard have been directed mainly toward the following questions: (1) To what degree have males and females accepted particular sex-role stereotypes as applicable to men (or to women) in general? (2) What are the traits or attributes of these stereotypes? (3) Is there a difference between the over-all favorability of the male and female stereotypes? (4) To what degree have males and females accepted sex role stereotypes as applicable to their own actual-self concepts? (5) Apart from the exploration of stereotypes and their personal applicability, are there differences in over-all favorability in the reported actual-self concepts of males and females? (6) Are there differences between male and female self concepts along specified content dimensions?

So far as the ideal-self concept is concerned, the studies have mainly concerned these questions: (1) In what respects, if any, do males and females feel that society's expectations of them differ? (2) What discrepancies, if any, occur between *S*s' perceptions of society's expectations of them and their personal ideals for themselves? (3) If such personal-social conflicts exist, do *S*s see themselves as conforming to their own ideals more than to society's expectations, or vice versa? Space precludes discussing researches on the ideal-self concept, which we have summarized elsewhere (Wylie, 1961).

The studies we consider here are arranged according to the questions we have stated concerning the actual-self concept.

Three studies by McKee and Sherriffs have explored questions concerning male and female stereotypes (McKee & Sherriffs, 1957, 1959; Sherriffs & McKee, 1957). When they used a generalized rating scale, they found that both male and female college students reported that males were superior to females. This finding was accentuated when no neutral response step was provided. Two other methods also led to the conclusion that both sexes have less favorable concepts of the female: (1) forced and unforced responses to adjective check lists; (2) coding for favorability some open-ended lists made by *S*s to describe males and females. There is some suggestion that this bias is stronger among females.

Lynn (1959) has referred to some studies of an earlier date than those reviewed here which suggest that there is a progressive increase from age 8 in the unfavorability of the female stereotype.

Is the female's self concept like the female stereotype? Is it less favorable than the male's self concept?

McKee and Sherriffs (1959) used empirical means for establishing sex stereotypes and found that Women's Real Self (a group measure) was more sex-typed than Men's Real Self. This was true despite the fact that the female stereotype was more undesirable than the male stereotype.

In the review mentioned above, Lynn (1959) reports some results which suggest that the female's acceptance of the unfavorable stereotype as personally applicable increases from age 8.

On the other hand, in the studies reviewed below, which were not particularly related to the question of stereotypes, there does not seem to be any clear trend in sex differences in self-favorability with age. We consider first the researches concerned with over-all self regard.

Amatora (1957) applied her 22-variable Child Personality Scale to 250 boys and 250 girls, with 100 *S*s at each age level 9 through 13 years of age. She presents a profile for each trait rather than statistical significance tests of any kind. On seven trait scales, girls at all five age levels rated themselves more favorably than did the boys at the respective age levels; on five scales, girls rated themselves more favorably than did the boys at every age level except 11 years. There were no scales on which the boys' self-ratings were consistently more favorable than girls' across four or five age levels. On all but two scales, boys' and girls' ratings came closer to one another at age 13 than they had been at age 12; but we cannot attach psychological significance to these age trends (even if they were known to be statistically significant) because *E* used different groups at each age level, and we cannot be sure they were matched across age levels on relevant variables. It does seem clear that the girls' self-ratings showed more over-all favorability across a wide variety of evaluative dimensions. (A published manual on this scale is referred to in Amatora [1956].)

Among 251 fourth- and sixth-grade children tested by Perkins (1958b), using a 50-item *Q*-sort, girls had significantly greater self-ideal congruence than did boys. (Some information on the construction of this instrument and its reliability is given in Perkins, 1958a, 1958b.)

In Engel's (1959) study, one group of boys and girls was tested in eighth grade and again in tenth grade, while the second group was tested in tenth grade and again in twelfth grade. The 172 *S*s *Q*-sorted items which had been prejudged for positive or negative tone, and self-sorts were scored for "positiveness" according to the prejudged favorability values of the items. In two of the comparisons, the boys had more positive self concepts, while in the other two comparisons, the girls had the more positive self concepts. Apparently none of these sex differences was statistically significant. (A microfilm reference on this instrument is cited.)

Turner and Vanderlippe (1958) obtained no sex differences in self-ideal congruence in 175 college student *S*s. They used Butler and Haigh's (1954) *Q*-sort items. (Some reliability and validity information is summarized in Wylie, 1961.)

Contrasting with the results of Turner and Vanderlippe, Jervis (1959) found slightly but significantly larger discrepancies between actual-self and ideal-self among 294 college women than among 556 college men. These larger discrepancies stemmed from the higher ideal-self descriptions of the women, as the actual-self descriptions of the sex groups were nearly identical. (Some reliability information but no validity information is given concerning the specially devised Self Description Inventory used in the study.)

Using still another technique, Kohn and Fiedler (1961) found results differing from either of the preceding studies. Forty high-school freshmen, 40 second-semester college freshmen, and 40 college seniors, all from upper-middle-class homes, received esteem scores obtained by summing their self-ratings from 20 six-point bipolar scales. According to a factor analysis these scales are highly evaluative in nature. At each age level, the females received higher esteem scores than did the males, and the total male-female difference was significant at better than the .05 level. (Some reliability information, but no validity information other than from the factor analysis is given.)

It might appear that, among children from 9–13 years of age, girls' self reports are more favorable than are boys' self reports while thereafter no clear trends with age are obtained. However, we must remember that methodological limitations characterized all of the studies, and that each investigator used a different instrument. This means that comparisons among the studies is impossible, either as a basis for general conclusions where there is apparent agreement, or to determine probable causes for apparent contradictions. Most importantly, we have no way of knowing whether a dimension of "over-all self-regard" is being indexed by any of these multi-item instruments; or even whether such a dimension is an operationally meaningful construct.

Among college students, the findings seem more definitely to confirm the occurrence of a commonly accepted stereotype of "women in general" which is less favorable than that for "men in general."

Are there interpretable sex differences along specified dimensions, if not with respect to over-all self-regard? In the study by Amatora (1957) cited above, a graphic profile is given for each of 22 traits, showing sex differences at each of five age levels for that trait. However, no significance tests for separate traits are given, nor can we make them from the published data.

In another study with children, Kagan, Hosken, and Watson (1961) prepared 66 pictures, six pairs to represent each of 11 trait dimensions. For example, a strong rabbit and a weak rabbit represented the strong-weak dimension. In a personal interview, each of 98 children, 6 to 8 years of age, indicated which picture in each pair represented himself, and (in a separate part of the interview) which picture in each pair represented "bad" and "good' respectively. Boys in comparison to girls labeled themselves stronger, larger, more dangerous, darker, more angular. Of these traits, two were labeled good and three bad. Girls and boys agreed on the evaluative ratings of the traits. (No information on the reliability and validity of the instrument is presented.)

Applying a 13-item "body-concept" scale to 306 college student *S*s, Calden, Lundy, and Schlafer (1959) found that females expressed less satisfaction with the attractiveness of their bodies and less satisfaction with their facial features than did males. Incidentally, the particular ways in which both male and female *S*s wished their physical characteristics could be changed seemed to coincide with the American cultural standard, as the latter might be judged from everyday observations. (No information is given on the reliability or validity of the instrument used.)

In a study which could also be classified as a research on insight, Talland (1958) examined the ranks which men and women in therapy groups estimated that other group members would assign to them on five traits: (a) leadership displayed in the group's work; (b) contribution to group discussion judged by its value; (c) dominance of, or influence upon group discussion without regard to its value; (d) general popularity in the group; (e) friendliness shown to group members in general. The ranks which others actually did assign men and women on each of these traits did not differ (except that women in mixed groups were judged to be more friendly than men). However, with respect to each of the traits, women on the average underestimated the rank they actually received, while men overestimated the rank they actually received. The differences were significant for each trait except Friendliness. *S*s were adult outpatients at a London hospital.

Using a modified Gough Adjective Check List, Sarbin and Rosenberg (1955) found that men exceeded women in checking such adjectives as resourceful, mature, logical, adventurous, realistic, deliberate, efficient. Women exceeded men in checking feminine, emotional, affectionate, pleasant, temperamental. Groups were not specified as being matched, however; and the greater response total of the men was not controlled in the statistical analysis. Furthermore, some of the multiple comparisons may yield significant differences by chance alone; and no cross-validation to check on this is reported. (See Wylie, 1961, for a summary of published reliability and validity information.)

In a somewhat similar study using a

much smaller *N,* Merenda and Clark (1960) used the Activity Vector Analysis, consisting of 81 words by which *S*s described themselves. Although they found some sex differences, their results warrant no conclusions because they give no assurance concerning comparability of sex groups, controls for possible differences in total response output between groups, or cross-validation of statistically significant findings from multiple comparisons.

Kosa, Rachiele, and Schommer (1962) obtained self-ratings along several dimensions from 455 native-white college students, divided into higher and lower socioeconomic groups. No significance tests are given for the sex comparisons; but using their data we find the following. Although low-socioeconomic-level females had insignificantly higher OSU Aptitude Test scores than did low-socioeconomic-level males, the mean of the females' estimates of their own ability is lower than the mean of the males' estimates of their own ability. Among upper-socioeconomic-level *S*s, the females had significantly higher aptitude scores than did the males, and again their mean self-rated ability is lower, although this latter difference is not significant. Altogether, this study makes possible 20 comparisons between the sexes (10 traits within each socioeconomic group). In addition to the one significant difference in self-rated ability, we find four other significant differences. Only two of these concerned the same trait at each socioeconomic level, viz., females at each level rated themselves as less temperamental than males rated themselves. Without cross-validation, we cannot say how many of these multiple comparisons are "significant" by chance alone.

Self-evaluations on ability dimensions have been explored by other investigators in addition to Kosa *et al.* (1962). In a study by Wylie (1963), 408 white boys and 331 white girls from seventh, eighth, and ninth grades estimated: (a) whether they were in the top half of their home rooms in the ability to do schoolwork; (b) whether they would have the ability to do college work. The groups were comparable on socioeconomic level, and the girls were slightly superior on mean IQ from the SRA Primary Mental Abilities Test. Sex comparisons were made at each of nine IQ levels. At the middle IQ levels, where there might be ambiguity in *S*s' self-knowledge concerning the questions asked, consistently more boys than girls gave self-favorable estimates. (No information is given on the reliability or validity of the questionnaire.)

Smith and Clifton (1962) examined sex differences in self concept concerning performances they had just made in five motor skills: walking, running, catching, throwing, standing broad jump. Unfortunately the volunteer samples of 23 male and 37 female college students could not be considered representative of their respective sex groups, because each was highly loaded with skilled sports performers. Thus, even though the male *S*s rated their performances more favorably than the female *S*s rated theirs, no general conclusions can be drawn concerning sex differences in this kind of self concept. (No information is given on the reliability or validity of the questionnaire.)

When we examine all the studies which explored sex differences along various fairly restricted self-concept dimensions, we quickly see their essential lack of comparability, since there is virtually no overlap among the dimensions studied by various researchers, and methods of exploring the dimensions vary widely. Perhaps the findings of Kosa *et al.* (1962) and of Wylie (1963) may be very roughly compared in that female *S*s had somewhat lower opinions of their academic ability despite their being equal or superior to a comparable male group on academic aptitude tests.

From a theoretical viewpoint, studies of sex differences along separate dimensions seem defensible and potentially fruitful. But more attention should be paid to the theoretical reason why girls and boys should be expected to differ in self concept with respect to the particular dimension chosen.

2. Effects on the Self Concept of Experimentally Induced Success or Failure

Two general assumptions underlie the studies in which *S* is made to feel he has failed or is personally inadequate: (1) The level of self-regard is learned through a combination of rewards and punishments for one's actions and self characteristics. The person learns some things about himself through success or failure in manipulating the physical environment and some things from the reactions of others to him. (2) A person's level of self-regard is of great importance in predicting his behavior. These assumptions imply the possibility of manipulating failure and success variables in the laboratory, and this is one of the few areas in which any truly experimental work has been done.

The experimenter may make the person fail or experience devaluation on any of a wide variety of tasks or traits. In practice, these have included specific puzzle tasks, alleged intelligence tests, alleged indicators of *S*'s emotional stability, and evaluation of *S*'s social characteristics and personal acceptability to others. The degree of importance which *S* assigns to the tasks or traits has evidently differed considerably from study to study. It seems reasonable that experimental effects would vary as a function of the type of induced failure or devaluation, and its importance to *S;* but these factors have not been systematically explored.

Another variable of probable relevance is the source of the alleged failure or devaluation. In some experiments *E* has judged *S*'s failure, presumably on the basis of norms, or *S* has discovered for himself that he cannot accomplish the task. In other experiments, friends, acquaintances, or participants in experimental discussion groups have supposedly judged the subject.

Self-concept theorists make several general assumptions about possible outcomes of failure, success, devaluation, or high valuation. These assumptions do not clearly imply specific predictions, unfortunately. It is expected that *S* will try to maintain or retrieve a favorable self-attitude. On the other hand, *S* supposedly strives to maintain his basic self concept, i.e., he will resist information which is discrepant from his longstanding views about himself. This may mean that he rejects highly favorable reports about himself if they are inconsistent with his self picture. Furthermore, a single artificial failure or success in an experimental setting would not necessarily be expected to have much effect in counteracting much previous learning about the self. Therefore null results are of possible theoretical interest, but without replication they are uninterpretable. Thus far, no study has been replicated.

If *S* fails to maintain a favorable self attitude in the face of induced failure or devaluation, he may lower his self-report. Some *E*s have predicted that he will lower it mainly or entirely on a scale strictly pertinent to the failed task. Others have suggested that he will also lower his self-report on other dimensions which are related to the task, or even lower a very global estimate of self-esteem. Some investigators have evidently assumed that failure on an academic task, for example, will lower self-esteem on an instrument tapping numerous nonacademic personality characteristics. Much remains to be done to develop an explicit rationale for predicting how widely and along what dimensions the lowering of self-regard should be expected to spread.

We also need to refine our rationale concerning the type of person who will respond to failure by lowering his self-report.

So far as measuring changes in self-regard is concerned, we are plagued with problems of interpretation. To what extent does *S*'s change represent mainly a shift in the range of the rating scale he tends to use for self and others, rather than representing a revision in his feelings about himself?

Perhaps *S* will try to preserve high self-regard by defensive behavior. He may devaluate the source of the unfavorable or failure information. He may claim that the task is unimportant, or the group is unappealing to him. He may blame others rather than himself for his failure. He may increase other behaviors which have yielded him self-esteem in the past. All these possibilities have been explored, and others could be hypothesized. The question arises: What type of person will be most likely to use one or another of these defensive maneuvers?

The available experiments in this area are not neatly classifiable according to the points of rationale just outlined. Each study is based on a somewhat different combination of these assumptions. Of the 19 studies we have examined, we choose four here as representative of the assumptions, methods, and problems in this area.

An experiment in which S's personality characteristics are devaluated—In an experiment by Harvey, Kelley, and Shapiro (1957), *Ss* were evaluated on five social characteristics, and the predicted outcomes concerned *Ss*' ways of defending themselves against unfavorable evaluations. The experimenters used a twelve-cell design, in which each *S* was experimentally exposed to evaluations of himself which were at one of four degrees of unfavorableness, and were attributed either to a stranger or to a close acquaintance. (Four of the twelve cells contained control *Ss* for the first two degrees of unfavorableness.) Experimental *Ss* were given an opportunity to (a) devaluate the source; (b) recall the source's evaluations as more favorable than they actually were; and/or (c) deny that the alleged source was responsible for the evaluation. Control *Ss* rated another *S*, acquaintance or stranger, twice. They were tested later for their perceptions of discrepancies between the source's alleged evaluations of them and their remembered self-ratings.

The results are complex and contain some puzzling exceptions. The general trend is for the above-mentioned three kinds of "defensive" reactions to the source to be greater the more informed the source and the more negative his evaluations of *S*. Experimental *Ss* showed changes in self-evaluation in the unfavorable direction under all conditions, which were significantly greater than changes in control *Ss*' self-ratings. However, there is no evidence that these changes were a function of either of the independent variables, acquaintance with source or degree of unfavorableness of the source's evaluations. The authors think that the changes in self-evaluation, then, probably do not represent real shifts in self concept, but may reflect merely the manner of *expressing* the self-evaluations (i.e., a shift to using a different range of the rating scale from that originally employed).

Experiments in which Ss were made to fail on experimental tasks—In a second group of experiments, *S* was made to fail on an experimental task. Usually the situation was set up so that his failure indicated lack of intellectual or perceptual-motor abilities. These experiments were concerned with the effects of failure upon *S*'s evaluation of his performance on the task, and upon his self-evaluations in other areas. Some of these investigations attempted to explore the conditions under which failure would affect self-evaluation. In this connection, both experimental conditions and the characteristics of the *Ss* have been examined in some of these experiments.

Howard and Berkowitz (1958) studied *Ss*' performance on a simulated air strategy problem which was presented to *S* as a test of "effective intelligence." The experimenters assumed that *S*'s reactions toward evaluations of his performance would be affected by a need for self-enhancement, and by a need for subjective certainty or accuracy. They utilized an analysis of variance design with two conditions of wanting to succeed at a task (as reported by *S*), and five conditions of evaluation of *S*s' performance by *O*s: (1) three *O*s giving moderately favorable evaluation, one giving high evaluation; (2) three *O*s giving moderately favorable evaluation, one giving low evaluation; (3) three *O*s giving moderately favorable evaluation; (4) one *O* giving high evaluation; (5) one *O* giving low evaluation. One dependent variable was *S*'s assessment of how accurate *O*s' evaluations of him were. An *O* whose evaluations deviated from the consensus of other *O*s was seen as probably being in error even if his evaluations were highly favorable. The magnitude of this effect depended upon the extent to which the deviate *O*'s evaluations frustrated *S*'s desire for a favorable evaluation. When the frustrating *O* was the only *O*, high-aspiration *S*s did not question his accuracy as much as when there were reality grounds for questioning *O*'s accuracy (i.e., when three other *O*s were more favorable). Thus both reality considerations and desire for self-enhancement were operative in *S*s' assessment of *O*s' accuracy. (We should note, however, that *S*'s *expected* performance correlated with his *desired* performance, so one cannot say to what extent the effects are associated with disruptions of wishes, expectations, or both.)

An experiment involving the effects of one failure upon other aspects of self-regard is that of Diggory and Magaziner (1959). They addressed their experiment to the following general questions: Will failure in regard to one characteristic lower the person's self-estimate about his other characteristics? Will it lower his global self-evaluation? If the effects of failure do spread in this way, is this spread dependent on the characteristic in which the person failed? They hypothesized that high self-evaluation is dependent on one's perception that his capacities are adequate to the achievement of his goals. If a person considers a given capacity particularly important (instrumental) to goal achievement, and if that capacity is devaluated in a failure experiment, the person will tend to lower his self-ratings on other capacities, and even to lower his global self-rating. But if a given capacity is not considered by a person to be instrumental to goal achievement, experimental failure with respect to this capacity will not affect the person's ratings of his other capacities or of his global adequacy.

To test this hypothesis, the experimenters asked male college students to rate themselves on five capacities and on their overall adequacy of functioning. Two groups were chosen, one containing *S*s who had rated themselves extremely low on one capacity, and one containing *S*s who had rated themselves extremely high on one capacity. *S*s were informed that they could get into an exclusive, desirable "Career Liaison" group if tests showed that they had all five supposedly equally important capacities to the required extent.

The *S*s were given the opportunity to rerate themselves on the five capacities in the light of the particular goal they were about to seek. These ratings were used as the initial (prefailure) ratings.

No check was made as to whether *S*s accepted the idea that all five capacities were equally important to achieving the goal of getting into and succeeding in the Career Liaison group. In any event, Diggory and Magaziner assumed that *S* would consider his highest rated capacity more instrumental to achieving the goal (or his lowest rated capacity least instrumental). They reasoned that *S* would think, in effect, "If I have any chance of getting in and succeeding, my highest capacity will be what gets me to this goal." A measurement problem arises here in that *S*'s view of the instrumental importance of a capacity is confounded with *S*'s view of his standing on that capacity. We shall point out below the way this confusion affects possible interpretations of their results.

S was tested on the capacity he had rated

very high (or very low), and he was told he had failed this test, so tests on the other capacities would not be necessary. *S* then rerated himself on all five capacities and on his global adequacy of functioning. As predicted, *S*s who failed on a capacity on which they initially rated themselves high lowered their self-ratings on the untested as well as the tested capacities. Those who failed on a capacity on which they had initially rated themselves low did not change as many self-ratings nor change them as much as did the former group. No significant effects on global ratings were found for either group.

The authors believe these results indicate that failure on a capacity which *S* sees as most instrumental to goal achievement will affect his other self-evaluations, while failure on a noninstrumental capacity will not affect his other self-evaluations. However, another interpretation also seems possible, as we now explain.

If *S* thinks a given capacity is low before failure, his failure on the test of this capacity may simply confirm his belief in the accuracy of his self-judgment (including all his prefailure self-ratings). Therefore he would tend to repeat his initial (prefailure) self-ratings. Failure on a high-scoring capacity may, on the other hand, raise a subject's doubts as to his general accuracy in the use of the rating scales. Hence he will tend to change all his ratings. In other words, as we said above, we need an operational definition of *S*'s view of the instrumental importance of a capacity which is independent of his initial self-rating value on that capacity.

The reader may wonder also whether statistical regression effects could account for the findings, as might be the case if the two groups were not initially matched on self-ratings for the four untested capacities. However, this has been taken care of, since the groups were said to be comparable on initial self-ratings of untested capacities.

It seems reasonable that the subject's characteristics will play a role in his reactions to failure or devaluation. In particular, *S*s who have generally poor self-regard may react to failure or stressful tasks with greater anxiety than do *S*s who have generally high self-regard. On the basis of this rationale, Solley and Stagner (1956) predicted that *S*s who have generally poor self-regard will show less accuracy and speed on a task, will give more physiological indicators of anxiety, and will make comments oriented toward self rather than toward the task, when the task induces failure or the threat of failure. In a well controlled 3×3 factorial design, the independent variables were: (1) *S*s' evaluations of self on Osgood Semantic Differential Scales; (2) the number of insoluble anagrams (0, 3, or 5) presented between two sequences of soluble anagrams; (3) affective quality of anagram words (negative, neutral, positive). The dependent variables were: (1) solution times; (2) the orientation of spontaneous comments toward self or toward task; (3) changes in palmar sweating from first to last soluble anagram. Findings relevant to the present discussion are: (a) *S*s with low evaluation of self showed greater increases in solution time after failure than did *S*s with high self-evaluation. (b) In the presence of insoluble anagrams, *S*s with low self-evaluation emitted more self-referent comments, while *S*s with high self-evaluation emitted more task-referent comments. (c) On negatively toned words, *S*s with low self-evaluation showed marked increases in palmar sweating with increasing numbers of insoluble anagrams, whereas high self-evaluating *S*s showed a slight decrement in this measure.

Summary—This is one of the few areas of self psychology in which any truly experimental work has been done. Synthesis of these experimental results is risky because each study involves a unique combination of assumptions, hypotheses, procedures, and measuring instruments. Therefore, the following summarizing statements, based on 19 studies we have examined, are offered quite tentatively. Fifteen of these are reviewed in detail in Wylie (1961).

It seems that *S*s will, under certain conditions, change their self-evaluations after experimentally induced success or failure. These changes are most likely to involve self-ratings on the experimental task itself, or on the characteristic which has been evaluated, and are least likely to involve reports on global self-regard. The latter seems to be affected little if any by a single experimental failure or evaluation. There is some evidence that changes in self-rating upward after success are more frequent than are changes downward after failure.

Numerous scaling and measurement problems make the changes which do occur difficult to interpret. Findings of no change in global self-regard after a single failure are congruent with self-concept theory, but such null findings cannot be clearly interpreted without experimental replication.

Whether or not changes in self-rating occur, there may be changes in "covert" self-evaluation. However, it remains to be demonstrated that the "covert" measures validly indicate covert self-evaluation.

Changes in self-evaluation have not been the only dependent variable studied. It seems that experimental failure may also lead to various defensive behaviors such as devaluing the source of failure information, failing to recall the low evaluations accurately, engaging in behaviors which have brought self-esteem in the past, or blaming others for one's failure. In addition, there may be performance decrements on the task which threatens *S* with failure, and concomitant anxiety reactions may be seen.

Changes or lack of changes in self-ratings after failure are probably a function of other variables within the experimental procedure or within the subject. There is limited evidence to suggest that the following may be found to be associated with changes in self-evaluation or with self-blame for failure: *S*'s personality characteristics, such as his "global" level of self-regard; *S*'s test anxiety; the particular characteristics which have been devalued in the experiment; the degree to which *S* values the source of his failure or success information and feels the source is well informed. It appears that *S* is influenced by reality considerations as well as by the desire for self-enhancement. Performance decrements and anxiety indicators on the experimental task may be greater in *S*s whose "global" level of self-regard is low.

3. Insightfulness of the Self Concept and "Adjustment"

Next to researches involving self-regard, the most numerous studies relevant to self-concept theory are those which concern "insight." This term has been used in the psychological literature with a number of literary and operational meanings, and most or all of the latter have involved evaluative traits.

The lines of thought which underlie the empirical studies performed to date fall mainly into two groups: In the classical Freudian and neo-Freudian view, lack of insight is alleged to be accompanied by defensiveness and/or maladjustment when the latter is defined in terms of *S*'s experience and/or an observer's diagnosis. So far as phenomenal theorists are concerned, it sometimes seems that they, too, hold this view. On the other hand, they occasionally seem to be saying that *S* will not become anxious (and hence defensive) unless and until he becomes at least dimly aware of the disparity between his phenomenal self and the views others hold of him (Rogers, 1951). Of course, a disparity of which *S* is unaware may render him more potentially vulnerable in the sense of increasing the likelihood that a discomfort-producing discrepancy will come to his attention. But until that eventuality does occur (i.e., until at least a dim awareness of the inappropriateness or incompleteness of the self concept develops), lack of insight presumably would not lead to anxiety or defensiveness. (It may, of course, lead to maladjusted or inappropriate behavior, as judged by an external observer.)

Many workers have indicated that there is

a great deal of surplus meaning to their concept of "insight" beyond that which their operational definitions cover. We take it for granted, then, that in this sense all operational definitions need to be improved. Our comments concern methodological problems of a more restricted nature.

The most commonly used insight measurements involve combinations of two classes of variables (*S*'s reports and *O*'s reports). It is evident that the problem of construct validity of such insight measurements is even more complicated and confused than was the question of construct validity of some of the measures of self-regard which we discussed earlier.

S's self reports—To understand insight measures, we need first of all to know something about the construct validity of *S*'s reports. Many of the problems here are the same as those already detailed in Section III of this chapter. In addition, some other difficulties crop up. Since *S*'s reports may be obtained under varying instructional sets, we need empirical information and process analyses to establish what *S* is doing under the varying sets, and to what extent the same or different constructs are being tapped.

A priori theoretical considerations make plausible the idea that, even with the clearest instructions, there can be no sharp separation on *S*'s part between his private-self concept and his social-self concept. On the other hand, the work of a number of investigators shows that there are significant differences in self-concept reports obtained under private-self and social-self instructions. This matter should be systematically explored further. In any event, when instructions to *S* are loose we certainly cannot know to what extent *S* is trying to give private-self or social-self reports. Therefore we cannot determine the degree to which idiosyncratic interpretations of the instructions influence individual *S*'s insight scores and the consequent findings.

Let us suppose for the moment that instructions to *S* tell him definitely to report his social-self concept, and that he is willing and able to express his social-self concept within the limitations of the technique *E* is using. Even under these conditions, *S*'s task in an insight study is more complicated than it is in some of the simpler self-regard studies. This is true because *S*, if he is to receive a nonartifactual insight score, must have some knowledge of the characteristics of the instrument itself. That is, he must know something about the general way *O*'s test scores distribute themselves (in the case of objective tests); or he must know something about the general rating behavior of *O* (in the case of rating scales). That is, of course, a version of the problem of stereotype and individual accuracy, discussed by Cronbach (1955), and Gage and Cronbach (1955). It has been surmounted to a certain extent in some insight studies by having *S* rank himself in a specified group. This procedure rules out (1) the effect of intra-*S* differences in knowledge of the characteristics of test score distributions; and (2) the possibilities that *O*s will vary from *S*s in elevation of all their ratings, as can happen with the use of rating scales.

Another special complication of *S*'s report of his social-self concept in an insight study is due to the fact that he may be trying to estimate any one or an unknown combination of the following factors: (a) each single *O*'s opinions; (b) how the *O*s' opinions will average out, if several are to be taken; (c) the degree to which each *O* will speak for himself or will vacillate between that and an expression of his (*O*'s) idea of how "generalized others" view *S*. Although instructions could presumably be written which would tell *S* what to aim for, this would not serve to control *O*s' individual or collective behavior to fit in with *S*'s expectations. Although some researchers have recognized some of these complications, no one has succeeded in devising means for coping with them.

Discriminant validity of discrepancy scores—A second source of serious trouble involves the discriminant construct validity of the two-part insight score. Let us assume for the moment that the Self and Other components of this two-part insight score have a high degree of validity as indices of *S*'s and *O*'s concepts concerning *S*. We must still demonstrate that individual differences in "insight" reflect something more than individual differences in self-reported self-regard. For example, suppose that the defensiveness of insightful *S*s is compared to the defensiveness of noninsightful *S*s, when insight is measured in terms of a discrepancy between *S*'s and *O*s' reports about *S*. Suppose further that *S*'s self ratings are not equated between insightful and noninsightful groups. This would mean that differences in insight are confounded with differences in self-regard. If correlations between "insight" and defensiveness are obtained in studies having this confounding, the correlations might be parsimoniously interpreted as meaning that defensiveness is associated with level of self-regard rather than with level of insight.

O's reports on S—Then there are many problems of construct validity of *O*'s reports. *O*'s statements of his own personal impressions of *S* are subject to the same pitfalls which we discussed in connection with *S*'s self-reports on self-regard measures. But when *O* presumes to say not only what he thinks of *S,* but to report what others think of *S,* the situation becomes more complicated. This is so because *O*'s opinions of others' opinions of *S* may be biased through insufficient knowledge, motivational distortions, etc. When *O* relies on tests, especially projectives, he is making many assumptions concerning the validity of these tests for inferring anything about *S*'s actual characteristics and/or for inferring anything about *S*'s self concept, conscious or unconscious. Some of these assumptions are poorly supported or completely unsupported.

When we try to combine *S* and *O* variables to make an insight score, we run into further pitfalls. One of these concerns the question whether lack of insight represents *S*'s failure to try to utilize a dimension corresponding to the one used by *O;* and/or *S*'s having a different view of himself on the same dimension used by *O*. For instance, in Sears's (1936) study, *S* was most probably rating himself in the private frame of reference. Therefore, if his rating did not correspond to the pooled *O*s' ratings, we cannot know whether (a) *S* could have predicted the pooled *O*s' ratings, but he was not trying to do so; *or* (b) *S* was trying to predict the pooled *O*s' ratings, but he was unable to do so. If the latter alternative is correct, we are then faced in some studies with the question: Is *S*'s failure due to lack of insight concerning his social-self characteristics, or is it due to various methodological difficulties we have just mentioned?

Errors of method in relating insight to a dependent variable—In addition to the problem of confounding of self concept and insight, we must note several other frequently repeated methodological errors.

The most common error involves artifactual contamination between the independent and dependent variables, in the following manner. In one way or another, all investigators have used some measure of "adjustment" as their dependent variable, and many have used self-reports of *S* as their index of adjustment. Now we know from many studies that evaluative self-reports tend to intercorrelate positively. We have also said that self-reports have not usually been held constant across groups which differed in insight. These facts imply that findings from such studies may simply be artifacts of the well-known tendency for two evaluative self-reports to correlate positively. An even more serious version of this artifact occurs in a number of studies in which *the same self-report instrument* enters into the definition of both the dependent and independent variables.

A related kind of artifact may be seen in studies where insight has been related to "projection," and projection has been measured partly through *S*s' ratings of others. We know from a number of studies that *S*s' evaluative self-ratings tend to correlate positively with the evaluative ratings which those *S*s assign to others. If the groups that differ in insight also differ in self-rating, the relationships between insight and projection may simply be an artifact of the tendency for *S*s' ratings of self and of others to correlate positively. Or in some cases (e.g., Sears, 1936) there is a contamination between the criteria used for assigning *S*s to insight groups (the independent variable) and the means used to measure projection (the dependent variable).

Although we have examined almost two dozen studies of "insight," we present here only a few involving insight and "projection," as they serve to illustrate typical procedures and problems in this area.

Projection is most commonly defined operationally as attribution of traits to others. In one study, *S* was said to "project" only if he consistently attributed more of an unfavorable trait to others than the group as a whole attributed to these same others (Wylie, 1957). In another study, however, the ratings *Ss* assigned to others were simply compared across insightful and noninsightful groups, without an attempt to see if *S's* ratings of others deviated from the pooled value for those others (Sears, 1936).

Sears did not hold self-ratings constant when making his comparisons between insightful and noninsightful groups. However, it is possible, using his published data, to compare groups in which self-rating is apparently at least approximately equated between groups, while insight varies. Thus Groups A and D both rate themselves favorably on a specified trait, but A lacks insight. Groups B and C both rate themselves unfavorably on the trait, but C lacks insight. In A *vs.* D comparisons, results for only two out of four traits show the noninsightful Group A members assigning more unfavorable ratings to others than do the insightful Group D members. In B *vs.* C comparisons, also, results for only two out of four traits show noninsightful Group C members assigning more unfavorable ratings to others than do insightful Group B members. Thus, when self-rating is held approximately constant, Sears's data do *not* support the contention that "projection" is associated with lack of insight.

His puzzling, partly positive findings appear to have been artifactual in the following way: To test his hypothesis, Sears held group rating constant and varied insight by varying self rating. When noninsightful Group A (self-rating good, rating from group bad) was compared to insightful Group B (self-rating bad, rating from group bad), he found noninsightful Group A members rating others more unfavorably than did insightful Group B members. This was artifactual because, in order to get into Group A in the first place, *S* had to place himself in the top half of the distribution (thus assigning poorer ratings than his own to at least half of the *S*s he rated). Also, in order to get into Group B, *S* had to rate himself in the bottom half of the distribution (thus assigning better ratings than his own to at least half of the *S*s he rated). When Sears compared noninsightful Group C (self-rating bad, rating from group good) to insightful Group D (self-rating good, rating from group good), he naturally obtained the puzzling finding that the *insightful* group attributed more *un*favorable ratings to others. In short, Sears used the same instrument as a basis for both independent and dependent variable scores; and his method yields the results it does because his way of forming comparison groups which differ in insight leads to an artifactual negative correlation between *S*s' self-rating and ratings *S*s assigned to others.

Rokeach (1945) studied the relations of "insight" and "projection" using college women's self- and group-ratings of beauty, made on a ten-point graphic rating scale. Recognizing some of the difficulties with Sears's method, he attempted to devise a more refined insight score. First he determined how much *S*'s self rating (B_{sr}) deviated from the average of the ratings *S* gave to her peers (B_{ar}). This difference was subtracted from the deviation between the average beauty rating S received from the group (B_s) and the grand mean for all Ss (which was 6.07). "Projection" was measured in terms of the average rating S assigned *to* others (B_{ar}). Thus it can be seen that B_{ar} entered into S's classification on the independent variable (insight), *and* into her projection score (the dependent variable).

Rokeach formed two main groups, according to the group ratings Ss received: Beautiful and Homely. Within each of these, using the method described above, he formed four subgroups: those who slightly and those who markedly over- and underestimated themselves. Although he obtained no statistically significant findings, he did obtain some regular trends within the Beautiful group. Even if these trends had been significant, they would apparently be artifactual, if the following reasoning is correct:

Considering first the Beautiful group, we may infer that group ratings were held approximately constant across the four subgroups, while "insight" was varied mainly in terms of varying Ss' self-ratings. That is, in the following formula, which expresses the design of the experiment, B_s was apparently approximately constant across all Beautiful subgroups which varied in insight, and of course 6.07 was always constant across such subgroups.

"Insight" was related to *"Projection"*
$(B_s - 6.07) - (B_{sr} - B_{ar})$ was related to B_{ar}

The major burden of the relationship would then reduce to

$(B_{sr} - B_{ar})$ related to B_{ar}

Whatever findings one might obtain would be most parsimoniously interpreted in one or both of the following ways: (1) covariation of the two scores due to the common variable B_{ar}, *or* (2) covariation between B_{sr} and B_{ar}. It would not be parsimonious to attribute variations in "projection" to variability in "insight" until it could be shown that neither of the above two possibilities would account for the findings.

When Wylie (1957) matched self-ratings very closely across experimental groups, and varied insight by varying others' ratings of S, she could find no consistent evidence that defensiveness was associated with "lack of insight." Defensiveness was measured in two ways: (1) consistent underestimation of others on a rating scale; (2) by a specially devised Rationalization-Projection Inventory pertaining to the traits being rated. The Rationalization-Projection Inventory had fairly good split-half reliability, and both it and underestimation-of-others did relate to absolute self-rating values and to certainty about self-ratings in a manner predicted by phenomenal theory. This implies that the null results with the insight variable were probably not due simply to errors of measurement.

Murstein's (1956) study enables us to compare the degree of "projection of hostility" shown by Ss who differ in insight but have approximately the same self concepts (self-ranking scores on hostility). He measured projection in two ways: (1) by means of a Rorschach hostility score based on content; (2) in terms of the favorability of S's rating of an examiner's interview behavior under two conditions: (a) the examiner gave S a favorable report on S's Rorschach, saying among other things, that it indicated that S was warm and friendly; (b) the examiner gave S an unfavorable report on S's Rorschach, saying among other things that it indicated that S was cold and hostile.

Four extreme groups of 20 Ss each were used, these being drawn from a pool of 536 Ss from 25 living groups who had ranked one another within their respective living groups with respect to friendliness (hostility). Groups 1 and 4 were nearly equal with respect to standard deviation equivalents of their self-rankings at a "friendly" point, but the living group ranked Group 4 members as "hostile," so Group 4 members lacked "insight." No significant differences in "projection" of hostility were found between these groups. Groups 2 and 3 were nearly equal with respect to standard deviation equivalents of their self-rankings at a "hostile" point, but Group 2 members lacked insight because the living group members had ranked them as "friendly." In this case, insightful Group 3 members showed significantly more hostile Rorschach scores.

When each of the four groups was divided into halves, which were matched on Group and Self scores, and one half received a "hostile" interpretation of their Rorschach record, while the others received a "friendly" interpretation, the following findings were obtained: (1) No main effect was found between either self-ranking score or group-ranking score and derogation of the examiner's interview behavior. (2) Regardless of group- or self-ranking scores, there was significantly greater derogation of the examiner when he was hostile in interpreting *S*'s Rorschach record. (3) A significant interaction effect occurred, thus: greatest derogation of the examiner was found among those who considered themselves friendly (whether or not they were insightful) and received a hostile interpretation of their Rorschachs.

The results seem to offer no support to the idea that lack of insight per se is associated with projection of hostility, when self-rankings of hostility are held approximately constant, and projection is measured either by a Rorschach score or by the *S*'s devaluation of a threatening person. The self-ranking, regardless of its insightfulness, was significantly associated with devaluation of a threatening person.

Conclusions concerning the relationship of insight to adjustment—In nineteen of the studies discussed in our earlier publication (Wylie, 1961), insightful *S*s are compared to noninsightful *S*s, when insight is measured in terms of a discrepancy between Self and Other reports about *S*. In at least sixteen of these studies, the self-ratings of the insightful groups are different from the self-ratings of the noninsightful groups. Thus, differences in insight are confounded with differences in self-regard in these sixteen studies. In fifteen of the sixteen studies where such confounding occurs, "insight" is reported to be related to "adjustment." In one of the fifteen investigations, self-regard was shown to be uncorrelated with the dependent variable. If there were no other methodological difficulties, we might parsimoniously interpret the results of the remaining fourteen by saying that the dependent variable is a function of self-regard, since self-regard was not held constant across groups differing in insight. Actually, in at least half of the studies, there is the additional difficulty that a contamination between independent and dependent variables occurs. That is, the *same instrument* was used in defining both dependent and independent variables. In still others, the findings could plausibly be a function of the correlation between two evaluative self-report instruments.

On the other hand, there are three studies in which the authors held self-regard constant across groups which differed in insight, or they presented their data in such a way that we can make comparisons across groups which had comparable levels of self-regard. Of these three studies, only one gave a possibly significant association between insight and a dependent variable. In short, there is no clear evidence that insight is significantly associated with adjustment or defensive behaviors. However, even the three relatively well-controlled studies do not cover a wide enough range of behavior characteristics and do not use sufficiently precise instruments to warrant our acceptance of the null hypothesis at this time.

Descriptive facts about the occurrence of insight—In addition to the central issues about the relation of insight to adjustment, published studies permit us to answer partially some descriptive questions about the occurrence of insight itself, and the variables of which it may be a function. We summarize here the descriptive facts which we report in more detail elsewhere (Wylie, 1961).

The typical but not unanimous finding is that *Ss*' self-ratings show low but significant correlations with the ratings which *Ss* receive from others. This seems to hold true for a wide variety of traits and persons but probably the correlations for some traits are higher than for other traits. Before definitive, clearly interpretable statements can be made about the degree of correspondence between self-ratings and ratings received from others, however, further research is necessary in which certain methodological difficulties are eliminated. For example, the influence of stereotype accuracy should be ruled out, the instructions to *S*s should make clear the frame of reference he is to use in making his self-ratings, and intertrait differences in variability among self-ratings should be taken into account.

There is considerable evidence that self-overestimation is more common than is self-underestimation. This holds true for a wide variety of traits and persons. Here, too, further research is needed before more definitive detailed statements can be made concerning the conditions of which underestimation is a function. For example, the roles of subject variables and of the objectivity and salience of traits remain to be explored in controlled research designs.

There is some limited evidence to suggest that there are consistent individual differences in the tendency toward overestimation, underestimation, or accurate estimation across a variety of traits. Detailed information on this matter remains to be established, however.

VI. CONCLUSIONS

This chapter considers both self theory and the state of research relevant to such theory.

Beginning with Freud, personality theorists have found it necessary or desirable to postulate constructs concerning the self. A number of recent theorists have laid so much emphasis on self-referent constructs that they are sometimes called self theorists. The self-referent constructs and laws have been introduced in an attempt to explain and predict human behavior more accurately than do behavioristic theories. Higher thought processes, certain complex aspects of motivated behavior, the supposed configurational properties of human behavior, and the uniqueness of each person's behavior are the sorts of phenomena which seem to some theorists to require self-referent constructs in order to make them understandable.

While constructs and laws concerning the self may seem to be needed for the above reasons, the way they have been presented has led to serious difficulties. The constructs have been stretched to cover so many inferred cognitive and motivational processes that their utility for analytic and predictive purposes has been greatly diminished. Internal inconsistency among "laws" apparently characterizes all personality theories which emphasize constructs concerning the self, although the vagueness of their statements often makes it impossible to identify inconsistencies with certainty. Partly as a result of these shortcomings in theorizing, the total accumulation of substantive research findings is very disappointing, especially in proportion to the great amount of effort which has obviously been expended.

What are the implications of this situation? One possibility is that theories which depend heavily on overgeneralized self-referent constructs should be abandoned as potentially fruitful scientific tools. Certainly if the construct system cannot be more precisely formulated, this alternative is the correct one.

But perhaps the constructs and hypotheses can be improved. It appears that more molecular inferred variables may have greater research utility. That is, such characteristics as self-actualization, self-differentiation, and self-consistency have not led to enlightening research. By contrast, such constructs as self-acceptance or self-esteem, especially when referring to specified attributes, have yielded more manageable and fruitful research procedures.

An additional alternative to abandoning self theories may be to improve their predictiveness by the addition of more variables, such as measures of the unconscious self concept, or objectively measurable stimuli or characteristics of *S*.

Not only are delimited constructs and internal consistency among postulates necessary, but "lower-order" hypotheses are required as well, if personality theories which stress the self are to become scientifically useful. Some psychologists have argued that general behavior theorists have been too molecular, and that they have failed to attack really significant aspects of human development and functioning. Even if one were to accept this allegation, it does not follow that stating vague, overarching, unverifiable generalizations will remedy the situation. As Morison (1960) reminds us, it may be satisfying to psychologists' needs to have a comprehensive theory, but it is probably more scientifically productive in the long run to begin one's work with limited but testable hypotheses.

We have suggested that self theorists might profitably seek connections with general behavior theories. This rapprochement might prove helpful in reformulating hypotheses concerning self constructs in such a way as to render them more testable. It might also suggest new hypotheses which are extensions from what is known in general psychology about learning, motivation, and perception.

The poor state of research findings is attributable not only to shortcomings in self theory, but also to problems of research design and measurement.

Corresponding to the need for more limited theoretical constructs is a requirement for more limited and well-analyzed measuring instruments. The instruments which have been applied thus far have tried to cover too much too soon, in a fashion parallel to the premature overinclusiveness of the theoretical constructs. Microanalysis of newly devised indices is badly needed. That is, one must undertake a slow accumulation of information in regard to reliability and construct validity at the item level, if any clear meaning can be attached to one's measures. It is particularly important to avoid the use of complex two-part indices until the component parts have been thoroughly explored. The experimental conditions leading to optimum validity must be ascertained, and this information systematically applied to researches which use self-concept measures. And of course scaling procedures should be systematically applied to the instruments so that one can get some idea of the psychological meaning of statistically significant changes or group differences.

Parallel to the need for more lower-order hypotheses is a requirement for more systematic, analytical research designs. For example, analysis of variance designs are called for because some of the apparent contradictions may be due to interaction of variables which are as yet unexplored in a systematic way by any presently available studies. Also, more use of the "transition experiment" described by Campbell (1957) would be highly desirable.

The wide use of R-R designs, in which two responses are correlated, is one of the main reasons why the substantive results in this field are generally inconclusive. Such R-R designs can, of course, never lead to "cause-effect" inferences. They may throw some light on theoretical questions, but often they have not been well enough controlled to do even that. Although it might seem that some kind of R-R design is uniquely demanded by self-concept theory, we have shown that this is not the case.

Finally, there have been a great many avoidable methodological difficulties at the design level. This is certainly a difficult area to work in, and it is understandable that artifacts cannot always be ruled out by those who pioneer. However, there are pertinent methodological precautions which have been worked out in other areas of psychology, and they can and should be applied to this one.

In short: It is true that personality theories which stress the self have addressed themselves to important, unanswered questions concerning human behavior. However, the empirical evidence supporting the theories is limited in proportion to the effort expended. This seems to be due in part to each of four factors: (1) the lack of proper scientific characteristics of the theories themselves; (2) the inevitable difficulties encountered in formulating relevant, well-controlled researches in a new area; (3) the understandable fact that individual researches in a new area are not part of a planned research program, and therefore cannot be easily synthesized; (4) avoidable methodological flaws. It seems that a crisis situation is at hand with regard to personality theories and researches which emphasize the self.

If theorists and researchers who are interested in this area decide to face the crisis and do what is necessary to put their work on a more solid footing, the process will be arduous and time-consuming. However, since the theories do concern themselves with important issues, it may well prove worthwhile to try to make the necessary changes in theory-building and methodology.

REFERENCES

Allport, G. W. The ego in contemporary psychology. *Psychol. Rev.,* 1943, 50, 451–478.

Allport, G. W. *Becoming: basic considerations for a psychology of personality.* New Haven: Yale Univer. Press, 1955.

Allport, G. W. *Pattern and growth in personality.* New York: Holt, Rinehart, & Winston, 1961.

Allport, G. W., & Odbert, H. S. Trait-names: a psycho-lexical study. *Psychol. Monogr.,* 1936, No. 211.

Amatora, Sister Mary. Validity in self-evaluation. *Educ. psychol. Measmt,* 1956, 16, 119–126.

Amatora, Sister Mary. Developmental trends in pre-adolescence and in early adolescence in self-evaluation. *J. genet. Psychol.,* 1957, 91, 89–97.

Angyal, A. *Foundations for a science of personality.* New York: Commonwealth Fund, 1941.

Ansbacher, H. L., & Ansbacher, Rowena R. (Eds.) *The individual psychology of Alfred Adler.* New York: Basic Books, 1956.

Bills, R. E., Vance, E. L., & McLean, O. S. An index of adjustment and values. *J. consult. Psychol.,* 1951, 15, 257–261.

Butler, J. M., & Haigh, G. V. Changes in the relation between self-concepts and ideal concepts consequent upon client-centered counseling. In C. R. Rogers & Rosalind F. Dymond (Eds.), *Psychotherapy and personality change.* Chicago: Univer. of Chicago Press, 1954. Pp. 55–75.

Calden, G., Lundy, R. M., & Schlafer, R. J. Sex differences in body concepts. *J. consult. Psychol.,* 1959, 23, 378.

Calkins, Margaret W. The self in scientific psychology. *Amer. J. Psychol.,* 1915, 26, 495–524.

Campbell, D. T. Factors relevant to the validity of experiments in social settings. *Psychol. Bull.,* 1957, 54, 297–312.

Campbell, D. T., & Fiske, D. W. Convergent and discriminant validation by the multitrait-multimethod matrix. *Psychol. Bull.,* 1959, 56, 81–105.

Cliff, N. The relation of adverb-adjective combinations to their components. Multilith technical report. Princeton, N.J.: Project Designation NR 150–088, October, 1956, Princeton University.

Cronbach, L. J. Processes affecting scores on "understanding of others" and "assumed similarity." *Psychol. Bull.,* 1955, 52, 177–193.

Cronbach, L. J., & Gleser, Goldine C. Assessing similarity between profiles. *Psychol. Bull.,* 1953, 50, 456–473.

Cronbach, L., & Meehl, P. E. Construct validity in psychological tests. *Psychol. Bull.,* 1955, 52, 281–302.

Diggory, J. C., & Magaziner, D. E. Self-evaluation as a function of instrumentally relevant capacities. *Bull. Ass. int. Psychol. appl.,* 1959, 8, 2–19.

Dudek, F. J. A comparison of scale values for adverbs determined by the constant-sum method and a successive intervals procedure. *Educ. psychol. Measmt,* 1959, 19, 539–548.

Edwards, A. L. *The social desirability variable in personality assessment and research.* New York: Holt, 1957.

Engel, Mary. The stability of the self-concept in adolescence. *J. abnorm. soc. Psychol.,* 1959, 58, 211–215.

English, H. B., & English, Ava C. *A comprehensive dictionary of psychological and psychoanalytical terms.* New York: Longmans, Green, 1958.

Fisher, S., & Cleveland, S. E. *Body image and personality.* Princeton, N.J.: D. Van Nostrand, 1958.

Freud, S. *An outline of psychoanalysis.* New York: Norton, 1949.

Fromm, E. Selfishness and self-love. *Psychiatry,* 1939, 2, 507–523.

Fromm, E. *Escape from freedom.* New York: Rinehart, 1941.

Gage, N. L., & Cronbach, L. J. Conceptual and methodological problems in interpersonal perception. *Psychol. Rev.,* 1955, 62, 411–422.

Garner, W. R., Hake, H. W., & Eriksen, C. W. Operationism and the concept of perception. *Psychol. Rev.,* 1956, 63, 149–159.

Guilford, J. P. *Psychometric methods.* (2nd ed.) New York: McGraw-Hill, 1954.

Hall, C. W., & Lindzey, G. *Theories of personality.* New York: Wiley, 1957.

Harvey, O. J., Kelley, H. H., & Shapiro, M. M. Reactions to unfavorable evaluations of the self made by other persons. *J. Pers.,* 1957, 25, 393–411.

Healy, W., Bronner, Augusta F., & Bowers, Anna M. *The structure and meaning of psychoanalysis.* New York: Knopf, 1930.

Hilgard, E. R. Human motives and the concept of the self. *Amer. Psychologist,* 1949, 4, 374–382.

Hill, W. F. Learning theory and the acquisition of values. *Psychol. Rev.,* 1960, 67, 317–331.

Horney, Karen. *Self analysis.* New York: Norton, 1942.

Horney, Karen. *Our inner conflicts.* New York: Norton, 1945.

Horney, Karen. *Neurosis and human growth.* New York: Norton, 1950.

Howard, R. C., & Berkowitz, L. Reactions to the evaluators of one's performance. *J. Pers.,* 1958, 26, 494–507.

Hull, C. L. *Essentials of behavior.* New Haven: Yale Univer. Press, 1951.

Humphreys, L. G. Note on the multitrait-multimethod matrix. *Psychol. Bull.,* 1960, 57, 86–88.

James, W. *Principles of psychology.* New York: H. Holt, 1890, 2 vols.

Jervis, F. M. The meaning of a positive self-concept. *J. clin. Psychol.,* 1959, 15, 370–373.

Jessor, R. Phenomenological personality theories and the data language of psychology. *Psychol. Rev.,* 1956, 63, 173–180.

Jung, C. G. *Psychological types.* New York: Harcourt, Brace, 1923.

Kagan, J., Hosken, Barbara, & Watson, Sara. Child's symbolic conceptualization of parents. *Child Develpm.,* 1961, 32, 625–636.

Klein, G. S., & Krech, D. The problem of personality and its theory. In D. Krech & G. S. Klein (Eds.), *Theoretical models and personality theory.* Durham, N.C.: Duke Univer. Press, 1952. Pp. 2–23.

Kohn, A. R., & Fiedler, F. E. Age and sex differences in the perception of persons. *Sociometry,* 1961, 24, 157–163.

Kosa, J., Rachiele, L. D., & Schommer, C. O. The self-image and performance of socially mobile college students. *J. soc. Psychol.,* 1962, 56, 301–316.

Lazarus, R. S. *Adjustment and personality.* New York: McGraw-Hill, 1961.

Lecky, P. *Self consistency: a theory of personality.* New York: Island Press, 1945.

Lynn, D. B. A note on sex differences in the development of masculine and feminine identification. *Psychol. Rev.,* 1959, 66, 126–136.

McClelland, D. C. *Personality.* New York: William Sloane, 1951.

McKee, J. P., & Sherriffs, A. C. The differential evaluation of males and females. *J. Pers.,* 1957, 25, 356–371.

McKee, J. P., & Sherriffs, A. C. Men's and women's beliefs, ideals, and self-concepts. *Amer. J. Sociol.,* 1959, 64, 356–363.

Maslow, A. H. *Motivation and personality.* New York: Harper, 1954.

May, R. I. The origins and significance of the existential movement in psychology. II. Contributions of existential psychotherapy. In R. May, E. Angel, & H. F. Ellenberger (Eds.),

Existence: a new dimension in psychiatry and psychology. New York: Basic Books, 1958. Pp. 3–91.

Merenda, P. F., & Clark, W. V. Multiple inferential selves of male and female college students. *J. psychol. Stud.*, 1960, 11, 206–212.

Morison, R. S. Gradualness, gradualness, gradualness. *Amer. Psychologist*, 1960, 15, 187–197.

Mullahy, P. *Oedipus: myth and complex*. New York: Hermitage, 1948.

Munroe, Ruth L. *Schools of psychoanalytic thought*. New York: Holt, Rinehart, & Winston, 1955.

Murphy, G. *Personality: a biosocial approach to origins and structure*. New York: Harper, 1947.

Murstein, B. I. The projection of hostility on the Rorschach and as a result of ego threat. *J. proj. Tech.*, 1956, 20, 418–428.

Nissen, H. W. The nature of the drive as innate determinant of behavioral organization. In M. R. Jones (Ed.), *Nebraska symposium on motivation*. Lincoln: Univer. of Nebraska Press, 1954. Pp. 281–321.

Perkins, H. V. Teachers' and peers' perceptions of children's self-concepts. *Child Develpm.*, 1958, 29, 203–220. (a)

Perkins, H. V. Factors influencing change in children's self-concepts. *Child Develpm.*, 1958, 29, 221–230. (b)

Progoff, I. *Jung's psychology and its social meaning*. New York: Grove, 1953.

Rank, O. *Will therapy and truth and reality*. New York: Knopf, 1945.

Rogers, C. R. *Client-centered therapy*. Boston: Houghton Mifflin, 1951.

Rokeach, M. Studies in beauty: II. Some determiners of the perception of beauty in women. *J. soc. Psychol.*, 1945, 22, 155–169.

Sarbin, T. R., & Rosenberg, B. G. Contributions to role-taking theory: IV. A method for obtaining a qualitative estimate of the self. *J. soc. Psychol.*, 1955, 42, 71–81.

Sears, R. R. Experimental studies in projection: I. Attribution of traits. *J. soc. Psychol.*, 1936, 7, 151–163.

Sherriffs, A. C., & McKee, J. D. Qualitative aspects of beliefs about men and women. *J. Pers.*, 1957, 25, 251–264.

Skinner, B. F. Are theories of learning necessary? *Psychol. Rev.*, 1950, 57, 193–216.

Smith, Hope M., & Clifton, Marguerite A. Sex differences in expressed self-concepts concerning the performance of selected motor skills. *Percept. mot. Skills*, 1962, 11, 71–73.

Snygg, D., & Combs, A. W. *Individual behavior: a new frame of reference for psychology*. New York: Harper, 1949.

Solley, C. M., & Stagner, R. Effects of magnitude of temporal barriers, type of goal, and perception of self. *J. exp. Psychol.*, 1956, 51, 62–70.

Spence, K. W. The nature of theory construction in contemporary psychology. *Psychol. Rev.*, 1944, 51, 47–68.

Stevens, S. S. On the psychophysical law *Psychol. Rev.*, 1957, 64, 153–181.

Stevens, S. S., & Galanter, E. H. Ratio scales and category scales for a dozen perceptual continua. *J. exp. Psychol.*, 1957, 54, 377–411.

Sullivan, H. S. *The interpersonal theory of psychiatry*. New York: Norton, 1953.

Symonds, P. M. *The ego and the self*. New York: Appleton, 1951.

Talland, G. A. Sex differences in self assessment. *J. soc. Psychol.*, 1958, 48, 25–35.

Thompson, Clara. *Psychoanalysis: evolution and development*. New York: Hermitage House, 1950.

Tolman, E. C. *Purposive behavior in animals and men*. Berkeley: Univer. of California Press, 1932.

Torgerson, W. S. *Theory and methods of scaling*. New York: Wiley, 1958.

Turner, R. H., & Vanderlippe, R. H. Self-ideal congruence as an index of adjustment. *J. abnorm. soc. Psychol.*, 1958, 57, 202–206.

Underwood, B. J. *Psychological research*. New York: Appleton-Century-Crofts, 1957.

Verplanck, W. S., & Skinner, B. F. In W. K. Estes, S. Koch, K. MacCorquodale, P. E. Meehl, C. G. Mueller, W. N. Schoenfeld, & W. S. Verplanck (Eds.), *Modern learning theory: a critical analysis of five examples*. New York: Appleton-Century-Crofts, 1954.

White, R. W. Motivation reconsidered: the concept of competence. *Psychol. Rev.*, 1959, 66, 297–333.

Wylie, Ruth C. Some relationships between defensiveness and self-concept discrepancies. *J. Pers.*, 1957, 25, 600–616.

Wylie, Ruth C. *The self concept*. Lincoln: Univer. of Nebraska Press, 1961.

Wylie, Ruth C. Children's estimates of their schoolwork ability as a function of sex, race, and socioeconomic level. *J. Pers.*, 1963, 31, 203–224.

CHAPTER 13 Theories of Consistency and the Study of Personality[1,2]

DAVID C. GLASS
Russell Sage Foundation and The Rockefeller University

In this chapter, we shall describe several related psychological theories and indicate their contributions to personality theory and research. The theories include Heider's (1944; 1946; 1958) balance theory and some of its recent modifications; Osgood and Tannenbaum's (1955) congruity theory; Abelson and Rosenberg's (1958; Rosenberg *et al.*, 1960) balance theory; and Festinger's (1957) theory of cognitive dissonance.[3] Since these theories all assume a tendency toward consistency in psychological functioning, we shall in the first section discuss the concept of consistency and indicate some of its antecedents in the older schools of psychology. In the second section, we shall discuss each of the consistency theories and attempt to evaluate them from the point of view of conceptual clarity and empirical verification. The third and final section of this chapter will deal with the implications of consistency theories, dissonance theory in particular, for the study of personality.

THE CONCEPT OF CONSISTENCY

THE TREND TOWARD CONSISTENCY

One of the older doctrines in psychology holds that man cannot tolerate inconsistency among his cognitions and that he continually strives to eliminate it. The existence of inconsistency makes him uncomfortable, makes him feel that something is wrong. The pressure to achieve consistency is based on the need to reduce the discomfort occasioned by the contradictory cognitions. This assumption of a trend toward consistency implies that a person will be motivated to seek consistency only in the presence of actual inconsistency. It does not imply that the person will seek out consistent cognitions in the absence of inconsistency, although the threat of imminent

[1] I wish to express my special indebtedness to Dr. Orville G. Brim, Jr., president of Russell Sage Foundation, whose cooperation and assistance enabled me to complete this chapter. My appreciation is also extended to Jack W. Brehm, John Neulinger, Helge H. Mansson, David A. Goslin, Polly Glass, and Margaret Dunn for their criticisms and comments on various drafts of the chapter. Thanks are also due to Milton J. Rosenberg and Philip G. Zimbardo for making relevant materials available prior to publication. Finally, I owe a debt of gratitude to Miss Laurel Leonard for her efficient typing of successive revisions of the manuscript.

[2] The survey of the literature for this chapter was concluded in January, 1965, including examination of then unpublished manuscripts.

[3] For purposes of simplicity we refer to these formulations as "consistency theories" and treat the terms imbalance, inconsistency, incongruity, and dissonance as equivalent.

inconsistency may, under certain conditions, arouse strong avoidance tendencies

When we speak of inconsistency, we are referring to more than just the logical or illogical relations that exist between cognitive and behavioral elements. Two elements are inconsistent if, *for any reason,* they do not fit together.[4] Cultural values, personal standards, or past experience may dictate that the two do not fit. For example, while there is nothing necessarily illogical about a man being a liberal and voting for Goldwater, this may be experienced psychologically as contradictory behavior. The knowledge that he is voting for Goldwater might be perfectly consistent in a logical sense if he does so because of the promise of some future "political favor." On the other hand, the knowledge that he, a liberal, is voting for a conservative may be inconsistent with his cognition that he is an honest person who behaves with integrity.

The presence of inconsistency gives rise to a state of tension in much the same way as do other drive states like hunger and thirst.[5] It is the existence of this psychological tension which motivates the person to eliminate inconsistency, thereby restoring what may be called a state of "dynamic equilibrium" (Lewin, 1935, p. 58). In this respect the tendency toward consistency may be viewed as homeostatic in character. The homeostatic assumption is of course not new, having formed the basis of much psychological theorizing over the past few decades (e.g., Lewin, 1935; Freud, 1933; Miller & Dollard, 1941; Fletcher, 1942; Hull, 1943; Stagner, 1951).

These theories have been attacked, however, for assuming a naive "hydraulic conception" of behavior (e.g., Scheerer, 1954, pp. 114–115), and more recent work on the reinforcing effects of intracranial stimulation (Olds & Milner, 1954) have called into question the necessity for employing such concepts as drive-arousal and drive-reduction. Even more troublesome for the concept of inconsistency reduction is the recent set of findings which indicate that intolerance for inconsistency may be higher for cognitions which convey antihedonic (i.e., drive-frustration) meanings rather than hedonic (i.e., drive-satisfaction) meanings (Rosenberg *et al.,* 1960; Rosenberg, 1963). Weiss (1964) goes still further and presents evidence suggesting that individuals will often seek the most satisfying set of cognitions even if this means the arousal of inconsistency. Anderson and Fishbein (1964) and Fishbein and Hunter (1964) also report data which run counter to consistency theory predictions. Indeed their results seem to support a contrasting theory of cognitive summation. Despite these negative findings, there is, as we shall see, quite compelling evidence on the other side. Moreover, homeostatic theories of consistency are useful in organizing existing knowledge as well as in generating interesting new knowledge; witness such recent theoretical papers and reviews of the experimental literature as McGuire's (1966b) "The current status of cognitive consistency theories," Rosenberg *et al.'s* (1960) *Attitude Organization and Change,* Brehm and Cohen's (1962) *Explorations in Cognitive Dissonance,* and (1968) *Theories of Cognitive Consistency: A Sourcebook,* edited by Abelson and his colleagues (1968).

The concepts of consistency and inconsistency are neither novel nor unique to psychology. As Zajonc (1960) has indicated, the concepts have appeared in almost all sciences at one time or another. The sociologist Sumner (1906), for example, spoke of a "strain toward consistency" among the cultural folkways, and Cannon (1939), a biologist, was the first to apply the concept of homeostasis to internal physiological activities. To say, then, that people are made uncomfortable by inconsistency and are motivated to eliminate the discomfort is really saying very little that is new. If this were the only contribution of the consistency theories, we might well dismiss them as

[4] Formal definitions of inconsistency will be presented later in the chapter, since the concept is defined somewhat differently in each theory.

[5] Throughout this chapter, we use the terms need, drive, and motive interchangeably, although we recognize that some psychologists prefer to distinguish between these concepts (Cofer & Appley, 1964).

trivial. The real contribution of these theories is of greater interest, however, and lies in their ability to specify the kinds of behavior to which inconsistency leads. For example, will inconsistency between an attitude and a contrary communication lead to attitude change or some other behavior? Maccoby and Maccoby (1961) enumerate some of the more frequently mentioned possibilities: (1) a strengthening of the original attitude by rejecting the source of the contrary communication; (2) a refusal to listen to the communication; and (3) a compartmentalization of the attitude so that inconsistency is made less salient. To these we should add still another, simply enduring the tension of inconsistency. That there are individual differences in this ability to tolerate inconsistency has been noted by several investigators (e.g., Festinger, 1957). The problem seems to be partly one of developing adequate measures of this characteristic, an issue we shall take up in a later section.

The fact that consistency and inconsistency are not novel concepts suggests that we consider some of their origins in the older schools of psychology. An examination of historical antecedents of the concepts should prove helpful in our discussion of contemporary formulations.

Historical Antecedents

Gestalt Theory

In the work of Wertheimer (1945) and others of the Gestalt school, we unquestionably have an anticipation of current theories of consistency. The Gestalt principles of organization such as proximity, similarity, and *prägnanz* are not unlike the principle of consistency. Both are concerned with organization of the psychological field, and both assume that the trend of behavior is toward a state of dynamic equilibrium. In at least one instance, we have explicit recognition of an equivalence between the two principles. Thus Jordan states that "... balanced [consistent] situations constitute strong *gestalten* and imbalanced [inconsistent] situations constitute weak *gestalten*" (1953, p. 281). It may be inferred from this that where imbalance exists, the individual will be motivated to restore a state of equilibrium or consistency among cognitive elements. The trend toward consistency, then, is akin to the tendency to overlook irregularities, and in general to strive to achieve the most "pregnant" gestalt.

Besides the organizing factors, Gestalt and consistency theories are not unalike in their emphasis on the dynamic quality of the psychological field. Köhler (1947), for example, speaks of the psychological field as a unitary system of interdependent subparts, a change in any one of which will affect the entire system in the direction of a balanced state. Similarly, Krech and Crutchfield (1948) maintain that imbalance in the psychological field produces tension which motivates the individual to restore consistency or equilibrium. They argue that any change in cognitive structure toward a balanced state occurs in such a way as to produce minimal change in the structure. This assumption also occurs in the "least effort principle" of Abelson and Rosenberg (1958), which states that the resolution of attitudinal inconsistency occurs in the direction involving minimal attitudinal reorganization.

In tracing the origins of the consistency principle to Gestalt theory, we have located inconsistency entirely within the stimulus field. This view is probably limited to Heider's (1946) formulation of the problem. Most consistency theorists, as we noted above, treat cognitive inconsistency as similar to deprivation states like hunger and thirst. Brehm and Cohen (1962) take exception to this interpretation. For them, inconsistency is not a general motive. They state that "discrepancies between other motives and their satisfaction result in behavior in the interests of discrepancy reduction; such behavior is not necessarily simply due to the fact that two stimuli or cognitions are 'inconsistent' with one another" (1962, p. 227). What they are suggesting is that inconsistency is a specific motivational state that always occurs when the individual commits himself to behavior which frustrates one of his other important motives. It is problematic whether this view would be accepted by other consistency theorists, although it appears more compatible with the dissonance formulation than with any of the others. Whatever consensus may ultimately develop, the important point for us is that the trend toward consistency may not be located solely in the stimulus field. The force for consistency may be the result of motivational dynamics operating within the individual.

This suggests that the origins of the consistency principle might also be found in more motivationally-based theories. We turn to an examination of such theories, a logical next step in any case, since our earlier discussion also stressed the homeostatic or drive-like character of consistency.

Conflict Theory

Current formulations about consistency can be traced in part to the motivational analysis of psychological conflict developed independently by Kurt Lewin (1935) and Neal Miller (1944). Though conflict theory and consistency theory presumably deal with different phases of the decision process (see below) it has been suggested that inconsistency may be coordinated to the three types of conflict described by Lewin and Miller: approach-approach conflict, approach-avoidance conflict, and avoidance-avoidance conflict (Brown, 1962). Take, for example, an approach-approach conflict in which a subject is placed between two positively valent objects or activities. This is a situation of conflict because locomotion toward one region will of necessity frustrate the need represented by the other region. We can also describe this situation as one involving inconsistency if we assume that the subject has already decided to locomote toward one region rather than the other. Commitment to one activity will of necessity frustrate the need that would be satisfied by the other activity. This is precisely what Brehm and Cohen mean when they define the arousal of dissonance as due to the incompatibility introduced by the individual's commitment to behave in a way which frustrates another strong motive. Like the principle of consistency, the conflict model assumes that conflict creates tension, and that the individual experiencing this tension will try to reduce it. One way in which he may do this is by changing the relative valences of the alternative objects.

A similar analysis can be made for the other types of conflict. This does not mean, as Brown (1962) has noted, that current views of consistency are "just conflict theory in a new guise" (p. 77). The principle of consistency may be operative in conflict theory, but it is used in a somewhat different way by contemporary models of consistency. Two differences may be noted here: (1) conflict theory deals with gross action tendencies, whereas consistency theories are concerned with cognitive reorganization; (2) conflict theory explores *pre*decisional behavior while consistency theories tend to emphasize *post*decisional processes. The latter point requires some comment since it has formed the basis of recent criticism directed against consistency theories, dissonance in particular (Jordan, 1963a).

Dissonance theory assumes that when a choice is made between two attractive alternatives, an inconsistency exists between the cognitions that the chosen alternative contains unattractive features and the unchosen alternative attractive features. To eliminate the inconsistency, one can increase the valence of the chosen alternative, and/or reduce the valence of the unchosen alternative. Brehm and Cohen (1962, pp. 236–242) point out that a similar claim can be made by conflict theory, although from this point of view, the cognitive revaluation will occur *prior* to the choice so that a choice between the options can in fact be made. Conflict theory thus emphasizes discrimination between alternatives in order to choose, whereas dissonance theory assumes postdecisional revaluation as a consequence of dissonance.

Empirical evidence relevant to this issue comes from a recent study by Davidson and Kiesler (in Festinger *et al.,* 1964). The authors reasoned that an adequate test of the conflict *versus* dissonance interpretation would require control over the making of implicit decisions before (and possibly during) postdecision revaluation of the alternatives. At the same time, the procedure should produce conditions favorable to predecision revaluation, so that if such a process exists it will be easily detected. Assuming that predecision revaluation is facilitated by adequate time for consideration of the alternatives, Davidson and Kiesler employed the following experimental procedure:

> ... Items of information relevant to [a] decision were given to subjects sequentially. In order to avoid implicit decisions, all subjects were told that later they would receive really important information [and that it would be impossible to make a "decent" decision until they had this information]. Half the subjects were given the items of information in rapid sequence, so that they had relatively little time to reflect on them [Short Deliberation Time]. The other half were given the items of information very slowly, so that there was considerable time for reflection and re-evaluation [Long Deliberation Time]. Re-evaluation was measured for half the subjects before the decision and for the other half, after the decision (Davidson & Kiesler, 1964, p. 11).

The results showed that before choice there was little revaluation in a direction favoring the alternative which was ultimately chosen. After choice there was substantial revaluation. It was also found that long-deliberation time had a greater impact on revaluation than short-deliberation time, suggesting that the more thoroughly the alternatives had been considered, the more effective was the dissonance reduction process after decision.

These data provide support for the position that predecision and postdecision processes are quite different. The Davidson-Kiesler experiment does not, however, settle the issue. Two arguments can be made which enable one to maintain that pre- and postdecision processes are actually identical. First, there was evidence to suggest that in the long-deliberation time condition some predecision revaluation occurred. Second, the subjects were probably suspending their decisions in anticipation of receiving more information of increasing importance. To this extent they may not have been in a conflict situation at all; hence it is understandable if there was no evidence of conflict resolution. The ambiguity of interpretation rests, in other words, on an uncertainty about whether the person was in conflict and also when the decision was made. Festinger *et al.* (1964) suggest that the dissonance-conflict issue can be resolved by a design that relies solely on postdecision measurement. Once the decision is made, the person can at least be said to have gone through the conflict situation.

The implementation of this line of reasoning fell to Jon Jecker (Jecker, 1964a) who carried out an experiment in which degree of conflict and degree of dissonance were manipulated orthogonally. He hypothesized that if a person, in the process of making a choice, is under the impression that he will get both alternatives, less conflict will be experienced than if he expects to get only the alternative he chooses. Regardless of whether he expects to receive both or one, if he in fact receives only the chosen alternative, dissonance should be present in the same amount. On the other hand, dissonance should be absent if both alternatives are actually received.

To test these ideas, Jecker recruited 88 female high school students, ostensibly for a market research study aimed at collecting information about how people were reacting to popular phonograph records. Each subject was shown fifteen records and asked to rate each one on a seven-point scale according to how much they wanted it. All subjects were then told they would receive gift records in exchange for their participation. In each experimental condition they were actually given a choice between two records they had rated as "moderately" attractive. To create High Conflict, subjects were told that the probability was very high (19 chances out of 20) that they would get only the record they chose. To create Low Conflict, they were told that the probability was very high (19 chances out of 20) that they would get both records. Within each condition, half the subjects rerated the records after they discovered they had received both records (No Dissonance condition); the remaining half rerated the records after discovering they received only the record they chose (Dissonance condition). On the assumption that the length of time it takes to make a decision is proportional to the severity of conflict, the data showed that the conflict manipulation was entirely successful. Subjects under High Conflict took 9.4 seconds to make their choice, while those under Low Conflict took only 6.7 seconds, a difference that was significant at the 5 per cent level.

The results of the attractiveness ratings showed that in the two dissonance conditions, there was substantial change in the direction of spreading the alternatives apart. The chosen alternative increased in attractiveness and the rejected alternative decreased in attractiveness. Corresponding changes under No Dissonance were negligible. Jecker concludes that if there is no postdecision dissonance aroused, then regardless of the degree of decisional conflict, there is little or no revaluation of the alternatives. On the other hand, when dissonance is aroused there is significant revaluation for both High and Low Conflict conditions.

The Davidson-Kiesler and Jecker experiments, taken together, provide evidence that revaluation of alternatives is a postdecisional phenomenon. The findings suggest that dissonance theory (and perhaps consistency theories in general) are applicable to postdecisional behavior. Whether conflict theory is a more appropriate model for predecisional phenomena is as yet unclear, but at least there is evidence that relatively little if any revaluation occurs prior to the making of a decision.

To summarize, we have traced the origins of the consistency principle to Gestalt and conflict theories. In the one case, inconsistency is treated as part of the dynamics of the stimulus field, therefore as part of the more general motivation for *prägnanz*. In contrast, most contemporary consistency theorists conceive of the need for consistency as a motivational state having homeostatic properties. It was this fact which led us to a consideration of the conflict theories of Lewin and Miller, and from this to the question of whether consistency (e.g., dissonance) and conflict theories deal with different phases of the decision process.

THEORIES OF CONSISTENCY

Despite the part that inconsistency has played in the older schools of psychology, our knowledge about the implications of inconsistency for psychological functioning is relatively limited. Only within the past fifteen years have psychologists really begun to concern themselves with the issue of psychological inconsistency—what it is and how people react to it (McGuire, 1966b). In this section we consider several of the current consistency models. Let it be said at the outset that these theories emphasize the specific inconsistencies which arise in connection with opinions and attitudes. An exception is Festinger's (1957) theory of cognitive dissonance, which attempts to state a more general theory of inconsistency. We will have more to say about this theory later in the section.

Heider's Theory of Balance

The formulation of Fritz Heider (1944; 1946; 1958) is unquestionably the earliest of the current theories of consistency. The theory is primarily concerned with the consequences of inconsistency in the way people view their relations with other people. There are three elements in Heider's theory: two persons, labeled P and O, and one impersonal entity, X, which can be a physical object, an idea, or an activity. The focus of the theory is on how the relations among the elements are cognitively experienced by P, with O being some other person.

The relations among P, O, and X can take two forms, an attitudinal or sentiment relation and a "unit" relation. By attitude Heider means a positive or negative relationship of P to O, or to X, symbolized as L or DL, respectively. For example, (*P* L *X*) means that P likes, approves, or loves X; (*P* DL *X*) means P dislikes, disapproves, or negatively evaluates X. The unit relation refers to the fact that persons are generally regarded as sources of acts, and as connected with objects. Thus objects (or acts) and persons can be related to one another through similarity, causality, ownership, or possession. U denotes a cognitive unit formation between two entities, and ~U a separation between entities. For example, (*P* U *X*) means that P owns X, or P made X; (*P* ~ U *X*), on the other hand, means P does not own X, or P did not make X.

Heider proposes that P's cognitive representation of the P-O-X triad is either balanced (consistent) or unbalanced (inconsistent). A balanced state exists where "all three possible relations are positive in all respects, or if two are negative and one positive" (Heider, 1946, p. 110). We have a balanced state where P likes O because O admires P's action, or P dislikes O because O derogates P's action. The first can be symbolized as (*P* L *O, O* L *X, P* U *X*); the second as (*P* DL *O, O* DL *X, P* U *X*).

The fundamental assumption of Heider's theory is that states of balance are preferred over states of imbalance. When imbalance exists, tension is produced which generates forces to restore balance. We have a state of imbalance, for example, where the P-O-X triad contains two positive relations (*O* U *X, P* L *O*) and one negative relation (*P* D L *X*). Balance can be restored by a change in either attitude relations or unit relations. A change in attitude could occur if P began to feel that O is really not so bad, thereby producing a triad of three positive relations. A change in unit relations could occur if P began to feel that O was not really responsible for X, thereby nullifying the unit between O and X and yielding two negative relations and one positive relation—a state of cognitive balance.

Cartwright and Harary (1956) have called attention to a number of ambiguities in Heider's formulation. The binary nature of the balance concept (i.e., states are either balanced or unbalanced) is a case in point. Since it is intuitively clear that some unbalanced structures are "more" balanced than others, a modification of the balance concept is indicated. Cartwright and Harary have made such a modification by using the mathematical theory of linear graphs. This permits a redefinition of balance in terms of degrees of balance ranging from 0 to 1. Moreover, the redefinition allows for a distinction between the complement of an L relation and its opposite. The opposite of liking, for example, is disliking, whereas its complement is the absence of liking, which can be disliking or a neutral attitude. Heider did not consider this difference in his original paper (1946), but graph theory enabled Cartwright and Harary to overcome the limitation.

The purpose and scope of this chapter do not warrant further discussion of these and similar modifications of the Heiderian model (e.g., Davis, 1963; Feather, 1964a). It is sufficient to note here that mathematical treatment provides a more rigorous conceptualization of certain aspects of the theory, and also generalizes it to more complicated cognitive structures involving any number of elements.

Also beyond the scope of this chapter is Newcomb's (1953; 1959) extension of balance theory to the problem of interpersonal communication. Whereas Heider is concerned with cognitive unit formation *within* the individual, Newcomb's interest is in communication *among* people. However, the concepts of an A-B-X system and a "strain toward symmetry" (Newcomb, 1959) parallel closely Heider's ideas of cognitive unit formation and forces toward balance. Newcomb's formulation has received support from a number of empirical studies (Newcomb, 1943, 1956, 1959, 1961, 1963a, 1963b; Festinger & Thibaut, 1951; Back, 1951; Steiner & Peters, 1958; Steiner, 1960; Broxton, 1963; Sampson & Insko, 1964), and ranks today among the major theoretical approaches to the study of interpersonal relations.

In our presentation of Heider's theory of balance we confined our discussion, by and large, to conceptual matters. However, a number of investigators have used balance theory as a point of departure for their empirical work (e.g., Deutsch, 1958; Deutsch & Solomon, 1959), and several studies have made explicit tests of the basic hypothesis of the theory. One of the first of these studies was designed to show evidence of tendencies toward balance in members of small discussion groups (Horowitz, Lyons, & Perlmutter, 1951). It was hypothesized that if P likes O, he will tend to see O's act, X, as positively valent in order to produce a balanced P-O-X unit. The results tended to confirm the prediction, subjects giving higher evaluations to events produced by group members whom they had rated as attractive.

One of the limitations of the Horowitz design is that it was a field study rather than an experiment. This places restrictions on the possibility of manipulation and control of relevant variables. A more precise test of the balance hypothesis requires an experimental design in which states of balance and imbalance are independently manipulated. An effort of this kind was made by Jordan (1953). Subjects were presented with 64 hypothetical situations in which the attitude and unit relations between each set of elements in the P-O-X unit were systematically varied. For example, a subject was presented with situations schematized as follows: "I dislike O; I like X; O has no sort of bond or relationship with X" (Jordan, 1953, p. 277). He was instructed to imagine himself in the situation playing the role of "I," and then to rate it on a 90-millimeter scale of experienced pleasantness. Half the situations were balanced and half unbalanced, the order of presentation being randomized for 288 subjects. Assuming unpleasantness reflects the tension aroused by imbalanced situations, the results supported Heider's hypothesis that imbalanced units produce a state of tension. The data showed a significant tendency for balanced situations to be rated as more pleasant than unbalanced ones.

However, Jordan's results are complicated further. He reports that negative units were rated as unpleasant even when balanced, and given balance, positive units were rated as more pleasant than negative units. It would appear that ratings of pleasantness are a function of balance plus positive relations between elements of a unit; unpleasantness is a function of imbalance *or* negative relations between elements in the unit. These results are not unlike those reported more recently by Rosenberg (1963), who found that degree of reported tension varies inversely with the "pleasantness" of the meaning conveyed by a set of inconsistent cognitions. When cognitions, even though inconsistent, forecast some gain to the person, they will be preferred to similarly inconsistent cognitions which suggest the possibility of loss.

More unequivocal support for the balance hypothesis comes from studies by Festinger and Hutte (1954), Kogan and Tagiuri (1958), Burdick and Burnes (1958), Morrissette (1958), Pilisuk (1962), Broxton (1963), Alexander (1964), and Sampson and Insko (1964). The Morrissette experiment is particularly important, since it represents the first attempt to test some of the Cartwright and Harary revisions of balance theory. Morrissette hypothesized that the magnitude of forces to restore balance varies inversely with the *degree* of balance in the cognitive unit, and, further, that the magnitude of tension in a person is also inversely related to the degree of cognitive balance. The design used to test these hypotheses was similar to Jordan's. Six hundred subjects were each presented with four hypothetical social situations. Within each, there was systematic variation of the unit and attitude relations between three or four persons, one of whom was the subject. Between some persons the attitude relations were not given, and the subject was asked to predict what he thought they would be. In addition, the subject answered three questions designed to measure the tension he would experience in the predicted configuration. The results supported both hypotheses. In social units in which U relations existed among all pairs of persons, subjects predicted attitude relations (either L or DL) which resulted in the highest degree of balance more frequently than would be expected by chance. Reported tension, moreover, decreased as the degree of balance of the structures increased.

The balance hypothesis assumes that forces toward balance arise because of a tension state aroused by the person's perception of imbalance. Jordan offered some evidence that imbalanced states are perceived as less pleasant than balanced ones. Morrissette made a more explicit attempt to measure tension, but unfortunately he relied exclusively on self-report measures. An improvement would be a behavioral, or at least a reliable physiological index of tension. Burdick and Burnes (1958) report an experiment in which GSR measures were obtained in the presence of balanced and imbalanced situations. The results indicated significantly greater tension (greater and larger GSR deflections) under imbalance than balance. One obvious difficulty with the experiment, however, is that GSR deflections may reflect psychological states other than imbalance, for example, anxiety or guilt.

In Heider's theory, and among the many studies designed to test it, resolution of imbalance is assumed to take one of three forms: (1) a change in attitude toward O, (2) a change in attitude toward X, (3) a separation of the unity between O and X. The difficulty with this formulation is that it fails to specify which of the alternative modes of imbalance resolution will occur. In a recent study by Pilisuk (1962), balance theory was modified so that more precise predictions could be made among the alternatives. Pilisuk suggests that certain relations, such as positive attitudes toward the self and toward significant others, are highly resistant to change. Imbalanced situations involving these attitudes are described as *central,* and central attitudes rarely change their positive sign. When imbalance exists between entities in a central group, the available modes of resolution are continuous tension or cognitive separation (e.g., rationalization). Pilisuk had subjects perform a task presented to them as a measure of social sensitivity and practical intelligence. The task was carried out in a group setting, the subject being told that other members would evaluate his performance. Prior sociometric ratings enabled the experimenter to include a close friend of the subject within each four-man group. A system of false feedback gave the experimenter an opportunity of playing the roles of all critics, one of whom sent negative criticism. In this way the subject was led to believe that his friend was the source of adverse criticism of his performance. A control group received criticism from apparent strangers. Both experimental and control subjects retained favorable estimates of their own performance despite the negative criticism. The experimental subjects, moreover, showed no sign of changing their attitudes toward the close friend. Instead, they used a number of rationalizations to explain the friend's behavior; e.g., he was joking or for some reason he was angry.

An earlier study by Harvey, Kelley and Shapiro (1957) reports a parallel set of findings. These authors presented subjects with unfavorable evaluations of themselves which deviated in varying degrees from the subjects' own self-evaluations. The evaluations were attributed either to acquaintances or to strangers. For the case in which the other's evaluation deviated only slightly from the subject's self-evaluation, the authors found a greater tendency to distort the communication in a favorable direction when it came from an acquaintance as compared to a stranger. For the high discrepancy conditions, the greatest amount of distortion occurred when the source was a highly regarded acquaintance. It was also found, as in the Pilisuk experiment, that subjects denied the acquaintance's causal responsibility for the negative evaluations. In this respect, they too engaged in cognitive separation or rationalization as a means of reducing imbalance.

Both sets of data, then, provide valuable additions to the predictive utility of balance theory. They suggest at least one condition which determines the mode of imbalance resolution. The specification of these conditions is a central issue in all consistency theories, but except for these experiments, and three or four others which have been specifically concerned with dissonance theory (e.g., Steiner & Rogers, 1963), there has been little direct work on the problem.

Evaluation of Balance Theories

The theories of balance contain several conceptual shortcomings that require comment. For one thing, there is no provision made for variation in the intensity of an attitude or unit relation (Zajonc, 1960). Hate is treated the same as mild dislike; love is considered the same as a favorable evaluation. Since amount of attitude change is doubtless affected by the intensity of the attitude, balance theories are deficient in neglecting to give the intensity dimension explicit theoretical status. In addition, there is no provision made for the existence of degrees of balance, hence no predictions regarding the amount of attitude change resulting from disequilibrium. Cartwright and Harary (1956) and Feather (1964a) attempt to handle this problem in their mathematical models but, it must be added, there is not yet appreciable experimental evidence in support of their formulations.

Another problem shared by balance theories is their failure to specify which relations will change following the arousal of imbalance (Brown, 1962). For example, take the case in which some individual, A, likes Nelson Rockefeller, but opposes prayer in the schools. If Rockefeller favors prayer, this is an imbalanced triad and, according to theory, A will alter one of the relations in the direction of establishing balance. But which relation will he change? Will he come to favor prayer, will he dislike Rockefeller, or will he dissociate the relation between Rockefeller and school prayer? None of the theories specifies which outcome will occur. Any one of the outcomes may occur, but which condition leads to which outcome is left indeterminate. What is obviously needed is a conceptual analysis of the factors determining the direction of imbalance resolution.

Related to the problem of form of imbalance reduction is the question of tolerance for imbalance. Balance theories recognize that an individual may simply tolerate the tension resulting from disequilibrium but few of them specify the personality and other variables which might lead to high or low tolerance for imbalance. Yet it seems reasonable to suppose that people have different thresholds for imbalance, hence a differential ability to withstand imbalance (Festinger, 1957; Cohen, 1960; Rosenberg *et al.,* 1960; Brehm & Cohen, 1962).

Balance theories are also deficient in not distinguishing between the complement and the opposite of a positive relation. The relation "DL" may be appropriate to describe my attitude toward the KKK, but it is certainly overstating the case to apply it to my attitude toward eggplant. It is for this reason that Cartwright and Harary distinguish between dislike and the absence of liking (e.g., a neutral attitude). But even with the distinction, it is sometimes difficult to tell when seemingly neutral actions represent dislike or simply no relation.

There is another and perhaps more critical aspect to the evaluation of theory, i.e., its predictive accuracy. What empirical evidence has in fact been generated in support of theories of balance? In 1960 Zajonc remarked that experimental confirmation had been rather limited. In the intervening four-year period, little has happened to warrant a change in this conclusion. Most of the research designed to test the balance hypothesis has been correlational in nature. Where experimental manipulation has been employed, it has dealt largely with subjects responding to hypothetical situations of imbalance. We do not condemn the use of hypothetical situations on the grounds that they are removed from the real world. Let anyone who takes this position enter the psychology laboratory and he will see intense involvement and affect aroused under so-called artificial conditions. However, we must also recognize that involvement may be represented on a dimension of arousal, and there is evidence for a curvilinear relationship between performance and arousal (e.g., Malmo, 1959). It may well be that hypothetical situations engage only the lower end of the arousal continuum, hence a person's responses may be different from those observed under higher levels of activation. Controlled experimentation is clearly a superior procedure, since it allows, through a variety of manipulative techniques, the engagement of larger segments of the arousal continuum. There is as yet little evidence of an experimental nature in support of balance theoretic hypotheses. There are of course exceptions like the work of Pilisuk, but, for the most part, there has been no systematic attempt to confirm the theories of balance. Even more serious perhaps is the absence of any attempt to disprove the theories, though Rosenberg (1963) and Weiss (1964) report evidence that the trend toward balance may not be as powerful a motive as the theory appears to assume. Another troublesome possibility is that situations defined as unbalanced may in fact remain stable and produce no pressures toward balance. Research on the types of cognitive structure that are more readily or less readily made inconsistent is relevant here (Zajonc, 1960, 1961).

Osgood and Tannenbaum's Theory of Congruity

Osgood and Tannenbaum (1955; Osgood, Suci, & Tannenbaum, 1957; Osgood, 1960) have developed a theory of consistency dealing with changes in attitudes[6] as a result of incongruity between the source of a communication and its content. There are two classes of elements in the theory, objects of attitudes and the bonds or linkages between them. Attitudinal objects include ideas, concepts, persons, and other social and nonsocial objects. The bonds are of two kinds: associative and dissociative. Associative bonds can be verbal expressions of approval or they can be actions which indicate approval. Dissociative bonds reflect expressions or actions of disapproval.

The paradigm of congruity research involves an individual who is confronted with an assertion regarding some relevant attitude object made by someone toward whom he also has an attitude. The attitudes of the individual toward object and source are typically measured on the semantic differential (Osgood, Suci, & Tannenbaum, 1957). These are 7-point scales (from $+3$ through 0 to -3) which reflect both the intensity and direction of the attitude. We can translate these operations into terms of the theory. If an individual, P, likes another individual, S, and some attitude object, X, and if S makes a positive statement about X, we have an associative bond between two positively valent objects. If S makes a nega-

[6] Following Brehm and Cohen (1962), we will henceforth use the general label "attitude change" to include changes in opinions, beliefs, values, and evaluations of people, objects, or behavior.

tive statement about X, we have a dissociative bond between two positively valent objects.

Congruity is said to exist if P likes S and X, and there is an associative bond between S and X. A case in point for a supporter of President Johnson would be for the President to extol the virtues of democracy. Congruity is also said to exist if P dislikes S and X, and there is an associative bond between S and X. This probably occurs for many Americans each time Mao Tse Tung praises Stalin. Still another form of congruity occurs where P likes X, dislikes S, and a dissociative bond exists between S and X.

The occurrence of associative and dissociative bonds other than those defining congruity lead to a state of disequilibrium or incongruity. Specifically, incongruity will occur if P's attitudes toward S and X are similar and the bond between S and X is dissociative, or if they are dissimilar and the bond is associative. Given the existence of incongruity, the theory hypothesizes that the individual will attempt to change his attitudes in the direction of increased congruity. The magnitude of these pressures will vary with the size of the discrepancy between attitudinal positions. Suppose, for example, an individual has an evaluation of Senator Goldwater represented by -3 on the attitude scale, and an evaluation of President Johnson of $+2$ on the scale. Suppose, further, that Senator Goldwater praises President Johnson. Congruity theory would predict a change in the individual's attitude toward each man to the point on the scale where they would be uniform. In our example the total amount of change would be five units.

The amount of change, however, will not be the same for each attitude. It is a basic assumption of the theory that while both attitudes are subject to forces of change, the more extremely polarized attitude (i.e., the one furthest from zero) will show the greater resistance to congruity pressures. The total amount of change, it is assumed, will be divided between the two attitudes in inverse proportion to their respective polarizations. The attitude toward Goldwater is more polarized than toward Johnson, since the former is at position -3 and the latter at $+2$. This means that of the five units of possible change, the attitude toward Johnson will show the greater change. The result would be a convergence or "regression" of the two attitudes to the same attitudinal position, thereby restoring congruity to the associative bond linking the attitude objects.

That the magnitude of attitude change is constrained by the extremity of its initial value is a principle supported by a number of experiments. Extreme attitudes have often been found to be less easily changed than moderate ones (e.g., Hovland, Harvey, & Sherif, 1957). The reason, presumably, is that the more polarized an attitude, the more correct the individual thinks it is; hence the less it tends to move toward congruence with the other attitude. The less polarized an attitude and, therefore, the less confident the individual is about its correctness, the more likely it is to change in the direction of congruity with the other attitude.

The principle of polarization assumes that the less extreme attitude will change whether it refers to the object or to the source. But this assumption is not intuitively reasonable. It certainly makes a difference if Johnson praises Goldwater or if Goldwater praises Johnson. The attitude toward the object should be more affected than the attitude toward the source. If Goldwater is praised by Johnson, one's attitude toward Goldwater should show more change than if Goldwater praised Johnson. Osgood and Tannenbaum agree with this line of reasoning and, accordingly, incorporate a correction in their theory to account for the fact that the object is expected to change more than the source. The correction, the Assertion Constant, is a value added to the change that would otherwise be predicted for the attitude toward the object. The constant is of the same sign as the predicted change, and is set at ± .17 on a 7-point bipolar scale. The value was suggested by results obtained in an experiment by Tannenbaum (1953), about which more will be said later.

Still another constraint on amount of attitude change is the factor of credulity. There is some evidence to indicate that people will not shift their attitudes if there is a large discrepancy between their evaluation of the attitude object and their evaluation of the source. Under these circumstances, people tend not to believe that the source made the assertion, thereby reducing incongruity and the consequent need to alter their attitudes (Harvey, Kelley, & Shapiro, 1957; Jones & Köhler, 1958; Brehm & Lipsher, 1959; Bergin, 1962; Aronson, Turner, & Carlsmith, 1963). Osgood and Tannenbaum include a correction for incredulity in their theory. This value is subtracted from the amount of attitude change that would otherwise be predicted by the model.

The main test of congruity theory, to date, is contained in Tannenbaum's doctoral dissertation (1953; Osgood & Tannenbaum, 1955; Zajonc, 1960; Brown, 1962). The experiment was concerned with six cognitive objects, three serving as sources of opinions (Labor Leaders, Chicago *Tribune,* and Senator Taft), and three as objects of opinions (Legalized Gambling, Abstract Art, and Accelerated College Programs). More than 400 college students evaluated the six objects on semantic differential scales. Some time later, they were asked to read "highly realistic" newspaper clippings containing statements made by the sources regarding the objects. Three source-object pairs were used in the newspaper stories: Labor Leaders-Legalized Gambling, Chicago *Tribune*-Abstract Art, and Senator Taft-Accelerated College Programs. Immediately after reading the stories, subjects rated, for a second time, each of the six objects.

Initial attitudes toward source and object were determined from before-test scores. On the basis of these scores, subjects were distributed into nine cells: those favoring both source and object, those feeling neutral toward source and object, those feeling antagonistic toward source and object, and so forth. Amount of attitude change was determined by subtracting before-scores from after-scores for each subject, a positive value indicating increased favorableness.

The results showed that when initial attitudes toward source and object were positive and the assertion in the newspaper story was also positive, no significant changes occurred. There were also no significant changes when initial attitudes toward source and object were negative and the assertion positive. It was found, however, that when a positively valued source made a positive assertion about a negatively valued object, the attitude toward the source became less favorable and toward the object more favorable. In general, the predicted positive and negative changes showed corresponding signs in the data, and predicted lack of change tended to yield obtained changes of small magnitude. Moreover, attitudes toward the object showed greater change than did attitudes toward the source, as predicted by the theory. The results also showed that amount of attitude change decreased with the extremity of the initial attitude.

The main assumptions of congruity theory appear to have received substantial support. The Tannenbaum experiment, however, remains the one major effort in this area. Zajonc (1960) summarizes several studies supporting the congruity principle, but none of these was *specifically* designed to test the theory. Additional support may be found in a paper by Osgood (1960), who cites several unpublished tests which confirm the congruity hypothesis. Other studies have reported evidence contrary to the congruity principle. Kerrick (1959) paired two written captions ("A Quiet Minute Alone" and "Exiled Communist") with each of five pictures (e.g., a profile of a well-dressed man on a park bench), and asked subjects to judge (on semantic differential scales) the meaning of the captions and pictures alone and then in combination. The results showed that if the caption and picture in isolation implied opposite meanings, the meaning of their combination was predictable from congruity theory. If the picture and caption implied similar meanings, their effects *summated* in combination. For example, combining a slightly "happy" picture with a slightly "happy" caption resulted in a very "happy" picture-caption combination, rather than a slightly "happy" combination as theory would predict. The significance of these findings remains unclear, although they certainly suggest that something other than congruity was operating in the experiment. Fishbein and his colleagues (e.g., Fishbein, 1963; Triandis & Fishbein, 1963; Fishbein & Hunter, 1964; Anderson & Fishbein, 1964) have very recently suggested an explanation of these results, in which attitude change is treated as a process of cognitive summation rather than cognitive balance. An assessment of these contrasting theories must await further experimentation.

Evaluation of Congruity Theory

The formal properties of congruity theory appear parsimonious, associative as well as dissociative relations being handled by the same principles of congruity, polarization, and credulity. There are, however, a number of instances of conceptual ambiguity. For one thing, the theory fails to specify alternatives to attitude change for reestablishing congruity. Congruity deals specifically with attitude change and, unlike theories of balance, makes no prediction about other possible responses to incongruity. A consequence of this concern with attitude change is that congruity theory has not been used extensively to analyze other psychological processes involving inconsistency. Some workers have suggested that the theory is capable of making predictions about interpersonal attraction and hostility (Brown, 1962; Secord, Backman, & Eachus, 1964; Pepitone, 1964), but there is a relative absence of data to support these claims.

Congruity theory is also deficient in not providing for variation in the intensity of a bond. It seems likely, as Brown (1962) has noted, that amount of change will depend on the intensity of the bond, but the theory does not say this. On the other hand, congruity does allow for variation in the intensity of an attitude relation. The inclusion of the intensity dimension permits the theory to make precise predictions regarding the extent and direction of attitude change. Indeed, it is precisely this ability to specify direction of change which gives congruity an advantage over the theories of balance. Take our earlier illustration of Nelson Rockefeller and prayer in the schools. A state of incongruity would occur if an individual evaluates Rockefeller as +2 and school prayer as −1, and Rockefeller then comes out in favor of school prayer. Given this state of incongruity, balance theories predict change toward the restoration of a balanced state; none of them, however, specifies which relation will change. Congruity, in contrast, predicts more change for the attitude toward prayer. This is because "prayer" is both the object of the assertion and the attitude object with the lesser degree of polarization.

There are of course other issues in congruity theory about which we might comment (cf. Brown, 1962). We have discussed those we believe to be most crucial to an evaluation of the formal structure of the theory. As for empirical evidence, it is certainly consonant with theoretical expectations. The chief problem is one of insufficient experimentation directly testing the theory. The validity of a theoretical formulation is not established by demonstrating that data collected for other purposes can be fitted to it. It is necessary to show that hypotheses derived from theory are supported by experimental evidence collected for the purpose of testing the theory.

Abelson and Rosenberg's Balance Theory

The Abelson-Rosenberg theory (1958; Rosenberg *et al.*, 1960) is very like the other models presented in this chapter.[7] It makes the now familiar assumption that the cognitive elements toward which people have attitudes can be assigned positive (+), negative (−), and neutral (o) signs. It further assumes that there are three relations between cognitive elements: Positive (p), negative (n), and null (o). Positive relations include "liking," "promoting," and "causing"; negative relations, "disliking," "opposing," and "preventing"; null relations, "indifference," "not affecting," and "unconnected with." The similarity of these distinctions and those adopted by Heider should be immediately apparent.

In addition to elements and relations, the Abelson-Rosenberg theory assumes that cognitive units are built out of pairs of elements connected by a relation. Examples of such units are: "I (A) support (p) Johnson for President" (B); "Goldwater (A) dislikes (n) the Social Security System" (B); and "The New York *Daily News* (A) is not interested in reporting (o) on recent archaeological discoveries" (B). These sentences, symbolically, are ApB, AnB, and AoB. If we replace the neutral A, B, ... terminology with the affectively significant signs, +, −, and o, we have twelve possible cognitive units; e.g., +p+, −n+, and so forth. Each unit may be classified as either balanced or unbalanced.

There is balance in a cognitive unit so long as elements of identical sign are linked by positive relations, and so long as elements of opposite sign are linked by negative relations. Specifically, a balanced unit can be any of the following: +p+, −p−, or +n−. An unbalanced unit is one in which elements of like sign are linked by negative relations and elements of unlike sign are linked by positive relations: e.g., +n+, −n−, or +p−. When two signed elements are connected by a null (o) relation, there is by definition no cognitive unit. Note that balance and imbalance are defined without reference to numbers. In this respect the Abelson-Rosenberg theory is akin to the Heider model, but different from congruity which requires matched values as well as matched signs. McGuire (1960b, chapter 24 of this volume) has gone even further in providing for a ratio-scaled index of a subject's beliefs. This technique permits the measurement of slight amounts of inconsistency, a technique which has obvious advantages over the cruder measures used by other consistency theories.

The Abelson-Rosenberg theory assumes, along with the other consistency models, that there is a tendency in man to reduce imbalance between attitudinal cognitions. However, the theory proposes two additional conditions that must exist before imbalance will produce change. First, the person must attend to the imbalance; undiscovered inconsistencies are not sufficient to motivate change. Second, the degree of imbalance must exceed the individual's "tolerance limit" for such imbalance. None of the other consistency theories explicitly emphasizes such preconditions, although the idea of a threshold for inconsistency is implicit in all of them.

Assuming the necessary conditions, it is hypothesized that the occurrence of imbalance will arouse pressures to restore balance. The restoration can take one of three forms: (1) a change in the signs and/or the relations; i.e., attitude change; (2) a redefinition of the cognitive elements; and (3) stopping thinking.

To illustrate the three modes of imbalance resolution, the authors take the issue of whether or not Yale University should admit "coeds." Suppose the elements in this domain are Having Coeds at Yale (C) and Getting Good Grades (G). For some students both elements may be positively valent, C+ and G+. If a particular student also believes that the presence of coeds would

[7] Abelson and Rosenberg have presented two versions of their theory. In their 1958 presentation, they do not provide their cognitive elements with signs, whereas the 1960 model makes such a provision. The theory as described here is the more recent version (Rosenberg & Abelson, in Rosenberg *et al.*, 1960, pp. 112–163).

interfere with (n) getting good grades, the cognitive unit would look like this: C + n G +. Assuming that the issue is hotly debated and the student is aware of the inconsistency, he will employ one of the above-mentioned techniques for reducing inconsistency. The first involves changing one of the two signs, either by weakening the desire for good grades or by opposing the admission of coeds. The student might also change the relation, by rationalizing that coeds do not really interfere with getting good grades.

A second possibility is for the student to differentiate "getting good grades" into "getting A's" and "getting C's." He could then reason that coeds may interfere with getting A's, but not with getting C's, and what he really wants is to get C's.

The final method for restoring balance is simply to stop thinking about the entire matter. With weak pressures to continue thinking and a structure highly resistant to change, the individual may well employ this method of achieving balance.

While the Abelson-Rosenberg theory allows for a variety of outcomes of imbalance, it does not specify which of the outcomes will occur in any given instance, nor does it predict unequivocally among the various changes of sign that could produce balance. A preliminary attempt has recently been made, however, to specify priorities among the three solutions. The authors suggest, for example, that the individual will try the first two methods, and if these fail because certain signs are resistant to change, he will then resort to "stopping thinking." They suggest further that if the individual adopts the first method, the preferred solution will be the one involving the least effort; i.e., the solution involving only one change in relation rather than multiple relation and sign changes. There is some evidence to support the "least effort principle" (Rosenberg & Abelson, 1960, pp. 123–163), but before turning to these studies, let us examine a variation of the Abelson-Rosenberg theory.

It has become traditional in psychology to characterize an attitude as a structure consisting of a *cognitive* as well as an *affective* component (Rosenberg *et al.*, 1960; Fishbein, 1963). Cognitions refer to beliefs about the relation between an attitude object and other objects of significance to the individual. Affect refers to the evaluative responses of the individual, how much he likes or dislikes a given attitude object. Rosenberg (1960b; 1965; Rosenberg *et al.*, 1960, pp. 60–61) has suggested that stable attitudes may be conceptualized as structures in which all of the affective-cognitive units or bands are balanced.[8] From this point of view, if the attitudinal object is positive, the related beliefs should reflect a positive relation between attitude object and other objects of positive affect, or a negative relation between the object and other objects of negative affect. If the attitudinal affect is negative, the related beliefs should reflect a positive relation between the object and other objects of negative affect, or a negative relation between the object and other objects of positive affect.

During the past decade, a number of studies have demonstrated a direct relationship between affective and cognitive dispositions toward an attitude object (e.g., Woodruff & DiVesta, 1948). These studies are deficient, however, in their measurement of cognitive aspects of attitudes. In an effort to improve the technique of measurement, Rosenberg (1956) developed an index of "cognitive structure." Each of 117 subjects was required to classify each of a set of 35 value statements (e.g., "having a steady income" or "all human beings having equal rights") in terms of (1) its importance to him as a source of satisfaction, and (2) its "perceived instrumentality," i.e., his estimate of whether the value would be achieved or blocked by a particular attitude object. In Rosenberg's study the object was "whether

[8] Rosenberg's initial work (1956) on affective-cognitive consistency preceded his collaborative efforts with Abelson. Subsequently, he has suggested that the two formulations may be treated within a common framework.

members of the Communist party should be allowed to address the public," but obviously any attitude issue could be used.

For the importance dimension, the subject was asked to rate each value on a 21-point scale in terms of how much satisfaction it would give him. For the "perceived instrumentality" dimension, the subject rated each value on an 11-point scale, where +5 represented "complete attainment of the value by allowing Communists to address the public," −5 represented "complete blocking," and 0 represented "neither attainment nor blocking." On the basis of these ratings, Rosenberg constructed an index consisting of the algebraic sum of the importance-instrumentality products for each of the values. The sum was assumed to reflect beliefs about the attitude object's value-attaining and value-blocking potential. The measure of attitudinal affect was less complex. Subjects were given a questionnaire containing the attitude issue and asked to check their first choice among five alternatives, ranging from "extreme approval" to "extreme opposition."

The major finding of the study was that the index of cognitive structure was significantly related to the measure of attitudinal affect. In both sign and magnitude, scores on the index were strongly associated with affective responses toward the attitude object. It was also found that perceived instrumentality was related to attitudinal affect under conditions where value importance was held constant. Conversely, a relationship was obtained between value importance and affect where perceived instrumentality was held constant. Similar results have been reported by Carlson (1956), Scott (1959a; 1959b), and Rosenberg and Oltman (1962). These studies appear to confirm the hypothesis of a relationship between affect toward an object and beliefs regarding that object. The results, however, are not entirely unequivocal. Rosenberg's technique of measurement was designed to provide independent indices of the cognitive and affective dimensions of an attitude. In point of fact, the measures of value importance and affect may well have been confounded, thereby resulting in a spuriously high relationship between affective and cognitive factors.

Rosenberg's (Rosenberg *et al.,* 1960, pp. 15–64; Rosenberg, 1965) main hypothesis, however, is concerned with more than simply the correlation between beliefs and feelings. He postulates that inconsistency between affective and cognitive components of an attitude produces forces toward restoring consistency. Restoration may again take a number of forms, but change in beliefs or affect is a primary concern of the theory. His prediction states that if a person undergoes a change in his beliefs about an object, his affect toward that object will show corresponding change. If there is change in the person's affect toward the object, his beliefs regarding the object will show corresponding change.

The most important requirement for testing this prediction is a set of manipulations which permit controlled variation of intra-attitudinal inconsistency. What is needed is an experimental operation by which affect can be manipulated independently of cognition and cognition independently of affect. The operation adopted by Rosenberg and his colleagues involved posthypnotic suggestions designed to change attitudinal affects. Several studies were conducted using this technique (Rosenberg & Gardner, 1958; Rosenberg, 1959; 1960a; 1960b), but we present only one of these in detail.

Eleven experimental and eleven control subjects were tested at two times for their affective and cognitive responses toward various social issues; e.g., Negroes moving into white neighborhoods, labor's right to strike, the U.S. being more conciliatory toward the U.S.S.R., and so forth (Rosenberg, 1960a). The measure of the cognitive response was essentially the same as the one employed in earlier studies by Rosenberg and described above as the cognitive structure index. The measure of affect consisted of a 16-point scale (ranging from "extremely in favor" to "extremely opposed") on which the subject evaluated the issues that subsequently received the hypnotic affect manipulation.

Between the two testing sessions, each experimental subject was hypnotized to a deep level. He was then given the suggestion that his affective responses toward each of two attitude issues would be changed upon awakening and that he would have no memory of this suggestion. The results showed a significant change not only in the subjects' affect toward the attitude objects, but also in their beliefs about the relationship between each of these objects and the values that were important to them. In a control group which received no affect manipulation, cognitive and affective responses remained stable from the first to the second administration of the attitude questionnaire.

The preceding studies were all specifically concerned with testing Rosenberg's thinking about the problem of affective-cognitive inconsistency. We noted, at the outset, that such inconsistency could be treated within the framework of the Abelson-Rosenberg balance theory. There is also substantial support for this theory and it is to this work that we now turn.

In an experiment by Rosenberg and Abelson (1960, pp. 123–163), each member of a group of Yale undergraduates was given a pamphlet which told him that he was to put himself into another person's position and "try to *be* this man." The assigned role was that of an "owner of a large department store." The role required the subject to adopt a specific attitude on each of several issues. Thus he was told to set a high positive value on "keeping sales at the highest possible volume in all departments of [the] store." Some subjects were told, in addition, to feel positively toward modern art and toward Fenwick, the manager of the rug department. A second group were required to feel negatively toward modern art but positively toward Fenwick. For a third group both modern art and Fenwick were to be negatively valued.

The assigned roles also involved beliefs about the relations among the three attitude objects (sales, modern art, and Fenwick). The subject was told that as the store owner he was to hold the following beliefs: (1) displays of modern art in department stores reduce sales volume; (2) Fenwick plans to mount such a display in the rug department; and (3) Fenwick in his tenure as rug department manager has increased the volume of sales. These three beliefs were supported by persuasive "paragraphs of facts."

In summary, each subject was assigned a role consisting of three cognitive relations. The relations were identical for all subjects, but the attitudes toward Fenwick and modern art were varied so as to create a state of imbalance in each role. In the first role, with all elements positively valent, it was the negative relation between modern art and sales that was unbalanced (+n+). In the second role, with modern art negatively valent, it was the relation involving the belief that Fenwick plans a modern art display that was unbalanced (+p−). In the third role, with both modern art and Fenwick negatively valent, it was the positive relation between Fenwick and increased rug sales that unbalanced (−p+).

Each of the three structures may be balanced in a number of different ways. The simplest or "least effortful" approach is to change the sign of the single unbalanced relation. In the first role, for example, changing the relation between modern art and sales volume from negative to positive would achieve balance. Alternatively, a subject could leave the negative relation intact, set a negative value on modern art, and change the relation between Fenwick and modern art to a negative one. The second resolution is obviously more complicated than the first, for it involves changing two aspects of the original structure rather than just one. The basic hypothesis of the experiment was: "The order of preference for paths toward restoring an unbalanced structure to balance will correspond to an ordering of the paths according to the number of sign changes required, from the least to the most" (Rosenberg *et al.*, 1960, p. 128).

To test this hypothesis, all subjects were asked to read three communications that were represented as coming from three different store officers. Each communication had something to say regarding the manager and the rug department. One communication argued, for example, that modern art displays actually increase sales, thereby reversing the unbalanced relation implied by the first role. Although each communication could restore balance, only one of them required a single sign change, the others involving two or three changes, depending on the role and the communication.

All subjects read the communications and then rated each one in terms of (1) how much it pleased him, (2) how much it persuaded him, and (3) how accurate it seemed to be. A composite "acceptability" index was computed by summing the three ratings. The main prediction was that subjects in each role would find most acceptable the communication that would restore balance through only one sign change. It was also predicted that of the two other communications, the one involving two sign changes to achieve balance would be preferred to the one involving three sign changes.

The data provided strong confirmation of both predictions. Imbalance resolution tended to follow a least effortful path. The communication advocating a single sign change was preferred to the others, and of the communications implying two and three sign changes, the former was preferred to the latter. The results showed, however, that not only did subjects look for a solution that required the least effort in order to restore balance, but they also sought the solution that maximized gain and minimized potential loss; i.e., the one that had the most pleasant consequences.

The main hypotheses of the Abelson-Rosenberg theory, then, have received substantial support. Admittedly, there are few other empirical studies directly testing the theory, but the results that have been reported are strongly confirmatory. An additional feature of the theory, as we already noted, is its concern with tolerance for inconsistency. Though such tolerance has frequently been observed (e.g., Zajonc, 1960), other consistency formulations have shown little interest in this fact. Hovland and Rosenberg (1960, pp. 215–221), in contrast, have suggested a number of variables that may influence whether or not specific inconsistencies will be tolerated. Some of these variables are personality characteristics of the individual; others are aspects of the situation within which the inconsistency occurs; and still others have to do with *content* aspects of the inconsistent cognitions. Rosenberg (1963) carried out a study designed to examine two such content variables and to show their effects upon the degree of tension aroused by inconsistent cognitions. The first variable concerned the hedonic or antihedonic aspect of inconsistent cognitions. The second variable was concerned with the personal-general dimension of inconsistent cognitions; i.e., whether the cognitions were those the individual could encounter regularly in his life (e.g., "an unpleasant neighbor") or whether they normally would not touch him directly (e.g., "victimization of the poor"). The procedure used in the study required subjects to judge how much they would be bothered by the inconsistency implied in each of sixteen hypothetical situations. Intolerance for inconsistency was found to be higher for cognitions conveying antihedonic meanings and lower for cognitions conveying hedonic meanings. Parallel results were reported for the personal-general variable. Inconsistent cognitions having personal reference aroused greater intolerance than those having more general reference. Almost identical results, it will be recalled, were obtained by Jordan (1953) and Weiss (1964), both of whom were mainly concerned with the hedonic-antihedonic dimension. The variables described here are almost certainly not the only content factors affecting responses to attitudinal inconsistency. Among others suggested by Rosenberg are initial complexity of the attitude before exposure to the inconsistency-arousing communication; the role of norms favoring the consistency standard; and the degree of visibility of the individual's expression of his attitudes. The question of tolerance for inconsistency will be considered in more detail later in the chapter.

Evaluation of Abelson and Rosenberg's Balance Theory

Among the more important criticisms of the Abelson-Rosenberg theory is its lack of precision in defining a balanced situation. There is no provision made for variation in the intensity of a person's attitudes; matched signs are all that is required for a state of balance to exist. This, we have seen, is a problem common to many of the consistency formulations and results in a decrement in predictive accuracy.

A second difficulty facing the theory concerns its failure to predict which outcome will occur in a given case of imbalance. It may be counted an advantage of the theory that it provides for several kinds of imbalance resolution, but it is deficient in not specifying the conditions under which each of these will occur. Hovland and Rosenberg (Rosenberg *et al.,* 1960, p. 288) recognize this problem and suggest that an important future research task is to spell out the conditions under which one or another type of inconsistency-reducing response will occur. An even more serious problem, perhaps, is the theory's inability to predict among the various changes in signs and relations by which attitude change will produce balance. The "least effort principle" represents an attempt at more precise specification, but this is hardly more than a first step. Congruity theory is more sophisticated in this matter, predicting one particular form of attitude change for a given instance of incongruity. (Dissonance theory, as will be shown later, allows for several kinds of imbalance resolution, but it too has difficulty in specifying which resolution will occur.)

The Abelson-Rosenberg theory does, however, have a number of very positive features. For one thing, it provides for a null relation, something that is notably lacking in many consistency theories. For another, it acknowledges a "threshold" for intolerance of inconsistency, hence the role of individual differences in reactions to inconsistency. Finally, the theory asserts that imbalance alone is not a sufficient condition for cognitive reorganization. A person must also be aware of the relevant cognitive elements and their relations before he will be motivated to change. This condition, while implicit in other consistency theories, is made manifest in the present model. We recognize that it is an open question whether responsiveness to inconsistency requires awareness. At the same time, however, it seems reasonable to assume that inconsistency will not be strongly motivating unless the individual is aware of it, or at least of some epiphenomenal aspect of it.

Turning from theory to experimental efforts made to test it, we can safely state that the present model has received substantial support. However, the studies themselves have certain methodological shortcomings. None of them employs deceptions designed to mask the experimenter's intent, hence the possibility that the subjects' reactions were artificial. The use of hypnotism as an alternative to deception may not always permit approximation of a real-life situation. It is well known, moreover, that not everyone can achieve deep hypnosis, and it may be that there are personality differences between those who can and those who cannot be hypnotized. If these differences are systematically related to the dependent variable, for example attitude change, this may seriously limit generalizability of the results. It is conceivable that there is a general factor of persuasibility (Hovland & Janis, 1959) which determines a person's susceptibility to hypnosis as well as to influence pressures designed to alter his attitudes (Hilgard, 1964). Attitude change in such a person may be attributable to his general persuasibility, a characteristic which would also make him vulnerable to hypnotic induction. Of significance, therefore, is the question of whether persons not susceptible to hypnosis would also show attitude change when confronted with a persuasive communication. Since the question is unanswerable using a hypnosis design, we can generalize results based on such designs only with considerable caution.

While not everyone can achieve deep hypnosis, most people can play a role satisfactorily. Brown (1962) considers the role-playing design superior to the technique of experimental deception, and it is quite true that deceptive measures may often result in biased results. But role-playing has serious limitations of its own. A role-playing subject may appear to respond more naturally than a subject who has been "conned," but it is problematic whether the former is quite as fully involved in the experimental situation. The engagement of a major part of a subject's arousal potential is a necessary prerequisite for approximating real-life reactions to inconsistency, for if motivation is low, between-conditions differences may not appear. A consequence of all this is a high proportion of Type II errors which inhibit rather than foster productive research. This, of course, cannot be said of the experiments by Abelson and Rosenberg, for these studies yielded results that were generally significant. We deem it a task of high priority, nonetheless, to replicate some of these studies relying on techniques (not necessarily deceptive) other than role playing and hypnosis. It may be that some role playing subjects react in terms of what they suspect the experimenter is interested in, namely, consistency-establishing responses. This possibility takes on added significance when we consider the recent work on experimenter-subject interaction as a source of bias in psychological research (Orne, 1962; T. M. Mills, 1962; Rosenthal, 1963; Rosenberg, 1965).

Festinger's Theory of Cognitive Dissonance

The theories discussed above have emphasized the specific inconsistencies which arise in connection with attitudes and their modification. An attempt to state a more general theory of inconsistency has been made by Festinger (1957) in his theory of cognitive dissonance. This formulation, because of its greater generality, has the advantage of being able to deal with a wide variety of psychological phenomena involving inconsistency. Thus the theory of cognitive dissonance has been useful in analyzing the social influence process, consequences of decisions, ego-defensive processes, and others.[9] Because of its ability to deal with such a broad range of issues, dissonance has generated more experimentation than the other theories of consistency. Even more important, for our purposes, is the fact that dissonance has more direct implications for the study of personality than the other less general models. For these reasons, we will give extended consideration to the theory in the discussion that follows.

Dissonance and Consonance Defined

The statement of the dissonance principle is quite simple: ". . . two elements [or cognitions] are in a dissonant relation if, con-

[9] Dissonance experiments have commonly been grouped into three categories (Festinger, 1957; Brehm & Cohen, 1962). The first, called "free choice" situations, involves a choice between alternatives which differ along some dimension of attractiveness. Dissonance in these studies is assumed to be a function of the proportion of cognitions favoring the rejected alternative. The second type of experiment is called a "forced compliance" situation, and involves a choice between engaging or not engaging in an act discrepant with prior attitudes. In the third type of study, "exposure" experiments, the subject is confronted with information inconsistent with his prior cognitions.

sidering these two alone, the obverse of one element would follow from the other" (Festinger, 1957, p. 13). The principle further holds that ". . . dissonance, being psychologically uncomfortable, will motivate the person to try to reduce the dissonance and achieve consonance" and ". . . in addition to trying to reduce it, the person will actively avoid situations . . . which would likely increase the dissonance" (Festinger, 1957, p. 3). The presence of dissonance, in other words, provides a source of motivation in much the same way as do other drive states like hunger and thirst.

The primary units of dissonance theory are cognitions and the relations between them. Festinger defines a cognitive element or cognition as any knowledge about the environment, oneself, one's behavior, or about one's beliefs. The use of the word "knowledge" may be ill-advised, since cognitive elements include things to which knowledge does not ordinarily refer, e.g., beliefs. Brown (1962) suggests that the elements might better be called propositions, whereas Brehm and Cohen (1962) consider them to be items of information. Whether cognitive elements refer to propositions, items of information, or knowledge is doubtless unclear in the Festinger formulation, but to belabor the issue seems to us pedantic.

More important is the question of whether a cognition is a single element or a cluster of elements (cf. Jordan, 1963a). For example, is the knowledge "Smoking is unhealthy" a single element, or a group of elements consisting of more specific knowledges? Festinger suggests that this question is presently unanswerable. This may be so, but we cannot agree with his next statement, ". . . it may be a question which does not need answering" (Festinger, 1957, p. 10). In any given situation, it is quite important to specify the number of cognitive elements involved, for the prediction of dissonance arousal often depends on the clarity of this specification. Take, for example, the cognition "I am an outstanding person." Is this cognition dissonant with the knowledge that one has just injured a close friend? Not necessarily. It is dissonant if the cognition "I am an outstanding person" means that the person thinks of himself as kind and considerate. It is not dissonant if the cognition implies only a favorable evaluation of one's intelligence and ability. Of course we recognize the danger of a *reductio ad absurdum*. One can also question whether the cognition "I am kind" is a single element or a group of elements. The criterion for deciding when we are dealing with a single element appears to be an empirical one, determined by the specification of the relationship between a given pair of cognitions.

The other major element in dissonance theory is the relationship between cognitions. A relationship is considered consonant if one cognition implies the other in a psychological sense (Brehm & Cohen, 1962). Psychological implication would occur if a person felt perfectly secure because he knew there were only friends in his immediate vicinity. In other words, implication means that holding a given cognition, A, leads to another cognition, B.

Two cognitions, A and B, are in a dissonant relationship if not-A follows from B. The two cognitions may not fit together because they are logically inconsistent, because cultural standards dictate that they do not fit, because of past experience, and so on. Cognitive elements that are neither consonant nor dissonant are said to be *irrelevant;* i.e., they have nothing to do with one another. For example, I believe that the Missouri River is a vast muddy stream and I also believe that the New York City subway system is inefficiently managed. Having nothing to do with each other, these cognitions bear an irrelevant relationship.

The Role of Commitment and Choice

In an extension of the original dissonance model, Brehm and Cohen (1962) have proposed that *commitment* to an action or point of view is a necessary condition for the arousal of dissonance. A person is said to be committed when his decision to do one thing rather than another unequivocally determines subsequent events, or when he actively performs an action that can be revoked only with great difficulty. The significance of commitment lies in the fact that it permits one to say when cognitions become relevant, hence either consonant or dissonant with each other. It is only when a person engages in a given behavior that the corresponding cognitions become relevant, and therefore either consonant or dissonant with knowledge of the committed behavior.

Though the conceptual meaning of commitment requires greater specification, there is some empirical evidence for the role of commitment in the arousal of dissonance. Brehm and Leventhal (1962, pp. 192–201) asked college students to judge the weight of each of a series of fifteen weights and then to predict, after each estimate, the average weight of the series. The weights alternated between light and heavy, but the eleventh weight was much heavier than the subject was likely to expect. This weight served as the discrepant information. In the High Commitment condition subjects were told, after judging the tenth weight, that their estimate of the average of the series at that point would determine whether or not they would win a $5.00 gift certificate, hence how well they performed. In the Low Commitment condition, subjects were told only that their judgment after the tenth trial was important. Within each of the commitment-treatments, some subjects were informed that the experiment was an important scientific study and that the experimenter was interested in how well they performed (High Importance). For the remaining subjects, ego-involvement was minimized and study presented as quite unimportant (Low Importance). It was hypothesized that dissonance would be greater under High Commitment as compared with Low, and would increase in magnitude as the importance of being accurate increased. It was expected that pressures to reduce dissonance would lead subjects to minimize the importance of the discrepant weight in estimating the series average. High Commitment-High Importance subjects, in other words, should show the least shift in their estimated average from before to after exposure to the discrepant (eleventh) weight. The results supported expectations. Other experiments have gone even further, suggesting that commitment to a discrepant position without actual behavior may be sufficient to produce cognitive dissonance (Rabbie, Brehm, & Cohen, 1959; Brehm & Cohen, 1959b; Brehm & Cohen, 1962, pp. 115–116; Brock & Blackwood, 1962).

Although commitment appears to be an important factor in the arousal of dissonance, the role of *choice* in the process of commitment has even greater significance. Brehm and Cohen (1962, p. 191) take the position that the arousal of dissonance is unequivocal in situations involving choice. The reason is that the act of choice implies commitment to one course of action rather than another, with the result that information inconsistent with the commitment becomes dissonant. The inconsistent information consists of knowledge that commitment implies a frustration of need satisfactions associated with the unchosen alternative(s).

The importance of choice in the dissonance process has been documented by a large number of experiments (Cohen, Terry, & Jones, 1959; Brehm & Cohen, 1959b; Brehm & Cohen, 1962, pp. 88–91, 210–217; Davis & Jones, 1960; Brock, 1962; Brock & Buss, 1962; Deutsch, Krauss, & Rosenau, 1962; Glass, 1964). Take the study by Cohen, Terry, and Jones. Yale undergraduates were interviewed on the issue of marriage before the age of 23, an ego-involving issue on the campus at that time. Subjects were then given high or low choice about whether or not to listen to a communication contrary to their own position. High Choice was induced by telling the subjects: "I'll leave it entirely up to you whether or not I [i.e., the experimenter] read it [the contrary communication] to you. Would you like to hear it?" If the subject said yes, he was asked, "Are you sure?" If he said yes, the experimenter asked again if he was sure. Only if he agreed a third time was the contrary communication read to him. In the Low Choice condition, subjects were simply told that the contrary communication would be read to them. After the choice manipulation, all subjects listened to the communication and their attitudes were remeasured. Among subjects who were extremely opposed to the position advocated by the communication, High Choice produced greater attitude change toward this position than did Low Choice. An experiment by Brehm (1959) has shown that a person need not know about the potentially dissonance-arousing event at the time of choice for it to create dissonance when it occurs. A discrepant event that is a *fait accompli* can affect the dissonance created by prior choice.

In each of these studies, the dissonance-arousing character of choice depended on its being made freely with only a minimum of pressure. The perception of choice is often difficult to induce in an experimental situation (e.g., Brehm & Cohen, 1959b). The act of making a choice can vary from complete volition, where the person believes he is personally responsible for his actions, to a situation in which commitment to discrepant behavior is induced through reward or punishment. Coercion or positive inducement provides justification for inconsistent behavior by enabling the person to appeal to these factors as a rationalization for his actions.

A number of experiments have shown that an increase in justification may induce the person to engage in discrepant behavior, but with the creation of only minimal dissonance. In the now classic study by Festinger and Carlsmith (1959), sixty female subjects performed a boring task and then were asked to tell the next subject (an experimental confederate) that the task was interesting and enjoyable. Justification for making this false statement was varied by offering to pay some subjects $1.00 (High Dissonance condition), and others $20 (Low Dissonance condition). A Control condition, in which the subjects were not asked to lie, was included to determine whether the experimental task was really experienced as unpleasant. It was found that Low Dissonance and Control subjects rated the task as unpleasant, whereas High Dissonance subjects evaluated it positively. Similar results were obtained in a replication by Cohen (in Brehm & Cohen, 1962, pp. 74–78) who used four rather than two levels of reward. In sum, the evidence suggests that if a person is induced to perform an act to which he is opposed, dissonance and consequent attitude change will occur to the extent that the incentive is just great enough to induce him to perform the act.

The evidence, however, is not entirely one-sided. A study by Janis and Gilmore (1965) found that incentive value had no effect on the arousal of dissonance, and Rosenberg (1965) reports evidence that attitude change varied directly rather than inversely with amount of reward. An earlier study by Leventhal and Brehm (1962) also yielded results contrary to dissonance theory expectations. These authors found that liking for instrumental activity increased rather than decreased with increments in reward magnitude. A parallel result was obtained in a more recent study by Leventhal (1964). Subjects were offered three levels of reward (credit points) for committing themselves to three hours of work at a highly repetitious task. Those offered a larger number of credit points (high reward) showed greater liking for the task than did subjects offered fewer points (low reward).

Though these findings seem to present some difficulty for dissonance theory, they should not be taken as conclusive. Other dissonance studies have demonstrated the effects of justification by varying the number (and kind) of reasons given to a person for engaging in discrepant behavior (Cohen, Brehm, & Fleming, 1958; Rabbie, Brehm, &

Cohen, 1959; Brehm, 1960; Brock & Blackwood, 1962; Freedman, 1963). In each of these experiments justification was found to act as a consonant cognition; it gave the subject a reason for acting as he did, thereby reducing or eliminating the dissonance.

It has recently been suggested that a two-process model may be necessary to reconcile the conflicting experimental findings. Leventhal (1964), for example, has proposed that as long as the total reward for engaging in discrepant behavior remains inadequate, increasing its size will only decrease the amount of dissonance aroused. Under these conditions, liking will be inversely related to reward magnitude. However, at a reward level which is considered just barely adequate by the individual, dissonance processes cease to operate. Raising reward level above this point will give rise to a direct relation between liking and reward magnitude. There is as yet little evidence to substantiate this line of reasoning, but it does suggest a fruitful line of further inquiry.

In the studies we have been discussing, justification was manipulated by offering rewards or by appealing to a subject's scientific and altruistic values. Coercion, too, can reduce perceived choice by providing justification for discrepant behavior. Knowledge that one will be punished for refusing to behave in a way contrary to one's attitudes is consonant with knowledge of the inconsistent behavior. Studies by Smith (1961), Brehm and Cohen (1962, pp. 84–88), Aronson and Carlsmith (1963), and Zimbardo *et al.* (1964a) provide evidence in support of this proposition.

We began this discussion with the assertion that choice is a necessary condition for the arousal of dissonance. But is volition really more than the inverse of justification? An experiment by Brehm and Cohen (1962, pp. 206–210) suggests an affirmative answer. The purpose of the experiment was to test whether dissonance depends on the coercive force itself or on the perception of choice arising from the circumstances surrounding the coercion. Subjects were induced to perform an unpleasant task by inappropriate threats made by the experimenter. It was assumed that such "illegitimate" coercion would result in a perception of choice about whether or not to participate, for compliance could not under these conditions be fully justified on the grounds of threat. The results showed a tendency, though nonsignificant, for High Coercion subjects to feel more volition than Low Coercion subjects. The data indicated, moreover, that the magnitude of dissonance was indeed a function of perceived choice, and not of coercion. Further support for this hypothesis comes from a study by Leventhal and Brehm (1962), who report that as pressure to choose between two alternatives increases, the magnitude of the post-decisional dissonance decreases.

The Magnitude of Dissonance

In discussing the role of commitment and choice in the arousal of dissonance, we indicated that these factors may also influence the magnitude of dissonance. The degree of dissonance is, in addition, a direct function of two other factors: (1) the importance of the relevant cognitions, and (2) the ratio of dissonant to consonant cognitions, where each cognitive element is weighted according to its importance to the person (Festinger, 1957, pp. 16ff.).

Let us examine each of these factors in greater detail. First, the "ratio" variable. Brehm and Cohen (1962) point out that this variable provides what is unique and non-obvious about dissonance theory. Take, for example, the finding cited above that performance of a disliked action produces little dissonance if there is substantial justification for the action, but a great deal of dissonance if there is little justification. An interpretation of this result is that under high justification more of the relevant cognitions are consonant than dissonant with performance of the act; under low justification, more of them are dissonant.

Several experiments support the hypothesis that dissonance varies with the ratio of dissonant to consonant cognitions (Brehm, 1956, 1960; Brehm & Cohen, 1959a; Raven & Fishbein, 1961; Cohen, 1962b; Brock, 1963). In the experiment by Brehm (1956), it was reasoned that a choice between alternatives will result in dissonance to the extent that the rejected alternative contains positive features and the chosen alternative contains negative or unattractive features. Female college students rated the desirability of eight consumer appliances, were then told they would receive one of the items as a reward, and were allowed to choose between two of them. After they received their gifts, they rerated all of the appliances. Some of the subjects made their choice between articles they had rated as about equally attractive, and other subjects between articles on which their ratings differed greatly. Higher dissonance was expected among the first group of subjects, since rejection of an equally attractive alternative results in a greater proportion of dissonance cognitions than rejection of a less attractive alternative. Dissonance could be reduced in these circumstances by increasing the desirability of the chosen alternative and/or by decreasing the desirability of the rejected alternative. The pre- to postchoice ratings confirmed the predictions, changes being greater for high as compared with low dissonance subjects.

Other relevant research comes from experiments concerned with dissonance resulting from effort. If a person continues to expend effort in order to reach a positively valent object, but does not reach it, he will presumably experience dissonance. His cognition that he is expending effort is dissonant with his cognition that he is unrewarded. One way to reduce dissonance is to attach extra value to performance of the unrewarded activity.[10] A number of experiments provide evidence of the effects of effort on dissonance arousal (Cohen, 1959; Aronson & Mills, 1959; Aronson, 1961; Yaryan & Festinger, 1961; Zimbardo, 1962). In the Cohen experiment, subjects were told they would have great difficulty in understanding a communication (High Effort) or that comprehension would be relatively easy (Low Effort). All subjects were initially opposed to the point of view advocated by the communication. It was expected that dissonance would be greater in the High Effort condition, hence greater attitude change. The results were in line with theoretical expectations. Although the findings of "effort" experiments are generally supportive of dissonance theory, they must in some cases be approached with caution—either because the data are equivocal (Aronson, 1961, 1963; Lott, 1963) or because they are open to a variety of alternative explanations (Jordan, 1963; Chapanis & Chapanis, 1964).

We noted at the beginning of this section that dissonance varies not only with the ratio of dissonant to consonant cognitions, but also with the importance of the relevant cognitions. In other words, the more important the inconsistent cognitions are to a person, the greater will be the dissonance between them.

A number of experiments have attempted to demonstrate the effects of importance on the magnitude of dissonance. Two of these failed to show the hypothesized effect (Mills, Aronson, & Robinson, 1959; Rosen, 1961). Other studies, however, have successfully shown that dissonance does in fact vary with importance (Cohen, Brehm & Latané, 1959; Zimbardo, 1960; Deutsch, Krauss, & Rosenau, 1962; Brehm & Leventhal, 1962, pp. 193–198; Brehm & Cohen, 1962, pp. 94–97). In the Zimbardo experiment, for example, pairs of friends were led to believe that they disagreed either a little or a great

[10] Lawrence and Festinger (1962) suggest that among rats, greater resistance to extinction under conditions requiring considerable effort may be due to the development of extra attractions for the effortful activity. These additional attractions reduce the dissonance aroused by engaging in unrewarded behavior. Mowrer (1963) takes issue with this interpretation, arguing that greater resistance to extinction under effort may be an artifact of the design of extinction experiments.

deal with respect to their judgments of a case study of juvenile delinquency. Importance of the judgments was varied by telling some pairs that their performance was a good indication of their social values, personality, and general philosophy of life (High Importance); other pairs were told that their judgments had little significance (Low Importance). Subjects could reduce dissonance by changing their judgments to agree with those of their friend. It was found that High Importance subjects changed significantly more than Low Importance subjects.

Discrepancy Size

The dissonance model recognizes degrees of dissonance, but it does not make explicit provision for variation in the magnitude of the relationship between dissonant cognitions. Any pair of cognitive elements are either consonant, dissonant, or irrelevant. Brehm and Cohen (1962, pp. 12–17) introduce a significant change, therefore, when they talk about the magnitude of dissonance varying with the *size of the discrepancy* between cognitive elements (for example, between a person's opinion and the contrary opinion expressed by a communicator). Many studies of attitude change have in fact relied on this assumption (e.g., Cohen, 1959; Zimbardo, 1960), but none of these have specified how attitude and attitudinal discrepancy may be conceptualized in the terms of dissonance theory.

Brehm and Cohen (1962, pp. 14–15) attempt to deal with this problem but succeed only in detailing some of the complex issues involved in relating the attitude construct to theory. They point out that an attitudinal position is usually a higher order derivative of the relevant cognitive elements and, as such, is not appropriate to the terms of dissonance theory. In order to predict whether dissonance will be aroused in a given situation, one needs to know all the consonant and dissonant cognitions summarized by the attitude construct. There are, however, difficulties involved in determining relevant cognitions. Take a person's attitude toward law. A measure of his attitude might consist of items concerning judicial procedure, ethics of the legal profession, issues of justice and retribution, the punitive character of law enforcement, and so on. Given such a multifaceted measure, how might dissonance occur? Obviously in connection with any one of the aspects of the attitude. But unless most of them were involved in the arousal of dissonance, we can hardly expect an appreciable effect on the attitude measure as a result of dissonance reduction. If, in fact, most of them were consonant with the event designed to produce dissonance, little attitude change would occur. It is difficult, in short, to relate the cluster of cognitive elements called "attitudes toward law" to a relevant but discrepant cluster of elements. We might isolate one of the dimensions, e.g., police practices, and ask what other cognitions are relevant to inducing a change in the first set of cognitions. Such a procedure would, of course, seriously limit the scope of one's research.

It is clear that dissonance theory must provide for discrepancy size, and one way to do this by rephrasing the dissonance principle, as Brehm and Cohen have done, so that the magnitude of dissonance is assumed to vary with degree of discrepancy. Still, one would hope for a more formal treatment of the problem. Jordan (1963) refers to this same weakness when he suggests that the difficulty encountered by Brehm and Cohen may stem from a failure to understand that a cognitive element is an inferred entity, and that nothing in cognition which can be recognized as an entity is a cognitive element. It is invariably a cluster of elements. Jordan may be correct, but we fail to see how this would solve the problem of giving explicit theoretical status to discrepancy size. Even if one is dealing with a cluster of elements, it is still necessary to select a specific cluster and then ask what other cognitions are relevant. The theoretical status of discrepancy size will remain equivocal until the relationship between attitudes and these relevant clusters is clarified.

Granted it seems reasonable to include discrepancy size in the dissonance formulation, what evidence is there that it actually affects the magnitude of dissonance? Several studies of attitude change support the assumption of a direct relationship between dissonance and degree of discrepancy (Cohen, 1959; Zimbardo, 1960; Allyn & Festinger, 1961; Bergin, 1962; Hill, 1963; Freedman, 1963). Other investigators find that the monotonic relationship holds only for highly involving issues (Carlson, 1956; Hovland, Harvey, & Sherif, 1957), or where the communicator has high credibility (Hovland & Pritzker, 1957). Indeed Festinger and Aronson (1960) suggest that the inconsistent results from these studies may be due to differential credibility of the communicator. They argue that when credibility is high, attitude change varies directly with discrepancy size. When credibility is low, the response shifts from attitude change to disbelief or derogation of the communicator, the degree of derogation varying directly with extent of disagreement. Support for this line of reasoning comes from a variety of social influence and attitude change experiments (Osgood & Tannenbaum, 1955; Harvey, Kelley, & Shapiro, 1957; Jones & Köhler, 1958; Brehm & Lipsher, 1959; Zimbardo, 1960; Allyn & Festinger, 1961; Bergin, 1962; Aronson, Turner & Carlsmith, 1963).

The Aronson *et al.* study, for example, showed that a highly credible communicator was more successful in inducing attitude change than a mildly credible communicator for all degrees of discrepancy (cf. Hovland & Pritzker, 1957). In addition, attitude change was found to increase as the degree of discrepancy increased. In contrast to this were the findings for the mildly credible condition. There, amount of attitude change increased up to the point of moderate discrepancy; as discrepancy became more extreme, attitude change decreased. It was also found that subjects derogated the mildly credible communicator to a greater extent than the highly credible communicator, although there were no significant differences in derogation among the discrepancy conditions. These data, then, support the prediction that credibility and discrepancy interact to produce attitude change. They do not support expectations concerning the derogation-discrepancy relationship. There may be a theoretical difficulty here, for Allyn and Festinger (1961) also found that derogation did not vary as a direct function of discrepancy size; and Brehm and Lipsher (1959) report that extreme discrepancy produced high rather than low perceived trustworthiness of the communicator. Cohen (1962a), moreover, has reported the occurrence of a "boomerang effect" under conditions of extreme discrepancy; i.e., a change in attitude in the direction opposite to that advocated.

Despite these ambiguities, Bergin (1962) has extended the Festinger-Aronson approach to the problem of psychotherapeutic interpretation. He asserts that what is meant by a "depth interpretation" is a statement by a therapist which is highly discrepant with the patient's self-concept. Therefore, deep interpretations should produce more change in self-concept than superficial interpretations, the change being greater the more respect the patient has for his therapist's competence. Bergin obtained strong support for this prediction in an experiment involving two levels of credibility and three degrees of discrepant interpretation.

The Reduction of Dissonance

To return to the original statement of the dissonance principle, it will be remembered that the existence of dissonance is assumed to be psychologically uncomfortable and this leads to attempts to reduce dissonance. The greater the magnitude of dissonance, the greater the pressures to reduce it. In the Festinger study (1957) and that by Brehm and Cohen (1962) admission is made that it is presently impossible to measure dissonance directly, that it can only be inferred from the subject's attempts at dissonance reduction. Of particular significance, therefore, are the observation and measurement of dissonance reductive behavior.

A person may reduce dissonance by changing one of his cognitions, adding new consonant cognitions, or by reducing the importance of all relevant cognitions. Changing a cognitive element might occur in the following situation. Suppose a man who is opposed to aggression injures another person whom he does not necessarily want to hurt. His knowledge that he has been aggressive is dissonant with his belief that aggression is bad. The man might achieve consonance in this situation by changing his beliefs, that is, by becoming more favorably disposed toward aggression. The reduction of dissonance by changing relevant cognitions has received by far the greatest amount of attention in the experimental literature. Brehm and Cohen (1962, pp. 306–307) report 37 different experiments on the subject as of 1962.

Cognitive change may reduce dissonance, but a more compelling case could be made for the theory if there was also evidence of accompanying changes in noncognitive aspects of behavior. A number of experiments provide such evidence. Brehm (in Brehm & Cohen, 1962, pp. 133–142) has shown that when a person commits himself to food or water deprivation and subsequently is given the opportunity to eat or drink as much as he wants, he not only reports feeling less hungry and thirsty, but also orders fewer food items and drinks less water. Aronson and Carlsmith (1963) have also reported a relationship between behavioral and cognitive change. College students who expected to do poorly on a test and then discovered they had done well changed a significant number of correct responses to incorrect responses when asked, on a pretext, to repeat the test. A similar result is reported by Cohen and Zimbardo (1962, pp. 143–151) for a situation involving delayed auditory feedback. In addition, task productivity has been shown to increase following compliance with a disliked supervisor (Weick, 1964), and Adams and Rosenbaum (1962) report that interviewers who felt they were being overpaid for their services interviewed more respondents than a comparable group who felt the salary was appropriate to their skills. These studies present a strong case for the correlation between cognitive and behavioral change following dissonance arousal.

The addition of new consonant cognitions is another mode of dissonance reduction. The man who injured another might find it difficult to change his beliefs or behavior, but he might be able to add the cognition that his victim provoked the attack and, therefore, he was justified in his aggression. Such rationalization would effectively reduce dissonance because even a person who does not believe in violence may engage in aggression under legitimate provocation. Support for this line of reasoning can be found in experiments by Davis and Jones (1960) and Glass (1964). Also relevant is an earlier study by Festinger, Riecken, and Schachter (1956). These investigators studied a group of religious fanatics called "Seekers," who claimed to have received a message from outer space informing them of a major flood. When the disaster did not occur, the "Seekers" became even more convinced of the validity of their beliefs, and began a campaign of intensive proselytizing. Presumably they reduced dissonance by seeking social support (i.e., new consonant cognitions) for their mystical beliefs (cf. Hardyck & Braden, 1962).

A third major technique for reducing dissonance involves decreasing the importance of the relevant cognitions. In our example of aggression, the man might decrease the importance of his stated opposition to aggression (Glass & Wood, 1968). Or, alternatively, he might minimize the attack, saying, in effect, "The pain I administered was really quite mild" (Brock & Buss, 1962).

There are of course numerous variations on these modes of dissonance reduction. For example, an analysis needs to be made of the extent to which selective forgetting of cognitive elements is used as a means of dissonance reduction (Festinger, 1957; Brehm & Cohen, 1962, pp. 92–97; Schlachet, 1965). Indeed Brehm and Cohen (1962) note that too little is known about how dissonance is reduced or how different modes of dissonance reduction interact. Jordan (1963) and Berkowitz (1963) make the same point, and Brown concludes that "unless many variables other than dissonance are specified, the theory does not predict one technique" (1962, p. 51). The situation is not, however, completely hopeless. Several attempts have been made to specify priorities among different modes of dissonance reduction (e.g., Raven, Anthony, & Mansson, 1960; Brehm & Cohen, 1962; Brock & Buss, 1962, 1964; Weick, 1964), and even in the original formulation (Festinger, 1957) it was suggested that the cognition least resistant to change will determine the way in which dissonance is reduced. Thus cognitions referring to attitudes are more easily changed than cognitions referring to the perception of the physical environment. An individual should have greater control over his attitudes than over the physical environment, since the latter often involves relatively immutable qualities such as form or size.

Experimental evidence has not always supported this line of reasoning. Take, for example, the experiment by Brock and Buss (1962) in which college students delivered electric shock to another person when they were on record as opposing such punishment. The authors found that a change in perception of the physical environment (minimization of the pain of electric shock) was a more favored avenue of dissonance reduction than a change in attitude toward the use of shock. However, the order in which the experimenters presented the avenues of dissonance reduction may have produced the results artifactually.

But there is still other evidence which seems to run counter to the idea of a hierarchy based on resistance to change. Self-referent cognitions, insofar as they reflect the individual's past performance, should be highly resistant to change (e.g., Harvey, Kelley, & Shapiro, 1957; Pilisuk, 1962), yet a number of studies report substantial modification of a person's self-concept following exposure to psychological test results (Bramel, 1962, 1963; Bergin, 1962; Secord, Backman, & Eachus, 1964; Glass, 1964). An explanation of these findings may depend on the strength of the individual's commitment to his self-concept. If the commitment is strong, defensive processes are invoked rather than just a strengthening of the original self-concept. If the discrepant information is equally resistant to change, dissonance may be reduced through a reaffirmation of the self-concept, or at least those aspects of it which are involved in the dissonance-producing situation.

How dissonance is reduced depends only partly on the resistance to change of relevant cognitive elements. There is also a consideration of multiple responses to a dissonance-producing stimulus. It has been suggested that if two alternative responses are possible only one will occur. Indeed, studies by Steiner and Peters (1958), Zimbardo (1960), and Steiner and Rogers (1963) indicate that plural responses may be contradictory, or at least the use of one response seems to make the alternative unnecessary. Steiner and Johnson (1964), however, report that dissonance-reducing responses may combine additively, thereby resulting in greater dissonance reduction than when only one response is used. Additional support for this point of view comes from experiments suggesting that cognitive and behavioral change act as mutually reinforcing avenues of dissonance reduction (Brehm, 1962; Brock & Grant, 1963; Weick, 1964). A number of studies of aggression and person perception have also demonstrated the complementary character of dissonance-reducing responses (Brock & Buss, 1962, 1964; Glass & Wood, 1967; Mirels & Mills, 1964). On balance, it would seem that multiple responses to dissonance are not incompatible and, perhaps, even mutually reinforcing.

Avoidance of Dissonance

The original statement of the dissonance principle assumes that in addition to tendencies to reduce or eliminate dissonance, there are "tendencies to avoid increases of dissonance or to avoid the occurrence of dissonance altogether" (Festinger, 1957, pp. 29–30). The avoidance of dissonant information occurs, for example, where a person initiates discussion with someone he thinks will agree with his opinions but avoids discussion with someone who may disagree.

A number of studies have demonstrated the occurrence of selective exposure to relevant information, but each was confined to showing that subjects seek new consonant information (e.g., Brodbeck, 1956; Adams, 1961; Maccoby, Maccoby, Romney, & Adams, 1961). Six studies were specifically designed to test the dissonance-avoidance hypothesis (Ehrlich, Guttman, Schönbach, & Mills, 1957; Festinger, 1957, pp. 126–131, 162–176; Cohen, Brehm, & Latané, 1959; Mills, Aronson, & Robinson, 1959; Rosen, 1961; Adams, 1961). Again it was found that subjects sought new consonant information, but there was no evidence that they tried to avoid dissonance-arousing information. Indeed, Rosen (1961) reports that subjects sometimes seek information which is contrary to their own viewpoints. It may be that people seek new information, whether consonant or dissonant (Chapanis & Chapanis, 1964). Feather (1962; 1963) seems to have obtained this kind of result, when he reports that cigarette smokers as compared with nonsmokers are more interested in information about smoking and lung cancer, regardless of whether it supports or does not support a positive relationship.

Two attempts have been made to explain lack of support for the dissonance-avoidance derivation (Brehm & Cohen, 1962; Festinger *et al.,* 1964). Brehm and Cohen suggest that one reason may be the salience of dissonant information immediately after the arousal of dissonance. Increased salience, they reason, would make it difficult for a person to avoid exposure to discrepant information. Experimental evidence for this point of view is, unfortunately, rather weak. Furthermore, the salience hypothesis is not explicitly derived from dissonance theory but is, rather, an instance of reformulation of theory to fit unanticipated results. Such reformulation is certainly legitimate, but in the present case, the new hypothesis seems to contradict theory. The arousal of dissonance should lead to attempts to reduce it, not to increase it as the salience hypothesis seems to suggest.

Festinger (1964, p. 96) offers another explanation for disconfirmation of the dissonance-avoidance derivation. He acknowledges that the original hypothesis may have been incorrectly stated, and that avoidance of dissonance-increasing information may occur only if the person feels unable to cope with the new information, or if there are no other reasons for exposure such as usefulness of the information. He suggests, therefore, that earlier studies (e.g., Mills *et al.,* 1959) were inadequately designed, insofar as they failed to control for the subject's self-confidence and the usefulness of the information to which the subject was exposed. If a person has confidence in his ability to cope with dissonant information, and if this information is useful in developing effective counterarguments, he should be willing to expose himself to such material in order to develop counterarguments. If he lacks confidence in his ability to counterargue, and if the dissonant information is not particularly useful, the person should avoid exposure to the dissonant information.

Support for these hypotheses comes from a recent experiment by Canon (1964, pp. 83–95). Subjects were led to believe they were taking part in a study of methods of teaching business policy. They were scheduled in groups of four to seven, but it was emphasized that they were to work independently. Each subject was given a booklet of case studies of business problems, and asked to indicate which of two solutions he would choose. After completing three of a total of four case studies, each subject was told privately whether or not he had made the correct choice. To create high confidence in their ability to cope with business problems, half the subjects were informed they had chosen correctly in each case and that, each time, the others had been incorrect. To create low confidence, the remaining subjects were informed they had chosen incorrectly while the others had been correct. Within each self-confidence treatment, half the subjects were assigned to a Highly Useful condition. Thus on the fourth case, they were told that instead of the usual feedback they would receive a series of questions posed from the point of view supporting the alternative they had not chosen. Their task was to combat these arguments by a written counterargument. To assist them in preparing their arguments, they were told they could read articles both supportive and nonsupportive of their own points of view. Each subject was given a list of descriptive titles of these articles and asked to rate them in terms of how much he wanted to read each one. Since the subjects would have to engage in rebuttal, it was assumed they would find it useful to have access to contradecisional information. The other half of the subjects were assigned to a Less Useful condition, in which they were to write a presentation of their position on the fourth case without having to engage in a rebuttal of opposing arguments. Presumably, they would see less usefulness in having access to contradecisional material.

The results were consistent with expectations. When contradecisional information was useful, and if the subject was confident that he could cope with it, there was a preference for reading such dissonance-increasing material. Conversely, when the dissonant articles were less useful, and if the subject had less confidence in his ability to deal with the material, there was a preference for consonant information. These results suggest that the potential usefulness of dissonant material interacts with the self-confidence of the person; i.e., the lower the self-confidence and the less the perceived usefulness, the greater is the tendency to avoid the dissonant material. We must regard as tentative, however, any conclusions based on these findings. For one thing, they involve only one experiment, and for another, the effect of the "usefulness" variable has not been successfully replicated (Jecker, 1964b). Festinger may be on the right track in proposing a new statement of the dissonance-avoidance hypothesis, but only further research will tell us how to phrase the new statement.

Evaluation of the Theory of Cognitive Dissonance

Cognitive dissonance has been the subject of a number of critical evaluations (Asch, 1958; Osgood, 1960; Jordan, 1963a, 1963b; Meyers, 1963; Stotland, 1963; Mowrer, 1963; Chapanis & Chapanis, 1964; Zimbardo, 1964c; Silverman, 1964a). We considered some of the evaluations of theoretical issues earlier in the section, but of dissonance experiments more needs to be said.

The most general criticism has been set forth by Chapanis and Chapanis (1964). These authors argue that the manipulations used in dissonance studies may not actually have produced dissonance, and if they did, there is no assurance that they did not also produce other internal states which could account for the findings. Thereupon follows a discussion of several experiments designed to buttress this argument. Take, for example, their discussion of the Aronson and Mills experiment (1959). In this study female college students were subjected to embarrassment in order to become members of a group discussing sexual matters. Upon learning that the group discussion was quite dull (dealing only with the sexual behavior of animals), subjects appeared to reduce dissonance by evaluating the discussion as more interesting than it really was. The Chapanises suggest several alternative explanations of this finding. The girls may have evaluated the discussion favorably because of the relief they felt when it turned out to be banal. Alternatively, the severity of initiation may have led to the feeling of successful accomplishment over a painful obstacle, and "there is no need to postulate a drive due to dissonance if a *pleasure principle* can account for the results quite successfully" (Chapanis & Chapanis, 1964, p. 5). But even the authors admit there is no way to check on the validity of these explanations, short of replication. The burden therefore is on the Chapanises (or their supporters) to design an experiment which permits comparison of their alternatives with the interpretation offered by Aronson and Mills. The Chapanises may be correct, but no amount of a priori theorizing can settle the question.

Silverman (1964a) has recently raised another objection to the Chapanises' position, namely that they actually provide incomplete alternative explanations, since there is no indication of how the intervening variables which they substitute for dissonance can account for the subjects' responses. How, for example, are the pleasurable effects stemming from embarrassment transmitted to a subject's evaluation of the group discussion? Until this question is answered (whether in terms of "generalization of affect" or some other process), dissonance theory offers the only complete explanation.

A more compelling set of criticisms can be found in the Chapanises' analysis of the Festinger-Carlsmith experiment. In this study, it will be recalled, subjects worked on a boring task and then told the next subject that participation was really enjoyable and interesting. One group of subjects received $1.00 for doing this, another group $20. The results showed that subjects rated the experiment as more enjoyable when anticipating only the $1 reward.

The Chapanises suggest that these results can be explained in terms of "incredulity" rather than dissonance. They argue that an offer of $20 to an undergraduate for thirty minutes' work is an implausible reward and may arouse his suspicions that the experimenter is up to some trick. Under these circumstances, subjects may evade giving their true feelings when asked to evaluate the experiment, for example, by circling the neutral point on the evaluation scale. This is what in fact occurred. Although the mean rating of the $20 group was significantly lower than that of the $1 group, it fell very close to the neutral point on the scale, −.05 on a bipolar 10-point scale.

The argument advanced by the Chapanises receives additional support from a recent replication of the Festinger-Carlsmith experiment (Janis & Gilmore, 1965). This study was based in part on the idea that an extraordinarily large reward may arouse some degree of suspiciousness about being exploited by the experimenter, or some degree of guilt about being "bought" to lie to a fellow student. Under these circumstances there is no way of knowing whether the large reward operates as a positive or negative incentive. If the $20 reward was so implausible as to arouse negative feelings in the subjects, the lower amount of attitude change in the $20 as compared with the $1 condition could well be attributed to the negative incentive value of high reward. Although the experiment designed to test this hypothesis showed that monetary reward had no effect on attitude change, comments by subjects in the $20 group indicated that high reward did arouse their suspicions.

There is, however, much stronger evidence against the incredulity interpretation. In another replication of the Festinger-Carlsmith study, Cohen (in Brehm & Cohen, 1962, pp. 74–78) assigned subjects to conditions differing in financial inducement ($0.50, $1.00, $5.00, or $10.00) for writing a counter-attitudinal essay. The results showed that the lower the incentive, the greater the attitude change toward the discrepant position, even where the difference in pay was only $0.50 *versus* $1.00. The relatively small reward of $1.00 is not likely to have aroused suspicion in Cohen's subjects.

In a recent critique of attitude change experiments, Rosenberg (1965) reasoned that the discrepancy between the small effort of writing an essay and the large reward offered as inducement may cause the subject to suspect the purpose of the study. These suspicions may in turn arouse his concern about making a favorable impression on the experimenter, i.e., arouse what may be called "evaluation apprehension." The subject may fear that if he can be easily induced to change his attitude, this may lower the experimenter's opinion of him. By maintaining his original position, on the other hand, the subject demonstrates that he is a person of integrity, thereby gaining approval from the experimenter. Evaluation apprehension, in other words, may interact with experimenter bias (Rosenthal, 1963) to guide the subject to respond in ways that will bring approval from the experimenter.

To control the effect of evaluation apprehension, Rosenberg carried out a replication of the Cohen study in which one experimenter induced dissonance and another did the attitude measurement. Subjects were male undergraduates at Ohio State University. They were asked to write essays against participation of the O.S.U. football team in the Rose Bowl game. (This was a hotly debated issue on the campus at the time of the experiment.) Three reward conditions were used: $0.50, $1.00, and $5.00. The results showed no significant difference between the attitudes of subjects in the $0.50 and $1.00 conditions. However, both groups were more favorable toward banning Rose Bowl participation than a Control (no-reward) group, and also less favorable than the $5.00 group. These data suggest that where evaluation apprehension is presumably eliminated, a reinforcement rather than a dissonance effect is obtained; the greater the reward the greater the attitude change. This finding, incidentally, is consistent with contemporary "learning theory" approaches to attitude change (e.g., Hovland, Janis, & Kelley, 1953; Scott, 1959a, 1959b).

Positive results notwithstanding, Rosenberg's idea of evaluation apprehension does not account for the Festinger and Carlsmith outcome. These investigators also separated the two parts of their experiment—one experimenter inducing dissonance and the other measuring cognitive change. There is, moreover, some doubt about the cogency of the apprehension concept as an explanation for the Cohen study. In order to draw unequivocal conclusions from Rosenberg's findings, it would be necessary to run a set of conditions like Cohen's, that is, in which there was no control for evaluation apprehension. Since the two experiments differ in a number of ways, one cannot be certain that Cohen's results would be replicated.

A number of attempts have been made to resolve the so-called "$20.00 misunderstanding," the most recent being a paper by Elliot Aronson (1966). He begins by suggesting that there are circumstances in which a positive relationship exists between reward and attitude change. However, in most experiments designed to show this effect, the situation is so complex that the relationship between high incentive and attitude change is obscured by opposing forces due to dissonance. To demonstrate a positive relationship between incentive and attitude change, a situation must be created in which dissonance is weak. Aronson proposes that one way to do this might be to manipulate the subject's commitment to the discrepant position by the device of assuring him complete anonymity. Under these conditions, the subject would not feel that he was falsely selling someone a bill of goods, hence commitment would be slight. Since dissonance would then be minimal, the argument continues, an incentive effect might emerge. For example, subjects might think harder in writing the discrepant essay and convince themselves more in a high reward condition than in a low reward condition. Conversely, if a subject makes a counter-attitudinal statement publicly, and if he knows that his audience is unaware of the fact that he was induced into doing it, commitment and therefore dissonance should be high. Aronson suggests that under these conditions, the dissonance effect would overcome any incentive effect, i.e., greatest attitude change would occur in the low reward condition. McGuire (1966a) has very recently proposed a somewhat different reconciliation between dissonance theory and "incentive theory," although the variable of commitment is also a critical factor in his argument. Thus the dissonance effect is predicted to the extent that the subject has not strongly committed himself to the counter-attitudinal position, e.g., has committed himself but not yet carried out the advocacy. Conversely, the incentive effect is predicted where commitment is strong, as where the agreed-to advocacy is actually carried out.

It is still too early to assess the validity of the Aronson and McGuire positions, though both of them refer to papers by Collins and Helmreich (e.g., Carlsmith, Collins & Helmreich, 1966) as providing support for their "commitment hypotheses." In the meantime, there are other avenues of possible reconciliation that should be explored. For example, a reassessment is needed of monetary reward as a technique for manipulating justification. Financial reward at best is a complex induction, and may be perceived quite differently by different subjects and by the same subject under different conditions. In some cases, it may result in a perception directly opposite to that intended by the investigator. In the face of such difficulty, sound experimental technique dictates that the subject be asked how he perceives the experimental situation, either directly or indirectly. This is done in part by the usual "checks on the effectiveness of the experimental manipulations." But this is not enough. A good deal more attention should be given to discovering the cognitions a subject holds about the experimental situation. Indeed, this is precisely one of the recommendations made by Chapanis and Chapanis.

In their comprehensive paper, the Chapanises consider a number of other dissonance experiments (e.g., Brehm, 1959; Aronson, 1961), but those we have discussed here should suffice to indicate the nature of their evaluation. Besides, a large part of the paper is devoted to a pair of dissonance-avoidance experiments (Festinger, 1957, pp. 126–131, 162–176; Cohen, Brehm, & Latané, 1959), though neither is really crucial to demonstrating the validity of dissonance theory. Indeed, the Chapanises tend to ignore much of the more crucial supporting evidence. For an extended discussion of this issue, the reader is referred to a recent paper by Silverman (1964a).

In general, we cannot agree with the conclusion of the Chapanises that dissonance experiments have yielded equivocal results. It is true that manipulations used in these experiments are often complex, but not so complex as to make all findings open to alternative explanations. It would be unwise to conclude that the entire theory is invalid even where such alternatives do exist. The alternative explanation might better be viewed as suggesting possible control conditions which help specify the limits of generality of a theory. Such controls are particularly important in dissonance experiments, for these often involve "correlated psychological processes" that must be ruled out in order to arrive at unequivocal interpretations (Brehm & Cohen, 1962, pp. 126–127, 157).

Our discussion has been mainly concerned with experimental design and manipulation. An equally important issue concerns possible inadequacies in the analysis of results. Among these alleged inadequacies, the Chapanises are most troubled by rejection of cases and refusal of subjects to participate, both widely acknowledged problems in dissonance experiments. Seven studies are cited as illustrative of the consequences of excluding subjects (Brehm, 1956, 1960; Ehrlich, Guttman, Schönbach, & Mills, 1957; Cohen, Brehm, & Fleming, 1958; Mills, 1958; Brehm & Cohen, 1959a; Brehm & Lipsher, 1959), and two as examples of the problem of subject-refusal (Cohen, Terry, & Jones, 1959; Rabbie, Brehm, & Cohen, 1959).

It ought to be noted, however, that the studies used to illustrate subject exclusion show no evidence of elimination of data on the basis of the dependent variable. Instead, they involve the accepted practice of preselecting subjects by some criterion that permits the investigator to test his hypotheses (cf. Silverman, 1964a). In our view such procedures do not constitute methodological errors. Moreover, a valid objection to subject exclusion requires that the critic show how the selection procedure accounts for the results in ways not proposed by the investigator. This the Chapanises fail to do, though in one instance (Brehm & Cohen, 1959a) they do provide what may be considered a legitimate set of criticisms. More often, however, the critique is unwarranted. Take the study by Cohen, Brehm, and Fleming (1958) in which subjects were eliminated in the course of an internal analysis of the data. In criticizing this procedure the Chapanises ignore an important consideration. The experiment was one of the earlier tests of dissonance theory, hence the manipulations were understandably somewhat less than effective. Under these circumstances, there is nothing wrong with categorizing the subjects on the basis of an *ad hoc* criterion in order to carry out a special analysis. Indeed in exploratory work an investigator is expected to make every effort to avoid Type II errors, including the use of internal analysis where between-conditions differences are statistically unreliable. These comments are not meant to imply, however, that Cohen *et al.* were justified in simply eliminating cases. It would certainly have been more appropriate to present data separately for those subjects who did and did not have initially extreme attitude scores.

In addition to the problem of subject exclusion, the Chapanises consider experiments in which subjects themselves refuse to participate. Though justified in emphasizing the serious nature of subject-refusal, the authors fail to offer a single criticism that has not been already discussed by Brehm and Cohen (1962, pp. 121–127). At this stage in the development of dissonance theory, the investigator may be forced to tolerate a certain amount of ambiguity in his research operations. Subject loss is an instance of such ambiguity. The difficulty will disappear, we feel certain, as the theory matures and the methodology becomes more sophisticated. Besides, there are more immediately pressing problems to which the dissonance theorist must address himself. We noted earlier, for example, that there is need for measures of dissonance that are independent of the dependent variable. There is, too, the perplexing problem of how to accurately specify the mode of dissonance reduction that will be adopted in a given situation. While we do not denigrate the importance of the subject-exclusion problem, these other issues would seem to have higher priority.

This completes our discussion of dissonance theory, and with it our presentation of the theories of consistency. In the next section, we shall consider the implications of these theories, dissonance in particular, for the study of personality.

CONSISTENCY AND THE STUDY OF PERSONALITY

In this section we distinguish between *personality structure* and *personality dynamics* (Sears, 1950; London & Rosenhan, 1964). Structural components are defined as stable features of personality organization that are employed to account for the similarities and consistencies in behavior over time and across situations. Dynamic components, on the other hand, include motivational processes, emotional states of the individual, and transitory situational factors. Although the distinction between structure and dynamics requires greater specification, two rather different approaches to personality have emerged which appear correlated with the distinction. One stresses manipulative experiments and is concerned with what we are calling dynamics. The other emphasizes assessment or psychometric devices (e.g., paper-and-pencil personality inventories) and deals largely with what we have referred to as structure. Our emphasis in this section will be on dynamics, since consistency theories are more concerned with the situational determination of behavior than with stable personality characteristics. We shall, however, give some attention to personality structure in our discussion of individual differences in reactivity to inconsistency, and also in our discussion of certain problems in the area of self-conception.

Of the many aspects of personality dynamics, consistency theories have addressed themselves to several, including self-concept and ego-defensive behavior, aggression, motivation, and personality development. We shall consider each of these areas in the discussion that follows, and attempt to show how personality processes are governed very much by the need to reduce inconsistency.

Self-Concept and Ego-Defensive Behavior

Festinger and Bramel (1962) have pointed out the conceptual similarity between psychoanalytic defense mechanisms and certain avenues of dissonance reduction. For example, the addition of cognitions consonant with a discrepant act seems very much like "rationalization." One reason for this similarity may be that the meaning of the concept of dissonance and the meaning of the psychoanalytic concept of conflict overlap. Festinger and Bramel elaborate on this point in some detail. The following is a paraphrase of their argument.

Psychoanalytic theory is concerned, for the most part, with situations in which a person's perception of some aspect of himself is discrepant with his values and standards, that is, his superego. Suppose a person who considers homosexuality a bad characteristic is suddenly exposed to information which would lead him to think that he has homosexual tendencies. His awareness of this information will arouse feelings of guilt and fear of punishment. In order to avoid further guilt, psychoanalytic theory asserts that the ego will initiate defensive measures, the most common being some form of denial of the threatening information.

Dissonance theory would approach this situation somewhat differently. It would first ask whether the cognition that one has homosexual tendencies is necessarily dissonant with the belief that such tendencies are bad. According to Festinger and Bramel, the answer is no, unless the person believes that he consistently lives up to his personal standards. For some people, knowledge that a trait is undesirable does not necessarily mean one does not possess it. Thus some people who are threatened in the psychoanalytic sense will also experience dissonance, whereas others will not.

Festinger and Bramel ask next whether psychoanalytic defense mechanisms can be used to reduce dissonance in the type of situation under discussion. They consider as an example the mechanism of projection. Imagine a person who has high self-esteem, that is, a preponderance of cognitions favorable to himself. Suppose that this person considers homosexuality a very bad thing. If he is suddenly confronted with information that he is sexually attracted to members of his own sex, this cognition will be dissonant with his cognitions concerning what a good person he is, and also dissonant with his belief that he is quite masculine.

One way to reduce dissonance would be to attribute homosexuality to persons who are liked and respected. If respected people possess the trait, perhaps homosexuality is not so bad after all. Then possession of the trait would no longer be dissonant with high self-esteem and dissonance would be reduced. Another possibility would be to ascribe the trait to members of one's reference group. This would allow the individual to conclude that he is no worse than average in the degree to which he possesses an undesirable trait.

These considerations suggest that defensive projection may indeed be used as a means of reducing dissonance. Some support for this hypothesis comes from studies by Deutsch and Solomon (1959); Gerard (1961); Jones, Gergen, and Davis (1962); Broxton (1963); Worchel and McCormick (1963); and Secord, Backman, and Eachus (1964). These studies leave a number of issues unresolved. A more definitive test of the "projection hypothesis" was carried out by Bramel (1962). He exposed volunteer college students to falsified personality test results intended either to increase or to decrease their general level of self-esteem. Subsequently, all subjects were given additional information implying they had strong homosexual tendencies.[11] It was hypothesized that for a subject in the Low Self-Esteem condition, this information would be dissonant with his conviction that homosexuality is bad, as well as contrary to his belief that he was not homosexual. For a subject in the High Self-Esteem condition, the information would, in addition, be dissonant with his favorable self-referent cognitions. The negative information, in other words, would produce more dissonance for the person with high than low self-esteem. In order to reduce dissonance, the subject could attribute homosexual tendencies to another subject with whom he was paired; the greater the dissonance, the greater the amount of such projection.

The results showed that subjects in the High Self-Esteem condition rated their partners as having significantly greater homosexual tendencies than did subjects in the Low Self-Esteem condition. High self-esteem subjects tended to evaluate their partners as having the same degree of homosexuality as themselves; low self-esteem subjects evaluated the other person as having less homosexuality than themselves. It would appear that more projection occurred where dissonance was high than low, even though the "threat" to the person was the same in both conditions.

Bramel had expected that projection would occur primarily where the subject liked and respected his partner. An internal analysis of the data confirmed this expectation. Further support comes from a second experiment (1963), in which Bramel systematically varied the stimulus properties of the other person. The results showed that college students who were induced to ascribe unfavorable traits to themselves attributed these traits to other students, but not to members of a disliked outgroup. The two experiments then suggest that dissonance-produced projection will occur primarily where the available social object is respected and/or similar to oneself.

Festinger and Bramel's (1962) use of dissonance to explain defensive projection makes no pretense at integrating dissonance and psychoanalytic theories. They seem to visualize the two theories as existing side by side insofar as both attempt to deal with defensive behavior (Brehm & Cohen, 1962, p. 166). The main advantage of the dissonance formulation over psychoanalysis is the former's greater predictive accuracy; i.e., the variables employed in the dissonance approach are more amenable to measurement and manipulation than those traditionally dealt with by psychoanalytic theory. It has been suggested, however, that there is something to be gained from an integration of the two theories. Brehm and Cohen (1962, pp. 168–171) have proposed one way of achieving such integration, but in our view, we are a long way from a theoretical rapprochement.

[11] While this study did not make explicit provision for the role of commitment and choice, it should be understood that the subjects were volunteers who got themselves into the dissonant situation through their own volition.

Festinger and Bramel deal with the relationship between self-concept and defensive projection. A number of other modes of defense may result from inconsistencies among self-referent cognitions. Pilisuk (1962), it will be recalled, found evidence of rationalization in an experiment designed to test derivations from Heider's balance theory. He found that subjects retained their favorable self-evaluations in the face of adverse criticism from a close friend by relying on a variety of rationalizations to explain their friend's behavior. It has also been found that people maintain a stable self-concept by employing direct forms of defensive denial (Edlow & Kiesler, 1966); by limiting cognitive input to information congruent with the self-concept (Stotland & Hillmer, 1962; Silverman, 1964b); by denying the implications of discrepant behavior (Brock & Buss, 1962); by denying that one voluntarily engaged in discrepant behavior (Brock & Buss, 1964); and by repressing the implications of discrepant behavior through selective recall (Buss & Brock, 1963; Schlachet, 1965).

Aronson (1960) has specifically incorporated the idea of a denial mechanism in his extension of dissonance theory to the issue of expectations regarding the nature of the self-concept. According to this author, the dissonance occasioned by exposure to discrepant information is due to the discrepancy between the expectation that one is a person of integrity and the cognition that one has not behaved with integrity. Events that confirm expectancies are consonant, hence sought out by the individual. Events that disconfirm expectancies are dissonant, therefore to be avoided or in some cases distorted in order to make them consonant. It is further assumed that the confirmation of expectancies is a central motive in all human organisms. Thus individuals will, under certain conditions, actually seek out failure, frustration, and other forms of deprivation in order to confirm self-referent expectancies. An interesting derivation from this hypothesis concerns the situation in which a person expects to perform poorly on some task. If the person actually gives a superior performance, he should experience dissonance rather than elation. Success disconfirms his expectations and therefore he tries to minimize the significance of his performance, perhaps even seeks failure, in an effort to reduce dissonance. On the other hand, if the person expects failure and fails, or expects success and succeeds, there should be no dissonance and consequent denial of the event.

Support for this derivation comes from an experiment by Aronson and Carlsmith (1962). Female subjects were given several sets of photographs to judge and were told that one of the three photographs on each card was that of a hospitalized schizophrenic. The test was presented as a measure of social sensitivity, the subject's task being to select the photograph of the schizophrenic. One hundred cards were used, grouped into five sets of twenty cards each. After a subject had made twenty judgments, the experimenter scored her performance and presented the next set of cards. For the first four sets, some subjects were led to believe they had performed extremely well, others very poorly. Thus it was assumed that when beginning the fifth set, some subjects would expect to score high while others would expect to score low. On the fifth set, half the subjects within each expectation condition had their expectancies confirmed, the other half disconfirmed. The experimenter then asked each subject to judge the fifth set again, giving as a pretext his need to record the time it took to complete that particular set. The dependent variable was the number of judgments a subject made on the repeated trial that differed from those she made on the first trial. This measure served as the operational definition of a subject's discomfort with her performance and consequent efforts to deny her performance.

The results strongly supported the predictions. Subjects who were given information which was inconsistent with their expectancies changed a significantly greater number of their responses than those given consistent information. For those whose performance was less than their expectations this finding is certainly straightforward. The results are less obvious when we consider subjects whose performance exceeded their expectations. This group also showed a strong preference for consistency, by seeking to maintain a belief in their own lack of ability rather than have their expectations of failure disconfirmed. Although this result is not a unique derivation from dissonance theory (cf. Lecky, 1945; Tolman, 1959) it is indeed startling. It takes on added significance when contrasted with work on achievement motivation (e.g., McClelland, Atkinson, Clark, & Lowell, 1953), and studies of self-judgment of ability through social comparison processes (Festinger, 1954). Defensive denial in the service of expectancy confirmation may well turn out to be an important feature of human behavior (cf. Adams & Rosenbaum, 1962; Adams, 1963).

The Aronson and Carlsmith experiment demonstrated defensive denial following a disconfirmed negative expectancy. It did not show that dissonance as evidenced by negative affect is the result of such disconfirmation. In a subsequent experiment (Carlsmith & Aronson, 1963), it was found that events which disconfirm expectancies are in fact perceived as unpleasant. For example, expecting a given solution to taste bitter made it seem less sweet to a subject after he had tested it and judged it to be sweet. Similarly, expecting a solution to taste sweet and discovering it was bitter made it seem more bitter. The authors suggest that these results apply to a larger class of events than just bitter and sweet solutions and, in general, there will be positive affect following expectancy confirmation, negative affect following disconfirmation. Most individuals should therefore attempt to avoid disconfirmation while showing a preference for events that imply confirmation. Support for this hypothesis comes from experiments by Aronson, Carlsmith, and Darley (1963), and Gerard, Blevans, and Malcolm (1964).

The expectancy disconfirmation model has recently come under attack. The array of data in support of the model is no longer as impressive as the early studies cited above seemed to suggest. Indeed, there are at least five papers presenting experiments which failed to replicate the original Aronson-Carlsmith study (Ward & Salvold, 1964; Lowin & Epstein, 1965; Waterman & Ford, 1965; Cottrell, 1965; Brock, Edelman, Edwards & Schuck, 1965). However, there is reason to believe that the particular dependent variable used in these experiments was of low validity (Bramel, 1968). Our own view is that the need to resolve inconsistency between expectations and performance is sometimes so strong that it will override powerful motives like achievement or failure-avoidance. There is, however, some ambiguity as to just why this occurs. It is not resonable to assume that the confirmation of expectancies always takes precedence over other motives. What is obviously needed is a specification of the conditions that produce striving for expectancy confirmation rather than for attainment of success. Brehm and Cohen (1962, p. 181) suggest that one condition may be the relative strength of the two motives which, in turn, depends on the person's commitment to one or the other motive. If the expectancy motive is stronger, the person can deny his achievement in order to restore consistency within the self-concept. If the person is strongly motivated to perform well, he can reduce dissonance by strengthening his achievement motivation and behavior, or by altering his expectations regarding the nature of his self-concept. The modification of expectancies is precisely what occurs when the individual attempts to reestablish consistency among self-referent cognitions by changing them in the direction advocated by a discrepant communication (Bergin, 1962).

The defensive processes we have been considering are for the most part intrapersonal in character. Some theorists (e.g.,

Secord & Backman, 1961; Sampson, 1963) have suggested that interpersonal processes may also be employed to restore consistency among self-attitudes. Take, for example, the approach set forth by Secord and Backman. Following the Heider and Abelson-Rosenberg models, these authors propose that cognitive stability or instability is a function of three factors: an aspect of the individual's self-concept, his interpretation of those elements of his behavior related to that aspect, and his perception of related aspects of the person with whom he is interacting. The individual strives to maintain consistency among these three components, a state that is achieved when the behavior of the individual and the other are consistent with relevant aspects of the individual's self-concept. Since congruency is continually being threatened by the changing nature of interpersonal relations, defenses are employed to reduce the incongruency occasioned by these changes. Secord and Backman suggest a number of such interpersonal defenses. For example, the individual may develop techniques for eliciting from the other behavior which is congruent with his self-concept or, alternatively, he may increase or decrease his liking for the other. These and similar processes are carefully described by the authors in an effort to extend the consistency principle into the interpersonal domain. Experimental support for the theory has not been extensive, although a number of studies do provide relevant evidence (Backman, Secord, & Pierce, 1963; Secord, Backman, & Eachus, 1964).

Interpersonal Aggression

In discussing Heider's theory of consistency, we saw that the tendency toward a balanced state underlies the empirical relationship between similarity of two attitude objects and liking of these objects. An individual will positively value others whose evaluation of him is similar to his own and negatively value those whose evaluation of him is dissimilar to his own. If the individual perceives himself in favorable terms, he will like those who evaluate him positively. If he views himself unfavorably, he will like those who evaluate him negatively. The balance hypothesis asserts that the individual will tend to adjust his attitudes toward the other person so as to make them consistent both with his own self-evaluation and the other's evaluation of him. If there is a discrepancy in evaluation, the individual may restore balance by developing a dislike for the other person. Support for this line of reasoning comes from several studies, including those by Harvey, Kelley, and Shapiro (1957); Deutsch and Solomon (1959); Jones, Gergen, and Davis (1962); Newcomb (1963b); Broxton (1963); Iwao (1963); and Secord, Backman, and Eachus (1964). Each of these studies has demonstrated that the individual may restore or preserve consistency among his cognitions by derogating the source of imbalance, that is, by being aggressive toward him. From this point of view, changes in the evaluation of others reflect attempts to make cognitions consistent with each other. The difficulty with these studies, and perhaps the formulations on which they are based, is that they do not go far enough. The results provide support for the consistency hypothesis, but of the many implications of inconsistency or of the conditions under which it will lead to aggression, nothing more is said.

A more ambitious and far-reaching approach to the study of aggression has been undertaken from the dissonance point of view (Davis & Jones, 1960; Brock & Buss, 1962, 1964; Iwao, 1963; Worchel & McCormick, 1963; Glass, 1964; Lerner, 1965). Of major concern to most of these investigators is the recurrent problem of the effect of the aggressive act on the aggressor's perception of his victim. It has been observed that there may be an increase in dislike of the victim where a person injures another whom he does not necessarily want to hurt (Buss, 1961; Berkowitz, 1962). The effect is particularly strong where the aggressor is unable to neutralize his behavior by explaining to the victim his reasons for being aggressive (Davis & Jones, 1960). The dissonance interpretation of these data is as follows: The "inappropriate" aggression induces dissonance in the aggressor which he reduces by increasing his dislike of the other person, thereby making his perception of the other consistent with his behavior. In other words, the aggressor appears to justify his actions by persuading himself that the victim deserved his fate.

Following Bramel's work on self-concept, we would expect the aggression to produce more dissonance in an aggressor with high self-esteem, since aggression is more discrepant with a positive than negative self-image. It follows that the higher the aggressor's self-esteem, the more he would dislike the other person after aggressing against him. Where he has low self-esteem, the act of aggression would produce minimal dissonance, hence little increase in dislike of the victim.

The possibility exists, however, that the aggressor will deny responsibility for his behavior, arguing that it was a consequence of situational pressures or coercion (Milgram, 1963; Brock & Buss, 1964). If a person feels he has no alternative except to behave in a manner discrepant with his beliefs, little if any dissonance is produced. If, on the other hand, he experiences the possibility of behaving in a manner consonant with his beliefs but still acts in a discrepant manner, relatively great dissonance is produced. In other words, the choice about whether or not to engage in the discrepant act is a necessary condition for the arousal of dissonance, precisely the point made by Brehm and Cohen (1962) in their extension of the dissonance formulation.

A number of experiments have shown the relevance of choice in aggression-produced dissonance (Davis & Jones, 1960; Brock & Buss, 1962, 1964). In the Brock and Buss (1962) study, it will be recalled, dissonance was produced by having students, who were opposed to using electric shock in research on humans, give high and low intensities of shock to a confederate under voluntary and nonvoluntary conditions. The dependent variable was the aggressor's change in rating of the painfulness of the shocks from before to after their administration. The more choice a subject had in carrying out such aggression, and the greater the intensity of shock, the greater was the dissonance and consequent minimization of the painfulness of shock.

Two recent studies by Glass (1964) and Glass and Wood (1968) provide further evidence relevant to the effects of dissonance on postaggression behavior. Both studies represent an extension of previous work on self-esteem into the domain of aggression, as well as a further test of the role of choice in arousing postaggression dissonance. The 1964 experiment, like the Brock and Buss study, examined the effects of inducing aggressive behavior in an individual who was opposed to such aggression, and under conditions where he had a choice of withdrawing from the experiment. If the individual chose to participate, the higher his self-esteem the greater the dissonance, since the act of injuring another was dissonant not only with his opposition to aggression but also with his self-image. It was expected that the aggressor would reduce dissonance by increasing his dislike of or unfriendliness toward the other person; the higher his self-esteem, the greater the increase in feelings of unfriendliness.

Sixty male undergraduates who were opposed to using electric shock on humans in scientific research were induced to administer seemingly painful shocks to another student, actually an experimental confederate. The subject played the role of an experimenter in a concept formation task and delivered electric shock to another student whenever the latter made an incorrect response (Buss, 1961). All subjects were given either choice or no choice about whether to administer the shocks. Half the subjects in each of these conditions had previously received falsified psychological test results aimed at increasing their general level of self-esteem (High Self-Esteem condition); the remaining half received comparable information designed to lower their self-esteem (Low Self-Esteem condition). Before and after the subjects delivered shock, they indicated their feelings of friendliness toward the confederate by responding to three intercorrelated items. The items asked: (1) "Would you admit Mr.——— (name of the confederate was written in here) into your circle of close friends?"; (2) "Would you like to participate in another study with Mr.———?"; (3) "Would you like Mr.——— as a roommate?" Each item was accompanied by a seven-point scale, ranging from "Definitely Yes" to "Definitely No." A total friendliness score was computed based on the sum of the scale points a subject checked for each item. The main dependent variable was the amount of change in this score from before to after administration of the shocks.

The data showed that for subjects in the Choice, High Self-Esteem condition, there was a significant increase in unfriendliness, whereas only minimal change appeared in the other three conditions. These findings suggest that choosing to engage in behavior discrepant with prior beliefs (that is, choosing to deliver shock) must imply a discrepancy with a positive self-image in order to arouse dissonance and consequent changes in friendliness.

It should be noted that unlike the Choice, High Self-Esteem condition, a decrement in friendliness did not appear in the Choice, Low Self-Esteem condition. In fact the mean change score showed an increase in friendliness, although not significantly different from zero. This finding was somewhat surprising since choosing to administer shock should arouse some (minimal) dissonance even if the person has low self-esteem. Apparently, however, the low self-esteem subject's decision to administer shock was consistent with his negative self-image, and the voluntary act of injuring another was not sufficiently discrepant to be dissonance-arousing. Some support for this position can be found in the results of previous experiments. Deutsch, Krauss, and Rosenau (1962) have demonstrated that for an act to arouse dissonance it must be not only voluntary but also inconsistent with a positive self-image. Also relevant here are recent studies by Malewski (1962) and Gerard (Gerard, Blevans, & Malcolm, 1964), both of whom found that postdecisional dissonance occurred only when the subject had a high self-evaluation. These comments should not be construed as implying that discrepant commitment in the absence of high self-esteem will produce only minimal dissonance. It seems reasonable to suppose that behavior discrepant with a negative self-concept (for example, where a person of low self-esteem performs an act of kindness) will also arouse cognitive dissonance. Of some relevance to this point is a very recent study by Walster (E. Walster, B. Walster, Abrahams & Brown, 1966) which shows that if an individual discovers he has accorded another person more respect than the other deserves, he will subsequently devalue the other.

A change in liking or feelings of friendliness is of course only one means of reducing postaggression dissonance. There are at least four other ways in which dissonance could be reduced. The aggressor might engage in self-derogation, thereby making his aggressive behavior consistent with the kind of person he is. We can assume, however, that there is strong resistance to self-derogation (Harvey, Kelley, & Shapiro, 1957; Bergin, 1962; Pilisuk, 1962; Secord, Backman, & Eachus, 1964), and that in the absence of explicit influence pressures this mode of dissonance reduction is not likely to occur.

Another way of reducing postaggression dissonance is pain minimization, or the judgment that electric shocks are less painful after administration than before. This was a major finding of the Brock and Buss (1962) study. In the Glass experiment, an effort was made to close off pain minimization as an avenue of dissonance reduction.

The confederate was instructed to behave as though he were experiencing great pain each time the subject depressed the "shock switch." It was expected that this procedure would make it difficult for the subject to maintain that the shocks did not hurt his victim. The ruse was successful, for there was little evidence of a drop in the subjects' ratings of the painfulness of shock.

In addition to self-derogation and pain minimization, subjects could reduce dissonance by becoming more favorable toward the use of shock in scientific research. A positive attitude would alter the psychological implication of administering shock so that the act would not necessarily be dissonant with a positive self-image. While evidence of attitude change was negligible, some change did occur. The possibility exists therefore that some of the subjects employed both attitude change and increased unfriendliness as complementary avenues of dissonance reduction.

Still another way of reducing dissonance would be to judge that one was obligated to administer shock, a cognition that is consonant with a positive self-concept. Brock and Buss found evidence of an increase in felt obligation (1962; 1964), despite the fact that subjects were given a choice about administering shock. In the Glass experiment, there was no evidence of denial of choice. The lack of consistency in these findings highlights, among other things, the insufficient specification of priorities between different modes of dissonance reduction.

In summary, the results show that from dissonance theory one can predict the direction of an aggressor's revaluation of his victim. At least under conditions of choice, the higher the self-esteem of the aggressor, the greater is his dislike of the victim.

It is not entirely clear from these findings whether postaggression increments in dislike are related to the aggressor's *initial* perceptions of his victim. Brehm and Cohen (1962) have suggested that where the injured person is a good friend, for example, barriers to derogation exist, making it difficult for the aggressor to reduce dissonance by means of increased dislike. Assuming the operation of such barriers, we may expect the use of alternative avenues of dissonance reduction. In a recent experiment, Glass and Wood (1968) deliberately manipulated the attractiveness of the victim in order to examine what effect this might have on the way in which dissonance was reduced.

The design of the experiment was similar to the Glass study. Forty male undergraduates were selected from a larger group because of their opposition to the use of electric shock in psychological research. Subjects were categorized as high or low in self-esteem, depending on whether they scored above or below the median on the Janis and Field Feelings of Inadequacy scale (in Hovland & Janis, 1959, pp. 55–68, 300–301). Within each self-esteem group subjects were randomly assigned to one of two experimental conditions. Those in the High Attraction condition were induced to administer electric shock to another person after receiving information aimed at increasing their feelings of attraction toward him. Those in the Low Attraction condition delivered the shocks without receiving such information. Before and after administration of shock, subjects indicated how much they liked their victim by rating him on twenty positive and negative personality characteristics (Davis & Jones, 1960). A total score was computed for each subject by algebraically summing the twenty ratings. At the end of the experiment, each subject indicated, for a second time, his attitude toward the use of shock on humans. The before-to-after change in ratings on each of these measures constituted the dependent variables used in the study.

The first hypothesis was as follows: Where a person chooses to carry out an aggression of which he disapproves and against a victim to whom he is attracted, the resulting dissonance will be reduced by adopting a more favorable attitude toward the aggression. The more self-esteem the aggressor has, the more the act of aggression will arouse dissonance and consequent attitude change. The second hypothesis predicted a replication of the results of the Glass experiment. That is, where the aggressor is not strongly attracted to his victim, postaggression dissonance will be reduced by an increase in dislike of the victim. In arriving at these predictions, it was assumed that alternative modes of dissonance reduction were not readily available. This was not an unreasonable assumption since the experiment was conducted under choice conditions, and a number of procedures were used to close off other ways of reducing dissonance.

The first hypothesis received support. High self-esteem subjects in the High Attraction condition showed the greatest amount of positive attitude change, whereas significantly less change was observed for low self-esteem subjects, and only minimal change occurred under Low Attraction. The second hypothesis received much weaker support. There was no evidence of a decrease in the subjects' overall evaluation of the confederate, although an analysis of each of the ratings revealed that on four of the twenty,[12] subjects changed significantly in the predicted direction. These significant findings may of course be due to chance fluctuation, but one hesitates to dismiss them on such grounds, since they do agree with the results obtained in the previous experiment. Besides, the failure to find a stronger devaluation effect may have been due to minimal dissonance arousal in the Low Attraction condition, an unintentional effect resulting from the experimental instructions used in that condition. At the beginning of the experiment, the subject was informed that the confederate did not fit his prior description of a desirable co-worker. These instructions were intended only to make the confederate appear less attractive than in the High Attraction condition, but they actually carry the implication that the confederate is somewhat undesirable. If the subject responded to this implication by developing an initial dislike for the confederate, the act of delivering shock is unlikely to have aroused more than minimal dissonance. Injuring another whom one dislikes is not strongly inconsistent with a positive self-image, or perhaps even with the belief that one is opposed to the use of shock. The data tended to support this interpretation. The mean of the subjects' initial attitudes toward the confederate was only slightly above the median, and significantly lower than the mean for the High Attraction condition.

What may we conclude from the results of the two experiments? In general, they suggest that the cognitive personality variable, self-esteem, is an important determinant of an aggressor's revaluation of his victim. Self-esteem, when viewed in the light of its role in arousing dissonance, leads to derivations which specify the effect of aggression upon the aggressor. If the victim is someone we like, attitude change in a direction favorable toward aggression appears to be a favored means of reducing dissonance. If the victim holds no strong attraction for us, we are likely to employ some other type of defense, for example increased dislike of the victim. The latter derivation takes on added significance when contrasted with the controversial "catharsis hypothesis" (e.g., Feshbach, 1956), and more recent work on aggression-anxiety (Hokanson, 1961; Berkowitz, 1962).

MOTIVATION

Studies of self-concept and ego-defensive processes, and work on the antecedents and consequences of aggressive behavior underscore the utility of the dissonance approach to the study of personality. The analysis of motivation is another area in personality research to which dissonance can be applied. It seems reasonable to assume, following Brehm and Cohen (1962), that cognitive

[12] The traits were: friendly and likeable, irresponsible, immature, and feels superior to others.

aspects of motivation are affected by dissonance in much the same way as other cognitions, such as self-attitudes. Thus motivational change may sometime result from the arousal of dissonance just as attitude change is a frequent consequence of dissonance. It should be clear, however, that our first concern is with cognitive aspects of motivation, and only secondarily with concomitant changes in behavior and physiological processes.

In the first of a series of studies on dissonance and motivation, Brehm (1962) proposed that dissonance can occur through a decision to deprive oneself of food when one is hungry. He hypothesized that the greater the drive and the less the justification for such deprivation, the greater will be the dissonance. One way to reduce dissonance is to minimize or eliminate the cognition that one is hungry. The less the reward for choosing to deprive oneself, the greater the reduction in cognized hunger from before to after commitment.

To test this hypothesis, male college students were asked to participate in a study of the effects of food deprivation on intellectual and motor functioning. They were told that they would be required to go without breakfast and lunch on the day of the testing session. Participation was voluntary, although each student was given "credit" toward his final grade in introductory psychology. When the subject arrived for the experiment, he was asked to indicate his hunger on a 61-point scale ranging from "Not at all" hungry to "Extremely" hungry. Next, the subject performed some intellectual and motor tasks requiring about fifteen minutes. After completing these tasks, the subject was induced to commit himself to further deprivation. He was asked to return for further testing in the evening which meant going without food until about 8 or 9 o'clock. To create High Dissonance, subjects were told that the evening session was voluntary and no additional credits would be given for participation. To create Low Dissonance, subjects were told that while participation was voluntary, $5.00 would be paid for the evening session. After a subject committed himself to going without dinner, he was asked to fill out the hunger rating scale for a second time. Finally, he was asked how many sandwiches and cartons of milk he wanted brought for his snack at the end of the evening session.

The results were in accord with theoretical expectations. High Dissonance (low incentive) subjects reduced their self-ratings of hunger significantly more than did Low Dissonance subjects from before to after commitment to further deprivation. The High Dissonance group also ordered significantly fewer food items than the Low Dissonance group. Though the results are positive, the study remains inconclusive, for there was considerable difference between the two groups in initial level of hunger. Internal analysis showed that the obtained effect was not due to simple regression, but there are, nonetheless, alternative interpretations of the data. It might be argued that the results were due to differential expectations set up by the incentive manipulations. Subjects offered $5.00 for further deprivation might conclude they ought to be very hungry, while those offered nothing might conclude they ought not to be hungry. A second study was conducted to eliminate such interpretations.

Thirsty subjects were induced to commit themselves to further deprivation of liquid by means of monetary incentives, and under conditions of high or low salience of water. The procedure was similar to that of the hunger experiment with two exceptions. To create a high dissonance commitment to liquid deprivation, the experimenter told the subject that participation was worth $10, "but, because of a departmental regulation, I can only offer you $1 for participating" (Brehm, 1962, p. 65). The reason subjects were told that deprivation was really worth $10 was to control their perceptions of how thirsty the experimenter thought they should be. Low Dissonance was created in much the same way except subjects were offered $5 for their participation. Salience of the goal object was manipulated by having a pitcher of water with paper cups on the testing desk throughout the experimental session. Half the subjects were exposed to these stimuli (High Salience), while the other half were exposed only to the materials necessary for the experiment (Low Salience). Self-ratings of thirst were measured on a 61-point scale before and after commitment to further deprivation. In addition, an attempt was made to measure consummatory effects by allowing subjects to drink as much water as they wanted at the end of the experimental session; i.e., after the commitment but before learning there would really be no further deprivation.

Brehm's hypotheses can be summarized as follows: The magnitude of dissonance is inversely related to the amount of incentive for further deprivation and directly related to the amount of initial thirst. Initial thirst is directly related to the salience of the goal object. A person will try to reduce dissonance by decreasing the cognized intensity of his thirst; the greater the dissonance, the greater will be the reduction in thirst.

Ten male and ten female subjects were included in each of the four experimental conditions. Since the incentive and salience manipulations were unsuccessful for females, only the results for males provide an adequate test of the predictions. The data generally supported expectations. Self-ratings of thirst were (nonsignificantly) higher in the High Salience condition as compared with the Low, and before-to-after changes in these ratings showed a decrease among High Dissonance subjects, an increase among Low Dissonance subjects ($p < .05$). The greatest decrement in thirst occurred in the High Dissonance, High Salience condition, as predicted. On the question of whether these motivational changes extended to actual behavior, there was a tendency for subjects showing the greatest decrease in thirst to consume the least amount of water.

Considered together, the hunger and thirst studies lend clear support to the hypothesis that cognitive aspects of motivation are affected by dissonance. The studies also suggest that dissonance may affect noncognitive aspects of motivation, for High Dissonance subjects ordered fewer food items and drank less water than their controls in the Low Dissonance condition. Additional support for the role of consummatory responses in dissonance reduction can be found in a recent doctoral thesis by Mansson (1965), and in an hypnosis experiment by Brock and Grant (1963). The latter results, however, must be viewed with caution since, as Brock and Grant readily admit, there were a number of alternative interpretations of their data.

Further evidence of the effect of dissonance on noncognitive aspects of motivation comes from two recent experiments by Brehm, Back, and Bogdonoff (1964). The experimental design was essentially a replication of the hunger study except that blood samples were taken at various times throughout the period of deprivation. These samples were analyzed for change in concentration of plasma-free fatty acids (FFA). Since FFA is directly related to length of food deprivation, it was predicted that subjects who committed themselves to deprivation for little justification would show less of an increment in FFA than those given high justification. To create High Justification, subjects were told that further participation in the study was highly important to science and the project was therefore willing to pay $25 for an additional eight-hour period of fasting. It was emphasized, however, that participation was entirely up to them. Low Justification was created by simply asking the subject if he would be willing to continue fasting for another eight hours. Fifteen subjects completed the experiment, eight in the High and seven in the Low Justification condition.

The results tended to support the predictions, although statistical tests were for the most part borderline in significance. On self-ratings of hunger, five out of the seven Low Justification subjects decreased their ratings from before to after commitment, whereas only one of the eight High Justification subjects did so. Changes in FFA level were computed by subtracting the resting level before commitment from the resting level at the end of the period of food deprivation, about six hours later. There were no between-conditions differences on this index. However, when subjects were divided on the basis of the median level of initial hunger, those in the Low Justification condition who were relatively hungry showed a smaller increase in FFA level than did hungry subjects in the High Justification condition. (The reverse was true for initially not-hungry subjects.) This result suggests that if subjects convince themselves they are sated during the period of deprivation, corresponding change occurs at the physiological level.

The second experiment by Brehm *et al.* was identical to the first, with two modifications. Monetary reward was omitted from the High Justification condition and, in addition, there was a third high-justification treatment in which food deprivation lasted a full twenty-four hours. The results failed to replicate the first set of findings. Even the predicted decrease in self-ratings of hunger following commitment did not occur. This may have been the result of an "anchoring effect," since initial ratings were very low in all three conditions. Mean FFA levels also failed to show the predicted effect, though internal analysis once again indicated that initially hungry subjects under Low Justification tended to increase less in FFA level than did subjects under High Justification.

It would be premature to conclude on the basis of these experiments that dissonance exerts an unequivocal influence on noncognitive aspects of motivation such as fat mobilization. The second study has a number of shortcomings, and, as we have seen, the positive results from both studies are based largely on internal analysis.

The experiments we have been considering open the way to an exploration of other problems in motivation, namely, the effect of dissonance manipulations on social motives such as achievement, fear, and affiliation. Philip Zimbardo has undertaken a program of research (designed originally in collaboration with the late Arthur R. Cohen) dealing directly with the effect of dissonance on behaviors assumed to result from social motivation. In the first of a series of experiments in this area, Cohen and Zimbardo (1962) hypothesized that if a person wants to achieve success but commits himself to a situation promising failure, he will reduce dissonance by decreasing the strength of the motive to avoid failure. A decrement in failure-avoidance motivation should be reflected in less concern with ensuring successful performance on future trials.

Twenty subjects were given instructions designed to arouse their need to succeed. The subjects were told that the study was concerned with ability to memorize and understand verbal materials under adverse conditions. The subjects were given a poem and asked to memorize it. Next, they recited the poem from memory and discussed its psychological implications under conditions of delayed auditory feedback (DAF). After a subject completed his interpretations of the poem, he was induced to commit himself to another 50-minute session with the DAF apparatus which, by now, he knew must lead to failure. Although the voluntary nature of further participation was emphasized, subjects were also told they would receive $2.00 for returning for the second session. To create High Dissonance, subjects were informed that it was highly probable they would do poorly in the second session. Low Dissonance was induced by telling the subjects they would probably perform not too badly. After agreeing to return each subject was shown the DAF equipment. He had been told in the initial session that the delay interval was extreme, 13 on a 15-point scale, and that a shorter delay would permit better performance. He was then allowed to choose the delay interval to be used in the second session. It was predicted that the more dissonance a subject experienced, the less he would lower the DAF interval.

The results supported the prediction. Nine out of ten subjects in the Low Dissonance condition decreased the DAF interval, whereas only two out of ten decreased it in the High Dissonance condition. This finding suggests that when committing himself to failure, the greater a subject's expectation of failure, the more the dissonance and the less the effort to avoid failure. (Brehm& Cohen [1962, pp. 30–31]; Glass, Canavan & Schiavo [1968], and Schlachet [1965], it might be noted, have reported related sets of findings.)

The preceding interpretation bears a strong similarity to Aronson's expectation model in which a person is assumed to seek out situations that confirm his expectations, while avoiding those that promise disconfirmation. High Dissonance subjects in the Cohen-Zimbardo study were expecting to fail, and by not decreasing the DAF dial they created a situation where their expectations of failure would be confirmed. This is similar to the technique used by Aronson and Carlsmith's subjects when they changed their responses on the social sensitivity test. Future research might well explore the possibility that the two studies reflect the same basic process. Indeed, the present experiment (and its replications) lend additional support to the idea that expectancy confirmation may often take precedence over the motivation to succeed.

Further support for the effect of dissonance on avoidance motivation comes from a later study by Zimbardo, Cohen, Weisenberg, Dworkin, and Firestone (1964b). In this experiment, five groups of subjects were used, three as control groups and two as dissonance groups. One control received low shock and the other two high shock during a serial-anticipation learning task. After reaching criterion, there was a short break in the experiment and then the learning trials were replicated with a matched list of words. During this next set of trials, two groups were kept at their initial level of shock and one was lowered from high to moderate, thereby creating high, moderate, and low shock groups. The procedure for the dissonance groups was identical to that for the controls except for two modifications. At the break in the experiment, subjects were given a choice about whether or not to participate in the second part of the study. To induce Low Dissonance, the experimenter gave the subjects a variety of reasons to support their commitment to further shock; e.g., the benefits accruing to science. High Dissonance subjects were given minimal justification for commitment. All dissonance subjects then received the same high level of shock during the second part of the study as they received during the first. Three dependent variables were employed: (1) the change in perceived painfulness of shock from before to after the break in the experiment; (2) the learning performance before and after commitment to further shock; (3) galvanic skin resistance to shocks administered during the first and second parts of the study.

It was assumed that when a subject voluntarily commits himself to further shock he experiences dissonance; the less the justification for commitment, the greater the dissonance. Dissonance can be reduced most directly by altering the perception of the intensity of pain, as in "The shock really doesn't hurt so much" (cf. Brock & Buss, 1962; Glass, 1964). If the experience of pain is actually altered, then instrumental and physiological behaviors affected by this experience should be modified accordingly. Thus the weaker effects of the pain stimulus should be reflected in improved learning performance and reduced physiological responsiveness.

The results strongly supported theoretical expectations. The High Dissonance group reported that shock was less painful following commitment than before, whereas the Low Dissonance group, like the control with high shock throughout, showed only a minor decrement in perceived painfulness. The learning data were equally consistent with theory. High Dissonance and high-to-moderate-shock controls improved on mean trials to criterion; Low Dissonance and high-shock-throughout controls did worse. The results on mean galvanic skin resistance also parallel those obtained with subjective evaluations and learning. The Low Dissonance group mirrored the high-shock-throughout controls, while the High Dissonance group behaved physiologically as if the shocks did not hurt as much after commitment as they had before.

Dissonance has also been demonstrated to have an effect on the motive for social reinforcement (Cohen, Greenbaum, & Mansson, 1963). Subjects who commit themselves to social deprivation for little reward experience greater dissonance than subjects who receive high reward. The greater the dissonance, the more will subjects justify their choice by reducing their need for social reinforcement. A decrease in such social motivation will be reflected in decreased responsivity in a verbal conditioning situation.

To test these ideas, Cohen and his colleagues assigned eighty subjects to one of four groups: (1) High Deprivation-Control, (2) Low Deprivation-Control, (3) High Deprivation-High Dissonance, and (4) High Deprivation-Low Dissonance. Deprivation was manipulated as follows: Subjects were given a series of cards on which were typed such questions as "Explain your purpose in coming to college." The subject was asked to give verbal responses to these questions while an experimenter (A) sat opposite him and listened. For twenty subjects assigned to the Low Deprivation condition, the experimenter said "Good" at the rate of five times per minute throughout the fifteen-minute interview period. For sixty subjects assigned to the High Deprivation condition, the experimenter said "Good" for the first five minutes and then said nothing for the remaining ten minutes of the interview. Following this, subjects were asked by a second experimenter (B) to commit themselves to what would probably be a disagreeable interview with still another experimenter. High Dissonance subjects were offered $1.00 for their commitment, Low Dissonance subjects $5. After they agreed to participate, experimenter B administered a hundred trials of reinforcement on a Taffel-type (Taffel, 1955) verbal conditioning task. This was similar to a task the subject had completed at the beginning of the experiment when his operant level was established. Reinforcement trials were followed by eighty trials of extinction. Control subjects were exposed to the same procedure except they were not asked to commit themselves to another interview.

High Dissonance subjects responded significantly less to social reinforcement than did control and Low Dissonance subjects. These findings occurred on two indices of verbal conditioning: (1) the mean of the reinforcement trials minus operant level, and (2) the mean of the extinction trials minus operant level. It seems clear that dissonance in the presence of motivation for social reinforcement can produce a reduction in such motivation as reflected in less conditioning of verbal behavior.

The experiments presented here have all assumed that motivation is affected by cognitive dissonance. In the hunger, thirst, and avoidance motivation studies, subjects chose to commit themselves to a situation promising deprivation of an important need. In each case, the commitment produced dissonance and consequent attempts to reduce dissonance through a decrease in the perceived intensity of the frustrated need. There was additional evidence showing that dissonance not only affects the cognized intensity of motivation, but also has an impact on non-cognitive aspects of motivation, such as consummatory behavior, learning, verbal conditioning, and physiological processes.

The occurrence of these two effects of dissonance raises the general problem of the relationship between cognitive and noncognitive aspects of motivation. A person could, for example, think of himself as having less need for social reinforcement and therefore condition less, even though his actual motivation remained high. Or, alternatively, dissonance could lead to an actual reduction in the person's motive strength, and this in turn could lead to a reduction in the cognized intensity of the motive. There are of course other possibilities, but these should give us an idea of the formidable complexities to which future research must address itself. Many of these issues will be discussed in a forthcoming book summarizing the experiments carried out within the Cohen and Zimbardo program of research (Zimbardo, 1968).

Perhaps of equal importance for future experimentation is a methodological problem which has plagued all studies in this area; that is, how to separate those effects that are attributable to dissonance from those that are attributable to the effects of other motivational processes (Brehm & Cohen, 1962). For example, when a person commits himself to a task on which he knows he will fail, he experiences dissonance and reduces his motivation to avoid failure. But he still has a need to succeed which remains unsatisfied. The effect of these two need states may cancel each other out, with the result that ambiguity exists regarding the specific effect of dissonance. What is needed is a baseline measure of need for achievement in the absence of commitment to deprivation of this need. The problem of adequate control groups for obtaining such a baseline is a methodological issue of major significance. We have seen two efforts to resolve the issue in the Cohen-Zimbardo experiments on learning and social deprivation. Both studies exercised exceptional care in establishing baseline indices of the frustrated need. In one case, three shock-control groups were used to determine the effect of pain on avoidance motivation in the absence of dissonance; in the second case, two social deprivation controls were used to establish that the operation did in fact produce a strong motivation for social reinforcers. If dissonance theory is to be given wider application to problems of social motivation, carefully controlled experiments must continue to characterize work in this area.

Dissonance research on motivation, and for that matter on personality in general, would also benefit from the development of dissonance measures that are independent of the dependent variables. In the typical dissonance study, the experimenter manipulates a set of stimulus conditions, *infers* that dissonance has been aroused, and then concludes that the results are due to the subjects' attempts to reduce dissonance (Berkowitz, 1963). There is no question that the dissonance position would be stronger if one could show, independently of change in the dependent variables, that dissonance was produced by the experimental manipulations. One possibility is the use of physiological indicators of dissonance, such as fat mobilization in the blood (Brehm, Back, & Bogdonoff, 1964), tonic or phasic skin conductance (Burdick & Burnes, 1958; Zimbardo *et al.,* 1964b; Glass & Mayhew, 1967), and electromyographic recordings (Horwitz, Glass & Niyekawa, 1964). There are of course a number of technical difficulties involved here, some of which may be insurmountable, given our present state of knowledge. Even more important is the perennial question of how to identify those physiological changes due to dissonance and those due to other motivational states.

Personality Development

Within the field of personality, a considerable amount of theory development and research effort has been devoted to the process of socialization and personality development. We know that in the course of his life an individual acquires behavior patterns and internalizes cultural and moral values. Our understanding of this process, however, is quite limited. The relevant theories come mainly from extensions of reinforcement-incentive models of learning (e.g., Sears, 1963; Bandura & Walters, 1963), from extensions of psychoanalytic theory (e.g., Dollard & Miller, 1950), or from sociological theories of role learning (e.g., Brim & Wheeler, 1966). The extent to which these theories can explain the socialization process has never been adequately tested.

Theories of consistency suggest a rather different approach to socialization, but here the problem is the more fundamental one of inadequate attention to the application of these theories to socialization. The neglect stems in part from the concern of consistency theorists with situational determination of behavior, almost to the exclusion of interest in stable personality characteristics. This is an unfortunate restriction, for our understanding of personality dynamics would benefit greatly from knowledge about the role of consistency in personality development.

Support for a consistency approach to personality development comes from a recent attempt to use dissonance theory to explain the process by which values become internalized (Festinger & Freedman, 1964). The paper is specifically concerned with one class of moral values, those pertaining to behavior that occurs with great frequency and which the culture defines as undesirable; e.g., stealing, cheating, and destructive aggression. An adult who has not internalized moral values proscribing such behavior is considered "deviant" and represents a failure of the socialization process. The central issue for any theory of socialization is to specify the conditions which determine whether or not moral values become internalized. Festinger and Freedman suggest that dissonance theory offers a possible solution to this problem. The following is a paraphrase of their argument.

Suppose a parent discovers that his four-year-old son has stolen something. The parent may punish the child in an effort to teach him that stealing is bad, and consequently to prevent a recurrence of the act. If the punishment is severe, and carries with it the implication of similar treatment if there is a recurrence, it will undoubtedly affect the child's behavior. The next time the child has an impulse to steal he will probably restrain himself. There will, however, be few attitudinal consequences for the child. The knowledge of the severe punishment that is being avoided is sufficient justification for not stealing.

A quite different state of affairs would result if the parent had punished the child only mildly. When the child refrains from stealing the next time he is tempted, the knowledge of the punishment which is avoided is barely sufficient justification for not taking the desired object. Under these circumstances, the child will provide his own additional justifications for restraining his behavior, and hence there will be attitudinal consequences.

Festinger and Freedman inquire into the nature of these consequences. One possibility is for the child to persuade himself that the object he did not steal was after all not very desirable. An experiment by Aronson and Carlsmith (1963; in Festinger & Freedman, 1964) provides evidence of this kind of effect. In a repeated-measurements design, 22 preschool children ranked each of several toys in terms of their degree of attractiveness. Each child was then threatened with either mild or severe punishment if he played with the second ranked toy during a play session. After leaving the child alone with the toys for ten minutes, the experimenter had the child rank the toys again. It was hypothesized that mild threat as compared with strong threat would arouse greater dissonance between the attractiveness of the second ranked toy and the child's avoidance of it during the play session. It was further hypothesized that the greater the dissonance, the greater would be the devaluation of the toy in an effort to reduce dissonance. The hypothesis was confirmed. However, most of the difference between strong and mild threat conditions was due to an increase in the attractiveness of the forbidden toy in the strong threat condition. This aspect of the results is not easily explained by dissonance theory, although Aronson and Carlsmith suggest that the increment in attractiveness was not due to severe threat, but to some other factor present in the experimental situation. Their explanation received some support from a "no-threat" control condition in which the experimenter took the critical toy with him when he left the room. In this condition, the attractiveness of the toy increased about as much as in the strong threat condition, indicating that the increase was not due to the strong threat itself. The dissonance-produced devaluation in the mild threat condition was considered, therefore, to be a response which somehow took precedence over a more general tendency for the forbidden toy to increase in attractiveness.

A change in the evaluation of an external object is only one means of reducing dissonance in the kind of situation under consideration. Festinger and Freedman suggest at least two other ways in which dissonance may be reduced. The child could exaggerate the severity of the threatened punishment, thereby providing additional justification for resisting temptation (cf. Zimbardo *et al.*, 1964b). Or the child could persuade himself that stealing is really very bad and this also provides justification for not stealing. It is this last mode of dissonance reduction which obviously leads to the development of moral values.

If this view of moral development is correct, then variations in reward should produce the same effect as variations in punishment. Other things being equal, a large reward for not engaging in forbidden behavior should provide sufficient justification for restraint. Small rewards should provide insufficient justification. An experiment by Mills (1958) provides evidence relevant to these considerations.

Sixth-grade students reported their attitudes concerning cheating before and after a contest in which they had an opportunity to cheat. The contest was so arranged that it was impossible to win without cheating and easy to win if the subject cheated. (Two contests were used in the experiment, but we discuss only one of them since both sets of results were virtually identical.) To induce high temptation to cheat, subjects were told that contest winners would receive $5.00 toward anything they might like to buy. In the low temptation condition, subjects were told that the names of the contest winners would be announced to the class, but nothing further was mentioned about prizes. The other variable included in the design was restraint against cheating. On the pretext that they might want to see how well they had done, Low Restraint groups were given the "correct" answers to the experimental task before their answer sheets were collected. They were told to "mark those you got right so you can keep track of your score." It was quite easy for these groups to cheat by changing answers while they were supposed to be correcting their papers. The answers given as correct were in fact incorrect, thereby enabling the experimenter to detect the cheaters. Subjects in the High Restraint groups were given an opportunity to learn their scores only after they had handed in their answer sheets, hence they had little opportunity to cheat.

Mills predicted that subjects who did not cheat would change their attitudes in the direction of feeling that cheating was bad, the amount of such change being greater in the high temptation condition than in the low temptation condition. A reverse effect would be observed among those who cheat, for dissonance is greatest when the violation occurs for little reward. The results supported the predictions. Cheaters in the low temptation condition became more lenient toward cheating, noncheaters in the high temptation condition became more severe. The other treatments produced a very slight change in the direction of a more severe attitude, but this may have been due to the effects of statistical regression. The findings concerning restraints against cheating were both ambiguous and of marginal significance.

The dissonance analysis of moral development is clearly an oversimplification. The social-interactive process introduces a number of complications as, for example, where a person's moral attitudes are fashioned as a reaction to his behavior in response to the actions of others. Take the situation in which a person sees someone else cheat and does nothing about it. Dissonance would exist between the person's knowledge that he had done nothing and the knowledge that he had suffered a loss through the other person's cheating, or between the first cognition and the knowledge that he had condoned an antisocial act. The person might reduce dissonance by persuading himself that cheating is not really so bad. On the other hand, if the person reported the cheater to an appropriate authority, his knowledge concerning this action would be dissonant with other values he holds; for example, one should not inform on others. One way the person could reduce this dissonance is by persuading himself that cheating is quite inexcusable.

Support for this line of reasoning comes from an experiment by Gumpert and Festinger (1964, pp. 235–240). A situation was created in which subjects observed someone else cheating. In one condition, they were induced to report the cheating behavior to the experimenter; in the other condition, there were no pressures to make such a report. It was hypothesized that dissonance would be greater in the former condition, hence subjects would show greater dislike of the cheater in an effort to reduce dissonance. The results supported the hypothesis. Subjects who reported the cheating showed a severe dislike of the cheater, while those who did not showed only mild dislike. In interpreting their results, the authors suggest that dislike reflects the subject's beliefs about the seriousness of cheating. On this assumption, the results seem to support the hypothesis concerning attitudinal consequences of behavior with respect to others who yield to temptation.

The dissonance approach to personality development has been the focus of our discussion because it is the one theory of consistency that has dealt specifically with this issue. However, a consistency theory of the socialization process should be able to say more than we have presented here. For example, something needs to be said about the effect of repeated experiences on the internalization of cultural values. Festinger and Freedman propose a rather complicated scheme to take account of the cumulative effects of dissonance reduction on moral development. There are no data presented to support their speculations, although a study by Aronson (1961) suggests that repeated and related dissonances tend to summate, thus increasing the magnitude of attempts to reduce dissonance. Cohen (in Brehm & Cohen, 1962, pp. 97–104), on the other hand, reports that repeated but *unrelated* dissonances may minimize the effect of a subsequent dissonance-arousing situation. The further exploration of these findings is an intriguing line for future research, and one which should enhance our knowledge of the socialization process.

Individual Differences in Reactivity to Inconsistency

In the preceding sections, we have attempted to evaluate the relevance of theories of consistency for the study of personality processes. In the present section, we turn to the related question of how individual differences influence the arousal and reduction of cognitive inconsistencies.

It has repeatedly been observed that people differ in their reactions to inconsistency-arousing situations (Festinger, 1957; Zajonc, 1960; Cohen, 1960; Rosenberg *et al.*, 1960; Brehm & Cohen, 1962; Feather, 1964a). Such differences may occur because people perceive the inconsistent situation differently, and it is likely that differential perception is in part a function of the individual's personality structure (e.g., Janicki, 1964). Individual differences might also be due to a differential threshold or tolerance for inconsistency, and the height of this threshold is undoubtedly affected by a variety of personality factors. Aronson and Festinger (1958) attempted to develop several instruments that would specifically measure tolerance for dissonance, including a personality inventory based on items from tests such as the MMPI, the CPI, and the F-scale. Of the five instruments that were developed, only the personality inventory effectively discriminated between subjects whose behavior indicated a high tolerance for dissonance and those whose behavior indicated a low tolerance for dissonance. It is not possible, however, to generalize these results, for the criterion of high tolerance was specific to the population studied by the authors.

Hovland and Rosenberg (1960, pp. 215–221; Rosenberg, 1963) have also suggested several classes of variables (including personality predispositions), which may influence the tolerance-for-inconsistency threshold. There is some support for their suggestions in studies of social influence, which indicate that a personality pattern characterized by chronic low self-esteem and general passivity disposes the individual to resolve inconsistencies by changing his attitude in the direction advocated by the contrary communication (McGuire, chapter 24 of this volume; Hovland & Janis, 1959; see Brehm and Cohen, 1962, pp. 259–261 for a dissonance interpretation of this result). Other studies report that high need for affiliation, authoritarianism, and measures of perceptual field dependence, and cognitive structure (concreteness-abstractness) correlate positively with general persuasibility (Burdick & Burnes, 1958; Hovland & Janis, 1959; Harvey, 1965). The results of these studies have been interpreted as providing evidence of variability in tolerance for inconsistency as a function of personality variables.

Additional factors responsible for differential reaction to inconsistency are the person's facility in restoring consistency, and his preference for one means of consistency restoration over another. It seems reasonable to assume that characteristic personality patterns are also associated with these factors. Steiner (1960), for example, has reported data which suggest that there may be sex differences in preference for dissonance-reducing responses. He found that males were more prone than females to reject a partner with whom they had disagreed. The study also reports that "maladjustment" (measured by the MMPI) among males involved response preferences which, among females, were associated with good adjustment. Similar findings were obtained in a later experiment by Steiner and Rogers (1963).

The preceding discussion suggests that there may be more than one source of difference between people's reactions to inconsistency. Regardless of the source one decides to emphasize in trying to understand the differences, a major task would be to specify precisely what personality factors influence the inconsistency process. This is often difficult to do, for personality "explanations" tend to be *ad hoc* and not theoretically coordinate with the specific inconsistency being manipulated in the experiment (Cohen, 1960; Brehm & Cohen, 1962). There is no reason why a randomly chosen personality variable should have implications for reactions to inconsistent situations. It is absolutely essential, therefore, that we isolate the personality constructs which seem coordinate with the particular cognitions involved in the inconsistency. To select an arbitrary variable from the pool of general personality traits is at best a dubious procedure.

But even if we could manage to isolate the relevant personality variables, we would still be confronted with difficulty. We refer here to the familiar criticism that the criterion variable, inconsistency, is not directly measurable. Thus the usual procedure is to create a situation containing inconsistent cognitions, and then to infer the existence of inconsistency-produced tension from attempts to restore consistency. Take as an example the dissonance experiment by Festinger and Carlsmith (1959). In this study, it will be recalled, a subject accepted money for saying something he believed to be untrue. According to theory he should have experienced dissonance. This was determined not by measuring dissonance directly, but by measuring attempts to reduce dissonance. Suppose we now wish to show that perceptual field dependency is related to the magnitude of dissonance. Having measured the field dependence-independence of a group of subjects, we place each of them in the dissonance arousal situation just described. We then measure their attempts to reduce dissonance, and correlate these measures with our index of perceptual style. It is at this point that our difficulties begin. First of all, several modes of dissonance reduction are usually operative in any given situation. In the example being discussed this means that subjects could reduce dissonance not only by changing their attitudes toward the experiment, but also by justifying their discrepant behavior. If the only way to measure dissonance is to measure attempts to reduce it, then clearly we must measure all attempts to reduce it. Without comprehensive measurement of this kind, it becomes impossible to assess the meaning of the correlation between field dependency and dissonance reduction.

But even if we could accomplish all this, we still would not necessarily be able to relate our personality measure to the magnitude of dissonance. The correlation may reflect a relationship with factors other than dissonance. As we indicated earlier, the personality variable may relate, either directly or through a mediating variable, to any of the independent variables controlling the perception of dissonance. It may also relate to one or more of the ways in which dissonance can be reduced, and finally, it may relate to the process by which the mode of dissonance reduction is selected. It ought to be clear, therefore, that the correlation between attempts to reduce dissonance and perceptual field dependency does not establish that field dependency has a direct effect on the magnitude of dissonance.

Despite these methodological problems, a number of studies of personality and inconsistency are worthy of attention. One group of experiments has been mainly concerned with the relation between authoritarianism (as measured by the F-scale or the E-scale) and inconsistencies in interpersonal perception (Steiner, 1954; Kenny & Ginsberg, 1958; Harvey, 1962; Steiner & Johnson, 1964; Newcomb, 1963b). In general, the results of these studies indicate that authoritarianism is positively related to the specific inconsistencies which arise in connection with the perception of others. It has been found, for example, that "authoritarian personalities" are intolerant of the ambiguity implied by an imbalanced interpersonal relationship (Newcomb, 1963b), and that this intolerance is also evident in a tendency to make "black" or "white" judgments and to be extreme in the evaluation of others (Steiner, 1954; Steiner & Johnson, 1964).

Additional evidence of these effects can be found in a more recent study by Feather (1964b). One hundred sixty-five male college students in an Australian university were asked to judge the logical validity of 24 religious syllogisms and 16 neutral syllogisms (cf. McGuire, 1960b, pp. 65–111). A Syllogism Evaluation score was computed for each subject by adding together the number of proreligious syllogisms marked sound and the number of antireligious syllogisms marked unsound. A Critical Ability score was also computed by summing the number of neutral syllogisms correctly answered by each subject. About a week later, a religious attitude scale was administered to all subjects. Two other tests were also administered on the assumption that each provided a measure of intolerance of inconsistency. The first test was Rokeach's (1960) Dogmatism Scale, a 40-item test designed to measure the extent to which a person's belief systems are "closed" rather than "open." The second test was an "intolerance of ambiguity" scale developed by Budner (1962). It consisted of 16 items designed to measure the degree to which a person perceives ambiguous (e.g., novel or insoluble) situations as sources of threat and unambiguous situations as desirable.

The results from the 131 subjects with proreligious attitudes provided statistically significant support for Feather's hypotheses, although the correlations were uniformly small in magnitude. The tendency to accept or reject relevant arguments in a manner consistent with one's attitude (i.e., a high Syllogism Evaluation score) was positively related to intolerance of ambiguity (+.21), negatively related to level of critical ability (−.24), and positively related to the strength of the proreligious attitude (+.22). (Dogmatism showed no relationship with the syllogism test scores.) The evidence that attitude intensity influences the acceptance of logical arguments is not a novel finding, although contrary results, it will be remembered, have also been found in the research literature. Of greater significance is the fact that personality variables like critical ability and intolerance of inconsistency affect the evaluation of arguments. The results for critical ability are consistent with the suggestion of Hovland and Janis (1959) that persuasibility may be related to more differentiated measures of intellectual ability than those customarily obtained from a general intelligence test. Also consistent with previous suggestions is the finding that intolerance of ambiguity is positively related to high Syllogism Evaluation scores (Festinger, 1957; Brehm & Cohen, 1962).

Evidence for the effects of personality variables other than authoritarianism comes from a number of dissonance experiments. The first is a study by Rosen (1961) which successfully replicated an earlier experiment by Mills, Aronson, and Robinson (1959). Dissonance was aroused in college students by giving them a choice between taking an essay or multiple-choice examination. After choosing, they were told they could read articles concerning either multiple-choice or essay examinations, and were then asked to indicate which they would most like to to read.The results showed that the articles selected tended to be those which supported the type of examination chosen.

Rosen also collected data relevant to two personality dimensions that might be related to the magnitude of dissonance. Reasoning that retention of dissonant cognitions in this experiment would imply a risk of being wrong, Rosen proposed that if a subject had an unusually strong desire to avoid such risks, he could be expected to try to avoid risks in other situations as well. It was hypothesized therefore that dissonance-reducing behavior would be related to cognitive variables known to be inversely linked to risk avoidance. Two such variables are decision certainty and width of categorizing. To measure these variables, Rosen had his subjects complete an abbreviated version of the Category Width Scale (Pettigrew, 1958), and also to indicate on five-point scales how certain they were of their judgments with respect to the range of each category of information. Category-width scores were computed by summing the weights for the ranges checked by each subject. Certainty scores were similarly obtained by summing the separate ratings.

The Category Width Scale measures the degree to which subjects are typically broad, medium, or narrow in the ranges they use for classifying objects. The scale is assumed to be related to risk taking: Those whose width is broad have a tolerance for Type I errors, where they risk negative instances in an effort to include a maximum of positive instances; those with narrow width are willing to make Type II errors by restricting category ranges in order to minimize the number of negative instances.

The results of Rosen's study showed that subjects who manifested the greatest dissonance reduction (that is, expressed a more extreme preference for reading articles consonant with their choice of examination) also tended to use narrower categories. This effect was significant for males but not for females, a result which takes on added significance when constrasted with evidence from other studies demonstrating sex differences in dissonance reduction (Steiner, 1960; Brock & Buss, 1962; Kogan & Wallach, 1964). Decision certainty showed no relationship to dissonance reducing tendencies.

Another piece of evidence relevant to the effect of personality variables on dissonance comes from a recent study by Steiner and Rogers (1963). Subjects were placed in a situation where their judgments were contradicted by an associate to whom they were somewhat attracted. The resulting dissonance could have been reduced in one of the following ways: (1) conformity to the contrary judgments of the associate; (2) rejection of the associate as incompetent; (3) devaluation of the importance of the experimental task; and (4) forgetting the number of disagreements. It was found that subjects tended to employ the four responses as alternative rather than supplementary means of dissonance reduction. As in an earlier experiment by Steiner (1960), marked sex differences were observed in preferences for dissonance-reducing responses. Females made less use of rejection than did males; in addition, they were more inclined to tolerate dissonance. These results appear to be consistent with descriptions of the changing female role in this culture. It is generally assumed that society forbids females from using overt rejection and devaluation as means of resolving conflict. At the same time, conformity, which is clearly the most submissive way of reducing conflict, is no longer regarded as entirely appropriate for emancipated women (e.g., Parsons, 1942). Since none of the four responses to dissonance is completely sanctioned for females, the only safe alternative in the Steiner and Rogers experiment was simply to tolerate the dissonance.

A related set of findings is reported by Brock and Buss (1962) in their study of postaggression revaluation of pain. When the victim was a male, it will be recalled, pain minimization was the dominant mode of dissonance reduction. With female victims the evidence showed that expression of great obligation to shock was used to reduce dissonance. Later experiments by these authors (Buss & Brock, 1963; Brock & Buss, 1964) provide additional confirmation of the fact that sex of the subject plays an important role in postaggression dissonance reduction.

In addition to showing the direct effect of sex differences, Steiner and Rogers (1963) have documented the influence of sex on the relationship between other personality variables and dissonance reduction. They report that among females, the Taylor Manifest Anxiety Scale correlates positively with conformity and tolerance of dissonance, and negatively with rejection. Among males, in contrast, anxiety scores correlate significantly only with underrecall of disagreements (−.31). These results suggest that the effect of anxiety on choice of a dissonance-reducing response depends on the sex of the subject. Anxious females tend to conform or to tolerate dissonance, but to avoid rejection. Anxious males tend not to emphasize the use of any single response, but they avoid the use of underrecall. Kogan and Wallach (1964) report what appears to be a parallel set of results for a postdecision dissonance situation. Females low in test anxiety were found to exhibit a consistent tolerance (or intolerance) for postdecisional dissonance, whereas for males, it was those low in defensiveness that showed this pattern of responses.

What can we conclude from our summary of research on personality structure and cognitive inconsistency? The area is clearly not well developed and offers a major challenge to further investigation. Any attempt to explore the relationship between personality predispositions and reactions to inconsistency must resolve two issues. The first is to specify whether it is the arousal or reduction aspects of the inconsistency process to which the personality variables will be related. Having done this, the next step is to search for personality variables that are theoretically coordinated to the type of inconsistency being studied. For example, if we assume that a basic proposition of dissonance theory is the fact of discrepant commitment, and prior choice in that commitment, then the personality variables we select ought to refer to differences between people in their commitment tendencies and ease of decision making (Brehm & Cohen, 1962). Thus the likelihood of dissonance arousal would be greater the more the person involved had personality predispositions related to ease of commitment or decision. The same is true if we deal with the reduction phase of the inconsistency process. Differences between people in cognitive style or ego-defensive behavior, for instance, might very well determine the mode of inconsistency reduction they adopt in a given situation (Glass, 1968; Glass, Canavan & Schiavo, 1968). One could go on to enumerate still other examples, but in the absence of data this seems unprofitable. The important point to emphasize here is that a search for relevant personality variables requires a clear description of their connection to the inconsistency-arousing variables and avenues of reduction.

CONCLUDING REMARKS

In this chapter, we have attempted to present a detailed summary of psychological theories of consistency and their applications to the study of personality. While many theorists in psychology might appropriately be discussed under the heading of consistency theories of personality (e.g., Lecky, 1945; Stagner, 1951; Rogers, 1951; Hunt, 1963), we have limited our discussion to the work of those men whose models are based primarily on the principle of consistency. Furthermore, our emphasis has been upon Festinger's theory of cognitive dissonance because this theory seems to us to have greater relevance for personality research than the other less general models. In our survey of dissonance studies of personality, we tried to indicate some of the benefits that would accrue from interrelating personality theory and dissonance theory. The increased refinement of personality constructs and the increased predictive accuracy of the dissonance model are examples of such benefits.

The extraordinary creativeness of dissonance theorists, and for that matter consistency theorists in general, cannot help being impressive. Yet like many innovators, their efforts are often crude and characterized by theoretical and methodological shortcomings. The main intention in this chapter, therefore, has been to present the reader with an overview of the major theories of consistency, and to convey our conviction that a "need for cognitive consistency" is a ubiquitous feature of human behavior with manifold implications for an understanding of personality.

REFERENCES

Abelson, R. P., & Rosenberg, M. J. Symbolic psycho-logic: A model of attitudinal cognition. *Behav. Sci.*, 1958, 3, 1–13.

Abelson, R. P., Aronson, E., McGuire, W. J., Newcomb, T. M., Rosenberg, M. J., & Tannenbaum, P. H. (Eds.), *Theories of Cognitive Consistency: A Sourcebook*. Chicago: Rand McNally, 1968.

Adams, J. S. Reduction of cognitive dissonance by seeking consonant information. *J. abnorm. soc. Psychol.*, 1961, 62, 74–78.

Adams, J. S. Toward an understanding of inequity. *J. abnorm. soc. Psychol.*, 1963, 67, 422–436.

Adams, J. S., & Rosenbaum, W. B. The relationship of worker productivity to cognitive dissonance. *J. appl. Psychol.*, 1962, 46, 161–164.

Alexander, C. N., Jr. Consensus and mutual attraction in natural cliques: A study of adolescent drinkers. *Amer. J. Sociol.*, 1964, 69, 395–403.

Allyn, J., & Festinger, L. The effectiveness of unanticipated persuasive communications. *J. abnorm. soc. Psychol.*, 1961, 62, 35–40.

Anderson, L. R., & Fishbein, M. Prediction of attitude from the number, strength, and evaluative aspect of beliefs about the attitude object: A comparison of summation and congruity theories. Paper read at the Midwest. Psychol. Assn., St. Louis, April, 1964.

Aronson, E. The cognitive and behavioral consequences of the confirmation and disconfirmation of expectancies. Application for Research Grant submitted to the National Science Foundation. Cambridge, Mass.: Harvard Univer., 1960.

Aronson, E. The effect of effort on the attractiveness of rewarded and unrewarded stimuli. *J. abnorm. soc. Psychol.,* 1961, 63, 375–380.

Aronson, E. Effort, attractiveness, and the anticipation of reward: A reply to Lott's critique. *J. abnorm. soc. Psychol.,* 1963, 67, 522–525.

Aronson, E. The psychology of insufficient justification: An analysis of some conflicting data. In S. Feldman (Ed.), *Cognitive consistency*. New York: Academic Press, 1966. Pp. 115–133.

Aronson, E., & Carlsmith, J. M. Performance expectancy as a determinant of actual performance. *J. abnorm. soc. Psychol.,* 1962, 65, 178–182.

Aronson, E., & Carlsmith, J. M. Effect of the severity of threat on the devaluation of forbidden behavior. *J. abnorm. soc. Psychol.,* 1963, 66, 584–588.

Aronson, E., Carlsmith, J. M., & Darley, J. M. The effects of expectancy on volunteering for an unpleasant experience. *J. abnorm. soc. Psychol.,* 1963, 66, 220–224.

Aronson, E., & Festinger, L. Some attempts to measure tolerance for dissonance. *USAF WADC tech. Rep.,* 1958, No. 58–942.

Aronson, E., & Mills, J. The effects of severity of initiation on liking for a group. *J. abnorm. soc. Psychol.,* 1959, 59, 177–181.

Aronson, E., Turner, J., & Carlsmith, J. M. Communicator credibility and communication discrepancy as determinants of opinion change. *J. abnorm. soc. Psychol.,* 1963, 67, 31–36.

Asch, S. E. Review of L. Festinger, *A theory of cognitive dissonance. Contemp. Psychol.,* 1958, 3, 194–195.

Back, K. W. The exertion of influence through social communication. *J. abnorm. soc. Psychol.,* 1951, 46, 9–24.

Backman, C. W., Secord, P. F., & Pierce, J. R. Resistance to change in the self-concept as the function of consensus among significant others. *Sociometry,* 1963, 26, 102–111.

Bandura, A., & Walters, R. H. *Social learning and personality development.* New York: Holt, Rinehart & Winston, 1963.

Bergin, A. E. The effect of dissonant persuasive communications upon changes in a self-referring attitude. *J. Pers.,* 1962, 30, 423–438.

Berkowitz, L. *Aggression: a social psychological analysis.* New York: McGraw-Hill, 1962.

Berkowitz, L. Social psychological theorizing. In M. H. Marx (Ed.), *Theories in contemporary psychology.* New York: Macmillan, 1963. Pp. 369–387.

Bramel, D. A dissonance theory approach to defensive projection. *J. abnorm. soc. Psychol.,* 1962, 64, 121–129.

Bramel, D. Selection of a target for defensive projection. *J. abnorm. soc. Psychol.,* 1963, 66, 318–324.

Bramel, D. Dissonance, expectancy, and the self. In R. P. Abelson, E. Aronson, W. J. McGuire, T. M. Newcomb, M. J. Rosenberg, & P. H. Tannenbaum (Eds.), *Theories of Cognitive Consistency: A Sourcebook.* Chicago: Rand McNally, 1968.

Brehm, J. W. Post-decision changes in the desirability of alternatives. *J. abnorm. soc. Psychol.,* 1956, 52, 384–389.

Brehm, J. W. Increasing cognitive dissonance by a fait-accompli. *J. abnorm. soc. Psychol.,* 1959, 58, 379–382.

Brehm, J. W. Attitudinal consequences of commitment to unpleasant behavior. *J. abnorm. soc. Psychol.,* 1960, 60, 379–383.

Brehm, J. W. Motivational effects of cognitive dissonance. In M. R. Jones (Ed.), *Nebraska symposium on motivation.* Lincoln: Univer. of Nebraska Press, 1962. Pp. 51–77.

Brehm, J. W., & Cohen, A. R. Re-evaluation of choice alternatives as a function of their number and qualitative similarity. *J. abnorm. soc. Psychol.,* 1959, 58, 373–378. (a)

Brehm, J. W., & Cohen, A. R. Choice and chance relative deprivation as determinants of cognitive dissonance. *J. abnorm. soc. Psychol.,* 1959, 58, 383–387. (b)

Brehm, J. W., & Cohen, A. R. *Explorations in cognitive dissonance.* New York: Wiley, 1962.

Brehm, J. W., & Leventhal, G. S. An experiment on the effect of commitment. In J. W. Brehm & A. R. Cohen, *Explorations in cognitive dissonance.* New York: Wiley, 1962. Pp. 192–201.

Brehm, J. W., & Lipsher, D. Communicator-communicatee discrepancy and perceived communicator trustworthiness. *J. Pers.,* 1959, 27, 352–361.

Brehm, M. L., Back, K. W., & Bogdonoff, M. D. A physiological effect of cognitive dissonance under stress and deprivation. *J. abnorm. soc. Psychol.,* 1964, 69, 303–310.

Brim, O. G., Jr., & Wheeler, S. *Socialization after childhood:*Two essays. New York: Wiley, 1966.

Brock, T. C. Cognitive restructuring and attitude change. *J. abnorm. soc. Psychol.,* 1962, 64, 264–271.

Brock, T. C. Effects of prior dishonesty on post-decision dissonance. *J. abnorm. soc. Psychol.,* 1963, 66, 325–331.

Brock, T. C., & Blackwood, J. E. Dissonance reduction, social comparison, and motivation as others' opinions. *J. abnorm. soc. Psychol.,* 1962, 65, 319–324.

Brock, T. C., & Buss, A. H. Dissonance, aggression, and evaluation of pain. *J. abnorm. soc. Psychol.,* 1962, 65, 197–202.

Brock, T. C., & Buss, A. H. Effects of justification for aggression and communication with the victim on postaggression dissonance. *J. abnorm. soc. Psychol.,* 1964, 68, 403–412.

Brock, T. C., Edelman, S. K., Edwards, D. C., & Schuck, J. R. Seven studies of performance expectancy as a determinant of actual performance. *J. exp. soc. Psychol.,* 1965, *1,* 295–310.

Brock, T. C., & Grant, L. D. Dissonance, awareness, and motivation. *J. abnorm. soc. Psychol.,* 1963, 67, 53–60.

Brodbeck, M. The role of small groups in mediating the effects of propaganda. *J. abnorm. soc. Psychol.,* 1956, 52, 166–170.

Brown, R. Models of attitude change. In R. Brown, E. Galanter, E. H. Hess, & G. Mandler, *New directions in psychology.* New York: Holt, Rinehart and Winston, 1962. Pp. 3–85.

Broxton, J. A. A test of interpersonal attraction predictions derived from balance theory. *J. abnorm. soc. Psychol.,* 1963, 66, 394–397.

Budner, S. Intolerance of ambiguity as a personality variable. *J. Pers.,* 1962, 30, 29–50.

Burdick, H. A., & Burnes, A. J. A test of "strain toward symmetry" theories. *J. abnorm. soc. Psychol.,* 1958, 57, 367–370.

Buss, A. H. *The psychology of aggression.* New York: Wiley, 1961.

Buss, A. H., & Brock, T. C. Repression and guilt in relation to aggression. *J. abnorm. soc. Psychol.,* 1963, 66, 345–350.

Cannon, W. B. *The wisdom of the body.* New York: Norton, 1939.

Canon, L. K. Self-confidence and selective exposure to information. In L. Festinger, *et al., Conflict, decision, and dissonance.* Stanford: Stanford Univer. Press, 1964. Pp. 83–96.

Carlsmith, J. M., & Aronson, E. Some hedonic consequences of the confirmation and disconfirmation of expectancies. *J. abnorm. soc. Psychol.,* 1963, 66, 151–156.

Carlsmith, J. M., Collins, B. E., & Helmreich, R. L. Studies in forced compliance: I. The effect of pressure for compliance on attitude change produced by face-to-face role playing and anonymous essay writing. *J. pers. soc. Psychol.,* 1966, *4,* 1–13.

Carlson, E. R. Attitude change through modification of attitude structure. *J. abnorm. soc. Psychol.,* 1956, 52, 256–261.

Cartwright, D., & Harary, F. Structural balance: A generalization of Heider's theory. *Psychol. Rev.,* 1956, 63, 277–293.

Chapanis, N. P., & Chapanis, A. Cognitive dissonance: Five years later. *Psychol. Bull.,* 1964, 61, 1–22.

Cofer, C. N., & Appley, M. H. *Motivation: Theory and research.* New York: Wiley, 1964.

Cohen, A. R. Communication discrepancy and attitude change: A dissonance theory approach. *J. Pers.,* 1959, 27, 386–396.

Cohen, A. R. Attitudinal consequences of induced discrepancies between cognitions and behavior. *Publ. Opin. Quart.,* 1960, 24, 297–318.

Cohen, A. R. A dissonance analysis of the boomerang effect. *J. Pers.,* 1962, 30, 75–88. (a)

Cohen, A. R. A study of discrepant information in bethrothal. In J. W. Brehm & A. R. Cohen, *Explorations in cognitive dissonance.* New York: Wiley, 1962. Pp. 78–81. (b)

Cohen, A. R., Brehm, J. W., & Fleming, W. H. Attitude change and justification for compliance. *J. abnorm. soc. Psychol.,* 1958, 56, 276–278.

Cohen, A. R., Brehm, J. W., & Latané, B. Choice of strategy and voluntary exposure to information under public and private conditions. *J. Pers.,* 1959, 27, 63–73.

Cohen, A. R., Greenbaum, C. W., & Mansson, H. H. Commitment to social deprivation and verbal conditioning. *J. abnorm. soc. Psychol.,* 1963, 67, 410–421.

Cohen, A. R., Terry, H. I., & Jones, C. B. Attitudinal effects of choice in exposure to counter-propaganda. *J. abnorm. soc. Psychol.,* 1959, 58, 388–391.

Cohen, A. R., & Zimbardo, P. G. An experiment in avoidance motivation. In J. W. Brehm & A. R. Cohen, *Explorations in cognitive dissonance.* New York: Wiley, 1962. Pp. 143–151.

Cottrell, N. Performance expectancy as a determinant of actual performance: A replication with a new design. *J. pers. soc. Psychol.,* 1965, 2, 685–691.

Davidson, J. R., & Kiesler, S. B. Cognitive behavior before and after decisions. In L. Festinger *et al., Conflict, decision, and dissonance.* Stanford: Stanford Univer. Press, 1964. Pp. 10–21.

Davis, J. A. Structural balance, mechanical solidarity, and interpersonal relations. *Amer. J. Sociol.,* 1963, 68, 444–462.

Davis, K., & Jones, E. E. Changes in interpersonal perception as a means of reducing cognitive dissonance. *J. abnorm. soc. Psychol.,* 1960, 61, 402–410.

Deutsch, M. Trust and suspicion. *Conflict Resolution,* 1958, 4, 265–279.

Deutsch, M., Krauss, R., & Rosenau, N. Dissonance or defensiveness? *J. Pers.,* 1962, 30, 16–28.

Deutsch, M., & Solomon, L. Reactions to evaluations by others as influenced by self-evaluation. *Sociometry,* 1959, 22, 93–112.

Dollard, J., & Miller, N. E. *Personality and psychotherapy.* New York: McGraw-Hill, 1950.

Edlow, D. W., & Kiesler, C. A. Ease of denial and defensive projection. *J. exp. soc. Psychol.,* 1966, 2, 56–69.

Ehrlich, D., Guttman, I., Schönbach, P., & Mills, J. Post-decision exposure to relevant information. *J. abnorm. soc. Psychol.,* 1957, 54, 98–102.

Feather, N. T. Cigarette smoking and lung cancer: A study of cognitive dissonance. *Aust. J. Psychol.,* 1962, 14, 55–64.

Feather, N. T. Cognitive dissonance, sensitivity, and evaluation. *J. abnorm. soc. Psychol.,* 1963, 66, 157–163.

Feather, N. T. A structural balance model of communication effects. *Psychol. Rev.,* 1964, 71, 291–313. (a)

Feather, N. T. Acceptance and rejection of arguments in relation to attitude strength, critical ability, and intolerance of inconsistency. *J. abnorm. soc. Psychol.,* 1964, 69, 127–136. (b)

Feshbach, S. The catharsis hypothesis and some consequences of interaction with aggressive and neutral play objects. *J. Pers.,* 1956, 24, 449–462.

Festinger, L. A theory of social comparison processes. *Hum. Relat.,* 1954, 7, 117–140.

Festinger, L. *A theory of cognitive dissonance.* Evanston: Row, Peterson, 1957.

Festinger, L., Allen, V., Braden, M., Canon, L. K., Davidson, J. R., Jecker, J. D., Kiesler, S. B., & Walster, E. *Conflict, decision, and dissonance.* Stanford: Stanford Univer. Press, 1964.

Festinger, L., & Aronson, E. The arousal and reduction of dissonance in social contexts. In D. Cartwright & A. Zander (Eds.), *Group dynamics.* (2nd ed.) Evanston: Row, Peterson, 1960. Pp. 214–231.

Festinger, L., & Bramel, D. The reactions of humans to cognitive dissonance. In A. Bachrach (Ed.), *The experimental foundations of clinical psychology.* New York: Basic Books, 1962. Pp. 254–279.

Festinger, L., & Carlsmith, J. M. Cognitive consequences of forced compliance. *J. abnorm. soc. Psychol.,* 1959, 58, 203–210.

Festinger, L., & Freedman, J. L. Dissonance reduction and moral values. In P. Worchel & D. Byrne (Eds.), *Personality change.* New York: Wiley, 1964. Pp. 220–243.

Festinger, L., & Hutte, H. A. An experimental investigation of the effect of unstable interpersonal relations in a group. *J. abnorm. soc. Psychol.,* 1954, 49, 513–522.

Festinger, L., Riecken, H. W., Jr., & Schachter, S. *When prophecy fails.* Minneapolis: Univer. of Minnesota Press, 1956.

Festinger, L., & Thibaut, J. Interpersonal communication in small groups. *J. abnorm. soc. Psychol.,* 1951, 46, 92–100.

Fishbein, M. An investigation of the relationships between beliefs about an object and the attitude toward that object. *Hum. Relat.,* 1963, 16, 233–239.

Fishbein, M., & Hunter, R. Summation versus balance in attitude organization and change. *J. abnorm. soc. Psychol.,* 1964, 69, 505–510.

Fletcher, J. M. Homeostasis as an explanatory principle in psychology. *Psychol. Rev.,* 1942, 49, 80–87.

Freedman, J. L. Attitudinal effects of inadequate justification. *J. Pers.*, 1963, 31, 371–385.

Freud, S. *New introductory lectures on psychoanalysis*. New York: Norton, 1933. (Translated from the German edition by W. J. H. Sprott.)

Gerard, H. B. Inconsistency of beliefs and their implications. Paper read at the Amer. Psychol. Ass., New York, September, 1961.

Gerard, H. B., Blevans, S. A., & Malcolm, T. Self-evaluation and the evaluation of choice alternatives. *J. Pers.*, 1964, 32, 395–410.

Glass, D. C. Changes in liking as a means of reducing cognitive discrepancies between self esteem and aggression. *J. Pers.*, 1964, 32, 531–549.

Glass, D. C., & Wood, J. D. The control of aggression by self esteem and dissonance. In P. G. Zimbardo (Ed.), *The cognitive control of motivation*. New York: Scott, Foresman, 1968 (in press).

Glass, D. C., Canavan, D. C., & Schiavo, S. Achievement motivation, dissonance and defensiveness. J. Pers., 1968 (in press).

Glass, D. C., & Mayhew, P. The effects of cognitive processes on psychophysiological reactivity to an aversive stimulus. Unpublished manuscript, The Rockefeller University, 1967.

Glass, D. C. Individual differences and the resolution of cognitive inconsistencies. In R. P. Abelson, E. Aronson, W. J. McGuire, T. M. Newcomb, M. J. Rosenberg, & P. H. Tannenbaum (Eds.), *Theories of Cognitive Consistency: A Sourcebook*. Chicago: Rand McNally, 1968.

Gumpert, P., & Festinger, L. Affective reactions toward people who violate rules. Cited in L. Festinger & J. L. Freedman, Dissonance reduction and moral values. In P. Worchel & D. Byrne (Eds.), *Personality change*. New York: Wiley, 1964. Pp. 220–243.

Hardyck, J. A., & Braden, M. Prophecy fails again: A report of a failure to replicate. *J. abnorm. soc. Psychol.*, 1962, 65, 136–141.

Harvey, O. J., Kelley, H. H., & Shapiro, M. M. Reactions to unfavorable evaluations of the self made by other persons. *J. Pers.*, 1957, 25, 393–411.

Harvey, O. J. Personality factors in resolution of conceptual incongruities. *Sociometry*, 1962, 25, 336–352.

Harvey, O. J. Some situational and cognitive determinants of dissonance reduction. *J. pers. soc. Psychol.*, 1965, *1*, 339–355.

Heider, F. Social perception and phenomenal causality. *Psychol. Rev.*, 1944, 51, 358–374.

Heider, F. Attitudes and cognitive organization. *J. Psychol.*, 1946, 21, 107–112.

Heider, F. *The psychology of interpersonal relations*. New York: Wiley, 1958.

Hilgard, E. R. The motivational relevance of hypnosis. In D. Levine (Ed.), *Nebraska symposium on motivation*. Lincoln: Univer. of Nebraska Press, 1964. Pp. 1–44.

Hill, A. H. Credibility, discrepancy, and latitude of communication as dimensions of dissonance influencing attitude change. *Aust. J. Psychol.*, 1963, 15, 124–132.

Hokanson, J. E. The effects of frustration and anxiety on overt aggression. *J. abnorm. soc. Psychol.*, 1961, 62, 346–351.

Horwitz, M., Glass, D. C., & Niyekawa, A. Muscular tension: Physiological activation or psychological act? In P. H. Leiderman & D. Shapiro (Eds.), *Psychobiological approaches to social behavior*. Stanford: Stanford Univer. Press, 1964. Pp. 59–91.

Horowitz, M. W., Lyons, J., & Perlmutter, H. V. Induction of forces in discussion groups. *Hum. Relat.*, 1951, 41, 57–76.

Hovland, C. I., Harvey, O. J., & Sherif, M. Assimilation and contrast effects in reactions to communication and attitude change. *J. abnorm. soc. Psychol.*, 1957, 55, 244–252.

Hovland, C. I., Janis, I. L., & Kelley, H. H. *Communication and persuasion*. New Haven: Yale Univer. Press, 1953.

Hovland, C. I., & Janis, I. L. (Eds.) *Personality and persuasibility*. New Haven: Yale Univer. Press, 1959.

Hovland, C. I., & Pritzker, H. A. Extent of opinion change as a function of amount of change advocated. *J. abnorm. soc. Psychol.*, 1957, 54, 257–261.

Hovland, C. I., & Rosenberg, M. J. Summary and further theoretical issues. In M. J. Rosenberg, C. I. Hovland, W. J. McGuire, R. P. Abelson, & J. W. Brehm, *Attitude organization and change*. New Haven: Yale Univer. Press, 1960. Pp. 198–232.

Hull, C. L. *Principles of behavior*. New York: Appleton-Century-Crofts, 1943.

Hunt, J. McV. Motivation inherent in information processing and action. In O. J. Harvey (Ed.), *Motivation and social interaction*. New York: Ronald, 1963. Pp. 35–94.

Iwao, S. Internal versus external criticism of group standards. *Sociometry*, 1963, 26, 410–421.

Janicki, W. P. Effect of disposition on resolution of incongruity. *J. abnorm. soc. Psychol.*, 1964, 69, 579–584.

Janis, I. L., & Gilmore, J. B. The influence of incentive conditions on the success of role playing in modifying attitudes. *J. pers. soc. Psychol.*, 1965, 1, 17–27.

Jecker, J. D. The cognitive effects of conflict and dissonance. In L. Festinger *et al.*, *Conflict, decision, and dissonance*. Stanford: Stanford Univer. Press, 1964. Pp. 21–30. (a)

Jecker, J. D. Selective exposure to new information. In L. Festinger *et al.*, *Conflict, decision, and dissonance*. Stanford: Stanford Univer. Press, 1964. Pp. 65–83. (b)

Jones, E. E., Gergen, K. J., & Davis, K. E. Some determinants of reactions to being approved or disapproved as a person. *Psychol. Monogr.*, 1962, 76, No. 2 (Whole No. 521).

Jones, E. E., & Köhler, R. The effects of plausibility on the learning of controversial statements. *J. abnorm. soc. Psychol.*, 1958, 57, 315–320.

Jordan, N. Behavioral forces that are a function of attitudes and of cognitive organization. *Hum. Relat.*, 1953, 6, 273–287.

Jordan, N. Fallout shelters and social psychology: The "theory" of cognitive dissonance. Unpublished manuscript, Hudson Institute, June, 1963. (a)

Jordan, N. The mythology of the nonobvious —Autism or fact? *Contemp. Psychol.*, 1963, 9, 140, 142. (b)

Kenny, D. T., & Ginsberg, R. The specificity of intolerance of ambiguity measures. *J. abnorm. soc. Psychol.*, 1958, 56, 300–304.

Kerrick, J. S. News pictures, captions, and the point of resolution. *Journ. Quart.*, 1959, 36, 183–188.

Kogan, N., & Tagiuri, R. Interpersonal preference and cognitive organization. *J. abnorm. soc. Psychol.*, 1958, 56, 113–116.

Kogan, N., & Wallach, M. A. *Risk taking: A study in cognition and personality*. New York: Holt, Rinehart and Winston, 1964.

Köhler, W. *Gestalt psychology*. New York: Liveright, 1947.

Krech, D., & Crutchfield, R. S. *Theory and problems of social psychology*. New York: McGraw-Hill, 1948.

Lawrence, D. H., & Festinger, L. *Deterrents and reinforcement*. Stanford: Stanford Univer. Press, 1962.

Lecky, P. *Self-consistency: A theory of personality*. New York: Island Press, 1945.

Lerner, M. J. The effect of responsibility and choice on a partner's attractiveness following failure. *J. Pers.*, 1965, *33*, 178–187.

Leventhal, G. S. Reward magnitude, task attractiveness, and liking for instrumental activity. *J. abnorm. soc. Psychol.*, 1964, 68, 460–463.

Leventhal, G. S., & Brehm, J. W. An experiment on volition of choice. In J. W. Brehm & A. R. Cohen, *Explorations in cognitive dissonance*. New York: Wiley, 1962. Pp. 210–217.

Lewin, K. *A dynamic theory of personality*. New York: McGraw-Hill, 1935.

London, P., & Rosenhan, D. Personality dynamics. In P. R. Farnsworth, O. McNemar, & Q. McNemar (Eds.), *Annu. Rev. Psychol.*, 1964, 15, 447–492.

Lott, B. E. Secondary reinforcement and effort: Comment on Aronson's "The effect of effort on the attractiveness of rewarded and unrewarded stimuli." *J. abnorm. soc. Psychol.*, 1963, 67, 520–522. (a)

Lott, B. E. Rejoinder. *J. abnorm. soc. Psychol.*, 1963, 67, 525–526. (b)

Lowin, A., & Epstein, G. F. Does expectancy determine performance? *J. exp. soc. Psychol.*, 1965, 1, 248–255.

Maccoby, Eleanor E., Maccoby, N., Romney, A. K., & Adams, J. S. Social reinforcement and attitude change. *J. abnorm. soc. Psychol.*, 1961, 63, 108–114.

Maccoby, N., & Maccoby, Eleanor E. Homeostatic theory in attitude change. *Publ. Opin. Quart.*, 1961, 25, 538–545.

Malmo, R. B. Activation: A neuropsychological dimension. *Psychol. Rev.*, 1959, 66, 367–386.

Malewski, A. The influence of positive and negative self evaluation on postdecisional dissonance. *Polish Sociol. Bull.*, 1962, 3–4, 39–49.

Mansson, H. H. The cognitive control of thirst motivation: A dissonance approach. Unpublished doctoral thesis, New York University, 1965.

McClelland, D., Atkinson, J. W., Clark, R. A., & Lowell, E. L. *The achievement motive.* New York: Appleton-Century-Crofts, 1953.

McGuire, W. J. Direct and indirect persuasive effects of dissonance producing messages. *J. abnorm. soc. Psychol.,* 1960, 60, 354–358. (a)

McGuire, W. J. A syllogistic analysis of cognitive relationships. In M. J. Rosenberg, C. I. Hovland, W. J. McGuire, R. P. Abelson, & J. W. Brehm. *Attitude organization and change.* New Haven: Yale Univer. Press, 1960. Pp. 65–111. (b)

McGuire, W. J. Inducing resistance to persuasion. In L. Berkowitz (Ed.), *Advances in experimental social psychology.* New York: Academic Press, 1964. Pp. 192–231.

McGuire, W. J. Attitudes and opinions. In P. R. Farnsworth, O. McNemar, & Q. McNemar (Eds.), *Annual review of psychology,* Vol. 17. Palo Alto, Calif.: Annual Reviews, 1966. (a)

McGuire, W. J. The current status of cognitive consistency theories. In S. Feldman (Ed.), *Cognitive consistency.* New York: Academic Press, 1966. Pp. 2–46. (b)

Meyers, A. E. Some connotations of cognitive dissonance theory. *Psychol. Rep.,* 1963, 13, 807–812.

Milgram, S. Behavioral study of obedience. *J. abnorm. soc. Psychol.,* 1963, 67, 371–378.

Miller, N. E. Experimental studies of conflict. In J. McV. Hunt (Ed.), *Personality and the behavior disorders.* Vol. I. New York: Ronald, 1944. Pp. 431–465.

Miller, N. E. Liberalization of basic S-R concepts: Extension to conflict behavior, motivation and social learning. In S. Koch (Ed.), *Psychology: A study of a science.* Vol. 2: *General systematic formulations, learning, and special processes.* New York: McGraw-Hill, 1959. Pp. 196–292.

Miller, N. E., & Dollard, J. *Social learning and imitation.* New Haven: Yale Univer. Press, 1941.

Mills, J. Changes in moral attitudes following temptation. *J. Pers.,* 1958, 26, 517–531.

Mills, J., Aronson, E., & Robinson, H. Selectivity in exposure to information. *J. abnorm. soc. Psychol.,* 1959, 59, 250–253.

Mills, T. M. A sleeper variable in small groups research: The experimenter. *Pacific Sociol. Rev.,* 1962, 5, 21–28.

Mirels, H., & Mills, J. Perception of the pleasantness and competence of a partner. *J. abnorm. soc. Psychol.,* 1964, 68, 456–459.

Morrissette, J. O. An experimental study of the theory of structural balance. *Hum. Relat.,* 1958, 11, 239–254.

Mowrer, O. H. Cognitive dissonance or counterconditioning?—A reappraisal of certain behavioral "paradoxes." *Psychol. Rep.,* 1963, 13, 197–211.

Newcomb, T. M. *Personality and social change.* New York: Dryden, 1943.

Newcomb, T. M. An approach to the study of communicative acts. *Psychol. Rev.,* 1953, 60, 393–404.

Newcomb, T. M. The prediction of interpersonal attraction. *Amer. Psychologist,* 1956, 11, 575–586.

Newcomb, T. M. Individual systems or orientation. In S. Koch (Ed.), *Psychology: A study of a science.* Vol. 3. *Formulations of the person and the social context.* New York: McGraw-Hill, 1959. Pp. 384–422.

Newcomb, T. M. *The acquaintance process.* New York: Holt, Rinehart, & Winston, 1961.

Newcomb, T. M. Persistence and regression of changed attitudes: Long-range studies. *J. soc. Issues,* 1963, 19, 3–14. (a)

Newcomb, T. M. Stabilities underlying changes in interpersonal attraction. *J. abnorm. soc. Psychol.,* 1963, 66, 376–386. (b)

Olds, J., & Milner, P. Positive reinforcement produced by electrical stimulation of septal area and other regions of rat brain. *J. comp. physiol. Psychol.,* 1954, 47, 419–427.

Orne, M. T. On the social psychology of the psychological experiment: With particular reference to demand characteristics and their implications. *Amer. Psychologist,* 1962, 17, 776–783.

Osgood, C. E. Cognitive dynamics in the conduct of human affairs. *Publ. Opin. Quart.,* 1960, 24, 341–365.

Osgood, C. E., Suci, G. J., & Tannenbaum, P. H. *The measurement of meaning.* Urbana: Univer. of Illinois Press, 1957.

Osgood, C. E., & Tannenbaum, P. H. The principle of congruity in the prediction of attitude change. *Psychol. Rev.,* 1955, 62, 42–55.

Parsons, T. Age and sex in the social structure of the United States. *Amer. sociol. Rev.,* 1942, 7, 604–616.

Pepitone, A. *Attraction and hostility.* New York: Atherton, 1964.

Pettigrew, T. F. Measurement and correlates of category width. *J. Pers.,* 1958, 26, 532–544.

Pilisuk, M. Cognitive balance and self-relevant attitudes. *J. abnorm. soc. Psychol.,* 1962, 65, 95–103.

Rabbie, J. M., Brehm, J. W., & Cohen, A. R. Verbalization and reactions to cognitive dissonance. *J. Pers.,* 1959, 27, 407–417.

Raven, B. H., Anthony, E., & Mansson, H. H. Group norms and dissonance reduction in belief, behavior, and judgment. Los Angeles: Univer. of California, 1960. (Tech. Rep. No. 4, Nonr 233 [54].)

Raven, B. H., & Fishbein, M. Acceptance of punishment and change in belief. *J. abnorm. soc. Psychol.,* 1961, 63, 411–416.

Rogers, C. R. *Client-centered therapy: Its current practice, implications, and theory.* Boston: Houghton Mifflin, 1951.

Rokeach, M. *The open and closed mind.* New York: Basic Books, 1960.

Rosen, S. Post-decision affinity for incompatible information. *J. abnorm. soc. Psychol.,* 1961, 63, 188–190.

Rosenberg, M. J. Cognitive structure and attitudinal affect. *J. abnorm. soc. Psychol.,* 1956, 53, 367–372.

Rosenberg, M. J. A disconfirmation of the description of hypnosis as a dissociated state. *Intl. J. clin. exp. Hypnosis,* 1959, 7, 187–204.

Rosenberg, M. J. Cognitive reorganization in response to the hypnotic reversal of attitudinal affect. *J. Pers.,* 1960, 28, 39–63. (a)

Rosenberg, M. J. A structural theory of attitude dynamics. *Publ. Opin. Quart.,* 1960, 24, 319–340. (b)

Rosenberg, M. J. Some content determinants of intolerance for attitudinal inconsistency. Unpublished manuscript (dittoed), The Ohio State Univer., 1963. (Now published in S. S. Tomkins & C. E. Izard (Eds.), *Affect, cognition, and personality.* New York: Springer, 1965. Pp. 130–147.)

Rosenberg, M. J. When dissonance fails: On eliminating evaluation apprehension from attitude measurement. *J. pers. soc. Psychol.,* 1965, 1, 28–42.

Rosenberg, M. J., & Abelson, R. P. An analysis of cognitive balancing. In M. J. Rosenberg, C. I. Hovland, W. J. McGuire, R. P. Abelson, & J. W. Brehm (Eds.), *Attitude organization and change.* New Haven: Yale Univer. Press, 1960. Pp. 112–163.

Rosenberg, M. J., & Gardner, C. W. Some dynamic aspects of posthypnotic compliance. *J. abnorm. soc. Psychol.,* 1958, 57, 351–366.

Rosenberg, M. J., Hovland, C. I., McGuire, W. J., Abelson, R. P., & Brehm, J. W. *Attitude organization and change.* New Haven: Yale Univer. Press, 1960.

Rosenberg, M. J., & Oltman, P. K. Consistency between attitudinal affect and spontaneous cognitions. *J. Psychol.,* 1962, 54, 485–490.

Rosenthal, R. On the social psychology of the psychological experiment: The experimenter's hypothesis as an unintended determinant of experimental results. *Amer. Scientist,* 1963, 51, 268–283.

Sampson, E. E. Status congruence and cognitive consistency. *Sociometry,* 1963, 26, 146–162.

Sampson, E. E., & Insko, C. A. Cognitive consistency and performance in the autokinetic situation. *J. abnorm. soc. Psychol.,* 1964, 68, 184–192.

Scheerer, M. Cognitive theory. In G. Lindzey (Ed.), *Handbook of social psychology,* Vol. I. Cambridge: Addison-Wesley, 1954. Pp. 91–142.

Schlachet, P. J. The effect of dissonance arousal on the recall of failure stimuli. *J. Pers.,* 1965, *33,* 443–461.

Scott, W. A. Attitude change by response reinforcement: Replication and extension. *Sociometry,* 1959, 22, 328–355. (a)

Scott, W. A. Cognitive consistency, response reinforcement, and attitude change. *Sociometry,* 1959, 22, 219–229. (b)

Sears, R. R. Personality. In P. R. Farnsworth & Q. McNemar (Eds.), *Annu. Rev. Psychol.,* 1950, 1, 105–118.

Sears, R. R. Dependency motivation. In M. R. Jones (Ed.), *Nebraska symposium on motivation.* Lincoln: Univer. of Nebraska Press, 1963. Pp. 25–64.

Secord, P. F., & Backman, C. W. Personality theory and the problem of stability and change in individual behavior. *Psychol. Rev.,* 1961, 68, 21–32.

Secord, P. F., Backman, C. W., & Eachus, H. T. Effects of imbalance in the self-concept on the perception of persons. *J. abnorm. soc. Psychol.,* 1964, 68, 442–446.

Silverman, I. In defense of dissonance theory: Reply to Chapanis and Chapanis. *Psychol. Bull.,* 1964, 62, 205–209. (a)

Silverman, I. Self-esteem and differential responsiveness to success and failure. *J. abnorm. soc. Psychol.,* 1964, 69, 115–119. (b)

Smith, E. E. The power of dissonance techniques to change attitudes. *Publ. Opin. Quart.,* 1961, 25, 626–639.

Stagner, R. Homeostasis as a unifying concept in personality theory. *Psychol. Rev.*, 1951, 58, 5–18.

Steiner, I. D. Ethnocentrism and tolerance of trait "inconsistency." *J. abnorm. soc. Psychol.*, 1954, 49, 349–354.

Steiner, I. D. Sex differences in the resolution of A-B-X conflicts. *J. Pers.*, 1960, 28, 118–128.

Steiner, I. D., & Johnson, H. H. Relationships among dissonance reducing responses. *J. abnorm. soc. Psychol.*, 1964, 68, 38–44.

Steiner, I. D., & Peters, S. C. Conformity and the A-B-X model. *J. Pers.*, 1958, 26, 229–242.

Steiner, I. D., & Rogers, E. D. Alternative responses to dissonance. *J. abnorm. soc. Psychol.*, 1963, 66, 128–136.

Stotland, E. Review of J. W. Brehm and A. R. Cohen, *Explorations in cognitive dissonance. Contemp. Psychol.*, 1963, 8, 419–420.

Stotland, E., & Hillmer, M. L., Jr. Identification, authoritarian defensiveness, and self-esteem. *J. abnorm. soc. Psychol.*, 1962, 64, 334–342.

Sumner, W. G. *Folkways.* New York: Ginn, 1906.

Tannenbaum, P. H. Attitudes toward source and concept as factors in attitude change through communications. Unpublished doctoral dissertation, Univer. of Illinois, 1953.

Taffel, C. Anxiety and the conditioning of verbal behavior. *J. abnorm. soc. Psychol.*, 1955, 51, 496–501.

Tolman, E. C. Principles of purposive behavior. In S. Koch (Ed.), *Psychology: A study of a science.* Vol. 2, *General systematic formulations, learning, and special processes.* New York: McGraw-Hill, 1959. Pp. 92–157.

Triandis, H. C., & Fishbein, M. Cognitive interaction in person perception. *J. abnorm. soc. Psychol.*, 1963, 67, 446–453.

Walster, E., Walster, B., Abrahams, D., & Brown, Z. The effect on liking of underrating and overrating another. *J. exp. soc. Psychol.*, 1966, *2*, 70–84.

Ward, W. D., & Sandvold, K. D. Performance expectancy as a determinant of actual performance. A partial replication. *J. abnorm. soc. Psychol.*, 1964, *67*, 293–295.

Waterman, A. S., & Ford, L. H. Performance expectancy as a determinant of actual performance: Dissonance reduction or differential recall. *J. pers. soc. Psychol.*, 1965, *2*, 464–467.

Weick, K. E. Reduction of cognitive dissonance through task enhancement and effort expenditure. *J. abnorm. soc. Psychol.*, 1964, 68, 533–539.

Weiss, W. Responses to certain types of communicated attitudinal structures. Paper read at the East. Psychol. Ass., Philadelphia, April, 1964.

Wertheimer, M. *Productive thinking.* New York: Harper, 1945.

Woodruff, A. D., & DiVesta, F. J. The relationship between values, concepts, and attitudes. *Educ. psychol. Measmt,* 1948, 8, 645–660.

Worchel, P., & McCormick, B. L. Self-concept and dissonance reduction. *J. Pers.*, 1963, 31, 588–599.

Yaryan, R., & Festinger, L. Preparatory action and belief in the probable occurrence of future events. *J. abnorm. soc. Psychol.*, 1961, 63, 603–606.

Zajonc, R. B. Balance, congruity, and dissonance. *Publ. Opin. Quart.*, 1960, 24, 280–296.

Zajonc, R. B. The process of cognitive tuning in communication. *J. abnorm. soc. Psychol.*, 1961, 61, 159–167.

Zimbardo, P. G. Involvement and communication discrepancy as determinants of opinion change. *J. abnorm. soc. Psychol.*, 1960, 60, 86–94.

Zimbardo, P. G. Self-persuasion: Improvisation or dissonance. In J. W. Brehm & A. R. Cohen, *Explorations in cognitive dissonance.* New York: Wiley, 1962. Pp. 30–31.

Zimbardo, P. G., Weisenberg, M., Firestone, I., & Levy, B. The effect of positive versus negative communicators on public conformity and private attitude change. Paper read at the East. Psychol. Ass., Philadelphia, April, 1964. (a)

Zimbardo, P. G., Cohen, A. R., Weisenberg, M., Dworkin, L., & Firestone, I. The dissonance effect of commitment to pain upon motivation and learning. Paper read at the Amer. Psychol. Ass., Los Angeles, September, 1964. (b) (Now published as The control of pain motivation by cognitive dissonance. *Science,* 1966, *151,* 217–219.)

Zimbardo, P. G. A reply to Jordan's attack on dissonance theory. *Contemp. Psychol.*, 1964, *9*, 332–333. (c)

Zimbardo, P. G. The cognitive control of motivation. New York: Scott, Foresman, 1968 (in press).

PART V

Personality Variables and Polar Types: The Current Status of Some Major Variables of Personality

CHAPTER 14 Research on the Achievement Motive[1]

ROBERT C. BIRNEY
Amherst College

In 1953 *The Achievement Motive* was published by D. C. McClelland, J. W. Atkinson, R. A. Clark, and E. L. Lowell. This book introduced a theory of motivation, a method for measuring motives through a modification of the Thematic Apperception Test (TAT) procedures, and a series of experimental and correlation studies establishing the construct validity of one motive: need for Achievement (n Ach). The term *n Ach* originated with Murray (1938) and remains part of his coding system for standard TAT protocol analysis. In Murray's system it is a term to be used in motivation coding and carries no implication for the particular data from which it is inferred. An observer may label his subject as having high n Ach; or he may code a statement of a hero figure in a TAT story for n Ach; or he may ask whether the behavioral pattern of his subject reflects a strong n Ach. Edwards (1954) has gone a step further and taken Murray's need descriptions to construct a series of self-descriptive statements which the subject himself may endorse, one of which is n Ach. This review is devoted solely to the n Ach construct as set out by McClelland and his associates and as measured by his modified TAT technique.

The Achievement Motive presented the measurement procedures, protocol scoring systems for n Ach, a series of studies designed to establish the nature of the psychometric characteristics of the scores, and a variety of exploratory studies of the role the motive played in behavioral processes of learning, performance, memory, perception, and cognition. These demonstrations of function contributed to a general confidence in the measurement system and inspired numerous additional exploratory studies. At the same time, more programmatic studies were begun. This second stage of the research is best reflected in *Motives in Fantasy, Action, and Society,* edited by J. W. Atkinson (1958a). Here we find the extension of the measurement technique to other motives, the use of n Ach as a variable in the study of social and cultural processes, and the new models for motivated behavior developed by Atkinson (1957) for choice situations and by McClelland for the study of society. Studies of the developmental sources of n Ach by Winterbottom (1953) and Rosen (1956); the role of n Ach as an

[1] Preparation of this article was supported by the Group Psychology Branch, Office of Naval Research, Contract Nonr 3591 (01).

ego mechanism (Knapp, 1958); n Ach in the female personality (Veroff, Wilcox, & Atkinson, 1953); and avoidance behavior in achievement situations (Moulton, 1952) also define areas of research which have developed programmatic character in the sense that sustained efforts to study these phenomena are continuously pursued.

The most recent reflections of the above diverging streams of interest are found in McClelland's *The Achieving Society,* H. Heckhausen's *Hoffnung und Furcht in der Leistungsmotivation,* and *A Theory of Achievement Motivation,* edited by Atkinson and N. T. Feather. Given the limitations of space faced by this review, we will focus on basic issues of measurement, construct validity, motivation theory, and n Ach as a motivational variable. The many studies appearing in the literature which use n Ach in the study of other problems will be given reference whenever possible, but those not given textual comment will have to be content with a reference listing.

Basic Assumptions

McClelland has summarized the "hypotheses which guided the research reported in *The Achievement Motive.* The measurement technique for motivation must . . . be at least partially dependent on the methods of measurement used to define two other main variables in psychological theory, namely, perception and learning." "Motives might be best measured in phantasy." "Motives could be experimentally aroused by manipulating external conditions." "Quite simply, then, our problem became one of attempting to arouse human motives experimentally and to measure the effects on phantasy" (in Guetzkow, 1951). It is important to emphasize at once the implications of the above statements. So long as fantasy codes remain sensitive to arousal conditions they reflect motivation, leaving the relations of these codes to other behavioral and self-report measures a matter of subsequent research. The definition of measures as motivational is not held to be a matter of high correlations with certain criteria variables with which motive measures "must" correlate. The correlation studies are simply seen as providing further refinement of the proper interpretation which motives play in behavior, however complicated these relationships may prove to be.

The only a priori assumption beyond that of arousal effects reflected in fantasy was that the fantasy contents would arrange themselves according to the adjustive problem-solving sequence used to describe overt behaviors. The basic hypotheses in the initial validation studies were that scoring categories of Need, Instrumental Activity, Goal Anticipation, Goal Affect, Blocks, both personal and environmental, and Press, both nurturant and hostile, would show systematic increases with increased arousal of the achievement motive. These ideas were put to the test, and most of the categories increased with motive arousal.

This empiristic attitude has been characteristic of the n Ach research throughout. Thus, the manner in which the motive is aroused, the nature of the thematic material scored, the psychometric properties of the scores, and the definition of motivation itself have all been evolved through research rather than pursued from some a priori basis. The great danger of such an attitude is that one may give too much weight to the chance finding; the only safeguard is successive replication of findings.[2]

Reliable increases in n Ach due to instructions and treatments prior to the administration of the measure have been reported in many studies (Ricciuti & Clark, 1954; Angelini, 1955; Lowell, 1950; Veroff, 1957; Anderson, 1962; Martire, 1956). The most effective procedure is one that begins with an experimenter who is clearly concerned with the success of the experiment; a task described to the *S*s as indicative of intelligence, future success, high potential, etc.; an

[2] For a more recent statement of assumptions and attitudes for basing the measurement of motivation on fantasy, see Veroff (1961).

absence of feedback of results on the task; and a following administration of the n Ach measure. The following instructions used by McClelland *et al.* (1953) to introduce a twelve-minute anagrams test give an example:

The tests which you are going to take indicate, in general, a person's level of intelligence. They were taken from a group of tests which were used to select Washington administrators and officer candidates for the OSS during the past war. Thus, in addition to general intelligence, they bring out an individual's capacity to organize material, his ability to evaluate situations quickly and accurately—in short, these tests demonstrate whether or not a person is suited to be a leader. The present research is being conducted under the auspices of the Office of Naval Research to determine just which individuals possess the leadership qualifications shown by superior performance on these tests.

Not all efforts to produce increases in n Ach have proved successful, and the effects of giving results on the prior tests which then vary the success-failure effect have proved complex. Apparently the so-called neutral administration consisting of straightforward presentation of the measure without prior tests or instructions is moderately achievement-cued, and there seem to be numerous ways in which uncontrolled arousal of the motive can occur.

Successful creation of the relaxed condition has usually depended upon an *E* who dresses as a casual student, implies ignorance of the measures, and has no official connection with the institution of which the *S*s are a part. These were Lowell's (1952) conditions. Birney (1958b) showed that substitution of an undergraduate as *E* in the place of a faculty person permitted a sharp drop in n Ach level. Failure to produce shifts from the Neutral to Aroused conditions are fairly common and indicate that a number of factors may act to equate the two conditions. Haber (1957) used very carefully controlled conditions but used the same *S*s under both conditions and failed to produce a differential effect, both the control and experimental groups showing increases in n Ach. Peak (1960) had a similar experience.

The use of prior arousal tasks with knowledge of results raises the risk that task incentives may prove arousing despite the introductory instructions. Murstein and Collier (1962) varied the probability of winning an ice cream certificate for seventh-grade students and obtained a uniformly high level of n Ach on a subsequent measurement regardless of the odds level. Tedeschi and Kian (1962) used the false-norm technique to produce a sense of failure on the arousal task and obtained an increase in n Ach from their Persian students but none from the U.S. students. They suspect that the Persians were more willing than the U.S. students to compare themselves to Harvard students whose "norms" were used.

Turek and Howell (1959) carefully controlled the order and proportion of successes and failures on a four-task series prior to writing the TAT stories. Failure followed by success produced increasing n Ach scores as the proportion of failures increased from one out of four tests to three out of four. The opposite arrangement of success followed by failure, total failure, or total success gave the same moderate level of n Ach. McClelland's original use of these conditions had also revealed little in the way of total score differences, but internal category differences did shift in a sensible fashion (1953, Chapter 5). It is probable here that the major difficulty lies in our understanding of the success-failure treatments themselves, and extensive questionnaire probing should be used to determine the *S*s' understanding of the results they have been given. An interesting example of the confusion such ignorance can create is found in a study by Lazarus, Baker, Broverman, and Mayer (1957). Subjects are "tested" for their ability to reproduce material from a tape recorder. "Instructions as to how the *S*s should handle the paragraph material and what they should write down were also left undefined." The results show that *S*s who presumably instructed themselves to record literally from the tape were the ones who later obtained the highest n Ach scores on a TAT which followed, while those who made "conceptual" recordings showed low n Ach. Since the high n Ach *S*s tended to be younger, the authors infer that n Ach is associated with a lower level of maturity. Actually, these data merely suggest that younger *S*s were more prone to see the situation as one having achievement cues, but in fact we do not know what arousal conditions prevailed.

Anderson (1962) induced failure on two successive administrations of a digit-symbol-substitution task but then "stated he would give them the opportunity to redeem themselves on a test of imagination." Two degrees of achievement arousal without prior tasks were also given, making three degrees of arousal for these eighth-grade boys and girls. Orderly increases in n Ach were obtained.

The recent analysis of the social psychology of the experiments by Rosenthal (1963) and Orne (1962) in which the actual results of experimental procedures are shown to be sensitive to experimenter-subject interaction, i.e., the subject acts as the *E* hopes he will, may be usefully applied to the n Ach measurement situation. It has long been obvious that the behavior of *E* and the situation itself may affect the arousal of achievement imagery. Recently, Klinger (1963) embarked on a series of studies using filmed sequences of action rather than arousing instructions and found the stories sensitive to film differences. He intends to extend the filming technique to include as much *E* behavior as possible in the hope of bringing this source of variance under control.

An overview of these studies of the arousal of achievement motivation indicates that successful studies tend to follow the same basic patterns of achievement task instruction, prior tasks with a minimum of feedback, and separate experimental groups.[3] Successive use of the same *S*s, failure to eliminate achievement situational cues, and various arousal techniques whose effects are not checked independently may simply affect most of the *S*s the same way and produce moderate-to-high levels of achievement scores without experimental distinction. As we shall see, however, several studies have shown that failure to produce shifts in scores may not mean a loss of score validity.

Score Characteristics

Scores for n Ach are compiled by summing the number of categories found in a story, provided the basic criterion of Imagery has been satisfied. Stories having no thematic content but reflecting the situation suggested by the picture cues alone ("Two men are working in an old shop") are scored zero, and stories having non-achievement themes are scored minus one. Studies of pictures (Atkinson, 1950; Birney, 1958a; Haber & Alpert, 1958; Jacobs, 1958) have shown that cue characteristics determine the *levels* of scores; that pictures differ in internal consistency; that the procedures for picture selection can successfully identify new pictures for use with various populations; and that efforts to manipulate picture cues as a variable have been relatively unsuccessful.

The chief difficulty encountered with the n Ach score has been its low coefficient of stability. Test-retest reliabilities have been low by the usual psychometric standards, varying from the low plus twenties with the same pictures to the mid-fifties for parallel forms of high cue value (Haber & Alpert, 1958). The highest values have been obtained where pictures have high cue value and the condition of testing is Relaxed (+.59) (Haber & Alpert, 1958); or where the administration halved the writing time and picture viewing time (Morgan, 1953).

[3] The general technique used here has since proved valuable in the development of motive measures for n Affiliation, n Power, n Sex, Threat Imagery (see Atkinson, 1958), need for Novelty (Maddi, 1962), and Hostile Press (Birney, Burdick, & Teevan, 1962).

The original battery of pictures when used either in parallel forms or on a repeat basis has consistently given lower values (Lowell, 1953; Reitman & Atkinson, 1958; Birney, 1959; Krumboltz & Farquhar, 1957).

From the outset it has been McClelland's position that "it is theoretically possible to have a test which will correlate highly with a number of other measures (high validity) but not with itself on a second administration (low reliability) if the first administration has somehow 'spoiled' the subject for this type of test" (1953, p. 194). Certainly it is true that ten years of subsequent research has demonstrated such is the case for these motive measures. Carefully controlled experiments continue to show numerous relationships between n Ach scores and behavior indices, having correlations higher than the test-retest coefficients, while there is no doubt that repeated administrations of the n Ach test change the behavior of the *S* on the test. This is a burden since it precludes many types of designs using the same *S*s under varying conditions, and it has especially impeded efforts to show changes in n Ach itself due to various treatment procedures. Clearly it would be better to have a measure displaying the same validities as the TAT n Ach score but possessing higher reliabilities. Efforts have been made to do so.

French (1955) designed a sentence-completion format scored with the n Ach categories which has proved to have similar validities and arousal characteristics as the TAT n Ach (French, 1958; French & Thomas, 1958). Himmelstein and Kimbrough (1960) report test-retest coefficients (alternate forms, seven-week interval) of +.37 for males and +.44 for females. However, despite the subsequent use of this device by Atkinson *et al.,* there have been no satisfactory tests of the actual relationship between the two n Ach measures. Himmelstein, Eschenbach, and Carp (1958) did include both the French Form I and the TAT in a test battery "administered within a period of two days as part of a larger testing program." Neither this description of the situation, which tells us nothing of the instructions, other tests and their possible effects, or the ordinal position of the tests, nor the interscorer reliability of +.71 inspires confidence in the reported zero order correlations, but a similar comparison of sentence completions and TAT themes by Lindzey and Heinemann (1955) has also reported zero order agreements for the n Ach themes of males. Under group administrations they did find a +.40 for females. Certainly if the French Test of Insight is to be used interchangeably, we need to know more of its relationship with n Ach TAT scores. Perhaps a carefully conducted study using the Relaxed vs. Aroused procedures, followed by testing with TAT pictures and French sentence completions integrated into a single instrument, would provide some of the controls needed.

Klinger (1963) used both the TAT and French measures, counterbalanced for order, and reports a −.07 relationship between their two n Ach scores.

Heckhausen (1963) reports success in scoring stories for both Hope of Success (HS) and Fear of Failure (FF). He validated a set of pictures having characteristics similar to those of McClelland but closer to typical settings of German society, demonstrated correlations of +.63 and +.62 between HS plus FF and n Ach with two samples of students, *N*s of 71 and 77, and used the two-score distributions as separate variables (see below). However, this remains a projective technique and shows reliability coefficients ranging from +.41 to +.59, depending on the combination of scoring systems.

Scoring of stories requires considerable training and practice, and deCharms (1958) has shown that the subjects themselves may be given sets of typical stories, asked to match their own stories to them, and the rank scores so obtained will divide large samples of subjects into thirds having close agreement to that obtained when actual scores are used.

Early in the program the relationship between self-description of motivation, called value Achievement (v Ach) and n Ach was found to range from low positive, +.234, P .05 (deCharms, Morrison, Reitman, & McClelland, 1955) to zero. Subsequent correlations between Edwards' Personal Preference Schedule for n Ach has shown the same pattern (Melikian, 1958). Although these self-report measures show much higher reliabilities, the nature of their correlates and their obvious sensitivity to direct suggestion, as contrasted with that of *S*s who fail to write stories obtaining high n Ach scores even when instructed to do so (McClelland, Atkinson, Clark, & Lowell, 1953), eliminate the possibility that these measurements have the same construct validity (McClelland, 1958a). Other problems of the scoring arise from the frequent positive correlation of total score with total length of stories. Veroff (1961) has an excellent discussion of the safeguards which must be taken if the sampling of *S*s permits verbal fluency or effects of the test procedure to influence scores.

In summary, the projective scores are most sensitive to subject arousal states. They provide ample discrimination when properly obtained to permit their use in controlled experimental settings. Long-range stability coefficients appear to fall in the range of +.25 to +.35 (Birney, 1959; Kagan & Moss, 1959; Feld, 1959) which provides enough stability to permit estimation of the presence of relationships. Because n Ach score reliability is low, Atkinson has repeatedly stated the necessity for experimenters to establish high scorer reliabilities with the manual materials and with themselves over time (1960).

THE EFFECTS OF n ACH ON PERFORMANCE

From the outset the major thrust of the research has been to learn more of generally important behavioral functions which are thought to have "theoretical interest." At first this meant devising laboratory situations having task-achievement cue values and attempting to demonstrate that the presence of achievement motivation as measured by n Ach scores affected task performance. Lowell (1953), Clark and McClelland (1953), Birney (1958b), Atkinson and Raphelson (1956), Atkinson and Reitman (1956), Wendt (1955), Brown (1953), and Burdick (1964) have demonstrated that *S*s scoring high in n Ach learn more rapidly, persist on familiar tasks, show more flexibility in problem-solving, attempt more problems, resist fatigue, get higher scores though not necessarily with fewer errors, and waste fewer responses when performing under variable ratio schedules. All of this research has a demonstrational cast to it, concentrating on learning and performance parameters to show that n Ach functions as we expect a motive to function, thus bolstering the claim of n Ach as a motive measure. However, studies by Atkinson and Reitman (1956) have also demonstrated that n Ach is an interactive variable quite capable of being masked or eliminated as a determinant of behavior if cognitive or ability factors have more relevance to the particular situation. Probably the most obvious example of this condition is found in the attempts to relate n Ach to academic achievement.

Academic Achievement

McClelland anticipated that any measure of motivation named n Ach would immediately arouse interest in its possibilities as a predictor which might provide the long-sought variance for the multiple regression equations devised to predict academic achievement. The failure of aptitude and achievement measures to account for much more than 30 per cent of the variance in college grades led some to the conclusion that "motivation" is the key to the problem here, but measures of motivation have been difficult to come by. Accordingly, we find a section in *The Achievement Motive* on college grades, but the opening lines reflect a basic wariness of the problem. "The relation of n Achievement score to college grades is obviously a point of very great practical importance. On the other hand, it is of dubious theoretical significance, since grades in college are affected by so many unknown factors" (McClelland *et al.*, 1953, p. 237). Subsequent studies have confirmed this judgment. The pattern on n Ach relationships to academic grades, behaviors, and levels shows wide variation, apparently depending on the control for the many other "unknown factors."

Morgan (1951) found that *S*s at the extreme upper level of the ACE (upper four per cent) at the University of Minnesota who differed in academic standing also differed reliably in n Ach, with the non-achievers being lowest in n Ach scores. Parish and Rethlingershafer (1954) used essentially the same design in a study of University of Florida students. Matching their samples of high and low achievers on age, geographical origin, socio-economic status, attendance, and past education, they administered the TAT individually and followed it with a questionnaire about academic behavior and attitudes. Both the individual administration and low-scorer agreements (scoring manuals were not available at the time) cast doubts on the comparability with other studies. The high achievers differed from the low achievers whose academic interests leaned toward applied subjects. The low achievers also had a history of past failures about which they now seemed to be indifferent, but there were no differences in n Ach as measured. With such a finding the main difficulty is presented by the non-achieving *S* with a high n Ach score. We shall hear more of him shortly.

Through this initial period of research on the n Ach measure a program was conducted at the Educational Testing Service to assess the feasibility of such a projective device providing valid predictors of grade averages. Ricciuti and Sadacca (1955) worked with a high school population (junior-year males), used two nine-picture forms of the test, and ran cross-validation studies against both pictures and scoring categories. Two groups were used, *N*s of 53 and 79, and gave roughly comparable results. The correlations were positive, +.18 and + .23, *P* .05, between n Ach and grade average, based on the past three quarters, adjusted for predicted standing from the Terman-McNemar IQ test. An earlier study using 147 high school juniors had yielded a coefficient of +.26 for the same adjusted average criterion.

This study of high school age *S*s was soon followed by Rosen's (1955) excellent analysis of the Achievement Syndrome from a sociological standpoint. Using Hollingshed's Index of Social Position he obtained a stratified sample of 120 high school sophomores from two large public, urban high schools. The five social-scale groups were found to reflect extreme differences in n Ach scores, in a positive direction; and a within-class comparison of *S*s high and low in n Ach shows a highly reliable relationship to general academic average (see Table 1).

Rosen's finding that n Ach is positively related to social class subsequently received support from a study by Veroff, Atkinson, Feld, and Gurin (1960), based on a national sample of adult respondents. At this point it appears that academic achievement shows a low positive relationship to the n Ach score among the fully representative high school samples, while the selected population of college students gives a more variable picture. In Ricciuti's (1954) first study, a sample of Naval officer candidates and a sample of college freshmen both yielded correlation coefficients of a zero order between academic average and n Ach scores. Two of the latest publications dealing with this problem continue to support this pattern. Bendig (1959a) reports a correlation of +.059 (*N* is 136 males) between n Ach and one-semester grades in the introductory course in psychology at the University of Pittsburgh. Littig and Yeracaris (1963) collected the TAT stories prior to an extensive interview of 400 heads-of-household selected in a probability cluster multi-stage sample.

TABLE 1

School Grades by Achievement Motivation and Social Class (Rosen, 1955)

	Social Class			
	I–II–III		IV–V	
Achievement Motivation Score	High	Low	High	Low
Average school grades	Per cent	Per cent	Per cent	Per cent
"B" or above	66	32	75	36
"C" or below	34	68	25	64
Number	(38)	(22)	(16)	(44)

The 190 males display a clear pattern of increasing education level with increasing n Ach scores.

Cole, Jacobs, and Zubok (1962) conducted two studies in which they found reverse relationships between n Ach and academic standing. In the first study, students in the honors program had low n Ach compared to a group of average performers with equal aptitude scores; and in the second study those students showing the least n Ach at admission as freshmen performed best academically by the end of the semester. The authors point to the disposition to respond to the Neutral cues of the testing session as the possible explanation of these findings.

Actually none of these findings depart from the original expectation that academic performance would be determined by many factors of which achievement motivation would be just one. It is McClelland's opinion that the motivation represented by the n Ach score is not particularly welcome in many academic settings. He suggests that high grades represent "skill in taking examinations, in following instructions, and finding solutions set by others" (1961a, p. 713). He accepts the fact that college grades may not be related to the n Ach score by suggesting that other evidence shows high scorers "like to solve problems set by themselves, rather than those set for them by others ..." (1961, p. 715). This position raises forcefully the issue of the interpretive basis from which evaluation of the "validity" of a construct is to proceed. McClelland is saying, in effect, that the meaning of Achievement Imagery in TAT stories is to be found in that matrix of variables which *do* relate to the scores. For an opposing position consider a recent study by Broverman, Jordan, and Phillips (1960).

These authors take the stance that self-reported behavior having achievement character, such as trying to find a better job, expressing a preference for more training, reading help-wanted ads, etc., constitutes striving for advancement and hence reflects achievement goal motivation. (No effort is reported to validate whether these reported behaviors actually occurred.) Scoring Feffer's Role-Taking task for four n Ach categories they find an inverse relationship between striving and their n Ach scores. By anchoring the analysis to the "validity" of the striving measure it then becomes necessary to argue that the n Ach score reflects fantasied achievement by "persons unable to express their achievement needs in life situations. ..." A similar type of argument was offered by Parish and Rethlingshafer (1954) who felt that sustained academic achievement was to be distinguished from situationally induced need states whose major effect might be upon apperception and laboratory tasks. Actually, there is no debate here if the point is being offered that high achievement may occur without n Ach motivation. McClelland's discussion of the origins of creative scientific work (1961b,

1962; Roe, 1953) make clear that any number of syndromes of actual striving and accomplishment may exist with little or no contribution from the achievement motive as measured by his method. However, the strategy of his research has been to assume that the score validation techniques previously described permit continuous testing of a slowly emerging conception of achievement motivation that may or may not fit some preconception of the criteria to which it is related. An example taken from the academic situation is Marlowe's (1959) report of a significant (+.33) relationship between n Ach (TAT) and ratings by fraternity brothers of each other as "achieving" vs. "non-achieving." He does not report the sociometric relationship to GPA, but we should expect it to be moderate at best. McKeachie's (1961) study of academic achievement provides an excellent example of the spirit in which one should study n Ach in the classroom. His results suggest that n Ach affects academic achievement most in the low achievement cue classroom, with considerable complexity introduced by teacher differences.

The conclusion seems clear that the experimenter must decide whether he is trying to predict academic achievement, in which case he must vigorously research the nature of predictors to his criteria, or whether he wishes to learn more of the function of n Ach in academic settings, which may dictate the creation of new criterion variables as Marlowe did. Experimenters who insist on treating projective n Ach scores as if they "obeyed" the standard canons of measurement will continue to find them contributing errors to their analyses (Mitchell, 1961; Bendig, 1959b).

Level of Aspiration

The literature on level of aspiration (LA) has consistently shown that clear results or norms cause LA to approximate the realities of the situation, and it was expected from the outset that motivation would be most influential under ambiguous results or prior to experience with the task at hand. Atkinson (1950) found that n Ach correlated +.45 with positive aspiration only for those *S*s in his course whose past grades conflicted with their general average, placing them in an ambiguous situation. Support for this functional relationship between motivation and cognition has also come from a study by Kausler and Trapp (1958), who found that *S*s with high n Ach displayed greater optimism at the outset of five trials of a Digit-Symbol-Substitution task, but as results were obtained, the difference in aspiration between high and low *S*s steadily approached zero. Kausler (1959) has also done one of the few experiments using LA as the independent variable which may have implications for the n Ach researcher. He reports that *S*s who were asked to make LA estimates out-performed those who were not asked, and one wonders whether *S*s with high n Ach may not give themselves such instructions when low n Ach *S*s do not. Furthermore, asking for LA could be achievement-arousing which might explain why Ricciuti and Schultz (1958) report no relationship between n Ach and LA for males who took the TAT after the LA task.

Earlier, Clark, Teevan, and Ricciuti (1956) found that students expressing extremes of aspiration about final examination grades had lower n Ach scores than those of moderate aspirations, and that these moderates wrote stories with negative subscores while the extremes used positive subscores. The suggestion that moderate aspiration reflects reality orientation toward achievement which realistically does involve obstacles, disappointment, and possible failure, which in turn appear in fantasy, has not been pursued by other experiments whose data could be so analyzed. Reitman and Williams (1961) repeated the above experiment and failed to replicate the results, using the Taylor Manifest Anxiety scale, they found FF patterns of aspiration associated with high anxiety.

Pottharst (1955) attempted to explore the

effects of success and failure on LA estimates of *S*s with high and low levels of n Ach. In the first session she gave the Digit-Symbol test under Neutral conditions (cooperative, female *E*), followed by the TAT. The same *S*s then returned for an individual, ego-arousing retest utilizing LA items followed by the TAT, report of results (Success-failure condition), and finally new LA estimates on the D-S with a final trial on which the *S* could shift to a maze-tracing task. The chief findings were that n Ach taken from the Neutral session showed a positive relationship to LA under the ego-aroused condition and for *S*s who chose to shift to the new task. Otherwise, LA was determined by the reality cues of success and failure with a subtle effect of n Ach found, i.e., an increase in performance following success and decrease following failure for high n Ach *S*s, and no change following success with an increase following failure for the low n Ach *S*s.

Diggory and Morlock (1961) used the French n Ach test and an individually administered card-sorting task with controlled scores producing one group of *S*s with high scores and another with low. Continuous plotting of scores and LA ("... try to get on the next trial") were kept in front of the *S*. They found that the high performance group gave larger positive LAs than the low performance group, and on the one trial where all *S*s were urged to make the top score, all LAs went up. The n Ach score shows no relation to LA but does relate to actual performance. Once again, the cognitive cues seem to override motivational effects on aspiration.

Mahone (1960) classified 135 college males as "realistic" or "unrealistic" in vocational aspiration according to *S*'s estimate of his ability, ability required for a vocation, actual ability as tested, and ability judged by a clinician. He found that *S*s with the high n Ach–low Test Anxiety pattern were most realistic, and those with the low n Ach–high Test Anxiety pattern most unrealistic. Burnstein (1963) used the aspiration indices of Clark, Teevan, and Ricciuti (1956) for occupational goals. Using the n Ach–TAQ patterns he found TAQ alone discriminated, with lowering aspirations as TAQ scores increased.

Heckhausen (1963) reports that FF *S*s set either very high or very low goals, and following failure do not change. His HS *S*s are more realistic and adjustive to outcomes. He also reports that initial goal-setting prior to results differs with those high in total n Ach starting with high aspiration and those with low n Ach starting low.

Memory

Further light was shed on the nature of n Ach by studies of memory. Atkinson (1953) used the task-interruption technique of Zeigarnik to induce failure and success and tested for the relationship between n Ach and recall under different levels of achievement arousal. Under Relaxed conditions *S*s moderate in n Ach remembered more incompleted tasks than completed ones, but this reversed itself for these *S*s under Achievement orientation.

These findings are taken to mean that motive arousal focuses attention on the possibility of personal accomplishment. "For them achievement orientation provides an incentive or challenge. They, therefore, recall more incompleted tasks as if they wanted to continue to strive to complete them. Here recall is instrumental to eventual success. For the middle n Ach group, Achievement orientation is a threat which leads to relatively greater avoidance of failures in recall since recall of failures would serve to re-integrate the pain of failure" (Atkinson, 1953, p. 271). Heckhausen (1963) has reported that his HS *S*s remember fewer completed tasks while the FF remember fewer incompleted.

Coopersmith (1960) required fifth- and sixth-grade children to recall tasks which had been previously failed or accomplished according to *E*'s intention and gave them a choice between one of each to repeat. The n Ach measure was gathered after the first encounter with the tasks and prior to the recall. He concluded that no clear relationship had emerged, though n Ach was related to other measures of self-esteem (see below).

Shifting from recall of possible successes or failures to materials dealing with these themes, Reitman (1961) allowed *S*s to read six stories for one minute each, following Achievement Arousal instructions concerning the task. Other tasks were then performed for thirty minutes preceding the memory test. *S*s from the middle third of the n Ach score distribution recalled proportionally more achievement success themes than either failure or neutral themes. This replicated a finding he had reported much earlier with fewer *S*s (Reitman, 1954). When he contrasted the Neutral instruction condition with the Achievement instruction in a second experiment, the relationship was reversed for the Neutral condition, with these *S*s recalling the failure stories better than the other *S*s. One analysis which has not been performed with this technique is to compare the categories of story components recalled with those written by the same *S*s. There is the possibility that recall of briefly exposed material is somewhat projective in its own right, and we could have here an example of congruence between reconstruction and construction of the unreal world by the same motivational processes.

Social Influence

Mention was made earlier of using n Ach as a variable in studies of other problems. These also make some contribution to the construct validity of the n Ach score. Studies of *social* influence have found that *S*s high in n Ach resist yielding to the majority (McClelland, Atkinson, Clark, & Lowell, 1953, p. 287); that movement toward a majority position by females who were told such movement was instrumental to being liked by others was least for those with high n Ach (Burdick, 1959); that depression of one's own task score in response to an appeal from a partner was most characteristic of the high n Aff–low n Ach pattern and least likely for the opposite, again with females (few males yielded at all) (Walker & Heyns, 1962); but that n Ach has no relationship to the Barron Independence Judgment Scale, a paper-and-pencil device validated on experimental induction of yielding (Liverant & Odell, 1959).

Summary

Researches of the kind described above have led to a progressive refinement of interpretation of the n Ach score. In *Motives in Fantasy, Action, and Society* Atkinson states "... when the situation seems to arouse in the person a cognitive expectancy (now to use Tolman's concept) that performance of the act will produce an effect he is generally interested in bringing about, his motive is aroused and manifested in overt performance of the Act." He then goes on to suggest that when this motive arousal takes place, we may say the individual has a state of motivation. Thus, measurement under Neutral conditions taps the general disposition for achievement motivation, i.e., the achievement motive. The research discussed so far implies that arousal of the achievement motivational state will affect task performance, memory, reaction to social influence, and level of aspiration, while the disposition to be aroused in academic settings shows some social bias but little over-all relationship to academic achievement. By concentrating on the problems inherent in learning more about the processes of the motivational states, Atkinson (1957) was led to propose a model of behavior within which n Ach could be studied. On the other hand, by concentrating on the problem of motive determination and dispositional sensitivity, McClelland (1961b) and others have been increasingly led to speak of "the n Achiever" or the person with high n Ach. We turn now to each of these diverging streams of research.

MOTIVATIONAL PROCESSES

Once demonstrations of the motivational significance of the n Ach score had been completed, efforts were begun to study the role of the motive in achievement situations demanding choice, aspiration, and judgment concerning possible outcomes. Since these aspects of behavior imply a balance of reward and cost, success and failure, hope and fear, it was necessary to organize what was known about the avoidance aspect of behavior in achievement situations, i.e., fear of failure. From the earliest studies this motivational construct had been part of the discussion, but efforts to measure it or isolate its effects on behavior had been equivocal. The *S*s with middle levels of n Ach in various experiments had displayed recognition thresholds suggesting sensitivity to failure and greater tendency to recall successes over failures under aroused achievement conditions. However, efforts to use categories of the n Ach system as a subsystem for fear of failure had not been encouraging (Clark & McClelland, 1953; Moulton, 1958).

Atkinson chose to assume that "a relatively low n Achievement score implies that the motive to avoid failure is relatively stronger than the motive to achievement within the individual" (1958, p. 571). One way an *S* may receive a low n Ach score is to write a story of escape or avoidance from work situations. However, a low n Ach may also occur when the *S* has written stories filled with other imagery, such as n Aff, etc., or if he rejects the instructions and writes elaborate descriptions of the pictures. There is no a priori reason why *S*s doing the latter will display "avoidance" patterns of behavior in achievement task situations. However, the model Atkinson (1957) proposed, using Motivation = f (Motive × Expectancy × Incentive), permits the use of approach and avoidance calculations in conjunction with the assumption that Expectancy and Incentive vary inversely and suggests that Hope of Success (high n Ach) will prefer moderate risks for moderate rewards while Fear of Failure (low n Ach) will prefer extreme risks, long or short odds, which produce uncertain rewards. The low n Ach *S* does this because "competitive achievement situations are unattractive to him ... he should avoid tasks of intermediate difficulty (*P* is .05) where the arousal of anxiety about failure is greatest."

Ideally we would prefer an independent measure of Fear of Failure (FF) rather than rely solely on low n Ach. Atkinson chose to experiment with the various Anxiety scales and settled on the Mandler-Sarason Test Anxiety Questionnaire (TAQ) which invites the respondent to describe himself as anxious (psychologically and physically) on a series of multiple-choice items. Using extreme criterion groups and ego-involving conditions, Sarason had shown that low scorers made better time, fewer errors, and expected to finish their task in contrast to those scoring high (1960). Raphelson (1957) used a measure of skin conductance (high conductance due to sweating implies anxiety) to determine the effect of his task procedures (tracking with feedback) and obtained his n Ach and TAQ measures *following* the task. The latter measures had a −.43 correlation,[4] suggesting low n Ach might be fear of failure; and he found that *S*s whose skin conductance rose (anxiety) during the insoluble task had gotten high TAQ scores and low n Ach while those whose skin conductance dropped did the opposite.

Raphelson and Moulton (1958) repeated the experiment but raised the uncertainty level of the task by eliminating the feedback with the intention of raising the anxiety level. Now the n Ach vs. TAQ r drops to .09. The content of the stories was ana-

[4] Subsequent correlations using TAQ scores from neutral administrations have been of a zero order (Atkinson & Litwin, 1960; Feather, 1961; Brody, 1963; Caron, 1963).

lyzed into Hope of Success and Fear of Failure components. These show that in the first, low uncertainty condition, high TAQ was accompanied by FF, and low TAQ by HS, while the relationship reversed under high uncertainty, indicating a shift to negative fantasy as the lows became anxious, and a shift to positive fantasy as the highs became anxious. The skin conductance showed more rapid adaptation for low n Ach than high n Ach groups and is taken to mean that under certain failure the lows successfully avoid arousal.

Vogel, Baker, and Lazarus (1958) also used GSR, pulse rate, and blood pressure measures in a study of performance under stress of continuous failure on a speed-of-estimation task. The n Ach measures followed, but the pictures were a repeat of three used earlier with the same *S*s. The Taylor Anxiety Scale and an inventory of study habits were also gathered in the earlier session. The first finding regarding n Ach was that following failure those *S*s attempting the fewest items had the highest n Ach. Secondly, those *S*s with low n Ach under both measures showed the greatest physiological reactivity. Finally, they also found that *S*s high on both measures reported high anxiety on the Taylor Anxiety scale. The authors suggest that low n Ach *S*s become involved on perpetual-motor tasks while high n Ach *S*s prefer abstract-conceptual tasks. Perhaps so, but this reviewer must note that studies using repeated measurement of n Ach with the *same* pictures introduce a variable about which very little is known.

On the face of it we must assume that *S*s reporting anxiety were experiencing it. These findings prompted a series of studies using patterns of n Ach and TAQ to test various deductions from Atkinson's model. Before reporting these, we should notice a shift in assumption which the concern with FF has occasioned. For study of the avoidance motivation in achievement situations, Atkinson and his associates combine the projective and non-projective measures. The former was carefully validated through experimental arousal techniques, while the latter is accepted for its ability to correlate with behavior as predicted. This is done on the ground that findings support the model whose key assumptions we must now reexamine.

In considering the state of satisfaction aimed for by n Ach, Atkinson suggests that *pride* of accomplishment is the end state. From this it follows that personal responsibility is a requisite for pride, and hence, the absolute value of some incentive or prize need not necessarily imply the winner may take pride in his prize. Rather, the key to pride is the degree of difficulty encountered in achieving the prize. Hence the high n Ach *S* should prefer increasing amounts of difficulty but being realistic he is willing to settle for those incentives appropriate to the 50-50 chance, rather than attempt the very difficult and finish empty-handed. A somewhat simpler explanation is possible. If an *S* is confronted by the inverse relationship of incentive and difficulty Atkinson uses, and given ten trials in which to maximize his payoff, it is evident that the best strategy is to choose tasks of intermediate difficulty. The fact that some *S*s do this and others do not could be due to interest in the task or the incentive, experience with problem-solving, and a whole variety of experiential factors less complicated than defensive processes.

The researches which follow bear on the question of n Ach vs. preference for risk, n Ach–TAQ patterns vs. risk, and in general illustrate the emerging role played by the incentive itself, and in particular the issues surrounding its measurement.

The basic pattern of these studies is to obtain the n Ach scores under Neutral conditions, and then subsequently involve the *S*s in tasks where the emphasis is on the incentive itself rather than the score as an indicator of personal ability. The *E* can vary the incentive, the degree of difficulty, and the variety of tasks. Some of these studies have used the French n Ach and a variety of populations so that strict comparability cannot be claimed with the earlier work.

Atkinson (1958c) used 124 females with the McClelland n Ach measure. The *S*s were working as part of the "psychology laboratory work this week." After being told that prizes of money would be available at odds from 1 of 10 to 1 of 30, the tasks were described as "sensitive to effort as to any particular skills or abilities so the person who tries hardest is likely to have the best score" (p. 291). Under the low incentive of $1.25 as the prize, performance was highest for the ⅓ and ½ conditions, but when the incentive moved to $2.50, all odds conditions showed an increase such that the differences between them are probably not significant. One can easily imagine that as the incentive condition increases, the greatest effort might come under the easiest, ¾, odds condition. Only under the low incentive condition do we find that the high n Ach group shows greater performance scores under the ⅓ and ½ conditions than the low n Ach. There are no differences between the groups at odds of ½. This suggests to Atkinson that *S*s high in n Ach may distort their expectancy of success and actually subjectively equate long odds with the intermediate 50-50 condition which maximizes payoff.

It is here that Atkinson most clearly states his assumption, "that difficulty of a task determines the incentive value of achievement" (1958, p. 305). Thus we see that the incentive for n Ach is pride in success, which is greatest when the odds are reasonably long (but not so long that the *S* cannot claim credit) and which varies independently from any prize or reward offered for performance.

Brody (1963) extended the "distortion" possibility by testing for effect of TAQ scores on estimates of *P*s when the *S* had to commit himself to a judgment, indicate his confidence level for that judgment, and then receive knowledge of results through a series of fifty trials. He found that high TAQ is associated with reports from the extreme quartiles of the confidence distribution, with the high n Ach–low TAQ vs. low n Ach–high TAQ contrast being the greatest. *S*s high in n Ach show the highest estimates of *P*s across trials, and the greatest level of confidence at the trial of decision. This means they approach the *P*s .50 level sooner than low n Ach *S*s. No report of the actual performance is given so we do not know if this optimism was justified. The *S*s were told the task was a test of decision-making ability without further elaboration, but apparently they wished to do well at the task because on the average the high n Ach–low TAQ groups waited until *P*s .78 before making their decision. This again indicates that some incentive beyond intermediate difficulty can operate with n Ach, in this case to produce caution.

McClelland (1958a) reported that young children classified on Aronson's n Ach measure showed a preference for moderate distance in a ring-toss game. Atkinson, Bastian, Earl, and Litwin (1960) used male undergraduates, *N* is 66, and found that those with high n Ach chose the intermediate risk alternatives in a shuffleboard game and expressed the greater expectancy when asked how many *S*s they expected to surpass. Inspection of group means in this study reveals that all *S*s were learning to shoot from the intermediate position, but the high n Ach *S*s learned more quickly and hence were reinforced more often. Oddly enough, under the highest incentive all odds of winning were *equally* preferred, rather than shifting to the most favorable. The low n Ach *S*s showed so little tendency to move toward the maximum payoff position that they were not reinforced much during the task, and one wonders about their motivation for the task itself. Again, Atkinson and Litwin (1960) report data for male students playing the ring-toss game in a relaxed coed setting, and all prefer the intermediate position with the high n Ach–low TAQ group showing a significantly greater preference over those *S*s with the low n Ach–high TAQ pattern. Intermediate must be defined here as relative to the group distribution and happens to be two-thirds of the available distance away from the pin. This illustrates that when games of physical skill are used, the *E* should be able to control the payoff, or failing that, should have norms which give good estimates of probability of success from each position. Subsequently these same high n Ach *S*s spent longer taking the course final examination and received higher grades than did the low n Ach group.

These experiments illustrate some of the difficulties in defining incentives. Atkinson (1957) suggests that difficulty per se has incentive character. However, these experiments may be interpreted from a straightforward reinforcement position which would also predict these results since *S*s adopting 50-50 strategies receive more payoffs. This throws us back to the issue of why high n Ach *S*s like these payoffs more than others, i.e., are more willing to take games seriously. What is needed are procedures which vary difficulty and value of payoff separately so that the n Ach incentive may emerge. A series of experiments by Feather (1959) has moved in this direction.

Feather first had sixth-grade boys scale (paired comparisons) the Life Saver flavors to equate for incentive value, then varied skill vs. chance, Achievement-orientation ("this is a test") vs. Relaxed-orientation ("this is a game"), and offered the *S*s two levels of difficulty and asked, "If you were to get one (prize) which one would you feel most pleased about getting?" and also, "Which one would you actually choose to try to get?" Under the Achievement-orientation the *S*s preferred to get their prize from the difficult task and said they would choose that task. However, under the Relaxed condition they were less unanimous about being pleased to win under difficult conditions and definitely chose the *easy* task as their strategy. Note that n Ach was not a variable in this experiment, but we are struck by the effect of "this is a test" vs. "this is a game." Could it be that these *S*s were aware that society has standards about how to reach a goal which differ for these two conditions? Perhaps pride in difficult achievement is associated with "testing" situations in a way that fun in winning games is not.

The same attention to control is found in Feather's (1961) experiment on persistence in the face of failure. College males were involved in a "test" of perceptual reasoning and given false norms which guaranteed their failure. An ingenious procedure permitted the *S* to estimate his chances of success continuously, and he was free to stop or continue at whatever point he felt was appropriate. Stopping permitted the *S* to attempt another task. Using the n Ach–TAQ patterns, Feather reports that those high in n Ach and low in TAQ persist when they believe the tasks easy and keep shifting tasks if they believe them difficult. Those of low n Ach–high TAQ do just the opposite. No mention is made of the other patterns. The fact that *S*s thought "anxious" avoid the experience of failure on "easy" tasks by persisting at difficult ones is taken as support for Atkinson's model. (This finding is not confounded by the presence of success since none was forthcoming under any condition.) Again another interpretation is possible. We have two strategies for maximizing outcomes: the first based on persistence at favorable odds (i.e., easy task) and the other based on persistence at the long shot (i.e., difficult) where the incentive is thought to be a good score on an important test of ability. Neither strategy is paying off. Both create a sense of difficulty and failure. If persistence is the basis of difficulty here, we have both groups valuing it but using it differently. Again the differences seem to lie in the problem-solving strategies.

Feather's latest study (1963) resulted in the finding of some relationship between estimates of *P*s and self-reported anxiety in achievement situations but a failure to find the expected relationship between n Ach and preference for moderate levels of *P*s. In this case *S*s were given norms to create expectation of success, but then they did the tasks and presumably experienced a sense of failure or success though these data are not reported. Immediately following, they filled out the Achievement Anxiety Test which has both positive and negative scales, permitting an assessment of debilitating and facilitating anxiety (Alpert & Haber, 1960). Four days later the n Ach measure was taken. Both these measures may have been affected by the experimental tests and warn us of the value of collecting the motive scores prior to task experiences of reinforcement. Again we find that as *S*s did the task they moved toward estimates of *P*s in the 50-50s, indicating the soundness of such payoff levels. There is some indication that *S*s high in debilitating anxiety made low *P*s estimates while those high on facilitating anxiety made high *P*s estimates. Essentially the finding is that *S*s who were optimistic during the task subsequently described themselves as facilitated by test anxiety, while those who were pessimistic described themselves as impaired. Whether these estimates are congruent with reality is not known. The failure of n Ach scores to relate to *P*s is thought to be due to the intrusion of "reality" estimates. Once again we are faced with the problem of the intrinsic incentive most appropriate to the motive, i.e., "pride" in accomplishment, and the extrinsic incentive of maximizing payoff for whatever reason.

Isaacson (1964) analyzed the course concentration of honoring and superior nonhonoring *S*s who had taken the French n Ach and TAQ at entrance. Using the ratio of grades obtained to student aptitude as an index of difficulty, independently checked against student attitudes toward the courses, he then contrasted course election patterns for the difference score distribution of transformed n Ach and TAQ scores. Those *S*s favoring n Ach, i.e., HS, uniformly preferred intermediate difficulty regardless of status as honors or nonhonors students. But those reporting anxiety, FF, showed a reversal, with nonhonoring men showing a slight preference for difficult courses while honors students definitely preferred the least difficult. Apparently these choices do not reflect past histories of success and failure. All of which raises the question of the incentive value of honors for these *S*s. The HS group shows again its preference for a reasonable strategy.

Berkun and Burdick (1963) have reported a study bearing on the issue of knowledge of results as a determinant of behavior for *S*s distinguished by n Ach–TAQ patterns. The test began with the TAQ for the 400 soldiers. Half the *S*s received "very good" and half received "very bad" reports of their performance on a test of reasoning following which they wrote the stories for the n Ach score. Next they heard a tape describing the test as a potent predictor of job success. A second test of reasoning was given without explanation, and this was followed by a series of attitude scales for affect, hostility toward *E*, evaluation of the reasoning test and *E*, and understanding about the experiment. The effect of the negative false reports was verified by increased reports of negative affect, expressed hostility toward *E*, and negative evaluation of *E* and the test. Since improvement occurred from the first test to the second, the increment becomes the dependent variable. And since *S*s knew their general level, we have an interaction possible between true score and reported score.

They found that *S*s reporting low TAQ respond to the second test with uniform increments, regardless of actual score or the false score received and regardless of n Ach level. However, those with high TAQ and low n Ach increase output if the report they receive is true, or if they are told they have done very poorly regardless of its truth, or if they are told they did well when in fact they had done poorly. These results suggest that knowledge of results affects the n Ach motive differentially depending on the level of TAQ scores. In the absence of anxiety n Ach had no effect as all *S*s simply tried harder the second time. Given anxiety, however, *S*s low in n Ach show sensitivity to failure even when it is not true, suggesting they may not have confidence in their own estimates of reality when challenged by a false report of failure. Those with high n Ach respond to the suggestion they have done well without regard to their actual performance. They seem to be more susceptible to *E*'s suggestion than those sensitive to failure, and this could be read to mean that they allow themselves to be unduly depressed by reported failure.

In sum, it seems that those low in TAQ worked to improve their score for incentives unknown, while those with high TAQ scores focus on *E* for information about accomplishment, with high n Ach *S*s tuned to hear of success and low n Ach *S*s tuned to hear of failure, both of which had the effect of reinforcing effort. This experiment is an excellent illustration of the complexities raised by efforts to vary the incentive variable beyond mere difficulty.

Sampson (1963) presents another way to test for the achievement incentive by placing the *S* in a situation where "the individual is faced with two conflicting needs or values—achievement vs. the need to avoid the unpleasant activity—with opposed or incompatible behavioral acts which lead to the satisfaction of these needs or values, i.e., doing well on a task in order to satisfy n Ach vs. doing poorly on the task in order to avoid the unpleasant activity." Using female *S*s and the French n Ach score, he convinced the *S*s that "their performance on the learning task (nonsense syllables) would determine which of the two 'creative' situations they would be placed.... This meant that those in the conflict condition who learned the syllables most rapidly would be placed in the shock condition (designing a shock schedule for mice) while those who learned most slowly would be placed in the feeding situation." In fact he found that the no-conflict situation yielded the more rapid learning with *S*s with high n Ach best while the conflict situation yielded uniformly slower learning regardless of n Ach. Being labeled "creative" has incentive value for female *S*s with n Ach but only when the instrumental expression of n Ach is constructive rather than destructive.

Smith (1964) examined the relationship between the relative strength measure of n Ach (French), TAQ, and Otis IQ scores, mid-term and final examination grades, and persistence in exam-taking. *S*s high on TAQ scored poorly on the Otis, r is $-.28$, P .01, spent more time on the final exam, r is $+.31$, and mid-term, r is $+.27$, a relationship which holds with intelligence partialled out. The n Ach measure showed no criterion relationships, nor did the usual n Ach–TAQ pattern groups. In the light of Feather's demonstration earlier (see p. 30) that perceived difficulty acts as a moderator, Smith then assumed that perceived difficulty would be inversely related to the Otis scores and analyzed the patterns according to high vs. low IQ groupings. Now he finds a replication of Atkinson and Litwin (see p. 29) as HS *S*s leave early if they have high Otis scores but stay longer than FF *S*s if they have low Otis scores. Smith's experience demonstrates very well the importance of expectancy as a variable.

Probably one of the most tightly designed efforts to test Atkinson's model is that of Caron (1963) who assumed that test anxiety would affect performance on a comprehension task but not on a task of rote learning, thus permitting a test for motive and expectancy effects under both conditions. He predicted motive effects, i.e., Hope of Success superior to Fear of Failure, for the comprehension task but not the rote; and he predicted *S*s whose *P*s is closest to .50 would be superior to those with extreme *P*s preference on the rote task; and since Fear of Failure affects the comprehension task we must predict success for the *P*s .50 and *P*f extreme pattern over its opposite. The *S*s were secondary school males in college preparatory courses whose subjective probabilities of success and failure were derived from the proportion of eight course grades exceeding their stated standard of grade success. This procedure did, in fact, support the assumption that High vs. Low academic groups differed in *Ps* and *Pf* for examination success.

The *Ss* attended three sessions: the first used to collect the n Ach and TAQ measures and the second to give the grade questionnaire and O'Connor's risk-taking scale; the third session asked the students to read a description of Atkinson's model. One group did so under Achievement instructions, i.e., they were to do their best so the Board of Education might get a fair estimate of their aptitude for psychological studies. The dependent variables are scores for definition and correct reproduction of symbols (rote scores) and scores for deductive transfer problems (comprehension scores). No support was found for the rote score hypothesis. *Ss* low in TAQ did outperform highs on the comprehension task as predicted, and the pattern of high n Ach–low TAQ was superior to low n Ach–high TAQ for both academic groups, with the high academic group superior to the low group. Caron concludes, "Perhaps the most reasonable assumption is that memorization and comprehension were equally demanding, but that individuals differ in the strength of these response dispositions. In this light the demonstrated deleterious effects of anxiety might be due not to reduced task directedness, as Atkinson, 1960, maintains, but to the fact that anxious subjects typically channel effort into less efficient components of tasks."

Caron ran a second group who were led to believe that the text would help them understand scores they were to receive from the risk-taking test they had taken. Calling this the Curiosity condition he finds that *Ss* who were both highly involved with the material (derived from a saliency test for the term "cowardly") and who had a high probability of understanding it (high Academic) very effectively absorbed both facts and principles in the Curiosity condition. High anxiety *Ss* performed well only on the Comprehension which was most relevant. The potency of the anxiety and academic variables suggests to Caron that "past experiments which have simply compared high n Ach, low Anxiety *Ss* with those having the reverse pattern (and which have also failed to assess Expectancy) may have obtained differences between these groups which were in fact due to differential Anxiety and/or Expectancy." He finally raises the issue which we have been attending throughout our review of tests generated from Atkinson's model and asks, "What is the precise relationship between generic motives, specific motives, and incentives?"

There is no question that the experiments prompted by the model have been dealing with this very issue or that we have a more or less consistent set of findings. However, there is considerable reason to doubt that Expectancy (difficulty) and Incentive are reciprocal as the model suggests; and there is good reason to suspend judgment regarding the extent to which Fear of Failure is a negative image of the n Ach calculus. The researches which combine a projective measure of positive motivation, n Ach, with a self-report measure of avoidance motivation, TAQ, may rest on hidden relationships between n Ach and Expectancy, as Caron suggests, or on unknown relationships between TAQ and Fear of Failure, projectively measured, which are just beginning to be examined.

Before proceeding to a look at these new efforts, let us summarize the empirical findings in this section. *Ss* high in n Ach have repeatedly shown the tendency to maximize payoff, or follow such strategy in various games or tests, and in general express greater optimism while they are doing so. These tendencies are strongest when various extrinsic incentives are of low potency. The role of self-reported anxiety is clearly important, especially as it differs in its effects on various levels of n Ach. At the low level of n Ach *Ss* reporting anxiety show pessimism about their chances, seem slow to learn the best payoff strategies, are sensitive to differing sources of feedback, and may be generally less efficient unless the "correct" path of action is clearly specified by the situation.

At high levels of n Ach many of these tendencies are attenuated, though at least one study (Berkun & Burdick, 1963) suggests a sensitization to "good news" rather than bad.

Projective Measures of Fear of Failure (FF)

Heinz Heckhausen's recent study (1963) presents an effort to measure Fear of Failure projectively, using the overt theme of Failure concern as his Imagery category and then proceeding to score the same categories used in n Ach, n Aff, and n Power as they relate to efforts to avoid or undo failure in achievement situations. This has been attempted several times in the U.S., and the reviewer has tried to use Heckhausen's system with protocols of college students, but the incidence of such imagery is too low to be useful. Heckhausen has added three pictures to the McClelland set, all of which involve the possibilities of authoritarian relationships ("in which the work of a person is checked or judged by an obvious superior . . .), and this may account for the suitable levels of Failure themes from his student populations (p. 51).

By scoring for both Hope of Success (HS) and Fear of Failure (FF), Heckhausen has been able to conduct a series of studies with the two score distributions. The table of correlations with the McClelland n Ach measure and between the HS and FF measures for two samples of students appears below (p. 74).

Heckhausen proceeds to test the construct validity of his measures in a wide variety of situations, using both secondary school level and college level students which we have cited where appropriate. Those related to performance will be treated here. In situations where clear information is available, the HS *Ss* overestimate failures while FF *Ss* overestimate success. These reactions reverse themselves as the feedback becomes ambiguous. On simple tasks requiring no special ability he finds the HS students slow and disinterested, but they display good study habits, work more quickly on complex problems, and respond to mild time pressure for problems requiring planning with better solutions than under no pressure. The FF students work speedily and well on simple tasks, show poor study habits, take more time on complex problems, and show a deterioration of solutions as time pressure increases. On maze problems the HS *Ss* show the greater gains with practice.

Without attempting to trace possible differences in motivational arousal techniques used in Germany, the above set of findings has a familiar ring. The HS students display

TABLE 2

Correlation between b Achievement after McClelland et al. and the Different Motivation Variables of the New Measuring Procedure (Heckhausen, 1963)

b Achievement	Hope of Success	Fear of Failure	Net Hope HS − FF	Total Motivation HS + FF
Students at a teachers college $N = 71$	+.73 <.001[a]	+.15	+.32 <.01	+.63 <.001
University students $N = 77$	+.60 <.001	+.21	+.27 <.01	+.62 <.001

[a] Significance level of product-moment coefficients

much of the behavior found for high n Ach, and the FF *S*s match those found for low n Ach.

A parallel attempt at creating a projective scoring system for Fear of Failure has met with success in the research of Birney, Burdick, and Teevan (1961). The key finding here is that arousal of failure or its expectation results in a marked increase of themes about figures who are the victims of a generally hostile press. That is, the story deals with someone who has been victimized by fortune, others, his own shortcomings, etc., and is now trying to escape or adapt to his condition. This scoring system, called Hostile Press (HosP), is being used in a program of research similar to that of Heckhausen. It is too early to tell whether the differences in the thematic content of the systems have revealed a cultural difference in failure-arousing cues. Apparently Heckhausen has not conducted a "shift" study to show that the failure conditions increase his FF scores, nor is it impossible that pictures can be found which elicit achievement failure themes from U.S. students. At any rate, current research with HosP has shown that *S*s high in the score prefer extremes of risk (Hancock & Teevan, 1964), display extremes of aspiration (Burdick, Birney, & Teevan, 1960), and show a loss of performance under pressure (Birney, Burdick, & Teevan, 1962).

In concluding this section on the programmatic efforts to research approach and avoidance achievement motivation, we must observe that despite the confusion of Fear of Failure measures there is no doubt that the general pattern of findings is congruent with the psychological literature on the subject and that current work is marked by sophisticated experimental design, refinement of procedure, and sensitivity to problems of measurement which will take us well beyond the demonstrational stage and into a period when we will learn much about the manner in which motives affect behavior. Atkinson's model has stimulated considerable research, and though it will undoubtedly experience modification, it points the way to the kind of careful hypothesis deduction which motivational research needs so badly.

THE n ACHIEVER

This final section of our review deals with the origins of n Ach, its cultural and social correlates, ego-processes thought to serve n Ach, and n Ach as a determinant of economic behaviors.

Development of n Ach

The capacity for arousal by achievement situations of achievement imagery must be learned at a very early age. Winterbottom (1953) studied the child-rearing techniques endorsed by mothers of boys whose teachers described their behavior and who were given the TAT. She found that boys who scored high on n Ach under both Relaxed and Aroused conditions received demands for independence of action at an earlier age than those scoring low; received rewards by display of physical affection; and did not differ from the lows in amount or nature of punishment received. Mothers rate these high n Ach sons as more skilled, and teachers see them as more motivated for success in school work, more independent, more popular, and more pleased with success. Mothers of high n Ach sons use fewer restrictions but impose them earlier. On a puzzle task the n Achiever less frequently asked for help, more often refused help that was offered, and less frequently accepted an invitation to rest. Finally, a content analysis of the stories suggested to Winterbottom that the n Achievers viewed achievement in a broad social context involving adults, competition, free from aggression and cheating, while those with low n Ach saw it in a specific and restricted sense.

Winterbottom's valuable start suggested that the social stratification basis of independence training should be investigated. Rosen's (1955) work cited earlier clearly revealed that secondary school sophomores displaying the most n Ach came from the middle class (Hollingshed Index). N Ach shows a positive correlation with academic average with social class partialled out, but not with aspiration to go to college. However, in this study, v Ach, i.e., self-ascribed achievement value, was associated with college aspiration. Douvan (1956) studied high school seniors and found that n Ach scores increased for working-class boys when a ten-dollar prize was offered but was uniformly high for middle-class boys under both monetary and achievement task instructions.

Rosen (1959) next cast a wider net and studied the appearance of n Ach in the TATs of sons of French-Canadian, Italian, Greek, Jewish, Negro, and White Protestant families, stratified by social class on Hollingshed's Index. He reports reliable differences between the groups for n Ach, for social class, and considerable support for Winterbottom's findings regarding the early beginnings of independence training as associated with the highest groups. The ordering of ethnic groupings was Greek, Jewish, Protestant, Italian, French-Canadian, and Negro, with both Negro and Catholic reliably below the others. Subsequently in 1962, Veroff, Feld, and Gurin reported a nationwide sample of religious information vs. n Ach and confirmed Rosen's basic findings. They also turned up a web of relationships between income, family size, and religious affiliation which suggests that the middle-aged Catholic with a high income and small family displayed more n Ach than other Catholics despite an emphasis on restrictive child-rearing practices. Strodtbeck (1958) compared a sample of boys, 14–17 (*N* is 24), matched for stratification from Jewish and Italian families, and found n Ach associated with academic achievement beyond aptitude prediction, with v Ach expressed by the father but not the mother or boy himself, and that v Ach was also associated with academic achievement.

These findings suggest the need to learn more about the actual family interaction surrounding independence training, and Rosen and D'Andrade (1959) have given us the best example yet of what must be done. They placed young boys (9–11) in achievement task situations in the home with the parents observing and being observed. First trial estimates by parents of what the boys could do were positively related to n Ach in their stories. Parents of high n Achievers selected more difficult tasks for the boys to do, and these boys performed best on the tasks and made the fewest requests for aid. The fathers of these boys set high standards but gave warm, nondirective help. The mothers also set high standards but were warmly demanding and urging without being specific in their demands. In this group the emphasis seemed to be on "achievement training" rather than independence training as Winterbottom had found with a younger group. Rosen (1962) conducted a similar study in Brazil. There he found the predominant family structure of male authoritarianism and maternal indulgence produces very little achievement motivation in young boys.

Argyle and Robinson (1962) administered a test battery of n Ach, Q-Ach (self-reported achievement behaviors), parental achievement demands, identification and general guilt reactions. One group of 59 male students yielded a test-retest reliability coefficient of +.44 after a one-year interval. Scorer agreement was low, and it is difficult to accept the administration of the tests during a school class period by a stranger as Relaxed, but the pattern of relationships suggests that n Ach is positively related to achievement demands, when identification is high, and to capacity for guilt. The n Ach–Q-Ach correlation is +.22, *P* .01.

Chance (1961) studied children in the first grade, and investigated the effects of independence training (as measured by Winterbottom's scale) on achievement with intellectual ability partialled out. She finds "that children whose mothers favor earlier demands for independence make poorer school progress relative to their intelligence level than children whose mothers favor later independence demands." She then suggests that there may be a distinction between instrumental act independence and emotional independence. However, this finding suggests that incipient n Ach in first-grade children may not be compatible with actual school achievement until the classroom has succeeded in making academic achievement instrumental to the satisfaction of n Ach.

In 1959 Feld reported once more on Winterbottom's sample of boys who were now 14–16. Retesting was possible for only 14 boys and 17 mothers of the original sample, so more were added to bring it up to the original number for the study of this age level. The n Ach measure and the TAQ were given the boys, and the mothers were again asked about achievement and independence. The test-retest correlation for n Ach was +.38 (*P* .10) for Winterbottom's Achievement condition scores, and zero order for those taken under the Relaxed condition. The placement of *S*s in the high and low n Ach groups across time showed 79 per cent agreement. The mothers' responses to the independence and achievement scales show negative correlation (−.39 and −.36 respectively) which implies a reversal of attitude toward these high school age sons. The TAQ scores proved to have negative relationships with early independence, −.75, and early low n Ach, −.63 and −.43 for the Relaxed and Achievement scores. In other words, adolescents who report anxiety in test situations are those who did not receive independence training at an early age and did not show n Ach at an early age. There is also some suggestion in the data that current maternal attitudes relate to the n Ach level of the boys when their earlier experience is partialled out. This study illustrates the type of longitudinal work that must be done to learn more about the genesis of n Ach.

Kagan and Moss (1959) scored standard TAT protocols for Achievement Thema, after McClelland's system, the protocols being given by boys and girls at ages 8–9, 11–12, and 14–16. They report very low levels of thema, but an increase with age, low positive stability over time, a generally positive relationship between n Ach and gain in IQ, and a relationship between n Ach and education of father for boys. Observing that parents of mentally retarded children do not stress early independence training, Jordan and deCharms (1959) predicted and found that these children have lower n Ach scores than their normal peers and seem quite free from overt fear of failure imagery if placed in special classes. They show that the lower scores are not due to low verbal fluency.

There emerges from these studies a sense of the origins of n Ach as rooted in early training for independence, subsequent harnessing of the dispositions so acquired for socially defined achievement situations, support of the n Ach by warm but demanding parental models, and considerable experience with emotional satisfaction in achievement situations. Certainly such a pattern does suggest that the n Achiever should be experienced in maximizing payoffs, relatively free from anxiety about failure, and therefore, efficient at those tasks he chooses to attempt.

Sex Differences

It was expected from the outset that important sex differences would appear in the achievement motive research. The basic validation studies used male populations, and the initial efforts by Veroff, Wilcox, and Atkinson (1950) to show increases in n Ach scores following the standard arousal procedures were unsuccessful with a population of secondary school females. A carefully designed study by Lesser, Krawitz, and Packard (1963), using college females, has revealed some of the complexities involving women. They varied instructions (Neutral vs. Achievement), pictures (male vs. female), and samples (first vs. fourth quartiles of academic average, matched for IQ and time in college). The instruction effect displayed an interaction with pictures such that the Achiever group increased in n Ach writing to female pictures but not males, while the non-Achievers increased on male pictures but not on female pictures. Clearly the locus of identification moderates the response to achievement situations.

Angelini (1955) studied Brazilian college women and found they did increase in n Ach under Achievement instructions and concludes that these highly selected females are more competitive than the U.S. college women.

French and Lesser (1964), suspecting the achievement relevance of the goals served by the task, designed a study of value orientation (intellectual vs. woman's role attitude scale), arousal condition (intellectual vs. woman's role), sex of stimulus figure, and college type (women's vs. coed), as they affected performance on the Neutral administration of the French Insight Test. A second session using carefully matched groups presented either the Scrambled-words test as the "best single index of intelligence we have," or the Social Skills test, "... a measure of your attainment of these skills...." They did find increases in n Ach "when arousal cues are related to goals achievement relevant for subjects but not otherwise." The strongest effects of motivation on performance were found using the female form of the Insight Test.

The pattern of findings emerging from these studies shows clearly that however similar the basic motivational dynamics may be for both sexes, the expression of those dynamics differs greatly according to the cues presented to the subjects. An earlier illustration of this was cited in McKeachie (1961).

Personality Processes

McClelland and Liberman (1953) had reported differential sensitivity of n Ach level to tachistoscopically flashed words related to success and failure. Moulton, Raphelson, Kristofferson, and Atkinson (1958) replicated the basic finding of positive relationship between n Ach and recognition of achievement words. Recognition of negative achievement terms was curvilinear in the original experiment and negatively related to n Ach in the Moulton study. These early experiments had no particular theoretical underpinning beyond testing the assumption that motivation may affect perception. Lately, more systematic efforts have been made. Wertheim and Mednick (1958) observed that children scoring "field dependent" on the Gottschalk embedded-figures test had parental relationships suggestive of low n Ach, and accordingly administered the TAT followed by the Field Independence Test to 42 college students of whom 31 were female. The entire sample yielded a —.40 relationship between n Ach score and field dependence. Honigfeld and Spigel (1960) suspected there might be sex differences and repeated the experiment with 15 males and 13 females, all college students. The women replicated the previous figure, —.42, but the men showed no relationship, the combined group correlation being —.24.

Similar processes were studied by Fisher (1961), who found that initial directional training of the movement of light under autokinetic conditions revealed that "subjects with low achievement scores manifest more right-directional movement than do high achievement subjects." Among females he found, in addition, that high n Ach accompanied more left-directional movement. The interpretation is interesting. All these *S*s were right-handed, and assuming more tonus on that side for immediate response, he suggests *S*s with high n Ach may be more future-oriented, more capable of foregoing immediate reward, and hence bring a lesser tonus for right-handed movement. We shall encounter the topic of delayed gratification subsequently.

The most systematic effort to research perceptual and aesthetic variables has been done by Knapp and his associates. Considering the possibility of n Ach as part of a syndrome, Knapp "speculate(s) that the future is already upon them while the past has not yet slipped away, the universe that confronts them is therefore teeming with opportunities for manipulation and achievement. If this interpretation is correct, we may tentatively propose a dynamic triad, relating 'parsimonious' time attitudes, achievement motivation, and asceticism of aesthetic taste which has historically found its manifestation in Puritanism." These speculations have led to a series of ingenious experiments. Using Scotch tartans which provide color differences while controlling for form, Knapp (1958) had 68 male college students express preference among a wide color range of plaids. As predicted, n Ach scores showed a positive relationship to preference for "blue" dominance, and a negative relationship to the "red." "We may now tentatively assert that the preference for somber bluish tartans and the dislike of red by individuals with high n Ach follows. For such persons require that their environment be 'soft' while they are 'hard'; they wish to exert their will effectively—to manipulate, not to be manipulated." Knapp and Garbutt (1958) next hypothesized "that persons with high n Ach would have an acute awareness of time as a medium in which achievement might be realized, that time would be deemed more than usually precious, and that time would therefore be viewed as moving rapidly." They created a list of time metaphors differing in their reference to swift movement ("a dashing waterfall"), and slow movement or stillness ("a quiet, motionless ocean"). Using 73 male college students they confirmed that *S*s high in n Ach preferred the swift movement metaphors to describe time. "Time, it appears to us, is conceived almost as a competitive force by the individual of high achievement motivation, a force which will deny him the joys of achievement and accomplishment unless carefully measured and cautiously controlled."

These two variables were combined in the next study by Green and Knapp (1959). Twenty-nine teachers, age 25–45, were required to estimate the time of appearance of a moving target passing behind a screen. *S*s expressing preference for somber plaids tended to anticipate the appearance of the target (r is $+.44$, P .05). Similarly, when asked to estimate the time since actual historical events, these *S*s showed a tendency to recall past events as nearer the present than they are ($+.42$, P .05). Heckhausen (1963) contrasts his HS and FF subjects on their sense of time as follows. HS *S*s "hold" in mind future tasks due at specific time intervals while FF are most mindful of those immediately due. HS is described as having large, futuristic time spans while FF are either very narrow or very large. HS sense time as a rapid movement toward a goal, or "forward-leading," while the FF prefer metaphors of goallessness.

The most recent experiment in this series used 73 college males matched on ability (Knapp & Green, 1960). The task was to estimate the length of four equal minutes while being subjected to a rather loud recording of Strauss' Blue Danube Waltz. The general tendency was to underestimate the intervals and increase each estimate until the fourth interval estimate actually approached the full minute. However, n Ach scores show a significant negative relationship to this increase. Two interpretations are offered, viz., that high n Ach is associated with resistance to distractibility and control of attention, or that high n Ach is a function of secondary ego control processes having the executive function of judgment and measurement of time. Knapp is currently extending these studies to test additional hypotheses concerning preferred modes of defense. One additional finding in support of Knapp's findings came when McClelland (1958) noted the colors children selected to perform a paper-and-pencil task and found that *S*s with high n Ach did choose colors from the blue-green portion of the spectrum.

Maddi and Berne (1964) tested for the effect of strong motivation on novelty of fantasy production and found no effect by n Ach or other motive scores.

Oddly enough, perhaps because of its psychometric characteristics, n Ach has not been the subject of many correlation studies with other well-known personality tests, and those reported do not appear promising (Cooper & Howell, 1961). An excellent example of the type of careful theorizing required for such studies is found in Becker (1960) who took the analysis of child-rearing patterns thought to contribute to manic-depressive dispositions, and linking them to the work on the origins of n Ach contrasted 24 remitted manic-depressives with 30 controls using n Ach, v Ach, F scale, and the Additions and X's-in-circles tasks used in experimental settings. Theorizing that achievement was valued as means of gaining approval, a series of hypotheses were framed describing the manic-depressive as a v Ach person who would not differ from the controls in n Ach or performance but who would describe himself as ambitious, believing in authoritarian ideology and traditional family roles and statuses. These hypotheses were confirmed. The effort of Cooper and Howell to contrast the three levels of n Ach on indices of neuroticism was not successful in its expectation that low n Ach implies neurotic disturbance.

It should be observed here that a blank area of research regarding n Ach exists if we turn to the individual case history. Schubert-Jäckel and Mehl (1962) encountered the expected difficulties of applying a measure with the reliability of n Ach to the study of individuals. They were able to replicate the basic arousal of imagery across *S*s, but individual analysis apparently did not confirm some of the relationships suggested by experimental analysis. The only case analysis reported by McClelland was that of Karl in *Personality,* 1951b. There is no question that a series of case studies using longitudinal and depth materials would add to our knowledge of n Ach, and McClelland has in preparation a follow-up study of the original sample of subjects used in the 1953 study.

What does the n Achiever think of himself? We have already seen he does not describe himself in v Ach terms, nor in the terms of Edwards PPS n Ach scale. Martire's (1956) early study using sensitivity to arousal of n Ach as his independent measure of "generalized" n Ach found the high n Achiever expressed a sense of wide discrepancy between his ideal and true self regarding various achievement-related traits, implying a striving toward a self not yet realized. Miller and Worchel (1956) test for the effects of n Ach and Self-Ideal discrepancy on performance under stress and found only the latter positively related to performance measures. Apparently persons at all levels of achievement motivation react to external demands for output in the same fashion.

Coopersmith (1960) combined self-esteem scores with teachers' ratings of behavior, self-esteem, and achievement. He tested the *S*s individually, failing them on half the tests, then gave the n Ach measure, following it with a measure of task recall, and finally choice of task to repeat. "Groups in which self-rated self-esteem was discrepant from behavior ratings tended to repeat failures; those in which the two measures agreed tended to repeat successes." It is the discrepant groups that are high in n Ach which showed a −.38 with repetition of successes. An interesting possibility here is that for some of these young children, fifth and sixth graders, their n Ach was appropriate to school tasks and was noted by the teacher but not themselves, while others may have gained confidence about themselves in situations not known to the teachers.

Cultural Effects on n Ach

McClelland was interested at the outset to learn whether the n Ach measure could generate sensible relationships among variables gathered from social and cultural indices. Kaltenbach and McClelland (1958) tested fifteen adult males nominated as "successful" in their life work, and subsequently rated as such by a large sample of peers. Positive relationships were found between n Ach and success-ranking and community service, but not for indices of income, occupation, education, etc. This means that n Achievers in various stations of life were none the less identifiable by behavior presumably associated with the presence of n Ach.

Crockett (1962) obtained n Ach scores from a nation-wide sample of over three hundred males. Using as his mobility index the discrepancy between the *S* and his father in socio-economic status, he found n Ach positively associated with upward mobility, as was n Aff, and established that the relationship held with education, age, and prestige of origin partialled out. Burnstein, Moulton, and Liberty (1963) find collateral support for the Kaltenbach-McClelland findings. They obtained n Ach scores from 116 male students and later had the *S*s give estimates of competence required for a job, prestige associated with the job, affect associated with having the occupation for the *S*, and v Ach as measured by combining the deCharms and Strodtbeck scales. The latter measure permits a pattern analysis of n Ach–v Ach, and the occupation items were converted into two sets of occupations yielding high prestige-low competence vs. low prestige-high competence, thus providing the independent and dependent variables. They found, as predicted, that the high n Ach–high v Ach group preferred the low prestige-high competence group while the low n Ach-low v Ach preferred the high prestige-low competence set. Obviously, both prestige and competence levels are incentives for occupational choice, and while the n Achiever is not averse to prestige, he will, if forced to make a choice, choose the job with the greatest demand for competence.

We have already cited findings relating to social class differences. Other studies have focused on processes within classes or cultures. Mischel (1961) tested 112 Trinidadian Negro children (68 M, 44 F), in the age group 11–14, and drawn from the lower middle and lower strata of society. Following the TAT, an aspiration question, a measure of acquiescence, and the Social Responsibility Scale, the *S*s were given their choice of a ten-cent candy bar (Immediate Reinforcement) or a promise of a 25-cent candy bar one week later (Delayed Reinforcement). He found n Ach positively related to preference for DelR and occupational responses to the open-ended aspiration measure.

Bradburn (1963) compared Turkish and American junior executives, classified into high and low father dominance, and found n Ach negatively associated with dominance as well as a much higher level of n Ach for the Americans. Kerckhoff (1959) also reported higher n Ach scores for white grade school children, living close to a Chippewa reservation, as opposed to the Indian children, with increased n Ach for those Indian children identifying most closely with the "white" society.

Merbaum (1962) tested white and Negro children in the elementary grades of a rural school system. Both groups came from lower societal strata, and they were tested by *E*s of the same race under a Neutral administration. The n Ach scores for the white children exceeded those of the Negroes with the difference increasing regularly with age. Among Negroes the girls had higher n Ach scores than the boys. Score differences were least for school scenes and greatest for neutral scenes.

Nuttal (1964) included two TAT pictures especially devised for the study in an extensive survey battery used with 196 Negro men and women drawn from a Negro district in Boston. There were marked differences in patterns of response for persons reared in the South as contrasted with the North or West, as well as sex differences. The summary states, "Positive r's between need for Achievement (n Ach) and occupational status, information, and seeing white as larger on the irradiation perceptual illusion were found. A negative r existed between n Ach and authoritarian child training attitudes. Father absence was linked to low n Ach. High n Ach northern men

(NM) tend to be less religious, more militant, better educated, have higher occupational status, and feel more victimized than low n Ach NM. High n Ach southern men (SM) have higher incomes, are more religious, deny feeling victimized by discrimination, repress their hostility, and are less educated than low n Ach SM. High n Ach women tend to join protest groups. High n Ach southern women (SW) express their own hostility and accept male violence while high n Ach northern women do not. No relation was found between n Ach and somatotype."

The institutional promotion of n Ach by the white rural middle class was studied by Straus and Houghton (1960) who scored editorials of the National 4-H Club News from 1924 to 1958. Compared to n Aff and Cooperation, n Ach dominates the editorials but they report a regression line of —.36, *P* .01, for n Ach through time, indicating a steady drop in this preoccupation.

The use of n Ach scores gathered from cultures beyond the one on which the validating studies were performed raises numerous issues. One might argue that the mere appearance of the achievement imagery does not assure it will show similar patterns of sensitivity to arousal, or of correlation. In *The Achieving Society,* whose central thesis appears in summary form in a paper delivered at the International Congress of Applied Psychology (1961c), McClelland marshals numerous data to satisfy both assumptions. Angelini (1955) did show the shift effects with Brazilian students. Lindzey (1961) has summarized the many questions raised by cross-cultural applications of projective methodology.

But McClelland's basic strategy is to take n Ach at face value, arguing that concern for competition with internalized standards of excellence must grow from a limited constellation of child-rearing practices and must culminate in reasonably clear sensitivity to cues, preferences for work conditions, and styles of performance. Accordingly he has set out to develop those criteria having meaning cross-culturally which can then be tested for relationships to n Ach, as it is found around the world. It is not possible to review *The Achieving Society* in this space, beyond saying that the book points toward the kind of research that must be done to cast a particular motivation dimension of behavior into its full cultural setting. The n Achiever emerges as one who desires to take personal responsibility for decisions where the risks are moderate and results of one's actions can be clearly known. Such a syndrome is found repeatedly in business and governmental situations of responsibility and seems to be the psychological essence of the term entrepreneur.[5]

Meyer and Walker (1961) contrasted a matched group of managers and specialists regarding attitudes and values toward performance appraisal and salary increase plans. In general, n Ach does not discriminate between the groups, but expressed preference for risk shows that those emphasizing moderate risks among managers show a preference for merit plans based on personal contributions, while those doing so among the specialists emphasize experience and rated performance. So we have n Achiever behavior without the imagery—suggesting the possibility of further developmental studies of n Ach throughout the career period.

Moving beyond the individual, McClelland also attempts to use n Ach as measured in cultural documents, especially those used in child-rearing, as a predictor to economic indices of national growth or decline. At this point the possibility of applied research emerges, namely, programs to indoctrinate or teach n Ach may be attempted in an effort to effect some current index of national achievement.

Burris (1958) demonstrated that counseling, focusing on achievement behaviors similar to the n Ach score categories, did produce an increase in n Ach scores over an

[5] For a comparison of Adlerian principles of achievement behavior to those emerging in n Ach research, see Angers (1960).

eight-week period marked by weekly 40-minute sessions of counseling. The *S*s were matched on ability and drawn from a self-improvement course devoted to reading and study skills. The counseling did not produce group differences in improvement in this course, but the over-all grade averages of the experimental counselees did increase.

The scope of the research programs involving studies of the achievement motive should now be apparent. There is nothing about these developments peculiar to the study of n Ach, there being no reason why similar programs could not be carried out for other dimensions or complexes of personality. Perhaps what is remarkable, in this cornucopian age of research, is that the study of n Ach has been programmatically pursued.

REFERENCES

Alpert, R., & Haber, R. N. Anxiety in academic achievement situations. *J. abnorm. soc. Psychol.*, 1960, 61, 207–215.

Angelini, A. L. Un nuovo methodo para avalier a motivacao humana. *Psicologia Educational*, 1955, #6.

Angers, W. P. Achievement motivation: an Adlerian approach. *Psychol. Rec.*, 1960, 10, 179–186.

Anderson, R. C. Failure imagery in the fantasy of eighth graders as a function of three conditions of induced arousal. *J. educ. Psychol.*, 1962, 53, 293–298.

Argyle, M., & Robinson, P. Two origins of achievement motivation. *Brit. J. soc. clin. Psychol.*, 1962, 1(2), 107–120.

Asch, S. E. Effects of group pressure upon the modification and distortion of judgments. In G. E. Swanson, T. M. Newcomb, & E. L. Hartley (Eds.), *Readings in social psychology*. New York: Holt, 1952.

Atkinson, J. W. Studies in projective measurement of achievement motivation. Unpublished doctoral dissertation, Univer. of Michigan, 1950. Cited in D. C. McClelland *et al.*, *The achievement motive*. New York: Appleton-Century-Crofts, 1953. Pp. 223 ff.

Atkinson, J. W. The achievement motive and recall of interrupted and completed tasks. *J. exp. Psychol.*, 1953, 46, 381–390.

Atkinson, J. W. Motivational determinants of risk-taking behavior. *Psychol. Rev.*, 1957, 64, 359–372.

Atkinson, J. W. *Motives in fantasy, action, and society*. Princeton, N.J.: Van Nostrand, 1958. (a)

Atkinson, J. W. Thematic apperceptive measurement of motives within the context of a theory of motivation. In J. W. Atkinson (Ed.), *Motives in fantasy, action, and society*. Princeton, N.J.: Van Nostrand, 1958. (b)

Atkinson, J. W. Towards experimental analysis of human motivation in terms of motives, expectancies, and incentives. In J. W. Atkinson (Ed.), *Motives in fantasy, action, and society*. Princeton, N.J.: Van Nostrand, 1958. (c)

Atkinson, J. W. Personality dynamics. In P. R. Farnsworth (Ed.), *Annual Review of Psychology*, 1960, 11, 255–290.

Atkinson, J. W., Bastian, J., Earl, R., & Litwin, G. H. The achievement motive, goal setting, and probability preferences. *J. abnorm. soc. Psychol.*, 1960, 60, 27–36.

Atkinson, J. W., & Feather, N. T. (Eds.) *A theory of achievement motivation*. New York: J. Wiley, 1966.

Atkinson, J. W., & Litwin, G. H. Achievement motive and test anxiety conceived as motive to approach success and motive to avoid failure. *J. abnorm. soc. Psychol.*, 1960, 60, 52–63.

Atkinson, J. W., & Raphelson, A. C. Individual differences in motivation and behavior in particular situations. *J. Pers.*, 1956, 24, 349–363.

Atkinson, J. W., & Reitman, W. R. Performance as a function of motive strength and expectancy of goal-attainment. *J. abnorm. soc. Psychol.*, 1956, 53, 361–366.

Becker, J. Achievement related characteristics of manic depressives. *J. abnorm. soc. Psychol.*, 1960, 60, 334–339.

Bendig, A. W. A preliminary factor analytic investigation of need achievement items. *J. psychol. Stud.*, 1959, 11, 32–38. (a)

Bendig, A. W. Comparative validity of objective and projective measures of need achievement in predicting students' achievement in introductory psychology. *J. gen. Psychol.*, 1959, 60, 237–243. (b)

Berkun, M. M., & Burdick, H. A. Effect of knowledge of test results on subsequent test performance as a joint function of need achievement and test anxiety. Unpublished paper presented at Amer. Psychol. Ass., August, 1963.

Birney, R. C. Thematic content and the cue characteristics of pictures. In J. W. Atkinson (Ed.), *Motives in fantasy, action, and society*. Princeton, N.J.: Van Nostrand, 1958. Pp. 630–643. (a)

Birney, R. C. The achievement motive and task performance: A replication. *J. abnorm. soc. Psychol.,* 1958, 56, 133–135. (b)

Birney, R. C. The reliability of the achievement motive. *J. abnorm. soc. Psychol.,* 1959, 58, 266–267.

Birney, R. C., Burdick, H., & Teevan, R. Analysis of TAT stories for hostile press thema. Paper read at East. Psychol. Ass., April, 1961.

Birney, R. C., Burdick, H., & Teevan, R. The effects of failure on fantasy. Paper read at Amer. Psychol. Ass., Sept., 1962.

Bradburn, N. N achievement and father dominance in Turkey. *J. abnorm. soc. Psychol.,* 1963, 67, 464–468.

Brody, N. N achievement, test anxiety, and subjective probability of success in risk taking behavior. *J. abnorm. soc. Psychol.,* 1963, 66, 413–418.

Broverman, D. M., Jordan, E. J., & Phillips, Leslie. Achievement motivation in fantasy and behavior. *J. abnorm. soc. Psychol.,* 1960, 60, 374–378.

Brown, J. S. Problems presented by the concept of acquired drives. In J. S. Brown *et al., Current theory and research in motivation: A symposium*. Lincoln: Univer. of Nebraska Press, 1953. Pp. 1–21.

Burdick, H., Birney, R. C., & Teevan, R. Motive correlates of level of aspiration strategies. Paper presented at East. Psychol. Ass., April, 1960.

Burdick, H. A. Three experiments in conformity. Paper presented at Amer. Psychol. Ass., April, 1959.

Burdick, H. A. Need for achievement and schedules of variable reinforcement. *J. abnorm. soc. Psychol.,* 1964, 3, 302–306.

Burnstein, E. Fear of failure, achievement motivation, and aspiring to prestigeful occupations. *J. abnorm. soc. Psychol.,* 1963, 2, 189–193.

Burnstein, E., Moulton, R., & Liberty, P., Jr. Prestige vs. excellence as determinants of role attractiveness. *Amer. sociol. Rev.,* 1963, 28, 212–219.

Burris, R. W. The effect of counselling on achievement motivation. Unpublished doctoral dissertation, Indiana Univer., 1958.

Caron, A. J. Curiosity, achievement, and avoidant motivation as determinants of epistemic behavior. *J. abnorm. soc. Psychol.,* 1963, 67, 535–549.

Chance, June E. Independence training and first graders' achievement. *J. consult. Psychol.,* 1961, 25, 149–154.

Clark, R. A., & McClelland, D. C. A factor analytic integration of imaginative performance and case study measures of the need for achievement. In D. C. McClelland *et al., The achievement motive*. New York: Appleton-Century-Crofts, 1953. Pp. 227–229.

Clark, R. A., Teevan, R., & Ricciuti, H. N. Hope of success and fear of failure as aspects of need for achievement. *J. abnorm. soc. Psychol.,* 1956, 53, 182–186.

Cole, D., Jacobs, S., & Zubok, B. The relation of achievement imagery scores to academic performance. *J. abnorm. soc. Psychol.,* 1962, 65, 208–211.

Cooper, Leslie M., & Howell, R. J. A reformulation of "fear of failure" and "hope of success" concepts as measured by McClelland's need achievement test. *J. soc. Psychol.,* 1961, 53, 81–85.

Coopersmith, S. Self-esteem and need achievement as determinants of selective recall and repetition. *J. abnorm. soc. Psychol.,* 1960, 60, 310–317.

Crockett, H. J., Jr. The achievement motive and differential occupational mobility in the United States. *Amer. Soc. Rev.,* 1962, 27, 191–204.

deCharms, R. A self-scoring projective measure of achievement and affiliation motivation. *J. consult. Psychol.,* 1958, 22, 172.

deCharms, R., Morrison, H. W., Reitman, W., & McClelland, D. C. Behavioral correlates of directly and indirectly measured achievement motivation. In D. C. McClelland (Ed.), *Studies in motivation*. New York: Appleton-Century-Crofts, 1955. Pp. 414–423.

Diggory, J. C., & Morlock, H., Jr. Level of aspiration and performance in relation to goal, n achievement and information about performance. Unpublished paper presented at East. Psychol. Ass., April, 1961.

Douvan, Elizabeth. Social status and success strivings. In J. W. Atkinson (Ed.), *Motives in fantasy, action, and society*. Princeton, N.J.: Van Nostrand, 1958. Pp. 509–517. Reprinted from *J. abnorm. soc. Psychol.*, 1956, 52, 219–223.

Edwards, A. L. *Edwards Personal Preference Schedule*. New York: Psychol. Corp., 1954.

Feather, N. T. Subjective probability and decision under uncertainty. *Psychol. Rev.*, 1959, 66, 150–164.

Feather, N. T. The relationship of persistence at a task to expectation of success and achievement-related motives. *J. abnorm. soc. Psychol.*, 1961, 63, 552–561.

Feather, N. T. The relationship of expectation of success to reported probability, task structure, and achievement-related motivation. *J. abnorm. soc. Psychol.*, 1963, 66, 231–238.

Feld, Sheila. Studies in the origins of achievement strivings. Unpublished doctoral dissertation, Univer. of Michigan, 1959.

Fisher, S. Achievement themes and directionality of autokinetic movement. *J. abnorm. soc. Psychol.*, 1961, 63, 64–68.

French, Elizabeth G. Some characteristics of achievement motivation. *J. exp. Psychol.*, 1955, 50, 232–236.

French, Elizabeth G. Development of a measure of complex motivation. In J. W. Atkinson (Ed.), *Motives in fantasy, action, and society*. Princeton, N.J.: Van Nostrand, 1958.

French, Elizabeth G., & Lesser, G. D. Some characteristics of the achievement motive in women. *J. abnorm. soc. Psychol.*, 1964, 68, 119–128.

French, Elizabeth G., & Thomas, F. H. The relation of achievement motivation to problem-solving effectiveness. *J. abnorm. soc. Psychol.*, 1958, 56, 45–48.

Green, H., & Knapp, R. H. Time judgment, aesthetic preference, and need for achievement. *J. abnorm. soc. Psychol.*, 1959, 58, 140–141.

Haber, R. N. The prediction of achievement behavior by an interaction of achievement motivation and achievement stress. Unpublished doctoral dissertation, Stanford Univer., 1957.

Haber, R. N., & Alpert, R. The role of situation and picture cues in projective measurement of the achievement motive. In J. W. Atkinson (Ed.), *Motives in fantasy, action, and society*. Princeton, N.J.: Van Nostrand, 1958. Pp. 644–663.

Hancock, J. G., & Teevan, R. Fear of failure and risk taking behavior. *J. Pers.*, 1964, 32, 200–209.

Heckhausen, H. *Hoffnung und Furcht in der Leistungsmotivation*. Meisenheim, Germany: Anton Hain, 1963.

Himmelstein, P., Eschenbach, A. E., & Carp, A. Interrelationships among three measures of need achievement. *J. consult. Psychol.*, 1958, 22, 451–452.

Himmelstein, P., & Kimbrough, W. W. Reliability of French's "Test of Insight." *Educ. psychol. Measmt*, 1960, 20, 737–741.

Honigfeld, G., & Spigel, I. M. Achievement motivation and field independence. *J. consult. Psychol.*, 1960, 24, 550–551.

Isaacson, R. I. Relation between n achievement, test anxiety, and curricular choices. *J. abnorm. soc. Psychol.*, 1964, 68, 447–452.

Jacobs, B., Jr. A method for investigating the cue characteristics of pictures. In J. W. Atkinson (Ed.), *Motives in fantasy, action, and society*. Princeton, N.J.: Van Nostrand, 1958. Pp. 617–629.

Jordan, T. E., & deCharms, R. The achievement motive in normal and mentally retarded children. *Amer. J. ment. Defic.*, 1959, 64, 457–466.

Kagan, J., & Moss, H. A. Stability and validity of achievement fantasy. *J. abnorm. soc. Psychol.*, 1959, 58, 357–364.

Kaltenbach, J. E., & McClelland, D. C. Achievement and social status in three small communities. In D. C. McClelland *et al.*, *Talent and Society*. Princeton, N.J.: Van Nostrand, 1958. Pp. 112–123.

Kausler, D. R. Aspiration level as a determinant of performance. *J. Pers.*, 1959, 27, 346–351.

Kausler, D. R., & Trapp, E. P. Relationship between achievement motivation scores and manifest anxiety. *J. consult. Psychol.*, 1958, 22, 448–450.

Kerckhoff, A. C. Anomie and achievement motivation. *Social Forces*, 1959, 37, 196–202.

Klinger, E. Eliciting achievement fantasy with motion picture stimuli. Paper read at Midwest. Psychol. Ass., 1963.

Knapp, R. H. N Achievement and aesthetic preference. In J. W. Atkinson (Ed.), *Motives in fantasy, action, and society*. Princeton, N.J.: Van Nostrand, 1958. Pp. 367–372.

Knapp, R. H., & Garbutt, J. T. Time imagery and the achievement motive. *J. Pers.,* 1958, 26, 426–434.

Knapp, R. H., & Green, H. B. The judgment of music-filled intervals and n achievement. *J. soc. Psychol.,* 1961, 54, 263–267.

Krumboltz, J. D., & Farquhar, W. W. Reliability and validity of n achievement. *J. consult. Psychol.,* 1957, 21, 226–231.

Lazarus, R. S., Baker, R. W., Broverman, D. M., & Mayer, J. Personality and psychological stress. *J. Pers.,* 1957, 25, 559–577.

Lesser, G. S., Krawitz, Rhoda N., & Packard, Rita. Experimental arousal of achievement motivation in adolescent girls. *J. abnorm. soc. Psychol.,* 1963, 66, 59–66.

Lindzey, G. *Projective techniques and cross-cultural research.* New York: Appleton-Century-Crofts, 1961.

Lindzey, G., & Heinemann, Shirley H. Thematic apperception test: Individual and group administration. *J. Pers.,* 1955, 24, 34–55.

Littig, L. W., & Yeracaris, C. A. Academic achievement correlates of achievement and affiliation motivations. *J. Psychol.,* 1963, 55, 115–119.

Liverant, S., & Odell, Miriam. Conformity and level of aspiration behavior.

Lowell, E. L. The effect of need for achievement on learning and speed of performance. *J. Psychol.,* 1952, 33, 31–40.

Lowell, E. L. A methodological study of projectively measured achievement motivation. Unpublished master's thesis, Wesleyan Univer., 1950. In D. C. McClelland *et al., The achievement motive.* New York: Appleton-Century-Crofts, 1953. Pp. 229–244.

McClelland, D. C. Measuring motivation in phantasy: the achievement motive. In H. Guetzkow (Ed.), *Groups, leadership, and men.* Pittsburgh: Carnegie Press, 1951. Pp. 191–205. (a)

McClelland, D. C. *Personality.* New York: Wm. Sloane Assoc., 1951. (b)

McClelland, D. C. Some consequences of achievement motivation. *Nebraska symposium on motivation.* Lincoln: Univer. of Nebraska Press, 1955. Pp. 41–72.

McClelland, D. C. Methods of measuring human motivation. In J. W. Atkinson (Ed.), *Motives in fantasy, action, and society.* Princeton, N.J.: Van Nostrand, 1958. (a) Pp. 7–42.

McClelland, D. C. Risk taking in children with high and low need for achievement. In J. W. Atkinson (Ed.), *Motives in fantasy, action, and society.* Princeton, N.J.: Van Nostrand, 1958. (b) Pp. 306–321.

McClelland, D. C. *The achieving society.* Princeton, N.J.: Van Nostrand, 1961. (a)

McClelland, D. C. Encouraging excellence. *Daedalus,* 1961, 90, 711–724. (b)

McClelland, D. C. The achievement motive in economic growth. *Proceedings of the 14th int. Congr. of applied Psychol.,* Copenhagen, 1961. (c)

McClelland, D. C. The psychodynamics of creative physical scientists. In H. E. Gruber, G. Terrell, & M. Wertheimer (Eds.), *Contemporary approaches to creative thinking.* New York: Atherton Press, 1962. Pp. 141–174.

McClelland, D. C., Atkinson, J. W., Clark, R. A., & Lowell, E. L. *The achievement motive.* New York: Appleton-Century-Crofts, 1953.

McClelland, D. C., & Liberman, M. The effect of need for achievement on recognition of need related words. Cited in D. C. McClelland *et al., The achievement motive.* New York: Appleton-Century-Crofts, 1953. Pp. 259–260.

McKeachie, W. J. Motivation, teaching, methods and college learning. *Nebraska symposium on motivation.* Lincoln: Univer. of Nebraska Press, 1961. Pp. 111–141.

Maddi, S. R., & Berne, Naomi. Novelty of productions and desire for novelty as active and passive forms of the need for variety. *J. Pers.,* 1964, 32, 270–277.

Maddi, S. R., Charles, A. M., Maddi, Dorothy-Anne, & Smith, Adrienne J. Effects of monotony and novelty on imaginative productions. *J. Pers.,* 1962, 30, 513–527.

Mahone, C. H. Fear of failure and unrealistic vocational aspiration. *J. abnorm. soc. Psychol.,* 1960, 60, 253–261.

Marlowe, D. Relationships among direct and indirect measures of the achievement motive and overt behavior. *J. consult. Psychol.,* 1959, 23, 329–332.

Martire, J. G. Relationships between the self-concept and differences in the strength and generality of achievement motivation. *J. Pers.,* 1956, 24, 364–375.

Melikian, L. H. The relationship between Edwards' and McClelland's measures of achievement motivation. *J. consult. Psychol.,* 1958, 22, 296–298.

Merbaum, Ann D. Need for achievement in Negro and white children. Unpublished doctoral dissertation, Univer. of North Carolina, 1962.

Meyer, H. H., & Walker, W. B. Need for achievement and risk preferences as they relate to attitudes toward reward systems and performance appraisal in an industrial setting. *J. appl. Psychol.,* 1961, 45, 251–256.

Miller, K. S., & Worchel, P. The effects of need achievement and self-ideal discrepancy on performance under stress. *J. Pers.,* 1956, 25, 176–190.

Mischel, W. Delay of gratification, need for achievement, and acquiescence in another culture. *J. abnorm. soc. Psychol.,* 1961, 62, 543–552.

Mitchell, J. W., Jr. An analysis of the factorial dimensions of the achievement motivation construct. *J. educ. Psychol.,* 1961, 52, 179–187.

Morgan, H. H. An analysis of certain structured and unstructured test results of achieving and non-achieving high ability college students. Unpublished doctoral dissertation, Univer. of Minnesota, 1951.

Morgan, H. H. Measuring achievement motivation with "picture interpretation." *J. consult. Psychol.,* 1953, 17, 289–292.

Moulton, R. W. Relationship of need for achievement to perceptual sensitivity under two degrees of motive arousal. Unpublished honors thesis, Univer. of Michigan, 1952.

Moulton, R. W. Notes for a projective measure of fear of failure. In J. W. Atkinson (Ed.), *Motives in fantasy, action, and society*. Princeton, N.J.: Van Nostrand, 1958. P. 571.

Moulton, R. W., Raphelson, A. C., Kristofferson, A. B., & Atkinson, J. W. The achievement motive and perceptual sensitivity under two conditions of motive-arousal. In J. W. Atkinson (Ed.), *Motives in fantasy, action, and society*. Princeton, N.J.: Van Nostrand, 1958. Pp. 350–359.

Murray, H. A. *Explorations in personality*. New York: Oxford Univer. Press, 1938.

Murstein, B. I., & Collier, H. L. The role of the TAT in the measurement of achievement as a function of expectancy. *J. proj. Tech.,* 1962, 26, 96–101.

Nuttall, R. L. Some correlates of high need for achievement among urban northern Negroes. *J. abnorm. soc. Psychol.,* 1964, 68, 593–600.

Orne, M. T. On the social psychology of the psychological experiment: with particular reference to demand characteristics and their implications. *Amer. Psychologist,* 1962, 17, 776–783.

Parish, J., & Rethlingershafer, D. A study of the need to achieve in college achievers and non-achievers. *J. gen. Psychol.,* 1954, 50, 209–226.

Peak, Helen. The effects of aroused motivation on attitudes. *J. abnorm. soc. Psychol.,* 1960, 60, 463–468.

Pottharst, Barbara C. The achievement motive and level of aspiration after experimentally induced success and failure. Unpublished doctoral dissertation, Univer. of Michigan, 1955.

Raphelson, A. C. The relationships among imaginative direct verbal and physiological measures of anxiety in an achievement situation. *J. abnorm. soc. Psychol.,* 1957, 54, 13–18.

Raphelson, A. C., & Moulton, R. W. The relationship between imaginative and direct verbal measures of test anxiety under two conditions of uncertainty. *J. Pers.,* 1958, 26, 556–567.

Reitman, E. E., & Williams, C. D. Relationships between hope of success and fear of failure, anxiety, and need for achievement. *J. abnorm. soc. Psychol.,* 1961, 62, 465–467.

Reitman, W. R. Selective recall of meaningful material as a function of achievement motivation. Unpublished master's thesis, Wesleyan Univer., 1954.

Reitman, W. R. Need, achievement, fear of failure, and selective recall. *J. abnorm. soc. Psychol.,* 1961, 62, 42–44.

Reitman, W. R., & Atkinson, J. W. Some methodological problems in the use of thematic apperceptive measures of human motives. In J. W. Atkinson (Ed.), *Motives in fantasy, action, and society*. Princeton, N.J.: Van Nostrand, 1958. Pp. 664–683.

Ricciuti, H. N. *The prediction of academic grades with a projective test of achievement motivation: I. Initial validation studies.* Princeton, N.J.: Educ. Testing Serv., 1954.

Ricciuti, H. N., & Clark, R. A. *A comparison of need achievement stories written by experimentally "relaxed" and "achievement-*

oriented" subjects: Effects obtained with new pictures and revised scoring categories. Princeton, N.J.: Educ. Testing Serv., 1954.

Ricciuti, H. N., & Sadacca, R. *The prediction of academic grades with a projective test of achievement motivation: II. Cross-validation at the high school level.* Princeton, N.J.: Educ. Testing Serv., 1955.

Ricciuti, H. N., & Schultz, D. G. *Level of aspiration measures and self-estimates of personality in relation to achievement motivation.* Princeton, N.J.: Educ. Testing Serv., 1958.

Roe, Anne. *The making of a scientist.* New York: Dodd, Mead, 1953.

Rosen, B. C. The achievement syndrome. *Amer. sociol. Rev.,* 1956, 21, 203–211.

Rosen, B. C. Race, ethnicity, and the achievement syndrome. *Amer. sociol. Rev.,* 1959, 24, 47–60.

Rosen, B. C. Socialization and achievement motivation in Brazil. *Amer. sociol. Rev.,* 1962, 27, 612–624.

Rosen, B. C., & D'Andrade, R. The psychosocial origins of achievement motivation. *Sociometry,* 1959, 22, 185–218.

Rosenthal, R. Experimenter attributes as determinants of subjects' responses. *J. proj. Tech.,* 1963, 27, 324–331.

Sampson, E. E. Achievement in conflict. *J. Pers.,* 1963, 31, 510–516.

Sarason, I. G. Empirical findings and theoretical problems in the use of anxiety scales. *Psychol. Bull.,* 1960, 57, 403–415.

Schubert-Jäckel, G., and Mehl, J. Assessment of achievement motivation. *Z. für Psychol.,* 1962, 166, 220–224.

Smith, C. P. Relationships between achievement-related motives and intelligence, performance level, and persistence. *J. abnorm. soc. Psychol.,* 1964, 68, 523–532.

Straus, M. A., & Houghton, L. W. Achievement, affiliation, and co-operation values as clues to trends in American rural society, 1924–1958. *Rural Sociol.,* 1960, 25, 394–403.

Strodtbeck, F. Family interaction, values and achievement. In D. C. McClelland *et al., Talent and society.* New York: Appleton-Century-Crofts, 1958. Pp. 135–194.

Tedeschi, J. W., & Kian, M. Cross-cultural study of the TAT assessment for achievement motivation: Americans and Persians. *J. soc. Psychol.,* 1962, 58, 227–234.

Turek, E. C., & Howell, R. J. The effect of variable success and failure situations on the intensity of need for achievement. *J. soc. Psychol.,* 1959, 49, 267–273.

Veroff, J. Development and validation of a projective measure of power motivation. *J. abnorm. soc. Psychol.,* 1957, 54, 1–8.

Veroff, J. Thematic apperception in a nationwide sample survey. In J. Kagan (Ed.), *Contemporary issues in thematic apperceptive methods.* Springfield, Ill.: Charles C Thomas, 1961. Pp. 83–118.

Veroff, J., Atkinson, J. W., Feld, Sheila, & Gurin, G. The use of thematic apperception to assess motivation in a nationwide interview study. *Psychol. Monogr.,* No. 499, 1960.

Veroff, J., Feld, Sheila, & Gurin, G. Achievement motivation and religious background. *Amer. sociol. Rev.,* 1962, 27, 205–217.

Veroff, J., Wilcox, Sue, & Atkinson, J. W. The achievement motive in high school and college age women. *J. abnorm. soc. Psychol.,* 1953, 48, 108–109.

Vogel, W., Baker, R. W., & Lazarus, R. S. The role of motivation in psychological stress. *J. abnorm. soc. Psychol.,* 1958, 56, 105–112.

Walker, E. L., & Heyns, R. W. *The anatomy for conformity.* Englewood Cliffs, N.J.: Prentice-Hall, 1962.

Wendt, H. W. Motivation, effort and performance. In D. C. McClelland (Ed.), *Studies in motivation.* New York: Appleton-Century-Crofts, 1955. Pp. 448–459.

Wertheim, J., & Mednick, S. A. The achievement motive and field independence. *J. consult. Psychol.,* 1958, 22, 38.

Winterbottom, Marian R. The relation of childhood training in independence to achievement motivation. Unpublished doctoral dissertation, Univer. of Michigan, 1953. In J. W. Atkinson (Ed.), *Motives in fantasy, action, and society.* Princeton, N.J.: Van Nostrand, 1958. Pp. 453–478.

CHAPTER 15 Leadership

EDWIN P. HOLLANDER AND JAMES W. JULIAN
State University of New York at Buffalo

While Cowley in 1928 could accurately capture the dominant theme of an era in saying that "the approach to the study of leadership has usually been and perhaps must always be through the study of traits" (p. 144), this venerable view has been widely supplanted by an emphasis upon the situational determinants of leadership and leader-follower interactions. Accordingly, the study of the personality characteristics of leaders engages much less attention today than was historically the case. As we write, in the mid-1960s, a concern for situational demands has prevailed over the older emphasis on leader attributes.

To our view, neither emphasis at the extreme proves fruitful in understanding influence processes represented in leader-follower relations. Our inclination is to look upon research embodying both of these concerns as more productive of an understanding of leadership phenomena. That there is a case to be made for this interrelated study we hope will become clear from the kinds of findings which we provide here. Our selective review is not intended to be encyclopedic but rather representative of some research which has investigated leader attributes and especially the interplay of personality and situational factors in leadership. We preface this review by a definitional statement concerning leadership which serves as a guide to our focus here.

A CURRENT CONCEPTION OF LEADERSHIP

Leadership in the broadest sense implies the presence of a particular influence relationship between two or more persons. In this view it is conceived as merely one representation of the more general phenomenon of interpersonal influence. The essence of the leader-follower relationship resides in a mutual dependence among persons involved in the pursuit of common goals. To specify this leader influence relationship we must simultaneously consider the interaction of three important determinants: (a) the "leader," with his personality, perceptions, and resources relevant to goal attainment; (b) the "followers," with their personalities, perceptions, and relevant resources; and (c) the situational context within which these variables function. To ignore entirely any of these factors destroys the inherently dyadic character of the phenomenon. As Gibb (1947) proposed: "Leadership is a concept applied to the personality-environment relation ..." (p. 267). A careful concern for human personality factors is clearly bound to the job of unraveling the complex interpersonal influence process.

Social influence, however, is not equivalent to leadership. Although a mutual dependence among group members certainly implies "influence" in the sense of altered response probabilities as a function of "others," this is not an exclusive property of leadership. Rather, leader influence suggests a positive contribution toward the attainment of group goals. "Leadership [is] the process of influencing the activities of an organized group toward goal setting and goal achievement" (Stogdill, 1950, p. 4). But when the individual *acts,* he necessarily *interacts* or *transacts* with elements of his environment (cf., e.g., Sells, 1963). He both gives something and gets something. Influence is in this very real sense two directional. This observation is quite pointed when placed in the context of the husband who comments: "I make all the decisions in my family, but naturally, I try to keep my wife happy."

To some degree therefore there is an error in speaking of an influence agent and an influence recipient as if distinct from one another. But how then are we to identify the leader? One answer is to consider the leader as the individual who is perceived by the interacting parties to yield the more valued resources needed for the attainment of a goal. Hence, to discuss "the leader" we must ask questions such as "of whom?" and "relative to what goals?" This kind of characterization can be readily translated into the current theoretical statements of Homans (1961), Hollander (1964), and others.

RECENT RESEARCH

The history of concern with leadership extends far back into philosophical thought. In the most widespread view, the leader was taken to be someone possessed of qualities which would make him achieve dominance in any situation. Such an idea finds its roots in the Aristotelian observation: "From the hour of their birth some (men) are marked out for subjection, and others for command" (Aristotle, *Politics,* i, 5).

The more recent situational trend of thinking and investigation regarding leadership phenomena was largely instigated by dissatisfactions felt with this traditional "trait" approach. One landmark in establishing this decisive emphasis upon the situation is found in the literature survey by Stogdill (1948) which revealed the disordered state of the quest for broad traits of leadership. Other distinctions also came along with this trend, including the recognition that some people are appointed as leaders and have their authority vested in them from above, while others are the choice of followers who provide them with a willing response. Furthermore, it became evident that distinctions were required between characteristics which led to the attainment of leadership and those which were effective in the maintenance of leadership.

The situational view gave attention to what had for so long been neglected, the varying demands for leadership imposed by the parameters of the situation. These parameters include the group's task, its structure, and its situational context (see Hemphill, 1949; Carter, Haythorn, Shriver, & Lanzetta, 1951). Pellegrin (1953) has revealed the kernel of this view in his statement that "it is the norms and activities of the group, we believe, that contribute the essential variables from one group leadership situation to another" (p. 15). As the dominant theme in the recent literature, the situational approach for the most part resists the intrusion of personality factors involved in leadership. There is therefore no need here to review findings which have accumulated concerning situational influences as such; moreover, recent books such as Hare's *Handbook of Small Group Research* (1962) and Cartwright and Zander's *Group Dynamics* (1960) can guide the reader to much of this work.

Even within the framework of the heavily

situational point of view, however, there has been differentiation of effort. Apart from the fact that to some there is persistent appeal in the study of leadership traits favoring the "great man" theory of leadership (see Jennings, 1960), there has been a movement toward recognizing the interaction of leaders and followers in terms of the positive weight given to certain personal characteristics *within* parameters of the situation. Thus, while many of the studies of leader attributes summarized by Jenkins (1947) and Stogdill (1948) were notable for failing to be concerned with these situational parameters, there still remains a distinctive requirement to study the personality characteristics of leaders given the appropriateness of these to a set of situational demands. No longer a quest for "universal traits," this effort would seek to reveal something about the context of interaction as it affects the response to leader characteristics. That there are distinctive needs in this direction is revealed, for example, by the review of small group research reported by McGrath and Altman (1966) where only sixteen of some 250 studies surveyed embodied personality attributes as variables of concern.

Several keys have been employed, then, in an attempt to understand the basis for "leadership." Leader performance was first partitioned into that source of variance explained by personality traits, leaving other sources unexplained. As if by reaction to disillusionment, social scientists then turned to situational factors as another major source of variance, largely ignoring any earlier gains from the trait approach. The more contemporary approach takes the position that, although some part of the variance can be attributed to leader personality, and some major part to situational variables, substantial gains are to be made by a further partitioning of the heretofore unexplained variance by examining the interaction effects of the important personality and situational variables previously identified. Our intention here is to review some of the findings which exemplify the study of personality variables in leadership research, giving special attention to studies which examine the moderating or interacting effects of both leader attributes and situational variables.

Leader Attributes

The more traditional approach to the study of personality and leadership rests upon findings such as those of Bell and French (1950). Making use of small discussion groups, they found that "... varying group membership in this situation accounts for at most a relatively small portion of the variation in leadership status. Leadership status seems to be rather highly consistent despite the situational changes involved" (p. 767). They point out, however, that this finding cannot be generalized to all types of groups since the task involved was of a particular variety and that certain characteristics of the subjects were fairly homogeneous. Nonetheless, this kind of result has been invoked to support the contention that there are characteristics of leadership which operate across varying situations. More recent results which make a similar point are reported by Cohen and Bennis (1962). They found after systematically shifting the communication networks of their groups that the sociometrically identified leaders remained fairly constant. Thus, they provide a further observation that personality factors contribute to the maintenance of leadership status within the group.

In a further study looking into personality variables related to leaderless group discussion (LGD) behavior (Bass, McGehee, Hawkins, Young, & Gebel, 1953), a significant correlation was found between leadership status and self-ratings on ascendance and social boldness as measured by the Guilford-Zimmerman Temperament Survey. Sociability was also found to bear a significant relationship to the LGD. In addition, Bass *et al.* (1953) found that authoritarian attitudes as assessed by the *F*-Scale correlated negatively with LGD scores. Although the authors explicitly recognized the situational bounds of the study, the usual inference drawn from it is that personality characteristics of leadership play a significant role in leadership emergence.

Relatedly, Borgatta, Couch, and Bales (1954) have presented results pertinent to a "great man" conception of the leader as one in whom inheres qualities which contribute to group effectiveness, including task competence, emotional supportiveness, and perceptiveness. Leaders were defined in terms of (a) intelligence, as measured by the SRA Primary Mental Abilities Test; (b) leadership ratings by co-participants; (c) participation or total activity rate in interaction; and (d) sociometric popularity. Across four discussion sessions, the 11 group participants who scored highest on a composite of these criteria were found to lead consistently more effective groups characterized by greater expression of positive affect and less tension. However, the task setting was essentially constant with only the participants varying across sessions.

Mann (1959) has reviewed much of this research relating personality variables to leadership, both defined quite broadly. As an overview of the area, his survey is an excellent source of general results. He identifies the seven major personality factors of intelligence, adjustment, extroversion, dominance, masculinity, interpersonal sensitivity, and conservatism and concludes that all but the last factor bear a significant positive relationship to leadership, and that conservatism is negatively related to leadership.

Some more recent studies continue in the traditional mode. Beer, Buckhout, Horowitz, and Levy (1959) used peer ratings to compare campus leaders with nonleaders on the three trait categories of self-acceptance, need achievement, and interpersonal skill. They found that campus leaders were rated to be more confident, more willing to take responsibility, more forceful, persuasive, and diplomatic. Borg (1960) using a sample of 819 air force officers, administered a test battery designed to assess individual skills on personality factors thought to predict roles in small group situations. His battery, when factor analyzed, yielded four predictor factors: assertiveness, power orientation, rigidity, and aggressive nonconformity. The officers were then divided into 60 small groups whose members rated one another with respect to each of six small group roles. The "assertiveness" factor was found to be most successful in predicting the leadership role with a correlation of .46. Borg interprets these findings as consistent with the similar results of Bass *et al.* (1953) and Cattell and Stice (1954), arguing for the importance of a type of "assertiveness leadership trait." Because of the possibly important similarities in task and samples, however, once again there is a question about the extent of generalizability.

Another series of investigations, though drawn from research done from a more situational view, is nonetheless relevant. These deal with "activity level" as a factor in leader performance. Strodtbeck (1951) observed that the relative participation rate of marital partners was an important predictor of which member would emerge as more dominant. Dominance in this study was measured by the number of decisions "won" by a spouse in their attempts to resolve differences of opinion. Further exemplifying this approach is a study by Riecken (1958), who constructed 32 four-man groups which were to discuss human relations problems. His results showed that members who spoke most were almost uniformly perceived as contributing more and were in fact more influential in getting the solution they suggested accepted by the group. A comparable finding was obtained by Kirscht, Lodahl, and Haire (1959) using three-person groups. They found that those who emerged as leaders manifested a high rate of participation in the discussion, in this case concerning a human relations problem, and they also tended to be members who were more task oriented. McGrath and Julian (1963) reported similar differences in participation rate for the appointed leaders of four-person negotiation groups. These studies give corroboration to the finding of Borgatta *et al.* (1954) and to the earlier work of Carter *et al.* (1951), which demonstrated across a number of tasks, i.e., reasoning, mechanical assembling, and discussion, that leaders tended to be those more likely to initiate action for the solution of a problem. On all three tasks, leaders were found to participate most frequently.

Personality and the Situation

As previously indicated, other studies have looked upon personality and situational variables specifically in terms of their moderating or interacting effects on leadership performance. An example is provided in a study by Maas (1950), who found that leaders who possessed the tendency to project blame showed desirable changes in their perception of members when they led relatively informal, unstructured groups; but those with a tendency to introject blame showed desirable changes in perception when they advised formal and clearly structured groups. The tendency to project or introject blame was evaluated from an intensive analysis of interview material. The leaders were 22 liberal arts college juniors serving as advisors of various youth groups sponsored by community agencies. These findings point to a clear interaction between the degree of formal group structure and the perceptual "set" or outlook of the leader.

In a military training situation, Hollander (1954) found a negative relationship between *F*-Scale scores of authoritarianism and leadership standing among officer candidates measured by peer nominations. Furthermore, it was found that the leadership nominees of those candidates "high" or "low" on authoritarianism did not differ significantly with respect to their authoritarianism scores. In both cases, those nominated "highest" on leadership had a significantly lower score on authoritarianism than those nominated "lowest" on leadership, and this held true even when the effects of intelligence were accounted for. Thus, even within a situation whose primary organizational structure has authoritarian properties, the less authoritarian group members were favored for positions of leadership.

While the studies by Maas and Hollander only infer something about leader behavior as it might affect responsiveness from others under given situational circumstances, other researchers have focussed directly on leader behavior as a variable to be measured. The previously noted study by Bass *et al.* (1953) illustrates this in terms of the leaderless group discussion. Also, Haythorn, Couch, Haefner, Langham, and Carter (1956) systematically created groups under four conditions involving leaders who scored high or low on the *F*-Scale paired with followers who had scored high or low on the *F*-Scale. Four-man groups were required to discuss specific human relations problems presented on film. Observations of behavior were recorded by several techniques involving ratings, interaction recording techniques, and postinteraction questions. The results indicated significant differences in the behavior evidenced by both leaders and followers who scored at either extreme of the *F*-Scale distribution. In addition, interaction analyses indicated that the behavior of leaders differed as a function of whether or not their followers were high or low on the *F*-Scale and that the behavior of followers depended on the *F*-Scale scores of their leaders.

Pepinsky, Hemphill, and Shevitz (1958) attempted to discern how leader behavior is shaped by others and how such shaping depends upon the personality needs of the leader. They preselected the leaders of 24 four-man groups on the basis of their achievement and affiliation needs. These motives were assessed by a combination of a self-report questionnaire and interview analysis. Under an acceptance condition, attempts to lead were rewarded by the other group members, and under conditions of rejection such attempts were disapproved by the others. Significant differences in leader behavior were found as a function of these two conditions. However, under the rejection condition, individuals with high need achievement were not found to attempt to lead with any greater frequency than individuals with high need affiliation.

Of related concern is the way in which group productivity is determined by the personality of the leader within a given situational context. Accordingly, Shaw (1955) studied the effects of an authoritarian style of leadership in three communication nets. These nets differed in their degree of "saturation" and "independence." In terms of work output, an authoritarian leadership style was superior to a nonauthoritarian style across communication nets, although authoritarian leaders were found to produce significantly lower morale across the 48 four-person groups in the study.

Berkowitz (1956) measured the ascendance of male undergraduate students with a Guilford-Zimmerman Temperament Survey and then placed high or low scorers in the central position of the "star" communication net. Although the groups differed initially in problem-solving performance, with the groups led by the high ascendant subjects initially more effective, by the third trial these differences had disappeared. Berkowitz interprets this effect as "position adaptation." Thus, the operation of particular personality variables depends crucially upon the stage of development and life history of the group.

Shaw (1959) reports an interaction between leader acceptance of authority and the degree of centralization of authority in two communication nets. The task involved solving simple arithmetic problems. Subjects were undergraduate male college students, and their acceptance of authority was measured with a modified *F*-Scale. High authoritarian leaders led groups which performed better under a centralized communication structure. Conversely, low authoritarian leaders led groups which performed better under a less centralized communication structure.

"Decision-time" has also been investigated (Dubno, 1963) as a characteristic of leadership. Dubno hypothesized that leader decision time interacted with group task conditions which emphasized leader speed or quality of group production. Although speed of decision had been found related to other personality factors such as rigidity and passivity (Block & Petersen, 1955), Dubno failed to find effects on group performance.

Fiedler and Meuwese (1963) present data from various military units analyzed to determine the moderating effects of group cohesiveness on the relationship between a leader's intelligence and group performance. Each sample was divided into cohesive and uncohesive groups, and a correlation between the leader's intelligence and group performance was calculated. The results indicated that the leader's intelligence quite consistently predicted group performance in cohesive groups but not in uncohesive groups.

The work of Fiedler and his co-workers also focuses on the contribution of leader characteristics to group productivity. Fiedler (1961) has nominated his assumed similarity between opposites (ASo) measure as a possible "leadership effectiveness" trait, and has reviewed studies that report a consistent relationship between this score and group productivity in a variety of task settings (1958). The measure derives from leader ratings of hypothetical good and poor coworkers.

The need to take account of important situational variables has been borne out in several studies of this series (cf. Fiedler, 1955; Godfrey, Fiedler, & Hall, 1959). In a more recent paper Fiedler (1962) summarized three laboratory studies and one field study relating leaders' least preferred co-worker (LPC) score to performance of the group or team on a task requiring creativity. The LPC measure reflects the favorability of the leader's rating of his least preferred co-worker; it is the major component of Fiedler's earlier ASo measure. Generally, he found consistent evidence for a positive relationship between leader LPC and group creativity under pleasant and relaxed group conditions and a negative relationship when the group operated under an unpleasant, stressful group climate. These studies further reflect the importance we have noted of viewing leader characteristics as they are moderated by certain properties of the situation. Most recently, Fiedler (1965) has presented a "contingency model" for predicting the contribution of the leader to group performance. Although handled from a more situational view, the model concentrates on describing the situational contingencies which influence the relationships between leader ASo (or LPC) and group productivity.

Still another feature of leadership which has been investigated concerns the leader's social perceptiveness. This characteristic has been variously measured, and in different kinds of groups, so that for the most part the results tend to be confusing. Hites and Campbell (1950), for example, found that leaders were not significantly better in their ability to estimate group opinion than were nonleaders. On the other hand, Chowdhry and Newcomb (1952) found that leaders were significantly better able to judge the group relevant opinions of members than were nonleaders. They interpreted these results to indicate that an important factor in the achievement of leadership status was the ability to assess others accurately.

Greer, Galanter, and Nordlie (1954) had army squad members estimate their own status within the group as well as the sociometric status of other squad members. The more popular individuals in the group were found to be more accurate in perceiving their own standing and the standing of others than were the less popular individuals. Squad leaders were also better judges of this hierarchy than were members. However, in a commentary on such studies, Campbell (1955) suggests that there is a spurious factor involved in the finding that leaders or other high status group members have better "insight." This arises, he says, from a statistical artifact in the means of computing the insight index, compounded by the fact that estimates tend to have much less variance than the true value of status and that most persons ascribe to themselves fairly high status.

Clarifying this issue somewhat, Talland (1954) conducted an experiment with therapy discussion groups and found that initially leaders were no better at predicting member opinions than were others. After discussion, however, group consensus moved closer to the leaders' opinions. Hence, the leaders were having a significant effect upon the development of the group's attitudes on matters of interest to the group, and this therefore suggested that the leaders' apparent superiority in estimating such attitudes was a function of the role they played in their development.

Using a different approach, Bell and Hall (1954) found that there were significant correlations between leadership scores from a leaderless group discussion situation and scores obtained on both the Dymond and Kerr tests of empathy. When these correlations were corrected for attenuation, they found that Kerr and leadership yielded a .37 value and Dymond and leadership a .25. These findings were interpreted in line with the view of the leader as one who is aware and is able to satisfy the needs of his group.

Mann (1959) has included much of this research concerned with "interpersonal sensitivity" in his survey of personality factors associated with leadership. "The overall trend of the results is positive; in 74% of the cases leaders are found to be more accurate in estimating various aspects of the opinions of other group members than nonleaders" (p. 250).

More recent findings tend to corroborate

this generalization. Showel (1960) found that in a military setting, rated leadership potential correlated significantly with interpersonal knowledge, even after the effects of general intelligence had been partialed out. Exline (1960), however, reported an interactive effect of group cohesiveness on accuracy of perception. In this study, only in cohesive groups was the leader a more accurate judge of opinion. Gallo and McClintock (1962) compared the leaders of campus organizations with nonleaders under the experimental conditions of group support or rejection. He found that once placed in a leadership position and given group support, campus leaders were more accurate in perceiving their status in the group than were nonleaders. In addition, such leaders were also found to become more hostile and aggressive when this support was withdrawn.

In this section we have covered findings that reveal the interactive relationship between characteristics of the leader as an influence agent and properties of the situation in which he functions. Among leader personality variables, we have attended to measures of dominance, assertiveness, authoritarianism, activity level, social perceptiveness, as well as modes of leader behavior. Regarding the situation, we have considered the task structure, communication patterns, and group responsiveness to be potent forces of which the investigator must take account in understanding the determinants of group productivity and member satisfaction. Further specification of the distinctive commerce between these variables appears to be a fruitful line for continuing investigation.

IN CONCLUSION

Commenting on the state of the literature, in the 1964 *Annual Review of Psychology,* Steiner has observed:

> Leadership is one of the most elusive terms in the language of group dynamics.... Leadership research places a strong emphasis upon the discovery of reasons why certain people (leaders, followers) produce specified acts at particular times; but, like other studies of group processes, investigations of leadership attempt to answer the questions: Who? What? To whom? When? (p. 437)

The present chapter has discussed attempts to answer these questions with particular emphasis on the personality characteristics of "who" in the context of these other factors.

Our review has revealed a growing body of research which takes account of the inherently dyadic nature of the leadership process. Such an approach is, to our view, likely to yield productive returns. A number of studies that investigate situational constraints on the effects of leader personality characteristics seem best to preserve the relational emphasis needed for an understanding of leadership. Nevertheless, some progress has been made in distinguishing general leadership attributes, and work toward this end continues. Several investigations with this concern have been included in the present discussion.

REFERENCES

Bass, B. M., McGehee, C. R., Hawkins, W. C., Young, P. C., & Gebel, A. S. Personality variables related to leaderless group discussion behavior. *J. abnorm. soc. Psychol.,* 1953, 48, 120–128.

Beer, M., Buckhout, R., Horowitz, M. W., & Levy, S. Some perceived properties of the difference between leaders and non-leaders. *J. Psychol.,* 1959, 47, 49–56.

Bell, G. B., & French, R. L. Consistency of individual leadership position in small groups of varying membership. *J. abnorm. soc. Psychol.,* 1950, 45, 764–767.

Bell, G. B., & Hall, H. E., Jr. The relationship between leadership and empathy. *J. abnorm. soc. Psychol.,* 1954, 49, 156–157.

Berkowitz, L. Personality and group position. *Sociometry,* 1956, 19, 210–222.

Block, J., & Petersen, P. Some personality correlates of confidence, caution, and speed in a decision situation. *J. abnorm. soc. Psychol.,* 1955, 51, 34–41.

Borg, W. R. Prediction of small group role behavior from personality variables. *J. abnorm. soc. Psychol.,* 1960, 60, 112–116.

Borgatta, E. F., Couch, A. S., & Bales, R. F. Some findings relevant to the great man theory of leadership. *Amer. sociol. Rev.,* 1954, 19, 755–759.

Campbell, D. T. An error in some demonstrations of the superior social perceptiveness of leaders. *J. abnorm. soc. Psychol.,* 1955, 51, 694–695.

Carter, L. F., Haythorn, W., Shriver, E., & Lanzetta, J. The behavior of leaders and other group members. *J. abnorm. soc. Psychol.,* 1951, 46, 589–595.

Cartwright, D., & Zander, A. (Eds.) *Group dynamics: Research and theory.* Evanston, Ill.: Row, Peterson, 1960.

Cattell, R. B., & Stice, G. F. Four formulae for selecting leaders on the basis of personality. *Hum. Relat.,* 1954, 7, 493–507.

Chowdhry, Kamla, & Newcomb, T. M. The relative abilities of leaders and non-leaders to estimate opinions of their own groups. *J. abnorm. soc. Psychol.,* 1952, 47, 51–57.

Cohen, A. M., & Bennis, W. G. Continuity of leadership in communication networks. *Hum. Relat.,* 1962, 14, 351–364.

Cowley, W. H. Three distinctions in the study of leaders. *J. abnorm. soc. Psychol.,* 1928, 23, 144–157.

Dubno, P. Decision time characteristics of leaders and group problem-solving behavior. *J. soc. Psychol.,* 1963, 59, 259–282.

Exline, R. V. Interrelations among two dimensions of sociometric status, group congeniality, and accuracy of social perception. *Sociometry,* 1960, 23, 85–101.

Fiedler, F. E. The influence of leader-keyman relations on combat crew effectiveness. *J. abnorm. soc. Psychol.,* 1955, 51, 227–235.

Fiedler, F. E. *Leader attitudes and group effectiveness.* Urbana, Ill.: Univer. of Ill. Press, 1958.

Fiedler, F. E. Leadership and leadership effectiveness traits. In L. Petrullo & B. M. Bass (Eds.), *Leadership and interpersonal behavior.* New York: Holt, Rinehart and Winston, 1961.

Fiedler, F. E. Leader attitudes, group climate, and group creativity. *J. abnorm. soc. Psychol.,* 1962, 65, 308–318.

Fiedler, F. E. The contingency model: A theory of leadership effectiveness. In H. Proshansky & B. Seidenberg (Eds.) *Basic studies in social psychology.* New York: Holt, Rinehart and Winston, 1965.

Fiedler, F. E., & Meuwese, W. A. T. Leader's contribution to task performance in cohesive and uncohesive groups. *J. abnorm. soc. Psychol.,* 1963, 67, 83–87.

Gallo, P. S., & McClintock, C. G. Behavioral, attitudinal, and perceptual differences between leaders and non-leaders in situations of group support and non-support. *J. soc. Psychol.,* 1962, 56, 121–133.

Gibb, C. A. The principles and traits of leadership. *J. abnorm. soc. Psychol.,* 1947, 42, 267–284.

Godfrey, Eleanor, Fiedler, F. E., & Hall, D. M. *Boards, management, and company success.* Danville, Ill.: Interstate, 1959.

Greer, F. L., Galanter, E. H., & Nordlie, P. G. Interpersonal knowledge and individual and group effectiveness. *J. abnorm. soc. Psychol.,* 1954, 49, 411–414.

Hare, A. P. *Handbook of small group research.* New York: Free Press, 1962.

Haythorn, W., Couch, A., Haefner, D., Langham, P., & Carter, L. F. The effects of varying combinations of authoritarian and equalitarian leaders and followers. *J. abnorm. soc. Psychol.,* 1956, 53, 210–219.

Hemphill, J. K. Situational factors in leadership. Ohio State Univer., *Educ. Res. Monogr.,* 1949, No. 32.

Hites, R. W., & Campbell, D. T. A test of the ability of fraternity leaders to estimate group opinion. *J. soc. Psychol.,* 1950, 32, 95–100.

Hollander, E. P. Authoritarianism and leadership choice in a military setting. *J. abnorm. soc. Psychol.,* 1954, 49, 365–370.

Hollander, E. P. *Leaders, groups, and influence.* New York: Oxford Univer. Press, 1964.

Homans, G. C. *Social behavior: Its elementary forms.* New York: Harcourt, Brace and World, 1961.

Jenkins, W. O. A review of leadership studies with particular reference to military problems. *Psychol. Bull.,* 1947, 44, 54–79.

Jennings, E. E. *The anatomy of leadership: Princes, heroes, and supermen.* New York: Harper & Brothers, 1960.

Kirscht, J. P., Lodahl, T. M., & Haire, M. Some factors in the selection of leaders by members of small groups. *J. abnorm. soc. Psychol.,* 1959, 58, 406–408.

Mann, R. D. A review of the relationships between personality and performance in small groups. *Psychol. Bull.,* 1959, 56, 241–270.

Maas, H. S. Personal and group factors in leaders' social perception. *J. abnorm. soc. Psychol.,* 1950, 45, 54–63.

McGrath, J. E., & Altman, I. *Small group research: A synthesis and critique of the field.* New York: Holt, Rinehart and Winston, 1966.

McGrath, J. E., & Julian, J. W. Interaction process and task outcome in experimentally-created negotiation groups. *J. Psychol. Stud.,* 1963, 14, 117–138.

Pepinsky, Pauline N., Hemphill, J. K., & Shevitz, R. N. Attempts to lead, group productivity, and morale under conditions of acceptance and rejection. *J. abnorm. soc. Psychol.,* 1958, 57, 47–54.

Pellegrin, R. J. The achievement of high status and leadership in the small group. *Soc. Forces,* 1953, 32, 10–16.

Riecken, H. W. The effect of talkativeness on ability to influence group solutions to problems. *Sociometry,* 1958, 21, 309–321.

Sells, S. B. An interactionist looks at the environment. *Amer. Psychologist,* 1963, 18, 696–702.

Shaw, M. E. A comparison of two types of leadership in various communication nets. *J. abnorm. soc. Psychol.,* 1955, 50, 127–134.

Shaw, M. E. Acceptance of authority, group structure, and the effectiveness of small groups. *J. Pers.,* 1959, 27, 196–210.

Showel, M. Interpersonal knowledge and rated leader potential. *J. abnorm. soc. Psychol.,* 1960, 61, 87–92.

Steiner, I. Group dynamics. In P. Farnsworth *et al.* (Eds.), *Annual review of psychology.* Vol. 15. Palo Alto, Calif.: Annual Reviews, 1964.

Stogdill, R. Personal factors associated with leadership: A survey of the literature. *J. Psychol.,* 1948, 25, 35–71.

Stogdill, R. Leadership, membership, and organization. *Psychol. Bull.,* 1950, 47, 1–14.

Strodtbeck, F. L. Husband-wife interaction over revealed differences. *Amer. sociol. Rev.,* 1951, 16, 468–473.

Talland, G. A. The assessment of group opinion by leaders, and their influence on its formation. *J. abnorm. soc. Psychol.,* 1954, 89, 431–434.

CHAPTER 16 Creativity

MORRIS I. STEIN
New York University

From about 1870 when Galton published *Hereditary Genius* (Galton, 1870) to about 1950 there were relatively few published scientific inquiries in the area of creativity. Since 1950, however, the number of publications almost equals all those that appeared earlier or at least since Galton's work (Guilford, 1962). This amazing proliferation of studies was stimulated by several factors—problems on the international and national levels and new developments within psychology. On the international level there was concern with maintaining the status of the United States as a world power. Consequently, funds became available for research that would aid in the understanding, selection, and utilization of the creative potential and abilities in scientific manpower. On the national level there were growing concerns with the problems of conformity and the eroding effects of experiences of the "organization man." And, in psychology, both psychoanalysts and psychologists became more interested in ego psychology and in the factors that made for mental health than in those that made for psychopathology; Guilford made important strides in the study of the structure of the intellect; and social psychologists became more involved in the study of individuals in large organizations.

Contemporary research in this area is not only vigorous but quite diverse. Investigators use several different criteria, study subjects in various fields of endeavor, and employ a multiplicity of techniques in their research. Both the number and variety of studies pose problems for a relatively brief presentation, especially since most studies have not been replicated. To delimit the area I shall first consider several procedural matters and then concentrate primarily on recent empirical investigations of several topics that have received much attention. More detailed summaries of the literature may be found elsewhere (Parnes & Harding, 1962; Stein, 1962; Stein & Heinze, 1960; C. W. Taylor, 1963b, 1964; C. W. Taylor & Barron, 1963).

DEFINITION

Creativity is a process with overlapping phases that take time. For Wallas (1926) it consists of preparation, incubation, illumination, and verification. The psychoanalyst, Kris (1952, 1953), regards it as consisting of inspiration, elaboration, and communication. The philosopher, Reichenbach (1938), differentiates between the "context of discovery" and the "context of justification."

And Stein (1953) uses the terms "hypothesis formation," "hypothesis testing," and the "communication of results."

A second characteristic of creativity is that it results in a novel product. ("Product" is used as synonymous with such terms as theory, art object, mechanical device, etc.) Novelty alone, however, is insufficient, for the product must be "tenable, useful, or satisfying" (Stein, 1953) in some significant way, it must be "adaptive" (MacKinnon, 1964), or contain an "effective surprise" (Bruner, 1962).

A third characteristic of creativity is that it occurs within a social context. The creative individual is a product of his time, although he may rise above it; he is almost always trained in or very well aware of the tradition, problems, data, and methods of his field. The products of his labor are reacted to or evaluated by significant others—scientific and professional colleagues, art, drama, and literary critics, or the power figures in an organization—all of whom may serve as "intermediaries" (Stein, 1963a) in the creative process. And finally, there is the broader audience or public who might agree or disagree with the intermediaries and who might either accept or reject the creative product.

The fact that creativity occurs in a social context is usually overlooked in studies that occur in the psychological laboratory or which use responses to psychological tests as criteria. But it is as true of these studies as it is of those concerned with subjects in real life situations. The differences, insofar as the social contexts of the two situations are concerned, lie in the persons doing the evaluation, the nature of the material being evaluated, and the complexity of social situations in which the behavior is manifest. The differences between these two types of social situations need to be made explicit, for they may be critical in affecting the results of cross-validation studies and in highlighting those psychological characteristics that are more important in one type of situation than in another.

CRITERIA

While there is much agreement that creativity is a process that takes time and results in novelty, and while there is some agreement that it occurs in a social context, there is still the criterion problem for those involved in empirical research. Who are the individuals to be selected for study from whom one can learn the psychological and social factors associated with creativity?

In contemporary research the following criteria have been used: statistical definitions which involve deviations or unique responses to psychological tests (e.g., Barron, 1955, 1957; Guilford, 1956, 1959a); number of citations or lines devoted to a person in general texts, histories, or biographies of "famous people" (e.g., J. M. Cattell, 1903; Galton, 1870; Lehman, 1953); judgments of professionally qualified people (e.g., MacKinnon, 1962; Roe, 1951; Stein, 1963c; C. W. Taylor, 1963a); generally acknowledged eminence, as in the cases of da Vinci and Shakespeare (e.g., Freud, 1948a; Sharpe, 1950a); number of products defined as creative (e.g., Rossman, 1931); and the pursuit of an activity such as painting or music which is assumed to require creative behavior (e.g., Eiduson, 1958; Rosen, 1955). There are as yet no "objective" or "ultimate" criteria, although the need for such has been discussed (Ghiselin, 1958; Harmon, 1958; McPherson, 1956).

There is an important difference between what has been called here the "definition of the creative process" and what has been called the "criteria" of creativity. By definition, creativity is a process, yet there are individuals who are studied who have been selected in terms of products they produced. Assume that all these persons have produced some form of novelty; there is no certainty that they did so through the creative process. Novelty may be arrived at through trial and error, problem-solving procedures, discovery, and serendipity. These procedures may share characteristics with the creative process, but they do not overlap in all respects. The relevance of this point to our later discussion is that subjects studied are not homogeneous as to process characteristics, but they are homogeneous insofar as their products have been evaluated by some group of significant others and have been regarded as containing unique and adaptive characteristics.

The differences in processes for arriving at novelty, and therefore the differences in the subjects studied, may also affect the level of correlations obtained between psychological characteristics studied and the criteria.

THEORIES AND HYPOTHESES

There has been a fair melding between theory and research in this area. Studies of cognitive functions have derived their hypotheses from association theory, gestalt theory, and psychoanalytic theory. Studies of the personality characteristics of creative individuals have derived their hypotheses from psychoanalytic or other dynamic theories, and studies of creativity in organizational settings have derived their hypotheses from sociological theory with emphasis on considerations involved in role, status, and communication. Nevertheless, it is still characteristic of the field that it is primarily empirical. Procedures and techniques that have been found useful in studies other than creativity have also been employed in this area without any specific hypotheses. Differentiating characteristics may then be interpreted after the fact to demonstrate their consistency with theory.

At this point there is no single generally accepted theory from which one might derive the characteristics of the creative individual. And there is some indication that when such a theory is developed, it will not be a theory of *the* creative individual but of creative *individuals*.

SUBJECTS AND PROCEDURES

Just as there has been diversity in criteria and orientations among investigators, so there have been differences in the work areas of subjects studied and in procedures employed. Subjects studied have been architects, artists (painters and sculptors), writers, mathematicians, biological, behavioral, and physical scientists, and engineers. In some studies subjects are homogeneous as to work area, but in others, especially in studies of scientists, they are quite heterogeneous. However, work areas differ in a variety of ways. They differ in terms of the level of abstraction involved and in the demands they make upon the person's resources. Psychological characteristics that are critical for one type of endeavor may not be so significant for another. It is apparent, therefore, that the obtained degree of relationship between a psychological variable and a criterion may be adversely affected when populations are so heterogeneous.

Another factor that may adversely affect results is that there is no assurance that an individual who has been selected for study because he represents a specific work area and is low on creativity in that area may not, in fact, be quite creative in other activities in his life. On any one test procedure, it is possible that such an individual may score similarly to his more creative colleagues. If there are enough such persons in a comparison group, few, if any, differentiating characteristics may be obtained.

Numerous techniques have been employed in studies of creativity. Use has been made of objective tests, projective tests, experimental situations, observations, and interviews. Relationships between data gathered by different techniques (for example, objective and projective) on the same personality variable are not yet completely known, and this, too, may make for differences between results reported. In view of the diversity of techniques employed, there is surprising agreement in the results, as shall be reported later.

With these procedural matters in mind to serve as proper cautions, let us now turn to several topics that have received much attention.

BIOGRAPHICAL CHARACTERISTICS

Age

Creativity (defined as man's "maximum productive rate for output of highest quality") rises to its highest point in his thirties and declines slowly thereafter (Lehman, 1953). A similar finding has been reported for inventors (Rossman, 1931). Scientists employed in industry are said to experience a decline in creativity after 40 (Stevens, 1951). This finding is rather interesting since productivity has been found to increase with age (Meltzer, 1956).

Several of the factors that may account for the relationships between age and creativity are (a) capacities involved in different fields—older people are at a disadvantage in fields requiring new learning and the unlearning of old material, while they may be at an advantage in fields requiring the accumulation of knowledge (Lehman, 1953); (b) the level of development of the field of work—discoveries may be made at a younger age in fields where significant contributions are related to consequent systematization of predictive knowledge, while older people are better off in fields where detailed phenomenological knowledge is most important (Manniche & Falk, 1957); (c) the assumption of new status—increased supervisory and administrative responsibility decreases the amount of time available for creative work (Bjorksten, 1946); (d) indirect effects of other factors related to age—with age there is a general diminution in physical vigor and capacity to resist fatigue, increase in family responsibilities as well as marital and sexual problems, an increase in the effects of nonrecognition and negative criticism, all of which may indirectly affect creativity (Lehman, 1953).

The negative effects of age, however, may be offset by both internal and external factors. Pelz (1964b), after studying a variety of research settings and using a variety of performance criteria, found saddle-shaped curves with twin peaks 10 to 15 years apart, rather than a single peak, in the relationship of age to creativity. These peaks occurred earlier in research-oriented than in product-oriented laboratories. And scientists who were more strongly involved in their work were more successful in resisting the effects of age than those who were only mildly involved in their work.

Early Life History

Life histories of creative individuals have been studied not only to highlight antecedent factors that may predispose the adult to creative work but also to focus attention on those characteristics that might be sought in younger persons with creative potential so that their future development might be facilitated.

There are studies (MacKinnon, 1960; Roe, 1952; Stein, 1957) in which there is reasonably good agreement about some of the early life history factors associated with creativity. Creative individuals, it has been found, grew up in environments that provided them with good bases for their later autonomous development and dedication to their work. Although their lives were not without complexity, and while the conditions of the complexity they experienced varied (e.g., early illness, death in the family, frequent movement from one area to another), they did not withdraw or react negatively to the complexity. Their early development provided them with sufficient resources so that they could weather difficulties and cope with problems involved in their future professional and scientific careers. Their parents provided them with encouragement, respect, and emotional support and also served as positive models for identification, since they were independent persons with a number of interests, some of which were directly related to their children's future activities. And if these sources of support or models were lacking in the immediate family, then they were to be found in the extended family or among teachers in school and college. Creative individuals were also provided with direction, either in terms of generalized values or orientations they were to follow or in terms of disciplinary actions that were to have more guidance than punitive value. In early life creative individuals did not socialize much with other children and frequently manifested interests that were the precursors of their future careers.

Biographical inventories have been developed and studied in relation to creativity. MacKinnon (1962) in his study of architects found a statistically significant correlation of .36 between autobiographical data obtained through interviews and experts' judgments of creativity. C. W. Taylor and Ellison (1963) report a biographical inventory that yielded an average cross-validity coefficient of .47 in two samples of government scientists involved in problems of propulsion for atmospheric and space flight. The items of this inventory, at the time of this writing, are not yet public, but it consists of four major sections: developmental history, parents and family life, academic background, and adult life and interests. Taylor reports that in various studies, the Adult Life and Interests section yielded consistently higher validity coefficients than the other sections of the inventory. The Parents and Family Life section held up least well, which is somewhat at variance with the experience of other investigators who found much significance in early parent-child relationships. Whether the differences in results between studies is a function of questions asked, procedures used, or types of subjects studied is still an open question. Nevertheless, Taylor, in addition to cross-validity coefficients reported above, also reports that his inventory was one of the best differentiators between high school students who participated in National Science Foundation programs that were oriented to research and those who participated in similarly sponsored programs that were oriented to academic-like activities. It was also one of the best predictors for ratings of research potential in a graduate student fellowship program at the University of Utah.

Results such as these are based on differences between groups of known creativity. However, both on theoretical grounds (Greenacre, 1957) and on the basis of empirical research (Roe, 1952), it is apparent that creativity is not always associated with one single constellation of antecedent factors. Different patterns of early experiences may be related to different types or styles of creativity in later life. Roe (1958) and Roe and Siegelman (1964) have presented a theory relating early experiences in the family to career choices and interests that may be helpful in this regard. Future efforts designed to delineate the various patterns of early life experiences might well improve the level of correlations obtained to date.

Education

Success in college, as manifested in the grade point average, is a poor predictor of future creativity of architects and research scientists (MacKinnon, 1960, 1961). It has also been found that the personality characteristics of students who get high grades are different from those that characterize creative adults (Holland, 1960). Hence, it is conceivable that one of the reasons why grades are poor predictors of future creativity is that creative adults, while they were in school, were too autonomous to accept on authority what they were taught and too self-directed to work at top level in courses that did not interest them. This hypothesis needs to be tested in future longitudinal research where grades and personality data are related to future creativity. In such research it would also be wise to utilize grade and creativity data to establish different groups of subjects—e.g., those high on both grades and creativity, those who are low on both, and two groups where one is higher on one than on the other. Such a breakdown of the subject population in a consequent investigation of the personality characteristics of the subjects in all four cells may tell us for what kinds of subjects grades will or will not predict future creativity.

In addition to grades, the teacher and

creativity have also been studied. Some teachers have played important roles in the lives of creative individuals and done remarkably well in producing students who were likely to be creative in their later years (Brandwein, 1955). In another study at the secondary school level (Getzels & Jackson, 1962), which will be described at greater length below, it was found that students who score higher on IQ tests than creativity tests (high IQ students) "are preferred over the average students by their teachers," but high creativity students (those who score higher on so-called tests of creativity than on intelligence tests) are not. Getzels and Jackson express surprise at their teachers' preferences, especially since the high IQ and high creative subjects do equally well in achievement. Their discussion of this problem implies that teachers prefer the high IQ to the high creativity students. This implication is not supported by an analysis of the data. While teacher preference scores for the high IQ students are higher than those obtained for the high creativity students, the difference between the two groups is not statistically significant (Wallach & Kogan, 1965). At the college level, teachers' assessments of the creativity of engineering students were found to be positively correlated with students' achievements in courses (MacKinnon, 1961). This positive relationship is contradictory with the results also reported by MacKinnon (1960, 1961) that grades are not good predictors of the creativity of employed architects and research scientists. It is this very contradiction that reflects the complexities of research in this area, for the contradiction may result from differences in fields studied, differences in raters used, etc. And, if a follow-up of the study of engineers corroborated the data obtained with employed architects and research scientists, then it would suggest that criteria of creativity used by teachers are different from criteria used by experts in the field. Further study might or might not support the hypothesis that teachers were not really rating their students' creativity but rather their students' capacity to learn what they had been taught.

At the elementary school level Torrance has conducted a series of extensive studies into the roles played by peers, teachers, and educational practices in the creative process. In their studies of the effects of peers on creativity, Torrance and his staff (1964) report: (a) When peers evaluate a work in terms of constructive possibilities rather than its defects, the former "tends to be more effective in producing originality, elaboration, sensitivity, and the like, especially in the fourth, fifth and sixth grades." (b) "Competition in grades one through six produces greater fluency, flexibility, and originality in creative thinking tasks. Practice and 'warm up' reduces but does not completely eliminate the advantage achieved by competition." (c) "If one member of a group is definitely superior to the others in creative thinking abilities, he almost always experiences pressures to reduce his productivity and/or originality and is frequently not given credit for the positive contribution he makes to the group's success." (d) "Homogeneous grouping for tasks requiring creative problem-solving reduces the social stress, enables less creative members to become more productive, and increases the enjoyment of members."

Insofar as teachers are concerned, Torrance *et al.* (1964) have this to say: (a) "... classroom teachers seem to want to reward creative thinking in their pupils, but many of them are unable to do so effectively because of their own personality characteristics, their perceptions of social expectations, and the like." (b) "In projecting plans for discussing with children their creative writing, beginning teachers seem to be preoccupied with the critical and remedial. When encouraged to develop strategies for talking with children which will encourage growth in creative writing, experienced teachers show a slight predominance of creative strategies over the critical and remedial." (c) "Teachers participating in in-service training programs for developing creative thinking, tend not to initiate any more creative activities than their colleagues under control conditions, but there is a fairly general tendency for their pupils to show greater growth in creative writing." (d) In one of his studies, Torrance compared pupils of teachers with strong creative motivations or attitudes with pupils of less strongly motivated teachers on tests of creative thinking administered four months apart and in a creative writing experiment carried out over a three-month period. There were few significant differences in pre- and post-test measures of creative thinking, but there were significant gains in creative writing. (e) Although "teachers may volunteer to carry out creative thinking activities, they tend to be inhibited in doing so, if the principal is not involved in the experiment and does not give his direct approval." This statement about the role of the principal is consistent with what one might infer from a study by Jex (reported in C. W. Taylor, 1963a) with high school science teachers. Jex gave a written creativity test to high school science teachers who came to the University of Utah to obtain a master's degree in science. Their scores correlated negatively with ratings they received from their supervisors or principals for their previous year's work. Both Torrance's and Jex's studies remind us that we must bear in mind that teachers themselves work in social systems and the degree to which their own creativity is rewarded may affect the degree to which they stimulate and reward the creativity of their students.

The possible effects of different teaching techniques on creativity has also come under investigation. Of their work in this area Torrance *et al.* (1964) report: (a) a study in which pupils were asked to write an imaginative story. In one set of conditions the primary reward was for originality, and the secondary reward was for correctness. In the second set of conditions the primary reward was for correctness and the secondary reward was for originality. When the primary reward was for originality, pupils "wrote more original and more interesting stories than their peers in the other condition and tended to write longer stories but made more errors." In another experiment Torrance alternated originality and fluency as primary and secondary rewards and found, again using a creative writing experiment, that when the primary reward was for originality, pupils "produced almost twice as many original ideas as their peers in the other condition and their fluency was not significantly reduced." (b) "The type of evaluated practice (criticism and correction, suggestions of other possibilities, and a combination of criticism and constructive possibilities) do not affect performance on similar subsequent tasks requiring creative problem-solving. Too frequent use of evaluation during the practice session, regardless of the type, seems to interfere with subsequent performance on similar tasks." (c) "Unevaluated ('off the record') practice tends to produce greater originality, elaboration, and sensitivity than evaluated practice in most instances, except at the sixth-grade level." (d) With graduate students in a course on personality development and mental hygiene, Torrance found that those who read and analyzed research in terms of constructive possibilities had more original ideas than those who analyzed it in terms of defects. (e) "More effective teachers in experimental mathematics courses ... report more trouble-shooting or hypothesis-making evaluative thinking and less criticism and praise than their less effective colleagues, effectiveness being determined by pupils learning as measured by pre- and post-tests." (f) "Teachers in various cultures evaluate creative personality characteristics differently as shown by their descriptions of the ideal pupil and the closeness of their evaluations to a model of the productive creative person seems to be related to the creative achievements of the culture." Torrance also reports that in all five cultures studied, Germany, India, Greece, Philippines, and the United States, there appears to be undue punishment "of the child who is courageous in his convictions, the intuitive thinker, the good guesser, the emotionally sensitive person, the individual who regresses occasionally, the visionary person, and the one who is unwilling to accept something on mere say-so without examination of evidence. Unduly great rewards may be going for being courteous, doing work on time, being obedient, being popular and well-liked, and being willing to accept the judgments of authorities." (g) It is therefore not surprising that analysis of stories by preadolescent children in different cultures about animals and persons with divergent characteristics revealed that approximately half of them preceived "some kind of pressure against divergent characteristics."

Despite the pessimism about the effects of the educational system on creativity, several explorations in the use of a variety of teaching techniques that might stimulate creativity among students are hopeful signs on the horizon. Brown (1964) has been exploring the possible value of developing in his students "creative and noncreative sub-selves" around symbols that might be utilized at some future date to call forth the appropriate sub-self. He has found that when the creative sub-self is called forth there is greater preference for complexity, and when the non-creative sub-self is called forth there is greater preference for simplicity. This is especially interesting since Barron (1953, 1958b) has found preference for complexity to be related to originality.

At the prenursery, nursery, kindergarten, and first-grade levels, Moore (1963) is utilizing automated and nonautomated equipment in a permissive atmosphere to help both ultra-rapid and ultra-slow learners gain intrinsic and extrinsic satisfaction from the learning process. Torrance and Gupta (1964) have developed a series of audio tapes and programmed materials to help stimulate creativity at the fourth-grade level because they observed a decline in creative thinking abilities at this grade (which will be reported later, pp. 912–13). They studied the effectiveness of the materials by comparing experimental and control groups in the fourth grade in three different states. Teachers in the experimental classes used the provided materials every two weeks, while teachers in the control group, some of whom had already worked out their own plans for encouraging creativity, were instructed to go ahead with whatever they had planned. To study the effects of the programmed materials Torrance and Gupta compared the subjects' scores on tests of creative thinking abilities developed by Torrance, which were administered at the beginning and at the end of the school term, and report that "the evidence is in favor of the experimental procedures." Torrance also learned that experience with the experimental procedures also affects the subjects' attitudes to school. There was a tendency for fewer of the experimental subjects to say they "hated" school than was true of the control subjects. The evidence on the degree to which both experimentals and controls participated in independent creative activities during vacation periods was inconclusive, but there was some evidence to suggest that, while the controls tended to participate in structured and academic activities, the experimentals favored activities that were more adventurous, nonacademic and more playful. Torrance also studied whether the use of his experimental procedures interfered with the acquisition of traditional educational skills. He reports that the experimental materials may have interfered with their acquisition in one school, "facilitated their acquisition in another, and made no difference in the third. It would appear," he suggests, "that whether the experimental materials interfere with, facilitate, or fail to affect the development of traditional educational skills depends upon the way in which the teacher uses the materials and how well he pursues his usual goals."

Two other findings are reported by Torrance. There was no difference between teachers in the experimental and control groups in their ability to identify creative talent as measured by the creativity tests used. And finally, differences were found in the subjects' career aspirations. Those in the experimental group chose a wider variety of occupations, and a larger proportion of them also chose creative occupations, unconventional occupations, and science occupations, while a larger proportion of their peers in the control groups chose occupations that were among the most popular for fourth graders.

While it is obviously too early to assess the effectiveness of these and other approaches in promoting the future creativity of the pupils and students that are in these programs, it is nevertheless possible that experiments such as those described may result in the effective nurturing of creative potential that may become manifest at some later date.

COGNITIVE CHARACTERISTICS

Empirical Studies

Intelligence

As one might expect, the relationship between creativity and intelligence has received a good deal of attention in the literature. We start with a presentation of the work of Terman and his associates on the intellectually gifted. Although there was no criterion of creativity in these studies, they are nevertheless presented here since they serve as the basis for Terman's and Cox's work on the IQ's of acknowledged geniuses and since they also serve as necessary background material for more recent studies in which investigators concerned themselves with individuals who scored differently on both intelligence tests and so-called creativity tests.

The Intellectually Gifted

The major effort in studying the characteristics of highly intelligent people is the monumental research of Terman and his associates (Burks, Jensen, & Terman, 1930; Terman, 1925, 1954a, 1954b; Terman & Oden, 1947). This work began with children who had IQ's of 120 and above on the National Intelligence Scale B, Form I and the Stanford-Binet. The study involved a rather intensive investigation of the pupils' interests, home backgrounds, physical statuses, anthropometric measurements, and character and personality characteristics, and the data were compared with information collected from a control group.

In 1925 Terman reported that the gifted children scored decisively higher than the control children in intellectual and social interests and did not differ materially in activity interests. A follow-up study two years later showed *"that the gifted children have not lost in educational or general ability, and that gains have far outbalanced losses with respect to such traits as social adaptability and breadth of interests"* (Terman, 1925). And even later (Burks *et al.*, 1930) this group was still achieving at high levels.

In the summary of the 1930 report (Burks *et al.*, 1930) Terman says, "It is to be hoped that the superstitions so commonly accepted relative to intellectually superior children have been permanently swept away by the factual data these studies have presented. It is simply not true that such children are especially prone to be puny, over-specialized in their abilities and interests, emotionally unstable, socially inadaptable, psychotic, and morally undependable; nor is it true that they usually deteriorate to the level of mediocrity as adult life is approached."

At the 25-year mark a comparison was made of subgroups ranked as the highest and lowest fifth of the entire group in success, defined as, "the extent to which a subject had made use of his superior intellectual ability" (Terman, 1954a). This comparison showed little difference between the groups in IQ; marked difference in the educational and occupational status of the family; no evidence of influence from such factors as age of parents, birth order, or size of family; greater breadth of interests among "high" subjects; marked contrast in drive to succeed and in all-round social adjustment. Not until high school had the two groups shown marked differences in achievement, but by the end of high school the difference had become very marked. The highs had been more accelerated in school and were favorable in opinion about acceleration.

When the subjects were close to 35 years of age (1945), the group had published 90 books or monographs and approximately 1,500 articles that appeared in scientific, scholarly, or literary magazines. More than 100 patents were granted to the group; nearly half of these went to two men. The group, however, is not regarded as containing anyone who manifested the promise of equalling Shakespeare, Goethe, Tolstoy, etc.

In the 1954 report which was devoted solely to the scientists and nonscientists in his group, Terman (1954b) says that, "their total contribution to science is many times the amount that could be expected from the same number of men picked at random in the general population," although no one in the group compares in status to those studied by Roe. On the basis of such data, Terman concludes, "The follow-up of these gifted subjects has proved beyond question that tests of 'general intelligence,' given as early as six, eight, or ten years, tell a great deal about the ability to achieve either presently or 30 years hence. Such tests do not, however, enable us to predict what direction the achievement will take, and least of all do they tell us what personality factors or what accidents of fortune will affect the fruition of exceptional ability" (Terman, 1954a). And once again, the importance of the *Zeitgeist* in determining "what talents will come to flower" is indicated.

A comparison of the most and least successful subjects in the population reflected the importance of background and personality characteristics. This study was based on two groups of subjects, 150 each, and the results indicated that, "In our gifted group success is associated with stability rather than instability, with absence rather than with presence of disturbing conflicts—in short with well-balanced temperament and with freedom from excessive frustrations" (Terman, 1954a).

Thus, Terman's material indicates that individuals of tested high IQ in the early grades in elementary school continue to maintain their intellectual superiority later in life. High intelligence alone, however, is not likely to lead to outstanding achievement, for, as Terman himself pointed out, there were critical background, personality, and social factors that accounted for differences between "more" and "less" successful groups in his own population. Unfortunately, there was no criterion of creativity in the above studies. Therefore, to learn about the relationship between intelligence and creativity let us turn to criterion-based studies.

Criterion-Based Studies

In criterion-based studies both the criteria and techniques used to estimate intelligence have varied. The kinds of subjects studied also varied. Thus, it should be noted that in studies where subjects have long since been dead, estimates of their IQ's have been high. However, in studies of living subjects a wide range of intelligence test scores have been obtained. In the latter studies the lack of a strong positive correlation may be a function of the restricted range of the criterion or the lack of specificity in the criterion. Another important factor that probably affects the relationship between intelligence and creativity in some situations is educational status. In these situations both educational level and the verbal aspects of intelligence may be related to obtaining the opportunity for creativity. Finally, it should be pointed out that the opinion is often explicit or implicit that in the general population a measure of IQ may be useful in weeding out individuals who are quite low in creativity but that above some as-yet-undetermined IQ level it may not be a matter of "how much" intelligence an individual has but how he uses what he possesses.

Using "historiometry," a method in which various primary and secondary sources are analyzed to estimate the IQ level an individual might have had to perform the various activities attributed to him, Terman (1917) decided that Galton was a boy prodigy and estimated that his IQ was not far from 200. The estimate was based on Galton's knowledge and capacities between the ages of three and eight.

Cox (1926) utilized the historiometric method in a larger study. In this study Cox asked, "What degree of *mental endowment* characterizes individuals of genius in their childhood and youth?" To answer this question Cox started with the list of 1000 eminent men assembled by Cattell and eliminated those who were of the hereditary aristocracy and nobility, and eminent men born before 1450; of those remaining, the men beyond the rank of 510 on the original list were also dropped. The remaining subjects were 282 eminent persons who lived between 1450 and 1850.

In addition to this group of 282, Cox included a group of 19 subjects whom she had used for preliminary study and who had appeared beyond the five-hundred-tenth name on the list. The professionals in the final group included: writers, statesmen and politicians, scientists, soldiers, religious leaders, philosophers, musicians, and revolutionary statesmen.

Cox made two IQ estimates for each of her subjects: one at the age of 17 and the other at the age of 26. The average IQ of her group was 155.

Cox also compared the men ranked highest with those ranked lowest in her group and found that the first ten and highest IQ's were "significantly above the average of a group of typical geniuses." She also emphasizes a point, which is quite germane in evaluating the data on intelligence, that the lowest IQ's "compensate for these low ratings by their relatively greater *balance* and *activity*"; and *"that high but not the highest intelligence, combined with the greatest degree of persistence, will achieve greater eminence than the highest degree of intelligence with somewhat less persistence."*

That intelligence alone is insufficient for creativity is supported by Roe's (1952) studies. Roe investigated the intelligence of her subjects using a specially designed Verbal-Spatial-Mathematical Test and obtained a rather large range of scores. Where comparable data were available, she found that some of her subjects did not score as high as the average Ph.D. She concludes by saying that, "It seems quite clear that, having chosen your general field, the particular kind of work you do in it is related in some degree to your particular capacities. How well you do in the field is partly a function of your capacity for that particular field, but even more a function of how hard you work at it." It should also be noted that Roe (1952) also found her groups to differ from each other on the three intellectual capacities studied. She reports that the social scientists and theoretical physicists were higher in verbal than nonverbal abilities; experimental physicists were the reverse of this; and anthropologists were relatively low in mathematical ability. That there were exceptions to the generalizations suggests that these abilities were a factor in vocational choice, but not a decisive one.

Drevdahl (1956) studied graduate and advanced undergraduate students in the sciences and the arts for whom faculty ratings on creativity were available. To both groups the Thurstone Primary Mental Abilities Test was administered and, while no statistically significant relationships between creativity and intelligence were obtained, the more creative group did score higher on the test of verbal meaning.

MacKinnon reports two studies in which he investigated the relationship between intelligence and creativity. In one (MacKinnon, 1959a) the subjects were industrial researchers working in the field of guided missiles and electronics who had been rated on a series of 17 variables by supervisors and peers. A factor analysis of the ratings yielded six factors and one of them, "General Competence," accounted for most of the variance. An investigation was then undertaken of the differences between more and less competent individuals on other data collected at the Institute for Personality Assessment and Research (IPAR) at the University of California at Berkeley. The results of this analysis indicated that the more competent researcher scored higher on standardized tests of mental functioning (tests not indicated), and in other assessment procedures the more competent individual revealed himself as possessing a high degree of intellectual efficiency and intellectual capacity.

MacKinnon (1964) also studied architects using the Terman Concept Mastery Test (a test of verbal intelligence with a high ceiling) and found that the relationship between creativity and intelligence was not significantly different from zero. Gough (1961) reports similar poor results with the same test in his study of industrial research scientists. In evaluating these results, as well as in all other studies of creativity, one needs to attend to the criterion. As McNemar (1964) argues, in criterion-based studies one must be aware of the range in the criterion. If the criterion is restricted in range then "little, if any, correlation can be expected for any and all predictors." Similarly, one must attend carefully to factors that make up the criterion. In commenting on MacKinnon's study of architects (MacKinnon, 1962), McNemar (1964) says, "If judged creativity reflects engineering-structural innovation, then intelligence would likely be a correlate; if judged creativity depends on new artistic designs, then the intelligence component would likely be of less importance."

Meer and Stein (1955) present a study that tells us more about the conditions under which intelligence and creativity may be related. These investigators found that scores on the Wechsler-Bellevue Intelligence Scale and the Miller Analogies Test were related to the creativity of industrial research chemists some of whom were Ph.D.'s and others of whom were not. When education was controlled for, the relationship between intelligence and creativity was obtained only for the non-Ph.D.'s. Furthermore, when measures of the opportunity for creativity in the research organization were obtained, it was found that among the non-Ph.D.'s in the high opportunity groups, the previously obtained relationship between intelligence and creativity was not found. Meer and Stein suggested, since it was the verbal subtests of the intelligence tests used that provided the significant correlations, that high capacity in the verbal aspects of intelligence may be related to obtaining the opportunity for creativity.

Guilford's Research

Guilford's (1950) research is based on the premise that "we must look well beyond the boundaries of the IQ if we are to fathom the domain of creativity," and the belief that the idea "that creative talent is to be accounted for in terms of high intelligence or IQ ... is not only inadequate but has been largely responsible for lack of progress in the understanding of creative people." Many investigators share this orientation. Some of them have, therefore, concentrated on the use of personality measures, but Guilford has concentrated on measures of the intellect which would tap abilities that are presumably not usually involved in tests of intelligence. He has developed a series of very interesting tests which other investigators have used or have adapted for their own purposes and which they often regard as tests of creativity. However, before these tests (or the Guilford-like tests) can be regarded as tests of creativity, they need to satisfy several conditions. First, the mental operations involved in them or the variables they purport to measure need to be of such a character that one would expect them to be related to creativity. And, by the same token, they must be meaningfully related to other psychological variables that one would also expect to be related to creativity. Secondly, the tests should relate to a criterion of creativity. And thirdly, since Guilford's tests are measures of the intellect, it has to be demonstrated that the former constitute a separate dimension that can be called creativity. In statistical terms, then, these tests should be highly correlated with each other and not significantly correlated with intelligence tests.

On the basis of factor-analytic investigations, Guilford regards the structure of intellect as composed of three major dimensions—*Content* (the medium in which thought occurs), *Operations* (the operation performed on the material), and *Products* (the results of the combination of the first two). In relating his studies of intellect to creativity, Guilford (1963) says, "although the most obvious aspects of creative thinking appear to depend on the abilities to do divergent-productive thinking and the abilities to effect transformations of information, with the abilities of fluency, flexibility, elaboration, and redefinition playing significant roles, with creative thinking put in its larger context of problem solving, we see that any or all kinds of abilities represented in the structure of intellect can play their useful roles, directly or indirectly."

The factors of the intellect, measured by tests developed by Guilford, are correlated with personality characteristics that might well be expected to relate to creativity. Guilford (1959b) reports that, "Individuals who are high on scores for ideational fluency are inclined to be more impulsive, more ascendant, and more confident and to have a stronger appreciation of creativity. Individuals who show more than ordinary signs of nervousness and depression are likely to be slightly lower on tasks requiring ideational fluency, but they show no handicaps on other types of fluency tests.... Those who score higher in tests of expressional fluency are inclined to be more impulsive, to appreciate aesthetic expression, and to like reflective thinking.... The original person tends to be more confident and tolerant of ambiguity and to like reflective and divergent thinking and aesthetic expression. The unoriginal person is inclined to be more meticulous and to feel a need for discipline.... The hypothesis that originality rests upon an attitude of unconventionality is not supported."

Guilford's work has stimulated a large number of investigators, some of whom have used Guilford's own tests or developed adaptations of them (referred to below as Guilford-like tests) for use in specific situations. One rather interesting development in this area has been undertaken by Torrance (1962b) who has studied the manner in which creative abilities, as measured by Guilford-like and other tests, vary in different cultures. Torrance administered both verbal and nonverbal tests of creative abilities to pupils in the first six grades in Australia, Western Samoa, Germany, India, segregated Negro schools in Georgia, and in middle-class white American schools. He found different developmental curves for each culture. Of special interest was the fact that for most of his measures of creative thinking he found "periods of decline rather than growth at about ages five, nine, thirteen and seventeen." These declines he regards as the "result of the stresses of cultural discontinuities and are accompanied by personality disturbances." As evidence for the effects of cultural discontinuity Torrance cites the new demands on the individual at each of the developmental stages posited by Sullivan (1953), as well as evidence he has obtained in working with and observing school children. Torrance says, "Using Harry Stack Sullivan's (1953) conceptualization of the stages of development of interpersonal skills, the drop at about age five occurs with the end of the childhood stage and the beginning of the juvenile stage with its demands for social accommodation, compromise, and acceptance of authorities outside the home. The second drop occurs with the onset of the preadolescent stage with its increased need for consensual validation, peer approval, identification with peers of the same sex, and conformity to peer norms. The third occurs at the onset of early adolescence with its increased anxieties, striving for approval of the opposite sex, and the like, all of which restrict many areas of awareness and impose new demands for conformity."

Some of the evidence for cultural discontinuity obtained from Torrance's own work with school children are as follows: At about age five "concerns about sex appropriateness and emphasis on sex differences become tremendously inhibiting." At about age nine when the child reaches the fourth-grade classroom, activity becomes more organized, children receive credit only for what they put on paper, they start doing homework, and they manifest "the inhibiting influence of their preoccupation with prevention and fear of making mental leaps." Teachers in the intermediate grades also behave differently with their pupils than teachers in the primary grades. The latter are "willing to sacrifice preoccupation with correctness and form for creative values." At age thirteen, when the pupil enters the seventh grade, he has to go to another school building, there is emphasis on promptness, deviations in appearance are discouraged, there is concern with approval from the opposite sex and there is an intensification of the pressure to be well-rounded socially and athletically. At seventeen, "High school seniors are faced with the immediacy of the transition to college, work, or military service.... There are new demands for grown-up behavior, sanctions against regression to childish thinking and behavior, and the like." Finally, as evidence for the possibility that personality disturbances occur at ages five, nine, thirteen, and seventeen, Torrance analyzed a sample of 100 letters written to him by parents about creative children who were in some kind of trouble because of their creativity. He found parents to be more frequently "disturbed about their thirteen-year-olds and nine-year-olds than any others. The five-year-olds and the seventeen-year-olds cause the next greatest concern."

To summarize what has been said: Guilford's tests and the variations thereof contain mental operations that one would expect to be associated with creativity. The personality variables they relate to are also of such a character that one would expect them to be related to creativity. Also, the manner in which the tests vary as a function of age and cultural factors is meaningful. The next question we come to is how well the tests relate to a criterion of creativity. A survey of the criterion-based literature indicates that they do not fare very well.

Chorness (1956) reports a study concerned with the prediction of creative expression among 50 students. The students were involved in a lecture-discussion and rated on "audience interest and reaction, degree of spontaneity, ability to transcend rote material, originality of expressions, and so on." These ratings yielded four factors, three of which were identified as *audience reactivity, native ideation,* and *problem sensitivity.* Ratings on originality and spontaneity did not load significantly on any dimension, but they were retained to see how they related to other test data.

After removing the effects of intelligence and studying the multiple correlations between the factor composites of the Guilford battery and criterion scores, Chorness says, "it would appear that the creativity tests can carry the burden of prediction," and that a test of controlled associations was the best predictor. The factor composite also predicted the students' grades better than did an intelligence test.

The positive results reported by Chorness cannot be generalized to other situations. Drevdahl (1956) in his study of advanced undergraduate and graduate students who were rated on creativity by their faculty found no significant differences on the following Guilford factors: redefinition, closure, ideational fluency, spontaneous flexibility, associational fluency, or sensitivity to problems. Word fluency and adaptive flexibility did not differentiate at the .05 level, but a low (significant) relationship between the criterion and scores on these factors was found. Originality scores did differentiate between the two groups.

Several other investigators also did not obtain very encouraging results with Guilford's tests. Gough (1961), for example, in his study of research scientists in which he used peer and supervisors' ratings of creativity found that "The Unusual Uses Test total score correlated −.05 with the criterion, but the quality score (rated quality of the uses suggested) correlated +.27. The Consequences total score and quality score correlated −.27 and −.12, respectively. The Matchsticks Problem Test correlated +.04, and the Gestalt Transformation Test gave a coefficient of +.27."

C. W. Taylor, Smith, Ghiselin, and Ellison (1961) have used the Guilford tests and report a lack of validity of any of the multiple scores taken from seven high level aptitude tests in a study of Air Force scientists. And C. W. Taylor, Cooley, and Nielson also found that such tests did not serve as good predictors of the creativity scores obtained by high school students engaged in a National Science Program for research activities. They did, however, predict ratings obtained by students in a similarly sponsored program that was devoted to more academic-like activities.

Adaptation of Guilford's procedures to the *specific field* in which an individual works seems to have some possible merit. Gough (1961) reports a New Scientific Uses Test that is modeled on Guilford's Unusual Uses Test and taps a laboratory worker's fluency of ideas with everyday laboratory materials. This test yields both a total score based on the number of uses suggested, as well as a quality score. While neither score correlated significantly with the criterion, in Gough's (1961) study of industrial researchers the quality score did make an important contribution to the multiple correlation. (In this study Gough also developed another adaptation of an old technique, a Scientific Word Association Test modeled on the Kent-Rosanoff Word Association Test, in which the stimulus words consist of objects and concepts known to scientists. An index which gives the subject credit for extremely unusual responses but which weights moderately unusual responses more highly yielded a significant correlation with a creativity criterion. A third adaptation, which did not fare as well as the other two, was a Scientific Incomplete Sentences Test that was scored both for infrequency and quality of completion. This test did not correlate significantly with a criterion.)

Thus, Guilford's tests do not fare very well in criterion-based studies. One of the possibilities for this is the ubiquitous criterion problem. Possibly more attention needs to be paid to the kinds of creative performance the tests are measuring and to relate them to criteria in areas where these performances are rewarded. Another possibility is that the value of the tests might be increased if they were integrated with measures of motivational, personality, and situational factors as moderator variables. Such combinations might overcome the objection that, while the tests may "measure the infrequency or originality of a subject's ideas in response to specific test items, they fail to reveal the extent to which the subject faced with real life problems is likely to come up with solutions that are novel and adaptive and which he will be motivated to apply in all of their ramifications" (MacKinnon, 1962).

Let us now turn to the third condition mentioned at the outset of this discussion: Do the tests tap a dimension which can be called creativity and which is separate from intelligence? To answer this question it is necessary to present studies among which are those that have utilized Guilford-like tests and which purport to have distinguished between intelligence *and* creativity.

Intelligence Tests and "Creativity Tests"

The basic research design of the studies reviewed in this section is one in which a population of subjects is tested with some intelligence test (or tests) and also either with Guilford's tests or adaptations of them. The subjects are then divided into two or four groups based on whether they scored high or low on the intelligence tests or high or low on the creativity tests. Differences between the groups on other measures are then studied.

Barron (1957) used the Terman Concept Mastery Test as his measure of intelligence. For his measure of what he called "originality" he used the following: Guilford's tests of Unusual Uses, Consequences B, Plot Titles B; Rorschach *O*+ responses, originality ratings of *TAT* stories, scores for infrequency of human movement responses to Rorschach-like ink-blots, scores for infrequency of correct anagram solutions, and an originality score based on a story composed by the subject. Using all these tests, Barron developed a composite originality score. The correlation between the intelligence and originality scores was .33. From a population of 343 Air Force captains, 15 were selected who were one standard deviation above the mean on the originality composite and, at the same time, one standard deviation below the mean on the Concept Mastery Test. This group was then regarded as high originality–low intelligence, and it was compared with a high intelligence–low originality group composed of 23 men who were one standard deviation above the mean on the Concept Mastery Test and one standard deviation below the mean on the originality composite score. Both groups described themselves with the Gough Adjective Check List, and the following adjectives appeared more frequently among the high originality–low intelligence group: "affected, aggressive, demanding, dependent, dominant, forceful, impatient, initiative, outspoken, sarcastic, strong, suggestible." For the low originality–high intelligence group, the following adjectives were found more frequently: "mild, optimistic, pleasant, quiet, unselfish."

Getzels and Jackson (1962) also studied the differences between "high creative" and "high IQ" individuals. Their subjects were drawn from a private school population whose education ranged from the sixth grade through the junior grade in high school. Their high creative subjects were in the upper 20 per cent on creativity (Guilford-like) tests but not on IQ tests. Their high intelligence subjects were in the upper 20 per cent on IQ tests but not in the upper 20 per cent on the creativity tests. They then studied a variety of characteristics of both populations. One of their findings was that, despite a 23-point difference in mean IQ, the two groups did not differ significantly from the total school population. Torrance (1962a) replicated these findings in six of eight school settings that included elementary schools, a high school, and two graduate schools. The results were not replicated in a parochial elementary school and in a small-town elementary school where the high IQ subjects scored significantly higher on an achievement test than did the high creative subjects. Torrance suggests that it is likely that no difference in scholastic achievement would be found between the high IQ and high creative groups in those school settings where the students "are taught in such a way that they learn creatively, and thus creative thinking abilities become important in learning." Where a difference is obtained (in favor of the high IQ subjects) it might be accounted for by the fact that the school setting has placed emphasis on "'traditional kinds of learning,'" including emphasis on authority and emphasis on memory and conformity to behavior norms. Torrance also suggests that an explanation might be found in the distribution of ability. In the two school situations where the Getzels-Jackson findings were not replicated, the average IQ of the high creative group was lowest of all schools studied. This suggests the possibility that creative thinking abilities may become important after an IQ of about 120. Yamamoto (1964) replicated the basic findings of Getzels and Jackson and Torrance with high school students in a study where he used the Lorge-Thorndike Intelligence Test and creativity tests developed by Torrance (1962a).

Getzels and Jackson (1962) also studied other characteristics of their two groups. They found, for example, that the families of the two groups differed and were important factors in the development of the children studied. "The overall impression of the high IQ family is that it is one in which individual divergence is limited and risks minimized, and the overall impression of the high creativity family is that it is one in which individual divergence is permitted and risks are accepted." Getzels and Jackson's finding on teacher preferences was previously discussed (p. 905).

The studies just reviewed are based on the assumption that tests of intelligence and creativity are statistically independent. But what is the relationship between intelligence and the so-called creativity tests? Guilford did not use a traditional measure of intelligence, so there is no evidence on the relationships between Guilford's tests and a more commonly used intelligence test. Guilford's own test battery, however, contains tests that are part of what he considers the general intelligence domain and other tests that are considered measures of divergent thinking and in which measures of creativity belong. Therefore, one can analyze the relationships within Guilford's own data to determine how distinct the creativity tests might be from the intelligence tests. Thorndike (1963) has done this analysis from which it appears that the variance that the divergent thinking tests have in common is the variance they share with the intelligence measures. In other studies which do report relationships between creativity tests and one or more traditional measures of creativity we find that the correlations are sufficiently high so as not to allow for the statement that there is independence between the creativity and intelligence dimensions. Barron (1957) reports a correlation of .33 between the various measures he used. Yamamoto (1964) found a correlation of .30 between his intelligence and creativity tests for the *total* school population from which he selected his subjects. (The correlations for separate grades ranged from .18 to .56.) For his *criterion* groups he found insignificant correlations. The Getzels and Jackson study has also come under critical review, and it too had not demonstrated independence between creativity and intelligence. Wallach and Kogan (1965) in their intensive analysis of this study say, "Five alleged tests of creativity were administered to large samples of students ranging in class from sixth grade through the end of high school. Four of the five creativity tests correlated significantly with IQ for the girls, and all five of these tests correlated significantly with IQ for the boys. Consider next the relationships among the instruments in the creativity battery—that is, the question of whether they define a unitary dimension of individual differences. The Getzels-Jackson results showed that the five creativity tasks were virtually no more strongly correlated among themselves than they were correlated with intelligence. To give some averages, for boys the mean correlation was .26 between the creativity battery and IQ, and was .28 among the tasks in the creativity battery; in the case of the girls, the corresponding mean correlations were .27 and .32. In sum, the creativity measures correlated with intelligence on the order of .3, and also correlated with each other on the order of .3. There was no evidence, in short, for arguing that the creativity instruments were any more strongly related to one another than they were related to general intelligence. The inevitable conclusion was that little warrant existed here for talking about creativity *and* intelligence as if these terms referred to concepts at the same level of abstraction. The creativity indicators measured nothing in common that was distinct from general intelligence." McNemar (1964) also studied the Getzels and Jackson data and reports, "From the published report I have ascertained (via the correlation-of-sums formula) that creativity and IQ correlate to the extent of .40 for the total of 533 cases." McNemar says further that "this *r* of .40 has been greatly attenuated because of three things: first, the usual measurement errors; second, the cases were highly selected on IQ (mean of 132); third, the IQs are a mixture from the Stanford-Binet, Henmon-Nelson, and Wechsler Intelligence Scale for Children (the use of regression-estimated Binet IQs from the other two scales aggravates rather than improves the mixture). We deduce that intelligence and the creativity tests used here have far more common variance than the authors believe." This last statement has been generalized by Wallach and Kogan (1965) who reviewed the literature in which Guilford's or Guilford-like tests were employed and concluded, "The measures that have been construed as indicators of creativity are not indicators of some single psychological dimension parallel to and distinct from the dimension of general intelligence defined by conventional intelligence test indices."

The fact that previously reviewed studies cannot support the conceptualization that there is a dimension of individual differences called "creativity" which is distinct from general intelligence does not mean that such a distinction cannot be found or does not exist. The study that set out to find this distinction and did so successfully is the one reported by Wallach and Kogan (1965) in which they studied the entire fifth grade population of a suburban middle-class public school.

Wallach and Kogan, as others in this area, concern themselves with associative processes. Their basic proposition is that essentials of the creative process are contained in two elements: "first, the production of associative content that is abundant and that is unique; second, the presence in the associator of a playful, permissive task attitude." Their operational definition of creativity is number and uniqueness of response where uniqueness is defined as a response given by only *one* subject. Equally important as their definition of creativity were the conditions under which they collected their data. Data were collected in an atmosphere that was free from time pressure and which was gamelike in orientation. They avoided an examination or test setting which was either explicit or implicit in other studies. The social conditions for collecting the data were therefore more congruent with descriptions of creative individuals of the conditions under which they worked than was true in other studies. The lack of time limits and the gamelike atmosphere in which the data were collected also gave the subjects adequate opportunity to manifest the creativity they possessed, for, as indicated in other studies, later responses are more unusual and remote than earlier responses (Christensen, Guilford, & Wilson, 1957), and creativity scores on a test of unusual uses are higher under relaxed conditions than they are under evaluational conditions (Dentler & Mackler, 1964).

In the Wallach and Kogan study five creativity tests were used. Three of them used verbal material and two of them consisted of visual materials. Each test yielded two measures—number of associations and uniqueness of associations. In four of the five procedures uniqueness of response was significantly related to number of responses. Furthermore, the six verbal indices of creativity were correlated with the four visual indices of creativity, which is regarded as "evidence for a unified dimension of individual differences that cuts across any verbal vs. visual type of distinction." The intelligence tests included measures of verbal, visual, and quantitative skills and covered a range of content. All but one of the intelligence tests were individually administered. The creativity tests were more highly correlated with each other (on the average, .4) than they were with the intelligence tests (on the average, .1). And the average correlation among the intelligence tests was .5. Thus, Wallach and Kogan achieved the necessary statistical independence to say they were studying intelligence *and* creativity.

Having established these two dimensions, the investigators then developed a single creativity index score and a single intelligence score. Distributions of both scores for both male and female pupils were obtained by dividing the distributions at the medians; four groups were established for each sex: high intelligence–high creativity; high intelligence–low creativity; low intelligence–high creativity; and low intelligence–low creativity. The manner in which each of the four groups within each sex differed from each other was studied through observations of two female observers, the pupils' conceptualizing activities, their capacity for physiognomic perception, their anxiety and defensiveness (dealt with both as dependent and independent variables), and clinical case studies.

The results of these investigations were as follows:

Behavioral observations—Observational data were obtained in nine areas (e.g., seeking attention in unsocialized ways, hesitancy in expressing opinions, seeking companionship, etc.) by two female observers two weeks prior to any testing. For the girls, variations in behavior were related to intelligence, creativity, and the interaction between them, while for the boys only the intelligence variable exerted any influence on the ratings. Variations in behavior by specific subgroups of girls were:

High creativity–high intelligence: The subjects in this group "... show the least doubt and hesitation of all the groups, show the highest level of self-confidence, and display the least tendency toward deprecation of oneself and one's work." In social relations these girls are both more active in seeking out others, and they are more actively sought out by others. This group has the highest level of attention span, concentration, and interest in academic work. But at the same time this group is also high in regard to disruptive, attention-seeking behavior, possibly because they are "brimming over with eagerness to propose novel, divergent possibilities in the classroom, in the face of boredom with the customary classroom routines."

High creativity–low intelligence: This group is the most disadvantaged of all in the classroom. They "are the most cautious and hesitant of all the groups, the least confident and least self-assured, the least sought after by their peers as companions, and in addition are quite avoidant themselves of the companionship of others.... In the academic sphere, they are the most deprecatory of their own work and the least able to concentrate and maintain attention." They are, however, equal to the high-high group in their disruptive attention-seeking behavior. Wallach and Kogan suggest that, "Most likely, however, the attention-seeking of these two groups is quite different in quality, given the highly different contexts of other behaviors in the two cases. While the disruptive behaviors of the high-high group suggest enthusiasm and overeagerness, those of the high creative–low intelligent group suggest an incoherent protest against their plight."

Low intelligence–low creativity: This "group possesses greater confidence and assurance, is less hesitant and subdued, and is considerably more outgoing toward peers in social relationships, than is the high creative–low intelligent group. The low-low group members appear to compensate for their poor academic performances by activity in the social sphere, while the high creative–low intelligent individuals, possessing seemingly more delicate sensitivities, are more likely to cope with academic failure by social withdrawal and a retreat within themselves."

High intelligence–low creativity: "... these girls show confidence and assurance. In terms of companionship patterns, however, an intriguing difference emerges. While sought quite strongly as a companion by others, the girl in this group tends not to seek companionship herself. She also is least likely to seek attention in disruptive ways and is reasonably hesitant about expressing opinions. Attention span and concentration for academic matters, in turn, are quite high. The impression that emerges, then, is of a girl who is strongly oriented toward academic achievement, is somewhat cool and aloof in her social behavior but liked by others anyway, and is unwilling to take the chance of overextending or overcommiting herself; there is a holding back, a basic reserve."

Among boys, the behavioral observations were related only to the intelligence dimension but not to creativity, and in this regard they were the same as those obtained for the girls—the high intelligent boy copes well with classroom requirements, and the low intelligent boy has difficulty.

Conceptualizing behavior—One of the tasks included in the conceptualizing study was one in which the pupils were asked to group pictures of everyday physical objects. Reasons for grouping the objects were also obtained. The results revealed that "... balanced usage of thematic or inferential conceptualizing styles seems to characterize the two high creativity subgroups, and especially the high-high group. An apparent distaste for thematic responding when other response options are available seems to characterize the high intelligence–low creativity subgroup. Finally, a possible inability to make more use of inferential conceptualizing, with a consequent concentration on thematic responding, appears to characterize the low-low subgroup."

Physiognomic perception—The results in this area revealed that "... both creativity and intelligence serve to augment physiognomic sensitivity, though one or the other of these thinking modes made a more substantial contribution dependent upon the physiognomic procedure at issue. In general, however, awareness of physiognomic properties tended to be maximal in the subgroup high in both creativity and intelligence, while such awareness tended to be minimal in the subgroup low in both creativity and intelligence. For the girls, the findings were similar in part to those just noted, but in part also suggested that under some conditions, noncongruent subgroups—those in which creativity and intelligence levels are different rather than similar—experience as much difficulty in making physiognomic attributions as members of the low-low subgroup."

Anxiety and defensiveness—Both anxiety (measured in terms of general and test anxiety) and defensiveness were treated as dependent and independent variables, and in both instances significant findings were obtained only for males and not for females. When the variables were treated as a function of creativity and intelligence, the results revealed that "... significant interaction effects were obtained for both general and test anxiety in boys. Highly intelligent–low creative boys were quite low, low intelligent–low creative boys were quite high, and the two highly creative subgroups were intermediate in admitted anxiety. The exceptionally low anxiety level for the boys of high intelligence and low creativity was explained on the basis of a neat match between their area of competence and the type of thinking emphasized in the classroom. In the case of defensiveness, a significant intelligence effect was obtained, the highly intelligent boys being less defensive."

When anxiety and defensiveness were treated as independent variables the results revealed that "For boys, test anxiety was inversely related to intelligence, and defensiveness was inversely related to creativity. Both findings were consistent with stated hypotheses. Results for girls were less clear-cut. In the case of intelligence, a significant interaction effect was obtained, largely as a consequence of an exceptionally low intelligence mean in girls high in both test anxiety and defensiveness. No significant effects for creativity were observed in girls, though the pattern of results was manifestly discrepant from the intelligence findings. A theoretical interpretation of the obtained sex differences was advanced based in part on prior published evidence indicating that anxiety and defensiveness may not mean the same thing in boys and girls."

Clinical studies—The observers prepared reports on their total experience with the children, discussions with current teachers, and examinations of reports of previous teachers. These reports revealed:

"High creativity–high intelligence: These children can exercise within themselves both control and freedom, both adultlike and childlike kinds of behavior.

"High creativity–low intelligence: These children are in angry conflict with themselves and with their school environment and are beset by feelings of unworthiness and inadequacy. In a stress-free context, however, they can blossom forth cognitively.

"Low creativity–high intelligence: These children can be described as 'addicted' to school achievement. Academic failure would be perceived by them as catastrophic, so that they must continually strive for academic excellence in order to avoid the possibility of pain.

"Low creativity–low intelligence: Basically bewildered, these children engage in various defensive maneuvers ranging from useful adaptations such as intensive social activity to regressions such as passivity or psychosomatic symptoms."

In summary, several investigators sought to differentiate between intelligence *and* creativity but statistical analysis of their data revealed that they were not successful. Wallach and Kogan, however, were able to achieve this differentiation both by virtue of the tests they utilized and the relaxed, non-evaluational conditions under which they administered the tests. They also demonstrated a variety of important differences between four groups of pupils who scored differently on both intelligence and creativity dimensions. This calls attention to another limitation in other studies where investigators concerned themselves only with two groups, high creative–low intelligent or high intelligent–low creative, but omitted the groups that were high on both dimensions and low on both dimensions.

Although one cannot expect any one study to investigate all problems, it would have been interesting to learn whether the behavioral differences that were found for girls but not for boys may have been effected by the use of female observers who gathered the data. It would also have been more interesting if Wallach and Kogan had been able to collect some external criterion data and information on teachers' attitudes, which had been studied by Getzels and Jackson and which yielded interesting results. One cannot help but wonder what will happen to the creativity of the pupils in this study, and in view of the time and effort already expended it is to be hoped that some longitudinal work will be possible. Finally, one should not lose sight of the creativity criterion in this study—number and uniqueness of response where uniqueness is a response given by only one child. How would this criterion fare with adults in a criterion-based study? In a study to be reported later (MacKinnon, 1962) we learn that too much weight assigned to rare responses may not result in the highest relationships with a criterion.

THINKING AND PROBLEM SOLVING

There have been several different approaches to the investigation of thought processes and problem-solving procedures associated with creativity. Some investigators have studied the process through which individuals created their products. Others have concerned themselves with tests that, in some ways, are similar to those developed by Guilford. And a third group has derived procedures that either implicitly or explicitly are based on associationistic, Gestalt, and psychoanalytic theories.

Studies of Process

Catharine Patrick (1935, 1937, 1938, 1941) studied the relevance of Wallas's (1926) analysis of the creative process in a series of studies in art, poetry, and science. Wallas had divided the process into the following stages: preparation, incubation, illumination, and verification. To obtain her data, Patrick in her study of poets, for example, presented them with a picture and asked them to write a poem. She then studied the development of the poem and, although she found some overlap in the stages, her findings generally substantiated Wallas's ideas. Eindhoven and Vinacke (1952) observed the behavior of artists and nonartists as they came to the laboratory to paint pictures. They claim they found no evidence for four distinct stages in the creative process, as one might assume on the basis of Patrick's work, but rather the "stages" are really aspects of the creative process that blend together throughout the work.

Tests

In an effort to obtain "an indicator" of a person's ability to produce a quantity of unique ideas in a given situation," Harris and Simberg (no date) constructed a test that consists of listing consequences to common situations, general reasoning, sensitivity to problems, practical judgment, and originality. Three types of scores are obtained with the test—quantity, quality, and uniqueness. The test has a reliability of .92 as measured by the Kuder-Richardson formula. Two forms of the test exist, and the validities reported are primarily with engineers.

Using this test at the AC Spark Plug Division of General Motors Corporation obtained the following results: (a) The total test and seven subscales differentiated at the .05 level or better between the two groups of 18 each (composed of experimental engineers, tool designers, methods analysts, suggestion supervisors, and process engineers) at General Motors who were separated in terms of supervisors' ratings of quantity of unique ideas. (b) The total test and all subparts differentiated significantly between engineers whose overall performance on creative tasks was rated satisfactory or unsatisfactory by their supervisors. (c) Combined quantity scores differentiated between matched pairs of hourly employees in terms of suggestions submitted to the company's suggestion plan. (d) Only two subtest scores differentiated between engineers who spent more than 50 per cent of their time on developmental work and whose supervisor said they had demonstrated ingenuity, inventiveness, plus many ideas, from a group of engineers who spent less than 30 per cent of their time in developmental work. (e) Significant differences were obtained between engineering students who received "A" 's and "B" 's in a course on product design. Students who received high instructor ratings also received higher test scores.

Bennett and Wesman (1949) report a *Test of Productive Thinking* with a reliability of .90. In this test the subject is presented with six hypothetical situations outside the range of his experience, and he is asked for probable consequences. The test is scored for number and quality of responses. D. W. Taylor (1963) studied electronic engineers and electronic scientists who were rated on creativity and productivity by supervisors and nonsupervisors and found that, while the *Strong Engineering Scale* and the *Terman Concept Mastery Test* did not yield significant correlations with the criterion, significant differences were found with the Test of Productive Thinking.

Other Studies Related to Theory

Associationism

MacKinnon (1962) found that a weighted score for unusualness of associations correlated +.50 with rated creativity among architects. To establish the weights, he used the Russell and Jenkins norms (1954). More weight was given in this study to associations given by more than one per cent to ten per cent of the population than to those given by less than one per cent of the population. This is noteworthy, since investigators who use association procedures and who do not find high relationships with their criteria may find that these negative results could be attributed to the fact that they assigned too much weight to or limited themselves solely to extremely rare or extremely unusual associations.

Associationism is central to Mednick's (1962) Remote Associates Test (RAT) in which the subject "is asked to form associative elements into new combinations by providing mediating connective links ... the combination must meet specified criteria that are experimenter imposed." For example, the subject is presented with three words, "rat," "blue," and "cottage." The correct associative link is "cheese" because it is present in the word pairs "rat-cheese," "blue-cheese," and "cottage-cheese." Two college forms of the test exist. Both have 30 items and the subject is allowed 40 minutes to complete the test. Reliability of the test is high: .92 in one study and .91 in another.

The RAT has been used in some studies to cast light on factors involved in the creative process, and in other studies it has been used to gather validity data. Houston and Mednick (1963) suggest that not only do creative individuals have a preference for novelty (Barron, 1958a) but a *need* for novelty. They suggest this on the basis of the following experiment. High and low scorers on the RAT were presented with pairs of words in which each pair contained a noun and a nonnoun. The subject was asked which he preferred. If a noun was selected the experimenter followed it with a novel association. Nonnoun selections were followed with a common association. The authors hypothesized that the novel associations should have a reinforcing effect for high RAT scorers to be manifest in the increased selection of nouns over the series of the pairs of words with which they were presented. Low RAT scorers were not expected to show this effect. The hypothesis was supported. The high RAT scorers significantly increased and the low RAT scorers significantly decreased their choice of nouns.

Martha Mednick, S. A. Mednick, and E. V. Mednick (1964) have used the RAT to learn something about the factors involved in the incubation phase[1] of the creative process. In one experiment they learned that performance on the RAT (which was regarded as the measure of creativity) was enhanced by specific priming. In a second experiment with a difficult remote associates task they replicated this result and also learned that length and placement of the time interval had no effect on performance, which they regard as casting doubt on the idea that dissipation of fatigue or inhibition is involved in the incubation phase. They also learned from this experiment that high RAT scorers scored significantly better than low RAT scorers after incubation, regardless of priming. While no significant interaction effect was found between creativity level and priming in this experiment, these investigators suggest that this possible interaction should be investigated further. The high RAT scorers in the second experiment performed better

[1] The incubation phase is that phase which follows a period of intensive work on a problem and in which no manifest work on the problem occurs. In descriptions of the creative process (e.g., Poincaré, 1954) the incubation phase is often regarded as facilitating the solution of the problem.

after incubation, and the subjects in the first experiment, who had scored higher on the RAT than the low scorers in the second experiment, had been more sensitive to associative priming. Furthermore, Mendelsohn and Griswold (1964) have shown that high RAT scorers use incidental cues to a larger extent than low RAT scorers in a problem-solving experiment. Since the associative priming technique used by Martha Mednick *et al.* appears similar to the use of incidental cues, the authors expect that the high creative person should be more sensitive than the low creative person to associative priming.

The RAT has also been used in the following validity studies: Mednick (1962) reports a correlation of .70 between number of correct RAT associations and creativity ratings by design instructors of students in a college of architecture. With first-year psychology graduate students, the RAT differentiated between those rated high and low by their instructors on creativity in research. In a study of architects it correlated .31 with scores on an originality scale in a questionnaire developed at IPAR and −.31 with a total conformity score based on Crutchfield's work (1955).

Martha Mednick (1963) obtained creativity ratings of graduate students in psychology from their research advisors one to two years after the students had taken the RAT. A significant correlation of .55 between ratings and RAT scores was found, but no significant correlation was found between creativity and Miller Analogies Test scores or grade point averages.

Less positive results have been reported in two other studies. C. W. Taylor (1963a) reports that the test did not correlate well with ratings obtained by high school students in a program of research sponsored by the National Science Foundation. He suggests that verbal tests such as the Remote Associates Test are probably better for fields that put more of a premium on verbal ability than do the sciences.

Andrews (1965) employed the Remote Associates Test with scientists employed in various laboratories. He found that the test was independent of performance when performance was based on the scientist's own report of his five-year output of patents, papers, and unpublished reports, on the judgments of the man's peers and superiors, and on the man's scientific and technical contribution and over-all usefulness to the organization. In only one rather small subgroup of scientists (N=14) did Andrews find a biserial correlation of .37 between scores on the Remote Associates Test and performance. This was a group that was high on self-confidence, highly motivated for its work, and was also high on status and influence in its organization. This finding, in which scores on an association test are combined with personality and social factors as moderator variables, is a highly suggestive lead that might well be followed up in future research.

Riegel, Riegel, and Levine (1966) tested Mednick's (1962) hypothesis that high creative subjects will yield flat response distributions by studying subjects' associations in a variety of tasks. The creativity criterion was subjects' scores on the Creative Personality Scale which is part of the Opinion Attitude and Interest Survey (Fricke, 1963). Mednick's hypothesis was confirmed. But the authors point out that "an interpretation of creativity in terms of associative processes appears more difficult than previously reported. Differences between the two groups [high and low creatives] are dependent on the type of tasks." The authors point to the need for looking at "classes and class relations of acquired conceptual structures."

Psychoanalysis

Hypotheses about the thought processes of creative persons have also been derived from psychoanalytic theory. Psychoanalytic theory differentiates between primary and secondary thought processes. The former is dominated by drives and the latter is controlled. A more elaborate statement of the characteristics of the two thought processes may be found in Rapaport (1951) and Kris (1952).

Pine (1959) related the quality of products produced in a literary task (stories told to the Thematic Apperception Test) and in a task of scientific hypothesis formation and found that quality of productions varied with the amount and control of drive content. Pine and Holt (1960) continued efforts in this direction and argued that the quality of an individual's productions should be related to his control over primary process material and to a combined score based on the expression of drive and the effectiveness of control. The quality of the production was not expected to be related to a score for the amount of drive expression alone. As their measure of quality of imaginative productions, Pine and Holt used: The Thematic Apperception Test, a Science Test, a Humor Test, the Rorschach Test, an Animal Drawing Test, and Guilford's Brick Uses and Consequences Tests. To assess expression of and control of primary process, the Rorschach Test was used, and responses were scored according to procedures developed by Holt (1959; Holt & Havel, 1960). Thirteen male and fourteen female students served as subjects.

The results of the study indicated that the amount of primary process expression and effectiveness of control over drive were independent. Quality scores based on the tests of imagination were unrelated to the amount of primary process expression but positively related to the effectiveness with which such expression was controlled.

Gestalt Psychology

Wertheimer (1945) has applied Gestalt theory to the analysis of the thought processes of several creative individuals, and his theoretical formulations were utilized by Blatt and Stein (1959) in studying the behavior of industrial research chemists whose creativity had been rated by their superiors, peers, and subordinates. One group of these subjects was regarded as "more" and the other as "less" creative. Blatt and Stein reasoned that a complex problem is composed of a universe of elements that have to be combined into one or more series of relationships which need to be coordinated before a solution is attained. In some problems, as in the one to be described later, some of the relationships are given and others need to be learned. The subject arrives at these latter relationships by analyzing their constituent elements. Theoretically, once the subject has attained all the necessary and sufficient information, the problem can be solved in a single coordinating step. At this point the subject's behavior changes from the *analysis* of constituent elements to the *synthesis* of information at his disposal. Consequently, the problem-solving process may be described as consisting of two major phases—an analysis phase and a synthesis phase. Ideally, the shift from analysis to synthesis occurs when the subject has been exposed to all the necessary and sufficient information for solving the problem. In an actual situation, however, mere exposure to various elements does not mean that the subject understands their significance. The shift from analysis to synthesis therefore occurs usually some time *after* all the necessary and sufficient information has been attained. Consequently, the analysis phase may be said to be composed of an initial phase and a lag phase. The initial phase extends from the beginning of the problem-solving process to that point at which the subject has been exposed to the necessary and sufficient information. It is followed by a lag phase that is concluded when the subject's predominant mode of activity shifts from analysis to synthesis. In the synthesis phase the subject is said to be primarily concerned with coordinating the obtained information. Using this model of the problem-solving process, it may be said that efficiency in problem solving may be defined as the *absence* of unnecessary questions.

The apparatus used to study the problem-solving behavior of the subjects was developed by John and Rimoldi (John, 1957). This is an electro-mechanical apparatus in which the subject is presented with a series of logical relationships which he must derive and then coordinate. A center light is to be activated by pressing the correct sequence of three critical buttons that can activate all the appropriate connections. The sequence of buttons actually pressed in arriving at the solution is automatically recorded on tape so that a complete protocol of the problem-solving behavior is available.

Eight more and nine less creative subjects participated in this study. Their protocols, the automatic tape-recorded sequences of the subjects' button presses, were analyzed in terms of a number of variables. The results indicated that ability to solve the problem (i.e., activating the center light through pressing an appropriate sequence of the three critical buttons) did not differentiate between the more and less creative subjects, but various characteristics of the problem-solving process did. The more creative men were significantly different from their less creative colleagues in that they had clearer analysis-to-synthesis shift points and asked a significantly larger proportion of their questions in the initial phase of the problem-solving process.

Imagery

In addition to intelligence, thinking, and problem solving, another of the cognitive characteristics studied in relation to creativity is imagery. Visual, kinesthetic, and auditory imagery were reported to be important characteristics among several composers (Agnew, 1922) and mathematicians (Hadamard, 1945). Roe (1951) also gathered systematic data on imagery in her interviews with high-level scientists and found that biologists and experimental physicists in her sample used mainly verbal or other symbolic images. Psychologists and anthropologists used verbal imagery mainly. The relationship between vocation and imagery was significant, and although the evidence is not clear on this point, Roe believes that the type of imagery an individual possesses influences his vocational choice rather than that the field of work develops a particular imagery in the person. Roe also suggests that men who did not follow the imagery pattern of their group tended to be different from their colleagues in other ways, e.g., early interests. Finally, she also points out that the imagery of her subjects was related to the verbal or nonverbal nature of their fathers' occupations.

Perception

Both perceptual processes and the preference for visual forms have been studied in relation to creativity. Stein and Meer (1954), in their study of more and less creative industrial research chemists, assumed that the more creative men would have greater personal resources and therefore would be more capable of developing better *Gestalten* (well-structured responses) with ambiguous visual stimuli (Rorschach cards) exposed tachistoscopically under varying conditions of difficulty (.01 of a second, .10 of a second, 3.0 seconds, and unlimited exposure). Using a weighting system for responses which would take into account the form level (structure) of the response and the frequency with which that response was given to the stimulus, Stein and Meer found a biserial correlation of +.88 between weighted scores and creativity ratings. Furthermore, the high and low creativity groups were significantly different from each other at each exposure level.

Perception goes through a series of developmental stages. One of its characteristics is that it shifts from a state where physiognomic factors are dominant to where the formal characteristics of the stimulus are focussed upon. Stein, with aid from Stern and Lane (Stern, Stein, & Bloom, 1956) developed a Physiognomic Cue Test based on this orientation. This paper-and-pencil test consists of 24 drawings or figures, each of which might be perceived in two alternate ways. For example, the subject is presented with two arcs, one above the other as if they were parts of a circle with spaces between them at either end, and he is asked whether he sees them as "two arcs" or an "open mouth." Each of the alternatives represents the ends of a six-point continuum. Since the first alternative, "two arcs," attends to the literal aspects of the stimulus, it is called a "form percept." The second, because it attributes animate characteristics to the stimulus, is called a "physiognomic percept." There are two sets of physiognomic percepts—feeling percepts and thing percepts.

Walker (1955) used this test with six mathematicians and twelve chemists who were rated high on creativity by their university colleagues and compared them with five mathematicians and eight chemists at a smaller university. The latter were not rated on creativity, but Walker assumed they were relatively less creative because they were at the smaller university. Using several of Thurstone's tests, Walker did not find any significant difference between his two groups. However, differences were obtained with the Physiognomic Cue Test. The control group scored higher on form perception, while the creative group scored higher on physiognomic perception. In his study of "more" and "less" creative Ph.D.'s involved in industrial research, Stein (unpublished) found trends that were in the same direction as those reported by Walker. Only when the chemists were equated for area of work were significant differences found, and then only for thing-physiognomic scores. Rosett, Robbins, and Sapirstein (1963) have recently found in a factor analysis of a test battery administered to college engineering students that the Physiognomic Cue Test loads on the same factor as scores on artistic and musical interests of the Thurstone Interest Schedule.

Among the studies of preferences for visual forms, there is the work of Brighouse (1939) and Barron and Welsh (1952). These investigators find contradictory results, but they also used different procedures and techniques. Brighouse, using geometric figures, found that artistically trained observers looked for unity and simplicity of organization, while untrained subjects preferred the "interestingness" of varied, involved, and complicated forms. Barron and Welsh (1952) also studied the preferences of artistically and nonartistically trained subjects but with free hand figures that varied on a simplicity-complexity dimension. They found that the artists disliked the simple-symmetric forms and preferred the complex-asymmetric forms more often than did the nonartists. Rosen (1955) corroborated these results, finding that both art students and art faculty preferred the more complex forms more than did nonartists but that the scores on this technique did not increase as a function of art training (i.e., there were no significant differences between art students and art faculty). Rosen also found that scores on the test correlated .40 with faculty ratings of originality for students' art products and .35 with grades in art school. Gough (1961) used the Barron-Welsh Art Scale in his study of industrial researchers, and with it he obtained a higher correlation (.41) with the criterion than he did with any of the other tests in the battery. Gough (1964) believes that this scale, which takes only ten minutes to administer, is "perhaps the most powerful single test yet discovered as a predictor of creative potential. . . ."

Summarizing the perceptual studies, we find process studies indicate creative individuals are more capable of integrated percepts and more free in suggesting hypotheses for poorly structured stimuli than are their less creative counterparts. Those studies concerned with the preference for visual forms have indicated that the more creative subjects show more preference for physiognomic percepts and complex forms. Where these perceptual data have been related to personality factors, it has been suggested that the more creative individuals are less defensive and less critical and take greater satisfaction in making order out of complexity than their less creative colleagues.

PERSONALITY CHARACTERISTICS

Almost from time immemorial man has tried to understand what motivates the creative individual to create and what there is in his personality makeup that differentiates him from other individuals. Answers have been numerous. As one might guess, they have varied with the Zeitgeist, the philosophical, sociological, or psychological orientations of the time. When man's behavior was believed to be affected by unknown external forces, spirits, demons, and the devil, his creativity was accounted for by the belief that he was possessed or that he had in some way obtained magical powers. Those investigators who regarded hereditary and constitutional factors as most critical in shaping individual differences turned to biological and physiological factors to learn about the mainsprings of creativity. When psychoanalysis came on the scene, studies of the creative individual emphasized the unconscious, psychosexual factors, sublimation, etc. And as psychoanalytic theory underwent revision, so views of the creative man were altered.

THEORIES

There are a number of theories of the creative individual's psychodynamics. Data and support for these theories are generally provided through case studies, since the theorists were or are engaged primarily in psychotherapeutic or other clinical-personality investigations. Although the theories have not been subjected to study in controlled investigations with large groups, they often serve as a fertile source for ideas to be tested or as a basis for interpreting results obtained in empirical investigations. The major theories are presented here in terms of their most significant critical elements, but this should not result in overlooking the fact that in a number of respects the theories do overlap. (In addition to primary sources, the reader may also wish to consult Stein and Heinze, 1960, and Raychaudhuri, 1965.)

1. *Creativity stems from some sort of pathology in the individual*—This view is not characteristic of contemporary theorists and is probably best expressed in the works of Lombroso (1891) and Lange-Eichbaum (1932). It is argued that, because creative individuals may also suffer from some sort of pathology, therefore creativity and pathology are dynamically related. The predisposition to insanity or the existing abnormality may sensitize the individual to aspects of his environment of which others are unaware. It is also argued that, while the creative person may share characteristics with the abnormal, he possesses characteristics essential to his creativity which remain unimpaired.

2. *Creativity stems from the sublimation of impulses*—Central to Freud's (1910, 1924, 1930, 1948a, 1948b) formulation is the sublimation of unconscious wishes, and among these, primarily, pregenital aggressive and libidinal impulses. Creativity provides for a discharge of tension and the release of the pain of unconscious conflict through the redirection of instinctual forces into socially acceptable form. Among others, Brill (1931), Bychowski (1951), and Kohut (1957) have utilized the sublimation concept in their respective studies of poetry, art, and music. The sublimation concept has, however, come under much criticism, and one rather penetrating critical review is presented by Levey (1939).

Since Freud's influence on studies of creativity has been so important, it is wise to mention some of his other contributions before turning to other theories. As Raychaudhuri (1965) points out, Freud contributed to our understanding by showing "(a) the unconscious and primary psychological processes as the mainspring of creative urge,

(b) the affinity of fantasy, dream and art-object, (c) the close relationship between 'Life-History' in the psychoanalytic sense and the work of art, (d) the omnipresence of certain themes known from fantasy life of the individual, such as the Oedipus themes, in the works of art. . . ."

3. *Creativity is viewed as a means of restitution that follows rage and fantasies of destruction*—The rage that initiates the aesthetic activity is directed toward some person who has thwarted the creative individual's need for love and approval. The rage and the impulse to destroy are directed toward the mother and are attended by guilt and dread of losing love. When the guilt has been alleviated by suffering and atonement, the artist achieves pity and love (inspired vision) and he seeks to come to terms with his environment. Through the artistic creation the damaged object or person is restored and perfected to satisfy the ideals of the mother. Thus, creative activity is both a denial of destructiveness and a means of identifying with the ideals of the person toward whom the rage was directed (Lee, 1947, 1950; Sharpe, 1930, 1950a, 1950b).

4. *Creativity is seen as a drive*—The motivation for creativity is seen as an integrative force (Hart, 1950), as a manifestation of the drive for self-actualization (Goldstein, 1939; Maslow, 1959; Rogers, 1959), or the urge toward competence (R. W. White, 1961).

5. *Creativity results from the stimulation of the archetype*—This is Jung's (1928) view of the creative process. For Jung the creative process is an "autonomous complex" and it involves an "unconscious animation of the archetype, and . . . a development and shaping of this image till the work is completed." By shaping the archetype, by raising it from the deepest unconscious and bringing it into relation with conscious ideas, the artist makes it possible for every man to find "the deepest springs of life which would otherwise be closed to him." The personal unconscious is involved in what Jung calls "symptomatic art," but symbolic art stems from the collective unconscious.

6. *Creativity is a function of compensation*—An individual, according to Adler, who suffers from defects in one area of his life may compensate for them by striving for creativity in others (Ansbacher & Ansbacher, 1956).

7. *Creativity is a manifestation of the need for mastery*—Alexander (1964) suggests that creativity stems from the urge to master tension-producing situations that may arise from conflict with external reality or from internal conflict. Alexander (1948) has also regarded creativity as resulting from the use of "surplus energy"—energy which is not expended in the satisfaction of impulse life or for selfish reasons.

8. *Creativity involves "regression in service of the ego"*—Although discussions of both unconscious and conscious factors in the creative process are to be found in a variety of psychoanalytic papers, the idea that during the creative process the ego regresses and makes use of unconscious material in a constructive fashion is best expressed by Kris (1952).

Empirical Studies

Contemporary empirical research on the personality characteristics of creative individuals has been quite vigorous. Subjects who come from a variety of fields have been studied with a variety of procedures—objective tests, projective tests, questionnaires, and interviews. What follows is a summary of research findings sketched in rather bold strokes.

Single Characteristics

The creative individual:

1. Is an achieving person. He scores higher on a Self-Description Test of need achievement (Stein, unpublished) than in a projective (TAT) measure of the same variable (McClelland, 1962), possibly because his achievement is fulfilled in actuality and need not be converted into fantasy. Gough (1964), using the California Personality Inventory, found that creative individuals score below average on a scale measuring conform-

ance motivation and the enhancement of form and structure but above average on achievement that stresses derivation of form and the modification of structure. Both scales are correlated in a student population but uncorrelated in creative individuals. This is also regarded as evidence for the complexity of the creative individual (Gough, 1964).

2. Is motivated by a need for order (Barron, 1958b).
3. Has a need for curiosity (Maddi, 1963; Maddi & Berne, 1964; Maddi *et al.,* 1964, 1965).
4. Is self-assertive, dominant, aggressive, self-sufficient. He leads and possesses initiative (Barron, 1955, 1957; R. B. Cattell & Drevdahl, 1955; MacKinnon, 1959a; Shannon, 1947; Van Zelst & Kerr, 1951). He is high on need power as measured by TAT-like pictures (McClelland, 1962).
5. Rejects repression, is less inhibited, less formal, less conventional, is bohemianly unconcerned, is radical, and is low on measures of authoritarian values (Barron, 1955; Blatt & Stein, 1957; R. B. Cattell & Drevdahl, 1955; Drevdahl, 1956; Van Zelst & Kerr, 1951). However, MacKinnon (1959a) finds that the creative individual is not "bohemian."
6. Has persistence of motive, liking and capacity for work, self-discipline, perseverance, high energy-output, is thorough (Blatt & Stein, 1957; Bloom, 1956; MacKinnon, 1959a; Peck, 1958; Roe, 1946a, 1949; Rossman, 1931; Shannon, 1947).
7. Is independent and autonomous (Barron, 1955; Blatt & Stein, 1957; Peck, 1958; Roe, 1953; Stein, 1957). Although independence has been an important factor in other groups studied, MacKinnon (1959a) did not find it to differentiate between groups of industrial engineers.
8. Is constructively critical, less contented, dissatisfied (Rossman, 1931; Shannon, 1947; Van Zelst & Kerr, 1951).
9. Is widely informed, has wide ranging interests, is versatile (Barron, 1957; MacKinnon, 1959b; R. K. White, 1931).
10. Is open to feelings and emotions. For him feeling is more important than thinking, he is more subjective, he possesses vitality and enthusiasm (MacKinnon, 1959a, 1959b; Peck, 1958; Shannon, 1947; Van Zelst & Kerr, 1951).
11. Is aesthetic in his judgment and value orientation (Blatt & Stein, 1957; Gough, 1964; MacKinnon, 1962; Roe, 1946a).
12. Is low in economic values (MacKinnon, 1962) or is a poor business man (Rossman, 1931). Blatt and Stein (1957), however, found with the Allport-Vernon-Lindzey Scale of Values that their more creative industrial research chemists did have higher economic values than their less creative colleagues. Using the same test but with a population of physicists, mathematicians, and electronic engineers, Gough (1961) did not find that any of the test's scales correlated with creativity.
13. Possesses freer expression of what has been described as feminine interests and lack of masculine aggressiveness (Blatt & Stein, 1957; Bloom, 1956; MacKinnon, 1959a, 1959b; Munsterberg & Mussen, 1953; Roe, 1946a, 1946b, 1946c).
14. Has little interest in interpersonal relationships, does not want much social interaction, is introverted, and is lower on social values, is reserved (Blatt & Stein, 1957; Bloom, 1956; MacKinnon, 1959a, 1959b; Munsterberg & Mussen, 1953; Roe, 1949). Nevertheless, Gough (1961, 1964) found in his study of industrial researchers that social sensitivity (as measured by the Chapin Social Insight Test) was correlated with creativity. In this study the predictive power of the Chapin Social Insight Test was exceeded only by the Barron-Welsh Art Scale.
15. Is emotionally unstable but capable of using his instability effectively, not well adjusted by psychological definition but adjusted in the broader sense of being socially useful and happy in his work (R. B. Cattell & Drevdahl, 1955; Roe,

1953). That creative individuals are not unstable has been found by MacKinnon (1959a) and Stein (unpublished). Blatt (1964), using a Self-Description Test developed by Stein (1963b), found that the self-descriptions of industrial research chemists who were regarded as "more" creative were more congruent with psychologists' conceptions of mental health than were the descriptions of "less" creative chemists. Gough (1964) regards the variability found in the creative individual's personal adjustment as a reflection of his complexity.

16. Sees himself as creative (Stein, unpublished; C. W. Taylor, 1963a). He is also more likely to describe himself in terms that investigators have found to be related to creativity than is true of less creative individuals. For example, MacKinnon in his study of architects (1962) found that his more creative group described themselves more frequently as "inventive, determined, independent, individualistic, enthusiastic, and industrious," while his less creative group described themselves more frequently as "responsible, sincere, reliable, dependable, clear thinking, tolerant, and understanding. In short, where creative architects more often stress their inventiveness, independence, and individuality, their enthusiasm, determination, and industry, less creative members of the profession are impressed by their virtue and good character and by their rationality and sympathetic concern for others." Considered in terms of their ideals, MacKinnon also found that the more creative group would like to be more sensitive, while the less creative groups would like to be more original and, at the same time, more self-controlled and disciplined.
17. Is intuitive and empathic. Test scales of "psychological-mindedness," intuitive preference, and need intraception correlate with creativity (Gough, 1964).
18. Is less critical of himself. He is less inclined to use negative and unfavorable adjectives and has a low self-criticality index on the Gough Adjective Check List (Gough, 1961).
19. Makes a greater impact on others. Gough (1961) found that assessment staff members who did not know criterion ratings of the subjects did differentiate between more highly and less highly rated research scientists. Some of the adjectives checked by assessors and which correlated positively with the criterion were: clear-thinking, interests wide, versatile, alert, and attractive. Among the adjectives that correlated negatively with the criterion were: undependable, pessimistic, commonplace, weak, and defensive.

Types

A listing of characteristics that differentiate more creative from less creative individuals, such as the one just presented above, may give the impression that there is only *one* picture of *the* creative individual. Such an impression is erroneous, for obviously the obtained results are based on group data.

Theoretically, following the principle of equifinality, there are many ways of arriving at the same goal. There are, therefore, several different constellations of personality characteristics that may characterize both more and less creative individuals. While creative individuals may fall more frequently into one category than into another, it would be erroneous to assume that there is only one set of characteristics that should be sought after in either studying creative individuals or in selecting individuals for creative pursuits.

Both MacKinnon and Stein provide data on this issue. Jung (1946) presented eight types and discussed their creative characteristics. MacKinnon (1959a), utilizing the Myers-Briggs Type Indicator (Briggs & Myers, 1957) which is based on Jung's system of personality types, has demonstrated how different types exist in various professional and scientific groups. Stein (1963b) has provided data that indicate that there are different personality types among industrial research chemists using a Self-Description Test based on Murray's (1938) system of needs. He has found that, while the frequency of more creative individuals may be larger in some types than in others, there is no single category yet obtained that contains only creative or noncreative individuals. What differentiates more from less creative individuals within the same personality type is a problem for future research.

As an aside, it should be pointed out that a type approach may help solve some of the problems involved in criteria of creativity. Gough and Woodworth (1960) developed a *Q*-sort deck for getting at stylistic variations in approaches to scientific and research activity. By combining data from the *Q*-sorts and assessment investigations at IPAR they developed eight research types that were named: (a) The Zealot, (b) The Initiator, (c) The Diagnostician, (d) The Scholar, (e) The Artificer, (f) The Esthetician, (g) The Methodologist, (h) The Independent. To differentiate among researchers in terms of these types might help curtail the heterogeneity of populations studied and might help clarify relationships between psychological variables and criteria as a function of style of work.

Types have a good deal of scientific merit and social utility. Insofar as the former is concerned, types yield a good deal more understanding of the data and may serve useful purposes in prediction. As to their social utility, they call attention to the fact that different kinds of individuals may manifest their creativity in different ways and different kinds of individuals may serve significant functions in a team endeavor oriented to creativity.

THE CREATIVE INDIVIDUAL IN GROUPS AND ORGANIZATIONS

Almost all of the studies considered above concerned themselves with the relationships between some psychological characteristic and creativity. But, since creativity occurs in a social context, attention has also been paid to the social factors within organizations which may affect the creativity of individuals in an effort to further our understanding of those social factors that may either facilitate or hinder the creativity of individuals, not only in specific organizations but also in the broader society. They may also be helpful in understanding why some techniques, tests, and procedures developed in the psychologist's laboratory and which are related to other test measures of creativity or faculty ratings of creativity do not necessarily cross-validate when utilized in studies of creativity in existing social organizations.

First we shall consider the effects of group interaction on the behavior of individuals in laboratory situations, and then we shall turn to a study of individuals in research organizations that count on the creativity of their personnel.

Crutchfield (1962) utilized a modification of the Asch (1952) experiment in which subjects were required to judge the length of lines under conditions where they had been led to believe that others had already made their judgments. The experimenter was interested in learning whether experimental subjects would, on certain critical trials where they were presented with wrong responses presumably developed by others, conform to the group pressure. In one study of industrial research scientists composed of physicists, mathematicians, and engineers where the scientist's originality had been rated by the assessment staff at IPAR, Crutchfield found that those rated high on originality were less conforming than those rated low. In a second study of 24 college seniors, who were differentiated in creativity by their faculty and who did not differ in intelligence test scores, those rated high in creativity were again less conforming than those not rated high. Finally, using a conformity scale based on an item analysis of a personality inventory used at IPAR where the criterion for the item analysis was conformity in the laboratory experiment, Crutchfield found that creative architects were less conforming than a group of architects not nominated for creativity. Crutchfield concludes that creativity in architects is related to the ability to resist group pressure, but he is also careful to point out that there is a range of individual differences in this respect.

Both Crutchfield's findings and the studies to be reported which were conducted in research organizations highlight the fact that creative individuals in social settings are capable, over the long run, of developing some "optimal balance" or coordination between their own autonomous strivings or personal values and those of the groups for and with whom they work. Scientists in industry may experience conflict between values that are necessary for success and those that are necessary for creativity (Stein *et al.*, 1958), but they are capable of resolving this conflict in some fashion so that it does not interfere too severely with their creativity.

That scientists do not put a premium on their autonomy above all else is also substantiated by Pelz's work (1964a) in which his criterion was actual scientific achievement (senior scientists', supervisors' and nonsupervisors' judgments of how much each man contributed to general scientific or technical knowledge in his field; it is not clear whether this criterion actually involved creativity, although it might have). Pelz asked, "If scientists say they want autonomy, does it follow that maximum autonomy results in maximum achievement, either scientific or practical?" The men he studied were scientists (both Ph.D.'s and non-Ph.D.'s) and engineers in a variety of government and industrial laboratories. Four echelons were established with whom the man could either consult or obtain direction for his work—the man himself, his immediate chief, his colleagues and subordinates, or individuals at higher executive levels. If autonomy was related to scientific or technical contribution, then fewer echelons should exert influence on a man's work. The over-all results, however, indicate that better performance occurred when influence on important decisions was shared with several persons at various levels in the organization. There were some exceptions to this finding. In development-oriented laboratories in which there were few Ph.D.'s, engineers who worked by themselves produced more patents than did others, but the data with regard to technical contribution were the same as the over-all finding. Another exception occurred among Ph.D.'s in research-oriented laboratories where individuals high on scientific contribution occurred among those who were involved with either four-echelon or one-echelon groups.

Pelz also studied the effects on his scientists' performance of both the influence they had on others and the number of echelons involved in their work. He found that maximum performance occurred when the scientist had both high influence and the involvement of others. If he lacked influence then multi-echelon involvement was helpful.

Finally, considering the people who might be involved in a scientist's activities, Pelz found that performance is best for Ph.D.'s in developmental laboratories when their goals are decided in consultation with their chief and lowest when the chief alone decides on their goals. A similar finding was found for some groups of non-Ph.D.'s. Among Ph.D. scientists in research laboratories, the most fruitful performance pattern occurred when decisions were made by the scientist himself in conjunction with his colleagues.

Using the same criterion of performance as did Pelz, Andrews (1964) contributes additional interesting data on the relationships to the criterion with scientists' motivation for their work, the manner in which they allot their time to various activities, as well as data regarding communication channels and status within the organization.

Scientists who were high on motivation

(defined as their involvement in their work, interest or excitement in their work, identification with their most important project, the importance of the challenge of their work) were high performers. This is consistent with Stein's (unpublished) report using a technique of role analysis (Stein, 1959) in which more creative industrial research chemists' assessments of their own skills and abilities were more congruent with their assessments of the requirements of their jobs than was true of their less creative colleagues. The more creative scientists also said that to be creative was more important to them than did less creative ones.

Andrews' data also show that status (defined as length of time the man had been in his technical division, the number of people officially reporting to him or his subordinates, and his annual income), too, is related to high performance. Status is no doubt related, either directly or indirectly, to the opportunity an individual has in a laboratory to implement his ideas. Stein's (unpublished) more creative industrial research chemists did say that they had more opportunity than did their less creative colleagues. But, interestingly enough, when both more and less creative chemists were presented with the fantasy question, "How creative do you think you would be if you had maximum opportunities?" the more creative men said that their creativity would be higher than did their less creative colleagues. These data suggest that more creative men have more confidence in their abilities, which probably facilitates achieving status and the opportunities that go with it for the continued manifestation of their creativity.

Finally, Andrews also found that adequacy of channels of communication (defined as number of people with whom the individual exchanged detailed information, coordination of activities between the individual and each of five colleagues, frequency of communication between the respondent and his administrative chief, and mean frequency of communication between the respondent and each of his five colleagues) was also related to scientific performance.

Pelz's (1963) data in an earlier study casts further light on the communication patterns that may be related to creativity. In this study Pelz used a sociometric technique to learn whether scientists' performance in a government laboratory was related to associating with people who were similar or different from themselves. He found that contact alone was not related to performance, nor was similarity, but when both of these were combined some rather interesting relationships were obtained. For scientists who were very similar to their colleagues, having contact only once or twice a week was related to maximum performance. A decline in performance was associated with more frequent contact. On the other hand, if scientists associated with people who were quite different from themselves in terms of values, then daily contact was found to be associated with high performance.

The previously discussed findings on adequacy of communication by Andrews may well account for the fact that there was greater agreement between the perceptions of more creative industrial research chemists and the top-level administrators in their companies as to what made for success (Stein *et al.*, 1958). This agreement might well facilitate their communication, and it might further aid them in their selection of the problems to which they can apply their creativity and so see their efforts rewarded as their final products are produced by the organization. Less creative individuals, not being tuned in on the organization's value system, might have difficulty not only in communication but also in the selection of appropriate problems.

This is not to suggest that creative individuals are "organization men." Several findings militate against such an argument. When asked about the kinds of working conditions in a laboratory which are important to them, a larger proportion of less than more creative industrial research chemists check "security." On the other hand, a larger proportion of the more creative ones check "the prestige of the laboratory." Furthermore, when the men were asked to recall what opportunities they were seeking when they first joined their companies, one of the items that differentiated between the more and less creative individuals was that more of the former said they wanted the opportunity to test their own ideas, while more of the latter said they wanted to work on the ideas of others and take care of routine matters. While a longitudinal study of industrial scientists at the beginning of their employment is necessary to check on this finding to avoid errors in recall, it nevertheless suggests the possibility that self-selection factors are involved in the opportunities the men seek and the orientations they develop. The last datum that can be cited against the "organization man" argument was that Pelz (1963) found that government scientists who were more oriented to their science than to their institution were regarded as having greater potential for doing outstanding research.

The weight of the data on scientists in organizational settings reflects the importance of considering the effects of socio-psychological factors on creativity. In an organizational setting the individual needs to coordinate, but not submerge, his own potentialities and abilities with the demands, requirements, and values of the situation in which he finds himself.

STIMULATING CREATIVITY

In addition to studies of the psychological and social factors related to creativity, a good deal of effort has been expended on attempts to stimulate creativity. A variety of procedures have been developed, such as *Brainstorming* (Osborn, 1953) and *Synectics* (Gordon, 1961), which are based on the assumption that evaluation too early in the creative process may inhibit ideas and in which it is formally agreed that there will be a separation in time between the verbalization of ideas and their evaluation. It is further assumed that in this permissive atmosphere that is free of criticism, more ideas and good ideas will come to the fore. Once these ideas are available, they can then be evaluated and implemented at a later date by the individual or individuals who thought of them or by others. The basic procedure can be utilized either by individuals or groups. When used by one person it is referred to as the "principle of deferred judgment" (Parnes, 1963), and when used by groups it is referred to as "brainstorming" or some other synonymous term.

A variety of studies have concerned themselves with the effectiveness of brainstorming. Most of these studies have been with student groups, and, while studies reported by Parnes and his associates at the Creative Education Foundation have favored brainstorming, those reported by others are either not so positive or negative.

Parnes and Meadow (1959) studied the effectiveness of a semester course in creative problem-solving in which brainstorming principles were used and found that it resulted in significant increments in two measures of quantity of ideas and in three out of five measures of quality of ideas. The effects were still evident in one group of students retested a year later.

Parnes and Meadow (1960) also report that more ideas of good quality were produced on Guilford-like tests by students trained in brainstorming procedures than by students who were not so trained. In addition, they also report that more ideas of good quality occur later in the brainstorming process than at the beginning. It does not appear, however, that the number of good ideas produced is a direct function of the total number of ideas produced (Hyman, 1961; Parloff & Handlon, 1964).

Parloff and Handlon (1964) believe that the production of good ideas in the brainstorming process is a function of lowering evaluative standards. They presented problems to dyads of female subjects and asked them to present their solutions. Solutions were to be produced under high-critical and low-critical conditions. Transcripts were made of the girls' conversations so that there was a record of all solutions produced. At the end of their deliberations, the girls were asked to submit their solutions in written form for evaluation. All solutions, whether written or not, were evaluated for how good they were. The results indicated that when all solutions (written or not) were tabulated, a significantly larger number of solutions were produced by dyads under low-critical conditions than under high-critical conditions. There was no significant effect of the experimental conditions on the number of good solutions produced. If anything, those girls who worked under the high-critical conditions tended to produce more good solutions. However, when solutions were written and presented for evaluation, it was found that the low-critical group not only presented more solutions but also more good solutions than the high-critical group, although, as indicated earlier, the latter had produced a slightly larger number of good solutions in their conversations. Since the high-critical groups submitted a smaller proportion of their good responses than did the low-critical groups, Parloff and Handlon believe that the brainstorming process may be productive of good ideas (defined as ideas presented for evaluation) because it allows the subject to pass judgmental responsibility on to others.

In industry, although there are no published reports of systematic investigations of brainstorming's effectiveness, there are reports of its usefulness. One brainstorming panel produced 61 ideas on how to increase long-distance telephone calls. After screening as to potential usefulness, 41 were sent to an operating committee, and it is reported that 16 of the ideas have been used (Bristol, 1958).

Since brainstorming is most popularly associated with delaying criticism or judgment in *groups,* there have been several studies comparing ideas produced by groups with those produced by individuals. Some contradictory results have been reported, and the literature suffers from the fact that when studies are repeated they are not replicated exactly. Nevertheless, some of the evidence suggests that groups may have inhibiting effects on the creativity of its individual members. This is based on the result found by some investigators that, when one totals the ideas of individuals who had worked alone but who used brainstorming principles, they produce more ideas than individuals who actually worked in groups on the production of ideas.

The paradigm for the efforts comparing individuals and groups is the work by D. W. Taylor *et al.* (1958), who studied 96 Yale seniors and juniors when presented with three problems. All students had had previous experience together in group discussion sections. One half of the students were divided into 12 four-man groups and were to brainstorm the problems together. These were called "actual" groups. The remaining half of the students were to brainstorm the problems individually, and later each of these men was randomly assigned to one of 12 four-man groups. These were called "nominal" groups. The number of different ideas produced by both nominal and actual groups was compared, and it was found that, on the average, the nominal groups produced twice as many ideas as the actual groups. Parnes (1963) followed the same experimental design as did Taylor, but replication in terms of procedures used, unfortunately, was not the same—there were differences in types and validity of problems used; nevertheless, he reports no significant differences between nominal and actual groups, and if anything, there was a trend in favor of the actual groups. He also reports from another experiment that, when his nominal groups were composed of individuals who had been asked to use conventional thinking procedures (which would presumably involve no deferment of judgment), they produced significantly fewer ideas than actual groups that did use brainstorming procedures.

Dunnette (1964) felt that the design employed by D. W. Taylor *et al.* (1958) could be improved upon. Rather than using *ad hoc* groups, he studied individuals that had had previous experience as functioning groups in real life situations. He selected groups of scientists and advertising personnel who had actually worked together and assumed that groups composed of individuals who had worked together would do better than when these individuals worked alone. Dunnette also felt that it would be a better experimental control if all subjects worked in both individual and group settings. All subjects were to use brainstorming principles whether they were in individual or group sessions, and equated problems were used for experimental purposes. The results of this study indicated that the pooled sum of individual efforts produced about one-third more different ideas than these same individuals produced in groups. Furthermore, when the ideas produced were rated for quality, no statistically significant results were obtained for scientists performing as individuals or in groups. For advertising personnel, however, the individual sessions produced more ideas of good quality than did the group sessions. Dunnette concludes that "brainstorming is most effective when undertaken by individuals working alone in an atmosphere free from the apparently inhibiting influences of group interaction." This result has support in some of the data presented by Tuckman and Lorge (1962) that group performance rarely exceeded the performance of the best member individually, and the performance of the best member of the group was often inhibited by the group.

A VIEW TO THE FUTURE

Research in the area of creativity has already produced a reasonable body of data. However, if they are not already, efforts in this area will soon be at the crossroads. On the one hand, the typical pattern of current research can be continued. If this is so then we shall see a proliferation of studies in which groups differentiated according to a specific criterion are shown to differ on some psychological or social variable. The value of such studies in the light of current knowledge is likely to be limited. It is no longer a problem whether one can or cannot differentiate between known groups. What we need is research that will further both our understanding and prediction of creativity.

To do so it is necessary to shift our emphasis from "What differentiates the creative from the noncreative subject?" or "What social factors affect creativity?" to a greater concentration on research which will help us define the characteristics of *different* situations in which *different* kinds of individuals will produce results that vary in level of creativity. Creativity, like all behavior, is a function of the transactional relationships between the individual and his environment (Stein, 1963c). The various fields in which creativity might occur differ in their requirements. The various organizational settings in which creativity might occur differ in the demands they make upon the individual. Consequently, while creative individuals may share various psychological characteristics in common, there will also be significant differences among them which may positively predispose them for their selected areas of endeavor and prepare them to cope constructively with the requirements of the situations in which they find themselves.

Insofar as the prediction problem is concerned, the fact that it has been possible to differentiate between known groups should not lead us to suspect that prediction will be equally effective. There are often critical differences between concurrent and predictive validity. Whether those psychological variables that differentiate between known groups are equally predictive, or whether new variables have to be investigated, is still an open question. And by the same token, information is necessary about the time period over which valid predictions can be made and the conditions of the social environment for which they can be made.

Finally, future developments in the area

of creativity are also dependent upon the growth of our knowledge in other areas of psychology including both individual and social factors. If we limit ourselves only to the area of personality for our present purposes then we need to call attention to the need for further knowledge about the factors that make for psychological growth, the characteristics that predispose an individual to seek out and accept change, and the ever-present need of determining the meaning of data related to the same personality but which have been obtained with different psychological procedures—especially when these do not agree. As these and other problems in the area of personality are resolved, we will also further both our understanding of and capacity to predict creativity.

REFERENCES

Agnew, M. The auditory imagery of great composers. *Psychol. Monogr.*, 1922, 31, 268–278.

Alexander, F. *Fundamentals of psychoanalysis.* New York: W. W. Norton, 1948.

Alexander, F. Neurosis and creativity. *Amer. J. Psychoanal.*, 1964, 24, 116–130.

Andrews, F. M. Scientific performance as related to time spent on technical work, teaching, or administration. *Admin. sci. Quart.*, 1964, 9, 182–193.

Andrews, F. M. Factors affecting the manifestation of creative ability by scientists. *J. Pers.*, 1965, 33, 140–152.

Ansbacher, H. L., & Ansbacher, Rowena R. (Eds.). *The individual psychology of Alfred Adler.* New York: Basic Books, 1956.

Asch, S. E. *Social psychology.* Englewood Cliffs, N.J.: Prentice-Hall, 1952.

Barron, F. Complexity-simplicity as a personality dimension. *J. abnorm. soc. Psychol.*, 1953, 48, 163–172.

Barron, F. The disposition toward originality. *J. abnorm. soc. Psychol.*, 1955, 51, 478–485.

Barron, F. Originality in relation to personality and intellect. *J. Pers.*, 1957, 25, 730–742.

Barron, F. The psychology of imagination. *Scient. Amer.*, 1958, 199, 150–166. (a)

Barron, F. The needs for order and for disorder as motives in creative activity. In C. W. Taylor (Ed.), *The second (1957) conference on the identification of creative scientific talent.* Salt Lake City: Univer. of Utah Press, 1958. (b)

Barron, F., & Welsh, G. S. Artistic perception as a possible factor in personality style: its measurement by a figure preference test. *J. Psychol.*, 1952, 33, 199–203.

Bennett, G. K., & Wesman, A. G. A test of productive thinking. *Amer. Psychologist*, 1949, 4, 282. (Abstract)

Bjorksten, J. The limitation of creative years. *Scient. Mon.*, 1946, 62, 94.

Blatt, S. J. An attempt to define mental health. *J. consult. Psychol.*, 1964, 28, 146–153.

Blatt, S. J., & Stein, M. I. Some personality, value, and cognitive characteristics of the creative person. *Amer. Psychologist*, 1957, 12, 406. (Abstract)

Blatt, S. J., & Stein, M. I. Efficiency in problem solving. *J. Psychol.*, 1959, 48, 193–213.

Bloom, B. S. Report on creativity research at the University of Chicago. In C. W. Taylor (Ed.), *The 1955 University of Utah research conference on the identification of creative scientific talent.* Salt Lake City: Univer. of Utah Press, 1956.

Brandwein, P. F. *The gifted student as future scientist.* New York: Harcourt, Brace, 1955.

Briggs, Katharine C., & Myers, Isobel B. *Myers-Briggs Type Indicator.* Privately printed, 1957.

Brighouse, G. Variability in preferences for simple forms. *Psychol. Monogr.*, 1939, 51, No. 5, 68–74.

Brill, A. A. Poetry as an oral outlet. *Psychoanal. Rev.*, 1931, 18, 357–378.

Bristol, L. H., Jr. The application of group thinking techniques to the problems of pharmaceutical education. *Amer. J. pharmaceut. Educ.*, 1958, 22, 146.

Brown, G. I. A second study in the teaching of creativity. Paper presented at the Amer. Educ. Res. Ass. Meetings, Chicago, February, 1964.

Bruner, J. S. The conditions of creativity. In H. E. Gruber, G. Terrell, & M. Wertheimer (Eds.), *Contemporary approaches to creative thinking.* New York: Atherton Press, 1962.

Burks, Barbara S., Jensen, Dortha W., & Terman, L. M. The promise of youth: follow-up studies of a thousand gifted children. In L. M. Terman (Ed.), *Genetic studies of genius.* Vol. 3. Stanford: Stanford Univer. Press, 1930.

Bychowski, G. Metapsychology of artistic creation. *Psychoanal. Quart.,* 1951, 20, 592–602.

Cattell, J. McK. A statistical study of eminent men. *Popular Sci. Mon.,* 1903, 62, 359–377.

Cattell, R. B., & Drevdahl, J. E. A comparison of the personality profiles (16PF) of eminent researchers with that of eminent teachers and administrators and of the general population. *Brit. J. Psychol.,* 1955, 46, 248–261.

Chorness, M. H. An interim report on creativity research. In C. W. Taylor (Ed.), *The 1955 University of Utah research conference on the identification of creative scientific talent.* Salt Lake City: Univer. of Utah Press, 1956.

Christensen, P. R., Guilford, J. P., & Wilson, R. C. Relations of creative responses to working time and instructions. *J. exp. Psychol.,* 1957, 53, 82–88.

Cox, Catharine M. The early mental traits of three hundred geniuses. In L. M. Terman (Ed.), *Genetic studies of genius.* Vol. 2. Stanford: Stanford Univer. Press, 1926.

Crutchfield, R. Conformity and character. *Amer. Psychologist,* 1955, 10, 191–198.

Crutchfield, R. S. Conformity and creative thinking. In H. E. Gruber, G. Terrell, & M. Wertheimer (Eds.), *Contemporary approaches to creative thinking.* New York: Atherton Press, 1962.

Dentler, R. A., & Mackler, B. Originality: some social and personal determinants. *Behav. Sci.,* 1964, 9, 1–7.

Drevdahl, J. E. Factors of importance for creativity. *J. clin. Psychol.,* 1956, 12, 21–26.

Dunnette, M. D. Are meetings any good for solving problems? *Personnel Adminis.,* March–April, 1964, 27, 12–29.

Eiduson, Bernice T. Artist and non-artist: a comparative study. *J. Pers.,* 1958, 26, 13–28.

Eindhoven, J. E., & Vinacke, W. E. Creative processes in painting. *J. gen. Psychol.,* 1952, 47, 139–164.

Freud, S. *Three contributions to the theory of sex.* New York: Nervous and Mental Disease Pub. Co., 1910.

Freud, S. *Civilization and its discontents.* Joan Riviere (Transl.). New York: J. Cope and H. Smith, 1930.

Freud, S. "Civilized" sexual morality and modern nervousness. *Collected papers.* Vol. 2. Joan Riviere (Transl.). London: Hogarth Press, 1948. (a)

Freud, S. *Leonardo da Vinci.* A. A. Brill (Transl.). London: Routledge & Kegan Paul, 1948. (b)

Freud, S. The relation of the poet to daydreaming. *Collected papers.* Vol. 4. Joan Riviere (Transl.). London: Hogarth Press, 1948. (c)

Fricke, B. G. *Opinion, attitude, and interest survey handbook.* Ann Arbor: Univer. of Michigan, Evaluation and Examination Division, 1963.

Galton, F. *Hereditary genius.* New York: D. Appleton, 1870.

Getzels, J. W., & Jackson, P. W. *Creativity and intelligence.* New York: Wiley, 1962.

Ghiselin, B. Ultimate criteria for two levels of creativity. In C. W. Taylor (Ed.), *The second (1957) conference on the identification of creative scientific talent.* Salt Lake City: Univer. of Utah Press, 1958.

Goldstein, K. *The organism.* New York: American Book, 1939.

Gordon, W. J. J. *Synectics.* New York: Harper, 1961.

Gough, H. G. Techniques for identifying the creative research scientist. In Proceedings of the Conference on "The Creative Person," Oct. 13–17, 1961, Univer. of Calif., Institute of Personality Assessment and Research.

Gough, H. G. Identifying the creative man. *J. Value Engng,* 1964, 2, 5–12.

Gough, H. G., & Woodworth, D. G. Stylistic variations among professional research scientists. *J. Psychol.,* 1960, 49, 87–98.

Greenacre, Phyllis. The childhood of the artist. Libidinal phase development and giftedness. *The psychoanalytic study of the child.* Vol. 12. New York: International Univer. Press, 1957.

Guilford, J. P. Creativity. *Amer. Psychologist,* 1950, 5, 444–454.

Guilford, J. P. The relation of intellectual factors to creative thinking in science. In C. W. Taylor (Ed.), *The 1955 University of Utah research conference on the identification of creative scientific talent.* Salt Lake City: Univer. of Utah Press, 1956.

Guilford, J. P. Three faces of intellect. *Amer. Psychologist,* 1959, 14, 469–479. (a)

Guilford, J. P. Traits of creativity. In H. H. Anderson (Ed.), *Creativity and its cultivation.* New York: Harper, 1959. (b)

Guilford, J. P. What to do about creativity in education. Paper presented at West. Reg. Conf. on Testing Problems of the Educ. Testing Serv., Los Angeles, May 4, 1962.

Guilford, J. P. Intellectual factors in productive thinking. Paper presented at Second Conference on Productive Thinking, conducted by the Project on the Academically Talented Student, of the Nat. Educ. Ass., Washington, D.C., May, 1963.

Hadamard, J. *An essay on the psychology of invention in the mathematical field*. Princeton, N.J.: Princeton Univer. Press, 1945.

Harmon, L. R. The development of a criterion of scientific competence. In C. W. Taylor (Ed.), *The second (1957) research conference on the identification of creative scientific talent*. Salt Lake City: Univer. of Utah Press, 1958.

Harris, R. H., & Simberg, A. L. *AC test of creative ability, examiner's manual*. Flint, Mich.: AC Spark Plug Division, General Motors Corp. (no date)

Hart, H. H. The integrative function in creativity. *Psychiat. Quart.*, 1950, 24, 1–16.

Holland, J. L. The prediction of college grades from personality and aptitude variables. *J. educ. Psychol.*, 1960, 51, 245–254.

Holt, R. R. Manual for the scoring of primary process manifestations in Rorschach responses (Draft 7). New York: Res. Cent. for Ment. Hlth, New York Univer., 1959. (Dittoed)

Holt, R. R., & Havel, Joan. A method for assessing primary and secondary process in the Rorschach. In Maria A. Rickers-Ovsiankina (Ed.), *Rorschach psychology*. New York: Wiley, 1960.

Houston, J. P., & Mednick, S. A. Creativity and the need for novelty. *J. abnorm. soc. Psychol.*, 1963, 66, 137–141.

Hyman, R. On prior information and creativity. *Psychol. Rep.*, 1961, 9, 151–161.

John, E. R. Contributions to the problem-solving process. *Psychol. Monogr.*, 1957, 71, No. 18.

Jung, C. G. On the relation of analytical psychology to poetic art. In C. G. Jung, *Contributions to analytical psychology*. New York: Harcourt, Brace, 1928.

Jung, C. G. *Psychological types*. New York: Harcourt, Brace, 1946.

Kohut, H. Observation on the psychological functions of music. *J. Amer. Psychoanal. Ass.*, 1957, 5, 389–407.

Kris, E. *Psychoanalytic explorations in art*. New York: International Univer. Press, 1952.

Kris, E. Psychoanalysis and the study of creative imagination. *Bull. NY Acad. Med.*, 1953, 334–351.

Lange-Eichbaum, W. *The problem of genius*. E. Paul & C. Paul (Transl.). New York: Macmillan, 1932.

Lee, H. B. On the esthetic states of the mind. *Psychiatry*, 1947, 10, 281–306.

Lee, H. B. The values of order and vitality in art. In G. Róheim (Ed.), *Psychoanalysis and the social sciences*. Vol. 2. New York: International Univer. Press, 1950.

Lehman, H. C. *Age and achievement*. Princeton: Princeton Univer. Press, 1953.

Levey, H. B. A critique of the theory of sublimation. *Psychiatry*, 1939, 2, 239–270.

Lombroso, C. *The man of genius*. London: Walter Scott, 1891.

McClelland, D. C. On the psychodynamics of creative physical scientists. In H. E. Gruber, G. Terrell, & M. Wertheimer (Eds.), *Contemporary approaches to creative thinking*. New York: Atherton Press, 1962.

MacKinnon, D. W. The creative worker in engineering. Paper read at Eleventh Annu. Industr. Engng Inst., Univer. of Calif., Los Angeles, and Univer. of Calif., Berkeley, February 6–7, 1959. (a)

MacKinnon, D. W. On becoming an architect. *Architectural Record*, August, 1959, 126, pp. 64-4 to 64-6 Western Section. (b)

MacKinnon, D. W. The highly effective individual. *Teachers Coll. Rec.*, 1960, 61, 367–378.

MacKinnon, D. W. Fostering creativity in students of engineering. *J. engng Educ.*, 1961, 52, 129–142.

MacKinnon, D. W. The nature and nurture of creative talent. *Amer. Psychologist*, 1962, 17, 484–495.

MacKinnon, D. W. The identification and development of creative potential. Paper read at Bowdoin College, Brunswick, Maine, May 2, 1964.

McNemar, Q. Lost: our intelligence? Why? *Amer. Psychologist*, 1964, 19, 871–882.

McPherson, J. H. A proposal for establishing

ultimate criteria for measuring creative output. In C. W. Taylor (Ed.), *The 1955 University of Utah research conference on the identification of creative scientific talent.* Salt Lake City: Univer. of Utah Press, 1956.

Maddi, S. R. Activation and the need for variety. Paper delivered at Knox College and Galesburg State Hospital, Galesburg, Ill., April, 1963.

Maddi, S. R., Andrews, S. L., & Hovey, R. D. Some structured self-report correlates of fantasy measures of the need for variety. *Res. Bull. 64-21.* Princeton: Educ. Testing Serv., 1964.

Maddi, S. R., & Berne, N. Novelty of productions and desire for novelty as active and passive forms of the need for variety. *J. Pers.,* 1964, 32, 270–277.

Maddi, S. R., Propst, Barbara S., & Feldinger, I. Three expressions of the need for variety. *J. Pers.,* 1965, 33, 82–98.

Manniche, E., & Falk, G. Age and the Nobel prize. *Amer. Scient.,* 1957, 2, 301–307.

Maslow, A. H. Creativity in self-actualizing people. In H. H. Anderson (Ed.), *Creativity and its cultivation.* New York: Harper, 1959.

Mednick, Martha T. Research creativity in psychology graduate students. *J. consult. Psychol.,* 1963, 27, 265–266.

Mednick, Martha T., Mednick, S. A., & Mednick, E. V. Incubation of creative performance and specific associative priming. *J. abnorm. soc. Psychol.,* 1964, 69, 84–88.

Mednick, S. A. The associative basis of the creative process. *Psychol. Rev.,* 1962, 69, 220–232.

Meer, B., & Stein, M. I. Measures of intelligence and creativity. *J. Psychol.,* 1955, 39, 117–126.

Meltzer, L. Scientific productivity in organizational settings. *J. soc. Issues,* 1956, 12, 32–40.

Mendelsohn, G. A., & Griswold, Barbara B. Differential use of incidental stimuli in problem solving as a function of creativity. *J. abnorm. soc. Psychol.,* 1964, 68, 431–436.

Moore, O. K. *Autotelic responsive environments and exceptional children.* Hamden, Conn.: Responsive Environments Foundation, 1963.

Munsterberg, Elizabeth, & Mussen, P. H. The personality structures of art students. *J. Pers.,* 1953, 21, 457–466.

Murray, H. A. *Explorations in personality.* New York: Oxford Univer. Press, 1938.

Osborn, A. F. *Applied imagination.* New York: Scribner's, 1953.

Parloff, M. B., & Handlon, J. H. The influence of criticalness on creative problem-solving in dyads. *Psychiatry,* 1964, 27, 17–27.

Parnes, S. J. The deferment-of-judgment principle: clarification of the literature. *Psychol. Rep.,* 1963, 12, 521–522.

Parnes, S. J., & Harding, H. F. *A source book for creative thinking.* New York: Scribner's, 1962.

Parnes, S. J., & Meadow, A. Effects of "brainstorming" instructions on creative problem-solving by trained and untrained subjects. *J. educ. Psychol.,* 1959, 50, 171–176.

Parnes, S. J., & Meadow, A. Evaluation of persistence of effects produced by a creative problem-solving course. *Psychol. Rep.,* 1960, 7, 357–361.

Patrick, Catharine. Creative thought in poets. *Arch. Psychol.,* 1935, 26, 1–74.

Patrick, Catharine. Creative thought in artists. *J. Psychol.,* 1937, 4, 35–73.

Patrick, Catharine. Scientific thought. *J. Psychol.,* 1938, 5, 55–83.

Patrick, Catharine. Whole and part relationships in creative thought. *Amer. J. Psychol.,* 1941, 54, 128–131.

Peck, R. F. What makes a man creative? *Personnel,* 1958, 35, 18–23.

Pelz, D. C. Relationships between measures of scientific performance and other variables. In C. W. Taylor & F. Barron (Eds.), *Scientific creativity: its recognition and development.* New York: Wiley, 1963.

Pelz, D. C. Freedom in research. *Int. Sci. Tech.,* February, 1964, 26, 54–66. (a)

Pelz, D. C. The "creative years" and the research environment. *IEEE Transactions on Engng Mgmt,* 1964, 11 (1), 23–29. (b)

Pine, F. Thematic drive content and creativity. *J. Pers.,* 1959, 27, 136–151.

Pine, F., & Holt, R. R. Creativity and primary process. *J. abnorm. soc. Psychol.,* 1960, 61, 370–379.

Poincaré, H. Mathematical creation. In B. Ghiselin (Ed.), *The creative process.* Berkeley: Univer. of Calif. Press, 1954.

Rapaport, D. Toward a theory of thinking. In D. Rapaport (Ed.), *Organization and pathology of thought.* New York: Columbia Univer. Press, 1951.

Raychaudhuri, M. Personality correlates of creativity: a review of psychodynamic studies. *Samiksa,* 1965, 19, 107–134.

Reichenbach, H. *Experience and prediction.* Chicago: Univer. of Chicago Press, 1938.

Riegel, K. F., Riegel, Ruth M., & Levine, R. S. An analysis of associative behavior and creativity. *J. Pers. soc. Psychol.,* 1966, 4, 50–56.

Roe, Anne. Artists and their work. *J. Pers.,* 1946, 15, 1–40. (a)

Roe, Anne. Painting and personality. *Rorschach Res. Exch.,* 1946, 10, 86–100. (b)

Roe, Anne. The personality of artists. *Educ. psychol. Measmt,* 1946, 6, 401–408. (c)

Roe, Anne. Psychological examinations of eminent biologists. *J. consult. Psychol.,* 1949, 13, 225–246.

Roe, Anne. A study of imagery in research scientists. *J. Pers.,* 1951, 19, 459–470.

Roe, Anne. *The making of a scientist.* New York: Dodd, Mead, 1952.

Roe, Anne. A psychological study of eminent psychologists and anthropologists, and a comparison with biological and physical scientists. *Psychol. Monogr.,* 1953, 67, No. 2.

Roe, Anne. Early differentiation of interests. In C. W. Taylor (Ed.), *The second (1957) research conference on the identification of creative scientific talent.* Salt Lake City: Univer. of Utah Press, 1958.

Roe, Anne, & Siegelman, M. *The origin of interests.* Washington, D.C.: American Personnel and Guidance Association, 1964.

Rogers, C. R. Toward a theory of creativity. In H. H. Anderson (Ed.), *Creativity and its cultivation.* New York: Harper, 1959.

Rosen, J. C. The Barron-Welsh Art Scale as a predictor of originality and level of ability among artists. *J. appl. Psychol.,* 1955, 39, 366–367.

Rosett, H., Robbins, H., & Sapirstein, M. R. Cognitive controls and education for creativity in the sciences. Paper presented at Conference on Education for Creativity in the Sciences, New York Univer., June 13–15, 1963.

Rossman, J. *The psychology of the inventor: a study of the patentee.* (rev. ed.) Washington, D.C.: Inventors Publishing Co., 1931.

Russell, W. A., & Jenkins, J. J. The complete Minnesota norms for responses to 100 words from the Kent-Rosanoff Word Association Test. Minneapolis: Univer. of Minnesota, Technical Report No. 11, Contract N8 onr-66216, Office of Naval Research, 1954.

Shannon, J. R. Traits of research workers. *J. educ. Res.,* 1947, 40, 513–521.

Sharpe, Ella F. Certain aspects of sublimation and delusion. *Int. J. Psycho-Anal.,* 1930, 11, 12–23.

Sharpe, Ella F. The impatience of Hamlet. In Ella F. Sharpe, *Collected papers on psychoanalysis.* Marjorie Brierley (Ed.). London: Hogarth Press, 1950. (a)

Sharpe, Ella F. Similar and divergent unconscious determinants underlying the sublimations of pure art and pure science. In Ella F. Sharpe, *Collected papers on psychoanalysis.* Marjorie Brierley (Ed.). London: Hogarth Press, 1950. (b)

Stein, M. I. Creativity and culture. *J. Psychol.,* 1953, 36, 311–322.

Stein, M. I. Creativity and the scientist. In National Physical Laboratories, *The direction of research establishments.* Part 3. London: Her Majesty's Stationery Office, 1957.

Stein, M. I. *Stein research environment survey.* New York: Abacus Associates, 1959.

Stein, M. I. *Survey of the psychological literature in the area of creativity with a view toward needed research.* Cooperative Research Project No. E-3. Washington, D.C.: Office of Education, 1962.

Stein, M. I. Creativity in a free society. *Educ. Horizons,* 1963, 41, 115–130. (a)

Stein, M. I. Explorations in typology. In R. W. White (Ed.), *The study of lives.* New York: Atherton Press, 1963. (b)

Stein, M. I. A transactional approach to creativity. In C. W. Taylor & F. Barron (Eds.), *Scientific creativity: its recognition and development.* New York: Wiley, 1963. (c)

Stein, M. I. Explorations in creativity. (Unpublished)

Stein, M. I., & Heinze, Shirley J. *Creativity and the individual.* New York: Free Press, 1960.

Stein, M. I., Heinze, Shirley J., & Rogers, R. R. Creativity and/or success: a study in value conflict. In C. W. Taylor (Ed.), *The second (1957) conference on the identification of creative scientific talent.* Salt Lake City: Univer. of Utah Press, 1958.

Stein, M. I., & Meer, B. Perceptual organization in a study of creativity. *J. Psychol.,* 1954, 37, 39–43.

Stern, G. G., Stein, M. I., & Bloom, B. S. *Methods in personality assessment.* New York: Free Press, 1956.

Stevens, R. The age problem in research workers: Viewpoint of the research administrator. *Scient. Mon.,* 1951, 62, 364–367.

Sullivan, H. S. *Interpersonal theory of psychology.* New York: Norton, 1953.

Taylor, C. W. A search for a creative climate. Talk given at Seventeenth Nat. Conf. on Admin. of Res., Estes Park, Colo., September, 1963. (a)

Taylor, C. W. *Creativity: progress and potential.* New York: McGraw-Hill, 1963. (b)

Taylor, C. W. *Widening horizons in creativity.* New York: Wiley, 1964.

Taylor, C. W., & Barron, F. (Eds.) *Scientific creativity: its recognition and development.* New York: Wiley, 1963.

Taylor, C. W., Cooley, G. M., & Nielsen, E. C. Identifying high school students with characteristics needed in research work. (Mimeographed)

Taylor, C. W., & Ellison, R. L. Biographical information and the prediction of multiple criteria of success in science. Report to Director of Personnel, NASA, August, 1963.

Taylor, C. W., Smith, W. R., Ghiselin, B., & Ellison, R. Explorations in the measurement and prediction of contributions of one sample of scientists. Report ASD-TR-61-96, Aeronautical Systems Division, Personnel Laboratory, Lackland Air Force Base, Texas, April, 1961.

Taylor, D. W. Variables related to creativity and productivity among men in two research laboratories. In C. W. Taylor & F. Barron (Eds.), *Scientific creativity: its recognition and development.* New York: Wiley, 1963.

Taylor, D. W., Berry, P. C., & Block, C. H. Does group participation when using brainstorming facilitate or inhibit creative thinking? *Admin. sci. Quart.,* 1958, 3, 23–47.

Terman, L. M. The intelligence quotient of Francis Galton in childhood. *Amer. J. Psychol.,* 1917, 28, 209–215.

Terman, L. M. Mental and physical traits of a thousand gifted children. In L. M. Terman (Ed.), *Genetic studies of genius.* Vol. 1. Stanford: Stanford Univer. Press, 1925.

Terman, L. M. The discovery and encouragement of exceptional talent. *Amer. Psychol.,* 1954, 9, 221–230. (a)

Terman, L. M. Scientists and nonscientists in a group of 800 gifted men. *Psychol. Monogr.,* 1954, 68, No. 7. (b)

Terman, L. M., & Oden, Melita H. The gifted child grows up. In L. M. Terman (Ed.), *Genetic studies of genius.* Vol. 4. Stanford: Stanford Univer. Press, 1947.

Thorndike, R. L. Some methodological issues in the study of creativity. In *Proceedings of the 1962 invitational conference on testing problems.* Princeton: Educ. Testing Serv., 1963.

Torrance, E. P. *Guiding creative talent.* Englewood Cliffs, N.J.: Prentice-Hall, 1962. (a)

Torrance, E. P. Cultural discontinuities and the development of originality in thinking. *Except. Child.,* 1962, 29, 2–13. (b)

Torrance, E. P., & Gupta, R. *Programmed experiences in creative thinking: development and evaluation of recorded programmed experiences in creative thinking in the fourth grade.* Minneapolis: Univer. of Minnesota, Bureau of Educ. Res., 1964.

Torrance, E. P., & Staff. *Role of evaluation in creative thinking, revised summary report.* Cooperative Research Project No. 725, U.S. Office of Education, Dept. of Health, Education, and Welfare. Minneapolis: Univer. of Minnesota, Bureau of Educ. Res., 1964.

Tuckman, J., & Lorge, I. Individual ability as a determinant of group superiority. *Hum. Relat.,* 1962, 15, 45–51.

Van Zelst, R. H., & Kerr, W. A. Some correlates of technical and scientific productivity. *J. abnorm. soc. Psychol.,* 1951, 46, 470–475.

Walker, D. E. The relationship between creativity and selected test behavior for chemists and mathematicians. Unpublished doctoral dissertation, Univer. of Chicago, 1955.

Wallach, M. A., & Kogan, N. *Modes of thinking in young children.* New York: Holt, Rinehart and Winston, 1965.

Wallas, G. *The art of thought.* New York: Harcourt, Brace, 1926.

Wertheimer, M. *Productive thinking.* New York: Harper, 1945.

White, R. K. The versatility of genius. *J. soc. Psychol.,* 1931, 2, 460–489.

White, R. W. Motivation reconsidered: the concept of competence. *Psychol. Rev.,* 1961, 66, 297–333.

Yamamoto, K. Role of creative thinking and intelligence in high school achievement. *Psychol. Rep.,* 1964, 14, 783–789.

CHAPTER 17 Affiliation and Social Comparison[1]

ROLAND RADLOFF
Naval Medical Research Institute

The focus of this paper is on affiliative behavior prompted by needs for self-evaluation. This area of inquiry has received increasing attention in recent years. A number of excellent laboratory experiments and field studies supported by a well-developed theoretical statement have resulted in interesting and provocative answers and questions on the subject of man's gregariousness. Basically this paper is a review, summary, and discussion of experiments leading to, included in, and stimulated by Schachter's book *The Psychology of Affiliation* (1959) and by "A Theory of Social Comparison Processes" (Festinger, 1954a), which is the theoretical foundation of Schachter's work and the present discussion as well.

Affiliation as a topic area is potentially overwhelming in magnitude and complexity. A list of causes and effects of man's association with his fellows would encompass nearly all of social psychology, much of psychology in general, and related social sciences as well. In pruning the topic of affiliation down to manageable size, Schachter (1959) divided needs leading to affiliation into two broad categories: (a) needs for which people qua people are irrelevant, that is, they are only incidental to need satisfaction, and (b) needs that can be satisfied only by some kind of contact with other persons, that is, people are, under normal circumstances, essential to the satisfaction of the need. Examples of the former type of need would be cravings for diversion, recreation, or excitement. Such desires might be satisfied by going to a ball game or to the local tavern, inviting friends over, or any of a long list of activities involving association with other people; but satisfaction could be obtained by a similarly long list of solitary activities such as watching TV, reading, or stargazing. These types of needs, ones for which people are useful but not essential, probably account for a great deal, if not the majority, of affiliative behavior. However, as Schachter (1959) observes, this is a peculiarly asocial sort of affiliation. Of greater interest and relevance to the present discussion are needs for the satisfaction of which other persons are essential. Examples of this type are needs for approval, friendship, support, prestige, and so on. To be sure, this distinction is far from clear cut; examples could be found which would be difficult to classify, and furthermore, many

[1] From Bureau of Medicine and Surgery, Navy Department, Research Task MF022.01.03-1002. The opinions and statements contained herein are the private ones of the writer and are not to be construed as official or as reflecting the views of the Navy Department or the Naval Service at large.

single instances of affiliative behavior may be prompted by the presence of a number of such motives, including, very likely, motives of both types. However, the emphasis is clear; in one case other people are incidental to the satisfaction of the needs while in the other they are, normally at least, essential. Difficult as these predispositions may be to disentangle in real life, the needs can be and have been isolated in laboratory studies. This paper will concentrate on laboratory studies dealing with a subclass of the latter type of needs—namely, needs for self-evaluation which can be satisfied principally by comparing oneself with other persons.

SOCIAL COMPARISON THEORY AND EVALUATION

As indicated above, the line of reasoning followed and the experiments to be cited in this paper are based on Festinger's theory of social comparison processes. Therefore, a brief review of the relevant postulates of the theory is necessary.

Hypothesis I of the theory of social comparison processes (Festinger, 1954a, p. 164) proposes that, "There exists in the human organism a drive to evaluate his opinions, abilities and [emotions]" (Schachter, 1959, p. 132). That is, humans desire accurate appraisals of their abilities; they want to know the correctness of their opinions and the appropriateness of their emotional reactions. If objective or physical standards exist, abilities and opinions can be evaluated by comparison with such standards. It is frequently the case, however, that objective standards do not exist or that a comparison with them is difficult or even dangerous. When objective standards are unavailable, opinions, abilities, and emotions in need of evaluation will be compared with the opinions, abilities, and emotions of other persons. This type of evaluation is called *social comparison,* and the information provided is called *social reality*.

Adequate evaluation by social comparison requires that the comparison persons be similar to the evaluator. For example, a civil rights worker would not evaluate the validity of his opinion regarding integration by comparing it with the opinions of members of the Ku Klux Klan. He would choose instead to judge it against opinions of his fellow civil rights enthusiasts. Similarly, a sand-lot ball player would judge his ability by comparisons with his peers rather than with Sandy Koufax. Finally, a person with normal emotional reactions would not knowingly judge the appropriateness of a particular emotional state by comparing himself with a psychotic manic depressive. To sum up, social comparison theory states: that agreement by others validates opinions subject to social reality tests; that emotional reactions of others support the appropriateness of one's own emotional reactions if they are similar; and that persons with similar abilities permit precise and accurate evaluations of one's own abilities. Further, persons with dissimilar attitudes, emotions, or abilities would tend to disturb and render invalid or unstable a person's evaluation of his own opinions, abilities, or emotions.

SOCIAL COMPARISON AND AFFILIATION

Through the process of social comparison, needs for evaluation of an opinion, ability, or emotion can result in affiliation, joining with others, or in pressures toward uniformity in existing groups. Theoretically derived by-products of pressures toward uniformity are rejection of others or dissolution of groups. The last named consequences are, of course, negative affiliation. Comparisons with other persons are made normally by talking to others or observing them face to face. The qualification normally is necessary since quasi-social comparisons are possible through other means such as reading others' opinions, telephone conversations, observing filmed or televised records of performances or emotional reactions, or through comparing one's salary or publication list with the credentials of others with similar training and experience in the same occupation.

Needs for accurate evaluation determine the types of others with whom one joins and the operation of pressures toward uniformity in existing groups. A person will tend to affiliate with persons similar to himself. He will tend to leave groups in which adequate or accurate evaluations of his opinions, abilities, and emotions are not available. Members of existing groups will exert pressures toward uniformity of opinions, abilities, or emotional reactions within the group. From an individual standpoint, these pressures toward uniformity will result in a tendency to change himself in the direction of the group norm, to change the attributes of others to make them similar to the self, to reject others who resist pressures to change, and to recruit similar others from outside the group.

It is not contended that persons associate and reject solely or even principally for reasons of social comparison. Rather, it is proposed that social comparison is an important reason for associating with people qua people. Similarly, the above discussion is not intended to imply that all opinions, abilities, and emotions or even all those subject to evaluation by social comparison arouse affiliative tendencies. Important abilities or opinions and relatively intense emotional reactions about which a person is uncertain are necessary for the arousal of affiliative tendencies. Thus there are thresholds of arousal and doubtless individual differences in those thresholds. It would be pointless, perhaps impossible, to specify any parameters of such thresholds at this time. Only the barest beginnings have been made in identifying individual differences in needs for social comparison. However, numerous experiments that will be cited in the following discussion demonstrate that social comparison needs are sufficiently sensitive to be manipulated reliably in the laboratory. The results of these studies in their entirety support the contention that needs for social comparison make a significant contribution to man's gregariousness.

DATA

Self-Evaluation and Affiliation

Festinger (1954a), in discussing the relationship between self-evaluation and affiliation, proposed that the drive for self-evaluation is an important source of affiliative behavior. However, Festinger presented no data bearing directly on the relationship since none were available. Experiments reported by Schachter (1959) were the first to demonstrate that the arousal of self-evaluative needs produces affiliation. Schachter's first study was a simple two-condition experiment employing the threat of electric shock as a fear stimulus. Subjects were run in groups of five and six. In one condition subjects were told that the shocks would be extremely painful, while in the second condition participants were told to anticipate only a mild tickling sensation. Following the fear arousing instructions, *S*s were given a choice of spending a waiting period, after which they were to be shocked, either alone or in the company of their fellows. Significantly more *S*s chose to wait with others in the high fear condition than in low fear. This experiment by itself did not, of course, demonstrate that needs for self-evaluation mediate the relationship between emotional arousal and affiliation. It was, however, the first step toward that result and is prototypic of a number of subsequent studies. Three additional experiments by Schachter and one by Wrightsman, all reported in detail in *The Psychology of Affiliation* (Schachter, 1959), were designed and executed to explain the relationship between emotional arousal and affiliation found in this first study.

Schachter's second experiment tested directionality of the affiliative tendency. Essentially the same manipulation was used as in the first study. *S*s were run alone instead of in groups, and two high fear conditions were run. In one condition *S*s were given the choice of waiting with others in a similar state of emotional arousal or waiting alone, while in the second condition they were given a choice between waiting with others who were in a different emotional state or waiting alone. *S*s chose to wait with others who were in the same state but not with dissimilar others. The first study had demonstrated that "misery loves company." This second study, as Schachter observed, indicates that "Misery doesn't love just any kind of company, it loves only miserable company" (Schachter, 1959, p. 24).

Two subsequent experiments eliminated a number of possible reasons for affiliation based on the opportunity to communicate. In a two-condition study, following the basic design of the original experiment, *S*s were instructed that, if they chose to wait together, they could not talk about the experiment. Opportunities to communicate were further restricted in another study in which *S*s were told that they could not talk about anything. In both experiments, *S*s in the high fear conditions chose to affiliate more than did those in the low fear conditions.

The experiment by Wrightsman (1960) tested the effects of waiting together on the evaluation of emotions. Wrightsman aroused fear in groups of *S*s who were then assigned to one of three treatment groups. In one condition, *S*s waited alone in separate rooms after receiving the fear-arousing instructions and prior to their anticipated painful experience. A second treatment group waited together but were not permitted to talk about anything, and they did not talk. *S*s in the third condition were allowed to talk about anything including the experiment, which they did. The dependent variable in Wrightsman's study was changes in pre-post waiting measures of self reports of fear. The social comparison prediction is that those groups that waited together should be more similar in level of emotional arousal than those groups that waited alone. Increasing similarity of emotional reaction was measured by an index of homogenization. As expected, there were no tendencies toward homogenization of affect in groups whose members waited alone. There were pre-post changes in self reports of fear for those who waited alone, but these changes were essentially random and did not reduce the range of variance of the level of anxiety within the group. In contrast, the groups waiting together, both the talk and the no-talk groups, did homogenize in levels of fear after waiting. That is, group members were more similar to each other in self reports on the post- compared to the pre-measure. There was also evidence of a rejection of dissimilar others among groups which waited together, since homogenization tended not to occur in groups in which the range of affect was large on the pre-measure.

In summary, the following are the major findings reported in Schachter's book. People choose to be with others when in a state of emotional arousal. The arousal must be above some threshold to produce affiliative tendencies. People choose to affiliate with others in a similar emotional state but not with others in a dissimilar emotional state. Affiliative tendencies are present whether or not talking with others is permitted. Finally, groups that wait together tend to become similar in emotional reactions. By analytically eliminating alternative explanations, Schachter proposed that needs for self-evaluation lead to affiliative behavior. He recognized at the close of his book that a definitive test of the anxiety-affiliation relationship remained to be provided, since his experiments had not manipulated evaluative needs directly.

As Festinger (1954a) has indicated, the need for social comparison is an intervening construct that is not directly observable. The experiments reported by Schachter did not prove the existence of a need of social comparison. His work, however, did demonstrate the utility of employing this hypothesized need as an explanatory concept in considering affiliation. Perhaps of equal importance, his work stimulated further studies in which needs for self-evaluation were manipulated, and expanded the investigation of the evaluation-affiliation relationship into the areas of opinion and ability evaluation and affiliation as well.

Subsequent work in the area of emotional evaluation will be considered first. In a series of three related studies, Gerard and Rabbie (1961; Gerard, 1963; Rabbie, 1963) investigated, among other aspects of the relationship, the effects of information about other persons, uncertainty regarding one's own reaction, and the direction of the affiliative tendencies. Their studies used the same fear-arousing stimulus as that used by Schachter, the fear of electric shock. One important difference in the Gerard and Rabbie studies compared with those of Schachter was that their *S*s received instructions while isolated from one another. They knew that others were present and taking part in the same experiment, but they could not see or hear them. This change in situation was not a whimsical variation; it was necessary to Gerard and Rabbie's experimental designs and aims, although it is difficult to judge the effects of the variation. It is quite possible that their being isolated while receiving instructions accentuated affiliative tendencies in Gerard and Rabbie's *S*s, since they were denied the possibility of evaluation by observing others when first being informed of their plight.

The first study of the three (Gerard & Rabbie, 1961) was a six-condition experiment. Two levels of fear were cross cut by three levels of information. A concept important to the work of Schachter was the notion that *S*s must be uncertain regarding their own emotional state in order for social comparison needs to be aroused. Gerard and Rabbie's findings provided strong support for this hypothesis. *S*s who received information regarding their own and others' emotional states, in the form of faked readings on dials in front of them, were significantly less eager to affiliate than were those who had no such information. An interesting additional finding is the fact that quasi-objective information about self reactions, the faked dial readings, did not decrease affiliative tendencies in the absence of information about others' reactions. Only information about self and others' reactions reduced the strength of affiliation. This study also replicated Schachter's findings that high fear subjects want to affiliate more than low fear.

The second study in this series (Gerard, 1963) investigated further the hypothesis regarding certainty of information. In this study certainty was manipulated by providing the subject with either a steady or a wavering meter reading to inform him of his own reactions. Information about the reactions of others was provided in the form of a steady meter reading purportedly showing the average of the reactions of the three other group members. In the uncertain condition there were four information conditions: no information (no dial); others similar to self; others higher than self; and others lower than self. In the certain condition only the first two of these treatments were used. Affiliative tendencies were higher in the uncertain condition than they were in the certain condition. Information that others were similar reduced affiliation under the certain condition but not under the uncertain. Affiliation with dissimilar others, uncertain condition only, tended to be reduced, significantly so toward others who were more fearful. This pattern of results gives strong support to the social comparison-affiliation hypothesis and suggests needs for anxiety reduction as well.

Rabbie (1961), in a study similar to the two reported above, manipulated uncertainty by instructions. *S*s were told that either all of them or only some of them would find the shocks exceedingly painful. As intended, this manipulation produced no differences in reported levels of fear. As predicted, the uncertain *S*s were significantly more affiliative than the certain *S*s. The opportunity to talk with others also resulted in stronger affiliation tendencies. Finally, additional support for the anxiety reduction hypothesis was provided by the finding that highly fearful others were rejected. This last finding is qualified by the fact that *S*s who were highly fearful rejected their high fear cohorts less than did those who were less frightened, a qualification which, of course, supports the hypothesis that similar others are desired for purposes of evaluation.

It is probably worth mentioning that GSR measures of emotionality in the Gerard and Rabbie studies demonstrated that appropriate physiological reactions were produced by the fear manipulations.

Two additional studies of emotional arousal, social comparison, and affiliation have been reported by Sarnoff and Zimbardo (1961) and by Zimbardo and Formica (1963). In design, these two studies followed the basic format of the original Schachter studies. Sarnoff and Zimbardo (1961) questioned the generality of the relationship between emotional arousal and affiliation. In a 2 × 2 experimental design they employed two levels of arousal of two emotions: fear, stimulated by threat of electric shock, and oral anxiety, stimulated by the anticipation of having to suck on various objects. Schachter's findings for fear were replicated, but as the authors predicted, high oral anxiety decreased affiliative tendencies. The prediction regarding oral anxiety and affiliation was derived from Freud. Sarnoff and Zimbardo succinctly summarized their position as follows: "The probability of the social comparison response is, thus, a function of: the kind of motive aroused, the intensity of the motive, the degree of novelty of the emotional experience, the response hierarchy associated with the specific motive, and certain attributes of those with whom the person is to affiliate" (1961, p. 362).

The study by Zimbardo and Formica (1963) employed the threat of electric shock as a fear-arousing stimulus. In support of the basic finding regarding fear and affiliation, high fear *S*s affiliated more than low fear. High fear *S*s affiliated more than low fear even when communication was restricted to topics irrelevant to the experiment. An interesting variation regarding similarity of others was tested. Others with whom the subject could choose to join were described alternatively as (a) subjects who had already completed the experiment or (b) subjects who were also waiting for the experiment to begin. Clearly, those who had already completed the experiment could provide cognitive clarity but could not provide emotional comparison, since they presumably would no longer be in a state of arousal. The findings strongly supported a social comparison explanation since affiliation was significantly greater toward those in a similar emotional state. Affiliative tendencies were taken beyond the paper and pencil stage by having subjects enter the room of their choice. All subjects went to the room they had checked as desiring. Finally, reasons for affiliating were solicited and analyzed. Reasons given indicated that *S*s were affiliating for reasons of social comparison in the high fear same state condition.

Opinion and Ability Evaluation

Most of the work on self-evaluation and affiliation has been done in the area of emotional evaluation. Only one experiment has tested the relationship for opinions and one for abilities. In addition, two field studies in the area of opinion comparison are relevant.

An experiment by Radloff (1961) demonstrated that uncertainty regarding an opinion arouses affiliative tendencies. In this five-condition experiment, opinions were solicited in four conditions. After giving their opinions, *S*s were provided with varying opportunities to evaluate them. In order of the quality of information provided, the four groups were given: no information, information regarding the opinions of inferiors, information pertaining to the opinions of peers, and information on the opinions of experts. In the fifth condition, opinions were not solicited nor was any information given on the opinions of others. *S*s were asked to volunteer to participate in discussion groups concerned with the opinion at issue. As predicted, there was a linear relationship between adequacy of evaluative information and desire to join a discussion group. That is, the less adequate evaluative information he had, the more likely an *S* was to want to discuss the topic with others. *Ss* who had not given an opinion on the subject had as little desire to discuss it as did those who had compared their opinions with those of experts. An analysis of free response reasons for wanting to join discussion groups showed that *Ss* theoretically in need of self-evaluation did in fact give significantly more reasons specifying social comparison needs than did those not in need of self-evaluation. Thus there is good evidence that needs for self-evaluation lead to affiliation for opinions as well as for emotions.

Additional evidence of the link between needs for opinion evaluation and affiliation is provided in a field study by Festinger, Riecken, and Schachter (1956). This study reported on a group that had predicted the destruction of the world by earthquake and flood. The prediction specified a date for the occurrence. Its fulfillment was of crucial importance to the group since many of the members had sold homes, closed businesses, and given up jobs in anticipation of the holocaust. Prior to disconfirmation of the prophecy, members of the group had shunned all contacts with persons outside the group. They resolutely refused to discuss their beliefs with outsiders. Following disconfirmation of the prophecy the group engaged in frantic proselyting. They attempted to convince anyone who would listen that their predictions were valid and that their faith had, in effect, saved the world. Their proselyting was predicted and is viewed by the authors as an attempt to gain social support for an opinion that had been shaken by a physical reality evaluation.

A subsequent study of a similar group (Hardyck & Braden, 1962) failed to find similar effects. The Hardyck and Braden group was about six times as large as the Festinger, Riecken, and Schachter group. Also, they had predicted destruction of the world by atomic holocaust rather than by earthquake and flood and had received support rather than ridicule from the outside community prior to disconfirmation of their prophecy. Existence of more adequate social support because of greater numbers and the absence of attack from the outside is cited by the authors as a possible reason for failure to replicate the Festinger, Riecken, and Schachter results. It should be noted that in these two studies, social reality was pitted against physical reality. According to social comparison theory physical reality is normally preferred over social reality as a basis for evaluating opinions. Only in very special and unusual circumstances, discussed by Festinger (Festinger, Riecken, & Schachter, 1956; Festinger, 1957) will social reality validation be sought when a physically real test has invalidated an opinion. In effect, the two studies cited posed the most stringent possible test of the link between opinion evaluation and affiliation via social comparison. Given these conditions, substantiation in one of two available tests is strong support for the hypothesis.

Only a single study has been published providing a direct test of the affiliation hypothesis regarding ability evaluation. Singer and Shockley (1965) found that subjects do affiliate when an ability is in need of evaluation. In a two-condition study subjects were given their scores on a perceptual task that had been made to seem an important ability by instructions. Following receipt of their scores, subjects were either given information allowing evaluation of their performance, a distribution of the scores of others, or were told that such information was unavailable. Subjects then chose between waiting alone or with others in their group for the continuation of the experiment. Subjects without information were significantly more affiliative than were those with information.

Other Data on Affiliation and Social Comparison

The evidence presented above supports directly the proposition that humans seek the company of others when self-evaluative needs are aroused and that this affiliative behavior is mediated by needs for social comparison. In this section other propositions related to affiliation which are derived from the relationship between self-evaluation and social comparison will be examined. Specifically, this section will be concerned with attempts to achieve adequate social comparison within existing groups. Affiliation in this context means the maintenance or viability of groups rather than their formation.

Rejection and Acceptance

Since persons in need of social reality join with others to satisfy their needs, it follows that, in existing groups, persons who do not satisfy social reality needs will tend to be rejected, while those who do satisfy such needs will tend to be accepted. Or stated more directly, we remain in the company of those who agree with us or are similar to us, and we shun those who disagree with or are dissimilar from us. There is abundant experimental evidence that dissimilar others are rejected and similar others are accepted for opinions, abilities, and emotions.

The classic study of opinion discrepancy and rejection (Schachter, 1951), predated the formulation of the theory of social comparison processes. However, since it is a study on which much of the reasoning of social comparison theory is based, it can be considered as having been designed to test the theory. Schachter organized discussion groups and observed their interaction in discussing a common topic. Confederates in the groups took various stands vis-à-vis the issue under discussion. In a counterbalanced design, three confederates took positions (a) deviant from the modal opinion of the group and maintained it throughout the discussion, or (b) deviant initially but changing toward the group norm as the discussion progressed, or (c) at the group norm initially, which position they maintained. In a 2 × 2 design, manipulation produced high and low cohesiveness and high and low relevance of topic. Sociometric measures taken after a 45-minute discussion revealed that the deviate was rejected, while "mode" and "slider" confederates were accepted. This differential acceptance was most pronounced in highly cohesive groups and in those in which the topic was relevant to the group goals.

Schachter's findings on deviation and rejection have been replicated in laboratory experiments by Arrowood and Amoroso (1965) and by Sampson and Brandon (1964). Other related findings have been reported by Fauquier and Vinacke (1964), Gerard and Greenbaum (1962), Walster and Walster (1963), Byrne (1962), and Byrne and Nelson (1965). Fauquier and Vinacke found that discussion groups with large opinion discrepancies changed less after exchanging opinions than did more homogeneous groups. That is, in social comparison terms, dissimilar others were rejected as comparison persons. Gerard and Greenbaum found that agreement by others increases confidence in one's own opinion and that others who agree are liked better than those who disagree. In the study by Walster and Walster, *S*s were attracted to dissimilar others only if they were assured that the dissimilar others would like them. The brace of studies by Byrne demonstrated a positive correlation between the number of similar attitudes held by a stranger and attraction to him. Numerous other findings could be cited regarding similarity and attraction. These particular studies have been chosen because the authors employed social comparison theory in the design of the study or in interpreting their results.

Field studies by Brock and Kipnis were designed specifically to test social comparison theory derivations on acceptance and rejection. Brock (1965) conducted an ingenious field experiment. It is of particular importance because of the rarity of field experiments in social psychology. The experimenters were paint salesmen who played roles of experts or of relatively naïve persons similar to the customers. Findings were that customers were significantly more inclined to accept advice on paint purchases from similar others than they were from expert others. Brock's results provide experimental evidence supporting correlational data on the power of similar others to influence marketing behavior reported by Katz and Lazarsfeld (1955) in their book *Personal Influence*. Taken together, these results provide strong support for the proposition that expert influence is frequently rejected because the experts are dissimilar from the buyer. Brock's results are especially compelling, since the expert had superior knowledge of a general nature. That some minions of Madison Avenue have accepted this proposition is demonstrated by an apparent increase in recent years of endorsements, in television commercials, of a variety of products by "just plain folks" rather than by the prototypic expert, the man in the white coat.

Kipnis (1961) in a longitudinal study of friendship tested hypotheses derived from social comparison theory. *S*s rated themselves and best friends on various traits. Among other findings, there was a tendency for friendships to be broken off if the best friend was rated negatively compared to the self. If the best friend was rated positively, there was more of a tendency to change self ratings over time to make oneself more similar to the friend.

For the abilities, Hoffman, Festinger, and Lawrence (1954) present data demonstrating that superior others are rejected as comparison persons if their superior ability is acknowledged. If others in the group are recognized as superior, average persons confine their comparisons of ability to others of their own ability. Zander and Havelin (1961) found rejection of others dissimilar in ability as measured by sociometric choice. While there was a tendency to be more attracted to groups with more competent members, the overriding tendency was to choose persons of similar ability. A study of ability comparison by Whitmyre, Diggory, and Cohen (1961) also showed a general tendency to choose others similar in ability. Howard and Berkowitz (1958) manipulated judgments ostensibly made by a group of peers who judged *S*s' performance (an ability evaluation). Members of judging groups who deviated from the consensus of their groups were thought to be in error by the *S*s. This was true even if the deviate's evaluation was favorable to the *S*. Further, judges who deviated from the group consensus were rejected sociometrically.

With reference to the emotions, several studies on affiliation have tested directionality of choices. The pioneering studies of Schachter (1959) demonstrated that others in a similar emotional state are sought out, while there is no desire for the company of others in a dissimilar state when fear is aroused. That this directionality holds even when the dissimilar others are persons with specific knowledge of the emotion-arousing situation was found by Zimbardo and Formica (1963). Experiments by Gerard (1963) and by Rabbie (1963) indicated that fearful *S*s tend to reject those who are more fearful, preferring the company of those who are similarly or less agitated.

Movement Towards Uniformity

Thus, humans tend to seek out others who are similar and to reject others who are dissimilar, but physical movement from group to group in search of similar others is probably a relatively rare phenomenon. That is, a person upon finding himself different from others in a group does not immediately pick up his opinion, ability, or emotion and leave. Nor does he readily expel divergent others from the group, although there are *tendencies* both to locomote and to reject. A person may be compelled, for a variety of reasons, to maintain membership in various groups. Similarly, he may be prevented from joining with others who would be more compatible. Various groups may be adequate on some dimensions and not on others; matters of economics, inertia, and the like will enter into a decision to stay or leave. For example, a man does not immediately quit his job if he finds that his co-workers all disagree with him on, say, a question of politics; nor does a homeowner precipitately dispose of his house if he finds that his neighbors' opinions on race relations are different from his. Such drastic steps have been taken, to be sure, but most instances of differences within groups give rise to less dramatic manifestations of pressures toward uniformity. Two such manifestations that have been investigated experimentally are the tendencies to change self and attempts to change others.

Studies of opinion comparison have used pre- and postmeasures assessing opinion change and frequency counts of influence attempts as indicators of pressures toward uniformity. Numerous studies could be cited exemplifying change of and attempts to change discrepant opinions in order to produce uniformity in groups, but only a few studies specifically designed to test hypotheses derived from social comparison theory will be cited here.

Schachter (1951), in a study using discussion groups, found that a disproportionately large number of comments were directed toward deviates. These communications were attempts to influence the deviate to accept the modal opinion of the group. Increasing group cohesiveness and the relevance of the issue increased the proportion of comments directed at the deviate up to a point. Sampson and Brandon (1964) found exactly the same results in similar discussion groups. Content analysis revealed that many of the excess comments directed at deviates were hostile or derogatory as deviation persisted. In both these studies deviates were steadfast because they were confederates of the experimenter.

Deviates who are *S*s rather than confederates tend to change their opinions toward the group norm as a result of influence attempts. This result has been found in studies by Raven (1959), Berkowitz (1957), and Arrowood and Amoroso (1965). A related phenomenon demonstrated by Brock and Blackwood (1962) is the tendency for deviates to support their own position by perceptually inflating the proportion of others who agree with them.

Variables affecting the strength of attempts to change others and the tendencies to change one's own position have also been investigated in many of the studies cited above. In brief, it has been found that influence attempts are more frequent and greater changes are produced by increasing the importance of the issue or its relevance to the group, by increasing the cohesiveness of the group, and by making expressions of opinion public.

With reference to the abilities, a study by Hoffman, Festinger, and Lawrence (1954) found that persons lower in ability attempt to affect the performance of a superior person so as to make him equal to others in the group. Brehm and Festinger (1957) demonstrated that increasing the importance of a task increased the tendency to perceive others as similar in ability.

Changes in emotional reaction were demonstrated by Wrightsman (1960). He found increases in the homogeneity of emotional reactions within a group as a result of waiting together. Schachter and Singer (1962) found that persons in an ambiguous emotional state produced behavior which agreed with those of a model. *S*s in the same physiological state, produced by the same drug, became either euphoric or angry depending upon the behavior of the model.

Summary

Let us summarize briefly the findings reported above. Experiments have demonstrated that people affiliate with others when they are uncertain about the appropriateness of their emotional reactions, the validity of their opinions, or the level of their abilities.

These affiliative tendencies are mediated by needs to evaluate those emotions, opinions, or abilities. When self-evaluative needs are aroused, there is a desire to join with others who are similar but not with dissimilar others. In existing groups, dissimilar others are rejected both as comparison persons and as future associates in general. Also, in existing groups, pressures are exerted on deviates to change toward the group norm, and deviates tend to yield to those pressures. A variety of factors have been found which affect these processes of affiliation, acceptance, rejection, and pressures toward uniformity. In general, the occurrence of all these processes is more likely: the greater the uncertainty regarding own and others' reactions, the greater the importance of the opinion or ability to the individual and the group, the higher the intensity of emotional arousal, the higher the group's cohesiveness, and the greater the relevance of the opinion or ability for the person or the group.

Discussion

The evidence is clear that social comparison processes do operate to produce affiliative behavior and to determine the composition and viability of groups. But how important are these processes in determining social behavior? This discussion will consider the potency of social comparison processes in determining the uniformity of groups as well as some forces which tend to counteract pressures toward uniformity.

Importance of Social Comparison

Social comparison theory's basic postulate is the existence of a drive for self-evaluation. The experiments reported above demonstrate the theoretical utility of such a drive. But granted that such a drive exists in humans and that it can explain research results, the question remains what purpose does it serve in nature and society? In discussing the existence of this drive for self-evaluation, Festinger (1954a and 1954b) indicates that it may have survival value and that it serves as a sort of social psychological "law of least effort." For example, "knowing" that a certain species of mushrooms is poisonous is valuable information. Most persons would be quite willing to accept the opinions of others (social reality) and would not submit the question to a physical reality test by eating them. Again, following Festinger, it is often quite convenient, saving of time and effort, to have a rather precise estimate of one's ability before committing oneself to a long and arduous test of that ability. Thus it is useful for a high school student to know the probability of his finishing college before he enrolls. An estimate of this probability can be obtained by social comparison tests of his intellectual ability, motivation, and similar factors. A poll conducted by potential candidates before committing themselves to a contest for office is another example of a vicarious test of ability and possibly opinions as well. Furthermore, for many opinions and for probably most emotions, the only definitions of validity or appropriateness are social reality definitions. Examples could be proliferated illustrating the utility of evaluation by social comparison, but a pervasive underlying basis for the need of accurate evaluation through consensual validation is provided by an analysis by Hebb and Thompson (1954).

In a brilliant and far-ranging chapter section entitled "A Theoretical Approach to Human Nature and Society," Hebb and Thompson derive the fact of uniformity of behavior in human societies by extrapolations from animal studies. Their analysis rests on the observation of a phylogenetic and ontogenetic correlation between intellectual ability and emotionality. Stated very briefly, studies of animal intelligence and emotionality indicate that the more intelligent and the more mature an organism, the more emotional it is as well. Increase in emotionality is defined as an increase in the variety of causes of emotional disturbance, an increase in the variety of emotional manifestations, and increases in duration of emotional reactions following brief stimulation. These results from animal studies lead to the inevitable conclusion that adult humans should be the most emotionally reactive of all organisms. Obviously such does not appear to be the case. Why not? Hebb and Thompson contend that civilized man's emotional stability is an illusion. It is achieved by society's insulating man in a cocoon of uniformity in order to protect him from a potentially destructive bombardment of emotional stimulation. As examples, they cite the treatment of corpses and the existence of stringent sex mores. Hebb and Thompson contend that the major goal of education in general, and moral training in particular, is to establish a uniformity of taboos, of emotional sensitivity, and of behavior in general. Uniformity is necessary because of man's deep-seated tendency to be disturbed emotionally by strange and unusual stimuli. According to their analysis, this tendency to be disturbed by the unfamiliar is wired into the organism, its locus being in the central nervous system.

Applying the Hebb and Thompson analysis to the drive for self-evaluation, we can conclude that humans need to evaluate, with considerable precision, their various states and reactions so that they will not behave in strange and unusual ways, so that they will not constantly disrupt the emotional equilibria of themselves and those around them. Stated another way, the range of possible reactions to the various stimuli in his environment is so great that the only way man can know how to react is to observe other humans.

Intra-group differences and changes in normative behavior over time are determined, according to Hebb and Thompson, by individual differences in emotional sensitivity and needs for an optimal level of arousal. Because of the simultaneous operation of these factors, some persons will periodically test the limits of the social code. In some cases this testing behavior will be punished, while in other instances it may be rewarded, and small changes in morals, customs, and styles will result.

Hebb and Thompson's analysis demonstrates that pressures toward uniformity and the relation of affiliation to similarity of others may be derived from studies of infrahuman behavior. Another indicator of the pervasive nature of the concepts developed in this paper is the frequency with which similar ideas have been advanced by other theorists. For example, affiliation based on similarity is basic to the balance theories of Newcomb (1953) and Heider (1958). Riesman's (1950) other-directed man behaves in accordance with social comparison principles. The comparison level concept developed by Thibaut and Kelley (1954) has overtones of social comparison processes. Bandura and Walters' (1963) studies of modelling behavior also employ concepts similar to social comparison. The power of the group (social reality) to influence perceptions of stimuli (physical reality) has been demonstrated in the work of Asch (1956). Other examples could be cited, but the above should be sufficient to demonstrate that the concepts employed here are central to the concerns of social psychology.

A further indication of the ubiquity of social comparison processes is the frequency with which their operation is observed in everyday life. The generality of the workings of self-evaluative processes can be illustrated by citing behavior ranging from that of a child in kindergarten, concerned over his inability to equal the performance of his peers, to a reported social rejection by the President of the United States of the Chairman of the Senate foreign relations committee because of a disagreement on foreign policy questions. The intensity with which pressures toward uniformity can operate is tragically illustrated by the fate of civil rights workers in some southern states who have been brutally murdered because of opinion discrepancies. The fact that the social reality of this set of beliefs, a way of life, has been challenged simultaneously by official agencies has doubtlessly prompted the fanatic defense of the beliefs.

Heterogeneity

Pressures toward uniformity would seem to require that face-to-face groups and definable communities will be relatively homogeneous with respect to abilities, opinions, and emotions. The extent to which they are or are not homogeneous could be the subject of a long discussion of uncertain outcome, so we will admit that observation indicates that groups are in reality less homogeneous than they should be, based on the above discussion. Why? What are the factors against uniformity? Several forces mitigating against complete uniformity can be identified. Some of these variables have been investigated experimentally while others have not. The order of presentation below is not intended to imply an order of importance.

Individual differences undoubtedly play a major role in producing heterogeneous groups. The banality of this truism may be softened somewhat by indicating the way in which individual differences apply to the present analysis. If it is true that uniformity of behavior is determined in part by emotional disturbances created by strange and deviant behavior, it follows that the less sensitive an organism is to such arousal, the less likely it will be to inhibit behavior productive of such disturbance. Thus, persons who are physiologically, neurologically, or by training and experience less susceptible to changes in emotional states will behave more frequently in a deviant or socially unacceptable manner. Schachter (1964) has demonstrated, for example, that psychopaths are unable to learn by punishment.[2]

Another important source of heterogeneity in groups stems from the fact that people congregate for a variety of reasons other than self-evaluation and that groups whose members are similar in some important respects may be quite dissimilar in others. The most common of such aggregates are work groups. Although, over time self-evaluative needs can be expected to operate in determining occupation and the level in the hierarchy a man occupies, different skill requirements within work groups may dictate heterogeneous composition. Also, mobility from group to group may be difficult in many cases, forcing interactions among persons of widely varying opinions and abilities. Furthermore, in western culture there are forces toward upward mobility that tend to counteract pressures toward uniformity for the abilities.

The attention-attracting value of deviancy in the matter of opinions is another force productive of group heterogeneity. Numerous studies have shown that communication is directed toward the deviate. If skillfully played, the role of devil's advocate, or less extreme variations on the theme, doubtless have reward value.

The operation of a principle called *need complementarity* may produce apparently heterogeneous groups. Need complementar-

[2] Individual differences have not been discussed extensively in this paper since to do them justice would have meant at least doubling its length and would have complicated the discussion greatly without providing much additional information. The individual difference variable most extensively considered in relation to affiliation and social comparison has been birth order. Schachter (1959) found a strong relationship between birth order and affiliation in his original studies. These findings have stimulated a great deal of work on the variable. Indeed, probably more work has accumulated in recent years on birth order than on affiliation and social comparison. Unfortunately, while birth order does appear to be intimately related to social behavior, the specific nature of its effects are not at all clear at present. For a recent review of this subject see Warren (1966).

Other individual difference variables have received some consideration in conjunction with social comparison analyses. Among these are n Affiliation (Byrne, 1962; Kissel, 1965; Sistrunk & McDavid, 1965), self-esteem (Stotland & Cottrell, 1961; Stotland, Thorley, Thomas, Cohen, & Zander, 1957; Zimbardo & Formica, 1963) and n Achievement (Sistrunk & McDavid, 1965).

ity appears, at a superficial level, to be at variance with principles of similarity in determining affiliation. Further consideration, however, indicates that need complementarity may be a special case of opinion similarity. To illustrate, a dominant-submissive dyad may be viewed as one in which both members agree on this fundamental aspect of the relationship. That is, A and B both agree that one will be dominant while the other is submissive.

IN CONCLUSION

In this chapter, affiliation has been considered within the framework of social comparison theory. It is recognized that this is a relatively narrow approach. This concentrated approach was taken because social comparison theory has been an area of recent and growing development. It represents an apparently new approach to affiliation. But most important, in the opinion of this writer, social comparison theory is the best developed, most clearly stated and testable theory in social psychology at this time. The evidence cited in this paper is, of course, subject to alternative explanations, but its major strength derives from the fact that the experiments producing it were designed to test hypotheses derived from the theory. Just as the present evidence is open to other interpretations, so also could other findings have been cited from studies not designed to test social comparison theory. However, a theory is best tested by studies designed for that purpose.

The case presented would doubtless be much stronger had the development of social comparison theory progressed at a steady rate. Immediately after its presentation the author turned his attention to the study of cognitive dissonance (Festinger, 1957). The appearance of dissonance theory seems to have enticed the research efforts of many able and productive scholars essentially out of the field of social psychology in general and probably away from the consideration of social comparison theory in particular. Nevertheless, tests of the theory have continued at a modest pace. In recent years it has received increasing attention, stimulated in large measure by Schachter's application of its postulates to emotional comparison and to affiliation.

But let us be clear as to what has been accomplished in relating social comparison to affiliation. Only a handful of studies directly linking ability and opinion evaluation to affiliation have appeared. Studies of emotional evaluation are more numerous, but they have dealt almost exclusively with fear. While, for example, common sense may support the notion that dissimilarities in senses of humor may lead to rejection (the overbearing "practical joker" or "sobersides") and similarity to acceptance, there is no experimental evidence. Furthermore, the relationship between affiliation and emotional reaction may be different for the different emotions. Still further, Schachter's (1964) recent work on the concept of emotion indicates that such studies might best await the clarification of the definition of emotion.

Thus the present evidence linking evaluation, social comparison, and affiliation is intriguing, having profound implications for human social behavior. But it is incomplete. Further experimental tests can be expected. Conceptual development of the theory may be anticipated also. For example, a distinction between evaluation and validation seems appropriate. This distinction is implicit in many of the studies reported here, but it has not as yet been made explicit. To date, social comparison theory has shown excellent promise. It has generated experimentally testable hypotheses. Its hypotheses as presently stated have been well substantiated by rigorous and sophisticated laboratory experiments. In the first five years following its publication, an average of only three papers per year were based wholely or in part on social comparison concepts. In the next five years, the average was ten per year, still a modest number. In a field as subject to fads and fashions as psychology, it is risky to project trends. However, if interest in social comparison theory continues to grow, its utilization can be expected to contribute significantly to an understanding of human affiliation.

REFERENCES

Arrowood, A. J., & Amoroso, D. M. Social comparison and ordinal position. *J. Pers. soc. Psychol.,* 1965, 2, 101–104.

Asch, S. E. Studies of independence and conformity: A minority of one against a unanimous majority. *Psychol. Monogr.,* 1956, 70, No. 9 (Whole No. 416).

Bandura, A., & Walters, R. H. *Social learning and personality development.* New York: Holt, 1963.

Berkowitz, L. Liking for the group and the perceived merit of the group's behavior. *J. abnorm. soc. Psychol.,* 1957, 54, 353–357.

Brehm, J., & Festinger, L. Pressures toward uniformity of performance in groups. *Human Relat.,* 1957, 10, 85–91.

Brock, T. C. Communicator-recipient similarity and decision change. *J. Pers. soc. Psychol.,* 1965, 1, 650–654.

Brock, T. C., & Blackwood, J. E. Dissonance reduction, social comparison and modification of others' opinions. *J. abnorm. soc. Psychol.,* 1962, 65, 319–324.

Byrne, D. Response to attitude similarity-dissimilarity as a function of affiliation need. *J. Pers.,* 1962, 30, 164–177.

Byrne, D., & Nelson, D. Attraction as a linear function of proportion of positive reinforcement. *J. Pers. soc. Psychol.,* 1965, 1, 659–663.

Deutsch, M., & Solomon, L. Reactions to evaluations by others as influenced by self-evaluations. *Sociometry,* 1959, 22, 93–112.

Fauquier, W., & Vinacke, W. E. Communication and opinion as a function of member attractiveness and opinion discrepancy. *J. soc. Psychol.,* 1964, 63, 295–308.

Festinger, L. A theory of social comparison processes. *Human Relat.,* 1954, 7, 117–140. (a)

Festinger, L. Motivations leading to social behavior. In M. R. Jones (Ed.), *Nebraska symposium on motivation.* Lincoln: Univer. of Nebraska Press, 1954. Pp. 191–219. (b)

Festinger, L. *A theory of cognitive dissonance.* Stanford: Stanford University Press, 1957.

Festinger, L., Riecken, H. W., and Schachter, S. *When prophesy fails.* New York: Harper Torchbooks, 1956.

Festinger, L., Torrey, Jane, and Willerman, B. Self-evaluation as a function of attraction to the group. *Human Relat.,* 1954, 1, 161–174.

Fishbein, M., Raven, B. H., & Hunter, Rhonda. Social comparison and dissonance reduction in self-evaluation. *J. abnorm. soc. Psychol.,* 1963, 67, 491–501.

Gerard, H. B. Emotional uncertainty and social comparison. *J. abnorm. soc. Psychol.,* 1963, 66, 568–573.

Gerard, H. B., & Greenbaum, C. W. Attitudes toward an agent of uncertainty reduction. *J. Pers.,* 1962, 30, 485–495.

Gerard, H. B., & Rabbie, J. M. Fear and social comparison. *J. abnorm. soc. Psychol.,* 1961, 62, 586–592.

Hardyck, Jane, & Braden, Marcia. Prophecy fails again: a report of a failure to replicate. *J. abnorm. soc. Psychol.,* 1962, 65, 136–141.

Hebb, D., & Thompson, W. The social significance of animal studies. In G. Lindzey (Ed.), *Handbook of social psychology.* Cambridge, Mass.: Addison-Wesley, 1954. Pp. 532–561.

Heider, F. *The psychology of interpersonal relations.* New York: Wiley, 1958.

Hoffman, P. J., Festinger, L., & Lawrence, D. H. Tendencies toward group comparison in competitive bargaining. *Human Relat.,* 1954, 7, 141–159.

Howard, R. C., & Berkowitz, L. Reactions to the evaluations of one's performance. *J. Pers.,* 1958, 26, 494–507.

Katz, E., & Lazarsfeld, P. F. *Personal influence.* Glencoe, Ill.: Free Press, 1955.

Kipnis, Dorothy M. Changes in self-concept in relation to perceptions of others. *J. Pers.,* 1961, 29, 449–465.

Kissel, S. Stress reducing properties of social stimuli. *J. Pers. soc. Psychol.,* 1965, 2, 378–384.

Newcomb, T. An approach to the study of communicative acts. *Psychol. Rev.,* 1953, 60, 393–404.

Rabbie, J. M. Differential preference for companionship under threat. *J. abnorm. soc. Psychol.,* 1963, 67, 643–648.

Radloff, R. Opinion evaluation and affiliation. *J. abnorm. soc. Psychol.,* 1961, 62, 578–585.

Raven, B. H. Social influence on opinions and the communication of related content. *J. abnorm. soc. Psychol.,* 1959, 58, 119–128.

Riesman, D. *The lonely crowd.* New Haven: Yale Univer. Press, 1950.

Sampson, E. E., & Brandon, Arlene C. The effects of role and opinion deviation on small group behavior. *Sociometry,* 1964, 27, 261–281.

Sarnoff, I., & Zimbardo, P. G. Anxiety, fear, and social affiliation. *J. abnorm. soc. Psychol.,* 1961, 62, 356–363.

Schachter, S. Deviation, rejection and communication. *J. abnorm. soc. Psychol.,* 1951, 46, 190–208.

Schachter, S. *The psychology of affiliation.* Stanford: Stanford Univer. Press, 1959.

Schachter, S. The interaction of cognitive and physiological determinants of emotional state. In L. Berkowitz (Ed.), *Advances in experimental social psychology.* Vol. 1. New York: Academic Press, 1964. Pp. 49–80.

Schachter, S., & Singer, J. E. Cognitive, social, and physiological determinants of emotional state. *Psychol. Rev.,* 1962, 69, 379–399.

Singer, J. E., & Shockley, V. L. Ability and affiliation. *J. Pers. soc. Psychol.,* 1965, 1, 95–100.

Sistrunk, F., & McDavid, J. W. Achievement motivation, affiliation motivation, and task difficulty as determinants of social conformity. *J. soc. Psychol.,* 1965, 66, 41–50.

Stotland, E., & Cottrell, N. B. Self-esteem, group interaction, and group influence on performance. *J. Pers.,* 1961, 29, 273–284.

Stotland, E., Thorley, S., Thomas, E., Cohen, A.R., & Zander, A. The effects of group expectations and self-esteem upon self-evaluation. *J. abnorm. soc. Psychol.,* 1957, 54, 55–69.

Thibaut, J., & Kelley, H. *The social psychology of groups.* New York: Wiley, 1959.

Walster, Elaine, & Walster, B. Effects of expecting to be liked on choice of associates. *J. abnorm. soc. Psychol.,* 1963, 67, 402–404.

Warren, J. R. Birth order and social behavior. *Psychol. Bull.,* 1966, 38–39.

Whitmyre, J. W., Diggory, J. C., & Cohen, D. The effects of liking, perceived ability and value of prize on choice of partners for a competition. *J. abnorm. soc. Psychol.,* 1961, 63, 198–200.

Wrightsman, L. S., Jr. Effects of waiting with others on changes in level of felt anxiety. *J. abnorm. soc. Psychol.,* 1960, 61, 216–222.

Zander, A., & Havelin, A. Social comparison and interpersonal attraction. *Human Relat.,* 1960, 13, 21–32.

Zimbardo, P., & Formica, R. Emotional comparison and self-esteem as determinants of affiliation. *J. Pers.,* 1963, 31, 141–162.

CHAPTER 18 Some Consequences of Taking Machiavelli Seriously[1]

RICHARD CHRISTIE
Columbia University
FLORENCE GEIS
University of Delaware

For almost ten years I[2] have been puzzling about the nature of individuals who are effective in manipulating others. Word of this hobby has gotten around so that it seems appropriate to dispel certain false rumors about the reasons for my curiosity. My usual response is that only those who are nonprejudiced study prejudiced people, that most analysts of economic trends are impecunious professors, etc.

The actual story is a bit more complicated. As was true of many of my generation of graduate students after World War II, I was both intrigued and perplexed by the research reported in *The Authoritarian Personality* (Adorno, Frenkel-Brunswik, Levinson, & Sanford, 1950). The embryonic John Birchers they described were so similar to many of the people I had grown up with that I had the lurking suspicion that most of their subjects were not California undergraduates but potential members of the Tulsa Rotary Club. There was one aspect of Shils' (1954) criticism of *The Authoritarian Personality* I could agree with. These right-wing people were not living in the world of social reality and in a broader social context were remarkably ineffective in dealing with the here and now. This agreement with Shils' position was somewhat shaken after observation of what happened at the 1964 Republican Convention in San Francisco. But the political ineptness of extremists in pursuit of vice was so reassuring that it was possible to win bets about the margin of Johnson's plurality in the 1964 election.

In 1954–55, two political scientists who were interested in political behavior, Robert Agger and Frank Pinner, and I were at the first year of the Center for Advanced Study in the Behavioral Sciences. This was a somewhat awesome experience. Every academician dreams of having a year in which he can sit on a hilltop and think Great Thoughts. When it suddenly happens, what have been described as panic reactions oc-

[1] This is a paper read at a symposium on Machiavellianism during the annual meetings of the American Psychological Association in Los Angeles on September 7, 1964.

[2] Throughout the discussion *I* refers to the senior author.

cur. One way of relieving anxiety is to form Work Groups so that anxiety can be shared and possibly dissipated. One of these work groups was composed of about ten relatively junior people who started a "True Believer" work group (the title came from the book by Eric Hoffer, 1951). The focus was upon zealots of the political right or left and religious extremists. Agger, Pinner, and I were impressed with a matter that, in retrospect, should have been obvious. Most empirical research had been done upon followers rather than leaders. This is perhaps paradoxical since most of the speculations to be found in the literature are about decision makers, or if you will, "leaders." We concluded that fewer people manipulate effectively than are manipulated, and it is easier to find subjects who are objects of manipulations than the converse. Most good manipulators are so busy manipulating that they are not members of the audiences captured by most researchers.

Our reflections led to four hunches which should not be dignified by being termed hypotheses but which seemed consistent with an "ideal type":

1. Manipulators are not basically concerned with morality in the conventional sense.
2. They are basically "cool" in interpersonal relationships. Once one becomes emotionally involved with another person it becomes difficult to treat him as an object to be manipulated.
3. Since those who manipulate are more concerned with means rather than ends, they might be of any ideological persuasion, but are more concerned with conning others than what they are conning them for.
4. Whether or not this behavior might suggest that those who display it should be candidates for a psychiatrist's couch, they do function successfully in the contemporary world. They should not display the type of irrationality commonly or technically viewed as neurotic or psychotic; if anything, they would be overrational in dealing with others.

Fortunately, the Center provided another resource. Almost everyone there was a manipulator in the behavioral sciences or the protege of one. We did a dastardly thing. We conducted unstructured interviews with those of our colleagues who had obtained their doctorates or served in departments with individuals who were generally identified as "operators" by most knowledgable behavioral scientists. It is a moot question whether we asked leading questions or whether the targets of our inquiry actually behaved in the way our respondents said. In any event, our hypothetical role descriptions were so closely matched by the descriptions of the behavior of the models that we were encouraged to continue our inquiries.

We were not the first to be intrigued with the ways in which people control others by psychological rather than physical means. Men have speculated about the characteristics of manipulators or operators since the dawn of recorded history. We thought it prudent to examine the writings of power theorists. This was educational. One of the more esoteric sources suggested by Harold Lasswell was Kung-sun Yang, who had written advice to guide rulers in China about the fourth century B.C. (Duyvendak, 1928). This was somewhat disappointing because it was not obvious to us why his writings were banned for centuries; he sounded like an early version of the late Senator Robert Taft.

It was easier to understand why the writings of Kautilya, or Chānakya, at approximately the same time were lost for over two thousand years. His advice to rulers suggests that India in 300 B.C. made the Florence of the Medicis a kindergarten playground in comparison. Among other things, he gave suggestions as to how to set up systems of internal and external spies, the best ways to bribe subordinates to test their loyalty, and ways of assuring that the ruler will not be stabbed in the back while busy in his harem (Shamasastry, 1923).[3] Parenthetically, when Kautilya's writings were uncovered at the beginning of this century, Indian intellectuals were delighted. This was evidence that Indians were not inherently as otherworldly and mystic as the British claimed (Brown, 1953).

It happened, not quite by chance, that I was reviewing a book, *The Psychology of Politics* (Eysenck, 1954) at the same time as dipping into the writings of power theorists. My objections to Eysenck's basic argument are spelled out in painful detail elsewhere (Christie, 1955; Christie, 1956a; Christie, 1956b), but the relevance to the present exposition is more general. Eysenck proposed a two-factor theory to explain political ideology. One factor was political Radicalism–Conservatism which was well established in his data. The other was Tough–Tender-mindedness which was not supported by his argument or his data. What was troubling was his identification of Communists and Fascists as "Tough-minded" and Conservatives and Socialists as "Tender-minded."

This conclusion seemed unlikely in terms of the experiences most people have had and in writings on political preference. There have been cases of wild-eyed impractical persons in the membership of all known political parties as well as hard-boiled, somewhat cynical "operators." People with diverse political ideologies reportedly took seriously the writings of various power theorists, especially Machiavelli, as a guide to actions which can hardly be described as tender-minded (Lerner, 1940). Gauss (1952) notes that: "As such it [*The Prince*] has a history of study and use by a long line of kings and ministers as diverse in aims and character as Richelieu, Christina of Sweden, Frederick of Prussia, Bismarck and Clemenceau." Despite their diverse ideologies these individuals were concerned with one common interest—the use of power in interpersonal relations.

The nub of the problem with Eysenck's interpretation was not his claim that hard-boiled manipulative attitudes were orthogonal to political ideology, but that the items he had chosen were selected from previous scales that were constructed in the 30's and 40's and had ideological content. What was essential was a group of nonideological items that would refer to interpersonal attitudes.

Many of the power theorists examined (Shang and Kautilya have been mentioned to indicate the scope of the search) gave advice on how to govern a kingdom, but the assumptions underlying the sort of people who would follow their advice seemed more implicit than explicit. The exception appeared to be Machiavelli. It was a revelation to reread *The Prince* and *The Discourses*. As an undergraduate these had impressed me as thoroughly detestable. After some years of experience with departmental chairmen, deans, college presidents, governmental officials, and foundation executives, my reaction was different. Some of them had apparently taken Machiavelli to heart or had independently discovered similar techniques of manipulating others.

Machiavelli also had a convenient habit of giving advice in what was essentially a series of short essays, each oriented around a specific point. This made it fairly easy to convert his precepts into statements that would fit into opinion inventories. For example, "Most men mourn the loss of their patrimony more than the death of their fathers" was edited to read, "Most men

[3] It is disconcerting for a nonexpert in a particular field to try to come to any firm conclusion about matters in which authorities disagree. Scholars specializing in early Chinese and Indian history disagree about who the writings attributed to Kung-sun Yang or Lord Shang were written by and when and whether such persons actually existed. Even greater division of opinion seems to exist about Kautilya or Chānakya. There seems little reason to doubt, however, that both the *Book of Lord Shang* and the *Arthaśāstra* represent extant speculations in the writings of Chinese and Indian power theorists in roughly the fourth century B.C.

forget more easily the death of their father than the loss of their property," on the grounds that it didn't change the basic meaning and the revision would be more meaningful to current populations. In an attempt to get around the problem of response set some statements were reversed, e.g., "Most men are cowards" became "Most men are brave." Some items which seemed congruent with Machiavelli were added, such as, "Barnum was probably right when he said there's a sucker born every minute."

The items were typed on cards, and fellow Fellows were asked to respond to them and then asked how they interpreted each item. This procedure had two results. One was that we edited the items for clarity of meaning. The second was that the extent of agreement or disagreement with Machiavelli on the part of the individual respondent had a higher than chance correlation with peer evaluations, made in a relatively closed society of operating ability.

There are several reasons for spending this amount of time on the development of the concept. With few exceptions the published rationale behind a given paper-and-pencil test is not spelled out. A second reason is that the use of the word "Machiavellianism" to describe the content of the scales has been questioned. Every statement that could be pruned from the translations of Machiavelli's writings that appeared to have a relevance to the way in which one person views another or others, ways of controlling or influencing their behavior, and even more philosophical ways of viewing the history of mankind, were thrown into the hopper. It may be possible to derive in logical fashion a philosophically tighter and more parsimonious set of axioms which condense Machiavelli's writings. Our concern was primarily with ways of identifying those individuals who gravitate to power positions in the contemporary rather than the Renaissance world, so we interpreted Machiavelli's writings in view of thousands upon thousands of responses to questionnaires and interviews.

The next step was empirical. Seventy-one statements were dittoed and given in a Likert format (agree strongly, agree somewhat, no opinion, disagree somewhat, disagree strongly) to three aggregates of undergraduates. They were not selected upon any scientific theory of sampling. They were simply as diverse a group as could be obtained at the time since the early work on this study did not fall within the scope of any foundation program and was done out of curiosity. The items were given to 518 students in sociology courses at the State University of Iowa, 427 in political science at the University of North Carolina, and 251 in psychology at Hofstra College on Long Island.[4]

Part-whole phi coefficients were computed separately on each sample. Surprisingly, 50 of the 71 items discriminated at the .05 level between high and low scorers in all three samples. Elation was somewhat dampened when it was found that statements lifted or modified from those enunciated by Machiavelli hundreds of years ago came through the item analysis more strongly than those we had devised.

A subsequent set of findings was also cause for reflection. The mean reliability on a 20-item scale (Mach IV) on nine samples was .79. Mach IV consisted of the best ten items worded in the Mach direction and the ten best worded in the opposite direction. A similarly long and counterbalanced revision of the *F* scale (Christie, Havel, & Seidenberg, 1958) had a mean reliability of only .68 on the same nine samples. This is interesting for several reasons. The *F* scale had gone through a number of revisions, reworking of items, retestings, and various other refinements, and it has proved to be one of the most popularly used and psychologically meaningful scales in recent times. The *F* scale is based upon a Freudian interpretation of behavior, Mach IV upon

[4] Gratitude is again expressed to Professors David Gold, Robert Agger, and Harold Yuker respectively for their cooperation in giving the preliminary scale to their classes.

an interpretation of Machiavelli. One is tempted to conclude that the dimension in which Machiavelli was interested is more relevant to current undergraduates than that of Freud, or that there is a greater internal consistency in Machiavelli's theorizing than in Freud's.

At that time, we were in a position of "have scale, will test." A problem soon confronted us. Budner (1962) found that correlations between Edwards' (1957) Scale of Social Desirability and Mach IV ran from —.35 to —.45 among male undergraduate samples. More disturbing were correlations of around —.75 among female undergraduates. Edwards' scale indicates the extent to which respondents are unwilling to attribute unpleasant personal characteristics (usually of a pathological nature, such as anxiety) to themselves. This finding suggested that those who have an unflattering view of others, and believe in manipulating them, are willing to admit unattractive personal idiosyncrasies in themselves. Another implication is that among the college females tested it is highly socially undesirable to admit to Machiavellian tendencies since the negative correlation approaches the reliabilities of the scales. This suggests that almost none of these young ladies felt it appropriate to admit even on anonymous questionnaires to such techniques as "white lies" or "flattery."

One alternative to get around the problem of the transparancy of items was to use a forced-choice technique. The one that seemed most relevant and hardest to see through was one Heineman (1953) had adapted from Stewart (1945). This procedure consists of putting items in triads in which one item is checked as being closest to one's own opinion or belief and a second as farthest from it. Only one of the three items in each triad is keyed as relevant to the behavioral dimension of interest. All items are rated independently for social desirability of endorsement. Both of the nonkeyed items are known to be unrelated to the psychological variable of interest; in Heineman's case it was manifest anxiety and in ours Machiavellian orientation. One of the two nonkeyed items, the matched one, has an independent rating of social desirability equivalent to the keyed item. The second nonkeyed item has a social desirability rating which is either higher or lower than the keyed and matched items. If the keyed and matched items are low in social desirability the buffer is high; if the keyed and matched items are high in social desirability the buffer is low. This is a sneaky technique. Roughly two thirds of the respondents we have tested check the buffer as most like them if it is relatively high in social desirability or least like them if it is relatively low. For scoring purposes, however, the crucial comparison is between the equally socially desirable (or undesirable) keyed and matched items.

This technique appears to be successful in eliminating the effect of social desirability upon the endorsement of Machiavellian tendencies since results with the forced-choice form indicate no substantial correlations with either Edwards' or Crowne and Marlowe's scales (1960) of social desirability.

Another sex difference also turns up with fair reliability. In undergraduate samples, we had initially found males scoring significantly higher than females on the more transparent Mach IV. The same pattern seems to be true of Mach V. The only samples on which college males do not score higher than females on Mach V are those from Pennsylvania State University as reported by Singer (1964). This appears to be a reliable finding for that University, since Virginia Boehm in a subsequent study of summer school students there replicated it. There is another matter that is relevant aside from the sex differences in mean scores. With but one or two exceptions, no studies have found predicted relationships between agreement with Machiavelli and predicted or other behavior among female subjects, but these are almost invariably found among male samples. Aside from Lucretia Borgia, most of Machiavelli's observations were of males (his titles suggest this: *The Prince* rather than *The Princess; The Discourses* rather than *The Gossip*).

One way of attempting to find out what a scale is measuring is to compare scores with those from other tests. An initial question is whether or not a new scale has a substantial correlation with older and presumably standardized tests. The most investigated measure of all is intellectual ability.

1. Mach IV and V do not correlate significantly with verbal scores of medical college students on the Medical College Admission Test;
2. Mach IV and V do not correlate with I.Q. measures given to students in the School of General Studies at Columbia University;
3. Mach V does not correlate with the aptitude battery given at Pennsylvania State University;
4. Mach IV does not correlate with the Navy's test of ability among a group of Naval enlisted men assigned to fire-control training;
5. No correlation was found between Mach IV and intelligence test scores among students in a private prep school in New York State;
6. No correlations were found between Mach IV and V scores and the ability test given by the Peace Corps among trainees;

But:

7. A positive correlation of +.16 (barely significant at the .05 level) was found with Mach IV by Wrightsman and Cook (1964) in a clutch of female students gathered from various institutes of higher education in the Nashville, Tennessee, area.

Of equal importance is the fact that only the Mach scales were constant; in seven cases different measures of IQ or ability were used. In only one case, (7), above, were the respondents recruited from different institutional settings. This might be relevant to a subsequent discussion of results for elite and nonelite settings.

Another way of interpreting a concept as a personality variable is to look at its relation to other variables measured by standardized inventories. The California *F* scale has been mentioned before. The *F* stands for potential fascism, and the argument has previously been made that the Mach scale is not ideologically oriented. It was reassuring to find that in the nine samples referred to earlier, there was no significant correlation between *F* and Mach IV or V. The average correlation was about —.10.

Some psychologists are surprised that there is not a positive correlation between the *F* and Mach scales. One possible reason is that those who are disenchanted with others should make high scores on both scales. A hunch is that there is a qualitative difference in agreeing with statements representing the two viewpoints. High scorers on both scales should agree with a simple statement, "Most people are no damn good." Underlying the *F* scale, however, is a moralistic and judging predisposition: "Most people are no damn good *but they should be*"; whereas a high Mach might say, "People are no damn good, why not take advantage of them." Those high in authoritarianism tend to evaluate others in moralistic terms, those high in manipulativeness in opportunistic terms.

The path of research is not always logical. Ideal samples for testing theoretically based hypotheses often do not exist or if they do they may be unavailable. There are, perhaps, some benefits in having to deal with the world as it is. For better or worse, by chance rather than choice, my burgeoning interest in Machiavelli coincided with a study of medical school students. They were given Mach scales in addition to hundreds of other questions which included choice of a medical specialty.

The major intended specialties ranked from highest to lowest, on a Mach IV scores, and as follows:

1. Psychiatry
2. Pediatrics
3. Internal Medicine
4. Obstetrics and Gynecology
5. Surgery

Although the difference in Mach scores between specialties was statistically significant, it was not predicted, and essentially it described the orientation of students in three elite medical schools who intended to specialize. (If it is at all relevant, the minority of the samples who wanted to be general practitioners had low scores.) Kurt Back and his associates administered Mach IV to students in eight medical schools carefully selected for their diversity. Again it was found that potential psychiatrists were highest and those opting for surgery and OBGY were lowest.

This particular finding interested Back (1959) and his colleagues enough to follow it up and give Mach IV to faculty members in medical schools as well as practitioners. Psychiatrists, in this case actual rather than potential, scored highest with surgeons and obstetricians being lowest.

Regularities in data, even if unpredicted, deserve attention. One post hoc interpretation is that a relationship appears to exist between the hypothesized number of hours a physician spends with an individual patient and Mach scores. Most patients, for example, are referred to surgeons by other doctors, have a diagnostic hour or two, are worked up in the hospital by a resident, and are under anaesthesia during treatment, while post-operative interchange with the surgeon is often perfunctory. If a nonrandom sample of mothers is correct, they frequently feel that they are part of an assembly line in obstetricians' offices.

At the other extreme, psychiatrists typically spend at least an hour a week with a patient and this process has been known to endure for years. Pediatricians are also likely to have a continuing relationship with the families that choose them.

Another aspect is the degree of interpersonal manipulation involved. By definition a psychiatrist is attempting to influence the behavior of his patients, i.e., manipulate them. A surgeon is an "operator" in the technical but not the popular sense.

Such speculations led to the hunch that individuals who were involved in formal social roles would tend to become "cooler" and more impersonal in dealing with others than persons whose life was spent in less formalized roles. This would fit with the finding that male college students, anticipating such roles, consistently made higher Mach scores than females (with the deviant exception of students at Pennsylvania State University). Data to date suggest that persons who are oriented toward social roles that involve the "conning" or manipulation of others are more in agreement with Machiavelli than those more oriented toward manipulation of things or pure ideas. (In this respect, it is not too surprising to find that graduate students in social psychology are more in tune with Machiavelli than any other aggregate of subjects yet tested.)

Some early findings which supported the hunch that people agreeing with Machiavelli succeeded in the world better than low scorers were by-products of research in which Mach scale items were included in questionnaires. Weinstock (1964) found a significant positive correlation between these items and the extent to which Hungarian refugees after the abortive rebellion in 1956 acculturated to American life. In this instance, however, it was difficult to disentangle cause and effect. Did more Machiavelli-like Hungarians find it easier to adapt to the United States, or did successful acculturation raise their scores? A similar problem of interpretation exists with data collected by Milbrath (1958) on Washington lobbyists. Those lobbyists who served more than one client were, as predicted, higher in agreement with items from Mach IV than those who had only one client. The most satisfying data were those obtained by Singer (1964) on freshmen at Pennsylvania State University. He correlated Mach V scores with grade point average and statistically controlled for ability, as measured by the admission test battery. A significant positive correlation was found among male undergraduates between Mach V scores at the beginning of college and first-semester grade point average. It should be noted that this relationship held only for males. Despite their aberrance in making comparatively high Mach scores, the coeds displayed the typical feminine pattern. Their Mach V scores did not correlate significantly with other behavioral measures. Singer did find a significant relationship, however, between ratings of physical attractiveness and grade point average, with ability held constant, among the female undergraduates.

Although we had not uncovered any relationship between IQ and Mach scores, the relationship between Mach and interpersonal role orientation intrigued us. An examination of Back's, Silverstein's (1959), and some of our own data indicated a significant positive relationship between the judged eliteness of medical schools and Mach scores of students. It is impossible to say whether highly manipulative students choose elite schools or elite schools tend to recruit them. The relationship between eliteness of schools and Mach scores was further investigated among a group of Peace Corps trainees. In this case, an index (known locally as the "fat cat" index) was computed. It was composed of four ratios: student/faculty, number of books in the library/students, annual budget/students, and number of scholarships/students. The average intercorrelation between these measures was roughly +.60 so that we felt justified in combining them.[5]

These trainees came from highly diverse colleges. The things they had in common were a bachelor's degree and the fact that they were going to teach in secondary schools in Nigeria and had been carefully screened. They could in no way be considered representative of the colleges they had attended. Our suspicion is that an Ivy League graduate who volunteers for the Peace Corps is probably lower on Mach than his classmates, whereas a volunteer from a state agricultural college is higher than his peers. Despite this possible built-in bias against the relationship between Mach scores and the fat-catness of the schools they had attended, a significant correlation of +.33 was found.

In candor, a failure to corroborate this finding was found in a different context. Graduating seniors from a private prep school had taken Mach IV. There was no relationship between their scores and Astin's (1962) Affluence ranking of the college at which they were accepted.

In a broader sense, some of the implications of bits and drabs of data collected haphazardly were provocative. The majority of attitude and personality inventories are correlated with measures of intelligence. The Mach scales were not (with the only marginally significant correlation among Tennessee female undergraduates). These results were all based upon captive audiences in such institutional settings as colleges or the Navy where a degree of homogeneity as far as age and institutional selective procedures were operative. What was more puzzling was the finding based upon samples collected for class training purposes: there seemed to be no relationship between years of education and Mach scores. This was especially interesting because the usual high negative correlations between education and *F*-scale scores were found and between education and anomia scores (this was based on a modification of a scale devised by Srole, 1960, which essentially gets at an attitude of normlessness or more starkly, despair).

As predicted, there was no correlation between the *F* and Anomia scales when response bias was controlled. Roberts and

[5] A more systematic study of college characteristics may be found in Astin (1962), who factor analyzed college characteristics and whose major factor, "Affluence," is closely related to our "fat cat" index.

Rokeach (1956) and Srole (1956) had found correlations of +.43 and +.41 on items worded in the positive direction (agreement being scored as high). The troublesome part was that Anomia and Mach did correlate positively despite a relatively successful attempt to correct for such technical artifacts as response set and the social desirability of items. It seemed incongruous that despair and interpersonal manipulation went hand in hand. Both, of course, involve a disenchanted view of the state of man, but Anomia implies passive acceptance of a deplorable state of affairs, while Machiavellianism implies making out the best way possible in an admittedly imperfect world.

Other bits of data led to speculations about the social conditions that might foster manipulative orientations. Back's data indicated that physicians on medical school staffs and in practice were less likely to endorse Machiavellian statements than students intending to go into medical specialties. Milbrath's sample of Washington lobbyists scored lower than samples of college students, and a wildly unrepresentive clutch of top-level but over 60-year-old business executives scored lower still.

There appeared to be at least one common denominator differentiating these groups and college students—age. In pondering the fact that older respondents tended to be lower on Mach scales than younger ones of comparable socio-economic status, several notions occurred:

1. Lazarsfeld, Berelson, and Gaudet (1944) have pointed to the fact that there are generational differences in voting. Those who first cast ballots for a presidential candidate in the 20's were more likely to persist in choice of Republican candidates; those first voting in the 30's were more likely to have first voted for and persist in voting for Democratic candidates. More recently, Newcomb (1963) found remarkable attitudinal consistency in a 25-year followup of former students at Bennington College. Although political ideology is involved in both instances, one inference is that values internalized at or about the time of attaining majority persist more frequently than not.
2. The weight of evidence indicates that individuals who spend more of their time interacting with others in a formal set of roles are more likely to be Machiavellian than those who do not. American society has been characterized by an increasing percentage of the population engaged in precisely these professional and service functions with a concomitant decrease in the proportion of people in farming and on the assembly line. If the postulated relationship is true, it can be hypothesized that a random sample of American adults in 1924 would have been less Machiavellian in orientation than in 1964, because of a less complex web of role sets.

If these two assumptions are made—that the prevalence of manipulative orientations is greater now than was true a generation or more ago, and that people's values tend to stabilize around those they acquire when 20 or so years of age—a prediction can be (and was) made. A representative sample of adults in the United States should be expected to show a negative correlation between age and Mach scores. To be more specific, the greatest change in the societal net of role relationships in the United States probably occurred at the time of the outbreak of World War II. If the preceding assumptions are true, it might be expected that not only is there a negative relationship with age but that the sharpest break should be between contemporary (as of 1963) adults 40 years of age or under who became adults in the early 40's, and those over 40.

These speculations were put to the test. Ten Mach IV items, ten from Mach V, and ten Anomia items were included in interviews of a representative nation-wide sample of 1482 American adults in 1963, in a study conducted by the National Opinion Research Center. Each respondent was presented a card with the question printed on it to peruse while the interviewer read the question aloud. The interviewer recorded the response.

The responses to these questions were factor analyzed using a varimax solution. Although there may be factor analysts who agree with one another, in general they appear to be a contentious lot. For our purposes, we made the assumption that whatever factor analytic technique was used (we tried several), basically it described the relationships among a number of responses to discrete items. A possible solution to the puzzling relationship between Anomia and Mach IV was suggested by the main factor in this sample. The items loading on this factor are presented in Table I. Naming factors is something of an art. We offer no apologies for calling this "anomic disenchantment"; anyone who consistently agrees with such items, and there were hundreds of people who did, has a dim view of their fellowmen and the society in which they live. It was not too surprising to find that those of lower socio-economic status, older persons, and those disadvantaged for other reasons scored higher on this factor scale.

Respondents who tended to agree with affirmatively worded Anomia items taken from Srole and items reflecting cynicism from the Mach scale apparently account for the positive correlations found between the Anomia and Mach scales.

The second factor is more relevant to the generational difference hypothesis. Items from the forced-choice Mach V scale designed to control for social desirability which hung together in this sample (Table II) appear to refer more to what might be termed interpersonal tactics—honesty is *not* the best policy in dealing with others, it *is* wise to flatter more important people, etc. The age categories in this representative nation-wide sample were coded by decades, i.e., 21–30, 31–40, 41–50, 51–60, and 60 and over. Those respondents who attained majority in or after 1941–42 fell in the first two aggregates. A one-way analysis of variance indicates a statistically significant negative relationship between age and scores on this factor. The

TABLE I

ANOMIC DISENCHANTMENT

Loading	Item No.	
—.62	14	It's hardly fair to bring a child into the world with the way things look for the future.
—.58	11	It is safest to assume that all people have a vicious streak and it will come out when they are given a chance.
—.58	8	Nowadays a person has to live pretty much for today and let tomorrow take care of itself.
—.55	15	The best way to handle people is to tell them what they want to hear.
—.54	16	Anyone who completely trusts anyone else is asking for trouble.
—.54	2	Next to health, money is the most important thing in life.
—.53	12	Generally speaking, men won't work hard unless they're forced to do so.
—.51	5	You sometimes can't help wondering whether anything is worthwhile anymore.
—.47	9	Most men forget more easily the death of their father than the loss of their property.
—.41	1	Most people in government are not really interested in the problems of the average man.
—.39	20	It is hard to get ahead without cutting corners here and there.

TABLE II

MACHIAVELLIAN TACTICS

Loading	Item No.		
.63	28	A.	It is best to give others the impression that you can change your mind easily.
		B.	It is a good working policy to keep on good terms with everyone.
		[a]C.	Honesty is the best policy in all cases.
.58	30	[a]A.	Barnum was probably right when he said that there's at least one sucker born every minute.
		B.	Life is pretty dull unless one deliberately stirs up some excitement.
		C.	Most people would be better off if they controlled their emotions.
.53	22	[a]A.	Never tell anyone the real reason you did something unless it is useful to do so.
		B.	The well-being of the individual is the goal that should be worked for before anything else.
		C.	Once a truly intelligent person makes up his mind about the answer to a problem he rarely continues to think about it.
.48	24	A.	The world would be a much better place to live in if people would let the future take care of itself and concern themselves only with enjoying the present.
		[a]B.	It is wise to flatter important people.
		C.	Once a decision has been made, it is best to keep changing it as new circumstances arise.
.39	26	[a]A.	All in all, it is better to be humble and honest than to be important and dishonest.
		B.	A man who is able and willing to work hard has a good chance of succeeding in whatever he wants to do.
		C.	If a thing does not help us in our daily lives, it isn't very important.

[a] Indicates items keyed to Machiavelli

single most significant difference between age groups is between those 40 or younger early in 1963 and those 41 or older.

Although it is gratifying to find confirmation in survey data of a hunch based upon assumptions that seemed reasonable but not firmly established, it should be reported that some expectations based upon more tenuous and even less firmly established assumptions were not supported. For example, we did not find any significant relation (in the statistical sense) between Mach score and education or socio-economic status, as measured by the Hollingshead SES index. This corroborated results from pilot studies which suggested no such relationship. What was shattering to the investigator's ego was the fact that a discrepancy score computed on the father's reported SES and that of the respondent did not indicate that respondents who were upwardly mobile in society were more in agreement with Machiavelli. Even a perverse hunch (that married female respondents whose husbands were higher on the social ladder than the respondent's father would score higher than ladies who did not marry "up") didn't work.

One of the advantages of data such as

these is that they jibe with previous findings and hunches based upon them just enough to convince one that something valid is being measured. At the same time, they are not in accord with other, less firmly grounded stereotypes about the prevalence of Machiavellian orientations in American society. It is easy to discount the finding that Machiavellian women (as measured by these scales) do not marry "up." After all, Mach scales do not seem to tap consistently anything meaningful which discriminates individual differences in behavior among women. But other problems are not so easily, or glibly, evaded. Why aren't upwardly-mobile males in this sample higher on the scale than SES-stable or downward-mobiles? Can an honest man get ahead as well in the American social system as a manipulator? Or are agreers with Machiavelli sons of those in the establishment so that they have nowhere to go socio-economically but to stay the same or go down in SES?

Partial light on this is cast by data collected in what we informally refer to as an "incubator for manipulation." We usually turn down requests to study samples unless they bear upon a problem which seems relevant. In this case we were invited to give the Mach scale to the entire student body of a prep school outside New York City. This was of interest for two reasons: (a) we had not given it to students below the freshman year of college, and (b) this school had some interesting characteristics. Its promotional literature stressed the number of graduates in the past few years who had been accepted in elite colleges. At the same time it gave the average college board scores of its graduates of these years. Despite the fact that they were intensively prepped, in both the literal and figurative sense, their mean college board scores hovered around the national average on verbal ability of the high school graduates of the standardization samples. In short, here was a sample of no brighter than average ability who were being coached to get into elite schools. Since their parents were willing to pay 1670 dollars a year for day students or 2670 dollars for boarding students, it might be inferred that the parents placed a great emphasis upon their sons' getting ahead. These fees do not reflect such other expenses as clothing, weekend expenses, or such extra-curricular activities as taking flying lessons at the school's private airport.

Since there were few full scholarships available, it is difficult to imagine that the parents would have a low socio-economic status as measured by any nationally based index. In short, if the students were not manipulation-oriented, one if not both of their parents must have been.

A preliminary analysis of these results indicates two things (Christie & Nachamie, 1964). There is a highly significant increase in score on Mach IV from the fifth and sixth graders continuing up to the upperclassmen. Second, the upperclassmen in this prep school make higher scores than students in some of the most competitive medical schools in the United States.

To return for a moment to the problem of why there was not the expected relationship between upward social mobility and Mach scores: it was suggested earlier that the relationship between manipulative orientation and professional preferences depended not so much on education level or the SES of an individual as on the interpersonal role context of such behavior. The occupational classifications used in the survey were designed to describe the social level rather than their role relations vis à vis others. Successful morticians and professors of classics might end up in the same SES category despite a different relationship with dead subjects, just as psychiatrists and surgeons whose patterns of interaction with others might be different.

In the terminology of sociologists, we had measures of statuses rather than of roles or role sets.

This finding prepared us to accept another that we had not anticipated. An analysis of size of place of residence by Mach scores did not yield a consistent relationship. This might seem to run counter to the general hypothesis that the greater the degree of urbanization, the greater the number of role-sets and the greater the Mach scores. Demographic data collected on respondents in the NORC sample were checked against 1960 census data and were found to fit amazingly closely. In 1960, however, the old differentiation between the city slicker and the rube did not fit neatly into census data on size of community. Many presumably successful manipulators did not live in populous metropolitan areas but had moved to less crowded suburbs, and many refugees from the countryside, especially unsuccessful members of minority groups, had moved to urban centers. This reciprocal migration probably diluted rural-urban differences that would have been found a generation or more ago, when city dwelling was associated with interpersonal "sharpness" and rural populations were "hicks" in the time before radio and television became accessible and commonplace among members of all social classes. In short, the blanketing effects of mass communications and the migration of social elites away from residence in census-defined cities and the countermovement of nonelites into core urban areas makes the simple equation of the more urban and complex society with interpersonal manipulation less likely than in times past.

In a less frenetic society the expected relationship holds. De Miguel's (1964) data on Spanish students in *collegios* and *institutos* indicate significant differences among *preuniversitario* students (16–18 years of age) in 15 schools located in different provinces in Spain. A plausible assumption is that students in this age group in Spain are living at home or near it. Unlike the presumably ambient sample of United States adults captured at one moment in time, the Spanish students were caught in their native habitat. One index of modernization in Spain is the degree of literacy in the various provinces. We computed a rank order correlation between this index for provinces and Mach scores on de Miguel's Spanish translation. It was .89. Students in Barcelona scored highest, those in Sevilla lowest.

It is difficult to compare absolute scores on the Mach scale in a Spanish translation with those in its American form. But leaving aside problems of translation, the samples of Spanish students collected by de Miguel do make lower Mach scores than most comparable American samples. This fits with American data since Spanish students are predominantly Catholic and we have found in a variety of samples that Catholic respondents in the United States score lower than those identifying themselves as Protestants or Jewish.

CONCLUSION

Unfortunately (or perhaps fortunately), time does not permit a thorough, organized summary of all the work done by various people who, like me, have had their curiosity aroused in trying to puzzle out why some people attempt to manipulate others. Most of the research that has been done stemmed from hunches or inductions based upon informal observations of successful manipulators, a translation of translations of power theorists from varied cultural settings, or attempts to reinterpret reports of studies that seemed relevant. In short, as mentioned at the beginning, this has been a hobby, and who can logically defend his hobby?

Actually the data described have dealt with only the beginnings of the idea, and a few of many attempts to investigate it. A second major approach has led to a series of laboratory studies. These will be described in a separate report.

Data collected to date indicate the following tentative conclusions:

1. There is a long historical tradition of interest in the individual characteristics of those who manipulate others and in those who permit themselves to be manipulated.
2. Translations of items relating to interpersonal manipulation appear to be relevant enough to differentiate reliably among respondents who are given an

opportunity to agree or disagree with them.

3. Endorsement of such items does not appear to be systematically correlated with known measures of psychopathology, political ideology, or social class.
4. Data to date suggest that the greater the involvement of an individual in a complex of formalized role relationships with others, the greater the endorsement of manipulative tactics.
5. Respondents in agreement with Machiavellian or manipulative statements seem to have greater success in meeting the demands of American society—including getting ahead in college.
6. College students who were selected as subjects for laboratory studies succeeded in out-manipulating their partners roughly in proportion to their agreement with Machiavellian precepts.[6]

Hobbies can be dangerous. Sometimes they tend to get out of hand. Sometimes they serve to arouse the curiosity of others to the extent that their feedback raises questions that were unanticipated but are relevant.

REFERENCES

Adorno, T. W., Frenkel-Brunswik, Else, Levinson, D., & Sanford, N. *The authoritarian personality*. New York: Harper & Brothers, 1950.

Astin, A. W. *Document No. 7262, ADI Auxiliary Publications Project,* Photoduplication Service. Washington: Library of Congress, 1962.

Back, Kurt. Personal communication, 1959.

Brown, D. MacKenzie. *The white umbrella.* Berkeley: Univer. of California Press, 1953.

Budner, S. Intolerance of ambiguity as a personality variable. *J. Pers.,* 1962, 30, 29–50.

Christie, R. Review of *The Psychology of Politics. Amer. J. Psychol.,* 1955, 68, 702–704.

Christie, R. Eysenck's treatment of the personality of communists. *Psychol. Bull.,* 1956, 55, 411–430. (a)

Christie, R. Some abuses of psychology. *Psychol. Bull.,* 1956, 53, 439–451. (b)

Christie, R., & Geis, Florence. *Studies in Machiavellianism.* New York: Academic Press (in press).

Christie, R., Havel, Joan, & Seidenberg, B. Is the *F* scale irreversible? *J. abnorm. soc. Psychol.,* 1958, 56, 143–159.

Christie, R., & Nachamie, S. Unpublished manuscript, 1964.

Crowne, D. P., & Marlowe, D. A new scale of social desirability independent of psychopathology. *J. consult. Psychol.,* 1960, 24, 349–354.

de Miguel, A. *Social correlates of Machiavellianism: The Spanish students.* Mimeographed draft, 1964.

Duyvendak, J. J. L. (Transl.) Kung-san Yang, *The Book of Lord Shang.* Chicago: Univer. of Chicago Press, 1928.

Edwards, A. L. *The social desirability variable in personality assessment and research.* New York: Dryden Press, 1957.

Eysenck, H. J. *The psychology of politics.* London: Routledge and Kegan Paul, 1954.

Gauss, C. Introduction to *The Prince.* New York: Oxford Press, 1952.

Heineman, C. E. A forced-choice form of the Taylor anxiety scale. *J. consult. Psychol.,* 1953, 17, 447–454.

Hoffer, E. *The true believer.* New York: Harper & Brothers, 1951.

Lazarsfeld, P. F., Berelson, B., & Gaudet, Hazel. *The people's choice.* New York: Duell, Sloan, and Pearce, 1944.

Lerner, M. Introduction to *The Prince* and *The Discourses.* New York: Modern Library, 1940.

Milbrath, L. W. Personal communication, 1958.

Newcomb, T. M. Persistence and regression of changed attitudes: Long-range studies. *J. soc. Issues,* 1963, 19, 3–14.

Roberts, A., & Rokeach, M. Anomie, authoritarianism, and prejudice: A replication. *Amer. J. Sociol.,* 1956, 61, 355–358.

Shamasastry, R. Kautilya's *Arthaśāstra.* (2nd ed.) Mysore: Wesleyan Mission Press, 1923.

Shils, E. A. Authoritarianism: "Right" and "left." In R. Christie & Marie Jahoda (Eds.), *Studies in the scope and method of "The Authoritarian Personality."* Glencoe, Ill.: Free Press, 1954.

[6] These laboratory studies are reported in detail in Christie and Geis (in press).

Singer, J. E. The use of manipulative strategies: Machiavellianism and attractiveness. *Sociometry,* 1964, 27, 128–150.

Silverstein, A. B. Personal communication, 1959.

Srole, L. Social integration and certain corollaries: An exploratory study. *Amer. Sociol. Rev.,* 1956, 21, 709–716.

Stewart, Naomi. Methodological investigation of the forced-choice technique, utilizing the officer description and the officer evaluation blanks. *AGO, Personnel Research Section, Report No. 701,* July, 1945.

Wrightsman, L. S., Jr., & Cook, S. W. Personal communication, 1964.

Wrightsman, L. S., Jr., Radloff, R. W., Horton, D. L., & Mecherikoff, M. Authoritarian attitudes and presidential voting preferences. *Psychol. Repts,* 1961, 8, 43–46.

CHAPTER 19 Conceptions of Normality[1]

WILLIAM A. SCOTT
University of Colorado

In medicine, the term "normal" usually denotes capacity for adaptation to ordinary environmental conditions (e.g., a climate in a moderate zone, an altitude of 0–10,000 feet, etc.) (Redlich, 1952, p. 553).

The term normal or healthy can be defined in two ways. Firstly, from the standpoint of furthering society, one can call a person normal or healthy if he is able to fulfill the social role he is to take in that society—if he is able to participate in the reproduction of society. Secondly, from the standpoint of the individual, we look upon health or normalcy as the optimum of growth and happiness of the individual (Fromm, 1941, p. 138).

Mental health consists of the ability to live (1) within the limits of bodily equipment; (2) with other human beings; (3) happily; (4) productively; (5) without being a nuisance (Preston, 1943, p. 112).

Let us define mental health as the adjustment of human beings to the world and to each other with a maximum of effectiveness and happiness.... It is the ability to maintain an even temper, an alert intelligence, socially considerate behavior, and a happy disposition (Menninger, 1937, p. 1).

[A mature person] participates and reflects, lives and laughs, according to some embracing philosophy of life developed to his own satisfaction and representing to himself his place in the scheme of things (Allport, 1937, p. 214).

It is the acceptance of one's own and only life cycle and of the people who have become significant to it as something that had to be and that, by necessity, permitted of no substitutions.... It is a sense of comradeship with men and women of distant times and of different pursuits, who have created orders and objects and sayings conveying human dignity and love (Erikson, 1955, p. 223).

In very simple terms, a mature and mentally healthy person is one who (1) respects and has confidence in himself and because he knows his true worth wastes no time proving it to himself and others; (2) accepts, works with, and to a large extent enjoys other people; (3) carries on his work, play, and his family and social life with confidence and enthusiasm and with a minimum of conflict, fear, and hostility (Rennie & Woodward, 1948, p. 334).

The continuum of psychological health and psychopathology can be conceptualized in terms of the degree of efficiency in meeting environmental requirements (Wishner, 1955, p. 70).

[A creatively mature person should possess] self-respect and good sense; personal courage, independence, and a sense of humor; good taste; a certain innocence of vision and spon-

[1] I am indebted, particularly, to Bruce P. Dohrenwend, O. Hobart Mowrer, Victor Raimy, and M. Brewster Smith for their many helpful comments on an earlier draft of this paper.

taneity of action; honesty of thought and behavior; social responsibility; and democracy in interpersonal relations. ... A Greek philosopher, considering such a compendium of qualities, would not hesitate to name it *virtue* (Barron, 1963, p. 38).

The normal mind is not one that is perfectly integrated and free from defects, arrests of development, or even from attitudes and habits similar to those characteristic of pathological conditions, but rather it is a mind that can compensate for its defects and weaknesses, that can correct its own errors and is able to curtail its pathological tendencies, or, in a single word, a mind that under ordinary circumstances can function normally (Burnham, 1924, p. 54).

The confusion in the area of criminal law arises because it is not recognized that the labelling of some acts as due to "illness" and some as due to "badness" is nothing but a purely social or conventional process (Hoffman, 1960, p. 209).

In a sense, the attempts to give meaning to the idea of mental health are efforts to grapple with the nature of man as he ought to or could be (Jahoda, 1958, p. 4).

To define in terms of adjustment what mental health really is, one would have to know what the essence of Man is, and the metaphysicians have not told us the secret (Redlich, 1952, p. 555).

In essence, we are proposing that there are, contentwise, many "normal" or "healthy" personalities. That which is common to each is the ability to function in relation to the norms of his particular societal setting (Zax & Klein, 1960, p. 446).

NORMALITY, MENTAL HEALTH, ADJUSTMENT, ETC.

When confronted with an unfamiliar object, one wishes at once to know: Is it benign or threatening? Pleasant or unpleasant? Good or bad? After several millenia of informal observation and nearly a century of empirical study, man still confronts himself as a stranger. Evaluation remains as one of the most salient considerations in attempting to understand man, individually or collectively. Is he good or bad, evil or benign, healthy or unhealthy? The search for more descriptive characterizations is likely to depend in any given instance on at least a tentative answer to the evaluative questions and, indeed, even to be impelled by a desire to understand more fully that which has already been recognized as desirable or undesirable.

Though it has another standard meaning, the term "normality"—in ethical, medical, and psychological usage—is most commonly understood in its evaluative sense, as indicating an appropriate, adaptive, or somehow desirable state, "... a standard worthy of emulation and possible of attainment for most persons" (English & English, 1958, p. 349). Psychologists frequently use the terms "mental health" and "adjustment" as approximate synonyms. Numerous contemporary writers (e.g., Freides, 1960; French & Kahn, 1962; Smith, 1961) have rejected such conceptions as theoretically or empirically deficient. Yet they persist in the psychologist's language as well as the layman's, serving at least the function of pointing to socially defined and professionally accepted problems that require more precise formulation.

"Mental health" ("normality" in its evaluative sense) is a human conception, a linguistic convention that is unlikely to fall into disuse for lack of a clear referent. The question, "What constitutes normality?" is best understood not as a question of fact, but rather as a question of conventional definition. The question, "How can mental health be attained?" can be answered only after a conventional definition of the state is determined. Our first object, therefore, shall be to study the various meanings of the concept as it appears in contemporary psychological writings. Clarification of a scientifically useful language takes place best in conjunction with relevant empirical study; so our second objective shall be to review some measures of "normality" that are frequently used in psychological research, with particular attention to their adequacy as measures and to the ways in which they relate to one another. Psychometric considerations alone are not sufficient to appraise a construct; but the construct can be pragmatically useful only to the extent that measures of it are valid and precise. So deficiencies in current measures should point the way either toward the development of new instruments or toward revision of the concepts that underlie them.

CRITERIA OF NORMALITY

It will be easier to appreciate the scope of concern and to highlight points at issue if analytical consideration is prefaced by a straightforward enumeration of various standards of personal well-being which have been proposed in the literature. The present classification is employed for the sake of convenience only; numerous others have been proposed (e.g., Jahoda, 1958; Scott, 1958).

General Adaptive Capacity

- Adaptability
- Flexibility
- Mastery of the environment
- Capacity to meet and deal with a changing world
- Capacity to formulate ends and implement them
- Successful behavior
- Modifiability of behavior, according to its favorable or unfavorable consequences

Capacity for Self-Gratification

- Genital sexuality (ability to achieve orgasm)
- Gratification of one's needs
- Enjoyment of life activities
- Ability to direct one's behavior to his own benefit
- Spontaneity of action
- Feeling of relaxed participation in the present moment

Competence in Interpersonal Roles

- Fulfilling one's social role
- Role-appropriate behavior
- Participation in social activities
- Using relevant help
- Adjustment in social relations
- Behavior eliciting social approval
- Interpersonal competence
- Commitment to others
- Social responsibility
- Steady employment
- Ability to work and love

Intellectual Capacity

- Accuracy of perception
- Efficient mental functioning
- Cognitive adequacy
- Good sense
- Rationality
- Contact with reality
- Knowledge of self
- Problem-solving capacity
- Intelligence
- Broad awareness and deep comprehension of human experience

Emotional and Motivational Control

- Frustration tolerance
- Ability to handle anxiety
- Morality
- Courage
- Self-control
- Resistance to stress
- Morale
- Conscience
- Ego strength
- Honesty
- Virtue

Wholesome Attitudes toward People

- Altruism
- Concern for others
- Trust
- Liking for people
- Warmth toward people
- Capacity for intimacy
- Empathy

Productivity

- Contribution to society
- Initiative

Autonomy

- Emotional independence
- Identity
- Self-reliance
- Detachment

Mature Integration

- Self-actualization
- Personal growth
- Unifying philosophy of life
- Balance between opposing forces
- Mutually compatible motives
- Self-utilization
- Ability to handle impulses, energies, and conflicts in an integrative way
- Maintaining consistency
- Complex level of integration
- Maturity

Favorable Attitudes toward Self

Sense of mastery	Favorable self-image
Satisfaction with one's accomplishments	Feeling of freedom and self-determination
Acceptance of self	Freedom from inferiority feelings
Self-respect	Happiness
Optimism	
Confidence in ability to meet and solve problems	

Such a list might be extended indefinitely and classified in numerous reasonable ways. Casual perusal of it generates several impressions: (a) The terms embody numerous cultural values, propounded in ethical systems independent of psychology, (b) they derive from a variety of perspectives on what constitutes the "good life," (c) anyone might object to inclusion of some of the qualities as criteria for mental health, and (d) anyone might propose additional criteria from his own favorite perspective. Rather than attempt to formulate some new and better list, we shall instead deal with the present composite in an analytic way—noting some major differences in perspective that are implicit in the various proposed meanings.

COMMONNESS VS. DESIRABILITY

One contemporary writer (Wishner, 1955) has proposed a seemingly reasonable terminological distinction: "abnormality" refers to deviation from a norm (average), without specifying its appropriateness, while "health" refers to appropriateness, without specifying the frequency of occurrence. Indeed, this proposed meaning of "normal" accords with the one given as the first dictionary usage (English & English, 1958). But the actuarial concept of normality is rarely used in the current psychological literature. Berg's (1961) "deviation hypothesis" proposes that various kinds of atypical responses tend to be found in the same individual; such atypicality may be culturally valued (as the medical profession), or culturally disvalued (as schizophrenia), or of no intrinsic evaluative significance (as the selection of unpopular alternatives in a paper-and-pencil test). But if diverse manifestations of atypicality tend to co-vary across individuals, then atypicality of any sort may provide an interesting focus of study. Berg seems to be almost alone among contemporary writers in his concern for nonevaluated actuarial atypicality. Other writers either ignore the phenomenon or explicitly reject its significance. Smith (1961) asserts, "We have come to see that statistical notions of normality are no real help in giving psychological meaning to mental health and mental illness: they beg the question or fail to come to grips with it." The alleged question-begging presumably lies in the failure to specify *what* norm the behavior deviates from (a physician is deviant from the "average" citizen but not from other physicians) and in the lack of standards for determining *what* sorts of deviations are relevant for adaptation.

Though the weight of numbers is clearly on the side of an evaluative, rather than an actuarial, definition of normality, one may readily note the limitations of both positions. A great many behaviors and states may be common—for example, unhappiness, ultimate senescence, and death—but few would treat these as instances of well-being. On the other hand, a great many states are undesirable—for example, inability to tolerate extremes of temperature, radiation, and lack of oxygen—but hardly regarded as evaluatively significant, because of their very commonness.

When typicality and desirability coincide, there is no problem as to which should constitute the standard of normality; but when the desirable is not typical, or the typical is not desirable, it is necessary to separate clearly the two considerations, and perhaps not even attempt to determine a unitary criterion. The average, per se, is rarely valued—even in regard to such traits as height and weight—unless it is seen as serving some other consequence deemed desirable—such as physical well-being, social acceptance, or ability to perform necessary social roles. If a trait is positively valued, then one usually prefers a maximal, rather than a moderate amount of it, other things being equal. Intellectual genius seems inherently desirable, unless it is accompanied by undesirable side-effects, such as social maladjustment; but it is the concomitant social disability, rather than the high intellectual ability per se, which is disvalued.

The effect of typicality seems to be to modulate social judgments of desirability, to limit the magnitude of praise for attainment and blame for nonattainment of the desirable. That which is desirable but rare (e.g., genius, exemplary courage, joy) is better than that which is desirable but common (capacity for orgasm, ability to hold a job). That which is undesirable but rare (e.g., pederasty, Mongolism) is worse than that which is undesirable but common (unkindness, lack of self-insight). It is as if the degree of praise or blame attached to a particular score on an evaluated trait depended on the standard normal deviation of that score in a frequency distribution.

Separation of typicality from desirability is almost impossible to achieve in either diagnostic or therapeutic judgments. Social psychological considerations tend to justify the fusion: an undesirable trait that is rare is likely to elicit more social disapproval than one that is common; it thus generates greater anxiety over the possibility of social rejection, which in turn may further incapacitate the individual.

HEALTH AND OTHER VALUES

Although the terms "normality" and "mental health" both denote an evaluative appraisal of human behavior, they suggest somewhat different frames of reference for the appraisal. "Mental health" explicitly draws a parallel to physical health, implying freedom from disease; "normality" includes this meaning, but also implies a variety of other evaluative criteria referring to standards of conduct and adjustment that have little to do with sickness and health in the organic sense. Around this difference in connotations revolves a controversy over how the processes of diagnosis and therapy for "mental disorders" are to be conceived (e.g., Mowrer, 1960, 1963; Szasz, 1960, 1961). Its ramifications extend to the present topic.

The disease-health model implies standards of adaptation which are universally shared; the vast proportion of variance in appraisals is attributed to differences among the people being described; some (relatively small) proportion is attributed to the circumstances of action—as, for example, when different degrees and kinds of physical fitness are required for different occupations. The value model may allow for substantial variation in standards and in circumstances of action, as well as in characteristics of the actor. Though the evaluators themselves may treat their own standards of appraisal as universal absolutes (Scott, 1965), the omniscient scientist recognizes their parochial character and is prepared to treat social norms as a variable entering into the determination of what constitutes adequate adaptation; even the evaluators may explicitly apply quite different standards depending on the role of the person who is judged.

It is well recognized that health itself is a value—implying, for instance, the desirability of human survival, rather than the survival of microbes and parasites (Redlich, 1952). But assent to this value is deemed practically universal, and there is reasonable consensus among the individual patient, the medical profession, and the wider society that pain and physical discomfort are undesirable, that regularity of survival functions (food intake, sleep, excretion) is desirable.

More than in the definition of "psychological health," actuarial considerations are likely to determine definitions of physical health. Though tender feet may be maladapted for walking barefoot, upright, on uneven ground; though inability to fly unaided or breathe under water may be inconvenient; these defects are not regarded as physical ailments, because they are universal in the species. Moreover, they are correctible by relatively convenient practices. Of course, one may probe the rationale further: Does poor vision, when corrected by glasses, constitute a physical ailment? Is the inability of a 70-year-old to run up stairs without shortness of breath to be designated as a physical disability? In the last analysis, these as well as other, less problematic, questions are matters of consensual definition. As Hoffman (1960) states the matter: "Organic medicine really faces the same problem as psychiatry, i.e., its definition of 'health' is essentially *not* arrived at by scientific inquiry, but rather by social agreement" (p. 208). Essential to the health-illness model is the requirement that close consensual agreement *can* be reached.

Most writers (e.g., Hoffman, 1960; Smith, 1961) would maintain that the "severe" forms of "mental illness" can be designated with sufficient consensus to justify application of the disease model. When behavior aberration threatens the person's own physical survival or the survival of others, this is often sufficient reason to designate the abnormality as a "disease"—providing, of course, that the behavior pattern is not a sanctioned, socially patterned action, such as warfare or prolonged fasting employed as a political technique. A vocal minority of writers, however, question the appropriateness of the health-illness model even when applied to the conventionally designated extreme of maladjustment. Mowrer (1960), for example, seems prepared to attribute all "mental illness" to guilt over violation of ethical standards (which he calls "sin"). And Szasz (1960) maintains that "the notion of mental illness has outlived whatever usefulness it might have had and ... now functions merely as a convenient myth ... whose function it is to disguise and thus render more palatable the bitter pill of moral conflicts in human relations" (p. 118).

The fact of consensus on the undesirability of the state and the fact that suffering is caused by some characteristic of the organism (e.g., his "sinfulness") constitute insufficient grounds, in the view of these authors, for the designation "illness." This is presumably because the abnormality consists of disordered conduct, rather than malfunctioning of a specific organ-system. The conventional application of the concept "illness" to such disorders serves to convey an attitude toward them—e.g., that the patient is blameless, should not be punished, is motivated to recover, etc.—but is hardly a better description than earlier conceptions that attributed the aberration to "sin" or malingering. Certainly one must agree with the implication of these authors that diagnostic terminology should do more than convey the attitudes of the user toward the phenomenon; it should bear some relation to etiology and treatment. But it would seem that, when professional and popular opinion are agreed on the undesirability of the state, then the designation "disease" (in the sense of malfunctioning) can be quite appropriate—particularly when one accepts the label as applicable to total organisms as well as to specific organs or tissues.

When reference is made to positive adaptation, rather than to malfunctioning, there is fairly wide agreement that optional, rather than absolute, values may be involved—values which are diverse and which may not command universal assent. It is perhaps this multiplicity of preferential (optional) criteria which has led some authors (e.g., Jahoda, 1958) to conceive of "mental health" as something quite different from the mere absence of "mental illness" in the usual sense. The definition of mental health involves a conception of "the good life" and thus poses a need to clarify the evaluative criteria appealed to (Smith, 1961). Current conceptions of "positive mental health" function predominately as substitutes for religious and ethical standards that provided norms of conduct in a prescientific era. On the one hand, this view may imply that one set of concepts has simply been substituted for another, discredited, set (this is essentially Mowrer's and Szasz's position). On the other hand, the contemporary language may signal an intent to take a more differentiated view of the problem of "good conduct"—a view that inquires "Good for what?" and treats the standards themselves as variables to be investigated.

Treating mental health as a question of ethics, it becomes clear that standards of normality depend for their definitions on the fundamental institutions of a society—family, religion, school, mythology, and so forth. To the objection that mental health cannot be scientifically defined within such a perspective (Freides, 1960; Hoffman, 1960), one may reasonably reply that the definition merely becomes more complex, in that it must encompass as variables characteristics of the evaluators and circumstances of action, as well as characteristics of the person being evaluated (Redlich, 1952; Eaton, 1951).

A problem remains with the ethical view of normality, however—namely, that it is too inclusive, identifying mental health with the attainment of any value that is culturally conceived as characterizing "the good life" (Smith, 1959, p. 674). There is little need for just a synonym, because it does not help to direct inquiry concerning how the good life can be attained. It does not help distinguish the potential contributions of psychology, sociology, and ethics in bringing about the desired state. Though it broadens the focus of inquiry into the condition of "normality," it does nothing to direct therapeutic action, until some broad consensus is achieved concerning what values (other than the absence of illness) are to be pursued. It leaves the psychologist either completely divorced from the major social concerns that support his activity or completely subservient to whatever definition of the good life happens to prevail in his microcosm.

One convenient resolution to the dilemma between the disease-health model and the ethical model of normality is to treat the two as applicable to different domains of phenomena. Illness may be conceived as a failure of functioning in some tissue or organ or in the total organism. Applied to the total organism, this means maladaptation that is primarily attributable to the person, rather than to characteristics of the environment to which adaptation is required. It implies that adaptation is both desirable and usual in the species, that some characteristic of the person impedes his adaptation, and that the characteristic would be dysfunctional under most reasonably conceivable conditions.

From such a perspective, it would appear quite paradoxical that current psychological usage defines "mental illness" (or "mental disorder") in such a way as to exclude "mental deficiency" (English & English, 1958, p. 317); it excludes the very condition that is likely to be most universally disabling, hence most akin to "illness" in the medical sense. There is some dispute over whether conditions variously referred to as "psychopathy," "personality disorders," and "character disorders" should be called "mental illness" or not (see Maughs, 1949; English & English, 1958, pp. 84, 383; Gough, 1948; Jahoda, 1958, p. 14; Lund & Glosser, 1957). The basis for the proposed distinctions seems to revolve around the age-old division of "mental" processes into "intellectual," "motivational," and "emotional," with disturbances attributed to the latter domain only having clear claim to the diagnosis "mental disorder" (i.e., "neurosis" or "psychosis"). Even this claim is disputed by some psychiatrists such as Szasz (1961), who asserts that hysteria in particular and "mental illness" in general is "a game characterized ... by the end-goals of domination and interpersonal control and by strategies of deceit" (p. 8). Sometime previously, Redlich (1952) challenged the classification of "neurosis" as an illness. In mild disorders, he said, symptoms "are expressions of certain maladjusted habits and are only labeled as symptoms through misunderstanding of their true nature or because their camouflage under the guise of illness is not recognized" (p. 566).

If "illness" refers to universally disabling characteristics of the person, "health" refers to those organismic characteristics that are deemed to *facilitate* adaptation to almost any reasonably conceivable circumstance. What constitutes a "reasonably conceivable circumstance" is a matter requiring consensus within the society or within a group of professional experts. The essential feature of the diagnosis "health" or "illness" is that the organismic trait is deemed universally adaptive or maladaptive.

Definitions of "mental health" rarely stumble on the distinction between "intellectual," "motivational," and "emotional" processes. They instead assume that healthy functioning of the total person demands general psychological adequacy; motivational, emotional, and intellectual criteria are thus intermixed. Barron (1963), for example, is explicit about the role that intellectual capacity plays in adequate functioning: "The more energy a person has at his disposal, the more fully will he become committed to the most complex possible integration.... Intelligence is a form of energy.... In the world of living forms it is the most intelligent form, not the most instinct-dominated, which succeeds" (p. 5). Indeed, Stoddard's very definition of intelligence, as quoted by English and English (1958, p. 268) is nearly as broad as the concepts "adaptation" and "mental health": "The ability to undertake activities that are characterized by difficulty, complexity, abstractness, economy, adaptiveness to a goal, social value, and the emergence of originals."

The health-illness model contrasts with other bases for judging the desirability or undesirability of organismic characteristics, bases that are deemed, even by the judges themselves, to depend substantially on the circumstances of adaptation. One suspects that most of the criteria for mental health enumerated above would fall into this latter, relativistic domain. The judge may deplore the circumstances under which honesty or empathy or social responsibility are *not* adaptive, but he must nevertheless recognize that such circumstances are "reasonably conceivable" and, indeed, frequently encountered in human society; hence the absence of these traits is not necessarily "sick" nor their presence necessarily "healthy."

Within this formulation, the value model is conceived as the more general, and the health-illness model as a special case within it. Health (as the capacity for adaptation to any circumstance) is conceived as a universal value, and illness (as inability to adapt to any circumstance) is seen as universally undesirable. Thus, use of these terms does not require explicit description of the circumstances of adaptation. But any other assertion concerning the adequacy or inadequacy of a person or trait should explicitly include a description of the particular adaptation problem posed. Needless to say, there will always be ambiguous cases in which one is not sure whether the "health" or "illness" designation is appropriate, because the "reasonably conceivable circumstances" criterion is too vague. Also, what constitute, for professional experts, "reasonably conceivable circumstances" may differ somewhat from one society to another and, as societies change over the centuries, notions of "reasonably conceivable circumstances" will probably change too; hence "health" and "illness" may take on new meanings. Perhaps the time will eventually come when honesty, empathy, and social responsibility are conceived as universally healthy traits, rather than just desirable within specified contexts.

PERFORMANCES VS. PSYCHOLOGICAL MEANS

Psychologists contribute to the definition of "the healthy person" in at least two ways: by espousing certain criteria of human performance and by attempting to establish links between psychological processes and the attainment of these criteria. The specifying of ends to be attained is an activity that they share with other goal-setters in the society—philosophers, teachers, religious institutions, and social reformers. For the most part, the behavioral goals espoused by psychologists are quite congruent with those of the surrounding culture—e.g., self-control, honesty, responsibility to others, self-reliance, mastery of the environment. Indeed, they are often adopted quite directly and with little question (Davis, 1938).

It is unlikely that psychologists will ever give up their prerogatives as human beings to set goals for their own and others' performance. However, it would seem that their unique contribution lies in theoretical elaboration and empirical testing of the relationships between psychological means and behavioral ends, especially focusing on those means which form the substance of established psychological theories. Traditional constructs such as "capacity" and "motivation" may, with elaboration, help in formulating some intra-personal determinants of complex adaptation. But it is likely that additional, human-specific concepts will be required as well. Wishner (1955), for example, suggests two classes of problem-oriented response, "diffuse" and "focused," that are differentially appropriate to his criterion of adjustment—efficiency in meeting environmental requirements. The notion of "ego disjunction" (Trehub, 1959), or conflict among motives, values, and interests may be useful in accounting for poor adaptation. Jahoda (1958, p. 64) has proposed a description of an optimal problem-solving process, that is said to maximize the chances for success, given favorable circumstances. Such traditional and novel concepts as these may be proposed as conditions of the person which mediate healthy adjustment—definition of the latter being taken as a postulate. It may even be possible to identify psychological conditions that seem relevant to almost any conceivable criterion of healthy functioning.

The identification of such means is ultimately an empirical problem. And here difficulties arise. First, of course, one must have empirical measures of the goal-states postulated as healthy and of the means-processes that facilitate or impede the goals—each independently defined. We are a long way from satisfactory operational definitions of the desired ends, let alone the constructs that serve as means.

Second, in the absence of systematic empirical evidence that a postulated means facilitates a desired end, many psychologists are prone to treat the allegedly mediating state itself as a criterion of healthy functioning. This is what seems to have happened in the case of "integration." From a concept that simply refers to mutually facilitative relations among component parts (motives, self-concepts, capacities, etc.), it has been converted into an inherently desirable state (Jahoda, 1958; Smith, 1950), apparently under the assumption that it generally facilitates adaptation, as defined by other criteria. Yet it is easy to conceive of simplistic, autistic modes of integration which would be quite maladaptive under most imaginable circumstances. The problem here is akin to that of distinguishing structural from functional abnormalities in physical medicine. A structural abnormality might, by itself, be of interest because unusual, but it becomes significant for health and illness only to the extent that it is associated, actually or potentially, with malfunctioning. Analogously, one would propose that deviations of psychological mediating states can reasonably be considered abnormal (in an evaluative sense) only if they result in behavioral malfunctioning.

One might object that this advocated role for the psychologist of theoretically and empirically relating means to ends deprives him of the opportunity for setting his own criteria of normality; that he becomes completely subservient to culturally established goals, that are arbitrary and nonultimate. It is, of course, conceivable that some psychologist will come up with a compelling criterion of human well-being that no philosopher, minister, or poet has ever thought of before. But the major problem in defining mental health would seem not to be so much one of proposing new criteria as of selecting among those that have already been proposed. Aside from appeals to popular consensus, which are open to anyone, the most convincing pressures for clarification are likely to be those based on empirical evidence—evidence that two proposed goals are mutually contradictory, or that the means to one goal are incompatible with the means to another, or that a single means facilitates the attainment of several different goals (see Smith, 1959). With such accumulated evidence, there would be a better chance of settling, by consensus, on a set of mutually consonant and realistically attainable goals of normal functioning. Maintaining a clear distinction between consensually established goals and empirically established means would appear to be an important ingredient of this quest.

THE UNIT OF REFERENCE

Jahoda (1958, p. 8) has observed that mental health may be defined either as referring to a relatively constant and enduring quality of personality or as a momentary function of personality and situation. In fact, most conceptions use the former unit of reference. Typical of these is the notion of mental health adopted by Lichtenberg, Cassetta, and Scanlon (1961) as "a quality of personality reflected in virtually every action of a person's life" (p. 620). Mental illness is seen by these authors as a generalized tendency of a person to deviate from what is appropriate. Such characterizations carry two implications: (a) That mental health and mental illness are pervasive states, manifest in most of a person's behaviors, and (b) that the states are relatively enduring, rather than transient. Such usage contrasts rather distinctly with conventional characterizations of physical health and illness. Physical illness is more likely to be seen as transitory and confined to a smaller locus than the total organism. Though chronic, pervasive states of physical illness are recognized, these are not the conditions most often treated by physical medicine; by contrast, psychiatrists are likely to conceive of the illnesses they treat as both chronic and pervasive.

Occasional departures from this general view are encountered. Birren, Jerome, and Chown (1961) have noted that the concept of the whole individual is exceedingly elusive and that empirical studies of adjustment tend to focus instead on isolated aspects of the person's behaviors. And Barron (1963, p. 4) speculates that temporary disorganization may occasionally be necessary in order for a person to achieve a more permanent, complex level of integration. But these are minority views; most psychologists tend to conceive of the "personality" as unitary—as either "sick" or "well" according to any particular specified criterion. One also suspects that they typically display an organismic (as opposed to a situational) bias, in attributing the major causes of behavior to relatively enduring characteristics of the "personality," conceived as a unitary entity.

It is possible to apply the concept "normal" to smaller units than the total personality. The units may be defined as traits, inferred from consistencies in a specified category of behaviors across various situations. Various traits do not necessarily display the degree of unity and interconnectedness that the several organ-systems of the body do; optimal functioning or malfunctioning with respect to one trait need not imply a similar characterization of the "total person." Though "total mental health" may be referred to elliptically as a summary, or average-value, of the healthiness of all traits, such a characterization would, in this view, have only poor predictive validity with respect to any particular adjustment problem that the person confronts—except, of course, for the few extreme individuals in whom pervasively poor or good functioning happened to be found.

Instead of inferring personality traits from consistent behaviors across situations, one may simply treat behaviors-in-situations as the units to be evaluated. Most evaluated behaviors occur in the context of role performance; thus behaviors-in-situations characterized as "healthy" or "unhealthy" might as frequently be attributed to the relatively enduring role structures as to the relatively enduring personality structures. Though most writers (e.g., Jahoda, 1958) would probably object to calling a situation either "healthy" or "unhealthy," this objection seems to stem from a desire to maintain linguistic convention, coupled with a tendency to regard as reasonable the adjustment demands that men typically confront. Indeed, it is behaviors-in-situations that are observed and designated "healthy" or "sick"; the attribution of these to a "healthy" or "sick" personality may be every bit as elliptical as attribution to a "healthy" or "sick" situation.

Reference to units smaller than the "total personality" simplifies the problem of operational definition that must precede objective research. It also permits one to treat as an hypothesis, rather than as an assumption, the proposition that the concept "normality" may be applied meaningfully to the total person—or, indeed, that the concept "total person" is a meaningful abstraction in the first place. It is still necessary, in any case, to recognize the inevitable interdependence between "qualities" and "performances"—between postulated "traits" of the person and his actions-in-situations. A "healthy" trait may contribute to healthy action; but conversely an action evaluated as healthy may enhance the person's self-concept and thereby increase the healthiness of his own behavior dispositions. (Healthy actions may also have salubrious effects on interpersonal situations, thereby enhancing the "health" of the role structure in some permanent way.)

SUBJECTIVE AND BEHAVIORAL CRITERIA

Among the values central to most conceptions of mental health is one which is distinctive in that it refers, not to overt behaviors or to relations with the environment, but to an essentially private, subjective feeling tone. This has been identified variously as happiness, morale, satisfaction with oneself, contentment, and so forth; here we shall use the general designation hedonic tone (euphoria vs. dysphoria), because this appears basic to the several subjective states. Of all the specific criteria proposed in the literature, this one is probably most closely associated with exposure to psychiatric treatment. By and large, persons under treatment (either self-referred or community-referred) are more dysphoric than those who are not. Yet, in the most inclusive and influential review of the topic (Jahoda, 1958), happiness is only grudgingly accepted as a criterion of mental health. "Only when happiness or well-being are clearly conceived of as personality predispositions, rather than momentary feeling states depending on circumstances, do these criteria appear useful" (Jahoda, 1958, p. 21).

Jahoda's principal objection to the happiness criterion seems to be simply that it may not be sufficient to warrant the appellation "mental health," or that happiness may conflict with some other, more important criterion. But exactly the same objection could be raised to any other criterion, depending on the perspective chosen. In one sense, most people tend to treat their own favored values as "absolutes"—as inherently and universally desirable states. Yet it seems probable that any so-called "absolute" could potentially be overridden by some other consideration. This is true of happiness no more, and no less, than for any valued state that may be conceived.

One manifestation of happiness which appears exceedingly important in our culture is satisfaction with oneself, or a positive self-regard. Indeed, this has become a major criterion of mental health and therapeutic effectiveness within the school of nondirective counselling (Rogers & Dymond, 1954). Satisfaction with self is to be distinguished from knowledge of self, or self-awareness.

It seems that the only thing in common between these two widely used criteria of psychological well-being is the word "self," which is misleading if used to refer to some objective entity. The "self" is in fact a cultural convention, a hypothetical construct that refers to no specifiable *thing*. It is an idea without a clear empirical referent. To say that a person's self-concept is accurate can mean nothing more than that it agrees with some other reasonable definition—such as the concept shared by his close friends or the concept developed by a psychologist following appropriate assessment. But a "reasonable definition" is not necessarily a uniquely appropriate definition when it comes to settling on hypothetical constructs. For purposes of communication, it is probably important that a person mean roughly the same thing by his notion of self as significant others around him do, but this is not to demand a self-concept that is "accurate" in some absolute sense.

Satisfaction is probably quite a different thing from accuracy, in any case. It is probably simply one of many possible manifestations of a pleasant hedonic tone. A pleasant emotional state (whatever it may be and however it may come about) is apt to be focussed on some object or event that is salient for the person. The "self" is commonly salient in Western society, or can be made so by appropriate questioning. Hence, the happy person, when asked, is likely to report satisfaction with self; he is also likely to report favorable sentiments toward a variety of other things or ideas that are significant for him—such as other people, a loved one, his work, or "God." The state of "high morale" typically describes a focus of satisfaction which is definitely *not* the self; the state of "joy" may be quite object-less. In any case, one suspects that it is the feeling tone that is basic; the object on which it is focussed depends on the circumstances—e.g., on what object is available—and on internalized cultural definitions of appropriate objects or concepts.

By contrast, "dissatisfaction with self" would appear to be just one manifestation of a general state of misery that may focus on various objects—being manifest as hate, misanthropy, xenophobia, guilt, despair, the feeling that others (rather than, or as well as, oneself) are inadequate. Frustration and anxiety, parallel to joy, may be felt simply as object-less dysphoria. One currently popular elaboration of a dysphoric state has been called "phrenophobia" (Raimy, 1963)—the feeling that one is "losing his mind." One suspects that this particular conviction is selected from among the many available in the culture by a person whose general hedonic tone is unpleasant. Negative convictions about the self are quite likely to induce a person to seek help—from a psychiatrist or other source—while negatively toned convictions about other objects may escape public attention, unless they are acted out irresponsibly.

All of which is to say that satisfaction with self—of either a short-term or long-term sort—seems an entirely appropriate consideration in defining "normality." But the self is probably just one of many possible foci for a generally positive or negative hedonic tone, and it is the hedonic tone, regardless of its focus, which should probably be conceived as basic to the definition.

SYMPTOMS VS. CRITERIA

In organic medicine there is a customary distinction made between symptom and pathology, the latter referring to an essentially morbid condition and the former referring to an indicator of morbidity that may not in itself be pathological. Usually it is assumed that the pathological condition constitutes the "underlying cause" of the symptom; this may imply that the symptom will necessarily persist until the pathology is removed. In any case, the diagnostic value of a symptom rests upon the extent to which it reflects a specific pathology or upon the degree of total organismic disability associated with it. A "symptom" that bears an uncertain relation to pathology (e.g., sneezing) is, by itself, of little diagnostic significance.

A comparable distinction is generally attempted in psychiatric diagnosis, but it appears not quite so successful for two reasons: First, because correspondences between "symptoms" and "pathologies" are less well established and, second, because what is "symptomatic" and what "pathological" often depends predominantly on the diagnostician's point of view. Conditions regarded by some as possibly symptomatic are treated as unquestionably pathological by others.

The status of childhood enuresis constitutes a case in point. This condition is frequently regarded as symptomatic of emotional disturbance. Yet a study of third-grade children reported by Tapia, Jekel, and Domke (1960) showed no association between bed-wetting (once a month or more) and teachers' or mothers' ratings of adjustment. Of course, the criterion ratings might be regarded by some as inappropriate validators, but at least the absence of any significant relationship in this large sample (830 families) raises serious question about the symptomatic importance of enuresis in children of this age.

To illustrate the indistinct line between symptom and pathology we may consider the case of psychological tests. A test is basically a device for eliciting responses, which may be regarded as symptomatic of some underlying personality state (for instance, psychopathology). Many tests (e.g., the MMPI) derive their diagnostic significance from comparisons of criterion groups, whose pathological status is presumably known. For other tests (such as the Rorschach inkblots and the Thematic Apperception Test), responses to be treated as diagnostic are less regularly validated against acceptable criteria. The attribution of guilt or feelings of rejection to the central figure of a TAT story, for example, is commonly accepted as evidence that the subject feels that way, or would feel that way under the circumstances described (e.g., Mussen & Jones, 1957; Miller & Swanson, 1960). In such instances, the elicited response is interpreted as symptomatic of, or even substituted for, the condition to be diagnosed, in the absence of evidence concerning an association between the two.

Even in the case of criterion-validated tests, there remains a problem in individual diagnosis. The association of test scores with a criterion may be of such low order that their diagnostic significance is exceedingly problematic in any individual case; many other conditions besides the assumed pathology might produce any given response pattern. Yet there are practitioners who treat the test responses themselves as *criteria* of normality (see Cartwright, Kirtner, & Fiske, 1963; Fairweather, Simon, Gebhard, Weingarten, Holland, Sanders, Stone, & Reahl, 1960, for example), much as the Stanford-Binet or Wechsler test is accepted as a criterion of intelligence. It would seem that, in contrast to definitions of intelligence (which may be entirely test-defined), definitions of mental health and illness usually refer to nontest behaviors—relating somehow to the person's adjustment in his everyday life. A reasonable aim of scientific psychology is to develop objective tests which correlate highly with what are at present essentially judgmental criteria, or to develop operational definitions via objective tests which can gain general acceptance as more valid than the judgmental criteria themselves (as many would claim is the case with intelligence tests). But until the tests are consensually accepted as criteria, either by definition or by virtue of their high correlation with other accepted standards, it would seem inappropriate to *substitute* performance on them for performance in the situations to which the definitions of normality refer.

Disregarding measures of elicited behavior, and focussing on emitted or "naturally occurring" behaviors—which are generally accepted as more appropriately definitional (rather than possibly symptomatic)—there is still room for dispute concerning what constitutes a symptom and what constitutes a criterion of pathology. The status of "anxiety" is illustrative: some (e.g., Freud, 1933, 1936; Horney, 1939) would regard the condition itself as inherently pathological; others (e.g., Mowrer, 1960) regard it simply as evidence of underlying repression or conflict, and it is the conflict, rather than the anxiety, which is pathological; yet others (Jahoda, 1958, p. 42; Miller & Dollard, 1941; Mowrer, 1939) conceive of anxiety as an internal organismic state (e.g., a drive) which may have either adaptive or maladaptive consequences, depending on the kind of problem faced and on how the person reacts to his own anxiety.

Maladjusted states recognized as "neurosis" and "psychosis" would be regarded by most as definitional. Yet Mowrer (1960, 1964) seems to take a different view, treating them as symptomatic of "immoral behavior." In less absolutistic terminology, one could conceive the causal sequence in somewhat the following terms: the person violates the normative standards of significant others (Mowrer's "sin"), these others reject him, he feels guilty or inadequate, and psychiatric symptoms ensue. Such a formulation is undoubtedly insufficient and fails to specify the conditions under which "sin" eventuates in "psychosis." The relevant point here, however, is that Mowrer treats the misbehavior as causative and the emotional disturbance as symptomatic, rather than the other way around as most contemporary formulations would do.

It seems that the distinction between "symptomatic" and "pathological" is more difficult to maintain in psychiatric than in organic discourse, for one man's symptom is another man's pathology. Even the therapeutic significance of the distinction may be questioned (Grossberg, 1964). "Dynamic theories" of psychology assert or imply that mere symptom removal is of little therapeutic value, since the underlying cause (the essential pathology) persists to be manifest elsewhere. Quite aside from empirical evidence concerning the efficacy of "symptom removal" (see Grossberg, 1964), the theoretical rationale itself may be criticized for failure to recognize the two-way interdependence between overt behaviors and "internal" states; either may "cause" or perpetuate the other. Even if some "underlying internal cause" were to persist following removal of a particular manifestation, it is quite possible that subsequent manifestations would turn out to be more personally satisfying and socially acceptable than their predecessors, hence less likely to be reasonably regarded as either symptoms or defining instances of pathology.

The foregoing considerations have centered around the definition of "mental illness" because this is the domain to which the distinction between symptom and criterion is usually applied. However, they have implications for the conception of mental health as well: The designation of what is, in itself, a "normal" or "desirable" state, of what is a "symptomatic" consequence of an inherently "normal" state, and of what is a condition likely to bring about a "normal" state, independently conceived, depends largely on one's value predilections. Unless social (or professional) consensus can be achieved on such matters, it would seem most appropriate simply to investigate the degree of empirical co-variation among a variety of proposed criteria, without concern for which of them may be the "most ultimate" (cf. Smith, 1959).

MEASURES OF NORMALITY

In contrast to the great variety of conceptual meanings attached to the concepts "normality," "adjustment," and "mental health," the range of commonly employed measures appears much more limited. To facilitate discussion, these measures may be classified into three gross types, corresponding to Cattell's (1957) classification of tests: self-reports, ratings by others, and overt behaviors "objectively" scored. There is also a fourth category, infrequently employed, consisting of discrepancies between self-reports and others' ratings.

Self-Report

Self-report instruments contribute by far the greatest number of operational definitions of "normality" appearing in the current literature. These may be used with two distinguishable intents: (a) to determine the degree to which the subject is happy or worried or satisfied with himself and his life, or (b) to assess the presence, or magnitude, of some trait which the researcher deems relevant to adjustment. The first kind of use provides a direct measure of "normality" conceived in subjective terms; the person is, by definition, normal to the extent that he is happy and content with himself. Single-question measures of this type have been employed by Gurin, Veroff, and Feld (1960), who asked a representative national sample of respondents how happy they were and how much they were inclined to worry; by Holtzman and Bitterman (1956), who had military recruits rate themselves on degree of adjustment; and by Storrow (1960), whose subjects rated their degree of self-improvement following psychotherapy.

Multiple-item scales or adjective check lists reflecting self-acceptance (satisfaction with self) have been used by numerous researchers, including Crowne, Stephens, and Kelly (1961); Suinn (1961); Strong (1962); Heilbrun (1963); Forsythe and Fairweather (1961); Fiedler, Dodge, Jones, and Hutchins (1958); Martin (1959); Cowen, Heilizer, and Axelrod (1957); and Dickey (1961). At least two variants on self-acceptance measures have been employed. One (see Bills, Vance, & McLean, 1951) consists in asking the subject first to describe himself (e.g., by checking a list of statements), then to indicate how content he is to be that way. The second variant—much more commonly used—presents a list of descriptive phrases, which the subject checks (or rates or sorts) according to two instructional sets: first, to describe himself, and second, to indicate how he would like to be (his "ideal self"). The measure of self-acceptance is the sum of absolute discrepancies between trait ratings under the two different sets.

The various multiple-item tests of self-acceptance are generally found to have quite high reliabilities (split-half or test-retest)—around .70 to .90 (Akeret, 1959; Strong & Feder, 1961; Fiedler *et al.,* 1958; Eastman, 1958; Dickey, 1961)—and to correlate moderately well (from about .40 to .80) with each other (Omwake, 1954; Strong & Feder, 1961; Strong, 1962; Crowne, Stephens, & Kelly, 1961)—though the magnitudes of interinstrument correlation appear to vary substantially depending on the instrument and on the population of subjects assessed.

When self-report tests are used for purposes other than to elicit direct expressions of self-acceptance, the researcher must himself determine whether or not the attribute assessed is a "healthy" one. Quite often an over-all "adjustment" score is defined by a priori designation of items as reflecting either "normal" or "abnormal" traits (see Cartwright & Roth, 1957; Strong, 1962; Crowne, Stephens, & Kelly, 1961; Fiedler *et al.,* 1958; Engel, 1959; Dickey, 1961). Alternatively, more restricted domains relevant to adjustment may be measured by clusters of self-report items, as in the case of the various scales derived from the MMPI (see, for example, Briggs, Wirt, & Johnson, 1961; Affleck & Garfield, 1960; Barron, 1963; Holtzman & Bitterman, 1956; Zuckerman & Monashkin, 1957; Engel, 1959; Fairweather *et al.,* 1960; Heilbrun, 1961), the California Psychological Inventory (Gough, 1957; Dinitz, Scarpitti, & Reckless, 1962; Nichols & Beck, 1960), the Bell Adjustment Inventory (Winthrop, 1959), Rogers' (1931) Adjustment Inventory, and Locke's Marital Adjustment Scale (Locke & Wallace, 1959; Luckey, 1960a, 1960b).

It is quite generally the case that these various a priori scales correlate substantially with each other and with measures designed to tap directly the subject's feeling of self-acceptance (see Cowen, Heilizer, & Axelrod, 1957; Fairweather *et al.,* 1960; Holtzman & Bitterman, 1956; Matarazzo, Matarazzo,

& Saslow, 1961; Forsythe & Fairweather, 1961; Engel, 1959; Cartwright & Roth, 1957; Strong & Feder, 1961; Block & Thomas, 1955; Van Evra & Rosenberg, 1963; Crowne, Stephens, & Kelly, 1961; Barron, 1963; Martin, 1959; Dickey, 1961; Heilbrun, 1963). This common finding may be variously interpreted. If the discrepancy between a subject's self and ideal ratings correlates highly with the discrepancy between the subject's self and the researcher's ideal (i.e., an a priori notion of "adjustment"), this at least indicates fair correspondence between the subject's and the researcher's conceptions of appropriate responses. Indeed, Cowen (1961) and Edwards (1957, 1961) have shown that there are very high correlations between pooled psychiatrists' or psychologists' judgments concerning the psychiatric "normality" of various traits and the pooled ratings of the "desirability" of these traits obtained from lay groups.

The substantial correlations between "adjustment" scores derived from different lists of traits might, in an earlier era, have been taken as evidence for the validities of all the instruments in assessing the intended property, adjustment. This interpretation must now be modified by the recognition that all such scores based on self-report share common instrument factors (e.g., the subject's tendency to perceive, or willingness to admit, defects in himself), which may be more important in determining the high correlations than the common trait factor ("adjustment") that they are deemed to represent (see Campbell & Fiske, 1959).

A third possible interpretation arises from the substantial correspondence between scores from instruments ostensibly measuring different attributes. Barron (1963), for example, reports that his Ego Strength scale from the MMPI correlates with certain psychiatric scales from that instrument (*Pt, D, Hs*) around −.75—about as high as the reliability of the Ego Strength scale itself. Matarazzo, Matarazzo, and Saslow (1961) found the Taylor Manifest Anxiety Scale correlating .82 with the psychiatric portion of the Cornell Medical Index. Martin (1959) reports a correlation of −.62 between the Manifest Anxiety Scale and items from the "lie" scales of the MMPI. Crowne, Stephens, and Kelly (1961) found that Edwards' (1957) Social Desirability scale correlated as well with various measures of self acceptance (about .55) as the latter did with each other. On what grounds, then, does one choose to call the common trait measured by these instruments "ego strength" as opposed to "psychasthenia," "anxiety" as opposed to "psychiatric symptoms," "self-acceptance" as opposed to "desire to appear in a favorable light"? It seems that these various terms, though intended to be quite distinct conceptually, are not well distinguished empirically. More thorough item analyses seem called for, to ascertain that items included in one scale actually correlate more highly with other items in their own scale than with items from a scale intended to measure a different trait. Until this is done, scale-naming must remain an arbitrary exercise, and the correspondence between differently named scales must remain uninterpretable.

The most careful interpretation that can presently be made is that various self-report instruments designed to assess traits that are "normal," either from the subject's or from the researcher's viewpoint, tend to correlate substantially.

Acceptance of Self and Acceptance of Others

One characteristic of "mentally healthy" persons which has received considerable attention in both the theoretical and the empirical literature is a liking for, or acceptance of, other people. This tendency is generally assessed by self-report measures, and there is nearly always a positive correlation found between acceptance of others and acceptance of self (Berger, 1952; Fey, 1955; McIntyre, 1952; Omwake, 1954; Phillips, 1951; Sheerer, 1949; Stock, 1949; Suinn, 1961). No relationship was found by

Zelen (1954) in his sample of sixth-grade pupils, but this exception is attributed by Suinn (1961) to the young age of Zelen's subjects. Reese (1961) found, among fourth, sixth, and eighth graders, that subjects low in self-acceptance tended to like their peers less well than subjects of moderate or high self-acceptance, but that the latter two groups did not differ significantly from each other in tendency to like or dislike others. Thus, a curvilinear relationship was suggested; but the results from other studies have not been analyzed in such a way as to permit this distinction, and one cannot tell from Reese's report whether his relationship represented a significant departure from linearity.

Compound Scoring

Self-report instruments can be scored in other ways besides a simple summation of all items into a total score. Trehub's (1959) measure of "ego disjunction," for example, is an index representing the degree to which presumably incompatible needs measured by the Edwards (1953) Personal Preference Schedule are of approximately equal (and high) strength. He found significantly higher "ego disjunction" among schizophrenics than among neurotics, and among neurotics than among normals. On the other hand, Jessor, Liverant, and Opochinsky (1963) found the degree of "need balance" to be positively correlated with measures of adjustment in a college population; "need balance" was defined as the possession of roughly equivalent levels of two different needs measured by Liverant's (1958) Goal Preference Inventory. Integration of these findings presumably requires a clearer conceptualization of "need-compatibility" (though Fordyce and Crow [1960] have since failed to replicate Trehub's findings). The relevant point here, however, is that such indices as these suggest more complex scoring of self-report inventories than simple summation of item responses. As such, they may be less vulnerable to contamination by unintended subject characteristics such as acquiescence or tendency to present oneself in a favorable light. Needless to say, their validity for measuring aspects of "normality" is as yet insufficiently demonstrated.

Ratings by Other People

Except for the definition of normality as satisfaction with self, most of the personal traits included under the rubric are ultimately dependent for their measurement on the judgments of other people. These judgments may come from the person's peers, from his supervisors, or from professionals (e.g., psychiatrists). They may refer to fairly specific traits, such as "emotional stability" and "self-confidence," or to global reactions of the rater to the person—e.g., "how much you like him." They may be based on specifically designated samples of behavior, such as are provided by a check list or by a situation test; more commonly they depend on intuitively integrated judgments reflecting whatever sample of contacts the rater has experienced and happens to recall. Not all of these sources, kinds, and bases of judgments would be regarded as equally valid. Nevertheless, one would expect some degree of correspondence among them, to the extent that they appraise a common characteristic of the subject.

It is not unusual to obtain fairly high inter-rater agreement (correlations between .60 and .80) when procedures are used to ensure that the raters attend to a common behavioral referent. Zuckerman and Monashkin (1957) established an inter-judge agreement of .77 in rating psychiatric patients' levels of adjustment from their hospital case histories; Reznikoff and Toomey (1958) made ratings on the extent of psychopathology from test protocols, which correlated .79 with each other and .57 with the therapist's rating; judges in a study by Rosenthal, Lawlor, Zahn, and Shakow (1960) rated "ego-intactness" of patients with a reliability of .80. Tuddenham (1959a) reports inter-rater agreements, based on observation of children's free play and on interviews, averaging around .60 or .70 for a variety of traits. The Lorr (1953) Psychiatric Scale and the Hospital Adjustment Scale (Ferguson, McReynolds, & Ballachey, 1953) were shown by Stilson, Mason, Gynther, and Gertz (1958) to have test-retest stabilities of .80 and .79, respectively, even when different raters were used on the two occasions. This same study showed a correlation of .57 between the two rating scales, when applied to a heterogeneous sample of patients. Ellsworth and Clayton (1959) report a correlation of .69 between a modified form of Lorr's (1953) scale and the MACC Behavioral Adjustment Scale (Ellsworth, 1962), also a correlation of .74 between change scores from these two instruments over a six-month period.

Inter-rater correspondence is less certain when each uses his own (different or unspecified) basis for rating. Epstein (1941) reports poor inter-teacher agreement in nominating "problem children." Tuddenham (1952) implies that teachers and pupils did not agree very well in nominating pupils on a variety of attributes, but detailed data are not presented. Therapists in Storrow's (1960) study did not agree significantly with the patients' relatives concerning the degree of improvement in therapy. Fairweather *et al.* (1960) found significant agreement of posthospital adjustment ratings by the patient's relative (or other person to whom he was discharged) with prior ratings of his behavior in group therapy, but not with ratings of his ward behavior or of his hospital job performance. An interesting exception to their general pattern of results was a *negative* (i.e., "wrong direction") correlation between ratings of excessive posthospitalization drinking and the other three inhospital ratings; this evidently resulted from the heterogeneous sample of subjects (alcoholics together with psychotics) and the heterogeneous nature of "posthospital adjustment." In the same study, ratings of ward behavior correlated with ratings of group therapy behavior, but neither correlated significantly with ratings of hospital job performance.

Barron (1963) obtained ratings on "soundness" of graduate students from their professors; for subjects rated by six or more professors, the reliability of mean ratings was .68, but this figure is based on pooled judgments: agreement between pairs of raters would necessarily have been lower. The mean professors' ratings on "soundness" correlated .41 with the assessment staff's (psychologists') ratings of soundness in these students. Tindall (1955) reports correlations among ratings by psychologists, deans, teachers, and cottage supervisors in a school for disturbed children averaging .53; these in turn correlated around .50 with measures of sociometric status derived from peer ratings. Perhaps the raters in this study had a more intimate acquaintance with their wards than is typical of other rating studies, and they were also more likely to share a common frame of reference concerning the manifestations of "good adjustment." In a similar setting, Rosengren and Davids (1961) found adult leaders' ratings of children's prestige to correlate negatively with prestige measured from peer ratings.

Adjustment ratings would appear to have the greatest chance for high reliability if (a) they are based on specified behaviors, (b) they come from raters who share a common definition of adjustment, (c) the scores provided by several raters are pooled into a single total (or mean) score, and (d) the sample of persons rated is selected so as to be heterogeneous with respect to level of adjustment. Unless one or more of these conditions are met, ratings of "normality" from persons other than the subject are unlikely to show high interjudge agreement.

Various indices of sociometric status can often be interpreted as measures of adjustment, if this quality is defined as acceptance of the person by his peers. Mouton, Blake, and Fruchter (1955) review numerous studies which show high concurrent and test-retest reliability of intragroup status, measured as the mean number of nominations received from other group members or as the mean rating on some scale of acceptance received by a subject. However, it should be noted that the measures of reliability are all based on *mean* ratings received—often from a very large number of other persons. These results should not be interpreted as indicating a high degree of agreement between any random pair of raters in the group. Scott (1965) has used the intraclass correlation coefficient (ρ) as a measure of the average agreement in ratings of college fraternity members. With respect to the attribute "How much you like them," ρs ranged from .04 to .34 over the ten fraternities studied, with a mean ρ of .15. This was significantly lower than the mean inter-rater agreement obtained on more "objective" qualities (studiousness and contribution to house activities); it also appeared that ratings of "liking" were strongly affected by mutuality—the tendency of pairs of members to reciprocate favorable or unfavorable ratings. Thus, while the *mean* rating received from one's peers in a sociometric task may provide a stable score (particularly when the number of peers is large), this does not necessarily imply a high level of inter-rater agreement concerning the likeableness of the persons rated. "Normality" assessed sociometrically is likely to depend as much on characteristics of the rater as on characteristics of the person rated.

Others' Ratings and Self-Reports

A number of assessment studies have included among their measures self-report instruments together with ratings of the subjects made either by their peers or by someone else (e.g., relative, friend, supervisor, or psychologist) with sufficient information to rate them. The results of such studies may provide two kinds of information relevant to the present problem. If the subject and his rater(s) are explicitly instructed to report the same trait—e.g., if both of them fill out the same inventory as applied to the one subject—the degree of correspondence between the two may be used as evidence concerning the validity of either (or both) measures. If the subject reports one measure of adjustment (say, self-acceptance) and the rater reports another (say, degree of liking for the subject), then the results may provide evidence concerning the degree of correspondence between the two different criteria for adjustment. This may be considered a "validating" study only to the extent that "normality" is regarded as a single trait, tapped comparably by the different measures. The distinction between the two types of studies is not always completely clear, however, for it is often hard to tell whether the two measures are aimed at a single trait or at different traits. If the subject, for example, takes the MMPI and is rated by his therapist on "level of adjustment" or on "severity of pathology," one is uncertain as to whether to treat a correlation between the two measures as an instance of convergent validation on a single trait or as a demonstration of co-variation between two different traits. The interpretation will depend largely on the theoretical stance of the investigator—whether he conceives "severity of pathology" as coterminous with the MMPI psychopathology scales or as a broader concept encompassing other behaviors and symptoms. Somewhat arbitrarily, we shall regard the traits as different unless they are similarly defined for both subject and rater. Thus, the foregoing example would be treated as a test of co-variation between two different traits; if the therapist had been set explicitly to rate the "degree of psychasthenic tendency," then the correlation between his ratings and the patient's *Pt* score would be treated as evidence for convergent validation.

Convergent Validation

As instances in which both subject and rater were set to report the same trait, we may cite six studies from the recent literature. They yield quite a range of validity coefficients, from substantial to nonsignificant. Winthrop (1959) had female college students fill out the Bell (1934) Adjustment Inventory for themselves, and it was also given to their best friends on campus with instructions to rate the subject. The correlation between subject- and friend-rated total adjustment score was .19 (nonsignificant), while correlations for the four subscales of the inventory (home, health, social, and emotional adjustment) ranged from .29 to .59 (all significantly different from zero at $p < .05$). When items on which either the subject or her friend indicated uncertainty (marking *?* rather than *Yes* or *No*) were eliminated from the scales, the correlation for total adjustment scores increased to .41 and the subscale correlations ranged from .48 to .66 (all $ps < .01$).

Considerably less confirmatory results were obtained in a similar study by Auble (1957). His subjects (female freshman college students) filled out the Heston (1949) Personal Adjustment Inventory during the first week of school. Several months later they were rated by faculty, dormitory heads, and counsellors on five-point rating scales summarizing the six subscales of the Inventory. The correlations between self-report Inventory subscales and pooled raters' judgments ranged from .03 to .35; only three of them were significantly different from zero. One would suspect that the discrepancy in correlations between Winthrop's and Auble's studies depended, at least to some extent, on the relatively poorer acquaintance of raters with subjects, on the time lapse, and on the difference in instruments filled out by subjects and raters which obtained in the latter study.

In a study by Holtzman and Bitterman (1956), subjects' ratings of their own adjustment did not correlate significantly with their peers' mean ratings of them on the same trait. Serot and Teevan (1961) found children's reports of their relations with their parents not to correspond with parents' reports of the same relationship. By contrast, Storrow (1960) reports significant relations between patients' self-ratings of degree of improvement following psychotherapy and (a) their therapists' ratings of improvement and (b) their relatives' ratings of improvement. (The possibility that these ratings were contaminated by the patients' communication with the two sources should not be overlooked.) And Neugarten, Havighurst, and Tobin (1961) found a correlation of .55 between a questionnaire measuring "life satisfaction" among older people and the researchers' ratings of their degree of "life satisfaction" from interview protocols.

At the risk of hasty generalization from too few instances, one might infer from these results that agreement between self-ratings and the ratings of others concerning a specified trait is most likely to appear when the trait is defined for both parties identically, and in some detail (e.g., by multiple-item scales). Otherwise, convergent validation is unlikely to occur.

Co-variation between Different Definitions of Normality

When self-ratings are scored to yield some over-all measure of self-acceptance and ratings by others refer to some different, global construct, such as "adjustment of the ratee" or "liking for the ratee," it is unusual for the two measures to correlate. In a report of four separate studies, Fiedler *et al.* (1958) found no significant correlations between three kinds of self-rating measures (a self-acceptance scale, a self-ideal discrepancy score, and the Taylor Manifest Anxiety Scale) on the one hand, and three kinds of ratings by other people (sociometric nominations and sociometric ratings by peers, disciplinary ratings by superior officers) on the other—although the several measures within each class (self-ratings or other-ratings) were significantly intercorrelated. Engel (1959) found no relationship between students' self-ratings (an a priori-scored *Q* sort) and either their teachers' or their peers' ratings on level of adjustment. A study by Reese (1961) reported school children's sociometric status (peer acceptance) positively correlated with an a priori measure of self-acceptance, but not with a measure based on self-ideal discrepancy. Miyamoto and Dornbusch (1956) and Zelen (1954) found positive correlations between self-acceptance and acceptance by peers, while Fey (1955) and McIntyre (1952) found no significant relationships. Iscoe and Garden (1961) found a negative correlation between girls' scores on the Children's Manifest Anxiety Scale (Castenada, McCandless, & Palermo, 1956) and their sociometric status, but no comparable correlation among boys.

Among one group of institutionalized boys (Tindall, 1955), scores on the Heston (1949) Personal Adjustment Inventory correlated .26 with peer-group sociometric status, but not with adult supervisors' ratings of adjustment; in another comparable group (Rosengren & Davids, 1961), self-esteem (rated by psychologists from subjects' self-descriptions) correlated *negatively* (i.e., in the "wrong" direction) with adult supervisors' ratings of prestige, and nonsignificantly with sociometric status, measured by peers' nominations of friends. Zuckerman and Monashkin (1957) report no significant correlation in a psychiatric patient group between a measure of self-ideal discrepancy and psychologists' ratings of adjustment from the patients' case histories.

A study of 96 psychiatric patients by Fairweather *et al.* (1960) included several self-report measures—a *Q* sort scored for self-ideal discrepancy, and five scales from the MMPI (Welsh's Repression, Welsh's Anxiety, Barron's Ego Strength, Simon's Inner Maladjustment, and the Schizophrenia scales). Four kinds of ratings by others were also obtained on hospital job performance, ward behavior, group therapy behavior, and posthospital adjustment (several ratings made six months later by the person with whom the patient was living). Out of 36 tetrachoric correlations between the two kinds of measures (self-report and other-report), the authors report only one significantly greater than zero. A later report of the same study (Forsythe & Fairweather, 1961) combines these self-report measures and other MMPI scales into a single cluster, and also combines three posthospital adjustment ratings and the group therapy rating into another cluster. The correlation between the two cluster scores was .25 ($p < .05$).

Butler and Haigh (1954) have reported that patients who were judged, following psychotherapy, to have shown substantial improvement tended to have reduced the discrepancy between self- and ideal-ratings, in comparison with an unimproved group. Comparably, Cartwright and Roth (1957) found that posttherapy measures from therapist and client tended to agree concerning the patient's level of adjustment. However, when change scores (i.e., the difference between pre- and posttherapy ratings) have been compared in these and other studies, essentially negative results were obtained. Cartwright and Roth (1957) found no correspondence between client-change scores and therapist-change scores. Cartwright, Kirtner, and Fiske (1963) reported changes in patients' self-ratings and changes in therapists' ratings of patient adjustment to be quite independent factors. In fact, Nichols and Beck (1960) obtained no correlations between changes in patients' scores on the California Personality Inventory (Gough, 1957) and the therapist's *posttherapy* rating of the degree of improvement shown by the patient. One suspects that, in those cases where posttherapy ratings of the therapist agree with patients' self-ratings (or with changes in self-ratings), there may have been some contamination resulting from communication between the two in the final interviews.

The inconsistent, and generally negative, pattern of these findings would seem to indicate that self-report measures of over-all adjustment have little in common with global ratings of adjustment provided by other persons. In view of the generally high reliabilities of the two kinds of measures, one is tempted to attribute the poor correspondence between them to two major sources: First, the traits rated by subjects themselves and the traits rated by others are usually not explicitly defined in comparable terms; hence the two sources of ratings may not be using comparable criteria for adjustment. This is to say that "adjustment" is not a single attribute, similarly reflected in self-ratings and in others' ratings. Such an interpretation implies, nevertheless, valid measures of the intended traits, either from the subject's or from the rater's standpoint. The second possible source of poor correlations may lie in the invalidity of the two separate classes of measures. Each of them tends to confound a particular attribute with a particular method of measurement. Self-acceptance is measured by self-report instruments, which may be affected predominantly by instrument-specific factors, such as acquiescence, degree of self-insight, desire to present oneself favorably, and other response-sets manifest in paper-and-pencil tests. Ratings of adjustment are measured somewhat more variously, but many of them provide poor specification of the attribute, hence are subject to "halo" effects, personal biases of the rater, and stereotypic inferences which may also be instrument-specific. Thus, intra-instrument reliability may reflect common methods components more than common trait components; the strengths of the former factors may be sufficient to overwhelm the latter, thus yielding no over-all correlation between the two kinds of tests. It is difficult, on the basis of present evidence, to choose between these two interpretations—that "different kinds of adjustment" are being measured by the two kinds of measures, or that neither kind of measure is a valid measure of "adjustment"—because of the confounding between trait and method inherent in present assessment procedures. It will be necessary to find other ways of measuring self-acceptance, which do not rely on direct self-report, and other ways of measuring acceptance by others or appraisals of adjustment, which do not rely on global ratings, before one can determine which interpretation to apply.

It may be objected that this application of Campbell and Fiske's (1959) multitrait-multimethod paradigm is unsound—that self-acceptance can *only* be measured by self-report and that acceptance by others can *only* be measured by *their* ratings of the subject. This is to say that "maximally different" measures of an attribute (Campbell and Fiske's standard of validity) can only be "minimally different." If so, then researchers must probably resign themselves to consistently low or nonsignificant correlations between self-acceptance and acceptance-by-others; for the differential instrument factors that reduce the correspondence almost certainly outweigh the common trait factors that contribute to it. "Normality" will necessarily appear as a "multidimensional" construct.

Sociometric Status and Acceptance of Others

The relationship between liking *for* others and reciprocated liking *by* others has been assessed in several studies, with generally positive results. Marks (1954) and Zelen (1954) found that the most popular school children tended themselves to choose more peers as friends. Among third-year medical students, Fey (1955) found a correlation of .20 ($p < .10$) between acceptance of others and acceptance by others; more importantly, acceptance by peers was correlated ($p < .05$) with the degree to which the subject *liked others better* than he liked himself. Reese (1961) obtained a correlation of .20 ($p < .001$) between popularity and liking for others in a study of fourth, sixth, and eighth graders. McIntyre (1952) found no significant correlation between these two "aspects of adjustment." Scott's (1965) study of ten college fraternities showed a general tendency toward correspondence for all organizations combined, but the correlation between sociometric status and liking for others was significant within only two of the organizations, considered individually. Taken together, these results seem to suggest a general "sociability" component of adjustment: people who like others tend to be well liked in return. While the proposition may seem commonsensical, it is one of the few in this area that have been demonstrated with measures that are not intercontaminated.

"ACCURACY" OF SELF-APPRAISAL

Accurate knowledge of oneself is a commonly proposed criterion for normality, but it is difficult to assess in the absence of some acceptable definition of what the "self" is "really like," independently of the person's own report. One criterion often used is the descriptions provided by other people who know the subject well. As indicated in a preceding section, self- and other-reports are likely to correspond, on the average, when the attribute is similarly and thoroughly defined for both raters. Such correspondence, however, is not necessarily high for individual subjects; its absence in individual cases might be regarded as evidence of poor (i.e., inaccurate) self-awareness.

Two studies have been encountered which related the discrepancy between self- and other-reports to some different measure of normality. Luckey (1960b) had both husbands and wives rate themselves and each other on Leary's (1956) Interpersonal Check List. The greater the agreement between the two ratings of the same person, the higher was that person's score on Locke's (1951) Marital Adjustment Scale. In a study of graduate students at the University of California, Barron (1963) had each subject rate himself on an adjective check list; he was also rated on the same check list by the assessment staff of psychologists conducting the study. The greater the agreement between subject and assessment staff, the more likely was the subject to have been rated high by his professors on "all-around soundness as a person."

There are undoubtedly other studies of this type reported in the literature. The superiority of the two cited here lies in their use of identical, detailed rating instruments for both subject and judge. Under these conditions, one would expect agreement between the two; thus, lack of agreement may reasonably be attributed to deficiency in either the subject's or the rater's judgment. The obtained correlations with the external criteria of normality suggest that at least some of the discrepancy was due to the subjects' "lack of self-insight"—i.e., their failure to see themselves as others saw them. It would nevertheless be appropriate in such studies to partial out of the correlation any contribution attributable to the *level* of rating given by the subject or the judge, so that this component does not confound the discrepancy score.

BEHAVIORAL MEASURES

"Objective measures of behavior" refers to those records of performance which are minimally susceptible to observer bias, maximally amenable to interobserver agreement. These may be records of a subject's performance in a controlled, directly observed, experimental situation; or they may be records of past behavior (e.g., school grades, criminal offenses, marital status), compiled by someone else, for some purpose other than assessing mental health. Since any behavior must be interpreted and recorded in order to be used as scientific data, the boundary between "objective behavior," on the one hand, and self-reports or informant ratings, on the other, is by no means distinct. For most objective measures, there would be clear consensus among observers as to whether or not the particular behavior had occurred; but there might be room for considerable disagreement as to whether or not the designated behavior was relevant to "normality."

Exposure to psychiatric treatment is the behavioral criterion of abnormality which is probably most widely used by laymen and scientific researchers alike. It is generally assumed that such treatment results either from extreme dissatisfaction with self or from publicly recognized deviancy that is attributed to "emotional" causes. Several studies have found both psychiatric patients and clients of counseling services expressing more negative self-appraisals than nonpsychiatric comparison groups (Chase, 1957; Rogers & Dymond, 1954; Heilbrun & Goodstein, 1961); this is also the essential significance of the MMPI "validation" studies (Hathaway & McKinley, 1945; Welsh & Dahlstrom, 1956). Yet an occasional exception appears (e.g., Fiedler *et al.,* 1958) to remind one that exposure to treatment depends on factors other than degree of illness, independently defined. It depends also on availability of psychiatric services (Adams, 1961), on the willingness of the troubled person to use those services (Gurin, Veroff, & Feld, 1960), and on the community's tolerance for deviant behavior (Freeman & Simmons, 1959).

It is hard to think of groups of persons who can be designated "exceptionally well adjusted" with the same degree of confidence that persons under psychiatric treatment can be considered maladjusted. Gough (1960) has attempted to validate the "positive end" of his Socialization Scale of the California Psychological Inventory (Gough, 1957) by showing that certain groups of "exemplary probity and rectitude" score higher on this scale than do groups of subjects who have not attained an exceptional degree of "social maturity, integrity, and rectitude." Unfortunately, he offers no explicit basis for designating the level of a group's social maturity, independent of its mean score on the Socialization Scale; hence, the "demonstrated" relationship amounts to a circularity. Nevertheless, this direction of research appears essential—defining "known groups" of superior adjustment and comparing their scores on other measures of "normality" with those of groups whose adjustment is deemed average or inferior.

More specific behavioral criteria include performances that can be evaluated by standards of excellence germane to a particular group's functioning. Grades in school or quality of products in an achievement-oriented setting may be considered germane. Marshall (1958) found that judged quality of performance in 4-H club work correlated positively with sociometric status within the clubs. Gronlund and Holmlund (1958) found that *high school grades* of students who had been best liked in grade school, seven years earlier, tended to be better than those of students least liked in grade school. However, Fiedler *et al.* (1958) report no replicated correlation between grades in college and any of their other criteria of adjustment—self-acceptance, sociometric status, visits to the Counseling Bureau, etc.

One rather ambiguous criterion of adjustment is implicit in certain studies of normative pressure within experimentally contrived groups. In the typical experiment (see Asch, 1952, pp. 450–501; Crutchfield, 1955) the subject is required to judge accurately the physical characteristics of presented stimuli, while other group members (confederates of the experimenter) produce a consensus of false judgments. If "accurate perception" is regarded as one criterion of normality, then resistance to the group norm may be considered appropriate behavior; if, on the other hand, consensual judgment and social reality testing are deemed normal, then yielding to group standards may be the more appropriate. Mangan, Quartermain, and Vaughan (1959, 1960) claim to have demonstrated a positive association between *yielding* to the group norm and one self-report measure of adjustment, the Taylor Manifest Anxiety Scale, but their data are inappropriately analyzed (i.e., they assume independence of successive judgments from the same subject); hence the conclusion is suspect. Tudenham (1959b) found no significant correlations between response to another type of conformity experiment and scores on the Socialization Scale of the California Psychological Inventory. The trouble with these kinds of experimental arrangements for assessing "normality" is that two rather different criteria, accuracy (or veracity) and consensual validation, are artificially pitted against one another. Instances of such clear opposition between behavior determinants are probably rather rare in natural human interactions; hence the import of even clear experimental findings for "real-life" adjustment would remain ambiguous.

Any of the foregoing behavioral measures of normality may be criticized on the grounds that the behavior observed results from other determinants besides the assumed central variable, adjustment—e.g., from general intelligence or specific skills, from the reactions of evaluators to the subject's performance, from motivation or opportunity to perform in the manner deemed desirable. Thus, though "objective behavior" may be presumed, a priori, superior to self-reports or ratings, because of its relative freedom from subject or rather bias, it still provides no infallible criterion. It would seem that some of the deficiencies of behavioral measures might be overcome if they were treated psychometrically in the same fashion as self-reports and rating scales—that is, as "additive probabilistic" indicators of the presumed underlying trait (see Scott & Wertheimer, 1962, p. 136). Since the response to any paper-and-pencil test item is influenced by a variety of factors other than the one intentionally assessed, psychometricians typically pool a number of such indicators into a multiple-item scale, under the assumption that such irrelevant effects will vary from one item to another and hence be "cancelled out" in the summation. A comparable approach to "objective behavior test" development would entail pooling of numerous behavioral indicators, each moderately or slightly correlated with the others, into an over-all score. Needless to say, this kind of assessment would be much more expensive and time-consuming than presently used self-report or rating instruments. Whether it would provide more valid predictors of adjustment remains to be seen.

UNTANGLING THE CONCEPTIONS OF NORMALITY

The need for assessing the relationships among various criteria of normality, under various circumstances of appraisal, has been recognized for some time now (Jahoda, 1958; Scott, 1958). Yet the present review has hardly begun to cover the enormous number of relevant studies already available, let alone attempt to report a systematic program of research designed to fill crucial gaps in our understanding of "adjustment." One reason for this incomplete and fragmentary state of affairs is the very scope of the concept, normality. Almost any evaluated trait constitutes, from someone's perspective, a criterion of normality. Psychological theories are replete with evaluated traits—authoritarianism, prejudice, mental deficiency, shallow affect, love, creativity, achievement, will, and so forth. These concepts are largely borrowed from the vernacular, and the scientific discipline has not yet advanced to the stage where it can offer compelling substitutes or, better yet, a sound, consistent reformulation of the entire language referring to human behavior. Thus, the psychologist who would study the adaptation of man to his social surroundings is confronted with a plethora of concepts, each serving to simplify understanding of the complex processes, in ways that are difficult to coordinate. It is not always clear when two or more evaluated traits are conceptualized as distinct; it is even rarer to find them distinctly measured. Thus one does not know what to make of certain empirical results that are purported to establish a relationship between two or more criteria of normality.

Taking the language and instruments as we find them, we may attempt a limited summary of the foregoing empirical results referring to the relationships among definitions of adjustment. All of the studies have been conducted in the United States and, for the most part, within fairly homogeneous subject-populations. Therefore, the following propositions should be regarded partly as tentative empirical generalizations, partly as hypotheses that require exploration, in a larger cross-cultural literature as well as in systematic studies explicitly designed to test them.

1. Favorableness of the self-concept can be assessed reliably with self-report inventories from which the person's evaluation of his perceived self is determined directly or inferred from group norms or from a priori judgments of the investigator. Summative scores derived from various instruments of these types tend to show substantial positive correlations with each other, indicating that they measure a great deal in common.
2. The concept of "self" can be broken down into components, each of which may be assessed by some type of self-report instrument. With appropriate selection of items, it is possible to develop reliable and distinguishable measures of different "aspects" of the "self." Though these will probably show some degree of mutual intercorrelation, insofar as they all refer to evaluated attributes similarly assessed (i.e., by self-report), it is possible that, for some purposes, "self-acceptance" might better be restricted to a more limited domain than the "total self."
3. Liking for oneself tends to be associated with liking for other people. Both of these attitudes may be expressions of a more general positive hedonic tone that can be focused on various objects significant to the person; however, not enough different objects have been considered in previous research to demonstrate such a general tendency. Moreover, measures of attitude toward the self and attitude toward others have thus far been obtained exclusively by means of self-report instruments, so the possibility that the correlations are due to instrument, rather than trait, factors cannot be precluded.
4. Evaluated traits can be rated by external observers, with substantial agreement, providing they know the subject reasonably well and rate him by means of multiple-item instruments that specify the behaviors from which the trait is to be inferred.
5. The correspondence between observers' ratings and self-ratings of evaluated traits can be reasonably high, providing both subject and observer use the same multiple-item instrument that defines the trait explicitly.
6. When the trait to be rated is grossly defined (as, for example, in the typical sociometric test), any two raters are likely to show only limited agreement—due, in part, to differing rater biases and to tendencies toward reciprocated ratings between pairs of persons. However, if many raters' appraisals are pooled into a summative score (comparable to the pooling of item scores in a multiple-item inventory), substantially reliable mean ratings can be achieved.
7. There is not likely to be much correspondence between subjects' self-ratings and observers' appraisals when the trait being rated is loosely or differently defined—e.g., when the subject rates overall self-satisfaction and the observer rates his degree of liking for the subject. This is probably because the two sources of ratings focus on different attributes or evaluate a common set of attributes differently.
8. One probable exception to this general lack of correspondence (Proposition 7) occurs when the subject's task is to report his degree of liking for others and the others' (his peers') task is to report their degree of liking for him. Under

these circumstances, one is likely to find a positive correlation between mean ratings given to others and mean ratings received from others.

9. When observers rate a subject on different evaluated traits that are all somehow relevant for over-all appraisal—e.g., if the evaluated traits are functionally relevant for group performance and maintenance—the mean ratings received by subjects on the several traits are likely to be positively intercorrelated. This result probably reflects, in part, "halo effects" or tendencies toward "cognitive balance" of the raters and, in part, covariance among the culturally valued traits across subjects, the traits being correlated with the person's acceptability to others.
10. There is unlikely to be much correspondence between "normality" as defined by self-reports or by others' ratings, on the one hand, and any single objective measure of "normal" behavior, on the other. This is probably due, in large part, to the fact that any single measure—be it a questionnaire item or an observed act—is not sufficiently reliable, does not sufficiently sample the domain of events encompassed by the concept, to permit substantial correlation with some other measure. Before one can tell whether measures of objective behavior *can* correlate with "normality," otherwise defined, it will be necessary to develop scales of objective behavior which approach the internal consistency and reliability of self-report and rating instruments now in use.
11. The magnitudes of all correlations—among various self-report measures, among observers' ratings of evaluated traits, among objective behavior scales, and between these several classes of measures—can be increased substantially by expanding the range of persons to be appraised. This simple psychometric theorem has implications for the problem of distinguishing among persons in the "relatively normal" range, after elimination of the seriously maladjusted (such as hospitalized psychotics, for example). Even conceptually distinct criteria (e.g., intelligence and popularity) will correlate across the phylogenetic scale, if the measures remain constant and humans do the rating. But, within a more limited range—even including "exceptionally well adjusted" persons—measures of seemingly similar attributes will necessarily show reduced co-variances. Thus, the degree of correspondence among various measures of normality depends substantially upon the population of subjects considered.

UNIDIMENSIONALITY VS. MULTIDIMENSIONALITY

One of the questions most frequently raised in discussions of this type is whether mental health is to be conceived as a unitary quality or as a collection of distinct characteristics—whether it makes sense to talk about the "over-all level" of a person's adjustment or whether one must confine his description to a particular trait or particular circumstance. Perhaps the most widely accepted resolution at present is that "mental health is multidimensional, rather than unidimensional," implying that there are "degrees of normality" to be discerned along several continua, largely independent of one another.

Let it be recognized, however, that the very notions of "continuum" and "dimension" are human constructs imposed on the observed events. Though the concepts "unidimensional" and "multidimensional" can be defined geometrically in fairly clear terms, it is by no means clear just what they are to mean psychometrically (see Scott, 1968). Unless error of measurement is specifically excluded, almost any collection of test items will prove to be "multidimensional" by factor analytic procedures, even if they measure the "same trait" over and over, with identical questions. Procedures for discounting errors of measurement—e.g., by item pooling, by repeated measures, or by estimating communalities—are by no means exact. As a consequence, any set of measures must necessarily be found to yield only *relatively similar* or *relatively disparate* results; any group of test items can be only *relatively unidimensional,* and the number of additional dimensions required to encompass them will depend on the larger set of items that are included with them in a common factor analysis.

In other words, it makes little sense to inquire, Is such-and-such a trait unidimensional? for it is, or is not, depending on what traits it is to be distinguished from, and depending on one's cutting point for distinguishing "similar" from "different." A more appropriate phrasing of the question would be: Can trait *X* be distinguished psychometrically from trait *Y*? Applied to the present topic, this question might take such forms as: Can normality be distinguished from intelligence or from general adaptive capacity? Can satisfaction with self be distinguished from acceptance by others?

There is little doubt that such distinctions *can* be made—even, probably, if specific instrument factors are somehow eliminated so that differences in the measures reflect "true" differences between the intended traits. But one would still wish to question the purpose of the distinction. Whether or not two or more conceivably distinguishable traits are to be treated as different will ultimately depend on the uses to which they are to be put in predicting or understanding some other domain of events. It makes little difference that various "aspects of intelligence" can be distinguished when one is comparing cats and humans with respect to their relative adaptabilities to the public school system. Yet the finding (Birren, 1961) that among adults (ages 25–64) the several subscales of the Wechsler Adult Intelligence Scale correlated about as highly with educational level as they did with each other challenges the utility of a "general intelligence" concept, distinct from education, for this population of subjects and suggests that more refined concepts may be necessary.

Thus it is with "mental health." If one wishes to distinguish hospitalized psychotics from nonhospitalized persons, then a variety of measures might correlate with each other and correlate comparably with the external variable (hospitalization). But if one wishes to distinguish the adjustment levels of eminent and mediocre scientists, then more refined differentiation of "adjustment" will probably be called for and the various definitions will probably be poorly intercorrelated.

It would seem that one appropriate strategy of research into problems of "normality," "mental health," and "adjustment" would consist of the following phases:

1. Conceptualizing the focal attribute in such a way that it is explicitly distinguished from other attributes that are regarded as different.
2. Specifying the population of persons within which variance in the attribute is to be sought.
3. Constructing (or adopting) measures of the focal attribute together with measures of the allegedly distinct attributes, utilizing a variety of assessment procedures, and determining whether the different measures of the same attribute correlate better with one another than they do with different measures of presumably distinct attributes.
4. Combining scores from the diverse, intercorrelated measuring instruments into a composite score, which reflects the "best" measure of the attribute, not systematically contaminated by irrelevant instrument factors.
5. Correlating composite scores on one attribute with composite scores on a different "aspect of adjustment" to see if the two attributes co-vary in the specified population.

6. Systematically varying the circumstances of appraisal and the norms of appraisors to determine the magnitudes of variance contributed by these sources in relation to the magnitude of intersubject variance.
7. Determining, for a specified set of relevant external variables, whether the several distinguishable "aspects of normality" correlate similarly or distinctively, and deciding on this basis whether it makes sense to subsume some or all of them under a single concept of "over-all adjustment."

Such a programmatic approach to assessing various conceptions of normality has not yet been attempted. Until it is, we shall be unprepared to proclaim either the distinctive appropriateness of one conception or the essential commonality of different conceptions.

REFERENCES

Adams, H. B. The influence of social variables, treatment methods, and administrative factors on mental hospital admission rates. *Psychiat. Quart.*, 1961, 35, 353–372.

Affleck, D. C., & Garfield, S. L. The prediction of psychosis with the MMPI. *J. clin. Psychol.*, 1960, 16, 24–26.

Akeret, R. U. Interrelationships among various dimensions of the self concept. *J. consult. Psychol.*, 1959, 63, 199–201.

Allport, G. W. *Personality*. New York: Holt, 1937.

Asch, S. E. *Social psychology*. Englewood Cliffs, N.J.: Prentice-Hall, 1952.

Auble, D. Validity measures for the Heston Personal Adjustment Inventory. *J. appl. Psychol.*, 1957, 41, 79–81.

Barron, F. *Creativity and psychological health*. Princeton, N.J.: Van Nostrand, 1963.

Bell, H. M. *The adjustment inventory*. Stanford: Stanford University Press, 1934.

Berg, I. A. Measuring deviant behavior by means of deviant response sets. In B. M. Bass & I. A. Berg (Eds.), *Conformity and deviation*. New York: Harper, 1961.

Berger, E. The relationship between expressed acceptance of self and expressed acceptance of others. *J. abnorm. soc. Psychol.*, 1952, 47, 778–782.

Bills, R. E., Vance, E. L., & McLean, O. S. An index of adjustment and values. *J. consult. Psychol.*, 1951, 15, 257–261.

Birren, J. E. Research on the psychology of aging: Concepts and findings. In P. H. Hoch & J. Zubin (Eds.), *Psychopathology of aging*. New York: Grune & Stratton, 1961.

Birren, J. E., Jerome, E. A., & Chown, Sheila M. Aging and psychological adjustment: Problem solving and motivation. *Rev. Educ. Res.*, 1961, 31, 487–499.

Block, J., & Thomas, H. Is satisfaction with self a measure of adjustment? *J. abnorm. soc. Psychol.*, 1955, 51, 254–259.

Briggs, P. F., Wirt, R. D., & Johnson, R. An application of prediction tables to the study of delinquency. *J. consult. Psychol.*, 1961, 25, 46–50.

Burnham, W. H. *The normal mind*. New York: D. Appleton, 1924.

Butler, J. M., & Haigh, G. V. Changes in the relation between self-concepts and ideal concepts consequent upon client-centered counseling. In C. Rogers & Rosalind Dymond (Eds.), *Psychotherapy and personality change*. Chicago: Univer. of Chicago Press, 1954.

Campbell, D. T., & Fiske, D. W. Convergent and discriminant validation by the multitrait-multimethod matrix. *Psychol. Bull.*, 1959, 56, 81–105.

Cartwright, D. S., Kirtner, W. L., & Fiske, D. W. Method factors in changes associated with psychotherapy. *J. abnorm. soc. Psychol.*, 1963, 66, 164–175.

Cartwright, D. S., & Roth, I. Success and satisfaction in psychotherapy. *J. clin. Psychol.*, 1957, 13, 20–26.

Castaneda, A., McCandless, B. R., & Palermo, D. S. The children's form of the Manifest Anxiety Scale. *Child Develpm.*, 1956, 27, 317–326.

Cattell, R. B. *Personality and motivation structure and measurement*. New York: World Book Co., 1957.

Chase, P. H. Self concepts in adjusted and maladjusted hospital patients. *J. consult. Psychol.*, 1957, 21, 475–497.

Cowen, E. L. The social desirability of trait descriptive terms: Preliminary norms and sex differences. *J. soc. Psychol.*, 1961, 53, 225–233.

Cowen, E. L., Heilizer, F., & Axelrod, H. S.

The correlates of manifest anxiety in perceptual reactivity, rigidity, and self concept. *J. consult. Psychol.,* 1957, 21, 405–411.
Crowne, D. P., Stephens, M. W., & Kelly, R. The validity and equivalence of tests of self-acceptance. *J. Psychol.,* 1961, 51, 101–112.
Crutchfield, R. S. Conformity and character. *Amer. Psychologist,* 1955, 10, 191–198.
Davis, K. Mental hygiene and the class structure. *Psychiatry,* 1938, 1, 55–65.
Dickey, Brenda. Attitudes toward sex roles and feelings of adequacy in homosexual males. *J. consult. Psychol.,* 1961, 25, 116–122.
Dinitz, S., Scarpitti, F. R., & Reckless, W. C. Delinquency vulnerability: A cross group and longitudinal analysis. *Amer. sociol. Rev.,* 1962, 27, 515–517.
Eastman, D. Self acceptance and marital happiness. *J. consult. Psychol.,* 1958, 22, 95–99.
Eaton, J. W. The assessment of mental health. *Amer. J. Psychiat.,* 1951, 108, 81–90.
Edwards, A. L. *Edwards Personal Preference Schedule.* New York: Psychological Corporation, 1953.
Edwards, A. L. *The social desirability variable in personality assessment and research.* New York: Dryden, 1957.
Edwards, A. L. Social desirability or acquiescence in the MMPI? A case study with the SD Scale. *J. abnorm. soc. Psychol.,* 1961, 63, 351–359.
Ellsworth, R. B. *The MACC Behavioral Adjustment Scale.* Beverly Hills, Calif.: West. Psychol. Serv., 1962.
Ellsworth, R. B., & Clayton, W. H. Measurement of improvement in "mental illness." *J. consult. Psychol.,* 1959, 23, 15–20.
Engel, Mary. The stability of the self-concept in adolescence. *J. abnorm. soc. Psychol.,* 1959, 58, 211–215.
English, H. B., & English, Ava C. *A comprehensive dictionary of psychological and psychoanalytical terms.* New York: Longmans, Green, 1958.
Epstein, L. J. An analysis of teachers' judgments of problem children. *Pedag. Seminary & J. genet. Psychol.,* 1941, 59, 101–107.
Erikson, E. H. Growth and crises of the "healthy personality." In C. Kluckhohn, H. A. Murray, & D. M. Schneider (Eds.), *Personality in nature, society, and culture.* New York: Knopf, 1955, pp. 185–225.
Fairweather, G. W., Simon, R., Gebhard, M. E., Weingarten, E., Holland, J. L., Sanders, R., Stone, G. B., & Reahl, J. E. Relative effectiveness of psychotherapeutic programs. *Psychol. Monogr.,* 1960, 74, No. 5.
Ferguson, J. T., McReynolds, P., & Ballachey, E. L. *Hospital Adjustment Scale.* Palo Alto, Calif.: Consult. Psychologists Press, 1953.
Fey, W. F. Acceptance by others and its relation to acceptance of self and others: A revaluation. *J. abnorm. soc. Psychol.,* 1955, 50, 274–276.
Fiedler, F. E., Dodge, Joan S., Jones, R. E., & Hutchins, E. G. Interrelations among measures of personality adjustment in nonclinical populations. *J. abnorm. soc. Psychol.,* 1958, 56, 345–351.
Fordyce, W. E., & Crow, W. R. Ego disjunction: A failure to replicate Trehub's results. *J. abnorm. soc. Psychol.,* 1960, 60, 466–448.
Forsythe, R. P., & Fairweather, G. W. Psychotherapeutic and other hospital treatment criteria: The dilemma. *J. abnorm. soc. Psychol.,* 1961, 62, 598–604.
Freeman, H. E., & Simmons, O. G. The social integration of mental patients. *Internat. J. soc. Psychiat.,* 1959, 5, 264–271.
Freides, D. Toward the elimination of the concept of normality. *J. consult. Psychol.,* 1960, 24, 128–133.
French, J. R. P., & Kahn, R. L. A programmatic approach to studying the industrial environment and mental health. *J. soc. Issues,* 1962, 18, No. 3, 1–47.
Freud, S. *New introductory lectures in psychoanalysis.* New York: Norton, 1933.
Freud, S. *The problem of anxiety.* (Engl. transl.) New York: Norton, 1936.
Fromm, E. *Escape from freedom.* New York: Farrar & Rinehart, 1941.
Gough, H. G. A sociological theory of psychopathy. *Amer. J. Sociol.,* 1948, 53, 359–366.
Gough, H. *California Psychological Inventory manual.* Palo Alto, Calif.: Consult. Psychologists Press, 1957.
Gough, H. Theory and measurement of socialization. *J. consult. Psychol.,* 1960, 24, 23–30.
Gronlund, N., & Holmlund, W. S. The value of elementary school sociometric status scores for predicting pupils' adjustment in high school. *Educ. Administ. & Supervis.,* 1958, 44, 255–260.
Grossberg, J. M. Behavior therapy: A review. *Psychol. Bull.,* 1964, 62, 73–88.

Gurin, G., Veroff, J., & Feld, Sheila. *Americans view their mental health*. New York: Basic Books, 1960.

Hathaway, S. R., & McKinley, J. C. *Manual for the MMPI*. New York: Psycholog. Corporation, 1945.

Heilbrun, A. B., Jr. The psychological significance of the MMPI *K* scale in a normal population. *J. consult. Psychol.,* 1961, 25, 486–491.

Heilbrun, A. B., Jr. Social value-social behavior inconsistency and early signs of psychopathology in adolescence. *Child Develpm.,* 1963, 34, 187–194.

Heilbrun, A. B., Jr., & Goodstein, L. Consistency between social desirability ratings and item endorsement as a function of psychopathology. *Psychol. Rep.,* 1961, 8, 69–70.

Heston, J. C. *Manual, Heston Personal Adjustment Inventory*. New York: World Book Co., 1949.

Hoffman, M. Psychiatry, nature, and science. *Amer. J. Psychiat.,* 1960, 117, 205–210.

Holtzman, W. H., & Bitterman, M. E. A factorial study of adjustment to stress. *J. abnorm. soc. Psychol.,* 1956, 52, 179–185.

Horney, K. *New ways in psychoanalysis*. New York: Norton, 1939.

Iscoe, I., & Garden, Joyce A. Field dependence, manifest anxiety, and sociometric status in children. *J. consult. Psychol.,* 1961, 25, 184.

Jackson, D. N., & Messick, S. Response styles on the MMPI: Comparison of clinical and normal samples. *J. abnorm. soc. Psychol.,* 1962, 65, 285–299.

Jahoda, Marie. *Current concepts of positive mental health*. New York: Basic Books, 1958.

Jessor, R., Liverant, S., & Opochinsky, S. Imbalance in need structure and maladjustment. *J. abnorm. soc. Psychol.,* 1963, 66, 271–275.

Leary, T. *Multilevel measurement of interpersonal behavior*. Berkeley, Calif.: Psychol. Consultation Serv., 1956.

Lichtenberg, P., Cassetta, Rhondda, & Scanlon, J. C. Mutual achievement strivings: A continuum for mental health. *J. abnorm. soc. Psychol.,* 1961, 63, 619–628.

Liverant, S. The use of Rotter's social learning theory in developing a personality inventory. *Psychol. Monogr.,* 1958, 72, No. 2.

Locke, H. J. *Predicting adjustment in marriage*. New York: Holt, 1951.

Locke, H. J., & Wallace, K. M. Short marital-adjustment and predictions tests: Their reliability and validity. *Marriage and family living,* 1959, 21, 251–255.

Lorr, M. Multidimensional scale for rating psychiatric patients. *U.S. Veterans Administ. tech. Bull.,* 1953, TB 10-507, 1–44.

Luckey, Eleanor B. Implications for marriage counseling of self perceptions and spouse perceptions. *J. counsel. Psychol.,* 1960, 7, 3–9. (a)

Luckey, Eleanor B. Marital satisfaction and its association with congruence of perception. *Marriage and family living,* 1960, 22, 49–54. (b)

Lund, F. H., & Glosser, H. J. The nature of mental illness: Diversity of psychiatric opinion. *Education,* 1957, 78, 154–166.

Mangan, G. L., Quartermain, D., & Vaughan, G. M. Relationship between Taylor *MAS* scores and group conformity. *Percept. mot. Skills,* 1959, 9, 207–209.

Mangan, G. L., Quartermain, D., & Vaughan, G. M. Taylor *MAS* and group conformity pressure. *J. abnorm. soc. Psychol.,* 1960, 61, 146–147.

Marks, J. B. Interests, leadership, and sociometric status among adolescents. *Sociometry,* 1954, 17, 340–349.

Marshall, Helen R. Prediction of social acceptance in community youth groups. *Child Develpm.,* 1958, 29, 173–184.

Martin, B. The measurement of anxiety. *J. gen. Psychol.,* 1959, 61, 189–203.

Matarazzo, Ruth G., Matarazzo, J. D., & Saslow, G. The relationships between medical and psychiatric symptoms. *J. abnorm. soc. Psychol.,* 1961, 62, 55–61.

Maughs, S. B. Psychopathic personality: Review of the literature, 1940–1947. *J. clin. Psychopath.,* 1949, 10, 247–275.

McIntyre, C. J. Acceptance by others and its relation to acceptance of self and others. *J. abnorm. soc. Psychol.,* 1952, 47, 624–625.

Menninger, K. A. *The human mind*. (2nd ed.) New York: Knopf, 1937.

Miller, D. R., & Swanson, G. E. *Inner conflict and defense*. New York: Holt, 1960.

Miller, N. E., & Dollard, J. *Social learning and imitation*. New Haven: Yale Univer. Press, 1941.

Miyamoto, S. F., & Dornbusch, S. M. A test of interactionist hypotheses of self-conception. *Amer. J. Sociol.,* 1956, 61, 399–403.

Mouton, Jane S., Blake, R. R., & Fruchter, B. The reliability of sociometric measures. *Sociometry,* 1955, 18, 7–48.

Mowrer, O. H. A stimulus-response analysis of anxiety and its role as a reinforcing agent. *Psychol. Rev.,* 1939, 41, 553–565.

Mowrer, O. H. "Sin," the lesser of two evils. *Amer. Psychologist,* 1960, 15, 301–304.

Mowrer, O. H. Payment or repayment? The problem of private practice. *Amer. Psychologist,* 1963, 18, 577–580.

Mowrer, O. H. *The new group therapy.* New York: Van Nostrand, 1964.

Mussen, P. H., & Jones, Mary C. Self-conceptions, motivations, and interpersonal attitudes of late- and early-maturing boys. *Child Develpm.,* 1957, 28, 243–256.

Neugarten, Bernice, Havighurst, R. J., & Tobin, S. S. The measurement of life satisfaction. *J. Geront.,* 1961, 16, 134–143.

Nichols, R. C., & Beck, K. W. Factors in psychotherapy change. *J. consult. Psychol.,* 1960, 24, 388–399.

Omwake, K. T. The relationship between acceptance of self and acceptance of others shown by three personality inventories. *J. consult. Psychol.,* 1954, 18, 443–446.

Phillips, E. L. Attitudes toward self and others: A brief questionnaire report. *J. consult. Psychol.,* 1951, 15, 79–81.

Preston, G. H. *The substance of mental health.* New York: Farrar & Rinehart, 1943.

Raimy, V. C. Phrenophobia and psychotherapy. Presidential address, Division of Clin. Psychol., APA, September, 1963.

Redlich, F. C. The concept of normality. *Amer. J. Psychother.,* 1952, 6, 551–569.

Reese, H. W. Relationships between self-acceptance and sociometric choices. *J. abnorm. soc. Psychol.,* 1961, 62, 472–474.

Rennie, T. A. C., & Woodward, L. E. *Mental health in modern society.* New York: Commonwealth, 1948.

Reznikoff, M., & Toomey, L. C. The weighted *Qsort.* A procedure for quantitatively estimating emotional disturbance and personality change. *J. consult. Psychol.,* 1958, 22, 187–190.

Rogers, C. R. Measuring personality adjustment in children nine to thirteen years of age. *Teachers college contributions to education,* 1931, No. 458.

Rogers, C. R., & Dymond, Rosalind F. *Psychotherapy and personality change.* Chicago: Univer. of Chicago Press, 1954.

Rosengren, W. R., & Davids, A. Self-esteem, social perception, and social status in a group of child psychiatric patients. *Percept. mot. Skills,* 1961, 13, 63–72.

Rosenthal, D., Lawlor, W. G., Zahn, T. P., & Shakow, D. The relationship of some aspects of mental set to degree of schizophrenic disorganization. *J. Pers.,* 1960, 28, 26–38.

Scott, W. A. Research definitions of mental health and mental illness. *Psychol. Bull.,* 1958, 55, 29–45.

Scott, W. A. *Values and organizations: A study of fraternities and sororities.* Chicago: Rand McNally, 1965.

Scott, W. A. Attitude measurement. In G. Lindzey & E. Aronson (Eds.), *Handbook of social psychology.* (Rev. ed.) Cambridge, Mass.: Addison-Wesley, 1968.

Scott, W. A., & Wertheimer, M. *Introduction to psychological research.* New York: Wiley, 1962.

Serot, Naomi M., & Teevan, R. C. Perception of the parent-child relationship and its relation to child adjustment. *Child Develpm.,* 1961, 32, 373–378.

Sheerer, E. T. An analysis of the relationship between acceptance of and respect for others in 10 counseling cases. *J. consult. Psychol.,* 1949, 13, 169–175.

Smith, M. B. Optima of mental health. *Psychiatry,* 1950, 13, 503–510.

Smith, M. B. Research strategies toward a conception of positive mental health. *Amer. Psychologist,* 1959, 14, 673–681.

Smith, M. B. "Mental Health" reconsidered: A special case of the problem of values in psychology. *Amer. Psychologist,* 1961, 16, 299–306.

Stilson, D. W., Mason, D. J., Gynther, M. D., & Gertz, B. An evaluation of the comparability and reliabilities of two behavior rating scales for mental patients. *J. consult. Psychol.,* 1958, 22, 213–216.

Storrow, H. A. The measurement of outcome in psychotherapy. *Arch. gen. Psychiat.,* 1960, 2, 142–149.

Strong, D. J. A factor analytic study of several measures of self concept. *J. counsel. Psychol.,* 1962, 9, 64–70.

Strong, D. J., & Feder, D. D. Measurement of the self concept: A critique of the literature. *J. counsel. Psychol.,* 1961, 8, 170–178.

Suinn, R. M. The relationship between self-acceptance and acceptance of others: A learning theory analysis. *J. abnorm. soc. Psychol.*, 1961, 63, 37–42.

Stock, D. An investigation into the interrelations between the self concept and feelings directed toward other persons and groups. *J. consult. Psychol.*, 1949, 13, 176–180.

Szasz, T. S. The myth of mental illness. *Amer. Psychologist,* 1960, 15, 113–118.

Szasz, T. S. *The myth of mental illness*. New York: Hoeber-Harper, 1961.

Tapia, F., Jekel, J., & Domke, H. A. Enuresis: An emotional symptom? *J. nerv. ment. Dis.*, 1960, 130, 61–66.

Tindall, R. H. Relationships among indices of adjustment status. *Educ. Psychol. Measmt,* 1955, 15, 152–162.

Trehub, A. Ego disjunction and psychopathology. *J. abnorm. soc. Psychol.*, 1959, 58, 191–194.

Tuddenham, R. D. Studies in reputation: I. Sex and grade differences in school children's evaluation of their peers. II. The diagnosis of social adjustment. *Psychol. Monogr.*, 1952, 66, No. 1.

Tuddenham, R. D. The constancy of personality ratings over two decades. *Genet. Psychol. Monogr.*, 1959, 60, 3–29. (a)

Tuddenham, R. D. Correlates of yielding to a distorted group norm. *J. Pers.*, 1959, 27, 272–284. (b)

Van Evra, Judy P., & Rosenberg, B. G. Ego strength and ego disjunction in primary and secondary psychopaths. *J. clin. Psychol.*, 1963, 19, 61–63.

Welsh, G. S., & Dahlstrom, W. G. (Eds.) *Basic readings on the MMPI in psychology and medicine*. Minneapolis: Univer. of Minnesota Press, 1956.

Winthrop, H. Self-images of personal adjustment vs. the estimates of friends. *J. social Psychol.*, 1959, 50, 87–99.

Wishner, J. The concept of efficiency in psychological health and in psychopathology. *Psychol. Rev.*, 1955, 62, 69–80.

Zax, M., & Klein, A. Measurement of personality and behavior changes following psychotherapy. *Psychol. Bull.*, 1960, 57, 435–448.

Zelen, S. Acceptance and acceptability: An examination of social reciprocity. *J. consult. Psychol.*, 1954, 18, 316.

Zuckerman, M., & Monashkin, I. Self-acceptance and psychopathology. *J. consult. Psychol.*, 1957, 21, 145–149.

CHAPTER 20 Defense Mechanisms

CHARLES W. ERIKSEN
University of Illinois
JAN PIERCE
State University of Iowa

DEFINITIONS AND CLASSIFICATIONS

In the broadest context, defense mechanisms are behaviors in response to stress or fear, but the term as used in personality and clinical psychology is restricted to mean responses elicited by fear or anxiety coming from specified sources or cues. These sources of anxiety are covert or, as Inglis (1961) conceives it, mediating reactions of the human organism. The laboratory rat can show defensive avoidance responses to the light or buzzer that has become a conditioned signal for shock, but only the human has the extensive capacity to contain these conditioned cues of anxiety within himself.

As has been noted, man is a time binder. Through his capacity for covert behavior in the form of thought, memory, consciousness, or mediating processes, he is capable of bringing not only the past but also the future to the immediate present. He can relive in the present anxiety- or fear-provoking experiences of the past, and he can anticipate in the present such experiences in the future. It is how man controls and responds to these internal signals that elicit anxiety that constitutes the phenomena of defensive mechanisms. They are man's way of controlling his thoughts by repression or avoidance, by engaging in rationalizations, or by other behaviors that have the capacity to reassure or reduce these internally stimulated fears.

Freudian Conceptions of Defenses

Most of the descriptive cataloguing of defensive mechanisms has been contributed by Freud and other psychoanalytic writers. As a consequence, the descriptions and conceptions of the defensive mechanisms are interwoven with other psychoanalytic concepts, and laboratory research frequently has been confounded with them.

Our current conceptions of defense mechanisms had their beginnings in 1895 when Freud first used the term *repression* to describe unconsciously motivated memory loss in hysterical patients. By 1926 he had arrived at the "modern" psychoanalytic formulation: *defense mechanisms* were *all* protective devices used by the ego against instinctual demands. Repression, which for a time had been a synonym for defense, was again defined specifically as unconscious forgetting or amnesia, and anxiety was given a central position as the cause rather than an effect of defensive behavior.

Currently there is disagreement among psychoanalytic writers on how to divide the defense mechanisms in meaningful ways, on what are or are not properly considered as defense mechanisms, and on other essentially classificatory problems. Fenichel (1945), for example, distinguishes between successful defenses (those which result in the termination of the anxiety-provoking impulse, such as sublimation) and unsuccessful defenses (those which require continuing enervating pathological activation to prevent the recurrence of the impulse). Included in Fenichel's unsuccessful category are most commonly discussed mechanisms: denial, projection, repression, reaction formation, isolation, and displacement. Freud distinguishes between repressive defenses (e.g., amnesia, reaction formation, and projection) and nonrepressive ones (e.g., regression and sublimation). White (1948) talks of primary defenses such as denial and repression as contrasted with secondary ones such as projection, reaction formation, displacement, and intellectualization. He sees the secondary defenses as fortifying and resolving inconsistencies left by the primary defenses. Distinctions are also sometimes made between general (i.e., characterological) and specific defenses, as well as between "normal" and "pathological" ones.

Another dichotomy is the familiar one used by Freud to distinguish between material that was never conscious, or by some interpretations, was repressed in early childhood (primal repression) and material that was once conscious but no longer is (repression proper or after expulsion). In this context, secondary repression is the repression of material that is cognitively associated with that of the repression proper.

Not all anxiety, according to Freudian theory, is dealt with by means of the classical defense mechanisms. Real anxiety (that resulting from genuine external dangers) is not. Defense mechanisms are created either by neurotic anxiety (fear of punishment for instinctual gratification) or by moral anxiety (which emanates from the superego). In specific terms these distinctions are not always sharp. The crucial point is that internal anxiety-provoking events such as thoughts and feelings are typically defended against, while external fear-arousing situations are not. Freud (1957) points out, in addition, that the existence of anxiety or tension is not sufficient in itself to motivate the classical defensive maneuvers. There must also be a threat to one's ego ideal or self-esteem. This explains for Freud why, in the case of unsatisfied hunger, "nothing in the nature of a repression seems ... to come remotely into question" (Freud, 1925). It is clear that contrary to popular belief, orthodox psychoanalytic defense mechanisms do not proceed from instinctual pressures alone.

A further distinction is made by Freud between the primal or traumatic anxiety of childhood, which originates from unfulfilled physiological need, separation from the mother, or threat of castration, and signal anxiety, which is the adult's fear that these repressed childhood traumas will recur. It is signal anxiety that motivates defense mechanisms.

Much of the support for the existence and operation of defensive mechanisms, and most particularly of repression, has come from clinical sources: failures in free association, inability to accept or understand interpretations made by the analyst, lateness, hostility, falling behind on the fee, premature termination, otherwise inexplicable lapses of memory, changes in the details of dreams or events upon retelling—in short, all of the myriad manifestations of resistance. That the repressed material still exists in the unconscious is demonstrated by reference to symptoms, dreams, slips of tongue, jokes, etc.

A list of defense mechanisms, even if restricted to those which are commonly mentioned by major psychoanalytic works, is impressive in its length: asceticism, amnesia, condemnation, conversion, creativity, denial, destruction in the id, displacement, externalization, fixation, identification, intellectualization, introjection, phobia, projection, rationalization, reaction formation, regression, repression, reversal, sublimation, turning against the self, undoing, etc. It is a motley grouping, and claims are virtually never made for its inclusiveness. Freud (1936) described repression as creating mental gaps which the other defense mechanisms fill by distorting reality in various ways. Other psychoanalytic writers differ in the importance they assign to repression. Some simply consider it to be frequent in occurrence, while others maintain that all defenses are essentially repressive.

If much psychoanalytic literature is devoted to describing the relationship between repression and the other defenses, more is devoted to detailing the relationships of the various defense mechanisms to each other. Phobia and sublimation are both seen in some quarters as forms of displacement. Projection is, or is not, considered synonymous with externalization. Isolation is a variety of intellectualization and/or a step beyond reaction formation. Repression is seen as an outgrowth of the more primitive mechanism of denial or, on the contrary, as the most primitive mechanism itself. Projection is divided into complementary and supplementary types, and complementary projection is then likened to rationalization. Asceticism is distinguished descriptively from repression. Still other segments of the classical defense literature place the defense mechanisms in developmental age sequence, explain the operation of the defense mechanisms in neurotic disorders, and call attention to their similarity to or differences from so-called normal mental processes (e.g., isolation vs. objectivity). Certain ubiquitous questions are asked and answered: Can sublimation be creative? How can one distinguish a reaction formation from genuine "goodness"? Is identification really a defense mechanism?

From the viewpoint of a behavioral scientist the psychoanalytic defense literature leaves much to be desired. The bulk of it was not written with experimental verification as a goal. At the descriptive level it is replete with surplus meaning. It has the advantages of a naturalistic, semiliterary descriptive system but lacks the operational definitions and specificity of terms required of a science of behavior. Because of this and because of its lack of concern with specifying the details of operation of defensive processes in terms of laboratory-derived concepts of learning, memory, perception, and motivation, Freudian concepts of defense cannot be directly translated to the experimental laboratory. Psychoanalytic theory has called attention to an important class of human behaviors and suggested research hypotheses, but further progress in understanding of these behaviors requires careful laboratory analysis and integration with the concepts and knowledge of experimental psychology.

EXPERIMENTAL STUDIES ON DEFENSIVE MECHANISMS

The majority of experiments on defense mechanisms have been designed to test Freudian ideas of repression, but we need not confine ourselves to examining these studies only from this point of view. To the extent that the methodology of an experiment is adequate in producing anxiety, conflict, or high arousal and the cues eliciting these states are covert, the study yields information on defensive processes. We might not find evidence of clear erasure of memory in the Freudian repression sense. Instead the results might indicate differential attention, differential rehearsal, or selection of other activities by the subject to avoid anxiety. Typically these alternative interpretations for repression phenomena have been considered as criticisms of the studies, but to the extent that they are valid, they also provide us with information on defensive behavior. They indicate how individuals respond to anxiety cues that are internal.

Some Methodological Considerations for Experiments on Defense Mechanisms

Before turning to an examination of the experimental results on repression and defensive mechanisms, it will be helpful first to consider certain logical criteria that must be met if an experiment is to prove capable of providing information on this topic. Many experiments have provided little information on defensive processes because of the experimenter's failure to insure that the material employed in the experiment was indeed anxiety-provoking for his subjects. Early studies on repression, for example, attempted to demonstrate the repressive process by showing that people remembered pleasant experiences more frequently than unpleasant ones or that words or nonsense syllables associated with pleasant odors were better recalled than those associated with unpleasant odors. Sears (1936) pointed out that such studies were inadequate because one cannot equate *unpleasant* with *anxiety-provoking*. Research for the most part has increased in sophistication from these early studies, but one still finds experimenters who make the highly dubious assumption that words such as *bitch, belly,* and *raped* are potent anxiety arousers for the majority of their college student subjects. It would seem clear that the first requisite for an experiment on defensive mechanisms would be an adequate demonstration that the stimuli employed in the experiment are actually anxiety-provoking for the individual subjects.

While defensive mechanisms are related to the broader context of responses to anxiety, the term is traditionally reserved for anxiety elicited by covert stimuli or cues. Thus, to qualify as an experiment on defensive mechanisms the experimental method must provide that the anxiety-provoking stimuli reside in the subject's thoughts or internal drive-produced stimuli. One would not expect to test the hypothesis that repression occurs by noting whether or not a subject represses the real situation of a charging lion. Similarly, repression would not be expected to occur in an experimental arrangement where the subject pronounces a nonsense syllable that is then followed by an electric shock. In neither situation is repression of the stimulus an adaptive or an effective response. Repression of the charging lion could be an effective reducer of anxiety for at the most a matter of seconds. Likewise, in the experimental arrangement, whether or not the subject pronounces the nonsense syllable or recalls it, he will be shocked. Thus, a minimum requirement of experimental methods is that avoidance, inhibition, or distortion of the anxiety-arousing covert cue will be effective; it will reinforce the subject by preventing anxiety.

A third requirement for experimental investigations in this area is one that is frequently overlooked. It requires that the experimental arrangement provide enough freedom for the subject to use defensive mechanisms without generating more anxiety than he avoids. One would not expect to elicit repression in a subject by pronouncing clearly and audibly a dirty anxiety-provoking word and then immediately asking the subject to reproduce the word. Even though the word might be highly effective in generating anxiety, the subject is under the motivation to behave in a reasonable manner. To fail to reproduce a word under these clear, unambiguous circumstances might well be expected to make him more anxious about his sanity and ability than the anxiety he avoids by forgetting the word. Satisfactory experimental conditions must be such that the subject is not placed in a conflict between anxiety elicited by the stimulus material and anxiety generated by failure to perform on the experimental task.

A final requirement is a provision in the

experimental arrangement for individual differences in the responses of the subjects. Individual differences are to be expected on several grounds; foremost is the clinical observation that different people use different types of defensive mechanisms. As Eriksen (1951b) has pointed out, the perceptual and memory consequences of a subject using a repressive or avoidant type of defense mechanism are apt to be quite different from those of a subject who employs projection or reaction formation. Whereas the use of the former defenses seems to rely for its effectiveness upon the avoidance of the anxiety-provoking thought or memory, the use of the latter mechanisms seems to be, at least clinically, characterized by a sensitization to the anxiety-related material. Thus the paranoid seems to be particularly sensitive in detecting in other people his own unacceptable impulses, and the person who engages in reaction formation is actively seeking out instances of the threatening impulse so that they can be campaigned against and denounced.

A second source for individual differences may lie in the differential effectiveness of the experiment in arousing anxiety in different subjects. Subjects may well differ in the amount of anxiety which is required in order to trigger their defenses. Inglis (1961) has suggested that an experimental situation that is stressful enough to activate the defenses in introversive subjects may be too mild a stress to produce defensive behavior in extraverts. An extensive literature indicates that as drive or arousal level increases, specific task performance reaches a maximum and then decreases. Inglis has suggested that as the level of stress in the experimental situation increases, the introversive subjects are brought past the point of drive level where their avoidant defenses are effective. With the collapse of these defenses a new manifestation of their behavior in the experimental situation occurs. For the extraverted subjects, on the other hand, as the stress level increases, their avoidant responses come into play. Studies investigating personality correlates of defensive behavior lend substance to Inglis's theorizing (Byrne, 1964). An experiment that is not prepared to take into account these individual differences in defensive behavior may well fail to find evidence of defense, because the combined effect of individual differences in defensive response is averaged out in the data.

Types of Laboratory Approaches

The laboratory methods that have been used for studying repression and other defensive behaviors may be conveniently classed into three broad types. The first of these involves *learning tasks* in which the dependent variable is either rate of acquisition or memory or both. Differential learning for neutral and emotional material is sought. A second approach makes use of *perceptual recognition* as the basic experimental task, and the dependent variable is some measure of the structuredness or clarity of neutral and affective material that is required before the subject can recognize these stimuli. The third approach has made use of *hypnotically induced conflicts* and subsequent investigation of these induced conflicts upon memory, associations, and autonomic nervous system behavior. Both the learning and the perceptual approaches may be further subdivided depending upon whether they experimentally produce anxiety and repressions in the subjects or depend upon learned anxieties and repressions that the subjects bring to the experimental situation with them. In the next section the logic underlying these different methodologies as well as the special problems they encounter is considered along with the results of representative experiments.

Experiments Employing Learning and Memory Tasks

Experiments that assume existing repressions—These experiments have in common a methodology that either assumes the existence of repression for certain types of stimuli in most subjects or, at a more sophisticated level, infers the existence of repression in a subject from his responses to a test. The experiment then consists of an attempt to show impaired learning and/or memory for stimulus material in the area of the detected or assumed repression. At the more sophisticated level the methodology is essentially a variation of the method of construct validation. On the basis of a specific clinical or personality theory, response-response relations are tied together by a theoretical construct. Blocking or other signs of affective disturbance for a stimulus word on a word association test, for example, are related via the concept of repression to the prediction that such a stimulus word would be more difficult to learn and recall if used in paired-associate learning. Or a discrepancy between a subject's self-concept and the way he is perceived by others would lead via Rogers' 1951 self theory to the expectation that the subject would be more apt to forget or repress material pertaining to this self-concept discrepancy. All the experiments employing this methodology rely upon theory at some level to justify their expectation that repression would be expected for the stimulus material they choose.

Freudian theory as well as a general knowledge of our culture would suggest that sexual ideation and drives would be likely sources of repression. Flanagan (1930) devised a list of paired associates in which the nonsense-syllable stimulus members when paired with the response syllables sounded like sexual words, e.g., piy-nis. He found poorer learning and recall of the sexual pairs than for neutral nonsense-syllable combinations. Williams (1951) assumed that aggressive ideation and impulses would also be expected to have a high incidence of repression and found decrements in learning of words pertaining to violence. Wilkinson and Cargill (1955) reported poorer recall of content from Oedipal theme stories than from neutral stories.

Kott (1955) elaborated upon this basic methodology by employing both a normal and a hospitalized anxious sample. Both groups of subjects were required to learn nonsense-syllable responses to sexual, unpleasant, and neutral word stimuli in a paired-associate procedure. Contrary to expectation, the hospitalized anxious subjects were more efficient in learning and retention of the nonsense-syllable associates to sexual words than to neutral and unpleasant words, while the reverse held true for the normal group.

Experiments employing this methodology shed little light upon the process of repression or upon defenses, particularly if negative results are obtained. They are limited by the tenuous assumption that the area of conflict chosen, whether sex, hostility, or some other area, is one involving repressions in the majority of their subjects. No independent operations are employed to substantiate this assumption, and in the case of negative results, one cannot be certain whether it is the absence of a repressivelike defense that is responsible or the failure of the assumption. Since the recall and learning of the emotional material is evaluated with reference to neutral material, these studies also encounter the problem of assuring that both classes of material are equally difficult for learning and retention, irrespective of emotional connotation. Thus, in the Wilkinson and Cargill study one can reasonably question whether the content of the Oedipal stories was equivalent to the neutral stories in interest value, difficulty, and other variables determining retention. In experiments such as that of Flanagan, one can ask whether the impaired learning obtained for the sexual nonsense pairs was not due to some reluctance on the part of the subjects to verbalize "dirty" words in the presence of the experimenter.

One methodological difficulty that is encountered in studies using the paired-associate procedure is whether the emotional word should be used as the stimulus (Jacobs, 1955; Kott, 1955; Truax, 1957) or response member of the associate pair (Eriksen,

1952a; Merrill, 1954). Truax defends his procedure, in which the emotional word is the stimulus member and a nonsense syllable is the response, by arguing that there is less likelihood of the subjects engaging in deliberate response suppression due to reluctance to verbalize the emotional word.

However, any gain that comes from eliminating response suppression by using the emotional word as the stimulus in the associate pair is more than counteracted by the fact that this order of pairing tends to vitiate the conditions under which one would expect avoidance defenses to operate. When the subject is presented the emotional word as the stimulus member, there is nothing he can do to avoid the anxiety that it may engender. In fact, the affect that is supposedly generated in the subject by this stimulus may very well serve as a distraction that impairs his learning performance, or it may lead to competing responses through internally produced cues which compete with his correct anticipation of the nonsense-syllable response. Since the act of repression is supposed to have the adaptive function of preventing the anxiety from coming to mind or being felt by the subject, there is little the subject can do in this procedure in an adaptive way except to learn as quickly as possible and get the unpleasant task over with.

On the other hand, if the nonsense material or neutral words are used as the stimulus members in the associate pairs, the subject is required to dredge up the emotional words from his own response repertoire. This procedure would seem to be maximally sensitive to any inhibiting influences on these emotional stimuli which may exist within the subject or any impoverishment they may have in his response hierarchies. It allows the repressive defense to be adaptive, since if the subject doesn't think of the emotional word, he avoids the associated anxiety.

Experiments using individual criteria of anxiety—More informative than the above studies are those experiments that have made use of personality theory and clinical lore to determine by independent tests or measures anxiety-eliciting stimuli in individual subjects. Clinical case histories, word-association tests, and other clinical diagnostic instruments have been employed in selecting stimuli that would be anxiety arousing. Most extensively used has been word association, perhaps because of the extensive clinical acceptance of this technique as a means of detecting psychological "sore spots" in the individual. Complex indicators such as blocking, long reaction-time, or peculiar responses, along with signs of autonomic nervous system disturbance, are assumed to result from the affective disturbance caused by the stimulus word or from lack of availability of associations due to repression in the content area. In relating performance on a word-association test to learning and memory procedures, this methodology takes a construct validation approach to the concept of repression. It draws upon a large number of observed relations of word-association procedures and relates them to learning and memory performance via the repression concept.

Experiments employing this methodology have generally been successful in demonstrating that words to which a subject shows disturbance on the word-association test take longer to learn or are harder to recall, or both, than words that do not elicit indications of disturbance. Among the better controlled of these studies are the experiments by Merrill (1954) and Levinger and Clark (1961).

For each subject in his experimental group, Merrill selected from a word-association list stimulus words that had elicited indications of disturbance, as well as a set of neutral or control words. For each experimental subject a control subject was selected who had shown neutral response or lack of disturbance for the words upon which his matched experimental subject had indicated disturbance. Both experimental and control subjects were required to learn the selected words as response members to nonsense-syllable stimuli in a paired-associate procedure. Although there were no significant differences between the experimental and control groups in the number of trials to reach the learning criterion, on two subsequent recall measures the experimental subjects showed poorer retention of the disturbing words relative to the neutral words. The control subjects recalled words from both groupings about equally well and at about the level of recall for neutral words shown by the experimental subjects.

Levinger and Clark (1961) introduced a modification in the usual procedure. Instead of forming paired associates from words producing disturbances on a word-association list, they required that the subject remember the responses he had given on a first administration of a word-association list when each of the stimulus words was now repeated. Subjects showed significantly higher GSRs while giving associations which they later failed to recall. Also, stimulus words rated highly emotional by the experimenters, and independently by the subjects, were far more likely to elicit associations that were later forgotten than were those stimuli rated low on emotionality.

Laffal (1955) has suggested that disturbance indicators on word-association tests occurred predominantly for stimulus words where a number of competing responses were available. Levinger and Clark examined the applicability of this explanation to their data. They found that when response variability was controlled, there were still appreciable relationships between their indices of the emotionality of a stimulus word and the tendency of their subjects to forget the associations they had previously given to it. They also employed a control for word frequency and found no relationship between the Thorndike-Lorge 1944 word counts and the emotionality of their stimuli.

Another well-controlled experiment using the word-association test is that of Jacobs (1955). Neutral and emotional stimulus words were selected for each subject, using reaction time and GSR as criteria for emotionality. When these words were subsequently used as the response terms in a paired associate learning task, significantly fewer correct associations occurred for the emotional words. Although Jacobs found a significant relationship between Thorndike-Lorge word frequency counts and number of correct associative responses, the difference between emotional and neutral words was still significant when this effect of familiarity was partialed out of the relationship.

In addition to the word-association test, the *Q* sort and other tests designed to detect areas of discrepancy in self-perception have been used. This line of investigation had its origin in Rogers' theory of self and self-consistency. As Rogers has stated: "Any experience which is inconsistent with the organization or structure of self may be perceived as a threat, and the more of these perceptions there are, the more rigidly the self structure is organized to maintain itself" (1951, p. 515).

Evidence that self-consistent material is better remembered than inconsistent material had been previously reported by Wallen (1942) and Shaw (1944). Both investigators found that subjects show better recall for personality trait ratings that agreed with their self ratings than they do for ratings that were in disagreement. It is difficult to evaluate these findings, however, since in both studies it is quite possible that a subject, when uncertain of a rating received on a trait, would put down his own evaluation. This bias in the subject's guessing procedure would give him a superior hit rate for items that were consistent with his self picture.

In a study that was directly influenced by Rogers' theorizing, Cartwright (1956) found that subjects were more apt to recall trait adjectives descriptive of themselves than trait adjectives they had previously rated as unlike themselves. He also found superior recall for objects the subjects had indicated they would be likely to own than for objects rated as unlikely to be owned by them. The interpretation of these findings in terms of defensive behavior hinges most critically upon the theoretical assumption of Rogers. The experiment contains no independent operations to show that the inconsistent items aroused anxiety, nor is there enough ancillary evidence of the kind that exists for the word-association test to justify making the assumption on the basis of Rogers' theory alone. A more simple interpretation of these findings would be in terms of the personal familiarity of the trait adjectives and items to the subject. It is not surprising that a subject would have greater familiarity with, and therefore better recall of, adjectives that he thinks are like himself than he would the large population of adjectives that are unlike himself. Similarly, there should be greater personal familiarity for objects he would be apt to own.

Experiments employing experimental induction of anxiety—The experiments we have considered so far are dependent upon theoretical assumptions and/or accumulated clinical lore in presenting their evidence for defensive avoidance. Even in the better designed studies we must still depend upon the assumption that materials inconsistent with the self or words eliciting long reaction-times on a word-association list are anxiety arousing for the subjects. A methodological improvement is obtained when the experiment contains adequate operations for attaching anxiety to specific cues or stimuli. The experiments considered in this section have this methodological advantage in common. They differ rather markedly, however, in the sophistication, adequacy, and convincingness of the experimental induction of anxiety.

A common procedure for producing anxiety has been through manipulated failure on a supposed test of intelligence. Here the assumption is made that the need to see themselves as intelligent is important to the self-esteem of the experimental sample involved. This assumption is probably justified when applied to certain samples: for example, premedical students who are competing with each other to gain admittance to a preferred medical school and who as yet have had inadequate opportunity in college to see how they can compete with a select group (Eriksen, 1954). It is quite dubious, however, when applied to a group of student nurses (Jourard, 1954) or to a group of randomly selected army inductees (Sandison, 1954). There is no convincing evidence that nonacademic people are made particularly anxious by suggestions that they aren't potential geniuses. Such studies are seriously defective when no control group is employed against which to show that the experimental threat actually elicited a change in performance.

Even when the experimental treatment seems adequate in inducing the desired anxiety, the methodology can still go awry. Zeller (1950) had subjects learn seminonsense material followed by a block-tapping test. On the tapping test the experimental subjects were made to feel that their performance was an intellectual failure. Following the block tapping the experimental subjects demonstrated poorer recall of the previously learned nonsense material than did the control group. When the experimental subjects were later informed of the artificial nature of the failure situation, an improvement in their recall was obtained.

The results of this study provide little information about cognitive avoidance. The recall decrement obtained for the experimental subjects seems more readily interpretable in terms of the heightened emotionality associated with the failure experience which might be expected to induce distraction. There is also the possibility that many subjects withdrew psychologically from the experiment as a result of this experience and did not exert themselves on a subsequent recall measure. Similarly, others may have been so overwhelmed with their failure and its implications for their future that they were too busy subjectively trying to rationalize or to explore what this meant in terms of their future goals to attend adequately the recall measures. These alternative interpretations to a repression process gain credence when it is noted that anxiety was not attached to the nonsense stimuli. Also the experimental procedure provided no way by which the subject could avoid anxiety by forgetting the nonsense words he had previously learned, since the occurrence of the nonsense syllables in his thoughts were not cues that elicited anxiety.

A variety of other methods have been used by experimenters in attempts to associate anxiety with certain stimulus material. Gould (1942) told subjects that their selections of certain tasks to perform indicated abnormalities about their personalities and subsequently found decremental memory for the tasks that had been associated with this undesirable attribute. Korner (1950) had subjects write a number of stories and told them that certain ones they had written indicated characteristics of abnormality. He found that the subjects showed decremental recall for the titles of these designated stories. Similarly, Flavell (1955) found that subjects showed a decrement in recall not only for nonsense syllables to which abnormality had been attributed but also for neutral nonsense syllables relative to the performance of a control group. The difference between the experimental and control groups' performance was partially dissipated after removal of the threat. However, since both neutral and emotionally associated nonsense syllables showed the recall decrement, it cannot be established whether the poorer performance on the first recall test of the experimental subjects was due to a cognitive avoidance or due to interference generated by anxiety and competing thoughts as may have been the case in the Zeller experiment.

Perhaps the most popular technique for experimentally inducing failure or anxiety involves the use of completed and interrupted tasks (Zeigarnik, 1927). Rosenzweig and Mason (1934) were the first to make use of this method in the study of repression. In a sample of children of heterogeneous ages they found that when interruption was indicative of failure, there was a tendency for the children with higher mental ages and higher ratings of pride to remember the completed tasks better than the incompleted ones. Subsequently, Rosenzweig (1943) administered a series of jigsaw puzzles to college students. One group was given the puzzles under a task-oriented condition, and a second group was told that the tasks measured intellectual abilities. All subjects were permitted to finish half of the puzzles but were interrupted on the remaining half. When asked to recall the different puzzles they had worked upon, the subjects under the task-oriented condition were found to recall the unfinished puzzles better than the finished ones while the group experiencing intellectual failure more frequently recalled completed puzzles. Rosenzweig, however, noted and commented on some characteristic individual differences in these recall patterns.

Glixman (1949), in an extensive and well-analyzed experiment, presented a series of twenty tests, similar to subtests on an intelligence scale, to college students under three degrees of stress. In the least stressful condition the subjects were told that the tasks were to be used in another experiment and that the experimenter wanted to find out how long it took people to complete them. The task was presented to the other two groups as an intelligence test, and the degree of stress was varied by emphasizing to one group that it was a measure of their individual abilities and would be related to and used as a predictor of their grade point averages. In subsequent recall, the number of incompleted tasks recalled decreased as the degree of stress increased. Recall of completed items showed a slight but nonsignificant decrease with increasing stress.

Experiments providing for individual differences—The evidence for cognitive avoidance or a repressionlike concept becomes more impressive in those procedures that take individual differences into account. Rosenzweig (1943) had noted apparent individual differences in completed-incompleted task recall under anxiety-inducing conditions, but his experiment did not have outside operations that would permit either the demonstration of consistency across situations or correlation with personality traits. Individual differences in defensive behavior can be shown by either of these methods.

Two experiments have shown individual consistency in defensive response under anxiety-provoking situations. Eriksen (1952b) found that subjects who recalled predominantly successful or completed tasks, when the tasks were performed under anxiety-provoking conditions, required significantly more trials to learn and to relearn words with long reaction-times on a word-association test. Subjects who tended to recall failed or incompleted tasks, on the other hand, learned the paired associates with the long reaction-time words as quickly as they did those with medium and short association-times. Not only did this finding substantiate consistent individual differences in defensive response but it also established this defensive process across the two basic tasks that have been employed in this research area.

Another experiment showing this consistency of defense across situations is that of Lazarus and Longo (1953). They had their subjects learn paired associates composed of nonsense syllables, but on half of the pairs a severe electric shock was administered one-third of the time, regardless of whether the subject correctly anticipated the correct response. On a recall test twenty-four hours later, subjects who in a previous experiment had shown a preponderant tendency to remember successful tasks rather than failed tasks showed an appreciable recall deficit for the nonsense-syllable pairs that had been shocked. However, subjects who had been predominantly failure recallers, showed a significant reverse tendency. No differences between these two groups of subjects were found on the learning trials.

A relationship between defensive behavior and personality variables was suggested by Rosenzweig (1943), when he reported that children rated high on pride were more apt to recall completed tasks when the tasks had been administered under self-esteem-involving orientation. Subsequently, Rosenzweig and Sarason (1942) found a positive relation between success recall and both impunitiveness and suggestibility. Alper (1948) related differences in success and failure recall under two differing degrees of stress to personality differences on a small group of subjects upon whom extensive clinical evaluations existed. She reported that subjects clinically characterized as strong egos tended to remember proportionally more successful items as the stress increased. Subjects characterized as weak egos tended to show a reverse pattern. Alper (1957) later confirmed her findings on a larger sample of subjects.

Clinical theory and lore provide considerable support for the expectation that cognitive avoidance of internally cued anxiety would be associated with the hysterias and with the extraversive personality. Eriksen (1954) related recall of completed and incompleted tasks administered under anxiety and neutral conditions to a measure of ego strength derived from the McReynolds concept choice test (1951) and to the hysteria and psychasthenia scales of the MMPI. In support of Alper's findings Eriksen found that under nonanxious conditions subjects with high scores on the ego strength scale tended to recall more incompleted than completed tasks, but under the anxiety administration this relationship was reversed. A significant positive correlation was found between hysteria and tendency to recall completed tasks under the anxiety condition and between psychasthenia and tendency to recall incompleted tasks. When the intercorrelation of these variables with the ego-strength score was partialed out, the correlation between completed task recall and hysteria was appreciably increased, but the correlation between incompleted task recall and psychasthenia was attenuated. It would appear, therefore, that at least two personality traits are associated with completed-incompleted task recall under anxiety-arousing conditions.

Evidence confirming the relation of the hysteria-psychasthenia dimension to cognitive avoidance has been supplied by Truax (1957). Using extreme groups on a dimension obtained by subtracting psychasthenia scale scores from hysteria scale scores, he found that subjects with high scores on this dimension required appreciably longer to relearn paired associates in which the stimulus member was a word that had been associated with experimentally produced failure. Subjects on the low end of the scale actually learned the paired associates with the failure words quicker than neutral pairs. In a second relearning session, after subjects had been informed of the artificial nature of the failure experience, differences between the high and low groups were eliminated.

In the same experiment Truax found no differences between learning or relearning of paired associates in which the stimulus member had been selected for emotionality upon the basis of performance on a word-association list. This finding would appear at variance with the numerous studies that have used the word-association technique with positive results. However, there is some reason to believe that this discrepancy is attributable to the method Truax used in obtaining emotional words. In the other studies long reaction-time was an important criterion in selecting words for emotionality, but Truax's emotional and neutral words both had short reaction-times but differed on the amount of GSR elicited.

Differential completed and incompleted task recall has also been related to need achievement by Atkinson (1953) and Atkinson and Raphelson (1956). High achievement motivation as measured from TAT stories was related to recall of more incompleted tasks as the anxiety associated with the administration of the tasks increased. Low need achievers showed the reverse tendency. A possible inverse relation between ego strength and high need achievement has been suggested by Alper (1957) which may account in part for these findings.

Indirect evidence of the relation of need achievement to success and failure recall has been provided by Caron and Wallach (1957). Their sample consisted of Harvard freshmen who were classified on the basis of whether they had attended a public high school or a private prep school. McArthur (1954, 1955) previously had obtained data indicating that Harvard undergraduates who came from public high schools were distinguished by higher achievement motivation than those from private prep schools. In the Caron and Wallach experiment, subjects from private schools recalled fewer incompleted items when the items were administered under the guise of an intelligence test than a matched group who were administered the items under neutral conditions. Subjects from public schools, on the other hand, were found to recall fewer completed items than subjects with the same background who had been administered the items under the neutral condition. In a footnote to their article, Caron and Wallach report that private school attendance was associated with low level of aspiration, indications of personal insecurity and social introversion as measured by Guilford's TDCR battery. Since the hysteria-psychasthenia scales employed by Eriksen (1954) and Truax (1957) have been shown to be related to Eysenck's introversion-extraversion dimension, and since level of aspiration is also loaded on that dimension, the results obtained by Caron and Wallach would seem to reflect some confirmation of the results of these other two studies.

In a subsequent paper, Caron and Wallach (1959) report the results of a factor analysis of a large battery of personality measures including various need achievement measures as well as the hysteria and psychasthenia scales from the MMPI and the modification of the McReynolds concept evaluation technique that had been used by Eriksen as a measure of ego strength. Included in the correlation analysis were the subjects' success and failure recall performance under the stressful conditions in the previous study as well as perceptual recognition thresholds for test- and nontest-related words. Five orthogonal factors were extracted and tentatively labeled neuroticism, intellectual flexibility, extraversion, "other" orientation, and perseverance for achievement. None of the factors was significantly related to success-failure recall, but the factor reflecting achievement orientation showed a significant relation to the differential perceptual recognition for test-related and neutral words. Subjects high on this factor tended to recognize the test (failure-associated) words more readily than the neutral ones, while low-scoring subjects showed the reverse tendency. Examination of the correlation matrix failed to show significant correlations for the hysteria or the psychasthenia scale with either perceptual recognition performance or success-failure recall. The same lack of relationship was found for the ego strength measure.

The failure of the Caron and Wallach study to confirm the results obtained by Truax and by Eriksen requires some comment for several reasons. As will be seen below in discussing the perceptual evidence for repression, a number of other investigators have found the relationship between the hysteria-psychasthenia dimension and differential perceptual recognition for threat and neutral words. Since the Caron and Wallach study is an unusually comprehensive and well-conducted experiment, an examination of this discrepancy in findings is merited.

Although Caron and Wallach described their selection of Harvard freshmen as random, this was far from the case. Their selection procedure involved randomly sampling the freshman names in the college and then sending a postcard inviting them to participate in an experiment on symbolic processes for which they would be paid. As the authors report, approximately half of the subjects contacted replied. There are some very marked personality differences associated with subjects who volunteer and those who do not. The approximately fifty per cent who responded to the request to participate could by no means be considered a random sample of Harvard freshmen. Even within the classifications of public high school vs. private prep school, one would expect important differences in the reasons why students from these two different groups would volunteer for the experiment. In view of such biases in selection of the samples and in view of the extensive evidence of marked personality differences as measured by questionnaires between volunteers and nonvolunteer populations, it seems most likely that the failure of Caron and Wallach to substantiate the personality relationships between success-failure recall and perception of threat and neutral words is attributable to biases operating on the samples involved in their study. Only slight bias would be needed to wipe out the relationships, since the findings of others suggest only about ten to fifteen per cent of the variance is attributable to these personality traits.

Perceptual Recognition Approaches

The use of perceptual techniques in investigations of defense mechanisms was an outgrowth of the New Look approach to perception. While its antecedents may be traced back twenty years or more, this motivational approach to perception may be said to have become a research enthusiasm in the early 1950's. The New Look orientation was that perception was adaptive and capable of reflecting the individual perceiver's needs and values. Two effects of needs upon perception were enunciated in a series of three articles by Bruner and Postman (1947a; 1947b) and Postman, Bruner, and

McGinnies (1948). The first of these effects was *perceptual vigilance,* a term which was used to describe the authors' findings that stimuli associated with experimentally produced anxiety had lower perceptual recognition thresholds than did neutral stimuli. It was postulated that stimuli important to the organism were enhanced in perception and recognized sooner.

The second effect was that of *perceptual defense,* which was related to the finding that stimuli associated with anxiety were sometimes found to have much higher perceptual recognition thresholds than neutral stimuli. Bruner and Postman (1947b) likened this concept of perceptual defense to the concept of repression where anxiety-provoking stimuli are defended against in perception or prevented from attaining conscious awareness in order to minimize anxiety.

Although the relation of perceptual defense to the concept of repression was noted by Bruner and Postman, they did little to relate systematically the concept to the experimental literature on defense mechanisms. With but few exceptions (Eriksen, 1951a; Lazarus, Eriksen, & Fonda, 1951), most of the early experiments on perceptual defense also failed to extend the concept to the clinical conceptions of defense mechanisms. The Freudians, however, had long recognized that repression had perceptual concomitants. Fenichel states, "(Repression) consists of an unconsciously purposeful forgetting or not becoming aware of internal impulses or *external events* which as a rule represent possible temptations or punishments for, or mere allusions to, objectionable instinctual demands" (italics supplied, 1945, p. 148). The theoretical basis for the approach was there; all that had been wanting was a method.

The essence of the method that Bruner and Postman drew attention to was the experimental control of stimulus ambiguity. Through the use of brief stimulus exposure by means of a tachistoscope, it was possible to vary the amount of stimulus information provided a subject from virtually nothing at very rapid exposures to complete stimulus information at slower exposures. The duration of exposure that a subject required for a need-related stimulus could be correlated with other measures of his needs or motivational states. The method was not limited to tachistoscopic presentations. Any technique by which the stimulus could be varied in degrees of ambiguity was satisfactory. Besides duration of exposure, experimenters have varied successfully luminance of the stimulus, masking of the stimulus with varying degrees of white noise, defocusing the stimulus material, using tactual recognition and even binocular rivalry arrangements. This use of experimentally varied stimulus ambiguity as a measure of an individual's needs had of course been anticipated by the clinical projective tests.

The experimental studies on the concepts of perceptual vigilance and defense are much too voluminous to be covered in the present chapter. Brown (1961) provides an excellent evaluative summary of this research; Eriksen (1963) has reviewed this literature with reference to defensive mechanisms, and Pierce (1963) with reference to form thresholds. Here we shall be concerned, for the most part, with those experiments that are better controlled and therefore more informative and/or which illustrate the development of methodological sophistication. As with the learning and memory experiments, these perceptual experiments will be classified into those which attempt to capitalize on existing anxieties and repressions in the subjects and those which experimentally attempt to condition or attach anxiety to specific cues.

Experiments employing existing anxiety cues—As was the case with the early mnemonic studies on repression, many of the experiments on perceptual defense have assumed that sexual or aggressive stimuli in general would elicit enough anxiety in the majority of subjects to produce defensive processes in perceptual recognition. A number of experiments used "taboo" words such as *bitch, belly,* and *Kotex.* It is not surprising that the results of these studies have been quite varied. Despite the early report by Bruner and Postman (1947b) of individual differences in perceptual recognition for anxiety-arousing stimuli, many experimenters have continued to make no allowance for a differential perceptual vigilance and perceptual defense reaction in their subjects. As Sears (1936) pointed out in criticizing the mnemonic studies using these simple designs, positive results are most readily attributable to differential stimulus familiarity on the part of the subject or to the subject's reluctance to verbalize socially taboo words and stimuli (see Howes & Solomon, 1951; Zajonc, 1962).

Negative results are also meaningless for a concept of defensive mechanism. Not only might some subjects showing a vigilance reaction tend to cancel out the subjects showing the defense reaction but the assumption that words like bitch and belly would generate enough anxiety in college sophomores to elicit the type of defensive process the clinician has in mind is naïve.

Some experiments have attempted to control for differences in stimulus familiarity by matching the taboo words with neutral words having the same frequency values in the Thorndike-Lorge (1944) word counts of written English. Eriksen (1963) has pointed out, however, that the Thorndike-Lorge word counts have highly questionable validity in estimating the familiarity of different English words among college students. The familiarity of taboo words is especially apt to be grossly underestimated. Consequently, matching such words with neutral words of equal Thorndike-Lorge frequency almost precludes obtaining a perceptual defense effect, if familiarity is, in fact, an important variable in perceptual recognition. Further, adjusting for familiarity in terms of word-count tables is an averaging technique that does not assure differential familiarity for individual subjects, a lapse that may account for their pattern of vigilance or defense.

Experiments using individual criteria for anxiety cues—Experimental designs in which an outside test or criterion is used to select anxiety-arousing stimuli for individual subjects have generally been successful in finding a sensitization or defensivelike effect in perceptual recognition. Bruner and Postman (1947b) determined the exposure durations necessary for their subjects to recognize words having varying reaction-times on a word-association test. For some of their subjects there was a monotonic relation between reaction time to the word and the duration of exposure necessary for its visual recognition. For other subjects the relationship was curvilinear with both short and long reaction-time words being recognized at shorter durations than words having medium reaction-times. Burner and Postman characterized the first pattern as illustrating perceptual defense and the second, perceptual vigilance.

Singer (1956) provided confirmation of the Bruner and Postman finding. Not only did he find these differences in perceptual recognition for words having different word-association reaction-times but he demonstrated that the subjects were consistent in their individual pattern of defense or vigilance in two testing situations separated by a two-week period. Different stimulus words on the recognition task were used in the two testing situations.

Eriksen (1951a) predicted that perceptual sensitization would occur for emotional or conflict material that was freely expressed in overt behavior. He found that patients rated as overtly aggressive on the ward and who freely expressed aggressive themes in TAT stories required shorter exposure durations for pictures depicting aggressive behavior than for neutral pictures.

Experiments recognizing individual differences—Unlike the mnemonic studies of defensive mechanisms, recognition of individual differences in response to covertly cued anxiety has characterized some of the research using perceptual recognition from the time of the earliest studies. Bruner and

Postman (1947b) described the difference in perceptual vigilance and defense in one of the earliest studies in the area. While their description of these two reactions was admittedly post hoc, the validity of the distinction was rather quickly supported.

Eriksen (1951a) selected hospitalized psychiatric patients on the basis of expectations that they would use avoidant-type defensive mechanisms. Positive relations were found between the amount of disturbance these patients indicated in a specific need area as assessed by a word-association technique and the exposure durations necessary for recognition of conflict-related pictures. A more extensive study was carried out by Lazarus, Eriksen, and Fonda (1951). Two groups of psychiatric outpatients, those characterized as using predominantly avoidant, repressive defenses and those using obsessive, ruminating defenses, were selected from case history and therapy session information. A sentence-completion test containing a number of sexual and aggressive stems was administered to both groups, and later the subjects were required to identify neutral, aggressive, and sexual sentences that were presented auditorily against varying degrees of white-noise background. For the repressor group, an inverse relation was found between the amount of blocking or distortion of sexual and/or aggressive sentence-completions and recognition accuracy for sentences from the corresponding emotional areas. For the sensitizer group, the relationship was in the opposite direction. On the sentence-completion test the repressors were more apt to block or to distort into an innocuous form sentences with sexual or aggressive stems, whereas subjects in the sensitizer group were more apt to express freely sexual or aggressive endings to these stems.

In a very similar experiment, Carpenter, Wiener, and Carpenter (1956) obtained confirming results. Sentence completions were judged by four clinical psychologists for indications of conflict and for the particular type of defense, repressive or sensitizing, used by the subject. Subjects characterized as using repressive defenses were found to have higher perceptual recognition thresholds for conflict-related material relative to neutral material, whereas sensitizers showed an opposite reaction.

Further evidence of the relation between clinically conceived defensive mechanisms and detection of conflicts with perceptual recognition behavior has been reported by Blum (1955) and Nelson (1955). Both investigators made use of the Blackie pictures not only to detect areas of anxiety but also to determine the type of defense mechanism employed by the subject in the particular conflict area. They were successful in relating perceptual recognition behavior to the clinically assessed areas of conflict and defense. Smock (1956), however, has raised some questions concerning Blum's procedure.

The Welsh *A* and *R* scales were used by Van de Castle (1960) to preclassify subjects as repressors or sensitizers. In a departure from the usual perceptual recognition technique, Van de Castle used a binocular rivalry situation in which emotional and neutral words were presented to different eyes. The dependent variable was the amount of time the subject reported each word as in view. A modified Rorschach technique patterned on the McReynolds concept choice procedure (1949) was used as a measure of each subject's aggressive conflicts. Aggression scores from this Rorschach index showed significant relationships to perception in the binocular rivalry situation. The behavior of the sensitizers was consistent with a vigilance attitude toward the emotional material, whereas that of the repressors was characterized by avoidance. Essentially the same general findings had been previously reported by Eriksen and Lazarus (1952) for relationships between auditory perceptual recognition and a very similar Rorschach index.

An extensive investigation of the relation between clinical assessments of defensive mechanisms and perceptual recognition has been reported by Shannon (1962). Case history and rating data were used to classify psychiatric patients into three groups, those using externalization, acting out, and internalization defenses. As predicted, externalizers and acter-outers had lower perceptual recognition thresholds for conflict-relevant stimuli than for matched control stimuli. Internalizers, on the other hand, had significantly higher recognition thresholds for the conflict-related pictures.

Since a hysteria-psychasthenia variable was found to differentiate success and failure recallers in some of the learning and memory experiments, it might be anticipated that this personality variable would be related to perceptual recognition behavior. Such a relationship has been reported by Mathews and Wertheimer (1958). Subjects scoring high on the psychasthenia scale from the MMPI had lower recognition thresholds for conflict words detected by word-association tests than did low-scoring subjects. Since high psychasthenia scores were related in the learning and memory studies with better recall of failures or threat-related stimuli and low scores with the opposite pattern, Mathews and Wertheimer's results supply an important linkage between the two methodologies. And since other investigators have found similar correlations on perceptual recognition tasks (Eriksen & Browne, 1956), this linkage would appear to be on firm footing.

Another important linkage between the two methodologies was provided in an experiment by Eriksen (1954). Subjects were first selected on the basis of a completed-incompleted task technique administered in the guise of an intelligence test for the experimental subjects. Subjects scoring on the two extremes of success-to-failure recall ratios were used in a later experimental session where their perceptual recognition thresholds were determined for neutral and conflict words as assessed by a word-association technique. Subjects in the success recall group showed positive correlations between word-association test reaction-times and perceptual recognition thresholds for conflict words relative to neutral words, whereas for subjects in the failure recall group, zero or negative correlations were obtained. Since similar consistency across tasks was also obtained by Caron and Wallach (1957), it would appear that, at least for extreme groups, there is a consistency in the subjects' type of response to anxiety as assessed by learning, memory, and perceptual recognition.

Experiments using induced anxiety—When anxiety is experimentally associated with specific stimuli in the laboratory, one can be more certain as to the meaning of the stimulus for individual subjects. Studies employing this methodology have for the most part confirmed the results reported above.

Postman and Solomon (1950) were the first to apply this methodology to perceptual recognition behavior. They administered a series of anagrams to their subjects in the guise of an intelligence test and manipulated the situation so that the subjects experienced a rather severe failure. Subsequently, the perceptual recognition threshold for the anagrams solutions, all of which had been told to the subject at the termination of the test, was compared with perceptual recognition for neutral words. Postman and Solomon found that some of their subjects showed significantly higher recognition thresholds for the failure-associated anagram solutions while other subjects showed a significant sensitization.

Although this study is of course limited by the post hoc conclusions of individual differences in defensive mode, the existence of these individual differences is consistent not only with the above surveyed research but also with further studies using induced anxiety. An improvement upon the Postman and Solomon experiment was made by Eriksen and Browne (1956). First, they selected high- and low-scoring subjects on the MMPI psychasthenia scale. Anagrams disguised as an intelligence test were again used to induce anxiety, but classmate stooges who feigned successful completion of all anagrams were included in the procedure to increase the degree of stress. When the exposure durations necessary for recognition of the anagram solutions and neutral words matched on frequency were subsequently determined, it was found that both high- and low-scoring psychasthenia subjects tended to recognize the anagrams solutions more quickly than the neutral words. This finding had been anticipated on the basis of a recency effect. The critical comparison showed that the low-scoring psychasthenia subjects showed significantly less gain due to recency than did the high-scoring subjects.

The findings from these two studies have been bolstered recently by Tempone (1962). Using a psychometrically improved measure of the hysteria-psychasthenia variable (Byrne, 1961), he selected forty repressors and forty sensitizers. The pseudo-intelligence test consisting of anagrams was administered with stooges employed to increase the plausibility and the stress. Half of both extreme groups were administered the anagrams under success conditions and the other half under failure conditions. The correct solution to each anagram was given to the subjects after each trial. Following this phase of the experiment, perceptual recognition was determined for the anagram solutions and comparable control words. The repressors and sensitizers who had experienced the success treatment did not differ in their perceptual recognition behavior, but for those who had undergone the failure experience the repressors showed significantly higher thresholds for the anagram solutions than did the sensitizing group. There was no difference in perceptual recognition for neutral words as a function of experimental treatment or personality classification.

Further evidence of individual consistency across memory and perceptual recognition tasks was found in the previously described study by Caron and Wallach (1957). As will be recalled, these investigators had studied memory for completed and incompleted tasks that had been administered under the convincing guise of an intelligence test. The group of subjects who were found to favor successful or completed items in their recall were subsequently found to show higher perceptual recognition thresholds for words pertaining to intelligence testing than for neutral words. Subjects who had favored incompleted or failed tasks in their recall showed a sensitization for the test-related words.

Hypnotic Induction of Repression and Conflicts

Various investigators have used hypnosis as a means of inducing conflicts or repressions in their subjects. While the subject is hypnotized the experimenter suggests an experience that the subject is supposed to have had at some prior time in his life, an experience over which he has considerable guilt and anxiety. It is further suggested that in the postamnesic period the subject will have no recall of this experience.

Bobbitt (1958), after inducing a conflict in her subjects under hypnosis, manipulated the degree of awareness of the conflict during the posthypnotic amnesic period and studied the effects of the varying degrees of awareness (repression) upon manifestations of the conflict on a word-association test. More recently, Reyher (1961) studied the perceptual recognition and somatic reactions to tachistoscopically presented words related to the induced conflict. He reported that the degree of repression was positively correlated with the proportion of somatic reactions to recognition of the critical words. Also, there were indications that levels of repression manifested themselves in different forms of somatic reactions.

The amount of information that studies using this methodology can supply on repression and other defensive processes is very limited. We have as yet a very limited understanding as to what constitutes hypnosis and what characterizes the hypnotic state. When hypnosis is used as a means of inducing a conflict in a subject in order to study the behavioral effects of repression, we are in the position of using a dependent variable to study another dependent variable. Only by making a number of very tenuous assumptions about the nature of hypnosis can inferences be drawn about repressive phenomena. The assumptions typically made are that under hypnosis the conflict induced is similar, if not identical, to the types of conflicts and repression that occur spontaneously in real-life situations. A very necessary control that has been lacking in these studies is the use of a hypnotically susceptible but nonhypnotized control group who is given the same suggestions and instructions but not the hypnosis. In other words, they are motivated to simulate the behavior of a person who has had the suggested conflict and has repressed or forgotten it. Only thus can we distinguish between repression and suppression. Until such controls are employed we have no evidence that the hypnotic trance has added anything to the behavior observed in these experiments. The importance of such a control has been increasingly indicated by current experiments (Barber, 1962; Orne, 1959; Sutcliffe, 1960) which have shown that most of the physiological manifestations obtained under hypnotic trance can be obtained equally well in nonhypnotized simulating subjects.

While suggesting conflicts and an attendant repression to subjects under hypnosis is of very dubious value in shedding light upon repression, the use of hypnosis nonetheless may shed some light on repressivelike phenomena through the study of posthypnotic amnesia. Subjects while hypnotized may be required to learn certain materials or to undergo an experience for which posthypnotic amnesia is suggested. At the occurrence of a prearranged signal the amnesia is removed. This phenomenon has obvious similarities to the concept of repression, even to the return of the repression when the postamnesic signal is supplied by the hypnotist.

Experiments on posthypnotic amnesia differ from the hypnotic conflict studies in that the primary phenomenon under investigation is the posthypnotic amnesia itself, not repression. Unfortunately, nearly all of the studies that have been performed on posthypnotic amnesia are unable to provide definite evidence as to the genuineness of the phenomena, since they lack the essential controls for hypnosis research as pointed out by Sutcliffe (1960).

One of the few studies that has exercised proper controls for hypnotizability and simulation is a recent experiment by Williamsen, Johnson, and Eriksen (1964). Two basic groups consisting of hypnotizable and nonhypnotizable subjects were employed. Each of these groups was subdivided into a hypnotized, simulating, and control group. Those subjects assigned to the hypnotized condition were given the standard hypnotic induction and then were asked to learn a list of six common words which they were told they would be unable to remember having learned after emerging from the trance until a cue was given by another experimenter. Simulating subjects who had previously, in a different session, experienced a trance induction if they were hypnotizable and an attempt at trance induction if not, were asked to simulate posthypnotic amnesia for the six words. The control subjects learned the six words with no instructions for amnesia. In a following session a second experimenter who was unaware of the treatment group to which a subject had been assigned, administered various measures of recognition and recall. Significant decrements in both recall and recognition measures were found for the hypnotized hypnotically susceptible group as compared to the control subjects. These differences disappeared immediately following the signal for termination of posthypnotic amnesia. The performance of the hypnotized subjects also differed significantly from that of the simulators whose performance was characterized by overplaying the posthypnotic amnesic role.

While the results of this study support the genuineness of the posthypnotic amnesic phenomenon, certain aspects of the results also suggest caution in equating the phenomenon with clinical repression. The posthypnotic amnesia of the hypnotized subjects was limited to direct measures of recognition and recall. They showed no reliable nor appreciable differences from the control subjects on a word-guessing task involving the amnesic words nor in the use of these words as responses on a word-association test. Differences on both these measures might have been anticipated if the posthypnotic amnesia was behaving as clinical repression is supposed to do.

EXPLANATIONS FOR DEFENSIVE PHENOMENA

The results from the learning, memory, and perceptual recognition experiments, taken as a whole, present an impressive amount of evidence for a distinctive class of behaviors in response to internally cued anxiety. This evidence is particularly impressive in those experiments where the anxiety was cued to specific stimuli under experimental control and where individual differences in response were related to independently assessed personality variables. Because these experiments have been essentially replicated, not once but several times, careful consideration is merited as to how these defensive processes are related to our more general, experimentally-derived knowledge of perceptual, learning, and memory phenomena.

Specifically, we need to look for the mechanisms or means by which the learning and perceptual recognition effects are produced. We need to account for the differences in the repressors and the sensitizers and to determine what factors may underlie this differential response to anxiety-arousing stimuli. And the repressor-sensitizer dimension needs to be considered in relation to and in the context of more general personality theory.

Traditional Freudian theory is of little help in answering the above questions or achieving these goals. It is a theory that is stated primarily at the naturalistic level and pays little attention to the specifics of how learning occurs or how the unconscious operates. Our knowledge in the areas of learning and perception has moved well beyond the naturalistic level, and adequate explanation now requires description of these experimentally observed defensive phenomena in the terms of the extant knowledge in these fields, couched in and related to current concepts.

There are two important theoretical assumptions that Freudian theory has made about the nature of repression which need be borne in mind as other explanations of the phenomena are examined. The first of these is that repression is an unconscious act. It differs from response or thought suppression in that this latter is considered a voluntary act. Suppression is a deliberate behavior that the individual engages in with the subjective feeling of awareness that he is avoiding thinking of certain topics or stimuli. Further, with suppression, the subject is assumed to be able to bring the anxiety-provoking thoughts to mind if the occasion makes this necessary. Repression, on the other hand, is considered to occur automatically without awareness on the subject's part that certain thoughts or covert responses are being suppressed. Except for rare moments of great emotional crisis where repression may break down, the repressed thoughts or material cannot be brought to mind unless the anxiety that was originally associated with them has been relieved or eliminated.

The second assumption is that repression is an active process, requiring the expenditure of psychic energy. A positive inhibiting force keeps the repressed responses or thoughts from occurring and gaining either covert (conscious) or overt expression. It is a different process of forgetting than associative interference or the replacing of an old response to a stimulus with a new response which becomes stronger and eventually is prepotent in the response hierarchy.

It is to be borne in mind that these are theoretical assumptions invoked by Freud to account for the clinically observed phenomena. They are not part of the phenomena. The adequacy of any explanation of defensive behaviors depends solely upon how well they account for the empirically observed phenomena, not how well they meet these theoretical criteria of Freudian repression. While it has been argued that the experimental demonstrations of defensive behavior are not synonymous with the behavior observed by the clinician, it would seem highly improbable that the defensive behaviors observed in the experiments summarized above differ qualitatively from those observed in the clinic.

Familiarity and Response Suppression

The oldest and most obvious explanations for the experimental results on defensive behavior are those of deliberate response suppression on the part of the subject and the differential familiarity he may have with the learning or perceptual recognition material. Sears (1936) has applied these criticisms to the learning and memory studies, and Howes and Solomon (1950) and Zajonc (1962) have applied them to the experiments using the perceptual recognition technique. As has already been noted, these are very plausible explanations for the results obtained in the simply designed studies on learning and memory and in the taboo-word perceptual experiments. Response suppression due to the social embarrassment to the subject of verbalizing a vulgar taboo word would appear to be a real factor in these experiments (Zajonc, 1962). But this explanation becomes strained if extended to cover the results of the experiments that used independent tests or techniques for selecting anxiety-provoking words for the individual subjects. Both the learning and perceptual studies that use word-association techniques for selection of anxiety-evoking stimuli typically did not use socially taboo words on the list. It seems unlikely that a subject would have social embarrassment for verbalizing words such as *blame* or *hate* in an experimental setting. Suppression as an explanation becomes completely implausible when extended to the results of the experiments that induced or conditioned the anxiety in the experimental situation. There is little basis for assuming any social embarrassment to be attached to verbalizing the innocuous name of an incompleted or failed task when asked to recall it, or to recognize it in a tachistoscopic exposure. Nor is there any clear theoretical basis for expecting that subjects high on the psychasthenia scale would show a facility for verbalizing anxiety-arousing stimuli whereas those who are high on hysteria and/or low on the psychasthenia scale would show social embarrassment for the same items.

Differences in familiarity between neutral and emotional stimuli have been used as an explanation for the differential learning and retention of these two classes of stimuli and also for the differential perceptual recognition. The most complete and sophisticated statement of this explanation was made by Howes and Solomon (1951), where they equated familiarity of a stimulus with its frequency of past occurrence. The argument has been that the more frequently a subject has experienced a stimulus in the past, the more familiar he will be with it. Therefore, the more readily he will learn and remember it, or the fewer cues he will require in order to recognize it when it is exposed under conditions of perceptual impoverishment.

As with the response suppression explanation, differential familiarity among stimuli may well account for the results obtained by the more simply designed learning and memory studies and the perceptual recognition studies using the taboo-word technique. But again, like response suppression, it begins to break down when it tries to encompass the results of the more adequately designed experiments. The experiments using the learning methodology and employing an outside criterion to detect anxiety-arousing material in individual subjects (e.g., Jacobs, 1955; Levinger & Clark, 1961; Merrill, 1954) provided adequate controls in their procedures for the possibilities of differential familiarity or frequency of past occurrence between their emotional and neutral stimuli.

Again, the most serious obstacle to a familiarity explanation comes from those experiments that experimentally conditioned anxiety to the stimuli (Caron & Wallach, 1957; Eriksen & Browne, 1956; Postman & Solomon, 1950; Tempone, 1962). This methodology permits control of differences in past experience among stimuli classified as emotional and neutral. Both the learning and the perceptual experiments employing this methodology have shown that differential learning, recall, and recognition performance for stimuli are associated not only with the anxiety conditioned to them but also related to broader personality variables. It is to be noted that the advocates of a familiarity explanation have restricted themselves to explaining the simpler learning designs and the taboo word perceptual recognition studies and have ignored the more adequately designed studies.

Covert Avoidance Conditioning

The frequency explanation is in an important sense a learning theory explanation for differences in the learning, recall, and perceptual recognition of neutral and emotional stimuli. It assumes that the more frequently a subject has been exposed to a stimulus in the past, the better he has learned that stimulus. But as an account of the phenomenon in terms of differential past learning it is markedly defective, since it implies that frequency of occurrence is the sole or primary determinant of learning. The typically small amounts of learning that can be shown by latent learning experiments argue strongly that the mere occurrence of a stimulus is not an effective determinant of whether it will be learned. It seems that for effective learning to occur, the subject somehow or other has to attend to or operate on the particular event or stimulus. One way of insuring that this occurs is through positive or negative reinforcement. When we expand an explanation of defensive mechanisms in terms of past learning to include differential reinforcement histories associated with the stimuli, we are then in a position to examine more adequately the results of the experiments in this area.

Dollard and Miller's (1950) main contribution in their treatment of defensive mechanisms in behavior theory terms was to conceive of covert responses such as thoughts, memories, and images as similar to overt responses and subject to the same laws of learning and reinforcement. Covert responses that are punished have a reduced probability of occurrence, whereas those that are rewarded increase in probability. How reward and punishment act to change the probability of occurrence of either covert or overt responses need not concern us at the moment. It is sufficient for the present to see how well we can integrate these covert defensive responses with our knowledge concerning overt responses.

In order to explain defensive behaviors in terms of the principles used to describe avoidance conditioning and the effects of punishment as Dollard and Miller have done, it is necessary to show that implicit, covert verbal behavior or thoughts are analyzable into stimulus-response sequences. It is also necessary to show that these stimulus-response sequences are learned and modified by the same principles of reinforcement that govern overt behavior. While Dollard and Miller give a most plausible account of covert behavior in these terms, experimental evidence for the fruitfulness and adequacy of the approach is needed.

This experimental support is contained in a study by Eriksen and Kuethe (1956). Their subjects were presented with a fifteen-item word-association list under the guise of taking part in an experiment to determine the limit of speed of associations. They were instructed to respond with the first word that came to mind as quickly as possible after the stimulus word was presented. During the first trial on the list the experimenter administered a strong electric shock immediately after each of five arbitrarily selected response words. The subjects were then given a number of further trials on the same fifteen stimulus words. Every time a subject responded with one of the five first-trial punished responses he received another electric shock. At the conclusion of this phase of the experiment subjects were informed that there would be no further shocks. They were then asked to chain associate to each of the stimulus words.

On the basis of postexperimental questioning, the subjects were classified into insightful and noninsightful groups, depending upon their ability to verbalize the basis for the electric shocks and what they had done to avoid receiving them. However, both groups were found to have shown a rapid and marked learning of avoidance behavior. Subjects in both classifications rather quickly changed their responses to the stimulus words that had elicited punished responses, whereas for the ten stimulus words that had not had punished responses the subjects continued to give these first trial responses throughout the experiment.

An analysis of the reaction times to stimuli having punished responses showed some interesting differences between the subjects in the two insight classifications. For subjects classified as insightful, reaction time to stimuli having had punished responses showed an increase for the first three trials through the list, but then reaction time began to decrease and by the final trial had reached a level that was not significantly nor appreciably different from that to the ten stimulus words that had not had shocked responses.

The noninsightful subjects, on the other hand, showed a progressive decrease in reaction time for both stimuli with punished responses and neutral stimuli throughout the experimental trials. These differences in reaction time corresponded with the subjects' verbalizations of what they had tried to do in the experiment. The insightful subjects reported that they had quickly learned not to give the punished response but had to pause when the stimulus occurred to think of a new response. They further reported that after several trials through the list the new association came to mind automatically, and there was no longer the subjective feeling of having to inhibit the punished response. The noninsightful subjects were unable to state how they avoided shock, and the progressive decrease in their reaction time would appear to have occurred by an automatic nonaware substitution of a new response for the punished one.

The results of this experiment would seem to demonstrate that associative connections can be modified by punishment in the same manner as overt responses. In other words, if a stimulus elicits a thought or association that is followed by punishment, the punished association would appear to be inhibited or replaced by a new association. Even in the insightful subjects where the change in response was accompanied by awareness of the mediational processes, the subjects' verbal reports, substantiated by the reaction-time data, indicate that the new association becomes automatic within a few trials.

A similar analysis can be applied to the perceptual recognition data and particularly perceptual defense. Eriksen and Browne (1956) have noted that the typical perceptual recognition experiment has more in common with guessing than with perceiving. What the subject perceives in the typical tachistoscopic exposure are some fragmentary parts of a word, an impression, perhaps, of word length and maybe a reasonably clear perception of one or two letters of the word. Subjects asked to describe exactly what they perceive on a tachistoscopic exposure of a word stimulus give responses such as, "It is a word that begins with s and has an o somewhere in the middle of it," or "I had the impression of maybe a word, a short word, and it looked like it had a tall letter at the end." In the typical recognition experiment, however, the subject is not asked to describe exactly what he perceives but is either implicitly or explicitly asked to respond in terms of whole English words or whole units depending upon the stimulus material employed. Now if we assume that the subject's actual perception is most adequately reflected when he is given the freedom of the English language to describe what he perceives, then the usual recognition experiment is essentially asking the subject to guess what word might fit the vague cues he receives in perception. In other words, the subject associates or tries to find a word that fits the fragmentary letter or impression of word length that corresponds with his actual perception.

When the perceptual recognition experiment is viewed as essentially a guessing task for the subject, we are in a position to account for the phenomena of perceptual defense in terms of the effects of punishment on the probability of occurrence of a response. It can be assumed that different words have different probabilities as responses to different cues. If for example the word *hook* is anxiety arousing or leads to self-devaluing thoughts in a subject due to previous experiences he has had, then "hook" would be expected to have a lower response probability to the fragmentary perception described by the subject as, "the impression of a short word that looks like it has an o in it and ends in a k." Look, took, or book might be expected to have higher probabilities to this particular cue. Thus, if this partial impression occurs in perception, "look" or "took" or "book" would have a higher probability of being elicited as a response than would the anxiety-associated "hook." But as the exposures lengthen, the subject's cues or perception changes and he gains more knowledge about the actual stimulus. Eventually the duration is long enough so that the actual perception is *hook*, in which "hook" has the greatest probability and occurs as the recognition response. The operation of such a process over a number of words will yield statistically higher recognition thresholds for anxiety-evoking words relative to neutral words.

The subject would not necessarily have to feel subjectively that he is searching for a word to fit the partial cues he actually perceives. The association of a response to these cues can be as immediate and automatic as the association "white" is to the stimulus word *black*. This associative connection in response to cues can be seen to underlie not only the perceptual recognition experiment but also the word-association test and may well account for the correspondence between perceptual recognition thresholds and word-association times.

Such an account of the concept of repression or cognitive avoidance is consistent with the clinical concept of the process. One of the defining operations for the detection of repression comes from the psychoanalytic free-association procedure. Here the analyst detects or suspects the operation of a repressive mechanism when the patient's associations show peculiar gaps and blockages or deviate from what the analyst considers to be a reasonable type of associative chain. A person has considerable latitude in the type of associative connections or trains of thought he subjectively experiences; he can be quite idiosyncratic without becoming too conspicuous to his fellows. In other words, there is room for avoidance in covert behavior. By learning to change directions of association, the person can effectively prevent the occurrence of covertly-stimulated anxiety, and it is only under the controlled condition of the clinician's couch that these peculiarities in associations become evident.

An important question is whether this cognitive avoidance is a conscious or unconscious process. If conscious, it corresponds to what Dollard and Miller call suppression, but in order to meet the criteria of Freudian repression and that advocated by Dollard and Miller for this process, this cognitive avoidance would have to occur at the unconscious level.

Unconscious Processes in Defense

The evidence that human adults learn without awareness has become increasingly negative. Dulany (1962) has shown convincingly that for learning to occur in the verbal conditioning experiments, it is not only necessary that the subject be able to verbalize the relationship between the correct response class and the reinforcement but also to verbalize the intention to perform in this manner. Spielberger (1962) has presented other evidence that the subject's performance in a verbal learning or conditioning experiment corresponds quite closely with his verbalizable statements concerning relationships between stimuli, responses, and reinforcement. Negative evidence for perceptual learning without awareness has been reported by Eriksen and Doroz (1963), and Chatterjee and Eriksen (1960, 1962), along with Branca (1957), have shown that autonomic conditioning does not appear to occur in human subjects without concomitant verbalizable mediational steps. In view of this negative evidence for unconscious learning in humans, it behooves us to question not only whether such a process occurs in cognitive avoidance but whether such a process is necessary to explain the data.

In the Eriksen and Kuethe experiment the noninsightful subjects appeared to have learned avoidance of the punished association unconsciously, by a process corresponding to repression. However, Martin and Dean (1964), in a series of replications of the Eriksen and Kuethe study, have raised serious doubts as to whether the noninsightful subjects can be described as having learned avoidance without awareness. By extensive and careful postexperimental questioning of their subjects, Martin and Dean found that unless a subject verbalized some hypothesis related to changing his response there was no evidence of learning. When they applied their more stringent criterion of unawareness, no evidence was found that unaware subjects avoided. Martin and Dean were successful in reproducing the differences in reaction time in certain of their replications, but more extensive analysis suggested that the differences observed in the reaction-time data for the insightful and noninsightful subjects in the Eriksen and Kuethe study may have had a complex relationship to the familiarity of the stimulus words to which shock was applied during the learning phase of the experiment.

The perceptual defense phenomenon has at times been ascribed to the operation of an unconscious discriminatory mechanism that serves to cue the avoidance responses, preventing conscious recognition of the anxiety-eliciting stimulus (Blum, 1955; Lazarus & McCleary, 1951). Not only does the behavior theory account of perceptual defense provided by Eriksen and Browne (1956) render the assumption of unconscious discrimination unnecessary to account for the phenomenon but a critical survey of the evidence for unconscious discriminating powers yields little support for belief in such a mechanism (Eriksen, 1958, 1960; Goldiamond, 1958). When methodological artifacts are eliminated, and misconceptions as to the nature of psychophysical thresholds are corrected (Pierce, 1963b), there is little convincing evidence that the human can discriminate more accurately or sensitively by autonomic or other nonverbal indicators than he can with a verbal response.

It may be argued that if the subject is aware that he is avoiding thinking of certain anxiety-arousing or unpleasant topics, then we are dealing only with suppression and not repression in the Freudian sense. This may be a valid argument, but it is also possible that the clinically observed phenomenon does not itself require the assumption of an unconscious automatic process, at least in the acquisition phase. In view of the extreme difficulty experimenters have had in producing convincing demonstrations of learning without awareness in the laboratory, the possibility must be seriously entertained that the clinical concept of repression is only a very well-learned, or overlearned, response suppression.

The clinical observations on repression in patients are obtained many years after the original repression has occurred. It may well be that at the time of the traumatic experience the patient was aware for a period of several days of engaging in a deliberate response suppression which after enough rehearsal became automatic. While human adults may not learn without awareness, each of us can attest to the knowledge that responses that have been overlearned seem capable of running off without our being aware of them. Many of our mannerisms, patterns of speaking, even complex motor skills, such as automobile driving, are capable of smooth execution for appreciable periods of time without our devoting subjective awareness to the specific task. Just as we can walk by a hot radiator and automatically avoid touching it, so perhaps can we automatically avoid thinking certain thoughts that lead to anxiety when the original avoidance learning has been well established.

The subjective train of thought has minimal constraints imposed upon it since it is not observable by others. This permits considerable freedom in the type of associative connections that a particular individual establishes. The thought of black might lead to the thought of white, which in turn leads to the thought of snow. Now if our particular individual had sometime in the past been responsible for a skiing accident in which a loved member of the family was killed, the thought of snow would be expected to lead to the thought of the accident, which in turn would reactivate the accident memories and lead to feelings of guilt. But since subjective associations are not rigidly constrained, it is quite possible for our individual to learn to think of night in response to the thought of black, which in turn leads to the association day, sunny, and off onto a completely different train of thought than would have occurred had the originally stronger associative connection taken place. Since this new associative train does not lead to the unpleasant state of affairs, it is expected that it would be reinforced and its probability of occurring would become greater.

Initially, this change in associative connections may have been accompanied by a deliberate response suppression, and the associative chain may have continued through to a much closer connection with the anxiety-arousing memory. But after suppression had been operating for a time, the new direction of thought became automatic, and through the short-circuiting of behavior chains, so well described by Dollard and Miller, the forking of thoughts or of associations occurs further away from the traumatic memory. Such a process would seem to account for the associative gaps that have been noted by clinicians in patients demonstrating repression.

Inhibition or New Learning

Whether we accept a concept of suppression or of repression, both concepts imply an active inhibitory process. The direct experimental evidence for such an active inhibitory factor in defensive phenomena is rather meager. An alternative interpretation for the elimination of a response is in terms of new learning where a new response becomes stronger or more dominant in the particular stimulus situation. The experimental studies on defensive mechanisms have provided little direct evidence on a choice of these two alternative explanations.

If the response is actively inhibited, removal of the anxiety that is responsible for the inhibition should lead to the reappearance of the response with little observable decrement. This is in keeping with the Freudian concept of repression. Experimental attempts to demonstrate this "return of the repressed" have not met with much success. In the experiments previously described by Zeller (1950) and Merrill (1954) an attempt was made to demonstrate this phenomenon. In both experiments an improvement in recall was found following removal of the anxiety, but due to weaknesses in experimental design, neither experiment is very convincing in showing that this increment in recall was due to the removal of inhibition. As was noted in discussing these experiments in the preceding sections, the material to be remembered was in no way associated with anxiety. Suppressing or repressing the learned material served no adaptive function for the subject since no anxiety was engendered by its conscious recall.

The best evidence of the effect of removal of anxiety upon recall is contained in the experiment by Caron and Wallach (1957). As will be recalled, these investigators studied the recall of completed and incompleted items administered under the guise of an intelligence test and, in addition, determined the perceptual recognition of neutral words and words related to an intelligence testing experience. Besides a control for individual differences in defensive behavior, Caron and Wallach employed several subgroups in their experiment who had the pseudo-nature of the intelligence test explained to them before recall for the items on this task was requested. They found that the explanation, with resulting catharsis and relief, did not change significantly the pattern of recall for failed and succeeded items from that of the subjects who recalled while still under the impression they had failed miserably on the intelligence test. From this finding Caron and Wallach concluded that the decrement in failed item recall by the repressor group and the decrement in successful item recall by the sensitizer group in their experiment was attributable to differences in the learning process rather than to differences in repression or inhibition of these respective items.

Unfortunately, this conclusion seems less certain when the performance on the perceptual recognition measure is considered. The data show that even the subjects who had the ruse explained to them showed differences in perceptual recognition for words pertaining to a testing situation, relative to neutral words. If the experimenter's explanation of the ruse and the group cathartic experience had been successful in removing all anxiety associated with the experimental stress, then patterns of defensive response to perceptual recognition of words associated with this stress experience would no longer be anticipated. The finding of such differences, however, makes it questionable whether the experimental removal of the stress was effective. In summary, the degree to which an inhibitory process is involved in defense mechanisms is still uncertain and needs to be more carefully delineated by future experimentation.

PERSONALITY CORRELATES OF DEFENSIVE BEHAVIORS

An important and intriguing question concerns the differences that have been observed between the repressor and the sensitizer in defensive reactions. Why should some subjects show a heightened sensitivity toward anxiety-associated material while others show a cognitive avoidance? Both responses can be considered defensive mechanisms since they are responses to the anxiety associated with covert cues. (Brown [1961] has grouped both the perceptual sensitization and the perceptual defense reaction under a general classification of perceptual defense.) It is interesting and natural to speculate on the relation of the clinically described mechanisms of defense to these experimentally observed extreme reactions to covertly cued anxiety. Indeed, the experiments of Lazarus, Eriksen, and Fonda (1951), Carpenter, Wiener, and Carpenter (1956), and Shannon (1962) have directly related these differences in experimentally produced behavior to clinically described differences in defensive mechanisms.

Psychoanalytic theory, substantiated by clinical observation, posits a relationship between repression and the hysteroid personality. Repression is supposed to be the primary or main defensive reaction of the hysteric. One might expect, then, to find a relation between personality traits associated with the hysteroid personality and tendencies to avoid in perception and memory. Just such a relation was suggested by Rosenzweig and Sarason (1942) when they reported a relation between impunitiveness and suggestibility, two traits associated with hysteria, and tendency to favor completed tasks in recall.

Eriksen (1954) speculated on the relationship of the hysteria-psychasthenia dimension and his measure of ego strength to Eysenck's factors (Eysenck, 1947) of introversion-extraversion and general neuroticism. The ego strength measure employed by Eriksen was very similar to a test that Eysenck had found highly saturated with his neuroticism factor. Similarly, the hysteria and psychasthenia scales of the MMPI seemed, from their pattern of reported relationships, to be similar to Eysenck's introversion-extraversion dimension. Eriksen's results suggested that both factors had an independent relationship with completed-incompleted task recall under conditions of anxiety arousal. Inglis (1961) has more thoroughly worked out this relationship and surveyed and ordered the research evidence in support of it.

While Eriksen and Inglis have sought to relate the differences in repressors and sensitizers to the factors of introversion-extraversion and general neuroticism, other investigators have been trying to devise improved scales for measuring these differential responses to threat or anxiety. Altrocchi, Parsons, and Dickoff (1960) selected three MMPI scales, depression, psychasthenia, and the Welsh Anxiety Scale, that previous research had suggested as likely measures of sensitization, and three other scales, Lie, *K,* and hysteria, as measures of repression. They computed a repression-sensitization index for subjects by subtracting the subject's total score on the latter three scales from his total score on the former three. With this index they found that repressors differed from sensitizers on self-ideal discrepancies, primarily due to the more negative self-concept that the sensitizers had. Altrocchi (1961) further found differences in interpersonal perception associated with scores on the repressor-sensitizer index which were shown to be due to the differences in self concepts between these two groups.

Some important psychometric refinements in the repressor-sensitizer index have been made by Byrne (1961). In an extensive program Byrne and his students have set about validating the improved repressor-sensitizer measure. An integrated review of not only the work in his own laboratory but also of the related work on the repressor-sensitizer dimension has been made by Byrne (1964).

An independent attempt to develop a measure of the repressor-sensitizer variable was undertaken by Ullmann (1958). Originally his scale was applicable only to neuropsychiatric patients, since it was based upon ratings of case history material using essentially the criteria that Shannon had employed in detecting his perceptual externalizers and internalizers (Shannon, 1962). Ullmann (1962) later undertook to construct a scale derived from MMPI items to measure this dimension that he termed facilitators-inhibitors. In subsequent studies the facilitation-inhibition scale of Ullmann has been found to correlate .76 with the repressor-sensitizer scale in one study (Byrne, 1961) and .94 for a psychiatric population in another (Ullmann, 1962). Despite their differences in derivation it would appear that both scales are measuring essentially the same personality characteristic.

Research employing one or the other of these scales has shown an interesting pattern of relationships with personality variables and performance that most clinical theorizing would expect to be related to a repressor-sensitizer difference. Ullmann and Limm (1962) found that sensitizers and facilitators showed greater appreciation for sexual and aggressive humor than did repressors. Gossett (1964) related the repressor-sensitizer scale to differential recall of successful and failed tasks administered under the guise of an intelligence or personality test, and Tempone (1962) related the scale to perceptual vigilance and perceptual defense in a well-controlled study. Numerous other correlations of the repressor-sensitizer facilitator-inhibition scale with various personality adjustment and task performance measures are summarized by Byrne (1964).

From the research surveyed by Byrne, it would appear that the pattern of relationships of the repressor-sensitizer and facilitator-inhibition scales with other personality and performance variables reflects, in a large part, an introversive-extraversive dimension. That more than an introversion-extraversion dimension is involved in the scales is shown by correlations of the scales with measures of maladjustment. Sensitizers tend to make more deviant responses on check lists (Byrne, 1961), are rated as more anxious in ward behavior (Ullmann & McReynolds, 1963), and more maladjusted as assessed by the California Psychological Inventory (Joy, 1963).

If repressors represent neurotic extraverts and sensitizers neurotic introverts as suggested by Inglis (1961), it would be anticipated that a curvilinear relationship would be obtained between the repressor-sensitizer scale and measures of maladjustment. However, as Byrne (1964) has pointed out, there is no suggestion of a curvilinear relationship between the repressor-sensitizer scale and the various measures of adjustment which have been studied. A possible basis for this failure to find curvilinearity may lie in the fact that the repressor-sensitizer and facilitator-inhibition scales are measuring both introversion-extraversion and neuroticism or emotional stability. Eriksen (1954) had found that both a measure of neuroticism and a measure of hysteria were independently related to differences in defensive responses. If both factors are involved in the repressor-sensitizer scale, it is possible to account for the positive linear relationship the scale shows with other self-report measures of adjustment.

The repressor-sensitizer scale has been shown to have a high correlation with the Edwards' social desirability scale (Joy, 1963; Liberty, Lunneborg, & Atkinson, in press). This tendency of the repressors to say socially desirable things about themselves, to have favorable self-concepts, and in general, to avoid thinking unpleasant thoughts, might well lead to a spurious indication of good adjustment on scales and measures that involve self-description or self-assessment. What is needed is evidence to show that the repressors' self-descriptions are at variance with the actual state of affairs.

Some support for a discrepancy between the repressors' self-descriptions or evaluations is found in a study by Lomont (1961). He found only a negligible correlation between the self-report measure of hostility and hostility as assessed by the Holtzman inkblots. However, when scores on the repressor-sensitizer scale were partialed out of the relationship, the correlation between the two measures of hostility increased to a significant .49. If the clinical assumption is true that the inkblots are capable of detecting an unacknowledged hostility, then Lomont's data would suggest that the repressors' self-report measures reflect an avoidance of recognition of the true state of affairs in their own personalities.

Further evidence that the repressors are overly favorable in their self-descriptions comes from an experiment by Lazarus and Alfert (1963). These experimenters recorded heart rate and skin conductance in an experimentally stressful situation. Subjects high on the *HY* scale refused to admit disturbance in their verbal reports but revealed it autonomically, while subjects low on the scale were apt to say they were more disturbed than their autonomic activity indicated.

The results of Lomont and of Lazarus and Alfert suggest that greater degrees of maladjustment may exist in the repressor subjects than appears from their self-reports on various adjustment inventories. However, much further research designed to get at the difference between self-description and underlying emotional state is required before we can be certain of this point.

We turn finally to an important question that remains. Why does one subject respond to internally cued anxiety by avoidance behavior where another seems to be particularly sensitive and preoccupied with anxiety-arousing thoughts?

Inglis (1961) has attempted to deal with this question, first, in terms of his conception of the repressors and sensitizers as neurotic extraverts and neurotic introverts and, second, in terms of the effects of increasing degrees of anxiety and stress upon performance. An inverted-*U* function has been frequently found to characterize the relationship of increasing degrees of drive level and/or anxiety and performance on specific tasks. For a certain range of drive level, performance improves as drive increases, but at some optimum point for the specific task, further increases in anxiety lead to a deterioration in performance. Inglis assumes that avoidance defenses characterize both neurotic introverts and extraverts, but like other performances the effectiveness with which they can be applied varies with drive or anxiety level. Inglis postulates that the neurotic introvert is more susceptible to anxiety-arousing situations. Thus in experiments on recall of completed-incompleted tasks or on perceptual recognition for emotional and neutral words, the neurotic introvert is apt to show avoidance defenses at very low stress levels. The neurotic extravert, on the other hand, is less susceptible to these minor degrees of stress. At the lower stress levels he responds with a vigilance-type reaction, but as the stress increases, the neurotic extravert begins to use avoidance defenses. As the stress increases, the neurotic introvert, on the other hand, reaches the point where the anxiety or drive level is too great for avoidant defenses to be effective and they break down with the resulting lack of defense or in some cases an apparent sensitization. As will be recalled, Bruner and Postman (1947a) had originally advanced this curvilinear relationship between perceptual recognition behavior and degree of stress or emotionality.

Inglis (1961), in reviewing the literature, finds some suggestive evidence to support this hypothesis, but convincing experimental evidence is lacking. What is required is an experiment that permits an assessment of just how much anxiety is aroused by the experimental task in each individual subject. As was noted earlier in this chapter, most of the techniques that have been employed are deficient in this respect. They merely allow a rather gross assumption that one treatment is on the average apt to be more stressful than another.

A different approach to the question of why sensitizers and repressors respond differentially to anxiety has been undertaken by Dulany (1957). He attempted to produce learning of perceptual vigilance and of perceptual defense. From the data he concluded that in a perceptual situation where one's perceptual response is followed by punishment, and competing perceptual responses are instrumental to avoidance of punishment, the punished response becomes weaker as compared with competing responses. In a situation where one's perceptual response is instrumental to avoidance of punishment and competing responses are punished, the avoidance response becomes stronger, leading to vigilance.

On the basis of Dulany's results, Byrne (1964) predicted that differential child-rearing practices would be used by the parents of repressors and sensitizers. In childhood, repressors would have experienced punishment in their attempts to express conflictual impulses, while sensitizers were permitted to express such material, at least at the verbal level. Thus child-rearing attitudes falling along a permissive-restrictive dimension would be expected to be related to the development of sensitizing vs. repressive mechanisms in the children. The predictions were not confirmed. While the repressors were found to indicate a childhood home atmosphere characterized by permissiveness, acceptance, and competence, the sensitizers were found to report restrictive and rejecting home atmospheres. The results are almost the reverse of the predictions. It would appear that the antecedents of perceptual and learning sensitization and defense will require considerable research before they are understood.

REFERENCES

Alper, Thelma G. Memory for completed and incompleted tasks as a function of personality: Correlation between experimental and personality data. *J. Pers.*, 1948, 17, 104–137.

Alper, Thelma G. Predicting the direction of selective recall: Its relation to ego strength and *N* achievement. *J. abnorm. soc. Psychol.*, 1957, 55, 149–165.

Altrocchi, J. Interpersonal perceptions of repressors and sensitizers in component analysis of assumed dissimilarity scores. *J. abnorm. soc. Psychol.*, 1961, 62, 528–534.

Altrocchi, J., Parsons, O. A., & Dickoff, Hilda. Changes in self-ideal discrepancy in repressors and sensitizers. *J. abnorm. soc. Psychol.*, 1960, 61, 67–72.

Atkinson, J. W. The achievement motive and recall of interrupted and completed tasks. *J. exp. Psychol.*, 1953, 46, 381–390.

Atkinson, J. W., & Raphelson, A. C. Individual differences in motivation and behavior in particular situations. *J. Pers.*, 1956, 24, 249–263.

Barber, T. X. Experimental controls and the phenomena of "hypnosis": A critique of hypnotic research methodology. *J. nerv. ment. Dis.*, 1962, 134, 493–505.

Blum, G. S. Perceptual defense revisited. *J. abnorm. soc. Psychol.*, 1955, 51, 24–29.

Bobbitt, Ruth A. The repression hypothesis studies in a situation of hypnotically induced conflict. *J. abnorm. soc. Psychol.*, 1958, 56, 204–211.

Branca, A. A. Semantic generalization at the level of the conditioning experiment. *Amer. J. Psychol.*, 1957, 70, 541–549.

Brown, W. P. Conceptions of perceptual defense. *Brit. J. Psychol.*, 1961, Monogr. Suppl.

Bruner, J. S., & Postman, L. Tension and tension-release as organizing factors in perception. *J. Pers.*, 1947, 15, 300–308. (a)

Bruner, J. S., & Postman, L. Emotional selectivity in perception and reaction. *J. Pers.*, 1947, 16, 69–77. (b)

Byrne, D. The repression-sensitization scale: Rationale, reliability, and validity. *J. Pers.*, 1961, 29, 334–349.

Byrne, D. Assessing personality variables and their alteration. In P. Worchel & D. Byrne (Eds.), *Personality change.* New York: Wiley, 1964. Pp. 38–68.

Caron, A. J., & Wallach, M. A. Recall of interrupted tasks under stress: A phenomenon of memory or of learning? *J. abnorm. soc. Psychol.*, 1957, 55, 372–381.

Caron, A. J., & Wallach, M. A. Personality determinants of repressive and obsessive reactions to failure stress. *J. abnorm. soc. Psychol.*, 1959, 59, 236–245.

Carpenter, B., Wiener, M., & Carpenter, Janeth T. Predictability of perceptual defense behavior. *J. abnorm. soc. Psychol.*, 1956, 52, 380–383.

Cartwright, D. S. Self-consistency as a factor affecting immediate recall. *J. abnorm. soc. Psychol.*, 1956, 52, 212–218.

Chatterjee, B. B., & Eriksen, C. W. Conditioning and generalization as a function of awareness. *J. abnorm. soc. Psychol.*, 1960, 60, 396–403.

Chatterjee, B. B., & Eriksen, C. W. Cognitive factors in heart rate conditioning. *J. exp. Psychol.*, 1962, 64, 272–279.

Dollard, J., & Miller, N. E. *Personality and psychotherapy.* New York: McGraw-Hill, 1950.

Dulany, D. E., Jr. Avoidance learning of perceptual defense and vigilance. *J. abnorm. soc. Psychol.*, 1957, 55, 333–338.

Dulany, D. E., Jr. The place of hypotheses and intentions: An analysis of verbal control in verbal conditioning. In C. W. Eriksen (Ed.), *Behavior and awareness.* Durham, N.C.: Duke Univer. Press, 1962. Pp. 102–129.

Edwards, A. L. *The social desirability variable in personality assessment and research.* New York: Dryden, 1957.

Eriksen, C. W. Some implications for TAT interpretation arising from need and perception experiments. *J. Pers.*, 1951, 19, 282–288. (a)

Eriksen, C. W. Perceptual defense as a function of unacceptable needs. *J. abnorm. soc. Psychol.*, 1951, 46, 557–564. (b)

Eriksen, C. W. Defense against ego threat in memory and perception. *J. abnorm. soc. Psychol.*, 1952, 47, 230–236. (a)

Eriksen, C. W. Individual differences in defensive forgetting. *J. exp. Psychol.*, 1952, 44, 442–447. (b)

Eriksen, C. W. Psychological defenses and "ego strength" in the recall of completed and incompleted tasks. *J. abnorm. soc. Psychol.*, 1954, 49, 45–50.

Eriksen, C. W. Unconscious processes. In M. R. Jones (Ed.), *Nebraska symposium on motivation*. Lincoln: Univer. of Nebraska Press, 1958. Pp. 169–227.

Eriksen, C. W. Discrimination and learning without awareness: A methodological survey and evaluation. *Psychol. Rev.*, 1960, 67, 279–300.

Eriksen, C. W. Perception and personality dynamics. In R. W. Heine & J. M. Wepman (Eds.), *Perspectives in personality theory*. Chicago: Aldine Publishing Co., 1963.

Eriksen, C. W., & Browne, C. T. An experimental and theoretical analysis of perceptual defense. *J. abnorm. soc. Psychol.*, 1956, 52, 224–230.

Eriksen, C. W., & Doroz, L. Role of awareness in learning and use of correlated extraneous cues on perceptual tasks. *J. exp. Psychol.*, 1963, 66, 601–608.

Eriksen, C. W., & Kuethe, J. L. Avoidance conditioning of verbal behavior without awareness: A paradigm of repression. *J. abnorm. soc. Psychol.*, 1956, 53, 203–209.

Eriksen, C. W., & Lazarus, R. S. Perceptual defense and projective tests. *J. abnorm. soc. Psychol.*, 1952, 47, 302–308.

Eysenck, H. J. *Dimensions of personality*. London: Kegan Paul, Trench, Trubner, and Co., 1945.

Fenichel, O. *The psychoanalytic theory of neurosis*. New York: Norton, 1945.

Flanagan, D. E. The influence of emotional inhibition on learning and recall. Unpublished master's thesis, Univer. of Chicago, 1930.

Flavell, J. H. Repression and the "return of the repressed." *J. consult. Psychol.*, 1955, 19, 441–443.

Freud, S. *The problem of anxiety*. (Eng. transl.) New York: Norton, 1936.

Freud, S. *Repression: An introduction*. 1914. (Standard Ed.) Vol. 14. London: Hogarth Press, 1957.

Freud, S. Repression. 1915. *Collected Papers*. Vol. 4. London: Hogarth Press, 1925.

Freud, S., & Breuer, J. *Studies on hysteria*. 1895. (Standard Ed.) Vol. 2. London: Hogarth Press, 1955.

Glixman, A. F. Recall of completed and incompleted activities under varying degrees of stress. *J. exp. Psychol.*, 1949, 39, 281–295.

Goldiamond, I. Indicators of perception: 1. Subliminal perception, subception, unconscious perception: An analysis in terms of psychophysical indicator methodology. *Psychol. Bull.*, 1958, 55, 373–411.

Gossett, J. T. An experimental demonstration of Freudian repression proper. Unpublished doctoral dissertation, Univer. of Arkansas, 1964.

Gould, R. Repression experimentally analyzed. *Character and Pers.*, 1942, 10, 259–288.

Guilford, J. P. *Inventory of factors STDCR*. Beverly Hills, Calif.: Sheridan Supply Co., 1940.

Holtzman, W. H. *The inkblot test*. Austin: Univer. of Texas, 1958.

Howes, D. H., & Solomon, R. L. A note on McGinnies' "Emotionality and perceptual defense." *Psychol. Rev.*, 1950, 57, 229–234.

Howes, D. H., & Solomon, R. L. Visual duration threshold as a function of word-probability. *J. exp. Psychol.*, 1951, 41, 401–410.

Inglis, J. Abnormalities of motivation and "ego functions." In H. J. Eysenck (Ed.), *Handbook of abnormal psychology*. New York: Basic Books, 1961.

Jacobs, A. Formation of new associations to words selected on the basis of reaction-time–GSR combinations. *J. abnorm. soc. Psychol.*, 1955, 51, 371–377.

Jourard, S. M. Ego strength and recall of tasks. *J. abnorm. soc. Psychol.*, 1954, 49, 51–58.

Joy, V. L. Repression-sensitization, personality, and interpersonal behavior. Unpublished doctoral dissertation, Univer. of Texas, 1963.

Korner, I. H. Experimental investigation of some aspects of the problem of repression: repressive forgetting. *Teach. Coll. Contr. Educ.*, 1950, No. 970.

Kott, M. G. Learning and retention of words of sexual and nonsexual meaning. *J. abnorm. soc. Psychol.*, 1955, 50, 378–382.

Laffal, J. Application of Guttman's scaling method to the TAT. *Educ. psychol. Measmt*, 1955, 15, 422–435.

Lazarus, R. S., & Alfert, Elizabeth. The short circuiting of threat by experimentally altering cognitive appraisal. Unpublished manuscript, Univer. of California, 1963.

Lazarus, R. S., Eriksen, C. W., & Fonda, C.

P. Personality dynamics and auditory perceptual recognition. *J. Pers.*, 1951, 19, 471–482.

Lazarus, R. S., & Longo, N. The consistency of psychological defense against threat. *J. abnorm. soc. Psychol.*, 1953, 48, 495–499.

Lazarus, R. S., & McCleary, R. A. Autonomic discrimination without awareness: A study of subception. *Psychol. Rev.*, 1951, 58, 113–123.

Levinger, G., & Clark, J. Emotional factors in the forgetting of word associations. *J. abnorm. soc. Psychol.*, 1961, 62, 99–105.

Liberty, P. G., Jr., Lunneborg, C. E., & Atkinson, G. C. Perceptual defense, dissimulation and response styles. *J. consult. Psychol.*, in press.

Lomont, J. F. The current status of repression. Unpublished doctoral dissertation, Univer. of Illinois, 1961.

Martin, R. B., & Dean, S. J. Word frequency and avoidance conditioning of verbal behavior. *J. abnorm. soc. Psychol.*, 1964.

Mathews, Anne, & Wertheimer, M. A "pure" measure of perceptual defense uncontaminated by response suppression. *J. abnorm. soc. Psychol.*, 1958, 57, 373–376.

McArthur, C. Personalities of public and private school boys. *Harv. educ. Rev.*, 1954, 24, 256–262.

McArthur, C. Personality differences between middle and upper classes. *J. abnorm. soc. Psychol.*, 1955, 50, 247–254.

McReynolds, P. The Rorschach concept evaluation technique. *Amer. Psychologist*, 1949, 4, 267. (Abstract)

McReynolds, P. Perception of Rorschach concepts as related to personality deviations. *J. abnorm. soc. Psychol.*, 1951, 46, 131–141.

Merrill, R. M. The effect of pre-experimental and experimental anxiety on recall efficiency. *J. exp. Psychol.*, 1954, 48, 167–172.

Murray, E. J. Conflict and repression during sleep deprivation. *J. abnorm. soc. Psychol.*, 1959, 59, 95–101.

Nelson, S. E. Psychosexual conflicts and defenses in visual perception. *J. abnorm. soc. Psychol.*, 1955, 51, 427–433.

Orne, M. T. The nature of hypnosis: Artifact and essence. *J. abnorm. soc. Psychol.*, 1959, 58, 277–299.

Pierce, Jan. Determinants of threshold for form. *Psychol. Bull.*, 1963, 60, 391–407. (a)

Pierce, Jan. Sources of artifact in the tachistoscopic perception of words. *J. exp. Psychol.*, 1963, 66, 363–370. (b)

Postman, L., Bruner, J., & McGinnies, E. Personal values as selective factors in perception. *J. abnorm. soc. Psychol.*, 1948, 43, 142–154.

Postman, L., & Solomon, R. L. Perceptual sensitivity to completed and incompleted tasks. *J. Pers.*, 1950, 18, 347–357.

Reyher, J. Posthypnotic stimulation of hypnotically induced conflict in relation to psychosomatic reactions and psychopathology. *Psychosom. Med.*, 1961, 23, 384–391.

Rogers, C. R. *Client-centered therapy.* Boston: Houghton Mifflin, 1951. P. 515.

Rosenzweig, S. An experimental study of "repression" with special reference to need-persistive and ego-defensive reactions to frustration. *J. exp. Psychol.*, 1943, 32, 64–74.

Rosenzweig, S., & Mason, G. An experimental study of memory in relation to the theory of repression. *Brit. J. Psychol.*, 1934, 24, 247–265.

Rosenzweig, S., & Sarason, S. An experimental study of the triadic hypothesis: Reaction to frustration, ego defense, and hypnotizability. 1. Correlational approach. *Charact. & Pers.*, 1942, 11, 1–20.

Sandison, R. L. Consistency of defense against psychological stress. Abstract of Ph.D. thesis, Department of Social Relations, Harvard Univer., 1954.

Sears, R. R. Experimental studies in projection: 1. Attribution of traits. *J. soc. Psychol.*, 1936, 7, 151–163.

Shannon, D. T. Clinical patterns of defense as revealed in visual recognition thresholds. *J. abnorm. soc. Psychol.*, 1962, 64, 370–377.

Shaw, F. J. Two determinants of selective forgetting. *J. abnorm. soc. Psychol.*, 1944, 39, 434–435.

Singer, B. R. An experimental inquiry into the concept of perceptual defense. *Brit. J. Psychol.*, 1956, 47, 298–311.

Smock, C. D. The relationship between test anxiety, "threat-expectancy," and recognition thresholds for words. *J. Pers.*, 1956, 25, 191–201.

Spielberger, C. D. Role of awareness in verbal conditioning. In C. W. Eriksen (Ed.), *Behavior and awareness.* Durham, N.C.: Duke Univer. Press, 1962.

Sutcliffe, J. P. "Credulous" and "skeptical" views of hypnotic phenomena: A review of certain evidence and methodology. *Int. J. clin. ex. Hypnosis,* 1960, 8, 73–101.

Sutcliffe, J. P. "Credulous" and "skeptical" views of hypnotic phenomena: Experiments on esthesia, hallucination, and delusion. *J. abnorm. soc. Psychol.,* 1961, 62, 189–200.

Tempone, V. J. Differential thresholds of repressors and sensitizers as a function of a success and failure experience. Unpublished doctoral dissertation, Univer. of Texas, 1962.

Thorndike, E. L., & Lorge, I. *The teacher's word book of 30,000 words.* New York: Columbia Univer. Press, 1944.

Truax, C. B. The repression response to implied failure as a function of the hysteria-psychasthenia index. *J. abnorm. soc. Psychol.,* 1957, 55, 188–193.

Ullmann, L. P. Clinical correlates of facilitation and inhibition of response to emotional stimuli. *J. proj. Tech.,* 1958, 22, 341–347.

Ullmann, L. P. An empirically derived MMPI scale which measures facilitation-inhibition of recognition of threatening stimuli. *J. clin. Psychol.,* 1962, 18, 127–132.

Ullmann, L. P., & Lim, D. T. Case history material as a source of the identification of patterns of response to emotional stimuli in a study of humor. *J. consult. Psychol.,* 1962, 26, 221–225.

Ullmann, L. P., & McReynolds, P. Differential perceptual recognition in psychiatric patients: Empirical findings and theoretical formulation. Paper read at Amer. Psychol. Ass., Philadelphia, August, 1963.

Van de Castle, R. L. Perceptual defense in a binocular-rivalry situation. *J. Pers.,* 1960, 28, 448–462.

Wallen, R. Ego-involvement as a determinant of selective forgetting. *J. abnorm. soc. Psychol.,* 1942, 37, 1–20.

White, R. B. *The abnormal personality.* New York: Ronald, 1948.

Wilkinson, F. R., & Cargill, D. W. Repression elicited by story material based on the Oedipus Complex. *J. soc. Psychol.,* 1955, 42, 209–214.

Williams, M. Rate of learning as a function of ego-alien material. *J. Pers.,* 1951, 19, 324–331.

Williamsen, J. A., Johnson, H. J., & Eriksen, C. W. Some characteristics of posthypnotic amnesia. *J. abnorm. Psychol.,* 1964.

Zajonc, R. B. Response suppression in perceptual defense. *J. exp. Psychol.,* 1962, 64, 206–214.

Zeigarnik, B. Untersuchungen zur Handlungs- und Affektpsychologie, Herausgegeben von K. Lewin. 3. Das Behalten erledigter und underledigter Handlungen. *Psychol. Forsch.,* 1927, 9, 1–85.

Zeller, A. F. An experimental analogue of repression. 2. The effect of individual failure and success on memory measured by relearning. *J. exp. Psychol.,* 1950, 40, 411–422.

CHAPTER 21 Human Reaction to Stress[1]

IRVING L. JANIS
Yale University
HOWARD LEVENTHAL
The University of Wisconsin

This chapter will present theoretical concepts, empirical generalizations, and explanatory hypotheses useful for the analysis of human behavior in stress situations. The focus is on major psychological determinants of stress behavior. Although considerable experimentation and field investigation are still required either to verify or disconfirm the propositions to be discussed, it is our expectation that most, if not all, of them are testable and will prove to contain some lasting "germs of truth."

Two strategies dominate the empirical investigation of stress behavior. One approach involves studying the effects of changes in stimulus conditions, while the other studies individual differences among people who are exposed to the same stress conditions. Both approaches are useful and will be drawn upon for evidence. Some recent studies will also be considered which use a combined approach, studying stress behavior as a function of the interaction between both the stimulus conditions and personal predispositions that take account of differences in the past history of the individual and/or latent personality characteristics. Therefore, we can expect to find three different types of general propositions or laws concerning stress reactions: (a) those that indicate how the average personality or most people would react to variations in the environmental situation in which a stressful event occurs; (b) statements about the characteristic reactions of particular types of personalities to stressful events in general; and (c) more complex assertions that specify how different types of personalities react to one type of stressful situation as against another.

We shall review some of the main findings which pertain to each of the three types of propositions. Without attempting an exhaustive survey of the literature, we shall select some of the major research studies that have contributed to our knowledge about the determinants of stress behavior and call attention to the main explanatory

[1] The senior author wishes to acknowledge the support of a grant from the National Institute of Mental Health (MH 08564), under which some of the experiments summarized in this chapter, and the accompanying theoretical analyses, were carried out. Several of the experiments by the second author and his associates which are discussed in this chapter were carried out under a separate grant (CH 00077-03) from the National Institute of Mental Health. The second author was affiliated with Yale University at the time this article was prepared.

concepts that have been used by research workers in this field. We shall also suggest some new concepts that may help to integrate existing findings and to focus subsequent research on relevant variables that have been neglected.

Definitions of "Stress"

There is no generally agreed upon definition of "psychological stress" among behavioral scientists. A wide variety of definitions can be seen in recent comprehensive reviews of the literature by Appley and Trumbull (1967); Basowitz, Persky, Korchin, and Grinker (1955); Lazarus (1961, 1966); Withey (1962). Selye's (1950) concept of physiological stress, which treats stress responses as specific reaction patterns elicited by a wide range of stimuli that interfere with "homeostasis," has been used by several writers (e.g., Menninger, 1954a, 1954b; Wolff, 1953) in an attempt to generate a parallel conception of psychological stress. This type of definition has not been widely accepted by psychologists, however, because the physiological term does not necessarily refer to the same type of phenomena as the psychological one. Withey (1962), for example, calls attention to three main obstacles to a definition of psychological stress parallel to that of physiological stress: (a) the psychologist has no adequate way of defining the psychological condition that corresponds to the homeostatic steady state; (b) defining stress in terms of the nonsatisfaction of needs requires specification of the tolerance limits for healthy and efficient functioning, which can be done more easily at the physiological than the psychological level; (c) in physiological stress, "the *structure* and *organization* of the organism determine the 'selection' and sequence of adaptive or defense processes," whereas in psychological stress, "it seems necessary to include the higher mental processes involving learned behaviors, intelligence level and other complicating factors."

Despite the above objections, which reflect the less advanced state of empirical knowledge about psychological than about physiological stress, there seems to be a fairly high degree of consensus as to the domain of behavioral events to which the term "psychological stress" refers. Thus, for most writers, the term designates a broad class of events involving interaction between extreme environmental stimuli and the adjustive capabilities of the organism. For example, in an excellent discussion of the problems entailed in assessing stress exposure and identifying the antecedent conditions, Basowitz *et al.* (1955, p. 7) state:

> ... We can conceive a continuum of stimuli differing in meaning to the organism and in their anxiety-producing consequences. At one end are such stimuli or cues, often highly symbolic, which have meaning only to single or limited numbers of persons and which to the observer may appear as innocuous or trivial. At the other end are such stimuli, here called stress, which by their explicit threat to vital functioning and their intensity are likely to overload the capacity of most organisms' coping mechanisms.
>
> ... Ultimately we can truly speak of a *stress situation* only when a given response occurs, but for schematic purposes as well as consistency with common usage, we may use the term stress to designate certain kinds of stimulating conditions without regard for response. Such stimuli are called stress because of their assumed or potential effect, although we well know that in any given case the organism's adaptive capacity, threshold, or previous learning may preclude any disturbance of behavior.

These authors propose that the term "stress" should be used to refer to those stimulus conditions that are likely to arouse the affective response of *anxiety*. But should the definition be so narrowly restricted? We know that sometimes exposure to a noxious event, such as an auto accident, will arouse anxiety in one person, shame in a second person, and anger in a third; moreover, the same person will display a variety of negative emotional responses, including undifferentiated affective states, many of which cannot be appropriately labeled as "anxiety" (Janis, 1958). Thus, it seems preferable to designate as a "stressful" event any change in the environment which typically —i.e., in the average person—induces a high degree of emotional tension and interferes with normal patterns of response. As Scott (1949, p. 61) puts it, "a stress situation ... may be defined as one in which adjustment is difficult or impossible but in which motivation is very strong."

Thus, while the concept of stress is not rigorously defined, it does focus on a broad class of emotional behaviors elicited by antecedent stimulation, ranging from clear-cut exposure to painful or injurious physical dangers to purely verbal statements or gestures that convey social disapproval. Moreover, a close examination of stress situations will undoubtedly suggest many common features that are responsible for the similarities of the stress reactions and for parallels in their consequences for adjustment.

"Stress" as an Intervening Variable

Our general approach, which we believe will help orient research toward the discovery of general behavioral laws, consists of equating stress with fear, grief, rage, and other negative emotional states elicited by aversive stimulation.

All negative emotional states can be expected to share a number of important functional characteristics, such as those postulated for "learnable drives" that can be attached to a variety of stimulus conditions and that can motivate instrumental actions appropriate for terminating or removing the organism from the stress-inducing stimuli (see Miller, 1951). If we wish to keep open the possibility that some general laws of this type might ultimately be warranted by the empirical evidence, it will be advantageous to regard the concept of "stress" as an intervening variable that has specifiable antecedents and consequences for adjustive behavior.

Three general classes of antecedent situations that are regarded as stressful have been delineated by Schwab and Pritchard (1949), all of which are capable of arousing negative emotional states and instigating avoidance activity or other marked changes in overt behavior:

1. *Mild stress* stimulation, the effects of which last from seconds to hours: e.g., annoying insects, public appearances before a large audience, missing a train, and other such minor occurrences in daily life;
2. *Moderate stress* stimulation, the effects of which last from hours to days: e.g., a period of overwork, a gastric upset, a visit of an unwelcome guest, the temporary absence of a loved person;
3. *Severe stress* stimulation, the effects of which last for weeks, months, or even years: e.g., prolonged separation from one's family, death of a loved one, drastic financial losses, illnesses, and surgical operations.

It is primarily the second and third types of stresses to which the general hypotheses and theoretical analyses in this chapter are directed. The first type, involving slightly annoying or mildly aversive stimuli, has been investigated in a large number of so-called stress experiments, but generalizations from these studies do not necessarily apply to the more intense stress stimuli. Since we are not concerned with all aspects of emotional behavior nor with all situations capable of eliciting negative emotional responses, we shall restrict our discussion to relatively powerful stress stimulation, focusing on situations that give rise to intense emotional states and that appear to have fairly dependable behavioral consequences.

BEHAVIORAL CONSEQUENCES OF SEVERE STRESS

In order to designate the major types of behavioral consequences, we shall briefly summarize findings from extensive studies of American soldiers in combat—a rich source of illustrative empirical observations of reactions to external danger.

Physiological Changes

Surveys of combat infantrymen and of combat air crew personnel during World War II show that the closer and the more frequently the men were exposed to actual combat dangers, the higher the incidence of physiological symptoms of fear (Shaffer, 1947; Stouffer, Suchman, DeVinney, Star, & Williams, 1949a; Stouffer, Lumsdaine, Williams, Smith, Janis, Star, & Cottrell, 1949b). The most frequently reported symptoms included tremors, sweaty hands, cold sweats, violent pounding of the heart, and stomach disturbances. Some of these symptoms result from innervation of striated muscles of the body and are referred to as "physical tension," while others involve changes in the visceral organs of the body which are innervated by the autonomic nervous system. Both types of physiological changes are prominent in the list of somatic manifestations of anxiety which characterize the traumatic neuroses that temporarily occur following exposure to harrowing combat situations. For example, a team of psychiatrists who examined 150 heavy bomber crew members shortly after they had completed their tour of combat duty reported that 95 per cent of the men had developed acute traumatic neuroses, the most frequent symptoms being palpitations of the heart, tremors, frequency of micturition, loss of appetite, and diarrhea, along with typical increases in maladjustive behavior such as irritability, loss of interest in social activities, and increased consumption of alcohol (Hastings, Wright, & Glueck, 1944).

The physiological symptoms observed in combat personnel correspond directly to those that have been studied intensively in the laboratory. Changes induced by fear stimuli have been recorded in muscle action potentials (e.g., Malmo, Wallerstein, & Shagass, 1953; Malmo & Smith, 1955) and in electrical changes denoting increased heart rate, galvanic skin responses, and respiration rate. However, these indices do not show uniform changes for all situations or for all subjects. For example, recent experimental research suggests that heart rate increases only when the stress situation evokes a tendency toward rejection or escape and decreases when the stress stimuli evoke heightened attentiveness to external stimuli (Lacey, Kagan, Lacey, & Moss, 1963). There are also indications that the viseral patterns for fear stimuli may differ from those for anger-inducing frustrations and that the fear reactions are related to secretions of adrenalin, while anger reactions are related to secretions of both adrenalin and nonadrenalin (Ax, 1953; Funkenstein, King, & Drolette, 1957).

Motivational and Affective Changes

Studies of military combat personnel also provide evidence of increased attentiveness to environmental cues and the acquisition of adaptive discriminations between the more and the less dangerous features of the environment. For example, with increased time in the front lines, combat infantrymen learned to take cover when the sounds emitted by projectiles were approaching close by but to ignore the equally impressive sounds of those traveling overhead. Green troops, on the other hand, were aroused by both types of cues (Janis, 1949b).

In conjunction with the characteristic physiological symptoms of intense emotional arousal and heightened sensitivity to warning signals, combat soldiers also displayed marked increases in subjective feelings of apprehensiveness and readiness to accept recommendations concerning safety regulations, such as those regarding "No Smoking," blackout precautions, and the like. These messages were accepted most readily from seasoned officers in the soldier's own unit but were also taken seriously if they came as strongly worded official communications from military headquarters.

In contrast to the increased vigilance, discrimination among danger cues, and heightened acceptance of safety precautions, all of which tend to be adaptive reactions to stress, there are also some well-known maladaptive changes, involving impairment of cognitive and judgmental processes. The latter reactions occur after unusually prolonged or unusually intense exposures to danger. For example, combat personnel who were kept on the front lines for an extraordinarily long period of time developed reactions of apathy, indifference, and depression, known as "the old sergeant syndrome," resulting in marked inefficiency in their military and self-protective performance (Sobel, 1947). Findings from morale surveys indicate that a high percentage of combat soldiers acknowledged that they became confused or rattled while carrying out dangerous missions and that their emotional excitement interfered with performance of essential combat tasks (Stouffer *et al.,* 1949b; Shaffer, 1947). Reports of psychiatric casualties also indicate that under conditions of very high fear, acute panic reactions occurred which disorganized cognitive functioning to such an extent that for several hours after a danger episode, the men acted in a psychoticlike manner. These reactions included misinterpreting unexpected stimuli as signs of danger, projecting aggressive impulses and fears onto fellow soldiers, taking cover in response to any loud noise, and performing other impetuous protective actions that actually increased the danger (Glass, 1953; Grinker & Spiegel, 1945a, 1945b; Kardiner & Spiegel, 1947; Menninger, 1948). Hypervigilance has been observed among combat infantrymen in isolated foxholes and among aerial gunners on combat flying missions. For example, the men sometimes became "trigger happy," firing in the direction of slight sounds or shadows, even though there were no objective signs that the enemy was in the vicinity (Stouffer *et al.,* 1949b). In the most extreme cases of hypervigilance, the man is likely to display such a high degree of suspiciousness toward his comrades and leaders that he has to be removed from his unit as a psychiatric casualty, usually with a diagnosis of temporary "paranoid state."

Transient reactions of cognitive impairment and paranoid anxiety, as well as other symptoms of extreme emotional arousal, are occasionally seen among people in nonmilitary settings, such as the victims of a natural disaster and surgical patients being brought to the operating room. For example, many men and women who go through the ordeals of the preoperative period in a relatively fearless manner will suddenly become hypervigilant when confronted by the unfamiliar apparatus and activity of the operating room, becoming agitatedly suspicious that something much more drastic might be done to them than they had been told, sometimes even to the point of suspecting that the surgeon might be a sadist (Janis, 1958). In a study of cognitive efficiency among clinically normal people confronted with the threat of major surgery, Wright (1954) reports a number of less dramatic signs of temporary impairment, such as decreased attention span and greater conceptual rigidity during the period of very high anticipatory fear before the operation.

Theoretical Concepts Bearing on Anticipatory Emotional Reactions

Most of the stresses faced by human beings occur in anticipation of danger rather than in direct confrontation with noxious stimuli. Long before the impact of actual danger there is usually a warning phase during which signs of the threat or warning communications arouse anticipatory emotions. Hebb and Thompson (1954) point out that many technological advances and culture patterns in modern society succeed in protecting people from direct confrontations with extreme physical danger or deprivation, often at the cost of making civilized man more susceptible to emotional disturbances arising from anticipatory signs that call forth protective actions. The emotional tensions engendered by anticipatory reactions are dealt with in a variety of ways by contemporary psychological theorists. Lazarus (1961) calls attention to some of the distinctive features emphasized by different theories, such as the associationist learning theory of J. Dollard and N. Miller; the phenomenological theories of K. Lewin, K. Goldstein, and C. Rogers; the classical psychoanalytic theory of Freud; and the neo-Freudian theories of E. Fromm, Karen Horney, and H. S. Sullivan. Lazarus notes that in spite of the divergencies among the various current theories of stress reactions, there is a basic model of stress which seems to run through all of them. This model involves the recognition that motivational conflict, whether generated by external or internal conditions, leads to the arousal of fear or anxiety, which in turn is dealt with by either successful coping with the sources of conflict or by avoidance mechanisms. The latter include both pathological and nonpathological modes of adjustment, which enable the person to ward off painful emotional tension.

A number of theorists postulate that all forms of intense negative affect, irrespective of marked differences in the conditions of arousal, will exhibit certain common functional properties. In line with this theoretical approach, we assume that some causes and consequences will prove to be characteristic of all instances of high emotional tension, whether it takes the form of fear, grief, guilt, anger, or disgust. For example, we expect all such unpleasant affective states to persist until the noxious stimuli or distressing cues are avoided in one way or another, either through the person's own efforts or through environmental changes. Furthermore, as tension mounts from a low to a high level, we expect to find some characteristic shifts in the average person's thoughts, fantasies, plans, and actions, all of which are likely to become more and more directed toward warding off or escaping from those environmental events that give rise to the distressing affective state. Carrying this set of expectations one step further, we entertain the general assumption that all negative emotional states are likely to share the major functional properties specified by those learning theorists who postulate that defenses, protective actions, and verbal reassurances are habitual modes of reaction which are acquired and remain effective by virtue of their contiguity with escape or avoidance of cues that arouse the disturbing state (Brown & Farber, 1951; Dollard & Miller, 1950; Lambert, 1954; Mowrer, 1950; Skinner, 1953).

A different approach to the theory of affective states is to be found in the writings of Freud and other psychoanalysts, whose primary concern has centered upon the problem of diagnosing and explaining pathological manifestations of anxiety, as against so-called normal or objective anxiety. Freud's conception of neurotic anxiety or morbid fear refers to a class of intense apprehensive reactions that cannot be explained as reactions to *external threat* stimuli. According to this view, it is the reactivation of *internal dangers,* associated with drive impulses subjected to social taboos during the individual's early years, that gives rise to neurotic anxiety, which in turn forms the underlying motivation for repression and other defense mechanisms. Thus, according to Freud (1936, p. 151), "neurotic anxiety" involves "danger from an instinctual demand"; whereas, "true" or "objective" anxiety occurs when there is "real danger ... which threatens from some external object."

There are two outstanding features of neurotic anxiety which are repeatedly emphasized in Freudian case studies and theoretical discussions: (a) the emotional symptoms are generally out of all proportion to the relatively mild or nonexistent external threat, which the patient claims to be the source of his concern; and (b) the neurotic emotional reaction remains uninfluenced by authoritative reassurances and other pertinent information about ways of coping with the external threat, as the neurotic individual continually develops new rationalizations in order to justify his fears. For example, a neurotic's morbid fear of cancer can be provoked merely by his noticing a slight pimple on his skin, which might touch off an unconscious longing for forbidden forms of masochistic or sexual gratification; the patient is likely to resist his physician's assurance that a biopsy is not needed by adducing rational-sounding counterarguments, such as the fact that public health messages warn everyone not to neglect the possible signs of early cancer.

Differences in the severity of the threat cues provoking emotional tension cannot always be relied upon, however, to differentiate neurotic from nonneurotic reactions. In a severe community disaster, the sight of oncoming danger can precipitate a neurotic panic state in predisposed personalities, and their symptoms are very difficult to distinguish from the panic states occasionally evoked in normal persons when they undergo a terrifying experience in the presence of seemingly inescapable danger. And, indeed, a normal person may temporarily become so terrified that he behaves like a neurotic or psychotic, making grossly unrealistic judgments and displaying uncontrolled actions that he would ordinarily renounce as foolish, shameful, or grossly inconsiderate of others. But he can, nevertheless, be rapidly "cured" by being given strong *reassurances* by trusted authority figures or by being *removed* from the harrowing danger situation (see Caplan, 1951; Fromm-Reichmann, 1943; Glass, 1953; Grinker & Spiegel, 1945a, 1945b). Not so for the neurotic personality whose anxiety reactions are precipitated by exposure to a disaster, since his underlying unconscious conflict remains relatively unaffected by reassurances or removal.

Functional Properties of Reflective Fear

Many psychologists have followed Freud's lead in distinguishing between "normal fear" or "objective anxiety" occurring when a person is aware of a known danger, and "neurotic anxiety" arising from inner dangers linked with a person's unconscious impulses. However, since the same external conditions that elicit normal fear can also elicit neurotic anxiety, criteria other than the eliciting stimuli must be used to differentiate normal from neurotic reactions. What are the criteria that will enable a consistent distinction to be made? A tentative answer to this question is given in an analysis of the antecedents and consequences of "reflective fear" (Janis, 1962). The term "reflective" was introduced to elaborate on Freud's distinction and is used in the sense of thoughtful or deliberative and in the sense of reflecting the realities of the external danger situation. Janis has specified four major functional properties that distinguish reflective from neurotic fear:

1. *Responsiveness to environmental cues* —Signs of potential or actual threat in the environment play a *determining* role in activating and perpetuating the reflective fear reaction; whereas they play a much more minor, "precipitating" role in neurotic anxiety, as reminders of past threats linked with forbidden impulses. Reflective fear is directly affected by changes in the external signs, increasing when there are warnings that the danger is increasing or is closer at hand and decreasing when there are creditable reassurances that the danger is lessening. The latter include the receipt of information indicating the disappearance of the threat agent and the availability of new resources for coping with the threat. In contrast to the relatively unmodifiable character of neurotic fear or anxiety, the presence or absence of these external signs will have the effect of lowering or raising the person's level of reflective fear by influencing his conscious *anticipations of personal vulnerability*. A person's level of reflective fear is also influenced by his previously acquired attitudes and preparatory sets, including those that are the product of past training in cultural traditions concerning where, when, and how danger is likely to appear. Thus, the relevant antecedent factors in the indi-

vidual's past life are those that affect his attention to and processing of relevant informational inputs from the environment.

2. *Arousal of need for vigilance*—A major behavioral consequence of the arousal of reflective fear is a heightened need for vigilance, resulting in increased attention to environmental events and greater readiness to take protective action in response to any cue indicating the onset of danger. On the cognitive side, this involves scanning the environment for signs of danger, attending to information pertinent to the danger, and planning alternative courses of action for dealing with emergency contingencies. On the action side, vigilance results in a lower threshold for executing precautionary measures and heightened muscular tension, sometimes followed by increased motor activity to avoid or ward off the anticipated danger. During an epidemic, for example, vigilance can take the form of focussing attention on feelings of physical discomfort and lower the threshold for taking precautionary actions, such as going to a clinic for a medical check-up.

3. *Arousal of need for reassurance*—Another consequence of reflective fear is a strong need for alleviating emotional tension by obtaining convincing reassurances. Like "vigilance," the "need for reassurance" is assumed to be positively correlated with the level of reflective fear and to have a marked influence on both cognitions and actions. Cognitively, a heightened need for reassurance can result in selective attention to and recall of communications that minimize the danger or that play up the protective resources available for coping with it. It can also lead to changes in attitudes, such as the adoption of a fatalistic outlook or a greater faith in divine protection, greater reliance on magical or superstitious practices for warding off bad luck, and the acceptance of new ideas that provide rationalizations for continuing on a business-as-usual basis. Changes in action include overt efforts to avoid exposure to distressing warnings and greater adherence to conventional morality in an effort to avoid offending the "powers that be."

The most extreme forms of reassurance are so called "blanket reassurances," those involving anticipations of total invulnerability. The person feels convinced either that the danger will never materialize in his vicinity ("It can't happen here") or that, if it does, he will be completely protected from it ("Others may suffer, but we shall be safe").

4. *Development of compromise defenses involving discriminative vigilance and reassurance*—Vigilance and reassurance needs are potentially conflicting tendencies, in that they can impel a person toward incompatible cognitions or actions (e.g., "I must watch out because something dangerous is likely to happen at any moment," *vs.* "I can relax and forget about it because the danger will not affect me"). Nevertheless, it is possible to develop *compromise defenses* which combine vigilance (anticipating danger, seeking information about it, remaining alert to signs of threat) and reassurance (expecting to be able to cope successfully with the danger or to be helped by others if the danger becomes extreme). For example, in Atlanta, Georgia, when large numbers of Negroes were suddenly afflicted by blindness and stomach pains from imbibing large quantities of poisoned whiskey, a number of well-educated members of the colored community became agitated by scare rumors about maltreatment of fellow Negroes and checked the reliability of the rumors by visiting the local hospital wards and the morgue (Powell, 1953). This type of investigative behavior, which is characteristic of compromise defenses, leads to emotional relief when the subsequent investigations fail to confirm the rumors. It differs sharply from the reactions of other individuals who, while aware of the danger and of their own stomach aches and other symptoms, failed to seek medical aid. In these cases, the threatening implications of the symptoms were denied and reassurance needs clearly dominated over vigilance needs.

The diagram in Figure 1 shows the three alternative modes of adjustment to threat specified in the foregoing assumptions about the distinctive functional properties of reflective fear. Since both vigilance and reassurance needs are aroused by warnings and other threat stimuli, we can expect behavior to take either of the two extremely divergent paths or to reflect a fusion of the two tendencies, as seen in discriminative vigilance.

It remains a task for subsequent theory and research to specify both the common and the differentiating characteristics of the different types of reflective emotion. In a recent paper, Janis and Leventhal (1965) indicate that the distinction between a *reflective* emotion (which is highly modifiable by informational inputs) and an *internally-aroused* emotion (which is relatively unmodifiable by the receipt of new information) can be applied to other negative affects, such as grief, guilt, and anger, as well as to fear. Reflective fear and other reflective emotions can be regarded as an integral part of normal adjustive behavior.

Considerable research is needed to find out what conditions will make one as against another of the three modes of adjustment to threat dominant when reflective fear is aroused. One important antecedent variable that needs to be taken into account from the outset is indicated in Figure 2, which represents the main causal sequences that are assumed to give rise to the alternative types of adjustive reactions evoked by threat cues. The key determinant represented in this figure is the content of the threat cues, which is assumed to have a direct effect on the level of reflective fear that is aroused.

With very mild warnings, which evoke a low level of reflective fear, blanket reassurance is likely to be the predominating response, leaving the person unmotivated to attend to subsequent threat cues or to prepare for action related to the onset of danger. Such under-reactions can lead to serious maladaptive behavior if the potential danger in fact turns out to be severe. While this pattern of under-reaction to severe threat resembles the denial pattern seen in psychotic patients, it does not necessarily imply preexisting emotional disorder. Under certain environmental conditions, such as when warning cues are quite ambiguous or when

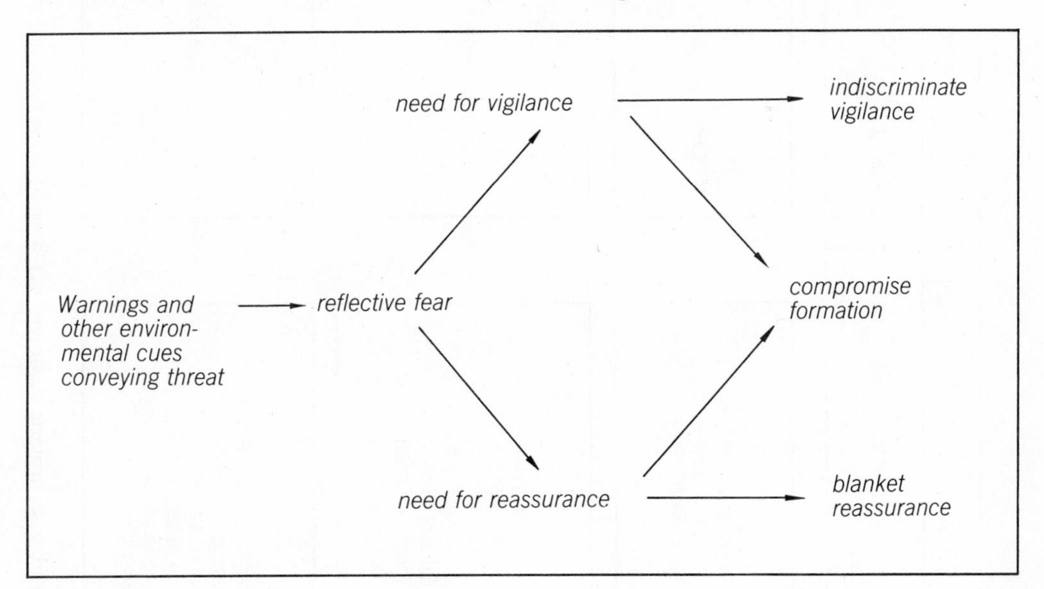

Figure 1. Hypothetical consequences of the arousal of reflective fear (Janis, 1962).

OBSERVABLE STIMULUS EVENTS	MEDIATING-PROCESS CONSTRUCTS		BEHAVIORAL CONSEQUENCES
Type of threat.	Immediate reaction (emotional R).	Type of defense.	Observable changes in attitudes and emotional symptoms.
(1) *Signs of low threat: danger is unlikely or not important.*	(2) *Mild reflective fear.*	(3) *Blanket reassurance: anticipated total invulnerability.*	(4) *Verbal denial of the threat or consistent expression of high optimism about being unaffected. No self-exposure to information or rumors about the danger. No planning or preparatory actions.*
(5) *Signs of moderate threat: danger appears likely and important but probably will not exceed resources available for coping with it.*	(6) *Moderate reflective fear.*	(7) *Discriminative vigilance and reassurance: anticipated partial vulnerability.*	(8) *Momentary rise in emotional tension to moderate or high level followed by sustained low level. Selective self-exposure to information. Evaluative set toward rumors and other relevant communications. Planning for emergency and precautionary measures. Development of danger-contingent reassurances.*
(9) *Signs of high threat: danger is likely and so grave that it might exceed resources available for coping with it.*	(10) *Strong reflective fear.*	(11) *Indiscriminate vigilance: anticipated high vulnerability.*	(12) *Chronically high level of emotional tension. Unselective self-exposure to information. Responsive to scare rumors and similar unauthoritative communications. Preoccupied with fantasies of being victimized. "Jittery" reaction to all potential signs of danger-onset.*

Figure 2. Schematic summary of "normal" psychological changes evoked by warnings or signs of external danger (Janis, 1967).

powerful reassurances are given by trusted authority figures, the potential threat will not be fully apprehended and blanket reassurances will then dominate. Such instances are reported in cases of hospitalized surgical patients who receive inadequate warnings or inappropriate reassurances regarding the magnitude of danger (Janis, 1958).

At the other extreme, when the threat appears unusually great or arrives precipitously under conditions where the person perceives his resources for coping to be poor, reflective fear may be so intense that vigilance dominates the behavioral picture. The indiscriminate vigilance reactions that ensue may be extremely maladaptive but are not necessarily indicative of neurotic anxiety. The range and variety of possible adjustive reactions to be expected when one or another of the alternative sequences predominates are indicated in the last column of Figure 2.

The Curvilinear Hypothesis

One of the main implications of the foregoing analysis of reflective fear is that we should not expect to find a linear relation between the probability of adaptive compromise defenses and the level of fear stimulation evoked by a given threat stimulus. According to the sequences shown in Figure 2, the following three propositions should characterize the main changes in behavior which occur as the intensity of fear stimulation increases: (a) at very low levels of fear arousal, the probability that a person will develop a compromise attitude is very low because of the tendency to remain indifferent and inattentive to threat cues (see box 4 in Figure 2); (b) as fear increases to a moderate level, the arousal of vigilance will motivate attention to and learning of available information bearing on the threat, which, in turn, will lead to a reality-tested compromise attitude (see box 8 in Figure 2); (c) when fear mounts to a high level, however, the probability that the person will develop a compromise attitude will again decrease because of the disruptive effects of strong emotional stimulation, resulting in indiscriminate vigilance, poor judgment, and extreme forms of defensive avoidance (see box 12 in Figure 2).

If all three hypotheses prove to be correct, the intensity of fear will be related to adequacy of performance by an inverted *U*-shape function, with maximal performance being achieved at some moderate level of fear arousal. This nonmonotonic type of function is, of course, by no means unfamiliar to psychologists. Brown (1961, p. 350) points out that recent neurophysiological discoveries have led Hebb, Malmo, Schlosberg, and other psychologists to consider just such a function on the basis of the presumption that the ascending reticular system may deliver insufficient stimulation to the cortex at low levels of emotional or motivational arousal and too intense bombardment of the cortex at high levels of arousal. If this presumption proves to be correct, an inverted *U*-shape function would be expected whenever the efficiency of any intellectual or motor performance is investigated in relation to the intensity of any type of emotional or motivational arousal. Optimal efficiency would always appear at some intermediate level, where the amount of arousal is neither too weak (as when the person remains unalert and lethargic) nor too strong (as when a person is terrified or enraged). (For a more extensive discussion of neurophysiological theories bearing on emotional and motivational aspects of behavior, see Chapters 7 and 10.)

These neurophysiological considerations are introduced here to indicate that the relation between fear arousal and adaptive behavior could prove to be a special case of a more general relation between the intensity of any form of motivational arousal and any type of intellectual or motor performance (see Duffy, 1962). But it still remains an open empirical question whether the inverted *U*-shape function does, in fact, provide an accurate description of the way in which the average person's attitudes and coping behavior will change as the intensity of fear increases.

Relation Between Level of Fear Arousal and Cognitive Efficiency

To test the three hypotheses relating fear to cognitive performances, two interrelated empirical questions must be answered: (a) Does arousal of a moderate degree of reflective fear induce a significant *gain* in cognitive efficiency in comparison to a low degree of arousal? (b) Does arousal of a *high* degree of reflective fear induce a significant *loss* in cognitive efficiency in comparison to a moderate degree of arousal?

While evidence bearing on the first question is fragmentary and equivocal, there is fairly consistent support for a positive answer to the second question. The field studies and clinical observations already mentioned indicate that very high fear arousal tends to be accompanied by indiscriminate vigilance in the presence of actual danger stimuli, which reduces the adequacy of a person's perceptions and judgments. In certain cases, such as the "trigger happy" soldier who unintentionally reveals his hidden location to the enemy by firing at shadows, the man becomes so excited by any unusual stimulus that he thoughtlessly engages in an inappropriate emergency action, which can actually increase the danger. Episodes of excited hypervigilance may be followed by swings to the opposite extreme of apathy and seemingly bland indifference to danger. The latter reaction, which is an outstanding component of "the old sergeant syndrome," is accompanied by covert signs of intense fear and other symptoms showing that the apathy is a defensive effort to deny the danger and ward off disturbing affect. Another symptomatic component is the moderate impairment in cognitive functioning, which enters into the apathetic soldier's indiscriminate ignoring of signs of danger (Kardiner & Spiegel, 1947; Sobel, 1949).

Laboratory experiments on changes in cognitive efficiency induced by conditions of stress provide considerable evidence indicating that some form of cognitive constriction is an immediate consequence of strong fear arousal. For example, a series of experiments by Luchins (1959), which assessed cognitive rigidity on "Einstellung" tests, showed that moderate rather than low or high levels of fear or anxiety were associated with relatively low scores on intellectual rigidity. His findings provide some support for the curvilinear (inverted *U*-shape) relationship.

Easterbrook (1959), in his review of research on the relation between emotional arousal and cognitive efficiency, concludes that high emotional tension is most disruptive of performance on the "most demanding" types of cognitive tasks, i.e., those requiring the utilization of the largest range and number of cues. His hypothesis predicts that for tasks where cues are relatively complicated, mild or moderate stress will facilitate performance by eliminating attention to peripheral and irrelevant cues. However, as tension mounts, the reduction of cue utilization would proceed to the point where relevant cues are also excluded. Thus, Easterbrook's hypothesis also predicts a nonmonotonic relation between level of fear arousal and cognitive efficiency. However, since the evidence he cites is open to a number of alternative interpretations, it does not provide a solid empirical foundation for the particular types of changes postulated for perceptual proficiency.

In a recent comprehensive review of stress experiments, Hall (1961) cites additional laboratory studies covering a variety of ego-involving threats, such as warnings of electric shock, academic failure experiences, reproof by a teacher, and "heckling" by fellow students. Some of the studies clearly indicate a temporary loss in cognitive performances when emotional tension is stimulated, but other experiments contradict these findings. Hall points out that inconsistencies in the outcomes may be due to different degrees of success in creating the deceptions used to manipulate the independent (arousal) variable. When the threats presented by the experimenters are not believed, they will stimulate little or no fear.

> It is quite possible that in many instances subjects were sufficiently sophisticated to "see through" the instructions which attempted to "ego involve" them. It does not seem too farfetched to assume that many college students do not always accept at face value instructions which indicate, for example, that the learning of a list of nonsense syllables is an indication of an individual's intelligence. It is also quite possible that the task required of the subject means so little to him that indications of his performance, which the investigator construes as success, or failure, or threat, are not similarly construed by the subject. It becomes important, then, to obtain some indication that the subject is truly "ego involved" (Hall, 1961, pp. 229–230).

To deal with this problem, Hall proposes that experimenters should be expected to present evidence of the degree to which emotional tension is aroused by their threat manipulations. But this requirement is not likely to be fulfilled adequately until there are further advances in the development of physiological and motor measures of emotional tension, and their relationship to verbal reports of affect, which are notoriously subject to "demand" and "counter-demand" characteristics in the laboratory setting.

Until less ambiguous experimental data become available, evaluation of the evidence at hand will require assessments somewhat akin to clinical judgments of the nature of the stress situation created by each experimenter and the likelihood that his attempted induction of emotion was successful. Thus, as Hall suggests, we must try to judge whether the studies that fail to show cognitive impairment under stress are generally the ones in which the experimenter failed to arouse a substantial degree of emotional tension. Were the subjects showing resistance to the experimenter's attempts to deceive them or did they actually believe they were being exposed to a genuine threat? If they did believe the experimenter, was the threat interpreted as a mild one (e.g., an unimportant form of reproof) of the type that evokes only a very low level of emotional tension, or was it interpreted as a moderate or strong one? While no definitive answer can be given to such questions, it is noteworthy that almost all the experimental evidence for perceptual or cognitive constriction under stress comes from studies in which relatively unambiguous and apparently realistic threats were made. In Osler's (1954) experiment, for example, fear was aroused by telling students to report to a school official because of a serious complaint that had been made about their behavior, while Beier (1951) and Cowen (1952) presented disturbing diagnostic statements about the subject's mental health based on a well-known personality test. So, too, in the previously mentioned study of cognitive rigidity in surgical patients by Wright (1954) and in the study of perceptual constriction in paratroopers by Korchin and Basowitz (1954), both of which entailed clear-cut threats of physical suffering or injury. All of these studies support the hypothesis that a temporary loss of perceptual or cognitive efficiency will occur under conditions of fairly strong threat. But it still cannot be said with certainty that the observed deficits are attributable primarily to the high level of fear evoked by the threat stimuli, as against other factors that might be associated with these stress conditions.

In summary, there is some evidence on the relation between cognitive efficiency and the level of reflective fear which makes the curvilinear hypothesis appear to be plausible. No single experiment has been carried out as yet, however, in which a series of values on the fear arousal continuum has been systematically varied from very low to very high levels. What is most clearly indicated by the existing evidence is that very high levels of fear arousal tend to impair perceptual and cognitive functions. But within the low and moderate sectors of the fear-arousal continuum, there is only very fragmentary evidence to support the prediction that cognitive efficiency will increase when fear is raised from zero to low or moderate levels.

Relation Between Level of Fear Arousal and Attitude Change

In the analysis of modes of adjustment to threat, as summarized in Figures 1 and 2, it was suggested that reality-oriented compromise attitudes will be most likely to predominate when reflective fear is aroused to a *moderate* degree rather than to a very low degree or a very high degree. This hypothesis has some direct implications for the effects of warning communications, such as those which call attention to public health hazards with the intention of promoting effective precautionary actions and adaptive attitude changes. If the hypothesis is correct, we should find an inverted *U*-shaped relation between the intensity of fear arousal and the acceptance of warning communications containing authoritative recommendations concerning plans, practices, or policies oriented toward avoiding potential dangers.

Evidence Bearing on the Curvilinear Hypothesis

The evidence from relevant communication experiments bearing on the curvilinear hypothesis remains incomplete and somewhat contradictory, although the findings provide some fruitful leads concerning the facilitating and interfering effects of fear arousal. No definitive conclusions can be drawn because the experiments on attitude change, like those on cognitive efficiency, have not yet investigated a sufficient series of points on the continuum of stressful stimulations. Nor have the experimenters been able to provide dependable evidence concerning the differences in intensity of fear arousal, if any, induced by different warning communications whose differential effects on attitudes have been compared.

One point that seems fairly clear from the available experimental evidence is that reduction in cognitive efficiency seldom, if ever, is a major source of failure to accept authoritative recommendations in public health messages and other warning communications, even when they contain horrifying details about potential or future dangers. However, some experiments indicate that under certain conditions strong threat appeals, as compared with parallel versions of the same communication containing milder appeals, can arouse various forms of psychological resistance that reduce the effectiveness of the communicator's message in the long run. The diminishing returns from increasing the intensity of fear was first suggested in an experiment by Janis and Feshbach (1953) which compared the effectiveness of three different forms of an illustrated lecture on dental hygiene, presented to equivalent groups of high school students. The strong fear-appeal version, which emphasized the threat of pain and disease, produced less attitude change and less change in dental hygiene practices than the mild threat version of the communication. On the basis of all the various findings from this experiment, the authors concluded that the resistances evoked by the strong fear-arousing communication could be explained in terms of the following "defensive avoidance" hypothesis: When fear is strongly aroused but is not fully relieved by the reassurances contained in a persuasive communication, the audience will become motivated to ignore, minimize, or deny the importance of the threat.

Several other studies give some indications of reduced acceptance with increased fear. For example, a study by Leventhal and Niles (1964) found somewhat less change in reported intentions to stop smoking among subjects given medium or strong fear-arousing communications than among subjects given a communication containing the same recommendations without any fear-arousing material. Evidence suggestive of a similar trend of reduced acceptance for high fear is also reported for the smoking and cancer issue by Janis and Terwilliger (1962). Haefner (1956), using communications concerning the suffering unexpectedly caused to Japanese fishermen exposed to fallout from U.S. H-bomb tests, found that a high guilt version of the communication favoring a test ban provoked more resistances than a milder form. Finally, an experiment by Nunnally and Bobren (1959) suggests reduced interest in fear-arousing communications if they are unaccompanied by statements suggesting apparently effective protective actions.

On the other hand, evidence from several other apparently similar experiments have reported more attitude change from high than from low threat messages. Berkowitz and Cottingham (1960), for example, found that among students who infrequently rode in cars, there was more acceptance of arguments in favor of seat belts after an illustrated talk that played up the risks of being seriously injured in automobile accidents than after an equivalent version which presented the same arguments in a nonthreatening context. Similar results were found in another study on the issue of automotive safety by Leventhal and Niles (1965). Subjects exposed to the greatest amount of fear-arousing material in technicolor movies focussing on the destructiveness of automotive accidents showed the greatest degree of acceptance of safety rules, such as "never drive after drinking." Leventhal, Singer, and Jones (1965) gave subjects different versions of a communication recommending tetanus inoculations and again found that subjects exposed to the more fear-arousing communications were the most favorable toward inoculations and expressed the strongest intentions to receive innoculations. Follow-ups on actual behavior (going to the health center for shots) showed no difference, however, between the groups exposed to high and low fear-arousing communications. But it was found that those subjects exposed to the specific recommendations as to where, when, and how to get the shots were more likely to obtain innoculations, irrespective of whether they had received the strong or mild fear-arousing version. Subjects in a control group exposed to specific recommendations only, with no exposure to any fear-arousing material, did not take any shots. Evidently, in this instance, some degree of fear-arousal was necessary along with the specific instructions in order for action to occur.

It is clear that there is no simple rule regarding the relation of the intensity of fear arousal evoked by warning communications and the degree of acceptance of protective recommendations. Some communication experiments, as we have seen, indicate that the use of strong threat appeals, as compared with milder ones, can arouse psychological resistance and interfere with acceptance of the communicator's recommendations; while other experiments indicate a gain in effectiveness which points to the potentially facilitating effects of fear arousal.

In view of the apparent inconsistencies among experimental studies on fear-arousing appeals, some further clarification is needed in order to take full account of the alternative ways of interpreting the experimental findings. The shortcomings of the measures of fear arousal which have been used so far make it difficult to test the implications of the curvilinear hypothesis derived from the analysis of the functional properties of reflective fear. What is required is some dependable way of assessing the level of arousal in relation to fixed points on the fear continuum. Perhaps a combination of affect measures, including content analyses of the subjects' verbal reports, records of facial expressions, and physiological indicators of autonomic responses during exposures to the communications, can be developed which will enable investigators to compare the degree of arousal from one experiment to another. Without such measures, we cannot be sure which of the following is being tested by any given experiment: (a) at very low levels of fear arousal, the average person remains unaffected by warning communications because he dismisses all information about the threat as inconsequential by means of blanket reassurances; (b) when a warning communication arouses a mild or moderate level of fear, the average person's vigilance and reassurance tendencies are stimulated, which is the optimal condition for developing compromise attitudes of the type required for sustained acceptance of whatever plausible safety measures are recommended by the communicator; (c) when a warning communication arouses a relatively high level of fear, the average person's state of intense emotional excitement will be characterized by preoccupation with hyperviligant speculations and ruminations which generate defensive maneuvers—such as denial, detachment, and minimizing rationalizations that interfere with acceptance of the safety measures recommended by the communicator. In the absence of absolute measures of the level of fear arousal, a very extensive experimental assessment is required in which measures of attitude change are obtained for a large series of points along the fear continuum, so that the investigator can observe the probability of acceptance of the same safety recommendations as a function of level of arousal, ranging from near zero to a very high degree of emotional excitement. No such experiment has, as yet, been carried out.

The Optimal Level of Fear Arousal

In reviewing the existing evidence on effects of fear arousal, Janis (1967) points out that it is inappropriate to expect to find any broad generalization about either a high or low threat version being generally more effective in inducing attitude change, because the optimal level of fear arousal will vary for different types of warning communications. There are numerous indications that the optimal level depends upon the relative weight of facilitating and interfering responses, which are evoked whenever a communication arouses fear. By the "optimal level" of fear is meant the point on the fear continuum where the facilitating effects of fear arousal are dominant over the interfering effects, beyond which the probability of acceptance of the communicator's recommendations will decrease. For example, many of the experiments we have just reviewed point to the perceived cogency of the recommended protective action as a critical factor in determining the optimal level, allowing a higher level of fear to produce acceptance of the recommendations.

A hypothetical diagram has been constructed—which is reproduced in Figure 3—in order to illustrate the notion that the optimal level of fear arousal for inducing acceptance can be shifted by a variety of content, situational, and dispositional factors that influence the relative balance of interfering and facilitating effects at any given point on the fear continuum. This diagram consists of a family of inverted *U*-shaped curves that relate fear arousal to acceptance, the optimal point on each curve falling at a different point on the fear dimension.

The first of the family of curves depicted in the diagram reaches the peak of acceptance at the low end of the fear continuum (optimal point A), and thereafter the degree of acceptance declines. The findings from the Berkowitz and Cottingham (1960) experiment can be interpreted as showing the rise in acceptance as fear arousal increases at the low end of the fear continuum. The no-threat version, which did not discuss automobile accidents, would presumably be at about the zero point on the *X*-axis, and consequently the degree of acceptance of the pro-seat belt recommendation would be represented on the *Y*-axis by the base level induced by the nonthreat material in the communication—the rational arguments, appeals to social norms, endorsement of the

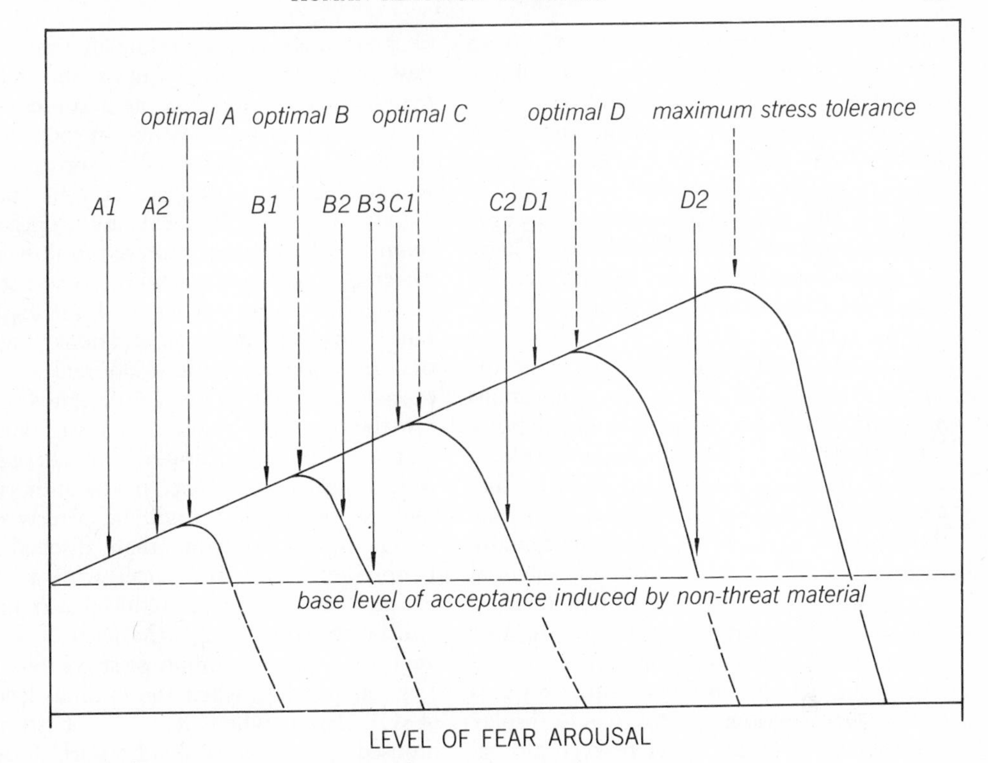

Figure 3. Hypothetical family of nonmonotonic curves representing the relation between level of fear arousal elicited by a communication and the degree of acceptance of the attitude or decision recommended (Janis, 1967).

conclusion by a prestigeful communicator, and other incentives that facilitate successful persuasion without implicating fear of dangerous consequences. The threat version used by Berkowitz and Cottingham introduced the added incentive of warding off fear of dangerous consequences and presumably induced a low intensity of arousal, which can be visualized as falling at point 1 or 2, which represents a gain in attitude change even though this point is below the optimal level for any of the other curves. The amount of acceptance on the *Y*-axis would be higher than the base level, and hence a mild fear-arousing version would be found to produce a greater degree of attitude change than a no-threat version.

A communication that is more capable of temporarily undermining the audience's normal invulnerability attitude and which gives cogent recommendations would be expected to generate an acceptance curve with a higher optimal point. Thus, for example, the dental hygiene communication in the Janis and Feshbach experiment, which vividly portrayed unfamiliar forms of damage to the teeth and gums, might have an optimal point at B in Figure 3. If we suppose that the minimal appeal—which proved to be the most effective version—aroused a level of fear at point 3, then the moderate appeal version would be placed at 4 and the strong appeal version at about 5. The three points obtained from this experiment could be regarded as delineating the descending portion of the curve which is labeled "optimal B." (In the absence of a fourth and fifth version of the same communication, containing less threat material than the minimal threat appeal, we cannot examine the entire curve to see if it rises from zero to an optimal point near point 3, as expected, before it begins to descend.) The tetanus study by Leventhal, Singer, and Jones (1965) might have elicited about equal intensities of fear but would be located on the ascending portion of a curve that has a higher optimal level (e.g., Curve C) if the audience tended to perceive the recommendations as being more adequate for preventing the danger.

It should be recognized that even the strong fear versions of the communications on dental hygiene, tetanus innoculations, lung cancer, and the like do not evoke a level of emotional arousal as high as that evoked by more immediate, personal threats. Most mass communications containing warnings and illustrations of potential threats probably elicit, at most, a level of fear that falls in the lower half of the fear arousal continuum. Any member of the audience, if told by his dentist that his gums show signs of serious disease, would display a considerably higher level of fear arousal (e.g., point 7 in Figure 3). The level of fear would be still higher (e.g., beyond optimal D) if the same person were told by his physician that he is a victim of lung cancer and that major surgery is urgently recommended.

In the operating room itself, in the presence of all the distressing sights of surgical equipment and gowned personnel, at the moment the person is asked by the anesthetist to position himself on the table for the anesthetic, the intensity of fear might approach the maximal level of stress tolerance. Still, as long as the patient realizes that he might be mutilated or annihilated if he does anything to make for errors, he can be expected to display an extraordinarily high level of acceptance, complying with every request to change his position, exposing his body, and breathing in the anesthetic, even though he knows that following these recommendations will entail pain and the risk of death. If, however, his fear becomes so intense that it exceeds the maximum level of stress tolerance, a decline in responsiveness to authoritative requests and recommendations would occur as a consequence of temporary impairments in perception, cognition, and control of motor impulses which characterize a state of acute panic.

Extremely fearful patients in the operating room have often been observed to shift from extreme compliance to a wild physical struggle against the surgeons and nurses (see Janis, 1958). These observations suggest that once the maximum optimal level is exceeded, the curve rapidly descends to below the base line, as depicted at the extreme right in Figure 3. Similarly, if there is a sudden loss of confidence in the authorities, the risk of obedience will be perceived as being more dangerous than disobedience (implying a shift to a curve with a lower optimal level), so that reduced acceptance will occur even though the level of fear is well below the maximum of stress tolerance (e.g., at point 8, when the optimal level is at C). Even when fear is not strongly aroused by warnings about future dangers, the recipients can be expected to scrutinize the communicator's arguments carefully, looking for obvious loopholes that they can seize upon to dismiss the communicator's statements about threats that require costly or unpleasant protective actions. But by introducing impressive new arguments that seal off the most obvious loopholes, the communicator may be able to prevent the recipient from using one or another form of defensive avoidance to escape from the distressing situation in which he momentarily finds himself as he thinks about the threats depicted in a fear-arousing communication. In terms of Figure 3, this would result in a shift in the optimal level. Thus, those experiments that employ communications conveying novel and realistic threats, combined with convincing reassurances that mesh with general beliefs about means for warding off danger, would be located on a curve that has a relatively high optimal level of fear.

The preceding discussion provides some

rough indications of how the model represented in Figure 3 might be useful for reconciling some of the apparently contradictory evidence from experiments on fear-arousing communications. But, obviously, such a model would have little value if it were used merely to explain away the divergences without generating any new predictions that could be tested. One such prediction, which would enable the model to be verified or falsified, is that whenever a shift in the optimal level is produced by closing off one or another loophole that enables the recipient to counteract the communicator's statements, there will be a *disproportionate* gain in the amount of attitude change. That is to say, whereas the addition of a good new argument would increase the degree of acceptance of the communication at all levels of fear, there will be a much greater increase when such an argument is given at a high level of fear, since it allows the optimal level to shift upwards (see Janis, 1967). An extraordinarily great increase in the amount of attitude change would be expected whenever something is added to a communication that succeeds in overcoming the interfering responses that had been preventing the facilitating responses stimulated by fear to become dominant. The same considerations apply to any communication device capable of shifting the optimal level of acceptance to a higher level, such as those suggested by recent experiments on the smoking and cancer issue —e.g., the use of dramatic film sequences that break through defenses against personal involvement with the cancer threat by eliciting empathiclike identification with a cancer victim (Leventhal & Niles, 1963; Niles, 1964).

In Figure 3, the overall increasing function (curve E) represents the assumption that when a warning stimulates a high level of fear, there will be a powerful motivation in the recipients to become vigilant, to take the threat seriously, and to seek for reassurance by adopting whatever recommended coping devices are felt to be successful in warding off danger. The decreasing portions of the curves represent the assumption that the facilitating effects of fear will be counteracted by other tension-reducing responses that can give rise to characteristic resistances, such as thinking up reasons why the communicator's statements about the threat are exaggerated or inapplicable to oneself. When the warning communication is altered in a way that prevents any such resistance from becoming dominant, there should be a tremendous gain from the removal of the interfering tendencies, allowing the full motivational gain from strong fear arousal to become manifested. Thus, the prediction is that a greater second order difference will be found from adding more effective devices that counteract resistances or from adding arguments that plug the loopholes in a strong fear-arousing version of a communication than in a milder threat version. These predictions, which have not yet been tested, will require a much more complex type of experiment than has hitherto been carried out.

Although the model cannot be evaluated until a number of such experiments are completed, there is some immediate heuristic value from postulating a family of curves like those represented in Figure 3, in that we can conceptualize a bit more clearly the need for orienting research on the effects of fear-arousing communications toward the goal of formulating and testing propositions that specify communication factors that make for a higher or lower *optimal* dosage of fear arousal (see Janis, 1968). Regardless of the accuracy of the particular functions implied by the family-of-curves model, the foregoing analysis clearly indicates that the optimal level of fear arousal for producing acceptance cannot be expected to remain fixed for all types of communication settings, for all contents, and for all types of audiences. Rather, we must expect the optimal level to vary over a considerable range, as a function of some well-known communication and predispositional variables—and also as a function of some that are not yet so well known or that have not yet been discovered.

The heuristic value of the model can be illustrated by recent experimental research on a new type of role-playing technique that was designed specifically for the purpose of inducing a relatively high optimal level by breaking down the usual defensive barriers that prevent people from taking seriously the personal implications of potential threats to their health. Janis and Mann (1965) developed and tested an "emotional" role-playing procedure that sets up a psychodramatic situation in which the subject plays the role of a medical patient who is suffering from the harmful consequences of cigarette smoking. In their initial experiment, 26 young women served as subjects, all of whom were smokers. They were not aware of the purpose of the study and had not been asked whether they wanted to try to cut down on smoking. In the experimental group, each subject was asked to play the role of a patient in a doctor's office at the time she is being informed that the diagnostic tests (X-rays, sputum analysis, etc.) indicate that she has cancer of the lung. The subject was asked to express her spontaneous personal responses, in the role-playing situation, as she received the bad news from the doctor. Among the five scenes acted out was one in which the cancer victim, while waiting for the physician to arrange for hospitalization, soliloquizes about the error she made in not having stopped smoking before it was too late. As expected, this role-playing procedure was a highly emotion-arousing experience.

Half of the subjects were assigned at random to a control condition in which they were exposed to the same instructions and information without engaging in any role playing. These subjects listened to a tape recording of an authentic session that had been conducted with one of the subjects in the experimental group.

The results showed that emotional role playing had a markedly greater effect than the control condition in modifying attitudes about smoking and in changing smoking habits, as reported by the subjects in follow-up interviews conducted two weeks later. There are some indications that this technique of emotional role playing provides unusual empathic experiences similar to those that occasionally lead to spectacular "conversions" among physicians, relatives, and friends of cancer victims. In contrast to the usual cognitive type of role playing, which many subjects carry out in a perfunctory way with a minimum of personal involvement, the emotional type of role playing seems to have greater success in breaking through the defensive facade. There are numerous indications suggesting that the high level of fear and vigilance aroused by the realistic quality of the experimental procedures may be a major factor responsible for the increased anti-smoking attitudes and the changes reported in smoking habits.

In a follow-up study, Mann and Janis (1968) found that over an 18-month period, the emotional role players continued to report a significantly greater decrease in number of cigarettes consumed than the passive control. This outcome suggests that a single one-hour session of emotional role playing might have a profound long-term effect upon smokers, including those who have no intention of cutting down on cigarette consumption, since the results suggest that significant changes in smoking habits may persist for years.

In a replication and extension of the earlier research, Mann (1967) compared three groups of men and women given different types of role-playing procedures: (a) the fear-arousing procedure that requires each subject to enact the role of a "cancer victim"; (b) a "cognitive" procedure that requires each subject to enact the role of a debater arguing against smoking; and (c) a "shame-arousing" procedure that requires each subject to enact the role of a helpless smoking "addict." The results showed that the fear-arousing type of emotional role playing was much more effective than either the cognitive or the shame-arousing type of role-playing procedure. Mann also investigated the effects of high vs. low opportunities for verbalization in each of the role-playing conditions. He found that the amount of attitude change produced by the fear-arousing type of emotional role playing was increased by giving subjects the opportunity for a great deal of verbalization while playing the role. The findings from Mann's study, like those from the Janis and Mann experiment, indicate that emotional role playing can function as a device for impressively "repackaging" information that is already available to the person, reducing the usual resistances that often prevent people from taking full account of public health information, thus leading to a change in self-image regarding personal vulnerability to the threat.

DETERMINANTS OF STRESS REACTIONS DURING CONFRONTATION WITH DANGER

One of the central research problems in the field of stress behavior is to determine the environmental conditions that induce indiscriminate vigilance and related maladaptive reactions to perceptable danger. Observations of military combat and large scale disasters (Janis, 1949b, 1951; Wolfenstein, 1957) reveal that hypervigilance, emotional shock, and panic can occur among clinically normal personalities when exposed to severe stress situations. But these are by no means invariable responses to danger. In many circumstances of oncoming danger, the same personalities can display either unperturbed complacency, apparently based on blanket reassurances, or adaptive precautionary behavior that implies the development of compromise defenses. What are the situational factors that influence the type of reaction evoked by confrontations with danger?

Perceived Entrapment

In those few instances where mass panics are known to have occurred, there were visible signs of clear and present danger accompanied by the apparent blocking of escape routes (Janis, Chapman, Gillin, & Spiegel, 1955). The two main conditions regularly associated with the outbreak of panic behavior appear to be: (a) awareness of oncoming physical danger for which no protection is available except escape to a safer place, and (b) awareness that presently open escape routes will be closed in the immediate future. It is this combination of cognitions, whether or not they are correct inferences about the objective situation, which is designated as "perceived entrapment" and which is most likely to lead to wild flight, trampling of fellow victims, and other uncontrollable, distraught reactions of the type referred to as "panic."

Separation from Primary Groups

Severe reactions of emotional shock occur more frequently among those survivors who are separated from families, relatives, and friends than among those who are not separated (Fritz & Marks, 1954). Separation prevents the reassurance normally experienced from the presence of members of primary groups and adds a gnawing concern about the safety of the absent loved ones which increases the person's apprehensiveness. Irrespective of whether it affects a person's chances of survival, the presence of other people will have a powerful effect on the control of his fear. In fact, the mere knowledge that trusted leaders are somewhere in the neighborhood can have a markedly dampening effect upon emotional excitement (see French, 1944; Stouffer *et al.*, 1949b; Wispe & Lloyd, 1955). In general, adults as well as children show marked efforts to avoid separation from families and other primary groups during peacetime as well as wartime crises (see Janis, 1958, pp. 89–93, 328–335). Studies of the air blitz in England and of the heavy bombing raids in Germany during World War II emphasize the extraordinary degree of dependency observed among civilian populations exposed to air war (Glover, 1942; Janis, 1951, pp. 159–165). Persons who remained in a threatened city became more fearful when separated from members of the family and also when friends or prestigeful persons in their community were evacuated. For young children, disruption of the family bond was considered the most traumatic factor in the prolonged stressful period of heavy air raids (Glover, 1942; Freud & Burlingham, 1944).

Parallel efforts to avoid separation from the military unit, observed among men exposed to the hazards of combat, have led many social psychologists and psychiatrists to infer that sustained contact with the primary group is a crucial factor in the soldier's morale (Glass, 1953; Grinker & Spiegel, 1945b; Shils & Janowitz, 1948; H. Spiegel, 1944; Stouffer *et al.,* 1949b). Time and again instances were observed of men failing to act in accordance with their own self-interests in order to ward off separation fears or guilt about "letting the other guys down." For example, soldiers who had performed well in combat sometimes refused to accept a promotion if it entailed being shifted to another group. Severe casualty cases, after being sent to a hospital in the rear, developed intense guilt feelings and sometimes went AWOL from a safely located hospital or replacement depot in order to return to the front lines in an attempt to rejoin their comrades (Smith, 1949). Combat flyers who were physically ill, or suffering from acute anxiety symptoms, avoided going on sick call and struggled against being withdrawn from combat flights because they did not want to be separated from their air crews (Janis, 1949a).

In recent experimental studies, Schachter (1959) has used experimental methods and objective behavioral indices to investigate the effects of stress on the momentary strength of affiliative tendencies. Female college students, upon arriving at the laboratory, were told that they would receive an electric shock. The shock was described as being either very mild and painless or severe and painful. The subjects were then informed of a ten-minute delay, supposedly needed to set up the equipment. Each subject was asked if she would prefer to wait alone in a private room, or in an equivalent room with another student. After answering questions about her preference for being alone or in the company of others and her subjective feelings in anticipation of the shock, the subject was given "dehoaxing" information, which ended the experimental session.

As expected, subjective reports indicated less fear for the low threat ("painless") condition than for the high threat ("painful") condition. Only 10 out of 30 girls (33⅓ per cent) chose to wait together in the low stress condition while 20 out of 31 (65 per cent) chose to do so in the high, thus indicating increased affiliative choice with increased threat.

In Schacter's second experiment, two groups of 10 girls each, all of whom were facing the same high threat, were given the choice of waiting either alone or with a number of other girls. One group was told that the other girls were facing the same threat, while the second group was told that the other girls were waiting to see their professors and advisors and were not in the experiment. When the girls "shared" the subjects' fate, 6 out of 10 chose to wait together, while 0 out of 10 chose to do so when the girls were not facing a similar plight. In a third experiment Schacter found that the affiliative tendency was not reduced when the choice was between waiting with fellow subjects to whom one could not talk or waiting alone.

Schacter concludes from these and other studies (e.g., Wrightsman, 1959) that two different motives or goals could account for his experimental findings: (a) evaluating one's own emotions and feelings by comparing one's reactions with those displayed by others; and (b) seeking direct fear reduction and reassurance simply from being in the presence of others who will be supportive because they are in a similar predicament. Other investigators have confirmed Schachter's finding that fear arousal increases preference for the company of others who share one's plight (see Chapter 17 by Radloff).

Rabbie (1963) found that affiliative tendencies, assessed by Schachter's method, increased as the threat became more ambiguous. However, when told about the emotional states of the others, subjects in the high fear condition were least interested in joining those in the same state of high fear. A post-experimental questionnaire showed they preferred companions who would provide reassurance and fear reduction and not those who would stimulate fear.

Sarnoff and Zimbardo (1961) present evidence suggesting a differential effect of reflective and neurotic fear upon affiliative choices. One experimental group of male college students was exposed to a realistic threat of painful shock. An equivalent group was given a task designed to arouse anxiety over unacceptable oral gratification. Each subject in the latter group was shown a series of rubber nipples, baby bottles, pacifiers, and breast shields and was told that he would be required to suck them as part of a taste experiment. Evidence from projective tests and questionnaires is reported to support the investigator's assumptions that the first type of manipulation would arouse reality-oriented fear, while the second would induce a neurotic type of anxiety. Using Schachter's technique to assess affiliative tendencies, the investigators found that in contrast to those facing the threat of painful shock, the subjects exposed to the "oral-gratification" threat preferred to remain alone. Since the latter threat could also involve the arousal of anticipatory shame, replications are needed to see if the same outcome occurs under conditions eliciting neurotic anxiety without shame. If confirmed, the results of the Sarnoff and Zimbardo experiment will represent a step toward differentiating the functional properties of reflective fear from those of neurotic emotional reactions stimulated by the arousal of repressed motives.

Earlier it was postulated that a tendency toward reassurance seeking was relatively unique to reflective fear. Being in the presence of others who are thought to be potentially helpful, protective, and capable of empathizing with one's own feelings of distress is clearly one form of this tendency. While this form of reassurance seeking can become a dominant mode of response to external threat, it is not necessarily dominant for all people. For example, nearly all the studies referred to found that the increase in affiliative choice following exposure to threat occurred mainly among first-born or only children. It is not known if the birth-order factor is related to the unreduced fear and hypervigilant behavior that occurs as a reaction to separation among the victims of community disasters.

In the previous discussion, the presence or absence of primary group members was considered from the standpoint of effects upon the current level of reflective fear: i.e., the social presence of significant others decreases fear, while their absence elevates fear. However, the primary group can function long before any confrontation with danger, in a way that influences the members' future susceptibility to fear arousal. Affiliative behavior may be acquired as a means of coping with fear on the basis of the group's role in preparing one for danger (Janis, 1963). For example, among members of military units facing common sources of combat danger, there appear to be many forms of "sharing of fear" (e.g., informal group discussions and interchanges of gallows humor). These interchanges, which occur when the group setting has reduced intense emotional states to more moderate levels of reflective fear, can then facilitate a working through process that enables each person to become psychologically prepared for facing subsequent painful reality situations. (See the discussion of "the work of worrying" below.) The essential point here is that the opportunity to talk about one's fear in a permissive group setting—and the opportunity to hear other members of the group verbalize fears similar to one's own—can facilitate the development of adaptive compromise defenses and have a long-range prophylactic effect.

It has also been suggested that separation from the group can arouse unconscious dependency needs related to reactivated childhood fears of abandonment (Janis, 1958, pp. 90–93, 324–325). Thus, temporary separation from highly valued people during periods of crisis can increase fear out of all proportion to the reality threat. Case studies indicate that these exaggerated fear reactions are augmented by rearousal of thoughts and images related to childhood episodes of illness or suffering in which temporary separation from the parents was apperceived as complete abandonment. Whether this hypothesis proves to be correct, or whether other factors are responsible for the augmentation of fear, will have to be determined by subsequent investigations. But the obvious importance of separation from significant persons and primary groups as determinants of emotion during crises and disasters suggests that we might obtain greater understanding of fear dynamics by investigating the history of separation reactions.

Witnessing Injury and Death

When confronting danger to oneself, the perception of other injured and suffering people can evoke intense empathic responses and can sometimes give rise to severe psychological trauma. In the wake of large-scale disasters, the incidence of acute emotional disturbances is extraordinarily high among those uninjured survivors who have witnessed mutilations, physical agony, and violent deaths. A content analysis of interviews of A-bomb survivors at Hiroshima and Nagasaki showed that a very high proportion of respondents (69 per cent of the 55 survivors in the Hiroshima sample and 64 per cent of the 46 in the Nagasaki sample) spontaneously mentioned disturbing perceptions of burned and maimed people (Janis, 1951, pp. 11–21). This far exceeded the frequency with which any other event that occurred during the atomic disasters was reported by the survivors as disturbing or frightening.

Similar data on the strong emotional impact created by exposure to the sight of death and suffering are also provided by morale surveys of combat soldiers (Stouffer *et al.*, 1949), by studies of peacetime disasters (Fritz & Marks, 1954; Wolfenstein, 1957), and by observations of people who are chronically ill on surgical wards (Janis, 1958; Leventhal, 1963). There is evidence suggesting that the degree of disturbance increases with the degree of exposure: for example, after a large-scale disaster uninjured rescue workers who had direct physical contact with the dead were found to show more symptoms of emotional disturbance than those who merely saw but did not handle the corpses (Fritz & Marks, 1954). Seeing injured and dying people seems to disrupt normal psychological defenses and beliefs that one is invulnerable to damage.

Near-Miss Episodes

Intense fear and its accompanying disruption of behavior resulting from entrapment, separation, and the sight of casualties tend to be short-lived reactions. Changes in the situation, such as the opening of escape routes, the removal of damaged bodies, and official announcements that the danger is over, soon lead to a return to normal emotional states. Persistent reactions of severe emotional shock, however, are likely to continue for days or even weeks if a person's exposure to danger was under conditions where he narrowly escaped serious injury or death (Fraser, Leslie, & Phelps, 1943; Glover, 1942; Janis, 1951; MacCurdy, 1943; Wolfenstein, 1957). Included in this "near-miss" category are all instances of victimization (personal damages or losses sustained by the individual) from exposure to the physical impact of disaster stimuli.

The available evidence suggests that the higher the degree of perceived victimization, the higher the probability of acute emotional shock. Extensive data on near-miss reactions have been obtained from clinical case studies and systematic correlational investigations of soldiers and civilians exposed to wartime dangers. For example, following the heavy air attacks against Britain in 1942, systematic follow-ups were made of all uninjured persons admitted to First Aid posts in one English city (Fraser *et al.*, 1943). Among these who had undergone the most severe near-miss experiences, 40 per cent had developed emotional disturbances that resulted in absence from work for at least three weeks. Among people who were less directly affected by the bomb explosions, the incidence of absenteeism was markedly less. A separate comparison was made between 61 uninjured survivors who subsequently developed neurotic symptoms and an equivalent group of 33 uninjured survivors examined at the same First Aid Post, but free of symptoms. Thirty per cent of the neurotic group had experienced destruction of their homes, death of a close friend, or some other form of serious personal loss during the air attack; whereas only 4 per cent of the nonneurotic group had undergone any such loss. In addition, the findings indicated that those who had been buried beneath debris were far more likely than others to develop temporary or persistent neurotic symptoms. Additional studies of British and German civilians during periods of heavy air attacks report the same relationship between direct personal involvement and persisting emotional symptoms (see Janis, 1951, pp. 103–116).

One of the few studies of peacetime disasters which provide systematic data on the effects of direct personal involvement is reported by Moore (1958). In his analysis of the social and psychological effects of tornado disasters in two Texas cities during 1953, he found more frequent symptoms of disturbance among persons forced to move because of serious damage to their homes than among those who were able to remain. His results also show a higher incidence of fear symptoms in the more extensively damaged of the two cities (which can be presumed to have had a much higher incidence of near-miss episodes).

In general, it appears that the incidence of transient emotional disorders (of sufficient intensity to create both considerable subjective suffering and impaired work productivity) can be predicted from objective indices of victimization, such as (a) the total incidence of nonfatal casualties, (b) the number of uninjured persons in buildings damaged during the impact phase of the disaster, (c) the number of homeless people, and (d) the number of families in which a fatality has occurred.

Mediating Processes in the Relation Between Perceived Victimization and Disruptive Fear Reactions

The prior discussion suggested four categories of events—entrapment, separation from primary groups, exposure to the sight of casualties, and near-miss experiences—that intensify reflective fear and produce behavioral disorganization. How are these categories related to the intervening psychological processes postulated for the arousal of reflective fear? Hypotheses concerning mediating processes would be especially useful if they were able to account for reactions to warnings and threat communications as well as to confrontations with danger itself. A number of such integrative hypotheses have been suggested, which also point to ways in which warnings are related to psychological preparation for actual danger episodes (Janis, 1968).

One way of accounting for the persistence of emotional disturbances following confrontations with danger is to assume that severe pain, sudden loss of physical support, and excessively loud sounds are unconditioned fear stimuli that, when paired with previously neutral cues (e.g., in the situation of being alone in the dark), can give rise to conditioned fear reactions of the Pavlovian type. But, while simple (nonverbal) instances of classical conditioned responses may develop as a result of near-miss experiences, there are undoubtedly other more complicated mediating response mechanisms that are responsible for both the intensity of reflective fear during a crisis and the maintenance or subsequent dissipation of the fear state. Thus, the emotional disturbances observed after a disaster cannot necessarily be traced to the presence of cues similar to those that were temporarily contiguous with the recent exposure to the terrifying (unconditioned) stimuli. The reappearance of emotional disturbances subsequent to the disaster may occur in situations that do not necessarily resemble the original danger episode. Verbal and other cognitive mechanisms seem to play a considerable role in determining the occurrence of disaster and postdisaster emotional reactions.

Some investigators (Hebb, 1946; Kessen & Mandler, 1961) have also pointed out that many stimuli that have the power to arouse fear have no history of association with threat-producing events. Hebb (1946) suggests that these reactions are the result of changes in stimulation which are significant departures from expected conditions. Although Hebb mainly cites observations of seemingly innate fear reactions, these expectations might include a wide range of previously learned beliefs concerning the constancy or continuity of the self and of various benign or protective features of the environment. When such expectations are formed during a normal life history, in which there have been relatively few exposures to severe threats or dangers of the type that can undermine self-confidence, the result may be rather powerful expectations of personal invulnerability to any serious danger.

In some analyses of normal psychological defenses, considerable emphasis is given to the illusion of personal invulnerability as a protective attitude for facing all situations of potential danger (Rado, 1942; Schmideberg, 1942). From her observations of individual reactions to the London air blitz, Schmideberg (1942) points out that "A person's conviction that nothing can happen to him is sometimes painfully shattered if something actually *does* happen to him. In that case the shock of being hurt or losing his property will be intensified by the shock of realizing his vulnerability." Having had the experience of being powerless to avert the direct impact of danger, the survivor can no longer convince himself that he is safe, since he is unable to dispel from his memory the image of the harrowing experience in which he was helpless.

Essentially the same type of changes in vulnerability attitudes has been described in communities exposed to the devastating impact of tornadoes, floods, industrial explosions, and other peacetime disasters (Moore, 1958; NORC, 1954; Tyhurst, 1957; Wolfenstein, 1957), and among hospital patients after severe illness, surgical operations, automobile crashes, and other accidents (Bernstein & Small, 1951; Deutsch, 1942; Diggory, 1956; Hamburg, 1953; Janis, 1958; Lindemann, 1941; Wittkower, 1952).

Thus, a critical aspect of the arousal of reflective fear involves breaking through expectations of invulnerability. Once the defenses are fractured, the intensity of the emotional reaction undoubtedly depends upon the expected or perceived magnitude of the danger. When danger is assumed to be very great and there is high expectation of personal vulnerability, reflective fear would be expected to be very high. As suggested in our prior discussion, we expect hypervigilance reactions to predominate when the person perceives himself as helpless to avert catastrophe. But so long as he does not perceive the danger as inescapable and overwhelming he will tend to take account of environmental supports and self-initiated techniques for controlling danger, which enables him to develop organized compromise defenses, even in the presence of severe threats that evoke relatively high levels of fear. The particular response to any given crisis or danger episode obviously can have far-reaching effects in shaping expectations and coping mechanisms for facing subsequent threats or dangers. So, too, exposure to warning communications can have a predisposing effect on reactions to subsequent crises or disaster.

The concept of personal invulnerability has some important implications for warning communications and other occurrences that take place before the onset of actual stress stimuli. For example, they help to explain why false alarms do not always result in desensitizing people and inducing them to ignore future warnings, as in the well-known story about the boy who cried "wolf, wolf." Killian (1954) interviewed the residents of Panama City, Florida, a short time after they had accidentally been given a false alarm about their community being in the path of a hurricane. The residents made very few complaints about having been misled by the false alarm and said that they would now be more inclined than ever to take emergency action in the event of new hurricane warnings. It is noteworthy that the hurricane had passed close enough to the community to provide ample evidence of its potential for destruction. We would expect just such marked increases in vigilance whenever a false alarm episode interferes with previously established expectations of blanket immunity ("It *can* happen to me—and it almost did"). Sensitizing effects of this type have been observed following other types of false alarms. For example, sustained vigilance sometimes occurs in medical patients after a harrowing experience of suspenseful waiting for the verdict concerning growths that proved to be noncancerous and after routine surgical operations that had evoked severe fright in the operating room (Janis, 1958).

In general, it is expected that attitudes of hypervigilance will be produced by information or danger episodes which interfere so drastically with anticipations of personal invulnerability that the person is no longer able to ward off strong reflective fear whenever he encounters new danger signs. Not all near-miss experiences necessarily have this effect, however, even though there is evidence indicating that maladaptive reactions are more likely to be produced by near-miss experiences than by remote-miss experiences. There appears to be a benign type of near-miss experience which merely breaks down blanket immunity reassurances and induces the person to become aware of his potential vulnerability, without rendering him incapable of evolving new danger-contingent reassurances. For example, after the San Angelo tornado, many survivors described themselves in interviews as having "learned a lesson" and reported that they now planned to build effective storm shelters before there were any more tornado warnings (Moore, 1958). Similar indications of new fear-reducing habits have been noted after other disasters and danger episodes (Janis, 1968).

Taking account of the concepts introduced earlier in the discussion of reflective fear, we can view the learning effects of a benign near-miss experience as resulting in the acquisition of a set of discriminatory compromise defenses, which has a twofold benign outcome: (a) in the normal course of events, when no warning signal is present, the person's level of fear remains very low, with blanket reassurance as the dominant reaction; and (b) when clear-cut warnings are perceived, the person's fear mounts to a moderate level, well above the threshold for discriminatory vigilance but below the threshold for hypervigilance.

In contrast, when a person has been emotionally shocked by a near-miss experience, the level of fear evoked by subsequent threat stimuli will frequently exceed the threshold for hypervigilance, and he will display inappropriately intense fear. If such reactions occur only at times when a person perceives clear-cut warning signals, his life adjustment may not be seriously impaired; but if they are also evoked at times when only very mild threat cues are present, the hypervigilance is much more disruptive and may be classified as a "traumatic neurosis."

Using "near-miss" and "remote-miss" as purely descriptive terms to designate, respectively, a high *vs.* low degree of proximity to actual danger stimuli in a stressful situation, we can say that the former is more likely to produce hypervigilance, whereas the latter is more likely to produce an attitude of blanket reassurance. Despite these differential tendencies, however, the effects of near-miss and remote-miss experiences can overlap to a considerable degree, and both types are capable of giving rise to adaptive compromise defenses. In short, the sustained effects of any given stressful episode, whether near-miss or remote-miss in character, can range over the entire continuum, motivating the development of blanket reassurances or compromise defenses or hypervigilance. Which type of outcome will ensue depends upon two main factors, according to the postulates presented in the analysis of reflective fear: (a) the type of information conveyed by the stress experience, and (b) the person's original level of fear in response to the threat stimuli (prior to the onset of the danger stimuli). When the information conveyed by the episode is of the type that breaks down expectations of personal invulnerability, the predicted poststress reaction to any recurrence of the threat will be: (a) maladaptive hypervigilance if the person's fear level initially was moderate or high, and (b) adaptive compromise defenses if the person's fear level initially was low. On the other hand, if the information conveyed by the episode is of the type that fosters expectations of personal invulnerability, the predicted poststress outcome will be: (a) blanket reassurance if the person's fear level initially was low, and (b) compromise defenses if the person's fear level initially was moderate or high.

The above-stated propositions serve to link the psychological impact of severe stress experiences with the impact of purely verbal warnings. We would expect that the effects of any pertinent informational input bearing on personal vulnerability to danger will depend upon the person's original level of fear, whether the information is conveyed by direct exposure to danger stimuli or by purely verbal warnings. We assume continuity between the two types of informational inputs in that the same type of emotional learning can be stimulated by both and will be facilitated or interfered with by essentially the same cognitive and motivational factors. Direct danger experiences, of course, are generally much more impressive than verbal messages, since one cannot easily ignore the relevant danger cues. In addition, direct exposure to danger stimuli entails more powerful rewards and punishments. Consequently, more drastic changes in habitual reactions to threat stimuli are likely to be produced by near-miss or even by remote-miss danger experiences than by purely verbal descriptions or predictions about oncoming dangers. But it is only in this respect that near-miss and remote-miss experiences take on special psychological significance, particularly when we are attempting to explain extreme changes in adjustive behavior, such as those observed in cases of severe emotional shock and sustained hypervigilance.

Effects of Preparatory Communications

The assumption that the same principles of learning operate, whether people are exposed to actual danger events or to purely verbal warnings about them, leads us to expect that when the appropriate conditions are present, the verbal messages can produce the same dramatic changes in emotionality as physical stress stimuli. That a purely verbal warning occasionally does so is a well-known fact to physicians who have the responsibility of communicating positive findings obtained from X-rays and medical tests to patients diagnosed as suffering from cancer or some other serious disease. When patients are told the truth by their physicians or learn it inadvertently from members of the family, some become as chronically hypervigilant as people who have been traumatized in a physical disaster and others become as depressed as those who have actually been bereaved (Bernstein & Small, 1951; Janis, 1958; Lindemann, 1941; Wittkower, 1949, 1952). Since the patient is familiar with the nature of the threat, a terse authoritative communication is sufficient for him to perceive his danger. Thus, it seems plausible to assume that although sensitization-inducing information is most likely to become salient during a near-miss disaster episode, such information can also occur and have the same effect during a predisaster warning period, during a remote-miss experience, or during a false alarm episode.

One of the main questions to be answered regarding preparatory communications is: what factors determine whether an advanced warning will instigate *effective* preparatory behavior, enhancing the recipients' ability to cope with subsequent stress? Some tentative answers to this question can be extracted from the available research literature.

Considerable evidence indicates that a significant determinant of emotional arousal is familiarity with the danger described in any warnings dealing with threats to physical safety, economic security, autonomy, social status, or other important values. If the danger is unfamiliar, or emanates from an unknown source, the warnings will generally go unnoticed unless information is presented which familiarizes the person with the *magnitude, probability of occurrence,* and *personal implications* of the danger. Evidence concerning the importance of prior familiarization that *personalizes* the meaning of the threat is provided by survey research studies on public reactions to warnings of common illnesses and public health hazards. Leventhal, Rosenstock, Hochbaum, and Carriger (1960) conducted a survey of public reactions to the Asian flu epidemic in the fall of 1957 and found marked differences in awareness that the epidemic was actually in progress, with relatively few people believing that they might actually fall ill with flu. The lack of awareness was probably due, in part, to the slow accumulation of cases; only a small percentage in each city was ill at any one time during the two-month period of the survey. The vast majority of people did not take account of repeated public health announcements or other warning signs showing the presence of the epidemic and failed to act to protect themselves by being vaccinated. But there was considerably greater sensitivity to warnings, including beliefs that an epidemic was present and that one could become ill, in families where illness had already struck. Thus, prior familiarity in the form of a near miss sensitized people to the threat and elicited vulnerability feelings.

Familiarity, of course, can sometimes *reduce* the intensity of fear reactions and promote indifference toward warnings and subsequent danger signs, particularly if the prior information minimizes the probability that the individual is currently vulnerable to danger. An experimental study by Janis, Lumsdaine, and Gladstone (1951), which dealt with reactions to a major "bad news" event, suggests that an advance warning can have a significant dampening effect even for a relatively impersonal type of threat that occurs many months later. In this study, high school students were presented with a radio program in June, 1949, that discussed Russia's ability to produce an atomic bomb. Unexpectedly, three months later, President Truman announced that Russia had succeeded in producing an atomic bomb explosion. The impact of this dramatic "bad news" event was attenuated as a result of the prior communication. An experimental group that had received the preliminary communication predicting the bad news event manifested less concern and showed less attitude change following President Truman's announcement than an equivalent control group that had received an irrelevant communication. The findings from this field experiment and from several laboratory investigations of human reactions to experimentally induced stress (e.g., Pronko & Leith, 1956; Laskin, 1955) support an "adaptation" hypothesis, which asserts that the intensity of the emotional reactions evoked by a stressful event will tend to be reduced by prior exposure to a preparatory communication that predicts and minimizes the event in advance.

There is also some experimental evidence indicating that prior information can have a marked influence on the way in which stress stimuli are interpreted, which seems to be especially applicable to modulating the effects of certain types of near-miss experiences, such as witnessing suffering and body damage to other people. An outstanding series of investigations by Lazarus and his co-workers (Lazarus, Speisman, Mordkoff, & Davison, 1962; Lazarus, 1964; Lazarus & Alfert, 1964) has shown that the subject's set or orientation can be manipulated in a way that significantly attenuates the intensity of the emotional reactions evoked by a documentary film showing young men undergoing mutilations of their genital organs during a subincision rite in a primitive society. Heart rate and galvanic skin reactions were recorded while male college students viewed the stressful film and a detailed mood adjective check list was administered afterward. In one of the studies (Lazarus & Alfert, 1964) three experimental conditions were compared. In one, the subincision film was presented without a sound track, and continuous recordings were made of physiological reactions. In a second experimental condition, the film was preceded by a short commentary that attempted to minimize the threatening aspects of the scenes that were about to be witnessed. The commentary was based on psychoanalytic concepts of denial and reaction formation and asserted that the apparently painful procedure was not disturbing to the young boys undergoing it and was, in fact, enjoyed by them. In a third condition the movie and the minimizing commentary were presented simultaneously. Analysis of the data from continuous recordings of physiological reactions during the film showed significant differences in degree of arousal among the three conditions. As compared with the two conditions where the film was preceded or accompanied by the denial materials, the film without any minimizing commentary yielded significantly higher scores for skin conductance and heart rate, as well as more verbal expressions of affective disturbance on the Nowlis mood adjective check list. Thus, the minimizing information presented either before or during exposure to the distressing scenes reduced the emotional impact.

Another aspect of emotional adaptation which bears more directly on the formation of effective compromise defenses for coping with subsequent stress is highlighted by various findings from Janis's study (1958) of the postoperative emotional behavior of surgical patients in relation to the magnitude and quality of their preoperative fear reactions. The following is one of the main conclusions that emerged from a combination of observations, based on his series of case studies and his correlational data from survey research. Persons who displayed a *moderate* degree of fear before the surgical operation were significantly *less* likely than others (those who were either extremely fearful beforehand or relatively free from preoperative fear) to display any form of emotional disturbance during the stressful period of postoperative convalescence. Of special interest is the comparison between the moderate group and the very low preoperative fear group. The patients who showed practically no preoperative fear turned out to be much more likely than the others to display disturbed reactions of anger and intense resentment, as well as various manifestations of high emotional tension during the stressful period of postoperative convalescence. (Discussion of the surgical patients who were extremely fearful before the operation will be postponed until a later section when we examine evidence bearing on chronic anxiety predispositions.)

Although in some instances the absence of preoperative fear may have been determined by personality predispositions, there were many cases whose lack of preoperative worry appeared to be attributable to the lack of adequate preparatory communications. In several cases, the interview data and the hospital records indicated that before and after an earlier operation, the patient's reactions had been markedly different. Neither the absence of fear while awaiting the operation nor the reactions of agitation and resentment to the stresses of postoperative convalescence could be regarded as "typical" for those personalities. For instance, one patient, a twenty-one-year-old woman had been given realistic information and reassurances by the physicians before an earlier abdominal operation (appendectomy). At that time she had been moderately worried beforehand, but showed excellent emotional adjustment after the operation. Two years later, she was admitted to the same hospital for another abdominal operation (cholecystectomy). This time she was told nothing by her physician except that "there's really nothing to it, it's a less serious operation than the previous one." The patient remained wholly unconcerned about the operation beforehand, apparently anticipating complete invulnerability, and then after the operation became markedly upset, negativistic, and resentful toward the nursing staff. The occurrence of a "pathogenic" denial defense in such a case certainly cannot be regarded as a chronic, invariant feature of the patient's personality; rather, it appears to be highly dependent upon the type of preoperative communications received from the surgeon or other medical authorities.

Failure to display fear before a major operation can be said to be "pathogenic" in that it is likely to result in maladjustment to the subsequent stresses during or immediately after the actual crisis. The failure to experience fear preoperatively results in a failure to worry and to develop reassurances contingent upon specific aspects of subsequent stress stimulation. When a patient fails to do the "work of worrying" beforehand, he remains unprepared for the distressing experiences that lie ahead of him—the postoperative pains, the discomforts, and the deprivations that invariably occur after surgery. When the stresses materialize, the patient either misinterprets these events or lacks the inner preparation necessary to reassure himself that he will not be mutilated or annihilated.

Correlational evidence on this point was obtained from a survey of a large sample of male surgery cases (Janis, 1958, pp. 357–360). The results showed that the men who were informed about specific unpleasant experiences beforehand were more likely than those who were uninformed to be worried or fearful before the operation but less likely to become angry or emotionally upset during the postoperative convalescent period. A significantly smaller percentage of the informed men subsequently expressed feelings of resentment or developed sustained changes of attitude in the negative direction toward the staff physicians or nurses.

These correlational data are based on retrospective reports and therefore cannot be accepted as conclusively valid evidence; but a number of studies of illness and disaster, reviewed by Janis and Leventhal (1965), provide additional observations consistent with these findings. For example, a quasi-experimental investigation by Prugh and his collaborators (Prugh, Staub, Sands, Kirschbaum, & Lenihan, 1953) and a parallel investigation by Jackson *et al.* (Jackson, Winkley, Faust, Germak, & Burtt, 1953) suggest that preparatory communications can have a marked influence in preventing depressive reactions and other adverse emotional sequelae of surgery and hospitalization among young children. In these studies, however, the effects of preparatory communications were confounded with those of other important variables that were also included in the same experimental programs, such as arranging to have the child's mother remain in the room during the most distressing periods. In addition, it was difficult for the experimenters to avoid unintentional errors from "observer contamination" in that the research workers who rated the children's behavior knew which ones were receiving the special experimental treatment and which ones were not. These methodological difficulties were partially surmounted in a recent experiment by Moran (1963) on children awaiting tonsillectomy. In this study an experimental group received preparatory communications—given to each parent as well as each child—while an equated control group received only the standard hospital care. The children and their parents in the experimental group were found to have fewer signs of emotional disturbance during convalescence, not only while in the hospital but also at home after discharge.

Similar findings from a carefully controlled field experiment with adult surgical patients at the Massachusetts General Hospital are reported by Egbert, Battit, Welch, and Bartlett (1964). These investigators designed their experiment specifically to test the implications of the correlational findings on the inverse relationship between preoperative information and postoperative disturbances reported by Janis (1958). Ninety-seven patients hospitalized for elective abdominal operations were assigned at random to the experimental and control groups, which proved to be well equated on age, sex, and type of operation. The patients in both groups had a visit from the anesthetist on the night before the operation and were given routine information about the time and duration of the operation, the nature of the anesthesia, and the fact that they would awaken in the recovery room. The patients in the control group were told nothing more, whereas those in the experimental group were given four additional types of information designed to facilitate the "work of worrying": (a) a description of postoperative pain—where they would feel it, how intense it would be, how long it was likely to last; (b) explicit reassurance that postoperative pain is a normal consequence of an abdominal operation; (c) advice to relax their abdominal muscles in order to reduce the pain, accompanied by special instructions about how to shift from one side to the other by the use of their arms and legs without tensing muscles in the sensitive area; and (d) assurance that they would be given pain-killing medication if they could not achieve a tolerable level of comfort. Neither the surgeons nor the ward nurses were told about this experiment so as to make sure that the patients in both groups would not receive any other differential treatment.

On the day of operation both groups required about the same amount of narcotics, but on each of the next five days the experimental group required significantly less narcotics. In fact, the requests for medication to relieve their pains were so infrequent from the well-informed patients that their postoperative narcotic requirements were reduced by about one-half, as compared with the uninformed control group. Blind ratings by a physician showed that the patients in the experimental group were more comfortable and in better emotional and physical condition than the controls. Further evidence of the more rapid improvement of the well-informed patients is provided by data on duration of hospitalization. Completely unaware of the experimental or control treatments received by the patients, the surgeons sent the well-informed patients home on an average of 2.7 days earlier than the uninformed patients ($p < .01$). This study provides systematic evidence in support of the conclusion, derived from the earlier studies, concerning the positive value of advance information about postoperative pain. In this case, the preoperative information was reiterated during the first few postoperative days, which may have contributed to the effectiveness of the preparatory communication. The results of this study not only show essentially the same positive outcome for adult surgical patients as the experiment by Moran with children but go a step further in suggesting that a brief form of emotional inoculation can speed up recovery during convalescence.

The various studies just cited provide

some empirical support for the conclusion that if preparatory communications stimulate "the work of worrying," the average person will become more highly motivated to develop an effective set of self-delivered reassurances before the onset of the stress situation and, therefore, will display higher stress tolerance when the crisis is actually at hand. Obviously, we cannot expect all preparatory communications to be effective in this respect. In the light of our earlier discussion of sensitization reactions to warnings, we would predict that preparatory communications will be effective only if they arouse vigilance and, at the same time, help to build up the person's self-concept of being capable of coping with the anticipated threat and of surviving the danger if it strikes. But until various pertinent communication variables are tested experimentally and evaluated under actual stress conditions, we cannot expect to have a dependable set of principles for successful "emotional inoculation."

PREDISPOSITIONAL DETERMINANTS

Research on experimentally induced stress and on fear-arousing communications indicates that there is a wide range of individual differences in sensitivity to threat and stress stimuli. Lazarus and Baker (1956) point out that the effects of stress sometimes remain undetected if the investigator fails to examine individual differences in response to the stressful situation. Illustrative examples are provided by the findings from the experiments by Lazarus and Erickson (1952) and Hardison and Purcell (1959). In both experiments no main effects were found in comparing the laboratory stress and the nonstress conditions, but there was, nevertheless, an increase in variability of response attributable to the stress condition. In the Hardison and Purcell experiment, improvements in performance under stress occurred in subjects rated as independent and flexible, while deficits appeared in a contrasting group rated as dependent and constricted. Interaction effects of this type, with no main effects for the stress manipulation itself, seem to be especially likely whenever the relatively mild stresses of laboratory research are being investigated. This does not imply, however, that we should not expect to find similar interactions, as well as main effects, when people are exposed to the more powerful stresses of disasters and illness.

Most of the pertinent evidence on predispositional factors currently at hand comes from a small number of studies comparing persons who are high or low on a given personality attribute in their responses to a given type of stress. While the data are fragmentary, we can extract a number of important leads concerning sources of individual differences that appear to be determinants of the intensity and quality of stress reactions.

In general, two types of predispositional factors seem to be relevant. One type has to do with *ego-involvement,* i.e., the degree to which the threat is relevant to the individual's personal goals, commitments, and ideology. The second type of predisposition involves *basic personality factors* that determine the individual's sensitivity to a much wider range of threat or stress stimuli.

Ego-Involvement in the Threat

An example of the first type of predispositional factor is provided by investigations comparing the reactions of smokers and nonsmokers to fear-arousing communications on smoking and lung cancer. The results of a number of studies indicate that smokers tend to be more resistant than nonsmokers to communications that call attention to the dangers of smoking (Cannell & MacDonald, 1965; Feather, 1962, 1963; Janis, 1959; Leventhal & Watts, 1966). The Leventhal and Watts study, for example, provides evidence suggesting that smokers are likely to develop a "blanket reassurance" type of attitude which functions as a defense against the arousal of fear when they are presented information on smoking and lung cancer. This study made use of fear-arousing movies on this topic. The heavy smokers were more likely than the others to believe they could not be vulnerable to a disease such as lung cancer and showed correspondingly less acceptance of the public health recommendations. A similar result was also reported for fear-arousing communications on automobile safety, with drivers being less influenced than nondrivers (Berkowitz & Cottingham, 1960).

From the various studies on ego involvement, it appears that those members of the audience for whom the threat is most applicable tend to become more vigilant and hence more *interested* than others in information about the threat; but they nevertheless show more reluctance than others to accept the conclusion that the danger is sufficiently great as to warrant protective action.

Additional material bearing on the role of ego involvement as a determinant of stress reactions can be found in the comprehensive review of the literature by Iverson and Reuder (1956) and in more recent discussions by Vogel, Raymond, and Lazarus (1959) and Lazarus (1966). The latter author reviews evidence that supports the expected relationship between the degree of emotional arousal induced by a threat of deprivation and the strength of the individual's need to avoid the deprivation.

Basic Personality Dispositions Influencing Responses to Danger

Whether or not a person is ego involved with a specific threat, he can be expected to overreact to any sign of danger if he has a high chronic level of anxiety. Even with relatively crude diagnostic techniques, it is possible to select persons who tend to display very high anxiety in the presence of all signs of oncoming danger, whether it involves potential pain, body damage, separation from family and friends, loss of status, or any other severe deprivation. Such an assessment should allow better-than-chance predictions as to *who* will display high, medium, or low emotional arousal in response to any given type of stress stimuli.

Evidence in support of the hypothesis that chronically anxious men overreact to stress is provided in a wartime study of volunteer paratroopers by Finan and his associates (reported in Janis, 1949). On the very first day of their preliminary-jump training, the volunteers' overt symptoms of fear were assessed in a comparatively mild military stress situation (being required to make a safe jump, while attached to a harness, from a 40-foot tower). None of these preliminary ratings were shown to any of the officer instructors involved in the actual paratroop training. Those volunteers who showed the most extreme fear reactions —overt hesitation to execute the jump command—proved to be much more likely than others to be "washed out" of the paratroop training program, primarily on the basis of subsequent refusal to jump from an airplane or other symptoms of low stress tolerance. These results provide systematic data in support of clinical case studies and psychiatric surveys which suggest that there are certain types of predisposed personalities who suffer from chronic anxiety and who consistently overreact to environmental threats and dangers (Menninger, 1948).

Research on surgical patients (Janis, 1958) also points to a certain type of hyperanxious personality who characteristically reacts with high anxiety to any sign of potential body damage. Such persons show a disproportionately high intensity of anticipatory fear both before the operation and again afterwards, often accompanied by symptoms of hypervigilance. They seem to react as though they were facing an enormous danger whenever they are told about even minor threats and dangers (e.g., penicillin injections). In these cases, the underlying source of anxiety evidently remains unconscious, and they fail to show the usual decrease in apprehensiveness when given reassuring communications by physicians or other authoritative persons. The chronically high level of fear and accompanying hypervigilance prevent these patients from developing discriminative vigilance reactions that could allow them to cope with the stress situation more adequately. In contrast, the findings cited in the preceding section indicated that those surgical patients who experienced moderate amounts of reflective fear before their operation developed danger-contingent reassurances, and responded more adaptively to the stresses of the postoperative period.

A follow-up study by Leventhal (1963) provides further evidence that predisposed individuals are more responsive to threat and danger cues both before and after surgery. But this study, as well as the earlier one by Janis (1958), relied exclusively on interview data and had no independent dispositional measure to predict hypervigilance. A recent study by Leventhal and Sharpe (1965), however, made use of the Welch dispositional anxiety scale and found a positive relationship with signs of emotional distress, obtained from direct observations of changes in facial expressions. The sample consisted of 71 maternity patients who were observed in the delivery rooms of a major hospital. Facial expressions were recorded by scoring the muscular activity in various regions of the face including the forehead, eyes, nose, and mouth. The data showed that specific changes in the face (particularly increases in furrows, creases, and V-formations of the forehead) showed significant increases with progress in labor. Women with high scores on the Welch anxiety scale exhibited a significantly greater number of these distress signs than did those low on the anxiety measure.

The assessment of sensitivity to stress is likely to be complicated at times by the occurrence of defensive personality tendencies that incline the individual to deny the presence of potential danger or to repress his negative affects. Some indications of these response patterns are provided in studies by Lazarus and his co-workers. In their studies of fear reactions to distressing sights of genital mutilations in a vivid documentary movie, Lazarus and Alfert (1964) compared the emotional reactions of subjects scoring high and low on various self-rating scales from the Minnesota Multiphasic Personality Inventory. When asked to give *self reports* on their affective states, the subjects who scored high on scales that purport to measure denial, repression, or repression-sensitization were less likely than others to say that they were disturbed by the stress stimulus. Nevertheless, on various *physiological* measures of arousal during exposure to the stressful stimulations, the deniers obtained higher scores than the non-deniers. The results suggest that since individuals may exhibit intense emotional reactions in different response systems, research on individual differences in stress reactions may be more productive if assessments are made of each person's predilection for one mode of emotional expression as against another. Similar considerations have been emphasized by Lacey (1959) concerning the need to investigate each individual's predominant "channel" for expression of affect among the various potential physiological changes that can be induced by stress stimuli.

Personality Dispositions Influencing Reactions to Warnings

Some indications of the ways in which predispositional characteristics are likely to interact with fear-arousing stimuli in producing adaptive behavior are provided by studies in which differentially frightening communications are exposed to equivalent groups of subjects whose personality attributes are assessed by personality tests. In the first study on personality differences in relation to acceptance or rejection of each of two versions of a fear-arousing communication, Janis and Feshbach (1953, 1954) divided their subjects into high- and low-anxiety subgroups. This was done on the basis of the subjects' answers to a personality inventory that dealt with somatic anxiety symptoms (e.g., questions about how often they suffered from pounding heart, trembling hands, cold sweats, damp and clammy hands, etc.). Acceptance of the dental hygiene recommendations given in both versions of the communication was found to be dependent upon the interaction of two variables: (a) the amount of fear-arousing material concerning the damaging consequences of neglecting one's teeth and (b) personality predispositions, as assessed by the somatic anxiety scale. Within the audience exposed to the *strong* threat-appeal version, those students with high-anxiety predispositions (i.e., manifesting many chronic anxiety symptoms) were *less influenced* than those with low-anxiety predispositions; whereas, within the equivalent audience exposed to the *minimal* threat version, the students with high-anxiety predispositions were *more influenced* than those with low-anxiety predispositions.

The findings were interpreted as indicating that an individual's threshold for fear or anxiety arousal will determine the degree to which he will be defensively resistant to a communication containing somewhat controversial recommendations bolstered by statements that depict *severe* threats. The high-anxiety students were more readily stimulated by the fear-arousing statements in the strong appeal version of the communication and were more likely to develop defensive reactions of the type that interfere with long-run acceptance. Thus, the strong-threat version appears to have exceeded the optimal level of fear arousal for the high-anxiety subjects but not for the low-anxiety subjects. On the other hand, the mild appeal was found to have a comparatively favorable effect on the high-anxiety students. These findings suggest that when a mild threat appeal is presented (e.g., one that refers to potential danger without "spelling out" any of the threatening details), the high-anxiety individuals, by virtue of their low threshold of anxiety arousal, will be more likely than others to display a slight increase in fear; if the emotional state does not become too intense, they will be more likely than their more placid neighbors to form compromise defenses and conform with the communicator's recommendations. But when confronted by a communication presenting severe threat statements, the high-anxiety individual will become emotionally disorganized or resort to habitual neurotic defenses, so that interfering responses predominate and prevent acceptance of the recommendations.

Several other experiments on fear-arousing communications provide comparative personality data similar to that obtained in the Janis and Feshbach experiment. These additional studies leave matters unclear, however, since the findings are somewhat inconsistent with each other and with the interaction outcome found by Janis and Feshbach. We shall briefly review these additional findings, which will serve not only to introduce an additional note of caution about the interaction hypothesis just discussed but also to call attention to some additional variables that may prove to be relevant as limiting conditions for any general propositions about the relationship between anxiety-proneness and acceptance of mild vs. strong fear-arousing communications.

An experiment that attempted to test the interaction of chronic neurotic anxiety with varied intensities of threat was carried out by Haefner (1956). He divided his subjects on the basis of the same somatic anxiety inventory that was used by Janis and Feshbach and compared their reactions to different versions of a communication advocating a ban on H-bomb testing. Haefner found no significant differences between high- and low-anxiety subjects on either the mild or strong threat versions of his communications. He points out that this negative finding might be attributable to the fact that he administered the personality test under nonprivate conditions, which could greatly reduce its validity. Nevertheless, the negative findings from his study raise a question about the generality of the interaction effect.

A somewhat mixed outcome has been reported by Goldstein (1959), who also used two different predispositional measures in an attempted replication of the Janis and Feshbach experiment. One measure was the somatic anxiety scale used in the original study; the other was Mainord's measure of avoidance tendencies as a habitual way of dealing with tension-producing material. The latter measure assesses the subjects' responses to a Sentence Completion test containing emotionally charged phrases that have aggressive and sexual connotations. High avoidance scores are obtained by those who characteristically fail to take account of the emotional implications of the sentence stems and avoid expressing any personal feelings in responding to them. Low scores, on the other hand, are obtained from those who readily acknowledge their conflicts and emotions. Essentially the same minimal and strong fear appeal versions of the dental hygiene communication were used as in the original experiment.

The results on the avoidance predisposition measure exactly parallel those previously obtained by Janis and Feshbach for their somatic anxiety scale. But despite the parallel outcomes, it remains unclear as to whether these findings can be interpreted as bearing on the same interaction hypothesis that was inferred from the Janis and Feshbach findings. Goldstein reports that the somatic anxiety measure used by Janis and Feshbach yield some differences in the same direction that were not large enough to be significant at the .05 level. However, he does present data which suggest that his measure of avoidance tendencies may be unrelated to the somatic anxiety scores. Goldstein's conclusion is that "While the patterns of results in both the present study and the Feshbach and Janis study are highly similar, they are not explicable by recourse to a common factor." Further study is needed, however, to determine whether there is a unitary personality factor or constellation tapped by the Janis and Feshbach somatic anxiety measure and the items in the avoidance tendency test.

Haefner (1964) and Singer (1965) have reported negative outcomes in recent studies designed to replicate more directly the Janis and Feshbach experiment. They found no interaction of anxiety dispositions, as assessed by the somatic anxiety scale, and responsiveness to fear-arousing appeals in dental hygiene communications. Both of these studies, and one by Leventhal and Singer (1966), report more overall acceptance for the strong than for the mild threat communication. There are also some observations (Leventhal & Singer, 1966; Singer, 1965) suggesting that the dental hygiene recommendations were perceived by the audience as highly effective means for warding off the danger. The latter factor may be important in contrasting these experimental outcomes with that from the Janis and Feshbach study, carried out about 15 years earlier. For more than a decade, fluoride toothpaste advertising and public endorsements by the American Dental Association have been attempting to increase the plausibility of the recommended practices for averting dental hygiene threats, perhaps with some considerable degree of success. This strengthening of the perceived effectiveness of the recommendations may eliminate the tendency for highly anxious subjects to reject the communications under high fear.

In another pertinent study, Niles (1964) used two predispositional measures and compared acceptance of recommendations to mild and strong fear-arousing communications on smoking and lung cancer. The first predispositional measure was the somatic anxiety scale used by Janis and Feshbach. The second, a "feelings of susceptibility" scale, was developed by Niles on the basis of survey research findings showing that subjects who felt themselves to be highly vulnerable to illness were more inclined than others to take preventive action (Hochbaum, 1958; Leventhal, Rosenstock, Hochbaum, & Carriger, 1960). The subjects, 192 Yale freshmen, all of whom were cigarette smokers, were divided into predispositional groups on the basis of each of the predispositional measures. No significant results were obtained for the somatic anxiety measure, but for the measure of perceived vulnerability to illness, there was an interaction outcome similar to that found by Janis and Feshbach. In response to a moderate fear-arousing movie, high-vulnerability subjects showed *more* attitude change than the low-vulnerability subjects (on intention to decrease cigarette smoking and to obtain chest X-rays); whereas, in response to a very strong fear version of the movie (containing a technicolor sequence depicting a cancer victim's lung operation), the high-vulnerability subjects showed *less* attitude change than the low-vulnerability subjects.

It is difficult to interpret this evidence because the somatic anxiety measure used in the dental hygiene study did not yield significant results, and yet the related measure dealing with perceived vulnerability yielded confirmatory results. Niles points out that the two predispositional measures correlate significantly ($r = .48$) and that both contain items concerning anxiety symptoms that are manifestly quite similar. Thus, many subjects high in vulnerability were also found to be high in somatic anxiety, and the divergent results therefore do not permit any definite conclusions as to whether chronic anxiety disposition interacts with intensity of fear arousal.

Responses to other questionnaire items reported by Niles suggest that high-vulnerability subjects, when exposed to the strong stimulus, regarded the threat as inevitable and impossible to prevent. Their intense fear reactions appear to have interfered with acceptance of the rational arguments about the benefits of giving up smoking and taking diagnostic tests. These findings on beliefs about the effectiveness of the recommended actions are congruent with the interpretation offered to the differences found between the more recent dental hygiene studies and the Janis and Feshbach study.

The results of the previously discussed Leventhal and Watts (1966) smoking and lung cancer experiment provide further suggestions regarding the interaction of disposition and treatment available. Subjects were divided on vulnerability and also on the basis of smoking habits. Light smokers reported greater fear than heavy smokers. Heavy smokers reported fear if they were high scorers on the vulnerability scale, while heavy smokers who did not regard themselves as susceptible to disease were less likely to report fear than any other subjects. There were no differences in reported fear level between high and low susceptibles among nonsmokers. Thus, the data suggest that vulnerability feelings influence the intensity of reflective fear only within the group of subjects (smokers) for whom the threat was most *relevant*. Moreover, smokers (who are actually more vulnerable to danger) took fewer X-rays after exposure to the high-fear film. In addition, high fear appears to have been more effective in producing success in cutting down smoking. The pattern of the findings suggested that subjects to whom the threat is most relevant are most eager to avoid contact with the danger agent. They do this by avoiding diagnosis (X-rays), which can lead to the danger of surgery, and by avoiding smoking, which can lead to death through lung cancer.

The behavior of smokers in the Leventhal and Watts (1966) study is similar to Niles's (1964) finding for her high-vulnerability subjects. (Since she did not classify her subjects on smoking behavior, the high-vulnerability *S*s could have been heavy smokers.) Other relations between the vulnerability variable and response to threat communications are being explored in new studies (Leventhal, Jones, & Trembly, 1966; Leventhal, Watts, & Pagano, 1967). It is yet to be determined whether increasing vulnerability feelings prior to exposure to a communication always reduces acceptance of protective actions or if it does so only when the communication creates a sense of helplessness or psychological entrapment. Moreover, it is not clear whether this sense of entrapment is induced by the perception that (a) effective protective action exceeds one's personal resources, (b) environmental sources of protection are unavailable, or (c) the recommended protective measures are in themselves associated with other serious dangers (see Leventhal, 1965). Furthermore, in recent discussions of reaction to threat communications (Leventhal & Singer, 1966; Leventhal, 1967; 1968a; 1968b) the question has also been raised as to whether the various cognitive adjustments involved in attitudinal and behavioral acceptance are merely correlated with fear reactions without being produced by them.

Evaluation of the Interaction Hypothesis

Taking account of additional psychiatric observations, Janis (1968) has suggested a possible explanation for the parallel outcomes from the various personality measures used by Janis and Feshbach (1954), Niles (1961), and Goldstein (1959), even though the measures may be uncorrelated with each other. Each of these measures might tap a somewhat different type of symptom of neurotic anxiety. The situation might be similar to that encountered in clinical work when symptoms of phobias, or hysterical conversion reactions, or obsessional worrying are used to diagnose people with severe neurotic anxiety (see Cameron, 1963). These various types of symptoms may be *disjunctive* in that a clinical investigator usually does not find the same patient having more than one of the three types of symptoms. But the presence of any one of these symptoms may be sufficient to categorize the individual as "psychoneurotic," rather than as "normal" or "psychotic," from which better-than-chance predictions can be made as to how this personality will respond to various future life situations. In the same way, a high score on a somatic anxiety scale (Janis & Feshbach), a vulnerability to disease scale (Niles), or a sentence completion test to measure avoidance tendencies (Goldstein) may serve to identify the presence of one or another form of neurotic anxiety, on a better-than-chance basis.

Although this possibility may seem plausible in the light of clinical observations, it will not be easy to devise systematic tests of the disjunctive conception of dispositional tendencies. Nor does this possible way of reconciling the findings from the three studies eliminate all the disparate findings. The best that can be said for the interaction hypothesis, in view of the conflicting evidence, is that it is worthwhile to continue to investigate differences in reactions to stress stimuli predicted by the hypothesis and to seek to discover limiting conditions that may bring better order into the observed differences reported so far.

That it would be premature to disregard the interaction hypothesis is indicated not only by some of the partially confirmatory data reported in the experiments just discussed but also by the strongly confirmatory evidence from a different type of stress experiment that was conducted with grade school children. Penny and McCann (1962) have reported findings closely paralleling those from Janis and Feshbach in their study of escape learning in third and fourth graders. The children were classified into high-anxiety and low-anxiety predispositional groups on the basis of the Sarason (Sarason, Davidson, Lighthall, Waite, & Ruebush, 1960) anxiety scale. They were then exposed to a laboratory situation in which a noxious, fear-arousing buzzer was sounded. At the beginning of each experimental session, a communication was given by the experimenter, with a specific recommendation for escaping from the distressing stimulation (viz., pull the lever all the way to the bottom immediately after the tone begins). The children were not told that the speed of their level-pressing response was being measured.

Two different intensities of the noxious tone were used, which corresponded to a relatively weak vs. a relatively strong fear-arousing stimulus. For the weak stimulus, high-anxiety subjects carried out the avoidance response recommended by the experimenter more rapidly than low-anxiety subjects; for the strong fear stimulus, the high-anxiety subjects responded less rapidly than the lows. This is essentially the same interaction outcome found by Janis and Feshbach (1954). Penny and McCann report, however, that the difference between the two groups under the strong fear condition appeared mainly during the first block of four trials; this difference disappeared as the number of trials increased to twenty, indicating a gradual adaptation to the fear stimulus.

The authors interpret their findings in terms of the Spence (1956) and Taylor (1956) theory, which postulates that anxiety acts as an irrelevant drive that energizes all existing habits. When a mildly noxious stimulus is presented, the higher drive level of the high-anxiety group would facilitate fast responding. But, when a stronger noxious stimulus is presented, the drive would become so powerful that older competing responses would be energized to a greater extent than new escape reactions and thus interfere with efficient performance. These interfering responses would include startle reactions and various forms of distraction and freezing behavior.

It will be noted that this interpretation, which relies primarily on evidence from animal and human learning research, predicts the same interaction outcome between anxiety level and strength of fear stimulus as that discussed in the preceding section. The Taylor and Spence theory differs, however, from the explanation formulated in terms of reflective vs. neurotic fear. For example, the latter theoretical approach leads to specific predictions, as we have seen, concerning the onset of human fear as being dependent upon cognitive changes from cues that convey information about personal vulnerability, even though it may be impossible to trace any association of the cues with pain, punishment, or any other previously experienced stress stimuli. It also has some implications for different types of sets and predispositions, on the assumption that the chronic level of reflective fear in response to any given type of threat will be highly susceptible to change via new informational inputs, whereas neurotic anxiety predispositions will be relatively unalterable. In contrast to the simpler postulates in the Spence-Taylor theory, defensive processes are taken into account which, if modified prior to the onset of the stress stimuli, are expected to alter in specifiable ways the intensity of fear arousal and the coping mechanisms that will come into play. In further attempts to verify the interaction hypothesis it should be possible to introduce some additional experimental manipulations to help determine which of the alternative theories provides a more adequate explanation of the observed differences between high- and low-anxiety subjects.

REFERENCES

Appley, M. H., & Trumbull, R. (Eds.) *Psychological stress: Issues in research.* New York: Appleton-Century-Crofts, 1967.

Ax, A. F. The physiological differentiation between fear and anger in humans. *Psychosom. Med.,* 1953, 15, 433–442.

Basowitz, H., Persky, H., Korchin, S., & Grinker, R. *Anxiety and stress.* New York: McGraw-Hill, 1955.

Beier, E. G. The effect of induced anxiety on flexibility of intellectual functioning. *Psychol. Monogr.,* 1951, 65, No. 9.

Berkowitz, L., & Cottingham, D. R. The interest value and relevance of fear arousing communications. *J. abnorm. soc. Psychol.,* 1960, 60, 37–43.

Bernstein, S., & Small, S. Psychodynamic fac-

tors in surgery. *J. Mt. Sinai Hospital,* 1951, 17, 938–958.
Brown, J. S., & Farber, I. E. Emotions conceptualized as intervening variables with suggestions toward a theory of frustration. *Psychol. Bull.,* 1951, 48, 465–495.
Brown, J. S. *The motivation of behavior.* New York: McGraw-Hill, 1961.
Cameron, N. *Personality development and psycho-pathology.* Boston: Houghton Mifflin, 1963.
Cannell, C., & MacDonald, J. The impact of health news on attitudes and behavior. *Journ. Quart.,* 1965, 33, 315–323.
Caplan, G. Mental hygiene work with expectant mothers. *Ment. Hygiene,* 1951, 35, 41–50.
Cowen, E. L. The influence of varying degrees of psychological stress on problem-solving rigidity. *J. abnorm. soc. Psychol.,* 1952, 47, 512–519.
Deutsch, H. Some psychoanalytic observations in surgery. *Psychosom. Med.,* 1942, 4, 105–115.
Diggory, J. Some consequences of proximity to a disease threat. *Sociometry,* 1956, 19, 47–53.
Dollard, J., & Miller, J. *Personality and psychotherapy.* New York: McGraw-Hill, 1950.
Duffy, Elizabeth. *Activation and behavior.* New York: Wiley, 1962.
Easterbrook, J. A. The effect of emotion on cue utilization and the organization of behavior. *Psychol. Rev.,* 1959, 66, 183–201.
Egbert, L. D., Battit, G. E., Welch, C. E., & Bartlett, M. K. Reduction of post operative pain by encouragement and instruction of patients. *New England J. Med.,* 270, 1964, 825–827.
Feather, N. T. Cigarette smoking and lung cancer: A study of cognitive dissonance. *Australian J. Psychol.,* 1962, 14, 55–64.
Feather, N. T. Cognitive dissonance, sensitivity, and evaluation. *J. abnorm. soc. Psychol.,* 1963, 66, 157–163.
Fenichel, O. *The psychoanalytic theory of neurosis.* New York: Norton, 1945.
Fraser, R., Leslie, I., & Phelps, D. Psychiatric effects of severe personal experiences during bombing. *Proc. Roy. Soc. Med.,* 1943, 36, 119–123.
French, J. R., Jr. Organized and unorganized groups under fear and frustration. *Iowa Stud. in Child Welf.,* 1944, 20, 229–308.
Freud, Anna, & Burlingham, Dorothy. *Infants without families.* New York: International Universities Press, 1944.
Freud, S. *The problem of anxiety.* (H. A. Bunker, Transl.) New York: Norton, 1936.
Fritz, C., & Marks, E. The NORC studies of human behavior in disaster. *J. soc. Issues,* 1954, 10, 26–41.
Fromm-Reichmann, Freida. Insight into psychotic mechanisms and emergency psychotherapy. *Med. Ann.,* 1943, 12, 107–112.
Funkenstein, D., King, S., & Drolette, Margaret. *Mastery of stress.* Cambridge, Mass.: Harvard Univer. Press, 1957.
Glass, A. Problem of stress in the combat zone. *Symposium on stress.* Washington: National Research Council and Walter Reed Army Medical Center, 1953, 90–102.
Glover, E. Notes on the psychological effects of war conditions on the civil population: Part III: The Blitz. *Int. J. Psychoan.,* 1942, 23, 17–37.
Goldstein, M. Relationship between coping and avoiding behavior and response to fear-arousing propaganda. *J. abnorm. soc. Psychol.,* 1959, 58, 247–252.
Grinker, R., & Spiegel, J. *Men under stress.* Philadelphia: Blakiston, 1945. (a)
Grinker, R., & Spiegel, J. *War neuroses.* Philadelphia: Blakiston, 1945. (b)
Haefner, D. Some effects of guilt-arousing and fear-arousing persuasive communications on opinion change. Unpublished Tech. Report. Aug. 15, 1956, Office of Naval Res., Contract No. N 6 ONR 241. (Mimeographed abridgement of unpublished doctoral dissertation, University of Rochester.)
Haefner, D. The use of fear arousal in dental health education. Paper read at the 92nd Annual Meeting of the American Public Health Association, Dental Health Section, October 7, 1964.
Hall, J. F. *Psychology of motivation.* Philadelphia: J. B. Lippincott, 1961.
Hamburg, D. Psychological adaptive processes in life-threatening injuries. *Symposium on stress.* Washington: National Research Council and Walter Reed Army Medical Center, 1953.
Hamburg, D., Artz, C., Reiss, E., Amspacher, W., & Chambers, R. Clinical importance of emotional problems in the care of patients with burns. *New England J. Med.,* 1953, 248, 355.

Hamburg, D., Hamburg, B., & De Groza, S. Adaptive problems and mechanisms in severely burned patients. *Psychiatry,* 1953, 16, 1–20.

Hardison, J., & Purcell, K. The effects of psychological stress as a function of need and cognitive control. *J. Pers.,* 1959, 27, 250–258.

Hastings, D., Wright, D., & Glueck, B. *Psychiatric experiences of the Eighth Air Force, first year of combat (July 4, 1942–July 4, 1943).* New York: Josiah Macy, Jr., Foundation, 1944.

Hebb, D. O. On the nature of fear. *Psychol. Rev.,* 1946, 53, 259–276.

Hebb, D. O., & Thompson, W. R. The social significance of animal studies. In G. Lindzey (Ed.), *Handbook of social psychology.* Cambridge, Mass.: Addison-Wesley, 1954.

Hochbaum, G. M. Public participation in medical screening programs: A socio-psychological study. Public Health Service Publication No. 572, Washington, D. C.: U. S. Gov't. Printing Office, 1958.

Iverson, M. A., & Reuder, M. E. Ego involvement as an experimental variable. *Psychol. Rep.,* 1956, 2, 147–181.

Jackson, K., Winkley, R., Faust, D., Germak, E., & Burtt, M. Behavior changes indicating emotional trauma in tonsillectomized children. *Pediatrics,* 1953, 12, 23–28.

Janis, I. L. Objective factors related to morale attitudes in the aerial combat situation. In S. Stouffer *et al., The American soldier, Vol. II: Combat and its aftermath.* Princeton, N. J.: Princeton Univer. Press, 1949. (a)

Janis, I. L. Problems related to the control of fear in combat. In S. Stouffer *et al., The American soldier, Vol. II: Combat and its aftermath.* Princeton: Princeton University Press, 1949. (b)

Janis, I. L. *Air war and emotional stress.* New York: McGraw-Hill, 1951.

Janis, I. L. *Psychological stress.* New York: Wiley, 1958.

Janis, I. L. Motivational factors in the resolution of decisional conflicts. In M. R. Jones (Ed.), *Nebraska symposium on motivation.* Lincoln: University of Nebraska Press, 1959.

Janis, I. L. Psychological effects of warnings. In C. W. Baker & D. W. Chapman (Eds.), *Man and society in disaster.* New York: Basic Books, 1962.

Janis, I. L. Group identification under conditions of external danger. *British J. Med. Psychol.,* 1963, 36, 227–238.

Janis, I. L. Psychodynamic aspects of stress tolerance. In S. Z. Klausner (Ed.), *The quest for self-control.* New York: The Free Press, 1965, 215–246.

Janis, I. L. Effects of fear arousal on attitude change: Recent developments in theory and experimental research. In L. Berkowitz (Ed.), *Advances in experimental social psychology.* New York: Academic Press, 1967.

Janis, I. L. *The contours of fear: Psychological studies of war, disaster, illness, and experimental stress.* New York: Mimeo., 1968.

Janis, I. L., Chapman, D. W., Gillin, J. P., & Spiegel, J. P. *The problem of panic.* Washington, D.C.: Fed. Civil Defense Admin. Bull., TB-19-2, 1955.

Janis, I. L., & Feshbach, S. Effects of fear-arousing communications. *J. abnorm. soc. Psychol.,* 1953, 48, 78–92.

Janis, I. L., & Feshbach, S. Personality differences associated with responsiveness to fear-arousing communications. *J. Pers.,* 1954, 23, 154–166.

Janis, I. L., & Leventhal, H. Psychological aspects of physical illness and hospital care. In B. Wollman (Ed.), *Handbook of clinical psychology.* New York: McGraw-Hill, 1965.

Janis, I. L., Lumsdaine, A. A., & Gladstone, A. I. Effects of preparatory communications on reactions to a subsequent news event. *Pub. Opin. Quart.,* 1951, 15, 487–518.

Janis, I. L., & Mann, L. Effectiveness of emotional role-playing in modifying smoking habits and attitudes. *J. exp. Res. Pers.,* 1965, 1, 84–90.

Janis, I. L., & Terwilliger, R. An experimental study of psychological resistances to fear-arousing communications. *J. abnorm. soc. Psychol.,* 1962, 65, 403–410.

Kardiner, A., & Spiegel, H. *War stress and neurotic illness.* New York: P. B. Hoeber, 1947.

Kessen, W., & Mandler, G. Anxiety, pain, and the inhibition of distress. *Psychol. Bull.,* 1961, 68, 396–404.

Killian, L. M. *Evacuation of Panama City before Hurricane Florence.* Washington, D.C.: National Academy of Sciences and National Research Council, Committee on Disaster Studies, 1954.

Korchin, Sheldon J., & Basowitz, Harold.

Perceptual adequacy in a life stress. *J. Psychol.,* 1954, 38, 495–402.

Lacey, J. I. Psychophysiological approaches to the evaluation of psychotherapeutic process and outcome. In E. A. Rubinstein & M. B. Parloff (Eds.), *Research in psychotherapy.* Washington, D.C.: American Psychological Association, 1959, 160–208.

Lacey, J. I., Kagan, J., Lacey, Beatrice, & Moss, H. A. The visceral level: Situational determinants and behavioral correlates of autonomic response patterns. In P. H. Knapp (Ed.), *Expression of the emotions in man.* New York: International Universities Press, 1963, 161–196.

Lambert, W. W. Stimulus-response contiguity and reinforcement theory in social psychology. In G. Lindzey (Ed.), *Handbook of social psychology, Vol. I, theory and method.* Cambridge, Mass.: Addison-Wesley, 1954.

Laskin, Eva R. Several methods of preparing individuals to resist social pressure to conform. Unpublished doctoral dissertation, Yale University, 1955.

Lazarus, R. S. *Adjustment and personality.* New York: McGraw-Hill, 1961.

Lazarus, R. S. A laboratory approach to the dynamics of psychological stress. *Amer. Psychologist,* 1964, 19, 400–411.

Lazarus, R. S. *Psychological stress and the coping process.* New York: McGraw-Hill, 1966.

Lazarus, R. S., & Alfert, Elizabeth. The short circuiting of threat by experimentally altering cognitive appraisal. *J. abnorm. soc. Psychol.,* 1964, 69, 195–205.

Lazarus, R. S., & Baker, R. W. Psychology. In E. Spiegel (Ed.), *Progress in neurology and psychiatry.* Vol. 2. New York: Grune and Stratton, 1956, 253–271.

Lazarus, R. S., & Eriksen, C. W. Psychological stress and personality correlates: Effects of failure stress upon performance. *J. exp. Psychol.,* 1952, 43, 100–105.

Lazarus, R. S., Speisman, J. C., Mordkoff, A. M., & Davison, L. A. A laboratory study of psychological stress produced by a motion picture film. *Psychol. Monogr.,* 1962, 76, 1–35.

Leventhal, H. Fear communications in the acceptance of preventive health practices. *Bull. N.Y. Academy of Medicine,* 1965, 41, 1144–1168.

Leventhal, H. Fear—*for your health. Psychol. Today,* 1967, 1, 54–58.

Leventhal, H. Experimental Studies of intervention in smoking. In E. Borgatta and R. Evans (Eds.), Smoking, health, and behavior. Chicago, Ill.: Aldine, 1969, 1968a.

Leventhal, H. Findings and theory in the study of fear communications. Mimeographed, 1968b.

Leventhal, H. Patient responses to surgical stress in regular and intensive care units. *Progr. Rep. Div. Hosp. Med. Facilities, U.S. Public Health Service,* 1963 (Mimeographed).

Leventhal, H., Jones, Susan, & Trembly, Grevilda. Sex differences in attitude and behavior change under conditions of fear and specific instructions. *J. exp. soc. Psychol.,* 1966.

Leventhal, H., & Niles, Patricia. A field experiment on fear arousal with data on the validity of questionnaire measures. *J. Pers.,* 1964, 32, 459–479.

Leventhal, H., & Niles, Patricia. Persistence of influence for varying durations of exposure to threat stimuli. *Psychol. Rep.,* 1965, 16, 223–233.

Leventhal, H., Rosenstock, I. M., Hochbaum, G. M., & Carriger, B. K. Epidemic impact on the general population in two cities. In I. M. Rosenstock, G. M. Hochbaum, H. Leventhal, *et al., The impact of Asian influenza on community life.* Public Health Service Publication No. 766, Washington, D.C., 1960, 53–77.

Leventhal, H., & Sharpe, Elizabeth. Facial expressions as indicators of stress. In C. Izard & S. Rompkins (Eds.), *Studies of emotion.* New York: Springer, 1965.

Leventhal, H., & Singer, R. P. Affect arousal and positioning of recommendations in persuasive communications. *J. pers. soc. Psychol.,* 1966, 4, 137–146.

Leventhal, H., Singer, R. P., & Jones, Susan. The effects of fear and specificity of recommendation upon attitudes and behavior. *J. pers. soc. Psychol.,* 1965, 2, 20–29.

Leventhal, H., & Watts, Jean. Sources of resistance to fear-arousing communications on smoking and lung cancer. *J. Pers.,* 1966, 34, 155–175.

Leventhal, H., Watts, Jean, & Pagano, Francia. The effects of fear and specificity of recommendations on smoking behavior. *J. pers. soc. Psychol.,* 1967, 6, 313–321.

Lindemann, E. Observations on psychiatric sequelae to surgical operations in women. *Amer. J. Psychiat.,* 1941, 98, 132–139.

Luchins, A. S., & Luchins, E. H. *Rigidity of behavior: A variational approach to the effect of Einstellung.* Eugene, Oregon: University of Oregon Books, 1959.

MacCurdy, J. *The structure of morale.* New York: Macmillan, 1943.

Malmo, R. B., Wallerstein, H., & Shagass, C. Headache proneness and mechanisms of motor conflict in psychiatric patients. *J. Pers.,* 1953, 22, 163–187.

Malmo, R. B., & Smith, A. A. Forehead tension and motor irregularities in psychoneurotic patients under stress. *J. Pers.,* 1955, 23, 391–406.

Mann, L. The effects of emotional role playing on smoking attitudes and behavior. *J. exp. soc. Psychol.,* 1967.

Mann, L., & Janis, I. L. A follow-up study on the long-term effects of emotional role playing. *J. per. soc. Psychol.,* 1968, 8, 339–342.

Menninger, K. Psychological aspects of the organism under stress. Part II: Regulatory devices of the ego under major stress. *J. Amer. psychoanal. assoc.,* 1954, 2, 280–310. (a)

Menninger, K. Regulatory devices of the ego under major stress. *Int. J. Psychoanal.,* 1954, 35, 412–420. (b)

Menninger, W. *Psychiatry in a troubled world.* New York: Macmillan, 1948.

Miller, N. Comments on theoretical models illustrated by the development of a theory of conflict. *J. Pers.,* 1951, 20, 82–100.

Moore, H. E. *Tornadoes over Texas.* Austin: University of Texas Press, 1958.

Moran, Patricia A. Experimental study of pediatric admissions. Master's report, Yale School of Nursing, 1963.

Mowrer, O. H. *Learning theory and personality dynamics.* New York: Ronald Press, 1950.

National Opinion Research Center. *Human reactions in disaster situations.* University of Chicago, 1954. (Mimeographed)

Niles, Patricia. The relationship of susceptibility and anxiety to acceptance of fear-arousing communications. Unpublished doctoral dissertation, Yale University, 1964.

Nunnally, J. D., & Bobren, H. M. Variables governing the willingness to receive communications on mental health. *J. Pers.,* 1959, 27, 38–46.

Osler, S. F. Intellectual performance as a function of two types of psychological stress. *J. exp. Psychol.,* 1954, 47, 115–121.

Powell, J. A poison liquor episode in Atlanta, Georgia. *Conference on field studies of reactions to disasters.* University of Chicago. NORC Report No. 47, 1953, 87–103.

Penny, R. K., & McCann, B. The instrumental escape conditioning of anxious and non-anxious children. *J. abnorm. soc. Psychol.,* 1962, 65, 351–354.

Pronko, N. H., & Leith, W. R. Behavior under stress: a study of its disintegration. *Psychol. Rep.,* 1956, 2, 205–222.

Prugh, D., Staub, E., Sands, H., Kirschbaum, R., & Lenihan, E. A study of the emotional reactions of children and families to hospitalization and illness. *Amer. J. Orthopsychia.,* 1953, 23, 70–106.

Rabbie, J. M. Differential preference for companionship under threat. *J. abnorm. soc. Psychol.,* 1963, 67, 643–648.

Rado, S. Pathodynamics and treatment of traumatic war neurosis (traumatophobia). *Psychosom. Med.,* 1942, 4, 362–368.

Sarason, S., Davidson, K., Lighthall, F., Waite, R., & Ruebush, B. *Anxiety in elementary school children.* New York: Wiley, 1960.

Sarnoff, I., & Zimbardo, P. G. Anxiety, fear and social affiliation. *J. abnorm. soc. Psychol.,* 1961, 62, 356–363.

Schacter, S. *The psychology of affiliation.* Stanford: Stanford Univer. Press, 1959.

Schmideberg, Melitta. Some observations on individual reactions to air raids. *Int. J. Psychoanal.,* 1942, 23, 146–176.

Schwab, R., & Pritchard, J. Situational stresses and extrapyramidal disease in different personalities. *Life stress and bodily disease.* Assoc. Research Nervous Mental Disease, 1949, 48–60.

Scott, J. Relative importance of social and hereditary factors in producing disturbances in life adjustment during periods of stress in laboratory animals. *Life stress and bodily disease.* Assoc. Research Nervous Mental Disease, 1949, 60–71.

Selye, H. *The physiology and pathology of exposure to stress.* Montreal: Acta, 1950.

Shaffer, L. Fear and courage in aerial combat. *J. consult. Psychol.*, 1947, 11, 137–143.

Shils, E., & Janowitz, M. Cohesion and disintegration in the Wehrmacht in World War II. *Publ. Opin. Quart.*, 1948, 12, 280–315.

Singer, R. P. The effects of fear-arousing communications on attitude change and behavior. Unpublished doctoral dissertation, University of Connecticut, 1965.

Skinner, B. F. *Science and human behavior.* New York: Macmillan, 1953.

Smith, M. B. Combat motivations among ground troops. In S. Stouffer *et al., The American soldier, Vol. II: Combat and its aftermath.* Princeton, N. J.: Princeton Univer. Press, 1949.

Sobel, R. Anxiety-depressive reactions after prolonged combat experience: The "old sergeant syndrome." *Bull. U. S. Army Med. Dept.*, 1949, 9, 137–146.

Spence, K. W. *Behavior theory and conditioning.* New Haven: Yale Univer. Press, 1956.

Spiegel, H. Psychiatric observations in the Tunisian campaign. *Amer. J. Orthopsychiat.*, 1944, 14, 381–385.

Stouffer, S., Suchman, E., DeVinney, L., Star, S., & Williams, R. *The American soldier, Vol. I: Adjustment during army life.* Princeton: Princeton Univer. Press, 1949. (a)

Stouffer, S., Lumsdaine, A., Williams, R., Smith, M., Janis, I., Star, S., & Cottrell, L., Jr. *The American soldier, Vol. II: Combat and its aftermath.* Princeton, N. J.: Princeton Univer. Press, 1949. (b)

Sullivan, H. S. *The interpersonal theory of psychiatry.* New York: Norton, 1953.

Taylor, Janet A. Drive theory and manifest anxiety. *Psychol. Bull.*, 1956, 53, 303–320.

Tyhurst, J. S. The role of transition states—including disasters—in mental illness. *Symposium on preventive and social psychiatry.* Washington: Walter Reed Army Institute of Research, 1957.

Vogel, W., Raymond, Susan, & Lazarus, R. Intrinsic motivation and psychological stress. *J. abnorm. soc. Psychol.*, 1959, 58, 225–233.

Wispe, L. G., & Lloyd, K. E. Some situational and psychological determinants of the desire for structured interpersonal relations. *J. abnorm. soc. Psychol.*, 1955, 51, 57–60.

Withey, S. Reaction to uncertain threat. In G. Baker & D. Chapman (Eds.), *man and society in disaster.* New York: Basic Books, 1962.

Wittkower, E. *A psychiatrist looks at tuberculosis.* London: National Association for the Prevention of Tuberculosis, 1949.

Wittkower, E. Psychological aspects of physical illness. *Canadian med. assoc. J.*, 1952, 66, 220–224.

Wolfenstein, M. *Disaster.* Glencoe, Ill.: The Free Press, 1957.

Wolff, H. *Stress and disease.* Springfield, Ill.: Charles C Thomas, 1953.

Wright, M. A study of anxiety in a general hospital setting. *Canadian J. Psychol.*, 1954, 8, 195–203.

Wrightsman, L. The effects of small-group membership on level of concern. Unpublished doctoral dissertation, University of Minnesota, 1959.

CHAPTER 22 Syndromes of Deviation

MAURICE LORR
The Catholic University of America

The aim of this chapter is to review critically the major syndromes of behavior disorders as derived by the method of factor analysis. Included will be the syndromes characterizing psychoses, neuroses, and personality disorders in both children and adults. No effort will be made to cover current theories concerning the origin or bases of the various disorders. Instead the review will be confined to a report on the dimensions of behavior deviation thus far isolated by statistical methods. However, before proceeding any further a brief sketch of the concepts regarded as central to the exposition will be offered.

In the field of psychiatric classification the concepts of *symptom, syndrome,* and *type* represent carry-overs from medicine of its conception of disease. The influence of Linnaeus and his eighteenth-century hierarchical scheme for plant classification is also evident. Consider conventional medical definitions of *symptom* and *syndrome.* The medical dictionary defines *symptom* as a sign of any change, either subjective or objective, occurring during disease and serving to point out its nature and location. The term *syndrome,* in physical medicine, refers to a group or complex of symptoms that tend with high frequency to occur together and indicate a disease. Moreover, a disease such as pneumonia is something you either have or do not have. All, or nearly all, signs and symptoms must be present before the syndrome is recognized as present.

The view taken here is that most of the functional disorders in clinical psychology and psychiatry represent deviations or excesses in attributes which, theoretically, everyone may exhibit. In abnormal psychology the concept of *syndrome* is more like the notion of a personality trait than a disease. Syndromes, like traits, are defined by a group of indicators that co-vary and represent the tendency to behave in a certain way. For example, anyone may manifest anxiety, depression, and paranoid tendencies. However, only a few manifest these tendencies to an excessive degree. The syndromes of the "behavior disorders" are thus distinctive dimensions or measurable magnitudes. Every individual can have a position on each dimension or continuum. In short, the syndrome is not an Aristotelian class concept or qualitative category but a continuous quantitative variable measurable in terms of degree. In this approach a symptom represents any deviant behavior, posture, attitude, or thought process. An associated characteristic of what may be called the dimensional approach is that all trait syndromes are conceived as present in an individual simultaneously. Every individual may be measured and described in terms of all existing syndromes, and his scores considered simultaneously represent a profile of his disorder.

The third concept requiring differentiation is that of *type*. The term is used here to refer to a class of persons satisfying a set of criteria for membership in a class. Psychiatric diagnosis is essentially a process of typing; each case is allocated to a single category. Cattell (1957), who has a similar view of types and typing, refers to a type as a "correlation cluster among people." However, others like Eysenck (1952) and Guilford (1959) use the term *type* to mean a group of correlated *traits* comparable to a second-order or third-order factor. Relatively little research has been reported on the isolation of psychotic or neurotic types as classes of persons. For a more general discussion the reader is referred elsewhere (Lorr, Klett, & McNair, 1963). Most investigators, including leaders like Eysenck and Cattell, have preferred to assume that such clinically defined classes as hysterics, psychopaths, obsessives, and dysthymics are adequately established. It would appear wiser, in the long run, not to accept clinically derived neurotic or psychotic types any more than clinically derived syndromes, without rigorous statistical evidence.

What can be said of the method for isolating syndromes of behavior deviation? The statistical method of factor analysis may be used both to isolate the functional unities in a body of data and to test for the existence of a set of hypothesized dimensions. The method is similar to what a clinician does when he interviews a cross-section of psychiatric patients, observes that certain behaviors and symptoms co-vary, and attaches a label to the complex. The major differences between the two operations are that in factor analysis, as compared to clinical practice, a specific mathematical model is employed, a larger number of characteristics are examined simultaneously, the search procedure is more rigorous and systematic, and the findings are open to a more objective check.

INTERVIEW-BASED PSYCHOTIC SYNDROMES

A recent review of factor analytic studies of psychotic syndromes (Lorr *et al.,* 1963) will serve as the principal guide in the area. The reports reviewed were all concerned primarily with behavior observations in the interview or on the ward. The first pioneer study was by Moore (1933); his data were later reanalyzed by Degan (1952). The doctoral dissertations of Dahlstrom (1949) and Guertin (1952) were also concerned with data descriptive of psychotic symptoms and behaviors. Following the development of his Psychiatric Rating Scale (PRS), Wittenborn published a series of factor analyses of ratings recorded on the PRS (Wittenborn, 1951; Wittenborn & Holzberg, 1951). Wittenborn (1962) has, in addition, reported a factor analysis of a revision of the PRS.

A series of studies were also reported by Lorr and his colleagues beginning in 1955 (Lorr, Jenkins, & O'Connor, 1955; Lorr, O'Connor, & Stafford, 1957). These studies were based on a rating schedule called the Multidimensional Scale for Rating Psychiatric Patients (MSRPP). A revision of the MSRPP, renamed the Inpatient Multidimensional Psychiatric Scale (IMPS), served as a basis for two subsequent factor analyses (Lorr, McNair, Klett, & Lasky, 1962; Lorr *et al.,* 1963).

There have been other reports, but these have either been defective technically or represent analyses of special groups. An adequate factorial experiment requires that all possible sources of trait variation in a domain be represented. A parallel requirement is the representation of all major sources of individual variation (Guilford, 1952). Thus factors isolated in samples representing only a fraction of a population will be different from those identified in broader samples and rarely generalizable to the domain as a whole. The Hamilton (1960) study of clinical syndromes in depressive states and the Grinker, Miller, Shabshin, Nunn, and Nunnally (1961) studies of depression fall into this category. Findings from such reports will be discussed here.

Lorr *et al.* (1963) list ten "confirmed" interview-based syndromes. Table 1 presents each of the syndromes and the investigators who, to varying degrees, have identified each. For convenience the labels for the syndromes are based on the IMPS analyses (Lorr *et al.,* 1963).

individual's speech and motor activities. There is also a lack of restraint in the expression of emotions and feelings. Mood level and self-esteem are usually high.

B. *Hostile Belligerence*—A tendency to complain, manifest hostility, and to express suspicion of others' intentions is evident in this syndrome.

C. *Paranoid Projection*—This syndrome is defined by beliefs that attribute a hostile and controlling intent to the world around the patient.

TABLE 1

STUDIES CONFIRMING THE TEN PSYCHOTIC INTERVIEW SYNDROMES

Syndrome	Study Authors									
	BSLHG	D(M)	G	LJO	LOS	LMKL	LKM	L(W)	W	WH
Excitement	x	x		x	x	x	x	x		x
Hostile Belligerence	x					x	x	x	x	x
Paranoid Projection			x	x	x	x	x	x		
Grandiose Expansiveness				x	x	x	x		x	x
Perceptual Distortion		x		x	x	x	x			
Anxious Intropunitiveness	x	x		x	x	x	x	x	x	x
Retardation and Apathy			x	x	x	x	x			
Disorientation		x				x	x			
Motor Disturbances		x		x	x	x	x			
Conceptual Disorganization		x	x	x	x	x	x			

Each syndrome may be regarded as a unitary pattern of response present to a greater or lesser degree in all patients. Further, it is assumed that the more severe the syndrome, the more probable that deviant behaviors will be manifested. Thus a low score implies a mild degree of disturbance. The names given the syndromes are somewhat arbitrary, but the intent is to describe the underlying reaction or response pattern.

A. *Excitement*—This syndrome is characterized by an excess and acceleration of the

D. *Grandiose Expansiveness*—This syndrome appears to represent a stage beyond paranoid projection. The individual characterized by this syndrome has found an explanation for his persecution. He is really an important personage with a divine mission and unusual powers.

E. *Perceptual Distortion*—Voices that threaten, accuse, and demand define this syndrome. Also included are visual, olfactory, and other types of hallucinations.

F. *Anxious Intropunitiveness*—Three elements appear to characterize this syndrome: anxiety, turning against the self, and lowered mood level. The individual experiences guilt and remorse and holds himself to blame for real or imagined faults.

G. *Retardation and Apathy*—This syndrome is defined by a slowing down and reduction of ideation, speech, and motor behavior. At the extreme there is apathy and disinterest.

H. *Disorientation*—This syndrome measures varying degrees of disorientation. As represented here, it probably is not due to brain injury but is indicative of autism or intense self-directed attention.

I. *Motor Disturbances*—Rigid bizarre postures, grimacing, and repetitive movements are the principal behaviors defining this syndrome.

J. *Conceptual Disorganization*—Disturbances in the stream of thought evidenced in irrelevant answers and incoherent or rambling speech characterize this syndrome. These are suggestive of a disorganization in thinking processes.

Brief descriptions of the rating scales defining the ten syndromes are given in Table 2. (See also IMPS Manual, Lorr, Klett, *et al.*, 1962.)

WARD-BASED PSYCHOTIC SYNDROMES

The syndromes defined by ward-observed behavior might be expected to be similar to many of the interview-based syndromes. However, the surrounding stimulus situations are relatively different. On the ward, as compared to the interview situation, a greater range of interpersonal behaviors may be exhibited by an individual in response to other patients, aides, and nurses. Further, it is necessary to establish empirically, rather than assume, a direct correspondence between two apparently similar behavior patterns. For these reasons the ward-observable behavior syndromes are listed separately from those derived on the basis of interview behaviors.

TABLE 2

BRIEF DESCRIPTIONS OF VARIABLES DEFINING THE PSYCHOTIC SYNDROMES

Scales Taken from IMPS	
Excitement	*Motor Disturbances*
Restraint	Rigid postures
Hurried speech	Overt tension
Elevated mood	Slovenly appearance
Attitude of superiority	Giggling
Self-dramatization	Grimacing
Loud speech	Repetitive movements
Overactivity	Talking to self
Excess of speech	Startled glances
Paranoid Projection	*Hostile Belligerence*
Delusional beliefs	Verbal hostility
Ideas of reference	Hostile attitude
Ideas of persecution	Irritability
Ideas of conspiracy	Blames others
People controlling	Bitter and resentful
Forces controlling	Complaints
Ideas of body destruction	Suspicious of people
Disorientation	*Grandiose Expansiveness*
As to place	Attitude of superiority
As to person	Extolling voices
As to season	Unusual powers
As to year	Great person delusion
As to age	Divine mission
Anxious Intropunitiveness	*Retardation and Apathy*
Blames self	Slowed speech
Anxiety (specific)	Lack of goals
Vague apprehension	Fixed fancies
Self-depreciation	Slowed movements
Depressed mood	Memory deficit
Guilt and remorse	Speech blocking
Suicidal thoughts	Apathy
Recurring thoughts	Whispered speech
Ideas of sinfulness	Failure to answer
Perceptual Distortion	*Conceptual Disorganization*
Hallucinatory voices	Irrelevant answers
Accusing voices	Incoherent answers
Commanding voices	Rambling answers
Visions	Neologisms
Other hallucinations	Stereotyped speech

TABLE 3

STUDIES CONFIRMING WARD BEHAVIOR SYNDROMES

	D(M)	GK	LJO	LOS	LO	L(W)	LKM	W
Hostile Belligerence (W)	x	x	x		x	x	x	x
Resistiveness (W)		x	x	x	x		x	
Overactivity (W)			x	x	x	x		
Paranoid Projection (W)					x		x	
Anxious Depression (W)					x		x	

There appear to be five syndromes that can be regarded as confirmed in two or more studies (see Table 3). However, a recently completed analysis (Lorr, Klett, & McNair, 1964) provides data for 11 syndromes.

The Hostile Belligerence (Ward) syndrome is characterized by use of obscene language, temper outbursts, belligerence towards others, and noisiness. The behavior pattern is one of overt aggressive behavior and lack of impulse control. Resistiveness (Ward) reflects the tendency to resist requests made, to do the opposite of what is requested, and to be obstructive. The Paranoid Projection (Ward) pattern, like its counterpart in the interview, represents a tendency to attribute hostility to the surrounding world. Characterizing this syndrome are numerous complaints and feelings of persecution. Anxious Depression (Ward) is characterized by manifest anxiety, dejection, fear, and fatigue and resembles the Anxious Intropunitive pattern found in the interview.

The previously cited study isolated six additional syndromes. Three positively correlated groupings were Seclusiveness (Ward), Retardation (Ward), and Apathy (Ward). The first syndrome is characterized by a relative absence of interpersonal relationships. The patient does not mix with others, has no friends, and rarely responds to or initiates any conversation. The Retarded patient is slow moving, whispers or speaks softly, and looks tired and worn out. The Apathetic patient shows a relative lack of interest in his surrounding environment. He ignores the activities around him, does not react to entertainment, and shows no interest in news or current events.

A second triad resembles closely three similarly labeled interview syndromes. Conceptual Disorganization (Ward) is characterized by speech that is difficult to understand, neologisms, rambling talk, and disorientation. The syndrome called Perceptual Distortion (Ward) is present when the patient talks to himself and seems to hear or see things not evident to others. Finally, Motor Disturbances (Ward) is marked, like its interview counterpart, by silly giggling, grimacing, and bizarre movements. While the similarity of these ward syndromes to those derived from interview data is great, it will still be necessary to demonstrate their equivalence experimentally in future multitrait and multimethod analyses. On the other hand, the convergence of findings in these two data-collecting milieus is encouraging.

HIGHER-LEVEL SYNDROMES

Once the major syndromes have been identified, interest shifts to the question of how the syndromes are related or organized. One conceptual scheme is a hierarchy consisting of graded categories beginning with specific symptoms that define first-order syndromes, which in turn define higher-order syndromes. Thurstone (1947) has developed the concept of higher-order factors that can be isolated from the correlations obtaining among the first-order factors. The second- or third-order composite variables provide definitions of more inclusive categories than the first-order. Eysenck (1952) has proposed a similar scheme for personality organization.

Degan (1952) factored the correlations among his nine first-order syndromes and isolated four second-order factors. These he labeled Mania, Hebephrenic Schizophrenia, Paranoid-Depressive Psychosis, and Catatonic Schizophrenia. Reanalysis of the Wittenborn and Holzberg data (Lorr, 1957) yielded three second-order factors labeled Anxious Intropunitiveness, Paranoid Belligerence, and Thinking Disorganization. Two analyses of IMPS (Lorr, McNair, *et al.,* 1962; Lorr *et al.,* 1963) each yielded three second-order factors. These syndromes were called Excitement *vs.* Retardation, Schizophrenic Disorganization, and Paranoid Process. Following a careful cross-study comparison, the last named investigators concluded that these three second-order factors could be regarded as replicated or confirmed. Table 4 presents the correlation between the first-order and the second-order syndromes identified in IMPS.

Syndrome X is a bipolar continuum defined by Excitement and Hostile Belligerence at one end and by Retardation and some Anxious Intropunitiveness at the other end. Naturally when one set of behaviors is present, the other behaviors are absent. The construct appears to correspond to the classical psychiatric notion of Mania *vs.* Depression. The second syndrome, Y, is most prominently characterized by Paranoid Projection, Perceptual Distortion (hallucinatory phenomena), and Grandiose Expansiveness. The behavior pattern implies a response tendency to attribute a controlling and malicious intent to persons around the disturbed individual. For the individual high on this continuum people persecute and try to control him, voices accuse and threaten him. These feelings and beliefs lead him to regard himself as important and superior. The third syndrome, Z, appears to represent a Schizophrenic Disorganization characterized by Disorientation, Motor Disturbances, Conceptual Disorganization, and Retardation.

TABLE 4

CORRELATIONS OF FIRST-ORDER WITH SECOND-ORDER SYNDROMES IN IMPS

	Second-Order Syndrome		
First-Order Syndrome	X	Y	Z
Excitement	.79	—.08	.06
Hostile Belligerence	.59	.10	—.26
Paranoid Projection	.15	.66	—.01
Grandiose Expansiveness	—.05	.43	—.04
Perceptual Distortion	.00	.67	.01
Anxious Intropunitiveness	—.29	.20	—.11
Retardation	—.42	—.10	.59
Disorientation	—.06	—.02	.63
Motor Disturbances	.14	—.01	.58
Conceptual Disorganization	.15	.22	.56

A third-order syndrome was also isolated in the IMPS data (Lorr *et al.,* 1963). Correlations of this syndrome TAU with X, Y, and Z were .15, .31 and .62. Thus TAU is principally defined by Schizophrenic Disorganization and Paranoid Projection. Examination of the correlations of the individual IMPS scales with TAU strongly supports the hypothesis that TAU represents Schizophrenia. Most prominent are irrelevant, incoherent, rambling, and stereotyped speech (Conceptual Disorganization). Next in importance are rigid posturing, grimacing, repetitive movements, and giggling (Motor Disturbances). Disorientation, talking to self, absence of insight, and memory deficit have lesser correlations with TAU. Voices, apathy, and speech blocking are also evident. Figure 1 diagrams the relations within the hierarchy.

SYNDROMES OF MALADJUSTMENT IN CHILDREN

Perhaps the earliest cluster analysis of children's behavior problems was reported

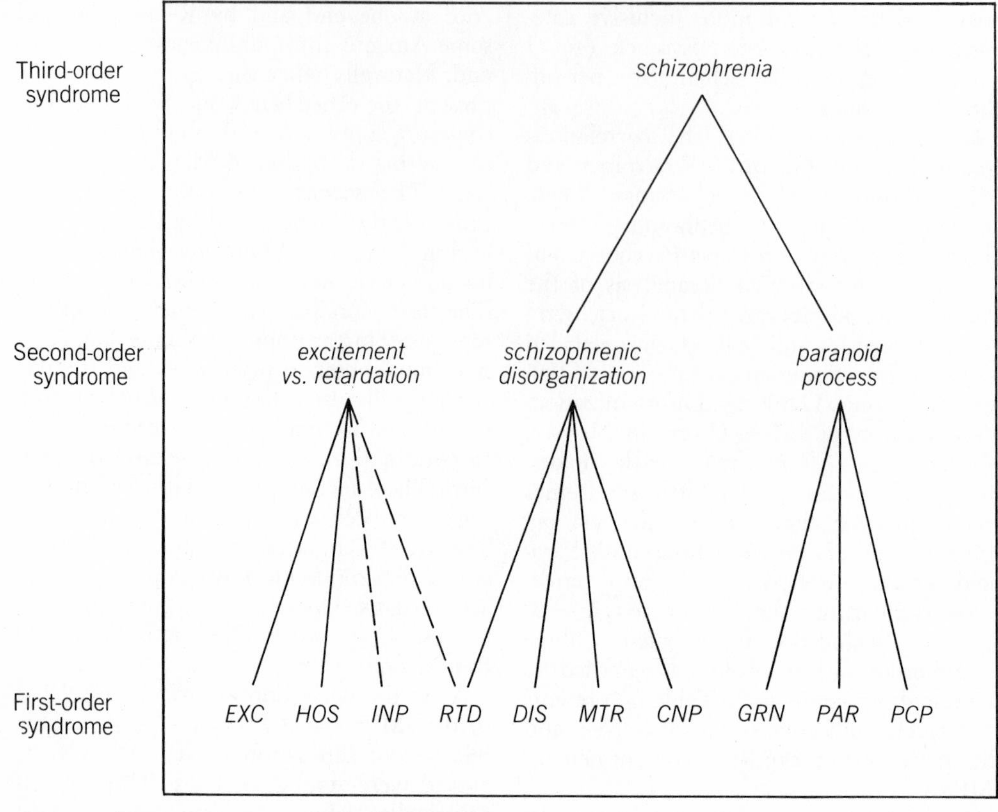

Figure 1. Relations among syndromes identified in IMPS. (A dotted line represents a negative correlation.)

by Hewett and Jenkins (1946). They described three principal syndromes among children referred to a child guidance clinic and related these syndromes to personality structure and background factors. The three syndromes isolated were Unsocialized Aggressive Behavior, Socialized Delinquent Behavior, and Overinhibited Behavior. Jenkins and Glickman (1946) confirmed the presence of these three major syndromes as well as two others in data reported by Ackerson (1942).

Lorr and Jenkins (1953) later reanalyzed the Ackerson data by factor methods, conducting parallel analyses for boys and girls. The same five correlated patterns were found to characterize both sexes with but small differences. Socialized Delinquency is characterized by truancy from home and school, police arrest, stealing, and staying out late nights. It is the pattern of the gang member who may be socialized with respect to his own group but antagonistic towards society at large. It is found in boys and girls who live in deteriorated and disorganized neighborhoods where traditions of disrespect for the law prevail. A related pattern of Unsocialized Aggressiveness is characterized by violence, fighting, temper tantrums, destructiveness, defiance, and incorrigibility. An Unsocialized Aggressive is distinguished by his lack of self-control, his hostility, and his inability to handle frustration. The lack of socialization of such a child is typically a product of parental rejection and lack of nurturance during his earliest years.

The third syndrome, called Overinhibited

Behavior, is a pattern of internal conflict. It is marked by inferiority feelings, a discouraged attitude, worry over specific fact, and staff notation of mental conflict. The pattern has been found to develop particularly in homes that offer little warmth and then only conditional upon conformity to standards difficult or impossible for the child to maintain. The fourth factor represents a schizoid syndrome. The characteristic markers are inefficiency or carelessness in work, study, or play, day "queerness"; the child is considered by others as mentally peculiar, erratic, or "crazy." The fifth syndrome is evidently a result of brain damage. There is a question of diagnosis of encephalitis, a question of change of personality, mental status, or behavior dating from a specific time or episode, and changeable, excitable moods.

The correlations among the above syndromes, when factored, yield two higher-level syndromes labeled Rebellion and Maladaptation. The first is defined by Socialized Delinquency and Unsocialized Aggressiveness. The second second-order syndrome is defined by Schizoid and to a lesser extent by Brain Injury and appears to represent a factor of maladaptation extending towards disorganization.

TABLE 5

CORRELATIONS OF FIRST-ORDER SYNDROMES WITH SECOND-ORDER SYNDROMES IN BOYS

	Second-Order Syndrome	
First-Order Syndrome	R	M
Socialized Delinquency	.46	—.05
Internal Conflict	.03	.17
Unsocialized Aggressiveness	.59	.20
Brain Injury	.24	.30
Schizoid	.00	.71

There have been several factor analyses of teacher behavior ratings of relevance here. Cattell and Coan (1957) secured ratings by eight teachers of a group of 198 children on 38 personality traits. The children who came from an urban community ranged in age from six to ten. Eleven of the factors appeared to be similar to those previously identified in older subjects. The factors of interest here were Guilt-Depression (O), Paranoid Trend (L), and Coasthenia (J). The factor O is defined by high ratings on fearful, worrying, anxious; easily upset; lacking in self-confidence and easily discouraged. The Paranoid factor (L) is characterized by suspicion of others, lack of popularity, aggressiveness, and untrustworthiness. Factor J is defined by aggressiveness, bullying; negativism, stubbornness, and disobedience; self-centered conceit.

In a similar study Digman (1963) secured teacher ratings of 102 first- and second-graders living in Hawaii on 36 personality traits. His findings (11 factors) were later rerotated by Cattell (1963). The Cattell interpretations will be used for the sake of consistency. The factor labeled *Schizothymia* is defined by negativism, stubbornness, disobedience; suspicion of others; aggressiveness, bullying; untrustworthiness; self-assertiveness. This places the factor somewhere between the earlier found factors L and J. A Guilt-Depression factor O is defined by high ratings on fearful, anxious, worrying; rigid; lacking in self-confidence, easily discouraged; poor health; easily upset; dependent. The two studies thus jointly support the presence of an anxiety factor and factors of hostility and suspicion.

An examination of the Jenkins syndromes in the context of the broader factors derived by Cattell and others in rating and questionnaire data suggests certain changes in approach. It is difficult to judge whether or not the behavior patterns found in children referred to guidance clinics are really unique to such individuals. It is more likely that they represent extremes on more general personality parameters that characterize all children. Thus studies are needed which will pool ratings of well-adjusted and problem children over the same variables.

RATER-BASED NEUROTIC SYNDROMES

Eysenck's study (1944) of 700 neurotic soldiers was one of the earliest efforts to factor symptoms and complaints of neurotics. Ratings were obtained on 39 variables, including intelligence. The first of the two factors extracted was characterized by items such as badly organized personality, abnormal before illness, little energy, narrow interests, and abnormality in parents. The second factor, bipolar in nature, opposed the hysteric (conversion symptoms, sex anomalies, lack of skill, hysterical attitudes, degraded work history, low IQ) and the dysthymic (anxiety, depression, obsessional traits, apathy, irritability, somatic anxiety, tremor and effort intolerance). Thus Eysenck appeared to confirm his hypothesis that people differ mainly with respect to (a) introversion-extraversion and (b) emotional instability or neuroticism. Slater (1945) obtained somewhat similar social history and symptom ratings on a group of 201 neurotic and nonneurotic officers on 13 traits. He also found a neurotic factor.

O'Connor (1953) in his study sought to identify the neurotic reaction types by means of a factor analysis of their present symptoms. Social history items were excluded. A group of 120 symptoms were abstracted from the case records of 300 male neurotic patients of a large mental hygiene clinic. The longer list was reduced to 34 on the basis of frequency of occurrence and apparent psychological importance. The tetrachoric correlations among the symptoms yielded eight interpretable factors or syndromes.

The first syndrome described as Obsessive-Compulsive Reaction is defined by obsessive thinking, compulsive behavior, fears, guilt feelings, self-consciousness, and phobias. A second factor appears to define an anxiety syndrome, physiological in nature. It is characterized by notations of hyperflexia, increased dermographia, hyperhidrosis, and guilt feelings. A third syndrome is labeled a Hostile Anxiety Reaction since it is characterized by feelings of hostility, bitterness, and irritability, as well as anxiety and suicidal thoughts. Inspection of the correlation table suggests that the latter two symptoms with this syndrome do not properly belong and would be removed by clarifying transformations. The factor most probably represents a hostility syndrome.

The fourth syndrome, called Acute Anxiety Reaction, is characterized by reports of breathing difficulty, apprehension, tremors, anxiety, and feeling of weakness. The fifth syndrome is readily recognized as Depressive Reaction. It is defined by depression, suicidal thoughts, phobias, crying spells, hyperhidrosis, apprehension, withdrawal, and lack of interest. The depressive pattern is surprisingly similar to that identified in psychotics, both defining an anxious type depression. The sixth factor, characterized by reports of vomiting, nausea, stomach pains, tension, and fears, is called a Gastro-Intestinal Reaction. The remaining two factors are doubtful in character. One is defined primarily by feelings of inadequacy and feelings of inferiority which are simply equivalent reports. The other syndrome is characterized by fatigue, dislike of crowds, lack of interest, and tachycardia.

In light of the O'Connor analysis Eysenck's factors are seen as likely second-order factors. However, Eysenck's factors are defined primarily by biographical variables. Thus the two studies are, strictly speaking, not comparable. Analysis of the correlations among the O'Connor first-order syndromes fails to reveal any clear-cut second-order groupings. Thus comparison at this level between the two studies is not feasible.

Another investigation of neurotic patterns (Lorr & Rubinstein, 1956) based on several preceding analyses (Lorr & Rubinstein, 1955) isolated ten factors. The sample consisted of 215 nonpsychotic outpatients newly accepted for psychotherapy. Each patient was rated on 61 scales by their therapists. A factor analysis of 50 of the scales revealed ten first-order factors, some of which represent personality traits rather than syndromes. Only the deviant behavior groupings or syndromes will be described.

Their factor B is defined by hostility, suspicion of others, resentment of authority, defensive attitude, inclination to blame others for difficulties, and resistiveness to regulation. This factor is quite similar to the O'Connor Hostility syndrome. A factor C is defined by manifest tension, anxiety, irritability, depressed mood, and sleep difficulties. The syndrome could be labeled Anxiety with depression and is most similar to but not identical with O'Connor's Depression syndrome.

The third factor (called D) is defined by feelings of inadequacy, lack of belief in self, inclination to give way and defer to others, and a need for approval. Questionnaires have yielded a similar pattern of Personal Inadequacy. A fourth factor (G) is characterized by distortions of reality in perception and thought, recurring thoughts, self-preoccupation, phobias, and ideas of reference. Compulsive acts also has a small correlation with G. The syndrome resembles the O'Connor Obsessive-Compulsive Reaction.

The remaining syndromes are narrower and usually categorized as psychophysiological disturbances. Factor H is characterized by complaints concerning stomach, intestinal, and bowel distress. The syndrome is probably the same as the O'Connor Gastro-Intestinal Grouping. A Cardiorespiratory syndrome defined by respiratory disturbances (asthma, hay fever) and cardiovascular symptoms (tachycardia, hypertension) is called factor I. The last factor (J) is characterized by guilt because of masturbation, conflict over sexual impulses, and concern over homosexual tendencies and impulses to perform irrational acts. The syndrome thus represents a Sexual Conflict.

TABLE 6

BEHAVIOR AND SYMPTOM SYNDROMES IN NEUROTICS

Syndrome	Study		
	O	LR_1	LR_2
Obsessive-Compulsive	+	+	+
Agitated Depression	+	+	+
Inadequacy	+	+	+
Hostility	+		+
Paranoid Trends		+	
Acute Anxiety	+		
Physiological Anxiety	+		
Gastro-Intestinal Symptoms	+	+	+
Cardio-Respiratory Symptoms		+	+
Sex Conflict		+	+

Table 6 summarizes the findings of three available studies of adult neurotic syndromes. As may be seen, seven of the patterns appear to be matched in at least two studies. It should be noted that the basic data are not unadulterated observations. When a patient comes to a clinic he reports his complaints and symptoms to the therapist, who in turn adds certain observations and inferences. Thus the ratings in the Lorr and Rubinstein studies and the case notations in the O'Connor analyses are a function both of patient self-reports and rater behavior observations.

A careful examination of the "syndromes" defined in the preceding section suggests certain important implications. Many of the "syndromes" are readily recognizable as extreme positions on traits that everyone exhibits. Everyone manifests from time to time anxiety, depression, and hostility to some degree. Further, the general patterns of expression are the same at mild levels in normals as they are at more extreme levels in neurotics. However, there are certain narrow groupings of behavior or complaint (patient self-report) patterns that evidently appear in their distinctive form only under limited conditions. Each individual, while capable of developing such, does not manifest or report such patterns. Illustrative of the psychotic patterns are panic states, phobias, and paranoid conditions. Similarly psychophysical patterns such as gastro-intestinal upsets and cardio-respiratory disturbances concomitant to emotional disturbances may be manifested but are not to be regarded simply as personality traits.

It is important to emphasize, as have Cattell and Scheier (1961), that clinical phenomena are best understood within a comprehensive framework of normal personality dimensions. Psychotherapists generally have always placed considerable stress on the comprehension of neurotic behavior within a framework of interpersonal behavior, defense mechanisms, and motivating conditions. Thus approached, neurotic behavior as well as other nonpsychotic "disorders" are perhaps best defined by the more general dimensions of temperament and personality.

CATTELL'S 16 PF FACTORS

Cattell and his colleagues report the confirmation of a second-order Anxiety questionnaire factor in six to eight studies (Cattell & Scheier, 1958; Cattell & Scheier, 1961). As may be seen in Table 7,

TABLE 7

AVERAGE CORRELATIONS OF 16 PF FIRST-ORDER FACTORS WITH ANXIETY (UI 24)

16 PF Subtest		Anxiety Factor	
		Adults	Children
Q_4+	More Ergic Tension	.67	.44
O+	More Guilt Proneness	.60	.50
Q_3—	Less Will Control	—.53	—.33
C—	More Emotionality	—.49	—.40
L+	More Suspicion	.45	—
H—	Less Venturesomeness	—.32	—.57

this anxiety variable is characterized by Q_4 (tense, driven); O (apprehensive, worrying, guilt-prone); Q_3— (casual, untidy, lacking control); C— (emotionally less stable, easily upset); L+ (suspicious, hard to fool); and H— (shy, restrained, timid). The claim for this factor, called UI (Universal Index) 24, is supported by positive correlations with independent ratings of global anxiety by psychiatrists and a correlation of .56 with an Anxiety-Tension self-checklist. Also of interest is a correlation of .85 with the well-known Taylor Manifest Anxiety Scale.

Becker (1961) reported an interesting confirmation of the second-order Anxiety factor in the Guilford-Martin and in the 16 PF questionnaires. Becker administered the Cattell 16 PF, Guilford's STDCR Inventory, the Guilford-Martin GAMIN Inventory, and the Guilford-Martin Personnel Inventory to a single group of 216 male and female psychology students. The cross-correlations of the 16 Cattell and the 12 Guilford-Martin scores revealed substantial agreements. In fact 4 of the Cattell scores defining UI 24 and 5 of the Guilford scores (D, C, I, N, O, and T) intercorrelated at least .74 or higher with each other after correction for attenuation. A factor analysis revealed an Anxiety vs. Emotional Stability factor defined by 5 Cattell Scores (Ergic Tension, Timidity, Lack of Will Control, Emotionality, and Suspicion) and 5 Guilford-Martin Scores (Depression, Emotional Instability, Lack of Objectivity, Nervous Tension, and Lack of Self-Confidence).

The 16 PF subtests defining the second-order Anxiety factor have been combined in the IPAT Anxiety Scale (40 items). The latter has been found to correlate highly with the Taylor Manifest Anxiety Scale in three studies (.85, .82, .75). Bendig (1959) obtained a correlation of .77 when relating the IPAT and the Eysenck Neuroticism Scale. This finding suggests that questionnaire factor UI 24 may be more than an anxiety continuum.

Indeed it may be asked, "What factors identify the clinical concept of neurosis?" Cattell and Scheier (1961) failed to find either first-order factors or second-order factors identifiable with neuroticism in the questionnaire domain. Cattell's approach to this problem has been to apply both a "trait and type definition" of neuroticism. For example, Cattell regards a factor as trait-defined in the area of neurosis, insofar as it involves responses clinicians agree have face valid content as neurotic signs or symptoms. A factor is type-defined if involved in, or contributing to, neurosis and if scores on them are significantly different for clinically judged neurotics as contrasted with normals. Furthermore, he regards the type-definition as the primary criterion. In this respect Cattell's view is similar to Eysenck's (1950) criterion-analysis approach. It should be evident, however, that this procedure assumes that clinically-derived types are valid. It also presupposes that such diverse groups labeled Anxiety Reaction, Depressive Reaction, Conversion Reaction, and Obsessive-Compulsive Reaction jointly define a homogeneous population and have in common a set of traits identifiable with neuroticism. Even if this presupposition were sound, why should such classes be exempt from the rigorous statistical analysis both advocate for symptoms and deviant behaviors? A sounder alternative approach is (a) to identify all trait-defined factors in the domain of neurosis and (b) to identify all homogeneous classes of patients (types) on the basis of score profiles on the trait-defined factors. The procedure proposed has been followed fruitfully in categorizing psychotics on the basis of their IMPS syndrome-profiles (Lorr, Klett, & McNair, 1963). For the above reasons, the Cattell-Scheier definition of neuroticism is not described here.

FACTORS IN THE MMPI

The Minnesota Multiphasic Personality Inventory (MMPI) is undoubtedly the most widely applied and researched questionnaire for the identification of the behavior disorders. There have been numerous factor analyses of the regular MMPI scales and of the 24 derived scales. Numerous studies have also been made on response sets, such as social desirability and acquiescence, in the MMPI. Discussion and review here will be confined to the higher-level factors identified and to the analyses of scale items. A major reason is that there is considerable item overlap or duplication in the various regular scales. Intercorrelations among existing factors are thereby magnified. Furthermore, as Comrey has shown, the individual scales may be highly complex factorially.

In the MMPI factor analyses there is essential agreement as to the first two factors, although the names assigned to these factors vary. The first factor, as in the Kassebaum, Couch, and Slater analysis (1959), may be labeled Ego Weakness vs. Ego Strength and is defined by Psychasthenia (Pt), Schizophrenia (Sc), Welsh's Anxiety Scale (A), and Navran's Dependency Scale (Dp). Of these scores only Welsh's A scale does not involve item overlap with other MMPI scales. The "pure" A scale, which best defined the first factor of an analysis of 16 MMPI based scales, involves the following: difficulty in concentration and in decision making; anxiety, guilt, and dysphoria; lack of energy and pessimism; and personal sensitivity. The similarity of these elements to those defining Cattell's Anxiety factor are noteworthy. A plausible hypothesis is that the first MMPI factor and Cattell's UI 24 are very much the same. The second MMPI factor is typically identified with Extroversion vs. Introversion.

A few analyses have been made which involve the MMPI scales, the 16 PF, and the Eysenck inventories. Bendig (1960) sought to relate various inventories measuring Anxiety, Neuroticism, Extraversion, and Falsification. He included the Maudsley Personality Inventory (MPI) which measures Neuroticism and Introversion-Extraversion. Also included were the following: Taylor's Manifest Anxiety Scale, Winne's Neuroticism Scale, Cattell's IPAT Anxiety Scales (Overt and Covert), the MMPI Lie Scale, and Cattell's Neurotic Inventory. The three orthogonal factors were labeled Emotionality, Falsification, and Sex. All of the neurotic and all of the anxiety scales defined the first Emotionality factor. Bendig suggests that Anxiety and Neuroticism as measured by these devices are really manifestations of a more general Emotionality factor. An alternative hypothesis is that these scales measure the same second-order factor Cattell calls Anxiety (UI 24). A related analysis has been reported by Gocka and Marks (1961). They factored the 16 PF subtest scores and a number of MMPI scale scores taken from a group of 84 hospitalized patients. Their first factor appeared to be identical with Cattell's Anxiety. It is characterized by the usual 16 PF scores as well as the Welsh Anxiety Scale and the MMPI Paranoia Scale.

Lingoes (1960) analyzed 8 Wiener and 28 rationally developed Harris subscales (1955) in four samples of subjects (patients and nonpatients, males and females). Seven factors were replicated in four analyses and four in three analyses. The more readily identifiable factors were: General Maladjustment, Denial of Social Anxiety, Loss of Control, Denial of Distrust and Hostility, Familial Discord, Inhibition, and Apathy. Subscales were formed by grouping together the items within each MMPI scale which seemed similar in content or which seemed to reflect a single trait. Judges reviewing the 69 items describing the best defining 7 subscales described the Maladjustment Factor as generalized anxiety, depression, guilt, pessimism, and worrying. The factor includes the majority of items from Comrey's Neuroticism factor. Lingoes regards it as equivalent to the Kassebaum, Couch, and Slater (1959) Ego Weakness *vs.* Ego Strength factor.

Peterson, Quay, and Cameron (1959) factored two questionnaire scales of demonstrated effectiveness in differentiating delinquents from nondelinquents. The subjects were 116 delinquents and 115 nondelinquents. Their five correlated factors were labeled Psychopathy, Neuroticism, Family Dissension, Inadequacy, and Scholastic Maladjustment. The Neuroticism factor resembled Comrey's factor of the same name.

Comrey has reported on an extended series of factor analyses of the items of each of the MMPI Scales (1957a, 1957b, 1957c, 1958a, 1958b, 1958c, 1958d). His subjects consisted of 360 cases (males and females, normals and psychiatric patients, hospitalized and nonhospitalized). The factors extracted were transformed by the Kaiser Varimax method. Table 8 presents a listing only of the factors that appeared to be replicated in the various analyses. Small factors and factors of mixed content are not listed. These analyses and the Lingoes study show clearly that the MMPI is factorially quite complex. The results also suggest a series of factorially homogeneous scales could be assembled and extended.

Two additional studies merit description. O'Connor, Lorr, and Stafford (1956) factored the Taylor MAS and obtained five correlated patterns. These patterns were described as Chronic Anxiety, Increased Physiologic Reactivity, Sleep Disturbances associated with inner strain, Sense of Inadequacy, and

TABLE 8

FACTORS REPLICATED IN COMREY'S ANALYSIS OF THE MMPI SCALE

Factor	MMPI Scale									
	D	Hy	Hs	Pt	Pa	Pd	Ma	Sc	F	K
Neuroticism	+	+		+	+	+				
Cynicism	+	+			+				+	+
Shyness		+				+	+		+	+
Euphoria						+			+	+
Family Dissension						+				+
Hostility	+									+
Poor Physical Health	+	+	+	+						
Depression	+						+			

Motor Tension. Direct comparison of these and the Comrey factors is restricted by the framework imposed. Comrey's factors are uncorrelated, while the O'Connor *et al.* factors are correlated. However, the Chronic Anxiety factor resembles the Comrey Neuroticism. The Depression Scale of the MMPI was also analyzed by O'Connor, Stefic, and Gresock (1957). They identified five correlated factors descriptive of Hypochondriasis, Cycloid Tendency, Hostility, Inferiority, and Depression. The first factor is probably the same as Comrey's Poor Physical Health. In fact all of the remaining factors appear to have counterparts in the Comrey studies.

OBJECTIVE TEST DEFINITION OF ANXIETY AND NEUROSIS

Cattell found that no single factor-dimension could be called neuroticism. In either first- or second-order structures, type-defined neurosis is complex. The clinical concept of Anxiety, on the other hand, appears to apply to a single second-order questionnaire factor (UI 24), and the same factor has an equivalent manifestation in a single first-order factor in objective test scores. The three tests that correlate substantially with first-order objective test factor UI 24 in more than a half dozen studies (Cattell & Scheier, 1961) are as follows: (a) more willingness to admit common frailties, (b) more tendency to agree, (c) more susceptibility to annoyance. Nine hypotheses concerning the essential nature of Anxiety were examined. The conclusion reached was that the above objective test factor came closest to involving behaviors classed clinically as anxious. Further, their evidence suggested that Free Anxiety is the most suitable title for this factor.

Cattell and Scheier have also identified a first-order factor in objective tests designated UI 23 which they identify with one aspect of neuroticism (Cattell & Scheier, 1958, 1961). The latest label given this factor is High Mobilization vs. Neurotic Regressive Debility. At the positive nonneurotic pole the factor expresses low motor-perceptual rigidity, good two-hand coordination, and good mobilization of personal habit resources generally. This factor, which has appeared in eight studies, is related to a similar factor identified in Eysenck's laboratory (1950, 1952). Type-defined neuroticism, on the other hand, is complex factorially for these investigators. Anxiety (UI 24) is only one of the dimensions that contribute to its characterization. In addition to Anxiety they have found that Low Cortical Alertness (UI 22—), Introversion (UI 32+), Subduedness (UI 19—), as well as Neurotic Debility (UI 23—) and others, are involved in the "Clinical Concept of Neuroticism."

It is curious that after expending a great deal of time and effort towards the isolation of the major personality dimensions, investigators reject their own findings as a basis for typing people. The present author believes it is unnecessary to accept a vague global concept, such as neuroticism, which has no single connotation. It would be more plausible to find all the major replicable types within the manifest behavior factors or the questionnaire factors. Types found among persons tagged as "neurotic" could then be compared with those found within "normals." Then it could be established whether their modal profiles are similar but vary in levels or whether some profiles are unique to those called neurotic.

SUMMARY

In this chapter an effort was made to describe the current status of knowledge about the major syndromes of behavior disorders as determined by factor analysis. Information concerning syndromes currently derives mainly from behavior ratings and questionnaires. Objective test measures have yet far to go, despite notable advances made by Eysenck, Cattell, and others. Considerable progress has been made in defining the principal syndromes in the psychoses through the use of refined rating schedules. Definition of the psychotic syndromes by means of self-report devices has been much less successful. Major obstacles are the defensive distortions of the psychotic and his use of response sets. However, the analyses of the MMPI by Comrey and Lingoes suggest that many of the behavior disorders can be assessed by questionnaires. Eysenck has made a beginning in objective test measurement of the psychoses, but an effort has yet to be made to measure the first-order syndromes. Now that criterion measures in the form of behavioral assessments are available, advances should be more rapid.

Progress in identification of the major neurotic and personality disorders has been substantial. The Cattell-Scheier second-order Anxiety factor seems well established, although its label may be in error. Findings at the first-order level, however, are not clear. Are the nonpsychotic disorders simply abnormalities in the sense of excesses or deviations in traits everyone has? The assertion implied has yet to be established. Paradoxically, success has been greatest in the questionnaire realm. Objective-tests of the neurotic disorders, as in the case of the psychoses, have been validated almost entirely at the higher-order levels. Also many have doubts and questions concerning the principal personality dimensions thus far isolated. Are these first-order dimensions actually bipolar? How many primary traits have been forced into bipolarity by virtue of arbitrary scale construction? Logical and verbal opposites are not necessarily psychological opposites. A given trait, such as dominance, need not have an opposite or may have several opposites, such as rebellion or autonomy.

Guttman (1954), Humphreys (1962), and others (Lorr & McNair, 1963; Leary, 1957) have pointed out that some models of the organization of the factors in a given domain are needful. Humphreys has indicated that the hierarchical model is not sufficiently general. For example, in approaches involving many traits and two or more methods of measurement (say ratings and questionnaires), it becomes impossible to define all of the second- and higher-order factors that are logically present. He suggests the use of Guttman's Facet theory to define tests. The simplex and the circumplex patterns (Guttman, 1954) may be more descriptive of personality than simple structure. The circumplex model has been applied successfully to psychotic syndromes (Lorr *et al.,* 1963) and interpersonal behavior (Lorr & McNair, 1963).

REFERENCES

Ackerson, L. *Children's behavior problems.* II. Relative importance and interrelations among traits. *Behavior Research Fund Monograph.* Chicago: Univer. of Chicago Press, 1942.

Becker, W. C. A comparison of the factor structure and other properties of the 16 PF and the Guilford-Martin Personality Inventories. *Educ. psychol. Measmt,* 1961, 21, 393–404.

Bendig, A. W. College norms for and concurrent validity of Cattell's IPAT Anxiety Scale. *Psychol. Newsltr,* 1959, 10, 263–267.

Bendig, A. W. Factor analyses of "anxiety" and "neuroticism" inventories. *J. consult. Psychol.,* 1960, 24, 161–168.

Cattell, R. B. The conceptual and test distinction of neuroticism and anxiety. *J. clin. Psychol.,* 1957, 13, 221–233.

Cattell, R. B. Teacher's personality description of six year olds: a check on structure. *Brit. J. educ. Psychol.,* 1963, 33, 219–235.

Cattell, R. B., & Coan, R. W. Child personality structure as revealed in teachers' ratings. *J. clin. Psychol.,* 1957, 13, 315–327.

Cattell, R. B., & Scheier, I. H. The objective test measurement of neuroticism. *Indian J. Psychol.,* 1958, 33, 217–233.

Cattell, R. B., & Scheier, I. H. *The meaning and measurement of neuroticism and anxiety.* New York: Ronald Press, 1961.

Comrey, A. L. A factor analysis of items on the MMPI hypochondriasis scale. *Educ. psychol. Measmt,* 1957, 17 (4), 568–77. (a)

Comrey, A. L. A factor analysis of items on the MMPI depression scale. *Educ. psychol. Measmt,* 1957, 17 (4), 578–85. (b)

Comrey, A. L. A factor analysis of items on the MMPI hysteria scale. *Educ. psychol. Measmt,* 1957, 17 (4), 586–92. (c)

Comrey, A. L. A factor analysis of items on the MMPI psychopathic deviate scale. *Educ. psychol. Measmt,* 1958, 18 (1), 91–98. (a)

Comrey, A. L. A factor analysis of items on the MMPI paranoia scale. *Educ. psychol. Measmt,* 1958, 18 (1), 99–108. (b)

Comrey, A. L. A factor analysis of items on the F scale of the MMPI. *Educ. psychol. Measmt,* 1958, 18 (3), 621–632. (c)

Comrey, A. L. A factor analysis of items on the K scale of the MMPI. *Educ. psychol. Measmt,* 1958, 18 (3), 633–640. (d)

Dahlstrom, W. G. An exploration of mental status syndromes by a factor analytic technique. Unpublished doctoral dissertation, Univer. of Minnesota, 1949.

Degan, J. W. Dimensions of functional psychosis. *Psychometr. Monogr.,* 1952, No. 6.

Digman, J. M. Principal dimensions of child personality as inferred from teacher's judgments. *Child develpm.,* 1963, 34, 43–60.

Eysenck, H. J. A factorial study of 700 neurotics. *J. Ment. Sci.,* 1944, 90, 851–861.

Eysenck, H. J. Criterion analyses—An application of the hypothetico-deductive method to factor analysis. *Psychol. Rev.,* 1950, 57, 38–53.

Eysenck, H. J. *The scientific study of personality.* New York: Macmillan, 1952.

Gocka, E. F., & Marks, J. B. Second-order factors in the 16 PF test and MMPI Inventory. *J. clin. Psychol.,* 1961, 17, 32–35.

Grinker, R. R., Jr., Miller, J., Sabshin, M., Nunn, R., & Nunnally, J. C. *The phenomena of depressions.* New York: Hoeber, 1961.

Guertin, W. H. A factor-analytic study of schizophrenic symptoms. *J. consult. Psychol.,* 1952, 16, 308–312.

Guilford, J. P. When not to factor analyze. *Psychol. Bull.,* 1952, 49, 26–37.

Guilford, J. P. *Personality.* New York: McGraw-Hill, 1959.

Guttman, L. A new approach to factor analysis: The radex. In P. F. Lazersfeld (Ed.), *Mathematical thinking in the social sciences.* Glencoe, Ill.: Free Press, 1954. Pp. 258–348.

Hamilton, M. A rating scale for depression. *J. Neurol. Neurosurg. & Psychiat.,* 1960, 23, 56–62.

Harris, R. E., & Lingoes, J. C. Subscales for the MMPI: An aid to profile interpretation. Langley Porter Neuropsychiatric Institute. San Francisco, California, 1955.

Hewitt, L. E., & Jenkins, R. L. *Fundamental patterns of maladjustment: The dynamics of their origin.* State of Illinois, 1946.

Humphreys, L. G. The organization of human abilities. *Amer. Psychol.,* 1962, 17, 475–483.

Jenkins, R. L., & Glickman, Sylvia. Common syndromes in child psychiatry: I. Deviant behavior traits. II. The schizoid child. *Amer. J. Orthopsychiat.,* 1946, 16, 244–261.

Kassebaum, G. G., Couch, A. S., & Slater, P. E. The factorial dimensions of the MMPI. *J. consult. Psychol.,* 1959, 23, 226–236.

Leary, T. *Interpersonal diagnosis of personality.* New York: Ronald Press, 1957.

Lingoes, J. C. MMPI factors in the Harris and the Wiener subscales. *J. consult. Psychol.,* 1960, 24, 74–83.

Lorr, M. The Wittenborn psychiatric syndromes: An oblique rotation. *J. consult. Psychol.,* 1957, 21, 439–444.

Lorr, M., & Jenkins, R. L. Patterns of maladjustment in children. *J. clin. Psychol.,* 1953, 9, 16–19.

Lorr, M., Jenkins, R. L., & O'Connor, J. P. Factors descriptive of psychopathology and behavior of hospitalized psychotics. *J. abnorm. soc. Psychol.,* 1955, 50, 78–86.

Lorr, M., Klett, C. J., & McNair, D. M. *Syndromes of psychosis.* Oxford: Pergamon Press, 1963.

Lorr, M., Klett, C. J., & McNair, D. M. Ward-observable psychotic behavior syndromes. *Educ. psychol. Measmt,* 1964, 24 (summer).

Lorr, M., Klett, C. J., McNair, D. M., & Lasky, J. J. *Inpatient multidimensional psychiatric scale, manual.* Palo Alto, Calif.: Consult. Psychol. Press, 1962.

Lorr, M., & McNair, D. M. An interpersonal behavior circle. *J. abnorm. soc. Psychol.,* 1963, 67, 68–75.

Lorr, M., McNair, D. M., Klett, C. J., & Lasky, J. J. Evidence of ten psychotic syndromes. *J. consult. Psychol.,* 1962, 26, 185–189.

Lorr, M., O'Connor, J. P., & Stafford, J. W. Confirmation of nine psychotic symptom patterns. *J. clin. Psychol.,* 1957, 13, 252–257.

Lorr, M., & Rubinstein, E. A. Factors descriptive of psychiatric outpatients. *J. abnorm. soc. Psychol.,* 1955, 51, 514–522.

Lorr, M., & Rubinstein, E. A. Personality patterns of neurotic adults in psychotherapy. *J. consult. Psychol.*, 1956, 20, 257–263.

Moore, T. V. The essential psychoses and their fundamental syndromes. *Stud. Psychol. & Psychiat.*, 1933, 3, 1–28.

O'Connor, J. P. A statistical test of psychoneurotic syndromes. *J. abnorm. soc. Psychol.*, 1953, 48, 581–584.

O'Connor, J. P., Lorr, M., & Stafford, J. W. Some patterns of manifest anxiety. *J. clin. Psychol.*, 1956, 12, 160–163.

O'Connor, J. P., Stefic, E. C., & Gresock, C. J. Some patterns of depression. *J. clin. Psychol.*, 1957, 13, 122–125.

Peterson, D. R., Quay, H. C., & Cameron, G. R. Personality and background factors in juvenile delinquency as inferred from questionnaire responses. *J. consult. Psychol.*, 1959, 23, 395–399.

Slater, P. The psychometric differentiation of neurotic from normal men. *Brit. J. Med. Psychol.*, 1945, 20, 277–279.

Thurstone, L. L. *Multiple factor analysis*. Chicago: Univer. of Chicago Press, 1947.

Wittenborn, J. R. A new procedure for evaluating mental hospital patients. *J. consult. Psychol.*, 1951, 15, 290–302.

Wittenborn, J. R. The dimensions of psychosis. *J. nerv. ment. Dis.*, 1962, 134, 117–128.

Wittenborn, J. R., & Holzberg, J. D. The generality of psychiatric syndromes. *J. consult. Psychol.*, 1951, 15, 372–380.

PART VI Changing Persons

CHAPTER 23 Counseling and Psychotherapy

RAYMOND J. CORSINI
Alcoholism Clinic
Honolulu, Hawaii

This discussion about counseling and psychotherapy is intended to be short and inclusive but must necessarily be individualistic. In an inchoate field—in which tempers and feelings run high; about which many feel that they alone have the full and final answer, but are criticized by others who feel equally sure of their omniscience; in which tradition and reputation are more important than evidence or ability; in which different names are given to similar concepts; in which people run in parallel and nonconverging lines; in which cross communication is blocked by special languages and closed groups; and about which some of the leading scientists in the field of human behavior have openly declared the whole business unscientific and unverified—no great degree of consensus can be expected.

About the only common agreement in this field is that counseling and psychotherapy are modes of learning (Shoben, 1954). The object of this process, patient or client, is expected to change amelioratively, internally (more subjective comfort, greater understanding, increased insight, greater self-acceptance, etc.), and to change externally (not so nervous appearing, complains less, sleeps better, does his work more satisfactorily, disturbs others less, has fewer complaints, and in general impresses others more favorably). All these beneficial changes are generally labeled "adjustment." To break down the changes into a finer grouping: changes are intended in *cognition,* such as insight; in *emotions,* such as self-acceptance; and in *behavior,* such as improved family relationships.

Man, in addition to the problems of adjustment to the demands of the environment, such as wind and weather; to demands of society, such as conformance; and to demands of his body, such as hunger and fatigue, is faced by problems relating to his interpretation of others and to his concept of himself (Burrow, 1950). An individual may have everything needed for physical contentment and survival: clothes, food, shelter, and the prospect of life-long physical security, but he may be miserable to the point that he will end his life. A person may be surrounded by a loving family and admiring friends and may have accomplished much more than 99 per cent of other people, yet may be in extreme distress due to feelings of inadequacy. A person may be in complete physical health, all of his organs may be in normal condition, but he may act like a paralyzed person, may appear not to see or to hear, or may operate in a grossly inadequate manner. Some physically normal people are almost completely unable to function; some function in grossly abnormal ways; some are so destructive to themselves or others that they are locked up like wild animals and even executed.

These states of "malfunctioning" which have been characterized by a variety of pejorative names such as psychoses, neuroses, or psychopathies seem to have their roots in inadequate, wrongful, and bizarre interpretations of past experiences and present conditions. They tend to be resistant to change. A person who is clearly wrong in his interpretations about life may hang on stubbornly to his beliefs. A person whose behavior evidently is harmful to himself and to others may nevertheless persist relentlessly in his patterns of behavior even against the advice of those he trusts.

Such "psychological" problems may be seen as homeostatic disturbances: imbalances between what is and what ought to be. The person who is "maladjusted" either knows that something is wrong and feels discomfort which he attempts to relieve in a variety of ways; and/or may have no understanding that he appears to be peculiar and unusual to others, who often attempt in various manners to bring him to normal functioning. In either case, whether it be the individual or the group outside, there is reference to some kind of standard or norm in judging persons' "normality" (Rennie, Srole, Opler, & Langner, 1957). The person who feels uncomfortable with himself because he feels inferior does not have this experience because he necessarily is inferior, but rather because he has some kind of expectation for himself. The person considered to be peculiar is not so regarded in terms of absolute norms, but rather relative to some peculiar and local standard of behavior.

As is true with physiological homeostasis, so too in psychological homeostasis the imbalance between what is and what ought to be becomes a motivator, and just as the body attempts to cure itself and to attain an optimal status, so too the "mind," to use a word in poor repute currently, has a tendency to normalize. The individual who is "maladjusted" tries to "straighten himself out" and those in a maladjusted person's milieu behave in such manners to "help him improve his condition." This apparently innate tendency for inner and outer adjustments has been accepted as fact by many personality theorists, who use a variety of terms in naming this force. Freud (1939) referred to *Eros,* or the Life Instinct; Adler (Ansbacher & Ansbacher, 1946) stated that the individual was motivated by the "as if" principle in which the person strives for personal superiority; Rogers (1942) and Goldstein (1939) discuss the organism's drive for *self actualization;* White (1959), summarizing a number of theorists' ideas, used the general concept of *competence*. Basic to our entire discussion is the notion that man has some kind of a need, most probably inherent in nature, to move from his present situation to a better one; to improve and develop; to grow and mature; to become more perfect. It is the function of the psychotherapist-counselor to assist nature, to help the individual employ this basic motivating force for amelioration of covert and overt behavior.

DEFINITIONS

The social sciences probably lag behind the natural sciences mostly due to the imprecision of words relative to numbers. Psychotherapy is plagued by the problem of definitions. The varieties of denotations and connotations of words cause considerable mischief and help to create the tower of Babel that psychotherapy is at this time. Two equally well-trained psychotherapists with equal experience meeting for the first time might seriously misunderstand one another even though using fairly common words due to the enormous variety of differences of shades of meaning that they may possess. We take the word *therapist* as an example. In one psychotherapeutic enclave, *therapist* refers to a "doctor"—one with a great deal of training—and the connotation of the term is quite favorable. However, in a different locale, the word *therapist* has quite a different meaning and an inferior connotation, since "doctors" who treat serious mental problems are *analysts,* while *therapists* are those who treat patients by means of music, work, etc.

Psychotherapy has been referred to as the art of persuasive communication (Frank, 1961). Since it consists of symbols, usually words, psychotherapy as art or as science is limited by the imprecision of language. A little anecdote may illustrate this point. Two therapists discussed a patient in his presence during "multiple therapy," and the word *transference* was used. The patient who took the word to mean "transferring" assumed that he was going to be changed from one therapist to another and became disturbed until, when he explained why he was upset, the special definition of this term was given.

One might assume that there is a fairly common amount of consensus about the meaning of the key words in the title of this chapter, but this too is not so. Rogers (1942) seems to use the two terms as equivalent, and one can also say that as far as he is concerned a counselor does not counsel. The more usual differentiation of these terms refers to subtle quantitative differences as shown in Table 1. In this concept counseling and psychotherapy shade into each other. Were one to listen to an interchange between two people in a helping professional relationship, experienced observers might well differ whether what was occurring should be labeled counseling or psychotherapy. However, as Brammer and Shostrom (1960) put it, a counselor tends to be educational, supportive, deals with specific situations, handles matters available to consciousness, and deals with "normals"; while the psychotherapist is more focused in his support and aims at reconstruction of the entire individual rather than with small-scale solutions. He emphasizes depth, is analytic, and tends to deal with seriously disturbed people. We have then those who equate counseling and psychotherapy and those who see them as quantitatively different processes.

TABLE 1

MAJOR PROCESSES IN COUNSELING AND PSYCHOTHERAPY WITH HYPOTHETICAL PER CENT DISTRIBUTION OVER TIME FOR TYPICAL COUNSELING AND PSYCHOTHERAPEUTIC SESSIONS

Processes	Counseling	Psychotherapy
Listening	20	40
Questioning	20	10
Evaluating	5	10
Interpreting	1	10
Supporting	5	10
Explaining	25	5
Informing	20	1
Advising	4	10
Ordering	0	4

Not merely to complicate what is already a confused situation, a third distinction is made in this paper. We are in need of a general term to refer to all kinds of professional symbolic helping functions: advising, guidance, counseling, and analysis. We suggest that all such ameliorative relationships be known as *psychotherapy,* and that within this general heading, more specific procedures be included. Thus, a ten-year analytic relationship is psychotherapy; and a one-hour guidance session is also psychotherapy. Accordingly, in this chapter psychotherapy refers to all varieties of symbolic helping relationships, but specific processes are named when necessary.

Another distinction should be made. Psychotherapy depends on the intention to help and not on the kind of results obtained. To say something is "therapeutic," meaning that it is good or valuable, etc., is incorrect. Therapy refers only to treatment and not to results. Along these lines a subtle and mischievous notion has taken root in the entire field of psychotherapy that "deep" processes are essentially better or more valuable than "superficial" processes which some may not class as therapy. Frequently, problems that can be solved simply by direct action methods are handled in a complex and unnecessarily complicated manner to make them conform to this notion of therapy.

We have referred to advising, guidance, counseling, and analysis as though they were four separable processes. Actually, in any formal ameliorative helping relationship what happens is a function of the need of the patient, the concepts of the therapist, the length of the helping relationship, the structure of the meetings, etc., and within any series of sessions and indeed within a single session the four processes may take place.

Dimensions of Therapy

It seems evident that there are different types (not merely schools) of counseling-psychotherapy with significant differences between them. But no one knows what the crucially important differentiating dimensions are.

Another problem in the semantics of psychotherapy has to do with confusing the general name of the process or of the school of thought with what actually happens in a relationship. Thus, what two therapists actually do in their work, even though they may share the same concepts, may be quite different. One man's nondirective therapy may well be another man's directive therapy.

In general, in the ensuing discussion, psychotherapy is viewed as a (a) formal, not incidental process; (b) based on a bilateral contract, usually, if both parties are of sound mind; (c) intended to help at least one of the people in the situation in terms of intellectual-emotional-behavioral changes; (d) which makes use of symbols as primary tools; and (e) which is based on some systematic internally consistent theory of personality. This definition is intended to differentiate purely educational processes (such as learning how to dance, which could have personality changes as an incidental consequence) and physiological processes (such as massage, hydrotherapy, electric shock therapy, etc., which also may have personality changes attendant on their employment). Psychotherapy, by our definition, is psychological treatment of psychological problems.

Classification of Psychotherapies

The psychotherapeutic pie may be cut in many ways. The most usual distinction is between (a) therapist-dominated or directive methods in which the patient is more or less the object of the therapist's ministrations and (b) patient-centered or nondirective therapies in which the therapist attempts to permit the patient's inner resources to develop. The writer prefers to call the first type of procedure *teaching* methods to indicate the relative dominance of the therapist in the learning experience and to call the second type *learning* methods to emphasize that the patient has the primary task of learning with little direct help.

To give some examples of other dichotomous classifications, Wolberg (1954) refers to *supportive* and *insight* therapies; Appel (1944) refers to *symptomatic-direct* and *reorganizational* therapies. Frank (1961) classifies the therapies into *directive* and *evocative*. Berne (1961) discusses the *parental* types and the *rational* types. As we see it, in the first instance in each of these four classifications, the essence of the therapy is directive-teaching; and in the latter instance it is nondirective-learning.

However, other important divisions can be made. Some therapies tend to be "deep" in the sense that deliberate attempts are made to uncover old material forgotten by the patient. Other methods tend to concentrate on here-and-now situations and so have no systematic concern for the past.

A third dimension in psychotherapy refers to the mode or avenue of approach. Some methods are essentially rational, and treatment is seen as a cognitive function. The patient is to remember, to analyze, to generalize, to understand, to gain insight, etc. The therapist sees himself as a kind of detective, uncovering clues; as a logician, giving arguments for and against conclusions; and in general operating rationally, thus leading his patient to operate in a calm, rational manner.

But another style is to depend on emotions to lead to improvement. The patient, instead of saying, "I think" or "I remember" tends to say "I feel" or "I want." The therapist attempts to generate a feeling of trust and of comfort, tries to convince the patient that he is worthwhile, gives the patient a feeling of unconditional regard, and in general operates to develop feelings of security and self-confidence by his all-accepting attitudes. Therapists who use this style tend to be quiet and do a great deal of listening.

Still another style of operating which minimizes cognition and emotions is an action approach in which the patient is to do certain things whether or not he understands them or feels like doing them. Here the therapist is a kind of trainer and demands action which may range from writing an autobiography to finger painting, playing an instrument, going on a trip, attending a meeting, etc. The basic idea is that if the person does the right and proper thing he will then gain understanding and security. Examples of the behavior approach are play therapy and therapeutic roleplaying.

It should be understood that these examples are ideal types. The pure psychoanalytic approach, as the name implies, is essentially a rational technique. The client-centered method is an example of an emotional approach. Psychodrama is a behavioral approach. In reality, in the application of these approaches there will be a complex interactive admixture of cognition, emotion, and action. Nevertheless, therapeutic approaches may be classified in terms of primary style components.

In summing the matter of classification, we thus can accept three major dimensions: teaching vs. learning approaches; historical vs. here-and-now procedures; and rational, emotional, and actional styles.

MALADJUSTMENT

The word *adjustment* has many denotations and connotations, but for the time being let it be considered as a measure of discrepancy between expectation and perceived reality. Thus, if a person is unhappy because he is not as handsome or as intelligent as he would like to be, he is maladjusted, since there is an imbalance between expectation and reality. Now, he may be considered very handsome by others but the imbalance between *his* perceptions is what amounts to *his* maladjustment. "Adjustment" then is the process of bringing together two conceptions of a person about himself regardless of the validity of either concept. It does not matter whether the final result is that the individual changes his expectation or his perception of reality. Thus, as a result of treatment, an individual may accept as fact that he is handsome (when in point of fact he may not be). Or, he may decide that it is not important to be handsome. In one case the expectation changed; in another case his perception of himself changed.

The other concept of "adjustment" refers to a convergence of observations and expectations on the part of others. Thus, a person may himself feel happy, at ease, comfortable, and so he is adjusted phenomenologically, and yet others may think that something is wrong with him. The most common example would be a psychosis, in which a person would have no realization that something is wrong with him, and he may in fact think that something is wrong with others, as occurs in classical cases of paranoia. In such cases, the individual may be at ease and adjusted as far as he is concerned, but others may disagree. This situation is a very ticklish social issue and presents grave philosophical, legal, and theoretical problems.

We can think of two scales, one called

expectation and the other *perception,* and view maladjustment as the discrepancy between the two. The question arises: How do such maladjustments arrive? As is true for almost everything in psychology, there are too many, not too few, answers. It would be too great a burden to try to explain all suggested causes of maladjustment, but we shall examine some causes suggested in terms of one specific public and private form of maladjustment: alcoholism. This series of suggestions may well give the reader some idea of the massive amount of theories available to the practitioner—and we present only a small sample.

Theories of Alcoholism

Maladjustment may be considered to have five major levels: (a) underlying causes, (b) precipitators, (c) reinforcers, (d) social expression, and (e) end results. We shall examine these five phases with respect to some theories of alcoholism.

Underlying Causes

Gibbins (1953): *the end product of poor family relationships, especially over-pampering by one parent; rejection by the other.* Zwerling (1959): *due to disruptive mother-child relationships.* Navratil (1957): *mother-child relationships characterized by deprivation or over-indulgence.* Abraham (1927): *children frustrated by mothers and forced to turn to fathers.* Adler (1941): *pampering which causes feelings of inferiority.* Schilder (1941): *insecurity due to early feelings of insecurity in family.*

Every one of these theories of alcoholism places the underlying causes in early childhood, and the mother-child relationship is stressed.

Precipitating Causes

Two people may have the same background of maternal rejection, and yet one may become maladjusted and the other may not, depending on precipitating causes. These are the causes that the individual himself tends to be aware of and the kinds the general public tends to attribute as the reason for maladjustments. Here are some theories with reference to precipitators of alcoholism.

Tiebout (1954): *feelings of social anomie with accompanying loneliness and ambivalent superiority-inferiority.* Adler (1941): *an overwhelming feeling of inferiority.* Schilder (1941): *a pervading sense of insecurity.* Lundquist (Burrow, 1927): *tension.*

As perceived in these theories the individual feels tense, insecure, lonely, unsure of himself, and turns to alcoholism as a means of surcease. However, the precipitators could be less evident to the individual, and motives can be quite hidden. Menninger (1938): *the alcoholic feels betrayed by the father and tries to get even with him by a kind of slow suicide.* Freud (1930): *alcoholism is an escape from homosexual wishes.*

Reinforcers

Whatever the symptoms of maladjustment—reluctance to participate in life, hypochondria, oversensitivity, alcoholism, criminalism, etc.—the individual somehow learns to behave in this particular maladjusted manner. One does not just fall into one of various classes of maladjustment: one selects, as it were, the kind of maladjustment one finally specializes in. How does one become an alcoholic?

Lundquist (Burrow, 1927): *alcohol gives temporary relief and the alcoholic tends to repeat the process when he is tense.* Navratil (1957): *the alcoholic who feels inferior usually marries an older, dominating and mothering woman who points out to him his inadequacies and contrasts her goodness with his badness, and he maintains his alcoholism in trying to escape her.* Meerloo (1952): *the alcoholic lives a drab existence but is able to get gratification through temporary superior behavior following alcoholic intake which reinforces drinking.* Knight

(1937): *the alcoholic considers himself manly when he is drinking; he defies society in a semi-acceptable manner*. Dollard and Miller (1950): *alcoholism depends on the relation of cue to response. When this relationship is strengthened, learning results. Alcoholism becomes a habit due to the reward properties it possesses when it leads to a temporary reduction of subjective negative feelings.* In general the theorists assume that alcoholism is in part a conditioned response to the reward properties of alcohol, i.e., its capacity to give temporary relief.

Social Expression

One may ask about any deviant behavior: why this one? It is well known that hysterical conditions, such as functional blindness and paralysis, have gone out of style. It is well known that alcoholism varies widely with cultural groups. Patterns of maladjustment are themselves culturally determined and individually learned. Zwerling (1959) points out that in the Orient, drug addiction, a passive method of submerging oneself, is the dominant means of escape, while in the west, alcoholism, a more aggressive mode of expression, is the rule. Shoben (1956) points out that in our society drinking is condoned and that the matter of maladjustment is quantitative rather than qualitative.

End Results

One may ask what is gained by maladjustment? Maladjustment is a form of adjustment, the form being disliked by the patient himself and/or others. Still it must have some logic, some purpose, some meaning. The end result of alcoholism is usually misery, as Dollard and Miller (1950) point out. Why then should the individual pursue so assiduously some end that appears to be evil in itself? The answer, as supplied by Meerloo (1952), is that at the time of the maladjustment process, there is a successful solution, i.e., escape from anxiety into ecstasy. Another reason for maladjustment patterns is that they provide a face-saving method of failing. Navratil (1957) indicates that the alcoholic can say in effect, "Don't expect too much from me, can't you see that I am drunk?" Menninger (1938) states that the end result is a kind of nirvana, a slow suicide, an escape from life.

However, learning theorists, who do not consider individuals as long-term oriented, state that the end result is but an incidental consequence, a kind of value statement by outside observers, for the affected individual operates in present time, is interested in immediate surcease of anxiety, and is trading present gratification for later misery, but he does not know and does not care for the future.

In this section we have considered one symptom of maladjustment, alcoholism, and have reviewed a variety of theories about causes, basic and precipitating, etc. As usual in this field, there are a variety of theories, none of which seem necessarily contradictory. One can formulate overall statements in many manners. For example, one might say the alcoholic has regressed to an oral dependent stage, a primary process geared to immediate gratification and loss of reality testing. Or, one might say that the individual has achieved a feeling of inferiority and operates in terms of his self concept of worthlessness. Or, one might say that the person is conditioned to respond positively to a stimulus material that gives him immediate gratification and freedom from anxiety. Whether there are essential differences between these formulations or whether they are different words for essentially similar concepts is a matter not to be settled here. The important point is that there are many good explanations for maladjustment.

Dimensions of Personality Theories

Hall and Lindzey (1957) have tabulated 18 dimensions of 17 theories of personality and find no agreement in terms of emphasis on any patterns of these factors. Using *high, medium,* and *low* to indicate degrees of emphasis, they point out that the concept of *purpose,* rated high in 13 systems, is rated medium in one system, and low in three systems. Unconscious determinants are strongly emphasized in only four systems, are considered to be of medium strength in nine systems, and have low valence in five systems. What explanation can be given for this diversity? Perhaps Pastore's (1949) theory that theoretical positions in science are affected by apparently extraneous factors, such as social class, also holds for personality theory. Such theories, especially when applied in psychotherapy, represent essentially philosophical, rather than scientific, points of views. Such theories are expressions of wishes, rather than of observations. Data supporting the validity of the theories can be explained as due to the unconscious deluding of oneself when one wants to prove a point as well as to the tremendous capacity of people to adjust to the desires of others. That is to say, as is well known, patients conform to their therapists' expectations. Thus, a patient with a Freudian analyst dreams Freudian dreams, and a patient with an Adlerian analyst dreams Adlerian dreams, the first emphasizing sex, the second emphasizing power. In this manner both therapists are separately convinced of the validity of their respective theories, since, after all, their conclusions come from clinical material.

There are some mighty strange relationships between theory and practice. To give two examples between theoretical antagonists: Slavson (1943) has developed what is essentially a nondirective method of handling disturbed youth, but he attempts to relate it to what seems to be completely inapplicable Freudian theory. Moreno (1952), who has done work with therapeutic role-playing under the name of Psychodrama, has attempted mightily and unsuccessfully to relate this to a theory of group association that goes under the name of Sociometry. In some cases, a theoretical position takes one minor point in somebody else's theory and makes this the central point of the new theory. Rank's (1952) separation anxiety is a case in point. While it can not be denied that this is a major problem for most people, it is difficult to conceive of an entire school of psychotherapy concentrating on this issue.

Most personality theories as applied to psychotherapy are really hidden philosophical systems, substitutes for the ethical commandments of conventional religions. The method of operating within psychotherapy becomes in essence a mode of operating in life. This is perhaps most clearly seen in the most restrictive of psychotherapeutic methods: Rogers' nondirective therapy, which in essence gives the patient maximum freedom and the therapist maximum restrictions. This procedure is essentially intended to create an Appolonian type of individual: kind, reserved, considerate. In contrast, Moreno's Psychodrama is intended to create a Dionysian type of person: aggressive, spontaneous, and uninhibited. The procedures involved in the classical psychoanalysis also become a kind of philosophical system: cautious, critical, analytic, suspicious individuals are created by psychoanalysis. It is as though the various authors of these systems were saying: *this is the way to be; act in this manner; become like me.* And indeed this is possibly what psychotherapy is really all about: the patient imitates the therapist; the therapist instructs the patient. The topic to be learned is life: philosophy, values, ways of thinking and feeling. The therapist is the model, the patient is to conform to this model.

Value of Personality Theories

Do personality theories help or hinder the development of psychotherapy as a profession, a method of helping humanity? Now, some people may throw the question out of consideration on at least two grounds. First, it is not important whether or not people are helped. The important thing is to establish a theory. Second, all proper practice is based on theory, and unless theories are permitted to flourish and develop, no proper practice can be had. But, if one asks this apparently innocent question, "Is psychotherapy an art or a science?" the prior question makes sense. Is psychotherapy, say, as some will contend, a part of science? If so, then personality theory has an important part in the practice of psychotherapy, and eventually we can expect that the various theories will be tested experimentally and clinically until finally we have the theories of personality amalgamating into the "laws" of personality. But suppose that personality and psychotherapy do not conform to science and are really more in the transcendent realm of art or philosophy. Then all attempts to capture the final and basic essence of behavior are bound to come to naught.

Personality theorists, especially those who come out of animal-experimental laboratories, have no doubts at all that in the last analysis man is a bundle of reflexes, some determined in utero, some affected by conditioning (Eysenck, 1960; Freud, 1928; Hebb, 1949; Wolpe, 1958). But this point of view has been challenged (Adler, 1927; Binswanger, 1956; Boss, 1963; Burrow, 1950), and as yet no one knows whether personality theory, like religion, is essentially a matter of philosophical choice, rather than scientific fact. But in any case, psychotherapy is currently an art, not a science. There is no evidence that current therapists are better than earlier ones. While today an average surgeon probably has far superior results to the best surgeon of a century ago, there is no evidence that current psychotherapists are any better than the earlier ones. Surgeons operate within the area of communicable science; psychotherapists do not. Just as Cotton Mather may have been a greater preacher than Billy Graham, and Michelangelo a greater artist than Dali, so too Sigmund Freud may have been a better psychotherapist than E. Lakins Phillips. Enrico Fermi learned from Einstein who in turn learned from Planck who in turn learned from Newton, etc. ..., but a person such as Ron Hubbard (1950) dares to start a whole system of psychotherapy and personality theory *ab initio*. Whether a system has elements of absurdum in it or not is not of the issue. A person starting a theory of physics without recourse to the past would be labeled a crank automatically. A person such as Moreno, who apparently did not borrow much from anyone in his system of personality, would not automatically be labeled a crackpot, even if his system were to be absurd. The standards of science as known in the *Naturwissenschaften* just do not apply to psychotherapy.

To revert to an earlier theme, a good part of the problem of personality theory as applied to psychotherapy is semantic. Is the concept of "superego" really meaningful? Is "transference" a real phenomenon? Why is "inferiority complex" a central issue to Adlerians but of little importance to Jungians? It would seem that psychotherapy as a part of personality theory requires some tightening of language, some condensation of terms, and some eliminations of competing words. We then may be able to see the elephant and not just parts of it.

An analogy can be made to four observers seeing the same mountain at the same time but from four vantage points: the man from the east, with his back to the sun, viewing the western slopes sees something quite different from the viewers at the west, the south and the north, and yet it is the same mountain seen on the same day by four apparently capable observers. And yet, others, even though they do get different impressions, do not necessarily get contradictory impressions. It seems that eventually personality theories will amalgamate, despite the almost hysterical attitude that some therapists have about "eclecticism" (Dreikurs, 1960).

THERAPEUTIC APPROACHES

We can distinguish two main dimensions with respect to therapeutic approaches. One dimension refers to the degree of direction the therapist assumes. The other dimension refers to the principal means of interaction with the patient: the therapeutic mechanisms employed, whether primarily intellectual, emotional, or behavioral. We could then, on a very rough basis, make a six-way classification: directive–intellectual therapists (Adlerians), directive–emotional (hypnotists), directive–behavioral (psychodrama), nondirective–intellectual (psychoanalysis), nondirective–emotional (Rogerians), and nondirective–behavioral (play-therapists). In the parentheses we indicate some typical therapeutic systems mainly using these approaches. It must be kept in mind that no therapist can be strictly contained at all times in any group, that most therapists vary from patient to patient in their approaches, and may vary from session to session, and even within sessions there may be variations.

What approach is employed depends on many factors, the most important of which, perhaps, is the therapist's style, his own manifest personality. One may ask why Freud developed his particular method of psychotherapy which involved doing a lot of listening, not looking at the patient, and trying to puzzle out the individual's complex mental gymnastics—much in the way of a puzzle-solver. Why did Rogers develop his particular system of psychotherapy: also listening a great deal to the patient, not caring to disagree with him, being kind and considerate? And, why did Moreno, with his tempestuous Psychodrama, develop a technique so different from these other two? The answer may be that these therapists' manifest personality dominated their procedures, that how they conduct psychotherapy is the way they have to because of their own nature (Corsini, 1956). Freud was a typical pedantic scientist (E. Jones, 1953); Rogers has been called a secular saint (Riesman, 1959); and Moreno is dynamic, gregarious, and highly socially developed. Thus, these three individuals each developed a system of psychotherapy consonant with their own manifest personality. So it may be that what therapy patients get is more a function of the kind of person that the therapist is, rather than a function of the theory he accepts.

This whole area of approach and the relationship between a therapist's personality and his mode of operating has not yet been fully explored; nor has there as yet been any amount of significant investigation of the preferred method of approach for patient-types. At the present time these are areas for speculation.

Dynamics of Therapy

Suppose the reader could put aside his doubts about the possible efficacy of psychotherapy by assuming that a formal one-to-one relationship between two people can have *some* effects on either of the two individuals, especially if the relationship is periodic, regular, and intensive. Let us also assume that the effects on the person called the "patient" were in the direction desired, namely, superior social functioning and better self-concept. What could be the reasons for these changes? What would be the dynamics of therapy?

Surprisingly, very little attention has been paid to this problem. In the general literature one finds a great many names of dynamic factors, such as abreaction, acting out, cognitive modifications, condensation, consensual validation, dramatization, empathy, perceptual restructuration, reconditioning, relationships, relaxation, suggestion, transference, and working-through, which are alleged to be mechanisms of psychotherapy. This list can be lengthened considerably and could conceivably contain several hundred words whose various connotations would cause confusion. Is it possible to find *the* basic dynamics of psychotherapy?

When a large number of articles on the mechanisms of group psychotherapy were summarized, three major dynamic areas of change emerged: those that depended on *cognitive* changes; those that were essentially *emotional-feeling* in nature; those that were *behavioral* (Corsini, 1957). Below we shall examine these dynamics in relation to individual therapy.

Intellectual Factors

Psychotherapy, as has already been pointed out, is a learning experience. The patient learns about himself and about others. Often he finds out what he really knew, but never believed. By interaction with the therapist who represents reality, and whose judgment he may accept over his own, he may discover some things about himself and others which he did not know before. He may gain insight and thus understand himself with respect to his relationships with others. Karpman's "objective psychotherapy" (1948) would be a good example of a system that focused on intellectual aspects. Patients are given assignments to write essays about certain broad problems and to write on specific issues. The therapist reads the material and formulates new questions, to which the patient is again to respond. If the therapist feels there was a disparity between the patient's views and reality, he might assign readings to the patient, and the patient might be asked to write further essays.

One may note in this system the absence of emotional relationships between the therapist and the patient. Psychotherapy is viewed as essentially a matter of proper thinking. Ellis's Rational-Emotive Psychotherapy (1962) is another example of a system of psychotherapy which concentrates primarily on proper thinking. The Adlerian system of psychotherapy also concentrates on patients' private logic and attempts to get them to direct their thinking along approved channels (Ansbacher & Ansbacher, 1946). The will-therapy method of Low (1952) is a further example, which concentrates on patients' use of language. Most forms of psychotherapy that go under the heading of guidance or counseling are primarily intellectual-cognitive in nature.

Emotional Factors

Some systems of psychotherapy emphasize emotional factors. Therapy is not envisaged as an exchange of information, the gaining of insights, or as primarily a cognitive function. Rather, therapy is seen as a matter of feeling expression and of emotional adjustment. Reassurance and suggestion are two of the most common techniques in this approach. Paul DuBois (Fiedler, 1950; Walker, 1957) was probably the first of the modern psychotherapists who emphasized persuasion, making use of his prestige as much as logic. Dejerine and Gaukler (Fiedler, 1950) stressed the importance of the emotions and initiated the use of repressive-inspirational techniques. Levy (1938) with his relationship therapy is an example of a system that concentrates on emotional factors. However, it is Rogers (1942, 1951) who seems to have made the greatest contribution to psychotherapy in terms of the importance of emotional factors. The therapist does all in his power to generate a feeling of unconditional positive regard for the patient, who in turn becomes encouraged by the relationship to express himself and to accept himself and others.

Within this general area, the dynamics of transference, ventilation, catharsis, abreaction and desensitization are found. The patient is seen as a feeling creature, forming relationships with the therapist, expressing himself fully, learning how to control his feelings, etc.

Behavioral Therapy

A third general set of dynamics may be formulated somewhat as follows: the patient is to be guided or persuaded or forced even to operate in certain ways which will eventually change the individual's thinking and his feelings. We operate from the outside in, rather than from the outside out. A fairly simple example would be music therapy as employed with psychotics or defectives. The environment is manipulated for these individuals; they are asked to operate in certain ways, such as striking sticks in unison, and as a result, changes occur within the individuals. While such music therapy cannot be considered a deep form of psychotherapy, nevertheless the essence of the direction of movement is expressed by the fact that manipulating the environment, by having music, or having the patient operate in certain ways without any great amount of explanation will have internal consequences.

The major approach along these lines is the use of conditioning techniques. Salter's conditioned reflex therapy (1949) is a highly directive procedure in which the patient is to give up practices that are considered unhealthy and to begin to operate in manners considered valuable. The reciprocal inhibition method of Wolpe (1958) depends on the patient unlearning unsuitable habit patterns. Eysenck's (1960) system is based similarly on reconditioning features.

Perhaps the clearest example of a method of psychotherapy that works from the outside in is Moreno's Psychodrama (1952) in which individuals explain their problems and then are asked to act them out to show how they deal with their problems. Later, the patient may be asked to operate, also on the level of action fantasy, in a socially adequate manner, perhaps after discussion, perhaps after observing others handle the same problem in a different manner. By operating in a better way in a therapeutic milieu, patients are often able to understand and to feel differently, coming more or less on their own to these changes in terms of their outside operations, even under the abnormal conditions of the psychodrama stage. This role assumption and its effects on behavioral changes are not as yet too well understood.

Sturm (1965) has made a pioneer effort to relate behavior therapy to learning theory. He suggests that these six learning principles operate in successful behavior therapy: (a) reciprocal inhibition, (b) systematic desensitization, (c) operant conditioning, (d) discrimination training, (e) shaping, and (f) emotive imagery. Principles (d) and (e) are essentially aspects of operant training, and all of them represent general learning principles.

THERAPEUTIC PROCESSES

Were one to observe a large number of therapists in the process of psychotherapy, and were one to classify their behaviors, undoubtedly the list found in Table 1 would cover more than 90 per cent of the observed behavior. The art of psychotherapy consists of the *what*—the functions used—and the *how*—the manner in which they are applied. Below we shall examine these various processes. The reader should realize that during the heat of treatment the therapist may shift rapidly, may use two or more of these functions simultaneously, and that some of these processes are rather difficult to separate out.

Listening

Perhaps a better term than listening is "attending" since the good therapist listens *and* looks. He sometimes gets visual clues from the patient. For example, the patient may state he feels fine, is comfortable, and yet he will shift about, rub his hands, his skin may glisten with perspiration, etc., and so give visual signs of distress. But ordinarily, most of the information that the therapist obtains is through his ears, and he listens not only for content, but also, and importantly so, for tone, since distress is rather easily conveyed by tonal variations.

Attending is a difficult task, demanding and fatiguing. The conscientious therapist attends carefully to all stimuli that his patient presents, and he tries to figure out not only what the person is saying, but what he is trying to say and what he is trying not to say. He listens dynamically, predicting what the patient will say, putting all items in a jigsaw puzzle mosaic until they begin to make some kind of sense. The experienced therapist is wary of making mistakes, or of coming to unwarranted assumptions, and he knows that the more he listens and the more that he is able to piece the elements together, the more likely he is to have the entire mosaic correct. One reason for listening is to get information about the patient, so that when the therapist begins to talk he will have enough data to enable him to make meaningful statements. The therapist knows that patients delude themselves, that they frequently try to confuse the therapist, and he waits carefully for "clues" that will give him insight into the patient. Slips of the tongue are a good example. A patient states, "My father drank to success—I mean excess," and the therapist believed him the first time. What Theodor Reik called "listening with the third ear" (1956) is something that all therapists learn to do.

But the therapist has other reasons for listening. One is that most patients like to talk, and they feel good if the therapist listens to them. They have a feeling of importance during the listening. So a good listener helps to dissolve resistance, the common enemy of all therapists. But an even more important reason for the therapist's being passive is that the patient cures himself, as it were, during the process of talking with an attentive listener. He may make a strong statement, repeat it, emphasize it, and look challengingly at the therapist, and then he may suddenly reverse himself and state he does not really believe what he said, and then begin to explore his new feelings and ideas. To a very great extent psychotherapy is autochthonous—the patient cures himself. Perhaps the most important part of classical analysis is the free association, simply the free expression of ideas and feelings. It is Carl Rogers, however, who has raised listening to an art, emphasizing the great importance of attending carefully and sympathetically, thus helping the patient to attain growth.

Questioning

Perhaps the second most common function of the therapist is questioning, which may be considered as a verbal stimulus intended to elicit another stimulus to which the therapist will attend. In a sense, questioning is an attempt by the therapist to obtain from his patient information which he requires to complete his picture. However, questions can have other purposes: they may serve as challenges, as criticisms, etc. A question is an aggressive statement: demanding an answer. Some therapists use questions to a great degree, hoping to shape the patient by means of Socratic type dialogue. Ellis (1962) is a prime exponent of this method. Such therapists use questions for confrontation, and the mode might go somewhat as follows: "Well, you agree that you are in condition X, and you have come to me for help, and I state that Y action is indicated, and you agree with that. Now, it seems to me that you should put Y action into effect. So we both agree on its necessity? Will you now do it?" In such instances the therapist acts as a goad, leading the patient on, and then finally putting the question to him.

Questioning can be a highly directive and demanding process. While one can ask very general questions: "How are things going?" "And what did you do?" etc., frequently a therapist who depends on questions starts the first of a long series in an attempt to direct the patient to a conclusion he has already formulated. Most eclectic therapists ask questions. Only the nondirective therapists tend to avoid them on the basis of principle.

Evaluating

Judging or evaluating occurs continuously throughout therapy. While listening and questioning or interpreting, the therapist is attempting to understand and to evaluate the patient, his situation, and his problem. The therapist will frequently stop to discuss the situation with his patient to attempt to come to some understanding with him about the gravity of the problem, what ought to be done, and in general take the patient on for a time as a kind of colleague with whom he can discuss the situation from a distance. The therapist may at such times disagree with his patient, express his private concerns, and may even tell the patient he does not believe him or agree with his conclusions.

This common evaluation process also becomes part of the general evaluation period. It must be kept in mind that the therapist is always evaluating or analyzing his patient: it is his task to get to understand the patient, and whatever he may do, even if it be some simple social act, can become grist for his mill of understanding.

It is during the evaluation period that therapists who employ evaluations are themselves tested, as it were, as well as their theories, because all the data obtained must somehow be summarized either in some clinical statement in the nature of a diagnosis or in terms of some final action statement. Whether or not the evaluation is correct is difficult to tell: the concurrence of the patient may not be too important. However, most successful therapists convince their patients that the interpretation they have come to and their summary and their course of action are good and worth heeding.

Interpreting

An interpretation has a slightly more restricted meaning than an evaluation. It usually refers to a limited explanation. The patient, for example, may present a dream, which to him is meaningless. The therapist may now attempt to make sense out of it, drawing on his theoretical resources. Or, the therapist may evaluate a particular action, trying to determine what the patient's motives may be. An interpretation represents the therapist's conclusion about the meaning of specific actions.

Therapists vary in their willingness to come to interpretations. Some will interpret at the drop of a hat. Others are much more conservative and want as much information as possible before coming to any conclusion. Some attempt to lead their patients to their own interpretations. Directive therapists tend to see themselves as detectives, who are to puzzle out the patient and his private logic; other therapists see the patient as the one who should do the puzzling, and it is the function of the therapist to lead the patient to his proper conclusions.

Supporting

Therapists tend to think of working with patients either on a deep or on a supportive level. The latter refers to a kind of handholding of the patient; reassuring him, listening to him, and giving encouragement. Some patients seem to wander in, ask for a bit of advice or guidance or comfort, and then go off again. Others, after having been in therapy for a while, come back, as it were, for a bit of kindness and then go on with their life again. While most psychotherapists take a helpful supportive stance toward all patients, some patients seem to call for only a bit of gentle reassurance. Supportive therapy is nothing more than a more complex form of saying: "You are all right; don't worry; you are a nice person; I like you; take it easy; everything will be all right."

Explaining

This word may seem to be similar to interpreting, but there is an important difference. Explaining refers to telling a person what he already knows but does not believe. It is a kind of refined nagging. Many patients know things but don't believe them. They seem to require strong emphasizing of simple and basic things. A therapist finds himself often in a situation of a parent who has to tell a grown person things that the person knows well enough. The therapist is put in a position of representing society, serving as a mirror, reporting to the patient what the patient knows. The therapist has to teach the patient how others react to his behavior, what is correct and incorrect, how to see social reality, etc. The therapist serves as a kind of measure of reality, informing the patient what is true and what is not true. To give an example: a patient informed the therapist casually that one of the reasons he had an inferiority feeling was because he was undersized. The therapist asked him how tall he was, and was told five feet ten inches. The therapist asked him how tall was the average American man, and was told about six feet. The therapist told him that statistics indicated the average man was about five-eight. The patient stated he knew this, but everybody he met was well over six feet. The therapist asked how tall the therapist was, and the patient said about "six feet." The therapist told the patient that he was five-eight. The patient refused to believe it. Only when both people were measured did the patient finally accept the fact that he was taller than the therapist. This incident was a crisis point in this interaction. Now, this seems like a kind of silly conflict, but frequently in therapy one minor, or apparently minor, confrontation may so affect the patient that he begins to get on the road to change.

Informing

Closely allied to explaining, but yet somewhat different, is giving the patient basic information. Most often the information has to do with how people think and feel. In educational and vocational guidance the information often is about basic facts. It frequently happens that people come to have strong opinions about matters, or have come to various decisions, which just are not in line with reality, or else that they have gaps in their knowledge and information. The therapist or counselor can serve as a resource person and give the patient-counselee data about the world which apparently he has not been able to obtain anywhere else.

Advising

We now come to a different order of relationships. The therapist or counselor not only may give interpretations and information but may take a more active role in suggesting that the patient do something or accept something as fact. The therapist who attempts to be persuasive, or who tries to influence the patient in his thinking or acting, may be said to be advising. In general, the more superficial the relationship, the greater the chance that the therapist will use advice as a tool. In an analytic type of relationship, the therapist is quite likely to avoid using advice or directly influencing the patient.

Ordering

The last of the procedures discussed here has to do with the therapist's demanding some behavior changes on the part of the patient. Some therapists will give their patients specific acts to perform and will rehearse them, or will nag them until they change their behavior. The idea is simply that some patients will not try to do what they can do unless they have some pressure applied to them. When they trust the therapist, and put themselves into his hands, they may begin to act in ways that they should, but only if he insists.

A variety of kinds of "assignments" can be given patients, ranging from as simple a procedure as writing an autobiography to going out on a date or canceling an ordered meal in a restaurant. Russian psychiatrists are much more inclined to use such procedures than therapists in the western societies. There are all kinds of risks in making demands on a patient, the most common of which is that the patient simply refuses, and the therapist-patient relationship may be broken. A clever therapist avoids such impasses and will ask a patient to do only that which he is fairly certain the patient will do with a bit of pressure.

THE THERAPIES

No one knows what is the most appropriate training for psychotherapists. Schofield (1964) estimates that one-third of a psychiatrist's graduate training, two-thirds of a psychologist's, and four-fifths of a social worker's are clearly related to psychotherapy. There has been considerable professional controversy about the various roles of individuals in psychotherapy with various professional groups claiming special competence. It should be emphasized that in most cases those who do psychotherapy tend to learn their skills after their formal graduate work, in private institutions, training centers, or on their own.

Just as we do not know the most appropriate training for psychotherapists, we do not know who should be trained in this field.

Fiedler reports the following: Good therapists are distinguished more by their years of experience rather than by their orientation or kind of training (Fiedler, 1950). When samples of therapeutic interaction of various orthodox Freudian, Rogerian, and Adlerian therapists were evaluated, differences between the schools were insignificant, but the experienced therapists in each of these systems were considered better than the inexperienced ones. Another research showed that the longer a therapist had been in his profession the more likely he was to go off on his own, as it were, to assume independence and no longer operate strictly within the limits in which he was trained. Specifically, nondirective therapists tended to show fewer tendencies to reflect and greater tendency to use other techniques as they developed (Jellinek *et al.*, 1955).

One comes to the general conclusion that if one wants to go to a therapist, it is more important that one selects an experienced individual with whom one is compatible rather than a person with a particular kind of training or a member of a particular school. One should ask, "who is the therapist?" rather than "what is his training?" or "what is his orientation?" In India, those seeking for truth and contentment attempt to find a *guru;* so too, those who want psychotherapy perhaps seek for a person whom they want to identify with and imitate. One sees clear evidence for identification in training programs. Neophytes imitate their teachers, sometimes not only their mannerisms but also their clothing styles. It may be that psychotherapy is more a process of introjection of the therapist's personality and values, rather than a process of development of one's basic inner patterns.

Other Therapies

In general the three professions of psychology, medicine, and social work provide the bulk of people who practice psychotherapy on a full-time basis. However, probably a large proportion of what can be called psychotherapy is provided by other individuals, mainly ministers and counselors. The great need for people to provide clinical services of the types described is such that people in these other professions are beginning to do more intensive psychotherapy and are developing programs of training and of self-evaluation.

Forms of Psychotherapy

There are four main forms of psychotherapy: self-, individual, group, and milieu. We shall discuss each of these with its informal analogue.

Self-Therapy

Used by Sigmund Freud, described by Karen Horney (1942), and highly recommended by Theodor Reik (1956), formal self-therapy can be considered a very difficult system that involves making an appointment with oneself, maintaining a schedule and an agenda, and systematically exploring one's self.

Informally people are continuously examining themselves, thinking about themselves, making plans, daydreaming, and in other ways analyzing themselves. When one is in some kind of trouble, one is highly likely to begin self-analysis. There seems to be little doubt that these meditative processes are very common and perhaps can be called the most common form of psychotherapy.

Individual Therapy

When the word *psychotherapy* is mentioned, most people think of individual psychotherapy, a dyadic relationship between one patient and one therapist. This is probably the most common form of formal psychotherapy. It gets its form mostly from the traditional one-to-one doctor-patient relationship. The major device in this form of treatment is a directed conversation between the patient and the therapist. Most counseling and guidance as well as case work is of this type.

Marriage, a partnership or a friendship is the social analogue of individual therapy in which a close, enduring and generally exclusive relationship is maintained for a common goal.

Group Psychotherapy

In the early years of this century, a number of individuals more or less independently began to work with groups of patients. Among the early innovators were Dr. J. H. Pratt (M. Jones, 1942), Trigant Burrow (1927), Paul Schilder (M. Jones, 1942), and J. L. Moreno (1952). A considerable number of different approaches have been employed, some showing great ingenuity (Corsini, 1957). While some people seem to regard group psychotherapy as a diluted form of individual therapy, there is no clear experimental evidence to support the contention that one form is superior to any other form or that individual psychotherapy is more suitable than group therapy. For some conditions of a social nature, such as delinquency, group methods seem to be preferred.

The analogue to group psychotherapy is the family, the social club, the "get together" in which relatively small groups meet on an intimate basis.

Milieu Therapy

A further extension of the concepts of group psychotherapy to a large living-in group on a 24-hour-a-day basis is known as milieu therapy, in which a whole environment is adapted to adjusting individuals. While milieu therapy has been tried in a number of mental hospitals, chiefly in Great Britain (M. Jones, 1942), little is actually known about its value, even though on a theoretic and humanistic basis there seems to be good reason for its employment.

Any corrective or educational institution such as a mental hospital, a prison or a college serves as an analogue to milieu therapy.

SOME SYSTEMS ANALYZED

Harper (1959) has described some 39 systems of psychotherapy. They represent possibly a small proportion of the identifiable schools of thought in this field, some of which have not been exposed to the public via the medium of print. It may be worth considering the basic propositions of some systems.

Will-Training

A relatively unimportant system of psychotherapy as far as general textbooks are concerned is one developed by Dr. A. A. Low (1952) which is currently being employed by some 50 or more ex-mental-hospital-patient groups in an organization known as *Recovery Incorporated*. Dr. Low developed this school of thought as a result of his dissatisfaction with other psychotherapeutic schools which he felt were too complicated and too difficult to understand. He wanted a system that worked, that was cheap, and that was simple. The system he developed was directed to a rather specific type of patient: psychotics in remission, who were to meet in members' homes and in other places for a kind of mutual treatment, using Dr. Low's book and various phonograph records he had made.

Low's theory and method deserve some attention. He felt that all behavior was dependent upon thinking: thus a person who thought incorrectly would behave incorrectly; therefore, if a person misbehaved, one could be sure his thinking was awry. This proposition is not too new, but he emphasized the prodromic importance of language in signaling errors in thinking, and he suggested that if one could treat a person's verbal utterances that occurred between the thought and the act, one could in this manner reach backward to the thoughts, changing them, and reach forward to the behavior, modifying it. That is to say, thinking leads to behavior, but words tell us about the thoughts and about the behavior, and so we affect thoughts and behavior by monitoring language. The method of psychotherapy known as will-training then consisted primarily of teaching people to watch their language and the language of others. If a person had a tendency to use "extreme" words, such as *never, always, impossible, urgent, miserable,* and *terrible,* he was warned by his peers of his sin of extremism. A person who stated as facts what were not facts, such as "I just can't stand it," was told that he was just not speaking the truth. A person who began to complain might be told that he was involved in the process of self-sabotage.

Low's semantic system of will-therapy is a self-contained school of psychotherapy and is an example of how it is possible to establish a whole school of thought on the basis of a central idea.

Hypnotherapy

A second school or systematic position is represented by hypnotherapy. The range of attitudes and opinions in this area goes from those therapists who never use hypnosis at all, whether because they do not understand how to do it or do not approve of its use, to those who employ it once in a while, to those who use it almost exclusively.

Despite the fact that the literature on hypnosis is extensive, with balanced scientific accounts, such as by Brenman and Gill (1947) and by Wolberg (1948), relatively little is known about the dynamics or the structural properties of hypnosis. A variety of theories of the hypnotic trance have been suggested, physiological and psychological, but none seems comprehensive or exclusive.

In general, methods of inducing trances are more or less alike. The therapist suggests that the patient is tired and sleepy and eventually the subject exhibits trance-like behavior, which can be graduated on a scale of suggestibility. Hypnosis is usually employed, albeit not too successfully, to get immediately to unconscious blocked areas causing troubles; as a means of removing symptoms; and as a way of inculcating into individuals certain concepts and ideas intended to change self- and other-perception, including changing basic philosophical ideas. While some cases are reported which indicate that such changes do happen, a more reasonable position is that the subject cooperates temporarily with the hypnotist and creates an illusion of permanent change. Hypnosis is a good means of relaxing people and of removing fears. The analgesic properties of hypnosis are well known, and hypnosis has been successfully used in dentistry, childbirth, and surgery.

In general, most psychotherapists have experimented with hypnosis, have become interested in it, and then, like Freud, drop it, realizing there really is no short-cut road to recovery.

Rational-Emotive System

An example of a brand-new school of psychotherapy is the Rational-Emotive system developed by Albert Ellis (1962). Ellis believes that practically all psychological problems arise out of irrational attitudes, due to the acceptance of false notions or values which are incorporated by the individual and then constantly fed back to the person by himself. These biased or prejudicial thoughts lead inevitably to emotional conditions. For Ellis, "Emotion is . . . largely a certain kind, a biased, prejudiced kind of thought." In other words a person who is a neurotic, who has personal problems that are not realistic, is a person who has certain illogical ideas and who needs to have his thinking straightened out. A prototype situation represents an individual who does not want to do something because he is afraid of being rejected. The therapist now points out to him that in order to get what one wants out of life one has to be ready to take the consequences of being hurt. The therapist then operates by arguing with the patient, leading him by Socratic-type questioning to logical conclusions which then can be compared to his behavior. By then pointing out the difference between the conclusion and the behavior, Ellis and those who operate in his school of thought now find the opportunity to demand that the patient act according to the conclusion logically arrived at.

Ellis's method of treatment is an example of a here-and-now therapy. One is interested in what the patient thinks right now and how he is currently operating, and not so much in the history of the patient which will indicate how he came to have such ideas. In summarizing Ellis's Rational-Emotive system, one can say that the therapist diagnoses the patient by having him expose his thinking. He learns how the patient maintains his mistaken ideas by irrational thinking and verbalizations. He discusses these ideas with the patient, trying to get him to come to logical conclusions, and then urges the patient to engage in activities designed to change his ideas and to attain superior social success.

Psychodrama

Another unique system of psychotherapy is represented by Psychodrama or therapeutic roleplaying. Psychodrama, like hypnosis, really has no theory. The writings of Moreno (1952) are of little help in understanding how Psychodrama works, and these writings do not touch on some of the structural problems of Psychodrama as a therapeutic method. Sturm (1965) hypothesizes that Psychodrama can best be explained by the concepts of learning theory as employed by behavior therapists.

Therapeutic roleplaying requires that the patient diagnose himself in the sense that he either selects or participates in the selection of a problem to be enacted. Once a problem has been defined by the patient, the therapist, either alone, in consultation with other assistants, or with the patient, establishes a situation to be enacted, and the patient, usually acting his own role, interacts with one or more therapeutic assistants. In a sense, the essence of the therapy is that the patient merely, on the Psychodrama stage, re-enacts his own reality situation but under neutral circumstances. Now, in many cases, this re-enactment has sufficient force to enable the individual to make striking changes, to gain insights, to calm down, and to begin to operate in a more efficient manner.

Therapy then is autochthonous—or self-generated. The reason is that the individual, without advice, without interpretations, without any efforts on the part of the therapist, seems to make rapid gains solely on the basis of re-enactment of past situations, or on the basis of enactment of anticipated situations. It is as though intellectual and emotional gains can be the consequent of acting out *per se*. In contrast with all other methods discussed so far, the internal dimensions of thinking and feeling are functions of behavior, rather than the other way around, which is the case in all other systems of psychotherapy discussed so far in this section. Socrates' injunction of "Know thyself" which may be considered the essence of conventional psychotherapy can be replaced by "Behave yourself." Just as subjective changes can affect objective behavior, so it seems that objective behavior changes can lead to subjective improvement.

Adlerian Family Counseling

Adlerian Family Counseling (Dreikurs *et al.*, 1959) has certain similarities both to Ellis's Rational-Emotive therapy and to therapeutic roleplaying. In this system, the problems of the parents and the problems of the children are determined by interviews and by observations. The locus of the treatment is the decision by the counselor about the causes of the problem—this is similar to Ellis's system. Then a solution is suggested to the adults, and the adults are led to accept the solution by logic and also by authority—this too fits in with Ellis's system—and then, the therapist gives parents certain instructions for them to act in particular manners but usually without theoretical explanation. They are told, in effect, to act a role, and to do it unquestioningly. This is somewhat similar to what the therapist suggests in roleplaying. Finally, after the patients have acted as they have been told and after they note the results of their behavior, they tend to generalize as to the reasons for any changes. This, also, as in therapeutic roleplaying, tends to occur after the fact. Patients who have done what they have been told to do and who experience success now learn to handle new situations on the basis of generalizations.

Reciprocal Inhibition

A relatively new system of psychotherapy of the behavior type has been suggested by Wolpe (Wolpe, 1938) which represents a different kind of thinking from the various methods discussed so far. Wolpe is concerned with persistent neurotic behavior which he views as learned unadaptive modes of functioning. The therapist's problem is to get the patient to unlearn these patterns and to replace them with superior ones. He uses conditioning theory and models himself against Hull's specific theoretical notions. He employs a here-and-now approach in which he first tries to find out what conditions generate anxiety and maladaptive responses. When the therapist knows what generates inappropriate fears, he tries to break the connections between the troubling situation and the anxiety. The basic principle is reciprocal inhibition, which means preventing anxiety attacks during the presence of the condition which formerly elicited them. In order for this to occur, when the precipitating condition occurs, an incompatible response must also occur. To give a simple example, if a patient reacts in a frightened manner to an object which is neutral to most people, say to a cat, the therapist tries to get the patient to respond in a favorable manner to some other stimulus and then produces the cat. By doing this over a number of times, presumably the original response to the cat is extinguished. This is due to the inhibiting circumstances of the present response taking precedence over the original response. One notes the identity of the theory to Jones's findings in getting a child no longer to respond with fear to a rabbit (Mary C. Jones, 1924).

The art of the method is finding methods of systematically desensitizing patients. The method can involve the following procedures: locating problem areas and setting a kind of hierarchy; then, teaching patients to relax. Hypnosis may be used, and also getting the patient to visualize a threatening situation. If the patient shows anxiety under these conditions of suggestion, a weaker stimulus situation is presented. Then, one suggests both the troubling situation and relaxation. When both occur, then the therapist goes along the list of troubling problem areas until the patient shows no more anxiety to any of the previously troubling areas.

One notes the mechanistic, conditioning types of treatment in the system, which has specific sectors of desensitization, is of the here-and-now type, and aims at specific areas. Presumably the individual may generalize and solve other problems concurrently through irradiation. This kind of treatment is quite similar to retraining animals and is offensive to those who have concepts of man which emphasize his rationality and uniqueness.

Adlerian Psychotherapy

We discuss Adlerian psychotherapy as a different approach from Adlerian Family Counseling because, in contrast to the latter in which individuals are told what to do without too much explanation, in Adlerian psychotherapy the essence of the therapeutic task is finding out the patient's hidden motivators or his "private logic." It is assumed that people who are maladjusted have certain basic attitudes toward self and others which interfere with normal social relationships. The person with these aberrant ideas is unaware of them and is only aware of the difficulties he has and of how unreasonable others are to him. The Adlerian analyst must first find out what the patient's hidden assumptions are and then lead the patient to understand them and to change his behavior. In this sense the position taken by Ellis is very similar to the Adlerian position.

The Adlerian therapeutic position is that behavior is consequent on thinking and that the locus of the therapy should be on the patient's concepts. Emotions are secondary factors, representing only the attempt of the patient to energize himself, or are means of affecting others. Behavior is secondary to thinking: once the patient is convinced how he should operate, he then is able to find means to operate successfully. These means of operating, which go under the name of *life style,* represent systematic means for obtaining goals. The organism is not pushed by his past, as seems evident in Wolpe's scheme of things, but rather operates holistically and teleologically in the pursuit of goals.

In further contrast to Wolpe's thinking, the individual is seen as actively and creatively creating his own personality. In contrast to some other depth personality systems, the person's unconscious is considered relatively unimportant; what the individual does is what he wills to do. He is to take responsibility for his actions.

Rogerian Nondirective Therapy

In client-centered counseling the locus of the therapy is in the patient. The therapist serves mostly as a catalyst. He is less active in some senses than in any of the other forms of therapy; he involves himself not at all in making decisions for the patient, does not order him to assume any systematic positions, does not make interpretations, does not give advice, does not even encourage. The basic view of Rogers (1951) is that the individual is responsible for his own therapy and that the therapist provides a climate in which the patient improves. By the therapist showing the patient that he understands him and by showing sympathy, it is expected that the patient will grow. The underlying force that leads to growth and improvement is a kind of basic life force which leads to self-maintenance and enhancement.

Existential Analysis

It is difficult to discuss existential analysis because it is much less concrete than any of the other systems taken up so far, and the various schools of thought usually included under this rubric seem at times to have little in relation to each other. One may consider existential analysis as a closer meeting between religion and psychotherapy, a rapprochement of the problems of man that religion has handled in the past by philosophers and psychologists.

Among those whose ideas are to be considered in this area, Ludwig Binswanger (1956) seems pre-eminent. He and Boss (1963) have attempted formal presentations about therapeutic procedures, even though both of these men, and others following in their tradition, seem to concentrate more on philosophical aspects of man rather than practical methods of treatment.

The difficulty in explaining existential psychotherapy lies in a number of basic facts: the first is that existentialism is a kind of philosophy—a point of view rather than a school of thought. Next, within the group of existentialists are a number of people who say very little in common and even contradict each other. We can refer to the Christians and the Buddhists—both religious groups, but with very little in common—even disagreeing on whether there is a God. But what do the existentialists have in common—more or less? First is a concern for the unique individual with his ineffable and private experience. Then, they all hold the concept that man is not determined, except in a very crude biological manner, and that he is the architect of his fate and therefore a responsible and a valuable human being. Man is aware: this is what makes him human; he *knows*. He is emerging, not determined; he never really is, but he is becoming. The important thing is unique reality, known as *phenomenology*. The person is aware of self and of his uniqueness. Moreover, the individual is concerned primarily with meaning, and he is operating in terms of motives, moving towards goals, formless and inchoate, but nonetheless powerful.

It is difficult to pin down how existential therapists operate, but essentially one gets the impression that they concern themselves primarily with appreciation of the individual and try to get inside him so as to understand him in all his uniqueness. Now, if one reads the above carefully, it may well be that one may say, "It looks as though I am an existentialist," since undoubtedly few therapists would deny the validity of the above remarks, except perhaps for dyed-in-the-wool pragmatic behaviorists who deny any inner reality. However, the difference may be quantitative in that the existentialists stress these private and unique feelings and attempt therapy via exposing the individual to himself, so that he can experience himself more thoroughly and honestly.

THE VALIDITY OF PSYCHOTHERAPY

A great many people suspect that psychotherapy is not a reality, that is to say that the so-called psychotherapeutic relationship is comparatively valueless. This suspicion is not held only by those who know nothing about psychotherapy, since negative attitudes toward psychotherapy as an entity are shared by people who have a great deal of information about the topic.

D. O. Hebb (1949), a former president of the American Psychological Association, writes, "It has not been shown that any specialized psychotherapy ... has any value in mental illness." Eysenck (1952) has manipulated some data and come to the conclusion that patients without psychotherapy do better than patients with psychotherapy. However, the compared groups are not really comparable. Borgatta (1964) has suggested that the regression effect may explain the reputed value of psychotherapy. Patients tend to go to a therapist when they are at the bottom and cannot really go much further in their despair. They would have gotten better anyway, but they attribute their improvement to the presence of the therapist. The most impressive evidence against this hypothesis comes from Grummon (1954), who tested a group of self-referred patients at two periods 60 days apart. The first testing was called the *pre-wait* period and took place when the patients first applied for counseling. The second testing took place 60 days later when the therapy was about to start. Changes over seven sets of tests were compared with a control tested group. If Borgatta's suggestion were valid, one would suspect that this self-referred group would have made superior scores on the second testing. However, no differences of any significance were found, and Grummon concluded there was no basis in terms of his data for accepting the hypothesis that motivation for therapy, or referral in and of itself, brings about constructive personality changes. In the same set of studies, Dymond (1954) concluded that perceptions of self indicate a somewhat less favorable self-impression after the 60-day waiting period, while very favorable self-impressions were attained following psychotherapy.

The old problem of idiographic and nomothetic psychology is raised here. The "hard nosed" scientist who will not accept evidence that is subjective and unique in nature, no matter how often repeated, can reject the concept of psychotherapy and will be supported by other scientists who believe only in what they cannot disbelieve. The "soft" scientist who accepts individual accounts will feel that the plethora of accounts about psychotherapy by patients and by therapists adds up to impressive evidence. We are forced back to our original statement about the purposes of psychotherapy, which we have concluded are two in nature: subjective comfort and objective improvement in behavior. The first cannot possibly be evaluated except by the individuals affected. Consequently, there is such a thing as psychotherapy simply because there are patients who say there is. That they may be wrong in fact has nothing to do with it, no more than whether or not a girl is really lovely when her fiance insists she is. Consensus has nothing to do with this kind of truth. The second can be evaluated. That is, evidence about greater efficiency for groups can be determined in the usual manner. The evidence for psychotherapy at this level is very weak, and even the Rogers-Dymond (1954) study, the most complete in this area, is not too impressive in this respect. We really do not know, even though a lot of people seem to be sure, whether or not psychotherapy has any social utility value. The behaviorist-psychologist en route to his therapist may well argue that there really isn't any evidence that what he is about to do has any value, but he feels better and that is why he goes.

REFERENCES

Abraham, K. C. *The psychological relation between sexuality and alcoholism.* London: Hogarth Press, 1927.

Adler, A. *Understanding human nature.* New York: Greenberg, 1927.

Adler, A. The individual psychology of the alcoholic patient. *J. crim. Psychopathol.,* 1941, 3, 74–77.

Ansbacher, H., & Ansbacher, Rowena. *The individual psychology of Alfred Adler.* New York: Basic Books, 1946.

Appel, K. E. Psychiatric therapy. In J. M. Hunt (Ed.), *Personality and the behavior disorders.* New York: Ronald, 1944.

Berne, E. L. *Transactional analysis in psychotherapy.* New York: Grove, 1961.

Binswanger, L. Existential analysis and psychotherapy. In Frieda Fromm-Reichman & J. L. Moreno (Eds.), *Progress in psychotherapy.* New York: Grune & Stratton, 1956.

Borgatta, E. F. Demonstrations of genuine placebo change. *Psychol. Rep.,* 1964, 14, 645–646.

Boss, M. *Daseinsanalyses and psychoanalysis.* New York: Basic Books, 1963.

Brammer, L. M., & Shostrom, E. L. *Therapeutic psychology.* Englewood Cliffs, N.J.: Prentice-Hall, 1960.

Brenman, Margaret, & Gill, M. M. *Hypnotherapy.* New York: International Universities Press, 1947.

Bromberg, W. *Man above humanity.* New York: Lippincott, 1956.

Burrow, T. The group method of analysis. *Psychoanal. Rev.,* 1927, 14, 268–280.

Burrow, T. *The neurosis of man.* New York: Harcourt, Brace, 1950.

Corsini, R. J., Freud, S., Rogers, C. R., and Moreno, J. L. *Group Psychother.,* 1956, 9, 274–281.

Corsini, R. J. *Methods of group psychotherapy.* New York: McGraw-Hill, 1957.

Dollard, J., & Miller, N. E. *Personality and psychotherapy.* New York: McGraw-Hill, 1950.

Dreikurs, R. Are psychological schools of thought outdated? *J. indiv. Psychol.,* 1960, 16, 3–10.

Dreikurs, R., Corsini, R., Sonstegard, M., and Low, R. *Adlerian family counseling.* Eugene, Ore.: Univer. of Oregon Press, 1959.

Dymond, Rosalind. Adjustment changes over therapy from Thematic Apperception Test ratings. In C. R. Rogers & Rosalind Dymond (Eds.), *Psychotherapy and personality change.* Chicago: Univer. of Chicago Press, 1954.

Ellis, A. *Reason and emotion in psychotherapy.* New York: Lyle Stuart, 1962.

Eysenck, H. J. The effects of psychotherapy: an evaluation. *J. consult. Psychol.,* 1952, 16, 319–324.

Eysenck, H. J. *Behavior therapy and the neuroses.* London: Pergamon, 1960.

Fiedler, F. E. A comparison of psychoanalytic, nondirective and Adlerian therapeutic relationships. *J. consult. Psychol.,* 1950, 14, 436–445.

Fiedler, F. E. The concept of an ideal therapeutic relationship. *J. consult. Psychol.,* 1950, 14, 239–245.

Frank, J. D. *Persuasion and healing.* Baltimore: Johns Hopkins Press, 1961.

Freud, S. *The future of an illusion.* New York: Liveright, 1928.

Freud, S. *Three contributions to the theory of sex.* Washington, D.C.: Nervous and Mental Disease Publishing House, 1930.

Freud, S. *An outline of psychoanalysis.* New York: Norton, 1939.

Gibbins, R. *Chronic alcoholism.* Brookside Monograph No. 1. Ontario: Alcoholism Research Foundation, 1953.

Goldstein, K. *The organism.* New York: American Book Co., 1939.

Grummon, D. L. Personality changes as a function of time in persons motivated for therapy. In C. R. Rogers & Rosalind Dymond (Eds.), *Psychotherapy and personality change.* Chicago: Univer. of Chicago Press, 1954.

Hall, C. S., & Lindzey, G. *Theories of personality.* New York: Wiley, 1957.

Harper, R. *Psychoanalysis and psychotherapy.* Englewood Cliffs, N.J.: Prentice-Hall, 1959.

Hebb, D. O. *The organization of behavior.* New York: Wiley, 1949.

Horney, Karen. *Self-analysis.* New York: Norton, 1942.

Hubbard, L. R. *Dianetics.* New York: Nelson, 1950.

Jellinek, E. M., *et al.* The craving for alcohol. *Quart. J. Stud. Alcohol.,* 1955, 16, 34–66.

Jones, E. *The life and works of Sigmund Freud.* New York: Basic Books, 1953.

Jones, Mary C. The elimination of children's fears. *J. exp. Psychol.,* 1924, 7, 382–390.

Jones, M. Group psychotherapy. *Brit. med. J.,* 1942, 2, 276–278.

Karpman, B. *Alcoholic women.* New Haven, Conn.: Associated Booksellers, 1948.

Knight, R. P. The dynamics and treatment of chronic alcohol addiction. *Bull. Menninger Clin.,* 1937, 1, 233–258.

Levy, J. Relationship therapy. *Amer. J. Orthopsychiat.,* 1938, 8, 64–69.

Low, A. A. *Mental health through will-training.* Boston: Christopher, 1952.

Mead, G. H. *Mind, self and society.* Chicago: Univer. of Chicago Press, 1934.

Meerlo, J. A. M. Artificial ecstasy. *J. nerv. ment. Dis.,* 1952, 15, 246–266.

Menninger, K. *Man against himself.* New York: Harcourt, Brace, 1938.

Moreno, J. L. *Who shall survive?* New York: Beacon House, 1952.

Mowrer, O. H. Some constructive features of the concept of sin. *J. counsel. Psychol.,* 1960, 7, 185–187.

Navratil, I. The role of the wife in alcoholism. *Alkohol. Politiikka Hels.,* 1957, 4, 119–124.

Pastore, N. *Nature-Nurture controversy.* New York: Kings Crown Press, 1949.

Pratt, J. H. The group method in the treatment of psychosomatic disorders. *Sociometry,* 1945, 8, 323–333.

Rank, O. *The trauma of birth.* New York: R. Brunner, 1952.

Reik, T. *Listening with the third ear.* New York: Grove, 1956.

Rennie, T. A. C., Srole, L., Opler, M. K., & Langner, T. S. Urban life and mental health. *Amer. J. Psychiat.,* 1957, 113, 831–837.

Riesman, D. Comments in S. W. Standal & R. J. Corsini (Eds.), *Critical incidents in psychotherapy.* Incident 15. Englewood Cliffs, N.J.: Prentice-Hall, 1959.

Rogers, C. R. *Counseling and psychotherapy.* New York: Houghton Mifflin, 1942.

Rogers, C. R. *Client-centered therapy.* Boston: Houghton Mifflin, 1951.

Rogers, C. R., & Dymond, Rosalind (Eds.) *Psychotherapy and personality change.* Chicago: Univer. of Chicago Press, 1954.

Salter, A. *Conditioned reflex therapy.* New York: Creative Age Press, 1949.

Schilder, P. The psychogenesis of alcohol. *Quart. J. Stud. Alcohol.,* 1941, 2, 277–292.

Schilder, P. *Introduction to a psychoanalytic psychiatry.* New York: International Universities Press, 1952.

Schofield, W. *Psychotherapy: purchase of friendship.* Englewood Cliffs, N.J.: Prentice-Hall, 1964.

Shoben, E. J. Counseling and the learning of integrative behavior. *J. counsel. Psychol.,* 1954, 1, 42–48.

Shoben, E. J. View on the etiology of alcoholism: the behavioristic view. In H. E. Kruse (Ed.), *Alcoholism as a medial problem.* New York: Hoeber-Harper, 1956.

Slavson, S. R. *An introduction to group therapy.* New York: Commonwealth Fund, 1943.

Sturm, I. E. The behavioristic aspect of psychodrama. *Group Psychother.,* 1965, 18, 50–64.

Tiebout, H. M. The ego factors in surrender in alcoholism. *Quart. J. Stud. Alcohol.,* 1954, 15, 610–621.

Walker, N. *A short history of psychotherapy.* London: Routledge & Kegan Paul, 1957.

White, R. W. Motivation reconsidered. *Psychol. Rev.,* 1959, 66, 297–333.

Wolberg, L. R. *Medical hypnosis.* New York: Grune & Stratton, 1948.

Wolberg, L. R. *The technique of psychotherapy.* New York: Grune & Stratton, 1954.

Wolpe, J. *Psychotherapy by reciprocal inhibition.* Stanford: Stanford Univer. Press, 1958.

Zilboorg, G., & Henry, G. W. *A history of medical psychology.* New York: Norton, 1941.

Zwerling, I. Psychiatric findings in an interdisciplinary study of 46 alcoholic patients. *Quart. J. Stud. Alcohol.,* 1959, 20, 543–544.

CHAPTER 24 Personality and Susceptibility to Social Influence[1]

WILLIAM J. McGUIRE
University of California, SD
La Jolla, California

The study of the personality correlates of susceptibility to social influence represents the interaction of two old and active fields of research, the area of personality dynamics (or individual differences) and the area of attitude change (or persuasive communication). Research on this topic of mutual interest by workers from each field has had a long history, or rather, if we may paraphrase Ebbinghaus (1908), a long past.

Among students of individual differences, this variable of persuasibility (at least in its rather simplified manifestation called "suggestibility") seems to have been the first dynamic dimension to receive scientific study. Certain abilities dimensions (such as the simple sensory-motor performances studied by Galton and J. McK. Cattell and the intelligence tests devised by Binet) received earlier sustained attention than any of the dynamic characteristics, but the only other dynamic dimension whose investigation is of similar antiquity is "imagery." Binet's preoccupation with hypnosis and suggestibility (1900) even preceded his contributions to intelligence testing (Boring, 1950). When Whipple published in 1910 the first *Manual of Mental and Physical Tests,* suggestibility was one of the few personality variables that warranted listing on the basis of availability of tests to measure it. A reason for this early preoccupation with suggestibility (aside from the intrinsic interest it arouses) may have been the key role it played in the controversy between the school of Salpêtrière (Charcot, Janet) and the School of Nancy (Liébault, Bernheim) regarding the nature of hysteria and, by implication, of all the neuroses (Wolf, 1964). Other possible sources of this interest include its apparent involvement in therapy and in hypnosis.

Opinion change researchers have shown no less preoccupation with personality correlates of susceptibility to influence. Lasswell (1948) proposed the interrogative formulation, "Who says what to whom, how, with what effect," as an inclusive analysis of persuasive communication. The "to whom" in this formulation singles out individual-difference factors as one of the five main classes of variables to be studied in opinion-change experimentation. An isomorphic analysis—in terminology derived from the communication engineers, "source-message-

[1] Preparation of this chapter was facilitated by grant G19799 received from the National Science Foundation, Division of Social Sciences.

channel-receiver-destination"—in the category of "receiver" likewise singles out personality variables (and other individual-difference dimensions) as one of the five key classes of independent variables in persuasive communication and opinion-change research.

This long-continued and extensive study of personality-influenceability relationships from several directions has by now provided us with a considerable corpus of empirical data. It can hardly be claimed that these data have provided a definitive theory for the area that leaves all major questions substantially answered. The motivation behind many of the individual experiments has been the testing of *ad hoc* hypotheses of little general theoretical relevance. As a result, it is hard to integrate the separate studies into an overall theory, and in many cases the results of separate studies even seem to be mutually contradictory. As we shall see, these apparent conflicts in results may often be due to unreported between-studies differences in situational parameters.

But while the existing body of findings is hardly definitive, we feel that it does allow the induction of some principles that could lead to a general theoretical framework. These principles help us to synthesize already determined personality-influenceability relationships and to suggest new hypotheses in this area. In the present chapter, we shall first evaluate the degree to which influenceability is a general trait. We shall then review four theoretical approaches that have given rise to research on influenceability. The section following will review the empirical findings in terms of six principles that we feel underlie much of the personality-influenceability data. Finally, we shall discuss briefly some methodological implications for future research in the area.

INFLUENCEABILITY AS A GENERAL TRAIT

To avoid from the outset misunderstandings as to the scope of this chapter, we should clarify that we are using "influenceability" in the very broad sense of covering any tendency of the person to change as a function of social pressure. We stress ideological change but not to the exclusion of other types of changes. Hence, we include changing one's opinion on a matter-of-fact or a matter-of-taste issue as a consequence of an argumentative message (rational or emotional) from some source. We also include changing one's judgment on an objective issue (like the relative lengths of lines) or on a subjective issue (the relative pleasantness of two paintings) after hearing the bare statement of a deviant judgment voiced by a peer or authority source. We include even movements (like body sway or eyelid closure) as a consequence of waking or hypnotic suggestion. Some will find this usage of "influenceability" objectionably overinclusive of processes they like to distinguish under such labels as suggestibility, compliance, conformity, indoctrination, persuasibility, attitude change. On the verbal issue, we feel apologetic for this admittedly overinclusive usage. We choose "influenceability" for economy of expression, as the most inclusive one-word label to refer to the generic class. In any case, terminology in the field is very fluid (Allport, 1935; Campbell, 1963; De Fleur & Westie, 1963).

More serious than the nominal objection is the worry that we are throwing together behavioral outcomes that are the resultants of quite different psychological processes. It might be felt that the several forms of susceptibility to social influence are quite different in their relations to personality variables. In anticipation of the remainder of the chapter, we can say that both theory and the empirical data do indicate that the various forms of susceptibility to influence are different from one another in their relations to personality. Indeed, it is these very differences that have compelled us to include the various types of influence situations within this review chapter. Otherwise, selecting one type by fiat would have resulted in an imbalanced and misleading coverage. Moreover, the changes in these personality relationships as we go from one type of influence situation to another tend to clarify the processes in each situation and allow the building of a more inclusive theory. In a sense, the whole is greater than the sum of its parts as regards heuristic and testing dividends. By considering personality-influenceability relations not just in one susceptibility situation but across a wide range of situations, we obtain information not only on first-order effects but on interaction effects as well.

Our contention here is that the data indicate that susceptibility to social influence in its myriad forms is indeed a (weak) general trait. The person's standing as to relative persuasibility in one situation tends to have a significant positive relationship to his standings on persuasibility in a very wide range of other social influence situations. Until this minimum degree of interrelation can be demonstrated, it makes little sense to examine how susceptibility in general is related to other personality dimensions. In this section, we shall present the evidence that there is such an overall trend to positivity among the various indices of susceptibility. In later sections (particularly in discussing principles 3 and 5) we shall take the opposite tack and point out that the intercorrelations, while predominantly positive, are usually quite low. We shall be arguing, then, that while there is an underlying general trait of susceptibility-to-influence, there are group and specific factors as well, so that many specifiable situational factors operate as moderator variables on the relationship between influenceability and personality.

The number and range of social influence situations that have been used in research are formidable. We shall attempt to reduce the problem to manageable size, without obscuring the essential complexities of the problem, by considering three general classes of influence situations to which we shall give the names *suggestion, conformity,* and *persuasion* situations. Each is operationally definable and distinguishable; each has received a great amount of research attention; and together they cover a wide range of social influence situations. (To give this *ad hoc* trichotomy a vague aura of theoretical imprimatur, we can point out that these classes have a superficial correspondence to the three processes of opinion change singled out by Kelman [Kelman, 1958, 1961; Kelman & Eagly, 1965]: compliance, identification, and internalization. The parallelism, however, breaks down when we bring to bear the full details of Kelman's analysis.) In the following section, we shall take up each of the three classes separately, operationally defining each and considering the homogeneity of influenceability tests falling within each class. Then we shall discuss the correlations of influenceability scores across classes.

Suggestibility as a General Trait

The longest continued attempt to determine the correlations among different forms of susceptibility to social influence has taken place with respect to our first-named class, suggestibility. As was pointed out at the start of the chapter, a large battery of suggestibility tests was in use even before the opening of this century (Binet, 1900). This field of inquiry, initiated disputatiously (Wolf, 1964), has fed on controversy ever since (Benton & Bandura, 1953). In this regard, the study of suggestibility has paralleled the history of research on the structure of intelligence, but with less solid data to serve as a basis for advancing the question. It is an interesting incident for the sociologist of science that Binet was the pioneer worker in both these seemingly unrelated fields which have developed so similarly. The state of the question with suggestibility is currently at about the stage of intelligence research in the 1920's. Hilgard's (1965) recent work sets the stage for the next leap forward.

Various types of suggestibility have been posited. The oldest question involves the extent to which waking and hypnotic suggestibility are correlated. Hull (1933), while stressing the essential similarity of waking and hypnotic suggestion, has with others distinguished between prestige (e.g., body sway) and nonprestige (e.g., progressive weights) suggestion. Others (Binet, 1900; Aveling & Hargreaves, 1921) have argued for a general suggestibility factor plus several group factors. The most actively debated current analysis is that suggested by Eysenck and Furneaux (1945) involving a fairly well-defined primary-suggestibility factor (hypnotizability, body sway, pendulum swing, etc.) and a less clear, secondary suggestibility factor (progressive weights, suggested false reports, odor suggestibility, etc.). They perceived some sign of a tertiary factor also. The distinction between the primary and secondary factors might be interpreted as a prestige vs. nonprestige induction, since the first set of tests usually involves explicit commands by an authority source, while the second set involves more of a task-induced expectation. However, a somewhat better-fitting distinction is that the first set of tests involves ideomotor acts, while the second set involves sensory hallucinations. Some trouble has been reported (Benton & Bandura, 1953) in replicating Eysenck and Furneaux's results, but there have been successful replications also (Stukát, 1958). The latter monograph contains an excellent review of the work on this problem. Another thorough review is found in Weitzenhoffer (1953). Hilgard (1965) reports a study by Lauer (1965) which shows one general factor throughout the hypnotic suggestibility tests, but as many as six secondary factors.

We feel that there is an underlying trait of general suggestibility, though all so-called suggestibility tests load on other factors as well. Hypnotizability and body-sway tests load heavily on this factor; progressive lines and heat illusion tests have lower loadings while other tests (false report) have very low loadings. In addition there are probably several other more specific dimensions, such as separate positive and negative hallucination factors and a "difficulty" factor, as suggested by Hilgard's (1965) Stanford group. The correlations tend to be predominantly positive, though their magnitudes are usually quite low, with a cluster of primary motor tests intercorrelating fairly highly, a cluster of secondary sensory tests with somewhat lower correlations and with even lower correlations between clusters (Stukát, 1958). The lowness of the between-test intercorrelations is partly ascribable to the discouraging low reliabilities of suggestibility tests. More reliable data are needed before the generality question can be answered with confidence. Such data probably await the development of longer tests, more precise scoring, and more standardized administration procedures (de Rivera, 1959) than hitherto, prescriptions which impose heavy burdens on subjects and experimenters alike. Hilgard's (1965) work shows what painstaking care can achieve.

Conformity as a General Trait

The second general type of social influence situation, which we call "conformity," also shows signs of a general factor, but again with considerable differences from situation to situation in loadings on other factors. By "conformity" situations here we mean those in which the individual is informed simply that a certain source (e.g., a peer participating in the study) holds a certain position on an issue. This source position is usually picked to be deliberately discrepant from the subject's as measured earlier (Zimbardo, 1960) or selected at an extremely unlikely erroneous position (Asch, 1956) or allowed to vary naturally (M. Sherif, 1935). The index of conformity is the extent to which the subject, after he hears the source's position, gives a similar position as his own judgment. For the situation to be called a "conformity" one in the present sense, it is required that the source give no arguments for his position and that he not give any explicit indication that he expects the subject to agree with him. Classic examples include the Sherif (M. Sherif, 1935) autokinetic studies and Asch's (1956) study on peer influence on the judgment of line lengths.

A number of investigators have demonstrated that "conformity" in one situation tends to be correlated with conformity in other situations. Rosner (1957) has shown that student nurses who conform to peers on one task tend to conform to other peers on other tasks at other times. Harper and Tuddenham (1964) show that conformity to strangers is much the same as conformity to acquaintances. Sears (1963) reports generality of various forms of dependency in children.

Asch (1956) also found that college students tend to get the same conformity scores early and late in the task. Blake, Helson, and Mouton (1956) also found considerable homogeneity of conformity. Abelson and Lesser (1959a) found that children who conformed to teacher's judgments were also likely to conform (as measured projectively) to mother's judgments. In some classes, the correlation between the two scores was as high as .90. Likewise, conformity to the teacher was highly related to the actual agreement of the child with his mother on a variety of issues. Frye and Bass (1958) and Beloff (1958) also found a close relationship between face-to-face "acquiescence" and general conventional "conformity" to social norms. Abelson and Lesser (1959b) found conformity to peers and to adults to be correlated in children 7–9 years old, though not in children 13 years old. In general, given that the sources are similarly evaluated by our subjects, the findings indicate that a person who conforms to one source on one issue will conform also to other sources and on other issues.

Correlation, of course, does not indicate identity. There tends to be an underlying conformity factor on which our various conformity tests load, so that we usually find significant positive correlation between them. But rarely do these correlations attain a magnitude that indicates even as much as a 50 per cent covariance between the two tests. In part, the lowness of the typical correlations reflects the unreliability of the tests; but also it indicates that scores on our conformity tests reflect reliable variance other than that on a common conformity factor. Ferguson (1944) does report an approximation to a unitary factor solution, but actually his correlations also were quite low on the average. Arguments for the specificity of conformity have been presented by Moeller and Applezweig (1957), Beloff (1958), Tuddenham (1959), and Hollander (1960).

Persuasibility as a General Trait

The third area of social influence situations, which we here call "persuasibility," refers to situations in which a source gives his position on an issue and (unlike the conformity situation) presents various arguments, based on emotional or rational considerations, why this position is correct. The subject is then asked his position on the issue and his susceptibility is measured by the degree it agrees with the source's (as compared to the subject's "before" score, or the score of a no-communication control group).

We deal with such persuasibility situations in various laboratory situations (e.g., the face-to-face group interaction studies summarized by Kelley and Thibaut, 1954; and the persuasive communication studies summarized by Hovland, 1954) and in various naturalistic situations such as political, advertising, and indoctrination campaigns using mass media (Hovland, Lumsdaine, & Sheffield, 1949) or personal influence (E. Katz & Lazarsfeld, 1955).

There is abundant evidence that persuasibility on one issue is positively related to persuasibility by other messages on other issues. Indeed, the attitude-change researcher takes it for granted that he is involved in a correlated-measures design when he carries out an experiment in which one subject receives several persuasive treatments, each on a different issue. The experienced investigator routinely uses different error terms for the among-subject and the within-subject treatments. Usually he finds that he was wise in doing so, since the among-subject variance is typically several times the within-subject variance.

One study will suffice to illustrate the magnitude of the relationships. Janis and Field (1956, reprinted in Janis & Hovland, 1959) gave a set of ten persuasive messages to about 185 high school students. Each was purportedly from a different newspaper reporter and they included a wide range of topics, each with a pro and con form. Each person's persuasibility for each message was scored 0 or 1 on the basis of a median split with respect to amount of change. Tetrachoric correlations were calculated between the impacts of each pair of messages, yielding 45 correlations in all. Only 6 negative correlations emerged. Of the 39 positive correlations 25 are significant at the .05 level. Again, we must caution that while there was a predominance of significant positive correlations, suggesting an underlying general factor, these correlations were not high (the highest was +.52), indicating that scores on these persuasibility tests are affected by many things besides this general common factor.

Between-Class Correlations

The previous sections have shown that there is a significant, though far from complete, overlap between susceptibility to social influence on one test and another when both fall within one of our three, somewhat arbitrary classes: suggestion, conformity, and persuasion. We now turn to the rather more demanding question of how highly the influenceability scores correlate when the tests come from different classes. As regards the correlation between suggestibility and conformity, Barry, Mackennon, and Murray (1931) and Moore (1964) found little correlation between hypnotic or waking suggestibility and conformity to majority opinion. On the other hand, Stukát (1958) found significant positive correlation between the two in a wide variety of experimental situations. Significant relationships between influenceability scores in conformity tests and in persuasibility tests have also been reported. Linton and Graham (1959; Linton, 1954) found a significant relation between conformity in a Sherif-type autokinetic test and persuasibility as measured by opinion change after reading a series of persuasive messages on such issues as requiring physician's prescriptions for the purchase of antihistamines. (The messages were those originally used by Hovland and Weiss, 1951.) Support for this relationship was also found by Abelson and Lesser (1959a, 1959b).

The general picture is much the same within class and across class: tests of susceptibility to social influence tend to show significant but low positive intercorrelations. Similar results could be cited with respect to other classifications of social influence situations, e.g., susceptibility on involving vs. noninvolving issues, on simple vs. complex issues, etc. The predominant positivity of the correlation matrix indicates that there is a detectible amount of communality underlying a wide range of tests of social influenceability, thus giving some support for the existence of a general persuasibility trait, such as the Yale group (Hovland, Janis, & Kelley, 1953; Hovland & Janis, 1959) has long sought to demonstrate. On the other hand, the intercorrelations between tests are sufficiently low (even allowing for the often low reliabilities of the individual test) to indicate a considerable degree of independence among the various forms of influenceability. It is quite possible that the relationship of a given personality variable to susceptibility will vary considerably among influence situations. A basic goal of this chapter is to present principles that will account for these situational variations in personality-influenceability relations.

PERSONALITY IMPLICATIONS OF THEORIES OF ATTITUDE CHANGE

We feel that currently active attitude researchers derive their inspiration from four rather different theoretical points of departure which may be characterized briefly as the learning, perceptual, consistency, and functional approaches to attitude change. The four do not constitute a set of opposed, mutually contradictory theories. Rather, they stress different aspects of the influence situation, sometimes yielding the same predictions, occasionally opposite ones, but more often simply yielding predictions about different variables. Hence these theories tend to supplement one another rather than to be mutually contradictory. Since they stress different processes underlying influenceability, they have different implications regarding personality-influenceability relations. These implications will be our focus of attention in the next four sections, each of which is devoted to one of the approaches. Our analysis here draws heavily from that of Brewster Smith (1968).

Learning Theory Approaches

The basic notion of learning theory approaches is that the opinion-change impact of a persuasive message is determined in part by the extent to which the target person learns (attends to and comprehends) its arguments. Hence, factors which affect learning will tend likewise to affect opinion change. In a later section of this chapter, when we discuss the "mediational" principle, we shall deal more fully with this role of learning in persuasion. As regards the three classes of social influence situations we considered above (suggestion, conformity, and persuasion), the role of learning will be appreciable only in the third, since in suggestion and conformity situations the message is so simple and repetitious that there will not be appreciable variance in learning among subjects drawn from the normal population (a point considered more fully in the later section on the "situational weighting" principle).

This learning approach was used heuristically by Hovland and other members of the Yale group to derive hypotheses about a number of persuasion phenomena. For example, studies on order effects in persuasion, such as the primacy-recency problem, frequently draw their inspiration from this learning approach (Hovland, 1957; Miller & Campbell, 1959; Insko, 1964; Anderson, 1965). The learning approach has implications regarding personality correlates of influenceability, because any individual-difference characteristic (like intelligence, anxiety, etc.) that has a predictable impact on the learning of complex persuasive communications will, by this theory, be related to attitude change in a comparable manner. This type of analysis will be frequently used in subsequent sections of this chapter.

One other sense in which there is a learning theory approach to influenceability is that the person's operant level of conforming is itself a function of learning. Miller and Dollard (1941) provided an early discussion of how social learning processes and experiences underlie the tendency to imitate. More recently Hoffman (1953), Abelson and Lesser (1959b), Harvey, Hunt, and Schroder (1961), Sears (1963), and McAllister (1965) have analyzed child-rearing practices that are likely to affect the person's learned characteristic level of compliance. Chapter 4 (by Levin and Fleischman) discusses the developmental approaches to personality more fully. These analyses introduce personality considerations, since in this theorizing, individual-difference characteristics serve as mediators between the antecedent conditions (childhood experiences) and the consequent behavior (conformity).

Because experimental data on attitude-change questions that arise from this type of analysis are sparse, we shall seldom advert to this theorizing in the remainder of the chapter; however, work along these lines is a likely direction of future research. The learning theory approaches to personality are considered more fully in Chapter 10 (by Daniel Berlyne).

Perceptual Theory Approaches

The crux of the perceptual approach to persuasion can be epitomized in Asch's (1952) statement that opinion change is not so much a change in the person's feelings about a given object, but rather a change in which object he is giving his feelings about. For example, if I uprate my judgment about the attractiveness of being a politician after hearing that my peers regard the profession as more attractive than I did initially, I am not really changing my feelings about any profession as a result of group pressure. Rather, I am reinterpreting what was meant by "politician." Johnson and Steiner (1965) have recently made an interesting application of this notion to provide an alternative explanation to a dissonance experiment. One of the earliest proponents of this perceptual approach to conformity was Sherif (M. Sherif, 1935) with his "frame of reference" notion. More currently he is using the approach in the work stemming from assimilation-and-contrast theory (M. Sherif & Hovland, 1961; C. Sherif, M. Sherif & Nebergall, 1965). Helson's (1964) adaptation-level theory, insofar as it deals with attitudes, is also in this tradition. Occasionally the learning and perceptual approaches can be brought into experimental confrontation (Anderson, 1965), but usually they supplement one another.

Personality considerations are introduced through the perceptual approach in a variety of ways. Proclivity to use perceptual distortion in resisting social influence has long been of interest (Cooper & Dinerman, 1951; Kendall & Wolf, 1949) and introduces questions of cognitive style and personality characteristics. Steiner (1960) has investigated the relationship between personality characteristics and the preference for using perceptual distortion (as opposed to other modes of conflict resolution) in handling social pressure situations. Assimilation-contrast theory isolates the person's "involvement" as a crucial variable in his perceptual and attitudinal responses to a persuasive message, and involvement is related to personality characteristics both as a general style and as cathected in particular issues. This involvement-conformity topic has given rise to a lively controversy (Zimbardo, 1960; Freedman, 1964; Greenwald, 1964). The long continued interest in stereotypes as a factor in racial prejudice is another illustration of the perceptual approach to attitudes and attitude change.

Consistency Theory Approaches

Unlike many other psychological approaches, consistency theories postulate that a person's attitude and behavior system have somewhat more internal structure than a bowl of oatmeal. In general, consistency theorists assume that the person behaves so as to maximize the internal consistency among his information, beliefs, and behavior. The consistency in question is not so much logical as "psycho-logical," to use the apt Abelson-Rosenberg (1958) phrase. In deriving heuristic value from this approach one views the person confronted with social pressure as acting as an honest broker, trying to arrive at a least-squares solution in minimizing discrepancies among the outside influences on the issue, his own already-formed beliefs on the given issue and on related issues, and his relevant behavioral possibilities. Illustrative of this approach are the various balance theories (Heider, 1946, 1958; Newcomb, 1953; Cartwright & Harary, 1956); Osgood and Tannenbaum's (1955) congruity theory; Festinger's dissonance theory (Festinger, 1957, 1964b;

Brehm & Cohen, 1962); Abelson-Rosenberg's (1958) affective-cognitive theory; and McGuire's wishful- vs. logical-thinking formulation (1960a, 1960b).

Personality considerations enter into the consistency approaches to influenceability in at least two ways. First, it seems likely that there are individual differences in sensitivity to and toleration of cognitive inconsistencies; for example, some people's cognitive compartments tend to be more logic-tight than others. Hence, we may derive hypotheses about personality correlates of such levels of toleration. Secondly, let persons be at a given level of felt inconsistency, there would be characteristic individual differences in preferred modes of inconsistency reduction. Again, we would use the consistency approach by looking for personality correlates of these characteristic preferences. The directions such thinking has taken are discussed in some detail in Chapter 13 (by David Glass). Since consistency can be restored by perceptual distortion and by learning new bolstering information (Abelson, 1959), this consistency approach makes contact at various places with the learning and perceptual approaches considered above.

The Functional Approaches

The general notion underlying the functional approaches is that the person's attitude often derives from his own need system rather than from information about the targets of the attitude. In the classic authoritarian personality syndrome (Adorno, Frenkel-Brunswik, Levinson, & Sanford, 1950), for example, some cases of antisemitism and other anti-minority attitudes are attributed to the person's having resolved a difficult hostility-to-father component of the Oedipal situation by a reaction formation such that he idealizes authority figures and in-groups and derogates the out-groups of his society. This functional, ego-service approach has been utilized by Smith, Bruner, and White (1956), DiVesta (DiVesta & Merwin, 1960; Woodruff & DiVesta, 1948) and especially by the Michigan group of Katz, Sarnoff, Stotland, McClintock, etc. Helen Peak (1955) and her group, who use the attitude-instrumentality-goal approach, can also be considered functional theorists.

Katz (1960; Katz & Stotland, 1959) reviewed various functions of attitudes, such as the expressive, instrumental, etc. However, the approach has yielded the richest personality interactions for influenceability in the case of ego-defensive functions. If attitudes are maintained in defense of one's ego, then the strategy for changing a person's attitude of, say, hostility to other ethnic groups should not be to provide the person with new, favorable information about that disliked group, as would be prescribed by the learning theory approach. Rather, the functionalist would predict that the attitude would most effectively be changed by altering its perceived utility for serving the person's psychological need. For example, Stotland, Katz, and Patchen (1959) have used the "self-insight" approach of presenting case history material to the prejudiced person to allow him (at least over time) to gain insight into the unflattering dynamics of his own prejudice, so as to produce a lowering (or at least a redirection of) this hostility. The personality implications of this approach to influenceability are rather obvious. One theoretically interesting but empirically questionable (Stotland & Patchen, 1961) derivation is the Michigan group's prediction that the self-insight approach will produce the most attitude change in persons with intermediate degrees of ego-defensiveness. In a later section of this chapter on the "combinatory" principle we consider in detail the conditions for such nonmonotonic relationships between personality and influenceability.

To recapitulate, the four theoretical approaches to attitude change discussed here are not logically distinct or mutually exclusive in their predictions. Rather, they constitute what we consider to be the four general notions from which attitude researchers draw heuristic inspiration in formulating hypotheses about personality correlates of influenceability. We would not urge that one approach is basically better than the others. Different researchers seem to resonate with different theories. Since creativity tends to be in short supply, the doctrinaire insistence that all march to the same drummer seems unwise.

From such diverse points of departure, several decades of attitude researchers have been accumulating a body of empirical results regarding personality-influenceability relationships. In the next section we shall educe from these results, without regard for the theoretical formulations that inspired them, six general principles about personality-influenceability relationships that we feel are the most useful generalizations to be derived from the existing body of theory and findings.

GENERAL PRINCIPLES UNDERLYING PERSONALITY-INFLUENCEABILITY RELATIONSHIPS

Six principles serve to summarize the considerations to which we wish to call attention in our analysis of obtained personality-influenceability interrelations. In outline they are as follows:

1. *The mediational principle*—Opinion change is not a direct response but the net outcome of a chain of behavioral steps. As a minimum it requires (a) adequate reception (through attention and comprehension) of the persuasive message; and (b) yielding to what is comprehended. The mediational role of reception is often overlooked, while that of yielding is overemphasized.

2. *The combinatory principle*—While each of the two behavioral steps (receptivity to the content of the persuasive message and tendency to yield to what is received) is positively related to influenceability, the relation of a given personality variable to one of these steps is often quite different from its relationship to the other. Hence its net relationship to the resultant influenceability can be complex and even nonmonotonic.

3. *The situational-weighting principle*—The relative importance of receptivity and of yieldingness in determining net influenceability will vary from situation to situation. Consequently, the relationship between a personality characteristic and influenceability will vary from situation to situation in a predictable way in accordance with these relative weights.

4. *The confounded-variable principle*—There tend to be cross-individual regularities in personality structure such that one trait tends to be associated with others. Hence an adequate prediction of how a personality variable will be related to influenceability requires that we consider its relation to other personality variables and the relations of these others to the two mediators of influenceability. It follows that influenceability may be differently related to a personality variable depending on whether the latter is varied by experimental manipulation to produce different acute levels or whether we take the subjects at their different chronic levels in a correlational study.

5. *The interaction principle*—In any social situation, personality factors are only one of several classes of relevant independent variables. It is highly likely that the personality factors will interact with variables of other classes (source, message, etc.) in affecting influenceability. Hence, although we should seek the most general relationships in mapping the domain of personality-influenceability interrelations, it is likely that these will tend to be interaction effects, rather than condition-free main effects of single personality variables. The relationship of a given personality characteristic to influenceability may change in size and even in direction as other aspects of the communication situation change.

6. *The compensation principle*—There is an optimal level of influenceability for ade-

quate adaptation to the human environment. Hence, it is implied by an adaptivity approach that there will tend to be compensatory mechanisms, such that a characteristic which tends in some ways to make an individual extremely open (or opaque) to influence will tend in other ways to have the reverse effect, resulting in a dynamic equilibrium. The pervasiveness of nonmonotonic relationships between personality and influenceability is one of the results.

Each of these six principles is in accord with common sense as well as congruent with obtained experimental results in its derivations. Yet, while they are rather obvious when our attention is called to them, the principles themselves and particularly some of their implications have often been overlooked, with the result that the various experimental results regarding influenceability relationships often seem implausible or mutually contradictory. The implications of these principles will become clearer when we explicate them in more detail in the sections that follow.

Principle 1: Persuasion as a Mediated Behavior

Our first principle states that opinion change is not a simple direct response but the residual outcome of a series of behavioral steps. The Yale group (Hovland, Janis, & Kelley, 1953) has long advocated a three-step process analysis of the behavior leading to opinion change: (a) attention to the communication, (b) comprehension of its contents, and (c) yielding to what is comprehended. Two further steps might be added: (d) retention of the position agreed with, and (e) action in accordance with the retained agreement, constituting in all a five-step stochastic process.

Researchers frequently overlook the fact that a personality characteristic could have an effect on influenceability by affecting any of the five links in the chain. Probably the error most frequently committed in this regard is overemphasis on the third step of the chain. This overemphasis results in inferring erroneously that a given personality variable will be related to influenceability simply insofar as it involves a tendency to yield to perceived interpersonal pressure. Many empirically determined relationships remain incomprehensible when viewed from this narrow perspective. As we shall discuss later, a given personality variable may make the person influenceable by being associated with a tendency to yield; but it may all the same protect him from persuasion at some other point in the chain (for example, by making him inattentive to the influencing message). The resultant multiple-mediated relationship between the personality variable and influenceability may be quite complex, as is illustrated below in our discussion of the combinatory principle.

It will not be necessary to analyze personality-influenceability relations in terms of the full five-step behavioral chain in order to demonstrate the necessity and utility of the multiple-process principle. Our first simplification will be to disregard the last two steps, retention and action. Considerable work has been done recently on the fourth step, retention of induced opinion change (McGuire, 1962; Papageorgis, 1963; Watts & McGuire, 1964), revealing the operation of complex psychodynamics in addition to passive forgetting. It seems highly likely, therefore, that personality factors affect this link in the chain. Likewise, there has been a considerable resurgence recently of the theoretical interest in the fifth step, as it involves the relationship between verbalized opinion change and gross overt action (Fishbein, 1966; Festinger, 1964a). This interest has been stirred by dissonance theorists (Festinger, 1957, 1964b; Brehm & Cohen, 1962) and by those working in the marketing and advertising areas (Howard, 1963; Steward, 1964). But since space is limited and since the interest in these topics has as yet resulted in only a little empirical research on influenceability correlates (Cohen, 1957; Steiner & Johnson, 1963; Steiner, 1960; Aronson & Festinger, 1958), we shall forego further discussion of the last two steps in this chapter. We shall make a second simplification of the behavioral chain by combining the first two steps, attention and comprehension, into one general step which we shall call "reception." Perhaps it will eventually become convenient to distinguish between the attention and comprehension steps, but at present it seems more economical to combine the two into a composite reception step.

We are left here with an oversimplified, two-step analysis of the behavioral process in social influence: reception of the message content and yielding to what is comprehended. Impoverished as it is, this analysis suffices for the exposition of our first principle. Understanding the relationship between personality and influenceability requires that we analyze the personality variable's effect on receptivity as well as on yieldingness (Walters & Parke, 1964). The reception mediator can be operationally defined and measured directly by a recall or recognition test of retention of the contents of the persuasive message. The person's yielding score can be measured by a covariance analysis that determines the discrepancy of his obtained opinion change from his predicted opinion change (predicted on the basis of his retention score and the overall correlation between retention and opinion change). The importance of considering the reception mediator in addition to the yielding mediator can be illustrated by reviewing the obtained results regarding the influenceability relationships of two of the most commonly studied dimensions of individual differences, intelligence and anxiety.

Intelligence and the Two Steps to Persuasion

If we analyzed the relationship between intelligence and influenceability simply in terms of the yielding mediator, the obtained results would be hard to explain. Looked at from this narrow point of view, one would expect a negative relationship between intelligence and influenceability. It would seem that the more intelligent the person, the more confidence he would have in his own opinion, the greater facility he would have in marshalling counterarguments against a persuasive attack, the greater his acumen in recognizing and criticizing flaws in the attacking arguments. All of these plausible assumptions imply that the more intelligent person would be more resistant to social influence, in that he would be less yielding to what he attended to and comprehended of the persuasive communication.

According to the multiple-mediator principle, however, the foregoing analysis is not adequate. We must also consider how intelligence is related to the reception mediator. While intelligence tends to protect the person from influence by making him less yielding to what he receives of the message, it with equal plausibility makes him more vulnerable to influence insofar as the initial reception steps of attention and comprehension are concerned. The more intelligent person will tend to be more interested in outside messages, have a longer attention span, be better able to comprehend its viewpoint, etc. Hence, intelligence could be positively or negatively related to influenceability depending on whether reception or yielding was the more important contributor to opinion-change variance in a given situation. We shall consider in connection with our third principle what situational characteristics are likely to make the relationship go in one direction or the other.

Actual findings indicate a negative relation between intelligence and influenceability in suggestion (Weitzenhoffer, 1953; Stukát, 1958) and conformity (Crutchfield, 1955) situations, both of which minimize the problem of reception by using a very simple, repetitively presented message. Even in suggestion situations, however, we find a curvilinear relationship if we span very low levels of intelligence. For example, there tends to be a nonmonotonic relation between age of children and suggestibility, with the peak suggestibility occurring at about 9 to 12 years (Barber & Calverly, 1963; Hilgard, 1965). Within the mentally deficient range, Sternlicht and Wanderer (1963) find a positive relation between mental age (or IQ) and suggestibility. On the other hand, where reception is made more of a problem, a positive relationship was found between intelligence and persuasion. For example, years of education were found to be positively related to the persuasive impact of indoctrination films shown to U.S. Army personnel in World War II (Hovland, Lumsdaine, & Sheffield, 1949, pp. 160 ff.). The most typical finding in a wider range of studies has been the absence of any overall significant relationship in either direction between intelligence and influenceability (Murphy, Murphy, & Newcomb, 1937, p. 930; Hovland, Janis, & Kelley, 1953, pp. 181–184; Janis & Hovland, 1959, Chs. 3, 4, 6, 9). There are, then, findings in some experiments of a positive relationship, in others of a negative, and in many of no appreciable relationship at all. One decision would be to accept the null hypothesis. However, it seems implausible that no relationship exists between two variables so basic as intelligence and influenceability. This mediational principle (and other principles discussed in this chapter) indicates some of the reasons why underlying relationships might exist and yet be obscured by mutual cancellations and interactions. These principles also indicate the experimental designs needed to test adequately for such underlying relationships.

Anxiety and the Two Steps to Persuasion

In specifying the relationship of anxiety to influenceability we meet with the same complexities as in the case of intelligence and influenceability, but with the directions of the complexities to a large extent reversed. If we commit the usual oversimplification of analyzing only the role of yielding as a mediator of the relationship, we would expect influenceability to be a positive function of anxiety. From this limited perspective, we would predict that, on the basis of the anxious person's being insecure, lacking in self-confidence, etc., he will be prone to yield to such social influence inductions as he received.

But the behavioral-chain principle requires us to consider also how anxiety would be related to the first step, receptivity. An anxious person would tend also to be withdrawn and preoccupied with his own troubles, little inclined to attend to outside communications, and sufficiently distracted by his personal problems so as to have difficulty in fully attending to and comprehending positions and arguments presented in the message (Janis, 1954; Buss, 1962). These "failings" would help to protect him from being influenced particularly when complex arguments are used. Hence, when we recognize opinion change as the outcome of a multistep process, we are led to the prediction that it may be negatively related to anxiety (to the extent that the reception mediator is involved) or positively related (to the extent that the yielding mediator is involved).

This analysis of the complexities involved in the anxiety-influenceability relationship already involves a major oversimplification. To enhance the contrast with intelligence, we are postulating a negative relation between anxiety and the reception mediator. In so doing we are considering anxiety only in its cue aspect, as an elicitor of task-interfering responses. The two-factor theory of anxiety postulates that anxiety also has drive value (Lazarus, Deese, & Osler, 1952; Brown, 1961) which would enhance learning, particularly for otherwise undermotivated subjects (e.g., subjects quite uninterested in the issues or in the contents of the persuasive message). According to this theory, our postulation of a negative relation between anxiety and the reception mediator would obtain only in the relatively high ranges of anxiety; over the full range of anxiety the relationship would be nonmonotonic (see the discussion on the combinatory principle, below) with an intermediate level of anxiety being optimal for reception. Hence the anxiety-influenceability relationship would be the outcome of a nonmonotonic relationship superimposed on a monotonically increasing relationship. It may also be necessary to consider still another effect involved with anxiety: the possibility that with increasing levels of induced anxiety, there will be an increase in hostility to the communicator (at least, when he is the source of the anxiety) and this hostility would furnish resistance to persuasion (Janis & Terwilliger, 1962). Furthermore, in addition to being a drive, anxiety is also a negative reinforcement (Freud, 1936). If the persuasive message uses fear-arousing appeals, the evoked anxiety would tend to punish any comprehension of the message. (It would be wise in these studies to adhere more closely to Freud's distinction between fear and anxiety (Sarnoff & Zimbardo, 1961; Janis & Leventhal, this volume, Ch. 22).)

The empirical results are, as might be expected, rather confusing. One study by Janis (1954) showed that students chronically high on neurotic anxiety symptoms were less persuasible than those chronically low, but his later studies have showed no relationship (Janis & Field, 1959b), or even the opposite relationship of other forms of anxiety (test and social) to persuasibility (Janis, 1955). Similarly confusing results were obtained in studies using experimental manipulation of anxiety levels. Janis and Feshbach (1954) found a negative relationship between anxiety arousal and opinion change, and Haefner (1956), Goldstein (1959), Kegeles (1963), and De Wolfe and Governale (1964) found some slight evidence in the same direction; Moltz and Thistlethwaite (1955) found no significant difference, while Berkowitz and Cottingham (1960), Insko, Arkoff, and Insko (1965), Leventhal and Niles (1964), and Leventhal, Singer, and Jones (1965) found positive relationships. All in all, the results constitute a remarkable show of impartiality on the part of Nature. The multiprocess, mediational principle leads us to expect and understand this confusion of seemingly contradictory results with influenceability. A similarly great but clarifiable confusion obtains in anxiety-learning studies (Brown, 1961). The next two principles will help us untangle some of the confusion and show when a positive and when a negative relation is likely to emerge.

Principle 2: The Combinatory Principle

The general theoretical situation that we are depicting is one common in the behavioral sciences: the independent variable (here, a personality characteristic) is related to the dependent variable (influenceability) through the mediation of two intervening variables (receptivity and yieldingness). Four primary relationships are therefore involved: the relationships of the personality variable to receptivity and yieldingness, and the relationships of receptivity and yieldingness to influenceability. The resultant relationship between personality and influenceability which we are trying to define is the outcome of these four. Our second principle, here under discussion, specifies what this resultant relationship will be in terms of the characteristics of the four mediating relationships.

The General Equation

We have already postulated in our first principle that opinion change is a positive function of reception and of yielding. The person changes insofar as he effectively receives the message and yields to the point received. The principle can be summed up in the following equation:

$$Pr\ (o) = Pr\ (\mathrm{R}) \times Pr\ (\mathrm{Y}) \times Pr\ (K) \quad [1]$$

where $Pr\,(o)$ represents the probability of opinion change; $Pr\,(R)$ the probability of effective reception; and $Pr(Y)$, the probability of yielding to what is received; and $Pr(K)$ a residual factor representing the probability of the other processes (retention, etc.) that effect opinion change but need not concern us in this exposition. (In the subsequent discussion we shall ignore this residual factor on the assumption that it is not consistently related to the personality characteristic that serves as the independent variable in the given study and that we aspire only to predict variations in $Pr(o)$, rather than its absolute level. (This "everything else equal" assumption is, of course, always dangerous.)

To simplify and generalize our formulations as regards scales and parameters, we have represented the variables as being measured in terms of their probabilities of reaching a given level. We can then trace back the relationship to the personality (individual difference) variable, I, by defining reception and yielding mediators in terms of this variable as follows:

$$Pr(R) = f(I) \quad [2]$$
$$Pr(Y) = F(I) \quad [3]$$

Whence, by substitution in [1] we obtain:

$$Pr(o) = f(I) \times F(I) \times Pr(K) \quad [4]$$

In discussing principle 1, we cautioned against the oversimplification of defining opinion change, $Pr(o)$, simply in terms of yielding, that is of $F(I)$ or $Pr(Y)$. Now, in this discussion of principle 2, we are trying to specify in what ways the $Pr(o)$ function is made more complex due to its being affected, not simply by $F(I)$ but by the combination of reception, $f(I)$, and yielding, $F(I)$.

Our discussion will be more concrete if we postulate the specific shapes of the mediator functions, $f(I)$ and $F(I)$. We shall assume that each is a monotonic, negatively accelerated function. That is, receptivity and yielding each increases (or decreases) continuously as the individual-difference variable, I, increases, but the increment in $Pr(R)$ and $Pr(Y)$ grows smaller for equal scale steps in I as we move up the I scale, so that reception and yielding tend to level off near asymptotes as I increases. To be more specific still, we shall say these functions are of the exponential families. It might seem rather arbitrary to make such specific assumptions, but it has several advantages. Choice of any specific type of relationship allows us to present a specific solution for at least that type. The exponential curve seems a particularly useful choice, since such a "growth" curve has proved very useful in describing biological and psychological relations. We seem naturally prone to adopt scales in measuring psychological variables that seem to yield exponential functions (McGuire, 1961). In fact, Sidman (1952) and Bakan (1954) have suggested that our group data tend to yield these exponential curves even when the individual curves show different shapes. A final excuse for choosing exponential (or any other) specific relationships for discussion is that our psychological scales are rather arbitrary in any case and, by a suitable scale transformation, we can always convert one obtained relationship to another. Hence, we shall derive specific solutions for the case where reception and yielding are each a negatively-accelerated, exponential function of our individual difference variable, and opinion change therefore is the product of two exponential curves.

Some Exponential Cases

Within these general specifications, there are two general classes into which the $Pr(o) = f(I) \times F(I)$ situation falls: one is the simple case where these two functions have the same sign; the other where they have opposite signs, i.e., one mediator increases and the other decreases as the personality variable, I, increases. We shall confine our discussion to the latter, more complex case for two reasons: this case is more interesting and it is more common. The interest derives from the fact that (as shown below) when the signs are different, influenceability tends to be a nonmonotonic function of the personality variable, and nonmonotonic relations are always interesting, if only because when not recognized they are likely to produce misleading results. The commonness may arise from considerations presented in our discussion of principle 6; the fact of the commonness of this nonmonotonic case is presented throughout the chapter. The simpler case, where both functions have the same sign, can in any case be easily derived from the following discussion of the more complex, opposite-sign situation.

Both of the variables discussed in the previous section, intelligence and anxiety, fit the opposite-sign paradigm, but as indicated above, the case with anxiety is probably more complex than represented. Hence, we shall use intelligence as our example to point out that when the personality variable has opposite effects on the two mediators, reception and yielding, it will tend to be nonmonotonically related to influenceability.

Figure 1 describes the case for intelligence where $f(I)$ is positive (i.e., the greater the person's intelligence, the better his attention to and comprehension of persuasive messages) and $F(I)$ is negative (i.e., the more intelligent, the smaller his proneness to yield). As discussed above, we define these relationships as negatively-accelerated exponential:

$$Pr(R) = f(I) = a - be^{-iI} \quad [5]$$
$$Pr(Y) = F(I) = c + de^{-jI} \quad [6]$$

where $Pr(R)$ stands for probability of reception, $Pr(Y)$ for probability of yielding, and I for intelligence (scaled so as to yield

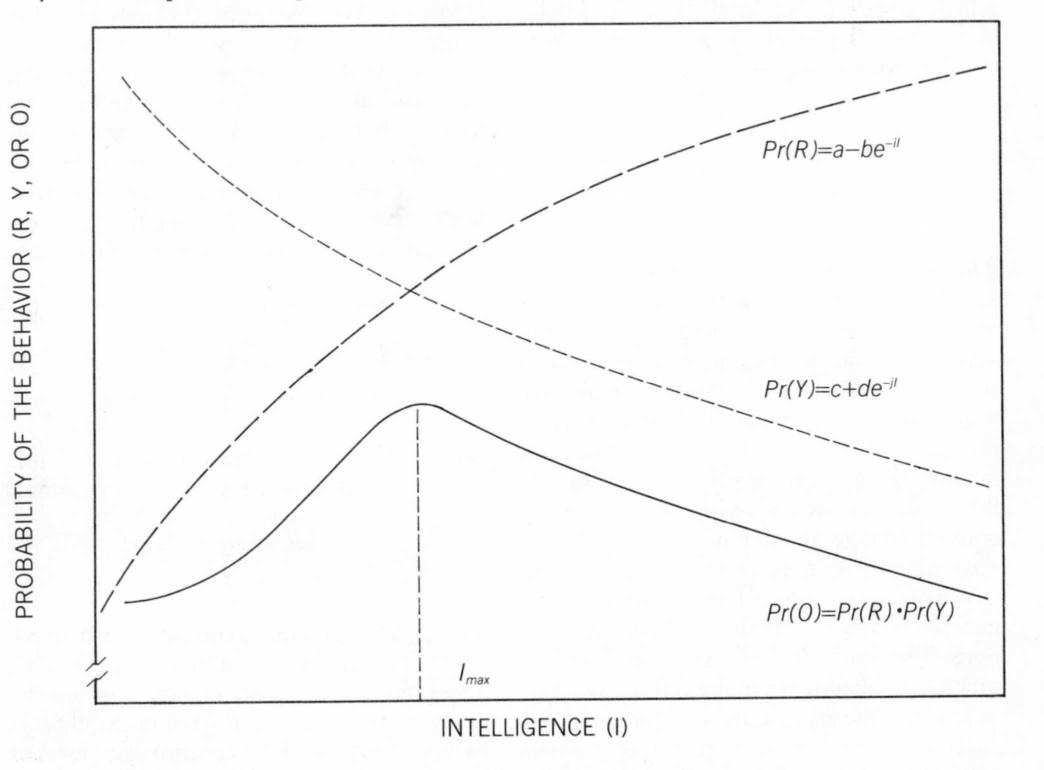

Figure 1. Nonmonotonic relation between a personality variable and influenceability due to the personality variable's having opposite effects on the two mediators, reception and yielding.

exponential functions for f and F), e is the natural logarithmetic base, and the other letters are the usual parameters of an exponential function. By substitution (and ignoring the $Pr(K)$ factor), the equation for the probability of opinion change becomes:

$$Pr(o) = (a - be^{-iI})\,(c + de^{-jI}) \quad [7]$$

It can be shown, rather laboriously, that $Pr(o)$ will be a nonmonotonic function of I, with maximum persuasion occurring at intermediate levels of intelligence, under a wide range of values of the parameters, particularly when $j \leq i$ (but even sometimes for $j > i$, if the values of the other parameters have certain relationships to one another). The general solution involves differentiating the above $Pr(o)$ expression with respect to intelligence level, I, setting the first derivative equal to zero and solving for I_{max}, which gives the "optimal" level of intelligence, i.e., the level at which maximum opinion change occurs.

$$I_{max} = \frac{ln\left[\frac{jd\,(a - be^{-iI})}{ib\,(c + de^{-jI})}\right]}{j - i} \quad [8]$$

The problem then becomes one of specifying the conditions (with respect to the parameters) which will yield an I_{max} value between 0 and ∞, i.e., with a finite positive value. Where such solutions exist, we shall have a nonmonotonic function such that there is a finite level of intelligence, greater than 0, at which maximum influenceability occurs, with a decline in opinion change as intelligence varies either upwards or down from this optimal level.

We can specify some fairly common parametric conditions which yield simple solutions. For example, our equation becomes much simplified if we make certain assumptions about the asymptotic and starting-point parameters, i.e., if we set limits on the values of a, b, c, and d. Specifically, we may assume that both functions traverse the whole probability interval, 0.00 to 1.00. Thus, we assume that if the person is dumb enough (and at least if his intelligence is 0) there is practically no possibility that he will effectively attend to and comprehend the message at some specified level; while if smart enough (and at least if his intelligence is infinite), such a level of reception is practically certain. Conversely with $Pr(Y)$, we assume that if the person is dumb enough, he is so gullible as to be practically certain to be influenced by what he attends to and comprehends, and if smart enough, practically certain to be uninfluenced by it. (This last assumption might seem unwarranted, but we regard it as tenable, because if the person were infinitely intelligent he would recognize any false argument as such and hence be uninfluenced by it, while any true argument he would have already considered and hence adjusted his opinion accordingly before he even received the message, and hence the message would produce no change. Perhaps, however, we had best leave the study of functioning at these extremely high levels of intelligence to the theologian rather than the psychologist.)

Under these assumptions that the functions traverse the whole range between 0.00 and 1.00, the above equations simplify to:

$$Pr(R) = f(I) = 1 - e^{-iI} \quad [9]$$

$$Pr(Y) = F(I) = e^{-jI} \quad [10]$$

$$Pr(o) = e^{-jI}(1 - e^{-iI}) \quad [11]$$

If we differentiate with respect to I this simplified expression for $Pr(o)$, we obtain:

$$I_{max} = \frac{ln(j + i) - ln(j)}{i} \quad [12]$$

for the level of intelligence at which maximum influenceability occurs. We see that under these conditions, the relationship between intelligence and influenceability is nonmonotonic with an intermediate level of intelligence optimal for opinion change. Should the scales be chosen so that $i = j$, that is, with the reception and yielding varying at the same rate as a function of intelligence, we get a further simplification:

$$I_{max} = \frac{ln2}{j} = 0.693\, j^{-1} \qquad [13]$$

where optimal intelligence depends on a single parameter, j, the growth rate of the mediator functions.

Empirical Evidence for the Nonmonotonic Case

We have discussed the combinatory principle in terms of progressively more stringent assumptions, producing cases capable of increasingly simpler solutions but having more and more narrow applicability. In the discussion of the principles that follow we shall go back to a more general case. For example, in our discussion of the situational-weighting principle which is taken up in the next section, we shall deal with how certain definable aspects of the persuasion situation affect all of the parameters in equation 7. Throughout the chapter we shall, however, be retaining the assumption that the personality variable affects the two mediators in opposite directions, thus tending to yield nonmonotonic relations between the personality variable, considered over its full range, and influenceability. Some broad theoretical considerations that would lead us to expect the wide empirical validity of this case are discussed in later sections, particularly in connection with the sixth "dynamic equilibrium" principle.

Aside from this question of why it is so, there is widespread empirical evidence that personality variables do in fact tend to be nonmonotonically related to influenceability. Indeed, considering that in most studies the personality characteristic varies over a rather narrow range (e.g., within the range of natural variation among college sophomores or as manipulated by rather mild laboratory inductions), it is surprising that so many nonmonotonic relations have been detected in experiments, even granting that over the full range of variation found in the population the relationship is nonmonotonic. Nonmonotonic effects seem particularly ubiquitous if we allow either influenceability or the personality variable to be a function of the other. One illustrative study by Appley and Moeller (1963) illustrates the ubiquity of nonmonotonic relationships between personality characteristics and influenceability. They obtained conformity scores for 41 college women (freshmen) in terms of the number of times they were influenced by a unanimously wrong majority of peers in an Asch-type (1956) situation. Scores were obtained for all subjects on 38 personality characteristics from three standardized self-report inventories: the Edwards (1954) EPPS, Gough's (1957) CPI, and Gordon's (1956) PP.

To measure the relationship between the personality variables and influenceability they partitioned their sample of 41 subjects into three groups: high, middle, and low conformers. They computed the mean scores of each of these three subgroups on each of the 38 personality variables. On only 5 of the 38 variables was a monotonic relation found. On 33 of the 38, the high and low subgroups lay on the same side of the middle personality group as regards conformity. These results do not, of course, constitute 38 independent tests, since the personality characteristics measured by these standardized inventories are far from orthogonal (Peterson, 1965). However, the results are impressive when we consider the overwhelming ratio of nonmonotonic effects despite the homogeneity of the sample.

These nonmonotonic effects are by no means confined to Appley and Moeller's female college students. Even confining ourselves to the single variable of self-esteem (which would operate much like the intelligence variable used as our example, above), recent studies can be cited showing nonmonotonic relationships between this personality variable and persuasibility in a wide variety of subjects and situations.

Gelfand (1962) showed such a relationship in fifth-grade boys and girls; Harvey and Consalvi (1960) in delinquent boys in a state training school; Cox and Bauer (1964) in middle-aged women belonging to a Catholic ladies' sodality; Silverman (1964) in elderly male residents in a VA domiciliary. We may cite, as a final example, one that involves an extremely different population and situation from the above, namely the individual-difference correlates of compliance with their Chinese captors of American prisoners during the Korean War (Segal, 1956, 1957; Schein, Hill, Williams, & Lubin, 1957). The over 3,000 U.S. Army repatriates were divided into three groups in terms of resistance to their captors' demands: collaborators (15 per cent of total) who were judged to have yielded to a degree that warranted disciplinary action by the U.S. Army upon release; the "neutrals" (80 per cent) who yielded only slightly or on whom there was no strong evidence one way or the other; and the resisters (5 per cent) who resisted to a degree that called for U.S. Army commendation after their release. These three groups were compared on an exhaustive series of demographic, biographical, and test variables. Although the differences were small, with variable after variable (age, education, length of service, information, vocabulary, comprehension, psychopathy, anxiety, marriage rates, participation in sports, etc.) the small differences were such that the two extreme groups, collaborators and resisters, tended again and again to be both on the same side of the neutrals, so that the overall relationship was nonmonotonic.

One interim conclusion that may be drawn at this point is that forms of analysis which are insensitive to nonmonotonicity (e.g., Pearson correlations, two-group designs subjected to chi-square or analysis of variance) are likely to be misleading in this area of research. Proper experimental design calls for many levels spread over a wide range on the independent (personality) variable, and the inferential statistics should involve analyses that provide a check of higher order trend components. We shall return to these methodological implications later in this chapter.

Principle 3: Situational Weighting

As was pointed out in the previous section, we frequently deal with personality variables whose relationship to influenceability is mediated by two processes that work in opposite directions. For example, intelligence was in the previous section analyzed as being positively related to influenceability via the reception mediator and negatively via the yielding mediator. Such a situation tends to result in a mutual cancellation. Hence, unless we make further specifications, no empirical outcome could refute the theoretical formulation. A finding of a positive, negative, or nonmonotonic relationship (or of no relationship at all) could be accounted for by the theory, provided that we are allowed complete freedom in choice of parameters.

The way out of this embarrassing richness of predictions—which tends to lose our theory its scientific status, since no empirical outcome could disconfirm it—is provided by the present principle. This situational-weighting principle specifies that we are not free to make any assumption we please about the importance of the mediators in a given situation. The weights of the mediators will tend to vary from situation to situation in predictable ways: different social influence situations vary greatly in the absolute and relative strains they put on reception and yielding. By specifying the weightings of these mediators, we can predict for a specific situation whether the resultant personality-influenceability relationship will be positive or negative. This predicted outcome depends on the relative contribution of the two mediators, reception and yielding, to the total opinion-change variance in the given situation. Where we cannot make absolute predictions about a given situation, it is often possible to make predictions about the difference between situations. To the extent that the situation allows considerable individual difference in attention and comprehension of the message, then the personality-receptivity relation is likely to be more important in mediating how the personality variable will be related to influenceability. To the extent that there is likely to be wide individual difference in yielding to whatever is comprehended, then the personality variable's relation to the yielding mediator is likely to be more important.

Need for Situational Analyses

It should in principle be possible by factor analyzing a series of social influence situations to determine each situation's loadings on a receptivity factor and a yielding factor. We could then define the standardized opinion change score, Z_{si}, of individual i in situation s by the equation:

$$Z_{si} = a_{sr} Z_{ri} + a_{sy} Z_{yi} \qquad [14]$$

where a_{sr} and a_{sy} would be the situation's loadings on the receptivity and yielding factors, and Z_{ri} and Z_{yi} the individual's standard factor scores on these two processes. The latter two scores would, in turn, depend on the individual's score on the personality variable and the personality variable's relation to the two mediators. By an unbiased ecological sampling of social influence situations, it seems reasonable to look for factors of reception and yielding that would approximate orthogonality. If, however, the two processes turn out to be oblique, then the suitable adjustment of the specification equations for their intercorrelation can easily be made. Equation 14 is obviously oversimplified and should be extended by adding additional terms to include other process factors (retention, etc.) that mediate influenceability and that are affected by the personality variable in question. Terms should also be added to deal with the unique factor variance and the unreliable variance.

To map out the personality-influenceability area adequately, we would need several matrices of scores. One matrix would give the factor loadings of a column of social influence situations on rows of mediation processes (reception, yielding, retention, action, etc.). A second matrix would give the weightings for columns of mediating processes on rows of personality variables. Each of these matrices would be discouragingly long if we included every situation and every personality variable that has received research attention. Fortunately, much work has been done already on reducing personality space to a few factors which together account for much of the obtained individual difference variance. Indeed, Peterson's (1965) analyses suggest that most of the measured variance on self-report inventories can be accounted for by as few as two factors. A similar paring down of influence situations is long overdue. There have been many factor analyses of the suggestibility area (e.g., Eysenck & Furneaux, 1945), but only a beginning of such work on conformity situations (Stukát, 1958) and persuasibility situations (Janis & Field, 1959a). Ideally, a group of subjects on whom we have multiple personality measures should be put through a wide range of influence situations, and we should obtain measures for each subject in each situation, not only of opinion change but also of the mediators, reception and yielding.

Situational Differences in Receptivity Demands

Even before formal empirical analyses of social influence situations (like the one just suggested) have been carried out, it is possible to hazard an a priori ordering in regard to loadings on reception and yielding of some of the commonly studied situations. Concerning reception loadings, the influence messages used in some situations are so obvious (and in others, so subtle) that there would be little individual-difference variance in reception. Other influence situations involve an intermediate level of subtlety and thus would have a high loading on reception variance. At one low variance extreme are the typical suggestibility situations (e.g., the simple and repetitive communications used in body-sway or hypnosis inductions) which put so little strain on attention and comprehension that almost all subjects sufficiently functional to get along in the ordinary environment would be near the asymptote of complete receptivity. In these situations, the effect of the personality variable on receptivity would be of little importance in determining its relation to influenceability. For the normal range of subjects, reception would be practically complete whether the individual was relatively high or low on general attention and comprehension proclivity.

Other influence situations are intermediate in the strain they put on receptivity. For example, persuasion situations using meaningful rational or emotional arguments, such as the World War II indoctrination program of the U.S. Army (Hovland, Lumsdaine, & Sheffield, 1949), political campaign speeches, and much advertising, put a more appreciable demand on attention and comprehension. Hence a wide range of individual differences in reception scores would result. In these situations the effect of the personality variable on reception would be of considerable importance in determining its relation to influenceability.

As a general principle, then, if situations are extremely hard or easy in terms of their strain on the sample's capacity for attention and comprehension, a personality variable will tend to affect influenceability mainly via its relation to yielding. In situations of intermediate difficulty, where there will be a wide range of individual differences in attention and comprehension, the personality variable's effect on influenceability will be determined to a considerable extent by its relation to receptivity as well as to yielding.

These various situations can be illustrated for the case where self-esteem is the personality variable. Let us make the reasonable assumption that self-esteem is negatively related to yielding: the higher the individual's self-esteem, the less (due to self-confidence, etc.) he will yield to influence attempts that he has effectively received at a given level. Hence, considered only as regards its relation to yielding, self-esteem would tend to have a monotonically decreasing relation to influenceability. We shall also assume that self-esteem is positively related to attention and comprehension, since lack of self-esteem is usually associated with distractibility, lack of intelligence, and social withdrawal, all of which tend to insulate the person from being influenced. Hence, if receptivity alone were considered, self-esteem would have a monotonically increasing relation to opinion change. In situations where both receptivity and yielding must be considered, then self-esteem would be nonmonotonically related to opinion change. Influenceability would first increase and then decrease as our range of individuals varied from low to high in self-esteem.

These relationships are illustrated in Figure 2 for the three situations discussed above: where the reception is easy, moderate, or hard. The strains on yielding are assumed to be intermediate and constant across the three illustrative situations. In simple suggestibility situations (e.g., Stukát, 1958) there would be high overall compliance and it would show a continuously decreasing relationship to self-esteem. In persuasion situations using very subtle, complex appeals (McGuire, 1960b; Stotland, Katz, & Patchen, 1959), the immediate overall persuasive impact would be small, and such as it is, it also would show a continuous decrease as self-esteem increased. In the more typical mass media advertising and face-to-face personal influence persuasion situations (Hovland, Lumsdaine, & Shef-

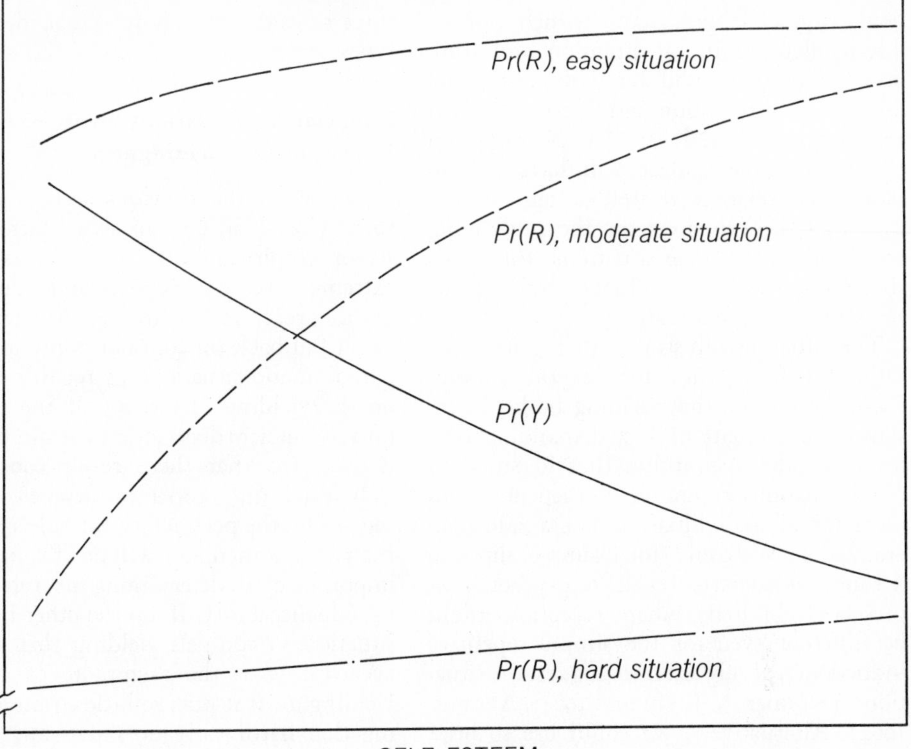

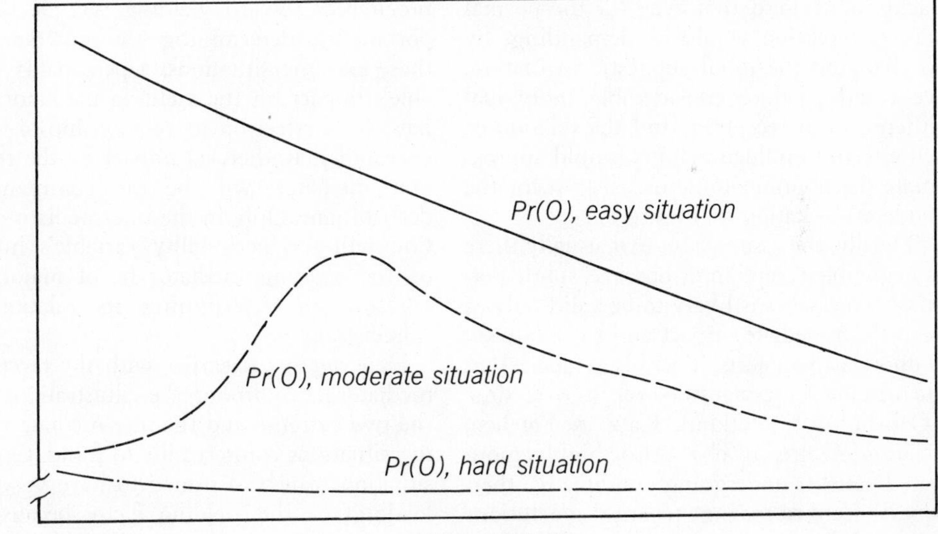

Figure 2. Effects of situational differences in comprehension difficulty on the resultant personality-influenceability relationship. Figure 2a: Three levels of reception difficulty as they affect the mediators (reception and yielding). Figure 2b: The three levels as they affect the resultant influenceability measure (opinion change).

field, 1949; Klapper, 1961) which put an intermediate strain on attention and comprehension, there will be wide individual differences in reception and hence there will be an intermediate level of overall opinion change and the impact will have a nonmonotonic relation to self-esteem. Figure 2a shows the functions for the underlying mediators in the three situations; Figure 2b shows the resultant influenceability functions in the three situations.

The situations illustrated in Figure 2 are rather artificial ones for several reasons. First, the proviso that yielding be held constant across situations is a demanding one. Secondly, the assumption that in suggestibility situations, reception is practically complete for all individuals is not a safe generalization. We could, for example, dip into a range of subjects (such as psychotics or preschool children) where reception might be different even for the simple repetitive induction typically used in suggestion situations (Kramer & Brennan, 1964; Abrams, 1964). Alternatively, we could use so brief an induction, or one sufficiently obscured by background noise, that even for the normal subject reception would be demanding. By so changing the usual suggestion situation, we could produce considerable individual differences in reception, and the relation of self-esteem to influenceability would approximate the nonmonotonic one shown for the moderate situation in Figure 2.

Thirdly, the assumption that usually there is negligible reception of obscure, subtle persuasive messages is likely to be valid only as regards immediate impact and for relatively unmotivated subjects. There is evidence that such indirect messages do seep in over time (Cohen, 1957; Stotland, Katz, & Patchen, 1959; McGuire, 1960b). Also, highly motivated patients undergoing nondirective therapy do seem to manage to draw conclusions from subtle messages. In such modifications of the "hard" situation, the relation of self-esteem to influenceability would also approximate the nonmonotonic one shown in the figure for the moderate situation. The three cases do serve, however, as ideal prototypes.

Situational Variations in Demands on Yieldingness

Just as in the previous section we ventured (in advance of an actual factor analysis of empirical data) to contrast certain extreme situations as to their loadings, a_{sr}, on the reception factor, so here we shall again fall back on common sense to classify paradigmatic situations as regards loadings on the yielding factor, a_{sy}. If the situation puts an intermediate level of strain on yieldingness (so that there result considerable individual differences in degree of yielding), then the personality variable's effect on the yielding mediator will be of considerable importance in determining its relationship to influenceability. If, on the other hand, the situation so compels yielding that virtually everyone is at the asymptote of complete yielding, or if it puts so little strain on yielding that hardly anyone shows any appreciable yielding, then the persons' individual proclivities toward yielding will be unimportant in determining the outcome. In these extreme situations, a personality variable's impact on the yielding mediator will have little effect on its relationship to influenceability. Rather, its impact on the reception mediator will be the commanding determinant. Only in the intermediate situation will the personality variable's impact on the yielding mediator be of major importance in determining its relation to influenceability.

Here again (as earlier with the reception mediator), commonplace illustrations for the two extreme and the intermediate yielding situations come readily to mind. Certain situations can be assumed to have very low loadings on the yielding factor because almost any normal subject will yield virtually completely to the message insofar as he receives it. Several components contribute to such a situation. Let the issue be a technical, matter-of-fact (rather than of-taste) one; let the source be expert and trustworthy; let the arguments be reasonable-sounding and dispassionate; and let the receiver have no strong preconception on the issue. Let us deal, in short, with the typical educational situation, such as is involved when a physics professor teaches the introductory course in his field. The question of the student's yielding to the teacher's position on the content he is trying to communicate hardly arises. We assume that insofar as the message is adequately attended to and comprehended, it will be accepted. In these educational situations, the personality variable's relation to opinion change will be determined almost entirely by its impact on the reception mediator, to the exclusion of its impact on yielding. The a_{sy} coefficient will be so small that the $a_{sy}Z_{yi}$ term will drop out of equation 14.

At the opposite extreme is the situation where a prejudiced nonexpert source gives impassioned arguments regarding a matter of taste on which the receiver has strong initial opinions. In this case we might assume that there would be relatively little yielding by any normal subject. With such a lack of individual differences in yielding, the situational loading on this factor (a_{sy} in equation 14) would once again be negligible. Hence in both of these opposite situations, where the message is extremely compelling or extremely unconvincing, the personality variable's relation to influenceability is mediated almost entirely by the reception process, with the loading on the yielding factor of only negligible importance.

In situations intermediate or mixed as regards the characteristics cited, there would be a wider range of individual differences in yielding. For example, the situation might involve a low credible source using reasonable and dispassionate arguments; or might deal with a matter-of-taste issue but one on which the receiver has no initial opinion; or might use arguments of intermediate reasonableness. These intermediate situations would have higher a_{sy} loadings on the yielding factor; hence the personality variable's relation to influenceability would be determined to an important extent by its relation to the yielding mediator.

Figure 3 summarizes the resultant relationships of our exemplar personality variable, self-esteem, to influenceability in the three types of situations. Figure 3a gives the hypothetical relationships for the underlying processes, and Figure 3b gives the relationships for the resultant persuasion in the three situations. In the very compelling situations, there will be high opinion change, with the amount increasing slightly with increasing self-esteem. In the very unconvincing situations, the amount of change will be small but, such as it is, will again rise monotonically as a function of self-esteem. In the intermediate situations, the relationship will be nonmonotonic, with opinion change at first increasing as a function of self-esteem up to a point and then, as self-esteem continues to increase, persuasibility will decline. We assume in all three cases that the reception variance is at a common intermediate level.

Propaganda vs. Education

This principle 3, dealing with situational weighting, offers a more precise basis for the frequently but vaguely made distinction between education and persuasion (or between information and propaganda). We say that a situation involves education or the communicating of information insofar as $a_{sr} > a_{sy}$, that is, insofar as the situation's loading on reception is large compared to its loading on yielding. Conversely, we say that the situation involves persuasion or propaganda to the extent that $a_{sy} > a_{sr}$. Hence, the relationship between the individual's personality and the amount of change produced in him by a message will vary considerably with the type of situation. In an "educational" situation, for example, self-esteem would tend to be related positively to the communication's impact; while in a "pure propaganda" situation, self-esteem will be negatively related to the impact. The

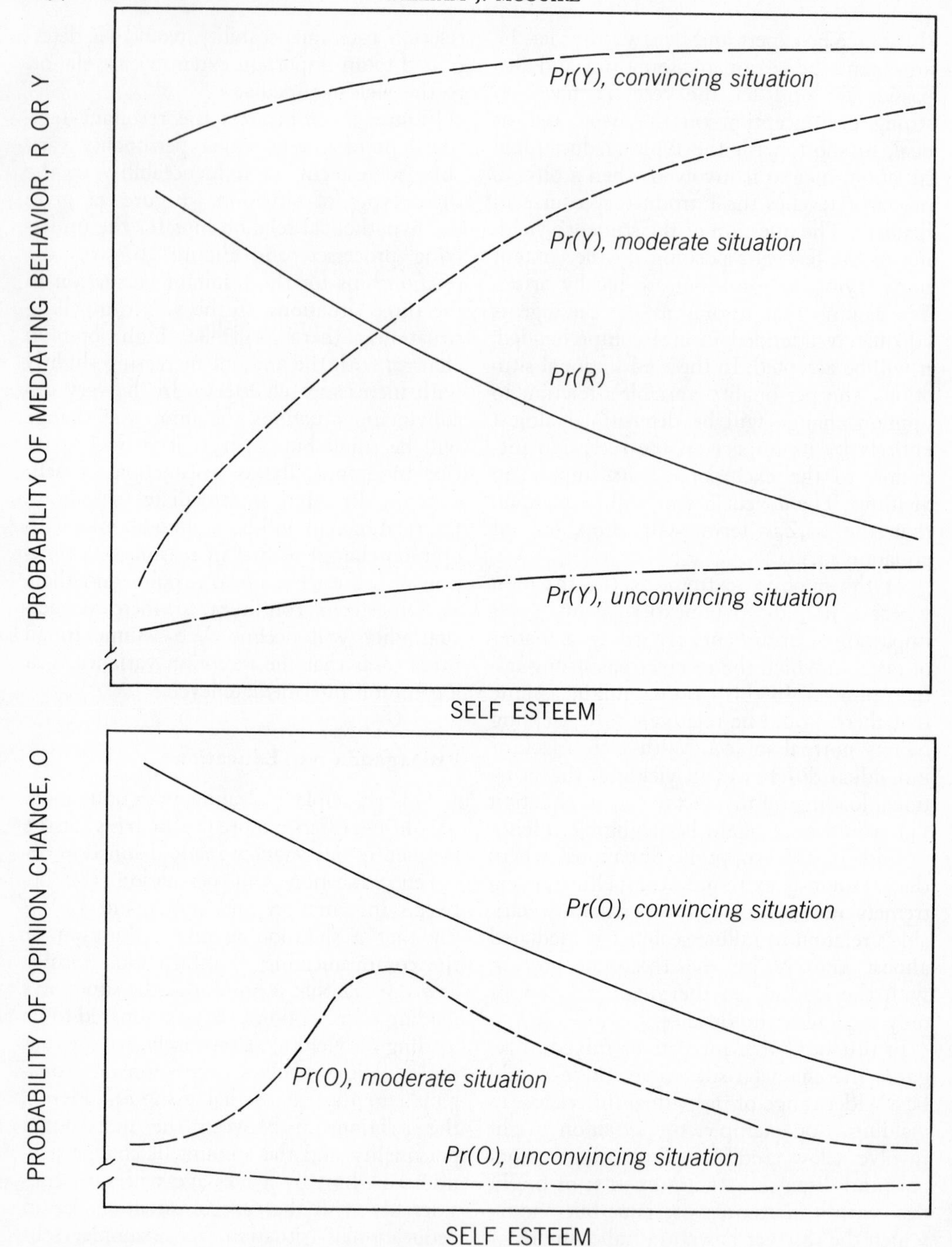

Figure 3. Effects of situational differences in plausibility on the resultant personality-influenceability relationship. Figure 3a: Three levels of plausibility as they affect the mediators (reception and yielding). Figure 3b: The three levels as they affect the resultant influenceability measure (opinion change).

point that is being stressed here is that most of the field and laboratory situations employed to study opinion change involve variance due to mediators, reception and yielding. Hence, it would be very misleading to regard the relationship of the personality variable to influenceability in the typically studied situations as if it were determined solely by the personality variable's impact on yielding.

Principle 4: Confounded Variables

Even when we consider the single personality variable's relation to influenceability in all the complexities introduced by the multiple mediators, we are still dangerously oversimplifying the situation. We must also consider the effects of other personality variables that are correlated with the one we are studying. Personality is more than a series of index numbers giving the individual's standing on orthogonal dimensions. It has a structure such that the personality dimensions we commonly deal with in psychological research (authoritarianism, anxiety, self-esteem, need for approval, etc.) tend to be intercorrelated. We recognize such confounding when the issue is explicitly raised, but all too frequently we try to test a hypothesized relationship between a specific personality variable and some dependent variable like influenceability, while ignoring the invalidity of the hypothesis' hidden assumption that "everything else is equal."

If among our subjects the given personality variable is correlated with other personality variables, then subgroups of subjects selected to represent different levels on the given variable will be contaminated in that the subgroups will tend to differ also with respect to the correlated variables. When the correlated personality variables are themselves related to influenceability (by having an impact on the mediating processes: attention, comprehension, yielding, etc.), any finding regarding our given variable's relations to influenceability must be re-examined in the light of the confounding. Any relationship found between the given variable and influenceability might be spurious, due to the correlated variable's producing the predicted effect on persuasibility; while if we found no relationship, there might actually have been one that was washed out by the correlated variables' having the opposite effect.

Heuristic Value of the Confounding Principle

Most of these problems can be illustrated by considering a conceptualized trait like depression. We might define this characteristic by responses to self-report questionnaire items dealing with lack of energy (at times I just seem to have no energy at all) and negative affect (I sometimes get disgusted with things in general). How will this depression variable relate to influenceability? We saw in connection with the previous principles that to answer this question we would do well to examine the possible impacts of depression on the various mediators of opinion change: attention, comprehension, yielding, etc. By the present "confounding" principle, we are stressing that we must also consider other personality traits with which depression is likely to be correlated and the impact of these related traits on the mediators of opinion change.

Depression is likely to be found in a syndrome that includes other traits related to the mediators. For example, it is likely to correlate negatively with self-esteem (as measured by items like "I often hesitate to do things because of fear of failure. At times I have felt completely useless and disgusted with myself."). The depressive's lack of self-esteem should make him more influenceable via the yielding mediator, since a person lacking in self-confidence would be more likely to give in when his own opinion is discrepant from another's. On the other hand, depression is likely (Bennis & Peabody, 1962) to co-vary positively with social withdrawal tendencies ("I often find my thoughts drifting when others are talking to me; sometimes I have to read a paragraph over again to get its meaning."). The depressive's withdrawal tendencies are likely to preserve him from being persuaded by interfering with the reception mediator.

TABLE 1

CORRELATIONS BETWEEN OPINION CHANGE AND PERSONALITY VARIABLES (BASED ON DATA FROM 72 COLLEGE STUDENTS)

Variables	1	2	3
1. Depression			
2. Withdrawal	+.35		
3. Self-Esteem	−.64	−.56	
4. Opinion change	−.27	−.39	+.10

$P_{.05} = .23$ $P_{.01} = .30$

The results of an experiment by the writer confirm these assumptions regarding the complexities involved. College students (N = 72) read a series of persuasive messages from authoritative sources. Each was about 700 words long, giving reasonable, semitechnical arguments on such issues as the adequacy of current expenditures on basic as compared to applied research. Persuasibility was measured by opinion change (in terms of responses to a self-report opinionnaire) from before to after the messages. Personality traits were assessed by self-report inventories containing ten items per trait, the items given above being examples of those used. The results are shown in Table 1. Our exemplar variable, depression, correlates −.27 with opinion change ($p < .05$). But the patterns of intercorrelation suggest that this relationship could be considered a spurious result of the fact that depressives are socially withdrawn ($r = +.35$) and withdrawal makes the person hard to persuade ($r = -.39$), presumably because of his poor message reception. If we partial out the effect of withdrawal, the correlation between depression and attitude change falls to an insignificant $r = -.15$. Conversely, we can argue that the relation between depression and persuasibility would be even more negative than it appears in Table 1 were it not for the suppressing effects of its negative correlation with self-esteem. Partialling out effect of self-esteem does indeed increase the (negative) correlation between depression and persuasibility so that it reaches the .01 level of significance. It is clear then, by both a priori analysis and empirical test, that a given personality-influenceability relationship is not determined by the given trait in isolation but emerges from a matrix of correlations involving other personality traits.

It is true, of course, that correlation does not mean causation. Our use of terms like *spurious, artifacts,* and *suppression,* above, were quite arbitrary. Granting that the correlation between depression and persuasibility vanishes when we partial out the effect of withdrawal, were we correct to call it "spurious?" Inevitably, the use of partial correlations raises the specter of throwing out the baby with the bath water. Perhaps its involvement with withdrawal was contained in the surplus meaning of the conceptual trait, depression. Hence, the correlation with withdrawal may have been the very reason for predicting that depression would be negatively related to persuasibility. Perhaps the withdrawal-persuasibility correlation is the one that should be called spurious. Perhaps if we partialled out the effect of all the confounding personality variables from our depression-persuasibility correlations, instead of partialling them out one-by-one as above, we would end up with a partial correlation much the same as the correlation with which we started. (Indeed this does happen with the Table 1 data when we partial out of the depression-persuasibility correlation the effects of both self-esteem and withdrawal.)

These considerations make it evident that casting a wider net to catch the confounding variables as well as the one of particular interest raises more questions than it answers. However, the broader approach suggested by this confounding principle under discussion does have two advantages for hypothesis formulation and testing. First, it has the heuristic value of promoting a search for other likely personality correlates of the given variable which might determine indirectly the latter's effect on influenceability. The above analysis of the relations between depression and persuasibility is an example of this heuristic use. A second advantage of the confounding principle is in the attention it draws and the light it casts on what might be called the "chronic vs. acute variations" problem (Spence, Farber, & Taylor, 1954; Brown, 1961, pp. 257 ff.). We shall consider this problem in the next section.

Chronic vs. Acute Levels

Hypothesis testing can involve two alternative procedures as regards tactics for varying the subject's level on the independent (personality) variable: the correlational approach vs. the manipulational approach. The correlational approach means taking the subjects at their various natural levels on the personality variable, exposing them to the social influence situations and measuring the relationship between the chronic personality level and the amount of opinion change effected. The manipulational approach takes the subjects and assigns them by some equitable (e.g., random) procedure to one of several alternative experimental conditions designed to induce different acute states on the personality variable, then exposes them to the influence situations, and measures the relationship between the acute, manipulated personality level and the amount of opinion change effected.

From the strictly methodological viewpoint, the question of which technique should be used in a given situation focuses on their relative sensitivity. Usually, it is tacitly assumed that both procedures, if they test the hypothesis at all, will yield the same answer, but depending on the situation, one or the other technique may fail to yield an answer because it does not produce a sufficient range of variation on the hypothesized personality variable. For example, if the hypothesis deals with the relationship between anxiety and influenceability, the sensitivity advantage might be claimed either for the correlational or for the manipulative approach on various grounds. It might be argued that a wider variation of anxiety is possible by the correlational method, since a wider range of anxiety exists in the natural environment than we can practically obtain by laboratory manipulation. On the other hand, if we are confined to sampling a restricted population (such as college sophomores), the reverse might be true: it might be possible by exposing half of our subjects to a very stressful situation to induce in them a higher level of acute anxiety than that at which any sizable subgroup of them chronically operate.

While the foregoing "range" consideration might, depending on the situation, favor either approach, a second consideration is more likely to be in favor of the correlational, chronic-level approach. This consideration has to do with the number of different levels that are achieved on the independent variable. Even if it is possible to bring "real fear" into the laboratory, it is prohibitively difficult to bring it in at many gradations. So long as we cling to the strict a priori operationism of considering only the manipulated levels, we cannot hope to design inductions that will produce more than three or so a priori orderable gradations of acute induced fear. This multilevel advantage of relying on chronic levels is a very important one when we expect the relationship of the personality variable to influenceability to be complex and even nonmonotonic. As was pointed out in connection with principle 2 above, such complex relationships are the rule rather than the exception.

A third consideration has to do with the relative validity with which we are varying the hypothesized personality characteristic via one or another of the two tactics. With the manipulated acute-level approach, the question of laboratory artificiality tends to arise. Perhaps laboratory stress situations designed to produce different levels of anxiety (Janis & Feshbach, 1953) do not vary what is meant by our construct of anxiety but something quite different (e.g., suspiciousness of the experimenter's intention or hostility or confusion). On the other hand, use of the correlational, chronic-level approach introduces worry about subjects' "self-selection" of their level such that the different levels of chronic anxiety might be associated systematically with differences in other variables (e.g., intelligence, withdrawal, etc.) that cause spurious relations to influenceability.

This last consideration raises a more fundamental issue that is particularly relevant to the confounding principle. The correlational chronic-level approach will result in varying the personality characteristic in its naturally confounded state. The manipulational, acute-level approach will result in a purer, more artificial variation of the characteristic in isolation from the company of confounding variables that tend to become associated with it in the natural environment. Hence, the choice between approaches involves an issue more fundamental than the methodological one of relative sensitivity. Where the naturally correlated variables affect the mediators of attitude change, different relationships of the given personality variable to influenceability might emerge, depending on whether acute or chronic variations are used.

If the size and even the direction of the relationship do depend on the tactic used for varying the personality characteristic, it might seem appropriate to ask which approach is better. However, the implication of the confounding principle under discussion here is that each approach has its uses and the outcome of each of them, as well as the difference between their outcomes, offers theory-relevant information. Each in isolation has its uses, and both together provide more information than the sum of their yields in isolation. The most clear and present danger in the availability of the two approaches is that the experimenter will do his theorizing (hypothesis formulation) in terms of one approach and his experimenting (hypothesis testing) in terms of the other. For example, he might theorize about the relationship between anxiety and influenceability in terms of the complex syndrome in which anxiety is naturally embedded, making use of chronic anxiety's acquired association with lack of self-esteem, social withdrawal, etc., to deduce its relation to influenceability. Then, he might test the prediction by inducing different levels of acute anxiety by experimental manipulation of threat, where the manipulated anxiety has not yet acquired the natural penumbra of associated variables. The outcome of the confusion of acute and chronic anxiety will tend to be misleading, as the empirical literature demonstrates all too clearly.

Empirical Results Using Chronic vs. Acute Levels

We can illustrate the consideration involved by examining the findings regarding self-esteem. In studies using acute levels of self-esteem, the subjects are typically manipulated as to an experimentally induced failure experience (e.g., the high self-esteem condition might consist of calling the subject "right" on 30 out of 35 trials during a prior test, and the low self-esteem condition might tell him he is right on only 5 of the 35 trials, as in Mausner and Block, 1957). Then all subjects are given a social influence induction, and the relationship of self-esteem to influenceability is ascertained by comparing the mean opinion-change scores in success vs. failure conditions. The success vs. failure manipulation varies self-esteem in isolation, as it would exist if the failure-prone person had no long experience adapting to his low self-esteem and hence had never learned to develop a set of rationalizations, evasive behaviors, and other defenses by which he would have adjusted to this chronic lack of self-esteem (Cohen, 1959). We would thus be manipulating a conceptually pure but "unnatural" variable of self-esteem. Not surprisingly, subjects put through the failure induction for which they are unprepared and to which they have no opportunity to adjust tend to be more susceptible to influence than groups of subjects given the success induction (Kelman, 1950; Mausner, 1954; Hochbaum, 1954; Samelson, 1957; Stukát, 1958). The increased susceptibility after failure tends to obtain even when the induced failure is given on a task irrelevant to the persuasion task (Gelfand, 1962). The opinion-change promoting effect of failure is augmented when the source of the influence attempt is shown himself to be successful (Mausner & Block, 1957).

Studies using the alternative, chronic-level approach measure the subjects as to preexisting chronic level of self-esteem (by *ad hoc* or standardized self-report inventories or by self-ideal discrepancy). Then all subjects are put in a social influence situation, and the relation of self-esteem to influenceability is ascertained by correlating the self-esteem scores with the opinion change or by partitioning the subjects by a median split into low vs. high chronic self-esteem groups and comparing the mean opinion change scores of the two groups. (Actually, the nonmonotonic relationship suggested in our previous discussion of combinatory principle 2 makes these types of analysis ill advised, since they assume a monotonic and even rectilinear relationship between the personality variable and influenceability. But we will not labor this point here.) This chronic self-esteem variable is embedded in a whole syndrome of correlated variables (depression, withdrawal, intelligence, ability to cope, etc.) in contrast to the relatively pure and artificial acute variation of isolated self-esteem by experimental manipulation. The effects of these correlated variables on the mediators of opinion change may result in obtaining a relationship of influenceability to chronic self-esteem that is considerably different from that of acute self-esteem.

Data on this question are still somewhat ambiguous. One chronic self-esteem study produced results similar to the acute self-esteem studies cited above. This was the Janis and Rife (1959) study that did find a strong negative relationship ($r = -.66$, $N = 56$) between influenceability and chronic self-esteem in institutionalized psychotics. Other chronic self-esteem studies have failed to show any significant relation, or have found a negative relationship that attains conventional significance levels only if we do a posteriori analyses of extreme cells (Janis & Field, 1959b; Lesser & Abelson, 1959, pp. 187–194; Leventhal & Perloe, 1962). Still other chronic self-esteem studies find nonmonotonic relationships (Linton & Graham, 1959; Appley & Moeller, 1963; Silverman, 1964; Cox & Bauer, 1964).

This chronic vs. acute level consideration becomes particularly interesting when the personality characteristic is varied by both approaches within the same experimental design. Several studies on self-esteem and influenceability have employed an approximation of an acute-chronic orthogonal design. One of these (Gelfand, 1962) is particularly interesting because it included in the design a third variable, subtlety of the influence induction, which is relevant to the previous principle involving situational weighting. Chronic self-esteem was measured by Sears' (1960) self-report inventory. Acute self-esteem was manipulated by preprogrammed success or failure experience on irrelevant tasks immediately before the social influence tests. (There was also a third, neither-success-nor-failure control group.) One influence score was from an Asch-type situation in which a peer gave preprogrammed deviant judgments prior to the subject's own judgment. In this conformity situation, the reception mediator is rather unimportant, since all Gelfand's subjects (normal fifth-graders) are likely with no difficulty to have comprehended the peer's choice. In this situation, the acute self-esteem level has a very strong negative relation to conformity ($p < .001$), while chronic self-esteem has no appreciable relation at all.

Her other social influence task follows the typical verbal conditioning technique (Taffel, 1955) with the experimenter's comment of "good" used to reinforce choice of certain pronouns in starting sentences. This is a much more subtle situation where there would be more individual differences in reception and where the social withdrawal tendencies associated with low self-esteem (Bennis & Peabody, 1962) would tend to furnish protection from influence. In this situation the most salient finding is a curvilinear relation ($p < .01$) such that those low on both chronic and acute self-esteem, as well as those high on both, show less compliance with the verbal reinforcement than do those on an intermediate level (the low-highs and the high-lows). A like result was obtained by Millman (1965) using anxiety as the personality variable and a rather subtle taped interview about China as the persuasion induction. She found that those high in both chronic and acute anxiety and those low in both were less persuasible than those in mixed conditions (low-highs and high-lows).

A third relevant study is that by Lesser and Abelson (1959) in which young children were given suggestions by teachers to make certain judgments. Influenceability was measured by degree of conformity to these suggestions. Chronic self-esteem was measured by the child's self-rating of his relative position in the class in terms of ability and popularity. Acute self-esteem was manipulated on a prior task where the teacher consistently agreed with the child's judgment or consistently disagreed with it. We are saying that this prior teacher behavior was perceived by the child as indicating his own success or failure, respectively. There were two replications of the study and both replications agreed on all the findings cited here. Lesser and Abelson found that there was more opinion change ($p < .05$) after the success experience than after failure. This is one of the few studies in which acute self-esteem was positively related to influenceability (the prior agreeing behavior of the teacher may have raised not only the child's self-esteem but his liking for the teacher, his interest in the tasks, etc.). Chronic self-esteem was related significantly negatively to influenceability. There were, however, interactions ($p < .05$) such that the effect of chronic self-esteem on influenceability was due entirely to the success condition. This interaction is in agreement with the results from the Gelfand (1962) study.

Perhaps reconciliation of the chronic and acute variation studies will be promoted by continuing the theoretical analysis of the Michigan group regarding preferences for the different defense mechanisms as a function of self-esteem (Cohen, 1959; Katz, 1960; Stotland & Hillmer, 1962). But these studies all agree in pointing up the implication of our principle 4 regarding confounding. Influenceability can differ greatly depending on whether we use acute or chronic variations in the characteristic. Furthermore, there tends to be an interaction effect on influenceability of the acute $\times$ chronic variables.

This whole discussion of the confounding principle as applied to personality-influenceability relationships has relied mainly on self-esteem as the illustration variable. The points could have been made with equal facility in terms of a number of other personality characteristics. One such alternative variable on which the data are particularly rich is anxiety. Acute anxiety is manipulated by some threatening or stressful experimental induction. The chronic, natural level anxiety is measured by, e.g., the Taylor Manifest Anxiety Scale. Other sections of this chapter (and McGuire, 1966) report a number of studies in which these anxiety variables are related to influenceability. There is also a growing literature on chronic vs. acute variations of anxiety, where learning and conditionability are the dependent variables, developing out of the Iowa work of Spence and his colleagues (Brown, 1961; Cofer & Appley, 1964).

Principle 5: Situational Interactions

Our discussion of the previous principles stressed that the relationships between a personality variable and influenceability will tend to be specific and vary with other aspects of the communication situation. This stress might seem to be in conflict with one of the main streams of persuasibility research. The Yale group (Hovland, Janis, & Kelley, 1953; Janis & Hovland, 1959) devoted a great deal of conceptual and empirical activity to teasing out topic-free personality correlates of "general, unbounded persuasibility." This work contrasted with other research that was designed to find personality correlates of susceptibility to persuasion toward specific ideological positions, such as the work of Hartley (1946), Adorno *et al.* (1950), and Bettelheim and Janowitz (1950) on susceptibility to antiminority propaganda or of Smith, Bruner, and White (1956) on proneness to acquire anti-Soviet attitudes. Hovland and his colleagues sought to find broader relationships between personality and influenceability, relatively unbounded by the specifics of the communication situation.

The Yale program of seeking transcendental relationships between personality and influenceability is appealing in that a scientific principle is useful in proportion to its generality, assuming that validity remains constant. The problem lies in this final qualification. Janis and Hovland themselves (1959, p. 15) point out that "boundedness" is a matter of degree. There are probably few influenceability relationships that are absolutely unbounded by other classes of communication variables. At best one may hope to uncover relationships that do not appreciably interact with certain classes of variables, but one should always be alert to the likelihood that ultimately there will be discovered some class of variables that do interact with the given personality variable in affecting influenceability. In an early section of this chapter we reviewed the empirical evidence that a general trait of influenceability does exist, but to a very limited extent.

Some dimensions of boundedness being practically inevitable, we feel that it is better research strategy to seek out the classes of communication variables that may limit a given personality-influenceability relationship, rather than to try to circumvent such limitations in the quest for relatively unbounded generalizations. Indeed if, as we maintain, a valid mapping of the personality-influenceability domain requires interaction formulations, then such formulations yield wider (albeit, more complex) generalizations than would delusively simple and transcendental main-effect formulations.

This principle that a given personality-influenceability relationship will be limited in size and even direction by other, interacting variables in the communication situation becomes useful to the extent that we have at our disposal a manageable and heuristically provocative classification of these other communication variables. Hence, we shall consider seriatim the five broad classes into which communication variables can be conveniently divided: source, message, channel, receiver, and destination. As we mentioned at the outset of this chapter, this classification has received wide usage in the communication areas. (Other systems have been suggested by Holland, 1959, and by Doob, 1961. Any of these classifications would serve to provide the heuristics for uncovering interaction variables.) Examples will be given to show how variables from each of the five classes interact with personality variables in determining influenceability. It will be seen that the relationship between a specific personality dimension and influenceability may vary drastically depending on the levels of these other, interactional variables at which our experimental parameters have been set. It will also be seen that these interactions between personality characteristics and other situational variables are in keeping with the implications of the previous four principles.

Interactions with Source Factors

Many studies have shown that the opinion-change impact of a given communication varies with the characteristics of the attributed source of the message. Kelman (1961) has exhaustively analyzed how these source effects operate through various psychodynamics involving credibility, likability, or power. Interactions between source characteristics and receiver personality variables in determining influenceability are inevitable, since personality plays a part in determining one's reference groups and hence how credible, likable, or powerful one perceives a given source to be. Hence, a personality variable may be positively or negatively related to the persuasive impact of a given message, depending on the source to whom the message is attributed. To cite an obvious case of the reference group consideration, Catholics will turn out to be more or less persuasible than Protestants, depending on whether the message is attributed to a Catholic or to a Protestant spokesman.

Source-personality interactions can occur also because certain personality traits are associated with higher sensitivity to source differentials. A number of studies have shown that the lower the self-esteem of the receiver, the more susceptible he is to differences in source status in regard to changing his judgment to agree with that source. This effect of self-esteem has been demonstrated in studies that manipulated the acute level of self-esteem, e.g., by induced failure experiences (Kelman, 1950; Mausner, 1954) or by rejection experiences (Kelley & Shapiro, 1954; Dittes & Kelley, 1956). Whether chronic level of self-esteem likewise interacts by sensitizing the person to differences in source status has not yet been demonstrated, and as was pointed out in the discussion of the fourth principle, there is reason to be cautious in assuming that it does so interact in the same way as does acute self-esteem.

One personality variable that seems extremely likely to interact with source factors in determining the opinion-change impact of a given communication is authoritarianism as measured by the California *F* scale (Adorno *et al.,* 1950). A number of studies have been done on the relationship between authoritarianism and influenceability, continuing even into the recent past, after the peak of substantive interest in the *F* scale had passed (Wright & Harvey, 1965). The relevant aspect of the authoritarian syndrome, as originally described by Adorno *et al.* (1950), is a tendency toward oversimplified categorization of people on the evaluative dimension into a few extreme groups, so that people are seen as being either very good or very bad. Hence, there would be more difference in the opinion-change impact of a positively vs. negatively valenced source with increasing authoritarianism in the receiver. Restating this interacting effect, authoritarianism is positively correlated with influenceability when the message is from positive sources, and negatively when from negative sources.

At first glance, the description of the syndrome might seem to imply that high authoritarian subjects would be more susceptible than low to differences in source factors. A closer scrutiny shows that this view is oversimplified. The relationship would tend to reverse when we consider the source differential where both sources have the same direction (sign) of evaluation but vary in degree: e.g., a mildly positive vs. a highly positive source. Authoritarians, seeing the world in blacks and whites, magnify differences between the good and the bad but overlook differences between gradations within goodness or badness. Hence, there would be less difference in opinion-change impact of moderately vs. strongly positive (or negative) sources with increasing authoritarianism in the receiver.

Over the whole range of source valence we would expect a second-order personality-influenceability interaction effect, involving the authoritarianism of the receiver and the sign of and size of the source valence. This theoretical analysis is indicative of the need to consider complex interactions in mapping the domain of personality-influenceability relationships. A study by Berkowitz and Lundy (1957) and an unpublished study by the writer touch on aspects of the above predictions, but it must be admitted that the formulation presented here has not yet been fully tested.

Whether dogmatism as measured by Rokeach's (1956, 1960) scale would function in the manner hypothesized for authoritarianism is not completely clear to this writer. It might be that all source differentials would be enhanced by dogmatism, but on the other hand the syndrome seems to include the same black vs. white polarizing tendency as does authoritarianism. Powell (1962) did find an enhancement of source differential associated with dogmatism. He used perceptual D^2 scores, rather than opinion change, as the dependent variable, but Rokeach's (1960, p. 396) formulation seems to imply a like finding would hold for opinion change also.

Another personality variable of the cognitive style type that might function as hypothesized above for authoritarianism is what has been called "category width" (Pettigrew, 1958), "leveling-and-sharpening" (Klein, 1958; Gardner, Holzman, Klein, Linton, & Spence, 1959), and "latitude of acceptance" (Sherif & Hovland, 1961). The implication of these partially overlapping formulations is that receivers high on category width (e.g., tendency to perceive the world in terms of a few, broad categories) will tend to be less affected by small source differences and perhaps more affected by wide differences than would subjects scoring low on the category-width scale (Zimbardo, 1960; Bergin, 1962; Aronson, Turner, & Carlsmith, 1963; Steiner & Johnson, 1965).

Interactions with Message Factors

The richest variety of independent variables in social influence research is found in this area of message factors. Included are (a) content variables, such as type of appeals, inclusions and omissions of material, amount of change advocated, etc.; and (b) structural variables, such as amount of material, order of presentation, etc. These subcategories themselves include many subdivisions of empirically investigated variables. Interactions of such a myriad of message factors with personality factors are so numerous that we can here only select rather arbitrarily a few to illustrate some general considerations. To promote at least geographical and theoretical diversity, we shall select one example from each of the two most active research centers, the Michigan and the Yale groups.

The functional approach (Katz, 1960) to attitude change advocated by the Michigan group (Katz, Sarnoff, McClintock, Stotland, etc.) directed the attention of these researchers to the role of ego-defensiveness as a personality variable related to susceptibility to influence inductions involving self-insight. In general, they expected a nonmonotonic relationship such that messages using self-insight appeals (attempting to reduce prejudice by depicting the unattractive psychodynamics underlying ethnic hostilities) would be more effective with subjects having intermediate levels of ego defensiveness than with subjects either high or low on this variable. The empirical validity of this formulation is still unclear (Stotland & Patchen, 1961), but the point that concerns us here involves a peripheral issue. In one study in their series (Katz, Sarnoff, & McClintock, 1956) it was demonstrated that this personality variable, ego-defensiveness, was related to influenceability either positively or negatively, depending on the kind of appeal used in the message. With the self-insight appeal that showed the unattractive psychodynamics underlying prejudice, there was a nonmonotonic relationship between ego-defensiveness and favorable change toward Negroes; with an informational appeal that presented Negroes in a sympathetic light, there was a positive relationship between ego-defensiveness and favorable change toward Negroes.

A finding of the Yale group illustrating an interaction between individual-difference variables and message variables comes from their research on "one-sided" vs. "two-sided" messages (Hovland, Lumsdaine, & Sheffield, 1949, Ch. 8). Two forms of a recording arguing that the war with Japan would not be won for a long time after the defeat of Germany were presented to American soldiers in World War II. The "one-sided" form ignored any arguments against the position being defended; the "two-sided" form mentioned incidentally or with refutations some of the opposition arguments. The less intelligent soldiers (those not completing high school) were more influenced than the more intelligent by the one-sided recording, but this relationship between intelligence and persuasibility was reversed with the two-sided message.

On the other hand, the Yale group failed to find any interaction between the intelligence variable and the message variable of implicit vs. explicit conclusion (Hovland & Mandell, 1952), although it would be predicted on the same theoretical basis as would the intelligence-sidedness interaction. Other researchers have indeed found some evidence for an interaction between intelligence and implicit-explicit conclusion (Cooper & Dinerman, 1951; Thistlethwaite, de Haan, & Kamenetsky, 1955). Still other interactions between personality and message variables in determining influenceability have been shown by Cohen (1957) and Lana (1961, 1964), both of whom deal with ordering variables within the message. The reasons for such interactions become clearer in the light of the earlier principles. In most of those discussed here, the personality variable's effect on the reception mediator is the crucial consideration.

A final example that we shall use to illustrate personality-message interaction in affecting influenceability has to do with the receiver's chronic anxiety level and the amount of fear aroused within the message. An interaction in this case would be predicted from our discussion of principle 2 on the basis of which an overall nonmonotonic relation between anxiety and influenceability would be expected, with maximum susceptibility coming at intermediate levels of anxiety. Hence, if the person is chronically low in anxiety, raising it by a high fear appeal would tend to increase opinion change; while to the extent that the person is already chronically high, inducing further anxiety by a high fear appeal in the persuasive message should become detrimental to opinion change. This detrimental interaction from compounding chronic anxiety with high fear appeals should become more pronounced as the influence situation puts a progressively greater strain on reception by the person, e.g., as we go from suggestibility and conformity situations to persuasion situations.

Empirical results tend to confirm this expected interaction. Niles (1964) found that low fear appeals were more effective than high on the smoking-cancer issue when the subjects were already worried about health, but for those who felt relatively invulnerable about illness, the high fear appeal produced more change. Berkowitz and Cottingham (1960) found some suggestion, by an internal analysis, that as initial concern about the issue went up, the persuasive efficacy of adding threat to the message went down. Goldstein (1959) found that an added fear appeal had a detrimental effect on persuasive impact for those who chronically reacted to threat by "avoidance," but not for "copers."

Interactions with Channel Factors

A great deal of research has been done on media and modality factors but this work has tended to be action-oriented, focused on determining "listenership" scores rather than on testing out relationships among variables. Hence, relative to the investment, the theoretically useful fallout has been disappointingly sparse. Still, some evidence has emerged regarding interaction effects on influenceability between individual-difference variables and channel factors, such as mass communications vs. face-to-face individual communication. Different channels of presentation put differing demands on the concentration power and interest levels of the receiver and on the amount of active participation required. Such differences as these (and others that cannot be reviewed here) make it inevitable that relationships between individual-difference variables and influenceability will change with different channel conditions. Thus Knower (1935), like many before and since, found women to be more influenceable than men, but showed further that this sex difference was more pronounced when the persuasive speech was heard by oneself in a face-to-face situation than when heard in a group situation.

In the adoption-of-innovations studies, it has been demonstrated that the channels of influence interacted with sociability of physicians in determining their susceptibility to communications urging them to adopt new drugs (Menzel & Katz, 1956). The unpopular physicians were more influenced by detail-men and mail from drug houses; while the more popular physicians were influenced mostly by journal articles and professional meetings. Hence, if we studied the persuasive impact of the pharmaceutical companies' campaigns, communicated through personalized channels, we would have to conclude that influenceability is negatively related to popularity; while if we studied the impact via the formal channels of professional communication, we would find a positive relationship between popularity and persuasibility. Once again, this interaction makes sense in terms of the earlier principles. The unpopular physicians are low in self-esteem and also tend to withdraw. The lack of self-esteem makes them prone to yield if they receive the message, but their withdrawal tendency protects them from receipt of messages. Hence, via channels where the source takes the initiative (drug house mail and visits from detail men), the unpopulars are most susceptible to influence; via channels with regard to which the recipient must take the initiative to expose himself (journal articles and meetings), the unpopulars are less influenceable.

Interactions with Receiver Factors: Sex as a Moderator Variable

Personality variables themselves constitute a large subclass of receiver factors, but what we wish to point out here is that these personality variables tend to interact with one another and with other kinds of receiver variables in determining influenceability. Studies abound which show that the relationship between a given personality variable and influenceability varies, depending on the individual's standing on some other personality variable. For example, the Berkowitz and Lundy (1957) study shows that the relationship between one personality variable and influenceability can vary in magnitude and even direction by varying the subjects' level on another personality dimension. Thus, the relationship between receivers' authoritarianism (California-F) and influenceability as measured by change toward a peer source is negative among persons with low self-esteem (or low interpersonal confidence) while the relationship becomes positive as the subsample changes to include those higher in self-esteem.

These interaction effects between one receiver factor and another are even more common when we consider individual-difference variables that interact simply to intensify rather than reverse a personality-influenceability relationship; that is, where one characteristic acts as a moderator variable to intensify the relationship between influenceability and another characteristic.

One such case that has attracted a considerable amount of research attention involves sex acting as the moderator variable for personality-influenceability relations. We already referred to the general finding that women tend to be more susceptible to social influence than men. What we refer to here, however, is another general finding that the correlations between personality characteristics and influenceability tend to be higher in males than in females. This finding of lower correlations for women than for men is not peculiar to the personality-influenceability area. Part of the lore of laborers in the experimental-personality vineyard is that if one wants to find strong relationships between personality variables and behavioral measures in college sophomores, one is wise to use male rather than female students as subjects. Typical of the results in the influenceability area is the finding by Janis and Field (1959b) that the correlations between personality variables and persuasibility were higher in men than in women for eight of the nine personality variables studied. None of the correlations in females was significant at even the .25 level, while in men most of the correlations were, and four of the nine were significant at the conventional .05 level. Similar results with hypnotizability were obtained by Hilgard, Lauer, and Melei (1965).

There could be a number of reasons why sex operates as a moderator variable such that personality-influenceability relationships tend to be attenuated in females. One possible explanation is that women respond more unreliably to personality inventories or opinionnaires, so that their lower intercorrelations should be "corrected" for attenuation (Block, 1963, 1964; Stephens & Crowne, 1964). While it has some a priori plausibility, this explanation conflicts with available data. Rather than being less reliable (e.g., in terms of test-retest changes in response), females tend to give more reliable self-ratings than males (Bain, 1931; Smith, 1933; Schofield, 1953).

This greater reliability in females raises suspicion of an opposite artifact: perhaps the females are more prone to response sets like social desirability or response styles like acquiescence (Rorer, 1965) which enhance reliability but reduce validity and lower correlations with behavioral variables. There are several paradoxical measurement situations in which validity and reliability tend to vary inversely (instead of positively, with the square root of the reliability as the upper limit for the validity coefficient). Possible cases of a paradoxical inverse relationship between reliability and validity are offered by forced-choice techniques, disguised items, skewed response distribution, and unfamiliar tests. Forced-choice items tend to yield less reliable (Cronbach, 1960) but more valid scores, at least for longer inventories (Appel, 1959), as compared with the traditional rating scales; both effects may be due to the fact that the forced-choice format is somewhat less susceptible to response biases, though the question has complexities that we cannot pursue here (Zavala, 1965). Likewise, items most likely to involve admission of undesirable characteristics and thus to have higher validity are likely also to have lower reliability, e.g., disguised items (Schofield, 1950), unpopular response categories (Mitra & Fiske, 1956; Osterweil & Fiske, 1956; Runkel, 1958), and unfamiliar tests (Windle, 1954, 1955; Schofield, 1953). Each of these operations can be interpreted as decreasing reliability and increasing validity by decreasing response biases, though the issue cannot be considered resolved at this stage of the field. Other interesting cases of inverse relationships between validity and reliability (of change scores) are described by Bereiter (1963).

This second possible explanation—that women provide more reliable personality scores but less valid ones, correlating less with objective measures of persuasibility because women are more prone to response sets—can be further evaluated by examining the data on sex differences in susceptibility to response sets and styles. There does seem to be a small but consistent tendency for females to give more socially desirable responses (Jackson & Pacine, 1961; Crowne & Marlow, 1964). On the other hand, the other widely studied response bias, acquiescence, has so far showed little relation to sex (Christie & Lindauer, 1963). In fact, males tend to obtain slightly higher acquiescence scores than females (Mahler, 1962; Hilgard, Lauer, & Melei, 1965) perhaps because the ARS items were initially (Couch & Keniston, 1960) selected on the basis of data from males.

This last point suggests still a third possibility of why personality variables tend to correlate with behavioral measures like influenceability less highly in females than in males. It has happened that many personality scales have been standardized mainly on a male population, with item selection based on discriminability among males. This state of affairs has obtained from the World War I neuroticism schedule which was incorporated in the Bernreuter Personality Inventory to such currently popular tests as the Taylor (1953) Manifest Anxiety Scale, the Couch-Keniston (1960) ARS, etc., if for no other reason than that male populations have in general been more accessible to test construction, in the form of military personnel, college students, prison inmates, and like groups. This selective sex bias is further augmented by the fact that the initial pool of items tends to be constructed by active psychologists, the large majority of whom are males, and hence construct items more suitable for picking up nuances of differences among male subjects than among females. This biased-origin explanation suggests a number of other likely moderator variables for personality-influenceability relationships. Test constructors and the populations used for selecting items tend to be homogeneous and nonrepresentative of the population as regards not only sex but also age, social class, educational level, and various "interests" as measured by the Strong Vocational Interest Blank and the Kuder Preference Record. The problem here is analogous to the current controversies over whether the homogeneous-background constructors of abilities tests can produce a truly "culture-free" intelligence test that is not biased against children from the lower economic strata and the nonwhite ethnic populations, and whether the homogeneous psychiatrists and clinical psychologists can properly appraise the normality of patients not from the educated, middle-class white population (Dohrenwend & Dohrenwend, 1965).

The previous three possible explanations of why sex operates as a moderator variable on personality-persuasibility interrelations (namely, sex differences in reliability, in susceptibility to response biases, and in test constructors) involved what might be called methodological artifacts, though admittedly the transition from methodological artifact to theoretical profundity is a gradual one. Indeed, one man's "methodological artifact" may be another's substantive explanation. A fourth possible explanation is more unambiguously a substantive one. This is the theory suggested by the Yale group (Janis & Hovland, 1959) that, in our society at least, it is a cultural norm that females be submissive, while the norm for males is less well defined. Hence, differential proclivities among individuals for independence behavior are submerged by the cultural norm in females but in males are left to determine each individual's operant level of independence behavior.

The validity of this explanation can be tested in terms of two corollaries that follow from it, namely, that there should be ontogenetic trends and cross-cultural trends in these sex differences. Some data are available on each of these points, but they are not adequate for a definitive answer. A study designed to test the ontogenetic trend corollary, for example, would involve testing for a triple interaction among age $\times$ sex $\times$ personality characteristic, with influenceability as the dependent variable. If the cultural-stereotype-in-women explanation is correct, we would expect the sex difference (higher personality-influenceability relations in men than in women) to increase with age. We do not know of any influenceability study where these three independent variables were varied over any sizable range within a single experimental design (though Abelson and Lesser, 1959b, did study sex and personality effects on persuasion in children ranging from 7 to 13 years of age). When we bring together the results of different studies (always a hazardous synthesis) we can find no evidence in support of the cultural hypothesis. For example, in the Yale studies, Lesser and Abelson (1959) found that even in young children (first graders), the relationships of personality and background variables to influenceability were higher, in the predicted direction, in boys than in girls for nine of the ten variables (though with only three of the ten variables did these sex differences reach the conventional levels of significance). Again in college students, as cited above, Janis and Field (1959b) found personality characteristics related to influenceability to a greater extent in men than in women for eight of their nine variables. Hence, we see no sign of a progressive sex differentiation with age as would be required by the cultural hypothesis. It is possible, of course, that the differential does depend on acculturation but that this effect reaches its asymptote by the time the children enter the first grade. Even though this cross-study comparison offers little support for the cultural hypothesis in terms of this crucial triple interaction effect, it does give some weak support in terms of a double interaction, sex × age, effect on influenceability. The sex difference such that women are more influenceable than men is found in college students (Janis & Field, 1959b) and in adolescents (King, 1959), but not in the first graders (Abelson & Lesser, 1959a).

There is as little support for the cross-cultural corollary as for this ontogenetic corollary. If the cultural-stereotype-in-women hypothesis is correct, then we would expect a triple interaction effect among sex × personality × culture on influenceability. We would predict that, as we sampled cultures that made progressively lesser submissiveness demands on women relative to men, the higher personality-influenceability correlations in men over women would tend to disappear. J. Rosenberg (1962) attempted to test this prediction in the apt setting provided by Israel. He gave a set of persuasive messages (on introducing TV in Israel, on permitting watering of private gardens, etc.) to male and female high school students drawn from four cultural groupings which could be completely ordered as to "traditionalism." They ranged from highly traditional groups typified by immigrants from Yemen to very low-traditional groups typified by kibbutz-reared Sabras. One relevant characteristic of traditionalism was a tendency to prescribe a higher degree of submissiveness for women than for men. According to the prediction, the second and third order effects (involving culture × sex, and culture × sex × personality) on persuasibility should diminish as we go from the Yemenites to the Sabras.

Unfortunately for the hypothesis, no such interactions involving culture were found. The sex differences appeared equally in all cultural groups, those to the "left" of the American college sophomore as well as those to the "right." There was a possible extenuating circumstance for the hypothesis, in that it might be argued that the use of high school students resulted in a nonequivalent sampling of the different cultural groups. Since almost all kibbutz children go to high school, while only some Yemenites send their children, it might be argued that the Yemenites' daughters who entered Rosenberg's sample may have represented only the most "liberated" segment of their population. Actually, Rosenberg did intend to take his subjects from among Army recruits, which in Israel samples the different subcultures more equitably, but these personnel were otherwise engaged at the time and were not available for testing.

Clearly, the cultural interpretation of sex differences in influenceability and in personality-influenceability relations has received little empirical support (though, of course, it has not been logically disproved either). Perhaps both main and interaction effects involving sex differences can be explained by one of the earlier discussed methodological "artifacts." However, such an explanation only pushes the question back one step and presents us with new questions, such as why are women more susceptible to response biases? Perhaps the hour has come to consider the genetic hypothesis. After religiously avoiding genetic interpretations of group differences for some decades, the field is nerving itself for a mature re-examination of the question (see Chapter 3). We can hardly claim at this point that we are forced by a process of elimination to accept the genetic interpretation. On the other hand, there is no reason in the present data to eliminate the possibility that women are indeed (a) genetically more susceptible to social influence and (b) genetically less variable among themselves in this regard than are men. There is evidence that social behavior of a comparable degree of complexity can be genetically determined (Scott & Fuller, 1965). It would be irresponsible to have left the question without at least mentioning this fifth possible explanation.

Interaction with Destination Factors

As destination factors, we include variables having to do with the specific target of the social influence, such as immediate vs. delayed opinion change, or changes on one vs. another type of issue. Earlier, we cited the Cohen (1957) study as showing an interaction, in regard to immediate persuasive impact, between the receiver variable of need for cognition and the message variable of clear vs. confusing order of presentation. The same study also shows an interaction between the need-for-cognition personality variable and the destination variable of immediate vs. delayed persuasive effect. For the clearly ordered message, the subjects with a high need for cognition showed a decay of persuasive effect from immediately after the message to a time three months later, while those with a low need for cognition showed a slight delayed-action effect, more change in the induced direction being shown three months after than immediately after the message.

Another type of receiver × destination interaction is shown in a study by Weiss and Fine (1956), where the personality variable was level of aggressiveness and the destination variable was the side of the issue that was being argued. Weiss and Fine manipulated aggressiveness by exposing the subject to different levels of failure and insult. They found that the higher-aggression group was more susceptible to persuasion when subsequent messages argued for punitive treatment of juvenile delinquents and less persuasible when the messages argued for a sympathetic attitude toward international allies. Again, we find that either a positive or a negative relationship could be demonstrated between this aggressiveness personality variable and persuasibility, depending on the level chosen for some interaction variable. Similarly with self-esteem, Leventhal and Perloe (1962) found that with dissimilar sources, high self-esteem receivers were more persuasible with optimistic messages, and low self-esteem receivers with pessimistic.

Evaluation

Before we leave this exposition of the interaction principle, some general remarks are in order. In the first place, this review, lengthy as it might seem, actually was extremely eclectic relative to the wealth of the available results. We chose to cite only one or two studies showing each type of interaction, to illustrate the extensiveness of the variable classes with which interactions must be expected. In each case, we could have multiplied examples at great length. We completely ignored higher than first order interactions, though these are often found (even in the studies cited). In most cases the interpretations will be obvious in terms of the preceding four principles. The occurrence of such interactions is the best evidence of the validity of these principles, and giving a theoretical account of the interactions is the best demonstration of the heuristic utility of the principles.

The moral is that we should not, in our quest for generality, seek absolute relationships between personality variables and influenceability. We may frequently find such relationships that are relatively source-free, or appeal-free, or issue-free, etc., but we should not hope to find relationships which are pervasive across all other aspects of the communication situation. Hence, we may generalize the personality-influenceability relationship found under a specific set of experimental conditions to other conditions only with fear and trembling. Obviously some generalization is necessary, since we are constructing a science. But it is to be expected that any simple relationship found will, if studied under a wide enough range of communication conditions, vanish and even reverse in some of the situations. What we have done here is to show a rough classification of the types of other variables with which generalization-limiting interactions might be sought.

The argument that we must make wide generalizations in terms of interactions rather than main effects receives a sour reception from many students of psychology, especially the young of heart to whom the world still seems simple and those with limited conceptual spans. The meaning of interaction effects can be grasped only with the exercise of considerable mental agility (and as we get to higher order interactions, even verbalizing them involves such imbedded syntax that many consider them unutterable). The unsophisticated student is inclined to say with annoyance of such interactions "Some people find a positive relationship between X and Y; others a negative relationship. The whole field is utterly confused. Is this supposed to be an objective science? No one agrees with anyone else. There are all sorts of contradictions." Even some practitioners shy away from interactions partly perhaps for poignant reasons of esthetics, partly because testing them involves us in statistical refinements like the disproportional-n problem and multiple error terms that we can often elude by staying with first-order effects. Still, if the universe to be described involves complexity, so must our theories and descriptions if they are to be valid.

However, the seeking of interaction effects strikes us as more than a necessary evil, enforced by the meanderings of a baroque creator. We regard their discovery as a sign of progress and would propose that the maturity of a science is directly proportional to how high an order interaction formulation is needed for the adequate prediction of its empirical variables. We regard the seeking after interaction effects as more than a necessary caution to the investigator exploring the limits of generalizability. Beyond this, it is a royal road to the discovery of new, more sophisticated formulations. The quest for interaction effects that limit one's main-effect finding constitutes an almost-mechanical heuristic whose creative use becomes progressively easier with one's research experience in a given area.

Wilhelm Weygandt, in organizing a medical congress at Hamburg in 1910, said, apropos of the inclusion of a session on psychoanalysis, that the topic was one not for scientific discussion but for a police action. Reversing his thinking, we would say that whenever responsible researchers come up with opposite findings regarding the relationship of a personality variable to influenceability, the "contradiction" is not a matter for a police action but for a theoretical advance in terms of a new interaction effect that will allow a higher order synthesis. It leads us to examine closely differences in experimental conditions of the two studies as regards supposedly irrelevant aspects of the communication situation, so as to tease out an interaction variable and reconcile the two studies in a higher theoretical synthesis that can be tested in a further study. Some guidance in where to look for these further interaction variables is given in our discussions of the other principles.

PRINCIPLE 6: THE COMPENSATION OR DYNAMIC-EQUILIBRIUM PRINCIPLE

In discussion of the previous five principles we have been repeatedly confronting, empirically and theoretically, the situations in which the relationship between the independent variable (some personality characteristic) and the dependent variable (susceptibility to social influence) is mediated by two opposing relationships, with the result that the overall personality-influenceability relationship is nonmonotonic. The actual occurrence of this case is quite widespread. We saw in the Appley and Moeller study, for example, that 33 of their 38 personality variables showed a nonmonotonic relation to conformity. We suspect this situation obtains fairly generally between personality characteristics and many other dependent variables besides influenceability. In this section we shall, however, restrict ourselves to the social influence area in trying to make explicit our thinking regarding why this situation is so general and explore the limits within which it obtains.

In general, our "explanation" of the prevalence of this situation is based on a functional analysis of the person's adaptation problem. In the case of susceptibility to social influence (as for many other behavioral dimensions, if we are to accept Aristotle's *Nicomachean Ethics*) there seems to be a golden middle range. The person should be open, but not too open, to outside influence if he is to thrive in the natural environment. It is intuitively plausible (and a common biological and engineering practice) that behavior can most satisfactorily be held at an optimal intermediate level by means of a dynamic equilibrium, i.e., in a steady state produced by the mutual cancellation of two opposing factors.

Maintaining behavior at a golden mean by a dynamic equilibrium situation has particularly obvious advantages for an organism adapting, ontogenetically and phylogenetically, to a complex and variable natural environment. It allows ready adjustment of fluctuations that occur in either direction. Variation thus becomes less costly, allowing for built-in trial-and-error oscillatory searchings that would permit readjustment to a changing environment. The dynamic equilibrium situation is also particularly apt for allowing a complex solution, in which the organism learns to switch its functioning to different optimal levels depending on the conditions.

Susceptibility to social influence is an area in which all of these circumstances obtain. An intermediate level seems optimal, since if the person were completely closed to influence from others, he would lose out on one of the most efficient sources of information about the environment and how to deal with it. On the other hand, if he were completely open to influence, he would hardly pursue any path to a goal before being diverted from it by some new social pressure. Hence, it is adaptive for him to be in a dynamic equilibrium where some of his personality proclivities make for openness, while others make him closed to social influence, resulting in his maintaining his influenceability within an intermediate range.

The easy fluctuation and return which are facilitated by the dynamic equilibrium adjustment are particularly adaptive with influenceability. We saw that such ease of fluctuations yielded two dividends: it permitted long-term secular trends to new levels of stabilization if environmental changes required it, and it permitted a complex solution where different equilibrium levels could be adopted under different sets of environmental conditions. As for openness to persuasion, an armchair ecological survey indicates a long-term ontogenetic trend, with the optimal level going downward over the lifespan, at least during the period from early childhood to maturity. The inexpensive searching fluctuations allowed by the dynamic equilibrium arrangement permit constant testing and a creeping readjustment downward with maturation, which is highly adaptive. The multilevel solution facilitated by the dynamic equilibrium arrangement also has a special utility in the case of influenceability. Such a solution permits the personality variable to function in interactions with other aspects of the influence situation in determining the characteristic level of influenceability. The person can, for example, function at one level with a credible source and at a lower level with a less credible source; at a higher level on a matter-of-fact issue than a matter-of-test one; at one level in the classroom and at another in political disputation.

We are presenting this dynamic equilibrium principle not as a proof of (or even evidence for) the preceding principles, which must stand or fall on the degree to which the hypotheses derived from them are confirmed by experimental outcomes. The functional reasoning, on which the present principle is based, is always hazardous. It rests on the following argument: that behavior in accord with a certain model would be adaptive in the existing environment; organisms seem fairly well adapted; therefore organisms might well behave as depicted in the model. The argument hardly compels assent. Among the more obvious possibilities of error in this functional approach are the following: behavior in accord with the model might be adaptive in the present environment; however, the contemporary social environment (which is the one on which we performed our hopefully correct ecological analysis) might be radically different from that in which people evolved and to which they adapted. Furthermore, the organism is no doubt generally adapted but is perhaps not adapted regarding the behavior in question. Also, even though behavior in accord with the model might be adaptive, it is still possible that the organism might have adapted along the lines of another model.

Hence, we are not offering this dynamic equilibrium principle as evidence but merely as a high order generalization, hardly testable by empirical outcomes in view of its tenuous multistep logical relation to any testable derivations. The principle serves mainly as a heuristic device for guiding our thinking. The hypotheses it suggests gain only a measure of plausibility from their relation to the principle. Rather than supporting any hypothesis, this plausibility at most makes the hypothesis a nominee for empirical testing.

Conclusions Based on the Six Principles

If it is safe to make any simple generalization about personality-influenceability relations, it is that no simple generalizations are valid. Our discussion of the preceding principles showed again and again that there are few, if any, simple personality-influenceability relations that are valid over a wide range of conditions. The compensation principle under discussion argues further that additional research is unlikely to "improve" this situation. As a golden-mean variable, influenceability is likely to be held at an optimal range by means of a dynamic equilibrium between opposing personality forces. Any valid theory of personality-influenceability relations must, therefore, hypothesize relations that are complex and situational-interacting or else must be of very narrow generalizability. The complexities are imposed on the theory, not by our failure to find the crucial key but by the complexities of the slice of reality we have chosen to describe.

METHODOLOGICAL REQUIREMENTS FOR PERSONALITY-INFLUENCEABILITY RESEARCH

We have concluded after a review of the complexities of personality-influenceability relations that we are confronted with a choice between two alternatives. Either we can back off from the stated problem and attempt to approach the total behavior sphere from another direction, one that might allow simpler description; or we can stay with the stated problem and develop modes of thinking and analysis adequate to deal with the complexities involved. Frequently we do not have the option of dropping the problem as formulated and seeking a new approach to the problem area. Rather, some external constraints hold us (as in writing this chapter) to the problem as formulated, however complex the solution is likely to be. In this case, it is necessary to approach the problem with a methodological sophistication commensurate with the complexities of the task. We feel that on the basis of the preceding consideration, an adequate approach to unraveling personality-influenceability relationships would involve at least the six improvements in methodological strategy discussed below.

Analysis of Social Influence Situations

As discussed in connection with principle 3, we need a dimensional analysis of social influence situations to determine aspects of situations that contribute to the attitude change variance. In terms of available computerized techniques, factor analysis seems the most attractive procedure in regard to information furnished per unit of scientist's input. Programs for a wide variety of direct and derived solutions (Harman, 1960) are available at many computer centers today (Cooley & Lohnes, 1962). Other methods that promise to be more powerful than factor analysis (Shepard, 1962a, 1962b, 1964; Kruskal, 1964) or to yield more meaningful solutions (Guttman, 1965, 1966) have also been computerized but are as yet unfamiliar or available only at special installations (Lingoes, 1965).

We feel it would be wise to select the set of influence situations to be analyzed according to an a priori classification scheme (Guttman, 1966) rather than throw together situations that happen to appear in the literature. (The dust-bowl empiricism would be better than nothing, however, particularly as a first step.) In terms of the five-step analysis presented above in connection with principle 1, we might select situations which differ as regards variance in attention, comprehension, yielding, retention, and overt action. A complete design, even if we restrict ourselves to two levels on each aspect (e.g., high vs. low on attention, etc.), would call for 32 situations. Since producing a reliable 32 × 32 matrix of correlations would require a sizable number of subjects (at least 150), each of whom would be given a persuasive induction in each situation, even this number of situations would begin to strain the limits of available resources. Moreover, the design of 32 influence situations, each having to meet five restrictions, would itself be a formidable task, even before the actual data collection. The main consolation in such an endeavor would be the foreknowledge that at least the analysis of the data would be relatively routine and simple in demands on human resources, thanks to the availability of computers and programs.

The results of a number of such multidimensional analyses, with some variations of the tests included and with the inclusion of marker variables, would begin to answer some of the issues raised earlier in this chapter. It should give us some idea of the extent to which the factors we conjectured to be of some importance do, in fact, contribute to the variance in susceptibility to social influence. Also, it should provide us with a set of social-influence situations of known characteristics from which we can, in designing an experiment to test a specific personality-influenceability hypothesis, choose the situations that provide the most appropriate test.

Measurement of Mediators

A basic assumption of the present approach is that opinion change is the outcome of a series of behavioral steps, each of which can serve as a mediator of personality-influenceability relationships. It is possible, in principle, to test a theoretical formulation of this type solely in terms of the ultimate dependent variable, the measured opinion change. However, it is much more efficient to test the theory, and particularly to correct its details and determine the parameters, if we can measure directly the successive mediators. Ideally, we would like to be able to expose the person to the social influence and take direct readings of each of the hypothesized steps: attention to the message, comprehension of its contents, yielding to what is comprehended, retention of this agreement, and action on the basis of the agreement. We already admitted, in discussing principle 1, that we shall seldom have the capacity to measure each of these directly. We proposed to get a measure after the second step via a test of comprehension of message content, without attempting to unravel the extent to which a failure at step 1 or 2 caused the failure of comprehension, and to get a further measure after step 3 via a test of opinion change.

We would thus have a measure of reception (attention plus comprehension) and of opinion change. The first would be in the form of a comprehensive test asking the person what was said in the persuasive message, regardless of his own agreement or disagreement with it. The second would be in the form of an opinionnaire, measuring the person's own belief on the issues on which the social influence was exerted. More precisely, the measures would be the scores on the comprehension test and opinionnaire as compared with some control level, e.g., the person's own before-message scores or the scores from a no-message control group. Two serious methodological questions arise in obtaining these control-to-experimental change scores. One involves the design problems involved in before-after and after-only designs, which have been subjected to penetrating examination recently (Campbell, 1957; Campbell & Stanley, 1963). The empirical results have been recently reviewed by McGuire (1966). The second is the computation of change scores with the unreliable and poorly scaled measures that are available to us in the personality-persuasibility area. Here, too, recent work has begun at last to explore the dimensions of the problem and to suggest tentative answers (Harris, 1963). The present chapter is not the place to do more than mention these methodological problems and procedures.

Given these measures of reception and opinion change we could then derive a measure of the yielding mediator by some form of covariance analysis. We could, for example, compute the within-condition correlation between reception and opinion change and on the basis of this correlation and of each person's reception score, calculate his predicted opinion-change score. His yielding score would then be the algebraic difference (or some better-scaled equivalent) between his predicted and obtained opinion-change scores. Such a procedure would leave us with each subject's reception, yielding, and net opinion-change scores, and we could test our hypothesis more thoroughly by relating the subject's personality scores to each of those dependent variables. We could thus determine the validity not only of the basic hypothesis but also of the hypothetical mediational processes as well.

Several objections can be raised against the proposed method of computing the yielding score. It assumes a linear relation between reception and yielding, which is unlikely to be the true relation. Furthermore, it assumes an independence between the reception and yielding mediators which is unlikely in view of our sixth principle positing a dynamic equilibrium in which reception and yielding might well operate as mutually countervalent forces. Finally, it is based on a commonsensical assumption of a simple sequence: first attention, then comprehension, then yielding, etc. Actually there is a fairly impressive body of data which requires us to give serious consideration to the possibility that the actual sequence is more complicated and can even reverse. We are referring here to notions such as perceptual defense, and distortion of perception, comprehension, or memory such that the person manages to understand the message as being more in agreement with his own initial opinion than it really was. At least two theories are currently designed to quantify such distortion of comprehension, adaptation-level theory (Helson, 1964) and Sherif and Hovland's assimilation-contrast theory (C. Sherif, M. Sherif, & Nebergall, 1965). Again, space restrictions will not permit us to do more than mention these developments in the present chapter. Hopefully, progress along these lines will allow us to adjust the person's obtained comprehension score for such initial-opinion distortion effects. The adjusted scores would then furnish an improved basis for deriving the yielding score.

Measurement of Related Variables

We pointed out in connection with principle 4 that the mediating processes that need concern us in the personality-influenceability area include not only the steps intervening between the exerted social influence and measured opinion change response but also the intercorrelations of the given personality variable of our hypothesis with the other personality variable. The given personality dimension is related to influenceability, not only via its direct impact on the various intervening steps but also indirectly via the impacts of these correlated personality dimensions on the successive steps. Hence, when we are collecting data on the specific personality dimension that is our independent variable, we should cast a wider net and also collect data on related personality dimensions.

There are, of course, a frighteningly large number of personality variables that one could measure. In any experiment, we would, for practical reasons, have to be selective about which additional variables to include in our net, in order to maximize the amount of information that could be obtained with our limited resources. As a criterion of the possible utility of another personality variable, we could ask whether there are a priori reasons to expect this additional dimension to be related to both (a) our independent (personality) variable; and (b) one or another of the mediating steps to opinion change (attention, comprehension, etc., as discussed under principle 1). Only to the extent that the additional personality variable is likely to be thus tied to both terms of our hypothesis need we be concerned with it.

A second criterion for inclusion is that we want each additional variable to add a maximum of new information not already furnished by the previous variables. An appropriate tactic toward this end would be to use as a set of additional variables those that emerged from an orthogonal solution to a factor analysis of personality space (e.g., Guilford & Zimmerman, 1949; Cattell, Saunders, & Stice, 1957).

Even with every effort to limit our measurement of correlated variables to a minimum, a heavy investment in time would be required. A standardized factorial personality test takes about three-quarters of an hour to administer, though Peterson (1965) has argued that this time could be shortened to a couple of minutes with little loss of information. Another five or ten more minutes would be required to measure the independent variable and such other highly relevant personality variables as happen not to coincide with the dimensions yielded by the standardized test. The main bother involved in this lengthy measurement procedure is the burden put on the subject and experimenter in the data collection stage. Such imposition might result in subject hostility, boredom, etc., that would reduce the validity and reliability of the scores on the dependent (opinion-change) variable if we gave the influence induction at the same session; or would cause systematic self-selection biases due to failures of the participants to show up the second time if we carried out the influence induction at a later session. Perhaps if the personality measuring session is going to be particularly onerous, we should apply the influence inductions and measurements in a subsequent session. This sequence would yield the additional dividend that we could then conveniently get a delayed measure of the persistence of the persuasive impact at the second session.

The lengthy personality measurement routine we have advised here would be bothersome at the data-analysis phase, as well as at data-collection. However, in this day of punched-card processing and computers, the irksomeness of data analysis tends to become a negligible consideration. Also, standardized tests are usually made up so that, by using one of the standardized answer sheets, obtaining scores on the multiple dimensions becomes relatively simple. One possibility not to be overlooked is that when we are selecting our subjects from a military or academic population, we may find that our subjects have already been scored on an appropriate personality inventory, either as part of some assessment procedure or when they participated in an earlier experiment.

A final methodological tactic suggested by the correlated variable problem is that we use both chronic and acute variations of the independent variable. As we discussed in connection with principle 4, the two procedures can yield different results, and the difference in results can be as theoretically informative as the separate results of each procedure. We should, of course, be able to clarify our thinking sufficiently to determine which form of variation is required by our theory. It is essential that this be done if practical considerations require us to restrict ourselves to only one form. However, it is attractive, wherever possible, to use both within a single experimental design, since we then get information not only on the separate effects of each but on the interaction between them. We also get an opportunity, albeit limited, to detect a nonmonotonic trend with such chronic and acute orthogonal designs. Even when we use only two levels (high vs. low) on each factor, inclusion of both kinds of variations allows us to plot at least three ordered points on the independent personality variable: high-high, low-low, and the two mixed low-high conditions in between them (e.g., Millman, 1965). While such results will be an ambiguous and shaky base for confident conclusions, they provide useful guidance for further research. The design becomes more interesting still if we also include a theory-relevant situational variable within the same design, adding another main effect and three interactions, each of which could be used to test a separate hypothesis. The utility of such complex factorial designs deserves discussion as a separate methodological consideration.

Complex Factorial Designs

A constant refrain in this chapter has been the conclusion that an adequate personality-influenceability theory would for the most part predict interactions rather than main effects. Should our knowledge of the area ever reach the point where we can posit the precise parameters of the relationships, it will be possible to make valid predictions about main effects in the mapped-out situations which might be of considerable practical utility. Even did we possess such knowledge of the parameters, the interactional approach would still be more attractive from the theoretical viewpoint, since multiple-factorial designs would offer the economy of testing predictions and specifying parameters not only on main effects of the separate variables but on the interaction between them.

Exploitation of the interactional approach imposes two types of methodological tactics upon us: one involving design, the other, analysis. In regard to design, it suggests we use multiple independent variables within the same experiment, varying each orthogonally to all the others. The multiple variables would include (a) several personality dimensions with some varied both as to chronic and acute level, as advised in the preceding section; (b) situational factors such as subtlety of the influence induction (to vary the reception mediator) and objectivity of the issue (to vary the yielding mediator). We could then test each of the main effects and also gain a rich theory-relevant informational harvest from the personality-situational interaction effects which would test the hypothesized role of the mediational processes.

As for analysis, we must utilize descriptive and inferential statistics that will detect and evaluate as many as possible of the higher order effects. The most obvious procedure towards this end is complex analysis of variance with sufficient replications to provide a residual error estimate even for the higher order interactions. Possibilities of confounding due to repeated measures must be faced either in the design or in the partition of the obtained residual variance into several error terms.

For some purposes, such as estimating the relative importance of the different independent variables, it might be appropriate to abandon analysis of variance for facet analysis or factor analysis. It is, of course, possible to get at the relative size of two effects by analysis of variance (as in Triandis & Triandis, 1962), analysis of co-variance, or other approaches utilizing deviations produced by one effect from trend lines described by another (e.g., Byrne & Rhamey, 1965). None of these methods is above criticism and probably it is vain to seek any test of the relative effects of two independent variables in this personality area until we have more meaningful scales of measurement for the personality dimensions than at present. We must also point out, in anticipation of the next methodological point, that the complex analysis of variance that we are suggesting will turn out to be even more complex than appears at first sight, since the nonmonotonic trends that are to be expected in this area require that we break down our various treatment effects into linear, quadratic, and cubic components.

When we have a poor measure of our dependent variable, opinion change, we are further limited as to possible analysis. For example, much of even the recent personality-persuasibility work (Janis & Hovland, 1959) has employed a gross median split on the dependent variable to dichotomize the subjects into high vs. low persuasibles, which restricts us to such insensitive forms of analysis as chi-square. Even with such gross statistical analysis some tests of interaction are possible, but they tend to be insensitive tests, and trend analysis becomes virtually impossible.

Designs and Analysis That Detect Nonmonotonic Trends

We have pointed out at many points in the preceding sections of this chapter that both theory and results indicate that many personality-influenceability relationships will be quite complex and depart considerably from straight line functions. This point has a number of implications for both experimental design and data analysis. Regarding design, it indicates that we should vary the personality variable over a wide range. If we are using chronic-level variations, we should endeavor to include in the sample some subjects functioning at very high and some at very low levels on the personality dimension. If we are using acute-level manipulations, we should include an induction that will place the subject at a very high level and another that will place the subject at a very low level. We would fail to meet the requirement, for example, with a dimension like self-esteem (or anxiety) if we used a sample of students from a good college with the likely result that the lower (higher) range of the dimension would be unrepresented in our sample. The generalization of results from an experiment on college students to the lower (or higher) range of the variable is likely to be invalid as to magnitude and even direction of the personality-influenceability relationship.

Besides requiring that we vary our independent variable over a wide range of the personality dimension, the likelihood of a nonmonotonic relationship requires that we measure its effect on opinion change at many steps within its total range. As was mentioned earlier in this chapter, it is very hard to meet this requirement with the acute-level tactic. It taxes our ingenuity to devise a series of graded inductions that produce many increasing steps of, for example, anxiety. With the chronic-level approach, we can get as many levels as our personality scale will reliably distinguish. Perhaps the tactic for assuring both a wide range of variation and many measurable steps in between is to use a heterogeneous sample and to expose them to a series of widely spaced inductions (e.g., from very reassuring to very anxiety-provoking, if anxiety is the personality dimension of our hypothesis), and then do an internal analysis on the basis of our check on the manipulation. That is, after the induction, each subject would be measured on a finely graded anxiety scale and placed at his obtained scale score on this independent (personality) variable regardless of his acute induction level. Internal analyses are always worrisome and particularly in this personality-influenceability area where, as we saw above, the confounding of chronic and acute levels is especially likely to produce misleading interpretations. However, for some time to come there will continue to be many experimental situations in which such a procedure will represent the lesser of evils.

Until recently, there was also a third requirement (or at least desideratum) imposed on our variation of the personality characteristic, and we shall mention it here to show that psychology, like the earth, does move. This additional requirement arose if we sought by efficient statistical techniques like trend analysis to test for nonmonotonic or other complex relations between the personality variable and influenceability. As discussed in connection with principles 2 and 6, such complex relationships tend to be the rule rather than the exception. Until recently, the computational techniques for trend analysis conveniently available to psychologists (McNemar, 1962; Edwards, 1960) were worked out only for the special case where the independent variable was varied over equal steps. This requirement (even where we could convince ourselves that our personality variable was adequately enough scaled so we could deal with the question at all) was a very onerous one. Quite often we can test our hypothesis more efficiently by crowding our gradations toward one end of the variable with just a few gradations extending toward the other extreme. For example, to test some of the Iowa school's (Brown, 1961) notions about chronic vs. acute anxiety effects we might want to test at only one or two levels at low chronic anxiety but test at more gradations toward the theoretically crucial high-anxiety end of the scale. Techniques for dealing with the unequal-interval case were available in the statistical literature and on occasion (Insko, 1964) utilized by psychologists working in the persuasibility area. More recently, however, these procedures for utilizing trend analysis with unequal intervals and unequal numbers of cases have been made more available to psychologists (Winer, 1962; Gaito & Turner, 1963; Gaito, 1965). These standardized procedures become particularly necessary when we deal, not simply with one-variable designs, but with the multiple-variable designs we have been urging in this chapter.

Given that we have designed our study to include many (though not necessarily equally spaced) levels of the independent variable, we have to use modes of data analysis appropriate to exploit the information furnished. Except over very narrow (and therefore likely to be misleading) ranges of the personality variable, descriptive statistics like the Pearson r which assume rectilinearity are inappropriate. Also chi-square and analysis of variance are inappropriate inferential statistics unless they are combined with some form of trend analysis that can pick up more complex components. At this point, personality study begins to be a science that specifies quantitatively relations to other variables such as influenceability. It is with this more accurate specification of relationships that our final methodological consideration deals.

Determining Quantitative Relationships

If, as we have sought to demonstrate in this chapter, the relationships in the personality-influenceability area cannot be described by straight lines or even monotonic lines, then it appears that a fundamental reevaluation of our statistical needs is in order. Currently, in our experimental work on personality, we emphasize inferential statistics that test qualitative hypotheses. If we find that the independent (personality) variable has a significant impact on the dependent variable (influenceability) by the usual methods such as chi-square or analysis of variance, we are simply confirming that there is some relationship between the two, i.e., that the sets of dependent variable scores obtained by our independent variable partition depart significantly from a straight horizontal line, with at most the general direction of the departure specified. If this field is to become a quantitative science, we must deal with null hypotheses more complex than a straight horizontal line.

In the preceding section we argued that as a matter of routine, we should incorporate trend analysis into our inferential statistics. Here we further propose that the field has reached a stage where we must give more attention to developing descriptive statistics adequate for the task and relatively less attention to gross quantitative inferential statistics. We should have sufficient respect for our data and awareness of our task to look to the data for more exact relationships between our dependent and independent variables. To this end, our data must be used for more precise and powerful purposes than to disprove a null hypothesis of no relationship. Rather, we should use them to fit the most appropriately shaped relationship and even to estimate the exact parameters involved. We are asking no more than that personality-influenceability research begin to move to the stage of development that the more advanced area of behavioral science attained a quarter-century or more ago, areas like vision (Hecht, 1934) and learning (Hull, Hovland, Ross, Perkins, & Fitch, 1940). Some may feel that these earlier attempts were less than completely successful, but the step has become more attractive now, and the road more open with the recently increasing availability to psychologists of the proper mathematical tools to do jobs like parameter estimation (Bush, 1963).

We feel that once researchers in the area become heartened by their mastery of such tools, so that they really can fit exact functions to their obtained data, there will be gains beyond just fuller exploitation of the current data. The possibilities opened up by these techniques of analysis may cause a noticeable rise in the level of the researcher's aspirations. As a result we should see more rigorous and precise theorizing, more controlled and careful data collection, more complete description of the experimental conditions. We will thereby gain a fuller mastery of the parameters of social influence situations and be able to describe more fully the relationships of personality variables to influenceability and to correct more precisely for the obscuring effects of extraneous factors. Progress will also become possible, at last, on the measurement problem of providing exact scales for personality variables. With such progress, we shall no longer be faced with the metaphysical task of deciding on the proper scale for a given variable in isolation. Rather, we can then use as the criterion for selecting a whole set of measurement scales the requirement that those scales yield the most simple total set of relationships among our personality variables and dependent variables such as influenceability. It must be admitted, however, that these last methodological prescriptions about parameter estimation and determination of exact quantitative relationships deal with a stage of theoretical, methodological, and empirical precision that still lies in the future.

Conclusion

We have emphasized in this chapter on personality and influenceability research that the more carefully we look at this area, the clearer it becomes that the underlying relationships are highly complex. We have tried to sketch out some of these complexities and also to outline some of the rather demanding methodological techniques needed to discover and test the complex theoretical principles likely to emerge. As Wilde's Algernon says, "The truth is rarely pure and never simple." He might have added, it is seldom discovered without painful effort.

REFERENCES

Abelson, R. P. Modes of resolution of belief dilemmas. *J. Conflict Resolution,* 1959, 3, 343–352.

Abelson, R. P., & Lesser, G. S. The measurement of persuasibility in children. In I. L. Janis & C. I. Hovland (Eds.), *Personality and persuasibility.* New Haven: Yale Univer. Press, 1959. Pp. 141–166. (a)

Abelson, R. P., & Lesser, G. S. A developmental theory of persuasibility. In I. L. Janis & C. I. Hovland (Eds.), *Personality and persuasibility.* New Haven: Yale Univer. Press, 1959. Pp. 167–186. (b)

Abelson, R. P., & Rosenberg, M. J. Symbolic psycho-logic: a model of attitude cognition. *Behavioral Sci.,* 1958, 3, 1–13.

Abrams, S. The use of hypnotic techniques with psychotics. *Amer. J. Psychotherapy,* 1964, 18, 79–94.

Adorno, T. W., Frenkel-Brunswik, Else, Levinson, D. J., & Sanford, R. N. *The authoritarian personality.* New York: Harper, 1950.

Allport, G. Attitudes. In C. Murchison (Ed.), *Handbook of social psychology.* Worcester, Mass.: Clark Univer. Press, 1935. Pp. 798–844.

Anderson, N. H. Primacy effects in personality impression formation using a generalized order effect paradigm. *J. abnorm. soc. Psychol.,* 1965, 2, 1–9.

Appel, V. An experimental test of the superiority and theory of forced-choice questionnaire construction. *Dissertation Abstr.,* 1959, 20, 1067.

Appley, M. H., & Moeller, G. Conforming behavior and personality variables in college women. *J. abnorm. soc. Psychol.,* 1963, 66, 284–290.

Aronson, E., & Festinger, L. Some attempts to measure tolerance for dissonance. USAF WADC Tech. Rep., 1958, No. 58–942.

Aronson, E., Turner, Judith, & Carlsmith, J. M. Communicator credibility and communicator discrepancy as determinants of opinion change. *J. abnorm. soc. Psychol.,* 1963, 67, 31–36.

Asch, S. E. *Social psychology.* Englewood Cliffs, N.J.: Prentice-Hall, 1952.

Asch, S. E. Studies of independence and conformity: a minority of one against a unanimous majority. *Psychol. Monogr.,* 1956, 70, No. 9 (Whole No. 416).

Aveling, F., & Hargreaves, H. L. Suggestibility with and without prestige in children. *Brit. J. Psychol.,* 1921, 12, 53–75.

Bain, R. Stability in questionnaire response. *Amer. J. Sociol.,* 1931, 37, 445–453.

Bakan, D. A generalization of Sidman's results on group and individual functions and a criterion. *Psychol. Bull.,* 1954, 51, 63–67.

Barber, T. X., & Calverley, D. S. "Hypnotic-like" suggestibility in children and adults. *J. abnorm. soc. Psychol.,* 1963, 66, 589–597.

Barry, H., Jr., Mackennon, D. W., & Murray, H. A., Jr. Studies in personality: A. Hypnotizability as a personality trait and its typological relations. *Hum. Biol.,* 1931, 13, 1–36.

Beloff, H. Two forms of social conformity: acquiescence and conventionality. *J. abnorm. soc. Psychol.,* 1958, 56, 99–104.

Bennis, W. G., & Peabody, D. The conceptualization of two personality orientations and sociometric choice. *J. soc. Psychol.,* 1962, 57, 203–215.

Benton, A. L., & Bandura, A. "Primary" and "secondary" suggestibility. *J. abnorm. soc. Psychol.,* 1953, 48, 336–340.

Bereiter, C. Some persisting dilemmas in the measurement of change. In C. W. Harris (Ed.), *Problems in measuring change.* Madison: Univer. of Wisconsin Press, 1963. Pp. 3–20.

Bergin, A. E. The effect of dissonant persuasive communications on changes in a self-referring attitude. *J. Pers.*, 1962, 30, 423–438.

Berkowitz, L., & Cottingham, D. R. The interest value and relevance of fear arousing communications. *J. abnorm. soc. Psychol.*, 1960, 60, 37–43.

Berkowitz, L., & Lundy, R. M. Personality characteristics related to susceptibility to influence by peers or authority figures. *J. Pers.*, 1957, 25, 385–397.

Bettelheim, B., & Janowitz, M. *Dynamics of prejudice: a psychological and sociological study of veterans.* New York: Harper, 1950.

Binet, A. *La suggestibilité.* Paris: Scheicher Frères, 1900.

Blake, R. R., Helson, H., & Mouton, Jane S. The generality of conformity behavior as a function of factual anchor, difficulty of task, and amount of social pressure. *J. Pers.*, 1956, 25, 294–305.

Block, J. The equivalence of measures and the correction for attenuation. *Psychol. Bull.*, 1963, 60, 152–156.

Block, J. Recognizing attenuation effects in the strategy of research. *Psychol. Bull.*, 1964, 62, 214–216.

Boring, E. G. *History of experimental psychology.* (2nd ed.) New York: Appleton-Century, 1950.

Brehm, J. W., & Cohen, A. R. *Explorations in cognitive dissonance.* New York: Wiley, 1962.

Brown, J. S. *The motivation of behavior.* New York: McGraw-Hill, 1961.

Bush, R. R. Estimation and evaluation. In R. D. Luce, R. R. Bush, & E. Galanter (Eds.), *Handbook of mathematical psychology.* Vol. 1. New York: Wiley, 1963. Pp. 429–469.

Buss, A. H. Two anxiety factors in psychiatric patients. *J. abnorm. soc. Psychol.*, 1962, 65, 426–427.

Byrne, D., & Rhamey, R. Magnitude of positive and negative reinforcement as a determinant of attraction. *J. pers. soc. Psychol.*, 1965, 2, 884–889.

Campbell, D. T. Factors relevant to the validity of experiments in social settings. *Psychol. Bull.*, 1957, 54, 297–312.

Campbell, D. T. Social attitudes and other acquired behavioral dispositions. In S. Koch (Ed.), *Psychology: a study of a science.* Vol. 6. New York: McGraw-Hill, 1963. Pp. 94–172.

Campbell, D. T., & Stanley, J. C. Experimental and quasi-experimental designs for research on teaching. In N. L. Gage (Ed.), *Handbook of research on teaching.* Chicago: Rand McNally, 1963. Pp. 171–246.

Cartwright, D., & Harary, F. Structural balance: a generalization of Heider's theory. *Psychol. Rev.*, 1956, 63, 277–293.

Cattell, R. B., Saunders, D. R., & Stice, G. *Handbook for the sixteen personality factor questionnaire.* Champaign, Ill.: Institute for Personality & Ability Testing, 1957.

Christie, R., & Lindauer, Florence. Personality structure. In P. R. Farnsworth (Ed.), *Annual review of psychology.* Vol. 14. Palo Alto, Calif.: Annual Reviews, 1963. Pp. 201–230.

Cofer, C., & Appley, M. *Motivation theory and research.* New York: Wiley, 1964.

Cohen, A. R. Need for cognition and order of communication as determinants of opinion change. In C. I. Hovland (Ed.), *The order of presentation in persuasion.* New Haven: Yale Univer. Press, 1957. Pp. 79–97.

Cohen, A. R. Some implications of self-esteem for social influence. In I. L. Janis & C. I. Hovland (Eds.), *Personality and persuasibility.* New Haven: Yale Univer. Press, 1959. Pp. 102–120.

Cooley, W. W., & Lohnes, P. R. *Multivariate procedures for the behavioral sciences.* New York: Wiley, 1962.

Cooper, Eunice, & Dinerman, Helen. Analysis of the film "Don't Be a Sucker": a study of communication. *Publ. opin. Quart.*, 1951, 15, 243–264.

Couch, A., & Keniston, K. Yeasayers and naysayers: agreeing response set as a personality variable. *J. abnorm. soc. Psychol.*, 1960, 60, 151–174.

Cox, D. F., & Bauer, R. A. Self-confidence and persuasibility in women. *Publ. opin. Quart.*, 1964, 28, 453–466.

Cronbach, L. J. *Essentials of psychological testing.* (2nd ed.) New York: Harper, 1960.

Crowne, D. P., & Marlow, D. *The approval motive.* New York: Wiley, 1964.

Crutchfield, R. S. Conformity and character. *Amer. Psychol.*, 1955, 10, 191–198.

De Fleur, M. L., & Westie, F. R. Attitude as a scientific concept. *Soc. Forces*, 1963, 42, 17–31.

de Rivera, J. The postural sway test and its correlates. Pensacola, Fla.: U.S. Naval

School of Aviation Medicine, Bureau of Medicine & Surgery, Res. Proj. MR005. 13-3001. Subtask 7, Rpt. No. 3. Nov. 12, 1959.

De Wolfe, A. S., & Governale, C. N. Fear and attitude change. *J. abnorm. soc. Psychol.,* 1964, 69, 119–123.

Dittes, J. E., & Kelley, H. H. Effects of different conditions of acceptance upon conformity to group norms. *J. abnorm. soc. Psychol.,* 1956, 53, 100–107.

DiVesta, F. J., & Merwin, J. C. Effects of need-oriented communication on attitude change. *J. abnorm. soc. Psychol.,* 1960, 60, 80–85.

Dohrenwend, B., & Dohrenwend, Barbara. The problem of validity in field studies of psychological disorder. *J. abnorm. Psychol.,* 1965, 70, 52–69.

Doob, L. W., *Communication in Africa.* New Haven: Yale Univer. Press, 1961.

Ebbinghaus, H. *Abriss der Psychologie.* Leipzig: Veit, 1908.

Edwards, A. L. *Edwards Personal Preference Schedule (Manual).* New York: Psychological Corp., 1954.

Edwards, A. L. *Experimental design in psychological research.* New York: Holt, Rinehart, and Winston, 1960.

Eysenck, H. J., & Furneaux, W. D. Primary and secondary suggestibility: an experimental and statistical study. *J. exp. Psychol.,* 1945, 35, 485–503.

Ferguson, L. W. An analysis of the generality of suggestibility to group opinion. *Charact. and Pers.,* 1944, 12, 237–243.

Festinger, L. *A theory of cognitive dissonance.* Stanford, Calif.: Stanford Univer. Press, 1957.

Festinger, L. Behavioral support for opinion change. *Publ. opin. Quart.,* 1964, 28, 404–417. (a)

Festinger, L. *Conflict, decision and dissonance.* Stanford, Calif.: Stanford Univer. Press, 1964. (b)

Fishbein, M. The relationship between beliefs, attitudes, and behavior. In S. Feldman (Ed.), *Cognitive consistency in relation to behavior.* New York: Academic Press, 1966.

Freedman, J. L. Involvement, discrepancy, and opinion change. *J. abnorm. soc. Psychol.,* 1964, 69, 290–295.

Freud, S. *The problem of anxiety.* New York: Horton, 1936.

Frye, R., & Bass, B. M. Social acquiescence and behavior in groups. Paper read at Midwest Psychol. Assoc. Convention, Detroit, Mich., May 3, 1958.

Gaito, J. Unequal intervals and unequal n in trend analyses. *Psychol. Bull.,* 1965, 63, 125–127.

Gaito, J., & Turner, E. Error terms in trend analysis. *Psychol. Bull.,* 1963, 60, 464–474.

Gardner, R. W., Holzman, P. S., Klein, G. S., Linton, Harriet B., & Spence, D. P. Cognitive control. *Psychol. Issues,* 1959, 1, No. 4.

Gelfand, D. M. The influence of self-esteem on the rate of verbal conditioning and social matching behavior. *J. abnorm. soc. Psychol.,* 1962, 65, 259–265.

Goldstein, M. J. The relationship between coping and avoiding behavior and response to fear-arousing propaganda. *J. abnorm. soc. Psychol.,* 1959, 58, 247–252.

Gordon, L. U. *Gordon personality profile (manual).* New York: Harcourt, Brace, 1956.

Gough, H. G. *California personality inventory (manual).* Palo Alto, Calif.: Consulting Psychologist Press, 1957.

Greenwald, H. The involvement-discrepancy controversy in persuasion research. Unpublished doctoral dissertation, Columbia Univer., 1964.

Guilford, J. P., & Zimmerman, W. S. *The Guilford-Zimmerman temperament survey (manual).* Beverly Hills, Calif.: Sheridan Supply Co., 1949.

Guttman, L. A general nonmetric technique for finding the smallest Euclidean space for a configuration of points. *Psychometrika,* in press.

Guttman, L. Order analysis of correlation matrices. In R. B. Cattell (Ed.), *Handbook of multivariate experimental psychology.* Chicago: Rand McNally, 1966.

Haefner, D. P. Some effects of guilt-arousing and fear-arousing persuasive communications on opinion change. Unpublished doctoral dissertation, Univ. of Rochester, 1956.

Harman, H. *Modern factor analysis.* Chicago: Univer. of Chicago Press, 1960.

Harper, B. W., & Tuddenham, R. D. The sociometric composition of the group as a determinant of yielding to a distorted norm. *J. Psychol.,* 1964, 58, 307–311.

Harris, C. W. *Problems in measuring change.* Madison: Univer. of Wisconsin Press, 1963.

Hartley, E. L. *Problems in prejudice*. New York: King's Crown Press, 1946.

Harvey, O. J., & Consalvi, C. Status and conformity to pressure in informal groups. *J. abnorm. soc. Psychol.*, 1960, 60, 182–187.

Harvey, O. J., Hunt, D. E., & Schroder, H. M. *Conceptual systems and personality organization*. New York: Wiley, 1961.

Hecht, S. The nature of the photoreceptor process. In C. Murchison (Ed.), *Handbook of general experimental psychology*. Worcester, Mass.: Clark Univer. Press, 1934. Pp. 704–828.

Heider, F. Attitudes and cognitive organization. *J. Psychol.*, 1946, 21, 107–112.

Heider, F. *The psychology of interpersonal relations*. New York: Wiley, 1958.

Helson, H. *Adaptation-level theory*. New York: Harper & Row, 1964.

Hilgard, E. R. *Hypnotic susceptibility*. New York: Harcourt, Brace, 1965.

Hilgard, E. R., Lauer, Lillian W., & Melei, Janet P. Acquiescence, hypnotic susceptibility & the MMPI. *J. consult. Psychol.*, in press.

Hochbaum, G. M. The relation between group members' self-confidence and their reactions to group pressure to uniformity. *Amer. sociol. Rev.*, 1954, 6, 678–687.

Hoffman, M. L. Some psychodynamic factors in compulsive conformity. *J. abnorm. soc. Psychol.*, 1953, 48, 383–393.

Holland, L. V. *Counterpoint: Kenneth Burke and Aristotle's theory of rhetoric*. New York: Philosophical Library, 1959.

Hollander, E. P. Reconsidering the issue of conformity in personality. In H. P. David & J. C. Brengelmann (Eds.), *Perspectives in personality research*. New York: Springer, 1960. Pp. 210–225.

Hovland, C. I. Effects of the mass media of communication. In G. Lindzey (Ed.), *Handbook of social psychology*. Cambridge, Mass.: Addison-Wesley, 1954. Pp. 1062–1103.

Hovland, C. I. (Ed.) *Order of presentation in persuasion*. New Haven: Yale Univer. Press, 1957.

Hovland, C. I., & Janis, I. L. Summary and implications for future research. In I. L. Janis & C. I. Hovland (Eds.), *Personality and persuasibility*. New Haven: Yale Univer. Press, 1959. Pp. 225–254.

Hovland, C. I., Janis, I. L., & Kelley, H. H. *Communication and persuasion*. New Haven: Yale Univer. Press, 1953.

Hovland, C. I., Lumsdaine, A. A., & Sheffield, F. D. *Experiments on mass communications*. Princeton, N.J.: Princeton Univer. Press, 1949.

Hovland, C. I., & Mandell, W. An experimental comparison of conclusion-drawing by the communicator and by the audience. *J. abnorm. soc. Psychol.*, 1952, 47, 581–588.

Hovland, C. I., & Weiss, W. The influence of source credibility on communication effectiveness. *Publ. opin. Quart.*, 1951, 15, 635–650.

Howard, J. A. *Marketing: executive and buyer behavior*. New York: Columbia Univer. Press, 1963.

Hull, C. L. *Hypnosis and suggestibility*. New York: Appleton-Century, 1933.

Hull, C. L., Hovland, C. I., Ross, R. T., Hall, M., Perkins, D. T., & Fitch, F. B. *Mathematico-deductive theory of rote learning*. New Haven: Yale Univer. Press, 1940.

Insko, C. A. Primacy vs. recency in persuasion as a function of the timing of arguments and measures. *J. abnorm. soc. Psychol.*, 1964, 69, 381–391.

Insko, C. A., Arkoff, A., & Insko, V. M. Effects of high and low fear-arousing communications upon opinions toward smoking. *J. exp. soc. Psychol.*, 1965, 1, 256–266.

Jackson, D. N., & Pacine, L. Response styles and academic achievement. *Educ. psychol. Measmt.*, 1961, 21, 1015–1028.

Janis, I. L. Personality correlates of susceptibility to persuasion. *J. Pers.*, 1954, 22, 504–518.

Janis, I. L. Anxiety indices related to susceptibility to persuasion. *J. abnorm. soc. Psychol.*, 1955, 51, 663–667.

Janis, I. L., & Feshbach, S. Effects of fear arousing communications. *J. abnorm. soc. Psychol.*, 1953, 48, 78–92.

Janis, I. L., & Field, P. B. A behavioral assessment of persuasibility: consistency of individual differences. In I. L. Janis & C. I. Hovland (Eds.), *Personality and persuasibility*. New Haven: Yale Univer. Press, 1959. Pp. 29–54. (a)

Janis, I. L., & Field, P. B. Sex differences and personality factors related to persuasibility. In I. L. Janis & C. I. Hovland (Eds.), *Per-*

sonality and persuasibility. New Haven: Yale Univer. Press, 1959. Pp. 55–68. (b)

Janis, I. L., & Hovland, C. I. (Eds.) *Personality and persuasibility*. New Haven: Yale Univer. Press, 1959.

Janis, I. L., & Rife, D. Persuasibility and emotional disorder. In I. L. Janis & C. I. Hovland (Eds.), *Personality and persuasibility*. New Haven: Yale Univer. Press, 1959.

Janis, I. L., & Terwilliger, R. An experimental study of psychological resistance to fear-arousing communication. *J. abnorm. soc. Psychol.*, 1962, 65, 403–410.

Johnson, H. H., & Steiner, I. Effort and subjective probability. *J. pers. soc. Psychol.*, 1965, 1, 365–368.

Katz, D. Functional approach to the study of attitude. *Publ. opin. Quart.*, 1960, 24, 163–204.

Katz, D., Sarnoff, I., & McClintock, C. Ego-defense and attitude change. *Hum. Relat.*, 1956, 9, 27–45.

Katz, D., & Stotland, E. A preliminary statement of a theory of attitude structure and change. In S. Koch (Ed.), *Psychology: Study of a science*. Vol. 3. New York: McGraw-Hill, 1959. Pp. 423–475.

Katz, E., & Lazarsfeld, P. F. *Personal influence*. Glencoe, Ill.: Free Press, 1955.

Kegeles, S. S. Some motives for seeking preventative dental care. *J. Amer. dental Assoc.*, 1963, 67, 110–118.

Kelley, H. H., & Shapiro, M. M. An experiment on conformity to group norms where conformity is detrimental to group achievement. *Amer. sociol. Rev.*, 1954, 19, 667–677.

Kelley, H. H., & Thibaut, J. Experimental studies of group problem solving and process. In G. Lindzey (Ed.), *Handbook of social psychology*. Cambridge, Mass.: Addison-Wesley, 1954. Pp. 735–785.

Kelman, H. C. Effect of success and failure on "suggestibility" in the autokinetic situation. *J. abnorm. soc. Psychol.*, 1950, 45, 267–285.

Kelman, H. C. Compliance, identification, and internalization: three processes of opinion change. *J. Conflict Resolution*, 1958, 2, 51–60.

Kelman, H. C. Processes of opinion change. *Publ. opin. Quart.*, 1961, 25, 51–78.

Kelman, H. C., & Eagly, Alice H. Attitude toward the communicator, perception of communication content, and attitude change. *J. abnorm. soc. Psychol.*, 1965, 1, 63–78.

Kendall, Patricia L., & Wolf, Katherine M. The analysis of deviant cases in communications research. In P. F. Lazarsfeld & F. N. Stanton (Eds.), *Communication research, 1948–1949*. New York: Harper, 1949.

King, B. T. Relationships between susceptibility to opinion change and child rearing practices. In I. L. Janis & C. I. Hovland (Eds.), *Personality and persuasibility*. New Haven: Yale Univer. Press, 1959. Pp. 207–224.

Klapper, J. T. *Effects of mass communication*. Glencoe, Ill.: Free Press, 1961.

Klein, G. Cognitive control and motivation. In G. Lindzey (Ed.), *Assessment of human motives*. New York: Rinehart, 1958.

Knower, F. H. Experimental studies of changes in attitudes. I. A study of the effect of oral arguments on changes of attitudes. *J. soc. Psychol.*, 1935, 6, 315–347.

Kramer, E., & Brennan, E. P. Hypnotic susceptibility of schizophrenic patients. *J. abnorm. soc. Psychol.*, 1964, 69, 657–659.

Kruskal, J. B. Multidimensional scaling by optimizing goodness of fit to a nonmetric hypothesis. *Psychometrika*, 1964, 29, 1–27.

Lana, R. E. Familiarity and the order of presentation in persuasive communications. *J. abnorm. soc. Psychol.*, 1961, 62, 573–577.

Lana, R. E. Three interpretations of order effects in persuasive communications. *Psychol. Bull.*, 1964, 61, 314–320.

Lasswell, H. D. The structure and function of communication in society. In L. Bryson (Ed.), *Communication of ideas*. New York: Harper, 1948.

Laver, Lillian W. Factorial components of hypnotic susceptibility. Ph.D. dissertation, Stanford Univer., 1965.

Lazarus, R. S., Deese, J., & Osler, S. F. The effect of psychological stress upon performance. *Psychol. Bull.*, 1952, 49, 293–317.

Lesser, G. S., & Abelson, R. P. Personality correlates of persuasibility in children. In I. L. Janis & C. I. Hovland (Eds.), *Personality and persuasibility*. New Haven: Yale Univer. Press, 1959. Pp. 187–206.

Leventhal, H., & Niles, Patricia. A field experiment on fear arousal with data on the validity of questionnaire measures. *J. Pers.*, 1964, 32, 459–479.

Leventhal, H., & Perloe, S. I. A relationship between self-esteem and persuasibility. *J. abnorm. soc. Psychol.,* 1962, 64, 385–388.

Leventhal, H., Singer, R. P., & Jones, S. H. The effects of fear and specificity of recommendation upon attitudes and behavior. *J. pers. soc. Psychol.,* 1965, 2, 20–29.

Lingoes, J. C. An IBM 7090 program for Guttman-Lingoes smallest space analysis. I. *Behav. Sci.,* 1965, 10, 183–184.

Linton, Harriet B. Autokinetic judgments as a measure of influence. *J. abnorm. soc. Psychol.,* 1954, 49, 464–466.

Linton, Harriet, & Graham, Elaine. Personality correlates of persuasibility. In I. L. Janis & C. I. Hovland (Eds.), *Personality and persuasibility.* New Haven: Yale Univer. Press, 1959. Pp. 69–101.

Mahler, I. Yeasayers and naysayers: a validity study. *J. abnorm. soc. Psychol.,* 1962, 64, 317–318.

Mausner, B. The effect of prior reinforcement on the interaction of observed pairs. *J. abnorm. soc. Psychol.,* 1954, 49, 65–68.

Mausner, B., & Block, Barbara L. A study of the additivity of variables affecting social interaction. *J. abnorm. soc. Psychol.,* 1957, 54, 250–256.

McAllister, Irma. Interference, immoderation, inconsistency, and dependency: differences in the behavior of mothers toward first and later-born children. Unpublished doctoral dissertation, Columbia Univer., 1965.

McGuire, W. J. Cognitive consistency and attitude change. *J. abnorm. soc. Psychol.,* 1960, 60, 345–353. (a)

McGuire, W. J. A syllogistic analysis of cognitive relationships. In M. J. Rosenberg & C. I. Hovland (Eds.), *Attitude organization and attitude change.* New Haven: Yale Univer. Press, 1960. Pp. 65–111. (b)

McGuire, W. J. A multiprocess model for paired-associate learning. *J. exp. Psychol.,* 1961, 62, 335–347.

McGuire, W. J. Persistence of the resistance to persuasion induced by various types of prior belief defenses. *J. abnorm. soc. Psychol.,* 1962, 64, 241–248.

McGuire, W. J. Attitudes and opinions. In P. R. Farnsworth (Ed.), *Annual review of psychology.* Vol. 17. Palo Alto, Calif.: Annual Reviews, 1966.

McNemar, Q. *Psychological statistics.* (3rd ed.) New York: Wiley, 1962.

Menzel, H., & Katz, E. Social relations and innovations in the medical profession: the epidemiology of a new drug. *Publ. opin. Quart.,* 1956, 19, 337–352.

Miller, N., & Campbell, D. T. Recency and primacy in persuasion as a function of the timing of speeches and measurement. *J. abnorm. soc. Psychol.,* 1959, 59, 1–9.

Miller, N. E., & Dollard, J. *Social learning and imitation.* New Haven: Yale Univer. Press, 1941.

Millman, Susan. The relationship between anxiety, learning and opinion change. Unpublished doctoral dissertation, Columbia Univer., 1965.

Mitra, S. F., & Fiske, D. W. Intra-individual variability as related to test score and items. *Educ. psychol. Measmt,* 1956, 16, 3–12.

Moeller, G., & Applezweig, M. H. A motivational factor in conformity. *J. abnorm. soc. Psychol.,* 1957, 55, 114–120.

Moltz, H., & Thistlethwaite, D. Attitude modification and anxiety reduction. *J. abnorm. soc. Psychol.,* 1955, 50, 231–237.

Moore, Rosemarie K. Susceptibility to hypnosis and susceptibility to social influence. *J. abnorm. soc. Psychol.,* 1964, *68,* 282–294.

Murphy, G., Murphy, Lois B., & Newcomb, T. N. *Experimental social psychology.* (Rev. ed.) New York: Harper, 1937.

Newcomb, T. M. An approach to the study of communicative acts. *Psychol. Rev.,* 1953, 60, 393–404.

Niles, Patricia. The relationship of susceptibility and anxiety to acceptance of fear-arousing communications. Unpublished doctoral dissertation, Yale Univer., 1964.

Osgood, C. E., & Tannenbaum, P. H. The principle of congruity in the prediction of attitude change. *Psychol. Rev.,* 1955, 62, 42–55.

Osterweil, J., & Fiske, D. W. Intra-individual variability in sentence completion responses. *J. abnorm. soc. Psychol.,* 1956, 52, 195–199.

Papageorgis, D. Bartlett effect and the persistence of induced opinion change. *J. abnorm. soc. Psychol.,* 1963, 67, 61–67.

Peak, Helen. Attitude and motivation. In M. R. Jones (Ed.), *Nebraska symposium on motivation.* Lincoln, Nebr.: Univer. of Nebraska Press, 1955. Pp. 149–188.

Peterson, D. R. Scope and generality of verbally defined personality factors. *Psychol. Rev.,* 1965, 72, 48–59.

Pettigrew, T. F. The measurement and correlates of category width as a cognitive variable. *J. Pers.,* 1958, 26, 532–544.
Powell, F. A. Open- and closed-mindedness and the ability to differentiate source and message. *J. abnorm. soc. Psychol.,* 1962, 65, 61–63.
Rokeach, M. Political and religious dogmatism: an alternative to the authoritarian personality. *Psychol. Monogr.,* 1956, 70, 18 (Whole No. 425).
Rokeach, M. *Open and closed mind.* New York: Basic Books, 1960.
Rorer, L. G. The great response-style myth. *Psychol. Bull.,* 1965, 63, 129–156.
Rosenberg, J. Persuasibility in personality and culture. Unpublished doctoral dissertation, Columbia Univer., 1962.
Rosner, S. Consistency in response to group pressure. *J. abnorm. soc. Psychol.,* 1957, 55, 145–146.
Runkel, P. J. Some consistency effects. *Educ. psychol. Measmt,* 1958, 18, 527–541.
Samelson, F. Conforming behavior under two conditions of conflict in the cognitive field. *J. abnorm. soc. Psychol.,* 1957, 55, 181–187.
Sarnoff, I., & Zimbardo, P. G. Anxiety, fear, and social affiliations. *J. abnorm. soc. Psychol.,* 1961, 62, 356–363.
Schein, E. H., Hill, W. F., Williams, H. L., & Lubin, A. Distinguishing characteristics of collaborators and resistors among American prisoners of war. *J. abnorm. soc. Psychol.,* 1957, 55, 197–201.
Schofield, W. Changes in response to the MMPI following certain therapies. *Psychol. Monogr.,* 1950, 64, No. 5.
Schofield, W. A further study of the effects of therapy on MMPI responses. *J. abnorm. soc. Psychol.,* 1953, 48, 66–77.
Scott, J. P., & Fuller, J. L. *Genetics and the social behavior of the dog.* Chicago: Univer. of Chicago Press, 1965.
Sears, Pauline S. The pursuit of self esteem: the middle childhood years. Paper read at annual Amer. Psychol. Assoc. convention, Chicago, Sept., 1960.
Sears, R. R. Dependency motivation. In M. R. Jones (Ed.), *Nebraska symposium on motivation.* Lincoln: Univer. of Nebraska Press, 1963. Pp. 25–64.
Segal, J. Factors related to the collaboration and resistance behavior of U.S. Army POWs in Korea. Tech. Rep. 33, Human Resources Research Office. Washington, D.C.: George Washington Univer., Dec., 1956.
Segal, J. Correlates of collaboration and resistance behavior among U.S. Army POWs in Korea. *J. soc. Issues,* 1957, 13, 31–40.
Shepard, R. N. The analysis of proximities: multidimensional scaling with an unknown distance function. I. *Psychometrika,* 1962, 27, 125–140. (a)
Shepard, R. N. The analysis of proximities: multidimensional scaling with an unknown distance function. II. *Psychometrika,* 1962, 27, 219–246. (b)
Shepard, R. N. Attention and the metric structure of the stimulus space. *J. math. Psychol.,* 1964, 1, 54–87.
Sherif, Carolyn W., Sherif, M., & Nebergall, R. E. *Attitude and attitude change.* Philadelphia: Saunders, 1965.
Sherif, M. A study of some social factors in perception. *Arch. Psychol.,* 1935, 27, No. 187. 60 pp.
Sherif, M., & Hovland, C. I. *Social judgment.* New Haven: Yale Univer. Press, 1961.
Sidman, M. A note on functional relations obtained from group data. *Psychol. Bull.,* 1952, 49, 263–269.
Silverman, I. Differential effects of ego threat upon persuasibility for high and low self-esteem subjects. *J. abnorm. soc. Psychol.,* 1964, 69, 567–572.
Smith, M. A note on stability in questionnaire responses. *Amer. J. Sociol.,* 1933, 38, 713–720.
Smith, M. B., Bruner, J. S., & White, R. W. *Opinions and personality.* New York: Wiley, 1956.
Spence, K. W., Farber, I. E., & Taylor, Elaine. The relation of electric shock and anxiety to level of performance in eyelid conditioning. *J. exp. Psychol.,* 1954, 48, 404–408.
Steiner, I. D. Sex differences in the resolution of A-B-X conflicts. *J. Pers.,* 1960, 28, 118–128.
Steiner, I. D., & Johnson, H. H. Authoritarianism and "tolerance for trait inconsistency." *J. abnorm. soc. Psychol.,* 1963, 67, 388–391.
Steiner, I. D., & Johnson, H. H. Category width and response to interpersonal disagreement. *J. pers. soc. Psychol.,* 1965, 2, 290–292.
Stephens, M. W., & Crowne, D. P. Correction for attenuation and the equivalence of tests. *Psychol. Bull.,* 1964, 62, 210–213.

Sternlicht, M., & Wanderer, Z. W. Hypnotic susceptibility and mental deficiency. *Int. J. clin. exp. Hypnosis,* 1963, 11, 104–111.

Steward, J. B. *Repetitive advertising in newspapers: a study in two new products.* Boston: Harvard Business School, 1964.

Stotland, E., & Hillmer, M. L., Jr. Identification, authoritarian defensiveness and self-esteem. *J. abnorm. soc. Psychol.,* 1962, 64, 334–342.

Stotland, E., Katz, D., & Patchen, M. The reduction of prejudice through the arousal of self-insight. *J. Pers.,* 1959, 27, 507–531.

Stotland, E., & Patchen, M. Identification and changes in prejudice and in authoritarianism. *J. abnorm. soc. Psychol.,* 1961, 62, 265–274.

Stukát, K.-G. *Suggestibility: a factorial and experimental study.* Stockholm: Almquist & Wiksell, 1958.

Taffel, C. Anxiety and the conditioning of verbal behavior. *J. abnorm. soc. Psychol.,* 1955, 51, 496–501.

Taylor, Janet A. A personality scale of manifest anxiety. *J. abnorm. soc. Psychol.,* 1953, 48, 285–290.

Thistlethwaite, D. L., de Hann, H., & Kamenetsky, J. The effects of "directive" and "nondirective" communication procedures on attitudes. *J. abnorm. soc. Psychol.,* 1955, 51, 107–113.

Triandis, H. C., & Triandis, Leigh M. A cross-cultural study of social distance. *Psychol. Monogr.,* 1962, 76, No. 21 (Whole No. 540).

Tuddenham, R. D. Correlates of yielding to a distorted group norm. *J. Pers.,* 1959, 27, 272–284.

Walters, R. H., & Parke, R. D. Social motivation, dependency, and susceptibility to social influence. In L. Berkowitz (Ed.), *Advances in experimental social psychology.* Vol. 1. New York: Academic Press, 1964. Pp. 232–277.

Watts, W. A., & McGuire, W. J. Persistency of induced opinion change and retention of inducing message content. *J. abnorm. soc. Psychol.,* 1964, 68, 233–241.

Weiss, W., & Fine, B. J. The effect of induced aggressiveness on opinion change. *J. abnorm. soc. Psychol.,* 1956, 52, 109–114.

Weitzenhoffer, A. M. *Hypnotism: an objective study in suggestibility.* New York: Wiley, 1953.

Whipple, G. M. *Manual of mental and physical tests.* Baltimore: Warwick, 1910.

Windle, C. Test-retest effects on personality questionnaires. *Educ. psychol. Measmt,* 1954, 14, 617–633.

Windle, C. Further studies in test-retest effects on personality questionnaires. *Educ. psychol. Measmt,* 1955, 15, 246–253.

Winer, B. J. *Statistical principles in experimental design.* New York: McGraw-Hill, 1962.

Wolf, Theta. Alfred Binet: a time of crisis. *Amer. Psychol.,* 1964, 19, 762–771.

Woodruff, A. D., & DiVesta, F. J. The relation between values, concepts and attitudes. *Educ. psychol. Measmt,* 1948, 8, 645–659.

Wright, J. M., & Harvey, O. J. Attitude changes as a function of authoritarianism and punitiveness. *J. pers. soc. Psychol.,* 1965, 1, 177–180.

Zavala, A. Development of the forced-choice rating scale technique. *Psychol. Bull.,* 1965, 63, 117–124.

Zimbardo, P. G. Involvement and communication discrepancy as determinants of opinion conformity. *J. abnorm. soc. Psychol.,* 1960, 60, 86–94.

Smith, M. B. Attitude change. In David L. Sills (Ed.), International Encyclopedia of the Social Sciences. New York: Macmillan, 1968, Vol. I, 459-467.

Author Index

Subject Index

PRINTED IN U.S.A.